RHS PLANT FINDER 2004-2005

DEVISED BY CHRIS PHILIP
AND REALISED BY TONY LORD

CONSULTANT EDITOR
TONY LORD

RHS EDITORS
JAMES ARMITAGE JANET CUBEY
MIKE GRANT CHRISTOPHER WHITEHOUSE

COMPILER
JUDITH MERRICK

A Dorling Kindersley Book

LONDON, NEW YORK, MUNICH, MELBOURNE, DELHI

Published by
Dorling Kindersley Ltd
80 Strand, London WC2R 0RL
A Penguin company

First edition April 1987
Seventeenth edition April 2004

British Library Cataloguing Publication Data.
A Catalogue record for this book is available from the British Library.

ISBN 1 4053 0348 4

Compiled by
The Royal Horticultural Society
80 Vincent Square,
London SW1P 2PE
Registered charity no: 222879

www.rhs.org.uk

Illustrations by Sarah Young
Maps by Alan Cooper

Produced for Dorling Kindersley Ltd by
COOLING BROWN
Printed and bound in England by Clays Ltd, St Ives Plc

The Compiler and the Editors of the *RHS Plant Finder* have taken every care, in the time available, to check all the information supplied to them by the nurseries concerned. Nevertheless, in a work of this kind, containing as it does hundreds of thousands of separate computer encodings, errors and omissions will, inevitably, occur. Neither the RHS, the Publisher nor the Editors can accept responsibility for any consequences that may arise from such errors.

If you find mistakes we hope that you will let us know so that the matter can be corrected in the next edition.

Front cover photographs from left to right: *Papaver orientale* 'Mrs Perry', *Malus pumila* 'Cowichan', *Canna* 'Striata'
Back cover photographs from top to bottom: *Acer palmatum* var. *dissectum* 'Garnet', *Geranium phaeum* 'Album', *Primula auricula* hort. 'Adrian', *Fritillaria imperialis*, *Cornus kousa* var. *chinensis* 'China Girl'
Spine: *Succisa pratensis*
Background: *Iris reticulata* 'Harmony'

See our complete catalogue at
www.dk.com

CONTENTS

INTRODUCTION

The *RHS Plant Finder* exists to put enthusiastic gardeners in touch with suppliers of plants. The book is divided into two related sections – PLANTS and NURSERIES. PLANTS includes an A–Z Plant Directory of some 72,000 plant names, against which are listed a series of nursery codes. These codes point the reader to the full nursery details contained in the NURSERIES section towards the back of the book.

The *RHS Plant Finder* is comprehensively updated every year and provides the plant lover with the richest source of suppliers known to us, whether you are looking for plants locally, shopping from your armchair or touring the country in search of the rare and unusual.

NEW IN THIS EDITION

This year several introductory sections of the book dealing with the naming of plants have been amalgamated in a new *Extended Glossary* section. We hope this will prove to be more helpful to you, the user of this book.

It is the intention of the editors that each future edition of the ***RHS Plant Finder*** will carry a unique essay on some aspect of plant naming or about a particular plant group. In this edition, Tony Lord has written the first such essay, *A Question of Plant Breeding*, on the breeding and selection of new plants by the amateur.

This edition contains few major changes to plant names. However, the appearance of a number of International Registers and Checklists in, for instance, *Brugmanisa*, *Hebe*, *Hemerocallis* and *Viola*, some of them freely available on the Internet, has helped corrections in these genera. One decision made by the RHS Advisory Panel on Nomenclature and Taxonomy has been to follow the current consensus of opinion in considering *Symphyandra* not to be distinct from *Campanula*. The main difference between the two, the presence of connate (fused) anthers in *Symphyandra*, derives from several groups within *Campanula* and is not felt to warrant treating the two as separate genera.

AVAILABLE FROM THE COMPILER

APPLICATION FOR ENTRY

Nurseries appearing in the *RHS Plant Finder* for the first time this year are printed in bold type in the *Nursery Index by Name* starting on p.907.

If any other nursery wishes to be considered for inclusion in the next edition of the *RHS Plant Finder* (2005-06), please write for details to the Compiler at the address below.

PLANTS LAST LISTED IN EARLIER EDITIONS

Plants cease to be listed for a variety of reasons. For more information turn to *How to Use the Plant Directory* on p.18.

A listing of the 24,000 or so plants listed in earlier editions, but for which we currently have no known supplier, is available from the Compiler. Please send a self-addressed A4 envelope stamped with £1.10 stamps.

LISTS OF NURSERIES FOR PLANTS WITH MORE THAN 30 SUPPLIERS

To prevent the *RHS Plant Finder* from becoming still larger, if more than 30 nurseries offer the same plant we cease to print the nursery codes and instead list the plant as having 'more than 30 suppliers'. This is detailed more fully in *How to Use the Plant Directory* on p.18.

If any readers have difficulty in finding such a plant, we will be pleased to send a full list of all the nurseries that we have on file as stockists. All such enquiries must include the full name of the plant being sought, as shown in the *RHS Plant Finder*, together with an A5 size SAE. For more than one plant, please send an A4 1st class SAE.

The above may all be obtained from:
The Compiler, *RHS Plant Finder*, RHS Garden Wisley, Woking, Surrey GU23 6QB

THE RHS PLANT FINDER ONLINE

The *RHS Plant Finder* is available on the Internet. Visit the Royal Horticultural Society's website **www.rhs.org.uk** and search the *RHS Plant Finder* database online.

TO AVOID DISAPPOINTMENT, WE SUGGEST THAT YOU ALWAYS

check with the nursery before visiting or ordering and always use the current edition of the book.

ACKNOWLEDGMENTS

For this year's edition, Judith Merrick, together with June Skinner, and assisted by Patty Boardman and Laura Pearce, co-ordinated the compilation of nursery information and plant data, while Richard Sanford kept track of the editing of plant names on the database. Rupert Wilson and Lynda Collett managed the Horticultural Database from which the book is produced – no mean feat during a year that involved the migration of the database from a DOS-based system to Windows.

The team at Wisley also acknowledges the help of Simon Maughan of RHS Publications in London, Dr Kerry Walter of BG-BASE (UK) Ltd., Max Phillips of Strange Software Limited and Alan Cooper, who produces the nursery maps.

The team of RHS botanists has been busy, in a year that has again seen staff changes; Jo Osborne emigrated and was replaced by Christopher Whitehouse, who joined James Armitage and Mike Grant (now Senior Botanist).

Once again this year we are indebted to our colleagues on the RHS Advisory Panel on Nomenclature and Taxonomy, along with the RHS International Registrars and the RHS Keeper of the Herbarium, Diana Miller, all of whom have provided much valuable guidance and information. Scores of nurseries have sent helpful information about asterisked plants which has proved immensely useful in verifying some of the most obscure names, as well as suggesting corrections to existing entries. Some of these suggested corrections remain to be checked and entered in our next edition and we are grateful for your patience while information is checked and processed, though those that contravene the Codes of Nomenclature may have to be rejected for reasons covered in the section on nomenclature. We are grateful, too, to our regular correspondents.

Actaea	J. Compton ('94)
Camellia	T.J. Savige, International Registrar, NSW, Australia ('96)
Cistus	R. Page ('97, '99 & '02)
Clematis	V. Matthews, International Registrar, RHS ('00-'04)
Conifers	P. Trehane, former International Registrar, RHS Wisley ('94 & '99)
Cotoneaster	Jeanette Fryer, NCCPG Collection Holder ('99)
Dahlia	R. Hedge, RHS Wisley ('96–'00 & '02)
Delphinium	Dr A.C. Leslie, International Registrar, RHS Wisley ('97–'00 & '02)
Dianthus	Dr A.C. Leslie, International Registrar, RHS Wisley ('91–'00 & '02)
Geranium	D.X. Victor, International Registrar ('03)
Hebe	Mrs J. Hewitt ('94–'99)
Hypericum	Dr N.K.B. Robson ('94–'97)
Ilex	Ms S. Andrews ('92–'98)
Iris	Mrs J. Hewitt ('95–'99 & '02)
Jovibarba & *Sempervivum*	P.J. Mitchell, International Registrar, Sempervivum Society ('98)
Lavandula	Ms S. Andrews ('92–'99)
Lilium	Dr A.C. Leslie, International Registrar, RHS Wisley ('91–'00 & '02)
Liriope	Dr P.R. Fantz ('99)
Meconopsis	Dr E. Stevens ('02 & '03)
Narcissus	Mrs S. Kington, International Registrar, RHS ('91–'00 & '02)
Ophiopogon	Dr P.R. Fantz ('99)
Rhododendron	Dr A.C. Leslie, International Registrar, RHS Wisley ('91–'00 & '02)
Sorbus	Dr H. McAllister ('01)

To all these, as well as to the many readers and nurseries who have also made comments and suggestions, we are once again extremely grateful.

Tony Lord, Consultant Editor, and Janet Cubey, RHS Principal Botanist, February 2004

EXTENDED GLOSSARY

This new glossary combines some of the helpful introductory sections from previous editions in an alphabetical listing. A fuller, more discursive account of plant names, *Guide to Plant Names,* and a detailed guide to the typography of plant names, *Recommended Style for Printing Plant Names,* are both available as RHS Advisory Leaflets. To request a copy of either please send an A4 SAE to The Compiler at the contact address given on page 4.

ADVISORY PANEL ON NOMENCLATURE AND TAXONOMY

This Panel advises the RHS on individual problems of nomenclature regarding plants in cultivation and, in particular, use of names in the *RHS Horticultural Database,* reflected in the annual publication of the *RHS Plant Finder.*

The aim is always to make the plant names in the *RHS Plant Finder* as consistent, reliable and stable as possible and acceptable to gardeners and botanists alike, not only in the British Isles but around the world. Recent proposals to change or correct names are examined with the aim of creating a balance between the stability of well-known names and botanical and taxonomic correctness. In some cases the Panel feels that the conflicting views on the names of some groups of plants will not easily be resolved. The Panel's policy is then to wait and review the situation once a more obvious consensus is reached, rather than rush to rename plants only to have to change them again when opinions have shifted.

The Panel is chaired by Dr Alan Leslie (RHS) and includes Susyn Andrews, Chris Brickell, Dr James Compton (University of Reading), Dr Janet Cubey (RHS), Mike Grant (RHS), Dr Christopher Grey-Wilson, Dr Stephen Jury (University of Reading), Sabina Knees, Dr Tony Lord, Piers Trehane and Adrian Whiteley.

AUTHORITIES

In order that plant names can be used with precision throughout the scientific world, the name of the person who coined the name of a plant species (its author, or authority) is added to the plant name. Usually this information is irrelevant to gardeners, except in cases where the same name has been given to two different plants. Although only one usage is correct, both may be encountered in books, so indicating the author is the only way to be certain about which plant is being referred to. This can happen equally with cultivars. Authors' names, where it is appropriate to cite them, appear in a smaller typeface after the species or cultivar name to which they refer and are abbreviated following Brummitt and Powell's *Authors of Plant Names.*

♀ THE AWARD OF GARDEN MERIT

The Award of Garden Merit (AGM) is intended to be of practical value to the ordinary gardener and is therefore awarded only after a period of assessment by the Society's Standing and Joint Committees. An AGM plant:

- must be available
- must be of outstanding excellence for garden decoration or use
- must be of good constitution
- must not require highly specialist growing conditions or care
- must not be particularly susceptible to any pest or disease
- must not be subject to an unreasonable degree of reversion

The AGM symbol is cited in conjunction with the **hardiness** rating. The RHS publication *AGM Plants 2004* gives the full list of AGM plants. Copies can be ordered from RHS Enterprises on (01483) 211320. Information about AGM plants is also available on the RHS website at www.rhs.org.uk.

BOTANICAL NAMES

The aim of the botanical naming system is to provide each different plant with a single, unique, universal name. The basic unit of plant classification is the species. Species that share a number of significant characteristics are grouped together to form a genus (plural genera). The name of a species is made up of two elements; the name of the genus followed by the specific epithet, for example, *Narcissus romieuxii.*

Variation within a species can be recognised by division into subspecies (usually abbreviated to subsp.), varietas (or variety abbreviated to var.) and forma (or form abbreviated to f.). Whilst it is unusual for a plant to have all of these, it is possible, as in this example, *Narcissus romieuxii* subsp. *albidus* var. *zaianicus* f. *lutescens*.

The botanical elements are always given in italics, with only the genus taking an initial capital letter. The rank indications are never in italics. In instances where the rank is not known it is necessary to form an invalid construction by quoting a second epithet without a rank. This is an unsatisfactory situation, but requires considerable research to resolve.

CLASSIFICATION OF GENERA

Genera that include a large number of species or with many cultivars are often subdivided into informal horticultural classifications or more formal Cultivar Groups, each based on a particular characteristic or combination of characteristics. Colour of flower or fruit and shape of flower are common examples and, with fruit, whether a cultivar is grown for culinary or dessert purposes. How such groups are named differs from genus to genus.

To help users of the *RHS Plant Finder* find exactly the plants they want, the majority of classifications used within cultivated genera are listed with codes and plants are marked with the appropriate code in brackets after its name in the Plant Directory. To find the explanation of each code, simply look it up under the genus concerned in the **Classification of Genera** starting on p.28. The codes relating to edible fruits are also listed here, but these apply across several genera.

COLLECTORS' REFERENCES

Abbreviations (usually with numbers) following a plant name refer to the collector(s) of the plant. These abbreviations are expanded, with a collector's name or expedition title, in the section **Collectors' References** starting on p.20.

A collector's reference may indicate a new, as yet unnamed range of variation within a species. The inclusion of collectors' references in the *RHS Plant Finder* supports the book's role in sourcing unusual plants.

The Convention on Biological Diversity calls for conservation of biodiversity, its sustainable use and the fair and equitable sharing of any derived benefits. Since its adoption in 1993, collectors are required to have prior consent from the country of origin for the acquisition and commercialisation of collected material.

COMMON NAMES

In a work such as this it is necessary to refer to plants by their botanical names for the sake of universal comprehension and clarity. However, at the same time we recognise that with fruit and vegetables most people are more familiar with their common names than their botanical ones. Cross-references are therefore given from common to botanical names for fruit, vegetables and the commoner culinary herbs throughout the Plant Directory.

CULTIVAR

Literally meaning cultivated variety, cultivar names are given to denote variation within species and that generated by hybridisation, in cultivation. To make them easily distinguishable from botanical names, they are not printed in italics and are enclosed in single quotation marks. Cultivar names coined since 1959 should follow the rules of the International Code of Nomenclature for Cultivated Plants (**ICNCP**).

CULTIVAR GROUP

This is a collective name for a group of cultivars within a genus with similar characteristics. The word Group is always included and, where cited with a cultivar name, it is enclosed in brackets, for example, *Actaea simplex* (Atropurpurea Group) 'Brunette', where 'Brunette' is a distinct cultivar in a group of purple-leaved cultivars.

Another example of a cultivar group is *Rhododendron polycladum* Scintillans Group. In this case *Rhododendron scintillans* was a species that is now botanically 'sunk' within *R. polycladum*, but it is still recognised horticulturally as a Group.

Cultivar Group names are also used for swarms of hybrids with the same parentage, for example, *Rhododendron* Polar Bear Group. These were formerly treated as **grex** names, a term now generally only used for orchids. A single clone from the Group may be given the same cultivar name, for example, *Rhododendron* 'Polar Bear'.

DESCRIPTIVE TERMS

Terms that appear after the main part of the plant name are shown in a smaller font to distinguish them. These descriptive elements give extra information about the plant and may include the **collector's reference**, **authority**, or what colour it is. For example, *Fritillaria thessala* SBEL 443, *Penstemon* 'Sour Grapes' M. Fish, *Lobelia tupa* dark orange.

FAMILIES

Genera are grouped into larger groups of related plants called families. Most family names, with the exception of eight familiar names, end with the same group of letters, *-aceae*. While it is still acceptable to use these eight exceptions, the modern trend adopted in the *RHS Plant Finder* is to use alternative names with *–aceae* endings. The families concerned are *Compositae* (*Asteraceae*), *Cruciferae* (*Brassicaceae*), *Gramineae* (*Poaceae*), *Guttiferae* (*Clusiaceae*), *Labiatae* (*Lamiaceae*), *Leguminosae* (split here into *Caesalpiniaceae*, *Mimosaceae* and *Papilionaceae*), *Palmae* (*Arecaceae*) and *Umbelliferae* (*Apiceae*). Also the traditionally large family *Liliaceae* is split into a number of smaller, more natural, families that as yet may be unfamiliar to readers.

GENERA

Genera used in the *RHS Plant Finder* are almost always those given in Brummitt's *Vascular Plant Families and Genera.* For spellings and genders of generic names, Greuter's *Names in Current Use for Extant Plant Genera* has also been consulted. See **Botanical Names**.

GREX

Particularly within orchids, hybrids of the same parentage, regardless of how alike they are, are given a grex name. Individuals can be selected, given cultivar names and propagated vegetatively. For example, *Pleione* Versailles g. 'Bucklebury', where Versailles is the grex name and 'Bucklebury' is a selected **cultivar**.

HARDINESS

Hardiness ratings are shown for **Award of Garden Merit** plants. The categories used are as follows:

H1 = plants requiring heated glass in the British Isles

H2 = plants requiring unheated glass in the British Isles

H3 = plants hardy outside in some regions of the British Isles or in particular situations, or which, while usually grown outside in summer, need frost-free protection in winter (eg. dahlias)

H4 = plants hardy throughout the British Isles

H1-2, H2-3, H3-4 = plants intermediate between the two ratings given

H1+3 = requiring heated glass; may be grown outside in summer

HYBRIDS

Some species, when grown together, in the wild or in cultivation, are found to interbreed and form hybrids. In some instances a hybrid name is coined, for example hybrids between *Primula hirsuta* and *P. minima* are given the name *Primula* × *forsteri*, the multiplication sign indicating hybrid origin. Hybrid formulae that quote the parentage of the hybrid are used where a unique name has not been coined, for example *Rhododendron calophytum* × *R. praevernum.* Hybrids between different genera are also possible, for example × *Mahoberberis* is the name given to hybrids between *Mahonia* and *Berberis.*

There are also a few special-case hybrids called graft hybrids, where the tissues of two plants are physically rather than genetically mixed. These are indicated by an addition rather than a multiplication sign, so *Laburnum* + *Cytisus* becomes +*Laburnocytisus.*

ICNCP

The ICNCP is the International Code of Nomenclature for Cultivated Plants. First published in 1959, the most recent edition currently dates from 1995.

Cultivar names that do not conform to this Code, and for which there is no valid alternative, are flagged I (for invalid). The commonest sorts of invalid name are generally those that are wholly or partly in Latin (not permissible since 1959, e.g. 'Pixie Alba', 'Superba', 'Variegata') and those that use a Latin generic name as a cultivar name (eg. *Rosa* 'Corylus', *Viola* 'Geranium'). Other articles of the Code have been discussed in previous editions of the *RHS Plant Finder* in a *Question of Nomenclature.* The next edition of the Code, which will be published in the spring of 2004, will become less restrictive with regard to certain articles and this will be implemented for the next edition of the *RHS Plant Finder* (2005), but is not reflected in this edition.

NOMENCLATURE NOTES

The **Nomenclature Notes**, starting on p.23, give further information for names that are complex or may be confusing. See also **Advisory Panel on Nomenclature and Taxonomy**.

PLANT BREEDERS' RIGHTS

Plants covered by an active grant of Plant Breeders' Rights (PBR) are indicated throughout the Plant Directory. Grants indicated are those awarded by both UK and EU Plant Variety Rights offices. Because grants can both come into force and lapse at any time, this book can only represent the situation at one point in time, but it is hoped that this will act as a useful guide to growers and gardeners. UK grants represent the position as of the end of December 2003 and EU grants as of the end of October 2003.

To obtain PBR protection, a new plant must be registered and pass tests for distinctness, uniformity and stability under an approved name. This approved name, under the rules of the **ICNCP**, established by a legal process, has to be regarded as the cultivar name. Increasingly however, these approved names are a code or "nonsense" name and are therefore often unpronounceable and meaningless, so the plants are given other names designed to attract sales when they are released. These secondary names are often referred to as selling names but are officially termed **trade designations**.

The *RHS Plant Finder* takes no responsibility for ensuring that nurseries selling plants with PBR are licensed to do so.

For further information on UK PBR contact:

Mr R Greenaway
Plant Variety Rights Office,
White House Lane,
Huntingdon Road,
Cambridge CB3 0LF
Tel: (01223) 342396
Fax: (01223) 342386.
Website: www.defra.gov.uk/planth/pvs/pbrguide.htm

For details of plants covered by EU Community Rights contact the Community Plant Variety Office (CPVO):

Office Communautaire des Variétés Végétales,
PO Box 62141,
3 Boulevard Maréchal Foch,
F-49021 Angers,
Cedex 02, France
Tel: 00 33 (02) 41 25 64 00
Fax: 00 33 (02) 41 25 64 10
Website: www.cpvo.eu.int

REVERSE SYNONYMS

It is likely that users of this book will come across names in certain genera that they did not expect to find. This may be because species have been transferred from another genus (or genera). In the list of **Reverse Synonyms** on p.33, the name on the left-hand side is that of an accepted genus to which species have been transferred from the genus on the right. Sometimes all species will have been transferred, but in many cases only a few will be affected. Consulting **Reverse Synonyms** enables users to find the genera from which species have been transferred. Where the right-hand genus is found in the Plant Directory, the movement of species becomes clear through the cross-references in the nursery code column.

SELLING NAMES

See **Trade Designations**

SERIES

With seed-raised plants, series have become increasingly popular. A series contains a number of similar cultivars, but differs from a **Cultivar Group** in that it is a marketing device, with cultivars added to create a range of flower colours in plants of similar habit. Individual colour elements within a species may be represented by slightly different cultivars over the years. Series names are styled similarly to **Cultivar Groups**.

SPECIES

See under **Botanical Names**

SUBSPECIES

See under **Botanical Names**

SYNONYMS

Although the ideal is for each species or cultivar to have only one name, anyone dealing with plants soon comes across a situation where one plant has received two or more names, or two plants have received the same name. In each case, only one name and application, for reasons of precision and stability, can be regarded as correct. Additional names are known as synonyms. Further information on synonyms and why plants change names is available in *Guide to Plant Names*. See the introduction to this glossary for details of how to request a copy.

See also **Reverse Synonyms**.

TRADE DESIGNATIONS

A **trade designation** is the name used to market a plant when the cultivar name is considered unsuitable for selling purposes. It is styled in a different typeface and without single quotation marks.

In the case of **Plant Breeders' Rights** it is a legal requirement for the cultivar name to appear with the trade designation on a label at the point of sale. Most plants are sold under only one trade designation, but some, especially roses, are sold under a number of names, particularly when cultivars are introduced from other countries. Usually, the correct cultivar name is the only way to ensure that the same plant is not bought unwittingly under two or more different trade designations. The *RHS Plant Finder* follows the recommendations of the **ICNCP** when dealing with trade designations and PBR. These are always to quote the cultivar name and trade designation together and to style the trade designation in a different typeface, without single quotation marks.

TRANSLATIONS

When a cultivar name is translated from the language of first publication, the translation is regarded as a **trade designation** and styled accordingly. We endeavour to recognise the original cultivar name in every case and to give an English translation where it is in general use.

VARIEGATED PLANTS

Following a suggestion from the Variegated Plant Group of the Hardy Plant Society, a (v) is cited after those plants which are "variegated". The dividing line between variegation and less distinct colour marking is necessarily arbitrary and plants with light veins, pale, silver or dark zones, or leaves flushed in paler colours, are not shown as being variegated unless there is an absolutely sharp distinction between paler and darker zones.

For further details of the Variegated Plant Group, please write to:

Mrs Bee Newbold,
Netherbury, 36 Worgret Road,
Wareham, Dorset BH20 4PN

VARIETY

See under **Botanical Names and Cultivar**

> *'The question of nomenclature is always a vexed one. The only thing certain is, that it is impossible to please everyone.'*
>
> W.J. BEAN – PREFACE TO FIRST EDITION OF *Trees & Shrubs Hardy in the British Isles*

A Question of Plant Breeding

The Horticultural Advisory Department at Wisley often receives enquiries from RHS members who think they have found a new plant, perhaps a seedling or a sport, in their garden: if it proves garden-worthy, what should they do to find a nursery outlet for it, perhaps even to take out plant breeders' rights (PBR)? To set the subject in context, it is perhaps worth examining the way new plants appear in the horticultural trade and assessing the amateur's role in this.

From its early years, every new edition of *Plant Finder* has included about 4,000-7,000 plants that were not in previous editions. Fifteen years ago, the vast majority of these, perhaps 75%, would have been species or cultivars that had lurked in cultivation for decades. Of the remainder, the majority would be new plants deliberately raised by nurseries, with "big" genera such as *Rosa* predominating. Recent years have seen a change, with many major nurseries and seed houses undertaking ambitious breeding programmes and amateurs becoming more aware that the lucky finds in their garden might have some potential and that plant breeding might not be so difficult after all. Now, the proportion of plants that are of very recent origin is higher, perhaps as much as 75%, and plants that have originated in the gardens of amateurs much more frequently find their way into the pages of the *RHS Plant Finder*.

Nowadays, every major seed house has to have its own set of, for instance, *Argyranthemum*, *Calibrachoa*, *Diascia*, *Osteospermum*, *Petunia* and *Verbena* cultivars, propagated by the 100,000 and sold as tiny, vegetatively propagated plants in plugs, to be grown on for sale in garden centres and even supermarkets. More genera are being added to the list each year, for instance *Angelonia*, *Sutera* and *Bidens*. This proliferation of new plants, most of them of a very high standard, makes the RHS Trials at Wisley all the more valuable, especially for genera such as *Calibrachoa* whose qualities and cultural foibles are not yet fully known to gardeners in these islands. The cut-flower trade has also been more active in producing many new cultivars, quite a number of which find their way into *RHS Plant Finder*, including the likes of *Alstroemeria*, *Aster*, *Chrysanthemum*, *Gypsophila*, *Solidago* and perpetual-flowering carnations.

Where does the amateur fit into all this? It is true that the more highly bred a hybrid cultivar of a genus such as *Rosa* or *Chrysanthemum* is, the less likely it is that any of its seed-raised offspring will be garden-worthy: the success rate for raising new roses from seed, even when the parents are chosen with exceptional care and knowledge, is extremely low. Better, then, for gardeners to concentrate on primary hybrids, the offspring of two species, usually of the same genus. Perhaps the majority of new plants raised by amateurs come about in this way: the parent plants grow near each other and, provided the hoe is used sparingly, any different-looking offspring can be allowed to grow on until they flower. This is how many of our best-loved and oldest garden plants arose, in times when there was virtually no knowledge of plant breeding and genetics: when botanic gardens were first created and related plants were grown together in Order Beds, sowing their seed often resulted in hybrids. This is how we believe the Dutch crocus, *C.* × *luteus* 'Golden Yellow' and the cabbage rose, *Rosa* × *centifolia*, came to appear in Holland in the late 16th century.

Two programmes that deservedly won the RHS's Reginald Cory Memorial Cup for plant breeding recently have aspects that could be applied to many simple projects to create new plants. Hector Harrison's pioneering work with *Diascia* accurately identified a genus that had been little used by breeders but that had great potential for producing attractive garden plants in a fairly wide range of flower colours. With only a small greenhouse, a garden of moderate size and boundless application and enthusiasm, Hector turned what had been a genus of relatively minor interest into an essential component of the summer garden. Since his death, even more stunning and floriferous cultivars have continued to appear, building on his pioneering work.

Dan Heims won the Cory Cup for his work on *Heuchera* but has applied his techniques to other genera and to intergeneric hybrids such as × *Heucherella*. He started by identifying good qualities in certain species that rarely if ever had been brought together in a hybrid cultivar. *Heuchera micrantha* was chosen for its ruffled leaves, rhizomatous forms, huge flower spikes and vigour and *H. richardsonii* for hardiness. Perhaps the most important parent was *H. americana*, selected for its shade tolerance, tall flower spikes, evergreen leathery foliage with silvery highlights and resistance to mildew and insects. Dan collected together an impressive range of variants of these chosen species and began to produce hybrids that were rigorously trialled before being named, patented, put into tissue culture production and marketed. The scale of this venture and the thoroughness of the process leading to large-scale production are not likely to be the prime objects of the amateur. However, the lessons of choosing suitable parent species and seeking out the very finest forms are equally relevant to gardeners who fancy having a bash at creating new plants on a much less adventurous scale.

Because they can differ substantially from any existing species, bigeneric hybrids offer exciting prospects for the plant breeder. Dan Heims's success with × *Heucherella* has already been touched on and there must be hundreds of other possible combinations of related genera. I often think that *Argyranthemum* might cross with some other genera once included in *Chrysanthemum* to produce plants with a wider range of colours and markings, perhaps being hardier too.

Another sort of new plant that gardeners might come across is the sport, a spontaneous mutation from the plant that bears it, differing in one or more characteristics. It might have a different flower colour, double instead of single blooms, variegated instead of all-green leaves or a dwarf habit, as is the case for witches' broom, a relatively common mutation on conifers. Sports seem to be more common on highly bred plants, such as roses, chrysanthemums and perpetual-flowering carnations and also occur frequently as a result of micropropagation. In fact, gardeners are as likely to spot promising new sports among the stock at a garden centre as in their own garden.

Whether the new plant is a deliberately-raised hybrid, a chance seedling or a new sport, the gardener's first task is to ensure it is safely in cultivation. Most new plants are lost before they are fully established, susceptible while young to a single chomp from a passing slug and plants are never more in need of conservation than when they are absolutely new. Propagation is advisable as soon as it is practicable. However, if the new cultivar seems to have exceptional potential, perhaps even for plant breeders' rights, it should not be given away or sold to anyone: this could jeopardize its chances of being granted PBR. Nor, regrettably, should it be left on view if you have a garden open day, to be spirited away by some unscrupulous gardener or nurseryman: tales of loss of control of an outstanding new plant in this way are not uncommon.

Once you have decided that you would like your new plant to be put into production by the nursery trade, perhaps to earn a royalty or flat fee, the time has come to contact a suitable firm that can offer a trialling agreement to protect your rights in the plant. Suitable firms, if they believe your plant is worthy, will deal with an application for PBR on your behalf. The RHS Horticultural Advisory team keeps a record of such firms and can provide addresses and contact details on request.

Especially if you think your plant has immense potential, it is not a good idea to ask just any nursery if they would like to take it on. The number of firms that have wide experience of trialling, marketing and obtaining PBR for new plants is relatively small; only these can protect your interests fully. Entering into an agreement with firms that might not have the experience or integrity to serve your interests to the full is risky. It is wise to enter into such arrangements with as much circumspection as if you were buying a house.

One example of such a firm is the British Association Representing Breeders (BARB) **(see below)**. BARB, as with others, will protect the discoverer's best interests, advising on and overseeing the whole process. They will put the discoverer in contact with a major nursery (a member of BARB) with a specialism in that genus. They will monitor dealings between discoverer and producer, so that both parties' interests are protected, making sure that only the chosen producer has access to the plant. After the plant has been trialled by the producer (usually for 2-4 years), they will assist with PBR and royalty collection for the following 25 years.

The trialling will assess the plant's commercial viability but will also look at the sort of factors that determine whether the plant can be granted PBR. To achieve this, it must pass a "DUS" test, so named from the three main criteria that it must meet – that is, that it must be distinct, uniform and stable. It will not be given PBR if it cannot be distinguished from a pre-existing cultivar, if there is significant variation within the batch under test or if, for instance, in a variegated plant, there is a significant amount of reversion to all green.

Of course, the majority of new plants will not be sufficiently commercial to make taking out PBR cost-effective. In this case, your plant might still find its niche in the nursery trade but, because the financial benefits are less, the need to find the most commercial nursery will be less pressing. You might be perfectly happy to place your plant with a nursery that you know will look after it and keep it in production for some time; you might also find one that is willing to give a royalty or flat fee, even without PBR.

The naming of your plant might be a cause for concern and it is true that the producer is likely to want a glamorous commercial name rather than one that commemorates, say, a friend or member of the family. It is preferable to follow the rules set out in *The International Code of Nomenclature of Cultivated Plants*, though names of plants with PBR are classed as "statutory names" and are exempt from the Code. Producers will be wary of taking on production of your plant if you insist on calling it 'Mrs H.C. Clutterbuck' when they want to call it 'Silver Wedding' or something else deemed to be more commercial. Nurseries have a good idea of the difference a catchy name can make to plant sales.

But it is *your* plant and if it is important to you, to the exclusion of financial gain, to commemorate someone dear to you in the name of the plant, then you should insist on it. But for all this, the very best plants will sell almost as many whatever they are called.

So if you would like to have a go at creating new plants, or if you think that plant that popped up at the bottom of the garden might be different, there are plenty of people to help you. Even spotting and evaluating chance sports and seedlings, in the pots at the garden centre if not at home, can result in some cracking good new varieties. Plant breeding does not have to be hard and can be great fun.

Tony Lord, January 2004

British Association Representing Breeders (BARB)
General Manager Ian Kennedy
35a Upper Market,
Fakenham,
Norfolk NR21 9BX
Tel: (01328) 851950
Fax: (01328) 851960.
Email: barb@barbuk.force9.co.uk

SYMBOLS AND ABBREVIATIONS

SYMBOLS APPEARING TO THE LEFT OF THE NAME

*	Name not validated. Not listed in the appropriate International Registration Authority checklist nor in works cited in the Bibliography. For fuller discussion see p.7
I	Invalid name. See *International Code of Botanical Nomenclature 2000* and *International Code of Nomenclature for Cultivated Plants 1995*. For fuller discussion see p.7
N	Refer to Nomenclature Notes on p.23
§	Plant listed elsewhere in the Plant Directory under a synonym
x	Hybrid genus
+	Graft hybrid genus

SYMBOLS APPEARING TO THE RIGHT OF THE NAME

✿	National Council for the Conservation of Plants and Gardens (NCCPG) National Plant Collection® exists for all or part of this genus. Provisional Collections appear in brackets. Full details of the NCCPG Plant Collections are found in the *National Plant Collections® Directory 2004–2005* available from: www.nccpg.com or NCCPG, RHS Garden, Wisley, Woking, Surrey GU23 6QP
🏆H4	The Royal Horticultural Society's Award of Garden Merit, see p.7
(d)	double-flowered
(F)	Fruit
(f)	female
(m)	male
(v)	variegated plant, see p.11
PBR	Plant Breeders Rights see p.9
new	New plant entry in this edition

For abbreviations relating to individual genera see **Classification of Genera** p.28
For **Collectors' References** see p.20
For symbols used in the **Nurseries** section see p.784

SYMBOLS AND ABBREVIATIONS USED AS PART OF THE NAME

×	hybrid species
aff.	affinis (allied to)
agg.	aggregate, a single name used to cover a group of very similar plants, regarded by some as separate species
ambig.	ambiguous, a name used by two authors for different plants and where it is unclear which is being offered
cl.	clone
cv(s)	cultivar(s)
f.	forma (botanical form)
g.	grex
sp.	species
subsp.	subspecies
subvar.	subvarietas (botanical subvariety)
var.	varietas (botanical variety)

IT IS NOT WITHIN THE REMIT OF THIS BOOK TO CHECK **that nurseries are applying the right names to the right plants or to ensure nurseries selling plants with Plant Breeders' Rights are licensed to do so.**

Please, never use an old edition

Plants

Whatever plant you are looking for, maybe an old favourite or a more unusual cultivar, search here for a list of the suppliers that are closest to you.

How to Use the Plant Directory

Nursery Codes

Look up the plant you require in the alphabetical Plant Directory. Against each plant you will find one or more four-letter codes, for example GKir, each code represents one nursery offering that plant. The first letter of each code indicates the main area of the country in which the nursery is situated. For this geographical key, refer to the **Nursery Codes and Symbols** on p.784.

Turn to the **Nursery Details by Code** starting on p.788 where, in alphabetical order of codes, you will find details of each nursery which offers the plant in question. If you wish to visit any nursery, you may find its location on one of the maps (following p.916). Please note, however, that not all nurseries, especially mail order only nurseries, choose to be shown on the maps. For a fuller explanation of how to use the nursery listings please turn to p.785. **Always check that the nursery you select has the plant in stock before you set out.**

Plants with more than 30 Suppliers

In some cases, against the plant name you will see the term 'more than 30 suppliers' instead of a nursery code. If we were to include every plant listed by all nurseries, the *RHS Plant Finder* would become unmanageably bulky. We therefore ask nurseries to restrict their entries to those plants that are not already well represented. As a result, if more than 30 nurseries offer any plant the Directory gives no nursery codes and the plant is listed instead as having 'more than 30 suppliers'. You should have little difficulty in locating these in local nurseries or garden centres. However, if you are unable to find such plants, we will be pleased to send a full list of all the nurseries that we have on file as stockists. To obtain a list, please see the Introduction on p.4.

Finding Fruit, Vegetables and Herbs

You will need to search for these by their botanical names. Common names are cross-referenced to their botanical names in the Plant Directory.

If you have Difficulty Finding your Plant

If you cannot immediately find the plant you seek, look through the various species of the genus. You may be using an incomplete name. The problem is most likely to arise in very large genera such as *Phlox* where there are a number of possible species, each with a large number of cultivars. A search through the whole genus may well bring success. Please note that, for space reasons, the following are not listed in the Plant Directory: annuals, orchids, except hardy terrestrial orchids; cacti, except hardy cacti.

Cross-references

It may be that the plant name you seek is a synonym. Our intention is to list nursery codes only against the correct botanical name. Where you find a synonym you will be cross-referred to the correct name. Occasionally you may find that the correct botanical name to which you have been referred is not listed. This is because it was last listed in an earlier edition as explained below.

Plants Last Listed in Earlier Editions

It may be that the plant you are seeking has no known suppliers and is thus not listed.

The loss of a plant name from the Directory may arise for a number of reasons – the supplier may have gone out of business, or may not have responded to our latest questionnaire and has therefore been removed from the book. Such plants may well be still available but we have no current knowledge of their whereabouts. Alternatively, some plants may have been misnamed by nurseries in previous editions, but are now appearing under their correct name.

To obtain a listing of plants last listed in earlier editions please see the Introduction on p.4.

Please, never use an old edition

USING THE PLANT DIRECTORY

The main purpose of the Plant Directory is to help the reader correctly identify the plant they seek and find its stockist. Each nursery has a unique identification code which appears to the right of the plant name. Turn to Nursery Details by Code (p.788) for the address, opening times and other details of the nursery. The first letter of each nursery code denotes its geographical region. Turn to the map on p.784 to find your region code and then identify the nurseries in your area.

Another purpose of the Directory is to provide more information about the plant through the symbols and other information. For example, if it has an alternative names, is new to this edition or has received the RHS Award of Garden Merit.

ABBREVIATIONS
To save space a dash indicates that the previous heading is repeated. If written out in full the name would be Euonymus alatus *'Fire Ball'.*

DESCRIPTIVE TERM
See p.8.

SYMBOLS TO THE LEFT OF THE NAME
Provides information about the name of the plant. See p.15 for the key.

NEW
Plant new to this edition.

SYMBOLS TO THE RIGHT OF THE NAME
Tells you more about the plant itself, e.g. (v) *indicates that the plant is variegated,* (F) *= fruit. See p.15 for the key.*

SELLING NAMES
See p.10.

Euonymus *(Celastraceae)*

	Name	Nursery codes
	B&L 12543	EPla EWes
	B&SWJ 4457	WPGP
	alatus ♀H4	More than 30 suppliers
	- B&SWJ 8794	WCru
	- var. ***apterus***	EPfP
	- Chicago Fire	see *E. alatus* 'Timber Creek'
	- 'Ciliodentatus'	see *E. alatus* 'Compactus'
§	- 'Compactus' ♀H4	More than 30 suppliers
	- 'Fire Ball'	EPfP
	- Little Moses = 'Odom' **new**	MBlu
•	- 'Macrophyllus' **new**	EPfP
	- 'Rudy Haag'	CPMA EPfP
	- 'Select'	see *E. alatus* 'Fire Ball'
§	- 'Timber Creek'	CPMA EPfP GKir MBlu NLar
	americanus	CBot EPfP GIBF MBlu NLar
	- narrow-leaved	EPfP NLar
	atropurpureus	EPfP GKir
	bungeanus	CMCN EPfP EPla NLar
	- 'Dart's Pride'	CPMA EPfP NLar
	- 'Fireflame' **new**	NLar
•	- var. ***mongolicus***	EPfP
	- 'Pendulus'	EPfP GKir MBlu
	- var. ***semipersistens***	CPMA EPla
	carnosus	EPfP NLar
	'Copper Wire' **new**	SPoG
	cornutus var. ***quinquecornutus***	CFil CPMA EBee EPfP GKir MAsh MBlu NLar SIFN WPGP WPat WCru
•	***cymosus*** B&SWJ 8989 **new**	
	'Den Haag'	EPfP
	echinatus	EPfP EPla
	- BL&M 306	SLon
	europaeus	CArn CCVT CDoC CDul CLnd CRWN CSam CWib EBee ECrN ELan EPfP EPla GIBF GKir LBuc MHer MSwo NLar NWea SCoo SRms SWvt SYvo WDin WFar WHar WHer WMou XPep
	- f. ***albus***	CBot CPMA CTho EPfP LTwo
	- 'Atropurpureus'	CMCN CTho EPfP GKir MBlu MBri NLar SIFN
	- 'Atrorubens'	CPMA
	- 'Aucubifolius' (v)	CFil EPfP WBcn
•	- 'Aureus'	CNat
•	- f. ***bulgaricus***	EPfP
	- 'Chrysophyllus'	EPfP MBlu
	- 'Howard'	EPfP
	- var. ***intermedius***	ENot EPfP MBlu NLar WWes
	- 'Miss Pinkie'	CEnd CMCN GKir
	- 'Red Cascade' ♀H4	More than 30 suppliers
	- 'Scarlet Wonder'	CPMA EPfP NLar
	- 'Thornhayes'	CTho
	farreri	see *E. nanus*
	fimbriatus	CBcs EPfP
	fortunei Blondy = 'Interbolwi' PBR (v)	More than 30 suppliers

♀H4
This plant has received the RHS Award of Garden Merit. See p.7.

CROSS-REFERENCES
Directs you to the correct name of the plant and the nursery codes. See p.18.

NURSERY CODE
A unique code identifying each nursery. Turn to p.788 for details of the nurseries.

MORE THAN 30 SUPPLIERS
Indicates that more than 30 Plant Finder nurseries supply the plant, and it may be available locally. See p.18.

PBR
Plant Breeders' Rights. See p.9.

SUPPLEMENTARY KEYS TO THE DIRECTORY

COLLECTORS' REFERENCES

Abbreviations following a plant name, refer to the collector(s) of the plant. These abbreviations are expanded below, with a collector's name or expedition title. For a fuller explanation, see p.8.

A&JW	A. & J. Watson
A&L	Ala, A.; Lancaster, Roy
AB&S	Archibald, James; Blanchard, John W; Salmon, M.
AC	Clark, Alan J.
AC&H	Apold, J.; Cox, Peter; Hutchison, Peter
AC&W	Albury; Cheese, M.; Watson, J.M.
ACE	AGS Expedition to China (1994)
ACL	Leslie, Alan C.
AGS/ES	AGS Expedition to Sikkim (1983)
AGSJ	AGS Expedition to Japan (1988)
Airth	Airth, Murray
Akagi	Akagi Botanical Garden
AL&JS	Sharman, Joseph L.; Leslie, Alan C.
ARG	Argent, G.C.G.
B L.	Beer, Len
B&L	Brickell, Christopher D.; Leslie, Alan C.
B&M & BM	Brickell, Christopher D.; Mathew, Brian
B&S	Bird P. & Salmon M.
B&SWJ	Wynn-Jones, Bleddyn; Wynn-Jones, Susan
BB	Bartholomew, B.
BC	Chudziak, W.
BC&W	Beckett; Cheese, M.; Watson, J.M.
Beavis	Beavis, Derek S.
Berry	Berry, P.
Berry & Brako	Berry, P. & Brako, Lois
BL&M	University of Bangor Expedition to NE Nepal
BM	Mathew, Brian F.
BM&W	Binns, David L.; Mason, M.; Wright, A.
Breedlove	Breedlove, D.
BR	Rushbrooke, Ben
BS	Smith, Basil
BSBE	Bowles Scholarship Botanical Expedition (1963)
BSSS	Crûg Expedition, Jordan 1991
Bu	Bubert, S.
Burtt	Burtt, Brian L.
C	Cole, Desmond T.
C&C	Cox, P.A. & Cox, K.N.E.
C&Cu	Cox, K.N.E. & Cubey, J.
C&H	Cox, Peter; Hutchison, Peter
C&K	Chamberlain & Knott
C&R	Christian & Roderick
C&S	Clark, Alan; Sinclair, Ian W.J.
C&V	K.N.E. Cox & S. Vergera
C&W	Cheese, M.; Watson, J.M.
CC	Chadwell, Christopher
CC&H	Chamberlain, David F.; Cox, Peter; Hutchison, P.
CC&McK	Chadwell, Christopher; McKelvie, A.
CC&MR	Chadwell, Christopher; Ramsay
CCH&H	Chamberlain, D.F.; Cox, P.; Hutchison, P.; Hootman, S.
CCH&H	Chamberlain, Cox, Hootman & Hutchison
CD&R	Compton, J.; D'Arcy, J.; Rix, E.M.
CDB	Brickell, Christopher D.
CDC	Coode, Mark J.E.; Dockrill, Alexander
CDC&C	Compton, D'Arcy, Christopher & Coke
CDPR	Compton, D'Arcy, Pope & Rix
CE&H	Christian, P.J.; Elliott; Hoog
CEE	Chengdu Edinburgh Expedition China 1991
CGW	Grey-Wilson, Christopher
CH&M	Cox, P.; Hutchison, P.; Maxwell-MacDonald, D.
CHP&W	Kashmir Botanical Expedition
CL	Lovell, Chris
CLD	Chungtien, Lijiang & Dali Exped. China 1990
CM&W	Cheese M., Mitchel J. & Watson, J.
CN&W	Clark; Neilson; Wilson
CNDS	Nelson, C. & Sayers D.
Cooper	Cooper, R.E.
Cox	Cox, Peter A.
CPC	Cobblewood Plant Collection
CPN	Compton, James
CSE	Cyclamen Society Expedition (1990)
CT	Teune, Carla
Dahl	Dahl, Sally

DBG	Denver Botanic Garden, Colorado
DC	Cheshire, David
DF	Fox, D.
DJH	Hinkley, Dan
DJHC	Hinkley China
DM	Millais, David
Doleshy	Doleshy, F.L.
DS&T	Drake, Sharman J.; Thompson
DWD	Rose, D.
ECN	Nelson, E. Charles
EDHCH	Hammond, Eric D.
EGM	Millais, T.
EKB	Balls, Edward K.
EM	East Malling Research Station
EMAK	Edinburgh Makalu Expedition (1991)
EMR	Rix, E.Martyn
EN	Needham, Edward F.
ENF	Fuller, E. Nigel
ETE	Edinburgh Taiwan Expedition (1993)
ETOT	Kirkham, T.S.; Flanagan, Mark
F	Forrest, G.
F&W	Watson, J.; Flores, A.
Farrer	Farrer, Reginald
FK	Kinmonth, Fergus W.
FMB	Bailey, F.M.
G	Gardner, Martin F.
G&K	Gardner, Martin F.; Knees, Sabina G.
G&P	Gardner, Martin F.; Page, Christopher N.
GDJ	Dumont, Gerard
GG	Gusman, G.
GS	Sherriff, George
Green	Green, D.
Guitt	Guittoneau, G.G.
Guiz	Guizhou Expedition (1985)
GWJ	Goddard, Sally; Wynne-Jones, Bleddyn & Susan
G-W&P	Grey-Wilson, Christopher; Phillips
H	Huggins, Paul
H&B	Hilliard, Olive M.; Burtt, Brian L.
H&D	Howick, C.; Darby
H&M	Howick, Charles; McNamara, William A.
H&W	Hedge, Ian C.; Wendelbo, Per W.
Harry Smith	Smith, K.A.Harry
Hartside	Hartside Nursery
HCM	Heronswood Expedition to Chile, 1998
HH&K	Hannay, S&S & Kingsbury, N
HLMS	Springate, L.S.
HM&S	Halliwell, B., Mason, M. & Smallcombe
HOA	Hoog, Anton
Hummel	Hummel, D.
HW&E	Wendelbo, Per; Hedge, I.; Ekberg, L.
HWEL	Hirst, J.Michael; Webster, D.
HWJ	Crûg Heronswood Joint Expedition
HWJCM	Crûg Heronswood Expedition
HWJK	Crûg Heronswood Expedition, East Nepal 2002
HZ	Zetterlund, Henrik
ICE	Instituto de Investigaciónes Ecológicas Chiloé & RBGE
IDS	International Dendrological Society
J&JA	Archibald, James; Archibald, Jennifer
J. Jurasek	Jurasek, J.
JCA	Archibald, James
JE	Jack Elliott
JJ	Jackson, J.
JJ&JH	Halda, J.; Halda, J.
JJH	Halda, Joseph J.
JLS	Sharman, J.L.
JMT	Mann Taylor, J.
JN	Nielson, Jens
JR	Russell, J.
JRM	Marr, John
JW	Watson, J.M.
K	Kirkpatrick, George
K&LG	Gillanders, Kenneth; Gillanders, L.
K&Mc	Kirkpatrick, George; McBeath, Ronald J.D.
K&P	Josef Kopec, Milan Prasil
K&T	Kurashige, Y.; Tsukie, S.
KC	Cox, Kenneth
KEKE	Kew/Edinburgh Kanchenjunga Expedition (1989)
KGB	Kunming/Gothenburg Botanical Expedition (1993)
KR	Rushforth, K.D.
KRW	Wooster, K.R. (distributed after his death by Kath Dryden)
KW	Kingdon-Ward, F.
L	Lancaster, Roy C.
L&S	Ludlow, Francis; Sherriff, George
LA	Long Ashton Research Station clonal selection scheme
LEG	Lesotho Edinburgh/Gothenburg Expedition (1997)
Lismore	Lismore Nursery, Breeder's Number
LM&S	Leslie, Mattern & Sharman
LP	Palmer, W.J.L.
LS&E	Ludlow, Frank; Sherriff, George; Elliott, E. E.
LS&H	Ludlow, Frank; Sherriff, George; Hicks, J. H.
LS&T	Ludlow, Frank; Sherriff, George; Taylor, George
M&PS	Mike & Polly Stone
M&T	Mathew; Tomlinson
Mac&W	McPhail & Watson
McB	McBeath, R.J.D.
McLaren	McLaren, H.D.
MDM	Myers, Michael D.
MESE	Alpine Garden Society Expedition, Greece 1999
MF	Foster, Maurice
MH	Heasman, Matthew T.
MK	Kammerlander, Michael

MP	Pavelka, Mojmir
MPF	Frankis, M.P.
MS	Salmon, M.
MS&CL	Salmon, M.; Lovell, C.
MSF	Fillan, M.S.
NJM	Macer, N.J.
NNS	Ratko, Ron
NS	Turland, Nick
NVFDE	Northern Vietnam First Darwin Expedition
Og	Ogisu, Mikinori
P&C	Paterson, David S.; Clarke, Sidney
P&W	Polastri; Watson, J. M.
PB	Bird, Peter
PC&H	Pattison, G.; Catt, P.; Hickson, M.
PD	Davis, Peter H.
PF	Furse, Paul
PJC	Christian, Paul J.
PJC&AH	P.J. Christian & A. Hogg
Polunin	Polunin, Oleg
Pras	Prasil, M.
PS&W	Polunin, Oleg; Sykes, William; Williams, John
PW	Wharton, Peter
R	Rock, J.F.C.
RB	Brown, R.
RBS	Brown, Ray, Sakharin Island
RCB/Arg	Brown, Robert, Argentina, 2002
RCB/Eq	Brown, Robert, Ecuador, 1988
RCB/TQ	Brown, Robert, Turkey 2001
RH	Hancock, R.
RMRP	Rocky Mountain Rare Plants, Denver, Colorado
RS	Suckow, Reinhart
RV	Richard Valder
S&B	Blanchard, J.W.; Salmon, M.
S&F	Salmon, M. & Fillan, M.
S&L	Sinclair, Ian W.J.; Long, David G.
S&SH	Sheilah and Spencer Hannay
Sandham	Sandham, John
SB&L	Salmon, Bird and Lovell
SBEC	Sino-British Expedition to Cangshan
SBEL	Sino-British Lijiang Expedition
SBQE	Sino-British Expedition to Quinghai
Sch	Schilling, Anthony D.
SD	Sashal Dayal
SDR	Rankin, Stella; Rankin, David
SEH	Hootman, Steve
SEP	Swedish Expedition to Pakistan
SF	Forde, P.
SG	Salmon, M. & Guy, P.
SH	Hannay, Spencer
Sich	Simmons, Erskine, Howick & Mcnamara
SLIZE	Swedish-Lithuanian-Iranian Zagros Expedition to Iran (May 1988)
SOJA	Kew / Quarryhill Expedition to Southern Japan
SS&W	Stainton, J.D.Adam; Sykes, William; Williams, John
SSNY	Sino-Scottish Expedition to NW Yunnan (1992)
T	Taylor, Nigel P.
T&K	Taylor, Nigel P.; Knees, Sabina
TS&BC	Smythe, T and Cherry, B
TSS	Spring Smyth, T.L.M.
TW	Tony Weston
USDAPI	US Department of Agriculture Plant Index Number
USDAPQ	US Dept. of Agriculture Plant Quarantine Number
USNA	United States National Arboretum
VHH	Vernon H. Heywood
W	Wilson, Ernest H.
WM	McLewin, William
Woods	Woods, Patrick J.B.
Wr	Wraight, David & Anke
Yu	Yu, Tse-tsun

NOMENCLATURE NOTES

These notes refer to plants in the Plant Directory that are marked with a 'N' to the left of the name. 'Bean Supplement' refers to W.J. Bean *Trees & Shrubs Hardy in the British Isles* (Supplement to the 8th edition) edited by D L Clarke 1988.

Acer davidii **'Ernest Wilson' and *A. davidii* 'George Forrest'**
These cultivars should be grafted in order to retain the characteristics of the original clones. However, many plants offered under these names are seed-raised.

Acer palmatum **'Sango-kaku'/ 'Senkaki'**
Two or more clones are offered under these names. *A. palmatum* 'Eddisbury' is similar with brighter coral stems.

Achillea ptarmica **The Pearl Group/ *A. ptarmica* (The Pearl Group) 'Boule de Neige' / *A. ptarmica* (The Pearl Group) 'The Pearl'**
In the recent trial of achilleas at Wisley, only one of the several stocks submitted as 'The Pearl' matched the original appearance of this plant according to Graham Stuart Thomas, this being from Wisley's own stock. At rather less than 60cm (2ft), this needed little support, being the shortest of the plants bearing this name, with slightly grey, not glossy dark green, leaves and a non-invasive habit. This has been designated as the type for this cultivar and only this clone should bear the cultivar name 'The Pearl'. The Pearl Group covers all other double-flowered clones of this species, including seed-raised plants which are markedly inferior, sometimes scarcely double, often invasive and usually needing careful staking. It has been claimed that 'The Pearl' was a re-naming of Lemoine's 'Boule de Neige' but not all authorities agree: all plants submitted to the Wisley trial as 'Boule de Neige' were different from each other, not the same clone as Wisley's 'The Pearl' and referrable to The Pearl Group.

Anemone magellanica
According to *The European Garden Flora*, this is a variant of the very variable *A. multifida*.

Anemone nemorosa **'Alba Plena'**
This name is used for several double white forms including *A. nemorosa* 'Flore Pleno' and *A. nemorosa* 'Vestal'.

Artemisia granatensis **hort.**
Possibly a variant of *A. absinthium*.

Artemisia ludoviciana **var. *latiloba* / *A. ludoviciana* 'Valerie Finnis'**
Leaves of the former are glabrous at maturity, those of the latter are not.

Artemisia stelleriana **'Boughton Silver'**
This was thought to be the first validly published name for this plant, 'Silver Brocade' having been published earlier but invalidly in an undated publication. However, an earlier valid publication for the cultivar name 'Mori' has subsequently been found for the same plant. A proposal to conserve 'Boughton Silver' has been tabled because of its more widespread use.

Aster amellus Violet Queen
It is probable that more than one cultivar is sold under this name.

Aster dumosus
Many of the asters listed under *A. novi-belgii* contain varying amounts of *A. dumosus* blood in their parentage. It is not possible to allocate these to one species or the other and they are therefore listed under *A. novi-belgii*.

Aster × frikartii **'Mönch'**
The true plant is very rare in British gardens. Most plants are another form of *A. × frikartii*, usually 'Wunder von Stäfa'.

Aster novi-belgii
See note under *A. dumosus*. *A. laevis* is also involved in the parentage of most cultivars.

Azara paraguayensis
This is an unpublished name for what seems to be a hybrid between *A. serrata* and *A. lanceolata*.

Berberis buxifolia **'Nana'/ 'Pygmaea'**
See explanation in Bean Supplement.

Berberis stenophylla **'Lemon Queen'**
This sport from 'Pink Pearl' was first named in 1982. The same mutation occurred again and was named 'Cream Showers'. The older name has priority.

Betula utilis **var. *jacquemontii***
Plants are often the clones *B. utilis* var. *jacquemontii* 'Inverleith' or *B. utilis* var. *jacquemontii* 'Doorenbos'

Blechnum chilense/B. tabulare
The true *B. tabulare* has an AGM and is grown in the British Isles but is probably not presently offered by nurseries. This name is often misapplied to *B. chilense*.

Brachyscome
Originally published as *Brachyscome* by Cassini who later revised his spelling to *Brachycome*. The original spelling has been internationally adopted.

Calamagrostis × acutiflora **'Karl Foerster'**
C. × *acutiflora* 'Stricta' differs in being 15cm taller, 10-15 days earlier flowering with a less fluffy inflorescence.

Caltha polypetala
This name is often applied to a large-flowered variant of C. *palustris*. The true species has more (7-10) petals.
Camassia leichtlinii **'Alba'**
The true cultivar has blueish-white, not cream flowers.
Camassia leichtlinii **'Plena'**
This has starry, transparent green-white flowers; creamy-white 'Semiplena' is sometimes offered under this name.
Camellia japonica **'Campbellii'**
This name is used for five cultivars including 'Margherita Coleoni' but applies correctly to Guichard's 1894 cultivar, single to semi-double full rose pink.
Campanula lactiflora **'Alba'**
This refers to the pure white flowered clone, not to blueish- or greyish-white flowered plants, nor to seed-raised plants.
Carex morrowii **'Variegata'**
C. oshimensis 'Evergold' is sometimes sold under this name.
Carya illinoinensis
The correct spelling of this name is discussed in *Baileya*, **10(1)** (1962).
Cassinia retorta
Now included within *C. leptophylla*. A valid infra-specific epithet has yet to be published.
Ceanothus **'Italian Skies'**
Many plants under this name are not true to name.
Chamaecyparis lawsoniana **'Columnaris Glauca'**
Plants under this name might be *C. lawsoniana* 'Columnaris' or a new invalidly named cultivar.
Chamaecyparis pisifera **'Squarrosa Argentea'**
There are two plants of this name, one (valid) with variegated foliage, the other (invalid) with silvery foliage.
Chrysanthemum **'Anastasia Variegated'**
Despite its name, this seems to be derived from 'Mei-kyo', not 'Anastasia'.
Clematis chrysocoma
The true *C. chrysocoma* is a non-climbing erect plant with dense yellow down on the young growth, still uncommon in cultivation.
Clematis montana
This name should be used for the typical white-flowered variety only. Pink-flowered variants are referable to *C. montana* var. *rubens*.
Clematis **'Victoria'**
There is also a Latvian cultivar of this name with petals with a central white bar.
Colchicum **'Autumn Queen'**
Entries here might refer to the slightly different *C.* 'Prinses Astrid'.
Cornus **'Norman Hadden'**
See note in Bean Supplement, p.184.
Cotoneaster dammeri
Plants sold under this name are usually *C. dammeri* 'Major'.
Cotoneaster frigidus **'Cornubia'**
According to Hylmø this cultivar, like all other variants of this species, is fully deciduous. Several evergreen cotoneasters are also grown under this name, most are clones of *C.* × *watereri* or *C. salicifolius*.
Crataegus coccinea
C. intricata, *C. pedicellata* and *C. biltmoreana* are occasionally supplied under this name.
Crocus cartwrightianus **'Albus'**
The plant offered is the true cultivar and not *C. hadriaticus*.
Dianthus fringed pink
D. 'Old Fringed Pink' and *D.* 'Old Fringed White' are also sometimes sold under this name.
Dianthus **'Musgrave's Pink' (p)**
This is the registered name of this white-flowered cultivar.
Elymus magellanicus
Although this is a valid name, Roger Grounds has suggested that many plants might belong to a different, perhaps unnamed species.
Epilobium glabellum **hort.**
Plants under this name are not *E. glabellum* but are close to *E. wilsonii* Petrie or perhaps a hybrid of it.
Erodium glandulosum
Plants under this name are often hybrids.
Erodium guttatum
Doubtfully in commerce; plants under this name are usually *E. heteradenum, E. cheilanthifolium* or hybrids.
Erysimum cheiri **'Baden-Powell'**
Plant of uncertain origin differing from *E. cheiri* 'Harpur Crewe' only in its shorter stature.
Fagus sylvatica **Cuprea Group/Atropurpurea Group**
It is desirable to provide a name, Cuprea Group, for less richly coloured forms, used in historic landscapes before the purple clones appeared.
Fagus sylvatica **'Pendula'**
This name refers to the Knap Hill clone, the most common weeping form in English gardens. Other clones occur, particularly in Cornwall and Ireland.
Fuchsia loxensis
For a comparison of the true species with the hybrids 'Speciosa' and 'Loxensis' commonly grown under this name, see Boullemier's Check List (2nd ed.) p.268.
Gentiana cachemirica
Most plants sold are not true to type.
Geum **'Borisii'**
This name refers to cultivars of *G. coccineum* Sibthorp & Smith, especially *G.* 'Werner Arends' and not to *G.* × *borisii* Kelleper.

Halimium alyssoides* and *H. halimifolium
Plants under these names are sometimes *H.* × *pauanum* or *H.* × *santae.*

***Hebe* 'C.P. Raffill'**
See note in Bean Supplement, p.265.

***Hebe* 'Carl Teschner'**
See note in Bean Supplement, p.264.

Hebe glaucophylla
A green reversion of the hybrid *H.* 'Glaucophylla Variegata' is often sold under this name.

***Hedera helix* 'Caenwoodiana' / 'Pedata'**
Some authorities consider these to be distinct cultivars while others think them different morphological forms of the same unstable clone.

***Hedera helix* 'Oro di Bogliasco'**
Priority between this name and 'Jubiläum Goldherz' and 'Goldheart' has yet to be finally resolved.

***Helleborus* × *hybridus* / *H. orientalis* hort.**
The name *H.* × *hybridus* for acaulescent hellebore hybrids does not seem to follow the *International Code of Botanical Nomenclature* Article H.3.2 requiring one of the parent species to be designated and does not seem to have been typified, contrary to Article 7 of the Code. However, the illustration accompanying the original description in Vilmorin's *Blumengärtnerei* 3(1): 27 (1894) shows that one parent of the cross must have been *H. guttatus*, now treated as part of *H. orientalis*. Taking this illustration as the type for this hybrid species makes it possible to retain *H.* × *hybridus* formally as a hybrid binomial (rather than *H. hybridus* as in a previous edition), as the Code's requirement to distinguish one parent is now met.

***Heuchera micrantha* var. *diversifolia* 'Palace Purple'**
This cultivar name refers only to plants with deep purple-red foliage. Seed-raised plants of inferior colouring should not be offered under this name.

Hosta montana
This name refers only to plants long grown in Europe, which differ from *H. elata.*

***Hydrangea macrophylla* Teller Series**
This is used both as a descriptive common name for Lacecap hydrangeas (German *teller* = plate, referring to the more or less flat inflorescence) and for the series of hybrids raised by Wädenswill in Switzerland bearing German names of birds. It is not generally possible to link a hydrangea described by the series name plus a colour description (e.g. Teller Blau, Teller Rosa, Teller Rot) to a single cultivar.

Hypericum fragile
The true *H. fragile* is probably not available from British nurseries.

***Hypericum* 'Gemo'**
Either a selection of *H. prolificum* or *H. prolificum* × *H. densiflorum.*

Ilex* × *altaclerensis
The argument for this spelling is given by Susyn Andrews, *The Plantsman*, 5(2) and is not superceded by the more recent comments in the Supplement to Bean's Trees and Shrubs.

Iris
Apart from those noted below, cultivar names marked 'N' are not registered. The majority of those marked 'I' have been previously used for a different cultivar.

***Iris histrioides* 'Major'**
Two clones are offered under this name, the true one pale blue with darker spotting on the falls, the incorrect one violet-blue with almost horizontal falls.

Juniperus* × *media
This name is illegitimate if applied to hybrids of *J. chinensis* × *J. sabina*, having been previously used for a different hybrid (P.A. Schmidt, *IDS Yearbook 1993*, 47-48). Because of its importance to gardeners, a proposal to conserve its present use was tabled but subsequently rejected.

***Lavandula angustifolia* 'Lavender Lady' / *L.* 'Cambridge Lady'**
Might be synonyms of *L. angustifolia* 'Lady'.

***Lavandula* × *intermedia* 'Arabian Night'**
Plants under this name might be *L.* × *intermedia* 'Impress Purple'.

Lavandula spica
This name is classed as a name to be rejected (*nomen rejiciendum*) by the *International Code of Botanical Nomenclature.*

***Lavandula* 'Twickel Purple'**
Two cultivars are sold under this name, one a form of *L.* × *intermedia*, the other of *L. angustifolia.*

Lavatera olbia* and *L. thuringiaca
Although *L. olbia* is usually shrubby and *L. thuringiaca* usually herbaceous, both species are very variable. Cultivars formally ascribed to one species or the other have been shown to be hybrids and are referable to the recently-named hybrid species *L.* × *clementii.*

***Lobelia* 'Russian Princess'**
This name, originally for a pink-flowered, green-leaved cultivar, is now generally applied to a purple-flowered, dark-leaved cultivar that seems to lack a valid name.

***Lonicera periclymenum* 'Serotina'**
See note in Bean Supplement, p.315.

Lonicera sempervirens* f. *sulphurea
Plants in the British Isles usually a yellow-flowered form of *L. periclymenum.*

***Malus domestica* 'Dummellor's Seedling'**
The phonetic spelling 'Dumelow's Seedling' contravenes the ICBN ruling on orthography, i.e. that, except for intentional latinizations, commemorative names should be based on the

original spelling of the person's name (Article 60.11). The spelling adopted here is that used on the gravestone of the raiser in Leicestershire.

***Meconopsis* Fertile Blue Group**

This Cultivar-group comprises seed-raised and intrinsically perennial tall blue poppies of as yet indeterminate origin (i.e. fertile forms other than the species *M. betonicifolia, M. grandis* and *M. simplicifolia*). The only cultivar so far established is *M.* 'Lingholm' (syns 'Blue Ice' and 'Correnie'). The bulk of seed-raised plants in cultivation and offered for sale are very likely to be *M.* 'Lingholm', although sometimes poorly selected. Many of these plants are currently being distributed erroneously as *M.* × *sheldonii* and as *M. grandis*.

***Meconopsis* George Sherriff Group**

This Cultivar-group comprises a number of sterile (almost invariably) clones of large blue poppies previously (and erroneously) known collectively as *M. grandis* GS600.

***Meconopsis grandis* ambig.**

See note under *M.* Fertile Blue Group. The true species has been recently reintroduced into cultivation in the British Isles but is still rarely offered.

***Meconopsis* Infertile Blue Group**

This cultivar-group comprises long-established sterile (almost invariably) clones of large blue poppies other than George Sherriff Group and often given the epithet × *sheldonii*.

***Meconopsis* × *sheldonii* ambig.**

See notes for *M.* Fertile Blue Group and *M.* Infertile Blue Group.

***Melissa officinalis* 'Variegata'**

The true cultivar of this name had leaves striped with white.

***Nemesia caerulea* 'Joan Wilder'**

The lavender blue clone 'Joan Wilder', described and illustrated in *The Hardy Plant,* **14**(1), 11-14, does not come true from seed; it may only be propagated from cuttings.

***Osmanthus heterophyllus* 'Gulftide'**

Probably correctly *O.* × *fortunei* 'Gulftide'.

***Papaver orientale* agg.**

Plants listed as *P. orientale* agg. (i.e. aggregate) or as one of its cultivars may be *P. orientale* L., *P. pseudo-orientale* or *P. bracteatum* or hybrids between them.

***Pelargonium* 'Lass o' Gowrie'**

The American plant of this name has pointed, not rounded leaf lobes.

Pelargonium quercifolium

Plants under this name are mainly hybrids. The true species has pointed, not rounded leaf lobes.

***Penstemon* 'Taoensis'**

This name for a small-flowered cultivar or hybrid of *P. isophyllus* originally appeared as 'Taoense' but must be corrected to agree in gender with *Penstemon* (masculine). Presumably an invalid name (published in Latin form since 1958), it is not synonymous with *P. crandallii* subsp. *glabrescens* var. *taosensis.*

Pernettya

Botanists now consider that *Pernettya* (fruit a berry) is not separable from *Gaultheria* (fruit a capsule) because in some species the fruit is intermediate between a berry and a capsule. For a fuller explanation see D. Middleton, *The Plantsman,* **12**(3).

***Picea pungens* 'Glauca Pendula'**

This name is used for several different glaucous cultivars.

Pinus ayacahuite

P. ayacahuite var. *veitchii* (syn. *P. veitchii)* is occasionally sold under this name.

***Pinus nigra* 'Cebennensis Nana'**

A doubtful name, possibly a synonym for *P. nigra* 'Nana'.

***Prunus laurocerasus* 'Castlewellan'**

We are grateful to Dr Charles Nelson for informing us that the name 'Marbled White' is not valid because although it has priority of publication it does not have the approval of the originator who asked for it to be called 'Castlewellan'.

Prunus serrulata* var. *pubescens

See note in Bean Supplement, p.398.

***Prunus* × *subhirtella* 'Rosea'**

Might be *P. pendula* var. *ascendens* 'Rosea', *P. pendula* 'Pendula Rosea', or *P.* × *subhirtella* 'Autumnalis Rosea'.

Rheum* × *cultorum

The name *R.* × *cultorum* was published without adequate description and must be abandoned in favour of the validly published *R.* × *hybridum.*

***Rhododendron* (azaleas)**

All names marked 'N', except for the following, refer to more than one cultivar.

***Rhododendron* 'Hinomayo'**

This name is based on a faulty transliteration (should be 'Hinamoyo') but the spelling 'Hinomayo' is retained in the interests of stability.

Rhus typhina

Linnaeus published both *R. typhina* and *R. hirta* as names for the same species. Though *R. hirta* has priority, it has been proposed that the name *R. typhina* should be conserved.

Rosa gentiliana

Plants under this name are usually the cultivar 'Polyantha Grandiflora' but might otherwise be *R. multiflora* 'Wilsonii', *R. multiflora* var. *cathayensis, R. henryi* or another hybrid.

***Rosa* 'Gros Choux de Hollande' hort. (Bb)**

It is doubtful if this name is correctly applied.

***Rosa* 'Jacques Cartier' hort.**
For a discussion on the correct identity of this rose see *Heritage Rose Foundation News*, Oct. 1989 & Jan. 1990.

***Rosa* 'Professeur Emile Perrot'**
For a discussion on the correct identity of this rose see *Heritage Roses,* Nov. 1991.

***Rosa* Sweetheart**
This is not the same as the Sweetheart Rose, a common name for *R.* 'Cécile Brünner'.

Rosa wichurana
This is the correct spelling according to the ICBN 1994 Article 60.11 (which enforces Recommendation 60C.1c) and not *wichuraiana* for this rose commemorating Max Wichura.

***Rubus fruticosus* L. agg.**
Though some cultivated blackberries do belong to *Rubus fruticosus* L. *sensu stricto,* others are more correctly ascribed to other species of *Rubus* section *Glandulosus* (including *R. armeniacus, R. laciniatus* or *R. ulmifolius)* or are hybrids of species within this section. Because it is almost impossible to ascribe every cultivar to a single species or hybrid, they are listed under *R. fruticosus* L. agg. (i.e. aggregate) for convenience.

Salvia microphylla* var. *neurepia
The type of this variety is referable to the typical variety, *S. microphylla* var. *microphylla.*

***Salvia officinalis* 'Aurea'**
S. officinalis var. *aurea* is a rare variant of the common sage with leaves entirely of gold. It is represented in cultivation by the cultivar 'Kew Gold'. The plant usually offered as *S. officinalis* 'Aurea' is the gold variegated sage *S. officinalis* 'Icterina'.

***Sambucus nigra* 'Aurea'**
Plants under this name are usually not *S. nigra.*

Sedum nevii
The true species is not in cultivation. Plants under this name are usually either *S. glaucophyllum* or occasionally *S. beyrichianum.*

***Skimmia japonica* 'Foremanii'**
The true cultivar, which belongs to *S. japonica* Rogersii Group, is believed to be lost to cultivation. Plants offered under this name are usually *S. japonica* 'Veitchii'.

Sorbus
Except for the following, *Sorbus* species marked N refer to names proposed by Dr Hugh McAllister for apomictic microspecies but not yet published.

***Sorbus multijuga* Sch 1132**
Though this is an accepted name, this collection was obtained from outside the usual range of this species.

***Spiraea japonica* 'Shirobana'**
Shirobana-shimotsuke is the common name for *S. japonica* var. *albiflora.* Shirobana means white-flowered and does not apply to the two-coloured form.

Staphylea holocarpa* var. *rosea
This botanical variety has woolly leaves. The cultivar 'Rosea', with which it is often confused, does not.

Stewartia ovata* var. *grandiflora.
Most, possibly all, plants available from British nurseries under this name are not true to name but are derived from the improved Nymans form.

***Thymus* Coccineus Group**
Thymes under this have dark crimson (RHS 78A) flowers whereas those of 'Alan Bloom' are purplish-pink (RHS 78C).

***Thymus serpyllum* cultivars**
Most cultivars are probably correctly cultivars of *T. polytrichus* or hybrids though they will remain listed under *T. serpyllum* pending further research.

***Thymus* 'Silver Posie'**
The cultivar name 'Silver Posie' is applied to several different plants, not all of them *T. vulgaris.*

***Tricyrtis* Hototogisu**
This is the common name applied generally to all Japanese *Tricyrtis* and specifically to *T. hirta.*

Tricyrtis macropoda
This name has been used for at least five different species.

Uncinia rubra
This name is also misapplied to *U. egmontiana* and *U. uncinata.*

Verbena
Entries marked (G) are considered by some botanists to belong to a separate genus, *Glandularia.* The principal differences are that verbenas have quadrangular, upright stems and terminal (rarely axillary) flowers in spikes or panicles of spikes; glandularias have cylindrical, creeping or semi-erect stems and flowers in terminal and axillary heads, sometimes elongating with age.

***Verbena* 'Kemerton'**
Origin unknown, not from Kemerton.

***Viburnum opulus* 'Fructu Luteo'**
See note below.

***Viburnum opulus* 'Xanthocarpum'**
Some entries under this name might be the less compact *V. opulus* 'Fructu Luteo'.

Viburnum plicatum
Entries may include the 'snowball' form, *V. plicatum* f. *plicatum* (syn. *V. plicatum* 'Sterile'), as well as the 'lacecap' form, *V. plicatum* f. *tomentosum.*

Viola labradorica
See Note in *The Garden*, **110(2)**: 96.

CLASSIFICATION OF GENERA

Genera including a large number of species or with many cultivars are often subdivided into informal horiticultural classifications or formal cultivar groups in the case of *Clematis* and *Tulipa*. The breeding of new cultivars is sometimes limited to hybrids between closely-related species, thus for *Saxifraga* and *Primula*, the cultivars are allocated to the sections given in the infrageneric treatments cited. Please turn to p.8 for a fuller explanation.

ACTINIDIA

(s-p) Self-pollinating

BEGONIA

(C) Cane-like
(R) Rex Cultorum
(S) Semperflorens Cultorum
(T) × *tuberhybrida* (Tuberous)

CHRYSANTHEMUM

(By the National Chrysanthemum Society)
(1) Indoor Large (Exhibition)
(2) Indoor Medium (Exhibition)
(3a) Indoor Incurved: Large-flowered
(3b) Indoor Incurved: Medium-flowered
(3c) Indoor Incurved: Small-flowered
(4a) Indoor Reflexed: Large-flowered
(4b) Indoor Reflexed: Medium-flowered
(4c) Indoor Reflexed: Small-flowered
(5a) Indoor Intermediate: Large-flowered
(5b) Indoor Intermediate: Medium-flowered
(5c) Indoor Intermediate: Small-flowered
(6a) Indoor Anemone: Large-flowered
(6b) Indoor Anemone: Medium-flowered
(6c) Indoor Anemone: Small-flowered
(7a) Indoor Single: Large-flowered
(7b) Indoor Single: Medium-flowered
(7c) Indoor Single: Small-flowered
(8a) Indoor True Pompon
(8b) Indoor Semi-pompon
(9a) Indoor Spray: Anemone
(9b) Indoor Spray: Pompon
(9c) Indoor Spray: Reflexed
(9d) Indoor Spray: Single
(9e) Indoor Spray: Intermediate
(9f) Indoor Spray: Spider, Quill, Spoon or Any Other Type
(10a) Indoor, Spider
(10b) Indoor, Quill
(10c) Indoor, Spoon
(11) Any Other Indoor Type
(12a) Indoor, Charm
(12b) Indoor, Cascade
(13a) October-flowering Incurved: Large-flowered
(13b) October-flowering Incurved: Medium-flowered
(13c) October-flowering Incurved: Small-flowered
(14a) October-flowering Reflexed: Large-flowered
(14b) October-flowering Reflexed: Medium-flowered
(14c) October-flowering Reflexed: Small-flowered
(15a) October-flowering Intermediate: Large-flowered
(15b) October-flowering Intermediate: Medium-flowered
(15c) October-flowered Intermediate: Small-flowered
(16) October-flowering Large
(17a) October-flowering Single: Large-flowered
(17b) October-flowering Single: Medium-flowered
(17c) October-flowering Single: Small-flowered
(18a) October-flowering Pompon: True Pompon
(18b) October-flowering Pompon: Semi-pompon
(19a) October-flowering Spray: Anemone
(19b) October-flowering Spray: Pompon
(19c) October-flowering Spray: Reflexed
(19d) October-flowering Spray: Single
(19e) October-flowering Spray: Intermediate
(19f) October-flowering Spray: Spider, Quill, Spoon or Any Other Type
(20) Any Other October-flowering Type
(22a) Charm: Anemone
(22b) Charm: Pompon
(22c) Charm: Reflexed
(22d) Charm: Single
(22e) Charm: Intermediate
(22f) Charm: Spider, Quill, Spoon or Any Other Type
(23a) Early-flowering Outdoor Incurved: Large-flowered
(23b) Early-flowering Outdoor Incurved: Medium-flowered
(23c) Early-flowering Outdoor Incurved: Small-flowered
(24a) Early-flowering Outdoor Reflexed: Large-flowered

(24b) Early-flowering Outdoor Reflexed: Medium-flowered
(24c) Early-flowering Outdoor Reflexed: Small-flowered
(25a) Early-flowering Outdoor Intermediate: Large-flowered
(25b) Early-flowering Outdoor Intermediate: Medium-flowered
(25c) Early-flowering Outdoor Intermediate: Small-flowered
(26a) Early-flowering Outdoor Anemone: Large-flowered
(26b) Early-flowering Outdoor Anemone: Medium-flowered
(27a) Early-flowering Outdoor Single: Large-flowered
(27b) Early-flowering Outdoor Single: Medium-flowered
(28a) Early-flowering Outdoor Pompon: True Pompon
(28b) Early-flowering Outdoor Pompon: Semi-pompon
(29a) Early-flowering Outdoor Spray: Anemone
(29b) Early-flowering Outdoor Spray: Pompon
(29c) Early-flowering Outdoor Spray: Reflexed
(29d) Early-flowering Outdoor Spray: Single
(29e) Early-flowering Outdoor Spray: Intermediate
(29f) Early-flowering Outdoor Spray: Spider, Quill, Spoon or Any Other Type
(29K) Early-flowering Outdoor Spray: Korean
(29Rub) Early-flowering Outdoor Spray: Rubellum
(30) Any Other Early-flowering Outdoor Type

CLEMATIS

Cultivar Groups as per Matthews, V. (2002) The International Clematis Register & Checklist 2002, Royal Horticultural Society, London.

(A) Atragene Group
(Ar) Armandii Group
(C) Cirrhosa Group
(EL) Early Large-flowered Group
(F) Flammula Group
(Fo) Forsteri Group
(H) Heracleifolia Group
(I) Integrifolia Group
(LL) Late Large-flowered Group
(M) Montana Group
(T) Texensis Group
(Ta) Tangutica Group
(V) Viorna Group
(Vb) Vitalba Group
(Vt) Viticella Group

DAHLIA

(By the National Dahlia Society with corresponding numerical classification according to the Royal Horticultural Society's International Register)

(Sin) 1 Single
(Anem) 2 Anemone-flowered
(Col) 3 Collerette
(WL) 4 Waterlily (unassigned)
(LWL) 4B Waterlily, Large
(MWL) 4C Waterlily, Medium
(SWL) 4D Waterlily, Small
(MinWL) 4E Waterlily, Miniature
(D) 5 Decorative (unassigned)
(GD) 5A Decorative, Giant
(LD) 5B Decorative, Large
(MD) 5C Decorative, Medium
(SD) 5D Decorative, Small
(MinD) 5E Decorative, Miniature
(SBa) 6A Small Ball
(MinBa) 6B Miniature Ball
(Pom) 7 Pompon
(C) 8 Cactus (unassigned)
(GC) 8A Cactus, Giant
(LC) 8B Cactus, Large
(MC) 8C Cactus, Medium
(SC) 8D Cactus, Small
(MinC) 8E Cactus, Miniature
(S-c) 9 Semi-cactus (unassigned)
(GS-c) 9A Semi-cactus, Giant
(LS-c) 9B Semi-cactus, Large
(MS-c) 9C Semi-cactus, Medium
(SS-c) 9D Semi-cactus, Small
(MinS-c) 9E Semi-cactus, Miniature
(Misc) 10 Miscellaneous
(O) Orchid-flowering (in combination)
(B) Botanical (in combination)
(DwB) Dwarf Bedding (in combination)
(Fim) Fimbriated (in combination)
(Lil) Lilliput (in combination)

DIANTHUS

(By the Royal Horticultural Society)

(p) Pink
(p,a) Annual Pink
(pf) Perpetual-flowering Carnation
(b) Border Carnation
(M) Malmaison Carnation

FRUIT

(B) Black (*Vitis*), Blackcurrant (*Ribes*)
(Ball) Ballerina (*Malus*)
(C) Culinary (*Malus, Prunus, Pyrus, Ribes*)
(Cider) Cider (*Malus*)
(D) Dessert (*Malus, Prunus, Pyrus, Ribes*)
(F) Fruit
(G) Glasshouse (*Vitis*)
(O) Outdoor (*Vitis*)
(P) Pinkcurrant (*Ribes*)
(Perry) Perry (*Pyrus*)
(R) Red (*Vitis*), Redcurrant (*Ribes*)
(S) Seedless (*Citrus, Vitis*)
(W) White (*Vitis*), Whitecurrant (*Ribes*)

GLADIOLUS

(B) Butterfly
(E) Exotic
(G) Giant
(L) Large
(M) Medium
(Min) Miniature
(N) Nanus
(P) Primulinus
(S) Small
(Tub) Tubergenii

HYDRANGEA MACROPHYLLA

(H) Hortensia
(L) Lacecap

IRIS

(By the American Iris Society)
(AB) Arilbred
(BB) Border Bearded
(Cal-Sib) Series *Californicae* × Series *Sibiricae*
(CH) Californian Hybrid
(DB) Dwarf Bearded (not assigned)
(Dut) Dutch
(IB) Intermediate Bearded
(La) Louisiana Hybrid
(MDB) Miniature Dwarf Bearded
(MTB) Miniature Tall Bearded
(SDB) Standard Dwarf Bearded
(Sino-Sib) Series *Sibiricae*, chromosome number 2n=40
(Spuria) Spuria
(TB) Tall Bearded

LILIUM

(Classification according to *The International Lily Register* (ed. 3, 1982) with amendments from Supp. 10 (1992), Royal Horticultural Society)

(I) Early-flowering Asiatic Hybrids derived from *L. amabile, L. bulbiferum, L. cernuum, L. concolor, L. davidii, L.* × *hollandicum, L. lancifolium, L. leichtlinii, L.* × *maculatum* and *L. pumilum*
(Ia) Upright flowers, borne singly or in an umbel
(Ib) Outward-facing flowers
(Ic) Pendant flowers
(II) Hybrids of Martagon type, one parent having been a form of *L. hansonii* or *L. martagon*
(III) Hybrids from *L. candidum, L. chalcedonicum* and other related European species (excluding *L. martagon*)
(IV) Hybrids of American species
(V) Hybrids derived from *L. formosanum* and *L. longiflorum*
(VI) Hybrid Trumpet Lilies and Aurelian hybrids from Asiatic species, including *L. henryi* but excluding those from *L. auratum, L. japonicum, L. rubellum* and *L. speciosum.*
(VIa) Plants with trumpet-shaped flowers
(VIb) Plants with bowl-shaped flowers
(VIc) Plants with flat flowers (or only the tips recurved)
(VId) Plants with recurved flowers
(VII) Hybrids of Far Eastern species as *L auratum, L. japonicum, L. rubellum* and *L. speciosum* (Oriental Hybrids)
(VIIa) Plants with trumpet-shaped flowers
(VIIb) Plants with bowl-shaped flowers
(VIIc) Plants with flat flowers
(VIId) Plants with recurved flowers
(VIII) All hybrids not in another division
(IX) All species and their varieties and forms

MALUS *SEE* FRUIT

NARCISSUS

(By the Royal Horticultural Society, revised 1998)
(1) Trumpet
(2) Large-cupped
(3) Small-cupped
(4) Double
(5) Triandrus
(6) Cyclamineus
(7) Jonquilla and Apodanthus
(8) Tazetta
(9) Poeticus
(10) Bulbocodium
(11a) Split-corona: Collar
(11b) Split-corona: Papillon

(12) Miscellaneous
(13) Species

NYMPHAEA

(H) Hardy
(D) Day-blooming
(N) Night-blooming
(T) Tropical

PAEONIA

(S) Shrubby

PELARGONIUM

(A) Angel
(C) Coloured Foliage (in combination)
(Ca) Cactus (in combination)
(d) Double (in combination)
(Dec) Decorative
(Dw) Dwarf
(DwI) Dwarf Ivy-leaved
(Fr) Frutetorum
(I) Ivy-leaved
(Min) Miniature
(MinI) Miniature Ivy-leaved
(R) Regal
(Sc) Scented-leaved
(St) Stellar (in combination)
(T) Tulip (in combination)
(U) Unique
(Z) Zonal

PRIMULA

(Classification by Section as per W.W. Smith & Forrest (1928) and W.W. Smith & Fletcher (1941-49))
(1) *Amethystina*
(2) *Auricula*
(3) *Bullatae*
(4) *Candelabra*
(5) *Capitatae*
(6) *Carolinella*
(7) *Cortusoides*
(8) *Cuneifolia*
(9) *Denticulata*
(10) *Dryadifolia*
(11) *Farinosae*
(12) *Floribundae*
(13) *Grandis*
(14) *Malacoides*
(15) *Malvacea*
(16) *Minutissimae*
(17) *Muscarioides*
(18) *Nivales*
(19) *Obconica*
(20) *Parryi*
(21) *Petiolares*
(22) *Pinnatae*
(23) *Pycnoloba*
(24) *Reinii*
(25) *Rotundifolia*
(26) *Sikkimensis*
(27) *Sinenses*
(28) *Soldanelloideae*
(29) *Souliei*
(30) *Vernales*
(A) Alpine Auricula
(B) Border Auricula
(Poly) Polyanthus
(Prim) Primrose
(S) Show Auricula
(St) Striped Auricula

PRUNUS *SEE* FRUIT

PYRUS *SEE* FRUIT

RHODODENDRON

(A) Azalea (deciduous, species or unclassified hybrid)
(Ad) Azaleodendron
(EA) Evergreen azalea
(G) Ghent azalea (deciduous)
(K) Knap Hill or Exbury azalea (deciduous)
(M) Mollis azalea (deciduous)
(O) Occidentalis azalea (deciduous)
(R) Rustica azalea (deciduous)
(V) Vireya rhododendron
(Vs) Viscosa azalea (deciduous)

RIBES *SEE* FRUIT

ROSA

(A) Alba
(Bb) Bourbon
(Bs) Boursault
(Ce) Centifolia
(Ch) China
(Cl) Climbing (in combination)
(D) Damask
(DPo) Damask Portland
(F) Floribunda or Cluster-flowered
(G) Gallica
(Ga) Garnette
(GC) Ground Cover
(HM) Hybrid Musk
(HP) Hybrid Perpetual
(HT) Hybrid Tea or Large-flowered

(Min) Miniature
(Mo) Moss (in combination)
(N) Noisette
(Patio) Patio, Miniature Floribunda or Dwarf Cluster-flowered
(Poly) Polyantha
(PiH) Pimpinellifolia hybrid (Hybrid Scots Briar)
(Ra) Rambler
(RH) Rubiginosa hybrid (Hybrid Sweet Briar)
(Ru) Rugosa
(S) Shrub
(T) Tea

SAXIFRAGA

(Classification by Section from Gornall, R.J. (1987). *Botanical Journal of the Linnean Society,* **95**(4): 273-292)
(1) *Ciliatae*
(2) *Cymbalaria*
(3) *Merkianae*
(4) *Micranthes*
(5) *Irregulares*
(6) *Heterisia*
(7) *Porphyrion*
(8) *Ligulatae*
(9) *Xanthizoon*
(10) *Trachyphyllum*
(11) *Gymnopera*
(12) *Cotylea*
(13) *Odontophyllae*
(14) *Mesogyne*
(15) *Saxifraga*

TULIPA

(Classification by Cultivar Group from *Classified List and International Register of Tulip Names* by Koninklijke Algemeene Vereening voor Bloembollenculture 1996)
(1) Single Early Group
(2) Double Early Group
(3) Triumph Group
(4) Darwinhybrid Group
(5) Single Late Group (including Darwin Group and Cottage Group)
(6) Lily-flowered Group
(7) Fringed Group
(8) Viridiflora Group
(9) Rembrandt Group
(10) Parrot Group
(11) Double Late Group
(12) Kaufmanniana Group
(13) Fosteriana Group
(14) Greigii Group
(15) Miscellaneous

VERBENA

(G) Species and hybrids considered by some botanists to belong to the separate genus *Glandularia*.

VIOLA

(C) Cornuta Hybrid
(dVt) Double Violet
(ExVa) Exhibition Viola
(FP) Fancy Pansy
(PVt) Parma Violet
(SP) Show Pansy
(T) Tricolor
(Va) Viola
(Vt) Violet
(Vtta) Violetta

VITIS *SEE* FRUIT

REVERSE SYNONYMS

The following list of reverse synonyms is intended to help users find from which genus an unfamiliar plant name has been cross-referred. For a fuller explanation see p.10.

Abelmoschus – Hibiscus
Abutilon – Corynabutilon
Acacia – Racosperma
Acca – Feijoa
× *Achicodonia – Eucodonia*
Achillea – Anthemis
Achillea – Tanacetum
Acinos – Calamintha
Acinos – Clinopodium
Acinos – Micromeria
Acmella – Spilanthes
Actaea – Cimicifuga
Actaea – Souliea
Aethionema – Eunomia
Agapetes – Pentapterygium
Agarista – Leucothoe
Agastache – Cedronella
Agathosma – Barosma
Agave – Manfreda
Agrostis – Eragrostis
Aichryson – Aeonium
Ajania – Chrysanthemum
Ajania – Dendranthema
Ajania – Eupatorium
Albizia – Acacia
Alcea – Althaea
Allardia – Waldheimia
Allocasuarina – Casuarina
Aloysia – Lippia
Althaea – Malva
Alyogyne – Anisodontea
Alyogyne – Hibiscus
Alyssum – Ptilotrichum
× *Amarygia – Amaryllis*
Amaryllis – Brunsvigia
Amomyrtus – Myrtus
Amsonia – Rhazya
Anacamptis – Orchis
Anaphalis – Gnaphalium
Anchusa – Lycopsis
Androsace – Douglasia
Androstoma – Cyathodes
Anemanthele – Oryzopsis
Anemanthele – Stipa
Anemone – Eriocapitella
Anisodontea – Malvastrum
Anisodus – Scopolia
Anomatheca – Freesia
Anomatheca – Lapeirousia
Anredera – Boussingaultia
Antirrhinum – Asarina
Aphanes – Alchemilla
Apium – Apium × *Petroselinum*
Arctanthemum – Chrysanthemum
Arctostaphylos – Arbutus
Arctotis – Venidium
Arctotis – × *Venidioarctotis*
Arenga – Didymosperma
Argyranthemum – Anthemis
Argyranthemum – Chrysanthemum
Armoracia – Cochlearia
Arnoglossum – Cacalia
Arundinaria – Pseudosasa
Asarina – Antirrhinum
Asarum – Hexastylis
Asparagus – Myrsiphyllum
Asparagus – Smilax
Asperula – Galium
Asphodeline – Asphodelus
Asplenium – Camptosorus
Asplenium – Ceterach
Asplenium – Phyllitis
Asplenium – Scolopendrium
Aster – Crinitaria
Aster – Doellingeria
Aster – Erigeron
Aster – Microglossa
Aster – Symphyotrichum
Astilboides – Rodgersia
Asyneuma – Campanula
Athanasia – Hymenolepis
Atropanthe – Scopolia
Aurinia – Alyssum
Austrocedrus – Libocedrus
Austromyrtus – Myrtus
Azorella – Bolax
Azorina – Campanula

Bambusa – Arundinaria
Bashania – Arundinaria
Bassia – Kochia
Beaucarnea – Nolina
Bellevalia – Muscari
Bellis – Erigeron
Bignonia – Campsis
Blechnum – Lomaria
Blepharocalyx – Temu
Bolax – Azorella
Bolboschoenus – Scirpus
Bonia – Indocalamus
Borago – Anchusa
Bothriochloa – Andropogon
Bouteloua – Chondrosum
Boykinia – Telesonix
Brachyglottis – Senecio
Brimeura – Hyacinthus
Brodiaea – Triteleia
Brugmansia – Datura
Brunnera – Anchusa
Buglossoides – Lithospermum
Bulbine – Bulbinopsis

Cacalia – Adenostyles
Calamagrostis – Stipa
Calamintha – Clinopodium
Calamintha – Thymus
Calibrachoa – Petunia
Callisia – Phyodina
Callisia – Tradescantia
Calocedrus – Libocedrus
Calomeria – Humea
Caloscordum – Nothoscordum
Calylophus – Oenothera
Calytrix – Lhotzkya
Camellia – Thea
Campanula – Campanula × *Symphyandra*
Campanula – Symphyandra
Cardamine – Dentaria
Carpobrotus – Lampranthus
Cassiope – Harrimanella
Cedronella – Agastache
Centaurium – Erythraea
Centella – Hydrocotyle
Centranthus – Kentranthus
Centranthus – Valeriana
Cephalaria – Scabiosa
Ceratostigma – Plumbago
Chaenomeles – Cydonia
Chaenorhinum – Linaria
Chamaecytisus – Cytisus
Chamaedaphne – Cassandra
Chamaemelum – Anthemis
Chamerion – Chamaenerion
Chamerion – Epilobium
Chasmanthium – Uniola
Cheilanthes – Notholaena
Chiastophyllum – Cotyledon
Chimonobambusa – Arundinaria
Chimonobambusa – Qiongzhuea
Chionohebe - Parahebe
Chionohebe – Pygmea
× *Chionoscilla – Scilla*
Chlorophytum – Diuranthera

Chrysanthemum – Dendranthema
Chrysopsis – Heterotheca
Cicerbita – Lactuca
Cissus – Ampelopsis
Cissus – Parthenocissus
× *Citrofortunella – Citrus*
Clarkia – Eucharidium
Clarkia – Godetia
Clavinodum – Arundinaria
Claytonia – Calandrinia
Claytonia – Montia
Clematis – Atragene
Clematis – Clematopsis
Cleyera – Eurya
Clinopodium – Calamintha
Clytostoma – Bignonia
Clytostoma – Pandorea
Cnicus – Carduus
Codonopsis – Campanumoea
Consolida – Delphinium
Cordyline – Dracaena
Cornus – Chamaepericlymenum
Cornus – Dendrobenthamia
Coronilla – Securigera
Cortaderia – Gynerium
Corydalis - Capnoides
Corydalis – Fumaria
Corydalis – Pseudofumaria
Cosmos – Bidens
Cotinus – Rhus
Cotula – Leptinella
Crassula – Rochea
Crassula – Sedum
Crassula – Tillaea
Cremanthodium – Ligularia
Crinodendron – Tricuspidaria
Crocosmia – Antholyza
Crocosmia – Curtonus
Crocosmia – Montbretia
Cruciata – Galium
Ctenanthe – Calathea
Ctenanthe – Stromanthe
× *Cupressocyparis – Chamaecyparis*
× *Cupressocyparis -* × *Cuprocyparis*
Cupressus – Chamaecyparis
Cyclosorus – Pneumatopteris
Cymbalaria – Linaria
Cymophyllus – Carex
Cyperus – Mariscus
Cypripedium – Criogenes
Cyrtanthus – Anoiganthus
Cyrtanthus – Vallota
Cyrtomium – Phanerophlebia
Cyrtomium – Polystichum
Cytisus – Argyrocytisus
Cytisus – Genista
Cytisus – Lembotropis
Cytisus – Spartocytisus

Daboecia – Menziesia
Dacrycarpus – Podocarpus
Dactylorhiza – Orchis
Dalea – Petalostemon
Danae – Ruscus
Darmera – Peltiphyllum
Datura – Brugmansia
Davallia – Humata
Delairea – Senecio
Delosperma – Lampranthus
Delosperma – Mesembryanthemum
Desmodium – Lespedeza
Deuterocohnia – Abromeitiella
Dicentra – Corydalis
Dichelostemma – Brodiaea
Dicliptera – Barleria
Dicliptera – Justicia
Diervilla – Weigela
Dietes – Moraea
Diplazium – Athyrium
Dipogon – Dolichos
Disporopsis – Polygonatum
Dracaena – Pleomele
Dracunculus – Arum
Dregea – Wattakaka
Drepanostachyum – Bambusa
Drepanostachyum – Chimonobambusa
Drepanostachyum – Gelidocalamus
Drepanostachyum – Thamnocalamus
Drimys – Tasmannia
Duchesnea – Fragaria
Dypsis – Chrysalidocarpus
Dypsis – Neodypsis

Echeveria – Cotyledon
Echinacea – Rudbeckia
Echinospartum – Genista
Edraianthus – Wahlenbergia
Egeria – Elodea
Elatostema – Pellionia
Eleutherococcus – Acanthopanax
Elliottia – Botryostege
Elliottia – Cladothamnus
Elymus – Agropyron
Elymus – Leymus
Ensete – Musa
Epipremnum – Philodendron
Epipremnum – Scindapsus
Episcia – Alsobia
Eranthis – Aconitum
Eremophila – Myoporum
Erepsia - Semnanthe
Erigeron – Haplopappus
Erysimum – Cheiranthus
Eucalyptus – Corymbia
Eupatorium – Ageratina
Eupatorium – Ayapana
Eupatorium – Bartlettina
Euphorbia – Poinsettia
Euryops – Senecio
Eustachys – Chloris
Eustoma – Lisianthus

Fallopia – Bilderdykia
Fallopia – Polygonum
Fallopia – Reynoutria
Farfugium – Ligularia
Fargesia – Arundinaria
Fargesia – Borinda
Fargesia – Semiarundinaria
Fargesia – Sinarundinaria
Fargesia – Thamnocalamus
Fatsia – Aralia
Felicia – Agathaea
Felicia – Aster
Fibigia – Farsetia
Filipendula – Spiraea
Foeniculum – Ferula
Fortunella – Citrus

Galium – Asperula
Gaultheria – Chiogenes
Gaultheria – Pernettya
Gaultheria – × *Gaulnettya*
Gelasine – Sisyrinchium
Genista – Chamaespartium
Genista – Cytisus
Genista – Echinospartum
Genista – Teline
Gethyum – Ancrumia
Geum – Sieversia
Gladiolus – Acidanthera
Gladiolus – Anomalesia
Gladiolus – Homoglossum
Gladiolus – Petamenes
Glechoma – Nepeta
Gloxinia – Seemannia
Gomphocarpus – Asclepias
Gomphocarpus – Asclepias
Goniolimon – Limonium
Graptopetalum – Sedum
Graptopetalum – Tacitus
Greenovia – Sempervivum
Gymnadenia – Nigritella
Gymnospermium – Leontice

Habranthus – Zephyranthes
Hacquetia – Dondia
× *Halimiocistus – Cistus*
× *Halimiocistus – Halimium*
Halimione – Atriplex
Halimium – Cistus
Halimium – Helianthemum
Halimium – × *Halimiocistus*

Halocarpus – Dacrydium
Hanabusaya – Symphyandra
Hedychium – Brachychilum
Helianthella – Helianthus
Helianthemum – Cistus
Helianthus – Coreopsis
Helianthus – Heliopsis
Helichrysum – Gnaphalium
Helicodiceros – Dracunculus
Helictotrichon – Avena
Helictotrichon – Avenula
Hepatica – Anemone
Herbertia – Alophia
Hermodactylus – Iris
Heterocentron – Schizocentron
Heteromeles – Photinia
Heterotheca – Chrysopsis
× *Heucherella – Heuchera*
× *Heucherella – Tiarella*
Hibbertia – Candollea
Hieracium – Andryala
Himalayacalamus – Arundinaria
Himalayacalamus – Chimonobambusa
Himalayacalamus – Drepanostachyum
Himalayacalamus – Drepanostachyum
Himalayacalamus – Thamnocalamus
Hippocrepis – Coronilla
Hippolytia – Achillea
Hippolytia – Tanacetum
Hoheria – Plagianthus
Homalocladium – Muehlenbeckia
Howea – Kentia
Hyacinthoides – Endymion
Hyacinthoides – Scilla
Hylomecon – Chelidonium
Hymenocallis – Elisena
Hymenocallis – Ismene
Hymenoxys – Dugaldia
Hymenoxys – Helenium
Hyophorbe – Mascarena
Hypoxis – Rhodohypoxis

Incarvillea – Amphicome
Indocalamus – Sasa
Iochroma – Acnistus
Iochroma – Cestrum
Iochroma – Dunalia
Ipheion – Tristagma
Ipheion – Triteleia
Ipomoea – Calonyction
Ipomoea – Mina
Ipomoea – Pharbitis
Ipomopsis – Gilia
Ischyrolepis – Restio
Isolepis – Scirpus
Isotoma – Laurentia
Isotoma – Solenopsis

Jamesbrittenia – Sutera
Jeffersonia – Plagiorhegma
Jovibarba – Sempervivum
Juncus – Scirpus
Jurinea – Jurinella
Justicia – Beloperone
Justicia - Duvernoia
Justicia – Jacobinia
Justicia – Libonia

Kalanchoe – Bryophyllum
Kalanchoe – Kitchingia
Kalimeris – Aster
Kalimeris – Asteromoea
Kalimeris – Boltonia
Kalopanax – Acanthopax
Kalopanax – Eleutherococcus
Keckiella - Penstemon
Keckiella – Penstemon
Kitagawia – Peucedanum
Knautia – Scabiosa
Kniphofia – Tritoma
Kohleria – Isoloma
Krascheninnikovia – Ceratoides
Kunzea – Leptospermum

Lablab – Dolichos
Lagarosiphon – Elodea
Lagarostrobos – Dacrydium
Lamium – Galeobdolon
Lamium – Lamiastrum
Lampranthus – Mesembryanthemum
Lavatera – Malva
Ledebouria – Scilla
× *Ledodendron – Rhododendron*
Ledum – Rhododendron
Leontodon – Microseris
Lepechinia – Sphacele
Lepidothamnus – Dacrydium
Leptecophylla – Cyathodes
Leptinella – Cotula
Leptodactylon – Gilia
Leucanthemella – Chrysanthemum
Leucanthemella – Leucanthemum
Leucanthemopsis – Chrysanthemum
Leucanthemum – Chrysanthemum
Leucocoryne – Beauverdia
Leucophyta – Calocephalus
Leucopogon – Cyathodes
Leucopogon – Styphelia
× *Leucoraoulia – Raoulia*
× *Leucoraoulia – Raoulia* × *Leucogenes*
Leymus – Elymus
Ligularia – Senecio
Ligustrum – Parasyringa
Lilium – Nomocharis
Limonium – Statice
Linanthus – Linanthastrum
Lindelofia – Adelocaryum
Lindera – Parabenzoin
Lindernia – Ilysanthes
Liriope – Ophiopogon
Lithodora – Lithospermum
Lobelia – Monopsis
Lophomyrtus – Myrtus
Lophospermum – Asarina
Lophospermum – Maurandya
Lotus – Dorycnium
Lotus – Tetragonolobus
Ludwigia – Jussiaea
Luma – Myrtus
× *Lycene – Lychnis*
Lychnis – Agrostemma
Lychnis – Silene
Lychnis – Viscaria
Lycianthes – Solanum
Lytocaryum – Cocos
Lytocaryum – Microcoelum

Macfadyena – Bignonia
Macfadyena – Doxantha
Machaeranthera – Xylorhiza
Machaerina – Baumea
Mackaya – Asystasia
Macleaya – Bocconia
Maclura - Cudrania
Macropiper – Piper
Magnolia – Parakmeria
Mahonia – Berberis
Mandevilla – Dipladenia
Mandragora – Atropa
Matricaria – Tripleurosperum
Maurandella – Asarina
Maurandya – Asarina
Melanoselinum – Thapsia
Melicytus – Hymenanthera
Melinis – Rhynchelytrum
Mentha – Preslia
Merremia – Ipomoea
Mimulus – Diplacus
Minuartia – Arenaria
Moltkia – Lithodora
Moltkia – Lithospermum
Morina – Acanthocalyx
Morina – Acanthocalyx
Mukdenia – Aceriphyllum
Muscari – Hyacinthus
Muscari – Leopoldia
Muscari – Muscarimia
Muscari – Pseudomuscari
Myrteola – Myrtus

Naiocrene – Claytonia
Naiocrene – Montia
Nectaroscordum – Allium
Nematanthus – Hypocyrta
Nemesia – Diascia × Linaria
Neolitsea – Litsea
Neopaxia – Claytonia
Neopaxia – Montia
Neoregelia – Nidularium
Nepeta – Dracocephalum
× *Niduregelia – Guzmania*
Nipponanthemum – Chrysanthemum
Nipponanthemum – Leucanthemum
Nolina – Beaucarnea
Nymphoides – Villarsia

Ochagavia – Fascicularia
Oemleria – Osmaronia
Oenothera – Chamissonia
Olsynium – Sisyrinchium
Onixotis – Dipidax
Onoclea – Matteuccia
Ophiopogon – Convallaria
Orchis – Anacamptis
Orchis – Dactylorhiza
Oreopteris – Thelypteris
Orostachys – Sedum
Oscularia – Lampranthus
Osmanthus – Phillyrea
Osmanthus – × *Osmarea*
Othonna – Hertia
Othonna – Othonnopsis
Ozothamhus – Helichrysum

Pachyphragma – Cardamine
Pachyphragma – Thlaspi
Pachystegia - Olearia
Packera – Senecio
Paederota – Veronica
Pallenis – Asteriscus
Papaver – Meconopsis
Parahebe – Derwentia
Parahebe – Hebe
Parahebe – Veronica
Paraserianthes – Albizia
Paris – Daiswa
Parthenocissus – Ampelopsis
Parthenocissus – Vitis
Passiflora – Tetrapathaea
Paxistima – Pachystema
Pecteilis – Habenaria
Pelargonium – Geranium
Peltoboykinia – Boykinia
Penstemon – Chelone
Penstemon – Nothochelone
Penstemon – Pennellianthus
Pentaglottis – Anchusa
Pericallis – Senecio
Persea – Machilus
Persicaria – Aconogonon
Persicaria – Bistorta
Persicaria – Polygonum
Persicaria – Tovara
Petrocoptis – Lychnis
Petrophytum – Spiraea
Petrorhagia – Tunica
Petroselinum – Carum
Phegopteris – Thelypteris
Phoenicaulis – Parrya
Photinia – Stransvaesia
Photinia – × *Stravinia*
Phuopsis – Crucianella
Phyla – Lippia
Phymatosorus – Microsorum
Phymosia – Sphaeralcea
Physoplexis – Phyteuma
Physostegia – Dracocephalum
Pieris – Arcterica
Pilosella – Hieracium
Platycladus – Thuja
Plecostachys – Helichrysum
Plectranthus – Coleus
Plectranthus – Solenostemon
Pleioblastus – Arundinaria
Pleioblastus – Sasa
Podophyllum – Dysosma
Podranea – Tecoma
Polygonum – Persicaria
Polypodium – Phlebodium
Polyscias – Nothopanax
Poncirus – Aegle
Potentilla – Comarum
Pratia – Lobelia
Prenanthes – Nabalus
Pritzelago – Hutchinsia
Prumnopitys – Podocarpus
Prunus – Amygdalus
Pseudocydonia – Chaenomeles
Pseudogynoxys – Senecio
Pseudopanax – Metapanax
Pseudopanax – Neopanax
Pseudosasa – Arundinaria
Pseudotsuga – Tsuga
Pseudowintera – Drimys
Pterocephalus – Scabiosa
Pteryxia - Cymopterus
Ptilostemon – Cirsium
Pulicaria – Inula
Pulsatilla – Anemone
Purshia – Cowania
Puschkinia – Scilla
Pyrrocoma – Aster
Pyrrocoma – Haplopappus
Reineckea – Liriope
Retama – Genista
Retama – Lygos
Rhamnus – Frangula
Rhapis – Chamaerops
Rhodanthe – Helipterum
Rhodanthemum – Argyranthemum
Rhodanthemum – Chrysanthemopsis
Rhodanthemum – Chrysanthemum
Rhodanthemum – Leucanthemopsis
Rhodanthemum – Leucanthemum
Rhodanthemum – Pyrethropsis
Rhodiola – Clementsia
Rhodiola – Rosularia
Rhodiola – Sedum
Rhododendron – Azalea
Rhododendron – Azaleodendron
Rhododendron – Rhodora
Rhododendron – Tsusiophyllum
Rhodophiala – Hippeastrum
× *Rhodoxis – Hypoxis* × *Rhodohypoxis*
× *Rhodoxis – Rhodohypoxis*
Rhus – Toxicodendron
Rhyncospora – Dichromena
Rosularia – Cotyledon
Rosularia – Sempervivella
Rothmannia – Gardenia
Ruellia – Dipteracanthus

Saccharum – Erianthus
Sagina – Minuartia
Sanguisorba – Dendriopoterium
Sanguisorba – Poterium
Sasa – Arundinaria
Sasaella – Arundinaria
Sasaella – Pleioblastus
Sasaella – Sasa
Sauromatum – Arum
Scadoxus – Haemanthus
Schefflera – Brassaia
Schefflera – Dizygotheca
Schefflera – Heptapleurum
Schizachyrium – Andropogon
Schizostachyum – Arundinaria
Schizostachyum – Thamnocalamus
Schizostylis – Hesperantha
Schoenoplectus – Scirpus
Scilla – Oncostema
Scirpoides – Scirpus
Sedum – Hylotelephium
Sedum – Sedastrum
Semiaquilegia – Aquilegia
Semiaquilegia – Paraquilegia
Semiarundinaria – Arundinaria
Semiarundinaria – Oligostachyum

Senecio – Cineraria
Senecio – Kleinia
Senecio – Ligularia
Senna – Cassia
Seriphidium – Artemisia
Shortia – Schizocodon
Sibbaldiopsis – Potentilla
Silene – Lychnis
Silene – Melandrium
Silene – Saponaria
Sinacalia – Ligularia
Sinacalia – Senecio
Sinningia – Gesneria
Sinningia – Rechsteineria
Sinobambusa – Pleioblastus
Sinobambusa – Pseudosasa
Siphocranion – Chamaesphacos
Sisymbrium – Hesperis
Sisyrinchium – Phaiophleps
Smallanthus – Polymnia
Smilacina – Maianthemum
Solanum – Lycianthes
Soleirolia – Helxine
Solenostemon – Coleus
× *Solidaster – Aster*
× *Solidaster – Solidago*
Sorbaria – Spiraea
Sparaxis – Synnotia
Sphaeralcea – Iliamna
Sphaeromeria – Tanacetum
Spirodela – Lemna
Stachys – Betonica
Stemmacantha – Centaurea
Stemmacantha – Leuzea
Stenomesson – Urceolina
Stewartia – Stuartia
Stipa – Achnatherum
Stipa – Agrostis
Stipa – Calamagrostis
Stipa – Lasiagrostis
Stipa – Nassella
Strobilanthes – Parachampionella
Strobilanthes – Pteracanthus
Succisa – Scabiosa
Sutera – Bacopa
Syagrus – Arecastrum
Syagrus – Cocos
Syncarpha - Helipterum
Syzygium – Caryophyllus

Talbotia – Vellozia
Tanacetum – Achillea
Tanacetum – Balsamita
Tanacetum – Chrysanthemum
Tanacetum – Matricaria
Tanacetum – Pyrethrum
Tanacetum – Spathipappus
Tecoma – Tecomaria
Telekia – Buphthalmum
Tetradium – Euodia
Tetraneuris - Actinella
Tetraneuris – Actinella
Tetraneuris – Hymenoxys
Tetrapanax – Fatsia
Thamnocalamus – Arundinaria
Thlaspi – Hutchinsia
Thlaspi – Noccaea
Thlaspi – Vania
Thuja – Thujopsis
Thymus – Origanum
Tiarella – × *Heucherella*
Tonestus – Haplopappus
Toona – Cedrela
Trachelium – Diosphaera
Trachycarpus – Chamaerops
Tradescantia – Rhoeo
Tradescantia – Setcreasea
Tradescantia – Zebrina
Trichopetalum – Anthericum
Tripetaleia – Elliottia
Tripogandra – Tradescantia
Tristaniopsis – Tristania
Triteleia – Brodiaea
Tritonia – Crocosmia
Tritonia – Montbretia
Trochiscanthes – Angelica
Tropaeolum – Nasturtium hort.
Tulipa – Amana
Tupistra – Campylandra
Tutcheria – Pyrenaria
Tweedia – Oxypetalum

Ugni – Myrtus
Utricularia – Polypompholyx
Uvularia – Oakesiella

Vaccaria – Melandrium
Vaccinium – Oxycoccus
Verbascum – Celsia
Verbascum – × *Celsioverbascum*
Verbena – Glandularia
Verbena – Lippia
Veronicastrum – Veronica
Vigna – Phaseolus
Viola – Erpetion
Vitaliana – Androsace
Vitaliana – Douglasia

Wedelia – Zexmenia
Weigela – Diervilla
Weigela – Macrodiervilla

Xanthophthalmum – Chrysanthemum
Xanthorhiza – Zanthorhiza
Xerochrysum – Bracteantha
Xerochrysum – Helichrysum

Yushania – Arundinaria
Yushania – Sinarundinaria
Yushania – Thamnocalamus

Zantedeschia – Calla
Zauschneria – Epilobium
Zephyranthes – × *Cooperanthes*
Zephyranthes – Cooperia

THE PLANT DIRECTORY

A

Abelia ✿ (*Caprifoliaceae*)

	biflora	MBri NLar WWes
	chinensis misapplied	see *A.* x *grandiflora*
§	***chinensis*** R. Br.	CBcs CPle EBee ECre EPfP MAsh NBlu SDnm SMer SPer SPla SPoG WBcn WFar WHCG WPat WSHC WTel
	dielsii	CPLG CTrw GQui
	'Edward Goucher'	CBcs CDoC CPle CTbh EBee ECrN EGra ELan EPfP LRHS MGos MRav MSwo NBea SEND SLim SPer SPlb SWvt WBVN WDin WFar WOld WPat WSHC
	engleriana	CPle EPfP MAsh SPoG WBcn WFar
	floribunda ♀H3	CBcs CFil CMac CPLG CPle CSBt CSam CTrw CWib ELan EPfP IDee LRHS MAsh SBrw SDnm SIgm SMur SPoG SSpi SSta STre WAbe WBcn WFar WOld WPat
§	x ***grandiflora*** ♀H4	More than 30 suppliers
	- 'Aurea'	see *A.* x *grandiflora* 'Gold Spot'
	- 'Compacta'	LRHS WFar
	- Confetti = 'Conti'PBR (v)	CBrm CChe CDoC COtt CSBt CSPN CWSG EBee EHoe ELan EPfP LAst LRHS MCCP MGos MLan NEgg SBod SLim SMur SPer SPoG SSta SWvt WDin WFar WWeb
	- dwarf	CDoC
§	- 'Francis Mason' (v)	More than 30 suppliers
§	- 'Gold Spot'	CBcs CDoC CTbh CWSG EPfP MAsh MWat SSto WBrE WOld WWeb
	- 'Gold Strike'	see *A.* x *grandiflora* 'Gold Spot'
	- 'Goldsport'	see *A.* x *grandiflora* 'Gold Spot'
	- 'Hopleys'PBR (v)	LRHS SBra SPoG
	- 'Panache' (v)	CPle MGos MRav
	- 'Prostrate White'	NLar
	- 'Sherwoodii'	WFar WPat
	- 'Sunrise'PBR (v)	CDoC CSBt EHoe ELan ENot EPfP LRHS NCGa SBod SBra SLim SMur SPer SPla
	- 'Variegata'	see *A.* x *grandiflora* 'Francis Mason'
	mosanensis	NLar
	rupestris hort.	see *A.* x *grandiflora*
	rupestris Lindl.	see *A. chinensis* R.Br.
	schumannii ♀H4	More than 30 suppliers
	- 'Saxon Gold'PBR	LAst NEgg SSto
	spathulata	WBcn WFar
	triflora	CAbP CBot CPLG CPle EBee EPfP LAst LRHS SLon WFar WPat
	zanderi	see *A. dielsii*

Abeliophyllum (*Oleaceae*)

	distichum	CAbP CBcs CBot CBrm CDoC CEnd CHar CMHG CWib EBee ECrN ELan ENot EPfP EWTr GKir LRHS MAsh MBri MGos NSti SPer SPla SSpi SSta SWvt WCFE WFar WPat WSHC
	- Roseum Group	CBcs CDoC CFil CPMA EBee ELan EPfP GBuc LAst LRHS MAsh MRav NSti SBrw SHBN SLon SPer SPoG SSpi WFar WPGP

Abelmoschus (*Malvaceae*)

§	***manihot***	EWin
	moschatus **new**	CSec

Abies ✿ (*Pinaceae*)

	alba	CDul GKir GTSp LCon MBar NWea WMou
	- 'Compacta'	CKen
	- 'King's Dwarf'	CKen
	- 'Microphylla'	CKen
	- 'Munsterland'	CKen
	amabilis	GKir GTSp LCon LRav
	- 'Spreading Star'	NLar
	arizonica	see *A. lasiocarpa* var. *arizonica*
	x ***arnoldiana***	GKir MBar NLar
	- 'Cyrille' **new**	MBlu
	balsamea	CDul GTSp LCon NWea WMou
	- Hudsonia Group ♀H4	CDoC CKen CMac ECho EHul EPot GKir IMGH LCon LLin LRHS MBar MGos NDlv NMen SLim SPoG WDin WEve
	- 'Jamie' **new**	CKen
	- 'Le Feber'	CKen
	- 'Nana'	CKen CRob EHul EOrn GKir LBee LCon LRHS MAsh NLar WDin
	- var. ***phanerolepis*** 'Bear Swamp'	CKen
	- 'Piccolo'	CKen EHul EMil IMGH NLar SLim SPoG WGor
	- 'Prostrata'	ECho EHul LLin LRHS WEve
	- 'Renswoude'	CKen
	- 'Tyler Blue' **new**	CKen
	- 'Verkade's Prostrate'	CKen
	borisii-regis	GTSp LCon
*	- 'Pendula'	CKen
	brachyphylla dwarf	see *A. homolepis* 'Prostrata'
	cephalonica	CDul GTSp LCon
	- 'Greg's Broom'	CKen
§	- 'Meyer's Dwarf'	CDoC EHul GKir IMGH LCon LLin LRHS MAsh MBar NLar SCoo SLim SPoG WEve
	- 'Nana'	see *A. cephalonica* 'Meyer's Dwarf'
	concolor ♀H4	CBcs CDul CTho EHul GKir GTSp GWCH ISea LCon LRHS MBar NWea SEND WDin
	- 'Archer's Dwarf'	CKen LCon MGos NLar SLim
I	- 'Argentea'	LCon NLar
	- 'Birthday Broom' **new**	CKen
	- 'Blue Spreader'	CKen MGos
§	- 'Compacta' ♀H4	CDoC CKen EBrs ECho EOrn GKir IMGH LCon LLin LRHS MAsh MBar MGos NEgg NLar SCoo SLim SPoG WEve WFar

	Name	Suppliers
	- 'Fagerhult'	CKen
	- 'Gable's Weeping'	CKen
	- 'Glauca'	see *A. concolor* Violacea Group
	- 'Glauca Compacta'	see *A. concolor* 'Compacta'
§	- 'Hillier's Dwarf'	CKen
	- 'Husky Pup'	CKen
	- Lowiana Group	LCon
	- - 'Creamy'	CKen
	- 'Masonic Broom'	CKen NLar
	- 'Mike Stearn'	CKen
	- 'Mora' **new**	CKen
	- 'Ostrov Nad Ohri'	CKen
	- 'Piggelmee'	CKen LLin SLim
	- 'Sherwood's Blue' **new**	ECho
*	- 'Swift's Silver'	LBee WBVN WEve
§	- Violacea Group	CDoC CKen LCon LLin MAsh MBar MBri WEve
	- 'Wattez Prostrate'	SLim WFar
	- 'Wattezii'	CKen LLin
	- 'Wintergold'	CKen EBrs NLar WEve
	delavayi	CMCN GKir GTSp
	- var. ***delavayi*** Fabri Group	see *A. fabri*
I	- 'Nana'	CKen
	- 'Nana Headfort'	see *A. fargesii* 'Headfort'
§	***fabri***	GTSp LCon
§	***fargesii*** **new**	GKir
	- var. ***faxoniana***	GKir
§	- 'Headfort'	LCon MBar NLar
	firma	GTSp
	forrestii	CKen GKir
	- var. ***ferreana*** SF 95168	ISea
	- - SF 95226	ISea
	- var. ***smithii*** **new**	GKir
	fraseri	CTri GIBF GKir MBar NWea SEND WMou
	- 'Blue Bonnet' **new**	CKen
	- 'Raul's Dwarf'	CKen
	grandis	CBcs CDul GIBF GKir LCon LRav MBar NWea SHBN WDin WEve WMou
	- 'Compacta'	CKen
	- 'Van Dedem's Dwarf'	CKen
	holophylla	CMCN GKir LCon
	homolepis	CDul CMCN GKir LCon NLar NWea
§	- 'Prostrata'	CKen
	koreana	More than 30 suppliers
	- 'Alpin Star' **new**	CKen
	- 'Aurea'	see *A. koreana* 'Flava'
	- 'Blaue Zwo'	CKen MAsh NLar
	- 'Blauer Eskimo'	CKen
	- 'Blauer Pfiff'	CKen GKir NLar SLim SPoG
	- 'Blinsham Gold'	CKen
	- blue	EHoe
	- 'Blue Emperor'	CKen NLar
	- 'Blue Magic'	CKen NLar
	- 'Blue 'n' Silver'	LLin NLar
	- 'Cis'	CKen NLar SCoo SLim
	- 'Compact Dwarf'	EPot LLin MBar MGos NLar
	- 'Crystal Globe'	CKen NLar
§	- 'Flava'	CKen ECho IMGH LLin MBar SCoo SLim SPoG WEve
	- 'Frosty'	NLar SLim
	- 'Gait'	CKen NLar
	- 'Golden Dream'	CKen
	- 'Golden Glow' **new**	NLar
	- 'Green Carpet'	CKen EBrs SLim
	- 'Inverleith'	CKen
	- 'Kohout'	CKen
	- 'Lippetal'	CKen
	- 'Luminetta'	CKen LRHS NLar SCoo SLim SPoG
	- 'Nadelkissen'	CKen
	- 'Nisbet'	CRez ECho GBin IMGH LLin NLar SLim WEve WGor
	- 'Oberon'	CKen CRob EHul LCon MAsh NLar
	- 'Piccolo'	CKen NLar
	- 'Pinocchio'	CKen NLar
	- 'Prostrata'	see *A. koreana* 'Prostrate Beauty'
§	- 'Prostrate Beauty'	CRez ECho EOrn IMGH LLin SPoG WEve WFar WGor
	- 'Silberkugel'	CKen SLim
	- 'Silberlocke' ♀H4	CDoC CKen CRob EBrs GKir LBee LCon LLin LRHS MAsh MBar MBlu MBri MGos NBea NEgg SCoo SLim SPer SPoG WEve WOrn
	- 'Silbermavers'	CKen
	- 'Silberperl'	CKen
	- 'Silberschmeltzer'	LLin
	- 'Silver Show'	CKen NLar
	- 'Starker's Dwarf'	CKen
	- 'Taiga'	NLar
	- 'Threave'	CKen
	- 'Tundra'	NLar
	- 'Winter Goldtip'	CRez LLin WEve
	lasiocarpa	CDul NWea
	- var. ***arizonica***	SCoo
I	- - 'Argentea'	NWea
	- - 'Compacta' ♀H4	CDoC CFee CKen CMac EBrs ECho EHul GKir IMGH LBee LCon LLin LRHS MAsh MBar MBri MGos SCoo SLim SPoG WBrE WEve WFar WGor
	- - 'Kenwith Blue'	CKen LLin NLar
	- 'Day Creek'	CKen
	- 'Duflon'	CKen
	- 'Green Globe'	CKen LLin MBar NLar WEve
*	- 'King's Blue'	CKen
	- 'Logan Pass'	CKen
	- 'Mulligan's Dwarf'	CKen
	- 'Prickly Pete' **new**	CKen
	- 'Roger Watson'	WEve
	- 'Toenisvorst'	CKen
	magnifica	LRav
I	- 'Nana'	CKen NEgg NLar
	- witches' broom	CKen
	nephrolepis	GIBF GKir
	nobilis	see *A. procera*
	nordmanniana ♀H4	CDul CTri EHul ENot EPfP GIBF GKir LBuc LCon LRHS MBar MGos NWea SEND WDin WEve WMou
	- 'Arne's Dwarf' **new**	CKen
	- 'Barabits' Compact'	LLin MBar MGos NLar
	- 'Barabits' Gold' **new**	LLin
	'Barabits' Spreader'	CKen LLin
	- subsp. ***equi-trojani***	GKir GTSp NWea
	- - 'Archer'	CKen
	- 'Golden Spreader' ♀H4	CDoC CKen EBrs ECho EOrn GKir IMGH LBee LCon LLin LRHS MAsh MBar MBri MGos NLar SCoo SLim SPoG WEve WFar
	- 'Jakobsen'	CKen
	- 'Pendula'	GKir
	- 'Silverspitze' **new**	CKen
	numidica 'Glauca'	CKen
	pindrow	GKir GTSp LCon
	pinsapo	GKir GTSp LCon LRHS MBar SEND
	- 'Aurea'	CKen CRob GKir LCon LLin NLar SLim WEve
I	- 'Aurea Nana'	CKen
	- 'Fastigiata'	MPkF
	- 'Glauca' ♀H4	CDoC CKen CTho EHul ELan GKir LCon LLin MBar MBlu NLar SCoo SLim SPoG WDin WEve WMou
	- 'Hamondii'	CKen

I - 'Horstmann' — CKen EBrs LCon LLin WEve
- 'Kelleriis' — LCon
- 'Pendula' — MPkF NLar WEve
- 'Quicksilver' — CKen
§ ***procera*** 🏆H4 — CBcs CDoC CDul EHul EPfP GIBF GKir LCon MBar NWea WBVN WDin WEve WMou
- 'Blaue Hexe' — CKen GKir NLar SLim SPoG
- Glauca Group — CDoC CMac CTho GKir LCon LLin LRHS MAsh MBar MBlu MBri MGos WEve WFar WGer
- 'Glauca Prostrata' — CRob GKir LBee LRHS MBar MGos SCoo WEve
- 'Sherwoodii' — CKen
recurvata — GKir
§ - var. ***ernestii*** — GKir
Rosemoor hybrid — CKen
sibirica — GKir NWea
squamata — GKir GTSp
veitchii — CBcs CDul GKir LCon MBar NWea
- 'Hedergott' — CKen NLar
- 'Heine' — CKen NLar
I - 'Pendula' — CKen
- 'Rumburg' — CKen

Abromeitiella (*Bromeliaceae*)

brevifolia 🏆H1 — CFil EPem WCot

Abrotanella (*Asteraceae*)

sp. — ECho

Abutilon ✿ (*Malvaceae*)

'Amiti' — MOak
'Amsterdam' — ERea
'Apricot Belle' — MOak
'Ashford Red' — CBcs WKif
'Boule de Neige' — CBot CHal ERea MOak
'Canary Bird' misapplied — see *A.* 'Golden Fleece'
'Canary Bird' 🏆H2 — CBot CHEx CHal ERea MLan MOak SHBN SYvo WKif WOld WWlt
'Cannington Carol' (v) 🏆H2 — ERea EWin MOak SDys
'Cannington Peter' (v) 🏆H2 — CHal MOak
'Cannington Sally' (v) — EWin MLan SWvt WWol
'Cannington Sonia' (v) — ERea
'Cynthia Pike' (v) — LRHS
I 'Eric Rose' — MTis
§ 'Feuerglocke' — MOak
Firebell — see *A.* 'Feuerglocke'
'Frances Elizabeth' — MOak
§ 'Golden Fleece' — ERea MOak
'Hinton Seedling' — CRHN MOak
x ***hybridum*** apricot **new** — CHEx
- red **new** — CHEx
indicum — CPLG
'J. Morris' — LRHS MAsh SPoG SSta
'Kentish Belle' 🏆H2-3 — CBcs CHEx CMHG CMac CPle CRHN CTbh EBee ECot ELan EPfP LSRN MOak NPal SBra SHBN SPer WFar
I 'Kentish Belle Variegatum' (v) — ELan SBrw
'Lemon Queen' — CHal
'Linda Vista Peach' 🏆H2 — MOak
'Louis Marignac' — MOak
'Marion' 🏆H2 — CHrt LRHS MOak SDys
'Master Michael' — CMac ERea
megapotamicum 🏆H3 — CBcs CBot CHEx CMHG CNic CPLG CPle CRHN CSBt CTrC EBee ELan EPfP EPla ERea GQui LRHS MAsh MGos MLan MOak MRav SPer SPoG SRms WFar WSHC XPep
- 'Compactum' — ENot
- 'Variegatum' (v) — CBcs CBrm CPLG CSBt ELan EPfP GQui LRHS LSRN MAsh MGos MOak SAga SBod SHBN SPer SPoG SSta SWvt WFar
- 'Wakehurst' **new** — WCot
- 'Wisley Red' — SBrw
x ***milleri*** 🏆H2 — CMac CPLG CRHN ERea MLan SHBN WCot
- 'Variegatum' (v) — CHEx CMHG CMac EWin LRHS MOak SEND
'Moonchimes' — MOak
'Nabob' 🏆H2 — CHal ERea LRHS MLan MOak MTis SLdr
'Orange Glow' (v) 🏆H2 — MOak
'Orange Vein' — CHal EShb
'Patrick Synge' — CMHG CPle ERea LPhx MOak
'Peaches and Cream' — LRHS
§ ***pictum*** — ERea
- 'Thompsonii' (v) — CHEx CHal ERea MJnS MOak WDyG
'Pink Lady' — ERea GQui
'Red Bells' — GQui MOak
'Rotterdam' — MOak
§ 'Savitzii' (v) 🏆H2 — CHal MOak SRms
sellowianum var. ***marmoratum*** — ERea
'Snowfall' — MOak
'Souvenir de Bonn' (v) 🏆H2 — CHal ERea EShb MLan MOak MTis SAga WCot
striatum hort. — see *A. pictum*
x ***suntense*** — CMHG CPLG CSBt EPfP ERea LHyd LRHS LSou MJnS MWgw NPer SPoG WTel
- 'Jermyns' 🏆H3 — EPfP LRHS MBri MFOX SLon
- 'Violetta' — CBcs CEnd CHEx MSte SPer
- white-flowered **new** — CBcs
theophrasti — MSal
variegated, salmon (v) — LAst
'Victory' — SSpi
vitifolium — CBot EBee ECot EPfP ERea IDee ISea MGos MHer NBid NEgg SAga SChu SPer WKif WOut
- var. ***album*** — CHEx CMHG CRHN EMan EPfP IDee ISea LHyd MLan MWgw SChu SEND SSpi WCru
- 'Buckland' — CHll
- 'Ice Blue' — CBot
- 'Simcox White' — WEas
- 'Tennant's White' 🏆H3 — CAbP CBot ELan EPfP ERea LRHS MBri NBur SDnm WCru
- 'Veronica Tennant' 🏆H3 — ERea MSte SDnm WKif

Acacia ✿ (*Mimosaceae*)

acinacea — SPlb
adunca — SPlb
alpina — WCel
armata — see *A. paradoxa*
baileyana 🏆H2 — CAlb CBcs CSBt CTrC ECot ELan EMil EPfP ERea EShb ESlt GQui LRHS MGol SBig SBrw SCoo SPlb SWvt WMul WPat
- var. ***aurea*** — SPlb
- 'Purpurea' 🏆H2 — CAbb CBcs CBos CDoC CEnd CFil CKno CTbh CTrC CWib EBee EMil EPfP ERea GQui IDee MGos MLan SBig SBrw SPer SPlb SPoG SWvt WFar WMul WPGP WPat
boormanii — ISea WCel
cultriformis — CPle CTrC ERea SEND
cyanophylla — see *A. saligna*
dealbata 🏆H2 — More than 30 suppliers
- subsp. ***subalpina*** — LRHS WCel WMul WPGP
Exeter hybrid — CSBt

filicifolia WCel
***floribunda* 'Lisette'** EPfP LRHS
frigescens WCel
julibrissin see *Albizia julibrissin*
juniperina see *A. ulicifolia*
karroo CArn CPLG WMul XPep
kybeanensis CTrC WCel
longifolia CAbb CBcs EAmu EPfP IDee SEND SPer SRms WGer
- subsp. ***sophorae*** GGar
macradenia SPlb
maidenii MGol
mearnsii WCel WMul
melanoxylon CDul CTrC IDee ISea LRHS WCel WHer
motteana ECot
mucronata CTrC EShb
***myrtifolia* new** EWll
obliquinervia WCel
§ ***paradoxa*** ♀H2 CTrC LRHS WPat
pataczekii EBee ENot EPfP ERea LRHS SSpi
podalyriifolia CDoC CFil WPGP
pravissima ♀H2-3 More than 30 suppliers
retinodes ♀H2 CAbb CBcs CDoC CPle EPfP ERea GQui IDee LRav MLan SEND WCFE WMul
riceana CTrC GQui IDee LRav WPat
rubida IDee LRav WCel WMul
§ ***saligna*** CSec EShb LRHS
sentis see *A. victoriae*
spectabilis SPlb
suaveolens SPlb
§ ***ulicifolia*** CPLG CSBt GGar
verticillata CBcs CHll
- riverine CTrC
§ ***victoriae*** ERea

Acaena (*Rosaceae*)

adscendens hort. see *A. magellanica* subsp. *magellanica*, *A. saccaticupula* 'Blue Haze'
adscendens misapplied see *A. affinis*
adscendens Vahl see *A. magellanica* subsp. *laevigata*
- 'Glauca' CMdw EMan NBir NFor SBla
§ ***affinis*** COIW ECha SDix
anserinifolia hort. see *A. novae-zelandiae*
§ ***anserinifolia*** (Forst. & Forst. f.) Druce ECha GGar
buchananii CSpe CTri EBee EDAr EGoo EPot GGar GTou IHMH MBar MLLN NBro NFor SRms WFar WGHP WPer
caerulea see *A. caesiiglauca*
§ ***caesiiglauca*** CBcs CTri GGar GTou NBid NFor NLon NMRc SBla SGar SVal WEas WGHP WPer
caespitosa EBee
fissistipula EHoe GGar WHer WMoo
glaucophylla see *A. magellanica* subsp. *magellanica*
inermis EBee EPot GTou MLLN NFla SPlb WGHP
- 'Purpurea' CAby CBcs CBrm EChP ECha EShb GGar MSph NJOw NLar SIng SPlb WHoo WMoo WWFP
macrocephala EBee
§ ***magellanica*** subsp. ***laevigata*** GGar GTou NLon WWpP
§ - subsp. ***magellanica*** EBee GTou LEdu
microphylla ♀H4 CSam CStu CTri EBee ECha GGar IHMH LBee LRHS MBar NJOw NMen SHFr SIng SPlb SRms SVal WGHP
- Copper Carpet see *A. microphylla* 'Kupferteppich'
- 'Glauca' see *A. caesiiglauca*
§ - 'Kupferteppich' CBrm EBee EHoe EMan GAbr GGar GKir IHMH MBri MRav MWgw NBir NChi NVic SIng WGHP WPat WPer WWpP
- 'Pewter Carpet' EGoo
- 'Pulchella' EMan LRHS
myriophylla EBee ECho EDAr EMFP MGGn
§ ***novae-zelandiae*** CTri EBee GGar GTou SDix WMoo WPer
ovalifolia EBee EDAr GTou
'Pewter' see *A. saccaticupula* 'Blue Haze'
pinnatifida GTou NBro
platycantha F&W 9293 WCot
profundeincisa see *A. anserinifolia* Druce
'Purple Carpet' see *A. microphylla* 'Kupferteppich'
'Purple Haze' **new** CSpe
saccaticupula MWgw NLar
§ - 'Blue Haze' COIW EBee ECha EDAr EPot GFlt GGar GKir GTou LRHS MBar MLLN NVic SIng SPer SPlb SRms SWvt WFar WGHP WHoo WMoo
sanguisorbae see *A. anserinifolia* Druce
viridior see *A. anserinifolia* Druce

Acalypha (*Euphorbiaceae*)

hispaniolae ♀H1 ERea ESlt MOak
hispida ♀H1 LRHS MBri
pendula see *A. reptans*
§ ***reptans*** CHal SPet

Acanthocalyx see *Morina*

Acantholimon (*Plumbaginaceae*)

sp. EMan
androsaceum see *A. ulicinum*
glumaceum MDHE MWat WPat
§ ***ulicinum*** ECho EPot

Acanthopanax see *Eleutherococcus*

ricinifolius see *Kalopanax septemlobus*

Acanthostachys (*Bromeliaceae*)

pitcairnioides EMan

Acanthus ✿ (*Acanthaceae*)

balcanicus see *A. hungaricus*
'Candelabra' **new** MBNS
caroli-alexandri EBla WHil
dioscoridis CBot EBla MAvo SMHy WHil WSel
- var. ***perringii*** CDes EBee LPio MAvo MSte NChi SBla SIgm SSpi WCot WFar WHil WPGP WSHC
- smooth-leaved SIgm
hirsutus CBot EMar EMon EWTr LPio MMil SIgm SPav SVal WCot WHil
- JCA 109.700 SBla
- f. ***roseus*** SBla SIgm WFar
- subsp. ***syriacus*** EHrv WHil
- - JCA 106.500 LPhx
§ ***hungaricus*** More than 30 suppliers
- AL&JS 90097YU EMon WPrP
- MESE 561 EPPr
- 'Architect' COIW EWll LRHS
longifolius see *A. hungaricus*
mollis More than 30 suppliers
- 'Feilding Gold' see *A. mollis* 'Hollard's Gold'
- free-flowering GCal WHil
- 'Hollard's Gold' More than 30 suppliers
- 'Jardin en Face' CBot

- 'Jefalba'	see *A. mollis* (Latifolius Group) 'Rue Ledan'
- Latifolius Group	EBee ECrN EMan EPfP LRHS MRav MSte SChu SPer SRms WHil WHoo WWpP
- - 'Rue Ledan'	EBee EMon LPhx MAnH SUsu WHil
- 'Summerdance'	WHil
- white-flowered **new**	CBct WSel
sennii	LPhx LPio SIgm
spinosus Υ^{H4}	More than 30 suppliers
- Ferguson's form **new**	WCot
- 'Lady Moore' (v)	EMon IBlr NLar SBch WHil WSPU
- 'Royal Haughty'	WHil
- Spinosissimus Group	CBct CMHG ECha EHrv ELan EMan EMon GCal LEdu LPhx LPio MAvo MMil MRav NChi SAga SBla SMad WCot WFar WHil WMnd WPop WTin
'Summer Beauty'	EVFa MBri NPro WCot WFar WGer WHil
syriacus	EMan GCal NLar NPro SAga SVal WCot WHil

Acca (*Myrtaceae*)

sellowiana (F)	CArn CBcs CBrm CDoC CMHG CPLG CPle CSBt CTri EBee ELan EPfP ERea ERom EUnu GQui IDee ISea LRHS LSpr MCCP SLim SPer SPlb SPoG SYvo WSHC XPep
- 'Apollo' (F)	CTrC ERea
- 'Coolidge' (F)	ERea
- 'Mammoth' (F)	CBcs ERea
- 'Triumph' (F)	CBcs ERea
- 'Variegata' (F/v)	ELan

Acer ✿ (*Aceraceae*)

HWJK 2040 from Nepal **new**	WCru
acuminatum	CMCN GKir WNor WWes
albopurpurascens	WWes
argutum	CMCN IMGH WCwm WNor
barbinerve	CMCN EPfP SHGN WNor WWes
x ***bornmuelleri***	WWes
buergerianum	CBcs CDul CMCN CMen CPMA ECrN GKir IMGH LRHS MPkF SBLw SBir SEND STre WCwm WGer WNor
- 'Goshiki-kaede' (v)	CPMA WWes
- 'Goshiki-kosode' (v)	WWes
- 'Integrifolium'	see *A. buergerianum* 'Subintegrum'
- 'Koshi-miyasama'	WWes
- 'Kyûden'	WWes
- 'Mino-yatsubusa'	MPkF WWes
- 'Miyasama-yatsubusa'	MPkF
- 'Naruto'	CMCN MPkF
- subsp. ***ningpoense***	WWes
- 'Shirley Debacq'	WWes
§ - 'Subintegrum'	CMCN WWes
* - 'Variegatum' (v)	CMCN
caesium	WWes
calcaratum	CMCN
campbellii B&SWJ 7685	WCru
* - var. ***fansipanense*** B&SWJ 8270	WCru
- - HWJ 569	WCru
§ - subsp. ***flabellatum*** B&SWJ 8057	WCru
- - var. ***yunnanense***	CDoC CFil ECrN GKir GTSp WCwm WHCr
- subsp. ***sinense***	see *A. sinense*
- subsp. ***wilsonii***	see *A. wilsonii*
campestre Υ^{H4}	More than 30 suppliers
- 'Carnival' (v)	CBcs CDul CEnd CMCN CPMA CWib EBee GKir LRHS MAsh MBlu MBri SMad SPer SPoG SWvt WCot WPGP WWes
- 'Elsrijk'	CAlb CCVT CLnd ENot SBLw
- 'Evenley Red'	MBlu
- 'Pendulum'	CEnd CTho GKir
- 'Postelense'	CEnd CMCN CPMA GKir MBlu MGos MPkF SLim WWes
- 'Pulverulentum' (v)	CDoC CEnd CMCN CPMA GKir MAsh SLim SMad SSta WBcn
- 'Queen Elizabeth'	CCVT SEND
- 'Red Shine'	ENot GKir MGos
- 'Royal Ruby'	CTho CWSG GKir GTSp MAsh MGos SSta
* - 'Ruby Glow'	CDoC CEnd CLnd GKir LRHS
- 'Silver Celebration' (v)	CPMA
- 'William Caldwell'	CEnd CTho LRHS
capillipes Υ^{H4}	CBcs CCVT CDul CMCN CRez CTho CWib ECrN EGFP ENot EWTr GKir LRHS MBar MDun NBea SBLw SBir SBrw SHGN WDin WFar WNor WOrn
- 'Candy Stripe'	GKir SLim SSpi SSta
- 'Gimborn'	WWes
- 'Golden Increase'	WWes
- 'Honey Dew' **new**	NLar
- var. ***morifolium***	see *A. morifolium*
cappadocicum	CDul CMCN CSam ECrN GKir GTSp LRHS MDun MLan NWea SBLw WDin WNor WWes
- 'Aureum' Υ^{H4}	More than 30 suppliers
- 'De Oirsprong'	WWes
- subsp. ***divergens***	MPkF
- var. ***mono***	see *A. pictum*
- 'Rubrum' Υ^{H4}	CLnd CMCN EBee ECrN ENot EPfP GKir LBuc LRHS MBlu MGos MRav SBLw SHBN SLim SPer WDin WFar WHer WOrn
- subsp. ***sinicum***	CEnd CFil CMCN EPfP WFar WPGP
- - GWJ 9360	WCru
§ - - var. ***tricaudatum***	CPLG
carpinifolium	CBcs CBrd CMCN CTho ECrN EWTr MPkF NLar WCwm WNor
- 'Esveld Select'	WWes
catalpifolium	see *A. longipes* subsp. *catalpifolium*
§ ***caudatifolium***	CFil CMCN CPle SBir WCwm WPGP
- B&SWJ 3531	WCru
- B&SWJ 6734	WCru
§ ***caudatum***	MDun SSpi
- GWJ 9279	WCru
- subsp. ***ukurunduense***	CMCN IArd MPkF WNor
cinnamomifolium	see *A. coriaceifolium*
circinatum	CBcs CDoC CDul CLnd CMCN CPMA CSam ECrN EPfP EShb EWTr LRHS MBlu MLan NBea NFor NLar SHBN SSpi SSta WDin WFar WNor
- 'Little Gem'	CPMA
- 'Monroe'	WWes
- 'Pacific Fire' **new**	CPMA
- 'Sunglow'	WWes
circinatum x ***palmatum***	GKir SIFN
cissifolium	CDoC CFil CLnd CMCN CTho EPfP GKir IArd IMGH LRHS WNor
x ***conspicuum*** 'Candy Stripe'	CPMA GKir SIFN
- 'Elephant's Ear'	CPMA EPfP NLar
I - 'Phoenix'	CEnd CMCN CPMA CTho EPfP GKir LRHS MBlu MBri NLar SIFN SSpi WPat
- 'Silver Ghost' **new**	MGos

§	- 'Silver Vein'	CDoC CDul CEnd CMCN CPMA EBee ECrN EPfP GKir LRHS MGos NLar SIFN SPur SSpi SSta
§	***cordatum***	WWes
§	***coriaceifolium***	WNor
	crataegifolium	CMCN IMGH WNor
	- 'Meuri-no-ôfu' (v) **new**	MPkF
	- 'Meuri-keade-no-fuiri' (v) **new**	MPkF
	- 'Veitchii' (v)	CDoC CMCN CPMA EPfP GKir MPkF NLar SIFN SSpi WBcn WWes
	creticum L., non F. Schmidt.	see *A. sempervirens*
	dasycarpum	see *A. saccharinum*
	davidii	CAbP CBcs CCVT CDoC CDul CFil CLnd CMCN CMHG CSBt ECrN ENot GIBF GKir ISea ITim LRHS MBar MGos MRav NBea SBLw SHBN SLim SPer WBVN WDin WFar WNor WOrn
	- B&SWJ 8183	WCru
	- 'Cantonspark'	MPkF WWes
N	- 'Ernest Wilson'	CBcs CMCN GKir LRHS MBlu NEgg NLar
N	- 'George Forrest' 🏆^{H4}	More than 30 suppliers
	- 'Hagelunie'	MPkF
	- 'Karmen'	CLnd CPMA GKir LRHS MBri MPkF SBir SIFN WWes
	- 'Madeline Spitta'	CMCN CPMA GKir MBlu MPkF SIFN
	- 'Purple Bark' **new**	SBir
	- 'Rosalie'	CDul EPfP GKir LRHS MBlu MBri SBir
	- 'Sekka'	WWes
	- 'Serpentine' 🏆^{H4}	CBcs CDoC CMCN CPMA CTho EPfP GKir LRHS MBlu MBri NEgg NLar SIFN SSpi SSta WFar WOrn
	- 'Silver Vein'	see *A.* x *conspicuum* 'Silver Vein'
	- variegated (v)	WWes
	diabolicum	CMCN GIBF WWes
	- f. ***purpurascens***	GIBF
	distylum	WCwm WWes
	divergens	CMCN
	elegantulum	CDoC CMCN WCwm WNor
	erianthum	CLnd CPne CTho WNor WWes
	fabri	CBcs CMCN WNor
	flabellatum	see *A. campbellii* subsp. *flabellatum*
§	***forrestii***	CBcs CMCN CTho EPfP IArd NBea WCwm WNor
	- 'Alice'	CBcs CDul CEnd CMCN CPMA GKir SIFN SSta WBcn
§	- 'Sirene'	CPMA
§	- 'Sparkling'	CPMA GKir LRHS MBri SBir
	x ***freemanii***	CMCN
	- 'Armstrong'	SBLw WFar WWes
	- Autumn Blaze = 'Jeffersred'	CBcs CCVT CDoC CDul CMCN EPfP LRHS MBlu SBLw SMad SPoG WDin WFar WOrn
	- 'Autumn Fantasy'	GKir MBlu
	- Celebration = 'Celzam'	LRHS WFar
§	- 'Elegant'	SBLw
	- Indian Summer = 'Morgan'	CEnd CPMA GKir LRHS SIFN WWes
	fulvescens	see *A. longipes*
	ginnala	see *A. tataricum* subsp. *ginnala*
	glabrum	WNor
	globosum	see *A. platanoides* 'Globosum'
	grandidentatum	see *A. saccharum* subsp. *grandidentatum*
	griseum 🏆^{H4}	More than 30 suppliers
	grosseri	CBcs CDul CMCN CTri EBee GKir IArd
	- var. ***hersii*** 🏆^{H4}	More than 30 suppliers
	- 'Leiden'	EPfP MBlu
	heldreichii	CMCN EPfP
	henryi	CBcs CLnd CMCN CTho ECrN ENot EPfP NLar WBVN WCwm WNor
	hookeri	CMCN
	hyrcanum	CMCN WWes
	- 'Alma Mater'	WWes
	japonicum	CMCN LRHS MBar SSta WNor
	- B&SWJ 5950	WCru
§	- 'Aconitifolium' 🏆^{H4}	More than 30 suppliers
	- 'Attaryi'	CMCN MPkF NLar
	- 'Aureum'	see *A. shirasawanum* 'Aureum'
	- 'Ezo-no-momiji'	see *A. shirasawanum* 'Ezo-no-momiji'
	- 'Fairy Lights'	WWes
	- 'Filicifolium'	see *A. japonicum* 'Aconitifolium'
	- 'Green Cascade'	CBdw CEnd CMCN CPMA ECho MPkF NLar SIFN SPoG WPGP WPat WWes
	- 'Kujaku-nishiki' (v)	WWes
	- 'Laciniatum'	see *A. japonicum* 'Aconitifolium'
	- f. ***microphyllum***	see *A. shirasawanum* 'Microphyllum'
§	- 'Mikasa-yama'	GKir LRHS
	- 'Ogurayama'	see *A. shirasawanum* 'Ogurayama'
	- 'Ô-isami'	CMCN EPfP GKir LRHS MPkF SIFN WWes
	- 'Ô-taki'	ECho
	- 'Vitifolium' 🏆^{H4}	CDoC CEnd CMCN CPMA CSBt ECho ELan EPfP GKir LRHS MBlu MPkF NEgg SCoo SIFN SPer SPoG SSpi SSta WPGP WPat
	kawakamii	see *A. caudatifolium*
	komarovii **new**	GIBF
	laevigatum	CMCN
	laxiflorum	CBcs
	leucoderme	see *A. saccharum* subsp. *leucoderme*
	lobelii Bunge	see *A. turkestanicum*
	lobelii Tenore	CTho WPGP WWes
§	***longipes***	CMCN
§	- subsp. ***catalpifolium***	CMCN
	- 'Gold Coin'	WWes
	macrophyllum	CFil CMCN CTho EPfP IDee ISea LHyd LRHS
	mandschuricum	CBcs EPfP IArd MPkF WCwm WDin WNor
§	***maximowiczianum***	CBcs CMCN CSam CTho ELan GIBF WFar WNor
	maximowiczii	CMCN ECrN LRHS WNor
§	***metcalfii***	WNor
	micranthum	CDoC CEnd CFil CMCN CPLG EPfP GKir IMGH MBlu MDun MPkF SHGN SIFN SSpi WCwm WNor WPGP
	miyabei	MPkF WWes
	mono	see *A. pictum*
	monspessulanum	CBcs CDul CFil CMCN CTho GKir IArd SEND XPep
§	***morifolium***	CCVT MPkF WWes
	morrisonense	see *A. caudatifolium*
	negundo	CDul CLnd CMCN CTho CWib ECrN NWea SBLw WNor
	- IDS 2000	WHCr
	- 'Argenteovariegatum'	see *A. negundo* 'Variegatum'
	- 'Auratum'	CMCN MBar SBLw WDin WPat
	- 'Aureomarginatum' (v)	LBuc WOrn
	- 'Aureovariegatum' (v)	CBcs MBar
	- subsp. ***californicum***	WNor WWes
	- - var. ***texanum***	WWes
§	- 'Elegans' (v)	CDul CEnd CLnd CMCN COtt

		ECrN ENot EPfP LRHS SHBN SPer WFar WWes
	- 'Elegantissimum'	see *A. negundo* 'Elegans'
	- 'Flamingo' (v)	More than 30 suppliers
	- 'Kelly's Gold'	CBcs CLnd CTho CWSG ENot LRHS MAsh MDun MGos NPro SCoo SCrf SLim SPoG WFar WOrn WWes
	- 'Sensation'	WWes
§	- 'Variegatum' (v)	CBcs CLnd ECrN ENot LAst LRHS SBLw SPer WDin WFar
	- var. ***violaceum***	CBcs CEnd CMCN WBcn WWes
	nikoense	see *A. maximowiczianum*
	nipponicum	WWes
	oblongum	CMCN
	- HWJK 2422	WCru
§	***obtusifolium***	WBcn WWes
	olivaceum	WWes
	oliverianum	CFil EPfP WNor WPGP WWes
	- subsp. ***formosanum***	WWes
	- - B&SWJ 6773	WCru
	- - B&SWJ 6797	WCru
	opalus	CMCN SSpi WCwm WWes
	orientale	see *A. sempervirens*
	Pacific Sunset = 'Warrenred'	GKir LRHS
	palmatum	More than 30 suppliers
	- 'Abigail Rose' **new**	CBdw
§	- 'Aka Shigitatsusawa'	CBcs CBdw CMCN CMac CMen CPMA GKir LRHS MGos MPkF NLar SIFN SMur SSpi SVil WFar WPat
	- 'Akane'	CBdw CMen MPkF
	- 'Akebono' **new**	CBdw
	- 'Akegarasu'	LRHS NLar
	- 'Alloys'	WWes
	- 'Alpine Surprise'	WWes
	- 'Ao Kanzashi' (v)	CBdw MPkF NLar
	- 'Aoba-jo'	CMen CPMA MPkF NLar
	- 'Aoshime-no-uchi'	see *A. palmatum* 'Shinobugaoka'
	- 'Aoyagi'	CEnd CMCN CMen CPMA EPfP GKir LAst LMil LRHS MAsh MBri SIFN WFoF WPat WWes
§	- 'Arakawa'	CEnd CMCN CMen ECho GKir SIFN WWes
	- 'Aratama'	CBdw CPMA SCoo WPat WWes
	- 'Ariake-nomura'	MPkF WWes
	- 'Asahi-zuru' (v)	CBcs CBdw CMCN CMen CPMA EBee ECho GKir LRHS MGos MPkF NLar SPer SPoG SVil WFar WFoF WPat WWes
	- 'Ashurst Wood'	SIFN
	- 'Atrolineare'	MPkF NBea WPat
	- f. ***atropurpureum***	CBcs CDoC CEnd CWSG EBee ENot EPfP EWTr GKir LBuc LHyd LRHS MBar MGos NBea NBee NBlu NWea SHBN SPer SReu WCFE WDin WFar WHar WPat WTel
	- 'Atropurpureum'	CBrm CCVT CDul CMen CSBt CTho CTri CWib EBee ECrN ISea LSRN MDun MSwo NEgg SBrw SLon SWvt WHil WWes
	- 'Atropurpureum Novum'	MPkF
	- 'Attraction'	CMCN WWes
	- 'Aureum'	CBdw CMCN CMen CWib ECho EPfP GKir LRHS MBlu MPkF NLar SIFN SSpi WFar WWes
	- Autumn Glory Group	CEnd CPMA SSpi WWes
	- 'Autumn Red'	LRHS
*	- 'Autumn Showers'	CEnd CPMA
	- 'Azuma-murasaki'	CPMA MPkF NLar WWes
	- 'Barrie Bergman'	CBdw CPMA WWes
*	- 'Beni K Sport'	CPMA
	- 'Beni-chidori'	CMen ECho WWes
	- 'Beni-gasa'	CPMA
	- 'Beni-hime'	CBdw CPMA NLar
	- 'Beni-hoshi' **new**	CBdw WPat
	- 'Beni-kagami'	CEnd CMCN CPMA EPfP GKir LRHS MBlu MGos NBea NLar WWes
	- 'Beni-kawa'	CBdw CPMA GKir MPkF SIFN SPur SSpi WPat WWes
	- 'Beni-komachi'	CBcs CEnd CMCN CMac CMen CPMA ECho EPfP GKir LMil LRHS MPkF SIFN SVil WPat WWes
	- 'Beni-maiko'	CBdw CEnd CMCN CMen CPMA CWib EPfP GKir LRHS MBri MPkF SCoo SIFN WPGP WPat WWes
	- 'Beni-otake'	CBcs CBdw CLnd CMCN CMen CPMA ECho EPfP LRHS MGos MPkF NLar SBod SIFN SMur SPer SVil WPat WWes
	- 'Beni-schichihenge' (v)	CBcs CBdw CEnd CMCN CMen CPMA CTbh EPfP GKir LRHS MAsh MPkF SCoo SIFN SMur SPoG SVil WPGP WPat
I	- 'Beni-shidare Tricolor' (v)	CBdw
	- 'Beni-shi-en' **new**	CBdw
	- 'Beni-shigitatsu-sawa'	see *A. palmatum* 'Aka Shigitatsusawa'
	- 'Beni-tsukasa' (v)	CBdw CEnd CMen CPMA ECho GKir LRHS MAsh MPkF SIFN SSpi SSta WPGP WPat WWes
	- 'Beni-tsukasa-shidare'	CBdw
	- 'Beni-ubi-gohon'	CPMA MPkF WWes
	- 'Beni-yatsubusa'	WWes
	- 'Beni-zuru'	CBdw
I	- 'Berry Broom' **new**	CBdw
	- 'Berry Dwarf'	CBdw WPat
	- 'Bloodgood' ♀H4	More than 30 suppliers
*	- 'Bonfire'	LRHS MAsh
	- 'Bonnie Bergman'	CPMA WWes
	- 'Boskoop Glory'	WWes
	- 'Brandt's Dwarf'	CBdw WPat
	- 'Burgundy Lace' ♀H4	CBcs CDoC CEnd CMCN CPMA CSBt CTbh CWib EMil GKir LRHS LSRN MAsh MBlu MBri MGos MPkF SBrw SCoo SIFN SPer SPoG WFar WPat
	- 'Butterfly' (v)	CBcs CDoC CEnd CMCN CPMA CTbh CWSG CWib EBee EPfP GKir LMil LRHS LSRN MBar MGos NBea SBrw SCoo SHBN SLdr SLim SPer SPoG SReu SSta WDin WFar WWes
	- 'Calico' **new**	CBdw CPMA
	- 'Carlis Corner' **new**	CPMA
I	- 'Carlis Corner Broom' **new**	CBdw
	- 'Carminium'	see *A. palmatum* 'Corallinum'
	- 'Chikuma-no'	MPkF
	- 'Chirimen-nishiki' (v)	CMCN MPkF
	- 'Chishio'	see *A. palmatum* 'Shishio'
	- 'Chishio-hime'	CBdw
	- 'Chitoseyama' ♀H4	CEnd CMCN CMen CPMA EBee ECho EPfP GKir LRHS MBar MBri MGos MPkF NEgg NLar SCoo SIFN SLim SMur SSpi SSta WFar WPat
	- 'Collingwood Ingram'	WWes
	- 'Coonara Pygmy'	CBdw CMCN CMen CPMA ECho LRHS MPkF SMur WFar WPat WWes
	- 'Coral Pink'	CBdw CPMA MPkF WWes
§	- 'Corallinum'	CEnd CMCN CMen CPMA MPkF NLar WPat
	- var. ***coreanum***	CMCN LMil SIFN WNor

	- - B&SWJ 4474	WCru
	- - B&SWJ 8606	WCru
	- - 'Korean Gem'	CPMA ECho
	- 'Crippsii'	CBcs CDoC CMen ECho EMil LRHS MBri MPkF SCoo SPoG WFar WPat WWes
	- 'Cynthia's Crown Jewel' **new**	CBdw
	- 'Demi-sec'	CBdw WWes
	- 'Deshôjô'	CBdw CMCN CMen MBar MBlu MGos MPkF SHBN
	- 'Deshôjô-nishiki' **new**	CBdw
	- 'Diana'	CMen MPkF NLar WWes
	- 'Diane Verkade'	CBdw
	- var. ***dissectum*** ♀^{H4}	More than 30 suppliers
	- - 'Ao-shidare'	CBdw CPMA WWes
	- - 'Ariadne' (v)	CBdw CPMA GKir MBri MPkF NLar SIFN WPat WWes
	- - 'Autumn Fire' **new**	CBdw CPMA
	- - 'Baby Lace'	CBdw CPMA
	- - 'Balcombe Green' **new**	SIFN
	- - 'Baldsmith'	CBdw CPMA
	- - 'Beni-fushigi'	CBdw MPkF NLar WPat WWes
	- - 'Beni-shidare Variegated' (v)	CMCN CPMA
	- - 'Berrima Bridge'	CBdw CPMA
	- - 'Bewley's Red' **new**	CBdw CPMA
	- - 'Brocade'	CBdw CMCN MPkF WPat WWes
	- - 'Chantilly Lace'	CBdw CPMA
	- - 'Chelwood' **new**	SIFN
	- var. ***dissectum*** 'Crimson Prince' **new**	CBcs SVil
	- - 'Crimson Queen' ♀^{H4}	More than 30 suppliers
	- - Dissectum Atropurpureum Group	CBcs CPMA CTri ELan ENot EPfP GKir LHyd LRHS MAsh MGos NBea NWea SHBN SLim SReu SSpi SSta WDin WFar WOrn WPat
	- - 'Dissectum Flavescens'	CBdw CEnd CMac CPMA MBlu
§	- - 'Dissectum Nigrum'	CPMA CWSG LRHS MPkF NBea NBee SSpi WPat
	- - 'Dissectum Palmatifidum'	CDoC CLnd LRHS MPkF SCoo SPer SVil WFar WPat WWes
	- - 'Dissectum Rubrifolium'	WWes
§	- - 'Dissectum Variegatum' (v)	CBcs CPMA EPfP LRHS MPkF SSta
	- - Dissectum Viride Group	CBcs CMCN CMen CPMA CSBt CWSG ELan EPfP LMil LRHS MAsh MDun MGos MSwo NBea NBlu NEgg SBod SBrw SLim SPer SPla SSta WFar WOrn
	- - 'Doctor Baker' **new**	CBdw
	- - 'Ellen'	CBdw CPMA WPat WWes
	- - 'Emerald Lace'	CPMA MBlu WWes
	- - 'Felice'	CBdw MPkF WPat
	- - 'Filigree' (v)	CBdw CMCN CMen CPMA EPfP GKir LMil LRHS MAsh MGos MPkF NLar SIFN SSpi WPat WWes
	- - 'Garnet' ♀^{H4}	More than 30 suppliers
	- - 'Goshiki-shidare' (v)	CEnd CMen CPMA MPkF WWes
	- - 'Green Globe'	CBdw LRHS NLar WWes
	- - 'Green Lace'	MPkF NLar
	- - 'Green Mist'	CBdw CPMA WWes
	- - 'Inaba-shidare' ♀^{H4}	CBcs CDoC CEnd CMCN CMen COtt CPMA CSBt CTbh CWib EBee EMil ENot EPfP GKir IMGH LMil LRHS MAsh MBar MBri MGos SBod SIFN SPer SSta WGer WPGP WPat
	- - 'Kiri-nishiki'	CMen CPMA ECho MPkF NLar
	- - 'Lemon Chiffon' **new**	CBdw
*	- - 'Lionheart'	CBdw CPMA ECho EMil LRHS MGos MPkF SBod SCoo SPer WFar WPat
	- - 'Nomura-nishiki' (v)	WWes
	- - 'Octopus'	CBdw CPMA
	- - 'Orangeola'	CBdw CEnd CPMA MPkF NLar SCoo SIFN WPat WWes
	- - 'Ornatum'	CDoC CMCN CMen COtt CWib ECho EPfP IMGH LMil MBar MDun MGos MPkF NBea NBlu NEgg SBrw SCoo WDin WFar WGer WHar
	- - 'Pendulum Julian'	CMCN MPkF NLar SIFN
	- - 'Pink Ballerina' (v) **new**	CPMA
	- - 'Pink Filigree'	CBdw WWes
	- - 'Raraflora' **new**	CBdw CPMA
	- - 'Red Autumn Lace'	CBdw WWes
	- - 'Red Dragon'	CBcs CBdw CDoC CMen CPMA ECho ECrN LRHS MGos MPkF NLar SBod WPat
	- - 'Red Feather' **new**	CPMA
	- - 'Red Filigree Lace'	CBdw CEnd CMCN CMen CPMA ECho EPfP GKir LRHS MBlu SIFN WPat
	- - 'Red Select'	ECho MPkF WWes
	- - 'Rilas Red' **new**	CBdw
	- - 'Seiryû' ♀^{H4}	More than 30 suppliers
§	- - 'Shôjô-shidare'	CBdw CEnd ECho LRHS NLar WWes
	- - 'Sunset'	CBdw CDul CMCN CPMA MDun MPkF WPat
	- - 'Tamukeyama'	CLnd CMCN CMen CPMA EMil LMil LRHS MDun MPkF NLar SBod SCoo SMur SSpi SVil WBVN WFar WPat
	- - 'Toyama-nishiki' (v)	CMCN CMen NLar SIFN
	- - 'Tumukeyama' **new**	CBcs
	- - 'Waterfall'	CMCN CPMA ECho
	- - 'Watnong'	CBdw CPMA
	- - 'Zaaling'	CPMA ECho
	- 'Dormansland' **new**	LMil SIFN
	- 'Dragon's Fire'	CBdw MDun
	- 'Eddisbury'	CEnd CMen CPMA MDun MPkF NBea NLar SSta WOrn WPat WWes
	- 'Edna Bergman'	CPMA
	- 'Effegi'	see *A. palmatum* 'Fireglow'
	- 'Eimini'	WPat WWes
	- 'Elegans'	ECho EPfP MPkF NLar SIFN WDin
	- 'Englishtown'	CBdw WPat WWes
	- 'Enkan'	CBdw CPMA MPkF NLar WPat WWes
	- 'Ever Red'	see *A. palmatum* var. *dissectum* 'Dissectum Nigrum'
	- 'Fall's Fire'	CBdw CPMA
	- 'Fascination' **new**	CBdw
	- 'Filigree Rouge'	CBdw WWes
	- 'Fior d'Arancio'	CPMA NBea WPat WWes
§	- 'Fireglow'	CBcs CDoC CEnd CLnd CMCN CMen CPMA CSBt CWib ECho EMil LRHS MBlu MGos MPkF NBea NBlu NEgg NLar SBod SCoo SIFN SPoG WFar WPGP WPat WWes
	- 'Fjellheim'	CBdw CPMA
	- 'Flushing'	WWes
	- 'Frederici Guglielmi'	see *A. palmatum* var. *dissectum* 'Dissectum Variegatum'
	- 'Garyū'	WWes
	- 'Gassho'	CBdw WWes
	- 'Geisha' **new**	CBdw
	- 'Gekkō-nishiki'	CBdw WWes
	- 'Germaine's Gyration'	CBdw
	- 'Glowing Embers'	WPat WWes
	- 'Golden Pond'	CBdw WWes
	- 'Goshiki-kotohime' (v)	CBdw CMCN CPMA MPkF WPat
	- 'Green Trompenburg'	CMCN CMen MPkF NLar SIFN
	- 'Groundcover'	CBdw WWes
§	- 'Hagoromo'	CMen ECho MPkF WFar
	- 'Hanami-nishiki'	CMen MPkF

	- 'Harusame' (v)	MPkF
	- 'Hatsushigure'	CBdw
	- 'Hazeroino' (v)	MPkF
	- 'Heartbeat'	CBdw CPMA WWes
	- 'Helena'	see *A.* 'Helena'
	- var. ***heptalobum***	CMCN WWes
§	- 'Heptalobum Elegans'	CMCN LRHS MBlu SHBN SSpi
	- 'Heptalobum Elegans Purpureum'	see *A. palmatum* 'Hessei'
	- 'Herbstfeuer'	CPMA
§	- 'Hessei'	CEnd CMCN ECho GKir LRHS MBlu NBea NLar WWes
	- 'Higasayama' (v)	CBcs CBdw CEnd CMCN CMen CPMA GKir LRHS MAsh MPkF NLar SCoo SIFN WPGP WPat WWes
	- 'Hime-shojo' **new**	CBdw
	- 'Hino-tori-nishiki' **new**	CMen
	- 'Hi-no-tsukasa'	CBdw
	- 'Hiryu'	WWes
	- 'Hôgyoku'	CMCN CPMA MPkF
	- 'Hondoshi'	CBdw WWes
	- 'Hoshi-kuzu'	CBdw
	- 'Hupp's Dwarf'	WWes
	- 'Ibo-nishiki'	CMen MPkF SIFN
	- 'Ichigyôji'	CEnd CMCN CPMA LMil LRHS SIFN WPGP WPat WWes
	- 'Improved Shishio'	see *A. palmatum* 'Shishio Improved'
	- 'Inazuma'	CBcs CMCN CMen ECho EPfP LRHS MPkF NLar SCoo WFar WWes
	- 'Irish Lace'	CBdw CPMA
	- 'Issai-nishiki'	MPkF
*	- 'Issai-nishiki-kawazu'	MPkF
	- 'Itami-nishiki'	CBdw WWes
	- 'Jane'	MPkF WWes
	- 'Japanese Sunrise'	CBdw CPMA WWes
	- 'Jerre Schwartz' **new**	WPat
	- 'Jirô-shidare'	EPfP LRHS MPkF NLar SIFN
	- 'Junihitoe'	see *A. shirasawanum* 'Jûnihitoe'
	- 'Kaba'	WWes
	- 'Kagero' (v)	MPkF WFar
§	- 'Kagiri-nishiki' (v)	CBdw CDul CMCN CMen CPMA CWSG ECho LRHS MGos MPkF NEgg SIFN SPur WFar WNor
	- 'Kamagata'	CBdw CEnd CMCN CMen CPMA EPfP GKir LMil LRHS MBri MGos MPkF NLar SBod SIFN SMur SSta SVil WPGP WPat WWes
	- 'Kandy Kitchen'	CBdw CPMA NLar WWes
	- 'Karaori'	WWes
	- 'Karaori-nishiki' (v)	CMen ECho MBlu MPkF NLar
	- 'Karasugawa' (v)	CBdw CMen CPMA MPkF NLar
	- 'Kasagiyama'	CBdw CEnd CMCN CMen CPMA LRHS MPkF NLar SIFN WPGP WPat
	- 'Kasen-nishiki'	CBdw CMen ECho MPkF
	- 'Kashima'	CEnd CMCN CMen CPMA ECho LRHS MBNS MPkF NLar WFar WWes
	- 'Kashima-yatsubusa'	CBdw
	- 'Katja'	CMen WWes
	- 'Katsura' ♀H4	CBcs CBdw CDoC CEnd CMCN CMen CPMA EPfP GKir LMil LRHS MAsh MBlu MBri MGos NBlu SBod SBrw SCoo SIFN SPer SPla SPoG SSpi SSta WFar WNor WOrn
	- 'Kenko-nishiki'	WWes
	- 'Ki-hachijô'	CMCN CMen CPMA EPfP NLar WWes
	- 'Kingsville Variegated' (v)	WWes
	- 'Kinran'	CMCN CMen ECho GKir LRHS MPkF WPat WWes
	- 'Kinshi'	CEnd CMCN CMen CPMA GKir LRHS MAsh MPkF NBea NLar SIFN SSta WPat
	- 'Kiyohime'	CBdw CDoC CMCN CMen ECho GKir MBlu MPkF NBea WFar WPat
	- 'Koba-shôjô' **new**	CBdw
	- 'Ko-chidori'	WWes
	- 'Kogane-nishiki'	WWes
	- 'Koko'	WWes
	- 'Kokobunji-nishiki' (v) **new**	CBdw
	- 'Komache-hime'	CBdw CPMA WPat
*	- 'Komaru'	NLar
	- 'Komon-nishiki' (v)	CBdw CPMA WPat WWes
	- 'Koriba'	CBdw CPMA MPkF NLar
	- 'Koshibori-nishiki'	CBdw
§	- 'Koshimino'	CPMA
	- 'Kotohime'	CBdw CMCN CMen CPMA MPkF NLar SCoo SIFN WWes
	- 'Koto-ito-komachi'	CBdw CMen CPMA ECho MPkF NLar WPat
	- 'Koto-maru'	CBdw MPkF
	- 'Koto-no-ito'	CBdw CMCN MPkF NLar WPat
	- 'Koya-san'	CBdw CMen MPkF
	- 'Koyô-ao-shidare' **new**	CBdw
	- 'Kurabu-yama'	CMCN CMen MPkF
	- 'Kurui-jishi'	CBdw MPkF NLar SIFN WPat
	- 'Kyra'	CMen MPkF WWes
	- 'Lemon Lime Lace'	CBdw WWes
	- 'Linearilobum'	CDoC EPfP GKir LHyd LMil LRHS MBlu MPkF NBea NLar SCam SCoo SSpi WFar WNor WPat
	- 'Linearilobum Atropurpureum'	LRHS WNor
	- 'Lin-ling'	LMil SIFN
	- 'Little Princess'	see *A. palmatum* 'Mapi-no-machihime'
	- 'Lozita'	WWes
	- 'Lutescens'	ECho MPkF
	- 'Lydia'	MPkF
	- 'Maiko'	CMen ECho MPkF
	- 'Mai-mori' (v)	CBdw WWes
	- 'Mama'	CMen ECho
§	- 'Mapi-no-machihime'	CBdw CEnd CMCN CMen CPMA ELan GKir LMil LRHS MAsh MBri MPkF SIFN SMur WPGP WPat
	- 'Marakumo'	MPkF
	- 'Margaret'	WWes
	- 'Margaret Bee'	WWes
	- 'Marjan'	NLar WWes
	- 'Masamurasaki'	WPat
	- 'Masukagami' (v)	CEnd CPMA MPkF NLar
	- 'Matsuga-e' (v)	MPkF
	- 'Matsukaze'	CMCN CMen COtt CPMA GKir SIFN WWes
	- 'Meihô-nishiki'	CBdw
	- 'Melanie'	SIFN SSpi
	- 'Meoto'	WWes
	- 'Mikasayama'	see *A. japonicum* 'Mikasa-yama'
	- 'Mikawa-yatsubusa'	CMCN CMen CPMA ECho LRHS MPkF NLar SVil WPat WWes
	- 'Milton Park' **new**	CBdw
	- 'Mimaye' **new**	CPMA
	- 'Mini Mondo'	WPat WWes
	- 'Mirte'	MPkF SIFN WFar WPat WWes
	- 'Misty Moon'	WWes
	- 'Mizuho-beni'	CPMA WPat
	- 'Mizu-kuguri'	CMCN MPkF NLar WPat
	- 'Momenshide'	CBdw WWes
	- 'Momoiro-koya-san'	MPkF NLar WPat
	- 'Mon Papa'	CPMA WWes
	- 'Mono-zigawa'	WWes
	- 'Monzukushi'	CMCN CPMA MPkF

	- 'Moonfire'	CMCN CPMA EPfP GKir LRHS MAsh NLar SIFN SSpi WWes
	- 'Mufuri'	WWes
*	- 'Muncaster' **new**	SIFN
	- 'Murasaki-hime' **new**	MPkF
	- 'Murasaki-kiyohime'	CBdw CEnd CMCN CMen CPMA ECho MPkF NLar WPat
	- 'Murasaki-shikibu'	CBdw
	- 'Mure-hibari'	CMCN CPMA MPkF SIFN WPat
	- 'Murogawa'	ECho
	- var. ***nakai***	WWes
	- 'Nanase-gawa'	MPkF
	- 'Nathan'	WWes
	- 'Nicholsonii'	CMCN EPfP LMil LRHS MPkF NLar SIFN WFar WPat WWes
	- 'Nigrum' ♀H4	CMCN WPat
	- 'Nishiki-gasane' (v)	MPkF
§	- 'Nishiki-gawa'	CEnd CMCN CMen CPMA GKir MPkF WPGP WWes
	- 'Nishiki-momiji'	CMen
	- 'Nomura' **new**	CPMA
	- 'Nomurishidare' misapplied	see *A. palmatum* var. *dissectum* 'Shôjô-shidare'
	- 'Nomurishidare' Wada	MAsh SSpi
	- 'Nuresagi'	CBdw CEnd CPMA
	- 'Ôgi-nagashi' (v)	CBdw WWes
	- 'Ôgon-sarasa'	CPMA
	- 'Ojishi'	CMen
	- 'Ô-kagami'	CEnd CMen CPMA ECho GKir LMil LRHS MPkF SCoo SHBN SIFN SPoG WPGP WPat
	- 'Okina'	CBdw WWes
	- 'Okukuji-nishiki'	CBdw CPMA
	- 'Okushimo'	CBdw CEnd CMCN CMen CPMA LRHS MBri MPkF NLar WPGP WPat WWes
	- 'Olga'	WWes
	- 'Omato'	CMen MPkF SIFN WFar
	- 'Omurayama'	CBcs CDoC CEnd CMCN CMen CPMA ECho EPfP LRHS MGos MPkF NBlu NLar SBod SCoo SMur SPer SPoG SSta SVil WFar WPat WWes
	- 'Orange Dream'	CBcs CBdw CDul CEnd CMCN CMen CPMA CWib GKir LBuc LMil LRHS LSRN MAsh MBar MBlu MBri MPkF NLar SBrw SCoo SIFN SPer SPoG WOrn WPGP WPat WWes
	- 'Oregon Sunset'	CBdw CMen MPkF WPat
	- 'Oridono-nishiki' (v)	CBcs CEnd CMCN CMen CPMA ELan EPfP LMil LRHS MAsh MBar MBlu MGos MPkF NBea NBee NEgg SCoo SIFN SSpi SSta WOrn
	- 'Ori-zuru'	WWes
	- 'Ôsakazuki' ♀H4	More than 30 suppliers
	- 'Ôshio-beni'	CPMA ECho NLar WWes
	- 'Ôshû-shidare'	CBdw CMen CPMA EPfP WFar WPat
	- 'Oto-hime'	CPMA ECho MPkF
	- 'Otome-zakura'	CMCN CMen MPkF WPat
I	- 'Paul's Variegated'	CBdw
	- 'Peaches and Cream' (v)	CBcs CBdw CPMA MPkF NLar WWes
	- 'Peve Multicolor'	CBdw MBri MPkF NLar
	- 'Phoenix'	CBdw MPkF
	- 'Pine Bark Maple'	see *A. palmatum* 'Nishiki-gawa'
	- 'Pixie'	CBdw CMCN CMen CPMA MPkF NLar WPat
	- var. ***pubescens*** B&SWJ 6886	WCru
	- 'Pung-kil'	CBdw MPkF
	- 'Purpureum'	WWes
	- 'Red Baron'	CPMA WWes
	- 'Red Flash'	LRHS WPat WWes
	- 'Red Jonas'	WPat WWes
	- 'Red Pygmy' ♀H4	More than 30 suppliers
	- 'Red Shadow'	SIFN
	- 'Red Spider' **new**	CPMA
	- 'Red Wood'	CDoC CPMA MPkF SVil WPat WWes
	- 'Reticulatum'	see *A. palmatum* 'Shigitatsu-sawa'
	- 'Ribesifolium'	see *A. palmatum* 'Shishigashira'
	- 'Roseomarginatum'	see *A. palmatum* 'Kagiri-nishiki'
	- 'Roseum Ornatum'	CBdw
	- 'Rough Bark Maple'	see *A. palmatum* 'Arakawa'
	- 'Royle'	CBdw WWes
I	- 'Rubrum Kaiser' **new**	CPMA
	- 'Ryuzu'	CPMA MPkF
	- 'Sagara-nishiki' (v)	CBdw CEnd CMen CPMA ECho WWes
	- 'Saint Jean'	CBdw
	- 'Samidare'	CPMA EPfP MPkF NLar WWes
	- 'Sandra'	CMen MPkF WWes
N	- 'Sango-kaku' ♀H4	More than 30 suppliers
	- 'Saoshika'	CMCN CPMA MPkF
	- 'Sa-otome'	MPkF
	- 'Satsuki-beni'	WWes
	- 'Sawa-chidori'	CBdw
	- 'Sazanami'	CEnd CPMA MBri MPkF NBea NLar WNor WPGP WPat
	- 'Scolopendriifolium'	LMil MPkF WFar WPat WWes
	- 'Seigai' **new**	CBdw MPkF
	- 'Seigen'	CBdw CEnd CMCN CMen CPMA ECho MPkF WPGP WPat
I	- 'Seigen Aureum'	CBdw CPMA
	- 'Seiun-kaku'	CBdw CPMA MBri WPat WWes
	- 'Sekimori'	CBdw CMCN CPMA SIFN
	- 'Sekka-yatsubusa'	CMCN CMen
	- 'Senkaki'	see *A. palmatum* 'Sango-kaku'
	- 'Septemlobum Elegans'	see *A. palmatum* 'Heptalobum Elegans'
	- 'Septemlobum Purpureum'	see *A. palmatum* 'Hessei'
	- 'Sessilifolium' dwarf	see *A. palmatum* 'Hagoromo'
	- - tall	see *A. palmatum* 'Koshimino'
	- 'Shaina'	CBcs CEnd CMen CPMA LRHS MBri MPkF NLar SVil WFar WPat WWes
	- 'Sharp's Pygmy'	CBdw CPMA MPkF WWes
	- 'Sherwood Flame'	CMCN CPMA CWib LRHS MAsh MBlu MGos NLar SCoo WFar WPat WWes
	- 'Shichigosan'	CMen
	- 'Shidava Gold'	CBdw CPMA GKir SIFN WPat
	- 'Shi-en' **new**	CBdw
	- 'Shigarami'	MPkF
	- 'Shigi-no-hoshi' **new**	CBdw
§	- 'Shigitatsu-sawa' (v)	CBcs CBdw CEnd CMCN CMen CPMA EMil GKir LRHS MGos MPkF NLar SIFN SPoG
	- 'Shigure-bato'	CMCN CPMA MPkF WPat WWes
	- 'Shigurezome'	CMCN MPkF WWes
	- 'Shikageori-nishiki'	LRHS MPkF
	- 'Shime-no-uchi'	CMCN CPMA LMil SIFN
	- 'Shindeshôjô'	CBcs CBdw CDoC CEnd CMCN CMen CPMA CSBt GKir LMil LRHS LSRN MAsh MBri MGos MLan NBea SBod SCoo SHBN SIFN SPer SPoG SReu SSta WFar WFoF WNor WPat
	- 'Shin-hikasa' **new**	CBdw
§	- 'Shinobugaoka'	CMCN CMen CPMA MPkF
	- 'Shinonome'	MPkF WWes
	- 'Shin-seyu'	WWes
§	- 'Shishigashira'	CBcs CDoC CMCN CMen COtt CPMA ECho EPfP LMil LRHS MBar MBlu MBri MDun MGos MPkF NLar SCoo SIFN SPoG WFar WPat

- 'Shishigashira-no-yatsubusa' **new**	CBdw
§ - 'Shishio'	CMCN CMen ECho GKir LAst LHyd LRHS MAsh MPkF SBig SSpi SVil WPat
§ - 'Shishio Improved'	CBdw CEnd CMCN CPMA CTho CWSG EPfP MBlu MGos MPkF NLar SIFN SPur SWvt
- 'Shôjô'	CMCN CPMA WFar WWes
- 'Shōjō-no-mai'	CBdw
- 'Shôjô-nomura'	CAbP CEnd CMen COtt CPMA LRHS MPkF NBea NLar WPGP WPat
- 'Skeeter's Broom'	CBdw CDoC LRHS MBri MPkF NBlu SBod SCoo SIFN SVil WPat
* - 'Sode-nishiki'	CBdw MPkF NLar
- 'Spreading Star'	WWes
- 'Stanley's Unknown'	WWes
- 'Stella Rossa'	CBdw CEnd CMCN CPMA LRHS MBlu MPkF NLar WPat WWes
- 'Suminagashi'	CDoC CMCN CMen LRHS MBri MDun MPkF SBod SIFN SMur SVil WPat
- 'Susan'	MPkF WWes
- 'Taiyō-nishiki'	CBdw
- 'Takao'	WWes
- 'Takinogawa'	LRHS MAsh
- 'Tamahime'	CMCN CMen CPMA ECho SIFN WWes
- 'Tana'	CBdw CMCN CPMA EPfP MPkF SIFN WFar WPat WWes
- 'Tarō-yama'	CBdw CPMA WPat
- 'Tatsuta'	ECho MPkF WWes
- 'Tennyo-no-hoshi'	MPkF NLar
- 'The Bishop'	WWes
- 'Tiny Tim'	CBdw CPMA WPat
- 'Trompenburg' ♀^{H4}	More than 30 suppliers
- 'Tsuchigumo'	CMCN CMen CPMA ECho MPkF
- 'Tsukushigata'	CMCN
- 'Tsuma-beni'	CBdw CMCN CMen CPMA EPfP LRHS MPkF WPat
- 'Tsuma-gaki'	CBdw CMCN CMen CPMA ECho EPfP MPkF NLar WPat WWes
- 'Tsuri-nishiki'	CBdw CPMA ECho WWes
- 'Ueno-homare'	CBdw MPkF SPoG WPat
- 'Ueno-yama'	CBdw CPMA
- 'Ukigumo' (v)	CBcs CBdw CEnd CLnd CMCN CMen CPMA CSBt CWSG ELan EMil LMil LRHS MBri MGos MPkF NBlu SBod SCoo SIFN SMur SPer SPoG SSta WPat
- 'Ukon'	CBdw CMCN CMen CPMA EMil MBri MPkF SVil
- 'Umegae'	CPMA
- 'Utsu-semi'	CPMA MPkF SIFN WWes
- 'Vanderhoss Red'	WWes
- 'Vens Broom'	WPat
- 'Vens Red' **new**	WPat
- 'Versicolor' (v)	CBdw CEnd CMCN CMen CPMA LRHS WWes
- 'Vic Broom'	CBdw WPat
- 'Vic Pink'	CBdw WPat
- 'Villa Taranto'	CBdw CDoC CEnd CMCN CMen CPMA CSBt EPfP GKir LMil LRHS MAsh MBlu MPkF NBea NLar SBrw SCoo SIFN SSpi SSta SVil WPGP WPat WWes
- 'Volubile'	CMCN CMen ECho EPfP LRHS MAsh SMur
- 'Wabito'	CMCN CPMA MPkF
- 'Waka-midori'	ECho
- 'Waka-momiji' (v)	CBdw
- 'Wakehurst Pink' (v)	CBdw CMCN CMen MPkF NLar WPat WWes
- 'Wendy'	CMen MPkF NLar WWes
- 'Wilson's Pink Dwarf'	CBdw CEnd CMen CPMA ECho EPfP MBri MPkF NLar WGer WPat
- 'Winter Flame'	CBdw CPMA MAsh NLar WPat
- 'Wolff's Broom'	CBdw WPat
- 'Wou-nishiki'	CBdw CMCN CMen CWib
- 'Yana-gawa'	CMen ECho
- 'Yasemin'	CBdw CMen CPMA MPkF NLar SIFN WWes
- 'Yashio' **new**	CBdw
- 'Yatsubusa'	WWes
- 'Yezo-nishiki'	CMCN CMen LRHS MPkF WFar
- 'Yūba e'	CMen WFar WPat
- 'Yû-fuji' **new**	CBdw
- 'Yûgure'	MPkF NLar WFar WWes
papilio	see *A. caudatum*
paxii	CMCN WWes
pectinatum	WWes
- subsp. ***forrestii***	see *A. forrestii*
- 'Sirene'	see *A. forrestii* 'Sirene'
- 'Sparkling'	see *A. forrestii* 'Sparkling'
pensylvanicum ♀^{H4}	More than 30 suppliers
- 'Erythrocladum'	CEnd CMCN CPMA EPfP GKir IMGH LRHS MAsh MBri MGos NBea NLar SLim SMad SPur SSpi SSta
pentaphyllum	CMCN CRez GKir LRHS SIFN SSpi
§ ***pictum***	CMCN CTho EPfP GIBF LRHS WNor WWes
- subsp. ***okamotoanum***	CMCN WWes
- - B&SWJ 8516	WCru
- 'Shufu-nishiki'	CMCN
platanoides ♀^{H4}	CBcs CCVT CDoC CDul CLnd CMCN CTri CWib ECrN ENot EPfP GKir LBuc MGos MSwo NBee NWea SBLw SPer WDin WFar WHar WMou WNor WWes
- 'Charles Joly'	WWes
- 'Cleveland'	CBcs
- 'Columnare'	CDul CLnd CMCN CWib ECrN GKir LRHS WOrn
- 'Crimson King' ♀^{H4}	More than 30 suppliers
- 'Crimson Sentry'	CDoC CDul CEnd CLnd CMCN COtt CWSG CWib EBee ECrN ENot EPfP GKir IArd LBuc LRHS MAsh MBlu MBri MGos MLan MRav NBee SLim SPoG WDin WFar WHar WOrn
- 'Cucullatum'	CMCN CTho
- 'Deborah'	CBcs CLnd CTho ENot WOrn WWes
- 'Dissectum'	CTho
- 'Drummondii' (v)	More than 30 suppliers
- 'Emerald Queen'	CLnd CWib ECrN SBLw SHBN WDin
- 'Faassen's Black'	GKir SBLw
§ - 'Globosum'	CLnd CMCN ECrN LBuc SBLw SWvt
- 'Goldsworth Purple'	CDul CLnd
- 'Laciniatum'	CEnd CMCN ECrN
- 'Lorbergii'	see *A. platanoides* 'Palmatifidum'
- 'Meyering'	WWes
- 'Olmsted'	WWes
§ - 'Palmatifidum'	CLnd
- Princeton Gold = 'Prigo'^{PBR}	CDoC EBee ECrN ELan ENot GKir LRHS MAsh SCoo SPoG
- 'Reitenbachii'	CDul WWes
- 'Royal Red'	CDul CWib ECrN ENot EWTr GKir MGos MRav WWes
- 'Ruby'	GKir
- 'Schwedleri' ♀^{H4}	CDul CMCN ECrN MGos NBee NWea SPer WDin
- 'Tharandt'	CMCN

	Plant	Suppliers
	- 'Walderseei'	CLnd
	pseudoplatanus	CBcs CCVT CDul CLnd CMCN CSBt CTri ECrN ENot GKir LBuc MBar MGos NBee NWea SBLw SPer WDin WFar WHar WMou
§	- 'Atropurpureum'	CDoC CLnd CTho NBee NWea SBLw WDin WGer
	- 'Brilliantissimum' ♀H4	More than 30 suppliers
	- 'Corstorphinense'	CMCN
	- 'Erectum'	WFar
	- 'Esk Sunset' (v)	CBcs LRHS MPkF WPat
	- 'Gadsby' **new**	GKir
	- 'Leopoldii' misapplied	see *A. pseudoplatanus* f. *variegatum*
	- 'Leopoldii' ambig. (v)	CBcs CDul CLnd CMCN CTho ECrN EGra ELan ENot GKir LAst MAsh NBee SBLw SEND SHBN SLim SPer SWvt WDin WFar WOrn WWes
	- 'Leopoldii' Vervaene **new**	SCrf
	- 'Nizetii' (v)	CMCN LRHS SBLw WWes
	- 'Prinz Handjéry'	CBcs CDul CEnd CLnd CMCN CTri CWib EBee GKir LRHS MAsh MBar MGos NWea SBLw SIFN SPer SPoG SSpi
	- 'Purpureum'	SEND
	- 'Simon-Louis Frères' (v)	CCVT CDul CEnd CLnd CMCN CWSG CWib EBee ECrN EPfP GKir LRHS MAsh MBar MBri MDun MGos NBea SCrf SIFN SLim SPer SWvt WFar WFoF WHar WOrn
	- 'Spaethii' misapplied	see *A. pseudoplatanus* 'Atropurpureum'
§	- f. ***variegatum*** (v)	NEgg
	- 'Worley'	CBcs CDul CLnd CMCN COtt CSBt CTho CTri EBee ECrN GKir LRHS MBar MRav NBee NWea SBLw SCrf SEND SHBN SLim SPer SWvt WDin WHar WOrn
	pseudosieboldianum	CFil CMCN GKir MBlu WNor
	- B&SWJ 8746	WCru
	- var. ***microsieboldianum*** B&SWJ 8766	WCru
	pubipalmatum	WNor
	pycnanthum	CMCN WWes
	robustum	CMCN WNor WWes
	rubescens	CPMA WPGP
	- B&SWJ 6710	WHCr
	- B&SWJ 6735	WCru WHCr
	- variegated seedlings (v) **new**	CPMA
	rubrum	CBcs CDoC CDul CLnd CMCN CSBt CTho CTri EBee ECho ECrN ELan EPfP EWTr GKir LRHS MGos MLan MWat NBea NWea SBLw SCoo SHBN SLim SPer WDin WFar WMoo WNor
	- 'Autumn Flame'	WWes
	- 'Bowhall'	CMCN SBir
	- 'Candy Ice' (v)	CPMA
	- 'Columnare'	CMCN EPfP
	- 'Fairview Flame' **new**	SPer
	- 'October Glory' ♀H4	CBcs CDoC CDul CEnd CLnd CMCN CPMA CTho CTri ELan EPfP GKir LRHS MAsh MBlu MBri MDun NWea SBir SCoo SIFN SMad SPer SPoG SSpi SSta WFar WPGP WPat
	- Red Sunset = 'Franksred'	CDoC CDul CEnd CMCN CPMA CTho EPfP GKir LRHS MBlu SBir SCoo SIFN SMad SSpi SSta WPGP
	- 'Scanlon'	CBcs CDoC CDul CEnd CMCN CPMA CTho GKir LRHS SBLw WOrn
	- 'Schlesingeri'	CEnd CLnd CMCN CMac CPMA EPfP NLar
	- 'Tilford'	GKir SBir SIFN SSta WWes
§	***rufinerve*** ♀H4	CBcs CCVT CDoC CDul CFil CLnd CMCN CTho CTri ECrN EPfP EPla EWTr GKir LRHS MAsh MBri MWat NBea NWea SBLw SBrw WBVN WDin WGer WNor WOrn WPGP WWes
	- 'Albolimbatum'	see *A. rufinerve* 'Hatsuyuki'
	- 'Albomarginatum'	see *A. rufinerve* 'Hatsuyuki'
	- 'Erythrocladum'	CPMA
§	- 'Hatsuyuki' (v)	CDoC CDul CEnd CMCN CPMA GKir LRHS SIFN WBcn WPGP
	- 'Winter Gold'	CPMA CTho GKir LRHS SIFN SPur SSpi
§	***saccharinum***	CBcs CCVT CDul CLnd CMCN CTri EBee ECrN ELan ENot EPfP EWTr LRHS MGos MLan NWea SBLw SHBN SPer WDin WFar WNor
	- 'Fastigiatum'	see *A. saccharinum* f. *pyramidale*
	- f. ***laciniatum***	CMCN EBee LRHS MBlu MGos SPer WDin
	- 'Laciniatum Wieri'	CDul CLnd CMCN CTho ECrN SBLw WDin
	- f. ***lutescens***	CDul CMCN CTho MBlu SBLw
§	- f. ***pyramidale***	CDoC CLnd CMCN ECrN SBLw SPer WDin
	saccharum	CAgr CBcs CDoC CDul CLnd CMCN CTho ECrN EPfP GKir IDee MBlu MLan NWea SBLw SPer WNor
	- subsp. ***barbatum***	see *A. saccharum* subsp. *floridanum*
	- 'Brocade'	MPkF WWes
§	- subsp. ***floridanum***	CMCN
§	- subsp. ***grandidentatum***	CMCN
§	- subsp. ***leucoderme***	CMCN
	- 'Louisa Lad'	WWes
	- subsp. ***nigrum***	CMCN
	- - 'Monumentale'	CMCN
	- subsp. ***skutchii***	CMCN
	schneiderianum	WWes
	seiboldianum 'Osiris'	WWes
§	***sempervirens***	CFil CMCN WPGP
	serrulatum B&SWJ 6760	WCru
§	***shirasawanum***	CMCN WNor
§	- 'Aureum' ♀H4	More than 30 suppliers
	- 'Autumn Moon'	CBdw CPMA MBri WWes
§	- 'Ezo-no-momiji'	CMCN CMen CPMA NLar WWes
	- 'Gloria'	WWes
§	- 'Helena'	NLar WWes
§	- 'Jûnihitoe'	WNor
§	- 'Microphyllum'	CMCN ECho WNor
§	- 'Ogurayama'	CBdw CPMA
	- 'Palmatifolium'	CBdw CMCN CPMA GKir SIFN
	- var. ***tenuifolium***	GKir WNor WWes
	sieboldianum	CMCN CMen CTho CTri ECho ECrN EPfP GKir GTSp MDun SSpi WHCr WNor
	- 'Isis'	WWes
	- 'Sode-no-uchi'	CMCN CMen SIFN WPat
	sikkimense subsp. ***metcalfii***	see *A. metcalfii*
§	'Silver Cardinal' (v)	CBcs CDoC CEnd CMCN CPMA EPfP GKir MBlu MBri MGos NLar SMad SPoG SSpi
	'Silver Vein'	see *A.* x *conspicuum* 'Silver Vein'
§	***sinense***	CMCN IArd WCwm WNor
	spicatum	CMCN EPfP NLar WNor

§	***stachyophyllum***	GIBF GQui GTSp WWes
§	***sterculiaceum***	CFil CMCN EBee WPGP
	syriacum	see *A. obtusifolium*
	takesimense **new**	WCru
	- B&SWJ 8500	WCru
	taronense	CMCN
	tataricum	CMCN WWes
	- IDS 97	WHCr
	- subsp. ***aidzuense***	WWes
	- 'Emerald Elf'	WWes
§	- subsp. ***ginnala***	CAgr CBcs CDul CLnd CMCN CTho CTri CWSG ECrN EPfP LRHS MGos NBea NWea SBLw SHBN SLim SPer WCwm WDin WMoo WNor
	- - 'Fire'	LRHS
	- - 'Flame'	CPMA CWSG ECrN ELan EPfP GBin GKir MGos SHBN SPoG
	- subsp. ***semenovii***	WWes
	tegmentosum	CMCN CPMA EPfP MBlu NLar WNor
	- B&SWJ 8421	WCru
	- subsp. ***glaucorufinerve***	see *A. rufinerve*
	tenuifolium	CMCN
	tetramerum	see *A. stachyophyllum*
	tonkinense	WWes
	trautvetteri	CMCN EPfP WNor
	triflorum ♀H4	CMCN CPMA CTho EPfP GKir IArd IMGH LRHS NLar SSpi WDin WFar WWes
	truncatum	CMCN MPkF WNor
	- 'Akaji-nishiki' (v)	LRHS
	- 'Akikaze-nishiki' (v)	CPMA GKir MPkF
	tschonoskii	GQui WNor WWes
	- subsp. ***koreanum***	CTho LRHS MPkF NLar WNor
§	***turkestanicum***	CDul CFil CMCN EBee WFar
	velutinum	CMCN WWes
	- var. ***vanvolxemii***	WPGP
	villosum	see *A. sterculiaceum*
	'White Tigress'	CTho LRHS MBlu WWes
§	***wilsonii***	CDul CMCN GIBF WNor
	x ***zoeschense***	CMCN
	- 'Annae'	CPMA SBLw WWes

Aceriphyllum see *Mukdenia*

x *Achicodonia* (*Gesneriaceae*)

'Dark Velvet'	WDib

Achillea ✿ (*Asteraceae*)

	ageratifolia ♀H4	EBla ECha ECtt LBee MTho NBre NJOw SRms WFar
	- subsp. ***serbica***	XPep
§	***ageratum***	CArn CHby CSev CWan ELau GBar GPoy MChe MGol MHer MSal NArg NPri NTHB SIde SRms WGHP WGwG WHer WJek WLHH WPer WWye
	- 'W.B. Childs'	CSli ECha ECtt ELan GBuc MArl MAvo MNrw NDov SHar WCot WEas
	'Alabaster'	CDes CKno CSli EBee GBuc LPhx
	Anthea = 'Anblo'[PBR]	CKno CSam EBee EBrs EMan EMar EWsh GKir GMaP GSki LRHS MLLN NChi NCob NLsd SRkn SRms WAul WFar XPep
§	'Apfelblüte'	CPrp CSBt CSli CWCL EBee EChP ECtt ELan EVFa GKir GSki LRHS MRav MTis MWgw NCGa NDov NGdn SSpe WCAu WCot WFar WMnd WPer WTel
	Appleblossom	see *A.* 'Apfelblüte'
	'Apricot Beauty'	CElw CFwr CPrp CSli EChP ECtt EMan EMar EPPr GBBs GMaP LBBr LSRN MBNS MBri NPro SHop SPoG SSvw SVil
	argentea misapplied	see *A. clavennae*, *A. umbellata*
	argentea Lamarck	see *Tanacetum argenteum*
	aurea	see *A. chrysocoma*
	'Bahama'	EPPr GBBs GBin GFlt LRHS NBro WWeb WWpP
	'Belle Epoque' ♀H4	CDes CSli WPGP
	'Bloodstone'	CSli EBee ECtt EMan EWes EWsh GBar GMac MRav WOut
	brachyphylla	EPot
	'Breckland Ruby' **new**	EPPr
	'Brilliant'	LRHS WWeb
	'Caroline' **new**	LRHS WWeb
	cartilaginea	CSli EPPr SPav WFar WMoo
	- 'Silver Spray'	EBee EMan NBre SDnm SPav WOut WWpP
	'Christine's Pink' ♀H4	CKno CSli EBee EMan EPPr
§	***chrysocoma***	ETow GAbr MWat WMoo WTel XPep
	- 'Grandiflora'	CHad CHar ECha ELan EMar NGdn
§	***clavennae***	CBrm ECtt EPot LPio MLLN MWat NRya SAga SBla SRms WAbe WCot WFar WPtf
	clypeolata Sibth. & Sm.	CSam EPPr LPio NBre NLar SMad SMar SPlb SRms WPer
	coarctata	NBir WPer XPep
	'Coronation Gold' ♀H4	CDoC CPrp CSam CWCL EBee EBla EBrs ECtt ELan ENot EPfP ERou GKir GMac GSki LRHS MBri MRav MWat SAga WCAu WEas WFar WGHP WMnd XPep
	'Credo' ♀H4	More than 30 suppliers
	crithmifolia	XPep
	decolorans	see *A. ageratum*
	erba-rotta subsp. ***moschata***	ECho NBro
	- subsp. ***rupestris***	MDHE
§	'Fanal'	More than 30 suppliers
	'Faust'	CDes CElw CHar CKno CMil CSli EBee EBla LPhx SMrm STes SUsu WPGP WPrP WWpP
	'Feuerland'	More than 30 suppliers
	filipendulina	NLRH NSti SWal WHrl WWpP
	- 'Cloth of Gold' ♀H4	More than 30 suppliers
	- 'Gold Plate' ♀H4	CDoC CHad EBee EBla EBrs EChP ECha ECtt ELan EPfP ERou GKir GSki MRav MWgw NEgg NOrc SHel SPav SPer SPoG SRms WCAu WCot WFar WGHP WMnd
	- 'Parker's Variety' ♀H4	EBee LRHS MLan NBre WFar
	Flowers of Sulphur	see *A.* 'Schwefelblüte'
	'Forncett Beauty'	CSli CStr MNFA SChu WHil
	'Forncett Bride'	CSli NBre NDov
	'Forncett Candy'	CSli NDov
I	'Forncett Citrus'	CSli EBee WPGP
	'Forncett Fletton'	CFir CSli CWCL EMan EMar EPPr EPfP EVFa GBri LPio MAvo MNrw NCob NGdn SAga STes WCAu WTMC
	'Forncett Ivory'	CSli MSte
	fraasii	MDKP
	glaberrima hybrid	EMan EPPr WCot
	'Gloria Jean'	EBee SHar
	'Gold and Grey'	CSli
	'Goldstar'	EBee NDov WFar
	grandifolia misapplied	see *Tanacetum macrophyllum*
§	***grandifolia*** Friv.	CElw CFwr COIW CSam EBee EChP GBuc LEdu LPhx MWgw NBro SMad SSvw WBor WFar WHer WMnd WMoo WOld WWye
	'Great Expectations'	see *A.* 'Hoffnung'

	'Grey and Gold'	SMrm
	'Hannelore Pahl'	EBee
	'Hartington White'	GBuc MWgw
	'Heidi' 🏆^{H4}	CSli GBri
	'Hella Glashoff' 🏆^{H4}	CDes CMea CSli EBee EBrs ECho EGoo LPhx MBri NCGa NDov WCot WHoo WWeb
§	'Hoffnung'	CPrp CSli CWCL EBee EBla ECtt EMan ERou GSki LRHS MBri MRav NCGa NPro SPer SSpe WCAu WMnd WPer
	'Huteri'	CLyd CPBP EBla ECtt EDAr EGoo EPfP EPot LBee MHer MRav NFor NJOw NLon SBla SChu SPoG WEas WFar WHil
	'Inca Gold'	CSli EBee EBla ECha ECtt EHrv EMan EMar EPPr EVFa GBuc LRHS MRav NBro NCob NGdn NPro SAga SBla SChu SPav WTMC WWpP
	'Jacqueline'	CFwr EBee
	'Joey' **new**	NRnb WHil
	'Judity' **new**	LRHS WWeb
	x ***kellereri***	MDHE NLar XPep
	x ***kolbiana***	EMan MWat NJOw NMen SRms WHoo WLin
§	- 'Weston'	ETow NBre
§	'Lachsschönheit' 🏆^{H4}	More than 30 suppliers
	x ***lewisii***	NMen
	- 'King Edward' 🏆^{H4}	CSam ECha EPfP GBin GMaP LPio LRHS NBir NJOw NPro SBla SChu SIng SPoG WFar
	ligustica	WCot
	'Lucky Break' 🏆^{H4}	EBla ECha SDix SMHy SUsu WWpP
	macrophylla	EBee
	'Marie Ann'	CWCL EBee EMan EMar ERou GBri LPio MBnl MBri NLar NPro NSti SSvw WCAu WHil
	'Marmalade'	CMdw CSli EBee LSou NDov WMnd WPGP
	'Martina' 🏆^{H4}	CDoC CKno CM&M CPrp CSli EBee EChP ECha ECrN ECtt EGoo EPPr EPfP GAbr GBuc LAst LPio LRHS MBnl MLLN MNFA NCGa NDov NGdn NOrc NPro SBla SOkh SVil
	'McVities'	More than 30 suppliers
	millefolium	CArn COld CWan ELau EUnu GBar GPoy GWCH MBow MHer NLan NMir SPlb WHer WJek WLHH WSel WWpP WWye XPep
	- 'Bright Cerise'	WFar
	- 'Carla Hussey'	WFar
	- 'Cassis'	CBrm EMag GFlt MTis NEgg NLsd SDnm SPav SPur SWal WWpP
§	- 'Cerise Queen'	More than 30 suppliers
	- 'Christel'	CDes CSli GBin MSph SUsu
	- 'Christine'	EMan GBin NBre
	- 'Colorado'	COIW CSam CWCL GAbr NChi NRnb SPav WHrl
	- dark red	CSli
	- 'Debutante'	WHil
	- 'Fire King'	CElw CHal
	- 'Kelwayi' 🏆^{H4}	CSli
	- Kirschkönigin	see *A. millefolium* 'Cerise Queen'
	- 'Lansdorferglut' 🏆^{H4}	CAby CKno CSli EBrs EPPr LRHS MBri MDKP MRav NDov NPro SUsu
	- 'Lavender Beauty'	see *A. millefolium* 'Lilac Beauty'
	- 'Lemon Curd'	LDai
§	- 'Lilac Beauty'	CElw CHar CSli CWCL EBrs EChP ECha EHrv EPPr ERou EWTr GMaP GSki LPio LRHS MAnH MAvo MRav NBir NDov NGHP NPri NSti SPav WFar WHoo WPer WSan WWpP XPep
*	- 'Lilac Queen'	CSli MArl
	- 'Lollypop'	LDai
	- 'Oertels Rose' **new**	WFar
	- 'Paprika'	More than 30 suppliers
	- 'Pink Trophy'	LBmB
	- 'Raspberry Ripple' **new**	GBin
	- 'Red Beauty'	CSli CWCL EMan ERou EWTr LRHS LSou NBro SBch SRms XPep
	- 'Red Velvet'	More than 30 suppliers
	- 'Rosie'	GAbr GBar
	- 'Rougham Beauty'	CSli
	- 'Rougham Cream'	CSli
	- 'Rougham White'	CSli
	- 'Ruby Port' **new**	WFar
	- 'Salmon Pink'	WFar
	- 'Salmon Queen'	WCra
	- 'Sammetriese'	CSli EBrs GBuc LPhx LRHS MSte SMad WCAu WCot WFar WGHP WHoo WTin WWpP
	- 'Schneetaler' **new**	GBin
	- 'Serenade'	EBee EBla
	- 'Summertime'	SBod SPav
	- 'Tickled Pink'	WPer
	- 'White Queen'	EBee EMar EWTr LBuc WPer
	- 'Yellowstone' **new**	EWes
	'Mondpagode' 🏆^{H4}	CHar CPrp CSli EBee EBla EChP EMan EMar EPPr EVFa LPhx LRHS MAvo MBNS NDov NPro SHel SUsu WCAu WPtf WWpP
*	'Moonbeam'	EBla
	'Moonshine' 🏆^{H3}	More than 30 suppliers
	'Moonwalker'	CAbP LRHS MLLN MWrn NLRH SIde SPav WBVN WFar WPer WWpP
	nobilis	XPep
	- subsp. ***neilreichii***	CSli EBla EChP EGoo EHrv EPPr EVFa GBri LPio LRHS MLLN MNFA NDov NSti SAga SPer WCAu WCot WHal WPrP WTin WWpP
	'Nostalgia'	EBee
	odorata	XPep
	'Old Brocade'	CHea CSli LPhx WPtf
	'Peardrop' **new**	NBre
	'Peter Davis'	see *Hippolytia herderi*
	pindicola subsp. ***integrifolia***	EWes
	Pink Island form	CKno
	'Pink Lady'	EBla EMan GBBs SGSe SPoG
	'Pink Temptation' **new**	WHil
	'Prospero'	CMea WCot WCra
	ptarmica	CArn ELau EMFW GBar MChe MGol MHer MSal NMir NPri SIde SPer WLHH WWye
*	- 'Ballerina'	MGol MWrn NBre NDov NLar
	- Innocence	see *A. ptarmica* 'Unschuld'
	- 'Major'	GMaP WCAu
	- 'Nana Compacta'	CSli EBla EChP ECha EMan EPPr GSki IGor LPio LRHS MLLN NBir NCGa SOkh SPlb SPoG SUsu WCAu WCFE WCot WOld
	- 'Perry's White'	CBre EBee ECha GCal LBmB LRHS NGHP WCot
	- 'Stephanie Cohen'	see *A. sibirica* 'Stephanie Cohen'
N	- The Pearl Group seed-raised (d)	CBcs ECha EGra ELan GKir GMaP NBlu NJOw NLsd NVic SPlb SPoG WFar WMoo WPer WTin WWpP
N	- - 'Boule de Neige' (clonal) (d)	CHal EBee GSki LSRN MBri NBre NCob NPer NSti SPer SPet SPla WFar WMnd

N	- - 'The Pearl' (clonal) (d) 𝕐H4	CDes CSBt EBee ENot EPfP ERou IHMH MRav MSte MWat MWgw NBPC NBid NBir NBro NCGa NEgg NGHP NLon SRms SWal WBor WBrk WCAu WCot WEas WFar WHer WHil WOld
§	- 'Unschuld'	NBir
I	'Rose Madder'	More than 30 suppliers
	'Rougham Bright Star'	CSli
	'Rougham Salmon'	CSli ERou
	'Sally'	EBee EGoo EPPr NBre
	'Sandstone'	see *A.* 'Wesersandstein'
§	'Schwefelblüte'	MRav NBir SBch SBla
	'Schwellenburg'	CDes CHar CSli
	sibirica	LPio
	- var. ***camschatica***	CSec CSli ECtt EMan EPfP EWTr
	'Love Parade'	GBar GSki LRHS MDKP MGol MNFA MRav MTis NEgg NJOw NLsd NSti SGSe SGar SPer SSvw SUsu WFar WMoo WSSM WSan WWpP
§	- 'Stephanie Cohen'	CPrp CStr EBee EMan EWTr MDKP MLLN MSph SOkh SPoG WCAu WCot WFar WTMC WWpP
	sintenisii **new**	WLin
	'Stephanie'	EBee EPPr
	'Summer Glory'	NCob
	Summer Pastels Group	CBrm CHrt CM&M COIW EGra EMil EShb GFlt GKir LRHS LSRN NArg NBir NBlu NOrc NRnb SECG SPav SPet SPoG SRms SWal WFar WMnd WPer WRha WWeb
	'Summerwine' 𝕐H4	More than 30 suppliers
	'Sunbeam'	LRHS WWeb
I	'Taygetea'	CSam CSli EBee EBla EChP ELan EMan EPPr EPfP EWTr GBBs GMaP MNFA MSte MTis MWgw NCGa SChu SDix SPer WCAu WCot WFar WKif WPer WSHC
	'Terracotta'	More than 30 suppliers
	'The Beacon'	see *A.* 'Fanal'
	tomentosa 𝕐H4	CTri ECha ECtt EPfP
§	- 'Aurea'	CHal EBla ELau IHMH NBlu NBre NBro NJOw SRms WPer
	- 'Maynard's Gold'	see *A. tomentosa* 'Aurea'
§	***umbellata***	EBee GBri WCot XPep
	- 'Weston'	see *A.* x *kolbiana* 'Weston'
	'Walther Funcke'	More than 30 suppliers
§	'Wesersandstein'	CDes CElw CFir CHar CKno CSli CWCL ECtt EPPr ERou GMaP LRHS MAvo MBnl MBri MLLN NBir NCGa NDov NPro STes SUsu WCAu WCot WFar WPGP WPer WTin WWhi
	'Wilczekii'	NChi SRms
	'Yellowstone'	LRHS SMer WWeb

x *Achimenantha* (*Gesneriaceae*)

'Inferno' 𝕐H1	WDib

Achimenes (*Gesneriaceae*)

'Ambroise Verschaffelt' 𝕐H1	LAma WDib
'Cattleya'	LAma
'Crummock Water'	WDib
erecta	WDib
'Harry Williams'	LAma
'Hilda Michelssen' 𝕐H1	WDib
'Himalayan Yellow Cloud'	LAma
'Little Beauty'	SWal WDib
'Maxima'	LAma
'Orange Delight'	WDib
'Peach Blossom'	LAma
'Purple King'	SWal
'Stan's Delight' (d) 𝕐H1	WDib
'Tarantella'	WDib
'Vivid'	LAma

Achlys (*Berberidaceae*)

californica	IBlr
japonica	GEdr WCru
triphylla	GBuc GGar IBlr WCru

Achnatherum see *Stipa*

Achyranthes (*Amaranthaceae*)

bidentata	CArn MSal

Acidanthera see *Gladiolus*

Acinos (*Lamiaceae*)

§	***alpinus***	CArn CBrm EMan ESis LTwo NJOw NLar SBla SHGN SPet SSvw WJek
§	***arvensis***	EUnu MHer MSal WBWf
§	***corsicus***	CStu ESis NLAp NWCA WHoo WPat

Aciphylla (*Apiaceae*)

aurea	CTrC GCal GCrs LTwo MCCP NJOw NLar NWCA SMad SPlb
congesta	GKev
crenulata	WCot
dieffenbachii	CFir
glaucescens	GCrs SMad
hectorii	EMan WCot
horrida	GCal WCot
kirkii	EMan WCot
monroi	GCal ITim LTwo NWCA WLin
pinnatifida	GCrs GGar GKev
similis	EMan
squarrosa	GCal WCot
subflabellata	EBee GCal

Acmella (*Asteraceae*)

§	***oleracea***	CArn EOHP MSal
	- 'Brede Mafane' **new**	EUnu

Acmena (*Myrtaceae*)

smithii	EShb

Acnistus (*Solanaceae*)

australis	see *Iochroma australe*

Acoelorrhaphe (*Arecaceae*)

wrightii	WMul

Aconitum ✿ (*Ranunculaceae*)

ACE 1449	GBuc
B&SWJ 2954 from Nepal	WCru
CC 4458	CPLG
GWJ 9393 from Northern India **new**	WCru
GWJ 9417 from Northern India	WCru
alboviolaceum	GCal
- var. ***albiflorum*** B&SWJ 4105	WCru
anglicum	see *A. napellus* subsp. *napellus* Anglicum Group
anthora	LPio MTis
arcuatum B&SWJ 774	WCru
austroyunnanense BWJ 7902	WCru
autumnale misapplied	see *A. carmichaelii* Wilsonii Group

	Name	Suppliers
	autumnale Rchb.	see *A. fischeri* Rchb.
	autumnale ambig.	NBir
	bartlettii B&SWJ 337	EBee GBin WCru
*	'Blue Opal'	EBee EWes SMHy
	'Blue Sceptre'	EBee EMan MBNS NLar WAul WCAu WSel
	'Bressingham Spire' ♀H4	More than 30 suppliers
	x ***cammarum*** 'Bicolor' ♀H4	More than 30 suppliers
	- 'Grandiflorum Album'	CAby ERou LPhx MSte
§	***carmichaelii***	CArn CBot CMea EBee EMan GAbr GIBF GKir GSki IBlr LLWP LRHS MBri MRav MWgw NBro NChi NFor NOrc SMrm SRms WFar WHoo WMoo WPnP WSel WTin
	- 'Arendsii' ♀H4	More than 30 suppliers
	- 'Pink Sensation'	EMan ERou EVFa LPio LTwo MBNS NBPC NGHP NSti SHop SUsu WHil
	- 'Royal Flush'	CFai CFir GCai GFlt LAst LRHS MSph NEgg NGdn SPoG WCot WPop WWeb
	- var. ***truppelianum*** HWJ 732	WCru
§	- Wilsonii Group	CAby CHar EBee EMar GGar LPhx LRHS MLLN MRav MSte MWat NChi NDov SBla SChu WFar WPGP WPer WSel WWye
§	- - 'Barker's Variety'	CKno CPou EBee EChP EMan EPfP GBuc GMac LPhx LPio MAnH NCGa NSti WAul WCot
	- - 'Kelmscott' ♀H4	EBee EMon GMac MRav MSte SAga SDix SMHy WFar WRHF
	- - 'Spätlese'	CAbP EBee EChP EMan EMar EVFa GCal MAnH MEHN MLLN NBPC NBir NDov NEgg NGdn SPer WCot WCra WLin WWhi WWlt
	- - 'The Grim Reaper'	EMon
	cilicicum	see *Eranthis hyemalis* Cilicica Group
	crassiflorum BWJ 7644 **new**	WCru
	'Eleonara'	CFir EBee EChP EMan EMar EPPr EPfP GBuc GKir LRHS MAvo MLLN NGHP NGby NLar NSti SSvw WAul WFar WMoo
	elliotii	GBin
	elwesii	GGar
	episcopale	CPLN WCru WFar
	aff. ***episcopale***	WSHC
	- CLD 1426	GBuc WFar
	ferox	EBee MLLN
	- HWJK 2217	WCru
	fischeri misapplied	see *A. carmichaelii*
§	***fischeri*** Rchb. **new**	CSpe EVFa GIBF
	fukutomei var. ***formosanum*** B&SWJ 3057	WCru
§	***hemsleyanum***	CBot CPLG CPLN CRHN GFlt ITim LRHS MDun NBid NCGa NChi NGHP SGSe SMad WBVN WBrE WCot WCru WFar WHoo WLin WOld WWhi
	- dark blue	CMea
	heterophyllum	LPhx
	hyemale	see *Eranthis hyemalis*
	'Ivorine'	More than 30 suppliers
	aff. ***jaluense*** B&SWJ 8741	WCru
	japonicum	WFar
	- subsp. ***subcuneatum*** B&SWJ 6228	WCru
	kusnezoffii **new**	GIBF
	lamarckii	see *A. lycoctonum* subsp. *neapolitanum*
	longecassidatum B&SWJ 4105	WCru
	- B&SWJ 8486	WCru
	lycoctonum	CAby EVFa GCrs MGol SRms WBVN WCAu
	- 'Dark Eyes'	CFir CMdw EBee LBuc MAnH MSph WCot
§	- subsp. ***lycoctonum***	MSal MWgw SRms
	- subsp. ***moldavicum***	EBee
§	- subsp. ***neapolitanum***	CBod EBee EChP ECtt ELan EMFP EMan EMar EPfP GCal GMaP GSki LRHS MBow MLLN MRav NGHP NLar SBla SSpi WFar WHlf WSan
§	- subsp. ***vulparia***	CArn CPrp EBee EMar GCal GKev GPoy MNFA MSal NDov NMRc SPoG WCot WEas WPer WSel WWhi WWye
	napellus	More than 30 suppliers
	- 'Albiflorus'	see *A. napellus* subsp. *vulgare* 'Albidum'
	- 'Bergfürst'	CAby EBrs LPhx LPio MBri NDov
	- 'Blue Valley'	EBee EChP EMan EPfP GBin NMyG NPro SHar WFar
	- 'Carneum'	see *A. napellus* subsp. *vulgare* 'Carneum'
	- 'Gletschereis' **new**	GBin
	- subsp. ***napellus*** **new**	GBin
§	- - Anglicum Group	CRow CSev CWan EBee EChP GBuc IBlr MGol MSal MSte NEgg SMac SSpi WBWf WCot WPen
	- 'Rubellum'	CFwr EBee EChP ELan EMan EMar ENot EPPr EPfP ERou EVFa LAst NBir NBro NOrc NPri SSvw WAul WBor WHoo WMnd WPnP
	- 'Schneewittchen'	EBee SSvw
	- 'Sphere's Variety'	NOrc
§	- subsp. ***vulgare*** 'Albidum'	More than 30 suppliers
§	- - 'Carneum'	EBrs EMan GCra GKir MLLN WCAu WHer WKif WLin WSel WWye
	napiforme	LPio WPGP WPnP
	- B&SWJ 943	WCru
	neapolitanum	see *A. lycoctonum* subsp. *neapolitanum*
	'Newry Blue'	CBos EMon ERou GBuc MFOX MRav MWhi NBir NEgg SRms WCAu WCra WFar WPer
	orientale hort.	see *A. lycoctonum* subsp. *vulparia*
	orientale ambig.	NPro
	paniculatum	EBee MBri
	- 'Roseum'	CFir LRHS MBNS MTis WFar
	'Pink Sensation' PBR	CFir CFwr IPot LSRN NLar
	proliferum B&SWJ 4107	WCru
	pseudolaeve	LPhx
	- B&SWJ 8663	WCru
	pyrenaicum	see *A. lycoctonum* subsp. *neapolitanum*
	ranunculifolius	see *A. lycoctonum* subsp. *neapolitanum*
	sczukinii	EMon
	seoulense B&SWJ 694	WCru
	- B&SWJ 864	WCru
	septentrionale	see *A. lycoctonum* subsp. *lycoctonum*
	'Spark's Variety' ♀H4	More than 30 suppliers
	spicatum	EBee
	'Stainless Steel'	More than 30 suppliers
	stoloniferum **new**	GIBF
	'Tissington Pearl'	MTis
	x ***tubergenii***	see *Eranthis hyemalis* Tubergenii Group
	uchiyamai B&SWJ 1005	WCru
	- B&SWJ 1216	WCru

- B&SWJ 4446	WCru
variegatum (v)	EBee
volubile hort.	see *A. hemsleyanum*
volubile Pall. **new**	NTHB
vulparia	see *A. lycoctonum* subsp. *vulparia*
'Wu To Di' SDR 928 **new**	GKev
yamazakii	WCru

Aconogonon see *Persicaria*

Acorus ✿ (*Acoraceae*)

calamus	CAgr CArn CDWL CRow CWat EHon ELau EMFW EPza GPoy LNCo LPBA MCCP MGol MSal NArg NBlu NPer WHer WPop WWpP
- 'Argenteostriatus' (v)	CBcs CRow CWat EBee EChP ECha ECtt EHon EMFW ENot EPfP EPza LNCo LPBA NOrc SHel SWal WMoo WPop WWpP
* ***christophii*** **new**	EWes SApp
gramineus	CPne LPBA MLan NPer WHer WTin WWpP
- 'Golden Delight' **new**	CKno EUnu SGSe
- 'Golden Edge' (v)	WMoo
- 'Hakuro-nishiki' (v)	More than 30 suppliers
I - 'Licorice'	CBgR EPPr EWin IFro LBuc LRHS MBNS MSal SHel WCHb WCot WLeb WPnP WWpP
- 'Masamune' (v)	EPla GCal SApp WBrk WTin
- 'Minimus Aureus'	CBgR CBre CWCL
- 'Oborozuki' misapplied	see *A. gramineus* 'Ogon'
- 'Oborozuki' (v)	CKno CPne CStu EPla SGSe WPrP
§ - 'Ogon' (v)	More than 30 suppliers
- var. ***pusillus***	EPla NBro
- 'Variegatus' (v)	More than 30 suppliers
- 'Yodo-no-yuki' (v)	EPla WDyG
'Intermedius'	NPer

Acradenia (*Rutaceae*)

frankliniae	CBcs CFil CMHG CPLG CPle CPne CTrC GGar IArd IDee LRHS SBrw SEND SSpi WFar WSHC

Acridocarpus (*Malpighiaceae*)

natalitius	CSec

Actaea (*Ranunculaceae*)

alba	see *A. pachypoda*, *A. rubra* f. *neglecta*
arizonica	CLAP EBee GCal LPhx SBri WCru
asiatica	CDes CLAP GBin WPGP
- B&SWJ 616	WCru
biternata	CLAP MSte
- B&SWJ 5591	WCru
cimicifuga	CDes CLAP GBin GCal GPoy
- B&SWJ 2966	WCru
cordifolia	CAby EMan ENot GMaP LPhx MLLN MSal NJOw WCru WPnP WWpP
- 'Blickfang'	GBin
dahurica	EBee GCal GKir MGol MSal NLar SBla
- B&SWJ 8426	WCru
- B&SWJ 8573	WCru
- B&SWJ 8653	GEdr
elata	WCru
erythrocarpa	see *A. rubra*
europaea	LPhx WCru
frigida B&SWJ 2657	WCru
heracleifolia	GKir GSki
- B&SWJ 8843	WCru
japonica	CLAP CMea CRow EBee EChP GCal GKir LPhx LRHS NSti WCot WFar
- B&SWJ 5828	WCru
- compact	GBin
mairei **new**	WCru
matsumurae 'Elstead Variety' ♀H4	CRow ECha GCal LPhx MRav NDov SOkh SSpi SUsu
- 'Frau Herms'	EBee GKir
- 'White Pearl'	More than 30 suppliers
§ ***pachypoda*** ♀H4	CDes CPom EBee ECGP ECha ELan EMan GBBs GBuc GCra GEdr GPoy GTou IBlr IGor MSal MSte MTis NArg NBid NCGa NLar NSti SSpi WBVN WCot WCru WMoo
- f. ***rubrocarpa***	ELan
podocarpa	GCal MSal SPlb SRms
racemosa ♀H4	CArn CRow CSam EBee EChP ELan EPfP ERou EVFa GBBs GCal GKir GPoy LRHS MLLN MSal NArg NBid NGdn SECG SPer WFar WMnd
§ ***rubra*** ♀H4	CBro CHid CMHG EBee EBrs EChP ECha ELan GBuc GCal GGar GIBF GKev GKir IBlr LRHS MSte NChi NSti SMad SPoG SSpi WCru WEas WFar WMoo WPGP
- ***alba***	see *A. pachypoda*, *A. rubra* f. *neglecta*
§ - f. ***neglecta***	EBee EChP EMan GBuc GEdr GKir NLar SMad SPoG SSpi WCru
simplex	CSam GKir LRHS MWgw NDov NPri
- B&SWJ 6355	WCru
- Atropurpurea Group	More than 30 suppliers
- - 'Bernard Mitchell'	CFir
- - 'Brunette' ♀H4	More than 30 suppliers
- - 'Hillside Black Beauty'	More than 30 suppliers
- - 'James Compton'	More than 30 suppliers
- 'Mountain Wave'	CLAP EBee WFar
- 'Pink Spike'	ERou NLar WCot WFar WMoo WPnP
§ - 'Prichard's Giant'	CLAP ECha GBuc GKir LPhx LRHS MBri MRav MSte NEgg WCot WFar
- ***ramosa***	see *A. simplex* 'Prichard's Giant'
- 'Scimitar'	LPhx SMeo
- 'Silver Axe'	GCal
§ ***spicata***	EBee GBuc GKir GPoy MFOX MSal MSte NLar NSti NWoo WCot WCru
- var. ***acuminata*** B&SWJ 6257	WCru
- var. ***rubra***	see *A. rubra*
taiwanensis	CLAP
- B&SWJ 343	CLAP
- B&SWJ 3413	WCru
yesoensis	GCal
yunnanensis ACE 1880	GBuc

Actinella see *Tetraneuris*

Actinidia (*Actinidiaceae*)

BWJ 8161 from China	WCru
arguta (m)	SHBN
- (f/F)	CAgr GIBF WPGP
- B&SWJ 569	WCru
- 'Issai' (s-p/F)	CBcs CPLN EBee ERea LBuc MGos
- 'Kiwai Vert' (f/F) **new**	CAgr
- LL#1 (m) **new**	CAgr
- LL#2 (f)	CAgr
- LL#3 (m)	CAgr
- 'Weiki'	MGos
callosa var. ***ephippioidea*** B&SWJ 1790	WCru

- var. ***formosana*** B&SWJ 3806	WCru
chinensis misapplied	see *A. deliciosa*
coriacea **new**	CPLN
§ ***deliciosa***	CPLG ERom MGos SLon WBVN WSHC
- (f/F)	ENot MRav SHBN
- (m)	ENot
- 'Atlas' (m)	ECrN MBri NLar SLim
* - 'Boskoop'	MWat
- 'Bruno' (f/F)	SLim
- 'Hayward' (f/F)	CBcs CDoC CHEx COtt EBee ECrN ELan EMil EPfP ERea LRHS MBri MGos NPal SHBN SPer SWvt WCru
- 'Jenny' (s-p/F)	CPLN CSBt ECrN LBuc LRHS MAsh MCoo MGos MLan SKee SPoG
- 'Solo'	CDoC
- 'Tomuri' (m)	CBcs CDoC CHEx COtt EBee ELan EMil EPfP ERea LRHS MGos NPal SHBN SPer SWvt WCru
hypoleuca B&SWJ 5942	WCru
kolomikta ♀H4	More than 30 suppliers
- (m)	CAgr MBlu
- B&SWJ 4243	WCru
- 'Tomoko' (F)	WCru
- 'Yazuaki' (m)	WCru
latifolia	CPLN
- B&SWJ 3563	WCru
petelotii HWJ 628	WCru
pilosula	CBcs CPLG CPLN CSPN GCal LEdu SCoo SLon WBcn WCru WPGP WPat WSHC
polygama (F)	CPLN WCru
- B&SWJ 5444	WCru
- B&SWJ 8525 from Korea **new**	WCru
purpurea (f/F)	CAgr
rubricaulis B&SWJ 3111	WCru
rufa	CPLN
- B&SWJ 3525	WCru
aff. ***strigosa*** HWJK 2367 **new**	WCru
tetramera	CPLN
- B&SWJ 3564	WCru

Actinotus (*Apiaceae*)

helianthi **new**	EMan

Adansonia (*Bombacaceae*)

gregorii	SPlb

Adelocaryum see *Lindelofia*

Adenia (*Passifloraceae*)

glauca **new**	LToo
spinosa **new**	LToo

Adenium (*Apocynaceae*)

obesum ♀H1	CRoM ESlt LToo MOak
- subsp. ***boehmianum*** **new**	LToo

Adenocalymma (*Bignoniaceae*)

comosum **new**	CPLN

Adenocarpus (*Papilionaceae*)

decorticans	CArn CTrC SPlb WSHC

Adenophora (*Campanulaceae*)

BWJ 7696 from China	WCru
'Afterglow'	see *Campanula rapunculoides* 'Afterglow'
'Amethyst'	CBos MAnH
* ***asiatica***	WFar
aurita	CBcs CFir CMdw CMea EChP EMan EPPr MLLN NCGa NChi NWoo WCot
bulleyana	CHar CWCL EBee EBrs EHyt ELan EMan EWTr GBuc GCra GIBF GKev LRHS MAnH MWgw NBid NChi NRnb SDnm SGSe SMac SPav SPet SPlb WCAu WCot WFar WPer
* ***campanulata***	WPer
coelestis	EBee EMan MMil NRnb
- ACE 2455	GBuc
- B&SWJ 7998	WCru
confusa	EMan LRHS MAnH MDKP NArg NLRH SPav WFar WHer WSHC
cymerae	MAnH MMil NRnb
divaricata	EMan WFoF
forrestii	NEgg WFar
grandiflora B&SWJ 8555	WCru
himalayana	GBri MNrw WPer
khasiana	CFir GMac LDai LTwo MAnH MDKP MMil MNrw NLar NRnb WPrP
koreana	EBee SPav
latifolia hort.	see *A. pereskiifolia*
latifolia Fischer	CWan GBri NBir WFar
liliifolia	CHar ECtt ELan EMan GCal GMac LRHS MAnH MWgw NCGa NPer NRnb NSti SMad SOkd SPav SRot WFar WTin
§ ***nikoensis***	CSec GIBF MMil MNrw NBid NRnb WPat
§ - var. ***stenophylla***	EBee GKev WCot
nipponica	see *A. nikoensis* var. *stenophylla*
§ ***pereskiifolia***	CWan GKev GMac NBre NEgg SEND SHar SPlb WCot WFar WPer
polyantha	CHar EBee EChP EHrv EMan GBuc LRHS MAnH MNrw SBod SRms WFar WPnP
polymorpha	see *A. nikoensis*
potaninii	CFir EBee EChP EHyt EMan GBuc LBBr MNrw NCGa NEgg NRnb NSti SBla SGar SPav SPoG WBVN WCHb WFar WHal WPnP
remotiflora B&SWJ 8562	WCru
stricta	LRHS
- subsp. ***sessilifolia***	GBuc NEgg SPla
sublata	NRnb WFar
takedae	MAnH NRnb
- var. ***howozana***	GKev MAnH NRnb WPrP
taquetii	GKev NEgg SOkd
- B&SWJ 1303	WCru
tashiroi	CNic CPrp EBee ECtt EPfP GBri GBuc GFlt MNrw NPro NRnb SBri SHel SMac WCHb
triphylla	EMan GCal GIBF NBir SPav WFar
- Brown 0204	CStu
- var. ***hakusanensis***	EBee
- var. ***japonica***	MAnH NRnb
- - B&SWJ 8835	WCru
uehatae	GKev MAvo
- B&SWJ 126	WCru

Adenostyles (*Asteraceae*)

alpina	see *Cacalia hastata*

Adiantum ✿ (*Adiantaceae*)

aethiopicum	NWoo WHer
§ ***aleuticum*** ♀H4	CBcs CFil CLAP EFer ELan EMon GBin MAvo NBid NBro WAbe WFib WHal WPGP WRic WTMC
- 'Imbricatum'	CBcs CLAP CPrp EChP ECha GBin

		LRHS MAvo NLar SBla SPla SRms WFar WFib
	- 'Japonicum'	CBos CDes CLAP CMil CPrp CWil EFtx ELan GCal MAsh MAvo MBri NBir NCGa SRms SSpi WCot WCru WFar WFib WHal WPGP WRic
	- 'Laciniatum'	SRms
*	- f. ***minimum***	CLAP SRms
	- 'Miss Sharples'	CAby CLAP CPrp ELan GCal LRHS MAsh MBnl MWgw NEgg NLar SRms WCru WFar WRic
	- 'Subpumilum' ♀H4	CLAP GBin MRav NWoo WAbe
	capillus-veneris	CHEx MMHG MWat SGSe WCot WFib
	- 'Mairisii'	see *A.* x *mairisii*
	cuneatum	see *A. raddianum*
	formosum	WRic
	hispidulum	SRms WRic
	jordanii **new**	CFil
§	x ***mairisii*** ♀H3	EFtx
*	***monocolor***	MBri
	pedatum misapplied	see *A. aleuticum*
	pedatum ♀H4	CBcs CFil CHEx CLAP EBee ECha EFer ELan EPfP EPza GMaP LPBA LRHS MBri MMoz SApp SChu SDix SPer SRot SSpi WBor WFar WPGP WTMC
	- var. ***aleuticum***	see *A. aleuticum*
	- Asiatic form	see *A. aleuticum* 'Japonicum'
	- 'Japonicum'	see *A. aleuticum* 'Japonicum'
	- 'Roseum'	see *A. aleuticum* 'Japonicum'
	- var. ***subpumilum***	see *A. aleuticum* 'Subpumilum'
	peruvianum	EFtx MBri WRic
	pubescens	MBri WRic
§	***raddianum*** ♀H2	CHal
	- 'Fragrans'	see *A. raddianum* 'Fragrantissimum'
§	- 'Fragrantissimum'	MBri
	- 'Fritz Lüthi' ♀H2	CHal MBri
	- 'Micropinnulum'	EFtx
	venustum ♀H4	CBos CFil CHEx CLAP CWil EFer EFtx EHyt EMon GCal NVic SDix SHFr SRms SSpi WAbe WCot WEas WFar WFib WIvy WPGP WRic

Adina (*Rubiaceae*)

rubella	IArd NLar

Adlumia (*Papaveraceae*)

fungosa	CSpe GFlt LRHS

Adonis (*Ranunculaceae*)

	amurensis misapplied	see *A.* 'Fukujukai', *A. multiflora*
	- 'Pleniflora'	see *A. multiflora* 'Sandanzaki'
	amurensis ambig.	CMea EBee ECho EPot GCrs GIBF LAma LTwo SCnR WCot
	annua	WBWf
	brevistyla	EHyt ETow GBuc NMen NSla
	'Fukujukai'	ECha WFar
§	***multiflora*** 'Sandanzaki' (d)	EBee EPot GBin MBri NLar SBod SPer WCot WFar
	sibirica	LAma
	sutchuenensis	LAma
	tianschanica	LAma
	vernalis	EHyt GPoy NSla SBla

Adoxa (*Adoxaceae*)

moschatellina	CRWN NMen WHer WPnP WShi WWye

Adromischus (*Crassulaceae*)

cooperi	EPem WEas
cristatus **new**	EPem
subdistichus **new**	EPem

Aechmea (*Bromeliaceae*)

sp.	XBlo
caudata **new**	EOas
'Covata' **new**	EOas
cylindrata **new**	EOas
distichantha **new**	EOas
- var. ***schlumbergeri***	CFir
fasciata ♀H1	LRHS MBri XBlo
gamosepala	EOas
ramosa **new**	XBlo
recurvata **new**	EOas
- var. ***benrathii*** **new**	EOas
- var. ***ortgiesii*** **new**	EOas
victoriana **new**	XBlo

Aegle (*Rutaceae*)

sepiaria	see *Poncirus trifoliata*

Aegopodium (*Apiaceae*)

podagraria 'Bengt'	EMon
- 'Dangerous' (v)	CHid CNat WCHb
- gold-margined (v)	EMon
- 'Variegatum' (v)	More than 30 suppliers

Aeonium (*Crassulaceae*)

	arboreum ♀H1	CAbb CHEx EPem EShb MWya WHal WRos
	- 'Atropurpureum' ♀H1	CHEx CSpe CTbh EAmu EPem EPfP ERea EShb IBlr MBri MLan MOak NPer SEND WCot
	- green-leaved	SEND
*	- 'Magnificum'	EBee EPfP EShb EWin EWll SAPC SArc
	- 'Variegatum' (v)	EShb EUJe EWll LPio NPer
	balsamiferum	CHEx CTrC EBee EPfP EWin EWll SAPC SArc SChr WCot
	'Blush'	EBee EWin
	canariense	CAbb CBrP CHEx EBee
	- var. ***palmense***	EBee EWin
§	- var. ***subplanum***	CTrC
	castello-paivae	EBee EShb EWin SChr
	cuneatum	CTbh MLan SChr SEND SPet
	decorum	SEND
*	- 'Variegatum' (v)	WCot
	'Dinner Plate'	CHEx
	'Dinner Plate' x ***haworthii*** **new**	CHEx
	x ***domesticum***	see *Aichryson* x *domesticum*
	glandulosum	SChr
	goochiae	CTbh EBee EWin
	haworthii ♀H1	CAbb CBrP CHEx CHal CTbh CTrC MLan SEND
	- 'Variegatum' (v)	EShb EWin SChr
	holochrysum	IBlr
	lindleyi	SChr
	- var. ***viscatum***	EBee EWin
*	***multiflora*** **new**	EWin
*	- 'Variegata' (v) **new**	EWin
	nobile	CBrP
	percarneum	EShb
	simsii	CHal CTbh EBee EWin SChr
	- variegated (v)	EPem
	spathulatum	CTrC
	subplanum	see *A. canariense* var. *subplanum*
	tabuliforme ♀H1	CSpe EPem
	- 'Cristatum'	EPem
	urbicum	CHEx
	'Zwartkop' ♀H1	More than 30 suppliers

Aeschynanthus (*Gesneriaceae*)

'Big Apple'	CHal EShb LRHS WDib

	Black Pagoda Group	LRHS WDib
	'Fire Wheel'	LRHS WDib
	hildebrandii	WDib
	'Holiday Bells' **new**	WDib
	'Hot Flash'	LRHS WDib
	'Little Tiger' **new**	LRHS
	lobbianus	see *A. radicans*
	longicalyx	LRHS WDib
§	***longicaulis*** ♀H1	LRHS WDib
	marmoratus	see *A. longicaulis*
	'Mona'	MBri
	parvifolius	see *A. radicans*
§	***radicans*** ♀H1	EBak LRHS MBri WDib
	'Scooby Doo' **new**	WDib
	speciosus ♀H1	CHal LRHS WDib

Aesculus ✿ (*Hippocastanaceae*)

	arguta	see *A. glabra* var. *arguta*
	x ***arnoldiana***	CDul CMCN SBir
	- 'Autumn Splendor'	EPfP
§	x ***bushii***	CMCN CTho MGos
	californica	CBcs CMCN CTho CTrw ECrN EPfP ERod IArd SSpi WPGP
	- 'Blue Haze'	SSpi
	x ***carnea***	CTri ELan MBar SBLw
	- 'Aureomarginata' (v)	CTho ERod SMad WPat
	- 'Briotii' ♀H4	More than 30 suppliers
	- 'Plantierensis'	CDul SBLw
*	- 'Variegata' (v)	CBcs CDul CMCN LRHS MGos WDin
	chinensis	CMCN NLar SMad
	'Dallimorei' (graft-chimaera)	SMad
§	***flava*** ♀H4	CFil CMCN CTho ECrN EPfP NWea SBLw SSpi WPGP
	- f. ***vestita***	CDoC CDul MBlu
	flava x ***pavia***	see *A.* x *hybrida*
	georgiana	see *A. sylvatica*
	glabra	CDul CMCN CTho EGFP GKir LRHS SSpi
§	- var. ***arguta***	CMCN GKir WDin
	- 'October Red'	MBlu WPGP
	glaucescens	see *A.* x *neglecta*
	hippocastanum ♀H4	More than 30 suppliers
§	- 'Baumannii' (d) ♀H4	CDoC CDul CLnd COtt EBee ECrN ENot EPfP ERod LRHS MGos MSwo NWea SBLw SHBN WDin WFar
	- 'Digitata'	CDul CMCN SBLw SMad
	- 'Flore Pleno'	see *A. hippocastanum* 'Baumannii'
	- 'Hampton Court Gold'	CBcs CDul CEnd CMCN
	- 'Honiton Gold'	CTho
	- 'Laciniata'	CBcs CDul CMCN ERod LRHS MBlu NLar
	- 'Monstrosa'	SMad
	- 'Pyramidalis'	CDul SBLw SMad
	- 'Wisselink'	CDul CLnd CMCN ECrN MBlu SMad
§	x ***hybrida***	SSpi
	indica	CDul CHEx CLnd CMCN CTho ECrN ELan EPfP GGGa GKir IArd IDee LRHS SMHT SSpi WDin WPGP
	- 'Sydney Pearce' ♀H4	CDoC CDul CEnd CMCN ERod MBlu MGos NLar SBir SMad SSpi WPGP
	x ***marylandica***	CDul
	memmingeri	SBir
	x ***mississippiensis***	see *A.* x *bushii*
	x ***mutabilis*** 'Harbisonii'	GTSp WWes
	- 'Induta'	CLnd CMCN EPfP GTSp IArd LRHS MBlu MBri NLar NSti SCoo SDix SMad SSpi WFar WWes
§	- 'Penduliflora'	CBcs CDul CEnd CTho EPfP LRHS MBlu
§	x ***neglecta***	CLnd CMCN
	- 'Autumn Fire'	MBlu
	- 'Erythroblastos' ♀H4	CBcs CDoC CDul CEnd CLnd CMCN CTho ECrN EMil EPfP ERod GKir IDee LRHS MBlu SBir SCoo SHBN SMad SSpi SSta WDin WPat
	parviflora ♀H4	CBcs CDul CFil CMCN CTri EBee ECrN ELan ENot EPfP EWTr IDee LRHS MBar MBlu MBri MGos MLan NBea NBlu NEgg SLPl SMad SPer SSpi SSta WDin WFar WOrn WPGP
§	***pavia*** ♀H4	CBcs CDul CMCN CTho EPfP GKir IDee ISea LRHS SSpi WDin WWes
	- 'Atrosanguinea'	CDul CEnd CLnd CMCN EBee EPfP ERod IMGH LRHS MBlu NPal SMad SSpi
	- var. ***discolor***	SBLw WDin
	- - 'Koehnei'	CDul CMCN LRHS MBlu NLar SCoo
	- 'Penduliflora'	see *A.* x *mutabilis* 'Penduliflora'
	- 'Purple Spring'	MBlu
	- 'Rosea Nana'	CMCN WPat
	splendens	see *A. pavia*
§	***sylvatica***	CMCN CTho GKir MBlu
	turbinata	CBcs CDul CLnd CMCN LRHS SSpi WBVN
	- var. ***pubescens***	MBlu WPGP
	wilsonii	CFil WPGP
	x ***woerlitzensis***	CLnd ISea WCwm

Aethionema (*Brassicaceae*)

	armenum	CSec GKev WLin
	coridifolium	WPer
	euonomioides	WLin
§	***grandiflorum*** ♀H4	CElw NArg NBro SBla SRms WPer
	- Pulchellum Group ♀H4	CLyd CSpe EPot GKev GKir NMen SGar
	iberideum	EHyt ETow MDKP MWat SRms
*	***kotschyi*** hort.	ECho NMen SBla WAbe
	oppositifolium	CLyd GTou MWat WAbe WHoo
	pulchellum	see *A. grandiflorum*
	spicatum **new**	WLin
	'Warley Rose' ♀H4	CLyd CWCL ELan EPot GKir NLAp NMen NWCA SIng SRms WPat
	'Warley Ruber'	CLyd CPBP NBir SBla WAbe

Afrocarpus (*Podocarpaceae*)

	falcatus	ECou GGar

Agalinis (*Scrophulariaceae*)

	linariodes	EMan

Agapanthus ✿ (*Alliaceae*)

	'Aberdeen'	CPne XDoo
I	'Adonis'	IBlr
	'African Moon' **new**	CPne
§	***africanus*** ♀H1	CAbb CElw EHrv EPfP EUJe EWTr GSki IBlr LRHS MBNS NArg NBlu SAPC SArc SBod SPav SPer WBor WBrE WFar WPer WPop XPep
*	- 'Albus' ♀H1	CBcs CDes CDoC CHad CHid EMan EPfP GSki IBlr IHMH LRHS MBNS NBlu SBod SEND SPav SPer WPer WPop XPep
*	- 'Big Blue'	CKno CPrp EBee GGar
	- 'Trebah' **new**	CTbh
*	'Albus'	CAvo CPLG GFlt GMaP IBal MGos MHer SAga
	'Amsterdam'	XDoo
	'Angela'	CPne
	'Anthea' **new**	CPne

'Aphrodite'	IBlr
'Arctic Star'	GSki
Ardernei hybrid	CDes CFil CPne EBee ECha EVFa EWes GCal IBlr LPio MSte NEgg SAga SRos SSpi SUsu WCot WPGP XDoo
'Baby Blue'	CLyd CPen IBal IBlr LRHS SMrm XDoo
'Ballyrogan'	IBlr LPio
'Basutoland'	EBrs LRHS
'Beatrice' **new**	CPne
'Beeches Dwarf'	EBee
'Ben Hope'	GBuc IBlr SDnm SPav WCot WHil XDoo
'Bethlehem Star'	CPne GSki SRos
'Bicton Bluebell'	IBlr
'Black Pantha' **new**	CFai CFir CSpe EHrv EUJe LAst MBNS MBnl MDKP NCob SPer SPoG WCot WPop
'Blue Baby'	LRHS SMur WFar
'Blue Bird'	CPne
'Blue Brush'	CPne CSBt EMil LSRN SCoo SPoG SVil
'Blue Cascade'	IBlr
'Blue Companion'	CPne CPrp IBlr
'Blue Diamond'	EHrv SRos
'Blue Dot'	EBee
'Blue Giant'	CBcs CBro CPen EBee ELan EWTr IBal IBlr LRHS MNFA MSte NEgg NGby SAga WDav WFar WPGP
'Blue Globe'	CM&M EBee EChP ERou GMaP IBal MBct NGdn STes WCAu WHil WMnd WTMC
'Blue Haze'	SRos
'Blue Heaven' PBR **new**	CPne
'Blue Imp'	CBro CPne GBuc GSki IBlr LRHS MMHG SApp XDoo
'Blue Moon'	CBro CHad CPen CPne EBee IBal IBlr LRHS SEND WCot
'Blue Nile'	CPne
'Blue Skies'	CBcs IBlr NCGa WTMC
'Blue Triumphator'	CHid EBee EPfP EWTr EWll GMaP IBlr LPio LRHS NGby SBod SMrm WCot XDoo
'Blue Velvet'	CPne
'Bressingham Blue'	CBro CPne CTri EBrs EMFP GCal IBlr LRHS MRav MSte NVic SChu SSpe WGer XDoo
'Bressingham Bounty'	EBrs
'Bressingham White'	CPne EBee ECtt EHrv EMan LPio LRHS MRav NCGa SOkh XDoo
'Buckingham Palace'	CBro CDes CFil CKno IBlr WPGP XDoo
'Cally Blue'	GAbr GCal
'Cambridge'	CPne
§ ***campanulatus***	CElw CFil CPLG CPrp CWCL EBee ELan EPfP EWTr GFlt GGar GSki IBlr IGor ISea LRHS MRav NCGa NCob SYvo WAbe WCot WFar WWpP XPep
- var. ***albidus***	CDes CHad CPne CWCL EBee ECha ELan EMar ENot EPfP EPza IBlr LRHS MNFA MRav MSte MWgw NGdn NSti NVic SChu SPer SSpi WCot WFar WHoo WPGP WWpP XDoo
- 'Albovittatus'	CBot CSam ECho EVFa
- bright blue	CWCL GCal
- 'Buckland'	IBlr
- 'Cobalt Blue'	EBla ECha
- 'Isis'	CAvo CBro CFil CFir CTri CWCL EBee EBla ECha EGra EMFP GBuc IBal IBlr LRHS SRos WCAu
- 'Meibont' (v)	WCot
- 'Oxbridge'	IBlr
- 'Oxford Blue'	CFil CPrp EBee EBrs GBri GBuc IBlr LRHS SRos WPGP
- subsp. ***patens*** 🏆H3	CPrp CSec EBee EBla EBrs EMan EPfP GBri GBuc LPio SSpi WHil WPGP
- - deep blue	CFir CPrp EBrs IBlr LRHS
- 'Premier'	CFil CPrp EBee EBrs IBlr WPGP
- 'Profusion'	CBro CWCL EBee EBrs ECha IBal IBlr LRHS SRos SSpi WFar
- 'Slieve Donard Variety'	IBlr WFar
- 'Spokes'	IBlr
- variegated (v)	EBla ECha NPer
- 'Wedgwood Blue'	CPrp EBrs IBal IBlr XDoo
- 'Wendy'	EBrs IBlr
- 'White Hope'	IBlr SRos
- 'White Triumphator'	WCot
'Castle of Mey'	CBro CFil EBee GBuc IBlr MTho SBla SPav SRos WPGP XDoo
'Catharina'	CPne XDoo
caulescens 🏆H1	CFil EBee IBlr IGor WBrE WPGP
- subsp. ***angustifolius***	CBrm IBlr WCot XPep
'Cedric Morris'	ERea IBlr SRos XDoo
'Chandra'	IBlr
'Cherry Holley'	CPne LPio SRos
'Clarence House'	CBro
coddii	CPLG EMan IBlr LPio LRHS SChu WCot WHil
'Columba'	CPne LAma XDoo
comptonii	CAvo CFil CMon CPou CPrp IBlr WCot
- subsp. ***comptonii***	CBrm
- subsp. ***longitubus***	CPne LPio WCot WHil
'Crystal Drop'	CPne
Danube	see *A.* 'Donau'
'Dark Star'	WFar
'Dawn Star'	XDoo
'Debbie'	CPne XDoo
'Delft'	IBlr
'Dell Garden'	LRHS
'Density'	IBlr
'Devon Dawn'	CPne
'Dnjepr'	GSki
'Dokter Brouwer'	CPen CPne EBee GSki MDKP NGby XDoo
§ 'Donau'	CBro CDoC CPen CPne EMan SMrm WFar XDoo
'Dorothy Kate' **new**	CPne
dyeri	CBro IBlr
'Ed Carman' (v)	WCot
'Elisabeth'	CPne
'Ethel's Joy'	CPen
'Eve'	EBee IBlr
'Evening Star'	CPne ECha GSki LRHS
'Exmoor' **new**	CPne
'Findlay's Blue'	CFil CLCN GBuc SMHy WPGP
'Gayle's Lilac'	More than 30 suppliers
'Gem' **new**	CPne
'Getty White' **new**	SGSe
'Glacier Stream'	CBro EBee GSki IPot
'Glenavon'	CAbb CFir CPne CPrp CTbh EBee EMil IBal NLar SApp SCoo SVil
'Golden Rule' (v)	CFir EHoe EVFa GBuc IBlr MAvo SSpi WPGP
'Harvest Blue' **new**	CPne
§ Headbourne hybrids	More than 30 suppliers
'Heavenly Blue' **new**	CPne
'Helen'	IBlr
'Holbeach'	CPne XDoo
'Holbrook'	CSam
'Hydon Mist'	XDoo
'Ice Blue Star'	CPne SRos

	'Ice Lolly'	CBro EBee
	inapertus	CBro CFil CMon IGor LRHS MHer SBla SMad SSpi WCot WPGP XPep
	- dwarf	IBlr
	- subsp. ***hollandii***	CAvo CPne GCal IBlr MSte WHil
	- - 'Lydenburg'	IBlr
	- - 'Zealot' **new**	IBlr
	- subsp. ***inapertus***	EChP ERea IBlr WCot
I	- - 'Albus'	IBlr
	- - 'Cyan'	IBlr
	- subsp. ***intermedius***	CFil EBee EChP GCal IBlr SSpi WCot
	- - 'Wolkberg'	IBlr
	- subsp. ***parviflorus***	IBlr
	- subsp. ***pendulus***	CFir EBrs ETow IBlr WPGP
	- - 'Graskop'	IBlr
	- - 'Violet Dusk' **new**	IBlr
	'Innocence'	IBlr
I	'Intermedius' van Tubergen	CPne GSki XDoo
	'Jack's Blue'	More than 30 suppliers
	'Jersey Giant'	LEdu
	'Jodie'	CPne
	'Johanna'	CPne
	'Jolanda' **new**	CPne
	'Kingston Blue'	CAby CMea CPne EBla ECha EHan EHrv ENot IBlr LRHS LSou SUsu WFar WPrP WSHC
	'Kirsty' **new**	CPne
	'Kobold'	CPne SBod WFar
	'Lady Edith'	IBlr
	'Lady Moore'	IBlr IGor SMHy
	'Latent Blue'	IBlr
	'Leicester'	EBee
	'Lilac Bells' **new**	CPne
	'Lilac Time'	CPne IBlr
	'Lilliput'	More than 30 suppliers
	'Loch Hope' ♀H3	More than 30 suppliers
	'Luly'	CPne
	'Mabel Grey'	CPne IBlr
	'Magnifico'	IBlr
	'Marcus'	CPne
	'Mariètte'	CPen CPne EBee XDoo
	'Marjorie'	CLCN CWCL SApp
	'Martine'	CPne
	'Mercury' **new**	CPne
	'Midnight'	CHad SAga
	'Midnight Blue' ambig.	CBos CDoC COIW ELan EPfP GBuc GSki IGor LPio LRHS MSte SMHy SPav WFar
	'Midnight Blue' P. Wood	GCal IBlr
	'Midnight Star'	CBro CPen CPne ECha ERea GSki IBal LRHS MSte SRos WFar WPrP XDoo
	mixed whites	WCFE
*	'Mooreanus' misapplied	CFil EPfP GCal IBlr WPGP
	'Morning Star'	CPne GSki SRos
	'Navy Blue'	More than 30 suppliers
	'New Blue'	CPen CPne EBee ENot IBal
	'Nikki' **new**	CPne
	'Norman Hadden'	IBlr
	nutans	IBlr LRHS WCot
	- 'Albus'	GCal
	'Nyx'	IBlr
	'Oslo'	CPne XDoo
	Palmer's hybrids	see *A.* Headbourne hybrids
	'Patent Blue'	IBlr
	'Penelope Palmer'	IBlr
	'Penny Slade'	SRos
	'Peter Pan'	CBcs CBro CElw CHid CMea COIW CPen CPne CPrp CSWP CWib EBee EChP ENot GBuc GGar GSki IBal LPhx LPio LRHS MRav SGSe WCAu WCFE WFar WPop WWeb XPep
	'Peter Pan American'	SMHy
	'Phantom'	CPne IBlr
	'Pinchbeck'	CPne XDoo
	'Pinocchio'	CFwr CPen GSki IPot MLan
	'Plas Merdyn Blue'	IBlr
	'Plas Merdyn White'	CFir CPne IBlr
	'Podge Mill'	CWCL IBlr
	'Polar Ice'	CFir CPne EBee GSki IBlr WFar WHil XDoo
	'Porcelain'	IBlr
	praecox	CFil CPrp EBee EBrs GAbr IBlr
	- 'Atlas'	IBlr
	- 'Bangor Blue'	IBlr
	- 'Blue Formality'	IBlr
I	- 'Blue Mercury'	IBlr
	- 'Dwarf White'	see *A.* white dwarf hybrids
	- 'Flore Pleno' (d)	CDes CFai CPne EBee ECha EHrv ELan EMan EMon IBlr MBNS SSpi WCot WFar WPGP WPrP
	- subsp. ***maximus*** 'Albus'	CPou EBrs IBlr SSpi
	- subsp. ***minimus***	CElw CPne GSki IBlr
	- - blue	ERea
I	- - 'Supreme'	IBlr
	- - white	ERea
	- 'Mount Stewart'	IBlr
	- 'Neptune' **new**	IBlr
§	- subsp. ***orientalis***	CSut EBee EHrv ERea GGar GSki IBlr NPal WPic XPep
	- - var. ***albiflorus***	CBro CPne CPou CSut GSki NArg
	- - 'Weaver'	CPne WHil
	- subsp. ***praecox***	IBlr IGor
	- - 'Silver Sceptre'	IBlr
	- - 'Variegatus' (v) ♀H1	CDes MBNS WSPU
	- 'Saturn' **new**	IBlr
	- Slieve Donard form	IBlr
	- 'Storms River'	XPep
	- 'Titan'	IBlr
	- 'Uranus' **new**	IBlr
	- 'Venus' **new**	IBlr
	- 'Vittatus' (v)	ERea WCot WFar
	'Proteus' **new**	EBee
	'Purple Cloud'	More than 30 suppliers
	'Queen Elizabeth The Queen Mother'	CPne
	'Rhône'	CPne IBlr
	rich blue	XDoo
	'Rosewarne'	CAbb CPne CPrp CTbh EBee IBlr NLar
	'Rotterdam'	CPne
	'Royal Blue'	CBro CWCL GBuc GMaP LPio MSte
	'Sandringham'	CDes CFil CPne IBlr WPGP XDoo
	'Sapphire'	IBlr
	'Sea Coral'	CBcs CDoC CFir CPne IBal LSRN
	'Sea Foam'	CBcs CPne IBal MBNS MSte NLar WCAu
	'Sea Mist'	CBcs CPne EBee EMil IBal
	'Sea Spray'	CBcs CKno CPne EBee EMil ENot GGar IBal XDoo
	'Septemberhemel'	XDoo
	'Silver Baby'	CAbb CPne EMil MSte
	'Silver Mist'	CPne IBlr
	Silver Moon = 'Notfred' (v)	ELan EMan ENot EPfP LBuc
	silver variegated (v)	SMrm
	'Sky' **new**	IBlr
	'Sky Rocket'	IBlr
	'Snow Pixie' **new**	SGSe
	'Snow Princess' **new**	IBal
	'Snowball'	CAby CBcs CDoC CFai COIW CPne CPrp EBee ERea GAbr IBal LSRN LSou MSte NBPC SGSe SVil WPop WWhi XDoo

Name	Suppliers
'Snowcloud'	CAbb CBro CPne CSBt EBee IBal NLar
I 'Snowdrops'	More than 30 suppliers
'Snowy Eyes'	EBee
'Snowy Owl'	EBee
'Starburst'	IBlr
'Stéphanie Charm'	XDoo
'Storm Cloud' (d)	CBro CFir
'Streamline'	More than 30 suppliers
'Summer Clouds'	EPfP IBal LRHS MBNS MWgw
'Summer Skies'	EPfP IBal LRHS
'Sunfield'	CPen CPne EBee GSki IBal LAma LRHS NPer WCAu WDav WGer WHil XDoo
'Super Star'	XDoo
'Sylvine'	XDoo
'Tall Boy'	IBlr
'Tarka' **new**	CPne
'Taw Valley' **new**	CPne
'Timaru'	More than 30 suppliers
'Tinkerbell' (v)	More than 30 suppliers
'Tiny Tim' **new**	SSpi
'Torbay'	CElw CPrp ECtt EWll IBlr XDoo
Tresco hybrid	CHEx
'Twilight'	IBlr
umbellatus L'Hérit.	see *A. africanus*
umbellatus Redouté	see *A. praecox* subsp. *orientalis*
'Underway'	CMon GCal IBlr
I 'Virgineus'	XDoo
'Wavy Navy' **new**	SGSe
white	CHEx CTbh GFlt GGar NCob
'White Christmas'	ERea
'White Dwarf'	see *A.* white dwarf hybrids
§ white dwarf hybrids	CBro CPen ECha EMan EPfP IBal LRHS MBri WFar WHil XDoo
'White Heaven'PBR **new**	CPne
'White Ice'	CBcs CPne EBee SApp XDoo
'White Starlet'	IBal XDoo
'White Superior'	CM&M CPne CSpe EBee EChP ERou GMaP LAst SHar SPet STes WCAu WMnd WTMC WWye
'White Swan' **new**	IBal
'White Umbrella'	WPrP
'Whitney'PBR	IBlr
'Windlebrooke'	EBee ECha XDoo
'Windsor Castle'	IBlr XDoo
'Windsor Grey'	CDes GFlt IBlr SSpi WPGP XDoo
'Winsome'	IBlr
'Wolga'	CPne
'Yolande' **new**	LAma
'Yves Klein'	IBlr
'Zachary' **new**	CPne
'Zella Thomas'	EBee LHyd XDoo

Agapetes (*Ericaceae*)

Name	Suppliers
'Ludgvan Cross' ♀H1-2	SBrw
serpens ♀H1	CHEx CKob CPLN CWib EShb SLon
- 'Nepal Cream'	SLon
- 'Scarlet Elf'	SBrw
smithiana var. ***major***	GGGa

Agarista (*Ericaceae*)

Name	Suppliers
§ ***populifolia***	WFar

Agastache (*Lamiaceae*)

Name	Suppliers
RCB/Arg X-1 **new**	WCot
anethiodora	see *A. foeniculum*
anisata	see *A. foeniculum*
'Apricot Sunrise'	EMan MSph SOkh
'Apricot Surprise'	WHer
aurantiaca	CSec
- 'Apricot Sprite'	CWCL EBee EWin EWll LDai MAnH MAvo MWrn SDnm SECG SPav SPoG SUsu WCHb WCot WFar WGwG WHil WPop WWeb WWpP
'Black Adder'	EBee
'Blue Fortune'	CBcs EBee ECha ECtt EMan EMil EMon ENot EPfP GBri IBal LBmB LPhx LRHS MLLN NCGa NDov SMer SMrm SOkh SPer WFar WPop WWeb
§ ***cana***	ECtt EMan EWTr LDai LPhx MAnH MLLN MSph MWrn WCHb WCot WFar
- 'Cinnabar Rose'	NBir WFar
- 'Purple Pygmy'	MSph
'Firebird'	More than 30 suppliers
foeniculum misapplied	see *A. rugosa*
§ ***foeniculum***	More than 30 suppliers
- 'Alabaster'	CBcs EBee EBrs EGoo ELau IHMH LPhx LRHS NDov SAga SBch WCHb WGHP
- 'Alba'	MLLN NGHP SHDw SPav WFar WHil
- 'Fragrant Delight'	SRms
'Globetrotter'	CSam EBee EMon LPhx NDov SUsu
'Glowing Embers'	ECtt ELan EMan ENot EPfP LRHS
'Hazy Days' **new**	LSou
'Heather Queen'	EOHP MAnH SRkn
§ ***mexicana***	EUnu LDai LSou MChe MSal SDnm SMHy SMrm SPav WGHP WGwG WJek WSan
- 'Carille Carmine'	EMan
- 'Champagne'	EMan WCHb
- 'Mauve Beauty'	LSou
- 'Red Fortune'PBR	EBee ENot EVFa MBri
- 'Rosea'	see *A. cana*
nepetoides	CArn CSec EMan EPPr LPhx MSal MWrn NLar NSti SDnm SPav SWal WCHb WWpP WWye
'New Blue'	EPfP
occidentalis	EMan LPhx
'Painted Lady'	CSpe EBee ECtt EMan EVFa EWin LPhx MNrw SMrm SUsu WCot WHil WWpP
pallidiflora var. ***pallidiflora***	EBee
- var. ***neomexicana*** 'Lavender Haze'	EMag
palmeri	EMan
'Pink Panther'	EBee ECtt EMan EShb LSRN WWpP
'Pink Pearl' **new**	WWeb
'Pink Pop' **new**	SPoG
pringlei	EBee EChP MWrn NLar SBri WCHb WMoo WWpP
'Purple Candle'	EBee EVFa EWes NCGa SPla
'Purple Haze'	EBee LPhx
rugosa	CAgr CArn CBod CBrm CFir CPne CSec EBee ELau EOHP EUnu GBar GPoy LPhx LRHS MAnH MLLN MSal SDnm SPav SSth SUsu SWal WGHP WJek WMoo WPer WSel WWye XPep
- B&SWJ 4187 from Korea **new**	WCru
- f. ***albiflora***	SDnm WCAu WGwG WLin
- - 'Honey Bee White'	EMag WWpP
- - 'Liquorice White'	EBee LRHS NBur NDov NLar SPav WGHP WWhi
- 'Golden Jubilee'	EGoo EMan LSou MAnH MCCP NLar SPoG WHil
- 'Honey Bee Blue'	EWll LRHS
- 'Liquorice Blue'	EChP ECrN EWTr LRHS MLan

	MWgw NBid NEgg NGdn NLar NLsd SAga SDnm SPav SPoG WFar WGHP WMoo WPer WWhi
- pink-flowered	CSam SUsu
rupestris	CSec CSpe EChP EMan EShb LPhx MWrn SPur WCot WKif
- 'Apache Sunset'	MAnH MWgw MWrn NTHB SDnm SGar SPav WPtf
scrophulariifolia	GIBF WCHb WWpP
'Serpentine'	EBee EMon LPhx
'Tangerine Dreams'	EBee ECtt EMan EWin LPhx SAga SBla WCot
'Tutti-frutti'	EBee ECtt EHrv EMan LDai LSRN SDnm SPav
urticifolia	CArn CSpe EBee LRHS MSal
- 'Alba'	CSec CSpe EBee WGHP WPer

Agathaea see *Felicia*

Agathis (*Araucariaceae*)

australis	CDoC LCon

Agathosma (*Rutaceae*)

ovata 'Igoda' **new**	EShb

Agave ✿ (*Agavaceae*)

americana ♀H1	More than 30 suppliers
- 'Marginata' (v) ♀H3-4	CBrP CHal CHll IBlr NPri SDnm WMul
- 'Mediopicta' misapplied	see *A. americana* 'Mediopicta Alba'
- 'Mediopicta' (v) ♀H1	CHEx SAPC SArc SBig WEas WMul
§ - 'Mediopicta Alba' (v) ♀H1	CBrP EAmu EOas SChr WMul
- 'Variegata' (v) ♀H1	More than 30 suppliers
attenuata	CAbb CBrP CHEx CTrC EAmu EOas EWll LRHS SAPC SArc WMul
bracteosa	EOas EPem SChr
§ ***celsii***	CBrP CHEx CTbh CTrC EOas SAPC SArc SChr
chrysantha	CTrC EOas SChr WLeb
deserti	CBrP
ferdinandi-regis	see *A. scabra* x *victoriae-reginae*
ferox	CBrP CTrC CWil EWll SBig WMul
filifera ♀H1	CBcs CHEx EOas EPem SChr WMul
geminiflora	WCot
ghiesbreghtii	CBrP
guiengiola	EOas
havardiana	CTrC
horrida	SChr
kerchovei	WCot
lechuguilla	EOas SChr
lophantha	WCot
- var. ***coerulescens***	EOas
§ - var. ***univittata***	EOas
mitis	see *A. celsii*
§ ***mitriformis***	WMul
neomexicana	CTrC SIgm
nizandensis	CHEx
palmeri	CTrC EPem IDee SChr
parryi	CDoC CTrC EOas EWll IDee LEdu SChr SIgm WCot WLeb WMul WPGP
- var. ***couesii***	see *A. parryi* var. *parryi*
- var. ***huachucensis***	EOas
§ - var. ***parryi***	CBrP CFir CFwr
parviflora ♀H1	CTrC EPyc SChr
aff. ***pelona***	EBee
potatorum ♀H1	SChr
salmiana	EAmu SBig WMul
- var. ***ferox***	EOas SAPC SArc SChr
scabra	EBee
scabra x ***victoriae-reginae***	SChr
schidigera	CBrP CFir EMan GCal
schottii	WCot
sisalana	WMul
striata	CTrC IDee XPep
stricta ♀H1	EOas WMul
I - 'Minor'	CBrP
toumeyana	SChr
univittata	see *A. lophantha* var. *univittata*
utahensis ♀H1	EOas SEND SIgm
- var. ***discreta***	SChr
- var. ***eborispina***	EOas
- var. ***nevadensis*** **new**	EOas
victoriae-reginae ♀H1	CBrP CTrC EWll SEND SWal WCot
xylonacantha	EOas SChr

Ageratina see *Eupatorium*

Ageratum (*Asteraceae*)

corymbosum	CHll CSpe

Aglaonema (*Araceae*)

§ ***crispum***	MBri
- 'Marie'	MBri
roebelinii	see *A. crispum*
'Silver Queen' ♀H1	MBri

Agonis (*Myrtaceae*)

flexuosa	CTrC
juniperina	LRav

Agrimonia (*Rosaceae*)

eupatoria	CArn COld CRWN EBee ELau EUnu GPoy MChe MHer NMir NPri SECG SIde WCHb WGHP WHer WWye
* - var. ***alba*** **new**	NBre
- 'Topas'	ELau
grandiflora	EBee
gryposepala	EBee
odorata misapplied	see *A. procera*
odorata (L.) Mill.	see *A. repens*
pilosa	CArn EBee ELau MSal
§ ***procera***	NEgg WBWf
§ ***repens***	CSec GBar MSal WCHb WMoo

Agropyron (*Poaceae*)

glaucum	see *Elymus hispidus*
magellanicum	see *Elymus magellanicus*
pubiflorum	see *Elymus magellanicus*
scabrum	see *Elymus scabrus*

Agrostemma (*Caryophyllaceae*)

coronaria	see *Lychnis coronaria*
githago	CHrt GWCH MBow NLsd WGwG WHer

Agrostis (*Poaceae*)

'Bamboo Green Giant' **new**	LIck
calamagrostis	see *Stipa calamagrostis*
§ ***canina*** 'Silver Needles' (v)	CBre EChP EGra EHoe EHul EMan EWes GCal GKir LRHS MMoz NBir WFar WRos
'Lago Lago'	EBee
nebulosa	EGoo EPza

Aichryson (*Crassulaceae*)

§ x ***domesticum***	CHal EBee EWin
- 'Variegatum' (v) ♀H1	CHal EBak EBee EWin WCot

Ailanthus (*Simaroubaceae*)

§ ***altissima***	CBcs CCVT CDul CHEx CLnd

	CPLG CTho EBee ECrN EMil ENot EPfP EWTr GKir MBlu NBlu NEgg SAPC SArc SBLw SDnm SPer SPlb SWvt WBVN WDin WNor
- var. ***tanakae*** B&SWJ 6777	WCru
glandulosa	see *A. altissima*

Ainsliaea (*Asteraceae*)

acerifolia B&SWJ 4795	WCru
fragrans	EBee
- var. ***integrifolia*** **new**	WPtf

Ajania (*Asteraceae*)

§ ***pacifica***	CHal EBee ECtt ELan EMFP EMan LDai LRHS MOak NBlu SMer SPoG WHer XPep
pallasiana	GIBF
tibetica JJH 9308103	NWCA

Ajuga (*Lamiaceae*)

ciliata var. ***villosior***	CFir GCal WOut
genevensis	EPPr EWTr LRHS WOut WWeb
- 'Tottenham'	WOut
incisa 'Bikun' (v) **new**	ENot SPoG
'Little Court Pink'	LRHS
metallica hort.	see *A. pyramidalis*
'Monmotaro San'	EMan
'Pink Spires'	NCot
§ ***pyramidalis***	CFee ECho WHer WMoo
- 'Metallica Crispa'	CRez EBee EMan EMar EPPr EWes GKir MBNS NLar NRya SBch SGSe SMer SPoG SWvt WFar WWeb WWpP
reptans	CAgr CNic CRWN ECtt ELau EMFW EWTr GPoy LGro LPBA MChe MHer MSal NMir SGar WFar WRHF WWpP
- f. ***albiflora*** 'Alba'	CArn CRow CWan ECtt EMan EPfP GCal GGar IHMH MNrw MRav NBro NSti SRms WCAu WCHb WFar WHil WMoo WWye
- - 'Silver Shadow'	GBBs WTin
- 'Arctic Fox' (v)	More than 30 suppliers
- 'Argentea'	see *A. reptans* 'Variegata'
§ - 'Atropurpurea'	CBcs COIW CRow CStu EBee ECha ELan ENot EPfP GGar GKir IHMH LGro LPBA LRHS MBow MWgw NArg NLon NVic SPer SPlb SRms SWvt WBrE WFar WMoo WWeb WWpP
- 'Braunherz'	More than 30 suppliers
- 'Brean Down'	CNat
- 'Burgundy Glow' (v)	More than 30 suppliers
§ - 'Catlin's Giant' ♀H4	More than 30 suppliers
- 'Chocolate Chip'	see *A. reptans* 'Valfredda'
- 'Delight' (v)	ECot SBod WEas
- 'Ebony'	EUJe LSRN SMac
- 'Ermine' (v)	EBee EChP EMan LAst MNrw NLar
- 'Evening Glow'	CFwr
- 'Flisteridge'	CNat
- 'Grey Lady'	EMan GBuc NLar SBch
- 'Harlequin' (v)	SWvt
- 'John Pierpoint'	SHar WCot
- 'Jumbo'	see *A. reptans* 'Jungle Beauty'
§ - 'Jungle Beauty'	CHid CSev EBee ECtt EMan EPfP IHMH MRav NCob SGSe
- 'Macrophylla'	see *A. reptans* 'Catlin's Giant'
§ - 'Multicolor' (v)	CArn CBcs CHEx COkL COIW EDAr ELan GGar IHMH LAst LGro LPBA MBar MRav NArg NBlu NFor SBod SPer SPlb SPoG SRms SWal SWvt WFar WMoo WTel
- 'Palisander'	EBee GSki LRHS MBNS NCob NLar NSti
I - 'Pat's Selection' (v)	CStr EMan
- 'Pink Elf'	CBre CChe CMHG CRow EMan MRav NBro SMac SUsu WFar WHoo WLin WWpP
- 'Pink Splendour'	CBre EBee NChi
- 'Pink Surprise'	CHid CNic CRow ECha ECtt EHoe EPfP GBar GBuc LAst LRHS MHer NCob NRya SSvw WEas WFar WMoo WTMC
- 'Purple Brocade'	CStr EHoe
- 'Purple Torch'	COIW EBee WEas WOut WTMC WWpP
- 'Purpurea'	see *A. reptans* 'Atropurpurea'
- 'Rainbow'	see *A. reptans* 'Multicolor'
- 'Rosea'	WHil WMoo
- 'Rowden Amethyst'	CRow
- 'Rowden Appleblossom'	CRow
- 'Rowden Blue Mist'	CRow
- 'Rowden Royal Purple'	CRow
- 'Silver Queen' **new**	SMac
- 'Tricolor'	see *A. reptans* 'Multicolor'
§ - 'Valfredda'	COkL CStu EBee EMan EMar ESis EWin EWll GBin LBBr LSou NCob NEgg NLar NPro SHar SPoG WCot WGwG WHrl WOut WWeb
- 'Vanilla Chip' (v)	EBee EMan
§ - 'Variegata' (v)	CBcs COkL ECtt EDAr EHoe EMFW LGro MHer NBid SBod SPer SPet SPoG SRms WCot WEas WFar WMoo WWpP

Akebia (*Lardizabalaceae*)

longeracemosa	CPLN NLar WCot
- B&SWJ 3606	WCru
x ***pentaphylla***	CPLN ELan EMil EPfP ERea GQui LRHS SBra WBcn WSHC
-B&SWJ 2829	WCru
quinata	More than 30 suppliers
- B&SWJ 4425	WCru
- 'Alba'	CBcs CSPN
- 'Amethyst Glow' **new**	SPoG
- cream-flowered	CPLN EPfP ERea LRHS SBra SPer SSta SWvt WCru
- variegated (v)	WCru WPat
- 'White Chocolate'	WCru
trifoliata	CBcs CHEx CPLN CRez EBee EPfP GKir LBuc LRHS MDun SLim WBcn
- B&SWJ 2829	WCru
- B&SWJ 5063	WCru

Alangium (*Alangiaceae*)

chinense	CBcs CFil EPla WBVN WBcn
platanifolium	CBot CFil CMCN CPLG IArd IDee MBlu NLar
- var. ***macrophyllum*** **new**	CBcs
- var. ***platanifolium***	NLar

Albizia (*Mimosaceae*)

chinensis **new**	CSec
distachya	see *Paraserianthes lophantha*
§ ***julibrissin***	CArn CSec CTrC EWin IDee LAst LRHS MGol SECG SHFr SPlb WDin WMul WPat
- f. ***rosea*** ♀H2-3	More than 30 suppliers
lophantha	see *Paraserianthes lophantha*

Albuca (*Hyacinthaceae*)

from Lesotho	GCal WAbe
altissima	CStu EBee WCot
batteniana	CFir

canadensis CStu
caudata CMon
clanwilliamigloria CDes WPrP
humilis CDes CMon CNic CStu EBee ECho ESis ETow NMen WAbe WPrP
juncifolia EMan
maxima WCot
nelsonii CFil CMon ERea LRHS WCot WHil
* ***pumila*** **new** NWCA WCot
setosa CMon
shawii CBro CDes CMon CPrp CStu EMan EMar ERos IFro NSla SAga SBla SOkd SPet SUsu WAbe WCot WPGP WPrP
spiralis CDes
trichophylla MDKP WCot
unifolia WCot
wakefieldii CMon

Alcea (*Malvaceae*)

'Antwerp' **new** SWal
'Arabian Nights' SPav
'Blackcurrant Whirl' NLsd SPav
ficifolia EChP EWTr GMac LSou MAnH MCCP MTis NLsd NPri SDnm SPav WHil WMoo
'Happy Lights' **new** SECG
pallida EMan SMar
'Park Rondel' EMon
'Peaches and Cream' NRnb
'Peaches 'n' Dreams' CWib MBri NRnb WHil
§ ***rosea*** CHrt CSim EUnu GWCH LAst MBow SECG WFar XPep
- 'Black Beauty' NBur
- Chater's Double Group pink (d) ECtt ENot EPfP GKir MBri MLan MWat NBlu NFor SRms SRob WRHF
- - (d) ECtt NPri SPer
- - red (d) ECtt NPri
- - salmon pink (d) EPfP NLsd
- - violet (d) SMar SPer
- - white (d) EPfP NPri SMar SPer
- - yellow (d) ECtt EPfP LAst NPri SPer
- 'Crème de Cassis' MAnH MSph NRnb SPav WRHF
- double apricot (d) NBur
- double pink (d) MHer
- double red (d) MHer
- double rose (d) EBee SPer
- double scarlet (d) SMar SPer
- double white (d) MHer
- double yellow (d) EBee MHer
- 'Lemon Light' NBur
- 'Nigra' More than 30 suppliers
- single COIW MWat MWgw WHil
- single pink LRHS NLsd
- single white WCAu
- Summer Carnival Group CWib SRms WGor
- 'Victoria Ann' (v) LSou
- yellow IHMH MMHG
§ ***rugosa*** CHad CSam CSim EMan EMar LRHS MSte MWat MWgw SDix SPav WHil WPGP
'The Watchman' **new** SECG

Alcea x *Althaea* (*Malvaceae*)

'Parkallee' EMan EMon GBri LPhx WCot
'Parkfrieden' EMan LPhx
'Parkrondell' EMan

Alchemilla ✿ (*Rosaceae*)

§ ***abyssinica*** CHid CNic WHrl
alpina misapplied see *A. conjuncta*, *A. plicatula*
alpina L. CFee CLyd CMea EBla EPfP GKir GTou LRHS MRav NChi NFor NGHP NLon NMir SBch SHel SIng SPet SRms WFar WKif WMoo WPer WWhi
aroanica EBee EBla
arvensis see *Aphanes arvensis*
* ***congesta*** **new** MBri
§ ***conjuncta*** More than 30 suppliers
elisabethae EBla ECGP EMon WCHb
ellenbeckii CFee CMCo EBee EBla EDAr EWsh GAbr GBar GGar GKir MBar MHer MTho NChi WCHb WFar WPGP WPer
epipsila CFwr EBee LPhx MSte NLar WPer
erythropoda ♀H4 More than 30 suppliers
faeroensis CMCo EBee NLon WPer
- var. ***pumila*** CLyd EBla EHyt NMen
filicaulis 'Minima' CNat
§ ***fulgens*** EWTr LEdu
glaucescens CNat EBla EMon GFlt
hoppeana misapplied see *A. plicatula*
hoppeana (Reichenb.) Dalla Torre GCal
iniquiformis EBee WPGP
lapeyrousei EBla EMon EPPr SIng
mollis ♀H4 More than 30 suppliers
I - 'Auslese' EPza LRHS WPop WWpP
* - 'Robusta' ECha EPla LRHS MTho NBur SEND SPlb WFar WMnd WMoo WPnP WWpP
* - 'Senior' EMil IHMH WMnd
- 'Thriller' EWin IBal NArg NBur WWeb
monticola WPer
pentaphylla EBla
§ ***plicatula*** WPer
psilomischa EBee EMon LRHS
robusta SWvt
saxatilis WPer
speciosa EBee
splendens misapplied see *A. fulgens*
straminea EMFP MRav
aff. ***venosa*** EPla
vetteri EBee EBla WHrl
vulgaris misapplied see *A. xanthochlora*
§ ***xanthochlora*** CArn EBee GBar GPoy MSal NLar SRms WFar WHer WPer

Aldrovanda (*Droseraceae*)

vesiculosa EFEx

alecost see *Tanacetum balsamita*

Alisma (*Alismataceae*)

plantago-aquatica CRow EHon EMFW LNCo LPBA NArg NPer WFar WPnP WPop WWpP
- var. ***parviflorum*** EMFW LPBA NArg SPlb WPop WWpP

Alkanna (*Boraginaceae*)

orientalis WCot
tinctoria MSal SAga
- HH&K 345 CMdw

Allamanda (*Apocynaceae*)

cathartica ERea LRHS MBri MJnS
- 'Birthe' MBri
- 'Cherry Red' **new** MJnS
- 'Grandiflora' CPLN
- 'Hendersonii' ♀H1 LRHS
'Jamaican Sunset' MJnS
neriifolia see *A. schottii*
§ ***schottii*** ♀H1 LRHS

Alliaria (*Brassicaceae*)

	petiolata	CAgr CArn GPoy NLan WHer

Allium ✿ (*Alliaceae*)

	aciphyllum	LAma WCot
§	***acuminatum***	CPom EBee EHyt GIBF GKir GSki NBir NMen
I	- 'Album'	ECho
	acutiflorum	CPom
	aflatunense misapplied	see *A. hollandicum*
	aflatunense B. Fedtsch.	EBee EMon EWTr GBBs MAnH SApp WBrE
	akaka	GCrs
	albidum	see *A. denudatum*
	albopilosum	see *A. cristophii*
	altaicum	GIBF
	altissimum 'Goliath'	EBee EMan WCot
	amabile	see *A. mairei* var. *amabile*
	ampeloprasum	CAgr CFil ECha GIBF LAma WHer WShi
	- var. ***babingtonii***	CAgr CArn CNat GPoy ILis LEdu MLLN WBWf WHer WShi
	amphibolum	EBee EHrv
	amplectens	EBee EHyt
§	***angulosum***	CAgr CAvo CMea EBee GIBF LAma MAnH MMil MSph SDix SMrm WCot WGHP
	angustitepalum	see *A. jesdianum* subsp. *angustitepalum*
	atropurpureum	CAby EBee EBrs EChP ECha EHrv ELan EMan EMon LAma LEdu LPhx LRHS MAnH MLLN MMHG SGar SPur
	atroviolaceum	GIBF
	azureum	see *A. caeruleum*
	balansae	SOkd
	'Beau Regard' 🏆^{H4}	LAma NDvn
	beesianum hort.	see *A. cyaneum*
	beesianum W.W. Smith	CLyd CPom GIBF GKir NBir NRya
	blandum	see *A. carolinianum*
	brevicaule	LRHS
	bucharicum	ERos
	bulgaricum	see *Nectaroscordum siculum* subsp. *bulgaricum*
§	***caeruleum*** 🏆^{H4}	More than 30 suppliers
	- ***azureum***	see *A. caeruleum*
	callimischon	CBro
	- subsp. ***haemostictum***	NMen SBla
	canadense	CArn EBee SHar
§	***carinatum***	WSan
§	- subsp. ***pulchellum*** 🏆^{H4}	More than 30 suppliers
	- - f. ***album*** 🏆^{H4}	CAvo CBro CHar CPom CSWP EBee EBrs EChP ECha EMon EPot ERos ERou LLWP LPhx LRHS MBow MNrw NChi NDov NMen NSti SSpi WBor WCot
	- - 'Tubergen' **new**	EBee EBrs
§	***carolinianum***	EBee GCrs GIBF MGol WCot
	cepa Aggregatum Group	ELau ILis
	- 'Kew White'	WCot
	- 'Perutile'	CArn GBar GPoy ILis LEdu MHer
	- Proliferum Group	CArn CBod CHby CPrp CSev CWan ELau GBar GPoy ILis LEdu MChe MHer NGHP SIde WCHb WGwG WHer WJek WLHH WSel
	- var. ***viviparum*** **new**	LAma
	cernuum	More than 30 suppliers
§	- 'Hidcote' 🏆^{H4}	CLAP EMon MBct MSte WBVN WGHP WKif
	- 'Major'	see *A. cernuum* 'Hidcote'
	- var. ***obtusum***	WCot
	- pink-flowered	CLyd CPLG EBrs GBBs GSki SIng
	cirrhosum	see *A. carinatum* subsp. *pulchellum*
	cowanii	see *A. neapolitanum* Cowanii Group
	crenulatum	EHyt
§	***cristophii*** 🏆^{H4}	More than 30 suppliers
§	***cyaneum*** 🏆^{H4}	CGra CLyd CPBP CPom CSec EBrs ERos GBBs GCrs GKir LBee LRHS NChi NJOw NMen NRya SBla SRot SUsu WCot
	cyathophorum	GBBs GCrs WBVN
§	- var. ***farreri***	CArn CBre CBro CLyd CNic CSec EBee EPot ERos GCrs GEdr GIBF GKir GSki LLWP MRav MSte NChi NLon NMen NRya WBVN WCot WPrP
	delicatulum	EBee
§	***denudatum***	EBee
	dichlamydeum	ERos
§	***drummondii***	ERos
	elatum	see *A. macleanii*
	ericetorum	ERos WCot
	eusperma	LAma WCot
	falcifolium	EBee EChP EPot GCrs LAma
	farreri	see *A. cyathophorum* var. *farreri*
	fasciculatum	LAma
	'Firmament'	CAvo CBro CMea EBee EChP EMan EMon LAma LBBr LRHS MAnH MSte WWhi
	fistulosum	CArn CBod CHby CWan EBee ELau EUnu GBar GPoy GSki ILis LAma LEdu MChe MHer NFor NGHP NPri SIde SWal WCHb WGwG WPer WWye
	- red	CBod CPrp NGHP
	- 'Red Welsh'	CAgr ILis SWal WJek WLHH
	flavum 🏆^{H4}	CArn CAvo CBro CPom EBrs ECha GIBF GKir GSki LAma MRav NSti SBch SHBN WBVN WGor WGwG
§	- 'Blue Leaf'	EBee EPot ERos MLLN NBir
	- subsp. ***flavum***	EBee ERou LEdu MBow MMHG MNrw
	- - var. ***minus***	EBee EHyt MTho NWCA
	- 'Glaucum'	see *A. flavum* 'Blue Leaf'
	- var. ***nanum***	CNic GEdr GKir NJOw
	- subsp. ***tauricum***	EBee ECho LPhx
	forrestii	CLyd CSec EBee GBin GCrs MDKP
	geyeri	EBee EHyt WCot
	giganteum 🏆^{H4}	More than 30 suppliers
	'Gladiator' 🏆^{H4}	CBro CFir CHar CPen EBee EChP ECtt EMan EMon ERou LAma LBBr LRHS MLLN MRav MSte NOrc SPer SPet WDav
	glaucum	see *A. senescens* subsp. *montanum* var. *glaucum*
	'Globemaster' 🏆^{H4}	CAvo CBro CFir CMea EBee EBrs ECtt EHrv ELan EMan ERou LAma LRHS MBri MMHG MSte NFor SPer WCot WCra WFar WHal
	'Globus'	EBee EMan ERou LAma LRHS MAnH
	goodingii	CNic CPom EHyt GCrs SSpi
	grisellum	EBee
	gultschense	GIBF
	guttatum subsp. ***dalmaticum***	EBee
	- subsp. ***sardoum***	ECho
	haematochiton	WCot
	'Hair'	see *A. vineale* 'Hair'
*	***hirtifolium*** var. ***album***	EBee LAma
	'His Excellency'	CFir EBee EBrs ECho EMan ERou LAma LRHS MAnH MSte
§	***hollandicum*** 🏆^{H4}	More than 30 suppliers

	Name	Suppliers
	- 'Purple Sensation' 🏆H4	More than 30 suppliers
	hookeri ACE 2430	WCot
	- var. ***muliense***	GEdr
	humile	CLyd WCot
	hyalinum pink	EBee EMan WCot
§	***insubricum*** 🏆H4	ECho ERos GCrs GEdr NBir NMen NSti SIng WAbe WDav
	jajlae	see *A. rotundum* subsp. *jajlae*
	jesdianum	CBro EMon
	- 'Akbulak'	LAma LRHS MSte WCot
	- subsp. ***angustitepalum***	EBee
	- 'Michael Hoog'	EBee ERou LAma LRHS WCot
	- 'Purple King'	EBee EMan ERou LAma LRHS MAnH MSte SPur WGHP
	- 'Shing'	EBee LAma LRHS
	- white-flowered	EBee ERou
	kansuense	see *A. sikkimense*
	karataviense 🏆H3	More than 30 suppliers
	- 'Ivory Queen'	CBro CElw CMea CStu EBee EBrs EChP ECtt EMar EMon EPfP GFlt GKev LAma LRHS MAnH MBow MCCP MDKP MNFA MSph MSte NJOw SPer SPlb WAul WDav WFar WWhi
	- 'Kara Tau'	LRHS
	karelinii **new**	EHyt
	komarovianum	see *A. thunbergii*
	ledebourianum	ECho
	lenkoranicum	EBee
	libani	WPer
	lineare	CPom IHMH
	'Lucy Ball'	EBrs ECtt EMan EMon EPot ERou LAma LRHS MAnH MLLN MSte NBir NLar SPet
§	***macleanii***	CArn EBee ELau EMan EMon LAma LRHS WDav
	macranthum	CLyd GBBs GEdr GFlt MSte
	macrochaetum	LAma
	mairei	CLyd EBee ERos GBBs LLWP LRHS MBar NMen NRya WGwG WTin
§	- var. ***amabile***	CLyd EBee ERos GCrs GEdr GIBF LTwo NChi NJOw NRya NSla WCot
	'Mars'	CFir ERou LRHS MAnH MLLN
	maximowiczii	ECho
	meteoricum	LRHS
	moly	CArn CBro EBee EBrs EPfP EUJe GBBs GFlt GSki LAma MBow MBri MRav NGHP NJOw NRya NSti SGar SRms WBor WCHb WCot WTin
	- 'Jeannine' 🏆H4	CBro CMea EBee ECho EPot GAbr LsAma LPhx MLLN
	'Mont Blanc'	CMea EBee ELan ERou LAma
	'Mount Everest'	CArn CAvo CBro CFir CHar EBee EBrs EChP EMan EMon EPot ERou LAma LBBr LRHS MLLN MSte NCGa SOkh SPer WCra WDav WShi
	multibulbosum	see *A. nigrum*
	murrayanum misapplied	see *A. unifolium*
	murrayanum Reg.	see *A. acuminatum*
	narcissiflorum misapplied	see *A. insubricum*
§	***narcissiflorum*** Villars	CLyd CPom GCrs GEdr GIBF WCot WDav
	neapolitanum	CAgr CArn EBee EPot EUnu LAma LRHS MBri NWCA SPer SRms WGwG
§	- Cowanii Group	CBro EBee EHrv ERos GIBF LRHS WCot WCra WLin
	- 'Grandiflorum'	CSam EBee LPhx LRHS MLLN WBrE
	nevskianum	EBee LAma MAnH
§	***nigrum***	CArn CAvo CBro CHar CSec EBee EBrs EHrv EMan EMon EPot GIBF LAma LPhx LRHS MLLN MRav NBir NJOw WCot
	noeanum **new**	CSec
	nutans	CBod EBee EHol EMar EUnu EWin IHMH LAma LEdu NGHP SHDw WHal WJek
	nuttallii	see *A. drummondii*
§	***obliquum***	CMil CSec EBee ECha ECho GSki LRHS MSte SUsu WCot WTin
	odorum L.	see *A. ramosum* L.
	oleraceum	WHer
§	***oreophilum***	CArn CAvo CBro CSam EBrs ECha ECtt EHrv EHyt EPfP GBBs GFlt GSki LAma LRHS MBow MLLN NJOw NRya SPer SRms WBor WCot WHoo WTin
	- 'Zwanenburg' 🏆H4	CBro EBee ECho EPot NMen WCot
	oreoprasum	LAma
	orientale	GIBF
	ostrowskianum	see *A. oreophilum*
	pallasii	EBee LAma
	pallens	CBre CHea MTho NBir
§	***paniculatum***	CAvo CNic CSec EChP EHyt MMil
	paradoxum	EBee LRHS NBir
	- var. ***normale***	CBgR CBro CMea EBee EHyt EMan EMon NJOw NMen WCot WDav
	pedemontanum	see *A. narcissiflorum* Villars
	peninsulare	EHyt
	platycaule	WCot
	platyspathum	EBee
	plurifoliatum	EBee LAma
	polyphyllum	see *A. carolinianum*
	polyrrhizum	EBee
	przewalskianum	EBee
	pulchellum	see *A. carinatum* subsp. *pulchellum*
	'Purple Giant' **new**	NDvn
	pyrenaicum misapplied	see *A. angulosum*
	pyrenaicum Costa & Vayreda	ELan EMan
	ramosum Jacquin	see *A. obliquum*
§	***ramosum*** L.	EBee LAma NBre NGHP WJek WPer
	'Rien Poortvliet'	CArn EBee EMan LAma LRHS
	rosenbachianum misapplied	see *A. hollandicum*
§	***rosenbachianum*** Regel	CArn CBro CHar CSec EBee EMan EMon EPot GIBF LAma MLLN WDav
	- 'Album'	EBee ECha ECho EPot LAma MLLN WCot WDav
	roseum	CAgr CArn CMea CPBP EBee ECtt ERos GFlt LAma LRav MAnH MDKP NCGa
§	- var. ***bulbiferum***	WCot
	- 'Grandiflorum'	see *A. roseum* var. *bulbiferum*
§	***rotundum*** subsp. ***jajlae***	EBee LLWP
§	***rubellum*** **new**	ERos
	rubens	CPom
	sarawschanicum	EBee
	- 'Chinoro'	IPot LRHS
	sativum	CArn EOHP MHer SIde WJek WSel WWye
	- 'Arno'	CPrp
	- 'Corail'	CPrp
	- 'Germinadour'	CPrp
	- golden	GPoy
	- var. ***ophioscorodon***	EBee GFlt GPoy ILis LAma MWgw
	- 'Printanor'	CBod
	- 'Solent White' **new**	NGHP SECG

	- 'Thermidrôme'	CBod
	saxatile	EBee ERos
	schmitzii	EMon
	schoenoprasum	More than 30 suppliers
	- 'Black Isle Blush'	GPoy MHer SMHy
	- 'Corsican White'	EMon
	- fine-leaved	ELau IHMH WGwG
	- 'Forescate'	CBod CM&M CPrp EBee ECha ELau EWes GBar GCal GSki LAma LRHS MLLN MRav SIde SPet SSpe SSvw WCHb
	- 'Forncett Forescate'	CBgR
	- 'Grolau'	EUnu
	- medium-leaved	ELau
	- 'Pink Perfection'	GPoy MHer SMHy
	- 'Polyphant'	CBre WCHb WRha WWpP
	- 'Shepherds' Crooks'	WThu
	- var. ***sibiricum***	CAgr GBar MBri SDix WSel WShi
	- 'Silver Chimes'	CMil CWan EBee MBri MRav SHDw WGHP WWpP
	- thick-leaved **new**	NPri
	- 'Wallington White'	GBar
	- white-flowered	CArn CPrp CSWP ECha ELau GMaP IHMH LEdu LPhx MChe MHer MSte NBir NCGa SIde SSvw WCHb WCot WEas WGHP WHer WWpP WWye
	schubertii	More than 30 suppliers
	scorodoprasum	CAgr GIBF SIde WCHb WJek
	- subsp. ***jajlae***	see *A. rotundum* subsp. *jajlae*
	- subsp. ***scorodoprasum*** **new**	LAma
	senescens	CAgr CArn CBro CTri EBee ECGP ERos EWsh GIBF IHMH LAma MHer MRav NChi NJOw SApp SBch SIng SRms SSpe SSvw WTin
	- var. ***calcareum***	IHMH
§	- subsp. ***montanum***	CBro CSpe ECha ECho EGoo EHol EMFP EPot LAma LEdu MAnH NBre NMen SDix SIng WAbe WCot WGHP WMoo
§	- - var. ***glaucum***	CArn CLyd CMea CPBP CPrp EBrs ECha EMan EMar EPla GEdr LEdu MNFA SAga SIng WCot WHer WPer WRos WTin WWye
	- subsp. ***senescens***	EBee EMon MLLN SUsu WPrP
	sibthorpianum	see *A. paniculatum*
	siculum	see *Nectaroscordum siculum*
	sieheanum	EBee
§	***sikkimense***	CPom EBee EBrs EMan ERos GIBF GKir LRHS MDKP NMen NSla NWCA SBla SSvw WCot WPer
	songpanicum	LAma WCot
	sphaerocephalon	More than 30 suppliers
	splendens	EBee ERos
	stellatum	CAgr EBee EBrs LRHS WGwG
	stellerianum	WPer
	- var. ***kurilense***	CLyd CNic
§	***stipitatum***	EChP EMon LAma LRHS MAnH MLLN WCot
	- 'Album'	CArn CBro EBee EMon EPot LAma LRHS
	- 'Glory of Pamir'	EMan LRHS
	- 'Violet Beauty'	EBee LAma SMeo WCot
	stracheyi	WCot
	strictum Ledeb.	see *A. szovitsii*
	strictum Schrad.	see *A. lineare*
	suaveolens	GIBF
	subhirsutum	CLyd EBee
	subvillosum	EBee ERos WCot
	'Summer Beauty'	see *A. senescens* subsp. *montanum*
	'Sweet Discovery' **new**	LAma
§	***szovitsii***	EBee
	tanguticum	EBrs LRHS
	textile	ERos
§	***thunbergii*** 🏆H4	EBee ECho GCrs GIBF NBir NDlv
	- 'Nanum'	EPot
	- 'Ozawa'	EBee NMen SBla SIng WCot
	tibeticum	see *A. sikkimense*
*	***tournefortii***	EBee ECho
	tricoccum	GIBF
	triquetrum	CAgr CAvo CStu EBee ELan EPfP EPot GGar IBlr ILis LAma LPhx MBow NBir NSti SYvo WCot WCru WGHP WHer WMoo WShi
	tuberosum	More than 30 suppliers
	- B&SWJ 8881	WCru
	- purple/mauve	CHby ELau GWCH WMoo
	turkestanicum	GIBF
§	***unifolium*** 🏆H4	CArn CAvo CBro CPom CSam EBee EHyt EPot GBBs LAma LLWP LPhx LRHS MAnH MBow MBri MLLN MNFA MNrw MRav NBir NSti SGar STes WAbe WBrE WCot WFar WPer
	ursinum	CArn CAvo CHby CWan GKir GPoy LAma MBow NArg NGHP NMir NTHB WAul WCHb WFar WJek WShi WWye
	'Valerie Finnis'	EBee SBla
	victorialis	GCal GIBF
	vineale	CArn EBee ECtt NMir WHer
	- 'Hair'	CFwr CRez EBrs EChP EMan EMar EPfP EUJe ITer LAma MWgw NJOw SOkh WHil WTMC
	violaceum	see *A. carinatum*
	'Violet Beauty'	see *A. stipitatum* 'Violet Beauty'
	virgunculae	EBee EHyt SBla SCnR SRot
	wallichii	CLyd CPou EMon GBuc GIBF LAma MBNS MGol NBir WCot WLin WTin
	- ACE 2458	WCot
	- CC&McK 1025	WCot
	- plum	GEdr
	'White Giant'	LPhx MSte
	'World Cup'	LRHS
	zaprjagajevii	LEdu
	zebdanense	EBee ERos LAma LRHS NJOw

Allocasuarina (*Casuarinaceae*)

monilifera	ECou GGar
nana	CTrC EShb IDee
zephyrea	CTrC

almond see *Prunus dulcis*

Alnus ✿ (*Betulaceae*)

cordata 🏆H4	More than 30 suppliers
cremastogyne	NLar
crispa	see *A. viridis* subsp. *crispa*
firma	CDul CMCN IArd IDee
formosana	GIBF
fruticosa	see *A. viridis* subsp. *fruticosa*
glutinosa	CBcs CCVT CDoC CDul CLnd CRWN CSBt CTri ECrN ENot EPfP GKir LBuc MGos NBee NBlu NWea SBLw SHBN SHFr WDin WMou WOrn
- 'Aurea'	CDul CEnd CLnd CTho ECrN LRHS MBlu MDun SBLw SPer
- var. ***barbata***	GIBF
- 'Imperialis' 🏆H4	CDoC CDul CEnd CLnd CPMA CTho EBee ELan ENot EPfP EWTr GKir LRHS MAsh MBri MDun

	NBee SBLw SPer SSpi WDin WMoo WOrn
- 'Laciniata'	CDoC CDul CTho ECrN MBlu MDun NBlu SBLw WFar WMoo
hirsuta	CMCN
- var. ***sibirica***	GIBF
x ***hybrida***	GIBF
incana	CDoC CDul CLnd CMCN CWib ECrN ENot GKir LBuc MBar MGos NWea SBLw SHBN SPer WDin WMou
- 'Aurea'	CBcs CDul CEnd CLnd CTho EBee ECrN ELan ENot EPfP EPla GKir IArd LRHS MBar MBlu MBri MGos SBLw SHBN SPer SPoG SSpi WDin WOrn
- 'Laciniata'	CDul CLnd CTho SBLw WBcn WDin WFar
- 'Pendula'	CLnd CTho SBLw
japonica	CLnd NLar
- var. ***arguta***	GIBF
lanata	CMCN WHCr
maximowiczii	NLar
nepalensis	WCwm
nitida	CMCN IArd IDee NLar
oregana	see *A. rubra*
orientalis	GIBF
rhombifolia	CMCN
§ ***rubra***	CAgr CCVT CDoC CDul CLnd CMCN CTho ECrN ELan ENot GKir NLar NWea SBLw WDin WMou
- 'Pinnatifida'	see *A. rubra* f. *pinnatisecta*
§ - f. ***pinnatisecta***	CLnd CMCN CTho
§ ***rugosa***	CMCN
serrulata	see *A. rugosa*
sinuata	see *A. viridis* subsp. *sinuata*
x ***spaethii***	CDoC CTho GKir LRHS SBLw SEND
subcordata	CLnd
viridis	CAgr CMCN ECrN NWea SBLw
- subsp. ***crispa***	GIBF
- - var. ***mollis***	CMCN
- subsp. ***fruticosa***	GIBF
§ - subsp. ***sinuata***	CAgr CMCN NWea

Alocasia ✿ (*Araceae*)

x ***amazonica*** ♀H1	ERea LRHS MBri XBlo
'Black Stem' **new**	MJnS
'Calidora'	MJnS
cucullata	CFir WMul
gageana	WMul
macrorrhiza	EAmu EUJe MJnS MOak SBig WMul
- 'Lutea'	MJnS SBig WMul
- 'Variegata' (v) ♀H1	EUJe MJnS SBig WMul
odora	CKob EAmu EUJe MJnS MOak WMul
'Portodora'	EAmu MJnS WMul
wentii	EAmu

Aloe (*Aloaceae*)

aculeata	WCot
arborescens	CAbb CHEx CTrC EShb EWll SChr WMul
- yellow-flowered	CTrC EOas
aristata ♀H1	CAbb CHEx CHal EOas EPem MBri SAPC SArc SChr SEND SPet SWvt WGwG WHer
barbadensis	see *A. vera*
barberae	WMul
bellatula **new**	LToo
branddraaiensis	WCot
brevifolia ♀H1	CRoM CTbh EOas SArc
broomii	EOas EPem EPfP SChr
camperi 'Maculata'	CTrC MBri SChr
ciliaris	EMan EOas ERea EShb SChr WCot
cooperi	CAbb
dawei	EPem
dichotoma	CAbb EShb
distans	SEND
dumetorum	EPem
ecklonis	CTrC EOas SChr SPlb
excelsa	SChr
ferox	CAbb CBrP CTrC EUnu MSal SBig SChr SEND SWal WMul
fosteri	EOas
globuligemma	WCot
greatheadii	CTrC SChr
- var. ***davyana***	CCtw EOas
humilis	CTrC EPem
imalotensis **new**	LToo
immaculata **new**	WCot
juvenna	EPem
littoralis	EPem
maculata	CHEx CRoM CTrC EOas
marlothii	CAbb EOas EPem EShb WCot WMul
mitriformis	NPri SChr SEND
mutabilis	CHEx CTrC SChr
parallelifolia **new**	LToo
plicatilis	CAbb CTrC EShb
polyphylla	EOas
pratensis	CFir CPLG CTrC SChr SPlb
- glaucous-leaved	EOas
prinslooi	EPem
ramosissima **new**	EShb
reitzii	CPLG CTrC EOas IDee
spectabilis	EOas
x ***spinosissima***	SChr
striata	EPem EShb XPep
striatula	CAbb CBrP CFil CHEx CTbh CTrC EAmu EBee EOas EPla EShb IBlr LPJP SAPC SArc SBig SChr WGer WMul WPGP XPep
- var. ***caesia***	IBlr
tenuior	EOas
thraskii	CAbb WMul
variegata (v) ♀H1	EShb SWal SWvt WEas
§ ***vera*** ♀H1	CArn CDoC CHby COld CSpe CTbh ELau EOHP EPem ERea EShb ESlt GPoy IFro ILis MSal NPer NPri NScw SBch SIde SWal WCot WGHP WGwG WHer
'Walmsley's Blue'	MBri

Alonsoa (*Scrophulariaceae*)

'Bright Spark'	CSpe EMan
meridionalis	LRav NJOw WWeb
- 'Shell Pink'	WWeb
'Pink Beauty'	CSpe NBur
'Snowflake'	LRav
unilabiata	CSpe
warscewiczii	CHll ELan SHFr WGwG
- pale-flowered	see *A. warscewiczii* 'Peachy-keen'
§ - 'Peachy-keen'	CSpe EMan SPet

Alopecurus (*Poaceae*)

alpinus	EBrs EHoe EMan EPPr LRHS NBur
- subsp. ***glaucus***	CBrm CPen CSLe EBee EHoe EPPr GBin MBri NSti SGSe SPer SPoG
borealis subsp. ***glaucus***	GCal
geniculatus	CRWN
lanatus	NBea
pratensis	EUJe NOrc
- 'Aureovariegatus' (v)	CWan EBee EHoe ENot EPPr EPla EPza EUJe GCal GKir GMaP GSki

	IHMH MBar MBnl MBri MMoz MSte MWgw NBid NFor NLon SApp SGSe SLim SPer WFar WMoo
- 'Aureus'	EChP ECha EGra GBin LRHS MRav MWhi NBro NGdn SPlb WFar WPer WRHF
- 'No Overtaking' (v)	EMan EMon EPPr WWpP

Alophia (*Iridaceae*)

drummondii	ERos
lahue	see *Herbertia lahue*

Aloysia (*Verbenaceae*)

chamaedrifolia	CPle XPep
citriodora	see *A. triphylla*
***polystachya* new**	GPoy
§ ***triphylla*** ♀H2	More than 30 suppliers

Alpinia (*Zingiberaceae*)

formosana	MOak
galanga	MGol WMul
japonica	LEdu MSal
- B&SWJ 8889	WCru
malaccensis B&SWJ 7196	WCru
nutans misapplied	see *A. zerumbet*
officinarum	CArn
purpurata	MJnS
- pink	MJnS
speciosa	see *A. zerumbet*
§ ***vittata*** (v)	MOak
§ ***zerumbet***	CKob MJnS MOak WMul
- 'Variegata' (v)	EAmu EUJe MJnS MOak WMul XBlo

Alsobia see *Episcia*

Alstroemeria ✿ (*Alstroemeriaceae*)

'Aimi'	CDoC COtt LRHS MBri SBai SWvt WFar
'Angelina'	LRHS SBai SVil SWvt
'Apollo' ♀H4	COtt GKir LRHS MBNS MBri SBai SPer SWvt
aurantiaca	see *A. aurea*
§ ***aurea***	CTri CWan EPfP EWin GGar ITer MDun MRav MWrn NLar SRms SSpi WCot WSHC
- 'Apricot'	GCal
- 'Cally Fire'	GCal
- 'Dover Orange'	CBod EChP EMan EPfP IGor LRHS MWgw NEgg SCoo SPoG
- 'Lutea'	CDoC EChP EWTr EWll LRHS MWrn SPlb
- 'Orange King'	CBod CDoC EBee ELan EPfP EWTr EWll LRHS NLar WBor WCot WTin
'Blushing Bride'	CBcs CDoC EMar MBNS MBri SBai SPer SVil SWvt
brasiliensis	EBee MDKP SSpi WCot WSHC
'Charm'	LRHS WFar
'Coronet' ♀H4	COtt LRHS MBNS
'Dandy Candy' **new**	CBrm NLar
'Desire' **new**	EBee
diluta subsp. ***chrysantha*** F&W 8700	WCot
Doctor Salter's hybrids	ECGP LTwo SRms SWal
'Eternal Love'	COtt
'Evening Song'	CDoC EMar LBuc LRHS MBNS MBri SBai SVil SWal SWvt
'Firefly'	LRHS
'Flaming Star'	CDoC EBee EMar LIck LRHS SBai SVil WCot
'Fortune'	LRHS
'Friendship' ♀H4	CBcs CDoC EBee EMar LBuc SBai SWal SWvt
garaventae	MDKP WCot
gayana	MDKP WCot
'Glory of the Andes' (v) **new**	EMan EMar LBuc
'Golden Delight'	COtt LIck LRHS MBri SBai SPla SVil
'Golden Queen' **new**	WFar
H.R.H. Princess Alice = 'Staverpi'PBR ♀H2	WFar
haemantha	MDKP
Hawera Seedlings	CDes EBee SMrm WCot
hookeri	ECho GCal MTho SCnR SIgm
- subsp. ***cummingiana***	LTwo WCot
- subsp. ***hookeri***	CFil
huemulina	MDKP
kingii	see *A. versicolor*
ligtu hybrids	CAvo CBcs CBrm CSBt EBee EChP ECha ELan EPfP GKir LAst LRHS MDun MNrw MWgw NBid NPer NVic SBla SPer SPoG SRms SWal SWvt WBVN WCAu WFar WHoo WTin WWol
- var. ***ligtu***	LPhx
'Lilac Wonder'	EBee
'Little Eleanor'	COtt EBee GKir LRHS NBlu WCot WFar
'Little Miss Charlotte'	COtt LRHS WFar
'Little Miss Christina'	MBNS SBai SVil SWvt
'Little Miss Gloria'	MBNS SVil SWvt
'Little Miss Isabel'	NBlu SBai
'Little Miss Lucy'	COtt
'Little Miss Matilda'	COtt
'Little Miss Rosalind'	MBNS NBlu SBai SVil SWvt
'Little Miss Rosanna'	COtt LRHS SVil
'Little Miss Sophie'	MBNS SBai SVil SWvt
'Little Miss Tara'	MBNS NBlu SVil SWvt
'Little Miss Veronica'	MBNS SBai SVil
'Lucinda'	CDoC LRHS MBri SBai SVil SWvt
magnifica	MDKP WCot
- subsp. ***magnifica***	WCot
- subsp. ***maxima***	WCot
'Marina'	LRHS MBNS
'Marissa'	LRHS
'Mars'	LRHS SWal
Meyer hybrids	MTho
'Moulin Rouge'	CDoC MBNS SBai SVil
'Orange Gem' ♀H4	COtt LRHS MBNS WFar
'Orange Glory' ♀H4	CBcs CDoC COtt IArd LRHS MBNS MBri SMrm SPla SWvt WCot WFar
'Oriana'	SBai SVil SWvt
pallida	CBro CFil CPBP SIgm
- JCA 2.028.500	WCot
patagonica	EHyt
- 'Maxi'	CPBP
pelegrina	EBee ECho LTwo MTho SIgm WCot
- 'Alba'	ELan SIgm
- var. ***humilis***	WCot
- 'Rosea'	ELan
'Perfect Love'	COtt
philippii	WCot
I 'Phoenix'	CDoC EBee EMar LRHS SBai SPla SVil SWvt WCot
'Pink Perfection'	LRHS NLar
'Polka'	CDoC EBee EMar LRHS MBNS SBai SPer SVil
presliana	EBee
- RB 94103	WCot
- subsp. ***australis***	CPou SIgm
Princess Aiko = 'Zapriko'	LIck SPla
Princess Angela = 'Staprilan'PBR	COtt LIck MBNS SCoo
Princess Beatrix = 'Stadoran'	WFar

Princess Carmina = 'Stasilva' CBcs
Princess Daniela = 'Stapridani'PBR CBcs SCoo SPoG
Princess Ella = 'Staprirange'PBR NLar
'Princess Ivana' CDoC EBee NLar SPoG
Princess Juliana = 'Staterpa' SPla SPoG
Princess Julieta = 'Zaprijul' EBee LIck
Princess Leyla = 'Stapriley'PBR CBcs CDoC MBNS
Princess Marilene = 'Staprilene'PBR COtt EBee MBNS
Princess Monica = 'Staprimon'PBR CBcs COtt EBee MBNS SPla
Princess Morana = 'Staprirana'PBR COtt
Princess Oxana = 'Staprioxa'PBR SCoo
Princess Paola = 'Stapripal'PBR COtt MBNS SCoo SPla
Princess Sarah = 'Stalicamp' MBNS
Princess Sissi = 'Staprisis'PBR COtt SPoG
Princess Sophia = 'Stajello'PBR SPoG
Princess Stephanie = 'Stapirag' CBcs NLar SPla
Princess Susana = 'Staprisusa'PBR EBee NLar SCoo
Princess VictoriaPBR see *A.* 'Victoria'
Princess Zavina = 'Staprivina'PBR CFir COtt MBNS NLar
§ ***psittacina*** CBro CFil CFwr CHar CSam CSev CStu EBee EBla EHrv ELan EPfP ERos EWTr EWoo GCal GCra LAst MBri MDun MSte NChi SIgm SSpi WCot WFar WPGP WSHC WTin
- 'Mona Lisa' EShb EWll LTwo WCot
- 'Royal Star' (v) CBro CHea EBee EBla EHol ELan EMan EMar EMon ENot EPPr EPfP EVFa LRHS NLar SIgm SPoG SUsu WCot WFar WHil WHoo WPrP WSHC
- variegated see *A. psittacina* 'Royal Star'
pulchella Sims see *A. psittacina*
pulchra CFil LTwo MDKP WCot
'Purple Rain' EMar MBri SBai SPer SVil SWvt
pygmaea EHyt MTho
'Red Beauty' (v) CDoC GKir LRHS MBNS MBri NBir SBai SPer SPlb SVil SWvt WCot
'Red Elf' CDoC GKir LRHS MBNS MBri SBai SVil SWvt WFar
'Regina'PBR see *A.* 'Victoria'
revoluta CFil
- F&W 8722 WCot
schizanthoides MDKP
'Selina' LRHS MBNS SVil WFar
'Short Purple' CDes
'Solent Candy' WFar
'Solent Crest' WFar
'Solent Dawn' WFar
'Solent Pride' WFar
'Solent Wings' WFar
'Sovereign' MDKP
'Spitfire' (v) CDoC EBee MBri SBai SVil SWvt
'Spring Delight' (v) EMan EVFa WCot
'Sunstar' LRHS
'Sweet Laura'PBR LTwo MMHG NOrc
'Tapestry' SWal
'Tessa' CDoC EBee LIck LRHS MBNS SBai WCot
umbellata WCot
'Verona' LRHS
§ ***versicolor*** GCrs
- BC&W 4624 GBin
§ 'Victoria'PBR WFar
werdermannii MDKP
var. ***flavicans*** F&W 956289
- var. ***werdermannii*** F&W 9585 MDKP
'White Apollo' EBee SPla WCot
'Yellow Friendship' ♀H4 CDoC COtt GKir LRHS MBNS NLar SPer SPlb SWvt WFar
'Yellow Queen' WFar
zoellneri F&W 9608 WCot

Althaea (*Malvaceae*)

armeniaca EBee EMan EMon LPio WCot
cannabina CFir CSpe EChP ELan EMon GBri GCal GQui MAnH MGol SOkh WBor WHal WHoo WOld WSHC WWhi XPep
officinalis CAgr CArn CPrp CSev CWan ELan EMon GBar GMac GPoy ILis ITer MChe MHer MSal SIde WPer WWye XPep
- ***alba*** EBee EChP NArg NLar WHer
§ - 'Romney Marsh' EWTr EWll GCal MRav NCot SMad WSHC
rosea see *Alcea rosea*
rugosostellulata see *Alcea rugosa*

Altingia (*Hamamelidaceae*)

gracilipes CFil CMCN

Alyogyne (*Malvaceae*)

hakeifolia CSpe ECou ERea
- 'Elle Maree' ERea LRHS
§ ***huegelii*** CSec EMan MOak WDyG
- 'Santa Cruz' CBcs CHll CMdw CPLG CSec CSpe ERea MSte SSpi WPGP WRos
'Melissa Anne' LRHS

Alyssoides (*Brassicaceae*)

utriculata CHrt WPer

Alyssum (*Brassicaceae*)

argenteum hort. see *A. murale*
corymbosum see *Aurinia corymbosa*
idaeum LRHS
montanum CArn ECha MWat NBir NBlu SPlb SRms WMoo
§ - 'Berggold' CBcs CHrt EPfP LRHS LRav SHGN
- Mountain Gold see *A. montanum* 'Berggold'
§ ***murale*** IHMH NLar
ovirense **new** CSec
oxycarpum SBla WAbe
purpureum WLin
repens subsp. ***repens*** GIBF
saxatile see *Aurinia saxatilis*
scardicum LTwo
serpyllifolium NWCA
spinosum CMea WFar XPep
§ - 'Roseum' ♀H4 CTri ECha EDAr EHyt ELan EPot GAbr LBee LRHS LSpr MWat NMen NWCA SBla WAbe WCot WPat WPer
- 'Strawberries and Cream' WAbe
stribrnyi CNic

wulfenianum	CNic GAbr LTwo NEgg NLar WMoo

Amana see *Tulipa*

x *Amarcrinum* (*Amaryllidaceae*)

memoria-corsii	CMon
- 'Howardii'	CFir EBee EMan LPio LRHS WCot

x *Amarine* (*Amaryllidaceae*)

'Fletcheri'	CMon
tubergenii	CAvo LPio
- 'Zwanenburg'	CAby EBee EMan WCot

x *Amarygia* (*Amaryllidaceae*)

parkeri	CMon
§ - 'Alba'	CAvo CBro CMon EBee ECho EMan LPio MSte SSpi WCot

Amaranthus (*Amaranthaceae*)

hypochondriacus	CSpe
'Pygmy Torch' ♀H3 **new**	

Amaryllis (*Amaryllidaceae*)

§ ***belladonna*** ♀H2-3	CAby CBcs CBro CFil CHEx CPne CStu EMan EMon EPfP LAma LRHS MBri MSte SChr SDnm SPav SPer SSpi WCot WGer
- 'Bloemfontein'	CAvo
- 'Johannesburg'	CAvo EMon LRHS WCot
- 'Kimberley'	CAvo CPne EMon
- 'Major'	CAvo
- 'Parkeri Alba'	see x *Amarygia parkeri* 'Alba'
- 'Purpurea'	EBee EBrs EMon WCot
- white-flowered	SSpi WCot
- 'Windhoek'	CAvo

Amelanchier ✿ (*Rosaceae*)

alnifolia	CTho EBee EPla LRHS WBcn
- 'Martin' (F) **new**	CAgr
- 'Obelisk'PBR	CAbP CDul EBee LBuc MAsh MGos NLar SPoG SSta
- pink-fruited	NLar
§ - var. ***pumila***	CTho GSki MSte SSta WDin WNor WTin
- 'Regent' (F) **new**	CAgr
- 'Smokey'	CDul NLar
* ***alpina***	EHyt
arborea	CPle CTho EGFP LRHS WNor
bartramiana	CTho LRHS SSta
- 'Eskimo'	NLar
canadensis (L.) Medik.	More than 30 suppliers
x ***grandiflora*** 'Autumn Brilliance'	CEnd GKir LRHS NLar
- 'Ballerina' ♀H4	More than 30 suppliers
- 'Cole's Select'	SReu
- 'Princess Diana'	CDoC NLar
- 'Robin Hill'	CBcs EBee ENot GKir LBuc LRHS MAsh MBlu MGos NEgg NLar SBLw SHBN SLim SMad WFar
- 'Rubescens'	CDul CEnd EBee GKir LRHS
'Honeywood' **new**	NLar
humilis	NLar
'La Paloma'	GKir MBri NLar SPoG
laevis	CBcs CDul CTri EPfP LRHS MGos SPer STre WGor
- 'Cumulus'	NLar
- 'Prince Charles'	NLar
- 'R.J. Hilton'	GKir MBri MGos MLan
- 'Snow Cloud'	CDoC
- 'Snowflakes'	CDoC CEnd CWSG EBee GKir LRHS MAsh MDun MGos NPro SLim SPoG WBVN
lamarckii ♀H4	More than 30 suppliers
ovalis	XPep
pumila	see *A. alnifolia* var. *pumila*
rotundifolia 'Edelweiss'	CDoC CEnd CPMA GKir MBlu MGos NEgg
- 'Helvetia'	CEnd EBee GKir LRHS WEas
spicata	ECrN GIBF

x *Amelasorbus* (*Rosaceae*)

jackii	MBlu

Amicia (*Papilionaceae*)

zygomeris	CBot CHEx CHll CMdw CPLG CPle CPom CSpe EHol EMan EMar EWes GBuc GCal SMrm SUsu WCot WSHC WWye

Ammi (*Apiaceae*)

majus	CArn EMan MSal NLsd SDix
visnaga	CArn CSpe GPoy LPio MSal

Ammobium (*Asteraceae*)

calyceroides	EMan

Ammocharis (*Amaryllidaceae*)

coranica	WCot

Ammophila (*Poaceae*)

arenaria	CRWN GFor GQui NBre SMar
breviligulata	GBin

Amomum (*Zingiberaceae*)

dealbatum	CKob MOak
subulatum	CKob MOak WMul

Amomyrtus (*Myrtaceae*)

§ ***luma***	CBcs CDoC CTbh CTri CTrw ELan EPfP GQui IDee SArc WFar WJek WPic

Amorpha (*Papilionaceae*)

canescens	CBcs CPle EMan IDee NSti SBrw SEND WBVN WSHC
fruticosa	CAgr CBcs CFil CPle EWTr LEdu MBlu MGol MNrw NLar SBrw SPlb WSHC
herbacea **new**	NLar
ouachitensis	NLar
paniculata **new**	NLar

Amorphophallus ✿ (*Araceae*)

bulbifer	CFil CKob EAmu EBee EUJe LAma LRHS MOak SBig WMul WPGP
kerrii	CKob
kiusianus	EShb
konjac	CFil CHEx CKob CMon CStu EUJe LEdu SSpi WPGP
nepalensis **new**	LAma
paeoniifolius	CKob EUJe MOak SBig WMul
rivieri	EBee GCal LAma WMul
stipitatus	SSpi
titanum	LAma
yunnanensis	CKob

Ampelocalamus (*Poaceae*)

scandens	CFil EPla WPGP

Ampelocissus (*Vitaceae*)

sikkimensis HWJK 2066 **new**	WCru

Ampelodesmos (*Poaceae*)

mauritanica	CBig CBrm CFwr CHar CHrt

	COIW CPen CSam EBee ECha EHoe EMan GFor LEdu LRav MCCP NChi NOGN SEND SMHy SMad SPlb SSvw XPep

Ampelopsis (*Vitaceae*)

aconitifolia	CPLN NLar NVic SBra
- 'Chinese Lace' **new**	SBra WPGP
***arborea* new**	CPLN
§ ***brevipedunculata***	CBcs CPLN CRHN ECrN ELan EShb LAst SCoo SGar SLim SPer SPoG WDin WFar
- 'Citrulloides' B&SWJ 1173	WCru
- var. ***maximowiczii*** 'Elegans'	CBcs CBrm CChe CHEx CMac CPLN CRHN CRez CWib EBee ELan EPfP LAst MBar MGos MRav MSwo NBlu SAdn SAga SBra SHBN SPer SPla SPoG SWvt WCot WDin WPat WSHC
glandulosa var. ***brevipedunculata***	see *A. brevipedunculata*
- 'Tricolor'	see *A. brevipedunculata* var. *maximowiczii* 'Elegans'
- var. ***hancei*** B&SWJ 3855	WCru
henryana	see *Parthenocissus henryana*
***humulifolia* new**	CPLN
***japonica* new**	GIBF
megalophylla	CBcs CBot CHEx CPLN EBee ELan EPfP EShb LRHS MBlu NCGa SMHy SPer SPoG WBVN WBcn WCot WCru WFar WNor WOVN
sempervirens hort. ex Veitch	see *Cissus striata*
sinica	CPLN
tricuspidata 'Veitchii'	see *Parthenocissus tricuspidata* 'Veitchii'

Amphicome see *Incarvillea*

Amsonia (*Apocynaceae*)

ciliata	CFee CFir CFwr ELan LPhx WCot WFar WPer
hubrichtii	CAby CMdw CPom EMan EPPr GCal MGol NDov NLar SIgm SMHy SMad
illustris	CPom EBrs EMan LRHS MGol MSte SHar SMHy WPer WTin
jonesii	SIgm
§ ***orientalis***	More than 30 suppliers
***peeblesii* new**	SIgm
tabernaemontana	More than 30 suppliers
* - ***galacticifolia* new**	EBee
- var. ***salicifolia***	CAby EBrs EChP GKir GSki LPhx LRHS MSte NDov WCAu WTin

Amygdalus see *Prunus*

Anacampseros (*Portulacaceae*)

***alstonii* new**	LToo
***dinteri* new**	LToo

Anacamptis (*Orchidaceae*)

laxiflora	CHdy
morio	CHdy WBWf
pyramidalis	CHdy EFEx WBWf WHer

Anacyclus (*Asteraceae*)

pyrethrum	GPoy
- var. ***depressus***	CTri ECtt EDAr ELan EPfP GKev GKir GMaP GTou IHMH LRHS MSte NBlu NFor NLAp NVic NWCA SBla SIng SPet SPlb WCFE WFar WHoo WPer
- - 'Garden Gnome'	CTri EWin NArg NJOw NPri SRms
- - 'Silberkissen'	WLin

Anadenanthera (*Mimosaceae*)

colubrina	MGol

Anagallis (*Primulaceae*)

arvensis	MHer MSal
linifolia	see *A. monellii* subsp. *linifolia*
§ ***monellii*** ♀H4	CNic SBla
§ - subsp. ***linifolia***	EHyt
- - 'Blue Light'	CSpe
- 'Skylover'	EMan LAst LSou MLan SPet
- 'Sunrise'	CPBP EHyt LAst SBla SUsu
tenella	SIng
- 'Studland'	CStu CWCL EBla EPot GAbr NJOw NMen NSla NWCA SBla SIng SPoG WAbe WHoo

Anagyris (*Leguminosae*)

foetida	XPep

Ananas (*Bromeliaceae*)

comosus (F)	CKob LRHS
- var. ***variegatus*** (v)	CKob MBri SMur

Anaphalis (*Asteraceae*)

CC 3725	WCot
alpicola	EPot NMen
margaritacea	CBcs COIW CSBt ECha ECrN ECtt EWTr GBin GGar GMaP IHMH ITer MBri MLLN NBid SMer SRms WFar WMoo
§ - var. ***cinnamomea***	EMon WEas
§ - 'Neuschnee'	CTri CWan GKir LBBr MWgw NArg NBPC NGdn NMir NPri SPla WFar WPer
- New Snow	see *A. margaritacea* 'Neuschnee'
§ - var. ***yedoensis*** ♀H4	CBre CTri EBee ECot NEgg SDix WBrE WCAu WTin
§ ***nepalensis*** var. ***monocephala***	ELan EMon NBre NSti WCAu
nubigena	see *A. nepalensis* var. *monocephala*
sinica 'Moon's Silver'	EBee
transnokoensis	EBee EWes
§ ***trinervis***	EBee NJOw
triplinervis ♀H4	More than 30 suppliers
- CC 1620	WCot
§ - 'Sommerschnee' ♀H4	CSLe EChP ECha ECot ECtt EPfP ERou LRHS MBri MNFA MRav MTis NEgg NFor NLon SChu SPer WMnd WMow WPer
- Summer Snow	see *A. triplinervis* 'Sommerschnee'

Anarrhinum (*Scrophulariaceae*)

bellidifolium	SPet SUsu

Anchusa (*Boraginaceae*)

angustissima	see *A. leptophylla* subsp. *incana*
§ ***azurea***	EUnu IHMH MGol NRnb WPer XPep
- 'Dropmore'	CTri EBee ELan EPfP GFlt LAst LRHS MAnH MEHN MGol MWgw NEgg NLon NOrc SPav SRms SSth WPer
- 'Feltham Pride'	CBrm CMdw CSBt CSam CSim EBee EWTr GKir GMaP MSte NBPC NLon NRnb SMar SPav SRms SWvt WFar WHil WHoo WPGP WPer WWeb WWhi
- 'Little John'	COtt ECot ERou SRms WTel
- 'Loddon Royalist' ♀H4	More than 30 suppliers

- 'Opal'	EBee ECGP EChP ECot EMan EPfP IGor LRHS MWat NCGa NEgg SBch SChu SPla SPoG WCAu
- 'Royal Blue'	LRHS
caespitosa hort. non Lam.	see *A. leptophylla* subsp. *incana*
capensis	CSec WHil WLin
- 'Blue Angel'	LRHS NJOw WWeb
cespitosa Lam.	ECho EHyt ELan EWes SBla SIng WAbe
italica	see *A. azurea*
laxiflora	see *Borago pygmaea*
§ ***leptophylla*** subsp. ***incana***	EBee ECGP LBuc LRHS MMHG MSte NEgg SBch SPet SPoG
- - F&W 9550	MDKP
myosotidiflora	see *Brunnera macrophylla*
officinalis	CArn EUnu LRHS MGol MSal SPav
sempervirens	see *Pentaglottis sempervirens*
undulata	SIgm

Ancylostemon (*Gesneriaceae*)

convexus B&SWJ 6624	WCru

Andrachne (*Euphorbiaceae*)

colchica	EMan WCot

Androcymbium (*Colchicaceae*)

europaeum MS 510 from Spain **new**	CMon
gramineum SB&L 26 from Morocco **new**	CMon
rechingeri SB&L 313 from Crete **new**	CMon

Andromeda (*Ericaceae*)

glaucophylla	CBrm MBar SBrw WDin
polifolia	CMHG EMil EPot GCrs GKev GKir NJOw SBrw WDin WFar
- 'Alba'	EBee ELan GKir LRHS MAsh MBar NLAp NRya SBod SBrw SPer SPlb SPoG SWvt WFar WPat
- 'Blue Ice'	CWib ELan ENot EPfP GKir LRHS MAsh NHar NLAp NMen SPer SPoG SSpi WAbe WFar WPat
- 'Compacta' ♀H4	CAlb CDoC CWib EBee EHoe EMil GCrs GKir LRHS MBar MBri NMen SPer SPoG SRms SWvt WBVN WFar WGwG WSHC
- 'Grandiflora'	ELan GKir ITim LRHS MAsh MBri SBod SPer
- 'Hayachine'	EPot ITim NLAp
- 'Kirigamine'	GKir LRHS MAsh MBri
- 'Macrophylla' ♀H4	ITim NDlv WAbe WPat
- 'Minima'	WThu
- 'Nana'	CSBt ELan EPfP GKir LRHS MAsh NMen
- 'Nikko'	CWib ITim WFar WPat
- 'Shibutsu'	NMen

Andropogon (*Poaceae*)

gerardii	CBig CBrm CKno CPen CRWN CWCL EBee EBrs EHoe EHul EMan EPPr EPla EPza GFor LPhx LRav MWhi SApp SMad WDyG WGHP WWpP
ischaemum	see *Bothriochloa ischaemum*
saccharoides	EBee
scoparius	see *Schizachyrium scoparium*
virginicus	CBig CBrm LPhx

Androsace (*Primulaceae*)

CD&R 2477 from China **new**	WCru
akbaitalensis **new**	EHyt
albana	EHyt
alpina	CGra WAbe
armeniaca var. ***macrantha***	EHyt
baltistanica	EHyt GCrs WAbe
barbulata	CNic CStu EPot
bulleyana	EHyt WAbe
carnea	CPBP
- ***alba***	LRHS NWCA WLin
- subsp. ***brigantiaca***	GCrs GKev GTou ITim NJOw NLAp NSla WAbe WHoo
- var. ***halleri***	see *A. carnea* subsp. *rosea*
- subsp. ***laggeri*** ♀H4	ECho GCrs GTou LTwo NSla WAbe
§ - subsp. ***rosea*** ♀H4	GKev
carnea x ***pyrenaica***	EHyt EPot NMen WAbe
chamaejasme	ECho
ciliata	GCrs GTou WAbe
cylindrica	CGra CPBP GCrs GTou ITim LRHS NMen NSla WAbe WFar
cylindrica x ***hirtella***	GKev GTou ITim LRHS WAbe
- (ENF strain)	WAbe
dasyphylla	EHyt GKev
delavayi	WAbe WLin
foliosa	GCrs
geraniifolia	CPLG EBee ECha GKev MFOX SRms WAbe WCru WLin
globifera	CPBP EHyt EPot NMen WAbe
hausmannii	GTou
hedraeantha	CLyd ITim MWat WAbe
x ***heeri***	EHyt
- white	SBla
helvetica	EHyt NLAp
himalaica	CGra CNic CPBP EHyt EPot SBla
hirtella	GTou ITim NLAp NMen
idahoensis	CGra WAbe
incana **new**	EHyt WAbe
jacquemontii	see *A. villosa* var. *jacquemontii*
kosopoljanskii **new**	EHyt
lactea	GCrs GTou WAbe
§ ***laevigata***	CGra GCrs NMen WAbe
- from Columbia River Gorge, USA	WAbe
- var. ***ciliolata***	GTou WLin
- 'Gothenburg'	EHyt WAbe WPat
lanuginosa ♀H4	CLyd CMea EHyt EPot GCrs GKev MWat NMen NWCA SBla SIng SRms WAbe WPat
- CC 1271	GKev
- 'Leichtlinii'	GKev
- 'Wisley Variety'	SIgm
limprichtii	see *A. sarmentosa* var. *watkinsii*
x ***marpensis***	EHyt EPot WAbe
mathildae	CGra EHyt GTou ITim NWCA WAbe
microphylla	see *A. mucronifolia* Watt
§ ***mollis***	CPBP EHyt EPot SIgm
mucronifolia hort.	see *A. sempervivoides*
§ ***mucronifolia*** G. Watt	EHyt EPot GTou NJOw
- Schacht's form	EHyt
mucronifolia x ***sempervivoides***	EHyt EPot NJOw
muscoidea	EHyt EPot
- C&R 188	GTou
- 'Breviscapa'	EPot
- f. ***longiscapa***	CGra CPBP EHyt NMen NWCA WAbe
- Schacht's form	EHyt GCrs SBla
§ ***nivalis***	WAbe WLin
x ***pedemontana***	ITim
primuloides	see *A. studiosorum*
pubescens	CGra ITim LRHS LTwo NMen WAbe
pyrenaica	CGra EHyt GTou ITim LRHS NMen NSla SIng WAbe

rigida	WAbe
- KGB 168	EPot
robusta	EHyt GCrs
- TJR 419-99	EHyt
- subsp. ***purpurea***	WAbe
rotundifolia	EHyt ETow GEdr GTou WCru
sarmentosa misapplied	see *A. studiosorum*
sarmentosa Wall.	EDAr EHyt ELan GKev GTou MWat NSla SRms WHoo WTel
- CC 407	LRHS
- from Namche, Nepal	EHyt WAbe
- 'Chumbyi'	see *A. studiosorum* 'Chumbyi'
- 'Salmon's Variety'	see *A. studiosorum* 'Salmon's Variety'
- 'Sherriffii'	CFee EPot GEdr MOne NLAp SIgm SRms WHoo
§ - var. ***watkinsii***	EPot NMen
- var. ***yunnanensis*** misapplied	see *A. studiosorum*
- var. ***yunnanensis*** Knuth	see *A. mollis*
selago	EPot WAbe
§ ***sempervivoides*** ♀H4	CLyd CMea ECha EDAr EHyt ELan EPot ESis GKev GMaP LRHS NDlv NLAp NMen NWCA SBla SIgm SOkd SRms WHoo WLin WPat
- 'Greystone'	EPot NMen
- scented	CWCL
- 'Susan Joan' (v)	CPBP EHyt GKev SBla WAbe
septentrionalis 'Stardust'	CBrm ECho NJOw
sericea	EHyt
spinulifera	GKev NLAp
strigillosa	WAbe
§ ***studiosorum*** ♀H4	CWCL EPot GAbr GEdr GKev NLAp
- 'Chumbyi'	EHol ETow GEdr LTwo MOne NWCA SBla SRms WPat
- 'Doksa'	CPBP EHyt EPot GCrs NMen SOkd WAbe
§ - 'Salmon's Variety'	CMea CTri ECho NRya SIgm WAbe
tapete	WAbe
- ACE 1725	EPot
vandellii	CGra CPBP EHyt EPot GTou ITim NSla WAbe WLin
villosa	WLin
- var. ***arachnoidea***	CPBP EHyt GKev
- - 'Superba'	NMen
- var. ***congesta***	EHyt
§ - var. ***jacquemontii***	ETow GCrs NMen SBla WLin
- - lilac	CPBP EPot WAbe
- - pink	EPot NLAp WAbe
- subsp. ***taurica***	CLyd EHyt
vitaliana	see *Vitaliana primuliflora*
watkinsii	see *A. sarmentosa* var. *watkinsii*
yargongensis	GKev WAbe
- ACE 1722	EPot
zambalensis	WAbe

Androstoma (*Epacridaceae*)

empetrifolia	EPot

Andryala (*Asteraceae*)

agardhii	NJOw WLin WPat
lanata	see *Hieracium lanatum*

Anemanthele (*Poaceae*)

lessoniana	More than 30 suppliers

Anemarrhena (*Anthericaceae*)

asphodeloides	CArn MSal WCot

Anemone ✿ (*Ranunculaceae*)

B&SWJ 1452	WCru
B&SWJ 6716 from Taiwan **new**	WCru
aconitifolia Michx.	see *A. narcissiflora*
aconitifolia ambig.	CSpe
altaica	GAbr MSal NEgg SRms
apennina ♀H4	CAvo CBos CLAP ECha GEdr IBlr WCru WTin
- var. ***albiflora***	CDes CFwr CLAP EBee ECha EPot ERos GEdr GMac IBlr LRHS MSte SMeo SOkh WPnP
- 'Ballyrogan Park'	IBlr
- double	ECha IBlr NDov SBla WCru
- 'Petrovac'	CLAP EBee IBlr LRHS WCot
baicalensis	EWll
baldensis	CSec ECho EPyc GCrs GKev GKir LBee LRHS NBre NBur NMen NOak NWCA SRms
barbulata	CAby CLAP EChP EKen EMan GAbr GBBs GBuc LPhx NLar WBVN
blanda ♀H4	GBBs GKir LAma MAnH MBri NBlu NChi SChu WFar WPer WPop WShi
- blue-flowered	CAvo CBro CMea CTbh CTri ELan ENot EPot GAbr GKir LAma LRHS MBri MNFA MWgw NLon SMrm SPoG SRms WBVN WFar
- blue shades	EBrs ECGP ECho EMar EPfP GEdr GKev GMaP IGor LPhx LRHS MAnH SMeo SPer WBrE WLin
- 'Charmer'	EMar EPot GKev NMen
- 'Ingramii'	LAma WCot
- 'Pink Charmer' **new**	ENot
- 'Pink Star'	CBro EPot LAma LRHS NBir
- 'Radar' ♀H4	CAvo CBro CDes CLAP CMea ECho EPot LAma MNrw NBir SVal WLin
- var. ***rosea*** ♀H4	CAvo CNic ECho ELan EPfP LAma MLLN MWgw SPer SPoG WFar WPer
- 'Violet Star'	EPot LPhx LRHS NLon SMeo WGHP
- 'White Splendour' ♀H4	CAvo CBro CElw CMea CTri EBrs ELan EMar ENot EPfP EPot GAbr GEdr GKev GKir LAma LPhx MNFA NBir NChi NLon NMen SChu SPer SPoG SRms WCot WFar WLin WPer
canadensis	CHar CNic CPMA CSpe EPPr EWsh GAbr GBBs GBuc GKir MNrw MSte MWrn NBur NCGa NEgg WBVN WCot WRos
caroliniana	EMFP GBuc GCrs GKir LRHS NEgg WCru
caucasica	SBla
chapaensis HWJ 631	WCru
coronaria 'Bicolor' **new**	CBgR
- De Caen Group	CMea EBrs EPfP LAma WFar
§ - - 'Die Braut'	GFlt SPer WFar WGHP
- - 'His Excellency'	see *A. coronaria* (De Caen Group) 'Hollandia'
§ - - 'Hollandia'	EBrs SMeo SPer
- - 'Mister Fokker'	EBrs GFlt LAma SMeo SPer WFar
- - The Bride	see *A. coronaria* (De Caen Group) 'Die Braut'
- - 'The Governor'	WFar
- Jerusalem hybrids	WFar
- Saint Bridgid Group (d)	EPfP LAma MBri SPet WFar WGwG
- - 'Lord Lieutenant' (d)	NBir NBur SMeo WFar
- - 'Mount Everest' (d)	GFlt NBir SMeo WRHF
- - 'The Admiral' (d)	EBrs NBir SMeo WFar
- 'Sylphide' (Mona Lisa Series)	NBir SMeo SPer WFar
crinita	GBuc WBVN WRHF
cylindrica	CFir CMHG CSam CSec EBee EChP MDKP MNrw NBre NLar

	Name	Suppliers
	davidii B&SWJ 7508	WCru
	decapetala	GCal MAnH NChi NRnb WBVN WLin
	demissa	EMan GBuc GKev NRya
	- BWJ 7785	WCru
	drummondii	CLyd EChP EMan GKev GSki LRHS NBur NChi WBVN WWeb
	elongata B&SWJ 2975	WCru
	eranthoides	CLAP EBee
	fasciculata	see *A. narcissiflora*
	flaccida	CBro CDes CLAP CMea EBee EHrv EPot GBuc GIBF GMac LPhx LRHS MSte SBch SBla WCot WCru WFar WHal WSHC WWhi
	x ***fulgens***	ECha SAga SIgm SVal
	- 'Annulata Grandiflora'	ECGP
	- 'Multipetala'	GEdr
	- Saint Bavo Group	ECGP
	globosa	see *A. multifida*
	'Guernica'	COlW ECho GBuc MAnH NRnb SRot WLin
	'Hatakeyama Double' (d)	CBos CDes GCal
	'Hatakeyama Single'	CDes GCal
	hepatica	see *Hepatica nobilis*
§	***hortensis***	LPhx NBre
	- ***alba***	CTbh
	- subsp. ***heldreichii***	CDes SBla
§	***hupehensis***	CBos EWll GBBs GKir GMaP IGor LRHS NOrc SVal WFar WRHF
	- BWJ 8190	WCru
	- f. ***alba***	CDes WGwG WPGP WWeb
§	- 'Bowles' Pink' 🏆^{H4}	CElw CMil CStr EPPr IGor MBri MWat WBrk WCru WPGP WTin WWhi
	- 'Crispa'	see *A.* x *hybrida* 'Lady Gilmour' Wolley-Dod
	- 'Eugenie'	CMil CStr EChP EMan EVFa GBuc GSki LRHS MBNS NBir
	- 'Hadspen Abundance' 🏆^{H4}	More than 30 suppliers
	- 'Hadspen Red' **new**	WFar
§	- var. ***japonica***	CBos CBrm CPou GCal LEdu NCob NFor
	- - B&SWJ 4886	WCru
	- - 'Bodnant Burgundy'	CBos CDes CPen CPrp EChP ECtt EMan IPot LRHS MCCP WCAu WHil WPGP
§	- - 'Bressingham Glow'	CMHG CPLG EBee EBrs ECtt ELan ENot EPfP EPza ERou GKir GSki LRHS MBri MMil MNrw MRav MWgw NBir NOrc NVic SHBN SPer SPet WAbb WCAu WFar WMnd
§	- - 'Pamina' 🏆^{H4}	More than 30 suppliers
	- - Prince Henry	see *A. hupehensis* var. *japonica* 'Prinz Heinrich'
§	- - 'Prinz Heinrich' 🏆^{H4}	More than 30 suppliers
§	- - 'Rotkäppchen'	CPar EBee EMan EMar EVFa EWTr GBin LRHS MRav NBur NGby NPro WAul WRHF WWeb
	- 'Ouvertüre'	WPGP
	- 'Praecox'	CBot CMea EHrv EPfP GBBs GBri GBuc GSki LRHS MAvo MBNS MBri MWgw NBir NCGa NGdn NPri NSti SWvt WAbb WBrk WCru WHal WHil WHoo WMnd WPnP WWeb
	- 'September Charm'	see *A.* x *hybrida* 'September Charm'
	- 'Splendens'	CAby CMHG EMan ENot GBBs GBuc LAst LRHS NEgg SPer SPur SWvt WAbb WFar WHal
	- 'Superba'	WKif
§	x ***hybrida***	MWat MWrn NChi NCob SChu SGar WCru WFar WMoo WWpP
	- 'Alba' hort. (UK)	see *A.* x *hybrida* 'Honorine Jobert'
	- 'Albert Schweitzer'	see *A.* x *hybrida* 'Elegans'
	- 'Andrea Atkinson'	CPrp EBee EChP EMan EPfP EVFa GBBs GBuc GSki LAst LGro LRHS MBri MLLN MNFA NBid NGdn NRnb SChu SMrm SPla WBrk WCot WCra WFar WHil WHoo WMnd WMoo
	- 'Bowles' Pink'	see *A. hupehensis* 'Bowles' Pink'
	- 'Bressingham Glow'	see *A. hupehensis* var. *japonica* 'Bressingham Glow'
§	- 'Elegans' 🏆^{H4}	CWCL EBee EMan MRav NBir WCAu WCru WHil WHoo
§	- 'Géante des Blanches'	CBos CHar CStr GKir GMac IGor LRHS MSph SHop SMrm WFar WHoo
§	- 'Honorine Jobert' 🏆^{H4}	More than 30 suppliers
§	- 'Königin Charlotte' 🏆^{H4}	More than 30 suppliers
	- 'Kriemhilde'	GCal GMac
	- 'Lady Gilmour' misapplied	see *A.* x *hybrida* 'Margarete'
§	- 'Lady Gilmour' Wolley-Dod	CFai CSpe EBee EChP ECtt EHol EHrv EPfP EVFa GCal GKir GMac LRHS MAnH MCCP MRav NBir NChi NGdn SAga SOkh SPoG WCAu WCru WFar WPnP
	- 'Loreley'	CMea CPrp EBee EChP EMan GBuc IPot MBNS MSte MWat SMrm WHil WHoo WWpP
	- 'Luise Uhink'	CPou IGor LRHS MDKP NBir SSpi WEas
	- 'Margarete' Kayser & Seibert	CFwr COlW CPLG CStr EBee ENot EPPr LAst LRHS NCGa STes WCot WCru WFar
	- 'Max Vogel'	see *A.* x *hybrida* 'Elegans'
	- 'Monterosa'	see *A.* x *hybrida* 'Margarete'
	- 'Montrose'	CPLG CPar CPou EChP EHrv EVFa EWes GCal GKir LRHS NBir NEgg SChu SRms WBor WCra WFar
	- 'Pamina'	see *A. hupehensis* var. *japonica* 'Pamina'
	- Prince Henry	see *A. hupehensis* var. *japonica* 'Prinz Heinrich'
	- 'Prinz Heinrich'	see *A. hupehensis* var. *japonica* 'Prinz Heinrich'
	- 'Profusion'	CTri LBuc LRHS MLan NBlu SHBN
	- Queen Charlotte	see *A.* x *hybrida* 'Königin Charlotte'
	- 'Richard Ahrens'	EBee EChP ECtt ERou GBuc GKir GMaP LRHS MNFA NDov NOrc NSti SAga SPla WCru WFar WLin WMnd WPnP WWeb
	- 'Robustissima'	More than 30 suppliers
	- 'Rosenschale'	CFwr EBee GCal LRHS MBri NCGa WCru WFar
	- 'Rotkäppchen'	see *A. hupehensis* var. *japonica* 'Rotkäppchen'
§	- 'September Charm' 🏆^{H4}	More than 30 suppliers
	- 'Serenade'	CPar EBee EBrs ECtt EMan EPfP ERou GBBs LRHS MBri MLLN NBPC NBir NEgg NRnb SHBN SPoG SSvw WAul WCAu WCot WFar WHil WMoo WWol
	- Tourbillon	see *A.* x *hybrida* 'Whirlwind'
§	- 'Whirlwind'	More than 30 suppliers
	- 'White Queen'	see *A.* x *hybrida* 'Géante des Blanches'
	- Wirbelwind	see *A.* x *hybrida* 'Whirlwind'
	imbricata **new**	CFwr
	japonica	see *A.* x *hybrida*, *A. hupehensis*
	keiskeana	WCru

	x ***lesseri***	CBro CFir CSpe EBee EChP ECha ECtt EDAr EHrv ELan ESis GBBs GKev MHer NChi NEgg NJOw SBla SGar SOkh SRms WAul WBVN WCru WFar WHoo WPat
	leveillei	More than 30 suppliers
§	x ***lipsiensis***	More than 30 suppliers
	- 'Pallida' ♀H4	CBos CHad EBee ECho ERos GBuc GCrs GEdr GKev IGor MAvo MNFA NPar WCot
	lyallii	EPPr GBuc
N	***magellanica*** hort. ex Wehrh.	see *A. multifida*
	mexicana B&SWJ 8414	WCru
	multifida misapplied red	see *A.* x *lesseri*
§	***multifida***	More than 30 suppliers
	- 'Major'	CFir CHar CLyd CMea LAst LPhx LRHS MBNS MBow NCob NLon NPro NWCA SAga SBla SMac WBVN WCFE WFar
	- pink	GBuc WSan
*	- 'Rubra'	EHrv EWll GAbr GBuc GGar LAst LPhx LRHS MBNS MNrw NBir NDlv NEgg NWCA SPet WLin WWeb
§	***narcissiflora***	EBee ECGP GBuc GKir IGor NBir NBre NChi SVal
	- var. ***citrina***	CWan SBla
	nemorosa ♀H4	More than 30 suppliers
N	- 'Alba Plena' (d)	CBro CHea CSWP CSam EBee ECha EPPr ERos ETow GBuc GEdr GGar GMac LRHS MTho NMen SIng SUsu WAbb WCot WCru WEas WFar WLin WPnP
	- 'Allenii' ♀H4	CBro CHea CLAP CSpe ECha EHyt ERos GEdr GKir GMaP ITim LPhx MAvo MNFA MRav NMen NPar NRya SIgm SIng SMac SSpi WCru WPGP WPnP
	- 'Atrocaerulea'	CLAP EBee GBuc IBlr NLar WCru
	- 'Bill Baker's Pink'	CDes CLAP
	- 'Blue Beauty'	CLAP CPom EBee EPot ERos ETow GBuc GMaP IBlr MAvo NMen SBch SSpi WCru
	- 'Blue Bonnet'	CElw CStu EBee ECho GBuc IGor ITim MAvo MNrw WCot
	- 'Blue Eyes' (d)	CAby CDes CLAP EBee ETow GBuc GCrs GEdr GMaP IBlr IGor MAvo MSte NBir NMen SBla SIgm WCot WCru WPGP
	- 'Blue Queen'	CStu GAbr GBuc
	- 'Bowles' Purple'	CBos CPom CStu EBee EPPr EPot ETow GBBs GBuc GMaP IBlr MAvo MNrw NDov NMyG NRya SIgm WCot WCru WFar WIvy WLin WPGP WTin
	- 'Bracteata'	CAvo EHrv ERos GEdr NDov NMen
	- 'Bracteata Pleniflora' (d)	CLAP CStu EBee ECha GBuc GMaP IBlr IGor MAvo MNFA MNrw NBir WCot WCru WFar
	- 'Buckland'	CDes CFil CFwr CLAP ECha EHrv IBlr WCru
	- 'Cedric's Pink'	CLAP EPPr ERos GBBs IBlr IGor MNrw WCru
	- 'Celestial'	EBee GBuc
	- 'Danica'	EBee
	- 'Dee Day'	CLAP EBee EHrv GBuc MAvo MNrw WCru
	- 'Flore Pleno' (d)	EBee EHyt GBBs GKir NBir NDov NMen WPGP
	- 'Gerda Ramusen' **new**	EHyt
	- 'Green Fingers'	CDes CLAP EBee ECho EHrv EPPr EPot GBuc GEdr GMaP IGor ITim LPhx MNrw NDov NGby NPar SCnR WCot WCru WIvy
	- 'Hannah Gubbay'	CLAP GBuc IBlr IGor MNrw MSte SSpi
	- 'Hilda'	CLAP EBee EPot ERos ETow GBuc GEdr MNFA MNrw NDlv NDov NMen NRya NSla SSpi WCru
	- 'Kentish Pink'	GBBs GBuc GCrs GMaP
	- 'Knightshayes Vestal' (d)	CLAP EBee MAvo MRav WCot WCru WIvy
	- 'Lady Doneraile'	CDes CLAP EBee ECha ETow GBuc NBir NLar NPar WCru WFar
	- 'Leeds' Variety'	EBee GCrs IGor ITim LPhx MAvo MNrw MTho NDov NSla SBla WCot
	- 'Lismore Blue'	EBee EPot
§	- 'Lismore Pink'	EHrv GEdr
	- 'Lychette'	CAby CAvo EBee ECha EHrv GBuc IBlr ITim LPhx MAvo NDov NSla NWCA SHar WCru WLin
	- 'Martin'	CStu
	- 'Monstrosa'	CDes EBee EPot GBuc WCot
	- 'New Pink'	CLAP IBlr
	- 'Parlez Vous'	CMil EBee EHrv EPPr MNrw NDov NMen WCru
	- 'Pentre Pink'	CBos IBlr MNrw MTho WBVN WCru WHal WIvy
	- 'Picos Pink'	EHrv SCnR
	- pink-flowered	CLAP LPhx WCru
	- 'Pink Carpet'	GBuc GEdr
	- 'Robinsoniana' ♀H4	More than 30 suppliers
	- 'Rosea'	CAvo CLAP GEdr GMac MNFA WCru
	- 'Royal Blue'	CAvo CDes CLAP CMil CNic CStu EBee ECha EHrv EPPr EPot ETow GBuc GEdr LAma MAvo MNFA NDov NMen SBla WCot WCru WFar WPnP WTin
	- 'Tinney's Blush'	SSpi
	- 'Tinney's Double' (d)	NPar
	- 'Tomas'	CDes EBee GBin GMac
	- 'Vestal' (d) ♀H4	More than 30 suppliers
	- 'Virescens' ♀H4	CAby CAvo CLAP CStu EBee EChP ECha EHrv EPPr EPot ERos GCrs GEdr GMaP NDov NPar NSla WHal WIvy WLin WPGP
	- 'Viridiflora'	CFil CFwr CLAP EBee EPfP GBuc LPhx MNrw MRav MTho NBir NSti SSpi WCot WCru WFar WSHC
	- 'Westwell Pink'	CBos CDes EBee MSte SIgm WCot WPGP
	- 'Wilks' Giant'	EBee WCot WCru
	- 'Wilks' White'	CLAP EBee GEdr LBuc WCru
	- 'Wyatt's Pink'	CBos CLAP CPom GBuc LPhx MAvo WCru WPnP WTin
	- 'Yerda Ramusem'	EBee ECho
	nemorosa x ***ranunculoides***	see *A.* x *lipsiensis*
	obtusiloba	CLAP GBuc GCrs GTou MTho SBla SRms WAbe
	- CLD 1549	GEdr
	- J&JA 4.044.010	NWCA
	- ***alba***	GMac SBla WAbe
I	- 'Sulphurea'	GEdr
	- yellow	GBuc SBla
	palmata	CFwr CLAP EPot MDKP NBre SMad SSpi WCru
	parviflora	CHea GBuc WGwG
	pavonina	CDes CSpe ECha ERos MAsh MBri MTho NBir SBla SIgm SRot SVal
	- 'Chapeau de Cardinal'	SBla
	- 'Grecian Sunset'	CDes MAsh
	polyanthes	GTou LRHS

- HWJK 2337	WCru
aff. ***polyanthes***	WCot
- ex ACE	SIgm
prattii	CFwr GEdr
pseudoaltaica	WCot WCru
- pale blue-flowered	CLAP
pulsatilla	see *Pulsatilla vulgaris*
quinquefolia **new**	WAbe WCot
ranunculoides ♀H4	More than 30 suppliers
- 'Frank Waley'	WCot
* - ***laciniata***	CLAP GBuc MSte NMen WCot
- 'Pleniflora' (d)	CAvo CBgR CDes CFwr CHea CLAP ECha EHrv EHyt EPot GBBs GCrs GMaP MRav NLar NMen SBla WCot WFar WIvy
- subsp. ***wockeana***	CBgR CDes CFwr EBee
riparia	see *A. virginiana* var. *alba*
rivularis	More than 30 suppliers
- B&SWJ 7611	WCru
- CLD 573	CDes WLin
- GWJ 1259	WCru
rupicola	GKev GMac NBir NWCA SRot SSpi
x ***seemannii***	see *A.* x *lipsiensis*
smithiana from China **new**	CFwr
stellata	see *A. hortensis*
sulphurea	see *Pulsatilla alpina* subsp. *apiifolia*
sylvestris	More than 30 suppliers
§ - 'Elise Fellmann' (d)	CDes CLAP EMan GBuc IGor SHar WCot
- 'Flore Pleno' (d) **new**	WCot
- 'Macrantha'	CLAP CPen CPrp EChP EMan EPfP GAbr GMac LAst SSpi WPGP
'Taiwan's Tiny Treasure'	WCru
tetrasepala	CLAP WPGP
§ ***tomentosa***	EBee ECha EMan EMar GGar GKev GSki IGor LRHS MAnH MWhi NArg SDix SRms WBVN WFar WGwG WWeb
§ - 'Albadura'	CFwr EPza GSki
- 'Robustissima'	see *A.* x *hybrida* 'Robustissima'
- 'Rose Beauty' **new**	NArg
trifolia	CAby CDes EBee ECha EHyt EMan EPPr EPot ERos GMac NDov SCnR SRms SSpi SUsu WCot WPGP WPat
- pink	CDes CLAP MSte WFar
- 'Semiplena' (d)	CAby CDes EBee WCot
trullifolia	EPfP ETow GBin GCra GCrs GEdr GFlt GGar GKev GMac ITim LRHS MMHG MRav SBla
- ***alba***	GBBs GTou
- var. ***coelestina***	CDes GBBs GBuc GCra GTou NBir
vernalis	see *Pulsatilla vernalis*
virginiana	CFir EBee EPPr EWll GAbr LDai MAnH MDKP MFOX MSte MWrn NBid NBur NRnb WBVN WFar WOut
§ - var. ***alba***	EKen NArg NLar NSti WBVN
vitifolia misapplied	see *A. tomentosa*
vitifolia DC.	GKev
- B&SWJ 2320	WCru
- B&SWJ 8202 from Vietnam **new**	WCru
- GWJ 9434	WCru
- HWJ 682	WCru
- HWJK 2044	WCru

Anemonella (*Ranunculaceae*)

thalictroides	More than 30 suppliers
- 'Alba Plena' (d)	GBuc
- 'Amelia'	GEdr NPar SOkd WAbe
- 'Betty Blake' (d)	GCrs GEdr
- 'Cameo'	EFEx SCnR WCru
- 'Charlotte' **new**	NHar
- 'Double Green' (d)	EFEx
- 'Flore Pleno' (d)	GCrs
- 'Full Double White' (d)	CWCL EFEx GEdr
- 'Green Hurricane' (d)	EFEx
- 'Jade Feather' **new**	CGra SBla
- f. ***rosea***	CElw CLAP CPom CWCL EPot GBuc GCrs GKir WCru WPrP
- - double pink (d)	SBla
- - 'Oscar Schoaf' (d)	CLAP WAbe
- semi-double pink (d)	CLAP
- semi-double white (d)	CLAP EHrv ETow GBuc NMen SBla SOkd SRot WCot
- 'Snowball' (d)	CGra
- 'Snowflakes' (d)	NPar
- 'White Bells' **new**	NHar

Anemonopsis (*Ranunculaceae*)

macrophylla	CBos CBro CElw CLAP EHyt EMan EPPr GBuc GCal GIBF IGor LPhx LRHS MNrw MSte MTho NLar SBla SOkd SSpi WAbe WCru WSHC

Anemopsis (*Saururaceae*)

californica	CDes EBee EMan EWes NLar WCru

Anethum (*Apiaceae*)

graveolens	CArn CHrt GPoy LRHS MBow MChe MHer MWat SECG SIde WPer WSel
- 'Dukat'	CSev ELau MChe NGHP
- fern-leaved	EOHP

Angelica (*Apiaceae*)

acutiloba	EBee EMan EWll GIBF NSti SBla SIgm WCot WFar
archangelica	More than 30 suppliers
- 'Corinne Tremaine' (v)	EBee EMan EMar EVFa NGHP NSti NTHB WCHb WCot
arguta	WCot
atropurpurea	CPLG CPom EChP ECtt EMan EVFa EWll EWsh GKev LEdu MAnH MHer MNrw NBur NCGa NGHP NLar NSti WCAu WCHb WFar WJek WMnd
cincta **new**	GIBF
dahurica	CArn EBee EUnu MSal
- B&SWJ 8603	WCru
decursiva	LPio MSal NDov
- B&SWJ 5746	WCru
florentii	GIBF WPGP
genuflexa **new**	GIBF
gigas	More than 30 suppliers
- B&SWJ 4170	WCru
* ***hispanica***	CArn CBod CHid CSpe EChP ELan EMFP EPyc EWll GBar GKir LEdu LPhx MCCP MHer MLLN NBir NGHP NTHB NVic SGar SIde SMad SPav SWal WCHb WCru WLin WPGP WSHC
japonica	LEdu
- B&SWJ 8816a	WCru
keiskei B&SWJ 8816b	WCru
leariloba	WLin
montana	see *A. sylvestris*
pachycarpa	CBct EBee EChP ELan EMan EOHP EUnu EWTr LPio MAvo MFOX NCGa NJOw SIgm SMad SPav WCot WFar WGwG WJek WPer WWpP WWye
pubescens	CSec LEdu MSte NDov
- B&SWJ 5593	WCru

	- var. ***matsumurae*** B&SWJ 6387	WCru
	razulii	EUnu
	sachalinensis	EBee GIBF
	saxatilis	EBee GIBF
	sinensis	EUnu GPoy WCHb
	'Summer Delight'	CRez CSpe EKen EMFP EMan ITer SPav SPoG WWpP
§	***sylvestris***	CAgr CArn CHrt CRWN GBar WCHb WHer WWpP
*	- 'Purpurea'	CKno CMil CSpe EWes GCal GKir SBla SDnm WGwG WPGP
	- 'Vicar's Mead'	EVFa LPhx MAnH NCGa NChi NDov SUsu WCHb WCot WHil
	taiwaniana	CRez CSec EBee ELan ITer WCot
	ursina	EUnu GIBF MAnH NBPC

angelica see *Angelica archangelica*

Angelonia (*Scrophulariaceae*)

sp.	CSpe
Angelface Blue Bicolour = 'Anstern' (Angelface Series)	LAst
angustifolia Angel Mist Series **new**	NPri
'Stella Gem'	LRHS

Anigozanthos (*Haemodoraceae*)

flavidus	CHEx CTbh CTrC ECre EOHP MBri SPlb
- 'Ember'	SVil
- 'Illusion'	SVil
- 'Opal'	SPoG SVil
- 'Pearl'	SPoG SVil
- 'Splendour'	SPoG SVil
- yellow	WBrE
manglesii ♀H1	CHEx GGar SPlb WBrE WDyG
rufus **new**	WCot

anise see *Pimpinella anisum*

Anisodontea (*Malvaceae*)

§	***capensis***	CBcs CPLG EBee EChP ELan EMan ERea GGar GKir LAst MBNS NBir SChu SLim SMrm SRkn SRms SWvt WDyG XPep
	- 'Tara's Pink'	EPfP LPhx MAsh MBNS SAga SMrm SPoG
	'Elegant Lady'	GFai
	huegelii	see *Alyogyne huegelii*
	x ***hypomadara*** misapplied	see *A. capensis*
§	x ***hypomadara*** (Sprague) D.M. Bates	ECtt SRms
	malvastroides	XPep
	scabrosa	CChe XPep

Anisodus (*Solanaceae*)

	carnioliciodes BWJ 7501 **new**	WCru
§	***luridus***	MGol MSal WWye

Anisotome (*Apiaceae*)

sp.	NSti
pilifera	EMan

Annona (*Annonaceae*)

cherimola (F)	XBlo
muricata (F)	XBlo

Anoiganthus see *Cyrtanthus*

Anomalesia see *Gladiolus*

Anomatheca (*Iridaceae*)

	cruenta	see *A. laxa*
	grandiflora	CHll ERos
§	***laxa*** ♀H2-3	More than 30 suppliers
	- var. ***alba*** ♀H2-3	CNic CPLG CPom CRHN CSpe CStu EHrv ELan ERos IBal MTho NMen SBch SSpi WAbe WBrk WCFE
	- ***albomaculata***	LRHS
	- blue	ERos SIng WAbe
	- 'Joan Evans'	CElw CNic CRHN CStu ECtt ELan ERos ITim LTwo NMen NWCA SRms WAbe WBrk WHrl
	- red spot	CPLG SGar WLFP
	viridis	CPLG CPou EBee ERos LRHS

Anopterus (*Escalloniaceae*)

glandulosus	IBlr WCru

Anredera (*Basellaceae*)

§	***cordifolia***	CFwr CPLN CRHN ECho EShb LEdu LRHS

Antennaria (*Asteraceae*)

	aprica	see *A. parvifolia*
	dioica	CBrm CTri GPoy MHer NBlu NFla NJOw NLon SPlb SRms WFar WRHF WWye
	- 'Alba'	EDAr EHoe
	- 'Alex Duguid'	GCrs GMaP LBee LRHS SBla
	- 'Aprica'	see *A. parvifolia*
§	- var. ***hyperborea***	LGro
	- 'Minima'	ECho EPot NBro NJOw NMen SIng WAbe
	- 'Nyewoods Variety'	EPot NLAp
*	- 'Rubra'	CTri ECha EDAr MHer NMen NPri SBla WDyG
	- ***tomentosa***	see *A. dioica* var. *hyperborea*
	'Joy'	SBla
	macrophylla hort.	see *A. microphylla*
§	***microphylla***	EDAr EHoe ESis LGro MBar NFla SRms WEas WPat WPer
	neglecta	ECho
§	***parvifolia***	CNic CTri MBar NLar SRms WAbe WMoo WPer
	- var. ***rosea***	see *A. microphylla*
	plantaginifolia	EBee
	'Red Wonder'	CMea NLar
§	***rosea*** ♀H4	CWCL ECho GBBs GKir NLAp NMen NVic SPlb SRms WFar

Anthemis ✿ (*Asteraceae*)

	from Turkey	LLWP
§	'Beauty of Grallagh'	ECtt ERou GBuc GCal GMac IGor MDKP MRav NCGa NGdn SDix SHel WCot WWpP
	'Cally Cream'	GCal
	'Cally White'	GCal
	carpatica	NBro WGHP WLin
	- 'Karpatenschnee'	CRez EBee NBre WDyG
§	***cretica*** subsp. ***cretica***	CLyd
	- - NS 754	NWCA
	frutescens	see *Argyranthemum frutescens*
	'Grallagh Gold' misapplied (orange-yellow)	see *A.* 'Beauty of Grallagh'
§	'Grallagh Gold'	EBla ECha ECtt EMon EWes LDai LPhx LRHS MBri MRav MWat NPer WCAu WFar WTel

§ ***marschalliana***	CPBP ECha EDAr EPot IHMH LBee MSte SMrm
montana	see *A. cretica* subsp. *cretica*
nobilis	see *Chamaemelum nobile*
punctata	CSLe
- subsp. ***cupaniana*** ♀H3-4	More than 30 suppliers
- - 'Nana'	EMon GKir NPer SHar
rudolphiana	see *A. marschalliana*
sancti-johannis	CPrp CWib EBee EBla ERou IGor LDai MBri MRav MSal NArg NPer SDix SPet SPoG SRms SUsu WFar WMnd WMoo WPer WWpP
'Sauce Béarnaise'	EMon WMnd
Susanna Mitchell = 'Blomit'	CHar CHea EBee EBla EChP ECtt EMan EPfP ERou EWll GKir GMaP GMac LRHS MMil MNrw MSph NBir NCGa NDov SBla SMrm WCAu WCra WMnd WSHC WTin WWeb WWhi XPep
'Tetworth'	CStr EBee EBla EChP ECha EHrv ELan EMan EMon EVFa EWin GBuc GMac MSte NCGa SChu SMad SUsu WCot WFar WPer WWpP
tinctoria	CArn CHby EBee ECha ELau EMon EPza GKir GPoy LRHS MBow MChe MHer NFor NLon NPer SPet SWvt WJek WWye
- from Judaea	EMon
- 'Alba'	EMan LPhx SChu WPer WWpP
* - 'Compacta'	EWes LPhx
- dwarf	EBee EBla EWin GMac SBla SBri SUsu WFar WWpP
- 'E.C. Buxton'	More than 30 suppliers
- 'Eva'	EMon LRHS MBNS NDov NLar WEas WWhi WWpP
I - 'Golden Rays'	EBee EWin MDKP NPro SDix
- 'Kelwayi'	CPrp CSBt CTri EBee ECtt EPfP ERou GKir GMaP LRHS MBNS NArg NBPC NBro NPer SMer SPer SPla SRms WFar WGHP WMnd WPer WWpP
- 'Lemon Maid'	CFir EPPr GCal SChu SMrm
- 'Pride of Grallagh'	see *A.* 'Beauty of Grallagh'
- 'Sauce Hollandaise'	More than 30 suppliers
- 'Wargrave Variety'	More than 30 suppliers
triumfettii	NPer
tuberculata	EMan LRHS NChi SBla
'White Water' **new**	WAbe

Anthericum (*Anthericaceae*)

algeriense	see *A. liliago* var. *major*
baeticum	EBee ERos
* ***fistulosum***	GSki
liliago	CAby CBro CFil CSec EBee EBrs ELan ERos EWTr GCal GKev GMaP GSki MAnH MAvo MLLN MRav MSte MWgw NCGa SBla SPer SSvw WPer
§ - var. ***major*** ♀H4	CAvo CDes EBee ECha EHrv GBuc IBlr IGor LPhx SSpi WPGP
ramosum	CDes EBee EBrs EChP ECha ELan EMan EPot ERos EWTr EWes GKev GSki LPhx LRHS MBrN MLLN NBid NBir NCGa NEgg NWCA SIng SMrm SOkd SUsu WLin WPer
- ***plumosum***	see *Trichopetalum plumosum*
saundersiae	CPne
undulatum	ERos

Antholyza (*Iridaceae*)

coccinea	see *Crocosmia paniculata*
crocosmioides	see *Crocosmia latifolia*
paniculata	see *Crocosmia paniculata*

Anthoxanthum (*Poaceae*)

odoratum	CArn CBig CRWN ELau GBar GIBF GPoy NBre WWye

Anthriscus (*Apiaceae*)

cerefolium	CArn CHrt CSev EOHP GPoy ILis MBow MChe MDun MHer NPri SECG WJek WLHH WPer WSel
sylvestris	CAgr CArn WShi
- 'Broadleas Blush'	CNat
- 'Hullavington' (v)	CNat
- 'Kabir'	CNat
- 'Moonlit Night'	EHoe
- 'Ravenswing'	More than 30 suppliers

Anthurium (*Araceae*)

amazonicum	MBri
andraeanum ♀H1	MBri
- 'Glowing Pink' **new**	XBlo
- 'Red Heart' **new**	XBlo
'Aztec' **new**	XBlo
crenatum **new**	XBlo
'Crimson'	XBlo
'Magenta'	XBlo
'Porcelaine White'	XBlo
scherzerianum ♀H1	MBri

Anthyllis (*Papilionaceae*)

barba-jovis	CSpe EMan XPep
hermanniae	XPep
- 'Compacta'	see *A. hermanniae* 'Minor'
§ - 'Minor'	EPot NLar WLin
montana	SBla
- subsp. ***atropurpurea***	LRHS
- 'Rubra' ♀H4	EChP ECho EDAr EMan EPot LTwo NMen
vulneraria	CFee EWin GTou MChe NMir NRya WBVN WBWf WHer
- var. ***coccinea***	CHar CMil CSpe EMan GAbr GGar GKev MCCP MLLN MSte MTho NSla NWCA SGar SPet WAbe WBVN WFar WHil
- subsp. ***pulchella*** **new**	GKev

Antigonon (*Polygonaceae*)

leptopus	MJnS

Antirrhinum (*Scrophulariaceae*)

asarina	see *Asarina procumbens*
barrelieri	CSpe EBee
braun-blanquetii	CHal EBee EMFP EMan ERou EWin MLLN STes WCAu WCot WHil WPtf
'Candy Stripe'	EMan
Chandelier Primrose Vein = 'Yaprim'PBR	LSou
Chandelier Rose Pink = 'Yarob'PBR **new**	LSou
glutinosum	see *A. hispanicum* subsp. *hispanicum*
graniticum	EBee
§ ***hispanicum***	NBir SBla
- 'Avalanche'	CHal ECtt EMan EWin LAst MLan NLon SPet
- subsp. ***hispanicum***	CSpe SRot WSPU XPep
§ - - 'Roseum'	CMea CPom CSpe EDAr EMan SPet
latifolium	XPep
majus	XPep
- 'Black Prince'	CHad CSpe EMan EShb MAnH SAga WMoo
- 'Candy Snap' (v)	LAst

	- subsp. ***majus***	EWll
	- 'Powys Pride' (v)	EWll
	- 'Taff's White' (v)	LRHS
	molle	CPom CSpe ECtt EHyt GKev MSte NBir NPer NWCA SAga SRot SUsu
	- pink	CSWP MSte
	'Night and Day' **new**	CSpe MAnH
I	'Pendula Lampion Appleblossom'	LAst LSou
I	'Pendula Lampion Purple'	LAst LSou
I	'Pendula Lampion Salmon/Orange'	LAst LSou
	pulverulentum	EHyt LPhx MArl SAga
	sempervirens	EMan EWin NGdn WHil
	siculum	EBee WMoo

añu see *Tropaeolum tuberosum*

Aphanes (*Rosaceae*)

§	***arvensis***	MSal WWye

Aphelandra (*Acanthaceae*)

	squarrosa	CHal LRHS MBri
I	- 'Citrina' **new**	XBlo

Aphyllanthes (*Aphyllanthaceae*)

	monspeliensis	CFee EBee ECho SBla

Apios (*Papilionaceae*)

§	***americana***	CAgr CMdw CPLN CPom CWan EBee EChP EMan EMon GBin LEdu MCCP NBir NSti SSpi WBVN WCot WCru WSHC
	tuberosa	see *A. americana*

Apium (*Apiaceae*)

	graveolens	CArn CBgR CBod CWan ELau EOHP GPoy MBow MHer MSal SIde WJek
	- (Secalinum Group) 'Par-cel'	MHer NGHP

Apium x *Petroselinum* (*Apiaceae*)

	hybrid	see *A. graveolens* Secalinum Group

Apocynum (*Apocynaceae*)

	cannabinum	CArn GPoy MGol MSal WWye

Aponogeton (*Aponogetonaceae*)

	distachyos	CDWL CRow CWat EHon ELan EMFW EPfP LNCo LPBA NArg NBlu NPer SCoo WFar WPnP WPop WWpP

apple see *Malus domestica*

apricot see *Prunus armeniaca*

Aptenia (*Aizoaceae*)

	cordifolia ♀H1-2	CSec CSev EOHP LRav NPer SChr SDnm SEND SPet WRos XPep
	- 'Variegata' (v)	EWin MRav

Aquilegia ✿ (*Ranunculaceae*)

	akitensis hort.	see *A. flabellata*, *A. flabellata* var. *pumila*
*	***alba variegata*** (v)	WEas
	alpina	CBot CMea EBee ECtt EDAr ELau EPfP ESis GKir GTou MHer MLan MRav NFor NJOw SPer SPet SRms WCAu WFar WMoo WPer
	- 'Alba'	CM&M NLon NOak
	'Alpine Blue'	NArg
	amaliae	see *A. ottonis* subsp. *amaliae*
	amurensis **new**	CLAP
	'Anja' (v)	WCot
	'Apple Blossom'	GKev LSou
	aragonensis	see *A. pyrenaica*
§	***atrata***	CPou GSki MDKP NEgg SBch SMHy WBVN WPer WWpP
	atrovinosa	EBee
	aurea misapplied	see *A. vulgaris* golden-leaved
	barnebyi	GKev NEgg
	bernardii	EWTr NJOw NOak WHil
	bertolonii ♀H4	EBee EHyt EPot GCrs GGar GKev GTou LBee LRHS NDlv NMen NOak SBla SRms WHoo WPat
	- ***alba***	WLin
	Biedermeier Group	EMil GKir IHMH LRHS MBNS MDKP NOrc NRnb WFar WPer WWpP
	'Black Majic' **new**	EMag
	'Blue Berry'	WPat
	'Blue Jay' (Songbird Series)	CFai ENot NPri SSvw SWvt
	'Blue Star' (Star Series)	CSim EBee ECtt LRHS WPer
	'Bluebird' (Songbird Series) ♀H2	GBBs NArg NPer SWvt
	buergeriana	MDKP NChi NEgg STes WPer
	- 'Calimero'	MDKP NGby NLar WHil
	- var. ***oxysepala***	see *A. oxysepala*
	'Bunting' (Songbird Series) ♀H2	EWll NLar SSvw SWvt
	'Burnished Rose'	EKen NPro NRnb WHil
	'Cally Spice' **new**	GCal
	canadensis ♀H4	CMHG CPom CSim EBee EBrs EDAr ELan GSki MHer MSte NBid NBir NBro NEgg NOak NWCA SGar SMac SRms SSpi SUsu WPer
	- 'Corbett'	GBuc
	- 'Little Lanterns'	CBgR EBee EMar EPPr GKev MDKP MSte NLar SMar WWeb
	- 'Nana'	CStu EPot GBuc MDKP NLAp WPat
	'Cardinal' (Songbird Series)	CFai ENot EWll MBri NLar NPri SPer SSvw SWvt
	cazorlensis	see *A. pyrenaica* subsp. *cazorlensis*
	'Chaffinch' (Songbird Series)	MBri
§	***chaplinei***	NBir NEgg SBch SIgm WEas
	chrysantha	CBot CHea CHrt CWan EBee GAbr GBin GCal GKev MLLN MNFA NOak SMar SRms WAbe WBrE WEas WLin WPer
	- var. ***chaplinei***	see *A. chaplinei*
I	- 'Flore Pleno' (d)	EMag MDKP NEgg
	- 'Yellow Queen'	CBot CHea COIW CSpe EBee EGoo EPfP GGar LAst MAvo MDKP NBre NLar NLsd NRnb SOkh SPla SPur SSvw SWal WHil WSan
	clematiflora	see *A. vulgaris* var. *stellata*
	coerulea ♀H4	EWTr GKev SIgm SRms WLin
	- 'Himmelblau' **new**	EGoo
	- 'Mrs Nicholls'	MBri
	- 'Rotstern' **new**	EGoo
	'Colorado' (State Series)	CFai EMar
	'Crimson Star'	CHea COIW CPen ENot EPfP GKir MDKP NCGa SPur WMoo
	'Debutante'	MDKP WGwG
	desertorum	CPom EBee MDKP SMac
	discolor	EPot EWTr GSki GTou LBee LRHS LTwo NEgg NMen NRnb WPat
	'Double Chocolate'	LRHS
	Double Rubies (d)	CHea NLsd NRnb SHar
	'Dove' (Songbird Series) ♀H2	CFai EWll MBri MHer NArg NLar NPri SHar SWvt WCra

I 'Dragonfly' CBcs EPfP GAbr MBri NBlu NJOw NMir SPer SPet SPur WFar

ecalcarata see *Semiaquilegia ecalcarata*

einseleana EBee NEgg

elegantula GCrs NEgg

'Firewheel' see *A. vulgaris* var. *stellata* 'Firewheel'

§ ***flabellata*** ♀[H4] CTri EBee GGar NEgg WPat WPer

- from Rebun-tō, Japan **new** CStu

§ - f. ***alba*** CTri ELan NEgg NWCA SBla WEas

* - - 'White Angel' NLar WPer

- 'Blue Angel' CBcs EDAr WPer

- Cameo Series CBrm EWll MAvo NArg NJOw WFar WGor WHil

- - 'Cameo Pink and White' MHer

- - 'Cameo Pink' MDKP

- - 'Cameo Rose' NBir

- Jewel Series CSpe ECho NBlu NLar SPet WHil WPer

- - 'Blue Jewel' SPla

- - 'Pink Jewel' EHyt SPla

- - 'White Jewel' GKev SPla

- 'Ministar' ECho EDAr EPfP EPyc GKir GSki LRHS MBNS MHer NCGa NVic SPet SRot WFar WHil WPer

- 'Nana Alba' see *A. flabellata* var. *pumila* f. *alba*

I - ***nana yezoense*** GFlt

§ - var. ***pumila*** ♀[H4] CBrm ECha EHyt EPfP EPyc GAbr GKev GTou MAvo MDKP MNFA NEgg SBla SIng WFar WHil WLin WPat WPer

§ - - f. ***alba*** ♀[H4] CBot ECha EWTr GKev LBee LRHS MBNS MFOX MSte SIng SRms WHil

- - f. ***kurilensis*** MSte

* - - 'Snowflakes' EHyt

flavescens WPer

formosa GGar MDKP NChi NEgg NPri WPer

- var. ***truncata*** GBin GBuc MLLN

§ ***fragrans*** CBot COIW EBee GBBs GBin GEdr MTho NEgg NOak NRnb SOkd STes WHil WHoo WLin WRha

- white-flowered ELan

glandulosa CMHG EBee GKev NDlv NEgg NLar SOkd WEas

glauca see *A. fragrans*

'Golden Guiness' EMag

'Goldfinch' (Songbird Series) CBot CFai ENot EWll NArg NBir NPri SWvt

grata MBNS MDKP NRnb

Harbutt's hybrids ERou

§ 'Hensol Harebell' ♀[H4] CPou CSWP GBuc MBow MWgw SHar SPer SRms WHoo WPtf

'Ice Blue' WCot

'Irish Elegance' EGoo WRha

japonica see *A. flabellata* var. *pumila*

'Jenny' MDKP

jonesii CGra ITim LBee WAbe

jonesii x ***saximontana*** GFlt GKev ITim

karelinii CPen MWrn NEgg SRob

'Koralle' COIW MDKP NRnb WFar

'Kristall' EBee ERou LAst MDKP NOak NRnb SSvw STes WHil

kuhistanica EBee

Langdon's Rainbow hybrids MAnH MDKP

laramiensis CGra CPBP MDKP NEgg WAbe

'Lavender and White' (Songbird Series) see *A.* 'Nuthatch'

'Little Plum' **new** WHil

longissima ♀[H4] CHar EBrs GBri GBuc MHer MLLN NEgg NRnb SBla SHar STes WEas WHoo

'Magpie' see *A. vulgaris* 'William Guiness'

'Maxi' COIW MDKP WHil

McKana Group ELan ENot EPfP GMaP LAst LRHS MWgw NEgg NFor NGdn NLon NOak NRnb NVic SPer SPlb SRms WCAu WMnd

'Mellow Yellow' ECtt EMag GBuc GKev MBNS MDKP NRnb SGSe SIgm WHil WMoo WPer WRos

'Milk and Honey' CBre EMag GBBs LSou MAvo MGol NArg NRnb WHil

moorcroftiana NEgg

- CC 1371 WCra

Mrs Scott-Elliot hybrids COIW CSBt EHol GAbr IGor LIck MLan NEgg SGar SPer WFar

Music Series ♀[H4] NOak SRms

nigricans see *A. atrata*

§ 'Nuthatch' (Songbird Series) CFai EMar NEgg WCra

'Olympia Red and Gold' COIW

olympica CPen EWes LPhx MDHE NEgg WPer

Origami Series **new** WHil

§ ***ottonis*** subsp. ***amaliae*** EBee GEdr NEgg WAbe WLin

§ ***oxysepala*** CPLG GCal GIBF NEgg WCru

- B&SWJ 4775 WCru

'Perfumed Garden' EBrs NArg

pubiflora WLin

'Purple Emperor' LRHS

§ ***pyrenaica*** GKev WLin

§ - subsp. ***cazorlensis*** NEgg

'Raspberry Ice' ITim

'Red Hobbit' CBrm CSpe ENot EVFa GAbr IBal ITim LRHS MAvo MDKP NBPC NJOw NWCA WFar WHil WHoo

'Red Star' (Star Series) CSim EBee ECtt ERou MDKP SHar WHil WPer

'Robin' (Songbird Series) CBot CFai NPri SWvt

rockii EBee GCal MBNS MDKP NEgg WHil WLin

- B&SWJ 7965 WCru

'Roman Bronze' see *Aquilegia* x *Semiaquilegia* 'Roman Bronze'

'Rose Queen' COIW CSim MDKP SSvw WHil WHoo

'Roundway Chocolate' CBot

saximontana CGra CStu EHyt GKev GTou ITim NLar NWCA WPer

§ 'Schneekönigin' WPer

scopulorum CGra EPot NEgg SBla WAbe

shockleyi GBuc

sibirica CPLG WPer

'Silver Queen' ELan MDKP MLan NLsd

'Simone's White' EBee

skinneri CHrt CSec EBee EBrs EChP EWTr EWsh GBBs GBin GFlt GSki ITer MBNS MBct MHer MWat NCGa NEgg NLsd NRnb SAga SHGN SPoG STes SWal WCru WMnd WMoo WRha WRos

- from Mexico CHar

Snow Queen see *A.* 'Schneekönigin'

Songbird Series CSpe LRHS MLLN NEgg NPri WFar

'Spring Magic Blue and White' (Spring Magic Series) MAvo WHil

stellata see *A. vulgaris* var. *stellata*

'Stoulton Blue' CHea EBee WSPU

'Sunburst Ruby' GAbr MBri MDKP NEgg NOak NPro SMad SPoG WHoo WMoo WRos

'Sweet Lemon Drops' EBee LSou NRnb STes WHil

'Sweet Rainbows' (d) GBBs LSou
thalictrifolia LPhx
transsilvanica EBee
triternata EBee GCal NEgg NWCA SIgm
viridiflora CBot CHar CSec CTri ECrN GBuc MHer MTho NRnb SBla SHGN SMHy WCru WEas WFar WHil WMnd WPer WPrP WWhi
- bronze-flowered SMHy
- hybrid SMHy
- yellow-flowered SMHy
vulgaris CArn CHrt CMHG CRWN EPfP GPoy LLWP MBow MChe MGol NBro SGar SPlb WBWf WCAu WGwG WMoo WPer WSSM WShi WTin WWye
- 'Adelaide Addison' ECha GBri GBuc GMac MFOX NEgg SBla WEas WFar
- var. ***alba*** CMea LLWP MNFA SEND WCAu WWhi
- 'Aureovariegata' see *A. vulgaris* Vervaeneana Group
- ***clematiflora*** see *A. vulgaris* var. *stellata*
- var. ***flore-pleno*** (d) EChP LLWP WPer
- - black-flowered (d) WCot
- - 'Blue Bonnet' (d) ERou WHil
- - blue-flowered (d) WCot
- - 'Burgundy' (d) CMil
- - Dorothy Series GBuc LRHS
- - - 'Dorothy Rose' (d) SAga
- - 'Double Pleat' blue/white (d) WHil WPer
- - 'Double Pleat' pink/white (d) NGdn WHil WPer
* - - 'Frilly Dilly Rose' (d) STes
* - - 'Frilly Dilly Sky Blue' (d) STes
- - 'Jane Hollow' (d) CPou
- - pale blue-flowered (d) LLWP NRnb
- - 'Pink Bonnet' (d) WMnd
- - pink-flowered (d) GGar
- - 'Powder Blue' (d) CHea
- - purple-flowered (d) LLWP
- - red-flowered (d) GGar
- - 'Strawberry Ice Cream' (d) CPen GBri NBro NBur
- - 'Tower Light Blue' (Tower Series) EGoo
- - 'Tower White' (Tower Series) (d) EGoo MWrn
* - - 'White Bonnet' (d) SRos
- - white-flowered (d) LLWP LPhx
§ - golden-leaved ECha ECho GKev
- Grandmother's Garden Group EWll
- 'Heidi' CBot EWll WPer
- 'Magpie' see *A. vulgaris* 'William Guiness'
- 'Miss Coventry' SMHy
- Munstead White see *A. vulgaris* 'Nivea'
§ - 'Nivea' ♀H4 CBot CNic CPou ECha LAst SBla SBri WHoo
- 'Pink Spurless' see *A. vulgaris* var. *stellata* pink-flowered
- 'Pom Pom Crimson' (Pom Pom Series) NBro NBur WCot
§ - var. ***stellata*** CHrt ELan EMan EPot EWsh GBuc GFlt GKev MBNS MWgw NArg NBro NEgg NLsd WLin WMoo WPer WWeb
- - Barlow Series (d) NJOw WFar
- - - 'Black Barlow' (d) CBcs CBod CFwr COIW EBee EChP ECtt EGoo ELan EMar EWll GFlt GGar GKir IBal MBri MDKP MNrw NCob NOrc SHBN SPer SPoG STes WAul WMnd WSan WWeb
- - - 'Blue Barlow' (d) CBgR CFwr EBee ECtt EMar EWll GCal GKir MBri SPer WMnd WPer WSan WWeb
- - - 'Christa Barlow' (d) EChP LRHS WWeb
- - - 'Nora Barlow' (d) ♀H4 More than 30 suppliers
- - - 'Rose Barlow' (d) CBgR EWTr GCal WMnd WWeb
- - - 'White Barlow' (d) CFwr
§ - - 'Firewheel' EBee EMag MDKP STes WMoo
- - 'Greenapples' (d) EBee EMan MAvo MCCP MDKP NRnb WCot WWhi
§ - - pink-flowered LLWP
- - purple-flowered LLWP
- - red-flowered ELan LLWP
- - 'Royal Purple' (d) GFlt LSou MBNS NBro SPoG WBVN
- - 'Ruby Port' (d) CAby CHrt COIW EBee GCal GGar GKir LAst LPhx MBri MNrw MRav MTis NChi NPri SHGN SPla SSvw STes SUsu WFar WMnd WPrP
- - 'Ruby Port' crimped (d) NDov WPnP WWol
- - 'Sunlight White' (d) WMnd WPer
§ - - white-flowered CSpe NBro WFar WHal
* - - 'Woodside Blue' ECtt MFOX
* - - 'Woodside Pink' MWgw
- variegated foliage see *A. vulgaris* Vervaeneana Group
§ - Vervaeneana Group (v) More than 30 suppliers
- - 'Graeme Iddon' (v) GBuc
- - 'Woodside' see *A. vulgaris* Vervaeneana Group
- - 'Woodside Blue' (v) COIW EGoo EWTr NRnb
- - 'Woodside Red' (v) NRnb
- - 'Woodside White' (v) EBee GKev MFOX NBir NRnb
- 'Warwick' (d) WCot
- 'Westfaeld' NOak
- 'White Spurless' see *A. vulgaris* var. *stellata* white-flowered
§ - 'William Guiness' More than 30 suppliers
- 'William Guiness Doubles' (d) WMnd
'White Rock' GFlt
'White Star' (Star Series) CSim EBee EPfP ERou LAst WHil WPer
Winky Series MAvo
- formula mixed **new** SMar
- 'Winky Blue and White' LAst WHil WWeb
- 'Winky Purple and White' WWeb
- 'Winky Red and White' IBal LAst WHil WWeb
yabeana CPen EBee GBin GFlt GGar MWrn SBri WHil
'Yellow Star' (Star Series) EGra SDix

Aquilegia x *Semiaquilegia* (*Ranunculaceae*)

blue WCru
§ 'Roman Bronze' EBee GBBs GKev LSou NEgg NOak NPro WCot WWhi WWpP

Arabis (*Brassicaceae*)

albida see *A. alpina* subsp. *caucasica*
alpina NEgg SPlb
§ - subsp. ***caucasica*** GAbr NBlu WFar WLin
- - 'Corfe Castle' ECtt
- - 'Douler Angevine' (v) LIck LSou NPri NPro SPoG
§ - - 'Flore Pleno' (d) ♀H4 CTri ECGP ECha ECtt ELan EWTr GMaP LGro MTho NWoo SRms WEas WFar
- - 'Pink Pearl' NBlu WFar
- - 'Pinkie' ECho
- - 'Rosea' CBrm NArg NBir NBlu NJOw NPri SRms WFar WMoo
§ - - 'Schneehaube' ♀H4 CTri ECho ECtt EPfP EShb GKir GMaP MBar NBlu NJOw NMir SPoG SRms WMoo WPer

- - Snowcap	see *A. alpina* subsp. *caucasica* 'Schneehaube'
- - 'Snowdrop'	MRav NArg NPri WFar
- - 'Variegata' (v)	CBrm ECtt EHoe ELan EPot GMaP LBee MBri MHer NEgg NFor NLon SPoG SRms WEas WFar
androsacea	GTou SRms
x ***arendsii*** 'Compinkie'	ECtt MBow NPri SPlb SRms
- 'Rosabella' (v)	LRHS MBNS
blepharophylla	CSec EPfP MWat SIng SPet SPoG WCot
§ - 'Frühlingszauber' ♀H4	CBcs GKir IHMH NBir NBlu NPri SPoG SRms WBVN WFar
- Spring Charm	see *A. blepharophylla* 'Frühlingszauber'
bryoides	GTou LRHS NMen
caerulea	CBrm
carduchorum	NMen
caucasica	see *A. alpina* subsp. *caucasica*
§ ***collina***	WMoo
§ - subsp. ***rosea***	IHMH
double white	CFee
'Doulier Anguine'	EPot WLin
ferdinandi-coburgi	WEas
- 'Aureovariegata' (v)	CTri ECtt EDAr EHoe GKir IHMH LGro NLon SPet SWvt
- 'Old Gold'	ECtt EDAr EPfP EPot GKir LBee MBar MHer NEgg NJOw NVic SBla SPoG SRms SWvt WAbe WCFE WFar WHoo
- 'Variegata'	see *A. procurrens* 'Variegata'
glabra	WPer
x ***kellereri***	NMen
lucida 'Variegata' (v)	NPro
§ ***procurrens*** 'Variegata' (v) ♀H4	CTri ECha ECtt ELan EPot EWes GKev GKir GTou LBee MBar MHer MWat MWgw NFor SBla SHFr SHGN SPlb SRms WAbe WFar WTel
rosea	see *A. collina* subsp. *rosea*
§ ***scabra***	CNat
§ ***soyeri*** subsp. ***coriacea***	NDlv
stelleri var. ***japonica*** **new**	CNic
stricta	see *A. scabra*
'Tu Tu' **new**	NLar

Arachniodes (*Dryopteridaceae*)

simplicior	NLar WCot WRic

Aralia ✿ (*Araliaceae*)

EDHCH 9720 from China **new**	WCru
armata B&SWJ 3137	WCru
bipinnata B&SWJ 6719	WCru
cachemirica	CDes CHad EBee EWes GCal GIBF NBid NLar SDix SSpi WHal WPGP
californica	EBee EPPr GCal GPoy LEdu MSal MSte NLar SSpi WCru
chapaensis HWJ 723	WCru
chinensis misapplied	see *A. elata*
chinensis L.	CAgr MBNS MSal
- BWJ 8102	WCru
continentalis	EBee EPPr GCal GIBF LEdu NLar
- B&SWJ 4152	WCru
- B&SWJ 8524	WCru
cordata	EBee EWes GAbr GCal LEdu MSal NEgg NLar
- B&SWJ 5511	WCru
decaisneana B&SWJ 3588	WCru
§ ***elata*** ♀H4	More than 30 suppliers
- B&SWJ 5480	WCru
- 'Albomarginata'	see *A. elata* 'Variegata'
- 'Aureovariegata' (v)	CBcs CDoC ELan ENot EPfP MBlu NLar NMoo NPal SBrw WCot WDin WGer WOrn WPat
- 'Golden Umbrella' (v)	CPen NLar
- 'Silver Umbrella'	CPen EPfP MGos NLar
§ - 'Variegata' (v) ♀H4	CBcs CBot CDoC CDul ELan ENot EPfP LRHS MBlu MGos NMoo NPal SBrw SHBN SPoG WCot WDin WGer WPat
foliolosa B&SWJ 8360	WCru
racemosa	CBrm EBee EMar GCal LEdu MLLN MNrw MSal MSte MWgw NLar SRms WFar WHal
sieboldii	see *Fatsia japonica*
spinosa	IArd MBlu NLar WHer

Araucaria (*Araucariaceae*)

angustifolia	LCon
§ ***araucana***	More than 30 suppliers
bidwillii	LCon
§ ***columnaris***	LCon
cunninghamii	LCon
excelsa hort.	see *A. heterophylla*
§ ***heterophylla*** ♀H1	CDoC CTbh EShb GTSp LCon LRHS MBri SAPC SArc WNor
imbricata	see *A. araucana*

Araujia (*Asclepiadaceae*)

angustifolia **new**	CPLN
sericifera	CHEx CMac CPLG CPLN CRHN CSpe CTbh EMil ERea EShb GQui ITer SBra SDnm SGar SPav SSpi WBor WSHC XPep

Arbutus ✿ (*Ericaceae*)

andrachne	CDul CTri EPfP SBrw XPep
x ***andrachnoides*** ♀H4	CAbP CBcs CDul CFil CMHG CPMA ELan EPfP GKir MAsh MWya SAPC SArc SBra SDnm SPer SReu SSpi SSta WHCG WPGP WPat XPep
glandulosa	see *Arctostaphylos glandulosa*
'Marina'	CAbP CDoC CDul CEnd CFil CPMA CSam EBee ELan EPfP LRHS MAsh MBlu MWya SEND SMad SPer SPoG SReu SSpi SSta WFar WPGP WPat
menziesii ♀H3	CBcs CDoC CEnd CFil CMCN CTho ECrN EPfP MAsh MGos MLan NLar SLon SMad SPer SPur SSpi WFar
unedo ♀H4	More than 30 suppliers
- 'Atlantic'	EBee EMil IArd MBri SBrw SPoG SSpi SWvt WGer WPat
- 'Compacta'	CBcs CDoC EBee GKir LPio LRHS MAsh MBri MGos WBcn WDin XPep
- 'Elfin King'	ELan SBrw SDnm SPoG SSpi SSta SWvt
- 'Quercifolia'	EPfP MWya NLar SDnm SReu SSpi SSta WPat
- f. ***rubra*** ♀H4	More than 30 suppliers

Archontophoenix (*Arecaceae*)

alexandrae	CRoM EAmu WMul
cunninghamiana ♀H1	CBrP CRoM CTrC EAmu EShb WMul

Arctanthemum (*Asteraceae*)

§ ***arcticum***	CKno EBee ECha EMFP NBre
- 'Roseum'	CFwr
- 'Schwefelglanz'	NCGa

Arcterica see *Pieris*

Arctium (*Asteraceae*)

lappa	CArn EUnu GBar GPoy MChe MHer MSal NMir SIde WHer
minus	MSal

Arctostaphylos (*Ericaceae*)

§ ***glandulosa***	SAPC SArc
x ***media*** 'Wood's Red'	GKir MBar WFar
myrtifolia	MBar
stanfordiana C&H 105	GGGa
uva-ursi	CArn CTri EBee GPoy GTSp MBar MCoo NBlu NLar NMen SHBN SPer SSta WDin
- 'Massachusetts'	GKir GQui MAsh SMur SReu SSta
- 'Snowcap'	MAsh WWes
- 'Vancouver Jade'	CDoC GKir LRHS LSRN MAsh MBar SBrw SCoo SPoG SReu SSta SWvt WWeb

Arctotheca (*Asteraceae*)

calendula	XPep

Arctotis (*Asteraceae*)

fastuosa	CHrt
- var. ***alba*** 'Zulu Prince'	MOak
x ***hybrida*** 'Apricot'	CAby CHEx EShb EWin LAst LSou SAga SMrm WWol
- 'China Rose'	SMrm
- cream-flowered	CHEx SAga
- 'Flame' ♀H1+3	CAby CBrm CHVG CSpe CWCL EShb EWin LAst LIck MBNS MLan MOak SMrm WEas WWol
* - 'Mahogany' ♀H1+3	CAby CHrt EShb LSou MBNS SAga SUsu WWol
- 'Red Devil'	CAby CHEx CSpe CWCL EWin LAst LIck MBNS SAga SMrm SPoG
- 'Wine'	CBrm CHEx CWCL EWin LAst LSou MBNS MLan SMrm
'Prostrate Raspberry'	CSpe SAga

Ardisia (*Myrsinaceae*)

crenata	LRHS MBri SMur
japonica B&SWJ 3809	WCru
- var. ***angusta***	SOkd WCot
maclurei B&SWJ 3772	LRHS

Areca (*Arecaceae*)

catechu	MBri

Arecastrum see *Syagrus*

Arenaria (*Caryophyllaceae*)

alfacarensis	see *A. lithops*
balearica	LBee LRHS SIng SPlb SRms WDyG
bertolonii	LRHS
festucoides	GTou
ledebouriana	EHyt MWat NLar
§ ***lithops***	CLyd WLin
montana ♀H4	More than 30 suppliers
pinifolia	see *Minuartia circassica*
pulvinata	see *A. lithops*
purpurascens	CPBP ECho EDAr EHyt EPot MBrN SBla SRms SRot
- 'Elliott's Variety'	WPat
tetraquetra	GCrs NMen
§ - subsp. ***amabilis***	EPot LRHS MBar NJOw NMen NSla NWCA
tschuktschorum **new**	GIBF
verna	see *Minuartia verna*

Arenga (*Arecaceae*)

engleri	EAmu WMul

Argemone (*Papaveraceae*)

grandiflora	ELan SBch SPav
hunnemanii **new**	EMan
mexicana	ELan SPav
pleiacantha	LRav SPav

Argyranthemum ✿ (*Asteraceae*)

'Anastasia'	LIck MAJR
'Apricot Surprise'	see *A.* 'Peach Cheeks'
'Beth' **new**	MAJR
'Blanche' (Courtyard Series)	IHMH MAJR
Blazer Eye (Daisy Crazy Series) **new**	LIck
Blazer Primrose = 'Supanova' (Daisy Crazy Series) **new**	MAJR
Blazer Rose = 'Supaglow' PBR (Daisy Crazy Series) **new**	LIck MAJR
Blazer Snow (Daisy Crazy Series) **new**	LIck
Blazer White = 'Supafield' (Daisy Crazy Series) **new**	MAJR
§ 'Blizzard' (d)	ECtt MAJR
Blushing Rose = 'Supaellie' (Daisy Crazy Series)	MAJR
'Bofinger'	MAJR
Boston yellow daisy	see *A. callichrysum*
'Bridesmaid'	MAJR
Bright Carmine = 'Supalight' PBR (Daisy Crazy Series)	LIck MAJR SVil
broussonetii	MAJR
Butterfly = 'Ulyssis' ♀H1+3	EWin LIck MAJR MBNS SVil WGor WWol
§ ***callichrysum***	MAJR
- 'Penny'	MAJR
'Camilla Ponticelli'	LIck MAJR
canariense hort.	see *A. frutescens* subsp. *canariae*
'Champagne'	MAJR
'Cheek's Peach'	see *A.* 'Peach Cheeks'
Cherry Love (Daisy Crazy Series) **new**	LIck MAJR SVil
'Christy Bell' **new**	MAJR
* ***compactum***	MAJR
'Comtesse de Chambord'	MAJR SPet
'Cornish Gold' ♀H1+3	CBcs LIck LSou MAJR MBNS
coronopifolium	MAJR XPep
Daisy Crazy Series **new**	LIck
'Donington Hero' ♀H1+3	ECtt LIck MAJR MHom
double white (d)	EWin LIck MAJR WWol
'Edelweiss' (d)	MAJR MHom
'Ella' PBR **new**	MAJR
'Flamingo'	see *Rhodanthemum gayanum*
§ ***foeniculaceum*** misapplied	CAby CSLe CTri ELan WKif
foeniculaceum misapplied pink	see *A.* 'Petite Pink'
§ ***foeniculaceum*** (Willd.) Webb & Sch.Bip.	CHal GMac MAJR
§ - 'Royal Haze' ♀H1+3	CHll MAJR NPer
'Frosty'	MAJR MBNS WWol
§ ***frutescens***	CHEx LIck LRHS MAJR
* - 'Album Plenum' (d)	SEND
§ - subsp. ***canariae*** ♀H1+3	ECtt LIck MAJR
- subsp. ***succulentum***	MAJR
- - 'Margaret Lynch'	MAJR
- 'Sugar Button' PBR (d) ♀H1+3	MAJR

	'Fuji Sundance'	LIck MAJR
	'George'	MAJR
	'Gill's Pink'	CPne ECtt GMac LIck MAJR MHom WPnn
	'Golden Treasure'	LIck MAJR
§	***gracile***	CHll
	- 'Chelsea Girl' ♀H1+3	CAby CHEx CHal CTbh ECtt LIck MAJR MHom MLan MSte WPnn
	'Gretel'PBR **new**	MAJR
	Gypsy Rose = 'M9/18D' **new**	LSou
	'Guernsey Pink'	LIck MAJR
	'Harvest Snow'	LAst MAJR MBNS
	'Henriette'PBR **new**	MAJR
	'Icknield Jubilee' **new**	LIck MAJR
	'Icknield Pink' **new**	MAJR
	'Icknield Pink 2000' **new**	LIck
	'Icknield Surprise' **new**	LIck MAJR
	'Icknield Sylvia' **new**	MAJR
	'Icknield Yellow' **new**	LIck MAJR
§	'Jamaica Primrose' ♀H1+3	CBot CHEx CPne CSpe ECtt LIck MAJR MHar SDix WPnn
	'Jamaica Snowstorm'	see *A.* 'Snow Storm'
	'Julie Anna' (d)	CBcs LAst MBNS
	'Julieanne' **new**	LAst LIck MAJR
	'Lemon Chiffon'	MAJR
	'Lemon Delight'	CHal LAst MAJR
	'Lemon Meringue' (d)	ECtt MAJR
	'Lemon Soufflé'	MAJR
	lemsii	LIck MAJR
§	'Levada Cream' ♀H1+3	LIck MAJR MHom
	'Libby Brett'	MAJR
	'Lilliput'	MAJR
§	***maderense*** ♀H1+3	CHal CHll CSam LRHS MAJR MSte SUsu
	- pale	MAJR
	'Maja Bofinger' **new**	EWin
	'Mary Cheek' (d) ♀H1+3	EWin LIck MAJR SPet WHoo
	'Mary Wootton' (d)	ECtt LIck MAJR MHom
	mawii	see *Rhodanthemum gayanum*
	'Mike's Pink'	MAJR
	'Millennium Star' **new**	LIck MAJR
	'Mini-snowflake'	see *A.* 'Blizzard'
§	'Mrs F. Sander' (d)	MAJR MHom
	'Nevada Cream'	see *A.* 'Levada Cream'
	ochroleucum	see *A. maderense*
	'Patches Pink' (d)	MAJR
§	'Peach Cheeks' (d)	CHal ECtt MAJR SPet
§	'Petite Pink' ♀H1+3	CHal ECtt EWin LAst MAJR MHom SEND
	Ping-Pong = 'Innping' (d) **new**	LIck
	'Pink Australian' (d)	LIck MAJR MHom
	'Pink Break'	MAJR
I	'Pink Dahlia'	MAJR
	'Pink Delight'	see *A.* 'Petite Pink'
	'Pink Pixie'	MAJR
	Pink Wonder = 'Supalily' (Daisy Crazy Series) **new**	MAJR
	pinnatifidium subsp. ***succulentum***	MAJR
	'Powder Puff' (d)	ECtt LIck MAJR
	'Primrose Petite' (Courtyard Series) **new**	LIck MAJR
	prostrate double pink	MAJR
§	'Qinta White' (d) ♀H1+3	GMac LIck MAJR
	'Rising Sun'	GMac LIck MAJR
	'Romance'	WWol
	'Rosa Dwarf'	MAJR
	'Royal Haze'	see *A. foeniculaceum* Webb 'Royal Haze'
	'Royal Yellow'	MAJR
	'Saimi'	MAJR
	'Saute'	MAJR
	'Serenade'	WWol
	'Silver Leaf'	MAJR
	'Silver Queen'	see *A. foeniculaceum* misapplied
	single pink-flowered	MAJR
§	'Snow Storm' ♀H1+3	CTbh LAst LIck MAJR MHom WPnn
	'Snowball'	MAJR
	'Snowflake' misapplied	see *A.* 'Mrs F. Sander'
	'Starlight'	MAJR
	Strawberry Pink = 'Suparosa'PBR (Daisy Crazy Series)	MAJR SVil
	'Sugar and Ice'PBR	MAJR
	'Sugar Baby'PBR	MAJR
	'Sugar Lace'	MAJR
	Sultan's Dream (Daisy Crazy Series) **new**	SVil
	Sultan's Lemon (Daisy Crazy Series) **new**	SVil
	'Summer Angel' (d)	MAJR
	'Summer Eyes'	MAJR
	'Summer Melody'PBR (d)	CBcs CSpe LIck MAJR
	'Summer Pink'PBR	LAst LIck SMrm WGor
	'Summer Stars'PBR (Daisy Crazy Series) **new**	LAst MAJR
	'Summer Stars Pink' (Daisy Crazy Series) (d)	CSpe MAJR
	'Summertime' **new**	MAJR
	'Sweety'	MAJR WPnn
	'Tenerife'	MSte
	'Tony Holmes'	MAJR
	'Tweeny' **new**	CSpe MAJR
	'Tweety' **new**	MAJR
	'Vancouver' (d) ♀H1+3	CHll CWCL ECtt EShb EWin LAst MHom SChu SPet WWol
	'Vara' **new**	EWin
*	'Vera'	MAJR
	'Wellwood Park'	MAJR
	'Weymouth Pink'	MAJR
	'Weymouth Surprise'	LIck MAJR
	White Blush = 'Supamorni' (Daisy Crazy Series) **new**	LIck MAJR
	White Crystal = 'Supagem' (Daisy Crazy Series) **new**	MAJR
	'White Spider'	ELan MAJR MHom
	'White Star' (d)	MAJR
	'Whiteknights' ♀H1+3	CSpe MAJR
	'Yellow Australian' (d)	LIck MAJR

Argyreia (*Convolvulaceae*)

	mollis **new**	CPLN
	nervosa	MGol

Argyrocytisus see *Cytisus*

Arisaema (*Araceae*)

	B&L 12160	MGol
	B&L 12161	MGol
	C&H 7026	NMen
	CC 3203	CPLG
	from China **new**	CFwr
	amurense	CFil CFir CHEx CLAP CStu EPot EUJe GCal GIBF GKir ITer LAma MLLN WCot WFar
	- B&SWJ 947	WCru
	- dark-flowered	WWst
	- green-flowered	WWst
§	- subsp. ***robustum***	CFil CStu EBee LRHS NMen WCot WWst
	- - B&SWJ 1186	WCru
	- subsp. ***serratum*** B&SWJ 711	WCru

	Name	Suppliers
*	***angustatum*** var. ***amurense***	EPot LAma
	- var. ***peninsulae***	GIBF
	- - B&SWJ 841	LAma WCru
*	- - f. ***variegatum*** (v) B&SWJ 4321	WCru
	- var. ***serratum***	see *A. serratum*
	asperatum	LAma MLul
	auriculatum	LAma
	bathycoleum	LAma
	biauriculatum	see *A. wattii*
	brevipes	CFwr LAma
	candidissimum ♀H4	More than 30 suppliers
	- green	LAma WCot
	- white	LAma WCot
	ciliatum	CBro CDes CFil CPom CStu EBla GEdr LAma MLLN MLul MNrw NLar SBla SRot SSpi WCot WIvy WSHC
	- var. ***liubaense***	CFwr CLAP EUJe MGol WWst
	- - CT 369	SCnR WCot
	clavatum	LAma
	concinnum	CFir CStu EMar EPot EUJe LAma MDun MGol MOak NLar
	- GG 94152	WCot
	- 'Sikkim' **new**	MGol
	consanguineum	CAby CBro CDes CFil CFwr CHEx CLAP CMea CPLG CPom CRow EPfP GBuc GCrs GGar GKir ITer ITim LAma MGol MTho SGar SSpi WCot WPGP
	- B&SWJ 071	WCru
	- CC 3635	WCot
	- CLD 1519	GKir
	- GG 92112	WCot
	- PJ 277	WCot
*	- bicolour	GCrs
	- 'J. Balis'	WCot
	- subsp. ***kelung-insulare*** B&SWJ 256	WCru
	- marbled leaf	MGol WCot
	- 'Qinling'	MGol WCot
	- silver-centred leaf **new**	ITer
	costatum	CFil CHEx CLAP EPot EUJe GBuc GEdr ITer LAma LRHS MDun MLul MOak NMen WCot WMul
	- CC 2924	WCot
	dahaiense **new**	LAma MLul WWst
	dilatatum	CFwr GFlt LAma
	dracontium	CLAP EUJe ITer LAma MDun MLul NLar NMen
	du-bois-reymondiae	LAma
	ehimense	LAma
	elephas	EUJe LAma MLul
	engleri	EUJe MLul
	- GG 98173	WCot
	erubescens	EPot ERos EUJe LAma NLar WCot
	exappendiculatum	CDes CFil SSpi WPGP
	fargesii	CLAP EPot EUJe LAma WCot WWst
	flavum	CBro CDes CFil CLAP CMea CStu EBee EHyt EPot GCal GIBF GKir ITer ITim LAma LRHS MLul MTho NMen NSla SSpi WBVN WCot WPGP
	- CC 1782	WCot WCra
	- CC 3946	MGol
	- subsp. ***abbreviatum***	EUJe LAma WCot
	- - GG 84193	WWst
*	- ***minus***	NWCA
	- tall	CLAP
	formosanum	LAma
	- B&SWJ 280	WCru
	- B&SWJ 390	CPou WCot
	- var. ***bicolorifolium*** B&SWJ 3528	WCru
	- f. ***stenophyllum*** B&SWJ 1477	WCru
§	***franchetianum***	EUJe GEdr ITer LAma MGol MLul WCot
	fraternum	WCot
	- CC 465	WCot
	galeatum	CFir EPot EUJe LAma MDun MGol MOak WCot WMul
§	***griffithii***	EPot EUJe GGar LAma LRHS MDun MLul NMyG SSpi WCru WMul
	- 'Numbuq' **new**	GCra
	hatizyoense	LAma MLul
	helleborifolium	see *A. tortuosum*
	heterophyllum	EUJe LAma
	- B&SWJ 2028	WCru
	- 'Baguo'	WCot
	ilanense B&SWJ 3030	WCru
	inkiangense	LAma
	intermedium	EMar EPot EUJe LAma MNrw NMen SSpi
	- CC 3102	WCot
	- GG 96283	WCot
	- var. ***biflagellatum***	ITer
	- - HWJCM 161	WCru
	- - PB 022	WCot
	iyoanum	LAma WCru
	jacquemontii	CBro CFil CLAP EBla ECho EHyt EPot EUJe GBuc GCrs GEdr GGar GKir ITim LAma LRHS NLar NMen WCot
	- B&SWJ 2719	WCru
	- GG 88172	WCot
	- GG 94120	WCot
	aff. ***jacquemontii***	ERou
	- MECCN 29	NMen
	- MECCN 76	NMen
	japonicum	see *A. serratum*
	jinshajiangense	LAma
	kishidae	LAma
	kiushianum	EFEx LAma SOkd WCot
	leschenaultii **new**	EUJe LAma
	lichiangense	GEdr LAma WCot
	lingyunense	CFir EPot LAma
§	***lobatum***	EUJe LAma
	maximowiczii	EBee GEdr LAma WCru
	meleagris	LAma
	multisectum	CFir
	negishii	LAma WCru
§	***nepenthoides***	CBro EMar EPot EUJe GBin GEdr GKev LAma MDun MGol MLul MNrw NMyG WCot WMul WSan
	- B&SWJ 2614b	WCru
	ochraceum	see *A. nepenthoides*
	omeiense	EBee LAma NLar
	onoticum	see *A. lobatum*
	polyphyllum B&SWJ 3904	WCru
	propinquum	CLAP EHyt EPot ERou EUJe GBin GKir LAma MDun NMen SSpi WCot WCru
	purpureogaleatum	see *A. franchetianum*
	rhizomatum	EUJe LAma MLul
	rhombiforme	LAma WCot
	ringens misapplied	see *A. amurense* subsp. *robustum*
	ringens (Thunberg) Schott	CDes EFEx EPot EUJe GIBF LAma MLul
	- f. ***praecox*** B&SWJ 1515	WCru
	- f. ***sieboldii*** B&SWJ 551	WCru
	robustum	see *A. amurense* subsp. *robustum*
	saxatile	EUJe LAma MLul
	sazensoo	GEdr LAma WCru

§ ***serratum***	CDes CFil GIBF LAma MNrw SBla WPGP
- AGSJ 249	WWst
- B&SWJ 5894	WCru
shihmienense	LAma
§ ***sikokianum***	CBro CDes EFEx EPot EUJe GEdr GIBF LAma LRHS MLul SOkd WCru
- var. ***serratum***	CFir
- variegated (v)	WCru
speciosum	CHEx CPLG ELan EPot EUJe GBuc GEdr GGar GSki LAma MDun MGol MOak NMen SSpi WFar WMul WPnP
- B&SWJ 2403	WCru
- CC 3100	WCot
- var. ***mirabile*** B&SWJ 2712	WCru
* - var. ***sikkimense***	LAma
stewardsonii **new**	NMen
taiwanense	CLAP SSpi WCot
- B&SWJ 269	WCru
- B&SWJ 356	CPou
- var. ***brevipedunculatum*** B&SWJ 1859	WCru
- f. ***cinereum*** B&SWJ 19121	WCru
- silver-leaved	WCot
tashiroi	GEdr LAma WCru
ternatipartitum	LAma WDav
- B&SWJ 5790	WCru
thunbergii	EFEx WCot
- subsp. ***autumnale*** B&SWJ 1425	WCru
- subsp. ***urashima***	CLAP EFEx GEdr GIBF LAma WWst
§ ***tortuosum***	CBro CFil CLAP EHyt EMar EPot ERos GBin GEdr GGar GIBF GKir ITer LAma MDun MLul MNrw MOak MTho NLar NWCA SBla WCot WPGP WPnP
- CC 1452	CPou
- var. ***helleborifolium*** CC 3641	WCot
- high altitude	EUJe GBuc NMen
- - B&SWJ 2386	WCru
- low altitude	WSan
- - B&SWJ 2298	WCru
tosaense	LAma
- B&SWJ 5761	WCru
- GG 91224	WCru
triphyllum	CFil CLAP CPom EMFP EPot EUJe GEdr GGar GSki ITer LAma LEdu LRHS MLul MSal MTho NWCA SMad SSpi WFar WPGP WPnP WSan
- subsp. ***triphyllum*** var. ***atrorubens***	CLAP
unzenense B&SWJ 6226	WCru
§ ***utile***	EUJe LAma MLul
- CC 3101	WCot
- HWJCM 161	WCru
verrucosum	see *A. griffithii*
- var. ***utile***	see *A. utile*
wattii	LAma MLul
yamatense	WCru
- subsp. ***sugimotoi***	GIBF LAma
- - B&SWJ 5092	WCru
yunnanense	CLAP EUJe LAma MGol WCot

Arisarum (*Araceae*)

proboscideum	More than 30 suppliers
- MS 958	EMar
vulgare	SIgm
- JRM 1396 from Crete **new**	CMon
- subsp. ***simorrhinum***	EBla WCot
- subsp. ***vulgare***	EBee WCot

Aristea (*Iridaceae*)

S&SH 88	SAga
ecklonii	CAby CBod CDoC CFil CHEx CPLG CPou CTbh EChP EMan GGar GSki IGor SChr SMar SSpi WCot WDyG WOut WPic
ensifolia	CMdw WPrP WSHC
grandis	CFir SMar WCot
§ ***major***	CCtw CFir CPen CPne CTrC EMan GGar GSki
- pink-flowered	CAbb CDes EBee WPGP
montana	CTrC
thyrsiflora	see *A. major*

Aristolochia ✿ (*Aristolochiaceae*)

baetica	CArn CPLN SSpi WCru
californica	LEdu
clematitis	CArn EChP GPoy LEdu MSal WCot WCru WWye
contorta	CBcs EBee GIBF SSpi
delavayi	CHEx CPLN
durior	see *A. macrophylla*
elegans	see *A. littoralis*
fimbriata	CStu
gigantea	CPLN SMur
gorgona **new**	CPLN
griffithii	CPLN
- B&SWJ 2118	WCru
heterophylla	see *A. kaempferi* f. *heterophylla*
kaempferi	CPLN
- B&SWJ 293	WCru
§ - f. ***heterophylla***	CPLN
- - B&SWJ 3109	WCru
§ ***littoralis*** ♀H1	CPLN CStu LRHS
§ ***macrophylla***	CBcs CBot CHEx CPLN EBee EShb GKir MRav NBlu NPal SBig SHBN SLim WCru WDin
manshuriensis	CPLN GIBF LEdu SSpi
- B&SWJ 962	WCru
onoei	CPLN
- B&SWJ 4960	WCru
paucinervis	CMon WCru
- AB&S 4393	WCot
ringens Vahl. non Link & Otto	CPLN
rotunda	CMon SSpi
sempervirens	CPLN CStu SSpi WSHC
sipho	see *A. macrophylla*
tomentosa	IDee ITer WCru
zollingeriana B&SWJ 7030	WCru

Aristotelia (*Elaeocarpaceae*)

chilensis 'Variegata' (v)	CBcs CSam CWib GQui LAst SEND SLim SPlb
fruticosa	CPne
- (f)	ECou
- (m)	ECou
- black-fruited (f) **new**	ECou
- white-fruited (f) **new**	ECou
serrata	ECou
- (f)	ECou
- (m)	ECou

Armeria (*Plumbaginaceae*)

§ ***alliacea***	CSpe ECha EPPr MWgw NJOw
- f. ***leucantha***	SRms WMoo
§ ***alpina***	MWat

	Bees' hybrids	SRms WAul WMoo
	'Bees' Ruby'	WPer
	caespitosa	see *A. juniperifolia*
	euscadiensis	CSpe EMFP
§	***girardii***	EPot NJOw
	Joystick Series	NArg
	- 'Joystick Lilac Shades'	IGor NLar
	- 'Joystick Red'	CWCL EShb MSph SBri WHil
	- 'Joystick White'	EGoo EShb WHil
§	***juniperifolia*** 🏆H4	CLyd CMea CNic ECtt EDAr ELan EPfP GMaP LBee LRHS MTho NMen NVic NWCA SIng SPoG SRms
	- 'Alba'	CMea EDAr ELan EPfP EPot GBin NMen NPri NRya SPoG SRms WAbe WLin
	- 'Beechwood'	LRHS
	- 'Bevan's Variety' 🏆H4	CTbh ECha ECtt ELan EPfP EPot ESis GCrs GGar GKir GMaP LRHS MWat NJOw NLAp NMen NPri NRya SBla SPoG SRms SRot WAbe WLin WPat
	- 'Brookside' **new**	EPot
	- dark-flowered	EWes SBla WAbe
	- rose-flowered	ITim
	- spiny dwarf	EPot
§	***maritima***	CArn EPfP EWTr GKir LAst LRHS MBar MBow NArg NBlu NFor NJOw SPet WFar WGwG WMoo XPep
	- 'Alba'	More than 30 suppliers
	- subsp. ***alpina***	see *A. alpina*
	- 'Bloodstone'	CTri ECot ELan MWat SPoG
	- 'Corsica'	CMea CTri ECha ECrN EPot MBNS NBir NRya SMer XPep
	- Düsseldorf Pride	see *A. maritima* 'Düsseldorfer Stolz'
§	- 'Düsseldorfer Stolz'	CElw CPBP ECha ECtt EDAr ELan EPfP GGar GKir ITim LRHS MBri NEgg NJOw NMen NPri SPoG WPat WWye
	- 'Glory of Holland'	EPot
	- 'Laucheana'	SHGN WHoo WMoo
I	- 'Rubrifolia'	CBgR CFir CFwr CMea CRez CSpe ECGP EHoe EMan EPPr EShb EWin MAvo MSph NEgg NJOw NLar SPoG WAbe
	- 'Ruby Glow'	CTri LBuc
	- 'Splendens'	CBcs CHrt COlW EMil ENot EPfP GGar GMaP GWCH LAst MBow MHer MWgw NBlu NMir NRya NVic SBch SPoG WFar WMoo WPer
	- 'Vindictive' 🏆H4	CMea CTri EDAr EPfP LGro
	morisii **new**	SBch
	'Nifty Thrifty' (v)	CBod CMea EBee EHoe ENot EShb EWes EWin LRHS NLAp NPri SCoo SIde SPoG SRot WMoo WPat
	'Ornament'	ECtt LRav NJOw SHGN SPoG WFar
	plantaginea	see *A. alliacea*
	pseudarmeria	CDes CHrt ELan MLan
	- 'Drumstick Red'	GBBs WPer
	- 'Drumstick White'	GBBs WPer
	- hybrids	CTri ELan MWgw NBlu NMir WRHF
	pungens	EBee
	setacea	see *A. girardii*
	tweedyi	CLyd GTou NLAp
	vulgaris	see *A. maritima*
	welwitschii	SRms
	'Westacre Beauty'	EWes

Armoracia (*Brassicaceae*)

§	***rusticana***	CArn CBod COld CPrp CSev ELau EUnu GAbr GPoy IHMH ILis MBri MHer MSal NPri NTHB SIde WGwG WHer WJek WLHH WSel WWye
	- 'Variegata' (v)	CPrp EBee ELau EMan EMar EMon GAbr GBar ITer LRHS MAvo MWrn NSti SMad SPla WCHb WCot WMoo WPnP WSel

Arnebia (*Boraginaceae*)

	echioides	see *A. pulchra*
	longiflora	see *A. pulchra*
§	***pulchra***	EBee EMan GCal LAst SBla SPoG

Arnica (*Asteraceae*)

	angustifolia	SRms
	subsp. ***alpina***	
	- subsp. ***iljinii***	NBir
	chamissonis Schmidt	see *A. sachalinensis*
	chamissonis Less.	CHby CHrt CWan EBee GBar MNrw MSal NBre NLar WHil WJek WPer WWye
	longifolia	NEgg
	montana	CArn CSam EUnu GBar GPoy GTou MChe MHer MLan SRms WPer WWye
	- yellow	MLan
§	***sachalinensis***	EBee GIBF
	- AER 0206	MGol

Aronia (*Rosaceae*)

	arbutifolia	CBcs CDul CTri EPfP EPla GBin GIBF GKir MBlu MWhi NBlu SHBN SLdr SLon WDin WOrn
	- 'Erecta'	EBee ECrN ELan EPfP LAst LEdu LPio MBNS MBlu MBri NLar SLPl SMac SPoG SRms SSpi WBor WFar
	melanocarpa	CAgr CDul CMCN CMHG EGra ELan EPfP EWTr GAbr GIBF GKir LEdu LRHS MAsh MBar MBlu MRav SSpi WDin WFar WHCG
	- 'Autumn Magic'	CBcs CDoC CFai CPMA EBee EPfP LAst LRHS MAsh MBlu NLar NMyG SCoo SPer
	- var. ***elata***	EPla
	- var. ***grandifolia*** **new**	CPMA
	- 'Hugin' **new**	CPMA
	x ***prunifolia***	CAgr CDoC CMHG EBee EWTr GKir LEdu WHCG
	- 'Aron' (F) **new**	CPMA
	- 'Brilliant'	CDoC COtt CTri EBee LRHS SCoo SPer SPur WBcn WWes
	- 'Nero' (F)	CAgr
	- 'Serina' (F) **new**	CPMA
	- 'Viking' (F)	CAgr EBee ECrN EPfP GKir LBuc MRav WDin WWes

Arrhenatherum (*Poaceae*)

	elatius subsp. ***bulbosum***	ECrN WFar
	- - 'Variegatum' (v)	CHrt EBee EChP EHoe ELan ENot EPza EUJe GBin GMaP LAst LEdu LRHS MBri MMoz MWgw MWhi NBid NGdn NOrc SHFr WFar WMoo WPer WSSM

Artemisia ✿ (*Asteraceae*)

	from Taiwan **new**	WHer
	RBS 0207 **new**	CPLG EPPr MAvo
§	***abrotanum*** 🏆H4	More than 30 suppliers
	absinthium	CAgr CArn CPrp CSLe CSev CWan EEls ELau GPoy MBar MBow MChe MHer MLLN MWgw NSti NTHB SIde SPer WGwG WPer WWye XPep

*	- 'Argentea'	XPep
	- 'Corinne Tremaine' (v)	WHer
	- 'Lambrook Giant'	EEls
	- 'Lambrook Mist' ♀H3-4	CSLe CSev EBee EChP EEls ELan EMan EPfP EPza GBri GMaP GMac LRHS MMil MRav NCiC NDov NWoo SBch WCAu WMnd
	- 'Lambrook Silver' ♀H4	CArn CBcs CPLG CSLe EBee ECha EEls EHrv EPfP ERou GBar GKir LRHS MHer MRav NBro NFor SBla SHBN SLim SPer SWvt WDin WEas WFar WMnd WPer XPep
	- 'Silver Ghost'	EEls
*	- 'Variegata' (v)	CBcs
	afra	CArn EBee EEls EMan EOHP EWin GBar IFro XPep
§	***alba***	CSev EEls EMan EMon EOHP GBar GPoy ILis MHer MSal NBur NSti SIde WMow WPer WRha XPep
§	- 'Canescens' ♀H4	More than 30 suppliers
	annua	EEls MGol MSal SIde WJek WWye
	anomala	EEls
	arborescens ♀H3	CArn CHEx CMHG CTri ECha ECrN EEls EWin SDix SPer WDin WHer XPep
	- 'Brass Band'	see *A.* 'Powis Castle'
	- 'Faith Raven'	CArn EEls ERou GBin GBuc NLar WCAu WFar WHer
	- 'Little Mice'	EBee NLar
	- 'Porquerolles'	CSLe EEls XPep
	arctica	EEls GIBF
	argyi	EEls
§	***armeniaca***	EEls XPep
	assoana	see *A. caucasica*
	atrata	EEls
	barrelieri	EEls
	brachyloba	CSLe MLLN WCHb
	californica	EEls IFro XPep
	campestris subsp. ***borealis***	EEls GIBF MChe WRha WSel
	- subsp. ***campestris***	EEls XPep
	- subsp. ***glutinosa***	XPep
	- subsp. ***maritima***	EEls XPep
	- - from Wales	EEls
	camphorata	see *A. alba*
	cana	see *Seriphidium canum*
	canariensis	see *A. thuscula*
	canescens hort.	see *A. alba* 'Canescens'
	canescens Willd.	see *A. armeniaca*
	capillaris	EEls MSal XPep
§	***caucasica*** ♀H3-4	CSLe EEls EWes GKir LGro LPhx MBrN MHer SBla SRms SRot WCHb WEas WJek WPer XPep
	- ***caucasica***	EEls ESis WFar
	chamaemelifolia	CArn EEls IGor MHer NBre WWye XPep
	cretacea	see *Seriphidium nutans*
	discolor Dougl. ex Besser	see *A. michauxiana*
	douglasiana	EEls
	- 'Valerie Finnis'	see *A. ludoviciana* 'Valerie Finnis'
	dracunculus	More than 30 suppliers
	- ***dracunculoides***	CArn CWan EEls EUnu GBar NPri WGHP
	ferganensis	see *Seriphidium ferganense*
	filifolia	EEls XPep
	fragrans Willd.	see *Seriphidium fragrans*
	frigida ♀H3-4	EBee EEls GBar ILis WHCG XPep
	genipi	EEls MSal
	glacialis	ECha EEls NLar XPep
	gmelinii	EBee EEls GBar GIBF
	gnaphalodes	see *A. ludoviciana*
	gorgonum	EEls
	gracilis	see *A. scoparia*
N	***granatensis*** hort.	MSte
	herba-alba	EEls XPep
	'Huntington'	EEls
	kawakamii B&SWJ 088	EEls WCru
	kitadakensis	EEls
	- 'Guizhou'	see *A. lactiflora* Guizhou Group
	kruhsiana **new**	GIBF
	laciniata	EEls
	lactiflora ♀H4	CPrp ECha ECtt EEls ELan ELau EMon ERou EVFa GBar GMaP MRav NFor NGdn NLon NOrc SDix SPer SRms WFar WMoo WTin WWpP
	- dark	see *A. lactiflora* Guizhou Group
	- 'Elfenbein'	GCal
§	- Guizhou Group	More than 30 suppliers
	- 'Jim Russell'	CDes CElw EBee EWes LPhx NBre NDov
	- ***purpurea***	see *A. lactiflora* Guizhou Group
	- 'Variegata'	see *A. vulgaris* 'Variegata'
	lagocephala	EEls EMan WCot
	lagopus	GIBF
	lanata Willd. non Lam.	see *A. caucasica*
	laxa	see *A. umbelliformis*
	longifolia	XPep
§	***ludoviciana***	CSLe CSec EBee EEls ELan ELau ERou GBar MBrN MEHN MGol MRav MWat NBid NLon NOak NOrc SGar SRms WBVN WWpP
N	- var. ***latifolia***	see *A. ludoviciana* subsp. *ludoviciana* var. *latiloba*
	- subsp. ***ludoviciana*** var. ***incompta***	ECha EEls EMan MRav WHer
§	- - var. ***latiloba***	EEls EHoe GBar GBuc GMac LRHS MRav NBro NOak NSti SBch SWvt WCot WCra WEas WHoo WPer WWpP
	- subsp. ***mexicana*** var. ***albula***	EEls WFar
	- 'Silver Queen' ♀H4	More than 30 suppliers
N	- 'Valerie Finnis' ♀H4	More than 30 suppliers
	manshurica	EBee EMan WCot
	maritima	see *Seriphidium maritimum*
§	***michauxiana***	EBee EEls NBur NSti WHer
	molinieri	EEls XPep
	mutellina	see *A. umbelliformis*
	niitakayamensis	EEls EOHP GBar XPep
	nitida	EEls
	norvegica	EEls
	nutans	see *Seriphidium nutans*
*	'Okra'	MMil
	palmeri hort.	see *A. ludoviciana*
	pamirica	EEls
	aff. ***parviflora***	EBee
	- CLD 1531	EEls
	pedemontana	see *A. caucasica*
	pontica	CArn EBee ECha ECrN EEls EHoe ELan GBar GGar GMaP GMac GPoy LRHS MBNS MHer MRav MWgw NBro NJOw NSti SDix SPer SSvw WFar WHoo WPer WWye XPep
	'Powis Castle' ♀H3	More than 30 suppliers
	princeps	CArn EEls MSal SIde
	procera Willd.	see *A. abrotanum*
	purshiana	see *A. ludoviciana*
	pycnocephala 'David's Choice'	EEls
	ramosa	EEls
	'Rosenschleier'	CBre EBee EMon EPPr EVFa LPhx NCGa WFar WPGP
	rutifolia	EEls
	sachalinensis **new**	WOut

	schmidtiana ♀H4	CFis ECha ECot EEls EMan GIBF GKir MGol MOne MWat NOrc SRms
	- 'Nana' ♀H4	More than 30 suppliers
§	***scoparia***	EEls
	selengensis	EEls
	splendens misapplied	see *A. alba* 'Canescens'
	splendens Willd.	EEls ELan LPhx NSti WEas
	stelleriana	ECha EEls EWTr GGar GIBF MFOX MHer MWgw NBro NFor NLon NSti SPet SRms WCAu WEas XPep
	- RBS 0207	EEls
N	- 'Boughton Silver'	More than 30 suppliers
N	- 'Mori'	see *A. stelleriana* 'Boughton Silver'
	- 'Nana'	EEls EMan SBla SWvt
	- 'Prostrata'	see *A. stelleriana* 'Boughton Silver'
	- 'Silver Brocade'	see *A. stelleriana* 'Boughton Silver'
	taurica	EEls
§	***thuscula***	EEls
	tilesii	EBee GIBF
	tridentata	see *Seriphidium tridentatum*
§	***umbelliformis***	EEls
	vallesiaca	see *Seriphidium vallesiacum*
	verlotiorum	EEls GBar
	vulgaris L.	CAgr CArn CPrp EEls ELau EUnu GBar GPoy GWCH IHMH MChe MGol MHer WHer WJek WLHH WWye
	- 'Cragg-Barber Eye' (v)	EBee EChP EEls EWin GSki NBid NPro SAga WCHb WHer WRha
	- 'Crispa'	ELau EMon
	- 'Obelisk'	EEls
	- Oriental Limelight = 'Janlim' (v)	More than 30 suppliers
	- 'Peddar's Gold' (v)	EChP EWin
§	- 'Variegata' (v)	EEls GBar GLil MHer NBir NMRc NPro NSti SMad WCHb WFar WHer WHil WJek WMoo WPer WRha
	x ***wurzellii***	EEls

Arthrocnemum (*Chenopodiaceae*)

	glaucum	XPep

Arthropodium (*Anthericaceae*)

	candidum	CBot CStu EBee ECha ECou GAbr GEdr ITim MBrN MWgw NWCA SHBN SRot WFar WHal WPer
	- 'Capri' **new**	EBee
	- ***maculatum***	GEdr LEdu SPlb
	- ***purpureum***	CBcs CPLG CPom CSec EBee EChP EMan EMar EPza GBri GCal GGar GKev LRHS MGGn MLan NJOw NLAp WCot WFar WGwG WPGP WPat
	cirratum	CHEx CPne CRHN ECou ERea GGar IDee LEdu MLan
	- 'Matapouri Bay'	CBcs CHEx CTrC EBee EMan EMil WPGP
	milleflorum	GGar NWCA WCot

Arthrostylidium (*Poaceae*)

	naibuense	CFil

artichoke, globe see *Cynara cardunculus* Scolymus Group

artichoke, Jerusalem see *Helianthus tuberosus*

Arum (*Araceae*)

	alpinum	CFil EUJe
§	***besserianum***	WWst
	'Chameleon'	CDes CLAP EMan EMar EMon EVFa MAvo MBct MMil MNrw MTho NBir SIgm SMad SPer SSpi WCot WFar WHal WHil WTin
§	***concinnatum***	CFil CStu EBee EMon EPot GIBF ITer LAma SChr SHar SSpi WCot WPrP
	- JCA	CStu
	- black-spotted **new**	EMar
	cornutum	see *Sauromatum venosum*
	creticum	CArn CBro CFir EBee EChP ECha EHyt EMan ETow GBuc GSki IBlr ITer MMil MNrw MRav MTho SCnR SDix SRot SSpi WBor WCot
	- MS 696	MNrw
	- FCC form	CFil EPot SBla WCot WPGP WPnP
	- 'Marmaris White' **new**	SCnR
	- white	MNrw MTho
	- yellow	NBir NPar WFar WIvy
	creticum x ***italicum***	MDKP WCot WFar
	cyrenaicum	CDes CFil CStu EBee EHyt MNrw MTho SSpi WCot WPGP
	- MS 696 from Crete **new**	CMon
§	***dioscoridis***	CDes CMon CStu EWes MMil MTho NLar WCot
	- JCA 195.197	WCot
	- MS&CL 524	ITer
	- var. ***cyprium***	EBee
§	- var. ***dioscoridis***	EBee ERos SSpi WCot
	- - JCA 195200	WPrP
	- - from Turkey **new**	CMon
	- var. ***liepoldtii***	see *A. dioscoridis* var. *dioscoridis*
	- var. ***philistaeum***	WWst
	- var. ***smithii***	see *A. dioscoridis* var. *dioscoridis*
	dracunculus	see *Dracunculus vulgaris*
	idaeum	SSpi
	italicum	CLAP EBee EWTr LAma MBri MTho NJOw NLar SBod SEND WAbe WCot WFar WPnP WSHC WShi
	- subsp. ***albispathum***	CDes CFil CHid CStu EMon LAma SSpi WCot WFar WPGP
	- black-spotted	EHyt WFar
	- 'Green Marble'	SBla WFar
	- subsp. ***italicum***	CStr EBee EBrs EPla EShb EUJe IHMH NJOw NWCA WTin
	- - 'Bill Baker'	EMon WFar
	- - 'Cyclops'	CHid CLAP MNrw WCot
§	- - 'Marmoratum' ♀H4	More than 30 suppliers
	- - 'Sparkler'	WCot
	- - 'Spotted Jack'	MNrw WCot WCru
	- - 'Tiny'	CFir EMon GCal SCnR
§	- - 'White Winter'	EBee ECGP EMon GBuc MAvo WCot WSPU
	- 'Nancy Lindsay'	EMar EMon
	- subsp. ***neglectum***	SChr
	- - 'Miss Janay Hall' (v)	EBee EVFa WCot
	- 'Pictum'	see *A. italicum* subsp. *italicum* 'Marmoratum'
	- 'Whitegate'	CMea
	jacquemontii	WWst
	korolkowii	WCot
	maculatum	CArn CRWN EPot GPoy LAma MBow MHer MRav MSal WHer WShi WWye
	- 'Painted Lady' (v)	EBee WCot
	- 'Pleddel'	MRav WCot
	- Tar Spot Group **new**	CNat
*	- 'Variegatum' (v)	GPoy
	nickelii	see *A. concinnatum*
§	***nigrum***	CDes EUJe WCot WGwG
	orientale	EHyt EPot ETow
	- subsp. ***amoenum***	MNrw
	- subsp. ***besserianum***	see *A. besserianum*
	palaestinum	CMon EMon

	petteri hort.	see *A. nigrum*
	pictum	CLAP EBee ERos GCra LAma LRHS SBla WCot WTin
	- PB 425 from Majorca **new**	CMon
	- 'Taff's Form'	see *A. italicum* subsp. *italicum* 'White Winter'
	purpureospathum	CDes CFil EHyt SSpi WCot WPGP
	- PB 49 from Crete **new**	CMon
	- PB 51 from Crete	CMon
§	***rupicola*** var. ***rupicola***	WWst
	- var. ***virescens***	SSpi WCot
	sintenisii	EBee WCot WWst
	'Streaked Spectre'	EMon

Aruncus ✿ (*Rosaceae*)

	aethusifolius ♕H4	More than 30 suppliers
	- 'Little Gem'	WCru
	asiaticus	EBee EBla
	dioicus	More than 30 suppliers
§	- (m) ♕H4	CDoC CRow ECha ELan ENot EPla GSki MBNS MRav MWgw NBro NFor NSti SGar SMad SPer SRms SSpi WFar WMoo WPer
	- Child of Two Worlds	see *A. dioicus* 'Zweiweltenkind'
	- 'Glasnevin'	CRow CSev EBee EBrs ECha ECtt MRav WFar
	- var. ***kamtschaticus***	EChP EKen EWes GIBF MCCP NBre NLar WWpP
	- - AER 0208	MGol
	- - B&SWJ 8624	WCru
	- - RBS 0208	NVic
	- 'Kneiffii'	More than 30 suppliers
§	- 'Zweiweltenkind'	CFwr CRez EBee EBla EBrs EHrv EWTr GCal GSki NBre NLar SMad
	'Horatio'	EBla EMon LPhx SMeo
	'Johannifest'	CDes EBee EBla EMon
	'Noble Spirit'	EBla EPPr LBuc MWrn NLar SCoo SGSe SWal WWeb
	plumosus	see *A. dioicus*
	sinensis	EBla EShb EWll NBre WFar
	sylvestris	see *A. dioicus*
	'Woldemar Meier'	EBla EMon

Arundinaria ✿ (*Poaceae*)

	amabilis	see *Pseudosasa amabilis*
	anceps	see *Yushania anceps*
	auricoma	see *Pleioblastus viridistriatus*
	chino	see *Pleioblastus chino*
	disticha	see *Pleioblastus pygmaeus* 'Distichus'
	falconeri	see *Himalayacalamus falconeri*
	fargesii	see *Bashania fargesii*
	fastuosa	see *Semiarundinaria fastuosa*
	fortunei	see *Pleioblastus variegatus*
	funghomii	see *Schizostachyum funghomii*
§	***gigantea***	WJun
	- subsp. ***tecta***	CBcs MGos
	hindsii	see *Pleioblastus hindsii*
	hookeriana misapplied	see *Himalayacalamus falconeri* 'Damarapa'
	hookeriana Munro	see *Himalayacalamus hookerianus*
	humilis	see *Pleioblastus humilis*
	japonica	see *Pseudosasa japonica*
	jaunsarensis	see *Yushania anceps*
	maling	see *Yushania maling*
	marmorea	see *Chimonobambusa marmorea*
	murielae	see *Fargesia murielae*
	nitida	see *Fargesia nitida*
	oedogonata	see *Clavinodum oedogonatum*
	palmata	see *Sasa palmata*
	pumila	see *Pleioblastus argenteostriatus* f. *pumilus*
	pygmaea	see *Pleioblastus pygmaeus*
	quadrangularis	see *Chimonobambusa quadrangularis*
	simonii	see *Pleioblastus simonii*
	spathiflora	see *Thamnocalamus spathiflorus*
	tessellata	see *Thamnocalamus tessellatus*
	vagans	see *Sasaella ramosa*
	variegata	see *Pleioblastus variegatus*
	veitchii	see *Sasa veitchii*
	viridistriata	see *Pleioblastus viridistriatus*
	'Wang Tsai'	see *Bambusa multiplex* 'Floribunda'

Arundo (*Poaceae*)

	donax	More than 30 suppliers
	- 'Golden Chain'	EBee EPPr EVFa EWes
	- 'Macrophylla'	CBig CFil CRow EPPr EPla LEdu LPJP SApp WPGP
	- 'Variegata'	see *A. donax* var. *versicolor*
§	- var. ***versicolor*** (v)	More than 30 suppliers
	- yellow variegated (v)	CKno EShb SEND SPoG
	formosana	CKno EMan EPPr
	pliniana	CFil CMCo CRow EPPr EPla LEdu WPGP

Asarina (*Scrophulariaceae*)

	antirrhiniflora	see *Maurandella antirrhiniflora*
I	***barclayana***	see *Maurandya barclayana*
	erubescens	see *Lophospermum erubescens*
	hispanica	see *Antirrhinum hispanicum*
	lophantha	see *Lophospermum scandens*
	lophospermum	see *Lophospermum scandens*
§	***procumbens***	CSec CStu CTri EBee EMan EPfP GBBs GKev GKir GTou MTho NRya SHFr SIng SRms SSpi WAbe WFar WGwG WPer
	'Victoria Falls'	see *Maurandya* 'Victoria Falls'

Asarum ✿ (*Aristolochiaceae*)

	albomaculatum B&SWJ 1726	WCru
	arifolium	CAby CDes CLAP EHrv GBBs NLar
*	***campaniforme***	CFwr CLAP GFlt LAma WCru
	canadense	CArn EBee EChP EMar EPot ERos EUJe GBBs GGar GLil GPoy GSki LRHS MSal NLar WCru
	caudatum	CAvo CDes CLAP CRow CStu ECha EHyt EMan EPPr GBuc LEdu NBro NLar NSti NWCA SRms WCot WCru WFar WPGP WPnP
	- white	CDes CLAP EHrv SSpi
	caudigerum	LAma
	- B&SWJ 1517	WCru
	caulescens	CLAP GFlt LAma LEdu WCru
	- B&SWJ 5886	WCru
	debile	LAma SSpi
	delavayi	CFwr LAma WCot WCru
	epigynum	LEdu
	- B&SWJ 3443	WCru
	- 'Silver Web'	CLAP WCru
	europaeum	More than 30 suppliers
	fauriei	WCru
	forbesii	WCot
	geophilum	CFwr
	hartwegii	CDes CLAP EBee EHyt EMan EMar EPot ERos EUJe GBuc WCot WCru WPGP
	- NNS 00-78	WCot
	heterotropoides	CFwr
	hirsutisepalum	CLAP
	hypogynum B&SWJ 3628	WCru
	infrapurpureum	WCot
	- B&SWJ 1994	WCru

kumageanum	WCot
lemmonii	EMan LEdu WCru
leptophyllum B&SWJ 1983	WCru
longirhizomatosum	CFwr WCru
macranthum	WCot
- B&SWJ 1691	WCru
maculatum B&SWJ 1114	WCru
magnificum	CFwr CLAP LAma WCru
maximum	CFwr CLAP EUJe LAma MLul WCot WCru WMul
minamitanianum	WCru
* ***naniflorum*** 'Eco Decor'	EHrv EUJe GCai LAst MBNS
pulchellum	EHrv EMan WCot WCru
rigescens	EHrv
shuttleworthii	CLAP NLar
sieboldii	CLAP WCru
splendens	More than 30 suppliers
taipingshanianum B&SWJ 1688	WCru
takaoi	SSpi
virginicum	EBee

Asclepias (*Asclepiadaceae*)

'Cinderella'	CSev LBuc SGar SIgm
curassavica	CHrt CSev EShb LRHS SHFr SPav SSpi WRos
§ ***fascicularis***	SIgm
fasciculata	see *A. fascicularis*
incarnata	CAgr CPom CSec CSev EBee EBrs ELan ERou GKir MRav NBre SMHy SPav SPer WAul WOld WPer WTMC
- 'Alba'	EChP ELan EMon
- 'Ice Ballet'	EBee EMan ERou EShb LBuc LRHS MCCP NEgg NTHB SAga SGSe SIgm SPav SPet SPoG WMnd WMoo
- 'Soulmate'	CFai EBee EChP EMar EPfP EWll LRHS LRav MLLN MMHG NJOw NTHB SGSe SPoG WMoo WWpP
ovalifolia **new**	EBee
physocarpa	see *Gomphocarpus physocarpus*
purpurascens	CArn EChP NEgg SPav
speciosa	CAgr EBee NLar
sullivantii	EMan NBre SPav
syriaca	CAgr CArn CPom EBee LRHS MSal MSte SPav
tuberosa	CAgr CArn CBcs EBee EBrs ELau EMan GKir GPoy LRHS MHer MNrw MSal NBir NEgg SDix SECG SGSe SMad SPet SPoG SSpi WGHP WMnd
- Gay Butterflies Group	NEgg NLar SMrm WMnd
- 'Hello Yellow'	LRHS SPoG
verticillata	NBre

Asimina (*Annonaceae*)

triloba (F)	CBcs IArd MBlu NLar SBrw SPlb WNor
- 'Davis' (F)	CAgr

Askidiosperma (*Restionaceae*)

chartaceum	CTrC
esterhuyseniae	WNor
paniculatum	CTrC

Asparagus (*Asparagaceae*)

asparagoides ♀H1	ERea EShb SEND
§ - 'Myrtifolius'	CHal SYvo
cochinchinensis B&SWJ 3425	ELau
crassicladus	EShb
densiflorus 'Mazeppa'	EShb
- 'Myersii' ♀H1	CHal ERea EUJe SRms
- Sprengeri Group ♀H1	CHal LRHS MBri
- - 'Variegatus'	EShb
falcatus	EShb SEND
filicinus var. ***giraldii*** **new**	WCot
officinalis	ERea SEND WFar
- 'Connover's Colossal' ♀H4 **new**	CWan
- 'Franklim'	CTri WFar
- 'Gijnlim' ♀H4	EMil NBlu
- 'Purple Jumbo'	EBee
plumosus	see *A. setaceus*
pseudoscaber 'Spitzenschleier'	EBee EMan EShb SMad
retrofractus	EShb WPGP
scandens	EShb
schoberioides B&SWJ 871	WCru
§ ***setaceus*** ♀H1	CHal EShb LRHS MBri
- 'Pyramidalis' ♀H1	MBri
suaveolens	EShb
verticillatus	SRms
virgatus **new**	CFil EShb WPGP

Asperula (*Rubiaceae*)

§ ***arcadiensis*** ♀H3	CLyd EHyt EPot SBla WAbe
aristata subsp. ***scabra***	ECha ELan EMan EMon
- subsp. ***thessala***	see *A. sintenisii*
cyanchica	MSal NLar
daphneola	CNic ECho EHyt EWes SBla WAbe
gussonei	CLyd CMea CStu EPot GCrs LRHS MWat NLAp NMen NWCA SBla WAbe WPat
hirta	CNic
lilaciflora var. ***caespitosa***	see *A. lilaciflora* subsp. *lilaciflora*
§ - subsp. ***lilaciflora***	CLyd CPBP EDAr NMen
nitida	ECho
- subsp. ***puberula***	see *A. sintenisii*
odorata	see *Galium odoratum*
orientalis	CSec WPGP
§ ***sintenisii*** ♀H2-3	CLyd CMea LBee LRHS NMen NWCA SBla WAbe WHoo
suberosa misapplied	see *A. arcadiensis*
suberosa Sibth. & Sm.	ECho
taurina subsp. ***caucasica***	NLar NSti WCHb
tinctoria	CArn EOHP GBar GPoy MChe MHer MSal SRms WCHb

Asphodeline (*Asphodelaceae*)

liburnica	CAvo CBro EChP ECha ELan EMan EMar ERos ERou GSki NEgg SAga SEND SSpi WCAu WCot WFar WPer
§ ***lutea***	More than 30 suppliers
§ - 'Gelbkerze'	GBBs LRHS WBVN
- Yellow Candle	see *A. lutea* 'Gelbkerze'
taurica	ECho NBre SVal WPer

Asphodelus (*Asphodelaceae*)

acaulis	EHyt SIgm SSpi WAbe WCot
§ ***aestivus***	CDes EBee ECha EMan GAbr GSki NBur SSvw WBVN WPer
albus	CArn CBot ECha GBuc GIBF GSki NBid SHop SPlb SRms WCot WPer
cerasiferus	see *A. ramosus*
fistulosus	MMHG NBir WPrP XPep
lusitanicus	see *A. ramosus*
luteus	see *Asphodeline lutea*
microcarpus	see *A. aestivus*
§ ***ramosus***	CBrm CMdw CPar EBee EChP EGoo EMan GSki MNrw MTho NEgg SIgm SMrm WBVN WCot WPer XPep

Aspidistra (*Convallariaceae*)

from China **new**	WCot
attenuata	CKob
- B&SWJ 377	WCru
caespitosa 'Jade Ribbons'	IBlr WCot
'China Star'	EBee IBlr WCot
'China Sun'	WCot
daibuensis	CKob IBlr
- B&SWJ 312b	WCru
elatior ♀H1	CBct CHEx CHal EBak EBee EShb IBlr LRHS MBri NPal SAPC SArc SEND SMad SYvo WCot
- 'Akebono' (v)	WCot
- 'Asahi' (v)	IBlr WCot
- 'Hoshi-zora' (v)	IBlr WCot
- 'Milky Way' (v)	CAby CBct CHid CKob EBee EMan EShb EWin IBlr MTho SEND WCot WHil
- 'Okame' (v)	WCot
- 'Variegata' (v) ♀H1	CBct CHEx CHal EBee ERea EShb IBlr IFro MTho NBir SMad SYvo WCot
leshanensis (v) **new**	IBlr
linearifolia 'Leopard'	IBlr WCot
lurida	ERea IBlr
- 'Amanogawa' (v) **new**	IBlr
- 'Fuji-no-mine' (v) **new**	IBlr
- 'Irish Mist' (v)	IBlr
saxicola 'Uan Fat Lady'	WCru
typica **new**	IBlr

Asplenium ✿ (*Aspleniaceae*)

adiantum-nigrum	LRHS SRms
bulbiferum ♀H1-2	CPLG CTrC ESlt SMur
bulbiferum* x *oblongifolium	EAmu
§ ***ceterach***	CLAP EBee EMil SRms WAbe WHer
dareoides	SOkd SRot SSpi WAbe WCot
ebenoides	WAbe
flaccidum	WRic
haurakiense **new**	WRic
hookerianum **new**	WRic
'Maori Princess'	CTrC
nidus ♀H1	LRHS MBri
oblongifolium	CTrC WRic
platyneuron	CDes WAbe
ruta-muraria	EFer SRms
§ ***scolopendrium*** ♀H4	More than 30 suppliers
- 'Angustatum'	CLAP CMil CWCL EPfP ERod EWTr GBin GEdr LRHS MAsh MAvo MBct MCCP MGos MMoz MWgw NLar NVic SGSe SMac SRms WCru WFar WPnP WPtf
- 'Capitatum'	MDun
* - 'Circinatum'	WPGP
- 'Conglomeratum'	SRms
- Crispum Group	CLAP CSBt CWCL EBee ECha EFer ELan EPza SApp SRms SRot WAbe WFib WPGP
- - 'Golden Queen'	CLAP
- 'Crispum Bolton's Nobile' ♀H4	NBro WFib WPGP
- Crispum Cristatum Group	CLAP EChP
- Crispum Fimbriatum Group	CLAP GQui
- Cristatum Group	CElw CFwr CHEx CLAP EHrv ELan EMar EPfP LRHS MBri MGos MMoz MRav MWgw NBid NDlv SNut SPer SPla SRms WFib WRic
- 'Cristatum'	CFwr CWCL ENot MAsh SApp SMac SPoG SRot SSto WBVN WBor
- Fimbriatum Group	CLAP WRic
- 'Furcatum'	CFwr CLAP GEdr NEgg WRic
- 'Kaye's Lacerated' ♀H4	CLAP EFer ELan SChu WRic
- Laceratum Group	CLAP SRms
- Marginatum Group	EFer WPGP
- - 'Irregulare'	SChu SRms WFib
- 'Muricatum'	CLAP ELan GBin NBid SChu SRms WFib WTin
- 'Ramocristatum'	CLAP
- Ramomarginatum Group	CLAP ELan SRms WAbe WFar WRic
- 'Sagittatocristatum'	SRms WPGP
- 'Sagittato-projectum Sclater'	WFib
* - 'Sagittatum' **new**	SRms
- 'Stagshorn' **new**	SRms
- Undulatum Group	CLAP CPLG EMFW EPfP MAsh NBid NBir NEgg NSti NVic SPla SRms SSpi WIvy WPnP WRic
- Undulatum Cristatum Group	CLAP MBri NDlv
septentrionale	SRms
trichomanes ♀H4	More than 30 suppliers
- Cristatum Group	SRms
- Grandiceps Group	EFer
- Incisum Group	CLAP NOrc
viride	SRms WFar

Astartea (*Myrtaceae*)

fascicularis	CPLG CTrC

Astelia (*Asteliaceae*)

alpina	IBlr
banksii	CBcs CDoC CPen ECou IBal LPio WAbe WDyG WMul
§ ***chathamica*** ♀H3	More than 30 suppliers
- 'Silver Spear'	see *A. chathamica*
cunninghamii	see *A. solandri*
fragrans	ECou GGar IBlr LEdu WCot WDyG WMul WPic
graminea	IBlr
grandis	CTrC IBlr LEdu WMul
'Lodestone'	CStu
'Luzulliea Johnsen'	LPBA
nervosa	CAbb CFil EBee ECou GCrs GKev IBlr LEdu SAPC SArc WMul WPGP WPat WPic
- 'Bronze Giant'	IBlr
- 'Westland'	CAbb CBcs CBod CDoC CKno CPen CTbh CTrC EBee EMan EMil GCal IBlr LEdu LPio SPoG SSpi WCot WLeb WMul
nivicola	IBlr
- 'Red Gem'	GCal IBlr LEdu
petriei	IBlr
§ ***solandri***	CHEx IBlr LEdu
trinervia	IBlr

Aster ✿ (*Asteraceae*)

acris	see *A. sedifolius*
§ ***albescens***	CPle GKev WLin
alpigenus var. ***alpigenus***	CPBP
- var. ***haydenii***	NBid
alpinus ♀H4	CHrt CTri EPfP GKev GKir IHMH MNrw MWgw NBlu NEgg NJOw NLon SBla SMar SPet SRms WBrk WFar WPer
- var. ***albus***	EHan EMil EPfP IHMH NBro WCAu WPer WWeb
- Dark Beauty	see *A. alpinus* 'Dunkle Schöne'
§ - 'Dunkle Schöne'	CBrm CHrt GAbr GKir LDai MHar NVic SMar SRms WPer WWeb
- 'Goliath'	ECho EHan GAbr NBro SMar SPlb WFar WWeb

	- 'Happy End'	CM&M EMil IHMH LDai NBro NLar SRms WFar WWeb
	- 'Pinkie'	CBrm EWTr GAbr GKev NBre NLar SMad SMar WWeb
	- 'Trimix'	ESis NArg NBir SRms WFar
	- violet	WPer
	- 'White Beauty'	NLon SRms
*	- 'Wolfii'	SRms
	amelloides	see *Felicia amelloides*
	amellus	LSou NFor NLon SPer WMoo
	- 'Blue King'	EWsh MLLN SWvt WCAu
	- 'Brilliant'	EBee EChP ECtt EMan GMac LSou MBNS MLLN MMil MNFA MRav MWat NDov NEgg WIvy WOld
	- 'Butzemann'	EBee GMac
	- 'Doktor Otto Petschek'	WFar
	- 'Forncett Flourish'	WOut
	- 'Framfieldii' ♀H4	WFar WOld
	- 'Jacqueline Genebrier' ♀H4	CHar CMil SChu WIvy WSHC
	- 'Joseph Lakin'	WFar
	- 'King George' ♀H4	More than 30 suppliers
	- 'Kobold'	LRHS WFar
	- 'Lac de Genève'	LRHS MRav NLar WCot WFar WOld
	- 'Lady Hindlip'	WFar
	- 'Moerheim Gem'	WIvy
	- 'Nocturne'	ERou WCot WIvy WOld
	- 'Peach Blossom'	WCAu
	- 'Pink Pearl'	WFar
	- Pink Zenith	see *A. amellus* 'Rosa Erfüllung'
§	- 'Rosa Erfüllung'	CDoC CHrt EBee ECtt ELan EMar EPfP ERou EVFa GBuc GKir GMaP MNFA MRav NDov NEgg NFor SChu SPla SWvt WCAu WCot WMnd WOld WPer
	- 'Rotfeuer'	NGby
	- 'Rudolph Goethe'	CHar EBee EMil ERou LRHS MLLN MMil MRav MWhi NRnb NVic SHBN STes WFar WMoo WOld WWye
	- 'Silbersee' **new**	NDov
	- 'Sonia'	EBee ECha MRav NGby NLar WCAu WFar
	- 'Sonora'	ECGP ERou MAnH MSte NDov SAga WHoo WKif WOld
	- 'Sternkugel'	WOld
	- 'Ultramarine'	WFar
	- 'Vanity'	GBuc WOld
§	- 'Veilchenkönigin' ♀H4	More than 30 suppliers
N	- Violet Queen	see *A. amellus* 'Veilchenkönigin'
	- 'Weltfriede'	WOld
	'Anja's Choice'	EBee EMon EPPr EWsh MAvo NBre NDov WCot WOld
	asper	see *A. bakerianus*
	asperulus	EBrs EPPr LPhx MBri MFOX NDov SBla SMeo SUsu
	'Bahamas'	MBri
§	***bakerianus***	WFar WPer
	'Barbados'	MBri
	capensis 'Variegatus'	see *Felicia amelloides* variegated
§	***carolinianus***	WOld
	'Cassandra'	MBri
	Cassy = 'Moercass'PBR	MBri
	'Chelsea'	MBri
	'Cirina Dark'PBR	MBri
	'Climax' misapplied	see *A. laevis* 'Calliope', *A. laevis* 'Arcturus'
	'Climax' ambig.	EVFa GBuc GCal LPhx MRav NRnb NSti SAga SMrm
	'Climax' Vicary Gibbs	CMdw WOld
	coelestis	see *Felicia amelloides*
	coloradoensis	CGra CPBP NSla
	'Connecticut Snow Flurry'	see *A. ericoides* f. *prostratus* 'Snow Flurry'
	'Coombe Fishacre' ♀H4	CHrt COIW CPrp EBee EChP EPPr ERou GBuc GCal MAvo MMil MOne MRav MSte NPar SAga SHel SOkh SPla SPoG SSvw SUsu WCot WFar WMnd WOld WTin
	cordifolius	WFar
	- 'Aldebaran'	LPhx
	- 'Chieftain' ♀H4	IGor LPhx MNFA MNrw WIvy WOld
	- 'Elegans'	CStr EBee IGor MBri MNFA MSte NSti WIvy WMnd WMoo WOld
	- 'Ideal'	EBee GMac WOld WPer
	- 'Silver Queen'	WHil WOld
	- 'Silver Spray'	CPrp EBee ERou GMaP GMac MLLN MNFA MWat NBre WOld WPer
	- 'Sweet Lavender' ♀H4	ERou GMac WOld
	corymbosus	see *A. divaricatus*
	'Cotswold Gem'	WCot
§	'Dark Pink Star'	WOld
	'Deep Pink Star'	see *A.* 'Dark Pink Star'
	delavayi	EBee SUsu WCot
	diffusus	see *A. lateriflorus*
	diplostephioides	EChP EMan EPPr EShb GCal NLar SMar WAul
§	***divaricatus***	More than 30 suppliers
§	- 'Eastern Star'	CBos NCGa WBVN WCot WOld
	- Raiche form	see *A. divaricatus* 'Eastern Star'
	drummondii	EBee
N	***dumosus***	WFar WPer
§	***elliottii***	WOld
	ericoides	CHrt EShb NBre NOrc NWCA WFar XPep
	- 'Blue Star' ♀H4	CPrp CSam CWCL EBrs GBuc IGor LRHS MBnl MFOX MLLN MSte NLar NSti SChu SHGN SPoG WBor WCAu WCot WMnd WOld
	- 'Brimstone' ♀H4	EPPr IGor MRav WOld
	- 'Cinderella'	COIW CPrp GBuc GMac MNFA NSti WOld
	- 'Cirylle'	LBmB
	- 'Constance'	WOld
	- 'Enchantress'	ERou
	- 'Erlkönig'	EBee EChP EGra EMan EPPr GAbr LAst LRHS MBnl MMil MNFA MRav MSte MWgw NCGa SChu SPla SSpe WMnd WOld WPer
	- 'Esther'	CHea EBee ECha ELan ERou MSte NLar SDix WOld
	- 'Golden Spray' ♀H4	GMaP MBow NLar NSti WFar WMnd WOld WOut
	- 'Herbstmyrte'	MLLN NGby
	- 'Hon. Edith Gibbs'	WOld
	- 'Maidenhood'	WOld
	- 'Monte Cassino'	see *A. pilosus* var. *pringlei* 'Monte Cassino'
	- 'Pink Cloud' ♀H4	More than 30 suppliers
	- f. ***prostratus***	EBee EMon EPot ESis LRHS SGar SHGN WFar
§	- - 'Snow Flurry' ♀H4	CMea CSam EBee ECha ECtt IGor LPhx MBnl MLLN MNFA MNrw SPla SUsu WBor WCAu WCot WEas WMnd WOld
	- 'Rosy Veil'	CHea GMac IGor MHom MNFA NBir NGdn WOld
	- 'Ruth McConnell'	NSti
	- 'Schneegitter'	CStr MLLN MSte WCot WFar
	- 'Schneetanne'	NRnb
	- 'Sulphurea'	MWat
	- 'Vimmer's Delight' **new**	WCot

	- 'White Heather'	CAby CPrp GMac IGor MNFA NLar WCot WIvy WMnd WOld WRHF
	- 'Yvette Richardson'	MHom MSte SMHy WOld
	falcatus var. ***commutatus*** **new**	WCot
	'Fanny's Fall'	see *A. oblongifolius* 'Fanny's'
	farreri	GKev
*	- 'Blue Moon'	MSph
§	***flaccidus***	EBrs LRHS WCot
	foliaceus from Montana	EPPr
	x ***frikartii***	EBee EHol ELan EPfP ERou LAst MRav SAga SChu SHBN SRms SWvt WEas WMnd WOld WPer WSHC
	- 'Eiger'	GMac WOld
	- 'Flora's Delight'	MRav WOld
	- 'Jungfrau'	CFis EBee MRav MSte NLar SOkh WOld WSHC WWhi
N	- 'Mönch' ♀H4	More than 30 suppliers
	- Wonder of Stafa	see *A.* x *frikartii* 'Wunder von Stäfa'
§	- 'Wunder von Stäfa' ♀H4	CEnd EBee ECtt ELan EMan EPfP GBuc GKir GMaP LRHS MAvo MBNS MNFA MRav NBlu NLar SChu WCAu WCot WMnd WOld WPGP WPnP WTel
	hayatae B&SWJ 8790 **new**	WCru
	'Herfstweelde'	CMil EBee EMon GBuc LRHS MAvo MSte NCGa SMad WFar WOld
	x ***herveyi***	EMan EMon LPhx LRHS MSph SAga WOld
	himalaicus	EShb GKev GTou SRms
*	'Hittlemaar'	WCot WCra
§	'Hon. Vicary Gibbs' (*ericoides* hybrid)	EBee GMac MNFA MSte WOld WOut
	hybridus luteus	see x *Solidaster luteus*
§	'Kylie' ♀H4	EMon EPPr ERou GBuc IGor LPhx MHom MSte NCGa SRGP WBor WCot WFar WOld WTin
	laevis	MSte NLar SMar WTin
§	- 'Arcturus'	CFir EBrs MHar MLLN MMil NCGa NMRc NRnb NSti SSvw WCot WFar
	- 'Blauhügel'	GCal
§	- 'Calliope'	More than 30 suppliers
	- var. ***geyeri***	MAvo MNrw
	- 'Nightshade' **new**	WOld
	lanceolatus Willd.	WCot
	- 'Edwin Beckett'	CBre EMan GMac MHom MNFA WOld
§	***lateriflorus***	EBee EWTr EWin WOld WPer
	- 'Bleke Bet'	WCot WOld
	- 'Buck's Fizz'	CHrt ELan NLar WOld
	- 'Datschi'	WFar
	- 'Delight'	MLLN
	- 'Horizontalis' ♀H4	More than 30 suppliers
	- 'Jan'	WOld
	- 'Lady in Black'	More than 30 suppliers
	- 'Lovely'	EBee EBrs LRHS MLLN MOne NRnb WOld
	- 'Prince'	More than 30 suppliers
	laterifolius 'Snow Flurry'	see *A. ericoides* f. *prostratus* 'Snow Flurry'
§	***linosyris***	GBin MSte NLar NSti SPer WHer WOld
	- 'Goldilocks'	see *A. linosyris*
§	'Little Carlow' (*cordifolius* hybrid) ♀H4	More than 30 suppliers
§	'Little Dorrit' (*cordifolius* hybrid)	EWsh MLLN NBro WHil WOld
	maackii	GIBF
	macrophyllus	CPou EBrs ELan EMon GFlt LRHS NLar WOld
	- 'Albus'	EMon EPPr GFlt WFar WIvy WOld
	- 'Twilight'	CHVG CMea EBrs EChP ECha ECtt EPfP EVFa GCal LLWP MLLN MNFA MSte NDov NSti SDix SRGP SSpe WCAu WCot WIvy WMnd WOld WTin
	'Midget'	NRnb
	mongolicus	see *Kalimeris mongolica*
	natalensis	see *Felicia rosulata*
	novae-angliae	ELau WMoo WOld
	- 'Andenken an Alma Pötschke'	More than 30 suppliers
	- 'Andenken an Paul Gerber'	EBee EMon ERou NGby WBrk WOld
	- 'Annabelle de Chazal'	WOld
	- Autumn Snow	see *A. novae-angliae* 'Herbstschnee'
	- 'Barr's Blue'	ECtt EMon ERou EWsh GCra LRHS MAvo MBNS MSte MWat NFla NSti SRms WBrk WCAu WFar WMoo WOld
	- 'Barr's Pink'	CBre EChP ECtt EMon ERou MRav NFla SEND SHel SHop WBrk WCAu WFar WHrl WOld WPer
*	- 'Barr's Purple'	ECtt WOld
	- 'Barr's Violet'	EPPr MAvo NFor NLon SHel SHop SRms WBrk WCot WHal WHoo WHrl WMoo WOld WPer WTin WWpP
	- 'Christopher Harbutt'	ERou NPro SRGP WOld
	- 'Colwall Galaxy' **new**	WOld
	- 'Colwall Orbit' **new**	WOld
	- 'Crimson Beauty'	CStr EMon EPPr MAvo MNFA MWat WBrk WOld
	- 'Dwarf Alma Pötschke'	WCot
	- 'Evensong'	WOld
	- 'Harrington's Pink' ♀H4	More than 30 suppliers
	- 'Helen Picton'	WOld
§	- 'Herbstschnee'	CPrp EChP ECtt EHrv EMon EPfP ERou GMac MNFA MRav MSte MWat NFor NSti SChu SHel SPer SPet SSpe WBor WBrk WCAu WFar WMnd WMoo WOld WPer WTin WWye
	- 'James Ritchie'	WHoo
	- 'John Davies'	WOld
	- 'Lachsglut'	WCot
	- 'Lou Williams'	WOld
I	- 'Lucida'	WBrk WHal
	- 'Lye End Beauty'	CPou ECtt EMon ERou LLWP LRHS MAvo MNFA MRav MSte NFor NLon SChu WCot WHoo WMoo WOld WTin
	- 'Marina Wolkonsky'	MAnH WCot
	- 'Millennium Star'	WOld
	- 'Miss K.E. Mash' **new**	ERou SRGP WBrk WOld
	- 'Mrs S.T. Wright'	ECtt EMon ERou GMac MAnH MBrN MHom MNFA MSte WFar WFoF WHal WOld
	- 'Mrs S.W. Stern'	WOld
	- 'Pink Parfait'	EBee GMac NGdn WCot WOld WWpP
	- 'Pink Victor'	CTri EPPr NLar SEND SHel WCra WWpP
	- 'Primrose Upward'	EWsh WCot WOld
	- 'Purple Cloud'	EMon ERou GMac MHer MNFA MWat MWgw NGdn WBrk WFoF WHal WOld
I	- 'Purple Dome'	More than 30 suppliers
	- 'Quinton Menzies'	CStr WOld
	- 'Red Cloud'	SMrm WOld
	- 'Rosa Sieger' ♀H4	CBre EMon ERou GMac LPhx MAvo MHom NGdn SChu SHel SUsu WBor WBrk WOld

	- 'Rose Williams'	WOld
	- 'Roter Stern'	ECtt ERou
	- 'Rubinschatz'	WOld
	- 'Rudelsburg'	EMon ERou
	- 'Sayer's Croft'	EMon MHom WBrk WCot WHoo WOld WOut WTin
	- September Ruby	see *A. novae-angliae* 'Septemberrubin'
§	- 'Septemberrubin'	CAby CMea EBee ECtt EMon ERou EWsh GFlt LPhx MAnH MNFA MRav MSte NEgg NSti SChu SMer SUsu WFar WMoo WOld WPnP WPrP
	- 'Treasure'	CBre EMon WFar WMoo WOld
	- 'Violetta'	CMea CStr EBee ECtt EMon LPhx LSou MAvo MHom MNFA MSte SHel WBrk WOld WTin WWye
	- 'W. Bowman'	WOld
	- 'Wow'	SMrm
N	***novi-belgii***	GWCH SPoG WHer WMoo
	- 'Ada Ballard'	EBrs ERou EVFa LRHS NBre NGdn NRnb SPer SPet WOld WWye
	- 'Albanian'	WOld
	- 'Alderman Vokes'	WOld
	- 'Alex Norman'	ERou WOld
	- 'Algar's Pride'	CHrt EBee ECtt ERou NBre NRnb SSvw WOld
	- 'Alice Haslam'	EBee ECtt EPPr GBri GKir IHMH LRHS MCCP MWgw NOrc NPri NRnb SPur WOld WPer
	- 'Anita Ballard'	WOld
	- 'Anita Webb'	ERou GBri NBir NBre NOak NRnb WOld
	- 'Anneke'	EBee EBrs WWeb
	- 'Apollo'	EBrs NBre NLar NPri
	- 'Apple Blossom'	WOld
	- 'Arctic'	ERou
	- 'Audrey'	ECtt EPPr ERou GKir GMaP LRHS MLLN MWgw NCGa NOrc SChu SHel SPla SRGP STes WOld WTel
	- 'Autumn Beauty'	WOld
	- 'Autumn Days'	WOld
	- 'Autumn Glory'	ERou WOld WWpP
	- 'Autumn Rose'	CHea WOld
	- 'Baby Climax'	WOld
	- 'Beauty of Colwall'	WOld
	- 'Beechwood Challenger'	ERou MOne NRnb WOld
	- 'Beechwood Charm'	WOld
	- 'Beechwood Rival'	EBee GFlt MOne MSte NBre NRnb
	- 'Beechwood Supreme'	ERou NRnb WOld
	- 'Benary's Composition' **new**	SECG SWal
	- 'Bewunderung'	NBre NRnb WOld
	- 'Blandie'	CHea CTri ERou EVFa MSte MWgw SHop WCAu WOld
	- 'Blauglut'	WOld
	- 'Blue Baby'	WPer WWye
	- 'Blue Bouquet'	ERou SRms WOld
	- 'Blue Boy'	WBrk WOld
	- 'Blue Danube'	CMdw WOld
	- 'Blue Eyes'	CElw CStr ERou SAga WOld WWye
	- 'Blue Gown'	CMdw ERou GCal NRnb WOld
	- 'Blue Lagoon'	GFlt LRHS MBnl MBri NOrc NRnb SPoG WBor WHil WOld
	- 'Blue Patrol'	ERou NBre NRnb WOld
	- 'Blue Radiance'	WOld
	- 'Blue Whirl'	ERou WOld
	- 'Bonanza'	WOld WTel
	- 'Boningale Blue'	WOld
	- 'Boningale White'	CStr ERou WOld
	- 'Bridesmaid'	WOld
	- 'Bright Eyes' **new**	SRGP
	- 'Brightest and Best'	WOld
	- 'Caborn Pink'	LLWP
	- 'Cameo'	WOld
	- 'Cantab'	WOld
	- 'Carlingcott'	ERou MOne WOld
	- 'Carnival'	CM&M ECtt ERou EVFa MMHG NBre NEgg NOrc SPer SSpe WOld
	- 'Cecily'	WOld
	- 'Charles Wilson'	WOld
	- 'Chatterbox'	COIW CPrp EBee EDAr LRHS MRav MWat NLar SChu SRms WOld WRHF
	- 'Chelwood'	EBee WOld
	- 'Chequers'	CBrm CM&M CStr ECot ERou MSte SRGP WOld
	- 'Christina'	see *A. novi-belgii* 'Kristina'
	- 'Christine Soanes'	NBre NRnb WOld
	- 'Cliff Lewis'	ERou MOne NBre NRnb WOld
	- 'Climax Albus'	see *A.* 'White Climax'
	- 'Cloudy Blue'	NRnb WOld
	- 'Colonel F. R. Durham'	ERou NRnb
	- 'Coombe Delight'	ERou NRnb
	- 'Coombe Gladys'	ERou NRnb WOld
	- 'Coombe Joy'	ERou NRnb WOld
	- 'Coombe Margaret'	WOld WOut
	- 'Coombe Pink'	ERou NBre NRnb
	- 'Coombe Queen'	WOld
	- 'Coombe Radiance'	ERou MSte WOld
	- 'Coombe Ronald'	ERou MWat WOld
	- 'Coombe Rosemary'	ECtt ERou LRHS NLar WBor WOld WRHF WTel
	- 'Coombe Violet'	MRav MWat WOld
	- 'Countess of Dudley'	WOld WPer
	- 'Court Herald'	WOld
	- 'Crimson Brocade'	CBcs ENot ERou LPhx MRav NLar SPoG WOld
	- 'Dandy'	EBee ECot ELan LRHS MOne NBir NGdn SChu WOld
	- 'Daniela'	WBrk WOld
	- 'Daphne Anne'	WOld
	- 'Dauerblau'	WOld
	- 'Davey's True Blue'	CTri EBee ERou MSte WOld
	- 'David Murray'	WOld
	- 'Dazzler'	WOld
	- 'Destiny'	WOld
	- 'Diana'	CNic ERou MOne WOld
	- 'Diana Watts'	ERou NBre NRnb WOld
	- 'Dietgard'	NRnb WOld
	- 'Dolly'	NBir WOld
	- 'Dusky Maid'	MBri WBor WOld
	- 'Elizabeth'	WOld
	- 'Elizabeth Bright'	WOld
	- 'Elizabeth Hutton'	WOld
	- 'Elsie Dale'	EBee WOld
	- 'Elta'	WOld
	- 'Erica'	CElw NBre NRnb WOld
	- 'Ernest Ballard'	ERou WOld
	- 'Eva'	WOld
	- 'Eventide'	CBcs CElw ENot ERou LPhx NOak SPer WMoo WOld WRHF
	- 'F. M. Simpson'	ERou EVFa
	- 'Fair Lady'	ERou MWat WOld
	- 'Faith'	WOld
	- 'Farncombe Lilac'	EBee EBrs
	- 'Farrington'	WOld
	- 'Fellowship'	CDes CFir CStr ERou EVFa IHMH LPhx MAvo MSte MWat SAga SPer SRms WBrk WCot WOld WTel
	- 'Fontaine'	WOld
	- 'Freda Ballard'	ECtt EPPr ERou EWll GMaP LRHS NGdn SRGP WBor WCAu WOld
	- 'Freya'	WOld
	- 'Fuldatal'	WOld WOut

- 'Gayborder Blue' WOld
- 'Gayborder Royal' CFir ERou MOne WOld
- 'Glory of Colwall' WOld
- 'Goliath' WOld
- 'Grey Lady' WOld
- 'Guardsman' ERou GKir WOld
- 'Gulliver' WOld
- 'Gurney Slade' CStr ERou GKir NRnb WOld
- 'Guy Ballard' ERou
- 'Harrison's Blue' EBee ERou EVFa LPhx NRnb SAga WBrk WOld WPer
- 'Heinz Richard' CM&M COIW EBee ECha MSte NBir NBre NEgg NGdn SBla SChu SPet WOld WWpP
- 'Helen' WOld
- 'Helen Ballard' CHea CStr ERou NRnb WBrk WOld
- 'Herbstgruss vom Bresserhof' EWTr NRnb
- 'Herbstpurzel' MOne
- 'Hilda Ballard' ERou NBre NRnb WOld
- 'Ilse Brensell' MOne MSte WOld
- 'Irene' WOld
- 'Isabel Allen' WOld
- 'Janet Watts' ERou WOld
- 'Jean' MWat WOld
- 'Jean Gyte' WOld
- 'Jenny' COIW CSBt EChP ECtt EDAr EMar EPfP GKir GMaP LRHS MBow MBri MHer MRav NBir NCGa NEgg NGdn SHBN SMer SPoG SRGP SRms STes WBrk WEas WMoo WOld WTel WWye
- 'Jollity' WOld
- 'Julia' MAvo WOld
- 'Karminkuppel' NBre NRnb WOld
- 'Kilmersdon' **new** GMaP
- 'King of the Belgians' WOld
- 'King's College' GKir WOld

§ - 'Kristina' COIW ECha ERou GKir LRHS MOne MRav SPet WCot WOld WTel WWpP
- 'Lady Evelyn Drummond' WOld
- 'Lady Frances' ENot WOld
- 'Lady in Blue' CBcs COIW CSBt EBee EChP ECtt ELan ENot EPfP EVFa GKir LRHS MBNS MBow MWgw NEgg NVic SMer SPer SPet SPoG SRms SSpe STes SWvt WFar WOld WPer WTel WTin
- 'Lady Paget' WOld
- 'Lassie' CElw CHea ERou LLWP MWat SBri WCot WOld
- 'Lavender Dream' WOld
- 'Lawrence Chiswell' WOld
- 'Lilac Time' WOld
- 'Lisa Dawn' WOld
- 'Little Boy Blue' ERou NBre NRnb SHBN WOld
- 'Little Man in Blue' WOld
- 'Little Pink Beauty' COIW CPrp ECtt ELan ERou EVFa GKir LRHS MBNS MRav NBid NEgg NMir NVic SPer SRGP SSpe STes WOld WTel
- 'Little Pink Lady' EBrs ERou WOld
- 'Little Pink Pyramid' NRnb SRms
- 'Little Red Boy' ERou WOld
- 'Little Treasure' WOld
- 'Lucy' WOld
- 'Madge Cato' WOld
- 'Malvern Castle' ERou
- 'Mammoth' MOne NRnb WOld
- 'Margaret Rose' NCiC NOrc WOld
- 'Margery Bennett' ERou GBri WOld
- 'Marie Ballard' CBcs CHea CSBt EBrs EChP ENot EPfP ERou EVFa GKir GMaP MWat NGdn NLon NOrc SHBN SPer SPoG SRms STes WBrk WCAu WEas WOld WPer WTMC WTel
- 'Marie's Pretty Please' WOld
- 'Marjorie' NRnb SPoG WOld
- 'Marjory Ballard' WOld

* - 'Mark Ballard' MOne NRnb
- 'Martonie' WOld WPer
- 'Mary Ann Neil' WOld
- 'Mary Deane' MSte WOld WPer
- 'Mauve Magic' WOld
- 'Melbourne Belle' NRnb WOld
- 'Melbourne Magnet' CHea ERou MOne WOld
- 'Michael Watts' ERou WOld
- 'Mistress Quickly' CRez ERou GBri MBri WOld
- 'Mount Everest' ERou LPhx WOld WPer
- 'Mrs Leo Hunter' NRnb WOld
- 'Nesthäkchen' ECho
- 'Nobilis' WOld
- 'Norman's Jubilee' ERou NBir NBre NRnb WOld WRHF
- 'Nursteed Charm' WOld
- 'Oktoberschneekuppel' ERou LRHS NRnb
- 'Orlando' ERou NRnb WOld
- 'Pamela' ERou WOld
- 'Patricia Ballard' CElw CPrp CSBt EBrs ERou GCra GKir MWat NLon SPer SRGP SSpe WBVN WCAu WFar WOld WPer WTel
- 'Peace' WOld
- 'Percy Thrower' ERou NRnb WOld
- 'Peter Chiswell' MBri WOld
- 'Peter Harrison' GMaP GMac NBir WOld WPer
- 'Peter Pan' CBcs CStu LSou WOld
- 'Picture' NBre NRnb WOld
- 'Pink Gown' WOld
- 'Pink Lace' ERou MBNS MLLN WOld WPer
- 'Pink Perfection' **new** MAnH
- 'Pink Pyramid' NRnb WOld
- 'Plenty' ERou MBri NBre NRnb WOld
- 'Porzellan' CElw CM&M COIW CStr EBee ECtt EMar EVFa MAvo NCGa NEgg WCot
- 'Pride of Colwall' CStr ERou MOne NBre NRnb WBrk
- 'Priory Blush' CHea ERou LPhx WOld
- 'Professor Anton Kippenberg' EBee EPfP ERou GKir GMaP IHMH LRHS MBow MHer MRav NRnb SPer SRGP WMoo WOld WTel
- 'Prosperity' ERou GKir NBre NMRc NRnb WOld

* - 'Prunella' ERou NBre NRnb WOld
- 'Purple Dome' EBrs ECha LPhx MBnl MCCP NEgg WOld
- 'Queen Mary' ERou WOld
- 'Queen of Colwall' WOld
- 'Ralph Picton' WOld
- 'Raspberry Ripple' ECot ERou NCiC WOld
- 'Red Robin' MWat
- 'Red Sunset' CBcs ERou SRms WOld
- 'Rembrandt' ECtt EVFa EWll GKir
- 'Remembrance' GKir NRnb WBrk WOld
- 'Reverend Vincent Dale' WOld
- 'Richness' ERou MFOX NRnb SAga WOld
- 'Robin Adair' WOld
- 'Roland Smith' WOld
- 'Rose Bonnet' CSBt EBee ENot MWat SHBN SPlb
- 'Rose Bouquet' WOld
- 'Rosebud' WOld
- 'Rosemarie Sallmann' MOne NRnb
- 'Rosenwichtel' EMar MWgw NCGa NLar NRnb WBrk WHil WOld

	- 'Royal Ruby'	EBee EBrs ECtt WOld
	- 'Royal Velvet'	ENot ERou NBre NRnb WOld
	- 'Rozika'	WOld
	- 'Rufus'	ERou WOld
	- 'Sailor Boy'	ERou NRnb WOld
	- 'Saint Egwyn'	WOld
	- 'Sam Banham'	EBee ERou WOld
	- 'Sandford White Swan'	ERou GBuc GKir MHom WBrk WEas WPer
	- 'Sarah Ballard'	ERou IHMH WOld
§	- 'Schneekissen'	CPrp CStu ECtt EGoo EPfP GMaP MHer MWgw NEgg NPri SEND SPer SPoG SRGP STes SWvt WOld WRHF
	- 'Schneezicklein'	GBin
	- 'Schöne von Dietlikon'	CKno WOld
	- 'Schoolgirl'	ERou GKir NBre NRnb WOld
	- 'Sheena'	ERou MBri WOld
	- 'Silberblaukissen'	GBin
§	- 'Silberteppich'	GMac
	- Silver Carpet	see *A. novi-belgii* 'Silberteppich'
	- Snow Cushion	see *A. novi-belgii* 'Schneekissen'
	- 'Snowdrift'	WOld
	- 'Snowsprite'	CBcs CSBt ELan EPfP MBow MWat NLar NOrc NPro SRGP WBrk WOld WTin
	- 'Sonata'	ERou GMaP NLon NOak NRnb WOld
	- 'Sophia'	CStr ERou NOak NRnb WBrk WOld
	- 'Starlight'	EBee ENot ERou GFlt LSou MBNS WFar WHil WMoo WOld
	- 'Steinebrück'	WOld
	- 'Sterling Silver'	ERou WOld
	- 'Sunset'	WOld
	- 'Susan'	WOld
	- 'Sweet Briar'	CElw WOld
	- 'Tapestry'	WOld
	- 'Terry's Pride'	WOld
	- 'The Archbishop'	WOld
	- 'The Bishop'	ERou WOld
	- 'The Cardinal'	ERou WOld
	- 'The Choristers'	WOld
	- 'The Dean'	ERou WOld
§	- 'The Rector'	WOld
	- 'The Sexton'	ERou WOld
	- 'Thundercloud'	EBee MOne NRnb WOld
	- 'Timsbury'	NBre NRnb WBrk WOld
	- 'Tony'	WOld
	- 'Tovarich'	WOld
	- 'Trudi Ann'	CStr NBir WOld
	- 'Twinkle'	NEgg WOld WOut
	- 'Victor'	MOne WOld
	- 'Vignem'	NSti
	- 'Violet Lady'	ERou WOld
	- 'Waterperry'	MWat
	- 'Weisses Wunder'	WOld WOut
	- 'White Ladies'	ERou GCra GMaP LLWP MWat NOrc SPoG
	- 'White Swan'	CPou ECtt EPPr LPhx NRnb WOld
	- 'White Wings'	MBri WOld
	- 'Winston S. Churchill'	CM&M COIW CTri EBee ELan ENot EPfP ERou GMaP LRHS MWat NOrc SHBN SPer SPlb SPoG SSpe WOld WPnP WTel
	oblongifolius	SUsu WOld
	- 'Fanny's'	EBee EMan MBnl MNFA SPoG WCot WFar WOld
	'Ochtendgloren' (*pringlei* hybrid) ♀H4	CPrp EPPr EVFa GBuc GKir GMac MAnH MAvo MBri MMil MNrw MSte NCGa SAga SMrm WCot WFar WOld WWye
	Octoberlight	see *A.* 'Oktoberlicht'
§	'Oktoberlicht'	EMon WOld
	oolentangiensis	EBee EPPr
	'Orchidee'	EBee
	pappei	see *Felicia amoena*
	'Pearl Star'	GMac WOld
	petiolatus	see *Felicia petiolata*
§	'Photograph' ♀H4	CStr EWes GCal MAvo MNFA MSte SMrm WFar WIvy WMnd WMoo WOld
§	***pilosus*** var. ***demotus*** ♀H4	EChP ECha EMon EWes MLLN MRav MSte WFar WOld WTin
§	- var. ***pringlei*** 'Monte Cassino' ♀H4	CHea CHid CPrp CSBt EBee EChP ECha EPfP ERou GAbr IHMH LPhx LRHS MAnH MBNS MLLN MRav NBPC NCGa SAga SPav SPer SRGP SUsu WCAu WFar WMnd WOld WTin
	- - 'October Glory'	WFar
I	- - 'Phoebe'	WOld
	- - 'Pink Cushion'	WCot
	'Pink Cassino'	WCAu
	'Pink Star'	CAby CMea CStr EMan GKir GMac LPhx MNFA MRav MWgw NSti SBch WBrk WFar WHoo WOld WTin
	'Plowden's Pink'	WOld
	'Prairie Lavender' **new**	WOld
	'Prairie Pink' **new**	WOld
	'Prairie Violet' **new**	WOld
	'Primrose Path' **new**	WCot
§	***ptarmicoides***	EBee EMon LPhx MLLN NBre WOld WPer
	puniceus **new**	NBre
	purdomii	see *A. flaccidus*
	pyrenaeus 'Lutetia'	CHea CSam EBee EChP ECha EMan EPPr GAbr GBuc GCal LRHS MAnH MNFA MSte NCGa NLar SBla WCAu WCot WFar WOld
	radula	EChP EMan GCal MAvo MNrw NBre NLar NSti SUsu WOld
	'Ringdove' (*ericoides* hybrid) ♀H4	CPrp EBee EPfP ERou GMac LRHS MBnl MNFA MNrw MWat MWgw NSti NVic SRGP STes WCAu WCot WIvy WOld
	'Rosa Star'	WOld
	rotundifolius 'Variegatus'	see *Felicia amelloides* variegated
	rugulosus 'Asrugo'	EBee
	x ***salignus***	WOld
	- Scottish form	WOld
	'Samoa'	MBri
§	***scaber***	EBee WCot WPGP
	scandens	see *A. carolinianus*
	schreberi	CHea EBee EPPr MHar MHom MLLN NCGa WCot WOld WWFP
§	***sedifolius***	EBrs ELan EMan MDKP MSte MWat NBid SBla SChu SDix SOkh SPla WEas WFar WMnd WOld WPer
	- 'Nanus'	CElw CSam EBee ERou LRHS MLLN MSte NBir NLar NSti SPer WCot WFar WMnd WOld WTin
	- 'Roseus' **new**	EBrs
	- 'Snow Flurries'	see *A. ericoides* f. *prostratus* 'Snow Flurry'
§	***sibiricus***	NLar WOld
	'Snow Flurry'	see *A. ericoides* f. *prostratus* 'Snow Flurry'
	'Snow Star'	WOld
	souliei	EBee EBrs WLin
	- B&SWJ 7655	WCru
	spathulifolius	NBir
	spectabilis	EBrs GAbr WOld
	subcaeruleus	see *A. tongolensis*

tataricus ECha WOld WWye
- 'Jindai' WCot WFar

thomsonii **new** WFar
- 'Nanus' CMdw GMaP LPhx MSte NBid NDov WCot WFar WOld WSHC

tibeticus see *A. flaccidus*
'Tonga' MBri
§ ***tongolensis*** EPfP GKir SRms WFar WWFP
- 'Berggarten' CHar EBrs GKir MBri MMil WFar WWeb
- 'Dunkleviolette' GBuc NBro SRms
- 'Lavender Star' GBuc
- 'Leuchtenburg' ERou
- 'Napsbury' CDes EBrs ECha ERou GKir LRHS WPGP
- 'Wartburgstern' CPrp CSam EChP EPfP LRHS MDKP MMil NGdn NPri SUsu WCFE WFar WMnd WPer

tradescantii misapplied see *A. pilosus* var. *demotus*
tradescantii L. EGra ELan EMan MBNS MBnl MRav MWgw NSti SHel SMad WCot WOld WTin
§ ***trinervius*** subsp. ***ageratoides***
- 'Asran' EWes SHGN SSvw WFar
- var. ***harae*** WOld
- 'Morea' **new** SSvw

tripolium EVFa MBow WHer
'Triumph' EBee WCot
turbinellus hort. ♀H4 EChP EMan EMon GBuc LPhx LRHS MAnH MBNS MBct MBri MNFA MSte SChu SDix SMHy WCot WFar WHoo WOld WTin
- hybrid CMea WWeb

turbinellus Lindl. EPPr SMar
umbellatus CBre EMon EPPr GBin NBre NCGa NSti SRms WCAu WCot WOld WTin
vimineus Lam. see *A. lateriflorus*
- 'Ptarmicoides' see *A. ptarmicoides*

§ 'White Climax' CMea LPhx MAnH MSte WBrk WCot WOld
yunnanensis WSHC
'Yvonne' CBre

Asteranthera (*Gesneriaceae*)

ovata CFil CFwr CPLN CPen GGGa GGar NCGa SSpi WAbe WCru WPGP WPrP WSHC

Asteriscus (*Asteraceae*)

'Gold Coin' see *Pallenis maritima*
maritimus see *Pallenis maritima*
§ ***spinosus*** CSec

Asteromoea (*Asteraceae*)

mongolica see *Kalimeris mongolica*
pinnatifida see *Kalimeris pinnatifida*

Asteropyrum (*Ranunculaceae*)

cavaleriei CDes GEdr WCot WCru

Asterotrichion (*Malvaceae*)

discolor **new** ECou

Astilbe ✿ (*Saxifragaceae*)

'America' CMHG ECtt GKir MBnl
'Amethyst' (x *arendsii*) CBcs CMHG EBrs EMFW EWTr GKir GSki LRHS MRav NBir NBlu SApp SBod SGSe SMac SPer WAul WCAu WFar WHoo WMoo WPop
'Anita Pfeifer' (x *arendsii*) CMHG EBrs GKir LPBA LRHS NLon WFar WPnP WWpP
'Aphrodite' (*simplicifolia* hybrid) CMCo CSam CWCL EChP ENot EVFa LAst MDKP NCGa NEgg NPro SChu SMac SSpi WBrE WGor
x ***arendsii*** CBrm CWat NBre NJOw SMac SPet WMoo WPer
astilboides CMHG SWvt
'Atrorosea' (*simplicifolia* hybrid) NCot SRms
'Avalanche' GAbr
Bella Group (x *arendsii*) NBre WMnd WRHF
'Bergkristall' (x *arendsii*) CMHG EMil
'Betsy Cuperus' (*thunbergii* hybrid) CMHG CMil EBee MRav MSte NPro SApp WCAu WWpP
biternata EBee EMon
'Bonn' (*japonica* hybrid) CBcs EBrs LPBA NBlu SCoo SRms
§ 'Brautschleier' (x *arendsii*) ♀H4 CM&M CMHG CMac CPrp CTri CWCL EBrs EChP ECtt ENot EPfP GCra MOne NGdn NPri WPnP WPtf
'Bremen' (*japonica* hybrid) CM&M CMHG EBrs GBin LPBA
'Bressingham Beauty' (x *arendsii*) More than 30 suppliers
Bridal Veil see *A.* 'Brautschleier'
§ 'Bronce Elegans' (*simplicifolia* hybrid) ♀H4 CBcs CMHG EBrs EChP ECha ENot EPfP EWTr GBBs GBuc GKir GMaP GSki LAst LRHS MBNS MDHE MDun MRav NOrc NPro SChu SMac SMer SPer WCAu WFar WHoo WMoo WPop
'Bronze Sprite' (*simplicifolia* hybrid) **new** WFar
'Bronzlaub' (x *arendsii*) CRez
* ***bumalda*** 'Bronze Pygmy' COIW EBee EWTr NArg STes
'Bumalda' (x *arendsii*) CFir CFwr CMCo COtt CRez CSam ENot EPPr GGar GMaP GSki LRHS NDlv NMyG NOrc NPro SPlb SSpi WAul WFar WMoo
'Carnea' (*simplicifolia* hybrid) CMHG NCGa
'Catherine Deneuve' see *A.* 'Federsee'
'Cattleya Dunkel' (x *arendsii*) CMHG WFar
'Cattleya' (x *arendsii*) CMHG CSam CWCL EBrs ECha MBnl NCGa NLar WFar WMoo
'Ceres' (x *arendsii*) CMHG
'Cherry Ripe' see *A.* 'Feuer'
chinensis CMCo CMHG CWat EBrs GKir GSki IBlr LRHS MBow NBre WLin WSHC WWeb
- B&SWJ 8178 WCru
- from Russia GCal
- var. ***davidii*** CMHG GSki
- - B&SWJ 8583 WCru
- - B&SWJ 8645 WCru
- 'Finale' EMFW EVFa GLil NArg NCGa NPro WFar WLin
- 'Frankentroll' CMHG
- 'Intermezzo' GMaP

§ - var. ***pumila*** ♀H4 More than 30 suppliers
- - 'Serenade' GSki LRHS MBri NGdn WFar
- 'Purple Glory' CMHG
- 'Purpurkerze' EBrs EChP EWTr GMaP LDai MBNS MBri MNrw NBPC NBid NBro SMrm WBor
- 'Spätsommer' CMHG
- var. ***tacquetii*** 'Rowden Sunstar' CRow
- var. ***taquetii*** EBrs EChP NBre NSti SRms
- - Purple Lance see *A. chinensis* var. *taquetii* 'Purpurlanze'

	Name	Suppliers
§	- - 'Purpurlanze'	CMHG CWCL EBrs ECha ECtt EGra EMFW EMan EPPr GCra GKir LLWP LPhx MBri MRav MWat NBir NDov NGdn NPro SPoG WCAu WCot WFar WMoo WWpP
§	- - 'Superba' ♀[H4]	CM&M CMHG CPLG CRow CTri CWCL EBrs ECha ENot EPfP GGar IHMH MCCP MLLN MSte NArg NBro SChu SDix SPer SPoG SRms STes WEas WFar WMoo WOld WPGP
	- 'Veronica Klose'	CMHG GKir NLar NPro SMrm WCAu
	- 'Vision in Red'[PBR]	MBNS MBnl MBri NFor NLar NMyG WBor
	- 'Visions'	CFai CMHG EBrs EChP EMan ENot LRHS MBNS MBri MSte NBro NGdn NMyG NPro STes WFar WLin
	Cologne	see *A.* 'Köln'
	'Crimson Feather'	see *A.* 'Gloria Purpurea'
	x ***crispa***	IBlr WFar
	- 'Gnom'	EMFW
	- 'Lilliput'	CLAP GBin GEdr GKir LRHS NLar NPro
§	- 'Perkeo' ♀[H4]	CBrm COtt EBrs ECha ELan EPfP GBBs GGar GKir GMaP GSki IMGH LRHS MDun MSte NBir NCGa NEgg NLar NMen NPro NSla SPoG SRms SSpi WAul WBVN WFar WMoo
	- 'Peter Pan'	see *A.* x *crispa* 'Perkeo'
	- 'Snow Queen'	LRHS NBir NMen NPro WFar
	'Darwin's Dream'	MBnl NLar NPri WFar
	'Darwin's Favourite' (x *arendsii*)	CWCL
	'Deutschland' (*japonica* hybrid)	More than 30 suppliers
§	'Diamant' (x *arendsii*)	CMHG EBrs LRHS MAvo MWrn NGdn WFar
	Diamond	see *A.* 'Diamant'
	'Drayton Glory'	see *A.* x *rosea* 'Peach Blossom'
	'Dunkellachs' (*simplicifolia* hybrid)	CM&M EBrs NPro WAbe WFar WSSM
	'Dutch Treat' (*japonica* hybrid) (v)	CMea
	'Düsseldorf' (*japonica* hybrid)	CMHG CSam CWCL EBrs GKir
	'Eden's Odysseus'	EBee EChP MOne WWpP
	'Elegans' (*simplicifolia* hybrid)	CMHG WFar
	Elizabeth Bloom = 'Eliblo'[PBR] (x *arendsii*)	EBee EBrs GSki LRHS MRav SVil WFar
	'Elizabeth' (*japonica* hybrid)	CMHG EBee
§	'Ellie van Veen' (x *arendsii*)	CFai CM&M CMHG CWCL EBrs EChP GBin MBri NPro
	'Ellie'	see *A.* 'Ellie van Veen'
	'Else Schluck' (x *arendsii*) **new**	ECha
	'Erica' (x *arendsii*)	CMHG CSBt CTri EWll GKir LRHS MBri MRav NPro WCAu WFar WMoo
	'Etna' (*japonica* hybrid)	CBcs CMHG CRez CSam CWCL EBee EGra EWTr GBri GSki MWrn NPro SRms WPnP WPop
	'Europa' (*japonica* hybrid)	CM&M CMHG CMac EBrs ECtt EMFW GKir LPBA MRav NEgg NOak SPla SPoG SSpe WFar WMoo
	'Fanal' (x *arendsii*) ♀[H4]	More than 30 suppliers
	'Fata Morgana' (x *arendsii* hybrid)	CMHG
§	'Federsee' (x *arendsii*)	CBcs CMHG CWCL EBrs ECha ELan EMil EVFa GKir LRHS NBro NGdn NPro WFar
§	'Feuer' (x *arendsii*)	CM&M CMCo CMHG CPrp CWCL EBrs ELan EPPr EPfP GKir LRHS MAvo MBnl NBid NCGa NOrc NPro NVic WBor WMoo
	Fire	see *A.* 'Feuer'
	'Flamingo'[PBR] (x *arendsii*)	MBNS MBnl MBri NCGa NPro
	'Gertrud Brix' (x *arendsii*)	CBcs NBir NGdn NPro SBod SPla
§	***glaberrima***	NMen
	- var. ***saxatilis*** ♀[H4]	CLyd CRow EBee EPfP GBin IFro IMGH NSla NWoo WAbe WHal
	- ***saxosa***	see *A.* 'Saxosa'
*	- - ***minor***	NJOw
	'Gladstone' (x *arendsii*)	see *A.* 'W.E. Gladstone'
§	'Gloria Purpurea' (x *arendsii*)	CMHG CTbh GKir LRHS MDun WMoo WWpP
	'Gloria' (x *arendsii*)	CMHG CTri GFlt LPBA LRHS MRav WFar
	Glow	see *A.* 'Glut'
§	'Glut' (x *arendsii*)	CFwr CMHG CWCL EBrs ECtt EGra EPPr GKir LRHS NMyG SRms WFar
	'Granat' (x *arendsii*)	CM&M CMHG CMac EMFW EWTr NBPC NBir NPro WMoo
*	Grande Group (x *arendsii*)	NBre
	grandis	CMHG WHer
	'Grete Püngel' (x *arendsii*)	CFwr ECha GBri MLLN WFar
	'Harmony' (x *arendsii*)	CMHG
	'Hennie Graafland' (*simplicifolia* hybrid)	CBcs CMHG COtt CWCL EBrs EChP EMan EMil GKir MBNS MDHE NCGa NLar NPro WLin
	Hyacinth	see *A.* 'Hyazinth'
§	'Hyazinth' (x *arendsii*)	CMHG CPLG CPrp EBrs EGra EMFW GMaP GSki LRHS LSou MLan NFor NGdn NPro SPoG WFar
	'Inshriach Pink' (*simplicifolia* hybrid)	CBcs CMHG EBrs EHoe ELan EMFW GBin GCrs GKir GLil LRHS MBri MDHE NBir NCGa NOak SAga SHGN WCot WFar WHal WLin
	'Irrlicht' (x *arendsii*)	CBcs CMHG CSBt EHon ELan EMFW EPfP EPla EWTr GGar GKir LBBr LPBA LRHS NFor SMac WAul WPnP WWpP
	japonica **new**	CPLG
	- var. ***terrestris***	see *A. glaberrima*
	'Jo Ophorst' (*davidii* hybrid)	CMHG EMan EPPr GSki LPBA LRHS MRav NGdn NLar NPro WWpP
	'Koblenz' (*japonica* hybrid)	CMHG CWCL MDKP
§	'Köln' (*japonica* hybrid)	CMHG EMil LPBA NMyG WFar WWpP
	koreana	GGar WCot
	- B&SWJ 8611	WCru
	- B&SWJ 8680	WCru
	'Koster'	LPBA
	'Kriemhilde'	CMHG
	'Kvele' (x *arendsii*)	CMHG GKir WFar WMoo
§	'Lachskönigin' (x *arendsii*)	CMHG
	'Lady Digby'	LPBA
	'Lilli Goos' (x *arendsii*)	CMHG
	'Lollipop'	MBNS MBnl MBri NPro WBor
	longicarpa B&SWJ 6711	WCru
	'Maggie Daley'	CM&M EBee LAst MBri NBro NPro WMoo WWeb
	'Mainz' (*japonica* hybrid)	CMHG ELan EMil LPBA MBow WWpP
	'Mars' (x *arendsii*)	CMHG
	microphylla	CMHG
	- pink	CMHG
	'Moerheimii' (*thunbergii* hybrid)	CMHG

'Moerheim's Glory' (x *arendsii*) CM&M LAst NGdn WWpP
'Mont Blanc' (x *arendsii*) CMHG
'Montgomery' (*japonica* hybrid) CMHG EBrs EChP GKir LRHS LSRN MBri MRav NFor NGdn SBch WBVN
'Obergärtner Jürgens' (x *arendsii*) CM&M EChP GBin WWpP
Ostrich Plume see *A.* 'Straussenfeder'
'Paul Gaärder' (x *arendsii*) CMHG
'Peaches and Cream' CFwr EBee GKir LRHS MMHG MRav NBro NLar WAul WPnP
'Peter Barrow' (*glaberrima* hybrid) SRms
'Pink Curtsy' (x *arendsii*) EBrs
'Pink Lightening'PBR (*simplicifolia* hybrid) CWCL EShb MBNS MBnl MTis NLar SMrm
Pink Pearl (x *arendsii*) see *A.* x *arendsii* 'Rosa Perle'
'Poschka' CFir NPro
I 'Poschka Alba' CFir NMyG NPro
'Professor van der Wielen' (*thunbergii* hybrid) CMHG CMil CWCL EBee EBrs ETow GCal GCra GGar GKir LAst MSte SDix SRms SSpi WCAu WFar
pumila see *A. chinensis* var. *pumila*
* 'Queen' LPBA
§ 'Queen of Holland' (*japonica* hybrid) MDun
'Radius' CM&M EBee GFlt NGdn
* 'Red Admiral' NFor NLon
Red Light see *A.* 'Rotlicht'
'Red Sentinel' (*japonica* hybrid) CBcs CFai CM&M CWCL EBrs EChP EMFW EMil GMaP LAst MOne MTis NBro NCGa NOrc NPro SGSe SMrm SPoG WBor WFar WSan WWeb
'Rheinland' (*japonica* hybrid) 🏆H4 CM&M CMHG CWCL EBrs EPfP GKir IHMH LPBA LRHS NArg NCGa NPri SPoG STes WCAu WEas WFar WHoo WPnP WWpP
'Rhythm and Blues' **new** WWeb
rivularis CMHG GBin WCot
- var. ***myriantha*** BWJ 8076a WCru
§ 'Rosa Perle' (x *arendsii*) CMHG CSam
§ x ***rosea*** 'Peach Blossom' CBcs CM&M CMHG EBrs EChP GBuc LPBA NArg NBir NEgg NPro NSti SPoG WFar WHoo WMoo WWeb WWpP
- 'Queen Alexandra' WFar
'Rosea' (*simplicifolia* hybrid) EBrs WFar
Rosemary Bloom = 'Rosblo' EBee
§ 'Rotlicht' (x *arendsii*) CMHG EBrs ECot GKir LRHS NLar NMyG NPro WFar WGor
Salmon Queen see *A.* 'Lachskönigin'
'Salmonea' (*simplicifolia* hybrid) CMHG
§ 'Saxosa' GGar SPla
Showstar Group (x *arendsii*) LRHS NBre
simplicifolia 🏆H4 CRow GKir SSpi WFar
- 'Alba' CMHG NEgg NPro
- Bronze Elegance see *A.* 'Bronce Elegans'
- 'Darwin's Snow Sprite' CMac CRez ECho EWTr GKir MBnl MBri MSte NLar NPri NPro WFar
- 'Jacqueline' EBee ECho NLar WFar
* - 'Nana Alba' NPro
- 'Praecox' NEgg
- 'Praecox Alba' CMCo CWan EBee EChP ENot NEgg SMac WHoo
'Snowdrift' (x *arendsii*) CAby CBrm CMHG CSBt CWat EBrs EPla GKir GMaP GSki LRHS MBNS MDKP NBir NCGa NFor NLon NOak NOrc NPro WFar
'Solferino' (x *arendsii*) CMHG
'Spartan' see *A.* 'Rotlicht'
'Spinell' (x *arendsii*) CWCL MDun NCGa NOrc WFar WPnP WWpP
'Sprite' (*simplicifolia* hybrid) 🏆H4 More than 30 suppliers
§ 'Straussenfeder' (*thunbergii* hybrid) 🏆H4 CM&M CMHG CTri CWCL EBrs EChP EMan EPfP EPla ETow GCal GFlt GKir GMaP LAst LRHS NBid NBir NBro NOrc SMac SPer SPla SPoG SSpi WAul WCAu WMoo WPnP
'Sugar Plum' (*simplicifolia* hybrid) EBee LAst NGdn
'Superba' see *A. chinensis* var. *taquetii* 'Superba'
thunbergii CPLG
- var. ***hachijoensis*** EBee
- var. ***terrestris*** B&SWJ 6125 WCru
'Venus' (x *arendsii*) CBrm CHar CPLG CSBt CSam EBrs ECha ECtt EGra EMFW EWTr GGar GKir GMaP LPBA MSte NOrc NVic SPer WCAu WFar WMoo
'Vesuvius' (*japonica* hybrid) CBcs EBrs GKir MDKP NBlu NBro NEgg NSti WLin WSan
§ 'W.E. Gladstone' (*japonica* hybrid) CWat GSki LBBr MSte NBlu NCGa NCiC NGby NPro WAbe WGor WWpP
'Walküre' (x *arendsii*) CMHG
'Walter Bitner' EPPr EVFa MBNS NLRH SVil
§ 'Washington' (*japonica* hybrid) CBcs EBee IHMH LAst MDKP NGdn SGSe SSpe
§ 'Weisse Gloria' (x *arendsii*) CMHG CTbh EBrs ECha EPPr EWTr LPBA MBnl MBow MLan NBPC NBro NEgg NMyG NOrc NSti SBod SPoG WBor WMoo WPop WTin
White Gloria see *A.* 'Weisse Gloria'
'White Queen' (x *arendsii*) NWoo
'White Wings'PBR (*simplicifolia* hybrid) NLar NPro
'William Reeves' (x *arendsii*) CMHG
'Willie Buchanan' (*simplicifolia* hybrid) CMHG CPrp ECtt EHoe ENot EPza EVFa GAbr GKir GMaP GSki LRHS MBar MDHE MWat NEgg NFor NMen SApp SChu SIng SPer SPla SRms SSpi WAbe WFar WMoo
'Zuster Theresa' (x *arendsii*) CMHG CWat EBee EBrs GKir LRHS MBNS MBnl NBro NFla WFar

Astilboides (*Saxifragaceae*)

§ ***tabularis*** More than 30 suppliers

Astragalus (*Papilionaceae*)

adsurgens **new** GKev
canadensis EMan GKir
danicus WBWf
glycyphyllos CAgr CArn WBWf
helmii **new** GIBF
membranaceus CArn ELau MSal
- var. ***mongholicus*** **new** MSal
polaris **new** GIBF

Astrantia ✿ (*Apiaceae*)

bavarica CCge EBee EMan EMar GCal MDKP WGwG WOut WWpP
'Bloody Mary' **new** CBgR GFlt MBNS NLar NRnb NSti SPer WHil
§ 'Buckland' More than 30 suppliers
carniolica EMon NEgg SBri WTel WWpP

	- ***major***	see *A. major*
	- var. ***rubra***	see *A. major* 'Rubra'
	- 'Rubra'	EBrs MWrn WPop WSHC WWpP
	- 'Variegata'	see *A. major* 'Sunningdale Variegated'
	'Hadspen Blood'	More than 30 suppliers
	'Helen' **new**	WCra
	helleborifolia misapplied	see *A. maxima*
§	***major***	More than 30 suppliers
	- 'Abbey Road' **new**	ENot MWrn WAul
*	- ***alba***	CBcs CMHG EBla ECha EHrv EMon GSki MBnl MRav MTis MWrn NBir NGdn NPer WMnd WWeb
	- 'Ann Cann'	CBct
	- 'Berendien Stam'	CCge EBee EMon MAvo WWpP
	- subsp. ***biebersteinii***	CCge EBla EMon NBir
	- 'Bo-Ann' **new**	EMan LBuc MAvo MWrn NCob NLar NSti WAul
	- 'Celtic Star'	CBct CElw CFai CFir CKno EBee EBla EChP ELan EMan MAvo MBNS MBnl MSph NCob NCot NEgg NGdn NMyG NOak SPla WCot WTMC WWhi
	- 'Claret'	More than 30 suppliers
	- 'Cyril James'	CBct
	- dwarf **new**	WFar
	- 'Elmblut'	EMon
	- 'Greenfingers' **new**	EWes
	- 'Gwaun Valley' **new**	WFar
	- 'Hillview Red'	CCge CElw EBee SHel
	- subsp. ***involucrata***	EBla EHrv GSki LRHS WFar
	- - 'Barrister'	CBct CSam GBuc SSpi WFar WOut WPGP
	- - 'Canneman'	CBct EBla EMon EWes LPhx MAvo MBct NSti SMrm SOkh WCot WFar WWpP
	- - 'Margery Fish'	see *A. major* subsp. *involucrata* 'Shaggy'
	- - 'Moira Reid'	CBct EBee EBla ECGP EMan GBri GCal IPot MAvo MNFA NBro NCob NDov SHar SUsu
	- - 'Orlando'	EBee WWpP
§	- - 'Shaggy' ♀H4	More than 30 suppliers
	- 'Jade Lady'	WFar
	- 'Lars'	More than 30 suppliers
	- 'Lars' seedlings	GCal
	- 'Little Snowstar' **new**	EHrv IBal NSti
	- 'Maureen'	NOak
	- 'Montelolor' **new**	WFar
	- 'Paper Moon' **new**	WFar
	- 'Primadonna'	CBct CCge CHea CKno EBla EHrv EMan ERou EWsh GSki MBNS MNFA MTis MWrn NArg NLar SIgm SPlb WFar WMnd WPer WWol
	- 'Prockter'	WCra WWpP
	- 'Roma'[PBR]	CBct CCge CHad COtt EBee EBla EHrv EMan EMon LPhx MAvo MBri MWrn NCGa NDov NOak SMHy SSpi SUsu WCAu WFar
	- 'Rosa Lee' **new**	CWCL EMan IBal MBnl MWrn NArg NCob NLar WAul WHil
	- var. ***rosea***	More than 30 suppliers
	- - George's form **new**	CBct EBla EMan EMar GCal LAst MAvo NCob NDov
	- 'Rosensinfonie'	EBee EBla GMaP GSki MBct MWrn NBro NOak NPro WFar WMnd WWpP
§	- 'Rubra'	More than 30 suppliers
	- 'Ruby Cloud'	CBct CCge CHea CHid EBee EBla EHrv EMan MNrw MRav MWgw MWrn NBro NRnb NSti WCAu WCra WFar WFoF WHil WLin
	- 'Ruby Wedding'	More than 30 suppliers
	- 'Starburst'	WFar
	- 'Sue Barnes' (v)	EMon
§	- 'Sunningdale Variegated' (v) ♀H4	More than 30 suppliers
	- 'Titoki Point'	WCot WWpP
	- 'Variegata'	see *A. major* 'Sunningdale Variegated'
§	***maxima*** ♀H4	More than 30 suppliers
	- 'Mark Fenwick'	NBir
*	- ***rosea***	CKno CWCL EBla ECtt LBmB MTis NBir NEgg NGdn SPet WHlf WSan WWol
	minor	CPrp WCru
	'Rainbow'	NLar
	rubra	see *A. major* 'Rubra'
	'Snow Star'[PBR]	CFir CWCL EBla EHrv EMan GBin IPot MAvo MBnl MBri MWrn
	'Warren Hills'	MAvo MWrn

Asyneuma (*Campanulaceae*)

	canescens	CSec ELan EMan MBNS NBre SGSe
	limonifolium	CPom
	prenanthoides	ELan
	pulvinatum	EHyt SIng WAbe

Asystasia (*Acanthaceae*)

	bella	see *Mackaya bella*
§	***gangetica***	CSev
	violacea	see *A. gangetica*

Athamanta (*Apiaceae*)

	turbith	SIgm
	vestina JCA 224300	SIgm

Athanasia (*Asteraceae*)

§	***parviflora***	GGar SPlb

Atherosperma (*Monimiaceae*)

	moschatum	CBcs CHII EShb WSHC

Athrotaxis (*Cupressaceae*)

	cupressoides	CDul CKen MBar
	laxifolia	CDoC CKen LCon MBar
	selaginoides	CDoC CDul

Athyrium ✿ (*Woodsiaceae*)

	'Branford Beauty'	CLAP WRic
	'Branford Rambler'	CLAP WRic
	filix-femina ♀H4	CBcs CBen CFil CSBt CTri CWCL ECha EFer ELan EMFW ENot EPfP ERod EUJe GMaP LLWP LPBA LRHS MAsh MBri NBro NOak NOrc SMac SPer SRms SRot WFib WPGP WShi
	- var. ***angustum*** 'Lady in Red'	CLAP WRic
	- 'Clarissimum'	WIvy
*	- ***congestum cristatum***	CLAP WFib
	- 'Corymbiferum'	GQui SRms
	- 'Crispum Grandiceps Kaye'	SRms
	- Cristatum Group	CLAP EFer EFtx ELan EMon EPza MMoz SBla WAbe WFib
§	- Cruciatum Group	CBos CFwr CLAP EGol ELan EMon EPfP MAsh MBct MMoz NOGN SPer SRms WCru WFib WMoo WRic
	- 'Fieldii'	CLAP SChu SRms WFib
	- 'Frizelliae' ♀H4	CElw CPrp CSBt CWCL EFer ELan EMon EPfP GEdr GMaP LPBA LRHS MBnl MBri MDun MLan

	NBid NCGa NOrc NSti SChu SPer SPlb SPoG SRms WFar WFib WGor WRic
- 'Frizelliae Capitatum'	CLAP WFib WPGP
- 'Frizelliae Cristatum'	SRms
- 'Grandiceps'	CLAP SRms
- 'Minutissimum'	CFil CLAP ECha EGol EHon ELan EMon LPBA MMoz SBla WPGP WWpP
* - 'Nudicaule'	SRms
- 'Percristatum'	EMon
- Plumosum Group	CFil CLAP GBri GQui WFib
- 'Plumosum Axminster'	CLAP EFer
- 'Plumosum Cristatum'	CLAP
- 'Plumosum Divaricatum' **new**	SRms
- 'Plumosum Percristatum'	GQui
- Red Stem	see *A. filix-femina* 'Rotstiel'
§ - 'Rotstiel'	CFwr CLAP EWTr MMoz NLar WFar WMoo WPnP
* - ***superbum*** 'Druery'	CLAP
- 'Vernoniae' ♀H4	CLAP ELan EMon LPBA SGSe SGar WRic
- 'Vernoniae Cristatum'	CLAP GBin WFib
- 'Victoriae'	CFwr GEdr LPBA NBid SGSe WCot
- Victoriae Group	see *A. filix-femina* Cruciatum Group
flexile	NWoo
'Ghost'	CLAP WRic
goeringianum 'Pictum'	see *A. niponicum* var. *pictum*
niponicum	CTbh SLdr
- f. ***metallicum***	see *A. niponicum* var. *pictum*
§ - var. ***pictum*** ♀H3	More than 30 suppliers
- - 'Applecourt' **new**	WRic
- - 'Burgundy Lace' **new**	EFtx WPtf
* - - 'Cristatoflabellatum'	CBos CLAP EBrs ELan EMon
- - 'Pewter Lace' **new**	EFtx
- - 'Red Beauty'	CFwr CLAP CRez EBee EFtx WRic
- - 'Silver Falls'	CFwr CLAP EFtx LAst LRHS MBnl MBow NCot SRot SSpi
- - 'Soul Mate' **new**	EFtx
- - 'Ursula's Red'	CFwr CLAP CRez EBee EFtx EMar EPPr ERou EShb EUJe GBin LAst LBuc LSou MBNS MBri MSte NArg NBir SHop SMrm SPer SPoG SRot WAul WCot WPnP WSan WWhi
- - 'Wildwood Twist'	CLAP EFtx
otophorum ♀H4	EMon NBid NVic SChu SRms WIvy WPGP WRic
- var. ***okanum***	More than 30 suppliers
vidalii	CFwr CLAP WFib WRic

Atractylodes (*Asteraceae*)

japonica	EFEx
macrocephala	CArn EFEx

Atragene see *Clematis*

Atriplex (*Chenopodiaceae*)

canescens	WDin XPep
cinerea	GGar
halimus	CArn CBcs CBot CSLe ECha EHoe EPPr LRHS MBlu MBri MRav NLar SLon SPer WCot WDin WHer WKif WSHC WTel WTin XPep
hortensis	MChe
- gold-leaved	WLHH
- var. ***rubra***	CArn CHad CSpe EGra ELan EOHP LSou MChe MHer NDov NGHP SIde WCHb WCot WEas WJek WWpP WWye
nummularia	XPep
portulacoides	see *Halimione portulacoides*

Atropa (*Solanaceae*)

bella-donna	CArn GBar GPoy MGol MSal WTin WWye
- var. ***lutea***	MGol MSal
mandragora	see *Mandragora officinarum*

Atropanthe (*Solanaceae*)

§ ***sinensis***	MSal

Aubrieta ✿ (*Brassicaceae*)

albomarginata	see *A.* 'Argenteovariegata'
'Alix Brett'	CMea CPBP ELan LRHS SPoG
'April Joy'	ECho ECot ELan
§ 'Argenteovariegata' (v) ♀H4	ECho ELan SBla SIgm WAbe WHoo
'Astolat' (v)	ECtt NLon NSla SBla SRms WEas
§ 'Aureovariegata' (v) ♀H4	CMea CNic ECho ECtt ELan GKir IHMH LRHS MHer NJOw NPer NWCA SBla WAbe WFar
'Belisha Beacon'	ECho ECtt MBri
Bengal hybrids	CNic STre WGor
Blaue Schönheit	see *A.* 'Blue Beauty'
'Blaumeise'	IHMH
§ 'Blue Beauty'	NBlu WRHF
'Blue Midnight'	EDAr
* 'Blue Mist'	ECho EDAr
'Blue Sky'	EDAr
§ 'Bob Saunders' (d)	CMea CNic ECtt LTwo SAga
'Bonfire'	ECho ECtt
'Bressingham Pink' (d) ♀H4	CMea ECho ECtt ELan EPfP LRHS SPoG
'Bressingham Red'	LRHS SIng SPoG
campbellii	ECho
canescens subsp. ***cilicica***	WLin
'Carnival'	NEgg
Cascade Series	NEgg WFar
- 'Blue Cascade'	ECho ECtt EPfP GKir NBlu SPlb SPoG WGor
- 'Lilac Cascade'	ECho SPoG
- 'Purple Cascade'	CTri CWib ECtt EPfP LRHS NBlu SCoo SPlb SPoG SRms WFar WGor
- 'Red Cascade' ♀H4	CTri CWib ECtt EPfP GKir NBlu SCoo SPlb SPoG
'Dantra'	ECho
deltoidea	SHGN
- 'Nana Variegata' (v)	CMea ECtt EPot NJOw WGor WLin
- Variegata Group (v)	ECtt GKir LRHS NMen NSla WFar WPat
'Doctor Mules' ♀H4	CSpe ECho LRHS SIng SRms WPat
'Doctor Mules Variegata' (v)	EPfP LAst MHer NArg NEgg NPri SIng SPoG SWvt
'Downers' **new**	GBin
'Dream'	SIng
'Elsa Lancaster'	EHyt EPot NMen NSla
'Fire King'	NLar
§ 'Frühlingszauber'	SRms WGor
'Gloriosa'	SIng
'Godstone'	ECho
'Golden Carpet'	SIng
'Golden King'	see *A.* 'Aureovariegata'
* 'Graeca'	NPri
'Greencourt Purple' ♀H4	ECho ELan MHer MWat SIng
'Gurgedyke'	ECho ELan SRms
'Hamburger Stadtpark'	ECho EDAr
'Harknoll Red'	EPot
'Hartswood'	SIng
'Hemswell Purity'PBR	see *A.* 'Snow Maiden'
'Hendersonii'	SRms
'J.S. Baker'	SRms
'Joy' (d)	ECho ECtt LTwo NSla SIng
'Kitte'	ECho GBin SPoG
'Leichtlinii'	ECho NJOw NLar

	'Lemon and Lime'	LRHS
	'Little Gem'	ECho
	'Lodge Crave'	SIng
	'Maurice Prichard'	ECtt LRHS
	'Mrs Lloyd Edwards'	ECho
	'Mrs Rodewald' ♀H4	ECho SRms
	'Novalis Blue'	SRms
	'Oakington Lavender'	ECho ELan
	parviflora	CStu
	'Pike's Variegated' (v)	ECho
	pinardii	EHyt NSla
	'Purple Charm'	SRms
	'Purple Emperor'	SIng
	'Red Carpet'	ELan EPot LGro LRHS MHer SIng SPoG SRms
	'Red Dyke'	SIng
	'Riverslea'	SIng
	'Rosanna Miles'	SIng
	'Rose Queen'	CMea CPBP LRHS SAga SMrm
	Royal Series	COIW
	- 'Royal Blue'	ECho LRHS NArg NEgg NJOw NPri WFar WMoo WPop
I	- 'Royal Lavender' **new**	WFar
I	- 'Royal Lilac' **new**	WFar
	- 'Royal Red'	MBow NJOw NPri SRms WFar WGor WMoo WPop
I	- 'Royal Rose' **new**	WFar
	- 'Royal Violet'	ECho LRHS MBow NArg NJOw WFar WPer
	'Schofield's Double'	see *A.* 'Bob Saunders'
	'Silberrand'	ECha ECtt NSla
§	'Snow Maiden'PBR	ECho ECtt LAst LRHS SPoG WPop
	'Somerfield Silver'	MBar
	'Somerford Lime' (v)	ECtt MBar
	Spring Charm	see *A.* 'Frühlingszauber'
	'Swan Red' (v)	EPot LAst NSla SPoG
	thessala	CPBP
	'Toby Saunders'	ECho
	'Triumphante'	ECho ECtt LRHS LTwo
	'Wanda'	ECho ELan SIng
	'Whitewell Gem'	NJOw SRms WMoo

Aucuba ✿ (*Aucubaceae*)

	japonica (f)	SMer
	- (m)	ENot SReu
	- 'Crassifolia' (m)	SAPC SArc
	- 'Crotonifolia' (f/v) ♀H4	More than 30 suppliers
	- 'Crotonifolia' (m/v)	MAsh NBlu SRms
	- 'Dentata'	CHEx WWes
	- 'Gold Dust' (f/v)	LRHS
	- 'Golden King' (m/v) ♀H4	CBcs CDoC CMac CSBt CTrw EBee ELan EPfP GKir LRHS MAsh MGos MTis MWat SLim SPla SPoG WBcn WFar WWeb
	- 'Golden Spangles' (f/v)	CBcs CDoC CHEx ECot SWvt
	- 'Goldstrike' (v)	EBee EHoe
	- 'Lance Leaf' (m)	SLon WCru
	- f. ***longifolia*** ♀H4	CMac SAPC SArc SDix WCru
	- - 'Salicifolia' (f)	CHEx EBee ENot EPla LRHS MRav NLar SLon SPla WBcn WCru WDin WFar WGer WPGP
	- 'Maculata' hort.	see *A. japonica* 'Variegata'
	- 'Marmorata'	EPla LRHS
	- 'Nana Rotundifolia' (f)	EPla
	- Pepper Pot = 'Shilpot' **new**	SSta
	- 'Pepperpot' (m/v)	CHEx EPfP MAsh SPoG
	- 'Picturata' (m/v)	CBcs CDul CHEx CMac CSBt EBee ELan LRHS MAsh MRav NEgg SAga SHBN SLim SPer SPoG WCFE WFar
	- 'Rozannie' (f/m) ♀H4	More than 30 suppliers
	- 'Speckles'	GSki
	- 'Sulphurea Marginata' (f/v)	CBcs CMac EMil EPla NPro SPoG WBcn
§	- 'Variegata' (f/v)	More than 30 suppliers
	- Windsor form (f)	EPla LRHS MBri WWes

Aurinia (*Brassicaceae*)

§	***corymbosa***	LTwo
§	***saxatilis*** ♀H4	ECho ENot EPfP GAbr GKir MBar MWat NBlu SIng SPlb STre WBVN WFar WTel
	- 'Citrina' ♀H4	CHal ECha ECho ECtt MWat SRms
	- 'Compacta'	CTri ECtt NLon
	- 'Dudley Nevill'	ECho EHol LRHS MWat SBla
	- 'Dudley Nevill Variegated' (v)	CRez ECha ECtt EWes MHer NBir SBla SIng
	- 'Flore Pleno' (d)	CFir EHol GEdr
	- Gold Ball	see *A. saxatilis* 'Goldkugel'
	- 'Gold Dust'	ECtt LGro SRms
	- 'Golden Queen'	ECtt MHer
§	- 'Goldkugel'	GKir IHMH LRHS NBlu SIng SPoG SRms
	- 'Silver Queen'	WEas
	- 'Variegata' (v)	EWin NPri SIng SPoG
	sinuata 'Pebbles'	LRav

Austrocedrus (*Cupressaceae*)

§	***chilensis***	CKen CPne CTho LRHS

Austromyrtus (*Myrtaceae*)

§	***dulcis***	ECou

Avena (*Poaceae*)

	candida	see *Helictotrichon sempervirens*
	sativa 'French Black' **new**	CSpe
	sterilis	SWal

Avenula see *Helictotrichon*

Ayapana see *Eupatorium*

Azadirachta (*Meliaceae*)

	indica	GPoy

Azalea see *Rhododendron*

Azara ✿ (*Flacourtiaceae*)

	alpina	CFil CPLG ISea
	dentata	CBcs CFil CHll CMac ERea IDee LAst SBrw WFar WSHC
	- 'Variegata'	see *A. integrifolia* 'Variegata'
*	***integerrima***	GQui
	integrifolia	CFil CRez SBrw
	- 'Variegata' (v)	CFil ERea SBrw SDnm SMur SPoG SSpi
	lanceolata	CBcs CFil CMCN CPLG CTri ECrN IDee ISea LAst LEdu NSti SBrw SLon WGer WPic
	microphylla ♀H3	More than 30 suppliers
	- 'Gold Edge' (v) **new**	WFar
	- 'Variegata' (v)	CBcs CDoC CFil CMac CPLG CPMA CPle CSBt CWib EBee EHoe ENot EPfP GQui IMGH ISea LAst MLan NSti SBrw SDnm SPoG SSpi SSta STre WCru WFar WGer WSHC
N	***paraguayensis***	GGar SDnm SPoG
	petiolaris	CFai CFil CPle EPfP SBrw WGer WPic
	serrata ♀H3	More than 30 suppliers
	uruguayensis	CPLG EBee

Azorella (*Apiaceae*)

	compacta	SPlb
	filamentosa	ECou

	glebaria misapplied	see *A. trifurcata*
	glebaria A. Gray	see *Bolax gummifer*
	gummifer	see *Bolax gummifer*
§	***trifurcata***	CPar CSpe CTri ECtt GAbr GEdr GKir GTou IHMH NLAp NWCA SBla SIgm WAbe WPer
	- 'Nana'	GGar MWat NJOw WPat

Azorina (*Campanulaceae*)

§	***vidalii***	CBot CSpe EBee ERea EShb IDee LPio MGol SAPC SAga SArc SGar WCot
	- 'Rosea'	CKob

B

Babiana (*Iridaceae*)

	ambigua	CMon CStu
	angustifolia	CPLG
	disticha	see *B. plicata*
	dregei	WCot
	ecklonii	CMon WCot
	framesii	CStu
	nana	CMon CStu WCot
	odorata	CPLG WCot
§	***plicata***	SYvo WCot
	pulchra	CMon
	pygmaea	CMon WCot
	ringens	CPLG
	rubrocyanea	CMon WCot
	sambucina	CStu WCot
	sinuata	CMon WCot
	stricta ♀H1-2	CPLG ECho WCot WRos
	- var. ***erectifolia*** **new**	WPrP
	- 'Purple Star'	CPLG ECho
	truncata	CMon CStu WCot
	tubulosa	WCot
	vanzyliae	CStu WCot
	villosa	WCot
	'Zwanenburg's Glory'	EMan

Baccharis (*Asteraceae*)

	genistelloides	SMad WCot
	halimifolia	CBcs CPle GQui LRav
	- 'Twin Peaks'	XPep
	patagonica	CTrC GGar LPhx LSpr SAPC SArc
	salicifolia **new**	WCot
	'Sea Foam'	EChP EKen EMan LSou NArg SHGN SMad

Bacopa (*Scrophulariaceae*)

	caroliniana	EOHP
	monnieri	EOHP EUnu
	'Snowflake'	see *Sutera cordata* 'Snowflake'

Baeckea (*Myrtaceae*)

	densifolia	ECou
	virgata	CBcs CTrC ECou SPlb

Baillonia (*Verbenaceae*)

	juncea	WSHC

Balbisia (*Geraniaceae*)

	peduncularis	WFoF

Baldellia (*Alismataceae*)

	ranunculoides	CRow EMFW EMan WWpP
	- f. ***repens***	EMan

Ballota ✿ (*Lamiaceae*)

	acetabulosa ♀H3-4	ECha ECrN EGoo EMan EWes EWin MGGn MWgw SDix WCot WKif XPep
	africana	MGGn
	'All Hallow's Green'	CFee EBee EGoo EMan EPza EWin GBuc LRHS MGGn NSti SBla SChu
	hirsuta	MGGn XPep
	nigra	CArn EBee GPoy GWCH MChe MGGn MHer MSal NMir SECG WMoo WWye XPep
§	- 'Archer's Variegated' (v)	EChP ECrN ECtt EMan ERou EWes MGGn
	- 'Intakes White'	MGGn MInt
	- 'Variegata'	see *B. nigra* 'Archer's Variegated'
	- 'Zanzibar' (v)	EMon MGGn
	pseudodictamnus ♀H3-4	More than 30 suppliers
	- B&M 8119	MGGn
	- from Crete	ECha
	- 'Candia'	MGGn MSph SBla

Balsamita see *Tanacetum*

Balsamorhiza (*Asteraceae*)

	sagittata	ECho

Bambusa ✿ (*Poaceae*)

	glaucescens	see *B. multiplex*
	gracilis	see *Drepanostachyum falcatum*
	gracillima	COtt
§	***multiplex***	EFul
	- 'Alphonso-Karrii'	CFil ENot GKir MMoz NMoo SBig WPGP
	- 'Elegans'	see *B. muliplex* 'Floribunda'
	- 'Fernleaf'	see *B. muliplex* 'Floribunda'
§	- 'Floribunda'	CHEx COtt EFul EShb NMoo
	- 'Golden Goddess'	NMoo
	- 'Wang Tsai'	see *B. muliplex* 'Floribunda'
	textilis	WJun
	ventricosa	NMoo SBig

banana see *Musa*

Banisteriopsis (*Malpighiaceae*)

	caapi	CPLN MGol

Banksia (*Proteaceae*)

	ashbyi **new**	WSAf
	canei	CTrC SPlb
	ericifolia var. ***ericifolia***	CTrC
	grandis	CBcs CCtw CTrC
	integrifolia	CCtw CTrC GQui
	marginata	CTrC ECou SPlb
	media	CTrC SPlb
	oblongifolia	CBcs CTrC SPlb
	occidentalis	CCtw
	paludosa	CTrC SPlb
	praemorsa **new**	WSAf
	robur	CAbb CTrC
	serrata	CCtw SPlb
	speciosa	CCtw SPlb
	spinulosa var. ***collina***	CCtw CTrC
	- var. ***spinulosa***	CBcs
	violacea	SPlb

Baptisia (*Papilionaceae*)

§	***alba***	CPom EMan SIgm
§	- var. ***macrophylla***	CMdw CPle EBrs LRHS MLLN NBir NDov NLar SMHy
	australis ♀H4	More than 30 suppliers
	- 'Caspian Blue'	MWrn NBPC SPla WHil WSHC
	- 'Exaltata'	ELan GBuc LRHS

- var. ***minor***	LPhx SMHy
§ ***bracteata*** var. ***leucophaea***	EBrs SIgm
lactea	see *B. alba* var. *macrophylla*
leucantha	see *B. alba* var. *macrophylla*
leucophaea	see *B. bracteata* var. *leucophaea*
pendula	see *B. alba*
'Purple Smoke'	EBrs IPot SMHy
tinctoria	CArn

Barbarea (*Brassicaceae*)

praecox	see *B. verna*
§ ***verna***	CArn GPoy MHer NGHP
vulgaris 'Variegata' (v)	CArn CBrm CHal ELan EMan IHMH LDai MDun MWrn NBid NBro NCob NSti SPav WCAu WCHb WCot WMoo
- 'Variegated Winter Cream' (v) **new**	LSou

Barleria (*Acanthaceae*)

suberecta	see *Dicliptera suberecta*

Barnadesia (*Asteraceae*)

caryophylla RCB/Eq T-5	WCot

Barosma see *Agathosma*

Bartlettina see *Eupatorium*

Bartsia (*Scrophulariaceae*)

alpina **new**	EMan

Basella (*Basellaceae*)

* ***atropurpurea*** **new**	EBee
rubra **new**	EShb EUnu

Bashania (*Poaceae*)

faberi Og 94053	EPla
§ ***fargesii***	CDoC CDul ENBC EPla ERod GKir MRav MWht SEND WJun
I ***qingchengshanensis***	CFil EBee EPla WJun WPGP

basil see *Ocimum*

Bassia (*Chenopodiaceae*)

scoparia	MSal

Bauera (*Cunoniaceae*)

rubioides var. ***alba***	ECou
- pink flowered	ECou

Bauhinia (*Caesalpiniaceae*)

alba	see *B. variegata*
corymbosa	CPLN
galpinii	EUnu SPlb
monandra	WMul
natalensis	EShb SPlb
tomentosa	EShb
vahlii	CSec
§ ***variegata*** (v)	LExo
yunnanensis	CPLN EShb

Baumea see *Machaerina*

bay see *Laurus nobilis*

Beaucarnea (*Dracaenaceae*)

recurvata ♀H1	CTrC EUJe LToo MBri
stricta	EOas

Beaufortia (*Myrtaceae*)

elegans **new**	EShb
sparsa	CTrC EShb
squarrosa	SPlb

Beaumontia (*Apocynaceae*)

multiflora **new**	CPLN

Beauverdia see *Leucocoryne*

Beckmannia (*Poaceae*)

eruciformis	WRos

Bedfordia (*Asteraceae*)

salicina	ECou

Beesia (*Ranunculaceae*)

calthifolia	EBee SSpi WCru WPGP WPrP
- DJHC 98447	CDes

Begonia ✿ (*Begoniaceae*)

from China	NShi
- BWJ 7840	WCru
- DJHC 98479	SSpi
from Ruwenzori, Uganda	NShi
from Sikkim, India	WCot
- B&SWJ 2692	EMan
from Vietnam	ER&R NShi
'Abel Carrière'	CHal ER&R NShi WDib
acerifolia	see *B. vitifolia*
acetosa	ER&R NShi
acida	ER&R NShi
aconitifolia	ER&R EShb NShi
acutifolia	ER&R NShi
'Aladdin'	ER&R
'Alamo III'	ER&R NShi
albopicta (C)	CHal EBak ER&R NShi
- 'Rosea'	CHal NShi WDib
alice-clarkiae	ER&R NShi
'Allan Langdon' (T)	CBla
'Alleryi' (C)	ER&R NShi
alnifolia	ER&R
'Alto Scharff' ♀H1	ER&R NShi
'Alzasco' (C)	ER&R NShi
'Amigo Pink' (C)	ER&R
'Amigo Variegated' (v)	ER&R
ampla	ER&R
'Amy' (T)	CBla
angularis	see *B. stipulacea*
'Anita Roseanna' (C)	ER&R NShi
'Ann Anderson' (C)	ER&R NShi
'Anna Christine' (C)	ER&R NShi
'Anniversary' (T)	CBla
§ ***annulata***	ER&R NShi
'Apollo' (T)	CBla
'Apricot Delight' (T)	CBla
'Aquarius'	ER&R NShi
'Arabian Sunset' (C)	ER&R NShi
'Argentea' (R)	EBak MBri NShi
x ***argenteoguttata*** (C)	CHal ER&R NShi
'Aries'	ER&R NShi
'Art Monday' (C)	NShi
'Arthur Mallet'	ER&R
'Aruba'	ER&R
'Autumn Glow' (T)	ER&R NShi
'Avalanche' (T)	ER&R NShi
'Axel Lange' (R)	NShi
'Aya' (C)	NShi WDib
'Baby Perfection'	NShi WDib
'Bahamas'	ER&R NShi
'Bantam Delight'	ER&R NShi
'Barbara Ann' (C)	ER&R
'Barbara Hamilton' (C)	ER&R
'Barbara Parker'	ER&R
'Barclay Griffiths'	ER&R NShi

Name	Suppliers
'Beatrice Haddrell'	CHal ER&R NShi WDib
* ***benichoma***	WDib
'Benitochiba' (R)	ER&R NShi
'Bernat Klein' (T)	CBla
'Bess'	ER&R NShi
'Bessie Buxton'	ER&R NShi
'Bethlehem Star'	ER&R NShi WDib
§ 'Bettina Rothschild' (R)	CHal ER&R NShi WDib
'Beverly Jean'	ER&R NShi
'Big Mac'	ER&R NShi
'Billie Langdon' (T)	CBla
'Bill's Beauty'	ER&R NShi
'Bishop's Irish Eyes' (C)	NShi
'Black Jack' (C)	ER&R NShi
'Black Knight' (R)	CHal NShi
'Black Raspberry'	ER&R NShi
'Black Velvet' **new**	NShi
'Blanc de Neige'	ER&R NShi
'Blue Vein'	ER&R
'Blue Wave'	NShi
'Bokit'	ER&R NShi WDib
boliviensis	NShi WCru
'Bonaire'	CHal
'Boomer' (C)	ER&R NShi
'Botato'	NShi
bowerae	CHal ER&R LRHS NShi
§ - var. ***nigramarga***	ER&R NShi
'Boy Friend'	ER&R NShi
bracteosa	ER&R
bradei	ER&R
brevirimosa	ER&R NShi
'Brown Lace'	NShi
'Brown Twist'	NShi WDib
'Bunchii'	ER&R NShi
'Burgundy Velvet'	ER&R NShi WDib
'Burle Marx' ♀^{H1}	CHal ER&R EShb NShi SDix WDib
'Bush Baby'	CHal NShi
'Butter Cup'	NShi
'Buttermilk' (T)	CBla
'Calico Kew'	ER&R
'Calla Queen' (S)	ER&R
'Can-can' (R)	see *B.* 'Herzog von Sagan'
'Can-can' (T)	CBla NShi
'Candy Floss'	NShi WCru
'Captain Nemo'	ER&R NShi
cardiocarpa	ER&R
'Carol Mac'	ER&R NShi
'Carol Wilkins of Ballarat' (T)	CBla
'Carolina Moon' (R)	ER&R NShi
carolineifolia	CHal NShi WDib
carrieae	ER&R NShi
x ***carrierei***	see *B.* Semperflorens Cultorum Group
'Cathedral'	ER&R NShi WDib
'Chantilly Lace'	CHal ER&R NShi
chapaensis	NShi
- HWJ 642	WCru
'Charles Chevalier'	ER&R NShi
'Charles Jaros'	ER&R NShi
'Charm' (S)	CHal ER&R NShi WDib
x ***cheimantha*** 'Gloire de Lorraine' **new**	NShi
'Cherry Feast'	CHal
'Cherry Jubilee' (C)	NShi
'Cherry Sundae'	ER&R
'Chesson'	ER&R NShi
'China Curl'	ER&R NShi
'China Doll'	NShi
'China Swirl'	NShi
chloroneura **new**	WDib
'Chocolate Box'	ER&R
'Chocolate Chip'	ER&R NShi
'Christine'	NShi
'Christmas Candy'	ER&R EShb WDib
'Christy White'	NShi
'Chumash'	ER&R NShi
'Cistine'	ER&R NShi
'Clara' (R)	MBri NShi
'Cleopatra' ♀^{H1}	CHal ER&R MRav NShi WDib
'Clifton'	ER&R NShi
coccinea (C)	ER&R NShi WDib
'Coconut Ice'	EShb LAst
compta	see *B. stipulacea*
'Comte de Lesseps' (C)	NShi WDib
conchifolia var. ***rubrimacula***	ER&R NShi
'Concord'	ER&R NShi
'Connee Boswell'	ER&R NShi WDib
convolvulacea	ER&R NShi
cooperi	ER&R NShi
'Coppelia' (T)	CBla
'Cora Anne'	ER&R
'Cora Miller' (R)	ER&R NShi
x ***corallina***	EBak
§ - 'Lucerna' (C)	CHal EBak ER&R LRav NShi
- 'Lucerna Amazon' (C)	CHal ER&R NShi
'Corbeille de Feu'	CHal ER&R NShi
'Cosie' (C)	NShi
'Cowardly Lion' (R)	ER&R NShi
'Cracklin' Rosie' (C)	ER&R NShi
crassicaulis	ER&R NShi
'Crestabruchii'	ER&R NShi
'Crimson Cascade'	CBla
'Crystal Brook'	ER&R NShi
* 'Crystal Cascade'	CBla
cubensis	ER&R NShi
cucullata	CHal ER&R NShi
'Curly Fireflush' (R)	ER&R NShi
'Curly Locks' (S)	CHal
'Dales' Delight' (C)	ER&R NShi
'Dancin' Fred'	ER&R NShi
'Dancing Girl'	ER&R NShi
'Dannebo'	MBri
'D'Artagnan'	ER&R NShi
'David Blais' (R)	NShi WDib
'Dawnal Meyer' (C)	ER&R NShi WDib
'De Elegans'	ER&R NShi WDib
'Decker's Select'	ER&R NShi
decora	ER&R NShi
deliciosa	ER&R NShi
'Delray Silver'	NShi
'Dewdrop' (R)	ER&R NShi WDib
diadema	ER&R NShi
'Di-anna' (C)	ER&R NShi
dichotoma	ER&R NShi
dichroa (C)	ER&R NShi
'Dielytra'	ER&R NShi
'Di-erna'	ER&R NShi
dietrichiana Irmsch.	ER&R
'Digswelliana'	ER&R
dipetala	ER&R
discolor	see *B. grandis* subsp. *evansiana*
domingensis	ER&R
'Don Miller'	ER&R NShi WDib
'Doublet Pink'	ER&R
'Doublet Red'	ER&R
'Doublet White'	ER&R
'Douglas Nisbet' (C)	ER&R
Dragon Wing Pink = 'Bepapink'^{PBR} **new**	EShb NShi
Dragon Wing Red = 'Bepared'^{PBR} ♀$^{H1+3}$	EShb NShi
dregei (T) ♀^{H1}	ER&R NShi
- 'Bonsai'	NShi STre
- 'Glasgow'	ER&R NShi

- var. ***macbethii***	NShi
'Druryi'	ER&R NShi
'Dwarf Houghtonii'	ER&R NShi
'Earl of Pearl'	ER&R NShi
* 'Ebony' (C)	CHal ER&R NShi
echinosepala	ER&R NShi
echinosepala* x *sanguinea	NShi
I 'Edinburgh Brevirimosa'	ER&R NShi
edmundoi	ER&R
egregia	ER&R
'Elaine'	ER&R NShi
'Elaine Ayres' (C)	ER&R NShi
§ 'Elaine Wilkerson'	ER&R NShi
'Elaine's Baby'	see *B.* 'Elaine Wilkerson'
'Elda'	ER&R NShi
'Elda Haring' (R)	ER&R NShi
'Elizabeth Hayden'	ER&R
'Elsie M. Frey'	ER&R
'Emerald Giant' (R)	ER&R NShi WDib
'Emerald Isle'	NShi
'Emerald Princess' **new**	NShi
'Emma Watson'	CHal ER&R NShi
'Enchantment'	ER&R
'Enech'	ER&R NShi
'English Knight'	ER&R NShi
'English Lace'	ER&R NShi
epipsila	ER&R
x ***erythrophylla***	EShb NShi
- 'Bunchii'	ER&R NShi
§ - 'Helix'	CHal ER&R NShi
'Essie Hunt'	ER&R
'Esther Albertine' (C) ♀H1	CHal ER&R NShi
'Eureka' (T)	CBla
'Evening Star'	ER&R NShi
'Exotica'	ER&R
'Fairy'	ER&R NShi
'Fairylight' (T)	CBla
feastii 'Helix'	see *B.* x *erythrophylla* 'Helix'
fernando-costae	ER&R NShi
'Festiva' (T)	CBla
§ 'Feuerkönigin' (S)	ER&R
'Filigree'	ER&R NShi
fimbriata Liebm.	WWol
'Fire Flush'	see *B.* 'Bettina Rothschild'
'Firedance' (T)	CBla
'Fireworks' (R)	ER&R NShi WDib
'Five and Dime'	ER&R NShi
'Flamboyant' (T)	ER&R MBri NShi
Flaming Queen	see *B.* 'Feuerkönigin'
'Flamingo'	ER&R NShi
'Flamingo Queen'	ER&R
'Flo'Belle Moseley' (C)	CHal ER&R NShi WDib
'Florence Carrell'	ER&R NShi
'Florence Rita' (C)	ER&R NShi
'Flying High'	ER&R
foliosa	CHal ER&R NShi WDib
- var. ***amplifolia***	CHal ER&R NShi
§ - var. ***miniata*** 'Rosea'	CDoC CHal LRHS
formosana	NShi
- B&SWJ 7041	WCru
'Frances Lyons'	ER&R NShi
'Freckles' (R)	ER&R NShi
'Fred Bedson'	ER&R NShi
'Fred Martin' (R)	NShi
friburgensis	ER&R
'Friendship'	ER&R NShi
'Frosty' (T)	NShi WDib
'Frosty Fairyland'	ER&R
'Frosty Knight'	ER&R NShi
'Fuchsifoliosa'	ER&R
fuchsioides ♀H1	CDoC EBak ER&R EShb EWin LIck MArl MOak NShi SDix SYvo WDib
- pink-flowered	GGar LAst NShi
- red-flowered	MOak WFar
- 'Rosea'	see *B. foliosa* var. *miniata* 'Rosea'
'Full Moon' (T)	CBla
fusca	ER&R NShi
'Fuscomaculata'	ER&R NShi
'Gaystar'	NShi
gehrtii	ER&R NShi
geranioides	ER&R EShb
glabra	ER&R
glandulosa	ER&R
glaucophylla	see *B. radicans*
'Glen Daniels'	NShi
'Gloire de Lorraine'	NShi
'Gloire de Sceaux'	ER&R NShi
goegoensis	ER&R NShi
'Gold Cascade'	CBla
'Gold Doubloon' (T)	CBla
'Goldilocks' (T)	CBla
'Good 'n' Plenty'	ER&R NShi
gracilis var. ***martiana***	NShi
'Granada'	ER&R NShi
grandis **new**	NShi
§ - subsp. ***evansiana*** ♀H3-4	CDoC CHEx CHal CSam CStu EBee ELan EMan EMon ER&R EShb GCal LEdu MLLN MOak MSte MTho MWrn NCiC NShi SBch SDix SGSe SMad SMrm SSpi WBrk WCot WCru WFar
- - var. ***alba*** hort.	CHal CMdw EMar EMon ER&R EShb GCal MOak MSte MTho SGSe SMad SSpi WCot WPGP
- - 'Claret Jug'	EBee EMan EMon WCot WPGP
- - hybrid **new**	ERos
- - 'Pink Parasol' **new**	WCru
- - 'Simsii'	NShi WFar
- 'Maria'	WCot
- 'Sapporo'	EMar EPPr GCal MSte SMrm WCru
* 'Great Beverly'	ER&R NShi
'Green Gold' (R)	NShi WDib
'Green Lace'	ER&R NShi
'Grey Feather'	ER&R NShi
griffithii	see *B. annulata*
'Gustav Lind' (S)	CHal ER&R EShb NShi
'Guy Savard' (C)	NShi WDib
'Gypsy Maiden' (T)	CBla
haageana	see *B. scharffii*
handelii	ER&R NShi
* 'Happy Heart'	ER&R NShi
'Harbison Canyon'	NShi
* 'Harry's Beard'	ER&R NShi
'Hastor'	ER&R NShi
hatacoa	ER&R NShi
- silver	CHal CSpe ER&R NShi
- spotted	ER&R NShi
'Hazel's Front Porch' (C)	ER&R NShi
'Helen Lewis'	ER&R NShi
'Helen Teupel' (R)	ER&R NShi WDib
'Helene Jaros'	ER&R NShi
'Her Majesty' (R)	ER&R
heracleifolia var. ***longipila***	ER&R NShi
- var. ***nigricans***	CHal NShi
- 'Wisley'	NShi
§ 'Herzog von Sagan' (R)	ER&R NShi
x ***hiemalis*** 'Elatior'	LRHS
hispida var. ***cucullifera***	ER&R NShi
'Holmes Chapel'	ER&R NShi
homonyma (T)	ER&R
'Honeysuckle' (C)	ER&R NShi
'Hot Tamale'	ER&R
'Hottentot'	NShi
hydrocotylifolia	ER&R NShi

hypolipara	ER&R NShi
(Illumination Series) 'Illumination Apricot'	WWol
- 'Illumination Rose'	SCoo WWol
- 'Illumination Salmon Pink' 🏆H2-3	SCoo
- 'Illumination White'	WWol
imperialis	ER&R NShi
imperialis x 'Bokit'	NShi WDib
incarnata (C)	ER&R NShi
- 'Metallica'	see *B. metallica*
'Ingramii'	ER&R NShi
'Interlaken' (C)	ER&R NShi
'Irene Nuss' (C) 🏆H1	ER&R NShi
'Ironstone' (R)	NShi
'Ivanhoe' (T)	CBla
'Ivy Ever'	ER&R NShi
'Jade'	NShi
'Jean Blair' (T)	CBla
'Jelly Roll Morton'	ER&R
'Joe Hayden'	CHal ER&R NShi
'John Tonkin' (C)	ER&R NShi
johnstonii	ER&R NShi
'Joy Porter' (C)	NShi
'Jubilee Mine'	ER&R
juliana	ER&R
'Jumbo Jeans'	ER&R NShi
'Jumbo Jet' (C)	ER&R NShi
'Kagaribi' (C)	ER&R NShi
kellermanii (C)	ER&R NShi
'Ken Lau Ren' (C)	NShi
keniensis	GCal
'Kentwood' (C)	ER&R NShi
kenworthyae	ER&R NShi
kingiana	NShi WDib
'Kit Jeans'	ER&R NShi
'Kit Jeans Mounger'	ER&R NShi
'Knutsford'	NShi
'Kookaburra' (T)	CBla
'Krakatoa'	CBla
'Kyoto'	NShi
'La Paloma' (C)	NShi WDib
'Lacewing'	ER&R NShi
'Lady Carol'	CHal
'Lady Clare'	ER&R NShi SDix
* 'Lady France'	ER&R MBri
'Lady Rowena' (T)	CBla
'Lady Snow'	CHal
'Lana' (C)	ER&R NShi
'Lancelot' (T)	CBla
'Langeana'	NShi
'Laurie's Love' (C)	ER&R
'Lawrence H. Fewkes'	ER&R
leathermaniae (C)	ER&R NShi
'Legia'	ER&R
'Lenore Olivier' (C)	ER&R NShi
'Leopard'	ER&R MBri NShi
'L'Escargot' **new**	WDib
'Lexington'	ER&R
'Libor' (C)	ER&R
'Lillian' (R)	NShi
'Lime Swirl'	ER&R NShi
limmingheana	see *B. radicans*
'Linda Dawn' (C)	ER&R NShi
'Linda Harley'	ER&R
'Linda Myatt'	ER&R NShi
lindeniana	ER&R NShi
listada 🏆H1	CHal ER&R MBri NShi WDib
'Lithuania'	ER&R
'Little Brother Montgomery' 🏆H1	CHal ER&R EShb GGar NShi SDix WDib
'Little Darling'	ER&R NShi
'Little Iodine'	NShi
'Lois Burks' (C)	CHal ER&R NShi WDib
'Loma Alta'	ER&R
'Looking Glass' (C)	ER&R NShi WDib
'Lospe-tu'	ER&R NShi
'Lou Anne'	CBla
'Lubbergei' (C)	ER&R NShi
'Lucerna'	see *B.* x *corallina* 'Lucerna'
'Lulu Bower' (C)	ER&R NShi
luxurians	CHll ER&R NShi WCot
- 'Ziesenhenne'	ER&R NShi
lyman-smithii	ER&R NShi
'Mabel Corwin'	ER&R NShi
'Mac MacIntyre'	NShi
macdougallii var. ***purpurea***	CHal NShi WDib
macduffieana	NShi
'Mac's Gold'	ER&R NShi
maculata 🏆H1	ER&R NShi
- 'Wightii' (C)	CHal CSpe ER&R NShi WDib
'Mad Hatter'	ER&R NShi
'Madame Butterfly' (C)	ER&R NShi
'Magic Carpet'	ER&R NShi
'Magic Lace'	ER&R NShi
'Majesty' (T)	CBla
'Manacris'	ER&R NShi
'Mandarin Orange' (C)	NShi
manicata	ER&R NShi WDib
'Maphil'	MBri NShi
'Mardi Gras' (T)	CBla
'Margaritae'	ER&R NShi
'Marmaduke' 🏆H1	CHal NShi WDib
'Marmorata' (T)	LRHS
'Martha Floro' (C)	ER&R
'Martin Johnson' (R)	ER&R NShi WDib
'Martin's Mystery'	ER&R NShi
masoniana 🏆H1	CHal ER&R ERea MOak NShi WDib
- light-leaved **new**	NShi
I 'Matador' (T)	CBla
'Maurice Amey'	ER&R NShi
'Maverick'	ER&R NShi
mazae	ER&R NShi
'Medora' (C)	ER&R NShi
'Melissa' (T)	CBla NShi
'Merry Christmas' (R) 🏆H1	ER&R NShi WDib
metachroa	ER&R
§ ***metallica*** 🏆H1	CHal ER&R EShb NShi
'Michaele'	ER&R
'Midnight Sun'	ER&R NShi
'Midnight Twister'	ER&R NShi
'Mikado' (R)	ER&R NShi
minor	ER&R
'Mirage' 🏆H1	ER&R NShi
'Miss Priss' (C)	NShi
mollicaulis	ER&R
'Moon Maid'	ER&R
* 'Moulin Rouge'	CBla
'Mr Steve' (T)	CBla
'Mrs Hashimoto' (C)	ER&R NShi
'Mrs Hatcher'	ER&R NShi
'Mrs Schinkle' (C)	NShi
multinervia	ER&R
'Munchkin' 🏆H1	CHal ER&R NShi WDib
* 'Mystic'	ER&R NShi
'Mystique'	ER&R NShi
'Nancy Cummings'	ER&R
natalensis (T)	ER&R NShi
'Nell Gwynne' (T)	CBla
'Nelly Bly'	ER&R
nelumbiifolia	ER&R NShi
nigramarga	see *B. bowerae* var. *nigramarga*
nigritarum	ER&R
* ***nitida alba***	ER&R

'Nokomis' (C)	ER&R NShi
'Norah Bedson'	ER&R NShi
'Northern Lights' (S)	ER&R NShi
obliqua	ER&R
obscura	ER&R
'Obsession'	ER&R
odorata	ER&R
'Odorata Alba'	ER&R NShi
odorata var. ***rosea***	NShi
olbia	ER&R
'Old Gold' (T)	ER&R
'Oliver Twist'	ER&R
'Ophelia' (T)	CBla
'Orange Cascade' (T)	CBla
'Orange Dainty'	ER&R
'Orange Pinafore (C)'	ER&R
'Orange Rubra' (C) ♀H1	CHal ER&R NShi
'Orococo'	NShi
'Orpha C. Fox' (C)	ER&R NShi
'Orrell' (C)	ER&R NShi
'Othello'	ER&R NShi
'Otto Forster'	ER&R NShi
oxyphylla	ER&R
'Pachea' (R)	NShi
paleata	ER&R NShi
palmata	CDes EBee EBla EMan EShb GCal NShi WPGP
- B&SWJ 2692 from Sikkim **new**	WCru
- from China **new**	EBla NShi
- var. ***palmata***	NShi SSpi
- - B&SWJ 7175	WCru
'Palomar Prince'	ER&R NShi
'Panasoffkee'	ER&R NShi
'Pantaloon'	NShi
'Panther'	ER&R
'Papillon' (T)	ER&R NShi
paranaensis	ER&R NShi
* 'Parilis'	ER&R NShi
partita	ER&R EShb NShi
'Passing Storm'	ER&R NShi
'Patricia Ogdon'	ER&R NShi
'Paul Harley'	ER&R NShi
'Paul Henry'	NShi
'Paul-bee'	ER&R NShi
paulensis	ER&R NShi
'Peace' (R)	NShi
'Peach Parfait' (C)	ER&R NShi
pearcei	ER&R NShi
'Pearl Ripple'	ER&R NShi
'Pearls' (C)	ER&R NShi
'Peggy Stevens' (C)	ER&R
peltata	ER&R NShi
* 'Penelope Jane'	ER&R
'Persephone' (T)	CBla
'Persian Brocade'	ER&R NShi
'Petite Marie' (C)	ER&R
'Phil Corwin' (R)	NShi
'Piccolo'	ER&R NShi
'Pickobeth' (C)	ER&R NShi
'Picotee' (T)	CSut
'Pinafore' (C) ♀H1	ER&R NShi
'Pink Basket'	NShi
'Pink Champagne' (R)	CBla NShi WDib
'Pink Frosted'	NShi
'Pink Jade' (C)	NShi
'Pink Lady' (R)	NShi WCru
'Pink Nacre'	CHal ER&R NShi
'Pink Parade' (C)	ER&R NShi
'Pink Parfan'	NShi
'Pink Shasta' (C)	NShi
'Pink Slate' (C)	NShi
'Pink Spot Lucerne' (C)	ER&R NShi SYvo
'Pink Taffeta'	ER&R NShi
plagioneura	ER&R
platanifolia var. ***acuminatissima***	ER&R
'Plum Rose'	ER&R NShi
plumieri	ER&R
polyantha	ER&R NShi
polygonoides	ER&R
popenoei	ER&R
'Posy Wahl' (C)	NShi
'Potpourri'	ER&R
'Président Carnot' (C)	ER&R NShi SYvo
'Pretty Rose'	ER&R
'Preussen'	ER&R NShi
'Primrose' (T)	CBla
'Princess of Hanover' (R)	ER&R NShi WDib
'Princessa Rio de Plata'	ER&R NShi
prismatocarpa	ER&R NShi
procumbens	see *B. radicans*
pustulata 'Argentea'	ER&R NShi
putii	NShi
- B&SWJ 7245	WCru
'Queen Mother' (R)	ER&R NShi
'Queen Olympus'	ER&R NShi WDib
'Quinebaug'	ER&R NShi
§ ***radicans*** ♀H1	CHal ER&R LRHS MBri NShi
'Raquel Wood'	ER&R NShi
'Raspberry Swirl' (R) ♀H1	CHal ER&R NShi WDib
ravenii	GCal NShi SSpi WCot
- B&SWJ 1954	WCru
'Raymond George Nelson' ♀H1	CHal ER&R NShi
'Razzmatazz' (R)	NShi WDib
'Red Berry' (R)	ER&R NShi
'Red Planet'	ER&R NShi WDib
'Red Reign'	ER&R NShi
'Red Robin' (R)	NShi WDib
'Red Spider'	ER&R NShi
'Red Undies' (C)	NShi WCru
'Red Wing' (R)	NShi
'Regal Minuet' (R)	NShi WDib
'Regalia'	ER&R
'Reine des Neiges' (R)	NShi
rex	LRHS MBri MRav NShi
- 'Orient'	ER&R NShi
'Richard Robinson'	ER&R
'Richmondensis'	ER&R EShb NShi
'Ricinifolia'	ER&R NShi
'Ricky Minter' ♀H1	ER&R ERea NShi
'Rip van Winkle'	ER&R NShi
'Robert Blais' (R)	NShi
'Robin' (R)	ER&R NShi
'Robin's Red' (C)	ER&R NShi
'Roi de Roses' (R)	ER&R NShi
roxburghii	ER&R NShi
'Roy Hartley' (T)	CBla
'Royal Lustre'	ER&R NShi
'Royalty' (T)	CBla
'Rubacon'	ER&R NShi
rubro-setulosa	ER&R
'Sabre Dance' (R)	ER&R NShi
'Sachsen'	ER&R NShi
'Saint Albans Grey'	NShi
salicifolia (C)	ER&R
sanguinea	ER&R NShi
'Scarlet Pimpernel' (T)	CBla
'Scarlett O'Hara' (T)	CBla ER&R
'Sceptre' (T)	CBla
scharffiana	ER&R
§ ***scharffii***	CHal EBak ER&R NShi SDix
'Scherzo'	CHal ER&R NShi WDib
'Scottish Star'	NShi
'Sea Captain'	NShi

	'Sea Coral' (T)	CBla
	'Sea Serpent'	NShi
	'Secpuoc'	ER&R
	semperflorens hort.	see *B.* Semperflorens Cultorum Group
§	Semperflorens Cultorum Group	MBri NShi
	'Serlis'	ER&R NShi
	serratipetala	CHal EBak ER&R MBri NShi WDib
	'Shamus'	ER&R NShi
*	***sheperdii***	CHal NShi WDib
	'Shiloh' (R)	ER&R NShi
*	'Shinihart'	ER&R NShi
	'Shoppy'	NShi
	'Sierra Mist' (C)	ER&R NShi
	'Silbreen'	NShi
	silletensis	GCal
	subsp. ***mengyangensis*** **new**	
	'Silver Cloud' (R)	ER&R NShi WDib
*	'Silver Dawn'	ER&R NShi
	'Silver Dollar'	NShi
	'Silver Dots'	NShi
	'Silver Giant' (R)	ER&R NShi
	'Silver Jewell'	NShi WDib
	'Silver King' (R) **new**	NShi
	'Silver Lace'	NShi WDib
	'Silver Mist' (C)	ER&R NShi
	'Silver Points'	ER&R NShi
	'Silver Queen' (R) ♀H1	NShi
	'Silver Sweet' (R)	ER&R NShi
	'Silver Wings'	ER&R NShi
	'Sinbad' (C)	ER&R NShi
	sinensis	EMan EMon NShi WCot
	- BWJ 8011	WCru
	aff. ***sinensis*** BWJ 8133 **new**	WCru
*	'Sir Charles'	ER&R
	'Sir John Falstaff'	ER&R NShi
	Skeezar Group	ER&R
	- 'Brown Lake'	ER&R NShi
*	'Snowcap' (C) ♀H1	ER&R EShb NShi WDib
	socotrana	ER&R
	solananthera ♀H1	CHal ER&R EShb GGar NShi WDib
	soli-mutata	NShi
	sonderiana	ERea EShb GCal
	'Sophie Cecile' (C) ♀H1	CHal ER&R NShi
	'Sophie's Jenny'	NShi
	'Speckled Roundabout'	NShi
	'Speculata' (R)	ER&R NShi
	'Spellbound'	ER&R NShi WDib
	'Spindrift'	ER&R NShi
	'Spotches'	ER&R NShi
	'Stained Glass' (R)	NShi WDib
	'Stichael Maeae'	ER&R
§	***stipulacea***	CHal ER&R NShi
	subvillosa (S)	ER&R
	'Sugar Candy' (T)	CBla
	'Sugar Plum'	ER&R NShi
	'Sun God'	NShi
	Superba Group (C) **new**	NShi
	'Superba Azella' (C)	NShi
	sutherlandii ♀H1	CAvo CHEx CHal EBak EOHP ER&R ERea ERos EShb LRHS MOak NBir NPer NShi SBch SDix SYvo WCot WCru WDib WEas WFar WHer
	- 'Papaya'	CSpe
	'Swan Song'	ER&R
	'Sweet Dreams' (T)	CBla
	'Sweet Magic'	CHal ER&R NShi
	'Swirly Top' (C)	ER&R NShi
	'Sylvan Triumph' (C)	ER&R NShi
	'Tahiti' (T)	CBla
	taiwaniana	NShi
	'Tapestry' (R)	ER&R NShi
	'Tar Baby' (T)	ER&R NShi
*	***taya***	WDib
	'Tea Rose'	ER&R NShi
	'Tequesta'	NShi
	teuscheri (C)	ER&R NShi
	'Texastar'	ER&R NShi WDib
	'The Wiz'	ER&R NShi
	thelmae	ER&R NShi
	'Think Pink'	NShi
	'Thrush' (R)	NShi
	'Thumotec'	ER&R
	'Thunderclap'	CHal ER&R NShi
	'Thurstonii' ♀H1	CHal ER&R EShb NShi
	'Tiger Paws' ♀H1	CHal ER&R MBri NShi
	'Tingley Mallet' (C)	ER&R NShi
	'Tiny Bright' (R)	ER&R NShi
	'Tiny Gem'	ER&R NShi
	'Tom Ment' (C)	ER&R NShi
	'Tom Ment II' (C)	ER&R
	'Tomoshiba'	ER&R
	'Tondelayo' (R)	ER&R NShi
	'Tornado' (R)	NShi
	'Tribute'	ER&R NShi
	'Trinidad'	ER&R NShi
	tripartita (T)	ER&R NShi WDib
	'Trout' (C)	NShi
	'Twilight'	ER&R NShi
	'Two Face'	ER&R NShi WDib
	ulmifolia	ER&R NShi
	undulata (C)	CHal ER&R NShi
	'Universe'	ER&R NShi
	'Venetian Red' (R)	NShi
	venosa	CHal ER&R NShi
	'Venus'	CHal ER&R NShi
	'Vera Wyatt'	NShi
	x ***verschaffeltii***	ER&R NShi
	versicolor	ER&R
	'Vesuvius' (R)	NShi WDib
	'Viaudii'	ER&R NShi
	'Viau-Scharff'	ER&R
§	***vitifolia*** Schott	ER&R NShi
	'Wally's World'	NShi
	'Weltoniensis'	ER&R NShi
	'Weltoniensis Alba' (T)	ER&R
	'White Cascade'	ER&R
	'Wild Swan'	NShi WCru
	williamsii **new**	NShi
	'Witch Craft' (R)	ER&R NShi
	'Withlacoochee'	ER&R NShi WDib
	wollnyi	ER&R
	'Wood Nymph' (R)	ER&R NShi
	'Yellow Sweety' (T)	CBla
	'Zuensis'	ER&R
	'Zulu' (T)	CBla

Belamcanda (*Iridaceae*)

chinensis	CArn CBro CMea EChP ECha ECrN EGra EMan ERos EShb EUnu GPoy LRHS MLLN MSal SDnm SIng SPav SPlb SRms SSto SYvo WBVN WBrE WCru WPer WWye
- 'Freckle Face' **new**	GBri IBal NArg
- 'Hello Yellow'	GBuc

Bellevalia (*Hyacinthaceae*)

ciliata **new**	ERos
dubia	EBee WCot
fominii	WWst
forniculata	GTou
gracilis	WCot

	hackelii	ERos
	hyacinthoides	CStu WCot
	kurdistanica	ERos
	longipes	WCot
	longistyla	WCot
§	***paradoxa***	CHar CMea CPom EChP EHrv EMan ERos ITim LTwo MAvo NJOw WCot
	- white-flowered **new**	ERos
	pycnantha hort.	see *B. paradoxa*
	romana	CNic CStu EBee ERos GBin LPhx MTho WCot
	sarmatica	EBee ERos WCot
	spicata	WCot
	tabriziana	ERos
	webbiana	ERos

Bellis (*Asteraceae*)

	perennis	NMir
	- 'Alba Plena' (d)	ECho ELan
	- 'Blue Moon'	WCHb
	- 'Dresden China'	ELan GAbr MTho NBlu WOut
	- Hen and Chickens	see *B. perennis* 'Prolifera'
	- 'Lower Minety' (v)	CNat
	- 'Miss Mason'	GAbr WOut
	- 'Parkinson's Great White'	GAbr
§	- 'Prolifera' (d)	WHer
	- 'Red Buttons'	NBlu
	- 'Robert'	GAbr
	- 'Rusher Rose'	EPfP
	- Rusher Series, mixed **new**	NBlu
	- 'Single Blue'	see *B. rotundifolia* 'Caerulescens'
	- 'Tasso Strawberries and Cream'	WRHF
§	***rotundifolia*** 'Caerulescens'	ELan GAbr NBir NBro SIng WCot WOut
	sylvestris	CArn

Bellium (*Asteraceae*)

*	***crassifolium canescens***	WPer
	minutum	MBNS MTho

Beloperone see *Justicia*

Bensoniella (*Saxifragaceae*)

	oregona	EBee EMon

Berberidopsis (*Flacourtiaceae*)

	beckleri	CFil CPLN WPGP
	corallina	More than 30 suppliers

Berberis ✿ (*Berberidaceae*)

	ACE 2237	EPot
	CC 4041	CPLG
	SDR 3055	GKev
	SDR 3256	GKev
	aetnensis	GIBF
	aggregata	GKir NBir SPer SRms WDin
	amurensis var. ***latifolia*** B&SWJ 4353	WCru
	x ***antoniana***	LRHS WBcn
	aquifolium	see *Mahonia aquifolium*
	- 'Fascicularis'	see *Mahonia* x *wagneri* 'Pinnacle'
N	***aristata*** ambig.	CArn CMCN
	aristata Parker	see *B. glaucocarpa*
	asiatica	CAgr CPLG GPoy
	bealei	see *Mahonia japonica* Bealei Group
	bergmanniae	SLPl
	'Blenheim'	WFar
	'Boughton Red'	MBri
	brevipedunculata	see *B. prattii*
	x ***bristolensis***	EPla SLon SPla SRms
	buxifolia	LEdu MRav SPoG WCFE
	- 'Nana' hort.	see *B. buxifolia* 'Pygmaea'
N	- 'Pygmaea'	CAbP CBcs CSBt EMil ENot EWTr GKir LRHS MBNS MBar MRav NEgg SLim SPer STre WDin WFar
	calliantha	CPle WBcn WFar
	candidula	EBee ECrN ENot EPfP GKir LAst MBar MGos MRav MSwo SLon SPer WDin WGwG
	- 'Jytte'	see *B.* 'Jytte'
	x ***carminea*** 'Barbarossa'	WDin
	- 'Buccaneer'	SPer
	- 'Pirate King'	CSBt EBee LRHS MRav SPer SWvt WPat
	chrysosphaera	WFar
§	***concinna***	IMGH
	congestiflora	CPle
	cooperi	GIBF
	coxii	GGar WCwm
	darwinii ♀H4	More than 30 suppliers
I	- 'Compacta' **new**	SPoG
	dictyophylla ♀H4	CPMA CPle EPfP EPla GKir MGos NLar SLon SPer SSpi WDin WPat WSHC
	dulcis 'Nana'	see *B. buxifolia* 'Pygmaea'
	empetrifolia	CPle NLon
	erythroclada	see *B. concinna*
	'Fireball'	CMac
	franchetiana var. ***macrobotrys***	GIBF
	x ***frikartii*** 'Amstelveen' ♀H4	CDoC CMac CSBt CSam EBee ELan ENot EPfP GKir LAst MBNS MRav NLar WDin WFar
	- 'Telstar'	ECrN LAst LBuc MRav NPro
	gagnepainii hort.	see *B. gagnepainii* var. *lanceifolia*
	gagnepainii C.K. Schneid.	CMac GKir LRav MRav NLon SLPl WBVN WTel
§	- var. ***lanceifolia***	CBcs CTri EBee ECrN ENot EPla GKir MBar MDun MGos MWhi NEgg NWea WDin WFar
	- - 'Fernspray'	EPfP EPla LRHS MRav SBod SRms
	- 'Purpurea'	see *B.* x *interposita* 'Wallich's Purple'
	'Georgei' ♀H4	CMHG CWib EPfP GKir GQui LRHS MAsh SMur SPoG SSpi WBcn
§	***glaucocarpa***	EPfP EPla
	'Goldilocks'	CAbP CFil CPMA CPSs EPfP GKir LAst LRHS MBlu MBri SPoG SSpi WBcn WGer WPGP
	gyalaica	GIBF
	x ***hybridogagnepainii*** 'Chenaultii'	CBcs ELan SPer
	hypokerina	CMac
	insignis	WFar
	- subsp. ***insignis*** var. ***insignis***	WFar
	- - B&SWJ 2432	WCru
§	x ***interposita*** 'Wallich's Purple'	CCVT ECrN EPfP MBar MDun MRav MSwo SPer WDin
	jamesiana	WCFE
	julianae ♀H4	CBcs CSBt EBee ECrN ELan ENot EPfP GKir LAst LRav MBar MGos MRav MSwo NEgg NLon NWea SCoo SHBN SHFr SLPl SPer SWvt WBVN WDin WFar WHCG WHar WSHC WTel
	- 'Mary Poppins'	EBee LRHS WSPU
§	'Jytte'	EBee MWhi WDin
	kawakamii	SLPl
	koreana	CDul CMCN EPfP EPla GIBF NLar
	lecomtei	GIBF
	lempergiana	CMCN
	lepidifolia	GBin

	linearifolia	CMac
	- 'Jewel'	SBrw
	- 'Orange King'	CBcs CDoC CMac EBee ECrN ELan ENot EPfP GKir LRHS MAsh MGos SCoo SHBN SIgm SPer SPoG WDin WFar WHar WPat
	'Little Favourite'	see *B. thunbergii* f. *atropurpurea* 'Atropurpurea Nana'
	x ***lologensis***	MGos WDin
	- 'Apricot Queen' ♀H4	CBcs CMac EBee EPfP GKir LRHS MAsh MGos MRav NBea NBlu NLar SCoo SHBN SPer SPoG WDin
	- 'Mystery Fire'	CDoC COtt EBee GKir LRHS MBlu MBri MDun MGos NBlu NEgg NLar SBrw SCoo SPoG SWvt WDin WFar WHar
	- 'Stapehill'	ELan EPfP GKir LRHS MAsh MBri SSpi WBcn
	lycium	MMil WHCr
	macrosepala var. ***macrosepala*** B&SWJ 2124	WCru
	x ***media*** Park Jewel	see *B.* x *media* 'Parkjuweel'
§	- 'Parkjuweel'	CBcs EBee EPfP GKir IArd MRav NLar SCoo WDin WFar
	- 'Red Jewel' ♀H4	CDoC CMac CSBt EBee EPfP LRHS MGos MWat NPro NScw SCoo SPer SPoG WDin WFar WMoo
	mitifolia **new**	NLar
	montana	WPat
	morrisonensis	CFil
	morrisonicola	GIBF
	aff. ***nepalensis***	GIBF
	nummularia	GIBF
	x ***ottawensis***	MWhi
	- 'Auricoma'	LRHS MRav
	- f. ***purpurea***	CWib EBee MGos SBod WDin WFar WHar
§	- - 'Superba' ♀H4	More than 30 suppliers
§	- 'Silver Miles' (v)	EHoe EPfP LRHS MRav SPoG WBVN WFar WPat
§	***panlanensis***	ENot MBar MMil MRav SLon WWes
	patagonica	NLon
	poiretii	CPLG NLar
	polyantha hort.	see *B. prattii*
§	***prattii***	CMHG GIBF MWat
	pruinosa	CDul CFil
	'Red Tears'	CPMA CSam LRHS MBlu MBri MGos MLan MRav NLar WHCG WMoo
	'Rubrostilla'	EBee NLon
	x ***rubrostilla*** 'Cherry Ripe'	CMac
	- 'Wisley'	EPfP LRHS
	sanguinea hort.	see *B. panlanensis*
	sargentiana	NFor NLon SLPl
	sherriffii	CPle WCwm
	sieboldii	WPat
	x ***stenophylla*** ♀H4	More than 30 suppliers
	- 'Claret Cascade'	EBee GKir LRHS MAsh MBri MGos NLar SPer SPoG WFar
	- 'Corallina'	WBcn
	- 'Corallina Compacta' ♀H4	CFee CLyd ELan EPfP EPot GKir LRHS MAsh NLAp NRya SChu SPoG SRms WAbe WPat
	- 'Cornish Cream'	see *B.* x *stenophylla* 'Lemon Queen'
	- 'Crawley Gem'	CMHG GBin LRHS MBar WFar
	- Cream Showers	see *B.* x *stenophylla* 'Lemon Queen'
	- 'Etna'	ELan LRHS MAsh SPoG
	- 'Irwinii'	CMac CTri GKir LAst MBar MGos MSwo SLon SPer WDin WFar WTel
N	- 'Lemon Queen'	WTel
	- 'Nana'	SRms WAbe
	- 'Pink Pearl' (v)	CMHG LRHS MGos
	temolaica ♀H4	CFil CPMA EPfP GKir LRHS MDun NEgg NLar NPen NSti SDnm SSpi SSta WDin WPGP WPat
	thunbergii ♀H4	CDoC CDul CSBt ENot GBin GKir LBuc MAsh MRav NEgg NWea SCoo SMer SPer SPlb WDin WFar
	- f. ***atropurpurea***	CBcs CCVT CTri EBee ENot EPfP EWTr GKir ISea LAst LBuc MAsh MBar MGos MSwo NBlu NEgg NFor NWea SCoo SPer SPoG WBVN WDin WFar WMoo
§	- - 'Atropurpurea Nana' ♀H4	More than 30 suppliers
	- - 'Bagatelle' ♀H4	CDoC COtt EBee ELan EMil ENot EPfP EPot GKir IArd LRHS LSRN MAsh MBar MBri MGos MRav MTis MWhi NEgg SLim SWvt WCFE WDin WFar WPat WWeb
	- - 'Carmen'	LRHS MGos
	- - 'Dart's Purple'	LRHS MBri WFar
	- - 'Dart's Red Lady'	CAlb CPLG CPMA CSBt CWib EBee ECrN ELan ENot EPfP ESis GKir LRHS MAsh MBri MRav NPro SCoo SLim SPer SPoG SWvt WDin WFar WPat
	- - 'Golden Ring' ♀H4	More than 30 suppliers
	- - 'Harlequin' (v)	CBcs CDoC CSBt EBee EHoe ELan EMil ENot EPfP GKir LRHS LSRN MAsh MBri MGos MRav NEgg SLim SPer SPla SPoG WBVN WDin WFar WHar WPat WWeb
	- - 'Helmond Pillar'	CDul CSBt CWib EBee ECrN EHoe ELan EMil ENot EPfP GKir LAst LRHS MAsh MBar MBlu MBri MGos MRav NBlu NEgg SLim SMad SPer SPoG SWvt WCFE WDin WFar WPat
	- - 'Red Chief' ♀H4	CBcs CBrm CMHG EBee ECrN EGra ELan ENot EPfP GKir LRHS MAsh MGos MRav NEgg SLim SLon SPer SPla SPoG SWvt WDin WFar WHCG WHar WMoo WPat WTel WWeb
	- - 'Red King'	MRav WDin
	- - 'Red Pillar'	CChe CDoC CPle EBee EHoe ELan GKir LRHS MAsh MBar MGos MWat SHBN SPla SPoG WDin WFar WPat
	- - 'Red Rocket'	EMil MBri MCCP NLar
	- - 'Rose Glow' (v) ♀H4	More than 30 suppliers
	- 'Atropurpurea Superba'	see *B.* x *ottawensis* f. *purpurea* 'Superba'
	- 'Aurea'	More than 30 suppliers
	- Bonanza Gold = 'Bogozam'PBR	CAbP CDoC COtt ELan EPfP GKir LRHS MAsh MRav NLar SMur SPoG WDin WFar WPat
	- 'Carpetbagger'	LBuc WHar
	- 'Coronita' **new**	MBri
	- 'Crimson Pygmy'	see *B. thunbergii* f. *atropurpurea* 'Atropurpurea Nana'
	- 'Erecta'	CMac EBee ENot EPfP LRHS MBar MGos MRav SPer WCFE WDin
	- 'Golden Torch'	CSBt ENot LSRN MBNS MBri SWvt WWeb
	- 'Green Carpet'	EBee LRHS MBar SPoG WFar
	- 'Green Mantle'	see *B. thunbergii* 'Kelleriis'
	- 'Green Marble'	see *B. thunbergii* 'Kelleriis'
§	- 'Kelleriis' (v)	CDoC EGra EPfP MBar NPro SLon SPoG WDin WFar
	- 'Kobold'	EBee ECrN ENot EPfP GKir LRHS

	MAsh MBar MGos SLim SPer SPla SPoG WFar
- 'Pink Queen' (v)	EBee ENot EPfP LAst MAsh MGos SPur WDin WFar WHar WPat
- 'Pow-wow'	CBcs MGos NLar WBcn
- 'Silver Beauty' (v)	CMHG EBee ELan LRHS MGos WDin
- 'Silver Carpet'	NLar
- 'Silver Mile'	see *B.* x *ottawensis* 'Silver Miles'
- 'Somerset'	CMac WBcn
* - 'Tricolor' (v)	CMac EHoe MRav WFar WPat
tischleri var. ***abbreviata***	GIBF
tsangpoensis	SLPl
valdiviana	CFil CPMA EPfP IArd SMad SSpi WPGP
veitchii	SLPl
verruculosa ♀H4	CBcs CTri EBee ENot EPfP GKir LAst MBar MGos MRav MSwo NLon NWea SCoo SGar SPer SRms WCFE WDin WFar
- 'Hard's Rob' **new**	NLar
virescens B&SWJ 2646D	WCru
vulgaris	CArn CNat GPoy WBWf
- 'Wiltshire Wonder' (v)	CNat
wilsoniae	CAgr CBcs CDul CFil CTri EBee ENot EPfP EPla GKir MBar MWhi NEgg NLon NWea SCoo SHBN SPer WCFE WDin WFar
- ACE 2462	EHyt
- L 650	WPGP
- blue	LRHS WBcn WFar WGer
- 'Graciella'	LRHS MMil NPro
- var. ***guhtzunica***	EPla EWes

Berchemia (*Rhamnaceae*)

polyphylla **new**	CPLN
racemosa	CPLN NLar WSHC
scandens **new**	CPLN

bergamot see *Citrus bergamia*

Bergenia ✿ (*Saxifragaceae*)

'Abendglocken'	EBee ECGP ECha ECtt EPfP GKir LGro LRHS MBri MNFA MWat NGdn NSti SChu SPla WCot WEas WFar
§ 'Abendglut'	More than 30 suppliers
'Admiral'	CBct ECha
* ***agavifolia***	CBct
'Apple Court White'	CBct
'Autumn Magic'	CBct LSou MSte SPoG
'Baby Doll'	More than 30 suppliers
'Bach'	SSpi
§ 'Ballawley' clonal ♀H4	CFir ECha IBlr IGor MRav NEgg SSpi WCAu WFar
'Ballawley Guardsman'	CBct EBee EHrv ERou
Ballawley hybrids	EBee LGro SDix
'Ballawley' seed-raised	see *B.* Ballawley hybrids
'Bartók'	SSpi
beesiana	see *B. purpurascens*
'Beethoven'	CBct CDes CLAP ECha EPla EVFa IGor MRav NBir NPar SSpi WCot WPGP WSHC
Bell Tower	see *B.* 'Glockenturm'
'Bizet'	CBct SSpi
'Borodin'	CBct
'Brahms'	CBct GBuc SSpi
'Bressingham Bountiful'	CBct WCot
'Bressingham Ruby' PBR	CBct EBrs ECGP ECha ECtt GKir LRHS MRav NBir NCGa NEgg SChu SHBN WCAu WCot WPGP
'Bressingham Salmon'	CBct CHar EBee EBrs ELan ENot EPfP ERou GMaP GSki LRHS MBri MRav NLar SHBN WCot WMnd
'Bressingham White' ♀H4	More than 30 suppliers
'Britten'	CMac SSpi
ciliata	CDes CFee CHEx CLAP EBrs EChP EPfP EShb GCal LEdu MRav MSte NBir NLar SBla SDix SSpi SUsu WCot WEas WKif WLin WPGP WSHC
- f. ***ciliata***	CBct WCot
- f. ***ligulata***	see *B. pacumbis*
- 'Wilton'	WCot
ciliata x ***crassifolia***	see *B.* x *schmidtii*
'Claire Maxine'	GCal
cordifolia	More than 30 suppliers
- 'Flore Pleno'	CBct
- 'Purpurea' ♀H4	CBcs CDoC CSBt ECha ELan EMFW ENot EPfP GKir GSki IHMH LBuc LGro LRHS MNFA MRav NBir SHBN SPer SPla SRms WCAu WFar WPnP
- 'Rosa Zeiten'	GBin
- 'Tubby Andrews' (v)	CBct EBla EVFa IFro MBrN MCCP MLLN NEgg NLar NPar NPro WHil
- 'Winterglut'	GMaP IBal ITim NBre SWvt WBor WHil
crassifolia	EBee EWTr NBre SRms
- DF 90028	EMon
- 'Autumn Red'	CBct ECha
- 'Orbicularis'	see *B.* x *schmidtii*
- var. ***pacifica***	CFil GIBF
* ***cyanea***	WCot
'David'	EMon EWes
delavayi	see *B. purpurascens* var. *delavayi*
'Delbees'	see *B.* 'Ballawley'
'Doppelgänger' **new**	SUsu
'Eden's Dark Margin'	CBgR ERou LAst
'Eden's Magic Carpet'	CFir
'Eden's Magic Giant'	EBee EChP ERou GBin
emeiensis	CDes NDov SBla
- hybrid	CBct MWat
'Eric Smith'	CBct CLAP ECha GCal GCra IGor MBri WCot
'Eroica'	CBct CSpe EChP ECha ELan EMon GBin MBri MRav NRnb NSti SHar WCAu WMnd
'Evening Glow'	see *B.* 'Abendglut'
'Frau Holle'	MBri
§ 'Glockenturm'	CBct GCal NEgg
'Hellen Dillon'	CBct
'Herbstblute'	EMon
'Jo Watanabe'	ECha MRav
'Lambrook'	see *B.* 'Margery Fish'
§ 'Margery Fish'	CBct EBee ECha
milesii	see *B. stracheyi*
§ 'Morgenröte' ♀H4	CBcs CBct EBee EBrs ECha EMil ENot EPfP GCra GKir GMaP IHMH LAst LRHS MBNS MGos MRav NSti SHBN SPer SRms SSvw SWvt WCot
'Morning Light'	LAst NPro NSti
Morning Red	see *B.* 'Morgenröte'
'Mozart'	CLAP
'Mrs Crawford'	CBct ECha
'Oeschberg'	CBct GCal WCAu
'Opal'	CBct
'Overture'	CBct EBee EHrv LAst NCob NEgg NGby SBla WCAu WCot WFar
§ ***pacumbis***	CLAP CPLG EBee GEdr LEdu MWgw NBid NBir NSti SDix SSpi WCot
- B&SWJ 2693	WCru
- CC 1793	SBch
- CC 3616	ITim MSph WCot

	'Perfect'	CBct WMnd
	'Pink Dragonfly'	GBin NEgg SMac
	'Profusion'	WCAu
	'Pugsley's Pink'	CBct ECha GCra SHBN
§	***purpurascens*** ♀H4	CMac EBrs EWTr GBuc GCrs GKir GMaP GSki IGor SDix SPer SSpi WCot
	- ACE 2175	WCot
	- CC 4461	GKev
	- SDR 1629	GKev
§	- var. ***delavayi*** ♀H4	MBri SRms WPnP
	- - CLD 1366	WPer
	aff. ***purpurascens*** ACE 2175	WCot
	'Purpurglocken'	GCal
	'Red Beauty'	MBow MGos NEgg NFla
	'Reitheim'	CBct
	'Rosi Klose'	CBct CFee EBee EChP ECha EMon EWes GAbr GBin GCal LAst MBri MNFA MRav NCob NMyG SBla SVil WCot WFar
	'Rotblum'	CBct ECtt EPfP GBin GMaP GSki GWCH MDun NBir NCob NGdn NOrc NPri NRnb NVic WFar WPer WRHF WWeb
§	x ***schmidtii*** ♀H4	CMac EBee EBrs ENot EWll IGor NBir SDix WCot
	'Schneekissen'	CBct EBee MAvo MNFA MRav WCAu
§	'Schneekönigin'	CBct ECha MRav
§	'Silberlicht' ♀H4	More than 30 suppliers
	Silverlight	see *B.* 'Silberlicht'
	'Simply Sweet' **new**	WCot
	Snow Queen	see *B.* 'Schneekönigin'
	'Snowblush'	SSpi
§	***stracheyi***	CBct ECha EGoo IGor MRav NBid SApp SDix WEas
	- Alba Group	CBct CDes ECha EPfP GCal MSte WSHC
	'Sunningdale'	CBcs CBct EBee ECha ELan EMFW EPfP GCra GKir GMaP GSki LRHS MLLN MRav NBir SChu SPer SSpi SWvt WCAu WMnd
	Winter Fairy Tales	see *B.* 'Wintermärchen'
§	'Wintermärchen'	CBct ECha ELan ENot EPfP GCra GKir GSki LRHS MGos MRav MSte MWgw NCGa NOrc NPro SPoG WCAu WCot WMnd

Bergeranthus (*Aizoaceae*)

sp. **new**	WThu
glenensis	EDAr
multiceps	SChr

Berkheya (*Asteraceae*)

macrocephala	EMon WCot
purpurea	CSpe EBee EMan GBri GGar IGor MAnH MBNS MDKP NArg SBch SIgm SPoG STes WCot WHil WRos WSHC

Berlandiera (*Asteraceae*)

lyrata	EMan GCal NJOw SPet

Berneuxia (*Diapensiaceae*)

thibetica	IBlr

Berula (*Apiaceae*)

erecta	EHon EMFW NPer WWpP

Berzelia (*Bruniaceae*)

galpinii	SPlb
lanuginosa	CSec CTrC GGar IDee

Beschorneria (*Agavaceae*)

sp.	CFil
calcicola **new**	CFil
septentrionalis	CFil CFir CTrC EAmu EBee EMan EOas SSpi WCot WPGP
tubiflora	CFil CHEx EBee EOas LEdu
tubiflora x ***yuccoides*** **new**	CFil
wrightii **new**	CFil
yuccoides ♀H3	CAbb CBcs CFil CHEx CPne CTrC EAmu EBee IBlr IDee ISea LEdu MAnH MSte SAPC SArc SChr SDnm SIgm SLim SMur WKif WMul WPGP XPep
- 'Quicksilver'	CBcs CBod CDoC CEnd CFil CKno CTbh CTrC EBee EMan MDun MSte NVic SDnm SPoG SSpi WCot WGer WPGP WPat

Bessera (*Alliaceae*)

elegans	CFir CFwr EBee EMan EPot LRHS MSte WCot

Beta (*Chenopodiaceae*)

trigyna	WCot
vulgaris	EWin WHer
- 'Bull's Blood'	CArn CSpe EMan EWin MSte WCot WJek
- subsp. ***cicla***	CArn
var. ***flavescens*** 'Bright Lights' ♀H3 **new**	
- - - 'MacGregor's Favourite' **new**	SBch
- - - 'Rhubarb Chard' ♀H3	WJek
- subsp. ***maritima*** **new**	CAgr

Betonica see *Stachys*

Betula ✿ (*Betulaceae*)

	Sich 543 **new**	GIBF
	alba L.	see *B. pendula*, *B. pubescens*
	albosinensis misapplied	see *B. utilis*
	albosinensis Burkill ♀H4	CBcs CCVT CDul CMCN CTri EBee EPfP GIBF GKir ISea MDun MGos NWea SBLw SPer WCwm WDin WFar WNor WOrn
	- 'Bowling Green'	CPMA CTho
	- 'China Ruby'	CDul CPMA GKir LRHS MBri SIFN SSpi
	- 'Chinese Garden'	CPMA CTho
	- clone F	see *B. albosinensis* 'Ness'
	- 'K.Ashburner'	CPMA CTho
	- 'Kansu'	CLnd CPMA GKir SIFN
§	- 'Ness'	CPMA CTho
	- var. ***septentrionalis*** ♀H4	More than 30 suppliers
	- - 'Purdom'	CLnd CPMA GKir SIFN
§	***alleghaniensis***	CDul CMCN GKir IArd IDee NLar NWea SPoG WDin
	alnoides	GIBF WNor
	apoiensis	GIBF SSta WNor
	- 'Mount Apoi'	CPMA SIFN
	austrosinensis	WNor
	borealis	see *B. pumila*
§	x ***caerulea***	CDul CPMA CTho LRHS NLar
	caerulea-grandis	see *B.* x *caerulea*
	chichibuensis	EPla GIBF SBir WHer
	chinensis	CMCN GIBF WNor
	'Conyngham'	CTho MBlu
	costata misapplied	see *B. ermanii* 'Grayswood Hill'

	costata Trautv.	CLnd CTho EBee ELan EPfP GKir GTSp LRHS SBLw STre WDin WOrn
*	- 'Fincham Cream'	ERea GKir SIFN
I	x ***cruithnei*** **new**	GIBF
	dahurica Pall.	CDul CMCN IArd LRHS WNor
	- B&SWJ 4247	WHCr
	- 'Maurice Foster'	CPMA CTho
	- 'Stone Farm'	CPMA CTho
	divaricata	GIBF
	ermanii	CBcs CCVT CDoC CDul CLnd CMCN CMHG CSBt CSam CTho CTri ECrN ELan ENot EPfP GKir GQui LRHS MAsh MBlu MGos MRav NBea NEgg NWea SBir WDin WFar WMoo WNor
	- from Kamtchatka **new**	GIBF
§	- 'Grayswood Hill' ♀H4	CDul CEnd CLnd CMHG CPMA CTho EBee GKir GQui LRHS MBri MGos NWea SCoo SHBN SIFN SLim SMad SPer SPoG SSpi WOrn
	- 'Hakkoda Orange'	CPMA CTho GKir LRHS MBlu SCoo
	- 'Moonbeam'	GKir SMad
*	- 'Pendula'	CPMA GKir SCoo SIFN
	- 'Polar Bear'	CPMA GKir LRHS MBri SIFN SMad WHCr
*	- ***ussuriensis***	GIBF
	'Fetisowii'	CLnd CMCN CTho GKir IMGH LRHS MBlu MBri SCoo SIFN SLim SSpi SSta
	fruticosa	see *B. humilis*
	glandulifera	see *B. pumila*
	globispica	EGFP EWTr GIBF SBir WCwm WNor
	gmelinii	see *B. ovalifolia*
	grossa	CDul CMCN GIBF IArd IDee
	'Haywood'	LRHS
	'Hergest'	COtt EBee EPfP GKir LRHS MAsh MBri MGos SCoo SLim WHCr
§	***humilis***	CMCN GIBF GKir GQui WDin
	- B&SWJ 8801	WCru
	insignis	GIBF
	'Inverleith'	see *B. utilis* var. *jacquemontii* 'Inverleith'
	jacquemontii	see *B. utilis* var. *jacquemontii*
	kamtschatica	see *B. humilis*
§	***kenaica***	CTho
	lenta	CMCN CTho EPfP NLar NWea WDin
	luminifera	CMCN CPMA IDee NLar
	lutea	see *B. alleghaniensis*
	mandshurica	GIBF IArd WHCr
§	- var. ***japonica***	CBcs CLnd EBee EWes GBin GIBF GKir NEgg NLar NPal WNor
	- - 'Whitespire'	CWSG
	- - 'Whitespire Senior'	CDul LRHS
	maximowicziana	CBcs CDoC CLnd CMCN CTho CWib EPfP EWTr GIBF IArd LRHS MDun NEgg WDin WNor
§	***medwedewii***	CDul CLnd CMCN CTho EBee ECrN EPfP EPla EWTr GEdr GIBF GQui NEgg NWea SBir SCoo
	- from Winkworth	CTho
	- 'Gold Bark'	CDoC MBlu
	megrelica	see *B. medwedewii*
	x ***minor***	GIBF
	nana	CDul EBee EMil ESis GIBF GKir MBar NScw NSla NWea SRms SSta STre WDin
	- subsp. ***exilis***	GIBF
	- 'Glengarry'	EPot ESis GBin LBee NLar
§	***neoalaskana***	WNor
	nigra	CBcs CCVT CDoC CDul CEnd CLnd CMCN CMHG CSBt CTho CTri ECrN GIBF GKir LRHS MAsh NEgg SBLw SSta WDin WGer WMou WNor WOrn
	- 'Heritage' ♀H4	CDoC CDul CEnd CLnd CMCN CPMA CTho EBee ECrN ENot GKir LRHS MBlu MRav SCoo SIFN SLim SSpi SSta WDin WFar WMoo WOrn
	- 'Little King' **new**	CPMA
	- Wakehurst form	EPfP GKir LRHS SPer
§	***ovalifolia***	GIBF
	papyrifera	CAgr CBcs CCVT CDul CLnd CMCN CSBt CTri EBee ECrN ELan ENot EPfP GIBF LBuc LRHS MAsh MBar MRav MSwo NBee NWea SHBN SPer SSta WDin WFar WNor WOrn
	- var. ***commutata***	EWTr WDin
	- subsp. ***humilis***	see *B. neoalaskana*
	- var. ***kenaica***	see *B. kenaica*
	- 'Saint George'	CPMA CTho LRHS
	- 'Vancouver'	CPMA CTho
§	***pendula*** ♀H4	More than 30 suppliers
	- var. ***aurea***	GIBF
	- 'Bangor'	CPMA GKir SIFN
*	- 'Boeugh's Variety'	CEnd GBin GKir
	- f. ***crispa***	see *B. pendula* 'Laciniata'
	- 'Dalecarlica' misapplied	see *B. pendula* 'Laciniata'
	- 'Dalecarlica' ambig.	CBcs CCVT CSBt ECrN ENot GTSp MDun MRav SCrf SLim WFar
	- 'Fastigiata'	CDoC CDul CLnd CSBt CTho EBee ECrN ELan MGos NWea SBLw SCoo SLim SPer WDin WFar WMoo WOrn
	- var. ***fontqueri***	GIBF
*	- 'Golden Beauty'	CDoC CTho CTri GKir LRHS MAsh MGos SCoo SLim SPer WDin WOrn
	- 'Golden Cloud'	ECrN
	- 'Gracilis'	CTho
§	- 'Laciniata' ♀H4	CDoC CDul CLnd CMCN CTho CTri CWSG CWib EBee ECrN ELan EPfP GKir LAst LRHS MAsh MBri MGos MRav MSwo NBea NBee NWea SBLw SPer SSpi SSta WDin WMou WWes
	- 'Long Trunk' **new**	GKir MBri
	- 'Purpurea'	CCVT CDul CLnd CMCN CSBt CTho CWib EBee ECrN ELan ENot GKir LAst LRHS MDun MGos MSwo NBea NBlu NEgg SBLw SCoo SIFN SPer WDin WFar WOrn
	- 'Silver Cascade'	MGos
	- 'Silver Grace'	ENot GKir
	- 'Tristis' ♀H4	More than 30 suppliers
	- 'Youngii'	More than 30 suppliers
	platyphylla Sukaczev	CMCN NWea
	- var. ***japonica***	see *B. mandshurica* var. *japonica*
	- var. ***kamtschatica***	see *B. mandshurica* var. *japonica*
	- subsp. ***platyphylla***	CMCN GIBF
	potaninii	GIBF
§	***pubescens***	CCVT CDul CLnd CRWN CTri ECrN EMil GKir NBee NWea SBLw SLPl WDin WFar WMou
	- 'Arnold Brembo'	CTho
	- subsp. ***carpatica***	see *B. pubescens* var. *glabrata*
	- - var. ***murithii***	see *B. pubescens* var. *glabrata*
§	- var. ***glabrata***	GIBF
§	***pumila***	GGar GIBF WCwm
	raddeana	GIBF WNor
	- 'Hugh McAllister'	CTho
I	***refugia*** **new**	GIBF
	resinifera	see *B. neoalaskana*

'Royal Frost' CPMA
schmidtii CMCN EWTr GIBF IArd WCwm
szechuanica CLnd WDin
- 'Liuba White' CPMA CTho
tianschanica GIBF MDun WNor
'Trost's Dwarf' CBcs EBee ECrN WDin
§ ***utilis*** CDul CMCN CMHG CSBt CTho EBee ECrN EMil ENot GKir ISea LRHS MAsh MBar MRav NBee NWea SSta WDin WFar WNor
- BL&M 100 CTho
- F 19505 CTho
- L 415 GKir
- McB 1257 CTho
- Sch 2168 MBri
- 'Fascination' CCVT CDul CPMA CRez EMil GKir LRHS MBri NWea SCoo SIFN SLim SMad SSpi
* - 'Fastigiata' CLnd CPMA GKir SIFN
- 'Forrest's Blush' CDul EBee GKir LRHS MBri SIFN
N - var. ***jacquemontii*** More than 30 suppliers
- - SF 00004 ISea
- - 'Doorenbos' ♀H4 CAlb CLnd CMCN CPMA CTho EBee GKir MBlu MGos NEgg SIFN SPoG SSta WDin WOrn
- - 'Grayswood Ghost' ♀H4 CEnd CLnd CMCN CMHG CPMA CTho ECrN ENot EPfP GKir LRHS MBri MDun SHBN SIFN SMad SPer SSpi WHCr
§ - - 'Inverleith' CDul CEnd CPMA EBee GKir LRHS MBri MDun MWya NWea SCoo SIFN SLim SSpi WFar WOrn
- - 'Jermyns' ♀H4 CDul CEnd CLnd CMCN CMHG CPMA CTho EBee ECot EPfP GKir LRHS MBlu MBri SCoo SIFN SMad SPoG SSpi WOrn
- - 'Silver Shadow' ♀H4 CDul CLnd CMCN CPMA CTho EPfP GKir LRHS MAsh MBlu MBri NWea SCoo SHBN SIFN SLim SPer SPoG SSpi SSta WHCr WOrn
- - 'Snowqueen' CDul CEnd CLnd CMCN COtt CPMA CSBt CWSG EPfP GKir LRHS MAsh MBri MDun MGos NWea SCoo SIFN SLim SPoG WHCr WOrn
- - 'Trinity College' CLnd CMCN CPMA EBee GKir LRHS MBri SIFN SSpi
- 'Knightshayes' CTho
- 'Moonbeam' CLnd CMCN CPMA GKir MBri SCoo SIFN SSpi WHCr
- var. ***occidentalis*** 'Kyelang' CPMA CTho
- 'Polar Bear' GKir
- var. ***prattii*** CEnd CTho GKir MDun
- 'Ramdana River' CTho MBlu
- 'Schilling' CEnd GKir LRHS MAsh
- 'Silver Queen' SSpi
- 'Thyangboche Monastery' MDun
- 'Wakehurst Place Chocolate' CPMA GKir LRHS MBri SCoo SIFN SMad SSpi WHCr
cf. ***utilis*** GWJ 9259 **new** WCru
- HWJK 2345 WCru
verrucosa see *B. pendula*

Biarum (*Araceae*)

arundanum PB 154 from Portugal **new** CMon
carratracense WCot
- SF 233 from Spain **new** CMon
davisii EHyt GCrs LAma SSpi WCot
dispar WCot
ditschianum PB 289 from Turkey **new** CMon
ochridense WCot
spruneri S&L 229 SSpi
tenuifolium CStu ECho ERos SSpi WCot
- AB&S 4356 GCrs
- PB 357 from Minorca **new** CMon
- subsp. ***abbreviatum*** from Greece **new** CMon
- subsp. ***idomenaeum*** from Crete **new** CMon

Bidens (*Asteraceae*)

atrosanguinea see *Cosmos atrosanguineus*
§ ***aurea*** CMil CStr EBee EBla ECtt EMon EPPr EVFa EWes GCal LAst LIck LRHS MAnH MDKP MNrw MOak NCGa SAga SBla SGar SPet STes WBor WFar WOld WWye
- cream MAnH MNrw MSte
- B&SWJ 9049 from Guatemala WCru
- 'Hannay's Lemon Drop' CFwr CHea CKno CMea CPen CSev CSpe CStr EBee EBla ECtt EVFa GBri MAnH MBnl MDKP MHar MNrw MSph MSte NCGa SPoG STes SUsu
ferulifolia ♀H1+3 ECtt NPer SChu SPet WWol
- Golden Flame = 'Samsawae' LAst
- 'Peters Goldteppich'PBR LAst SPoG
heterophylla Ortega see *B. aurea*
heterophylla hort. CFwr CHad CKno ECtt MRav SCoo SHGN SOkh SPoG WFar WMoo WWlt
- CD&R 1230 CHad
humilis see *B. triplinervia* var. *macrantha*
integrifolia EChP SMad
Peter's Gold Rush = 'Topteppichi' **new** LSou
pilosa EBee
'Sundens' **new** LAst
§ ***triplinervia*** var. ***macrantha*** EBee

Bignonia (*Bignoniaceae*)

capreolata CPLN SBra WCot WSHC XPep
§ - 'Atrosanguinea' CPLN LRHS
- 'Dragon Lady' **new** WCot
- 'Tangerine Beauty' SSpi
lindleyana see *Clytostoma calystegioides*
unguis-cati see *Macfadyena unguis-cati*

Bilderdykia see *Fallopia*

Billardiera (*Pittosporaceae*)

longiflora ♀H3 More than 30 suppliers
- 'Cherry Berry' CBcs EBee ECou ELan ERea IArd LPio LRHS MCCP SBra SBrw SLim SMur SPer SPoG SSpi SWvt WSHC
- ***fructu-albo*** CBcs CPle EBee ELan EWes GGar ITer LRHS SBrw SLim SPoG SSpi
- red-berried CPle GGar
scandens ECou

Billbergia (*Bromeliaceae*)

Mibbs Whelan Group CFir
morelii CFir
nutans CHEx CHal EBak EOHP EShb ESlt GFlt IBlr IDee MBri SChr SRms WGwG WHer WMul XPep
- var. ***schimperiana*** **new** EShb

*	- 'Variegata' (v)	EShb ESlt WCot WGwG
	pyramidalis ♀H1 **new**	XBlo
I	- 'Variegata' (v)	IBlr
	'Santa Barbara' (v)	EOas
	x ***windii*** ♀H1	CHEx CHal EBak ESlt SRms
	zebrina **new**	EOas

Bismarckia (*Arecaceae*)

nobilis	EAmu SBig

Bistorta see *Persicaria*

Bixa (*Bixaceae*)

orellana	ELau MGol

blackberry see *Rubus fruticosus* agg.

blackcurrant see *Ribes nigrum*

Blechnum (*Blechnaceae*)

	alpinum	see *B. penna-marina* subsp. *alpinum*
	brasiliense ♀H1	WRic
	capense	CTrC
N	***chilense*** ♀H3	CAby CBcs CDes CFil CHEx CLAP CWil ECha EPfP GCra GGar IBlr NVic SAPC SArc SChu SDix SGSe SSpi WAbe WCot WCru WMoo WMul WPGP WRic
	discolor	CLAP CTrC IDee WRic
	- 'Silver Lady'	CTrC WMul
	durum	CTrC WRic
	fluviatile	CLAP CTrC IDee SGSe WMul WRic
	gibbum	EAmu LRHS MBri WMul
	magellanicum misapplied	see *B. chilense*
	minus	WRic
	minus x ***wattsii***	WRic
	novae-zelandiae	CTrC GGar WMul WRic
	nudum	EAmu EExo EPfP MCCP NMoo WRic
	penna-marina ♀H4	CElw CFil CLAP CPLG CWil EFer EMon EUJe GAbr GGar GMaP LEdu MBri NRya NVic NWCA SChu SDix SGSe SIng SRms SRot SSpi WEas WMoo WRic WWye
§	- subsp. ***alpinum***	CFil CLAP ECha GEdr SGSe WAbe WMoo
	- 'Cristatum'	CFil CLAP GAbr GGar SRms
	procerum	CTrC GGar WAbe WRic
	punctulatum	WRic
	spicant ♀H4	More than 30 suppliers
	- 'Cristatum'	WRic
	tabulare misapplied	see *B. chilense*
N	***tabulare*** (Thunb.) Kuhn ♀H1	CFil EFtx WPGP WRic
	vulcanicum	CLAP WRic
	wattsii	EAmu

Blepharocalyx (*Myrtaceae*)

cruckshanksii	CPLG LRHS
- 'Heaven Scent'	CSam EBee LAst MCCP NLar WBor

Blephilia (*Lamiaceae*)

'Cherokee'	EBee
ciliata	EBee IFro MSal

Bletilla ✿ (*Orchidaceae*)

	Brigantes g.	CHdy
*	***formosana alba***	CHdy
	hyacinthina	see *B. striata*
	ochracea	LAma WCot
	Penway Dragon g.	CHdy
*	**Penway Imperial g.**	CHdy
	Penway Paris g.	CHdy EMan
	Penway Starshine g.	CHdy
	Penway Sunset g.	WCot
§	***striata***	CBct CDes CFwr CPom EBee EBla ERea ERos GSki IBlr IHMH LAma LEdu MSal NCGa NMen SBla SChr WFar WPGP
	- ***alba***	see *B. striata* var. *japonica* f. *gebina*
	- 'Albostriata'	CBct CDes EBee EBla ELan EMan IBlr LAma NCGa WCot
	- var. ***japonica***	EPot
§	- - f. ***gebina***	CBct CDes EBee EPot GSki IBlr IHMH LAma LEdu LRHS SBla SChr SSpi WCot WFar
	- - - variegated (v)	EPot NMen WCot
	Yokohama g.	CHdy EBla

Bloomeria (*Alliaceae*)

crocea var. ***aurea***	ERos LRHS

blueberry see *Vaccinium corymbosum*

Blumenbachia (*Loasaceae*)

insignia **new**	EUnu

Bocconia (*Papaveraceae*)

cordata	see *Macleaya cordata*
microcarpa	see *Macleaya microcarpa*

Boehmeria (*Urticaceae*)

nivea	MSal
sylvatica **new**	NLar

Boenninghausenia (*Rutaceae*)

albiflora	EMan WCot
- B&SWJ 1479	WCru
- pink-flowered B&SWJ 3112 **new**	WCru
japonica B&SWJ 4876	WCru

Boesenbergia (*Zingiberaceae*)

longiflora	CKob

Bolax (*Apiaceae*)

	glebaria	see *Azorella trifurcata*
§	***gummifer***	EPot SBla WAbe

Bolboschoenus (*Cyperaceae*)

	caldwellii	EPPr
§	***maritimus***	CRWN LPBA WFar

Boltonia (*Asteraceae*)

asteroides	CFee CSam EBee ECtt EHrv EMon GCra GFlt GMac GSki LRHS NGdn NSti SPer SPoG WBVN WCAu WDyG
- var. ***latisquama***	EBee EPPr GMaP MBrN MRav MSte MWat SSvw WBor WFar WHal WWFP
- - 'Nana'	CBre EBee EGoo EMan LRHS MLLN MRav MWgw NChi WBVN WMoo WPer
- - 'Snowbank'	EBla EBrs ELan EMan EWTr EWsh
- 'Pink Beauty'	CBre EBla EMon LPhx NArg
- var. ***recognita***	EBee EMon LRHS
decurrens	EBee
incisa	see *Kalimeris incisa*

Bomarea (*Alstroemeriaceae*)

from Mexico	SSpi
acutifolia B&SWJ 9094	WCru

	boliviensis RCB/Arg P-18 new	WCot
	caldasii ♀H1	CDes CFil CFir CHEx CPLN CRHN CTbh EBee ERea LSou SIgm SSpi WBGC WBor WPGP WSHC
	edulis	ERea
	hirtella	CFil CHEx CPLN CRHN EBee EShb SSpi WCot WHil WPGP WSPU
	- B&SWJ 9017	WCru
	isopetala	CFil SSpi
	kalbreyeri	WCot
	multiflora	CFil CFir CPLN EShb
	- JCA 13761	SSpi
	ovata	ERea
	patacocensis	CPle
	- JCA 13987	WCot
	salsilla	CFil CPLN GCal SBla SIgm WCot WPGP WSHC

Bongardia (*Berberidaceae*)

	chrysogonum	CAvo EBee EHyt EPot LRHS WCot

Bonia (*Poaceae*)

	solida	CBig CHEx ERod MMoz MWht NPal SEND WJun WMul

Boophone (*Amaryllidaceae*)

	disticha new	LToo

borage see *Borago officinalis*

Borago (*Boraginaceae*)

	alba	EOHP MChe WCHb
	laxiflora	see *B. pygmaea*
	officinalis	CArn CBod CHrt CSev CWan EChP ELau EPfP GKir GPoy LRHS MBow MChe MHer NGHP NLsd NPri NVic WCot WGwG WHer WPer WSel WWye
	- 'Alba'	CBre CHrt CSev EChP ELau ILis MBow MHer NGHP SBch SDnm SIde WCHb WGwG WHer WJek WLHH WPer WRha WSel WWpP
	- 'Bill Archer' (v)	CNat
§	***pygmaea***	CArn CCge CHid CPLG CSev EChP ELan EOHP GBar MAnH MHar MHer MTho NGHP NLar NMRc NSti STes WCHb WGwG WMoo WOld WWpP

Boronia (*Rutaceae*)

	denticulata	ECou
	heterophylla	CBcs CPLG CSWP ECou SBrw
	- white-flowered	ECou
	megastigma	ECou
	- 'Brown Meg'	CBcs
	pinnata	ECou
	serrulata	ECou

Bossiaea (*Papilionaceae*)

	aquifolium new	LToo

Bothriochloa (*Poaceae*)

	barbinodies	CKno
§	***bladhii***	EPPr
	caucasica	see *B. bladhii*
§	***ischaemum***	CBig EHoe EMan EPPr GFor LRav WGHP WWpP

Botryostege see *Elliottia*

Bougainvillea (*Nyctaginaceae*)

	'Ailsa Lambe'	see *B.* (Spectoperuviana Group) 'Mary Palmer'
	'Alabama Sunset'	CWDa
	'Alexandra'	MBri
	'Apple Blossom'	see *B.* 'Elizabeth Doxey'
	'Audrey Grey'	see *B.* 'Elizabeth Doxey'
	'Aussie Gold'	see *B.* 'Carson's Gold'
	'Begum Sikander'	CWDa ERea
	'Betty Lavers'	ERea
§	'Blondie'	CWDa
	'Bridal Bouquet'	see *B.* 'Cherry Blossom'
	'Brilliance'	CWDa ERea LRHS
	'Brilliant' misapplied	see *B.* x *buttiana* 'Raspberry Ice'
	x ***buttiana*** 'Afterglow'	CWDa
	- 'Ametyst'	MBri
	- 'Asia'	ERea
	- 'Audrey Grey'	see *B.* 'Elizabeth Doxey'
	- 'Barbara Karst'	CWDa ERea
	- 'Chitra'	ERea
	- 'Coconut Ice'	CWDa
	- 'Daphne Mason'	ERea
§	- 'Enid Lancaster'	LRHS
	- 'Golden Glow'	see *B.* x *buttiana* 'Enid Lancaster'
	- 'Golden McClean'	CWDa
§	- 'Jamaica Red'	ERea
	- 'Killie Campbell' ♀H1	ERea
§	- 'Lady Mary Baring'	ERea
§	- 'Louise Wathen'	CWDa MJnS
§	- 'Mahara' (d)	CWDa ERea
	- 'Mahara Double Red'	see *B.* x *buttiana* 'Mahara'
	- 'Mahara Off-white'	see *B.* 'Cherry Blossom'
	- 'Mahara Pink'	see *B.* 'Los Banos Beauty'
§	- 'Mardi Gras' (v)	CWDa ERea
§	- 'Miss Manila'	CWDa ERea
§	- 'Mrs Butt' ♀H1	CWDa ERea
	- 'Mrs McClean'	ERea
§	- 'Poultonii'	ERea
§	- 'Poulton's Special' ♀H1	ERea
§	- 'Rainbow Gold'	ERea
§	- 'Raspberry Ice' (v)	ERea MJnS
	- 'Ratana Red' (v)	ERea
§	- 'Rosenka'	CWDa ERea
§	- 'Roseville's Delight' (d)	ERea LRHS
§	- 'Scarlet Glory'	ERea
§	- Texas Dawn = 'Monas'	ERea
	- 'Tiggy'	ERea
	'California Gold'	see *B.* x *buttiana* 'Enid Lancaster'
	Camarillo Fiesta = 'Monle' (*spectabilis* hybrid)	CWDa ERea
	'Captain Caisy'	CWDa ERea
§	'Carson's Gold' (d)	CWDa ERea
§	'Cherry Blossom'	CWDa ERea
§	'Chiang Mai Beauty'	ERea
§	'Closeburn'	ERea
	'Crimson Lake' misapplied	see *B.* x *buttiana* 'Mrs Butt'
	'Dauphine'	see *B.* 'Los Banos Beauty'
	'David Lemmer'	CWDa ERea
	'Delicate'	see *B.* 'Blondie'
	'Dixie'	ERea
	'Donya'	CWDa ERea
	'Double Yellow'	see *B.* 'Carson's Gold'
	'Durban'	see *B. glabra* 'Jane Snook'
§	'Elizabeth Angus'	CWDa ERea
§	'Elizabeth Doxey'	ERea
	'Elizabeth' (*spectabilis* hybrid)	ERea
*	'Elsbet'	CWDa
	'Enchantment'	see *B.* (Spectoperuviana Group) 'Mary Palmer's Enchantment'
	'Fair Lady'	see *B.* 'Blondie'
	'Flamingo Pink'	see *B.* 'Chiang Mai Beauty'
	'Floribunda'	CWDa ERea
	'Gillian Greensmith'	ERea
	glabra ♀H1	ERea MBri XPep
§	- 'Doctor David Barry'	CTbh CWDa ERea

§ - 'Harrissii' (v) CWDa ERea LRHS
§ - 'Jane Snook' CWDa ERea
§ - 'Magnifica Traillii' ERea
- 'P J Weeping Beauty' ERea
- 'Peggy Redman' (v) ERea
§ - 'Pride of Singapore' ERea
§ - 'Sanderiana' ERea WMul
'Gloucester Royal' CWDa
'Glowing Flame' (v) CWDa ERea
'Golden Doubloon' see *B.* x *buttiana* 'Roseville's Delight'
'Golden Glow' see *B.* x *buttiana* 'Enid Lancaster'
'Golden MacLean' see *B.* x *buttiana* 'Golden McLean'
'Golden Tango' CWDa ERea
'Harrissii' see *B. glabra* 'Harrissii'
'Hawaiian Scarlet' see *B.* 'San Diego Red'
'Hugh Evans' see *B.* 'Blondie'
'Indian Flame' see *B.* 'Partha'
'Isabel Greensmith' CWDa ERea
'Jamaica Orange' CWDa ERea
'Jamaica Red' see *B.* x *buttiana* 'Jamaica Red'
'James Walker' ERea
'Jane Snook' see *B. glabra* 'Jane Snook'
§ 'Jennifer Fernie' ERea
'Juanita Hatten' CWDa ERea
'Kauai Royal' see *B.* 'Elizabeth Angus'
'Klong Fire' see *B.* x *buttiana* 'Mahara'
'La Jolla' ERea
'Lady Mary Baring' see *B.* x *buttiana* 'Lady Mary Baring'
'Lavender Girl' CWDa ERea
'Lemmer's Special' see *B.* 'Partha'
'Limberlost Beauty' see *B.* 'Cherry Blossom'
'Little Caroline' CWDa
'Lord Willingdon' misapplied see *B.* 'Torch Glow'
§ 'Los Banos Beauty' (d) CWDa ERea
'Mahara Double Red' see *B.* x *buttiana* 'Mahara'
'Mahara Off-white' see *B.* 'Cherry Blossom'
'Mahara Orange' see *B.* x *buttiana* 'Roseville's Delight'
'Mahara Pink' see *B.* 'Los Banos Beauty'
'Mahara White' see *B.* 'Cherry Blossom'
'Manila Magic Red' see *B.* x *buttiana* 'Mahara'
'Mardi Gras' see *B.* x *buttiana* 'Mardi Gras'
'Mariel Fitzpatrick' ERea
'Mary Palmer's Enchantment' see *B.* (Spectoperuviana Group) 'Mary Palmer's Enchantment'
* 'Michael Lemmer' CWDa
'Mini-Thai' see *B.* 'Torch Glow'
'Mrs Butt' see *B.* x *buttiana* 'Mrs Butt'
'Mrs Helen McLean' see *B.* x *buttiana* 'Mrs McLean'
'Mrs McLean' see *B.* x *buttiana* 'Mrs McLean'
Natalii Group CWDa ERea
'Nina Mitton' CWDa ERea
'Orange Glow' see *B.* Camarillo Fiesta = 'Monle'
'Orange King' see *B.* x *buttiana* 'Louise Wathen'
'Orange Stripe' (v) ERea
'Pagoda Pink' see *B.* 'Los Banos Beauty'
§ 'Partha' CWDa
'Penelope' see *B.* (Spectoperuviana Group) 'Mary Palmer's Enchantment'
pink-bracted ESlt
'Pink Champagne' see *B.* 'Los Banos Beauty'
'Pink Clusters' CWDa ERea
'Pixie' see *B.* 'Torch Glow'
'Poultonii' see *B.* x *buttiana* 'Poultonii'
'Poultonii Special' see *B.* x *buttiana* 'Poulton's Special'
'Pride of Singapore' see *B. glabra* 'Pride of Singapore'
'Princess Mahara' see *B.* x *buttiana* 'Mahara'
'Purple Robe' CWDa ERea
'Rainbow Gold' see *B.* x *buttiana* 'Rainbow Gold'
'Raspberry Ice' (v) see *B.* x *buttiana* 'Raspberry Ice'
'Ratana Orange' (v) ERea
'Red Diamond' ERea
'Red Fantasy' (v) ERea
'Red Glory' CWDa ERea
'Reggae Gold' (v) CWDa ERea MJnS
'Robyn's Glory' see *B.* x *buttiana* Texas Dawn = 'Monas'
'Rosenka' see *B.* x *buttiana* 'Rosenka'
'Royal Purple' CWDa ERea
'Rubyana' CWDa ERea
§ 'San Diego Red' ERea ESlt
'Sanderiana' see *B. glabra* 'Sanderiana'
'Scarlet Glory' see *B.* x *buttiana* 'Scarlet Glory'
Scarlett O'Hara see *B.* 'San Diego Red'
'Singapore Pink' see *B. glabra* 'Doctor David Barry'
'Singapore White' CWDa ERea
'Smartipants' see *B.* 'Torch Glow'
'Snow Cap' see *B.* (Spectoperuviana Group) 'Mary Palmer'
spectabilis 'Speciosa Floribunda' ERea
- 'Wallflower' CWDa
§ Spectoperuviana Group (v) ERea
§ - 'Mary Palmer' CWDa LRHS
§ - 'Mary Palmer's Enchantment' CWDa ERea
- 'Mischief' CWDa
§ - 'Mrs H.C. Buck' CWDa ERea
'Summer Snow' CWDa
Surprise see *B.* (Spectoperuviana Group) 'Mary Palmer'
'Tango' see *B.* x *buttiana* 'Miss Manila'
* 'Tango Supreme' CWDa
'Temple Fire' see *B.* 'Closeburn'
'Thai Gold' see *B.* x *buttiana* 'Roseville's Delight'
* 'Tom Thumb' CWDa
'Torch Glow' EAmu ERea
'Tropical Bouquet' CWDa
'Tropical Rainbow' see *B.* x *buttiana* 'Raspberry Ice'
* 'Turkish Delight' CWDa ESlt
'Variegata' see *B. glabra* 'Harrissii'
'Vera Blakeman' CTbh CWDa ERea ESlt MJnS
'Wac Campbell' (d) CWDa
* 'White Cascade' CWDa ERea

Boussingaultia (*Basellaceae*)

baselloides see *Anredera cordifolia*

Bouteloua (*Poaceae*)

curtipendula CBig CRWN EBee EChP EMan EPPr GFor LEdu LRav NBre
§ ***gracilis*** CBig CBrm CHrt CRWN EBee EChP EMon EPPr EPza EWsh GFlt GFor MBNS MLLN MWgw NBea NBlu NJOw SGSe SUsu SWal WPGP WPer XPep

Bouvardia (*Rubiaceae*)

x ***domestica*** EShb
longiflora ERea EShb LRHS

Bowenia (*Boweniaceae*)

serrulata CBrP

Bowiea (*Hyacinthaceae*)

volubilis CHal EBee WCot

Bowkeria (*Scrophulariaceae*)

citrina CPle
cymosa **new** CSec SPlb
verticillata **new** CPLG CPle

Boykinia (*Saxifragaceae*)

	aconitifolia	CAbP CSec EBee EBla EBrs GBuc GGar GTou MLLN MRav NLar NRya SMad SSpi WCru WMoo WPtf WSHC
	elata	see *B. occidentalis*
	heucheriformis	see *B. jamesii*
§	***jamesii***	CGra EDAr NJOw SOkd
	major	WBor WCru
§	***occidentalis***	EBee GFlt GGar WCru WMoo WPat WPtf
	rotundifolia	EBee GBuc NBir WCru WMoo WPnP WWpP
	- JLS 86269LACA	EMon
	tellimoides	see *Peltoboykinia tellimoides*

boysenberry see *Rubus* Boysenberry

Brachychilum see *Hedychium*

Brachychiton (*Sterculiaceae*)

acerifolius	CHEx EShb
bidwillii	EShb
discolor	EShb
rupestris	ESlt

Brachyelytrum (*Poaceae*)

japonicum	GFor GIBF

Brachyglottis ✿ (*Asteraceae*)

§	***bidwillii***	WGer
	- 'Basil Fox'	WAbe
	brunonis	CPle
§	***buchananii***	WSHC
	- 'Silver Shadow'	GGar MWgw
§	***compacta***	ECou EPfP LRHS MAsh NPro SPer SPoG WBcn WEas
	compacta x ***monroi***	ECou LRHS
	'County Park'	ECou
	'Drysdale'	ELan EPfP GGar GKir LRHS MAsh MBri MRav NPri SLon SPoG SWvt
§	(Dunedin Group) 'Moira Reid' (v)	EBee EGoo
§	- 'Sunshine' ♀H4	More than 30 suppliers
	'Frosty'	ECou
	greyi misapplied	see *B.* (Dunedin Group) 'Sunshine'
§	***greyi*** (Hook. f.) B. Nord.	EBee EPfP ISea MBar MWhi NLon
§	***huntii***	CHEx GGar
	laxifolia misapplied	see *B.* (Dunedin Group) 'Sunshine'
	'Leith's Gold'	CTrC
§	***monroi*** ♀H4	CBcs CSBt CWib EBee ECou EGoo EHoe EHol ELan EOHP EPfP GGar GKir LAst MAsh MBar MLLN MRav NLon SLon SMer SPoG WBrE WDin WEas XPep
	- 'Clarence'	ECou
	repanda	CBcs CHEx CPle CTrC IDee
	- 'Purpurea'	CHEx EShb
	- var. ***rangiora***	LEdu
	repanda x ***greyi***	CDoC CHEx CPle EShb EWin GGar SAPC SArc SPoG
§	***rotundifolia***	CDoC CHEx CPle EPfP GGar GTSp NLar WEas
	'Silver Waves'	ECou
§	***spedenii***	GGar GTou
I	'Sunshine Improved'	SWvt WSPU
	'Sunshine Variegated'	see *B.* (Dunedin Group) 'Moira Reid' (v)
	'Walberton's Silver Dormouse' **new**	SPoG

Brachypodium (*Poaceae*)

pinnatum	EHoe
retusum	XPep
sylvaticum	CBig CPen EHul GCal GFor NBre

Brachyscome (*Asteraceae*)

'Blue Mist'	SPet
formosa	ECou
'Lemon Mist'	LAst
'Metallic Blue'	LIck SVil
'Mini Mauve Delight'	SVil
'Mini Yellow'	NPri
multifida	MBri NPri
'Pink Mist'	LAst SPet
rigidula	ECou GKev MDHE
'Strawberry Mousse'	LAst SPet
'Tinkerbell'	LSou SPoG

Brachystachyum (*Poaceae*)

densiflorum	ENBC EPla NLar

Bracteantha see *Xerochrysum*

Brahea (*Arecaceae*)

armata	CAbb CBrP CRoM EAmu EExo EPfP NPal SAPC SAin SArc SChr SPer WMul
edulis	CBrP CRoM EAmu SBig WMul

Brassaia see *Schefflera*

Brassica (*Brassicaceae*)

	japonica	see *B. juncea* var. *crispifolia*
§	***juncea*** var. ***crispifolia***	CArn WJek
	oleracea	WHer
*	***rapa*** var. ***japonica***	CArn WJek
*	- var. ***purpurea***	WJek

Breynia (*Euphorbiaceae*)

nivosa 'Rosea Picta' (v)	ESlt

x *Brigandra* (*Gesneriaceae*)

calliantha	SOkd

Briggsia (*Gesneriaceae*)

aurantiaca	SOkd

Brillantaisia (*Acanthaceae*)

subulugurica	GFai

Brimeura (*Hyacinthaceae*)

§	***amethystina*** ♀H4	CAvo CFwr CPom EBrs EHyt ERos GBin GCrs GKev LPhx LRHS
	- 'Alba'	CAvo ERos GKev LPhx LRHS
§	***fastigiata***	ERos

Briza (*Poaceae*)

maxima	CHrt CKno COIW EChP EGoo EHoe EPla EPza MFOX NGdn SSth SWal WGwG WHal WHer WRos WWye
media	More than 30 suppliers
- 'Limouzi'	CElw CFir CKno EBee EBrs EHoe EHrv EMan EMon EPPr GCal LRHS MAvo MMoz MSph NSti SDys SHel SOkh SPoG WDyG WPrP WWpP
minor	EPza SWal WRos
subaristata	CSec GKev MAnH WHal WWpP
triloba	CPen CRez EChP EHoe EMan EPPr EUJe EWes EWsh GBin MBri MMHG NOGN SWal WGwG WHal WMoo WPrP WRos WWpP

Brodiaea (Alliaceae)

§ **californica** CNic EBee ECho ERos NMen WCot
capitata see *Dichelostemma capitatum*
coronaria WCot
'Corrina' see *Triteleia* 'Corrina'
elegans CMon ERos WCot
ida-maia see *Dichelostemma ida-maia*
jolonensis ERos
laxa see *Triteleia laxa*
§ **minor** WCot
pallida WCot
peduncularis see *Triteleia peduncularis*
purdyi see *B. minor*
stellaris CMon EHyt
terrestris CMon
- subsp. **terrestris** NMen

Bromus (Poaceae)

carinatus B&SWJ 9100 WCru
inermis 'Skinner's Gold' (v) CAby CBrm CWCL EBee EGra EHoe EHul EMan EMar EWes LBBr MBri NSti SPer SPoG WCot
ramosus EHoe

Broussonetia (Moraceae)

kazinoki CBcs EBee IArd NLar WDin
papyrifera CAbP CBcs CDoC CFil CMCN ELan IDee MBri SMad SPer SSpi WDin WPGP WSPU
- 'Laciniata' NLar

Bruckenthalia see Erica

Brugmansia ✿ (Solanaceae)

'Apricot Goldilocks' WVaB
§ **arborea** CArn CHEx EHol LExo MGol SRms WVaB
§ - 'Knightii' (d) ♀H1 CHEx CHal EBak EHol ELan EPfP ERea ESlt LRHS MJnS MOak WMul WVaB
aurea CHEx LRHS WVaB
'Butterfly' WVaB
'Canary Bird' **new** MJnS
x **candida** CHEx EBak ERea WMul WVaB
- 'Blush' ERea
- 'Culebra' MGol WVaB
§ - 'Grand Marnier' ♀H1 CBot CHEx CHll ECot ELan EPfP ERea ESlt MJnS WVaB
- 'Maya' WVaB
- 'Ocre' WVaB
- 'Plena' see *B. arborea* 'Knightii'
- 'Primrose' ERea
- 'Tiara' (d) WVaB
§ - 'Variegata' (v) CKob ERea MJnS MOak WCot WVaB
§ **chlorantha** MJnS
I 'Citronella' WVaB
x **cubensis** 'Charles Grimaldi' MJnS WVaB
'Dark Rosetta' **new** MJnS
'Desiree' (d) **new** MJnS
'Full Rosea Magic' (d) **new** MJnS
'Golden Cornet' **new** MJnS
'Golden Lady' WVaB
'Goldrichter' WVaB
'Herrenhäuser Gärten' MJnS WVaB
'Herzenbrucke' **new** MJnS
hybrids WMul
'Igea Pink' **new** WVaB
§ x **insignis** CHll
- 90-95 WVaB
- 'Glockenfontäne' WVaB
§ - pink-flowered CHEx EPfP
- 'Pink Delight' WVaB
'Jacob' **new** WVaB
'Jean Pasko' WVaB
'Logee's Orange' WVaB
'Loreley' WVaB
'Marrakesch' WVaB
meteloides see *Datura inoxia*
'Mia' **new** WVaB
'Mobishu' **new** EShb
'Morning Sun' **new** MJnS
* pink-flowered LIck WFar WWol
'Rosabelle' WVaB
rosei see *B. sanguinea* subsp. *sanguinea* var. *flava*
'Rosenrot' WVaB
'Roter Vulkan' WVaB
'Rothkirch' WVaB
§ **sanguinea** CHEx CHll EBak EShb LExo MGol MOak MSal WMul
- 'Feuerwerk' WVaB
- red-flowered CHEx
- 'Rosea' see *B.* x *insignis* pink
- 'Sangre' WVaB
§ - subsp. **sanguinea** var. ***flava*** CHEx WMul WVaB
- 'White Flame' WVaB
§ **suaveolens** ♀H1 CHEx CHll CHrt ELan ERea LExo MGol SPlb WMul WVaB
- pink-flowered WVaB
- **rosea** see *B.* x *insignis* pink
- 'Variegata' (v) CKob ERea EShb WMul
suaveolens x **versicolor** see *B.* x *insignis*
'Sunrise' **new** MJnS
'Variegata Sunset' see *B.* x *candida* 'Variegata'
versicolor misapplied see *B. arborea*
§ **versicolor** Lagerh. ERea WVaB
- 'Ecuador Pink' EPfP ERea MJnS WVaB
- 'Lachs' WVaB
- 'Pride of Hanover' WVaB
'White Marble' WVaB
yellow-flowered LIck WFar WWol
* 'Yellow Trumpet' EPfP

Brunfelsia (Solanaceae)

calycina see *B. pauciflora*
jamaicensis CSpe
nitida **new** ERea
§ **pauciflora** ♀H1 ELan EShb ESlt LRHS MBri

Brunia (Bruniaceae)

albiflora SPlb

Brunnera (Boraginaceae)

§ **macrophylla** ♀H4 More than 30 suppliers
- 'Alba' see *B. macrophylla* 'Betty Bowring'
§ - 'Betty Bowring' CDes CLAP CPom EBee ECha EVFa GBuc LPhx MHar NCob NLar NSti SBla WCot WFar WHal WPnP WTin
- 'Blaukuppel' EMon
§ - 'Dawson's White' (v) More than 30 suppliers
- 'Gordano Gold' (v) EBee EHoe EVFa WHal
- 'Hadspen Cream' (v) ♀H4 More than 30 suppliers
- 'Jack Frost'PBR More than 30 suppliers
- 'Langford Hewitt' (v) CLAP WPrP
- 'Langtrees' More than 30 suppliers
* - 'Marley's White' LBuc
- 'Silver All Over' **new** WCot
- 'Variegata' see *B. macrophylla* 'Dawson's White'

sibirica	CDes EMon

x *Brunscrinum* (*Amaryllidaceae*)

'Dorothy Hannibel'	CMon

Brunsvigia (*Amaryllidaceae*)

bosmaniae **new**	CMon LToo
radulosa	WCot
rosea 'Minor'	see *Amaryllis belladonna*

Bryonia (*Cucurbitaceae*)

dioica	GPoy MSal

Bryophyllum see *Kalanchoe*

Buchloe (*Poaceae*)

dactyloides	CBig CPen CRWN GFor NBre

Buddleja ✿ (*Buddlejaceae*)

HCM 98.017 from Chile **new**	WPGP
agathosma	CBot CFil CPle SLon WEas WKif WLav WPGP WSHC XPep
albiflora	CPle SLon WLav
alternifolia ♀H4	More than 30 suppliers
- 'Argentea'	CBot CDoC CPMA CPle EBee ELan EPfP LPio MBNS MRav NLar NSti SHBN SPer SPla SPoG SSpi WCot WHCG WLav WPat WSHC XPep
asiatica ♀H2	CBot CPle ERea EShb ESlt SBrw SLon WBcn WLav
- B&SWJ 7214	WCru
auriculata	CBcs CBot CFil CMCN CPSs CWib EHol EPfP ERea GQui LAst MRav NSti SDix SLon SPoG WCru WHCG WLav WPGP WPat XPep
australis	CPle SLon
* 'Butterfly Ball'	SLon WBVN WBcn
caryopteridifolia	CFai EHol SLon
colvilei	CDoC CDul CFil CPle CTrw EPfP GKir IDee LAst MRav SBrw SDnm WBor
- B&SWJ 2121	WCru
- GWJ 9399	WCru
- 'Kewensis'	CBot CFil CPLG CRHN CSam NEgg NLar NSti SBra SLon WCru WCwm WLav WPGP WSHC
cordata	SLon
coriacea	CPle SLon
§ ***crispa***	CBcs CBot CPSs CPle ECha ELan EPfP LRHS MRav NSti SAga SBra SBrw SDnm SHBN SSpi WCot WEas WFar WHCG WKif WPGP WSHC XPep
- L 1544	CFil
- Moon Dance = 'Hulmoon' **new**	SPoG
crotonoides amplexicaulis	SLon
curviflora f. ***venenifera*** B&SWJ 6036	WCru
davidii	CArn GWCH NWea SGar SHFr STre WDin
- B&SWJ 8083	WCru
- from Beijing, China	CDul SLon
- Adonis Blue = 'Adokeep'	ENot WWeb
- 'African Queen'	SLon SPer SRGP
- var. ***alba***	CNic CWib SHBN WWpP
- 'Autumn Beauty'	CPle
- 'Black Knight' ♀H4	More than 30 suppliers
- 'Blue Horizon'	CSam SEND SLon SRGP WCot WLav WMoo WRHF
- 'Border Beauty'	GKir MAsh
- Camberwell Beauty = 'Camkeep' **new**	ENot
- 'Castle School' **new**	CSam
§ - 'Charming'	CDul WMoo WSHC WWlt
- 'Croyde' **new**	CSam
- 'Dartmoor' ♀H4	More than 30 suppliers
- 'Dart's Ornamental White'	EBee MRav
- 'Dart's Papillon Blue'	SLPl
- 'Dubonnet'	SLon WLav
- 'Ecolonia'	MAsh
- 'Empire Blue' ♀H4	CAlb CBcs CDoC CDul CSBt EBee ECrN ECtt ENot EPfP GKir LRHS MAsh MBri MRav MWat NPer NWea SPer SPlb SRGP WDin WFar WTel WWeb WWlt
- 'Fascinating'	CTri MRav WLav
- 'Flaming Violet'	SLon WLav
- 'Glasnevin Hybrid'	SDix SPer WLav
- 'Gonglepod'	SLon
- 'Harlequin' (v)	More than 30 suppliers
- 'Ile de France'	CBcs CWib GKir NWea SBod SRms WLav
- Masquerade = 'Notbud'PBR (v)	ENot MBri MGos MRav SLon WGor WWes
§ - 'Nanho Blue' ♀H4	More than 30 suppliers
- 'Nanho Petite Indigo'	see *B. davidii* 'Nanho Blue'
- Nanho Petite Plum	see *B. davidii* 'Nanho Purple'
- 'Nanho Petite Purple'	see *B. davidii* 'Nanho Purple'
§ - 'Nanho Purple' ♀H4	CAlb CDoC CMHG CTri CWib EBee ELan ENot EPfP GKir LRHS LSRN MAsh MBar MRav SLim SLon SPer SPla SPlb SPoG SRGP WHar WSHC
- var. ***nanhoensis***	CPle EBee EWTr SEND SIde SIgm SPer WHCG WLav
- - ***alba***	ELan EPfP GKir MAsh MBar SPer SRms WFar WWeb
- - blue-flowered	SLon SPer
- 'Orchid Beauty'	MBNS WLav
- 'Orpheus'	WLav
- 'Peace'	CChe CDoC CPLG CSBt EBee ENot EPfP MBri MRav NPer SPer SPoG WLav
- Peacock = 'Peakeep'	ENot
- 'Pink Beauty'	GKir NArg SHBN SRGP WHCG
- 'Pink Charming'	see *B. davidii* 'Charming'
- 'Pink Pearl'	SLon WLav
- 'Pink Spreader'	MAsh WBcn
- 'Pixie Blue'	MAsh NLar SRGP WWeb
- 'Pixie Red'	MAsh NLar NPri SLon WBcn WWeb
- 'Pixie White'	MAsh MBNS NLar SRGP WLav
- Purple Emperor = 'Pyrkeep'	ENot
- 'Purple Friend'	WLav
- 'Royal Purple'	SLim
- 'Royal Red' ♀H4	More than 30 suppliers
- 'Santana' (v)	CDul CFai LRHS SPoG WCot WPat
- 'Summer Beauty'	CWib EMil GKir LRHS MGos MRav WBcn WLav
- 'Variegata' (v)	LRHS SMrm WLav
- 'White Ball'	EBee LRHS MBNS NEgg NLar SLon
- 'White Bouquet'	CCVT CSBt EBee EPfP GKir LAst LRHS MAsh MHer MSwo MWat NWea SEND SMer SPer SRGP SReu WLav WRHF WTel
- 'White Butterfly'	LRHS SLon
- 'White Cloud'	ECrN GQui SRms WGwG
- 'White Harlequin' (v)	CRow SLon WBcn WCFE WEas
- 'White Profusion' ♀H4	CAlb CBcs CSam EBee ECtt ELan EPfP LRHS MBar MGos MRav NBlu NFor NLon NWea SHBN SLim SPla

	SWvt WCFE WDin WEas WFar WHCG WHar WMoo
- 'White Wings'	SLon WLav
§ ***delavayi***	CPLG CPle ERea WCru
fallowiana misapplied	see *B.* 'West Hill'
fallowiana Balf. f.	CBcs CPle ELan IFro LRHS NFor NLon WLav
- ACE 2481	LRHS
- BWJ 7803	WCru
- CLD 1109	CFil
- var. ***alba*** ♀H3	CBot CDoC EBee ECrN ELan EPfP LRHS MRav SBrw SLon SPer SPoG WBcn WEas WFar WPGP WSHC WWeb XPep
farreri	CBot CPle MSte
forrestii	CBot CHEx CPle WCru
globosa ♀H4	More than 30 suppliers
- RCB/Arg C-11	WCot
- 'Cally Orange'	GCal
- 'Lemon Ball'	WLav
glomerata	EShb XPep
heliophila	see *B. delavayi*
indica	CPle SLon
japonica	CPle IFro
- B&SWJ 8912	WCru
x ***lewisiana*** 'Margaret Pike'	CBot SLon
limitanea	SLon
lindleyana	More than 30 suppliers
'Lochinch' ♀H3-4	More than 30 suppliers
loricata	CBot CFai CFil CFis CPle CWib ERea GQui IDee MSte SGar SIgm SLon SPlb SSpi WCot WEas WLav WPGP XPep
macrostachya	CFil CPle WPGP
- HWJ 602	WCru
§ ***madagascariensis*** ♀H1	CPle CRHN EShb WCot XPep
marrubiifolia	XPep
megalocephala B&SWJ 9106	WCru
myriantha	CFai GQui XPep
* - f. ***fragrans***	WCot
nappii	CFil SLon
nicodemia	see *B. madagascariensis*
nivea	CBot CMCN CPLG IFro WLav XPep
- B&SWJ 2679	WCru
- BWJ 8146	WCru
- pink-flowered	SLon
- var. ***yunnanensis***	CPle MSte WCFE
officinalis ♀H2	CBot CPLG CPle CRHN EHol ERea XPep
paniculata	SLon
parvifolia MPF 148	WLav
§ x ***pikei*** 'Hever'	CHal CPle GQui SPer
'Pink Delight' ♀H4	More than 30 suppliers
'Pink Perfection'	WFar
saligna	CPle CTrC SLon XPep
'Salmon Spheres'	CPle
salviifolia	CBcs CBot CFil CRHN CSWP CSam EBee ELan GGar GQui IFro LAst NSti SBrw SDnm SIgm SWal WGwG WHer WLav XPep
- white-flowered	CRHN
stenostachya	CPLG CPle
sterniana	see *B. crispa*
'Thai Beauty' **new**	CPLN
tibetica	see *B. crispa*
tubiflora	CBot ERea SLon WLav
venenifera B&SWJ 895	WCru
§ 'West Hill'	SLon WLav
x ***weyeriana***	CDul CRHN CSam EBee ECtt EPfP GQui MNrw MSwo MTis NBir SGar SPlb SWvt WBVN WBor WBrE WDin WFar WHCG WLav WMoo WTel WWpP
- 'Golden Glow' (v)	CSBt CTri EBee ECrN EPfP LSRN NFor NLon SHel SLon WBrE WLav
- 'Lady de Ramsey'	SEND WPer
- 'Moonlight'	CPLG CPle IFro MSph SLon WLav WSel
- 'Sungold' ♀H4	CBrm CHrt CPle CWib EBee ELan EPfP GKir GQui MAnH MBlu MCCP MGos MLLN MRav NBlu NEgg NVic SBod SLon SPer SRGP WBVN WCot WHar WLav XPep
'Winter Sun' **new**	SLon

Buglossoides (*Boraginaceae*)

§ ***purpurocaerulea***	CCge CFwr CHll CMHG CPom EBee ECha ELan EMan EMar LRHS MSal MSte MWhi NBid NFla SPet WAul WFar WSHC WWye

Bukiniczia (*Plumbaginaceae*)

cabulica	CSpe

Bulbine (*Asphodelaceae*)

annua misapplied	see *B. semibarbata*
caulescens	see *B. frutescens*
§ ***frutescens***	CHll CPLG EMan LToo NBur SGSe WBrk WJek XPep
- 'Hallmark'	XPep
latifolia **new**	EShb
§ ***semibarbata***	CPom

Bulbinella (*Asphodelaceae*)

angustifolia	ECho EMan GCrs
cauda-felis	WCot
eburnifolia	WCot
elata	WCot
floribunda	CPLG CWCL IBlr
gibbsii var. ***balanifera***	ECho GCrs GKev
hookeri	CPom EBee EBrs EMan EUnu GAbr GCrs GFlt GGar GKev ITim NDlv NLAp SRms SYvo
latifolia	EBee
nutans	CDes ECho
setosa	CPne
talbotii	WCot

Bulbinopsis see *Bulbine*

Bulbocodium (*Colchicaceae*)

vernum	EBee EBrs EHyt EPot ERos GCrs LAma MBri MWgw NJOw
- white-flowered	ECho

bullace see *Prunus insititia*

Bunias (*Brassicaceae*)

orientalis	CAgr EUnu MSal

Bunium (*Apiaceae*)

bulbocastanum	CAgr LEdu

Buphthalmum (*Asteraceae*)

§ ***salicifolium***	CHrt CSam CSev EBee ELan EPfP GKir MBri MNFA MRav NBid NBlu NBro NGdn NOrc SHGN SRms WCAu WCot WFar WHil WPer WWpP
- 'Alpengold'	ECha GKir GMaP GSki MNFA NBre NLar SIgm
- 'Dora'	EGra EMan WCot
- 'Sunwheel'	EWll LRHS NPri SRms WWpP

	speciosum	see *Telekia speciosa*

Bupleurum (*Apiaceae*)

	angulosum	CFil EBee SBla SIgm SMrm SSpi WFar
	- copper	see *B. longifolium*
	baldense **new**	WBWf
	benoistii	SIgm
	candollii GWJ 9405 **new**	WCru
	falcatum	CAby CArn EBee EChP ECha EMan EPPr MLLN MSal NDov SChu WBWf WCot WFar WTin
	fruticosum	CBcs CBot CFil CPLG CPle ECtt EHol EPfP SBrw SChu SDix SDnm SIgm SMad SSpi SSta WCot WCru WDin WEas WPat XPep
*	***griffithii***	MSal
	- 'Decor' **new**	CSpe
§	***longifolium***	CElw CFee CSpe EBee EChP GBBs GBin GBuc MFOX MNrw NCGa NChi NLar SMrm WCot WHoo WWhi
	- short bronze	WCru
	- subsp. ***aureum***	LPhx MAvo NGby NLar
	longiradiatum B&SWJ 729	WCru
	ranunculoides	EBee SIgm
	rotundifolium	MSal NDov WGwG
	spinosum	NLar SIgm SMad
	stellatum	LRHS
	tenue	CArn
	- B&SWJ 2973	WCru
	- var. ***humile*** B&SWJ 6470	WCru

Bursaria (*Pittosporaceae*)

	spinosa	ECou GQui SBrw

Butia (*Arecaceae*)

	bonnetii	WMul
	capitata	CAbb CBrP CHEx CPHo CRoM CTrC EAmu EExo EUJe LEdu LPJP NPal SAPC SAin SArc SBLw SChr WMul
	yatay	CRoM SBig WMul

Butomus (*Butomaceae*)

	umbellatus ♀H4	CBen CDWL CFwr CRWN CRow CWat EBee ECha ECtt EHon EMFW ENot EPfP GAbr GIBF LNCo LPBA MCCP MRav NArg NPer WFar WMoo WPnP WPop WTin WWpP
	- 'Rosenrot'	CRow
	- 'Schneeweisschen'	CRow

butternut see *Juglans cinerea*

Buxus ✿ (*Buxaceae*)

	aurea 'Marginata'	see *B. sempervirens* 'Marginata'
	balearica ♀H4	CFil EPla SLon WPGP WSHC WSPU XPep
	bodinieri	EPla
	- 'David's Gold'	WPen WSHC
	'Green Gem'	NGHP WSel
	'Green Velvet'	EPfP
	harlandii hort.	EPla SRiv
	- 'Richard'	STre
	japonica 'Nana'	see *B. microphylla*
§	***microphylla***	CAlb CSWP MHer NWea SIng STre WBVN
	- 'Asiatic Winter'	see *B. sinica* var. *insularis* 'Winter Gem'
§	- 'Compacta'	CFil NLAp SRiv WCot WPat
	- 'Curly Locks'	EPla MHer
	- 'Faulkner'	CAlb EBee ELan EMil EPfP EPla LBuc LRHS MBNS MBlu MBri SPoG SRiv WBcn
	- 'Golden Triumph' **new**	SPoG
	- 'Green Pillow'	SRiv
	- var. ***insularis***	see *B. sinica* var. *insularis*
	- var. ***japonica*** 'Morris Midget'	IArd
	- - 'National'	MHer WPGP
	- 'John Baldwin'	SRiv WBcn
	- var. ***koreana***	see *B. sinica* var. *insularis*
	- var. ***riparia***	see *B. riparia*
	- 'Winter Gem'	see *B. sinica* var. *insularis* 'Winter Gem'
§	***riparia***	EPla
	sempervirens ♀H4	More than 30 suppliers
§	- 'Angustifolia'	MHer SMad
	- 'Argentea'	see *B. sempervirens* 'Argenteovariegata'
§	- 'Argenteovariegata' (v)	EPfP GKir MRav NGHP WBcn WFar WSHC
	- 'Aurea'	see *B. sempervirens* 'Aureovariegata'
	- 'Aurea Maculata'	see *B. sempervirens* 'Aureovariegata'
	- 'Aurea Marginata'	see *B. sempervirens* 'Marginata'
	- 'Aurea Pendula' (v)	EPla SLon WBcn WWye
§	- 'Aureovariegata' (v)	CBcs CSBt ECrN EPfP GBar ISea MBar MBow MGos MHer MRav NSti SChu SMer SPer SRiv WDin WFar WMoo WTel WWye
	- 'Bentley Blue'	MBNS
	- 'Blauer Heinz'	ELan EMil LRHS MHer SRiv WBcn WSel
§	- 'Blue Cone'	CHar
	- 'Blue Spire'	see *B. sempervirens* 'Blue Cone'
	- clipped ball	CWib EPfP LEar NBlu NGHP SRiv WFar
	- clipped pyramid	CWib EPfP LEar NBlu NGHP SRiv
	- clipped spiral	NBlu SRiv
§	- 'Elegantissima' (v) ♀H4	More than 30 suppliers
	- 'Gold Tip'	see *B. sempervirens* 'Notata'
§	- 'Graham Blandy'	MHer SRiv WBcn
	- 'Green Balloon'	LBuc
	- 'Greenpeace'	see *B. sempervirens* 'Graham Blandy'
	- 'Handsworthiensis'	EBee ECrN EMil LEar SEND SPer
	- 'Handsworthii'	CTri NWea SRms
	- 'Japonica Aurea'	see *B. sempervirens* 'Latifolia Maculata'
	- 'Kingsville'	see *B. microphylla* 'Compacta'
	- 'Kingsville Dwarf'	see *B. microphylla* 'Compacta'
	- 'Lace'	NSti
§	- 'Langley Beauty'	WBcn
	- 'Langley Pendula'	see *B. sempervirens* 'Langley Beauty'
	- 'Latifolia Macrophylla'	SLon SPoG WSel
§	- 'Latifolia Maculata' (v) ♀H4	CAbP CChe CDoC CWib EBee EPfP EPla LEar LRHS NEgg NGHP NPer SPoG SRiv STre WJek
	- 'Lawson's Golden'	MAsh
	- 'Longifolia'	see *B. sempervirens* 'Angustifolia'
§	- 'Marginata' (v)	CBrm ECtt EPla GBar GKir MHer MRav NSti SHBN SHFr SLon WBrE WHar WSel
	- 'Memorial'	MHer SRiv
	- 'Myosotidifolia'	CFil CMHG EPla NPro SRiv WPGP
	- 'Myrtifolia'	CBot EPla MHer SLon
§	- 'Notata' (v)	CBcs CSBt CSWP GKir SHel SPlb
	- 'Parasol'	MHer
	- 'Pendula'	CMHG EPla GKir SLon
	- 'Prostrata'	NWea WBcn
*	- 'Pygmaea' **new**	SBla

	- 'Pyramidalis'	EBee NBee WFar
	- 'Rosmarinifolia'	MRav
	- 'Rotundifolia'	CLnd EBee MHer SIde WDin
	- 'Silver Beauty' (v)	EMil MGos
	- 'Silver Variegated'	see *B. sempervirens* 'Elegantissima'
	- 'Suffruticosa' ♀H4	More than 30 suppliers
	- 'Suffruticosa Variegata' (v)	ECrN EOHP NEgg NWea SRms SWvt
	- 'Vadar Valley' **new**	SLon
	- 'Vardar Valley'	NPro SRiv
*	- 'Variegata' (v)	ELan ENot LRHS SLon
	- 'Waterfall'	WBcn
§	***sinica*** var. ***insularis***	EPla
	- - 'Filigree'	EPla WSel
	- - 'Justin Brouwers'	MHer SRiv
	- - 'Tide Hill'	SRiv WBcn WSel
§	- - 'Winter Gem'	ENot MHer MRav NLar SLPl
	wallichiana	CFil EBee EPla WPGP

C

Cacalia (*Asteraceae*)

	atriplicifolia	EBee LRHS
	corymbosa HWJK 2214 **new**	WCru
	delphiniifolia	GEdr
	- B&SWJ 5789	WCru
§	***hastata***	EMan
	muhlenbergii	MSal
	robusta **new**	GIBF
	suaveolens	EBee

Caesalpinia (*Caesalpiniaceae*)

	gilliesii	CBcs CBot SPlb XPep
	- RCB/Arg N-1	WCot
	pulcherrima	SPlb

Caiophora (*Loasaceae*)

	RCB/Arg M-1	WCot

Caladium (*Araceae*)

§	***bicolor*** (v)	MBri
	- 'Postman Joyner'	MOak
	'Blaze'	MOak
	'Candidum' (v)	MOak
	'Carolyn Whorton' (v)	MOak
	'Fannie Munson' (v)	MOak
	'Festivia' (v)	MOak
	'Flash Rouge'	MOak
	'Galaxy'	MOak
	'Gingerland' (v)	MOak
	x ***hortulanum***	see *C. bicolor*
	'June Bride' (v)	MOak
	'Kathleen'	MOak
§	***lindenii*** (v)	MJnS
	'Lord Derby' (v)	MOak
	'Miss Muffet'	MOak
	'Mrs F. M. Joyner' (v)	MOak
	'Red Frill' (v)	MOak
*	'Scarlet Pimpernell'	MOak
	'Symphonie Rose'	MOak
	'White Christmas' (v)	MOak
	'White Queen' (v)	MOak

Calamagrostis (*Poaceae*)

N	x ***acutiflora*** 'Karl Foerster'	More than 30 suppliers
	- 'Overdam' (v)	More than 30 suppliers
	- 'Stricta'	EPPr EWsh GKir LPhx
	argentea	see *Stipa calamagrostis*
§	***arundinacea***	More than 30 suppliers
§	***brachytricha***	More than 30 suppliers
	emodensis	CBig CBod CBrm CFwr CKno CMil CPen CSam CWCL EBrs EPPr EPla MMoz NOak SYvo WGHP WPGP
§	***epigejos***	CBig CHrt CNat EMan EPPr EWsh GBin GFor LPhx NBre NOGN WDyG WRos WWpP
	splendens misapplied	see *Stipa calamagrostis*
	varia	EHoe EPPr

Calamintha (*Lamiaceae*)

	alpina	see *Acinos alpinus*
§	***ascendens***	CSec EBee MLLN SGar WBWf WGHP WMoo
	clinopodium	see *Clinopodium vulgare*
	cretica	CLyd WPer
§	***grandiflora***	CAgr CArn CSam CSev EBee ECha ELan GGar GPoy LEdu MHer MRav MWgw NCGa NPer SAga SBla SMad SPet SPlb SSvw WBVN WCAu WCru WFar WMoo WTin WWeb WWhi WWye
	- 'Elfin Purple'	EPfP
	- 'Variegata' (v)	CPLG EBee ELan EMan ERou EVFa GGar LSou MAnH MMil NPri SMar SPoG WCHb WFar WWpP
§	***menthifolia***	CPom NBre NLar SHGN WJek WOut
	- HH&K 163	GBri
§	***nepeta***	More than 30 suppliers
	- subsp. ***glandulosa***	CSec EBee NEgg SHGN WGHP WLin WMoo
	- - ACL 1050/90	LRHS WHoo
	- - 'White Cloud'	CHea CSec CSpe EHrv ELan ERou GBar GBuc LLWP MRav MSte NBir WCAu WMoo WWye XPep
	- 'Gottfried Kuehn'	MRav WCAu
§	- subsp. ***nepeta***	CSev ELan EMon EPfP ERou GBar IHMH MBri MHer MRav MWat NSti SHel SPer SUsu WCHb WEas WFar WTin WWpP
	- - 'Blue Cloud'	CHea CSam CSec EBee EChP ECha EHrv GKev ILis LPhx NBir NDov SAga SBla SOkh WCAu WCHb WGHP WMoo WWpP XPep
	- 'Weisse Riese' **new**	LPhx
	nepetoides	see *C. nepeta* subsp. *nepeta*
	officinalis misapplied	see *C. ascendens*
	sylvatica	see *C. menthifolia*
I	- 'Menthe'	EBee
	vulgaris	see *Clinopodium vulgare*

calamondin see x *Citrofortunella microcarpa*

Calamovilfa (*Poaceae*)

	longifolia	EBee

Calandrinia (*Portulacaceae*)

	colchaguensis	WGwG
	depressa	CSec
	discolor	LRHS
	grandiflora	CSec MLLN
*	***ranunculina***	CPBP
	sibirica	see *Claytonia sibirica*
	umbellata	NJOw WPer
*	- ***amarantha***	EDAr
	- 'Ruby Tuesday'	NPri

Calanthe (*Orchidaceae*)

	amamiana	EFEx
	arisanenesis	EFEx
	aristulifera	EFEx LAma

	bicolor	see *C. discolor* var. *flava*
	caudatilabella	EFEx
	discolor	EFEx LAma WCot
§	- var. ***flava***	CLAP LAma
	hamata	EFEx
	japonica	EFEx
	Kozu hybrids	LEdu
	mannii	EFEx
	nipponica	EFEx LAma
	reflexa	EBee EFEx LAma
§	***sieboldii***	EBee EFEx LAma WCot
	striata	see *C. sieboldii*
	tokunoshimensis	EFEx
	tricarinata	EFEx LAma

Calathea (*Marantaceae*)

	crocata ♀H1	LRHS MBri
	'Greystar'	MBri
	louisae 'Maui Queen'	MBri
§	***majestica*** ♀H1	LRHS
	makoyana ♀H1	MBri XBlo
	metallica	MBri
	oppenheimiana	see *Ctenanthe oppenheimiana*
	ornata	see *C. majestica*
	picturata 'Argentea' ♀H1	MBri
	roseopicta ♀H1	LRHS MBri
*	***stromata***	XBlo
	veitchiana	MBri
	warscewiczii	MBri
	'Wavestar'	MBri
	zebrina ♀H1	MBri XBlo
	'Zoizia' **new**	XBlo

Calceolaria (*Scrophulariaceae*)

	acutifolia	see *C. polyrhiza*
	alba	CPLG EMan GKev LSou
	arachnoidea	CSec NWoo SPav
	bicolor	WCot
§	***biflora***	CSec EDAr EHol EHyt GGar GTou LEdu MHer NWCA
	- 'Goldcrest Amber'	MBow WPer
	'Briga Elite' **new**	EWin
	'Camden Hero'	MOak
	chelidonioides	GGar MTho WLin
	corymbosa **new**	GKev
	crenatiflora	NWoo
	falklandica	SPav SRms WHer WPer
	fothergillii	GKev NArg
	'Goldcrest'	EPfP GKev NBlu SRms
	'Hall's Spotted'	NWCA
§	***integrifolia*** ♀H3	CFis CHal CPLG EBee ECtt ELan SChu SEND SGar SIng SPer SRms WAbe
	- var. ***angustifolia***	MOak
	- bronze	SPer WAbe
	'John Innes'	ECho LRHS SChr WCot WRha WWeb
	'Kentish Hero'	CHal MOak NPer SChu
	mexicana	CPLG CSec SHFr
	petiolaris **new**	CSec
	plantaginea	see *C. biflora*
§	***polyrhiza***	ECho EHyt NRya
	rugosa	see *C. integrifolia*
	Sunset Series	EPfP IHMH NBlu
	tenella	ECtt EDAr NLAp NMen NWCA WAbe
	uniflora	GKev
	- var. ***darwinii***	ECho EHyt GEdr GKev GTou
	'Walter Shrimpton'	ECho EPot EWes SIng WAbe

Caldcluvia (*Cunoniaceae*)

paniculata	ISea

Calea (*Asteraceae*)

zacatechichi	MGol

Calendula (*Asteraceae*)

sp.	EPPr
meuselii	CFee
officinalis	CArn EDAr ELau GPoy GWCH MChe MHer MSal NLsd SIde SPav WGwG WJek WLHH WSel WWye
- 'Fiesta Gitana' ♀H4	CPrp WJek WWpP

Calibrachoa (*Solanaceae*)

(Million Bells Series) Million Bells Cherry = 'Sunbelchipi'PBR	LAst LSou
- Million Bells Lemon = 'Sunbelkic'	LAst LSou WWol
- Million Bells Red = 'Sunbelre'	LAst NPri WWol
- Million Bells White **new**	LSou
- Million Bells Terracotta = 'Sunbelkist'	LAst WWol
- Million Bells Trailing Blue = 'Sunbelkubu'PBR	WWol
- Million Bells Trailing Fuchsia = 'Sunbelrkup' ♀H3	WWol
- Million Bells Trailing Lavender Vein = 'Sunbelbura'	LAst WWol
- Million Bells Trailing Pink = 'Sunbelkupi'PBR ♀H3	LAst
- Million Bells Trailing White = 'Sunbelkuho'PBR	LAst
(Superbells Series) Superbells Candy White = 'USCALI48' **new**	LAst LSou NPri SPoG
- Superbells Imperial Purple = 'USCALI100' **new**	LAst LSou SPoG
- Superbells Indigo = 'USCALI51' **new**	LAst LSou
- Superbells Magenta = 'USCALI17'	LAst LSou NPri
- Superbells Pink = 'USCALI11' ♀H3 **new**	LAst LSou
- Superbells Red = 'USCALI28' **new**	LAst LSou SPoG
- Superbells Royal Blue = 'USCALI14'	LAst LSou NPri
- Superbells Strawberry Pink = 'USCALI47' **new**	LAst LSou

Calicotome (*Papilionaceae*)

spinosa	XPep

Calla (*Araceae*)

aethiopica	see *Zantedeschia aethiopica*
palustris	CRow CWat EHon EMFW EPfP LNCo LPBA MCCP NBlu NPer SPlb WFar WPnP WWpP

Calliandra (*Mimosaceae*)

emarginata 'Minima'	LRHS

Callianthemum (*Ranunculaceae*)

anemonoides	GCrs GKev SBla WAbe
kernerianum **new**	GCrs NMen

Callicarpa (Verbenaceae)

americana	NLar
- var. ***lactea***	CMCN
bodinieri	NBir WFar
- var. ***giraldii***	GBin GIBF MRav SMac WDin WWeb
- - 'Profusion' ♀H4	More than 30 suppliers
cathayana	CMCN NLar
dichotoma	CPLG CPle ELan EPfP GIBF LRHS NLar WBcn WFar
- f. ***albifructa***	GIBF
- 'Issai'	MBNS NLar WBcn
- 'Shirobana'	WBcn
aff. ***formosana*** B&SWJ 7127	WCru
japonica	CPle NLar WWes
- B&SWJ 8587	WCru
- f. ***albibacca***	NLar
- 'Heavy Berry'	WBcn
- 'Koshima-no-homate' **new**	NLar
- 'Leucocarpa'	CBcs CMac CPLG EBee ELan EPfP LRHS MRav NLar NVic SPer WBcn WFar
- var. ***luxurians***	NLar
- - B&SWJ 8521	WCru
kwangtungensis	CMCN NLar
mollis	NLar
shikokiana **new**	NLar
x ***shirasawana*** **new**	NLar

Callirhoe (Malvaceae)

involucrata	EMan GBri NBur NWCA SUsu WHrl

Callisia (Commelinaceae)

elegans ♀H1	CHal
§ ***navicularis***	CHal
repens	CHal MBri

Callistemon ✿ (Myrtaceae)

acuminatus	XPep
'Awanga Dam' **new**	ECou
citrinus	CHll CSBt EBee ECot ECou ERom EShb GGar GSki IFro ITim LAst SMer SPlb WBrE WDin WHar
- 'Albus'	see *C. citrinus* 'White Anzac'
- 'Firebrand'	CDoC LRHS MAsh SMur
- 'Splendens' ♀H3	CBcs CBrm CDoC CDul CHEx CMac CTrC CWib EGra ELan EPfP GQui IArd MAsh MBri MGos NBlu NPal SBra SBrw SHBN SHFr SPer SPoG SReu SSta SWvt WFar
§ - 'White Anzac'	ELan EPfP SBra SPoG
glaucus	see *C. speciosus*
laevis hort.	see *C. rugulosus*
linearis ♀H3	CBcs CMac CSBt CTrC CTri ECou ECrN ELan EPfP EPla LExo LRHS LRav LSRN MDun MHer SCoo SLim SLon SPlb SRms SSpi SWvt WMul WNor
macropunctatus	SPlb
'Mauve Mist'	CDoC CHEx LRHS MAsh
pachyphyllus	ECou
pallidus	CHEx CMHG CMac CPLG CWib ECou ELan EPfP GGar IDee ITim LRHS MRav SBrw SMur SPer SPlb SPoG SSta
paludosus	see *C. sieberi* DC.
'Perth Pink'	CBcs CDoC ELan EShb SBra SBrw SPoG
phoeniceus	ECou
pinifolius	SPlb
§ ***pityoides***	CPLG CTrC ECou XPep
- from Brown's Swamp, Australia	ECou
'Red Clusters'	CAlb CDoC CTrC ELan ERea IArd LAst MAsh MDun NLar SBrw SMer SMur SWvt
rigidus	More than 30 suppliers
§ ***rugulosus***	EGra IArd LRHS NCob XPep
salignus ♀H3	CBcs CBrm CDoC CHEx CSBt CTrC CTri ECrN EPfP GSki ISea LExo MHer SBrw SEND SHFr SLim SYvo WBVN WDin WSHC XPep
sieberi misapplied	see *C. pityoides*
§ ***sieberi*** DC.	CBcs CBrm CDoC CMHG CTrC ECou ELan EPfP EShb GGar GSki NBir NPal SBra SPlb SPoG SSpi WFar
§ ***speciosus***	CDul CTrC MDun SMur SPlb SPoG WAbe
subulatus	CDoC CTrC ECou MCCP NLar SAPC SArc SBrw SPlb SWal WMoo
- 'Crimson Tail'	MDun NEgg
viminalis	CBcs CHEx CTrC SGar SPlb
- 'Captain Cook'	CAlb ECou ERea EShb LAst LRHS MJnS NLar
- 'Little John'	CBcs CWSG IArd SPoG WGer XPep
'Violaceus'	CRez LRav XPep
viridiflorus	CTrC ECou GGar GQui LExo MCCP MHer SBrw WCru
- 'County Park Dwarf'	ECou
- 'Sunshine'	ECou
'White Anzac'	see *C. citrinus* 'White Anzac'

Callitriche (Callitrichaceae)

autumnalis	see *C. hermaphroditica*
§ ***hermaphroditica***	EMFW EPfP WPop
§ ***palustris***	EHon
stagnalis	NArg
verna	see *C. palustris*

Callitris (Cupressaceae)

rhomboidea	CTrC

Calluna ✿ (Ericaceae)

vulgaris	GWCH LRHS MBow
- 'Alba Aurea'	MBar
- 'Alba Elata'	CNCN MBar
- 'Alba Elongata'	see *C. vulgaris* 'Mair's Variety'
- 'Alba Jae'	MBar
§ - 'Alba Plena' (d)	CSBt LRHS MBar
- 'Alba Pumila'	MBar
§ - 'Alba Rigida'	LRHS MBar
- 'Alexandra' PBR ♀H4	LRHS SPoG
- 'Alicia' (L.)Hull PBR ♀H4	CBcs LRHS SPoG
- 'Alison Yates'	MBar
- 'Allegro' ♀H4	EPfP LRHS MBar
- 'Alportii'	CBrm MBar
- 'Alportii Praecox'	CNCN LRHS MBar
- 'Amethyst' PBR	CBcs MBar SPoG
- 'Amilto'	CNCN
- 'Andrew Proudley'	MBar
- 'Anette' (L.) Hull PBR ♀H4	LRHS MBar
- 'Annemarie' (d) ♀H4	CNCN CSBt EPfP LRHS MBar SCoo SPlb
- 'Anthony Davis' ♀H4	CNCN MBar
- 'Applecross' (d)	CNCN
- 'Arabella' PBR	LRHS
- 'Argentea'	MBar
- 'Arina'	CNCN LRHS MBri
- 'Arran Gold'	CNCN MBar
- 'August Beauty'	CNCN
- 'Aurea'	LRHS

- 'Barnett Anley' CNCN
- 'Battle of Arnhem' CNCN MBar
- 'Beechwood Crimson' CNCN
- 'Beoley Crimson' CNCN LRHS MBar
- 'Beoley Gold' ♀H4 CBrm CNCN CSBt CTri EPfP GKir LRHS MBar MBri MGos
- 'Beoley Silver' CNCN MBar NBlu
- 'Blazeaway' CBrm CNCN CTri EPfP GKir LRHS MBar MBri
- 'Bognie' CNCN
- 'Bonfire Brilliance' CNCN CSBt MBar
- 'Boreray' CNCN
- 'Boskoop' CBrm CNCN LRHS MBar MBri
- 'Braemar' CNCN
- 'Bray Head' CNCN MBar
- 'Bunsall' CNCN
- 'C.W. Nix' CSBt MBar
- 'Californian Midge' LRHS MBar
- 'Carole Chapman' MBar
- 'Catherine Anne' LRHS
- 'Coccinea' MBar
- 'Con Brio' CBcs CNCN LRHS
- 'Coral Island' MBar
- 'County Wicklow' (d) ♀H4 CBcs CNCN CTri EPfP GKir LRHS MBar MBri MGos NBlu
- 'Cramond' (d) CNCN LRHS MBar
- 'Crimson Glory' LRHS MBar NBlu NDlv
- 'Crimson Sunset' CNCN
- 'Cuprea' CNCN EPfP LRHS MBar MBri
- 'Dainty Bess' LRHS MBar MSwo
- 'Dark Beauty'PBR (d) ♀H4 CNCN EPfP ESis GKir LRHS MBar NDlv
- 'Dark Star' (d) ♀H4 CBcs CBrm CNCN EPfP LRHS MBar MGos SCoo
- 'Darkness' ♀H4 CBcs CNCN CSBt CTri EPfP GKir LRHS MBar MBri SCoo
- 'Darleyensis' MBar
- 'Dart's Gold' MBar
- 'David Eason' CNCN
- 'David Hutton' MBar
- 'Dirry' CNCN
- 'Doctor Murray's White' see *C. vulgaris* 'Mullardoch'
- 'Drum-ra' MBar SRms
- 'Dunnet Lime' SPlb
- 'Dunwood' MBar
- 'E. Hoare' MBar
- 'Easter-bonfire' CNCN NBlu
- 'Elegant Pearl' MBar
- 'Elegantissima' CBcs
- 'Elkstone White' CNCN MBar
- 'Elsie Purnell' (d) ♀H4 CNCN CSBt EPfP LRHS MBar MGos SPlb

§ - 'Finale' MBar
- 'Fire King' MBar
- 'Firebreak' MBar
- 'Firefly' ♀H4 CBrm CNCN CSBt EPfP LRHS MBar MBri NBlu
- 'Flamingo' CBcs CNCN CSBt LRHS MBar MBri MSwo
- 'Flore Pleno' (d) MBar
- 'Foxhollow Wanderer' CNCN MBar
- 'Foxii Floribunda' LRHS MBar
- 'Foxii Lett's Form' see *C. vulgaris* 'Velvet Dome', 'Mousehole'
- 'Foxii Nana' CNCN ESis LRHS MBar NBlu NDlv
- 'Fred J. Chapple' CNCN LRHS MBar MBri NBlu
- 'French Grey' CNCN
- 'Gerda' LRHS
- 'Glencoe' (d) LRHS MBar MBri
- 'Glenfiddich' CSBt MBar
- 'Glenlivet' MBar
- 'Glenmorangie' MBar
- 'Gold Flame' LRHS MBar
- 'Gold Haze' ♀H4 CBcs CNCN CTri GKir LRHS MBar MBri NBlu SCoo
- 'Gold Knight' EPfP LRHS MBar
- 'Gold Kup' MBar
- 'Gold Mist' LRHS NDlv
- 'Golden Carpet' CNCN CSBt ESis LRHS MBar MBri MGos NDlv
- 'Golden Feather' CNCN CSBt LRHS MBar
- 'Golden Fleece' CNCN
- 'Golden Rivulet' LRHS MBar MSwo
- 'Golden Turret' CNCN LRHS
- 'Goldsworth Crimson' CSBt
- 'Goldsworth Crimson Variegated' (v) CNCN MBar
- 'Grasmeriensis' MBar
- 'Great Comp' MBar
- 'Grey Carpet' CNCN LRHS MBar
- 'Guinea Gold' CNCN LRHS MBar MBri

§ - 'H.E. Beale' (d) CNCN CSBt CTri EPfP GKir LRHS MBar MBri MGos
- 'Hamlet Green' CNCN MBar
- 'Hammondii' CNCN
- 'Hammondii Aureifolia' CNCN LRHS MBar MBri SPlb
- 'Hammondii Rubrifolia' LRHS MBar MBri
- 'Hibernica' MBar
- 'Hiemalis' MBar
- 'Highland Cream' CNCN
- 'Highland Rose' CNCN LRHS SPlb
- 'Hillbrook Orange' MBar
- 'Hirsuta Typica' CNCN
- 'Hookstone' MBar

§ - 'Hugh Nicholson' CNCN
- 'Humpty Dumpty' MBar
- 'Ineke' CNCN MBar
- 'Inshriach Bronze' CNCN MBar
- 'Iris van Leyen' CNCN LRHS MBar
- 'Isle of Hirta' CNCN MBar
- 'Isobel Frye' MBar
- 'Isobel Hughes' (d) MBar
- 'J.H. Hamilton' (d) ♀H4 CBrm CNCN CTri GKir LRHS MBar MBri MGos SRms
- 'Jan Dekker' CNCN LRHS MBar NBlu
- 'Janice Chapman' MBar
- 'Joan Sparkes' (d) CNCN LRHS MBar
- 'John F. Letts' CSBt LRHS MBar SRms
- 'Johnson's Variety' CBcs CNCN MBar
- 'Joy Vanstone' ♀H4 CNCN CSBt EPfP GKir LRHS MBar MBri MGos
- 'Kerstin' ♀H4 CBcs LRHS MBar MSwo NBlu SPlb
- 'Kinlochruel' (d) ♀H4 CNCN CSBt CTri EPfP GKir LRHS MBar MBri MGos NBlu SPlb SRms
- 'Kirby White' CNCN LRHS MBar MBri NBlu NDlv SPlb
- 'Kirsty Anderson' LRHS
- 'Kit Hill' MBar
- 'Kuphaldtii' MBar
- 'Kynance' CNCN MBar
- 'Lambstails' MBar
- 'Leslie Slinger' LRHS MBar
- 'Lime Glade' CNCN
- 'Llanbedrog Pride' (d) MBar
- 'Loch Turret' MBar MBri
- 'Loch-na-Seil' MBar
- 'Long White' CNCN MBar
- 'Lyle's Late White' CNCN
- 'Lyle's Surprise' MBar

§ - 'Mair's Variety' ♀H4 CBrm LRHS MBar
- 'Marion Blum' MBar
- 'Marleen' (L.)Hull CNCN MBar
- 'Masquerade' MBar
- 'Melanie' LRHS MBar MSwo
- 'Minima' MBar
- 'Minima Smith's Variety' MBar

	Name	Suppliers
	- 'Mirelle'	CNCN
	- 'Molecule'	MBar
§	- 'Mousehole'	CNCN LRHS MBar
	- 'Mousehole Compact'	see *C. vulgaris* 'Mousehole'
	- 'Mrs Pat'	CNCN LRHS MBar
	- 'Mrs Ronald Gray'	CNCN MBar
§	- 'Mullardoch'	MBar
	- 'Mullion' ♀H4	MBar
	- 'Multicolor'	CNCN GKir LRHS MBar NDlv SRms
	- 'Murielle Dobson'	MBar
§	- 'My Dream' (d) ♀H4	CNCN CSBt EPfP LRHS MBar SCoo
	- 'Nana Compacta'	CNCN LRHS MBar SRms
	- 'Naturpark'	MBar
	- 'October White'	CNCN
	- 'Orange and Gold'	LRHS NBlu
	- 'Orange Queen'	CNCN CSBt CWCL LRHS MBar
	- 'Öxabäck'	MBar
	- 'Oxshott Common'	CNCN GQui MBar
	- 'Pearl Drop'	MBar
	- 'Pepper and Salt'	see *C. vulgaris* 'Hugh Nicholson'
	- 'Peter Sparkes' (d) ♀H4	CNCN CSBt CWCL EPfP LRHS MBar MBri MGos SRms
	- 'Pewter Plate'	MBar
	- 'Pink Beale'	see *C. vulgaris* 'H.E. Beale'
	- 'Prostrate Orange'	CNCN ESis MBar
	- 'Purple Passion'	EPfP
	- 'Pygmaea'	MBar
	- 'Pyramidalis'	LRHS
	- 'Pyrenaica'	MBar
	- 'Radnor' (d) ♀H4	CBcs CNCN CSBt LRHS MBar
	- 'Radnor Gold' (d)	MBar
	- 'Ralph Purnell'	CNCN MBar
	- 'Red Carpet'	CNCN LRHS MBar
	- 'Red Favorit' (d)	CBcs LRHS
	- 'Red Haze'	CBrm CNCN EPfP LRHS MBar
	- 'Red Pimpernel'	CNCN EPfP MBar
	- 'Red Star' (d)	CNCN LRHS MBar
	- 'Richard Cooper'	MBar
	- 'Rigida Prostrata'	see *C. vulgaris* 'Alba Rigida'
	- 'Robert Chapman' ♀H4	CBrm CNCN CSBt CTri GKir LRHS MBar MBri
	- 'Roland Haagen' ♀H4	MBar
	- 'Roma'	LRHS MBar
	- 'Romina'	CNCN MSwo
	- 'Ronas Hill'	CNCN
	- 'Rosalind' ambig.	CNCN CSBt EPfP LRHS MBar
	- 'Rosalind, Underwood's' l	LRHS
	- 'Ruby Slinger'	CNCN LRHS MBar
	- 'Ruth Sparkes' (d)	CNCN LRHS MBar
	- 'Saint Nick'	MBar
	- 'Sally Anne Proudley'	CNCN MBar
	- 'Salmon Leap'	CBrm MBar
	- 'Sampford Sunset'	CSam
	- 'Sandy'PBR	CBcs SPoG
	- 'Schurig's Sensation' (d)	CNCN LRHS MBar MBri
	- 'Serlei'	LRHS MBar
	- 'Serlei Aurea' ♀H4	CNCN CSBt EPfP LRHS MBar
	- 'Serlei Grandiflora'	MBar
	- 'Shirley'	MBar
	- 'Silver Cloud'	CNCN MBar
	- 'Silver King'	CNCN LRHS MBar
	- 'Silver Knight'	CNCN CSBt EPfP GKir LRHS MBar MBri MGos SPlb
	- 'Silver Queen' ♀H4	CNCN GKir LRHS MBar MBri SRms
	- 'Silver Rose' ♀H4	CNCN LRHS MBar
	- 'Silver Spire'	CNCN MBar
	- 'Silver Stream'	LRHS MBar
	- 'Sir John Charrington' ♀H4	CBcs CNCN CSBt EPfP ESis GKir LRHS MBar MBri MGos NBlu
	- 'Sirsson'	MBar MBri
	- 'Sister Anne' ♀H4	CNCN CSBt EPfP LRHS MBri NBlu NDlv SRms
	- 'Skipper'	MBar
	- 'Snowball'	see *C. vulgaris* 'My Dream'
	- 'Soay'	MBar
	- 'Spicata Aurea'	CNCN MBar
	- 'Spitfire'	CNCN ESis LRHS MBar
	- 'Spring Cream' ♀H4	CBcs CNCN GKir LRHS MBar MBri SPoG
	- 'Spring Glow'	CNCN LRHS MBar MBri
	- 'Spring Torch'	CBcs CNCN CSBt CWCL GKir LRHS MBar MBri NBlu SCoo SPoG
	- 'Springbank'	MBar
	- 'Strawberry Delight' (d)	EPfP
	- 'Summer Orange'	CNCN CSBt LRHS MBar
	- 'Sunningdale'	see *C. vulgaris* 'Finale'
	- 'Sunrise'	CNCN CSBt EPfP LRHS MBar MGos NBlu
	- 'Sunset' ♀H4	CNCN CSBt LRHS MBar SRms
	- 'Tenuis'	MBar
	- 'Tib' (d) ♀H4	CSBt LRHS MBar MBri NBlu NDlv SRms
	- 'Tom Thumb'	MBar
	- 'Tricolorifolia'	CNCN EPfP GKir LRHS
	- 'Underwoodii'	LRHS MBar
§	- 'Velvet Dome'	LRHS MBar
	- 'Velvet Fascination' ♀H4	CBcs CNCN EPfP GKir LRHS MBar MGos
	- 'White Bouquet'	see *C. vulgaris* 'Alba Plena'
	- 'White Carpet'	MBar
	- 'White Coral' (d)	EPfP MGos
	- 'White Lawn' ♀H4	CNCN LRHS MBar MSwo NBlu NDlv SRms
	- 'White Mite'	LRHS MBar
	- 'White Princess'	see *C. vulgaris* 'White Queen'
§	- 'White Queen'	MBar
	- 'White Star' (d)	LRHS
	- 'Whiteness'	CNCN MBar
	- 'Wickwar Flame' ♀H4	CBcs CNCN CSBt EPfP LRHS MBar MBri MGos NBlu SPlb
	- 'Winter Chocolate'	CNCN CSBt EPfP LRHS MBar MBri MSwo NDlv
	- 'Yellow Dome'	CNCN

Calocedrus (*Cupressaceae*)

	Name	Suppliers
§	***decurrens*** ♀H4	CBcs CDoC CDul CLnd CMac CTho CTri EHul EOrn EPfP GKir LCon LRHS MBar MBlu MBri MGos NWea SLim SPer WEve WMou
	- 'Aureovariegata' (v)	CBcs CKen EBrs EHul LCon LRHS MAsh MBar MBlu MBri NLar SCoo SLim WEve WFar
	- 'Berrima Gold'	CKen EBrs EPfP GKir LRHS MGos NLar SLim WEve
§	- 'Depressa'	CKen
	- 'Intricata'	CKen NLar SLim
	- 'Maupin Glow' (v) **new**	SLim
	- 'Nana'	see *C. decurrens* 'Depressa'
	- 'Pillar'	CKen NLar
	formosana **new**	WPic
	macrolepis	EMon

Calocephalus (*Asteraceae*)

	Name	Suppliers
	brownii	see *Leucophyta brownii*

Calochortus (*Liliaceae*)

	Name	Suppliers
	albus var. ***rubellus***	ECho LAma
	argillosus	EHyt
	- J&JA 1151500	CPBP
	barbatus	EPot
	catalinae	EHyt
	gunnisonii **new**	EHyt
	luteus	EPot LAma WLin
	- 'Golden Orb'PBR	EChP ECho LRHS
	purpureus **new**	CStu

	splendens	LAma
	striatus JA 93-21	EHyt
	superbus	EChP ECho EPot LRHS
	uniflorus	EPot WCot
	venustus	EChP EPot LAma LRHS WLin

Calomeria (*Asteraceae*)

§	***amaranthoides***	WJek

Calonyction see *Ipomoea*

Calopogon (*Orchidaceae*)

	tuberosus	SSpi

Calopsis (*Restionaceae*)

	paniculata	CBig CPne CTrC IArd IDee WMul

Caloscordum (*Alliaceae*)

§	***neriniflorum***	EBur WAbe

Calothamnus (*Myrtaceae*)

	quadrifidus	EShb
	validus	CPLG SPlb

Caltha ✿ (*Ranunculaceae*)

	'Auenwald'	CLAP CRow SSpi
	'Honeydew'	CLAP CRow GBuc
	laeta	see *C. palustris* var. *palustris*
	leptosepala	CLAP CRow EBee NWCA
	natans	CRow
	palustris ♀H4	More than 30 suppliers
	- var. ***alba***	More than 30 suppliers
	- var. ***barthei***	CFir EBee GEdr SSpi
	- 'Flore Pleno' (d) ♀H4	More than 30 suppliers
	- var. ***himalensis***	MGol WCot WWpP
	- 'Marilyn'	CLAP GBuc
	- 'Multiplex' (d)	CFwr COtt GBuc GGar
§	- var. ***palustris***	CBen CBre CRow ECha EHon ELan EMFW EMon EWTr GGar LPBA NArg SSpi WCra WFar WPnP WPop WWpP
	- - 'Plena' (d)	COlW CRow CWat ENot EPfP LNCo LRHS SMac WFar WWpP
	- var. ***polypetala***	CDWL LNCo NPer WPnP
	- var. ***radicans***	CRow GCrs SSpi
	- - 'Flore Pleno' (d)	CRow
	- 'Semiplena' (d)	EMon
	- 'Stagnalis'	CRow WWpP
	- Trotter's form	GBuc
	- 'Tyermannii'	CRow
	- 'Yellow Giant'	CDWL
N	***polypetala*** hort.	see *C. palustris* var. *palustris*
N	***polypetala*** Hochst. ex Lorentz.	CLAP CWat EBee EWll GBuc LNCo SGSe WBor
	sagittata	CLAP CRow
	- JCA 2.198.200	SSpi
	scaposa	GKev
	'Susan'	CRow

Calycanthus (*Calycanthaceae*)

	fertilis	see *C. floridus* var. *glaucus*
	- 'Purpureus'	see *C. floridus* var. *glaucus* 'Purpureus'
	floridus	CAgr CArn CBcs CDul CMCN CPMA CPle CTho CWib EBee ECrN ELan EPfP EWTr IDee LAst LEdu LRHS MBNS MBlu MDun SBrw SDnm SMur SPlb SPoG WDin
§	- var. ***glaucus***	CPle EPfP LBuc MGos NBlu NLar WSHC
§	- - 'Purpureus'	CBcs CPMA MBlu NLar WBcn
	- var. ***laevigatus***	see *C. floridus* var. *glaucus*
	- var. ***oblongifolius***	NLar
	occidentalis	CAgr CArn CBcs CMCN CPle CWib ECrN EMil EPfP IDee MBlu SBrw SGar SHGC SIgm SMur SSpi

Calystegia (*Convolvulaceae*)

	affinis **new**	CPLN
	collina subsp. ***venusta***	WCot
§	***hederacea*** 'Flore Pleno' (d)	CPLN EBee EChP ECha ELan EMon MCCP MTho NCGa NLar NSti SMad SSvw WCot WFar WHer
	japonica 'Flore Pleno'	see *C. hederacea* 'Flore Pleno'
	macrostegia subsp. ***cyclostegia***	WCot
	silvatica 'Incarnata'	EMon EWes
	soldanella	XPep
	- NNS 99-85	WCot

Calytrix (*Myrtaceae*)

	tetragona	SPlb

Camassia ✿ (*Hyacinthaceae*)

	biflora	CTbh EBee
	- F&W 8669	WCot
	cusickii	More than 30 suppliers
	- 'Zwanenburg'	LRHS MSte WCot WDav
	esculenta Lindl.	see *C. quamash*
	fraseri	see *C. scilloides*
	howellii	EBee
	leichtlinii misapplied	see *C. leichtlinii* subsp. *suksdorfii*
	leichtlinii (Baker) S.Watson	ISea SSto
N	- 'Alba' hort.	see *C. leichtlinii* subsp. *leichtlinii*
*	- 'Alba Plena'	NBir
	- Blue Danube	see *C. leichtlinii* subsp. *suksdorfii* 'Blauwe Donau'
§	- subsp. ***leichtlinii*** ♀H4	More than 30 suppliers
	- 'Magdalen' **new**	CAvo
N	- 'Plena' (d)	ECha MSte
	- 'Semiplena' (d)	CAvo CBro CFai CFwr CMea CMil EBee EChP EMan EMon EPot GEdr MDun MSte NMen SAga WAul WCot WDav WHoo WLin
§	- subsp. ***suksdorfii***	CAvo EBee GBBs GBuc LRHS MSph NBPC WAul
§	- - 'Blauwe Donau'	EBee LAma LRHS MSte WDav
	- - Caerulea Group	More than 30 suppliers
	- - 'Electra'	ECha SMHy SUsu
§	***quamash***	More than 30 suppliers
	- 'Blue Melody' (v)	CBro CMea EBee EMan EMon EPPr EPot GBuc GMac LRHS MCCP MDun MWgw NMen
	- 'Orion'	CBro CMea EBee EMon GBuc GMac MAvo WAul WCot
§	***scilloides***	EBee MBri WRos

Camellia ✿ (*Theaceae*)

	'Auburn White'	see *C. japonica* 'Mrs Bertha A. Harms'
	'Bacciochi' **new**	NLar
	'Barbara Clark' (*saluenensis* x *reticulata*)	MGos SCog WCwm
	'Barbara Hillier' x ***japonica*** 'Juno'	CDoC
	'Bertha Harms Blush'	see *C. japonica* 'Mrs Bertha A. Harms'
	'Black Lace' (*reticulata* x *williamsii*) ♀H4	CBrm CCtw CTbh CTrh CTri MAsh MBri NLar SCam SCog SPer SPoG WBVN WBcn WMoo
	'Bonnie Marie' (hybrid)	CBcs SCam SCog
	brevistyla	CBcs
*	'Chatsworth Belle'	CTrh
	'China Lady' (*reticulata* x *granthamiana*)	MBri
	'Cinnamon Cindy' (hybrid)	SCog

	Name	Suppliers
	'Contessa Lavinia Maggi'	see *C. japonica* 'Lavinia Maggi'
*	'Cornish Clay'	ISea
	'Cornish Snow' (*cuspidata* x *saluenensis*) ♀H4	CDoC CSBt CSam CTbh EPfP ISea LHyd MGos SBrw SCam SCog SHBN SPur SSpi SSta WFar
	'Cornish Spring' (*japonica* x *cuspidata*) ♀H4	CBcs CCtw CDoC CSBt CTbh CTrh ENot EPfP LHyd NVic SCog WBcn WCot
	'Corsica'	SHBN
	cuspidata	LHyd
	'Czar'	see *C. japonica* 'The Czar'
	'Dainty Dale' (hybrid)	SCam SSta
	'Delia Williams'	see *C.* x *williamsii* 'Citation'
	'Diana's Charm'	CDoC LSRN
	'Doctor Clifford Parks' (*reticulata* x *japonica*) ♀H2	LHyd SCog
	'Donckelaeri'	see *C. japonica* 'Masayoshi'
	'Extravaganza' (*japonica* hybrid)	CBcs CTrh IArd MBri SCog WBcn
	'Faustina Lechi'	see *C. japonica* 'Faustina'
	'Felice Harris' (*sasanqua* x *reticulata*)	MBri SCog
	'Fire 'n' Ice'	SCog
	'Forty-niner' (*reticulata* x *japonica*)	CBcs SCog
	'Fragrant Pink' (*rusticana* x *lutchuensis*)	CTrh WBcn
	'Francie L' (*saluenensis* x *reticulata*) ♀H3-4	CDoC CTrh EPfP LHyd NBlu SCam SCog SSta
	'Freedom Bell' (hybrid) ♀H4	CCtw CMHG CTrh ENot GGGa ISea LHyd SBrw SCam SCog WBcn
	'Gay Baby' (hybrid)	MGos
	grijsii	CTrh LHyd
	handelii	CBcs
§	***hiemalis*** 'Bonanza'	CTrh SCam
	- 'Chansonette'	SCam
§	- 'Dazzler'	CBcs CSBt LHyd SCam SCog
	- 'Kanjirô'	CTrh LHyd SCam
	- 'Showa Supreme'	SCam
§	- 'Sparkling Burgundy' ♀H3	CBcs CBrm ENot EPfP LHyd SBrw SCam SCog
	'Hooker' (hybrid)	CDoC
	'Howard Asper' (*reticulata* x *japonica*)	SCam
	'Ice Follies'	SCog
	'Imbricata Rubra'	see *C. japonica* 'Imbricata'
	'Innovation' (x *williamsii* x *reticulata*)	CBcs ISea SCam
	'Inspiration' (*reticulata* x *saluenensis*) ♀H4	CBcs CDoC CMHG CMac CSBt CTrh CWSG EPfP GGGa GKir ISea LHyd MBri MGos NBlu SBod SBrw SCam SCog SHBN SSpi
	japonica 'Aaron's Ruby'	CBcs COtt
	- 'Ace of Hearts'	MBri
	- 'Ada Pieper'	CTrh
	- 'Adelina Patti' ♀H4	CBcs CCtw CMHG CTbh CTrh LHyd SCog
	- 'Adolphe Audusson' ♀H4	More than 30 suppliers
	- 'Adolphe Audusson Special'	CBcs
§	- 'Akashigata' ♀H4	CDoC CTrw ENot EPfP SBrw SCam SCog SSta WCot WCwm
§	- 'Akebono'	CTrw
	- 'Alba Plena' ♀H4	CTrh CWSG EGra ENot LHyd SBod SCog WFar
	- 'Alba Simplex'	CBcs CMac ELan EPfP SBod SBrw SCam SCog SHBN SMer SPer SSpi SSta
	- 'Alexander Hunter' ♀H4	LHyd SBod SCam SCog
	- 'Alexis Smith'	CBcs
§	- 'Althaeiflora'	CBcs CDoC SCam
	- 'Ama-no-gawa'	LHyd
	- 'Anemoniflora'	CBcs CDoC ELan SCam WFar
	- 'Angel'	CBcs SCam SCog
	- 'Annette Gehry'	CBcs
	- 'Annie Wylam' ♀H4	CTrh LHyd SCog
I	- 'Apollo' Paul	CBcs CSam CTrh EPfP MAsh MGos MSwo NBlu SCam SCog SHBN WBcn
§	- 'Apple Blossom' ♀H4	CBcs CMac ELan
	- 'Arajishii'	see *C. rusticana* 'Arajishi'
*	- 'Augustine Supreme'	CMac
	- 'Australis' ♀H4	CTrh
	- 'Ave Maria' ♀H4	CBrm CTrh
	- 'Baby Sis'	SCam
	- 'Ballet Dancer' ♀H4	MGos SCam SCog WBcn
	- 'Baron Gomer'	see *C. japonica* 'Comte de Gomer'
	- 'Baronne Leguay'	SCam
	- 'Beau Harp'	SCam
	- 'Bella Romana'	SCam
	- 'Benidaikagura'	SCam
	- 'Benten' (v)	CTrw
	- 'Berenice Boddy' ♀H4	CBcs CTrh SCam
	- 'Berenice Perfection'	CMHG LHyd LRHS WFar
	- 'Betty Foy Sanders'	CTrh
	- 'Betty Sheffield'	COtt MAsh MGos SCog SHBN WFar
	- 'Betty Sheffield Pink'	SCam
	- 'Betty Sheffield Supreme'	CBcs
	- 'Billie McCaskill'	SCam
	- 'Black Tie'	LHyd SCog
	- 'Blackburnia'	see *C. japonica* 'Althaeiflora'
	- 'Blaze of Glory'	CTrh NLar SCog WBcn
§	- 'Blood of China'	CBcs CCtw CSBt CWSG LRHS MAsh NLar SCam SCog WCwm WMoo
	- 'Bob Hope' ♀H4	CBcs CDul CTrh LRHS MGos
	- 'Bob's Tinsie' ♀H4	CDoC CMHG CSBt CTrw ENot EPfP ISea LRHS
§	- 'Bokuhan' ♀H4	CCtw CDoC EPfP SCog
	- 'Bright Buoy'	CDoC
	- 'Brushfield's Yellow' ♀H4	CAlb CBcs CDoC CMHG COtt CSBt EPfP GKir IArd IMGH ISea LHyd MBri MDun MGos SCam SCog SPer SSta WFar
§	- 'C.M. Hovey' ♀H4	CMHG CMac CTrh EPfP MAsh SCam SHBN WBcn
	- 'C.M. Wilson'	CMac SCog
N	- 'Campbellii'	CDoC
	- 'Campsii Alba'	LRHS SMer
	- 'Can Can'	CBcs SCam SCog
	- 'Cara Mia'	CBcs SCam
	- 'Carolina Beauty' **new**	CDoC
	- 'Carter's Sunburst' ♀H4	CBcs CTrh EPfP SCam SCog
	- 'Chandleri Elegans'	see *C. japonica* 'Elegans'
	- 'Charlotte de Rothschild'	CTrh CTri
	- 'Cheryll Lynn'	CTrh
	- 'Christmas Beauty'	SCam
	- 'Cinderella'	SCog
	- 'Clarise Carleton'	CTrh GGGa LHyd MBri
	- 'Clarissa'	SCam
§	- 'Coccinea'	LRHS
	- 'Colonel Firey'	see *C. japonica* 'C.M. Hovey'
	- 'Commander Mulroy' ♀H4	CTrh MBri WBcn
	- 'Compton's Brow'	see *C. japonica* 'Gauntlettii'
§	- 'Comte de Gomer'	ELan EPfP LRHS SCam WBcn
	- 'Conspicua'	CBcs
§	- 'Coquettii' ♀H4	CBcs MAsh
	- 'Coral Beauty'	WFar
	- 'Coral Pink Lotus'	SCam
	- 'Coral Queen'	SCam
	- 'Countess of Orkney'	WBcn
	- 'Dahlohnega'	CTrh SPer
	- 'Daikagura'	CBcs

- 'Dainty' CBcs WBcn
- 'Daitairin' see *C. japonica* 'Dewatairin'
- 'Dear Jenny' CBcs
- 'Debutante' CBcs CDoC CMac CTrh LHyd LRHS MAsh SCam WBcn
- 'Desire' 🏆H4 CBcs CMHG CTrh ENot MDun SCam SPoG
- 'Devonia' CBcs EPfP LHyd LRHS SCog

§ - 'Dewatairin' (Higo) SCam SCog
- 'Dixie Knight' CDoC LRHS MGos SCam SCog
- 'Dobreei' CMac
- 'Doctor Burnside' CBcs CMHG CTrh SCog
- 'Doctor Olga Petersen' SCog
- 'Doctor Tinsley' 🏆H4 CDoC LRHS SCam WBcn
- 'Dona Herzilia de Freitas Magalhaes' SCam WBcn
- 'Dona Jane Andresson' SCam
- 'Donckelaeri' see *C. japonica* 'Masayoshi'
- 'Donnan's Dream' CTrh
- 'Doris Ellis' **new** CMHG
- 'Double Rose' (d) SCog
- 'Drama Girl' 🏆H2 CBcs CDoC CTrw SBod SCam SCog
- 'Dream Time' CBcs
- 'Duc de Bretagne' ISea SCog
- 'Duchesse Decazes' CBcs MBri
- 'Edelweiss' MGos SCam SCog
- 'Effendee' see *C. sasanqua* 'Rosea Plena'
- 'Eleanor Hagood' CBcs WBcn

§ - 'Elegans' 🏆H4 CBcs CDoC CMac ENot EPfP ISea LRHS MAsh NBlu SBod SBrw SCam SCog SHBN SPer SReu SSta WBcn WFar
- 'Elegans Champagne' WBcn
- 'Elegans Splendor' WBcn
- 'Elegant Beauty' see *C.* x *williamsii* 'Elegant Beauty'
- 'Elisabeth' WFar
- 'Elizabeth Dowd' CBcs SCog
- 'Elizabeth Hawkins' CTrh LHyd MAsh
- 'Ella Drayton' SCog
- 'Emmett Barnes' LHyd SCam
- 'Emmett Pfingstl' SCam WBcn
- 'Emperor of Russia' LHyd LRHS
- 'Erin Farmer' CBcs
- 'Eugène Lizé' SCam
- 'Evelyn' SCam
- 'Eximia' NBlu SCam
- 'Fanny' SCam
- 'Fashionata' SCam

§ - 'Faustina' MAsh

§ - 'Fimbriata' SCam
- 'Fimbriata Alba' see *C. japonica* 'Fimbriata'
- 'Finlandia Variegated' SCam SCog
- 'Fire Dance' CTrh
- 'Fire Falls' 🏆H4 CMHG
- 'Flame' CBcs
- 'Flashlight' EPfP

§ - 'Fleur Dipater' SCam SPoG
- 'Flowerwood' SCam SCog WFar
- 'Forest Green' ELan LRHS
- 'Fortune Teller' CBcs
- 'Fred Sander' CBcs CDoC CWSG SCam SCog SMer
- 'Frosty Morn' CBcs
- 'Furo-an' MAsh SCam

§ - 'Gauntlettii' CBcs
- 'Geisha Girl' SCam SCog

§ - 'Gigantea' NBlu SCam
- 'Giuditta Rosani' CDoC
- 'Giuseppina Pieri' LHyd
- 'Gladys Wannamaker' SCog
- 'Glen 40' see *C. japonica* 'Coquettii'
- 'Gloire de Nantes' 🏆H4 CBcs NBlu SCam SCog WBcn
- 'Gold Tone' SCam

* - 'Golden Wedding' (v) LRHS
- 'Grace Bunton' CBcs MGos SCam SCog
- 'Granada' SCog
- 'Grand Prix' 🏆H4 CDoC CTrh CTrw LHyd LRHS MGos SCam SCog
- 'Grand Slam' 🏆H2 CBcs CBrm CDoC CDul CMac CTrh EPfP LRHS MAsh SCam SCog WBcn
- 'Guest of Honor' CBcs
- 'Guilio Nuccio' 🏆H4 CBcs CDoC EPfP IArd LRHS MBri MGos SCam SCog SMer SPer SPur
- 'Gus Menard' SCam
- 'Gwenneth Morey' CBcs EPfP SCam
- 'H.A. Downing' SCam

§ - 'Hagoromo' 🏆H4 CTrh ELan EPfP LRHS SBrw SCog SHBN SPer WBcn WFar

§ - 'Hakurakuten' 🏆H4 CMHG CTrh EHol IArd ISea SBod SCam SCog
- 'Hanafûki' SCam SCog
- 'Hanatachibana' SCam WBcn
- 'Hatsuzakura' see *C. japonica* 'Dewatairin'
- 'Hawaii' CBcs CDul CSBt CTrh LRHS SCam SCog
- Herme see *C. japonica* 'Hikarugenji'
- 'High Hat' CBcs LHyd

§ - 'Hikarugenji' SCog
- 'Hime-otome' SCam
- 'Hinomaru' CMac LRHS
- 'Holly Bright' CTrh
- HTB 4 **new** SCam
- HTB 10 **new** SCam

§ - 'Imbricata' ENot ISea SCog
- 'Imbricata Alba' SBrw SCam
- 'Incarnata' SCam
- 'Italiana Vera' MAsh
- 'J.J. Whitfield' CMac
- 'Jack Jones Scented' CMHG
- 'Janet Waterhouse' CBcs WFar

§ - 'Japonica Variegata' (v) WBcn
- 'Jean Clere' MGos SCog WBcn
- 'Joseph Pfingstl' 🏆H4 CCtw MAsh SCam SCog
- 'Joshua E. Youtz' LHyd LRHS SCog
- 'Jovey Carlyon' (hybrid) CDoC
- 'Joy Sander' see *C. japonica* 'Apple Blossom'

§ - 'Julia Drayton' LRHS
- 'Julia France' SCog
- 'Juno' CBcs SCam

I - 'Jupiter' Paul 🏆H4 CBcs CDul CMac CTbh CTrh CTri CTrw EPfP ISea LHyd LSRN MAsh MGos SBrw SCog SHBN
- 'Justine Heurtin' SCam

§ - 'K. Sawada' SCam SCog
- 'Katie' MDun SCog
- 'Kellingtoniana' see *C. japonica* 'Gigantea'
- 'Kenny' CBcs
- 'Kentucky' SCam
- 'Kewpie Doll' CTrh
- 'Kick-off' CBcs CTrh WBcn
- 'Kimberley' CBcs CCtw CDoC EPfP SCog WBcn
- 'King Size' **new** CDoC
- 'King's Ransom' CMac MAsh

§ - 'Kingyo-tsubaki' SSta
- 'Kitty Berry' CTrh
- 'Kokinran' SCam

§ - 'Konronkoku' 🏆H4 CCtw CDoC CTrh SCog WBcn
- 'Kouron-jura' see *C. japonica* 'Konronkoku'
- 'Kramer's Beauty' NBlu SCog SPoG
- 'Kramer's Supreme' CDoC CWSG MGos NLar SBod SCam SCog WFar
- 'La Pace Rubra' SCam

	- 'Lady Campbell'	CTri SCam
	- 'Lady Clare'	see *C. japonica* 'Akashigata'
	- 'Lady Erma'	CBcs
	- 'Lady Loch'	CTrh MBri MGos
	- 'Lady McCulloch'	SCam
	- 'Lady Vansittart'	CBcs CDoC CSam ELan ENot EPfP ISea LHyd LRHS MAsh NBlu SCog SPer WBcn
§	- 'Lady Vansittart Pink'	NBlu SCam SHBN
	- 'Lady Vansittart Red'	see *C. japonica* 'Lady Vansittart Pink'
	- 'Lady Vansittart Shell'	see *C. japonica* 'Yours Truly'
	- 'Latifolia'	SCam
	- 'Laurie Bray'	WFar
§	- 'Lavinia Maggi' ♀H4	CTbh CTrh ELan ENot EPfP LHyd LRHS MAsh MGos NBlu SBrw SCam SCog SHBN SMer SPer SReu SRms SSta WBVN
	- 'Lavinia Maggi Rosea'	SCam
§	- 'Le Lys'	SCam
	- 'Lemon Drop'	CTrh
	- 'Lily Pons' ♀H4	CTrh LHyd WBcn
	- 'Lipstick'	CTrh LHyd
	- 'Little Bit'	CBcs CDoC CMHG CTrh SCam SPer
	- LOR 280 **new**	SCam
	- 'Lotus'	see *C. japonica* 'Gauntlettii'
	- 'Lovelight' ♀H4	CTrh ISea
	- 'Ludgvan Red' **new**	SCam
	- 'Lulu Belle'	SCog
	- 'Ma Belle'	CMHG
	- 'Mabel Blackwell'	SCam
	- 'Madame de Strekaloff'	CMac SCam
	- 'Madame Lebois'	CBcs SCam
	- 'Madame Martin Cachet'	CMHG SCog
	- 'Madge Miller'	LRHS
	- 'Magic Moments' **new**	SCam
	- 'Magnoliiflora'	see *C. japonica* 'Hagoromo'
	- 'Magnoliiflora Alba'	see *C. japonica* 'Miyakodori'
	- 'Maiden's Blush'	CMac
	- 'Margaret Davis'	CDoC CSBt CTbh EPfP IMGH LHyd LSRN MAsh MGos SCam SPoG
	- 'Margaret Davis Picotee' ♀H4	CBcs CMHG CTbh CTrh CTrw SCog SPer SSta WBcn
	- 'Margaret Rose'	SCam
	- 'Margherita Coleoni'	CBcs LHyd SHBN
	- 'Marguérite Gouillon'	ISea LHyd SCam
	- 'Marian Mitchell'	SCam
	- 'Mariann'	CTrh
	- 'Marie Bracey'	CBcs SCam
	- 'Marinka'	CBcs
	- 'Marjorie Magnificent'	LHyd LRHS MAsh
	- 'Mark Alan'	CDoC
	- 'Maroon and Gold'	WBcn
	- 'Mars' ♀H4	MGos SBrw SCam SCog
	- 'Mary Costa'	CBcs CTrh WFar
	- 'Mary J. Wheeler'	CTrw
§	- 'Masayoshi' ♀H4	CSBt LHyd SCog
§	- 'Mathotiana'	LRHS
	- 'Mathotiana Alba' ♀H4	CBcs CDoC CMac CSBt EPfP LRHS LSRN MGos NBlu SBrw SCam SCog SPer
	- 'Mathotiana Purple King'	see *C. japonica* 'Julia Drayton'
§	- 'Mathotiana Rosea' ♀H4	CBcs CMac SBrw SCam SHBN SPer
	- 'Mathotiana Supreme'	SCam SCog
	- 'Matterhorn'	CTbh CTrh LRHS WBcn
	- 'Mattie Cole'	LHyd SCam
	- 'Mercury' ♀H4	CBcs CMac COtt CWSG GGGa SBrw SCog SHBN
	- 'Mercury Variegated'	CMHG
	- 'Midnight'	CBcs CDoC CMHG MAsh SCam WFar
	- 'Midnight Magic'	CTrh
	- 'Midnight Serenade'	CCtw CTrh
	- 'Midsummer's Day'	CBcs
§	- 'Mikenjaku'	ENot LRHS MAsh SBrw SCam SCog
	- 'Minnie Maddern Fiske'	SCam
	- 'Miriam Stevenson'	SCam
	- 'Miss Charleston'	CBcs CTbh LHyd SCog
	- 'Miss Lyla'	SCam
	- 'Miss Universe'	CTrh
	- 'Mississippi Beauty'	CTrh
§	- 'Miyakodori'	EPfP LRHS
	- 'Monsieur Faucillon'	CBcs
	- 'Monte Carlo'	CDoC SCam SCog
	- 'Moonlight Bay'	SCog
	- 'Moshe Dayan'	MAsh SCam SMer
§	- 'Mrs Bertha A. Harms'	SCam
	- 'Mrs D.W. Davis'	CBcs CTrw EPfP SCam SCog
	- 'Mrs Sander'	see *C. japonica* 'Gauntlettii'
	- 'Mrs William Thompson'	SCam
I	- 'Mutabilis'	WBcn
	- 'Nagasaki'	see *C. japonica* 'Mikenjaku'
	- 'Nigra'	see *C. japonica* 'Konronkoku'
	- 'Nobilissima'	CBcs CDoC CMac CTrh CTri ENot EPfP ISea LRHS NLar SBrw SCam SCog SHBN SPer WBVN WBcn WFar
	- 'Nuccio's Cameo'	CDoC CTrh MAsh
	- 'Nuccio's Gem' ♀H4	CMHG ELan LHyd LRHS SBrw SCog SSta
	- 'Nuccio's Jewel' ♀H4	CCtw CDoC COtt CTrh CWSG IMGH LHyd LRHS SCog SPer SPoG WBcn WMoo
	- 'Nuccio's Pearl'	CBcs CCtw SCam SCog SMer WBVN WBcn WMoo
	- 'Onetia Holland'	CBcs CBrm CDoC CTbh CTrw LSRN SCam SCog
	- 'Optima'	SCog
	- 'Optima Rosea'	CBcs ENot WBcn
	- 'Paulette Goddard'	SCam
	- 'Paul's Apollo'	see *C. japonica* 'Apollo' Paul
	- 'Peachblossom'	see *C. japonica* 'Fleur Dipater'
	- 'Pearl Harbor'	SCam
	- 'Pink Champagne'	SBod
	- 'Pink Clouds'	CBcs SCog
	- 'Preston Rose'	CBcs CDoC WBcn
	- 'Primavera'	CTrh LHyd SCam SCog
	- 'Princess Baciocchi'	CBcs SCam
	- 'Princess du Mahe'	CMac
	- 'Professor Sargent'	WCwm
	- 'Purple Emperor'	see *C. japonica* 'Julia Drayton'
	- 'R.L. Wheeler' ♀H4	CBcs CDoC CSBt CTrw LHyd LSRN MAsh SCog
	- 'Rafia'	SCam
	- 'Red Dandy'	CDoC MGos SCam SCog
	- 'Red Elephant'	SCam
	- 'Reg Ragland'	CMHG SCam SCog
	- 'Robert Strauss'	SCam
	- 'Roger Hall'	CDoC CTbh ENot ISea SCam SCog SPoG WCwm
	- 'Rôgetsu'	SCam
	- 'Roman Soldier'	CBcs
	- 'Rosularis'	SCam SCog SPur
	- 'Rubescens Major' ♀H4	CBcs ISea LHyd SBrw SCam
	- 'Ruddigore'	CTrh LRHS
	- 'Saint André'	CMac
	- 'Sally Harrell'	SCam
	- 'San Dimas' ♀H4	CTrh SCam SCog WBcn
	- 'Saturnia'	CCtw CDoC COtt MAsh
	- 'Sawada's Dream'	ISea SCog
	- 'Scented Red'	CCtw SCam SCog
	- 'Scentsation' ♀H4	CMHG COtt SCog
	- 'Sea Foam'	LHyd SCam SSta

	- 'Sea Gull'	CTrh SCam
	- 'Seiji'	CMac
	- 'Shin-akebono'	see *C. japonica* 'Akebono'
§	- 'Shiragiku'	SPer
	- 'Shiro Chan'	SCam WBcn
	- 'Shirobotan'	ENot GQui MGos SCam SCog SPur
	- 'Silver Anniversary'	CBcs CBrm CDoC CMHG CSBt CTrh ELan ENot GQui ISea LHyd LRHS LSRN MAsh MBri MGos NBlu SCam SCog SPer SPoG SReu SSta WBVN
	- 'Silver Moon'	see *C. japonica* 'K. Sawada'
	- 'Silver Ruffles'	SCam
	- 'Simeon'	SCam
	- 'Sleigh Ride'	WBcn
	- 'Snow Chan' **new**	CMHG
	- 'Souvenir de Bahuaud-Litou' ♀H4	CBcs SCam SCog
	- 'Spencer's Pink'	CBcs CTrw SCam
	- 'Spring Fever'	SCam
	- 'Spring Formal'	CTrh
	- 'Spring Frill'	SCam SCog
	- 'Strawberry Blonde'	SCog
	- 'Sugar Babe'	SCog
	- 'Sunset Glory' **new**	CMHG
	- 'Sweetheart'	SCog
	- 'Sylva' ♀H4	GGGa SSpi
	- 'Sylvia'	CMac LRHS
	- 'Tammia'	COtt EPfP SCam
	- 'Teresa Ragland'	SCam
§	- 'The Czar'	CBcs CTrw ISea SCog
	- 'The Mikado'	CDoC SCog
	- 'Theo's Mini'	SCam
	- 'Tickled Pink'	CDoC SCam
	- 'Tiffany'	CBcs CDoC LHyd LRHS SCam SHBN
	- 'Tiki'	MBri
	- 'Tinker Bell'	CDoC MBri SCog
	- 'Tom Thumb' ♀H4	CTrh ISea SCam SRms SSta
	- 'Tomorrow'	CBcs CDoC CTrw LRHS MAsh SCam SCog
	- 'Tomorrow Park Hill'	SCog
§	- 'Tomorrow Variegated'	SCam
	- 'Tomorrow's Dawn'	CBcs SCam
	- 'Touchdown'	SCam
	- 'Tregye'	CBcs
	- 'Trewithen White'	CSam
§	- 'Tricolor' ♀H4	CBcs CDoC CMHG CMac CSBt CTrh EPfP LHyd MAsh NBlu SBrw SCam SCog SHBN WBrE WFar
	- 'Twilight'	LRHS
	- 'Victor de Bisschop'	see *C. japonica* 'Le Lys'
	- 'Victor Emmanuel'	see *C. japonica* 'Blood of China'
	- 'Ville de Nantes'	SSta WBcn
	- 'Ville de Nantes Red'	WBcn
	- 'Virginia Carlyon'	CBcs CCtw CDoC
	- 'Virginia Robinson'	SCam
	- 'Vittorio Emanuele II'	CTrh
	- 'Warrior'	COtt SCam SCog
	- 'White Giant'	CBcs
	- 'White Nun'	CBcs SCog
	- 'White Swan'	CMac COtt CSBt MAsh
	- 'Wilamina' ♀H4	CMHG CTrh NBlu
	- 'Wildfire'	SCam
	- 'William Bartlett'	CTrh
	- 'William Honey'	CTrh
	- 'Winter Cheer'	SCog
	- 'Wisley White'	see *C. japonica* 'Hakurakuten'
§	- 'Yours Truly'	CBcs CMac CTrh LHyd LRHS MDun SCam WBcn
§	- 'Yukishiro'	CTrw
	'John Tooby'	COtt LBuc
	'Jury's Yellow'	see *C.* x *williamsii* 'Jury's Yellow'
	'Lasca Beauty' (*reticulata* x *japonica*)	SCam
	'Lavender Queen'	see *C. sasanqua* 'Lavender Queen'
	'Leonard Messel' (*reticulata* x *williamsii*) ♀H4	CBcs CDoC CDul CMHG CTrh ENot EPfP GGGa LHyd MAsh MDun MGos NBlu SBrw SCam SCog SHBN SMer SPer SReu WCwm
	lutchuensis	CTrh SCam
	'Madame Victor de Bisschop'	see *C. japonica* 'Le Lys'
§	***maliflora*** (d)	CBcs
	'Maud Messel' (x *williamsii* x *reticulata*)	SCam
	'Milo Rowell'	SCam
	'Nicky Crisp' (*japonica* x *pitardii*)	LHyd
	'Nijinski' (*reticulata* hybrid)	CDoC ISea
	oleifera	CTrh NLar SCam SCog WFar
	'Paolina Guichardini' **new**	NLar
	'Paradise Little Liane'PBR	CBcs SCam SCog
	'Pink Spangles'	see *C. japonica* 'Mathotiana Rosea'
	pitardii	SCog
	'Polar Ice' (*oleifera* hybrid)	CDoC SCam SCog
	'Polyanna' (hybrid)	CDoC SCog
	'Portuense'	see *C. japonica* 'Japonica Variegata'
	'Quintessence' (*japonica* x *lutchuensis*)	SCog
	reticulata 'Mary Williams'	CBcs
	- 'Miss Tulare'	LHyd
	- 'Nuccio's Ruby'	LHyd
	- 'William Hertrich'	CBcs
	'Royalty' (*japonica* x *reticulata*) ♀H3	CBcs
§	***rusticana*** 'Arajishi'	CBcs CDul CMac COtt SCam SCog SCoo WFar
	saluenensis 'Exbury Trumpet'	CCtw
	- 'Trewithen Red'	CTrw
	'Salutation' (*reticulata* x *saluenensis*)	CBcs ISea SCam SCog
	sasanqua Thunb.	CDul CSBt CSam ISea
	- 'Baronesa de Soutelinho'	SCam SCog
	- 'Ben'	SCog
	- 'Bettie Patricia'	SCog
	- 'Bonanza'	see *C. hiemalis* 'Bonanza'
	- Borde Hill form	SCam
	- 'Crimson King' ♀H3	GQui SBrw SCam SHBN WBcn
	- 'Dazzler'	see *C. hiemalis* 'Dazzler'
	- 'Flamingo'	see *C. sasanqua* 'Fukuzutsumi'
	- 'Flore Pleno'	see *C. maliflora*
	- 'Fragrans'	SCog
	- 'Fuji-no-mine'	CTrh
§	- 'Fukuzutsumi'	CSBt ISea SBrw SCam SCog WCwm
	- 'Gay Sue'	CTrh LHyd SCam
	- 'Hiryû' **new**	SCam
	- 'Hugh Evans' ♀H3	CBcs COtt CTbh CTrh CTri LHyd SBrw SCam SCog SSta
	- 'Jean May' ♀H3	CDoC ENot EPfP LHyd SBrw SCam SCog SPer SSta WBcn
	- 'Kenkyô'	SCam SCog SSta
§	- 'Lavender Queen'	SCam
	- 'Little Pearl'	LHyd
	- 'Maiden's Blush'	CSBt ISea SCam SCog WFar
	- 'Mignonne'	CTrh
	- 'Narumigata'	CBcs CDoC CMac CTbh CTrw ENot EPfP LHyd MAsh SBrw SCam SCog SSta WSHC
	- 'New Dawn'	SCam
	- 'Nyewoods'	CMac
	- 'Papaver'	SCam SCog

	Name	Suppliers
	- 'Paradise Blush'	CBcs SCam SCog
	- 'Paradise Glow'	CBcs SCam SCog
	- 'Paradise Hilda'	CBcs SCog
	- 'Paradise Pearl'	CBcs SCam SCog
	- 'Paradise Petite'^{PBR}	SCog
	- 'Paradise Venessa'^{PBR}	CBcs SCog
	- 'Peach Blossom'	CBcs LHyd
	- 'Plantation Pink'	CBrm ENot SCam SCog SPer
	- 'Rainbow'	ISea SCam SCog SPoG SSta WBcn WFar
	- 'Rosea'	SCam SSta
§	- 'Rosea Plena'	CBcs CMac CTbh CTrw SCog
	- 'Sasanqua Rubra'	CMac
	- 'Sasanqua Variegata' (v)	SCam SSta
	- 'Setsugekka'	SCam SCog
I	- 'Shishigashira'	CTrh SCam
	- 'Snowflake'	SCam SCog SSta
	- 'Sparkling Burgundy'	see *C. hiemalis* 'Sparkling Burgundy'
	- 'Winter's Joy' **new**	SCam
	- 'Winter's Snowman'	CDoC SCam SCog
	'Satan's Robe' (*reticulata* hybrid)	CDoC NBlu SCam SCog WFar
	'Scented Sun'	CTrh
	'Scentuous' (*japonica* x *lutchuensis*)	WBcn
	'Show Girl' (*sasanqua* x *reticulata*)	LHyd SBod SCog WBcn
§	'Shôwa-wabisuke' (wabisuke)	CTrh WBcn
§	***sinensis***	EShb SCam
	'Snow Flurry' (*oleifera* hybrid)	CDoC SCam SCog
	'Splendens'	see *C. japonica* 'Coccinea'
	'Spring Festival' (*cuspidata* hybrid) $\mathbb{Y}^{H4}$	CBcs CDoC CMHG ENot LHyd WMoo
	'Spring Mist' (*japonica* x *lutchuensis*)	CMHG CTrh LHyd SCam
	'Strawberry Parfait'	NBlu SPoG
	'Swan Lake' (hybrid)	ISea
	'Tarôkaja' (wabisuke)	SCam
	thea	see *C. sinensis*
	'Tinsie'	see *C. japonica* 'Bokuhan'
	'Tiny Princess' (*japonica* x *fraterna*)	CBcs
	'Tom Knudsen' (*reticulata* x *japonica*) $\mathbb{Y}^{H3}$	CTrh SCam
	'Tomorrow Supreme'	see *C. japonica* 'Tomorrow Variegated'
	transnokoensis	CCtw CTrh SCam
	'Tricolor Sieboldii'	see *C. japonica* 'Tricolor'
	'Tristrem Carlyon' (*reticulata* hybrid) $\mathbb{Y}^{H4}$	CBcs CCtw CDoC SPoG
	tsaii	CPLG
	'Valley Knudsen' (*saluenensis* x *reticulata*)	SCog
	x ***vernalis*** 'Hiryû'	SCog
	- 'Star Above Star' **new**	CMHG
	- 'Yuletide'	SCam
	x ***williamsii*** 'Anticipation' $\mathbb{Y}^{H4}$	CBcs CDoC CMHG CSBt CSam CTbh CTrh CTrw CWSG ENot EPfP GGGa GKir ISea LHyd LRHS MAsh MBri MDun MGos MSwo NBlu SBrw SCam SCog SHBN SPer SSpi WBcn WFar
	- 'Anticipation Variegated'	GGGa
	- 'Ballet Queen'	CBcs CDoC CSBt GKir MGos SPoG WFar
	- 'Ballet Queen Variegated'	SCog
	- 'Bartley Number Five'	CMac
	- 'Beatrice Michael'	CBcs CMac
	- 'Bow Bells'	CDoC CDul CMac CTrh GKir LHyd LRHS NBlu SCam SSta
	- 'Bowen Bryant' $\mathbb{Y}^{H4}$	CTbh CTrw GGGa SCog
	- 'Bridal Gown'	LHyd
	- 'Brigadoon' $\mathbb{Y}^{H4}$	CDoC CMHG CTrh CTrw EPfP GGGa GKir LHyd LRHS MBri MDun MGos SBrw SCog
	- 'Burncoose'	CBcs
	- 'Burncoose Apple Blossom'	CBcs
	- 'C.F. Coates'	CDoC SCog SSta
	- 'Caerhays'	CBcs
	- 'Carolyn Williams'	CBcs SCam
	- 'Celebration'	CBcs
	- 'Charlean'	SCam
	- 'Charles Colbert'	WBcn
	- 'Charles Michael'	CBcs
	- 'China Clay' $\mathbb{Y}^{H4}$	CBcs EPfP LHyd LRHS SBod SCog WBcn
§	- 'Citation'	CBcs CMac CTrw
	- 'Contribution'	CTrh
	- 'Crinkles'	SCam SSta
	- 'Daintiness' $\mathbb{Y}^{H4}$	LHyd LRHS
	- 'Dark Nite'	CMHG
	- 'Debbie' $\mathbb{Y}^{H4}$	More than 30 suppliers
	- 'Debbie's Carnation'	CMHG
	- 'Donation' $\mathbb{Y}^{H4}$	More than 30 suppliers
	- 'Dream Boat'	CBcs LHyd
	- 'E.G. Waterhouse'	CBcs CDoC CMHG CSBt CTrh CTri CTrw ENot EPfP GKir LHyd MAsh SBod SCam SCog SSta WBcn WCot WCwm
	- 'E.T.R. Carlyon' $\mathbb{Y}^{H4}$	CBcs CCtw CDul CTrh CTri ENot EPfP LHyd LRHS NLar SCog SPoG WBVN
§	- 'Elegant Beauty' $\mathbb{Y}^{H4}$	CBrm CDoC CSBt CTrh CTrw CWSG MDun SBod SCam SCog SPur WBVN WCwm
	- 'Elizabeth Anderson'	CTrh
	- 'Ellamine'	CBcs
	- 'Elsie Jury' $\mathbb{Y}^{H3}$	CBcs CDoC CMac CSBt CTbh CTri CTrw CWSG GKir GQui LHyd LRHS MGos NBlu SBod SCam SCog WBVN WBcn
	- 'Exaltation'	SCog
	- 'Francis Hanger'	CBcs CDoC CTrh LHyd MDun SCam SCog SSpi
	- 'Free Style'	SCam
	- 'Galaxie' $\mathbb{Y}^{H4}$	CBcs ISea SCog
	- 'Garden Glory'	GGGa
	- 'Gay Time'	CBcs
	- 'George Blandford' $\mathbb{Y}^{H4}$	CBcs CMHG CMac SCam
	- 'Glenn's Orbit' $\mathbb{Y}^{H4}$	CBcs CDoC CTrw SCam WBcn
	- 'Golden Spangles' (v)	CBcs CDoC CMac CSBt ELan EPfP GKir LHyd LRHS MGos SCam SPer SReu SSta WBcn
	- 'Gwavas'	CBcs CDoC CTbh LHyd MAsh SCog
	- 'Hilo'	CTbh CTrw
	- 'Hiraethlyn'	CBcs LHyd SCam
	- 'J.C. Williams' $\mathbb{Y}^{H4}$	CBcs CMac CSam CTri CTrw CWSG ENot EPfP ISea LHyd SBrw SCog SSpi
	- 'Jenefer Carlyon'	CCtw CDoC
	- 'Jill Totty'	CTrh
	- 'Joan Trehane' $\mathbb{Y}^{H4}$	CTrw
	- 'Julia Hamiter' $\mathbb{Y}^{H4}$	CBcs CTrw
§	- 'Jury's Yellow' $\mathbb{Y}^{H4}$	CBcs CDoC CRez CSBt CTbh CTrh CTri CTrw ELan ENot EPfP GGGa GKir GQui ISea LHyd LRHS LSRN MAsh MGos NBlu SCam SCog SHBN SPoG SSta WBVN WBcn WFar
	- 'Laura Boscawen'	CTrh LHyd
	- 'Les Jury' $\mathbb{Y}^{H4}$	CDoC CMHG CSBt CTrh LSRN SCog SPer

- 'Margaret Waterhouse'	CBcs COtt SCam SCog
- 'Mary Christian' 🏆H4	CBcs COtt EPfP LHyd SCam SSta
- 'Mary Jobson'	CBcs CDoC SCam
- 'Mary Phoebe Taylor' 🏆H4	CBcs CDoC CTbh CTrw CWSG ENot GKir SCam SCog SHBN
- 'Mildred Veitch'	CSBt
- 'Mirage'	CTrh
- 'Moira Reid'	CDoC
- 'Monica Dance'	CBcs CTbh
- 'Muskoka' 🏆H4	CBcs CMHG CTrh ISea SBrw WCwm
- 'New Venture'	CBcs
- 'November Pink'	CBcs EHol
- 'Phillippa Forward'	CMac
- 'Rendezvous'	CDoC SCam SCog
- 'Rose Parade'	LHyd MAsh
- 'Rose Quartz'	MAsh
- 'Rosemary Williams'	CBcs SCam
- 'Rosie Anderson'	LRHS
- 'Ruby Bells'	CMHG
- 'Ruby Wedding'	CBrm CDoC CSBt CTrh ENot GQui LHyd SCog SPer SPoG WBVN WBcn
- 'Saint Ewe' 🏆H4	CBcs CDoC CSBt CTbh CTrh CTri CTrw EPfP GGar ISea LHyd MBri MGos SBrw SCam SCog SHBN SMer SPer
- 'Sayonara'	SCog
- 'Senorita' 🏆H4	CDoC CTrh LHyd SCam SCog
- 'Simon Bolitho'	CTbh LHyd
- 'Taylor's Perfection'	CTrw
- 'The Duchess of Cornwall'	CCtw CDoC
- 'Tiptoe'	CDoC CTrh LHyd MBri
- 'Twinkle Star'	CDoC
- 'Water Lily' 🏆H4	CBcs CDoC CTrh CTrw EPfP MGos SBrw SCam SPur WBcn
- 'Wilber Foss' 🏆H4	CBcs CDoC CMHG CTrh LHyd SCam SCog
- 'William Carlyon'	CWSG
- 'Wynne Rayner'	NBlu SCam
- 'Yesterday'	NBlu
'Winter's Charm' (*oleifera* x *sasanqua*)	SCog
'Winter's Dream' (*biemalis* x *oleifera*)	SCog
'Winter's Interlude' (*oleifera* x *sinensis*)	CDoC SCog
'Winter's Joy'	SCog
'Winter's Toughie' (?*oleifera* x *sasanqua*)	SCam SCog
'Winton' (*cuspidata* x *saluenensis*)	CBcs CDoC SCam
'Wirlinga Belle'	SCog
'Yoimachi' (*fraterna* x *sasanqua*)	CTrh
'Yukihaki'	see *C. japonica* 'Yukishiro'

Campanula ✿ (*Campanulaceae*)

from Iran	EPPr NBre WPGP
abietina	see *C. patula* subsp. *abietina*
§ ***alliariifolia***	More than 30 suppliers
- 'Ivory Bells'	see *C. alliariifolia*
allionii	see *C. alpestris*
§ ***alpestris***	ECho GTou
alpina	MDKP NBur
americana	MAnH SPav
ardonensis	NSla
argaea	EChP MAnH MWrn
argyrotricha	NBur
armena	CNic CSec EBee EBur ELan EWTr EWin GBuc MAnH NCGa NLar NLsd
arvatica	CLyd EPot ETow GMaP LRHS MDKP NMen WAbe WPat
- 'Alba'	CLyd GMaP NMen NSla WPat
aucheri	see *C. saxifraga* subsp. *aucheri*
§ 'Balchiniana' (v)	WEas
barbata	GBin GKev GTou ITim MAnH MMHG NBur NLAp NWCA SMar WMoo WPer
- var. ***alba***	GAbr NBur
bellidifolia	NBir NBre NGdn
***bellidifolia* x *tridentata* new**	GKev
§ ***betulifolia*** 🏆H4	CSam EHyt ITim NBur WLin
- JCA 252.005	SBla
'Birch Hybrid' 🏆H4	CMHG CNic ECho ECtt EDAr ELan EPfP GKir GMaP LBee LRHS NJOw WFar WTel
bononiensis	GBBs SPoG SRms WLin
'Bumblebee'	CGra CNic CPBP EHyt SBla
'Burghaltii' 🏆H4	CElw CHar CMil CPom EBee ECGP ECha EHrv ELan EMon GMac LRHS MAnH MSte SBch SBla SSpi WCot WFar WPer WWhi
calaminthifolia	EBur
§ ***carnica***	ECho EVFa MSte
carpatha	SBla
carpatica 🏆H4	ECho EPfP GKir ITim MBar MBri MCCP MDKP MWgw NBro NGdn NLon SBch SPlb SRms
- f. ***alba***	GKev MCCP MWgw NFor NGdn SPlb WSSM
- - 'Bressingham White'	GKir SBla
§ - - 'Weisse Clips'	COkL EBee ECtt EDAr ELan ENot EPfP GGar GKir GMaP GTou LAst MDun NBlu NGdn NJOw SPer SPla SPoG SRms SWvt WFar WPat WPer WWeb
§ - 'Blaue Clips'	More than 30 suppliers
- blue	MRav
- Blue Clips	see *C. carpatica* 'Blaue Clips'
- 'Blue Moonlight'	EBur GKir LRHS SMer
- 'Chewton Joy'	CLyd CTri GKir LRHS
- dwarf	EPot
- 'Harvest Moon'	GMaP
- 'Karpatenkrone'	EBee
- 'Kathy'	GBuc
- 'Maureen Haddon'	GKir LRHS
- 'Queen of Somerville'	NJOw
- 'Silberschale' **new**	EWTr
- 'Suzie'	SBla
- var. ***turbinata***	EHyt GKev MTho NSla SRms
- - f. ***alba*** 'Hannah'	LRHS
- - 'Förster'	GBuc GKir LRHS MTho SBla SMer WHoo
- - 'Georg Arends'	CLyd CNic
- - 'Isabel'	LRHS
- - 'Jewel'	EHyt LRHS
- - 'Wheatley Violet'	LRHS SBla
- White Clips	see *C. carpatica* f. *alba* 'Weisse Clips'
§ ***cashmeriana***	EBur GIBF MAnH NBur WGwG
- SEP 386	EHyt
- 'Blue Cloud'	CWib MAnH MBri WCFE
celsii	ITim
cenisia	EHyt
cephallenica	see *C. garganica* subsp. *cephallenica*
cervicaria	EBee
§ ***cespitosa***	CGra
§ ***chamissonis***	NBur NSla SBla WPat
§ - 'Major'	CPBP EDAr EPot ESis EWes LBee NBur
- 'Oyobeni'	NBur NLAp WLin

	Name	Suppliers
§	- 'Superba' ♀H4	EBur ECho ELan MTho NBur NMen NSla
	choruhensis	CGra ITim NBur
§	***cochlearifolia*** ♀H4	CSpe CTri EDAr ELan EPfP EPot ESis GKir GMaP GTou MDun MTho NJOw SPet SSvw STre WFar WHoo WLin WPer WTel WWhi
	- var. ***alba***	CNic CSpe EDAr EWTr GMaP LRHS MHer NChi NRya SBch SBla SIng SRms WAbe WHoo WLin WPer
	- - 'Bavaria White'	ITim MWgw WGwG
	- - double white (d)	WPat
	- - 'White Baby' (Baby Series)	ECtt EPfP GAbr GGar NBlu NPri SPoG
	- 'Bavaria Blue'	ECho ITim MWgw NLRH NWCA WGwG
	- 'Blue Baby' (Baby Series)	ECho ECtt EPfP GGar MHer NPro SBch SPoG SRms
	- 'Blue Tit'	GBuc
	- 'Blue Wonder'	COtt EPot
	- 'Cambridge Blue'	LRHS NBur WAbe
	- 'Elizabeth Oliver' (d)	CGra CStu CWCL EDAr EHyt ELan EPot GBuc GCal GMaP LAst LRHS MBri MHer MTho NLAp NWCA SBla SIng SOkd SPlb SPoG SRms WAbe WCru WFar WHoo WPat
	- 'Flore Pleno' (d)	ECtt NLAp
	- 'Miss Willmott'	CLyd EBur MTho NBir
	- 'Oakington Blue'	LRHS SBla
	- var. ***pallida*** 'Miranda'	LRHS WIvy
	- - 'Silver Chimes'	ITim
	- 'Tubby'	CLyd ECho GKev LRHS MHer MTho NJOw SRms
	- 'Warleyensis'	see *C.* x *haylodgensis* 'Warley White'
	collina	CTri GSki LTwo NBur NJOw SIgm WCFE WPer
	'Covadonga'	CMea CPBP ECGP LRHS LTwo
	cretica	EBee EMag ETow MAvo MWrn SGSe WOut WSPU
	'Crystal'	ECtt MAnH MAvo MNrw SUsu
	dasyantha	see *C. chamissonis*
	dolomitica **new**	LTwo
	'E.K.Toogood'	CElw CPBP EBee ECtt GKev MWat NBro NLAp NVic SBla SMac SRms WWpP
	elatines	EBrs
	'Elizabeth'	see *C. takesimana* 'Elizabeth'
	ephesia	CSec
	eriocarpa	see *C. latifolia* 'Eriocarpa'
§	'Faichem Lilac'	CHar EBee ECtt GKev LSou LTwo MAnH NChi NLar NLsd NPro NRnb STes
	fenestrellata	ITim MTho NBro NJOw SRms
	finitima	see *C. betulifolia*
	foliosa	NBur WPer
	formanekiana ♀H2-3	EBee EBur EChP EMag EMan GBBs LPio NBur
	fragilis	EBur ECho EHyt
	- subsp. ***cavolinii***	EHyt
	- 'Hirsuta'	ECho
	garganica ♀H4	EGra EPfP EPza GAbr GBBs GMaP GSki MDKP MRav NFla NFor NLon SMar SPet SWvt WCot WFar WMoo WPer
	- 'Aurea'	see *C. garganica* 'Dickson's Gold'
	- 'Blue Diamond'	EDAr ELan NBlu SBla WAbe
§	- subsp. ***cephallenica***	CElw NBro NJOw
§	- 'Dickson's Gold'	More than 30 suppliers
	- 'Major'	ECho IHMH LAst NJOw SPoG
	- 'W.H. Paine' ♀H4	CLyd ECho ECtt EDAr LRHS MDKP NMen NSla WAbe WHoo
§	'Glandore'	NPro
	glomerata	CBot CElw CRWN EDAr EGra EPza GKir GTou LSRN MBNS MBow MBrN NBid NBro NLan NMir SOkh SPet SRms STes SWal WBrk WFar WWye
	- var. ***acaulis***	CPrp CStu CWan EBee EMan EPfP ERou GAbr GKir LRHS MBNS NArg NJOw NWCA SPet SPla WFar WPer WWeb
	- var. ***alba***	More than 30 suppliers
§	- - 'Alba Nana'	EBee LAst
§	- - 'Schneekrone'	EBrs ECha EPfP ERou NLon NOak WFar
	- 'Caroline'	More than 30 suppliers
*	- 'Compacta Alba'	EPza
	- Crown of Snow	see *C. glomerata* var. *alba* 'Schneekrone'
	- var. ***dahurica***	CTri EBee MAnH NLar SMar SPet WPer
	- 'Joan Elliott'	CCge EChP ECha EMan GBuc IPot LRHS MRav MWat NGdn SPet WAul
	- 'Nana Alba'	see *C. glomerata* var. *alba* 'Alba Nana'
	- 'Superba' ♀H4	More than 30 suppliers
	- 'White Barn'	ECha NOak
	grossekii	EBee EChP EHrv EWll LTwo MFOX NEgg NRnb SPoG WBVN WOut
	hakkiarica	CGra
	'Hallii'	LRHS NWCA
	Hannay's form	CHar
	x ***haylodgensis*** *sensu stricto* hort.	see *C.* x *haylodgensis* 'Plena'
§	- 'Marion Fisher' (d)	CGra EDAr SBla WAbe WCot WHoo WLin
§	- 'Plena' (d)	EBee EDAr ELan EPot LAst LBee LRHS NBro NMen NWCA SBla SRms WAbe WBVN WCot WEas WHoo WKif WPat
§	- 'Warley White' (d)	EBur ELan
	- 'Yvonne'	EDAr NEgg SPoG WFar
	'Hemswell Starlight'	CLyd NPro
	hercegovina 'Nana'	CPBP EHyt SBla WAbe
	'Hilltop Snow'	CGra CPBP EHyt WAbe
	hofmannii	CWan EBur ELan EPyc GIBF MAnH MTho MWhi NLar NLsd NPri SGSe SYvo WFar WRha WWpP
	hypopolia	EPfP
§	***incurva***	CSpe EBur EMan EPot EWTr GAbr GBBs MAnH MNrw NOak NSti WLin WOut WPer
	- ***alba***	NBPC
	x ***innesii***	see *C.* 'John Innes'
	isophylla ♀H2	ECho MBri SPet
	- 'Alba' ♀H2	ECho
	- 'Flore Pleno' (d)	EBur
	- 'Mayi' ♀H2	CSpe
	- 'Mayi' misapplied	see *C.* 'Balchiniana'
	- 'Variegata'	see *C.* 'Balchiniana'
	jaubertiana	CGra EHyt
	'Joe Elliott' ♀H2-3	CStu ECho LRHS
§	'John Innes'	CLyd
	kemulariae	ESis NBur NJOw SRms WPer
	- ***alba***	ITim
	'Kent Belle' ♀H4	More than 30 suppliers
	'Kifu' **new**	ENot LBuc LRHS SPoG
	lactiflora	More than 30 suppliers
	- ***alba***	see *C. lactiflora* white
N	- 'Alba' ♀H4	EBee EBla EBrs EChP EMil ERou GAbr GKir GMaP GMac MAvo MDKP STes
	- 'Avalanche' **new**	EBrs

	Name	Suppliers
	- 'Blue Avalanche'	EBee SMrm SOkh
	- 'Blue Cross'	COtt EBrs EMag GMac LRHS MAnH WTel
	- 'Blue Lady'	EBee EChP WFar
	- 'Dixter Presence' **new**	SMHy
	- dwarf pink	SPet WWpP
	- 'Favourite' **new**	CFir CSpe ERou NFla NGdn SSpe STes
	- 'Loddon Anna' ♀H4	More than 30 suppliers
	- 'Pouffe'	EBee EBla EChP ECha ECtt ELan EMan EPfP EVFa GKir GMaP GMac LRHS MDKP MRav MWrn NBro NCGa NGdn SPer SPet SPla SWvt WFar
	- 'Prichard's Variety' ♀H4	More than 30 suppliers
	- 'Senior'	EMil LPio MDKP
	- 'Superba' ♀H4	GKir
	- 'Violet'	WPer WPop
§	- white-flowered	CBot ECha LAst MAnH NBir NBur NCot SChu SPer WPer
	- 'White Pouffe'	EBee EChP ELan EPfP GKir GMaP GMac GSki LRHS MRav NCGa NChi NLar SMer SPer SPla STes WFar
	lanata	CSec
	lasiocarpa	CGra EBur ITim LRHS NBur WFar
§	***latifolia***	CArn EBee EChP ECha GAbr GBBs GGar LRHS MAnH MNFA MWgw NBid NFor NLsd NMir NOrc NSti NVic SBla SMer SPer SRms WBWf WCAu WCra WFar WMoo
	- var. ***alba***	EBee ELan GAbr GBBs MAnH MAvo MBri MSte NGdn SBla SPav SPer SRms SSpi WFar WMnd
	- - 'White Ladies'	NBur
*	- 'Amethyst'	EBee SDnm SPav WMnd
	- 'Brantwood'	CFwr EBee EBrs EChP ENot ERou GAbr GMac MAnH MRav MWat MWhi NBPC NChi NOak SDnm SMer SPav SPer SRms STes WMnd
	- 'Buckland'	CHea SBla SPav
§	- 'Eriocarpa'	EBee MAnH NBur
	- 'Gloaming'	EBee EMan ERou NBur SMeo WHil
	- var. ***macrantha***	EBee ELan EPfP ERou GLil GMaP LRHS MAnH MBri MHer MSte NBPC NCGa NJOw NRnb NSti SPav SSvw SWvt WCot WMnd WMoo WPer WWeb WWye
	- - 'Alba'	CAby CM&M CMil ECha ECtt EHrv EMan ERou GMaP LPhx LRHS MAnH MRav MSte NCGa SSvw WCAu WCot WMnd WMoo WPer WWFP
	- 'Misty Dawn' **new**	WFar
	- 'Roger Wood'	MAnH MWgw WCot
§	***latiloba***	CBre CElw CMHG GKir LGro NChi NLsd NWoo SBch WBrk WCot WFar
	- 'Alba' ♀H4	CBre CElw CHar ELan EPPr EPfP GAbr GCal GMaP MDKP NChi NGdn SBch SGar SHel WBrk WEas WRHF
	- 'Hidcote Amethyst' ♀H4	More than 30 suppliers
	- 'Highcliffe Variety' ♀H4	CHea EBee EChP ELan EMan EPfP GBuc GCra GFlt MAnH MFOX MRav NCGa NSti SPla WCot WEas WKif WMnd
*	- 'Highdown'	MLLN WFar
	- 'Percy Piper' ♀H4	CSam EBee EBrs ELan EWsh GBBs GBuc GKir LRHS MFOX MRav MSph NBre NBro NFor NLar NLon WFar WOut
	- 'Splash'	CElw CFee EBee ECtt MAvo WCot
	lingulata	ITim
	linifolia	see *C. carnica*
	longestyla	WCot
	'Lynchmere'	ETow
	makaschvilii	EBrs ECtt EMan GFlt GIBF GMac IGor ITim LRHS MAnH MSph MWhi MWrn NBPC NBur NLar NLsd NRnb SAga SBod SGSe SIgm STes WCHb WHil WHrl WPer
	'Marion Fisher'	see *C.* x *haylodgensis* 'Marion Fisher'
	massalskyi **new**	EHyt
	medium	LAst MAnH NBlu NRnb
§	- var. ***calycanthema***	EBla ERou
	- 'Cup and Saucer'	see *C. medium* var. *calycanthema*
	- white-flowered	MAnH
	mirabilis 'Mist Maiden'	CLyd EPot ETow LRHS WFar
	morettiana	GKev
	muralis	see *C. portenschlagiana*
	'Mystery Blue'	EMan EPfP ERou
	nitida	see *C. persicifolia* var. *planiflora*
	- var. ***planiflora***	see *C. persicifolia* var. *planiflora*
	'Norman Grove'	CLyd EPot
	ochroleuca	CMea EBee EChP GBBs GCal ITim LRHS MAnH NBPC NBur NCGa SGSe SHGN SPoG STes WCFE WHal WHrl WLin WMoo
	- 'White Beauty'	CWib
	- 'White Bells'	MWhi NRnb SPet WMnd
	odontosepala	CElw EMon
	'Oliver's Choice'	WHrl
	olympica hort.	see *C. rotundifolia* 'Olympica'
§	***ossetica***	CElw EBee ECtt ELan EMan MAnH MWrn NCiC
	pallida subsp. ***tibetica***	see *C. cashmeriana*
	parviflora Lam.	see *C. sibirica*
	patula	NLar WBWf
§	- subsp. ***abietina***	MAnH NBre NLar
	'Paul Furse'	ECtt LRHS MDKP MLLN NBre NLar SHar STes WCot WSSM WTin
	pelviformis	MNrw
	pendula	CFir CSec CWan EBee EChP EPfP EWes GBuc GKev MAnH MBNS MNFA NJOw NLar SHGN WFar WWeb
	persicifolia	More than 30 suppliers
	- var. ***alba***	More than 30 suppliers
§	- 'Alba Coronata' (d)	CFir CStr EMon EVFa GAbr GBri LRHS NBir WEas WFar
	- 'Alba Plena'	see *C. persicifolia* 'Alba Coronata'
	- Ashfield double ice blue (d) **new**	NBre
	- 'Beau Belle'	EBee EChP EMan ERou MAvo MBNS NCot NLar STes WHil WSan
§	- 'Bennett's Blue' (d)	CSev EBee EBla EChP ECtt ELan EPla EVFa GBri GBuc GSki LAst LPio LRHS MBnl MCCP MNFA MRav NCiC NEgg NRnb NSti SPer SPla SRms WCAu WCra
	- blue-flowered	LAst MBow MRav NLsd NRnb SGSe SPlb WEas WFar
	- blue and white-flowered **new**	WHil
	- 'Blue Bell'	MWat WSSM
	- 'Blue Bloomers' (d)	CElw CHar CHea CLAP CMil EBee EChP EMon EVFa EWes GBri GMac LLWP MAnH MNFA MRav MSph WCot WPnP WRHF WWeb
	- blue cup-in-cup (d)	EBla MBnl MDKP WFar WLin
	- 'Boule de Neige' (d)	CHea CM&M EBee EBla ECtt NOak WEas WMnd
	- 'Caerulea Coronata'	see *C. persicifolia* 'Coronata'
*	- 'Caerulea Plena' (d)	EWsh MBNS

	Name	Suppliers
§	- 'Chettle Charm'[PBR] ♀H4	More than 30 suppliers
§	- 'Coronata' (d)	GCra NEgg SPer WBrE
	- 'Cristine'	MDKP
	- cup and saucer blue (d)	CAby GCra
§	- cup and saucer white (d)	CElw EBla ELan GMaP WFar WPer WWye
§	- double blue (d)	NBir NBro WEas
	- double white (d)	ELan NChi WMoo
	- 'Eastgrove Blue'	NCob
	- 'Fleur de Neige' (d) ♀H4	CSam ECtt LRHS MLLN MSph NCob NOak WAul WCot WHoo WWpP
	- 'Flore Pleno'	see *C. persicifolia* double blue
	- 'Frances' (d)	CLAP EMon GBri
	- 'Frank Lawley' (d)	LRHS
	- 'Gawen' **new**	WCot
	- 'George Chiswell'[PBR]	see *C. persicifolia* 'Chettle Charm'
	- 'Grandiflora Alba'	GBuc MAnH SMrm
	- 'Grandiflora Caerulea'	NLar
§	- 'Hampstead White' (d)	EChP ECtt EHrv ERou GBri GBuc GSki LRHS MNFA MTis MWgw NBro NGdn NSti SAga SChu SMrm SPla STes WCAu WEas WHer WMnd
	- 'Hetty'	see *C. persicifolia* 'Hampstead White'
	- 'Kelly's Gold'	More than 30 suppliers
	- 'Kent Blue'	CSec
	- 'La Belle'	EBee EChP EMan EPyc ERou MTis NCot NLar STes WCAu WHil
	- 'Moerheimii' (d)	EBee ERou MBnl MDKP NBir STes WCAu WHil
	- var. ***nitida***	see *C. persicifolia* var. *planiflora*
	- 'Peach Bells'	MBNS NOak
	- 'Perry's Boy Blue'	NPer
§	- var. ***planiflora***	CPBP EBee ETow GTou ITim SBla WAbe
§	- - f. ***alba***	GFlt SBch WAbe
	- 'Pride of Exmouth' (d)	CCge CHar CHea CM&M CSam EBee EChP ECtt EHrv ELan EMan GBuc LAst LRHS MArl MBnl MBri MCCP MNFA MWgw NLon NOak SPet WBrk WCFE WCot WCra
	- 'Rearsby Belle' (d)	MDKP
	- subsp. ***sessiliflora***	see *C. latiloba*
	- 'Snowdrift'	ELan SRms
	- 'Telham Beauty' misapplied	CHea COtt CSBt CWCL EBee ECtt ELan ENot EPfP EPza ERou GAbr GKir LRHS MAnH MRav MSte NRnb SGSe SMer SMrm SPer SPla SRms SWvt WMnd WPer WWeb WWpP
	- 'Tinpenny Blue'	WTin
	- 'White Bell'	MWat MWrn NEgg
	- 'White Cup and Saucer'	see *C. persicifolia* cup and saucer white
	- 'White Queen' (d)	NBur WMnd
	- 'Wortham Belle'	see *C. persicifolia* 'Bennett's Blue'
	petrophila	CGra EHyt NSla
§	'Pike's Supremo' (d)	NBir
	pilosa	see *C. chamissonis*
	piperi 'Townsend Ridge'	CGra
	- 'Townsend Violet'	CGra
	planiflora	see *C. persicifolia* var. *planiflora*
§	***portenschlagiana*** ♀H4	More than 30 suppliers
	- 'Lieselotte'	CElw GBuc GMaP WPat
	- 'Major'	WFar
	- 'Resholdt's Variety'	CMea CSam EDAr EPfP GMaP LBee LRHS MRav WPer
	poscharskyana	More than 30 suppliers
	- 'Blauranke'	EGoo EWes
	- 'Blue Gown'	GMaP MAnH
	- 'Blue Waterfall'	EBrs LRHS MAnH WFar WWpP

	Name	Suppliers
	- 'E.H. Frost'	CBre CElw EBee ECtt EDAr EPPr EPfP ESis EWTr GKev GMaP LAst MAnH MBow MWat NBro NJOw NRya SAga SRms SWvt WBrk WFar WMoo WPer WTel WWpP
	- 'Lilacina'	CElw EPPr SHel SIng
	- 'Lisduggan Variety'	CElw CNic EBee EBur ECtt EDAr EPPr EWes GKir GMaP GMac NBro NCGa NLsd SBch SBla WCot WFar WMoo WPer WWpP
	- 'Stella' ♀H4	CWCL ECha ECtt ENot LRHS MAvo MRav NBro NJOw SChu SDix SPer SWvt WFar WMoo WWpP
	- variegated (v)	EHoe IBlr
	- white	ELan LAst MDKP WFar
	prenanthoides	see *Asyneuma prenanthoides*
	primulifolia	CHar CSec EBee EBrs ECtt ELan EMan GAbr GBBs IFro LRHS MAnH MMil MNrw MSte NCGa SBod SMad SRms WCHb WMoo WPer WTin
	- 'Blue Oasis'	CMHG EBee NBPC NJOw NRnb WMnd WWeb
	x ***pseudoraineri***	EBur EDAr EHyt EWes NMen
	'Puff of Smoke'	WCot
	pulla	CLyd CPBP CSpe EBur ECtt EDAr EHyt ELan ESis GKev GMaP LAst MTho NRya SBla SIng SPoG SRot WAbe WFar WPat
	- ***alba***	EBur ECtt EDAr EHyt LBee LRHS SBla WPat
	x ***pulloides***	CLyd EDAr
	- 'G.F. Wilson' ♀H4	EBur ECho ECtt LTwo WRHF
	punctata	More than 30 suppliers
	- f. ***albiflora***	CM&M EBee GKir LRHS MAnH MLLN MNrw NChi WFar
	- - 'Nana Alba'	CStr LRHS MWrn NBur WFar
	- 'Alina's Double' (d)	CStr EBee EVFa MNrw WCot
	- var. ***hondoensis***	CHar EPPr IGor MBrN MNrw SAga WHrl WWpP
	- hose-in-hose (d)	CDes EBla MAnH NLar WFar
	- 'Hot Lips'	More than 30 suppliers
	- var. ***microdonta***	EBrs LRHS
	- - B&SWJ 5553	WCru
	- 'Millennium'	MAvo WCot WFar
	- 'Milly'	CDes CStr CStu EBee EMon MDKP WPGP
	- 'Mottled'	NBre NRnb
*	- 'Nana'	EChP
	- 'Pantaloons' (d)	EBla SBch SHar WCot WCra
	- 'Pink Chimes'	CPou EBee EPPr LSou NEgg NPri NPro SBch
	- 'Pink Eclipse'	WFar
	- 'Reifrock'	SMrm
	- 'Rosea'	LPio SRms WFar WSan
	- f. ***rubriflora***	More than 30 suppliers
	- - 'Beetroot'	CFwr EBee EBla EChP EMon GBri MAnH MCCP MFOX NBur NChi SSpi WPGP
	- - 'Bowl of Cherries'[PBR]	CFwr CPou CRez EBee EBla EMan EPPr ERou EShb GGar LIck LSou LTwo MMHG NEgg NLar NPri NSti SHar SPav SUsu WPop
	- - 'Cherry Bells'	CElw CFir EBee EBla ECtt EMan EPfP GMac IPot LAst LBmB MAnH MAvo MCCP MNrw MTis NCot NLar NRnb SHar SPav SPet WCAu WCot WSan WWol
	- - 'Vienna Festival' **new**	MBnl NLar NSti
	- - 'Wine 'n' Rubies'	CElw ECtt EHrv EMan MAvo MDKP MNrw SBch SHar SPav SUsu WCot

- var. ***takesimana***	see *C. takesimana*
- 'Wedding Bells'	More than 30 suppliers
- white hose-in-hose (d)	EBee GMac MAnH MAvo MNFA MNrw SAga WBrk WCot WFar
pusilla	see *C. cochleariifolia*
pyramidalis	CBot CSpe EBee ELan EPfP EShb GIBF GWCH MAnH MBNS MCCP MHer MRav NLsd NOrc NRnb SDnm SPav SPlb WPer
- 'Alba'	CSpe CWib EBee ECtt ELan EPfP GWCH LPio NBre SDnm SPav SPlb WBrE WPer
- lavender blue	NRnb
raddeana	CElw CLyd ITim MDKP NEgg NJOw NLAp NLar WBrk WFar WLin
raineri ♀H4	EPot GKev LRHS NLAp NMen NWCA SBla WAbe
- 'Nettleton Gold' **new**	EPot
§ ***rapunculoides***	EBee EGoo NBre NRnb WHer
§ - 'Afterglow'	EBee MAvo WCot WFar
- 'Alba'	CStr EMon MAvo
rapunculus	ILis MLLN MWgw
recurva	see *C. incurva*
reiseri	NBur
rhomboidalis Gorter	see *C. rapunculoides*
rigidipila	NBur
rotundifolia	CArn CRWN EPfP GAbr GIBF GWCH MBow MHer NBid NLan NMir NRya SHGN SIde SPlb SWal WBrk WJek WPer WPop
- var. ***alba***	EBee MAnH
- 'Jotunheimen'	CPBP EHyt
§ - 'Olympica'	EBee EBur EMan EPfP GEdr IGor MBNS NBur NJOw NLar NPri WCot WFar WHoo
- 'White Gem'	MAnH NChi
rupestris	EBur LTwo
'Samantha'	CSpe EBee EBla EMan EVFa LAst MCCP SBch SHar SMrm SPoG WCot
'Sarastro'	More than 30 suppliers
sarmatica	CSec EMag EMan EMon EWTr GAbr GBuc MAnH MBrN MNFA MSte MWhi NBPC NBid NJOw NOak NRnb NSti SMad SRms STes WCAu WCHb WMnd WPen WPer
sartorii	EBur EMan ITim
saxifraga	EBur ITim NBur NLAp NMen SIgm
§ - subsp. ***aucheri***	EBur EHyt NLAp WAbe
scabrella	CGra
scheuchzeri	EPot
shetleri	CGra GKev
§ ***sibirica***	EMan NBur SSvw WPer
- white	NLar
siegizmundii	GMac ITim NBur
'Sojourner'	CGra EHyt
speciosa	EBee EChP MWhi NBre
'Stansfieldii'	CGra EBur EPot NMen WPat
stevenii	CGra EHyt
'Summer Pearl'	CStu LAst MBNS NEgg
§ 'Swannables'	CPou EBee ECtt EMan EWsh GMac LTwo MAnH MNFA NCGa NChi
§ ***takesimana***	More than 30 suppliers
- B&SWJ 8499	WCru
* - ***alba***	EBee EBla EBrs GKir LPio MAnH MDKP NEgg SHar SMad WMoo WOut
- 'Beautiful Trust' PBR	CFai CLAP CSpe EBee EBla GMac LAst MAvo NBPC NSti SGSe SHar WCru WLFP WOVN
§ - 'Elizabeth'	More than 30 suppliers
- 'Elizabeth II' (d)	MAvo MTho WCot
- purple-flowered	SOkh
teucrioides	NWCA
thessala	WAbe
thyrsoides	EBee EMag EMan EWll GKev GTou LPio NBPC NBre NBur NRnb NSti SDnm SPav SSpi WHal WPer
- subsp. ***carniolica***	SGar
'Timsbury Perfection'	CGra
tommasiniana ♀H4	EHyt LRHS NBur SBla
trachelium	CMHG EBee EBrs EChP EMag EPfP GAbr MAnH MBNS MBow MNrw MRav MWgw MWrn NBPC NEgg NJOw NLan SGar SSpi WCAu WFar WHer WMnd WMoo WPer
- var. ***alba***	CLAP EBee EBrs EChP EWTr GAbr LRHS MAnH MMHG MNrw MWhi MWrn NLsd NPar STes WBrE WCot WFar WHrl WMnd WMoo WPer
- 'Alba Flore Pleno' (d)	CDes CFir CHar CHea CLAP CMil CStr EVFa LPhx LPio MAnH SBch SBla STes WCot WFar
- 'Bernice' (d)	More than 30 suppliers
- hose-in-hose **new**	NPar
- lilac-blue	NOrc NRnb
- 'Snowball'	EVFa LAst LSRN SPoG SVil
tridentata	GKev
troegerae	GKev LRHS SBla
'Tymonsii'	CPBP EBur ECho EHyt LRHS NBir NJOw
'Van-Houttei'	CElw CHar CMil CStr EBee GMac NLar SAga SBch WCot WFar WLin WPer
versicolor G&K 3347	EMon
vidalii	see *Azorina vidalii*
waldsteiniana	CPBP GKev LRHS LTwo NBur NWCA WFar
wanneri	CSec EBur EChP EMan EPfP LRHS MAnH NCGa NLar SPet
'Warley White'	see *C.* x *haylodgensis* 'Warley White'
'Warleyensis'	see *C.* x *haylodgensis* 'Warley White'
witasekiana	EBee
x ***wockei*** 'Puck'	EBee EBur ECtt EHyt EPot LRHS NLar NWCA WAbe WPat
zangezura	CSec CWan EBee EBur EChP EMan EShb GKev MAnH MLLN MWrn SGar SHFr SHGN SSvw
'Zierlotte'	NJOw
zoysii	LRHS SBla
zoysii x ***pulla*** **new**	CGra

Campanula x *Symphyandra* see *Campanula*

Campanumoea see *Codonopsis*

Camphorosma (*Chenopodiaceae*)

monspeliaca	XPep

Campsis (*Bignoniaceae*)

RCB/Arg L-8 **new**	WCot
atrosanguinea	see *Bignonia capreolata* 'Atrosanguinea'
grandiflora	CArn CBcs CPLN CSPN CTbh EBee ELan ENot EPfP GSki IMGH LRHS SPer SWvt WCFE XPep
radicans	CArn CBcs CBrm CDul CMac CRHN CSBt CStu CWib EBee ECrN ELan EPfP GQui LAst LRHS LSRN MSwo NBlu SHBN SLon SPlb WBVN WBrE WDin XPep

	- 'Flamenco'	CDoC CStu EBee ELan EShb GQui GSki LAst LRHS MAsh SAdn SBra SCoo SHGC SLim SPoG SWvt WCot
§	- f. ***flava*** ♀H4	CBcs CDoC CHEx CStu CTbh ELan ENot EPfP IMGH LRHS LSRN MAsh MBri MCCP MGos NBlu NPal NSti SBra SLim SPet SPoG SSta SWvt XPep
	- 'Indian Summer'	CBcs CTbh ENot MAsh MBlu MGos NLar SLim WCot
	- 'Yellow Trumpet'	see *C. radicans* f. *flava*
	x ***tagliabuana*** Dancing Flame = 'Huidan'PBR	NLar
	- 'Madame Galen' ♀H4	More than 30 suppliers

Camptosema (*Leguminosae*)

rubicundum **new**	CPLN

Camptosorus see *Asplenium*

Campylandra see *Tupistra*

Campylotropis (*Papilionaceae*)

macrocarpa	NLar WCot

Canarina (*Campanulaceae*)

canariensis ♀H1	CFil CStu EShb WCot WPGP
eminii **new**	CPLN

Candollea see *Hibbertia*

Canna ✿ (*Cannaceae*)

	'Adam's Orange'	CHEx
	'Aida' (Grand Opera Series)	MJnS
	'Alaska' ♀H3 **new**	SHaC
	'Alberich'	CSam SHaC
	altensteinii	SHaC XBlo
	'Ambassador'	IPot LAma MOak WHil
	'America'	EBee LAma WCot
	'Amundsen' ♀H3 **new**	SHaC
	'Angel Pink'	MJnS
	'Annaeei' ♀H3	EAmu MOak SHaC
	'Anthony and Cleopatra' (v)	WCot
I	'Aphrodite' van Klaveren ♀H3 **new**	SHaC
	'Apricot Dream'	EShb MBri MOak SHaC
	'Apricot Frost' **new**	MJnS
	'Apricot Ice'	MOak SHaC
	'Aranyálom'	LAma SHaC
	'Argentina'	SHaC
	'Aristote'	SHaC
	'Assaut'	EUJe SAPC SArc SHaC
	'Atlantis'	XBlo
I	***aurea*** **new**	CHEx
	'Australia'	MJnS MOak SHaC WCot XBlo
	'Black Knight'	CFir CSpe CTbh EAmu EBee EChP ELan EShb EUJe IPot LAma LAst MJnS MOak MSte SPet SWal WCot WMul WWlt XBlo
	'Bonfire'	CHEx SHaC
	'Bonnezeaux'	SHaC
	brasiliensis	CHll CRHN WCot
	'Brillant'	ELan LAma SHaC WDyG
	'Caballero' **new**	EAmu EBee SHaC
	'Caliméro' **new**	SHaC
	'Canary'	XBlo
	'Carnaval' **new**	SHaC
	'Centenaire de Rozain-Boucharlat'	CHEx SHaC
	'Centurion'	LAma
	'Cerise Davenport'	CFir MOak
	'Champigny'	SHaC
	'Chaumes' **new**	SHaC
	'Cherry Red'	EShb SHaC
	'Chinese Coral'	CHEx LAma
	'Chouchou' **new**	SHaC
I	'Citrina' **new**	XBlo
§	'City of Portland'	CPLG ELan LAma MBri MOak SChr SHaC
*	'Cleopatra'	EAmu EBee LAma MBri MJnS SHaC SPet WGwG
*	'Cléopâtre' **new**	SHaC
	coccinea	MOak
§	'Colibri'	EBee LAma SHaC
	'Conestoga'	MOak
	'Confetti'	see *C.* 'Colibri'
	'Corail' **new**	SHaC
	'Corrida' **new**	SHaC
	'Creamy White'	CHEx XBlo
	'Crimson Beauty'	LAma LAst MOak SHaC
	Crozy hybrids	LRav
	'Delaware' ♀H3	MOak
	'Délibáb'	CSam CTbh EBee EChP EShb IPot LAma MJnS SHaC SPet SWal WDyG
	'Di Bartolo'	MJnS SHaC XBlo
	'Dollar' **new**	SHaC
	'Dondoblutrot' **new**	SHaC
	'Durban' orange-flowered	see *C.* Tropicanna = 'Phasion'
	'E. Neubert' **new**	SHaC
	edulis	CHEx MOak
	- purple-leaved	MOak
§	x ***ehemanii*** ♀H3	CHEx CKob CRHN CSev EUJe MJnS MOak SAPC SArc SChr SDix SHaC WMul WPGP
	'Ember'	XBlo
	'Emblème'	SHaC
	'Empire' **new**	MOak
	'En Avant'	CHEx LAma SHaC SPlb
	'Endeavour'	CDWL CHEx EUJe LPJP MOak SHaC WMul WPGP
	'Erebus' ♀H3	CDWL EUJe MOak SDix SHaC
	'Ermine'	WCot
	'Étoile du Feu'	SHaC XBlo
	'Eureka'	MOak
	'Evening Star'	LAma SHaC
	'Extase'	SHaC XBlo
	'Fatamorgana'	LAma SHaC
	'Felix Ragout'	LAma SHaC
*	'Felix Roux'	SHaC
	'Feuerzauber' **new**	SHaC
	Firebird	see *C.* 'Oiseau de Feu'
	flaccida	CDWL SHaC WMul
	'Flame'	XBlo
	'Flammèche'	SHaC
§	'Florence Vaughan'	EShb MJnS SHaC
	'Fournaise'	SHaC
	(Futurity Series) 'Pink Futurity'	MOak
	- 'Red Futurity'	MOak
	- 'Rose Futurity'	MOak
	'Gaiety'	MOak
	'Gamay' **new**	SHaC
	'Gemini' **new**	MJnS
	'General Eisenhower' ♀H3	SHaC
	x ***generalis***	SHaC SHGC
	glauca	EUJe MOak SDix SHaC WWpP
	'Gnom'	SHaC
*	'Gold Ader'	LAma
	'Gold Dream'	LAma
	'Golden Girl'	SHaC
	'Golden Inferno'	XBlo
	'Golden Lucifer'	CHEx CSpe ELan LAma MJnS
	'Gran Canaria' **new**	EAmu SHaC
	'Grand Duc'	MOak SHaC

	Name	Suppliers
	'Grande'	CFir MJnS MOak SHaC
	'Heinrich Seidel'	CHEx SHaC
	'Hercule'	CHEx SHaC
	'Horn'	SHaC
	hybrids	ELan
	'Ibis' **new**	SHaC
§	***indica***	CHEx CSev EFul EUJe IFro MGol MOak SAPC SArc SHaC SPlb SYvo
	- 'Purpurea'	CHEx ECha EUJe LEdu MOak SChr SDix SHaC SPlb WCot WDyG WMul WPGP
	- 'Russian Red' ♀H3 **new**	SHaC
	'Ingeborg' ♀H3	LAma SHaC
	'Intrigue'	MOak SHaC
	iridiflora misapplied	see *C.* x *ehemanii*
	iridiflora Ruiz & Pav.	CDWL CSpe
	'Italia' **new**	EAmu SHaC
	'Jivago'	SHaC
	'Journey's End' **new**	SHaC
	'Kansas City' (v)	MJnS WCot
	'King City Gold' **new**	MOak
I	'King Humbert' (blood-red)	CBcs CHEx EPfP LAma LAst MGol MJnS MOak SYvo WCot WHil XBlo
	King Humbert (orange-red)	see *C.* 'Roi Humbert'
	'King Midas'	see *C.* 'Richard Wallace'
	'Königin Charlotte'	EBee SHaC
	'La Bohème' (Grand Opera Series)	LAma
	'La Gloire'	SHaC
	'La Quintinie' **new**	SHaC
	'La Source' **new**	SHaC
	'La Traviata'	MOak
	'L'Aiglon'	SHaC
	'Lenape' ♀H3	MOak
	'Leo' **new**	MJnS
	'Lesotho Lill'	CHll SHaC
	'Libération'	EAmu SHaC
	'Liberté'	see *C.* 'Wyoming'
	'Lippo's Kiwi'	MOak
	'Lolita' **new**	SHaC
	'Louis Cayeux' ♀H3	SDix SHaC
	'Louis Cottin'	CHEx EChP EPfP LAma SChr SHaC WWol
	'Lucifer'	CBcs CHEx CSpe EAmu EPfP LAma LAst LRHS MJnS MLan MOak NPer SHaC SPet SPlb SYvo WBrE WHil WWol
	lutea	CHEx XBlo
	'Madame Angèle Martin'	EAmu EShb MOak SHaC XBlo
	'Madame Paul Casaneuve'	SHaC
	'Madras' **new**	SHaC
	'Maggie' **new**	SHaC
	'Malawiensis Variegata'	see *C.* 'Striata'
	'Marabout' **new**	SHaC
	'Margaret Strange' **new**	SHaC
	'Marvel'	LAma LAst
	'Meyerbeer'	SHaC
	'Monet'	ECho EPfP
	'Montaigne' **new**	SHaC
	'Mrs Oklahoma'	LAma MOak SHaC
	'Musifolia' ♀H3	CHEx CKob EAmu EUJe LPJP MJnS MOak SChr SDix SHaC WDyG WMul XBlo
	'Mystique' ♀H3	MOak SDix SHaC
	'Ointment Pink' **new**	XBlo
§	'Oiseau de Feu'	LAma SHaC
	'Oiseau d'Or'	SHaC
	'Orange Beauty'	EAmu MOak
	'Orange Blush'	MOak
	'Orange Futurity'	MJnS MOak
	'Orange Perfection'	CFir CHEx CSam LAma LAst MOak SHaC
	'Orange Punch'	MBri MJnS SHaC WCot
	'Orchid'	see *C.* 'City of Portland'
	'Osric' **new**	CSpe
	'Pacific Beauty' **new**	WCot
	'Pallag Szépe' **new**	SHaC
	'Panache'	CHEx CTrC MOak SHaC WCot WDyG WMul
	'Panama' **new**	SHaC
	'Passionata' **new**	SHaC
	'Peach Blush'	CTbh
	'Pearlescent Pink' **new**	XBlo
	'Perkeo'	LAma LAst MOak SHaC SPet WWol
	'Petit Poucet'	SHaC
§	'Pfitzer's Salmon Pink'	CHEx SHaC
	'Picadore'	SHaC
	'Picasso' ♀H3	CBcs CHEx CPLG CSam CTbh EAmu EBee EPfP LAma LAst MGol MJnS MLan SHaC SPet SWal SYvo XBlo
	'Pink Beauty' **new**	MOak
	'Pink Champagne' **new**	XBlo
	'Pink Perfection' **new**	SHaC
	'Pink Sunburst' (v)	CKob CSpe MJnS SHaC SPlb
	'Pink Sunrise' **new**	MOak
	'Plantagenet'	SHaC
	'Plaster Pink' **new**	XBlo
	'President'	CHEx CRHN CSut ECho LAma LAst MOak SHaC SPet SPur WBrE XBlo
	'President Carnot' **new**	SHaC
	'Pretoria'	see *C.* 'Striata'
	'Primrose Yellow'	SHaC
	'Prince Charmant'	SHaC
	'Princess Di'	MBri MOak SHaC
	'Pringle Bay' (v)	SHaC XBlo
	'Puck'	SHaC
	'Ra' ♀H3	CDWL MOak SHaC
	'Red Wine'	MOak SHaC
§	'Richard Wallace'	CPLG CSam CSut CTbh LAma LAst MJnS MOak SAPC SArc SHaC SPlb SYvo WCot WMul XBlo
	'Robert Kemp'	EAmu LAma SHaC
§	'Roi Humbert'	CSam EShb MSte SHaC WMul
	'Roi Soleil' ♀H3	CHEx LAma SHaC WPGP
	'Roitelet'	CHEx SHaC
I	'Rosa'	MBri SHaC
	'Rosalinde' **new**	SHaC
	'Rosemond Coles'	CBcs CHEx CSam CSut EPfP LAma MJnS MLan MOak SHaC SWal SYvo WMul
	'Saladin'	SHaC
	'Salmon Pink'	see *C.* 'Pfitzer's Salmon Pink'
	'Salsa' **new**	SHaC
	'Saumur' **new**	SHaC
	'Savennieres' **new**	SHaC
	'Schwäbische Heimat' ♀H3 **new**	SHaC
	'Sémaphore'	MAvo MJnS SHaC SPur
	'Shenandoah' ♀H3	SHaC
	'Singapore Girl'	MOak SHaC
	'Snow Dragon' **new**	MJnS
	'Snow-White'	XBlo
	speciosa	XBlo
	'Stadt Fellbach'	MOak SHaC
	'Strasbourg'	CSam LAma NPer SHaC WMul WPGP
	'Strawberry Pink' **new**	XBlo
	'Striata' misapplied	see *C.* 'Stuttgart'
§	'Striata' (v) ♀H3	CHEx CKob CSev CSpe CTbh EBee EShb EUJe LAst LPJP MJnS MOak NVic SHBN SHaC SPet SYvo WCot WDyG WHal WMul WSPU XBlo

'Striped Beauty' (v)	CDWL CTrC EAmu EShb EUJe MOak SHaC
§ 'Stuttgart' (v)	CSpe EAmu EPfP MAvo MJnS MOak SHaC WCot WHal WMul
'Summer Gold' **new**	XBlo
'Sundance' **new**	SHaC
'Südfunk'	EAmu SHaC
'Tafraout'	SHaC
'Talisman'	MJnS SHaC XBlo
'Taney'	CDWL EUJe SHaC
'Tangelo' **new**	MOak
'Tango'	SChr
'Taroudant'	SHaC
'Tashkent Red'	CHad
'Tchad'	SHaC
'Tirol'	IPot MJnS MOak WMul
'Tricarinata'	CHEx
'Triomphe' **new**	SHaC
'Tropical Rose'	CPLG EAmu LRHS SRms WCot
'Tropical Sunrise' **new**	MJnS
Tropicanna = 'Phasion' (v) ♀H3	CFwr CHEx CHll CKob COtt CSpe CTbh CTrC EBee ELan EPfP EUJe EWes LAst LPJP MJnS MOak NPer NVic SDix SHBN SHaC SPoG WCot WGwG WHal WMul XBlo
'Vainqueur'	SHaC
'Valentine' **new**	WCot
'Vanilla Pink' **new**	XBlo
* 'Variegata' (v)	LAma LRHS WCot WMul
'Verdi' ♀H3	CSpe EUJe LAma MJnS SChr SHaC
'Virgo' **new**	MJnS
'Viva' **new**	SHaC
warscewiczii	MOak SYvo WCot
'Whithelm Pride' ♀H3 **new**	SHaC
'Wine 'n' Roses'	MBri SHaC
'Wintzer's Colossal' **new**	MJnS
'Woodbridge Pink'	XBlo
§ 'Wyoming' ♀H3	CBcs CHEx CSam CTbh EUJe LAma LAst MCCP MJnS MOak MSte NVic SHaC SWal SYvo WCot WMul WPGP XBlo
'Yellow Humbert' misapplied	see *C.* 'Richard Wallace', *C.* 'Cleopatra', *C.* 'Florence Vaughan'
'Yellow Humbert'	LAma LAst MGol MJnS MOak SHaC

Cannomois (*Restionaceae*)

virgata	CBig

Cantua (*Polemoniaceae*)

buxifolia	CAbb CBcs CFee CPLG CPle ECre EShb GQui SIgm WCot WPGP

Cape gooseberry see *Physalis peruviana*

Capparis (*Capparaceae*)

spinosa	WJek XPep
- var. ***inermis***	EUnu XPep

Capsicum (*Solanaceae*)

annuum	CSim MBri
- var. ***annuum*** (Longum Group) cayenne **new**	LRav
- - - habanero **new**	LRav
- - - jalapeno **new**	LRav
- - 'Oda' **new**	LRav
- - 'Othello' **new**	LRav
- - 'Purple Prince' **new**	LRav
- - 'Purple Tiger' **new**	LRav
baccatum **new**	CSim
chinense **new**	CSim
frutescens **new**	CSim
- Tabasco Group **new**	LRav
pubescens **new**	CSim EUnu

Caragana (*Papilionaceae*)

arborescens	ECrN EPfP GKir MBar NBee NWea SBLw SEND SPer SPlb WBVN WDin XPep
- 'Lorbergii'	CEnd CLnd EPfP GBin GKir IMGH LRHS MBlu SCoo SPer WBcn WFoF
- 'Nana' **new**	NLar
- 'Pendula'	CDul CWib EBee ECrN EGra ELan ENot EPfP GKir LAst LRHS MAsh MBar MBlu NBlu NEgg NPri SBLw SCoo SLim SPer SPoG WDin
- 'Walker'	CBcs CDul CEnd CWib EBee ELan EMil ENot EPfP GKir LRHS MAsh MBar MBlu MBri MGos NEgg SBLw SCoo SLim SPer WOrn
aurantiaca	MBar
frutex 'Globosa'	NBlu
jubata	NLar
microphylla	WNor
nubigena **new**	WLin

caraway see *Carum carvi*

Cardamine ✿ (*Brassicaceae*)

alba	WEas
asarifolia misapplied	see *Pachyphragma macrophyllum*
asarifolia L.	CLAP
bulbifera	CLAP EPPr IBlr LEdu NRya WBWf WCru WSHC
californica	EBee EMan NRya WCru WMoo
concatenata	CLAP NLar SSpi SVal WCru WHal
diphylla	CLAP EBee LEdu MLLN NLar SSpi WCot WCru WFar
- 'Eco Cut Leaf'	CDes WCru WPGP
- 'Eco Moonlight' **new**	SSpi
enneaphylla	CLAP IBlr LEdu NDov NGby SSpi SVal WCot WCru
glanduligera	CDes CElw EBee LEdu NDov SCnR SSpi WCru WPGP
§ ***heptaphylla***	CLAP EBee EBrs ELan GBin IBlr MBri MRav SSpi WCru
- Guincho form	CDes CLAP GBin IBlr
- white-flowered	CLAP GCal WCot
§ ***kitaibelii***	CLAP EBee ECha GBin IBlr LEdu NPol SCnR SIng SSpi WCru
latifolia	see *C. raphanifolia*
lineariloba	IBlr
macrophylla	CLAP SDys SSpi WCot WCru WFar
- B&SWJ 2165a	WCru
maxima	LEdu WCru
§ ***microphylla***	CLAP EHyt GCrs LEdu NDov WAbe WCot WCru
pachystigma	EBee
- NNS 98-149	WCot
pentaphylla ♀H4	CPom EBee EBrs ELan EMar EPPr EPla ERos GBBs GBuc GCrs GGar GKir IBlr LRHS MBri MDun MNFA MRav NBir NDov SBla SSpi SVal WCot WCru WPnP WTin
* - 'Alba'	EWTr
- bright pink	CLAP NPol WCot
pratensis	CArn CRWN EBee EMFW ENot EWTr GFlt MBow MHer NLan NMir NOrc NPri SIde WFar WHer WMoo WShi WWpP WWye
- 'Edith' (d)	CDes CLAP EBee EPPr GBuc MNrw NChi WPrP
- 'Flore Pleno' (d)	CBre CFee CWan EBee ECha ELan EMan GKir IFro ITer LRHS MBct

	MFOX MHer MNrw MTho NBid NBir NBro NDov NLar SBla WEas WFar WHoo WMoo WOut WSHC WWhi
- 'Improperly Dressed'	CNat
- 'William' (d)	CMea EMan EPPr GBuc MNrw WFar WMoo WPnP WPrP
quinquefolia	CDes CElw CLAP CMea CPom EBee EBrs ECha EHrv EMan EMar GBuc IBlr NDov SBla SDys SSpi SUsu WBrk WCot WCru WFar WPGP WRha WWye
§ ***raphanifolia***	CBre CDes CLAP CPom CRow EBrs ECha EMan GBuc GCal GGar IBlr LEdu MRav NBid NBro SSpi WBor WMoo WPGP WPnP WTin
trifolia	CDes EBee EBrs ECha EHrv EPPr GBuc GCal GCrs GEdr GGar GMaP IBlr IFro LRHS MBar MRav NBir NBro NLon NRya NVic WCot WCru WFar WHer WMoo WTin WWye
* - ***digitata***	MTho
waldsteinii	CAby CDes CElw CLAP CPom EBee ECho EHrv LToo NDov SBla SCnR SRot SSpi WCru WHoo WIvy WTin WWhi
yezoensis	CDes IBlr SSpi
- B&SWJ 4659	WCru

cardamon see *Elettaria cardamomum*

Cardiandra (*Hydrangeaceae*)

alternifolia	CLAP
- B&SWJ 5719	WCru
- B&SWJ 5845	WCru
- B&SWJ 6354	WCru
formosana	CLAP
- B&SWJ 2005	WCru
- B&SWJ 3632	WCru

Cardiocrinum (*Liliaceae*)

cathayanum	CFil WCot WPGP
cordatum B&SWJ 4841	WCru
- var. ***glehnii***	CLAP GEdr SSpi
- - B&SWJ 4758	WCru
- red-veined	CLAP GEdr SSpi
giganteum	CBcs CBct CBot CBro CFil CHEx EPot EPza EUJe EWTr GAbr GBuc GEdr GGar GKir GMaP IBlr LAma MBri MDun SMad SSpi WCot WCru WFar WHer WMul WPGP
- B&SWJ 2419	WCru
- var. ***yunnanense***	CFil CLAP CPom EPfP GAbr GBuc GEdr GGGa GGar IBlr NBid NLar SSpi WCru WPGP
- - CD&R 2491	WCru

cardoon see *Cynara cardunculus*

Carduus (*Asteraceae*)

benedictus	see *Cnicus benedictus*

Carex (*Cyperaceae*)

from Uganda	GBin GCal MMoz SApp
RBS 0214 **new**	MAvo
acuta	CBig GFor NBre
acutiformis	CRWN GFor GKir NBre
alba	CBrm EPPr GFor WDyG
albida	CHrt EBrs EHul EMan EPla GKir LRHS SWal WWpP
albula	MMoz WHoo
appressa	CBig SApp
arenaria	EPPr GBin GFor NBre NNor
atrata	CCol CHrt EBee EBrs EHoe EKen EPPr EPla ESis GKir LRHS MAnH WDyG WHrl
aurea	EPPr GFor GKir NBre
baccans	CBig CBrm EPPr EShb GCal LRav NOak WDyG
bebbii	EPPr
berggrenii	CHrt EBee EBrs EChP ECou ECrN EHoe EHul ELan EMon EUJe GFor GKir GSki ITim LPBA LRHS MBnl MWhi NBro NCob NWCA SPer SPlb SWal WMoo WPer WTin WWye
bicknellii	EPPr
binervis	CRWN
boottiana	EWes
brunnea	EHoe EPPr EWes NBlu
- 'Jenneke'	CBrm CFwr CKno CPen EBee LBuc LRHS MAvo SGSe SPoG
- 'Variegata' (v)	CBrm CPLG EHoe EPPr MMoz NGdn SApp
buchananii ♀H4	More than 30 suppliers
- 'Viridis'	EHoe ELan EMan EPza GBin LRHS MMoz WHer
'Caldwell Blue'	SSpi
caryophyllea 'The Beatles'	EBee EChP EGoo EHoe EPPr EPla ESis MMoz NBir NBro
chathamica	CAby CBig CKno CRez EMan EPPr MMoz
'China Blue'	CRez MMoz SApp
comans	COIW CWCL EBrs EFul EHoe EMon EPPr GCal GFor GKir GSki LRHS MAnH NBro NOak NPol SHel
- bronze	More than 30 suppliers
- 'Bronze Perfection' **new**	GBin
- 'Dancing Flame'	CPrp CWCL EBee GBin LBBr MCCP SVil SWal
- 'Frosted Curls'	More than 30 suppliers
- 'Small Red'	see *C. comans* 'Taranaki'
§ - 'Taranaki'	CTbh CWCL EBee EMan EPPr EPza EUJe GKir MBNS MBri MMoz NGdn SWal WPtf
conica 'Hime-kan-suge'	see *C. conica* 'Snowline'
§ - 'Snowline' (v)	More than 30 suppliers
coriacea	CBig
- from Dunedin, New Zealand	EPPr
crinita	EPPr MNrw WWpP
cristatella	EBee EPPr
crus-corvi	EPPr
curta	CRWN
dallii	EBee ECou EWes GBin MAnH MMoz NLar WWeb
davisii	EPPr
demissa	CRWN EBee EHoe EPPr WWye
depauperata	CRWN EHoe EMon WWye
digitata	CRWN WWye
dioica	CRWN
dipsacea	More than 30 suppliers
dissita	CBig LEdu
divulsa subsp. ***divulsa***	CRWN
- subsp. ***leersii***	EPPr
dolichostachya 'Kaga-nishiki' (v)	CAby CMil CPen CRez EBee EMan EMon EPPr LAst LBBr LEdu LRHS MMoz SAga SGSe WCot WPnP WPrP WPtf
duthiei	EBee GCal WCot
- KEKE 494	MMoz WPGP
echinata	CRWN GIBF
elata	EPPr
§ - 'Aurea' (v) ♀H4	More than 30 suppliers

	Name	Suppliers
	- 'Bowles' Golden'	see *C. elata* 'Aurea'
	- 'Knightshayes' ♀H4	CKno CPen EMan EWes GBin MMoz SGSe WCot
	'Evergold'	see *C. oshimensis* 'Evergold'
	fascicularis	CBig EPPr
	ferruginea	GBin
	firma 'Variegata' (v)	EHyt MTho MWat NMen NWCA SChu SIng WAbe
§	***flacca***	CBig CHrt CRWN EHoe EMan EPPr EWin GBin GFor GKir NBre SWal WGwG WPer
	- 'Bias' (v)	CNat EBrs EMan EMon EPPr EPla GKir LRHS MMoz WDyG WRHF
§	- subsp. ***flacca***	EBee EPza EWes MMoz NSti SGSe WPGP WWye
	flagellifera	More than 30 suppliers
	- 'Auburn Cascade'	CMil GCal NPro SApp SMac
	- 'Coca-Cola'	CKno CPen EUJe GCal MAvo MBnl NOak SGSe
	- 'Rapunzel'	MMoz WPGP
	flava	EHoe EPPr GFor SMar WWpP
	fortunei	see *C. morrowii*
	fraseri	see *Cymophyllus fraserianus*
	fraserianus	see *Cymophyllus fraserianus*
	geminata	CBig
	glauca Scopoli	see *C. flacca* subsp. *flacca*
	glauca Bosc. ex Boott	CBig CKno EPla EUJe SHel WCot WPGP
	'Golden Falls' **new**	ENot NPri SPoG
	granularis	EPPr
	grayi	CBig EBee EHoe EMon EPPr EPla GCal GFlt GFor GKir LEdu LRHS MBlu MTho NCGa NOak SGSe WCot WDyG WPer WSan WWye
	- 'Morning Star'	EPza
§	***hachijoensis***	EMon LAst LRHS WFar
	- 'Evergold'	see *C. oshimensis* 'Evergold'
	halleriana	XPep
	'Happy Wanderer'	SLPl
	hirta	CRWN EPPr
	hispida	CBig EPPr WMoo WRos
	hordeistichos	EBee EPPr
	hostiana	CRWN
	hystricina	EPPr
§	'Ice Dance' (v)	CMea EBee EPPr GGar MMoz NCGa NLar NOak SWvt WCot WPGP WPop WPrP WWpP
	kaloides	EBee EHoe EMan EMon EUJe LRHS MAvo
	'Kan-suge'	see *C. morrowii*
	longebrachiata	CBig
	longibracteata	see *C. myosurus*
	lupulina	CPen EPPr GBin NBPC
	lurida	CBig CPen EPPr EPza GBin MAvo MBNS NBre NLar WWpP
	macloviana	EPPr
	macrocephala	EPPr GFor NBre
	'Majken'	EBee GFor NBre
	maorica	CBig LEdu
	maritima	CRWN
	Milk Chocolate = 'Milchoc'PBR (v)	CHar CKno CPen EUJe MAvo SApp WLeb
*	***mimosa***	EPPr
	molesta	EPPr
	montana	EBrs EPPr GKir LRHS
	morrowii hort.	see *C. oshimensis*, *C. hachijoensis*
§	***morrowii*** Boott	MWhi
	- 'Evergold'	see *C. oshimensis* 'Evergold'
	- 'Fisher's Form' (v)	CFwr CHar CHrt CKno CTri EBee EHoe EPPr EPla EPot EUJe EWsh GKir LEdu LRHS MMoz MRav NGdn NMir SApp SGSe SMac SWvt WCot WFar WPGP WPer WWye
	- 'Gilt' (v)	EMon EPPr LRHS
	- 'Nana Variegata' (v)	CTri NBir NWoo WPGP
	- var. ***temnolepis*** 'Silk Tassel'	EPPr WCot
N	- 'Variegata' (v)	More than 30 suppliers
	muehlenbergii	EPPr
	multifida	EPPr
	muricata subsp. ***muricata***	EPPr
	muskingumensis	More than 30 suppliers
	- 'Ice Fountains' (v)	EPPr LIck
	- 'Little Midge'	EBee EBrs EMan EPPr GBin GKir LRHS WWpP
	- 'Oehme' (v)	CHar CKno CWCL EBrs EMan EMon EPPr EPla EPyc EShb GBin GCal LRHS MAvo NBid SUsu WCot WDyG WTin
	- 'Silberstreif' (v)	CBrm CKno CPen EBee EMon NLar SApp
	- 'Wachtposten'	GCal
§	***myosurus***	GGar
	'Mystery'	GGar
	nigra	CRWN EHon EPPr EUJe GSki NLar WWpP
§	- 'On-line' (v)	EPPr MAnH MMoz SApp WBrk WWpP
	- 'Variegata'	see *C. nigra* 'On-line'
	No. 1, Nanking (Greg's broad leaf) **new**	MMoz
	No. 4, Nanking (Greg's thin leaf)	EPPr MAvo SApp
	normalis	EPPr
	obnupta	EBee EPPr
	obtrubae	CRWN
	ornithopoda 'Aurea'	see *C. ornithopoda* 'Variegata'
§	- 'Variegata' (v)	CBrm ECtt EHoe EHul EPla EPot GFor MBrN MMoz MWhi NBro NGdn WCot WFar WMoo WTin WWye
§	***oshimensis***	WCot
§	- 'Evergold' (v) ♀H4	More than 30 suppliers
	- 'Evergold Compact'	SMac
	- 'Variegata' (v)	EPot IHMH NBir
	ovalis	CRWN WRos
	pallescens	EPPr WWye
	- 'Breckland Frost' (v) **new**	EPPr
	- 'Wood's Edge' (v)	CNat EPPr
	panicea	CKno CRWN CWCL EBee EHoe EPPr EPla MMoz SApp SGSe WFar WWpP
	paniculata	CBig CRWN GFor NBre
	pauciflora	GKir
	pendula	More than 30 suppliers
	- 'Cool Jazz' (v)	MAvo
	- 'Moonraker' (v)	CBot CFil CWCL EBee EHoe EPPr EPla LEdu MAvo MBNS SApp WCot WLeb WPtf WWpP
	petriei	CWCL ECha EMag EWes GBuc GGar LAst LLWP MAvo MBNS MMoz NBPC NVic SWal SYvo WCot WFar WHoo WPer WTin
	phyllocephala	EHoe EPza WCot WDyG WRos
	- 'Sparkler' (v)	More than 30 suppliers
	pilulifera 'Tinney's Princess' (v)	CNic EBrs EMan GKir LRHS SOkd WCot
	plantaginea	CAby CFil EBee EBrs EHoe EMon EPPr EPla GBin LEdu NBea SApp WCot WDyG WFar WHil WMoo WPGP
	platyphylla	WWye
	projecta	EPPr
§	***pseudocyperus***	CElw CRWN EHoe EHon EPPr EPla EPza GBin GFor GIBF GKir LPBA

	MBow MMoz MNrw NArg NBlu NGdn NPer SRms WFar WLeb WMoo WPer WPnP WWpP WWye
pulicaris	CRWN
reinii	WPrP WWpP
remota	CBig CRWN EPPr GBin GFor GKir LRHS NBre WPer WWye
riparia	CBig CRWN EMFW EPPr GFor LPBA MBow MMoz MWhi NPer SWal WFar WPop WRos WShi
- 'Bowles' Golden'	see *C. elata* 'Aurea'
- 'Variegata' (v)	CDWL CRow EBee EBrs ECha EGra EHoe EHon EMFW EMag EMon EPPr EPla GCal GMaP LPBA LRHS MAvo MMoz NArg NBro SAga SApp WAbb WCot WFar WHal WMoo WPop WWpP
rostrata	CRWN NArg
* ***saxatilis*** 'Variegata' (v)	EHoe EMan
scoparia	EPPr
secta	CBig EBee ECou EHoe EPPr GFor GGar GMaP MNrw NBre WDyG WMoo WPer WRos
- from Dunedin, New Zealand	EPPr
- var. ***tenuiculmis***	see *C. tenuiculmis*
shortiana	EPPr
siderosticha	CFil ECrN SLPl WPGP WPer
- 'Elaine West' (v)	EBee WCot
- 'Golden Fountains' **new**	WCot
- 'Kisokaido' (v)	EMan EMon WCot
- 'Old Barn'	EPPr
- 'Shima-nishiki' (v)	CBcs CElw CMil CPen CPrp EBee EHoe EMan EMar EPPr EPfP EPla EPza EUJe GBin LAst MBri MCCP MMoz NPro SMac SPoG WBor WCot WLin
- 'Variegata' (v)	More than 30 suppliers
'Silver Sceptre' (v)	More than 30 suppliers
'Silver Streams' **new**	ENot NPri
solandri	CPen CSam CTrC EBee EChP ENot EWsh LEdu MAvo NLar SApp SHel SWal WMoo WWpP
'Spiky Lollipops'	GFlt
spissa	CHrt EBrs MAvo MNrw
sprengelii	EPPr
stipata	EPPr
stricta Gooden.	see *C. elata*
stricta Lamarck	CBrm EPPr EPla
- 'Bowles' Golden'	see *C. elata* 'Aurea'
'Supergold'	EBee
sylvatica	CRWN EBee EPfP GFor WWye
tasmanica	CBig
tenuiculmis	CBrm CKno CWCL EBee EBrs EChP EHoe EMan EMon EPPr EPza EUJe EWTr EWsh GBin GFor GWCH LAst LRHS MAvo MWhi NSti WTin WWpP
tereticaulis	WCwm
testacea	More than 30 suppliers
- 'Old Gold'	CPrp EBee EPPr EWes LBBr MBnl MCCP NOak SMer SPlb SVil WBrE WFar WLeb
texensis	EPPr
trifida	CHEx CHrt EKen EPPr EPza GCal GFor GGar ITim LRHS MMoz MNrw SMad WCot WDyG WFar WWpP WWye
- 'Chatham Blue'	CAlb CKno CMHG EChP GBin NBPC NBir
tuckermanii	EPPr
typhina	EPPr
umbrosa	CBig
- subsp. ***sabynensis*** 'Thinny Thin' (v)	EMon EPPr
uncifolia	ECou
utriculata	EPPr
virgata	CBig
viridula subsp. ***viridula***	CRWN NArg
vulpina	CBig EPPr GFor NBre
vulpinoidea	EPPr
'Yellow Tassels' RBS 0213 **new**	ITer

Carica (*Caricaceae*)

goudotiana	CKob EUnu
x ***heilbornii*** (F)	CKob
papaya (F)	CKob EUnu
pubescens	CKob
quercifolia	CKob EUnu

Carissa (*Apocynaceae*)

grandiflora	see *C. macrocarpa*
§ ***macrocarpa*** (F)	ERea EShb ESlt MWya

Carlina (*Asteraceae*)

acanthifolia	CArn NSla SIgm
- subsp. ***cyanara*** JJA 274.101	NWCA
acaulis	CAby CArn ELan EPfP GAbr GEdr NEgg NPri NWCA SDnm SPav SPlb SRms WFar WGwG WJek WPer
- subsp. ***acaulis***	GPoy
- bronze	CAby CSam EMan EWll LDai LPhx SPav WHil
- var. ***caulescens***	see *C. acaulis* subsp. *simplex*
§ - subsp. ***simplex***	EBee ECGP EChP ECha EMan EShb GBuc GGar GKir GMaP LRHS SMar WCAu WCot WFar WJek WPer
- - bronze	NBre NChi NSla SMad WLin
vulgaris	NBre WPer
- 'Silver Star'	EMan

Carmichaelia (*Papilionaceae*)

'Abundance'	ECou
'Angie'	ECou
angustata 'Buller'	ECou
appressa	ECou GGar
- 'Ellesmere'	ECou
§ ***arborea***	ECou
- 'Grand'	ECou
astonii	ECou
- 'Ben More'	ECou
- 'Chalk Ridge'	ECou
australis	ECou
- 'Bright Eyes'	ECou
- 'Cunningham'	ECou
- Flagelliformis Group	ECou
- 'Mahurangi'	ECou
- Ovata Group	ECou
- 'Solander'	ECou
'Charm'	ECou
'Clifford Bay'	ECou
corrugata	ECou
'Culverden'	ECou
curta	ECou
enysii	EHyt
exsul	ECou
fieldii 'Westhaven'	ECou
flagelliformis 'Roro'	ECou
glabrata	CHEx CPLG CPle
'Hay and Honey'	ECou
juncea Nigrans Group	ECou
kirkii	ECou
'Lilac Haze'	ECou
monroi	ECou

- 'Rangitata'	ECou
- 'Tekapo'	ECou
nana	ECou
- 'Desert Road'	ECou
- 'Pringle'	ECou
- 'Waitaki'	ECou
nigrans 'Wanaka'	ECou
odorata	CPLG ECou
- Angustata Group	ECou
- 'Green Dwarf'	ECou
- 'Lakeside'	ECou
- 'Riverside'	ECou
ovata 'Calf Creek'	ECou
'Parson's Tiny'	ECou
petriei	ECou SMad
- 'Aviemore'	ECou
- 'Lindis'	ECou
- 'Pukaki'	ECou
- Virgata Group	ECou
'Porter's Pass'	ECou
'Spangle'	ECou
'Tangle'	ECou
uniflora	ECou
- 'Bealey'	ECou
'Weka'	ECou
williamsii	ECou SIgm
'Yellow Eyes'	ECou

x *Carmispartium* (*Papilionaceae*)

astens	see x *C. hutchinsii*
§ ***hutchinsii***	ECou
- 'Butterfly'	ECou
- 'County Park'	ECou GCal
- 'Delight'	ECou
- 'Pink Beauty'	ECou
- 'Wingletye'	ECou

Carpenteria (*Hydrangeaceae*)

californica 🏆H3	CFwr CMCN CPMA CSBt ELan ENot EPfP GKir GQui IMGH MBri MGos MLan NPal NSti SBrw SHBN SHGC SMur SPla SReu SSpi SSta WAbe WDin WHCG WPat WSHC
- 'Bodnant'	LPio LRHS MBri MGos SBra SBrw SPoG SSpi WGer WPGP
- 'Elizabeth'	CAbP CPMA EPfP GKir LRHS MAsh MBri SBra SBrw SMur SPer SPoG SSpi SSta WPat
- 'Ladhams' Variety'	CBcs CPMA EPfP MRav NEgg NLar SBra SBrw SSpi WKif WSPU

Carpinus ✿ (*Corylaceae*)

betulus 🏆H4	More than 30 suppliers
* - 'A. Beeckman'	SBLw
- 'Columnaris'	CLnd CTho GKir LRHS SBLw
* - 'Columnaris Nana'	CMCN
§ - 'Fastigiata' 🏆H4	CBcs CCVT CDoC CDul CEnd CLnd CMCN CSBt CTho CWib EBee ECrN ELan ENot EPfP GKir LBuc LRHS MBar MBri MGos NBee NBlu NWea SBLw SPoG WDin WFar WOrn
- 'Frans Fontaine'	CDoC CDul CMCN CTho EBee ENot GKir IArd IMGH LAst MBlu MBri MGos NBlu SBLw SCoo SLim SPer SSta
- 'Horizontalis'	CMCN
- 'Incisa'	GKir
- 'Pendula'	CDul CEnd CLnd CTho EBee GKir MBlu SBLw SIFN WDin
- 'Purpurea'	CDul CEnd EWTr NLar SBLw
- 'Pyramidalis'	see *C. betulus* 'Fastigiata'
- 'Quercifolia'	CDul SBLw
caroliniana	CLnd CMCN NEgg WNor
cordata	CMCN SBir WCwm WDin
coreana	CLnd CMCN CTho WDin WNor
fangiana	CEnd CFil CLnd CTho GKir WPGP
fargesii	see *C. viminea*
henryana	CMen SBir WDin WHCr WNor
japonica 🏆H4	CEnd CMCN CMen CTho EPfP GKir IDee LRHS MBlu SIFN SMad WDin
laxiflora	CMen WFar WNor WPGP
- var. ***longispica*** B&SWJ 8772	WCru
- var. ***macrostachya***	see *C. viminea*
orientalis	CMCN WNor
polyneura	CMCN SBir WNor
pubescens	GKir
x ***schuschaensis***	GKir
shensiensis	CFil CMCN
tschonoskii	CMCN
turczaninowii 🏆H4	CBcs CDul CMCN CMHG CMen CTho GKir IDee NLar NPal NWea SBir SHGN STre WDin WNor
§ ***viminea***	CDul CEnd CMCN CTho EPfP GKir SSpi WNor

Carpobrotus (*Aizoaceae*)

acinaciformis	SChr
§ ***edulis***	CAgr CDoC CHrt CTbh EShb EUnu EWin SAPC SArc SChr SEND WHer
- var. ***edulis*** **new**	CHEx
- var. ***rubescens*** **new**	CHEx
muirii	EShb EWin
quadrifidus	CTrC
rossii	GGar
sauerae	CTrC

Carpodetus (*Escalloniaceae*)

serratus	CBcs CTrC

Carthamus (*Asteraceae*)

tinctorius	MChe MSal SPav

Carum (*Apiaceae*)

carvi	CArn CBod CHrt CWan GPoy GWCH MChe MHer NPri NVic SECG SIde WHer WJek WLHH WPer WSel
copticum	EUnu MSal
petroselinum	see *Petroselinum crispum*
roxburghianum	EUnu

Carya ✿ (*Juglandaceae*)

aquatica	CTho
cordiformis	CMCN CTho EPfP
glabra	CMCN
N ***illinoinensis*** (F)	CAgr CBcs CMCN SSpi
- 'Carlson no. 3', seedling **new**	CAgr
- 'Colby', seedling **new**	CAgr
laciniosa (F)	CTho EGFP EPfP LRHS SSpi
- 'Henry' (F)	CAgr
- 'Keystone', seedling (F)	CAgr
myristiciformis	EGFP
ovalis **new**	EGFP
ovata (F)	CAgr CLnd CMCN CTho EPfP MBlu SSpi WDin WWes
- 'Grainger', seedling (F) **new**	CAgr
- 'Neilson', seedling (F) **new**	CAgr
- 'Weschke', seedling (F) **new**	CAgr

- 'Yoder no. 1', seedling (F) **new**	CAgr
pallida	CMCN

Caryophyllus see *Syzygium*

Caryopteris ✿ (*Verbenaceae*)

x ***clandonensis***	EBee ECtt ENot MWat NBir WCFE WDin WFar WHCG WHar WSHC WTel WWye
- 'Arthur Simmonds' ♀H4	CSam CTri EBee ECha EPfP SPer WGor
- 'Blaue Donau'	EBee LAst SPoG
- 'Dark Night'	CHar LRHS MSph SPoG WBcn WHil
- 'Ferndown'	CDoC CWib EBee ECrN EPfP EWTr LRHS MGos NLar SPer SPla SReu SRms SSpi WWeb
- 'First Choice' ♀H3-4	CAbP CSpe ECrN ELan EPfP LRHS LSRN MAsh MBri MWat NLar SChu SMad SMrm SMur SOkh SPer SPoG WBcn WHil WOVN
- Grand Bleu = 'Inoveris'PBR	CDul CSBt CTbh EBee ELan ENot LBuc LSRN MAsh MBNS MBri MRav NCGa SPoG SPur
- 'Heavenly Baby'	MAsh
- 'Heavenly Blue'	More than 30 suppliers
- 'Kew Blue'	More than 30 suppliers
- 'Longwood Blue'	ELan EPfP LRHS WBcn
- 'Moody Blue' (v)	EPfP SPoG
- 'Pershore'	EBee MTis MWgw WSPU
- 'Summer Gold'	MAsh MRav SPoG
- 'Summer Sorbet' (v) **new**	CBcs LRHS
- 'Worcester Gold' ♀H3-4	More than 30 suppliers
divaricata	EBee EMon
- 'Electrum'	EMan EMon MDKP
- 'Jade Shades'	EBee EMon WPGP WSHC
§ ***incana***	CMCN CPle ECrN EPfP MWhi SLon SPer SPoG WSHC XPep
- 'Blue Cascade'	ENot MRav
- 'Sunshine Blue' **new**	ENot MGos
- weeping	CPle EBee ELan GBuc GCal MSte MTis NLar SAdn WLeb WPat WSPU
mastacanthus	see *C. incana*
mongolica	XPep
odorata **new**	EShb

Caryota (*Arecaceae*)

'Hymalaya'	CRoM WMul
mitis ♀H1	EAmu SBig WMul

Cassandra see *Chamaedaphne*

Cassia (*Caesalpiniaceae*)

corymbosa	see *Senna corymbosa*
grandis **new**	CSec
marilandica	see *Senna marilandica*
obtusifolia	see *Senna obtusifolia*

Cassinia (*Asteraceae*)

aculeata	GGar
leptophylla	GGar SPer
- subsp. ***fulvida***	CBcs ECou EHoe GGar GKir GTou IFro MBar NLon SPer WBcn
- subsp. ***vauvilliersii***	CDoC CPLG GGar NLon SPer
- - var. ***albida***	CBcs EGoo LRHS SPer WBcn
N ***retorta***	CDoC ECou
'Ward Silver'	CBot CHar CRez ECou EHoe EWes GSki IArd NLon WGer

Cassinia x *Helichrysum* (*Asteraceae*)

* hybrid	WKif WSHC

Cassiope ✿ (*Ericaceae*)

* 'Askival'	EPot
'Askival Arctic Fox'	GCrs
'Askival Freebird'	see *C.* Freebird Group
'Askival Snowbird'	GCrs ITim
'Askival Snow-wreath'	see *C.* Snow-wreath Group
'Askival Stormbird'	GCrs ITim
'Badenoch'	ECho GCrs GEdr GKir NDlv NLAp
'Bearsden'	CMHG MBar NDlv
'Edinburgh' ♀H4	CMHG ECho EPfP GCrs GEdr GKir MBar NDlv NMen WPat
ericoides **new**	GIBF
§ Freebird Group	GCrs ITim
'Kathleen Dryden'	GCrs
lycopodioides ♀H4	GTou MBar
- 'Beatrice Lilley'	EPot GCrs GEdr GKir GTou ITim LTwo MBar NDlv SRms WPat
- 'Jim Lever'	GCrs ITim WAbe
- ***minima***	GEdr
- 'Rokujô'	GKir ITim
'Medusa'	GTou WPat
mertensiana	ECho GTou MBar NDlv NJOw SRms
- 'California Pink'	GKev
- var. ***californica***	EPot GKir
- var. ***gracilis***	CMHG GEdr GKir
- - dwarf	ITim
'Muirhead' ♀H4	CMHG ECho EPot GCrs GEdr GKir GTou ITim MBar MDun NDlv NLAp NMen NRya SRms WAbe WPat
'Randle Cooke' ♀H4	CMHG ECho EPot GCrs GEdr GKir GTou MBar MDun NDlv NLAp SRms WPat
selaginoides LS&E 13284	GCrs ITim WAbe
§ Snow-wreath Group	GCrs ITim
§ ***stelleriana***	GCrs
tetragona	GKir GTou MBar NLar SRms
- var. ***saximontana***	ITim
wardii	GGGa
- 'George Taylor'	GGGa GKir
wardii x ***fastigiata*** Askival strain	GCrs

Castanea ✿ (*Fagaceae*)

'Bouche de Betizac' (F)	CAgr
crenata **new**	CAgr
henryi	CBcs
'Layeroka' (F)	CAgr
'Maraval'	CAgr LRHS NWea
'Maridonne' (F)	CAgr
'Marigoule' (F)	CAgr SKee
'Marlhac' (F)	CAgr
'Marsol' (F)	CAgr
mollissima	CBcs CMCN ISea
x ***neglecta***	CTho LRHS
'Précoce Migoule' (F)	CAgr
pumila	CAgr CMCN
'Rousse de Nay' (F)	CAgr
sativa ♀H4	More than 30 suppliers
§ - 'Albomarginata' (v) ♀H4	CDoC CDul CEnd CTho EBee EPfP GKir IMGH LRHS MBlu MBri MDun MGos NBea SBLw SCoo SPer WDin WWes
- 'Anny's Red'	MBlu
- 'Anny's Summer Red'	CDul LRHS MBri
- 'Argenteovariegata'	see *C. sativa* 'Albomarginata'
- 'Aspleniifolia'	CBcs CDul MBlu
- 'Aureomarginata'	see *C. sativa* 'Variegata'
- 'Belle Epine' (F)	CAgr
- 'Bournette' (F)	CAgr
* - 'Doré de Lyon'	CAgr

- 'Herria' (F) **new** CAgr
- 'Laguépie' (F) CAgr
- 'Marron Comballe' (F) **new** CAgr
- 'Marron de Goujounac' (F) CAgr
- 'Marron de Lyon' (F) CAgr CDul CEnd CLnd CTho EPfP MBlu MCoo NWea SKee
- 'Marron de Redon' (F) **new** CAgr
- 'Numbo' (F) CAgr
- 'Pyramidalis' WDin
§ - 'Variegata' (v) CBcs CLnd CMCN ECrN ELan EMil EPfP EWTr LRHS MAsh SCoo
- 'Verdale' (F) **new** CAgr
seguinii LEdu LRHS
'Simpson' CAgr
'Vignols' (F) CAgr

Castilleja (*Scrophulariaceae*)

christii **new** CPBP
miniata GKev WAbe

Casuarina (*Casuarinaceae*)

cunninghamiana ECou

Catalpa ✿ (*Bignoniaceae*)

bignonioides ♀H4 More than 30 suppliers
- 'Aurea' ♀H4 More than 30 suppliers
- 'Nana' CRez ECrN EUJe LRHS SBLw
- 'Purpurea' see *C.* x *erubescens* 'Purpurea'
- 'Variegata' (v) CTho EPfP LRHS MRav SLim SSta WPat
bungei CLnd CTho EGFP NPal SHGN WNor
- 'Purpurea' ELan
x ***erubescens*** SBLw
§ - 'Purpurea' ♀H4 More than 30 suppliers
fargesii CFil CLnd
- f. ***duclouxii*** CTho EPfP MBlu NLar WPat
ovata CMCN CPle CTho EGFP
speciosa CBcs CLnd CMCN CPle CTho EPfP LRHS SBLw SPer
- 'Pulverulenta' (v) CDoC CDul CEnd CMCN EMil LRHS MDun MGos NLar SPer

Catananche (*Asteraceae*)

caerulea More than 30 suppliers
- 'Alba' CMea COlW EBee EBla EChP ECha EPfP ERou GKir LRHS NBid NBir NPri SPer SPoG WGwG WMoo WPer
- 'Amor White' CSim LRav
- 'Bicolor' CM&M ECrN EMan LRHS MAnH MHer MNrw SHGN STes WFar WHoo WMoo
- 'Major' ♀H4 EBee EChP ECrN LRHS SRms WEas
caespitosa SBla

Catha (*Celastraceae*)

edulis CArn MGol WJek

Catharanthus (*Apocynaceae*)

roseus ♀H1 GPoy MBri MSal
- Ocellatus Group MBri

Cathaya (*Pinaceae*)

argyrophylla CFil

Caulokaempferia (*Zingiberaceae*)

linearis CKob

Caulophyllum (*Berberidaceae*)

thalictroides CArn CLAP EBee GBBs GBuc GEdr LEdu LRHS MGol MSal WCot WCru WFar WPnP
- subsp. ***robustum*** CLAP WCru

Cautleya ✿ (*Zingiberaceae*)

sp. EMan
cathcartii B&SWJ 2281 WCru
- B&SWJ 2314 CBct
- 'Tenzing's Gold' **new** WCru
§ ***gracilis*** CBct CKob CLAP EBee EUJe IBlr LEdu MOak SBig WMul
- B&SWJ 7186 WCru
- CC 1751 WCot
lutea see *C. gracilis*
spicata CBct CDoC CHEx CKob EBee EUJe GBin GFlt IBlr LPio SBig WCot
- B&SWJ 2103 WCru
- CC 3676 ITer
- 'Crûg Canary' **new** WCru
- 'Crûg Cardinal' **new** CLAP
* - var. ***lutea*** CBct CPne EUJe EVFa MOak
- 'Robusta' CAvo CHEx CLAP CMdw CPne EAmu EBee EMan EShb EVFa GCal GCra IBlr LEdu MGol SGSe SMad WBor WCot WCru WMul WPGP

Cayratia (*Vitaceae*)

§ ***thomsonii*** **new** WCru

Ceanothus ✿ (*Rhamnaceae*)

'A.T. Johnson' CDul EBee ECrN MWya SHBN SLim SPer SRms
americanus CArn CPle MSal
arboreus SAPC SArc
- 'Owlswood Blue' LRHS
- 'Trewithen Blue' ♀H3 More than 30 suppliers
'Autumnal Blue' ♀H3 More than 30 suppliers
'Basil Fox' LRHS
'Blue Buttons' LRHS
* 'Blue Carpet' CWSG
'Blue Cushion' CBcs CDoC CPMA CWSG EBee ECtt GGar LAst LRHS MGos MRav SMer SWvt
'Blue Dreams' WFar
'Blue Jeans' IArd LRHS WAbe WLeb
* 'Blue Moon' LRHS
'Blue Mound' ♀H3 More than 30 suppliers
'Blue Sapphire' PBR CAlb CBcs CDoC CFwr CRez CSBt CWSG EBee EMil EPfP LAst MAsh NLar SPer SPoG SWvt WPGP
'Burkwoodii' ♀H3 CAlb CBcs CDoC CDul CMac CSBt CTri CWSG ENot EPfP GKir LRHS MAsh MBri MDun MGos MRav NBea NLon SHBN SPer SPoG SWvt WFar
'Cascade' ♀H3 CAlb CBcs CTri CWSG ENot GKir LRHS MBri MGos MWat NLon NSti SCoo SLon SPer SPlb WHCG XPep
'Centennial' **new** LRHS MBri
'Concha' ♀H3 More than 30 suppliers
§ ***cuneatus*** var. ***rigidus*** EHol LRHS SRms WAbe WSHC
- var. ***rigidus*** 'Snowball' ELan EPfP LRHS WBcn
'Cynthia Postan' CAbP CBcs CMHG CSBt CWSG EBee ECrN EPfP IArd LRHS MBlu MRav MWat NLar SCoo SDix WWeb
'Dark Star' ♀H3 CBcs CBrm CChe CDoC CMHG CPMA CSPN CTbh CWSG EBee EPfP EWll LRHS SPla SSta SWvt WPat

	'Delight'	CBcs EBee ELan EPfP EPla EWTr LRHS MGos MRav NBlu NLar SWvt WAbe WDin WFar
	x ***delileanus***	CBcs
	- 'Gloire de Versailles' ♀H4	CBcs CBot CDoC CMac CSam CTri CWSG CWib EBee ECrN ELan ENot EPfP ISea LRHS MGos MRav MSwo MWat NBPC NEgg NScw SHBN SPer SPla SPoG SWvt WDin WFar WSHC
	- 'Henri Desfossé'	CPle EHol ELan IMGH LRHS MRav NCGa SPer WDin WKif
	- 'Indigo'	WKif
	- 'Topaze' ♀H4	CBcs CRez CWSG EBee ELan EMil EPfP LRHS MRav SLon WDin WHar WKif
	dentatus misapplied	see *C.* x *lobbianus*
	dentatus Torr. & A.Gray	ENot GBin MAsh MGos SPer
	- var. ***floribundus***	CSBt EBee ELan LRHS SDix
*	- 'Superbus'	EBee
	'Diamond Heights'	see *C. griseus* var. *horizontalis* 'Diamond Heights'
	'Edinburgh' ♀H3	EPfP LRHS MGos WFar
	'El Dorado' (v)	SPoG
	'Fallen Skies'	LRHS
	foliosus	CTrw
	var. ***austromontanus***	
	'Frosty Blue'	LRHS
	'Gentian Plume'	LRHS
	gloriosus	CFai EBee EWes LRHS
	- 'Anchor Bay'	COtt EBee ELan EPfP IArd LRHS SLon WWeb
	- 'Emily Brown'	CAlb CBcs CDoC CSPN ELan MRav MWat NLar WFar
§	***griseus*** var. ***horizontalis*** 'Diamond Heights' (v)	LRHS MGos NPri SPer WFar
	- - 'Hurricane Point'	WBcn WFar
	- - 'Silver Surprise'PBR (v)	CAlb CBcs CFai CRez CSPN ELan ENot EPfP MGos MWat NLar NPri SHBN SLim SPer SPoG WOVN
	- - 'Yankee Point'	More than 30 suppliers
	impressus	CBcs CMHG CSBt CTri ECrN ELan EPfP LRHS MAsh MRav SMer SPer SPla SWvt WCFE WFar WWeb XPep
N	'Italian Skies' ♀H3	More than 30 suppliers
	'Joyce Coulter'	CBcs ISea
	'Julia Phelps'	CMHG EBee WEas WSPU
	'Ken Taylor'	LRHS
§	x ***lobbianus***	CBcs CTri ECtt EHol MRav NJOw SPlb WDin WFar
	- 'Russellianus'	MWya SHBN
	x ***pallidus***	CFai WBcn
	- 'Golden Elan' (v)	WBcn
	- 'Marie Simon'	CBcs CBot CBrm CChe CWib EBee ECrN EHol ELan EMil ENot EPfP LAst LRHS MGos NBlu NJOw NLon SCoo SPoG SRms SSta SWvt WCFE WDin WFar WKif WSHC WWeb
	- 'Marie Simon Variegated' (v)	CPMA
	- 'Perle Rose'	CBcs CMac CPle EBee EPfP LRHS SHBN SPla WKif WSHC
	papillosus var. ***roweanus***	CPle
	'Pershore Zanzibar'PBR (v)	CAlb CBcs CChe CSBt CSPN CWSG EBee EHoe ENot EPfP LAst LRHS MGos MRav MSwo MTis MWat MWgw MWya NPri SAdn SHBN SPer SPoG SWvt WSPU WWeb
	'Pin Cushion'	CDoC CWSG CWib EPfP LRHS MBri MWgw WBcn WSPU
	'Point Millerton'	see *C. thyrsiflorus* 'Millerton Point'
	prostratus	CPle MAsh SHBN SMad WAbe
	'Puget Blue' ♀H4	More than 30 suppliers
	purpureus	CPle WWeb
	'Ray Hartman'	SMad WBcn XPep
	repens	see *C. thyrsiflorus* var. *repens*
	rigidus	see *C. cuneatus* var. *rigidus*
	'Sierra Blue'	EBee SHGC
	'Snow Flurries'	see *C. thyrsiflorus* 'Snow Flurry'
	'Snow Showers'	NBPC
	'Southmead' ♀H3	CAlb CDoC CTri EBee ECrN ECtt EGra ELan EMil EPfP GBuc LRHS MAsh MGos MSwo MWat NBPC NBlu NEgg NPri WBrE WDin WHCG WMoo
	thyrsiflorus	CBcs CMac CTri CWSG CWib EPfP LRHS MAsh SHBN SPer SRms SWvt WDin WFar WHar WTel
	- 'Borne Again' (v)	WBcn WWpP
§	- 'Millerton Point'	CChe CDul CRez CWSG EBee EMil EPfP LAst LRHS MBlu NLar SCoo SLim SPoG WGwG WWpP XPep
§	- var. ***repens*** ♀H3	More than 30 suppliers
	- 'Skylark' ♀H3	CBrm CDoC CDul CMHG CWSG ECtt ELan ENot EPfP EPla GKir ISea LAst LRHS MAsh MBri MGos NPri NPro SDix SLim SReu SSpi SSta WFar WPat WWeb
§	- 'Snow Flurry'	CBcs CWib ECrN ECtt EMil EPfP LAst MGos MSwo MWat WFar WSPU
	'Tilden Park'	LRHS
	x ***veitchianus***	CMac CSBt EBee ELan LRHS MBar SPer
	velutinus	MSal
	'Victoria'	EGra LBuc NLar XPep
	'White Cascade'	EHol LRHS
	'Zanzibar'PBR	see *C.* 'Pershore Zanzibar'

Cedrela (*Meliaceae*)

	sinensis	see *Toona sinensis*

Cedronella (*Lamiaceae*)

§	***canariensis***	CArn CBod CHby CHrt CSec CSev EShb EUnu GBar GGar GPoy IFro ILis MBow MChe MHer MSal NGHP NTHB SIde WCHb WGHP WHer WPer WSel WWye XPep
	mexicana	see *Agastache mexicana*
	triphylla	see *C. canariensis*

Cedrus (*Pinaceae*)

	atlantica	CDul CLnd CMen CSBt ECrN EHul EWTr GKir LCon MBar NWea SEND SHGC WBVN WEve WMou
	- 'Aurea'	CMac LLin MBar MGos NLar SCoo SSta WDin WHar
	- 'Fastigiata'	CDoC CDul CMac EHul LCon MBar MBri MGos NLar SCoo SLim SPoG WEve
	- Glauca Group ♀H4	More than 30 suppliers
	- - 'Silberspitz'	CKen
	- 'Glauca Fastigiata'	CKen CMen ECho WEve
	- 'Glauca Pendula'	CDoC CDul CKen CMen EBrs ECrN EHul EOrn EPfP GKir IMGH LCon LRHS MBar MBlu MBri MGos NBee NBlu NEgg SBLw SHBN SLim SMad SSta WDin WEve WFar WOrn
	- 'Pendula'	CDul CMac ECho GBin MAsh SHBN
	brevifolia	ECho GKir LCon LLin MBar MGos NLar WEve

- 'Epstein' MBar
- 'Hillier Compact' CKen GTSp
- 'Kenwith' CKen

deodara ♀H4 More than 30 suppliers
- 'Albospica' (v) LCon LLin SWvt
- 'Argentea' MBar MGos NLar
- 'Aurea' ♀H4 CDoC CDul CSBt CTho ECho ECrN EHul ENot EOrn EPfP GFlt GKir IMGH LCon LLin LRHS MBar MBri MGos NBlu NEgg SBLw SLim WDin WEve WFar WOrn
- 'Blue Dwarf' CKen LLin NLar WEve
- * - 'Blue Mountain Broom' CKen
- 'Blue Snake' CKen NLar
- 'Blue Triumph' WEve
- 'Cream Puff' CSli EBrs ECho LLin MAsh MBar MGos
- 'Dawn Mist' (v) LLin
- 'Devinely Blue' **new** CKen
- 'Feelin' Blue' CDoC CKen COtt CRob CSli EBrs EHul ENot EPla GKir IMGH LBee LCon LLin LRHS MAsh MBar MBri MGos MLan SCoo SHBN SLim SPoG SWvt WEve WFar
- 'Gold Cone' MGos
- 'Gold Gowa' **new** NLar
- 'Gold Mound' CKen CSBt MAsh WEve
- 'Golden Horizon' CDoC CKen CMen CRob CSBt EHul EOrn EPla GKir IMGH ISea LBee LCon LLin LRHS MAsh MBar MBri MGos NBlu SCoo SHBN SLim SPoG SWvt WDin WEve WFar
- 'Karl Fuchs' CDoC GKir LRHS MAsh MBri NBlu NLar SCoo SMad WGor
- 'Kashmir' CSli NLar
- 'Kelly Gold' GKir NLar
- 'Klondyke' MAsh
- 'Mountain Beauty' CKen
- 'Nana' CKen
- 'Nivea' CKen
- 'Pendula' CDoC EHul MBar MGos WEve WGor
- 'Polar Winter' SMad
- 'Pygmy' CKen
- 'Raywood's Prostrate' CKen
- 'Robusta' WEve
- 'Roman Candle' CSli ECho EOrn SHBN WEve
- 'Scott' CKen
- 'Silver Mist' CKen
- 'Silver Spring' MAsh MGos NLar

* 'Home Park' CKen

libani ♀H4 More than 30 suppliers
- 'Comte de Dijon' EHul LLin LRHS NLar SLim SPoG
- 'Fontaine' **new** NLar
- Nana Group CKen ECho MAsh
- 'Pampisford' **new** NLar
- 'Sargentii' CDoC CKen EHul EOrn IMGH LCon LLin LRHS MBar MGos SHBN SLim WEve
- 'Taurus' MBar NLar

Celastrus (*Celastraceae*)

angulatus GIBF WPGP
glaucophyllus CPLN
var. ***rugosus*** **new**
orbiculatus CBcs CDoC CFwr CMac CPLN EBee ELan GBin LRHS MRav NSti SBrw SHGC SLon SReu SSta WBor WFar WSHC
- 'Diana' (f) NBea NLar SSta
- 'Hercules' (m) NBea NLar
- Hermaphrodite Group ♀H4 CBrm CSam GSki SBra SDix SPer SSpi
- var. ***papillosus*** B&SWJ 591 WCru
- var. ***punctatus*** B&SWJ 1931 WCru

rosthornianus GIBF
scandens CMac EBee IMGH NLar NScw SMur SPlb WDin
- (f) CPLN
- (m) CPLN

Celmisia (*Asteraceae*)

adamsii IBlr
allanii IBlr SOkd
alpina GAbr IBlr SOkd
- large-leaved IBlr

angustifolia EPot GCrs GEdr IBlr ITim
- silver-leaved IBlr

argentea EPot GCrs GGar GTou IBlr ITim NDlv NLAp WAbe
armstrongii ECho IBlr
asteliifolia IBlr
Ballyrogan hybrids IBlr
bellidioides EPot EWes GCrs GEdr IBlr MDKP NLAp NMen
bonplandii IBlr
brevifolia IBlr ITim
cordatifolia **new** GKev
coriacea misapplied see *C. semicordata*
coriacea Raoul see *C. mackaui*
coriacea (G. Forst.) Hook. f. GCal GKev IBlr MDun
costiniana IBlr
dallii IBlr
'David Shackleton' IBlr
densiflora GCrs GKev IBlr
- silver-leaved IBlr

discolor IBlr
durietzii IBlr
glandulosa IBlr
gracilenta GCrs IBlr ITim NLAp NSla SOkd SRot
- CC 563 NWCA

graminifolia IBlr
haastii IBlr
'Harry Bryce' IBlr
hectorii GCrs GKev IBlr ITim SOkd WLin
hectorii* x *ramulosa WAbe
holosericea IBlr
hookeri GCal IBlr
inaccessa IBlr
incana GCrs IBlr SOkd
Inshriach hybrids IBlr NHar
insignis IBlr
Jury hybrids IBlr
latifolia IBlr
- large-leaved IBlr

longifolia GGar SSpi
- large-leaved IBlr
- small-leaved IBlr

lyallii GKev
§ ***mackaui*** GGar IBlr
* ***macmahonii hadfieldii*** **new** GKev
markii IBlr
monroi IBlr
morganii IBlr
petiolata **new** GKev
philocremna **new** GKev
prorepens GKev IBlr
pugioniformis IBlr SOkd
ramulosa EPot GEdr GGar ITim NLAp SIng SOkd
§ - var. ***tuberculata*** GCrs GTou IBlr NSla

saxifraga	CStu IBlr ITim WAbe
§ ***semicordata***	GBuc IBal IBlr ITim NSla
- subsp. ***aurigans***	GKev IBlr
- subsp. ***stricta***	GFlt GKev IBlr
sericophylla	GKev IBlr
- large-leaved	IBlr
sessiliflora	EPot GKev GTou IBlr ITim NArg NWCA
- 'Mount Potts'	IBlr
spectabilis	CTrC IBlr MDun WAbe WHil
- 'Eggleston Silver' **new**	NEgg
- subsp. ***magnifica***	IBlr
- subsp. ***spectabilis*** var. ***angustifolia***	IBlr
spedenii	IBlr
tomentella	IBlr
traversii	IBlr LRHS WWeb
verbascifolia	GKev IBlr
viscosa	IBlr
§ ***walkeri***	GCrs GGar GTou IBlr
webbiana	see *C. walkeri*

Celosia (*Amaranthaceae*)

argentea var. ***cristata***	MBri
- - Plumosa Group	MBri

Celsia see *Verbascum*

x *Celsioverbascum* see *Verbascum*

Celtis (*Ulmaceae*)

australis	CAgr CBcs CDul EGFP LRHS SBLw SCoo
bungeana	CMCN IDee NLar
julianae	NLar WCwm WNor
occidentalis	CAgr CTho ELan GIBF LRHS NBlu WBVN
- var. ***pumila***	WNor
sinensis	EGFP NLar WNor
trinervia	GIBF

Cenolophium (*Apiaceae*)

denudatum	CDes CHrt EBee ECha SIgm WPGP

Centaurea ✿ (*Asteraceae*)

from Turkey	WPGP
HH&K 271	NBid
alba	EBee WCra
alpestris	CMHG EChP ECho NEgg NGby NLar
argentea	CBot
atropurpurea	NLar
bella	More than 30 suppliers
- 'Katherine' (v)	MAvo
benoistii	CDes CHad CKno EBee LPhx MRav NDov SIgm SUsu WHrl WPGP
'Black Ball'	CSpe NLsd
'Blue Dreams'	EMon MLLN SUsu
candidissima hort.	see *C. cineraria*
'Caramia'	EBee SMeo SSvw SUsu
cheiranthifolia	CDes CElw EChP ECha ECtt EMon EPPr NBir SBch WFar
§ - var. ***purpurascens***	EMon
§ ***cineraria***	EMan MOak SRms WCot WEas WWpP
- subsp. ***cineraria*** ♀H3 **new**	EBee
cyanus	CArn GWCH MBow MHer NArg NPri WBWf WFar WGwG WJek
dealbata	CBot COIW CPrp CTri EBee EPfP GAbr IHMH LAst LRHS MBow MHer NArg NBPC NBlu NBro NMir NOrc NVic WBor WCot WFar WMoo WPer WWeb WWhi WWpP
- 'Steenbergii'	CAbP CMHG EBee EChP ELan ERou EVFa GCal GGar GKir LRHS MNFA NBid NOak NPer NSti SBch SGSe SPer SPoG SSpe WAbb WCot WFar WHoo WMnd
declinata	NLon
fischeri	CDes EBee EMon MAvo
glastifolia	EMon GCal MLLN WCot WPGP
gymnocarpa	see *C. cineraria*
'Hoar Frost'	CMil EMon
hypoleuca 'John Coutts'	More than 30 suppliers
jacea	EMan EShb GAbr MBow NBid NLar SYvo WCAu WCot WPer WSSM
'Jordy' **new**	IPot
kotschyana	CDes EBee NBid WPGP
macrocephala	More than 30 suppliers
marschalliana	NBid
mollis	NBid
montana	More than 30 suppliers
- 'Alba'	More than 30 suppliers
§ - 'Carnea'	CAby CElw CPom EBee EChP ECha EMon GCra GMaP LLWP LPhx MAnH MNFA NChi NLar SMeo STes WCAu WFar WMoo
- 'Coerulea'	CBot WBVN
- 'Gold Bullion'	CDes CFai EBrs ECGP ECtt EMon EPPr EVFa EWes GBuc LDai MAvo MBri MCCP NBid NBir NSti SMad SPoG SSvw SUsu WBcn WBor WCAu WCra
- 'Grandiflora'	EBee WHlf
- 'Joyce'	CDes CElw EMon
- 'Lady Flora Hastings'	CBot CBre CDes CElw CKno CSam CSpe EBee GMac SBla WPGP
- 'Ochroleuca'	EGoo EMon GBuc MLLN NBre WBcn
- 'Parham'	CElw CMHG CPrp CSev EBee EMan ERou GCal LLWP LRHS MNFA MRav NEgg NFla NSti SChu SHel SPer SPet SPla SPlb WMnd
- 'Purple Prose'	EMon WBcn
- 'Purpurea'	CDes EBee
- 'Rosea'	see *C. montana* 'Carnea'
* - ***violacea***	IBlr
- 'Violetta'	CPom NBir WFar WMoo
nervosa	see *C. uniflora* subsp. *nervosa*
nigra	CArn COld CRWN EBee MBow MOne NLan NMir NPri SRob WMoo
- var. ***alba***	CArn CBre NBid WWye
- subsp. ***rivularis***	ECha NBid
orientalis	CMdw CRez CSam EBee EChP EMar LPhx MHar MMHG MNFA NLar SBla SIgm SSvw WPer
pannonica subsp. ***pannonica***	CPom NBid WSHC
- HH&K 259	CStr
pestalozzae	EHyt
phrygia	EBee EMan GAbr MNrw NBid NLar WPer WRos
- subsp. ***pseudophrygia***	NBid
pulcherrima	EBee EChP ECha EMan EMon EWTr GCal MAnH MAvo MLLN NBre NOak NSti SUsu WPer XPep
'Pulchra Major'	see *Stemmacantha centauriodes*
rhenana **new**	WOut
rothrockii	EMan
rupestris	CMHG EBee EChP LPhx NEgg NJOw NLar SAga SBla SGar WPer WWeb

	ruthenica	CHea EBee EChP EMan LPhx MNFA MSte NGdn NLar SBch SMad WCot
*	- 'Alba'	MSte
	salonitana	EMon
	scabiosa	CArn CRWN EMag GWCH MBow MChe MHer MWhi NBid NJOw NLan NMir NPri SPoG WPer
	- f. ***albiflora***	ECGP EMan EMon EPza LAst LRHS STes
	simplicicaulis	CKno CNic CSam EBee ECrN EMan EVFa GAbr GBri MBct MTho NMen SBch SBla SIgm SRms SRot WCot WEas WHoo WPGP WPer WSHC WWhi WWpP
	stenolepis	CStr
	subsp. ***razgradensis*** HH&K 297	
	thracica	EBee LPhx SAga WCot
§	***triumfettii***	CBrm NJOw SBla
	subsp. ***cana*** 'Rosea'	
	- subsp. ***stricta***	CBgR CDes CKno CPrp CSLe EBee EMon GAbr GBuc MSte WPGP
§	***uniflora*** subsp. ***nervosa***	NBid NBro WPer

Centaurium (*Gentianaceae*)

	erythraea	CArn GPoy MChe MHer MSal NJOw NLar SECG WWye
*	***littorale*** 'Alba' **new**	CSec
	scilloides	CStu LRHS MTho NMen NSla WAbe

Centella (*Apiaceae*)

§	***asiatica***	CArn EBee EOHP GPoy ILis MGol MSal WJek

Centradenia (*Melastomataceae*)

floribunda	LAst SYvo
grandifolia **new**	LBmB
inaequilateralis	CHal ECtt EMan EWin MBri SHFr
'Cascade'	SPet

Centranthus (*Valerianaceae*)

	macrosiphon	NLsd
§	***ruber***	CArn CBot COIW CRWN CSBt ECtt ELau EPfP ERou EWTr GGar GMac GPoy GWCH MBow MHer MTis NBPC NFor NPer SECG SPer SRms STes SWvt WFar WMoo WWye XPep
*	- 'Alba Pura'	NBPC
§	- 'Albus'	More than 30 suppliers
	- 'Atrococcineus'	ECha EMan SPoG WPer
	- var. ***coccineus***	More than 30 suppliers
	- mauve	LPhx MAnH NDov XPep
	- 'Roseus'	NEgg WMoo WOVN
	- 'Snowcloud'	COIW CSev EKen EWTr NLsd WHil
	- 'Swanage'	CNat
	'White Cloud'	WJek

Cephalanthera (*Orchidaceae*)

falcata	EFEx
longibracteata	EFEx

Cephalanthus (*Rubiaceae*)

occidentalis	CBcs CDul CPle CWib EBee EDAr EMil IFro IMGH LRav MBNS MBlu MGos NBlu SBrw SPer SPoG SSpi WBVN WFar

Cephalaria (*Dipsacaceae*)

	from Nepal 2800m	CSam
	HWJ 695	LPhx
§	***alpina***	COIW EBee EBla ECha EDAr EHrv EMan EPfP GKir IBal IHMH LAst LRHS MHer MNrw NEgg NLar NRnb SOkh SRms WBVN WFar WPer
	- 'Nana'	CMil EMon NMen NWCA
	ambrosioides	MLLN
	dipsacoides	CFee CKno CSec EBee EBla EChP ECha GFlt LDai LPhx MFOX MGol MHer NLar NRnb SMHy SPoG WMoo
§	***flava***	EBee GKir
	galpiniana **new**	SPlb
	- subsp. ***simplicior***	CSec EBee
§	***gigantea***	More than 30 suppliers
	graeca	see *C. flava*
	leucantha	CHea COIW EMan GBuc MLLN MSph NBre NLar STes WMoo
	litvinovii	CElw EMon
	oblongifolia	NRnb SPoG
	radiata	NDov
	tatarica	see *C. gigantea*
	tchihatchewii	EBee MLLN

Cephalotaxus (*Cephalotaxaceae*)

fortunei	CDoC CDul SLon
- 'Prostrate Spreader'	EHul
harringtonii	CDoC ECho IDee LEdu SMur
- B&SWJ 5416	WPGP
- var. ***drupacea***	CDoC GIBF
- 'Fastigiata'	CBcs CDoC CKen EHul ENot EOrn GKir IArd LCon LLin LRHS MAsh MBar MBri SCoo SLim SPoG WDin WFar WGer
- 'Gimborn's Pillow'	MBar
- 'Korean Gold'	CKen NLar SLim
- 'Prostrata'	MBar

Cephalotus (*Cephalotaceae*)

follicularis	SHmp

Cerastium (*Caryophyllaceae*)

alpinum	SRms
- var. ***lanatum***	CMea ECho ETow EWes MDKP NJOw WPer
arvense	NDlv
candidissimum	NLar XPep
grandiflorum **new**	EShb
tomentosum	CBrm CHal CTri ECrN ENot EPfP GAbr GKir GWCH IHMH LGro MHer NBlu NDlv NFor NJOw NPri SPer SPet SPlb SPoG WFar WPer XPep
- var. ***columnae***	CNic ECha ECho ECrN EHoe EPfP EWes SIng WCot

Ceratoides (*Chenopodiaceae*)

lanata	see *Krascheninnikovia lanata*

Ceratonia (*Caesalpiniaceae*)

siliqua	CAgr CFil EUnu LExo MSal XPep

Ceratophyllum (*Ceratophyllaceae*)

demersum	CBen CRow EHon EMFW EPfP LNCo NArg SLon WPop WWpP

Ceratostigma ✿ (*Plumbaginaceae*)

	abyssinicum	ELan
	'Autumn Blue'	EPfP WBcn
	griffithii	More than 30 suppliers
	- SF 149/150	ISea
	- 'Album'	CPle
§	***plumbaginoides*** ♀H3-4	More than 30 suppliers

willmottianum ♀H3-4	More than 30 suppliers
- Desert Skies = 'Palmgold'PBR	CBcs CFwr CRez CSBt EBee ELan EPfP GBuc LRHS MGos SCoo SHGC SHop SMad SPer SPoG SSta SWvt WPat WWeb
- Forest Blue = 'Lice'PBR	CAbP CBcs CDoC CFwr CSBt CWSG ECrN EGra ELan ENot EPfP LRHS MAsh MRav NPri SCoo SHBN SMer SPer SPla SPoG SReu WPat WWeb

Ceratotheca (*Pedaliaceae*)

triloba	SUsu
* - ***alba*** **new**	SUsu

Cercidiphyllum ✿ (*Cercidiphyllaceae*)

japonicum ♀H4	More than 30 suppliers
- 'Heronswood Globe'	CMCN CPMA EPfP MBlu NLar
- f. ***pendulum*** ♀H4	CBcs CDul CEnd CLnd CMCN CPMA CWSG EBee EPfP GKir LBuc LRHS MAsh MBlu NBea NEgg NLar SCoo SHBN SLim SMad SPer SSpi WDin WOrn WWes
- - 'Amazing Grace'	CTho LRHS
- Red Fox	see *C. japonicum* 'Rotfuchs'
§ - 'Rotfuchs'	CBcs CEnd CMCN CPMA CTho EBee EPfP GKir LRHS MAsh MBlu MDun MGos NEgg NLar NPal SIFN SLim SMad SSpi WBcn WPGP
- 'Ruby'	CPMA MBlu
I - 'Strawberry'	EBee EPfP MBlu NLar
magnificum	CBcs CDul CEnd CFil CMCN EPfP MBlu NLar SSpi WPGP
- Og 95.144	CFil EPla
- f. ***pendulum***	see *C. japonicum* f. *pendulum*

Cercis (*Caesalpiniaceae*)

canadensis	CAgr CBcs CBrm CDul CHEx CLnd CMCN EMil EPfP GIBF IFro MGos SLim SPer WHCG WMul WNor WPat
- f. ***alba***	LRHS
- - 'Royal White'	EPfP MBlu NLar
- 'Appalachian Red' **new**	MBlu NLar
- 'Covey' **new**	NLar
- 'Flame' **new**	ENot
- 'Forest Pansy' ♀H4	More than 30 suppliers
* - 'Gigantea'	IArd NLar
- 'Lavender Twist' **new**	NLar
§ - var. ***occidentalis***	CAgr LRav NLar SSpi
- 'Pauline Lily' **new**	NLar
- 'Rubye Atkinson'	NLar
chinensis	IFro LRHS NLar SPer SSta WDin WMoo
* - f. ***alba***	CLnd
- 'Avondale'	CBcs CDoC CEnd CPMA CWib EBee EMil EWes IArd LRHS MBlu MGos NEgg NLar SBrw SCoo SLim SMur SPoG SSpi SWvt WPGP
griffithii	IArd NLar
occidentalis	see *C. canadensis* var. *occidentalis*
racemosa	NLar
reniformis 'Oklahoma'	CBcs CPMA EBee IArd MBlu NLar
- 'Texas White'	CBcs CPMA NLar SLim
siliquastrum ♀H4	More than 30 suppliers
- f. ***albida***	CBot CTho ECrN EPfP LRHS SBrw SSpi
- 'Bodnant'	EPfP MBlu NLar
- 'Rubra'	WPat
yunnanensis	IFro

Cercocarpus (*Rosaceae*)

montanus var. ***glaber***	NLar

Cerinthe (*Boraginaceae*)

glabra	NJOw SPlb
major	EUJe WBor WEas WSan
- 'Kiwi Blue'	CHll MDKP
- 'Purpurascens'	More than 30 suppliers
- 'Yellow Gem'	NLar
minor	CSec WGwG
retorta	CSec

Ceropegia (*Asclepiadaceae*)

barklyi	CHal
linearis subsp. ***woodii*** ♀H1	CHal EShb IBlr MBri SRms
pubescens GWJ 9441	WCru

Ceroxylon (*Arecaceae*)

alpinum	CPHo LPJP

Cestrum (*Solanaceae*)

aurantiacum	ERea EShb
x ***cultum***	CHll
- 'Cretan Purple'	CHll CPle EPfP ERea SMur SSpi SUsu
§ ***elegans***	CHEx CHal CHll CPLG CSev EUJe IDee LRHS MOak WCot WDin WWlt
fasciculatum	CBcs SIgm SMad SUsu
'Newellii' ♀H2	CAbb CBcs CHEx CMHG CPLG CSev CWib EBak ELan EPfP ERea SDnm SGar SIgm SSpi WBor WPic WSHC
nocturnum	CBcs CDoC CHal CHll CPLN CPle EBak ERea EShb ESlt LRHS SHBN XPep
parqui ♀H3	CAbb CBcs CHEx CHll CMHG CPLG CPle EBee ECha ELan EPfP ERea EShb MOak SDix SDnm SGar SLon SMad SMrm SMur SUsu SYvo WCot WKif WPic WSHC WWlt XPep
- hybrid	SSpi
- 'Orange Essence'	WCot
psittacinum	CPLG
purpureum misapplied	see *Iochroma cyaneum* 'Trebah'
purpureum (Lindl.) Standl.	see *C. elegans*
roseum	CPLG CSev
- 'Ilnacullin'	CFee CPLG CSec ERea IDee
violaceum misapplied	see *Iochroma cyaneum* 'Trebah'

Ceterach (*Aspleniaceae*)

officinarum	see *Asplenium ceterach*

Chaenomeles (*Rosaceae*)

x ***californica***	CAgr CTho EPfP EPla LEdu SMad WBcn WHer
§ ***japonica***	ECrN ENot MBar NFor WDin WFar XPep
- 'Cido' **new**	NEgg
- 'Orange Beauty'	NEgg WFar WMoo
- 'Sargentii'	CBcs CMac NEgg NLar
'John Pilger'	NPro SLon
lagenaria	see *C. speciosa*
'Madame Butterfly'	COtt GKir SPoG
maulei	see *C. japonica*
sinensis	see *Pseudocydonia sinensis*
§ ***speciosa***	CSam ISea MBar NFor NWea WNor
- 'Apple Blossom'	see *C. speciosa* 'Moerloosei'
- 'Aurora'	LRHS
- 'Brilliant'	EPfP
- 'Contorta'	SPoG
- 'Falconnet Charlet' (d)	MRav
- 'Geisha Girl' ♀H4	More than 30 suppliers

	- 'Grayshott Salmon'	MCCP NCiC NPro WFar WLeb
§	- 'Moerloosei' ♀H4	More than 30 suppliers
	- 'Nivalis'	More than 30 suppliers
	- 'Port Eliot'	WBcn WWeb
	- 'Rosea Plena' (d)	SPoG WBcn
	- 'Rubra Grandiflora'	WBrE
	- 'Simonii' (d)	CBcs EBee EHol ENot EPfP LRHS MGos MRav NEgg NWea WFar
	- 'Snow'	CChe CSBt MRav MSwo MWat NPro WCot
	- 'Umbilicata'	SPer SRms WWes XPep
	- 'Winter Snow'	ENot
	- 'Yukigoten'	LRHS NLar WBcn
	x ***superba***	NFor STre
	- 'Boule de Feu'	CTri CWib ECtt GKir
	- 'Cameo' (d)	CBot CChe ECrN EPfP LAst LRHS MBri MRav SLPl SPoG WWeb
	- 'Coral Sea'	NLon
	- 'Crimson and Gold' ♀H4	More than 30 suppliers
	- 'Elly Mossel'	CBcs CMac CSBt CWib GKir MAsh NBlu SMer WFar
	- 'Fire Dance'	CMac CWib EBee ECrN ECtt ENot IMGH MRav MSwo SPoG
	- 'Hollandia'	MGos
	- 'Issai White'	LRHS WBcn
	- 'Jet Trail'	CBcs CSBt EBee ELan ENot EPfP EWTr LAst LRHS MGos MRav MSwo NBlu NPro SLPl SMac SPoG SSta WFar
	- 'Knap Hill Scarlet' ♀H4	CBrm CDoC EBee ECot EPfP GKir LRHS MAsh MRav NEgg SEND SLim SMac SPer SPoG SRms WDin WFar
	- 'Lemon and Lime'	EBee ELan ENot EPfP MAsh MGos MRav NSti SPer WBcn
	- 'Nicoline' ♀H4	CBcs CDoC EBee EPfP GKir LRHS MAsh MBri MRav NLon NPri SBra SPoG WDin WFar
	- 'Pink Lady' ♀H4	More than 30 suppliers
	- 'Red Joy'	SPoG WBcn
	- 'Red Trail'	ENot MRav
	- 'Rowallane' ♀H4	EBee ECrN ELan ENot EPfP IMGH MRav SHBN WRHF
	- 'Salmon Horizon'	EWTr MGos WBcn
	- 'Texas Scarlet'	WBcn
	- 'Tortuosa'	MBNS SPoG WBcn
	- 'Vermilion'	MAsh MBNS

Chaenorhinum (*Scrophulariaceae*)

§	***origanifolium***	CNic ESis GKev LIck NBlu NEgg NWCA SBch SPlb XPep
	- 'Blue Dream'	CSpe EBee ECtt EMan NArg NBur NPri SPet SPoG SWvt WFar WMoo WPer WWeb
	- 'Summer Skies' **new**	NPri

Chaerophyllum (*Apiaceae*)

	azoricum **new**	SIgm
	hirsutum	CRow ELan
	- 'Roseum'	More than 30 suppliers

Chamaebatiaria (*Rosaceae*)

	millefolium	NLar

Chamaecyparis ✿ (*Cupressaceae*)

	formosensis	CKen
	funebris	see *Cupressus funebris*
	lawsoniana	CDul EHul MBar NWea WBVN WDin WEve WMou
	- 'Albospica' (v)	ECho EHul GKir MBar SBod WFar
	- 'Albospica Nana'	see *C. lawsoniana* 'Nana Albospica'
	- 'Albovariegata' (v)	ECho EHul EOrn LBee LRHS MBar
	- 'Allumii Aurea'	see *C. lawsoniana* 'Alumigold'
	- 'Allumii Magnificent'	CBcs MAsh
§	- 'Alumigold'	CDoC CSBt CWib GKir MAsh MBar MGos SBod SCoo SMer SPoG WDin
	- 'Alumii'	CMac CTri ECrN EHul GKir MAsh MBar NWea SPoG
	- 'Annesleyana' **new**	NEgg
	- 'Argentea'	see *C. lawsoniana* 'Argenteovariegata'
§	- 'Argenteovariegata' (v)	CDoC CMac ECho GKir SLim SPoG
	- 'Aurea'	CDul
I	- 'Aurea Compacta'	ECho
	- 'Aurea Densa' ♀H4	CFee CKen CMac CNic CRob CSBt CTri ECho EHul EOrn EPfP GKir MAsh MBar MGos NEgg SBod SPoG STre WEve WGor
	- 'Aureovariegata' (v)	MBar WBcn
§	- 'Barabits' Globe'	MBar
	- 'Barry's Gold'	EOrn
	- 'Beacon Silver'	WBcn
§	- 'Bleu Nantais'	CKen CMac CRob CSBt EHul EOrn GKir LBee LCon LRHS MAsh MBar MGos MWat SBod SCoo SHBN SLim SPoG WCFE WEve WFar
	- 'Blom'	CKen EHul MBri
§	- 'Blue Gown'	EHul LBee MBar MGos SRms
§	- 'Blue Jacket'	MBar NWea
	- Blue Nantais	see *C. lawsoniana* 'Bleu Nantais'
	- 'Blue Surprise'	CKen EHul EOrn MBar WFar
	- 'Brégéon'	CKen
	- 'Broomhill Gold'	CBrm CDoC CMac CRob CSBt EHul ENot GKir LCon LLin LRHS MAsh MBar MBri MGos MWat SBod SCoo SLim SPer SPla SPoG WCFE WDin WEve
	- 'Buckland Gold'	CDoC
*	- 'Burkwood's Blue'	MBar
	- 'Caudata'	CKen MBar NLar WBcn
	- 'Chantry Gold'	ECho EHul
§	- 'Chilworth Silver' ♀H4	CRob CSBt CTri EHul EOrn EPot GKir LBee LRHS MAsh MBar SBod SCoo SHBN SLim SPer SPoG SRms WBVN WDin WFar
	- 'Chingii'	EHul
	- 'Columnaris'	CBcs CDoC CMac ENot EPfP GKir LBee LRHS MBar MBri MGos NBlu NEgg NWea SCoo SHBN SLim SPoG WCFE WFar
	- 'Columnaris Aurea'	see *C. lawsoniana* 'Golden Spire'
N	- 'Columnaris Glauca'	CSBt CWib EHul EOrn GKir LCon MAsh MGos NEgg SBod SPer WDin WFar WTel
	- 'Crawford's Compact'	CMac
	- 'Cream Crackers'	ECho EHul
	- 'Cream Glow'	CDoC CKen CRob GKir LRHS NLar SCoo SLim SPoG WFar WGor
	- 'Croftway'	EHul
	- 'Dik's Weeping'	CDoC MBri WEve
	- 'Dorset Gold'	CMac
	- 'Duncanii'	EHul
	- 'Dutch Gold'	EHul GKir MAsh
	- 'Dwarf Blue'	see *C. lawsoniana* 'Pick's Dwarf Blue'
	- 'Eclipse'	CKen
	- 'Elegantissima' ambig.	CKen CMac
	- 'Ellwoodii' ♀H4	CMac CSBt CTri CWib EHul ENot EPfP GKir LCon LRHS MAsh MBar MGos NBlu NEgg NWea SBod SCoo SLim SMer SPer SPoG WCFE WDin WFar WMoo WTel
I	- 'Ellwoodii Glauca'	EGra SPlb

	- 'Ellwood's Empire'	EHul LRHS MBri SPoG WEve
	- 'Ellwood's Gold' ♀H4	More than 30 suppliers
	- 'Ellwood's Gold Pillar'	CRob CSBt ECho EHul ENot EOrn GKir LBee LCon MAsh MGos NEgg SCoo SLim SPla SPoG WFar WPat
§	- 'Ellwood's Nymph'	CKen CRob EOrn LLin MAsh MBar SCoo SHBN SLim SPoG WFar WGor
	- Ellwood's Pillar = 'Flolar'	CChe CDoC CKen CMac CRob CSBt EGra EHul EOrn EPfP GKir LBee LCon LRHS MAsh MBar MBri MGos MWat NBlu NEgg SBod SLim SPla SPoG WBrE WCFE WDin WFar
	- 'Ellwood's Pygmy'	CMac ECho GKir MBar
	- 'Ellwood's Silver'	MAsh WFar
	- 'Ellwood's Silver Threads'	CMac EGra GKir
*	- 'Ellwood's Treasure'	ECho
	- 'Ellwood's Variegata'	see *C. lawsoniana* 'Ellwood's White'
§	- 'Ellwood's White' (v)	CKen CMac CSBt EHul EPfP LRHS MBar SHBN WFar WMoo
I	- 'Emerald'	CKen MBar
	- 'Emerald Spire'	CMac MAsh
	- 'Empire'	WFar
	- 'Erecta Argenteovariegata' (v)	WEve
	- 'Erecta Aurea'	ECho EHul LBee LRHS MGos
	- 'Erecta Filiformis'	MBar
§	- 'Erecta Viridis'	CMac GKir MBar NEgg NWea WDin WFar
	- 'Ericoides'	EHul GKir NEgg
	- 'Erika'	MBar
	- 'Filiformis Compacta'	EHul
	- 'Fleckellwood'	CRob CWib ECho EHul GKir MAsh MBar SMer SPoG WEve
	- 'Fletcheri' ♀H4	CBcs CMac CWib EHul GKir LBee LCon LRHS MAsh MBar NWea SBod SHBN SMer SPer SPoG WDin WFar
	- 'Fletcheri Aurea'	see *C. lawsoniana* 'Yellow Transparent'
	- 'Fletcher's White'	ECho EHul LRHS MBar WBcn
	- 'Forsteckensis'	CKen CSli EHul EOrn GKir LLin LRHS MBar NWea SLim SPoG SRms WEve WFar WGor
	- 'Fraseri'	MBar NWea WDin
	- 'Gimbornii' ♀H4	CDoC CMac ECho EHul EOrn GKir LBee LCon MAsh MBar MBri SBod SCoo SLim SPoG SRms WCFE WFar
	- 'Glauca'	CDul
	- 'Glauca Spek'	see *C. lawsoniana* 'Spek'
	- 'Globosa'	MGos
	- 'Globus'	see *C. lawsoniana* 'Barabits' Globe'
	- 'Gnome'	CDoC CMac CRob EHul ENot EOrn GEdr LLin MBar MGos SBod SCoo SLim SPoG
	- 'Gold Flake'	MBar MGos
	- 'Gold Lace' **new**	SPoG
	- 'Gold Splash'	MBar
	- 'Golden King'	MBar NWea
§	- 'Golden Pot'	CBrm CDoC CMac CRob CSBt CWib EGra EHul ENot EOrn GKir LBee LCon LRHS MBar MGos MWat SCoo SMer SPoG WDin WFar
§	- 'Golden Queen'	EHul
	- 'Golden Showers'	EHul
§	- 'Golden Spire'	GKir LRHS MAsh MBar NEgg WFar
	- 'Golden Triumph'	EHul
	- 'Golden Wonder'	CMac EHul LBee LRHS MBar MGos NEgg NWea SCoo SPoG SRms WDin WEve WFar
	- 'Goldfinger'	CDoC
	- 'Grant's Gold'	EHul
	- 'Grayswood Feather'	CDoC CRob CSBt ECho EGra EHul GKir LBee LRHS MAsh MBar MGos SLim SMer WEve
	- 'Grayswood Gold'	EHul EOrn LBee LRHS MBar WEve
	- 'Grayswood Pillar' ♀H4	CDul CMac ECho EHul EOrn GKir LRHS MBar MGos
*	- 'Grayswood Spire'	CMac
	- 'Green Globe'	CDoC CKen CRob CSBt CSli EHul EOrn ESis GKir LBee LCon LLin LRHS MAsh MBar MGos SAga SBod SCoo SLim SPoG WDin WEve
§	- 'Green Hedger' ♀H4	CMac CSBt CTri EHul GKir LBuc MBar NBlu NEgg SBod SRms WFar
§	- 'Green Pillar'	CBrm CRob CSBt CWib LBee LCon LRHS MBar NEgg SHBN SPoG
	- 'Green Spire'	see *C. lawsoniana* 'Green Pillar'
	- 'Greycone'	LRHS
	- 'Hillieri'	MBar
	- 'Hogger's Blue Gown'	see *C. lawsoniana* 'Blue Gown'
	- 'Howarth's Gold'	LRHS MBri
	- 'Ilona'	WBcn
	- 'Imbricata Pendula'	CKen IDee SLim
	- 'Intertexta' ♀H4	EHul WBcn WEve
	- 'Ivonne'	EHul MGos NBlu NEgg SCoo WEve WOrn
	- 'Jackman's Green Hedger'	see *C. lawsoniana* 'Green Hedger'
	- 'Jackman's Variety'	see *C. lawsoniana* 'Green Pillar'
	- 'Kelleriis Gold'	EHul MBar NEgg
	- 'Kilmacurragh' ♀H4	CMac ECho GKir MAsh MBar MGos NWea
	- 'Kilworth Column'	CRob LLin MGos SPoG
	- 'Kingswood'	LRHS MGos WEve
	- 'Knowefieldensis'	CMac EHul ENot LLin WBcn
	- 'Lane' hort.	see *C. lawsoniana* 'Lanei Aurea'
	- 'Lanei'	CSBt CWib LCon MAsh NEgg SCoo WDin
§	- 'Lanei Aurea' ♀H4	CMac ECho EHul GKir MBar MGos NWea WBVN WFar
	- 'Lemon Pillar'	SPoG WBcn WDin WEve WOrn
	- 'Lemon Queen'	CSBt ECho EGra EHul LBee LRHS SPoG WEve WGor
	- 'Limelight'	EHul MGos
	- 'Little Spire' ♀H4	CDoC EOrn GKir LBee LCon LLin LRHS MBar MBri MGos SCoo SLim SPoG WEve WGor
	- 'Lombartsii'	EHul WBcn WFar
	- 'Lutea' ♀H4	CMac ECho EHul MGos NWea SBod
§	- 'Lutea Nana' ♀H4	CMac ECho EHul MAsh MBar MGos NLar
§	- 'Lutea Smithii'	MBar NWea
	- 'Luteocompacta'	LBee LRHS SHBN
	- 'Lycopodioides'	EHul MBar SPoG WBcn
*	- 'MacPenny's Gold'	CMac
	- 'Miki'	WEve
	- 'Milford Blue Jacket'	see *C. lawsoniana* 'Blue Jacket'
§	- 'Minima' (Murray) Parl.	MBar NEgg SRms WCFE
	- 'Minima Argentea'	see *C. lawsoniana* 'Nana Argentea'
	- 'Minima Aurea' ♀H4	More than 30 suppliers
	- 'Minima Densa'	see *C. lawsoniana* 'Minima'
	- 'Minima Glauca' ♀H4	CMac CSBt EHul ENot EPfP GKir LRHS MAsh MBar MGos NEgg NWea SBod SCoo SHBN SLim SPer SPla SPoG WDin WEve WFar
	- 'Moonlight'	MBar MGos
	- 'Moonshine' **new**	SPoG
*	- 'Moonsprite'	LLin LRHS SCoo SLim WEve
	- 'Nana'	MBar
§	- 'Nana Albospica' (v)	CBrm CRob EGra EHul EOrn GKir LBee LCon LRHS MBar SCoo SLim SPoG WFar WGor

§ - 'Nana Argentea' CKen CMac ECho EHul EOrn EPfP WFar WGor
- 'Nana Lutea' see *C. lawsoniana* 'Lutea Nana'
- 'New Silver' SPoG
- 'Nicole' SLim SPoG
- 'Nidiformis' EHul LBee LRHS MBar NWea SCoo SRms
- 'Nyewoods' see *C. lawsoniana* 'Chilworth Silver'
- 'Nymph' see *C. lawsoniana* 'Ellwood's Nymph'
- 'Parsons' CDoC
§ - 'Pelt's Blue' ♀H4 CDoC CKen CSBt EGra EHul ENot LBee LCon LRHS MBar MBri MGos NEgg SCoo SHBN SLim SPoG WDin WFar WOrn
- 'Pembury Blue' ♀H4 CDoC CDul CMHG CMac CSBt CWib ECrN EHul EOrn EPfP GKir LBee LCon LRHS MAsh MBar MGos MWat NWea SBod SCoo SHBN SLim SPer SPoG WDin WFar
- 'Pendula' CDoC MBar
§ - 'Pick's Dwarf Blue' EHul MBar MBri SPoG WGor
- Pot of Gold see *C. lawsoniana* 'Golden Pot'
- 'Pottenii' CMac CSBt ECrN EHul GKir LBee LCon LRHS MAsh MBar MGos NWea SBod SHBN SMer SPoG WDin WEve WFar
- 'Pygmaea Argentea' (v) ♀H4 CKen CMac CWib EGra EHul ENot EOrn EPfP GKir LBee LCon LLin LRHS MAsh MBar MBri MGos NEgg SBod SCoo SLim SPoG SRms WCFE WDin WEve WFar
- 'Pygmy' CNic ECho EHul MBar NLar SCoo SLim
- 'Rijnhof' EHul LBee LLin SLim WBcn
- 'Rogersii' MBar SRms WFar
- 'Romana' MBri NBlu
- 'Royal Gold' ECho EHul EOrn
- 'Silver Queen' (v) CKen MBar NWea WBcn
- 'Silver Threads' (v) CMac CRob EGra EHul GKir LBee LRHS MAsh MBar MWat SBod SPoG WBVN WFar
- 'Silver Tip' (v) EHul SCoo SLim SPoG
- 'Slocock' SHBN
- 'Smithii' see *C. lawsoniana* 'Lutea Smithii'
- 'Snow Flurry' (v) EHul ENot WFar
- 'Snow White'PBR (v) CDoC CRob CSBt EHul ENot GKir LBee LCon LRHS MAsh MBar MBri MGos SCoo SLim SPla SPoG WFar WGor
- 'Somerset' CMac MBar
§ - 'Spek' CBcs MBar
- 'Springtime'PBR CDoC CRob ECho EHul EOrn LBee LCon LRHS MAsh SCoo SLim SPoG WGor
- 'Stardust' ♀H4 CDoC CMac CRob CSBt CTri CWib EHul ENot GKir LCon LRHS MAsh MBar MBri MGos NBlu NEgg SBod SCoo SHBN SLim SMer SPer SPoG WDin WOrn
- 'Stewartii' CDul CMac CTri ENot GKir MBar NBlu NEgg NWea SBod SCoo SHBN SMer
- 'Stilton Cheese' MBar
* - 'Summer Cream' EHul
- 'Summer Snow' (v) CBcs CDoC CDul CMac CRob EHoe EHul ENot EPfP GKir LBee LLin LRHS MAsh MBar MGos NEgg SBod SCoo SLim SPla SRms WEve WFar
- 'Sunkist' SLim WFar
- 'Tamariscifolia' CDoC ECho EHul MBar SBod SPoG WCFE WDin WFar
- 'Tharandtensis Caesia' EOrn MBar WFar
- 'Tilford' EHul
- 'Treasure' (v) CRob CSli EHoe EHul EOrn EPfP LBee LCon LRHS MAsh MBar SCoo SLim SPoG WEve WFar
- 'Triomf van Boskoop' MBar
- 'Van Pelt's Blue' see *C. lawsoniana* 'Pelt's Blue'
- 'Versicolor' (v) MBar
- 'Waterfall' SMad
- 'Westermannii' (v) CMac EHul GKir LCon LLin SBod SCoo SLim WBcn
- 'White Edge' WFar
- 'White Spot' (v) CDoC EHul GKir LBee LRHS MBar MBri NBlu NEgg SLim SPoG WBVN WFar
- 'Winston Churchill' CBcs CDul CSBt GKir MBar MGos NWea SBod
- 'Wisselii' ♀H4 CDoC CKen CMac CRob EGra EHul GKir LBee LCon LLin LRHS MAsh MBar NBlu NWea SBod SRms WDin WFar
- 'Wisselii Nana' CKen EHul
- 'Wissel's Saguaro' CDoC CKen LCon LRHS NLar
- 'Witzeliana' CSBt ECho EOrn LRHS MBar MGos SCoo WOrn
- 'Wyevale Silver' MBar
- 'Yellow Cascade' ECho
- 'Yellow Queen' see *C. lawsoniana* 'Golden Queen'
- 'Yellow Success' see *C. lawsoniana* 'Golden Queen'
§ - 'Yellow Transparent' CMac CSli LBee MBar SBod SHBN SPoG WEve
- 'Yvonne' CRob ECho GKir LLin LRHS MAsh MBar SCoo SLim SPoG WEve

leylandii see x *Cupressocyparis leylandii*

nootkatensis MBar
- 'Aurea' ECrN GKir SCoo WDin WEve
- 'Aureovariegata' (v) EHul SLim WBcn
- 'Compacta' CDul CTri MBar
- 'Glauca' CTho LCon MBar NWea WEve
- 'Gracilis' EHul
- 'Green Arrow' CKen NLar SLim
- 'Jubilee' SCoo SLim
- 'Lutea' CMHG CMac CTri MBar NWea SLim
- 'Nidifera' MBar
- 'Pendula' ♀H4 CDoC CKen ELan EOrn EPfP GKir LCon LLin LRHS MAsh MBar MBri MGos NBlu NWea SLim SPer WCFE WDin WEve WMou WOrn
- 'Strict Weeper' CKen SLim
- 'Variegata' (v) LRHS MBar SLim WBcn

obtusa 'Albospica' (v) ECho EHul
- 'Albovariegata' (v) CKen
- 'Arneson's Compact' CKen
- 'Aurea' CDoC
- 'Aureovariegata' see *C. obtusa* 'Opaal'
- 'Aurora' CKen EOrn LCon SPoG WEve
* - 'Autumn Gold' MBar
- 'Bambi' CKen EOrn LLin MGos NLar WEve
- 'Barkenny' CKen
- 'Bartley' CKen
- 'Bassett' CKen
- 'Bess' CKen
- 'Brigitt' CKen
- 'Buttonball' CKen
- 'Caespitosa' CKen
- 'Chabo-yadori' CDoC EHul EOrn LBee LCon LLin LRHS MBar MGos SCoo SLim SPoG WFar
- 'Chilworth' CKen LCon MBar MGos NLar
- 'Chima-anihiba' CKen

	Name	Suppliers
	- 'Chirimen'	CKen NLar SBla
	- 'Clarke's Seedling'	CDoC NLar
	- 'Confucius'	CRob EHul
	- 'Contorta'	EOrn MBar NLar
§	- 'Coralliformis'	CMac ECho EOrn LLin MBar SMur WBcn
§	- 'Crippsii' ♀H4	CBcs CDoC CMHG CMac ECho EHul EOrn GBin LCon LLin LRHS MBar MGos SBod SCoo SLim SPoG
	- 'Crippsii Aurea'	see *C. obtusa* 'Crippsii'
	- 'Dainty Doll'	CKen EOrn NLar
	- 'Densa'	see *C. obtusa* 'Nana Densa'
	- 'Draht'	CDoC MBar NLar SCoo SLim SPoG WBcn WEve
	- 'Draht Hexe' **new**	CKen
	- 'Elf'	CKen
	- 'Ellie B'	CKen EOrn
	- 'Ericoides'	CKen ECho EOrn
	- 'Erika'	ECho EOrn WBcn
	- 'Fernspray Gold'	CDoC CKen CMac CRob CTri EHul ENot EOrn GKir LCon LLin MAsh MBar NEgg SBod SCoo SLim SPla WFar
	- 'Flabelliformis'	CKen
	- 'Gnome'	CKen
	- 'Gold Fern'	CKen WFar
	- 'Gold Tip' **new**	EOrn
	- 'Golden Fairy'	CKen EOrn WEve
	- 'Golden Filament' (v)	CKen
	- 'Golden Nymph'	CKen EOrn MGos NLar
	- 'Golden Sprite'	CKen MGos NLar WEve
	- 'Goldilocks'	ECho EHul WBcn
	- 'Gracilis Aurea'	CKen
	- 'Graciosa'	see *C. obtusa* 'Loenik'
	- 'Green Diamond'	CKen
	- 'Hage'	CKen EOrn LCon
	- 'Hypnoides Nana'	CKen EOrn
	- 'Intermedia'	CKen EOrn MGos
	- 'Ivan's Column'	CKen
	- 'Junior'	CKen
	- 'Juniperoides'	CKen EOrn
	- 'Juniperoides Compacta'	CKen EPot
	- 'Kamarachiba'	CDoC CKen LCon LLin LRHS MAsh NLar SCoo SLim SPoG WBcn WEve WFar
	- 'Kanaamihiba'	MBar NLar
	- 'Konijn'	EHul EOrn
	- 'Kosteri'	CDoC CKen CMac CRob EHul EOrn LBee LLin MAsh MBar MGos NDlv NEgg SCoo SHBN SLim WEve
	- 'Leprechaun'	NLar
	- 'Little Markey'	CKen EOrn
§	- 'Loenik'	ECho EOrn MBar WBcn
	- 'Lycopodioides'	ECho EOrn
	- 'Lycopodioides Aurea'	SLim
	- 'Marian'	CKen
§	- 'Mariesii' (v)	CKen EHul EOrn LBee SHBN
	- 'Minima'	CKen MGos NEgg SMer
	- 'Nana' ♀H4	CKen CMac CRob ECho LBee LCon LRHS MBar MGos WEve
	- 'Nana Albospica'	ECho
	- 'Nana Aurea' ♀H4	CDoC CMac CRob EHul EOrn EPfP GKir MAsh MBar MGos SHBN SMer SPla WBrE WFar
	- 'Nana Compacta'	EOrn
§	- 'Nana Densa'	CDoC CKen CMac NLar WEve
	- 'Nana Gracilis' ♀H4	CDoC CKen CMen CSBt CSli EHul ENot EOrn EPfP GKir IMGH LCon LLin MAsh MBar MBri MGos NBlu SBod SHBN SLim SMer SPla SPoG STre WDin WEve WFar
I	- 'Nana Gracilis Aurea'	EHul SMur WEve
I	- 'Nana Lutea'	CDoC CKen CRob CSBt EHul EOrn EPfP GKir LBee LCon LLin LRHS MAsh MBar MGos NDlv SBod SCoo SLim SPla SPoG WGer
	- 'Nana Pyramidalis'	ECho
	- 'Nana Rigida'	see *C. obtusa* 'Rigid Dwarf'
	- 'Nana Variegata'	see *C. obtusa* 'Mariesii'
§	- 'Opaal' (v)	MBar WBcn
	- 'Pygmaea'	CNic CSBt EHul EOrn ESis LCon LLin MBar MGos SBod SCoo SLim SPoG WEve
	- 'Pygmaea Aurescens'	MBar NEgg
	- 'Reis Dwarf'	LLin
	- 'Repens'	ECho EOrn WBcn
§	- 'Rigid Dwarf'	CDoC CKen EHul EOrn IMGH LBee LCon LRHS MBar SCoo SPoG WEve
	- 'Saffron Spray' **new**	CKen
*	- 'Saint Andrew'	CKen
	- 'Snowflake' (v)	CDoC CKen CRob EOrn SPoG WBcn WEve WFar WGor
	- 'Snowkist' (v)	CKen
	- 'Spiralis'	CKen ECrN MBar
	- 'Stoneham'	CKen GKir LCon MBar
	- 'Tempelhof'	CKen CSBt EHul EOrn GKir LCon LLin LRHS MAsh MBar MGos NDlv NEgg SBod SCoo SLim WEve
	- 'Tetragona Aurea'	CBcs CBrm CMac ECho EGra EHul EOrn GKir IMGH LCon LLin LRHS MBar MGos SCoo SLim SPer SPoG WEve
	- 'Tonia' (v)	CDoC CKen EHul EOrn MAsh SCoo SLim WEve WGor
	- 'Topsie'	CKen
	- 'Torulosa'	see *C. obtusa* 'Coralliformis'
	- 'Tsatsumi Gold'	CDoC CKen NLar SLim
	- 'Verdon'	CKen
	- 'Winter Gold'	WEve
	- 'Wissel'	CKen EOrn
	- 'Wyckoff'	CKen
	- 'Yellowtip' (v)	CKen EHul MAsh MBar MGos NLar WBcn WEve
	pisifera 'Aurea Nana' misapplied	see *C. pisifera* 'Strathmore'
	- 'Avenue'	EHul
	- 'Baby Blue'	CKen EPfP LLin SCoo SLim WEve
	- 'Blue Globe'	CKen EOrn
	- 'Boulevard' ♀H4	More than 30 suppliers
	- 'Compacta'	ECho EOrn NDlv
	- 'Compacta Variegata' (v)	ECho EHul EOrn MBar NDlv
	- 'Curly Tops'	CRob ECho GTSp LCon LLin MGos SCoo SLim SPoG WBcn WEve WGor
	- 'Devon Cream'	CRob LBee LRHS MAsh MBar NEgg WFar
	- 'Filifera'	CMac CSBt GKir MBar SCoo SLim SPoG WFar
	- 'Filifera Aurea' ♀H4	CKen CMac CSBt CWib EGra EHul EOrn GKir LBee LCon LLin LRHS MAsh MBar NEgg NWea SBod SCoo SPoG SRms WCFE WDin WEve WFar
	- 'Filifera Aureovariegata' (v)	CMac EHul LLin MBar SCoo SLim SPoG
	- 'Filifera Nana'	EHul EOrn GKir MBar NDlv SLim SPoG STre WDin WFar
	- 'Filifera Sungold'	see *C. pisifera* 'Sungold'
	- 'Fuiri-tsukomo'	CKen
*	- 'Gold Cascade'	MGos
	- 'Gold Cushion'	CKen
	- 'Gold Dust'	see *C. pisifera* 'Plumosa Aurea'
	- 'Gold Spangle'	EHul EOrn MBar NEgg SBod WFar
	- 'Golden Mop' ♀H4	CKen ECho EHul MAsh NDlv
	- 'Green Pincushion'	CKen

	- 'Hime-himuro'	CKen
	- 'Hime-sawara'	CKen EOrn
	- 'Margaret'	CKen
	- 'Nana'	CKen EHul EPfP ESis LLin MAsh MBar NDlv SBod SMer WFar
I	- 'Nana Albovariegata' (v)	CDoC CNic ECho EOrn LLin LRHS MAsh MBar SPoG WFar
§	- 'Nana Aureovariegata' (v)	CDoC CMac CRob CSBt EGra EHul IMGH LBee LCon LLin LRHS MAsh MBar NDlv NEgg SCoo SLim SPoG WEve WFar
I	- 'Nana Compacta'	CMac SRms
	- 'Nana Variegata' (v)	ECho LBee LRHS MBar SCoo SLim WFar
I	- 'Parslorii'	CKen
	- 'Pici'	CKen
	- 'Plumosa Albopicta' (v)	ECho MBar
§	- 'Plumosa Aurea'	CKen EHul GKir MBar NWea WDin WFar
	- 'Plumosa Aurea Compacta'	CKen CMac NDlv
I	- 'Plumosa Aurea Compacta Variegata' (v)	CMac NEgg
	- 'Plumosa Aurea Nana'	CRob MAsh MBar MGos NDlv SMer WFar
I	- 'Plumosa Aurea Nana Compacta'	CMac
	- 'Plumosa Aurescens'	CDoC CMac
§	- 'Plumosa Compressa'	CDoC CFee CKen CRob ECho EHul EOrn ESis LBee LCon MBar NDlv NEgg SCoo SLim SPoG WFar WGor
	- 'Plumosa Densa'	see *C. pisifera* 'Plumosa Compressa'
	- 'Plumosa Flavescens'	EHul LRHS MBar NDlv SCoo
I	- 'Plumosa Juniperoides'	CKen EHul EOrn LLin MBar NDlv SLim WFar WGor
	- 'Plumosa Purple Dome'	see *C. pisifera* 'Purple Dome'
I	- 'Plumosa Pygmaea'	ECho MGos NDlv WGor
§	- 'Plumosa Rogersii'	CRob EHul EOrn LRHS MBar SBod WGor
	- 'Pompom' **new**	CRob
§	- 'Purple Dome'	CRob ECho EHul EOrn MBar
	- 'Rogersii'	see *C. pisifera* 'Plumosa Rogersii'
	- 'Silver and Gold' (v)	EHul MBar
	- 'Silver Lode' (v)	CKen EOrn
	- 'Snow' (v)	CKen CMac EOrn MBar SMer
	- 'Snowflake'	CKen EHul
	- 'Spaan's Cannon Ball'	CKen
§	- 'Squarrosa'	MBar WDin WFar
	- 'Squarrosa Dumosa'	CKen EHul MBar
I	- 'Squarrosa Dwarf Blue' **new**	SPoG
	- 'Squarrosa Intermedia'	EHul MBar
I	- 'Squarrosa Lombarts'	CMac CSBt ECho EHul EOrn LBee MBar
	- 'Squarrosa Lutea'	CKen MAsh MBar
	- 'Squarrosa Sulphurea'	CSBt EGra EHul EOrn EPfP LBee LCon LRHS MAsh MBar NEgg SLim SPla STre WBVN WDin WFar
	- 'Squarrosa Veitchii'	see *C. pisifera* 'Squarrosa'
§	- 'Strathmore'	CKen EHul LLin MBar WDin
§	- 'Sungold'	CDoC CKen CRob CSBt CTri EGra EHul ENot LCon LLin LRHS MAsh MBar NBlu NDlv NEgg NWea SBod SCoo SLim SPla SPoG WEve
	- 'Tama-himuro'	CKen WBcn
*	- 'Tsukibeni'	WBcn
*	- 'White Brocade'	CMac
	- 'White Pygmy'	EOrn
	thyoides 'Andelyensis'	CMac CRob CSBt ECho EHul EOrn GKir LLin MBar NDlv SCoo SPoG WEve WFar
	- 'Andelyensis Nana'	CKen
	- 'Aurea'	EHul MBar WBcn
	- 'Conica'	CKen MAsh
	- 'Ericoides' ♀H4	CDoC CKen CMac CRob CTri ECho ECrN EHul EOrn GKir LBee LLin MBar MWat SBod SPlb SPoG WDin WEve WFar
§	- 'Glauca'	EOrn
	- 'Kewensis'	see *C. thyoides* 'Glauca'
	- 'Little Jamie'	CKen
	- 'Red Star'	see *C. thyoides* 'Rubicon'
§	- 'Rubicon'	CKen CMac CRob CSBt EHul ENot EOrn EPfP LBee LCon LLin LRHS MAsh MBar MGos NDlv NEgg SLim SPla SPoG WEve WFar WGer
	- 'Schumaker's Blue Dwarf'	WBcn
	- 'Top Point'	CDoC CRob ENot EOrn LBee LCon MAsh SCoo SLim SPoG WEve
	- 'Variegata' (v)	ECho EHul MBar
	- 'Winter Wonder'	EHul SPoG

Chamaecytisus (*Papilionaceae*)

§	***albus***	GKir GQui SPer WDin
§	***hirsutus***	CFil WPGP WWeb
	palmensis **new**	CSec
	prolifer	CPLG
§	***purpureus***	CWCL EGra ELan EPfP GKir MAsh MBar MRav MSwo NBlu NWea SHBN SPer WBVN WDin WFar WPat
	- f. ***albus***	CBcs EPfP MBar SHBN SPer WBcn
§	- 'Atropurpureus' ♀H4	CBcs LAst SPer WTel
	- 'Incarnatus'	see *C. purpureus* 'Atropurpureus'
	- 'Lilac Lady'	MAsh
§	***supinus***	CPLG SRms

Chamaedaphne (*Ericaceae*)

§	***calyculata***	CBcs GIBF LRHS LTwo SPer WSHC
	- 'Angustifolia' **new**	NLar
	- 'Nana'	CBcs CMHG EBee MBar NLar SPer

Chamaedorea (*Arecaceae*)

	elegans ♀H1	MBri
	glaucifolia	WMul
	metallica misapplied	see *C. microspadix*
	metallica O.F. Cook ex H.E. Moore ♀H1	EAmu SBig
§	***microspadix***	CPHo CRoM GTrC EExo LPJP WMul
	oblongata **new**	WCot
	radicalis	CBrP CPHo EAmu EExo LPJP WMul

Chamaemelum (*Asteraceae*)

§	***nobile***	CArn CHby CHrt CPrp CSev CWan EDAr ELau EPfP GBar GKir GMac GPoy IHMH MBow MBri MHer NGdn NJOw SPlb SRms WJek WPer WSel WWye
	- dwarf	GBar
	- dwarf, double-flowered (d)	GBar NLRH
	- 'Flore Pleno' (d)	CBre CMea CPrp CSev ECha EDAr ELau EOHP EPfP GBar GPoy MBri MHer MRav NBro NCot NDov NGHP NGdn NWCA SIde SRms WFar WGwG WHal WJek WPer XPep
	- 'Treneague'	More than 30 suppliers

Chamaenerion see *Chamerion*

Chamaepericlymenum see *Cornus*

Chamaerops (*Arecaceae*)

excelsa misapplied	see *Trachycarpus fortunei*
excelsa Thunb.	see *Rhapis excelsa*
humilis ♀H3	CAbb CBcs CBrP CFil CHEx CRoM CTbh CTrC CWSG EBee EPfP EUJe LPJP LRHS MJnS NBlu NMoo NPal NScw SAPC SAin SArc SChr SEND SPlb SPoG WGer WMul WPGP XPep
§ - var. ***argentea***	CBrP CPHo CTrC EAmu EExo LPJP NPal WMul
- var. ***cerifera***	see *C. humilis* var. *argentea*
- 'Vulcano'	EAmu MBri MGos WMul

Chamaespartium see *Genista*

Chamaesphacos (*Lamiaceae*)

ilicifolius misapplied	see *Siphocranion macranthum*

Chamelaucium (*Myrtaceae*)

uncinatum	EShb ESlt

Chamerion (*Onagraceae*)

§ ***angustifolium***	GBar GWCH SPer
- 'Album'	More than 30 suppliers
- 'Isobel'	CSpe MLLN MRav WAbb WCot
- 'Stahl Rose'	CAby CBot CHid CMea CPom EBee EPPr EWes LPhx MWat SMrm SSpi WPGP WSHC
dodonaei	ELan EMan MAnH MLLN MTho NEgg WEas WFar WMoo
fleischeri	CNic

Chasmanthe (*Iridaceae*)

aethiopica	CPou GGar SYvo
bicolor	CPou CStu WCot WHil
floribunda	CHEx ERea LRHS WCot
- var. ***duckittii***	EBee ECho EPfP LRHS WCot WPGP

Chasmanthium (*Poaceae*)

§ ***latifolium***	More than 30 suppliers

Cheilanthes (*Adiantaceae*)

argentea	CLAP WAbe WRic
distans	SRms
eatonii	WAbe
- f. ***castanea*** **new**	WAbe
eckloniana **new**	WAbe
lanosa	CLAP EBee EWes SRms WCot
lindheimeri	WCot
myriophylla	WAbe
§ ***nivea***	WAbe
sieberi **new**	WAbe
siliquosa NNS 00-83	WCot
sinuata	CLAP
tomentosa	CLAP SRms WAbe WCot WRic

Cheiranthus see *Erysimum*

Cheiridopsis (*Aizoaceae*)

derenbergiana	EMan WCot

Chelidonium (*Papaveraceae*)

japonicum	see *Hylomecon japonica*
majus	CArn CRWN GPoy MChe MGol MHer MSal WCHb WHer WShi WWye
- 'Chedglow' (v) **new**	CNat
- 'Flore Pleno' (d)	CBre EBee EMag MGol NBro WBor WCHb WCot WHer
- var. ***laciniatum***	EMon GBar NSti WCot
- 'Laciniatum Flore Pleno' (d)	EMar IBlr

Chelone (*Scrophulariaceae*)

barbata	see *Penstemon barbatus*
§ ***glabra***	More than 30 suppliers
- 'Black Ace'	SSpi
lyonii	EChP LAst LEdu MBow NGdn NLar NRnb SBri SHFr WCAu WMoo WPer WSan WShi
- 'Hot Lips'	WCot
obliqua	More than 30 suppliers
- var. ***alba***	see *C. glabra*
- 'Forncett Foremost'	GQui
- 'Ieniemienie'	EMon
- 'Pink Sensation'	EBee
* - ***rosea***	CHar EBee LRHS MMHG WGwG

Chelonopsis (*Lamiaceae*)

longipes **new**	CPom
moschata	CDes CPom EBee ECha EMan MHar NGby WCot WDyG WMoo WPGP
yagiharana	CAby CBod CFai CFir EBee EWTr GGar LPio MBri MCCP MDKP MMHG NBid NLar NSti SMrm WHil WPnP

Chenopodium (*Chenopodiaceae*)

ambrosioides	EUnu WJek
bonus-henricus	CAgr CArn CBod CHby CWan EUnu GBar GPoy GWCH ILis LRHS MChe MHer NTHB SIde WCHb WHer WSel WWye
botrys	MSal
giganteum	ILis WJek
nuttaliae **new**	EUnu

cherimoya see *Annona cherimola*

cherry, duke see *Prunus* x *gondouinii*

cherry, sour or morello see *Prunus cerasus*

cherry, sweet see *Prunus avium*

chervil see *Anthriscus cerefolium*

chestnut, sweet see *Castanea*

Chiastophyllum (*Crassulaceae*)

§ ***oppositifolium*** ♀H4	More than 30 suppliers
- 'Frosted Jade'	see *C. oppositifolium* 'Jim's Pride'
§ - 'Jim's Pride' (v)	More than 30 suppliers
simplicifolium	see *C. oppositifolium*

Chiliotrichum (*Asteraceae*)

diffusum	CWib GAbr GGar GKir GSki
- 'Siska'	CBcs IArd SMad WCot WWes

Chimaphila (*Ericaceae*)

maculata	SSpi

Chimonanthus (*Calycanthaceae*)

fragrans	see *C. praecox*
§ ***praecox***	More than 30 suppliers
- 'Brockhill Goldleaf' **new**	SBra
* - 'Fragrance'	ERea

- 'Grandiflorus' ♀H4 — CEnd ENot EPfP MBri SPoG SSta WPat
- var. ***luteus*** ♀H4 — CEnd CPMA ECrN ELan ENot EPfP LPio MBri MRav SPer SSta
- 'Trenython' — CEnd
yunnanensis — NLar

Chimonobambusa (*Poaceae*)

falcata — see *Drepanostachyum falcatum*
hejiangensis — EPla
hookeriana — see *Himalayacalamus falconeri* 'Damarapa'
macrophylla f. ***intermedia*** — EPla
§ ***marmorea*** — CAbb CFil EPla ERod MMoz NMoo SBig WDyG WJun WMul WPGP
- 'Variegata' (v) — CFil EFul EPla ERod SLPl WJun WPGP
§ ***quadrangularis*** — CBcs CDoC CFil CHEx EFul EPfP EPla ERod LEdu MAsh MMoz MWht NMoo SBig WJun WPGP
- 'Nagaminea' (v) — EPla
- 'Suow' (v) — CFil EPla WPGP
- 'Tatejima' new — EPla
§ ***tumidissinoda*** — CAbb CFil CMCo EPla ERod MMoz SBig WDyG WJun WPGP

Chinese chives see *Allium tuberosum*

Chiogenes see *Gaultheria*

Chionanthus (*Oleaceae*)

foveolatus new — EShb
retusus — CBcs CMCN EPfP IDee MPkF NLar SBrw SLon SSpi WDin
virginicus — CBcs CDoC CDul CEnd CFil CMCN CPMA ELan EPfP EWTr GKir IArd IDee IMGH LRHS MBlu MBri SBrw SMad SPer SSpi SSta WDin WHCG WOrn WPGP

Chionochloa (*Poaceae*)

conspicua — CBig CFil CKno EBee EChP EKen EMan EWsh GCal GFor GIBF GKev GSki LEdu MAnH MWhi NBir NFor NOGN WHer WPGP WWpP WWye
- subsp. ***conspicua*** — GGar WCot
- subsp. ***cunninghamii*** — CPLG
- 'Rubra' — see *C. rubra*
flavescens — EBee EHoe EPza GSki
flavicans — CAby CBrm CKno CTrC EChP EMan EWsh GFor MAnH SMad SMar
pallens new — CBig GKev
rigida — LEdu
§ ***rubra*** — More than 30 suppliers
- subsp. ***cuprea*** — GBin GGar GKev

Chionodoxa ✿ (*Hyacinthaceae*)

§ ***forbesii*** — CBro CMea CNic EPfP EPot LRHS NBir NJOw NLon SPer SRms WHer WPer WPnP WShi WWpP
- 'Alba' — ECho LAma
- 'Blue Giant' — CFwr EPot LRHS WDav
- 'Rosea' — LAma
- Siehei Group — see *C. siehei*
gigantea — see *C. luciliae* Gigantea Group
luciliae misapplied — see *C. forbesii*
luciliae Boiss. ♀H4 — CAvo CBro EPfP EPot LAma MBri
- 'Alba' — CBro CFwr CRez EBrs ECho LPhx LRHS SPer WLin
§ - Gigantea Group — ECho ELan EPot LAma LPhx NJOw
- - 'Alba' — EPot GCrs
'Pink Giant' — CAvo CBro CFwr EBrs EPfP EPot GFlt LAma LRHS MAvo MMHG WCot WDav WHil
sardensis ♀H4 — CBro ECho EPot LAma LRHS MMHG WLin WRHF WShi
§ ***siehei*** ♀H4 — CBro
'Valentine Day' — EPot

Chionographis (*Melanthiaceae*)

japonica — EFEx WCru

Chionohebe (*Scrophulariaceae*)

armstrongii — EPot ITim
§ ***densifolia*** — EPot GAbr GCrs ITim NLAp
pulvinaris — GCrs ITim NLAp NSla

x *Chionoscilla* (*Hyacinthaceae*)

§ ***allenii*** — ECho EPot

Chirita (*Gesneriaceae*)

'Aiko' — LRHS WDib
'Chastity' — LRHS WDib
'Diane Marie' — LRHS WDib
dielsii new — CFir
heterotricha — LRHS WDib
'Keiko' — LRHS WDib
* ***latifolia*** x ***linearifolia*** new — WDib
linearifolia — LRHS WDib
linearifolia x ***sinensis*** — EShb LRHS WDib
longgangensis — LRHS WDib
'New York' — LRHS WDib
sinensis ♀H1 — CHal LRHS WDib
- 'Hisako' — LRHS WDib
'Stardust' — LRHS WDib
tamiana — LRHS WDib

x *Chitalpa* (*Bignoniaceae*)

tashkentensis — CBcs CEnd CMCN EBee EPfP IMGH MBlu MWya NLar SCoo WPGP XPep
- 'Summer Bells' — CDoC LRHS

chives see *Allium schoenoprasum*

Chlidanthus (*Amaryllidaceae*)

fragrans — CStu ECho

Chloranthus (*Chloranthaceae*)

fortunei — CLAP LEdu SBla WCot WCru
henryi — SSpi
japonicus — CLAP SSpi WCru
oldhamii — CLAP LEdu SSpi
- B&SWJ 2019 — WCru WPrP
serratus — CLAP WCru

Chloris (*Poaceae*)

distichophylla — see *Eustachys distichophylla*
virgata — CWCL

Chlorogalum (*Hyacinthaceae*)

pomeridianum — WCot

Chlorophytum (*Anthericaceae*)

bowkeri new — EShb
comosum — EShb SEND
- 'Mandanum' (v) — CHal
- 'Variegatum' (v) ♀H1+3 — CHal LRHS MBri SRms
- 'Vittatum' (v) ♀H1+3 — CHEx EShb SRms SWal
intermedium B&SWJ 6447 — WCru
krookianum — CFir WCot
macrophyllum — EShb
§ ***majus*** — WCot

nepalense WCot
- B&SWJ 2393 WCru

Choisya (*Rutaceae*)

'Aztec Pearl' ♀H4 More than 30 suppliers
dumosa var. ***arizonica*** SIgm SLon
- var. ***mollis*** SLon
Goldfingers = 'Limo'PBR More than 30 suppliers
ternata ♀H4 More than 30 suppliers
- 'Brica'PBR see *C. ternata* Sundance = 'Lich'
- Moonshine = 'Walcho'PBR EBee LRHS NLar SPoG
- MoonsleeperPBR see *C. ternata* Sundance = 'Lich'
§ - Sundance = 'Lich'PBR ♀H3 More than 30 suppliers

Chondropetalum (*Restionaceae*)

hookerianum **new** CFil
mucronatum CBig CCtw CTrC EAmu
tectorum More than 30 suppliers

Chondrosum (*Poaceae*)

gracile see *Bouteloua gracilis*

Chonemorpha (*Apocynaceae*)

fragrans **new** CPLN

Chordospartium (*Papilionaceae*)

muritai ECou
- 'Huia Gilpen' ECou
- 'Ron Feron' ECou
- 'Wayne Nichols' ECou
stevensonii CPle ECou EPfP NLar SMad WBVN WSHC
- 'Duncan' ECou
- 'Kiwi' ECou
- 'Miller' ECou

Chordospartium x *Corallospartium* (*Papilionaceae*)

C. stevensonii x ***Corallospartium*** **new** ECou
- x ***C. crassicaule***, 'Coral Spears' **new** ECou

Chorisia (*Bombacaceae*)

speciosa EAmu WMul

Chorizema (*Papilionaceae*)

cordatum ♀H1 CSec ECou
dicksonii CSec
diversifolium ERea
ilicifolium CAbb CSPN CSec ERea SBra

Chronanthus see *Cytisus*

Chrysalidocarpus see *Dypsis*

Chrysanthemopsis see *Rhodanthemum*

Chrysanthemum ✿ (*Asteraceae*)

'Alec Bedser' (25a) WWol
'Alehmer Rote' (29Rub) EMon
'Alex Young' (25b) WWol
'Alexandra' NHal WWol
'Allouise' (25b) ♀H3 NHal WWol
alpinum see *Leucanthemopsis alpina*
'Amber Gigantic' (1) NHal WIvo
'Amber Matlock' (24b) NHal
'Anastasia'PBR (28) CHid ECtt EMon EPPr GMac MNrw MRav NMRc NSti SChu SRms WCot WFar WPer WRHF
N 'Anastasia Variegated' (28/v) EMon
'Anastasia White' (28) WCot WIvy
'Anne, Lady Brocket' EMon EWsh GBuc MNrw
'Annie Lea' (25b) NHal
'Apollo' (29K) EMon EWll LPhx
'Apricot' (29Rub) CPrp EBee EChP EPPr GKir MNrw MRav
'Apricot Chessington' (25a) NHal
'Apricot Courtier' (24a) NHal
'Apricot Enbee Wedding' (29d) see *C.* 'Bronze Enbee Wedding'
'Apricot Harry Gee' (1) WIvo
arcticum L. see *Arctanthemum arcticum*
argenteum see *Tanacetum argenteum*
'Arona Gran' (25b) NHal
'Astro' NHal
'Autumn Days' (25b) NHal
'Balcombe Perfection' (5a) NHal WWol
balsamita see *Tanacetum balsamita*
Barbara = 'Yobarbara'PBR (22) EPfP NHal
'Beacon' (5a) ♀H2 NHal
'Beppie' (29e) WWol
'Beppie Bronze' (29) WWol
'Beppie Purple' (29) WWol
'Beppie Red' (29) WWol
'Beppie Yellow' (29) WWol
'Bernadette Wade' (23a) NHal
Beth = 'Yobeth'PBR (22c) WWol
'Bethanie Joy' (25b) **new** WWol
'Big Wheel'PBR (22) LAst
'Bill Wade' (25a) NHal
* 'Billy Bell' (25a) NHal WWol
'Blenda' CHrt
'Bo-peep' (28) EMon
'Boulou Pink' **new** WWol
'Boulou White' **new** WWol
Bravo = 'Yobra'PBR (22c) ♀H3 EPfP NHal
* 'Breitner's Supreme' MNrw WCAu
'Brennpunkt' WMnd
'Brierton Terry' (7b) **new** WWol
'Bright Eye' (28) WMnd WPer WWol
'Brightness' (29K) SChu SUsu
'Bronze Beauty' (25b) WFar
'Bronze Cassandra' (5b) ♀H2 NHal
'Bronze Dee Gem' (29c) NHal
§ 'Bronze Elegance' (28b) CSam EBee EMon ENot MLLN NBir NGdn NSti SPla SRms WEas WIvy WMnd
§ 'Bronze Enbee Wedding' (29d) ♀H3 NHal
'Bronze Margaret' (29c) ♀H3 NHal
'Bronze Matlock' (24b) NHal
'Bronze Max Riley' (23b) ♀H3 NHal
'Bronze Mayford Perfection' (5a) ♀H2 NHal WWol
'Bronze Mei-kyo' see *C.* 'Bronze Elegance'
'Bruera' (24b) NHal
'Bryan Kirk' (4b) WWol
'Carlene Welby' (25b) NHal
'Carmine Blush' (29Rub) EBee MNrw WCot
I 'Cassandra' (5b) ♀H2 NHal
'Cawthorne' (29d) WWol
'Cerise Mayford Perfection' WWol
'Cezanne' WWol
'Cherry Chessington' (25a) NHal
'Cherry Margaret' (29c) NHal
'Chessington' (25a) NHal

	Name	Suppliers
	'Chesterfield' (13b)	WWol
	'Christopher Lawson' (24b)	NHal
	cinerariifolium	see *Tanacetum cinerariifolium*
	'Clapham Delight' (23a)	NHal
	'Clara Curtis' (29Rub)	More than 30 suppliers
	coccineum	see *Tanacetum coccineum*
	'Conjora' (22c)	LAst WWol
	'Constable'PBR **new**	WWol
	'Contralto' (22)	WCot
	'Copper Margaret' (29c)	CHrt
	'Cornetto' (25b)	NHal
	'Corngold' (5b)	NHal
	corymbosum	see *Tanacetum corymbosum*
	'Cossack' (2)	WWol
	'Cottage Apricot'	CHea EChP EWoo MBNS MNrw WEas
	'Cottage Pink'	see *C.* 'Emperor of China'
	'Cottage Yellow'	MSte WCot WHoo
	'Courtier' (24a)	NHal
	'Cream Duke of Kent' (1)	WIvo
	'Cream Jessie Habgood' (1)	WIvo
	'Cream Margaret' (29c) ♀H3	NHal
	'Cream Patricia Millar' (14b)	NHal
	'Creamist' (25b) ♀H3	WWol
	'Crimson Gala'PBR	WWol
	Dana = 'Yodana' (25b) ♀H3	NHal
	'Daniel Cooper' (29Rub)	MNrw
	'Dark Red Mayford Perfection' (4b) ♀H2	WWol
	'Darlington Anniversary' (25b)	WWol
	'Darren Pugh' (3b)	NHal WWol
	'David McNamara' (3b)	WWol
	Debonair = 'Yodebo'PBR (22c) ♀H3	EPfP
	'Dee Gem' (29c) ♀H3	NHal
	'Delta Dark Cerise'	WWol
	'Delta Orange' (29)	WWol
*	'Delta Pink' (29)	WWol
	'Delta Rose' (29c)	WWol
*	'Delta White' (29)	WWol
	'Delta Yellow' (29)	WWol
§	'Doctor Tom Parr' (28)	ELan EMon IGor LPhx SUsu WPtf
	'Doreen Statham' (4b)	NHal
	'Dorothy Stone' (25b)	NHal
	'Dorridge Beauty' (24a)	WWol
	'Dorridge Crystal' (24a)	NHal WWol
	'Dorridge Vulcan' (23b)	WWol
	'Duchess of Edinburgh' (30)	CPrp CSam EBee EBrs EChP ECtt ELan EMon GKir LRHS MBri MRav MTis NCGa SSvw WCAu
	'Duke of Kent' (1)	NHal WIvo
	'Ed Hodgson' (25a)	NHal
	'Edelgard'	WWhi
	'Edelweiss' (29K)	EMon GMac WCot
	'Egret' (23b)	NHal
	'Elaine Johnson' (3b)	NHal
	'Elegance' (9c)	WWol
	'Elegance Yellow' (9e)	WWol
	'Elizabeth Burton' (5a)	WWol
	'Elizabeth Lawson' (5b)	NHal
	'Elizabeth Shoesmith' (1)	NHal WIvo
	'Ellen' (29c)	CHrt NHal
*	'Emma Jane' (25a)	WWol
§	'Emperor of China' (29Rub)	CAby CElw CSam EChP ECha EMon ENot EPPr GCal IGor LPhx LRHS MNrw MRav MSte NCGa SChu SSvw WBor WCAu WCot WFar WMnd
	'Enbee Wedding' (29d) ♀H3	NHal
	Ernst	WWol
	'Esther' (29Rub)	EMon
*	'Evesham Vale' (24b)	WWol
	'Fieldfare' (22)	NHal
	'Firecracker'PBR (22)	WWol
	'Fitton's Reward' (1)	WIvo
	foeniculaceum hort.	see *Argyranthemum foeniculaceum* misapplied
	foeniculaceum (Willd.) Desf.	see *Argyranthemum foeniculaceum* (Willd.) Webb & Sch.Bip.
	'Foxtrot'PBR	LAst
	'Fred Shoesmith' (5a)	WWol
	frutescens	see *Argyranthemum frutescens*
	'Gala'PBR (22)	LAst
	'Gambit' (24a)	NHal
	'Geof Brady' (5a)	NHal WWol
	'George Griffiths' (24b) ♀H3	NHal
	'Gigantic' (1)	WIvo
	'Gladys' (24b)	EBee EChP ELan EWoo
	'Gladys Emerson' (3b)	NHal
	'Glen Kelly' (2) **new**	WWol
	'Gold John Wingfield' (14b)	NHal
§	'Gold Margaret' (29c) ♀H3	NHal
	'Golden Cassandra' (5b) ♀H2	NHal
	'Golden Courtier' (24a)	NHal
	'Golden Gigantic' (1)	NHal WIvo
	'Golden Lady' (3b) **new**	WWol
	'Golden Margaret'	see *C.* 'Gold Margaret'
	'Golden Mayford Perfection' (5a) ♀H2	NHal WWol
	'Golden Plover' (22)	NHal
	'Golden Seal' (7b)	EMon GBuc
	'Goldengreenheart' (29Rub)	MNrw
	'Gompie Bronze'	NHal
I	'Gompie Rose'	NHal
	'Goodlife Sombrero' (29a) ♀H3	NHal
	'Grace Wade' (25b)	NHal WWol
§	***grandiflorum***	SRms
	'Green Boy' (10b)	WWol
*	'Green Envy' (10b)	WWol
	'Green Nightingale' (10)	WWol
	'Green Satin' (5b)	WWol
	'Hanenburg'	NHal WWol
*	'Happy Days' (15b)	WWol
	haradjanii	see *Tanacetum haradjanii*
	'Harold Lawson' (5a)	NHal
	'Harry Gee' (1)	NHal WIvo WWol
	'Harry Woolman' (3b)	NHal
	'Hazy Days' (25b)	NHal
	'Heather James' (3b)	NHal
	'Heide' (29c) ♀H3	NHal
	'Helen Gravestock' (4a)	WWol
	'Herbstrubin'	IGor
	'Hesketh Knight' (5b)	NHal
	'Hilda Veal' **new**	WIvo
	'Holbein'PBR (22) **new**	WWol
	Holly = 'Yoholly' (22b) ♀H3	NHal
	'Honey Enbee Wedding' (29d)	NHal
	'Horningsea Pink' (19d)	WBor
	hosmariense	see *Rhodanthemum hosmariense*
	'Innocence' (29Rub)	CSam EChP ELan EMon IGor MNrw MRav NCGa NGdn NSti SPla
*	'Iris Morris' (4b)	WWol

'Ivor Mace' (1) WIvo
'Jan Horton' (3b) WWol
'Janice'PBR (7a) LAst
'Jante Wells' (28) EMon WEas WTel
'Jessie Cooper' see *C.* 'Mrs Jessie Cooper'
'Jessie Habgood' (1) WIvo
'Jimmy Motram' (1) WIvo
'John Harrison' (25b) NHal
'John Hughes' (3b) NHal
'John Wingfield' (14b) NHal
'Julia' (28) GMac
'Julie Lagravère' (28) EMon WPtf WWhi
'Kay Woolman' (13b) NHal WWol
'Kenneth Roy' (15a) NHal
x ***koreanum*** see *C. grandiflorum*
'Lady in Pink' (29Rub) GBuc
'Lakelanders' (3b) NHal
'Lameet' (29) WWol
'Lancashire Fold' (1) WIvo
'Lancashire Lad' (1) WIvo
'Laser' (24b) WWol
'Laureate' WWol
'Le Bonheur Red' NHal WWol
'Leading Lady' (25b) WWol
'Lemon Margaret' (29c) ♀H3 NHal
'Leo' (28) EMon
leucanthemum see *Leucanthemum vulgare*
'Lilac Chessington' (25a) NHal
Linda = 'Lindayo'PBR (22c) WWol
'Lizzie Dear' (25b) NHal
'Long Island Beauty' (6b) ♀H2 WTel
'Lorna Wood' (13b) NHal
'Lucy' (29a) NHal
'Lundy' (2) NHal
'Luv Purple' NHal
'Lynn Johnson' (15a) NHal
Lynn = 'Yolynn'PBR (22c) ♀H3 NHal
macrophyllum see *Tanacetum macrophyllum*
'Malcolm Perkins' (25a) NHal
'Malcolm Sargeant' (23b) **new** WWol
'Mancetta Comet' (29a) NHal
'Mandarin' (5b) NCGa
maresii see *Rhodanthemum hosmariense*
'Margaret' (29c) ♀H3 NHal
'Margaret Howells' (5a) **new** WWol
'Marion Hayselden' (25a) **new** WWol
'Mark Woolman' (1) NHal WIvo
'Mary Stoker' (29Rub) CElw CPrp CSam EBee EBrs EChP ECha ECtt ELan EMon GBri GMac LRHS MBri MNrw MRav MSte MTis MWgw NCGa NSti SSvw STes SUsu WAul WBor WCAu WEas WFar WHoo
'Matador' (14a) NHal
'Matlock' (24b) NHal
mawii see *Rhodanthemum gayanum*
'Max Riley' (23b) ♀H3 NHal
maximum misapplied see *Leucanthemum* x *superbum*
maximum Ramond see *Leucanthemum maximum* (Ramond) DC.
'Maxine Johnson' (25b) NHal
'May Shoesmith' (5a) ♀H2 NHal
'Mayford Perfection' (5a) ♀H2 NHal
'Megan Woolman' (3b) WWol
'Mei-kyo' (28b) CMea EBee EMon IGor LBBr MLLN MRav MWgw SPla SRms WBor WFar
'Membury' (24b) NHal
'Mermaid Yellow' LAst
'Michelle Preston' (13b) NHal
'Migoli' WWol
'Millennium' (25b) **new** NHal
'Minstreel Dark' (9) WWol
'Minstreel Red' (9) **new** WWol
'Minstreel Soft Pink' (9) **new** WWol
'Miral White' WWol
'Moonlight' (29d/K) MRav
morifolium SSpi
§ 'Mrs Jessie Cooper' (29Rub) CAby ELan GMac MNrw MSte NBir SChu SSvw WCot WHoo WHrl WTin
'Mrs Jessie Cooper No.1' MSph WTin
'Mrs Jessie Cooper No.2' **new** WTin
'Music' (23b) NHal
'Myss Goldie' (29c) NHal
'Nancy Perry' (19Rub) CSam ELan EMon MNrw MRav SChu SSvw
§ ***nankingense*** WFar
'Nantyderry Sunshine' (28b) ♀H4 CSam EBee ENot LBBr LRHS MNrw MWgw SPla WCot WDyG WEas WMnd WPer WRha
'Nell Gwyn' (29Rub) MNrw
'Netherhall Moonlight' EMon LPhx
Nicole = 'Yonicole'PBR (22c) ♀H3 NHal
nipponicum see *Nipponanthemum nipponicum*
'Orange Allouise' (25b) NHal WWol
'Orange Enbee Wedding' (29d) NHal
'Oury' EMon
pacificum see *Ajania pacifica*
'Pandion' WWol
'Parkfield Tigger' (29c) NHal
parthenium see *Tanacetum parthenium*
'Pat Davison' (25b) NHal
'Paul Boissier' (30Rub) EMon LPhx MAnH NSti WMnd
'Payton Dale' (29c) ♀H3 NHal
'Payton Glow' (29c) NBir
'Payton Toffee' (29c) **new** NHal
'Peach Courtier' (24a) NHal
'Peach Enbee Wedding' (29d) ♀H3 NHal
'Peach John Wingfield' (14b) NHal
'Pearl Celebration' (24a) NHal
'Peggy Anne' (1) WIvo
'Pennine Bullion' NHal WWol
I 'Pennine Coconut' (29) WWol
'Pennine Digger' (29c) WWol
'Pennine Drift' NHal WWol
'Pennine Eagle' (29c) WWol
'Pennine Gift' (29c) NHal
'Pennine Ginger' (29c) ♀H3 NHal
'Pennine Goal' (29c) ♀H3 WWol
'Pennine Grant' WWol
'Pennine Jane' WWol
'Pennine Marie' (29a) ♀H3 NHal
'Pennine Oriel' (29a) ♀H3 NHal
'Pennine Pageant' (29d) NHal
'Pennine Passion' (29c) WWol
'Pennine Perfecta' (29d) WWol
'Pennine Pilot' WWol
'Pennine Point' WWol
'Pennine Polo' (29d) ♀H3 NHal WWol
'Pennine Port' WWol
'Pennine Ranger' (29d) NHal

Cultivar	Suppliers
'Pennine Romeo' (19c)	NHal
'Pennine Splash' (29d)	NHal
'Pennine Sunlight' (19d)	WWol
'Pennine Swan' (29c)	NHal
'Pennine Toy'	NHal WWol
'Pennine Volcano'	WWol
'Perry's Peach'	MNrw NPer SUsu
'Peter Rowe' (23b)	NHal
'Peterkin'	ECtt EMon GMac MNrw MWgw
'Phil Houghton' (1)	WIvo WWol
'Pink Duke' (1)	NHal
'Pink Duke of Kent' (1)	WIvo
'Pink John Wingfield' (14b)	NHal
'Pink Progression'	GMac MWgw NBir
'Pink Spider' (10a) **new**	WWol
'Polar Gem' (3a)	NHal
'Polaris' (9c)	EWII
* 'Pompon Bronze' (28)	WWol
* 'Pompon Pink' (28)	WWol
* 'Pompon Purple' (28)	WWol
* 'Pompon Yellow' (28)	WWol
'Primrose Allouise' (24b) 🏆H3	NHal
'Primrose Chessington' (25a)	NHal
'Primrose Courtier'	see *C.* 'Yellow Courtier'
'Primrose Dorothy Stone' (25b)	NHal
'Primrose Dorridge Crystal' (24a)	NHal
'Primrose Enbee Wedding' (29d) 🏆H3	NHal
'Primrose Jessie Habgood' (1)	WIvo
'Primrose John Hughes' (3b)	NHal
'Primrose Mayford Perfection' (5a) 🏆H2	NHal WWol
'Primrose West Bromwich' (14a)	NHal
'Promise' (25a)	NHal
'Purleigh White' (28b)	GMac MNrw NSti SPla WBor WRha
'Purple Chempak Rose' (14b)	NHal
'Purple Glow' (5a)	NHal
'Purple Margaret' (29c)	NHal
Radiant Lynn = 'Radiant Yolynn'PBR (22c)	NHal WWol
'Ralph Lambert' (1)	NHal WIvo
'Raquel' (29K)	EPfP
'Red Balcombe Perfection' (5a)	NHal WWol
'Red Bella' (29c)	NBir
'Red Pennine Gift' (29c)	NHal
'Red Regal Mist' (25b)	WWol
'Red Shirley Model' (3a)	NHal
'Red Wendy' (29c) 🏆H3	CHrt
'Regal Mist' (25b)	WWol
'Regalia' (24b) 🏆H3	WWol
'Rehange'	EMon
'Rene Green' (25b)	WWol
'Revert'PBR	WWol
'Riley's Dynasty' (14a)	NHal
'Rita McMahon' (29d)	NHal
Robin = 'Yorobi'PBR (22c)	NHal
'Romantika'	GMac
'Romany' (2)	CElw WEas
'Rose Enbee Wedding' (29d)	NHal
'Rose Mayford Perfection' (5a) 🏆H2	NHal WWol
'Rose Patricia Millar' (14b)	NHal
Rose Pink Debonair = 'Rosepink Yodebo'PBR (22c)	LAst
roseum	see *Tanacetum coccineum*
'Royal Command' (29Rub)	EMon MNrw
'Rubaiyat'	WWol
rubellum	see *C. zawadskii*
'Ruby Enbee Wedding' (29d) 🏆H3	NHal
'Ruby Mound' (29c/K)	CAby LPhx LRHS MNrw WEas
'Ruby Raynor' (29Rub)	MNrw
'Rumpelstilzchen'	CMdw CMea EBee MNrw WPer
'Salmon Allouise' (25b)	NHal
'Salmon Chessington' (25a)	NHal
'Salmon Enbee Wedding' (29d) 🏆H3	NHal
'Salmon Harry Gee' (1)	WIvo
'Sam Vinter' (5a)	NHal
'Sarah Louise' (25b)	NHal
'Sarah's Yellow'	CSam
Shelley = 'Yoshelley' (22b)	WWol
'Shepherd'PBR	WWol
'Shirley Primrose' (1)	NHal WIvo
'Silver Gigantic' (1)	WIvo
sinense	see *C. morifolium*
'Skylark' (22a)	NPri
'Smokey' (29)	NHal
Soft Lynn = 'Soft Yolynn' (22c)	NHal
'Sonnenschein'	EWTr
'Sophie Elizabeth' (24a)	NHal
'Southway Shiraz' (29d)	NHal
'Southway Snoopy' (29d)	NHal
'Southway Spree' (29d)	NHal
'Southway Stomp' (29d)	NHal
'Southway Strontium' (29d)	NHal
'Spartan Fire'	WWol
'Spartan Glory' (25b)	WWol
'Spartan Leo' (29c)	WWol
'Spartan Linnet'	WWol
'Spartan Moon' (25b)	WWol
'Spartan Raspberry' (29d) **new**	WWol
'Spartan Seagull'	WWol
'Spartan Star' (29d) **new**	WWol
'Spartan Sunrise' (29c)	WWol
'Spartan Torch'	WWol
'Stockton' (3b) 🏆H2	NHal
'Streamer' ambig.	WWol
Sundoro = 'Yosun' (22d)	NHal
Sunny Linda = 'Sunny Lindayo' (22c) 🏆H3	WWol
Sunny Robin = 'Sunny Yorobin'PBR	WWol
'Sutton White' (25a)	WWol
'Swansong' (24a) **new**	WWol
'Syllabub'PBR	LAst
'Taiga White'	WWol
'Tapestry Rose' (29K)	CMea EChP EMon IGor MNrw
Target = 'Yotarget' (22)	NHal
'Thoroughbred' (24a)	NHal WWol
'Tightrope'PBR 🏆H3	WWol
'Tom Parr'	see *C.* 'Doctor Tom Parr'
'Tom Snowball' (3b)	NHal
'Tracy Waller' (24b)	NHal
'Trapeze'	WWol
'Turner' 🏆H3 **new**	WWol
uliginosum	see *Leucanthemella serotina*
'Uri' **new**	LPhx
'Vagabond Prince'	CSam MSte WHoo
'Venice' (24b)	NHal

'Wedding Day' (29K)	EMon EWin GBuc MNrw WCAu WTin
'Wedding Sunshine' (29K)	LRHS
welwitschii	see *Glebionis segetum*
'Wembley' (24b)	NHal
'West Bromwich' (14a)	NHal
'Westland Regal'	WWol
§ ***weyrichii***	EBee ECtt GKev MTho NJOw NWCA SBla SPet SPoG SRms
'Whitby' (5b)	NHal
'White Allouise' (25b) ♀H3	NHal
'White Beppie' (29e)	WWol
'White Bouquet' (28)	WWol
'White Cassandra' (5b)	NHal
'White Enbee Wedding' (29d)	NHal
'White Gloss' (29K)	LRHS
'White Lancashire Fold' (1)	WIvo
'White Margaret' (29c) ♀H3	NHal
'White Pearl Celebration' (24a) **new**	ENot
'White Skylark' (22)	NHal
'White Spider' (10a)	WWol
'White Tower'	MNrw
'Windermere' (24a)	NHal
'Winning's Red' (29Rub)	EMon LPhx MNrw MSph SMad
'Woolman's Century' (1)	WWol
'Woolman's Prince' (3a)	WWol
'Woolman's Star' (3a)	NHal
'Woolman's Venture' (4b)	NHal
'Yellow Allouise' (25b)	NHal
'Yellow Beppie' (29e)	WWol
§ 'Yellow Courtier' (24a)	NHal
'Yellow Duke of Kent' (1)	WIvo
'Yellow Egret' (23b)	NHal
'Yellow Ellen' (29c)	NHal
'Yellow Fred Shoesmith' (5a)	WWol
'Yellow Hazy Days' (25b)	NHal
'Yellow Heide' (29c) ♀H3	NHal
'Yellow John Hughes' (3b) ♀H2	NHal
'Yellow John Wingfield' (14b)	NHal
'Yellow Margaret' (29c) ♀H3	NHal
'Yellow May Shoesmith' (5a)	NHal
'Yellow Mayford Perfection' (5a) ♀H2	NHal
'Yellow Pennine Oriel' (29a) ♀H3	NHal
'Yellow Phil Houghton' (1)	WIvo WWol
'Yellow Ralph Lambert' (1)	NHal WIvo
'Yellow Whitby' (5b)	NHal
§ ***yezoense*** ♀H4	CSam CStu EBee ELan WEas
- 'Roseum'	CSam NSti WBor
§ ***zawadskii***	EWTr NCGa NWCA WFar

Chrysocoma (*Asteraceae*)

ciliata JJH 9401633	NWCA
coma-aurea	EMan NWCA

Chrysogonum (*Asteraceae*)

virginianum	CHal CMea EBee EBrs ECha EMan EMar EShb EWes LRHS MAvo MRav SBch SPer SPet WFar WMoo

Chrysopogon (*Poaceae*)

gryllus	CBig CBrm EBee GCal GFor SApp WPGP

Chrysopsis (*Asteraceae*)

mariana	EMon WOld
villosa	see *Heterotheca villosa*

Chrysosplenium (*Saxifragaceae*)

alternifolium	EMFW ESis IHMH MCCP
davidianum	CBre CPLG CSam EBee ECha EMan EPot GEdr GFlt GKev ITer LSpr MNFA NBir NSla WBor WCot WCru WGer WMoo WPrP WPtf
- SBEC 231	NWoo
forrestii **new**	GKev
lanuginosum var. ***formosanum*** B&SWJ 6979	WCru
macrophyllum	WCru
macrostemon	EPot
var. ***shiobarense***	
- - B&SWJ 6173	WCru
oppositifolium	EBee WHer WShi

Chrysothemis (*Gesneriaceae*)

pulchella ♀H1	CHal

Chusquea ✿ (*Poaceae*)

breviglumis hort.	see *C. culeou* 'Tenuis'
coronalis	WJun
culeou ♀H4	More than 30 suppliers
- 'Breviglumis'	see *C. culeou* 'Tenuis'
§ - 'Tenuis'	CFil EPla ERod WJun WNor
cumingii	WJun
gigantea	CFil EPla MMoz SBig WMul
macrostachya	CFil EPla WPGP
montana	CFil EPla
pittieri	WJun
quila	CFil MMoz
ramosissima	CFil
sulcata	WJun
uliginosa	WJun
valdiviensis	WJun

Cicerbita (*Asteraceae*)

sp.	ECtt
B&SWJ 5162	WCru
B&SWJ 6588	WCru
BWJ 7891 from China	WCru
§ ***alpina***	GFlt MSph NBid NLar SGar SPlb WBWf WRos
macrorhiza B&SWJ 2970	WCru
plumieri	EMan WCot WFar WPtf WRos
- 'Blott' (v)	LSpr

Cichorium (*Asteraceae*)

intybus	More than 30 suppliers
- f. ***album***	CBod CPrp EBee EBla EChP ECha ECrN EMag EMan EPfP GMac LRHS MRav NGdn NSti SPoG WCAu WCHb WHil
- 'Roseum'	CBod CBot CHad CPrp CSpe EBee EBla ECGP EChP ECha ECot ELan EMag EPfP EVFa GFlt GMac LRHS MBow MRav NGdn SPer SPoG WCAu WCHb

Cimicifuga see *Actaea*

americana	see *Actaea podocarpa*
foetida	see *Actaea cimicifuga*
ramosa	see *Actaea simplex* 'Prichard's Giant'
rubifolia	see *Actaea cordifolia*

Cineraria (Asteraceae)

	maritima	see *Senecio cineraria*
	saxifraga	EShb

Cinnamomum (Lauraceae)

	camphora	CBcs CHEx ERea
	japonicum	CFil WPGP
	micranthum	CFil WPGP

Cionura (Asclepiadaceae)

	oreophila	CPLN GCal WPGP WSHC

Circaea (Onagraceae)

	lutetiana	MSal WHer WShi
	- 'Caveat Emptor' (v)	CHid EBee EMan EMon NBid WCot WHer WHil

Cirsium (Asteraceae)

	acaule	NBre
	diacantha	see *Ptilostemon diacantha*
	dissectum	WBWf
	eriophorum	NLar WBWf
	falconeri	NBur
	helenioides	see *C. heterophyllum*
§	***heterophyllum***	CPom EChP EMan EMon GBri LDai MNFA NBre NBur NEgg NLar SHar SUsu WCot WPGP WTin
	japonicum 'Early Pink Beauty'	LDai
	- 'Pink Beauty'	CMHG NEgg
	- 'Rose Beauty'	EBrs GBin LRHS MBri NBlu SPur
	kamtschaticum **new**	GIBF
	'Mount Etna' **new**	EBla EMar LRHS
	oleraceum	LEdu NBid NLar
	palustre	WBWf
	purpuratum	EMan EVFa MNrw WCot WPGP
	- JCA 4.192.500	CDes
	rivulare 'Atropurpureum'	More than 30 suppliers

Cissus (Vitaceae)

	adenopoda **new**	CPLN
	antarctica 🏆H1	CTrC LRHS MBri
	discolor	CHal CPLN EShb
	pedata B&SWJ 2371	WCru
	rhombifolia 🏆H1	MBri
	- 'Ellen Danica' 🏆H1	CHal LRHS
§	***striata***	CBcs CDoC CDul CHEx CPLG CTrC EMil EPla EShb IMGH LRHS MRav SBra SLim SWvt WCru WSHC WWeb

Cistus ✿ (Cistaceae)

	x ***aguilarii***	CBcs CChe CPLG CSBt CTri EPfP SIgm WSHC XPep
	- 'Maculatus' 🏆H3	CDoC CHar CSam EBee ELan EPfP GGar GKir LRHS LSRN MAsh MSwo NCGa SDys SLPl SLdr SPer SPla SPoG WAbe WBrE WCFE WGer WHCG WKif WWeb XPep
	albanicus	see *C. sintenisii*
	albidus	CArn CFil EGoo SSpi XPep
	- f. ***albus***	XPep
	algarvensis	see *Halimium ocymoides*
	'Ann Baker'	SLPl SUsu WAbe XPep
	'Anne Palmer'	see *C.* x *fernandesiae* 'Anne Palmer'
	x ***argenteus*** 'Blushing Peggy Sammons'	CDoC CSBt LPhx LSRN MAsh WSPU XPep
	- Golden Treasure = 'Nepond' (v)	EBee ENot EPfP MGos SLim
	- 'Paper Moon'	LSRN XPep
§	- 'Peggy Sammons' 🏆H3	CBot CDoC CSLe CSam EBee ECha EGra ELan ENot EPfP GKir IMGH LRHS LSRN MRav NSti SIgm SLim SMer SPer SPoG SWvt WBor WBrE WFar WHar WSHC WTel XPep
	- 'Silver Ghost'	CDoC XPep
	- 'Silver Pink' ambig.	More than 30 suppliers
	- 'Stripey'	XPep
	atriplicifolius	see *Halimium atriplicifolium*
	'Blanche'	see *C. ladanifer* 'Blanche'
	x ***bornetianus*** 'Jester'	CSBt SHop SPla WAbe XPep
	'Candy Stripe' (v)	MBNS WBcn
	x ***canescens***	XPep
	- f. ***albus***	CWib SIgm WEas WHCG WKif XPep
	'Chelsea Pink'	see *C.* 'Grayswood Pink'
	chinamadensis	XPep
	x ***chnoodophyllus***	XPep
	x ***clausonis***	XPep
§	***clusii***	CHar MAsh SPla XPep
	- subsp. ***multiflorus***	XPep
	x ***corbariensis***	see *C.* x *hybridus*
	creticus	CDoC LAst MWgw NBlu SGar SPoG WBVN
	- subsp. ***corsicus***	XPep
	- subsp. ***creticus***	CFil CMHG CTrC EBee ELan EPfP LRHS MBri MSte SCoo SPer WAbe WBcn WGer XPep
	- - f. ***albus***	XPep
§	- - - 'Tania Compton'	WAbe
*	- - 'Ano Moulia'	XPep
*	- - 'Bali'	XPep
	- - 'Lasithi'	WAbe
	- subsp. ***eriocephalus***	XPep
*	- - 'Michel Valantin'	XPep
	- subsp. ***incanus***	WHCG
	- var. ***tauricus***	XPep
	x ***crispatus***	XPep
§	- 'Warley Rose'	EWTr NSti SHBN SHop SIgm WKif WWeb XPep
	crispus misapplied	see *C.* x *pulverulentus*
§	***crispus*** L.	EGoo SIgm WEas XPep
	- 'Prostratus'	see *C. crispus* L.
	- 'Sunset'	see *C.* x *pulverulentus* 'Sunset'
§	x ***cyprius*** 🏆H4	CArn CBrm CDul EBee ECrN ECtt ELan EPfP MGos MRav MWat SDix SEND SHBN SLPl SRms WBrE WDin WFar WWeb XPep
	- f. ***albiflorus***	MSte WBcn XPep
	- var. ***ellipticus*** f. ***bicolor***	XPep
	- - 'Elma' 🏆H3	CMHG ELan EPfP LRHS MAsh SIgm SPla WEas WGer WHCG WPGP XPep
§	x ***dansereaui***	CHar CMHG CSam CWib EBee ECrN ENot EPfP MRav MSte WFar WWpP XPep
	- 'Albiflorus'	see *C.* x *dansereaui* 'Portmeirion'
	- 'Decumbens' 🏆H4	CBrm CMHG CTrC CTri ELan ENot EPfP LSRN MAsh MBNS MDun MRav MSwo MWgw NCGa NFor NLon SArc SCoo SHBN SIgm SMer SPer SPla SPoG WAbe WDin WGer WHCG XPep
	- 'Jenkyn Place'	CDoC EBee MBNS MBri SIgm SLPl SPoG SUsu WBor XPep
	- 'Little Gem'	LRHS XPep
§	- 'Portmeirion'	WFar XPep
	x ***dubius***	XPep
	x ***escartianus***	XPep
	x ***fernandesiae***	XPep
§	- 'Anne Palmer'	CDoC EPfP LSRN SIgm WAbe WFar
	x ***florentinus*** misapplied	see x *Halimiocistus* 'Ingwersenii'
§	x ***florentinus*** Lam.	CAbP CHar SChu XPep
*	- 'Béziers'	XPep

	- 'Fontfroide'	WAbe WWeb
*	- 'Tramontane'	XPep
	formosus	see *Halimium lasianthum* subsp. *formosum*
	x ***gardianus***	XPep
	'Gordon Cooper'	WAbe XPep
§	'Grayswood Pink' ♀H4	More than 30 suppliers
	x ***heterocalyx*** 'Chelsea Bonnet'	CFai CFil EBee MSte SCoo SIgm SLim WBrE WPGP WPen WWeb XPep
	heterophyllus	XPep
	hirsutus Lam. 1786	see *C. inflatus*
	- var. ***psilosepalus***	see *C. inflatus*
	x ***hybridus***	More than 30 suppliers
*	- 'Donadieu'	XPep
	- Gold Prize (v)	MBri
	incanus	see *C. creticus* subsp. *incanus*
§	***inflatus***	CPLG EBee NWoo SEND WHar WHer XPep
	ingwerseniana	see x *Halimiocistus* 'Ingwersenii'
	'Jessamy Beauty'	SHop SLPl SUsu WAbe WBcn XPep
	'Jessamy Bride'	SLPl XPep
	'Jessamy Charm'	XPep
	'John Hardy'	NLar
	ladanifer misapplied	see *C.* x *cyprius*
	ladanifer L. ♀H3	CDoC CFil CSBt CTri ECha ECrN ELan EPfP EWTr IMGH LEdu LRHS MRav MSal MSwo NEgg NLon SChu SECG SGar SPer WEas WFar WHar WSHC WTel XPep
	- var. ***albiflorus***	CBcs SSpi XPep
*	- - 'Bashful'	XPep
§	- 'Blanche'	LRHS SHop SIgm WKif XPep
§	- 'Paladin'	SHop XPep
	- Palhinhae Group	see *C. ladanifer* var. *sulcatus*
	- 'Pat'	ELan EPfP LRHS MAsh
	- var. ***petiolatus***	XPep
	- - f. ***immaculatus***	XPep
§	- var. ***sulcatus***	CDoC CHar CPle EWTr LRHS MSte WFar
	- - f. ***bicolor***	SPoG XPep
	- - f. ***latifolius***	XPep
	- var. ***tangerinus***	XPep
	lasianthus	see *Halimium lasianthum*
	laurifolius ♀H4	CDoC CFil CHar EBee ENot EPfP LPio MGos MNrw MRav NBir NEgg NSti SLPl SLon SPer SPoG WHar WOut XPep
	- subsp. ***atlanticus***	XPep
§	x ***laxus*** 'Snow White'	CAbP CDoC EPfP LRHS MDun MSte NLon NPer NPro NSti SChu SLPl SLim SLon SPer SPoG SSpi SUsu WKif WLeb XPep
	x ***ledon***	SLPl WWeb XPep
	libanotis	CHar CPle NLon XPep
	x ***longifolius***	see *C.* x *nigricans*
	x ***loretii*** misapplied	see *C.* x *dansereaui*
	x ***loretii*** Rouy & Foucaud	see *C.* x *stenophyllus*
	x ***lucasii***	XPep
	x ***lusitanicus*** Maund	see *C.* x *dansereaui*
	'May Snow' **new**	MBNS
	'Merrist Wood Cream'	see x *Halimiocistus wintonensis* 'Merrist Wood Cream'
	x ***mesoensis***	XPep
	monspeliensis	CAbP CPle EBee EPfP GGar LPio LRHS SPer SSpi WFar XPep
	- CMBS 62	WPGP
	- 'Densifolius'	XPep
	- 'Vicar's Mead'	CDoC MBNS SPla SPoG XPep
	munbyi	XPep
§	x ***nigricans***	EBee EWin SLPl WCot XPep
	x ***oblongifolius***	XPep
	- 'Barr Common'	LRHS
	x ***obtusifolius*** misapplied	see *C.* x *nigricans*
	x ***obtusifolius*** Sweet	CAbP EPfP EWes MAsh SLPl WEas XPep
	- 'Thrive'	MBri SCoo
	ochreatus	see *C. symphytifolius* subsp. *leucophyllus*
	ocymoides	see *Halimium ocymoides*
	osbeckiifolius	SIgm XPep
	'Paladin'	see *C. ladanifer* 'Paladin'
	palhinhae	see *C. ladanifer* var. *sulcatus*
	parviflorus misapplied	see *C.* 'Grayswood Pink'
	parviflorus Lam.	CBot NSti SChu WCFE WSHC XPep
	x ***pauranthus***	XPep
*	- 'Natacha'	XPep
	'Peggy Sammons'	see *C.* x *argenteus* 'Peggy Sammons'
	x ***penarcleusensis***	XPep
	x ***picardianus***	XPep
	x ***platysepalus***	LPhx SHop SLPl XPep
	populifolius	CBot CBrd CMHG ECha GKev LTwo SPer WAbe WHer WPGP
	- var. ***lasiocalyx***	see *C. populifolius* subsp. *major*
§	- subsp. ***major*** ♀H3	CPle EPfP LSRN XPep
	- subsp. ***populifolius***	XPep
	pouzolzii	XPep
	psilosepalus	see *C. inflatus*
§	x ***pulverulentus***	CDul CPLG CTri EBee ECha EPfP MMHG MWgw SChu WAbe WDin WSHC
*	- Delilei Group	XPep
*	- - 'Fiona'	XPep
§	- 'Sunset' ♀H3	More than 30 suppliers
	- 'Warley Rose'	see *C.* x *crispatus* 'Warley Rose'
§	x ***purpureus*** ♀H3	More than 30 suppliers
	- 'Alan Fradd'	CBcs CTbh EBee ENot EPfP LRHS LSRN MAsh MDun MGos MSwo MWgw SCoo SEND SLim SMrm SPla SPoG WFar WGer XPep
	- var. ***argenteus*** f. ***stictus***	WAbe WSPU XPep
	- 'Betty Taudevin'	see *C.* x *purpureus*
	- var. ***holorhodos***	XPep
	x ***ralletii***	XPep
	- f. ***subcreticus***	XPep
	x ***rodiaei*** 'Jessica'	CDoC NLar WAbe WSPU XPep
	rosmarinifolius	see *C. clusii*
	'Ruby Cluster'	CDoC WLeb XPep
	sahucii	see x *Halimiocistus sahucii*
	salviifolius	CAbP CArn CPle EMil ISea LRHS NWCA SSpi WCFE WFar WHCG WWeb XPep
	- 'Avalanche'	CRez MAsh MRav NPro WAbe
	- 'Gold Star'	SPoG XPep
*	- 'Ivoire'	XPep
	- 'Prostratus'	ELan LPhx LRHS SPoG WHCG WPGP
*	- 'Sirocco'	XPep
*	- 'Villeveyrac'	XPep
	salviifolius x ***monspeliensis***	see *C.* x *florentinus*
	x ***sammonsii*** 'Ida'	XPep
	'Silver Pink' misapplied	see *C.* 'Grayswood Pink'
§	***sintenisii***	XPep
	x ***skanbergii*** ♀H3	CBcs CHar CSBt CSLe CTri CWib EBee ELan ENot EPfP LRHS MGos MRav MWat NBir SCoo SDix SHBN SIgm SPer SPla SPoG WEas WFar WLin XPep
*	- 'Akamas'	XPep
§	'Snow Fire' ♀H4	CAbP CDoC CSBt ENot EPfP LRHS MAsh MBri NPro SCoo SHop SIgm SLPl SPla SPoG SSpi SUsu WAbe WGer WLeb WSPU XPep
§	x ***stenophyllus***	CWib EBee EGra SPer XPep

- var. ***albiflorus***	XPep
* - - 'Mistral'	XPep
* - 'Elise'	XPep
symphytifolius	CSLe WPGP XPep
§ - subsp. ***leucophyllus***	XPep
- - MSF 98.019	WPGP
'Tania Compton'	see *C. creticus* subsp. *creticus* f. *albus* 'Tania Compton'
x ***tephreus***	XPep
'Thrive'	see *C.* x *obtusifolius* 'Thrive'
tomentosus	see *Helianthemum nummularium* subsp. *tomentosum*
x ***verguinii***	EWin LRHS SIgm XPep
- f. ***albiflorus***	XPep
- var. ***albiflorus*** misapplied	see *C.* x *dansereaui* 'Portmeirion'
* - 'Salabert'	XPep
villosus	see *C. creticus* subsp. *creticus*
wintonensis	see x *Halimiocistus wintonensis*

Citharexylum (*Verbenaceae*)

spicatum	CPLG CPle

x *Citrofortunella* (*Rutaceae*)

floridana 'Eustis' (F)	ERea
- 'Lakeland' (F)	ERea
ichangquat **new**	EZes
§ ***microcarpa*** (F) ♀H1	CDoC CTbh EPfP ERea MBri WBVN WMul
§ - 'Tiger' (v/F) ♀H1	EPfP ERea
- 'Variegata'	see x *C. microcarpa* 'Tiger'
mitis	see x *C. microcarpa*
swinglei 'Tavares' (F)	ERea

citron see *Citrus medica*

x *Citroncirus* (*Rutaceae*)

citandarin	MJnS
citremon	EZes MJnS
'Curafora' **new**	EZes
US119	EZes MJnS
'Venasca' **new**	EZes
webberi 'Morton'	EZes MJnS
- 'Rusk'	MJnS

Citrullus (*Cucurbitaceae*)

colocynthis	CArn

Citrus ✿ (*Rutaceae*)

amblycarpa Djeruk lime (F)	ERea
aurantiifolia Indian lime (F)	ERea
- key lime (F)	CDoC
aurantium 'Bouquet de Fleurs'	ERea
- var. ***myrtifolia*** 'Chinotto' (F)	ERea
- 'Seville' (F)	ERea
- 'Willowleaf' (F)	SPer
bergamia bergamot	CKob ERea
calamondin	see x *Citrofortunella microcarpa*
deliciosa	see *C.* x *nobilis*
hystrix **new**	CKob ERea
Ichang lemon (F)	EZes MJnS
ichangensis (F)	EZes
japonica	see *Fortunella japonica*
junos	EZes
kumquat	see *Fortunella margarita*
'La Valette'	CKob EPfP ERea ESlt
latifolia (F/S)	CWSG EPfP ERea ESlt SPer
limettoides (F)	CArn
limon (F)	CHEx WMul
- 'Fino' (F)	EPfP
§ - 'Garey's Eureka' (F)	CDoC CKob CWSG EPfP ERea
- 'Imperial' (F)	ERea
- 'Lemonade' (F)	ERea
- 'Lisbon' (F)	ERea
- 'Quatre Saisons'	see *C. limon* 'Garey's Eureka'
- 'Toscana'	CWSG EPfP ERea
- 'Variegata' (F/v) ♀H1	ERea
- 'Villa Franca' (F)	ERea
x ***limonia*** 'Rangpur' (F)	ERea
madurensis	see *Fortunella japonica*
maxima (F)	ERea
medica 'Cidro Digitado'	see *C. medica* var. *digitata*
§ - var. ***digitata*** (F)	CKob ERea ESlt
- 'Ethrog' (F)	ERea ESlt
- var. ***sarcodactylis***	see *C. medica* var. *digitata*
§ x ***meyeri***	CHEx CWSG MJnS
- 'Meyer' (F) ♀H1	CBcs CKob CWSG EPfP ERea ESlt GTwe LRHS MJnS SPer
microcarpa Philippine lime	see x *Citrofortunella microcarpa*
mitis	see x *Citrofortunella microcarpa*
§ x ***nobilis*** (F)	CWSG
- 'Blida' (F)	ERea
- 'Ellendale' (F)	EPfP
- 'Murcott' (F)	EPfP ERea
- Ortanique Group (F)	EPfP
- 'Silver Hill Owari' (F)	ERea
- Tangor Group (F)	ERea
x ***paradisi*** 'Foster' (F)	ERea
- 'Golden Special' (F)	ERea
- 'Star Ruby' (F/S)	ERea ESlt
'Ponderosa' (F)	ERea
reticulata (F)	CWSG SArc WMul
- Mandarin Group (F)	CBcs CDoC
- - 'Clementine' (F)	CDoC ERea
- - 'De Nules' (F/S)	ESlt
- - 'Encore' (F)	ERea
- - 'Fortune' (F)	ESlt
- 'Miyagawa'	ERea
- Satsuma Group	see *C. unshiu*
- 'Variegata' (F/v) **new**	WMul
sinensis (F)	ERea SAPC SArc WMul
- 'Egg' (F)	ERea
- 'Embiguo' (F)	ERea
- 'Harwood Late' (F)	ERea
- 'Jaffa'	see *C. sinensis* 'Shamouti'
- 'Lane Late' (F)	EPfP
- 'Malta Blood' (F)	ERea ESlt
- 'Moro Blood' (F)	ERea
- 'Navelina' (F/S)	CDoC ERea ESlt
- 'Parson Brown' (F)	ERea
- 'Prata' (F)	ERea
- 'Ruby' (F)	ERea
- 'Saint Michael' (F)	ERea
- 'Sanguinelli' (F)	ERea
§ - 'Shamouti' (F)	ERea
- 'Thomson' (F)	ERea
- 'Valencia' (F)	CWSG ECot ERea
- 'Valencia Late' (F)	ERea ESlt
- 'Washington' (F/S)	ERea GTwe
x ***tangelo*** 'Seminole' (F)	ERea
§ ***unshiu*** (F)	ERea
- 'Clausellina' (F/S)	ERea ESlt
volkameriana	ERea

Cladium (*Cyperaceae*)

mariscus	GFor

Cladothamnus see *Elliottia*

Cladrastis (*Papilionaceae*)

	kentukea	CArn CBcs CDul CLnd CMCN CPne CTho ELan EPfP LRHS MBlu NLar SHBN SSpi WBVN WDin WNor
	- 'Perkins Pink'	CMCN MBlu
	- 'Rosea'	see *C. kentukea* 'Perkins Pink'
	lutea	see *C. kentukea*
	sinensis	CFil CMCN EPfP MBlu SSpi WPGP

Clarkia (*Onagraceae*)

*	***repens***	CSpe

Clausia (*Brassicaceae*)

	aprica **new**	CGra CPBP

Clavinodum (*Poaceae*)

§	***oedogonatum***	EPla WJun

Claytonia (*Portulacaceae*)

	acutifolia **new**	GIBF
	alsinoides	see *C. sibirica*
	australasica	see *Neopaxia australasica*
	caroliniana	EBee LAma NLar
§	***nevadensis***	EMar
	parvifolia	see *Naiocrene parvifolia*
§	***perfoliata***	CArn CPLG GPoy ILis WCHb WHer
§	***sibirica***	CAgr CArn CElw CNic CSec EEls EMag EMan NBid WBVN WBWf WGHP WRHF WWye
	- 'Alba'	CElw NBid
	virginica	EHrv LAma WFar WMoo

Clematis ✿ (*Ranunculaceae*)

	B&SWJ 599	WCru
	BWJ 7630 from China	WCru
	BWJ 8169 from China	WCru
	RCB TQ-H-7	WCot
	WJS 8910 from Japan	WCru
	'Abundance' (Vt) 🏆H4	CDoC CElw CPev CRHN CSPN EPfP ERob ESCh ETho GAbr GLbr LRHS MAsh MBri MRav NBea NTay SBra SDix SHBN SPer SPet SPoG WBGC WTel
	addisonii	CBcs CSPN EBee ERob ESCh MWhi NHaw WBGC
	aethusifolia	CSPN ERob
	afoliata	CBcs CPev CSPN CStu EBee ECou ERob ETho WBGC
	afoliata x ***forsteri***	ECou
	'Aino' (Vt)	ERob
	'Akaishi' (EL)	ERob ESCh ETho NBrk NTay
	akebioides	CPLG EHyt GKev LRHS SBra SHBN SLim WCru
	'Akemi' (EL)	ERob
	Alabast = 'Poulala'[PBR] (EL) 🏆H4	CSPN ERob ESCh ETho MBNS MWgw NHaw NTay SBra SCoo SLim SPoG WBGC
	'Alba Luxurians' (Vt) 🏆H4	More than 30 suppliers
	'Albatross'	ENot ERob ESCh
	'Albiflora' (A)	CSPN ECtt ESCh NBrk NSti WBGC
I	'Albina Plena' (A/d)	ESCh SLim WBGC
	'Aleksandrit' (EL)	ERob
	'Alice Fisk' (EL)	CSPN ERob ESCh ETho LSRN MSwo NBea NBrk NHaw NTay SBra SHBN SPoG WBGC WGor
	'Alionushka' (I) 🏆H4	More than 30 suppliers
	'Allanah' (LL)	CRHN EPfP ERob ESCh ETho GKir LAst LSRN MGos MSwo NBea NHaw NTay SBra SCoo SLim SPoG WBGC WFar
§	***alpina*** 🏆H4	CMac CPev ECtt EPfP ESCh GIBF GKev GKir GSki MBar MDun MWhi NBlu NHaw NPer SHBN SLim SPlb WBVN WCot WFar
	- 'Albiflora'	see *C. sibirica*
	- 'Columbine White'	see *C.* 'White Columbine'
	- 'Jan Lindmark'	see *C.* 'Jan Lindmark'
	- 'Mary Whistler'	ESCh
I	- 'Odorata' (A)	CSPN ERob LBuc MGos NBea NHaw
I	- 'Pamela Jackman' (A)	CDoC CSPN CWSG EBee EHan ELan ESCh GKir LAst LRHS LSRN MAsh MDun MGos NBea NCGa NEgg NSti NTay SBra SCoo SDix SLim SPer SPoG SWvt WBGC WFar
	- subsp. ***sibirica***	see *C. sibirica*
	'Alpinist' (LL)	ERob
	'Amelia Joan' (Ta)	ERob MWat
	'Ameshisuto' (EL)	ETho
	'Amethyst Beauty' (A)	ERob
	'Anders' (A/d)	ESCh
	'André Devillers'	see *C.* 'Directeur André Devillers'
I	'Andromeda' (EL)	CSPN EBee ERob ESCh ETho NBrk NHaw NTay SBra WFar
	'Anita' (Ta)	EMil ERob ESCh ETho NHaw SBra SLim SPoG WBGC
	'Anna' (EL)	ERob ESCh NTay
	'Anna Carolina' **new**	ESCh
	'Anna Herman' (EL)	ERob ESCh
	Anna Louise = 'Evithree'[PBR] (EL) 🏆H4	CSPN EBee ERob ESCh ETho LRHS MBri NTay SBra SCoo SLim SWCr WBGC
	'Annabel' (EL)	CSPN ERob MAsh
	'Annemieke' (Ta)	ERob ESCh MGos SBra WBGC
	'Annie Treasure'	ERob WBGC
	Anniversary = 'Pynot'[PBR] (EL)	ENot ERob ESCh LSRN NBrk SCoo
	anshunensis	see *C. clarkeana*
	'Anti' (LL)	ESCh
	'Aoife' (Fo)	ETho
	'Aotearoa' (LL)	ERob ESCh
	'Aphrodite'	CRHN ERob WBGC
	apiifolia	CPev ERob MWhi
	- B&SWJ 4838	WCru
	'Apple Blossom' (Ar) 🏆H4	More than 30 suppliers
	'Apulejus' (A) **new**	NBrk
	'Arabella' (I) 🏆H4	More than 30 suppliers
	Arctic Queen = 'Evitwo'[PBR] (EL) 🏆H4	CSPN EBee EHan ENot ESCh ETho GKir LRHS LSRN MBNS NPri SCoo SLim SPer SPoG SWCr WBGC WFar WWes
	armandii	More than 30 suppliers
	- 'Enham Star' (Ar)	LRHS MBri MGos
	- 'Little White Charm' (Ar)	CSPN ERob MBlu NLar SHBN SPoG
	- 'Meyeniana'	see *C. armandii* 'Little White Charm'
§	- 'Snowdrift' (Ar)	CBcs CPev CSBt CSPN CSam CWSG ELan EPfP ERob ESCh ETho LRHS LSRN MAsh MGos MLan NSti NTay SHBN SPer SPoG SRms WBGC
	x ***aromatica***	CElw CSPN EBee ELan EPfP ERob ESCh ETho LAst LFol LRHS MBNS MBri MWgw NBea NSti NTay SBra SCoo SPoG SWCr WBGC
§	'Asagasumi' (EL)	ERob ESCh LBuc NBrk NTay
	'Asao' (EL)	CElw CRHN EBee ELan EPfP ERob ESCh ETho GLbr LAst LRHS MAsh MGos MRav NBPC NBea NTay SBra SLim SPer SPoG SWCr WBGC WOrn
	'Ascotiensis' (LL)	CElw CPev CSPN EBee EPfP ESCh

ETho LRHS MAsh NBea NHaw NPri NTay SBra SDix SLim SPer SPoG SWCr WBGC WFar
'Ashva' **new** — ESCh ETho
§ 'Aureolin' (Ta) — CSPN CWSG EPfP ERob ESCh GKir LRHS MAsh MBar MGos NBrk NPri SBra SCoo SLim SPoG WBGC WPGP
australis — ERob ITim
'Bagatelle' (EL) — CRHN CSPN ERob ESCh NBrk NHaw NTay SBra SCoo SLim WBGC
'Ballerina in Blue' (A/d) — ERob ESCh NBrk NHaw
'Ballet Skirt' (A/d) — ERob ESCh LBuc LRHS MBri MGos NHaw NLar SLim SPoG SWCr WBGC
'Bałtyk' (EL) — CSPN ERob ESCh NBrk
'Barbara' (LL) — ETho
'Barbara Dibley' (EL) — CPev CTri CWSG ERob ESCh LRHS MAsh MBNS MSwo NBea NTay SBra SCoo SDix SLim SPoG WBGC
'Barbara Harrington'[PBR] **new** — ENot
'Barbara Jackman' (EL) — CPev EBee ECtt ENot ERob ETho GKir LRHS LSRN MAsh MBar MGos MSwo NBea NEgg NTay SBra SCoo SLim SPer SPoG SWCr WBGC WFar WFoF
'Barbara Wheeler' — ERob
barbellata — EHyt ERob
'Basil Bartlett' (Fo) — ECou ERob ESCh
'Beata' (LL) — ESCh
'Beauty of Richmond' (EL) — CWSG ERob ESCh
'Beauty of Worcester' (EL) — CPev CSPN CWSG ELan EPfP ESCh ETho GKir LAst LRHS LSRN MAsh MBar MSwo MWgw NBea NHaw NTay SBra SCoo SDix SLim SPer SPoG WBGC WFar WWeb
'Bees' Jubilee' (EL) — More than 30 suppliers
'Bella' (EL) — EBee ERob ESCh ETho NHaw
'Belle Nantaise' (EL) — CElw CPev ERob ESCh LRHS MAsh NBea NTay SBra SCoo SPet WBGC
'Belle of Woking' (EL) — More than 30 suppliers
'Benedictus' (EL) — ESCh
'Bessie Watkinson' — ERob ESCh
§ 'Beth Currie' (EL) — CSPN ERob ESCh NTay SCoo SPoG
'Betina' — see *C.* 'Red Beetroot Beauty'
'Betty Corning' (Vt) ♀H4 — CHad CRHN CSPN EBee ELan EMil EPfP ERob ESCh ETho LRHS MBri MGos MWgw NBea NBrk NTay SBra SLon SWCr WBGC WTel WWhi
'Betty Risdon' (EL) — ERob ESCh ETho MAsh NBrk
'Big Bird' (A/d) — ERob ESCh LBuc NBrk
§ 'Bill MacKenzie' (Ta) ♀H4 — More than 30 suppliers
Black Madonna — see *C.* 'Czarna Madonna'
'Black Prince' (Vt) — CRHN ELan ERob ESCh ETho NBrk NTay WBGC
'Black Tea' (LL) — ERob
§ 'Błękitny Anioł' (LL) ♀H4 — CElw CRHN CSPN EHan ERob ESCh ETho GMac LRHS MGos MWgw NBea NBrk NPri NTay SBra SCoo SPer SPet SPoG SWCr WBGC
Blue Angel — see *C.* 'Blekitny Aniol'
'Blue Belle' (Vt) — CElw CPou CRHN ELan ESCh LRHS NBea NBrk NSti NTay SBra SPet SPoG SWCr WBGC WFar
'Blue Bird' (A/d) — CBcs CPLN CWSG EBee ECtt ESCh MAsh NBea NCGa SBra SLim SPer SPoG WBGC
'Blue Boy' (I) — see *C.* × *diversifolia* 'Blue Boy'
'Blue Boy' (L/P) — see *C.* 'Elsa Späth'
'Blue Dancer' (A) — CElw EPfP ERob ESCh ETho GKir IBal MGos NBea NBrk NTay SPet SWCr WBGC WWes
'Blue Eclipse' (A) — CSPN ERob ESCh NBrk WBGC
'Blue Eyes' (EL) — CSPN EBee ERob ESCh NBrk NHaw NTay
'Blue Gem' (EL) — ERob ESCh SBra SLim SPoG
'Blue Light'[PBR] (EL/d) — CSPN EHan ELan ENot ERob ESCh ETho LBuc MGos NLar NTay SBra WBGC WFar
Blue Moon = 'Evirin'[PBR] (EL) — ENot ESCh ETho LAst LRHS LSRN MBNS MWgw NBea NLar NPri NTay SBra SCoo SWCr WFar
'Blue Pirouette' **new** — ESCh
Blue Rain — see *C.* 'Sinee Dozhd'
'Blue Ravine' (EL) — EBee EPfP ERob ESCh ETho GLbr MGos NBPC NBrk NLar NTay SBra SCoo WBGC
'Blue Stream' (A) — ESCh
'Blue Tapers' (A) — ERob ESCh NHaw
'Blushing Ballerina' (A/d) — ERob ESCh NTay
× ***bonstedtii*** (H) — ESCh
§ - 'Campanile' (H) — CPev ERob ESCh NBir NBrk
- 'Crépuscule' (H) — ERob ESCh GCal NBrk NTay SRms WBGC WCot
'Boskoop Beauty' (EL) — ERob ESCh NBrk
'Bowl of Beauty' (Ar) — ERob MGos
'Bracebridge Star' (EL) — ECtt ERob ESCh
brachiata — ESCh
brachyura — ERob
'Bravo' (Ta) — ERob WBGC
brevicaudata — GIBF
'Brocade' (Vt) — CPev CRHN CSPN ERob ESCh ETho
'Broughton Bride' (A) — ERob ESCh ETho NBrk
'Broughton Star' (M/d) ♀H4 — More than 30 suppliers
§ 'Brunette' (A) — CSPN ELan EPfP ERob ESCh ETho MGos NBrk NHaw NTay SBra SWCr WBGC
buchananiana Finet & Gagnep. — see *C. rehderiana*
buchananiana DC. — CPLG EBee ERob
- B&SWJ 8333a — WCru
'Burford Bell' (V) — ERob WBGC
'Burford Princess' (Vt) — ERob
I 'Burford Variety' (Ta) — ERob ESCh NTay WBGC
'Burford White' (A) — CSPN EPfP ERob ESCh NBrk NLar NTay WBGC
'Burma Star' (EL) — CElw CPev EHan EPfP ERob ESCh ETho NBea NBrk NHaw NTay SBra WBGC
'C.W. Dowman' (EL) — ERob ETho
'Caerulea Luxurians' (Vt) — CRHN ERob ESCh NTay WBGC
calycina — see *C. cirrhosa*
§ ***campaniflora*** — CBot CElw CMea CNic CPev CRHN CSPN CStu EHyt ERob ETho MWhi NBea NBrk NWCA SBra SDix WBGC WPGP
- 'Lisboa' (Vt) — ERob NBrk SBra
'Campanile' — see *C.* × *bonstedtii* 'Campanile'
'Candida' (EL) — ESCh
'Candleglow' (A) — CElw CSPN NBrk
'Candy Stripe' — ERob ESCh GKir NTay SCoo SLim
'Capitaine Thuilleaux' — see *C.* 'Souvenir du Capitaine Thuilleaux'
'Cardinal Wyszynski' — see *C.* 'Kardynał Wyszyński'
'Carmencita' (Vt) — CRHN CSPN EBee ERob ESCh ETho NBrk NHaw NTay SBra SCoo WBGC WFar
'Carnaby' (EL) — CRHN CSPN CWSG EBee ELan EPfP ERob ESCh ETho LAst LRHS MAsh MBar MBri MGos NBea NTay SBra SCoo SLim SPet SPoG SWCr WBGC WPGP

	'Carnival Queen'	CSPN CWSG ERob ESCh NBrk NTay
	'Caroline' (LL)	CHad CPev CSPN EBee ERob ESCh ETho LBuc NBea NBrk NHaw NTay SBra WBGC
	'Caroline Lloyd' (Vt)	ERob
§	x ***cartmanii*** hort. 'Avalanche'^{PBR} (Fo/m) 🏆^{H3}	CSPN EHan ELan ERob ESCh GBin LBuc LRHS NPri NTay SBla SHBN SLim SMur SPoG WCot
	- 'Joe' (Fo/m)	More than 30 suppliers
	- 'Snow Valley'^{PBR} (Fo)	MAsh SBla
	- 'White Abundance'^{PBR} (Fo/f)	ESCh MAsh NTay SBla
	'Celebration'^{PBR}	ESCh
	'Chalcedony' (EL)	CPev CSPN ERob ESCh ETho MAsh MGos NBrk NTay SBra WBGC
	'Charissima' (EL)	CBcs CElw CPev CSPN CSam EHan EPfP ERob ESCh ETho MGos NTay SBra SCoo SPet WBGC WFar
	chiisanensis	CBcs CSPN ERob MWhi NBrk NEgg SBra WBGC WHrl
	- B&SWJ 4560	WCru
	- B&SWJ 8706	WCru
	- 'Lemon Bells' (A)	ELan LRHS MAsh SCoo SMur SPoG SWCr
	- 'Love Child' (A)	CBcs CElw CSPN ELan ERob ESCh ETho LBuc MBlu NBrk NTay SBra SCoo SLim SPer WBGC WCot
	chinensis misapplied	see *C. terniflora*
	chinensis Osbeck	ERob
	'Chinook'	ESCh LRHS
	'Christian Steven' (LL)	CSPN ERob ESCh
	chrysantha	see *C. tangutica*
	- var. ***paucidentata***	see *C. hilariae*
	chrysocoma misapplied	see *C. spooneri*, *C.* x *vedrariensis*
N	***chrysocoma*** Franch.	CPev EPfP ERob MBNS MBar NBPC SBra WCru
	- ACE 1093	CPou
	- B&L 12237	NBea
	'Cicciolina' (Vt)	ERob NBrk NTay
§	***cirrhosa***	CBot CPev CTri ELan LRHS MAsh MGos MWhi NTay SArc SWCr WBGC
	- var. ***balearica***	More than 30 suppliers
	- 'Ourika Valley' (C)	ERob NLar WFar
	- var. ***purpurascens*** 'Freckles' (C) 🏆^{H3}	More than 30 suppliers
	- - 'Jingle Bells' (C)	CElw CRHN EBee EHan EPfP ERob ESCh ETho LRHS MAsh NHaw NTay SBra SCoo SLim SMur SPoG SWCr WBGC WFar
	- - 'Lansdowne Gem' (C)	CSPN CWib LBuc MBlu WBcn
	- subsp. ***semitriloba***	ERob
	- 'Wisley Cream' (C) 🏆^{H3}	More than 30 suppliers
	'Citra'	see *C.* 'Claudius'
§	***clarkeana***	ETho
	'Claudius' (A)	ERob ESCh NBrk NTay WSHC
	'Clochette Pride' (A/d)	ERob
	coactilis	ERob
	'Colette Deville' (EL)	ERob ESCh NTay
	columbiana	ERob
§	- var. ***tenuiloba***	SOkd
	- - 'Ylva' (A)	EHyt WAbe
	'Columbine' (A)	CPev CWSG EBee ETho LBuc MAsh MBar MSwo NBea SCoo SDix SLim SPer SPoG WBGC
	'Columella' (A)	ERob ESCh NBrk NHaw NLar
	'Comtesse de Bouchaud' (LL) 🏆^{H4}	More than 30 suppliers
	confusa HWJK 2200 **new**	WCru
	connata	CPLN ERob ESCh GQui NBrk SBra
	- GWJ 9386	WCru
	- HWJCM 132	WCru
	aff. ***connata*** HWJK 2176 from Nepal **new**	WCru
	- GWJ 9431 from West Bengal **new**	WCru
	'Constance' (A) 🏆^{H4}	CElw CSPN EBee EPfP ERob ESCh ETho LRHS NBrk NHaw NSti NTay SBra SCoo SPer SRms SWCr WBGC WBor WPGP
	'Continuity' (M)	ERob NTay SBra SDix SLim SPla WSHC
	'Corona' (EL)	CPev CSPN ELan EPfP ERob LAst LRHS MAsh MBar NBea NHaw NTay SBra SCoo SLim SPet SPoG WBGC WFar
	'Corry' (Ta)	ERob ESCh NBrk
	'Côte d'Azur' (H)	CFwr CRez ERob ESCh GCal MAvo MCCP NBPC NBrk NLar WBGC
	'Cotton Candy'	ERob
	'Countess of Lovelace' (EL)	CBcs CSPN CWSG EBee EHan ELan EPfP ERob ESCh ETho LRHS MAsh MBar MBri MGos MWgw NBea NEgg NTay SBra SCoo SDix SLim SPer SPet SPoG SWCr WBGC
	County Park hybrids (Fo)	ECou
	'Cragside' (A)	ETho
	crassifolia B&SWJ 6700	WCru
§	'Crimson King' (LL)	ERob ESCh NBrk NHaw NTay SBod WGor
§	***crispa***	CPou CSPN EHyt ERob ESCh MWhi NBea
*	- 'Cylindrica'	ERob NBrk
	Crystal Fountain = 'Fairy Blue' (EL/d)	ESCh ETho LRHS NPri SCoo
	x ***cylindrica***	CSPN EBee ESCh NBrk WBGC
	'Czarna Madonna' (EL)	ERob
I	'Danae' (Vt)	CRHN ERob WBGC
	'Daniel Deronda' (EL) 🏆^{H4}	More than 30 suppliers
	'Dark Secret' (A)	CSPN ERob ESCh NBrk
	'Dawn' (EL)	CPev CSPN ERob ESCh ETho LRHS MAsh NBea NTay SBra SCoo SLim SPer SPoG SWCr WBGC WGwG
	'Débutante' (EL)	ESCh ETho
	delavayi var. ***limprichtii*** BWJ 7727 **new**	WCru
	'Denny's Double' (EL/d)	CSPN CWSG ERob ESCh ETho MAsh NBrk NRib NTay WBGC
	'Diana' (LL)	ERob ESCh ETho
	dioscoreifolia	see *C. terniflora*
§	'Directeur André Devillers' (EL)	ERob ESCh
	x ***diversifolia***	CElw CRHN EBee ESCh GKir GLbr LRHS MBNS MGos MSte NBPC NBrk NHaw SBra SDix SGar SHBN SPer SPet WBGC
	- 'Amy' (I)	ERob
	- 'Blue Boy' (I)	CBgR CElw CRHN CSPN EBee EPfP ERob ESCh ETho MBri MGos NBrk NHaw NTay SBra SPet WBGC
	- 'Floris V' (I)	ERob ESCh NBrk NTay SHar
	- 'Heather Herschell' (I)	CBgR CElw CPev CSPN ERob ESCh ETho NBrk NLar SPet WBGC
	- 'Hendersonii' (I)	CHad CPev CSam EBee EChP EHyt ELan EMar EPfP ERob ESCh ETho GSki LAst LRHS MAsh MRav MSwo MTis MWgw NBea NBir NGdn NLar NSti NTay SDix SLim SPoG WBGC
	- 'Hendryetta' (I) **new**	ESCh ETho SPoG
	- 'Lauren' (I)	ERob
	- 'Olgae' (I)	CPev CSPN ESCh MBow MDKP NBea NBrk NTay SBra SDix SLim WBGC

Name	Suppliers
'Docteur Le Bêle' (LL)	ERob NBrk NTay
'Doctor Ruppel' (EL)	More than 30 suppliers
'Doggy' (Vt)	ERob
'Dominika' (LL)	CSPN ERob ESCh ETho NBrk NHaw NTay SBra WBGC
'Dorath'	ERob ESCh NBrk WBGC
'Dorota' (EL)	ERob
'Dorothy Tolver' (EL)	ERob ESCh ETho WBGC
'Dorothy Walton'	see *C.* 'Bagatelle'
'Dovedale' (M)	CPev ESCh
'Dubysa' **new**	ESCh
'Duchess of Albany' (T)	More than 30 suppliers
'Duchess of Edinburgh' (EL)	More than 30 suppliers
'Duchess of Sutherland' (EL)	CPev ERob ESCh LRHS MGos NBea NHaw NTay SBra SDix SPet WBGC
'Dulcie'	NHaw
x ***durandii*** 🏆^{H4}	More than 30 suppliers
'Early Sensation' (Fo/f)	More than 30 suppliers
'East Malling' (M)	ERob ESCh NHaw
'Edith' (EL) 🏆^{H4}	ECtt EPfP ERob ESCh ETho LRHS MAsh NBea NBrk NHaw NTay SBra SLim WBGC WGor
'Edomurasaki' (EL)	ERob ESCh ETho NBrk WBGC
'Edouard Desfossé' (EL)	ERob ESCh MAsh NTay SBra
'Edward Prichard'	CSPN EBee EPfP ERob ESCh MAsh NBea NBrk NHaw SBra WBGC
'Eetika' (LL)	ERob ESCh ETho NBrk
'Ekstra' (LL)	EBee ERob ESCh ETho NBrk
'Eleanor' (Fo/f)	ECou ESCh
Eleanor of Guildford = 'Notpy'^{PBR} (EL)	ENot ERob ESCh
'Elf' (Vt)	CPev
'Elfin' (Fo/v)	ECou
'Elizabeth' (M) 🏆^{H4}	More than 30 suppliers
§ 'Elsa Späth' (EL)	More than 30 suppliers
'Elten' (M)	CSPN ERob ESCh NBrk
'Elvan' (Vt)	CBgR CPev CRHN ERob ESCh NBrk NHaw NLar NTay SPet WBGC
'Emerald Stars'	ESCh
'Emilia Plater' (Vt)	CRHN CSPN ERob ESCh ETho MBri NBea NBrk NHaw NTay SBra WBGC WBcn
'Emogi'	ESCh
'Empress of India' (EL)	ERob ESCh MWgw WBGC
'Entel' (Vt)	ERob ETho NBrk NHaw WBGC
'Erik' (A)	ESCh
x ***eriostemon***	see *C.* x *diversifolia*
'Ernest Markham' (LL) 🏆^{H4}	More than 30 suppliers
'Esperanto' (LL)	EBee ESCh
'Etoile de Malicorne' (EL)	ERob ESCh LRHS NBea NTay WBGC WGor
'Etoile de Paris' (EL)	ERob ESCh ETho MWgw NTay SBra WBGC
Etoile Nacrée	see *C.* 'Sakurahime'
'Etoile Rose' (Vt)	CPev CRHN CSPN CTri ELan EPfP ERob ESCh ETho GKir LAst LRHS LSRN MAsh MWgw NBea NTay SBra SCoo SDix SLim SMur SPer SPoG SWCr WBGC WFar WPGP WSHC
'Etoile Violette' (Vt) 🏆^{H4}	More than 30 suppliers
'Europa' (EL)	ERob
'Eva' (LL)	ERob ESCh NBrk
Evening Star = 'Evista'^{PBR}	EPfP ERob ESCh ETho MWgw NTay SBra SLim SPoG WFar
'Eximia'	see *C.* 'Ballerina in Blue'
'Fair Rosamond' (EL)	CPev EBee EPfP ERob ESCh LRHS MAsh NBea NHaw NTay SBra SDix SLim WBGC

Name	Suppliers
'Fairy' (Fo/f)	ECou ESCh
'Fairy Queen' (EL)	ERob ESCh ETho SBra
fargesii var. ***souliei***	see *C. potaninii* var. *potaninii*
x ***fargesioides***	see *C.* 'Paul Farges'
fasciculiflora	CBot CMHG CRHN CSPN ERob IDee LRHS SSpi WBcn
- L 657	CFil SAga WCru WPGP
'Fascination'^{PBR} (I)	ESCh ETho LRHS MAsh SBra
fauriei	ERob
finetiana hort.	see *C. paniculata* J.G. Gmel.
'Firefly' (EL)	ERob ESCh MGos
'Fireworks' (EL)	COtt CSPN EBee ECtt ENot EPfP ESCh ETho LAst LRHS LSRN MAsh MBri MGos NBea NPri NTay SBra SLim SPoG SWCr WBGC WFoF WGor
'Flamingo' (EL)	CWSG ERob MGos
flammula	More than 30 suppliers
- var. ***flavescens***	ERob
- 'Ithaca' (F/v)	ERob
- 'Rubra Marginata'	see *C.* x *triternata* 'Rubromarginata'
'Floral Feast' (A/d)	CSPN ESCh LRHS NBea NBrk NTay SCoo SLim SPoG
'Floralia' (A/d)	see *C.* 'Floral Feast'
florida	CSPN ERob ESCh ETho
- 'Bicolor'	see *C. florida* var. *sieboldiana*
- var. ***flore-pleno*** (d)	CPev CSPN ELan EPfP ESCh ETho LAst LRHS MAsh MWgw NBea NEgg NRib NTay SBod SBra SHBN SMad SPer SPla SPoG SWCr WBGC WCot WFar
- Pistachio = 'Evirida'^{PBR} (LL)	COtt CSPN EHan EPfP ESCh ETho IBal LBuc MBNS NLar NTay SLim SPer SPoG SRkn SWCr
- var. ***sieboldiana*** (d)	More than 30 suppliers
foetida	CBcs CSPN
foetida x ***petriei***	ECou
'Fond Memories' (EL) **new**	ETho
forrestii	see *C. napaulensis*
§ ***forsteri***	CBcs CSPN ERob ESCh ETho IDee LFol NBrk SBra SSpi WPGP
forsteri x ***indivisa***	WCru
forsteri x ***parviflora***	ESCh
'Foxtrot' (Vt)	CRHN ERob ESCh MAsh NBrk WBGC
'Fragrant Joy' (Fo/m)	ECou ESCh
'Fragrant Spring' (M)	CSPN ECtt ERob ESCh ETho MGos NBlu NBrk NHaw NLar SBra SLim WBGC WBcn WFar
'Frances Rivis' (A) 🏆^{H4}	More than 30 suppliers
'Francesca' (A)	ESCh MGos NBrk
'Frankie' (A) 🏆^{H4}	CSPN ELan ENot ERob ESCh ETho LRHS NTay SBra SCoo SLim SWCr WBGC
'Frau Mikiko' (EL)	ERob ESCh
'Freda' (M) 🏆^{H4}	More than 30 suppliers
'Fryderyk Chopin' (EL)	CSPN ERob ESCh ETho NHaw NTay
'Fuji-musume' (EL) 🏆^{H4}	CSPN EHan ERob ESCh ETho MAsh NBrk NHaw NLar NTay SBra SCoo SLim WBGC WFar
'Fujinami' (EL)	ERob
fusca hort.	see *C. japonica*
fusca Turcz.	CPLN ERob MWhi WIvy
- B&SWJ 4229	WCru
§ - var. ***fusca***	ESCh ETho GIBF
- var. ***kamtschatica***	see *C. fusca* var. *fusca*
- var. ***umbrosa*** B&SWJ 700	WCru
fusijamana	ERob
'G. Steffner' (A)	ERob ESCh NBrk
'Gabrielle' (EL)	CSPN ERob ESCh LBuc NHaw NTay SBra SLim WBGC

Name	Suppliers
'Gazelle'	ESCh LRHS
'Gekkyuuden'	ERob
'Gemini'	ENot ERob ESCh
'General Sikorski' (EL)	CBcs CElw CMac CRHN CSPN CSam CWSG ECtt ELan EPfP ESCh ETho LAst LRHS LSRN MAsh MBri MGos NBea NTay SBra SCoo SDix SHBN SLim SPer SPet SPoG SWCr WBGC
gentianoides	ERob WAbe WCot
'Georg' (A/d)	ERob ESCh MBri MGos NHaw WBGC
'Georg Ots' (LL)	ERob ESCh
'Giant Star' (M)	ESCh NCGa NLar NPer
'Gillian Blades' (EL) ♀H4	CRHN CSPN EBee EHan ELan ENot EPfP ERob ESCh ETho IBal LAst LRHS MAsh NBea NBrk NHaw NPri NTay SBra SCoo SLim SPoG SWCr WBGC
'Gipsy Queen' (LL) ♀H4	More than 30 suppliers
'Gladys Picard' (EL)	ERob ESCh NTay SLim WBGC WFar
glauca Turcz.	see *C. intricata*
glaucophylla	CPLN
'Glynderek' (EL)	ERob ESCh NTay SBra
'Golden Harvest' (Ta)	ERob ESCh NLar SBra WBGC WFar
Golden Tiara = 'Kugotia'PBR (Ta) ♀H4	CSPN ENot ERob ESCh ETho LRHS MBri MGos MWgw NBea NBrk NPri NTay SBra SPoG WBGC WCot
'Gornoe Ozero' (EL)	ERob ESCh
'Gothenburg' (M)	EBee ERob ESCh NBea NHaw SBra WBGC WFar
gouriana	ERob
- subsp. ***lishanensis*** B&SWJ 292	WCru
'Grace' (Ta)	CRHN CSPN EBee ERob ESCh ETho NBrk NHaw NLar WBGC
gracilifolia	ERob ESCh NBrk NLar WBGC
- var. ***dissectifolia***	ERob
'Grandiflora Sanguinea' (Vt)	ERob SLim
'Grandiflora Sanguinea' Johnson	see *C.* 'Södertälje'
grata hort.	see *C.* x *jouiniana*
grata Wall.	CElw CPLG CPev EHyt ERob NBrk WCot
- B&SWJ 6774	WCru
'Gravetye Beauty' (T)	More than 30 suppliers
'Green Velvet' (Fo/m)	ECou
grewiiflora B&SWJ 2956	WCru
'Guernsey Cream' (EL)	CSPN CSam CWSG EBee EHan EMil ESCh ETho LAst LRHS MAsh MBri MWgw NBea NEgg NTay SBra SCoo SDix SHBN SLim SPet SPoG SWCr WBGC WFar WWeb WWes
'Guiding Star' (EL)	ERob NHaw SBra
'H.F. Young' (EL)	CElw CPev CSPN CWSG EBee ELan EPfP ERob ESCh ETho GKir GMac LRHS MAsh MBar MBri MGos MWgw NBea NTay SBra SDix SHBN SLim SPer SPet WBGC WTel
'Hagley Hybrid' (LL)	More than 30 suppliers
'Hainton Ruby' (EL)	ERob ESCh
'Haku-ôkan' (EL)	CPev CSPN EBee EHan EPfP ERob ESCh ETho LRHS MAsh NBea NTay SBra SCoo SLim SPoG WBGC
'Hakuree' K. Ozawa (I)	ESCh ETho
'Hanaguruma' (EL)	CSPN ERob ESCh ETho NBea NBrk NHaw NTay WBGC WFar
'Hanajima' (I)	EHyt ERob ESCh ETho NBrk
'Hania'	ETho
Harlow Carr = 'Evipo004'	ESCh LRHS MAsh MBri
'Harmony' (EL/d)	ERob ESCh
'Haruyama' (EL)	ESCh
Havering hybrids (Fo)	ECou
'Helen Cropper' (EL)	ERob ESCh ETho NBrk
'Helios' (Ta)	CSPN CSpe ENot EPfP ERob ESCh ETho GMac LRHS MGos NBea NBrk NSti NTay SBra SCoo SPoG WBGC WCot
'Helsingborg' (A) ♀H4	CBcs CSPN CTbh EBee ECtt ELan ENot EPfP ERob ESCh ETho LAst LRHS NBea NEgg NPri NSti NTay SBra SCoo SPla SPoG SWCr WBGC WTel WWes
hendersonii Henderson	see *C.* x *diversifolia* 'Hendersonii'
hendersonii Koch	see *C.* x *diversifolia* 'Hendersonii'
hendersonii Stand.	see *C.* x *diversifolia*
I 'Hendersonii' (I)	ERob ETho GKir LRHS LSRN MSte NTay SPet SWCr WBGC
'Hendersonii Rubra' (Ar)	CSPN
henryi	CDul CPLN ENot LSRN MWgw
- B&SWJ 3402	WCru
'Henryi' (EL) ♀H4	More than 30 suppliers
henryi var. ***morii*** B&SWJ 1668	WCru
heracleifolia	CAby CBcs CPou EChP ECtt EGra EHol ESCh GKir GSki LPio MFOX NLar SWCr WBGC WMoo
- Alan BloomPBR	see *C. tabulosa* Alan Bloom = 'Alblo'
- 'Blue Dwarf'	ESCh ETho MGos NBrk
I - 'Cassandra' (H)	EHyt EMar EPfP ESCh GCal MAvo NBrk
- 'China Purple' (H)	CFai ERob GBri NBrk NLar WHil
- var. ***davidiana***	see *C. tubulosa*
- 'Roundway Blue Bird' (H)	CBot ESCh LRHS NHaw
'Herbert Johnson' (EL)	CPev ESCh NBrk SBra
hexapetala misapplied	see *C. recta* subsp. *recta* var. *lasiosepala*
hexapetala Forster	see *C. forsteri*
hexasepala	see *C. forsteri*
'Hikarugenji' (EL)	CSPN ERob ESCh NBrk NHaw NTay
§ ***hilariae***	ERob
§ ***hirsutissima***	WIvy
- var. ***scottii***	ERob WIvy
'Honora' (LL)	CSPN ERob ESCh MGos NTay SBra WBGC
'Horn of Plenty' (EL)	EHan ERob ESCh LRHS NBea NBrk NHaw NTay SBra SLim SPoG WBGC
'Huldine' (LL) ♀H4	More than 30 suppliers
'Huvi' (LL)	ERob ESCh NTay
'Hybrida Sieboldii' (EL)	CRHN EBee ERob ESCh ETho NBea NBrk NTay SBra SLim WBGC WCot
Hyde Hall = 'Evipo009'	ESCh LRHS MAsh MBri SPer
'Hythe Chiffchaff' (Fo)	EHyt
'Hythe Egret' (Fo)	EHyt LTwo SIng
ianthina	CPLN EHyt EPfP ERob ESCh SBra WPGP WSHC
- var. ***kuripoensis***	ERob ETho
- - B&SWJ 700	WCru
'Ice Maiden' (EL)	ESCh
'Ice Queen'	ESCh MAsh NBrk
'Ideal' (EL)	ERob ESCh
'Ilka' (EL)	ERob ESCh
'Imperial' (EL)	ERob ESCh ETho NBrk NHaw
indivisa	see *C. paniculata* J.G. Gmel.
'Inglewood' (EL)	ERob NTay
Inspiration = 'Zoin'PBR (I)	CSPN ELan ERob ESCh ETho LBuc MAsh MGos NBrk NTay SBra SCoo WBGC

	Name	Suppliers
	integrifolia	More than 30 suppliers
I	- 'Alba'	CBcs CElw CHad CSPN ECtt EHan EMar ESCh ETho GBuc LAst LRHS LSRN MDKP NBea NBir NBrk NHaw NSti NTay SBra SCoo SLim SOkh SPer SPet SPoG WBGC WCru
	- 'Budapest' (I)	ERob ESCh LBuc MWgw NHaw SBra WBGC
I	- 'Finnis Form' (I)	SChu
	- 'Hendersonii' Koch	see *C.* x *diversifolia* 'Hendersonii'
	- var. ***latifolia***	ERob ESCh
	- 'Olgae'	see *C.* x *diversifolia* 'Olgae'
	- 'Ozawa's Blue' (I)	EMar ESCh LRHS NSti
§	***intricata***	CBcs CSPN EHyt EPfP ERob MGos
	- 'Harry Smith' (Ta)	ERob ESCh
	- 'Vince Denny'	ESCh ETho
	'Iola Fair' (EL)	CSPN ERob ESCh ETho NHaw NTay
	'Ishobel' (EL)	ERob ESCh NBrk
	'Iubileinyi-70' (LL)	EBee ERob ESCh NBrk
	'Ivan Olsson' (EL)	CSPN ERob ESCh ETho NBrk
	'Izumi' H. Hayakawa (LL)	ESCh
	'Jackmanii' (LL) ♀H4	CBcs CMac CRHN CTri EBee ENot EPfP ERob ESCh ETho GKir LRHS LSRN MAsh MGos NBea NEgg NWea SBod SBra SCoo SLim SPer SPet SPoG SWCr WBGC WFar WTel
	'Jackmanii Alba' (EL)	CPev ELan EPfP ERob ESCh ETho LAst LRHS LSRN MAsh MBar NBea NBrk NTay SCoo SLim SPet SPoG SWCr WBGC
	'Jackmanii Rubra' (EL)	CPev ERob ESCh MAsh NBea SLim WBGC
	'Jackmanii Superba' ambig. (LL)	More than 30 suppliers
	'Jackmanii Superba' misapplied	see *C.* 'Gipsy Queen'
	'Jacqueline du Pré' (A) ♀H4	CElw CHad CPev CSPN EBee EHan ELan EPfP ERob ESCh ETho MGos NBea NHaw NTay SBra SPet WBGC
	'Jacqui' (M/d)	ERob ESCh ETho LRHS MGos NBrk NHaw NLar SBra SCoo SLim SPoG WBcn
	'James Mason' (EL)	CPev CSPN EHan ESCh NBea NHaw NTay SBra SCoo WBGC
	'Jan Lindmark' (A/d)	EBee ERob ESCh ETho LRHS MAsh MGos NBea NBir NSti NTay SBra SCoo SLim SWCr WBGC WCru WFar
§	'Jan Paweł' (EL)	CMac CWSG EBee ECtt ELan EPfP ESCh ETho GKir LRHS MAsh NBea SBra SCoo SLim SPer SPet SPoG
	'Jānis Ruplēns Number 1'	ERob
§	***japonica***	CPLN CPev CSPN CSec ERob ESCh NBrk NHaw SBra WBGC
	- B&SWJ 5017	WCru
§	- var. ***obvallata***	ESCh
	aff. ***japonica*** B&SWJ 8900	WCru
	'Jasper'	ERob ESCh
	'Jenny Caddick' (Vt)	CSPN ERob ESCh ETho NHaw NTay
	'Jenny Keay' (M/d)	EBee ERob ESCh ETho LBuc NBrk SBra SCoo
	'Jim Hollis' (EL)	ERob
	'Joan Baker' (Vt)	ERob
	'Joan Gray' (EL)	ERob ESCh
	'Joan Picton' (EL)	CWSG ESCh MAsh NBea NBrk NRib NTay SBra
	'John Gould Veitch' (EL)	ERob ESCh
	'John Gudmundsson' (EL)	ERob ESCh
	'John Huxtable' (LL) ♀H4	CDoC CPev CRHN ENot EPfP ERob ESCh ETho LRHS NBea NBrk NHaw NPri NTay SBra SCoo SLim SPoG SWCr WBGC WGor
	John Paul II	see *C.* 'Jan Paweł II'
	'John Treasure' (Vt)	CRHN ETho WBGC
	'John Warren' (EL)	CWSG ERob ESCh ETho LRHS MAsh NTay SBra SCoo SLim WBGC
	'Jorma' (LL)	ERob ESCh
	Josephine = 'Evijohill'PBR (EL) ♀H4	COtt CSPN EHan EPfP ESCh ETho GKir LAst LRHS LSRN MBNS NLar NPri NTay SBra SCoo SPer SPoG SRkn SWCr
§	x ***jouiniana***	EBee ERob ESCh MBlu MWya SPer WBGC WGwG WSHC
	- 'Chance' (H)	ESCh NBrk NTay
	'Julka' (EL)	ETho
	'June Pyne'	ESCh ETho LRHS NPri
	'Juuli' (I)	ERob ESCh ETho NBrk
	'Kaaru' (LL)	CRHN CSPN ERob ESCh ETho NBrk WBGC
	'Kacper' (EL)	CSPN ESCh ETho MGos NBrk NTay
	'Kaiu' (V)	ERob ESCh
§	'Kakio' (EL)	CElw EBee ERob ESCh ETho GKir LAst LSRN MAsh MGos NBea NTay SBra SLim SPer SPoG SWCr WBGC WFar
	'Kalina' (EL)	ERob ESCh NBrk NHaw
	'Kamilla' (EL)	ERob ESCh
§	'Kardynal Wyszyński' (EL)	CRHN EBee ERob ESCh ETho MAsh MGos NBea NBrk NTay SBra SCoo WBGC
	'Kasmu' (Vt)	ERob ESCh ETho NBrk WBGC
	'Kasugayama' (EL)	ERob
	'Katharina' (EL)	ERob ESCh
	'Kathleen Dunford' (EL)	ERob ESCh LAst LRHS LSRN MAsh NBea NHaw NTay SCoo SLim WBGC
	'Kathleen Wheeler' (EL)	CPev ERob ESCh ETho NBea NTay SCoo SDix SLim WBGC
	'Kathryn Chapman' (Vt) **new**	ESCh
	'Keith Richardson' (EL)	CPev ERob ESCh NBea NBrk NTay WBGC
	'Ken Donson' (EL) ♀H4	CElw EBee EPfP ERob ESCh MGos NBrk NTay SPet
	'Kermesina' (Vt) ♀H4	CElw CHad CPev CRHN CSam EBee ELan EPfP ESCh ETho GKir LRHS MAsh MBri MGos NBPC NBea NSti NTay SBra SCoo SDix SLim SPer SPet SPoG SWCr WBGC WBVN WSHC
	'Ketu' (LL)	ERob
	'Kiev' (Vt)	ERob ESCh
	'King Edward VII' (EL)	EBee EPfP ERob ESCh LRHS NBea NBrk NTay SBra WBGC WGor
	'King George V' (LL)	ERob ESCh NBrk
	'Kinokawa' (EL)	ERob
	'Kiri Te Kanawa' (EL)	CPev CSPN EBee EHan ERob ESCh ETho LAst LSRN MAsh NBea NBrk NHaw NTay SBra SLim WBGC
	kirilovii	ERob
	'Kirimäe' (LL)	ERob ESCh
	'Kjell' (EL)	ERob ESCh
	'Klaara' (EL)	ERob
	'Kommerei' (LL)	ERob ESCh ETho NBrk
	'Königskind' (EL)	CSPN ERob ESCh ETho NBrk NTay WBGC
	koreana	ERob NBea WSHC
	- var. ***lutea***	CElw ESCh NBrk
	'Kosmicheskaia Melodiia' (LL)	CSPN ERob ESCh NBrk NTay
	'Kotkas' (LL)	ERob
	'Kuba' (LL)	ERob ESCh NBrk
	kweichowensis	ETho

	'Küllus' (LL)	ERob ESCh ETho NTay
	ladakhiana	CPev CSPN EPfP ESCh ETho GQui MWhi NBea NBir NHaw SBra WCru
	'Lady Betty Balfour' (LL)	CElw CPev CSPN CWSG ERob ESCh ETho GKir LRHS MAsh MBNS MBri NTay SBra SCoo SDix SGar SLim SPet SPoG WBGC WFar
	'Lady Bird Johnson' (T)	CPev EBee ERob ESCh ETho NBrk NTay SBra SCoo SLim SPoG WBGC
	'Lady Caroline Nevill' (EL)	CPev ERob ESCh MAsh NBea NTay SWCr WBGC
	'Lady Catherine' (EL/d)	ERob
	'Lady Londesborough' (EL)	CPev EBee EPfP ERob ESCh LRHS NBea NBrk NHaw NTay SCoo SDix SLim WBGC
	'Lady Northcliffe' (EL)	CPev CSPN CTri CWSG EHan EPfP ERob ESCh ETho LRHS MAsh NBea NTay SBra SDix SLim SPoG SWCr WBGC
	'Lambton Park' ♀H4	CRHN EBee EPfP ERob ESCh ETho LRHS NBea NBrk NTay WBGC
	lasiandra	CPLN ERob NHaw
	- B&SWJ 6775	WCru
	- white-flowered	ERob
	lasiantha B&SWJ 6252	WCru
	'Last Dance' (Ta)	CRHN ERob ESCh
	Lasting Love = 'Grażyna'	ESCh MAsh NBrk
	'Lasurstern' (EL) ♀H4	More than 30 suppliers
	'Laura' (LL)	ERob ESCh NBrk NHaw
	'Laura Denny' (EL)	ESCh ETho MAsh NBrk
	'Lavender Lace'	ERob ESCh MAsh
	'Lawsoniana' (EL)	CElw CRHN CWSG ESCh LAst MAsh MBar NBea NBlu NBrk NTay SLim SPet WBGC
	'Leione'	ESCh
	'Lemon Chiffon' (EL)	CSPN EBee ERob ESCh ETho NBrk NHaw NTay SBra
	aff. ***leschenaultiana*** B&SWJ 7202 **new**	WCru
	Liberation = 'Evifive'PBR (EL)	ERob ESCh ETho LAst LRHS NTay SBra SCoo SLim SPoG SWCr WBGC
§	***ligusticifolia***	ERob GSki NHaw
	'Liisu' (LL)	ESCh
	'Lilacina Floribunda' (EL)	CBcs EBee ESCh LRHS MBNS MBar NBea NBrk NHaw SBra WBGC
	'Lilactime' (EL)	ERob ESCh NBea NBrk NHaw NTay SBra
	'Lincoln Star' (EL)	CPev CRHN EPfP ERob ESCh GKir LAst LRHS MAsh MBar MGos NBea NBrk NEgg NPri NTay SBra SCoo SDix SLim SPer SPet SPoG WBGC
	'Lincolnshire Lady' (A)	NTay
	'Little Bas' (Vt)	CRHN CSPN ERob ESCh NBrk NHaw NLar NTay
	'Little Butterfly' (Vt)	CRHN ERob ESCh NHaw NTay
	'Little Nell' (Vt)	CElw CPev CRHN CSPN ELan ERob ESCh ETho GKir LRHS MAsh MWgw NBea NBrk NTay SBra SCoo SDix SLim SPer SPet SPoG WBGC WFar
	'Lord Herschell'	CElw CPev ERob ETho
	'Lord Nevill' (EL)	CPev CWSG EPfP ERob ESCh ETho LRHS MAsh NBea NBlu NTay SBra SDix WBGC WFar
	'Louise Rowe' (EL)	EBee ELan ERob ESCh ETho LRHS MAsh MGos NBea NHaw NTay SBra SCoo SLim SPet SPoG WBGC
	loureiroana HWJ 663	WCru
	'Love Jewelry'	ESCh ETho
	'Lucey' (LL)	ESCh NBrk
	'Lucie' (EL)	NBea WBGC
	'Lunar Lass' (Fo/f)	CRez CStu ECho EHyt EPfP ESCh ETho ITim LBee NLAp NSla SIng WAbe WPGP
	'Lunar Lass' x ***foetida*** (Fo)	ECou
I	'Lunar Lass Variegata' (Fo/v)	ECho
	'Luther Burbank' (LL)	ERob ESCh NTay
§	'M. Johnson' (A)	ERob
§	'M. Koster' (Vt)	CDoC CElw CRHN CSam EBee EPfP ESCh ETho LRHS MBri MSwo NBea NHaw NTay SBra SLim SPer SPet SPoG WBGC
	'Macrantha' (F)	ERob
	macropetala (d)	CBcs CElw CPev CSBt EBee ELan ENot EPfP ERob ESCh ETho GKir LAst LRHS MAsh MBar MGos NBPC NBea NBlu SDix SGar SLim SPer SPet SWCr WBGC WFar WOrn
	- 'Alborosea'	see *C.* 'Blushing Ballerina'
	- 'Blue Lagoon'	see *C. macropetala* 'Lagoon' Jackman 1959
§	- 'Chili' (A/d)	ERob NBrk
	- 'Harry Smith'	see *C. macropetala* 'Chili'
	- 'Lagoon' Jackman 1956	see *C. macropetala* 'Maidwell Hall' Jackman
§	- 'Lagoon' Jackman 1959 (A/d) ♀H4	CSPN ERob ETho LRHS LSRN MAsh MSwo MWgw NBea NBrk NSti SBra SCoo SLim SMur SPoG SWCr WBGC WCru
§	- 'Maidwell Hall' Jackman (A/d)	CSPN CTri CWSG EBee ECtt EPfP ERob ESCh ETho LRHS LSRN MAsh MGos NBea NBrk SBra SCoo SHBN SWCr WBGC WCru WPGP WSHC WTel
	- 'Wesselton' (A/d)	CSPN ERob ESCh ETho MBri MGos NBrk NHaw NTay WBGC
	- 'White Moth'	see *C.* 'White Moth'
	'Madame Baron-Veillard' (LL)	CPev ECtt ESCh LAst LRHS MBar MWgw NBrk NTay SBra SCoo SDix SLim SWCr WBGC
	'Madame Edouard André' (LL)	CPev CRHN CSPN EPfP ERob ESCh LRHS LSRN MAsh NBea NTay SBra SCoo SDix SLim SPoG SWCr WBGC
	'Madame Grangé' (LL) ♀H4	CPev CRHN CSPN EPfP ESCh ETho LRHS MAsh NBea NBrk NHaw NTay SBra SCoo SDix SLim SPoG SWCr WBGC
	'Madame Julia Correvon' (Vt) ♀H4	More than 30 suppliers
	'Madame van Houtte' (EL)	ERob ESCh
	'Magnus Johnson'	see *C.* 'M. Johnson'
	'Majojo' (Fo)	GEdr
	'Mammut' (EL)	ERob ESCh
§	***mandschurica***	ERob ETho GCal NLar SBra
	- B&SWJ 1060	WCru
	marata	WCot
	'Marcel Moser' (EL)	CPev ERob ESCh NBrk NTay SDix
	'Margaret Hunt' (LL)	CSPN ELan ERob ESCh ETho LRHS NBea NBrk NHaw NTay SBra SPla
	'Margaret Jones' (M/d)	ERob ESCh NBrk NHaw SBra WBGC
	'Margaret Wood' (EL)	ERob ESCh NTay
	'Margot Koster'	see *C.* 'M. Koster'
	'Maria Louise Jensen' (EL)	ESCh NTay SBra WBGC
	'Marie Boisselot' (EL) ♀H4	More than 30 suppliers
	'Marjorie' (M/d)	More than 30 suppliers
	'Markham's Pink' (A/d) ♀H4	More than 30 suppliers
	marmoraria ♀H2-3	EHyt ENot EPot ESCh GCrs LRHS NLAp NSla SBla SIng WAbe WFar
	- hybrid (Fo)	ITim LBee WThu
	marmoraria x ***cartmanii*** hort. 'Joe' (Fo)	MGos

	Name	Suppliers
	'Marmori' (LL)	ERob ESCh ETho NBrk
	'Mary-Claire' (EL/d)	ERob ESCh
§	'Maskarad' (Vt)	CSPN ERob ESCh NBrk SBra SWCr WBGC
	Masquerade (Vt)	see *C.* 'Maskarad'
I	'Masquerade' (EL)	ETho LRHS MBri NTay SMur
	'Matilda' (EL) **new**	ESCh
	'Matka Siedliska' (EL)	CSPN ERob ESCh NTay
§	'Matka Teresa' (EL)	ERob
	'Matka Urszula Ledóchowska' (EL)	ERob
	'Maureen' (LL)	CPev CSPN CWSG ETho MAsh NBrk
	mauritiana	ERob
	maximowicziana	see *C. terniflora*
	'Mayleen' (M) 🏆H4	CElw CHad CPou CSBt CWSG EBee ECtt ERob ESCh ETho GLbr LRHS MAsh MBri MGos NBea NPri NTay SAga SBra SHBN SLim SPer SPet SPoG SWCr WBGC WFar WPen
	'Medley'	ESCh LRHS
	'Meeli' (LL))	EBee ESCh NBrk
	'Meloodia' (LL)	WBGC
	'Memm' (A/d)	ERob
I	'Mercury'	ETho NHaw
	'Mia' (EL/d)	ERob
	'Michelle' (I)	ERob
	microphylla	ECou
	'Mikelite' (Vt)	ERob ESCh NBrk NHaw
	'Mikla' (LL)	ERob
	'Miniseelik' (LL)	ERob ESCh ETho NBrk
	'Minister' (EL)	ESCh ETho NBrk SCoo
	'Minuet' (Vt) 🏆H4	CHad CRHN CSPN EPfP ERob ESCh ETho GKir GLbr LRHS MSwo NBPC NBea NTay SBra SCoo SDix SLim SPer SPla SPoG SWCr WBGC WSHC WTel
	'Miriam Markham' (EL)	CPev ERob ESCh NBea NBrk NHaw SBra SPoG WBGC
	'Miss Bateman' (EL) 🏆H4	More than 30 suppliers
	'Miss Crawshay' (EL)	CPev ERob ESCh NHaw NTay SLim WBGC
N	***montana***	CBcs CElw CPLG CPev CSBt EBee ECtt ENot ESCh GKir MBar MGos NBea SBod SBra SDix SHBN SLim SPet SPoG SSta WBGC WFar
	- B&SWJ 6724 from Taiwan **new**	WCru
	- B&SWJ 6930	WCru
	- BWJ 8189b from China	WCru
	- HWJK 2156 from Nepal **new**	WCru
	- ***alba***	see *C. montana*
	- 'Alexander' (M)	CPou CWSG ERob LRHS MBNS MGos NTay SCoo SWCr WBrE WCru
	- var. ***grandiflora*** 🏆H4	More than 30 suppliers
I	- 'Lilacina' (M)	ESCh MAsh SBra WPen
	- 'Peveril' (M)	CPev CSPN ERob ESCh NBrk SBra
	- var. ***rubens*** E.H.Wilson	More than 30 suppliers
	- - 'Brookfield Clove' (M)	ERob
I	- - 'Odorata' (M)	EBee EPfP ERob ESCh ETho GSki LFol MGos MWgw NTay SCoo SLim SPoG WBGC WGor
	- - 'Pink Perfection' (M)	CDoC CElw CWSG EBee ECtt ELan EPfP ERob ESCh LAst LRHS LSRN NBea NBlu NBrk NTay SBra SCoo SLim SPer SPet SPoG SWCr WBGC WFar
	- - 'Tetrarose' (M) 🏆H4	More than 30 suppliers
I	- 'Rubens Superba' (M)	CMHG CWSG EBee ECtt ESCh GKir LBuc NCGa SHBN SLim WFar
	- var. ***sericea***	see *C. spooneri*
	- var. ***wilsonii***	CElw CPev CSPN CSam EBee ECtt ELan EPfP ERob ESCh ETho GGar LAst LRHS LSRN MBar MSwo NBea NEgg NTay SBra SDix SPet SPoG SWCr WBGC WBVN WBrE WFar WWhi
	'Monte Cassino' (EL)	CRHN CSPN ERob ESCh ETho MAsh NBrk NTay SPet WBGC
	'Moonbeam' (Fo)	EBee ECou EHyt ELan EMar EPot ESCh GEdr GKir ITim MGos MSte MTis NBrk NLAp NSla NTay SBla SBra SLon WAbe WCot
§	'Moonlight' (EL)	CElw CPev CSPN ERob ESCh LAst MAsh NBrk NTay SBra WBGC
	'Moonman' (Fo)	EHyt ETho SIng WAbe
	Morning Cloud	see *C.* 'Yukikomachi'
	Mother Theresa	see *C.* 'Matka Teresa'
	'Mrs Bush' (LL)	ERob ESCh LRHS NBea WBGC WWes
	'Mrs Cholmondeley' (EL) 🏆H4	More than 30 suppliers
	'Mrs George Jackman' (EL) 🏆H4	CPev CSPN ERob ESCh ETho MAsh MBri MGos NBea NBlu NBrk NTay SBra SCoo SLim SPla WBGC
	'Mrs Hope' (EL)	CPev ERob ESCh NBea NBrk SBra WBGC
	'Mrs James Mason' (EL)	CPev ERob ESCh ETho NBea NHaw NTay SBra SLim WBGC
	'Mrs N.Thompson' (EL)	More than 30 suppliers
	'Mrs P.B.Truax' (EL)	EHan ERob ESCh LRHS NBea NTay SBra SCoo SDix SLim WBGC
	'Mrs. P.T. James' (EL)	ERob ESCh
	'Mrs Robert Brydon' (H)	CBgR EPfP ERob IPot MWgw NBrk NEgg NTay SCoo SGar SLim SPur STes WBGC WCot
	'Mrs Spencer Castle' (EL)	CPev CSPN ERob ESCh NTay SBra WBGC
	'Mrs T. Lundell' (Vt)	CSPN EBee ERob ESCh ETho NBea NBrk NTay
	'Multi Blue' (EL)	More than 30 suppliers
	'My Angel'PBR (Ta)	CSPN ELan ESCh MGos NHaw NLar NTay SPoG WBGC
	'Myôjô' (EL)	CSPN ERob ESCh LRHS SBra SCoo SLim SPoG WBGC
	'Myôkô' (EL)	SLim
	'Nadezhda' (LL)	ERob ESCh ETho NBrk NTay
§	***napaulensis***	CBcs CPLN CPev CSPN CSec ERob ESCh ETho LFol LRHS NBea NTay SBra SLim SPoG WBGC WCru WFar WGwG WSHC
I	'Natacha' (EL)	CElw EBee ERob ESCh ETho NBea NBrk NHaw NTay SBra SCoo SLim SPet SPoG WBGC
	'Negritianka' (LL)	CSPN ERob ESCh LBuc MBri NBrk NHaw NTay WBGC
	'Negus' (LL)	ERob ESCh
	'Nelly Moser' (EL) 🏆H4	More than 30 suppliers
	Nettleton seedlings	EPot
	'New Dawn' (M)	CSPN ERob ESCh NEgg NHaw SBra WBGC
	'New Love'PBR (H)	CBgR CSPN ENot ERob ESCh ETho LAst LBuc LPio MBlu MGos NHaw NLar NSti NTay SBra WCAu WHil
	New Zealand hybrids (Fo)	ECou
	'Nikolai Rubtsov' (LL)	CSPN ERob ESCh ETho NTay
	'Niobe' (EL) 🏆H4	More than 30 suppliers
	'Norfolk Queen' (EL)	ESCh
	'North Star'	see *C.* 'Põhjanael'
	'Nuit de Chine' (EL)	ERob ESCh NBrk
	obscura	ERob

Name	Suppliers
obvallata	see *C. japonica* var. *obvallata*
§ ***occidentalis***	NEgg
- subsp. ***grosseserrata*** **new**	EHyt
ochotensis	CSPN ERob GIBF SDys
- 'Carmen Rose' (A)	ERob
'Odoriba' (V)	ESCh ETho
'Ola Howells' (A/d)	ERob ESCh NBrk
'Olga' (M)	ERob ESCh
'Olimpiada-80' (EL)	ERob ESCh
'Omoshiro' (EL)	ESCh NBrk
'Oonagare' **new**	ESCh
Opaline	see *C.* 'Asagasumi'
orientalis misapplied	see *C. tibetana* subsp. *vernayi*
- 'Orange Peel'	see *C. tibetana* subsp. *vernayi* 'Orange Peel'
orientalis L.	CPLG EBee ESCh GSki LRHS SBra SCoo SReu WFar
- var. ***orientalis***	CStr ERob
* - 'Rubromarginata' (Ta)	CPev
- var. ***tenuifolia***	ERob
- var. ***tenuiloba***	see *C. columbiana* var. *tenuiloba*
'Otto Fröbel' (EL)	CSPN ERob ESCh NBrk NTay
'Paala' (EL)	ERob
'Paddington' (EL)	ERob ETho
'Pagoda' (Vt) ♀H4	CDoC CElw CPev CRHN EBee EPfP ESCh ETho LAst LRHS MAsh MBri MWgw NBea NSti NTay SBra SCoo SLim SPla SPoG SRms SWCr WBGC
'Päkapikk' (LL)	ERob
'Pamela' (F)	CSPN ERob ESCh ETho LBuc NHaw NTay WBGC
'Pamela Jackman'	see *C. alpina* 'Pamela Jackman'
'Pamiat Serdtsa' (I)	ERob ESCh ETho WBGC
'Pamina' (EL) **new**	ETho
'Pangbourne Pink' (I) ♀H4	CElw CHad CSPN EBee EHan EPfP ERob ESCh ETho GBuc LRHS MAsh MWgw NBPC NBea NBrk NHaw NTay SBra SCoo SLim SWCr WBGC WCru
paniculata Thunb.	see *C. terniflora*
paniculata J.G. Gmel.	CPev CSPN ESCh GGar LRHS SBra WPGP WSHC
- var. ***lobata***	MWgw NLar WBGC
'Paola' (EL/d)	ESCh
'Paradise Queen' (EL)	ESCh MWgw NLar
'Parasol' (EL)	CSPN ERob ESCh NBrk NTay
parviflora DC.	see *C. campaniflora*
parviflora ambig.	ERob
parviloba var. ***bartlettii*** B&SWJ 6788	WCru
'Pastel Blue' (I)	CPev ERob ESCh ETho LRHS NBea
'Pastel Pink' (I)	CPev ERob ESCh ETho WBGC
'Pastel Princess' (EL)	ERob NHaw NTay
'Pat Coleman' (EL)	ESCh ETho
patens	NBea
- from China	ERob ESCh
- from Japan	ERob ESCh
- 'Korean Moon' (EL)	WCru
§ - 'Manshuu Ki' (EL)	More than 30 suppliers
- 'Nagoya' (EL)	ESCh
- 'Sanda' (EL)	ESCh
- 'Yukiokoshi' (EL)	ERob ESCh ETho
Patricia Ann Fretwell = 'Pafar' (EL)	CPev CSPN ERob ETho LRHS NBea
§ 'Paul Farges' (Vt) ♀H4	CBcs CSPN CStu EBee ERob ETho MBlu MWgw NBrk NSti NTay SBra SLim WBGC WTel WWeb
'Pauline' (A/d)	CWSG EBee ERob ESCh ETho LRHS NBea NBrk NTay SBra SCoo SLim SWCr WBGC
'Pearl Rose' (A/d)	CWSG ERob
'Pendragon' (Vt)	ERob ESCh
'Pennell's Purity' (LL)	ERob ESCh ETho NBrk NHaw NTay
'Percy Picton' (EL)	ESCh MAsh
'Perle d'Azur' (LL)	More than 30 suppliers
'Perrin's Pride' (Vt)	ERob ESCh LRHS MGos NBrk NTay SBra SWCr WBGC
'Peter Pan' (EL)	ERob
peterae	ERob
- var. ***trichocarpa***	ERob
Petit Faucon = 'Evisix'[PBR] (I) ♀H4	EBee ECtt EHan ENot EPfP ERob ETho GMac IBal LAst LRHS LSRN MAsh MBNS MBri MWgw NBea NPri NTay SBra SCoo SLim SPoG SRkn SWCr WBGC WPGP
petriei	ECou LPio MBow SOkd
- 'Princess' (Fo/f)	ECou
- 'Steepdown' (Fo/f)	ECou
'Peveril Peach'	CPev ESCh
'Peveril Pearl' (EL)	CElw CPev ERob ESCh ETho NTay
'Peveril Pendant'	CPev
I 'Phoenix' (EL)	ESCh
Picardy = 'Evipo024'	LRHS
I 'Picton's Variety' (M)	CPev CTri EBee ERob ESCh ETho NHaw SBra SHBN WBGC
pierotii	ERob
'Piilu' (EL)	CSPN ELan ERob ESCh ETho LBuc LRHS MBri NBrk NHaw NPri NTay SBra SCoo SLim SPoG WBGC
'Pink Champagne'	see *C.* 'Kakio'
'Pink Fantasy' (LL)	CPev CRHN CSPN CTri CWSG ERob ESCh ETho LRHS MAsh MBar NBea NBrk NTay SBra SCoo SLim SPoG SRkn SWCr WBGC
'Pink Flamingo' (A) ♀H4	CElw CMHG CSPN EBee ECtt ELan ENot EPfP ERob ESCh ETho LRHS LSRN MWgw NBPC NEgg NPri NSti NTay SCoo SLim SMur SPet SPoG SRkn SWCr WBGC
'Pink Pearl' (EL)	ESCh NBrk NTay
'Pirko' (Vt)	ERob ESCh
§ ***pitcheri***	CPLG CPev ERob ESCh ETho NBrk
'Pixie' (Fo/m)	CElw CSPN CStu CTbh ECou EHyt ELan ENot EPfP ESCh ETho LRHS MGos MWgw NHaw NLar NTay SBra SCoo SPet SPoG SWCr WBGC
I 'Pleniflora' (M/d)	ESCh MGos NBrk NHaw SBra
§ 'Plum Beauty' (A)	CSPN ERob ESCh WBGC
§ 'Põhjanael' (LL)	CSPN CWSG ERob ESCh ETho MGos NBea NBrk SCoo SLim WBGC
'Pointy' (A)	ESCh NTay
'Polish Spirit' (LL) ♀H4	More than 30 suppliers
§ ***potaninii***	CCge CRHN CSPN ECtt EShb GCra GIBF MWhi NEgg WSHC
§ - var. ***potaninii***	CPev ERob NBea NTay SDix
- var. ***souliei***	see *C. potaninii* var. *potaninii*
'Praecox' (H) ♀H4	More than 30 suppliers
* 'Prairie'	LRHS
'Prairie River' (A)	ERob
Pretty in Blue = 'Zopre'[PBR] (F)	ESCh ETho NTay SBra SHBN
'Pribaltika' (LL)	ERob ESCh WBGC
'Primrose Star'[PBR]	see *C.* 'Star'
'Prince Charles' (LL) ♀H4	CElw CHad CPou CRHN CSPN CTri EBee ELan EPfP ESCh ETho LRHS LSRN NBea NBir NTay SBra SCoo SDix SLim SPer SPet SPoG SWCr WBGC WSHC
'Prince Philip' (EL)	ERob ESCh NBrk NTay SBra WFar
§ 'Princess Diana' (T) ♀H4	CBcs CElw CHad CPev CRHN CSPN CWSG EBee EHan ELan

		ERob ESCh ETho LBuc LSRN MAsh MBlu MGos MSwo MWgw NBea NBrk NHaw NTay SBra SLim SPet SPoG SWCr WBGC
§	'Princess of Wales' (EL)	EPfP ERob ESCh LRHS LSRN MBNS NLar NPri SBra WBGC WSHC
	'Prins Hendrik' (EL)	ERob WGor
	'Prinsesse Alexandra'PBR **new**	ESCh NTay
	'Propertius' (A)	ERob ESCh ETho NBrk NHaw
	'Proteus' (EL)	CPev CSPN EHan ELan EPfP ESCh ETho GKir LAst LRHS MAsh MBNS NBea NTay SBra SCoo SDix SLim SPer SPet SPoG WBGC
	'Pruinina'	see *C.* 'Plum Beauty'
	'Pulmapäev' (LL)	ERob ESCh
	'Purple Haze'	CRHN
	'Purple Spider' (A/d)	CBcs CElw CSPN EBee ERob ESCh ETho GKir LBuc LSRN MBlu MWgw NBea NHaw NTay SBra SCoo SLim SPer SPet SPoG WBGC WWhi
	'Purple Treasure' (V) **new**	ESCh
	'Purpurea Plena Elegans' (Vt/d) ♀H4	More than 30 suppliers
	quadribracteolata	ECou
	- 'Nancy's Lookout'	ECou
	'Queen Alexandra' (EL)	ERob ESCh
	'Radar Love' (Ta)	GBin NLar
	'Radost' (EL)	ERob
	'Ragamuffin' (EL/d)	ENot ERob ESCh
	'Rahvarinne' (LL)	ERob ESCh
	ranunculoides CD&R 2345	WCru
	recta	CFee CHad CPev CSPN EChP ECtt EPfP ERob ETho EWTr GKev GKir GSki LPio LRHS MAsh MLLN MNrw MWhi NBea NEgg NLar SPer WBGC WPer WWye
§	- 'Lime Close' (F)	MSte SMrm
I	- 'Peveril' (F)	CPev ERob ESCh LAst LRHS MSte NBrk SCoo WBGC WCra
	- 'Purpurea' (F)	More than 30 suppliers
§	- subsp. ***recta*** var. ***lasiosepala***	CSPN ERob WHil
	- Serious Black	see *C. recta* 'Lime Close'
	- 'Velvet Night' (F)	CSpe ECtt ERob ESCh ETho LAst MBri MDun MTis NEgg SPoG WBGC
	'Red Ballon' (Ta)	ERob ESCh LBuc
	'Red Beetroot Beauty' (A)	CSPN ERob ESCh LBuc MAsh NBrk
	'Red Cooler'	see *C.* 'Crimson King'
	'Red Five' (T)	CPev
	'Red Pearl' (EL)	ERob ESCh ETho MGos NTay
§	***rehderiana*** ♀H4	More than 30 suppliers
	- BWJ 7700	WCru
	- CC 3601	CPLG
	'Reiman' (LL)	ERob
	reticulata	ERob
	'Rhapsody' F. Watkinson (LL) ♀H4	CPev CSPN ENot EPfP ERob ETho LRHS MAsh MBri MGos NBrk NHaw NTay SBra SCoo SPoG WBGC WFar
	'Richard Pennell' (EL) ♀H4	CPev EBee EHan ERob ESCh ETho LRHS MAsh MBri NBea NBrk NPri NTay SBra SDix SLim SWCr WBGC
	'Ristimägi' (LL)	ERob
	'Rodomax' (A)	ERob ESCh
	'Roko' (LL)	ERob
	'Roko-Kolla' (LL)	CSPN EBee ERob ESCh ETho NBea NBrk SBra WWes
	'Romantika' (LL)	CSPN EBee ELan ERob ESCh ETho MAsh NBea NHaw NTay SBra SCoo SLim SPer SPoG WBGC
	'Roogoja' (LL)	ERob ESCh
	'Rooguchi' (I)	EBee ERob ESCh ETho LRHS NBrk
	'Rosa Königskind' (EL)	ERob ESCh
I	'Rosea' (I) ♀H4	CBcs CBot CPev CSPN EBee EHan EMar EPfP ERob ESCh ETho LAst LRHS LSRN MBri MSte MSwo MTho MWgw NBea NBrk NChi NSti NTay SCoo SLim SOkh WBGC WCra
	'Rosea' (Vt)	ERob
	'Rosebud' (M/d)	EBee ESCh NCGa NLar NPer
	Rosemoor = 'Evipo002'	ESCh LRHS MAsh MBri SPer
	'Rosy O'Grady' (A) ♀H4	EBee ELan ESCh ETho MAsh MBar MBri MGos NBea NSti NTay SCoo SLim SPer WBGC
	'Rosy Pagoda' (A)	EBee ELan EPfP ERob ESCh LRHS LSRN MBri NBea NBir NHaw WBGC WTel
	'Rouge Cardinal' (LL)	More than 30 suppliers
	'Royal Velours' (Vt) ♀H4	More than 30 suppliers
	Royal Velvet = 'Evifour'PBR (EL)	CSPN EPfP ESCh ETho LAst MBri MWgw NTay SBra SCoo SLim WBGC
	'Royalty' (EL) ♀H4	CElw CSPN ELan EPfP ERob ESCh LRHS MAsh NBea NBir NPri NTay SBra SCoo SDix SLim SPer SPet SPoG SWCr WBGC
	'Rozalia' (EL)	ESCh
	'Rubra' (Vt)	LBuc NBrk
	'Ruby' (A)	CMHG CPev CSPN CWSG EBee ELan EPfP ESCh ETho LRHS MAsh MGos NBea NEgg NSti SBra SChu SCoo SDix SHBN SLim SPer SPet SPoG WBGC WTel
	'Ruby Glow' (EL)	EPfP ERob ESCh NTay WBGC
	'Rüütel' (EL)	ERob ESCh ETho MAsh NBrk NHaw NTay SBra SCoo SLim SPoG WBGC
	'Saalomon' (LL)	ERob
	'Sakala' (EL)	ERob ESCh
	'Sakurahime' (EL)	ERob ESCh
	'Sally Cadge' (EL)	ERob ESCh
	'Salmon Blush' (A/d)	NBrk
	'Samantha Denny' (EL)	CSPN ERob ESCh ETho MAsh NBrk NHaw NRib WBGC
	'Sander' (H)	CSPN ERob ESCh WBGC
	'Sandra Denny' (EL)	ESCh ETho NBrk
	'Sano-no-murasaki' (EL) **new**	ESCh
	'Satsukibare' (EL)	ERob ESCh MGos NBrk WBGC
I	'Saturn' (LL)	ERob ESCh NBea SPla WBGC
	'Scartho Gem' (EL)	CPev EPfP ERob ESCh NBea NPri NTay SCoo WBGC
	'Sealand Gem' (EL)	CPev ERob ESCh ETho LAst NBea NHaw NTay SBra SCoo SLim WBGC
	'Seeryuu' (I) **new**	ETho
	'Semu' (LL)	CSPN ERob ESCh ETho NBrk
	'Serenata' (EL)	ERob ESCh
	serratifolia	CElw CPev EHyt ERob ESCh ETho GFlt GIBF MDKP MLLN MWhi NTay SDix WBGC WFar
	- from Korea B&SWJ 8458	WCru
	'Sheila Thacker' (EL)	ESCh ETho
I	'Sherriffii' (Ta)	ERob ESCh
	'Shirakihane'	NBrk
	'Shirayukihime' (LL)	CSPN ESCh
§	'Shiva' (A)	CElw ERob NBrk WBcn
	'Shorty' (Ta)	ERob
	'Sho-un' (EL)	EBee ERob ESCh NTay SBra
	'Shropshire Blue'	ERob WBGC
	'Sialia' (A/d)	ERob ESCh NBrk
	sibirica	CBcs CPev ERob NTay SPla WBVN

- 'Altai' (A)	ESCh
- var. ***tianschanica*** 'Riga' (A)	ERob NTay WBGC
'Signe' (Vt)	see *C.* 'Kasmu'
'Siirus' (EL)	ERob
'Silmakivi' (EL)	ERob ESCh
'Silver Lady' **new**	SPoG
'Silver Moon' (EL)	CSPN EHan ERob ESCh ETho MAsh NBea NTay SBra WBGC
§ 'Simplicity' (A)	CBgR CSPN ERob ESCh NBrk SPet
simsii Small	see *C. pitcheri*
simsii Sweet	see *C. crispa*
§ 'Sinee Dozhd' (I)	CSPN ERob ESCh LBuc MGos NBrk NTay WBGC
'Sinee Plamia' (LL)	ERob ESCh NHaw
'Sir Garnet Wolseley' (EL)	ERob ESCh MAsh NBrk NTay SDix WBGC
'Sir Trevor Lawrence' (T)	CPev CSPN EBee ERob ESCh ETho LAst LRHS MAsh NBea NHaw NSti NTay SBra SCoo SDix SLim SPer SPoG SWCr WBGC
'Sizaia Ptitsa' (I)	ERob ESCh ETho NBrk
'Snow Queen' (EL)	CElw CSPN EBee EHan EPfP ESCh ETho GMac LRHS MBri MGos MSwo NBea NTay SBra SPet WBGC WTel
'Snowbird' (A/d)	CPev CSPN ERob ESCh MAsh NHaw SBra
'Snowdrift'	see *C. armandii* 'Snowdrift'
§ 'Södertälje' (Vt)	CRHN ERob ESCh ETho NBea NTay SBra SCoo SPoG
'Solweig' (EL)	ERob
songarica	ERob ESCh LRHS NBrk NTay SBra WHil
'Souvenir de J.L. Delbard' (EL)	ERob ESCh NBrk SBra
§ 'Souvenir du Capitaine Thuilleaux' (EL)	CPev ESCh GKir LAst MAsh MGos NBea NBlu NTay SBra SCoo SLim SPoG WBGC
'Special Occasion' (EL)	CSPN ENot ERob ESCh ETho LBuc MBNS NBea NHaw NLar NPri NTay SBra SCoo SLim WBGC WFar
§ ***spooneri***	CElw CPev CTri CWSG ECtt ELan ERob ESCh GKir GQui LRHS MAsh MWgw NBrk NTay SBra SCoo SLim SLon SRms WCru WFoF
§ 'Spooneri Rosea' (M)	CTbh CTrw ERob ESCh NBrk
'Sputnik' (I)	CSPN ERob ESCh NBrk NTay
stans	CAby CHea CPLG CPou ERob ESCh ETho GSki IFro ITer LRHS MWhi NLar SHel SIng WBGC
- B&SWJ 4567	WCru
- B&SWJ 6345	WCru
- 'Rusalka' (H)	ERob
§ 'Star'PBR (M/d)	CDoC COtt CSPN EHan EPfP ERob ESCh ETho LAst LBuc LRHS MBlu MGos MSwo MWgw NBrk NLar NPri SBra SCoo SPer SPoG WBGC WFar WWhi
'Star of India' (LL)	CElw CPev CRHN EBee EPfP ERob ESCh ETho LRHS MAsh MGos NBea NTay SBra SCoo SDix SLim SPer SPoG SWCr WBGC
'Starfish' (EL)	ERob ESCh NHaw NTay
'Stasik' (LL)	ERob ESCh
'Strawberry Roan' (EL)	ESCh
Sugar Candy = 'Evione'PBR (EL)	EMil ERob ESCh LAst MBri NPri NTay SBra SCoo SLim WBGC WWes
Summer Snow	see *C.* 'Paul Farges'
'Sundance'	CSPN EBee ERob ESCh
'Sunrise'PBR (M/d)	COtt CSPN EHan ESCh ETho MAsh MSwo NBrk NHaw NLar SBra SPoG WFar
'Sunset' (EL) 🏆H4	EHan ERob ESCh LRHS MBri NBea NEgg NTay SBra SMur SWCr WBGC
'Suruga' (EL) **new**	ESCh
'Susan Allsop' (EL)	CPev ERob ESCh WBGC
'Suzanne'	LRHS
'Sylvia Denny' (EL)	CWSG EBee ELan EPfP ERob ESCh ETho GKir LAst LRHS LSRN MAsh MBar NBea NBrk NRib NTay SBra SCoo SLim SPer SPoG WBGC
'Sympatia' (LL)	ERob ESCh NHaw NTay WBGC
'Syrena' (LL)	ESCh NHaw
szuyuanensis B&SWJ 6791	WCru
§ 'Tage Lundell' (A)	CElw CSPN EBee ERob ETho MGos NBea NBrk NTay SPet WBGC
'Tango' (Vt)	CElw CRHN EBee ERob ESCh NBrk SBra WBGC
tangutica	More than 30 suppliers
- subsp. ***obtusiuscula*** 'Gravetye Variety' (Ta)	ERob ESCh MWgw
'Tapestry' (I)	CPev ERob SBra
'Tartu' (EL)	CSPN ERob ESCh
tashiroi	ERob ESCh ITer
- B&SWJ 1423	WCru
- purple-flowered B&SWJ 7005	WCru
- 'Yellow Peril'	WCru
'Tateshina' (EL)	NTay
'Teksa' (LL)	ERob ESCh
'Tentel' (LL)	ERob ETho
tenuiloba	see *C. columbiana* var. *tenuiloba*
§ ***terniflora***	CBcs CPev EBee EHol EPfP ESCh ETho LFol LRHS NBrk NHaw NSti SBra SLim SPer WCru
- B&SWJ 5751	WCru
- var. ***mandshurica***	see *C. mandschurica*
- var. ***robusta***	see *C. terniflora* var. *terniflora*
§ - var. ***terniflora***	ERob ESCh LFol
'Teruko'	ERob
'Teshio' (EL)	CSPN ERob ESCh ETho LBuc NBrk NHaw SBra SLim SPoG WBGC
texensis	CBcs ETho IFro
- 'The Princess of Wales'	see *C.* 'Princess Diana'
'The Bride' (EL)	CSPN ERob ESCh ETho LBuc NBea NBrk NHaw NTay SBra SLim WBGC
'The Comet' (EL)	ERob
'The Dubliner' **new**	ENot
'The First Lady' (EL)	CSPN ERob ESCh ETho LBuc MAsh NTay SCoo SLim WBGC
'The President' (EL) 🏆H4	More than 30 suppliers
'The Princess of Wales' (L)	see *C.* 'Princess of Wales' (L)
'The Princess of Wales' (T)	see *C.* 'Princess Diana' (T)
'The Vagabond' (EL)	CSPN CWSG ELan ERob ESCh ETho MAsh MGos NBea NBrk NHaw NTay SBra WBGC
'The Velvet' (EL)	ERob
'Theydon Belle'	ESCh
thunbergii hort.	see *C. terniflora*
'Thyrislund' (EL)	CSPN ESCh ETho
'Tibetan Mix' (Ta)	CSPN ERob ESCh
§ ***tibetana***	CPev MBar MNrw NEgg NHaw SCoo SLim SPer
- CC 4167	MGol
§ - subsp. ***vernayi***	CMHG EHyt EPfP ERob GKir MSte NLon NSti SBra SPoG SWCr WCru
- - CC&McK 193	NWCA
- - var. ***laciniifolia***	ERob ESCh WBGC
- - LS&E 13342	see *C. tibetana* subsp. *vernayi* 'Orange Peel'

§	– – var. ***vernayi*** 'Orange Peel' LS&E 13342	CBcs CDoC CElw CPev ENot EPfP ERob ESCh GKir GMac LAst LBuc LRHS MBNS MBri NBrk SBra SGar SLim SPoG WBGC WFar
	Timpany NZ hybrids (Fo)	ITim NLAp
	'Tinkerbell'	see *C.* 'Shiva'
	'Titania' (EL)	ERob ESCh NBrk
	'Toki' (EL)	ESCh
	tongluensis	CPLN
	- GWJ 9358	WCru
	- HWJCM 076	WCru
	- HWJK 2368	WCru
	tosaensis B&SWJ 8900 **new**	WCru
	'Treasure Trove' (Ta)	CSPN ESCh LBuc WBGC
	'Trianon' (EL)	ERob ESCh NBrk
	'Triibu' (LL)	ESCh
	'Triinu' (Vt)	ERob
	'Trikatrei' (LL)	ESCh NBrk
§	x ***triternata*** 'Rubromarginata' ♀H4	More than 30 suppliers
	'Tsuzuki' (EL)	CSPN ERob ESCh ETho NBea NTay
	tubulosa	CHad CPev CPle CSPN EBee ESCh ETho SRms
§	- Alan Bloom = 'Alblo'[PBR] (H)	EBrs GBri GKir LRHS NLar
I	- 'Alba' (H)	ERob
	- 'Wyevale' (H) ♀H4	CPev CSPN CStr EChP ELan ENot EPfP ERob ETho GKir LRHS MAvo MBlu MRav MWat MWgw NBea NTay SBra SCoo SDix SLim SMad SPer SPla SRkn WBGC WCot WEas WHil
	'Tuchka' (EL)	ERob
	'Twilight' (EL)	CSPN ESCh ETho MAsh NTay SBra SCoo SLim SPoG WBGC
	'Ulrique' (EL)	ERob
	uncinata	CPev ERob SDix
	- B&SWJ 1893	WCru
	- var. ***ovatifolia***	ERob
	'Unity' (M)	ESCh
	urophylla	CPLN ERob SSpi
	- 'Winter Beauty'	ESCh SHBN SPoG
	urticifolia	ESCh
	- B&SWJ 8640	WCru
	- B&SWJ 8651	WCru
	'Valge Daam' (LL)	ERob ESCh ETho NHaw NTay SLim
	'Vanessa' (LL)	CRHN ERob ESCh ETho NBrk
	'Vanilla Cream' (Fo)	ECou
	x ***vedrariensis***	NBrk
	- 'Hidcote' (M)	ERob ESCh SBra WBGC
	- 'Highdown' (M)	ERob NBrk SBra
	- 'Rosea'	see *C.* 'Spooneri Rosea'
	veitchiana	ERob
	'Velutina Purpurea' (LL)	ERob
	'Venosa Violacea' (Vt) ♀H4	CElw CRHN CSPN CTbh EBee EHan ELan EPfP ERob ESCh ETho LAst LRHS LSRN MAsh NBea NSti SBra SCoo SDix SPer SPet SPla SWCr WBGC WFar
	'Vera' (M)	CElw CSPN EBee ECtt ERob ESCh ETho LRHS NBea NBir NBrk NTay SBra SCoo SLim SPla SPoG WBGC WCru
	vernayi	see *C. tibetana* subsp. *vernayi*
	'Veronica's Choice' (EL)	CPev CRHN CSPN EHan ELan ERob ESCh LRHS MGos NBea NHaw NTay SBra WBGC
	versicolor	ERob ESCh WIvy
	verticillaris	see *C. occidentalis*
	'Vetka' (LL)	ERob
	Victor Hugo = 'Evipo007' **new**	ESCh ETho NLar
N	'Victoria' (LL) ♀H4	CPev CRHN CSPN ERob ESCh ETho LAst LRHS MAsh NBea NHaw NTay SBra SCoo SDix SLim SPoG SWCr WBGC
	'Ville de Lyon' (LL)	More than 30 suppliers
	Vino = 'Poulvo'[PBR] (EL)	ERob ESCh LRHS MBri NHaw NTay SBra SCoo SPoG WBGC
I	'Viola' (LL)	CSPN EBee ERob ESCh ETho MAsh MBri NBea NBrk NHaw NTay WBGC WBcn
	'Violet Charm' (EL)	CWSG ERob ESCh NBrk NTay SBra
	'Violet Elizabeth' (EL)	ESCh NBrk SBra
	'Violet Purple' (A)	ERob ESCh MGos NHaw
	'Violetta' (EL)	ERob ESCh
	viorna	CPLN EHyt ERob ESCh WIvy WSHC
	virginiana Hook.	see *C. ligusticifolia*
	virginiana misapplied	see *C. vitalba*
§	***vitalba***	CArn CPev CRWN ERob ESCh ETho MBar MHer NHaw NTay SECG WGwG WHer
	viticella ♀H4	CElw CPev CWib ERob ESCh ETho MBNS MBri NBea NBlu NHaw SBra SDix WBGC WTel
§	- 'Flore Pleno' (Vt/d)	CPev CRHN ERob ESCh ETho LAst LRHS NBrk NHaw SBra WBGC
	- 'Hågelby White' (Vt)	ERob ESCh
	- 'Hanna' (Vt)	ERob ESCh ETho
	- 'Mary Rose'	see *C. viticella* 'Flore Pleno'
	Vivienne	see *C.* 'Beth Currie'
	'Vivienne Lawson' (LL)	ERob ESCh NTay
	'Voluceau' (Vt)	CPou CRHN ELan ERob ESCh LAst MGos NBea NTay SBra SLim SPer WBGC
	'Vostok' (LL)	ERob ESCh NBrk
	'Vyvyan Pennell' (EL)	More than 30 suppliers
	'W.E. Gladstone' (EL)	CPev CRHN ERob ESCh ETho GKir LRHS MAsh NBea NTay SBra SDix WBGC
	'W.S. Callick' (EL)	ERob ESCh NTay
	'Wada's Primrose'	see *C. patens* 'Manshuu Ki'
	'Walenburg' (Vt)	ERob ESCh NBrk NHaw SBra
	'Walter Pennell' (EL)	CPev CWSG ESCh ETho NBea NTay SBra SCoo SLim WBGC WGor
	'Warszawska Nike' (EL) ♀H4	CElw CRHN EBee EHan ELan ENot EPfP ERob ESCh ETho LAst MAsh MBri MGos MWgw NBea NBlu NBrk NTay SBra SCoo SHBN SPer SPet SPoG WBGC
	'Warwickshire Rose' (M)	CElw CRHN CSPN CWSG ECtt EHan ERob ESCh ETho GKir LSRN MAsh NBea NBrk NHaw NTay SBra SPoG WBGC WCot WFar WPGP WSHC WWeb WWhi
	'Waterperry Star' (Ta)	ERob MWat
	'Western Virgin' (Vb)	ERob NTay
	'Westerplatte' (EL)	CSPN EHan EPfP ERob ESCh ETho LAst LBuc LRHS MAsh NBea NBrk NHaw NScw NTay SBra WBGC WFar
	'White Columbine' (A) ♀H4	EPfP ERob ESCh ETho LAst NBea NSti WBGC
	'White Lady' (A/d)	EPfP ERob ESCh GKir NHaw NTay SBra WBGC
	'White Moth' (A/d)	CElw CSPN CWSG ELan EPfP ESCh ETho LRHS MGos MRav NBrk NEgg NHaw NTay SBra SLim SPer SPet SPla SPoG SRms WTel
§	'White Swan' (A/d)	CSPN EPfP ERob ESCh LRHS MAsh MBri MGos NBea NPri NSti SCoo SDix SLim SPer SPla SPoG WBGC WFoF
	'White Tokyo' (A/d)	MGos

'White Wings' (A/d)	CBcs EBee ERob ESCh ETho LAst MWgw NBrk SWCr
'Wilhelmina Tull' (EL)	CSPN ERob ESCh NBrk
'Will Goodwin' (EL) ♀H4	CBcs EBee ELan EPfP ERob ESCh ETho GMac LAst LRHS MAsh MBri NBea NBrk NPri SBra SLim SWCr WBGC
'William Kennett' (EL)	CPev CWSG EBee ELan EPfP ESCh ETho LAst LRHS MBNS MBar MBri MGos MWgw NTay SBod SBra SDix SLim SPet SPoG SWCr WBGC
williamsii	ESCh
'Willy' (A)	More than 30 suppliers
Wisley = 'Evipo001'	ESCh LRHS MAsh MBri SPer
'Xerxes' misapplied	see *C.* 'Elsa Späth'
'Yaichi' (EL) **new**	ESCh
'Yatsuhashi'	ERob
'Yellow Queen' Holland	see *C.* 'Manshuu Ki'
'Yellow Queen' Lundell/ Treasures	see *C.* 'Moonlight'
'Yorkshire Pride' (EL)	ERob ESCh
§ 'Yukikomachi' (EL)	CSPN ERob ESCh ETho NBrk NHaw NTay WBGC
'Yuki-no-yoso'oi' (EL)	ERob
yunnanensis	ERob
'Yvette Houry' (EL)	ERob ESCh NHaw NLar NTay WBGC
'Zingaro' (Vt)	ERob
'Zolotoi Iubilei' (LL)	ERob

Clematopsis see *Clematis*

Clementsia see *Rhodiola*

Clerodendrum (*Verbenaceae*)

bungei	More than 30 suppliers
- 'Herfstleu'	MGos
- 'Pink Diamond'PBR (v)	ENot EPfP MGos NSti SMad SPoG
§ ***chinense*** var. ***chinense*** (d) ♀H1	ERea
- 'Pleniflorum'	see *C. chinense* var. *chinense*
fragrans var. ***pleniflorum***	see *C. chinense* var. *chinense*
* ***mutabile*** B&SWJ 6651	WCru
myricoides 'Ugandense' ♀H1	CHII CKob CMdw CPLN CSpe ELan ERea EShb ESlt
philippinum	see *C. chinense* var. *chinense*
x ***speciosum***	CPLN ERea
thomsoniae ♀H1	ELan LRHS MBri
trichotomum	More than 30 suppliers
- B&SWJ 4896A	WCru
- 'Carnival' (v)	CBcs CDul CFil CPMA EBee ELan EPfP EWes GKir IArd LRHS MAsh MBlu MBri NLar SBrw SLim SLon SMad SMur SPer SPoG SSta WBcn
- var. ***fargesii*** ♀H4	More than 30 suppliers
- white calyx B&SWJ 4896	WCru

Clethra (*Clethraceae*)

acuminata	EPfP NLar
alnifolia	CBcs CBrm CDul CEnd CMCN CMHG CPLG CSBt CTbh CTrC ECrN EPfP EWTr GKir IDee MBar SMur SPer SRms SSpi WCFE WDin WFar
- 'Anne Bidwell'	NLar
- 'Creel's Calico' (v)	NLar
- 'Fern Valley Pink' **new**	NLar
- 'Hokie Pink' **new**	NLar
- 'Hummingbird'	CEnd EBee ELan EPfP GKir LRHS MAsh MBlu MBri MWgw NLar SBrw SMur SPoG SSpi SWvt WBcn WFar WGer
- 'Paniculata' ♀H4	CDoC CPLG EPfP SMac SPoG SPur WFar
- 'Pink Spire'	CBcs CDoC EBee ECrN EPfP EWTr IDee MRav NBlu NEgg SBrw SCoo SMac SPoG WBVN WDin WFar WOrn
- 'Rosea'	CBot CTri GKir GQui IMGH MBar MBlu MGos SHBN SPer WFar
- 'Ruby Spice'	CBcs CBrm CEnd CMHG CPLG ELan EMil EPfP GKir IMGH LAst LRHS MAsh MBlu NEgg SBrw SMur SPer SRkn SSpi SSta SWvt WBVN WBcn
- 'September Beauty'	NLar
arborea	CBcs CFil CHEx CMHG CPLG GCal
barbinervis ♀H4	CBcs CFai CMCN CPLG EPfP IDee IMGH MBlu NLar SBrw SPer SPoG WBVN WDin WFar WSHC
- B&SWJ 5416	WPGP
- B&SWJ 8915	WCru
delavayi Franch.	CDoC CPLG EPfP GGGa GQui NLar
- C&H 7067	GGGa
fargesii	EPfP IMGH MGos NLar
monostachya	NLar
pringlei **new**	NLar SSpi
tomentosa	WWes
- 'Cottondale'	NLar SSpi

Cleyera (*Theaceae*)

fortunei	see *C. japonica* 'Fortunei'
- 'Variegata'	see *C. japonica* 'Fortunei'
§ ***japonica*** 'Fortunei' (v)	CFil CHal CMac CWib SBrw WFar
- var. ***japonica***	CFil EMil WPGP
- var. ***wallichii***	CFil WPGP

Clianthus (*Papilionaceae*)

maximus	ECou
§ ***puniceus*** ♀H2	More than 30 suppliers
§ - 'Albus' ♀H2	CBcs CBot CHEx CHII CPLG CTrw CWib EMil EPfP ERea EShb SBra SBrw SGar SPer
- 'Flamingo'	see *C. puniceus* 'Roseus'
- 'Kaka King'	CBcs
- 'Red Admiral'	see *C. puniceus*
- 'Red Cardinal'	see *C. puniceus*
§ - 'Roseus'	CBcs CPLG EMil ERea LRHS SBra SBrw SPer
- 'White Heron'	see *C. puniceus* 'Albus'

Clinopodium (*Lamiaceae*)

acinos	see *Acinos arvensis*
ascendens	see *Calamintha ascendens*
calamintha	see *Calamintha nepeta*
georgianum	SSpi
grandiflorum	see *Calamintha grandiflora*
§ ***vulgare***	CArn CRWN EBee EMag EMan EPPr EUnu GBar MAnH MBow MHer NGHP NLsd NMir SECG SIde WCAu WGHP WHer WMoo WOut WPtf

Clintonia (*Convallariaceae*)

andrewsiana	CBro CLAP GBin GBuc GCrs GGGa GKir SSpi WCru
borealis	SCnR WCru
udensis	WCru
- from Ussuri **new**	GIBF
umbellulata	CLAP WCru
uniflora	CLAP

Clitoria (*Papilionaceae*)

ternatea	EMan

Clivia ✿ (*Amaryllidaceae*)

caulescens	ERea
x ***cyrtanthiflora***	ERea
gardenii	ERea
miniata ♀H1	CBcs CHal LRHS MLan SChr SMur SRms WCot
- 'Aurea' ♀H1	CSpe
- var. ***citrina*** ♀H1	ECho WSAf
- - 'New Dawn'	ERea
- hybrids	ERea LAma MBri NPal SEND WBVN
- 'Striata' (v)	ERea
nobilis ♀H1	ERea

Clytostoma (*Bignoniaceae*)

§ ***calystegioides***	CHll CPLN CRHN ERea

Cneorum (*Cneoraceae*)

tricoccon	CKob SSpi XPep

Cnicus (*Asteraceae*)

§ ***benedictus***	CArn GPoy MHer MSal SECG SIde SPav

Cobaea (*Cobaeaceae*)

pringlei	CPLN ERea WSHC
scandens ♀H3	CSpe CTbh ELan EWin LRav SGar SMur WPen
- f. ***alba*** ♀H3	ELan EShb SMur WPen

cobnut see *Corylus avellana*

Coccothrinax (*Arecaceae*)

argentata	WMul
argentea (Lodd. ex Schult.f.) Sarg. ex Becc.	EAmu

Cocculus (*Menispermaceae*)

§ ***orbiculatus***	CPLG CPLN
- B&SWJ 535	WCru
trilobus	see *C. orbiculatus*

Cochlearia (*Brassicaceae*)

armoracia	see *Armoracia rusticana*
glastifolia	MSal
officinalis	MHer MSal WHer

Cocos (*Arecaceae*)

plumosa	see *Syagrus romanzoffiana*
weddelliana	see *Lytocaryum weddellianum*

Coddia (*Rubiaceae*)

rudis	EShb

Codiaeum ✿ (*Euphorbiaceae*)

variegatum var. ***pictum*** 'Excellent' (v)	LRHS
- - 'Petra' (v)	LRHS MBri

Codonanthe (*Gesneriaceae*)

gracilis	EBak WDib
'Paula'	WDib

x *Codonatanthus* (*Gesneriaceae*)

'Golden Tambourine'	WDib
'Sunset'	WDib
'Tambourine'	WDib

Codonopsis ✿ (*Campanulaceae*)

CC 4471	CPLG
SDR 1867	GKev
affinis HWJCM 70	WCru
- HWJK 2151	WCru
benthamii	NChi
- GWJ 9352	WCru
bhutanica	MGol WCot
bulleyana	NLar WCot WLin WSan
cardiophylla	GCal ITim NLar
celebica HWJ 665	WCru
clematidea	CHar CNic CSpe EBee ECGP EChP ECha ECtt EPfP GCal GIBF GKev GTou LPhx MCCP MDun MTho MWgw NBid NChi SBla SGSe SMad SPet SPlb SRms SWvt WCru WFar WKif
- 'Lilac Eyes'	MCCP NSti WRHF
convolvulacea misapplied	see *C. grey-wilsonii*
convolvulacea Kurz	CPLN CPne GBuc GFlt IGor MTho NSla WCru WHoo WLin WPGP
- B&SWJ 7812	WCru
- B&SWJ 7847	WCru
- CC 4471	MGol
- 'Alba'	see *C. grey-wilsonii* 'Himal Snow'
- Forrest's form	see *C. forrestii* Diels
dicentrifolia	EMan GKev ITim
- EMAK 1708	EHyt
- HWJCM 267	WCru
forrestii misapplied	see *C. grey-wilsonii*
§ ***forrestii*** Diels	CPLN EHyt GKev ITim WCot WCru
- BWJ 7776	WCru
§ ***grey-wilsonii*** ♀H4	CAby CBro CDes CLAP CPLN EChP ECho GCrs GEdr SBla WCot
- B&SWJ 7532	WCru
§ - 'Himal Snow'	CLAP EHyt GCrs GEdr GKev IMGH ITim MDKP SBla WCot
handeliana	see *C. tubulosa*
§ ***javanica*** B&SWJ 380	WCru
- B&SWJ 8145	WCru
kawakamii B&SWJ 1592	WCru
§ ***lanceolata***	CAby CPLN CPne GCal ITim
- B&SWJ 562	WCru
- B&SWJ 5099	WCru
lancifolia B&SWJ 3835	WCru
macrocalyx **new**	NChi
mollis	EChP GSki NBre NLar WFar
nepalensis	see *C. grey-wilsonii*
obtusa	GKev NChi WCot
ovata	CFir CLyd EHyt GBuc GKev MTho NBro NChi SBla SIgm SRms WCot
§ ***pilosula***	EBee EOHP GPoy MNrw MSal MTho WCot
rotundifolia CC 1770	WCot
§ - var. ***angustifolia***	GKev MDKP
- var. ***grandiflora*** **new**	GKev
silvestris	see *C. pilosula*
subsimplex	CLyd
tangshen misapplied	see *C. rotundifolia* var. *angustifolia*
tangshen Oliv.	CAby CArn CPLN GKev MNrw MSal MTho SHFr
thalictrifolia **new**	GKev
- MECC 93	WCru
§ ***tubulosa***	LRHS
ussuriensis	see *C. lanceolata*
vinciflora	CNic CPne EHyt GEdr IGor SBla WCot WCru
- BWJ 7847	WCru
viridiflora	CNic
viridis HWJK 2435	WCru

Coix (*Poaceae*)

lacryma-jobi	MSal

Colchicum ✿ (*Colchicaceae*)

	agrippinum ♀H4	CAvo CBro CFee CMon ECha EHyt EPot GCal GKev LAma MRav NBir NMen NRya NSla SSpi WTin
	'Antares'	ECha LAma LLWP NBir
	atropurpureum	CBro EPot GEdr LAma
	- Drake's form	EPot
	'Attlee'	LAma
	'Autumn Herald'	LAma
N	'Autumn Queen'	LAma
§	***autumnale***	CArn CAvo CBro CFee EPot GKev GPoy ITim LAma LRHS NMen NRya WFar WShi
*	- 'Albopilosum'	NBir
	- 'Alboplenum'	CBro EBrs EPot LAma WTin
	- 'Album'	CAvo CBgR CBro EBrs EHyt EPot GAbr GEdr GKev LAma LLWP LRHS NBir SPer WFar WHoo WPnP WShi WTin
	- var. ***major***	see *C. byzantinum*
	- var. ***minor***	see *C. autumnale*
	- 'Nancy Lindsay' ♀H4	CBro EBrs ECho EPot SRot
	- 'Pannonicum'	see *C. autumnale* 'Nancy Lindsay'
§	- 'Pleniflorum' (d)	CBro EPot GEdr GKev LAma
	- 'Roseum Plenum'	see *C. autumnale* 'Pleniflorum'
	baytopiorum	EHyt EPot GEdr
	- PB 224 from Turkey **new**	CMon
	'Beaconsfield'	GEdr
§	***bivonae***	CBro ECha LAma
	Blom's hybrid	WTin
§	***boissieri***	ERos SSpi
	- MFF 2192	WCot
	bornmuelleri misapplied	see *C. speciosum* var. *bornmuelleri* hort.
	bornmuelleri Freyn	CBro EPot GEdr LAma
	bowlesianum	see *C. bivonae*
§	***byzantinum*** Ker Gawl. ♀H4	CBro ECho EPot GKev LAma LRHS MBri NBir SOkd WTin
	- ***album***	see *C. byzantinum* 'Innocence'
	- 'Innocence'	CBro EPot
	cilicicum	CBro EPot LAma LRHS
	- 'Purpureum'	EBrs LAma
	'Conquest'	see *C.* 'Glory of Heemstede'
	corsicum	ERos LAma NMen SSpi
	- from Corsica **new**	CMon
	cupanii	SOkd
	- from Crete **new**	CMon
	'Daendels'	LAma
	davisii	GEdr
	- from Turkey **new**	CMon
	'Dick Trotter'	EPot LAma
	'Disraeli'	CBro GEdr
	doerfleri	see *C. hungaricum*
	'E.A. Bowles'	GEdr LAma LRHS
§	***giganteum***	EBrs EPot GEdr LAma
§	'Glory of Heemstede'	GKev LAma
	'Harlekijn' **new**	GEdr
	hierosolymitanum	LAma
§	***hungaricum***	CBro EPot LAma
	- f. ***albiflorum***	CMea EHyt
	illyricum	see *C. giganteum*
	'Jolanthe' **new**	WWst
	kesselringii	WWst
	kotschyi	LAma
	laetum hort.	see *C. parnassicum*
	'Lilac Bedder' **new**	EPot GKev
	'Lilac Wonder'	CBro EHyt EPot GKev LAma LRHS MBri SPer WCot WHoo
	lingulatum	WTin
§	***longiflorum***	LAma
	lusitanum	LAma
	- AB&S 4353 from Morocco **new**	CMon
	- B&S 469 from Spain **new**	CMon
	luteum	LAma
	macrophyllum	LAma
	micranthum	EHyt LAma
	neapolitanum	see *C. longiflorum*
*	- subsp. ***micranthum*** AB&S 4493 from Morocco **new**	CMon
	'Oktoberfest'	EPot
§	***parnassicum***	CBro ECha
	peloponnesiacum	CMon
	'Pink Goblet' ♀H4	CBro EHyt LAma
	'Prinses Astrid'	LAma
	procurrens	see *C. boissieri*
	pusillum MS 715 from Crete **new**	CMon
	- MS 718 from Crete	CMon
	- MS 833 from Crete	CMon
	'Rosy Dawn' ♀H4	CBro ECha EHyt EPot LAma
	sibthorpii	see *C. bivonae*
	speciosum ♀H4	CAvo CBro ECho EHyt EPot GEdr LAma LRHS NBir SSpi WCot WPnP
	- 'Album' ♀H4	CAvo CBro CFee EBla EBrs ECha ECho EHyt EPot ETow GEdr LAma LPhx LRHS MBri NBir SSpi WCot
	- 'Atrorubens'	ECha LAma LRHS
I	- var. ***bornmuelleri*** hort.	GEdr GKev
	- var. ***illyricum***	see *C. giganteum*
	- 'Maximum'	LAma
	szovitsii Fisch. & B. Mey.	WWst
	tenorei ♀H4	ECho EPot GKev LAma NBir WCot
	'The Giant'	CBro EBrs EPot GKev LAma LRHS WCot
	troodi ambig.	ERos
	troodii Kotschy from Cyprus **new**	CMon
	variegatum	CBro LAma
	'Violet Queen'	CBro EPot GAbr LAma LPhx LRHS
	'Waterlily' (d) ♀H4	CAvo CBro CLyd EBrs ECho ELan EPot GAbr GKev LAma LPhx LRHS MBri NBir WCot WHoo
	'William Dykes'	GEdr LAma
	'Zephyr'	LAma

Coleonema (*Rutaceae*)

	album	XPep
	pulchrum	CHEx CSpe NSti WCot XPep
	'Sunset Gold'	CPLG CSpe CTrC

Coleus see *Plectranthus, Solenostemon*

Colletia (*Rhamnaceae*)

	armata	see *C. hystrix*
	cruciata	see *C. paradoxa*
§	***hystrix***	CBcs CHEx CTri GBin GGar SAPC SArc SLon SMad
	- 'Rosea'	CBcs CPle
§	***paradoxa***	CBcs CHEx CPle EBee IDee LPJP NLar SAPC SArc SIgm SMad
	spinosissima	CPle

Collinsonia (*Lamiaceae*)

	canadensis	CArn EBee ELan EMan MSal WWye

Collomia (*Polemoniaceae*)

	debilis	EHyt NPol
	- var. ***larsenii***	see *C. larsenii*
	grandiflora	EMan NPol WCot
§	***larsenii***	GTou
	mazama	NPol WLin

Colobanthus (*Caryophyllaceae*)

canaliculatus CPBP EPot NMen

Colocasia (*Araceae*)

affinis var. **jeningsii** EAmu EUJe MOak
antiquorum see *C. esculenta*
§ **esculenta** 🏆H1 CDWL CHEx EAmu EUJe MJnS MOak SDix SSpi WMul XBlo
- 'Black Magic' EAmu EUJe MJnS MOak SBig WCot WMul XBlo
- 'Black Ruffles' **new** MJnS
- 'Bun-long' MJnS
- burgundy stem SBig WMul
- 'Elepaio Keiki' MJnS
- 'Fontanesii' EAmu MJnS SSpi WMul
- 'Hilo Beauty' **new** XBlo
- 'Illustris' MJnS
- 'Japanese Cranberry' **new** MJnS
- 'Nigrescens' EAmu
- 'Palau Keiki' MJnS
- 'Silver Splash' **new** EAmu
- 'Ulaula Kumu-oha' MJnS
fallax **new** SSpi
formosana B&SWJ 6909 **new** WCru
gigantea EAmu SBig WMul
'Nancyana' MJnS

Colquhounia (*Lamiaceae*)

coccinea CArn CHEx CHal CTrC EShb GQui MRav SIgm WCru WHer WHil WPGP WSHC WWye
§ - var. **vestita** CBcs CFil CPle CWib EPfP GGar IMGH MSte SBra SDnm SEND WBor
- - B&SWJ 7222 WCru

Columnea (*Gesneriaceae*)

'Aladdin's Lamp' CHal WDib
'Apollo' WDib
x **banksii** 🏆H1 CHal EOHP WDib
'Bold Venture' WDib
§ 'Broget Stavanger' (v) WDib
'Chanticleer' 🏆H1 CHal MBri WDib
I 'Firedragon' WDib
'Gavin Brown' WDib
gloriosa EBak
hirta 🏆H1 MBri WDib
- 'Variegata' see *C.* 'Light Prince'
'Inferno' WDib
'Katsura' MBri WDib
I 'Kewensis Variegata' (v) 🏆H1 MBri
§ 'Light Prince' (v) WDib
'Merkur' WDib
microphylla 'Variegata' (v) MBri
I 'Midnight Lantern' WDib
'Rising Sun' WDib
'Robin' WDib
schiedeana CHal EShb MBri WDib
'Stavanger' 🏆H1 CHal EBak WDib
'Stavanger Variegated' see *C.* 'Broget Stavanger'
Yellow Dragon Group CHal

Colutea (*Papilionaceae*)

arborescens CArn CBcs CPLG EBee ELan ENot GKir LRHS MBlu MGos MSal NWea SHBN SLon SPer SPlb SPoG WDin WHer XPep
§ **buhsei** NLar SLPl
x **media** LRav MAvo MBlu WGwG WOut
- 'Copper Beauty' CBcs MGos MRav SPer WPat
orientalis CPle LAst XPep
persica misapplied see *C. buhsei*

Comarum see *Potentilla*

Combretum (*Combretaceae*)

paniculatum CPLN

Commelina (*Commelinaceae*)

coelestis see *C. tuberosa* Coelestis Group
communis EMan
dianthifolia EBrs EMan GCal GCrs GKev GKir MTho NWCA SPet SRms WPer
tuberosa ELan EMFP EPfP ERos MAvo MLan MSte NSti
- 'Alba' ELan MLLN MSte WPer
- 'Axminster Lilac' WPer
§ - Coelestis Group EBrs EChP ECha EMan EVFa EWin GKev IGor MLLN SPet SRms WFar WPGP WPer WPtf WSHC
- - 'Hopleys Variegated' (v) EMan

Commidendrum (*Asteraceae*)

robustum RCB/Arg P-17 **new** WCot

Comptonia (*Myricaceae*)

peregrina NLar WCru WRos

Conandron (*Gesneriaceae*)

ramondoides B&SWJ 8929 WCru

Conanthera (*Tecophilaeaceae*)

bifolia **new** CMon
campanulata CMon

Congea (*Verbenaceae*)

tomentosa **new** CPLN

Conicosia (*Aizoaceae*)

pugioniformis CTrC SChr

Conioselinum (*Apiaceae*)

morrisonense B&SWJ 173 WCru

Conium (*Apiaceae*)

maculatum CArn MGol MSal

Conoclinium (*Asteraceae*)

greggii **new** SIgm

Conopodium (*Apiaceae*)

majus CRWN WShi

Conradina (*Lamiaceae*)

verticillata WPat

Consolida (*Ranunculaceae*)

§ **ajacis** MSal
ambigua see *C. ajacis*

Convallaria ✿ (*Convallariaceae*)

japonica see *Ophiopogon jaburan*
keiskei CLAP EBla GIBF
majalis 🏆H4 More than 30 suppliers
§ - 'Albostriata' (v) CBct CFil CFwr CLAP CRow EBla EBrs ECha EHrv ELan EMan EPfP EVFa GKir LRHS MRav MTho MWrn NBir SGSe SIng SMac SOkh WCHb WCot WCru WEas WHer WPGP

- 'Berlin Giant' — EBee EBla NRya
- 'Blush' **new** — CAvo
- 'Dorien' — CBct CBre CFir EBee EChP
- 'Flore Pleno' (d) — CBct EBla EHrv MTho SGSe WCot
- 'Fortin's Giant' — CAvo CBct CBro CLAP CMea CRow EBla EMon EPla EPot GEdr MRav NEgg NGby SIng SMad WCot WPGP WSel
- 'Gerard Debureaux' (v) — see *C. majalis* 'Green Tapestry'
- 'Golden Slippers' — NPar
§ - 'Green Tapestry' (v) — CRow EMon EVFa
- 'Haldon Grange' (v) — CLAP EBee EMon
- 'Hardwick Hall' (v) — CAvo CBct CLAP CMdw CRow EBla ECha EHoe EHrv EPla EPot EVFa NPar WCot WSan
- 'Hofheim' (v) — CRow EBee WTMC
- 'Prolificans' — CAvo CBct CBro CFir CLAP CMdw CRow EBee EBrs EMon ERos MRav NPar SIng
- var. ***rosea*** — More than 30 suppliers
- 'Variegata' (v) — CAvo CBro CHar EBla EPla ERou GCrs NMen SChu SMad WHil WSel
- 'Vic Pawlowski's Gold' (v) — CLAP CPLG CRow CStu SBla WCHb

montana — LRHS
transcaucasica — EBee WCot

Convolvulus (*Convolvulaceae*)

althaeoides — CBot CHad CHrt CPle ECGP EChP ELan LPhx LRHS MNrw MTho NBir SBch SBla SHFr SMad SPer WAbb WEas WHal WPGP WPtf
§ - subsp. ***tenuissimus*** — CSWP CSpe EBee EMan EWes MBri MHer NCGa WCFE WCot
§ ***boissieri*** — CFir CGra EHyt NWCA SBla WAbe
cantabricus — CHll EChP MDKP NSla
cneorum ♀H3 — More than 30 suppliers
- 'Snow Angel' — SPoG SSta SVil SWvt WCot WWeb
elegantissimus — see *C. althaeoides* subsp. *tenuissimus*
floridus **new** — CSec
incanus — WCru
lineatus — ECho EHyt LRHS MTho NMen NWCA SMrm SOkd
mauritanicus — see *C. sabatius*
nitidus — see *C. boissieri*
oleifolius — XPep
§ ***sabatius*** ♀H3 — More than 30 suppliers
- dark — CSpe ELan EMan LIck MOak MSte SMrm SUsu
suendermannii ambig. **new** — SOkd

x *Cooperanthes* see *Zephyranthes*

Cooperia see *Zephyranthes*

Copernicia (*Arecaceae*)

alba — SBig
prunifera — EAmu

Coprosma ✿ (*Rubiaceae*)

acerosa — GGar
- 'Live Wire' (f) — ECou
areolata (m) — ECou
atropurpurea (f) — ECou NWCA
- (m) — ECou
'Autumn Orange' (f) — ECou
'Autumn Prince' (m) — ECou
baueri misapplied — see *C. repens*
'Beatson's Gold' (f/v) — CBcs CBot CChe CHal CMHG EBee ELan EMil EPfP ERea GGar GQui ISea SAga SBrw SPoG STre WDin WSHC
'Blue Pearls' (f) — ECou
'Brunette' (f) — ECou
§ ***brunnea*** — CTrC ECou
- 'Blue Beauty' (f) — ECou
- 'Violet Fleck' (f) — ECou
'Bruno' (m) — ECou
cheesemanii (f) — ECou
- (m) — ECou
- 'Hanmer Red' (f) — ECou
- 'Mack' (m) — ECou
- 'Red Mack' (f) — ECou
'Chocolate Soldier' (m) — ECou
'Coppershine' — CBcs CPLG CTbh CTrC ERea MOak
crassifolia x ***repens*** (m) — ECou
crenulata **new** — WPic
x ***cunninghamii*** (f) — ECou
x ***cunninghamii*** x ***macrocarpa*** (m) — ECou
'Cutie' (f) — ECou
depressa — ECou
- 'Orange Spread' (f) — ECou
'Evening Glow'PBR (f/v) — CAlb CDoC COtt ECou LRHS MAsh
'Green Girl' (f) — ECou
'Hinerua' (f) — ECou
'Indigo Lustre' (f) — ECou
'Jewel' (f) — ECou
'Karo Red'PBR (v) — CDoC COtt CTrC LRHS MAsh SPoG
x ***kirkii*** 'Gold Edge' **new** — ECou
- 'Kirkii' (f) — ECou ERea STre XPep
- 'Kirkii Variegata' (f/v) — CBcs CBot CDoC CHal CStu CTrC EBee ECou ECrN ERea GQui IFro MOak SBrw STre WBrE WSHC WWeb
'Kiwi' (m) — ECou
'Kiwi-gold' (m/v) — ECou ERea
'Lemon Drops' (f) — ECou
linariifolia (m) — ECou
lucida (f) — ECou
- 'Mount White' (m) — ECou
- 'Wanaka' (f) — ECou
macrocarpa (f) — CTrC ECou
- (m) — ECou
nitida (f) — ECou
parviflora (m) — CTrC ECou
- purple fruit (f) — ECou
- red fruit (f) — ECou
- white fruit (f) — ECou
'Pearl Drops' (f) — ECou
'Pearl's Sister' (f) — ECou
'Pearly Queen' (f) — ECou
petriei — ECou WThu
- 'Don' (m) — ECou
- 'Lyn' (f) — ECou
'Pride' — CDoC CTrC
propinqua (f) — ECou
- (m) — ECou
- var. ***latiuscula*** (f) — ECou
- - (m) — ECou
'Prostrata' (m) — ECou
pseudocuneata (m) — ECou
pumila Hook.f. pro parte — EPot
'Rainbow Surprise'PBR (v) — CAlb COtt CPLG LRHS MAsh SPoG WWeb
§ ***repens*** — CPLG EShb XPep
§ - (f) — ECou
- (m) — CBcs ECou SEND
- 'Apricot Flush' (f) — ECou
- 'County Park Plum' (v) **new** — ECou

- 'County Park Purple' (f)	ECou ERea
- 'Exotica' (f/v)	ECou
- 'Marble King' (m/v)	ECou
- 'Marble Queen' (m/v) ♀H1-2	CHll ECou EShb WCot WFar
- 'Orangeade' (f)	ECou
- 'Painter's Palette' (m)	CBcs ECou WDin
- 'Picturata' (m/v) ♀H1-2	ECou ERea EShb
- 'Pink Splendour' (m/v)	CBcs CDoC ECou ERea EShb WDin
- 'Rangatiri' (f)	ECou
- 'Silver Queen' (m/v)	ECou
- 'Variegata' (m/v)	ECou
rigida	ECou
- 'Ann' (f)	ECou
- 'Tan' (m)	ECou
robusta	CTrC ECou
- 'Cullen's Point' (f)	ECou
- 'Sally Blunt' (f)	ECou
- 'Steepdown' (f)	ECou
- 'Tim Blunt' (m)	ECou
- 'Variegata' (m/v)	ECou
- 'William' (m)	ECou
- 'Woodside' (f)	ECou
rotundifolia	ECou
'Roy's Red' (m)	CDoC EBee ECou
rugosa (f)	ECou
I 'Snowberry' (f)	ECou
'Taiko'	CTrC
tenuifolia (m)	ECou
'Translucent Gold' (f)	ECou
'Violet Drops' (f)	ECou
virescens (f)	ECou
'Walter Brockie'	CHll CTrC
'White Lady' (f)	ECou
'Winter Bronze' (f)	ECou

Coptis (*Ranunculaceae*)

japonica var. ***dissecta*** B&SWJ 6000	WCru
- var. ***major***	WCru
quinquefolia B&SWJ 1677	WCru

x *Coralia* (*Papilionaceae*)

'County Park'	ECou
'Essex'	ECou
'Havering'	ECou

Corallospartium (*Papilionaceae*)

crassicaule	ECou
- 'Jack Sprat'	ECou
- var. ***racemosum***	ECou

Cordyline (*Agavaceae*)

australis ♀H3	More than 30 suppliers
- 'Albertii' (v) ♀H3	CBcs MBri NMoo NPri SAPC SArc WCot
- 'Atropurpurea'	CDoC ECrN ENot GKir SSto WDin WFar
- 'Black Night' **new**	CTrC
- 'Black Tower'	CBcs CDoC CHll EBee ELan LRHS MGos
- 'Coffee Cream'	CTrC EAmu EBee ELan EPfP LRHS MLan MWgw SPer WDin WFar WGer
- 'Karo Kiri'	CTrC
- 'Krakatoa'	ENot
- 'Peko' PBR	WCot
- 'Pink Champagne' **new**	MAsh
- 'Pink Stripe' (v)	CBcs CBrm CDoC COtt EBee ELan ENot EPfP ISea LRHS LSRN MAsh MCCP NPri SHGC SLim SNew SPla SSto SWvt WFar
- 'Purple Heart'	CTrC WPat
- 'Purple Tower'	CBrm CDoC CHEx COtt CTrC EAmu EBee EChP EMil ENot EPfP LRHS MCCP SLim SNew SPoG WCot
- Purpurea Group	CBcs CBot CChe CDul CHar CMHG CTbh CTrC CWSG EBee ENot EPfP ISea LAst LRHS MGos NBlu SBLw SEND SGar SHBN SPer SPlb WFar WGer
- 'Red Robin'	LRav
- 'Red Sensation'	CHEx CTrC EGra GKir ISea LRHS SHGC SWvt
- 'Red Star'	More than 30 suppliers
- 'Sparkler' **new**	CBcs
- 'Sundance' ♀H3	More than 30 suppliers
- 'Torbay Dazzler' (v) ♀H3	More than 30 suppliers
* - 'Torbay Razzle Dazzle'	CTrC
- 'Torbay Red' ♀H3	CAbb CBcs CBrm CDoC CMHG COtt CTbh CTrC CWSG EBee ELan EPfP ISea LRHS LSRN MAsh MBri MJnS SPla SWvt WFar WWeb
- 'Torbay Sunset'	CDoC COtt CTrC ELan LRHS
- 'Variegata' (v)	CBot
'Autumn'	CTrC WFar
banksii	CTrC LEdu WPic
'Dark Star'	CDoC MCCP MDun MWgw
fruticosa 'Atom'	MBri
- 'Baby Ti' (v)	MBri
- 'Calypso Queen'	MBri
- 'Kiwi'	MBri
- 'New Guinea Black'	CTrC EChP ELan NCot NSti WCot
- 'Orange Prince'	MBri
- 'Red Edge' ♀H1	MBri
- 'Yellow King'	MBri
x ***gibbingsiae*** 'Red Fountain'	EBee ENot
'Green Goddess'	CBcs CTrC
§ ***indivisa***	CAgr CBrP CFil EAmu EBak GGar IDee ITim LEdu LRHS MBri NJOw SBig SPlb WGer WMul WPGP
- 'Perkeo'	EBee
'Jurassic Jade' **new**	CBcs CTrC
kaspar	CHEx ISea LEdu SAPC SArc
- bronze	LEdu
parryi 'Purpurea'	NPal
pumilio	LEdu
§ ***stricta***	CHEx MBri
terminalis	see *C. fruticosa*

Coreopsis ✿ (*Asteraceae*)

auriculata Cutting Gold	see *C. auriculata* 'Schnittgold'
- 'Nana'	NBre WFar
§ - 'Schnittgold'	CSam CWan EBee MWgw NBlu NLRH WFar WPer
- 'Superba'	EBrs LRHS
'Baby Gold'	EBee EPfP MBNS MTis NBlu NFla NNor SWvt WFar WWeb
Baby Sun	see *C.* 'Sonnenkind'
gladiata **new**	WCot
'Goldfink'	GKir GSki LRHS MBrN MRav SRms
grandiflora	SRob SUsu XPep
- 'Astolat'	CStr EMon MNFA SPet SUsu
- 'Badengold'	EBee EMil IHMH
- 'Bernwode' (v)	EBee EMan NBPC NLar SGSe
I - 'Calypso' (v)	CFwr EWes LBmB LRHS SCoo SPoG WWeb
- 'Domino'	EBee NOak SHGN
- 'Early Sunrise' ♀H4	CSBt CSam ECrN ECtt EGra EPfP ERou EWTr GMaP LRHS MHer MWat NBir NEgg NLsd NMir NPer SGar SPet SPoG SWvt WFar WGwG WPer WWFP

- Flying Saucers = 'Walcoreop'PBR	EBee EChP GBri GKir LRHS NLar SCoo SPoG
- 'Kelvin Harbutt'	CStr EMan ERou
- 'Mayfield Giant'	CSBt EBee EMan ERou EShb LRHS MFOX MNrw MWgw NBPC NPri SChu SPer SPoG SRms SWvt
lanceolata	NSti
- 'Sterntaler'	CFir CPen EBee EMil ERou GAbr GKir IHMH LRHS MBri MNFA MSph NCGa NPri NVic SPet SWvt WMoo WPer WWeb
- 'Walter'	MBri MCCP MMHG
'Limerock Ruby'PBR	EBrs EVFa GBri MNrw NLar SPer
maximiliani	see *Helianthus maximiliani*
palmata	MDKP WWpP
rosea	NLar WFar WPer
- 'American Dream'	More than 30 suppliers
- f. ***leucantha***	CStr
- 'Sweet Dreams'PBR	EBrs GBri SPer WCot WFar
§ 'Sonnenkind'	CPen EBee ECtt EMil GMaP IHMH LRHS MHer MWgw NBro NJOw WPer
Sun Child	see *C.* 'Sonnenkind'
'Sunburst'	COtt EBee GSki LRHS MWgw NOak WPer WWpP
'Sunray'	CBcs CDoC COlW CSBt CWib EBee ECtt GKir IHMH LAst LRHS LSRN MBri MNrw MWgw NBPC NGdn NOak SPet SPlb SPoG SRms SWvt WFar WMnd WMoo WPer WWeb WWye
'Tequila Sunrise' (v)	CFai EBee EChP EHoe EMan EVFa MBNS NSti WCot
tinctoria	MSal
tripteris	CAby CPou EBrs EChP EMan EMon GBin LPhx MDKP MSte SAga SGSe SHar SMad SSvw WMoo WPer
- 'Pierre Bennerup'	EMon
verticillata	EBee ECha ECrN EHrv ENot EPfP IHMH LRHS MBrN MDun MHer MWat NPer SDix SRms WFar WHal WTin
- 'Golden Gain'	CTri EBee ECtt EMan EPla GBri GKir GSki LRHS MArl MLLN MMil NGdn WMnd
- 'Golden Shower'	see *C. verticillata* 'Grandiflora'
§ - 'Grandiflora' 🏆H4	CBcs CPrp CTri EBee EBrs ELan EPfP EPza ERou GMaP GSki MNFA MRav NCGa NFor NGdn NLon NOak NVic SBla SChu SMad SPer SPla SSpe WCAu WCot WFar WMnd WOld
- 'Moonbeam' 🏆H4	More than 30 suppliers
- 'Old Timer' 🏆H4 **new**	SDix SMHy
- 'Zagreb' 🏆H4	More than 30 suppliers

coriander see *Coriandrum sativum*

Coriandrum (*Apiaceae*)

sativum	CArn CSev EOHP GPoy ILis LRHS MChe MHer NBlu NVic SIde WLHH WPer
- 'Leisure'	CBod CSev MBow NPri
- 'Santo'	ELau NGHP WJek

Coriaria ✿ (*Coriariaceae*)

arborea	WCru
intermedia B&SWJ 019	WCru
japonica	IDee NLar WCot WCru
- B&SWJ 2833	WCru
- subsp. ***intermedia*** B&SWJ 3877 **new**	WCru
kingiana	ECou WCru
§ ***microphylla***	WCru
- B&SWJ 8999	WCru
myrtifolia	CFil GSki NLar WCru WFar XPep
napalensis	WCru
- BWJ 7755	WCru
pteridoides	WCru
ruscifolia	LEdu WCru
- HCM 98178	WCru
sarmentosa	GCal WCru
terminalis	CDes EMan EPfP GBuc GCal NLar
var. ***xanthocarpa***	SSpi WCot WCru WPGP
- - GWJ 9204	WCru
- - HWJK 2112c	WCru
thymifolia	see *C. microphylla*

Coris (*Primulaceae*)

monspeliensis	EMan XPep

Cornus ✿ (*Cornaceae*)

alba	CAgr CCVT CDoC CDul CLnd ECrN ENot EWTr GKir IHMH ISea MAsh MDun MHer MRav NWea SRms WDin WMou
* - 'Albovariegata' (v)	ENot
- 'Argenteovariegata'	see *C. alba* 'Variegata'
- 'Aurea' 🏆H4	More than 30 suppliers
- 'Elegantissima' (v) 🏆H4	More than 30 suppliers
- 'Gouchaultii' (v)	CBcs EBee ECrN EPfP EWTr GKir MAsh MBar MRav NBlu NPri SPer SRms WDin WFar
- 'Hedgerow'	WPat
- 'Hessei'	LRHS MRav
- 'Hessei' misapplied	see *C. sanguinea* 'Compressa'
- Ivory Halo = 'Bailhalo'PBR	EBee ENot EPfP GKir LRHS MAsh MBNS MBri MGos MRav NMoo NPri NWea SPer SPoG WGer
- 'Kesselringii'	More than 30 suppliers
- 'Red Gnome'	MAsh WPat
- 'Siberian Pearls'	CBcs EBee ELan GKir MBlu MGos NEgg NMoo SSta
§ - 'Sibirica' 🏆H4	More than 30 suppliers
- 'Sibirica Variegata' (v)	CAlb CDoC CMac EBee EPfP EPla EWTr GKir LRHS LSRN MAsh MBar MBlu MGos NCGa NEgg NPri SHBN SLim SPer SSpi SSta SWvt WFar
- 'Spaethii' (v) 🏆H4	More than 30 suppliers
§ - 'Variegata' (v)	CBcs LAst SPer
- 'Westonbirt'	see *C. alba* 'Sibirica'
alternifolia	CMCN COtt EBee ELan GIBF GKir MDun SSpi WPat
§ - 'Argentea' (v) 🏆H4	More than 30 suppliers
- 'Silver Giant' (v) **new**	CPMA
- 'Variegata'	see *C. alternifolia* 'Argentea'
amomum	CAbP CBcs EBee GIBF NLar WBcn WWpP
- subsp. ***obliqua***	CFil WPGP
angustata	CTho GIBF LRHS SPer SSpi
§ 'Ascona' (Stellar Series)	CBcs CEnd CPMA ELan EPfP IMGH LRHS MBlu MBri NEgg NLar SSpi SSta SWvt WPat
'Aurora' (Stellar Series)	CPMA MBlu MPkF NLar
§ ***canadensis*** 🏆H4	More than 30 suppliers
candidissima	see *C. racemosa*
capitata	CAgr CBcs CDoC CMac CPne CSBt CTho CTri EPfP GIBF LRHS MWya NArg SEND SSpi WCru WCwm WFar WMoo WPat WPic
- subsp. ***emeiensis***	SSpi
§ Celestial = 'Rutdan' (Stellar Series)	CPMA MPkF NLar
'Centennial' **new**	LRHS
'Constellation' (Stellar Series)	CPMA

	controversa	CBcs CDul CLnd CMCN CTho CTri ECrN ELan EMil EPfP EWTr MBar MBlu MDun NDlv SHBN SLPl SPer SReu SSpi SSta SWvt WDin WHar WOrn WPGP
§	- 'Frans Type'	CBcs CBot CEnd ELan EMil ERom LSRN MBlu MBri SHBN SReu SSta WDin WHCG WPat
I	- 'Marginata Nord'	CTho NLar NPal
	- 'Pagoda'	MBlu NLar NPal SBrw SSpi
	- 'Variegata' (v) ♀H4	More than 30 suppliers
	- 'Variegata' Frans type (v)	see *C. controversa* 'Frans Type'
	- 'Winter Orange' **new**	NLar
	'Eddie's White Wonder' ♀H4	More than 30 suppliers
	florida	CCVT CDul CLnd CMCN CTho EPfP GIBF ISea LRHS MBar NBlu SPer WBVN WNor
	- 'Alba Plena' (d)	CPMA NLar
	- 'Andrea Hart'	CPMA
	- 'Apple Blossom'	CMac CPMA ECho
	- Cherokee Brave = 'Comco'	CPMA CWib LRHS NCGa NLar SSpi SSta
	- 'Cherokee Chief' ♀H4	CAbP CBcs CEnd CPMA CTri CWib ECho EPfP GKir IArd IMGH LRHS MGos MPkF NLar SHBN WDin WOrn WPat
	- 'Cherokee Daybreak' (v)	CBcs COtt CWib MPkF
	- 'Cherokee Princess'	CPMA EPfP LRHS MAsh MPkF NCGa SMur SSpi SSta
	- 'Cherokee Sunset' (v)	CBcs MPkF NLar
	- 'Cloud Nine'	CBcs CDoC CPMA EMil MGos MPkF NCGa NLar SLdr SPoG SSpi WOrn WPat
	- 'Daybreak' (v)	CEnd CPMA MGos SPer WPat
	- 'First Lady'	CBcs CMac CPMA EBee ECho SSpi
	- 'G.H. Ford' (v)	CPMA
	- 'Golden Nugget'	CPMA
	- 'Junior Miss'	CEnd CPMA EMil
	- 'Junior Miss Variegated' (v)	CPMA
	- 'Marzelli' Rainbow (v)	CAbP CBcs COtt CPMA CWib EPfP GKir LRHS MAsh MBri MGos MPkF NEgg SHBN SPla SSta WDin WPat
	- 'Moonglow'	CPMA
	- 'Pendula'	CPMA
	- f. ***pluribracteata*** (d)	NLar
	- 'Purple Glory'	CPMA
	- 'Red Giant'	CAbP CPMA ELan EPfP LRHS MAsh SMur SPoG SSpi
	- 'Royal Red'	CPMA MPkF
	- f. ***rubra***	CBcs CSBt CTri CWib EBee ELan EPfP GKir LAst LRHS MGos SBLw SSta WFar WGer WNor WPat
	- 'Spring Day' **new**	ECho
	- 'Spring Song'	CMac CPMA ECho LRHS
	- 'Springtime' **new**	CPMA
	- 'Stoke's Pink'	CEnd COtt CPMA ECho GKir
	- 'Sunset' (v)	CEnd CPMA CWib MGos SHBN WPat
	- 'Sweetwater'	CEnd CPMA EMil
	- 'Tricolor'	see *C. florida* 'Welchii'
	- 'Variegata'	SSpi
	- 'Weaver's White'	MPkF
§	- 'Welchii' (v)	CEnd CPLG CPMA SSpi
	- 'White Cloud'	CPMA EBee MPkF
	- 'Xanthocarpa' **new**	MPkF
	'Gloria Birkett'	SSpi
	'Greenlight'	NPro WGHP
	hemsleyi	EPla
	hessei misapplied	see *C. sanguinea* 'Compressa'
	hongkongensis	CBcs IDee
	'Kelsey Dwarf'	see *C. sericea* 'Kelseyi'
	'Kenwyn Clapp' **new**	CPMA
	kousa	CDoC CDul CHEx CMCN CPne CTbh CTho ECrN ELan EPfP ERom GKir ISea LRHS MBar MDun MLan NBlu NEgg NFor NLon SHBN SPer SPlb WDin WFar WHCG WHar
	- B&SWJ 5494	WCru
	- 'All Summer' **new**	CPMA
	- 'Autumn Rose'	CPMA EPfP NLar
	- 'Beni-fuji'	CPMA
I	- 'Big Apple' **new**	CPMA
	- 'Blue Shadow'	CPMA
	- 'Bonfire' (v)	CPMA
	- 'Bultinck's Beauty'	LRHS SSpi
	- 'Bultinck's Giant'	NLar
	- 'Bush's Pink' **new**	CPMA
	- 'China Dawn' (v) **new**	CPMA
	- var. ***chinensis*** ♀H4	More than 30 suppliers
	- - 'Bodnant Form'	CDul CEnd CPMA GKir
	- - 'China Girl'	CAbP CBcs CEnd CPMA CWib ELan EPfP EWTr GKir LBuc LRHS MAsh MBlu MBri MGos MSwo MWya SHBN SLim SSpi SSta WDin WOrn WPGP WPat
	- - 'Greta's Gold' (v)	CPMA
	- - 'Milky Way'	CMCN CPMA CWib LBuc MBlu MPkF NLar SHBN
	- - 'Snowflake'	CPMA
	- - Spinners form	CPMA
	- - 'Summer Stars'	NLar
	- - 'White Dusted'	EPfP
	- - 'White Fountain'	MBlu MPkF NLar
	- - 'Wieting's Select'	CPMA MPkF
	- 'Claudine'	CPMA
	- 'Doubloon'	CPMA SPer
	- 'Dwarf Pink' **new**	CPMA
	- 'Ed Mezitt'	CPMA
	- 'Elizabeth Lustgarten'	CPMA SSpi SSta
	- 'Galilean' **new**	CPMA
I	- 'Girard's Nana' **new**	CPMA
	- 'Gold Cup' (v)	CPMA MPkF
	- 'Gold Star' (v)	CAbP CBcs CEnd CMCN CMac CPMA CTho CWib ELan EPfP LBuc LRHS MBlu MGos NEgg SHBN SPla SSpi
	- 'Highland' **new**	CPMA
	- 'John Slocock'	MAsh SSpi
	- 'Kreus Dame' **new**	MPkF
	- 'Lustgarten Weeping'	LRHS NLar SSpi
	- 'Madame Butterfly'	CEnd CPMA LRHS MAsh SSpi SSta
	- 'Milky Way Select' **new**	CPMA
	- 'Minuma'	NLar
	- 'Miss Petty' **new**	MPkF
	- 'Moonbeam'	CPMA MPkF
	- 'Mount Fuji'	NLar
	- 'National'	CPMA MBlu MGos MPkF WPat
	- 'Nicole'	CDoC EBee WDin
	- 'Peve Foggy' **new**	NLar
	- 'Peve Limbo' (v) **new**	MPkF NLar
	- 'Polywood' **new**	CPMA
	- 'Radiant Rose'	CPMA MPkF
	- 'Rasen'	NLar
	- 'Rel Whirlwind' **new**	CPMA
	- 'Rosea'	CPMA
	- 'Samaratin' **new**	MPkF
	- 'Satomi' ♀H4	More than 30 suppliers
	- 'Schmetterling'	CPMA
	- 'Snowboy' (v)	CBcs CEnd CPMA LRHS NLar
	- 'Southern Cross'	CPMA
	- 'Steeple' **new**	CPMA
	- 'Summer Majesty'	CPMA
	- 'Sunsplash' (v)	CPMA CTho

	Name	Suppliers
	- 'Temple Jewel' (v)	CPMA LRHS SSpi
	- 'Teutonia' **new**	MPkF
	- 'Tinknor's Choice' **new**	CPMA
	- 'Trinity Star' **new**	CPMA
	- 'Triple Crown'	CPMA
	- 'Tsukubanomine'	CPMA NLar
	- 'U.S.A.' **new**	MPkF
	- 'Weaver's Weeping'	CPMA MPkF
	- 'Wolf Eyes' (v) **new**	CPMA MBlu MPkF
	macrophylla	CHEx CMCN EPfP IArd SMad WCwm
	mas	More than 30 suppliers
	- 'Aurea' (v)	CAbP CPMA EBee ELan EPfP GKir MAsh MBri MRav NEgg SBrw SLim SPer SSpi SSta WDin WPat
§	- 'Aureoelegantissima' (v)	CEnd CFil CPMA CWib EBee LRHS MAsh NLar SBrw SPer SSpi WFar WPGP WPat WSHC
	- 'Elegantissima'	see *C. mas* 'Aureoelegantissima'
	- 'Golden Glory' ♀H4	CBcs CPMA MBlu NCGa NLar
	- 'Jolico'	CPMA NLar
	- 'Spring Glow' **new**	NLar
	- 'Variegata' (v) ♀H4	CBcs CBot CMCN CPMA CTho EBee EPfP GKir LRHS MAsh MBlu MGos NPal SBrw SPer SPoG SSpi WDin WFar WPat
N	'Norman Hadden' ♀H4	CAbP CDoC CDul CEnd CMCN CMac CPMA CSBt CTho EPfP GKir LAst LRHS MAsh MRav MWya SBrw SHBN SHFr SPer SSpi SSta WAbe WBor WDin WFar WPGP WPat
	nuttallii	CBcs CDul CPLG CTho CTri CWib ECrN ELan EPfP EWTr IMGH ISea LAst LRHS MDun MWya NBlu NWea SHBN SPer WDin WFar WNor
	- 'Ascona'	see *C.* 'Ascona'
	- 'Barrick'	CPMA
	- 'Colrigo Giant'	CPMA MPkF SSpi
	- 'Gold Spot' (v)	CMac CPMA EPfP LRHS MGos WPat
	- 'Monarch'	CBcs CPMA CTho NLar
	- 'North Star'	CPMA NLar
	- 'Pink Blush' **new**	MPkF
	- 'Portlemouth'	CEnd CPMA LRHS MAsh NLar SSpi WPat
	- 'Zurico' **new**	MPkF
§	***occidentalis***	EPla
	officinalis	CMCN CTho EPfP LRHS MBri NLar SPoG WCwm WDin
	'Ormonde'	CPMA ECho LRHS NLar SSpi
	paucinervis	GIBF
	'Pink Blush'	CPMA
	'Porlock' ♀H4	CDul CMCN CPMA EPfP GKir LRHS MBri MWya NLar SSpi WDin
	pubescens	see *C. occidentalis*
	pumila	CPMA NLar WDin
§	***racemosa***	NLar WFar
	rugosa	WNor
	x ***rutgersiensis*** 'Ruth Ellen'	see *C.* Ruth Ellen = 'Rutlan'
	Ruth Ellen = 'Rutlan' (Stellar Series)	CPMA NLar
	sanguinea	CBcs CCVT CDul CLnd CRWN CTri ECrN ENot EPfP GKir LBuc MRav MSwo NFor NLon NWea SPer WDin WGwG WHar WMou XPep
	- 'Anny's Winter Orange'	MBlu
§	- 'Compressa'	EBee NLar WSPU WWes
	- 'Magic Flame'	MBri
	- 'Midwinter Fire'	More than 30 suppliers
§	- 'Winter Beauty'	CDoC CSBt CWib EBee EPfP MBlu MWgw NEgg SHBN SLon WFar WPat WSPU
§	***sericea***	CArn
	- 'Budd's Yellow'	GKir MBri MGos
	- 'Cardinal'	MBri MGos
§	- 'Flaviramea' ♀H4	More than 30 suppliers
	- 'Hedgerow Gold'	SPoG SSpi WCot
	- 'Kelseyi'	CAlb CBgR CMac CRez EBee EHyt ENot EPla ESis GKir MBNS MBar MRav NPri NPro SBod SLPl SMac SPer SPoG WWpP
	- Kelsey's Gold = 'Rosco'	SLon WPat
	- 'Sunshine'	CSpe NPro
§	- 'White Gold' (v) ♀H4	CDoC CPMA EBee ECrN EHoe ENot EPla LRHS MBri MRav MSwo NPro SLon SPer SPoG WBcn WDin WFar WMoo
	- 'White Spot'	see *C. sericea* 'White Gold'
	Stardust = 'Rutfan' (Stellar Series) **new**	CPMA
	Stellar Pink = 'Rutgan' (Stellar Series)	CPMA CWib MPkF NLar
	stolonifera	see *C. sericea*
	- 'White Spot'	see *C. sericea* 'White Gold'
	suecica	GIBF
	walteri	CMCN NLar WCwm WFar
	wilsoniana **new**	GIBF

Corokia (*Escalloniaceae*)

	Name	Suppliers
	buddlejoides	CDoC CMHG CWib ECou GGar SBrw SPer WCru WFar
	'Coppershine'	CMHG
	cotoneaster	CAbP CMac CSBt CTri CTrw ECou ELan EMan ENot EPfP EPot MAsh MGos SBrw SIgm SLon SMad SMur SPer SPoG WBrE WCot WFar WPat WSHC WWes
	- 'Boundary Hill' **new**	ECou
	- 'Brown's Stream' **new**	ECou
	- 'Hodder River' **new**	ECou
	- 'Little Prince'	GGar
	- 'Ohau Scarlet'	ECou
	- 'Ohau Yellow'	ECou
	- 'Swale Stream'	ECou
	- 'Wanaka'	ECou
	macrocarpa	CDoC ECou ISea SDix WSHC
	x ***virgata***	CAbP CBcs CDoC CMHG CMac CTrC CTri EBee ECou ECrN ELan EPfP LRHS MBlu MCCP MWhi NScw SAPC SArc SPer SPlb SWvt WBVN WCru WSHC
	- 'Bronze King'	CBrm CDoC CPLG CTrC ECrN SBrw SPer
	- 'Bronze Lady'	ECou
	- 'Cheesemanii'	ECou GGar
	- 'County Park Lemon'	ECou
	- 'County Park Orange'	ECou
	- 'County Park Purple'	ECou
	- 'County Park Red'	ECou
	- 'Envy' **new**	ECou
	- 'Everglades' **new**	ECou
	- 'Frosted Chocolate'	CBcs CDoC CTrC EBee ECou EPfP MGos SBrw WBcn WDin WFar
	- 'Geenty's Green' **new**	ECou
	- 'Havering'	ECou
	- 'Mangatangi'	MGos
	- 'Pink Delight'	CDoC CRez ECou EPfP SBrw WBor
	- 'Red Wonder'	CBrm CDoC CMHG CPen CTrC EBee ECrN GGar LRHS MWgw SAga SBrw SEND SMac SPoG SSpi WDin
	- 'Sandrine' **new**	ECou

	- 'Sunsplash' (v)	CBcs CDoC CTrC EBee ECou MGos SAga SBrw SPoG
	- 'Virgata'	CChe CTrC ECou MGos
	- 'Wingletye' **new**	ECou
	- 'Yellow Wonder'	CBcs CMHG CPen CTrC EBee ECot ECou ECrN EMan GGar MGos SBrw SPoG WDin

Coronilla (*Papilionaceae*)

	comosa	see *Hippocrepis comosa*
	emerus	see *Hippocrepis emerus*
	glauca	see *C. valentina* subsp. *glauca*
	minima	SBla SIgm XPep
	valentina	CDoC CMac CRHN CSPN EMil SBra SDix XPep
§	- subsp. ***glauca*** ♀H3	CBot CDul CFee CHar CMac CPle CSBt CSam CWib EBee ELan ENot EPfP ERea LAst LRHS MWhi SAga SBrw SGar SPer SPoG SRms SUsu WAbe WCot WHCG XPep
	- - 'Brockhill Blue' **new**	SBra
	- - 'Citrina' ♀H3	More than 30 suppliers
*	- - 'Pygmaea'	WCot
	- - 'Variegata' (v)	More than 30 suppliers
§	***varia***	CAgr CArn CStr NLar NPri SPet XPep

Correa (*Rutaceae*)

	alba	CBcs CDoC CPLG CTrC ECou EPfP SBrw SMur WGwG XPep
	- 'Pinkie' ♀H2	CBcs CPLG ECou SDys SHGN WCot
	backhouseana ♀H2	CAbb CBcs CDoC CPLG CPle CSam CTri EBee ECre EPfP GGar GQui SAga SBrw SGar SLon WCot WGwG WPat WSHC WSPU
	- 'Peaches and Cream' **new**	SRkn
	baeuerlenii	CMHG CPLG
	decumbens	CAbb CPLG CPle CTrC ECou ESlt GSki SDys SMur
	'Dusky Bells' ♀H2	CBcs CDoC CHll CSWP CTrC CTri ECou EPfP MOak SBra SBrw SMur WCot
	'Dusky Maid'	CPLG
	'Federation Belle'	ECou
	glabra **new**	ECou
	- red-flowered **new**	ECou
	'Gwen'	ECou
	'Harrisii'	see *C.* 'Mannii'
	'Inglewood Gold' **new**	ECou
	'Ivory Bells'	ECou SDys
	lawrenceana	CDoC CTrC ECou GQui SBrw SEND WAbe
§	'Mannii' ♀H2	CBcs CPLG CPom CSev ECou EPfP SBrw SPoG WSHC
	'Marian's Marvel' ♀H2	CAbb CMHG CPLG ECou GQui SDys WAbe
	'Peachy Cream'	CDoC SBrw SMur
	'Pink Mist' **new**	ECou
	'Poorinda Mary'	ECou
	pulchella ♀H2	CDoC CTri GQui
§	***reflexa*** ♀H2	CDoC CPLG CPle ECou WAbe WCot
	- var. ***nummulariifolia***	WAbe
	- var. ***reflexa***	CPLG
	- var. ***scabridula*** 'Yanakie'	CPle
*	- ***virens***	CPLG WEas
*	***spectabilis***	CPLG
I	***viridiflora***	GQui

Cortaderia ✿ (*Poaceae*)

	RCB/Arg K2-2	WCot
	RCB/Arg Y-1	WCot
	argentea	see *C. selloana*
	fulvida misapplied	see *C. richardii*
§	***fulvida*** (Buchanan) Zotov	CBcs CBig EBee EWes EWin GFor MNrw SMad SPur WDin WKif
	richardii misapplied	see *C. fulvida*
§	***richardii*** ♀H3-4	CAby CBcs CBig CKno CMCo CSec EHoe EPPr EPla EPza EWes GAbr GGar GMaP IBlr NVic SAPC SArc SMad SWal WCot WCru WMnd WWpP
	- BR 26	GGar
§	***selloana***	CBcs CBig CDul CHEx CTri ECrN EHul ENot EPfP EUJe GFor GKir MBar MRav NBir NBlu NFor SAPC SArc SPlb WMoo WMul
§	- 'Albolineata' (v)	CBcs CBrm CKno EBee EHoe EPza EWes EWsh MBri MCCP MGos MWht NOak SEND SLim SPoG SSta SSto SWvt WLeb WMoo WPat
§	- 'Aureolineata' (v) ♀H3	CBrm CDoC CMac CMil CSam CWCL EHoe ELan ENot EPfP EWsh GKir LRHS MAsh MCCP MGos MMoz SHBN SLim SPer SPoG SSto WFar WLeb WMoo WPGP WPat
	- 'Cool Ice' **new**	CPen
	- 'Elegans'	CBig
	- 'Gold Band'	see *C. selloana* 'Aureolineata'
	- 'Monstrosa'	SMad
	- 'Patagonia'	EHoe EPPr
	- 'Pink Feather'	EPfP EPza GKir SAdn SApp SHBN SPer WFar WWeb
	- 'Pumila' ♀H4	More than 30 suppliers
	- 'Rendatleri'	CBcs CBig CDoC ELan ENot EPfP EWsh GKir LRHS MAsh SCoo SLim SPer WDin
	- 'Rosea'	CBig EBee EPfP EUJe GFor GSki IHMH LRHS MBar MGos NBlu NGdn WFar WMoo
	- 'Senior'	IHMH
	- 'Silver Comet'	GKir
	- Silver Feather = 'Notcort'	ENot
	- 'Silver Fountain'	ELan EPfP LRHS MAsh SHGC
	- 'Silver Stripe'	see *C. selloana* 'Albolineata'
	- 'Splendid Star' (v) **new**	MAsh MBri SPoG
	- 'Sunningdale Silver' ♀H3	More than 30 suppliers
	- 'White Feather'	EPza IHMH MWhi NGdn SApp WFar WWeb

Cortiella (*Apiaceae*)

	aff. ***hookeri*** HWJK 2291 **new**	WCru

Cortusa (*Primulaceae*)

	altaica	GKev
	brotheri	NEgg NWCA WLin
	matthioli	CPom EPfP GBBs GGar GKev GKir GTou ITim MBow NEgg NMen NWCA SRms WFar WLin WRos WWhi
	- 'Alba'	GBuc GKev NEgg NLar NMen NWCA SRms
	- subsp. ***pekinensis***	CFir CLyd GBuc GKev NJOw NLar NMen SRms
	turkestanica	ECho NArg

Corydalis ✿ (*Papaveraceae*)

	from Sichuan, China	CPom EMan MDKP NCot
	alexeenkoana subsp. ***vittae***	see *C. vittae*
	x ***allenii***	GCrs WWst
	- 'Enno' **new**	WWst
	ambigua hort.	see *C. fumariifolia*

	angustifolia	NDlv
	- white	WWst
	anthriscifolia	CLAP
	'Blackberry Wine'	CDes CHll CLAP CSpe GBri MDKP
§	***blanda*** subsp. ***parnassica***	EHyt
	'Blue Panda'	see *C. flexuosa* 'Blue Panda'
	bracteata	GCrs
	- white	WWst
	bulbosa misapplied	see *C. cava*
	bulbosa (L.) DC.	see *C. solida*
	buschii	CDes CLAP CPom EBee EHyt ERos GCrs GEdr NDov NRya SBla SChu SCnR WPGP WPrP WWst
	calcicola **new**	GKev
	cashmeriana	GCrs GEdr GKev GTou SBla WAbe WHal
	- 'Kailash'	CLAP EMon GBuc MAvo NLar
	caucasica	ERos GBuc LAma NMen
	- var. ***alba*** misapplied	see *C. malkensis*
§	***cava***	CLAP CPom EBee EChP ECho EPot GGar LAma MWgw NJOw SHGN
	- ***albiflora***	EPot SBla
	- subsp. ***marschalliana***	WWst
	var. ***purpureo-lilacina*** **new**	
	chaerophylla	IBlr
	- B&SWJ 2951	WCru
	cheilanthifolia	CHrt CMea CPLG CRow CSpe ECha ECtt EDAr EHrv EHyt EPfP GAbr GEdr GSki LPhx LRHS MBri NEgg NWCA SGar SPet SRms WCot WEas WKif WPGP WPnP WPnn WTin
	curviflora	EPot
	- subsp. ***rosthornii***	SMHy
	- - DJHC 0615	SMHy
	decipiens Schott, Nyman & Kotschy	see *C. solida* subsp. *incisa*
I	***decipiens*** hort. ♀H4	CFwr CPom ECho EPot GAbr MWgw WPrP
I	- purple-flowered	EBee ECho
§	***densiflora***	WWst
	'Early Bird'	EWes
	elata	More than 30 suppliers
	- 'Blue Summit'	CLAP EBrs MSte SBla
	elata x ***flexuosa*** clone 1	CLAP CPom GBin GCrs GEdr WCot WPrP
	erdelii	WWst
	flexuosa ♀H4	CFee CMil CPLG CPne CSpe EBee ECrN EDAr EMar EPfP EPot EVFa IFro LAst MArl MNrw MTho NCob NRnb SChu SGar SMac WAbe WBor WCFE WFar WSHC WWpP
	- CD&R 528	EHyt MRav NRya SAga
	- 'Balang Mist'	CLAP SBla SMrm SOkh SUsu
	- 'Blue Dragon'	see *C. flexuosa* 'Purple Leaf'
§	- 'Blue Panda'	EBee EPfP EWes GBuc GMaP IBlr LRHS MDun NHar NLar SBla SSpi WWol
	- 'China Blue'	More than 30 suppliers
	- 'Golden Panda' (v)	CBct GFlt LAst LSou MBNS NHar NLar SPoG WPrP WWol
	- 'Nightshade'	CElw EBee EBrs ECtt EMan GBuc MAvo NBid NCob WBrk WCot WFar WIvy WPrP
I	- 'Norman's Seedling'	EBee EPPr WCot WPGP
	- 'Père David'	More than 30 suppliers
	- 'Purple Leaf'	More than 30 suppliers
§	***fumariifolia***	EPot LAma MTho
	glauca	see *C. sempervirens*
	glaucescens	WWst
	- 'Pink Beauty'	WWst
	gorodkovii **new**	GIBF
	gracilis	WWst
	haussknechtii	EHyt
	henrikii	EHyt GCrs
	incisa B&SWJ 4417 **new**	WCru
	integra	WWst
	'Kingfisher'	NHar SBch WAbe
	kusnetzovii	EHyt GCrs
	ledebouriana	NMen
	leucanthema	CLAP CPom
	- DJHC 752	CDes
	- 'Silver Sceptre'	SSpi
	linstowiana	CPom CSec EDAr EHyt EMan EMon EPPr IBlr LPhx NRnb NWCA
	- CD&R 605	CLAP
§	***lutea***	CBcs CRWN EBee EChP EDAr EMar EPfP GBuc IBlr IFro LGro MBow MTis NCob NPer NVic SEND SHFr SPoG SRms WCot WMoo
	lydica **new**	WWst
	magadanica	GIBF
§	***malkensis*** ♀H4	CMea CPom EHyt ERos ETow GBin GBuc GCrs NBir NMen SBla SCnR
	nariniana **new**	WWst
	nemoralis	CFwr
	nobilis	CPom MLLN SHBN
	nudicaulis	WWst
	ochotensis B&SWJ 3138	WCru
	- B&SWJ 917	WCru
§	***ochroleuca***	CDes CElw CHrt CRow CSec CSpe EChP EMar EPot GAbr GCrs MTho NCot NJOw NPol SBch WFar WMoo
	ophiocarpa	EBee EGoo EHoe ELan EMan EMar GBBs GCal GIBF IBlr MBNS MRav MWhi NBur NRnb SHGN SPoG SWal WFoF WMoo
	ornata	WWst
	pachycentra	EPot
	paczoskii	EBee EHyt ERos GBuc GKir LRHS NDlv NMen
*	***pallescens***	NRnb
	pallida	NRnb
	- B&SWJ 395	WCru
	parnassica	see *C. blanda* subsp. *parnassica*
	paschei	EHyt
	popovii	GCrs MTho
	pseudofumaria alba	see *C. ochroleuca*
	pumila	EPot ETow WLin
	rosea	IBlr
	ruksansii	WWst
	scandens	see *Dicentra scandens*
	schanginii	WLin
	- subsp. ***ainii*** ♀H2	EHyt NMen
	- subsp. ***schanginii***	EHyt GCrs
	scouleri	NBir
	seisumsiana	WWst
§	***sempervirens***	EMan GIBF NLsd SPet WRos WSan
	- ***alba***	ECho WFoF WGwG
	siamensis B&SWJ 7200 **new**	WCru
	smithiana	EDAr GKev WFar WTin
	- ACE 154	GBuc
§	***solida***	CBro CPom CStu EBrs EChP ELan EPot EWTr GAbr GCrs IBlr ITim LAma LRHS MBow MRav NJOw NLAp NMen NRya NWCA WBVN WCot WFar WPnP WShi WTin
	- pink and red shades	CFwr
	- 'Ballade'	WWst
	- 'Cantata'	GCrs WWst

- 'Cat's Paw' WWst
- 'Christina' WWst
- compact WWst
- 'Evening Dream' WWst
- 'First Kiss' WWst
- 'Harkov' GCrs
- 'Highland Sunset' GCrs
§ - subsp. ***incisa*** 🏆H4 CMea ECho EHyt GCrs LRHS MNrw MTho WPrP WShi
- - 'Vermion Snow' **new** WWst
- 'Kissproof' WWst
- 'Margaret' WWst
- 'Merlin' **new** WWst
- 'Moonlight Shade' WWst
- Nettleton seedlings EPot
- 'Pink Discovery' WWst
- 'Pink Smile' WWst
- 'Pink Splash' WWst
- 'Pussy' WWst
- 'Rozula' WWst
- 'Snowlark' GCrs WWst
§ - subsp. ***solida*** CFwr CLAP EHyt EPot NBir NDov NMen NRya WLin WTin
- - from Penza, Russia GBuc GCrs SBla
- - 'Alba' NSla
- - 'Beth Evans' CMea CRez EBrs EHyt EPot GBin LTwo NMen SCnR SRot WCot WWst
- - 'Blue Dream' WWst
- - 'Blue Giant' WWst
- - 'Blushing Girl' WWst
- - 'Charles Archbold' NPar
- - 'Dieter Schacht' 🏆H4 ECho EHyt GCrs LAma NMen NPar WCot
- - 'Evening Shade' WWst
- - 'George Baker' 🏆H4 CBro CMea CPom CRez EBee EBrs ECho EHyt EPot ETow GBuc GCrs GEdr GSki IPot LAma LBee LRHS LTwo MTho NDov NMen NSla SCnR SOkd SOkh SUsu WCot WLin WWst
- - 'Highland Mist' GCrs
- - 'Lahovice' EHyt GCrs NMen
- - 'Munich Sunrise' EHyt
- - 'Prasil Sunset' EHyt
- - 'Sixtus' WWst
- - 'White Knight' GCrs
- 'Spring Bird' WWst
- subsp. ***subremota*** WWst
- f. ***transsylvanica*** see *C. solida* subsp. *solida*
- 'White King' WWst
- 'Yaroslavna' WWst

'Spinners' CAby CDes CElw CLAP EPPr LPhx SBch SMeo SSpi SUsu WPGP
taliensis CPom CSec GKev
- ACE 2443 EPot
tauricola EPot GCrs
tomentella GEdr GKev SIng
'Tory MP' CAby CDes CHid CKno CLAP CSam EBee GEdr MDKP MNrw NChi NHar WHoo WLin WPGP WPrP
trachycarpa **new** EPot
transsylvanica see *C. solida* subsp. *solida*
triternata 🏆H4 EHyt EPot
turtschaninovii CFwr GIBF WWst
- 'Blue Gem' **new** WWst
- 'Vladivostok' **new** WWst
verticillaris EHyt
§ ***vittae*** EHyt
wendelboi EHyt GCrs
- subsp. ***congesta*** WWst
wilsonii EHyt GEdr GKev IBlr IGor MTho NRnb NWCA SBla WEas
zetterlundii GBuc NDlv

Corylopsis ✿ (*Hamamelidaceae*)

from Chollipo, South Korea LRHS SSpi
§ ***glabrescens*** CPMA GIBF IDee IMGH LRHS NLar SBrw SMur WNor WWes
- var. ***gotoana*** EPfP LRHS SMur SSpi SSta
- - 'Chollipo' MAsh SPoG SSta
glandulifera **new** NLar
himalayana NLar
multiflora SSpi SSta
pauciflora 🏆H4 More than 30 suppliers
platypetala see *C. sinensis* var. *calvescens*
- var. ***laevis*** see *C. sinensis* var. *calvescens*
sinensis EBee GIBF NEgg SSta
§ - var. ***calvescens*** CBcs CPMA LRHS NLar SBrw
§ - - f. ***veitchiana*** 🏆H4 CBcs CPMA ELan EPfP IArd IDee LRHS NLar SBrw SMur SPoG WDin
- - - purple CPMA
- 'Golden Spring' **new** NLar
§ - var. ***sinensis*** 🏆H4 CBcs CBrm CDoC CMHG CPMA CWSG EPfP IMGH LAst SBrw SLon SReu WDin WFar
- - 'Spring Purple' CAbP CBcs CMac CPMA EPfP EWTr IArd LRHS MBri NLar SBrw SPla SPoG SSpi SSta WDin WPGP
spicata CBcs CPMA CSBt EWTr GIBF IDee LRHS MBlu NBlu NEgg SBrw SLim
- 'Red Eye' NLar
veitchiana see *C. sinensis* var. *calvescens* f. *veitchiana*
willmottiae see *C. sinensis* var. *sinensis*

Corylus ✿ (*Corylaceae*)

avellana (F) CBcs CCVT CDoC CDul CLnd CRWN CTri ECrN ENot EPfP ERea GKir LAst LBuc LRHS MAsh MBar MBow MBri NWea SKee SPer WDin WHar WMou WOrn
- 'Anny's Red Dwarf' **new** WPat
- 'Aurea' CDul CEnd CLnd COtt CSBt CTho EBee ECrN ELan ENot EPfP EWTr GKir LBuc LRHS MAsh MBlu MBri MGos MRav NEgg NWea SIFN SLim SPer SPoG SSta SWvt WDin WFar
- 'Bollwylle' see *C. maxima* 'Halle'sche Riesennuss'
- 'Casina' (F) CAgr CTho
- 'Contorta' More than 30 suppliers
- 'Corabel' (F) **new** CAgr MCoo
- 'Cosford Cob' (F) CAgr CDoC CDul CSBt CTho CTri ECrN ERea GKir GTwe LBuc LRHS MBlu MBri MGos SKee SPer
- 'Fortin' (F) ECrN
§ - 'Fuscorubra' (F) ECrN GKir MRav MSwo SAga SIFN
- 'Gustav's Zeller' (F) **new** CAgr MCoo
§ - 'Heterophylla' CEnd CTho EPfP GKir GTSp NLar SIFN WMou WWes
- 'Laciniata' see *C. avellana* 'Heterophylla'
- 'Merveille de Bollwyller' see *C. maxima* 'Halle'sche Riesennuss'
- 'Nottingham Prolific' see *C. avellana* 'Pearson's Prolific'
- 'Pauetet' (F) **new** CAgr
§ - 'Pearson's Prolific' (F) ECrN ENot ERea GTwe LBuc SKee
- 'Pendula' GKir MBlu SBLw SCoo SIFN WBcn
- 'Purpurea' see *C. avellana* 'Fuscorubra'
- 'Red Majestic' PBR MBri MPkF
- 'Webb's Prize Cob' (F) CDoC ERea GTwe MBlu SBLw SKee WMou
chinensis EGFP

	colurna ♀H4	CAlb CDul CLnd CMCN CTho ECrN ENot EPfP GKir LRHS MGos NBee NWea SBLw SLPl SPer WDin WMou
	x ***colurnoides*** 'Laroka' (F)	ECrN
	Early Long Zeller	see *Corylus* 'Lang Tidlig Zeller'
	ferox GWJ 9293 **new**	WCru
§	'Lang Tidlig Zeller' **new**	MCoo
	maxima (F)	CDul CLnd ECrN GTwe MSwo NWea WDin
	- 'Butler' (F)	CAgr CDul CTho CTri ERea GTwe LRHS MBri SKee
	- 'Ennis' (F)	CAgr ERea GTwe LRHS SKee
	- 'Fertile de Coutard'	see *C. maxima* 'White Filbert'
	- 'Frizzled Filbert' (F)	ECrN EMil ENot
	- 'Frühe van Frauendorf'	see *C. maxima* 'Red Filbert'
	- 'Garibaldi' (F)	MBlu
	- 'Grote Lambertsnoot'	see *C. maxima* 'Kentish Cob'
	- 'Gunslebert' (F)	CAgr CSBt CTho ECrN ERea GKir GTwe LRHS MBri SKee
	- Halle Giant	see *C. maxima* 'Halle'sche Riesennuss'
§	- 'Halle'sche Riesennuss' (F)	CAgr ERea GTwe SKee
§	- 'Kentish Cob' (F)	CAgr CBcs CDoC CSBt CTho CWSG ECrN ENot EPfP ERea GKir GTwe LBuc LRHS MBlu MBri MGos NBee NPri SFam SKee SPer SRms WHar WOrn
	- 'Lambert's Filbert'	see *C. maxima* 'Kentish Cob'
	- 'Longue d'Espagne'	see *C. maxima* 'Kentish Cob'
	- 'Monsieur de Bouweller'	see *C. maxima* 'Halle'sche Riesennuss'
	- 'Purple Filbert'	see *C. maxima* 'Purpurea'
§	- 'Purpurea' (F) ♀H4	More than 30 suppliers
§	- 'Red Filbert' (F)	CEnd CTho CWSG ENot ERea GKir GTwe IMGH LRHS MBlu MBri SCoo SKee SLim SPoG
	- 'Red Zellernut'	see *C. maxima* 'Red Filbert'
	- 'Spanish White'	see *C. maxima* 'White Filbert'
§	- 'White Filbert' (F)	CDoC ENot ERea GTwe MBri SKee WHar
	- 'White Spanish Filbert'	see *C. maxima* 'White Filbert'
	- 'Witpit Lambertsnoot'	see *C. maxima* 'White Filbert'
	sieboldiana var. ***mandshurica***	CMCN NLar
	'Te Terra Red'	CMCN GKir MBlu SBLw SIFN SMad SSpi WMou
	'Tonda di Giffoni' **new**	MCoo

Corymbia see *Eucalyptus*

Corynephorus (*Poaceae*)

	canescens	CBig CPen CRez CStr EHoe EMan ENot EPza EUJe GFor MBar MCCP NBir NJOw WHrl

Corynocarpus (*Corynocarpaceae*)

	laevigatus	CHEx ECou MBri

Cosmos (*Asteraceae*)

§	***atrosanguineus***	More than 30 suppliers
	bipinnatus 'Purity' **new**	CSpe
	- 'Sonata Pink'	SPoG
	- 'Sonata White'	SPoG
	peucedanifolius	CSpe
	sulphureus	MSal

costmary see *Tanacetum balsamita*

Costus (*Costaceae*)

	amazonicus	MOak
	barbatus	WMul
	curvibracteatus	MOak
	erythrophyllus	MOak
	speciosus	CKob MOak WMul
I	- 'Variegatus' **new**	MOak
	stenophyllus	MOak

Cotinus (*Anacardiaceae*)

	americanus	see *C. obovatus*
§	***coggygria*** ♀H4	More than 30 suppliers
	- 'Foliis Purpureis'	see *C. coggygria* Rubrifolius Group
	- Golden Spirit = 'Ancot' PBR	CAbP CDul CHad CRez CSBt CWib EBee EHan ELan ENot EPfP GKir LAst LBuc LSRN MAsh MBri MGos MRav NPri NSti SCoo SHBN SLim SPer SPoG WOVN
	- 'Kanari' **new**	NLar
	- 'Notcutt's Variety'	EBee ELan ENot EPfP GKir MGos MRav NSti WWes
	- 'Pink Champagne'	CPMA EPfP NLar
	- 'Red Beauty'	CBcs LRHS
	- 'Royal Purple' ♀H4	More than 30 suppliers
§	- Rubrifolius Group	CAlb CBcs CDul CMac EBee EPfP GKir LRHS NFor SChu SPer SWvt WDin WFar
	- 'Smokey Joe'	MAsh SSta
	- 'Velvet Cloak'	CAbP CBcs CPMA EBee ELan ENot EPfP GKir LRHS MAsh MBri MGos MRav NLar SLon SPer SPla WHCG
	- 'Young Lady' **new**	EPfP MBlu SPer
	'Flame' ♀H4	CAbP CBcs CDul CPMA EBee EPfP LAst LRHS MAsh MBlu MBri MGos MRav NEgg SLim SPla SPoG SSpi WHCG WPat
	'Grace'	More than 30 suppliers
§	***obovatus*** ♀H4	CMCN CMHG ELan ENot EPfP IArd IDee MBlu MRav NLar SHBN SPer SSpi SSta WPat WWes

Cotoneaster ✿ (*Rosaceae*)

	CC&McK 465	NWCA
	acuminatus	SRms
	acutifolius	GIBF
	adpressus ♀H4	EPfP GKir MGos MSwo MWgw NFor NLar NLon
§	- 'Little Gem'	ECho EWTr LRHS NLar SRms
	- var. ***praecox***	see *C. nanshan*
	- 'Tom Thumb'	see *C. adpressus* 'Little Gem'
	affinis	SRms
	albokermesinus	SRms
	amoenus	SLPl SRms
	- 'Fire Mountain'	LRHS NPro WFar
§	***apiculatus***	EBee GKir SRms
§	***ascendens***	SRms
	assadii	SRms
	assamensis	SRms
§	***astrophoros***	MBlu NEgg SIng
	atropurpureus	SRms
§	- 'Variegatus' (v) ♀H4	More than 30 suppliers
	boisianus	SRms
	bradyi	SRms
	brickellii	SRms
§	***bullatus*** ♀H4	CDul CLnd CTri EPfP GKir MGos NFor NLon SEND SRms WCwm WOrn WSHC WTel
	- 'Bjuv'	SRms
	- 'Firebird'	see *C. ignescens*
	- f. ***floribundus***	see *C. bullatus*
	- var. ***macrophyllus***	see *C. rehderi*
	- 'McLaren'	SRms
	bumthangensis	SRms
	buxifolius blue-leaved	see *C. lidjiangensis*
	- 'Brno'	see *C. marginatus* 'Brno'

	- f. ***vellaeus***	see *C. astrophoros*
	calocarpus	GIBF
	camilli-schneideri	SRms
	canescens	SRms
	cavei	SRms
	cinerascens	SRms
	cinnabarinus	SRms
§	***cochleatus***	CPLG EBee EPot GIBF GKir LAst MBar MGos NEgg NLon NMen SRms WEas WLin
§	***congestus***	CRez CSBt CWib EBee GKir LRHS MBar MGos MRav MSwo NFor NLon SPer SPlb SRms WDin WHar
	- 'Nanus'	CLyd CMHG CTri ELan EOrn LRHS MOne NBid NFor NLAp WBVN WPat
	conspicuus	CBcs SRms
	- 'Decorus' ♀H4	CAlb CCVT CDoC CSBt CWSG EBee EHol ENot EPfP GKir LRHS MBar MGos MRav MSwo MWhi NEgg NFor NLon NWea SLim SPer SPlb SPoG SWal WBVN WDin WTel WWes
	- 'Flameburst'	LRHS SHBN
	- 'Leicester Gem' **new**	SRms
	- 'Red Alert'	SRms
	cooperi	SRms
	cornifolius	SRms
	crispii	SRms
	cuspidatus	SRms
N	***dammeri*** ♀H4	More than 30 suppliers
§	- 'Major'	LAst LBuc NBlu SRms WCFE
§	- 'Mooncreeper'	LRHS MBNS MBri SCoo
	- 'Oakwood'	see *C. radicans* 'Eichholz'
	- var. ***radicans*** misapplied	see *C. dammeri* 'Major'
	- var. ***radicans*** C.K.Schneid.	see *C. radicans*
	- 'Streib's Findling'	see *C.* 'Streib's Findling'
	delavayanus **new**	SRms
	dielsianus	GIBF NWea SRms
	distichus var. ***tongolensis***	see *C. splendens*
	divaricatus	EPfP NWea SLon SRms WFar
	duthieanus 'Boer'	see *C. apiculatus*
	elatus	SRms
	elegans	SRms
	emeiensis	SRms
	'Erlinda'	see *C.* x *suecicus* 'Erlinda'
	estonicus **new**	SRms
	falconeri	MGol SRms
	fastigiatus	SRms
	flinckii	SRms
	floccosus	CSBt GKir LRHS NWea SRms
	floridus	SRms
	forrestii	GIBF SRms
	franchetii	More than 30 suppliers
	- var. ***sternianus***	see *C. sternianus*
	frigidus	CDul NWea SRms
N	- 'Cornubia' ♀H4	More than 30 suppliers
	- 'Fructu Luteo'	GKir MBri WWes
	- 'Notcutt's Variety'	EBee ELan ENot EPfP MRav WWes
§	- 'Pershore Coral'	WSPU
	- 'Saint Monica'	MBlu
	gamblei	SRms WCwm
	ganghobaensis	SRms
	glabratus	SLPl SRms
	glacialis	SRms
	glaucophyllus	SEND SRms
§	***glomerulatus***	MBar SRms
	gracilis	SRms
	granatensis	SRms
	harrovianus	NLar SLPl SRms
	harrysmithii	EMFP GIBF
	hebephyllus	NLar
	- var. ***hebephyllus*** **new**	SRms
I	***hedegaardii*** 'Fructu Luteo' **new**	SRms
	henryanus	CDoC SRms
	- 'Anne Cornwallis'	WBcn
	'Herbstfeuer'	see *C. salicifolius* 'Herbstfeuer'
	'Highlight'	see *C. pluriflorus*
	hillieri	SRms
§	***hjelmqvistii***	LBuc SRms
	- 'Robustus'	see *C. hjelmqvistii*
	- 'Rotundifolius'	see *C. hjelmqvistii*
	hodjingensis	SRms
	horizontalis ♀H4	More than 30 suppliers
	- 'Peitz'	SRms
	- 'Variegatus'	see *C. atropurpureus* 'Variegatus'
	- var. ***wilsonii***	see *C. ascendens*
	hualiensis	SRms
	humifusus	see *C. dammeri*
	hummelii	CDul CPle SRms
§	'Hybridus Pendulus'	More than 30 suppliers
§	***hylmoei***	SLPl SRms
	hypocarpus	SRms
	ignavus	SLPl SRms
	ignescens	LRHS SRms
	ignotus	SRms
	incanus	SRms
	induratus	SLPl SRms
	insculptus	SRms
	insolitus	SRms
	integerrimus	SRms
§	***integrifolius*** ♀H4	CMHG EBee EPfP EPla GKir LRHS MBar MWhi NBlu NMen SCoo SRms STre WMoo
	kangdingensis	SRms
	konishii ETE 233 **new**	GIBF
	lacteus ♀H4	CBcs CDul CTri EBee ELan ENot EPfP EPla EWTr GKir LBuc LRHS MBri MGos MRav NBlu NEgg NWea SCoo SEND SHBN SLon SPer SPla SPoG SRms WCFE WDin WFar XPep
	- 'Variegatus' (v)	CEnd
	lancasteri	SRms
	langei	SRms
	laxiflorus	SRms
	lesliei	SRms
§	***lidjiangensis***	SRms WCot
§	***linearifolius***	CLyd EHol GKir LRHS MWht
	lucidus	SRms
	ludlowii	SRms
	magnificus **new**	SRms
§	***mairei***	SRms
	marginatus	SRms
§	- 'Blazovice' **new**	EMFP SRms
§	- 'Brno' **new**	SRms
	marquandii	EPla SRms
§	***meiophyllus***	SRms
	meuselii	SRms
	microphyllus misapplied	see *C. purpurascens*
	microphyllus Wall. ex Lindl.	CTri EBee ENot GIBF MBar MGos NFor NScw NWea SDix SHBN SPoG STre WDin WTel
	- var. ***cochleatus*** (Franch.) Rehd. & Wils.	see *C. cochleatus*
	- 'Donard Gem'	see *C. astrophoros*
	- 'Ruby'	SRms
	- 'Teulon Porter'	see *C. astrophoros*
	- var. ***thymifolius*** misapplied	see *C. linearifolius*
	- var. ***thymifolius*** (Lindl.) Koehne	see *C. integrifolius*
	milkedandai	SRms

	miniatus	SRms
	mirabilis	SRms
	moliensis Yu 14196	GIBF
	monopyrenus	SRms
	'Mooncreeper'	see *C. dammeri* 'Mooncreeper'
	morrisonensis new	SRms
	moupinensis	EBee SRms
	mucronatus	SRms
	multiflorus Bunge	SRms
§	***nanshan***	EBee NLar NWea SRms WSPU
	- 'Boer'	see *C. apiculatus*
	newryensis	SRms
	niger	GIBF
	nitens	SRms
	nitidifolius	see *C. glomerulatus*
	nitidus var. ***parvifolius***	SRms
	nohelii	GIBF SRms
	notabilis	SRms
	nummularioides	SRms
	nummularius	SRms
	obscurus	SRms
	obtusus	SRms
	omissus	GIBF SRms
	otto-schwarzii	SRms
	pangiensis new	SRms
	pannosus	SLPl SRms WFar
	- 'Speckles'	SRms
	paradoxus	SRms
	parkeri	SRms
	pekinensis	SRms
	permutatus	see *C. pluriflorus*
	perpusillus	SRms WFar
	'Pershore Coral'	see *C. frigidus* 'Pershore Coral'
§	***pluriflorus***	SRms
	poluninii	SRms
	polycarpus	SRms
	praecox 'Boer'	see *C. apiculatus*
§	***procumbens***	SRms WDin
	- 'Queen of Carpets'	CDoC EBee GKir LRHS LSRN MAsh MBNS MGos MRav SCoo SLim SPoG SRms SWvt
	- 'Seattle'	SRms
	- 'Streib's Findling'	see *C.* 'Streib's Findling'
	prostratus	SRms
	- 'Arnold Forster'	SRms
	przewalskii	SRms
	pseudo-obscurus	SRms
§	***purpurascens***	CDul ENot MDun SCoo WBcn WFar
	pyrenaicus	see *C. congestus*
	qungbixiensis	SRms
	racemiflorus	SRms
§	***radicans***	LRHS
§	- 'Eichholz'	EBee GKir IArd LRHS MGos WWeb
§	***rehderi***	NLar SRms
	roseus	GIBF SRms
	'Rothschildianus'	see *C. salicifolius* 'Rothschildianus'
	rotundifolius	EBee SLon SRms
	'Royal Beauty'	see *C.* x *suecicus* 'Coral Beauty'
	rufus	SRms
	rugosus	SRms
	salicifolius	CLnd EMil GKir MSwo NLon SRms WDin WFar
	- Autumn Fire	see *C. salicifolius* 'Herbstfeuer'
§	- 'Avonbank'	CDoC CEnd MAsh NLar WSPU
	- 'Bruno Orangeade'	SRms
	- 'Elstead'	MRav
	- 'Exburyensis'	CBcs CDoC EBee EPfP GKir LRHS MAsh MBri MGos MRav SCoo SHBN SPla WDin WFar WHCG
	- 'Gnom'	EBee ELan EPfP GKir LRHS MAsh MBar MBlu MGos MRav MWht NFor NLon SPer SPoG SRms WDin WFar
§	- 'Herbstfeuer'	EBee EHol GKir LAst MGos MRav MSwo SRms WDin WFar WRHF
	- 'Merriott Weeper'	CDoC
	- Park Carpet	see *C. salicifolius* 'Parkteppich'
§	- 'Parkteppich'	NWea SPer
	- 'Pendulus'	see *C.* 'Hybridus Pendulus'
	- 'Repens'	CDoC CWib EHol EPfP NLon NScw NWea SPer SPoG SRms SSto WDin WFar
§	- 'Rothschildianus' ♀H4	More than 30 suppliers
	- var. ***rugosus*** hort.	see *C. hylmoei*
	- 'Scarlet Leader'	LRHS
	salwinensis	SLPl SRms
	sandakphuensis	SRms
	saxatilis	SRms
	scandinavicus	SRms
	schantungensis	SRms
	schlechtendalii 'Blazovice'	see *C. marginatus* 'Blazovice'
	- 'Brno'	see *C. marginatus* 'Brno'
	schubertii	SRms
	serotinus misapplied	see *C. meiophyllus*
	serotinus Hutchinson	CAbP SLPl SRms
	shannanensis	SRms
	shansiensis	LRHS SRms WBcn
	sherriffii	SRms
	sikangensis	GBin SLon SRms
	simonsii ♀H4	CDoC CDul CLnd CTri EBee ELan EPfP GKir LBuc LRHS MBar MGos NScw NWea SCoo SPoG SRms WDin WFar WHar
§	***splendens***	GIBF SRms WFar
	- 'Sabrina'	see *C. splendens*
	spongbergii	SRms
	staintonii	SRms
§	***sternianus*** ♀H4	EPfP LRHS MBar SLPl SRms
	- ACE 2200	EPot
	'Streib's Findling'	MAsh
	suavis new	SRms
	subacutus	SRms
	subadpressus	SRms
§	x ***suecicus*** 'Coral Beauty'	CCVT CDoC CTri CWSG CWib EBee ELan ENot EPfP GKir LAst LBuc LGro LRHS MAsh MBar MGos MSwo NBlu NEgg NLon SAga SLim SPla SPoG SRms SWal WDin WFar
§	- 'Erlinda' (v)	CEnd CWib EBee MBar NLar SCoo SRms
	- 'Ifor'	SLPl SRms
	- 'Juliette' (v)	CWib LSRN MBar NBlu NLar NPro SCoo SLim SPoG WFar WOrn
	- 'Skogholm'	CBcs CSBt CWSG CWib EBee GKir LRHS MBar MGos NWea SCoo SPer SRms WDin WFar WHar
	taoensis	SRms
	tardiflorus	SRms
	tauricus	SRms
	teijiashanensis	SRms
	tengyuehensis	SRms
	thimphuensis	SRms
	tomentosus	SRms
	trinervis	SRms
	- 'Bruno'	SRms
	turbinatus	SRms
	uralensis new	SRms
	uzbezicus	SRms
	'Valkenburg'	SRms
	vandelaarii	SRms
	veitchii	NLar SRms
	verruculosus	SRms
	villosulus	EHol SRms
	vilmorinianus	SRms
	wardii misapplied	see *C. mairei*

wardii W.W. Sm. — EWTr GIBF SRms
x ***watereri*** — CCVT CDul CSBt CWib EBee EMil LRHS MAsh MSwo NEgg NWea WDin WJas WTel
- 'Avonbank' — see *C. salicifolius* 'Avonbank'
- 'Coral Bunch' — MBri
- 'Corina' — SRms
- 'Cornubia' — see *C. frigidus* 'Cornubia'
- 'John Waterer' ♀H4 — EPfP WFar
- 'Pendulus' — see *C.* 'Hybridus Pendulus'
- 'Pink Champagne' — CAbP LRHS SPer
wilsonii **new** — SRms
yakuticus — SRms
yallungensis — SRms
yinchangensis — SRms
zabelii — GIBF SRms

Cotula (*Asteraceae*)

C&H 452 — NWCA
atrata — see *Leptinella atrata*
- var. ***dendyi*** — see *Leptinella dendyi*
coronopifolia — CSev CWat LPBA NBlu NPer WPop WWpP
§ ***hispida*** — More than 30 suppliers
lineariloba — ECha EWes LBee LRHS
minor — see *Leptinella minor*
'Platt's Black' — see *Leptinella squalida* 'Platt's Black'
potentilloides — see *Leptinella potentillina*
pyrethrifolia — see *Leptinella pyrethrifolia*
rotundata — see *Leptinella rotundata*
sericea — see *Leptinella albida*
serrulata — see *Leptinella serrulata*
squalida — see *Leptinella squalida*

Cotyledon (*Crassulaceae*)

chrysantha — see *Rosularia chrysantha*
gibbiflora var. ***metallica*** — see *Echeveria gibbiflora* var. *metallica*
oppositifolia — see *Chiastophyllum oppositifolium*
orbiculata — CHEx CStu SDix SIgm
- B&SWJ 723 — WCru
- var. ***oblonga*** — EBee EMan SChr WCot WEas
- var. ***orbiculata*** **new** — EShb
simplicifolia — see *Chiastophyllum oppositifolium*
tomentosa — EShb
subsp. ***ladismithensis*** **new**
undulata — WEas

Cowania see *Purshia*

Coxella (*Apiaceae*)

dieffenbachii — GCal

Crambe (*Brassicaceae*)

cordifolia ♀H4 — More than 30 suppliers
maritima ♀H4 — More than 30 suppliers
- 'Lilywhite' — CAgr ILis LPio WCot
orientalis — WCot
tatarica — EMan NLar WPer

cranberry see *Vaccinium macrocarpon, V. oxycoccos*

Craspedia (*Asteraceae*)

alpina from Tasmania — GGar

Crassula (*Crassulaceae*)

anomala — SChr
arborescens — see *C. atropurpurea* var. *arborescens*
argentea — see *C. ovata*
arta **new** — EPem
§ ***atropurpurea*** var. ***arborescens*** — EPem EShb EUJe SRms STre
'Buddha's Temple' **new** — EShb
coccinea — CHEx CTrC EShb WOld
columella **new** — EPem
dejecta **new** — EShb
elegans subsp. ***elegans*** **new** — EPfP
falcata ♀H1 — EShb IBlr MBri
lactea — CHal STre
'Morgan's Pride' **new** — EShb
multicava — CHEx
muscosa — EShb SChr STre
obtusa — SRot
orbicularis — EPem
§ ***ovata*** ♀H1 — CHEx CHal EBak EOHP EPem EPfP EUJe MBri NPer SWal
- 'Gollum' — EPem EPfP
- 'Hummel's Sunset' (v) ♀H1 — CHal EPem STre SWal
- 'Minima' — EPem
* - ***nana*** — STre
* - 'Variegata' (v) — CHal EBak WCot
pellucida subsp. ***marginalis*** — CHal
* - - 'Variegata' (v) — CHal
peploides — SChr
perforata — CHal
- 'Variegata' (v) — CHal
portulacea — see *C. ovata*
rupestris ♀H1 — MBri
- subsp. ***marnieriana*** **new** — EPem
§ ***sarcocaulis*** — CHEx CHal CStu CTri ELan ESis GEdr GGar GMaP GTou ITim MTho NJOw NMen NVic NWCA SIgm SIng SPlb SPoG SRms SRot STre WAbe WEas WPat WSHC
- ***alba*** — CHal NJOw SHFr STre WPer
- 'Ken Aslet' — SPet STre
schmidtii — CHal MBri
sedifolia — see *C. setulosa* 'Milfordiae'
sediformis — see *C. setulosa* 'Milfordiae'
setulosa 'Milfordiae' — CTri GKir MBar MWat NBir NJOw NLAp
socialis — CHal WPat
tetragona — SEND
* ***tomentosa*** 'Variegata' (v) — EShb EWin
'Très Bon' — STre

Crataegus ✿ (*Rosaceae*)

arnoldiana — CAgr CEnd CLnd CTho CTri EBee ECrN EPfP GKir LRHS MAsh MBri MCoo MGos NWea SCoo SEND SFam SLPl SMad SPoG WOrn
'Autumn Glory' — CEnd CLnd EBee ECrN GKir LRHS WFar
azarolus — CAgr
champlainensis — CLnd CTho
chlorosarca — GIBF
chungtienensis — CMCN EBee GKir
- ACE 1624 — SSpi
coccinea ambig. — NWea
coccinea L. — CAgr CLnd CTho EPfP GKir LRHS MBri MCoo SCoo
cordata — see *C. phaenopyrum*
crus-galli misapplied — see *C. persimilis* 'Prunifolia'
crus-galli L. — CCVT CDoC CDul CLnd CTho EBee ECrN EPfP GKir LBuc LRHS MAsh SPer WDin WJas
- var. ***pyracanthifolia*** — CLnd CTho

- thornless **new**	MBlu
douglasii	GIBF
x ***durobrivensis***	CAgr CLnd CTho GKir
ellwangeriana	CAgr CLnd CTho ECrN GKir SDix
eriocarpa	CLnd
flabellata	CEnd GIBF GKir SSpi
gemmosa	CEnd CLnd GKir MBlu MCoo NLar NWea
greggiana	CLnd
x ***grignonensis***	CBcs CCVT CDul CLnd ECrN EMil MAsh SBLw SPer WJas
jonesiae	EPfP
laciniata	see *C. orientalis*
§ ***laevigata***	CDul NWea WMou
- 'Coccinea Plena'	see *C. laevigata* 'Paul's Scarlet'
- 'Crimson Cloud'	CDoC CEnd CLnd CWSG CWib EBee ECrN ELan ENot EPfP GKir LBuc LRHS MAsh MBri MGos MSwo NWea SCoo SCrf SLim SLon SPer WJas WOrn
- 'Flore Pleno'	see *C. laevigata* 'Plena'
- 'Gireoudii' (v)	CDul CEnd CPMA CWib GKir GTSp LAst MBlu MGos NLar NSti WPat
- 'Mutabilis'	CLnd GKir SBLw SHBN
§ - 'Paul's Scarlet' (d) ♀H4	More than 30 suppliers
- 'Pink Corkscrew'	CTho GKir MBlu MGos NLar SMad WCot WPat WWes
§ - 'Plena' (d)	CBcs CDoC CDul CLnd CSBt CTho CTri CWib ECrN GKir LAst LRHS MSwo MWat NBee NWea SBLw SCrf SFam SHBN SLim SPer WDin WOrn
- 'Punicea'	GKir
- 'Rosea Flore Pleno' (d) ♀H4	More than 30 suppliers
x ***lavalleei***	CCVT CDul CLnd CTri EBee ECrN ENot GKir LRHS MSwo NEgg NWea SCoo SFam SPer SPur WDin
- 'Carrierei' ♀H4	CDoC CTho ECrN EPfP GKir LRHS MAsh MBlu MBri NWea SBLw SCoo
maximowiczii	GIBF
mexicana	see *C. pubescens* f. *stipulacea*
mollis	CAgr CTho ECrN EPfP NWea
monogyna	CBcs CCVT CDoC CDul CLnd CRWN ELan ENot EPfP GKir GWCH LAst LBuc LRHS MBar MBri MGos NBlu NWea SPer WDin WMou
§ - 'Biflora'	CDul CEnd CTho CTri ECrN GKir LRHS MAsh MCoo MGos NWea SCoo SLim SPoG WSPU
- 'Compacta'	MBlu NLar SMad
- 'Ferox'	CTho
- 'Flexuosa'	MGos
- 'Praecox'	see *C. monogyna* 'Biflora'
- 'Stricta'	CCVT CDul CLnd CSBt CTho EBee ECrN EPfP SBLw
- 'Variegata' (v)	CDul ECrN WBcn
x ***mordenensis*** 'Toba' (d)	CDul CLnd CTho SBLw
neofluvialis	GIBF
orientalis	CDul CEnd CLnd CMCN CTho CTri EBee ECrN EPfP GIBF GKir IArd LRHS MAsh MBlu MBri MCoo MGos NWea SCoo SHBN SLPl SLim SMad SPer SSpi WJas WMou
oxyacantha	see *C. laevigata*
pedicellata	see *C. coccinea* L.
§ ***persimilis*** 'Prunifolia' ♀H4	More than 30 suppliers
- 'Prunifolia Splendens'	CCVT IDee SBLw
§ ***phaenopyrum***	CDul CLnd CMCN CTho EPfP GIBF GKir MGos SLPl SMad SSpi
pinnatifida	MAsh SMad
- var. ***major***	CEnd EPfP GKir MCoo NWea SCoo
- - 'Big Golden Star'	CAgr CTho ECrN GKir LRHS MBri
'Praecox'	see *C. monogyna* 'Biflora'
prunifolia	see *C. persimilis* 'Prunifolia'
§ ***pubescens*** f. ***stipulacea***	CDul CTho SSpi
punctata	CTho SLPl
sanguinea	GIBF
schraderiana	CAgr CLnd CTho GKir SCoo
succulenta	GKir SMad
var. ***macracantha***	
tanacetifolia	CAgr CDul CLnd CTho ECrN GKir LRHS MBlu SPoG SSpi
uniflora	GIBF
viridis 'Winter King'	CDoC GKir LRHS MAsh MBlu MCoo
wattiana	CTho

x *Crataemespilus* (*Rosaceae*)

grandiflora	CDul CTho GKir LRHS

Crawfurdia (*Gentianaceae*)

speciosa	GEdr
- B&SWJ 2138	WCru

Cremanthodium (*Asteraceae*)

sp.	EMan WCot
aff. ***ellisii*** HWJK 2262 **new**	WCru
§ ***reniforme*** **new**	GKev
- GWJ 9407	WCru

Crenularia see *Aethionema*

Crepis (*Asteraceae*)

aurea	EBee GAbr NJOw NWCA
incana ♀H4	CFee CMea CPom EGoo EMan GBri GKir GSki LPhx LRHS MAvo MTho NBid NChi NSla NWCA SIng SRms WAbe WCot WPat
- 'Pink Mist' **new**	WWeb
rubra	CSpe EMan LPio LRHS

Crinitaria see *Aster*

Crinodendron (*Elaeocarpaceae*)

§ ***hookerianum*** ♀H3	More than 30 suppliers
- 'Ada Hoffmann'	CPLG MBlu NLar
patagua	CBcs CPLG CPle CRez CSam CWib GGar GQui IArd IDee LRHS MDun SBrw SPer WAbe WFar WSHC

Crinum (*Amaryllidaceae*)

amoenum	MOak
asiaticum var. ***sinicum***	CDes EUJe
§ ***bulbispermum***	CFil CFir EBee ELan LToo SSpi WCot WPic
- 'Album'	EMan
§ ***campanulatum***	CMon
capense	see *C. bulbispermum*
'Carolina Beauty'	WCot
'Elizabeth Traub' **new**	WCot
'Ellen Bosanquet'	CDes CFir WCot
'Hanibal's Dwarf'	CDes WCot
macowanii	WCot
moorei	CDes CFir CMon EBee SChr WPGP
- f. ***album***	CAvo CFil WCot WMul
§ x ***powellii*** ♀H3	More than 30 suppliers
- 'Album' ♀H3	CAvo CBct CDes CHEx CMon CTri EBrs ECha ELan EMan EUJe EWes LAma LPio LRHS MOak MRav SSpi WCot WCru WFar WPGP WPic
- 'Harlemense'	SSpi

- 'Longifolium' — see *C. bulbispermum*
- 'Roseum' — see *C.* x *powellii*

variabile — WCot
yemense — CMon WCot

Criogenes see *Cypripedium*

Crithmum (*Apiaceae*)

maritimum — CArn CWan EMan GPoy MSal NLar NTHB SECG SIgm WJek WWye XPep

Crocosmia ✿ (*Iridaceae*)

'African Glow' — ENot
'Alistair' **new** — EGra EMar
'Amberglow' — CElw CFwr CHar CMea CPrp EWoo IBlr MBNS MLan NPer WFar WSSM WWpP
'Anniversary' — IBlr SSpi
aurea misapplied — see *Crocosmia* x *crocosmiiflora* 'George Davison'
aurea ambig. — NBir
aurea Planchon — CPou CSec IBlr SSpi
- JCA 3.100.000 — WCot
- var. ***aurea*** — GCal IBlr
- var. ***maculata*** **new** — IBlr
- var. ***pauciflora*** **new** — IBlr

'Auriol' **new** — IBlr
'Bicolor' **new** — IBlr WHil
Bressingham Beacon = 'Blos' — EBrs GGar GKir IBlr LRHS WRHF
'Bressingham Blaze' — CBre CMHG CPrp EBrs GCal GKir IBlr LRHS WCot
'Cadenza' — IBlr
'Carnival' — IBlr
'Cascade' — IBlr
'Chinatown' — IBlr WHil
'Comet' Knutty — GBuc IBlr SIgm SSpi WWhi
§ x ***crocosmiiflora*** — CHEx COIW EGra EPla IBlr LAst NLon NOrc SIng SPlb SRms WBrk WCot WFar WMoo WRHF WSSM WShi WWpP WWye
- 'A.E. Amos' — EGra EMar
- 'A.J. Hogan' — GBin IBal IBlr WHil
- 'Amber Sun' **new** — IBlr
- 'Apricot Queen' — IBlr
- 'Autumn Gold' **new** — IBlr
- 'Baby Barnaby' — CBos CBre IBlr WPGP
- 'Babylon' — More than 30 suppliers
- 'Burford Bronze' — CPrp IBlr WHil
- 'Buttercup' — IBlr NFla WBor WFar
- 'Canary Bird' — CBro CCge CPrp CRow CSam EBrs ECtt EGra EMar GAbr GKir GMac IBal IBlr LRHS NBPC NGdn WBrk WHil WRHF
- 'Cardinale' **new** — IBlr
- 'Carmin Brillant' ♀H3-4 — More than 30 suppliers
- 'Citronella' J.E. Fitt — CBro CCge CFwr CHar CPLG CPrp CSam CTri EBrs EChP EGra EHrv EMar EPfP GKir GMaP LRHS MAvo NGdn WBVN WRha WWpP
- 'Columbus' — CFwr CM&M EBee EBrs EChP GMac IBal LRHS NRnb SAga WBor WCAu WFar WMnd
- 'Colwall' — IBlr
- 'Constance' — CBre CBro CElw CFwr CSam EBrs EChP EGra EPot ERou GGar GKir IBal IBlr LRHS MBNS MBri MNrw NBid NCot NGdn NRnb SRos WFar WHil
I - 'Corona' — CPrp IBlr MAvo WHil
- 'Corten' — IBlr
§ - 'Croesus' — EGra GBri IBlr MRav WCot
- 'Custard Cream' — CMil CPrp CSpe GBin GKir IBlr LRHS MAvo SRos WFar WHil
- 'D.H. Houghton' — IBlr
- 'Debutante' — CBos CMil CPrp EBrs EGra IBlr MAvo WCot WLin WSHC WWhi WWpP
- 'Dusky Maiden' — More than 30 suppliers
§ - 'E.A. Bowles' — CPou EBrs GCal IBlr WCot
- 'Eastern Promise' — CBre CMea CPrp GKir IBlr SMrm WLin
- 'Elegans' — CBre CElw ECtt IBlr
§ - 'Emily McKenzie' — More than 30 suppliers
- 'Etoile de Feu' — IBlr
- 'Fantasie' — CFwr EBee MBNS
- 'Firebrand' — CBos IBlr
- 'Flamethrower' — IBlr
§ - 'George Davison' Davison — More than 30 suppliers
§ - 'Gerbe d'Or' — More than 30 suppliers
- 'Gloria' — CPen IBlr
§ - 'Golden Glory' — CHar CPrp CSam CTbh EBrs EHrv ELan GFlt GKir GMaP IBal IBlr MAvo MSwo NBid NBir NChi NEgg SPlb SPoG SRos WBrE WCot WCra WFar WHil WLin WPop WWpP
- 'Golden Sheaf' — GBri IBlr NGdn SDys SUsu
- 'Goldfinch' — IBlr WHil
- 'Hades' — CPrp IBlr MAvo WHil
- 'Harvest Sun' **new** — IBlr
- 'His Majesty' — CBro CPne CPou CPrp CSam CSpe GKir IBal IBlr LRHS SDys WFar WHil WPer WWhi
§ - 'Jackanapes' — CBos CFwr CMil CPrp CRow EBrs EGra EHrv EPfP GCal GGar GKir IBlr LRHS MBri SDys SUsu WCot WHil WWeb WWhi WWpP WWye
- 'James Coey' J.E. Fitt — CHad CHar COIW CPrp CRow EChP ECha EHrv EPfP ERou EVFa GCal GGar GMac GSki LAma LAst LRHS MDun NDov NGdn SIng SWvt WFar WMoo
* - 'Jesse van Dyke' — IBlr
§ - 'Jessie' — CElw CFwr EBrs GGar IBlr WCot WPer WWpP
- 'Kapoor' **new** — IBlr
- 'Kiautschou' — EBee EGra GMac IBlr MAvo SDys WHil
- 'Lady Hamilton' — More than 30 suppliers
- 'Lady McKenzie' — see *C.* x *crocosmiiflora* 'Emily McKenzie'
- 'Lady Oxford' — CPrp EBrs EGra EMan EMar GGar IBlr LRHS WHil
- 'Lutea' — EBrs ECtt EGra EMar IBlr
- 'Marjorie' — LAma WCot WOut
- 'Mephistopheles' — CPrp IBlr MAvo WHil
- 'Météore' — CFwr EBee EBrs EMar GGar LAst MBNS NOrc WWeb
- 'Morgenlicht' — CPen ECtt IBlr WCot WRHF
- 'Mrs David Howard' **new** — SApp
§ - 'Mrs Geoffrey Howard' — CHVG CMea CSam EBrs ECtt EGra GBri IBlr NCGa SUsu WCru WPGP WWhi
- 'Mrs Morrison' — see *C.* x *crocosmiiflora* 'Mrs Geoffrey Howard'
- Newry seedling — see *C.* x *crocosmiiflora* 'Prometheus'
- 'Nimbus' — CBos CPrp GBri IBlr WCot WHil
§ - 'Norwich Canary' — More than 30 suppliers
- 'Olympic Fire' **new** — IBlr
I - 'Pepper' — IBlr
- 'Polo' — CFwr
- 'Princess' — see *C.* x *crocosmiiflora* 'Red Knight'

- 'Princess Alexandra' IBlr
- 'Prolificans' IBlr
§ - 'Prometheus' CPrp IBlr WHil
§ - 'Queen Alexandra' J.E. Fitt EChP ECha IBlr LAma NCGa SOkh WHal WMoo WPer
- 'Queen Charlotte' CPrp IBlr
- 'Queen Mary II' CAvo CBos CPar CPrp EGra EMan EMar GBin IBal IBlr WFar WHil WWpP
- 'Queen of Spain' CCge CPrp EBrs GGar GKir IBlr LRHS MBri MDKP MLLN SOkh WHil
- 'Rayon d'Or' IBlr
- 'Red King' CFwr CHar EBla EBrs IBlr LAst SGSe WFar
§ - 'Red Knight' CM&M EGra IBlr MAvo WCot
- 'Rheingold' see *C.* x *crocosmiiflora* 'Golden Glory'
- 'Rose Queen' IBlr
- 'Saint Clements' **new** IBlr
- 'Saracen' CMil EBee EChP EMan GCal IBal IBlr IPot LAst MAvo MBNS MBnl NDov NEgg SIgm SMrm SOkh SPla SSpi WCot WFar
- 'Sir Matthew Wilson' EBee EBrs GBri IBlr WCot
- 'Solfatare' ♀H3 More than 30 suppliers
- 'Solfatare Coleton Fishacre' see *C.* x *crocosmiiflora* 'Gerbe d'Or'
- 'Star of the East' ♀H3 More than 30 suppliers
- 'Starbright' **new** IBlr
§ - 'Sulphurea' CPLG CPou CRow CSam EBee EGra GGar GKir IBlr LAma SDix SIng WBrk WCot WEas WHal WHil WPer
- 'Sultan' CBro CCge CElw EBee IBlr LPio SOkh WFar WPGP
- 'Venus' CAby CBre CFwr CPen CPou EBee EBrs ECtt EGra EMar EShb GBuc IBlr LRHS MBow NFla SRos STes WFar WLin WOut
- 'Vesuvius' W. Pfitzer CElw GCal GKir IBlr WFar
'Culzean Peach' GAbr GCal GMac IBlr MAvo MRav NBir SMrm WCot WOut
'Darkleaf Apricot' see *C.* x *crocosmiiflora* 'Gerbe d'Or'
'Diademe' **new** CSam
'Eclatant' IBlr
'Eldorado' see *C.* x *crocosmiiflora* 'E.A. Bowles'
'Elegance' **new** IBlr
'Ellenbank Firecrest' **new** GMac
'Emberglow' More than 30 suppliers
'Fandango' IBlr
'Festival Orange' IBlr MAvo
'Fire King' misapplied see *C.* x *crocosmiiflora* 'Jackanapes'
'Fire Sprite' IBlr
'Firebird' EBrs GBuc IBlr IGor LRHS MBri SIgm SRos WCot
'Firefly' IBlr
'Fireglow' ECtt EGra EMar IBlr WFar WPer
'Flaire' **new** IBlr
fucata 'Jupiter' see *C.* 'Jupiter'
'Fugue' **new** IBlr
* 'Fusilade' IBlr
'George Davison' hort. see *C.* x *crocosmiiflora* 'Golden Glory', 'Sulphurea'
Golden Fleece Lemoine see *C.* x *crocosmiiflora* 'Gerbe d'Or'
'Goldsprite' IBlr
'Highlight' IBlr MAvo WHil
§ 'Honey Angels' More than 30 suppliers
'Honey Bells' WBrk
'Irish Dawn' CPrp GBin IBlr
Jenny Bloom = 'Blacro'PBR CHar CM&M EBrs ECtt GBin GBuc GKir GSki LRHS NBir SMHy STes
'John Boots' CPen CPrp EBee EBrs EChP EHrv EPot GBuc IBlr LBBr MBNS NRnb SMrm WBor WCot WFar
§ 'Jupiter' CBot CBre CPou CWCL EBee EBrs EGra EMar GBuc GMac IBlr LRHS NChi SApp WCot WFar WHil WLin WOld WWpP
'Kiaora' IBlr
'Lady Wilson' hort. see *C.* x *crocosmiiflora* 'Norwich Canary'
'Lambrook Gold' CAvo IBlr
'Lana de Savary' CPen CPrp EBee EMan GBin GCal IBal IBlr WCot WLin
'Late Cornish' see *C.* x *crocosmiiflora* 'Queen Alexandra' J.E. Fitt
'Late Lucifer' CHEx CTri GCal IBlr LSRN SDix
§ ***latifolia*** IBlr WHil
- 'Castle Ward Late' CBos CPou CRow ECha EGra GAbr GBuc GCal GCra IBlr MNFA MSte WMoo WSHC WWpP
- 'Vulcan' T.Smith EBee GKir IBlr
'Lord Nelson' CPrp WHil
'Loweswater' WCot
'Lucifer' ♀H4 More than 30 suppliers
'Malahide Castle' IBlr
'Mandarin' IBlr
§ 'Marcotijn' EBee EBrs EChP ECtt EGra EMan EMar GCal GGar IBlr IGor MAvo MNFA NLon
'Mars' CElw CFwr CPrp EBee EBla EBrs ECtt EGra EMar EWes GBuc GCal GGar GMac IBlr LRHS NFla SPlb WBor WCAu WFar WOld WPGP WPer
§ ***masoniorum*** ♀H3 More than 30 suppliers
- 'Amber' **new** IBlr
- 'Auricorn' IBlr
- 'Dixter Flame' IBlr LPio SDix
- 'Fernhill' IBlr
- 'Flamenco' GKir IBlr
- 'Minotaur' IBlr
- 'Quantreau' **new** IBlr
- red CHar IBlr
- 'Rowallane Apricot' **new** IBlr
- 'Rowallane Orange' IBlr MAvo
- 'Rowallane Yellow' ♀H3-4 CBos CPen EBrs ECha EGra GBri GKir IBlr IGor LRHS MBri SMHy SRos WCot WHil WWpP
- 'Tropicana' **new** IBlr
mathewsiana IBlr
'Merryman' WWpP
'Mistral' CFwr CMea CPrp EBee EBrs EChP GBuc IBlr LRHS MAvo MNrw NRnb WBor WCot WFar WLin WMoo WWpP
'Moira Reed' EGra EMar IBlr
'Mount Stewart' see *C.* x *crocosmiiflora* 'Jessie'
'Mount Usher' CFir CMdw EGra GCal IBlr MAvo WFar WOut
'Mr Bedford' see *C.* x *crocosmiiflora* 'Croesus'
Old Hat see *C.* 'Walberton Red'
'Orange Devil' CBre IBlr MBri WWpP
'Orange Lucifer' WWpP
'Orange Spirit' WFar
'Orangeade' CHar EBee EBrs ECtt EGra EMar GBin GBri IBal IBlr SUsu
* 'Orangerot' SGSe
§ ***paniculata*** CBcs CElw CHEx COIW CPou EBee EBla EChP ECtt ERou GAbr GGar LRHS MNFA MNrw NBid

	NOrc SAPC SChu SPet WBrk WCot WMoo WPen WShi WTin
- brown/orange	IBlr
- 'Cally Greyleaf' **new**	GCal
- 'Major'	CTri IBlr
- red	CPLG CStu GKir IBlr SWvt
* - 'Ruby Velvet'	IBlr
- triploid	IBlr
aff. ***paniculata***	ECtt IBlr
pearsei	IBlr
'Phillipa Browne'	WCot
'Plaisir'	CAby CBos CFwr EBee EBrs EPot IBlr MBNS WCra WFar
§ ***pottsii***	CFee CHVG CRow EBrs EChP ECtt EPla GBin GMac IBlr MAvo WFar
- CD&R 109	CBre CPou
- 'Culzean Pink'	CHVG CPom CPrp EBrs EGra GBin GBuc GFlt GKir IBal IBlr LRHS NCob WHil WLin WPGP
- deep pink	IBlr IGor WSHC
- 'Grandiflora'	IBlr
- 'Lady Bangor'	ECtt IBlr
'Roman Gold' **new**	IBlr
rosea	see *Tritonia disticha* subsp. *rubrolucens*
'Rowden Bronze'	see *C.* x *crocosmiiflora* 'Gerbe d'Or'
'Rowden Chrome'	see *C.* x *crocosmiiflora* 'George Davison' Davison
'Rubygold'	IBlr
'Sabena'	MAvo
'Saffron Queen' **new**	IBlr
'Saturn'	see *C.* 'Jupiter'
'Scarlatti'	IBlr WHil
'Severn Sunrise' ♀H3-4	More than 30 suppliers
'Shocking'	IBlr
'Son of Lucifer'	WFar
'Sonate'	ECtt NCot NGby SPlb WPer
'Spitfire'	CBot CMil CPne CRow CSam EBrs EChP ECha ECtt EGra ELan EMar GAbr GBuc GGar GKir GMac GSki IBlr LRHS MArl MRav MWgw NDov SChu SPla SRos SWvt WEas WFar
'Starfire' **new**	EGra EMar
'Sunset'	GSki
'Sunzest'	WFar
'Tangerine Queen'	CPen EBrs ECtt EGra EMar IBal IBlr WCot WWpP
* 'Tiger'	CElw IBlr
'Vic's Yellow'	SGar SMrm SSpe
* 'Voyager'	CFwr CPrp EBee EBrs EPot GKir IBlr LRHS MAvo MBow NFla WHil
I 'Vulcan' A.Bloom	CMdw CPen EBrs EGra GGar IBal IBlr LRHS SAga WCot WFar WHil WWhi
§ 'Walberton Red'	CFwr EBrs IBlr MAvo MBri SAga SApp SUsu WCot
Walberton Yellow = 'Walcroy'PBR	SApp SMHy SSpi WCot
'Zeal Giant'	EGra EMar IBlr WHil
'Zeal Tan'	CBos CElw CPen CSam EBee ECGP EChP EGra EHrv ELan EMan EMar EPPr EVFa GBin GCal IBlr LAst MAvo MBNS MBnl MDKP MLLN NEgg SPla WBrk WCAu WCot WWhi WWlt
Zeal unnamed	EBee EGra IBlr

Crocus ✿ (*Iridaceae*)

abantensis	EPot ERos
adanensis	ERos
alatavicus	EPot WWst
albiflorus	see *C. vernus* subsp. *albiflorus*
§ ***ancyrensis***	EPot LAma
- 'Golden Bunch'	EBrs EPfP LPhx LRHS NJOw WLin WShi
§ ***angustifolius*** ♀H4	EBrs EPot ERos GIBF LAma
- 'Minor'	EPot LAma
antalyensis	EPot
asturicus	see *C. serotinus* subsp. *salzmannii*
asumaniae	ECho EPot ERos
aureus	see *C. flavus* subsp. *flavus*
banaticus ♀H4	CBro EHyt EPot ERos GCrs GEdr LAma MS&S WWst
- ***albus***	ERos
baytopiorum	EPot ERos
biflorus	LAma
- subsp. ***adamii***	ERos
- subsp. ***alexandri***	EPot ERos LAma LRHS
§ - subsp. ***biflorus***	ERos LAma
§ - - 'Parkinsonii'	EPot ERos
- subsp. ***crewei***	ERos
- subsp. ***isauricus***	ERos
- subsp. ***melantherus***	ERos
- - JCA 341.353	WCot
- 'Miss Vain'	CAvo EPot LAma LRHS
- var. ***parkinsonii***	see *C. biflorus* subsp. *biflorus* 'Parkinsonii'
- subsp. ***tauri***	WWst
- subsp. ***weldenii*** 'Albus'	EPot ERos LAma
- - 'Fairy'	CBro EPot ERos LAma LRHS
'Big Boy'	EHyt
boryi	EHyt
cambessedesii	ERos SBla SCnR
§ ***cancellatus*** subsp. ***cancellatus***	ERos LAma
- var. ***cilicicus***	see *C. cancellatus* subsp. *cancellatus*
- subsp. ***mazziaricus***	CNic ERos
- subsp. ***pamphylicus***	ERos
candidus var. ***subflavus***	see *C. olivieri* subsp. *olivieri*
§ ***cartwrightianus*** ♀H4	LAma
- 'Albus' misapplied	see *C. hadriaticus*
- 'Albus' Tubergen ♀H4	EPot ERos
chrysanthus 'Advance'	CBro EPfP EPot LAma SPer WLin
- 'Alionka' **new**	WWst
- 'Ard Schenk'	EPot LAma LRHS NJOw WLin
- 'Aubade'	EPot
- 'Blue Bird'	CBro EPot LAma LRHS MSte
- 'Blue Pearl' ♀H4	CAvo CBro CMea EBrs EPfP EPot LAma LPhx LRHS MBri MSte NBir NJOw SPer WShi
- 'Blue Peter'	LAma
- 'Brass Band'	LAma LRHS
- 'Cream Beauty' ♀H4	CAvo CBro CMea EBrs EPfP EPot LAma LPhx LRHS MBri MSte NBir NJOw SPer
- 'Dorothy'	EPot LAma LRHS
- 'E.A. Bowles' ♀H4	ECho LAma
- 'E.P. Bowles'	CBro EPot LAma LRHS MBri
- 'Early Gold' **new**	WWst
- 'Ego' **new**	WWst
- 'Elegance'	LAma LRHS
- 'Eye-catcher'	EPot LAma LRHS
- var. ***fuscotinctus***	EPot LAma MBri WLin
- 'Gipsy Girl'	CAvo CBro EPot LAma LRHS MBri NJOw
- 'Goldilocks'	EBrs EPot LAma LRHS
- 'Goldmine' **new**	WWst
- 'Herald'	EPot LAma LRHS MSte
- 'Jeannine'	EPot
- 'Ladykiller' ♀H4	CAvo CBro EPot LAma LRHS MBri MSte
- 'Little Amber' **new**	WWst
- 'Moonlight'	LAma LRHS

	Name	Suppliers
	- 'Nida' **new**	WWst
	- 'Prins Claus'	EPot LAma
	- 'Prinses Beatrix'	EBrs EPot LAma LRHS
	- 'Romance'	CAvo CBro EPot LAma LRHS WLin
	- 'Saturnus'	EPot LAma
	- 'Skyline'	CBro EPot LRHS
	- 'Snow Bunting' 🏆H4	CAvo CBro EPfP EPot LAma LPhx LRHS NBir WShi
	- 'Spring Pearl'	CBro LAma LRHS
	- 'Sunspot'	EPot
	- 'Uschak Orange'	EPot WWst
	- 'White Beauty'	LAma
	- 'White Triumphator'	LAma NBir
	- 'Zenith'	EPot LAma
	- 'Zwanenburg Bronze' 🏆H4	EPfP EPot LAma LRHS MSte WLin
	'Cloth of Gold'	see *C. angustifolius*
	clusii	see *C. serotinus* subsp. *clusii*
	corsicus 🏆H4	EPot ERos LAma
	dalmaticus	EPot LAma
	- 'Petrovac'	WWst
	danfordiae	ERos ETow
	'Dutch Yellow'	see *C.* x *luteus* 'Golden Yellow'
	etruscus 🏆H4	ERos
	- 'Rosalind'	EPot WLin
	- 'Zwanenburg'	EPot LAma
	flavus	see *C. flavus* subsp. *flavus*
§	- subsp. ***flavus*** 🏆H4	EPot GIBF LAma LRHS WCot WShi
	fleischeri	EPot ERos LAma
	gargaricus	ERos SCnR
	- subsp. ***gargaricus***	ERos SOkd
	'Golden Mammoth'	see *C.* x *luteus* 'Golden Yellow'
	goulimyi 🏆H4	CBro EPot ERos LAma LRHS NMen SIgm SSpi WCot
	- 'Albus'	see *C. goulimyi* subsp. *goulimyi* 'Mani White'
§	- subsp. ***goulimyi*** 'Mani White' 🏆H4	EHyt ERos
	- subsp. ***leucanthus***	EHyt
	graveolens	EPot
	'Haarlem Gem'	LAma
§	***hadriaticus*** 🏆H4	ERos LAma WCot
	- var. ***chrysobelonicus***	see *C. hadriaticus*
	imperati 🏆H4	ERos
	- subsp. ***imperati*** 'De Jager'	CAvo CPBP EPot LAma LRHS
	- subsp. ***suaveolens***	ERos
	x ***jessoppiae***	ERos WWst
	karduchorum	EPot LAma
	korolkowii	ERos GIBF LAma LRHS
	- 'Golden Nugget'	GCrs
	- 'Kiss of Spring'	EPot
	- 'Yellow Tiger'	WWst
	kosaninii	EPot ERos
	kotschyanus 🏆H4	ECho NRya
	- 'Albus'	ECho EHyt LRHS
§	- subsp. ***kotschyanus***	CBro EPot LAma
	- var. ***leucopharynx***	LRHS
	laevigatus 🏆H4	LAma
	- from Crete	EHyt
	- 'Fontenayi'	CBro EHyt EPot LAma LEdu WPnP
	'Large Yellow'	see *C.* x *luteus* 'Golden Yellow'
	longiflorus 🏆H4	CBro EPot ERos GEdr WCot
§	x ***luteus*** 'Golden Yellow' 🏆H4	EBrs EPfP LAma WShi
§	- 'Stellaris'	EPot ERos
	malyi 🏆H2-4	ERos
	'Mammoth Yellow'	see *C.* x *luteus* 'Golden Yellow'
	mathewii	EPot
	medius 🏆H4	CBro EPot ERos LAma
	michelsonii	WWst
	minimus	EHyt EPot ERos LAma LRHS
	niveus	CAvo CBro EHyt EPot ERos LAma SOkd SSpi WCot
	nudiflorus	CBro EPot ERos LAma NMen WCot
	ochroleucus 🏆H4	CBro EPot ERos LAma LRHS MMHG
	olivieri	ERos LAma
	- subsp. ***balansae*** 'Zwanenburg'	CMea EPot
§	- subsp. ***olivieri***	EHyt EPot ERos LAma LRHS
	pallasii subsp. ***pallasii***	ERos
	pestalozzae	EHyt ERos
	- var. ***caeruleus***	EPot ERos
	pulchellus 🏆H4	CPBP ECho EPot ERos GCrs LAma MBow NWCA WBor
	- ***albus***	EPot
	'Purpureus'	see *C. vernus* 'Purpureus Grandiflorus'
	reticulatus subsp. ***reticulatus***	EPot
	rujanensis	ERos
	salzmannii	see *C. serotinus* subsp. *salzmannii*
	sativus	CArn CAvo CBod CBro ELan EOHP EPfP EPot GPoy LAma LPhx LRHS MBri MMHG MSal NBir NGHP
	- var. ***cartwrightianus***	see *C. cartwrightianus*
	scepusiensis	see *C. vernus* subsp. *vernus* var. *scepusiensis*
	scharojanii	EHyt EPot
§	***serotinus*** subsp. ***clusii***	CBro EPot LAma
§	- subsp. ***salzmannii***	CBro EPot ERos LAma LRHS
	sibiricus	see *C. sieberi*
§	***sieberi*** 🏆H4	EPot ERos
§	- 'Albus' 🏆H4	CAvo CBro ECho EHyt EPot LAma LRHS MSte WLin
	- subsp. ***atticus***	EHyt LAma LRHS
	- 'Bowles' White'	see *C. sieberi* 'Albus'
	- 'Firefly'	CBro EPot LAma LRHS WLin
	- 'Hubert Edelsten' 🏆H4	EHyt EPot ERos LAma
	- subsp. ***sublimis*** 'Tricolor' 🏆H4	CAvo CBro EBrs ECho EHyt EPfP EPot ERos GCrs LAma LRHS NMen
	- 'Violet Queen'	CAvo CBro EPot LAma LRHS MBri MSte
	speciosus 🏆H4	CAvo CBro CPBP EPot LAma LRHS NBir WCot WHoo WShi
	- 'Aitchisonii'	CBro CPBP EPot LAma LRHS
	- 'Albus' 🏆H4	CBro EPot LRHS
	- 'Artabir'	CBro EPot LRHS
	- 'Cassiope'	EPot LAma LRHS
	- 'Conqueror'	CBro LAma LRHS
	- 'Oxonian'	EPot LAma LPhx LRHS
	x ***stellaris***	see *C.* x *luteus* 'Stellaris'
	susianus	see *C. angustifolius*
	suterianus	see *C. olivieri* subsp. *olivieri*
	tommasinianus 🏆H4	CAvo CBro CMea EBrs ECho EPot LAma LLWP MBri MRav NBir SRms WShi
	- f. ***albus***	EHyt EPot LAma LRHS
	- 'Barr's Purple'	EPot LAma LRHS
	- 'Eric Smith'	CAvo
	- 'Lilac Beauty'	EPot LAma
	- var. ***pictus***	CAvo EPot ERos LAma NMen
	- var. ***roseus***	CMea EHyt EPot ERos LAma LPhx NMen WCot
	- 'Ruby Giant'	CAvo CBro CNic EHyt EPfP EPot LAma LRHS NBir SPer WLin WShi
	- subsp. ***tommasinianus***	GIBF
	- 'Whitewell Purple'	CAvo CBro ECho EPot LAma LPhx LRHS MBri NBir WShi
	tournefortii 🏆H2-4	CBro EPot ERos LAma WCot
	vallicola	EHyt EPot
§	'Vanguard'	CAvo CBro EBrs EPot LAma LPhx
	veluchensis	EPot
§	***vernus*** subsp. ***albiflorus***	EPot ERos LAma

- 'Enchantress'	EPot LAma
- 'Flower Record'	EPfP EPot NBir
- 'Glory of Sassenheim'	EPot
- 'Graecus'	EPot ERos
- 'Grand Maître'	LAma
- 'Haarlem Gem'	EPot
- 'Jeanne d'Arc'	CAvo CBro EBrs EPfP EPot LAma LPhx NBir WLin WShi
- 'King of the Striped'	EBrs WLin
- 'Negro Boy'	EPot
- 'Paulus Potter'	EPot
- 'Pickwick'	CAvo EPfP EPot LAma NBir WShi
§ - 'Purpureus Grandiflorus'	CBro EPot LAma
- 'Queen of the Blues'	CAvo CBro EPot LPhx WLin
- 'Remembrance'	EBrs EPfP EPot LAma LPhx NBir WShi
- 'Snowstorm'	LAma
- 'Striped Beauty'	LAma
- 'Twinborn'	EPot
- 'Vanguard'	see *C.* 'Vanguard'
- subsp. ***vernus*** 'Grandiflorus'	see *C. vernus* 'Purpureus Grandiflorus'
§ - - Heuffelianus Group	CPBP EPot GCrs WWst
- - - 'Dark Eyes' **new**	WWst
- - var. ***neapolitanus***	ERos
- - 'Oradea'	WWst
§ - - var. ***scepusiensis***	EPot ERos
- 'White Christmas'	EPot
* ***versicolor***	EHyt
- 'Picturatus'	CMea EBrs EPot ERos LAma LRHS
vitellinus **new**	WWst
'Yellow Mammoth'	see *C.* x *luteus* 'Golden Yellow'
'Zephyr' ♀H4	CBro EPot ERos LAma LRHS
zonatus	see *C. kotschyanus* subsp. *kotschyanus*

Croomia (*Stemonaceae*)

heterosepala	WCru

Crowea (*Rutaceae*)

exalata x ***saligna***	CPLG

Crucianella (*Rubiaceae*)

maritima	XPep
stylosa	see *Phuopsis stylosa*

Cruciata (*Rubiaceae*)

§ ***laevipes***	CNat NMir

Cryptantha (*Boraginaceae*)

paradoxa **new**	CPBP

Cryptanthus (*Bromeliaceae*)

bivittatus ♀H1	CHal
- 'Roseus Pictus'	CHal
bromelioides	MBri

Cryptogramma (*Adiantaceae*)

crispa	EFer SRms WHer

Cryptomeria (*Cupressaceae*)

fortunei	see *C. japonica* var. *sinensis*
japonica ♀H4	CDul CMen ECho GIBF GKir ISea LCon NBea STre WEve WNor
- Araucarioides Group	CDoC EHul IArd LCon NLar
- 'Bandai'	LBuc
- 'Bandai-sugi' ♀H4	CKen CMac CMen ECho EHul EOrn EPfP LCon LLin LRHS MBar MGos NDlv SCoo SLim SPla STre WEve WGor
- 'Barabits Gold'	MBar MGos
- 'Compressa'	CDoC CFee CKen CSli EHul ENot EPfP ESis LBee LLin LRHS MAsh MBar MGos SCoo SLim
§ - 'Cristata'	CDoC CMac ECho ELan EOrn LCon MBar NEgg NPal SCoo SPoG
* - 'Cristata Compacta'	EOrn
- Elegans Group	CBcs CBrm CDul CMac CSBt CTri EHul ELan ENot EOrn EPfP GKir LCon LLin MBar MGos MWat NEgg SHBN SLim SPer SPoG WDin WFar WOrn
- 'Elegans Aurea'	CBcs CDoC CTri EHul LCon LLin MAsh MBar SPoG STre WDin WEve
- 'Elegans Compacta' ♀H4	CDoC CRob CSBt CWib EHul EOrn GBin IMGH LBee LCon LRHS MAsh MBNS MBar MBri SCoo SLim SPoG WBVN WEve
- 'Elegans Nana'	LBee LRHS SRms
- 'Elegans Viridis'	ELan LBuc LRHS MBar SCoo SLim SPer SPoG
- 'Globosa'	EOrn SLim
- 'Globosa Nana' ♀H4	ECho EHul ERom LBee LCon LLin LRHS MBar NDlv NEgg SCoo SHBN SLim SPoG WFar WGor
- 'Golden Promise'	CDoC CRob EOrn LLin MAsh MBri SCoo SLim SPoG WEve WGor
- Gracilis Group **new**	LCon
- 'Jindai-sugi'	CMac MBar NDlv NLar WEve
- 'Kilmacurragh'	CDoC CKen EHul MBar NWea SLim
- 'Knaptonensis' (v)	CDoC
- 'Kohui-yatsubusa'	CKen ECho
* - 'Konijn-yatsubusa'	CKen
- 'Koshiji-yatsubusa'	EOrn MBar
- 'Koshyi'	CKen
- 'Little Champion'	CKen NLar SLim
- 'Little Diamond'	CKen
- 'Littleworth Dwarf'	see *C. japonica* 'Littleworth Gnom'
§ - 'Littleworth Gnom'	LLin
- 'Lobbii Nana' hort.	see *C. japonica* 'Nana'
§ - 'Mankichi-sugi'	NLar
- 'Monstrosa'	MBar
- 'Monstrosa Nana'	see *C. japonica* 'Mankichi-sugi'
- 'Mushroom' **new**	MGos
§ - 'Nana'	CDoC CMac CTri EHul ENot EOrn EPfP LCon LLin LRHS SCoo SLim SPoG WFar
- 'Pipo'	CKen
- 'Pygmaea'	LLin MBar MGos SRms
- 'Rasen-sugi'	COtt LBuc LCon LLin MBar NEgg NPal SCoo SLim SMad SPoG
- 'Sekkan-sugi'	CBcs CDul CSli EHul EOrn LBee LCon LLin LRHS MAsh MBar MGos NEgg NLar SCoo SLim SPoG WEve WFar
- 'Sekka-sugi'	see *C. japonica* 'Cristata'
§ - var. ***sinensis***	CMCN LAst NOGN
* - - 'Vilmoriniana Compacta'	EOrn
§ - 'Spiralis'	CDoC CKen CMac CRob EHul EOrn EPfP LBee LCon LLin LRHS MAsh MBar SCoo SLim SPer SPla SPoG WEve WFar
§ - 'Spiraliter Falcata'	CDoC LBuc MBar NLar
§ - 'Tansu'	CKen ECho EHul EOrn LCon LLin MBar
- 'Tenzan-sugi'	CDoC CKen LLin MAsh SOkd
- 'Tilford Cream'	MAsh
- 'Tilford Gold'	EHul ENot EOrn LLin MBar MGos NDlv NEgg WBcn WEve WFar
- 'Toda' **new**	CKen
- 'Vilmorin Gold'	CKen EOrn WEve WFar
- 'Vilmoriniana' ♀H4	CDoC CKen CMHG CMen CRob CSli CTri EHul ENot EOrn EPfP

		EPot IMGH LBee LCon LLin LRHS MAsh MBar MGos SCoo SHBN SIng SLim SPer SPoG WDin WEve WFar
	- 'Winter Bronze'	CKen
	- 'Yatsubusa'	see *C. japonica* 'Tansu'
	- 'Yore-sugi'	see *C. japonica* 'Spiralis', *C. japonica* 'Spiraliter Falcata'
	- 'Yoshino'	CKen SLim
	sinensis	see *C. japonica* var. *sinensis*

Cryptotaenia (*Apiaceae*)

	canadensis	MRav
	japonica	CAgr CPou EUnu GIBF MHer MSal NRnb WHer WJek
	- f. ***atropurpurea***	CFwr CHar CSpe ECha EHoe EMag EMan EMon EWTr GCal GGar GMac ITer LDai LPhx LRHS LSpr MNFA MNrw NSti NVic SBla WCHb WCru WEas WFar WWhi

Ctenanthe (*Marantaceae*)

§	***amabilis*** ♀H1	CHal
	lubbersiana ♀H1	CHal XBlo
§	***oppenheimiana***	LRHS XBlo

Ctenium (*Poaceae*)

	concinnum	CBig

Cucubalus (*Caryophyllaceae*)

	baccifer	EBee GFlt GIBF NLar WPer WPrP WRos

Cudrania see *Maclura*

cumin see *Cuminum cyminum*

Cuminum (*Apiaceae*)

	cyminum	CArn EUnu SIde

Cunninghamia (*Cupressaceae*)

	konishii	CFil
§	***lanceolata***	CBcs CDoC CDul CFil CMCN CTho GKir IArd IDee LCon LLin LRHS MBlu SCoo SLim SMad SPoG SSta STre WEve WNor WPGP
§	- 'Bánó'	CMac EOrn
	- 'Compacta'	see *C. lanceolata* 'Bánó'
	- 'Little Leo'	CKen
	sinensis	see *C. lanceolata*
	unicaniculata	see *C. lanceolata*

Cunonia (*Cunoniaceae*)

	capensis	CPLG CTrC EShb

Cuphea (*Lythraceae*)

	blepharophylla	LRav
	caeciliae	CHal CPne MOak WBor
	cyanaea	CMHG CPLG MLLN MOak SDix SUsu
	glutinosa	ITer
	hirtella	EShb MOak SDys
	aff. ***hookeriana*** B&SWJ 9039	WCru
	hyssopifolia ♀H1	CHal CHll ESlt MBri MOak SRms STre SWvt
	- 'Alba'	LIck MOak STre SWvt
	- 'Riverdene Gold'	EMan
	- 'Rosea'	LIck SWvt
§	***ignea*** ♀H1	CHal ELan EShb MBri MLLN MOak SRms SUsu WWlt
	- 'Variegata' (v)	CHal MOak
§	***llavea*** 'Georgia Scarlet'	EBee EShb EUJe EWin LAst LIck MOak NPri SPoG SUsu
	- 'Tiny Mice'	see *C. llavea* 'Georgia Scarlet'
	macrophylla hort.	CHll MOak
	melvilla	ERea
	platycentra	see *C. ignea*
	viscosissima	SUsu

x *Cupressocyparis* ✿ (*Cupressaceae*)

§	***leylandii*** ♀H4	CBcs CChe CDoC CDul CMac EHul ENot EPfP GKir LBuc LRHS MAsh MBar MBri MGos NBlu NEgg NWea SLim SPer SWvt WDin WEve WHar WMou
§	- 'Castlewellan'	CBcs CChe CDoC CDul CMac EHul ENot EPfP ERom GKir LBuc LRHS MAsh MBar MBri MGos NBlu NEgg NWea SLim SPer SWvt WDin WEve WFar WHar WMou
	- 'Douglas Gold' **new**	CRob
	- 'Galway Gold'	see x *C. leylandii* 'Castlewellan'
	- 'Gold Rider' ♀H4	CDoC EHul ENot LBee MAsh MBar MBri MGos NEgg NMoo SCoo SLim SPer SWvt WDin WEve WHar
§	- 'Harlequin' (v)	LRHS MBar SLim SWvt
	- 'Herculea'	CDoC MAsh
	- 'Hyde Hall'	CTri EPla LBee
	- 'Naylor's Blue'	CMac SEND
	- 'New Ornament'	SMad
	- 'Olive's Green'	EHul SWvt
	- 'Robinson's Gold' ♀H4	CMac EHul GQui LBee MBar NWea SLim WEve WFar WHar
	- 'Silver Dust' (v)	MBri SRms WFar
	- 'Variegata'	see x *C. leylandii* 'Harlequin'
	- 'Winter Sun'	WCFE
	notabilis	WCwm
	ovensii	EHul WCwm

Cupressus (*Cupressaceae*)

§	***arizonica***	MAsh MBri
	var. ***arizonica*** 'Arctic'	
	- 'Conica Glauca'	MBar
§	- var. ***glabra***	ECrN
	- - 'Aurea'	CRob ECho EHul LCon LLin MBar SLim WEve
	- - 'Blue Ice' ♀H3	CBcs CDoC CDul CMHG CRez CRob CTho EBrs EHul EOrn LCon LLin LRHS MAsh MBar MBri MGos SCoo SLim SPer SPoG SWvt WEve WFar WGer
	- - 'Blue Pyramid'	WEve
	- - 'Compacta'	CKen
	- - 'Conica'	CKen SBod
I	- - 'Fastigiata'	CBcs CDoC ECrN EHul LCon MBar
	- - 'Glauca'	ECho MBlu NBlu
*	- - 'Lutea'	EOrn SPoG
	- 'Pyramidalis' ♀H3	CMac ECho EPfP LRHS SCoo WEve
I	- 'Sulfurea'	CKen MAsh NLar WEve
	cashmeriana ♀H2	CBcs CDoC CTho ECho EPla ERea LCon LLin LRHS NPal SLim SPoG WEve WFar WNor WPGP
	duclouxiana	CMHG WCwm
	dupreziana	WCwm
§	***funebris***	CMCN
	gigantea	CDoC
	glabra	see *C. arizonica* var. *glabra*
	- 'Arctic'	see *C. arizonica* var. *arizonica* 'Arctic'
	goveniana	MBar
	- var. ***abramsiana***	WCwm
	guadalupensis	CMHG
	- var. ***forbesii***	WCwm
	lusitanica	WCwm

- var. ***benthamii*** 'Knightiana'	WCwm
- 'Brice's Weeping'	CKen
- 'Brookhall' **new**	IDee
- 'Glauca Pendula'	CKen EPfP MBri WCwm WEve
- var. ***lusitanica*** **new**	CMCN
- 'Pygmy'	CKen
macrocarpa	CCVT CDoC CDul CSBt CTrC EHul SEND
- 'Barnham Gold'	SBod SRms
- 'Compacta'	CKen
- 'Conybearii Aurea'	WEve
- 'Donard Gold'	CMac CSBt ECho EOrn MBar
- 'Gold Spread'	CDoC CRob ECho EHul EOrn LBee LCon LLin LRHS SCoo SLim SPoG WBcn WEve WFar
- 'Goldcrest' ♀H3	CBcs CDoC CDul CMac CSBt CTrC EBee ECrN EHul ELan EOrn EPfP LBee LCon LRHS MBar MBri MGos NBlu SBod SLim SPer SPoG STre SWvt WCFE WDin WEve WFar
- 'Golden Cone'	CKen CSBt ECho LRHS WEve
- 'Golden Pillar' ♀H3	CDoC CMac CRob CTrC ECho EHul EOrn LBee LRHS MAsh MBar MBri NEgg SLim SPoG SWvt WDin WFar WGer
- 'Golden Spire'	WFar
- 'Greenstead Magnificent'	LCon LRHS MAsh SCoo SLim
- 'Horizontalis Aurea'	EHul MBar WBcn
- 'Lohbrunner'	CKen
- 'Lutea'	CDoC CMac CTrC ECho
- 'Pygmaea'	CKen
- 'Sulphur Cushion'	CKen
- 'Wilma'	ECho EHul ENot LBee LCon LLin LRHS MAsh MGos NBlu NEgg SCoo SLim SPoG SWvt WBcn WEve
- 'Woking'	CKen
sempervirens	CBcs CDul CMCN CPMA CSec ECrN EHul ELan ERom ISea LLin WEve WFar WMul
- 'Garda'	CDoC
- 'Green Pencil'	CKen EBrs EPfP LRHS
- 'Pyramidalis'	see *C. sempervirens* Stricta Group
- var. ***sempervirens***	see *C. sempervirens* Stricta Group
§ - Stricta Group ♀H3	CArn CMCN CSWP ECho ECrN EHul EPfP LCon LLin NBlu NLar SAPC SArc SBLw SCoo WCFE WEve WOrn
- 'Swane's Gold'	CBcs CDoC CFee CKen EBrs ECho EHul EOrn EPfP LBee LCon LLin LRHS MAsh NPal SCoo SLim SPoG WEve WFar
- 'Totem Pole'	CDoC CKen CSBt CTho EHul EOrn EPfP LBee LCon LLin LRHS MAsh MGos NEgg SCoo SEND SLim SPoG WBcn WEve WGor
torulosa	CDoC EGFP IDee
- CC 3687	WHCr

x *Cuprocyparis* (*Cupressaceae*)

leylandii	see x *Cupressocyparis leylandii*

Curculigo (*Hypoxidaceae*)

capitulata **new**	XBlo

Curcuma (*Zingiberaceae*)

alismatifolia	ECho
- 'Chiang Mai Dark Pink'	CKob
- 'Chiang Mai Pink'	CKob
- 'Chiang Mai White'	CKob
- 'Lady of the Dawn'	CKob
- 'Noi White-pink'	CKob
- 'Siam Violet'	CKob
- 'Tropic Snow'	CKob
amada	CKob EUJe MOak
angustifolia	CKob EUJe MOak
aromatica	CKob EUJe MOak
I ***aurantiaca***	CKob MOak
'Blue Top'	CKob
'Cobra'	CKob
cordata	MOak
- 'Amethyst'	CKob
elata	CKob
gracillima 'Chiang Mai Chocolate'	MOak
- 'Chiang Mai Chocolate Zebra'	CKob
- 'Peacock'	CKob
harmandii	CKob
'Khmer Giant'	CKob
leucorhiza	EUJe
longa	CKob EUJe GPoy MOak MSal
ornata	CKob
parviflora 'White Angel'	CKob
petiolata 'Emperor' (v)	CKob
'Prachinburi'	CKob
'Precious Patumma'	CKob
'Red Fire'	CKob
'Red Giant'	CKob
'Ribbon'	CKob
roscoeana	CKob LAma MOak
'Ruby'	CKob
'Siam Diamond'	MOak
'Siam Ruby'	CKob MOak
siamensis 'Chiang Mai Delight'	CKob
- 'Dwarf Chiang Mai Delight'	CKob
thorelii 'Chiang Mai Snow'	CKob MOak
- 'Dwarf Chiang Mai Snow'	CKob
zedoaria	CKob EUJe GPoy LAma LRHS MOak WMul

Curcumorpha (*Zingiberaceae*)

longiflora	MOak

currant see *Ribes*

Curtonus see *Crocosmia*

Cuscuta (*Convolvulaceae*)

chinensis	MSal

Cussonia (*Araliaceae*)

paniculata	CKob EShb SIgm WMul
spicata	CKob EShb WMul
transvaalensis	CKob EShb

custard apple see *Annona cherimola*

Cyananthus (*Campanulaceae*)

delavayi	GKev
integer misapplied	see *C. microphyllus*
integer Wallich 'Sherriff's Variety'	WIvy
lobatus ♀H4	ECho EHyt EMan GBuc GMaP NJOw NSla SBla
- 'Albus'	EPot EWes GEdr SBla WIvy
- giant	EPot GCrs GEdr GTou SBla
lobatus x ***microphyllus***	EPot NWCA WAbe
macrocalyx	EMan GEdr SBla WIvy WLin
§ ***microphyllus*** ♀H4	EPot GEdr GMaP NJOw NSla SBla WAbe
sherriffii	EHyt EPot GEdr GKev

Cyanella (*Tecophilaeaceae*)

lutea	CMon ECho

	orchidiformis	CMon

Cyanotis (*Commelinaceae*)

	somaliensis ♀H1	CHal

Cyathea (*Cyatheaceae*)

	australis	EAmu EUJe GQui WFib WMul WRic
	brownii	EAmu WMul WRic
	cooperi	CBcs EAmu WFib WRic
*	- 'Brentwood'	WRic
	cunninghamii	LRav WRic
	dealbata	CAbb CBcs CBrP CTrC EAmu EUJe GQui IDee MGos WMul WRic
	dregei	SPlb WRic
	incisoserrata	WRic
	medullaris	CAbb CBcs CTrC EAmu MGos WMul WRic
	robusta	WRic
	smithii	CBcs CTrC EAmu EFtx EUJe IDee WMul WRic
	tomentosissima	EAmu WRic

Cyathodes (*Epacridaceae*)

	colensoi	see *Leucopogon colensoi*
	empetrifolia	see *Androstoma empetrifolia*
	fasciculata	see *Leucopogon fasciculatus*
	fraseri	see *Leucopogon fraseri*
	juniperina	see *Leptecophylla juniperina*
	parviflora	see *Leucopogon parviflorus*
	parvifolia	see *Leptecophylla juniperina* subsp. *parvifolia*

Cycas (*Cycadaceae*)

	cairnsiana	CRoM
	circinalis	CRoM
	media	CRoM
	panzihihuaensis	CBrP
	platyphylla	CRoM
	revoluta ♀H1	CAbb CBrP CDoC CHEx CRoM CTrC CWSG EAmu EPfP ESlt LRHS LToo MBri NMoo NPal SAPC SArc SChr SEND WMul WNor
	revoluta x ***taitungensis***	CBrP
§	***rumphii***	CBrP EAmu LRHS
	taitungensis	CBrP CRoM
	thouarsii	see *C. rumphii*

Cyclamen ✿ (*Primulaceae*)

	africanum	CBro CElm CLCN EJWh GFlt ITim LAma LRHS MAsh NWCA STil
	alpinum	CBro CLCN CWCL EJWh EPot LAma LRHS MAsh STil
	balearicum	CBro CElm CLCN EJWh LAma LRHS MAsh NMen STil
	cilicium ♀H2-4	CBro CElm CLAP CLCN CMea EBla ECtt EHyt EJWh EPot ERos GIBF ITim LAma LRHS MBri MHer MS&S MTho NMen SBla SSpi STil WFar WIvy WNor WPat
	- f. ***album***	CBro CLCN CWCL CWoo EHyt EJWh EPot ERos ITim LAma LRHS MAsh STil WLFP
	- patterned leaf	NBir
	colchicum **new**	STil
§	***coum*** ♀H4	More than 30 suppliers
	- from Meryemana, Turkey **new**	CElm
	- from Turkey	ERos
	- var. ***abchasicum***	see *C. coum* subsp. *caucasicum*
	- 'Broadleigh Silver'	CElm
§	- subsp. ***caucasicum***	EPot ERos ETow LAma SSpi STil
I	- - 'Album'	GBBs NMen
	- subsp. ***coum***	CBro MAsh
	- - f. ***albissimum***	WLFP
	- - - 'George Bisson' **new**	CElm
	- - - 'Golan Heights'	CElm MAsh STil WLFP
	- - 'Atkinsii'	CBro
	- - f. ***coum*** 'Linnett Jewel'	WLFP
	- - - 'Linnett Rose'	WLFP
	- - - Nymans Group	CLAP CWCL MAsh SBla
	- - - Pewter Group ♀H2-4	CWCL ECGP ERos MAsh MTho NPar SBla SSpi WCot WIvy
	- - - - bicoloured	EJWh
	- - - - 'Blush'	CElm STil
	- - - - 'Maurice Dryden'	CAvo CBro CLAP CPBP CStu CWCL ECGP EHrv GBuc GCrs ITim LAma LRHS MAsh STil WAbe WCot WIvy WLFP
	- - - - red	CLCN GBBs LAma WLFP WPat
	- - - - 'Tilebarn Elizabeth'	CElm EHrv MAsh STil WHoo
	- - - - white	GBuc MAsh
	- - - plain-leaved red	STil
	- - - 'Roseum'	CElm CWCL EBrs GBuc LAma STil
	- - - Silver Group	CBro CElm CWoo EHrv GCrs LRHS MAvo NSla SSpi WAbe WPGP
	- - - - bicolor	WLFP
	- - - - red	CAvo EPot MTho STil WHoo
	- - - - 'Silver Star'	WLFP
	- - - - 'Sterling Silver'	WLFP
	- - magenta	CElm CWCL
	- - f. ***pallidum*** 'Album'	CAvo CElm EPot ERos ITim LAma MAsh SIng STil WAbe WCot WHoo WNor WPat
	- - - 'Marbled Moon'	MAsh STil WLFP
	- dark pink	CAvo CLAP EDAr ITim WHoo
	- 'Elm Tree Special' **new**	CElm
	- marbled leaf	CWCL EDAr ITim WHoo
	- 'Meaden's Crimson'	CElm EPot WLFP
	- plain-leaved	CElm CLAP EBla EPot ITim WAbe WLFP
	- red	CLAP CStu EDAr WHoo
	- scented	ITim
	creticum	CLCN CWCL EJWh ITim LAma MAsh STil
	creticum x ***repandum***	see *C.* x ***meiklei***
	cyprium	CBro CFwr CLCN CWCL EHyt EJWh ITim LAma LRHS MAsh NJOw STil WCot WIvy
	- 'E.S.'	CWCL MAsh STil
	elegans	EJWh MAsh STil WLFP
	europaeum	see *C. purpurascens*
	fatrense	see *C. purpurascens* subsp. *purpurascens* from Fatra, Slovakia
	graecum	CBro CElm CFil CLCN CStu CWoo EBla EHyt EJWh EPot ESis LAma LRHS MAsh NMen SIgm SRot SSpi STil WIvy
	- f. ***album***	CBro CElm CWCL EJWh EPot LAma LRHS MAsh SSpi STil
	- subsp. ***anatolicum***	STil
	- subsp. ***candicum***	MAsh STil
	- subsp. ***graecum*** f. ***graecum*** 'Glyfada'	STil
	- silver-leaved **new**	CElm
§	***hederifolium*** ♀H4	More than 30 suppliers
	- arrow-head	CLAP
	- var. ***confusum***	MAsh STil WCot WLFP
	- var. ***hederifolium*** f. ***albiflorum***	More than 30 suppliers
§	- - - 'Album'	CElm GBBs
	- - - Bowles' Apollo Group	CLCN SIgm WLFP
§	- - - - 'Artemis'	CWCL STil
	- - - - 'White Bowles' Apollo'	see *C. hederifolium* var. *hederifolium* f. *albiflorum* (Bowles' Apollo Group) 'Artemis'

	- - - 'Cotswold White'	WCot
	- - - 'Daley Thompson'	WLFP
	- - - 'Linnett Longbow'	WLFP
	- - - 'Linnett Stargazer'	WLFP
	- - - 'Nettleton Silver'	see *C. hederifolium* var. *hederifolium* f. *albiflorum* 'White Cloud'
	- - - 'Perlenteppich'	EDAr GMaP NMyG WLFP
	- - - 'Tilebarn Helena' **new**	STil
§	- - - 'White Cloud'	CElm CLAP EBla EHyt EPot ITim MAsh NEgg NSla STil WIvy WLFP
	- - f. ***hederifolium*** Bowles' Apollo Group	CLAP CWCL ECGP MAsh SBla SSpi STil WCot
	- - - 'Fairy Longbow'	WLFP
	- - - 'Fairy Rings'	CElm MAsh WLFP
	- - - 'Oliver Twist'	WLFP
	- - - red	NEgg
	- - - 'Rosenteppich'	EDAr EShb GBuc GMaP MAsh WLFP
	- - - 'Ruby Glow'	CElm CWCL MAsh WCot WLFP WPat
	- - - 'Silver Cloud'	CBro CLAP CLCN GBuc MAsh NBir SSpi STil WAbe WCot WHoo WIvy WLFP WPGP WTin
	- - - 'Silver Foil'	WLFP
	- - - 'Silver Shield'	WLFP
	- - - 'Stargazer'	MAsh WLFP
	- - 'Tilebarn Silver Arrow' **new**	STil
	- long-leaved **new**	CElm
	- scented	CLCN STil
	- silver-leaved	CAby CWoo EBla ECGP EPfP EPot GBBs GBin GCrs LRHS MAsh SBla SRot STil WLFP
	hederifolium x ***africanum***	ECho EHyt ITim
	x ***hildebrandii***	WIvy
	ibericum	see *C. coum* subsp. *caucasicum*
	intaminatum	CBro CLCN CPBP CSWP CWoo EJWh EPot ERos ITim LAma LRHS MAsh NMen SChr STil WIvy WPat
	- 'E.K. Balls'	CWCL SSpi
	- patterned-leaved	EJWh MAsh STil WLFP
	- pink	CWCL MAsh NMen STil
	- plain-leaved	MAsh STil
	latifolium	see *C. persicum*
	libanoticum	CBro CElm CLCN CWCL EJWh ERos ITim LAma LRHS MAsh NMen SBla SSpi STil WCot WLFP
§	x ***meiklei***	CBro CLCN
	mirabile ♀H2-3	CBro CElm CLCN CWCL CWoo EBla EJWh LAma LRHS MAsh NMen SSpi STil WAbe WIvy
	- silver-leaved **new**	CElm
	- 'Tilebarn Anne'	MAsh STil
	- 'Tilebarn Jan'	STil
	- 'Tilebarn Nicholas'	CElm CWoo EBla MAsh STil
	neapolitanum	see *C. hederifolium*
	orbiculatum	see *C. coum*
	parviflorum	EJWh LAma MAsh STil
	peloponnesiacum ♀H2-3	EJWh ERos MAsh
*	- subsp. ***peloponnesiacum***	CBro CLCN CWoo SSpi STil WLFP
	- 'Pelops' **new**	CElm
*	- subsp. ***rhodense***	CLCN LAma MAsh SSpi STil WLFP
*	- subsp. ***vividum***	STil
	- white-flowered	STil
§	***persicum***	CBro CElm CFil CLCN EJWh LAma LRHS MAsh NMen SChr STil
	- CSE 90560	STil
	- var. ***persicum*** f. ***puniceum*** from Lebanon	STil
	- - - 'Tilebarn Karpathos'	CElm STil
	pseudibericum ♀H2-3	CBro CElm CLCN CWCL CWoo EJWh GCrs LAma LRHS MAsh SBla SIng SSpi STil WLFP
	- 'Roseum'	CLCN MAsh NMen STil WLFP
§	***purpurascens*** ♀H4	CBro CElm CFil CLCN EBee EJWh GBuc LAma LRHS MAsh MS&S NMen SBla SSpi STil WBor WHoo WIvy WPat
	- f. ***album***	SBla
	- var. ***fatrense***	see *C. purpurascens* subsp. *purpurascens* from Fatra, Slovakia
	- 'Lake Garda'	CFil MAsh SSpi WPGP
§	- subsp. ***purpurascens*** from Fatra, Slovakia	EHyt STil
	- silver-leaved	CElm STil WLFP
	- - from Limone, Italy	SBla
	repandum	CAvo CBro CElm CFil CLCN EHrv EHyt EJWh EPot ERos LAma LRHS MAsh NMen SBla SSpi STil WHer WLFP
	- JCA 5157	SSpi
	- subsp. ***repandum*** f. ***album***	CElm CLAP CLCN EJWh MAsh SBla STil
	rohlfsianum	CBro CWCL EJWh LRHS MAsh SSpi STil
	x ***saundersii***	CLCN EJWh MAsh STil
	x ***wellensiekii***	MAsh STil

Cyclosorus (*Thelypteridaceae*)

	pennigerus	WRic

Cydonia ✿ (*Rosaceae*)

	japonica	see *Chaenomeles speciosa*
	oblonga 'Agvambari' (F)	SKee
	- 'Aromatnaya' (F)	ERea
	- 'Champion' (F)	CBcs SKee WJas
	- 'Early Prolific' (F)	ECrN
	- 'Ekmek' (F)	SKee
	- 'Isfahan' (F)	SKee
	- 'Leskovac' (F)	MGos
	- 'Ludovic' (F)	WJas
§	- 'Lusitanica' (F)	CDoC CDul ERea GTwe SKee WJas
	- 'Meech's Prolific' (F)	CAgr CCVT CLnd CTho CTri ECrN ERea GKir GTwe LRHS MBlu MGos MWat SFam SKee SPer
	- pear-shaped (F)	CDul ECrN
	- Portugal	see *C. oblonga* 'Lusitanica'
	- 'Seibosa' (F)	SKee
	- 'Shams' (F)	SKee
	- 'Sobu' (F)	SKee
§	- 'Vranja' Nenadovic (F) ♀H4	CAgr CCVT CDoC CDul CEnd CLnd CMac CSBt CTho CTri EBee ECrN EPfP ERea EWTr GTwe LAst LBuc LRHS MBri MGos SCrf SFam SKee SPer WDin WJas

Cymbalaria (*Scrophulariaceae*)

	aequitriloba 'Alba'	GGar
§	***hepaticifolia***	EDAr LRHS NLar WCru WPer
	- 'Alba'	CNic
§	***muralis***	ECtt IHMH MBar MHer MWat NJOw NPri WGor XPep
	- 'Albiflora'	see *C. muralis* 'Pallidior'
§	- 'Globosa Alba'	CHal EDAr MDHE NWCA
	- 'Kenilworth White'	WMoo
	- 'Nana Alba'	NJOw NPri SIng WPer
§	- 'Pallidior'	EWin SIng
	- 'Rosea'	WFar
§	***pallida***	CMea LRHS NSla SBla SPlb WCru WFar WMoo WPer
§	***pilosa***	ECtt EMan NJOw NLar

Cymbopogon (*Poaceae*)

	citratus	CArn CBod COld CSev CWan

	EUnu GPoy LRav MChe MGol MSal NGHP NPri NTHB SHDw SIde WCHb WJek WLHH
flexuosus	CBig GWCH MGol MHer
martini	CArn GPoy MGol MSal
nardus	CArn GPoy MSal

Cymophyllus (*Cyperaceae*)

fraserianus	CDes CHEx GBin

Cymopterus (*Apiaceae*)

***bulbosus* new**	GKev
***gilmanii* new**	GKev
hendersonii	see *Pteryxia hendersonii*

Cynanchum (*Asclepiadaceae*)

acuminatifolium	EMan GCal

Cynara (*Asteraceae*)

§ ***cardunculus*** ♀H3-4	More than 30 suppliers
* - 'Cardy'	EBee EChP EMan EShb EWin MWat NCGa SMrm WWhi
- dwarf	WCot
* - 'Florist Cardy'	IGor MFOX NLar WCot WWpP
§ - Scolymus Group	CAgr CBcs CHEx CKno CWan EBee EBrs EDAr EHoe ENot EPfP EWes GCal GPoy IGor ILis LRHS LSRN MBri MLan MRav NEgg SDnm SMrm SPav SPer SPoG WFar WHer WHoo
- - 'Gigante di Romagna'	WHer
- - 'Green Globe'	CBod CPrp CSBt CSev EBee MWat NPer NVic SWal
- - 'Gros Camus de Bretagne'	MAvo WCot
- - 'Gros Vert de Lâon'	CBcs ECha ELan IBal WCot WPGP
- - 'Large Green'	EWin NLar
- - 'Purple Globe'	CArn CPrp CSBt
- - 'Romanesco' **new**	EWin
- - 'Violetto di Chioggia'	CSev MSph WHer WHil
- 'Vert de Vaux en Velin'	LPio
scolymus	see *C. cardunculus* Scolymus Group

Cynodon (*Poaceae*)

aethiopicus	CBig EHoe LPhx SWal
dactylon 'Santana'	XPep

Cynoglossum (*Boraginaceae*)

amabile ♀H4	NCGa WTMC
- f. ***roseum*** 'Mystery Rose'	WPGP
creticum	WOut
dioscoridis	CBot EChP NLar WPer
nervosum	CArn CBot EBee ECtt ELan EMan EMil EPPr EPfP GMac LRHS MNFA MRav MTis MWgw NChi NEgg NGdn NWCA SHGN SPer SPet WCHb WCot WPnn WTMC
officinale	CArn MChe MHer MSal SECG WCHb WHer WWye

Cynosurus (*Poaceae*)

cristatus viviparous **new**	CNat

Cypella (*Iridaceae*)

§ ***coelestis***	CMon CPom EBee EMan WCot
herbertii	CMon CNic CPom LAma
peruviana	CMon CPom EMan EShb
plumbea	see *C. coelestis*

Cyperus (*Cyperaceae*)

§ ***albostriatus***	CHEx CHal MBri
alternifolius misapplied	see *C. involucratus*
alternifolius L.	LPBA WWpP
- 'Compactus'	see *C. involucratus* 'Nanus'
'Chira'	EChP MBNS SWal WWpP
§ ***cyperoides***	MBri
diffusus hort.	see *C. albostriatus*
§ ***eragrostis***	CArn CBrm CElw CFwr CHad CHal CMea CMil CPLG CRow CSec EBrs ECrN EHoe EPPr GFor GKir ITer MCCP NArg NOGN SDix SPlb SWal WAbb WMoo WPop WWhi WWpP
esculentus	CArn CBig IBlr LRav
fuscus	EKen EPPr MDKP WFar WHal WMoo
§ ***giganteus***	CDWL
glaber	EMan EPGN EPza EShb EUJe GFor MBar NBre SMar
haspan misapplied	see *C. papyrus* 'Nanus'
§ ***involucratus*** ♀H1	CBen CHEx CHal CRow CWCL EBak EHon ERea EShb EUJe GFor LPBA MBri NArg NBea SArc SGSe SWal SYvo WFar WMul WPop WWpP WWye
- 'Gracilis'	EBak MBri
§ - 'Nanus'	LPBA SWal
- 'Variegatus' (v) **new**	MJnS
longus	CFwr CHad EBee EHoe EHon EMFW EMon EPPr EPza GIBF LNCo LPBA MBar NArg NBlu NPer SMad SWal WFar WHal WPop WPrP WWpP
papyrus ♀H1	CHEx CHal CKno CMCo CTrC EAmu ERea EShb ESlt EUJe MBri MJnS SAPC SArc SLdr SUsu WHal WMul XBlo
- 'Mexico'	see *C. giganteus*
§ - 'Nanus' ♀H1	CDWL CHEx ERea ESlt WMul XBlo
rotundus	CRow EChP MCCP SBch SWal WWpP
sumula hort.	see *C. cyperoides*
ustulatus	CTrC EPPr MMoz
vegetus	see *C. eragrostis*
'Zumila'	WMul

Cyphomandra (*Solanaceae*)

betacea (F)	CHEx CPLG LRav
- 'Goldmine' (F)	ERea
- 'Oratia Red' (F)	ERea
***corymbiflora* new**	EUnu

Cyphostemma (*Vitaceae*)

juttae	CRoM LToo

Cypripedium (*Orchidaceae*)

Aki g.	CHdy XFro
- 'Light' **new**	GCrs
x ***andrewsii***	GCrs LAma XFro
calceolus	CFir CHdy EHrv MDun WCot
debile	EFEx
Emil g.	CHdy XFro
***farreri* new**	EFEx
***fasciolatum* new**	EFEx
flavum	WCot
§ ***formosanum***	EFEx LAma SSpi
Gisela g.	CHdy GCrs LAma XFro
- 'Yellow'	GCrs LAma XFro
guttatum var. ***yatabeanum***	see *C. yatabeanum*
henryi	EFEx LAma
himalaicum	EFEx
Inge g. new	XFro
Ingrid g. new	XFro
§ ***japonicum***	EFEx LAma

- var. ***formosanum***	see *C. formosanum*
Karl Heinz g.	CHdy
kentuckiense	WCot
macranthos	CHdy EFEx EHrv LAma WCot
- green-flowered	EFEx
- var. ***hotei-atsumorianum*** hort.	EFEx
- var. ***rebunense***	EFEx
- var. ***speciosum***	EFEx
margaritaceum	EFEx
Michael g. **new**	LAma XFro
montanum	EFEx LAma
parviflorum	CHdy
§ - var. ***pubescens***	CHdy LAma
Philipp g.	GCrs XFro
pubescens	see *C. parviflorum* var. *pubescens*
Rascal g.	CHdy
reginae	CLAP EHrv LAma LAst MDun SSpi WCot
Sabine g. **new**	XFro
segawae	CHdy EFEx LAma
tibeticum	EFEx
Ulla Silkens g.	GCrs LAma XFro
wardii **new**	EFEx
§ ***yatabeanum***	EFEx GIBF

Cyrilla (*Cyrillaceae*)

parvifolia	SSpi
racemiflora	NLar WBcn

Cyrtanthus (*Amaryllidaceae*)

'Alaska'[PBR]	CBro LRHS WCot
§ ***brachyscyphus***	CDes CMon EBee ERos EShb GGar MTis SHFr WCot WSPU
breviflorus	CDes SIgm WPGP
contractus	CDes
'Edwina'	ECho EShb
§ ***elatus*** 🏆H1	CBro CHal CSev CSpe CStu EMan ERea EShb LAma LRHS MCCP NCiC SYvo WCot WGwG WHer
- 'Cream Beauty'	WCot
- hybrid **new**	CMon
- pink	CSpe
* - 'Snow Queen' **new**	WCot
'Elizabeth'	ECho
falcatus 🏆H1	CMon EBee
flanaganii	CDes
loddigiesianus	CDes
§ ***luteus***	WAbe
mackenii	CDes CPen CPne WGwG
- var. ***cooperi***	CMon WCot
montanus	EBee WCot
obliquus	CMon WCot
* ***ochroleucus*** 'Stutterheim Variety'	WCot
parviflorus	see *C. brachyscyphus*
* 'Pink Diamond'	CBro LRHS
purpureus	see *C. elatus*
sanguineus	CFil CMon ECho WCot WPGP
- 'Horseshoe Falls' **new**	CMon
smithiae	CDes
speciosus	see *C. elatus*

Cyrtomium (*Dryopteridaceae*)

§ ***caryotideum***	CLAP GQui WRic
§ ***falcatum*** 🏆H3	CFwr CHEx CHal CLAP CMHG ELan EUJe EWTr GCal GMaP IBal MDun NOrc NSti SEND SMer SPla SPoG SRms SRot WFar WMoo WPnP WRic
* - 'Muricatum'	ELan
- 'Rochfordianum'	CBcs WFib
§ ***fortunei*** 🏆H4	More than 30 suppliers
- var. ***clivicola***	CFwr CPrp EChP EPfP NDlv NLar NVic SGSe SRot WRic
lonchitoides	CLAP
macrophyllum	CFil CLAP WCru WRic

Cystopteris ✿ (*Woodsiaceae*)

bulbifera	CLAP GQui
diaphana	WRic
dickieana	CLAP EBee EMon GBin NVic SRms WCot WFib WRic
fragilis	EBee ECha EFer GQui NBro SRms WRic
- 'Cristata'	CLAP
* ***gracilis***	WFib
moupinensis B&SWJ 6767 **new**	WCru
tennesseensis	WRic

Cytisus (*Papilionaceae*)

albus misapplied	see *C. multiflorus*
albus Hacq.	see *Chamaecytisus albus*
'Amber Elf'	COtt GKir LRHS MBri SPoG
'Andreanus'	see *C. scoparius* f. *andreanus*
'Apricot Gem'	MBar MGos NLar WBcn WCot WFar
ardoinoi 🏆H4	ECho
battandieri 🏆H4	More than 30 suppliers
- 'Yellow Tail' 🏆H4	CEnd LRHS WPGP WSPU
x ***beanii*** 🏆H4	CPLG EBee ELan EPfP GKir LRHS MAsh MBar SLon SRms SSto WDin WFar
'Boskoop Ruby' 🏆H4	CBrm CDoC CHar CRez CSBt EBee EGra EPfP GGar GKir LAst LRHS NBlu SPer SWvt WFar WRHF
'Burkwoodii' 🏆H4	CBcs CDoC CDul CHar CSBt CWSG EBee EGra ELan ENot EPfP GKir LAst LRHS LSRN MRav MSwo MWat MWhi SPoG WFar
canariensis	see *Genista canariensis*
'Compact Crimson'	CDoC SPoG
'Cottage'	EPot WAbe WBcn
'Daisy Hill'	CSBt
'Darley Dale Red' **new**	EWTr
§ ***decumbens***	CLyd NLar SSto WLin
'Donard Gem'	CDoC WWeb
'Dorothy Walpole'	WFar
'Dragonfly'	WBVN
'Dukaat'	GKir SHBN WBcn
'Firefly'	CBcs CSBt EBee NBlu NLar
'Fulgens'	CSBt EPfP MBar SPer WWeb
'Golden Cascade'	CBcs CDoC ELan LAst LRHS
'Golden Sunlight'	CSBt ENot EPfP SHBN WBVN
'Goldfinch'	CBcs CDoC CHar CSBt CWSG EBee ELan ENot GKir MAsh MBri MSwo NBlu NPri WRHF
hirsutus	see *Chamaecytisus hirsutus*
'Hollandia' 🏆H4	CBcs CDoC CHar CWSG EBee EPfP GKir LRHS MBar MGos MRav NEgg NPri SHBN SPer WDin WFar
x ***kewensis*** 🏆H4	CBrm CSBt CWSG EBee ELan ENot EPfP GKir LRHS MAsh MBar MBri MGos MRav NEgg SHBN SPer SPoG SReu SRms WDin
- 'Niki'	EBee EPfP LRHS MAsh MGos SPer SPoG SSta WGer
'Killiney Red'	EBee ECrN ELan GKir MBri NEgg
'Killiney Salmon'	CTri EBee LSRN MRav NBlu SSto WFar
'La Coquette'	CDoC CMHG EBee EGra LRHS MAsh MBar MWat NBlu SPlb SPoG
'Lena' 🏆H4	CAlb CDoC EBee EGra ENot EPfP GKir LAst LRHS MAsh MBar MBri

	MGos MRav MWat NEgg NPri WFar WRHF WWeb
leucanthus	see *Chamaecytisus albus* (Hacq.) Rothm.
'Luna'	CAlb EBee LRHS
maderensis	see *Genista maderensis*
'Maria Burkwood'	EPfP NBlu NEgg SHBN
'Minstead'	CDoC EBee ELan EPfP GGar SPer SPoG
monspessulanus	see *Genista monspessulana*
'Moyclare Pink'	CMHG
§ ***multiflorus*** 🏆H4	GKir LRav SRms
nigrescens	see *C. nigricans*
§ ***nigricans***	CPle ECrN NEgg WPGP
- 'Cyni'	ELan IArd LAst LRHS MAsh SPer SSpi SSta
'Palette'	LAst LRHS MBar
'Porlock'	see *Genista* 'Porlock'
x ***praecox***	CBrm CPSs CSBt EWTr LAst NBlu NEgg WFar WWeb
- 'Albus'	CDoC CHar EBee ECrN ELan ENot EPfP GKir LAst LRHS MAsh MBar MGos MRav MWat NBlu NEgg SEND SHBN SPer WFar WHCG WWeb
- 'Allgold' 🏆H4	More than 30 suppliers
- 'Canary Bird'	see *C.* x *praecox* 'Goldspeer'
- 'Frisia'	CBcs EWTr MBar
§ - 'Goldspeer'	CSBt EBee SEND
- 'Lilac Lady'	LRHS
§ - 'Warminster' 🏆H4	EBee ENot EPfP GKir LRHS MAsh MBar MBri MGos MRav MWat NWea SPer SRms
'Princess'	LRHS WBcn
procumbens	NBid SOkd
purgans	NLon
purpureus	see *Chamaecytisus purpureus*
'Queen Mary'	WBcn
racemosus hort.	see *Genista* x *spachiana*
'Red Beacon' **new**	WBcn
Red Favourite	see *C.* 'Roter Favorit'
'Red Wings'	GKir NEgg SPer
§ 'Roter Favorit'	EPfP MBar NScw WGor
scoparius	CAgr CArn CRWN EBee ECrN ENot GWCH MCoo NWea SRms WDin
§ - f. ***andreanus*** 🏆H4	CBgR CDoC EGra ENot EPfP GKir MGos NLon NWea SPoG WFar
- - 'Splendens'	CBcs SSto
- 'Cornish Cream'	CBgR CDoC ECot EPfP GKir SPer WWeb
§ - subsp. ***maritimus***	GSki MMHG NLon SLPl
- var. ***prostratus***	see *C. scoparius* subsp. *maritimus*
- 'Vanesse'	NBlu
x ***spachianus***	see *Genista* x *spachiana*
supinus	see *Chamaecytisus supinus*
'Windlesham Ruby'	CDoC CPLG EBee ELan ENot EPfP GKir LAst LRHS MBar NBlu NLar SPer WDin WFar WWpP
'Zeelandia' 🏆H4	CBcs EBee ENot EPfP GKir LAst LRHS MBar MRav MWat NBlu NPri SEND SPer WFar WWeb

D

Daboecia ✿ (*Ericaceae*)

§ ***cantabrica*** f. ***alba***	CPLG CSBt MBar MBri
- - 'Alba Globosa'	EPfP MBar MSwo
- - 'David Moss' 🏆H4	MBar WBan
- 'Arielle' 🏆H4	WBan
- 'Atropurpurea'	CNCN CSBt GKir
- 'Barbara Phillips' 🏆H4	MBar
- 'Bicolor' 🏆H4	CNCN
- 'Blueless'	EPfP
- 'Celtic Star'	WBan
- 'Charles Nelson' (d)	MBar
- 'Cinderella'	CNCN MBar
- 'Covadonga'	MBar
- 'Cupido'	CNCN
- 'Donard Pink'	MBar
- 'Hookstone Purple'	MBar
- 'Lilac Osmond'	MBar
- 'Pink'	see *D. cantabrica* 'Donard Pink'
- 'Pink Lady'	MBar
- 'Polifolia'	CNCN SRms
- 'Porter's Variety'	MBar
- 'Praegerae'	CNCN CTri GKir MBar
- 'Purpurea'	MBar
- 'Rainbow' (v)	CNCN MBar
- 'Rosea'	MBar
- subsp. ***scotica*** 'Bearsden'	MBar
- - 'Cora'	CNCN MBar
- - 'Goscote'	MGos
- - 'Jack Drake' 🏆H4	CNCN MBar MBri NDlv
- - 'Silverwells' 🏆H4	CBcs CNCN MBar MBri NDlv
- - 'Tabramhill'	CNCN MBar
- - 'William Buchanan' 🏆H4	CNCN GKir MBar MBri NDlv
- - 'William Buchanan Gold' (v)	CNCN MBar MBri
- 'Snowdrift'	MBar
- 'Waley's Red' 🏆H4	GQui MBar

Dacrycarpus (*Podocarpaceae*)

§ ***dacrydioides***	ECou LEdu
- 'Dark Delight'	ECou

Dacrydium (*Podocarpaceae*)

bidwillii	see *Halocarpus bidwillii*
cupressinum	CAbb CBcs CDoC CTrC SMad
franklinii	see *Lagarostrobos franklinii*
laxifolium	see *Lepidothamnus laxifolius*

Dactylis (*Poaceae*)

glomerata 'Variegata' (v)	CPen EBee ECGP ECrN EMan EMon ENot EPPr IBlr IHMH MBlu MCCP NBid NBro NGdn WFar

Dactylorhiza (*Orchidaceae*)

aristata	EFEx
x ***braunii***	ECha
- dark **new**	ECha
Calibra g. (*elata* x *majalis*)	CHdy
§ ***elata*** 🏆H4	CDes CLAP GCra GCrs GMaP GQui IBlr LAma LPhx MBri MDun SMHy SSpi WCot
- 'Lydia'	CLAP GCrs
Estella g. (*elata* x *foliosa*)	CHdy
§ ***foliosa*** 🏆H4	CBro CDes CElw CFir CLAP CRow EPot ERos ETow GCra GCrs IBlr MAvo MDun MTho NLAp WCot WFar WOld
foliosa x ***saccifera***	CHdy
§ ***fuchsii***	CHdy CMil EPot ERos GBuc GCrs GKev MGos MNrw NMen NRya NSla SCnR SSpi SUsu WHer WTin
- 'Bressingham Bonus'	GCrs
x ***grandis***	CHdy SMHy
incarnata	CFir CHdy
§ ***maculata***	CHdy CHid EChP EHrv ELan EMan ENot EPfP GAbr LAma MDun NGdn NLAp WCot WFar WHer

- 'Madam Butterfly' CBro GFlt
maderensis see *D. foliosa*
Madonna g. (*majalis* x *sambucina*) CHdy
§ ***majalis*** CHdy CLAP LAma SSpi WFar
- subsp. ***praetermissa*** see *D. praetermissa*
mascula see *Orchis mascula*
§ ***praetermissa*** CFir CFwr CHdy CLAP EPot SSpi WFar
purpurella CLAP NRya SUsu WCot WFar WSan
saccifera CHdy

Dahlia ✿ (*Asteraceae*)

'A la Mode' (LD) CWGr
'Abba' (SD) CWGr
'Abridge Alex' (SD) CWGr
'Abridge Ben' (MinD) CWGr
'Abridge Florist' (SWL) CWGr
'Abridge Fox' (MinD) CWGr
'Abridge Primrose' (SWL) CWGr
'Abridge Taffy' (MinD) CWGr
'Adelaide Fontane' (LD) CWGr
'Admiral Rawlings' CHad MAJR WWlt
'Aimie' (MinD) CWGr
'Akita' (Misc) WAba
'Alan Sparkes' (SWL) CWGr
'Albert Schweitzer' (MS-c) CWGr
'Alden Regal' (MinC) CWGr
'Alfred C' (GS-c) CWGr
'Alfred Grille' (MS-c) CWGr EPfP LRHS
'Alf's Mascot' WAba
'Aljo' (MS-c) CWGr
'All Triumph' (MinS-c) CWGr
'Allan Snowfire' (MS-c) NHal WAba
'Allan Sparkes' (SWL) ♀H3 LAyl
'Alloway Cottage' (MD) CWGr NHal
'Alltami Apollo' (GS-c) CWGr
'Alltami Classic' (MD) CWGr
'Alltami Corsair' (MS-c) CWGr
'Alltami Cosmic' (LD) CWGr
'Alltami Ruby' (MS-c) CWGr
'Almand's Climax' (GD) ♀H3 CWGr WAba
'Alpen Beauty' (Col) CWGr
'Alpen Fern' (Fim) CWGr
'Alpen Flame' (MinC) CWGr
'Alpen Mildred' (SS-c) CWGr
'Alpen Sun' (MinS-c) CWGr
'Alva's Doris' (SS-c) ♀H3 CWGr LAyl
'Alva's Lilac' (SD) CWGr
'Alva's Supreme' (GD) ♀H3 CWGr NHal WAba
'Amanda Jarvis' (SC) CWGr
'Amanjanca' (MinS-c) CWGr
'Amaran Candyfloss' (SD) CWGr
'Amaran Pentire' (SS-c) CWGr
'Amaran Relish' (LD) CWGr
'Amaran Royale' (MinD) CWGr
'Amaran Troy' (SWL) CWGr
'Amber Banker' (MC) CWGr
'Amber Festival' (SD) CWGr NHal
'Amber Vale' (MinD) CWGr
'Amberglow' (MinBa) CWGr LAyl
'Amberley Jean' (SD) CWGr
'Amberley Joan' (SD) CWGr
'Amberley Nicola' (SD) CWGr
'Amberley Victoria' (MD) CWGr
'Ambition' (SS-c) CWGr NHal
'Amelia's Surprise' (LD) CWGr
'American Copper' (GD) CWGr
'Amethyst' (SD) CWGr
'Amgard Coronet' (MinD) CWGr WAba
'Amgard Rosie' (SD) CWGr
'Amira' (SBa) CWGr NHal WAba
'Amorangi Joy' (SC) CWGr
'Amy Campbell' (MD) NHal
'Ananta Patel' (SD) CWGr
'Anchorite' (SD) CWGr
'Andrea Clark' (MD) NHal
'Andrew Lockwood' (Pom) CWGr
'Andrew Mitchell' (MS-c) CWGr NHal WAba
* 'Andries' Amber' (MinS-c) LBut
'Andries' Orange' (MinS-c) CWGr LBut
'Anglian Water' (MinD) NHal
'Anja Doc' (MS-c) CWGr
'Anniversary Ball' (MinBa) CWGr LAyl
'Apache' (MS-c/Fim) CWGr
'Appetizer' (SS-c) CWGr
I 'Appleblossom' (Col) CWGr
'Apricot Beauty' (MS-c) LAyl
'Apricot Honeymoon Dress' (SD) CWGr WAba
'Apricot Jewel' (SD) LAyl
'Apricot Parfait' (SS-c) CWGr
'April Dawn' (MD) CWGr
'Arab Queen' (GS-c) CWGr
'Arabian Night' (SD) CAvo CBcs CPen CSpe CWGr EBee EChP ECtt EHrv ELan EMan EPfP ERou EUJe LAst LPio LRHS MAvo MMil MNrw MSte NCob NEgg SPav SWal WAba WCot
'Arc de Triomphe' (MD) CWGr
'Arnhem' (SD) CWGr
'Arthur Godfrey' (GD) CWGr
'Arthur Hankin' (SD) CWGr
'Arthur Hills' (SC) CWGr
'Arthur's Delight' (GD) CWGr
'Asahi Chohje' (Anem) ♀H3 CBgR CWGr
'Aspen' (MS-c) CWGr
'Athelston John' (SC) CWGr
'Atilla' (SD) CWGr
'Audacity' (MD) CWGr LAyl
'Audrey R' (SWL) CWGr
'Aurora's Kiss' (MinBa) CWGr LBut NHal
'Aurwen's Violet' (Pom) CWGr LAyl NHal
australis CFil
'Autumn Choice' (MD) LAyl
'Autumn Lustre' (SWL) ♀H3 CWGr
'Avoca Salmon' (MD) **new** NHal
'Awaikoe' (Col) CWGr
'B.J. Beauty' (MD) LAyl NHal WAba
'Babette' (S-c) LBut
'Baby Fonteneau' (SS-c) CWGr
'Baby Royal' (SD) CHad
'Babylon' (GD) EPfP
'Bacchus' (MS-c) CWGr
'Bach' (MC) CWGr LRHS
'Bagley Blush' (MinD) **new** WAba
'Bahama Red' **new** CBgR
'Balbas' **new** WAba
'Balcombe' (SD) CWGr
'Ballego's Glory' (MD) CWGr
'Bambino' (Lil) CWGr
'Banker' (MC) CWGr
'Bantling' (MinBa) CWGr EPfP
'Barb' (LC) CWGr
'Barbara' (MinBa) CWGr
'Barbara Schell' (GD) CWGr
'Barbara's Pastelle' (MS-c) CWGr
'Barbarossa' (LD) CWGr
'Barbarry Ball' (SBa) CWGr
'Barbarry Banker' (MinD) CWGr LAyl
'Barbarry Bluebird' (MinD) NHal
'Barbarry Cadet' (MinD) CWGr
'Barbarry Carousel' (SBa) CWGr WAba

'Barbarry Cascade' (SD) CWGr
'Barbarry Challenger' (MinD) CWGr
'Barbarry Choice' (SD) WAba
'Barbarry Clover' (SB) CWGr
'Barbarry Coronet' (MinD) WAba
'Barbarry Cosmos' (SD) CWGr
'Barbarry Dominion' (MinD) CWGr
'Barbarry Flag' (MinD) CWGr
'Barbarry Gem' (MinBa) CWGr
'Barbarry Ideal' (MinD) CWGr
'Barbarry Monitor' (MinBa) CWGr
'Barbarry Noble' (MinD) CWGr
'Barbarry Olympic' (SBa) CWGr
'Barbarry Oracle' (SD) CWGr WAba
'Barbarry Orange' (SD) WAba
'Barbarry Pinky' (SD) CWGr
'Barbarry Polo' (MinD) **new** CWGr
'Barbarry Red' (MinD) CWGr
'Barbarry Ticket' (SD) WAba
'Barbarry Token' (SD) WAba
'Barbarry Triumph' (MinD) CWGr
'Barbetta' (MinD) CWGr
'Barbette' (MinD) CWGr
'Baret Joy' (LS-c) CWGr NHal WAba
'Bargaly Blush' (MD) NHal
'Baron Ray' (SD) CWGr
'Barry Williams' (MD) CWGr
'Bart' (SD) CWGr
'Barton Memory' (S-c) **new** NHal
'Baseball' (MinBa) CWGr
'Bassingbourne Beauty' (SD) CWGr
'Bayswater Red' (Pom) CWGr
I 'Bea' (SWL) WAba
'Beach Boy' (SD) CWGr
'Beacon Light' (SD) CWGr
I 'Beatrice' (MinBa) CWGr
'Bedford Sally' (MD) CWGr
'Bednall Beauty' (Misc/DwB) ♀H3 CBgR CHll CSpe CWGr EBee ECtt EHrv EMan EMil ERou EShb EUJe EVFa EWes EWin SChu SDys SPav SUsu WAba WCot WDyG
'Bell Boy' (MinBa) CWGr
'Bella S' (GD) CWGr
'Belle Epoque' (MC) CWGr
'Belle Moore' (SD) CWGr
'Bell's Boy' (MS-c) WAba
'Ben Huston' (GD) WAba
'Berger's Rekord' (S-c) CSut CWGr LRHS
'Berliner Kleene' (MinD/DwB) CWGr LRHS
'Bernice Sunset' (SS-c) CWGr
'Berolina' (MinD) CWGr
'Berwick Banker' (SBa) CWGr
'Berwick Wood' (MD) CWGr NHal
'Bess Painter' (SD) CWGr
'Betty Ann' (Pom) CWGr
'Betty Bowen' (SD) CWGr
'Biddenham Fairy' (MinD) CWGr
'Biddenham Strawberry' (SD) CWGr
'Bill Homberg' (GD) WAba
'Bingley' (SD) CWGr
'Bingo' (MinD) CWGr
'Bishop of Auckland' **new** WHlf
'Bishop of Canterbury' **new** WHlf
'Bishop of Lancaster' **new** WHlf
'Bishop of Llandaff' (Misc) ♀H3 More than 30 suppliers
'Bishop of Oxford' **new** WHlf
'Bishop of York' **new** WHlf
'Bitter Lemon' (SD) CWGr
'Black Fire' (SD) CWGr LAyl
'Black Monarch' (GD) CWGr NHal
'Black Narcissus' (MC) CWGr WWlt
'Black Spider' (SS-c) CWGr
'Black Tucker' (Pom) CWGr
'Blaze' (MD) CWGr
'Blewbury First' (SWL) CWGr
'Bliss' (SWL) CWGr WAba
'Bloemfontein' (SD) LRHS
'Bloodstone' (SD) CWGr EVFa
'Bloom's Amy' (MinD) CWGr
'Bloom's Graham' (SS-c) CWGr
'Bloom's Kenn' (MD) CWGr
I 'Blossom' (Pom) CWGr
'Blue Beard' (SS-c) CWGr
'Blue Diamond' (MC) CWGr
'Bluesette' (SD) CWGr
'Blyton Crystal' (SD) NHal
'Bob Fitzjohn' (GS-c) CWGr
'Bonaventure' (GD) NHal
'Bonesta' (SWL) **new** CWGr
'Bonne Espérance' (Sin/Lil) CWGr
'Bonny Blue' (SBa) CWGr
'Bonny Brenda' (MinD) CWGr
'Boogie Woogie' (Anem) CWGr
'Bora Bora' (SS-c) CWGr
'Border Princess' (SC/DwB) CWGr
'Brackenhill Flame' (SD) CWGr WAba
'Brackenridge Ballerina' (SWL) CWGr LAyl NHal WAba
'Brandaris' (MS-c) CWGr
'Brandysnap' (SD) CWGr
'Brian R' (MD) CWGr
'Brian's Dream' (MinD) NHal
'Bride's Bouquet' (Col) CWGr
'Bridge View Aloha' (MS-c) ♀H3 CWGr WAba
'Bridgette' (SD) CWGr
'Bristol Petite' (MinD) CWGr
'Bronze Glints' (MS-c) WAba
'Brookfield Delight' (Sin/Lil) ♀H3 CWGr LBut
'Brookfield Dierdre' (MinBa) CWGr
'Brookfield Judith' (MinD) NHal
'Brookfield Rachel' (MinBa) CWGr
'Brookfield Rene' (Dwf MinD) CWGr
'Brookfield Snowball' (SBa) CWGr
'Brookfield Sweetie' (DwB/Lil) CWGr
'Brookside Cheri' (SC) CWGr
'Bryce B. Morrison' (SD) CWGr
'Bud Flanagan' (MD) CWGr
* 'Buttercup' (Pom) CWGr
'Buttermere' (SD) CWGr
'By George' (GD) CWGr
'Caer Urfa' (MinBa) WAba
'Café au Lait' (LD) CWGr EBee NLar
'Calgary' (SD) CWGr
'Camano Ariel' (MC) CWGr
'Camano Choice' (SD) CWGr
'Camano Passion' (MS-c) CWGr
'Camano Poppet' (SBa) CWGr
'Camano Regal' (MS-c) CWGr
'Cameo' (WL) CWGr LBut NHal
'Campos Hush' (SS-c) CWGr
'Campos Philip M' (GD) CWGr
* 'Canary Fubuki' (MD) CWGr

'Candy' (MS-c) CWGr
'Candy Cane' (MinBa) CWGr
'Candy Cupid' (MinBa) ♀H3 CWGr LBut WAba
'Candy Hamilton Lilian' (SD) CWGr
'Candy Keene' (LS-c) NHal
'Capulet' (SBa) CWGr
'Cara Tina' (Dwf O) CWGr
'Careless' (SD) CWGr
'Carolina Moon' (SD) CWGr LAyl NHal
'Carstone Ruby' (SD) NHal
'Carstone Sunbeam' (SD) CWGr
'Carstone Suntan' (MinC) CWGr NHal
'Castle Drive' (MD) CWGr
'Catherine Ireland' (MinD) CWGr
'Cerise Prefect' (MS-c) CWGr
'Cha Cha' (SS-c) CWGr
'Chanson d'Amour' (SD) CWGr
'Chantal' (MinBa) CWGr
'Charles de Coster' (MD) CWGr
'Charlie Kenwood' (MinD) CWGr
'Charlie Two' (MD) CWGr LAyl LBut NHal WAba
'Charlotte Bateson' (MinBa) CWGr
'Chat Noir' (MS-c) CWGr
'Chee' (SWL) CWGr
'Cheerleader' (GS-c) CWGr
'Cherokee Beauty' (GD) CWGr
'Cherry Wine' (SD) CWGr
'Cherrywood Millfield' (MS-c) CWGr
'Cherrywood Stoddard' (MD) CWGr
'Cherrywood Turnpike' (SD) CWGr
'Cherrywood Wilderness' (MD) CWGr
'Cherubino' (Col) CWGr
'Cherwell Goldcrest' (SS-c) CWGr LAyl NHal WAba
'Cherwell Lapwing' (SS-c) NHal
'Cherwell Siskin' (MD) **new** WAba
'Cherwell Skylark' (SS-c) NHal
'Chessy' (Sin/Lil) ♀H3 CWGr EPfP LAyl LRHS WAba
'Chic' (MinBa) WWeb
'Chilson's Pride' (SD) CWGr
'Chiltern Amber' (SD) CWGr
'Chiltern Fantastic' (SC) CWGr
'Chiltern Herald' (MS-c) CWGr
'Chiltern Sylvia' (MinS-c) CWGr
'Chimacum Topaz' (MS-c) CWGr
'Chimborazo' (Col) CWGr LAyl SDix
'Chorus Girl' (MinD) CWGr
'Christine' (SD) CWGr
'Christmas Star' (Col) CWGr
'Christopher Nickerson' (MS-c) CWGr
'Christopher Taylor' (SWL) CWGr NHal WAba
I 'Cindy' (MinD) WAba
'Clair de Lune' (Col) ♀H3 CBgR CWGr EBee EWin LAst NHal SPav WAba
'Claire Diane' (SD) CWGr
'Claire Louise Kitchener' (MWL) **new** CWGr
'Clara May' (MS-c/Fim) CWGr
'Clarence' (S-c) CWGr
'Classic A.1' (MC) CWGr LAyl
'Classic Elise' (Misc) CWGr
'Classic Masquerade'PBR (Misc) CBgR EBee EPfP WWol
'Classic Poème'PBR (Misc) EBee
'Classic Rosamunde'PBR (Misc) CBgR EBee
'Classic Summertime' (Misc) CWGr EBee EPfP WWeb WWol
'Classic Swanlake'PBR (Misc) EBee
'Clint's Climax' (LD) WAba
'Cloverdale' (SD) CWGr
coccinea (B) CBgR CFil CHll CWGr EBee EMan EUJe EWin MSte NCob SChu SDix SPav WAba WCot WDyG WPGP WSHC
- B&SWJ 9126 WCru
- var. ***palmeri*** CFil MCCP
coccinea* x *merckii (B) EMan EWes
'Cocktail' (S-c) CWGr
'Colac' (LD) CWGr
'Color Spectacle' LS-c CWGr
'Coltness Gem' (Sin/DwB) CWGr
'Comet' (Misc Anem) CWGr
'Como Polly' (LD) CWGr
'Conchos' **new** WAba
I 'Concordia' (SD) CWGr
'Connie Bartlam' (MD) CWGr
'Connoisseur's Choice' (MinBa) CWGr
'Constance Bateson' (SD) CWGr
'Contraste' (Misc) CWGr
'Copper Queen' (MinD) NHal
* 'Coral Puff' LRHS
'Coral Relation' (SC) CWGr
'Coral Strand' (SD) CWGr
'Cornel' (SBa) CWGr LAyl LBut NHal WAba
'Corona' (SS-c/DwB) CWGr
'Coronella' (MD) CWGr
'Corrie Vigor' (SS-c) NHal
'Corrine' (SWL) WAba
'Cortez Silver' (MD) CWGr
'Cortez Sovereign' (SS-c) CWGr
'Corton Bess' (SD) CWGr
'Corton Olympic' (GD) CWGr
'Cottesmore' (MD) CWGr
'Country Boy' (MS-c) CWGr
'Crazy Legs' (MinD) CWGr
'Cream Alva's' (GD) ♀H3 CWGr
'Cream Delight' (SS-c) CWGr
'Cream Klankstad' (SC) CWGr
'Cream Linda' (SD) CWGr
'Cream Moonlight' (MS-c) CWGr WAba
'Cream Reliance' (SD) CWGr
'Crève Coeur' (GD) CWGr
'Crichton Cherry' (MinD) CWGr
'Crichton Honey' (SBa) CWGr
'Crossfield Allegro' (SS-c) CWGr
'Crossfield Anne' (MinD) CWGr
'Crossfield Ebony' (Pom) CWGr
'Crossfield Festival' (LD) CWGr
'Croydon Ace' (GD) CWGr
'Croydon Jumbo' (GD) CWGr
'Croydon Snotop' (GD) CWGr
'Crushed Velvet' (MinD) CWGr
'Cryfield Bryn' (SS-c) NHal
'Cryfield Jane' (MinBa) CWGr
'Cryfield Keene' (LS-c) CWGr
'Cryfield Max' (SC) CWGr
'Cryfield Rosie' (SBa) CWGr
'Curate' (Misc) CWGr
'Curiosity' (Col) CWGr LAyl NHal
'Currant Cream' (SBa) CWGr
'Cyclone' (MD) CWGr
'Cycloop' (SS-c) CWGr
'Cynthia Chalwin' (MinBa) CWGr
'Cynthia Louise' (GD) CWGr WAba

	Name	Suppliers
	'Czardas'	GCal
	'Daddy's Choice' (SS-c)	CWGr
	'Dad's Delight' (MinD)	CWGr
	'Daleko Adonis' (GS-c)	CWGr
	'Daleko Gold' (MD)	CWGr
	'Daleko Jupiter' (GS-c)	CWGr NHal WAba
	'Daleko Tangerine' (MD)	CWGr
	'Dana Champ' (MinS-c)	CWGr
	'Dana Dream' (MinS-c)	CWGr
	'Dana Iris' (SS-c)	CWGr
	'Dana Sunset' (SC)	CWGr
	'Dancing Queen' (S-c)	CWGr
	'Danjo Doc' (SD)	CWGr
	'Danum Cherry' (SD)	CWGr
	'Danum Chippy' (SD)	CWGr
	'Danum Fancy' (SD)	CWGr
	'Danum Gail' (LD)	CWGr WAba
	'Danum Julie' (SBa)	CWGr
	'Danum Meteor' (GS-c)	CWGr WAba
	'Danum Rebel' (LS-c)	CWGr
	'Danum Rhoda' (GD)	CWGr
	'Danum Salmon' (MS-c)	CWGr
	'Danum Torch' (Col)	CWGr
	'Dark Desire'[PBR] (Sin/DwB)	CAvo MBri
	'Dark Stranger' (MC) 🏆H3	CWGr
	'Darlington Diamond' (MS-c)	CWGr
	'Darlington Jubilation' (SS-c)	CWGr
	'Davar Hayley' (SC)	CWGr
	'Davenport Anita' (MinD)	CWGr
	'Davenport Honey' (MinD)	CWGr WAba
	'Davenport Lesley' (MinD)	CWGr
	'Davenport Sunlight' (MS-c)	CWGr NHal
	'Dave's Snip' (MinD)	WAba
	'David Digweed' (SD)	CWGr NHal
	'David Howard' (MinD) 🏆H3	More than 30 suppliers
	'David Shaw' (MD)	CWGr
	'David's Choice' (MinD)	CWGr
	'Dawn Chorus' (MinD)	CWGr
	'Dawn Sky' (SD)	LAyl
	'Daytona' (SD)	CWGr
	'Deborah's Kiwi' (SC)	CWGr NHal WAba
	'Debra Anne Craven' (GS-c)	CWGr NHal WAba
	'Decorette' (DwB/SD)	CWGr
	'Decorette Bronze'	CWGr
I	'Decorette Rose'	CWGr
	'Deepest Yellow' (MinBa)	CWGr
	'Denise Willow' (Pom)	WAba
	'Dentelle de Venise' (MC)	CWGr
	'Deuil du Roi Albert' (MD)	CWGr
	'Deutschland' (MD)	CWGr
	'Devon Joy' (MinD)	CWGr
I	'Diamond Rose' (Anem/DwB)	CWGr
	'Dinah Shore' (LS-c)	CWGr
	dissecta	CFil
	'Doc van Horn' (LS-c)	CWGr
	'Doctor Anne Dyson' (SC)	CWGr
	'Doctor Arnett' (GS-c)	CWGr
	'Doctor Caroline Rabbitt' (SD)	CWGr
	'Doctor John Grainger' (MinD)	CWGr
	'Doktor Hans Ricken' (SD)	WAba
	'Don's Delight' (Pom)	CWGr
	'Doris Bacon' (MinBa)	CWGr
	'Doris Day' (SC)	CWGr LBut NHal
	'Doris Knight' (SC)	LBut
	'Doris Rollins' (SC)	CWGr
	'Dottie D.' (SBa)	CWGr
	'Downham Royal' (MinBa)	CWGr
	'Drummer Boy' (LD)	CWGr
	'Duet' (MD)	CWGr EPfP LRHS
	'Dusky Harmony' (SWL)	CWGr LBut
	'Dutch Baby' (Pom)	CWGr WAba
	'Dutch Boy' (SD)	CWGr
	'Dutch Triumph' (LWL)	CWGr
	'Earl Haig' (LD)	CWGr
	'Earl Marc' (SC)	CWGr LBut
	'Early Bird' (SD)	CWGr
	'Easter Sunday' (Col)	CWGr
	'Eastwood Moonlight' (MS-c)	CWGr NHal WAba
	'Eastwood Star' (MS-c)	CWGr WAba
	'Ebbw Vale Festival' (MinD)	CWGr
	'Ebony Witch' (LD)	CWGr
	'Edge of Gold' (GD)	CWGr
	'Edgeway Joyce' (MinBa)	CWGr
	'Edinburgh' (SD)	CWGr WAba
	'Edith Holmes' (SC)	CWGr
	'Edith Mueller' (Pom)	CWGr
	'Eileen Denny' (MS-c)	CWGr
	'Eisprinzessin'	CWGr
	'El Cid' (SD)	CWGr
	'El Paso' (SD)	CSut CWGr
	'Eleanor Fiesta' (MinS-c)	CWGr
	'Elgico Leanne' (MC)	CWGr
	'Elizabeth Hammett' (MinD)	CWGr WAba
	'Elizabeth Snowden' (Col)	CWGr WAba
	'Ella Britton' (MinD)	CPen EBee LRHS MWgw
	'Ellen Huston' (Misc/DwB) 🏆H3	CBgR CWGr LRHS MBri NHal WWeb
	'Elma E' (LD)	CWGr NHal WAba
	'Elmbrook Chieftain' (GD)	CWGr
	'Elmbrook Rebel' (GS-c)	CWGr
	'Embrace' (SC) **new**	NHal
	'Emma's Coronet' (MinD)	CWGr WAba
	'Emmie Lou' (MD)	CWGr
	'Emory Paul' (LD)	CWGr
	'Emperor' (MD)	CWGr
	'Engadin' (MD)	CWGr
	'Engelhardt's Matador' **new**	WCot
	'Enid Adams' (SD)	CWGr
	'Eric's Choice' (SD)	CWGr
	'Ernie Pitt' (SD)	CWGr
	'Esau' (GD)	CWGr
	'Esther'	MBri
	'Eunice Arrigo' (LS-c)	CWGr
	'Eveline' (SD)	CBgR CWGr EPfP LRHS
	'Evelyn Foster' (MD)	CWGr
	'Evelyn Rumbold' (GD)	CWGr
	'Evening Lady' (MinD)	CWGr
	excelsa (B)	CHII
	'Exotic Dwarf' (Sin/Lil)	CWGr NHal WCot
	'Explosion' (SS-c)	CWGr
	'Extase' (MD)	CWGr LRHS
	'Fabula' (Col)	CWGr
	'Facet' (Sin/Lil)	WAba
	'Fairway Pilot' (GD)	CWGr
	'Fairway Spur' (GD)	CWGr LAyl NHal
	'Fairy Queen' (MinC)	CWGr
	'Falcon's Future' (MS-c)	CWGr
	'Fascination' (SWL/DwB) 🏆H3	CBcs CBgR CBos CHad CWCL CWGr EVFa LAyl LSou MAJR NEgg NHal SChu WWeb
	'Fascination Aus' (Col)	CWGr
	'Fashion Monger' (Col)	CWGr NHal
	'Fata Morgana'	CWGr
	'Fermain' (MinD)	CWGr WAba
	'Fern Irene' (MWL)	CWGr
	'Ferncliffe Illusion'	CWGr
	'Fernhill Champion' (MD)	CWGr

Cultivar	Suppliers
* 'Fernhill Suprise' (SD)	CWGr LBut
'Festivo' (Dwf Col)	CWGr
'Feu Céleste' (Col)	CWGr
'Fidalgo Blacky' (MinD)	CWGr
'Fidalgo Bounce' (SD)	CWGr
'Fidalgo Climax' (LS-c/Fim)	CWGr
'Fidalgo Magic' (MD)	CWGr WAba
'Fidalgo Snowman' (GS-c)	CWGr NHal
'Fidalgo Splash' (MD)	CWGr
'Fidalgo Supreme' (MD)	CWGr LAyl
'Figurine' (SWL) ♀H3	CWGr WAba
'Fille du Diable' (LS-c)	CWGr
'Finchcocks' (SWL) ♀H3	CWGr LAyl
'Fire Magic' (SS-c)	CWGr
* 'Fire Mountain' (MinD/DwB)	NHal
'Firebird' (Sin)	LRHS WAba
'Firebird' (MS-c)	see *D.* 'Vuurvogel'
'First Lady' (MD)	CWGr
'Fleur Mountjoy' (Col) **new**	CWGr
'Flevohof' (MS-c)	CWGr
'Floorimoor'	CWGr
'Flutterby' (SWL)	CWGr
'Forncett Furnace' (B)	GCal
'Forrestal' (MS-c)	CWGr
'Frank Holmes' (Pom)	CWGr WAba
'Frank Hornsey' (SD)	CWGr
'Frank Lovell' (GS-c)	CWGr WAba
'Franz Kafka' (Pom)	CWGr
'Frau Louise Mayer' (SS-c)	CWGr
'Fred Wallace' (SC)	CWGr
'Freelancer' (LC)	CWGr
'Freestyle' (SC)	CWGr
'Freya's Paso Doble' (Anem) ♀H3	CWGr LAyl
'Freya's Thalia' (Sin/Lil) ♀H3	LAyl
'Friendship' (S-c)	CWGr
'Fringed Star' (MS-c)	LRHS
'Frits' (MinBa)	CWGr
'Funny Face' (Misc)	CWGr WAba
'Fusion' (MD)	CWGr
'G.F. Hemerik' (Sin)	CWGr
'Gala Parade' (SD)	CWGr
'Gale Lane' (Pom)	CWGr
'Gallery Art Deco'PBR (SD) ♀H3	CWGr NHal WWol
'Gallery Art Fair'PBR (MinD)	WWol
'Gallery Art Nouveau'PBR (MinD) ♀H3	CWGr NHal WWol
'Gallery Cézanne'PBR (MinD)	CWGr WWol
'Gallery Leonardo'PBR (SD) ♀H3	CWGr WWol
'Gallery Rembrandt'PBR (MinD) **new**	CWGr
'Gallery Singer'PBR (MinD)	CWGr WWol
'Gamelan' (Dwf Anem)	CWGr
'Garden Festival' (SWL)	CWGr LAyl
'Garden Party' (MC/DwB) ♀H3	CWGr LAyl
'Garden Princess' (SC/DwB)	CWGr
'Garden Wonder' (SD)	EPfP LPio LRHS WWol
'Gargantuan' (GS-c)	CWGr
Gateshead Festival	see *D.* 'Peach Melba' (SD)
'Gaudy' (GD)	CWGr
'Gay Mini' (MinD)	CWGr
'Gay Princess' (SWL)	CWGr LAyl
'Geerlings' Cupido' (SWL)	WAba
§ 'Geerlings' Indian Summer' (MS-c) ♀H3	NHal
'Geerlings' Yellow' (SS-c)	CWGr
'Gemma Darling' (GD)	CWGr
'Gemma's Place' (Pom)	CWGr
'Genève' (MD)	CWGr
'Geoffrey Kent' (MinD) ♀H3	NHal
'Gerald Grace' (LS-c)	CWGr
'Gerlos' (MD)	CWGr
'Gerrie Hoek' (SWL)	CWGr LBut LRHS
'Gill's Pastelle' (MS-c)	CWGr WAba
'Gina Lombaert' (MS-c)	CWGr LRHS WAba
* 'Ginger Willo'	CWGr
'Giraffe' (Misc)	CAby CWGr
'Gitts Perfection' (GD)	CWGr
'Gitty' (SBa)	CWGr
'Glad Huston' (Dwf SS-c)	CWGr
'Glenbank Honeycomb' (Pom)	CWGr
'Glenbank Paleface' (Pom)	CWGr
'Glenbank Twinkle' (MinC)	CWGr
'Glengarry' (SC)	CWGr
'Glenplace' (Pom)	NHal
'Globular' (MinBa)	CWGr
'Gloria Romaine' (SD)	CWGr
'Glorie van Heemstede' (SWL) ♀H3	CWGr LAyl LBut LPio LRHS NHal WWol
'Glorie van Naardwijk' (SD)	CWGr
'Glory' (LD)	CWGr
'Glow Orange' (MinBa)	CWGr
'Go American' (GD)	CWGr NHal
'Gold Ball' (MinBa)	CWGr
'Gold Crown' (LS-c)	CSut
'Gold Standard' (LD)	CWGr
'Goldean' (GD)	CWGr
'Golden Emblem' (MD)	CWGr SWal
'Golden Fizz' (MinBa)	CWGr
'Golden Glitter' (MS-c)	CWGr
'Golden Heart' (MS-c)	CWGr
'Golden Horn' (MS-c)	CWGr
'Golden Jubilee' (D)	EPfP
'Golden Leader' (SD)	CWGr
'Golden Scepter' (Pom)	EPfP WAba
'Golden Symbol' (MS-c)	CWGr WAba
'Golden Turban' (MD)	CWGr
'Golden Willo' (Pom)	CWGr
'Goldie Gull' (Anem) **new**	NHal
'Goldilocks' (S-c)	CWGr
'Goldorange' (SS-c)	CWGr
'Good Earth' (MC)	CWGr
'Good Hope' (MinD)	CWGr
'Good Intent' (MinBa)	CWGr
'Goshen Beauty' (SWL)	CWGr
'Goya's Venus' (SS-c)	CWGr
'Grace Nash' (SD)	CWGr
'Grace Rushton' (SWL)	CWGr
'Gracie S' (MinC)	NHal
'Grand Prix' (GD)	CWGr
'Grand Willo' (Pom)	WAba
'Grenadier' (SWL)	CBgR EBee EMan ERou EUJe EWin LPio SDix SDys SPav WAba WCot
'Grenidor Pastelle' (MS-c)	CWGr LBut NHal WAba
'Gretchen Heine' (SD)	CWGr
'Grock' (Pom)	CWGr
'Gunyu' (GD)	CWGr
'Gurtla Twilight' (Pom)	CWGr NHal
'Gypsy Boy' (LD)	CWGr LAyl
'Gypsy Girl' (SD)	CWGr
'Hallwood Asset' (MinD)	CWGr
'Hallwood Coppernob' (MD)	CWGr
'Hallwood Satin' (MD)	CWGr
'Hallwood Tiptop' (MinD)	CWGr
'Hamari Accord' (LS-c) ♀H3	LAyl NHal WAba

'Hamari Bride' (MS-c) ♀H3 CWGr LAyl
'Hamari Girl' (GD) CWGr NHal
'Hamari Gold' (GD) ♀H3 CWGr NHal WAba
'Hamari Katrina' (LS-c) CWGr LRHS WAba
'Hamari Rosé' (MinBa) ♀H3 CWGr LAyl NHal
'Hamari Sunshine' (LD) ♀H3 CWGr NHal
'Hamilton Amanda' (SD) CWGr
'Hamilton Lillian' (SD) ♀H3 CWGr WAba
'Hans Radi' (Misc) WAba
'Hans Ricken' (SD) CWGr
'Happy Caroline' CWGr LRHS
* 'Haresbrook' EBee EMan ERou EShb EUJe EWin LAst MSte NGdn SDys SPav WAba WCot WPop
'Harvest Amanda' (Sin/Lil) ♀H3 LBut
'Harvest Brownie' (Sin/Lil) LBut
§ 'Harvest Imp' (Sin/Lil) LAyl
§ 'Harvest Inflammation' (Sin/Lil) ♀H3 LBut
§ 'Harvest Samantha' (Sin/Lil) ♀H3 LAyl LBut
'Haseley Bridal Wish' (MC) CWGr
'Haseley Goldicote' (SD) CWGr
'Haseley Miranda' (SD) CWGr
'Haseley Triumph' (SD) CWGr
'Haseley Yellow Angora' (SD) CWGr
'Hayley Jayne' (SC) CWGr WAba
'Helga' (MS-c) CWGr
'Helma Rost' (SS-c) CWGr
'Henri Lweii' (SC) CWGr
'Henriette' (MC) CWGr
'Herbert Smith' (D) CWGr
'Hexton Copper' (SBa) CWGr
'Hi Ace' (LC) CWGr
'Hidi' (SS-c) CWGr
'Higherfield Champion' (SS-c) CWGr
'Highness' (MinS-c) CWGr
'Hildepuppe' (Pom) CWGr
'Hillcrest Amour' (SD) CWGr
'Hillcrest Bobbin' (SBa) CWGr
'Hillcrest Camelot' (GS-c) CWGr
'Hillcrest Carmen' (SD) CWGr
'Hillcrest Contessa' (MinBa) CWGr
'Hillcrest Delight' (MD) NHal
'Hillcrest Desire' (SC) ♀H3 CWGr LAyl WAba
'Hillcrest Divine' (MinD) WAba
'Hillcrest Fiesta' (MS-c) CWGr
'Hillcrest Hannah' (MinD) NHal
'Hillcrest Heights' (LS-c) CWGr WAba
'Hillcrest Kismet' (MD) NHal
'Hillcrest Margaret' WAba
'Hillcrest Pearl' (MD) CWGr
'Hillcrest Regal' (Col) ♀H3 CWGr WAba
'Hillcrest Royal' (MC) ♀H3 NHal SDix
'Hillcrest Suffusion' (SD) CWGr
'Hillcrest Ultra' (SD) CWGr
'Hill's Delight' (MS-c) CWGr
'Hindu Star' (MinBa) CWGr
'Hit Parade' (MS-c) CWGr
'Hockley Maroon' (SD) CWGr
'Hockley Nymph' (SWL) CWGr
'Holland Festival' (GD) CWGr
'Homer T' (LS-c) CWGr
'Hondp' **new** WAba
'Honey' (Anem/DwB) CWGr LRHS WAba
'Honeymoon Dress' (SD) CWGr
'Honka' (Misc) ♀H3 CWGr
'Hot Chocolate' CWGr ECho EPfP NLar SChu WWol
'Hugh Mather' (MWL) CWGr
'Hulin's Carnival' (MinD) CWGr
'Hy Clown' (SD) CWGr
'Hy Fire' (MinBa) CWGr
'Ice Queen' (SWL) CWGr
'Ida Gayer' (LD) CWGr
'I-lyke-it' (SS-c) CWGr
'Imp' see *D.* 'Harvest Imp'
imperialis (B) CHEx CHll CWGr EMon EShb EWes GCal LPio MJnS MOak WAba WBVN WDyG WHal WMul
- B&SWJ 8997 WCru
- 'Alba' (B) CWGr
I - 'Tasmania' (B) GCal
'Impression Flamenco' CWGr LRHS
'Impression Fortuna' (Dwf Col) CWGr
'In Green' MBri
'Inca Concord' (MD) CWGr
'Inca Dambuster' (GS-c) CWGr NHal
'Inca Glamour' (LD) CWGr
'Inca Matchless' (MD) CWGr
'Inca Metropolitan' (LD) CWGr
'Inca Panorama' (MD) CWGr
'Inca Royale' (LD) CWGr
'Inca Vanguard' (GD) CWGr
'Inca Vulcan' (GS-c) CWGr
'Indian Summer' (SC) CWGr WAba
'Inflammation' see *D.* 'Harvest Inflammation'
'Inglebrook Jill' (Col) CWGr LAyl
'Inland Dynasty' (GS-c) CWGr
'Inn's Gerrie Hoek' (MD) CWGr
'Irene Ellen' (SD) WAba
'Irene van der Zwet' (Sin) CWGr EPfP
'Iris' (Pom) WAba
'Irisel' (MS-c) CWGr
'Islander' (LD) CWGr
'Ivanetti' (MinBa) NHal
'Ivor's Rhonda' (Pom) **new** WAba
'Jack Hood' (SD) CWGr
'Jackie Magson' (SS-c) CWGr WAba
'Jackie's Baby' (MinD) WAba
'Jacqueline Tivey' (SD) CWGr
'Jacqui'PBR **new** WAba
'Jaldec Jerry' (GS-c) CWGr
'Jaldec Joker' (SC) CWGr
'Jaldec Jolly' (SC) CWGr
'Jamaica' (MinWL) CWGr
'Jamie' (SS-c) CWGr
'Jan van Schaffelaar' CWGr
'Janal Amy' (GS-c) NHal WAba
'Jane Cowl' (LD) CWGr
'Jane Horton' (Col) CWGr
* 'Janet Becket' (LC) CWGr
'Janet Clarke' (Pom) CWGr
'Janet Howell' (Col) **new** CWGr
'Janet Jean' (SWL) CWGr
'Japanese Waterlily' (SWL) CWGr
'Jason' (SS-c) WAba
'Jazzy' (Col) CWGr
'Je Maintiendrai' (GD) CWGr
'Jean Fairs' (MinWL) CWGr LBut
'Jean Marie'PBR (MD) CWGr LRHS
'Jean Melville' (MinD) CWGr
'Jeanette Carter' (MinD) ♀H3 CWGr
'Jeanne d'Arc' (GC) CSut CWGr
'Jeannie Leroux' (SS-c/Fim) CWGr
'Jean's Carol' (Pom) CWGr
'Jennie' (MS-c/Fim) CWGr

	Cultivar	Suppliers
	'Jescot Buttercup' (SD)	CWGr
	'Jescot India' (MinD)	CWGr
	'Jescot Jess' (MinD)	CWGr LBut
	'Jescot Jim' (SD)	CWGr
	'Jescot Julie' (O)	CWGr LAyl
	'Jescot Lingold' (MinD)	CWGr WAba
	'Jescot Nubia' (SS-c)	CWGr
	'Jescot Redun' (MinD)	CWGr
	'Jessica' (S-c)	CWGr
	'Jessie G' (SBa)	CWGr
	'Jessie Ross' (MinD/DwB)	CWGr
	'Jet' (SS-c)	CWGr
	'Jill Day' (SC)	CWGr LBut
*	'Jill's Blush' (MS-c)	CWGr
	'Jill's Delight' (MD)	CWGr
	'Jim Branigan' (LS-c)	CWGr NHal WAba
	'Jim's Jupiter' (LS-c)	WAba
	'Jive'	CWGr
	'Joan Beecham' (SWL)	CWGr
	'Jocondo' (GD)	CWGr NHal
	'Johann' (Pom)	CWGr NHal
	'John Prior' (SD)	CWGr
	'John Street' (SWL) ♀H3	CWGr
	'John's Champion' (MD)	CWGr
	'Jomanda' (MinBa) ♀H3	LBut NHal WAba
	'Jorja' (MS-c)	CWGr
	'Jo's Choice' (MinD)	CWGr LBut
	'Joy Donaldson' (MC)	CWGr
	'Joyce Green' (GS-c)	CWGr
	'Joyce Margaret Cunliffe' (SD)	CWGr
	'Juanita' (MS-c)	CWGr
	'Judy Tregidden' (MWL)	NHal
	'Julie One' (Misc Dbl O)	CWGr
	'Julio' (MinBa)	CWGr
	'Jura' (SS-c)	CWGr
	'Just Jill' (MinD)	CWGr
	'Kaftan' (MD)	CWGr
	'Kaiserwalzer' (Col)	CWGr
	'Karenglen' (MinD) ♀H3	LBut NHal WAba
	'Kari Quill' (SC)	CWGr
	'Karma Amanda' (SD)	CWGr WAba
	'Karma Bon Bini'[PBR] (SC)	WAba
	'Karma Corona'[PBR] (SC)	CWGr WAba
	'Karma Lagoon'[PBR]	CWGr WAba
	'Karma Maarten Zwaan'[PBR] (SWL)	WAba
	'Karma Naomi'[PBR]	WAba
	'Karma Sangria'[PBR]	CWGr WAba
	'Karma Serena'[PBR]	WAba
I	'Karma Thalia'	WAba
	'Karma Ventura'[PBR] (SD)	WAba
	'Karma Yin-Yang' (SD)	WAba
	'Karras 150' (SS-c)	CWGr
	'Kate Mountjoy' (Col) **new**	CWGr
	'Kate's Pastelle'	WAba
	'Kathleen's Alliance' (SC) ♀H3	NHal
	'Kathryn's Cupid' (MinBa) ♀H3	CWGr SWal WAba
	'Kathy' (SC)	CWGr
	'Katie Dahl' (MinD)	CWGr NHal
	'Katisha' (MinD)	CWGr
	'Kay Helen' (Pom)	CWGr
	'Kayleigh Spiller' (Col) **new**	CWGr
	'Keith's Choice' (MD)	CWGr NHal WAba
	'Kelsea Carla' (SS-c)	CWGr NHal WAba
	'Kelvin Floodlight' (GD)	CWGr EPfP
	'Kenn Emerland' (MS-c)	CSut
	'Kenora Canada' (MS-c)	CWGr WAba
	'Kenora Challenger' (LS-c)	CWGr NHal WAba
	'Kenora Christmas' (SBa)	CWGr
	'Kenora Clyde' (GS-c)	CWGr
	'Kenora Fireball' (MinBa)	NHal
	'Kenora Jubilee' (LS-c)	NHal
	'Kenora Lisa' (MD)	CWGr WAba
	'Kenora Moonbeam' (MD)	CWGr
	'Kenora Ontario' (LS-c)	CWGr
	'Kenora Peace' (MinBa)	CWGr
	'Kenora Sunset' (MS-c) ♀H3	CWGr LAyl LBut NHal
	'Kenora Superb' (LS-c)	CWGr NHal WAba
	'Kenora Valentine' (LD) ♀H3	CWGr LAyl NHal
	'Kenora Wildfire' (LD)	CWGr
	'Ken's Choice' (SBa)	NHal
	'Ken's Coral' (SWL)	CWGr NHal
	'Ken's Flame' (SWL)	CWGr
	'Ken's Rarity' (SWL)	NHal
	'Keri Blue' (SWL)	CWGr
	'Kidd's Climax' (GD) ♀H3	CWGr NHal WAba
	'Kilmorie' (SS-c)	NHal
	'Kim Willo' (Pom)	CWGr
	'Kimberley B' (MinD)	CWGr
	'Kim's Marc' (SC)	LBut
*	'Kingston' (MinD)	CWGr
	'Kismet' (SBa)	CWGr
	'Kiss' (MinD)	CWGr
	'Kiwi Brother' (SS-c)	CWGr
	'Kiwi Cousin' (SC)	CWGr
	'Kiwi Gloria' (SC)	NHal WAba
	'Klondike' (MS-c)	CWGr WAba
*	'Kogano Fubuki' (MD)	CWGr
	'Korgill Meadow' (MD)	CWGr
	'Kotare Jackpot' (SS-c)	CWGr
	'Kung Fu' (SD)	CWGr
I	'Kyoto' (SWL)	CWGr WAba
	'L.A.T.E.' (MinBa)	CWGr NHal WAba
	'La Cierva' (Col)	CWGr
	'La Gioconda' (Col)	CWGr
	'Lady Kerkrade' (SC)	CWGr
	'Lady Linda' (SD)	CWGr LBut NHal WAba
	'Lady Orpah' (SD)	CWGr
	'Lady Sunshine' (SS-c)	CWGr
	'L'Ancresse' (MinBa)	CWGr LAyl NHal WAba
	'Larkford' (SD)	CWGr
	'Last Dance' (MD)	CWGr
	'Laura Marie' (MinBa)	CWGr
*	'Laura's Choice' (SD)	CWGr
	'Lauren's Moonlight' (MS-c)	CWGr NHal WAba
	'Lavendale' (MinD)	CWGr
	'Lavender Chiffon' (MS-c)	CWGr
	'Lavender Freestyle' (SC)	CWGr
	'Lavender Leycett' (GD)	CWGr
	'Lavender Line' (SC)	CWGr NHal
	'Lavender Nunton Harvest' (SD)	CWGr
	'Lavender Perfection' (GD)	CSut CWGr EPfP
	'Lavender Prince' (MD)	CWGr
	'Lavengro' (GD)	CWGr
	'Le Castel' (D)	CWGr
	'Le Patineur' (MD)	CWGr
	'Leander' (GS-c)	CWGr
	'Lecta' (MS-c)	CWGr
	'Lemon' (Anem)	CWGr WAba
	'Lemon Cane' (Misc)	CWGr WAba
	'Lemon Elegans' (SS-c) ♀H3	CWGr LBut NHal WAba
	'Lemon Meringue' (SD)	CWGr
*	'Lemon Puff' (Anem)	CWGr
	'Lemon Symbol' (MS-c)	CWGr
	'Lemon Zing' (MinBa)	NHal WAba
*	'Lenny' (MinD)	CWGr
	'Lexington' (Pom)	CWGr
	'Leycett' (GD)	CWGr
	'Libretto' (Col)	CWGr

	Name	Suppliers
*	‘Life Force’ (GD)	CWGr
	‘Life Size’ (LD)	CWGr
	‘Light Music’ (MS-c)	CWGr
	‘Lilac Athalie’ (SC)	CWGr
	‘Lilac Shadow’ (S-c)	CWGr
§	‘Lilac Taratahi’ (SC) ♀H3	CWGr NHal
	‘Lilac Time’ (MD)	EPfP LRHS SWal
	‘Lilac Willo’ (Pom)	CWGr
	‘Lillianne Ballego’ (MinD)	CWGr
	‘Linda’s Chester’ (SC)	CWGr LBut
	‘Linda’s Diane’ (SD)	CWGr
	‘Lisa’PBR	CWGr
	‘Lismore Canary’ (SWL)	NHal
	‘Lismore Carol’ (Pom)	CWGr NHal
	‘Lismore Chaffinch’ (MinD)	NHal
	‘Lismore Moonlight’ (Pom)	CWGr LAyl NHal
	‘Lismore Peggy’ (Pom)	CWGr
	‘Lismore Robin’ (MinD)	NHal
	‘Lismore Sunset’ (Pom)	CWGr WAba
	‘Lismore Willie’ (SWL) ♀H3	LBut NHal WAba
	‘Little Dorrit’ (Sin/Lil) ♀H3	CWGr LBut
	‘Little Glenfern’ (MinC)	CWGr
	‘Little Jack’ (MinS-c)	CWGr
	‘Little John’	CWGr
	‘Little Laura’ (MinBa)	CWGr
	‘Little Reggie’ (SS-c)	CWGr
	‘Little Robert’ (MinD)	CWGr
	‘Little Sally’ (Pom)	CWGr
	‘Little Scottie’ (Pom)	CWGr
	‘Little Shona’ (MinD)	CWGr
	‘Little Snowdrop’ (Pom)	CWGr
	‘Little Tiger’	CWGr
	‘Little Treasure’	EPfP
I	‘Little William’ **new**	EPfP
	‘Liz’ (MS-c)	CWGr
	‘Lois Walcher’ (MD)	CWGr
	‘Lombada’ (Misc)	CWGr
	‘Long Island Lil’ (SD)	CWGr
	‘Longwood Dainty’ (DwB)	CWGr NHal
	‘Loretta’ (SBa)	CWGr
	‘Loud Applause’ (SC)	CWGr
	‘Louis V’ (LS-c)	CWGr
	‘Louise Bailey’ (MinD)	CWGr
	‘Lucky Devil’ (MD)	CWGr
	‘Lucky Number’ (MD)	CWGr
	‘Ludwig Helfert’ (S-c)	CWGr EPfP LRHS
	‘Lupin Dixie’ (SC)	CWGr
	‘Lyn Mayo’ (SD)	CWGr
	‘Lyndsey Murray’ (MinD)	CWGr
	‘Ma Folie’ (GS-c)	CWGr
	‘Mabel Ann’ (GD)	CWGr LAyl WAba
I	‘Madame de Rosa’ (LS-c)	NHal
	‘Madame J. Snapper’	EShb
	‘Madame Simone Stappers’ (WL)	CWGr EBee
	‘Madame Vera’ (SD)	CWGr LBut
	‘Madelaine Ann’ (GD)	CWGr
	‘Magenta Magic’ (Sin/DwB)	NHal
	‘Magic Moment’ (MS-c)	CWGr
	‘Magnificat’ (MinD)	CWGr
	‘Maisie Mooney’ (GD)	CWGr
	‘Majestic Athalie’ (SC)	CWGr
	‘Majestic Kerkrade’ (SC)	CWGr
	‘Majjas Symbol’ (MS-c)	CWGr
	‘Malham Honey’ (SD)	CWGr
	‘Malham Portia’ (SWL)	WAba
	‘Maltby Fanfare’ (Col)	CWGr
	‘Maltby Whisper’ (SC)	LAyl
	‘Mandy’ (MinD)	CWGr
	‘March Magic’ (MinD)	CWGr
	‘Margaret Ann’ (MinD)	CWGr LAyl LBut
	‘Margaret Brookes’ (LD)	CWGr
	‘Margaret Haggo’ (SWL)	LAyl NHal

	Name	Suppliers
	‘Marie’ (SD)	CWGr
	‘Marie Schnugg’ (Misc) ♀H3	CWGr
	‘Mariposa’ (Col)	CWGr WAba
	‘Mark Damp’ (LS-c)	CWGr
	‘Mark Hardwick’ (GD)	NHal
	‘Mark Lockwood’ (Pom)	CWGr WAba
	‘Market Joy’ (SS-c)	CWGr
	‘Marla Lu’ (MC)	CWGr
	‘Marlene Joy’ (MS-c/Fim)	CWGr NHal WAba
	‘Maroen’PBR (Misc)	CWGr
	‘Mars’ (Col)	CWGr
	‘Marshmello Sky’ (Col)	CWGr
	‘Martin’s Red’ (Pom)	CWGr
	‘Martin’s Yellow’ (Pom)	NHal WAba
	‘Marvelous Sal’ (MD)	NHal
	‘Mary Eveline’ (Col)	LAyl NHal WAba
	‘Mary Hammett’ (MinD)	WAba
	‘Mary Jennie’ (MinS-c)	CWGr
	‘Mary Lunns’ (Pom)	CWGr
	‘Mary Magson’ (SS-c)	CWGr
	‘Mary Partridge’ (SWL)	CWGr
	‘Mary Pitt’ (MinD)	CWGr
	‘Mary Richards’ (SD)	CWGr
	‘Mary’s Jomanda’ (SBa)	NHal
	‘Master David’ (MinBa)	CWGr
	‘Master Michael’ (Pom)	CWGr
	‘Match’ (SS-c)	CWGr
	‘Matilda Huston’ (SS-c)	CWGr NHal
	‘Matisse’ **new**	EPfP
	‘Matt Armour’ (Sin)	CWGr
	‘Maureen Hardwick’ (GD)	CWGr
	‘Maureen Kitchener’ (SWL) **new**	CWGr
	‘Maxine Bailey’ (SD)	CWGr
	‘Maya’ (SD)	CWGr
	‘Meiro’ (SD)	CWGr
	‘Melanie Jane’ (MS-c)	CWGr
	‘Melody Dixie’PBR (MinD)	CWGr
	‘Melody Dora’PBR	CWGr
	‘Melody Gipsy’PBR (SS-c)	WWeb
	‘Melody Swing’PBR	CWGr
	‘Melton’ (MinD)	CWGr
	merckii (B)	CBgR CHad CMdw CSpe CWGr EBee EBrs EGoo EWes GCal GMac LRHS MNrw MSte SChu SMad WAba WDyG WPGP WSHC
	- ***alba*** (B)	CFil CHad MSte WCru
	- compact (B)	CBos CFil EBee EMan WPGP
	- ‘Edith Eddleman’ (B)	CFil
	‘Meredith’s Marion Smith’ (SD)	CWGr
	‘Mermaid of Zennor’ (Sin)	CFir CWGr EBee EMan ERou NCot WCot
	‘Merriwell Topic’ (MD)	CWGr
	‘Miami’ (SD)	CWGr
	‘Michael J’ (MinD)	CWGr
	‘Michigan’ (MinD)	CWGr
	‘Mick’ (SC)	CWGr
	‘Midas’ (SS-c)	CWGr
	‘Midnight’ (Pom)	CWGr
	‘Mies’ (Sin)	CWGr
	‘Mignon Silver’ (Dwf Sin)	CWGr
	‘Mingus Gregory’ (LS-c)	CWGr
	‘Mingus Kyle D’ (SD)	CWGr
	‘Mingus Nichole’ (LD)	CWGr
	‘Mingus Tracy Lynn’ (SS-c)	CWGr
	‘Mingus Whitney’ (GS-c)	CWGr
	‘Mini’ (Sin/Lil)	CWGr LBut
	‘Mini Red’ (MinS-c)	CWGr
	‘Minley Carol’ (Pom) ♀H3	CWGr LAyl NHal WAba
	‘Minley Linda’ (Pom)	CWGr
	‘Minnesota’ (LD)	WAba

	Cultivar	Suppliers
	'Miramar' (SD)	CWGr
	'Miss Blanc' (SD)	CWGr
	'Miss Rose Fletcher' (SS-c)	CWGr
	'Miss Swiss' (SD)	CWGr
	'Misterton' (MD)	CWGr
	'Mistill Beauty' (SC)	CWGr
	'Mistill Delight' (MinD)	CWGr
	'Mom's Special' (LD)	CWGr
	'Mon Trésor' (MS-c)	CWGr
	'Monk Marc' (SC)	CWGr LBut
	'Monkstown Diane' (SC)	CWGr
	'Monrovia' (MinBa)	CWGr
	'Moonfire' (Misc/DwB) 🏆H3	More than 30 suppliers
	'Moonglow' (LS-c)	CWGr
	'Moor Place' (Pom)	NHal WAba
	'Moray Susan' (4)	CWGr WAba
	'Moret' (SS-c)	CWGr
	'Morley Lady' (SD)	CWGr
	'Morley Lass' (SS-c)	CWGr
	'Morning Dew' (SC)	CWGr
	'Mount Noddy' (Sin)	CWGr
	'Mrs A. Woods' (MD)	CWGr
	'Mrs Black' (Pom)	CWGr
	'Mrs Geo Le Boutillier' (GD)	CWGr
	'Mrs H. Brown' (Col)	CWGr
	'Mrs McDonald Quill' (LD)	CWGr NHal
	'Mrs Silverston' (SD)	CWGr
	'Mummies Favourite' (SD)	CWGr
	'Murdoch'	CBgR CPen EBee ECtt EMan EPfP ERou EWin SDys SPav WAba WCot
	'Muriel Gladwell' (SS-c)	CWGr
	'Murillo'	MBri
	'Murray May' (LD)	CWGr
	'Musette' (MinD)	CWGr
	'My Beverley' (MS-c)(Fim)	NHal
	'My Joy' (Pom)	CWGr
	'My Love' (SS-c)	CSut LRHS
	'My Valentine' (SD)	CWGr
	'Mystery Day' (MD)	CSut CWGr EPfP
	'München' (MinD)	CWGr
	'Nancy H' (MinBa)	CWGr
	'Nankyoko'	CWGr
	'Nargold' (MS-c/Fim)	CWGr LAyl
	'Natal' (MinBa)	CAby CWGr EPfP
	'National Vulcan' (MinD)	CWGr
	'Nationwide' (SD)	CWGr WAba
	'Neal Gillson' (MD)	CWGr
	'Nellie Birch' (MinBa)	CWGr
	'Nellie Geerlings' (Sin)	CWGr
	'Nenekazi' (MS-c/Fim)	CWGr LAyl
	'Nepos' (SWL)	CWGr LBut
	'Nescio' (Pom)	CWGr EPfP WAba
	'Nettie' (MinBa)	CWGr
	'New Baby' (MinBa)	CWGr LRHS
	'New Dimension' (SS-c)	CWGr EPfP
	'New Look' (LS-c)	CWGr
	'Newsham Wonder' (SD)	CWGr
	'Nicola' (SS-c)	CWGr
	'Nicola Jane' (Pom) 🏆H3	NHal
	'Nicolette' (MWL)	CWGr
	'Night Life' (SC)	CWGr
I	'Night Queen' (Pom)	EPfP
	'Nijinsky' (SBa)	CWGr
	'Nina Chester' (SD)	CWGr
	'Nonette' (SWL)	CWGr EVFa WAba WCot
	'Norbeck Dusky' (SS-c)	CWGr
	'Noreen' (Pom)	CWGr NHal
	'North Sea' (MD)	CWGr
	'Northland Primrose' (SC)	CWGr
*	'Nuit d'Eté' (MS-c)	CWGr LPio
	Nunton form (SD)	CWGr
	'Nunton Harvest' (SD)	CWGr
	'Nutley Sunrise' (MC)	CWGr
	'Nymphenburg' (SD)	CWGr
	'Oakwood Diamond' (SBa)	CWGr LBut
	'Old Boy' (SBa)	CWGr
	'Omo' (Sin/Lil) 🏆H3	LAyl LBut WAba
	'Onesta' (SWL)	CWGr
	'Only Love' (MS-c)	CWGr
	'Onslow Michelle' (SD)	CWGr
	'Onslow Renown' (LS-c)	CWGr
	'Opal' (SBa)	CWGr
	'Optic Illusion' (SD)	CWGr
	'Opus' (SD)	CWGr
	'Orange Berger's Record' (MS-c)	CWGr
	'Orange Fire' (MS-c)	CWGr
	'Orange Jewel' (SWL)	CWGr
	'Orange Keith's Choice' (MD)	CWGr NHal
	'Orange Mullett' (MinD/DwB)	CBos CWGr
	'Orange Nugget' (MinBa)	CWGr LRHS
I	'Orange Queen' (MC)	CWGr
	'Orange Sun' (LD)	CWGr
	'Oranjestad' (SWL)	CWGr
	'Orel' (Col)	CWGr WAba
	'Oreti Classic' (MinD) **new**	NHal
	'Orfeo' (MC)	CWGr
I	'Orion' (MD)	CWGr
	'Ornamental Rays' (SC)	CWGr LBut
	'Othello' (MS-c)	CWGr
	'Otto's Thrill' **new**	EPfP
	'Pacific Argyle' (SD)	NHal
	'Pacific Revival' (Pom)	NHal
	'Paint Box' (MS-c)	CWGr
	'Palomino' (MinD)	CWGr
	'Pamela' (SD)	CWGr
	'Park Princess' (SC/DwB)	CWGr LRHS NHal
	'Parkflamme' (MinD)	CWGr
	'Paroa Gillian' (SC)	CWGr
	'Party Girl'	NHal
	'Paso Doble' misapplied (Anem)	see *D.* 'Freya's Paso Doble'
	'Pat Mark' (LS-c)	CWGr NHal
	'Pat 'n' Dee' (SD)	CWGr
	'Pat Seed' (MD)	CWGr
	'Patricia' (Col)	NHal
	'Paul Critchley' (SC)	CWGr
	'Paul's Delight' (SD)	CWGr
	'Peace Pact' (SWL)	CWGr WAba
	'Peach Athalie' (SC)	CWGr
	'Peach Cupid' (MinBa) 🏆H3	CWGr LBut WAba
§	'Peach Melba' (SD)	NHal
	'Peaches and Cream'PBR	CWGr WWol
	'Pearl Hornsey' (SD)	CWGr
	'Pearl of Heemstede' (SD) 🏆H3	LAyl NHal
	'Pearl Sharowean' (MS-c)	WAba
	'Pearson's Ben' (SS-c)	CWGr
	'Pearson's Mellanie' (SC)	CWGr
	'Pecos'PBR **new**	WAba
	'Pembroke Pattie' (Pom)	CWGr
	'Pennsclout' (GD)	CWGr
	'Pennsgift' (GD)	CWGr
	'Pensford Marion' (Pom)	WAba
	'Perfectos' (MC)	CWGr
	'Periton' (MinBa)	CWGr
	'Peter' (MinD)	CWGr
I	'Peter' (LD)	LRHS
	'Peter Nelson' (SBa)	CWGr
	'Petit Bôt' (SS-c)	CWGr
	'Petit Byoux'	CWGr

'Philis Farmer' (SWL) CWGr
I 'Phoenix' (MD) CWGr WAba
'Pianella' (SS-c) CWGr
'Pim's Moonlight' (MS-c) CWGr
'Pineholt Princess' (LD) CWGr
'Pinelands Pam' (MS-c) CWGr LAyl NHal
'Pink Attraction' (MinD) CWGr
'Pink Breckland Joy' (MD) CWGr
'Pink Carol' (Pom) CWGr
'Pink Giraffe' (O) CWGr
'Pink Honeymoon Dress' (SD) CWGr
'Pink Jupiter' (GS-c) NHal
'Pink Katisha' (MinD) CWGr
'Pink Kerkrade' (SC) CWGr
'Pink Loveliness' (SWL) CWGr
'Pink Newby' (MinD) CWGr
'Pink Pastelle' (MS-c) Y[H3] CWGr NHal WAba
'Pink Preference' (SS-c) CWGr
'Pink Robin Hood' (SBa) CWGr
'Pink Sensation' (SC) Y[H3] LBut
'Pink Shirley Alliance' (SC) LAyl
'Pink Suffusion' (SD) WAba
'Pink Sylvia' (MinD) CWGr
'Pink Worton Ann' (MinD) CWGr
'Piperoo' (MC) CWGr
'Piper's Pink' (SS-c/DwB) CWGr LAyl
I 'Pippa' (MinWL) LBut
'Playa Blanca' LRHS
'Playboy' (GD) CWGr
'Plum Surprise' (Pom) CWGr
'Polar Sight' (GC) CWGr
'Polly Bergen' (MD) CWGr
'Polly Peachum' (SD) CWGr
'Polventon Supreme' (SBa) CWGr
'Polyand' (LD) CWGr
'Pontiac' (SC) CWGr LAyl
'Pooh' (Col) NHal
'Pop Willo' (Pom) CWGr
I 'Poppet' (Pom) CWGr WAba
'Popular Guest' (MS-c/Fim) CWGr
'Porcelain' (SWL) Y[H3] LBut
'Potgieter' (MinBa) CWGr
'Pot-Pourri' (MinD) CWGr
'Prefect' (MS-c) CWGr
'Prefere' CWGr LRHS
'Preference' (SS-c) CWGr SHop
'Preston Park' (Sin/DwB) Y[H3] CBgR CWGr LAyl MAJR NHal
Pride of Berlin see *D.* 'Stolze von Berlin'
'Pride of Holland' (LC) CWGr
'Prime Minister' (GD) CWGr
'Primeur' (MS-c) CWGr
'Primrose Accord' (LS-c) CWGr
'Primrose Diane' (SD) WAba
'Primrose Pastelle' (MS-c) NHal WAba
'Primrose Rustig' (MD) CWGr
'Prince Valiant' (SD) CWGr
'Princess Beatrix' (LD) CWGr
'Princess Marie José' (Sin) CWGr
'Pristine' (Pom) CWGr
'Procyon' (SD) CSut CWGr EPfP LRHS
'Prom' (Pom) CWGr
'Promise' (MS-c/Fim) CWGr
'Punky' (Pom) CWGr
'Purbeck Lydia' (LS-c) CWGr
'Purbeck Princess' (MinD) CWGr
I 'Purity' (SS-c) CWGr
'Purper R'O'Sehen' CWGr
'Purpinca' (Anem) CWGr WAba
'Purple Cottesmore' (MWL) CWGr
'Purple Gem' CWGr LRHS
'Purple Sensation' (SS-c) CWGr
'Purple Tai Hei Jo' (GD) CWGr
'Pussycat' (SD) CWGr
'Quel Diable' (LS-c) CWGr
'Quick Step' CWGr
'Rachel's Place' (Pom) CWGr
'Radfo' (SS-c) CWGr WAba
'Radiance' (MC) CWGr
'Raffles' (SD) CWGr LAyl
'Ragged Robin'[PBR] (Misc) CAvo MBri WKif
'Raiser's Pride' (MC) NHal WAba
'Raspberry Ripple' (SS-c) CWGr
'Rebecca Lynn' (MinD) CWGr
'Red Admiral' (MinBa) CWGr
'Red Alert' (LBa) CWGr
'Red Arrows' (SD) CWGr
'Red Balloon' (SBa) CWGr
'Red Beauty' (SD) CWGr
'Red Cap' (MinD) CWGr
'Red Carol' (Pom) CWGr
'Red Diamond' (MD) CWGr NHal
'Red Highlight' (LS-c) CWGr
'Red Kaiser Wilhelm' (SBa) CWGr
'Red Majorette' (SS-c) CWGr
'Red Pimpernel' (SD) CWGr
'Red Pygmy' (SS-c) CWGr
'Red Riding Hood' (MinBa) CWGr
'Red Schweitzer' (MinD) CWGr
'Red Sensation' (MD) CWGr
'Red Sunset' (MS-c) CWGr
'Red Triumph' (SD) CWGr
'Red Velvet' (SWL) CWGr LAyl
'Red Warrior' (Pom) CWGr
'Reddy' (Dwf Lil) CWGr
'Reedly' (SD) CWGr LBut
'Reese's Dream' (GD) **new** CWGr
'Regal Boy' (SBa) CWGr WAba
'Reginald Keene' (LS-c) NHal
'Reliance' (SBa) CWGr
'Rembrandt (USA)' (Dwf Sin) CWGr
'Renato Tozio' (SD) CWGr
'Requiem' (SD) CBos CSut CWGr WAba
'Reverend P. Holian' (GS-c) CWGr
'Rhonda' (Pom) CWGr NHal
'Richard Howells' (MinD) CWGr
'Richard Marc' (SC) CWGr
'Richard S' (LS-c) NHal
'Riisa' (MinBa) CWGr WAba
'Risca Miner' (SBa) CWGr WAba
'Rita Easterbrook' (LD) CWGr
'Roan' (MinD) CWGr
'Robann Royal' (MinBa) CWGr
'Robbie Huston' (LS-c) CWGr
'Robert Too' (MinD) CWGr
I 'Roberta' (SD) WAba
'Robin Hood' (SBa) CWGr WAba
'Rockcliffe' (MinD) WAba
'Rockcliffe Gold' (MS-c) CWGr
'Rokesly Mini' (MinC) CWGr
'Rokewood Candy' (MS-c) CWGr
* 'Rokewood Opal' (SC) CWGr
'Roodkapje' (Sin) CWGr
'Rosalinde' (S-c) CWGr
'Rose Cupid' (MinBa) CWGr
'Rose Jupiter' (GS-c) CWGr LRHS NHal
'Rose Tendre' (MS-c) CWGr
'Rosella' (MD) CSut CWGr EPfP LRHS
'Rosemary Webb' (SD) CWGr
'Rossendale Luke' (SD) CWGr WAba
'Rosy Cloud' (MD) CWGr
'Rothesay Castle' (MinD/DwB) CWGr

	Name	Suppliers
	'Rothesay Herald' (SD/DwB)	CWGr
	'Rothesay Reveller' (MD)	CWGr
	'Rothesay Robin' (SD)	CWGr WAba
	'Rothesay Rose' (SWL)	CWGr
	'Rothesay Snowflake' (SWL)	CWGr
	'Rotonde' (SC)	CWGr
	'Rotterdam' (MS-c)	CWGr
I	'Roxy'	CM&M CWGr EBee EMan EMil ENot EPfP ERou EUJe EVFa LAst LAyl LRHS MBri MMil MWgw NGdn NVic SPav SPla WAba WCot WWeb WWol
	'Royal Blood'[PBR] (Misc)	CAvo MBri
	'Royal Visit' (SD)	CWGr
	'Royal Wedding' (LS-c)	CWGr
	'Ruby Red' (MinBa)	CWGr
	'Ruby Wedding' (MinD)	CWGr
	'Ruskin Belle' (MS-c)	CWGr
I	'Ruskin Buttercup'	CWGr
	'Ruskin Charlotte' (MS-c)	CWGr LAyl NHal WAba
	'Ruskin Delight' (SS-c)	CWGr
	'Ruskin Diana'	LBut NHal WAba
	'Ruskin Dynasty' (SD)	CWGr
	'Ruskin Emil' (SS-c)	CWGr
	'Ruskin Gypsy' (SBa)	CWGr
	'Ruskin Impact' (SD)	WAba
	'Ruskin Lilo' (SD)	WAba
*	'Ruskin Marigold' (SS-c)	CWGr LAyl LBut NHal
	'Ruskin Myra' (SS-c)	NHal
	'Ruskin Orient' (SS-c)	CWGr
	'Ruskin Petite' (MinBa)	CWGr
	'Russell Turner' (SS-c)	CWGr
	'Rustig' (MD)	CWGr WAba
	'Rusty Hope' (MinD)	CWGr
	'Rutland Water' (SD)	CWGr SUsu
	'Ryecroft Jan' (MinBa) **new**	NHal
	'Ryedale King' (LD)	CWGr
	'Ryedale Pinky' (SD)	CWGr
	'Ryedale Rebecca' (GS-c)	CWGr
	'Ryedale Sunshine' (SD)	CWGr WAba
	'Safe Shot' (MD)	CWGr
	'Sailor' (MS-c)	CWGr
	'Saint Croix' (GS-c)	CWGr
	'Saint Moritz' (SS-c)	CWGr
*	'Saladin' (Misc)	CWGr
	'Salmon Carpet' (MinD)	CWGr
	'Salmon Hornsey' (SD)	CWGr
	'Salmon Jupiter' (LS-c) **new**	WAba
	'Salmon Keene' (LS-c)	NHal WAba
	'Salmon Symbol' (MS-c)	WAba
	'Sam Hopkins' (MWL/SWL) **new**	NHal
	'Sam Huston' (GD)	LAyl NHal WAba
	'Samantha'	see *D.* 'Harvest Samantha'
	'Sans Souci' (GC)	CWGr
	'Santa Claus' (SD)	CWGr
	'Sarabande' (MS-c)	CWGr
	'Sarah G' (LS-c)	CWGr
	'Sarah Jane' (LD)	CWGr
	'Sarah Louise' (SWL)	CWGr
	'Sarum Aurora' (SD)	CWGr
	'Sascha' (SWL) **new**	NHal
	'Sassy' (MinD)	CWGr
	'Satellite' (MS-c)	CWGr
	'Saynomore' (SWL)	CWGr
	'Scarborough Ace' (MD)	CWGr
	'Scarlet Comet' (Anem)	CWGr
	'Scarlet Rotterdam' (MS-c)	CWGr WAba
	'Scaur Pinky' (MinD) **new**	NHal
	'Scaur Princess' (SD)	CWGr
	'Scaur Snowball' (MinD) **new**	NHal
	'Scaur Swinton' (MD)	CWGr LAyl NHal
	'Schloss Reinbek' (Sin)	CWGr
	'Schweitzer's Kokarde' (MinD)	CWGr
	'Scura' (Dwf Sin)	CBgR CWGr
	'Seattle' (SD)	CWGr LRHS
	'Seikeman's Feuerball' (MinD)	WAba
	'Senzoe Brigitte' (MinD)	CWGr
	'Severin's Triumph' (LD)	CWGr
	'Shandy' (SS-c)	CWGr EVFa LAyl NHal
	'Shannon' (SD)	CWGr EPfP
	'Sharon Ann' (LS-c)	CWGr
	'Sheila Mooney' (LD)	CWGr
	sherffii	CHad CHal CWGr MCCP MNrw
	sherffii* x *coccinea	CHad
	'Sherwood Monarch' (GS-c)	CWGr
	'Sherwood Standard' (MD)	CWGr WAba
	'Sherwood Sunrise' (SD)	CWGr
	'Sherwood Titan' (GD)	CWGr
	'Shiloh Noelle' (GD)	CWGr
	'Shining Star' (SC)	CWGr
	'Shirley Alliance' (SC)	WAba
	'Shooting Star' (LS-c)	CWGr
	'Shy Princess' (MC)	CWGr
	'Siedlerstolz' (LD)	CWGr
	'Siemen Doorenbos' (Anem)	WAba
	'Silver City' (LD)	CWGr NHal
	'Silver Slipper' (SS-c)	CWGr
	'Silver Years' (MD)	CWGr
	'Sir Alf Ramsey' (GD)	LAyl NHal WAba
*	'Sisa' (SD)	CWGr
	'Skipley Spot' (SD)	CWGr
	'Skipper Rock' (GD)	CWGr
	'Sky High' (SD)	CWGr
	'Small World' (Pom) ♀H3	LAyl NHal WAba
	'Smokey'	CWGr EPfP LRHS
	'Smoky O' (MS-c)	CWGr
	'Sneezy' (Sin)	CWGr LRHS
	'Snip' (MinS-c)	CWGr WAba
	'Snoho Barbara' (MS-c)	CWGr
	'Snoho Christmas'	CWGr
	'Snoho Tammie' (MinBa)	CWGr
	'Snow Cap' (SS-c)	CWGr
	'Snow Fairy' (MinC)	CWGr
	'Snow White' (Dwf Sin)	CWGr
	'Snowflake' (SWL)	CWGr WAba
	'Snowstorm' (MD)	CSut
	'Snowy' (MinBa)	CWGr
	'So Dainty' (MinS-c) ♀H3	CAby CWGr LAyl WAba
	'Sondervig' (SD)	CWGr
	'Song of Olympia' (SWL)	CWGr
	'Sonia'	CWGr
	'Sorrento Fiesta' (SS-c)	WAba
	'Sorrento Girl' (SS-c)	WAba
	'Sorrento Style' (SD)	WAba
	'Soulman'	CWGr
	'Sourire de Crozon' (SD)	CWGr
	'Souvenir d'Eté' (Pom)	CWGr
	'Spartacus' (LD)	CSut
	'Spassmacher' (MS-c)	CWGr
	'Spectacular' (SD)	CWGr
	'Spencer' (SD)	CWGr
	'Spennythorn King' (SD)	CWGr
	'Spikey Symbol' (MS-c)	CWGr
	'Sprinter'	CWGr
	'Star Child' (Misc)	CWGr WAba
	'Star Elite'	CWGr LRHS
	'Star Spectacle' (MS-c)	CWGr
	'Star Surprise' (SC)	CWGr
	'Starry Night' (MinS-c)	CWGr
	'Star's Favourite' (MC)	CWGr

	'Star's Lady' (SC)	CWGr
	'Stefan Bergerhoff' (Dwf D)	CWGr
	'Stella J' (SWL)	CWGr
	'Stella's Delight' (SD)	CWGr
	'Stellyvonne' (LS-c/Fim)	CWGr
	'Stephanie' (SS-c)	CWGr
§	'Stolz von Berlin' (MinBa)	CWGr EPfP WAba
	'Stoneleigh Cherry' (Pom)	LAyl
	'Stoneleigh Joyce' (Pom)	CWGr
	'Storm Warning' (GD)	CWGr
	'Stylemaster' (MC)	CWGr
	'Sue Mountjoy' (Col) **new**	CWGr
	'Sue Willo' (Pom)	CWGr
	'Suffolk Fantasy' (SWL)	CWGr
	'Suffolk Punch' (MD)	CBgR CWGr LAyl LBut
	'Suitzus Julie' (Lil)	CWGr
	'Summer Festival' (SD)	CWGr
	'Summer Night' (SC)	CAby CHad ECGP LAyl NHal
	'Summer's End'	CWGr
	'Sungold' (MinBa)	CWGr
	'Sunlight Pastelle' (MS-c)	CWGr WAba
*	'Sunny Boy' (MinBa)	CWGr LRHS WAba
	'Sunray Glint' (MS-c)	CWGr WAba
	'Sunray Silk' (MS-c)	CWGr
	'Sunset' (SD) **new**	WAba
I	'Sunshine' (Sin)	LAyl WWeb
	'Sunshine Paul' (MD) **new**	WAba
	'Sunstruck' (MS-c)	CWGr
	'Super Rays' (MC)	CWGr
	'Super Trouper' (SD)	CWGr
	'Superfine' (SC)	CWGr WAba
	'Sure Thing' (MC)	CWGr
	'Susan Willo' (Pom)	CWGr
	'Susannah York' (SWL)	CWGr
	'Suzette' (Dwf SD)	CWGr
	'Swallow Falls' (SD)	CWGr
	'Swan Lake' (SD)	LPio MBri WWol
	'Swanvale' (SD)	CWGr
	'Sweet Content' (SD)	CWGr
	'Sweet Sensation' (MS-c)	WAba
	'Sweetheart' (SD)	CBgR LRHS WAba
	'Swiss Miss' (MinBa/O)	CWGr
I	'Sylvia' (SBa) **new**	WAba
	'Sylvia's Desire' (SC)	CWGr WAba
	'Symbol' (MS-c)	CWGr
	'Sympathy' (SWL)	WAba
	'Syston Harlequin' (SD)	CWGr
	'Syston Sofia' (MinBa)	CWGr
	'Tahiti Sunrise' (MS-c)	CWGr
	'Tally Ho' (Misc) ♀H3	CBgR CM&M CWGr EBee EMan ENot ERou EUJe LPio LRHS MBri MSph MWgw NCob SDys SPav SPla WAba WCot WWhi WWol
	'Taratahi Lilac'	see *D.* 'Lilac Taratahi'
	'Taratahi Ruby' (SWL) ♀H3	CWGr LBut NHal WAba
	'Tartan' (MD)	CWGr
	'Teesbrooke Audrey' (Col)	LAyl NHal WAba
	'Temptress' (SC)	CWGr
	'Tender Moon' (SD)	CWGr
	tenuicaulis **new**	CWGr
	'Thames Valley' (MD)	CWGr
	'That's It!' (SD)	CWGr
	'The Baron' (SD)	CWGr
	'Thelma Clements' (LD)	CWGr
	'Theo Springers' (SD)	CWGr
	'Thomas A. Edison' (MD)	CSut CWGr EPfP
	'Thoresby Jewel' (SD)	CWGr
	'Tiara' (SD)	CWGr
	'Tiffany Lynn' (Misc)	CWGr
	'Tiger Eye' (MD)	CWGr
	'Tiger Tiv' (MD)	CWGr
	'Tina B' (SBa)	CWGr
	'Tinker's White' (SD)	CWGr
	'Tioga Spice' (MS-c/Fim)	CWGr NHal
	'Toga' (SWL)	CWGr
	'Tohsuikyou' (Misc)	CWGr WAba
	'Tommy Doc' (SS-c)	CWGr WAba
	'Tommy Keith' (MinBa)	CWGr
	'Tomo' (SD)	LAyl NHal
	'Top Affair' (MS-c)	CWGr
	'Top Totty' (MinD) **new**	NHal
*	'Topaz Puff'	LRHS
*	'Toto' (DwB)	CWGr NHal
	'Townley Class' (SD)	CWGr
I	'Tranquility' (Col)	NHal
	'Trelawny' (GD)	WAba
	'Trelyn Kiwi' (SC)	WAba
	'Trengrove Autumn' (MD)	CWGr
	'Trengrove d'Or' (MD)	CWGr
	'Trengrove Jill' (MD)	CWGr LAyl
	'Trengrove Millennium' (MD) **new**	CWGr NHal
	'Trengrove Tauranga' (MD)	CWGr
	'Trengrove Terror' (GD)	CWGr
	'Trevelyn Kiwi' (S-c)	NHal
	'Trevor' (Col)	CWGr
	'Tropical Sunset'	CWGr
	'Tsuki-yorine-shisha' (MC)	CWGr
	'Tsuki-ytori-no-shisha' (MC) **new**	WAba
	'Tu Tu' (MS-c)	CWGr
	'Tui Avis' (MinC)	CWGr
	'Tui Orange' (SS-c)	CWGr WAba
	'Tui Ruth' (SS-c)	CWGr
	'Tujays Lemondrop' (SD)	NHal
	'Tula Rosa' (Pom)	CWGr
	'Tutankhamun' (Pom)	CWGr
	'Twiggy' (SWL)	CWGr LRHS
	'Twilight Time' (MD)	CWGr EPfP LPio LRHS WWol
	'Twyning's Candy' **new**	CWGr
	'Twyning's Chocolate' **new**	CWGr
	'Uchuu' (GD)	CWGr
	'Union Jack' (Sin)	CWGr WAba
	'United' (SD)	CWGr
	'Usugesho' (LD)	CWGr
	'Vader Abraham' (MinD)	CWGr
	'Vaguely Noble' (SBa)	CWGr
	'Valentine Lil' (SWL)	CWGr
	'Vancouver' (Misc)	CWGr
	'Vanquisher' (LS-c)	CWGr
	'Variace' (MinBa)	CWGr
	'Vesuvius' (MD)	CWGr
	'Vicky Crutchfield' (SWL)	LBut
	'Vicky Jackson' (SWL)	CWGr
	'Victory Day' (LC)	CWGr
	'Vidal Rhapsody' (MS-c)	CWGr
	'Vigor' (SWL)	CWGr
	'Vinovium' (MinBa)	CWGr
	'Violet Davies' (MS-c)	CWGr
	'Vivex' (MinBa)	CWGr
	'Volkskanzler' (Sin)	CWGr
	'Vrouwe Jacoba' (SS-c)	CWGr
	'Vulcan' (LS-c)	CWGr
	'Vuurvogel' (MS-c)	CSut CWGr
	'Walter Hardisty' (GD)	CWGr
	'Walter James' (SD)	CWGr
	'Wanborough Gem' (SBa)	CWGr
	'Wanda's Aurora' (GD)	NHal
	'Wanda's Capella' (GD)	CWGr NHal WAba
	'Wanda's Moonlight' (GD)	CWGr
	'Wandy' (Pom) ♀H3	CWGr WAba
I	'War of the Roses'	WHer
	'Warkton Willo' (Pom)	CWGr
	'Warmunda'	LRHS
	'Washington'	CWGr

'Waveney Pearl' (SWL) CWGr
'Welcome Guest' (MS-c) CWGr WAba
'Welsh Beauty' (SBa) CWGr
'Wendy' (MinBa) CWGr
'Wendy Spencer' (MinD) CWGr
'Wendy's Place' (Pom) CWGr
'Weston Aramac' (SS-c) CWGr
'Weston Forge' (SC) CWGr
'Weston Miss' (MinS-c) CWGr NHal
'Weston Nugget' (MinC) CWGr WAba
'Weston Pirate' (MinC) ♀H3 **new** NHal
'Weston Princekin' (MinS-c) CWGr
'Weston Spanish Dancer' (MinC) ♀H3 CWGr LBut NHal WAba
'Whale's Rhonda' (Pom) WAba
'Wheel' (Col) WAba
'White Alva's' (GD) ♀H3 CWGr LAyl NHal
'White Aster' (Pom) EPfP
'White Ballerina' (SWL) **new** NHal
'White Ballet' (SD) ♀H3 CWGr LAyl LBut NHal
'White Charlie Two' (MD) NHal
'White Hunter' (SD) CWGr
'White Klankstad' (SC) CWGr
'White Knight' (MinD) NHal
'White Linda' (SD) CWGr NHal
'White Mathilda' (Dwf) CWGr
'White Merriwell' (SD) CWGr
'White Moonlight' (MS-c) LAyl LBut NHal WAba
'White Nettie' (MinBa) CWGr
'White Pastelle' (MS-c) WAba
'White Perfection' (LD) CSut CWGr EPfP
'White Polventon' (SBa) CWGr NHal
'White Rustig' (MD) CWGr
'White Star' CWGr LRHS
'White Swallow' (SS-c) NHal
'Wicky Woo' (SD) CWGr
'Wildwood Marie' (SWL) CWGr
'Willemse Glory' (Misc Orch) CWGr
'William 'B'' (GD) CWGr
'Williamsburg' (MS-c) CWGr
'Willo's Borealis' (Pom) CWGr NHal
'Willo's Flecks' (Pom) WAba
'Willo's Night' (Pom) CWGr
'Willo's Surprise' (Pom) CWGr NHal
'Willo's Violet' (Pom) CWGr NHal WAba
'Willowfield Kay' (MS-c) WAba
'Willowfield Matthew' (MinD) NHal WAba
'Willowfield Mick' (LD) CWGr LAyl NHal WAba
'Winholme Diane' (SD) CWGr NHal WAba
'Winkie Colonel' (GD) CWGr
'Winnie' (Pom) CWGr
'Winsome' (SWL) CWGr
'Winston Churchill' (MinD) CWGr LBut
'Winter Dawn' (SWL) CWGr
'Wise Guy' (GD) CWGr
'Wisk' (Pom) CWGr
'Wittem' (MD) CWGr
'Wittemans Superba' (SS-c) ♀H3 CWGr LAyl NHal SDix
'Wootton Cupid' (MinBa) ♀H3 CWGr LBut NHal WAba
'Wootton Impact' (MS-c) ♀H3 NHal
'Wootton Phebe' (SD) CWGr
'Wootton Tempest' (MS-c) CWGr
'Worton Bluestreak' (SS-c) CWGr
'Worton Revival' (MD) CWGr
'Worton Superb' (SD) CWGr
'Wundal Horizon' (LS-c) CWGr
'Yellow Abundance' (SD) CWGr
'Yellow Baby' (Pom) CWGr
I 'Yellow Bird' (Col) CWGr
'Yellow Frank Hornsey' (SD) WAba
'Yellow Galator' (MC) CWGr
'Yellow Hammer' (Sin/DwB) ♀H3 CBgR CWGr LAyl NHal SChu
'Yellow Linda's Chester' (SC) CWGr
'Yellow Pages' (SD) CWGr
'Yellow Pet' (SD) CWGr
'Yellow Snow' (MD) CWGr
'Yellow Spiky' (MS-c) CWGr
'Yellow Star' (MS-c) CWGr
'Yellow Symbol' (MS-c) CWGr LBut
'Yellow Twist' CHad
'Yelno Enchantment' (SWL) CWGr LAyl
'Yelno Firelight' (SWL) CWGr
'Yelno Harmony' (SD) ♀H3 CWGr LBut
'Yelno Petite Glory' (MinD) CWGr
'York and Lancaster' (MD) CWGr EMon IGor
'Yorkie' (MS-c) CWGr WAba
'Yoro Kobi' (DwB) NHal
'Yukino' (Col) CWGr
I 'Yvonne' (MWL) WAba
'Zagato' (MinD) CWGr
* 'Zakuro-fubuki' (MD) CWGr
'Zakuro-hime' (SD) CWGr
I 'Zelda' (LD) CWGr
'Zest' (MinD) CWGr
'Zing' (LS-c) CWGr
'Zorro' (GD) ♀H3 CWGr NHal WAba
'Zurich' (SS-c) CWGr

Dais (*Thymelaeaceae*)

cotinifolia EShb

Daiswa see *Paris*

Dalea (*Papilionaceae*)

candida SUsu
purpurea SUsu

Dalechampia (*Euphorbiaceae*)

dioscoreifolia CPLN ERea ESlt

Dampiera (*Goodeniaceae*)

diversifolia ECou
lanceolata ECou
teres ECou

damson see *Prunus insititia*

Danae (*Ruscaceae*)

§ ***racemosa*** CBcs CFil EBee ELan EMon ENot EPfP EPla ETow GCal IDee LRHS MGos MRav SAPC SArc SBrw SPer SRms SSpi SSta WCot WDin

Danthonia (*Poaceae*)

californica CBig

Daphne ✿ (*Thymelaeaceae*)

acutiloba CFil CPMA EPot ERea GAbr GIBF GKev GKir SAga SSpi
albowiana CFil CPMA CPle EWes SAga SBla SSpi WCru
'Allison Carver' (v) CPMA
alpina CPMA EHyt GAbr GKev SBla
altaica CPMA
arbuscula ♀H4 CPMA EPot NMen SBla SIgm

	- subsp. ***arbuscula*** f. ***albiflora***	SBla
	- f. ***radicans***	CPMA
	bholua	CAbP CHll CPMA ECho ERea LRHS MGos MWya SPoG SReu SSpi SSta WAbe WCru WPat
I	- 'Alba'	CBcs CEnd CFil CLAP CPMA EPfP GAbr GKir LTwo MAsh MGos NLar SBla SCoo SMur SPoG SSpi SSta WCru WPGP
	- 'Darjeeling'	CBrm CFil CLAP CPLG CPMA EPfP LRHS MAsh SLon SSpi SSta WPGP
	- var. ***glacialis***	WCru
	- - 'Gurkha'	CFil CPMA ELan ENot EPfP SBla SSpi WPGP
	- 'Glendoick'	EPfP GGGa MAsh
	- 'Jacqueline Postill' ♀H3	More than 30 suppliers
	- 'Peter Smithers'	CLAP EPot SBla SCoo SReu SSpi SSta
	- 'Rupina La' SCH 2611	SBla
	blagayana	CBcs CFil CPMA EPot GAbr GCrs GGGa GKev GKir MDun MWya NEgg SBla SIgm SRms SSpi WFar
	- 'Brenda Anderson'	ITim SBla
	'Bramdean'	see *D.* x *napolitana* 'Bramdean'
	x ***burkwoodii*** ♀H4	CBcs EBee ECho ECrN EPot GKir MWya SAga SHBN SLon WBrE WDin WGwG
	- 'Albert Burkwood'	CBcs CPMA GKir LTwo MDun NLar NWea WBrE
	- 'Astrid' (v)	CBcs CPMA EBee ENot LRHS MGos MLan SCoo SMrm SMur SPoG SSta WDin WWes
	- Briggs Moonlight = 'Brimoon' (v)	LRHS
§	- 'Carol Mackie' (v)	CBcs CPMA GAbr GGGa GKir LRHS LTwo MDun MGos NLar SIgm SSta
	- 'G.K. Argles' (v) ♀H4	CBcs CFil CPMA ERea GKir LAst LRHS LSRN MAsh MBri MDun MGos MLan MWya WBrE WFar WWes
I	- 'Gold Sport' **new**	MWya
	- 'Gold Strike' (v)	CPMA
	- 'Golden Treasure' **new**	LRHS SBla
	- 'Lavenirei'	CPMA NLar
	- 'Somerset'	CBcs CDul CEnd CFil CPMA CWSG ELan ENot EPfP GKir LRHS MDun MGos MSwo NBlu NWea SAga SBla SHBN SIng SLim SPer SPla SPoG SReu SSta WDin WOrn
§	- 'Somerset Gold Edge' (v)	CPMA
§	- 'Somerset Variegated' (v)	LAst SAga WPat
I	- 'Variegata' (v)	EBee ENot WPat
	- 'Variegata' broad cream edge	see *D.* x *burkwoodii* 'Somerset Variegated'
	- 'Variegata' broad gold edge	see *D.* x *burkwoodii* 'Somerset Gold Edge'
	- 'Variegata' narrow gold edge	see *D.* x *burkwoodii* 'Carol Mackie'
	caucasica	CPMA SBla
	circassica	SBla
	cneorum	CBcs CFil CPMA ENot EPfP LRHS MGos NMen SMur SSpi WDin WPat
	- f. ***alba***	CPMA SBla
	- 'Blackthorn Triumph'	CPMA SBla
	- 'Eximia' ♀H4	CBcs CPMA EPot GAbr MDun MGos MLan SBla SHBN SIng SRms SSpi SUsu
	- 'Grandiflora'	see *D.* x *napolitana* 'Maxima'
	- 'Lac des Gloriettes'	CPMA
	- 'Puszta'	CPMA SAga WCru
	- var. ***pygmaea***	CPMA EPot SBla
	- - 'Alba'	CPMA SBla
	- 'Rose Glow'	CPMA
	- 'Ruby Glow' **new**	EPot MWya
	- 'Stasek' (v)	CPMA SBla
	- 'Variegata' (v)	CBcs CPMA ECho EPot MGos MMil NWCA SHBN SIng
	- 'Velký Kosir'	CPMA WAbe
	- var. ***verlotii*** x ***arbuscula***	CPMA
	collina	see *D. sericea* Collina Group
	'Fragrant Cloud' (aff. acutiloba)	EWes CPMA SBla WBcn
	genkwa	LRHS SBla
	giraldii	CPMA EHyt MDun SIgm SSpi
	aff. ***giraldii***	GKir NMen
	x ***hendersonii***	CEnd CPMA EPot
	- 'Appleblossom'	CPMA GEdr SBla
	- 'Aymon Correvon'	CPMA SBla
	- 'Blackthorn Rose'	SBla
	- 'Ernst Hauser'	CPMA EPot GAbr GEdr GKir LTwo MDun SBla SSpi SUsu WAbe
	- 'Fritz Kummert'	CPMA SBla WAbe
	- 'Kath Dryden'	SBla
	- 'Marion White'	SBla
	- 'Rosebud'	CPMA SBla
	x ***houtteana***	CBot CPMA LTwo MDun MGos MWya NBir SPoG WBcn
	x ***hybrida***	CEnd CPMA ECho SBla
	japonica 'Striata'	see *D. odora* 'Aureomarginata'
	jasminea	CPMA ECho NMen SBla
	jezoensis	CPMA GIBF LRHS SBla SSta WCru
	juliae	CPMA SBla
	kamtschatica **new**	GIBF
	kosaninii	GKev
	laureola	CFil CPMA CSWP EPfP GKev MGos MSte NBir NPer WCFE WGwG WPGP WWye
	- var. ***cantabrica***	SChu
	- 'Margaret Mathew'	CPMA EPot
	- subsp. ***philippi***	CBcs CBgR CPMA CPle CWSG EBee ELan EPfP GKir LRHS MAsh NDlv NMen SChu SHBN SPer SSpi SSta WCru WFar
	'Leila Haines' x ***arbuscula***	see *D.* x *schlyteri*
	longilobata	CPle NSla
	- 'Peter Moore'	SBla
	x ***manteniana***	MGos
	- 'Manten'	CPMA EPot GEdr LRHS LTwo MDun MWya SPoG
	x ***mauerbachii*** 'Perfume of Spring'	CPMA SBla
	'Meon'	see *D.* x *napolitana* 'Meon'
	mezereum	More than 30 suppliers
	- f. ***alba***	CFil CPMA CPle CWib EBee EHyt EPfP GAbr GIBF GKir LRHS MBar MDun MGos NChi NEgg SBla SHBN SPer SRms WCru WPat WTin
	- - 'Bowles' Variety'	CBot CPMA EPot GAbr
	- 'Rosea'	SRms
	- var. ***rubra***	CBcs CDul CFil CPMA CSBt CWSG CWib EBee ELan EPfP EWTr GKir MGos MSwo NBlu SBod SPer SPoG WCru WDin WOrn
	x ***napolitana*** ♀H4	CPMA EBee ECho EMil EPot GAbr GGGa GKir MDun MGos NLar NMen SHBN SOkd SPoG SSpi SUsu WAbe WBrE
§	- 'Bramdean'	CPMA EPot MDun MWya SBla
§	- 'Maxima'	MGos
§	- 'Meon'	CEnd CPMA EBee EPot GEdr LTwo MWya NMen SBla WAbe WPat

	odora	CBcs CPMA CPle CSBt EPot ERea LRHS LSpr MGos MSwo NMen SChu SSta WDin
§	- f. ***alba***	CEnd CPMA ERea LRHS MGos
I	- 'Aureamarginata Alba' (v)	CPMA ECrN
§	- 'Aureomarginata' (v) ♀H3-4	More than 30 suppliers
	- 'Clotted Cream' (v)	CPMA
	- 'Geisha Girl' (v)	EBee ELan ERea MAsh MGos SBla SSpi
	- var. ***leucantha***	see *D. odora* f. *alba*
	- 'Marginata'	see *D. odora* 'Aureomarginata'
	- var. ***rubra***	CFir LRHS LTwo
	- 'Sakiwaka'	CPMA LTwo
	- 'Walberton' (v)	GKir LRHS MGos SPoG WBcn
	oleoides	CPMA EPot SBla SSpi
	- subsp. ***kurdica*** **new**	GKev
	petraea	SBla WAbe
	- 'Alba'	see *D. petraea* 'Tremalzo'
	- 'Grandiflora'	GCrs NMen SBla WAbe
§	- 'Tremalzo'	SBla
	pontica ♀H4	CBcs CFil CPMA CPle EHyt EPfP EPla GKir MAsh NLar NMen SDix SPoG SSpi SSvw WCot WCru WGwG WPGP
	pseudomezereum	WCru
	retusa	see *D. tangutica* Retusa Group
	'Richard's Choice'	CPMA
	x ***rollsdorfii*** 'Arnold Cihlarz'	CPMA EPot
	- 'Wilhelm Schacht'	CPMA EPot SBla
	'Rosy Wave'	CPMA SAga SBla
§	x ***schlyteri***	CPMA SBla
§	***sericea***	CPMA SBla
§	- Collina Group	CPMA EPfP SBla SPoG SRms SSpi
	- Collina Group x ***petraea***	SSta WAbe
	sureil GWJ 9200 **new**	WCru
	x ***susannae*** 'Anton Fahndrich' x ***sericea*** **Collina Group**	CPMA NLar
	- 'Cheriton'	CPMA EHyt EPot GEdr LTwo NLar SBla SSta WBcn
	- 'Tichborne'	CPMA NMen SBla
	tangutica ♀H4	More than 30 suppliers
	- SDR 1944	GKev
§	- Retusa Group ♀H4	CPMA EHyt EPot GAbr GCrs GGGa GKev GKir ITim MAsh MBri NEgg NLAp NMen NRya SHBN SIgm SRms SSpi WCru WSHC
	- - SDR 3024	GKev
	x ***thauma***	NMen SBla
	x ***transatlantica***	SBla
	'Beulah Cross' (v) **new**	
	- 'Jim's Pride'	SBla
	'Valerie Hillier' **new**	LRHS
	x ***whiteorum*** 'Beauworth'	CPMA LRHS LTwo SBla SIgm WAbe
	- 'Kilmeston'	CPMA LTwo NMen
	- 'Warnford'	CPMA

Daphniphyllum (*Daphniphyllaceae*)

	calycinum	NLar SSpi
	glaucescens B&SWJ 4058	WCru
	- subsp. ***oldhamii*** var. ***oldhamii*** B&SWJ 7056	WCru
	- - var. ***kengii*** B&SWJ 6872	WCru
§	***himalaense*** subsp. ***macropodum***	CBcs CFil CHEx CMCN CWib EBee EPfP NLar SAPC SArc SBrw SDix SLPl SMad SSpi WCru WFar WPGP
	- - B&SWJ 2898	WCru
	- - B&SWJ 581	WCru
	- subsp. ***macropodum*** dwarf	WCru
	- - B&SWJ 6809 from Taiwan	WCru
	- - B&SWJ 8763 from Cheju-Do	WCru
	humile	see *D. himalaense* subsp. *macropodum*
	teijsmannii B&SWJ 3805	WCru

Darlingtonia (*Sarraceniaceae*)

	californica ♀H1	CFil CSWC EEls EFEx LHew MCCP SHmp WSSs

Darmera (*Saxifragaceae*)

§	***peltata*** ♀H4	More than 30 suppliers
	- 'Nana'	CCol CHEx EBee ECha EVFa GBuc GKir MBri MTis NLar WCot WFar WMoo WPnP WWpP

Dasylirion (*Dracaenaceae*)

	sp.	SBLw
	- from Coahuilla, Mexico	EOas
§	***acrotrichum***	SAPC SArc XPep
	glaucophyllum	EAmu WMul
	gracile	see *D. acrotrichum*
	leiophyllum	XPep
	longissimum	CAbb CBrP CTrC EAmu EOas EShb SChr WMul XPep
	serratifolium **new**	EAmu
	texanum	CTrC EOas XPep
	wheeleri ♀H1	CBrP CRoM CTrC EAmu EOas EShb SChr XPep

date see *Phoenix dactylifera*

Datisca (*Datiscaceae*)

	cannabina	CArn EBee ECha EMag EMan GCal GFlt LPhx LPio MGol NBPC NLar SMrm WCot WHil WMoo WPGP

Datura (*Solanaceae*)

	arborea	see *Brugmansia arborea*
	chlorantha	see *Brugmansia chlorantha*
	cornigera	see *Brugmansia arborea*
§	***inoxia*** ♀H3	EBak MGol MSal
	metel	LExo MGol
	- 'Belle Blanche'	MGol
	- 'Triple Yellow' **new**	LExo
	meteloides	see *D. inoxia*
	rosea	see *Brugmansia* x *insignis* pink
	rosei	see *Brugmansia sanguinea*
	sanguinea	see *Brugmansia sanguinea*
	stramonium	CArn LExo MGol MSal
	- var. ***chalybaea***	MSal
	- var. ***inermis***	MSal
	suaveolens	see *Brugmansia suaveolens*
	versicolor	see *Brugmansia versicolor* Lagerh.
	- 'Grand Marnier'	see *Brugmansia* x *candida* 'Grand Marnier'

Daucus (*Apiaceae*)

	carota	CArn CHrt CRWN MBow NMir WHer
	- 'Jane's Lace'	CNat

Davallia (*Davalliaceae*)

	canariensis ♀H1	CFil
§	***mariesii*** ♀H3	CFil WAbe WCot
	tasmanii	CFil WRic

Davidia (*Cornaceae*)

	involucrata ♀H4	More than 30 suppliers

- 'Sonoma' **new**	MBlu
- var. ***vilmoriniana*** 🏆H4	CBcs CDoC ELan EPfP EWTr IMGH LRHS MAsh MCCP MDun MGos NBlu NEgg SHBN SPer SPoG WOrn

Daviesia (*Papilionaceae*)

brevifolia	SPlb

Decaisnea (*Lardizabalaceae*)

fargesii	More than 30 suppliers
- B&SWJ 8070	WCru
insignis	CFil CPLG WNor WPGP

Decodon (*Lythraceae*)

verticillatus	EMon

Decumaria (*Hydrangeaceae*)

barbara	CBcs CMac CPLN EBee EMil LRHS NSti SBra SHBN SLim SLon SPer SSta WCru WFar WSHC
- 'Vicki' **new**	NLar
sinensis	CPLN EPfP SBra SLon SSpi WCru WSHC

Degenia (*Brassicaceae*)

velebitica	EHyt WLin

Deinanthe (*Hydrangeaceae*)

bifida	CDes CLAP CPLG GEdr LEdu WCru
- B&SWJ 5012	WCru
- B&SWJ 5436	GEdr
- B&SWJ 5655	WCru
bifida* x *caerulea	CLAP
caerulea	CDes CLAP GEdr IGor MHar SBla WCru WPGP
- pale-flowered **new**	GEdr

Delonix (*Caesalpiniaceae*)

regia	CSec XBlo

Delosperma (*Aizoaceae*)

HWJK 2179 from Nepal **new**	WCru
HWJK 2263 from Nepal	WCru
LEG 037	CStu
§ ***aberdeenense*** 🏆H1	CHEx
ashtonii	CStu EDAr GEdr WAbe WPer
'Basutoland'	see *D. nubigenum*
congestum	EShb EWll NJOw
cooperi	CStu EChP ECtt EDAr EWll GEdr ITim NJOw NLAp SChr SIng WFar WPat WPer XPep
***ecklonis* new**	EWin
lineare	NBir XPep
lydenburgense	CHEx CTrC SChr
§ ***nubigenum***	CHEx CHal ECtt EDAr ELan EPfP EPot ESis EWin GAbr GEdr GGar ITim LRHS NJOw SPoG WPer
sutherlandii	EDAr EWin EWll NJOw NLAp
- 'Peach Star' **new**	EWin

Delphinium ✿ (*Ranunculaceae*)

'Abendleuchten'	LPhx
'After Midnight'	CNMi
'Agnes Brookes'	ERou
'Ailsa' **new**	CNMi
'Alice Artindale' (d)	CBos CDes CHad EMon IFro LPhx SAga SBla SMrm WCot WPGP WSan
'Alie Duyvensteyn'	ERou
'Alison Claire' **new**	CNMi
ambiguum	see *Consolida ajacis*
'Ann Woodfield'	CNMi
'Anne Kenrick'	CNMi
'Anne Page'	ERou
'Apollo' **new**	NRnb
Astolat Group	More than 30 suppliers
'Atholl' 🏆H4	NRnb
'Baby Doll'	CNMi
Belladonna Group	EShb
- 'Atlantis' 🏆H4	ECha ENot ERou LPhx LRHS MBri SBla SMeo SMrm SOkh WCot
- 'Ballkleid'	EBee ERou
- 'Capri'	EBee
- 'Casa Blanca'	CSim EShb GMaP LRHS MAnH NCGa NLar SBla SMrm WMnd WPer
- 'Cliveden Beauty'	CBot EBee GBri MAnH MRav MSte NCGa NChi NLar NPri SBla WMnd WPer
- 'Delft Blue' **new**	EBee
- 'Moerheimii'	ERou LRHS SMrm
- 'Oriental Blue' **new**	MAnH
- 'Peace'	LRHS
- 'Piccolo'	ECha ENot ERou LBmB LRHS SMrm
- 'Pink Sensation'	see *D.* x *ruysii* 'Pink Sensation'
- 'Völkerfrieden' 🏆H4	EBrs ERou LRHS MBri MRav NGby NPri NPro SOkh
x ***bellamosum***	CBot CSim LRHS MAnH MWgw NCGa NLar WPer
'Berghimmel'	LRHS NGby
'Beryl Burton'	CNMi ERou
Black Knight Group	More than 30 suppliers
'Black Pearl'	EBee ENot
'Blackberry Ice'	CNMi
'Blauwal'	CFir EBee
'Blondie'	CNMi
Blue Bird Group	CBcs CSBt CTri EBee ELan EPfP GKir GLil GMaP LRHS MAnH MBri MRav MWat MWgw NEgg NFor NLar NLon NMir NPri SMer SPer SPla SPoG WCAu WFar WHil WHoo WWeb
'Blue Butterfly'	see *D. grandiflorum* 'Blue Butterfly'
'Blue Dawn' 🏆H4	CBla CNMi ERou
Blue Fountains Group	CSBt EPfP GKir LRHS LSRN MBri NBre SPer SPet SPoG SRms WBVN
Blue Jade Group	CBla ERou
'Blue Jay'	CBcs CTri EBee ENot EPfP LRHS LSRN MBow MWgw NBir NLar NPri SPer SPoG WCAu
'Blue Lagoon'	CBla CNMi
'Blue Mirror'	NArg SRms
'Blue Nile' 🏆H4	CBla CNMi ERou
'Blue Oasis'	CNMi
'Blue Skies'	MAnH NLar NRnb
Blue Springs Group	NGdn NLar
'Blue Tit'	CBla CNMi ERou
'Bruce' 🏆H4	CNMi ERou WCFE
'Butterball'	CBla CNMi NRnb
Cameliard Group	CBcs CSBt EBee ECtt ELan EWTr LRHS MWat MWgw NLar NLon NPri SPer SPoG
'Can-can' 🏆H4	CNMi ERou
cardinale	EHrv NBre
'Carl Topping'	ERou
cashmerianum	MTho WSHC
'Cassius' 🏆H4	CBla CNMi ERou
caucasicum	see *D. speciosum*
ceratophorum	WCru
var. ***ceratophorum*** BWJ 7799 **new**	

	Name	Suppliers
	'Chelsea Star'	CBla CNMi ERou
	'Cher'	CNMi
	'Cherry Blossom'	EWTr GAbr NLar
	'Cherub' ♀^{H4}	CBla ERou
	chinense	see *D. grandiflorum*
	'Christel'	EBee ERou IPot
	'Circe'	ERou
	'Clack's Choice'	CNMi ERou
	'Claire' ♀^{H4}	CNMi
	Clear Springs Series	EHan LIck NArg NBre
	- 'Clear Springs Rose Pink'	NArg
	'Clifford Lass'	CNMi NRnb
	'Clifford Pink'	CBla
	Connecticut Yankees Group	MAnH NArg NBre SRms
	'Conspicuous' ♀^{H4}	CBla CNMi ERou
	'Constance Rivett' ♀^{H4}	ERou
	'Coral Sunset' (d) **new**	EBee ERou SHBN
	'Corinth' **new**	CNMi
	'Cream Cracker'	CNMi
	'Cressida'	ERou
	'Cristella'	ERou
	'Crown Jewel'	CBla ERou WCFE
	'Cupid'	CBla CNMi ERou
	'Darling Sue'	CNMi
	'Darwin's Blue Indulgence'[PBR]	EBee NSti SMrm
	'Darwin's Pink Indulgence'[PBR]	EBee NSti
	delavayi	GKev SBla WCot WRos
	- B&SWJ 7796	WCru
*	'Delfy Blue'	NBre
	'Demavand'	CNMi
	'Dolly Bird'	CBla ERou
	'Dreaming Spires'	SRms
	drepanocentrum **new**	WLin
	'Duchess of Portland'	NRnb
	'Dunsden Green'	CNMi
	dwarf dark blue	LRHS
	dwarf lavender	LRHS
	dwarf pink	LRHS
	dwarf sky blue	LRHS
	'Eelkje'	ERou
	'Eileen Joan' **new**	CNMi
	elatum	CArn GCal MAnH NGdn SRms SSth
	'Elizabeth Cook' ♀^{H4}	CNMi
	'Elmfreude'	EBee
	'Emily Hawkins' ♀^{H4}	CNMi ERou NRnb
	'Eva Gower'	ERou
	'F.W. Smith'	SSth
	'Fanfare'	CBla CNMi ERou NRnb
	'Father Thames'	ERou
	'Faust' ♀^{H4}	CBla CNMi EBee ERou NRnb
	'Fenella' ♀^{H4}	CBla CNMi WCFE
	'Filique Arrow'	CFir
	'Finsteraarhorn'	EBee ERou WCot
	'Florestan'	CNMi
	'Foxhill Nina'	CNMi
	'Franjo Sahin' **new**	CNMi
	Galahad Group	More than 30 suppliers
	'Galileo' ♀^{H4}	CNMi
	'Garden Party'	CBla
	'Gemma'	CNMi
	'Gillian Dallas' ♀^{H4}	CBla CNMi ERou NRnb
	'Giotto' ♀^{H4}	CNMi
	glaciale HWJK 2299 **new**	WCru
	'Gletscherwasser'	LPhx
	'Gordon Forsyth'	CBla CNMi ERou
	'Gossamer'	CNMi NRnb
§	***grandiflorum***	NCob
§	- 'Blauer Zwerg'	EPfP IBal MCCP SHGN
§	- 'Blue Butterfly'	CBot CSpe EBrs EBur LRHS MAnH MWgw SBla SCoo SPer SPlb SPoG WPer WSHC WWeb
	- Blue Dwarf	see *D. grandiflorum* 'Blauer Zwerg'
*	- 'Tom Pouce'	CBot NGdn
	- 'White Butterfly'	CBot
	Great Expectations Group **new**	MAnH
	'Grey Wagtail' **new**	CNMi
	Guinevere Group	CBcs CSBt CWib EBee ECtt EPfP EWTr LRHS MAnH MBow MBri MRav MWgw NBPC NBir NFor NLar NLon NPri SPer SPla SPoG WFar
	'Guy Langdon'	CNMi ERou
	'Harlekijn'	ERou
	'Harmony'	ERou
	'Heavenly Blue'	NLar
	'Holly Cookland Wilkins'	CNMi
	'Horizon' **new**	MAnH WWpP
	Ivory Towers Group	ECtt
	'Jenny Agutter'	CNMi
	'Jill Curley'	CNMi
	'Joan Edwards'	CNMi
	'Joyce Roffey'	ERou
	'Kasana'	CNMi
	'Kathleen Cooke'	CNMi
	'Kennington Calypso'	CNMi
	'Kennington Carnival'	CNMi
	'Kennington Classic'	CNMi
	'Kestrel'	CNMi ERou
	King Arthur Group	CBcs CMHG CSBt EBee ECtt EHol ELan ENot EPfP GKir LSRN MBri MRav MWat MWgw NBPC NEgg NLar NPri SMer SPer SPoG WFar WHoo
	'Lady Guinevere'	ERou
§	'Langdon's Royal Flush' ♀^{H4}	CBla CNMi
	'Lanzenträger'	SMeo
	'Layla' **new**	CNMi
	'Leonora'	CNMi ERou
	likiangense	ETow WLin
	'Lillian Basset' **new**	CNMi
	'Loch Leven' ♀^{H4}	CBla CNMi ERou
	'Loch Lomond' **new**	NRnb
	'Loch Nevis'	CNMi
	'Lord Butler' ♀^{H4}	CBla CNMi NRnb
	'Lorna'	ERou
	'Lucia Sahin' ♀^{H4}	CNMi
§	***luteum***	EHyt GKev SIgm WIvy
	maackianum	GCal
	Magic Fountains Series	CBrm CSam EHan GAbr GKir GMaP NCob NJOw NPri SPlb SPoG WFar WGor WHil
	- 'Magic Fountains Cherry Blossom' **new**	NBre
	- 'Magic Fountains Dark Blue'	EPfP GAbr GMaP LSRN MBow NArg NLar NLsd WBVN WFar
	- 'Magic Fountains Deep Blue'	CBrm NLar
	- 'Magic Fountains Lavender'	WBVN WWeb
	- 'Magic Fountains Lilac Rose'	EChP NArg NLar NVic WFar WWeb
	- 'Magic Fountains Pure White'	EChP EPfP NArg NLar WBVN WFar WWeb
	- 'Magic Fountains Sky Blue'	EChP LRHS NArg NVic WFar
	'Margaret Farrand'	ERou
	'Marie Broan'	CNMi
	menziesii	CSec ERos GIBF MAnH
	'Mèrel'[PBR]	EBee MBri

'Michael Ayres' ♀H4	CBla CNMi ERou NRnb
micropetalum CNDS 031	WCru
'Mighty Atom'	CBla CNMi ERou NRnb
'Min' ♀H4	CNMi ERou NRnb
'Molly Buchanan'	CBla CNMi ERou
'Moonbeam'	CBla CNMi
'Morning Cloud'	CNMi
'Mother Teresa'	ERou
'Mrs Newton Lees'	EBee ERou
'Mrs T. Carlile'	ERou
'Mulberry Rose' **new**	MAnH
'Mystique'	CBla ERou
'Ned Rose'	ERou
'Ned Wit'	ERou
New Century hybrids	CBcs LRHS
'Nicolas Woodfield'	CNMi
'Nimrod'	CBla ERou
'Nobility'	CBla ERou
nudicaule	EDAr EPfP MBNS SPoG SRot
- 'Laurin'	NRnb SGar WFar
- var. ***luteum***	see *D. luteum*
'Olive Poppleton' ♀H4	CBla CNMi
'Oliver' ♀H4	CNMi NRnb
'Our Deb' ♀H4	CNMi
'Ouvertüre'	EBee
oxysepalum	CSec MAnH WGwG
Pacific hybrids	ENot EPfP GKir LRHS LSRN MHer NArg NBlu NJOw NLar SGar SPet SRms SWal SWvt
'Pagan Purples' (d) **new**	NArg
'Pandora'	CBla CNMi
'Parade'	ERou
'Patricia Johnson'	CNMi ERou
Percival Group	LRHS NLar NLon
'Pericles'	CBla CNMi NRnb
'Perlmutterbaum'	LPhx SMeo
'Pink Petticoat' (d) **new**	EMon
'Pink Ruffles'	CBla CNMi
'Polar Sun'	NRnb
Princess Caroline = 'Odabar'PBR	CBcs MBri
'Purity'	ERou NRnb
'Purple Ruffles'	ERou
'Purple Triumph'	ERou
'Purple Velvet'	CBla CNMi
'Pyramus'	ERou
'Rainbow Select' **new**	NRnb
'Rakker'	ERou
Red Caroline = 'Bartwentyfive'	CBcs MBri
requienii	CSec MAnH MTho MWgw NBir SBch WCot WEas WOut WWFP
'Rona'	CNMi
'Rosemary Brock' ♀H4	CNMi ERou NRnb
'Royal Flush'	see *D.* 'Langdon's Royal Flush'
'Royal Velvet'	NRnb
'Rubin'	LPhx
'Ruby'	CBla
§ x ***ruysii*** 'Pink Sensation'	CDes CFir EMon ENot ERou GBri NLar NPro STes WFar WPGP
'Sabrina'	CBla
'Samantha'	ERou
'Sandpiper' ♀H4	CNMi
'Sarita' **new**	EBee SMrm
'Schildknappe'	EBee
§ ***semibarbatum***	SIgm
'Sentinel'	CNMi
'Shimmer'	CBla ERou
siamense B&SWJ 7278	WCru
'Silver Jubilee'	CNMi ERou
'Silver Moon'	ERou
'Sir Harry Secombe'	CNMi
'Skyline'	CBla CNMi ERou
'Snowdon'	CNMi
'Solomon'	ERou
'Sommerabend'	LPhx
'South Seas' **new**	CNMi
* 'Space Fantasy'	SBla
§ ***speciosum***	NMen SBla
'Spindrift' ♀H4	CNMi NRnb
stapeliosmum B&SWJ 2954	WCru
- B&SWJ 2960	GEdr
staphisagria	CArn CHrt ECGP EOHP MGol MSal SSth
'Stardust' **new**	ENot
'Strawberry Fair'	CBla CNMi EBee ERou
'Summer Haze'	ERou
Summer Skies Group	CBcs CMHG CSBt EBee ECtt ELan EPfP EWTr LRHS MBri MWat MWgw NBir NEgg NLar NLon NPri SMer SPer SPoG WBrE WCAu WFar WHoo WWeb
'Summerfield Diana'	CNMi
'Summerfield Miranda' ♀H4	CNMi
'Summerfield Oberon'	CNMi WCot
'Sungleam' ♀H4	CBla CFir CNMi ERou
'Sunkissed' ♀H4	CNMi
sutchuenense B&SWJ 7867	WCru
tatsienense	GKev SRms WCru WSHC
- 'Album'	EWes
- 'Blue Ice'	EHyt
tenii B&SWJ 7693	WCru
- BWJ 7906	WCru
'Tessa'	ERou
'Thundercloud'	ERou
'Tiddles' ♀H4	CBla
'Tiger Eye'	CNMi
'Tiny Tim' **new**	CNMi
'Titania'	CBla
tricorne	CLAP
'Turkish Delight'	CBla ERou
'Vanessa Mae'	CNMi
'Venus Carmine'	LRHS
'Vespers'	CBla
vestitum	GKev NBir SBch
viridescens **new**	WCot
viscosum HWJK 2268 **new**	WCru
'Walton Beauty'	CNMi
'Walton Benjamin'	CNMi
'Walton Gemstone' ♀H4	CBla CNMi
'Watkin Samuel'	ERou
'West End Blue'PBR	MBri
'White Ruffles'	CBla CNMi
'Wishful Thinking'PBR	SMrm
Woodfield strain	WHrl
'Yvonne'	ERou
zalil	see *D. semibarbatum*

Dendranthema ✿ (*Asteraceae*)

nankingense	see *Chrysanthemum nankingense*
pacificum	see *Ajania pacifica*

Dendriopoterium see *Sanguisorba*

Dendrobenthamia see *Cornus*

Dendromecon (*Papaveraceae*)

rigida	CBcs CFil EPfP LRHS NLar SMad SMur SSpi WPGP

Dennstaedtia (*Dennstaedtiaceae*)

punctilobula	CLAP WCot WRic

Dentaria see *Cardamine*

microphylla	see *Cardamine microphylla*
pinnata	see *Cardamine heptaphylla*
polyphylla	see *Cardamine kitaibelii*

Deparia (*Woodsiaceae*)

pycnosora	WRic

Derris (*Papilionaceae*)

elliptica	CPLN

Derwentia see *Parahebe*

Deschampsia (*Poaceae*)

cespitosa	CBig CBrm CHrt CNat COlW CRWN EPPr EPfP EWTr GFor ITim MBar NArg NBre NNor SPlb SPoG SYvo WCFE WDin WGHP WGwG WMoo WPer WPnP WTin WWpP
- subsp. ***alpina***	LRHS
- Bronze Veil	see *D. cespitosa* 'Bronzeschleier'
§ - 'Bronzeschleier'	CKno CMea EBee EBrs EHoe ELan EMag ENot EPla EPza EUJe EWsh GBri GCal GKir GMaP LPhx MBnl MSte MWgw NGdn SApp SPer SPla WCAu WGHP WMoo
- brown **new**	SApp
- 'Fairy's Joke'	see *D. cespitosa* var. *vivipara*
- 'Fose' **new**	SApp
- Gold Dust	see *D. cespitosa* 'Goldstaub'
- Golden Dew	see *D. cespitosa* 'Goldtau'
- Golden Pendant	see *D. cespitosa* 'Goldgehänge'
- Golden Shower	see *D. cespitosa* 'Goldgehänge'
- Golden Veil	see *D. cespitosa* 'Goldschleier'
§ - 'Goldgehänge'	CSam ECtt EHoe EHul EMan EPPr EPfP EPla MMHG NBir NPro SLPl
§ - 'Goldschleier'	CBig CBrm CFwr EBee EBrs ECGP EChP ECha EHoe EMon EPPr EPla EWsh GKir GMaP LPhx NGdn NJOw SApp SWal WGHP WMoo WPGP
§ - 'Goldstaub'	EBee EPPr
§ - 'Goldtau'	CBig CHar EHoe EHul EMon EPGN EPPr EPla EPza GKir GMaP LPhx LRHS MBnl MMoz MRav MWgw MWhi NGdn NOrc SApp SGSe SHel SLPl SPer SPla SPoG SUsu WCot WGHP
- 'Morning Dew'	EMag WFar
- 'Northern Lights' (v)	More than 30 suppliers
- subsp. ***paludosa***	EPPr
- 'Schottland'	GBin
§ - var. ***vivipara***	CKno EBee ECtt EHoe EMon EPPr EPla EUJe LRHS MWgw NBid NBro NOGN SGSe SWal WRos WWpP
- 'Willow Green'	GCal MRav SCoo SPoG
elongata	CBig
flexuosa	CBig CBrm COlW CPen EHoe EMon EPPr EWTr GFor GIBF MBri NBir SMar WPer
- 'Tatra Gold'	More than 30 suppliers
holciformis	CBig

Desfontainia (*Loganiaceae*)

§ ***spinosa*** ♀H3	More than 30 suppliers
- 'Harold Comber'	CMac MDun WCru WGer
- f. ***hookeri***	see *D. spinosa*

Desmanthus (*Mimosaceae*)

illinoensis	EBee EMan MGol MSal

Desmodium (*Papilionaceae*)

callianthum	CMac EPfP LRHS WSHC
canadense	CPLG EBee EMan EShb MGol NLar WCot
§ ***elegans*** ♀H4	CBcs CFil CHEx CHar CPle EBee EPfP MGol NLar SSpi WCru WHer WPGP WSHC
praestans	see *D. yunnanense*
tiliifolium	see *D. elegans*
§ ***yunnanense***	CHEx CPle EPfP LRHS SSpi WSHC

Desmoschoenus (*Cyperaceae*)

spiralis	CTrC

Deutzia ✿ (*Hydrangeaceae*)

calycosa	CFil GQui
- B&SWJ 7742	WCru
- Farrer 846	SMHy
- 'Dali'	CFil
- - SBEC 417	SDys WPGP
chunii	see *D. ningpoensis*
compacta	CFil SLon WFar WPGP
- 'Lavender Time'	GSki MBNS WCFE
cordatula	CFil
- B&SWJ 6917	WCru
coreana BWJ 8588	WCru
corymbosa	CDoC CFil GKir
crenata 'Flore Pleno'	see *D. scabra* 'Plena'
- var. ***heterotricha*** BWJ 8896	WCru
- var. ***nakaiana***	WPat
- 'Pride of Rochester' (d)	CBcs CMCN CTri CWib EHol ENot GKir MBar MDun MRav NArg SLon SMac SPoG WDin WHar
§ - var. ***pubescens***	CFil
aff. ***crenata*** BWJ 8879	WCru
discolor 'Major'	CPLG
x ***elegantissima***	ENot MRav SRms
- 'Fasciculata'	EPfP SPer WLeb
- 'Rosealind' ♀H4	CBcs CTri EBee ECrN ECtt ENot EPfP EWTr LRHS MRav NCGa NEgg NLon NSti SPoG SRms SSpi WCot WKif WLeb WSHC
glabrata B&SWJ 617	GQui WCru
glomeruliflora	CFil
- B&SWJ 7748	WCru
gracilis	CAlb CDoC CHar CSBt EBee ELan EPfP EWTr GQui MBar MRav MSwo MWat SPer WDin WFar WGwG WMoo
- B&SWJ 5805	WCru
- 'Carminea'	see *D.* x *rosea* 'Carminea'
§ - 'Marmorata' (v)	CPMA SLon WHCG
- 'Nikko'	CAbP CBcs CPBP CPLG EBee EHyt EWTr EWes GKir LRHS MBar MGos MHer NBlu NJOw NPro SPlb WDin WHCG WKif WSHC
- 'Rosea'	see *D.* x *rosea*
- 'Variegata'	see *D. gracilis* 'Marmorata'
grandiflora **new**	CBrm
hookeriana	GGGa WFar
- KW 6393	WPGP
x ***hybrida*** 'Contraste'	CPLG SPer
- 'Joconde'	CPLG ECtt GKir WFar WKif
- 'Magicien'	CAlb CBrm CDoC CDul CHar CMHG CPLG CSBt CSam CWib ENot EPfP GKir GQui MAsh MBri MRav MSwo SHBN SLon SPer SWvt WFar WHCG WHar WKif WPat
- 'Mont Rose' ♀H4	CAlb CBrm CDoC CDul CPLG EBee ELan EPfP EWTr GKir IMGH LAst LBuc LRHS MAsh MBar MGos MRav MSwo NCGa NLon SPer

	SPoG SWvt WCFE WDin WFar WHCG WMoo WSHC
- 'Strawberry Fields' 🏆H4	CBot CFai CFil CHar CPLG CTri EBee ELan EMil EPla GKir LAst LBuc LRHS LSRN MBar MBlu MBri MDun MTis NPro SBod SLon WKif WPGP
'Iris Alford'	SLon
x ***kalmiiflora***	CPLG CPMA CSBt CTri EHol GKir GQui LRHS MBar MBri MDun MRav MWhi NEgg NFor SLPl SPer SRms WMoo
x ***lemoinei***	CBot
longifolia	CFil
- 'Veitchii' 🏆H4	CDul CPLG CPle CSBt GQui MRav SMHy WCFE
§ - 'Vilmoriniae'	MRav
x ***magnifica***	CBcs ECrN EHol ELan EPfP GQui LRHS MBri SRms WDin WHCG WHar
- 'Rubra'	see *D.* x *hybrida* 'Strawberry Fields'
monbeigii	CPLG WBcn WKif
§ ***ningpoensis*** 🏆H4	CBcs CPLG EBee GQui SBch SLPl SPer SSta WBcn WPGP
parviflora var. ***barbinervis*** B&SWJ 8427	WCru
'Pink Pompon'	see *D.* 'Rosea Plena'
pubescens	see *D. crenata* var. *pubescens*
pulchra	CBot CFai CFil CHar CMCN CPom ECha EPfP GKir MRav NPro SLon SMac SPer SSpi WFar WHCG WPGP
- B&SWJ 3870	WCru
- B&SWJ 6908	WCru
aff. ***purpurascens*** BWJ 8007	WCru
§ x ***rosea***	CBot CDul CPle CTrw CWib EBee ENot EPfP LAst LRHS MBar MWat NArg NLon SHBN SMer SRms WFar WKif
- 'Campanulata'	CPLG EBee ENot EPfP NEgg
§ - 'Carminea'	CAlb CChe MDun MRav MSwo NCGa SPlb SRms SSta WDin WFar WMoo
§ 'Rosea Plena' (d)	CBot CDoC CHar CPLG CSBt CWib EPfP GKir LRHS MAsh MDun MGos NBlu NEgg SLim SPoG SSta WCFE WFar WGwG WPat
scabra	CDul GKir NPro
§ - 'Candidissima' (d)	CMHG ECrN GKir GQui MRav NLar SMer SPer WCFE
- 'Codsall Pink'	MBri MRav
§ - 'Plena' (d)	CChe CPLG ECtt ELan EPfP GKir IMGH LRHS MDun MRav NEgg SHBN SPer SPur WMoo
- 'Punctata' (v)	CFai EHoe SRms WFar
- 'Variegata' (v)	CDul SLim
aff. ***scabra*** B&SWJ 8924	WCru
setchuenensis	CFil EPfP GGGa GKir GQui SSpi WHCG WPat WSHC
- var. ***corymbiflora*** 🏆H4	CBcs CBot CDoC CDul CFil CTri EPfP GKir LRHS MTis NEgg SPoG WBcn WFar WKif WPGP
staminea	CFil
taiwanensis	NLar WPGP
- B&SWJ 6858	WCru
'Tourbillon Rouge'	EBee WDin
x ***wellsii***	see *D. scabra* 'Candidissima'
x ***wilsonii***	SRms

Dianella ✿ (*Phormiaceae*)

brevipedunculata	CWil
caerulea	CWil EBee EBla ECou ELan GBuc IGor NBir
- var. ***petasmatodes***	EMan WCot
- 'Variegata'	see *D. tasmanica* 'Variegata'
intermedia	CTrC IBlr WCot WPic
- 'Variegata' (v)	IBlr
nigra	CFil CFir CPou CWil ECou IFro LEdu NCGa WFar WHer
revoluta	CFir CWil ECou IBlr
tasmanica	More than 30 suppliers
§ - 'Variegata' (v)	CBct CFir CPen CSpe CStu ECou ELan EMan EPfP GFlt GQui IBlr LPio MSte WCot WOld

Dianthus ✿ (*Caryophyllaceae*)

ACW 2116	CLyd LBee WPer
'A.A. Sanders' (b) **new**	SAll
acicularis **new**	EHyt
'Activa' (pf)	SBai
'Adam James' (b) **new**	SAll
'Admiral Lord Anson' (b)	WKin
'Alan Titchmarsh' (p)	CSBt ENot EPfP EWll MMHG NEgg NLar SBai SPoG WWol
'Albatross' (p)	SChu
'Aldridge Yellow' (b) **new**	SAll
'Alegro'	SHay
'Alfred Galbally' (b) **new**	SAll
'Alfriston' (b) 🏆H4 **new**	SAll
'Alice' (p)	EPfP SAll SHay WKin
'Alice Forbes' (b)	SAll SHay
'Alice Lever' (p)	EPot WAbe
'Alloway Star' (p)	EMFP WKin
'Allspice' (p)	CLyd MRav SBch SChu SSvw WEas WHoo WKin
'Allspice Sport' (p)	WKin
Allwoodii Alpinus Group (p)	CBrm ECho NJOw SRms WBor
'Allwood's Crimson' (pf)	SAll SHay
alpinus 🏆H4	CLyd EHyt GKev GKir GTou ITim LRHS NBlu NEgg NJOw NMen NWCA SPet SRms WPer
- 'Albus'	CPBP LRHS WAbe
§ - 'Joan's Blood' 🏆H4	ECho NMen NWCA SBla SIng WAbe WHoo
- 'Millstream Salmon'	CLyd
'Alyson' (p) **new**	SAll
amurensis	LPhx LRHS MAnH NDov SIgm SSvw WPer
- 'Andrey'	GCal SHar
- 'Siberian Blue'	GBin
anatolicus	CLyd CTri LBee LRHS MHer NDlv SSvw WPer XPep
'Andrew Morton' (b) **new**	SAll
'Angelo' (b) **new**	SAll
'Annabelle' (p)	EMFP LAst LRHS SChu
'Annette' (pf)	EDAr EWin GKev LRHS MBNS NWoo
'Anniversay' (p)	SBai
'Apollo' (b)	GAbr
'Apricot Chace' (b)	SHay
'Arctic Star' (p)	CMea CTri EDAr MBNS NCGa NEgg NLar SPet SPoG
arenarius	CNic EWTr GKev MHer NEgg NJOw SHel SPlb SSvw WPer
'Arevalo' (pf)	SHay
'Argus'	IGor SChu WKin
* 'Arlene' (b) **new**	SAll
armeria	WBWf WHer WOut WPer
arpadianus	MDHE
- var. ***pumilus***	NWCA
'Arthur' (p)	EMFP WKin
'Arthur Leslie' (b) **new**	SAll
§ x ***arvernensis*** (p) 🏆H4	CNic ECha EPot GAbr WLin

	Name	Suppliers
	'Atletico' **new**	SBai
	'Audrey's Frilly'	SChu WKin
	'Aurora' (b)	SHay
	'Autumn Tints' (b) **new**	SAll
	'Auvergne'	see *D.* x *arvernensis*
	'Avenarius' (p) **new**	SAll
	'Avon Dasset'	EDAr LBuc
	'Baby Treasure' (p)	CLyd ECho SRot
	'Badenia' (p)	CLyd LRHS SChu SIgm
	'Bailey's Celebration' (p)	EBee ENot SBai
	'Bailey's Festival' (p)	SBai
	barbartus 'Newport Pink' **new**	NArg
	barbatus	CHrt GWCH
	- 'Bodestolz' **new**	LSou
	- Nigrescens Group (p,a) ♀H4	CBre CHad CHrt CMea CSpe LPhx NArg
	- 'Oeschberg' **new**	NArg
I	- 'Sooty' (p,a)	EChP ELan GBri LSou MWrn NArg NDlv
	'Barleyfield Rose' (p)	CLyd SBla SIng
	'Bath's Pink'	LRHS
§	'Bat's Double Red' (p)	EMFP IGor SAll SChu SSvw SWal WKin
	'Beauty of Cambridge' (b) **new**	SAll
	'Beauty of Healey' (p)	EMFP WKin
	'Becka Falls' (p)	SHay
	'Becky Robinson' (p) ♀H4	NLsd SAll SHay
	'Bella' **new**	CPBP
	'Belle of Bedfordshire' (b) **new**	SAll
	'Belle of Bookham' (b) **new**	SAll
	'Berlin Snow'	CLyd CPBP EPot ESis ITim
	'Bet Gilroy' (b)	SHay
	'Betty Buckle' (p)	SChu
	'Betty Miller' (b) **new**	SAll
	'Betty Morton' (p) ♀H4	COkL ECtt MSph SBla SSvw WKif WKin WThu
	'Betty Tucker' (b)	SHay
	'Binsey Red' (p)	EMFP SSvw WKin
	Black and White Minstrels Group	CElw CLyd WKin
	Blakeney seedling (p)	WKin
*	'Blue Carpet'	WPer
	'Blue Hills' (p)	CLyd ECho ELan GCrs GKev SChu
	'Blue Ice' (b)	SAll SHay
	'Blush'	see *D.* 'Souvenir de la Malmaison'
	'Bobby' (p) **new**	SAll
	'Bobby Ames' (b)	SHay
	'Bookham Fancy' (b)	SAll SHay
	'Bookham Grand' (b)	SHay
	'Bookham Heroine' (b) **new**	SAll
	'Bookham Lad' (b)	SAll
	'Bookham Perfume' (b)	SHay
	'Bookham Sprite' (b)	SAll
	'Border Special' (b) **new**	SAll
	'Bourboule'	see *D.* 'La Bourboule'
	'Bovey Belle' (p) ♀H4	CBcs LRHS MBNS SBai SHay
	'Boydii' (p)	CLyd
	'Bransgore' (p)	CLyd
	'Bremen'	COkL
	'Bressingham Pink' (p)	ECtt
	'Brian Tumbler' (b) **new**	SAll
	'Bridal Veil' (p)	EMFP GAbr SAll SBch SChu SSvw WKin
	'Brilliance' (p)	MBow
	'Brilliant'	see *D. deltoides* 'Brilliant'
	'Brilliant Star' (p) ♀H4	CPBP EDAr EMFP LBee SPet WWol
	'Brimstone' (b)	SHay
	'Brympton Red' (p)	ECha EMFP MRav SBch SBla SChu SSvw WEas WKif WKin

	Name	Suppliers
	'Bryony Lisa' (b) ♀H4 **new**	SAll
§	'Caesar's Mantle' (p)	WKin
	caesius	see *D. gratianopolitanus*
	'Callander' (b) **new**	SAll
	callizonus	EPot
	'Calypso Star' (p) ♀H4	ECtt EDAr EWin GBuc GMaP MBNS NCGa NEgg NLar SPet SPoG
	'Camelford' (p)	SChu WKin
	'Camilla' (b)	CLyd EGoo EMFP SSvw WKin
	'Can-can' (pf)	ECtt
	'Candy Clove' (b)	SAll SHay
	'Carinda' (p)	SHay
	'Carlotta' (p)	SHay
	'Carmen' (b)	SHay
	'Carmine Letitia Wyatt'PBR (p) ♀H4	EMFP SPoG
	'Caroline Bone' (b)	SHay
	'Caroline Clove' (b)	SHay
	carthusianorum	CBrm CHad CKno EPot EWTr IGor LPhx MAnH MSte NDlv NDov SAga SGar SMeo SSvw STes WEas WOut WPer XPep
	caryophyllus	CArn GBar GWCH WHer
	'Casser's Pink' (p)	GBuc
	'Catherine Glover' (b)	SAll
*	'Catherine Tucker'	WEas
	'Cecil Wyatt' (p)	EMFP EPfP NEgg NLar WMnd
§	'Cedric's Oldest' (p)	SChu WKin
	'Charcoal'	WCot
	'Charles' (p) **new**	SAll
	'Charles Edward' (p)	SAll
	'Charles Musgrave'	see *D.* 'Musgrave's Pink'
	'Charm' (b)	SHay
	'Chastity' (p)	SBla SChu WHoo WKin
	Cheddar pink	see *D. gratianopolitanus*
	'Cheerio' (pf)	SHay WWol
	'Cherry Clove' (b) **new**	SAll
	'Cherry Moon'	LRHS
	'Cherry Pie' (p)	ENot EPfP NEgg WMnd
	'Cherryripe' (p)	SHay
	'Cheryl'	see *D.* 'Houndspool Cheryl'
	'Chetwyn Doris' (p) ♀H4	SBai
	'Chianti' (pf)	MBNS NGdn
	'China Doll' (p)	SBai
	chinensis (p,a)	GKev WHer
	'Chris Crew' (b) ♀H4	SAll
	'Christine Hough' (b) **new**	SAll
	'Christopher' (p)	LRHS SAll SHay
	'Circular Saw' (p)	SChu
	'Clare' (p)	SAll SHay
	'Claret Joy' (p) ♀H4	CBcs EBee EDAr EMFP EPfP LAst SAll
	'Clarinda' (b) **new**	SAll
	'Clifford Pink'	WKin
	'Clunie' (b)	SAll SHay
§	'Cockenzie Pink' (p)	EMFP GAbr IGor SAll SSvw WEas WKin
	'Constance' (p)	SAll
	'Constance Finnis'	see *D.* 'Fair Folly'
	'Consul' (b) **new**	SAll
	'Conwy Silver'	NHar WAbe
	'Conwy Star'	CPBP WAbe
	'Copperhead' (b)	SHay
	'Corleone' (pf)	SBai WWol
	'Coronation Ruby' (p) ♀H4	SAll SBai SHay
	corsicus	XPep
	'Coste Budde' (p)	CLyd IGor WEas WKin WSHC
	'Cotton Chace' (b)	SHay
	'Cranborne Seedling' (p)	WKin
	'Cranmere Pool' (p) ♀H4	CBcs CMea EBee ECtt EDAr ELan EPfP LAst LRHS MBNS MBow NPri SBai SHay SMrm SPoG WCra WFar WMnd WWol

	Name	Suppliers
	cretaceus	NWCA
	'Crimson Ace' (p)	SHay
	'Crimson Chance' (p)	NSla
	'Crimson Joy' (p) 🏆H4	EDAr SPoG
	'Crimson Tempo'PBR (pf)	SBai SHay WWol
	'Crimson Velvet' (b)	SHay
	crinitus	NJOw SHFr
	cruentus	LPhx MSte SSvw
	'Dad's Choice' (p)	SBai
	'Dad's Favourite' (p)	EMFP IGor SAll SChu SHay SRms SSvw WEas WHer WKin WWhi
	'Daily Mail' (p)	CBcs EBee SBai SChu WWol
	'Dainty Dame' (p) 🏆H4	CSpe CTri EBee EDAr ESis GBuc GMaP LRHS MSte MWgw NJOw SBla SChu SPoG SRot
	'Damask Superb' (p)	IGor WKin
	'Daphne' (p) **new**	SAll
	'Dark Tempo' (pf)	SHay
	'Dartington Laced'	WKin
	'David' (p)	COkL SAll SHay
	'David Russell' (b) 🏆H4 **new**	SAll
	'Dawlish Charm' (p)	SBai
	'Dawlish Joy' (p)	EDAr EMFP ENot
	'Dawn' (b)	SAll SHay
	'Daydream' (pf)	SBai SHay WWol
	'Deep Purple' (pf)	SHay
	'Delphi' (pf)	SHay WWol
	deltoides 🏆H4	CArn CElw CSev ECha ELau EPfP GBar GKev GWCH SECG SHGN SPlb SRms WBWf WFar WJek WSel
	- 'Albus'	CNic ECGP ECha EPfP GBar IHMH NBlu NEgg NPri SSvw WMoo WPer WRos WSel
	- 'Arctic Fire'	NGdn NLsd WMoo WWpP
	- 'Bright Eyes'	ECho
§	- 'Brilliant'	CTri GTou MDun MFOX NPri NVic SAll SRms WGor WHrl WWpP
	- 'Broughty Blaze'	NRya
	- 'Dark Eyes'	EWes
	- 'Erectus'	EPfP NLon
	- Flashing Light	see *D. deltoides* 'Leuchtfunk'
§	- 'Leuchtfunk'	CElw CHrt COkL ECtt EPfP GGar GKir GTou LAst LGro LRHS NBPC NEgg NMir SPoG WFar WPer WRos
	- 'Microchip'	NJOw SPet WFar
	- 'Nelli' (p)	GAbr SSvw WMoo
	- red	NBlu
	- 'Vampir' **new**	NLsd WWpP
	'Denis' (p)	ELan
	'Desert Song' (b) **new**	SAll
	'Devon Blush' (p)	EBee
	'Devon Charm' (p)	LRHS
	'Devon Cream'PBR (p)	CSBt EBee EMFP LRHS NEgg WCra WMnd WWol
	'Devon Dove'PBR (p) 🏆H4	CMea EBee EPfP LAst NEgg NPri WRHF
	'Devon General'PBR (p)	CTri EBee ECtt EMFP SPoG
	'Devon Glow'PBR (p) 🏆H4	EBee EMFP EPfP LRHS NEgg SPoG WCAu
	'Devon Joy' (p)	LRHS
	'Devon Magic'PBR (p)	SPoG WFar
	'Devon Maid' (p) 🏆H4	EBee EPfP
	'Devon Pearl'PBR (p)	EBee EMFP WMnd
	'Devon Velvet'PBR	EBee NLar
	'Devon Wizard'PBR (p) 🏆H4	CHar EMFP ENot LRHS NPri SPoG WCAu WFar
	'Dewdrop' (p)	CMea CTri EBee ECtt EDAr EPot ESis EWin LRHS MHer NBir NGdn NPro SAll SChu WAbe WFar WKin WPer
	'Diana'	see *D.* Dona = 'Brecas'
	'Diane' (p) 🏆H4	EDAr ELan EMFP NEgg SAll SHay SPla WMnd WWol
	'Dianne' (pf)	EDAr
	'Diplomat' (b) **new**	SAll
	'Doctor Archie Cameron' (b)	SHay
§	Dona = 'Brecas' (pf)	LRHS SHay
	'Donnet's Variety'	WEas
	'Dora'	LRHS SChu
	'Doris' (p) 🏆H4	More than 30 suppliers
	'Doris Allwood' (pf)	CSBt SAll SHay
	'Doris Elite' (p) **new**	SAll
	'Doris Galbally' (b)	SAll
	'Doris Majestic' (p) **new**	SAll
	'Doris Ruby'	see *D.* 'Houndspool Ruby'
	'Doris Supreme' (p)	SAll SHay
	'Dover' (pf) **new**	SBai
§	'Dubarry' (p)	CTri CWan ECtt WGor WPer
	'Duchess of Westminster' (M)	SAll
	'Dusky' (p)	WKin
	'Dwarf Vienna'	COkL
	'E.J. Baldry' (b)	SHay
	'Earl of Essex' (p)	EMFP SHay SSvw WKin
	'Ebor II' (b)	SAll
	'Edenside Scarlet' (b)	SHay
	'Edenside White' (b) **new**	SAll
	'Edna' (p) **new**	SAll
	'Edward Allwood' (pf) **new**	SAll
	'Eileen' (p) **new**	SAll
	'Eileen Lever' (p)	CNic CPBP EPot ITim MDHE SBla WAbe WLin
	'Eleanor's Old Irish'	WCot WTin
	'Elfin Star' (p)	EDAr MSte SPet
	'Elizabeth' (p)	WEas
	'Elizabeth Patrick' (b) **new**	SAll
	'Elizabeth Pink'	SMrm
	'Elizabethan' (p)	CAby CFee GAbr GMac SBla WKin
*	'Elizabethan Pink' (p)	CCge SAll
	'Emile Paré' (p)	SChu WKin
	'Emjay' (b) **new**	SAll
	'Emma James' (b) **new**	SAll
	'Emperor'	see *D.* 'Bat's Double Red'
	'Empire'	SHay
	'Enid Anderson' (p)	SChu WKin
	'Enid Burgoyne'	WKin
	erinaceus	EHol EPot GKev GTou LRHS MOne NJOw SRot WAbe WPer
	- var. ***alpinus***	CLyd EPot
	'Erycina' (b)	SAll
	'Ethel Hurford'	WHoo WKin
	'Eudoxia' (b) **new**	SAll
	'Eva Humphries' (b)	SAll SHay
	'Evening Star' (p) 🏆H4	CPBP EDAr EWin LBee MWgw SPet SPoG
	'Excelsior' (p)	NFor NLon SSvw
	'Exquisite' (b)	SAll
§	'Fair Folly' (p)	SAll SChu SSvw WEas WKin
	'Falcon' (pf)	SBai SHay WWol
	'Fanal' (p)	NBir WKin
	'Fancy Schubert' (pf)	SBai
	'Farida'PBR (pf)	SBai SHay
	'Farnham Rose' (p)	SChu SSvw
	'Fenbow Nutmeg Clove' (b)	CWan SChu WKin WMnd
	'Fettes Mount' (p)	CLyd EWin GAbr GMac SChu SSvw WCot WKin WSPU
	'Feuerhexe' (p)	LRHS NPro
	'Fiery Cross' (b)	SAll SHay
	'Fimbriatus' (p)	WHoo WKin
	'Fingo Clove' (b) **new**	SAll
	'Fiona' (p) **new**	SAll
	'Fireglow' (b) **new**	SAll

	'Firestar' (p) **new**	LBee WWol
	'First Lady' (b) **new**	SAll
	'Flame' (p)	SHay
	'Flanders' (b) ♀H4 **new**	SAll
	'Fleur' (p) **new**	SAll
	'Forest Glow' (b) **new**	SAll
	'Forest Sprite' (b)	SAll
	'Forest Treasure' (b)	SAll
	'Forest Violet' (b) **new**	SAll
	'Fortuna' (p) **new**	SAll
	'Fountain's Abbey' (p)	IGor WKin
	'Fragrans' (pf)	NJOw
	'Fragrant Ann' (pf) ♀H1	SHay
*	***fragrantissimus***	LRHS
	'Frances Isabel' (p)	SAll
	'Frances Sellars' (b)	SHay
	'Frank's Frilly' (p)	WKin
	'Freckles' (p)	SHay
	'Freda' (p)	SAll
	freynii	CLyd EPot EWes MDHE NDlv NLAp SBla WAbe
N	fringed pink	see *D. superbus*
	'Fusilier' (p)	CElw CMea CTri ECtt EDAr EMFP EPfP GKir LRHS MBar MSte MWgw NBlu NCGa NEgg NPri NWCA SAll SChu SHay WBVN WFar WKin
	'G.W. Hayward' (b)	SHay
	'Gail Graham' (b) **new**	SAll
	'Garland' (p)	CTri LRHS WGor
	'Garnet' (p)	COkL SChu
	'Gaydena' (b) **new**	SAll
	'George Allwood' (pf)	SAll
	giganteus	CSpe IBlr MBct MSte NJOw WKin
	'Gingham Gown' (p)	NBir SBla SPoG
	'Gipsy Clove' (b)	SHay
	glacialis	GTou SSvw
*	- ***elegans*** **new**	GKev
	'Gloriosa' (p)	WKin
	'Gold Flake' (p)	SHay
	'Gold Fleck'	EPot LBee SChu
	'Golden Sceptre' (b) ♀H4	SAll
	'Grana' **new**	SBai
	'Grandma Calvert' (p) **new**	SAll
	graniticus	GKev
	'Gran's Favourite' (p) ♀H4	CBcs CMea CSBt CTri EBee ECtt EDAr EMFP ENot EPfP LAst LRHS MBow MWat NPri SAll SBai SBla SChu SHay SPlb SPoG SRms WCra WEas WFar WKin WWol
§	***gratianopolitanus*** ♀H4	CArn CElw CSLe CTri EPfP EPot GKev GTou LRHS MBow MFOX MHer MNrw MRav NBid NJOw NWCA SPet SRms WBWf WKin WWye
	- from Cheddar	CLyd
	- 'Albus'	CLyd EPot
	- 'Flore Pleno' (d)	EMFP MInt SSvw
§	- 'Tiny Rubies' (p)	ECho WAbe WKin
	'Gravetye Gem' (b)	SRms
	'Gravetye Gem' (p)	WKin
	'Green Lanes' (p) **new**	CHll
	'Grenadier' (p)	ECho ELan
	'Grey Dove' (b) ♀H4 **new**	SAll
	'Gwendolen Read' (p)	SHay
	'Gypsy Star' (p)	CMea EBee ECho EDAr EWin GMaP MBNS NCGa NEgg SPet SPoG
	haematocalyx	CPBP GKev NWCA SSvw WAbe WPer
	- 'Alpinus'	see *D. haematocalyx* subsp. *pindicola*
§	- subsp. ***pindicola***	CGra CLyd EHyt ITim NLAp WAbe WPat
	'Hannah Louise' (b) ♀H4	SAll
	'Hare Hope Clove' (b) **new**	SAll
	'Harkell Special' (b) **new**	SAll
	'Harlequin' (p)	ECtt EMFP WPer
	'Harmony' (b)	SAll SHay
	'Harry Oaks' (p)	WKin
	'Havana' (pf)	SHay
	'Haytor'	see *D.* 'Haytor White'
	'Haytor Rock' (p) ♀H4	EBee EPfP SHay SPoG WCra
§	'Haytor White' (p) ♀H4	EBee EDAr EMFP ENot EPfP LAst LRHS NLon SAll SBai SChu SHay SRms WCFE WCot WEas WWhi
	'Hazel Ruth' (b) ♀H4	SAll
I	'Heath' (b)	WKin
	'Heidi' (p)	EPfP
	'Helen' (p)	SAll SHay
	'Helena Hitchcock' (p)	SAll
	'Herbert's Pink' (p)	WKin
	'Hereford Butter Market'	EBee SChu WKin
	'Hidcote' (p)	CLyd CTri EBee ELan LRHS MWat NMen SBla SHay WKin
	'Hidcote Red'	ECho LBee LRHS
	'Highland Fraser' (p)	SAll SChu SRms WEas WKif
	'Highland Queen' (p)	WKin
	'Hoo House' (p)	WKin
	'Hope' (p)	EMFP SChu SSvw WKin
	'Horsa' (b)	SAll SHay
	'Hot Spice'PBR (p) ♀H4	EMFP EWll WWol
§	'Houndspool Cheryl' (p) ♀H4	COkL CTri EBee EMFP EPfP LRHS MBow SAll SRms WFar WWol
§	'Houndspool Ruby' (p) ♀H4	EBee EMFP EPfP MBNS SAll SBai WCAu WEas WWol
	'Ian' (p)	CBcs SAll SBai SHay
	'Ibis' (b)	SHay
	'Icomb' (p)	CLyd SRms WHoo WKin WPer
	'Imperial Clove' (b)	SHay
	'Ina' (p)	SRms
	'Incas' (pf) ♀H1	SHay
	'Inchmery' (p)	EMFP NFor SAll SChu SHay SSvw WEas WHoo WKin WTin
	'India Star'PBR (p) ♀H4	CPBP CTri EDAr LAst NEgg SPet
	'Indios' (pf) ♀H1	SHay
	'Ine' (p)	COkL
	'Inglestone' (p)	CTri SBla WLin WPer
	'Inshriach Dazzler' (p) ♀H4	CLyd CMea ECtt EDAr EWin GKir GMaP LBee MHer NDlv NPri NRya SBla SIng SPoG WAbe WKin WLin
	'Inshriach Startler' (p)	CLyd CMea
	'Ipswich Pink' (p)	ENot LGro LRHS SRms
	'Irene Della-Torré' (b) ♀H4	SAll
	'Irene Hobbah' (b) **new**	SAll
I	'Ivonne' (pf)	SHay
	'Ivonne Orange' (pf)	SHay
	'Jack Hodges' (b) **new**	SAll
	'James Michael Hayward' (b)	SHay
	'James Portman' (p)	WMnd WWol
	'Jane Austen' (p)	SChu WKin WPer
	'Jane Barker' (b) **new**	SAll
	'Jane Coffey' (b)	SAll SHay
	'Jane Hammond' (b) **new**	SHay
	'Janet Walker' (p) **new**	GMaP
	japonicus	CSpe NWCA
	- f. ***albiflorus*** **new**	CSec
	'Jenny Wyatt' (p)	SHay
	'Jess Hewins' (pf)	SAll
	'Joan Schofield' (p)	CLyd EDAr NBlu NLRH SHel SPoG
	'Joan Siminson' (p)	WKin
	'Joan's Blood'	see *D. alpinus* 'Joan's Blood'
	'John Ball' (p)	EMFP SSvw WKin
	'John Grey' (p)	WKin
	'Jolene' (b) **new**	SAll
	'Joseph Griffiths' (b) **new**	SAll

'Joy' (p) ♀H4	ECho ECtt EDAr EMFP ENot EPfP LAst LRHS SAll SHay SPoG
'Julian' (p) **new**	SAll
'Julie Ann Davis' (b) **new**	SAll
'Kathleen Hitchcock' (b) ♀H4	SAll
'Kesteven Chamonix' (p)	WPer
'Kesteven Kirkstead' (p) ♀H4	CSWP MNrw
'King of the Blacks' (p,a)	ELan
'Kiro' **new**	SBai
kitaibelii	see *D. petraeus* subsp. *petraeus*
knappii	ELan EPfP MLLN NDov NVic SRms SSvw WMoo WPer XPep
- 'Yellow Harmony' (p,a)	LRHS MBNS SGar
'Komachi' (pf)	SBai
'Kristina' (pf) **new**	SBai
§ 'La Bourboule' (p) ♀H4	CMea CTri EChP EDAr ELan EPot GAbr GKir ITim LBee LRHS MBar MWat NMen NPri SBla SRms WFar WKin WLin WPat
'La Bourboule Albus' (p)	CTri EDAr EPot GCrs ITim SBla WFar WGor
'Laced Hero' (p)	IGor SChu WKin
'Laced Joy' (p)	CElw EDAr SAll SChu SHay
'Laced Monarch' (p)	CBcs EBee ECtt EDAr LRHS NLar SAll SBai SChu SPlb SPoG WKin WWol
'Laced Mrs Sinkins' (p)	SAll SPer
'Laced Prudence'	see *D.* 'Prudence'
'Laced Romeo' (p)	EMFP SAll SChu SHay WKin
'Laced Treasure' (p)	SAll
'Lady Granville' (p)	IGor SAll SSvw WKin
'Lady Green'[PBR] **new**	SBai
'Lady Salisbury' (p)	EMFP WKin
§ 'Lady Wharncliffe' (p)	EMFP IGor SBch WKin
'Lancing Monarch' (b)	SHay
'Laura' (p)	SAll SHay
'Lavastrom'	SBla SOkd WAbe
'Lavender Clove' (b)	SAll
'Lawley's Red' (p)	WKin
'Leiden' (b)	SAll
'Lemsii' (p) ♀H4	ECho ECtt EMFP NMen NVic WPer
'Leslie Rennison' (b)	SAll SHay
'Letitia Wyatt' (p) ♀H4	CMea EBee EDAr EMFP ENot SPoG WCra
'Leuchtkugel'	ECho LTwo
leucophaeus var. ***leucophaeus*** **new**	EPot
'Liberty' (pf)	SBai SHay
'Lily Lesurf' (b) **new**	SAll
'Linfield Dorothy Perry' (p) ♀H4 **new**	SAll
'Linfield Isobel Croft' (p) **new**	SAll
'Lionheart' (p)	LRHS WCra
'Lipstick' (pf)	SHay
'Lisboa' (pf)	SHay
'Little Ben' (p) **new**	SAll
'Little Gem' (pf)	WKin
'Little Jock' (p)	CPBP EDAr ELan EPot GKir GMaP LBee LRHS MBar MHer MRav NJOw SAll SBla SChu SHay SPlb SPoG SRms WEas WFar WKin WLin WPat
'Little Miss Muffet' (p)	CHll
'Liz Rigby' (b)	SAll
'London Brocade' (p)	SSvw WKin
'London Delight' (p)	EMFP SHay WKin
'London Glow' (p)	SAll WKin
'London Lovely' (p)	SAll SHGN SSvw WKin
'London Poppet' (p)	NDlv SAll SSvw WKin
'Loveliness' (p)	CBre
lumnitzeri	EHyt GCal LTwo WPer XPep
'Lustre' (b)	SAll SHay
'Mab'	WKin
'Mabel Appleby' (p)	SHel
'Madame Dubarry'	see *D.* 'Dubarry'
'Madonna' (pf)	SHay WKin
'Maisie Neal' (b) ♀H4 **new**	SAll
'Malaga' (pf) ♀H1	SHay
'Mambo' (pf) ♀H4	SBai SHay WWol
'Mandy' (p) **new**	SAll
'Manningtree Pink'	see *D.* 'Cedric's Oldest'
'Margaret Stewart' (b) **new**	SAll
'Marion Robinson' (b) ♀H4 **new**	SAll
'Marmion' (M)	SAll
'Mars' (p)	ECtt ELan GAbr NDlv SChu WAbe WFar
'Marshmallow' (p)	EBee NEgg NLar
'Marshwood Melody' (p)	SBai
'Marshwood Mystery' (p)	WKin
'Mary Simister' (b)	SAll
* 'Mary's Gilliflower'	EMFP WKin
'Matador' (b)	SHay
'Matthew' **new**	WHoo
'Maudie Hinds' (b)	SAll
'Maybole' (b)	SAll SHay
'Maythorne' (p)	SRms
'Melocoton' **new**	SBai
'Mendip Hills' (b)	SAll SHay
'Mendlesham Belle' (p) ♀H4	EMFP
'Mendlesham Frilly' (p)	EMFP
'Mendlesham Glow' (p)	EMFP
'Mendlesham Maid' (p) ♀H4	EMFP
Mendlesham Minx = 'Russmin'[PBR] (p)	CLyd EBee EDAr EMFP GBuc LBee NBlu SPet
'Mendlesham Miss' (p)	EMFP
'Mendlesham Moll' (p)	EMFP
'Mendlesham Saint Helen's' (p)	EMFP
'Mendlesham Spice' (p)	EMFP
'Mendlesham Sweetheart' (p)	EMFP
'Merlin'	CPen
'Merlin Clove' (b)	SHay
'Messines Pink' (p) **new**	SAll SSvw
'Michael Saunders' (b) ♀H4	SAll
microlepis	CGra EHyt GCrs ITim NMen NWCA SBla WAbe WLin
- f. ***albus***	CGra EHyt NSla WAbe
* - var. ***degenii***	CPBP GKev NWCA
- 'Leuchtkugel'	ECho ITim WAbe
- var. ***musalae***	CLyd CMea CPBP EHyt LTwo MDHE NMen WAbe
'Mike Briggs' (b) **new**	SAll
'Miniver'	SHay
'Miss Sinkins' (p)	EDAr GKir SPet SPla
'Monica Wyatt' (p) ♀H4	EMFP EPfP GKir LRHS NEgg SBai SChu SHay SPoG
monspessulanus	GKev NDlv NWCA SSvw WMoo WPer
'Montrose Pink'	see *D.* 'Cockenzie Pink'
'Moortown Plume'	WKin
Morning Star = 'Devon Winnie' **new**	LBee WWol
'Moulin Rouge' (p) ♀H4	EBee ENot MBow SChu SHGN SPoG WWol
'Mrs Clark'	see *D.* 'Nellie Clark'
'Mrs Gumbly' (p)	WKin
'Mrs Holt' (p)	EMFP
'Mrs Jackson' (p)	CLyd
'Mrs Macbride' (p)	WKin
'Mrs N. Clark'	see *D.* 'Nellie Clark'

	'Mrs Perkins' (b) **new**	SAll
	'Mrs Roxburgh'	WKin
	'Mrs Sinkins' (p)	More than 30 suppliers
	'Murray Douglas' (p)	SSvw
	'Murray's Laced Pink' (p)	WKin WSPU
N	'Musgrave's Pink' (p)	ECha MRav SAga SAll SBch SBla SChu SHay SSvw WEas WKin
	'Musgrave's White'	see *D.* 'Musgrave's Pink'
	myrtinervius	CLyd ECho EHyt EWTr GBin NLar SBch SHGN SRms WPer
	- subsp. ***caespitosus***	EHyt NHar
	- - MESE 433	WAbe
	'Nan Bailey' (p)	SBai
	'Nancy Lindsay' (p)	SSvw
	'Napoleon III' (p)	WKif
	nardiformis	SSvw WPer
	'Natalie Saunders' (b) 🏆H4	SAll
	'Nautilus' (b)	SAll SHay
	neglectus	see *D. pavonius*
§	'Nellie Clark' (p)	CLyd SChu
	'Nelson'[PBR]	SHay
	'Neon Star'[PBR] (p)	EDAr EMFP SPoG WWol
	'New Tempo' (pf)	SBai SHay
	'Night Star' (p) 🏆H4	EChP EMFP EWin LIck MNrw NBlu NCGa NEgg SChu SPet WWol
	nitidus	CLyd GKev NBir SSvw WPer
	nivalis	NWCA
	noeanus	see *D. petraeus* subsp. *noeanus*
	'Nonsuch' (p)	WKin
	'Northland' (pf)	SAll SHay
	'Nyewoods Cream' (p)	CMea CTri CWan EMFP EPot GAbr GKev GKir LBee LRHS MBar MHer MRav NMen NPri SIng WPat WPer WTin
§	'Oakington' (p)	CTri LRHS MRav NPri NWCA SChu WKin WTel
	'Oakington Rose'	see *D.* 'Oakington'
	'Oakwood Gillian Garforth' (p) 🏆H4	SBai
	'Oakwood Romance' (p) 🏆H4	NLon
	'Oakwood Splendour' (p) 🏆H4	MBNS
	'Old Blush'	see *D.* 'Souvenir de la Malmaison'
	'Old Dutch Pink' (p)	IGor SChu SSvw WKin
	'Old Fringed Pink' (p)	WKin
	'Old Fringed White' (p)	EMFP
	'Old Irish' (p)	IGor WKin
	'Old Mother Hubbard' (p)	CFee CHll
	'Old Red Clove' (p)	WCot WEas
§	'Old Square Eyes' (p)	MNrw SAga SAll SBla SChu SHay SMrm SSvw WEas WKin
	'Old Velvet' (p)	GCal SAll SChu WKin
	'Oliver' (p) **new**	SAll
	'Opera'	SHay
	'Orange Maid' (b) **new**	SAll
	'Oscar' (b) **new**	SAll
	'Osprey' (b)	SHay
	'Paddington' (p)	SChu SSvw WKin
	'Painted Beauty' (p)	EMFP NBir
	'Painted Lady' (p)	CLyd IGor SAll SChu WKin
	'Paisley Gem' (p)	SChu SSvw WKin
	'Patricia' (b)	SHay
	'Paul Hayward' (p)	SHay
§	***pavonius*** 🏆H4	CElw CLyd EHyt EWes GKev GTou NLar NWCA SIgm WPer
	- ***roysii***	see *D.* 'Roysii'
	'Pax' (pf)	SBai SHay WWol
	'Peach' (p)	SHay
	'Perfect Clove' (b)	SHay
	'Peter Wood' (b) 🏆H4 **new**	SAll
§	***petraeus***	EWes NWCA
§	- subsp. ***noeanus***	CLyd GBin GKev LTwo WPer
	- - ***albus***	GCrs
	- subsp. ***orbelicus*** **new**	EHyt
§	- subsp. ***petraeus***	SSvw WPer
	'Petticoat Lace' (p)	SHay
	'Phantom' (b)	SHay
	'Pheasant's Eye' (p)	EMFP SAll SSvw WHer WKin
	'Philip Archer' (b)	SHay
*	'Picton's Propeller' (p)	GBuc
	'Pike's Pink' (p) 🏆H4	CSLe CTri EBee EDAr ELan EPfP LBee LRHS MHer MRav NMen SAll SBla SChu SHay SPet SPoG SRms SSvw WAbe WBVN WEas WKin WLin WTel
	pindicola	see *D. haematocalyx* subsp. *pindicola*
	'Pink Bizarre' (b)	SHay
*	'Pink Dona' (pf)	SHay
	'Pink Dover' (pf)	SBai
	'Pink Fantasy' (b) **new**	SAll
	'Pink Jewel' (p)	CLyd CMea ECha EDAr EPot GKev LBee LRHS MHer NMen SAll SChu WEas
	'Pink Mrs Sinkins' (p)	ECha EMFP MHer SAll SChu WKin
	'Pink Pearl' (p)	EDAr SAll SPoG
	'Pixie' (b)	EPot
	'Pixie Star'[PBR] (p) 🏆H4	EDAr SPoG WWol
	plumarius	NJOw NMir SAll SRms SSvw WGor WHer WMoo WPer WSSM
	- 'Albiflorus'	WPer
	pontederae	EWTr NDlv WPer
	'Portsdown Fancy' (b)	SHay
	'Prado' (pf) 🏆H4	SHay
	'Prado Refit' (pf)	WWol
	'Pretty'	LRHS
	'Primero Dark' (pf)	SBai
	'Prince Charming' (p)	CLyd ELan EPot NEgg NPri SRms WPer
	'Princess of Wales' (M)	SAll
	'Priory Pink' (p)	SAll
§	'Prudence' (p)	SAll WKin
	'Pudsey Prize' (p)	CLyd CPBP EHyt EPot WLin
	'Pummelchen' (p)	ITim WAbe
	'Purple Jenny' (p) **new**	SAll
	'Purple Pacal' (pf)	SHay
	pygmaeus	NBro
*	- 'Pink Frills'	NEgg
*	***pyrenaicus*** 'Cap Béar'	XPep
	'Queen of Hearts' (p)	CTri LRHS NWCA WPer
§	'Queen of Henri' (p)	ECtt EDAr GEdr GMaP LBee LRHS MHer SBla SChu SHar WBVN WFar WKin
	'Queen of Sheba' (p)	SChu SSvw WKif WKin
	'Rachel' (p)	ECtt WPat
	'Raggio di Sole' (pf)	SBai WWol
	'Rainbow Loveliness' (p,a)	CSec SAll SRms WHil WRHF
	'Ralph Gould' (p)	ECho
	'Rebecca' (b) **new**	SAll
	'Red and White' (p)	WKin
	'Red Dwarf' 🏆H4	MSte SPet SPoG
	'Red Velvet'	CLyd LRHS
	'Reine de Henri'	see *D.* 'Queen of Henri'
	'Renoir' (b)	SHay
	'Revell's Lady Wharncliffe'	see *D.* 'Lady Wharncliffe'
	'Riccardo' (b) 🏆H4	SAll
	'Richard Gibbs' (p)	MOne
	'Richard Pollak' (b) **new**	SAll
	'Rififi' (pf) **new**	SBai
	'Rivendell' (p)	CLyd CPBP NMen WAbe
	'Robert Allwood' (pf)	SAll
	'Robert Baden-Powell' (b)	SHay
*	'Robin Ritchie'	WHoo WKin WWhi
	'Robin Thain' (b)	SHay
	'Robina's Daughter'	GAbr

	'Roodkapje' (p)	SSvw WKin
	'Rose de Mai' (p)	CLyd CSam CSev EMFP SBch SChu SSvw WHoo WKin
	'Rose Joy' (p) ♀H4	EBee EMFP EPfP SHay
	'Rose Monica Wyatt'PBR (p) ♀H4	WWol
	'Rosealie' (p)	SHay
	'Royalty' (p)	SHay
§	'Roysii' (p)	NDlv WPer
	'Rubin' (pf)	WEas
	'Ruby'	see *D.* 'Houndspool Ruby'
	'Ruby Doris'	see *D.* 'Houndspool Ruby'
	'Rudheath Pixie' (b) **new**	SAll
	'Rudheath Ruby' (b) **new**	SAll
	'Saint Edith' (p)	WKin
	'Saint Nicholas' (p)	EMFP SChu SSvw WKin
	'Saint Winifred'	SChu WKin
	Salamanca = 'Kosalamana' (pf)	SBai SHay
	'Sally Anne Hayward' (b)	SHay
	'Sam Barlow' (p)	COkL EGoo SAll SChu SHay SSvw WKin WWye
	'Sangria' (pf) **new**	SBai
	sanguineus **new**	SMHy
	'Santa Claus' (b)	SAll SHay
	'Santorini'	SHay
	'Scania' (pf)	SHay
	'Scarlet Fragrance' (b)	SHay
	'Schubert' (pf)	WWol
*	***scopulorum perplexans***	EPot
	'Sean Hitchcock' (b) **new**	SAll
	seguieri	EShb SSvw WMoo WPer
	serotinus	EPot EShb GKev SSvw WCot
	Shiplake seedling (p)	WKin
	'Shot Silk' (pf)	SAll
	'Show Aristocrat' (p) **new**	SAll
	'Show Beauty' (p) **new**	SAll
	'Show Glory' (p) **new**	SAll
	'Show Harlequin' (p) **new**	SAll
	'Show Portrait' (p)	NFor NLon
	'Show Satin' (p) **new**	SAll
	simulans	CLyd EHyt
	'Sir Cedric Morris'	see *D.* 'Cedric's Oldest'
	'Sir David Scott' (p)	WKin
*	'Six Hills'	WPat
	'Snowfire'	SChu
	'Snowshill Manor' (p)	WPer
	'Solar Chiaro' (pf)	SBai
	'Solar Giallo Oro' (pf)	SBai
	'Solomon' (p)	SSvw WKin
	'Solomon's Hat' (p)	WKin
	'Sops-in-wine' (p)	EChP ECha EMFP GBuc GCal MNrw SAll SBch SChu SHay SMrm WKin WSSM
	'Southmead' (p)	ECho
§	'Souvenir de la Malmaison' (M)	SAll
	'Spangle' (b) **new**	SAll
	'Spangled Star' (p)	MBNS
	'Spencer Bickham' (p)	EMFP MNrw WKin
	'Spinfield Volcano' (b) **new**	SAll
	'Spirit' (pf)	SBai SHay
	'Spring Beauty' (p)	NBir WHer
	'Spring Star' (p)	ECtt EWin NLar NPri
	'Square Eyes'	see *D.* 'Old Square Eyes'
	squarrosus	EPot GKir NWCA
*	- ***alpinus***	ECho ITim
	- 'Nanus'	ELan EWes LBee LRHS
	'Squeeks' (p)	SChu
	'Stan Stroud' (b)	SHay
I	'Star' **new**	SBai
	'Starry Eyes'	EPot NBlu NCGa
	'Storm' (pf)	SAll
	'Strathspey' (b)	SAll SHay
	'Strawberries and Cream' (p)	CHar CSBt EBee ECtt EMFP LAst LRHS NEgg NOrc SHay SPla SPoG WMnd WRHF WWol
	'Strawberry Kiss' **new**	LRHS WWeb
*	***strictus*** subsp. ***pulchellus***	EHyt GCrs NSla SOkd
§	***subacaulis***	GAbr NLar
	- subsp. ***brachyanthus*** 'Murray Lyon' **new**	WThu
	suendermannii	see *D. petraeus*
	'Summerfield Adam' (p) **new**	SAll
	'Summerfield Amy Francesa' (p) **new**	SAll
	'Summerfield Blaze' (p) **new**	SAll
	'Summerfield Debbie' (p) **new**	SAll
	'Summerfield Emma Louise' (p) **new**	SAll
	'Summerfield Rebecca' (p) **new**	SAll
	'Sunray' (b)	SAll SHay
	'Sunstar' (b)	SAll SHay
§	***superbus***	CHrt CSpe EGoo EShb EWTr LPhx MSal WHer WKin WMoo WPer
	- 'Crimsonia'	SHGN WHrl WPer WPtf
	- var. ***longicalycinus***	MNrw MSte WHer
I	- 'Primadonna'	WPer WPtf
*	- 'Rose'	WPer
	- 'Snowdonia'	WPer
	- subsp. ***speciosus***	CSec
	'Susan' (p)	SAll
	'Susannah' (p) **new**	SAll
*	'Susan's Seedling' (p) **new**	SAll
	'Swanlake' (p)	SAll SHay
	'Sway Belle' (p)	CBcs SBai
	'Sway Delight' (p)	SBai
	'Sway Sorbet' (p)	SBai
	'Sweet Sue' (b)	SAll SHay
	'Sweetheart Abbey' (p)	EMFP GBuc IGor SChu SSvw WKin
	sylvestris	EPot SSvw
	'Syston Beauty' (p)	WKin
	'Taff Glow' (b) **new**	SAll
	'Tamsin' (p) ♀H4	SBla WKin
	'Tamsin Fifield' (b) ♀H4 **new**	SAll
	'Tatra Blush'	GCal GMac
	'Tatra Bull's-eye' (p)	GCal
	'Tatra Fragrance'	CMdw GCal
	'Tatra Ghost'	GCal
	'Tayside Red' (M)	SAll
	'Tempo' (pf) ♀H1	SBai SHay WWol
	'Terranova'PBR	SHay
	'Terry Sutcliffe' (p)	WKin
	the Bloodie pink	see *D.* 'Caesar's Mantle'
	'The Saboteur' (b) **new**	SAll
	'Thomas' (p)	CSLe SChu SMrm WEas
	'Thomas Lee' (b) **new**	SAll
	'Thora' (M)	SAll
I	'Tickled Pink'	COtt WWeb
	'Tiny Rubies'	see *D. gratianopolitanus* 'Tiny Rubies'
	'Toledo' (p)	WKin
	'Treasure' (p)	SHay
	'Trevor' (p) **new**	SAll
	'Tundra'PBR (pf)	SBai SHay
	turkestanicus	NBir
	'Tweedale Seedling'	GBuc
	Tyrolean trailing carnations **new**	SAll
	'Uncle Teddy' (b) ♀H4	SAll

'Unique' (p)	EMFP SAll SChu SSvw WHoo WKin
'Ursula Le Grove' (p)	EMFP IGor SChu SSvw WKin
'Valda Wyatt' (p) 🏆H4	CBcs EBee ELan EMFP EPfP GKir LAst LRHS MBow NEgg SAll SBai SChu SHay SPla SPoG WMnd
'Violet Clove' (b)	SHay
'W.A. Musgrave'	see *D.* 'Musgrave's Pink'
'W.H. Brooks' (b) **new**	SAll
'Waithman Beauty' (p)	CTri ECtt GAbr MBar SAll WHoo WKin WPer WTin WWye
'Waithman's Jubilee' (p)	SAll SRms
'Warden Hybrid' (p)	CMea CPBP CTri ECtt EDAr EPfP EWin GAbr LRHS NBlu SHGN SHay SPoG WAbe WLin
'Wedding Bells' (pf)	SAll
'Weetwood Double' (p)	CFee WSPU
'Welcome' (b)	SHay
weyrichii	CLyd ECho NMen
'Whatfield Anona' (p)	ELan SAll
'Whatfield Beauty'	EChP ECho ECtt EDAr ELan LRHS SAll
'Whatfield Brilliant' (p)	GKir
'Whatfield Can-can' 🏆H4	CLyd CMea COkL CPBP ECho ECtt EDAr EMFP EWin GKir GMaP LRHS NCGa NEgg NJOw NPri SAll SPoG WAbe
'Whatfield Cerise'	CLyd
'Whatfield Cream Lace'	GAbr NWCA
'Whatfield Cyclops'	CLyd CPBP EDAr LRHS SAll SChu WKin
'Whatfield Dawn'	CLyd ECho ELan GKev
'Whatfield Dorothy Mann' (p)	ECho ELan SAll
'Whatfield Fuchsia' (p)	CLyd SAll
'Whatfield Gem' (p)	CLyd CPBP ECtt ELan EMFP EWin GCal GMac LAst LRHS MSte MWgw NJOw NPri SAll WFar WKin WPer
'Whatfield Joy' (p)	CLyd ECtt EDAr ELan EPfP EPot EWin GAbr LBee LRHS MHer NMen NPri SAll WPat
'Whatfield Magenta' (p) 🏆H4	CLyd ELan EPfP EPot ESis GAbr GKir LBee LRHS NJOw NWCA SAll SChu SPoG WAbe WEas
'Whatfield Mini' (p)	EDAr SAll SRms WPer
'Whatfield Miss' (p) **new**	SAll
'Whatfield Misty Morn' (p)	CLyd ECho ELan SAll
'Whatfield Peach' (p) **new**	SAll
'Whatfield Pom Pom' (p)	CLyd
'Whatfield Pretty Lady' (p)	ECho ELan SAll
'Whatfield Rose' (p)	ECho EPot
'Whatfield Ruby' (p)	CLyd ELan GKir LRHS NWCA SAll WPer
'Whatfield Supergem'	CLyd ECho ECtt ELan EPot
'Whatfield White' (p)	CLyd ECho ECtt ELan LRHS SAll SRms
'Whatfield White Moon' (p)	ECho
'Whatfield Wisp' (p)	CM&M CPBP CTri ELan EWin GAbr GEdr MRav NBir NMen NWCA WFar
I 'White and Crimson' (p) **new**	SAll
'White Joy'[PBR] (p) 🏆H4	EDAr EMFP ENot SPoG WWol
'White Ladies' (p)	ELan ENot SAll WKin
'White Liberty'[PBR] (pf)	SHay
'Whitecliff' (b)	SAll SHay
'Whitehill' (p) 🏆H4	ECho MHer NMen NWCA NWoo WPat
'Whitesmith' (b) 🏆H4 **new**	SAll
'Whitford Belle' (p)	SBai
'Widecombe Fair' (p) 🏆H4	CMea CTri EBee ECtt EDAr ELan LRHS NLar NLon SAll SPoG SRms
* 'Wild Velvet' (p)	WKin
'William Brownhill' (p)	EMFP SChu SSvw WKin
'Winnie Lesurf' (b) **new**	SAll
'Winsome' (p)	SHay
'Yorkshireman' (b)	SHay
'Zebra' (b)	SAll SHay
zederbaueri	NWCA
'Zoe's Choice' (p) 🏆H4	COkL

Diapensia (*Diapensiaceae*)

lapponica var. ***obovata***	GIBF WAbe

Diarrhena (*Poaceae*)

americana **new**	EPPr
japonica	EPPr GFor WDyG
* ***mandschurica***	EPPr
obovata **new**	EPPr

Diascia ✿ (*Scrophulariaceae*)

anastrepta	MHom
- HWEL 0219	NWCA
'Appleby Appleblossom'	GCal SChu
'Appleby Apricot'	NDov NGdn
'Apricot' hort.	see *D. barberae* 'Hopleys Apricot'
Apricot Delight = 'Codicot' (Sun Chimes Series)	LIck NPri
* 'Aquarius'	SChu
'Baby Bums'	SPoG WWol
barberae	ELan
- 'Belmore Beauty' (v)	CCge ECtt EMan EPyc EWes EWin LSou MHer NFla SChu
- 'Blackthorn Apricot' 🏆H3-4	EChP ECha ECtt EDAr EHyt ELan EPfP GBuc GKir IHMH LAst LRHS MBow MHer MSte MWgw NRya SBla SChu SMrm SPav SPer SPlb SPoG SWvt WCAu WFar WPer WSHC
- 'Crûg Variegated' (v)	EMan
§ - 'Fisher's Flora' 🏆H3-4	EPyc NBro NDov NMen WFar
- 'Fisher's Flora' x 'Lilac Belle'	ECtt EDAr SHFr
§ - 'Hopleys Apricot'	EPfP
§ - 'Ruby Field' 🏆H3-4	CMea ECha ECtt EDAr ELan EPfP GKir LAst LRHS MDun MHer MWgw NGdn NRya SBla SPer SPla SPoG SRms SWvt WCFE WFar
Blue Bonnet = 'Hecbon'	EChP ECtt EMan GMac SChu SWvt WFar
'Blush'	see *D. integerrima* 'Blush'
Blush Delight = 'Codiush' (Sun Chimes Series)	LIck
'Coldham'	ECtt EMan SDys
Coral Belle = 'Hecbel'[PBR] 🏆H3-4	CHar ECtt EHyt EMan EPfP EWes EWin GMac LAst LRHS LSou MBow MDun MSte MTis NEgg NLon SChu SIng SPav WEas WFar WPer
cordata misapplied	see *D. barberae* 'Fisher's Flora'
cordifolia	see *D. barberae* 'Fisher's Flora'
'Dainty Duet'	SChu
'Dark Eyes' 🏆H3-4	MSte SChu
Eclat = 'Heclat'[PBR]	ECtt WFar
elegans misapplied	see *D. fetcaniensis*, *D. vigilis*
'Elizabeth' 🏆H3-4	MMil WSPU
'Emma'	NLon SChu SUsu SWvt
felthamii	see *D. fetcaniensis*
§ ***fetcaniensis***	CMHG CPne EPfP EWin MHom NEgg WBVN WBrk WCFE WHal
- 'Daydream'	LRHS WLin WWeb
flanaganii misapplied	see *D. vigilis*
flanaganii Hiern	see *D. stachyoides*
'Frilly' 🏆H3-4	ECtt MSte SChu
'Hector Harrison'	see *D.* 'Salmon Supreme'

'Hector's Hardy' ♀H3-4	MSte
Ice Cracker = 'Hecrack'	CElw CMea EChP ECtt EHyt ELan EMan EShb EWin GMac LAst MBow NFla NGdn SHGN SPav WWol
Ice Cream = 'Icepol' **new**	LAst LSou
Iceberg = 'Hecice'[PBR]	CHar CSpe NLar NPri SWvt
§ ***integerrima*** ♀H3-4	CPne CSam ECha ELan EMan LLWP MHom SChu SGar SIgm SPla WCot
- 'Alba'	see *D. integerrima* 'Blush'
§ - 'Blush'	CAby CSam CSpe EGoo EMan GMac MSte NEgg SAga SGar SHGN SMrm
- 'Ivory Angel'	see *D. integerrima* 'Blush'
integrifolia	see *D. integerrima*
'Jack Elliott'	see *D. vigilis* 'Jack Elliott'
'Jacqueline's Joy'	CMea EMan MSte NFla NGdn NPer SBch SChu SMrm WFar
'Joyce's Choice' ♀H3-4	CStr EWes EWin MSte NGdn SBri WFar WHoo
'Kate'	LRHS NDov SChu
'Katherine Sharman' (v)	ECtt EMan EWes EWin LRHS LSou MBNS NGdn SAga WWol
'Lady Valerie' ♀H3-4	CStr EWes EWin MSte WPer
'Lilac Belle' ♀H3-4	CCge CMea CPne ECtt EHyt ELan EPfP LAst LRHS MHar MHer MWgw NEgg NGdn NLon SMrm SPla SPlb SPoG WFar WHoo WPer
'Lilac Mist' ♀H3-4	NLon NPer NWoo SChu
Little Dancer = 'Pendan'[PBR]	LAst LSou NLar NPri SGar SIng WGor
'Louise'	GBuc
'Lucy' x ***mollis***	SChu SDys SUsu
'Miro'	MBow NLar WWol
patens	CHll
Pink Delight = 'Codiink'	LIck
Pink Panther = 'Penther'[PBR]	ECtt NEgg NLar SCoo SPav SPoG SWvt
'Pink Queen'	ECtt SRms
* 'Pisces'	SChu
Prince of Orange = 'Hopor' **new**	EShb LAst LSou WGor
Red Ace = 'Hecrace'[PBR]	EChP EPfP EWin LAst NEgg NPer SGar SIng SPav SPoG SWvt
Redstart = 'Hecstart'	ECtt EPfP EWin LAst MBow NFla NGdn NPri SChu SPet SWvt WFar WWol
rigescens ♀H3	More than 30 suppliers
§ - 'Anne Rennie'	EBee EMan SPoG
- pale	see *D. rigescens* 'Anne Rennie'
rigescens x ***lilacina***	CCge CElw
I 'Rosa'	WWol
'Ruby Field'	see *D. barberae* 'Ruby Field'
'Rupert Lambert' ♀H3-4	CElw CStr EMon GBuc LLWP MHom NDov SBri SChu WLin WPer
§ 'Salmon Supreme'	ECtt ELan EPfP EWin LPhx NGdn NPer NPri SChu SRms WFar WMoo WPer
'Selina's Choice'	GBuc SChu
§ ***stachyoides***	ELan SBch
Sun Chimes Peach = 'Codipeim' **new**	LAst
Susan = 'Winsue'[PBR]	WFar
Sydney Olympics = 'Hecsyd'	EMan
tugelensis	WFar
'Twinkle' ♀H3-4	CPBP ECtt EPfP EWes GCal LAst NBir NGdn NPer NPri SChu SCoo SPet WFar
* 'Twins Gully'	GCal SMrm
* ***variegata*** (v)	MBNS
§ ***vigilis*** ♀H3	CFee CMHG CPLG CSam EChP ECha EDAr EPfP EWin GCal LPhx MTis MWgw NBro NEgg NLon SAga SChu SDix SGar
§ - 'Jack Elliott'	EWin MDun SPla WCFE
'White Cloud'	SChu WSPU

Diascia x *Linaria* see *Nemesia caerulea*

Dicentra ✿ (*Papaveraceae*)

CC 4450 **new**	CPLG
'Adrian Bloom'	CWCL EChP ECtt EHrv EPfP EPla GSki LRHS MBNS MWgw NBid NCob NSti SCoo SGSe SWvt WFar WMnd WMoo WPnP
'Angel Heart' **new**	MBNS NBro NGdn NLar SPer
'Bacchanal' ♀H4	More than 30 suppliers
'Boothman's Variety'	see *D.* 'Stuart Boothman'
'Bountiful'	CMHG GKir GMaP GSki LRHS MLLN MNFA MRav MWgw NArg NGdn NLon NSti SChu SPer SPet SPla SWvt WMnd WRHF
'Brownie'	GBuc
canadensis	CLAP EBee GBuc GSki MTho NSti SSpi WCot WCru
'Candy Hearts' **new**	WHlf
'Coldham'	SMac WCru WSHC WTin
cucullaria	More than 30 suppliers
- 'Pittsburg'	CBos EBee SCnR SSpi WCot
'Dragon Heart' **new**	MBNS NBro NGdn NLar WCot
eximia hort.	see *D. formosa*
eximia (Ker Gawl.) Torr.	MTho MWat NEgg
- 'Alba'	see *D. eximia* 'Snowdrift'
§ - 'Snowdrift'	CLAP CM&M EChP ECtt EHrv ELan ENot EPfP GKir IHMH LRHS MBri MDun MTho NGdn NRnb SPoG SRms SSpi WFar WHoo WMnd WMoo WPnP WPrP
§ ***formosa***	More than 30 suppliers
- *alba*	CPLG CRow CTri ECha GAbr GMaP MWrn NBir NFor NLon NMRc NSti NVic SChu SPla SRms STes WCAu WCru WFar WLin
* - 'Aurora'	CBct CBre EBee EChP EWTr GBin GFlt GSki LRHS MBri MCCP MRav MWgw NCGa NGdn NRnb SPoG SWvt WFar WMnd WSan
- 'Cox's Dark Red' **new**	GCrs
- dark	WMoo
- 'Furse's Form'	GBin
- 'Gold Leaf'	EVFa
- subsp. ***oregana***	CLAP CRow EBee EPPr GAbr GCal GCrs GKir NChi NMen SBla SSpi WAbb WCru
- - NNS 00-233	WCot
- - 'Rosea'	EPPr NPar SSpi
- 'Rosemoor' **new**	NLon
- 'Spring Gold'	ECha WMoo
'Ivory Hearts' **new**	NCob WHlf
'King of Hearts'	More than 30 suppliers
'Langtrees' ♀H4	More than 30 suppliers
lichiangensis	CPLN WCru
- GWJ 9376	WCru
'Luxuriant' ♀H4	CBcs CSBt EBee EChP ECtt ELan ENot EPfP GAbr GKir GSki LRHS MBri MLLN MTis NCob SAga SMer SPer SPoG SRms STes SWvt WBVN WCot WFar WMnd WMoo WPnP WSan
macrantha	CDes CFil CLAP CRow EBee ECha EPfP GBuc GCra GFlt LAma MTho SBla SMad SSpi WCru WPGP WSHC

	macrocapnos	CAby CBcs CFir CPLN CRow CSec EBee EChP EPfP GBuc GQui IDee LRHS MDKP MTho NSti WBGC WBrE WCru
	'Pearl Drops'	CElw CRow EChP EHrv ELan EVFa GBuc GGar GKir GMaP LRHS LSpr MBri MRav NBid NEgg NGdn NOak SMac SOkh SPer SPla SRms WAbb WEas WHoo WMoo WTin WWhi
	peregrina	GIBF GTou NMen SOkd WAbe
§	***scandens***	CBrm CMHG CMil CRHN CRow CSpe CStu EBee EPfP GCal IFro MCCP MTho MWgw NCob NLar SGSe SHGN SMac SPoG SSpi SUsu WSHC WSPU WWhi
	- B&SWJ 2427	WCru
	- CC 3223	WRos
	- 'Shirley Clemo'	CPLG
	'Silversmith'	CFil
	Snowflakes = 'Fusd'	EWes GKir LRHS MCCP MRav NDov
	spectabilis ♀H4	More than 30 suppliers
	- 'Alba' ♀H4	More than 30 suppliers
	- 'Gold Heart'PBR	CHad CPen EBee EHan EMan ENot EPfP GBri GKir MRav NCGa NLar NSti SPer SPoG WFar
	'Spring Morning'	CElw CMHG CMil CPLG CPrp CRow CSam EHrv EPPr EPfP IBlr NSti SChu SSpi WEas WRHF
§	'Stuart Boothman' ♀H4	More than 30 suppliers
	thalictrifolia	see *D. scandens*
	torulosa B&SWJ 7814	WCru

Dichelostemma (*Alliaceae*)

§	***capitatum***	ETow
	- NNS 95-213	WCot
	congestum	CAvo EBee EBrs EMan EPot ERos LRHS WCot
	- NNS 97-75	SIgm
§	***ida-maia***	CAvo CBro EBee EBrs EPot LRHS
	- 'Pink Diamond'	CBro EBee EPot
	multiflorum	WCot
	pulchellum	see *D. capitatum*
	volubile	WCot
	- NNS 95-220	WCot

Dichocarpum (*Ranunculaceae*)

dalzielii	EBee WCot

Dichondra (*Convolvulaceae*)

§	***micrantha***	EShb
	- 'Emerald Falls' **new**	LSou NPri
	- 'Silver Falls'	COtt CSpe EShb LSou NPri SCoo SGar SPoG WPtf
	repens misapplied	see *D. micrantha*
	repens J.R. Forst & G. Forst.	XPep

Dichopogon (*Anthericaceae*)

strictus	CMon

Dichotomanthes (*Rosaceae*)

tristaniicarpa	CFil

Dichroa (*Hydrangeaceae*)

febrifuga	CAbb CBcs CDoC CFil CHII CKob CMil CPLG CWib EWes MAvo SLon WCot WCru WOVN WPGP
- B&SWJ 2367	WCru
- pink	CHEx
aff. ***hirsuta*** B&SWJ 8207 from Thailand	WCru
versicolor B&SWJ 6565	WCru

Dichromena see *Rhynchospora*

Dicksonia ✿ (*Dicksoniaceae*)

antarctica ♀H3	More than 30 suppliers
fibrosa ♀H3	CAbb CBcs CTrC EAmu EExo EUJe IDee SChr WMul WRic
sellowiana	WRic
squarrosa ♀H2	CAbb CBcs CTrC EExo ERea EUJe NBlu NMoo SAPC SArc SPoG WMul WRic
youngiae	WRic

Dicliptera (*Acanthaceae*)

§	***suberecta***	CBcs CDes CHal CHll CMdw EBee EHol EMan ERea EShb MOak SHFr SIgm SRkn WCot WDyG WPGP XPep

Dictamnus ✿ (*Rutaceae*)

	albus	More than 30 suppliers
§	- var. ***purpureus*** ♀H4	More than 30 suppliers
*	- ***turkestanicus*** **new**	GCal
	caucasicus	EBee SMHy
	fraxinella	see *D. albus* var. *purpureus*

Dictyolimon (*Plumbaginaceae*)

macrorrhabdos	GKev WCot

Dictyosperma (*Arecaceae*)

album	CRoM

Didymochlaena (*Dryopteridaceae*)

	lunulata	see *D. truncatula*
§	***truncatula***	CHal MBri

Dieffenbachia (*Araceae*)

'Camille' (v) ♀H1	LRHS
'Compacta' (v)	LRHS

Dierama ✿ (*Iridaceae*)

	CD&R 192	CRow
	CD&R 278	WHil
	ambiguum	CPne CStu SHFr
	argyreum	CElw CFil GKev IBlr
	'Ariel'	IBlr
	'Ballerina' **new**	CFir
	'Black Knight'	CPen IBlr
	'Blush'	IBlr
	'Candy Stripe'	CRow GBri GSki MCCP STes
	'Castlewellan' **new**	WCra
	'Cherry Chimes'	CPen ENot IBal LBuc
	cooperi	CElw CFwr CPne CPrp GBri IBlr SPoG WHil
	- 'Edinburgh White'	WLFP
	'Coral Bells'	GCal
	'Donard Legacy'	GBri IBlr
§	***dracomontanum***	More than 30 suppliers
	- dwarf lilac	MAnH
	- dwarf pale pink	CM&M WWeb
	- dwarf pink	CBot CPne
	- Wisley Princess Group **new**	LRHS
	dubium	IBlr
	ensifolium	see *D. pendulum*
	erectum	CLAP IBlr MAnH
	'Fairy Bells'	CPen ENot
	floriferum	CBro EBee IBlr
	galpinii	CAby CFil CLAP GAbr GSki MAnH MWrn NLar STes WCot WPGP
	grandiflorum	IBlr
	'Guinevere'	More than 30 suppliers
	igneum	More than 30 suppliers

Plant	Suppliers
- CD&R 278	CPou
'Iris'	IBlr
jucundum	CPne EBee EPot GBri GBuc MLLN
'Knee-high Lavender'	CSpe SAga
'Lancelot'	CElw CFir CKno CLAP EBee EMan EPPr GBuc GEdr GMaP GSki IBal IBlr IPot LAst MBnl MDun NEgg NLar NSti SPla SVil WCot WKif WPop WWhi
latifolium	CFwr CHid EBee EChP GAbr GSki IBlr SIgm SMad WSan
luteoalbidum	CDes CLAP CStu EBee WPGP
'Mandarin'	IBlr
medium	CFil CMil CPen EBee GSki LPio LRHS SMrm SUsu WCot WPGP WWpP
'Milkmaid'	CPrp IBlr
mossii	CFil EBee IBlr MWrn NLar SPlb
nixonianum	IBlr
'Oberon' **new**	EBee
'Pamina'	IBlr
'Papagena'	IBlr
'Papageno'	IBlr
pauciflorum	More than 30 suppliers
- CD&R 197	CPBP MDKP
§ ***pendulum***	More than 30 suppliers
- var. ***pumilum*** **new**	EShb
pictum	IBlr
Plant World hybrids	MWrn NPri
'Pretty Flamingo'	IBlr
'Puck'	CDes CPen EBee GCal IBlr IGor ITim MLLN WPGP
pulcherrimum	More than 30 suppliers
- var. ***album***	More than 30 suppliers
- - B&SWJ 2827	WCru
- 'Angel Gabriel'	WWpP
- 'Blackbird'	More than 30 suppliers
- brick shades **new**	WHil
- dark pink	WHil
- dwarf	GCal GSki WWhi
- 'Falcon'	IBlr
- 'Flamingo'	CPrp IBlr
- 'Merlin'	More than 30 suppliers
- 'Miranda' **new**	WCot
- 'Pearly Queen'	CRow
- 'Peregrine'	WPGP
- pink	CDWL CTbh EPza GBBs NBPC NBid WBVN WWhi
- 'Red Orr'	ITim
- 'Redwing'	IBlr
- Slieve Donard hybrids	CLAP CSam EChP ECtt EMan GBri GCal ITim LRHS MAnH MAvo MFOX MHer MTis MWrn NArg SPet SPoG WCot WCra WHrl WPnP WSSM WSan WWpP
pumilum hort.	see *D. dracomontanum*
'Queen of the Night'	IBlr
reynoldsii	CAbb CDes CFil CFwr CHid CPne EBee EMan EVFa GAbr GBuc GSki IBlr ITim MAnH MCCP MHar MLLN MWrn SGar SHGN SMad SPlb SSpi STes WHil WHoo WLFP WPGP
'Rich Pink'	CPen
robustum	CFil CLAP CPou EBee GBri IBlr WBVN WPGP
'Sarastro'	CPrp IBlr
'September Charm'	IBlr
sertum	CBro
'Snowgoose' **new**	WCra
'Tamino'	IBlr
'Tiny Bells'	GCal
'Titania'	CPen IBlr
trichorhizum	CLAP EBee EKen EVFa GAbr GBri GSki IBlr MNrw MWrn NLar SAga SHGN SMad STes
'Tubular Bells'	IBlr
'Violet Ice'	IBlr
'Westminster Chimes'	CDes IBlr WPGP

Diervilla ✿ (*Caprifoliaceae*)

Plant	Suppliers
lonicera	CHar MTis SLon SMac WFar
middendorffiana	see *Weigela middendorffiana*
rivularis	CPle
§ ***sessilifolia***	CBcs CHar CPle ECrN EPfP IMGH LAst MRav SGar SLon WBVN WCot WFar WSHC WTin WWpP
- 'Butterfly'	GKir LRHS
x ***splendens***	CAbP CCge CMHG CPLG CPle CWib EBee EHoe ELan EPfP LAst LRHS MBNS MBar MRav MSwo SBrw SGar SLPl SMac SPer SPla SPoG SSta WBcn WDin

Dietes (*Iridaceae*)

Plant	Suppliers
bicolor	CAbb CDes CHEx CMon CPne CTrC EMan ERea EShb LEdu LPio SDnm SGSe
* ***compacta*** **new**	CPen
grandiflora	CAbb CArn CDes CFee CFwr CMon CPne EBee EMan ERea EShb LEdu LPio LRHS NEgg SBch SGSe WWye
* - 'Reen Lelie'	CMdw
§ ***iridioides***	CDes CNic CPLG CPne CSWP CSec EBee EShb GBin GGar LEdu LRHS MSte WPGP

Digitalis ✿ (*Scrophulariaceae*)

Plant	Suppliers
ambigua	see *D. grandiflora*
apricot hybrids	see *D. purpurea* 'Sutton's Apricot'
cariensis	EBla SPav
ciliata	CFir EBee EChP ELan MLLN SPav WCot
davisiana	CBot EBla EChP GBuc MWgw NOak NRnb SPav WCHb WHrl WMoo WPer WPnP
dubia	CBot EBla EPfP MAnH NBir NLar SBla SDnm SPav WAbe WOut
'Elsie Kelsey'	GBin MAnH MBri NArg NLsd NRnb SDnm SPav WCra WPen WWpP
eriostachya	see *D. lutea*
ferruginea ♀H4	More than 30 suppliers
- 'Gelber Herold'	CBot EBee EChP ERou EWin GMaP LPhx LRHS MAnH MSte NBre NDov NLar NRnb SMac WGor
- 'Gigantea'	CBot EBee EMan ERou EWTr GCal LRHS MBNS MWgw NEgg NPri NRnb NSti WSel
- var. ***schischkinii***	CPLG CSec EBla EWTr GCal MBNS NLar NRnb SDnm SPav WLin WPGP
'Flashing Spires'	see *D. lutea* 'Flashing Spires'
* ***floribunda***	CSec EBee SPav
fontanesii	EChP EPPr EWTr GBuc NBur
'Foxley Primrose'	MBri
x ***fulva***	MLLN NBir
'Glory of Roundway'	CBot CDes CPom EBee MEHN MFOX MHer SSvw WCot WFar
§ ***grandiflora*** ♀H4	More than 30 suppliers
- 'Carillon'	CBot CHea CPom CSam CWan EBee EChP ENot EShb LDai LPhx MBNS MSte MTis NLar NPri WGor WPer
- 'Carlyon' **new**	SOkd

- 'Dwarf Carillon'	ECtt
- 'Temple Bells'	EBee EBla EMag WPer
heywoodii	see *D. purpurea* subsp. *heywoodii*
'John Innes Tetra'	CBot CSam EChP EShb LRHS MBNS WPGP
kishinskyi	see *D. parviflora*
laevigata	More than 30 suppliers
- subsp. ***graeca***	EBee WGor
- white-flowered	NRnb
lamarckii hort.	see *D. lanata*
lamarckii Ivanina	EBee SIgm WLin
§ ***lanata***	More than 30 suppliers
- 'Café Crème' **new**	LSou
leucophaea	EGoo EMar
§ ***lutea***	More than 30 suppliers
§ - subsp. ***australis***	EBla LDai SDnm SHFr SPav WHil
§ - 'Flashing Spires' (v)	EKen EMan GBri LSou NEgg NRnb
- 'Yellow Medley'	WCot
x ***mertonensis*** ♀H4	More than 30 suppliers
- 'Summer King'	CBot ECtt MBow NGHP WGor WSel
micrantha	see *D. lutea* subsp. *australis*
nervosa	EBla SPav
obscura	CBot CFir CPom EBee EBla EChP EHrv ERou EWTr LAst LRHS MWgw NBir NCob NGHP NPri SBla SDnm SIde SIgm SPav SSpi WCHb WGor WHil WMnd WPer
* - 'Dusky Maid'	WCra
- subsp. ***laciniata*** **new**	SSpi
orientalis	see *D. grandiflora*
§ ***parviflora***	More than 30 suppliers
- 'Milk Chocolate'	EPfP MHer NEgg NRnb SIde SPet SSvw WSel
purpurea	CArn CHrt EBee ECtt EDAr ELau EUnu GPoy MBow MHer NArg NBlu NCGa NCob NFor NLRH NLan NMir NPri SECG SIde SPlb SPoG WMoo WPer WWFP WWpP WWye
- f. ***albiflora***	More than 30 suppliers
- - 'Anne Redetzky'	EBee EChP ECtt ENot LBuc LSou MAnH NSti SCoo SOkd SPoG
- - unspotted	CWan EMar
* - 'Campanulata Alba'	CBot
- 'Chedglow' (v)	CNat WCHb
- dwarf red	MBNS WGor
- Excelsior Group	CBcs CBot CCge CHrt CSBt CTri ENot EPfP ERou GMaP MBri MWat NMir NVic SMer SPer SPoG SRms SWvt WFar WGor WWeb
- - primrose	ERou SPer
- - (Suttons; Unwins) ♀H4	ECtt MRav
- - white	ERou
- Foxy Group	CBot CWib ECtt EHrv GKir MBNS NArg NJOw NLsd SPet SPoG SRms WFar WPer WSan WWeb
- - 'Foxy Apricot'	CBot SPla SWvt
- - 'Foxy Pink'	EBee SPla SSpi
- - 'Foxy Primrose'	CBot EChP
- Giant Spotted Group	CBot COtt EBee ECtt EHrv EMag EPfP GKir LRHS SCoo WPer
- Glittering Prizes Group	LRHS
- Gloxinioides Group	CBot EBee ELan ENot EPfP MAnH NCob SHFr
- - 'Isabellina'	CBot WPer
- - 'The Shirley' ♀H4	ECtt WGor
* - ***heptandra***	CNat
§ - subsp. ***heywoodii***	CBot CDes CHrt CSec EBee EChP ELan ENot GBuc MAnH SDnm SPav WCHb WMoo WPer
- - 'Pink Champagne'	ENot
- - 'Silver Fox' **new**	CSec MBri SMar
- 'Jellito's Apricot' **new**	CSam
- subsp. ***mariana***	EBee
- subsp. ***nevadensis***	CBot
- 'Pam's Choice'	CSpe EMag EMar EPyc EWin MAnH MWrn SSth WHrl WMnd
- peloric	WCHb
- 'Primrose Carousel'	EBee ECtt EMag EWin MAnH MBct MWat MWrn NEgg NLsd SMar SSth
- 'Snow Thimble'	CBot ENot EShb EWin GAbr MAnH MNFA MWgw NCGa NJOw NLar NVic WHil WWeb
§ - 'Sutton's Apricot' ♀H4	More than 30 suppliers
* - 'Sutton's Giant Primrose'	CBot EMan EWll MAnH MWrn WSSM
- 'Tinkerbell'	EMag NArg
'Saltwood Summer'	COtt NPro SCoo
sibirica	CSec EBee EChP GBuc LPhx NEgg NRnb WCHb WPer WTMC
* ***spaniflora***	EChP LPhx NEgg NLar NRnb WGwG
* ***stewartii***	CHar CSec CWan EChP ECtt ELan EWes GAbr GBBs GIBF LDai MAnH MAvo MBNS MDKP MFOX NBur NCGa NChi NRnb SBod SGSe SPav SPer WLin WMoo WWpP
thapsi	CArn CBot CSec CWan EBla EChP ECtt EWTr MBNS MLLN NBur NPri SBla SBod SDnm SIde SMac SPav WCHb WMoo WPer WWFP
- JCA 410.000	EBee
trojana	ECtt GBuc LRHS SGar
viridiflora	CPom EBee EBla ECtt EDAr MBNS MDKP MWhi NBro SGSe SGar SPav WCHb WFar WPer

dill see *Anethum graveolens*

Dionaea (*Droseraceae*)

muscipula	CSWC LRHS MCCP WSSs
- 'Akai Ryu'	WSSs
- 'Royal Red'	CSWC
- shark-toothed **new**	CSWC
- 'Spider'	CSWC

Dionysia (*Primulaceae*)

afghanica **new**	EHyt
'Annielle'	EHyt
archibaldii	EHyt
aretioides ♀H2	WAbe
- SLIZE 035	EHyt
- 'Bevere'	EHyt WAbe
- 'Gravetye'	ECho
- 'Paul Furse'	EHyt
- 'Phyllis Carter'	ECho
- 'Susan Tucker'	EHyt
bazoftica T4Z **new**	EHyt
bryoides H 1986	EHyt
- SLIZE 236	EHyt
- 'Woodside' **new**	EHyt
'Charlson Drew'	EHyt
'Charlson Gem'	EHyt
'Charlson Jake'	EHyt
'Charlson Moonglow' **new**	EHyt
'Charlson Petite'	EHyt
'Charlson Stuart'	EHyt
'Charlson Thomas'	EHyt
'Chris Grey-Wilson' **new**	EHyt
'Cinderella'	EHyt
curviflora	EHyt
- SLIZE 213	EHyt
'Emmely'	EHyt WAbe
'Eric Watson'	EHyt
'Ewesley Gamma'	EHyt

'Ewesley Iota' EHyt
'Ewesley Kappa' EHyt
'Ewesley Mu' EHyt
'Ewesley Theta' EHyt
'Francesca' EHyt
freitagii EHyt
gaubae **new** EHyt
'Gotborg' **new** EHyt
'Ina' EHyt
involucrata white **new** CGra
iranshahrii SLIZE 213 EHyt
janthina EHyt
- SLIZE 265 EHyt
lamingtonii EHyt
'Liberty' **new** EHyt
'Luna' **new** EHyt
'Lycaena' **new** EHyt
'Markus' EHyt
michauxii EHyt
- SLIZE 254 EHyt
'Monika' EHyt WAbe
'Nan Watson' EHyt
'Nocturne' EHyt
odora **new** EHyt
'Orion' EHyt
'Pascal' **new** EHyt
'Rhapsodie' EHyt
'Schneeball' EHyt
tapetodes ENF 92-5 EHyt
- farinose ECho
- 'Peter Edwards' EHyt
termeana T4Z **new** EHyt
viscidula GWH 1305 EHyt
'Yellowstone' **new** EHyt
zagrica SLIZE 176 EHyt

Dioon (*Zamiaceae*)

califanoi CBrP
caputoi CBrP
edule ♀H1 CBrP CRoM WMul
- var. ***angustifolium*** CBrP
mejiae CBrP
merolae CBrP
rzedowskii CBrP
spinulosum CBrP EAmu SBig WMul

Dioscorea (*Dioscoreaceae*)

batatas CPLN LEdu MGol MSal
discolor **new** CPLN
elephantipes ♀H1 EShb
japonica CSec EShb ITer WBVN
nipponica MSal
quinqueloba WCru
villosa CArn MSal

Diosma (*Rutaceae*)

ericoides LBuc SWvt
- 'Pink Fountain' LBuc
- 'Sunset Gold' LBuc SCoo
hirsuta 'Silver Flame' LBuc

Diosphaera (*Campanulaceae*)

asperuloides see *Trachelium asperuloides*

Diospyros (*Ebenaceae*)

austroafricana SPlb
duclouxii CBcs CFil
kaki (F) CBcs CMCN EPfP ERom NLar WDin
lotus CAgr CBcs CFil CLnd CMCN CTho ECre LEdu NLar SPlb WFar WPGP
- (f) **new** CAgr
- (m) **new** CAgr
lycioides **new** EShb SPlb
rhombifolia CFil WPGP
virginiana (F) CAgr CBcs CMCN CTho EPfP LEdu NLar SSpi

Dipcadi (*Hyacinthaceae*)

glaucum CDes
lividum WPGP
serotinum AB&S 4308 from Morocco **new** CMon
- var. ***lividum*** AB&S 4311 from Morocco **new** CMon

Dipelta (*Caprifoliaceae*)

floribunda ♀H4 CBcs CBot CBrm CDul CFil CMCN CPMA EBee ELan EMil EPfP GKir LRHS MBlu NLar SBrw SLon SPer SSpi SSta WPGP
ventricosa CAbP CBcs CFil CMCN CPMA CPle EPfP GKir LRHS MBlu NLar SLon SSpi WFar WPGP
yunnanensis CBcs CFil CPLG CPMA CTri ELan EMil EPfP IArd IDee LRHS NLar SBrw SSpi SSta WPGP WPat WWes

Diphylleia (*Berberidaceae*)

cymosa CAby CLAP EBee ECha EMan GEdr LPhx MSal SSpi WCot WCru WTin
grayi CLAP GEdr WCru
sinensis CLAP GEdr WCru

Dipidax see *Onixotis*

Diplacus see *Mimulus*

Dipladenia see *Mandevilla*

Diplarrhena (*Iridaceae*)

Helen Dillon's form IBlr SUsu
§ ***latifolia*** CFil CHar EMan GBBs GGar IBlr SGSe WAbe
moraea CAbP CDes CElw CFil CMea CPLG CWCL EBee EBrs EMan GAbr GCal GSki IBlr ITim LPio LRHS MDun NCGa SSpi WAbe WBrE WCot WPGP WSHC
- ***minor*** GBBs IBlr
- 'Slieve Donard' IBlr
- West Coast form see *D. latifolia*

Diplazium (*Woodsiaceae*)

wichurae **new** EPPr

Diplotaxis (*Brassicaceae*)

muralis CArn WJek

Dipogon (*Papilionaceae*)

§ ***lignosus*** CPLN

Dipsacus ✿ (*Dipsacaceae*)

§ ***fullonum*** CArn CHrt CPrp CWan GBar IFro MBow MChe MHer MWgw NBid NDov NLsd NMir NPri NVic SBch SIde SWal WHer WJek WWpP WWye
inermis CPom EBee ECha EMon GBar IFro LPhx NBid NDov NLar WFar WHer
japonicus EBee MSal
- HWJ 695 WCru
pilosus CPom NDov WBWf
sativus NLar WHer
strigosus LPhx
sylvestris see *D. fullonum*

Dipteracanthus see *Ruellia*

Dipteronia (*Aceraceae*)

sinensis — CBcs CFil CMCN IArd LRHS NLar SBrw SSpi WBcn WNor WPGP

Disanthus (*Hamamelidaceae*)

cercidifolius ♀H4 — CAbP CBcs CFil CMCN EPfP IDee LRHS MAsh MGos NEgg NLar SBrw SSpi

Discaria (*Rhamnaceae*)

chacaye — CFil LEdu WPGP

Diselma (*Cupressaceae*)

archeri — CDoC CKen CNic MBar NLar SCoo
- 'Read Dwarf' **new** — CKen

Disphyma (*Aizoaceae*)

crassifolium — SChr

Disporopsis (*Convallariaceae*)

B&SWJ 3891 from Philippines — WCru
* **aspera** — CDes CLAP WCru WPGP
fuscopicta — CLAP EHrv EPPr WCru WTin
longifolia — CLAP
- B&SWJ 5284 — WCru
* **luzoniensis** B&SWJ 3891 — WCru
'Min Shan' — CBct
§ **pernyi** — More than 30 suppliers
- B&SWJ 1490 — WCru WFar
- 'Bill Baker' — MAvo
* **punctata** — SBla

Disporum (*Convallariaceae*)

bodinieri — LEdu
cantoniense — CDes CLAP CPom GEdr SSpi WCru WFar WPGP
- B&L 12512 — CLAP SBla
- B&SWJ 1424 — WCru
- DJHC 98485 — CDes
I - 'Aureovariegata' — WCot
- var. **cantoniense** f. **brunneum** B&SWJ 5290 — WCru
- 'Green Giant' **new** — CDes
- var. **kawakamii** B&SWJ 350 — WCru
flavens — CBct CBos CDes CFil CLAP CPom CStu EBee EMan EPfP GKir LPhx MDun NBid SBla SOkh SSpi SUsu WFar WPGP WSHC
- B&SWJ 872 — WCru
* **flavum** — EBrs LRHS SOkd
hookeri — CLAP EPot GGar GKir NMen WCot WCru
- var. **oreganum** — EBee GCrs GTou IBlr WCru
lanuginosum — EBee GCrs GEdr SSpi WCot WCru
leucanthum — SMHy
- B&SWJ 2389 — WCru
lutescens — WCru
maculatum — CBct CLAP EBee LPhx SBla SMac WCru
megalanthum — CDes CLAP EHrv SSpi WCot WCru
- CD&R 2412b — EPPr
nantauense — CStu LEdu SSpi WPGP
- B&SWJ 359 — CBct EBee WCot WCru
sessile — CHEx GFlt WCru
I - 'Aureovariegatum' (v) — WCru
- 'Cricket' **new** — GEdr
I - 'Robustum Variegatum' — EBee
- 'Variegatum' (v) — More than 30 suppliers
- 'White Lightning' (v) **new** — WCot
shimadae B&SWJ 399 — WCru
smilacinum — WCru
- B&SWJ 713 — WCru
* - 'Aureovariegatum' (v) — WCot WCru
- 'Choyo' — WCru
- double-flowered (d) — GCrs GEdr WCru
- pink — WCru
smithii — CAvo CBct CMea CStu EPot ERos GBuc GCrs GFlt GKir ITim LEdu NBir NMen SSpi WCot WCru WPGP
- 'Riele' **new** — SBla
taiwanense B&SWJ 1513 — WCru
trabeculatum 'Nakafu' **new** — WCru
uniflorum — LEdu WCru
- B&SWJ 651 — WCru
viridescens — LEdu SSpi WCru
- B&SWJ 4598 — WCru

Distictis (*Bignoniaceae*)

buccinatoria — CPLN

Distylium (*Hamamelidaceae*)

myricoides — CFil CMCN WFar
racemosum — CBcs CFil EBee EPfP GSki LRHS MBlu NLar SHBN SLon SMur SReu SSta WBVN WBcn WFar WSHC

Diuranthera see *Chlorophytum*

Dizygotheca see *Schefflera*

Dobinea (*Podoaceae*)

vulgaris B&SWJ 2532 — WCru

Dodecatheon (*Primulaceae*)

alpinum — GEdr NLAp SRms
- JCA 11744 — SBla
- subsp. **majus** — NSla
amethystinum — see *D. pulchellum*
'Aphrodite' — EBee EMan MBri NLar WAul WTMC
austrofrigidum — WCot
clevelandii — ETow
- subsp. **insulare** — LRHS NWCA
- subsp. **patulum** — GBuc LRHS
conjugens — CNic CPom
cusickii — see *D. pulchellum* subsp. *cusickii*
dentatum ♀H4 — CElw CPBP CPLG GBuc LRHS MDKP MTho NSla WAbe WFar
- subsp. **ellisiae** — GCrs
frigidum — WAbe
§ **hendersonii** ♀H4 — CBro CNic GBuc NMen NPar SBch SRms
integrifolium — see *D. hendersonii*
§ **jeffreyi** — CElw CMHG EBee GSki LRHS MBri NBid NDlv NMen NMyG NWCA SBla WAbe WFar
- 'Rotlicht' — SRms WPer
* x **lemoinei** — WAbe
§ **meadia** ♀H4 — More than 30 suppliers
- from Cedar County — WAbe
- f. **album** ♀H4 — CBcs CBro CFwr CMea CSWP CStu CTri EBee EChP ELan EPfP GSki LAma LPhx LRHS MNFA MTho NMen SBla SPer SRms SWvt WPnP WWhi
- 'Aphrodite' — EChP
* - 'Goliath' — GSki NLar WMoo
- membranaceous — WAbe
I - 'Purple Rose' **new** — NEgg

- 'Queen Victoria'	CFwr GSki MAvo NGby SMeo WFar WPnP
pauciflorum misapplied	see *D. pulchellum*
pauciflorum (Dur.) E.Greene	see *D. meadia*
poeticum	ETow MDKP SBla
§ ***pulchellum*** ♀H4	CBro CNic GCrs GKev GSki LRHS MNrw NMen NRya
§ - subsp. ***cusickii***	LRHS NWCA SRms
- subsp. ***pulchellum*** 'Red Wings'	CFwr CMea EBee EPot GCrs GEdr MBri MDKP NMen NSla NWCA SMeo WHoo WPnP WSan
- ***radicatum***	see *D. pulchellum*
- 'Sooke's Variety'	CStu WAbe
radicatum	see *D. pulchellum*
redolens	EBee NHar WAbe
tetrandrum	see *D. jeffreyi*

Dodonaea (*Sapindaceae*)

RCB/Eq P2-1	WCot
viscosa	CArn CBrm CTrC ECou SPlb XPep
- (f)	ECou
- (m)	ECou
- 'Picton' (f)	ECou
- 'Purpurea' (m)	ECou
- 'Purpurea'	CAbb CBcs CBrm CDoC CPLG CPne ECou EMan ERea EShb IArd ISea LRav WGer XPep
- 'Purpurea' (f)	ECou
- 'Red Wings' (f)	ECou

Doellingeria (*Asteraceae*)

scabra	see *Aster scaber*

Dolichos (*Papilionaceae*)

lignosus	see *Dipogon lignosus*
purpureus	see *Lablab purpureus*

Dombeya (*Sterculiaceae*)

burgessiae	IDee

Dondia see *Hacquetia*

Doodia (*Blechnaceae*)

aspera	GQui WPrP
§ ***caudata***	WRic
media	GQui WRic
squarrosa	see *D. caudata*

Doronicum ✿ (*Asteraceae*)

austriacum	NBid NBre
carpetanum	CSam
caucasicum	see *D. orientale*
§ x ***excelsum*** 'Harpur Crewe'	CPSs CPrp EBee LEdu MNFA MRav NPer NVic WCAu WEas
'Finesse'	EBee EPfP EWin LRHS NBre SRms WCot WMoo
'Little Leo'	CMHG COIW ELan EMan ENot ERou EVFa GMaP LRav MBow MHer NBlu NCGa NEgg NLar NVic SMac SPet SPoG WBrE WCot WHil WWeb
'Miss Mason' ♀H4	LRHS
§ ***orientale***	CWan EBee EChP EPfP EVFa EWsh LRHS NBid NBlu NEgg NFla NJOw SPer SPoG STes WWpP
- 'Goldcut'	NBre NGdn
- 'Magnificum'	CHrt CSBt CSam EBee EMar EPfP EWTr GKir GMaP LAst LRHS MHer NArg NLon NLsd NMir NPri SECG SGSe SMer SPer SRms WFar WMnd
pardalianches	CHrt CMea ECha GGar IHMH WRHF
plantagineum 'Excelsum'	see *D.* x *excelsum* 'Harpur Crewe'
'Riedels Goldkranz'	MWhi

Doryanthes (*Doryanthaceae*)

palmeri	CHEx

Dorycnium see *Lotus*

Doryopteris (*Adiantaceae*)

concolor var. ***kirkii*** **new**	EFtx
pedata	MBri

Douglasia see *Androsace*

idahoensis	see *Androsace idahoensis*
laevigata	see *Androsace laevigata*
nivalis	see *Androsace nivalis*
vitaliana	see *Vitaliana primuliflora*

Dovea (*Restionaceae*)

macrocarpa	CBig CFil CPne

Dovyalis (*Flacourtiaceae*)

caffra (F)	CPle XBlo

Doxantha see *Macfadyena*

Draba (*Brassicaceae*)

acaulis	CSec EHyt
aizoides	CSec ELan GKir LRHS MWat NBlu NPri SIng SPlb SPoG SRms
aizoon	see *D. lasiocarpa*
altaica **new**	GIBF
aurea var. ***leiocarpa*** **new**	CSec
bertolonii Boiss.	see *D. loeseleurii*
bruniifolia	EBur EWes LRHS MTho NWCA
- subsp. ***heterocoma*** var. ***nana*** **new**	WLin
- subsp. ***olympica***	NLar
bryoides	see *D. rigida* var. *bryoides*
cappadocica	EHyt
compacta	see *D. lasiocarpa* Compacta Group
cretica	NMen
cuspidata	EPot
dedeana	ECho EHyt EWes
densifolia	WLin
§ ***glabella***	NLAp
hispanica	NMen
hyperburea **new**	GIBF
kotschyi **new**	GKev
§ ***lasiocarpa***	NArg NBlu NJOw
§ - Compacta Group	ECho NRya NWCA
§ ***loeseleurii***	MMHG
longisiliqua ♀H2	SIng
- EMR 2551	EPot
mollissima	EPot GTou
oligosperma	NWCA
- subsp. ***subsessilis***	WLin
ossetica	EHyt
paysonii var. ***treleasei***	CSec WAbe
polytricha	EHyt GTou WLin
repens	see *D. sibirica*
rigida	MTho NLar
§ - var. ***bryoides***	EHyt NWCA WAbe
- var. ***imbricata*** f. ***compacta***	EPot
sakuraii	EDAr
scardica	see *D. lasiocarpa*
shiroumana **new**	CSec
§ ***sibirica***	CNic
ussuriensis **new**	GIBF
ventosa	GTou WAbe
yunnanensis	WLin

Dracaena ✿ (*Dracaenaceae*)

congesta	see *Cordyline stricta*
draco 🏆H1	CArn CTrC IDee
fragrans	MBri
- (Compacta Group) 'Compacta Purpurea'	MBri
- - 'Compacta Variegata' (v)	MBri
- (Deremensis Group) 'Lemon Lime' (v) 🏆H1	LRHS MBri
- - 'Warneckei' (v) 🏆H1	MBri
- - 'Yellow Stripe' (v) 🏆H1	MBri
* - ***glauca***	MBri
- 'Janet Craig'	MBri
- 'Massangeana' (v) 🏆H1	MBri
indivisa	see *Cordyline indivisa*
marginata (v) 🏆H1	LRHS MBri
- 'Colorama' (v)	MBri
sanderiana (v) 🏆H1	LRHS MBri
* ***schrijveriana***	MBri
steudneri	MBri
stricta	see *Cordyline stricta*

Dracocephalum (*Lamiaceae*)

altaiense	see *D. imberbe*
argunense	CPBP GEdr GKir LBee LPhx LRHS NLAp SAga SBla SGar SRms SRot WCru WPat WPer
* - 'Album'	NEgg
- 'Blue Carpet' **new**	CBgR
- 'Fuji Blue'	CBrm CFwr EPPr NEgg NLar
- 'Fuji White'	CBrm CPBP EMan EPPr LPhx NEgg SBla SHGN WPer WWeb
'Blue Moon' **new**	CSpe
botryoides	CPBP CSec EMan GFlt NJOw NLar NWCA SHGN WMoo WPer
bungeanum **new**	GKev
foetidum **new**	GKev
forrestii	EPot
grandiflorum	CBod CMHG CMdw CPom EChP EMFP GKev LPhx LTwo MMHG NEgg NLar SAga SBla WCAu WFar WMoo WWeb
hemsleyanum	LTwo NLAp WPat
§ ***imberbe***	MLLN WOut
isabellae	EBrs NLar
mairei	see *D. renatii*
moldavica	CSec EUnu SIde
nutans	CSec NLar WPer
prattii	see *Nepeta prattii*
§ ***renatii***	CSec
rupestre	CFwr GBri MBri NLAp WPat
ruyschianum	CMdw EBrs EChP ELan EMan GEdr LPhx LRHS MLLN MRav NLAp NLar NWCA
sibiricum	see *Nepeta sibirica*
tanguticum	NLar WWeb
* ***tataricum***	EBee
virginicum	see *Physostegia virginiana*
wendelboi	MLLN NBir

Dracophyllum (*Epacridaceae*)

pronum	ITim

Dracunculus (*Araceae*)

canariensis	CStu ITer WCot
muscivorus	see *Helicodiceros muscivorus*
§ ***vulgaris***	CFwr CHid CMea CPom CSec CSpe EBee EBrs EHrv EMan EMon EPot EUJe LEdu LRHS MAvo MCCP MRav NJOw SDix SEND SMad SSpi WCot

Dregea (*Asclepiadaceae*)

macrantha **new**	EShb
§ ***sinensis***	CBcs CBot CHEx CPLN CSam ELan EPfP ERea EShb EWes GQui LRHS MAsh SBra SPoG WCot WCru WFar WPGP WSHC
- 'Brockhill Silver' **new**	SSpi
- 'Variegata' (v)	WCot

Drepanocladus (*Amblystegiaceae*)

revolvens	EMFW

Drepanostachyum (*Poaceae*)

§ ***falcatum***	CAbb EShb MGos WJun
falconeri hort.	see *Himalayacalamus falconeri*
hookerianum	see *Himalayacalamus hookerianus*
§ ***khasianum***	CFil EBee EPla WPGP
§ ***microphyllum***	EPla WJun

Drimiopsis (*Hyacinthaceae*)

maculata	CMon CStu LToo WCot
maxima **new**	CMon

Drimys (*Winteraceae*)

aromatica	see *D. lanceolata*
colorata	see *Pseudowintera colorata*
granatensis	CFil WPGP
§ ***lanceolata***	More than 30 suppliers
- L 1737	CFil
- (f)	CTrC ECou GGar GTSp NCGa
- (m)	CDoC CTrC ECou GGar GTSp
- 'Mount Wellington'	GCal
- 'Suzette' (v) **new**	MBlu
* ***latifolia***	CBcs CHEx
winteri 🏆H4	CBcs CDoC CDul CFil CHEx CMac CPle CSBt CSam CTrw ELan EPfP GGar IArd NBea SAPC SArc SBrw SHBN SLim SPer SPoG WBrE WCwm WDin WFar WGer WPic WSHC
- var. ***andina***	CFil EPfP GGGa SSpi WPGP
§ - var. ***chilensis***	CFil CPLG EBee EPfP ISea SSpi WCru WPGP
- Latifolia Group	see *D. winteri* var. *chilensis*

Drosanthemum (*Aizoaceae*)

hispidum	CStu ECtt EDAr ELan EPfP EPot ITim LRHS MTho NMen NWCA SIng SPlb SPoG WPat XPep

Drosera (*Droseraceae*)

admirabilis	LHew
aliciae	CSWC EBla SHmp
andersoniana	EFEx
ascendens **new**	LHew
binata	SHmp
§ - subsp. ***dichotoma***	CSWC
- var. ***multifida*** **new**	LHew
- 'Multifida'	MCCP
browniana	EFEx
bulbigena	EFEx
bulbosa subsp. ***bulbosa***	EFEx
- subsp. ***major***	EFEx
callistos	LHew
capensis	CSWC LRHS MCCP SHmp
- 'Albino'	MCCP
- red	CSWC
dichotoma	see *D. binata* subsp. *dichotoma*
dichrosepala	LHew
erythrorhiza	EFEx
- subsp. ***collina***	EFEx

- subsp. ***erythrorhiza*** EFEx LHew
- subsp. ***magna*** EFEx
- subsp. ***squamosa*** EFEx
filiformis var. ***filiformis*** CSWC
gigantea EFEx
graniticola EFEx
heterophylla EFEx
intermedia 'Carolina Giant' MCCP
loureiroi EFEx
macrantha EFEx
- subsp. ***macrantha*** EFEx
macrophylla subsp. ***macrophylla*** EFEx
mannii **new** LHew
marchantii subsp. ***prophylla*** EFEx
menziesii subsp. ***basifolia*** EFEx
- subsp. ***menziesii*** EFEx
- subsp. ***thysanosepala*** EFEx
modesta EFEx
nidiformis **new** LHew
orbiculata EFEx
peltata CSWC EFEx
platypoda EFEx
ramellosa EFEx
rosulata EFEx
rotundifolia EBla SHmp
salina EFEx
scorpioides CSWC
slackii LHew
stelliflora LHew
stolonifera subsp. ***compacta*** EFEx
- subsp. ***humilis*** EFEx
- subsp. ***porrecta*** EFEx
- subsp. ***rupicola*** EFEx
- subsp. ***stolonifera*** EFEx
tubaestylus EFEx
zonaria EFEx

Drosophyllum (*Droseraceae*)

lusitanicum LHew

Dryandra (*Proteaceae*)

formosa CTrC EShb SPlb

Dryas (*Rosaceae*)

ajanensis **new** GIBF
drummondii EPot SBla WAbe
grandis GIBF
§ ***integrifolia*** CMea NMen
- 'Greenland Green' WAbe
octopetala 🏆H4 CMea CTri EDAr EPfP GIBF GKev GKir GMaP GTou MWat NChi NFor NLAp NLon NRya NVic SBla SPoG SRms WAbe
- var. ***lanata*** GIBF
- 'Minor' 🏆H4 EDAr LBee LRHS NMen NWCA NWoo WAbe
x ***suendermannii*** 🏆H4 EHol EPfP GKir GMaP GTou LRHS MCCP NLAp NMen SPoG WBVN
tenella Pursh see *D. integrifolia*

Dryopteris ✿ (*Dryopteridaceae*)

from Emei Shan, China WPGP
aemula SRms
§ ***affinis*** 🏆H4 CBrm CFil CFwr CLAP EBee ECha EMFW EMon EPfP ERod EWTr GMaP LPBA MMoz SPer SRms SSto WFib WRic
§ - subsp. ***borreri*** MBri SRms
- subsp. ***cambrensis*** EFer
- - 'Insubrica' EFer
- 'Congesta' CLAP GKir
- 'Congesta Cristata' CLAP CWCL EDAr EFer EPfP GMaP LPBA MBri MRav NSti SPla SRot
- Crispa Group CLAP ENot GBin LAst LRHS MMoz
- 'Crispa Barnes' MAvo WPGP
§ - 'Crispa Gracilis' 🏆H4 CFwr CLAP EFer EFtx ELan ENot EPPr ERod GBin MAsh MCCP NBir SMac WRic
* - 'Crispa Gracilis Congesta' CPrp ENot IBal SGSe SMac WFib
§ - 'Cristata' 🏆H4 More than 30 suppliers
- 'Cristata Angustata' 🏆H4 CFwr CLAP EFer ELan EMon GBin MAsh MMoz MWgw NBid NDlv SRms WFib WMoo WPGP WPrP WRic
- 'Cristata The King' see *D. affinis* 'Cristata'
- 'Grandiceps Askew' EFer SRms WFib
- 'Pinderi' CLAP EFer ELan GBin MBri SRms WRic
- Polydactyla Group CLAP GQui MDun MRav SPer WFar
- 'Polydactyla Dadds' CFwr CLAP EFtx MBri SMac WBor
- 'Polydactyla Mapplebeck' 🏆H4 CLAP EUJe GBin LPBA NBid SRms WRic
- 'Revolvens' CLAP EFer SRms
ardechensis **new** EFer
atrata misapplied see *D. cycadina*
x ***australis*** CLAP WRic
austriaca hort. see *D. dilatata*
bissetiana WRic
blanfordii CFil WPGP
borreri see *D. affinis* subsp. *borreri*
buschiana CLAP EFtx NLar SMac
carthusiana CBgR CFil CLAP EFer GBin NLar SRms WPtf WRic
celsa WRic
championii CLAP WRic
clintoniana CFil CFwr CLAP EFer WPGP WRic
x ***complexa*** 'Ramosissima Wright' CLAP
- 'Stablerae' CLAP EFtx GBin GQui WFib WPGP WRic
- 'Stablerae' crisped WFib
crassirhizoma CLAP WRic
crispifolia NVic
cristata CFwr CLAP EBee EFer EMon EPfP EPza MLan NBlu WCru WMoo WRic
§ ***cycadina*** 🏆H4 More than 30 suppliers
dickinsii EMon
§ ***dilatata*** 🏆H4 CRWN ECha EFer ELan EMon EPfP ERod MAsh MSte MWgw SGSe SRms WFib WRic WShi WWye
- 'Crispa Whiteside' 🏆H4 CFil CFwr CLAP CPrp CWCL EBee EFer EMon ERod IBal MAsh MAvo MBct MBri NBlu NLar SMac SPlb SRms WFib WPGP WRic
- 'Grandiceps' CLAP CMHG CWil EFer EMon SChu WFib
- 'Jimmy Dyce' CLAP
- 'Lepidota Crispa Cristata' CLAP LRHS MWgw
- 'Lepidota Cristata' 🏆H4 CFwr CLAP CMHG CWCL EFer EFtx ELan EMon ERod GBin IMGH MAsh MBct NVic SGSe SRms WCru WFib WMoo WPrP WRic
- 'Lepidota Grandiceps' CFwr CLAP
* - 'Recurvata' CLAP MBct WRic
erythrosora 🏆H4 More than 30 suppliers
I - 'Prolifera' see *D. erythrosora* var. *prolifica*
§ - var. ***prolifica*** 🏆H4 CFwr CLAP EChP GCal IBal MAsh MBct MSte NBir NCiC NDlv NRib NSti SPla WCot WFib WRic

expansa EMon
I ***felix-mas*** 'Parsley' **new** CLAP
filix-mas ♀H4 CSBt CTbh CTri CWCL ECha EMFW ENot EPfP EPza ERod EUJe GKir GMaP LPBA LRHS MAsh MBow MMoz MRav SGar SMac SPer SRms SSto WFar WShi WWye
- 'Barnesii' CFwr CLAP EFer ERod GBin MSte NDlv NLar SMac SPlb SPoG WRic
* - 'Corymbifera Crispa' EFer
- 'Crispa' CLAP EHon SRms WFib
- 'Crispa Congesta' see *D. affinis* 'Crispa Gracilis'
- 'Crispa Cristata' CFwr CLAP CPrp EFer EFtx EGol ELan EMon ERod GMaP MAsh MBnl MBri MDun MWgw NBid NBir NSti SChu SGSe SMac SPoG SRms WAul WFib WGor WRic WWpP WWye
- 'Crispatissima' NVic
- 'Cristata' ♀H4 CFil CFwr CLAP EFer EHon ELan GKir MMoz NOak NOrc SRms WFib WMoo WWye
- Cristata Group EFer WFib WRic
- - 'Fred Jackson' CLAP WFib
* - 'Cristata Grandiceps' EFer
- 'Cristata Jackson' CLAP SPlb
- 'Cristata Martindale' CFwr CLAP GQui NBid SRms WFib
- 'Depauperata' CFil CLAP SChu WPGP
- 'Euxinensis' CLAP
* - 'Furcans' CLAP
- 'Grandiceps Wills' ♀H4 EMon NBid SChu WFib
- 'Linearis' CMHG EFer EHon ELan EMon EWTr LPBA MGos NEgg SGSe SRms
- 'Linearis Congesta' CFil WPGP
- 'Linearis Cristata' WRic
- 'Linearis Polydactyla' CBrm CFwr CLAP CPrp CSBt CWCL EBee EFer EPfP GBin IMGH MAsh MBct MBri MMoz MWgw NBlu SLdr SPoG WFar WIvy WMoo
* - Polydactyla Group MGos MRav
- 'Rich Beauty' WBor
formosana EFer
goldieana CFwr CLAP CMHG EFer GBin GMaP NBir NCob NEgg NLar SPoG SSpi WCru WFar WMoo WPnP WRic
hirtipes see *D. cycadina*
'Imperial Wizard' CFir
marginalis CFwr CLAP EBee GBin GCal MMoz NLar NOGN SPoG WCru WMoo WRic
oreades SRms WAbe
pacifica CLAP
paleacea CLAP
pseudofilix-mas WRic
pseudomas see *D. affinis*
pycnopteroides WRic
x ***remota*** SRms WRic
sieboldii CFil CFwr CHEx CLAP CPrp ELan EMon ERod GCal IMGH MAsh MBri MSte NDlv NOGN SChu SGSe SMad SRms SSpi WCot WCru WFib WMoo WPGP WRic
stewartii CLAP
tokyoensis CFwr CLAP CRez EFer GBin GCal NEgg NLar SMac WRic
uniformis CLAP ELan EMon LPBA
- 'Cristata' CLAP
wallichiana ♀H4 More than 30 suppliers

Duchesnea (*Rosaceae*)

chrysantha see *D. indica*
§ ***indica*** CAgr CBgR CSWP CSec EUnu GAbr IGor ITer MRav WBrk WMoo
§ - 'Harlequin' (v) EMag EMan GBar ITer MCCP MTho
* - 'Snowflake' (v) CRow EBee WMoo
- 'Variegata' see *D. indica* 'Harlequin'

Dudleya (*Crassulaceae*)

abramsii subsp. ***affinis*** NNS 01-156 WCot
cymosa ETow SIgm
- JCA 11777 CNic
- subsp. ***paniculata*** NNS 98-221 WCot
- subsp. ***pumila*** WCot
farinosa CHEx
lanceolata EMan WCot
pulverulenta SIgm
saxosa subsp. ***aloides*** NNS 99-141 WCot
verityi NNS 01-159 WCot

Dugaldia (*Asteraceae*)

hoopsii see *Hymenoxys hoopesii*

Dunalia (*Solanaceae*)

australis see *Iochroma australe*
- blue see *Iochroma australe* 'Bill Evans'
- white see *Iochroma australe* 'Andean Snow'

Duranta (*Verbenaceae*)

§ ***erecta*** EShb LRHS
plumieri see *D. erecta*
repens see *D. erecta*

Duvernoia see *Justicia*

aconitiflora **new** CPLG

Dyckia (*Bromeliaceae*)

'Morris Hobbs' EMan WCot
* ***parviflora*** EPem
remotiflora SChr
velascona **new** CHEx

Dymondia (*Asteraceae*)

margaretae SBla WAbe
* ***repens*** XPep

Dypsis (*Arecaceae*)

§ ***decaryi*** EAmu WMul XBlo
decipiens CBrP EExo WMul
lutescens ♀H1 LRHS MBri

Dyschoriste (*Acanthaceae*)

thunbergiiflora GFai

Dysosma see *Podophyllum*

E

Ebenus (*Papilionaceae*)

cretica XPep

Ecballium (*Cucurbitaceae*)

elaterium CArn CFil LEdu MSal SIde WPGP

Eccremocarpus (*Bignoniaceae*)

scaber CBcs CDul CHrt CRHN EBee ELan EMil ENot EPfP GAbr GKev GKir

		LIck MBri MEHN MNrw MWgw NPer SBrw SGar SLim SRms SYvo WBrE
	- apricot-flowered	EMar
	- 'Aureus'	EPfP GKev NLar SLon
	- 'Carmineus'	CBrm EBee EPfP GGar MFOX NLar SGar
	- orange-flowered	EBee MAsh
I	- 'Roseus'	MAsh
	- 'Tresco Cream' **new**	CSpe

Echeveria ✿ (*Crassulaceae*)

	affinis	MBri
	agavoides ♀H1	WBrE
*	- 'Metallica'	MBri
*	'Black Prince'	EMan NPer WCot WDyG
	'Crûg Ice'	WCru
	x ***derosa***	EPfP
	- 'Worfield Wonder' ♀H1	WEas
	elegans ♀H1	CHEx CHal EBee EOas EPfP EWin MBri SAPC WBrE WDyG WGwG
	elegans x ***elegans*** var. ***hernandonis***	EBla
§	***gibbiflora*** var. ***metallica*** ♀H1	WEas
	glauca	see *E. secunda* var. *glauca*
	harmsii ♀H1	CHal CSWP
	'Hens and Chicks' **new**	CHEx
	'Mahogany'	MAvo SUsu
	'Meridian' **new**	CHEx
	'Paul Bunyon'	CHal MAvo
	peacockii	EBee EPfP EUJe EWin SPet SPoG SWal WRos
	'Perle d'Azur'	CHEx WCot
	pulidonis ♀H1 **new**	EPfP
	pulvinata ♀H1	CHal
	rosea **new**	WCot
	runyonii 'Topsy Turvy' **new**	CHEx EPfP
	secunda	CAbb STre SWal
§	- var. ***glauca*** ♀H1	CHEx CStu EBee ELan EPfP EShb EWin LPJP MAvo NBir NBlu SArc STre SUsu WCot WGwG
*	- - 'Gigantea'	NPer
	setosa ♀H1	EPfP
	- var. ***ciliata*** **new**	EShb

Echinacea ✿ (*Asteraceae*)

	angustifolia	CArn CBod CCge EBee EBla EChP EMan EMar EPPr EPfP EWTr GPoy LPio LRHS MAnH MBNS MHer MLLN MSal MWgw NGHP NSti STes WCot WHer WSel WWye
	'Art's Pride' **new**	CFir EBee EHrv EPPr GFlt GSki MAnH MBnl MBri MDKP NCob NDov NSti SPoG STes WCot WPop WTMC
	atrorubens	EUnu
	pallida	More than 30 suppliers
	paradoxa	More than 30 suppliers
§	***purpurea***	More than 30 suppliers
	- 'Alba'	CBot CCge EBla EUJe IHMH MBri NBlu
	- 'Augustkönigin'	CKno EBee EHrv EVFa GBin GSki MAnH MBnl MSph MSte NBir NCob NDov NEgg NLar NRnb WCot WPop WWlt WWpP
	- Bressingham hybrids	EBla EBrs ELan EMar LRHS MRav SChu SPer SPet WFar
	- dark-stemmed	CAby GBBs LPhx MAnH SAga
	- 'Indiaca' **new**	EMan GFlt MBri NArg NGHP
	- 'Kim's Knee High'PBR	More than 30 suppliers
	- 'Kim's Mop Head'	More than 30 suppliers
	- 'Leuchtstern'	CBrm EBee GSki MAnH NBir NCGa NDov NGdn NRnb WPer
	- 'Little Giant' **new**	CKno MBnl SHar
	- 'Magnus' ♀H4	More than 30 suppliers
	- 'Maxima'	EBee EBrs EHrv EVFa LRHS MAnH MBnl MNFA NCob NDov SMad WBVN WCot
	- 'Pink Flamingo'	WWhi
I	- 'Primadonna Deep Rose' **new**	GFlt
	- 'Razzmatazz'PBR (d) **new**	EPfP IPot MBri MCCP MNrw NArg SHBN SPer SPoG WSan
	- 'Robert Bloom'	EBee EBla EBrs EHrv EMil LPhx MAnH MBNS MNFA MSph NCob NRnb SMad SVal WCot WWhi
	- 'Rubinglow'	CKno CWCL EBee EBla EChP ECtt EHrv IBal LAst MBNS MBnl MSph MSte NBir NCob NDov NGHP NLar NRnb SPoG SWvt WCAu
	- 'Rubinstern' ♀H4	More than 30 suppliers
	- 'Ruby Giant' ♀H4	CBos CFir CKno CM&M CMea CMil EBee ECtt EHrv ERou GSki LIck LSou MAnH MDKP MSph NCob NDov NEgg NGHP NRnb NSti SHar SPla SPoG SSpe SVil WCot WHlf WTMC
	- 'The King'	LRHS NRnb SSpe WWeb
	- 'Verbesserter Leuchtstern'	MAnH NGHP NLar
	- 'Vintage Wine' **new**	CFwr CWCL EBee GBri IPot LBuc MBnl NCob NGHP NLar NSti SPoG
	- 'White Lustre'	EBee EChP ECha EPfP EShb EVFa GSki MBNS NDov NGHP NLar SHBN SPav WCAu WCot WFar WLin WWhi
	- 'White Swan'	More than 30 suppliers
	'Ruby Glow' **new**	SSpe
	simulata	SUsu
	tennesseensis	CArn CBrm EBee EUnu GPoy MAnH MNFA
	- 'Rocky Top' **new**	CKno CSam EHrv EMan EMar EPPr EWTr GBri GSki LBuc MBri NBre NDov NGHP NGdn SPur STes WAul WCot WHil WPtf WSel
	'Vintage Wine' **new**	IBal SHBN

Echinops (*Asteraceae*)

	RCB/TQ H-2	WCot
	albus	see *E.* 'Nivalis'
§	***bannaticus***	CSec GSki NBid SMar WFar WTel
*	- 'Albus'	EPfP EWll LAst LRHS NGdn NSti SPoG
§	- 'Blue Globe'	COlW CWan EBee EChP EMan EPfP ERou GCal GMaP GSki IBal LAst LRHS LSRN NCGa NChi NVic SCoo SIgm WBrE WFar WMnd WPer WWeb
	- 'Blue Pearl'	CM&M EBee
	- 'Taplow Blue' ♀H4	CBcs CHad CPrp CSev ELan ERou EVFa EWTr GKir GSki LAst LRHS LSRN MBNS MBow MRav MWat NGdn NPer SBla SEND SMer SPer SPla SPoG SWvt WCAu WFar WMnd WTel
	commutatus	see *E. exaltatus*
§	***exaltatus***	MWgw NBir
	maracandicus	GCal WCot
	microcephalus HH&K 285	CPom
§	'Nivalis'	CBre ECha ERou MWgw SEND
	niveus	IFro
*	***perringii***	GCal
	ritro hort.	see *E. bannaticus*
§	***ritro*** L. ♀H4	More than 30 suppliers

- 'Moonstone'	CRow
- subsp. ***ruthenicus*** ♀H4	CBrm ECGP EGra ELan EWTr GBuc IGor MHar SIgm WCot WPGP
- - 'Platinum Blue'	CKno EBee EMan MBNS MBri NLar SPet WMnd
- 'Veitch's Blue' misapplied	see *E. ritro* L.
- 'Veitch's Blue'	More than 30 suppliers
setifer B&SWJ 8416	WCru
sphaerocephalus	EMan GFlt IBlr NBid NBre NBur SBla SIgm SPlb WPer WWpP
- 'Arctic Glow'	More than 30 suppliers
tjanschanicus	EMan EWll GIBF MHar NBPC NLar WBVN WCAu

Echinospartum see *Genista*

Echium (*Boraginaceae*)

albicans	EWll
amoenum	CFir
boissieri	CSec ELan WHil WOut
§ ***candicans*** ♀H2-3	CAbb CBcs CCtw CFir CHEx CPLG CSec CTbh CTrC EAmu ECre EShb ESlt EUnu IDee NBur SAPC SArc SBch SChr SRob WCHb WFar
decaisnei	CSec
fastuosum	see *E. candicans*
giganteum	EWll
italicum	CSec MAnH NLar SIde WHil
lusitanicum subsp. ***polycaulon***	CSec GBBs MSph NEgg NLar WGwG WHil WOut
nervosum	CTrC EBee
§ ***pininana*** ♀H2-3	More than 30 suppliers
- 'Pink Fountain'	CTbh ELan LSou NLar NRnb WHil
- 'Snow Tower'	CEnd ELan EUnu MAnH NRnb
pininana x ***wildpretii***	EUnu MAnH
pinnifolium	see *E. pininana*
rossicum	GIBF SPlb
russicum	CFir CPLG CSam CSec EChP EMan EPyc EWll GIBF IFro LPhx MAnH MNFA NBPC NCGa NChi NLar SDnm SGSe SIde SIgm SPav SSpi WAul WBVN WCHb WCot WWeb
x ***scilloniense***	SYvo
simplex	CSec
sordidum **new**	CPLG
tuberculatum	CFir EBee EChP IDee LPhx NBur NLar SBod WHil WOut
vulgare	CArn CTbh EChP EGoo ELan EOHP MBow MChe MHer MSal NLar NMir NPri SECG SIde WBrE WCHb WGwG WHer WJek WPnn WSel WWye
- Drake's form	CCge MAnH MSph SGar
wildpretii ♀H2-3	CTrC EWll
- subsp. ***wildpretii***	CSec SPav
- subsp. ***trichosiphon***	CSec

Eclipta (*Asteraceae*)

alba	see *E. prostrata*
§ ***prostrata***	MSal

Edgeworthia (*Thymelaeaceae*)

§ ***chrysantha***	CBcs CPMA CWib EPfP LBuc SMur SPer SPoG WSHC
- B&SWJ 1048	WCru
I - 'Grandiflora'	CPMA NLar
- 'Red Dragon'	CPMA LBuc NLar
- f. ***rubra*** hort.	see *E. chrysantha* 'Red Dragon'
gardneri	NLar WCot
papyrifera	see *E. chrysantha*

Edraianthus (*Campanulaceae*)

croaticus	see *E. graminifolius*
dalmaticus	EPot SBla
dinaricus	NSla WLin
§ ***graminifolius***	CPBP ECho ECtt EPot GKev NLAp NMen SPet WFar WPer
- ***albus***	see *E. graminifolius* subsp. *niveus*
§ - subsp. ***niveus***	CSec
montenegrinus **new**	GKev
§ ***pumilio*** ♀H4	CGra CLyd EHyt GKev LRHS NMen NSla NWCA SBla SOkd SRms WLin
§ ***serpyllifolius***	EPot NMen
§ - 'Major'	NMen SBla WAbe
- 'Minor' **new**	GKev
tenuifolius	CPBP NJOw
- 'Albus' **new**	GKev

Ehretia (*Boraginaceae*)

dicksonii	CFil CHEx CPLG WPGP

Ehrharta (*Poaceae*)

thunbergii	EPPr

Eichhornia (*Pontederiaceae*)

crassipes	CWat EMFW LPBA NArg SCoo
- 'Major'	NPer

Elaeagnus ✿ (*Elaeagnaceae*)

angustifolia	CAgr CBcs CBot CDul ECrN EPfP LRHS MBar MBlu MCoo MRav SHBN SPer SRms WBVN WDin WFar XPep
- Caspica Group	see *E.* 'Quicksilver'
argentea	see *E. commutata*
§ ***commutata***	CAgr CBcs CBot CMCN EBee ECrN EGra EHoe ENot EPfP IMGH MBlu MWgw MWhi NFor NLar NLon SPer WDin
x ***ebbingei***	More than 30 suppliers
- 'Coastal Gold' (v)	CAbP CAlb CBcs CDoC CDul COtt EBee EMil ENot LBuc LRHS LSRN MAsh MGos SLim SRms WWes
- 'Gilt Edge' (v) ♀H4	More than 30 suppliers
* - 'Gold Flash' **new**	MGos
- Gold Splash = 'Lannou' (v)	CDoC CDul CTrC CWSG EGra EPfP MAsh SArc SPoG SWvt
- 'Limelight' (v)	More than 30 suppliers
- 'Salcombe Seedling'	LRHS NLar
glabra	EPfP
- 'Reflexa'	see *E.* x *reflexa*
macrophylla	EPfP NFor SSpi WMoo
multiflora	CDul CFil GIBF IDee SPer WPGP
parvifolia	EBee ENot EPfP
pungens	ERom NBir
- 'Argenteovariegata'	see *E. pungens* 'Variegata'
- 'Aureovariegata'	see *E. pungens* 'Maculata'
- 'Dicksonii' (v)	CBcs CTrC CWib EBee LRHS NLar SLon SPer SRms WBcn WFar
- 'Forest Gold' (v)	CAbP ELan EPfP LRHS MAsh
- 'Frederici' (v)	CBcs CBrm CDoC CMHG CMac CTrC EBee EHoe ELan EPfP EPla MAsh MGos MRav SHBN SLim SPer SPla SPoG WBor WDin WHCG WPat WWeb
- 'Goldrim' (v) ♀H4	COtt EBee EPfP LRHS MGos SHBN SLim WDin
- 'Hosuba-fukurin' (v)	MAsh SPoG
§ - 'Maculata' (v)	More than 30 suppliers
§ - 'Variegata' (v)	CBcs CMac CPLG LRHS NBir SHBN SPer WGer WHCG
§ 'Quicksilver' ♀H4	More than 30 suppliers
§ x ***reflexa***	CBcs CFil WBcn WHCG WPGP

x ***submacrophylla***	see *E.* x *ebbingei*
umbellata	CAgr CBcs CBrm CPle CTho EBee ECrN EPfP EWTr MBlu NLar SMad SPer WBcn WHCG WMou WRHF WSHC XPep

Elatostema (*Urticaceae*)

repens var. ***pulchrum*** ♀H1	CHal MBri
- var. ***repens***	CHal
rugosum new	CHEx

elderberry see *Sambucus nigra*

Elegia (*Restionaceae*)

capensis	CAbb CBig CCtw CDoC CFil CFir CFwr CHEx CPLG CPen CTrC CWil EBee EShb EUJe GGar IDee SPlb WDyG WMul WNor WPGP
cuspidata	CBig EShb LRav
equisetacea	CBig WNor
filacea	CBcs CBig
fistulosa	CBig EBee
grandis	CBct CBig
grandispicata	CBig
persistens	CBig
racemosa	CCtw
spathacea	CFil CFir

Eleocharis (*Cyperaceae*)

sp.	LNCo
acicularis	ELan EMFW EPza IHMH NArg WWpP
dulcis variegated (v)	CRow WWpP
palustris	CRWN EMFW
sphacelata	GGar

Elettaria (*Zingiberaceae*)

cardamomum	CArn EAmu EShb GPoy LEdu MBri MSal SHDw WJek WMul

Eleusine (*Poaceae*)

coracana 'Green Cat'	CFwr

Eleutherococcus (*Araliaceae*)

hypoleucus B&SWJ 5532	WCru
nikaianus B&SWJ 5027	WCru
pictus	see *Kalopanax septemlobus*
sciadophylloides B&SWJ 4728	WCru
senticosus	GIBF GPoy LEdu
- B&SWJ 4528	WCru
septemlobus	see *Kalopanax septemlobus*
sessiliflorus	GIBF
- B&SWJ 8457	WCru
§ ***sieboldianus***	MRav WDin WFar
§ - 'Variegatus' (v)	CBot EBee ECrN EGra EHoe ELan EPfP LAst MBlu MGos MRav NEgg NPal SMur SPoG WHer WSHC

Elingamita (*Myrsinaceae*)

johnsonii	ECou

Elisena (*Amaryllidaceae*)

longipetala	see *Hymenocallis longipetala*

Elliottia (*Ericaceae*)

bracteata	see *Tripetaleia bracteata*
* ***paniculata latifolia***	NLar
pyroliflorus	CStu

Ellisiophyllum (*Scrophulariaceae*)

pinnatum	WMoo
- B&SWJ 197	WCru WDyG WPrP

Elodea (*Hydrocharitaceae*)

canadensis	EHon EMFW
crispa	see *Lagarosiphon major*

Elsholtzia (*Lamiaceae*)

ciliata	CArn MSal
fruticosa	CArn WWye
stauntonii	CArn CBcs CBot CBrm CPLG EBee ECha ECre EMan EOHP EPPr GPoy IDee MFOX MHer MTis NJOw SBrw SLPl SPer SPoG WBor WWye XPep
- 'Alba'	CArn CBot LRav WWye

Elymus (*Poaceae*)

arenarius	see *Leymus arenarius*
californicus	CBig
canadensis	CRWN CWCL EHoe EPPr GFor NBre SWal WMoo
- f. ***glaucifolius***	CFir GCal SLim
cinereus from Washington State, USA	CDes EPPr
elongatus new	SApp
giganteus	see *Leymus racemosus*
glaucus hort.	see *E. hispidus*
§ ***hispidus***	CBod CBrm COIW CSLe CWCL EGoo EHoe EPPr ESis EUJe GFor LRHS MBlu MBri MMoz MWrn NCGa NDov NSti SPer SPla SPoG SUsu WCFE WCot WPrP WRos WWhi
N ***magellanicus***	More than 30 suppliers
- 'Blue Sword'	NBPC
riparius	EPPr
§ ***scabrus***	SMrm
sibiricus	EPPr
solandri	EWes GBin GFor GGar MAvo WHrl
- JCA 5.345.500	WPGP
tenuis	SMad
villosus	EPPr
- var. ***arkansanus***	EPPr NOGN WWpP
virginicus	EBee EPPr

Embothrium ✿ (*Proteaceae*)

coccineum	CFil CPLG CPne CSec EPfP EShb LRHS SPlb SReu WBrE WNor WPGP WPat
- Lanceolatum Group	CDoC CEnd CPLG CSBt CTbh CTho ELan EPfP GGar GKir LRHS MAsh MDun MLan NPal SBrw SHBN SPer SPoG SSpi SSta WCot WDin WFar WPat WPic
- - 'Inca Flame'	CBcs CDoC COtt CPMA CSBt ELan EPfP ISea LRHS MDun NLar SBrw SHGC SMur SPoG SSta SWvt WPat
- - 'Ñorquinco' ♀H3	CBcs CDoC CPLG GGar LRHS SSpi WCru
- Longifolium Group	IArd IBlr ISea SBrw

Eminium (*Araceae*)

spiculatum new	WCot

Emmenopterys (*Rubiaceae*)

henryi	CBcs CFil CMCN EBee EPfP IArd NLar SBrw SMad SPoG SSpi WPGP

Empetrum (*Empetraceae*)

luteum	MBar
nigrum	GIBF GPoy MBar NLar
- var. ***japonicum***	GTou
rubrum	WWes

Encelia (*Asteraceae*)

farinosa	XPep

Encephalartos ✿ (*Zamiaceae*)

altensteinii	CBrP
caffer **new**	CBrP
cycadifolius	CBrP
ferox **new**	SBig
friderici-guilielmi **new**	CBrP
horridus	CBrP
lanatus **new**	CBrP
lebomboensis	CBrP
lehmannii	CBrP
natalensis	CBrP
umbeluziensis **new**	CBrP
villosus	CBrP

Endymion see *Hyacinthoides*

Engelmannia (*Asteraceae*)

pinnatifida	EBee

Enkianthus ✿ (*Ericaceae*)

campanulatus ♀H4	More than 30 suppliers
- var. ***campanulatus*** f. ***albiflorus***	LRHS NLar SMur SSpi
I - 'Hollandia' **new**	CPMA
- var. ***palibinii***	EPfP GGGa GKir LRHS MAsh MGos NLar SBrw SSpi SSta WBrE WNor
- 'Red Bells'	CBcs CDoC COtt EPfP GBin GKir LRHS MDun MGos NEgg SBrw SSpi SSta SWvt WFar
- var. ***sikokianus***	CAbP EPfP GGGa LRHS MBlu MDun NLar SSpi
- 'Tokyo Masquerade'	CPMA NLar
* - 'Variegatus' (v)	LRHS MAsh SPoG
- 'Wallaby'	NLar
cernuus	CBcs GKir
- f. ***rubens*** ♀H4	EPfP GGGa LRHS NBea NEgg NLar SSpi WDin WNor WPic
chinensis	EPfP GGGa GKir IMGH LRHS MAsh SBrw SPoG SSpi WNor
deflexus	CFil LRHS SSpi WPGP
- GWJ 9225	WCru
perulatus ♀H4	CBcs CFil CRez EPfP GKir MBar NEgg SBrw SPoG WFar WWes

Ennealophus (*Iridaceae*)

fimbriatus RCB/Arg P-16 **new**	WCot

Ensete (*Musaceae*)

glaucum	CKob EAmu EShb EUJe LExo MJnS WMul
- from China	CKob
- from Thailand	CKob
- 'Vudu Vudu'	CKob
superbum	CKob WMul XBlo
- from Thailand	CKob
§ ***ventricosum*** ♀H1+3	CBot CDoC CHrt CKob EAmu ESlt EUJe LExo MGol MJnS SAPC SArc WMul XBlo
- B&SWJ 9070	WCru
§ - 'Maurelii'	CBrP CHEx CKob EAmu EShb EUJe LExo MJnS SAPC SArc WMul WPGP
- 'Montbeliardii'	CKob
- 'Rubrum'	see *E. ventricosum* 'Maurelii'

Entelea (*Tiliaceae*)

arborescens	CHEx ECou EShb

Eomecon (*Papaveraceae*)

chionantha	More than 30 suppliers

Epacris (*Epacridaceae*)

paludosa	ECou GCrs GGGa
petrophila	GCrs GGGa
serpyllifolia **new**	ECou

Ephedra (*Ephedraceae*)

sp.	GCrs SAPC SArc
distachya	GPoy MSal NFor NLon WWye
equisetina	MSal
gerardiana	IFro
- KR 0853	EPla
- var. ***sikkimensis***	CStu EPla NLar WOld WPer
§ ***major***	WHer
minima	NWCA
nebrodensis	see *E. major*
nevadensis	EUnu GPoy MSal
sinica	MSal
viridis	CArn ELau EShb EUnu MSal

Epidendrum (*Orchidaceae*)

§ ***ibaguense***	CHal

Epigaea (*Ericaceae*)

gaultherioides	GGGa
repens	GGGa

Epilobium (*Onagraceae*)

angustifolium	see *Chamerion angustifolium*
- f. ***leucanthum***	see *Chamerion angustifolium* 'Album'
californicum hort.	see *Zauschneria californica*
canum	see *Zauschneria californica* subsp. *cana*
crassum	GBuc NWoo WGwG
dodonaei	see *Chamerion dodonaei*
fleischeri	see *Chamerion fleischeri*
garrettii	see *Zauschneria californica* subsp. *garrettii*
N ***glabellum*** hort.	CHea CSpe ECtt EMan GKir GMaP GMac LRHS NBir SUsu WAbe WEas WWhi
hirsutum 'Album'	NSti SPoG
- 'Pistils at Dawn'	CNat
- ***roseum***	WRha
- 'Well Creek' (v)	EMan MLLN NBid WCHb WCot WHrl
microphyllum	see *Zauschneria californica* subsp. *cana*
obcordatum	CStu NEgg
rigidum	SSpi
rosmarinifolium	see *Chamerion dodonaei*
septentrionale	see *Zauschneria septentrionalis*
villosum	see *Zauschneria californica* subsp. *mexicana*
'White Wonder Bells' PBR **new**	WRHF

Epimedium ✿ (*Berberidaceae*)

from Jian Xi, China **new**	CFwr
from Yunnan, China	CPom
acuminatum	CDes CElw CFil CLAP EBee EFEx EHyt GLil LPio MDun SChu SMac WPGP WSHC
- L 575	EHrv MSte SBla SSpi WPnP
- 'Galaxy'	CLAP CPMA
'Akakage'	GLil
'Akebono'	CDes CLAP EBee GLil NLar WPGP
alpinum	CFis CMac EMon EPPr GBBs GBuc GKir SBch WMoo WSHC

'Amanagowa'	CLAP CPMA SBla
Asiatic hybrids	CElw CLAP SChu WPnP
'Beni-chidori'	GLil WPGP
'Beni-kujaku'	CPMA EBee GBuc GLil WPGP
brachyrrhizum	CDes CPMA WPGP
brevicornu	CLAP CPMA CPom
- Og 88.010	SBla
- f. ***rotundatum***	CDes CLAP CPMA
- - Og 82.010	SBla
'Buckland Spider'	CDes CLAP SBla
campanulatum	CPMA
- Og 93.087	SBla
x ***cantabrigiense***	CBro CPom ECtt EPPr EPla GKir GLil LRHS MRav SMac WHlf
chlorandrum	CDes CLAP
creeping yellow **new**	NLar STes
cremeum	see *E. grandiflorum* subsp. *koreanum*
davidii	CDes CPMA CPom EBee ECha GBri GCrs MDun MSte NLar SMac SSpi WFar WHal WHoo WPGP WSHC
- EMR 4125	CElw CLAP EHrv SBla
diphyllum	CFwr CPom EHrv SAga WBVN WHal
- dwarf white	GLil
dolichostemon	CElw CLAP CPMA MSte
ecalcaratum	CDes CLAP CPMA CPom WPGP
- Og 93.082	SBla
elongatum	CFwr CLAP
'Enchantress'	CLAP CPMA CPom EHrv GBuc MSte SSpi WHal
epsteinii	CDes CLAP CPMA CPom WPGP
- CPC 940347	SBla
fangii	SSpi
fargesii	CDes CFwr EHrv WPGP
- 'Pink Constellation'	CLAP CPMA CPom SBch
- - Og 93.023	SBla
flavum	CDes CLAP CPMA EHrv
franchetii	CPom SSpi
- 'Brimstone Butterfly'	CDes CLAP CPMA MDun SSpi WPGP
- - Og 87.001	SBla
'Genpei'	GLil
§ ***grandiflorum*** ♀H4	CBcs CElw CFis CTri EHrv ELan EPfP EWTr GAbr GEdr GKir NBir NCGa NMen SBla SPer WBor WCra WFar WPnP
- 'Album'	CBos CFwr CLAP
- var. ***coelestre***	GLil
- 'Crimson Beauty'	CLAP CPMA ECha GBuc MRav SAga SChu SMac SUsu WHal WHoo WSHC
- 'Crimson Queen'	CDes EBee WPGP
- 'Freya'	CBos
- 'Jennie Maillard'	SUsu
- 'Koji'	WSHC
§ - subsp. ***koreanum***	CFil CLAP ECha EFEx GLil
- - 'La Rocaille'	CDes CLAP
- lilac	CLAP WFar
- 'Lilacinum'	CDes SBla
- 'Lilafee'	More than 30 suppliers
- 'Mount Kitadake'	CLAP GLil SMHy SOkh SSpi
- 'Nanum' ♀H4	CBos CDes CLyd CPMA CPom EBee EHrv ETow NMen NWCA SBla SChu SSpi WAbe WPGP
- 'Pallidum'	EBee
- pink	EHrv
- 'Purple Prince'	EBee
- 'Queen Esta'	CDes SBla
- 'Red Beauty'	CLAP GAbr MSte
- 'Rose Queen' ♀H4	More than 30 suppliers
§ - 'Roseum'	CFwr CHid CLAP GBri NMen SGSe WSHC
- 'Rubinkrone'	GBin GLil GMaP WOVN
- 'Saturn'	CDes CPMA SBla
- 'Shikinomai'	CPMA
- 'Sirius'	CDes CPMA SBla
- f. ***violaceum***	CFir CLAP CPMA SBch SBla SChu SMac WSHC
- 'White Beauty'	WSHC
- 'White Queen' ♀H4	CFir CPMA EChP EHrv NOak SBla SOkh SSpi
- 'Yellow Princess'	CDes CLAP CPMA SBla
higoense	SIgm
ilicifolium	CDes
- Og 93.020	SBla
'Kaguyahime'	CDes CLAP EBee EHrv MSte SBla
latisepalum	CDes CLAP CPMA EBee EHrv WPGP
leptorrhizum	CDes CLAP CPMA EBee EHrv EMon GCrs GLil SDys WHal WPGP WSHC
- Og Y 44	EHyt SAga SDys SSpi
- 'Mariko' Og 93.009	SBla
lishihchenii Og 96.024	SBla
'Little Shrimp'	CLAP CLyd CPMA CTri GBuc NLar WPat
macranthum	see *E. grandiflorum*
membranaceum	CLAP CPMA CPom WHal
myrianthum	CDes CPMA
ogisui	CDes CLAP CPMA CPom EHrv MSte WPGP
- Og 91.001	SSpi
x ***omeiense***	WBcn
- 'Akame'	CDes CLAP CPMA WPGP
- - Og 82.001	SBla
- 'Emei Shan'	see *E.* x *omeiense* 'Akame'
- 'Pale Fire Sibling'	CPom
- 'Stormcloud'	CDes CLAP CPMA SMac
pauciflorum	CPMA CPom
x ***perralchicum*** ♀H4	CBro CPMA CTri EBee EMon GBuc GKev GKir MNFA NLon SGar SLPl SSpi WBVN WPnP WSHC
- 'Frohnleiten'	More than 30 suppliers
- 'Lichtenberg'	CFwr EBee
- 'Nachfolger'	CFwr EBee
- 'Wisley'	CElw CPMA CSam EHrv EWes SBla
perralderianum	CFil CHEx CSam EBee ELan GKir GMaP LGro MDun SRms SSpi WPGP WPnP
'Pink Elf'	SPla
pinnatum	GLil GMaP MDun WHal WRha
§ - subsp. ***colchicum*** ♀H4	More than 30 suppliers
- - L 321	SBla
- - 'Black Sea'	CLAP EHrv GLil IBlr NLar
- ***elegans***	see *E. pinnatum* subsp. *colchicum*
platypetalum	CLAP CPMA CPom EBee
pubescens	CPMA CPom EHrv SAga
pubigerum	CFwr CHid CPMA EBee ECha EWTr GAbr GBuc GEdr GKir GLil NEgg NPri WCAu WLin
rhizomatosum	CLAP CPom EBee WPGP
- Og 92.114	CPMA SBla
x ***rubrum*** ♀H4	More than 30 suppliers
sagittatum	CLAP EFEx GLil
'Sasaki'	GBuc
sempervirens	CLAP CPMA WHal
- white-flowered **new**	CLAP
x ***setosum***	CFil CPMA EBee ECha EHrv GAbr MDun MSte NLar SMac SSpi WHal WSPU
'Shiho'	GLil
stellulatum 'Wudang Star'	CDes CLAP CPom EBee EHrv EHyt EWes MDun SMac WPGP WSPU
'Sunset'	GLil

'Tama-no-genpei'	CPMA
x ***versicolor***	CPLG LAst WMoo
- 'Cupreum'	CPom SMHy SMac SSpi
- 'Neosulphureum'	CBro CLAP CM&M EMon EPPr SAga SBla SSpi
- 'Sulphureum' ♀H4	More than 30 suppliers
- 'Versicolor'	CLAP CPom EHrv SAga SBla SMHy
x ***warleyense***	More than 30 suppliers
- 'Orangekönigin'	CPom EBee GBuc LPio MMil MRav NSti SLPl SPla WBor WCAu WMoo WPnP
wushanense	CLAP CPMA
- 'Caramel'	CDes CLAP CPMA CPom EBee EHrv WPGP
- - Og 92.009	SBla
x ***youngianum***	CBcs
- 'Lilacinum'	see *E.* x *youngianum* 'Roseum'
- 'Merlin'	CBos CFir CLAP CPMA ECha EHrv EPfP NLar NMyG NSti SBch SBla SChu SOkh
- 'Niveum' ♀H4	More than 30 suppliers
§ - 'Roseum'	More than 30 suppliers
- 'Tamabotan'	CDes GBuc GLil SBla
- 'Typicum'	CLAP EBee EHyt WSHC
- white	NMen WLin
- 'Yenomoto'	CLAP CPMA
zhushanense	CFwr

Epipactis (*Orchidaceae*)

gigantea	More than 30 suppliers
- 'Enchantment'	CHdy
- 'Serpentine Night'	IBlr
* **Lowland Legacy g.** 'Edelstein'	CHdy
* - 'Frankfurt'	CHdy
palustris	CBod CHdy EBla EMan GEdr IPot WHer
'Renate'	CHdy
royleana	SBla
Sabine g.	CHdy
* - 'Frankfurt'	CHdy NMen SBla
thunbergii	EFEx

Epipremnum (*Araceae*)

§ ***aureum*** ♀H1	CHal EBak MBri
§ ***pinnatum***	LRHS MBri
- 'Marble Queen' (v)	CHal LRHS

Episcia (*Gesneriaceae*)

'Country Kitten'	CHal
cupreata	CHal
§ ***dianthiflora***	CHal SRms WDib
'Pink Panther'	CHal
'San Miguel'	CHal WDib

Equisetum ✿ (*Equisetaceae*)

arvense	CArn MSal
'Bandit'	CNat CRow EMon SMad
x ***bowmanii***	CNat
* ***camtschatcense***	CDes CMCo CNat CRow ITer SMad
x ***dycei***	CNat
fluviatile	CNat EUJe NLar
hyemale	CBrm CDWL CKno CMCo CMil CNat CTrC EBla EPfP EPla EPza EUJe NPer NSti SPlb SSpi WCot WDyG WFar WHal WMoo WPrP WWhi WWpP
§ - var. ***affine***	CNat CRow EBee ELan EMan EMon EPla MBlu NLar SMad SSpi WHal WOld WWye
- var. ***robustum***	see *E. hyemale* var. *affine*
palustre	GWCH
ramosissimum	CFwr EMFW LPBA MCCP NArg
var. ***japonicum***	NFor WPop WWpP
scirpoides	CDWL CMCo CMil CNat CPen CTbh CTrC EFer EMFW EMon EPfP EPla EPza EUJe LPBA MCCP NPer SPlb WMoo WPrP WWpP
sylvaticum	CNat
telmateia	CNat
variegatum	EBee NVic WCot

Eragrostis (*Poaceae*)

RCB/Arg S-7	WCot
airoides	CHar CKno CMea CSam CWCL EBee EChP EKen EMan ESis EWsh GAbr LAst LPhx MAnH MAvo NOak NPro SGSe SMad WCot WHrl WMoo WPGP WPnP WRos WWpP
chloromelas	CStr EMan EPPr LPhx MSte WCot WGHP WPGP
curvula	More than 30 suppliers
- S&SH 10	MSte WPGP
- 'Totnes Burgundy'	CBig CDes CKno CPen CStr CWCL EPPr MAvo MMoz MNrw NOak WHrl WPGP
elliottii	CBrm EMan EPPr
gummiflua	CBig EMan
'Silver Needles'	see *Agrostis canina* 'Silver Needles'
spectabilis	CBig CBrm CFwr CStr
trichodes	CBig CBrm CKno CPen CWCL EBee ECGP EGoo EMan EPPr EPza GFor NBre SMar WPer

Eranthis (*Ranunculaceae*)

§ ***hyemalis*** ♀H4	CBro CHar CMea EBrs ELan EMon EPfP EPot GAbr GBBs GFlt GKev LAma LRHS MBri WBVN WCot WFar WPop WShi
§ - Cilicica Group	CBro ELan EMon EPot GEdr GFlt IBal LAma WCot
- 'Orange Glow'	EHyt
§ - Tubergenii Group	EPot
- - 'Guinea Gold' ♀H4	CBro ECho EHyt GCrs SOkd
pinnatifida	EFEx GCrs WCru
stellata	GFlt

Ercilla (*Phytolaccaceae*)

volubilis	CAbb CFee CPLG CPLN CRHN EBee NSti NVic SBrw WCot WCru WPic WSHC

Eremophila (*Myoporaceae*)

§ ***debilis***	ECou
maculata	CPLG ECou
'Yellow Trumpet'	ECou

Eremurus (*Asphodelaceae*)

§ ***aitchisonii***	GIBF LAma
- 'Albus' **new**	WCot
* ***brachystachys*** **new**	CMon
* 'Brutus'	EBee ERou IPot LAma MSte
bungei	see *E. stenophyllus* subsp. *stenophyllus*
elwesii	see *E. aitchisonii*
'Emmy Ro'	EBee ERou GBin LAma LRHS MSte SPur
'Helena'	EBee LAma SPur
himalaicus	CBot EBee EBrs EHrv ELan EPot ERou EWTr GIBF LAma LRHS MHer MSte SPer WCot WCra
'Image'	EBee ERou IPot MBNS
x ***isabellinus*** 'Cleopatra'	More than 30 suppliers

- 'Obelisk'	CMea CRez EBee ELan ERou LAma LRHS WCot
- 'Pinokkio'	CRez EBee EBrs EPot ERou IPot LAma MHer NFor NLar WPGP
- Ruiter hybrids	CMea CSWP EBrs EChP ECot ELan EMon ENot EPfP ERou LAma LAst LRHS MLLN MNFA MWgw SPer SPet WAul WFar WPop WWol
- Shelford hybrids	CAby CBcs EBee ELan EMon EWTr EWsh LAma LRHS MLLN MNrw NArg WFar
- 'Tropical Dream'	EChP
'Jeanne-Claire'	EBee LAma NLar SPur
'Joanne'	EBee LAma NLar
lactiflorus	WCot
'Line Dance' **new**	LAma
'Moneymaker'	CPLG EBee EPot ERou IPot LAma LRHS
'Oase'	CAvo CMea EBee EChP EHrv ELan ERou EWTr LAma LRHS MSte NLar SPer WCot WCra
olgae	GIBF
'Rexona'	CRez EBee ERou LAma
robustus ♀H4	CAvo CBcs CBot CMea EBee EBrs EHrv ELan EMon ENot EPot ERou EWTr LAma LPio LRHS MAvo MHer MSte NLar SIgm SPer SPlb WAul WBVN WCot WCra WFar WWFP
'Roford'	ERou LAma
'Romance'	CAvo CMea CRez EBee EMon EPot ERou LAma LRHS MSte WLin
'Rumba' **new**	LAma
'Samba' **new**	LAma
stenophyllus ♀H4	CAby CBgR CBro EChP EPot ERou LRHS SMrm SPoG WCot WFar WPGP
§ - subsp. ***stenophyllus***	CAvo CMea EBee EHrv EMon ENot EPfP ERou GMaP LAma MAvo MHer MLLN MNrw MRav MWgw NArg NBPC NFor NPer NPri SPer WFar WGHP WPop
'Tap Dance' **new**	LAma
'Yellow Giant'	EBee ERou WCot

Erepsia (*Aizoaceae*)

inclaudens	SChr

Erianthus see *Saccharum*

Erica ✿ (*Ericaceae*)

alopecurus **new**	SPlb
arborea	CNCN SAPC SLon SPlb
§ - 'Albert's Gold' ♀H4	CBcs CNCN CSBt CTri CWCL ELan EPfP GKir LRHS MAsh MBar MBri MSwo NBlu SBrw SPer SPla SPoG WBan
- var. ***alpina*** ♀H4	CDoC CNCN CTri ENot EPfP GAbr GKir LRHS MBar SBrw SPer SPoG
- 'Arbora Gold'	see *E. arborea* 'Albert's Gold'
- 'Arnold's Gold'	see *E. arborea* 'Albert's Gold'
- 'Estrella Gold' ♀H4	CDoC CNCN CSBt CTri ELan EPfP LRHS MAsh MBar MGos SBrw SPer SPla SPoG WBan
australis ♀H4	CBcs LRHS MBar
- 'Castellar Blush'	CNCN SBrw
- 'Mr Robert' ♀H3	CNCN EPfP LRHS MBar
- 'Riverslea' ♀H4	CNCN CTri LRHS MBar SBrw WBcn
caffra	CTrC SPlb
canaliculata ♀H3	CBcs SBrw
carnea	ELan
- 'Adrienne Duncan' ♀H4	CNCN GKir MBar MBri NDlv WTel
- 'Alan Coates'	CNCN MBar
- 'Altadena'	CNCN MBar
- 'Ann Sparkes' ♀H4	CNCN CSBt CTri EPfP GKir LGro MBar MBri MSwo SPla
- 'Atrorubra'	CNCN MBar
- 'Aurea'	CNCN CSBt LGro MBar MBri NDlv
- 'Barry Sellers'	LRHS
- 'Bell's Extra Special'	WMoo
- 'Beoley Pink'	CNCN
- 'Carnea'	CNCN MBar
- 'Cecilia M. Beale'	CNCN MBar
- 'Challenger' ♀H4	CNCN EPfP MBar MBri MGos SCoo SPer SPla
- 'Clare Wilkinson'	CNCN
- 'December Red'	CBcs CNCN CSBt EPfP MBar MBri MSwo SPer SPla WBan
- 'Eileen Porter'	CNCN MBar WBcn
- 'Foxhollow' ♀H4	CBrm CNCN CSBt CTri EPfP GKir IArd LGro MBar MBri MGos MSwo MWat SPer SPla WBan WMoo WTel
- 'Foxhollow Fairy'	CBcs CNCN MBar SRms
- 'Golden Starlet' ♀H4	CBrm CNCN CTri CWCL EPfP LGro MBar MGos NBlu SPer SPla WBan
- 'Gracilis'	MBar NDlv
- 'Heathwood'	CNCN MBar SCoo SPla SRms
- 'Hilletje'	CNCN
- 'Ice Princess' ♀H4	CBrm CNCN EPfP SCoo SPer SPla WBan WBcn
- 'Isabell' ♀H4	CNCN EPfP LRHS SCoo SPla WBan WBcn
- 'Jack Stitt'	MBar
- 'James Backhouse'	CNCN CTri
- 'Jean'	CNCN LRHS
- 'Jennifer Anne'	CNCN MBar
- 'John Kampa'	CNCN MBar
- 'King George'	CNCN CSBt CTri GKir MBar SPer WTel
- 'Lesley Sparkes'	CSBt MBar
- 'Lohse's Rubin'	NDlv
- 'Loughrigg' ♀H4	CNCN CSBt CTri GKir MBar SPla WTel
- 'March Seedling'	CNCN EPfP MBar MBri SPer WTel
- 'Mrs Sam Doncaster'	CNCN MBar
- 'Myretoun Ruby' ♀H4	CBcs CNCN CSBt CTri EPfP GKir LGro MBar MBri MGos NBlu NDlv SPer SPla WTel
- 'Nathalie' ♀H4	CNCN LRHS MSwo SCoo WBan WBcn
- 'Pink Beauty'	see *E. carnea* 'Pink Pearl'
- 'Pink Cloud'	CNCN
- 'Pink Mist'	LRHS
§ - 'Pink Pearl'	CNCN MBar
- 'Pink Spangles' ♀H4	CBcs CNCN CSBt CTri GKir MBar MBri MGos MSwo WMoo WTel
- 'Pirbright Rose'	CNCN MGos
- 'Porter's Red'	LRHS MBar WBan
- 'Praecox Rubra' ♀H4	CBcs CNCN EPfP GKir LGro MBar
- 'Prince of Wales'	CNCN CSBt
- 'Queen Mary'	CNCN
- 'Queen of Spain'	MBri
- 'R.B. Cooke' ♀H4	CBrm CNCN EPfP MBar MBri SCoo SPla
- 'Rosalie' ♀H4	CBcs CBrm CNCN EPfP IArd LRHS MSwo SCoo SPer SPla WBan WBcn WMoo
- 'Rosea'	SPlb
- 'Rosy Gem'	CNCN MBar
- 'Rotes Juwel'	LRHS
- 'Rubinteppich'	CNCN
- 'Ruby Glow'	CNCN CSBt GKir MBar MSwo NDlv SPla WTel
§ - 'Sherwood Creeping'	MBar

	- 'Sherwoodii'	see *E. carnea* 'Sherwood Creeping'
	- 'Smart's Heath'	CNCN
	- 'Snow Queen'	CNCN MBar WMoo
	- 'Spring Cottage Crimson'	MBar
	- 'Spring Day'	MSwo
	- 'Springwood Pink'	CBcs CBrm CNCN CSBt CTri MBar MBri WMoo WTel
	- 'Springwood White' ♀H4	CBcs CBrm CNCN CSBt CTri EPfP GKir MBar MBri MGos MSwo MWat SPer SPla WMoo WTel
I	- 'Startler'	LRHS MBar
	- 'Sunshine Rambler' ♀H4	CNCN MBar
	- 'Thomas Kingscote'	CNCN MBar
	- 'Tybesta Gold'	CNCN
	- 'Urville'	see *E. carnea* 'Vivellii'
	- 'Viking'	CNCN
§	- 'Vivellii' ♀H4	CNCN CSBt CTri GKir MBar MBri MWat NDlv WTel
	- 'Walter Reisert'	CNCN
	- 'Wanda'	MBar
	- 'Westwood Yellow' ♀H4	CNCN CSBt CWCL GKir MBar MBri MGos SPer SPla WMoo
	- Whisky	see *E. carnea* 'Bell's Extra Special'
	- 'Whitehall'	LRHS
	- 'Winter Beauty'	CNCN GKir MGos NDlv
	- 'Winter Snow'	SCoo WMoo
	- 'Wintersonne'	CBcs EPfP LGro
	ciliaris 'Aurea'	CNCN MBar SRms
	- 'Camla'	MBar
	- 'Corfe Castle'	CNCN MBar
	- 'David McClintock'	CNCN MBar
	- 'Mrs C.H. Gill' ♀H4	CNCN
	- 'Stoborough' ♀H4	CNCN MBar
	- 'White Wings'	CNCN
	cinerea f. ***alba*** 'Alba Major'	CNCN CSBt MBar
	- - 'Alba Minor' ♀H4	CNCN MBar MBri NBlu
	- - 'Celebration'	MBar NBlu
	- - 'Domino'	CNCN MBar
	- - 'Hookstone White' ♀H4	CNCN MBar NDlv
	- - 'Nell'	MBar
	- - 'Snow Cream'	MBar
	- - 'White Dale'	MBar
	- 'Ann Berry'	CNCN MBar
	- 'Apricot Charm'	CNCN CSBt MBar MSwo
	- 'Ashgarth Garnet'	MBar
	- 'Atropurpurea'	CNCN MBar NDlv
	- 'Atrorubens'	GKir MBar SRms
	- 'Atrosanguinea'	CNCN MBar
	- 'Baylay's Variety'	MBar
	- 'Blossom Time'	MBar
	- 'C.D. Eason' ♀H4	CBcs CNCN CSBt CTri EPfP GKir MBar MBri NBlu
§	- 'C.G. Best' ♀H4	CNCN ECho MBar
	- 'Caldy Island'	MBar
	- 'Cevennes'	CNCN MBar
	- 'Cindy' ♀H4	CNCN MBar
	- 'Coccinea'	CNCN
	- 'Colligan Bridge'	MBar
	- 'Constance'	MBar
	- 'Contrast'	LRHS MBar
	- 'Daphne Maginess'	CNCN
	- 'Duncan Fraser'	CNCN MBar
	- 'Eden Valley' ♀H4	CNCN GKir MBar NBlu SRms
	- 'Fiddler's Gold' ♀H4	CNCN MBar MBri NBlu NDlv
	- 'Foxhollow Mahogany'	MBar
	- 'G. Osmond'	MBar
	- 'Glasnevin Red'	MBar
	- 'Glencairn'	MBar
	- 'Golden Charm'	CNCN
	- 'Golden Drop'	CNCN CSBt GKir MBar MBri MSwo
	- 'Golden Hue' ♀H4	CNCN MBar NDlv
	- 'Graham Thomas'	see *E. cinerea* 'C.G. Best'
	- 'Grandiflora'	MBar
	- 'Guernsey Lime'	MBar
	- 'Hardwick's Rose'	CNCN MBar
	- 'Harry Fulcher'	CNCN MBri
	- 'Heidebrand'	MBar
	- 'Honeymoon'	MBar
	- 'Jack London'	CNCN
	- 'Janet'	MBar
	- 'Joseph Murphy'	CNCN MBar
	- 'Josephine Ross'	MBar
	- 'Joyce Burfitt'	CNCN
	- 'Katinka'	CNCN MBar MSwo
	- 'Knap Hill Pink' ♀H4	CNCN MBar
	- 'Lady Skelton'	MBar
	- 'Lilac Time'	MBar
	- 'Lilacina'	MBar
	- 'Lime Soda' ♀H4	CNCN MBri
	- 'Maginess Pink'	CNCN
	- 'Michael Hugo'	CNCN
	- 'Miss Waters'	MBar
	- 'Mrs Dill'	MBar
	- 'Mrs E.A. Mitchell'	CNCN LRHS SPlb
	- 'Mrs Ford'	MBar
	- 'My Love'	CNCN MBar MBri
	- 'Newick Lilac'	MBar
	- 'Next Best'	MBar
	- 'P.S. Patrick' ♀H4	CNCN GKir MBar
	- 'Patricia Maginess'	CNCN
	- 'Pentreath' ♀H4	CNCN MBar MBri
	- 'Pink Foam'	MBar
	- 'Pink Ice' ♀H4	CNCN CTri EPfP GKir MBar MBri MSwo NBlu NDlv
	- 'Plummer's Seedling'	MBar
	- 'Providence'	LRHS
	- 'Purple Beauty'	CNCN MBar NBlu
	- 'Purple Robe'	LRHS
	- 'Pygmaea'	MBar
	- 'Rock Pool'	MBar
	- 'Romiley'	MBar MBri
	- 'Rosy Chimes'	CNCN MBar
	- 'Ruby'	CNCN MBar
	- 'Sandpit Hill'	MBar
	- 'Schizopetala'	CNCN MBar
	- 'Sea Foam'	CNCN MBar
	- 'Sherry'	CNCN MBar
	- 'Splendens'	CNCN
	- 'Startler'	MBri
	- 'Stephen Davis' ♀H4	CNCN GKir MBar MBri NBlu
	- 'Summer Gold'	CNCN LRHS NDlv
	- 'Tom Waterer'	MBar
	- 'Velvet Night' ♀H4	CNCN CSBt CWCL GKir MBar MBri SRms
	- 'Victoria'	MBar
	- 'Violetta'	CNCN
	- 'Vivienne Patricia'	MBar
	- 'Windlebrooke' ♀H4	CNCN MBar
	curviflora	SPlb
	x ***darleyensis***	WTel
	- 'Ada S. Collings'	CBrm CNCN MBar
	- 'Alba'	see *E.* x *darleyensis* 'Silberschmelze'
	- 'Arthur Johnson' ♀H4	CBcs CNCN CSBt CTri MBar MBri SRms
	- 'Aurélie Brégeon'	CBcs
	- 'Cherry Stevens'	see *E.* x *darleyensis* 'Furzey'
§	- 'Darley Dale'	CBcs CNCN CSBt EPfP MBar MBri NBlu SCoo SPer WMoo
	- 'Dunwood Splendour'	MBar
§	- 'Furzey' ♀H4	CNCN CSBt EPfP GKir MBar MBri MGos NDlv SCoo SPer SRms WTel
	- 'George Rendall'	CBrm CNCN CSBt CTri CWCL EPfP GKir SCoo SPla

- 'Ghost Hills' ♀H4 — CBcs CBrm CNCN CSBt EPfP MBar MSwo SCoo SPer
- 'J.W. Porter' ♀H4 — CBcs CNCN EPfP MBar NDlv SCoo SPla WTel
- 'Jack H. Brummage' — CNCN CSBt CTri GKir IArd MBar MBri MGos MSwo SPla WTel
- 'James Smith' — MBar
- 'Jenny Porter' ♀H4 — CNCN CSBt EPfP MBar MBri WBan
- 'Kramer's Rote' ♀H4 — CNCN CSBt CTri EPfP GKir MBar MBri MGos NBlu NDlv SPer SPla WBan WMoo
- 'Margaret Porter' — CBcs CNCN CSBt EPfP SPer SPla WTel
- 'Mary Helen' — CBcs CBrm CNCN CSBt EPfP LRHS NBlu SCoo SPer SPla WBan WBcn WMoo
- Molten Silver — see *E.* x *darleyensis* 'Silberschmelze'
- 'N.R. Webster' — CNCN
- 'Pink Perfection' — see *E.* x *darleyensis* 'Darley Dale'

§ - 'Silberschmelze' — CBcs CNCN CSBt CTri EPfP GKir MBar MBri MGos MSwo NBlu NDlv SPer WMoo WTel
- 'Spring Surprise'PBR — EPfP
- 'White Glow' — CNCN CSBt CTri SPla
- 'White Perfection' ♀H4 — CBcs CNCN CSBt EPfP IArd MBar MBri SCoo SPla WMoo

erigena 'Alba' — MBar
- 'Brian Proudley' — CNCN MBar
- 'Brightness' — CBcs CNCN CSBt EPfP GKir MBar MBri MSwo MWat NDlv SCoo WTel
- 'Ewan Jones' — CNCN MBar
- 'Golden Lady' ♀H4 — CNCN CSBt MBar MBri MSwo SCoo
- 'Hibernica Alba' — MBar
- 'Irish Dusk' ♀H4 — CNCN CSBt CTri EPfP GKir MBar MBri MGos SCoo SPer SPla SRms
- 'Irish Salmon' — CNCN CSBt MBar NDlv
- 'Irish Silver' — MBar MBri
- 'Nana Alba' — CNCN MBar
- 'Rosea' — MBar
- 'Rubra' — NDlv
- 'Superba' — CNCN MBar MGos WMoo
- 'W.T. Rackliff' ♀H4 — CBcs CNCN CSBt EPfP GKir MBar MBri MGos MSwo NBlu SCoo SPla

§ x ***griffithsii*** 'Heaven Scent' — CNCN LRHS WBan
- 'Jaqueline' — SPla WBan WBcn
- 'Valerie Griffiths' — LRHS MBar SCoo WBcn WMoo

'Heaven Scent' — see *E.* x *griffithsii* 'Heaven Scent'

x ***krameri*** — SDys

lusitanica ♀H3 — CBcs CNCN MBar SBrw
- 'George Hunt' — CNCN ELan LRHS SBrw SPer SPla
- 'Sheffield Park' — ELan LRHS SPer SPoG WBcn

mackayana 'Ann D. Frearson' (d) — CNCN
- 'Doctor Ronald Gray' — CNCN MBar MBri
- 'Galicia' — CNCN
- 'Plena' (d) — CNCN MBar
- 'Shining Light' — SDys

manipuliflora — MBar
- 'Aldeburgh' — CNCN

multiflora — XPep

x ***oldenburgensis*** 'Ammerland' — SDys

patersonia — SPlb

x ***praegeri*** — see *E.* x *stuartii*

scoparia new — SBrw

§ - subsp. ***scoparia*** 'Minima' — MBar
- - 'Pumila' — see *E. scoparia* subsp. *scoparia* 'Minima'

spiculifolia — ITim MBar
- 'Balkan Rose' — CStu GCrs

straussiana — SPlb

§ x ***stuartii*** — MBar
- 'Irish Lemon' ♀H4 — CNCN CSBt EPfP MBar MSwo
- 'Irish Orange' — CBcs CNCN CSBt GKir MBar NBlu

§ - 'Stuartii' — CNCN

subdivaricata — CTrC

§ ***terminalis*** ♀H4 — CNCN MBar SRms
- ***stricta*** — see *E. terminalis*
- 'Thelma Woolner' — CNCN MBar SBrw

tetralix — SRms
- 'Alba Mollis' ♀H4 — CNCN CSBt MBar MBri
- 'Bala' — CNCN
- 'Bartinney' — MBar
- 'Con Underwood' ♀H4 — CNCN CSBt GKir MBar MBri MSwo SRms
- 'Delta' — MBar
- 'Foxhome' — MBar
- 'Hailstones' — MBar
- 'Hookstone Pink' — CNCN GKir MSwo
- 'Ken Underwood' — CNCN MBar
- 'L.E. Underwood' — MBar
- 'Melbury White' — CNCN MBar
- 'Morning Glow' — see *E.* x *watsonii* 'F. White'
- 'Pink Pepper' — NLAp
- 'Pink Star' ♀H4 — CNCN MBar

§ - 'Ruby's Variety' — MBar
- 'Ruby's Velvet' — see *E. tetralix* 'Ruby's Variety'
- 'Ruth's Gold' — CNCN MBar
- 'Silver Bells' — CSBt MBar
- 'Tina' — CNCN

umbellata — CNCN MBar

vagans 'Alba Nana' — see *E. vagans* 'Nana'
- 'Birch Glow' ♀H4 — CNCN EPfP GKir
- 'Cornish Cream' ♀H4 — CNCN CWCL EPfP MBar WMoo
- 'Cream' — CNCN
- 'Diana Hornibrook' — CNCN MBar
- 'Fiddlestone' — CNCN MBar
- 'French White' — CNCN MBar
- 'George Underwood' — MBar
- 'Golden Triumph' — MBar WBan
- 'Grandiflora' — CNCN MBar
- 'Holden Pink' — CNCN
- 'Hookstone Rosea' — MBar
- 'Ida M. Britten' — MBar
- 'Kevernensis Alba' ♀H4 — MBar
- 'Lilacina' — CNCN MBar
- 'Lyonesse' ♀H4 — CNCN CTri MBar MBri MGos MSwo SRms
- 'Miss Waterer' — MBar
- 'Mrs D.F. Maxwell' ♀H4 — CBcs CNCN CSBt CTri GKir MBar MBri MGos MSwo SRms WBan

§ - 'Nana' — MBar
- 'Pallida' — CNCN
- 'Peach Blossom' — MBar
- 'Pyrenees Pink' — CNCN MBar
- 'Rubra' — CNCN MBar
- 'Saint Keverne' — CNCN CSBt CTri GKir IArd MBar WBan WMoo
- 'Summertime' — CNCN MBar
- 'Valerie Proudley' ♀H4 — CNCN CSBt GKir MBar MBri MGos MWat SRms
- 'Viridiflora' — CNCN MBar
- 'White Lady' — MBar
- 'White Rocket' — CNCN MBar
- 'Yellow John' — CBcs CNCN MBar NBlu WBan

x ***veitchii*** 'Exeter' ♀H3 — CNCN CSBt ELan EPfP LRHS MBar SBrw SPer SPoG WBcn
- 'Gold Tips' ♀H4 — CNCN CSBt EPfP MBar MBri SBrw
- 'Pink Joy' — CNCN MBri SBrw

verticillata — CTrC

x ***watsonii*** 'Dawn' ♀H4 — CNCN MBar MBri

§	- 'F. White'	MBar
	- 'Gwen'	CNCN MBar
	- 'H. Maxwell'	CNCN
	x ***williamsii*** 'Gold Button'	MBar
	- 'Gwavas'	CNCN MBar
	- 'Ken Wilson'	SDys
	- 'P.D. Williams' ♀H4	CNCN MBar

Erigeron ✿ (*Asteraceae*)

	from Bald Mountains	NWCA
	from Big Horn	NLAp
	'Adria'	EBee EChP GBuc LRHS NEgg NGdn SPer WMnd WWpP
	aliceae NNS 00-280 **new**	WCot
§	***alpinus***	EHol GKev GKir GTou LRHS SPoG
	angulosus **new**	GKev
	aurantiacus	EDAr EHol EPfP MBNS MHer MWgw NBre NBro NChi NJOw NOak SGSe SPet
§	***aureus***	NSla WAbe
	- NNS 96-87	NWCA
§	- 'Canary Bird' ♀H4	CPBP EHyt EPfP NBir NMen SIng SPer WAbe
*	'Azure Beauty'	EBee EPfP LRHS NPro
	Azure Fairy	see *E.* 'Azurfee'
§	'Azurfee'	CBot CSBt ELan EPfP EWTr GAbr GKir GMaP MBNS MHer NBir NEgg NOak SGSe SGar SPer SPla SPoG SWvt WMoo WPer WSSM
	Black Sea	see *E.* 'Schwarzes Meer'
	'Blue Beauty'	LRHS SRms
	'Charity'	LRHS MRav WBrE
	chrysopsidis	CPBP
	var. ***brevifolius*** **new**	
	- 'Grand Ridge'	CPBP EHyt EPfP EPot LRHS LTwo NWCA SBla WLin
	compositus	CPBP CTri ITim SRms WPer
§	- var. ***discoideus***	EBur GBin GKir NJOw NMen SPlb WPer
	- 'Mount Adams Dwarf'	EHyt
	- 'Rocky'	ECho ECtt SPoG SRot WRHF
	Darkest of All	see *E.* 'Dunkelste Aller'
	deep pink	CHEx
	'Dignity'	EBee ELan NBro SSpe WCot WFar WPGP WWpP
	'Dimity'	CMea ECha EDAr MBri WAbe WBrk WFar WHal
§	'Dunkelste Aller' ♀H3	CSam EBee ECtt ELan ENot EPfP ERou GKir GMaP LRHS MBri MRav MWgw NGdn SPer SPoG SRms SWvt WBrE WCAu WFar WMnd
*	***ereganus*** **new**	NBre
	'Felicity'	ERou
	flettii	NJOw WPat WPer
	'Foersters Liebling' ♀H4	CStr EBee EPfP GKir LRHS MWat NFla NGdn SPet WCot
	formosissimus	GBin
	'Four Winds'	ECtt EDAr ELan EWes LRHS MRav NGdn NJOw NMen NWCA WPer
	'Gaiety'	WWpP
	glaucus	CHrt CSBt EHol EWTr EWll GAbr GGar IHMH NLon SIng SMad WBrk WCot WFar WHoo WWeb
	- 'Albus'	EGoo EShb EWTr LRHS WMow WPer
	- 'Elstead Pink'	CTri EBee EChP ELan NEgg SAga SPla WFar WMow WSHC
	- pink	SPla
*	- 'Roger Raiche'	SMrm
	- 'Roseus'	CBcs CHal ERou NLon
	- 'Sea Breeze'	COIW GBin MBNS NEgg NLar NPri SPoG WCot
	'Goat Rocks'	GCrs
	howellii	NBre
§	***karvinskianus*** ♀H3	More than 30 suppliers
	leiomerus	LBee LTwo
	linearis	NMen
	'Mrs F. H. Beale'	EBee
	mucronatus	see *E. karvinskianus*
	'Nachthimmel'	EBee ECGP EMan LAst NGdn SPet WWpP
	nanus	NWCA WPer
§	***peregrinus***	NOak
	philadelphicus	CElw IGor NBir NBro WSHC
	'Pink Beauty'	ECtt
	Pink Jewel	see *E.* 'Rosa Juwel'
	pinnatisectus	NWCA WPer
	'Profusion'	see *E. karvinskianus*
	'Prosperity'	EBee
	pyrenaicus hort.	see *E. alpinus*
	'Quakeress'	CElw CSam EBee ECtt EMan EPfP GKir GMaP GMac LAst LRHS MRav NBro SMrm SSpe SUsu WCot WEas WFar WRHF WTel WWpP
§	'Rosa Juwel'	CSBt CTri ECtt ENot EPfP GFlt GKir GMaP IBal LAst LRHS MBNS MHer MRav MTis NBir NEgg NJOw NOak SEND SPer SPla SPoG SRms SWvt WMnd WMoo WPer
	'Rose Jewel' **new**	WWeb
	'Rotes Meer'	EBee ELan LRHS WCot
	rotundifolius	see *Bellis rotundifolia*
	'Caerulescens'	'Caerulescens'
	salsuginosus misapplied	see *Aster sibiricus*,
	salsuginosus (Richardson) A. Gray	see *E. peregrinus*
§	'Schneewittchen'	CM&M EBee EChP ECtt ELan EMan EPfP LAst MRav MWat MWgw NCGa NVic SPet SPla SPoG SWvt WCAu WWpP
§	'Schwarzes Meer'	ERou GKir LRHS NGdn WCot WFar
	scopulinus	CPBP EHyt ITim LRHS NJOw
	simplex	CPBP LRHS MWat NMen
	'Sincerity'	WFar
	'Snow Queen'	WFar
	Snow White	see *E.* 'Schneewittchen'
	'Sommerneuschnee'	ECha GBin WMnd
	speciosus	SMer
	- 'Grandiflora' **new**	NBre
	- var. ***macranthus***	SIgm
	'Strahlenmeer'	EBee LRHS WBrk WMnd
	'The Jewel'	CBot
	thunbergii var. ***glabratus*** B&SWJ 8790	WCru
	trifidus	see *E. compositus* var. *discoideus*
	uncialis var. ***conjugans***	CGra
	uniflorus	LTwo SRms
	'Unity'	WWpP
	vagus	LTwo
	'White Quakeress'	CElw CMea ERou GBuc MAnH MRav MWrn WCot WRHF
	'Wuppertal'	EBee LRHS MRav NBro NEgg NGdn WMnd WWpP

Erinacea (*Papilionaceae*)

§	***anthyllis*** ♀H4	SIng SOkd XPep
	pungens	see *E. anthyllis*

Erinus (*Scrophulariaceae*)

	alpinus ♀H4	CMHG CMea CSec CTri ECtt EPfP GFlt GKev GKir GMaP GTou MWat NBlu NFor SBch SIng SPet SPoG SRms WEas WFar WPer
	- var. ***albus***	CBot CNic GTou NLar NMen SIng SRms WHoo WPer

	- 'Doktor Hähnle'	CNic EDAr GFlt LRHS MCCP NLAp NLar NMen SIng SRms WHoo

Eriobotrya (*Rosaceae*)

	deflexa	CFil CHEx CKob IDee
	- 'Coppertone' **new**	SCoo
	japonica (F) ♀H3	More than 30 suppliers

Eriocapitella see *Anemone*

Eriocephalus (*Asteraceae*)

	africanus	EUnu SPlb WJek

Eriogonum (*Polygonaceae*)

	cespitosum	CGra SBla WLin
	- subsp. ***douglasii***	see *E. douglasii*
§	***douglasii***	WLin
	flavum	GEdr WPer
	jamesii	WPat
	niveum subsp. ***niveum*** **new**	WLin
	ovalifolium var. ***depressum***	GKev
	- var. ***nivale***	SBla
	umbellatum	EPot EShb LRHS NLAp
	- var. ***humistratum***	SBla WLin
	- var. ***porteri***	NWCA
	- var. ***torreyanum***	CMea EPot WLin WPat
	- var. ***umbellatum***	LBee
	wrightii	WLin

Eriophorum (*Cyperaceae*)

	angustifolium	CBrm COIW CRWN CWat EHoe EHon EMFW ENot EPla EPza GFor LPBA MCCP NArg SPlb WHer WMoo WPer WPnP WWpP
	latifolium	LPBA WWpP
	vaginatum	CAby CKno CRow EHoe GFor SGSe WWpP

Eriophyllum (*Asteraceae*)

	lanatum	CFis CHal EBee ECha EHan EPfP EShb LPhx MDKP MEHN MWat NArg NBid NBre SAga SBla WWeb

Eriophyton (*Lamiaceae*)

	wallichii **new**	GKev

Eritrichium (*Boraginaceae*)

	howardii **new**	CGra
	rupestre var. ***pectinatum***	NSla
	sericeum **new**	GIBF
*	***sibiricum***	EMan LRav

Erodium ✿ (*Geraniaceae*)

	absinthoides	LRHS MDHE
	- from Genoa	MDHE
	- var. ***amanum***	see *E. amanum*
§	***acaule***	GSki NCiC NLar WFar
	'Almodovar'	MDHE
	alpinum	MDHE
§	***amanum***	EBee LRHS MDHE WAbe
	'Ardwick Redeye'	GCal MDHE
	balearicum	see *E.* x *variabile* 'Album'
§	'Bidderi'	CElw MDHE MOne NChi WAbe
	'Burnside Silver'	MDHE
	'Carla'	MDHE
	'Carmel'	MDHE WAbe
	'Caroline'	CElw MDHE WHoo
	carvifolium	CElw GKev GKir LRHS MDHE NFla NWCA SBch WFar WWpP
§	***castellanum***	CLyd EBee ETow GCrs GKir LTwo NBro NFla NMen NSti SBch SBla SRms
	- 'Cupidon'	MDHE
	- 'Dujardin'	LPhx MDHE
	- 'La Féline'	MDHE
	- 'Logroños Real'	MDHE SIgm
	'Catherine Bunuel'	MDHE MOne
	celtibericum	MDHE
	- 'Javalambre'	MDHE
	- 'Peñagolosa'	MDHE SIgm
	'Cézembre' **new**	MDHE MOne
	chamaedryoides	see *E. reichardii*
§	***cheilanthifolium***	SHBN
	- 'David Crocker'	EPot
	chrysanthum	More than 30 suppliers
	- pink	CSpe ECha LPhx NCot NMen SBla SMrm SRot SUsu
	corsicum	CNic EBur EHyt ETow MDHE MTho NMen NWCA SRot WAbe XPep
	- 'Album'	EHyt LAst LTwo MDHE WAbe
§	'County Park'	CLyd CMea ECha ECou EDAr MOne NMen NRya SBla SChu SHBN SRms WAul
	crispum x ***saxatile***	MDHE
	daucoides misapplied.	see *E. castellanum*
	'Eileen Emmett'	MDHE WAbe
§	***foetidum***	ETow MDHE MWat NMen NSla XPep
	- 'Couvé' **new**	MDHE
	- 'Pallidum'	see *E.* 'Pallidum'
	- 'Roseum'	GCal MWat
	'Fran's Choice'	see *E.* 'Fran's Delight'
§	'Fran's Delight'	CElw CMea CSpe GMaP MDHE NMen WHoo WSHC
	'Fripetta'	MDHE MOne
	'Géant de Saint Cyr'	EMan EMon
N	***glandulosum*** ♀H4	EDAr EPfP GCal MDHE MHer SBla SRms WKif WPat WSHC
	- 'Marie Poligné'	MDHE
	gruinum	EMan LPhx WPat WSan WWpP
	guicciardii	EDAr MDHE
	guttatum misapplied	see *E.* 'Katherine Joy'
N	***guttatum***	CDes EBee EChP EPot LPio MWat SIng SRms WHal WPer WSHC
	'Helen'	MDHE
	x ***hybridum*** misapplied	see *E.* 'Sara Francesca'
	x ***hybridum*** Sünderm.	WAbe WHal
	hymenodes L'Hér.	see *E. trifolium*
	'Julie Ritchie'	CMea MDHE WHoo
	'Katherine Joy'	CLyd CNic EBee EWes MDHE MHer MOne NDlv NLAp NRya SRot WAbe
	x ***kolbianum***	MDHE NDlv SMrm SUsu WAbe WHoo
	- 'Nadia'	MDHE
	- 'Natasha'	CLyd CMHG CNic EPot EWes GKir LBee LRHS MAvo MDHE MHer NChi NMen SChu SPoG WAbe WFar WKif
	'La Belette'	MDHE
	'Las Meninas'	SUsu
	'Lilac Wonder'	MDHE MOne
	x ***lindavicum***	MDHE NChi
	- 'Charter House'	LPio MDHE
	macradenum	see *E. glandulosum*
	manescaui	More than 30 suppliers
	'Maryla'	MDHE WAbe
	'Merstham Pink'	GMaP MDHE NChi NDlv NLar SBla SIng SRms WLin
	'Nunwood Pink'	MDHE MOne NWCA
§	'Pallidum'	CHal CSam
	'Parma'	MDHE

	pelargoniiflorum	CSpe EPfP EWTr GFlt GSki MAnH MTho NBro NChi NDov NLar NRnb SRms STes WEas WFar WKif WPGP WPer WWFP WWpP
	'Pequenito'	MDHE
	'Peter Vernon'	NWCA
	petraeum subsp. ***crispum*** misapplied	see *E. cheilanthifolium*
	- subsp. ***glandulosum***	see *E. glandulosum*
	- subsp. ***petraeum***	MHer SBla
	'Pickering Pink'	MDHE NDlv NMen SRot
	'Pippa Mills' **new**	CElw
	'Princesse Marion'	MDHE
*	'Purple Haze'	CSpe MMil NEgg SPoG SRms SRot
§	***reichardii***	CElw ECtt GSki LRHS MDHE MHer MTho NLAp SPet SPoG SRms WAbe WTel
	- JR 914	MDHE
	- JR 962	MDHE
	- ex coll	NWCA
	- albino	MDHE NJOw
	- 'Album'	EHyt EWTr NEgg NWoo SPet SPoG WHoo
	- 'Bianca'	EChP
	- 'Pipsqueak'	MDHE SRot WAbe
*	- 'Rubrum'	CElw MDHE
	'Robertino'	MDHE
	'Robespierre'	LPhx MDHE
	'Robin'	MDHE
	'Rock et Rocaille'	MDHE
	rodiei	EBee MDHE
	rodiei x ***glandulosum***	MDHE
	romanum	see *E. acaule*
§	***rupestre***	EBee ECho ECtt GMaP MDHE MOne NDlv NWCA SBla SRms SRot
	'Santamixa'	MDHE
§	'Sara Francesca'	MDHE
	'Sarck'	MDHE
	sibthorpianum **new**	WLin
	'Spanish Eyes'	GKir MAvo MDHE MOne NChi SMrm SRot SUsu WAbe WCot
	'Stephanie'	CFis CLyd EWes GMaP LBee LPio LRHS MAvo MDHE MHer NChi NDlv SIgm SRot
	supracanum	see *E. rupestre*
	'Tiny Kyni'	MDHE WAbe
	trichomanifolium misapplied	see *E. cheilanthifolium*
	trichomanifolium L'Hér.	EWes LBee LRHS MHer NJOw
§	***trifolium***	CHrt ELan EPfP MHer NCiC NSla NSti SBri SGar SIng SSpi WCru WHal WHoo WTMC XPep
§	x ***variabile***	CBrm ECtt EHyt MDHE SIng
§	- 'Album'	CNic EDAr EPot ESis EWin GBuc LBee MBar MDHE MHer MTho NEgg NPri NWCA SBla SHFr SRms SRot WAbe WBrk WPat WPer WTel
I	- 'Bishop's Form'	CMea ECtt EDAr EHyt EMar EPfP EPot ESis LAst LPio LRHS MBar MDHE MHer NBro NEgg NMen NPri NWCA SBla SGar SPoG SRms SRot WAbe WHoo WPat
	- 'Derek'	ECho
	- 'Flore Pleno' (d)	CStu ECtt EDAr EHyt ELan EWTr EWes MDHE NJOw NMen SHFr SIng SRms SUsu WFar WPer
	- 'Red Rock'	EWes SIng
	- 'Roseum' 🏆H4	CBot CNic ECho ECtt EDAr ELan GSki LBee LRHS MDHE NLAp NWCA SIng SRms WBrk WFar WPer
	'Veinina'	MDHE
I	'Westacre Seedling'	EWes MDHE
	'Whiteleaf'	MDHE
	'Whitwell Beauty' **new**	NWCA
	'Whitwell Superb' **new**	CDes NWCA
	x ***willkommianum***	MDHE NFla NWCA

Erpetion see *Viola*

Eruca (*Brassicaceae*)

vesicaria	CWan MBow
- subsp. ***sativa***	CArn CSpe ELau GPoy MBow MChe MHer MSal NGHP SIde WJek WLHH WSel

Eryngium ✿ (*Apiaceae*)

	CD&R	EWes
	CDPR 3076	CFil WPGP
	PC&H 268	MAvo MSph NLar
	RB 94054	ITer MSph
	RCB/Arg R-5	WCot
	RCB/TQ A-3	WCot
§	***agavifolium***	More than 30 suppliers
	alpinum 🏆H4	More than 30 suppliers
	- 'Amethyst'	EBee GBuc IPot LPhx LRHS MAvo MBri MSte NBro NLar SMrm
	- 'Blue Star'	CBcs CBot CHar CSpe EBee EChP EHrv EPfP ERou GAbr GBBs GCal LAst LPhx MAvo MSte NCGa NEgg NJOw NLon SPet SPla SRkn SSpi WHoo WPer WSan WTel WTin WWeb
	- 'Holden Blue'	EBee GMac
	- 'Slieve Donard'	see *E.* x *zabelii* 'Donard Variety'
	- 'Superbum'	CBot CMea CSpe EBee ECtt EHrv GAbr GBri GBuc GSki MAnH MBnl MNrw NBPC NCob NEgg NJOw NLar NLon SBla SGar SMad SPla SRms WSan
	amethystinum	CBot CMdw EChP EHrv EMan GSki LPhx LPio MNrw SChu SIgm SPla WBVN WCAu WPer WSHC
	biebersteinianum	see *E. caeruleum*
	'Blue Jackpot'	EWes NCGa SCoo SGSe SPoG SVil
	bourgatii	More than 30 suppliers
	- Graham Stuart Thomas's selection	More than 30 suppliers
	- 'Oxford Blue' 🏆H4	CBot COIW EHrv LPio MHer NCGa SGSe SGar SPer SSpi STes SWvt WEas WHoo WOld
	- 'Picos Amethyst' **new**	EBee EVFa SGSe SHar SPoG SVil WOVN
	- 'Picos Blue'^{PBR}	CBot EBee EHrv EVFa IPot LPhx SHar SMrm SPoG SVil SWvt WHoo WPGP WWhi
	bromeliifolium misapplied	see *E. agavifolium*
§	***caeruleum***	EBee GBuc MNrw NEgg WOut
	campestre	CAgr CBot EWll MDKP MHer NChi NGby NLar SIgm WFar WPer
	carlinae	LPhx MAnH NDov
	caucasicum	see *E. caeruleum*
	creticum	MAvo NBir NBro NChi WTin
	Delaroux	see *E. proteiflorum*
	dichotomum	EMon EPPr GFlt NChi
	ebracteatum	CFil CHad EBla LPhx LPio MWrn SIgm WCot
	- CDPR 3139B	CHad
	- var. ***poterioides***	CAby CFil LPhx MAnH SMad
§	***eburneum***	CBot CFil CSec ECha EMag EPfP EWTr EWes GBuc GMaP LEdu LPio LRHS MAnH MWgw MWrn NBro NChi NEgg WCot WFar WPic

aff. ***eburneum*** **new** WPGP
foetidum CArn GPoy
§ ***giganteum*** ♀H4 More than 30 suppliers
- 'Silver Ghost' ♀H4 More than 30 suppliers
glaciale WLin
- JJA 461.000 NWCA
horridum CFil EWes LEdu LPhx LPio LRHS MEHN MNrw SAPC SArc SIgm WCAu WFar WMnd WPGP WTin WWhi
- HCM 98048 WCru
'Jos Eijking'PBR EBrs EMan ENot GKir GMac LRHS MRav NLar
maritimum CArn CBot CPom CPou EGoo GPoy LEdu LPhx MAvo MHer NLar SIgm SPlb WCot WFar WSel
Miss Willmott's ghost see *E. giganteum*
monocephalum CFil EBee WPGP WTin
x ***oliverianum*** ♀H4 CHad CMea EBla ECGP EHrv ELan GBuc GMac LPio LRHS MAvo MNFA SBch SDix SIgm SPoG SUsu WCAu WWhi
§ ***pandanifolium*** CBct CFil CHEx CHar CHrt CMHG CSec EBee EMan EPfP EVFa EWes GCal IBlr ITer MAnH MMil SAPC SArc SMad SPav SPer SPoG SWvt WBor WBrE
- 'Physic Purple' CAby CFil LPhx SDix SMHy SPet
paniculatum CFil EBee WPGP
pectinatum B&SWJ 9109 WCru
petiolatum MNrw
planum More than 30 suppliers
- 'Bethlehem' ♀H4 EBee EMan GCal LRHS MBNS NBro WHlf
§ - 'Blauer Zwerg' CKno LRHS NFla SPla WFar WHlf
- 'Blaukappe' CBot CFir CHar COIW CWCL EBrs ERou GBBs GBri LDai LPhx LRHS MAnH MWat MWrn NLar SMrm WFar WGwG WHil WMnd WWhi WWpP
* - 'Blue Candle' WFar WHlf
- Blue Dwarf see *E. planum* 'Blauer Zwerg'
- 'Blue Ribbon' CSam EBee EMan GBBs LAst LRHS LSou NEgg WCAu
- 'Flüela' CKno CM&M CSam EBee ECtt EMan EShb EWes GCal GMaP IPot LRHS MBow MNFA MWgw NBid NBro SPet SPla WCAu WFar WHrl WTin
- 'Hellas' **new** LBuc NBid WHil WSan
- 'Seven Seas' CFir CM&M EVFa LAst LRHS MRav MWgw NBro SChu SPla WCAu WCot WPer
- 'Silverstone' EBee GCal GMaP LDai LRHS MBnl NBro NOrc NPri NSti WCAu
- 'Tetra Petra' LPio MAvo NBPC NEgg SRkn WPer
- violet blue GCal
§ ***proteiflorum*** CAby CBot COIW EWll GCal GSki ITer LPhx LPio LRHS MAnH MAvo MSph MWrn NJOw SMHy WCot WCru
serbicum GCal
serra CAby EBee EBrs EPyc EWes GBuc LDai LRHS NChi WBor
- RB 90454 MDKP
spinalba CBot GSki LPio SIgm
tricuspidatum EBee EBrs ECtt LRHS WPer
x ***tripartitum*** ♀H4 More than 30 suppliers
* - 'Electric Blue' EBee
* ***umbelliferum*** GKev
variifolium More than 30 suppliers
venustum CAby LPhx MAnH SIgm
yuccifolium CArn CBct CBot CBrm CFil CHEx EChP EMag ERou EUnu EWes GCal GKir LEdu LPio MAnH NLRH NVic SDix SDnm SIgm SPav SPet SWvt WBrE WFar
- 'Green Sword' MBnl MWgw
x ***zabelii*** ELan ETow GCal GMac LPhx MAvo NBir NDov SMrm WEas
- 'Donard Variety' CDes CFir GCal GKir GMac IBlr IPot ITim LAst LRHS MDKP NPri WHil
- 'Forncett Ultra' CDes SMHy
- 'Jewel' CMdw MAvo SApp SMHy SUsu
- 'Spring Hill Seedling' **new** MAvo
- 'Violetta' CBos ELan GBuc IGor MSte NGby SMHy WFar WHoo WPen

Erysimum (*Brassicaceae*)

from Madeira CPLG
alpinum hort. see *E. hieraciifolium*
'Anne Marie' ELan SOkh
'Apricot Delight' COtt EShb EWin SCoo
'Apricot Twist' More than 30 suppliers
arkansanum see *E. helveticum*
§ ***asperum*** IFro
bicolor WCot
'Bowles' Mauve' ♀H3 More than 30 suppliers
'Bowles' Purple' CBrm EChP LAst NCob SRms SWvt WBVN
'Bowles' Yellow' ECtt ERou GBuc NLar
'Bredon' ♀H3 CFis CHar EBee EChP EPfP EWin GKir LRHS LSou MAsh NBlu NPer NPri SBch WHil WHoo WKif
'Butterscotch' CFee GKir MMHG NCob WEas WHoo WTin WWhi
'Butterscotch Variegated' (v) GBri NCob WCot
candicum XPep
capitatum CLyd NMen
- 'Chilli Pepper Red' **new** NWCA
cheiri CArn GWCH MBow MHer SECG WCot
- 'Bloody Warrior' (d) CBot CElw EChP ECtt ELan GBri GBuc NPer WCAu WEas
- 'Harpur Crewe' (d) CElw CFee CTri EChP ECtt ELan EPfP EPot ERou EShb GKir GMaP LRHS MTho MTis NLon NPer SChu SMrm SRms WHoo WPnn
- 'Jane's Derision' CNat
'Chelsea Jacket' EChP EHol EPfP ERou EWin GBri LDai WEas
concinnum see *E. suffrutescens*
'Constant Cheer' CElw CSpe EBee EChP ECtt EGoo ELan EMan ENot EPfP ERou EWTr GBuc GGar GMaP LRHS MEHN MTis NFla NPer SUsu SWvt WCAu WKif WMnd WRha WWhi
'Cotswold Gem' (v) CElw COtt EBee EChP EHoe EMan EPPr EPfP EVFa GBri LAst LDai MBnl MHer MSph NCob NEgg NPer NSti SAga SBri SHBN SMrm SPoG STes SWvt WCot
'Cream Delight' **new** EWin
'Dawn Breaker' **new** WCot
'Devon Gold' see *E.* 'Plant World Gold'
'Devon Sunset' CElw GBri MSte NLsd SAga SChu WBcn WHil WWhi
'Dorothy Elmhirst' see *E.* 'Mrs L.K. Elmhirst'
dwarf lemon WHoo
'Ellen Willmott' GBin NLsd
'Fragrant Sunshine' SPoG
* ***gelidum*** var. ***kotschyi*** NWCA SBla
* 'Gingernut' NPer
'Glowing Embers' SOkh

'Golden Gem'	EWin IHMH NBlu NDlv SPoG WPer
'Golden Jubilee'	CHar ECho LIck SIng
'Hector Harrison'	COtt
§ ***helveticum***	GTou IFro NPri SOkd SRms WRHF
§ ***hieraciifolium***	CNic EHol NFla NLAp
'Jacob's Jacket'	CStu EBee ECtt NPer SChu WEas
'Jaunty Joyce' **new**	GBri
'John Codrington'	CElw GBri GBuc MHer NFor NGdn NPer SChu SUsu WKif
'Joseph's Coat'	CElw
'Jubilee Gold'	EWll
'Julian Orchard'	CElw CSpe ECtt MHar NCiC SChu SSth
kotschyanum	CGra CLyd CPBP ECtt EHyt ETow LBee MDHE MOne NMen NWCA SRms WPat
'Lady Roborough'	CFee GBuc
linifolium	EBur EMag SHGN SRms WBVN WGor XPep
§ - 'Variegatum' (v)	CArn CBrm CSBt EBee ECtt ELan EPfP EPot ERou LRHS NLsd NPer SAga SPer SPoG SRot WHoo WPGP
'Little Kiss' **new**	SECG
'Mayflower'	NCob
'Miss Hopton'	WEas WLin
'Moonlight'	ECtt EPot GAbr GBuc GMaP LBee MHer MTho NCGa NDov NFla NFor SBla SChu SOkd SRms SSvw WBVN
§ 'Mrs L.K. Elmhirst'	NPer SOkh WCot
mutabile	CBgR CFwr CTri EGoo LPhx MBow MRav NBir SIde
- 'Variegatum' (v)	WEas
'Orange Flame'	CMea CNic ECtt EPot EWin LAst LBee LSou MBar MHer NPer NWCA SAga SIng SPoG WPer WRHF WSan
'Orange Queen' **new**	WWeb
'Parish's'	CBgR CMdw CSpe EChP ECtt EWTr MRav MSph SAga SChu SMrm
perofskianum	WEas
Perry's hybrid	NPer
'Perry's Peculiar'	NPer
'Perry's Pumpkin'	NPer
§ 'Plant World Gold'	CElw
'Plant World Lemon'	CElw EWin LIck LSou MEHN SRot WPop WSan
§ ***pulchellum***	ECha MWat SRot
- 'Variegatum' (v)	GGar WBrE
pumilum DC.	see *E. helveticum*
rupestre	see *E. pulchellum*
'Rushfield Sunrise'	CElw
* 'Rushfield Surprise'	NLar
'Ruston Royal' **new**	EWin
§ ***scoparium***	ECha
'Sissinghurst Variegated'	see *E. linifolium* 'Variegatum'
'Sprite'	CLyd CTri ECtt EDAr EPot ESis IHMH NPer SBch
§ ***suffrutescens***	XPep
'Sweet Sorbet'	CHVG CHar EBee EChP EPfP EWin LAst MSte NPri SPav SPoG WSan
'Variegatum' ambig. (v)	CBcs CRez
'Walberton's Fragrant Sunshine'	COtt LRHS MBri SCoo
'Wenlock Beauty'	LDai MTis NFor NGdn SChu SRms WHoo WMnd WWhi
wheeleri	EMag NBur
witmannii	SSth

Erythraea see *Centaurium*

Erythrina (*Papilionaceae*)

x ***bidwillii***	SSpi
caffra	WMul
crista-galli	CAbb CBcs CBot CHEx CSpe ELan ERea GQui LRHS MLan SMur SPlb SSpi WCot WMul WPat WSHC
- 'Compacta'	SMad
flabelliformis	MGol
herbacea	EMan SSpi
- pink-flowered	SSpi

Erythronium ✿ (*Liliaceae*)

albidum	CAby CBro CLAP EBee EPot GBuc GCrs GFlt GKev LAma SSpi
americanum	CAby CArn CLAP CWoo EBee EPot GBuc GCrs GEdr GKev IBlr LAma MLLN MS&S NMen SSpi WCru
'Beechpark'	IBlr
'Blush'	GBuc IBlr
'Californian Star' **new**	IBlr
californicum ♀H4	CAby CLAP CWoo EHyt SCnR WAbe WCru
- J&JA 1.350.209	CWoo
- J&JA 13216	CLAP
- Plas Merdyn form	IBlr
§ - 'White Beauty' ♀H4	More than 30 suppliers
caucasicum	CLAP
citrinum	CWoo GBuc NMen WLin
- J&JA 1.350.410	CWoo
- J&JA 13462	CLAP CWoo
'Citronella'	CBro CLAP EBee EChP EHrv ERos GBuc IBlr ITim LAma LRHS MS&S NArg NDlv NJOw NMen NMyG SSpi WAbe WCru WFar WPnP
cliftonii hort.	see *E. multiscapoideum* Cliftonii Group
dens-canis ♀H4	More than 30 suppliers
- JCA 470.001	CLAP
- 'Charmer'	EPot WWst
- 'Frans Hals'	CLAP EPot ERos GBuc GCrs GEdr GGar LAma MNFA MTho WAbe WCru
- from Slovenia	CLAP
- - WM 9615	MPhe
- 'Lilac Wonder'	EBee EPot GEdr LAma LRHS MTho WAbe WLin WWst
* - 'Moerheimii' (d)	IBlr WWst
- var. ***niveum***	ERos IBlr
- 'Old Aberdeen'	CLAP IBlr
- 'Pink Perfection'	EBee ERos GCrs GGar LAma LRHS WAbe WCru
- 'Purple King'	EBee EPot ERos GCrs GEdr LAma MDun NCGa SPur WCru
- 'Rose Queen'	CAby CAvo CBro CFwr CPLG EBee EBrs EHyt EPot ERos GBuc GCrs GGar LAma LRHS MDun MTho NJOw
* - 'Semi-plenum' (d)	IBlr
- 'Snowflake'	CLAP CMea ECha EHyt EPot ERos GCrs GEdr GGar LAma MDun MNFA NBir NMen WAbe WCru WLin
- 'White Splendour'	CBro EBrs ERos IBlr
elegans	SBla SSpi
'Flash'	IBlr
§ ***grandiflorum***	GBuc GCrs GEdr GKir NMen
- J&JA 11394	CLAP
- M&PS 007	CLAP SSpi
- M&PS 96/024	NMen
- subsp. ***chrysandrum***	see *E. grandiflorum*
helenae	CLAP CWoo IBlr
- J&JA 11678	WWst
hendersonii	CLAP CWoo EHyt LAma MS&S WAbe
J&JA 1.351.301	CWoo

- J&JA 12945	CLAP CWoo SSpi
- JCA 11116	CLAP
hendersonii x ***citrinum*** **new**	IBlr
howellii	CLAP GCrs SSpi
- J&JA 13428	WWst
- J&JA 13441	CLAP
japonicum	EBee EFEx EPot GBBs GBuc LAma MPhe SPer WCru
'Jeanette Brickell' **new**	IBlr
'Jeannine'	GBuc GEdr IBlr WCru
'Joanna'	CLAP IBlr LAma NMen
'Kondo'	CFwr EBee EHyt EPfP EPot ERos GBBs GBuc GCrs GEdr GGar GMaP IBal IBlr ITim LAma LRHS MAvo MDun MS&S MTho NBir NJOw NMen SPer WAbe WCru WFar WHil WPnP
'Margaret Mathew'	IBlr
mesochoreum	IBlr
§ ***multiscapoideum***	CLAP CWoo MPhe WCot
- JCA 12700	SSpi
§ - Cliftonii Group	CLAP MPhe
- - J&JA 13525	CLAP SSpi
oregonum	CLAP CWoo ETow GBuc MS&S SBla WCot WCru
- subsp. ***leucandrum***	CLAP MPhe
- - J&JA 13494	CWoo SSpi
'Pagoda' ♀H4	More than 30 suppliers
purdyi	see *E. multiscapoideum*
revolutum ♀H4	CAby CAvo CBro CFir CLAP CMea CWoo EPot GBuc GCrs GFlt GGar GKev GMaP IBlr ITim MS&S SBla SCnR SOkd SRot SSpi WAbe WCru
- 'Guincho Splendour'	IBlr
- Johnsonii Group	CNic CWoo SSpi WAbe WCru
- 'Knightshayes Pink'	CAby CLAP GBuc IBlr
- 'Pink Beauty'	WNor
- Plas Merdyn form	IBlr
- 'Rose Beauty'	GKev NMen
- 'White Beauty'	see *E. californicum* 'White Beauty'
'Rippling Waters'	IBlr
'Rosalind'	IBlr
sibiricum	GCrs GKev SPer
- from China **new**	CFwr
- from Ussuri **new**	GIBF
- 'Lady in Red' **new**	WWst
- white	WWst
'Sundisc'	ECha IBlr MS&S MTho NMen WAbe
tuolumnense ♀H4	CBro CLAP EBee EHrv EMon EPot ERos GBuc GCrs GGar GKev GMaP IBlr LAma MCCP MS&S NMen WAbe WCot
- EBA clone 2	WAbe
- EBA clone 3	WAbe
- 'Spindlestone'	IBlr
umbilicatum	GCrs IBlr

Escallonia ✿ (*Escalloniaceae*)

'Alice'	SLPl SPer
'Apple Blossom' ♀H4	More than 30 suppliers
§ ***bifida*** ♀H3	CFee CPle SDix WBcn WFar WSHC
'C.F. Ball'	CBcs CSBt CTri EBee EHol ELan GGar LBuc MSwo NBlu NEgg NScw NWea SEND SLim SRms WAbe WBVN WDin WFar WMoo WTel
'Compacta Coccinea'	CBcs
'Dart's Rosy Red'	SLPl
'Donard Beauty'	SRms WFar
'Donard Radiance' ♀H4	More than 30 suppliers
'Donard Seedling'	More than 30 suppliers
'Donard Star'	CSBt CWib ENot EPfP LAst MRav NWea SLPl WCFE
'Donard Surprise'	NFor NLon
'Donard White'	COkL
'Edinensis'	CBcs ECtt ENot EPfP MBar MRav NLar SBch SEND SLim WDin WFar WGer WMoo
'Erecta'	EPfP LAst SHGN
x ***exoniensis***	SRms
'Gwendolyn Anley'	CMHG SLPl SPer WFar
'Hopleys Gold'PBR	see *E. laevis* 'Gold Brian'
illinita	SPoG
'Iveyi' ♀H3	More than 30 suppliers
§ ***laevis***	CDoC CTrw WFar
§ - 'Gold Brian'PBR	CDul CMHG CSBt EBee EHoe ELan ENot EPfP LRHS LSRN MAsh MGos MWat NScw SCoo SHop SMer SPer SWal WFar WHar
- 'Gold Ellen' (v)	CBcs CChe CTri CWSG EBee ELan EMil EPfP LAst LRHS MAsh MCCP MGos MRav MSwo SAga SCoo SEND SLim SPer SPla SPoG SWvt WCot WMoo WWeb
Lanarth no.1	CBcs
'Langleyensis' ♀H4	CBcs CPLG CSBt CTri CWib NLon NWea WDin WFar WHar
leucantha	WKif
mexicana	CBot WFar
x ***mollis***	SPer
montevidensis	see *E. bifida*
'Newry'	SPer
organensis	see *E. laevis*
'Peach Blossom' ♀H4	CBcs CDoC CDul CPle CSam CWib EBee ECrN ELan EMil EPfP GKir LRHS MAsh MBNS MBri MGos MSwo NCGa NEgg NLon SCoo SHBN SLPl SLim SPer SPoG WFar
'Pink Elf'	ECtt LRHS MSwo NLon
'Pride of Donard' ♀H4	CBcs CDoC CSBt EPfP GGar LRHS MAsh NBlu NCGa NPri SRms SSto WBrE
'Red Dream'	CChe CWSG EBee LRHS MAsh MBri MGos MSwo NBlu NScw SCoo SPoG SRms SWvt WFar WGer
'Red Elf'	CBrm EBee ECrN ECtt ELan ENot EPfP GKir LAst LRHS MAsh MBar MBri MRav MSwo MWat NEgg NLon SCoo SGar SLPl SPer SPlb SPoG SRms SWvt WFar WWeb
'Red Hedger'	CDoC CSBt CWib LRHS MTis SCoo
'Red Robin' **new**	SPoG
resinosa	CBcs CPle IFro SAPC SArc WHCG
revoluta	WKif
rubra 'Crimson Spire' ♀H4	CAlb CBcs CBrm CChe CDul COkL CSBt CTri CWSG CWib ENot EPfP GGar GKir LRHS LSRN MAsh MBNS MRav MWat NJOw SBod SHBN SLim SPer SPlb SPoG SRms WMoo WWeb
- 'Ingramii'	CSBt CWib NWea SHBN
§ - var. ***macrantha***	More than 30 suppliers
* - - ***aurea***	NScw
- 'Pygmaea'	see *E. rubra* 'Woodside'
§ - 'Woodside'	ECrN EHol EPfP SIng SRms SSto WHCG
'Saint Keverne'	CBcs
'Silver Anniversary'	MSwo WBcn
'Slieve Donard'	EBee ECrN ENot EPfP MRav NEgg NWea SLPl SLim SLon SRms WFar

Eschscholzia (*Papaveraceae*)

I ***caespitosa*** 'Sundew' **new**	ENot

californica ♀H4 GKev XPep
- 'Jersey Cream' CSpe
- var. ***maritima*** XPep
lobbii **new** CSpe

Eucalyptus ✿ (*Myrtaceae*)

acaciiformis LRav
aggregata GTSp LRav SAPC SArc SPer WCel WMul
alpina LRav SPlb
amygdalina GGar
approximans LRav WCel
subsp. ***approximans***
archeri CBrm CCVT CDoC CDul EPfP GKir GQui GTSp LSou MBNS WCel WOVN WPGP
baeuerlenii LRav
barberi LRav
§ ***bridgesiana*** CMCN LRav MHer
caesia SCoo SPlb
calycogona LRav
camaldulensis LRav SPlb
camphora CTho LRav WCel
cinerea CTrC GQui LRav SBig SPlb WCel
citriodora CHrt CWib GQui LRav MHer NGHP SPlb SWal WCel WNor
coccifera CBcs CCVT CDoC CHEx CSBt CTho EBee ECrN EGra ELan EPfP GGar GKir LRHS MCCP MLan NBea NBlu NPri SBig SEND SPlb SPoG WBVN WCel WDin WMul WNor WPGP
cordata CCVT LRav NEgg WCel
crenulata CTrC GQui LRav WCel
crucis subsp. ***crucis*** SPlb
cypellocarpa CMCN SPlb
dalrympleana ♀H3 CAbb CBcs CCVT CDoC CDul CMHG EBee ECrN ELan ENot EPfP EWes GKir LAst LRHS MGos MSwo NBea NEgg SBig SCoo SPer SPoG SRms WBrE WCel WDin WMul WPGP WWeb
dalrympleana × ***fraxinoides*** LRav
deanei WCel
debeuzevillei see *E. pauciflora* subsp. *debeuzevillei*
delegatensis CMHG GTSp LRav WCel WMul
- subsp. ***tasmaniensis*** GGar WNor
divaricata see *E. gunnii* subsp. *divaricata*
dives LRav
elata **new** CMCN
erythrocorys SPlb
eximia SPlb
* - ***nana*** LRav WGwG
forrestiana **new** LRav
fraxinoides LRav SPlb WCel
gamophylla SPlb
glaucescens CCVT CMHG CTho ECrN EPfP EWes GKir GQui LRHS NEgg NPri SAPC SArc SPer WBVN WCel WGer WMul WPGP
globulus CHEx ISea LRav MSal WCel WFar WMul
goniocalyx EPfP WCel
§ ***gregsoniana*** CCVT CDoC LRav SPlb WBVN WCel WPGP
gunnii ♀H3 More than 30 suppliers
- subsp. ***divaricata*** CCVT EPfP GQui LRHS LRav MBri WCel WGer
- 'Silver Rain' **new** LRav
johnstonii CAgr CDul CMHG ECrN GGar LRav SPer WCel
kitsoniana GGar LRav WCel
kruseana SPlb
kybeanensis CCVT GQui GTSp LRav SCoo WCel
lacrimans WCel
leucoxylon WCel
- subsp. ***megalocarpa*** SPlb
ligustrina LRav WCel
'Little Boy Blue' CWib
macarthurii LRav WCel
macrocarpa SPlb
macroryncha SPlb
mannifera subsp. ***elliptica*** LRav WCel
- subsp. ***praecox*** LRav
mitchelliana LRav WCel WDin
moorei WCel
* - ***nana*** LRav MHer MWat WNor
neglecta EPfP LRav NBlu WCel
nicholii CAbb CBrm CCVT CDul ECrN EPfP EWes GKir GQui GTSp MGos SCoo SPoG WCel WGer WMul WOVN WPGP
niphophila see *E. pauciflora* subsp. *niphophila*
nitens CCVT CLnd GKir LRav NBlu SAPC SArc SBig SCoo SPlb WCel WMul WOrn
§ ***nitida*** CMHG GGar WCel WNor
nova-anglica CMHG CTho LRav
obliqua GGar
ovata GGar
parvifolia ♀H4 CBcs CCVT CDoC CDul CLnd EPfP EShb GKir LRHS LRav NEgg SCoo SEND WBVN WCel WMul
pauciflora CCVT CDoC CSBt EBee ELan EPfP MGos NEgg SEND SPer WBrE WCel WMul WNor
- subsp. ***acerina*** WCel
§ - subsp. ***debeuzevillei*** CBrm CCVT CDoC CLnd CMHG CTho EPfP EWes GKir GQui LRHS MBri MGos NBlu SAPC SArc SBig WCel WMul WPGP WWeb
- subsp. ***hedraia*** WCel
- var. ***nana*** see *E. gregsoniana*
§ - subsp. ***niphophila*** ♀H4 More than 30 suppliers
- - 'Pendula' CCVT GTSp LRHS WCel WPGP
- subsp. ***pauciflora*** LRav
perriniana CCVT CDul CLnd CMHG CSBt EBee ECrN ELan EPfP GKir LRHS MBri MGos NEgg SBig SCoo SPer SPlb SPoG WBVN WCel WDin WFar WMul WNor WOrn WPGP
pulchella LRav
pulverulenta CDul CEnd CSLe EBee GTSp LRHS LRav SPlb WGer WHer
- 'Baby Blue' LRav WCel
regnans GGar WMul
risdonii GGar LRav WNor
rodwayi GGar LRav
rubida CMHG LRav WCel
scoparia LRav
sideroxylon SPlb
- 'Rosea' SPlb
simmondsii see *E. nitida*
stellulata LRav NEgg WCel
stricklandii **new** LRav
stricta LRav
stuartiana see *E. bridgesiana*
sturgissiana LRav
subcrenulata CCVT CMHG EPfP GGar GKir GQui GTSp LRav MBNS WCel WOrn

tenuiramis	LRav
tetraptera **new**	LRav
torquata	SPlb
urnigera	CCVT CDoC GKir LRHS MBNS SCoo WCel WDin
vernicosa	CBrm CCVT GGar WCel
viminalis	CArn CHEx GGar LRav WCel WDin
youmanii	LRav

Eucharidium see *Clarkia*

Eucharis (*Amaryllidaceae*)

§ ***amazonica*** ♀H1	LAma LRHS MLan MOak SPav
grandiflora hort.	see *E. amazonica*

Eucodonia (*Gesneriaceae*)

'Adele'	WDib
andrieuxii 'Naomi'	WDib
§ ***verticillata*** **new**	CSpe

Eucomis ✿ (*Hyacinthaceae*)

§ ***autumnalis*** ♀H2-3	CAbb CAvo CBro CHEx CPne CPou CRHN CSWP CTbh EBee ENot EPot EUJe GBin GSki LAma LPio LRHS MAvo MCCP MDun SDnm SPav SPlb WPGP WTin
- subsp. ***amaryllidifolia***	CFil WPGP
- subsp. ***autumnalis***	CFil WPGP
- subsp. ***clavata***	CFil EBee SSpi
- 'White Dwarf'	CStu EShb SPer
bicolor ♀H2-3	More than 30 suppliers
- 'Alba'	CAvo CPLG EAmu EBee EBrs EPot GSki LPio LRHS SDnm
- 'Stars and Stripes'	WCru
§ ***comosa***	CAvo CBrm CBro CHEx CHll CPne CRHN EBee EBrs EChP ENot GAbr GSki LAma LEdu LRHS MDun SDnm SPav SYvo WCru WEas WHil
- 'First Red'	CPou
- purple-leaved	SBla SIgm
- 'Sparkling Burgundy'	More than 30 suppliers
'Frank Lawley' **new**	EBee
hybrid	SDix
'John Treasure'	SMHy
'Joy's Purple'	CPen
montana	CCtw CFil WPGP
pallidiflora ♀H4	CFil CHEx EBee LEdu WPGP
pole-evansii	CFil CFir CHEx CPLG EBrs ECGP EMar EPza EUJe GBin GCal LRHS MLLN MMil SMrm WCot WCru WHil WPGP
- bronze	CPne
- 'Burgundy'	EBla
- 'Purpurea'	GCal
punctata	see *E. comosa*
regia	CFil CPLG LToo
* ***reichenbachii***	WCot
'Royal Burgundy'	SPer
'Swazi Pride'	EBee
undulata	see *E. autumnalis*
vandermerwei	CPen
zambesiaca	CPen EBee ENot GBin GCal LPio
'Zeal Bronze'	CBcs CDes CDoC CFil CMHG CStu EBee EPfP GCal LPio MAsh MCCP NSti SPav WCot WCru WPGP

Eucommia (*Eucommiaceae*)

ulmoides	CBcs CFil CMCN EPfP NLar SMad

Eucrosia (*Amaryllidaceae*)

stricklandii **new**	CMon

Eucryphia ✿ (*Eucryphiaceae*)

'Castlewellan'	ISea
cordifolia	CAbP CFil CMac CTho CTrw CWib ISea SSpi WDin
- Crarae hardy form	GGGa
cordifolia x ***lucida***	CBcs ELan ISea NEgg NPen SSpi WDin WPGP WPat
glutinosa ♀H4	CBcs CDul CTho ECrN ELan EPfP GKir IMGH LHyd LRHS MAsh MBar MBri MDun NBea NBir NEgg SBrw SHBN SPer SSpi SSta WDin WFar WNor WPat
- Plena Group (d)	WPat
x ***hillieri*** 'Winton'	CMHG GQui SSpi
x ***intermedia***	CSam CTrC CWSG ECrN ELan EPfP GGGa LRHS NPal NPri NVic SHBN SRms SSpi WDin WFar WPat
- 'Rostrevor' ♀H3	CBcs CDul CMHG CPMA CSBt CWib ELan EPfP GQui IArd IMGH ISea LHyd LRHS LSRN MAsh MDun MGos NCGa SBrw SLon SPer SReu SSta WFar WPat WPic WSHC
lucida	CDoC CFil CTbh CTrC ELan EPfP GGar GSki GTSp IArd IMGH ISea SBrw SPer WFar WNor
- 'Ballerina'	CPMA ISea LRHS NVic SCoo SPoG SSpi SSta WFar
- 'Gilt Edge' (v)	CFil ISea SSpi
- 'Leatherwood Cream' (v)	ISea SBrw
- 'Pink Cloud'	CBcs CDoC CEnd CFil CPMA CTbh CWSG ELan EPfP GQui IMGH ISea LRHS LSRN MDun NPri SBrw SDnm SMur SPer SPoG SSpi SSta SWvt WFar WPGP
- 'Pink Whisper'	ISea
- 'Spring Glow' (v)	ISea
milliganii	CAbP CDoC CFil CPMA CTrC EPfP GGar GQui ISea MBlu MDun SHBN SRms SSpi WPGP
moorei	CBcs CFil ELan GQui ISea SSpi
x ***nymansensis***	CFil CWib ECrN EMil ENot NEgg SAPC SArc SDnm SReu SRkn SRms SSpi WBrE WFar WHCG
- 'George Graham'	GGGa IMGH ISea
- 'Mount Usher'	ISea
- 'Nymansay' ♀H3	More than 30 suppliers
'Penwith' misapplied	see *E. cordifolia* x *E. lucida*
'Penwith' ambig.	CDoC CPMA GQui NEgg NLar SBrw SPer SSpi WBrE WDin WFar WGer WMoo

Eugenia (*Myrtaceae*)

myrtifolia	ERom
smithii	ECou

Eumorphia (*Asteraceae*)

prostrata	CTrC

Eunomia see *Aethionema*

Euodia (*Rutaceae*)

daniellii	see *Tetradium daniellii*
hupehensis	see *Tetradium daniellii* Hupehense Group

Euonymus (*Celastraceae*)

B&L 12543	EPla EWes
B&SWJ 4457	WPGP
alatus ♀H4	More than 30 suppliers
- B&SWJ 8794	WCru
- var. ***apterus***	EPfP

	- Chicago Fire	see *E. alatus* 'Timber Creek'
	- 'Ciliodentatus'	see *E. alatus* 'Compactus'
§	- 'Compactus' ♀H4	More than 30 suppliers
	- 'Fire Ball'	EPfP
	- Little Moses = 'Odom' **new**	MBlu
*	- 'Macrophyllus' **new**	EPfP
	- 'Rudy Haag'	CPMA EPfP
	- 'Select'	see *E. alatus* 'Fire Ball'
§	- 'Timber Creek'	CPMA EPfP GKir MBlu NLar
	americanus	CBot EPfP GIBF MBlu NLar
	- narrow-leaved	EPfP NLar
	atropurpureus	EPfP GKir
	bungeanus	CMCN EPfP EPla NLar
	- 'Dart's Pride'	CPMA EPfP NLar
	- 'Fireflame' **new**	NLar
*	- var. ***mongolicus***	EPfP
	- 'Pendulus'	EPfP GKir MBlu
	- var. ***semipersistens***	CPMA EPla
	carnosus	EPfP NLar
	'Copper Wire' **new**	SPoG
	cornutus	CFil CPMA EBee EPfP GKir MAsh
	var. ***quinquecornutus***	MBlu NLar SIFN WPGP WPat
*	***cymosus*** B&SWJ 8989 **new**	WCru
	'Den Haag'	EPfP
	echinatus	EPfP EPla
	- BL&M 306	SLon
	europaeus	CArn CCVT CDoC CDul CLnd CRWN CSam CWib EBee ECrN ELan EPfP EPla GIBF GKir LBuc MHer MSwo NLar NWea SCoo SRms SWvt SYvo WDin WFar WHar WHer WMou XPep
	- f. ***albus***	CBot CPMA CTho EPfP LTwo
	- 'Atropurpureus'	CMCN CTho EPfP GKir MBlu MBri NLar SIFN
	- 'Atrorubens'	CPMA
	- 'Aucubifolius' (v)	CFil EPfP WBcn
*	- 'Aureus'	CNat
*	- f. ***bulgaricus***	EPfP
	- 'Chrysophyllus'	EPfP MBlu
	- 'Howard'	EPfP
	- var. ***intermedius***	ENot EPfP MBlu NLar WWes
	- 'Miss Pinkie'	CEnd CMCN GKir
	- 'Red Cascade' ♀H4	More than 30 suppliers
	- 'Scarlet Wonder'	CPMA EPfP NLar
	- 'Thornhayes'	CTho
	farreri	see *E. nanus*
	fimbriatus	CBcs EPfP
	fortunei Blondy = 'Interbolwi'^{PBR} (v)	More than 30 suppliers
	- 'Canadale Gold' (v)	CDoC COkL EBee ENot EPla LRHS MAsh MGos MWhi SPer WCFE WDin
	- 'Coloratus'	EHol EPfP MBar MSwo SHBN SLon SPer WDin
	- 'Dart's Blanket'	CDul ECrN ELan ENot EPla MRav MWhi NScw SLPl SSta WDin WFar
	- 'Emerald Cushion'	EBee SPer
	- 'Emerald Gaiety' (v) ♀H4	More than 30 suppliers
	- 'Emerald 'n' Gold' (v) ♀H4	More than 30 suppliers
	- 'Emerald Surprise' (v) ♀H4	ENot EPfP LRHS MBri
	- 'Gold Spot'	see *E. fortunei* 'Sunspot'
	- 'Gold Tip'	see *E. fortunei* 'Golden Prince'
§	- 'Golden Pillar' (v)	EHoe EHol EPla ESis WFar
§	- 'Golden Prince' (v)	ENot EPfP EPla LRHS MBar MRav MSwo NPro SLim SRms WFar WGor
	- 'Harlequin' (v)	CBcs COtt CSBt CWSG EBee EHoe ELan ENot EPfP EPla LBuc LRHS LSRN MAsh MBar MGos MRav NPro SAga SHBN SLim SPer SPla SRms SWvt WCot WFar
	- 'Kewensis'	CWib EPfP LAst MBar MRav NVic SAPC SArc SBod SLon SPoG WCru WFar
	- 'Minimus'	CTri EPla ESis MGos NPro WFar
*	- 'Minimus Variegatus' (v)	ECho SPlb
§	- var. ***radicans***	CPLN WWpP
	- 'Sheridan Gold'	COkL CTri ECtt EHoe EPla MRav SHBN
	- 'Silver Gem'	see *E. fortunei* 'Variegatus'
	- 'Silver Pillar' (v)	CPLG ECrN EHoe ENot LRHS WFar
	- 'Silver Queen' (v)	More than 30 suppliers
	- 'Sunshine' (v)	CAbP ELan LRHS MAsh NEgg
§	- 'Sunspot' (v)	CBcs CChe CMHG CWSG ECrN ECtt EGra ELan EPla LRHS MBar MGos MSwo SLim SPer SRms WBrE WDin WFar WHar WTel
	- 'Tustin' ♀H4	EPla SLPl
§	- 'Variegatus' (v)	CMHG MBar NFor NSti SPer SRms STre WCot WDin
	- var. ***vegetus***	EPla
	- 'Wolong Ghost'	SSpi
	frigidus	EPfP GIBF WPGP
	grandiflorus	CPMA EPfP GIBF GKir MBlu NLar SIFN SSpi WFar
	- 'Red Wine'	CPMA CTho EBee EPfP LRHS MBri NLar SLim WPat
	- f. ***salicifolius***	CPMA EPfP MBri NLar
	hamiltonianus	CMCN EPfP GKir SSpi WFar
I	- 'Calocarpus' **new**	MBlu SIFN
	- 'Coral Chief' **new**	SLon
	- 'Fiesta'	MBri
	- subsp. ***hians***	see *E. hamiltonianus* subsp. *sieboldianus*
	- 'Indian Summer'	CPMA EBee EPfP GKir LRHS MBlu MBri NLar SIFN SPur SSpi SSta WBcn
	- 'Koi Boy'	CPMA GKir LRHS MAsh SIFN
	- var. ***lanceifolius*** **new**	WPic
	- 'Miss Pinkie'	CDul CPMA EBee GKir LRHS MAsh MGos SCoo SIFN SSpi SSta
	- 'Pink Delight'	CPMA MBri
	- 'Poort Bulten'	MBlu NLar
	- 'Popcorn' **new**	EPfP MBlu
	- 'Rainbow'	CPMA MBri NLar
	- 'Red Chief' **new**	EPfP
	- 'Red Elf'	CPMA EPfP GKir MBri
	- 'Rising Sun' **new**	MBlu MBri
§	- subsp. ***sieboldianus***	CDul CMCN CPMA CTho EBee EPfP GIBF GKir MBri MRav SLPl WFar
	- - 'Calocarpus'	EPfP GKir MBri NLar
	- - 'Coral Charm'	CPMA EPfP NLar SMur
	- - Semiexsertus Group	EPfP
*	- - var. ***yedoensis*** f. ***koehneanus***	EPfP
	- 'Snow'	EPfP MBlu NLar
	- 'Winter Glory'	CPMA EPfP GKir LRHS MBlu MBri NLar WWes
	- var. ***yedoensis***	see *E. hamiltonianus* subsp. *sieboldianus*
	hibarimisake	see *E. japonicus* 'Hibarimisake'
	japonicus	CDoC CDul CTrC ECrN ENot EPfP LRHS SAPC SArc SPer WDin XPep
	- 'Albomarginatus'	CBcs CTri MBar NBlu SEND SRms
	- 'Aureopictus'	see *E. japonicus* 'Aureus'
	- 'Aureovariegatus'	see *E. japonicus* 'Ovatus Aureus'
§	- 'Aureus' (v)	CBcs CBrm CDoC CDul CMHG CSBt CWib EBee ECrN EGra ENot LRHS MSwo MWat NBlu SCoo SHBN SHFr SLon SPer SSto WDin WHar WTel WWeb

	- 'Bravo'	CDoC EBee ECrN EGra EHoe EMil LAst LRHS NLar SCoo SPer SPoG SWvt WDin WFar
	- 'Chedju' (v)	WBcn
	- 'Chollipo' ♀H4	ELan EPla LRHS MAsh
	- 'Compactus'	SAPC SArc SCoo
	- 'Duc d'Anjou' misapplied	see *E. japonicus* 'Viridivariegatus'
	- 'Duc d'Anjou' Carrière (v)	CBcs CHrt EHoe ELan EPla EWes MRav SPoG
	- 'Francien' (v) **new**	SPoG
	- 'Golden Maiden'	ELan EPfP LRHS MAsh SLim SPoG SWvt
	- 'Golden Pillar'	see *E. fortunei* 'Golden Pillar'
	- 'Green Spider' **new**	SPoG
	- 'Grey Beauty'	EBee NLar SCoo
§	- 'Hibarimisake'	EPla SBla
	- 'Kathy'PBR	NScw SPoG
§	- 'Latifolius Albomarginatus'	CDul CTbh EHoe EHol ELan EPfP EPla LRHS MRav MSwo SPer SPoG WDin WWeb
	- 'Luna'	see *E. japonicus* 'Aureus'
	- 'Macrophyllus'	ECrN
	- 'Macrophyllus Albus'	see *E. japonicus* 'Latifolius Albomarginatus'
	- 'Maiden's Gold'	COtt CSBt
	- 'Marieke'	see *E. japonicus* 'Ovatus Aureus'
	- 'Microphyllus'	CDoC CMac EMil SAga STre WFar WGwG
§	- 'Microphyllus Albovariegatus' (v)	More than 30 suppliers
§	- 'Microphyllus Aureovariegatus' (v)	CDoC CMea CSLe EGra EHyt EMil EPfP MWhi NLar WCFE WCot WPat
	- 'Microphyllus Aureus'	see *E. japonicus* 'Microphyllus Pulchellus'
§	- 'Microphyllus Pulchellus' (v)	CBcs CDoC CMHG CSBt CWSG EBee ECrN ENot EPfP EPla MBar MRav NDlv NJOw SPoG SWvt WDin WHCG WWeb
	- 'Microphyllus Variegatus'	see *E. japonicus* 'Microphyllus Albovariegatus'
§	- 'Ovatus Aureus' (v) ♀H4	More than 30 suppliers
	- 'Président Gauthier' (v)	CDoC EBee ECrN MGos SCoo SWvt WDin
	- 'Pulchellus Aureovariegatus'	see *E. japonicus* 'Microphyllus Aureovariegatus'
	- 'Robustus'	EPfP EPla
	- 'Royal Gold'	SPoG
	- 'Silver Krista' (v) **new**	SPoG
	- Silver Princess = 'Moness'	NArg SHBN WRHF
	- 'Susan'	EPla
§	- 'Viridivariegatus' (v)	LRHS MAsh
	kiautschovicus	EPfP EPla GKir
	- 'Berry Hill'	EPfP NLar
	- 'Manhattan' **new**	NLar
	latifolius	CMCN CPMA CTho EPfP NLar WDin
	maackii	GIBF
	macropterus	EPfP EPla NLar
	maximowiczianus	EPfP GIBF MBlu NLar
	morrisonensis	EPfP
	- B&SWJ 3700	WCru
	myrianthus	CPMA EPfP GKir MBlu NLar
§	***nanus***	CNic CWib EHol EPfP EPla NLar SSpi WSHC
	- var. ***turkestanicus***	EPfP EPla SLon SRms WFar
	obovatus	EPfP
	occidentalis	EPfP
	oresbius	CPMA EPfP
	oxyphyllus	CMCN CPMA CTho EPfP GKir MBri NLar WCru WDin WWes
	- 'Waasland' **new**	NLar
	pauciflorus	EPfP
§	***pendulus***	CHEx CHll CPLG
	phellomanus ♀H4	CDul CEnd CTho EBee EHol EPfP GIBF GKir LRHS MAsh MBar MBlu MBri MRav NLar SHBN SIFN SMac SPoG WDin WFar WPGP WPat
	- 'Silver Surprise' (v)	CPMA EPfP GKir NLar
	Pierrolino = 'Heespierrolino' **new**	SPoG
§	***planipes*** ♀H4	More than 30 suppliers
	- 'Dart's August Flame' **new**	NLar
	- 'Gold Ore' **new**	EPfP NLar
	- 'Sancho' **new**	NLar
	radicans	see *E. fortunei* var. *radicans*
	'Rokojô'	CLyd NWCA
	rongchuensis **new**	EPfP
	rosmarinifolius	see *E. nanus*
	sachalinensis hort.	see *E. planipes*
	sachalinensis (F. Schmidt) Maxim. from Ussuriland	GIBF
	sacrosanctus	EPfP
	sanguineus	CPMA CTho EPfP LRHS NLar SSpi
	tanakae	GIBF
	tingens	CFil EPfP GIBF GKir
	vagans	EPfP
	- L 551	EPla SLon
	velutinus	EPfP NLar
	verrucosus	CPMA EPfP EPla GKir NLar SIFN WWes
	vidalii	EPfP
	yedoensis	see *E. hamiltonianus* subsp. *sieboldianus*

Eupatorium (*Asteraceae*)

	B&SWJ 9052 from Guatamala	WCru
	RCB/Arg P-1	WCot
	RCB/Arg Q-2	WCot
§	***album***	ERou NBid WPer
	- 'Braunlaub'	EBee EChP EMan EMon EPza EWTr GKir LPio LRHS MNFA NGdn NSti SSpi WCAu WHrl WMnd
	altissimum	CBot MSal SRms
	arnottianum **new**	WCot
	- RCB/Arg L-2	WCot
	aromaticum	CRow CSev EBee MLLN MRav NBro WCHb WPer WWye
	atrorubens	CPLG ERea EShb GCal
	cannabinum	CArn EBee EHon ELan EMFW GBar GFlt GGar GPoy LPBA MBNS MBow MHer MRav MSal NBir NGHP NMir NPer NRnb SECG SPav SRob SSpi WGwG WPer WWpP WWye
	- 'Album'	EMon SMHy
	- 'Flore Pleno' (d)	More than 30 suppliers
	- 'Not Quite White'	LNCo
	- 'Spraypaint'	CNat EPPr WWpP
*	- 'Variegatum' (v)	EBee EMan EVFa WCot WPop
	capillifolium	EShb LPio LSou MLLN SAga SArc SDix SMrm WCot WDyG WPGP
	- 'Elegant Feather'	CAby CHea CSpe EMan EVFa EWes LPhx MDKP SHar SMad SUsu
	coelestinum	CPLG EMan EShb EWes GCal MDKP SMad WFar WWpP
*	***cyclophyllum***	EMan
	fistulosum	CSec MGol
*	- 'Atropurpureum'	CKno EPza EShb IBal MAnH NJOw WPer WSSM WWeb
	fortunei	CArn SSpi
*	- 'Variegatum' (v)	CKno EBee EMan EVFa LSou WCot WPGP

	glechonophyllum **new**	MDKP
§	***ligustrinum*** 🏆H3	CBcs CDoC CPLG CPle CRHN CSam CTbh CTri CWib ECha ELan EMan ISea LRHS NCGa SAga SBrw SDix SLim SPer WCHb WCot WFar WHCG WMnd WSHC
	lindleyanum	EBee
	maculatum	see *E. purpureum* subsp. *maculatum*
	madrense	CSam
	'Massive White'	GCal
	micranthum	see *E. ligustrinum*
	occidentale NNS 94-53	WCot
	perfoliatum	CAgr CArn EBee GPoy MNrw MSal NLar SPav WPer WWye
	purpureum	More than 30 suppliers
	- 'Album'	EPPr GKir LPhx MLLN WWpP
	- 'Bartered Bride'	EBrs GCal GKir
§	- subsp. ***maculatum***	CAby CSam EBee ECGP EHrv EMon MDKP NGHP NGdn NLar NLon SBri SSpi STes WFar WHil WHrl WOut WPer WWpP
	- - 'Album'	EMon EWTr GBin NBir NSti SMad
	- - 'Atropurpureum' 🏆H4	More than 30 suppliers
	- - 'Berggarten'	GCal
	- - 'Gateway'	CRow ECtt WTin
	- - 'Glutball'	EBee EBrs GCal NChi SMad WWpP
	- - 'Riesenschirm'	CKno EBee EBrs GCal LPhx LRHS MSph MSte
	- 'Purple Bush'	CHad CKno CSam EBee ECha EWTr LPhx MDKP NCGa NDov NEgg SMad SSvw WGHP WWpP
	rugosum	EBee ELan EPfP GBar GIBF GKir LPhx MGol NLar SDys SPav WCHb WTin
	- ***album***	see *E. album*
	- 'Brunette'	EHrv
	- 'Chocolate' 🏆H4	More than 30 suppliers
*	'Snowball'	SMrm
	triplinerve	MSte
*	***variabile*** 'Variegatum' (v)	EMan EVFa EWes MDKP SMad WCot WWpP
	weinmannianum	see *E. ligustrinum*

Euphorbia ✿ (*Euphorbiaceae*)

	RCB/TQ J-4 **new**	WCot
	'Abbey Dore'	WCot
	altissima	MSte
	amygdaloides	CNic ECtt GKir NBlu NLsd SSpi
	- 'Bob's Choice' **new**	EWes
	- 'Brithembottom'	CSam
	- 'Craigieburn'	CDes CSam EBee EChP EMan EVFa EWes GBri GCal GCra LRHS MAvo NDov SUsu WCra WPGP WWeb
§	- 'Purpurea'	More than 30 suppliers
	- 'Red Shank'	CMea SBla
§	- var. ***robbiae*** 🏆H4	More than 30 suppliers
	- - dwarf	EPot GCal
	- - 'Pom Pom'	CDes EMan WPGP
	- - 'Redbud'	EBee EMan EPla EWes SLPl
	- var. ***robbiae*** x ***characias***	see *E.* x *martini*
	- 'Rubra'	see *E. amygdaloides* 'Purpurea'
	- 'Signal' **new**	EMon
	- 'Variegata' (v)	GBuc SHBN SMad
	- 'Welsh Dragon'	EBee
	- 'Winter Glow' **new**	CSpe
	- yellow-leaved **new**	WCot
	aureoviridiflora **new**	LToo
	baselicis	CMea EKen EMan EShb GBBs LSou MAnH MAvo MGol NPro SIgm
	biglandulosa	see *E. rigida*
	biumbellata	NWit
	'Blue Haze'	SBla
	brittingeri	NWit
	- Baker's form	EPPr
	broteroi	WCot
	bulbispina **new**	LToo
	canariensis	EPfP
	capitata	CLyd
	capitulata	ELan EPot EWes MTho NWit
	ceratocarpa	CFis CFwr EBee EPPr EVFa EWes EWin GBuc NWit SIgm SMad WCot WSHC
	characias	CBcs CBot CHEx CHrt COIW ECtt EPfP EUJe EUnu GKir MDun MRav NEgg NOak NPer NPri NVic SPer SRms SSpi WAul WCot WFar WMnd WPer XPep
	- Ballyrogan hybrids	IBlr
	- 'Black Pearl'	CBcs CFwr CMHG CTbh EChP EPfP GKir IPot LAst MAvo MBNS MCCP MDun MSte NCGa NEgg NSti SDnm SHBN SHop SMer SPav SPoG SSpi SWvt WCra WFar WOVN WPop
	- 'Blue Wonder'	CM&M CSpe EBee EPfP GBin GCal GMaP LRHS MAvo MCCP MDun MSte NEgg NLar NWit SDnm SPav SPoG SSpi SVil WCot WCra WGer WWeb
	- subsp. ***characias***	EBee EHrv GMaP LBBr MGos WCru
	- - 'Blue Hills'	ECtt EMan GBin GBuc GCal MSph NBlu NWit SMrm
	- - 'Burrow Silver' (v)	More than 30 suppliers
	- - 'Green Mantle'	IBlr
	- - 'H.E. Bates'	NBir
	- - 'Humpty Dumpty'	More than 30 suppliers
	- - 'Percy Picton'	CMil
	- - 'Perry's Winter Blusher'	ECtt NWit
	- dwarf	SMrm
	- 'Forescate'	CSWP EBee EMil EPfP EWin LRHS MNFA MRav MSte NCGa NGdn NWit SDnm SPav WFar WMnd
	- 'Giant Green Turtle'	CMil
	- 'Goldbrook'	CHad CSam EHoe EMan LAst LRHS MBNS MRav MSph MSte MWgw SHBN SSpi
	- 'Portuguese Velvet' 🏆H4	CDes CSam CSpe EChP ECha EGra EHrv ELan EMar EWTr EWsh GBri LPhx MAnH MRav NCGa NDov SChu SIgm SPav SPoG SSpi WCot WCra WMnd WPen WSHC WWFP WWeb WWhi
	- Silver Swan = 'Wilcott'[PBR] (v)	ELan EMan ENot EPfP ERou LBuc MGos NPri NSti SBra SHGC SPoG SSpi
	- 'Sombre Melody'	IBlr
	- 'Spring Splendour'	EWes NWit
	- 'Starbright'	EBee NWit
	- 'Whistleberry Jade'	CFwr NWit
	- subsp. ***wulfenii*** 🏆H3-4	More than 30 suppliers
	- - 'Bosahan' (v)	CBcs GCra NWit
	- - 'Emmer Green' (v)	CDes CPen CSpe EBee ECtt EHrv EMan EMon EWes GBri GMaP NWit SBla SHBN SPav SUsu WCot WFoF
	- - 'Jayne's Golden Giant' **new**	SMad
	- - 'Jimmy Platt'	EVFa MTho SRms WBrE WCot WPic WWhi
§	- - 'John Tomlinson' 🏆H3-4	CDes CHar EBee ECha EGra EHrv EVFa EWes GAbr GBin GMaP MFOX MRav NEgg SDnm SMrm SPav SUsu WCot

	Name	Suppliers
	- - Kew form	see *E. characias* subsp. *wulfenii* 'John Tomlinson'
	- - 'Lambrook Gold' ♀H3-4	CSam EBee ECtt EPfP LRHS MBri MRav MWat NPer SMad SVal WFar WGer
	- - 'Lambrook Gold' seed-raised	see *E. characias* subsp. *wulfenii* Margery Fish Group
	- - 'Lambrook Yellow'	EBee EMon EWsh GBuc LPio SMur SVal WSPU
§	- - Margery Fish Group	EMan LRHS MLLN NBir SPer
	- - 'Perry's Tangerine'	EVFa EWes NPer NWit
§	- - 'Purple and Gold'	CFwr CM&M EBee EVFa EWes GMaP SHBN SWvt WBrE WCot
	- - 'Purpurea'	see *E. characias* subsp. *wulfenii* 'Purple and Gold'
	- - 'Silver Shadow' **new**	SBla
	- - 'Thelma's Giant'	NWit
	clavarioides **new**	EHyt
	- var. ***truncata***	WCot
	cognata	NWit
	- CC&McK 607	EWes
	- CC&McK 724	GBin
	conifera	CBos
	'Copton Ash'	CSpe EBee NLsd NWit
	corallioides	CBrm ECha EMan IBlr LRHS NBPC NPer NSti SHFr SIgm SPav SRms WBrE WHer WPnP WWpP XPep
§	***cornigera*** ♀H4	CElw CFil CFwr CHad EBee ECha EPfP GBBs GBin GCal GMac IBlr LPio LRHS MBri MNFA MRav MTis NBid NCGa NDov NGdn NLar NSti SSpi WHoo WPGP WPen WSHC
	- 'Goldener Turm'	EChP GBin
	corollata	EShb SIgm
	croizatii **new**	LToo
	cylindrifolia	LToo
	var. ***tubifera*** **new**	
	cyparissias	CArn CBcs CHrt EChP ECha EDAr ELan GAbr GKir LRHS MRav NBir NFor NGdn NJOw NLon NMen NSti NVic NWCA SPav SPer SRms WEas WFar WFoF WPer WTin XPep
	- 'Baby'	WFar
	- 'Betten'	see *E.* x *gayeri* 'Betten'
	- 'Bushman Boy'	GBri IBlr
	- 'Clarice Howard'	see *E. cyparissias* 'Fens Ruby'
	- clone 2	WCot
§	- 'Fens Ruby'	More than 30 suppliers
	- 'Orange Man'	CWan EBee EBrs EChP EDAr EMon EPPr EPfP ERou EWes GBin GBri IBlr LRHS MWgw NBPC NBro NSti SPav SPla SWvt WFar
	- 'Purpurea'	see *E. cyparissias* 'Fens Ruby'
	- 'Red Devil'	CBre IBlr NWit SChu
	- 'Tall Boy'	EMon EWes GBri IBlr XPep
	dendroides	SIgm SSpi WCot
	denticulata	SBla
	'Despina' **new**	NLar
§	***donii***	EWes GGar IBlr NWit SDix SVal WCru WPer
	dulcis	CBre CStu ECtt NBro NOak NWit WEas
	- 'Chameleon'	More than 30 suppliers
	'Efanthia' **new**	LSou NLar NPri
	enopla **new**	EPem
	epithymoides	see *E. polychroma*
§	***erubescens***	WLin
	esula Baker's form	NWit
	Excalibur = 'Froeup' PBR ♀H4	CFwr CMil COIW CTrC EMan GBin GBuc LRHS MAvo MBNS MBri MCCP MRav MSte MWgw NBir NCGa NSti SHBN SPoG SSpi WFar WSHC WWhi
	flavicoma **new**	SSpi
	fragifera	EBee NWit
	fulgens ♀H1	EShb
	'Garblesham Enchanter'	EPPr NWit
§	x ***gayeri*** 'Betten'	EMan GCal
	glauca	CFee CFir ECou SSpi WCot
	'Golden Foam'	see *E. stricta*
	gottlebei **new**	LToo
	griffithii	CHll GKev GKir NBro SPav SSpi WFar WGer WMoo WTel
	- 'Dixter' ♀H4	More than 30 suppliers
	- 'Dixter Flame'	EGra MBri NWit
	- 'Fern Cottage'	CElw EBee EHrv EWes GAbr SMrm SUsu WHal
	- 'Fireglow'	More than 30 suppliers
	- 'King's Caple'	CFwr CRez MBNS NWit SWal WCru
	- 'Robert Poland'	MBri
	- 'Wickstead'	EBee EMar WBrE
	'Hale Bop'	CFwr
	hyberna	CFis GBri IBlr MLLN NMen NWit SChu
	iharanae **new**	LToo
	jacquemontii	EMan GIBF LPio MNrw MRav NChi NWit SIgm
	'Jade Dragon'	CSpe
	jolkinii	GKev
	x ***keysii***	MBri
	lactea 'Grey Ghost' **new**	LToo
	lathyris	CArn CBre EMar MDun MHer NBid NLar NPer NRnb SIng SRms WBrk WEas WWye
	longifolia misapplied	see *E. cornigera*
	longifolia D. Don	see *E. donii*
	longifolia Lamarck	see *E. mellifera*
	macrostegia	see *E. erubescens*
	margalidiana	EWes
	x ***martini*** ♀H3	More than 30 suppliers
	- 'Baby Charm'	CPen
	- dwarf	CFir GCal
	- 'Red Dwarf'	CMil MSph
§	***mellifera*** ♀H3	More than 30 suppliers
	milii ♀H1	CHal EBak SHFr
	- 'Koenigers Aalbäumle'	MBri SHFr
*	- 'Variegata' (v)	CHal
	- yellow-flowered	CHal ECtt
	millii var. ***millii*** **new**	LToo
I	'Mini Martinii'	LBuc NLar
	myrsinites ♀H4	More than 30 suppliers
	nereidum	EWes NWit
	nicaeensis	CDes CFil EMan EMon GCal LPhx NWit SBla SMad SSpi WCra WPGP XPep
	- subsp. ***glareosa***	NWit
	oblongata	CFil EMan ERou EWes GBuc IBlr LRHS NWit WCHb
	pachypodioides **new**	LToo
	palustris ♀H4	More than 30 suppliers
	- 'Walenburg's Glorie'	CAby CMHG EBee EChP ECha ELan EWTr GBin LRHS MBri MNrw MRav NSti NWit SMad WCra WRHF
	- 'Zauberflöte'	CHrt LPBA SRms WFar WWpP
	x ***paradoxa***	NWit
	paralias	WHer XPep
	x ***pasteurii***	CFil CFir CPLG CPom EWes MAnH SIgm WMul WPGP
	pekinensis	MSal NWit
	pilosa 'Major'	see *E. polychroma* 'Major'
	piscatoria **new**	CFil WPGP
	pithyusa	CBot CNic CSam CSpe EBee EChP ECha ECtt ELan EMan EPfP EVFa LAst LRHS MArl NGdn SChu SHBN XPep

§ ***polychroma*** ♀H4 More than 30 suppliers
§ - 'Candy' CSam EBee EChP ECha ECtt EHrv ELan EPfP ERou EVFa GCal LRHS MAvo MCCP MDun MTis SPla WCot WFar WHoo WLin WMnd WPop
- 'Emerald Jade' GBri IBlr NWit WPGP
§ - 'Lacy' (v) More than 30 suppliers
§ - 'Major' ♀H4 CMHG CPLG ECha EVFa GCal LPhx LPio MBri SAga WCot WEas
- 'Midas' CFee MAvo MNrw NLar NWit SMHy SMrm
- 'Orange Flush' WHoo WTin
- 'Purpurea' see *E. polychroma* 'Candy'
* - 'Senior' EMil GBin LBmB MCCP WMnd
- 'Sonnengold' EBrs EVFa EWes GCal WSHC
- 'Variegata' see *E. polychroma* 'Lacy'
portlandica CNic MBri NWit WHer
- 'Dolce Vita' **new** EShb
§ x ***pseudovirgata*** CFis EMan IBlr NWit
pugniformis MBri
pulcherrima LRHS MBri
'Purple Preference' EPPr NWit
Redwing = 'Charam'PBR ♀H4 ECtt ELan EMan ENot EPfP LRHS MGos MRav NPri NSti SBra SCoo SHGC SPoG SSpi
reflexa see *E. seguieriana* subsp. *niciciana*
resinifera EOas
§ ***rigida*** CBot CBro CDes CFil EBee EChP EGoo EHrv ELan EMan EPfP EPyc EVFa EWes GCal GMaP LPhx MAnH MAvo MLLN NSti SBla SIgm SMrm SSpi WCot WHoo WKif WPGP WSHC
- 'Sardis' NWit
robbiae see *E. amygdaloides* var. *robbiae*
'Rosies Surprise' **new** MTho
rothiana GWJ 9479a **new** WCru
sarawschanica EBee EMan GBin LPhx NWit WCot
schillingii ♀H4 More than 30 suppliers
seguieriana ECha EMan GBin NBir NLar WPer
§ - subsp. ***niciciana*** EMan EMon EWsh MArl NBir SBla SUsu WCra WHoo
serrata XPep
serrulata see *E. stricta*
sikkimensis ♀H4 CFee CMHG CMea CPLG CSam CSpe CWCL EBee ECha EGra EWTr GAbr GBBs MAvo MBri NBid NEgg SIgm SMrm SPav SRms WCot WCru WEas WFar WWye
- GWJ 9214 WCru
soongarica MSte NWit
spinosa NWit SIgm SMad XPep
§ ***stricta*** EMan GBri IBlr MCCP NLsd WBWf WBrk WRos WTin
stygiana CBot CFil CFir CFwr CSam LEdu LPhx MAvo MSte NWit SAga SSpi WCru WPGP WSHC
- 'Devil's Honey' NWit
* ***submammillaris*** 'Variegata' (v) MBri
terracina WCot
tirucalli **new** EShb
umfoloziensis **new** LToo
uralensis see *E.* x *pseudovirgata*
viguieri ♀H1 **new** LToo
villosa GBin NWit
§ ***virgata*** EMFP EWes NSti NWit SPav WCot
x ***waldsteinii*** see *E. virgata*
wallichii misapplied see *E. donii*
wallichii Kohli see *E. cornigera*
wallichii Hook. f. CDes CPLG CSam EBee EBrs EMan GCal GKir IBlr LRHS MBri NBid NOrc WHil WPGP WSHC
- 'Lemon and Lime' LSou MWhi

Euptelea (*Eupteleaceae*)

franchetii see *E. pleiosperma*
§ ***pleiosperma*** CMCN EPfP IArd NLar SSpi
polyandra CFil CMCN EPfP IArd NLar

Eurya (*Theaceae*)

japonica CFil WPGP
- 'Variegata' misapplied see *Cleyera japonica* 'Fortunei'

Euryops (*Asteraceae*)

§ ***acraeus*** ♀H4 CBot CHea CMea CPle CSBt ELan EPot GKev GTou LRHS MDun MWat NFor NLon NMen NWCA SAga SIng WAbe WLin
candollei WAbe
§ ***chrysanthemoides*** CBcs CHEx ERea MMil MSte
- 'Sonnenschein' CHal EBee EWin SPet
decumbens CNic NJOw WLin
evansii see *E. acraeus*
linearis GGar WWFP
pectinatus ♀H2 CBcs CDoC CHEx CPLG CSLe CSam CTbh CTrC CTri ERea EShb ESlt GGar MMil MNrw MRav SGar SHBN SMrm WCFE WHer WWye XPep
tysonii CPle CStu CTrC GEdr GGar SPlb WCot
virgineus CBcs CBrm CTrC GGar IDee LRav NWCA WGer WWFP

Euscaphis (*Staphyleaceae*)

japonica CPle NLar

Eustachys (*Poaceae*)

§ ***distichophylla*** EPPr MAvo WCot

Eustephia (*Amaryllidaceae*)

darwinii **new** CMon

Eustoma (*Gentianaceae*)

§ ***grandiflorum*** LRHS MBri
russellianum see *E. grandiflorum*

Eustrephus (*Philesiaceae*)

latifolius ECou

Eutaxia (*Papilionaceae*)

obovata ECou

Evolvulus (*Convolvulaceae*)

convolvuloides ERea
§ ***glomeratus*** 'Blue Daze' ERea
pilosus 'Blue Daze' see *E. glomeratus* 'Blue Daze'

Ewartia (*Asteraceae*)

planchonii GKev

Exacum (*Gentianaceae*)

affine ♀H1+3 LRHS MBri
- 'Rococo' MBri

Exochorda (*Rosaceae*)

alberti see *E. korolkowii*
giraldii CPle WGwG
- var. ***wilsonii*** CRez CSam EBee EPfP GBin GKir IMGH LRHS LSRN MAsh MBNS MBlu NLar SBrw SLim SPoG SSta SWvt
§ ***korolkowii*** WBcn

	x ***macrantha***	EBee
	- 'The Bride' ♀H4	More than 30 suppliers
	racemosa	EHol EPfP ISea MGos NBlu NLar SHBN SPer WDin WHCG
	serratifolia	EPfP NLar
	- 'Northern Pearls'	CPMA
	- 'Snow White'	CPMA EBee LBuc MBlu MDun

F

Fabiana (*Solanaceae*)

	imbricata	CAbP EMil EPfP GGar GQui LRHS SBra SBrw SLon SPer SPoG
	- 'Prostrata'	EBee EPfP GCal LRHS SBrw SSpi WAbe
	- f. ***violacea*** ♀H3	CBcs CFee CPLG CSBt CTri EBee EHol EMil EPfP GQui LRHS MBar SBrw SPer WKif XPep
	nana F&W 9364 **new**	EHyt

Fagopyrum (*Polygonaceae*)

	cymosum	see *F. dibotrys*
§	***dibotrys***	EBee ECha ELan EPPr LEdu MGol NSti WMoo

Fagus ✿ (*Fagaceae*)

§	***crenata***	CMCN CMen WDin WNor
	- 'Mount Fuji'	SBir
	engleriana	CMCN SBir
	grandifolia	CMCN
	- subsp. ***mexicana***	SBir
	japonica	CMCN LRHS
	lucida	CMCN
	orientalis	CMCN CTho ECrN LRHS
	sieboldii	see *F. crenata*
	sylvatica ♀H4	More than 30 suppliers
§	- 'Albomarginata' (v)	CLnd CMCN GKir
	- 'Albovariegata'	see *F. sylvatica* 'Albomarginata'
	- 'Ansorgei'	CDul CEnd CLnd CMCN CTho GKir MBlu SCrf
N	- Atropurpurea Group	More than 30 suppliers
	- - Swat Magret'	GKir
	- 'Aurea Pendula'	CEnd CMCN GKir MBlu SBLw SMad
	- 'Bicolor Sartini'	MBlu
	- 'Birr Zebra'	CEnd
	- 'Black Swan'	CEnd CMCN ENot GKir MBlu SBLw SBir WGor
	- 'Bornyensis'	SBir
	- 'Brathay Purple' **new**	MBlu
	- 'Cochleata'	CMCN GKir LRHS
	- 'Cockleshell'	CDul CMCN CTho LRHS MBlu
	- 'Comptoniifolia'	see *F. sylvatica* var. *heterophylla* 'Comptoniifolia'
	- 'Cristata'	CMCN MBlu
§	- 'Dawyck' ♀H4	CBcs CCVT CDoC CDul CLnd CMCN COtt CSBt CTho EBee ECrN ELan EMil ENot EPfP GKir LRHS MBar MGos MRav NWea SBLw SLim SPer WDin WOrn
	- 'Dawyck Gold' ♀H4	CAbP CAlb CBcs CDoC CDul CEnd CLnd CMCN COtt CTho CTri ENot GKir IMGH LRHS MAsh MBar MBlu MRav MSwo NBea NEgg NWea SBLw SBir SLim SPer WDin WFar WOrn
	- 'Dawyck Purple' ♀H4	More than 30 suppliers
	- 'Fastigiata' misapplied	see *F. sylvatica* 'Dawyck'
	- 'Felderbach'	LRHS MBlu SBir
	- 'Franken' (v)	MBlu
	- 'Frisio'	CDul CEnd CMCN
	- 'Grandidentata'	CMCN LRHS
	- 'Greenwood'	CDul CMCN MBlu
*	- 'Haaren'	CMCN GKir
	- var. ***heterophylla***	CLnd CSBt CTho ISea NWea WOrn
	- - 'Aspleniifolia' ♀H4	CDoC CDul CEnd CMCN COtt EBee ELan EMil ENot EPfP GKir IMGH LRHS MAsh MBar MBri NEgg SBLw SBir SCoo SPer WDin WMou WNor
§	- - 'Comptoniifolia'	SBir
	- - f. ***laciniata***	CMCN LRHS MBlu
	- 'Horizontalis'	CMCN
	- f. ***latifolia***	SBLw
	- 'Luteovariegata' (v)	CEnd CMCN NLar
	- 'Mercedes'	CMCN GKir MAsh MBlu SBir
	- 'Miltonensis'	CDul LRHS SMad
N	- 'Pendula' ♀H4	CBcs CCVT CDoC CDul CEnd CLnd CMCN CSBt CTho EBee ECrN ELan EWTr GKir IMGH MBar MRav MSwo NBlu NWea SBLw SBir SCrf SPer WDin WHar WMou WOrn
	- 'Prince George of Crete'	CDul CEnd CMCN CTho LRHS
	- 'Purple Fountain' ♀H4	CDoC CEnd CMCN COtt EBee ELan EMil GKir LRHS MAsh MBar MBlu MBri MGos NBee SBLw SLim SPoG WOrn
	- Purple-leaved Group	see *F. sylvatica* Atropurpurea Group
	- 'Purpurea Nana'	CMCN LRHS
	- 'Purpurea Pendula'	CBcs CDul CEnd CMCN CSBt CTho CTri CWib EBee ECrN ELan ENot EPfP LRHS MBar MGos MSwo MWat NBee NBlu NEgg NWea SBLw SCoo SCrf SLim SPer WDin WFar WHar
§	- 'Purpurea Tricolor' (v)	CDoC CDul CEnd CMCN ECrN GKir LRHS MBar MGos MWya NBea NBee NBlu NEgg SBir SCoo SCrf SHBN SLim SPer WDin
	- 'Quercifolia'	CDul CMCN MBlu
I	- 'Quercina'	CMCN LRHS
	- 'Red Obelisk'	see *F. sylvatica* 'Rohan Obelisk'
	- 'Riversii' ♀H4	CBcs CDoC CDul CEnd CLnd CMCN CSBt CTho CTri CWib ELan EMil ENot EPfP GKir LRHS MBri MGos MRav NBlu NEgg NWea SBLw SHBN SLim SPer WDin WFar WHar WOrn
	- 'Rohan Gold'	CDul CEnd CLnd CMCN EBee GKir LRHS MBlu
	- 'Rohan Obelisk'	CEnd CMCN EBee ELan IArd LRHS MBlu MGos SBir WOrn
I	- 'Rohan Pyramidalis'	CDul CEnd CMCN LRHS
	- 'Rohan Trompenburg'	CMCN LRHS MBlu
	- 'Rohan Weeping'	MBlu
	- 'Rohanii'	CAbP CBcs CDoC CDul CEnd CLnd CMCN COtt CTho CTri EBee ECrN ELan EMil EPfP IMGH LRHS NBee NEgg SCrf SHBN SPer WDin WFar WOrn
	- 'Roseomarginata'	see *F. sylvatica* 'Purpurea Tricolor'
	- 'Rotundifolia'	CDoC CDul CTho MBlu
	- 'Silver Wood'	CMCN LRHS
	- 'Spaethiana'	CMCN LRHS
	- 'Striata'	CMCN GKir LRHS SBir
	- 'Tortuosa Purpurea'	CMCN CTho MBlu
	- 'Tricolor' (v)	CBcs CLnd CSBt CWib EBee ELan MAsh SBLw WDin
	- 'Tricolor' misapplied	see *F. sylvatica* 'Purpurea Tricolor'
	- 'Viridivariegata' (v)	CMCN

- 'Zlatia'	CBcs CDoC CDul CLnd CMCN CSBt CTho CWib ELan EPfP GKir LRHS MAsh MBar MGos MSwo NBee NEgg NWea SBLw SBir SHBN SPer WDin WOrn

Falkia (*Convolvulaceae*)

repens	CFir WCot

Fallopia (*Polygonaceae*)

aubertii	see *F. baldschuanica*
§ ***baldschuanica***	More than 30 suppliers
- Summer Sunshine = 'Acofal'PBR	MCCP
baldschuanicum 'Pink Flamingo' **new**	NPri
x ***bohemica*** 'Spectabilis' (v)	CRow EMon
§ ***japonica*** var. ***compacta***	CRow NLar NPri SPoG WFar WMoo
- - 'Fuji Snow'	see *F. japonica* var. *compacta* 'Milk Boy'
- - 'Midas'	IBlr
§ - - 'Milk Boy' (v)	CRow EMan EShb EWes IBlr ITer SMad
- - 'Variegata'	see *F. japonica* var. *compacta* 'Milk Boy'
- 'Crimson Beauty'	CRow
§ ***multiflora***	CArn CPLN EOHP EUnu MSal
- var. ***hypoleuca***	EBee SPoG
- - B&SWJ 120	WCru
sachalinensis	CRow EBee EWes GIBF NLar

Faradaya (*Verbenaceae*)

splendida **new**	CPLN

Farfugium (*Asteraceae*)

formosanum B&SWJ 7125	WCru
§ ***japonicum***	CHEx MTho
- B&SWJ 884	WCru
- 'Argenteum' (v)	CFir SDnm WCot WFar WSan
- 'Aureomaculatum' (v) ♀H1	CAbb CFir CHEx CKob EBee EChP EHoe EMan EPfP MBNS MCCP MTho SDnm SMad SPav WFar WHal WHer WMul WSan
- 'Crispatum'	CAbP CAbb CBod CFir CHid CKob CPen EBee EChP ELan EPPr EPfP EUJe EWll GFlt LEdu MCCP MDun MFOX NSti SDnm SMad SPav SPer SPoG WCot WFar WMul WTMC
- var. ***giganteum***	CHEx
- 'Kagami-jishi' (v)	WCot
- 'Kinkan' (v)	WCot
I - 'Nanum'	CHEx
- 'Ryuto'	WCot
- 'Tsuwa-ubki'	WCot
tussilagineum	see *F. japonicum*

Fargesia (*Poaceae*)

from Jiuzhaigou, China	WJun
albocerea	CFil EPla ERod WJun
angustissima	CFil EPla
contracta	EPla
denudata	CFil ENBC EPla SBig WJun
- L 1575	MMoz MWht WPGP
dracocephala	CAbb CBrm CDoC CFil EPfP EPla GBin GCal LEdu MAvo MBrN MMoz MWht NGdn SBig SEND SLPl WJun WMoo WMul WNor WPGP
edulis	WJun
ferox	CFil EPla
frigida	EPla WJun
fungosa	CFil EPla WJun WPGP
§ ***murielae*** ♀H4	More than 30 suppliers
- 'Amy' **new**	NLar
- 'Bimbo'	CFil CHEx CTrC EPfP EPza GBin MWht WJun WMul
- 'Grüne Hecke'	MWht
- 'Harewood'	CWSG GBin MAsh MBri MCCP MMoz MWht SWvt WFar
- 'Joy' **new**	NLar
- 'Jumbo'	More than 30 suppliers
- 'Kranich'	CFil MBri NLar WPGP
- 'Mae'	GBin MWht
- 'Novecento'	ELan
- 'Simba' ♀H4	More than 30 suppliers
I - 'Willow'	MGos
murieliae 'Little John' **new**	ENBC
§ ***nitida***	More than 30 suppliers
* - from Jiuzhaigou, China	CFil EPla WPGP
- 'Anceps'	EPla MWht NPri
- 'Eisenach'	CAbb CFil CTbh EPla LRHS MBri MMoz NGdn WFar WMoo WPGP
- Gansu 2	EPla WPGP
- 'Great Wall' **new**	MBri
- 'Nymphenburg' ♀H4	CFil CFwr CPMA ENBC EPla EPza GKir LRHS MBar MBri MMoz MWhi MWht NLar NPri SBig WFar WMoo WMul WPGP
- 'Wakehurst'	EPla EPza MWht NLar
papyrifera	WJun
robusta	CAbb CBrm CEnd CFil EFul ENBC EPfP EPla MBrN MBri MMoz MWht NGdn NLar NMoo SBig SLPl WJun WMul WNor
- 'Pingwu'	MBri NLar
- 'Red Sheath'	CFil EPla ERod MMoz MWht SEND WJun WPGP
- 'White Sheath' **new**	ENBC
- 'Wolong' **new**	CDoC
rufa	CAbb CBrm CFil ENBC ENot EPfP EPla EShb MAvo MBar MBrN MBri MCCP MMoz MWht NLar SBig WJun WMul WNor WPGP
scabrida	WJun
spathacea misapplied	see *F. murielae*
utilis	CAbb CFil EPla ERod LEdu MAvo MMoz MWht NLar SEND WJun WNor WPGP
yulongshanensis	CFil EPla MWht

Farsetia (*Brassicaceae*)

clypeata	see *Fibigia clypeata*

Fascicularia (*Bromeliaceae*)

andina	see *F. bicolor*
§ ***bicolor***	More than 30 suppliers
§ - subsp. ***canaliculata***	CFil EOas IBlr LEdu WCot WPGP
kirchhoffiana	see *F. bicolor* subsp. *canaliculata*
pitcairniifolia misapplied	see *F. bicolor*

x *Fatshedera* (*Araliaceae*)

lizei ♀H3	CBcs CBot CChe CDoC CDul CHEx EBee EGra EPfP EPla GKir GQui LRHS MRav MWat NPal SAPC SArc SBra SDix SLon SMac SPer SPla SPlb SPoG SWvt WCFE WDin WFar
§ - 'Annemieke' (v) ♀H3	CHEx CSWP EBee EPfP MRav SBra SMac SMad SPer SPoG
§ - 'Aurea' (v)	EHoe ELan EPfP LRHS SBra SEND
- 'Aureopicta'	see x *F. lizei* 'Aurea'
- 'Lemon and Lime'	see x *F. lizei* 'Annemieke'
- 'Maculata'	see x *F. lizei* 'Annemieke'

- 'Pia' CSWP
* - 'Silver Prusca' EPla
- 'Variegata' (v) ♀H3 CAbb CBcs EBee ELan EPfP LAst LRHS SBra SEND SHGN SMac SMer SPer SPla SPoG SWvt WDin WFar

Fatsia (*Araliaceae*)

§ ***japonica*** ♀H4 More than 30 suppliers
- 'Moseri' CAbP CMdw CSam CTrC EChP ECtt EUJe GBin IBal MSte NGdn NLar SMad SWvt WCot WWhi
- 'Murakumo-nishiki' (v) NPal SPer
- 'Variegata' (v) ♀H3 CBcs EBee ENot EPfP LRHS LSRN MBri MGos MRav NPal SArc SHBN SPer
papyrifera see *Tetrapanax papyrifer*
polycarpa CHEx SSpi
- B&SWJ 7144 WCru

Fauria see *Nephrophyllidium*

Feijoa see *Acca*

Felicia (*Asteraceae*)

§ ***amelloides*** CAby CHEx CHal ERea LRHS MLan SChu SGar SPlb
- 'Astrid Thomas' CSpe
- 'Read's Blue' CHal CSpe EWin LIck SDnm SPet XPep
- 'Read's White' CHal ERea EWin MOak SDnm SPet
- 'Santa Anita' ♀H3 CHal CTri ECtt ERea LIck MOak
§ - variegated (v) CHal CTbh ECtt ERea EWin IHMH LAst LIck MBNS MBri MOak MSte NPer NPri SHFr SPet
- variegated, white-flowered (v) EWin LIck
§ ***amoena*** CTri MOak SRms
- 'Variegata' (v) CTri SChu
capensis see *F. amelloides*
- 'Variegata' see *F. amelloides* variegated
coelestis see *F. amelloides*
drakensbergensis ETow
echinata **new** CPLG
erigeroides CHal
filifolia WWFP XPep
- blue LAst
fruticosa **new** CHll
natalensis see *F. rosulata*
pappei see *F. amoena*
§ ***petiolata*** EMan EWin MOak NSti SGar WCot WEas WWFP
§ ***rosulata*** CPBP EHyt EMon GAbr GCrs GKir MHer MTho NBro NJOw SRms SRot
uliginosa EDAr EWes GEdr GGar GTou IHMH LRHS MTho

fennel see *Foeniculum vulgare*

fenugreek see *Trigonella foenum-graecum*

Ferraria (*Iridaceae*)

crispa var. ***nortieri*** **new** CMon
ferrariola **new** CMon
uncinata CMon

Ferula (*Apiaceae*)

assa-foetida CArn EBee LDai MSal WJek
chiliantha see *F. communis* subsp. *glauca*
§ ***communis*** CArn CMea EBee ECGP ECha EWTr GKir LEdu NBid NLar NSti SDix SDnm SMad SPav SPlb SPoG SUsu WCAu WCot WJek WPGP WPrP WSHC
- 'Gigantea' see *F. communis*
§ - subsp. ***glauca*** CSpe EMan LPhx SDix SGar SIgm WCot WPGP XPep
'Giant Bronze' see *Foeniculum vulgare* 'Giant Bronze'
tingitana SMad
- 'Cedric Morris' ECha LPhx SDix SIgm SMHy WCot

Ferulago (*Apiaceae*)

sylvatica EBee

Festuca (*Poaceae*)

actae CBig LEdu WHrl
amethystina CBig CBrm CHrt CKno CWCL EHoe EMon EPot EPza EVFa EWsh GFor GIBF IPot LRHS MBnl MNrw MWhi NCGa NCiC NGdn NOak SPer SWal WMoo WPer WRos WTin
- 'Aprilgrün' EHoe EPPr
arundinacea CRWN EWTr
californica CBig EBee EPPr
coxii WCot
curvula subsp. ***crassifolia*** EPla
'Eisvogel' EBee
'Emerald' **new** CHEx
erecta EHoe
eskia CKno CWan EHoe EHul EPPr GKir LRHS MWhi SPer SPla WCot WDyG WPer
filiformis EHoe EMon
'Fromefield Blue' CSLe EChP EHul
§ ***gautieri*** CBrm GBin GCal GFor GIBF MBar NBre NGdn WFoF
- 'Pic Carlit' EMon GBin
gigantea CBig GFor NBre
glacialis EHoe
glauca More than 30 suppliers
I - 'Auslese' CPLG GFor NGdn WSSM
- 'Azurit' CBig CPrp EBee EChP EGra EHoe EPPr EPza EVFa EWes EWsh LAst MBnl NLar SIng SPoG
§ - 'Blaufuchs' ♀H4 More than 30 suppliers
§ - 'Blauglut' CBig EBrs EHoe EHul ENot EPfP EPla EPza GKir GSki LRHS MWgw SHel WCra
- Blue Fox see *F. glauca* 'Blaufuchs'
- Blue Glow see *F. glauca* 'Blauglut'
- 'Boulder Blue' CKno
- 'Elijah Blue' More than 30 suppliers
- 'Golden Toupee' More than 30 suppliers
- 'Harz' CBrm EHoe EHul EMil EPla GKir LBuc MBNS MBar NBea NCGa SApp SGSe WPnP
* - ***minima*** IHMH
- 'Pallens' see *F. longifolia*
- Sea Urchin see *F. glauca* 'Seeigel'
§ - 'Seeigel' CBig EBee EHoe GKir MBnl MMoz NPro
- 'Seven Seas' see *F. valesiaca* 'Silbersee'
- 'Silberreiher' EPPr
- 'Uchte' CWCL
'Hogar' EHoe EVFa
idahoensis CBig
§ ***longifolia*** EPPr
mairei EHoe EMon EPPr LRHS SMHy SWal WCot WDyG
novae-zelandiae CPen CWCL EBee EPPr NNor
ovina CWan EHoe GFor NBre NGdn WPer
- subsp. ***coxii*** EHoe
- var. ***duriuscula*** CRWN
* - 'Tetra Gold' SWvt

paniculata EHoe EPla EWsh
- subsp. ***spadicea*** EPPr
pulchella CBig
punctoria EHoe EWsh SIng WMoo
rubra CBig CRWN
- var. ***nankotaizanensis*** B&SWJ 3190 WCru
scoparia see *F. gautieri*
'Siskiyou Blue' **new** CKno
tatrae CBrm EBee GBin WCot
valesiaca NOak WFar
- var. ***glaucantha*** CBig EWII GFor GWCH MBri MWhi NBre NGdn NLar XPep
§ - 'Silbersee' CBig EBee ECha EHoe ENot EPot ESis EUJe EWsh LRHS MBar MBnl MNrw MSte SIng SRms WFar
- Silver Sea see *F. valesiaca* 'Silbersee'
violacea EBee EChP EHoe EMan EPPr EPza GFlt GFor MBNS NLar NOak SIng SPer SWal WRos WWpP
vivipara CNat CPrp EGoo EHoe EMon LEdu NBid SBch WRos WWhi
* 'Willow Green' CBod SLim SPlb

Fibigia (*Brassicaceae*)

§ ***clypeata*** SGar
- 'Select' CSpe
triquetra GKev

Ficus ✿ (*Moraceae*)

afghanistanica ERea
australis misapplied see *F. rubiginosa* 'Australis'
benghalensis MBri WMul
benjamina ♀H1 CHal LRHS MBri SRms
- 'Exotica' CHal LRHS MBri
- 'Golden King' (v) LRHS MBri
- 'Starlight' (v) ♀H1 LRHS MBri SMur
capitola 'Long' ERea
carica (F) CWSG EGra MBri SArc
- 'Abbey Slip' (F) CHEx
* - 'Acanthifolia' XPep
- 'Adam' (F) ERea
- 'Alma' (F) ERea
- 'Angélique' (F) ERea
- 'Beall' (F) ERea
- 'Bellone' (F) ERea
- 'Bifère' (F) ERea
- 'Black Ischia' (F) ERea
- 'Black Mission' (F) ERea
- 'Boule d'Or' (F) ERea
- 'Bourjassotte Grise' (F) ERea
- 'Brown Turkey' (F) ♀H3 More than 30 suppliers
- 'Brunswick' (F) CAgr CWib ERea GBon GTwe LRHS MCCP MCoo NGHP SLim SPoG WCot
- 'Castle Kennedy' (F) ERea GTwe
- 'Col de Dame Blanc' (F) ERea
- 'Conandria' (F) ERea
- 'Figue d'Or' (F) ERea
- 'Goutte d'Or' (F) ERea
- 'Grise de Saint Jean' (F) ERea
- 'Grise Ronde' (F) ERea
- 'Grosse Grise' (F) ERea
- 'Kaape Bruin' (F) ERea
- 'Kadota' (F) ERea
* - 'Laciniata' (F) SMad
- 'Lisa' (F) ERea
- 'Longue d'Août' (F) ERea
- 'Malcolm's Giant' (F) ERea
- 'Malta' (F) ERea GTwe
- 'Marseillaise' (F) ERea GTwe
- 'Negro Largo' (F) ERea
- 'Newlyn Coombe' **new** CHEx
- 'Newlyn Harbour' (F) CHEx
- 'Noir de Provence' see *F. carica* 'Reculver'
- 'Osborn's Prolific' (F) ERea SWvt
- 'Panachée' (F) ERea
- 'Pastilière' (F) ERea
- 'Peter's Honey' (F) ERea
- 'Petite Grise' (F) ERea
- 'Pied de Boeuf' (F) ERea
- 'Pittaluse' (F) ERea
- 'Précoce de Dalmatie' ERea
- 'Précoce Ronde de Bordeaux' (F) ERea
§ - 'Reculver' (F) ERea
- 'Rouge de Bordeaux' (F) ERea
- 'Saint Johns' (F) ERea
- 'San Pedro Miro' (F) ERea
- 'Snowden' (F) ERea
- 'Sollies Pont' (F) ECrN ERea
- 'Sugar 12' (F) ERea
- 'Sultane' (F) ERea
- 'Tena' (F) ERea
- 'Trojano' (F) ERea
- 'Verte d'Argenteuil' (F) ERea
- 'Violette Dauphine' (F) ERea
- 'Violette de Sollies' (F) ERea
- 'Violette Sepor' (F) ERea
- 'White Genoa' see *F. carica* 'White Marseilles'
- 'White Ischia' (F) ERea
§ - 'White Marseilles' (F) CWib ECrN EHol EPfP ERea LRHS MCoo NGHP SKee
cyathistipula MBri
deltoidea var. ***diversifolia*** MBri
elastica LRHS SEND
- 'Doescheri' (v) ♀H1 NScw
- 'Robusta' MBri
foveolata Wallich see *F. sarmentosa*
lyrata ♀H1 MBri
microcarpa STre
- 'Hawaii' (v) CHal
pumila ♀H1 CBcs CHEx CHal EBak LRHS MBri XPep
- 'Minima' CFee
- 'Sonny' (v) MBri
- 'Variegata' (v) CHEx CHal MBri
radicans 'Variegata' see *F. sagittata* 'Variegata'
religiosa WMul
§ ***rubiginosa*** 'Australis' MBri
- 'Variegata' (v) ♀H1 CHal
§ ***sagittata*** 'Variegata' (v) MBri
§ ***sarmentosa*** MBri

fig see *Ficus carica*

filbert see *Corylus maxima*

Filipendula ✿ (*Rosaceae*)

alnifolia 'Variegata' see *F. ulmaria* 'Variegata'
camtschatica CFir CMCo CRow EBee ELan GIBF GKir MDun NBid NLar NMir NPol WFar WMoo WPGP
- 'Rosea' SMad
digitata 'Nana' see *F. multijuga*
formosa B&SWJ 8707 WCru
hexapetala see *F. vulgaris*
- 'Flore Pleno' see *F. vulgaris* 'Multiplex'
'Kahome' CMCo CRow EBee EBrs EChP GBuc GGar GKir GMaP GMac IPot LAst LRHS NBir NGdn NLar NMir NOrc NSti SMac SMer SPla SVil WBor WFar WGHP WHoo WMoo WWpP
kiraishiensis B&SWJ 1571 EBee WCru

§	***multijuga***	CRow GCal GGar GSki WBor WFar WMoo
	palmata	ECha GCal GSki WFar WMoo WWpP
	- 'Digitata Nana'	see *F. multijuga*
	- dwarf	CLAP GSki
	- 'Elegantissima'	see *F. purpurea* 'Elegans'
	- 'Nana'	see *F. multijuga*
	- ***purpurea***	see *F. purpurea*
	- 'Rosea'	ERou IBlr NBir WCHb
	- 'Rubra'	CTri GSki MRav NGdn WGwG
	- ***rufinervis*** B&SWJ 8611	WCru
	- - B&SWJ 941	WCru
§	***purpurea*** ♀H4	CKno CRow CSBt EPfP GCra GGar GKir GSki LPBA LRHS MBri MWrn WCru WFar WMoo
	- f. ***albiflora***	EBee LPhx MBri NPri WMoo WPnP WWpP WWye
§	- 'Elegans'	CHea CRow EChP ECha EMan EMil ERou EWsh GCal GGar GMac LAst MSte NBid NSti SSpe WFar WMoo
	- 'Nephele'	SMHy
	- 'Pink Dreamland'	EBee EPPr LPhx SAga WWpP
*	- 'Plena' (d)	NLar
	- 'White Dreamland'	EBee
	'Queen of the Prairies'	see *F. rubra*
§	***rubra***	CRow EWTr GAbr LAst NBid NWoo WBVN WCra WFar WWpP
§	- 'Venusta' ♀H4	More than 30 suppliers
	- 'Venusta Magnifica'	see *F. rubra* 'Venusta'
§	***ulmaria***	More than 30 suppliers
	- 'Aurea'	More than 30 suppliers
	- 'Flore Pleno' (d)	CBre CMil CRow EBee EBrs GKir GSki LAst LRHS MRav NBid NGdn SIde SPer WCot WFar WPnP WTin
	- 'Rosea'	CDes EBee IBlr WPGP WWpP
§	- 'Variegata' (v)	More than 30 suppliers
§	***vulgaris***	CArn CFee CRWN CTri CWan ECtt GBar LAst LPBA MChe MDun MSal MWgw NArg NBlu NBro NMir NOrc WBWf WGHP WPer WWpP WWye
	- 'Alba'	EBee
	- 'Devon Cream' **new**	SBla
	- 'Flore Pleno' (d)	see *F. vulgaris* 'Multiplex'
	- 'Grandiflora'	EPPr WCot
§	- 'Multiplex' (d)	More than 30 suppliers
	- 'Plena'	see *F. vulgaris* 'Multiplex'
	- 'Rosea'	EBee

Firmiana (*Sterculiaceae*)

simplex	CHEx EShb WMul

Fittonia (*Acanthaceae*)

albivenis Argyroneura Group ♀H1	CHal LRHS
- - 'Nana' **new**	CHal
- Verschaffeltii Group ♀H1	CHal

Fitzroya (*Cupressaceae*)

cupressoides	CDoC CMac CTho IArd LCon LRHS MBar SCoo SLim SPoG

Foeniculum (*Apiaceae*)

	vulgare	CAgr CArn CHby CPrp CWan EChP ECha ELan ELau EPfP GBar GMaP GPoy MBow MChe MHer MSal MWat NGHP NPri SIde SPer SPlb WBrE WGwG WMoo WPer WSel WWye XPep
	- 'Bronze'	see *F. vulgare* 'Purpureum'
	- var. ***dulce***	CSev SIde
§	- 'Giant Bronze'	ELan GKir LPhx WBrE
§	- 'Purpureum'	More than 30 suppliers
	- 'Smokey'	ECha MRav

Fontanesia (*Oleaceae*)

phillyreoides	CBcs CMCN

Fontinalis (*Sphagnaceae*)

sp.	LPBA
antipyretica	WFar WPop

Forestiera (*Oleaceae*)

	neomexicana	see *F. pubescens*
§	***pubescens***	CFil

Forsythia ✿ (*Oleaceae*)

	'Arnold Dwarf'	CDul NLar SRms
	'Beatrix Farrand' ambig.	CTri CWSG EBee ECtt GKir LRHS MGos NEgg NFor NWea SIng SPer SRms WMoo WRHF WTel
§	Boucle d'Or = 'Courtacour'PBR	COtt SLim
	'Fiesta' (v)	CWSG EBee EPfP GKir LAst LRHS MAsh MBar MGos MRav MSwo NEgg NLon NWea SHBN SLim SPer SPoG WCot WDin WFar WWpP
	giraldiana	MSwo SLon SRms WBcn
	Gold CurlPBR	see *F.* Boucle d'Or = 'Courtacour'
	Gold TidePBR	see *F.* Marée d'Or = 'Courtasol'
	'Golden Bells'	CDul EMil LRHS
	'Golden Nugget'	ELan EPfP LRHS MAsh SCoo SLon SMer SPer SPoG WCFE
	'Golden Times' (v)	CBcs EHoe EWes LBuc LRHS LSRN MAsh MGos NLar NPro SCoo SPoG SWal SWvt WBcn WCot WDin WFar
	'Golden Times Allgold'	WBcn
	x ***intermedia*** 'Arnold Giant'	MBlu
	- 'Densiflora'	NWea
	- 'Goldzauber'	NJOw NWea
	- 'Lynwood' variegated	CWib
	- 'Lynwood Variety' ♀H4	More than 30 suppliers
	- 'Minigold'	ECtt EPfP LAst LRHS MGos MSwo MWat NBlu NEgg SRms WBVN WRHF WTel
	- 'Spectabilis'	CDul CRez EBee EPfP GKir LBuc MAsh MBar NWea SCoo SPer WDin WFar WTel
	- 'Spectabilis Variegated' (v)	LRHS MBNS NPro
	- 'Spring Glory'	EBee ECtt LRHS MHer NWea
	- 'Variegata' (v)	NSti NWea SPer
	- Week-End = 'Courtalyn'PBR ♀H4	CWSG ENot EPfP LBuc MAsh MBri MGos NWea SHGC SLim SLon SMer SPlb SPoG WDin WFar
	'Josefa'	WBcn
	koreana 'Ilgwang' (v)	CPMA
§	Marée d'Or = 'Courtasol'PBR ♀H4	COtt CWSG EBee ENot LRHS MGos MRav NLar SMer SPoG WDin
	Mêlée d'Or = 'Courtaneur'PBR	LRHS SCoo SPer
	Melissa = 'Courtadic'	NLar NWea
	'Northern Gold'	EPfP
	ovata	GIBF
	- 'Tetragold'	CBcs MBar NEgg NWea
	'Paulina'	NLar
	spectabilis 'Yosefa'	ELan MAsh
	suspensa	CArn CBcs CTri CWib ENot EPfP LRHS MBar MSal MWat NVic NWea SHBN SPer WTel
	- f. ***atrocaulis***	CDul CPle

- var. ***fortunei*** NEgg
- 'Nymans' EBee EPfP GKir MBri MRav NSti NWea SLPl WMoo
§ - 'Taff's Arnold' (v) CFai CPLG CPMA WBcn WSPU WWpP
- 'Variegata' see *F. suspensa* 'Taff's Arnold'
'Swingtime' (v) EGra
'Tremonia' EBee NFor SLon WGwG
viridissima NFor NWea
- 'Bronxensis' EHyt EPot GEdr NBir NLar NVic NWea SMad SRot WAbe
- 'Weber's Bronx' NLar NWea

Fortunearia (*Hamamelidaceae*)

sinensis **new** NLar

x *Fortucitroncirus* (*Rutaceae*)

citrangequat 'Thomasville' EZes MJnS

Fortunella (*Rutaceae*)

x ***crassifolia*** 'Meiwa' (F) ♀H1 ERea
'Fukushu' (F) ♀H1 ERea ESlt
§ ***japonica*** (F) SAPC SArc
§ ***margarita*** (F) CBcs CDoC CWSG MBri
- 'Nagami' (F) ERea ESlt

Fothergilla (*Hamamelidaceae*)

gardenii CBcs CPMA ELan EPfP EWTr GKir MBlu MBri NEgg NLar SPer SSpi WDin
- 'Blue Mist' CAbP CBrm CDoC CEnd CPMA CWSG ELan EPfP GKir LRHS MBri SBrw SLim SMad SPer SPla SReu SSpi SSta WDin WFar WPat
- 'Suzanne' NLar
major ♀H4 CBcs CDul CEnd CPMA CWib EBee ELan EPfP EWTr GKir LRHS MBri MGos MLan NBlu NEgg SHBN SPoG SReu SSpi WDin WFar WNor WPat
- Monticola Group CDoC CEnd CPMA CSBt CWSG EBee ELan ENot EPfP IMGH LRHS MAsh MBar MBri MDun NDlv NPal SBrw SChu SHBN SLim SPer SRkn SSpi SSta SWvt WBrE WFar
'Mount Airy' CMCN CPMA EPfP IArd IMGH NLar SSpi

Fragaria (*Rosaceae*)

from Taiwan WHer
alpina see *F. vesca* 'Semperflorens'
x ***ananassa*** 'Alice'PBR (F) CSut
- 'Aromel' (F) ♀H4 CSBt CWSG GTwe LRHS
- 'Bogota' (F) LRHS
- 'Bolero'PBR (F) CSBt CSut MBri SKee
- 'Calypso'PBR (F) CSBt
- 'Cambridge Favourite' (F) ♀H4 CTri CWSG GKir GTwe LRHS MBri MCoo SKee
- 'Cambridge Late Pine' (F) CWSG LRHS
- 'Cambridge Rival' (F) LRHS
- 'Cambridge Vigour' (F) CWSG GTwe LRHS
- 'Darselect'PBR (F) CSBt
- 'Elsanta'PBR (F) CSBt CWSG GKir GTwe IArd LRHS NPri SPer
* - 'Emily' (F) GTwe LRHS NPri SPer
- 'Eros'PBR (F) GTwe NPri SKee
- 'Florence'PBR (F) GTwe LRHS SKee SPer
- 'Fraise des Bois' see *F. vesca*
* - 'Franny Karan' (F) WGor
- 'Gorella' (F) LRHS
- 'Hapil'PBR (F) ♀H4 CSBt GTwe LRHS NPri
- 'Honeoye' (F) ♀H4 GTwe LRHS MBri SKee SPer
- 'Kimberly'PBR CSBt
- 'Korona'PBR (F) CSut
- 'Kouril' (F) LRHS
- 'Laura' (F) LRHS
- 'Pantagruella' (F) LRHS
- 'Pegasus'PBR (F) ♀H4 CTri GTwe LRHS
- Pink Panda = 'Frel'PBR (F) EBee EChP ECtt EGra ELan EWsh GKir LBuc LEdu LRHS MRav NEgg NLar SHFr SIng SPer SPoG SSto WCAu WEas WFar
- pink-flowered CFee
- Red Ruby = 'Samba'PBR CTbh EBee EChP GKir LRHS MNrw NEgg NGdn NLar SIng SPoG WCAu
- 'Redgauntlet' (F) GTwe LRHS
- 'Rhapsody'PBR (F) ♀H4 GTwe LRHS
- 'Royal Sovereign' (F) GTwe LRHS
- 'Serenata' (F) NBur
- 'Sophie'PBR (F) CSBt LRHS
- 'Symphony'PBR (F) ♀H4 SKee
- 'Talisman' (F) LRHS
- 'Tamella' (F) LRHS
- 'Totem' (F) GTwe
§ - 'Variegata' (v) CArn CMea CSev EBee EMan EMon ENot EPPr EPla EPza LDai LRHS MCCP MHar MRav MWgw SPoG WMoo WRha
- 'Viva Rosa' (F) MBNS
'Bowles' Double' see *F. vesca* 'Multiplex'
chiloensis (F) CAgr EMon GAbr ILis LEdu
- 'Chaval' CHid ECha EGoo EHrv EMon EPPr MRav MWgw WMoo
- 'Variegata' misapplied see *F.* x *ananassa* 'Variegata'
* - 'Variegata' ambig. (v) WEas
indica see *Duchesnea indica*
'Lipstick' EBee EWsh NLar NPro WRos
moschata **new** CAgr
nubicola GPoy
'Variegata' see *F.* x *ananassa* 'Variegata'
§ ***vesca*** (F) CAgr CArn CRWN CWan EMag EPfP EWTr GPoy LRHS MBow MHer NGHP NLon NMir NPri SECG SIde SPer SPet SPlb WBWf WGHP WGwG WJek WPer WShi WWye
- 'Alexandra' (F) CArn CBod CPrp ELau EWin GAbr IHMH LRHS MBow MChe NVic SECG SIde WCHb
- 'Flore Pleno' see *F. vesca* 'Multiplex'
- 'Fructu Albo' (F) CAgr CArn CBgR CBre CRow IHMH NLar WMoo WPer WWpP
- 'Golden Alexandra' **new** EMag WHer
- 'Mara des Bois'PBR (F) GTwe MBri
- 'Monophylla' (F) CRow EMon IGor LRHS SIde WHer
§ - 'Multiplex' (d) CRow CSev EMon GAbr ILis MInt MRav NGHP NLar SMac WCHb WHer WWye
§ - 'Muricata' CPou CRow EOHP IGor ILis ITer LEdu WHer WWye
* - 'Pineapple Crush' WHer
- 'Plymouth Strawberry' see *F. vesca* 'Muricata'
- 'Rügen' (F) CHal IGor
§ - 'Semperflorens' (F) EUnu ILis WHer WRHF
- 'Variegata' misapplied see *F.* x *ananassa* 'Variegata'
* - 'Variegata' ambig. (v) EHoe EHrv GAbr MBct NGHP SMac SMar WFar WHrl WPer WSel
virginiana CAgr
viridis **new** CAgr

Francoa (*Saxifragaceae*)

appendiculata CAbP CRez EBla EMFP EMan EWTr LPio MDKP SGar SOkh WCAu WFar WHer WMoo WPic WPnP

	– red-flowered	CKno EBee
	Ballyrogan strain	IBlr
	'Confetti'	CAby CDes CKno CPLG EBee EMan EPPr GBin LAst LPhx LPio MAnH MAvo MFOX MNrw NEgg SPoG SWal WCot WFar WPGP WTMC
	'Purple Spike'	see *F. sonchifolia* Rogerson's form
§	***ramosa***	CMCo CTri EChP EHrv EMan GBri GBuc IBlr LRHS MBct MBow MLan MNrw MTis MWat NBro NEgg SAga SDix SHGN SOkh SPav WCru WFar WMoo
*	– 'Alba'	CSpe
	sonchifolia	More than 30 suppliers
	– 'Alba'	MDKP NRnb SHar SMrm SUsu WFar
	– 'Doctor Tom Smith'	WCot
	– 'Molly Anderson'	EBee MAvo
§	– Rogerson's form	More than 30 suppliers

Frangula see *Rhamnus*

Frankenia (*Frankeniaceae*)

laevis	CTri SRms WRHF XPep
thymifolia	CBrm CNic EPot ESis GGar LRHS MBar MHer MWat SPlb WFar WPer WTel WTin XPep

Franklinia (*Theaceae*)

alatamaha	CBcs CPMA EPfP LHyd MBlu SSpi WFar WNor

Frasera (*Gentianaceae*)

fastigiata **new**	GKev

Fraxinus ✿ (*Oleaceae*)

	americana	CDul CMCN EGFP EPfP SBLw WDin
	– 'Autumn Purple'	CDul CEnd CTho ECrN EPfP GKir LRHS MAsh MBlu SBLw
	– 'Rosehill'	CTho
	angustifolia	CMCN CTho EGFP
	– 'Elegantissima'	CTho
	– var. ***lentiscifolia***	CTho
§	– 'Monophylla'	CLnd CTho
§	– subsp. ***oxycarpa***	GIBF
	– 'Raywood' ♀H4	More than 30 suppliers
*	– 'Variegata' (v)	MGos
	anomala	GIBF
	bungeana	CMCN EGFP
	chinensis	CDul CLnd CMCN CTho GIBF
	– subsp. ***rhyncophylla***	GIBF GKir
	elonza	CLnd
	excelsior	CBcs CCVT CDoC CDul CLnd CRWN CSBt CTri CWib ECrN ENot EPfP GKir LAst LBuc MBar MGos NBee NWea SBLw SHBN SHFr STre WDin WMou WOrn
	– 'Allgold'	CEnd
	– 'Aurea'	SBLw
	– 'Aurea Pendula'	CDul CEnd CMCN CRez CWib ECrN EPfP GKir LRHS MAsh MBlu SBLw
	– 'Crispa'	MBlu NEgg NLar SBLw
	– f. ***diversifolia***	CDul CLnd CTho WMou
	– 'Globosa'	SBLw
	– 'Jaspidea' ♀H4	More than 30 suppliers
	– 'Nana'	EMon SBLw WPat
	– 'Pendula' ♀H4	CAlb CCVT CDoC CDul CEnd CLnd CTho EBee ECrN ENot EPfP GKir LRHS MBlu MBri NBee NEgg NWea SBLw SHBN SLim SPer WDin WJas WMou WOrn
	– 'R.E. Davey'	CDul CNat
	– variegated (v)	CDul ECrN
	– 'Westhof's Glorie' ♀H4	CCVT CDoC CLnd ECrN ENot MDun NEgg SBLw WDin WJas WOrn
	holotricha	CTho
	insularis var. ***henryana***	CDul CFil CMCN WPGP
	latifolia	EGFP GIBF
	longicuspis	GIBF
	mariesii	see *F. sieboldiana*
	nigra	CMCN
	– 'Fallgold'	CEnd
	ornus ♀H4	CCVT CDul CLnd CMCN CTri ECrN ELan ENot EPfP EWTr GKir IMGH LRHS MBri MSwo NWea SBLw SPer SSpi SSta WDin WFar WMoo WOrn
	– 'Arie Peters'	CDul SBLw
	– 'Mecsek'	MBlu
	– 'Obelisk'	MBri
	– 'Rotterdam'	SBLw
	oxycarpa	see *F. angustifolia* subsp. *oxycarpa*
	pennsylvanica	CDul CLnd CMCN GIBF
	– 'Aucubifolia' (v)	CTho
	– 'Summit'	CTho
	– 'Variegata' (v)	CLnd CTho EBee GKir LRHS MAsh MBri SSta
	quadrangulata	NWea WDin
§	***sieboldiana***	CDoC CDul CFil CLnd CMCN CPMA EPfP GKir MBlu NLar SSpi WPGP WPat
	'Veltheimii'	see *F. angustifolia* 'Monophylla'
	velutina	CDul CLnd CTho SLPl
	xanthoxyloides **new**	ISea

Freesia (*Iridaceae*)

	alba Watson	see *F. caryophyllacea*
	alba (G.L. Mey.) Gumbl.	CMon
	andersoniae **new**	CMon
§	***caryophyllacea***	CMon
	laxa	see *Anomatheca laxa*

Fremontodendron (*Sterculiaceae*)

'California Glory' ♀H3	More than 30 suppliers
californicum	CSBt CTri EBee ELan EMil MBri MLan MWat NBlu SHBN SLim SPlb WCFE WDin WNor
'Ken Taylor'	LRHS
mexicanum	XPep
'Pacific Sunset'	CDul CPMA EBee ENot EPfP LRHS MGos MRav SBra SBrw SMur SPer SPoG
'Tequila Sunrise'	CBcs CPMA EBee GBin ISea MGos MRav MSph NLar SBrw SRkn

Freylinia (*Scrophulariaceae*)

	cestroides	see *F. lanceolata*
§	***lanceolata***	CTrC
	tropica	CHll GFai

Fritillaria ✿ (*Liliaceae*)

	acmopetala ♀H4	CAvo CBro CPom EHyt EPot ERos GBuc GCrs GEdr GIBF LAma LPhx LRHS MAnH MS&S MSte MTho NJOw NMen NWCA SSpi WCot WCra WLin WSel
	– LB 410 from Greece **new**	CMon
	– 'Brunette' **new**	GCrs MSte
	– subsp. ***wendelboi***	EPot LAma LPhx WCot WDav
§	***affinis***	GCrs GKir ITim LAma MS&S NMen SBla SSpi WCot
§	– var. ***gracilis***	LAma

	Name	Suppliers
	- 'Sunray'	GCrs GEdr SSpi
§	- var. ***tristulis***	ERos ITim NMen
	- 'Vancouver Island'	ECho EPot
*	***albidiflora***	LAma
	alburyana	EHyt EPot
	alfredae	ITim WWst
	subsp. ***glaucoviridis*** **new**	
	arabica	see *F. persica*
	assyriaca	EPot NJOw
	aurea	EHyt EPot GCrs MS&S NMen
	- 'Golden Flag'	EPfP GEdr GKev LTwo WDav
	biflora	GIBF WCot
	- 'Martha Roderick'	CBro LAma MS&S SBla
§	***bithynica***	CBro GEdr ITim LAma MS&S
	- PB 316 from Turkey **new**	CMon
	bucharica	NMen
	- 'Nurek Giant'	WWst
	camschatcensis	CAvo CBro EBrs ECha EFEx EHyt EPfP EPot EUJe GAbr GBBs GCrs GEdr GFlt GIBF GKir LAma LPhx MS&S MTho NBir NDov NJOw NMen SSpi WAbe WCru WDav WLin
	- from Alaska	GCrs
I	- ***alpina aurea***	GCrs
	- 'Aurea'	GBuc GKir NMen SSpi
	- black-flowered	GBuc GKir SOkh
	- f. ***flavescens***	EFEx GEdr LAma
	- green-flowered	NMen
I	- ***multiflora*** (d)	CFir NMen
	carduchorum	see *F. minuta*
	carica	EHyt EPot MS&S NMen
	- brown-flowered	EPot
	- subsp. ***serpenticola***	EHyt EPot
	caucasica	EHyt GIBF LAma NMen
	cirrhosa	EPot GEdr GKir WWst
	- brown-flowered	GEdr GKir NMen
	- green-flowered	GEdr GKir NMen
	citrina	see *F. bithynica*
§	***collina***	ENot WWst
	conica	EPot GCrs NMen WCot
	crassifolia	GIBF LAma MS&S WCot
	- subsp. ***crassifolia***	CGra EHyt
§	- subsp. ***kurdica***	EHyt EPot GCrs GIBF NMen SSpi WLin
	- - 'Talish' **new**	WWst
	davisii	EBrs EHyt EPot EUJe GCrs GEdr GKev LAma LPhx NMen SSpi WCot WDav WLin
	delphinensis	see *F. tubiformis*
	eastwoodiae	SSpi
	eduardii	WWst
	ehrhartii	EPot SBla
	elwesii	EHyt EPot GCrs GEdr NMen WCot
	ferganensis	see *F. walujewii*
	forbesii from Turkey **new**	CMon
	frankiorum **new**	WWst
	gentneri	SSpi
	glauca	LAma MS&S NMen WCot
	- 'Goldilocks'	EPot LRHS NMen WCot WDav
	graeca	CAvo CBro EPot GBuc GCrs GEdr MTho NMen WDav WLin
	- subsp. ***graeca***	EHyt
	- subsp. ***ionica***	see *F. thessala*
§	***grayana***	MS&S
	- tall	WCot
	gussichiae	EPot GCrs MS&S NMen
	hermonis subsp. ***amana***	EBrs EHyt EPot GCrs GEdr GKev LAma LTwo NJOw NMen WCot WLin
	- - yellow-flowered	EPot
	hispanica	see *F. lusitanica*
	hupehensis	LAma
	imperialis	ECGP GIBF MBri
	- 'Argenteovariegata' (v)	LAma
	- 'Aureomarginata' (v)	LAma LRHS MBri
	- 'Aurora'	EBee EBrs EPot GBBs GKev LAma LRHS NBPC NGHP NPer SPer WFar WHil
	- var. ***inodora*** **new**	EBee GCrs
	- 'Lutea'	CAby CAvo CSam EBrs ELan EPfP LRHS MSte NBPC NFor
	- 'Lutea Maxima'	see *F. imperialis* 'Maxima Lutea'
	- 'Maxima'	see *F. imperialis* 'Rubra Maxima'
§	- 'Maxima Lutea' Υ^{H4}	CBro EBee EMon EPfP EPot LAma LRHS SPer WHil
	- 'Orange Brilliant'	EBee MSte
§	- 'Prolifera'	EBee LAma LRHS WCot
	- 'Rubra'	CAvo CSam EMon GBBs GKev LAma NBPC NBir SPer WFar WHil
§	- 'Rubra Maxima'	CAby CBro EBee EBrs ENot EPfP EPot LAma LRHS MSte
	- 'Slagzwaard'	EBee
	- 'Sulpherino'	EBee EMon LAma LRHS
	- 'The Premier'	EPot LAma LRHS
	- 'William Rex'	CMea EBee EPot LAma
	involucrata	EHyt GKir LAma MS&S SSpi
	ionica	see *F. thessala*
	japonica	EFEx GEdr
	var. ***koidzumiana***	
	karadaghensis	see *F. crassifolia* subsp. *kurdica*
I	***karelinii***	WWst
	kittaniae	EHyt
	kotschyana	EPot GCrs NMen WWst
	lanceolata	see *F. affinis* var. *tristulis*
	latakiensis	EPot WWst
§	***latifolia***	EPot GEdr LAma
	- var. ***nobilis***	see *F. latifolia*
§	***lusitanica***	LAma MS&S NMen SBla SSpi
	lutea Bieb.	see *F. collina*
	meleagris	More than 30 suppliers
	- var. ***unicolor*** subvar. ***alba*** Υ^{H4}	CAvo CBro CFwr ECho EPot GBri GBuc GFlt LAma LRHS MBri MS&S NLAp NRya SPer WAul WCot WPnP WShi
	- - - 'Aphrodite'	EMar EPot GBuc NBir
	meleagroides	WCot WWst
§	***messanensis***	EHyt GCrs LAma MS&S SBla WLin
	- subsp. ***gracilis***	EHyt GCrs MS&S WLin WWst
	- subsp. ***messanensis***	CBro
	michailovskyi Υ^{H2}	More than 30 suppliers
§	***minuta***	EPot GCrs MS&S NMen
	montana	EPot GIBF NMen
	nigra hort.	see *F. pyrenaica*
	obliqua	EHyt WCot
	olivieri	GCrs
§	***orientalis***	WWst
	pallidiflora Υ^{H4}	CAvo CBro CLAP CMea EBee EBrs EHyt EMon EPot ERos GEdr GFlt GIBF ITim LAma LPhx MS&S MSte MTho NBir NMen NSla NWCA SSpi WCru WLin WPnP
§	***persica***	EBee ECtt EHrv ENot EPfP EPot GBBs GFlt GIBF LAma LPhx LRHS MBow MBri MLan MWgw NBPC NJOw NMen SPer WCra WSel
	- 'Adiyaman' Υ^{H4}	CAvo CBro EBrs ELan EMon LPhx WDav
	- 'Ivory Bells' **new**	EMon
	phaeanthera	see *F. affinis* var. *gracilis*
	pinardii	EHyt EPot NMen WWst
	pluriflora	WWst
	pontica	CAvo CBro CLAP EHyt EPot ERos GBuc GCrs GEdr GKir ITim LAma MLLN MS&S MTho NLAp NMen

		NSla SBla SPer SSpi WCot WCru WLin WPnP
	- Prasil form	WWst
	- subsp. ***substipilata*** **new**	GIBF
	przewalskii	EPot
	pudica	EBrs EHyt GCrs GEdr GKir ITim LAma MS&S MTho NJOw NMen SSpi WLin
*	- 'Fragrant'	EPot GCrs NMen
	- 'Giant'	EPot
	- 'Richard Britten'	GCrs NMen
	puqiensis	LAma
	purdyi	GKir MS&S SSpi
§	***pyrenaica*** ♀H4	CBro CLAP CNic EHyt EPot ERos ETow EUJe GCra GCrs GEdr GIBF LAma MS&S NMen NSla SBla SChu SSpi WCot WCru WDav WTin WWst
	- 'Lutea'	NSla WCot
	- 'Old Gold' **new**	GCrs
	raddeana	EBrs EPot LAma WCot
	recurva	GIBF SSpi
	- 'Sensational'	LAma
	rhodocanakis	EHyt NMen WWst
	- subsp. ***argolica***	NMen WWst
	roderickii	see *F. grayana*
	roylei	GIBF
	rubra major	see *F. imperialis* 'Rubra Maxima'
	ruthenica	ERos GCrs GIBF MS&S NMen SBla
	sewerzowii	GCrs WWst
	sibthorpiana	CBro EPot NMen WCot
	spetsiotica	EHyt
	sphaciotica	see *F. messanensis*
	stenanthera	CBro EHyt EPot LAma NMen
	straussii **new**	WWst
	stribrnyi	WWst
	tachengensis	see *F. yuminensis*
	tenella	see *F. orientalis*
§	***thessala***	EHyt GBuc GIBF MS&S MTho NMen WCot WDav
	thunbergii	CAvo EBee EHyt EMar GCrs GEdr NMen SMeo WDav WWst
	tortifolia	LAma NMen
§	***tubiformis***	EHyt GEdr GKir NMen
	usuriensis	LAma
	uva-vulpis	More than 30 suppliers
	verticillata	CBro CMea EBee ECha EHrv EPot GCrs GEdr GIBF LAma MS&S MTho NMen WCru
§	***walujewii***	EPot LAma
	whittallii	EPot MS&S NMen
§	***yuminensis***	LAma WCot
	zagrica	EHyt

Fuchsia ✿ (*Onagraceae*)

	'A.M. Larwick'	CSil EBak EKMF
	'A.W. Taylor'	EBak
	'Aad Franck' **new**	WP&B
	'Aalt Groothuis'	WP&B
	'Abbé Farges' (d)	CDoC CLoc CSil CWVF EBak ECtt EKMF EPts MWhe NDlv SLBF SPet WFFs WP&B
	'Abigail'	CWVF EKMF WFFs WP&B
	'Abigail Storey' **new**	CSil
	'Abundance'	CSil
	'Acclamation' (d)	GLbr WP&B
	'Achievement' ♀H4	CDoC CLoc CSil EKMF LCla MJac NDlv SPet
	'Ada Perry' (d)	ECtt
	'Adagio' (d)	CLoc
	'Adinda'	CDoC EKMF LCla MWar SLBF WP&B
	'Admiration'	CSil EKMF
	'Adrienne'	GLbr MJac SVil
	'Ahehee' (d)	WP&B
	'Ailsa Garnett'	EBak
	'Aintree'	CWVF
	'Airedale'	CWVF MJac
	'Aladna's Sanders'	CWVF GLbr WP&B
	'Alan Ayckbourn'	CWVF
	'Alan Titchmarsh' (d)	CDoC EKMF EPts LCla MWar SLBF
	'Alaska' (d)	CLoc EBak EKMF GLbr WP&B
	'Albertus Schwab'	LCla
	'Albion'	WP&B
	'Alde'	CSil CWVF
	'Alderford'	SLBF WP&B
	'Alf Thornley' (d)	CWVF MWhe
	'Alfred Rambaud' (d)	CDoC CSil
	'Algerine'	SLBF
	'Ali' (d)	EKMF
	'Ali Harder' **new**	WP&B
	'Alice Ashton' (d)	EBak EKMF
	'Alice Blue Gown' (d)	CWVF
	'Alice Doran'	CDoC CSil EKMF LCla SLBF
	'Alice Hoffman' (d) ♀H3-4	More than 30 suppliers
	'Alice Mary' (d)	EBak EMan
	'Alice Stringer'	ECtt
	'Alice Sweetapple'	CWVF
	'Alice Travis' (d)	EBak
	'Alipat'	EBak EKMF
	'Alison Ewart'	CLoc CWVF EBak MJac MWhe SPet
	'Alison Patricia' ♀H3	CWVF EBak EKMF EMan GLbr LAst LCla MJac MWar SLBF WFFs WP&B
	'Alison Reynolds' (d)	CWVF LCla
	'Alison Ruth Griffin' (d)	MJac
	'Alison Ryle' (d)	EBak
	'Alison Sweetman' ♀H1+3	CSil CWVF EKMF MJac MWhe
	'Allure' (d)	CWVF
	'Alma Hulscher'	CWVF
	Aloha = 'Sanicomf' (Sunangels Series)	SLBF
§	***alpestris***	CDoC CSil EBak LCla WFFs
	- Berry 64-87	EKMF
	'Alton Water' (d/v)	MWar
	'Alwin' (d)	CSil CWVF GLbr MWar MWhe
	'Alyce Larson' (d)	CWVF EBak MJac
	'Amanda Bridgland' (d)	EKMF
	'Amanda Jones'	EKMF MWhe
	'Amazing Maisie' (d)	MWar WP&B
	'Ambassador'	EBak SPet
	'Ambriorix'	WP&B
	'Amilie Aubin'	CLoc CWVF EBak EKMF WP&B
	'America'	CWVF
	'American Flaming Glory' (d)	GLbr WP&B
	'Amethyst Fire' (d)	CSil
	'Amigo'	EBak
§	***ampliata***	EKMF LCla
	'Amy' **new**	MJac
	'Amy Lou'	MWar WFFs
	'Amy Lye'	CLoc CSil EBak EKMF
	'Amy Ruth'	CWVF
§	'Andenken an Heinrich Henkel'	CDoC CLoc CWVF EBak ECtt EKMF MOak MWhe
	'André Le Nostre' (d)	CWVF EBak
	'Andreas Schwab'	LCla
	andrei	CDoC LCla
	- Berry 4637	EKMF
	'Andrew'	CDoC EBak EKMF
	'Andrew Carnegie' (d)	CLoc
	'Andrew George'	MJac
	'Andrew Hadfield'	CWVF EKMF MWar SLBF WFFs
	'Andrew Simmons' **new**	WP&B
I	'Andromeda' De Groot	CSil
	'Angela Leslie' (d)	CLoc CWVF EBak EKMF

Name	Suppliers
'Angela Rippon'	CWVF MJac
'Angel's Flight' (d)	EBak
'Anita' (d)	CLoc CSil CWVF EKMF EPts LAst MJac MWar MWhe SLBF WFFs WGor WP&B
'Anjo' (v)	CWVF
'Ann Adams' (d)	MJac
'Ann Howard Tripp'	CDoC CLoc CWVF MBri MJac MWhe WP&B
'Ann Lee' (d)	EBak
'Anna' **new**	WP&B
'Anna Louise' **new**	EKMF
'Anna of Longleat' (d)	CWVF EBak EMan MJac SPet
'Annabel' (d) ♀H3	CDoC CHrt CLoc CSil CTri CWVF EBak EKMF EMan EPts GLbr LAst LCla LVER MBri MJac MWar MWhe SLBF SPet SSea WFFs WP&B
'Annabelle Stubbs' (d)	GLbr LAst
'Anneke de Keijzer'	LCla
'Annie Earle'	EKMF
'Anniek Geerlings'	WP&B
'Another Storey' **new**	CSil
'Anthea Day' (d)	CLoc
'Anthony Heavens'	SLBF WFFs WP&B
'Antigone'	SLBF WP&B
'Anton Schreuder' (d)	WP&B
apetala DG 1044	EKMF
'Aphrodite' (d)	CLoc CWVF EBak
'Applause' (d)	CLoc CWVF EBak ECtt EKMF EPts LVER SPet
'Apple Blossom'	EKMF
aprica hort.	see *F.* x *bacillaris*
aprica Lundell	see *F. microphylla* subsp. *aprica*
'Aquarius'	MWhe
'Aquillette'	WP&B
'Arabella'	CWVF MWhe
'Arabella Improved'	CWVF
arborea	see *F. arborescens*
§ ***arborescens***	CBcs CDoC CHEx CLoc CSil CWVF EBak EKMF EPts EShb LCla LRHS SYvo
'Arcadia Gold' (d)	CWVF ECtt MWhe
'Arcadia Lady'	MJac
'Arcady'	CLoc CWVF
'Ariel'	CDoC CSil WFFs
'Arlendon'	CWVF
'Army Nurse' (d) ♀H4	CDoC CLoc CSil CWVF EKMF EPts LVER MWhe NBir NDlv SLBF SPet WFFs
'Aronst Hoeck' **new**	WP&B
'Art Deco' (d)	WP&B
'Arthur Baxter'	EBak
'Ashley'	CDoC LCla
'Ashley and Isobel'	CWVF
'Ashtede'	LCla SLBF
'Athela'	EBak
'Atlantic Star'	CWVF EKMF MJac
'Atlantis' (d)	CWVF MJac
'Atomic Glow' (d)	EBak
'Aubergine'	see *F.* 'Gerharda's Aubergine'
'Audrey Hepburn'	CWVF EKMF
'August Cools'	WP&B
'Augustin Thierry' (d)	EKMF MWhe
'Aunt Juliana' (d)	EBak
'Auntie Jinks'	CDoC CSil CWVF EBak ECtt LAst LCla MJac MWhe SPet WFFs
'Aurora Superba'	CLoc CSil CWVF EBak EKMF
'Australia Fair' (d)	CWVF EBak
§ ***austromontana***	EBak
'Autumnale' ♀H1+3	CDoC CHEx CLoc CWVF EBak ECtt EKMF EMan EPts LAst LCla LRHS LVER MWhe NVic SLBF SMrm SPet SPoG SSea
'Avalanche' (d)	CLoc CSil EBak EKMF SLBF
'Avocet'	CLoc EBak
'Avon Celebration' (d)	CLoc
'Avon Gem'	CLoc CSil
'Avon Glow'	CLoc
'Avon Gold'	CLoc
ayavacensis	LCla
- Berry 3601	EKMF
'Azure Sky' (d)	EKMF MJac
'Babette' (d)	EKMF
'Baby Blue Eyes'	CDoC CSil CWVF EKMF SLBF WFFs
'Baby Blush' **new**	CSil
'Baby Bright'	CDoC CWVF EPts SLBF WFFs WP&B
'Baby Chang'	CSil LCla MWhe
'Baby Pink' (d)	CWVF
'Baby Thumb' (d)	CSil EPts
§ x ***bacillaris***	CAbb CBrm CChe CDoC CSil EBak EWes EWin MBlu SLBF SPoG SRms
§ - 'Cottinghamii'	CDoC CSil EKMF IDee WSHC
- 'Oosje'	see *F.* 'Oosje'
§ - 'Reflexa'	CAbP CTrC GQui LAst LSou WFFs
'Bagworthy Water'	CLoc
'Baker's Tri'	EBak
'Bali Hi'	WP&B
'Balkon'	CWVF
'Balkonkönigin'	CLoc EBak ECtt
'Ballerina'	CDoC
'Ballerina Blue'	GLbr LAst
'Ballet Girl' (d) ♀H1+3	CLoc CSil CWVF EBak ECtt EKMF EShb GLbr LCla SLBF SPet
'Bambini'	CWVF EPts
'Banks Peninsula'	GQui
'Barbara'	CLoc CSil CWVF EBak EKMF EPts MJac MWar MWhe SPet WEas
'Barbara Evans'	MWar
'Barbara Pountain' (d)	CWVF LVER
'Barbara Windsor'	CWVF EPts LAst MJac
'Baron de Ketteler' (d)	CSil EKMF
'Barry M. Cox'	CSil WP&B
'Barry's Queen'	CSil EBak SPet
'Bart Comperen' **new**	WP&B
'Bashful' (d)	CDoC CSil EPts LCla LRHS NDlv SPet
'Beacon'	CDoC CLoc CSil CWVF EBak EKMF EMan EPts LAst LCla MBri MJac MWhe NBlu NDlv SPet WFFs WTel
'Beacon Rosa'	CDoC CLoc CSil CWVF EKMF EMan EPts LCla MBri MJac MWhe NDlv SLBF SPet
'Beacon Superior'	CSil
'Bealings' (d)	CDoC CLoc CWVF ECtt EMan GLbr MBri WFFs WP&B
'Beatrice Burtoft'	EKMF
'Beau Nash'	CLoc
'Beautiful Bobbie' (d)	SLBF
'Beauty of Bath' (d)	CLoc EBak
'Beauty of Cliff Hall'	EKMF
'Beauty of Clyffe Hall'	CSil EBak
'Beauty of Exeter' (d)	COtt CWVF EBak EKMF
'Beauty of Prussia' (d)	CDoC CLoc CSil CWVF ECtt
'Beauty of Swanley'	EBak
'Beauty of Trowbridge'	CDoC CWVF LCla
'Becky'	WP&B
'Becky Jane'	CSil
'Bel Cinette'	WP&B
'Belijn'	WP&B
'Belinda Jane'	WP&B
'Bella Forbes' (d) ♀H1+3	CLoc CSil EBak EKMF
'Bella Rosella' (d)	CSil CWVF ECtt EKMF EPts GLbr LAst MJac SCoo SLBF

	'Belle de Spa' **new**	WP&B
	'Belsay Beauty' (d)	CWVF MJac
	'Belvoir Beauty' (d)	CLoc
	'Belvoir Lakes'	ECtt
	'Ben de Jong'	LCla MJac
	'Ben Jammin'	CDoC CLoc CSil CWVF EPts LAst LCla LSou MJac MWar WFFs WGor WP&B
I	'Béranger' Lemoine 1897 (d)	CSil EBak EKMF
	'Berba's Happiness' (d)	CWVF
	'Berba's Inge Mariel' (d)	ECtt
	'Berba's Trio'	WP&B
	'Berliner Kind' (d)	CSil CWVF EBak EKMF
	'Bermuda' (d)	CSil CWVF
	'Bernadette' (d)	CWVF
	'Bernie's Big-un' (d)	MJac
	'Bernisser Hardy'	CDoC CSil EKMF EPts LCla WFFs
	'Bert de Jong'	WP&B
	'Bertha Gadsby'	EKMF
	'Beryl Shaffery'	WP&B
	'Berys' **new**	EKMF MWar
	'Berys Elizabeth' **new**	SLBF WP&B
	'Bessie Kimberley'	LCla MWar
	'Beth Robley' (d)	CWVF
	'Betsy Ross' (d)	EBak
	'Bettina Stubi' **new**	WP&B
	Betty = 'Goetzbet' (Shadowdancer Series)	LAst NEgg
	'Betty Jean' (d)	MWar WP&B
	'Beverley'	CSil CWVF EBak EKMF EPts SPet WFFs
	'Bewitched' (d)	EBak
	'Bianca' (d)	CWVF WP&B
	'Bicentennial' (d)	CDoC CLoc CSil CWVF EBak EKMF EPts LAst LSou LVER MJac MWar MWhe SPet SSea
	'Big Slim'	WP&B
	'Bilberry Sorbet' **new**	WP&B
	'Billy Green' ♈H1+3	CDoC CLoc CWVF EBak ECtt EKMF EPts LCla LRHS MJac MWar MWhe SLBF SPet WFFs
	'Bishop's Bells' (d)	CWVF
	'Bittersweet' (d)	CDoC ECtt
	'Black Beauty' (d)	CSil CWVF
	'Black Prince'	CDoC CSil CWVF MWar
	'Blackmore Vale' (d)	CWVF
	'Blacky' **new**	GLbr LAst
I	'Blanche Regina' (d)	CWVF MJac MWhe
	'Bland's New Striped'	EBak EKMF EPts SLBF
	'Blauer Engel'	WP&B
	'Blaze Away' (d)	MBri
	'Blood Donor' (d)	EKMF MJac
	'Blowick'	CDoC CWVF EMan MBri MJac MWhe SPet WFFs
	'Blue Beauty' (d)	CSil EBak EKMF
	'Blue Boy' **new**	WP&B
	'Blue Bush'	CSil CWVF EKMF EPts MJac NDlv
	'Blue Butterfly' (d)	CWVF EBak
	'Blue Eyes' (d)	CDoC GLbr SPet
	'Blue Gown' (d)	CDoC CLoc CSil CWVF EBak EKMF GLbr LRHS LVER MWhe NDlv SPet WP&B
	'Blue Ice'	CSil MWhe
	'Blue Lace' (d)	CSil
	'Blue Lagoon' ambig. (d)	CWVF
	'Blue Lake' (d)	CSil CWVF ECtt LVER
	'Blue Mink'	EBak
	'Blue Mirage' (d)	CWVF EKMF GLbr MJac
	'Blue Mist' (d)	EBak
	'Blue Pearl' (d)	CWVF EBak
	'Blue Pinwheel'	EBak
	'Blue Satin' (d)	COtt MWhe
	'Blue Tit'	CSil LCla
	'Blue Veil' (d)	CLoc CSil CWVF EKMF GLbr LVER MJac MWar SVil
	'Blue Waves' (d)	CLoc CSBt CSil CWVF EBak MJac MWar MWhe SPet
	'Blush o' Dawn' (d)	CLoc CWVF EBak EKMF EPts LVER SPet WP&B
	'Blythe' (d)	SLBF
	'Bob Pacey'	CWVF
	'Bobby Boy' (d)	EBak
	'Bobby Dazzler' (d)	CWVF ECtt EKMF
	'Bobby Shaftoe' (d)	EBak MWhe
	'Bobby Wingrove'	EBak
	'Bobby's Girl'	EPts
	'Bobolink' (d)	EBak
	'Bob's Best' (d)	CWVF EPts LVER MJac
	'Boerhaave'	EBak
	boliviana 'Alba'	see *F. boliviana* Carrière var. *alba*
	boliviana Britton	see *F. sanctae-rosae*
§	***boliviana*** Carrière	CAbb CDoC CHEx CLoc CSil CWVF EBak EKMF LCla MOak SHFr SYvo
§	- var. ***alba*** ♈H1+3	CDoC CLoc CSil EBak EKMF EPts LCla MOak WP&B
	- var. ***boliviana***	CRHN LRHS
	- f. ***puberulenta*** Munz	see *F. boliviana* Carrière
	'Bon Accorde'	CLoc CSil CWVF EBak EKMF EPts MJac
	'Bon Bon' (d)	CWVF EBak
	'Bonita' (d)	CWVF MJac WP&B
	'Bonnie Lass' (d)	EBak
	'Bonny' (d)	CLoc
	'Bora Bora' (d)	CWVF EBak EKMF WP&B
	'Borde Hill' (d)	EPts SLBF
	'Border Princess'	EBak
	'Border Queen' ♈H3-4	CBgR CDoC CLoc CSil CWVF EBak EKMF EMan EPts LCla MBNS MJac MWar SPet WFFs
	'Border Raider'	MWar SLBF WP&B
	'Border Reiver'	EBak
	'Börnemann's Beste'	see *F.* 'Georg Börnemann'
	'Bouffant'	CLoc
	'Bougie Humpary' **new**	WP&B
	'Bountiful' ambig.	GLbr
I	'Bountiful' Munkner (d)	CLoc CWVF EKMF MWhe SPet
	'Bouquet' (d)	CSil EKMF
	'Bow Bells'	CDoC CLoc CWVF MJac MWhe SPet
	'Boy Marc'	LCla WP&B
	'Braamt's Glorie'	WP&B
	bracelinae	EKMF
	'Brancaster' **new**	SLBF
	'Brandt's Five Hundred Club'	CDoC CLoc EBak SPet
	'Brechtje'	WP&B
	'Breckland'	EBak
	'Breeders' Delight'	CSil CWVF MBri WP&B
	'Breeder's Dream' (d)	EBak
	'Breevis Blauwtje'	WP&B
	'Breevis Homerus' **new**	WP&B
I	'Breevis Iris'	WP&B
	'Breevis Karna'	WP&B
I	'Breevis Lowi'	WP&B
I	'Breevis Paradoxa' **new**	WP&B
	'Breevis Rex' **new**	SLBF
	'Brenda' (d)	CLoc CSil CWVF EBak
	'Brenda Pritchard' (d)	ECtt LVER
	'Brenda White'	CDoC CLoc CWVF EBak EPts
	'Brentwood' (d)	EBak
	brevilobis	CSil WP&B
	- Berry 4445	EKMF
	'Brian A. McDonald' (d)	CWVF
	'Brian C. Morrison'	EKMF LCla WP&B
	'Brian G. Soanes'	EBak

	'Brian Hilton'	MWar
	'Brian Kimberley'	EKMF LCla MWar
	'Bridal Veil' (d)	EBak
	'Bridesmaid' (d)	CWVF EBak SPet
	'Brigadoon' (d)	CLoc EBak
	'Bright Lights' **new**	EKMF
	'Brightling'	WP&B
	'Brighton Belle'	CDoC CSil CWVF EWll WP&B
	'Brilliant' ambig.	CWVF NDlv
I	'Brilliant' Bull	CDoC CLoc CSil EBak EKMF LCla MGos MWhe
	'Briony Caunt'	CSil EKMF
	'British Jubilee' (d)	CWVF EKMF
	'Brixham Orpheus'	CWVF
	'Brodsworth'	CSil EKMF NDlv
	'Bronze Banks Peninsula'	CSil EKMF
	'Brookwood Belle' (d)	CWVF EPts LCla MJac SLBF WFFs
	'Brookwood Dale'	MWhe
	'Brookwood Joy' (d)	CWVF MJac
	'Brookwood Lady'	MWhe
	'Brutus' ♀H4	CDoC CLoc CSil CWVF EBak EBee EKMF EMan EPts LAst LCla LRHS MHar MWat MWhe NDlv SPet SWal WP&B
	'Bryan Breary'	LCla
	'Bubba Jack'	SLBF
	'Buddha' (d)	EBak
	'Bugle Boy'	EPts LCla MWar SLBF
	'Bunny' (d)	CWVF EBak
	'Burnt Hill'	SLBF WP&B
	'Burstwick' **new**	CSil
	'Burton Brew'	MJac
	'Buster' (d)	EKMF LCla MWar SLBF
I	'Buttercup'	CLoc CWVF EBak
	'C.J. Howlett'	CSil EBak EKMF
	'Caballero' (d)	EBak
	'Caesar' (d)	CWVF EBak
	'Caitlin Isabelle'	WP&B
	'Caledonia'	CSil EBak EKMF
	'California'	WP&B
	'Callaly Pink'	CWVF
	'Cambridge Louie'	CSil CWVF EBak MBri MWar MWhe SPet WFFs
	'Cameron Ryle'	WP&B
	campii	EKMF LCla
	campos-portoi	CDoC CSil LCla
	- Berry 4435	EKMF
	'Cancun' (d)	MJac
	'Candlelight' (d)	CLoc EBak
	'Candy Stripe'	CLoc
	canescens misapplied	see *F. ampliata*
	canescens Bentham	EKMF
	'Canny Bob'	MJac
	'Canopy' (d)	CWVF
	'Capri' (d)	CSil CWVF EBak
	'Caprice'	WP&B
	'Cara Mia' (d)	CLoc CSil CWVF SPet
	'Caradela'	CLoc EKMF MJac MWar
	'Cardinal'	CLoc EKMF WP&B
	'Cardinal Farges' (d)	CLoc CSil CWVF EKMF SLBF SPet SSea WFFs WP&B
	'Carillon van Amsterdam'	MWhe
	'Carioca'	EBak
	'Carisbrooke Castle' (d)	EKMF
	'Carl Drude' (d)	CSil
	'Carl Wallace' (d)	EKMF MJac
	'Carla Johnston' ♀H1+3	CDoC CLoc CWVF EKMF EPts LCla LVER MBri MJac MWar MWhe WFFs WP&B
	'Carleton George'	MWar
	'Carmel Blue'	CDoC CLoc CSil EKMF LAst LCla LSou MWar MWhe NBlu SPet WFFs WGor
	'Carmen' Lemoine (d)	CDoC CSil EKMF WP&B
	'Carmine Bell'	CSil EKMF
	'Carnea'	CSil CWib
	'Carnival' (d)	CWVF
	'Carnoustie' (d)	EBak
	'Carol Grace' (d)	CLoc
	'Carol Lynn Whittemore' (d)	SLBF WP&B
	'Carol Nash' (d)	CLoc
	'Carol Roe'	EKMF
	'Caroline'	CLoc CWVF EBak EPts MWhe
	'Caroline's Joy'	MJac MWhe SPet SVil
	'Cascade'	CDoC CLoc CSil CWVF ECtt EKMF EMan EPts MBri MJac MWhe SPet SSea WBVN WP&B
	'Caspar Hauser' (d)	CSil CWVF GLbr SLBF WP&B
	'Catharina'	LCla
	'Catherine Bartlett'	CWVF EKMF
	'Cathie MacDougall' (d)	EBak
	'Cecil Glass'	EKMF
	'Cecile' (d)	CDoC CWVF ECtt EKMF EPts GLbr LAst LCla LVER MJac MWhe SLBF WP&B
	'Celadore' (d)	CWVF LVER MJac
	'Celebration' (d)	CLoc CWVF MWar
	'Celebrity' **new**	WP&B
	'Celia Smedley' ♀H3	CDoC CLoc CSil CWVF EBak EKMF EPts LAst LCla LVER MBri MJac MWar MWhe SLBF SPet WFFs WP&B
	'Celine'	MWar
	'Centerpiece' (d)	EBak
	'Ceri'	CLoc
	'Chameleon'	CDoC SPet
	'Champagne Celebration'	CLoc
	'Chancellor'	CWVF
	'Chandleri'	CWVF EKMF SLBF
	'Chang' ♀H1+3	CDoC CLoc CSil CWVF EBak EKMF LCla LRHS MWar MWhe SLBF WFFs
	'Chantry Park'	CDoC LCla WFFs
	'Charles Edward'	CSil EKMF
	Charlie Dimmock = 'Foncha'PBR	GLbr LAst MWhe
	'Charlie Gardiner'	CWVF EBak MWhe
	'Charlie Girl' (d)	EBak
	'Charlotte Clyne'	MJac
	'Charming'	CDoC CLoc CSil CWVF EBak EKMF MJac MWar NDlv SPet
	'Chase Delight' (v)	CDoC
	'Checkerboard' ♀H3	CDul CHrt CLoc CSil CWVF EBak ECtt EKMF EPts LCla LVER MJac MWar MWhe SLBF SPet SSea WFFs WP&B
	'Cheeky Chantelle' (d)	SLBF WP&B
	'Cheers' (d)	CWVF EKMF MWhe
	'Chelsea Louise'	EPts
	'Chenois Godelieve'	WP&B
I	'Cherry' Götz	GLbr LAst WP&B
	'Cherry Pie'	CSil
	'Cheryl'	MJac
	'Chessboard'	CLoc
	'Cheviot Princess'	WP&B
	'Chillerton Beauty' ♀H3	CDoC CLoc CSil CTri CWVF ECtt EKMF EPts LCla LRHS MJac MWhe SLBF SPer SPet WMnd
	'China Doll' (d)	CWVF EBak MWhe
	'China Lantern'	CLoc CSil CWVF EBak WFFs
	'Chor Echo'	WP&B
	'Chris Nicholls'	CSil EKMF
	'Christ Driessen'	WP&B
	'Christine Bamford'	CDoC CSil CWVF WFFs
	'Christine Shaffery' (d)	WP&B

	'Churchtown'	CWVF
	cinerea	LCla
	- Berry 004-86	EKMF
	'Cinnabarina'	CLoc SLBF
*	'Cinnamon'	WP&B
	'Cinque Port Liberty' (d)	MWar SLBF
	'Cinvenu' **new**	LCla
	'Cinvulca'	LCla
	'Circe' (d)	CWVF EBak EKMF
	'Circus'	EBak
	'Circus Spangles' (d)	CDoC COtt ECtt EKMF GLbr LAst MWar
	'Citation'	CDoC CLoc CSil CWVF EBak
	'City of Adelaide' (d)	CLoc MWhe
	'City of Leicester'	CSil CWVF LCla SPet
	'Claire de Lune'	CDoC CWVF EBak WP&B
	'Claire Evans' (d)	CLoc CWVF
	'Claire Oram'	CLoc
	'Clare Frisby'	EKMF WP&B
	'Claudia' (d)	GLbr LAst LCla MJac MWar
	'Cliantha' (d)	LCla MJac MWar MWhe
	'Clifford Gadsby' (d)	EBak
	'Cliff's Hardy'	CSil EKMF LCla SPet
	'Cliff's Unique' (d)	CWVF EPts
	'Clifton Beauty' (d)	CWVF MJac
	'Clifton Belle'	CWVF
	'Clifton Charm'	CSil EKMF EPts LCla MJac
	'Clipper'	CSil CWVF
	'Cloth of Gold'	CLoc CWVF EBak MJac MWhe SPet
	'Cloverdale Jewel' (d)	CDoC CWVF EBak ECtt LCla MWhe SPet
	'Cloverdale Joy'	EBak
	'Cloverdale Pearl'	CWVF EBak EKMF EMan ENot EPfP MJac MWhe SPet WFFs
	'Coachman' ♀H4	CLoc CSil CWVF EBak EKMF EMan EPts LCla MWar MWhe SLBF SPet WBVN
	coccinea	CDoC CSil EKMF EPts LCla
	'Codringtonii' **new**	CSil
	x ***colensoi***	CDoC CSil ECou EKMF LCla SHFr
	'Collingwood' (d)	CLoc CWVF EBak
	'Colne Fantasy' (v)	CDoC EKMF EPts
	'Come Dancing' (d)	CDoC CWVF ECtt LCla SPet
	'Comet' Banks	CWVF
I	'Comet' Tiret (d)	CLoc EBak SPet
	'Comperen Libel' **new**	WP&B
	'Conchilla'	EBak
	'Condor'	WP&B
	'Connie' (d)	CSil EBak EKMF
	'Conspicua'	CSil CWVF EBak EKMF WP&B
	'Constable Country' (d)	CWVF
	'Constance' (d)	CDoC CLoc CSil CWVF EKMF LCla MJac MWar MWhe NDlv SLBF SPet SWal WFFs
	'Constance Comer'	MJac
	'Constellation' ambig.	CWVF
I	'Constellation' Schnabel (d)	CLoc EBak
	'Contramine' **new**	WP&B
	'Coombe Park'	MJac
	'Copycat'	CSil
	'Coq au Vin' (d)	WP&B
	'Coquet Bell'	CWVF EBak
	'Coquet Dale' (d)	CWVF EBak
	'Coquet Gold' (d/v)	ECtt
	'Coral Baby'	LCla SLBF
	'Coral Rose'	CSil
	'Coral Seas'	EBak
§	'Coralle'	CDoC CLoc CWVF EBak EKMF EMan EPts LCla MJac MWar MWhe SLBF WFFs WP&B
	'Corallina'	CDoC CLoc CSil EBak EHol EKMF LVER MWhe SPet WFar
I	'Corallina Variegata' (v)	CSil
*	***cordata*** B&SWJ 9095 **new**	WCru
	cordifolia hort.	see *F. splendens*
	cordifolia Benth.	CBcs EBak EKMF MOak WP&B
	'Core'ngrato' (d)	CLoc CWVF EBak
	coriacifolia	EKMF LCla
	'Cornelia Smith'	WP&B
	'Cornwall Calls' (d)	EBak
	'Corrie Palm' **new**	MWar
	'Corsage' (d)	CWVF
	'Corsair' (d)	EBak
	corymbiflora misapplied	see *F. boliviana*
	corymbiflora alba	see *F. boliviana* var. *alba*
	corymbiflora Ruíz & Pav.	CDoC EBak EKMF EPts
	- Berry 4688	EKMF
	'Cosmopolitan' (d)	EBak
	'Costa Brava'	CLoc EBak
	'Cotta 2000'	EKMF LCla
	'Cotta Bella' (d)	EKMF
	'Cotta Bright Star'	CWVF EKMF LCla
	'Cotta Carousel'	EKMF LCla
	'Cotta Christmas Tree'	EKMF LCla SLBF
	'Cotta Fairy'	CWVF EKMF
	'Cotta Vino'	EKMF
	'Cottinghamii'	see *F.* x *bacillaris* 'Cottinghamii'
	'Cotton Candy' (d)	CLoc CWVF ECtt LCla MWhe
	'Countdown Carol' (d)	EPts
	'Countess of Aberdeen'	CLoc CSil CWVF EBak EKMF SLBF
	'Countess of Maritza' (d)	CLoc CWVF
	'County Park'	ECou EWes
	'Court Jester' (d)	CLoc EBak
	'Cover Girl' (d)	EBak EPts MWhe SPet
	'Coxeen'	EBak
	'Crackerjack'	CLoc EBak
	crassistipula	LCla
	- Berry 3553	EKMF
	'Crescendo' (d)	CLoc CWVF
	'Crinkley Bottom' (d)	EPts LVER MJac SLBF
	'Crinoline' (d)	EBak
	'Crosby Serendipity'	CLoc
	'Crosby Soroptimist'	CWVF MWar MWhe
	'Cross Check'	CWVF EMan MBri MJac
	'Crusader' (d)	CWVF
	'Crystal Aniversary' (d)	CWVF
	'Crystal Blue'	EBak GLbr
	'Cupid'	CSil EBak
	'Curly Q'	EBak SPet
	'Curtain Call' (d)	CLoc CWVF EBak
	x ***cuzco***	EKMF LCla
	cylindracea misapplied	see *F.* x *bacillaris*
	cylindracea Lindl.	CSil LCla WP&B
	cylindracea (m) BRE 43908 **new**	EKMF
	'Cymon' (d)	CWVF MWhe
	cyrtandroides	CSil
	- Berry 4628	EKMF
	'Dainty'	EBak
	'Dainty Lady' (d)	EBak
	'Daisy Bell'	CDoC CLoc CSil CWVF EBak ECtt EKMF LCla MJac SPet WP&B
	'Dalton'	EBak
	'Dana Samantha'	EPts
	'Dancing Bloom'	EPts
	'Dancing Elves' **new**	WP&B
	'Dancing Flame' (d) ♀H1+3	CHrt CLoc CWVF EBak EKMF EMan EPts GLbr LAst LCla LVER MBri MJac MWar MWhe SLBF SPet WP&B
	'Daniel Austin' (d)	MJac
	'Danielle Frijstein'	WP&B
	'Danielle's Dream' (d)	WP&B
	'Danish Pastry'	CWVF SPet
	'Danny Boy' (d)	CLoc CWVF EBak EKMF MWhe WP&B

	'Danny Kaye' (d)	WP&B
	'Daphne Arlene'	CSil WP&B
	'Dark Eyes' (d) ♕H4	CLoc CSil CWVF EBak EKMF EMan EShb GLbr LAst LVER MBri MJac MWhe SLBF SPet SSea WFFs WP&B
	'Dark Lady'	MWhe
	'Dark Mystery' (d)	SLBF WP&B
	'Dark Night' (d)	CSil
	'Dark Secret' (d)	EBak
	'Dark Treasure' (d)	CDoC EKMF
	'Daryn John Woods'	WP&B
	'Dave's Delight'	EKMF WP&B
	'David'	CDoC CLoc CSil CWVF EKMF EOHP EPts LCla LSou MWhe NDlv SLBF WFFs WGor WP&B WSPU WWeb
	'David Alston' (d)	CLoc CWVF EBak
	'David Lockyer' (d)	CLoc CWVF
	'David Savage' (d)	LCla
	'Dawn'	EBak
	'Dawn Carless' (d)	WP&B
	'Dawn Fantasia' (v)	CLoc EKMF EPts MWar
	'Dawn Redfern'	CWVF
	'Dawn Sky' (d)	EBak SVil
	'Dawn Star' (d)	CWVF GLbr LAst LVER MJac MWhe
	'Day by Day'	CSil
	'Day Star'	EBak
	'De Groot's Beauty' (d)	WP&B
	'De Groot's Moonlight'	WP&B
	'De Groot's Pipes'	WP&B
	'De Groot's Regenboog'	WP&B
	'De Groot's Tricolore' **new**	WP&B
	'De Vondeling'	WP&B
	'Debby' (d)	EBak
	'Deben Petite'	EWll LCla
	'Deborah Street'	CLoc
§	***decussata*** Ruíz & Pav.	CDoC EBak LCla
	- Berry 3049	EKMF
	'Dee Copley' (d)	EBak
	'Deep Purple' (d)	CDoC CLoc CWVF ECtt EKMF GLbr LAst MJac SCoo SLBF WGor WP&B
	'Delilah' (d)	CWVF MJac
	'Delta's Angelique'	WP&B
	'Delta's Bride'	SLBF WP&B
	'Delta's Dream'	CWVF WP&B
	'Delta's Groom'	LCla WP&B
	'Delta's K.O.' (d)	GLbr
	'Delta's Matador'	LAst
	'Delta's Night'	WP&B
	'Delta's Paljas'	WP&B
	'Delta's Parade' (d)	EPts GLbr LCla
	'Delta's Pim' **new**	WP&B
	'Delta's Robijn'	WP&B
	'Delta's Song'	WP&B
	'Delta's Symphonie' (d)	CWVF WP&B
	'Delta's Wonder'	CSil WP&B
	'Demi van Roovert'	WP&B
§	***denticulata***	CDoC CLoc CWVF EBak EKMF EPts LCla MOak SLBF WP&B
	dependens **new**	EKMF
	'Derby Imp'	CWVF WFFs
	'Desire'	GLbr WP&B
	'Desperate Daniel'	EKMF EPts LCla
	'Devonshire Dumpling' (d)	CDoC CLoc CSil CWVF EBak ECtt EKMF EMan EPts GLbr LAst LCla LVER MBri MJac MWar SLBF SPet WP&B
	'Diablo' (d)	EBak
	'Diamond Celebration' (d)	EKMF GLbr MWar
	'Diana' (d)	CDoC EBak
	'Diana Wills' (d)	CWVF MWhe
	'Diana Wright'	CSil EKMF WSPU
	'Diane Brown'	CWVF EKMF MWhe
§	'Die Schöne Wilhelmine'	WP&B
	'Dilly-Dilly' (d)	CWVF ECtt
	'Dimples' (d)	CSil MBri
	'Dipton Dainty' (d)	CLoc EBak
	'Dirk van Delen'	MWhe
	'Display' ♕H4	CDoC CLoc CSil CWVF EBak EBee ECtt EKMF EMan EPts LAst LCla LVER MBri MJac MWhe NDlv NPer SLBF SPet SSea WFFs
	'Doc'	CDoC CSil EPts NDlv SPet
	'Doctor'	see *F.* 'The Doctor'
	'Doctor Foster' ♕H4	CDoC CLoc CSil CTri EBak EKMF ENot EPts NDlv WEas
	'Doctor Judith' (d)	CWVF
	'Doctor Mason'	CWVF
	'Doctor Olson' (d)	CLoc EBak
	'Doctor Robert'	CWVF EPts MBri MJac MWhe
	'Doctor Topinard'	CLoc EBak EKMF
	'Dodo'	WP&B
§	'Dollar Princess' (d) ♕H4	CDoC CHrt CLoc CSil CWVF EBak EBee ECtt EKMF EMan EPts GLbr LAst LCla MBri MJac MWar MWhe NDlv NPer SChu SLBF SPet SPlb SWal WFFs WFar
	'Dolly Daydream' (d)	EKMF
	'Dominique' (d)	EKMF
	'Dominyana'	EBak EKMF LCla
	'Don Peralta'	EBak
	'Dopey' (d)	CDoC CSil SPet
	'Doreen Redfern'	CLoc CWVF MJac SPet
	'Doreen Stroud'	CWVF
	'Doris Coleman' (d)	EMan
	'Doris Deaves'	SLBF
	'Doris Hobbs'	WP&B
	'Doris Joan'	SLBF
	'Dorothea Flower'	CLoc CSil CWVF EBak EKMF
	'Dorothy'	CSil EKMF LCla SLBF SPet
	'Dorothy Ann'	SLBF WP&B
	'Dorothy Cheal'	CWVF
	'Dorothy Day' (d)	CLoc
	'Dorothy Hanley' (d)	CSil EKMF EPts LAst LSou MAsh MJac MWhe SLBF SPoG WFFs WGor WWeb
	'Dorothy Shields' (d)	CWVF MJac
	'Dorrian Brogdale'	LCla WP&B
	'Dorset Delight' (d)	CWVF WP&B
	'Dove House'	EKMF
	'Drake 400' (d)	CLoc
	'Drama Girl'	CWVF
	'Drame' (d)	CDoC CSil CWVF EBak EKMF LCla NDlv SPet
	'Drum Major' (d)	EBak
	'Du Barry' (d)	EBak
	'Duchess of Albany'	CLoc CSil EBak
	'Duchess of Cornwall' (d)	CSil
I	'Duke of Wellington' Haag (d)	CLoc
	'Dulcie Elizabeth' (d)	CWVF EBak MJac SPet
	'Dunrobin Bedder'	CSil
	'Dusky Beauty'	CWVF
	'Dusky Rose' (d)	CDoC CLoc CWVF EBak MJac MWhe
	'Dusted Pink' (d)	CWVF
	'Dutch Kingsize'	WP&B
	'Dutch Mill'	CLoc CWVF EBak
	'Duyfken'	CWVF
	'Dying Embers'	CLoc
	'Dymph Werker van Groenland'	LCla
	'East Anglian'	CLoc EBak
	'Easter Bonnet' (d)	CLoc CWVF

'Ebanflo' EBak MWar
'Ebbtide' (d) CLoc EBak WP&B
'Echo' CLoc CWVF LRHS
'Ector's Isle Cora' **new** WP&B
'Ectors Nursery' WP&B
'Ed Largarde' (d) CWVF EBak EKMF
'Edale' EKMF
'Eden Lady' CDoC CLoc SPet
'Eden Princess' CWVF MJac MWhe
'Edith' ambig. NDlv
'Edith' Brown (d) CSil EKMF LCla SLBF
'Edith Emery' (d) CDoC SPet
'Edna May' CWVF
'Edna W. Smith' CWVF ECtt
'Eileen Drew' **new** SLBF
'Eileen Raffill' EBak
'Eileen Saunders' CSil EBak
'Eileen Storey' EKMF WP&B
'Eisvogel' WP&B
'El Camino' (d) CWVF WBVN
'El Cid' CLoc CSil EBak EKMF
'Elaine Ann' EPts MJac
'Elaine Taylor' (d) **new** MJac
'Eleanor Clark' WP&B
'Eleanor Leytham' CDoC CWVF EBak EKMF LCla
'Eleanor Rawlins' CSil EBak EKMF
'Elf' CSil
'Elfin Glade' CLoc CSil CWVF EBak EKMF WMnd
'Elfrida' (d) CSil EKMF NDlv
'Elfriede Ott' CLoc EBak MWhe WP&B
'Eline Brantz' GLbr
'Elisabeth Schnedl' (d) **new** SLBF
I 'Elizabeth' Whiteman EBak EKMF
'Elizabeth Broughton' EKMF
'Elizabeth Tompkins' (d) MJac
'Elizabeth Travis' (d) EBak
'Ellen Morgan' (d) CWVF EBak
'Ellie Jane' EPts
'Elma' CSil LCla
'Elsa' (d) CWVF ECtt LRHS SPet
'Elsie Maude' (d) CWVF
'Elsie Mitchell' (d) CWVF MWhe SPet
'Elsstar' WP&B
'Elysée' CSil EKMF
§ 'Emile de Wildeman' (d) CSil CWVF EBak EKMF LVER SPet
'Emile Zola' **new** CSil
'Emily' MJac
'Emily Austen' CWVF EKMF
'Emma Alice' (d) CWVF
'Emma Louise' (d) CWVF
'Emma Margaret' **new** SLBF
'Empress of Prussia' ♀H4 CDoC CLoc CSil CWVF EBak ECtt EKMF EMan EPts GLbr LAst LRHS NDlv SLBF SPet WMnd
'Enchanted' (d) CWVF EBak MWar
encliandra subsp. ***encliandra*** CDoC EKMF LCla
* - var. ***gris*** CSil LCla
- subsp. ***microphylloides*** Berry & Brako 7592 **new** EKMF
§ 'Enfant Prodigue' (d) CDoC CLoc CSil EKMF SDix SMrm WMnd
'English Rose' (d) CWVF
'Enid Joyce' SLBF
'Enstone' see *F. magellanica* var. *molinae* 'Enstone'
'Erecta' MBNS NPri
'Erica Julie' (d) MWhe
'Eric's Everest' (d) EKMF
'Eric's Hardy' (d) CSil
'Eric's Majestic' (d) EKMF MJac
'Erika Köth' LCla
'Ernest Rankin' CSil
'Ernie Bromley' CSil CWVF SLBF
'Errol' (d) CLoc
'Estelle Marie' CLoc CSil CWVF EBak MBri MWar MWhe SLBF SPet WP&B
'Eternal Flame' (d) CSil CWVF EBak EPts MBri MWhe
'Ethel May' MJac
'Ethel Wilson' CSil
'Eureka Red' (d) CWVF GLbr LAst
'Eurydice' (d) CLoc
'Eusebia' (d) MJac
'Eva Boerg' CHrt CLoc CSil CTri CWVF EBak ECtt EKMF EMan LAst LCla MBri MWar SPet SWal WFFs WKif
'Evanson's Choice' CDoC
'Evelyn Stanley' (d) CWVF
§ 'Evelyn Steele Little' EBak
'Evening Sky' (d) EBak
'Evensong' CLoc CWVF EBak MWhe
excorticata CBcs CDoC CHEx CPLG CPle CRHN CSil CTrw EKMF LCla SPlb WPat WSHC
'Exmoor Woods' CSil WBcn
'Fabian Franck' CDoC LCla
'Falklands' (d) CSil EKMF
'Falling Stars' CLoc CWVF EBak ECtt MWhe
'Fan Dancer' (d) EBak
'Fancy Free' (d) MBri
'Fancy Pants' (d) CLoc CWVF EBak
'Fanfare' CDoC EBak EKMF EWll LCla
'Fascination' see *F.* 'Emile de Wildeman'
'Fashion' (d) EBak
'Favourite' EBak
'Feltham's Pride' CWVF
'Fenman' CWVF EPts
'Fergie' (d) LCla
'Festival' (d) MWhe
'Festival Lights' SLBF
'Festoon' EBak
'Fey' (d) CWVF EKMF GLbr WP&B
'Ffion' EPts
'Fiery Spider' EBak WP&B
'Finn' CWVF EPts
'Fiona' CLoc CWVF EBak SPet
'Fire Mountain' (d) CLoc CSil ECtt SSea
Firecracker = 'John Ridding'PBR (v) CHEx CLoc SAga SPoG
'Firelite' (d) EBak
'Firenza' (d) CWVF
'First Kiss' CWVF
'First Lady' (d) CWVF
'First Lord' CWVF
'First Success' CDoC CWVF EKMF LCla
'Flair' (d) CLoc CWVF
'Flame' EBak
'Flamenco Dancer' (d) CLoc CWVF ECtt GLbr LAst
'Flash' ♀H3-4 CDoC CLoc CSil CTri CWVF EBak EKMF EPts LCla MAsh MJac MWhe NDlv SLBF SPet
'Flashlight' CDoC CSil CWVF LAst LSou MJac NDlv WFFs
'Flashlight Amélioré' CSil
'Flat Jack o' Lancashire' (d) CSil ECtt EKMF SLBF
'Flavia' (d) EBak
'Flirt' WP&B
'Flirtation Waltz' (d) CLoc CSil CWVF EBak EKMF EMan EPts LVER MJac MWhe SPet
'Flocon de Neige' CSil EBak EKMF
'Floral City' (d) CLoc EBak
'Florence Mary Abbott' EMan
'Florence Taylor' CWVF
'Florence Turner' CSil EBak EKMF MWhe

'Florentina' (d)	CLoc CWVF EBak EKMF
'Florrie's Gem' (d)	SLBF
'Flowerdream'	CWVF
'Flyaway' (d)	EBak
'Fly-by-night' (d)	CWVF
'Flying Cloud' (d)	CLoc CSil CWVF EBak EKMF MBri
'Flying Scotsman' (d)	CDoC CLoc CWVF EBak EKMF EPts LVER MJac SVil
'Fohnhimmel' (d)	WP&B
'Folies Bergères' (d)	EBak
'Foolke'	CSil EBak EPts
'Forfar's Pride' (d)	CSil MWar
'Forget-me-not'	CLoc CSil CWVF EBak EKMF WP&B
'Fort Bragg' (d)	CWVF EBak
'Forward Look'	CDoC MWhe WP&B
'Fountains Abbey' (d)	CWVF EMan
'Four Farthings' (d)	EKMF WP&B
'Foxgrove Wood' ♀H3-4	CSil CWVF EBak EKMF EPts SLBF WFFs
'Foxtrot'	CWVF
'Foxy Lady' (d)	CWVF EKMF WP&B
'Frances Haskins'	CSil MWhe
'Frank Lawrence'	LCla
'Frank Saunders'	CWVF LCla
'Frank Unsworth' (d)	CHrt CWVF ECtt EKMF EPts MJac SPet
'Frankie's Magnificent Seven' (d)	EPts
'Frau Hilde Rademacher' (d)	CDoC CSil CWVF EBak EKMF EMan GLbr LVER SLBF SWal
'Fred Hansford'	CSil CWVF SLBF
'Fred's First' (d)	CDoC CSil EKMF
'Freefall'	EBak
'Friendly Fire' (d)	CLoc
'Frosted Flame'	CDoC CLoc CSil CWVF EBak EKMF LCla MJac MWar MWhe SPet SSea WP&B
'Frozen Tears'	WP&B
'Frühling' (d)	CSil EBak EKMF
'Fuchsiade '88'	CLoc CSil CWVF EBak EKMF MWhe
'Fuchsiarama '91'	CWVF WP&B
'Fuji-San'	CDoC EPts LCla
'Fuksie Foetsie'	CDoC CSil
fulgens ♀H1+3	CDoC EKMF GCal IFro LCla MOak MWhe
* - var. ***minuata***	EKMF
* - 'Variegata' (v)	CDoC CLoc CSil EKMF EPts LCla WP&B
'Fulpila'	LCla WP&B
furfuracea	EKMF
'Für Elise' (d)	EBak
'Gala' (d)	EBak
'Garden News' (d) ♀H3-4	CDoC CLoc CSil CWVF ECtt EKMF EPts GLbr LAst LCla LRHS LVER MGos MJac MWar MWhe NDlv NPer SLBF SPet SWal WFFs WFar WP&B
'Garden Week' (d)	CWVF MWhe WP&B
'Gartenmeister Bonstedt' ♀H1+3	CDoC CLoc CTbh CWVF EBak EKMF EPts LCla LRHS SPet SSea WP&B
'Gary Rhodes' (d) **new**	MJac
'Gay Anne' (d)	EKMF
'Gay Fandango' (d)	CLoc CWVF EBak ECtt LCla SPet WFFs
'Gay Future'	EKMF
'Gay Parasol' (d)	CLoc LAst MJac
'Gay Paree' (d)	EBak WP&B
'Gay Senorita'	EBak
'Gay Spinner' (d)	CLoc
gehrigeri	EBak EKMF LCla
'Gemma Fisher' (d)	EPts
Gene = 'Goetzgene'PBR (Shadowdancer Series)	LSou
'Général Monk' (d)	CDoC CSil CWVF EBak ECtt EKMF EMan EPts GLbr LAst LVER MBri WP&B
'Général Voyron'	CSil
'Genii' ♀H4	More than 30 suppliers
'Geoffrey Smith' (d)	CSil ECtt EKMF EPts
§ 'Georg Börnemann'	CDoC CLoc CWVF EBak
'Georgana' (d)	MWhe WP&B
'George Barr'	EKMF LRHS WFFs
'George Bartlett'	CLoc WFFs
'George Johnson'	CDoC SPet
'George Travis' (d)	EBak
'Georges Remy'	WP&B
'Gerald Drewitt'	CSil
§ 'Gerharda's Aubergine'	CLoc CSil CWVF EKMF WP&B
'Gerharda's Kiekeboe'	EKMF WP&B
§ 'Gesneriana'	CDoC CLoc EBak
'Giant Pink Enchanted' (d)	CLoc EBak
'Gilda'	CWVF MJac
'Gillian Althea' (d)	CDoC CWVF
'Gillian's Gem' (d)	SLBF
'Gilt Edge' (v)	CLoc
'Gina Bowman' **new**	LCla
'Gina's Gold' (d)	WP&B
Ginger = 'Goetzginger'PBR (Shadowdancer Series)	LSou NEgg
'Gipsy Princess' (d)	CLoc
'Girls' Brigade'	CWVF EKMF
'Gitana'	WP&B
'Gladiator' (d)	EBak EKMF LCla
'Gladys Cecilia' (d)	SLBF
'Gladys Godfrey'	EBak
'Gladys Lorimer'	CWVF EPts
'Gladys Miller'	CLoc
glazioviana	CDoC CSil CTbh CWVF EKMF LCla SLBF SWal WP&B
'Glenby' (d)	CWVF
'Glendale'	CWVF
'Glitters'	CWVF EBak EPts
§ 'Globosa'	CAgr CSil EBak EKMF EUnu
'Gloria Johnson'	EKMF
'Glow'	CSil EBak EKMF
'Glowing Embers'	EBak
Glowing Lilac (d)	CSil ECtt EMan EPts
'Glyn Jones' (d)	EKMF
'Gold Brocade'	CSil SPet SPoG SWal
'Gold Crest'	EBak
'Gold Leaf'	CWVF
'Golden Anniversary' (d)	CLoc CWVF EBak EKMF EMan GLbr LVER MJac WP&B
'Golden Arrow'	CDoC LCla WFFs WP&B
'Golden Border Queen'	CLoc
'Golden Dawn'	CLoc CWVF EBak ECtt SPet
'Golden Eden Lady' (v)	MWhe
'Golden Girl'	SLBF
'Golden Herald'	CSil SLBF
'Golden La Campanella' (d/v)	CLoc ECtt MBri
'Golden Lena' (d/v)	CSil CWVF EMan
'Golden Margaret Roe' (v)	CSil
'Golden Marinka' (v) ♀H3	CLoc EBak ECtt EKMF LAst LRHS LSou MBri SPet WFFs
'Golden Melody' (d)	CSil
'Golden Monique' **new**	WP&B
'Golden Swingtime' (d)	CHrt CSil ECtt EPts MBri MJac SPet SSea WP&B
'Golden Treasure' (v)	CLoc CSil CWVF ECtt EKMF MBri MWar
'Golden Vergeer' (v)	EKMF SLBF
'Golden Wedding'	EKMF
'Goldsworth Beauty'	CSil LCla

	'Golondrina'	CSil CWVF EBak
	'Goody Goody'	EBak
	'Gooseberry Hill'	WP&B
	'Gordon Boy' (d)	CSil
	'Gordon Thorley'	CSil EKMF MWhe
	'Gordon's China Rose'	LCla
	'Gorgeous Gemma' (d)	WP&B
	'Gottingen'	EBak EKMF WP&B
	'Governor 'Pat' Brown' (d)	EBak
	'Grace Darling'	CWVF EBak MWhe
	gracilis	see *F. magellanica* var. *gracilis*
	'Graf Witte'	CDoC CSil CWVF EKMF EPts NDlv SPet
	'Grand Duchess'	WP&B
	'Grand Duke' (d)	CWVF
	'Grandad Hobbs' (d)	LCla
	'Grandma Hobbs'	LCla
	'Grandma Sinton' (d)	CLoc CWVF EMan MBri MWhe
	'Grandpa George' (d)	CSil LCla
	'Grandpa Jack' (d)	SLBF
	'Grayrigg'	CDoC CSil EKMF EPts LCla NDlv
	'Great Ouse' (d)	EPts
	'Great Scott' (d)	CLoc
	'Green 'n' Gold'	EBak
	'Greenpeace'	EKMF SLBF WP&B
	'Greta'	CDoC MWar WFFs
	'Gretna Chase'	MBri MWhe
	'Grey Lady' (d)	CSil
	'Grietje'	WP&B
	'Groene Boelvaar' (d)	WP&B
	'Groene Kan's Glorie'	CDoC
	'Grumpy'	CDoC CSil CWVF EPts LRHS MBri MLan MWhe SPet
	'Gruss aus dem Bodethal'	CLoc CWVF EBak EKMF EPts WP&B
	'Guinevere'	CWVF EBak
	'Gustave Doré' (d)	CSil EBak EKMF
	'Guy Dauphine' (d)	EBak
	'Gwen Burralls' (d)	EKMF
	'Gwen Dodge'	LCla WP&B
	'Gypsy Girl' (d)	CWVF
*	'H.C. Brown'	LCla
	'H.G. Brown'	CSil EBak EKMF MWhe
	'Halsall Beauty' (d)	MBri
	'Halsall Belle' (d)	MBri
	'Halsall Pride' (d)	MBri
	'Hampshire Beauty' (d)	MJac
	'Hampshire Blue'	CDoC CWVF
	'Hampshire Prince' (d)	LVER
	'Hampshire Treasure' (d)	CWVF
	'Hanna' (d)	WP&B
	'Hannah Gwen' (d)	EKMF
	'Hannah Louise' (d)	EPts
	'Hannah Rogers'	MWar
	'Hans Callaars'	WP&B
	'Happy'	CDoC CSil CWVF EPts LCla SPet
	'Happy Anniversary'	CLoc
I	'Happy Anniversary' (d/v)	EKMF
	'Happy Fellow'	CDoC CLoc CSil EBak NDlv WFFs
	'Happy Wedding Day' (d)	CDoC CLoc CWVF ECtt EKMF EPts GLbr LAst MJac MWhe SCoo SPet WP&B
	'Hapsburgh'	EBak
	'Harbour Lites' **new**	SLBF
	'Harlow Car'	CDoC CWVF EKMF EPts
	'Harlow Perfection'	EKMF
I	'Harmony' Niederholzer	EBak
	'Harnser's Flight'	CSil
	'Harrow Pride' (d)	CSil
	'Harry Dunnett'	EBak
	'Harry Gray' (d)	CLoc CSil CWVF EBak ECtt EMan EPts GLbr LAst LCla MBri MJac MWhe NBlu SPet SSea
	'Harry Pullen'	EBak
	'Harry Taylor' (d)	EPts
	'Harry's Sunshine' **new**	SLBF
	'Hartis Phönix' **new**	WP&B
	'Hartis Schwarzer' **new**	SLBF
	hartwegii	CDoC CSil EKMF LCla
	'Hathersage' (d)	EBak
	'Hathor'	WP&B
	hatschbachii	CDoC CSil EPts LCla
	- Berry 4464	EKMF
	- Berry 4465	EKMF
	'Haute Cuisine' (d)	CLoc EMan LVER MWhe
	'Hawaiian Princess' (d)	ECtt
	'Hawaiian Sunset' (d)	CWVF LCla SLBF
	'Hawkshead' ♀H3-4	CDoC CLoc CSil CWVF ECha EKMF ELan EPfP EPts GCal GQui LCla LRHS MBri MGos MJac MWhe NChi SChu SGar SLBF SMrm SPet SPoG SWal WBcn WMnd WP&B
I	'Hazel' (d)	CWVF GLbr MWhe
	'Heart Throb' (d)	EBak
	'Heavenly Hayley' (d)	SLBF
	'Hebe'	EBak MWhe
I	'Hedens Montana'	WP&B
	'Heidi Ann' (d) ♀H3	CDoC CLoc CSil CWVF EBak EKMF EMan EPts LAst LCla MBri MWhe NDlv SLBF SPet SSea SWal WFFs
	'Heidi Blue' (d)	SLBF
	'Heidi Joy' **new**	CSil
§	'Heidi Weiss' (d)	CDoC CLoc CSil CWVF MBri SPet
	'Heinrich Henkel'	see *F.* 'Andenken an Heinrich Henkel'
	'Heinzelmännchen'	WP&B
	'Heirloom' (d)	ECtt EKMF
	'Helen Clare' (d)	CLoc CWVF EBak
	'Helen Gair' (d)	CWVF
	'Helen Nicholls' (d)	EKMF
	'Hella' **new**	WP&B
	'Hellen Devine'	CWVF
	'Hello Dolly'	CLoc
	'Hemsleyana'	see *F. microphylla* subsp. *hemsleyana*
	'Henkelly's Elegantie'	WP&B
	'Henkelly's Sam' **new**	WP&B
	'Henkelly's Stippelke'	WP&B
	'Henning Becker'	CWVF WP&B
	'Henri Poincaré'	EBak EKMF
	'Herald' ♀H4	CDoC CSil CWVF EBak EKMF MHar NDlv SLBF SWal
	'Herbé de Jacques'	see *F.* 'Mr West'
	'Heritage' (d)	CLoc CSil EBak EKMF
	'Herman de Graaff' (d)	EKMF WP&B
	'Hermiena'	CLoc CSil CWVF MWar MWhe SLBF WFFs WP&B
	'Heron'	CSil EBak EKMF
	'Herps Bonang' **new**	WP&B
	'Hertogin van Brabant' (d)	WP&B
	'Hessett Festival' (d)	CDoC CWVF EBak MWhe
	'Heston Blue' (d)	CWVF EKMF
	'Hettenheuvel'	WP&B
	'Hetty Blok' (d)	WP&B
	'Heydon'	CWVF
	'Hi Jinks' (d)	EBak
	hidalgensis	see *F. microphylla* subsp. *hidalgensis*
	'Hidcote Beauty'	CDoC CLoc CSil CWVF EBak MWhe SLBF SPet WFFs
	'Hidden Treasure'	MWar WP&B
	'Hier Ben Ik'	LCla
	'Highland Pipes'	CSil EKMF LCla
	'Hilda Fitzsimmons' **new**	WP&B
	'Hilda May Salmon'	CWVF

'Hindu Belle' EBak
'Hinnerike' CSil CWVF EPts LCla WP&B
'Hiroshige' LCla
'His Excellency' (d) EBak
'Hobo' (d) CSil MWar WP&B
'Hobson's Choice' (d) CWVF SLBF
'Hokusai' WP&B
'Holly Hobit' NMRc
'Holly's Beauty' (d) CDoC CLoc EKMF EPts GLbr LAst MWar WP&B
'Hollywood Park' (d) EBak
'Horatio' ECtt MJac
'Hot Coals' CLoc CSil CWVF ECtt EKMF EPts LCla MJac MWar MWhe WP&B
'Howard Hebdon' **new** EKMF
'Howlett's Hardy' CDoC CLoc CSil CWVF EBak ECtt EKMF EPts LRHS MBri NLar WMnd WP&B
'Hula Girl' (d) CWVF EBak EKMF MJac MWar MWhe SPet
'Humboldt Holiday' (d) EKMF
'Huntsman' (d) CDoC ECtt GLbr LAst MWhe
'Ian Brazewell' (d) CLoc
'Ian Leedham' (d) EBak
'Ian Storey' **new** CSil
'Ice Cream Soda' (d) EBak
'Ice Maiden' ambig. (d) WP&B
'Iceberg' CWVF EBak
'Icecap' CWVF EKMF MBri
'Iced Champagne' CLoc CWVF EBak GLbr MJac
'Ichiban' (d) CLoc WP&B
'Icicle' (d) WP&B
'Ida' (d) EBak
'Igloo Maid' (d) CLoc CWVF EBak EKMF MWhe SPet
'Illusion' WP&B
'Impala' (d) CWVF
'Imperial Fantasy' (d) CWVF
'Impudence' CLoc EBak SPet
'Impulse' (d) CLoc
'Indian Maid' (d) CWVF EBak LVER WP&B
inflata EKMF
'Insulinde' CDoC CFee CWVF EPts LCla MJac MWar SLBF WFFs WP&B WWol
'Interlude' (d) EBak
'Iolanthe' CWVF
'Irene L. Peartree' (d) CWVF LCla
'Irene Sinton' (d) **new** MJac SVil
'Iris Amer' (d) CLoc CWVF EBak
'Irish Dawn' MWar
'Irving Alexander' (d) WP&B
'Isabel Erkamp' WP&B
'Isabel Ryan' CSil
'Isis' ambig. WP&B
'Isis' Lemoine CSil
'Isle of Mull' CDoC CSil SPet WP&B
'Italiano' (d) CWVF MJac
'Ivana van Amsterdam' **new** WP&B
'Ivy Grace' CSil
'Jack Acland' CWVF ECtt
'Jack Shahan' ♀H3 CDoC CLoc CSil CWVF EBak EKMF EMan LAst LCla MBri MJac MWar MWhe SPet SSea WFFs
'Jack Stanway' (v) CSil CWVF EKMF EPts MWar
'Jack Wilson' CSil
'Jackie Bull' (d) CWVF EBak
'Jackpot' (d) EBak
'Jackqueline' CSil CWVF
'Jadas Mam' WP&B
'Jam Roll' (d) LVER
'Jamboree' (d) EBak
'James Lye' (d) CWVF EBak EKMF
'James Travis' (d) CDoC CSil EBak EKMF LCla
'Jandel' CWVF
'Jane Humber' (d) CWVF EKMF
'Jane Lye' EBak
'Janet Williams' (d) CSil
'Janice Ann' EKMF LCla MWar WFFs WP&B
'Janice Perry's Gold' (v) CLoc EShb MJac SLBF
'Janie' (d) MAsh
'Jap Vantveer' LCla WP&B
'Jaunty Jack' SLBF
'Jean Baker' CSil
'Jean Campbell' EBak
'Jean Clark' WP&B
'Jean Frisby' CLoc
'Jeane' EKMF NEgg
'Jeangil' WP&B
'Jennifer' EBak
'Jennifer Hampson' (d) CSil
'Jennifer Lister' (d) CSil EKMF
'Jenny Brinson' (d) WP&B
'Jenny May' CLoc EPts WP&B
'Jenny Sorensen' CWVF EKMF LCla
'Jess' LCla SLBF WP&B
'Jessie Pearson' CWVF
'Jessimae' CWVF SPet
'Jester' Holmes (d) CLoc CSil
'Jet Fire' (d) EBak
'Jezebel' WP&B
'Jiddles' LCla SLBF
'Jill Harris' WP&B
'Jill Whitworth' CDoC
'Jim Coleman' CWVF
'Jim Dodge' (d) EPts
'Jim Hawkins' EBak
'Jim Muncaster' CWVF EKMF
jimenezii EKMF LCla WP&B
– hybrid EKMF
'Jimmy Carr' (d) EKMF
'Jimmy Cricket' LCla
'Jingle Bells' MWhe
'Jinlye' EKMF
'Joan Barnes' (d) CDoC CSil CWVF
'Joan Cooper' CLoc CSil CWVF EBak EKMF SLBF
'Joan Goy' CWVF EKMF EPts MJac MWhe
'Joan Jones' (d) **new** MJac
'Joan Knight' CLoc
'Joan Leach' CSil
'Joan Margaret' (d) MJac
'Joan Morris' SLBF
'Joan Pacey' CWVF EBak EKMF
'Joan Paxton' (d) LCla
'Joan Smith' EBak
'Joan Waters' (d) CWVF
'Jo-Anne Fisher' (d) EPts
'Joan's Delight' **new** WP&B
'Joe Kusber' (d) CSil CWVF EBak MJac
'Joe Nicholls' (d) EKMF
'Joel' CLoc SLBF WP&B
'John Bartlett' CLoc
'John E. Caunt' CSil EKMF
'John Green' **new** EKMF
'John Grooms' (d) CLoc MJac
'John Lockyer' CLoc CWVF EBak
'John Maynard Scales' CDoC CWVF LCla MJac MWhe WP&B
'John Quirk' (d) SLBF
'John Stephens' EPts
'John Suckley' (d) EBak
'John Wright' CSil EKMF LCla
'Johnny' (d) CLoc
'Jomam' ♀H3 CLoc CWVF MWar WP&B
'Jon Oram' CLoc CWVF
'Jon Vincent' (d) **new** SLBF
'Jopie' (d) WP&B

	Name	Suppliers
	'Jose's Joan' (d)	CWVF
	'Joy Bielby'	EKMF
	'Joy Patmore'	CLoc CSil CWVF EBak EKMF EPts LCla MBri MWar MWhe SLBF SPet WP&B
	'Joyce'	WP&B
	'Joyce Adey' (d)	CWVF
	'Joyce Maynard' (d)	MJac
	'Joyce Sinton'	CWVF EMan MBri
	'Joyce Wilson' (d)	EPts LCla
	'Jubilee Quest'	LCla MWar
	'Judith Coupland'	CWVF
	'Juella' **new**	WP&B
	'Jules Daloges' (d)	EBak EKMF
	'Julia' (d)	EKMF WP&B
	'Julie Ann'	MWar
	'Julie Horton' (d)	WP&B
	'Julie Marie' (d)	CSil CWVF MJac
	'June Gardner'	CWVF EKMF
	'Jungle'	LCla WP&B
I	'Juno' Kennett	EBak
	juntasensis	EKMF WP&B
	'Jupiter Seventy'	EBak
	'Just a Tad' (d)	SLBF
	'Justin's Pride'	CDoC CSil EKMF
	'Jülchen'	CWVF WP&B
	'Kaboutertje'	EKMF
	'Kaleidoscope' (d)	EBak
	'Kallinga'	WP&B
	'Karen Bielby'	EKMF
	'Karen Isles'	LCla
	'Karen Louise' (d)	CLoc
	'Karin de Groot'	EKMF
	'Karin Siegers'	CSil
	'Kate Taylor' (d) **new**	SLBF
	'Kate Wylie'	MWar
	'Kath van Hanegem'	CSil EPts LCla SLBF WP&B
	'Kathleen Muncaster' (d)	EKMF WP&B
	'Kathleen Smith' (d)	ECtt EKMF
	'Kathleen van Hanegan'	CLoc MWar
	'Kathy Louise' (d)	EMan WP&B
	'Kathy's Pipes'	EKMF
	'Kathy's Prince'	ECtt EKMF
	'Kathy's Sparkler' (d)	EKMF
	'Katie Elizabeth Ann' (d)	MWar
	'Katie Rogers'	EPts
	'Katinka'	CWVF EPts LCla
	'Katjan'	CSil EKMF SLBF
	'Katrien Michiels'	WP&B
	'Katrina' (d)	CLoc EBak
	'Katrina Thompsen'	CLoc CWVF EKMF EPts MWar SLBF
	'Katy James'	EKMF MWar
	'Keepsake' (d)	CLoc EBak
	'Kegworth Carnival' (d)	CWVF
	'Kegworth Supreme'	MJac
	'Kelsey's Kisses' **new**	WP&B
	'Ken Goldsmith'	CWVF EPts SWal
	'Ken Jennings'	CWVF MJac
	'Ken Shelton'	SLBF
	'Kenny Dalglish' (d)	CSil EKMF
	'Kenny Holmes'	CWVF
	'Kenny Walkling'	SLBF
	'Kernan Robson' (d)	CLoc CWVF EBak
	'Kerry Anne'	EPts
	'Kevin R. Peake' (d)	MWar
	'Keystone'	EBak
	'Kim Nicholls' **new**	EKMF
	'Kim Wright' (d)	MWhe
	'Kimberly' (d)	EBak
	'King of Bath' (d)	EBak
	'King of Hearts' (d)	EBak
	'King's Ransom' (d)	CLoc CSil CWVF EBak LRHS MWhe SPet
	'Kiss 'n' Tell'	CWVF MJac MWhe
	'Kit Oxtoby' (d)	CHrt CWVF ECtt EKMF EMan GLbr LCla LVER MJac SVil WFFs WP&B
	'Kiwi' (d)	EBak
	'Klassic'	LCla SLBF
	'Knockout' (d)	CWVF EKMF
	'Kolding Perle'	CWVF EKMF SPet
	'Königin der Nacht'	WP&B
	'Kon-Tiki' (d)	CLoc EKMF SPet
	'Koralle'	see *F.* 'Coralle'
	'Krimar'	WP&B
	'Krommenie'	WP&B
	'Kwintet'	CWVF EBak LCla MJac SPet
	'Kyoto'	CWVF
	'La Bianca'	EBak
	'La Campanella' (d) 🏆H3	CDoC CLoc CSil CWVF EBak ECtt EKMF EMan EPts GLbr LAst LCla LSou MBri MJac MWar MWhe NVic SPet WFFs
	'La Fiesta' (d)	EBak
	'La France' (d)	EBak EKMF
	'La Neige' ambig.	CWVF
	'La Neige' Lemoine (d)	EBak EKMF
	'La Porte' (d)	CLoc CWVF
	'La Rosita' (d)	EBak SLBF
	'La Traviata' ambig.	WP&B
I	'La Traviata' Blackwell (d)	EBak
	'La Violetta' (d)	MWhe
	'Lace Petticoats' (d)	EBak EKMF
	'Lady Boothby'	CDoC CHEx CSil CWVF EBak EKMF EShb LRHS SLBF SMrm SPet SPoG WP&B
	'Lady Framlingham' (d)	EPts
	'Lady Heytesbury'	EKMF MJac
	'Lady in Grey' (d)	EKMF LAst MJac
	'Lady Isobel Barnett'	CDoC CLoc CSil CWVF EBak EKMF MBri MJac MWar MWhe SPet WP&B
	'Lady Kathleen Spence'	CWVF EBak MWhe SPet
	'Lady Patricia Mountbatten'	CWVF EKMF EMan MJac
	'Lady Ramsey'	EBak
	'Lady Rebecca' (d)	CLoc
	'Lady Thumb' (d) 🏆H3	More than 30 suppliers
	'Lady's Smock'	EKMF
	'Laing's Hybrid'	CWVF EBak
	'Lakeland Princess'	EBak
	'Lakeside'	CWVF EBak
	'Laleham Lass'	EKMF
	'Lambada'	GLbr LAst MJac MWar MWhe WFFs
	'Lancambe'	CSil
	'Lancashire Lad' (d)	GLbr LAst MWar WP&B
	'Lancashire Lass'	CWVF MBri
	'Lancelot'	EBak
	'Land van Beveren'	MWar SLBF WFFs WP&B
	'Lark'	CWVF EPts WP&B
	'L'Arlésienne' (d)	CLoc
	'Lassie' (d)	CDoC CLoc CWVF EBak
	'Laura' ambig.	CWVF
I	'Laura' (Dutch)	CLoc CSil EPts LCla MWar SLBF
I	'Laura' Martin (d)	EKMF MWhe
	'Laura Cross' **new**	MWar
	'Lavender Kate' (d)	CLoc CWVF EBak
	'Lavender Lace'	MWhe
	'Lazy Lady' (d)	CWVF EBak
	'Le Postier'	WP&B
	'Lea de Smedt' **new**	WP&B
	'Lea's Aubergine'	WP&B
	'Lechlade Apache'	CDoC LCla MWar
	'Lechlade Chinaman'	CDoC EKMF WFFs
	'Lechlade Debutante'	LCla
	'Lechlade Fire-eater'	CDoC LCla WP&B

	'Lechlade Gorgon'	CDoC CWVF EKMF LCla SLBF
	'Lechlade Magician'	CDoC CSil EKMF EPts LCla SLBF WFFs WSPU
	'Lechlade Maiden'	CWVF LCla
	'Lechlade Martianess'	LCla
	'Lechlade Potentate'	LCla
	'Lechlade Tinkerbell'	LCla
	'Lechlade Violet'	CDoC CSil EKMF
	lehmanii	LCla
	'Leicestershire Silver' (d)	MJac
	'Leila' (d)	WP&B
	'Len Bielby'	CDoC CWVF LCla
	'Lena' (d) 🏆H3	CDoC CLoc CSil CTri CWVF EBak EKMF EPts GLbr LAst LVER MBri MJac MWhe NDlv SPer SPet SSea WEas WP&B WWol
	'Lena Dalton' (d)	CLoc CWVF EBak MWhe
	'Leonhart von Fuchs'	WP&B
	'Leonora'	CDoC CLoc CSil CWVF EBak EKMF LCla MBri MWhe SLBF SPet
	'Lesley'	CWVF
	'Lett's Delight' (d)	CWVF EPts
	'Letty Lye'	EBak
	'Leverhulme'	see *F.* 'Leverkusen'
§	'Leverkusen'	CDoC CLoc EBak LCla MJac MWhe
	'Li Kai Lin'	CSil
	'Liebesträume' ambig.	WP&B
I	'Liebesträume' Blackwell (d)	EBak
	'Liebriez' (d) 🏆H3-4	CSil EBak EKMF EPts NDlv SPet SWal
	'Liemers Lantaern'	CWVF
	'Lieze Brantze'	WP&B
	'Likalin'	CWVF
	'Lilac'	CSil EBak
	'Lilac Dainty' (d)	CSil
	'Lilac Lustre' (d)	CLoc CWVF EBak SPet
	'Lilac Princess'	MJac
	'Lilac Queen' (d)	EBak
	'Lilian'	EKMF
	'Lillian Annetts' (d)	CDoC CWVF EKMF LAst LCla MJac MWar SLBF WFFs
	'Lillibet' (d)	CLoc CWVF EBak
	'Lime Lite' (d)	MJac
	'Linda Goulding'	CWVF EBak MWhe
	'Linda Grace'	EKMF EPts MJac MWar
	'Linda Mary Nutt'	MWar
	'Linda Rosling' (d)	EKMF
	'Lindisfarne' (d)	CLoc CWVF EBak EKMF MJac SPet
	'L'Ingénue'	WP&B
	'Linlithgow Lass'	MWar SLBF
	'Lionel'	CSil
	'Lisa' (d)	CDoC EPts WP&B
	'Lisa Jane'	MWhe
	'Lisa Rowe' (d)	WP&B
	'Lisi'	WP&B
	'Little Annie Gee'	MWar
	'Little Baby'	EKMF
	'Little Beauty'	CDoC CSil CWVF EKMF MWhe WP&B
	'Little Boy Blue'	EPts
	'Little Brook Gem'	SLBF
	'Little Catbells'	SLBF
	'Little Gene'	EBak
	'Little Jewel'	SPet
	'Little Nan' **new**	SLBF
	'Little Orphan Annie'	LCla
	'Little Ouse' (d)	CWVF MWhe
	'Little Snow Queen'	WP&B
	'Little Witch'	EKMF LCla SLBF
	'Liz' (d)	CSil EBak EKMF
	Liza = 'Goetzliza'PBR (Shadowdancer Series)	LAst LSou
	'Lochinver' (d)	CWVF
	'Loeke's Marie-Lou'	WP&B
	'Loeky'	CLoc CWVF EBak SPet
	'Logan Garden'	see *F. magellanica* 'Logan Woods'
	'Lolita' (d)	CWVF EBak
	'London 2000'	LCla MJac SLBF WP&B
	'London in Bloom'	SLBF WP&B
	'Lonely Ballerina' (d)	CLoc CWVF
	'Long Wings'	EKMF LCla
	'Lonneke'	WP&B
	'Lord Byron'	CLoc EBak EKMF
	'Lord Derby'	CSil
	'Lord Jim'	LCla
	'Lord Lonsdale'	CWVF EBak EPts LCla MWhe WP&B
	'Lord Roberts'	CLoc CSil CWVF
	'Lorelei'	EPts
	'Lorna Fairclough'	MJac
	'Lorna Swinbank'	CLoc CWVF
	'Lottie Hobby' 🏆H1+3	CDoC CLoc CSil CWVF ECtt EKMF EPfP EPts LCla LRHS MHar MOak MWhe SPet WFFs
	'Louise Emershaw' (d)	CWVF EBak MJac
	'Louise Nicholls'	EKMF SLBF
	'Lovable' (d)	EBak
	'Loveliness'	CLoc CWVF EBak EKMF MWhe
	'Lovely Blue' (d)	WP&B
	'Lovely Les' (d)	LCla
	'Lovely Linda'	SLBF
	'Love's Reward' 🏆H1+3	CLoc CWVF EKMF EPts LCla MJac MWar MWhe SLBF WP&B
	'Lower Raydon'	EBak
I	'Loxensis'	CDoC CWVF EBak EKMF LCla
	- Berry 3233	EKMF
	- DG 1001	EKMF
	loxensis misapplied	see *F.* 'Speciosa', *F.* 'Loxensis'
	'Loxhore Calypso'	EKMF
	'Loxhore Fairy Dancer'	CSil LCla
	'Loxhore Herald'	CSil
	'Loxhore Lullaby'	CSil
	'Loxhore Mazurka'	CSil WFFs WP&B
	'Loxhore Minuet'	CSil LCla
	'Loxhore Operetta'	CSil
	'Loxhore Posthorn'	CSil LCla
	'Lucinda'	CWVF
	'Lucky Strike' (d)	CLoc EBak
	Lucy = 'Goetzlucy' (Shadowdancer Series)	EBak
	'Lucy Locket'	MJac
	'Lukas'	WP&B
	'Lunter's Trots' (d)	WP&B
	'Luscious Lisa' **new**	WP&B
	'Lustre'	CWVF EBak
	'Lutz Bogemann'	WP&B
§	***lycioides*** Andrews	EBak EKMF
I	'Lycioides'	LCla
	'Lye's Elegance'	CSil EKMF
	'Lye's Excelsior'	EBak
	'Lye's Own'	EBak SPet
	'Lye's Perfection'	EKMF
	'Lye's Unique' 🏆H1+3	CDoC CLoc CSil CWVF EBak EKMF EPts LCla MJac MWar MWhe SLBF SPet WFFs
	'Lynette' (d)	CLoc
	'Lynn Ellen' (d)	CWVF EBak
	'Lynne Marshall'	CSil
	'Lyric'	WP&B
	'Maartje'	WP&B
	'Mabel Greaves' (d)	CWVF WP&B
	'Machu Picchu'	CLoc CWVF EKMF EPts LCla WP&B
	macrophylla	WMoo
	- BEA 922539	EKMF

	Name	Suppliers
	- Berry 3080	EKMF
	- Berry 80-539	EKMF
	- Berry 80-541	EKMF
	- Dahl, S.	EKMF
	macrostigma	EKMF
	'Madame Aubin'	EKMF
	'Madame Butterfly' (d)	CLoc
	'Madame Cornélissen' (d) ♀H3	More than 30 suppliers
	'Madame Eva Boye'	EBak EKMF
	'Madeleine Sweeney' (d)	MBri
	'Maes-y-Groes'	CSil EKMF
	magdalenae	EKMF WP&B
	magellanica	CAby CDoC COld CWib EKMF EMil GGar NFor NLon NPer NWea SPer WFar WPnn WRha WSSM
	- 'Alba'	see *F. magellanica* var. *molinae*
I	- 'Alba Aureovariegata' (v)	CDoC EPfP LAst MBri SPer WBcn WFar
	- 'Alba Variegata' (v)	CSil NPol
	- 'Americana Elegans'	CDoC CSil
	- 'Comber'	CSil
	- var. ***conica***	CDoC CSil EKMF
	- 'Derek Cook'	WBcn
	- var. ***discolor***	CSil
	- 'Exmoor Gold' (v)	CSil WBcn
	- 'Fire Gold'	LRHS
§	- var. ***gracilis*** ♀H3	CDoC CHEx CLoc CSil CTri CWVF EKMF LRHS MWhe SCoo WPnn
	- - 'Aurea'	CDoC CSil CWVF EHoe EKMF ELan ENot EPfP GAbr GQui ISea LAst LCla LRHS MRav MWhe SAga SCoo SDix SLBF SPer SPet SPla WFar
§	- - 'Tricolor' (v)	CDoC CSLe CSil EHol EKMF EPts EWes EWin GAbr LCla LRHS SLBF SRms WCFE WPnn WWpP
	- - 'Variegata' (v) ♀H3	CSil EBak EBee EKMF ENot EPfP LCla LRHS LSou MGos MRav SAga SChu SDix SIng SPer SPet SPoG WBVN WPnn
	- 'Lady Bacon'	EKMF MSte
§	- 'Logan Woods'	CDoC CSil EKMF GCal ISea SLBF WBcn WSPU
	- 'Longipedunculata'	CDoC CSil EKMF
	- var. ***macrostema***	CSil EKMF
§	- var. ***molinae***	More than 30 suppliers
§	- - 'Enstone' (v)	CBrm CSBt EHoe EKMF EMil EPts
	- - 'Enstone Gold'	EKMF
	- - 'Golden Sharpitor' (v)	CBgR LAst LSou MDKP WGor
§	- - 'Sharpitor' (v)	More than 30 suppliers
	- var. ***myrtifolia***	CDoC CSil EKMF
*	- var. ***prostrata***	CSil
	- var. ***pumila***	CBgR CDoC CSil ETow EWes GCal LAst SBla SHGN SIng SMHy SPer SRot
§	- 'Thompsonii'	CDoC CSil ECGP EKMF GCal SBch SMHy
§	- 'Versicolor' (v)	More than 30 suppliers
	'Magenta Flush'	CWVF
	'Magic Flute'	CLoc CWVF MJac
	'Maharaja' (d)	EBak
	'Major Heaphy'	CWVF EBak EKMF MWhe
	'Malibu Mist' (d)	CWVF LVER WP&B
	'Mama Bleuss' (d)	EBak
	'Mancunian' (d)	CSil CWVF
I	'Mandarin' Schnabel	EBak
	'Mandi'	EWll LCla MWar
	'Mantilla'	CDoC CLoc CSil CWVF EBak EKMF MJac MWhe
	'Maori Pipes'	CSil
	'Marcia'PBR (Shadowdancer Series)	LAst LSou
	'Marcus Graham' (d)	CLoc CWVF EBak EKMF MWar MWhe SCoo SVil WP&B
	'Marcus Hanton' (d)	CWVF LCla
	'Mardi Gras' (d)	EBak
	'Margam Park'	LCla
	'Margaret' (d) ♀H4	CDoC CLoc CSil CTri CWVF EBak EKMF ENot EPts ISea LCla LVER MWar MWhe NDlv SLBF SPet SWal WP&B
	'Margaret Berger' (d)	SLBF
	'Margaret Brown' ♀H4	CDoC CLoc CSil CTri CWVF EBak EKMF LCla MHar MWhe NDlv SLBF SPet SWal WFFs
	'Margaret Davidson' (d)	CLoc
	'Margaret Ellen'	WP&B
	'Margaret Hazelwood'	EKMF
	'Margaret Pilkington'	CWVF MWar SSea
	'Margaret Roe'	CDoC CSil CWVF EBak EKMF MJac SPet SWal
	'Margaret Rose'	MJac
	'Margaret Susan'	EBak
	'Margaret Tebbit'	LAst MJac WGor
	'Margarite Dawson' (d)	CSil
	'Margery Blake'	CDoC CSil EBak
	'Margrit Willimann'	WP&B
	'Maria Landy'	CWVF EKMF EMan LCla MJac MWar WFFs
	'Maria Merrills' (d)	EMan
	'Marie Helene Meus'	WP&B
	'Marielle van Dummelen' **new**	WP&B
	'Mariken'	WP&B
	'Marilyn Olsen'	CWVF EPts LCla
	'Marin Belle'	EBak
	'Marin Glow' ♀H3	CLoc CSil CWVF EBak MWhe SLBF SPet
	'Marinka' ♀H3	CLoc CSil CWVF EBak ECtt EKMF EMan EPts GLbr LAst LCla LVER MBri MJac MWar MWhe SLBF SPet SSea WFFs
	'Marion Hilton'	MWar SLBF
	'Mark Kirby' (d)	CWVF EBak EKMF WP&B
	'Marlies de Keijzer'	LCla SLBF
	'Martin Beye' **new**	WP&B
	'Martina' **new**	SLBF
	'Martin's Inspiration'	LCla MWar
	'Martin's Midnight' (d)	WP&B
	'Martin's Umbrella'	WP&B
	'Martin's Yellow Surprise'	CLoc LCla SLBF
	'Martinus' (d)	WP&B
	'Marton Smith'	MWhe
	'Marty' (d)	EBak
	'Mary' ♀H1+3	CDoC CLoc CSil CWVF EKMF EPts LCla LRHS MLan MWar MWhe SLBF WP&B
	'Mary Ellen Guffey' (d)	SLBF
	'Mary Jones' (d)	EKMF
	'Mary Lockyer' (d)	CLoc EBak
	'Mary Poppins'	CWVF
	'Mary Reynolds' (d)	CWVF
	'Mary Shead' (d)	MWar
	'Mary Thorne'	CSil EBak EKMF
	'Mary's Millennium'	CWVF
	'Masquerade' (d)	CWVF EBak EMan
	'Matador'	CSil
	'Maureen Ward'	EKMF
	'Mauve Beauty' (d)	CSil CWVF EKMF NDlv
	'Mauve Lace' (d)	CSil
	'Max Jaffa'	CSil CWVF
I	'Maxima'	EKMF WP&B
	'Maybe Baby'	GLbr
	'Mayblossom' (d)	CWVF ECtt SPet
	'Mayfayre' (d)	CLoc

	Name	Suppliers
	'Mayfield'	CWVF MWhe
	'Mazda'	CWVF
	'Meadowlark' (d)	CWVF EBak ECtt EKMF
	'Mechtildis de Lechy'	WP&B
	'Meditation' (d)	CLoc CSil
	'Melanie'	CDoC WP&B
	'Melissa Heavens'	CWVF
	'Melody'	EBak MWhe SPet
	'Melody Ann' (d)	EBak
	'Melting Moments' (d)	EKMF WP&B
	'Menna'	WP&B
	'Mephisto'	CSil CWVF
	'Mercurius'	CSil WP&B
	'Merlin'	CDoC CSil EKMF LCla
	'Merry Mary' (d)	CWVF EBak EKMF
I	'Mexicali Rose' Machado	CLoc
	'Michael' (d)	CWVF EPts
	'Michael Swann' **new**	MWar
	'Michael Wallis' **new**	EKMF LCla SLBF
	michoacanensis misapplied	see *F. microphylla* subsp. *aprica*
	michoacanensis Sessé & Moç. B&SWJ 8982	WCru
	'Micky Goult' ♀H1+3	CLoc CWVF EKMF EPts LCla MJac MWhe SPet WFFs WP&B
	'Microchip'	CSil LCla
	microphylla	CBrd CDoC CElw CLoc CPLG CSil CTbh CWVF EBak GCal GGar MLan MWhe SLon STre WBor WCru WEas WFFs
	- B&SWJ 9101	WCru
§	- subsp. ***aprica***	LCla
	- - BRE 69862	EKMF
§	- subsp. ***hemsleyana***	CDoC CPLG CSil EKMF LCla MHar MWhe SWal WOut
§	- subsp. ***hidalgensis***	CSil CTbh EKMF LCla
	- subsp. ***microphylla***	CSil EKMF
§	- subsp. ***minimiflora***	CTbh
	- subsp. ***quercetorum***	CDoC CSil EKMF LCla
	- 'Sparkle' (v)	WCot
	'Midas'	CWVF MBri
	'Midnight Sun' (d)	CSil CWVF EBak EPts
	'Midwinter'	LAst
	'Mieke Meursing' ♀H1+3	CLoc CWVF EBak ECtt EKMF GLbr MJac MWhe SPet
	'Mien Kuypers'	WP&B
	'Miep Aalhuizen'	LCla WP&B
	'Mike Foxon' **new**	EKMF
	'Mike Oxtoby'	CWVF EKMF
	'Mikey's Reward' **new**	WP&B
	'Mildred Wagg'	MWar
	'Millennium' **new**	CLoc EPts SCoo
	'Millie Butler'	CWVF
	'Ming'	CLoc
	'Miniature Jewels'	LCla SLBF
	minimiflora Hemsley	see *F. microphylla* subsp. *minimiflora*
	'Minirose'	CDoC CSil CWVF EPts MJac MWar MWhe
	'Minnesota' (d)	EBak
	'Mipan'	SLBF
	'Mischief'	CSil
	'Miss California' (d)	CDoC CLoc CWVF EBak ECtt MBri MWhe WFFs
	'Miss Great Britain'	CWVF
	'Miss Lye'	CSil EKMF
	'Miss Muffett' (d)	CSil SIng
	'Miss Vallejo' (d)	EBak
	'Mission Bells'	CDoC CLoc CSil CWVF EBak EKMF EPts SPet WFFs
	'Misty Blue' (d)	CSil
	'Misty Haze' (d)	CWVF LVER

	Name	Suppliers
	'Moira Ann'	ECtt
	'Molesworth' (d)	CSil CWVF EBak EKMF MJac MWhe SPet
	'Mollie Beaulah' (d)	CSil CWVF ECtt EKMF WP&B
	'Money Spinner'	CLoc EBak
	'Monique Comperen' **new**	WP&B
	'Monsieur Thibaut' ♀H4	CSil EKMF ENot SPet
	'Monte Rosa' (d)	CLoc CWVF
	'Monterey'	MWhe
	'Montevideo' (d)	CWVF
	'Monument' (d)	CSil
	'Mood Indigo' (d)	CSil CWVF LVER WP&B
	'Moon Glow'	LAst MJac WP&B
	'Moonbeam' (d)	CLoc MWhe
	'Moonlight Sonata'	CLoc CWVF EBak SPet
	'Moonraker' (d)	CWVF
	'More Applause' (d)	CLoc EKMF LVER MWhe WP&B
	'Morecott' (d)	CWVF
	'Morning Light' (d)	CLoc CWVF EBak SPet
	'Morning Mist'	EBak
	'Morning Star'	MBri
	'Morrells' (d)	EBak
	'Moth Blue' (d)	CSil CWVF EBak SPet
	'Mountain Mist' (d)	CWVF EKMF
	'Moyra' (d)	CWVF EKMF
	'Mr A. Huggett'	CLoc CSil CWVF EKMF EPts LCla MWhe SPet
	'Mr P.D. Lee'	MWhe
	'Mr W. Rundle'	EBak WP&B
§	'Mr West' (v)	CSil EHoe EKMF SPet
	'Mrs Churchill'	CLoc
	'Mrs John D. Fredericks'	CSil
	'Mrs Lawrence Lyon' (d)	EBak
	'Mrs Lovell Swisher' ♀H4	CDoC CSil CWVF EBak EPts LCla MJac MWhe SPet WP&B
	'Mrs Marshall'	CSil CWVF EBak SLBF SPet
	'Mrs Popple' ♀H3	More than 30 suppliers
	'Mrs W. Castle'	CSil EKMF
	'Mrs W.P. Wood' ♀H3	CDoC CLoc CSil CWVF EKMF EPts MBri WFFs WP&B
	'Mrs W. Rundle'	CLoc CSil CWVF EBak EKMF LRHS MWhe SLBF SPet WP&B
	'Multa'	LAst MJac WFFs
	'Muriel' (d)	CLoc CWVF EBak ECtt EKMF
	'My Delight'	CWVF
	'My Fair Lady' (d)	CLoc CWVF EBak SPet
	'My Honey'	CSil
	'My Mum'	LCla SLBF WP&B
	'My Reward' (d)	CWVF
	'Naaldwijk 800'	WP&B
	'Nancy Darnley' (d)	EKMF
	'Nancy Lou' (d)	CDoC CLoc CWVF EPts LAst LCla LVER MJac MWhe SLBF SPet WFFs
	'Nanny Ed' (d)	CWVF MBri
	'Naomi Eggli' **new**	WP&B
	'Natalia' **new**	WP&B
	'Natasha Sinton' (d)	CLoc CSil CWVF ECtt EKMF EMan LAst LVER MBri MJac MWhe SLBF SPet WFFs WP&B
	'Native Dancer' (d)	CWVF EBak WP&B
	'Naughty Nicole' (d)	SLBF WP&B
	'Nautilus' (d)	EBak EKMF
	'Navy Blue'	CSil
	'Neapolitan' (d)	CDoC EPts MWhe SLBF
	'Neil Clyne'	MWhe
	'Nell Gwyn'	CLoc CWVF EBak
	'Nellie Nuttall' ♀H3	CLoc CSil CWVF EBak EKMF EPts MWar MWhe SLBF SPet WFFs
	'Neopolitan'	CLoc CSil WFFs
	'Nettala'	CDoC WP&B
	'Neue Welt'	CSil CWVF EBak EKMF
	'New Fascination' (d)	EBak
	'New Millennium'	GLbr LVER

'Newmel'	MWar
'Nice 'n' Easy' (d)	LVER MBri MJac
'Nicki's Findling'	CDoC CSil CWVF EKMF EPts LCla MJac WFFs
'Nicola'	CLoc EBak
'Nicola Jane' (d)	CDoC CSil CWVF EBak EKMF EPts LCla MBri MJac MWhe SLBF SPet SWal WP&B
'Nicola Storey' **new**	WP&B
'Nicolette'	CWVF MJac
'Nightingale' (d)	CLoc CWVF EBak
§ ***nigricans***	CDoC EKMF LCla
nigricans x ***gehrigeri***	EKMF
'Nina Wills'	EBak
'Niobe' (d)	EBak
'Niula'	CDoC EKMF LCla
'No Name' (d)	EBak
'Nonchalance'	LCla
'Nora' (d)	WP&B
'Norfolk Ivor' (d)	WP&B
'Normandy Bell'	CWVF EBak SPet
'North Cascades' (d)	WP&B
'Northern Dancer' (d)	EKMF GLbr
'Northumbrian Belle'	EBak
'Northumbrian Pipes'	LCla WP&B
'Northway'	CLoc CWVF MJac MWhe SPet
'Norvell Gillespie' (d)	EBak
'Novato'	EBak EPts
'Novella' (d)	CWVF EBak
'Nuance'	LCla WP&B
'Nunthorpe Gem' (d)	CDoC CSil
obconica	CSil EKMF LCla
'Obcylin'	EKMF LCla SLBF
'Obergärtner Koch'	EKMF LCla SLBF
'Ocean Beach'	EPts
'Oddfellow' (d)	CDoC
'Oetnang' (d)	CTri SCoo
'Old Somerset' (v)	LCla WP&B
'Olive Moon' (d)	WP&B
'Olive Smith'	CWVF EPts LCla MJac MWar MWhe WP&B
'Olympia'	EKMF MWhe
'Olympic Lass' (d)	EBak
'Onward'	CSil EKMF WFFs
§ 'Oosje'	CDoC CSil LCla SLBF WFFs
'Opalescent' (d)	CLoc CWVF
'Orange Crush'	CLoc CWVF EBak MJac MWhe SPet
'Orange Crystal'	CWVF EBak EKMF MJac MWhe SPet
'Orange Drops'	CLoc CSil CWVF EBak EKMF EPts MWhe SPet
'Orange Flare'	CLoc CWVF EBak MWhe SLBF
'Orange King' (d)	CLoc CSil CWVF EMan
'Orange Mirage'	CLoc CSil CWVF EBak LAst LVER MWhe SPet WFFs
'Orangeblossom'	SLBF
'Oranje van Os'	CWVF MJac MWhe
'Orchid Flame'	WP&B
'Orient Express'	CDoC CWVF LAst MJac MWhe SWal WFFs WP&B
'Oriental Flame'	EKMF
'Oriental Sunrise'	CWVF MWhe
'Ornamental Pearl'	CLoc CWVF EBak
'Orwell' (d)	CWVF WP&B
'Oso Sweet'	CWVF
'Other Fellow'	CSil CWVF EBak EKMF EPts LCla MJac MWhe SLBF SPet
'Oulton Empress'	SLBF
'Oulton Fairy'	SLBF
'Oulton Red Imp'	LCla SLBF
'Oulton Travellers Rest'	SLBF
'Our Darling'	CWVF MWhe
'Our Debbie' **new**	MWar
'Our Nan' (d)	MJac
'Our Ted'	EKMF EPts WP&B
'Our William'	SLBF WP&B
'Overbecks'	see *F. magellanica* var. *molinae* 'Sharpitor'
'Overbecks Ruby'	GBuc
'Pabbe's Torreldöve'	WP&B
'Pacemaker'	MGos
pachyrrhiza	EKMF
'Pacific Grove' Greene	see *F.* 'Evelyn Steele Little'
'Pacific Grove' Niederholzer (d)	EBak
'Pacific Queen' (d)	CLoc EBak
'Pacquesa' (d)	CDoC CWVF EBak EPts MWhe SPet
'Padre Pio' (d)	CWVF EBak MJac
'Pallas'	CSil
pallescens	EKMF LCla
'Paloma'PBR	GLbr LAst
'Pam Plack'	CSil EKMF LCla
'Pamela Knights' (d)	EBak
'Pam's People'	LCla
'Pan'	MWar WP&B
'Pan America' (d)	EBak
'Panache' (d)	LCla
'Pangea'	LCla WP&B
paniculata ♀H1+3	CDoC CEnd CRHN CTbh CWVF EBak EGra EKMF EPts LCla SHFr SLBF WCru
'Panique'	CSil LCla
'Pantaloons' (d)	EBak
'Pantomine Dame' (d)	CWVF
'Panylla Prince'	CDoC EPts LCla
'Papa Bleuss' (d)	CLoc CWVF EBak
'Papoose' (d)	CDoC CSil EBak EKMF GLbr LCla WFFs
'Papua' (d)	SLBF WP&B
'Parkstone Centenary' (d)	CWVF
'Party Frock'	CDoC CLoc CWVF EBak LVER SPet
'Party Time' (d)	CWVF
parviflora hort.	see *F.* x *bacillaris*
§ ***parviflora*** Lindley	EBak
'Pastel'	EBak
'Pat Meara'	CLoc EBak
'Patatin Pataton' (d)	WP&B
'Pathétique' (d)	CLoc
'Patience' (d)	CWVF EBak MJac SWal
'Patio King'	EKMF
'Patio Princess' (d)	CWVF EPts LAst LCla MBri MJac MWhe SSea WFFs WGor
'Patricia' Wood	CSil EBak
'Patricia Bervoets' (d)	WP&B
'Pat's Smile' **new**	SLBF
'Patty Evans' (d)	CWVF EBak
'Patty Sue' (d)	MBri
'Paul Berry'	CSil EKMF LCla WP&B
'Paul Cambon' (d)	EBak EKMF
'Paul Kennes' **new**	WP&B
'Paul Roe' (d)	MJac
'Paul Storey'	CSil EKMF WP&B
'Paula Jane' (d)	CDoC CLoc CWVF GLbr LAst LCla MBri MJac MWar MWhe SLBF WFFs WGor WP&B
'Pauline Rawlins' (d)	CLoc EBak
'Paulus'	WP&B
'Peace' (d)	EBak
'Peaches 'n' Cream'	LCla
'Peachy' (d)	CDoC EKMF GLbr LAst MJac SCoo WP&B
'Peachy Keen' (d)	EBak WP&B
'Peacock' (d)	CLoc
'Pearly Gates'	CWVF

Name	Suppliers
'Pearly King' (d)	CWVF
'Pee Wee Rose'	CSil EBak EKMF MAsh
'Peggy Burford' **new**	LCla
'Peggy Cole'	EPts
Peggy = 'Goetzpeg' (Shadowdancer Series)	LAst LSou
'Peggy King'	CDoC CSil EBak EKMF LCla MWhe SPet
'Peloria' (d)	CLoc EBak
'Pennine'	MBri
'People's Princess'	MJac
'Peper Harow'	EBak
'Pepi' (d)	CLoc CWVF EBak SPet
'Peppermint Candy' (d)	CWVF EPts GLbr LAst
'Peppermint Stick' (d)	CDoC CLoc CSil CWVF EBak EKMF EMan LRHS LVER MBri MJac MWhe SPet
'Perky Pink' (d)	CWVF EBak EPts MWhe SPet
'Perry Park'	CWVF EBak MBri MJac
'Perry's Jumbo'	NBir NPer
perscandens	CSil EKMF LCla MWhe
'Personality' (d)	EBak
'Peter Bellerby' (d)	EKMF
'Peter Bielby' (d)	CWVF EKMF LCla MWar
'Peter Boor' **new**	SLBF
'Peter Crookes'	CWVF
'Peter Grange'	EBak
'Peter James' (d)	CSil EKMF
'Peter Pan'	CSil CWVF SIng
'Peter Sanderson'	MJac
petiolaris	CDoC LCla
- Berry 3142	EKMF
'Petit Four'	CWVF WP&B
'Petite' (d)	EBak
'Phaidra'	LCla
'Pharaoh'	CLoc
'Phénoménal' (d)	CSil CWVF EBak EKMF EPts GLbr LRHS WP&B
'Philippe' **new**	WP&B
'Phillip Taylor'	MJac
'Phyllis' (d) ♀H4	CDoC CLoc CSil CWVF EBak EKMF EPts LCla MHar MJac MWhe NDlv SLBF SPet WFFs WFar WP&B WTel
'Phyrne' (d)	CSil EBak EKMF
'Piet G. Vergeer'	WP&B
'Piet van der Sande'	LCla
pilaloensis	EKMF
x ***pilcopata***	LCla
'Pinch Me' (d)	CWVF EBak EKMF LVER SPet
'Pink Aurora'	CLoc
'Pink Ballet Girl' (d)	CLoc EBak ECtt
'Pink Bon Accorde'	CLoc CWVF
'Pink Cloud'	CLoc EBak
'Pink Cornet'	LCla
'Pink Darling'	CLoc EBak MWhe
'Pink Dessert'	EBak
'Pink Domino' (d)	EKMF
'Pink Fairy' (d)	CWVF EBak SPet
'Pink Fandango' (d)	CLoc
'Pink Fantasia'	CDoC CLoc CSil CWVF EBak EKMF EPts LAst LCla MJac MWar MWhe WP&B
'Pink Flamenco' (d) **new**	SLBF
'Pink Flamingo' (d)	CLoc EBak
'Pink Galore' (d)	CLoc CSil CWVF EBak EKMF EMan GLbr LAst LCla LVER MBri MJac MWhe SPet SSea WP&B
'Pink Goon' (d)	CDoC CSil EKMF LCla LRHS NDlv SLBF
'Pink Jade'	CWVF EBak
'Pink la Campanella'	CWVF EBak EMan GLbr LAst MBri MWar MWhe WBVN WGor
'Pink Lace' (d)	CSil SPet
'Pink Lady' Ryle-Atkinson	MWhe
'Pink Marshmallow' (d) ♀H1+3	CDoC CHrt CLoc CSil CWVF EBak EKMF EMan GLbr LAst LCla LVER MJac MWar SLBF SPet SSea
'Pink Panther' (d)	EKMF MJac WFFs
'Pink Pearl' Bright (d)	CSil EBak EKMF LVER
'Pink Picotee'	MJac
'Pink Profusion'	EBak
'Pink Quartet' (d)	CLoc CWVF EBak SPet
'Pink Rain'	CSil CWVF EKMF EPts MJac WFFs WP&B
'Pink Slippers'	CLoc
'Pink Spangles'	CWVF EMan MBri
'Pink Surprise' (d)	MJac
'Pink Temptation'	CLoc CWVF EBak
'Pink Trumpet'	WP&B
'Pinkmost' (d)	ECtt EKMF
'Pinto de Blue' (d)	EKMF LCla MWar WP&B
'Pinwheel' (d)	CLoc EBak
'Piper' (d)	CDoC CSil CWVF
'Piper's Vale'	LCla MJac SLBF SWal WFFs
'Pippa Rolt'	EKMF EPts
'Pirbright'	CWVF EKMF
'Pixie'	CDoC CLoc CSil CWVF EBak EKMF MJac NDlv SLBF SPet
'Playford'	CWVF EBak
'Plenty'	CSil EBak
'Plumb Bob' (d)	CWVF
'Poermenneke'	WP&B
'Pole Star'	CSil
'Pop Whitlock' (v)	CWVF EKMF SPet WP&B
'Popely Pride' (d)	WP&B
'Poppet'	CWVF
'Popsie Girl'	MWar SLBF
'Port Arthur' (d)	CSil EBak
'Postiljon'	CWVF EBak MJac SPet WFFs
'Powder Puff' ambig.	CWVF ECtt MBri SPet
'Powder Puff' Hodges (d)	CLoc LVER
I 'Powder Puff' Tabraham (d)	CSil
'Prelude' Blackwell	CLoc CSil
I 'Prelude' Kennett (d)	EBak EKMF
'President'	CDoC CSil EBak EKMF LCla WFFs
'President B.W. Rawlins'	EBak
§ 'President Elliot'	CPLG CSil EKMF MWhe
'President George Bartlett' (d)	CSil EKMF EPts LAst LCla MAsh MJac MWar SLBF WFFs
'President Jim Muil' **new**	SLBF WP&B
'President Joan Morris' (d)	EKMF SLBF
'President Leo Boullemier'	CDoC CSil CWVF EBak ECtt EKMF LCla MJac SPet WFFs
'President Margaret Slater'	CLoc CSil CWVF EBak EMan LCla MJac MWhe SPet
'President Moir' (d)	SLBF WP&B
'President Norman Hobbs'	CWVF EKMF MWar
'President Roosevelt' (d)	CDoC ECtt
'President Stanley Wilson'	CWVF EBak ECtt EPts SPet
'Preston Guild' ♀H1+3	CDoC CLoc CSil CWVF EBak EKMF LRHS MWar MWhe NPer SLBF SPet WFFs
'Prickly Heat' **new**	WP&B
'Pride of the West'	CSil EBak EKMF
'Pride of Windsor' **new**	SLBF
'Prince of Orange'	CLoc CSil CWVF EBak EKMF
'Princess Dollar'	see *F.* 'Dollar Princess'
'Princess of Bath' (d)	CLoc
'Princess Pamela' (d)	SLBF
'Princessita'	CSil CWVF EBak ECtt EMan MJac MWhe SPet
procumbens	More than 30 suppliers
- 'Argentea'	see *F. procumbens* 'Wirral'
- 'Variegata'	see *F. procumbens* 'Wirral'
§ - 'Wirral' (v)	CDoC CHEx CLoc CSil CStu EKMF WBor WCot

	'Prodigy'	see *F.* 'Enfant Prodigue'
	'Profusion' ambig.	EKMF MWhe
	'Prosperity' (d) $\mathbb{Y}^{H3}$	CDoC CLoc CSil CWVF EBak EBee EKMF ENot EPfP EPts LCla LRHS LVER MJac MWar MWhe NDlv SPet SWal
	'Pumila'	CPLG CWib ECha EKMF ELan EPfP EPts SPet SWal
	'Purbeck Mist' (d)	CWVF EKMF
	'Purperklokje'	CSil CWVF EBak LCla WP&B
	'Purple Ann'	EKMF
	'Purple Emperor' (d)	CLoc
	'Purple Heart' (d)	CLoc EBak
	'Purple Lace'	CSil
	'Purple Patch'	MBri
	'Purple Pride'	MBri
	'Purple Rain'	CLoc CSil EKMF EPts
	'Purple Splendour' (d)	CDoC CSil
	'Pussy Cat'	CLoc CWVF EBak WP&B
	'Putney Pride'	EPts
	'Put's Folly'	CWVF EBak MJac WFFs
	putumayensis	CSil EBak
	'Quasar' (d)	CDoC CLoc CSil CTbh CWVF EKMF EPts GLbr LAst LCla LRHS LSou LVER MJac MWhe SLBF SPet WBVN WP&B
	'Queen Elizabeth II'	EKMF LCla
	'Queen Mabs'	EBak
	'Queen Mary'	CLoc CSil EBak EKMF
	'Queen of Bath' (d)	EBak
	'Queen of Derby' (d)	CSil CWVF LCla
	'Queen Victoria' Smith (d)	EKMF
	'Queen's Park' (d)	EBak
	'Query'	CSil EBak WP&B
	'R.A.F.' (d)	CLoc CSil CWVF EBak ECtt EKMF EPts GLbr LCla MWar SLBF SPet WP&B
	'Rachel Craig' (d)	MWar
	'Rachel Sinton' (d)	EMan LAst MBri
	'Radcliffe Beauty'	MWhe
	'Radcliffe Bedder' (d)	CSil EKMF
	'Radings Gerda'	LCla
	'Radings Karin'	CDoC WP&B
	'Radings Mia'	LCla
	'Radings Michelle'	CSil CWVF LCla
	'Rahnee'	CWVF
	'Rainbow'	CWVF
	'Ralph Oliver' (d)	WP&B
	'Ralph's Delight' (d)	CWVF EKMF LAst MJac WP&B
	'Rambling Rose' (d)	CLoc CWVF EBak ECtt MJac
	'Rams Royal' (d)	CDoC LVER MJac
I	'Raspberry' (d)	CLoc CWVF EBak LCla MWhe
	'Raspberry Sweet' (d)	CWVF
	'Ratae Beauty'	CWVF
	'Ratatouille' (d)	EKMF
	ravenii	CSil LCla
	'Ravensbarrow'	CSil WP&B
	'Ravenslaw'	CSil EKMF
	'Ray Redfern'	CWVF
	'Razzle Dazzle' (d)	EBak
	'Reading Show' (d)	CSil CWVF EKMF EPts LCla
	'Rebecca Williamson' (d)	CWVF MJac MWhe WP&B
	'Rebeka Sinton'	CLoc EBak MBri
	'Red Ace' (d)	CSil
	'Red Imp' (d)	CSil
	'Red Jacket' (d)	CWVF EBak
	'Red Petticoat'	CWVF
	'Red Rain'	CWVF LCla WP&B
	'Red Ribbons' (d)	EBak
	'Red Rover'	MWar
	'Red Rum' (d)	CSil SPet
	'Red Shadows' (d)	CLoc CSil CWVF EBak MJac
	'Red Spider'	CLoc CSil CWVF EBak EKMF EMan LAst MWar MWhe SCoo SPet WGor WP&B
	'Red Sunlight'	EPts
	'Red Wing'	CLoc
	'Reflexa'	see *F.* x *bacillaris* 'Reflexa'
	'Reg Gubler'	SLBF
	'Regal'	CLoc
	regia	CSil EHol
	- var. ***alpestris***	see *F. alpestris*
	- subsp. ***regia***	CDoC CSil EPts LCla
	- - Berry 4450	EKMF
	- - Berry 77-87	EKMF
	- - Berry 87-87	EKMF
	- subsp. ***reitzii***	CDoC CSil LCla
	- - Berry 04-87	EKMF
	- - Berry 67A-87	EKMF
	- subsp. ***serrae***	CSil
	- - Berry 11-87	EKMF
	- - Berry 4504	EKMF
	- - Berry 49-87	EKMF
	'Remember Eric'	EKMF
	'Remembrance' (d)	CSil EKMF EPts LCla SLBF
	'Remus' (d)	CSil
	'Remy Kind' (d)	WP&B
	'Rene Schwab'	LCla
	'Rensina'	WP&B
	'Requiem'	CLoc
	'Reverend Doctor Brown' (d)	EBak
	'Reverend Elliott'	see *F.* 'President Elliot'
I	'Rhapsody' Blackwell (d)	CLoc
	'Rhombifolia'	CSil
	'Ria V.D. Leest' **new**	WP&B
	'Rianne Foks'	WP&B
§	'Riccartonii' $\mathbb{Y}^{H3}$	More than 30 suppliers
	'Richard John Carrington'	CSil
	'Ridestar' (d)	CLoc CWVF EBak EMan MJac MWhe
	'Rijs 2001'	MWar SLBF
	'Rina Felix'	WP&B
	'Ringwood Market' (d)	CSil CWVF ECtt EKMF EPts LCla MJac SCoo SPet
	'Robbie'	EKMF WP&B
	'Robin Hood' (d)	CSil NDlv
	'Rocket'	WP&B
	'Rocket Fire' (d)	CWVF EPts GLbr LAst
	'Rodeo'	WP&B
	'Roesse Blacky'	EKMF WP&B
	'Roesse Esli'	WP&B
	'Roesse Femke'	WP&B
	'Roesse Marie'	GLbr WP&B
	'Roesse Procyon' **new**	WP&B
	'Roesse Tricolor'	GLbr WP&B
	'Roger de Cooker'	CLoc SLBF WP&B
	'Rohees Alchita'	GLbr
	'Rohees Alioth' (d)	GLbr WP&B
	'Rohees Azha'	GLbr WP&B
	'Rohees Canopus'	WP&B
	'Rohees Emperor' (d) **new**	SLBF
	'Rohees Izar'	WP&B
	'Rohees King'	WP&B
	'Rohees Ksora' (d)	WP&B
	'Rohees Leada' (d) **new**	SLBF
	'Rohees Maasym'	WP&B
	'Rohees Menkar'	GLbr
	'Rohees Metallah'	WP&B
	'Rohees Minkar'	WP&B
	'Rohees Mira'	WP&B
	'Rohees Naos'	WP&B
	'Rohees Nekkar'	GLbr WP&B
	'Rohees New Millennium' (d)	LCla SLBF WP&B
	'Rohees Nunki'	WP&B

Name	Suppliers
'Rohees Queen'	WP&B
'Rohees Rana'	WP&B
'Rohees Reda' (d)	WP&B
'Rohees Rotanev'	WP&B
'Rohees Sadir'	WP&B
'Rohees Segin'	WP&B
'Rohees Zaurak' **new**	WP&B
'Rolla' (d)	CWVF EBak EKMF
'Rolt's Bride' (d)	EKMF
'Rolt's Ruby' (d)	CSil EKMF EPts
'Roman City' (d)	CLoc WP&B
'Romance' (d)	CWVF
'Romany Rose'	CLoc
'Ron Chambers Love'	MWar
'Ron Ewart'	EKMF MWhe
'Ronald L. Lockerbie' (d)	CLoc CWVF
'Ron's Ruby'	CSil LCla MWhe WP&B
'Roos Breytenbach'	CDoC EKMF LAst LCla MJac WFFs WP&B
'Rosamunda'	CLoc
'Rose Aylett' (d)	EBak
'Rose Bradwardine' (d)	EBak
'Rose Churchill' (d)	MBri MJac
'Rose Fantasia'	CDoC CLoc CSil CWVF EKMF EPts LAst LCla MJac MWar MWhe SLBF WFFs WP&B
'Rose Marie' (d)	CLoc
'Rose of Castile'	CDoC CLoc CSil EBak EKMF LCla LRHS MJac MWhe WFFs
'Rose of Castile Improved' 🏆H4	CSil CWVF EBak EKMF LCla MJac MWar SPet WP&B
'Rose of Denmark'	CLoc CSil CWVF EBak LAst MBri MJac MWar MWhe SCoo SPet SWal WGor WP&B
'Rose Reverie' (d)	EBak
'Rose Winston' (d)	LAst SCoo
rosea hort.	see *F.* 'Globosa'
rosea Ruíz & Pav.	see *F. lycioides* Andrews
'Rosebud' (d)	EBak WP&B
'Rosecroft Beauty' (d)	CSil CWVF EBak MWhe
Rosella = 'Goetzrose' (Shadowdancer Series)	WP&B
'Rosemarie Higham'	EShb MJac
'Rosemary Day'	CLoc
'Roslyn Lowe' (d)	CDoC
'Ross Lea' (d)	CSil
'Roswitha'	SLBF
'Rosy Bows'	CWVF
'Rosy Frills' (d)	CWVF LCla MJac MWhe
'Rosy Morn' (d)	CLoc EBak
'Rosy Ruffles' (d)	EKMF
'Rough Silk'	CLoc CSil CWVF EBak
'Roy Castle' (d)	CWVF
'Roy Sinton'	LAst
'Roy Walker' (d)	CLoc CWVF LVER MJac
'Royal and Ancient'	CWVF
'Royal Mosaic' (d)	CDoC CWVF GLbr LAst MJac WP&B
'Royal Orchid'	EBak
'Royal Purple' (d)	CSil EBak EKMF GLbr MBri
'Royal Serenade' (d)	CWVF
'Royal Touch' (d)	EBak WP&B
'Royal Velvet' (d) 🏆H3	CLoc CSil CWVF EBak EKMF EMan EPts GLbr LAst LCla LVER MJac MWar MWhe SLBF SPet
'Royal Wedding'	LCla
'Rubra Grandiflora'	CWVF EBak EKMF LCla SLBF
'Ruby Wedding' (d)	CSil CWVF EKMF GLbr SLBF WP&B
'Ruddigore'	CWVF WP&B
'Ruffles' (d)	CWVF EBak
§ 'Rufus' 🏆H3-4	CDoC CLoc CSil CTri CWVF EBak EHol EKMF EPts LCla LRHS MHar MJac MWar MWhe NDlv SLBF SPet
'Rufus the Red'	see *F.* 'Rufus'
'Rummens Trots'	WP&B
'Ruth'	CSil
'Ruth Brazewell' (d)	CLoc
'Ruth King' (d)	CWVF EBak ECtt
'Sailor'	EPts MJac WFFs
'Sally Bell'	CSil
'Salmon Cascade'	CSil CWVF EBak ECtt EKMF EMan EPts LCla MJac MWhe SLBF WP&B
'Salmon Glow'	CWVF MJac MWhe
'Samba'	GLbr LAst
'Sam's Song' (d)	MJac
'Samson' (d/v)	EBak
'San Diego' (d)	CSil CWVF
'San Francisco'	EBak
'San Leandro' (d)	EBak
'San Mateo' (d)	EBak
§ ***sanctae-rosae***	EBak EKMF EPts LCla WP&B
'Sandboy'	CWVF EBak
'Sanguinea'	CSil EKMF
'Sanrina'	EKMF
'Santa Cruz' (d)	CSil CWVF EBak EKMF GLbr LCla MWhe NDlv SLBF SWal
'Santa Lucia' (d)	CLoc EBak
'Santa Monica' (d)	EBak
'Santorini Sunset' **new**	WP&B
'Sapphire' (d)	CSil EBak
'Sara Helen' (d)	CLoc EBak
'Sarah Eliza' (d)	SCoo
'Sarah Elizabeth'	GLbr
'Sarah Jane' (d)	CSil EBak
'Sarah Louise'	CWVF
'Sarong' (d)	EBak
'Satellite'	CLoc CWVF EBak EKMF SPet WP&B
'Saturnus'	CSil CWVF EBak SPet
scabriuscula	CDoC EKMF LCla
scandens	see *F. decussata*
'Scarcity'	CDoC CSil CWVF EBak EKMF MWhe SPet SWal WFFs
'Scarlet Cascade'	EKMF
'Schiller' ambig.	EKMF
'Schimpens Glorie' (d)	WP&B
'Schlosz Bentheim'	WP&B
'Schneckerl' (d)	SLBF
'Schneeball' (d)	CSil EBak EKMF
'Schneewitcher'	EKMF EPts
'Schneewittchen' Hoech	CSil EKMF
'Schneewittchen' Klein	CSil EBak
'Schönbrunner Schuljubiläum'	EBak
I 'Schöne Wilhelmine'	see *F.* 'Die Schöne Wilhelmine'
'Scotch Heather' (d)	CWVF
'Sea Shell' (d)	CWVF EBak
'Seaforth'	EBak EKMF
'Sealand Prince'	CDoC CWVF ECtt EKMF LCla
'Sebastopol' (d)	CLoc
'Seppe' **new**	WP&B
serratifolia Hook.	see *F. austromontana*
serratifolia Ruíz & Pav.	see *F. denticulata*
sessilifolia	LCla
'Seventh Heaven' (d)	CLoc CWVF GLbr LAst MJac
'Severn Queen'	CWVF
'Shady Blue'	CWVF
'Shangri-La' (d)	EBak WP&B
'Shanley'	CWVF WP&B
'Shannon So Special' (d) **new**	SLBF
'Sharon Allsop' (d)	CWVF MWhe
'Sharon Caunt' (d)	CSil EKMF
'Sharon Leslie' **new**	SLBF

	'Sharonelle'	EKMF
	'Sharpitor'	see *F. magellanica* var. *molinae* 'Sharpitor'
	'Shauna Lindsay'	LCla
	'Sheila Crooks' (d)	CWVF EBak EMan MJac WP&B
	'Sheila Kirby'	CWVF MJac
	'Sheila Mary' (d)	EKMF
	'Sheila Steele' (d)	CWVF
	'Sheila's Love'	MJac
	'Sheila's Surprise' (d)	SLBF
	'Shekirb' (d)	MJac
	'Shelford'	CDoC CLoc CWVF EBak EKMF EMan EPts LCla MJac MWar MWhe SLBF SSea WFFs WP&B
	'Shell Pink'	CSil
	'Shirley Halladay' (d)	EKMF LCla
	'Shirley'[PBR] (Shadowdancer Series)	LAst LSou
	'Shooting Star' (d)	EBak
	'Showfire'	EBak
	'Showtime' (d)	CWVF
	'Shy Lady' (d)	SPet
	'Siberoet'	WP&B
	'Sierra Blue' (d)	CLoc CWVF EBak
	'Silver Anniversary' (d)	EKMF
	'Silver Dawn' (d)	CSil CWVF EKMF EPts SLBF
	'Silver Dollar'	MWhe
	'Silver Pink'	CSil
	'Silverdale'	CDoC CSil EKMF MWhe
	'Simmari'	GLbr WP&B
	'Simon J. Rowell'	LCla
	'Simone Delhommeau'	WP&B
	'Simple Simon'	CSil
	simplicicaulis	EBak EKMF LCla
	'Sincerity' (d)	CLoc
	'Sint Bartholomeus' (d)	WP&B
	'Sinton's Standard'	MBri
	'Siobhan'	CWVF
	'Siobhan Evans' (d) **new**	MWar
	'Sir Alfred Ramsey'	CWVF EBak MWhe
	'Sir Matt Busby' (d)	EKMF EPts GLbr LAst MJac WP&B
	'Sir Steve Redgrave' (d) **new**	MJac
	'Siren' Baker (d)	EBak
	'Sissy Sue'	WP&B
	'Sister Ann Haley'	EKMF EPts
	'Sister Sister' (d)	SLBF WP&B
	'Six Squadron'	EKMF
	skutchiana	CPLG SMrm
	'Sleepy'	CSil EPts MBri SPet WFFs
	'Sleigh Bells'	CLoc CSil CWVF EBak EKMF MWhe SPet WP&B
	'Small Pipes'	CWVF EKMF LCla WP&B
	'Smokey Mountain' (d)	MJac MWar
	'Smoky' (d)	GLbr
	'Smouldering Fires'	WP&B
	'Sneezy'	CSil EPts MWhe
	'Snow Burner' (d)	CDoC CWVF LAst WP&B
	'Snow White' (d)	CSil SPet
	'Snowbird' (d)	MWar SLBF WP&B
§	'Snowcap' (d) ♀H3-4	CDoC CLoc CSil CWVF EBak EKMF EPts GKir GLbr LAst LCla LVER MBNS MBri MGos MJac MWar MWhe NPer SIng SLBF SPet SPla SWal WFFs WFar WP&B
	'Snowdon' (d)	CWVF
	'Snowdrift' Colville (d)	CLoc
	'Snowdrift' Kennett (d)	EBak
	'Snowfall'	CWVF
	'Snowfire' (d)	CLoc CSil CWVF ECtt EKMF MJac MWhe SCoo WP&B
	'Snowflake'	EKMF LCla SLBF WBor
	'Snowstorm' (d)	ECtt SPet
	'So Big' (d)	EKMF
	'Sofie Michiels' **new**	WP&B
	'Softpink Jubelteen'	WP&B
	'Son of Thumb' ♀H4	CDoC CLoc COkL CSil CWVF EKMF EMan EPfP EPts LAst MAsh MBar MBri MGos MJac MWhe NDlv SIng SLBF SPet WFFs WFar WP&B
	'Sonata' (d)	CLoc CWVF EBak
	'Sophie Louise'	EKMF EPts MWar WP&B
	'Sophie's Silver Lining'	MJac SVil
	'Sophie's Surprise'	WP&B
	'Sophisticated Lady' (d)	CLoc CWVF EBak ECtt EKMF EPts LVER SPet
	'Soroptimist International'	MWar
	'South Gate' (d)	CHrt CLoc CWVF EBak EKMF EMan EPts GLbr LAst MBri MJac MWar MWhe SPet WFFs WP&B
	'South Lakeland'	CSil
	'South Seas' (d)	EBak
	'Southern Pride'	SLBF
	'Southlanders'	EBak
	'Southwell Minster'	EKMF
	'Space Shuttle'	CLoc EKMF LCla MWhe SLBF
	'Sparky'	CDoC CWVF EPts LCla MWar MWhe WFFs WP&B
§	'Speciosa'	EBak EKMF LCla MWhe SWal
	'Spice of Life' (d)	CWVF
	'Spion Kop' (d)	CDoC CWVF EBak EKMF GLbr LAst MJac MWar MWhe SPet WGor
§	***splendens*** ♀H1+3	CAby CDoC CLoc CSec CTbh EBak EKMF EPts LCla NPer
	- 'Karl Hartweg'	CDoC
	'Spring Bells' (d)	MWhe
	'Squadron Leader' (d)	CWVF EBak EPts LVER
	'Stanley Cash' (d)	CLoc CSil CWVF EKMF LVER MWar SPet
	'Star Wars'	MBri MJac MWar MWhe SVil WP&B
	'Stardust'	CWVF EBak MJac MWhe
	'Steirerblut'	WP&B
	'Stella Ann'	CSil CWVF EBak EPts LCla WP&B
	'Stella Didden' (d)	WP&B
	'Stella Marina' (d)	CLoc EBak
I	'Stephanie Wheat'	MWar
	'Stewart Taylor'	MJac
	steyermarkii DG 1057	EKMF
	'Straat Magelhaen'	LCla
	'Straat Malakka'	LCla
	'Straat Napier'	WP&B
	'Straat of Plenty' **new**	LCla
	'Strawberry Delight' (d)	CLoc CWVF EBak ECtt EKMF LVER MJac MWhe SPet
	'Strawberry Mousse' (d)	LVER
	'Strawberry Sundae' (d)	CLoc CWVF EBak
	'Strawberry Supreme' (d)	CSil EKMF
	'String of Pearls'	CLoc CWVF EKMF MJac SLBF SPet WP&B
	'Stuart Joe'	CWVF EKMF
	'Student Prince'	CWVF
	'Sue'	SLBF
	'Sugar Almond' (d)	CWVF
	'Sugar Blues' (d)	CDoC EBak
	'Summer Bells' **new**	WP&B
	'Summerdaffodil'	SLBF WP&B
	'Sunkissed' (d)	COtt EBak
	'Sunningdale'	CDoC CWVF LCla
	'Sunny'	COtt
	'Sunny Smiles'	CSil CWVF EKMF SPet
	'Sunray' (v)	CLoc CTbh CWVF EBak EHoe EKMF ENot LRHS MAsh MBNS MWar MWat NEgg NMRc NSti SPla SPoG SWal WP&B

	Name	Suppliers
	'Sunset'	CLoc CSil CWVF EBak MWhe SPer
	'Sunset Boulevard' (d)	CDoC
	'Supersport' (d)	CDoC WP&B
	'Superstar'	CWVF EPts WP&B
	'Susan' (d)	COtt LAst
	'Susan Drew'	SLBF
	'Susan Ford' (d)	CWVF SPet
	'Susan Green'	CDoC CSil CWVF EBak EKMF EMan MJac MWar MWhe SPet
	'Susan McMaster'	CLoc
	'Susan Olcese' (d)	CWVF EBak
	'Susan Skeen'	MJac WP&B
	'Susan Travis'	CLoc CSil CWVF EBak EKMF MWhe SPet
	'Swanley Gem' 𝕐H3	CLoc CWVF EBak EKMF MWhe SLBF SPet
	'Swanley Pendula'	CLoc
	'Swanley Yellow'	CWVF EBak
	'Sweet Gilly' (d) **new**	SLBF
	'Sweet Leilani' (d)	CLoc EBak
	'Sweet Sarah'	SLBF
	'Sweet Sixteen' (d)	CLoc
I	'Sweetheart' van Wieringen	EBak
	'Swingtime' (d) 𝕐H3	CLoc CSil CWVF EBak EKMF EMan EPts GLbr LAst LCla LVER MGos MJac MWar MWhe SLBF SPet WP&B
	'S'Wonderful' (d)	CLoc EBak
	sylvatica misapplied	see *F. nigricans*
	sylvatica Benth.	EKMF LCla
	'Sylvia Barker'	CWVF LCla MJac MWar WFFs
	'Sylvia Noad'	MWar
	'Sylvia Rose' (d)	CWVF
	'Sylvia's Choice'	EBak
	'Sylvy'	MWhe
	'Symphony'	CLoc CWVF EBak
	'T.S.J.'	LCla
	'Taatje'	WP&B
	'Taco'	LCla
	'Taddle'	CWVF EMan MJac SLBF SPet
	'Taffeta Bow' (d)	CLoc EKMF LVER
	'Taffy'	EBak WP&B
	'Tahoe'	WP&B
	'Tamerus Hoatzin' **new**	WP&B
	'Tamworth'	CLoc CWVF EBak MJac
	'Tangerine'	CLoc CSil CWVF EBak MWhe
	'Tanja's Snowball' **new**	WP&B
	'Tantalising Tracy' (d)	SLBF WP&B
	'Tanya'	CLoc EKMF SPet
	'Tanya Bridger' (d)	EBak
	'Tarra Valley'	LCla MWhe
	'Task Force'	CWVF
	'Tausendschön' (d)	CLoc ECtt
	'Ted Perry' (d)	CWVF
	'Temptation' ambig.	CWVF ECtt SPet
	'Temptation' Peterson	CLoc EBak
	'Tennessee Waltz' (d) 𝕐H3	CDoC CLoc CSil CWVF EBak EKMF EMan EPts GLbr LCla LRHS LVER MJac MWar MWhe SChu SLBF SPer SPet WEas WP&B
	'Tessa Jane'	CSil
	tetradactyla misapplied	see *F.* x *bacillaris*
	'Texas Longhorn' (d)	CLoc CSil CWVF EBak EKMF WP&B
	'Texas Star'	WP&B
	'Thalia' 𝕐H1+3	CDoC CHEx CHrt CLoc CSil CTbh CWVF EBak ECtt EKMF EPts LAst LCla LRHS LVER MBri MJac MOak MWar MWhe NBlu SLBF SPet SPla SPoG SWal WEas WFFs WP&B
	'Thamar'	CDoC CLoc CSil CWVF EPts MWhe WFFs WP&B
	'That's It' (d)	EBak WP&B
	'The Aristocrat' (d)	CLoc EBak
§	'The Doctor'	CLoc CSil CWVF EBak EKMF MWhe
	'The Jester' (d)	EBak
	'The Madame' (d)	CWVF EBak
	'The Tarns'	CSil CWVF EBak EKMF NCiC
	'Theresa Drew'	SLBF
	'Therese Dupois'	CSil
	'Théroigne de Méricourt'	EBak EKMF
	'Thilco'	CSil EKMF
	'Thistle Hill' (d)	CSil EKMF
	'Thompsonii'	see *F. magellanica* 'Thompsonii'
	'Thornley's Hardy'	CSil EMan SPet
	'Three Cheers'	CLoc EBak
	'Three Counties'	EBak
	'Thunderbird' (d)	CLoc CWVF EBak
	thymifolia	CWVF GQui SHFr SHGN SIng WKif
	- subsp. ***minimiflora***	CSil EKMF LCla
	- subsp. ***thymifolia***	CDoC CSil EKMF LCla WKif
	'Tiara' (d)	EBak
	'Tickled Pink' **new**	MWar
	'Tiffany' Reedstrom (d)	EBak
	'Tijl Uilenspiegel'	WP&B
	'Tilla Dohmen'	WP&B
	tillettiana	EKMF
	'Tillingbourne' (d)	CSil EKMF LCla
	'Tillmouth Lass'	EKMF
	Tilly = 'Goetztil' (Shadowdancer Series)	LAst
	'Timlin Brened'	CSil CWVF EBak MWhe
	'Timothy Titus'	LCla MWar SLBF
	'Tina's Teardrops' (d)	WP&B
	'Ting-a-ling'	CDoC CLoc CSil CWVF EBak MWhe SLBF SPet WP&B
	'Tinker Bell' ambig.	CDoC
	'Tinker Bell' Hodges	EBak
I	'Tinker Bell' Tabraham	CSil EKMF WP&B
	'Tintern Abbey'	CWVF
	'Tjinegara'	LCla
	'Toby Bridger' (d)	CLoc EBak
	'Tolling Bell'	CWVF EBak MJac MWhe SPet WP&B
	'Tom Goedeman'	LCla
	'Tom H. Oliver' (d)	EBak
	'Tom Knights'	CDoC EBak MWhe SPet
	'Tom Thorne'	EBak
	'Tom Thumb' 𝕐H3	More than 30 suppliers
	'Tom West' misapplied	see *F.* 'Mr West'
	'Tom West' Meillez (v)	More than 30 suppliers
	'Tom Woods'	CWVF MWhe
	'Tony Porter' (d)	MJac
	'Tony's Treat' (d)	EPts
	'Topaz' (d)	CLoc EBak
	'Topper' (d)	CWVF EMan
	'Torch' (d)	CLoc CWVF EBak
	'Torchlight'	CWVF EPts LCla
	'Torvill and Dean' (d)	CLoc CWVF EKMF EPts LAst LRHS LVER MJac MWhe SPet WGor WWeb
	'Tosca'	CWVF
	'Trabant'	WP&B
	'Tracid' (d)	CLoc CSil
	'Tracie Ann' (d)	EKMF WP&B
	'Trail Blazer' (d)	CLoc CSil CWVF EBak MJac SPet
	'Trailing King'	WP&B
	'Trailing Queen'	CSil EBak EKMF MJac WP&B
	'Trase' (d)	CDoC CSil CWVF CWib EBak EKMF EPts GLbr LVER SWal WP&B
	'Traudchen Bonstedt'	CDoC CLoc CSil CWVF EBak EKMF EPts LCla MWhe SLBF SPet WFFs WP&B
	'Traviata'	see *F.* 'La Traviata' Blackwell

'Treasure' (d) EBak
'Tresco' CSil WBcn
'Treslong' WP&B
I 'Triantha' WP&B
'Tricolor' see *F. magellanica* var. *gracilis* 'Tricolor'
'Tricolorii' see *F. magellanica* var. *gracilis* 'Tricolor'
'Trientje' LCla
'Trimley Bells' EBak
'Trio' (d) CLoc
triphylla EBak EKMF LCla LRHS
- 'Dominica' WP&B
'Trish's Triumph' **new** EPts
'Tristesse' (d) CLoc CWVF EBak
'Troika' (d) EBak EKMF
'Troon' CWVF
'Tropic Sunset' (d) MBri MWhe
'Tropicana' (d) CLoc CWVF EBak
'Troubador' Waltz (d) CLoc
'Troutbeck' CSil
'Trudi Davro' CHrt GLbr LAst MJac
'Trudy' CSil CWVF EBak EKMF SPet SWal
'True Love' GLbr WP&B
'Truly Treena' (d) SLBF
'Trumpeter' ambig. CDoC CWVF WP&B
'Trumpeter' Reiter CLoc EBak EKMF EPts LAst LCla MJac MWhe
'Tsjiep' CDoC
'Tubular Bells' EKMF LCla WP&B
'Tumbling Waters' (d) LVER
'Tuonela' (d) CLoc CWVF EBak MWhe WP&B
'Turandot' GLbr
'Turkish Delight' LAst MJac MWar SVil WFFs WP&B
'Tutti-frutti' (d) CLoc
'Twinkletoes' EPts
'Twinkling Stars' CSil CWVF MJac WP&B
'Twinney' CWVF
'Twinny' EKMF EPts LCla MWar SLBF
'Twirling Square Dancer' (d) WP&B
'Twist of Fate' (d) CSil EKMF
'Two Tiers' (d) CSil CWVF EKMF WP&B
'U.F.O.' CWVF
'Uillean Pipes' WP&B
'Ullswater' (d) CWVF EBak LVER
'Ultramar' (d) EBak
'Uncle Charley' (d) CDoC CLoc CSil EBak EKMF
'Uncle Jinks' SPet
'Uncle Steve' (d) EBak
'University of Liverpool' MJac
'Upward Look' EBak EKMF
'Valda May' (d) CWVF
'Valentine' (d) EBak
'Valerie Ann' (d) EBak SPet WFFs
'Valerie Hobbs' (d) LCla
'Valerie Tooke' (d) LCla
'Valiant' EBak
'Vanessa' (d) CLoc
'Vanessa Jackson' CLoc CWVF MJac MWhe
'Vanity Fair' (d) CLoc EBak
vargasiana CDoC
'Variegated Brenda White' (v) EKMF
'Variegated la Campanella' (d/v) MWhe
'Variegated Lottie Hobby' (v) CSil EKMF EPts LCla
'Variegated Pixie' CSil EKMF
'Variegated Procumbens' see *F. procumbens* 'Wirral'
'Variegated Snowcap' (d/v) MWhe
'Variegated Superstar' (v) MBri
'Variegated Swingtime' (v) EBak LAst
'Variegated Vivienne Thompson' (d/v) MBri
'Variegated Waveney Sunrise' (v) MBri
'Variegated White Joy' (v) EKMF
'Veenlust' LAst MJac WP&B
'Vendeta' LCla
'Venus Victrix' CSil EBak EKMF MWhe SLBF
venusta CDoC EBak EKMF LCla
'Versicolor' see *F. magellanica* 'Versicolor'
'Vesuvio' EKMF
'Vicky' EKMF
'Victorian' (d) CSil
'Victory' Reiter (d) EBak
'Vielliebchen' CDoC CSil
'Vincent van Gogh' WP&B
'Violet Bassett-Burr' (d) CLoc EBak
'Violet Gem' (d) CLoc
'Violet Lace' (d) CSil
'Violet Rosette' (d) CWVF EBak
Violette = 'Goetzviolet' (Shadowdancer Series) LAst LSou
'Viva Ireland' EBak ECtt
'Vivien Colville' CLoc EKMF
'Vobeglo' CWVF
'Vogue' (d) EBak
'Voltaire' CSil EBak EKMF
'Voodoo' (d) CDoC CLoc CSil CWVF EBak EKMF EMan EPts GLbr LAst LSou SLBF SPet SSea
'Vrijheid' **new** WP&B
vulcanica CDoC EKMF LCla
- subsp. ***hitchcockii*** EKMF
'Vyvian Miller' CWVF MJac
'W.P. Wood' CSil
§ 'Wagtails White Pixie' CSil EBak
'Waldfee' CDoC CSil EKMF LCla MWhe
'Waldis Alina' **new** SLBF
'Waldis Geisha' (d) SLBF
'Waldis Lea' WP&B
'Waldis Ovambo' SLBF
'Waldis Simon' SLBF
'Wally Yendell' (v) WFFs WP&B
'Walsingham' (d) CWVF EBak WP&B
'Walton Jewel' EBak
'Walz Banjo' WP&B
'Walz Beiaard' WP&B
'Walz Bella' LCla WP&B
'Walz Blauwkous' (d) CWVF
'Walz Cello' WP&B
'Walz Epicurist' WP&B
'Walz Fanclub' LCla WP&B
'Walz Floreat' WP&B
'Walz Fluit' LAst MJac WP&B
'Walz Fonola' **new** WP&B
'Walz Freule' CWVF EKMF MJac
'Walz Gitaar' WP&B
'Walz Gong' WP&B
'Walz Harp' CDoC CWVF LCla WP&B
'Walz Hoorn' WP&B
'Walz Jubelteen' CDoC CLoc CSil CWVF EKMF EMan EPts LCla MJac MWar MWhe SLBF SSea WP&B
'Walz Kattesnoor' WP&B
'Walz Klarinet' WP&B
'Walz Lucifer' LCla SLBF WP&B
'Walz Luit' CDoC
'Walz Mandoline' (d) CWVF WP&B
'Walz Nugget' WP&B
'Walz Panfluit' LCla
'Walz Parasol' WP&B
'Walz Pauk' (d) WP&B
'Walz Piano' WP&B

'Walz Piston' WP&B
'Walz Polka' LCla WP&B
'Walz Spinet' WP&B
'Walz Telescope' WP&B
'Walz Triangel' (d) CSil EKMF WP&B
'Walz Trombone' WP&B
'Walz Trommel' (d) WP&B
'Walz Tuba' WP&B
'Walz Wipneus' WP&B
'Wapenveld's Bloei' CDoC LCla SLBF WFFs
'War Dance' (d) MWhe
'War Paint' (d) CLoc EBak
'War Pipes' LCla
'Warton Crag' CWVF
'Water Nymph' CLoc SLBF SSea WP&B
'Wave of Life' CWVF EKMF MWhe
'Waveney Gem' CDoC CSil CWVF EBak EKMF EMan LCla MJac MWar SLBF SPet WFFs
'Waveney Queen' CWVF
'Waveney Sunrise' CWVF MJac MWar MWhe SPet
'Waveney Unique' CWVF
'Waveney Valley' EBak MJac
'Waveney Waltz' CWVF EBak MJac MWar
'Welsh Dragon' (d) CLoc CWVF EBak WP&B
'Wendy' Catt see *F.* 'Snowcap'
'Wendy Atkinson' (d) EKMF
'Wendy Harris' (d) MJac
'Wendy Leedham' (d) ECtt EKMF
'Wendy van Wanten' EPts WP&B
'Wendy's Beauty' (d) CLoc EPts GLbr MJac SVil WP&B
'Wentworth' CWVF
'Wessex Belle' (d/v) CWVF
'Wessex Hardy' CSil EKMF
'Westham' LCla
'Westminster Chimes' (d) CLoc CWVF MWhe SPet
'Wharfedale' CSil MJac SLBF WFFs
'Whickham Blue' CWVF
'Whirlaway' (d) CLoc CSil CWVF EBak EKMF
'White Ann' (d) see *F.* 'Heidi Weiss'
'White Clove' CDoC CSil LCla
'White Fairy' GLbr WP&B
'White Galore' (d) CWVF EBak EMan LVER SPet
'White Général Monk' (d) CDoC CSil GLbr LAst
'White Gold' (v) EBak
'White Heidi Ann' (d) CSil MWhe
'White Joy' EBak
'White King' (d) CLoc CSil CWVF EBak EKMF EMan GLbr LVER MWhe SPet
'White Lace' CSil
'White Lady Patricia Mountbatten' EMan
'White Pixie' ♀H3-4 CDoC CSil EKMF EPts LCla LVER MJac NDlv SPer SPet WP&B
'White Pixie Wagtail' see *F.* 'Wagtails White Pixie'
'White Queen' ambig. CWVF
'White Queen' Doyle EBak MWhe
'White Spider' CLoc CWVF EBak MWhe SPet
'White Veil' (d) CWVF
'White Water' WP&B
'Whiteknights Amethyst' CDoC CSil EKMF WBcn
'Whiteknights Blush' CDoC CMdw CSil CStr EPts GCal GQui SMrm WBcn
'Whiteknights Cheeky' CWVF EBak EPts LCla
'Whiteknights Green Glister' CDoC CSil EKMF
'Whiteknights Pearl' ♀H1+3 CBot CDoC CSil CWVF ECha ECtt EKMF EPts LCla MAsh SHGN SLBF SMHy SPet WFFs
'Whiteknights Ruby' CSil EKMF LCla WFFs WP&B
'Whitton Starburst' LCla
'Wicked Queen' (d) CDoC CSil
'Widow Twanky' (d) CWVF WP&B
'Wigan Pier' (d) LCla MWar SLBF WFFs
'Wight Magic' (d) MJac
'Wild and Beautiful' (d) CWVF EKMF SPet
'Wilf Langton' MWar
'Wilhelmina Schwab' LCla
'Will van Brakel' WP&B
'William Caunt' EKMF
'Willie Tamerus' WP&B
'Willy Winky' CSil
'Wilma van Druten' LCla WP&B
'Wilma Versloot' WP&B
'Wilson's Colours' EPts
'Wilson's Joy' MJac WFFs
'Wilson's Pearls' (d) SLBF SPet
'Wilson's Sugar Pink' EPts LCla MJac MWhe
'Win Oxtoby' (d) CWVF EKMF
'Windmill' CWVF
'Wine and Roses' (d) EBak
'Wings of Song' (d) CWVF EBak
'Winston Churchill' (d) ♀H3 CHrt CLoc CSil CWVF EBak EKMF EMan EPts GLbr LAst LVER MBri MJac MWar MWhe NVic SCoo SPet SPlb SSea SWal WFFs WP&B WWeb
'Winter's Touch' EKMF
'Woodnook' (d) CWVF
'Woodside' (d) CSil
wurdackii EKMF
'Ymkje' EBak
'Yolanda Franck' CDoC CSil
'Youth' EKMF
'Yuletide' (d) CSil
'Yvonne Schwab' LCla
'Zara' MWhe WP&B
'Zellertal' WP&B
'Zets Bravo' CDoC
'Ziegfield Girl' (d) EBak WP&B
'Zulu King' CDoC CSil WFFs
'Zwarte Dit' WP&B
'Zwarte Snor' (d) CWVF GLbr

Fumana (*Cistaceae*)

ericoides XPep
thymifolia XPep

Fumaria (*Papaveraceae*)

lutea see *Corydalis lutea*
officinalis CArn MSal
purpurea **new** WBWf

Furcraea (*Agavaceae*)

bedinghausii CAby CBct CFil CHll CTrC EOas WMul WPGP
longaeva CAbb CCtw CHEx CPne CTrC EBee EOas MOak SAPC SArc SChr SDix WCot WPGP
selloa var. ***marginata*** (v) CDoC

G

Gagea (*Liliaceae*)

lutea EPot WBWf
pratensis EPot

Gahnia (*Cyperaceae*)

filum GGar
xanthocarpa **new** GGar

Gaillardia (*Asteraceae*)

aristata hort. see *G.* x *grandiflora*
aristata Pursch **new** SMar

	- 'Maxima Aurea'	CWCL EBee LRHS WCAu WWeb
	'Bijou'	CBrm EBee NVic NWCA SWvt
	'Bremen'	EBee LRHS NNor NPri
	'Burgunder'	More than 30 suppliers
	'Dazzler' $\mathbb{Y}^{H4}$	CSBt EBee ECtt ELan ENot EPfP ERou EVFa GKir LRHS MBri MWgw NLar NVic SPer SPoG WCAu WGor WPer
	'Dwarf Goblin'	LAst SPet
§	'Fackelschein'	SRms WHer XPep
	'Fanfare'	COtt MBri SCoo SPer SPoG
	Goblin	see *G.* 'Kobold'
§	'Goldkobold'	ELan ERou MBri MHer
§	x ***grandiflora***	ECrN GKev
	- 'Aurea'	LRHS
	- 'Aurea Plena' (d)	EBee
§	'Kobold'	More than 30 suppliers
	'Mandarin'	LRHS SRms
*	new giant hybrids	MWat WFar
	'Sundance Biocolour' **new**	LSou
	'Sundance Red' **new**	EMag
	'Tokajer'	EBee EPfP NLar WCAu
	Torchlight	see *G.* 'Fackelschein'
	Yellow Goblin	see *G.* 'Goldkobold'

Galactites (*Asteraceae*)

	tomentosa	CHrt CSpe EHrv ELan EMan EMar LDai LPhx LRHS MBct MBri NBPC NBur NDov SDnm SGar SPav SPer WEas WWeb
	- white	NBur WMnd

Galanthus ✿ (*Amaryllidaceae*)

	x ***allenii***	CBro EHyt WIvy
§	***alpinus***	CLAP LAma
	- var. ***alpinus***	CAvo CBro EHyt LAma LFox MTho NMen
	- - late-flowering	LRHS
	- var. ***bortkewitschianus***	LFox
§	***angustifolius***	CBro EHyt
	antarctica **new**	WThu
	'Armine'	CAvo LFox
	'Atkinsii' $\mathbb{Y}^{H4}$	CAvo CBro CElw CLAP EHrv EHyt EMon EPot ETow GAbr GCrs GKev LAma LFox LRHS MRav NBir SChr WPGP WShi WTin WWye
	'Backhouse Spectacles'	GFlt
	'Barbara's Double' (d)	CLAP EHyt
	'Benhall Beauty'	CAvo LFox
	'Bertram Anderson'	LFox
	'Brenda Troyle'	CAvo CBro CLAP EHrv EPot GCrs GEdr IGor LFox NPol WIvy
	byzantinus	see *G. plicatus* subsp. *byzantinus*
	caucasicus hort.	see *G. elwesii* var. *monostictus*
	caucasicus (Bak.) Grossh.	see *G. alpinus* var. *alpinus*
	- 'Comet'	see *G. elwesii* 'Comet'
	- var. ***hiemalis***	see *G. elwesii* var. *monostictus* Hiemalis Group
	'Clare Blakeway-Phillips'	CLAP
	'Colesborne'	EHrv
	corcyrensis spring-flowering	see *G. reginae-olgae* subsp. *vernalis*
	- winter-flowering	see *G. reginae-olgae* subsp. *reginae-olgae* Winter-flowering Group
	'Cordelia' (d)	CAvo CLAP EHyt EMon EPot LFox LRHS
	'Cowhouse Green' **new**	EHrv
	'Desdemona' (d)	CLAP EPot GCrs LFox WCot WIvy
	'Dionysus' (d)	CBgR CBro CLAP EHrv EHyt EPot ERos GCrs LFox MHom NBir
§	***elwesii*** $\mathbb{Y}^{H4}$	CBro ECho ELan EMon ENot EPfP EPot ERos ERou GFlt GKev IGor LAma LFox LRHS NBir NMen NPol SRms WCot WShi
	- 'Athenae'	GCrs
	- 'Cedric's Prolific' **new**	ECha
§	- 'Comet'	CAvo EMon
	- 'Daphne's Scissors'	WIvy
	- 'David Shackleton'	EHrv
	- Edward Whittall Group	CLAP
	- var. ***elwesii***	GCrs
	'Fred's Giant' **new**	
	- - 'Kite'	NPol
	- - 'Magnus'	CLAP
	- - 'Maidwell L'	CAvo EHrv LFox
*	- 'Flore Pleno' (d)	ENot LFox
	- 'Helen Tomlinson' **new**	MBri
	- 'J. Haydn'	CElw LAma
	- 'Kyre Park'	EMon
§	- var. ***monostictus*** $\mathbb{Y}^{H4}$	CAvo ECho EHrv EHyt EMon ETow WIvy
	- - from Ukraine **new**	MPhe
	- - 'G. Handel'	LAma
*	- - 'Green Tips'	NPol
	- - 'H. Purcell'	CElw LAma
§	- - Hiemalis Group	CBro ECha EHrv EMon LAma LRHS WCot
	- - 'Barnes' **new**	EHrv
	- 'Selborne Green Tips'	EMon
	- 'Zwanenburg'	EMon LRHS
	'Faringdon Double' (d) **new**	EHrv
	fosteri	CBro EHrv EHyt ERou LAma LRHS SCnR
	'Galatea'	CAvo CLAP EHrv EMon LFox LRHS MHom WIvy
	'Ginns'	CLAP LFox
§	***gracilis***	CBro CLAP ERos ETow LFox MTho NPol WIvy
	- 'Highdown'	CElw CLAP EHyt
	- 'Vic Horton' **new**	WThu
	graecus misapplied	see *G. gracilis*
	graecus Orph. ex Boiss.	see *G. elwesii*
	Greatorex double (d)	CLAP
	'Greenfields' **new**	CAvo
	'Hill Poë' (d)	CBro IGor LFox
	'Hippolyta' (d)	CAvo CBro CElw CLAP ECha EHrv EPot LFox SOkd WIvy
	x ***hybridus*** 'Merlin'	CAvo CElw IGor LFox MHom NPol WIvy
	- 'Robin Hood'	CFee CLAP EHrv EHyt ERos GCrs LFox SBla
§	***ikariae*** Bak.	CElw EPot ERos IGor LAma WFar
	- subsp. ***ikariae*** Butt's form	NPol
	- Latifolius Group	see *G. platyphyllus*
	- subsp. ***snogerupii***	see *G. ikariae*
	'Imbolc'	CAvo
	'Jacquenetta' (d)	CAvo CBro CDes CElw CLAP EHrv EHyt GCrs MHom WPGP
	'John Gray'	CBro EMon GCrs LFox LRHS NPol
	'Ketton'	CAvo CBro CElw LFox LRHS WIvy
	'Kingston Double' (d)	CAvo CLAP
	'Lady Beatrix Stanley' (d)	CAvo CBro CElw CLAP ECha EHrv EMon EPot ERos LAma LFox LRHS MTho
	lagodechianus	LRHS WWst
	latifolius Rupr.	see *G. platyphyllus*
	'Lavinia' (d)	CAvo CElw CLAP EHyt
	'Lerinda' **new**	EHrv
	'Limetree'	CLAP EHrv LFox NPol
	'Little Ben'	GFlt
	'Little John' **new**	EHrv
	lutescens	see *G. nivalis* Sandersii Group
	'Lyn' **new**	EHrv

'Magnet' ♀H4	CAvo CBro CFee CLAP EHyt EPot GAbr GCrs GEdr IGor LAma LFox NPol SOkd WCot WPGP
'Mighty Atom'	CDes CFee EHrv GCrs LFox
'Moccas'	EPot
* 'Mrs Backhouse' **new**	SOkd
'Mrs Backhouse No. 12' **new**	EHrv
'Mrs Thompson'	EHrv WCot WIvy
'Neill Fraser'	LFox
nivalis ♀H4	CBro CNic CTri EBrs ELan ENot EPfP EPot GFlt ITim LAma LFox LRHS MBow MBri NJOw NRya SHFr SPer SRms WBrk WCot WFar WShi WWFP
- 'Anglesey Abbey'	CAvo EMon
- var. ***angustifolius***	see *G. angustifolius*
- 'April Fool'	LFox MHom
- 'Bitton'	CBro CLAP LFox NPol
- 'Chedworth' **new**	CAvo
- dwarf	LFox
- subsp. ***imperati***	WBrk
- 'Lutescens'	see *G. nivalis* Sandersii Group
- 'Melvillei'	EMon
- f. ***pleniflorus*** 'Blewbury Tart' (d)	CAvo CLAP
- - 'Flore Pleno' (d) ♀H4	CBro CStu CTri EPfP EPla EPot GAbr GFlt LAma LFox LRHS NRya SPer SRms WBrk WCot WFar WGwG WShi WWye
- - 'Hambutt's Orchard' (d)	LFox
- - 'Lady Elphinstone' (d)	CBgR CBro CLAP CRow EHrv GCrs GFlt LAma LFox MRav MTho NPol WIvy
- - 'Pusey Green Tip' (d)	CAvo CBro CElw CLAP EPot GCrs LFox SIgm WPGP WTin
- Poculiformis Group	CLAP EMon LRHS
§ - Sandersii Group	CAvo CBro EPot NPol
§ - Scharlockii Group	CAvo CBro EHyt EMon EPot IGor LAma LFox LRHS SBla
- 'Tiny'	EPot GCrs
- 'Tiny Tim'	EHyt NPar NRya
- 'Virescens'	CLAP SBla
- 'Viridapice'	CAvo CBro ECha EHyt EMon EPot ERou GCrs GEdr LAma LFox LRHS NMen NPol SIgm WCot WIvy WPGP WShi
- 'Warei'	LFox
'Ophelia' (d)	CAvo CBro ETow GCrs IGor LFox NPar
peshmenii	EHyt EPot SCnR WWst
§ ***platyphyllus***	CBro LAma LFox WTin
plicatus ♀H4	CElw CFee ECho EHrv EMon EPot GEdr GFlt LFox LRHS NMen WShi
- from Ukraine **new**	MPhe
- 'Augustus'	CAvo CFee EHrv EHyt ERos GCrs LFox WIvy
- 'Bowles' Large'	ERos MHom
§ - subsp. ***byzantinus***	CBro EHyt ERos LFox
- - 'Ron Ginns'	LFox
- 'Colossus'	CAvo
- 'Edinburgh Ketton'	EHrv
- 'Florence Baker' **new**	EHrv
- large	GFlt NPol
- 'Sally Passmore'	CAvo
- 'Sophie North'	CLAP GCrs
- 'The Pearl' **new**	EHrv
- 'Three Ships'	EHrv
- 'Warham'	CBro EHrv EPot GEdr WPGP
- 'Washfield Warham'	ECha EMon LRHS
- 'Wendy's Gold'	EMon GCrs LRHS
reginae-olgae	CBro EBrs EHrv EHyt ERos LAma MRav SSpi WCot
- WM 9901	MPhe
- WM 9908	MPhe
§ - subsp. ***reginae-olgae*** Winter-flowering Group	CBro LAma LFox
§ - subsp. ***vernalis***	EHyt EMon EPot LRHS
rizehensis	EHrv EPot
'S. Arnott' ♀H4	CBro CElw CLAP EBrs ECha ECho EHyt ELan EPot GAbr GBuc GEdr IGor LAma LFox LRHS NBir NMen NRya SBla SIgm WLin WPGP WTin
'Saint Anne's'	WIvy
'Sally Ann'	LFox
'Scharlockii'	see *G. nivalis* Scharlockii Group
'Shaggy'	EHyt
'Silverwells' **new**	GEdr
§ 'Straffan'	CAvo CBro EHyt EPot GEdr IGor LAma LFox LRHS MHom NPol
'The Apothecary' **new**	EHrv
'The Linns'	GCrs
'The O'Mahoney'	see *G.* 'Straffan'
'Titania' (d)	CBro EHrv EHyt
'Tubby Merlin'	LFox WIvy
'William Thomson'	EMon LFox
'Winifrede Mathias'	CLAP LFox
'Wisley Magnet' **new**	ECha
woronowii ♀H4	CAvo CBro CElw CLAP EMon ENot ETow GCrs GKev LAma LRHS WCot

Galax (*Diapensiaceae*)

aphylla	see *G. urceolata*
§ ***urceolata***	CMac GCrs IBlr SOkd SSpi WSHC

Galega (*Papilionaceae*)

bicolor	IBlr MLLN NBir SRms SSth STes WFar
'Duchess of Bedford'	CFir CFwr CStr MTis
x ***hartlandii***	IBlr MRav WHoo WWhi
- 'Alba' ♀H4	EBee EHrv EMar EMon EVFa EWes GBar GBri GCal IBlr LPhx MArl NDov SAga SMHy SOkh WCot WHoo WPrP WSHC WWhi
- 'Candida'	NBir
- 'Lady Wilson' ♀H4	CStr ECtt EMan EVFa EWes MArl MRav WCot WFoF WHoo WPen
- 'Spring Light' (v)	ECtt EMan EWes
'Her Majesty'	see *G.* 'His Majesty'
§ 'His Majesty'	CBos CKno ECtt EMan GBri MArl MRav NGby SAga WCot WFar WHoo WPGP WWlt
officinalis	More than 30 suppliers
- 'Alba' ♀H4	CMdw COIW CPom CPrp CStr EBee ECtt ELan ELau EMan EPfP MBrN MHer NLsd SBch SWal WCHb WFar WHer WHil WHrl WMoo WWye
- Coconut Ice = 'Kelgal'[PBR] (v)	MBri SPer SPoG WHer
orientalis	CDes EBee ECtt GFlt GMaP LPhx LRHS MArl MLLN MRav SBch SMac WAbb WCot WMoo WPGP WSHC WWlt

Galeobdolon see *Lamium*

Galium (*Rubiaceae*)

aristatum	ECha EMan MLLN SBch
cruciata	see *Cruciata laevipes*
mollugo	CArn CRWN MSal SIde WCHb
§ ***odoratum***	More than 30 suppliers
verum	CArn CRWN GPoy GWCH MBow MChe MHer MSal NLan NMir NPri SIde WCHb WHer

Galtonia (*Hyacinthaceae*)

candicans ♀H4	More than 30 suppliers
princeps	CAvo CBro EBee EBrs ECha ERos ERou GBuc LPio SMac
regalis	ERos GCal GEdr LPio
viridiflora	More than 30 suppliers

Galvezia (*Scrophulariaceae*)

speciosa	XPep

Gardenia (*Rubiaceae*)

augusta	see *G. jasminoides*
florida L.	see *G. jasminoides*
globosa	see *Rothmannia globosa*
grandiflora	see *G. jasminoides*
§ ***jasminoides*** ♀H1	CBcs EBak LRHS MBri
- 'Kleim's Hardy'	ELan EPfP LRHS MAsh SPoG SSta
thunbergia	EShb

garlic see *Allium sativum*

Garrya ✿ (*Garryaceae*)

congdonii **new**	NLar
elliptica	CAgr CBcs CDul ECrN ENot GKir ISea LRHS LSRN MBri MGos NEgg NFor NWea SPet SPlb SReu WFar WHar WPat
- (f)	ECrN LAst MSwo SWvt WPat
- (m)	CCVT CDoC CSBt EHol GGar NBlu SLim SPoG WFar
- 'James Roof' (m) ♀H4	More than 30 suppliers
fremontii	NLar WBVN
x ***issaquahensis*** 'Glasnevin Wine'	CAbP CDoC CPMA ELan EPfP IMGH ISea LRHS MAsh MBlu NEgg NLar NPal NSti NVic SCoo SMur SPoG SSta WFar
- 'Pat Ballard' (m)	CPMA EPfP LRHS NLar
x ***thuretii***	MGos NLar WFar

Garuleum (*Asteraceae*)

woodii JCA 324000	CPBP

Gasteria ✿ (*Aloaceae*)

batesiana ♀H1 **new**	EPem
liliputana	EPem
* ***multipluncata***	EPem
verrucosa	EOas EPem EShb

x *Gaulnettya* see *Gaultheria*

Gaultheria ✿ (*Ericaceae*)

adenothrix	WAbe
cardiosepala	GEdr
cumingiana B&SWJ 1542	WCru
cuneata ♀H4	GEdr LRHS MBar NDlv NLAp SPer SPoG
- 'Pinkie'	GKir LRHS
hispidula	GGGa
hookeri	IBlr
itoana	GEdr MBar NDlv NLAp
'Jingle Bells'	MGos
macrostigma BR 67	GGar
miqueliana	GEdr
mucronata	EPfP MBar NWea WDin
- (m)	CBcs CDoC CSBt CTri CWSG EPfP GKir LAst MAsh MBar MBri MGos NBlu SPer SPoG SRms
- RB 94095	GTou
- 'Alba' (f)	MBar MGos SLon
- 'Bell's Seedling' (f/m) ♀H4	CBcs CDoC CDul CTri CWSG EPfP GGar GKir LRHS MAsh MGos NLRH SHBN SPer SPoG SReu SSta
- 'Cherry Ripe' (f)	GKir SHBN
- 'Crimsonia' (f) ♀H4	EPfP GKir LRHS MBar MDun SHBN SPer SPur SReu SRms
- 'Lilacina' (f)	CBcs WGwG
- 'Lilian' (f)	CSBt CWSG ENot EPfP GKir GSki LAst SHBN SPer
- Mother of Pearl	see *G. mucronata* 'Parelmoer'
- 'Mulberry Wine' (f) ♀H4	CSBt CTri EPfP GKir LRHS SPoG
§ - 'Parelmoer' (f)	ENot GKir LAst SPer SPoG SPur
- 'Pink Pearl' (f) ♀H4	SRms
- pink-berried (f)	NBlu
- 'Rosea' (f)	MBar MGos
- 'Rosie' (f)	SBod
§ - 'Signaal' (f)	CBcs CBrm ENot EPfP GKir GWCH LAst LRHS MGos SPer
- Signal	see *G. mucronata* 'Signaal'
§ - 'Sneeuwwitje' (f)	CBcs CWSG ENot EPfP GKir GSki LAst LRHS SHBN SPer SPur
- Snow White	see *G. mucronata* 'Sneeuwwitje'
- 'Thymifolia' (m)	EPfP SHBN
- 'White Pearl' (f)	GKir
- white-berried (f)	NBlu
- 'Wintertime' (f) ♀H4	CBrm MGos SRms
* ***mucronifolia*** dwarf	NWCA
nana	see *G. parvula*
nummularioides	GEdr GGGa
§ ***parvula***	GCrs
'Pearls'	GCrs
phillyreifolia	CMHG
'Pink Champagne'	SSta
* ***poeppigii racemosa***	SSta
procumbens ♀H4	More than 30 suppliers
pumila	GAbr GCrs LEdu MBar NMen
schultesii	WThu
shallon	CAgr CBcs CDoC CSBt EBee GBar GKir MBar MDun MGos SBrw SHBN SPer SRms SWvt WDin WFar
sinensis lilac-flowered **new**	NHar WThu
tasmanica	ECou GAbr MBar
tetramera	IDee
trichophylla	GGGa
x ***wisleyensis***	LRHS SLon SRms SSta
- 'Pink Pixie'	CMHG GKir LRHS MAsh MBar MGos NLar SBrw SPer SSta
- 'Wisley Pearl'	CBcs CDoC GKir IBlr IDee MBar MGos NLar SBrw SReu WFar
yunnanensis	SReu

Gaura (*Onagraceae*)

lindheimeri ♀H4	More than 30 suppliers
- 'Cherry Brandy'	EBee EVFa EWin GBin MSph NLar SPer WFar
- compact red	EVFa
- 'Corrie's Gold' (v)	CBcs CWSG EBee EChP ECha ECtt EDAr EHoe ELan EPfP ERou EVFa LAst LPhx LRHS MHer MLLN NBlu NPri SAga SGar SPav SPer SPet SPoG WMnd XPep
- 'Crimson Butterflies'PBR	CBcs CHea COtt EBee EPfP EShb EVFa LAst LSRN NCGa SPoG WHil
§ - 'Heather's Delight'PBR **new**	SHar
- In the PinkPBR	see *G. lindheimeri* 'Heather's Delight'
- 'Jo Adela' (v)	EBee ELan EMan EPfP
- Karalee Petite = 'Gauka' **new**	CSpe LAst NPri
- Karalee Pink **new**	MBri
- Karalee White = 'Nugauwhite' **new**	CHVG CWCL LAst MBri NPri
- 'Madonna'	EBee
- 'My Melody' (v)	EBee EWin LSou SPoG
- short	LSou SGar

	- 'Siskiyou Pink'	More than 30 suppliers
	- 'The Bride'	CSim CTri EBee ECrN EWTr LRHS LSou MAnH MArl MRav MWat NGdn SMar SMrm SPav SPla STes SWal SWvt WBVN WHil WMnd
	- 'Val's Pink'	WHoo WSPU
	- 'Whirling Butterflies'	CKno CSpe CWCL EBee ECtt ELan EMan EMil EPfP EVFa GMaP IBal LPio NJOw SBod SCoo SMad SMrm SPav SPoG WMnd XPep
	- 'White Heron'	EChP IBal MNrw
I	'Variegata' (v)	ENot LIck

Gaylussacia (*Ericaceae*)

	baccata	NLar
	brachycera	GGGa

Gazania (*Asteraceae*)

	'Acajou' **new**	CWCL
	'Aztec' 🏆H1+3	CHal EWin SUsu
	'Bicton Cream'	CHal
	'Bicton Orange'	CHVG COIW
	'Blackberry Ripple'	COIW LAst NCiC SAga SCoo
	'Christopher'	CHal GGar MOak MSte SAga SCoo
I	'Christopher Lloyd'	CHVG COIW LAst
	'Cookei' 🏆H1+3	CSpe MSte SAga WCot
	'Cornish Pixie'	CHal
	cream	CHal NCiC
	'Cream Beauty'	MSte
	'Cream Dream'	LAst MOak
	Daybreak Series	WFar
	'Diane' **new**	CWCL
	double bronze	CHal
	'Garden Sun'	MLan
*	***grayi***	CHal
*	'Hazel'	MSte
	(Kiss Series) 'Kiss Bronze Star'	LIck SGar
I	- 'Kiss Pomegranate'	LIck
	- 'Kiss Rose'	CBrm SGar
	- 'Kiss Yellow'	LIck SGar
	krebsiana	XPep
	linearis 'Colorado Gold'	CFir
	'Lydie' **new**	CWCL
	'Magic'	LAst NPri SCoo
	'Northbourne' 🏆H1+3	GGar MSte
	'Orange Beauty'	CHEx ELan
	'Red Velvet'	CHEx CSpe MSte SAga
§	***rigens***	LRHS
	- var. ***uniflora*** 🏆H1+3	MSte XPep
	- 'Variegata' (v) 🏆H1+3	ELan LAst LSou MOak SPoG WCot
	'Silverbrite'	CHal
	splendens	see *G. rigens*
	'Talent'	CBrm CHal
	'Torbay Silver' **new**	CHEx

Geissorhiza (*Iridaceae*)

	corrugata **new**	CStu
	imbricata	CStu

Gelasine (*Iridaceae*)

	azurea	see *G. coerulea*
§	***coerulea***	CMon EBee EMan WCot

Gelidocalamus (*Poaceae*)

	fangianus	see *Drepanostachyum microphyllum*

Gelsemium (*Loganiaceae*)

	rankinii	CPLN WSHC
	sempervirens 🏆H1-2	CArn CFwr CHll CMCN CPLN CRHN ERea EShb IDee MSal NCGa SBra
	- 'Flore Pleno' (d)	CPLN ERea
	- 'Pride of Augusta'	CMCN

Genista (*Papilionaceae*)

	aetnensis 🏆H4	CBcs CDul CEnd CHEx CMCN CSBt CTbh CTri EBee ECrN ELan ENot EPfP LRHS MDun MRav SAPC SArc SDix SHBN SMad SPer SPoG SRms SSpi SSta WBVN WDin WSHC XPep
§	***canariensis***	CPLG CSBt CWib ERea NBlu WBrE
	cinerea	WCFE
	decumbens	see *Cytisus decumbens*
	delphinensis	see *G. sagittalis* subsp. *delphinensis*
	'Emerald Spreader'	see *G. pilosa* 'Yellow Spreader'
	fragrans	see *G. canariensis*
	hispanica	CBcs CCVT CDul CSBt CTri EBee ECrN ELan ENot EPfP GKir LRHS MBar MGos SHBN SLim SPer SPoG SRms SWvt WCFE WDin WFar WHar WTel XPep
	humifusa	see *G. pulchella*
	lydia 🏆H4	More than 30 suppliers
	maderensis	WPic
	monosperma	see *Retama monosperma*
§	***monspessulana***	XPep
	pilosa	CTri EPot ESis ISea MBar MDun MWhi NMen WBVN
	- 'Lemon Spreader'	see *G. pilosa* 'Yellow Spreader'
*	- ***major***	NMen
	- var. ***minor***	GKir GTou ITim NLar NLon NMen
	- 'Procumbens'	CMea MDKP WPat
	- 'Vancouver Gold'	CBcs CSBt CTrC ELan ENot EPfP LRHS MAsh MGos MRav SMad SPer SPoG SRms WDin WFar WGor
§	- 'Yellow Spreader'	CBcs CMHG CSBt EHol EPot GEdr IArd MSwo NJOw
§	'Porlock' 🏆H3	CAlb CBcs CDoC CSPN CWSG MRav SEND WDin WWeb
§	***pulchella***	CTri SBla
	sagittalis	CTri EPfP MDKP NBir NFor NLar NLon NWCA SBla SPer WBVN WTin
§	- subsp. ***delphinensis*** 🏆H4	NMen
	- ***minor***	see *G. sagittalis* subsp. *delphinensis*
§	x ***spachiana*** 🏆H1	CTri
	tenera 'Golden Shower'	CPLG SLPl
	tinctoria	CAgr CArn GBar GPoy GWCH ILis MChe MGol MHer MSal NFor NLon SIde WHer WWye
	- 'Flore Pleno' (d) 🏆H4	CLyd MGos NMen NPro SRot
	- 'Humifusa'	EPot GEdr NWCA
	- 'Moesiaca'	ITim
	- var. ***prostrata***	LBee
	- 'Royal Gold' 🏆H4	CWSG CWib EBee ENot EPfP MGos MRav SHBN SPer SPlb SPoG
	villarsii	see *G. pulchella*

Gentiana ✿ (*Gentianaceae*)

§	***acaulis*** 🏆H4	More than 30 suppliers
	- f. ***alba***	GKev WThu
	- 'Alboviolacea'	NLar
	- Andorra form	WAbe
	- 'Belvedere'	GCrs NMen WAbe
	- 'Coelestina'	EHyt EPot GCrs
	- 'Dinarica'	see *G. dinarica*
	- 'Holzmannii'	GKev WAbe
	- 'Krumrey'	EHyt EPot GKev
	- 'Max Frei'	CStu GCrs
I	- 'Maxima Enzian' **new**	EPot

Plant	Suppliers
- 'Rannoch'	EPot NMen
- 'Stumpy'	EPot
- 'Trotter's Variety'	EPot WAbe
- 'Undulatifolia'	EPot
- 'Velkokvensis'	EHyt
affinis	GAbr NWCA
'Alex Duguid'	GEdr
'Alpha'	see *G.* x *hexafarreri* 'Alpha'
'Amethyst'	CWrd EPot GCrs GMaP NLAp SIng WAbe
andrewsii SDR 2263	GKev
angustifolia	GCrs
- 'Rannoch'	GKev
'Ann's Special'	CWrd
asclepiadea ♀H4	More than 30 suppliers
- var. ***alba***	CFil CHea GAbr GBuc GFlt GKev GMaP IGor LRHS MDKP MTho NChi SPer SRms WAbe WCru WTin
- 'Knightshayes'	GKev NLAp
- pale blue-flowered	CFil WPGP
- 'Phyllis'	CFir EBee GBuc GKev
- 'Pink Cascade'	GKev SIgm
- 'Pink Swallow'	GBuc
- 'Rosea'	CDes EBee GAbr GBuc GMaP MDKP MNrw NChi WPGP
- yellow-flowered	ELan
atuntsiensis	GKev
'Barbara Lyle'	CWrd WAbe
bavarica var. ***subacaulis***	SPlb
bellidifolia	GTou
x ***bernardii***	see *G.* x *stevenagensis* 'Bernardii'
bisetaea	GKev SRms
'Blauer Diamant'	GCrs
'Blue Flame'	GCrs
'Blue Heaven'	WAbe
'Blue Sea'	CWrd
'Blue Shell'	CWrd
'Blue Silk'	CWrd EPot EWes GCrs GMaP NLAp SBla SIng WAbe
boissieri **new**	GKev
burseri	CSec
- var. ***villarsii***	GIBF
cachemirica ambig.	GTou WPat
'Cairngorm'	CWrd GAbr GCrs GEdr GKir GMaP NDlv
Cambrian hybrids	CWrd
'Cambrian White' **new**	WAbe
x ***caroli***	SBla WAbe
chinensis **new**	GKev
'Christine Jean'	CWrd GCrs GTou NDlv SIng
clausa	GIBF
clusii	EPot GCrs GKev WAbe
- ***alba***	GKev WAbe
- subsp. ***clusii*** **new**	WLin
- subsp. ***costei***	WAbe
- pink **new**	GKev
'Compact Gem'	EPot GCrs GEdr NLAp WAbe
crassicaulis	GAbr
§ ***cruciata***	GAbr GTou MTho SBch
- subsp. ***phlogifolia***	GIBF
§ ***dahurica***	GAbr GCal LRHS SBch SBla SSto
'Dark Hedgehog'	GEdr
decumbens	GAbr
dendrologi **new**	WHil
depressa	MTho WAbe
'Devonhall'	GEdr WAbe
§ ***dinarica***	CLyd GKev MTho
- 'Col. Stitt' **new**	WThu
- 'Frocheneite' **new**	WThu
divisa	GKev
Drake's strain	CWrd GKir LRHS
'Dumpy'	CPBP CWrd EPot GEdr WAbe WPat
'Dusk'	CWrd GCrs
'Eleanor'	GCrs
'Elizabeth'	CWrd GCrs GEdr GMaP NDlv
'Ettrick'	GEdr
'Eugen's Allerbester' (d)	CWrd NHar
'Excelsior' **new**	NHar
farreri	EWes GKir NSla WAbe
- 'Duguid'	GEdr
- hybrids	WAbe
'Fasta Highlands'	NBir
fetissowii	see *G. macrophylla* var. *fetissowii*
freyniana	CSec SOkd
gelida	GAbr GKev
Glamis strain	GCrs GEdr NDlv
'Glen Isla'	EWes
'Glen Moy'	GMaP
§ ***gracilipes***	ECho LRHS MWat SPlb SRms
- 'Yuatensis'	see *G. macrophylla* var. *fetissowii*
grossheimii	CSec GIBF GKev
x ***hascombensis***	see *G. septemfida* var. *lagodechiana* 'Hascombensis'
'Henry'	WAbe
x ***hexafarreri***	CWrd GCrs
§ - 'Alpha'	GMaP
'Indigo' **new**	WAbe
Inshriach hybrids	CWrd GCrs GMaP
'Inverleith' ♀H4	CWrd EDAr EWes GCrs GEdr GKir IHMH SPlb WGor
'Joan Ward'	CWrd
'John Ward'	CWrd
kesselringii	see *G. walujewii*
'Kirriemuir'	CWrd EWes GCrs NDlv
kochiana	see *G. acaulis*
kurroo var. ***brevidens***	see *G. dahurica*
lagodechiana	see *G. septemfida* var. *lagodechiana*
ligustica	GCrs
lucerna	CWrd GCrs GEdr
lutea	GAbr GCal GIBF GKir GPoy NBid NChi SRms WAul WWye
x ***macaulayi*** ♀H4	CWrd EDAr GCrs GEdr GKir SIng SRms WHoo
- 'Elata'	CWrd GCrs NDlv
- 'Kidbrooke Seedling'	CTri CWrd EDAr EWes GCrs GEdr GKir GMaP GTou NLAp NRya WAbe
- 'Kingfisher'	CTri CWrd EDAr GAbr GEdr GKir NBir NFor NLAp SBla SIng WAbe
§ - 'Praecox'	CWrd EDAr GCrs GEdr GKir GTou NDlv NLAp
§ - 'Wells's Variety'	CWrd GCrs GEdr
§ ***macrophylla*** var. ***fetissowii***	ECho GAbr GKev
makinoi 'Royal Blue'	CFai CWCL GBin GBri IDee IPot NSla WMnd
'Margaret'	WAbe
'Maryfield'	GEdr
'Melanie' **new**	NHar
'Merlin'	GCrs
'Multiflora'	CWrd
* ***nepaulensis***	GIBF
nipponica	GIBF
§ ***nubigena***	CSec GIBF
occidentalis	EPot GKev NLAp
olivieri	EHyt
orbicularis	GKev
oreodoxa	CWrd GCrs GTou
ornata	GKev
paradoxa	CLyd GAbr GEdr GKev NDlv NLAp NSla SIgm SOkd WPat
- 'Blauer Herold'	NCGa NJOw
phlogifolia	see *G. cruciata*
phyllocalyx **new**	GKev
platypetala	SOkd

pneumonanthe GIBF NSla SPlb SSpi
prolata GCrs GKev SOkd WAbe
przewalskii see *G. nubigena*
pumila WAbe
subsp. ***delphinensis***
punctata EBee ITim NLAp
purdomii see *G. gracilipes*
purpurea GCal GIBF
'Robyn Lyle' WAbe
'Royal Highlander' CWrd
'Saphir Select' EDAr GEdr
saxosa CLyd CPBP EHyt EPot GCrs GEdr GKev GKir GTou ITim NBir NLAp NWCA SIgm WAbe WLin
scabra EDAr WWye
§ - var. ***buergeri*** GKev
- 'Ishusuki' SBla SOkd
- var. ***saxatilis*** see *G. scabra* var. *buergeri*
- 'Zuikorindo' NCGa NLar
'Sensation' CStu GEdr
septemfida 🏆H4 EHyt ELan GCrs GEdr GKev GKir LBee LRHS MBri MHer MTho MWat NBir NBlu NLAp NRya NWCA SBla SIng SPlb SRms WHoo WPat
- 'Alba' NBir
§ - var. ***lagodechiana*** 🏆H4 EDAr EHyt GAbr GCal NLAp SRms WBVN WFar
- - 'Doeringiana' ECho NMen
§ - - 'Hascombensis' ECho
'Serenity' CWrd GEdr WAbe
setigera GKir
'Shot Silk' CPBP CSam CWrd EDAr EWes GCrs GEdr GMaP SIng SUsu WAbe
sikkimensis GEdr
'Silken Giant' WAbe
'Silken Seas' WAbe
'Silken Skies' GBuc WAbe
sino-ornata 🏆H4 CTri EDAr GCrs GEdr GGar GKev GKir LRHS MBri NBlu NLAp NMen SBla SIng SPer SRms WAbe WBVN WFar
- CLD 476B GEdr
- 'Alba' CWrd GKir WFar
- 'Angel's Wings' CWrd EDAr GCrs GEdr GKir GTou
- 'Bellatrix' CWrd
- 'Blautopf' CWrd
- 'Brin Form' CWrd SIng SRms WAbe
- 'Downfield' CWrd GCrs NDlv
- 'Edith Sarah' GCrs GEdr SBla SRms
- 'Mary Lyle' CWrd GEdr WAbe
- 'Praecox' see *G.* x *macaulayi* 'Praecox'
- 'Starlight' NHar
I - 'Trotter's Form' CWrd EWes NDlv NRya
- 'Weisser Traum' CWrd
- 'White Wings' CWrd EWes GCrs LRHS NDlv
siphonantha **new** CSec
'Soutra' GEdr
x ***stevenagensis*** 🏆H4 CLyd CTri CWrd LRHS SIng
§ - 'Bernardii' CWrd EDAr GCrs GEdr SIng WAbe
- dark CWrd WAbe WPat
- 'Frank Barker' CWrd WAbe
stragulata GCrs GKev WAbe
straminea GAbr MDKP WCot
'Strathmore' 🏆H4 CStu CTri EDAr EHyt EWes GAbr GCrs GEdr GKir GMaP LRHS NLAp NRya SIng SPlb WAbe
'Susan Jane' GTou
syringea **new** WAbe
tenella **new** GIBF
ternifolia EDAr GCrs
- 'Cangshan' GCrs GEdr WAbe
- 'Dali' GEdr GKev NBir
tibetica CArn EBee EUnu GCal GIBF GPoy MAnH NBid SBch WCAu WEas WGwG WTin WWye
aff. ***tibetica*** CC 3935 MGol
trichotoma GKev WAbe
triflora EPot GBuc GCrs GKev WFar WPGP
- 'Alba' GBuc GKev
- var. ***japonica*** GBri GBuc GCal
- 'Royal Blue' CRez EBee GCal NGby
Tweeddale strain GCrs
verna CPBP CWCL EBee EHyt ENot EPfP EWes GKev GKir ITim LRHS MTho NMen NRya NSla SBla SIng WAbe WBWf WPat
- SDR 1316 GKev
- 'Alba' GCrs ITim WAbe WPat
- subsp. ***balcanica*** CLyd ELan GTou MTho NLAp SRms WPat
- subsp. ***oschtenica*** NSla WAbe
- slate blue WPat
- subsp. ***tergestina*** EDAr
'Violette' CWrd GCrs GEdr
waltonii ECho EWes
§ ***walujewii*** GAbr
wellsii see *G.* x *macaulayi* 'Wells's Variety'
wutaiensis see *G. macrophylla* var. *fetissowii*

Gentianella (*Gentianaceae*)

amarella WBWf

Gentianopsis (*Gentianaceae*)

grandis GKev NLar

Geranium ✿ (*Geraniaceae*)

from China **new** CFwr
from Pamirs, Tadzhikistan EPPr WPnP
from Sikkim NWCA
aconitifolium misapplied see *G. palmatum*
aconitifolium L'Hér. see *G. rivulare*
'Alan Mayes' CSev EBee EBla EPPr MNFA MSte NCot NSti WCra WWpP
'Alaska' CBgR
albanum CElw EBee EChP EGra EMan EMar EPPr EWsh GAbr GSki LLWP MNrw MTis NCot NSti SDix SRGP WCru WMoo WTMC WWpP
- 'Pink and Stripes' CDes
albiflorum CCge CMCo EChP EPPr IMGH LRHS MNFA MWhe SRGP WCru WMoo WPnP WWpP
'Amanda's Blush' **new** SMrm
anemonifolium see *G. palmatum*
'Ann Folkard' 🏆H4 More than 30 suppliers
'Ann Folkard' x ***psilostemon*** **new** LSRN
'Anne Thomson' More than 30 suppliers
x ***antipodeum*** CMHG SRms
- 'Chocolate Candy'PBR CFai EPfP GBri LAst WFoF WWeb
§ - Crûg strain CSpe EHrv EMan EPot EVFa GKir GSki LRHS MCCP MDKP MDun NBPC SHBN WCru
- 'Crûg's Dark Delight' WCru
- 'Elizabeth Wood' CCge EMan NBro
- 'Persian Carpet' NLar
- 'Sea Spray' CCge ECtt EMar EWes GBuc GGar GSki IPot LAst LPio LRHS MNrw MSte MWgw MWhe NBro NGdn NSti SPoG WCru WMnd WTMC WWpP
- 'Stanhoe' CSpe EBee ECtt GBin LRHS MWgw SBch SHar SRot WFar

Plant	Suppliers
- 'Stanhoe' purple-leaved **new**	CBrm EVFa
aristatum	CDes CPou EBee EBla EChP EPPr EWes MNFA MNrw MRav MSph MTis NBir NCot SPav SRGP STes WCra WCru WMoo WPnP WTMC WWpP
- NS 649	NWCA
armenum	see *G. psilostemon*
asphodeloides	CBre CElw CHid EBee EChP GAbr GKir GSki IFro LLWP MBNS MNFA MNrw NArg NBid NCot NGdn NSti SPav SRGP WBrk WCra WCru WFar WHCG WMnd WMoo WTin WWpP
- subsp. ***asphodeloides*** 'Prince Regent'	CHid CStr EMan EPPr MNFA SBch WCra WPtf WWpP
- - white-flowered	CCge EBla EMan EPPr SRGP WFar WMoo WWpP
- subsp. ***crenophilum***	CElw WWpP
- 'Starlight'	NBid SHel WCra WPtf
atlanticum Hook. f.	see *G. malviflorum*
'Aya'	LPio
'Baby Blue'	see *G. himalayense* 'Baby Blue'
'Bertie Crûg'	CDes CHar CPrp CSpe EBee EBla EHrv EPPr GBin LTwo NArg NBir NEgg NLAp NSti SCoo SIng SPoG SRms SRot SWvt WCru WHoo WPat WPop WWpP
biuncinatum	IFro WPnP
Black Beauty = 'Nodbeauty'	CHad CPen ELan ENot IPot MGos NPri SCoo SDnm SPav SPer
'Black Ice'	GBuc SHel WCru
'Blue Cloud'	CDes CElw CMea EBla ECGP EGra EMar EPPr GMaP GMac LPhx MAvo NBir NChi NCot NMRc SHel SRGP SSvw SUsu WCra WMoo WPnP WTMC WWpP
'Blue Pearl'	CCge EBee EPPr EVFa MAvo MMil NBir NSti SHel SRGP SUsu SVil WCra WPnP WWpP
§ 'Blue Sunrise'	CCge EBee EBla ELan GKir LAst LPio LRHS MCCP MSte NEgg NLar NLsd NSti SAga SPla SPoG SRkn SRms WCra WFar WWpP
'Bob's Blunder'	CCge CElw CM&M CSpe EBee EBla ECtt EMan EVFa MBNS MBnl MEHN NEgg SPla SWvt WCot WCru WFar WGor WPop WWhi WWlt
bohemicum	CCge EBla EMan GSki MAnH NCot NWCA SRGP WBrk WCru WHer WWpP
- 'Orchid Blue'	CCge EPfP EShb LRHS SWvt WFar WPop
'Brookside'	More than 30 suppliers
brycei	MNrw
'Buckland Beauty'	CDes CElw EBee EPPr SBch SBla SSpi
'Buxton's Blue'	see *G. wallichianum* 'Buxton's Variety'
caeruleatum	EBla EMon EPPr SHel SUsu WWpP
caffrum	CCge CHVG CMCo EBee EMan GBuc GSki MNrw NChi NCot NSti NWCA SRGP SWal WCru WOut WWpP
californicum	CElw GBuc WCru
canariense	see *G. reuteri*
candicans hort.	see *G. lambertii*
§ x ***cantabrigiense***	More than 30 suppliers
- 'Berggarten'	CDes CElw EBee EPPr SHel SRGP WPtf WWpP
- 'Biokovo'	More than 30 suppliers
- 'Cambridge'	More than 30 suppliers
- 'Karmina'	CElw CMCo EBee EBla EChP EPPr EPla GKir GSki IHMH MBnl NRnb SBch WHoo WMoo WPnP WTMC WWpP
- 'Show Time'	CMCo EBla WWpP
- 'St Ola'	More than 30 suppliers
- 'Westray' PBR	CCge CHid CTbh EBee EChP EPPr EVFa GAbr GBin GKir GLbr MCCP MDun MSte NBlu NEgg NGdn NPro SPoG SRms SSpi STes SVil SWvt WWeb
cataractarum	CCge MLLN WCru
- subsp. ***pitardii***	SRGP
'Chantilly'	CElw CMCo CSam EBee EBla EGra EMan EPPr GBuc MAvo MNrw NBir NPro SUsu WCru WMoo WPGP WPnP WTMC WWpP
'Chocolate Pot'	NArg
christensenianum	EPPr
- B&SWJ 8022	WCru
cinereum	CCge EBee EBla GKir NSla WBrE
- 'Album'	WCru
- 'Apple Blossom'	see *G.* x *lindavicum* 'Apple Blossom'
- 'Ballerina'	see *G.* (Cinereum Group) 'Ballerina'
I - 'Heather'	CCge EBee EBla EChP EMan EPPr LRHS MAvo MBNS MMHG MWhe NBro NGdn NSti
- hybrids	WCru
- 'Janette'	COtt EBla LAst LRHS
- subsp. ***nanum***	see *G. nanum*
- 'Purple Pillow'	EBee EBla EShb EVFa IPot LSRN LTwo MAvo MBNS MBri MTis NBro NSti SHBN SMrm SPur STes SUsu WCra WHoo
- 'Rothbury Gem'	EBla NLar WCra
§ (Cinereum Group) 'Ballerina' ♀H4	More than 30 suppliers
- 'Carol'	CCge EBee EBla EChP EHoe EMan EMar EPPr EVFa EWes GKir LAst MAvo MWhe NBro NGdn NLar NSti SVil SWvt WCra WPnP
- 'Laurence Flatman'	More than 30 suppliers
- 'Sugar Babe' PBR	CCge
'Claridge Druce'	see *G.* x *oxonianum* 'Claridge Druce'
clarkei 'Kashmir Green'	CFwr EPPr WMoo
- 'Kashmir Pink'	More than 30 suppliers
- 'Kashmir Purple'	More than 30 suppliers
§ - 'Kashmir White' ♀H4	More than 30 suppliers
- 'Mount Stewart'	IBlr WCru
'Coffee Time'	WWpP
collinum	EPPr GAbr GBuc MNrw NBir NCot SRGP WBrk WCru WPnP WTMC WWpP
aff. ***collinum*** **new**	CDes
'Coombland White'	CCge CDes CElw CSpe EBee EBla EPPr IFro LPio MBri MMil MNFA MNrw NCot NSti SRGP STes SVil WCot WCra WCru WHoo WMoo WPop WWeb WWpP
Crûg strain	see *G.* x *antipodeum* Crûg strain
'Cyril's Fancy'	EBee EBla EChP EPPr MAvo MNFA NLsd SUsu WPtf WWpP
dahuricum	WCru
dalmaticum ♀H4	More than 30 suppliers
- 'Album'	CNic EBla ECtt EDAr EHyt ELan EPPr EPot GBBs GKir MHer MRav MTho MWhe NChi NRya SIng SRGP SRms SRot WAbe WCra WCru WFar WHCG WPat WWpP

	- 'Bressingham Pink'	WPnP
	- 'Bridal Bouquet'	GBri NChi NMen NSla SBla WAbe WHer
	dalmaticum* x *macrorrhizum	see *G.* x *cantabrigiense*
	delavayi hort.	see *G. sinense*
	delavayi Franch.	CDes WCru
	- B&SWJ 7582	WCru
	'Derek Cooke'	WCra
	'Dilys'	CElw CStr EBee EBla EChP EGra EPPr LPio MAvo MNFA MNrw MSte NBir NCot NGdn NSti SBla SHel SRGP SUsu WCra WCru WFar WHal WMoo WPnP WTMC WWpP
	dissectum	CHll MSal
	'Distant Hills'	EBee EBla EPPr SUsu WPtf
	'Diva'	CCge CElw CMCo CSam EBee EBla EPPr GBBs MMil MNrw NSti SRGP SVil WCru WPnP WTMC WWpP
	donianum HWJCM 311	WCru
	'Dusky Crûg'	CBod CCge CElw EBee EHrv EPPr GCai LAst MBNS MNrw MWhe NCot NSti SPoG WCru WFar WPop WWlt
	'Dusky Gem'	SUsu
	'Dusky Rose'	CFai ELan EMan ENot EPfP GKir LRHS MBNS
	'Eleanor Fisher'	SUsu
	'Elizabeth Ross'	CElw EPPr LPio LRHS MAvo MNrw SBch WCra WCru WRha WTMC WWhi WWpP
	'Elworthy Blue Eyes' **new**	CElw
	'Elworthy Dusky'	CCge
	'Elworthy Eyecatcher' **new**	CElw
	'Emily'	SRGP
	endressii ♀H4	More than 30 suppliers
	- 'Album'	see *G.* 'Mary Mottram'
	- 'Beholder's Eye'	CCge CHid COlW EBla EPPr GAbr LBBr MNFA MSte NCot NSti SHel WPnP WPtf WTMC WWpP
	- 'Betty Catchpole'	EPPr
	- 'Castle Drogo'	EBee EBla ECtt EPPr SRGP WTMC WWpP
	- dark	GBBs
	- 'Prestbury White'	see *G.* x *oxonianum* 'Prestbury Blush'
	- 'Priestling's Red'	CElw CMCo EGra EMar NCot
I	- 'Rose'	WPer WPnP WWpP
	- white-flowered	SSpi WPtf
	erianthum	CCge EMan GAbr GBuc GKev GMaP GMac NLar SRGP WCru WWpP
	- 'Calm Sea'	CCge CDes EBla GBuc SUsu WCru WMoo WTMC
	- f. ***leucanthum*** 'Undine' **new**	SUsu
	- 'Neptune'	EPPr SChu SUsu WCra WCru
	eriostemon Fischer	see *G. platyanthum*
§	***farreri***	CCge CLyd EBla EHyt GBri GBuc GCal GCrs LRHS MNrw NBir SBla WCru WEas
	glaberrimum	WCru
	goldmannii	SSpi
	gracile	EChP EPla GBuc GMaP LSou MNrw NBir SRGP WBrk WCru WMoo WPnP WTMC WWpP
	- 'Blanche'	CElw EBee EPPr WWpP
	- 'Blush'	CElw CMCo EBee EMan EPPr WWpP
	grandiflorum	see *G. himalayense*
	- var. ***alpinum***	see *G. himalayense* 'Gravetye'
	'Grasmere'	EGra
	'Gwen Thompson'	WOut

	gymnocaulon	CCge CElw CM&M CMCo CMHG EBee EBla EMan EPPr LRHS MNFA NSti SRGP STes WCru WMnd WWpP
	gymnocaulon* x *platypetalum	EBee
	'Harmony'	EPPr
	harveyi	CBrm CElw CMea EBee EBla EMan EPPr EWes GSki LGro LPhx NWCA WCru WHoo WKif WPGP WPat
	hayatanum	NCot WTMC
	- B&SWJ 164	CBod EBee WCru WMoo WWpP
§	***himalayense***	More than 30 suppliers
	- CC 1957 from Tibetan border	EPPr
	- ***alpinum***	see *G. himalayense* 'Gravetye'
§	- 'Baby Blue'	CElw EBee EBla EBrs EPPr EVFa GBuc GCal GCra GKir IFro MAvo MBri MNFA MNrw NCot NLsd NSti WCra WCru WEas WMoo WPnP WTMC WWpP
	- 'Birch Double'	see *G. himalayense* 'Plenum'
	- 'Devil's Blue'	WPtf WWpP
	- 'Frances Perry'	CCge SMur
§	- 'Gravetye' ♀H4	More than 30 suppliers
	- 'Irish Blue'	CElw CMCo EBee EBla EChP ECtt EGra EPPr GAbr GBuc GCal MBri MNFA MSte NPol NSti WAbb WCAu WCra WCru WHal WMoo WTMC WTin WWpP
	- ***meeboldii***	see *G. himalayense*
	- 'Pale Irish Blue'	GCal
§	- 'Plenum' (d)	More than 30 suppliers
	hispidissimum	CFee
	ibericum misapplied	see *G.* x *magnificum*
	ibericum Cav.	CCge CNic CSBt CTri EBla NLar SMac SPav SRGP STes WFar WWpP
	- 'Blue Springs'	EGra
	- subsp. ***ibericum***	EBee EPPr MTis
	- subsp. ***jubatum***	CElw EBee EBla EPPr GCal GKir GMac MNFA MNrw NCot NSti SRms WCru WMoo WPnP WTMC WWpP
	- - 'White Zigana'	CDes CFwr
	- subsp. ***jubatum* x *renardii***	GCal SWvt
	- var. ***platypetalum*** Boissier	see *G. platypetalum* Fisch. & C.A. Mey.
	- var. ***platypetalum*** hort.	see *G.* x *magnificum*
	ibericum* x *renardii	NSti
	incanum	CCge CHll CSev EBee EMag EMan ETow EWes IFro MNrw NBir SGar SMrm SRGP WCot WWpP XPep
	- var. ***multifidum***	GGar SUsu WCru WFar
	- white	SRGP
	'Incognito' **new**	MAvo
	'Ivan'	CCge CElw CMCo EBee EBla EBrs EMan EPPr GBuc LPhx LRHS MBNS SDix SIgm SRGP WCot WCru WMoo WPGP WPnP WWpP
	'Jack of Kilbryde' **new**	GCrs
	'Jean Armour'	SRGP WCru WTMC
	'Jean's Lilac'	see *G.* x *oxonianum* 'Jean's Lilac'
	'Jennifer' **new**	NCot
	'Johnson's Blue' ♀H4	More than 30 suppliers
	'Jolly Bee'[PBR]	CElw CFai EBee EChP EHrv EMan EPyc MAvo MBNS MTis NSti SHBN SPoG STes SUsu WCot WPnP WPtf WTMC
	'Joy'	CMCo CSam CSpe CStr EBla EGra EPPr GBuc IFro LRHS MAvo MNrw MRav NBir NChi NCot NDov SPoG SRGP STes SUsu SVil WCra WCru

	Name	Suppliers
		WMoo WPGP WTMC WWeb WWpP
	'Kahlua'	EHrv EMan EPfP MBNS NLar WPop
§	'Kashmir Blue'	CCge CHar EChP ECha EGra EPPr ERou EWsh GKir GMaP MAvo MBnl MNFA NCot NSti SHel WCAu WMoo WPnP
§	'Kate'	CElw EBla EPPr WCru
	'Kate Folkard'	see *G.* 'Kate'
§	'Khan'	CMCo CMil EBee EBla EPPr IFro MNrw NCot NPro SDys SMHy SRGP SUsu WCra WCru WWpP
	kishtvariense	CMCo EBee EBla EMag EMan EPPr GCal LPio LRHS MNFA MNrw MRav NCot NSti SSpi WCru WOVN WPnP
	koraiense	CBod CCge EBla EMan NSti WMoo WWpP
	- B&SWJ 797	WCru
	- B&SWJ 878	WCru
	koreanum	CCge CFil EBla GBuc GIBF GKir LRHS MNFA NCot SSpi SUsu WFar WMoo WPGP WTMC
	- B&SWJ 602	WCru
	kotschyi **new**	EBla
§	- var. ***charlesii***	EBee EBla EPPr
	krameri	EBla EMan
	- B&SWJ 1142	EBla WCru
§	***lambertii***	CCge EBla EWes GBuc LPio MNrw NBir NChi WTMC
	- 'Swansdown'	EBla EChP EMan GBuc MNrw WCra WCru WPtf WSHC
	lanuginosum	EChP
	libani	CDes EBee EPPr GBuc GCal LLWP MTho MWhe NCot NSti WBrk WCot WCra WCru WEas WPnP WTMC WTin WWpP
	libani* x *peloponnesiacum	CBos CCge CDes EBee
	'Libretto'	CElw WCru
§	x ***lindavicum*** 'Apple Blossom'	CCge CLyd CNic EBla EBrs EDAr GBuc GKir GSki LRHS MSte NChi SBla SRGP SRot WAbe WHCG WLin
	- 'Gypsy'	SBla
	- 'Lissadell'	SBla
	linearilobum subsp. ***transversale***	EPPr SRot WCru
§	'Little David'	EPPr MAvo SRGP SUsu WWpP
	'Little Devil'	see *G.* 'Little David'
	'Little Gem'	CBrm CCge CMea EBee EBla GKir LRHS NChi NDov SUsu WCra WCru WFar WTMC WWpP
	lucidum	MSal NSti NVic
	'Luscious Linda' **new**	MBNS NSti SPer WHlf
	'Lydia'	SRGP
§	***macrorrhizum***	More than 30 suppliers
	- AL & JS 90179YU	CHid EPPr
	- JJH 7003/95	EBee
	- 'Album' ♀H4	More than 30 suppliers
	- 'Bevan's Variety'	More than 30 suppliers
	- 'Bulgaria'	EPPr WTMC WWpP
	- 'Czakor'	More than 30 suppliers
I	- 'De Bilt'	CFwr WWpP
	- 'Freundorf'	GCal MNFA
	- 'Ingwersen's Variety' ♀H4	More than 30 suppliers
	- 'Lohfelden'	CDes EPPr EVFa GBuc MNFA NChi SHel SRGP WCra WMoo WWpP
	- 'Mount Olympus'	see *G. macrorrhizum* 'White-Ness'
	- 'Mount Olympus White'	see *G. macrorrhizum* 'White-Ness'
	- 'Pindus'	CPrp EBee EBla EBrs EPPr GAbr LRHS MNFA NCot NMRc NSti SHel SPoG SRGP SUsu WCru WFar WMoo WPnP WTMC WWpP
	- 'Ridsko'	CElw CFee CMCo EBee EPPr GBuc GCal MNFA NBro SBch SRGP WCru WTMC WWpP
	- ***roseum***	see *G. macrorrhizum*
	- 'Sandwijck'	CCge CFwr EPPr WWpP
	- 'Snow Sprite'	CCge CMea COIW EPPr EPyc EVFa GSki LSou MAnH MCCP NCot NLsd NPro SBri SPoG STes WHrl
	- 'Spessart'	CCge EBee EBla EChP ELan EPPr EPfP GKir LAst NCGa WBVN WCra WCru WFar WOVN WTMC WWFP WWpP
	- 'Variegatum' (v)	CElw EBee EBla EChP ECha EHrv ELan EVFa GKir GLbr GMaP LRHS MDun MNFA MTho NBid NBir NLsd NSti SGSe SPer SPoG SRms WCot WEas WFar WHCG WTMC WWpP
	- 'Velebit'	CCge EPPr MSte SRGP WCru WMoo WTMC WWpP
§	- 'White-Ness'	CBod CCge CElw CLAP CPrp EGoo EMon EPPr EPfP GMaP MWhi NBPC NBir NDov NPro SHel SRGP SRms SUsu WBrk WCot WCru WFar WHal WMoo WPGP WPnP WTMC WWpP
	macrostylum	CDes CPou EBee SSpi WBVN WCot WCru WPGP WPer WPnP
	- MP 8103D	WCot
	- 'Leonidas'	see *G. tuberosum* 'Leonidas'
	maculatum	CArn CElw CSev EBee EBrs ECha EGra EPfP EWTr GCal GPoy LLWP LRHS MNFA MRav MSal NSti SMac WCAu WCra WCru WHal WHoo WPnP WWpP WWye
	- from Kath Dryden **new**	EPPr
	- f. ***albiflorum***	CElw CMea EBla EMan EMon EPPr GCal LPhx MAnH MNrw NBid NSti SRGP SSpi STes SUsu WBrk WCot WCra WCru WMoo WPen WPnP WTMC WWpP
	- 'Beth Chatto'	More than 30 suppliers
	- 'Elizabeth Ann' **new**	WCot
	- 'Espresso'	More than 30 suppliers
	- purple-flowered	EPPr WWpP
	- 'Shameface'	EBee EPPr MSte SDys SGar SHel SOkh
	- 'Vickie Lynn'	CFwr
	maderense ♀H2	More than 30 suppliers
	- white-flowered **new**	CTrC MAnH
§	x ***magnificum*** ♀H4	More than 30 suppliers
	- 'Peter Yeo'	EPPr NSti WWpP
	- 'Rosemoor'	CCge CFwr CHid CSpe EBee EBla EChP ELan EPPr EPfP IPot MSte NCot NPro NSti SBch WBrk WCot WCra WMnd WPtf WTMC WWpP
	magniflorum	IFro MRav NBid NEgg WCru
§	***malviflorum***	CDes CElw CMHG ECha ELan EMar EPPr EVFa GKir LLWP LPhx LRHS MBow MNFA MNrw MTho SBla SRms SSpi WAul WCot WCra WCru WFar WHoo WPnP WTin
	- from Spain	EPPr EWes WSHC
	- pink	CDes CMil EBee EVFa SBla WCru WMoo WPnP
§	'Mary Mottram'	CDes CMCo EBee EPPr NBir NCot NSti SRGP WCot WEas WWpP
	maximowiczii	CElw EBee SBch
	'Maxwelton'	WTMC
	'Menna Bach'	WCru WPnP
	'Meryl Anne'	WPtf
	microphyllum	see *G. potentilloides*
	molle	NLRH

	Name	Suppliers
	x ***monacense***	CMCo EBee EBla ELan EMar EPla GGar GKir GSki LRHS MWgw MWhe NSti SMac WBrk WCru WHer WMnd WMoo WPnP WWpP
	- var. ***anglicum***	CCge EBla EBrs EChP ECtt EPPr GKir GMaP MNFA MRav MWhe NSti WMoo WPnP WWpP
	- 'Anne Stevens' **new**	NCot
	- 'Breckland Fever'	EBee EPPr
	- 'Claudine Dupont'	EPPr WCot
	- dark-flowered	WMoo
	- var. ***monacense***	EBla WFar
§	- - 'Muldoon'	CHar CSev EBla EChP EMag EPPr EPla GKir GSki LRHS MBow MRav NBPC NBir NEgg NOak STes WFar WHCG WMoo WPer WPnP WTMC
	moupinense	CFwr EBee
	'Mourning Widow'	see *G. phaeum* var. *phaeum*
	multisectum	WCru WTMC
§	***nanum***	NWCA
	napuligerum misapplied	see *G. farreri*
	napuligerum Franch.	NSla
	'Natalie'	CDes CElw EBee EBla EPPr MAvo NChi WCot WCra WPGP
	nepalense	CMCo NCot SHel SRGP SRms WMoo WWpP
	'New Dimensions' **new**	MGos
	'Nicola'	CCge CElw EBee EBla EPPr MNFA NCot SAga SHel WCra WTMC WWpP
	'Nimbus'	More than 30 suppliers
	nodosum	More than 30 suppliers
	- dark	see *G. nodosum* 'Swish Purple'
	- 'Julie's Velvet'	CDes MAvo MSte WHoo WTin WWhi WWpP
	- pale	see *G. nodosum* 'Svelte Lilac'
	- 'Pascal'	EBee
	- 'Saucy Charlie'	SHel
	- 'Silverwood' **new**	SBch
§	- 'Svelte Lilac'	CElw EBee EBla ECGP EMan EPPr EPfP GCal MNFA MSte NFor NLon SHel SRGP WCAu WCot WCru WFar WMoo WPnP WWpP
§	- 'Swish Purple'	CBos CElw CHar CMil EBee EBla EPPr MAvo MNFA MSte NCiC SHel SRGP WCru WFar WMoo WPGP WPnP WWpP
	- 'Whiteleaf'	CBos CElw EBee EBla EMag EPPr MAvo NPro SBch SBla SUsu WCru WFar WMoo WPnP WTMC WWpP
	- 'Whiteleaf' seedling	EBla EMan SHel
	'Nora Bremner'	SRGP SUsu
	'Nunnykirk Pink'	EMan GCal MAvo
	'Nunwood Purple'	EBee EPPr NCot SUsu WPtf WTMC
	ocellatum	CBre CCge
	oreganum	CCge CMCo ECGP
§	***orientalitibeticum***	More than 30 suppliers
	'Orion'	CBre CCge CElw CM&M CMCo EBla ECGP EChP EPPr GBuc LRHS MAvo MBnl MNFA MSte NChi NCot NGby NSti SMHy SSvw STes SUsu WCru WPnP WPtf WWeb WWpP
	'Orkney Blue'	WCru
	'Orkney Dawn'	WCru
	'Orkney Pink'	More than 30 suppliers
	ornithopodon	CDes IFro NCot
	'Out of the Blue'	WOut
	x ***oxonianum***	NCot NEgg WCru WMoo
	- 'A.T. Johnson' 🏆H4	More than 30 suppliers
	- 'Anmore' **new**	SRGP
	- 'Breckland Brownie'	CElw EBla EPPr EVFa NCot SRGP WWpP

	Name	Suppliers
	- 'Breckland Sunset'	EBee EPPr MAvo NCot SHel SRGP WPnP WTMC WWpP
	- 'Bregover Pearl'	CBre CElw CMCo EBee EBla EChP EPPr MNFA NCot SRGP WMoo WTMC WWpP
	- 'Bressingham's Delight'	CMCo EBee EBla ECtt EWsh GKir LRHS NCot SRGP WCra WTMC WWpP
I	- 'Buttercup'	EMan EPPr NCot WWpP
I	- 'Cally Seedling'	EBee EPPr EWes GCal NPro
§	- 'Claridge Druce'	More than 30 suppliers
	- 'Coronet'	CCge EBee EPPr MNFA SRGP WBrk WMoo
	- 'David McClintock'	CCge CElw EBee EMan EPPr GBin MNFA NSti SHel SRGP WFar WMoo WTMC WWpP
	- 'Dawn Time'	WWpP
	- 'Diane's Treasure' **new**	NCot
	- 'Dirk Gunst'	CElw
	- 'Elsbeth Blush'	EBee EBla NCot
	- 'Elworthy Misty'	CElw EBee EPPr NCot SBch WWpP
	- 'Frank Lawley'	CElw CFis CMCo EBee EBla EChP EPPr EVFa GBuc GCal GCra GMac LLWP MNFA NBid NPro NSti SHel SMrm SRGP WBrk WCra WMoo WTMC WWpP
§	- 'Fran's Star' (d)	EBee EBla EGoo EVFa WBrk WCru WTMC
	- 'Hexham Pink'	CCge EBee NChi NPro WTMC WWpP
	- 'Hollywood'	CCge CElw CMCo EBee EBla EChP ELan EPPr GBBs GBuc GMac LRHS MBri MSte MTho NCot NPer SRGP SRms SSpe WBor WBrk WCra WFar WMoo WPnP WTMC WWpP
I	- 'Jean's Lilac'	NCot
	- 'Julie Brennan'	CElw EBee EPPr GAbr GBin GCal GMac MNFA NGdn NSti SRGP WCra WMoo WWpP
	- 'Julie Searle' **new**	SRos
	- 'Kate Moss'	EBee EPPr GCai GKir MBnl MNFA NSti WCra WTMC WWpP
	- 'Katherine Adele' **new**	MBnl NLar NSti
§	- 'Kingston'	EBee EPPr WWpP
	- 'Klaus Schult' **new**	LPio
	- 'Königshof'	CMCo EBee EPPr WWpP
	- 'Kurt's Variegated'[PBR] (v)	see *G.* x *oxonianum* 'Spring Fling'
	- 'Lace Time'	CBre CElw CMCo CSev EBee EBla EPPr GBBs GMac MNFA MNrw MTis MWhe NCot NEgg NOak SBch SCoo SPoG SRms WMoo WPnP WSSM WTMC WWpP
	- 'Lady Moore'	CMCo EBee EBrs EPPr EPla GBuc MNrw NBro NCot SRGP WBor WCra WMoo WPnP WTMC WWpP
	- 'Lambrook Gillian'	CCge CElw CFis EBee EPPr MNFA NCot SBch SRGP WBrk WPnP WPtf WTMC WWpP
	- 'Lasting Impression'	EBee EBla EPPr NCot SRGP WWpP
	- 'Miriam Rundle'	CElw EBrs EPPr MNFA MNrw NCot SRGP WCru WMoo WPnP WTMC WWpP
	- 'Moorland Jenny'	CElw WMoo
	- 'Moorland Star'	WMoo
	- 'Old Rose'	CBrm EBee EPPr GCal GKir LRHS MNFA NCot SRGP WCra WCru WPnP WTMC WWpP
	- 'Pat Smallacombe'	CElw EPPr NCot SRGP WCru WMoo WTMC
	- 'Phoebe Noble'	CBre CElw CMCo CMil EBee EBla EChP EPPr GKir IFro LRHS MAvo MNFA MNrw MWgw NCob NCot

		NSti SAga SRGP SUsu WCAu WCra WMoo WPnP WTMC WWpP
	- 'Phoebe's Blush'	EBee EBla EPPr GFlt GMac MNFA SHel WTMC WWpP
	- 'Pink Lace'	CCge LSou NCot
§	- 'Prestbury Blush'	CBre CElw EBee EPPr MNFA SRGP WCru WMoo WTMC WWpP
	- 'Prestbury White'	see *G.* x *oxonianum* 'Prestbury Blush'
	- 'Raspberry Ice' **new**	EWes
	- 'Rebecca Moss'	CMil CSev EBee EBla EChP EMar EPPr GBuc GKir GMac LRHS MNFA MSte NCot NLsd NSti SHBN SRGP WCra WCru WFar WPnP WTMC WWpP
	- 'Red Sputnik'	CMCo EBee EPPr MAvo WWpP
	- 'Rose Clair'	CElw CHid CMCo EBee EBla GKir LAst LRHS MNFA NBir NSti SChu SGar SHel SMer SPet SRms WBrk WCra WCru WEas WMnd WMoo WPer WTMC WWpP
I	- 'Rosemary'	SBch WWpP
	- 'Rosemary Verey'	SHel
	- 'Rosenlicht'	CBos CElw CSev EBee EBla EPPr LRHS MNFA MRav NLar SChu SRGP SSpi WCAu WCra WCru WMnd WMoo WPGP WPnP WWpP
	- 'Rosewood' **new**	SRos
	- 'Sherwood'	CBod EBla EChP ECtt EPPr GCal GKir IFro MTho MWgw NBro NCob NCot NEgg NLsd NPro NRnb NVic SApp SGar SHel SRGP WCAu WCra WFar WLin WMoo WPnP WWpP
§	- 'Spring Fling'^{PBR} (v)	CBct CCge CElw CRez EBee EBla EChP EHrv EPPr EVFa GFlt GSki LAst MBNS MHar NCot NGdn NSti SPla SPoG SRGP STes SVil WCot WWeb WWpP
	- 'Stillingfleet'	see *G.* x *oxonianum* 'Stillingfleet Keira'
§	- 'Stillingfleet Keira'	NCot NSti
	- 'Summer Surprise'	CElw CFwr EBee EPPr EWes SHel SRGP WCru WPnP WTMC WWpP
	- 'Susan'	EBee EBla EPPr EWes
	- 'Susie White'	CElw CMCo EBee EPPr MAvo WCru WWpP
*	- f. ***thurstonianum***	More than 30 suppliers
	- - 'Armitageae'	EBee EPPr MNFA NCot SHel SRGP WTMC WWpP
	- - 'Crûg Star'	CCge CElw
	- - 'Peter Hale'	CMea
	- - 'Southcombe Double' (d)	More than 30 suppliers
§	- - 'Southcombe Star'	EBee EBla EPPr GAbr GCal IPot MNFA NBro NGdn NLon NSti SHel SRGP WBrk WCru WFar WMoo WPer WPnP WTMC WWpP
	- 'Trevor's White'	EBee EBla EChP EPPr MBnl MNFA MNrw NCot SBch SRGP SUsu WCAu WCru WTMC WWpP
	- 'Wageningen'	CBre CElw CMCo EBee GCal GKir GMac LRHS MNFA NCot NGdn NPro SAga SRGP SRms WBrk WCra WCru WHer WMoo WTMC WWpP
	- 'Walter's Gift'	More than 30 suppliers
	- 'Wargrave Pink' 🏆^{H4}	More than 30 suppliers
	- 'Waystrode'	CMCo EBee EBla EPPr SRGP WTMC WWpP
	- white-flowered	EBla
	- 'Whitehaven'	EBee NCot
	- 'Winscombe'	CElw CMCo EBee EChP GCal LGro LLWP LRHS MRav MTho MWgw NCob NCot NSti WCru WMnd WMoo WWpP
	x ***oxonianum***	EHrv
	x ***sessiliflorum*** subsp. ***novae-zelandiae*** 'Nigricans'	
	'Pagoda'	CCge MNrw NCot
§	***palmatum*** 🏆^{H3}	More than 30 suppliers
	palustre	CElw EBee EBla EChP EMar EPPr LLWP MBow MNFA MNrw NBro NCot NSti SRGP STes WCra WFar WMoo WPnP WTMC WTin WWpP
	papuanum	SBla WCru
	'Patricia'	More than 30 suppliers
	peloponnesiacum	CDes CStr EBee EPPr GFlt GGar WFar
	- NS 660	CElw
	phaeum	More than 30 suppliers
	- 'Album'	More than 30 suppliers
	- 'Alec's Pink'	EBla LLWP SHar WOut WTMC
	- 'All Saints'	CElw EBee EMon SUsu WTMC
	- 'Aureum'	see *G. phaeum* 'Golden Spring'
	- black-flowered	see *G. phaeum* var. *phaeum*
	- 'Blauwvoet'	CFwr WTMC
	- 'Blue Shadow'	CDes CElw EPPr NCot WTMC WWpP
	- 'Calligrapher'	CElw EChP EPPr SRGP SUsu WCra WMoo WTMC WWpP
	- 'Chocolate Chip'	CFwr CMCo WTMC
	- dark-flowered	CElw
	- 'David Bromley'	EMon WCru WPrP WPtf WTMC
	- 'Geele Samobor'	WTMC
	- 'George Stone'	EPPr
§	- 'Golden Spring'	CCge CElw EPPr GBBs NChi NCot NPro SBch SRGP WTMC
	- 'Hannah Perry'	CElw CHad EBee EPPr LLWP MBnl WTMC
	- var. ***hungaricum***	EBee EPPr WCru WTMC WWpP
	- 'Klepper'	CFwr CMCo WTMC
	- 'Lily Lovell'	More than 30 suppliers
	- 'Little Boy'	CElw CMCo EBee EMon EPPr NCot WTMC
	- var. ***lividum***	CBre CElw CFee EBee EChP EMar EWTr GMaP LLWP LRHS MBow MRav MWgw NCot NEgg SPer SRGP SRms STes WCra WCru WFar WPer WPnP WTMC WWhi WWpP
	- - 'Joan Baker'	CBre CElw CMil COlW CSam EBee EChP EPPr GBuc LLWP LPio LRHS MBow MNFA MWhe NChi NCot NGdn NSti SBla SOkh SRGP SUsu WCra WCru WFar WMoo WPnP WTin WWpP
	- - 'Majus'	CCge CElw EBee ECtt EMon EPPr EPfP GKir LLWP LPhx MNFA MWgw NLsd NSti SBch WFar WGHP WMoo WPnP WTMC
	- 'Marchant's Ghost'	LPhx SMHy WTMC
	- 'Margaret Wilson' (v)	CBos CDes CElw CFir EBee EBla EChP EPPr EVFa EWes LPio MAvo MBNS NCot SRGP SUsu WCot WTMC WWpP
	- 'Mierhausen'	CElw CMCo EBee EPPr EShb NCot WPtf WTMC WWpP
	- 'Moorland Dylan'	WMoo WTMC
	- 'Mourning Widow'	see *G. phaeum* L. var. *phaeum* black-flowered
	- 'Mrs Charles Perrin'	CBgR CCge CElw EBee EPPr STes WTMC
	- 'Night Time'	EPPr EVFa LLWP MNFA
	- 'Our Pat'	EBee
§	- var. ***phaeum*** black-flowered	CMil EChP EPPr GBin GCal IBlr MWhe NCob NCot NDov SGar

	Name	Suppliers
		SRGP SRms WCra WCru WMoo WPGP WWpP
	- - 'Langthorns Blue'	CCge CDes CElw CMCo CMea CSev EBee ELan EPPr MNFA MNrw SRGP WCra WTMC WWpP
	- - 'Samobor'	More than 30 suppliers
I	- 'Ploeger de Bilt'	EPPr WTMC
	- purple-flowered	MDun
	- 'Rachel's Rhapsody'	EPPr NCot
	- 'Raven'	CFwr WTMC
	- red-flowered	MRav WTMC
I	- 'Rise Top Lilac'	CMCo EBee NCot WPGP WTMC
	- 'Rose Air'	CMCo EChP EGoo EPPr MNFA SRGP WCra WMoo WPnP WTMC WWpP
	- 'Rose Madder'	CCge CElw CHad CM&M EPPr EVFa GBuc GCal LLWP LPhx MNFA MNrw MSte NChi NCot SBch SHBN WCru WMoo WWpP
	- 'Saturn'	EBee WTMC
	- 'Silver Fox'	WRha
I	- 'Small Grey'	EPPr WTMC
	- 'Springtime'PBR	EChP EVFa
	- 'Stillingfleet Ghost'	CElw EBee EBrs EPPr LRHS NCot NLsd NPro NSti WPGP WTMC
	- 'Taff's Jester' (v)	CCge CElw CStr EWes NSti SApp SRGP WCot WHer WTMC WWpP
	- 'Thorn's Blue'	LRHS
§	- 'Variegatum' (v)	More than 30 suppliers
	- 'Walküre'	EBee EPPr MAvo WTMC
	- 'Zit Factory'	WTMC
	'Philippe Vapelle'	More than 30 suppliers
	'Pink Delight'	CElw EBee LPhx LPio WWpP
	'Pink Spice'PBR	EBla ECtt MRav
	'Pink Splash' **new**	LSou
§	***platyanthum***	CCge EChP EPPr GCal GGar GKir MAnH MNrw SBri SRGP WBrk WCru WHCG WMoo WPer WWpP
	- giant	EPPr SGar
	- var. ***reinii***	WCru
	- - f. ***onoei***	EBee WCru
	platypetalum misapplied	see *G.* x *magnificum*
	platypetalum Franch.	see *G. sinense*
§	***platypetalum*** Fisch. & C.A. Mey.	EChP EPPr EWsh GKir LRHS MAvo NBir NSti SRms WCru WTMC WWpP
	- 'Georgia Blue'	EBee MSte SSpi WCru WFar WPtf
	- 'Turco'	GBin
§	***pogonanthum***	CDes EBee GBuc GCal IFro MNrw NBir WCru WMoo
	polyanthes	CFwr CMCo GBuc GTou MSph NEgg WTMC
	- CC 3329	WRos
	- HWJCM 276	WCru
	- from China **new**	CFwr
	aff. ***polyanthes***	SOkd
§	***potentilloides***	CCge EBee GSki NBir SRGP WBrk WWpP
	pratense	CArn CBre CMCo CRWN EBee EBla ECtt ELan EPPr GKir GMaP LRHS MBow NBPC NCot NLan NMir NPri SPer SPlb SRms STes WBVN WFar WGHP WMoo WPer WPnP WWye
	- CC&McK 442	CMCo GTou
	- from Tibetan border	MAnH
I	- 'Bittersweet'	CHar EBee EBla EChP EMon EPPr
	- 'Cluden Sapphire'	CAbP EBla GKir MWhi NCot NPro WCru WFar
	- 'Flore Pleno'	see *G. pratense* 'Plenum Violaceum'
I	- 'Himalayanum'	NLar
	- 'Hocus Pocus'	CFai EBee EChP EHrv EPfP EVFa MBNS MTis NLar NSti WCra WPtf
	- 'Janet's Special'	WHoo
	- 'Lilac Lullaby'	EBee
	- Midnight Reiter strain	More than 30 suppliers
	- 'Mrs Kendall Clark' ♀H4	More than 30 suppliers
	- 'New Dimension'	EBee ENot EPfP GBin LBuc LRHS NSti
	- 'Okey Dokey' **new**	CFwr
	- pale form	EBee WPnP
	- 'Plenum Album' **new**	NCot NGdn SPoG WPop WTMC
	- 'Plenum Caeruleum' (d)	More than 30 suppliers
	- 'Plenum Purpureum'	see *G. pratense* 'Plenum Violaceum'
§	- 'Plenum Violaceum' (d) ♀H4	More than 30 suppliers
	- var. ***pratense*** f. ***albiflorum***	CBot CElw CSam EPPr GMaP IFro MAnH MBow MHer MNrw NBid NCot NEgg NOrc NSti WCra WCru WHCG WMnd WMoo WPnP WTMC WWpP
	- - - 'Galactic'	CCge EBee EChP EPPr GKir NBir WCra WCru WMoo WPnP
	- - - 'Plenum Album' (d)	CDes CElw CSpe CStr EBee EPPr MBnl NEgg NLar NSti SPer STes WCot WPnP
	- - - 'Silver Queen'	CBre CHar EBee EBla EChP ECtt EPPr MAnH MBow MNrw NBir NMRc SRGP WFar WMoo WPGP WPnP WSSM WTMC WWpP
	- - - 'Whimble White'	WWhi
	- 'Purple Heron'	CDes CKno CSpe EBee EBla EChP ECtt EPPr EUJe EVFa IBal IPot LAst LSRN MBri MCCP MNrw MSph MSte NBPC NEgg NGdn NLar SPla STes WCot WFar WGor
	- 'Purple-haze'	CCge EMag GBuc GFlt GSki ITer LSou MAnH MCCP MWhi NCob NLar WHoo WHrl
	- 'Rectum Album'	see *G. clarkei* 'Kashmir White'
§	- 'Rose Queen'	EBee EBla MAnH MNrw MRav NBir NEgg NLar SRGP SSpi WCra WCru WPnP WTMC WWpP
	- 'Roseum'	see *G. pratense* 'Rose Queen'
	- 'Splish-splash'	see *G. pratense* 'Striatum'
	- 'Stanton Mill'	NBid
	- var. ***stewartianum***	EBee MRav WPnP
	- - 'Elizabeth Yeo'	CCge EBee EBla EPPr MAnH SGar SUsu WCru WTMC WWpP
§	- 'Striatum'	More than 30 suppliers
	- 'Striatum' dwarf	WCru
	- 'Striatum' pale	CBre
§	- Victor Reiter Junior strain	More than 30 suppliers
	- 'Wisley Blue'	CMCo EBee EBla EPPr MSte SHel SRGP WHal
	- 'Yorkshire Queen'	EBee EPPr NGdn WCru
	pratense x ***himalayense*** **new**	NEgg
	'Prelude'	CCge CDes CElw EBee EPPr IFro NBir NCot NPro WCra WTMC
	procurrens	CBre CElw COIW CPLG CSev EChP EMar EPPr GAbr GCal GGar GKir IMGH LLWP LRHS MLLN NBid NGdn NSti WBrk WCru WFar WHCG WMoo WPnP WRos WWpP
	pseudosibiricum	EBee
§	***psilostemon*** ♀H4	More than 30 suppliers
	- 'Bressingham Flair'	CMCo EBee EBla EBrs EChP ECtt EGra EPfP GAbr GCal GKir GSki LRHS MMil MNFA MRav NBid NGdn NLar NOrc SChu SMer SRms WCAu WCru WFar WMoo WSHC WTMC

Name	Suppliers
- 'Fluorescent' **new**	ENot MWhi
- 'Goliath'	EPPr SUsu
- hybrid	CElw
pulchrum	CElw CHid CMCo CSpe EBee EMan EPPr LPio MAnH MNrw MWhi NSti SGar SIgm SRGP SSpi STes SWal WCot WCru WPer WRos WWpP
punctatum hort.	see *G.* x *monacense* 'Muldoon'
- 'Variegatum'	see *G. phaeum* 'Variegatum'
pusillum	MSal
pylzowianum	CCge CMCo EBee GGar MRav NBid NJOw NRya SBch WCra WCru WFar WMoo WPnP WTel
pyrenaicum	CCge CElw CRWN CSev EBee EWsh GAbr MBow NEgg NSti WBrk WTMC WWpP
- f. ***albiflorum***	CPrp EBee EBla EChP EGra GAbr GBBs LLWP MNFA MNrw MTho NBir NCot NEgg NSti WBrk WCra WPer WWpP
- 'Barney Brighteye' **new**	CCge
- 'Bill Wallis'	More than 30 suppliers
- Gordon's strain **new**	NEgg
- 'Isparta'	CElw EBee EChP EPPr IFro LPhx LPio MAnH SBch SMHy SRGP SUsu WBrk
- 'Summer Sky'	CCge MAnH NCot NLsd SPav SRGP WPtf WWpP
- 'Summer Snow'	EBee EPyc MAnH NCot NLar SPoG WLin WWpP
'Rambling Robin'	EBee EMan EPPr EWes MMil WCot WCru WPGP WWpP XPep
'Ray's Pink'	CCge MAnH NPro WWpP
rectum	EPPr WCru
- 'Album'	see *G. clarkei* 'Kashmir White'
'Red Admiral'	NCot
'Red Dwarf'	CCge CElw EPPr WMoo
'Red Propellers' **new**	LSou MAnH
reflexum	CHid CSev EBla EChP EPPr WFar WHCG WTMC WWpP
refractoides	CFwr
refractum from China **new**	CFwr
regelii	CBos CCge CElw CMCo CSam EPPr GMac MNFA SChu WCra WCru WMoo WPnP WWpP
renardii ♀H4	More than 30 suppliers
- 'Beldo'	EBee
- blue	see *G. renardii* 'Whiteknights'
- 'Tcschelda'	CFai CMil EBee EBla EChP EMil GBBs LPio MAnH NCGa NCot SBod SPla SRms SUsu WCra WFar WPnP WWhi WWpP
§ - 'Whiteknights'	CElw CFee EBla EGra GBuc GSki MAnH MAvo NBir NPro WCru WEas
- 'Zetterlund'	CElw CMCo EBee EBla EHrv EMar EPPr GKir LLWP LRHS MAvo MLLN MNFA MWhe NLsd WBrk WCAu WCru WFar WMoo WTMC
retrorsum	CCge
§ ***reuteri***	CCge ELan IDee LDai LPio NArg SBod SChr SDnm SGar SPav SRGP SRob WCru WPnP
'Richard John'	CCge
richardsonii	CCge EBee EBla EChP EPPr GCal MAvo MNrw NBir NDov SRGP SRms WCru WPnP WPtf WTMC WWpP
I 'Rise Top Lilac' **new**	CCge
x ***riversleaianum***	WCru
- 'Mavis Simpson'	More than 30 suppliers
- 'Russell Prichard' ♀H4	More than 30 suppliers
§ ***rivulare***	CCge CMCo EBee EBla GAbr GKir GSki MNFA NCot NSti STes WHCG WMnd WPnP WPtf
- 'Album'	EBla
robertianum	CArn EPPr GWCH MChe MHer SECG SRms WWpP
§ - 'Album'	CBgR EBla EPPr NSti SHar SRms
- f. ***bernettii***	see *G. robertianum* 'Album'
- 'Celtic White'	CBgR CBre CCge EMag EMon EPPr GCal GSki MHer SPav SRGP WOut WPnP WWpP
robustum	EPPr GSki IFro MNrw MSph NBPC NBro NChi NCot SIgm SMad SPav SRGP STes WCot WCru WFar WHal WHer WPGP WSHC WWpP XPep
- Hannays' form	CCge CSev CSpe CStr EBee WPGP
- 'Norman Warrington'	WHer
robustum x ***incanum***	CCge CMea CSpe MAnH MSph WCru
'Rosie Crûg'	CCge CHid EBee EChP EMan NLar SWvt WCru WWhi
rosthornii	WCru
Rozanne = 'Gerwat' PBR	CCge CFir CKno CMil EBee EBrs EPPr EVFa GKir IPot LAst LSRN MBNS MWgw MWhe NCob NDov NSti SMac SPer SPoG STes SVil WCot WCra WFar
rubescens	see *G. yeoi*
rubifolium	EMan GGar MNFA SSpi WCru WTMC
ruprechtii (Grossh.) Woronow	CCge CElw EBee EMag EPPr MAvo MNrw NCot SRGP WPer WPnP WWpP WWye
'Salome'	More than 30 suppliers
sanguineum	More than 30 suppliers
- Alan Bloom = 'Bloger' PBR	ECtt GKir LRHS SIng WCra WTMC
- 'Album' ♀H4	More than 30 suppliers
- 'Alpenglow'	EPPr SHel SRGP
- 'Ankum's Pride'	CCge CM&M EBee EBla ECGP EChP EDAr EMon EPPr EVFa GMac IPot LRHS MMil MNFA NChi NCot NGdn NSti SAga SBla SGSe SUsu WCra WCru WMoo WPnP WTMC WWpP
- 'Apfelblüte'	CRez EBee SSvw
- 'Aviemore'	EPPr SHel
- 'Barnsley'	CElw EBee EPPr NBro NPro WTMC WWpP
- 'Belle of Herterton'	CMCo EBee EPPr MSte NBid NPro SUsu WCru WTMC WWpP
- 'Bloody Graham'	EPPr MWhe SHel WMoo
- 'Canon Miles'	EBee EPPr IPot LPio
- 'Catforth Carnival'	EPPr
- 'Cedric Morris'	CElw CFil EBee EBla EChP ECha EGra EPPr GCra LPio MAvo MTho NBid SAga SHel SRGP SUsu WCot WCru WPnP WTMC WWpP
- 'Compactum' **new**	CFwr
§ - 'Droplet'	SUsu WPnP WWpP
- 'Elsbeth'	CCge CElw CMCo CMil EBee EBla EChP ECtt EGra EPPr EWes GBuc NCot NEgg NGdn NSti SHel SPoG SRGP WCra WCru WFar WHal WMoo WPnP WTMC WWpP
- 'Feu d'Automne'	EPPr
- 'Fran's Star'	see *G.* x *oxonianum* 'Fran's Star'
- 'Glenluce'	More than 30 suppliers
- 'Hampshire Purple'	see *G. sanguineum* 'New Hampshire Purple'
- 'Holden'	CElw CNic EPPr SHel WWpP
- 'Inverness' **new**	CFwr EPPr
- 'Joanna'	SHel

	- 'John Elsley'	CElw CMCo CPrp EBee EBla EChP ECtt EHoe EPPr GKir LLWP LRHS MMil MWhe NBro NCot NGdn NLar SHel SRGP SSpe SSpi WBVN WCAu WCra WMnd WPer WPnP WTMC WWpP
	- 'John Innes' **new**	CFwr
	- 'Jubilee Pink'	CElw EBla GCal SBla WCra WCru WTMC
	- var. ***lancastrense***	see *G. sanguineum* var. *striatum*
	- 'Leeds Variety'	see *G. sanguineum* 'Rod Leeds'
§	- 'Little Bead'	EBla NMen WCru WPnP WWpP
	- 'Max Frei'	More than 30 suppliers
	- 'Minutum'	see *G. sanguineum* 'Droplet'
	- 'Nanum'	see *G. sanguineum* 'Little Bead'
§	- 'New Hampshire Purple'	CBgR CBos EBee EChP EPPr LSou NBro NGdn NLar NSti SSvw WCAu WCra WTMC WWpP
	- 'Nyewood'	EBee EMon EPPr IMGH MLLN SEND SRGP WCru WWpP
I	- 'Plenum' (d)	EPPr
	- var. ***prostratum*** (Cav.) Pers.	see *G. sanguineum* var. *striatum*
	- 'Purple Flame'	see *G. sanguineum* 'New Hampshire Purple'
§	- 'Rod Leeds'	CBgR CBos EBee LPio MSte NCot NPro NSti WCAu WHal WPnP WTMC WWpP
	- 'Sandra'	SRGP
	- 'Sara'	WPnP
	- 'Shepherd's Warning' ♀H4	CMea CSev EBla ECtt EDAr EPPr EVFa GKir LRHS MLLN MRav NBir NLar SRGP SUsu WCru WHCG WHoo WTel WTin WWpP
	- 'Shepherd's Warning' seedlings	GCal
§	- var. ***striatum*** ♀H4	More than 30 suppliers
	- - deep pink	CSBt CWCL GBBs MSwo SWvt
	- - 'Reginald Farrer'	EBee GBuc WCru
	- - 'Splendens'	CElw CSev EBla ELan ENot EPPr LBee MRav MWat NBid NChi NCot WCru WEas WPnP WTin WWhi WWpP
	- 'Vision'	CCge CFwr EBla LRHS NArg NCot SGar WPer WPnP WWpP
	- 'Vision Light Pink' **new**	WPtf
	- 'Westacre Poppet'	EPPr EWes
	'Sarah Louisa'	NPar
	'Sea Fire'	CCge CElw CWCL MNrw
	'Sea Pink'	CElw MNrw WHal
	'Sellindge Blue'	CElw NCot WCra
	sessiliflorum	ECou
I	- subsp. ***novae-zelandiae*** 'Nigricans'	CBrm CCge CHar EBla ECha EHrv ELan GAbr GGar LLWP MHer NBid NJOw NWCA SRGP WCru WEas WFar WHCG WPnP WTMC WWpP
§	- - 'Porter's Pass'	CMea CWib EHoe EWes GBuc GFlt LAst MCCP MNrw NBir SBch SPlb WCru WFar WHoo WTMC WWpP
	- - red-leaved	see *G. sessiliflorum* subsp. *novae-zelandiae* 'Porter's Pass'
*	- 'Rubrum'	CCge CSec GSki
	'Sheilah Hannay'	CSpe CStr SHar
	shensianum	CFwr
	shikokianum	EBee EChP EShb GKev MAnH MCCP NLar SPer SRGP WWpP
	- var. ***kaimontanum***	EBee EBla WCru
	- var. ***quelpaertense***	CDes EBee EBla NChi WHal WPGP
	- - B&SWJ 1234	WCru
	- var. ***yoshiianum***	CCge CElw GBuc GKev WCru WMoo WPat WTMC
	- - B&SWJ 6147	WCru
	'Shocking Blue' **new**	NSti
	sibiricum	EBla
*	Silver Cloak Group	ECre GSki LSou MCCP WCot WCra
	'Silver Shadow'	ENot LDai NScw WPop
§	***sinense***	CElw CFwr EBee EBla EChP EMar GCal ITer LRHS MNFA MNrw NLar NSti SRGP WCra WCru WHCG WHer WMnd WMoo WPer WTMC WWhi WWpP
	- B&SWJ 7870	WCru
	'Sirak'	More than 30 suppliers
	soboliferum	CBod CBos EBee EBla ELan EMan EPPr GMac LRHS MHar NBir NDlv NSti SPla SRGP WCra WCru WHal WMoo WWpP
	- Cally strain	GCal MSte
	'Southcombe Star'	see *G.* x *oxonianum* f. *thurstonianum* 'Southcombe Star'
	'Spinners'	More than 30 suppliers
	stapfianum var. ***roseum***	see *G. orientalitibeticum*
	'Stephanie'	CDes CElw EBee EPPr GGar NDov NLsd WCra WWpP
	'Strawberry Frost'	EBla EChP LTwo MBNS WCAu
	subcaulescens ♀H4	More than 30 suppliers
	- 'Guiseppii'	CTbh EBla EChP ECtt EPPr GKir GSki MNrw MRav MWhe NBro NCot NDov NGdn NPri SPla SRGP WCra WFar WPnP WWeb
	- 'Splendens' ♀H4	CSpe CTri EBee EBla ECtt EDAr EPPr EPfP GLbr LRHS MBNS MDun MTis MWhe NLon NSla NSti SHBN SPla SRms WCra WFar WPat WPnP WWpP
*	- 'Violaceum'	EPPr NEgg
	'Sue Crûg'	More than 30 suppliers
	'Summer Cloud'	EBee EBla EPPr MAvo NCot SHel SRGP WCra WHrl
	Summer Skies = 'Gernic'PBR (d)	CCge CFir CStr EPPr IFro LRHS LSpr MAnH MBnl MMHG MWgw NBro NCot NDov NGdn NLar SPer WCot WCra WFar WPnP WTMC
	suzukii	IFro WPtf
	- B&SWJ 016	WCru
	swatense	MLLN WCru
	sylvaticum	CM&M CRWN EBee EBla GKir MBow MSal NBid SSpi WBVN WBrk WHal WMoo WOut WPer WShi WTMC
	- f. ***albiflorum***	CBre CCge CElw CMil EBee ELan EMar MWhe NSti SSpi WCru WTin
	- 'Album' ♀H4	More than 30 suppliers
	- 'Amy Doncaster'	More than 30 suppliers
	- 'Angulatum'	CElw EBee EPPr LPhx MNFA SHel WMoo WWpP
I	- 'Birch Lilac'	CElw EBee EBla EChP EPPr EPfP EWTr GBuc GCal GKir LRHS MAvo WCra WFar WMoo WPnP WTMC WWpP
	- 'Blue Ice'	EBla EPPr GBin WWpP
*	- 'Heron'	CCge
	- 'Immaculée'	EPPr MRav
	- 'Kanzlersgrund'	CElw EPPr
	- 'Lilac Time'	EBla EPPr WWpP
	- 'Mayflower' ♀H4	More than 30 suppliers
	- 'Meran'	CCge EPPr
	- f. ***roseum***	CCge EBee EPPr GGar GKir NLar
	- - 'Baker's Pink'	CCge CElw CMil EBee EBla EPPr MRav NCot SRGP SSpi WCra WCru WFar WHCG WMoo WPnP WTMC WTin WWhi WWpP
I	- 'Silva'	CElw EBee ECtt EMan EPPr MAvo MNFA MRav NCot WCru WWpP
	- subsp. ***sylvaticum*** var. ***wanneri***	CCge EBee EPPr MRav WCru WTMC WWpP

	'Terre Franche'	EPPr GBin MAvo NGby NLar NSti SSpi SSvw WFar
	'Thorn's Blue' **new**	CCge
§	***thunbergii***	CCge CHid EBee GGar GSki LAst MBow NBid NJOw NOak NSti WBrk WPer WPnP WWpP
	- dark	CSev EMar
	- 'Jester's Jacket' (v)	CCge EKen EMan MAvo MCCP NPro NSti SPoG WBrk WCru WHrl WMoo WOut WTMC WWpP
	- pink	EPPr SRGP WCru WTMC
	- white	EPPr SRGP WTMC
	thurstonianum	see *G.* x *oxonianum* f. *thurstonianum*
	'Tidmarsh'	EBee
	'Tinpenny Mauve'	WHoo WTin
	'Tiny Monster'	CDes CFwr EBee EBla EWes MAvo MBnl NSti
	transbaicalicum	CCge CFwr EPPr MBow MNrw SRGP
	traversii	CCge CLyd GGar MDKP WRos
	- 'Big White'	WPnP
	- var. ***elegans***	CFee CSpe ECtt GGar IGor LPhx MNrw SRGP WCru WEas WHCG WKif WPGP WSSM
	tuberosum	CBro CElw CHid EBee EBla EBrs ECha ELan EPot EVFa EWTr EWsh LLWP LPhx LRHS MBow MHer MNFA MTho MWhe NBir NBro NGdn NSti WFar WPnP
	- var. ***charlesii***	see *G. kotschyi* var. *charlesii*
§	- 'Leonidas'	EBee EBrs LPhx LRHS WCot WPnP
	- subsp. ***linearifolium***	WCru
	- pink-flowered	WCru WHoo WPnP
	'Vera May'	SUsu
	'Verguld Saffier'	see *G.* 'Blue Sunrise'
	versicolor	More than 30 suppliers
	- 'Kingston'	see *G.* x *oxonianum* 'Kingston'
	- 'Knighton'	EBee
§	- 'Snow White'	CCge CElw CMCo EChP EGoo EPPr MNFA MNrw MWhe NCot NDov SRGP WCra WCru WMoo WPnP WTMC WWpP
	- 'The Bride'	CMea EGra EMan EMar
	- 'White Lady'	see *G. versicolor* 'Snow White'
	'Victor Reiter'	see *G. pratense* Victor Reiter Junior strain
	violareum	see *Pelargonium* 'Splendide'
	viscosissimum	EBla GSki SRGP STes WMnd
	- var. ***incisum***	CMCo EWsh MCCP STes WOut WTMC WWpP
	- rose pink	NBir
	wallichianum	CBod CBos CBot CCge CMCo CPou CStr ECGP IFro LRHS NBir NChi NSti SBla WFar WMoo WTMC
§	- 'Buxton's Variety' ♀H4	More than 30 suppliers
	- 'Chadwell's Pink'	CCge NEgg
	- 'Chris' **new**	EBee EPPr SRGP SUsu
	- 'Martha'	EBee
	- pale blue	CElw
	- 'Pink Buxton' **new**	SPoG
	- pink-flowered	EBla EMan GBuc GKir LPio NCot WCra WCru WWpP
	- 'Rosie'	SRGP
	- 'Syabru'	CCge CElw CMea EBee EBla EMar EMil EVFa GBuc GSki MAnH MNrw NCot NLar NPro SAga SSpi WBVN WFar WMoo
	'Wednesday's Child'	WFar
	'Welsh Guiness'	WCru WTMC
	wilfordii misapplied	see *G. thunbergii*
	wilfordii Maxim.	CCge EBee
	Wisley hybrid	see *G.* 'Khan'
	wlassovianum	More than 30 suppliers
	- 'Blue Star'	CCge GKir MRav NPro WFar WTMC WWpP
	yeoi	CCge CSpe EPPr MNrw NBir NBro SRGP WBrk WCru WHal WOut WSHC WTMC
	yesoense	EBla EPPr GBin GGar MDKP NBir NSti SRGP WCru WFar WOut
	- var. ***nipponicum***	WCru
	- white-flowered	EBee MNFA NWCA
	yoshinoi	CMCo EBee EBla EMan EWes GAbr GIBF GSki LLWP MSte MWhi NCot NLar SRGP SWal WMoo WPGP WTMC WWpP
	yunnanense misapplied	see *G. pogonanthum*
	yunnanense Franchet	CFir CFwr IFro
	- BWJ 7543	WCru

Gerbera (Asteraceae)

	gossypina	NWCA

Gerrardanthus (Cucurbitaceae)

	macrorhiza **new**	ERea

Gesneria (Gesneriaceae)

	cardinalis	see *Sinningia cardinalis*
	x ***cardosa***	see *Sinningia* x *cardosa*
*	***macrantha*** 'Compacta'	EShb

Gethyum (Liliaceae)

	atropurpureum **new**	CMon
	cuspidatum F&W 8233	WCot

Geum ✿ (Rosaceae)

	'Abendsonne'	MAvo
	aleppicum	CFee SBri WMoo
	alpinum	see *G. montanum*
	'Apricot Beauty'	EBee
	'Beech House Apricot'	More than 30 suppliers
	'Bell Bank'	CElw GBri MAvo MFOX MRav NBir NBre NChi NCot NDov NGby NPro WMoo
	'Birkhead's Cream'	NBir
	'Birkhead's Creamy Lemon'	MAvo
	'Blazing Sunset' (d)	CElw EBee ECtt LSou MBNS MDKP MRav MSph MWrn NArg NDlv NPro SHGN SOkh WHil WPnP
N	'Borisii'	More than 30 suppliers
	bulgaricum	EBee GKir LRHS MRav NBir NLar NPro NRya WPnP WPrP WSSM WTMC WTin
	'Caitlin' **new**	EMon
	calthifolium	EBee EPPr GKir MCCP MLLN MRav NBro
	canadense	NArg
	capense	LSou MAvo NPro SHGN
	- JJ&JH 9401271	EBee EWes
§	***chiloense***	EBee EBla NArg
	- P&W 6513	GBri MSte NWCA
	- 'Farncombe'	WCot
	coccineum hort.	see *G. chiloense*
	coccineum ambig.	EBla WRha
	coccineum Sibth. & Sm. MESE 374	EBee
	- 'Cooky' **new**	LSou
	- 'Werner Arends'	CBos CMHG CSev EBee EBla GCal MBnl MRav NBro SBri WFar WMoo
	'Coppertone'	More than 30 suppliers
	'Dingle Apricot'	CFir ECtt EMan EVFa GCal MAvo MNrw MRav MWgw NBir
	'Dolly North'	CFir EBee EMan ERou GBri GGar LRHS MAvo MBNS MBri MNrw

		MRav NBro WAul WCAu WHal WPrP WTMC WTin
I	'Elaine's Variety'	MAvo
	elatum	EBee
I	'Farmer John Cross'	CBre CDes CElw EBee EBla ECtt MAvo MHar MNrw NCot SBri WCra WHal WLin WMoo WPGP
	fauriei* x *kamtschatica	EBee
	'Feuerball' **new**	NBre
	'Feuermeer'	EBee EBla MSte NPro SBri
	'Fire Opal' ♀H4	CAby CDes CSam EBee MAvo MNrw MSph NBir NBre WMoo WPGP
	'Flames of Passion' PBR	EBee EChP EMan EVFa GBin GFlt IPot MAvo MBNS MBnl NArg NLar SPoG SUsu WAul WCAu WCot WCra WHil
	'Georgeham'	WWhi
	'Georgenburg'	More than 30 suppliers
	glaciale **new**	GIBF
	- album	NBre
	'Herterton Primrose'	ECtt MAvo
*	***hybridum luteum***	NSti
	x ***intermedium***	CBre EBee EMan EMon EPPr GBri LRHS MAvo MNrw NLar NPro SBri SChu SHGN WBWf WFar WMoo WPtf WTMC
	- 'Diane'	MAvo NBre
	'Karlskaer'	CElw EBee EBla EChP ECtt EPfP EVFa EWes GBin GCal LPio MAvo MBnl MBri MHar MNrw SAga SBri SOkh SUsu WCot WHil WMoo WPGP WPnP WTin
	'Lady Stratheden' ♀H4	More than 30 suppliers
	'Lemon Drops'	More than 30 suppliers
	'Lemon Frilled' **new**	NArg
	'Lionel Cox'	More than 30 suppliers
	macrophyllum	EBee EMan GBar NBre WMoo
	magellanicum	EBee EBla
	'Mandarin'	CFir CMdw EBla GCal
	'Marika'	CBre CHid CRow EBee EBla LRHS MNrw NBre SBri SChu WMoo
	'Marmalade'	EBla EChP ECtt GAbr LPhx MAvo MBnl MHar MNrw NPro SAga SBri SDys SMHy SUsu WCra WMoo WWhi
§	***montanum*** ♀H4	EBee EBla GKir GTou ITim NArg NBir NBro NDlv NPri NRya SPet SRms WBrk WMoo WPat WPer
	- 'Diana' **new**	EMon NDov
	- 'Maximum'	MNrw
	'Moorland Sorbet'	WMoo
	'Mrs J. Bradshaw' ♀H4	More than 30 suppliers
	'Mrs W. Moore'	CDes ECtt GBri MAvo MBnl MLLN MNrw NBir NChi NCot NPro WMoo WPGP WTMC
	'Nordek'	EMan GMac MAvo NCot SBri WPtf WWhi
*	'Orangeman'	MNrw
	parviflorum	GGar LEdu MLLN NBro
	'Paso Doble'	NLsd NPro SBri WRHF WRos WSan
§	***pentapetalum***	GEdr MNrw WAbe
	- 'Flore Pleno' (d)	WAbe
	'Pink Frills'	CElw EBla ECha NDov SMHy
	ponticum **new**	GIBF WOut
	'Present'	EBee EBla MAvo NBre SBri WPGP
I	'Primrose'	NPro WTMC
	'Prince of Orange'	CElw EBla GAbr IGor MNrw NBre WFar WMoo WRha
	'Prinses Juliana'	More than 30 suppliers
	pyrenaicum	EBla
	quellyon	see *G. chiloense*
I	'Rearsby Hybrid'	MAvo MRav
	'Red Wings'	CBre CM&M EBla EMan GCal MBNS MRav NBro SUsu
	x ***rhaeticum***	EBee ECtt ETow MNrw WMoo
	'Rijnstroom'	EBee EBla EChP ELan EWTr MBnl NBro SUsu WAul WCra WHil WPtf
	rivale	More than 30 suppliers
	- 'Album'	More than 30 suppliers
	- 'Barbra Lawton'	EBla MAvo MDKP
	- 'Cream Drop'	EBla EVFa NChi NGby NLsd NPro NWoo SBri
	- cream, from Tien Shan, China	CFee
*	***- islandicum***	EBee
	- lemon	EMan
	- 'Leonard's Double' (d)	CPrp MAvo WFar WMoo WTMC
	- 'Leonard's Variety'	More than 30 suppliers
	- 'Marmalade'	MSph NBPC NChi NLsd SOkh
	- 'Oxford Marmalade'	CElw SApp
	- 'Snowflake'	NChi
	rossii **new**	GIBF
	'Rubin'	CElw CHad EBee MBNS MNrw NBro NDov NGdn SChu SSpe SUsu WAul WTMC
	'Sigiswang'	CDes GAbr GMac MAvo MNrw MRav MSte NCot NPro SBri WLin WMoo WPGP
I	'Starker's Magnificum'	WCot
	'Tangerine'	GGar LSou MAvo MNrw MRav NPro
	'Tinpenny Orange'	WTin WWhi
	x ***tirolense***	EBee EBla MAvo NBre SBri
	triflorum	CNic CPBP EBee EBla EChP EHrv EMan EPla GKir GTou ITer LPhx LPio LRHS MBri MCCP MNrw MRav MTis NLar SRot SWal WFar WTin WWhi
	- var. ***campanulatum***	EDAr EHyt ETow GBri NPro NRya
	urbanum	CArn ELau GBar GWCH IHMH MBow MChe NLan NMir NPri SECG WBWf WHer WMoo
	- from Patagonia	EBla MAvo MDKP
	- 'Checkmate' (v)	EMon ITer
	'Wagonwheel' **new**	NChi
	'Wallace's Peach' **new**	SWal
	'Werner Arends'	see *G. coccineum* 'Werner Arends'

Gevuina (*Proteaceae*)

avellana	CBcs CHEx CTrw EBee SSpi WPGP

Gilia (*Polemoniaceae*)

aggregata	see *Ipomopsis aggregata*
californica	see *Leptodactylon californicum*
'Red Dwarf'	NPol
tricolor	NPol

Gillenia (*Rosaceae*)

stipulata	CHea CWCL EBee EMon LPhx NLar SVal
trifoliata ♀H4	More than 30 suppliers
- 'Pixie'	CFil EBee WPGP

Ginkgo ✿ (*Ginkgoaceae*)

	biloba ♀H4	More than 30 suppliers
	- B&SWJ 8753	WCru
	- 'Anny's Dwarf'	MBlu
	- 'Autumn Gold' (m)	CBcs CEnd CMCN EPfP MBlu MGos SIFN SMad WPGP
I	- 'Barabits Nana'	CMCN SIFN SMad
	- 'Chotek'	MBlu
	- 'Doctor Causton' (f) **new**	CAgr
	- 'Doctor Causton' (m) **new**	CAgr
	- 'Fairmount' (m)	CMCN MBlu SIFN

- 'Fastigiata' (m) CMCN MGos NLar SBLw
- 'Hekt Leiden' CMCN
- 'Horizontalis' CMCN EPfP MBlu SIFN
- 'Jade Butterflies' CBcs MPkF NLar
- 'King of Dongting' (f) CMCN GKir MBlu WMou
- 'Mariken' MPkF SLim
- Ohazuki Group (f) CAgr
- Pendula Group CBcs CEnd CMCN CRez CTho EPfP NPal SIFN SLim
- 'Princeton Sentry' (m) MBlu
I - 'Prostrata' CPMA
- 'Saratoga' (m) CBcs CDoC CEnd CMCN CPMA CTho EMil MGos SIFN WPGP
- 'Tit' CMCN EPfP MGos SIFN
- 'Tremonia' CMCN EPfP LRHS MBlu SIFN
- 'Troll' **new** SCoo
- 'Tubifolia' CMCN MBlu SIFN
- 'Umbrella' CMCN SIFN
- Variegata Group (v) CMCN CPMA MBlu NLar SLim

ginseng see *Panax ginseng*

Gladiolus (*Iridaceae*)

acuminatus WCot
alatus CFil
'Alexander S' (L) **new** MSGs
'Amanda Mahy' (N) CBro
'Amsterdam' (G) MSGs
'Anchorage' (L) MSGs
'Andre Viette' EBee EMan WCot
angustus WCot
'Anna Leorah' (L) MSGs
antakiensis CPou
'Antique Lace' (L) **new** MSGs
I 'Antique Rose' (M) MSGs WCot
'Anyu S' (L) **new** MSGs
'Arabella' (P) WCot
'Atom' (S/P) CBro EBee EBrs
atroviolaceus WCot WPGP
'Aubrey Lane' (M) MSGs
'August Days' (L) MSGs
aurantiacus WCot
aureus WCot
'Bangladesh' (M) **new** MSGs
'Beautiful Angel' MSGs
'Beauty Bride' (L) MSGs
'Beauty of Holland'PBR (L) MSGs
'Bizar' EPfP
'Black Lash' (S) MSGs
'Black Pearls' (S) MSGs
blandus var. ***carneus*** see *G. carneus*
'Blue Conqueror' (L) LRHS
'Blue Frost' (L) EBrs
'Blue Tropic' **new** EPfP
bonaespei CDes WCot
'Bono's Memory' LRHS
'Bradley W' (M) MSGs
'Burgundy Queen' (M) MSGs WCot
byzantinus see *G. communis* subsp. *byzantinus*
caeruleus CPou
callianthus CSWP EBla EPfP EPyc GFlt LPio MSte SPet WFar WHil WWhi
cardinalis CAby CDes CFil CMea CPne CPrp EBla EMan GCal IBlr LPio SAga SIgm SSpi WCot WCru WPGP
carinatus CDes WCot
carinatus* x *orchidiflorus EBee WCot
carmineus CFil WCot
§ ***carneus*** CFil CPou EBee EMan GCal LRHS SMeo
'Carquirenne' (G) MSGs
'Carved Ivory' (M) MSGs
caryophyllaceus CFil CPou
'Century Mark' (G) **new** MSGs
ceresianus JCA 3.256.409 **new** WCot
'Charm' (N/Tub) CAvo CBro EBee EBla
'Charming Beauty' (Tub) ECho
'Charming Lady' (Tub) ECho
'Chlöe' (M) MSGs
'Christabel' (L) ERos
'Cindy' (B) ECho EPfP
citrinus see *G. trichonemifolius*
'Clarence's Choice' (L) MSGs
'Clemence' (Min) **new** MSGs
x ***colvillii*** CPne EVFa IBlr
- 'Albus' EBrs NJOw SOkh
'Comet' (N) EBee EBrs LPio WPnP
communis LAma
§ - subsp. ***byzantinus*** ♀H4 More than 30 suppliers
- subsp. ***communis*** SSpi
'Coral Butterfly' (L) MSGs
'Côte d'Azur' (G) MSGs
crassifolius CFir GBuc LPio WCot
'Cream Perfection' (L) **new** MSGs
'Creamy Yellow' (S) **new** MSGs
cunonius CFil
§ ***dalenii*** CPou CSam ERos GCal IBlr LPio SSpi WCot
- green **new** CDes
- hybrids WCot
- orange CDes
* - f. ***rubra*** CFil WCot
- yellow CDes CFil EBee
debilis **new** CFil
'Desirée' (B) MSGs SPet
'Dominick C' (S) MSGs
'Doris Darling' (L) MSGs
'Drama' (L) MSGs
'Dusk' (S) **new** MSGs
ecklonii CFil WHil
'Elegance' (G) MSGs
'Elvira' (N) EBee EBla ECho LAma WPGP
'Emerald Spring' (S) WCot
'Emir' (S) MSGs
equitans CFil
'Esperanto' (M) MSGs
'Esta Bonita' (G) MSGs
'Eunice Ann' MSGs
'Fashion Romance' MSGs
'Felicta' (L) **new** MSGs
ferrugineus **new** CFil
'Fidelio' (L) LAma
'Fireball II' (L) MSGs
'Flamenco' (L) MSGs
flanaganii EBee GKir SSpi WCot
'Flevo Amico' (S) WCot
'Flevo Bambino' (S) MSGs
'Flevo Candy' (S) MSGs
'Flevo Clown' (S) MSGs
'Flevo Cosmic' (Min) GBri LPio MSGs WCot
'Flevo Eclips'PBR (G) MSGs
'Flevo Eyes'PBR (L) MSGs
'Flevo Fire'PBR (M) MSGs
'Flevo Jive' (S) MSGs
'Flevo Junior' (S) WCot
'Flevo Maitre' (L) MSGs
'Flevo Party' (S) MSGs
'Flevo Smile' (S) MSGs WCot
'Flevo Sunset'PBR (L) MSGs
'Flevo Touch' (S) **new** MSGs
'Flevo Vision' (L) MSGs
floribundus CFil
'Flowersong' (L) LAma

	***fourcadei* new**	CFil
	'Friendship' (L)	LRHS
	garnieri	SSpi
	geardii	WCot
	'Gladiris' (L)	MSGs
	'Golden Melody' (M)	MSGs
	'Golden Sunset' (L)	MSGs
	'Good Luck' (N)	CBro
	gracilis	CFil WCot
	***grandiflorus* new**	CFil
	grandis	see *G. liliaceus*
	'Green Star' (L)	MSGs
	'Green with Envy' (L)	MSGs
	'Green Woodpecker' (M)	EBee LAma LRHS
	gueinzii	CFil
	'Halley' (N)	CBro ECho
	'Hastings' (P)	WCot
	'Hunting Song' (L)	LAma
	'Huron Darkness' (L)	MSGs
	'Huron Frost' (L) **new**	MSGs
	'Huron Glow' (L)	MSGs
	'Huron Jewel' (M) **new**	MSGs
	'Huron Silk' (L)	MSGs
	huttonii* x *tristis	CPou
	- x - var. ***concolor***	WCot
	hyalinus	WCot
	'Ice Cap' (L)	MSGs
	'Ice Follies' (L)	MSGs
	illyricus	CBrm CFil CSam GBuc GCal SSpi WBWf WPGP
	- 'Mallorca'	CFil
	imbricatus	EPot ERos GBuc GCrs
	'Impressive' (N)	SPet
§	***italicus***	CFil EBee ELan GCal GKir LPhx LPio MSte
	'Iva May' (L) **new**	MSGs
	'Ivory Priscilla'PBR (L)	MSGs
	'Jarni Tani' (L) **new**	MSGs
	'Jayvee' (S)	MSGs
	'Jean K' (M) **new**	MSGs
	'Jim S' (G)	MSGs
	'Jupiter' (B)	LRHS
	kotschyanus	EBee GCrs GKir SSpi
	'Kristin' (L)	MSGs
	'Kytice' (L)	MSGs
	'Lady Barbara' (P)	MSGs
	'Lady Caroline' (P)	MSGs
	'Lady Eleanor' (P)	WCot
	'Lady in Red' (L)	MSGs
	'Lady Lucille' (M)	MSGs
	'Laura Maria' (S) **new**	MSGs
	'Lavender Masterpiece' (L)	MSGs
I	'Lavender Rose' (L) **new**	MSGs
	'Lemon Drop' (S) **new**	MSGs
	lewisiae	SSpi
§	***liliaceus***	CDes WCot
	'Lime Green' (P)	LRHS
	'Linne' (S) **new**	MSGs
	'Little Jude' (P)	MSGs WCot
	'Little Wiggy' (P)	WCot
	'Loulou' (G)	MSGs
	'Lowland Queen' (L)	MSGs
	***maculatus* new**	CFil
	'Maggie' (S)	EPfP
	'Marj S' (L)	MSGs
	'Mascagni' (M) **new**	EPfP
	'Mi Mi' (S) **new**	MSGs
	'Mileesh' (L)	MSGs
	***miniatus* new**	CFil
	'Mirella' (N)	MRav
	'Miss America' (M)	MSGs
	'Miss Gwendoline' (S) **new**	MSGs
	'Miss Henriette' (P) **new**	MSGs
	***monticola* new**	CFil
	mortonius	CFil GCal SIgm
	'Mother Theresa' (M)	MSGs
	'Mr Chris' (S)	MSGs
	'Mrs Rowley' (P)	GBri
§	***murielae*** ♀H3	CAby CAvo CBro CFwr CMea EBee EBrs LAma LPhx SMeo STes WGwG WHoo WRHF
	'Murieliae'	see *G. murielae*
	'My Love' (L)	LAma
	natalensis	see *G. dalenii*
	'Nathalie' (N)	EBee EBrs LPio WHil WPnP
	'New Parfait' (L)	MSGs
	'New Wave'PBR (L)	MSGs
	'Nicholas' (S)	MSGs
	'Nikita' (P) **new**	MSGs
	'Nola' (S)	MSGs
	'Nova Lux' (L)	CSut EBrs EPfP LAma LRHS
	'Nymph' (N)	CAvo CElw EBee EBla EBrs EChP ITim LAma LDai LPio MBow MDun SPur WHil WPnP
	'Ocean Breeze' (S)	MSGs
	ochroleucus	CFil
	'Of Singular Beauty' (G)	MSGs
	'Olympic Torch' (L)	MSGs
§	***oppositiflorus***	CDes CFil CPou
	- subsp. ***salmoneus***	see *G. oppositiflorus*
	orchidiflorus	CFil CPou CSWP
	'Orlando' (L)	MSGs
	'Oscar' (G)	CSut LAma LRHS
	palustris	ERos
	papilio	More than 30 suppliers
	- 'David Hills'	WCot
§	- Purpureoauratus Group	CBro CSam EBee EMan ERos GKir IBlr SRms
	- ruby-flowered **new**	CHad
	- yellow-flowered	SMad
	pappei	CDes CFil EBee WPGP
	'Peach Royale' (L)	MSGs
	***permeabilis* new**	CFil
	'Perth Ivory' (M)	MSGs
	'Perth Pearl' (M)	MSGs
	'Peter Pears' (L)	CSut LAma LRHS
	'Phyllis M' (L)	MSGs
	'Pink Elegance' (L)	MSGs
	'Pink Elf' (S)	MSGs
	'Pink Lady' (L)	MSGs
	'Pinnacle' (L)	MSGs
	'Plum Tart' (L)	LRHS SMeo
	'Pop Art'	LRHS
	'Praha' (L)	LAma
	'Pretty Woman' (L)	MSGs
	primulinus	see *G. dalenii*
	'Princess Margaret Rose' (Min)	LAma
	'Prins Claus' (N)	CBro EBee EBla LAma LRHS SPet
	'Priscilla' (L)	LAma
	'Pulchritude' (M)	MSGs
	punctulatus var. ***punctulatus***	ERos
	'Purple Prince' (M)	WCot
	purpureoauratus	see *G. papilio* Purpureoauratus Group
	quadrangularis	SSpi
	'Ramona'	CFil
	'Rasmin' (L)	MSGs
	'Red Alert' (L) **new**	MSGs
	'Red Beauty'	LRHS
	'Red Ruffles' (L)	MSGs
	'Revelry' (S) **new**	MSGs
	'Robert S' (L) **new**	MSGs
	'Robinetta' (*recurvus* hybrid) ♀H3	CBro CElw EBee EBla EChP ECho EPfP LAma LDai SPur

	rogersii	CDes CFil
	'Roma' (L) **new**	MSGs
	'Rose Elf' (S)	MSGs
	'Sabu'	LRHS
	'Sailor's Delight' (L)	MSGs
	'Samson' (L)	MSGs
	saundersii	CFil WCot WPGP
	segetum	see *G. italicus*
	'Serafin' (Min)	LRHS
	sericeovillosus	IBlr
	'Sharkey' (G)	MSGs
	'Show Chairman' (L)	MSGs
	'Showstar' (L)	MSGs
	'Silver Shadow'[PBR] (S)	EPfP
	'Smoky Joe' (L) **new**	MSGs
	splendens	CDes CFil WCot
	'Spring Green'	EPfP
	'Starfish' (S) **new**	MSGs
	'Starry Night' (L)	MSGs
	'Stromboli' (L)	MSGs
	'Sue' (P) **new**	MSGs
	'Sunset Fire' (G)	MSGs
	'Super High Brow' (G)	MSGs
	'Tan Royale' (P)	MSGs
	'Tantastic' (S)	MSGs
	'The Bride' (x *colvillii*) ♀H3	CAvo CBro CHad CMil EBee EBla ECho EVFa ITim LAma LDai MWgw
	'Tickatoo' (P)	WCot
	'Tiger Eyes' (S)	MSGs
	'Topaz' (L)	MSGs
	'Trader Horn' (G)	LAma
§	***trichonemifolius***	CFil SSpi
	tristis	CBro CElw CFil CMea CPLG CPne CPou ECha ELan EMan EVFa LPio NCGa SAga SSpi SUsu WAbe WHal WPGP WPrP WWhi
	- var. ***concolor***	CFil CPLG EMan ERos EVFa WCot WHer
	'Ultimate' (S)	MSGs
	undulatus	CDes CSWP ERos SSpi WCot
	usyiae	CPou WCot
	venustus **new**	CFil
	'Victoria' (M)	LRHS
	'Violetta' (M)	ECho EMan MSGs
	virescens	CFil CPou SSpi WCot
	watermeyeri **new**	CFil
	watsonioides	CPou ERos SSpi WCot
	watsonius **new**	CFil
	'Whistle Stop' (S)	MSGs
	'White City' (P/S)	LRHS
	'White Darling' (L)	MSGs
	'White Friendship' (L)	LAma
	'White Prosperity' (L)	CSut LRHS

Glandularia see *Verbena*

Glaucidium (*Glaucidiaceae*)

	palmatum ♀H4	EFEx EHyt ETow GCrs GEdr GIBF GKev NSla WAbe WCru
	- 'Album'	see *G. palmatum* var. *leucanthum*
§	- var. ***leucanthum***	EFEx GCrs

Glaucium (*Papaveraceae*)

§	***corniculatum***	CAby CHar EBee EChP EKen LPhx MAnH MLLN MWgw NLar SEND SPav SPoG WCot WEas
	flavum	CHrt CSpe ECha EGoo ELan EMFP GKev GKir LRHS MHer NLar SPav XPep
	- ***aurantiacum***	see *G. flavum* f. *fulvum*
§	- f. ***fulvum***	ECha EMFP EMan SChu SDix SMHy WHil
	- orange	see *G. flavum* f. *fulvum*
	- red	see *G. corniculatum*
	phoenicium	see *G. corniculatum*

Glaux (*Primulaceae*)

	maritima	WPer

Glebionis (*Asteraceae*)

	coronaria	CArn WJek
	segetum	GWCH MBow WHer

Glechoma (*Lamiaceae*)

	hederacea	CArn GBar GPoy MHer NMir WHer WWye XPep
	- 'Barry Yinger Variegated' (v)	EBee WCot
	- 'Rosea'	GBar WWye
§	- 'Variegata' (v)	CHal EWin IHMH ILis LRHS MBri SPet

Gleditsia (*Caesalpiniaceae*)

	caspica	SMad
	japonica	EPfP
	macrantha	EGFP
	sinensis	EGFP NLar
	triacanthos	CAgr CDul CWib ECrN LEdu MGol SBLw SPlb WBVN WNor
	- 'Bujotii'	SBLw
	- 'Calhoun' **new**	CAgr
	- 'Elegantissima' (v) **new**	SPer
	- 'Emerald Cascade'	CDul CEnd EBee LRHS
	- f. ***inermis***	CAgr SBLw WNor
	- 'Millwood' **new**	CAgr
	- 'Rubylace'	CBcs CDul CEnd CMCN COtt CTri EBee ECrN ELan ENot EPfP EWTr LBuc LRHS MAsh MBar MBlu MDun MGos MRav MSwo SHBN SPer SSpi WCot WDin WFar WOrn
	- 'Shademaster'	ENot MRav SBLw
	- 'Skyline'	SBLw
	- 'Sunburst' ♀H4	More than 30 suppliers

Glehnia (*Umbelliferae*)

	littoralis **new**	CPom GFlt

Globba (*Zingiberaceae*)

	andersonii	CKob MOak
*	***cathcartii***	CKob MOak
	'Compact Golden'	CKob
	'Emerald Isle'	LRHS
	marantina	CKob LAma MOak
	'Mount Everest' **new**	LAma
	'Pink Superior Compact'	CKob
	'Purple Compact'	CKob
	'White Rain'	CKob
	'White Superior Compact'	CKob
	winitii	EShb LRHS
	- 'Burmese White'	CKob
	- 'Golden Dragon'	MOak
	- 'Mauve Dancing Girl'	MOak
	- 'Purple Dancing Girl'	CKob
	- 'Red Leaf'	MOak
	- 'Violett'	MOak
	- 'White Dancing Girl'	CKob
	- 'White Dragon'	MOak WMul

Globularia (*Globulariaceae*)

	alypum	XPep
	bellidifolia	see *G. meridionalis*
	bisnagarica	GEdr WLin
	cordifolia ♀H4	CBrm CNic CTri EDAr EPot GEdr LBee LRHS MTho NMen SAga SBla WFar WHoo WPat

- NS 696	NWCA
incanescens	LBee LRHS
§ ***meridionalis***	CFee CLyd CPBP EPot ESis EWTr EWes GEdr MWat NLAp NMen NWCA SAga SBla WPat
- 'Alba'	NMen
- 'Hort's Variety'	CNic CTri NMen WAbe
nana	see *G. repens*
nudicaulis	NLAp SBla
- 'Alba'	WIvy
punctata	GMaP LRHS NChi NJOw NWCA SRms
pygmaea	see *G. meridionalis*
§ ***repens***	CLyd CNic EHyt EPot MTho NLAp NMen WPat
spinosa	NWCA WLin
stygia	NMen
trichosantha	CFee EBee EDAr NRya SPet SRms WFar WLin WPer

Gloriosa (*Colchicaceae*)

lutea see *G. superba* 'Lutea'

rothschildiana	see *G. superba* 'Rothschildiana'
superba ♀H1	CAby LAma MBri
§ - 'Lutea'	CBct CHal LAma LRHS
§ - 'Rothschildiana'	CBcs CHal CRHN CStu EPfP LAma LRHS MOak SRms

Glottiphyllum (*Aizoaceae*)

nelii **new**	CStu

Gloxinia (*Gesneriaceae*)

sylvatica	CHal CSpe WDib

Glumicalyx (*Scrophulariaceae*)

flanaganii	GCrs GEdr WAbe WHil
- HWEL 0325	NWCA
montanus	CFee EMan IDee MHar NWCA
nutans	CStu

Glyceria (*Poaceae*)

aquatica variegata	see *G. maxima* var. *variegata*
maxima	CRWN EMFW GFor LNCo NPer SPlb WPop
§ - var. ***variegata*** (v)	More than 30 suppliers
spectabilis 'Variegata'	see *G. maxima* var. *variegata*

Glycyrrhiza (*Papilionaceae*)

echinata	CAgr CArn MSal NLar
§ ***glabra***	CAgr CArn CBod CHby CWan ELau EShb GPoy GWCH MHer MSal NBPC NLar NTHB SECG SIde WHer WJek WWye XPep
glandulifera	see *G. glabra*
uralensis	CArn ELau GPoy MHer MSal
yunnanensis	LPhx WSHC

Glyptostrobus (*Cupressaceae*)

pensilis	CFil

Gmelina (*Verbenaceae*)

philippensis **new**	CPLN

Gnaphalium (*Asteraceae*)

'Fairy Gold'	see *Helichrysum thianschanicum* 'Goldkind'
trinerve	see *Anaphalis trinervis*

Godetia see *Clarkia*

Gomphocarpus (*Asclepiadaceae*)

§ ***physocarpus***	CArn EWll NLar WCot WCra

Gomphostigma (*Buddlejaceae*)

virgatum	CDes CMdw CPLG CPle CTrC EMan EPPr EShb EVFa LPio LRHS MLLN MSte SPlb SSvw WCot WHrl WSHC
- 'White Candy'	SHGN

Goniolimon (*Plumbaginaceae*)

§ ***incanum***	XPep
- 'Blue Diamond'	CM&M EBee NBre
§ ***tataricum***	EMan MWrn NBre NLar
§ - var. ***angustifolium***	EBee NBlu SRms WPer
- 'Woodcreek'	MWgw NBre NLar

Goodenia (*Goodeniaceae*)

scaevolina **new**	CSec
scapigera **new**	CSec

Goodyera (*Orchidaceae*)

biflora	EFEx
pubescens	EFEx LRHS WCru
schlechtendaliana	EFEx

gooseberry see *Ribes uva-crispa*

Gordonia (*Theaceae*)

axillaris	CHll

Gorodkovia (*Cruciferae*)

jacutica **new**	GIBF

Gossypium (*Malvaceae*)

herbaceum	MSal

granadilla see *Passiflora quadrangularis*

granadilla, purple see *Passiflora edulis*

granadilla, sweet see *Passiflora ligularis*

granadilla, yellow see *Passiflora laurifolia*

grape see *Vitis*

grapefruit see *Citrus* x *paradisi*

Graptopetalum (*Crassulaceae*)

bellum ♀H1	CStu SChr
§ ***paraguayense***	CHal EOas

Gratiola (*Scrophulariaceae*)

officinalis	CArn CWan EHon EMFW EMan MHer MSal WSel WWpP WWye

Greenovia (*Crassulaceae*)

aizoon	ETow
§ ***aurea***	SIng WCot

Grevillea ✿ (*Proteaceae*)

alpina	CFee CPLG CPle EBee GQui SMur
- 'Olympic Flame'	CAbb CBcs CDoC CPLG CSBt CTbh CTrw CWib SPoG
australis var. ***brevifolia***	CPLG
banksii	CPLG
- 'Canberra Hybrid'	see *G.* 'Canberra Gem'
- var. ***forsteri***	SPlb
'Bonnie Prince Charlie'	CPLG
§ 'Canberra Gem' ♀H3-4	CAbb CBcs CDoC CDul CPLG CPle CWSG ECou LRHS LSRN MAsh MBri SBrw SCoo SDix SIgm SPoG SRkn SSpi SWvt WAbe WBrE WCru WFar WGer WPat WSHC
'Clearview David'	CAbb CPLG ESlt

'Cranbrook Yellow'	CDoC CPLG
crithmifolia	CPLG
curviloba	CPLG
johnsonii	ESlt
juniperina	CBcs CPLG GGar
- 'Molonglo'	CPLG
- f. ***sulphurea***	CBcs CDoC CFil CHll COtt CPLG CSBt CTrw EPfP GQui SBrw SIgm SPer SPlb WAbe WPat WSHC
lanigera	CPLG
- 'Mount Tamboritha'	CBcs CDoC CMHG CPLG CTrC WFar
- prostrate	SIgm WPat
longistyla	SPlb
paniculata	SPlb
'Poorinda Peter'	CPLG
'Poorinda Rondeau' **new**	CPLG
robusta ♀H1+3	CHal CTrC SBrw SMur SPlb
'Robyn Gordon'	ESlt
'Rondeau'	CEnd EShb ESlt
rosmarinifolia ♀H3	More than 30 suppliers
- 'Desert Flame'	CPLG
- 'Jenkinsii'	CPLG
§ x ***semperflorens***	CDoC CEnd CPLG CRez CWib
'Sid Reynolds'	CPLG
'Spider Man'	ESlt
thelemanniana	CPLG ECou ESlt
- 'Silver' **new**	CPLG
thyrsoides	CBcs CPLG
tolminsis	see *G.* x *semperflorens*
tridentifera	CPLG
victoriae	CPLG SSpi
williamsonii	ECou SIgm WPat

Greyia (*Greyiaceae*)

sutherlandii	CKob CTrC SGar SPlb

Grindelia (*Asteraceae*)

§ ***camporum***	EBee EChP GBar MSal NLar SPlb WCot WPer
chiloensis	CAbb ECha SDix SIgm SMad WCot WPat
integrifolia **new**	CSam
robusta	see *G. camporum*
'Setting Sun'	WCru
squarrosa	GBar
stricta	CArn

Griselinia (*Griseliniaceae*)

littoralis ♀H3	More than 30 suppliers
- 'Bantry Bay' (v)	CAbP CAlb CDoC CWSG EBee EHoe ELan GGar LRHS MAsh MSwo NCGa SAga SEND SLim SPer SPoG SSto SWvt WCru WFar
- 'Brodick Gold'	CPLG GGar GTSp
- 'Crinkles'	CPMA SLon
- 'Dixon's Cream' (v)	CBcs CSBt EPfP GQui IArd MAsh SAga SLon SPoG WCru
- 'Green Jewel' (v)	CBcs CEnd CPMA CWib NLar SPla SPoG WLeb
- 'Variegata' (v) ♀H3	More than 30 suppliers
scandens	WSHC

guava, common see *Psidium guajava*

guava, purple or strawberry see *Psidium littorale*

Gueldenstaedtia (*Papilionaceae*)

himalaica B&SWJ 2631	WCru

Gundelia (*Asteraceae*)

tournefortii	EBee

Gunnera (*Gunneraceae*)

arenaria	GGar
chilensis	see *G. tinctoria*
dentata	WGwG
flavida	EBee EBla EShb GGar GSki NWCA SGSe
hamiltonii	CFwr CRez CStu EBee EBla ECha ECou GGar NBir SBch WWpP
magellanica	More than 30 suppliers
- 'Muñoz Gamero'	WShi
- 'Osorno'	SSpi WPGP
manicata ♀H3-4	More than 30 suppliers
monoica	GGar GSki IBlr
prorepens	CFee CStu EBee EBla ECha EPza GEdr GKev GSki IBlr LEdu NBir SGSe SSpi WMoo WWpP WWye
scabra	see *G. tinctoria*
§ ***tinctoria***	CAlb CDWL CFil CHEx CMHG CPLG CRow CWib EBee EBla ECha EHon ELan EPfP EPla EPza EUJe GGar MDun NCot NGdn SDix SSpi SWvt WBVN WCot WFar WMul WPGP WWpP
- 'Nana'	IBlr

Guzmania (*Bromeliaceae*)

'Gran Prix'	MBri
'Surprise'	see x *Niduregelia* 'Surprise'
'Vulkan'	MBri

Gymnadenia (*Orchidaceae*)

conopsea	EFEx

Gymnocarpium (*Woodsiaceae*)

dryopteris ♀H4	CLAP EFer EFtx EMar EMon EPot GGar GMaP MBri MMoz NLar NWCA SDix SGSe SRms WFib WNor WRic
- 'Plumosum' ♀H4	CFil CFwr CLAP CWCL EFtx EPla ERod GBin GQui MWgw NBid NLar NVic SChu SPoG WFib WHal WMoo WOut
oyamense	CLAP EFer
robertianum	CLAP EFer

Gymnocladus (*Caesalpiniaceae*)

chinensis	WNor
dioica	CBcs CDul CFil CLnd CMCN CTho ELan EPfP LEdu LRHS MBlu MBri NEgg SPer SSpi WDin WGer WNor WPGP

Gymnospermium (*Berberidaceae*)

§ ***albertii***	WCot
altaicum	GCrs

Gynandriris (*Iridaceae*)

setifolia	CMon
sisyrinchium	CMon EBee EMan
- purple-flowered AB&S 4447 from Morocco **new**	CMon

Gynerium (*Poaceae*)

argenteum	see *Cortaderia selloana*

Gynostemma (*Cucurbitaceae*)

pentaphyllum B&SWJ 570	WCru

Gynura (*Asteraceae*)

§ ***aurantiaca*** 'Purple Passion' ♀H1	MBri

sarmentosa hort.	see *G. aurantiaca* 'Purple Passion'

Gypsophila (*Caryophyllaceae*)

acutifolia	ELan EMon
aretioides	EPot LRHS NJOw NMen NSla NWCA WRos
§ - 'Caucasica'	EBur EHyt EPot LTwo NDlv SIng WAbe
- 'Compacta'	see *G. aretioides* 'Caucasica'
briquetiana	NLAp WPat
cerastioides	CTri ECtt EMan EWTr GAbr GBBs GGar GTou LRHS MRav NDlv NLAp NLon NMen NWCA SPlb SRms WHoo WPer WPnn
dubia	see *G. repens* 'Dubia'
fastigiata	EBee EMan WPer
- 'Silverstar' **new**	LSou
(Festival Series) 'Festival Pink'	EBee GKir LRHS SHar WFar
- 'Happy Festival'	LRHS
- 'White Festival'PBR	EBee NLar WFar
gracilescens	see *G. tenuifolia*
'Jolien' (v)	EBee ELan WCot WHil WWeb
muralis 'Garden Bride'	LIck SWvt
- 'Gypsy Pink' (d)	LIck SWvt
nana 'Compacta'	CLyd
oldhamiana	EBee EShb MLLN
pacifica	EBee ECtt EMag EShb NBre NBro NLar WPer
paniculata	EBee GKir GWCH LAst NBre NFor NMir SECG SRms
- 'Bristol Fairy' (d) ♀H4	CSBt CWCL EBee ELan EMan ENot EPfP ERou GKir LRHS MAvo MBri MDun NEgg NLar NOrc SOkh SPoG SSto SWvt WBrE WCAu
- 'Compacta Plena' (d)	EBee EChP ECtt ELan EPfP GCal GMaP MRav MWgw NDov NEgg NLar NVic SPet SPla SRms WPer
- 'Flamingo' (d)	CBcs CFwr EBee ECha ECot ERou MAvo MBri NLar SCoo SPer
- 'Magic Gilboa'	COtt
- 'Magic Golan'	COtt
- 'Pacific Pink'	EBee LAst
- 'Perfekta'	CBcs SPer
§ - 'Schneeflocke' (d)	GKir GMaP MWat NBre NLar NPri SRms SSto WPer
- Snowflake	see *G. paniculata* 'Schneeflocke'
§ ***petraea***	EPot GKev WLin
repens ♀H4	ECtt EMil GKir GTou LBee MHer MWat MWrn NJOw SBch SHGN SPlb SWvt WFar WPer
- 'Dorothy Teacher'	CLyd CMea ECtt LBee SIng WEas WGor
§ - 'Dubia'	CLyd ECha ECtt EDAr EHol ELan EPot ESis MHer SIgm SRms WLin WPer WSHC
- 'Fratensis'	ECtt ELan ESis ITim NMen
- Pink Beauty	see *G. repens* 'Rosa Schönheit'
§ - 'Rosa Schönheit'	EBee ECha EPot LRHS NLar
- 'Rose Fountain'	WPat
- 'Rosea'	CMea CTri CWib ECtt EPfP GAbr GKir GMaP LAst MWat NFor NOak NWCA SAga SBla SGSe SPet SPoG SRms SUsu SWvt WBrE WFar WHal WHoo WTin
- white	CM&M CWib ELan EPfP EWin LAst NFor SPet SWvt WPer
§ 'Rosenschleier' (d) ♀H4	CMea CWCL EBee EChP ECha ECtt EGoo ELan ENot EPfP GKir MRav MWat NDov NJOw SIgm SPer SRms SUsu SWvt WCAu WEas WHoo WSHC WTin
'Rosy Veil'	see *G.* 'Rosenschleier'
§ ***tenuifolia***	CLyd EHyt EPot ITim LBee NDlv NMen SBla
transylvanica	see *G. petraea*
Veil of Roses	see *G.* 'Rosenschleier'
violacea **new**	GIBF

Haastia (*Asteraceae*)

pulvinaris	ITim

Habenaria (*Orchidaceae*)

radiata	see *Pecteilis radiata*

Haberlea (*Gesneriaceae*)

ferdinandi-coburgii	CLAP CStu EPot NWCA
- 'Connie Davidson' **new**	NMen
rhodopensis ♀H4	CDes CElw CNic CStu EBee EHyt GCrs GEdr GFlt GGar GKev MSte MWat NLAp NMen NSla NWCA SBla SIng SRms SSpi WAbe WPGP WPat WTin
- 'Virginalis'	CElw CLAP CStu SBla SOkd

Habranthus ✿ (*Amaryllidaceae*)

andersonii	see *H. tubispathus*
brachyandrus	CBro SRms
gracilifolius	CBro CStu ERos
martinezii	CBro CMon CStu EHyt
§ ***robustus*** ♀H1	CBro CDes CMon EBee EPot LAma LRHS SIgm WCot
texanus	CBro CFil CMon ERos WAbe
§ ***tubispathus*** ♀H1	CBro CMon CStu EBee ERos NWCA WCot WPrP

Hacquetia (*Apiaceae*)

epipactis ♀H4	More than 30 suppliers
§ - 'Thor' (v)	CDes EBee EMon GCrs LTwo SBla SRot
- 'Variegata'	see *H. epipactis* 'Thor'

Haemanthus (*Amaryllidaceae*)

albiflos ♀H1	CHEx CHal CMon CStu EOHP ITer LAma LToo SRms WCot
amarylloides subsp. ***polyanthes***	ECho LToo
barkerae	ECho
coccineus ♀H1	CMon ECho LToo
humilis	ECho
katherinae	see *Scadoxus multiflorus* subsp. *katherinae*
'König Albert' **new**	CMon
natalensis	see *Scadoxus puniceus*
pauculifolius	ECho
pubescens subsp. ***leipoldtii***	ECho
sanguineus	ERea

Hakea (*Proteaceae*)

§ ***drupacea***	CTrC EShb
epiglottis	CTrC ECou
laurina	SPlb
lissocarpha	CTrC
§ ***lissosperma***	CDoC CFil CTrC ECou EPla SPlb WPGP
microcarpa	SLon
nodosa	CTrC
platysperma **new**	SPlb
§ ***salicifolia***	IMGH LRHS SPlb
- 'Gold Medal' (v)	CTrC

	saligna	see *H. salicifolia*
	***scoparia* new**	CTrC
	sericea hort.	see *H. lissosperma*
	suaveolens	see *H. drupacea*
	teretifolia	CTrC IDee

Hakonechloa (*Poaceae*)

	macra	CAby CFil CKno EBee EBrs EHoe EMon EPla LPhx MMoz MRav MWgw NOGN SMad SWal WCot WDyG WPGP
§	- 'Alboaurea' ♀H4	More than 30 suppliers
*	- 'Albolineata'	CKno CWan EBee EMon LEdu WDyG
	- 'Albovariegata' **new**	GKev
	- 'Aureola' ♀H4	More than 30 suppliers
*	- 'Mediopicta' (v)	SApp
*	- 'Mediovariegata' (v)	CFil EPPr EPla SSpi WPGP
	- 'Variegata'	see *H. macra* 'Alboaurea'

Halenia (*Gentianaceae*)

	elliptica	GKev

Halesia (*Styracaceae*)

§	***carolina***	More than 30 suppliers
	diptera	CBcs CMCN MBlu
	- var. ***magniflora***	MBlu
	monticola	CBcs CLnd CMCN ELan EPfP GKir LRHS MAsh SPer SReu SSpi WFar WNor
	- var. ***vestita*** ♀H4	CAbP CDoC CFil CPMA CTho EBee EPfP GKir IMGH LRHS MBlu NLar NVic SBrw SHBN SPer SSpi WDin WFar WHCG WPGP WPat
	- - f. ***rosea***	CBcs CPLG EPfP MBlu
	tetraptera	see *H. carolina*

x *Halimiocistus* (*Cistaceae*)

	algarvensis	see *Halimium ocymoides*
§	'Ingwersenii'	CBcs CDoC ELan EWes MAsh SPer SPoG SRms
	revolii misapplied	see x *H. sahucii*
	revolii (Coste & Soulié) Dansereau	XPep
§	***sahucii*** ♀H4	CDoC CSBt EBee ECha ELan ENot EPfP LAst MAsh MBNS MRav MSwo MWat NBlu SDys SGar SHBN SPer SPoG SWvt WAbe WCFE WDin WFar WKif WWeb XPep
	- 'Ice Dancer' (v)	CDoC EBee ENot EPfP LAst MAsh NLar NLon SPer SWvt
	'Susan'	see *Halimium* 'Susan'
§	***wintonensis*** ♀H3	CBcs CChe CDoC CSBt EBee ECrN ELan EPfP LRHS MAsh MRav SHBN SPer SPla SRms SSpi WCFE WHar WSHC WWeb XPep
§	- 'Merrist Wood Cream' ♀H3	CBcs CDoC CSBt CSam EBee ELan ENot EPfP LAst LRHS MAsh MRav MSwo MWgw NBir NLon NSti SChu SPer SPla SSpi SSta SWvt WAbe WDin WFar WPat WSHC XPep

Halimione (*Chenopodiaceae*)

§	***portulacoides***	EEls XPep

Halimium ✿ (*Cistaceae*)

N	***alyssoides***	LSRN
§	***atriplicifolium***	LRav SUsu XPep
§	***calycinum***	EBee ELan ENot EPfP LRHS LSRN MAsh MBri MSwo NBlu SCoo SLim SPer SPoG SSpi SWvt WAbe WBrE WDin WWeb XPep
	commutatum	see *H. calycinum*
	formosum	see *H. lasianthum* subsp. *formosum*
	halimifolium misapplied	see *H.* x *pauanum*, *H.* x *santae*
	halimifolium Willk.	EBee WBrE XPep
§	***lasianthum*** ♀H3	CBcs CHar CPLG CSBt CWib EBee EChP ELan ENot EPfP LRHS MAsh MBri MRav SLim WBrE WCFE WEas WLin
	- 'Concolor'	CDoC CWib EMil MAsh MSwo SWvt WDin
§	- subsp. ***formosum***	CHar WSHC XPep
	- - 'Sandling'	EGoo ELan EPfP LRHS MAsh WAbe
	- 'Hannay Silver'	LSRN SPla WAbe
	libanotis	see *H. calycinum*
§	***ocymoides*** ♀H3	CBcs CChe CDoC CTrC CWib EBee EGoo ELan EPfP LRHS LSRN MAsh MMHG MSwo MWat SLon SPer WBrE WHar WLin XPep
§	x ***pauanum***	EBee LRHS NPro WAbe WBcn WSPU XPep
§	x ***santae***	LPhx XPep
	'Sarah'	LSRN SPoG XPep
§	'Susan' ♀H3	CDoC EBee ELan EPfP LRHS LSRN LSou MAsh MMHG NLon SCoo SLim SPer SPoG WAbe
§	***umbellatum***	LPhx LRHS NLar SPer WDin WHCG WKif WPat
	verticillatum	XPep
	wintonense	see x *Halimiocistus wintonensis*

Halimodendron (*Papilionaceae*)

	halodendron	CBcs EBee MBlu NBlu SPer WDin

Halleria (*Scrophulariaceae*)

	lucida	CSec WBor

Halocarpus (*Podocarpaceae*)

§	***bidwillii***	CDoC ECou

Haloragis (*Haloragaceae*)

	erecta	CPle CSev
	- 'Rubra'	CBrm WCot WPer
	- 'Wellington Bronze'	CPLG CSpe EBee ECtt EMan EUnu EWsh GBBs GGar GSki ITer LEdu LRHS MBNS MCCP SBod SBri SDys SMad SUsu SWal WEas WHer WMoo WSHC WWpP

Hamamelis ✿ (*Hamamelidaceae*)

	'Brevipetala'	CBcs CEnd GKir MBri
	x ***intermedia*** 'Advent'	NLar
	- 'Allgold'	MBri
	- 'Angelly'	MAsh MBlu MBri NLar
	- 'Aphrodite'	EPfP LRHS MAsh MBlu MBri MGos SSpi
	- 'Arnold Promise' ♀H4	More than 30 suppliers
	- 'Aurora'	MBri SSpi
	- 'Barmstedt Gold' ♀H4	CWib EPfP GKir LRHS MAsh MBlu MBri MGos MRav SBrw SReu SSpi SSta
	- 'Carmine Red'	MGos WNor
	- 'Copper Beauty'	see *H.* x *intermedia* 'Jelena'
	- 'Diane' ♀H4	CBcs CDoC CDul CEnd CSBt CWSG CWib ELan ENot EPfP GKir ISea LRHS MAsh MBri MGos NBea NEgg SBrw SHBN SLim SPer SPoG SReu SSpi SSta SWvt WDin WFar WPGP
	- 'Doerak'	NLar
§	- 'Feuerzauber'	CDul CMac GKir LBuc MGos MSwo NBlu SPer WDin WOrn
*	- 'Fire Cracker'	CSBt

- 'Girard's Orange' EPfP
- 'Harry' LRHS MAsh MBri NLar
- 'Hiltingbury' LRHS MAsh SSpi
§ - 'Jelena' ♀H4 More than 30 suppliers
- 'Livia' **new** MAsh NLar
- Magic Fire see *H.* x *intermedia* 'Feuerzauber'
- 'Moonlight' CDul
- 'Nina' MAsh
- 'Orange Beauty' CBcs EPfP MGos NLar
- 'Orange Peel' EPfP LRHS MAsh MBri NLar SSpi
- 'Pallida' ♀H4 More than 30 suppliers
- 'Primavera' CWSG ECrN EPfP MLan SPla
- 'Ripe Corn' EPfP LRHS MAsh MBri SSpi
- 'Robert' MBri
- 'Rubin' LRHS MAsh
- 'Ruby Glow' CBcs ECho GKir ISea MGos NLar SPer SPoG WDin
- 'Sunburst' EPfP MBri SSta
- 'Vesna' EPfP LRHS MBlu MBri SSpi
§ - 'Westerstede' COtt CWSG ENot LBuc LRHS MGos MRav NBlu NLar NWea SLim WDin WHar

japonica WFar
- 'Arborea' WNor
- 'Robin' CDul

mollis ♀H4 CBcs CDul CEnd CSBt CWSG ELan ENot EPfP GKir ISea MBar MBri MGos MSwo NBea NEgg NWea SHBN SLim SPer SReu SSpi SSta WDin WFar WPGP WPat
- 'Boskoop' NLar
- 'Coombe Wood' MBri
- 'Jermyns Gold' EPfP SBrw
- 'Select' see *H.* x *intermedia* 'Westerstede'
- 'Superba' LRHS
- 'Wisley Supreme' ELan LRHS MAsh MBri SSpi

'Rochester' NLar

vernalis GIBF WDin
- 'Lombart's Weeping' NLar
- purple MBlu NLar
- 'Purpurea' CBcs
- 'Sandra' ♀H4 CBcs CMCN EPfP GIBF GKir LBuc LRHS MBri MGos MRav SHBN SLon SPer SPoG SReu SSpi SSta WCot

virginiana CBcs ECrN GBin GIBF GPoy IDee MDun WDin WFar

Hanabusaya (*Campanulaceae*)

§ ***asiatica*** CHar CPom NChi WFar

Haplocarpha (*Asteraceae*)

rueppellii NBro SRms SRot WPer

Haplopappus (*Asteraceae*)

brandegeei see *Erigeron aureus*
coronopifolius see *H. glutinosus*
§ ***glutinosus*** CMHG ECha ECtt EPot GEdr MMil MTho NLar NWCA SPlb SPoG SRms XPep
lyallii see *Tonestus lyallii*
microcephalus WPer
prunelloides GEdr
- var. ***mustersii*** CPBP
- - F&W 9384 WCot
pygmaeus see *Tonestus pygmaeus*
rehderi EBee NJOw SPet WFar

Hardenbergia (*Papilionaceae*)

comptoniana ♀H1 CSec CSpe
- 'Rosea' CSpe ERea
violacea ♀H1 CAbb CHll CPLN CRHN CSPN CSpe CTbh CTrC ELan EMil ERea ESlt GKir GQui LRHS SLim SMur SPer WCot
- f. ***alba*** CBcs CPLN EShb
§ - - 'White Crystal' ERea ESlt
- 'Happy Wanderer' EBee EMil ERea LRHS
- f. ***rosea*** CBcs EBee ESlt

Harpephyllum (*Anacardiaceae*)

caffrum (F) XBlo

Harrimanella see *Cassiope*

Hastingsia (*Hyacinthaceae*)

alba GBuc
- NNS 98-310 WCot
- NNS 98-311 WCot

Haworthia ✿ (*Aloaceae*)

attenuata **new** SWal
'Black Prince' **new** EPfP
cymbiformis **new** EPfP
- var. ***umbraticola*** EPem
fasciata EPfP
glabrata var. ***concolor*** **new** EPfP
radula **new** EPfP
reinwardtii ♀H1 CHal
tortusa EPem

hazelnut see *Corylus*

Hebe ✿ (*Scrophulariaceae*)

albicans ♀H4 CChe CPLG CWCL EBee ECou ELan ENot EPfP ESis GKir GLbr LAst LRHS MBar MBri MGos MRav MWgw NBlu NEgg NLon SHBN SPer SPoG SSto WFar WHCG WTel
- 'Cobb' ECou
- 'Cranleigh Gem' ECou
- prostrate see *H. albicans* 'Snow Cover'
- 'Red Edge' see *H.* 'Red Edge'
§ - 'Snow Cover' ECou EWes
- 'Snow Drift' see *H. albicans* 'Snow Cover'
- 'Snow Mound' ECou
§ - 'Sussex Carpet' ECou
§ 'Alicia Amherst' EHol SPer SRms SSto SWal
allanii see *H. amplexicaulis* f. *hirta*
'Amanda Cook' (v) EHoe MCCP NPer
amplexicaulis CNic
- clone 4 STre
- f. ***hirta*** NDlv
§ 'Amy' ESis MAsh MBri NBur NPer SHBN SHop SPer WSHC
x ***andersonii*** CDul COkL
§ - 'Andersonii Variegata' (v) CSpe NBur SPla SRms SWal
- 'Argenteovariegata' see *H.* 'Andersonii Variegata'
anomala misapplied see *H.* 'Imposter'
anomala (Armstr.) Cockayne see *H. odora*
'Aoira' see *H. recurva* 'Aoira'
§ ***armstrongii*** CMHG EHoe GGar GKir MBar NLon WDin WPer
'Arthur' ECou
'Autumn Beauty' COkL WBrE
'Autumn Glory' More than 30 suppliers
'Autumn Queen' NLon
azurea see *H. venustula*
'Azurens' see *H.* 'Maori Gem'
'Baby Blush'PBR CAbP ELan MAsh
'Baby Marie' CAbP CLyd COtt CSBt EBee ECot ECou EHoe ELan EPfP ESis GKir LRHS MAsh MGos MSwo NJOw NLon NMen NPer SCoo SLim SPla

		SPoG SRms SRot SSto SWvt WGwG
	'Balfouriana'	WHCG
	barkeri	ECou
	'Beatrice'	ECou NDlv
	'Beverley Hills'PBR	LRHS MAsh
§	***bishopiana***	ECou ELan ENot ESis LRHS MAsh NBlu SBod SCoo SPoG SSto
	'Blue Clouds' ♀H3	ECou ESis LAst MBNS MSwo MWat NDlv SAga SPer WCFE
	'Blue Star'	LRHS MAsh NBlu SPoG
	bollonsii	GGar MSte
	'Boscawenii'	MGos
	'Bouquet' **new**	SPoG
§	'Bowles' Hybrid'	COkL CSBt ECou ESis EWin LRHS MSwo NLon SRms WAbe
	'Bowles' Variety'	see *H.* 'Bowles's Hybrid'
	brachysiphon	CTrC ENot EPfP EWin GWCH MGos MWhi SPer WDin WHCG
	brevifolia	ECou
	breviracemosa	ECou
	'Brill Blue'	see *Veronica* x *guthrieana*
	buchananii	ECou ESis GGar GKir GTou MBar MGos MHer MTho NBur NDlv NLon NPer WPer
	- 'Christchurch'	ECou
§	- 'Fenwickii'	WHoo
§	- 'Minor' ambig.	CLyd EPot ESis GBin GCrs MBar NBir NDlv NWCA SIng
	- 'Ohau'	ECou
	- 'Sir George Fenwick'	see *H. buchananii* 'Fenwickii'
	buxifolia misapplied	see *H. odora*
	buxifolia (Benth.) Cockayne & Allan	EBee ENot GGar GLbr NWea WDin
N	'C.P. Raffill'	ECou
§	'Caledonia' ♀H3	CSBt ECou ENot EPfP ESis GGar GLbr LRHS MAsh MBri MGos MSte MWhi NBlu NDlv NJOw NLon NPer SCoo SPer SPoG SWal WFar WPat
	'Candy'	ECou
§	***canterburiensis***	ECou GGar
N	'Carl Teschner'	see *H.* 'Youngii'
	'Carnea'	CElw
	'Carnea Variegata' (v)	ESis SBod SPer WOut
	carnosula	EHoe EWin GGar GTSp LRHS MGos NBir NLon SPer WPer
	catarractae	see *Parahebe catarractae*
	'Celine' **new**	SPoG
I	'Chalk's Buchananii'	SBla
	'Champion' **new**	SPoG
*	'Charming White'	ENot EPfP LRHS MBNS SWal
	chathamica	CNic ECou GGar MHer
	'Christabel'	ECou ESis EWin
	ciliolata* x *odora	GGar
	'Clear Skies'	CAbP ECou MAsh SPoG
	colensoi 'Glauca'	see *H.* 'Leonard Cockayne'
	'Colwall'	ECho
	'County Park'	ECou ECtt EWes NLon NMen WMow
	'Cranleighensis'	SSto
	'Cupins'	CLyd
	cupressoides	CFis CMHG GKir MBar NDlv NLon SEND WDin
	- 'Boughton Dome'	CTri ECou EHoe EPfP ESis EWin GTou MGos MTho NLAp NMen WAbe WEas WHoo WPer WSHC
	- 'Nana'	ECou NJOw
	darwiniana	see *H. glaucophylla*
	'Dazzler'PBR (v)	CAbP CSBt EBee ELan ENot LRHS MBNS NBlu SPoG
	decumbens	CLyd CNic ECou EWes GGar
	'Diana'	ECou

	dieffenbachii	GGar
	diosmifolia	CAbP CBot CDoC CPle ECou ELan ESis NBlu WAbe
	- 'Marie'	ECou ESis
	divaricata	ECou
*	- 'Marlborough'	ECou
	- 'Nelson'	ECou
	x ***divergens***	NDlv
	'Dorothy Peach'	see *H.* 'Watson's Pink'
	'E.A. Bowles'	ECou
	'E.B. Anderson'	see *H.* 'Caledonia'
	'Early Blue'	CSpe NBir
	'Edinensis'	COkL ECou GKir NJOw NLon WSHC WSPU
	'Edington'	CElw CHal LRHS SPer WCFE
	elliptica	CDul COkL ECou
	- 'Anatoki'	ECou
	- 'Charleston'	ECou
	- 'Kapiti'	ECou
	- 'Variegata'	see *H.* x *franciscana* 'Variegata'
	'Emerald Dome'	see *H.* 'Emerald Gem'
§	'Emerald Gem' ♀H3	Dul EBee ECou ENot EPfP ESis GGar GKir GLbr LAst LRHS MAsh MBar MBri MGos MHer MSwo MWat MWgw NDlv NMen NWCA SLim SPer SPlb SPoG WAbe WBVN WFar
	'Emerald Green'	see *H.* 'Emerald Gem'
	epacridea	EWes GTou
§	'Eveline'	COkL CSBt EHol ELan LRHS NBir NLon SPer WCot
	evenosa	LRHS NDlv
	'Eversley Seedling'	see *H.* 'Bowles's Hybrid'
	'Fairfieldii'	CPLG EHol MMil WTin
	'First Light'PBR	NArg NBlu NEgg NPro SCoo SPoG
	'Fragrant Jewel'	CPle SEND SWal
	x ***franciscana***	ECou LRHS
§	- 'Blue Gem' ambig.	CDul COkL EBee GGar GLbr LRHS MGos NBir NPer NWea SPer SPlb SRms SSto SWal WGer WHar XPep
	- 'Purple Tips' misapplied	see *H. speciosa* 'Variegata'
	- 'Variegata'	see *H.* 'Silver Queen'
I	- 'White Gem'	SRms
	'Franjo'	ECou
	'Gauntlettii'	see *H.* 'Eveline'
	'Gibby'	ECou
N	***glaucophylla***	ECou GLbr SBod
	- 'Clarence'	ECou GGar
I	'Glaucophylla Variegata' (v)	CNic CTri ECou ESis GLbr NBir NDlv SPer SWal WCot WKif
	'Goldrush' (v) **new**	SPoG
	'Great Orme' ♀H3	More than 30 suppliers
	'Green Globe'	see *H.* 'Emerald Gem'
	'Greensleeves'	ECou ESis GGar LRHS MBar NDlv
	'Gruninard's Seedling'	GGar
	haastii	EPfP NLar NLon
	'Hagley Park'	CSBt EPfP LRHS MMil SAga SOkh WHCG
§	'Hartii'	MRav SPer
	'Heartbreaker'PBR (v)	ELan MAsh MGos NBlu SCoo SPoG
	hectorii	GTou
	'Highdownensis'	COkL
	'Hinderwell'	NPer
	'Hinerua'	ECou GGar NJOw NNor
	'Holywell'	SBod
	hookeriana	see *Parahebe hookeriana*
	hulkeana ♀H3	CBot CMdw CStr CWCL EMan MHer MMil NBir NLon SAga SIgm SSpi SWal WEas WHCG WHoo WKif WTin
	'Ian Young' **new**	ITim
§	'Imposter'	CNic SRms SWal
	insularis	ECou

	'Jack's Surprise'	EBee EWin
	'James Stirling'	see *H. ochracea* 'James Stirling'
	'Jane Holden'	WSHC
	'Janet'	COkL SGar
	'Jannas Blue'	EPfP
	'Jasper'	ECou ESis
	'Joan Lewis'	ECou ESis
	'Joanna'	ECou
	'Johny Day'	CDul MBNS
	'Joyce Parker'	NDlv
	'Judy'	ECou
	'June Small'	CNic
	'Karo Golden Esk'	ECou NEgg
	'Kirkii'	EMil ENot EPfP EWin SCoo SPer
	'Knightshayes'	see *H.* 'Caledonia'
	'La Séduisante'	CDul CElw CSBt ECou GKir SCoo SEND WKif WSHC
	'Lady Ann' (v) **new**	NArg SPoG
	'Lady Ardilaun'	see *H.* 'Amy'
	laevis	see *H. venustula*
	laingii	CNic
	latifolia	see *H.* x *franciscana* 'Blue Gem'
	'Lavender Spray'	see *H.* 'Hartii'
§	'Leonard Cockayne'	WSHC
	'Lindsayi'	ECou NDlv NJOw
§	'Loganioides'	CFai GAbr GGar MHer NLon
	'Lopen' (v)	ECou EGra EWes
	'Louise'	COkL NLsd SGar
	lyallii	see *Parahebe lyallii*
	lycopodioides	EWes
	- 'Aurea'	see *H. armstrongii*
	mackenii	see *H.* 'Emerald Gem'
	macrantha ♀H3	EPfP GAbr GCrs GGar LRHS NLon NMen SPer SRms WAbe
	macrocarpa	ECou LRHS SPoG
	- var. ***latisepala***	ECou
§	'Maori Gem'	GGar SCoo SSto
	'Margery Fish'	see *H.* 'Primley Gem'
	'Margret' PBR ♀H4	COtt CSBt EBee EMil ENot EPfP ESis GKir LAst LRHS MAsh MBNS MGos MSwo NMen SCoo SHBN SPer SPoG SSto
	'Marjorie'	CBcs CDul CSBt ECtt ENot EPfP GLbr LRHS MGos MRav MSwo NDlv NFor NPer NWea SBod SPer SSto SWal WDin WTel
	matthewsii	ECou
	'Mauve Queen'	EHol
	'Mauvena'	SPer
	'McCabe'	NJOw
	'McKean'	see *H.* 'Emerald Gem'
	'Mcewanii'	ECou NDlv
	'Megan'	ECou
	'Mercury'	ECou
	'Midsummer Beauty' ♀H3	ECou ENot EPfP GGar GKir LRHS MGos MRav NBir NLon SBod SHBN SPer SPlb SSto SWvt WDin WFar
	'Milmont Emerald'	see *H.* 'Emerald Gem'
	'Miss Fittall'	ECou
	'Monica'	ECou NDlv
*	'Moppets Hardy'	SPer
	'Mohawk' PBR	COtt MBri MGos SCoo SPoG
§	'Mrs Winder' ♀H4	More than 30 suppliers
	'Mystery'	ECou ELan SWal
	'Mystery Red'	ENot ESis MAsh MBNS SPoG
	'Nantyderry'	CHal GBri MWgw SPla SWal WOut
§	'Neil's Choice' ♀H4	ECou MBNS MSte SCoo SPoG STre
	'Netta Dick'	ECou
	'Nicola's Blush' ♀H4	More than 30 suppliers
	'Northumbria Beauty'	NLon
	'Northumbria Gem'	NLon
	obtusata	ECou SCoo
	ochracea	MGos NBlu
§	- 'James Stirling' ♀H4	CSBt EBee EHoe ELan ENot EPfP ESis GGar GKir GTou LRHS MAsh MBar MBri MGos MSwo MTho NBir NFor NJOw SLim SPer SPlb SPoG STre SWvt WDin WFar WMoo
	'Oddity'	ECou
§	***odora***	ECou ENot EPfP MRav MWhi WBrE WCFE
I	- 'Nana'	EPfP EWin MBar
	- 'New Zealand Gold'	CNic ECou ESis EWin GKir LRHS MBNS NDlv SCoo SEND SLon SSto SWal SWvt
*	- var. ***patens***	WHCG
	- prostrate	SOkd
	- 'Stewart Island'	ECou
	- 'Summer Frost'	CRez MBNS NPri SCoo SPoG SWal
	- 'Wintergreen'	MRav
	'Oratia Beauty' ♀H4	ESis MAsh MRav MWgw
	'Orphan Annie' PBR (v)	CSBt EBee ENot MGos NBlu SCoo SPoG
	'Oswego'	ECou
	'Otari Delight'	CMHG
	parviflora hort.	see *H.* 'Bowles's Hybrid'
§	***parviflora*** (Vahl) Cockayne & Allan	GGar
	- 'Holdsworth'	SDys
	- 'Palmerston'	ECou
	- var. ***angustifolia***	see *H. stenophylla*
	- var. ***arborea***	see *H. parviflora* (Vahl) Cockayne & Allan
*	'Pascal' ♀H4	COkL ECou ELan EPfP MAsh MBNS MBri MRav NPri SCoo SPoG
	'Pastel Blue' **new**	SPoG
	pauciramosa	ESis SRms SWal
	'Paula'	ECtt NBlu
	'Pearl of Paradise' PBR	SPoG
	perfoliata	see *Parahebe perfoliata*
	'Perry's Rubyleaf'	NPer
	'Petra's Pink'	ENot LRHS
	'Pewter Dome' ♀H4	CDoC CSBt ECou ECtt EGra EHoe EPfP MGos MRav NBee NDlv NEgg NLon SBod SDix SPoG SRms STre WBrE
	pimeleoides	ECou NJOw
	- 'Glauca'	NLon NPer
	- 'Glaucocaerulea'	ECou NDlv SPer
	- 'Quicksilver' ♀H4	CSBt CSLe CTri EBee ECou EHoe ELan ENot EPfP ESis GGar GKir GMaP LRHS MBar MGos MRav MSwo NBir NMen NPer SCoo SPer SPoG SWal WBrE WCot WFar WGwG WPat
	- var. ***rupestris***	ECou
	pinguifolia	ECou NDlv SPlb WFar
	- 'Hutt'	ECou
	- 'Pagei' ♀H4	More than 30 suppliers
	- 'Sutherlandii'	CDoC CNic ENot ESis GLbr LEdu LRHS MBar MWhi NBee NDlv SCoo SSto WFar
	'Pink Elephant' (v) ♀H3	CAbP CSBt EBee ELan ENot EPfP LAst LRHS MAsh SCoo SPer SPla SPoG SWvt
	'Pink Fantasy'	LRHS MRav
	'Pink Goddess'	CAbP MBNS
	'Pink Paradise' PBR	EBee ELan ENot EPfP LAst LRHS MBNS NBlu NPri SBod SPoG SSto
	'Pink Payne'	see *H.* 'Gauntlettii'
	'Pink Pixie'	LSou MBri SCoo
	'Porlock Purple'	see *Parahebe catarractae* 'Delight'
§	'Primley Gem'	ESis LRHS

	propinqua	MHer NLAp NMen
	- 'Minor'	NDlv
*	'Prostrata'	CNic CSBt NDlv
	'Purple Emperor'	see *H.* 'Neil's Choice'
	'Purple Paradise'[PBR]	EPfP MBNS MBri SPoG
	'Purple Picture'	ECtt
	Purple Pixie[PBR]	see *H.* 'Mohawk'
	'Purple Princess'	MBNS
	'Purple Queen'	CSBt EBee ELan EPfP GGar GLbr MBNS SHFr SPla WAbe
	Purple Shamrock = 'Neprock'[PBR] (v)	CSBt ENot EPfP MAsh MBNS MBri SCoo SPer SPoG SWal
	'Purple Tips' misapplied	see *H. speciosa* 'Variegata'
	'Rachel'	ENot
	rakaiensis ♀H4	More than 30 suppliers
	ramosissima	GTou
	raoulii	GBri NWCA SBla WAbe
	- 'Mount Hutt'	GTou
§	***recurva***	CNic CSam CTri EBee ECou EPfP ESis GAbr GGar GKir LAst LRHS MTis NBee SHFr SPoG SRms WBrE WCot WDin
§	- 'Aoira'	COkL ECou NDlv
	- 'Boughton Silver' ♀H3	ELan ENot EPfP LRHS MAsh MBNS MWgw SPoG
	- 'White Torrent'	ECou
§	'Red Edge' ♀H4	More than 30 suppliers
	'Red Ruth'	see *H.* 'Gauntlettii'
	rigidula	ECou ESis SWal
	'Ronda'	ECou
	'Rosie'[PBR]	EPfP MBNS MMHG NBee NMen SCoo
	'Royal Purple'	see *H.* 'Alicia Amherst'
	salicifolia	CChe COkL ECou ELan ENot EPfP GAbr GGar LAst LGro MRav NEgg NJOw SHBN SPer SPlb SPoG SRms SWal WFar WHCG WTel
	- BR 30	GGar
	'Sapphire' ♀H4	CDoC COkL EBee ECou ENot ESis GGar GKir MAsh MBNS MBar MGos NBlu NLsd SCoo SPoG SSto WGer
	'Sarana'	ECou
	selaginoides hort.	see *H.* 'Loganioides'
	'Shiraz'	MBNS SCoo
	'Silver Dollar' (v)	CAbP CM&M CSBt EHoe ELan ENot EPfP MAsh MBNS MGos NPri SPer SPoG SSto SWvt
§	'Silver Queen' (v) ♀H2	CDul CSBt CWSG EBee ECou EGra ELan ENot EPfP GGar LRHS MAsh MBar MGos MRav NJOw NPer SPer SSto SWal WHar
	'Simon Délaux'	CSBt ECou LRHS NCiC SAga SPer SSto SUsu
	'Snow Mass'	GLbr
	- 'Rangatira'	ECou
	- 'Ruddigore'	see *H. speciosa* 'La Séduisante'
§	- 'Variegata' (v)	CHal IBlr NPer SSto WEas
	'Spender's Seedling' misapplied	see *H. stenophylla*
	'Spender's Seedling' Hort.	ECou EPfP EWin GAbr LRHS NBee SEND SPoG SRms STre
	'Spring Glory'	LRHS
§	***stenophylla***	ECou EShb EWes EWin SAPC SArc SDix SHFr SUsu
	- 'White Lady'	GGar
	stricta	ECou
	- var. ***egmontiana***	ECou
	- var. ***macroura***	ECou
	subalpina	CSBt ECou ESis MTis
	subsimilis	SBla
	'Summer Blue'	ENot EPfP ESis
	'Summer Snow'	NBir
	'Sussex Carpet'	see *H. albicans* 'Sussex Carpet'
	'Sweet Kim' (v)	COtt ENot SPoG
	'Tina'	ECou
	'Tiny Tot'	CLyd EHyt MTho
	'Tom Marshall'	see *H. canterburiensis*
	topiaria ♀H4	CAbP CSBt EBee ECou EMil EPfP ESis GGar GKir GLbr LAst MBrN MBri MSwo MTis MWgw SCoo SPer SPla SPoG STre WAbe WGwG
	townsonii	ECou SAga SCoo
	traversii	ECou MSte SRms
	- 'Mason River'	ECou
	- 'Woodside'	ECou
	'Tricolor'	see *H. speciosa* 'Variegata'
	'Trixie'	CNic ECou
	'Twisty'	LSou MAsh MBNS SPoG
	urvilleana	ECou
	'Valentino' **new**	MAsh
	'Veitchii'	see *H.* 'Alicia Amherst'
§	***venustula***	ECou GGar IArd WPer
	- 'Sky Blue'	ECou
	- 'Patricia Davies'	ECou
	vernicosa ♀H3	CNic ECou EPfP ESis GLbr MBar MBri MGos MHer MWgw NBee NDlv NJOw NLon SCoo SIgm SPer SPlb SPoG SRot STre SWvt WAbe WHCG
	'Vogue'	COkL EPfP SPoG
	'Waikiki'	see *H.* 'Mrs Winder'
	'Wardiensis'	CMHG
	'Warleyensis'	see *H.* 'Mrs Winder'
§	'Watson's Pink'	COkL ECou GGar SPer WKif
	'White Diamond'	SPer
	'White Gem' (*brachysiphon* hybrid) ♀H4	ECou ESis MGos NBee NDlv NPer SPer SWal WBVN WFar WRHF
	'White Heather'	ESis LRHS NBir
	'White Spreader' **new**	EWin
	'Willcoxii'	see *H. buchananii* 'Sir George Fenwick'
	'Wingletye' ♀H3	CNic ECou ESis GGar LRHS MBri MWgw MWhi NDlv NEgg NNor WAbe WPer WTel
	'Winter Glow'	COtt ESis EWin LSou SWal
	'Wiri Blush'	SWvt
	'Wiri Charm'	CAbP CBcs CDoC CDul COtt CSBt ENot EPfP ESis GGar GLbr MLan MRav MTis SHBN SSto WBVN WGer WGwG WOut
	'Wiri Cloud' ♀H3	CAbP CSBt EPfP ESis EWin GGar MSwo MTis NBee SSto SWal WGwG
	'Wiri Dawn' ♀H3	CAbP CBcs COtt CSBt ELan EPfP ESis EWes EWin GGar LSou SHBN SSto SWvt WHrl WRHF
	'Wiri Gem'	EWin LRHS MRav
	'Wiri Image'	CBcs CDoC COtt CSBt ESis EWin LRHS
	'Wiri Joy'	LRHS
	'Wiri Mist'	CBcs COtt CTrC ESis EWin GGar LRHS NBlu
	'Wiri Prince'	EWin
	'Wiri Splash'	CDoC COtt CSBt CTrC ESis EWin GGar LRHS SHBN SSto WGwG WRHF
	'Wiri Vision'	COtt CSBt LRHS
§	'Youngii' ♀H3-4	More than 30 suppliers

Hebenstretia (*Scrophulariaceae*)

dura	CPBP

Hedeoma (*Lamiaceae*)

hyssopifolia **new**	LPhx

Hedera ✿ (*Araliaceae*)

	Name	Suppliers
	algeriensis	see *H. canariensis* hort.
§	***azorica***	EShb WFar WFib
	- 'Pico'	WFib
§	***canariensis*** hort.	CDoC CDul SAPC SArc WFib
	- 'Algeriensis'	see *H. canariensis* hort.
	- var. ***azorica***	see *H. azorica*
	- 'Cantabrian'	see *H. maroccana* 'Spanish Canary'
§	- 'Gloire de Marengo' (v) ♀H3	More than 30 suppliers
	- 'Marginomaculata' ♀H3	CDoC EPfP EShb LRHS MAsh SMad SPoG WFib WWeb
	- 'Montgomery'	MWht
	- 'Ravensholst' ♀H3	CMac NLon NSti WFib
	- 'Variegata'	see *H. canariensis* hort. 'Gloire de Marengo'
	chinensis	see *H. nepalensis* var. *sinensis*
	- typica	see *H. nepalensis* var. *sinensis*
§	***colchica*** ♀H4	ENot EPfP LRHS SPer WCFE WDin WFar WFib
	- 'Arborescens'	see *H. colchica* 'Dendroides'
	- 'Batumi'	MBNS
§	- 'Dendroides'	WCot
	- 'Dentata' ♀H4	EPla MRav MWhi WFib
	- 'Dentata Aurea'	see *H. colchica* 'Dentata Variegata'
§	- 'Dentata Variegata' (v) ♀H4	More than 30 suppliers
	- 'Golden Ice Cream' (v) **new**	SPoG
	- 'My Heart'	see *H. colchica*
	- 'Paddy's Pride'	see *H. colchica* 'Sulphur Heart'
§	- 'Sulphur Heart' (v) ♀H4	More than 30 suppliers
	- 'Variegata'	see *H. colchica* 'Dentata Variegata'
	cristata	see *H. helix* 'Parsley Crested'
§	***cypria***	WFib
	'Dixie'	NLar
	helix	CArn CCVT CRWN CTri MBar MGos NBlu NWea SHFr WDin WHer XPep
	- 'Abundance'	see *H. helix* 'California'
	- 'Adam' (v)	COkL CWib ECrN LAst MBri MTho WFib
	- 'Amberwaves'	WFib
§	- 'Angularis'	ECot
	- 'Angularis Aurea' ♀H4	EHoe EPfP MWht NBir SHBN WFib
	- 'Anita'	CBgR CHal ECrN GBin WFib
§	- 'Anna Marie' (v)	CMac COkL LRHS MBri WFib
	- 'Anne Borch'	see *H. helix* 'Anna Marie'
	- 'Annette'	see *H. helix* 'California'
	- 'Arborescens'	CAlb CNat ENot MAsh NPal WCot WDin
	- 'Ardingly' (v)	MWhi WFib
	- 'Asterisk'	WFib
	- 'Atropurpurea'	CNat EPPr EPla GBin MBar WDin WFib
	- 'Aurea Densa'	see *H. helix* 'Aureovariegata'
§	- 'Aureovariegata' (v)	CNic
	- 'Baby Face'	WFib
	- var. ***baltica***	WFib
	- 'Barabits' Silver' (v)	EGoo EPla
	- 'Bill Archer'	WFib
	- 'Bird's Foot'	see *H. helix* 'Pedata'
	- 'Blue Moon'	WFib
	- 'Bodil' (v)	SHFr
	- 'Boskoop'	WFib
	- 'Bowles Ox Heart'	WFib
	- 'Bowles Shield'	CNic
	- 'Bredon'	ECrN
	- 'Brigette'	see *H. helix* 'California'
§	- 'Brokamp'	MWht SLPl WFib
	- 'Bruder Ingobert' (v)	WHrl
	- 'Buttercup'	More than 30 suppliers
	- 'Buttercup' arborescent	MAsh SPoG
	- 'Caecilia' (v) ♀H4	CBcs CBrm ELan EPfP LAst LRHS MAsh MSwo NLar NSti SLim SWvt WCot WFar WFib WWeb
N	- 'Caenwoodiana'	see *H. helix* 'Pedata'
	- 'Caenwoodiana Aurea'	WFib
	- 'Calico' (v) **new**	WFib
§	- 'California'	MBri NSti
	- 'California Gold' (v)	WFib
	- 'Calypso'	WFib
	- 'Carolina Crinkle'	CBgR MWhi WFib
	- 'Cathedral Wall'	WFib
§	- 'Cavendishii' (v)	MAsh SRms WBcn WFib
§	- 'Ceridwen' (v) ♀H4	CRHN EBee MBri SPlb WFib WWeb
	- 'Chalice'	ECrN WFib
	- 'Chedglow Fasciated'	CNat WFar
	- 'Cheeky'	WFib
	- 'Cheltenham Blizzard' (v)	CNat
	- 'Chester' (v)	MBri WFar WFib
	- 'Chicago'	CWib WFib
	- 'Chicago Variegated' (v) **new**	WFib
	- 'Chrysophylla'	EPla MSwo
	- 'Clotted Cream' (v) **new**	WFib
	- 'Cockle Shell'	WFib
§	- 'Congesta' ♀H4	EPla MTho SRms STre WCot WFib
	- 'Conglomerata'	CBcs ELan EPla MBar MBri NBir NBlu NEgg NFor SPer SRms WDin WFib WTel WTin
	- 'Conglomerata Erecta'	CSWP NLon NVic SRms WCFE WFib
	- 'Courage'	WFib
	- 'Crenata'	WFib
	- 'Crispa'	MRav NFor NLon
	- 'Cristata'	see *H. helix* 'Parsley Crested'
	- 'Cristata Melanie'	see *H. helix* 'Melanie'
	- 'Curleylocks'	see *H. helix* 'Manda's Crested'
	- 'Curley-Q'	see *H. helix* 'Dragon Claw'
	- 'Curvaceous' (v)	WCot WFib
	- 'Cyprus'	see *H. cypria*
	- 'Dainty Bess'	CWib
	- 'Dead Again'	WCot
§	- 'Dealbata' (v)	CMac WFib
	- 'Deltoidea'	see *H. hibernica* 'Deltoidea'
	- 'Discolor'	see *H. helix* 'Minor Marmorata', *H. helix* 'Dealbata'
	- 'Domino' (v)	EWes
§	- 'Donerailensis'	CBgR MBlu WFib WPer
	- 'Don's Papillon'	CBgR CNat
	- 'Dovers'	WFib
§	- 'Dragon Claw'	ECrN EPla WFib
	- 'Duckfoot' ♀H4	CBgR CDoC CHal CSWP ECrN MTho MWhi NSti WFar WFib WOut
	- 'Dunloe Gap'	see *H. hibernica* 'Dunloe Gap'
	- 'Egret'	WFib
	- 'Eileen' (v)	WFib
	- 'Elfenbein' (v)	WFib
	- 'Emerald Gem'	see *H. helix* 'Angularis'
	- 'Emerald Jewel' **new**	WFib
	- 'Erecta' ♀H4	CAlb EBee EMFP EPfP EPla MBar MGos MTho MWhi NBlu NGHP SHGN SMac SPer SPlb SPoG WCot WDin WFar WFib WPat WPrP WWye XPep
	- 'Ester' (v) **new**	WFib
§	- 'Eva' (v)	ECrN MBri MGos NBir WDin WFib
	- 'Fanfare'	WFib
	- 'Fantasia' (v)	ECrN WFib
	- 'Feenfinger'	WFib
	- 'Ferney'	WFib

	- 'Filigran'	ECrN NLar SMad WFib WHer
	- 'Flashback' (v)	WFib
	- 'Flavescens'	WFib
	- 'Fleur de Lis'	ECrN
	- 'Fluffy Ruffles'	ECrN WFib
*	- 'Francis'	MBri
I	- 'Francis Ivy'	WFib
	- 'Fringette'	see *H. helix* 'Manda Fringette'
	- 'Frizzle'	ECrN WFib
	- 'Frosty' (v)	WFib
	- 'Gavotte'	EPPr MTho MWht WFib
	- 'Gertrud Stauss' (v)	MBri
	- 'Ghost'	WFib
	- 'Gilded Hawke'	WFib
	- 'Glache' (v)	SHFr WFib
	- 'Glacier' (v) ♀H4	More than 30 suppliers
	- 'Glymii'	EPla SLPl WFib
	- 'Gold Harald'	see *H. helix* 'Goldchild'
	- 'Gold Ripple'	EHoe
§	- 'Goldchild' (v) ♀H3-4	CBcs CDoC COkL CSam EBee ECrN ENot EPfP EPla LAst LRHS MAsh MBar MBri MGos MRav MSwo MTho MWhi NBir SAga SHFr SLim SPer SPoG SWvt WDin WFib WTel
	- 'Goldcraft' (v)	WFib
	- 'Golden Ann'	see *H. helix* 'Ceridwen'
*	- 'Golden Arrow'	ELan LRHS MAsh SPoG
	- 'Golden Curl' (v)	EPfP SCoo WWeb
	- 'Golden Ester'	see *H. helix* 'Ceridwen'
	- 'Golden Gate' (v)	ECrN LAst MBri WFib
	- 'Golden Gem'	NPro
	- 'Golden Girl'	WFib
	- 'Golden Ingot' (v) ♀H4	COkL ECrN ELan EPla GAbr MBar MWhi WFib
	- 'Golden Kolibri'	see *H. helix* 'Midas Touch'
	- 'Golden Mathilde' (v)	CHal COkL
	- 'Golden Pittsburgh' (v)	WFib
	- 'Golden Snow' (v)	MBri WFib
	- 'Goldfinch'	WFib
	- 'Goldfinger' **new**	WFib
	- 'Goldheart'	see *H. helix* 'Oro di Bogliasco'
	- 'Goldstern' (v)	CBgR EHoe MWhi MWht WFib
	- 'Goldwolke' (v)	SLPl
	- 'Gracilis'	see *H. hibernica* 'Gracilis'
§	- 'Green Feather'	EGoo
	- 'Green Finger'	see *H. helix* 'Très Coupé'
§	- 'Green Ripple'	CBcs CSBt CTri CWib EBee ECrN ENot GKir LRHS MBar MGos MRav MSwo MWht NBro NCiC NLon SEND SLim SPer SPlb WBor WDin WFar WFib
	- 'Greenman'	WFib
	- 'Hahn's Green Ripple'	see *H. helix* 'Green Ripple'
	- 'Halebob' **new**	WFib
	- 'Hamilton'	see *H. hibernica* 'Hamilton'
	- 'Harald' (v)	CWib EBee LAst MBri NSti SCoo WDin WFib
	- 'Harlequin' (v)	COkL WFib
*	- 'Hazel' (v)	WFib
	- 'Hedge Hog'	WFib
	- 'Heise' (v)	WFib
	- 'Heise Denmark' (v)	WFib
	- 'Helvig'	see *H. helix* 'White Knight'
	- 'Henrietta'	CStr WFib
	- 'Hester'	WFib
	- subsp. ***hibernica***	see *H. hibernica*
	- 'Hispanica'	see *H. maderensis* subsp. *iberica*
	- 'Hite's Miniature'	see *H. helix* 'Merion Beauty'
	- 'Holly'	see *H. helix* 'Parsley Crested'
	- 'Hullavington'	CNat
	- 'Humpty Dumpty'	CPLG MBar
	- 'Ice Cream' **new**	MBlu

	- 'Ideal'	see *H. helix* 'California'
	- 'Imp'	see *H. helix* 'Brokamp'
	- 'Ingelise' (v) **new**	WFib
	- 'Ingrid' (v) **new**	WFib
	- 'Irish Lace'	WFar
	- 'Ivalace' ♀H4	CBcs CNat CRHN EBee ECha ECrN EPfP EPla MAsh MNrw MRav MSwo MWhi MWht NBid NSti SRms WDin WFib WTin
	- 'Jake'	CHal WFib
	- 'Jake's Gold'	WBcn
	- 'Jasper'	WFib
	- 'Jersey Doris' (v)	WFib
	- 'Jerusalem'	see *H. helix* 'Schäfer Three'
	- 'Jessica' **new**	SCoo
	- 'Jester's Gold'	ELan ENot EPfP EPla LRHS MBri MGos
	- 'Jubilee' (v)	COkL ECrN WCFE WFar WFib
	- 'Kaleidoscope'	WFib
	- 'Kevin'	WFib
	- 'Knülch'	MWat WFib
	- 'Kolibri' (v)	CDoC CHal COkL CRHN EBee EMil EPfP LAst MBar MBri MWht WFib
§	- 'Königer's Auslese'	CRHN SLPl WFib
	- 'Kurios'	CNat
	- 'Lalla Rookh'	MRav WBcn WFib WHrl
	- 'Lemon Swirl' (v)	WFib
	- 'Leo Swicegood'	CBgR CSWP MWhi WFib
	- 'Light Fingers'	SPoG WFib WHrl
	- 'Limey'	WFib
	- 'Little Diamond' (v)	CDoC CTri EHoe ELan EPfP LRHS MAsh MBar MBri MGos MWht SHBN SLon SPoG SWvt WDin WFib WHrl
	- 'Little Luzii' (v)	WFib
	- 'Little Witch'	EPla
	- 'Liz'	see *H. helix* 'Eva'
	- 'Lucille'	WFib
	- 'Luzii' (v)	EBee ECrN EHoe MBar MGos NLon NSti SGar SHBN WFib
	- 'Maculata'	see *H. helix* 'Minor Marmorata'
§	- 'Manda Fringette'	MTho
§	- 'Manda's Crested' ♀H4	CSWP ECrN NLar WFib
	- 'Maple Leaf' ♀H4	WFib
	- 'Maple Queen'	MBri
	- 'Marginata' (v)	SRms
	- 'Marginata Elegantissima'	see *H. helix* 'Tricolor'
	- 'Marginata Minor'	see *H. helix* 'Cavendishii'
I	- 'Marmorata' **new**	WFib
	- 'Masquerade' (v)	WGor
	- 'Mathilde' (v)	EBee LRHS MWht WFib
	- 'Maxi' **new**	SCoo
	- 'Meagheri'	see *H. helix* 'Green Feather'
§	- 'Melanie' ♀H4	ECha ECrN EPla LRHS WCot WFib
	- 'Meon'	WFib
§	- 'Merion Beauty'	EMFP WFib
§	- 'Midas Touch' (v) ♀H3-4	COtt CWib EPfP MBri NLar WFib
	- 'Midget'	CRow
	- 'Mini Ester' (v)	EPfP MBri
	- 'Mini Heron'	LAst MBri
	- 'Mini Pittsburgh'	COkL LAst
	- 'Minikin' (v)	WFib
	- 'Minima' misapplied	see *H. helix* 'Spetchley'
	- 'Minima' Hibberd	see *H. helix* 'Donerailensis'
	- 'Minima' M. Young	see *H. helix* 'Congesta'
§	- 'Minor Marmorata' (v) ♀H4	CHal MTho WFib WSHC
	- 'Mint Kolibri'	EHoe MBri WBcn
	- 'Minty' (v)	EMFP EPla LRHS MWht SCoo WFib
*	- 'Minutissima'	EPla WBcn
	- 'Miss Maroc'	see *H. helix* 'Manda Fringette'
	- 'Misty' (v)	WFib

	- 'Needlepoint'	EHoe
	- 'New Ripples'	MWht
	- 'Nigra Aurea' (v)	WFib
	- 'Norfolk Lace'	EWes
	- 'Northington Gold'	WBcn
	- 'Obovata'	WFib
	- 'Olive Rose'	CStr MTho
N	- 'Oro di Bogliasco' (v)	More than 30 suppliers
	- 'Ovata'	WFib
§	- 'Parsley Crested' ♀^{H4}	CMac CSBt EBee ECrN EPfP MBar NSti SGar SPer SPoG SRms WBVN WFar WFib
	- 'Patent Leather'	WFib
N	- 'Pedata'	CSWP EPfP MSwo WFib
	- 'Perkeo'	CHal EGoo WFib
	- 'Perle' (v)	NBir
	- 'Persian Carpet'	WFib
	- 'Peter' (v)	WFib
	- 'Peter Pan'	WFib
*	- 'Pin Oak'	EHoe LBuc WFar
	- 'Pink 'n' Curly' **new**	WFib
	- 'Pink 'n' Very Curly'	WCot
§	- 'Pittsburgh'	LAst WFib
	- 'Plume d'Or'	CHal MTho WFib
§	- f. ***poetarum***	CNat EPla MBlu WBcn WFib
	- - 'Poetica Arborea'	ECha SDix
	- 'Poetica'	see *H. helix* f. *poetarum*
	- 'Preston Tiny'	NBir
	- 'Raleigh Delight' (v)	WCot
	- 'Rambler'	NBir
	- 'Ray's Supreme'	see *H. helix* 'Pittsburgh'
	- subsp. ***rhizomatifera***	WFib
	- 'Ritterkreuz'	WFib
	- 'Romanze' (v)	WFib
	- 'Russelliana'	WFib
	- 'Rüsche'	EGoo
	- 'Sagittifolia' misapplied	see *H. helix* 'Königers Auslese'
	- 'Sagittifolia' Hibberd	see *H. hibernica* 'Sagittifolia'
	- 'Sagittifolia Variegata' (v)	COkL EBee ECrN LRHS MAsh MBri NBea WFib
	- 'Sally' (v)	WFib
	- 'Salt and Pepper'	see *H. helix* 'Minor Marmorata'
§	- 'Schäfer Three' (v)	CWib WFib
	- 'Shadow'	WFib
	- 'Shamrock'	COkL MBri MWht WFib
	- 'Silver Butterflies' (v)	WFib
	- 'Silver King' (v)	MRav MWht NBir WFib
	- 'Silver Queen'	see *H. helix* 'Tricolor'
	- 'Spectre' (v)	MTho WHer
§	- 'Spetchley' ♀^{H4}	CHal CNic CSWP EPla EPot GCal MBar MRav MTho MWhi NPer SMad WBcn WCFE WCot WFib WPat WPrP WTin
	- 'Spiriusa'	WFib
	- 'Stuttgart'	CWil WFib
	- 'Sunrise'	WFib
	- 'Suzanne'	see *H. nepalensis* var. *nepalensis* 'Suzanne'
	- 'Tamara' **new**	SCoo
	- 'Tango'	ECrN
	- 'Tanja'	WFib
	- 'Teardrop'	ECrN
	- 'Telecurl'	CBgR WFib
	- 'Tenerife'	WFib
	- 'Tiger Eyes'	CBcs WFib
	- 'Tony'	COkL
	- 'Topazolite' (v)	WFib
§	- 'Très Coupé'	CBcs CDoC CSWP EBee ECrN EGoo ISea LRHS MAsh MTho SAPC SArc SCoo SPoG WDin
§	- 'Tricolor' (v)	CBcs CTri EBee EPfP LRHS MGos MWht SBra SHBN SPoG WCFE WFib WTel
	- 'Trinity' (v)	WFib
	- 'Tripod'	CBcs EMFP WFib
	- 'Triton'	MBar MTho WFib
	- 'Troll'	EMFP WFib
	- 'Tussie Mussie' (v)	WFib
	- 'Ursula' (v)	CSWP EShb LPBA WFib
	- 'Very Merry'	LPBA
	- 'White Heart'	ENot MGos
§	- 'White Knight' (v) ♀^{H4}	MBri WFib
	- 'White Kolibri'	MBri
	- 'White Mein Herz' (v)	GBin WFib
	- 'William Kennedy' (v)	WFib
	- 'Williamsiana' (v)	CBcs WFib
	- 'Woeneri'	MWht SLPl WFib
	- 'Wonder'	WFib
	- 'Yab Yum' (v)	CBcs WBcn
	- 'Yellow Ripple'	COkL LPBA WBcn
	- 'Zebra' (v)	WFib
§	***hibernica*** ♀^{H4}	CBcs CNat CSBt ENot GKir LBuc LRHS MBar MRav MSwo MWhi NBea NBlu NWea SBra SPer SPoG SRms WDin
	- 'Anna Marie'	see *H. helix* 'Anna Marie'
	- 'Aracena'	EPla SLPl
	- 'Betty Allen'	WFib
§	- 'Deltoidea' ♀^{H4}	EPla MBri MWht WFib
I	- 'Digitata Crûg Gold'	WCru
§	- 'Dunloe Gap'	EPla
§	- 'Gracilis'	WFib
§	- 'Hamilton'	WFib
	- 'Lobata Major'	SRms
	- 'Maculata' (v)	EPla SLPl WBcn WSHC
	- 'Palmata'	WFib
	- 'Rona'	WFib
§	- 'Sagittifolia'	COkL CTri EPfP GBin LRHS MAsh MBar NLon SHFr SRms WFar
	- 'Sulphurea' (v)	WFib
	- 'Tess'	EPla
	- 'Variegata' (v)	COkL MBar
	maderensis	WFib
§	- subsp. ***iberica***	WFib
	maroccana 'Morocco'	WFib
§	- 'Spanish Canary'	WFib
	nepalensis	WBcn WFib
§	- var. ***nepalensis*** 'Suzanne'	MBar WFib
§	- var. ***sinensis***	MWht WFib
	- - L 555	EPla
	pastuchovii	EShb WBcn WFib
	- from Troödos, Cyprus	see *H. cypria*
	- 'Ann Ala'	WFib
§	***rhombea***	WCot WFib
	- 'Eastern Dawn'	WFib
	- 'Japonica'	see *H. rhombea*
I	- f. ***pedunculata*** 'Maculata'	CWib
	- var. ***rhombea*** 'Variegata' (v)	WFib

Hedychium ✿ (*Zingiberaceae*)

	B&SWJ 3110	WPGP
	B&SWJ 7155	WPGP
	'Anne Bishop'	CFil CKob MJnS
	aurantiacum	CBcs CFil CPne EAmu EBee LEdu MJnS WMul WPnP
	chrysoleucum	CHEx EShb LAma LPio MJnS
	- B&SWJ 8116	WCru
	coccineum ♀^{H1}	CBcs CFil CKob EAmu EShb EUJe LAma LExo LRHS MJnS MNrw MOak WMul
	- var. ***angustifolium***	CFil CRHN EBee EPfP WHal WPGP
I	- - 'Peach'	MOak

- var. ***aurantiacum***	CBct CHEx LAma
- 'Tara' ♀H3	More than 30 suppliers
coronarium	CAvo CBct CDes CHEx CKob CRHN EAmu EBee EShb EUJe LExo LRHS MJnS MOak MSte SYvo WCot WMul
- B&SWJ 8354	WCru
- 'Andromeda'	WMul
- var. ***flavescens***	see *H. flavescens*
- gold- spotted	CKob
- var. ***maximum***	CFir
- 'Orange Spot'	EAmu
coronarium* x *gardnerianum	MJnS WMul
'Dave Case'	CKob
densiflorum	CBct CBrd CDes CFil CHEx CHll CKob CPne EAmu EBee ECha EShb EUJe IBlr MLLN MOak SDix SSpi WCru WMul WPGP
- LS&H 17393	CFil
- SCH 582	CFil
- 'Assam Orange'	CAvo CBct CBrm CDoC CFil CHEx CKob CPne CSam EAmu EBee GCal LEdu LPio MAvo MJnS MNrw MOak MSte SChr SDix SSpi WBVN WCru WMul WPGP
- 'Sorung' **new**	CFil
- 'Stephen'	CBct CBrd CDes CFil CHEx CKob EAmu EBee LPio MNrw MSte SSpi WMul WPGP
'Doctor Moy'	CKob MJnS
'Double Eagle'	CFil CKob
'Elizabeth'	CDes CFil CKob MJnS WMul
ellipticum	CFil CHEx CKob CPLG EAmu EBee EShb EUJe LAma LEdu MJnS MNrw MOak WCru WMul
- B&SWJ 7171	WCru
'Filigree'	CDes CFir CKob
§ ***flavescens***	CBct CFil CKob CPne EAmu EBee EShb EUJe LAma LEdu LExo LRHS MJnS MNrw MOak SChr WCru WMul WPGP WPnP
- B&SWJ 7900	WCru
forrestii	CDes CFil CHEx CKob EAmu EShb GCal IBlr ITer LPJP LPio MJnS MNrw MOak MSte SAPC SArc SSpi WCru WKif WMul WPGP
- var. ***latebracteatum*** HWJ 604 **new**	WCru
gardnerianum ♀H1	More than 30 suppliers
- B&SWJ 7155	WCru
- var. ***pallidum***	CKob
'Gold Flame'	CDes CFil CFir CKob MNrw MOak WPGP
gracile	CFil CKob EAmu EShb EUJe MOak
greenii	CBcs CBct CDoC CFil CFir CHEx CKob CRHN CSam EShb EUJe LEdu LPio LRHS MJnS MNrw MOak MSte SArc SBig SChr SDix SYvo WBor WCot WCru WMul WPGP WPnP
griffithianum	MNrw
'Hardy Exotics 1'	CHEx
horsfieldii	CKob CRHN
hybrid from Great Dixter	CKob MJnS
'Kinkaku'	CFil CKob WPGP
'Lemon Sherbet'	CFir CKob
'Luna Moth'	CDes CFil CKob EBee EUJe WMul
maximum	CKob WMul
'Nikasha-cho' **new**	EBee
'Orange Brush'	CKob
pink-flowered	CDes
'Pink Flame'	CKob
'Pink Sparks'	CFil CKob
'Pink V'	CFil CKob
'Pradhan'	CFir CHEx
x ***raffillii***	CKob MJnS MNrw
'Shamshiri'	CKob
spicatum	CDes CFil CFir CHEx CKob CMdw CPLG CPne EBee EChP EMan EShb EUJe GPoy LEdu MNrw MOak MSte SSpi WCFE WMul
- B&SWJ 2303	WCru WPGP
- B&SWJ 5238	WCru
- BWJ 8116	WCru
- CC 1705	CKob
- CC 3249	WCot
- CC 3650	ITer
- 'Tresco' **new**	CKob
'Telstar 4'	CHEx
thyrsiforme	CFil CKob CPne EAmu EBee EUJe MOak WCru WMul
'Twengwainran'	MOak
villosum	EBee LAma WMul
yunnanense	CDes CFil CHEx CKob EAmu MNrw SBig WCot WCru WPGP
- L 633	CKob

Hedysarum (*Papilionaceae*)

coronarium	CArn CBcs CPle CSpe EHrv ELan EPfP MAnH MBrN NLsd SPet SSpi SYvo WCot WCra WKif
hedysaroides	EBee WCot
multijugum	CBcs IDee MBlu SPer WCot WSHC
nitidum	EBee

Hegemone (*Ranunculaceae*)

lilacina **new**	GKev

Heimia (*Lythraceae*)

salicifolia	CArn CBrm CPle EMan EUnu IDee LRav MBlu MGol MSal SGar WWye
- RCB/Arg P-7	WCot

Helenium ✿ (*Asteraceae*)

'Autumn Lollipop'	GFlt SPav WMnd WWpP
autumnale	CSam CTri EGoo LDai LSRN MAnH MBNS MSal NChi NEgg NJOw SPet SSvw SWvt WBVN WFar WMoo
- 'All Gold'	SWvt
- 'Praecox'	MWrn
- 'Sunset Shades'	GBBs
'Baronin Linden'	CSam
'Baudirektor Linne' ♀H4	CSam GKir LRHS WWpP
'Biedermeier'	CSam CWCL EBee EBrs ECtt EVFa LRHS MLLN MNFA MTis NGdn SPer SPla SUsu
bigelovii	CSam SGSe
'Blütentisch' ♀H4	CPrp CSam EBee EChP EMan GMaP GMac MBnl MMil MNFA MWgw NCGa NVic SPoG SPur WHal WMnd WWpP
'Bressingham Gold'	CElw CSam WWpP
'Bruno'	CAby CFwr CHar CWCL EBrs ELan ERou EVFa GKir GMac GSki LRHS MArl MMil MRav NRnb SChu SHop SOkh WWpP
'Butterpat' ♀H4	CHad EBee EBrs EChP ECtt EGra EHrv EPfP ERou GCra GKir GMaP IBal LRHS MMil MRav NBPC NCGa NPri NSti SBla SChu SHop WHlf WSan WWpP
'Chipperfield Orange'	CElw CHad CSam EGra ERou GBri MArl MMil MRav NBre NGdn NVic WOld WWpP

	'Coppelia'	EBrs GKir NBir NGdn WOld WTel
	Copper Spray	see *H.* 'Kupfersprudel'
	'Crimson Beauty'	CSam ECtt ELan EPfP LRHS MLLN MRav
	Dark Beauty	see *H.* 'Dunkelpracht'
	'Die Blonde'	LPhx NBre NDov SMHy WWpP
§	'Dunkelpracht'	More than 30 suppliers
	'Feuersiegel' ♀H4	CSam LPhx NBre NDov WOld WWpP
	'Fiesta'	CSam
	'Flammendes Käthchen'	CSam EBrs LPhx LRHS NBre NDov SAga WGHP WWpP
	'Flammenspiel'	CFwr CSam EBrs EChP ECtt GFlt LRHS MNFA MRav MSph WWpP
	flexuosum	CSam EBee MWrn NBre NChi
	'Gartensonne' ♀H4	CSam WWpP
	'Gay-go-round'	CSam
	'Gold Fox'	see *H.* 'Goldfuchs'
	'Gold Intoxication'	see *H.* 'Goldrausch'
	Golden Youth	see *H.* 'Goldene Jugend'
§	'Goldene Jugend'	CElw CMea CSam ECtt ELan MRav SSpe WCot WEas WWpP
§	'Goldfuchs'	CSam CWCL WCot WWpP
§	'Goldlackzwerg'	WHlf
§	'Goldrausch'	CHar CSam MDKP MWat WHlf WWpP
	'Helena'	MAnH NEgg NLsd NRnb
	hoopesii	CMHG CPrp EHrv EPfP EPza GKir GMaP GSki IHMH LRHS MBNS MBow MNrw MRav NArg NBir NEgg NJOw NLRH NPri NSti SPer SPet SRms SWvt WFar WMnd WMoo WPer
	'Indianersommer'	CElw CFwr CSam CWCL EBee EChP ECtt EHrv EMan GMaP GMac LDai MBNS MBnl MLLN MOne MSph MWgw NBPC NCGa NLar NOrc SMHy SMer SUsu WFar WHil WWpP
	'July Sun'	NBir SSpe
	'Kanaria'	CAby CBre CHea CPrp EBee EBrs EMil ERou EWll LRHS MCCP MNFA MRav NCob SPur WLin WMnd WOld WWpP
	'Karneol' ♀H4	CSam EBrs LRHS SOkh WWpP
	'Kleiner Fuchs'	CSam EChP NLar WWpP
	'Kokarde'	CSam
	'Königstiger'	CFwr CSam EBee EBrs LRHS MBri WWpP
	'Kugelsonne'	WWpP
§	'Kupfersprudel'	CFwr
	'Kupferzwerg'	CSam CWCL LPhx NBre NDov SAga SOkh WEas WGHP
	'Mahogany'	see *H.* 'Goldlackzwerg'
	'Margot'	CDes CSam CWCL WCAu WWpP
	'Meranti'	CSam
	'Moerheim Beauty' ♀H4	More than 30 suppliers
	'Orange Beauty' **new**	WHlf
	Pipsqueak = 'Blopip'	CHea EBrs ECtt EMan GBri LRHS
	'Potter's Wheel'	CDes CSam EBee WCot WWpP
	puberulum	SGSe SPav WOut
	'Pumilum Magnificum'	CDes CKno CPrp CSam CWCL EHol EPfP GLil GSki LEdu LRHS MBnl MNFA MWat NFla SPer WFar WPGP WTel
	'Rauchtopas'	CSam
	Red and Gold	see *H.* 'Rotgold'
	'Red Army' **new**	MBri NGdn NRnb SSpe
	'Red Glory' **new**	CFwr
	'Ring of Fire' ♀H4	CSam
	'Riverton Beauty'	CSam CStr EBee ERou SUsu
	'Riverton Gem'	CSam CWCL ECtt
§	'Rotgold'	CFwr ECtt ENot GFlt LSRN MHer MWrn NArg NEgg NJOw NOak NPri NRnb SGar SPoG SRms STes WFar WMoo WPer WPop WWeb
	'Rubinkuppel'	CSam LPhx NDov SChu SUsu
	'Rubinzwerg' ♀H4	More than 30 suppliers
	'Sahin's Early Flowerer' ♀H4	More than 30 suppliers
	'Septemberfuchs'	WWpP
	'Septembergold'	CSam
	'Sonnenwunder'	CSam ECha GKir WOld WWpP
	'Sunshine'	WBrk WSan
	'The Bishop'	More than 30 suppliers
	'Vivace'	CSam
	'Waldhorn'	LRHS MSph
	'Waldtraut' ♀H4	More than 30 suppliers
	'Wesergold' ♀H4	EBee EChP SPoG
	'Wonnadonga'	CFwr
	'Wyndley'	More than 30 suppliers
	'Zimbelstern'	CDes CElw CFwr CMdw CMil CSam EBee EBrs ECha ERou GKir LPhx LRHS MNFA MRav NDov SAga SOkh WAul WFar WWpP

Heliamphora (*Sarraceniaceae*)

	nutans	SHmp

Helianthella (*Asteraceae*)

§	***quinquenervis***	CStr EMan GCal GFlt NLar WFar

Helianthemum ✿ (*Cistaceae*)

	'Alice Howarth'	CFul MDHE WHoo
	alpestre serpyllifolium	see *H. nummularium* subsp. *glabrum*
	'Amabile Plenum' (d)	CFul EPfP GAbr GCal MBNS NLar SIgm
	'Amber'	GAbr
	'Amy Baring' ♀H4	CFul CTri GAbr GKir LRHS WPer
	'Annabel'	CFul COkL EPfP GAbr GKir IGor MWya SBla SChu SMer WBVN WPer WTel
	apenninum	CFul MDHE SRms XPep
	'Apricot'	CFul WBcn
	'Apricot Blush'	CFul WAbe
	'Avalanche' **new**	CFul
	'Baby Buttercup'	CFul CLyd CMea GAbr
	'Banwy Copper'	WBVN
	'Beech Park Red'	CFul ECtt ESis LBee LRHS MDHE MHer SAga SChu SIgm WAbe WHoo WKif
	'Ben Afflick'	CFul COkL GKir LBee LRHS MBNS MDHE SIgm SRms
	'Ben Alder'	CFul COkL GAbr MDHE MHer
	'Ben Attow'	CFul
	'Ben Dearg'	CFul CMea COkL ECtt GAbr MDHE SRms
	'Ben Fhada'	CBcs CFul CMea COkL COlW CTri ECtt EPfP GAbr GKir GMaP LBee LRHS MDHE MHer NEgg NLon NPri SBla SPoG SRms WAbe WBrE WCFE WPer
	'Ben Heckla'	CFul COkL CSam CTri ECtt EPfP GAbr GKir IHMH ITim LRHS MDHE MSte SBla WPer WTel
	'Ben Hope'	CFul COkL ECtt EPfP GAbr MDHE NLon
§	'Ben Ledi'	CBcs CBrm CFul COkL ECtt EPfP GAbr GMaP IHMH LRHS MBar MDHE MHer MWgw NChi NLon NPri NSla NVic SPoG SRms WAbe WHoo WPer
	'Ben Lomond'	CFul COkL GAbr
	'Ben Macdhui'	CFul COkL GAbr

	'Ben More'	CBcs CFul COkL COlW ECtt EWin GAbr GKir GTou LRHS MDHE MSwo MWat NBir NLon NPri SIng SPoG SRms WBrE
	'Ben Nevis'	CFul COkL CTri ECha GAbr MDHE SBla SRms WTel
	'Ben Vane'	CFul COkL COlW GAbr LRHS MDHE WBcn
	'Bentley'	CFul
	'Birch White'	MDHE
	'Bishopsthorpe'	CFul
	'Boughton Double Primrose' (d)	CFul ELan EWes GKir GMaP GMac LRHS SBla SChu SIgm SMer WEas WHoo WSHC WSel WTin
	'Brilliant'	NBir
	'Bronzeteppich' **new**	CRez
	'Broughty Beacon'	CFul COkL GAbr MDHE WGor
	'Broughty Orange'	WSel
	'Broughty Sunset'	CFul COkL CSam GAbr MDHE NBir SIgm WHoo WSel
	'Bunbury'	CFul CMea COlW CStr GAbr IHMH MBrN MDHE MWhi NBir SPoG SRms
	'Butterball' (d)	CFul MDHE
	canum	SBla
	'Captivation'	CFul COkL EGoo GAbr
	caput-felis	XPep
	'Cerise Queen' (d)	CFul CTri ECha GAbr GKir LRHS MSwo SDix SIgm SRms WBVN WHoo
	chamaecistus	see *H. nummularium*
	'Cheviot'	CFul CMea ECha GAbr MDHE NBir SAga WEas WHoo WPer WSHC
	'Chichester'	CFul
	'Chocolate Blotch'	CFul CMea CRez ECtt GAbr GKir LRHS MHer NChi NLon SChu SEND SPla SRms WPer
	'Coppernob'	CFul
	'Cornish Cream'	CFul GAbr LBee LRHS
	croceum	LTwo
	cupreum	CFul GAbr
	'David'	CFul EGoo
	'David Ritchie' **new**	WHoo
	'Diana'	CMea SAga
	'Die Braut'	CFul
	double apricot (d)	GAbr
	double cream (d)	ECha MDHE WFar
	double pale pink (d)	SIgm
	double pale yellow (d)	NWoo
	double pink (d)	ECha NWoo WFar
	double primrose (d)	GAbr MDHE
	double red (d)	NChi
	'Elisabeth'	CFul EGoo
	'Ellen' (d)	CMea
	'Etna'	CFul STre
	'Everton Ruby'	see *H.* 'Ben Ledi'
	'Fairy'	CFul GAbr LTwo MDHE
§	'Fire Dragon' ♀H4	CFul CMea COkL ECha ECho EPfP GAbr GKev GKir GMaP LRHS MDHE MWgw MWhi NBir NEgg NWCA SAga SBla SChu SIgm SPoG SRms WAbe WHil WLin XPep
	'Fireball'	see *H.* 'Mrs C.W. Earle'
	'Firegold'	WAbe
	'Flame'	CFul COkL
	'Georgeham'	CFul ECtt EPfP LBee LRHS MDHE NBir SBla SMer SPoG SRms WEas WGor WHoo WPer
	'Gloiriette'	CFul
§	'Golden Queen'	CFul COkL ECtt EPfP GAbr ITim LRHS MAvo MBNS MSwo MWhi NLar SChu SPoG WFar WPer WSan
	'Henfield Brilliant' ♀H4	CBrm CFul COkL CPBP CPLG CSpe ECho EPfP GAbr GKir LRHS MDHE NBir SIng SMad SMer SPla SPoG SRms WEas WHoo WLin WPer WSHC WSel WTel
	'Hidcote Apricot'	CFul GAbr MDHE NEgg
	'Highdown'	CFul GAbr SRms
	'Highdown Apricot'	MDHE SPoG WRHF
	'Highdown Peach'	GAbr
	'Honeymoon'	CFul GAbr MDHE SBla WHil WSel
	'John Lanyon'	CFul MDHE
	'Jubilee' (d) ♀H4	CFul COkL COlW CTbh ECtt ELan GAbr LAst MDHE NBir NChi NLon SBla SDix SPoG SRms WAbe WEas WSel WTel
I	'Jubilee Variegatum' (v)	CFul GAbr NLon
	'Karen's Silver'	CFul WAbe
	'Kathleen Druce' (d)	CFul COkL EWes GAbr MWat WHoo
	'Kathleen Mary'	CMea
	'Lawrenson's Pink'	CFul ECGP GAbr
	'Lemon Queen'	CFul WBcn
I	'Linton Rose'	NBir
	'Lucy Elizabeth'	CFul COkL GAbr
	lunulatum	CFul CLyd CMea ECtt LRHS MDHE NMen SIgm WAbe WPat
	'Magnificum'	CFul EHol MDHE MWat
§	'Mrs C.W. Earle' (d) ♀H4	CFul COkL COlW CTri ECGP ECho ECtt ELan GAbr MBow MDHE MWya NPri SBla SDix SGar SPoG SRms WAbe WHoo WSel
	'Mrs Clay'	see *H.* 'Fire Dragon'
	'Mrs Croft'	WPer
	'Mrs Hays'	CFul GAbr MDHE
	'Mrs Jenkinson'	CFul WTel
	'Mrs Lake'	CFul GAbr WBcn
	'Mrs Moules'	CFul SRms
	mutabile	CFul SPlb
§	***nummularium***	GPoy MBow MDHE MHer NArg NMir SECG SHGN WPat WWye XPep
§	- subsp. ***glabrum***	CFul CNic EHyt GAbr MDHE NJOw NLAp WPat
	- subsp. ***pyrenaicum*** **new**	GKev
§	- subsp. ***tomentosum***	CFul GAbr MDHE MWat
	oelandicum	GAbr NWCA SRms
	- subsp. ***alpestre***	CFul CLyd NJOw NMen WPer
	- subsp. ***piloselloides***	CLyd
	'Old Gold'	CFul GAbr GKir LRHS MDHE SIgm SRms WAbe WLin WPer WSel WTel
I	'Orange Phoenix' (d) **new**	CRez LSou NEgg
	'Ovum Supreme'	CFul GAbr
	'Pershore AGS' **new**	WBcn
	'Pershore Orange' **new**	CFul
	pilosum	SIgm
	'Pink Beauty'	WHil
	'Pink Glow'	CFul WPer
	'Praecox'	CFul CMea CTri GAbr LBee LRHS SIgm SMer SRms WHoo WPer WTel
	'Prima Donna'	CFul NBir
	'Prostrate Orange'	CFul SRms
	'Raspberry Ripple'	CFul CHar ELan EPfP EPot GAbr GKir LRHS MAvo MWrn SIng SPoG SRms WAbe WBVN WHoo
	'Razzle Dazzle' (v)	CFul LAst SRms
	'Red Dragon'	GKir WAbe
	'Red Orient'	see *H.* 'Supreme'
	'Regenbogen' (d)	ECha GAbr GCal SBla
§	'Rhodanthe Carneum' ♀H4	More than 30 suppliers
	'Rosakönigin'	CFul ECtt GAbr MDHE MHer WAbe WLin
	'Rose of Leeswood' (d)	CBrm CFul CMea CPBP CTri GMaP LBee LRHS MDHE NEgg NLon

		SAga SBla SIgm SPoG SRms WEas WHoo WKif WSHC WSel
	Rose Queen	see *H.* 'Rosakönigin'
	'Rosenburg'	GAbr
	'Roxburgh Gold'	CFul SRms
	'Rushfield's White'	CFul WBcn
	'Saint John's College Yellow'	CFul CSam GAbr LRHS MDHE WFar
	'Salmon Beauty'	CFul
	'Salmon Bee'	CFul
	'Salmon Queen'	CElw CFul COkL ECtt GAbr GKir LBee LRHS MDHE NPri SRms WPer WRHF WSel
*	***scardicum***	CFul CMea
	'Schnee' (d)	CFul ECha EGoo
	serpyllifolium	see *H. nummularium* subsp. *glabrum*
	'Shot Silk'	CFul COkL CPBP EWes MDHE
	'Snow' **new**	WBcn
	'Snow Queen'	see *H.* 'The Bride'
	'Southmead'	CFul COkL GAbr
	'Sterntaler'	CFul GAbr MDHE SRms
	'Sudbury Gem'	CFul COkL COlW EChP ECha ESis EWin GAbr GKir LRHS SMer WRHF WTel
	'Sulphureum Plenum' (d)	CFul ECtt EPfP
	'Summertime'	CFul
	'Sunbeam'	CSam GAbr MDHE SRms
	'Sunburst'	CFul GAbr
§	'Supreme'	CFul ELan EPfP EWes LBee LRHS MAvo SDix SIgm SRms WSel WWeb
	'Tangerine'	CFul ECha GAbr
	'Terracotta'	CRez
§	'The Bride' 🏆^{H4}	CBcs CFul CMea ECha ELan EPfP GAbr GKir GMaP LRHS MBow MDHE MHer MSte MWat MWgw NVic SBla SChu SDix SIng SMer SPoG SRms WAbe WEas WHoo WSel WWeb
	'Tigrinum Plenum' (d)	CFul CPBP ESis EWes LRHS MDHE SBla
	'Tomato Red'	CFul ECha NSla
	tomentosum	see *H. nummularium*
	umbellatum	see *Halimium umbellatum*
	'Venustum Plenum' (d)	CFul WEas
	'Voltaire'	CFul COkL ECtt EPfP GAbr MDHE NPri NVic
	'Watergate Rose'	CFul MWat NBir
	'Welsh Flame'	WAbe
	'Windermere'	SIgm
	'Windmill Gold'	CFul COkL LBee WBcn
	'Wisley Pink'	see *H.* 'Rhodanthe Carneum'
	'Wisley Primrose' 🏆^{H4}	More than 30 suppliers
	'Wisley White'	CFul COkL CTri ECha ECtt EGoo EPfP NLon WHoo
	'Wisley Yellow'	CBrm
	'Yellow Queen'	see *H.* 'Golden Queen'

Helianthus ✿ (*Asteraceae*)

	RCB/Arg CC-3 **new**	WCot
	angustifolius	CFwr WPer
	atrorubens	EBee EVFa LRHS MRav NBro WFar WGHP
	'Capenoch Star' 🏆^{H4}	CElw CPrp CStr EBee ECha ECtt EMan ERou GBuc LRHS MArl MBri MLLN MRav NBro NCGa NLar SDix SMrm SPoG WFar WOld WWpP
	'Capenoch Supreme'	EMan
	decapetalus	CStr MDKP NFla WWye
	- 'Maximus'	SRms
	- Morning Sun	see *H.* 'Morgensonne'
	x ***doronicoides***	SRms
	giganteus 'Sheila's Sunshine'	CBre CElw CStr GBri MAvo MHar MNFA MSte NDov WOld
	grosseserratus	LPhx
	'Gullick's Variety' 🏆^{H4}	CBre CHea CStr EBee ECtt EPfP IBlr LLWP LPhx MAnH MBnl NBro NChi NEgg NSti STes WBrk WOld WWpP
	hirsutus	EBee
	x ***kellermanii***	CStr EBee EMon LPhx MWgw NDov SAga
§	x ***laetiflorus***	EBee ELan MDKP NLar NOrc
*	- 'Superbus'	IBlr
§	'Lemon Queen' 🏆^{H4}	More than 30 suppliers
	'Limelight'	see *H.* 'Lemon Queen'
§	'Loddon Gold' 🏆^{H4}	CElw ECtt ELan EMan EPfP ERou GAbr IBlr LPhx LRHS MAvo MBnl MBri MRav MTis NEgg NVic SAga WBVN WBrE WBrk WCot WCra WFar WWpP WWye
§	***maximiliani***	EBee EShb LRHS MAnH MDKP MSte SPav SWal WWpP XPep
	'Miss Mellish' 🏆^{H4}	NRnb WCot WHoo
	mollis	CStr EShb SPav WPer
	'Monarch' 🏆^{H4}	CElw CFwr CStr EMan ERou LPhx MDKP MRav MWgw SAga SDix SVal WOld WWpP
	'Morgensonne'	CStr EHrv MAvo MDKP MWat NRnb WCot
	x ***multiflorus*** 'Meteor'	EBee NChi
	occidentalis	IBlr LRHS WPer
	orgyalis	see *H. salicifolius*
	quinquenervis	see *Helianthella quinquenervis*
	rigidus misapplied	see *H.* x *laetiflorus*
§	***salicifolius***	CFwr CStr EBee EBrs EMan EMon EPPr EVFa LRHS MSte NCGa NSti SDix SGSe SMad SMrm SSpe WAul WBVN WCot WFar WHrl WMnd WTin WWye XPep
	- 'Low Down'	CFwr EBrs GBri LBuc LRHS
	scaberrimus	see *H.* x *laetiflorus*
	'Soleil d'Or'	ECtt EGra WCAu WHal
	strumosus	WCot
	'Triomphe de Gand'	CHea CStr GBri LPhx MRav MWat WFar WOld
	tuberosus	EBee EUnu GPoy WOld
	- 'Fuseau'	LEdu
	- 'Garnet'	LEdu
	- 'Sugarball'	LEdu

Helichrysum (*Asteraceae*)

	from Drakensberg Mountains, South Africa	CNic NWCA
	acutatum	GCal
	adenocarpum **new**	SPlb
	alveolatum	see *H. splendidum*
	ambiguum	CFis CSLe NLon SIgm WBcn
	angustifolium	see *H. italicum*
	- from Crete	see *H. microphyllum* (Willd.) Cambess.
	arenarium	ECho
§	***arwae***	EHyt EPot LBee NLAp WAbe
	bellidioides	CTri ECha GAbr GGar LRHS NLAp SMer WCru
	bellum	NWCA
	chionophilum	EPot NWCA
	'Coco'	see *Xerochrysum bracteatum* 'Coco'
§	***conglobatum***	XPep
	cooperi	EHyt
	coralloides	see *Ozothamnus coralloides*
	'County Park Silver'	see *Ozothamnus* 'County Park Silver'

	Plant	Suppliers
	'Dargan Hill Monarch'	see *Xerochrysum bracteatum* 'Dargan Hill Monarch'
	depressum	EHyt
	doerfleri	XPep
	'Elmstead'	see *H. stoechas* 'White Barn'
	fontanesii	SPer WHer XPep
	frigidum	CPBP EHyt EPot ITim LRHS
	heldreichii	EPot
	- NS 127	NWCA
	hookeri	see *Ozothamnus hookeri*
	hypoleucum	GGar WHer
§	***italicum*** ♀H3	CArn CBcs CSLe CWan EChP ECha EGra ELau EShb ESis GPoy IHMH LGro MBar MBow MHer MWgw NGHP SECG SPet SRms WDin WGHP WGwG WHCG WWye XPep
	- from Crete	NWCA
	- 'Dartington'	CBod EOHP EWin MHer NGHP SIde WJek WSel
I	- 'Glaucum'	CWib
	- 'Korma'PBR	CAbP EBee ELan ENot EPfP EWTr EWin MAsh MBNS NGHP SIde SLon SPoG WJek
	- subsp. ***microphyllum***	see *H. microphyllum* (Willd.) Cambess.
	- 'Nanum'	see *H. microphyllum* (Willd.) Cambess.
§	- subsp. ***serotinum***	CChe EBee EGoo EPfP GGar GPoy MRav SLim SMer SPla SRms STre SWal SWvt WDin WPer WSel WTel XPep
	lanatum	see *H. thianschanicum*
	ledifolium	see *Ozothamnus ledifolius*
	marginatum misapplied	see *H. milfordiae*
	marginatum DC. JJ&JH 9401733	NWCA
	microphyllum misapplied	see *Plecostachys serpyllifolia*
§	***microphyllum*** (Willd.) Cambess.	ETow EVFa GBar MHer NBlu NWoo SIde SIgm WJek WSel XPep
§	***milfordiae*** ♀H2-3	EDAr EPot GEdr NLAp NMen NWCA SIng SRms WAbe WPat
	montanum	NWCA
	orientale	EPot SMer SPoG XPep
	pagophilum	CPBP EHyt EPot
	- JJ&JH 9401304	NWCA
§	***petiolare*** ♀H2	CSLe EBak ECtt EWin MOak NBlu SGar
	- 'Aureum'	see *H. petiolare* 'Limelight'
	- 'Goring Silver' ♀H2-3	CHal MOak NPri SPet
§	- 'Limelight' ♀H2	CHal ECtt EWin MOak NBlu NPri SPet
	- 'Roundabout' (v)	LSou MOak
	- 'Variegatum' (v) ♀H2	CHal ECtt NPri SPet SPoG
	petiolatum	see *H. petiolare*
	plumeum	ECou EPot
	populifolium misapplied	see *H. hypoleucum*
	rosmarinifolium	see *Ozothamnus rosmarinifolius*
	'Ruby Cluster'	SPer WFar
	rupestre	XPep
§	'Schwefellicht'	CSLe EBee ECha EPPr EPfP ERou EVFa LRHS MNFA MWgw NFla NLon NVic SChu SMer SPer SPet WCAu WEas WKif WSHC
	selago	see *Ozothamnus selago*
	- var. ***tumidum***	NSla
	serotinum	see *H. italicum* subsp. *serotinum*
	serpyllifolium	see *Plecostachys serpyllifolia*
	sessile	see *H. sessilioides*
§	***sessilioides***	EPot NLAp NSla NWCA WAbe
§	***sibthorpii***	CSev EHyt LRHS NWCA
	'Skynet'	see *Xerochrysum bracteatum* 'Skynet'
§	***splendidum*** ♀H3	CStu EHoe EPfP NBro NFor SLon SPer WBrE WDin WPer XPep
	aff. ***splendidum***	MWgw
	stoechas	CArn XPep
§	- 'White Barn'	WCot
	Sulphur Light	see *H.* 'Schwefellicht'
§	***thianschanicum***	EBee ENot EShb SRms XPep
	- Golden Baby	see *H. thianschanicum* 'Goldkind'
§	- 'Goldkind'	EPfP GKir IHMH NBir NBlu NPri
	thyrsoideum	see *Ozothamnus thyrsoideus*
	trilineatum	see *H. splendidum*
	tumidum	see *Ozothamnus selago* var. *tumidus*
	virgineum	see *H. sibthorpii*
	woodii	see *H. arwae*

Helichrysum x *Raoulia* (Asteraceae)

	Plant	Suppliers
	H. sp. x ***R. bryoides*** **new**	GKev

Helicodiceros (Araceae)

	Plant	Suppliers
§	***muscivorus***	CDes CFir CHid CMon WCot

Heliconia ✿ (Heliconiaceae)

	Plant	Suppliers
	aemygdiana **new**	LExo
	angusta 'Holiday' **new**	MJnS
	- 'Yellow Christmas' **new**	MJnS
	bihai	WMul
	caribaea 'Purpurea'	XBlo
	'Fire and Ice'	WMul
	'Golden Torch'	MJnS XBlo
	indica 'Spectabilis' **new**	XBlo
	latispatha 'Orange Gyro'	MJnS XBlo
	- 'Red Gyro' **new**	XBlo
	metallica	XBlo
	rostrata	MJnS XBlo
	stricta 'Dwarf Jamaican'	MJnS

Helictotrichon (Poaceae)

	Plant	Suppliers
	pratense	EHoe MAvo
§	***sempervirens*** ♀H4	More than 30 suppliers
	- var. ***pendulum***	EBee EMon EPPr GBin MAvo
	- 'Saphirsprudel'	CKno CMdw EPPr GBin WCot WPGP

Heliophila (Brassicaceae)

	Plant	Suppliers
	carnosa	SPla
	longifolia	CSpe

Heliopsis ✿ (Asteraceae)

	Plant	Suppliers
	helianthoides	CFwr CStr EBrs EMon LRHS NBre
	- 'Limelight'	see *Helianthus* 'Lemon Queen'
	- var. ***scabra***	EBee EHan EWTr MDKP WMnd
	- - 'Asahi' **new**	MBnl MBri
	- - Ballerina	see *H. helianthoides* var. *scabra* 'Spitzentänzerin'
	- - 'Benzinggold' ♀H4	MRav SMrm
	- - Golden Plume	see *H. helianthoides* var. *scabra* 'Goldgefieder'
§	- - 'Goldgefieder' ♀H4	EMan EPfP LRHS MBnl MBri
	- - Goldgreenheart	see *H. helianthoides* var. *scabra* 'Goldgrünherz'
§	- - 'Goldgrünherz'	CFwr EBrs MSph SOkh WAul
	- - 'Hohlspiegel'	EMan GBin
	- - 'Incomparabilis'	MWgw WCAu
	- - 'Light of Loddon' ♀H4	MWat SVal
	- - 'Mars'	CFwr
§	- - 'Sommersonne'	CFwr CSBt ECtt ERou MBow MRav NArg NJOw NLRH NLsd NPer SPer SRms STes WCAu WFar WMnd WWeb WWpP
§	- - 'Spitzentänzerin' ♀H4	CFwr MBri

- - Summer Sun	see *H. helianthoides* var. *scabra* 'Sommersonne'
- - 'Venus'	CFwr GBri LAst MTis NBid NGdn NRnb NVic SSpe WCAu WFar
Loraine Sunshine = 'Helhan'PBR (v)	EMan LRHS

Heliotropium ✿ (*Boraginaceae*)

§ ***arborescens***	CArn EPfP MHom MOak
- 'Chatsworth' 🏆H1	CAby CHad CPle CSev EHol EMan ERea EShb MAJR MHom MOak MSte SDnm WFar WPen
- 'Dame Alice de Hales'	CHal ERea MAJR MHom MOak
- 'Gatton Park'	CMdw ERea MAJR MHom MOak SMrm
- 'Lord Roberts'	ERea MAJR MHom MOak
- 'Marine'	EWin LIck SGar SPav SUsu WGor
- 'Mrs J.W. Lowther'	MAJR MOak
- 'Nagano'PBR **new**	EWin
- 'Netherhall White'	ERea
- 'P.K. Lowther'	ERea WEas
- 'President Garfield'	MOak SMrm WFar
- 'Princess Marina' 🏆H1	CMdw CSev CSpe EMan ERea LAst LRHS LSou MAJR MSte SPav WEas
* - 'The Queen'	ERea
- 'The Speaker'	ERea MAJR MHom MOak
- 'White Lady'	CHal CPLG CSev EHol ERea EShb EWin LSou MAJR MHom MOak
- 'White Queen'	MAJR MHom
'Chequerboard' **new**	ERea
'Fowa' **new**	ERea
peruvianum	see *H. arborescens*
'Seifel' **new**	ERea

Helipterum see *Syncarpha*

anthemoides	see *Rhodanthe anthemoides*
'Paper Cascade'PBR	see *Rhodanthe anthemoides* 'Paper Cascade'

Helleborus ✿ (*Ranunculaceae*)

abschasicus	see *H. orientalis* subsp. *aschasicus*
§ ***argutifolius*** 🏆H4	More than 30 suppliers
- from Italy	EHrv MGos
- 'Janet Starnes' (v)	MAsh
- 'Little 'Erbert'	MAsh
- mottled-leaved	see *H. argutifolius* 'Pacific Frost'
§ - 'Pacific Frost' (v)	CLAP CMil EVFa MAsh MCCP NEgg NPro SPoG SSth
- 'Silver Lace'PBR	CBcs CFir CMil CTbh CWCL ELan EPfP EVFa EWTr GKir MCCP MGos MSte NBir NEgg NSti SPer SPoG SSth
atrorubens misapplied	see *H. orientalis* Lam. subsp. *abchasicus* Early Purple Group
atrorubens Waldst. & Kit.	CLCN EBee MHom NBlu NEgg NPar WAbe
- WM 9028	NRar
- WM 9319	NRar
- WM 9805 from Croatia	MPhe
- from Slovenia	GBuc
- - WM 9028	MPhe
- - WM 9216	WCru
- - WM 9216	MPhe
- - WM 9617	SSth
x ***ballardiae***	CLAP MAsh MPhe WAbe WFar
- double-flowered (d) **new**	CLAP
'Black Beauty' **new**	GKev
bocconei subsp. ***bocconei***	see *H. multifidus* subsp. *bocconei*
colchicus	see *H. orientalis* Lam. subsp. *abchasicus*
corsicus	see *H. argutifolius*
croaticus	CLCN SSth WFar
- from Croatia	GBuc
- WM 9313	MPhe
- WM 9416	MPhe
- WM 9810 from Croatia	MPhe
cyclophyllus	EPfP GBin GBuc GEdr GKir LRHS MHom MPhe SSpi WFar
- JCA 560.625	CLCN SSpi
dumetorum	CLCN EBee GBuc MHom NLar WCru WFar WPGP
- WM 9209 from Hungary	MPhe
- WM 9209 from Slovenia	MPhe
- WM 9627 from Croatia	MPhe
§ x ***ericsmithii***	CElw CLAP CMil CPMA EChP EHrv ENot GBin GFlt GKir LRHS LTwo MAsh MBNS MBri MSte NDov SBla SVil WAbe WCot WFar
foetidus 🏆H4	More than 30 suppliers
- from Italy	GBin WCot
- 'Chedglow'	CNat
- 'Chedglow Variegated' (v)	CNat
- 'Curio' (v)	CNat
- 'Gold Bullion'	MCCP
- 'Green Giant'	MAsh MTho WCru
- 'Miss Jekyll's Scented'	ITer
- 'Ruth'	MAsh MPhe
- scented	MHom
- 'Sopron'	CLAP EBee ITer MAsh NLar WCru
- Wester Flisk Group	More than 30 suppliers
N x ***hybridus***	More than 30 suppliers
- 'Agnes Brook'	WFib
- 'Alys Collins'	WFib
- Anderson's red hybrids	CLCN
- anemone-centred	CLAP CPLG EHrv NRar WFar WLFP
- 'Angela Tandy'	WFib
- 'Antique Shades' **new**	WFar
- 'Apple Blossom'	EHrv WFar
- apricot	CLAP CLCN EHrv GBuc SPla WFar WLFP WTin
- 'Aquarius'	CLCN
- Ashwood Garden hybrids	EHrv ENot EPPr GKir LRHS MAnH MAsh MGos MRav SCoo SHBN WCra WPop
- Ashwood Garden hybrids, anemone-centred	EPfP MAsh
- Ashwood Garden hybrids, double (d)	MAsh
- 'Baby Black'	ECot
- Ballard's Group	CLAP EBee EChP GEdr GKir ITer MBnl MBri NCGa NRar SPoG WCot WCru WFar WMnd WPnP
- black-flowered	CLAP CLCN EHrv EPPr GBuc NRar WCru WFar WHoo WTin
- 'Blowsy' seedlings	CLCN
- 'Blue Lady'	CBot COIW EBee EChP ENot EPfP EShb GBin GEdr GFlt LAst MBNS MGos MNrw MSte SPoG WWeb
- 'Blue Wisp'	WLFP
- blue-grey-flowered	CLCN EHrv GKir
- Blumen Group **new**	MBri
- Bradfield hybrids	EHrv
- Bradfield hybrids, anemone-centred	EHrv
- Bradfield Star Group	EHrv
- 'Button'	WLFP
- Caborn hybrids	LLWP
- 'Carlton Hall'	WFib
- 'Cheerful'	NBir WCru WLFP
- 'Cherry Davis'	WFib
- 'Citron'	CLAP WLFP
* - 'Compact Cream'	NRar

- cream-flowered CLAP CPMA MCCP WFar WTin
- 'David's Star' (d) CFir
- deep red-flowered CLAP GKir WFar WTin
- double-flowered (d) CLAP NRar WCot WFar WHoo WLFP
- 'Dove Cottage Double Pink' NDov
- Draco strain CLCN
- 'Dusk' WCru WLFP
- 'Elizabeth Coburn' WFib
- 'Fibrex Black' WFib
- 'Fred Whitsey' WFib
- Galaxy Group NPar
- 'Garnet' WFar WLFP
- 'Gertrude Raithby' WFib
- 'Gladys Burrow' WFib
- green-flowered CLCN ITer MBNS WCru WFar
- 'Green Ripple' **new** WFar
- 'Greencups' WCru WLFP
- 'Hades' WLFP
- 'Hades' seedling WCru
- Hadspen hybrids CHad
- 'Harvington Apricots' **new** SPoG
- 'Harvington Picotee' **new** SPoG
- 'Harvington Pink' GKir LRHS MHer NLar SPoG
- 'Harvington Red' GKir LRHS MHer NLar SPoG
- 'Harvington Shades of the Night' MHer NLar SPoG
- 'Harvington Speckled' GKir LRHS MHer SPoG
- 'Harvington White' GKir LRHS MHer NLar SPoG
- 'Harvington Yellow' GKir LRHS MHer NLar SPoG
- 'Harvington Yellow Speckled' MHer NLar SPoG
- 'Hazel Key' WFib
- 'Helen Ballard' GKev WLFP
- 'Helena Hall' WFib
- 'Ian Raithby' WFib
- 'Ingot' WLFP
- ivory-flowered CLCN WFar
- 'John Raithby' WFib
- Joy hybrids EBee EChP ENot GFlt
- Kaye's garden hybrids CSBt EPfP LAst MWgw NBPC NFla WMnd
- Kochii Group CAvo ECha GKir WCru
- 'Lady Charlotte Bonham-Carter' WFib
- 'Lady Macbeth' EWes
- Lady Series COtt
- large, pink-flowered WTin
- 'Le Max Creme' EBee EChP
- 'Limelight' ECha
- 'Little Black' ECho ELan EWes
- 'Lynne' WLFP
- 'Maia' WLFP
- maroon-flowered NRar SPla WCru WFar
- 'Mary Petit' WFib
- 'Massive White' NPar
- 'Maureen Key' WFib
- 'Metallic Blue' CFai CMil EBee MBNS MNrw SHBN
- 'Moonshine' **new** GCai
- 'Mrs Betty Crawford' **new** CPen
- 'Mrs Betty Ranicar' (d) **new** ENot GBin LBuc MBNS NLar SPer SPoG
- 'Mystery' WCru
- 'Orion' WLFP
- 'Pamina' EHrv WLFP
- Party Dress Group (d) EHrv SBla WFar
- 'Pebworth White' WFib
- 'Philip Ballard' WCru WLFP
- 'Picotee' CLAP EHrv GBuc GKir NDov NRar SPla SPoG SSth WCot WCru WFar WHoo WLFP
- pink-flowered CLAP CLCN CPMA EGra GBuc MBNS MCCP NEgg NRar SPla SSth WAbe WCru WFar WHoo WTin
- 'Pink Lady' EBee ENot GBin WWeb
- plum-flowered CLAP CLCN EGra EHrv SSth WFar WTin
- 'Plum Stippled' ECha
- 'Pluto' WLFP
- primrose-flowered CLAP GBuc GKir MBNS NRar SPla SSth WAbe WCru WFar WTin
- purple-flowered CLAP CLCN CPMA ECha NRar SSth WAbe WBor WCru WFar WHoo

* - 'Purpurascens' ENot MCCP
- 'Queen of the Night' CLAP
- 'Ray Peters' WFib
- 'Red Lady' CBot CTbh EBee ENot GBin IBal MBNS MGos MSte SHBN SPer SPoG SPur WCot WWeb
- 'Red Mountain' MBNS
- red, double-flowered (d) **new** GBin

I - 'Rosa' WLFP
- 'Rosina Cross' WFib
- 'Seamus O'Brien' MPhe
- 'Shades of Night' EHrv GKir LRHS
- 'Sirius' seedlings CLCN
- slaty blue-flowered CLAP EHrv GBuc GKir NRar SSth WCot WCru WFar
- slaty purple-flowered NRar SAga WFar WHrl
- 'Smokey Blue' NBPC NEgg
- smokey purple-flowered WFar
- 'Snow Queen' EHrv
- 'Speckled Draco' CPLG
- spotted CAvo CLAP CLCN EChP EPfP GAbr GKir LAst MBnl MCCP NEgg SBla WCot WCru WHoo WTin WWol
- 'Spotted Lady' ENot GBin MNrw SHBN
- spotted, cream CLAP NBir SAga SSth WTin
- spotted, green CLAP SSth WFar WTin
- spotted, ivory CLAP
- spotted, light purple LAst
- spotted, pink CLAP NBPC NBir NDov NFla NRar SAga SPla WFar WHoo WTin
- spotted, pink, double (d) **new** GBin
- spotted, primrose CLAP SAga WFar WTin
- spotted, white EChP NBir NDov NRar SPla SSth WAbe WCru WFar WTin
- spotted, white, double (d) **new** GBin
- 'Sunny' WCru WLFP
- 'Sunny' seedlings CLCN
- 'Sylvia' WLFP
- 'Titania' WLFP
- 'Tommie' WLFP
- 'Tricastin' **new** CFir
- 'Ursula Key-Davis' WFib
- 'Ushba' CLAP WLFP
- 'Ushba' seedlings CLCN GCal NBir
- 'Victoria Raithby' WFib
- 'Violetta' WCru
- white-flowered ECha EGra ITer NRar SAga SSth WCFE WCru WFar WHoo WTin

	- white, double-flowered (d) **new**	GBin NPar
	- 'White Lady'	CBot COIW EBee ENot GEdr MGos MWrn SHBN SPer SPoG WCot WWeb
	- 'White Lady Spotted'	CBot CBrm EBee GMac MSte NGHP SPoG WWeb
	- white-veined	EGra WFar
	- 'William'	WLFP
	- yellow-flowered	NDov SSth WCru WFar WHoo WHrl WTin
	- 'Yellow Lady'	CBot EBee EChP MNrw MSte SPer SPoG WCot WWeb
	- Zodiac Group	CLCN ENot EPfP GBuc LBuc NPar
	lividus ♀H2-3	CBot CBro CHar CLAP CLCN EHyt ELan EPfP EWes GKir LRHS MAsh MPhe NBir SBla SIgm WAbe WCru WFar
	- Anne Watson strain	NRar
	- subsp. ***corsicus***	see *H. argutifolius*
	Marion White Group	SBla
	multifidus	CLCN EBee EPfP NBir SPer WFar
§	- subsp. ***bocconei***	CLCN EHrv MHom WFar
	- - from Italy WM 9719	MPhe
	- subsp. ***hercegovinus***	EHrv MDun SBla SIgm WFar
	- - WM 0020	MPhe
	- subsp. ***istriacus***	CBro GBuc WFar
	- - WM 9225	WCru
	- - WM 9322	MPhe
	- - WM 9324	MPhe
	- subsp. ***multifidus***	EHrv MHom
	- - WM 9104	MPhe
	- - WM 9529	MPhe
	- - WM 9748 from Croatia	MPhe
	- - WM 9833	MPhe
	niger ♀H4	More than 30 suppliers
	- Ashwood marble leaf **new**	MAsh
	- Ashwood silver leaf **new**	MAsh
	- Ashwood strain	CLAP MAsh
	- Blackthorn Group	EHrv GKir SBla
I	- 'Crûg Hybrid'	WCru
	- double (d) **new**	LAst
	- Harvington hybrids	EHrv GKir LRHS MHer
	- 'Louis Cobbett'	EHyt
§	- subsp. ***macranthus***	EBee NCGa NGHP
	- ***major***	see *H. niger* subsp. *macranthus*
	- 'Maximus'	CLAP EBee EChP EWes NCGa
	'Nell Lewis'	MAsh
	- 'Potter's Wheel'	CPMA EBee ECot ELan ENot EVFa GBuc LRHS MRav SBla SPla WCru
	- 'Praecox'	EBee EWes SHBN SPur SVil WWeb
	- Sunrise Group WM 9519	MPhe
	- Sunset Group WM 9113	GBuc MPhe
	- 'White Magic'	CBcs CPMA GMaP LBuc MGos MNrw SBla WCru
	- Wilder strain **new**	MAsh
	x ***nigercors*** ♀H4	EHrv ENot ETow GBin GKir LPio LRHS MAsh MBri WAbe WCot
	- 'Alabaster'	NBir
	- double-flowered (d) **new**	CFai EHrv WCot WTMC
	- 'Pink Beauty' **new**	LBuc SHBN
	- 'Vulcan Beauty' **new**	LBuc SHBN
	x ***nigristern***	see *H.* x *ericsmithii*
	odorus	CAvo CBcs CLCN EBee EHrv MPhe WFar WPGP
	- WM 0312 from Bosnia **new**	MPhe
	- WM 9202	WCru
	- WM 9310	GBuc
	- WM 9415	MPhe
	- WM 9728 from Hungary	MPhe
N	***orientalis*** misapplied	see *H.* x *hybridus*
	orientalis Lam.	CBcs CLCN CPne EBrs EPot EWTr EWes GFlt MPhe NBlu NEgg WWeb
§	- subsp. ***abchasicus***	EBee GEdr ITim SRms
§	- - Early Purple Group	CAvo CBre CTri GCal LPio LRHS MBow WFar WWol
	- subsp. ***guttatus***	EBee EWTr GGar NEgg SMac SPla SRkn SSpi WCru
	purpurascens	CLCN EBee EHrv EPot GBuc GEdr GKir LRHS MBNS NBir SBla SIgm SPer SSth WAbe WBrE WFar WPnP WPop
	- from Hungary	WCAu
	- WM 9211 from Hungary	MPhe WCru
	- WM 9412	MPhe WCru
	Snowdon strain	CSBt ENot EPfP GCai LBuc NEgg SHBN
	x ***sternii***	CBos CBot CBro CDes CSam CSpe ELan EPfP EPot GAbr GBin GKir GMaP IFro ITer ITim LRHS MGos MHer NCGa NEgg NLar SPla WAbe WEas WFar WHoo WMnd WTin WWeb
	- Ashwood strain	MAsh
	- 'Beatrice le Blanc'	MAsh
	- Blackthorn Group ♀H3-4	CElw CKno CPMA CSpe EHrv ENot EPfP GBuc GKir ITer MBri MRav MSte SBla SMac SPoG SRkn SSpi WBrk WCru WFar WHoo WPGP
	- Blackthorn dwarf strain	CLAP EBee GBuc SHBN
	- Boughton Group	GBin MAsh
	- 'Boughton Beauty'	CAby CAvo CHar CLAP EBee EHrv EHyt ELan GBuc MTho
	- Bulmer's blush strain	LRHS MAsh
	- Cally strain	GCal
	- dwarf	WFar
	- pewter	CSpe
	thibetanus	CLAP EFEx EHrv GBuc GEdr GKev LAma MMil MPhe SBla SSpi WCru
	torquatus	CBro CLCN EBee EHrv MHom MPhe MTho SSth WFar WTin
	- WM 9820 from Bosnia	MPhe
	- WM 9106 from Montenegro	GBuc MPhe WCru
	- Caborn hybrids	LLWP
	- 'Dido' (d)	WFar
	- double-flowered hybrids (d)	CBos WFar
	- double-flowered, from Montenegro (d)	WFar
	- hybrids	ECGP EHrv SBla WFar
	- Party Dress Group	see *H.* x *hybridus* Party Dress Group
	- semi-double (d)	WFar
	- Wolverton hybrids	SBla WFar
	vesicarius	CDes EBee EHrv EWes SSpi
	viridis	EBee ECha EHrv EPfP GKir LRHS SRms WBWf WCAu WCru WFar WGwG WTin
	- subsp. ***occidentalis***	CBro MHom
	- - WM 9401	MPhe
	- - WM 9502 from Germany	MPhe
	- subsp. ***viridis*** WM 9723 from Italy	MPhe
	'White Beauty'PBR **new**	ENot LBuc

Helonias (*Liliaceae*)

bullata	EBee GEdr IBlr WCot

Heloniopsis (*Melanthiaceae*)

acutifolia B&SWJ 218	WCru
japonica	see *H. orientalis*
kawanoi	CLAP NMen SIgm SOkd WAbe WCru
§ ***orientalis***	CBro CLAP EHyt GBuc GCal GCrs GEdr LRHS NMen NSla SBch SIgm SOkd SSpi WCot WCru
§ - var. ***breviscapa***	CFil WCru WPGP
- variegated (v)	WCru
- var. ***yakusimensis***	see *H. kawanoi*
umbellata	CLAP
- B&SWJ 1839	WCru

Helwingia (*Helwingiaceae*)

* ***asiatica***	CFil
chinensis	CPle CSam NLar SSpi
himalaica	CFil EBee WPGP
japonica	EFEx NLar WFar

Helxine see *Soleirolia*

Hemerocallis ✿ (*Hemerocallidaceae*)

'Aabachee'	CCol SApp
'Absolute Zero'	SDay SRos
'Adah'	SDay
'Added Dimensions' **new**	SApp
'Addie Branch Smith'	EGol SDay
'Admiral'	WCAu
'Admiral's Braid'	EWoo
'Adoration' **new**	SPer
'Ah Youth' **new**	SApp
'Alan'	EChP ECtt MNFA MRav WFar
'Alan Adair'	MAnH
'Alaqua'	CFir CMil IBal MBNS MFOX MNrw NRnb SApp SHBN WCAu WSan
'Albany'	CCol
'Alec Allen'	SRos
'Alien Encounter'	SPol
'All American Baby'	EBee MBNS SPol
'All American Plum' **new**	CWrd EMar EPfP IBal WAul
'All Fired Up'	CCol SPol
altissima	CHEx EMon EPla LPhx MNFA MNrw SDix SMeo SMrm
'Always Afternoon'	CCol CWrd EChP EMar EWoo GBri GLil MBNS NCGa NLar SApp SDay WAul WCAu
'Amadeus'	SApp SDay
'Amazon Amethyst'	WCAu
'Ambassador'	CBgR
'Amber Classic'	SApp
'Amber Star'	LPBA
'American Revolution'	CPar CPen CSpe EBee ECtt EHrv EWll MBNS MCCP MSte NEgg SApp SDnm SHBN SMad SPav SRos WAul WCAu WCot WPnP WTin WWhi
'Amersham'	GSki MNFA SApp
'Andrea Nicole'	CCol
'Andrew Christian'	SPol
'Angel Artistry'	SApp SDay
'Angel Curls'	EGol
'Angel Unawares'	SApp WTin
'Ann Kelley'	MSte SApp SDay
'Annie Golightly'	SDay
'Annie Welch'	CFai ECGP EPla LBBr MBNS MMil
'Antarctica' **new**	SApp
'Antique Rose'	CKel SDay
'Anzac'	COIW ECha ECtt EHrv EPla ERou GKir GMac LRHS MBow MNFA NGdn NPri SAga SApp SPav SWvt WFar WMoo WTMC
'Apache Uprising'	SRos
'Apple Court Chablis'	SApp
'Apple Court Champagne'	SApp
'Apple Court Ruby' **new**	SApp SPol
'Apple Crisp' **new**	SApp
'Après Moi'	EMar EMil LAst MBNS MLLN NLar WCAu
'Apricot Angel'	SApp
'Apricot Beauty' (d)	EMar NPri WHlf
'Apricotta'	WCot WPnP
'Arctic Snow'	CCol EChP EHoe EMar EPfP EWoo MLan MNrw NLar SDnm SMer SPav SPoG SRos SUsu WAul WSan
'Ariadne'	SBla
'Arriba'	MNFA NBro
'Artistic Gold'	LAst WTin
'Asiatic Pheasant'	CCol
'Aten'	CCol MNFA NPri WAul
'Atlanta Bouquet'	SRos
'Atlanta Fringe' **new**	SApp
'Atlanta Full House'	SDay
'August Flame' **new**	SSpi
'August Orange'	MNFA
'Autumn Minaret'	CCol
'Autumn Red'	EMar MBNS NBir NOak WCot
'Ava Michelle'	SApp SDay
'Avant Garde'	SPol
'Awakening Dream'	SRos
'Awesome Blossom'	CPen CWrd NArg
'Aztec Furnace'	SDay
'Baby Darling'	SDay
'Baby Talk'	CFir LRHS
'Baja'	MNFA WFar
'Bald Eagle'	CMCo SChu
§ 'Bali Hai'	EMar ENot GFlt LRHS MBNS NGdn NRnb WHrl
'Ballerina Girl'	SRos
'Ballet Dancer'	ERou
'Banbury Cinnamon' **new**	MBNS
'Bandolero' (d)	EBee
'Bangkok Belle'	SDay
'Banned in Boston' **new**	EWoo
'Barbara Mitchell'	CCol EChP MBNS MNFA NCGa SApp SDay WAul
'Barbary Corsair'	SApp SDay
'Barley Hay' **new**	MSte
'Baronet's Badge'	SPol
'Baroni'	ECha GBin
'Battle Hymn'	WCAu
'Bayou Ribbons'	MBNS
'Beat the Barons'	SPol SRos
'Beautiful Edgings'	SRos
'Beauty Bright'	WCAu
'Beauty to Behold'	SApp SDay SRos
'Becky Lynn'	CCol ECtt EWoo MBNS WAul WHoo
'Bed of Roses'	MNFA
'Bedarra Island'	SDay
'Bejewelled'	EGol EPla NMoo SApp
'Bela Lugosi'	CMil CPar CWan EBee EChP EMar EPfP EWTr EWoo GBin GMac LSRN MBNS MBri MDun MMil NBro SDnm SHBN SPav SPer WAul WBVN WCot WCra WHrl WPop WSan
'Beloved Returns' ♀H4	WCAu
'Benchmark'	MNFA SApp SRos
'Berlin Lemon' ♀H4	MNFA
'Berlin Maize'	SApp

Cultivar	Suppliers
'Berlin Oxblood'	MNFA
'Berlin Red' 🏆H4	CPrp EBee ECha EMar EPla MBNS MMil MNFA NGdn SApp SChu
'Berlin Red Velvet' 🏆H4	MNFA
'Berlin Tallboy'	SApp
'Berlin Watermelon' **new**	MBNS
'Berliner Premiere'	MNFA
'Bernard Thompson'	EMar MNFA SApp
'Bertie Ferris'	EBee SRos
'Bess Ross'	CMHG MNFA WCAu
'Bess Vestale'	ENot MNFA
'Best of Friends'	GKir
'Bette Davis Eyes'	SApp SPol SRos
'Betty Benz' **new**	SRos
'Betty Lyn' **new**	SApp
'Betty Warren Woods' **new**	SRos
'Betty Woods' (d)	SRos
I 'Big Apple' **new**	SApp SRos
'Big Bird'	CMCo CPar EChP MBNS SApp SHBN SHar
'Big Smile'	EBee EMar IPot MBNS MNrw NArg
'Big Snowbird'	SRos
'Big World'	MNFA
'Bill Norris'	SApp SRos
'Bird Bath Pink'	SPol
'Bitsy'	EGol MNFA MOne MSte SPet SSpe WCot WMnd
'Black Emmanuella'	EMar
'Black Eyed Stella'	CKel MBNS
'Black Knight'	SRms
'Black Magic'	CBro CHad CHar CPLG CTri EGol ELan EPla ERou GMaP GMac LRHS LSRN MNFA MRav MWgw NBir NGdn SChu SGSe SPer WCAu WHer WMoo
'Black Plush'	CCol SRos
'Black Prince'	CRez EBee EUJe EWll MBNS NBro SOkh WAul WCAu WMow
'Blackberry Candy'	GBri MBNS SMrm WAul WCAu
'Blaze of Fire'	WCAu
'Blessing'	SRos
'Blonde Is Beautiful'	SRos
'Bloodspot'	SDay
'Blue Happiness'	SDay
'Blue Moon' **new**	SApp
'Blue Sheen'	CCol CFir EBee ECtt EGol EMar LAst LRHS MBNS MCCP NGdn NOrc NPri WCAu WFar WMoo WWeb
'Blueberry Candy'	MBNS WAul WSan
'Blushing Belle'	CFai CMil ECGP EChP EMar LRHS MAnH MBNS MNFA NBro SApp
'Bold Courtier'	WCAu
'Bold One'	SRos
'Bold Tiger'	SDay
'Bonanza'	More than 30 suppliers
'Boney Maroney' **new**	SApp
'Booger'	SRos
'Booroobin Magic' **new**	EWoo
'Born Yesterday' **new**	SApp
'Boulderbrook Serenity'	SDay
'Bourbon Kings'	CMHG EGol EMar ERou MBNS SPav WCAu
'Bowl of Roses'	SApp WCAu
'Brand New Lover'	SApp
'Brass Buckles'	see *H.* 'Puddin'
'Brenda Newbold'	SPol
'Bridget'	ELan
'Bright Banner'	WCAu
'Bright Spangles'	SApp SDay SRos WEas
'Brilliant Circle'	SApp
'Broadway Valentine' **new**	SApp
'Brocaded Gown'	CCol ELan SApp SDay SRos
'Brookwood Wow' **new**	SApp
'Brunette'	MHar SAga SApp SHop
'Bruno Müller'	MNFA SApp
'Bubbly'	SApp SDay SRos
'Bud Producer' **new**	SPol
'Buffy's Doll'	EBee EMar MBNS MNFA SApp SDay SRos
'Bumble Bee'	EMar GKir MBNS NRnb SApp
'Buried Treasure'	MNFA
'Burning Daylight' 🏆H4	EBee EBrs ECtt EHol EHrv EMar EPfP EPla ERou GSki LRHS MBow MNFA MNrw MRav SPer SRms WCot WFar
'Bus Stop'	SApp SPol
'Butterfly Ballet'	SDay SRos
'Butterscotch' **new**	WFar
'Buzz Bomb'	CWat ECGP EHrv EMFW EMar GMac GSki LRHS LSRN MHar MNFA NCob NGdn SApp SChu SPer SRos WCAu
'California Sunshine'	SRos
'Camden Glory' **new**	SApp
'Camden Gold Dollar'	EGol SApp SRos
'Cameron Quantz' **new**	SApp
'Cameroons'	CCol SDay
'Canadian Border Patrol'	EMar EPfP EWoo IBal MBNS NLar SPol WHil
'Canary Feathers'	SApp
'Canary Glow'	CSBt CTri ERou SRos WFar
'Candide'	SApp
'Cantique'	SApp
'Capernaum Cocktail'	SPol
'Captive Audience'	SRos
'Caramea'	EMar MBNS WFar
'Caroline'	WHrl
'Carolipiecrust'	SApp
'Cartwheels' 🏆H4	EBee EGra EHrv EMFW EMar EPfP EPla ERou GMaP LRHS MBNS MMil MNFA NBro NRnb SBch SPer SRos WCAu WFar WMoo WTin
'Casino Gold'	SRos
'Castle Strawberry Delight' **new**	SPol
'Catherine Neal'	CCol SRos
'Catherine Woodbery'	More than 30 suppliers
'Cathy's Sunset'	CSam EBee ECtt EMar EPla EVFa MBNS MWat MWgw NBro NGdn NRnb SVil
'Cedar Waxwing'	CHea EGol MSte
'Cee Tee' **new**	SRos
I 'Cenla Crepe Myrtle' **new**	EWoo
'Cerulean Star'	SApp
'Champagne Memory'	SApp
'Chance Encounter'	CCol MBNS
'Chantilly Lace'	CMHG NGdn
'Charbonier'	MNFA
'Charles Johnston'	CKel CM&M EChP LAst NRnb SApp SDay SRos WAul WTMC
'Charlie Pierce Memorial'	EWoo SRos
'Chartreuse Magic'	EGol EPla ERou SChu SPer
'Cherry Brandy' **new**	EWoo
'Cherry Cheeks'	ECtt EGol ELan EPfP ERou GKir LRHS MBNS MBri MRav NFla NRnb SApp SPav SRos SVil WAul WCAu WCot WFar WWeb
'Cherry Eyed Pumpkin'	SRos
'Cherry Kiss'	SRos
'Cherry Smoke'	SApp
'Chesieres Lunar Moth'	SApp SPol
'Chester Cyclone' **new**	SDay
'Chestnut Lane'	SApp
'Chic Bonnet'	SPer

'Chicago Apache'	CFir COtt EBee EChP EMar ENot EPfP MBNS MNFA MSte NBir NCGa NRnb SApp SDay SRos SUsu WAul
'Chicago Arnie's Choice'	WSan
'Chicago Blackout'	CFir COIW COtt CSpe EBee EChP EGol EPfP MBNS NRnb SApp WAul WCAu
'Chicago Cattleya'	CFir EChP EGol LAst MRav NRnb SApp WAul
'Chicago Cherry'	NRnb WWpP
'Chicago Fire'	EBee EGol EPfP MBNS SHar WWye
'Chicago Heirloom'	CFir COtt EChP EGol EWTr NRnb WAul WCAu
'Chicago Jewel'	CFir EGol NRnb NSti WAul WWpP
'Chicago Knobby'	EMar MBNS
'Chicago Knockout'	CFir COtt EBee EGol EPfP EWoo MBNS NRnb SPer WAul WCAu
'Chicago Peach'	EChP IPot NBir WCAu
'Chicago Peach Parfait'	WSan
'Chicago Petticoats'	EGol SApp WAul
'Chicago Picotee Lace'	EChP EGol EPfP GKir NGdn SApp WAul WCAu
'Chicago Picotee Memories'	EBee MBNS
'Chicago Picotee Queen'	MNFA SApp
'Chicago Princess'	EGol
'Chicago Rainbow'	IPot MBNS WAul WSan
'Chicago Rosy'	EGol
'Chicago Royal Robe'	CWat EBee EGol EPla ERou GKir LLWP MBNS MNFA MRav MSte NBid NCGa SPer SWal WCot WTin WWhi
'Chicago Ruby' **new**	SApp
'Chicago Silver'	CFir COIW COtt EGol IPot MBNS WCAu
'Chicago Star'	SRos
'Chicago Sunrise'	CHad CSBt EBee EBrs EGol EMar ENot EPla GMaP IBlr LRHS MBNS MBri MNFA MRav NGdn NMoo NOrc NRnb SAga SApp SRos SUsu SWvt WPer WPop WWeb
'Chicago Violet'	WCAu
'Chief Sarcoxie' ♀H4	SApp SRos WCAu
'Child of Fortune' **new**	SApp
'Children's Festival'	More than 30 suppliers
'China Bride'	SApp SRos
'Chinese Autumn'	SApp SRos
'Chinese Cloisonne'	CKel
'Chinese Coral'	WBcn
'Chorus Line'	SApp SDay SRos
'Chosen Love'	SApp
'Chris Taylor' **new**	CCol
'Christmas Carol'	SApp
'Christmas Is'	CCol EGol EMar LPhx MBNS MBri MNFA SApp SDay SDnm SMrm SPav WAul WCAu
'Christmas Island'	NCGa WHil
'Churchill Downs'	MNFA
'Ciao'	MHar SApp
citrina	ELan EWTr GIBF LRHS MNFA MSte MWgw NFla NGdn WTin XPep
'Civil Law' **new**	SDay
'Civil Rights'	SRos
'Classic Simplicity'	WCAu
'Classic Spider' **new**	SApp
'Claudine'	SApp
'Cleopatra'	CPar
'Cloth of Gold'	WCot
'Clothed in Glory'	MBNS
'Colonial Dame'	WTin
'Colour Me Yellow' **new**	SApp
'Comanche Eyes'	SApp

'Coming Up Roses'	SApp SRos
'Condilla' (d)	SApp
'Constitutional Island'	WCAu
'Contessa'	CBro EBrs EHon WWpP
'Cool It'	EMar LPio LRHS MBNS NArg NCGa NRnb SApp
'Cool Jazz'	EMar SApp SDay SRos
'Copper Dawn' **new**	SApp
'Coral Crab' **new**	SApp
'Coral Dawn'	CKel
'Coral Mist'	CCol CSBt MBNS NRnb
'Corky' ♀H4	More than 30 suppliers
'Corsican Bandit'	CM&M SDay
'Cosmic Hummingbird'	EWoo SApp SDay
'Country Club'	EChP EGol LAst MBNS SApp WCAu WSan WWpP
'Country Fair Winds'	CCol
'Country Melody'	SDay SRos
'Court Magician'	EWoo SApp SRos
'Cranberry Baby'	SDay SRos WHoo WTin
'Crazy Pierre'	SPol
'Cream Drop'	CPrp EChP ECtt EGol EMar GMaP GMac LRHS MRav NBro NCiC NOrc SApp SChu SDnm SPav SPer SSpe WAul WCAu WCot WCra WMoo WTMC WTel WTin
'Creative Art'	SRos
'Creative Edge'	ERou EWoo MBNS SDnm SPav
'Crimson Icon'	MSte SDay WTin
'Crimson Pirate'	CBre CCol CTbh EBee EMar EMil EPPr ERou GKir LRHS LSRN MBNS MLan MNFA MSph NBir NBlu NCGa NOrc NPro SApp SPlb WCAu WHrl WTin
'Crimson Wind' **new**	SApp
'Croesus'	SRms WCAu
'Crystalline Pink' **new**	SRos
'Cupid's Bow'	EGol
'Cupid's Gold'	SDay SRos
'Curly Ripples' **new**	SApp
'Custard Candy'	EChP MBNS MBri NBir SApp SRos SUsu WAul WCAu
'Cynthia Mary'	EMar LRHS MBNS MNFA NBro WFar
'Dad's Best White'	EMar
'Daily Dollar'	GKir LRHS NGdn SApp
'Dainty Pink'	EGol
'Dallas Spider Time'	MNFA
'Dallas Star'	SApp SPol
'Dan Tau'	CKel
'Dance Ballerina Dance'	SDay SRos
'Dancing Dwarf'	SApp SDay
'Dancing Shiva'	SApp SDay
'Dancing Summerbird'	SPol
'Daring Deception'	CFir CKel EWoo LAst MBNS SApp WAul WCAu
'Daring Dilemma' **new**	EWoo
'Dark Angel'	EWoo
'Dark Elf'	SApp SDay
'Darrell'	SDay
'David Kirchhoff'	EBee EWoo MBNS SApp WAul WCAu
'Dazzle' **new**	SApp
'Decatur Imp'	EGol
'Dee Dee Mac' **new**	SApp
'Delicate Design'	SApp
'Delightsome'	SRos
'Demetrius'	MNFA SApp
'Desdemona' **new**	CMil
'Designer Gown'	SApp
'Designer Jeans' **new**	SPol SRos
'Destined to See'	CFir CPar CWan EBee EMar GBin MBNS MDun NCob NCot NEgg SPav SPer WBVN WCot WSan

'Devil's Footprint'	SDay SPol
'Devon Cream'	SChu
'Devonshire'	SApp SRos
'Dewberry Candy'	SRos
'Diamond Dust'	CCol EBee EChP EMar EPla EWTr LPhx LRHS MBNS MNFA MSte NLar SApp SChu SPer WTin
'Dido'	CTri ERou GBuc
'Diva Assoluta'	SApp
'Divertissment'	CCol SApp
'Doll House' **new**	SRos
'Dominic'	CPar EMar MBNS SApp SRos WMoo
'Dorethe Louise'	SDay SRos
'Dorothy McDade'	COIW EGol ENot
'Double Action' (d) **new**	SPol
'Double Coffee' (d)	SApp SPav
'Double Confetti' (d) **new**	SApp
'Double Corsage' (d) **new**	SApp
'Double Cream' (d)	WCot
'Double Cutie' (d)	CMCo MBNS NLar SChu SDay WAul
'Double Daffodil' (d)	WCAu
'Double Dream' (d)	EMar
'Double Firecracker' (d)	CBcs CWrd EMar EUJe IBal MBNS NBro WCra WHlf WSan
'Double Grapette' (d) **new**	SApp
'Double Oh Seven' (d)	SApp
'Double Pink Treasure' (d) **new**	SApp
'Double Pompon' (d)	WCAu
'Double River Wye' (d)	CBos CCol CFir COIW EChP ECtt EGol EMar EMil IPot MBNS MNrw NPri SApp SHBN SHar SRos WCot WHoo WMnd WPop WTin WWye
§ 'Doubloon'	COIW ERou GBuc MWgw WCAu
'Dragon Dreams' **new**	SApp
'Dragon King'	SPol
'Dragon Mouth'	EGol
'Dragon's Eye'	CCol EWoo SApp SDay
'Dragon's Orb'	CKel
'Dream Baby'	NBre
'Dream Legacy'	WAul
'Dreamy Cream'	SRos
'Dresden Doll'	SPer
'Driven Snow' **new**	SApp
'Druid's Chant' **new**	EWoo
'Duke of Durham' **new**	SApp
'Dum Needlepoint' **new**	SPol
dumortieri	CAvo CBro CSam ECha EGol EGra EHrv ELan EMar EPla GGar MNFA MNrw MRav NBid NBir NSti NVic SPer SSpe WCAu WCot WTin WWpP
- B&SWJ 1283	WCru
- from Ussuri **new**	GIBF
'Dutch Beauty'	EMar EPla WFar WTMC
'Dutch Gold'	CFai MNrw NBro
'Earlianna'	SPol
'Earth Angel' **new**	SApp
'Easy Ned'	SDay SRos
'Ed Murray'	CSBt EUJe MNFA SRos WAul WCAu
'Ed Ra Hansen' **new**	CCol
'Edelweiss'	EWTr SDay WBcn
'Edgar Brown'	EWoo MBNS
'Edge Ahead'	CCol MBNS NRnb
'Edge of Darkness'	CWrd EBee EChP EPfP MBNS NLar NSti SDnm SPav SPoG WCAu WCra WHil WSan
'Edna Spalding'	EBrs SApp SDay SRos
'Eenie Allegro'	CBro CCol EChP EGol ENot IBal MBNS SOkh SPla WMnd
'Eenie Fanfare'	COtt EGol GKir LRHS MBNS MNFA NBir WAul WCra
'Eenie Gold'	LRHS
'Eenie Weenie'	CBro CFee EBla ECtt EGol EMar EPla ERos GKir IBal LRHS MBNS MBri MSwo NArg NBro NBur SAga SApp SChu SHBN SPer SRms WPer WTMC WWye
'Eenie Weenie Non-stop'	ECha EPPr
'Eggplant Escapade'	SPol
'Egyptian Ibis'	EWoo MBNS
'El Desperado'	CPar CWrd EBee EMar EWoo MBNS MDun MLLN MNrw NArg NCGa NCob NCot NEgg NRnb SDnm SPav SPoG SUsu WBVN WCAu WCot WCra WHoo WSan WWlt
'El Padre' **new**	SApp
'Elaine Strutt'	EGol MBNS MNFA NCGa SApp SDay SRos SWvt WCot
'Eleanor Marcotte'	SDay
'Elegant Candy'	CCol CKel CPen ENot MBNS NRnb SApp SRos WSan
'Elegant Greeting'	ERou MBNS NOak
'Elizabeth Ann Hudson'	MNFA SDay
'Elizabeth Salter'	EBee MBNS SApp SRos SUsu WCAu
'Elizabeth Yancey'	EGol
'Elva White Grow'	SDay
'Emerald Enchantment' **new**	SApp
'Emily Anne' **new**	SApp
'Emily Jaye' **new**	SApp
'Emperor Butterfly'	SApp
'Emperor's Dragon'	CCol
'English Toffee'	SApp
'Entransette' **new**	SApp
'Erin Prairie'	SApp
esculenta	SMad
'Esther Walker'	WBcn
'Etched Eyes' **new**	EWoo
'Eternal Blessing'	SRos
'Ethel Smith' **new**	SApp
'Evelyn Claar'	EChP
'Evelyn Lela Stout' **new**	SApp
'Evening Bell'	SApp
'Evening Glow' **new**	SApp SRos
'Ever So Ruffled'	SRos
exaltata	GIBF
'Exotic Love'	SDay
'Eye Catching' **new**	EWoo
'Eye-yi-yi'	SPol
'Faberge' **new**	SApp
'Fabulous Prize'	SApp SRos
'Fairest Love'	EMar MBNS
'Fairy Charm'	SApp
'Fairy Tale Pink'	CCol MNFA SApp SDay SRos
'Fairy Wings' **new**	SPer
'Faith Nabor'	EMar SRos
'Fall Guy'	SApp
'Fan Dancer'	EGol
'Fandango'	MNFA SPer
'Farmer's Daughter'	SApp SRos
'Fashion Model'	SApp WPer
'Fazzle' **new**	SApp
'Feelings'	SApp
'Femme Osage'	SRos
'Ferris Wheel' **new**	SApp
'Festive Art'	EWoo MBNS SRos
'Finlandia'	MNFA
'Fire Dance'	SRos
'Fire from Heaven' **new**	SApp
'Fire Tree'	SPol

‘Firestorm’	SApp
‘First Formal’	SPer
‘Flames of Fantasy’	SRos
‘Flaming Sword’	EBee GBuc LRHS NBlu
flava	see *H. lilioasphodelus*
‘Fleeting Fancy’	SRos
‘Flint Lace’ **new**	SApp
‘Floyd Cove’	SDay
‘Fly Catcher’	EMar SRos
‘Fooled Me’	SRos
forrestii	EBee
- ‘Perry’s Variety’	CCol EMon
‘Forsyth Lemon Drop’	SDay
‘Forsyth White Sentinal’ **new**	SRos
‘Fortune’s Dearest’ **new**	EWoo
‘Forty Second Street’	CFir CWrd EBee EWTr MBNS MLLN SMrm WHlf WSan
‘Fragrant Bouquet’	SRos
‘Fragrant Pastel Cheers’	SDay SRos
‘Frances Fay’	SRos WAul WCAu
‘Frandean’	MNFA
‘Frank Gladney’	MNFA SApp SRos
‘Frans Hals’	More than 30 suppliers
‘French Doll’ **new**	SApp
‘French Porcelain’	SDay
‘Frosted Encore’	SApp
‘Frozen Jade’	SRos
‘Full Reward’	WCAu
fulva	CTri EGra ELan IBlr LRHS MHar MWgw NBir NLon SHBN SRms WBVN WBrk WWpP
N - ‘Flore Pleno’ (d)	CAvo CFee CHar CMHG CStu EChP ECtt EGol EHon ELan EMon EPfP IBlr MFOX MRav NBir NBro NGdn NSti SHBN SPav SPer SRms WCAu WEas WMoo
N - ‘Green Kwanso’ (d)	CHar CPLG CRow CSWP ECGP ECha EGra EMon EPla GFlt IBlr MHer MMHG NVic SMad SPla WAul WBrk WFar WPnP WRha WTin WWpP
- ‘Kwanso’ ambig. (d)	EBrs NOrc
- var. ***littorea***	EPla SSpi
- var. ***rosea***	EBrs EMon MNFA SMHy
- ‘Variegated Kwanso’ (d/v)	CBot CRow ELan EMon EPPr EShb EVFa GCal IBlr MRav MTho NBir SBla SPav SPoG WBcn WCot WFar WHer WWlt
I ‘Funky Fuchsia’	SPol
‘Gadsden Goliath’	SPol
‘Gadsden Light’	CCol
‘Gala Gown’	SApp
‘Garden Plants’	SRos
‘Gaucho’	MNFA
‘Gay Rapture’	SPer
‘Gemini’	SRos
‘Gentle Country Breeze’	SApp SRos
‘Gentle Shepherd’	More than 30 suppliers
‘George Cunningham’	CSev ECtt EGol EHrv ELan EPla ERou MNFA MRav NBir SChu SRos SUsu WCAu WFar
‘Georgette Belden’	MBri
‘Georgia Cream’ (d)	MBNS
‘German Ballerina’	SPol
‘Giant Moon’	CMHG ELan EPla ERou LRHS SChu SRms WFar WHal
‘Gingerbread Man’	MBNS SApp
‘Girl Scout’	SApp
‘Glacier Bay’ **new**	CBgR EWoo
‘Glazed Heather Plum’ **new**	SApp
‘Gleber’s Top Cream’ **new**	SApp
‘Glomunda’	SApp
‘Glory’s Legacy’	SRos
‘Glowing Gold’	WCAu
‘Gold Crest’	MNFA
‘Gold Elephant’ **new**	SDay
‘Gold Imperial’	EWll NBre
‘Golden Bell’	NGdn
‘Golden Chance’	WCAu
‘Golden Chimes’ 🏆H4	More than 30 suppliers
‘Golden Empress’ **new**	SApp
‘Golden Ginkgo’	LRHS MBri MNFA SApp WSPU
‘Golden Nugget’	MBNS
‘Golden Orchid’	see *H.* ‘Doubloon’
‘Golden Peace’	SRos
‘Golden Prize’	EPla MNFA NGdn NPri SApp SDay SRos WCot WFar
‘Golden Scroll’	SApp SDay SRos
Golden Zebra = ‘Malja’[PBR] (v)	ENot EPfP NSti SPoG
‘Goldeneye’ **new**	SApp
‘Good Looking’	EGol
‘Grace and Favour’	SDay SPol
‘Graceful Eye’	SApp SRos
‘Grand Masterpiece’	CM&M CSpe EBee EChP IPot NGdn NRnb SPet
‘Grand Palais’	SApp SRos
‘Grape Magic’	EGol SRos WTin
‘Grape Velvet’	CHar CPar CSpe EGol MBNS MCCP MFOX MHar MNFA NRnb NSti SApp SHar SOkh WAul WCAu WMnd WWye
‘Great Northern’	SApp
‘Green Dragon’	SDay
‘Green Drop’	WFar
‘Green Eyed Giant’	MNFA
‘Green Eyed Lady’ **new**	SDay
‘Green Flutter’ 🏆H4	CSev EChP EPfP EWTr GCal LPhx LPio LRHS LSRN MBNS MBri MNFA NBir NCGa NGdn NSti SApp SRos
‘Green Glitter’	MNFA
‘Green Gold’	CMHG MNFA
‘Green Puff’	NBir SDay
‘Green Valley’	MNFA
‘Groovy Green’ **new**	SDay
‘Grumbly’	ELan WPnP
‘Guardian Angel’	WTin
‘Gusto’	WCAu
‘Halo Light’	MNFA
‘Hamlet’	SDay
‘Happy Returns’	CHid COtt CTri ECha EGol ELan EMar EWoo IBal IFro LAst MAnH MBNS MBri MHar MNFA NEgg NGdn SApp SDay SRos SSpe WAul WCAu WTin
‘Harbor Blue’	CCol
‘Harvest Hue’	SDay
‘Hawaiian Punch’	EGol
‘Hawaiian Purple’	EGol
‘Hawk’	SApp SPol
‘Hazel Monette’	EGol
‘Heartthrob’	WCAu
‘Heather Green’	SApp
‘Heavenly Treasure’	SApp SRos
‘Heidi Eidelweiss’	CPLG
‘Heirloom Lace’	WBcn WCAu WFar
‘Helle Berlinerin’ 🏆H4	MNFA SApp SPol
‘Her Majesty’s Wizard’	SPol
‘Hercules’	NBre
‘Hey There’	SRos
‘High Energy’	SApp
‘High Tor’	GCal GQui MNFA SHar
‘Highland Belle’ **new**	SApp
‘Highland Lord’ (d)	SDay

'Holiday Mood' ELan ERou SApp
'Holly Dancer' SPol
'Honey Jubilee' SPol
'Hope Diamond' CCol SDay WCAu
'Hornby Castle' CBro EBrs LRHS WPer
'Hot Ticket' SApp SRos
'Hot Wire' SRos
'Houdini' EChP EGol WCAu WMnd WWye
'House of Orange' SApp SPol
'Howard Goodson' MNFA
'Humdinger' SRos
'Hyperion' CPrp CSev CTri ECha ECtt EGol EPfP GKir LAst LPio MLan MNFA MRav NGdn SApp SChu SHBN SPer SPla SUsu WCAu WTMC WWye
'Ice Carnival' CKel EPfP ERou EWTr LRHS MBNS MNFA NGdn NOrc SPet SVil
'Ice Castles' CTri SApp
'Ice Cool' SApp SRos
'Icecap' SChu WAul WFar WPnP WWpP
'Icy Lemon' SRos
'Ida Duke Miles' SDay SRos
'Ida Munson' EGol
'Ida's Magic' WAul
'Imperator' EPla LPBA
'Imperial Lemon' **new** SApp
'In Depth' (d) EPfP MBNS NCGa NLar WCot
'Indian Paintbrush' EChP EWoo GKir MBri NBir SPol SVil WCAu
'Indigo Moon' **new** SApp
'Inner View' EChP ECtt EWoo MBNS NLar NRnb SApp STes WAul WMnd
'Inspired Edge' MBNS
'Inspired Word' SRos
'Invicta' SRos
'Iridescent Jewel' SDay
'Irish Elf' GBuc GMac SApp WTin
'Iron Gate Glacier' MBNS
'Isle of Capri' **new** SRos
'Isleworth' **new** EWoo
'Jake Russell' MBNS MNFA
'James Marsh' CCol CPar EBee EChP EPfP EWes MBNS MBri MNFA MNrw NRnb NSti SApp SRos SSpe WAul WCAu WMnd
'Janet Gordon' SPol SRos
'Janice Brown' CCol CKel EChP EMar EWoo MBNS MNFA NLar SApp SRos WCAu
'Jan's Twister' CCol SApp SDay
'Jason Salter' NCGa SApp SDay WAul
'Java Sea' EBee
'Jay Turman' SApp
'Jedi Brenda Spann' **new** SApp
'Jedi Dot Pierce' SApp SRos
'Jedi Irish Spring' **new** SApp
'Jedi Rose Frost' SApp
'Jedi Rust Frost' **new** SApp
'Jenny Wren' EMar EPPr EPla EVFa GSki LRHS MBNS MNFA NBro NEgg SSpe SUsu WAul WCAu
'Jerusalem' **new** SRos
'Jesse James' **new** SApp
'Jo Jo' WCAu
'Joan Senior' More than 30 suppliers
'Jocelyn's Oddity' **new** SApp
'Jock Randall' MNFA
'Jockey Club' (d) MBNS
'John Bierman' SRos
'John Robert Biggs' SApp
'Joie de Vivre' **new** EWoo
'Jolyene Nichole' SApp SRos
'Journey's End' SDay
'Jovial' SApp SDay SRos
'Judah' SApp SDay SRos
'Justin June' CCol
'Kate Carpenter' SRos
'Kathleen Salter' EWoo SRos
'Katie Elizabeth Miller' SRos
'Kazuq' SApp
'Kecia' MNFA
'Kelly's Girl' SRos
'Kent's Favorite Two' **new** SRos
'Kimmswick' **new** SApp
'Kindly Light' CCol MNFA SRos WCAu
'King Haiglar' CCol EGol LPhx SApp SRos
'Kiwi Claret' **new** EWoo
N 'Kwanso Flore Pleno' see *H. fulva* 'Green Kwanso'
N 'Kwanso Flore Pleno Variegata' see *H. fulva* 'Variegated Kwanso'
'Lacy Marionette' SApp
'Lady Cynthia' CSBt
'Lady Fingers' CCol SAga
'Lady Hillary' **new** SApp
'Lady Inma' **new** SApp
'Lady Mischief' EWoo SApp
'Lady Neva' CCol SApp
'Ladykin' SApp SRos
'Lake Norman Spider' SApp
'Lark Song' EBrs EGol WBcn WFar
'Lauren Leah' **new** SRos
'Lavender Bonanza' WCAu WCFE
'Lavender Deal' EMar
'Lavender Flushing' **new** SApp
'Lavender Illusion' SApp
'Lavender Memories' SDay
'Lavender Silver Cords' SPol
'Lavender Spider' SApp
'Leebea Orange Crush' EMar
'Lemon Bells' ♀H4 EBee ECha EMFW EMar EPPr EPfP GMaP GSki MBNS MNFA MWgw NBro NCGa NGdn SApp SChu SDay SRos SVil WCAu
'Lemon Mint' EGol SRos
'Lemonora' **new** SDay
'Lenox' SDay SRos
'Leonard Bernstein' SApp SRos
'Light the Way' ECha
'Lil Ledie' **new** SApp
§ ***lilioasphodelus*** ♀H4 More than 30 suppliers
– 'Rowden Golden Jubilee' (v) CRow
'Lillian Frye' EGol
'Lilting Belle' CCol
'Lilting Lady' SApp SDay
'Lilting Lady Red' **new** SApp
'Lilting Lavender' CCol
'Lime Frost' SRos
'Linda' ERou EWll MRav SRos
* 'Liners Moon' EGol
'Lipstick Print' **new** SRos
'Little Angel' **new** SApp
'Little Audrey' SApp
'Little Baby Mine' **new** EWoo
'Little Bee' MBNS
'Little Beige Magic' EGol
'Little Big Man' SDay
'Little Bugger' MBNS NEgg NGby NLar
'Little Bumble Bee' CFir COIW EGol EMar MBNS MNFA SApp WCAu WTin
'Little Business' EWoo MBNS MNFA SApp SDay
'Little Cadet' MNFA
'Little Cameo' EGol
'Little Carpet' MBNS
'Little Carrot Top' WCAu

'Little Cranberry Cove'	EGol
'Little Dandy'	EGol
'Little Deeke'	MHar MNFA SApp SDay SRos
'Little Fantastic'	EGol
'Little Fat Dazzler'	SApp SDay SRos
'Little Fellow'	MBNS
'Little Fruit Cup' **new**	SApp
'Little Grapette'	CBro CHad CPrp EGol EMar MBNS MNFA NLar NSti SApp SBod SRos WAul WBcn WCAu WHrl WTin
'Little Greenie'	SDay
'Little Gypsy Vagabond'	SDay SRos
'Little Lassie'	MBNS
'Little Lavender Princess'	EGol
'Little Maggie'	MHar MSte SApp SDay
'Little Missy'	EMar EMil LAst MBNS MMHG SPet WHoo WSan
'Little Monica'	SApp SDay
'Little Pumpkin Face'	EGol
'Little Rainbow'	EGol
'Little Red Hen'	ECGP EMar GBuc LRHS MBNS MNFA NBro NEgg NGdn SBch SDay WCAu
'Little Show Stopper' **new**	NBro SMrm WSan
'Little Sweet Sue'	MNFA
'Little Sweet Talk' **new**	SRos
'Little Tawny'	WCAu
'Little Toddler'	SApp SDay
'Little Violet Lace'	GSki SApp SDay
'Little Wart'	EGol MNFA SDay
'Little Wine Cup'	More than 30 suppliers
'Little Wine Spider' **new**	SApp
'Little Witching Hour' **new**	EWoo
'Little Women'	SDay
'Little Zinger'	SDay
'Littlest Clown' **new**	SDay
'Lochinvar'	ENot GBuc MRav SRos
'Long Stocking'	SPol
'Longfield Purple Edge'	EBee MBNS
'Longfield's Beauty'	MBNS NCGa
'Longfield's Glory'	CCol MBNS NCGa
'Longfield's Maxim' (d) **new**	WHlf
'Longfield's Pride'	MBNS WBor
'Longfield's Purple Eye'	MBNS NCGa NLar
'Longfield's Twins'	CWrd MBNS WCot
longituba	CPLG
- B&SWJ 4576	WCru
'Look Away' **new**	SApp
'Lord of Lightning' **new**	EWoo
'Love Glow'	CFir
'Loving Memories' **new**	SApp
'Lowenstine'	SApp
'Lucretius'	MNFA
'Luke Senior Junior' **new**	SApp
'Lullaby Baby'	CCol EGol ELan MBNS NOrc SApp SDay SRos STes
luna	NOak
'Lusty Lealand'	CHea CPar EGol EMar MBNS SRos
'Luxury Lace'	CPrp EChP ECtt EGol ELan EMar EPfP EPla GKir LRHS MNFA MTis NBir NGdn SMrm SPer SRos WAul WCAu WCFE WFar WMoo WPnP WTMC WTin WWhi
'Lyn Wright' **new**	EWoo
'Lynn Hall'	EGol EMar MBNS
'Mabel Fuller'	MRav SPer
'Mae Graham'	SApp
'Maggie Fynboe' **new**	SPol
'Magic Carpet Ride'	SPol
'Mahogany Magic'	SRos
'Malayasian Masquerade' **new**	SApp
'Malaysian Monarch'	SRos
'Maleny Bright Eyes' **new**	EWoo
'Maleny Charmer' **new**	EWoo
'Maleny Miter' **new**	EWoo
'Maleny Piecrust' **new**	EWoo
'Maleny Sizzler' **new**	EWoo
'Maleny Tapestry' **new**	EWoo
'Maleny Think Big' **new**	EWoo
'Maleny Tiger' **new**	EWoo
'Mallard'	CWat ECtt EGol EHrv EMar EPla LLWP LRHS MRav MTis SApp SRos WBcn WCra WPer WTMC
'Manchurian Apricot'	SRos
'Marble Faun'	SApp SRos
'Margaret Perry'	CFee WAul
'Marion Caldwell' **new**	SPol
'Marion Vaughn' ♀H4	CSev EBee ECot EGol EHrv ELan EPfP EVFa GMaP GSki LRHS MMil MNFA NLon NSti SBch SChu SDix SPer SRos SSpi WFar
'Mariska'	SApp SDay SRos
'Mark My Word'	SApp
'Marse Connell'	SRos
'Mary Ethel Anderson' **new**	EWoo
'Mary Todd'	EBee EGol MBNS MNFA SApp WCAu
'Mary's Gold'	SDay SPol SRos
'Matador Orange'	EWsh
'Matt'	SRos SWal
'Mauna Loa'	CCol EBee EMar MBNS MNFA MNrw NBre NRnb SApp WAul WCAu WCot
'May Hall' **new**	CMCo
'May May'	SApp SPol
'Mayan Poppy' **new**	EWoo
'Meadow Mist'	EGol
'Meadow Sprite'	SRos
'Medieval Guild'	SApp
'Mega Stella'	SApp
'Melody Lane'	CMCo EGol MNFA
'Meno'	EGol
'Mephistopheles' **new**	EWoo
'Merlot Rouge'	WAul
'Merry Maker's Serenade' **new**	EWoo
'Metaphor'	SApp SDay
'Michele Coe'	CM&M EBee EGol EHrv EMar LRHS MBNS MNFA NBro NCGa NEgg NGdn SApp SChu SPav SRos WCAu WMoo
middendorffii	CAvo EBee EBrs EMon GCal GIBF GLil GMaP MNFA NFla NGdn NSti WCAu WFar WPnP WWpP
- 'Elfin'	EMon
- var. ***esculenta***	EMon
- 'Major'	CFee
'Midnight Love' **new**	EWoo
'Midnight Magic'	SDay
'Mikado'	LRHS
'Milady Greensleeves'	CCol SDay SRos
'Milanese Mango' **new**	EWoo SDay
'Mildred Mitchell' **new**	LBuc WSan
'Millie Schlumpf'	SApp SRos
'Ming Lo'	SDay
'Ming Porcelain'	SApp SDay SRos
'Mini Pearl'	CM&M EChP EGol EPfP GKir LRHS MBri SApp SChu SDay SPer SRos WPer WWye
'Mini Stella'	CBro ECtt ENot IBal MBNS NOrc SMac WAul WBcn WFar WPnP
miniature hybrids	SRms WPer
minor	CBro EBrs EGol EMon GCal NGdn SOkd SRms

Name	Suppliers
'Missenden' 🏆^{H4}	MNrw SApp SRos
'Mission Moonlight'	COtt EGol MHar WCAu
'Missouri Beauty'	CCol CPar EBee ERou LRHS MBNS NOrc NPri SApp SOkh WWeb
'Missouri Memories' **new**	EWoo SRos
'Mister Lucky' **new**	EWoo
'Mojave Mapeor' **new**	SApp
'Mokan Cindy'	EMar
'Moment of Truth'	MBNS
'Monica Marie'	SRos
'Moon Witch'	SRos
'Moonbeam' **new**	SApp
'Moonlight Mist'	CCol SApp SRos
'Moonlit Caress'	EBee EWoo MBNS WAul
'Moonlit Crystal'	CSpe SApp
'Moonlit Masquerade'	CCol CPen EChP EMar ERou EWTr LPio MBNS MBri MCCP MLLN NCGa NOrc NRnb SApp SDnm SPav SPer SRos WAul WCAu WHrl WSan
'Moontraveller'	WCot
'Mormon Spider'	SApp
'Morning Sun'	EMar MBNS WCot
'Morocco' **new**	SPol
'Morocco Red'	CBro CTri ELan EPla GSki MMil NGdn
'Morrie Otte' **new**	SPol
'Mount Joy' **new**	SPer
'Mountain Beauty' **new**	EWoo
'Mountain Laurel'	LRHS MNFA MRav SApp WFar
'Mr Ted' **new**	CCol
'Mrs B.F. Bonner'	WAul
'Mrs David Hall'	CMdw
'Mrs Hugh Johnson'	CHad CSev ECot GCra LAst MSte SHBN WWpP
'Mrs John J. Tigert'	ERou
'Mrs Lester'	SDay
multiflora	EMon MNFA SMHy WCot
'Mumbo Jumbo' **new**	SApp
'My Belle'	SApp SRos
'My Darling Clementine'	SApp SDay
'My Melinda'	SDay
I 'My Sweet Rose' **new**	SRos
'Mynelle's Starfish'	SPol
'Mysterious Veil'	EGol
'Nacogdoches Lady'	CCol
'Nairobi Dawn' **new**	SRos
'Nairobi Night' **new**	EWoo
nana	CFir EPot
'Nanuq'	SApp SDay SRos
'Naomi Ruth'	EGol LAst MBNS SApp WCAu WTin
'Nashville'	CBro ELan ERou IBlr MMil
'Natural Veil' **new**	SPol
'Neal Berrey'	SApp SRos
'Nefertiti'	CM&M CMCo EChP LAst NBir SPer WCAu WSan
I 'Neon Rose' **new**	SRos
'Netsuke'	SApp
'New Swirls' **new**	SApp
'Neyron Rose' 🏆^{H4}	CHea EGol EPfP EPla ERou GSki MBNS MNFA NEgg NGdn SChu SRos WCAu WMoo
'Night Beacon'	ECtt EGol EMar EWes EWoo IBal LBBr MBNS MBri MNrw NCGa NLar SApp SDay SRos WCAu WHrl
'Night Raider'	SApp SDay SRos
'Nigrette'	LPBA WWpP
'Nile Crane'	ERou MBNS MNrw SApp SPer WAul
'Nile Grave' **new**	SApp
'Nile Plum'	SApp
'Nivia Guest'	SApp SDay
'Nob Hill'	CMdw EGol EPla GBin MNFA SApp SRos
'Noble Warrior' **new**	EWoo
'Nordic Night'	CCol
'North Star'	SApp
'Norton Orange'	MNFA WFar
'Nova' 🏆^{H4}	CPrp MNFA SApp SRos
'Ocean Rain'	SApp SRos
x ***ochroleuca***	SSpi
'Old Tangiers'	SRos
'Olive Bailey Langdon'	EGol SApp SRos
'Olympic Showcase'	SRos
'Omomuki'	SApp SRos
'Oom Pah Pah'	ECha
'Open Hearth'	CCol SRos
'Orange Dream'	SDay
'Orange Prelude' **new**	SApp
'Orange Velvet'	SApp SRos
'Orangeman' hort.	EMar EPla GSki LRHS MBNS
'Orchid Beauty'	ECha WMoo
'Orchid Candy'	CWrd MBNS NBir
'Orchid Corsage'	SApp SDay
'Oriental Ruby'	EGol MNFA
'Outrageous'	SApp SRos
'Paige Parker'	EGol
'Paige's Pinata'	EBee MBNS
'Paint Your Wagon' **new**	SApp
'Paintbrush'	CRez
'Painted Lady'	MNFA SApp
'Palace Guard'	MNFA
'Pandora's Box'	More than 30 suppliers
'Pantaloons' **new**	SApp
'Pantherette'	SApp
'Paper Butterfly'	CCol CKel SRos
'Paradise Pink'	NPri
'Paradise Prince'	EGol
'Pardon Me'	CM&M CMHG EGol ELan GMaP IBal LPio MBNS MNFA NCGa NGdn SApp SRos WAul WBor WCAu
'Pas de Deux' **new**	SApp
'Pastel Ballerina'	SRos
'Pastel Classic'	SApp SRos
'Pastilline'	SPol
'Pat Mercer' **new**	SApp
'Patchwork Puzzle'	EWoo SRos
'Patricia Fay'	SApp
'Patsy Bickers'	CCol SApp
'Peach Petticoats'	SRos
'Peacock Maiden'	SApp SDay
'Pear Ornament'	SRos
'Pearl Lewis'	SDay
'Pemaquid Light'	CMHG
'Penelope Vestey'	EBla EMar GBuc LRHS MBNS MNFA NCGa NGdn SApp SRos
'Penny's Worth'	EBrs EGol GKir MBNS NOrc WAul WCot WFar
'Persian Princess'	CMCo WBcn
'Persian Ruby'	SPol
'Petite Ballerina'	SDay
'Piano Man' **new**	EMar SMrm WAul
'Piccadilly Princess'	SRos
'Pink Attraction'	SApp
'Pink Ballerina'	EGol
'Pink Charm'	COIW EBee EChP ECha EMar GBBs GMaP LPBA LRHS MNFA MWgw NBro NGdn NLon NOrc SChu SHBN SRos WCAu
'Pink Cotton Candy'	SRos
'Pink Damask' 🏆^{H4}	More than 30 suppliers
'Pink Dream'	EMar IPot LRHS MBNS MNFA NBir WCAu
'Pink Glow'	CM&M

'Pink Heaven' EGol
'Pink Lady' ERou MNrw MRav NBur SHBN SRms
'Pink Lavender Appeal' EGol WCAu
'Pink Prelude' CCol EBee EChP EMar EWll LRHS MBNS MNFA NBro SChu
'Pink Puff' ERou MAvo MBNS NBir NCGa NLar SDay
'Pink Salute' SRos
'Pink Sundae' ECha MTis
'Pink Super Spider' MNFA SRos
'Pinocchio' MBNS
'Pirate Treasure' **new** MBNS
'Pirate's Patch' SPol SRos
'Pirate's Promise' **new** EWoo
'Pixie Pipestone' CCol SApp
'Pocket Size' **new** SApp
'Pompeian Purple' EGol
'Pony' EGol SDay SRos
'Ponytail Pink' EGol
'Pookie Bear' SApp
'Prague Spring' MNFA
'Prairie Belle' CSWP MBNS SApp WCAu WFar WWhi
'Prairie Blue Eyes' CCol EChP EGol LRHS MBNS MNFA NPri NRnb SApp SPlb SRos WAul WBcn WCAu WCot WMnd WTMC
'Prairie Charmer' IPot
'Prairie Moonlight' SRos
'Prairie Queen' IPot
'Prairie Sunset' WCAu
'Prelude to Love' EMar
'Pretty Mist' MBri
'Pretty Peggy' MNFA
'Primrose Mascotte' NBir
'Prince Redbird' SDay SRos
'Princess Blue Eyes' **new** SPol
'Princess Eden' **new** SApp
'Princess Ellen' SApp
'Princeton Point Lace' SApp
'Princeton Silky' **new** SRos
'Prize Picotee Deluxe' SRos
'Prize Picotee Elite' SRos WTin
'Protocol' SDay
§ 'Puddin' SDay WAul
'Pudgie' **new** SApp
'Pumpkin Kid' SApp SRos
'Puppet Show' SDay
'Pure and Simple' SDay SPol
'Purple Bicolor' CRez
'Purple Corsage' **new** SApp
'Purple Pinwheel' SPol
'Purple Rain' CHea EUJe MBNS SApp SRos SWvt
'Purple Rain Dance' **new** SPol
'Purple Waters' CCol EPfP EWll LRHS MBNS MWgw NArg NOrc NPri WAul WPnP
'Pursuit of Excellence' SRos
'Pyewacket' SApp
'Queen of May' SApp WCot
'Queens Fancy' **new** SApp
'Queen's Gift' SApp
'Queensland' **new** SApp
'Quick Results' SApp SRos
'Ra Hansen' **new** SDay
'Radiant Ruffles' WCAu
'Raging Tiger' SDay
'Rainbow Candy' MBNS WSan
'Raindrop' EGol SSpe
'Rajah' EGra EMar MBNS NBro WWeb
'Raspberry Candy' EChP EMar MBNS MNrw NBro NCGa NOrc SApp WAul WCAu WHrl
'Raspberry Pixie' EGol MNFA SPol
'Raspberry Wine' MHar
'Real Wind' CCol MNFA SApp SRos
'Red Flag' CCol
'Red Joy' SApp
'Red Precious' 🏆H4 EGol MNFA MNrw SApp SRos
'Red Ribbons' CCol SDay SPol SRos
'Red Rum' EWll GLil MBNS MTis NBro WPnP WPop WWhi
'Red Volunteer' SRos
'Regal Centre' **new** EWoo
'Regency Dandy' **new** SApp
'Respighi' **new** SApp
'Return Trip' **new** SPol
'Ribonette' **new** WSan
'Riley Barron' **new** SDay
'Ringlets' MNFA
'Riptide' SApp
'Robin Coleman' MNFA
'Rocket City' ELan SRos
'Roger Grounds' CCol SApp SPol
'Romantic Rose' EMar MBNS
'Romany' LPBA
'Ron Rousseau' SApp
'Root Beer' SRos WBcn WCAu WTin
'Rose Emily' SApp SDay SRos
'Rose Festival' WCAu
'Rose Fever' **new** EWoo
'Rose Roland' **new** NBre
'Rosella Sheridan' SRos
'Rosewood Flame' **new** SRos
'Royal Braid' CPen EChP ENot EPfP EWoo MBNS MNrw NCGa NLar NOrc SApp SPer WAul WCot WSan
'Royal Charm' SRos
'Royal Corduroy' SRos
'Royal Prestige' SApp
'Royal Robe' CPLG CTri LPhx
'Royal Saracen' SDay
'Royalty' GCra NGdn WWpP
'Ruby Spider' CCol SDay
'Rudolf Seyer' MBNS
I 'Ruffled Antique Lavender' WCAu
'Ruffled Apricot' CKel MBNS NFla SDay SPav SRos WCAu
'Ruffles and Lace' CCol
'Russell Prichard' ERou
'Russian Easter' SRos
'Russian Rhapsody' CKel SApp SRos
'Rutilans' CFee
'Sabie' SApp
'Sabine Baur' EBee EMar EWoo IBal IPot WAul WCra
'Sabra Salina' SRos
* 'Sagamore' **new** SApp
'Saintly' **new** EWoo
'Salmon Sheen' MNFA SDay SPer SRos
'Sammy Russell' More than 30 suppliers
'Sandra Walker' EGol LAst
'Sari' SApp
'Satin Clouds' EGol
'Satin Glass' MNFA
'Satin Glow' ECha
'Scarlet Chalice' **new** SApp
'Scarlet Flame' ECha WMoo
* 'Scarlet Oak' LRHS MBri MNFA NLon SRos
'Scarlet Orbit' EWoo SApp SRos
'Scarlet Ribbons' SPol
'Scarlock' MNFA
'Scatterbrain' CKel
'Schoeppinger Anfang' EBee
'Schoolgirl' EBrs
'Scorpio' CBgR CCol MNFA

'Scotland' IBal SApp
'Searcy Marsh' EGol
'Sebastian' SApp SRos
'Secret Splendor' SPol
'Seminole Wind' EWoo
'Serena Sunburst' SRos
'Serene Madonna' CFir
'Serenity Morgan' **new** EPfP LBuc
'Shaman' SApp SRos
'Sherry Fair' **new** SApp
'Sherry Lane Carr' SPol SRos
'Shogun' **new** MBNS
'Shooting Star' SPla
'Show Amber' MBNS SApp SRos
'Significant Other' **new** SApp
'Silent Sentry' **new** CFir
'Silken Fairy' EGol
'Silken Touch' SApp
'Siloam Amazing Grace' **new** SApp SDay SRos
'Siloam Angel Blush' SDay
'Siloam Baby Talk' CM&M EChP EGol EMar LAst NBir SApp SRos WAul WHoo WPnP WTin
'Siloam Bo Peep' EGol MNFA SApp WAul WTMC
'Siloam Brian Hanke' SRos
'Siloam Button Box' EBee EChP EGol EWoo WAul WSan
'Siloam Bye Lo' EGol SDay WHil
'Siloam Cinderella' EGol SDay SRos
'Siloam David Kirchhoff' EWoo MBNS SDay SRos
'Siloam Doodlebug' EGol SRos
'Siloam Double Classic' (d) CCol EGol SRos WHlf
'Siloam Dream Baby' EPPr EPza GBri MBNS NCGa
'Siloam Edith Sholar' EGol
'Siloam Ethel Smith' EGol SDay SRos
'Siloam Fairy Tale' EChP EGol
'Siloam Flower Girl' SDay
'Siloam French Doll' CCol MBNS NRnb
'Siloam French Marble' SRos
'Siloam Frosted Mint' SApp
'Siloam Gold Coin' SApp SDay
'Siloam Grace Stamile' CFir SApp SRos
'Siloam Harold Flickinger' SRos
'Siloam Jim Cooper' SRos
'Siloam Joan Senior' ECtt EGol MBNS SDay
'Siloam John Yonski' SDay
'Siloam June Bug' EGol ELan MNFA SApp WCAu
'Siloam Justine Lee' MBNS
'Siloam Kewpie Doll' EGol
'Siloam Little Angel' EGol SApp
'Siloam Little Girl' EGol SDay SRos
'Siloam Mama' SApp SRos
'Siloam Merle Kent' SApp SDay SRos
'Siloam New Toy' EGol
'Siloam Nugget' SApp
'Siloam Orchid Jewel' EGol
'Siloam Paul Watts' **new** SRos
'Siloam Peewee' EGol WCAu
'Siloam Penny' **new** SApp
'Siloam Pink' LAst
'Siloam Pink Glow' EGol WAul
'Siloam Pink Petite' EGol
'Siloam Plum Tree' EGol SApp
'Siloam Pocket Size' EGol MSte
'Siloam Powder Pink' **new** SApp
'Siloam Prissy' EGol SApp
'Siloam Purple Plum' EGol
'Siloam Ra Hansen' **new** SApp
'Siloam Red Ruby' EGol
'Siloam Red Toy' EGol MNFA SDay
'Siloam Red Velvet' EGol
'Siloam Ribbon Candy' EGol SApp SDay
'Siloam Rose Dawn' SApp SRos
'Siloam Rose Queen' SDay
'Siloam Royal Prince' CM&M EChP EGol EPfP MNFA NRnb SApp SDay
'Siloam Shocker' EGol
'Siloam Show Girl' CCol CMCo CRez EGol GKir MBNS NCGa SApp WAul
'Siloam Sugar Time' EGol
'Siloam Tee Tiny' EGol
'Siloam Tinker Toy' EGol
'Siloam Tiny Mite' EGol SDay
'Siloam Toddler' EGol
'Siloam Tom Thumb' EGol EMar MBNS WCAu
'Siloam Ury Winniford' EGol EMar MBNS MCCP MNFA SApp WAul WHoo WPnP WTin
'Siloam Virginia Henson' COtt EGol MNFA SApp SOkh SRos WCAu
'Siloam Wendy Glawson' **new** SApp
'Silver Ice' SApp SRos
'Silver Trumpet' EGol
'Silver Veil' WFar
'Sir Blackstem' SApp SRos
'Sir Modred' MAnH
'Sirocco' EChP WTin
'Slender Lady' SRos
'Smoky Mountain Autumn' EWoo SApp SRos
'Smoky Mountain Bell' **new** SApp
'Smuggler's Gold' **new** SApp
'Snappy Rhythm' MNFA
'Snowed In' EWoo SRos
'Snowy Apparition' EWTr EWll MNFA MSte SApp SMrm
'Snowy Eyes' EGol EMar GBuc IPot MBNS NCGa NRnb SApp WCAu
'So Lovely' SApp
'Solid Scarlet' SRos
'Someone Special' SDay SPol SRos
'Song Sparrow' GKir GMac LRHS SApp WPer WWye
'Sovereign Queen' EGol
'Spacecoast Starburst' EBee EMar MBNS WCAu
'Spanish Glow' SRos
'Speak of Angels' **new** SApp
'Spider Breeder' SApp
'Spider Miracle' CCol MNFA
'Spiderman' SApp SRos WCAu
'Spilled Milk' SPol
'Spiral Charmer' **new** SApp
'Spode' SApp
'Spring Ballerina' SApp
'Stafford' More than 30 suppliers
'Starling' CFir CPar EChP EGol EUJe MNFA MSte SApp WAul WCAu
'Stars and Stripes' MNFA
'Startle' **new** EWoo MBNS WSan
'Statuesque' **new** WFar
'Stella de Oro' More than 30 suppliers
'Stoke Poges' 𝕐^{H4} CBro CSev EBee EChP EGoo EMFW EMar EPPr EPfP EPla LAst LRHS MBNS MMil MNFA NEgg NGdn SApp SChu SDay SRos STes WCAu
'Stoplight' CCol EMar SApp SDay SPol SRos
'Strawberry Candy' CM&M EChP EMar EPfP EWoo LAst LSRN MBNS MBri NCGa NGdn NOrc NRnb SApp SOkh SPer SPoG SRos WAul WCAu WHoo WHrl
'Strawberry Fields Forever' EWoo MBNS SPol
'Strawberry Swirl' MNFA
I 'Streaker' B. Brown (v) WCot
'Streaker' McKinney MNFA

'Strutter's Ball'	CPar EChP EWoo IPot MNFA NGdn NRnb SApp SDay SPer SRos WAul WCAu WCot WHoo WMnd
'Sugar Cookie'	EWoo SApp SDay SRos
'Summer Interlude'	WCAu WMoo
'Summer Jubilee'	SApp SDay
'Summer Wine'	More than 30 suppliers
'Summertime'	WBcn
'Sunday Gloves'	EGol SRos
'Sunstar'	CCol
'Super Purple'	CKel SApp
'Superlative'	SApp SRos
'Susan Weber' **new**	SApp SRos
'Suzie Wong'	MNFA SChu SRos
'Svengali'	SDay SPol
'Sweet Harmony'	CCol
'Sweet Pea'	EGol
'Taffy Tot'	SApp
'Taj Mahal'	WFar
'Tall Boy' **new**	SApp
'Tang'	EBee MAvo MBNS MNFA NOrc WCAu
'Tangerine Tango' **new**	EWoo
'Tango Noturno'	SApp SPol
'Tapestry of Dreams' **new**	EWoo
'Tarantula' **new**	SApp
'Tasmania' **new**	SPer
'Techny Peach Lace'	SRos
'Techny Spider'	SRos
'Tejas'	CElw EMil MBNS SPer
'Tender Shepherd'	EGol WCAu
'Tetraploid Stella de Oro'	SDay
'Tetrina's Daughter' ♀H4	EPfP SApp SRos
'Texas Sunlight'	EWTr WAul
'Thai Silk' **new**	SApp
'Theresa Hall' **new**	WFar
'Thumbelina'	ECha MNFA
§ ***thunbergii***	EBee ECha EMon MNFA MNrw SMac SSpi WCAu
'Thy True Love'	SApp
'Tigerling'	SRos
'Time Lord'	SApp SDay
'Timeless Fire'	SApp SRos
'Tinker Bell'	MSte SRos
'Tiny Talisman'	SApp
'Tom Collins'	SRos
'Tom Wise'	SRos
'Tomorrow's Song' **new**	SApp
'Tonia Gay'	SApp SRos
'Tootsie'	SDay
'Tootsie Rose'	SRos
'Torpoint'	EMar LRHS MBNS MNFA NCob
'Towhead'	EBee EGol ENot MRav
'Toyland'	CMCo CSev EChP EGol EMar EPPr EPfP GSki MBNS NBir NGdn NLon NPri SSpe SUsu
'Trahlyta'	CPar SApp SPol SRos
'Trond' **new**	SDay
'Tropical Heat Wave' **new**	SApp
'Troubled Sleep' **new**	EWoo
'True Glory'	SApp
'True Grit' **new**	SApp
'Tuolumne Fairy Tale'	SPol
'Tuscawilla Blackout'	SApp SRos
'Tuscawilla Tigress'	EMar NCGa SRos WAul
'Tuxedo' **new**	SApp SPol
'Twenty Third Psalm'	WTin
'Two Faces of Love' **new**	SPol
'Uniquely Different'	SPol
'Upper Class Peach'	SRos
'Uptown Girl'	SRos
'Valiant'	EMar MBNS
'Vanilla Candy' **new**	SRos
'Varsity'	EBrs EGol NBir SPer SRos WCAu
'Veiled Beauty'	WCAu
'Vera Biaglow'	SApp SDay SPol SRos
'Vespers'	CAbP WFar WPnP
vespertina	see *H. thunbergii*
'Vi Simmons' **new**	SRos
'Victoria Aden'	CBro IBal
'Victorian Collar' **new**	SApp
'Victorian Ribbons'	SPol
'Video'	SApp SRos
'Vino di Notte'	SRos
'Vintage Bordeaux'	ELan SApp WAul
'Violet Hour'	SDay
'Viracocha' **new**	SApp
'Virgin's Blush'	SPer
'Vision of Beauty' **new**	SApp
* 'Vohann'	CMdw SApp SRos
'Walking on Sunshine'	SApp SRos
'Wally Nance'	SDay
'Water Witch'	EGol SApp
'Waxwing'	WPer
'Wayside Green Imp'	EGol SApp SOkh
'Wayside Green Lamp'	MNrw MSte
'Wedding Band'	SRos
'Wee Chalice'	EGol
'Welchkins'	WAul
'Welfo White Diamond' **new**	SApp SPol
'Well of Souls' **new**	CCol
'Wendy Glawson' **new**	SApp
'Whichford' ♀H4	CBro CHad CM&M CSam EBee EBrs ECGP ECtt EGol ELan ETow LAst LPhx LRHS MNFA NCob NLon SChu SMHy SPer SPla SRos WCAu
'Whiskey on Ice' **new**	SApp
'White Coral'	EMar LRHS LSRN MNFA NBro NEgg WCAu
'White Dish'	EGol
'White Edged Madonna'	EMar GFlt WHrl
'White Pansy' **new**	SRos
'White Temptation'	CFir CM&M EBee EChP EGol EPfP EWoo MNFA NGdn SApp SDay SRos WAul WCAu WHoo
'White Tie Affair'	SApp
'Whooperee'	SRos
* 'Wide Eyed'	EPla MNFA
'Wild about Sherry'	SPol
'Wild Mustang'	CCol MBNS
'Wild One' **new**	SApp
'Wild Welcome'	WCAu
'Wildfire Tango' **new**	SApp
'Wilson Spider' **new**	SApp SPol
'Wind Frills'	CCol SApp SDay
'Wind Song'	SApp SRos
'Window Dressing'	COIW EGol GMac
'Windsor Castle' **new**	SApp
'Windsor Tan'	WCAu WCFE
'Wine Bubbles'	EGol SApp
'Wine Merchant'	MNFA
'Wineberry Candy'	CPar CWrd EPfP MBNS NLar WCAu
'Winnetka'	WCAu
'Winnie the Pooh'	SDay
'Winsome Lady'	ECha WHrl
'Winter Olympics'	SDay
'Wishing Well'	SChu
* 'Witch Hazel'	COtt WCAu
'Women's Work'	SApp
'Wood Duck'	COtt SApp
'Wren'	COtt
'Xia Xiang'	SDay SRos
'Yabba Dabba Doo'	CCol SPol

'Yearning Love' **new**	SApp
'Yellow Angel' **new**	SApp
'Yellow Explosion'	SApp
'Yellow Lollipop'	MNFA SApp SDay SRos
'Yellow Mantle'	MNFA
'Yellow Spider' **new**	SApp
'Yesterday Memories'	SRos
'Young Countess' **new**	CMCo
'Zagora'	WCAu
'Zampa'	SDay
'Zara'	SPer

Hemigraphis (*Acanthaceae*)

§ ***alternata***	EShb
colorata	see *H. alternata*

Hemiorchis (*Zingiberaceae*)

pantlingii	CKob MOak

Hepatica ✿ (*Ranunculaceae*)

acutiloba	CArn CBro CLAP EBee EPot GBuc GCrs GEdr GKir LAma MAsh NBir NLar SIgm WCru WPnP
'Akane'	EBee
americana	CLAP EBee EHrv GBuc GCrs MAsh NBir NLar SBla WCru WPnP
angulosa	see *H. transsilvanica*
'Baien'	EBee
henryi	EPot LAma MAsh WCru
insularis	CLAP SBla
- B&SWJ 859	WCru
'Isaribi' **new**	EBee
'Kasumino' **new**	EBee WHil
maxima	GEdr MAsh
- B&SWJ 4344	WCru
x ***media*** 'Ballardii'	GKir IBlr
- Blackthorn Group **new**	SBla
- 'Harvington Beauty'	CFwr CLAP GBuc IBlr MAsh NBir
'Moeharu'	EBee
§ ***nobilis*** ♀H4	More than 30 suppliers
- blue-flowered	CDes GAbr GBuc GEdr LPio MAsh NSla NWCA SBla SRot WAbe WCru
- 'Cobalt'	CLAP NMyG NSla WAbe WHil
- dark blue-flowered	CLAP
- double pink-flowered	see *H. nobilis* 'Rubra Plena'
- var. ***japonica***	CArn CBro EBee GBuc GCrs LAma MAsh NBir SBla SIgm WCru
- 'Landquart Marble' **new**	WHil
- large, pale blue-flowered **new**	WHil
- lilac-flowered	MTho SBla
- mottled leaf	EHrv MTho
- 'Pearl Grey'	NPar
- Picos strain	SBla
- pink-flowered	CLAP EHyt EPot ETow GCrs MAsh MS&S NLar NWCA SBla SOkd SRot
- var. ***pubescens***	MAsh
* - var. ***pyrenaica***	GBuc MAsh
* - - 'Apple Blossom'	CLAP GCrs MAsh NBir
* - 'Pyrenean Marbles'	CLAP
- red-flowered	WHil
I - Rene's form **new**	WFar
- var. ***rubra***	CLAP NMen NSla
§ - 'Rubra Plena' (d)	ECha GCrs NSla
- violet-flowered	SBla
- white-flowered	CLAP CNic EHyt GCrs LPio MAsh MS&S NMen NSla SBla SRot WCru WHil WIvy
'Noubeni'	EBee
'Noumurasaki'	EBee
'Oboroyo'	EBee
* ***pyrenaica*** white-flowered J&JA 0.566.055 **new**	NWCA
'Ryokka'	EBee
'Saikaku'	EBee
'Sakuragari'	EBee
'Sayaka'	EBee
'Syungyou'	EBee
'Syunsai'	EBee
§ ***transsilvanica*** ♀H4	CBro CLAP EBee EHyt EPot GAbr GCrs GKir LAma LRHS MAsh MS&S NMen SBla SPer WAbe WAul WCru WTin
- 'Ada Scott'	WSHC
* - ***alba***	SBla
- 'Blue Jewel'	CFir CLAP CRez GCrs GEdr WPnP
- 'De Buis'	CBod CFwr CLAP EBee EPot GCrs GEdr LPhx LPio MAvo MDun NLar SUsu WPnP
- deep blue-flowered	IBlr
- 'Eisvogel'	CLAP EPot GEdr GKir NMen NPar
- 'Elison Spence' (d)	ECha IBlr NPar SBla
- Jan/Feb flowering	NPar
- 'Lilacina'	ECha GEdr NPar
- 'Loddon Blue'	IBlr NPar
- pink-flowered	CLAP EPot SBla
triloba	see *H. nobilis*
'Umezono'	EBee
'Wakana'	EBee
yamatutai	MAsh SBla
'Yukikomachi' **new**	EBee

Heptacodium (*Caprifoliaceae*)

jasminoides	see *H. miconioides*
§ ***miconioides***	More than 30 suppliers

Heptapleurum see *Schefflera*

Heracleum (*Apiaceae*)

candicans	EMan
- BWJ 8157	WCru
dulce	EBee GIBF
lanatum 'Washington Limes' (v)	EBee EMan EPPr ITer WCot
lehmannianum	EBee EMan GBin NSti WCot
minimum 'Roseum'	CPom WPat
moellendorfii	EBee GIBF
sibiricum **new**	GIBF
sosnowskyi **new**	GIBF
- RBS 0231	ITer
sphondylium pink	CNat
wilhelmsii **new**	GIBF

Herbertia (*Iridaceae*)

§ ***lahue***	CDes CFil CStu LRHS WCot WPGP

Hereroa (*Aizoaceae*)

odorata	EShb EWin

Hermannia (*Sterculiaceae*)

althaeoides	CPBP
candicans	see *H. incana*
erodioides	WAbe
- JCA 15523	CPBP
§ ***incana***	CHal MOak
§ ***pinnata***	CPBP CSec
pulchella **new**	CPBP WAbe
stricta	CPBP NWCA WAbe

Hermodactylus (*Iridaceae*)

§ ***tuberosus***	CAby CAvo CBro CMea CTri EBee EBrs ECGP ECha EMan EUJe LAma LPhx LPio LRHS MLul SBch SMeo SOkh STes WCot WTin
- MS 821	WCot

Herniaria (*Illecebraceae*)

glabra	CArn EOHP GBar GPoy MSal NGHP NJOw SIde WHer WLHH WWye

Herpolirion (*Anthericaceae*)

novae-zealandiae	ECou

Hertia see *Othonna*

Hesperaloe (*Agavaceae*)

funifera	EOas XPep
parviflora	CTrC EBee EMan LPio SBig SChr SIgm WCot WMul XPep

Hesperantha (*Iridaceae*)

§ ***baurii***	CLyd CPBP CStu EBee EMan EPot GBuc NLar NMen SSpi WAbe
coccinea	see *Schizostylis coccinea*
cucullata	EBee
* - 'Rubra'	NWCA
grandiflora **new**	ECho
huttonii	EBee EMan MWrn NBir NCGa NEgg
mossii	see *H. baurii*
petitiana	GCal
woodii	CDes CFir

Hesperis (*Brassicaceae*)

lutea see *Sisymbrium luteum*	
matronalis	More than 30 suppliers
- ***alba***	see *H. matronalis* var. *albiflora*
§ - var. ***albiflora***	CCge CHrt CPrp CSpe CTri EBee ELau EMar EPfP ERou GFlt GMaP LRHS MAnH MBow NDov NGHP NPri SIde SPer SPoG SSvw WBrk WCAu WFar WGwG WMnd WMoo WPer WWye
- - 'Alba Plena' (d)	CAbP CCge CElw CMea EBee ECtt ELan EMan EVFa LRHS MNrw NBir SPoG WBrk WCAu WCot WFar
- double-flowered (d)	EChP GKir MBri
- 'Frogswell Doris'	IFro MAvo
- 'Lilacina Flore Pleno' (d)	CCge CElw
steveniana	SMrm

Hesperochiron (*Hydrophyllaceae*)

pumilus **new**	GKev

Heterolepis (*Asteraceae*)

aliena	GFai SGar

Heteromeles (*Rosaceae*)

arbutifolia	see *H. salicifolia*
salicifolia	CAgr EShb

Heteromorpha (*Apiaceae*)

arborescens	SPlb

Heteropappus (*Asteraceae*)

altaicus	WPer

Heteropyxis (*Myrtaceae*)

natalensis	EShb

Heterotheca (*Asteraceae*)

mariana	see *Chrysopsis mariana*
pumila	NWCA
§ ***villosa***	EMan SPet
- 'Golden Sunshine'	EBee

Heuchera ✿ (*Saxifragaceae*)

'Amber Waves'[PBR]	More than 30 suppliers
§ ***americana***	EBee ECha GBar MHar MMil MRav NBir
- Dale's strain	CBct CChe EBla ECha EMan GKir IBal IFro LRHS MNrw NGdn NLar SMar SPlb SPur SWvt WGor WHrl WMnd WPnP WTMC WWeb
- 'Harry Hay'	CDes EPPr MSte
- 'Ring of Fire'	CBcs COtt EBee EBla EPfP GBri IArd IBal LRHS LSRN MAvo MBow MDun MSte NCGa NMyG NPri NSti SApp SDnm SPav SPla SPoG SWvt WCot WFar WPnP
'Amethyst Myst'	CFai CM&M COIW EBee EBla EMan ENot EPfP GAbr GBBs GSki LRHS MBNS MBnl NCob NEgg NLar NMyG NPri SDnm SPav SPer SPoG SRkn SRot WCot WFar WGor WPnP
'Beauty Colour'	More than 30 suppliers
'Black Beauty'	CBcs GCai LSou NPri SRot
* 'Black Velvet'	EPfP MCCP NOrc
'Blackbird' ♀H4	EDAr MBNS NPro SApp SDnm SPav SRkn SSto SWvt WMnd
'Blood Vein'	MBNS MWrn
'Blushing Bride' **new**	NRnb
Bressingham hybrids	CWib ENot GKir LRHS NArg NBir NBlu NMir SPer SPet SRms WFar WMoo WPer WSSM
x ***brizoides***	IHMH NJOw
- 'Gracillima'	EBee
'Burgundy Frost' ♀H4	WCot
Cally hybrids	GCal
'Can-can' ♀H4	More than 30 suppliers
'Canyon Chimes'	COtt
'Canyon Duet'	COtt
'Canyon Pink'	NRnb NSti
'Cappuccino'	CBct CHar CTbh EBee EChP ECtt EMan IBal MBNS MBnl MBow MDHE MLLN NBro NPri NRnb SDnm SPav SWvt WCFE WFar WHlf WLin WWeb WWol WWpP
'Cascade Dawn'	CMHG EBee ECtt EMan GBuc IBal LAst LRHS LSRN MRav MSte NBir NLar NPri SPav SPer WBrk WCot WFar WGwG
'Champagne Bubbles'[PBR]	GCai MBNS NPri WHlf
Charles Bloom = 'Chablo'	EBrs
'Cherries Jubilee'[PBR]	CFir EBee EBla GMaP LRHS MBNS MBnl MLLN MSph NCGa NEgg NPri SHar SPav SVil WBrk WCot WCra WGor WHlf
'Chiqui'	SUsu
chlorantha	EBee GCal
'Chocolate Ruffles'[PBR]	More than 30 suppliers
'Chocolate Veil' ♀H4	CPen EPfP SHar WWeb
'City Lights' **new**	GCai
coral bells	see *H. sanguinea*
'Coral Bouquet'	EBee EMan LAst LBuc MBNS MLLN SHar WCot
'Coral Cloud'	EBla MRav
'Crimson Curls'	LRHS SWvt WHlf
'Crispy Curly'	EMan MBNS MWrn NBur NRnb
cylindrica	EBee MBNS MRav MSte MWgw NBre WPer
- var. ***alpina***	EHyt NWCA
- 'Brownfinch'	SMHy
- 'Greenfinch'	CFee ECha ELan ENot EPfP ERou GCal GKev GKir GTou IBal IHMH LRHS MHer MRav MTis NBir NDov

		NLsd NOrc SPav SPoG WFar WGHP WMnd WPer WSSM
	- 'Hyperion'	ECtt
	'Dennis Davidson'	see *H.* 'Huntsman'
	'Diana Clare'	ECtt
	'Dingle Mint Chocolate'	ECtt EVFa
	Ebony and Ivory = 'E and I'[PBR]	More than 30 suppliers
I	'Eco Magnififolia'	CLAP EBee
	'Eden's Aurora'	EBee EChP WMnd
	'Eden's Joy'	EChP MBNS
	'Eden's Mystery'	ECtt WWeb
	elegans	NMen
	'Emperor's Cloak'	CHar ECtt EKen EMil LSou MAnH MGol NArg NBur NDlv NLar NLon SWvt WMoo WSan
	'Emperor's Cloak' green **new**	NArg
	'Firebird'	NBir NVic
	Firefly	see *H.* 'Leuchtkäfer'
	'Fireworks'[PBR] 🏆H4	CPen EBee EMan EPPr GBBs GBin MBNS MBnl MLLN NCob NDov NLar SHar SPla STes WBor WBrk WCot WGor WHoo
	'Florist's Choice'	CAbP EBee EMan MBNS NRnb SHar WBor WCot WHoo
	glauca	see *H. americana*
	'Green Ivory'	EBee EMan LRHS MRav NGdn NSti SBch
	'Green Spice'	GBin LSou MBNS NPri SPav SRot
	'Green Spire'	WGwG
	'Greenfinch'	see *H. cylindrica* 'Greenfinch'
	grossulariifolia	MBNS WPer
	'Helen Dillon' (v)	CHid EBee EBla ECtt EMan GBri IBal LAst MLLN MRav NBir NPri SPla SPoG SWvt WFar WPnP WWhi WWpP
	'Hercules'[PBR]	EBee EChP ECtt MBNS
	hispida	EBee EMan MSte WPer
§	'Huntsman'	EChP ECha ELan EMan GBri GBuc MBNS MRav WBcn WFar WMnd WPen
	'Ibis'	EBee
	'Lady in Red'	MBNS
	'Lady Romney'	GCal
§	'Leuchtkäfer'	CFee CWat EBee EChP ECtt EMFW GBuc GMaP IBal LAst LRHS MHer MRav MWrn NBir NEgg NMir NOrc NPri SBla SPer SPlb SRms WFar WMnd WMoo WPer WPnP
	'Lime Rickey' **new**	GCai SHar
	'Magic Wand'[PBR] 🏆H4	CAbP EBee LRHS MBNS SHar SUsu WCot
	'Marmalade' **new**	GCai SHar
	'Mars'	EBee MBNS MBnl NSti SPav
	maxima	EMon
	'Mercury'	EChP MBNS SPav
	'Metallica'	GKev MWrn NLar
	micans	see *H. rubescens*
	micrantha	EBee GCal SRms
	- var. ***diversifolia***	EBee EBrs EPla LRHS SPla WCAu
	Bressingham Bronze = 'Absi'[PBR]	WFar
N	- - 'Palace Purple'	More than 30 suppliers
	- 'Martha Roderick' **new**	WCot
§	- 'Ruffles'	EPPr LRHS
	'Mini Mouse'	EBee
	'Mint Frost'[PBR]	COtt EBee ECtt EHan ELan EMar ENot GAbr GBin GBri GKir GSki LAst LRHS MGos MLLN MRav NMRc NPri NRnb SDnm SPav SPoG SWvt WCAu WCot WFar WOVN WWlt
	'Monet'	see *H. sanguinea* 'Monet'
	'Mother of Pearl'	ECtt
	'Neptune'	EBee EChP EPfP IPot MBNS SPav SPoG
	Neueste hybrids **new**	LRav
	'Northern Fire'	MBNS
	'Oakington Jewel'	EBla EBrs ELan EMan LRHS
	'Obsidian' **new**	CPen GCai MBnl MSte NRnb SPer SPoG WHlf
	'Painted Lady'	GBuc
	'Palace Passion'	WBrE
*	'Palace Purple Select'	CTri CWib EDAr IBal ITim LAst NJOw SMac SWvt
	parishii NNS 93-384	NWCA
	'Persian Carpet'	CHEx EBee ECha ECtt EMan EMar EPza GKir GSki IBal LRHS MDun MLLN MNFA NBir NGdn NPri SDnm SWvt WBVN WCot WFar
	'Petite Marbled Burgundy'	COtt CStr EBee ECtt EDAr EVFa GBri IBal LAst LTwo MDHE MNFA MSte NDov NLar NPri NSti SUsu SWvt WCot WFar WGwG WLin WWhi
	'Petite Pearl Fairy'	CAbP CBct COtt EBee EHoe EVFa GBin GSki MBri MDHE MSte NGdn NLar SOkh SPla SWvt WAul WCot WFar WGor WHoo WLin WWhi
	'Petite Pink Bouquet'	CBct EBee EChP ECtt EMan EPPr EVFa IBal MBNS MBnl NLar NPro SPla WCot WWeb
	'Petite Ruby Frills' **new**	WWeb
	'Pewter Moon'	EBee ELan EMil EPfP EUJe GKir IHMH LRHS MGos MRav NBir NLon NPri SChu SDnm SSto WBrk WFar WMnd WPnP WTin
	'Pewter Veil'[PBR]	EBee EMan ENot EPfP EUJe LAst NArg NCGa NPri SPer SPoG WFar WPnP WWol
	pilosissima	EBee NBre
§	'Pluie de Feu'	CFir CWCL EBrs EChP ECtt EPfP GBri LBmB MBNS MRav SSto
	'Plum Fairy'	CM&M
	'Plum Pudding'[PBR]	More than 30 suppliers
	'Prince'	CPen EBrs ENot EPfP LSRN MBNS SApp SMac SPoG SRkn SWvt WPtf
	'Prince of Silver'	EBee IBal MBNS
	pringlei	see *H. rubescens*
*	x ***pruhonicana*** Doctor Sitar's hybrids	SRms
	pubescens	EBee GBri
	pulchella	CPBP CSam EBee EDAr GFlt IBal ITim LRHS MBNS MHer MWrn NJOw SRms SUsu
	- JCA 9508	NMen NWoo
	'Purple Petticoats' 🏆H4	CBcs EPfP GCai MDun MLLN NCGa NCob NDlv NGdn NLar NPri SHar SRot WCot
	'Quick Silver'	CMea EBla GSki MAvo MDHE NBir SWvt WFar
	'Quiqui' **new**	SMHy
	'Rachel'	More than 30 suppliers
	Rain of Fire	see *H.* 'Pluie de Feu'
	'Raspberry Ice' **new**	NRnb
	'Raspberry Regal' 🏆H4	CMHG EBee ECtt EMan GAbr MLLN MRav MSph NBir NEgg NSti SWvt WAul WCra WFar WLin WSSM
	'Red Spangles'	EBrs EPfP LRHS MBNS MWrn NBir WCAu
	'Regina' 🏆H4	CAbP CSpe EBee ECtt EPfP GKir IBal LSRN MBNS MBri MDHE NBro NCGa SHar SPoG SWvt WFar WWeb

richardsonii	MNrw
'Robert'	LAst MBNS SChu WCAu
Rosemary Bloom = 'Heuros'PBR	LRHS
§ ***rubescens***	CAbP EBee EDAr EHyt MTho NBro NMen SIng WPer
'Ruby Veil'	EBee GKir SPoG WGor
'Ruffles'	see *H. micrantha* 'Ruffles'
'Sancyl'	SRms
§ ***sanguinea***	CAgr CSBt EDAr LRHS NBir NFor SECG WGHP WPer
- 'Alba' 🏆H4	EMon EVFa WBcn
- 'Geisha's Fan'	EDAr EKen GCai IBal MBnl MTis NGdn SHar SPer SWvt WWol
§ - 'Monet' (v)	EBee EChP EMan ENot MBNS NSti
- var. ***pulchra*** **new**	GKev
- 'Sioux Falls'	EChP EWes MWgw NBre WPnP
§ - 'Snow Storm' (v)	CBrm EBee ELan EPfP IBal MBar MGos MHer MRav SPlb WFar WMnd
- 'Taff's Joy' (v)	EMon EWes
- 'Vivid Crimson'	MWrn
- 'White Cloud' (v)	EBee SRms WPer WPnP
'Sashay' 🏆H4 **new**	GCai
'Saturn'	EBee EChP MBnl NOrc NSti
'Schneewittchen'	EMan EPfP EWTr LRHS MRav
'Scintillation' 🏆H4	ECtt LRHS SRms
'Shamrock' **new**	GCai
'Silver Indiana'PBR	LSRN SPoG
'Silver Lode' **new**	NRnb
'Silver Scrolls'PBR	More than 30 suppliers
'Silver Shadows'	GCai SHar
'Silver Streak'	see x *Heucherella* 'Silver Streak'
'Snow Angel' **new**	CFir
'Snow Storm' (v)	see *H. sanguinea* 'Snow Storm'
'Stormy Seas'	More than 30 suppliers
'Strawberries and Cream' (v)	EHrv WHer
'Strawberry Candy'	CBcs CRez EBee GBBs GCai LSou NCGa NEgg NPri SPer SPoG SRkn WLin
'Strawberry Swirl'	CBcs CHar CMHG EBee EBla ECtt ENot EUJe GMaP LAst MLLN MMil MRav MSte NBir NDov NLar NPri NSti SPoG SWvt WAul WCAu WCot WFar WOVN WWhi
'Swirling Fantasy'	CFai EBee EChP EMan EPfP EShb IBal MBnl WAul
'Titania'	EBee
'Van Gogh'	EBee LSRN MBNS SMac SPoG
'Veil of Passion'PBR	SHar
'Velvet Cloak'	EHan
'Velvet Night'	CKno EBee EBrs EMan EPfP EWsh IBal LBBr LRHS MBNS NBir NRnb SHar SHop WFar WPtf WSan
'Venus'	EWTr MBNS MTis SPur WAul WCot
'Vesuvius'PBR	NRnb SHar
villosa	ECha MRav
- 'Autumn Bride'	EWTr MWrn
- var. ***macrorhiza***	EShb GCal WMnd
- 'Royal Red'	ECha GBuc
'Wendy Hardy'	WCot
'White Marble'	SHar
'Winter Red'	NOrc SPur WCAu
'Yeti'	WPnP
'Zabelliana'	GBri GCal

x *Heucherella* (*Saxifragaceae*)

alba 'Bridget Bloom'	EBla EChP ECha ELan ENot GKir GMaP LGro MRav NOrc NPri SPer SRms WCAu WFar WHoo WMnd
§ - 'Rosalie'	CFee CMHG EBee EBla ECha EMar EWTr LRHS MBNS MBri MRav MSte NBir NBro NDov NJOw NPro SPlb WBrk WFar WMnd WMoo WTin
'Burnished Bronze'	CBct CSBt EBee EBla EMan GCai GKev LSou MBnl MLLN MSte NBro NCGa NEgg NGdn NLar SDnm SHar SPav SPoG SRot SUsu SWvt WFar WGor
'Chocolate Lace'	EBee MBri MLLN NRnb SHar
'Dayglow Pink'PBR	CBct EBee EBla EPPr GAbr GCai GMaP NBro NCGa NEgg SGSe SHar SRkn SRot WFar WGor WMoo WSan
'Heart of Darkness' **new**	NRnb
'Kimono' 🏆H4	CWCL EBee ECtt EKen EMan EPPr GCai GKev GMaP LAst LSou MAvo MBnl MBri MLLN MSte NBro NCGa NEgg NGdn NLar NPri NRnb SBch SHar SRot WCot
'Ninja'PBR	see *Tiarella* 'Ninja'
'Pearl Kohl' (v)	CCol
'Pink Frost'	EBla
'Quicksilver'	CBcs CBct EBee EBla EChP EHrv GAbr GCai GLil GMaP IPot LAst MBnl MSte NDov NGdn NPri SPer SSpi SWvt WCAu WCot WFar WMoo WWhi
'Ring of Fire'	CHar IPot WFar
§ 'Silver Streak'	CMHG EBee EBla EChP EPPr EUJe GAbr GKir IPot LSRN MBnl MSte NBro NCGa NPri SPla SWvt WCot WCra WFar WWpP
'Sunspot' (v)	ENot GCai LBuc LRHS SHar SPoG WCot
tiarelloides 🏆H4	EBee EMan EMil EPfP LRHS NLon SVal WMnd
'Viking Ship'PBR	More than 30 suppliers

Hexastylis see *Asarum*

Hibanobambusa (*Poaceae*)

'Kimmei'	EBee
tranquillans	CMCo EFul EPla MBrN MMoz WJun
- 'Shiroshima' (v) 🏆H4	CAbb CAlb CDoC CFil CPMA EAmu EBee ENBC ENot EPla EPza ERod IFro MBrN MCCP MMoz MWhi MWht NMoo NVic SApp SBig WJun WMul WNor WPGP

Hibbertia (*Dilleniaceae*)

aspera	CPLG CPle CRHN WFar WSHC
§ ***cuneiformis***	CPle ERea MAsh WPat
pedunculata	ECou
procumbens	ITim NLAp WAbe
§ ***scandens*** 🏆H1	CBcs CHEx CHll CRHN ECou ELan ERea GQui WMul
stricta	ECou
tetrandra	see *H. cuneiformis*
* ***venustula***	ECou
volubilis	see *H. scandens*

Hibiscus ✿ (*Malvaceae*)

acetosella 'Red Shield' **new**	CSpe EShb
cannabinus	CSec SIde
coccineus	EShb MSte SSpi
fallax	CHll
huegelii	see *Alyogyne huegelii*
leopoldii	SRms
manihot	see *Abelmoschus manihot*
'Moesiana'	MBri
moscheutos	CArn CFir CHEx MSte

- 'Galaxy'	EShb
panduriformis **new**	CSec
paramutabilis	SMad
radiatus	EShb
rosa-sinensis	EBak LRHS MBri
- 'Casablanca'	MBri
- 'Cooperi' (v) ♀H1	CHal
- 'Holiday'	MBri
- 'Kardinal'	MBri
- 'Koeniger'	MBri
- 'Tivoli'	MBri
sabdariffa	MSal
sinosyriacus	EPfP LRHS
- 'Autumn Surprise'	SBrw
- 'Lilac Queen'	LRHS SBrw WBcn
- 'Ruby Glow'	MGos WPGP
syriacus	SPet WFar WNor
- 'Admiral Dewey' (d)	MGos SPla
- 'Aphrodite'	CPMA EBee ENot MRav
- 'Ardens' (d)	CEnd CSBt EBee EPfP LRHS MGos NLar SPer WBcn
- Blue Bird	see *H. syriacus* 'Oiseau Bleu'
- 'Boule de Feu' (d)	ELan
- 'Bredon Springs' ♀H4	EBee ENot WBcn
- 'Coelestis'	SPer
- 'Diana' ♀H4	CDul EBee EMil ENot EPfP LRHS MBNS MRav SLon WBcn
- 'Dorothy Crane'	CEnd EBee ENot LRHS MGos MRav SBra WWes
- 'Duc de Brabant' (d)	CSBt EMil EPfP LRHS SHBN SPer WBcn
- 'Elegantissimus'	see *H. syriacus* 'Lady Stanley'
- 'Hamabo' ♀H4	CBcs CDul CSBt EBee EMil ENot EPfP LAst LRHS LSRN MBri MGos MRav MSwo MWat NBlu NLar NPri SCoo SHBN SLim SPer SPla SPlb SPoG SWvt WDin WFar
- 'Helene'	ELan ENot LRHS LSRN MBlu MBri MRav WBcn
- 'Jeanne d'Arc' (d)	SLon
§ - 'Lady Stanley' (d)	EBee LRHS SCoo SPer WBcn
- Lavender Chiffon = 'Notwoodone'PBR ♀H4	EBee ELan ENot EPfP LRHS MGos MRav NPri SPer SPoG
- 'Lenny' ♀H4	EBee ENot MGos MRav
- 'Leopoldii'	NBlu
- 'Marina'	CRez EPfP
- 'Meehanii' misapplied	see *H. syriacus* 'Purpureus Variegatus'
§ - 'Meehanii' (v) ♀H4	CDul CEnd CSBt ENot EPfP LRHS MAsh MBri MGos SCoo SLim SPer SPla SPoG SSta WBcn
- 'Monstrosus'	WBcn
§ - 'Oiseau Bleu' ♀H4	More than 30 suppliers
- Pink Giant = 'Flogi'	CBcs CDul CMHG EBee ELan EPfP LRHS MBri MGos NBlu SLon SPer WDin
- 'Purpureus Plenus' (d)	SLim
- 'Purpureus Variegatus' (v)	CSBt SLim SPoG WBcn
- 'Red Heart' ♀H4	CEnd CSBt EBee ELan ENot EPfP LAst LRHS MAsh MBNS MBri MCCP NBlu NLar NPri SBra SPer SPla SPoG SRms SWvt WDin
- 'Rosalbane'	MBri
- 'Roseus Plenus' (d)	SLim WBcn WDin
- Russian Violet = 'Floru'	CEnd COtt ELan EMil EPfP LRHS MBri MGos MRav
- 'Sanchon Yo' **new**	ENot
- 'Speciosus'	ENot MRav SLon SPer
- 'Stadt Erlenbach'	MGos
- 'Totus Albus'	CSBt EMil NBlu SPoG
- 'Variegatus'	see *H. syriacus* 'Purpureus Variegatus'
- White Chiffon = 'Notwoodtwo'PBR ♀H4	EBee ELan ENot EPfP LRHS LSRN MGos MRav SPer SPoG
- 'William R. Smith' ♀H4	ELan LAst LRHS MRav MSwo SHBN SLon SPer SSta WDin WWes
- 'Woodbridge' ♀H4	CBcs CEnd CSBt CTri EBee ELan EMil ENot EPfP LAst LRHS MAsh MBri MGos MRav MSwo NBlu NEgg NPri SHBN SLim SPer SPla SPlb SPoG SSpi SWvt WCot WDin WFar
trionum	CSpe SBch WKif
- 'Sunny Day'	ELan

hickory, shagbark see *Carya ovata*

Hieracium (*Asteraceae*)

aurantiacum	see *Pilosella aurantiaca*
bombycinum	see *H. mixtum*
britannicum **new**	WOut
brunneocroceum	see *Pilosella aurantiaca* subsp. *carpathicola*
§ ***glaucum***	WEas
§ ***lanatum***	CSpe EHol MDKP NBir SUsu WEas WRos
maculatum	see *H. spilophaeum*
§ ***mixtum***	GKev
pilosella	see *Pilosella officinarum*
praecox	see *H. glaucum*
§ ***spilophaeum***	EBee EGra EHoe EMag EMar GGar LRHS NBid NPer NWCA WMoo WPer WRos
- 'Leopard' (v)	EMan NJOw SGar SMar WWeb
umbellatum	WOut
villosum	CSpe EBee EHoe LRHS MDun NBro NPri WCot WHer WRos
waldsteinii	MDKP
welwitschii	see *H. lanatum*

Hierochloe (*Poaceae*)

occidentalis	CBig
odorata	CBig ELau EMan EMon EPPr GAbr GFor GPoy MGol SMar SSvw WPtf WSSM
redolens	GAbr

Hieronymiella (*Amaryllidaceae*)

aurea RCB/Arg M-4 **new**	WCot

Himalayacalamus (*Poaceae*)

asper	CFil EPla ERod WPGP
§ ***falconeri***	CBrm CFil EBee EFul EPfP EPla MAsh MMoz SDix SDys WPGP
§ - 'Damarapa'	CFil EPla MMoz WDyG WJun
§ ***hookerianus***	CAbb CFil EPla WJun
porcatus	CFil EBee WPGP

x *Hippeasprekelia* (*Amaryllidaceae*)

'Red Beauty' **new**	CFwr

Hippeastrum ✿ (*Amaryllidaceae*)

BC&W 5154	CStu
x ***acramannii***	CMon GCal
advenum	see *Rhodophiala advena*
'Apple Blossom'	LAma MBri SGar
aulicum **new**	CMon
'Beautiful Lady'	LAma
'Bestseller' ♀H1	LAma
bifidum	see *Rhodophiala bifida*
'Blossom Peacock' (d) **new**	EBrs
'Calimero' **new**	EBrs
'Christmas Gift'	EBrs LRHS

'Dutch Belle'	LAma
'Fairy Tale'	MBri
'Fantastica'	LAma
'Floris Hekker' **new**	EBrs
'Hercules'	MBri
'Inca'	LAma
'Jewel' (d)	EBrs LRHS MBri
'Jungle Star' **new**	EBrs
'Lady Jane'	MBri
'Lemon Lime'	EBrs LAma LRHS
'Lima'	LAma
'Ludwig's Goliath'	LAma
'Mary Lou' (d)	EBrs LAma
papilio ♀H1	CMon LAma
* - 'Butterfly'	LRHS
'Papillon'	LAma
pardinum CDPR 3001 **new**	CFil
'Pasadena'	LRHS
'Philadelphia' (d) **new**	EBrs
'Picotee'	LAma LRHS
puniceum **new**	CMon
reticulatum	CMon
var. ***striatifolium*** **new**	
rutilum var. ***fulgidum*** **new**	CMon
* 'San Antonio Rose'	WCot
stylosum	CMon
'Toughie'	CDes EMan MSph WCot
vittatum **new**	CBgR CMon
'White Dazzler'	LAma
'Yellow Pioneer'	LAma

Hippocrepis (*Papilionaceae*)

§ ***comosa***	CRWN SSpi XPep
§ ***emerus***	CMHG CPLG CTri ELan EPfP ERea LAst MGos MMil NLar STre WHCG WSHC XPep

Hippolytia (*Asteraceae*)

§ ***herderi***	EMan EOHP EShb

Hippophae (*Elaeagnaceae*)

rhamnoides ♀H4	CArn CBcs CCVT CDul CLnd CRWN CSBt CTri EBee ELan ENot EPfP GIBF GKir GPoy LBuc MBar MBlu MCoo MRav NWea SPer SPlb SPoG WDin WFar WHCG WMou XPep
- 'Askola' (f)	MGos
- 'Frugna' (f) **new**	CAgr
- 'Hergo' (f)	CAgr
- 'Hikal Dafo' (m) **new**	CAgr
- 'Juliet' (f) **new**	CAgr
- 'Leikora' (f)	CAgr ELan MBlu MGos SPer
- 'Pollmix' (m)	ELan MBlu MGos SPer
- 'Romeo' (m) **new**	CAgr
salicifolia	CAgr LEdu
- GWJ 9221	WCru

Hippuris (*Hippuridaceae*)

vulgaris	CBen EHon EMFW IHMH NArg NPer WFar WWpP

Hiptage (*Malpighiaceae*)

benghalensis **new**	CPLN

Hirpicium (*Asteraceae*)

armerioides	NWCA

Histiopteris (*Dennstaedtiaceae*)

incisa	CFil WRic

Hoheria ✿ (*Malvaceae*)

§ ***angustifolia***	CFil CTho ECou EPfP SBrw SSpi
'Borde Hill'	CPMA EPfP SBrw SPer SSpi SSta WHCG
glabrata	CBcs CFil ECou EPfP GGar IMGH NPal SBrw WPGP
- 'Silver Stars'	EPfP
'Glory of Amlwch' ♀H3	CFil CPMA CSam CTho EPfP GCal LRHS SBrw SSpi WCru WKif WPGP
'Hill House'	CHll
§ ***lyallii*** ♀H4	CBcs CDoC CPLG ECou ELan EPfP IDee LSRN SBrw SHBN SPer SSpi SSta WBor WDin
microphylla	see *H. angustifolia*
populnea	CBcs CBot CPle
- 'Alba Variegata' (v)	CBcs CDoC CTrC SMad
- 'Moonlight'	SPoG
- 'Osbornei' **new**	SBrw
- 'Sunshine' (v)	SMur
'Purple Delta' **new**	ECou
sexstylosa	CAbb CBot CDoC CDul CHEx CHid CMHG CTri ELan EPfP IMGH ISea MDun SBrw SLon SPer SSta SWvt WGer
- 'Pendula'	CBcs WDin
- 'Stardust' ♀H4	CAbP CDul CEnd CFil CMCN CPLG CPMA CTho ELan EPfP LRHS MAsh MBri MGos NLar NPal SBrw SMad SMur SPer SPoG SReu SSpi WFar WPGP WPat WSHC
* - 'Starshine'	ERea
* - 'Sunburst' **new**	NEgg

Holboellia (*Lardizabalaceae*)

angustifolia **new**	NLar
coriacea	CBcs CBot CHEx CHll CPLN CRHN CRez CSam CTbh EPfP LRHS MDun MGos SAPC SArc SBra SHGC SPer SSta WCFE WCot WCru
fargesii	CPLN
- DJHC 506	WCru
grandiflora	CPLN
- B&SWJ 8223	WCru
latifolia	CBrm CHEx COtt CPLN CRHN CSBt CSam CTbh CTri EPfP ERea LRHS SAPC SArc SBra SEND SLim SPer SPoG WFar
- HWJK 2014	WCru
- SF 95134	ISea

Holcus (*Poaceae*)

mollis 'Albovariegatus' (v)	More than 30 suppliers
- 'White Fog' (v)	CChe CPen EBee EHul ENot EUJe MBlu MBri SApp SGSe WFar

Holmskioldia (*Verbenaceae*)

sanguinea **new**	EShb

Holodiscus (*Rosaceae*)

discolor	CAgr CDul CFil CPLG CPle EBee ELan EWes GKir GQui LRHS MBlu MBri MRav MTis NBlu NSti SBrw SHBN SLon SMad SPer SPlb SPoG SSpi SSta WBVN WDin WHCG WPat
- var. ***ariifolius***	EPfP
- var. ***discolor***	CBcs
dumosus	NLar WPGP WPat

Homalocladium (*Polygonaceae*)

§ ***platycladum***	CHal CPle LEdu

Homalomena (*Araceae*)

pendula **new**	EAmu

Homeria (*Iridaceae*)

breyniana	see *H. collina*
- var. ***aurantiaca***	see *H. flaccida*
§ ***collina***	ERos
§ ***flaccida***	LAma
ochroleuca	CMon LAma

Homoglossum see *Gladiolus*

Hordeum (*Poaceae*)

brachyantherum	CBig
chilense	EBee
jubatum	CBig CHrt CKno CWCL EChP EGoo EHoe EKen EPla EPza EUJe EWes GFlt GKev LIck LRHS MAvo MBnl NChi NDov NGdn SIng SPoG SUsu WRos WWye
- from Ussuri **new**	GIBF

Horkelia (*Rosaceae*)

fusca subsp. ***capitata***	EBee

Horkeliella (*Rosaceae*)

purpurascens	EBee
- NNS 98-323	WCot

Horminum (*Lamiaceae*)

pyrenaicum	CMHG EBee ELan EMan GAbr NJOw SBla SRms WBVN WFar WMoo WPer WTin
- pale blue	MAvo MDKP MSte

horseradish see *Armoracia rusticana*

Hosta ✿ (*Hostaceae*)

AGSJ 302	CDes
'A Many-Splendored Thing' **new**	IBal
'Abba Dabba Do' (v)	CBdn EBee EGol EMic EPGN LRHS NMyG SApp
'Abby' (v)	CBdn EGol EMic EPGN IBal NMyG SApp WWye
'Abiqua Ariel'	CBdn EMic SApp
'Abiqua Blue Crinkles'	CBdn EMic NBir
'Abiqua Drinking Gourd'	CBdn EGol EMic EPGN GBin GKir GSki IBal LRHS MHom NMyG SApp
'Abiqua Ground Cover'	EGol
'Abiqua Moonbeam' (v)	CBdn CRez CWin EMic EPGN IBal MSwo NMyG SApp
'Abiqua Recluse'	EGol LRHS SApp
'Abiqua Trumpet'	CBdn EGol IBal NGdn NMyG SApp
'Abiqua Zodiac'	CBdn
aequinoctiiantha	EGol
albomarginata	see *H. sieboldii* 'Paxton's Original'
§ 'Albomarginata' (*fortunei*) (v)	CBcs CBdn CHar EGol EMic GKir MBar MNrw NBir NMyG SGSe SHBN SPer SPoG SWvt
'Alex Summers'	EBee IBal
'Allan P. McConnell' (v)	CBdn EGol EMic EPGN GCra LBuc WHal WIvy
'Allegan Fog' (v)	EGol IBal
'Alligator Shoes' (v)	EGol IBal
'Alpine Aire'	EMic
'Alvatine Taylor' (v)	CBdn EGol
'Amanuma'	EGol EMic IBal MHom
'Amber Maiden' (v)	EGol
'Amber Tiara'	EMic
'American Dream' (v)	CBdn EGol EMic EPGN IBal NMyG
'American Halo' **new**	SMrm
'American Sweetheart' **new**	IBal
'Amy Elizabeth' (v)	CBdn EGol EMic IBal
'Angel Feathers' (v)	EGol
'Ann Kulpa' (v)	CBdn EMic EPGN IBal
'Anne' (v)	CBdn EGol IBal
'Anne Arett' (*sieboldii*) (v)	EPGN
'Antioch' (*fortunei*) (v)	CBdn EGol EMic GAbr IBal IHMH MIDC MRav MSte NMyG NRnb WFar WWye
'Aoki' (*fortunei*)	EMic EPGN
'Aphrodite' (*plantaginea*) (d)	CFir CWin EBee EBrs EGol EMic EPGN IBal MBNS MBri MHom MSte NCGa NCob NLar SApp SPoG WCot
'Apple Court' **new**	SApp
'Apple Green'	EMic IBal
'Apple Pie' **new**	SApp
'Aqua Velva'	EGol LRHS
'Archangel'	EGol
'Argentea Variegata' (*undulata*)	see *H. undulata* var. *undulata*
'Aristocrat' (Tardiana Group) (v)	CBdn EGol EPGN IBal NMyG SApp
'Aspen Gold' (*tokudama* hybrid) **new**	SApp
'August Beauty'	CBdn EMic
'August Moon'	More than 30 suppliers
aureafolia	see *H.* 'Starker Yellow Leaf'
'Aureoalba' (*fortunei*)	see *H.* 'Spinners'
'Aureomaculata' (*fortunei*)	see *H. fortunei* var. *albopicta*
* 'Aureomarginata' ambig. (v)	CPrp CSBt EGra GAbr GKir NEgg
§ 'Aureomarginata' (*montana*) (v)	CBdn CBos CSBt EGol EHoe ELan EMic EPGN EWsh GCal GMaP IBal MBri NEgg NLar NMyG SGSe SPla SSpi SUsu WBVN WFar WTin WWpP
§ 'Aureomarginata' (*ventricosa*) (v) ♀H4	CBdn CBro EBrs ECha EGol EMic EPfP IBal LRHS MBri MIDC MWgw NGdn NVic SApp WBVN WFar WTin WWye
'Aureostriata' (*tardiva*)	see *H.* 'Inaho'
'Aurora Borealis' (*sieboldiana*) (v)	EGol EPGN
'Austin Dickinson' (v)	EGol EMic IBal
'Azure Snow'	CBdn EGol LRHS WBcn
'Babbling Brook'	EGol
'Baby Bunting'	CBdn EGol EMic EPGN IBal MBNS MIDC NBro NLar NMyG NPro
'Ballerina'	EGol
'Banana Boat' (v)	EGol IBal
'Banyai's Dancing Girl'	EGol EMic
'Barbara Ann' (v)	CBdn EMic EPGN MBri
'Barbara White'	EGol
'Bea's Colossus'	SApp
'Beauty Substance'	CBdn EGol EMic EPGN EVFa NMyG
bella	see *H. fortunei* var. *obscura*
'Bennie McRae'	EGol
'Betcher's Blue'	EGol
'Betsy King'	EBee EGol MRav NMyG
'Bette Davis Eyes'	EGol
'Betty'	EGol
'Bianca' **new**	SApp
'Big Boy' (*montana*)	EGol GKir
'Big Daddy' (*sieboldiana* hybrid) (v)	More than 30 suppliers
'Big Mama'	EBee EGol EUJe IBal LRHS MBNS NLar
'Bigfoot'	EGol
'Bill Brinka' (v)	EGol
'Bill Dress's Blue' **new**	IBal
'Birchwood Blue'	EGol

	'Birchwood Elegance'	CBdn SApp
§	'Birchwood Parky's Gold'	CBdn CMHG EGol EMic EPGN EPfP GKir GMaP IHMH LRHS MBNS MIDC NCob NOak SApp SHBN SMrm WWye
	'Birchwood Ruffled Queen'	EGol EMic
	'Bitsy Gold'	EGol IBal
	'Bitsy Green'	EGol
	'Black Beauty'	EGol EPGN
	'Black Hills'	CBdn EBee EGol IBal LRHS NMyG
	'Blackfoot' **new**	EGol
	'Blaue Venus'	EGol
§	'Blonde Elf'	EGol EMic EPGN IBal MBNS NEgg NGdn NMyG SApp
	'Blue Angel' misapplied	see *H. sieboldiana* var. *elegans*
	'Blue Angel' (*sieboldiana*) ♀H4	More than 30 suppliers
	'Blue Arrow'	CBdn EGol EPGN SApp
	'Blue Belle'(Tardiana Group)	CBdn EGol EMic MSte NGdn NLar NPro WHoo WTin
	'Blue Blazes'	LRHS
	'Blue Blush'(Tardiana Group)	CBdn EGol EPGN WTMC
	'Blue Boy'	CBdn EGol EMic EWes NMyG
	'Blue Cadet'	CBcs CBdn CTbh EGol EMic GKir GSki IBal IHMH LAst LPBA MBar NBir NLar NMyG NOak NRnb SApp SBod SGSe WCAu WCra WFar WMnd WWpP
	'Blue Canoe' **new**	IBal SApp
	'Blue Chip' **new**	CBdn
	'Blue Cup' (*sieboldiana*)	CBdn MRav
	'Blue Danube' (Tardiana Group)	CBdn EGol EMic MHom
	'Blue Diamond'(Tardiana Group)	CBdn CMHG CWin EGol EMic EPGN WFar WPop
	'Blue Dimples'	CBdn CWin EGol IBal IPot LRHS MBNS
	'Blue Edger'	CBdn NBir
	'Blue Heart' (*sieboldiana*)	EMic LPio
	'Blue Ice' (Tardiana Group)	CBdn EGol EPGN IBal
	'Blue Impression'	EMic
	'Blue Jay' (Tardiana Group)	CBdn EGol
	'Blue Lady'	CBdn EMic
	'Blue Mammoth' (*sieboldiana*)	CBdn EGol EMic EPGN LRHS
	'Blue Moon'(Tardiana Group)	CBdn EGol EPGN EPfP ERos IPot LPBA LPhx MBNS MHom MIDC NMyG WAul
	'Blue Mouse Ears' **new**	CBdn EGol EMic IBal
	'Blue Seer' (*sieboldiana*)	CBdn EGol
	'Blue Shadows' (*tokudama*) (v)	CBdn CWin EPGN GFlt IBal LPio LRHS MIDC MWgw NMyG SApp SHBN
	'Blue Skies' (Tardiana Group)	CBdn EGol MHom SApp
§	'Blue Umbrellas' (*sieboldiana* hybrid)	CBdn EBrs EGol EHan ELan EMic EPGN EPfP GSki IBal IPot LRHS MBri MHom NGdn NLar NMyG
	'Blue Velvet'	CBdn
	'Blue Vision'	EPGN LRHS
	'Blue Wedgwood' (Tardiana Group)	CBdn CBro CPrp EBee EGol ELan EMic ENot GKir IBal LAst LPBA MIDC NMyG SApp SChu SPla SPoG WCFE WHil WTMC WWpP
	'Blütenwunder' **new**	SApp
	'Bobbie Sue' (v) **new**	EGol
	'Bold Edger' (v)	CBdn EGol EPGN
	'Bold Ribbons' (v)	CBdn EGol EMic GAbr WTin
	'Bold Ruffles' (*sieboldiana*)	EGol LRHS SApp
	'Bonanza'	EMic
	'Border Bandit' (v)	EGol
	'Borsch 1'	CBdn
	'Borwick Beauty' (*sieboldiana*) (v)	CBdn EMic NGdn NLar NMyG
	'Bountiful'	EGol EMic
	'Bouquet'	EGol
	'Brenda's Beauty' (v) **new**	EGol
	'Bressingham Blue'	CBdn CHVG CPrp CWin EBee EBrs ECtt EGol IBal LRHS MIDC MRav NMyG SPoG SWvt WCAu WFar WMnd WTMC WWpP
	'Brigadier'	EGol
	'Bright Glow' (Tardiana Group)	EGol
	'Bright Lights' (*tokudama*) (v)	CBdn CRez CWin EGol EMic EPGN GBBs IBal LAst NMyG WTMC WWye
	'Brim Cup' (v)	CBdn CWin EGol EMic EPGN EWTr GKir IBal MBNS MBri MIDC NBro NGdn NMyG NOrc NRnb SApp
	'Brooke'	EGol EMic NMyG
	'Brother Ronald' (Tardiana Group)	CBdn EGol EMic LRHS SApp
	'Bruce's Blue'	EGol GSki
	'Buckshaw Blue'	CBdn EGol EPGN ETow MDKP NBir NGdn NPro SSpi WBcn WTMC
	'Bunchoko' **new**	IBal
	'Butter Rim' (*sieboldii*) (v)	EGol
	'Cadillac' (v)	CBdn MIDC
	'Caliban' **new**	SApp
I	'Calypso' (v)	CBdn EGol EMic EPGN
	'Camelot' (Tardiana Group)	CBdn EGol EMic LRHS NGdn
	'Canadian Blue'	WTMC
	'Candy Hearts'	CBdn CMHG CSam EGol EMic EPGN MHom WTin
	capitata B&SWJ 588	WCru
	- MSF 850	CFil
	'Captain Kirk' (v) **new**	CBdn IBal NMyG
	caput-avis	see *H. kikutii* var. *caput-avis*
	'Carnival' (v)	CBdn EGol EMic EPGN IBal MIDC NEgg
	'Carol' (*fortunei*) (v)	CBdn CWin EBee EGol EMic EWsh IBal LAst MBNS MSte NEgg NMyG SApp WHal
	'Carolina Blue' **new**	IBal
	'Carousel' (v)	EGol
	'Carrie Ann' (v)	see *H.* 'Carrie'
§	'Carrie' (*sieboldii*) (v)	EGol
	'Cascades' (v)	CBdn EGol EMic EPGN
	'Cat's Eyes' (v) **new**	CBdn EGol EMic EPGN IBal
	'Celebration' (v)	EGol ELan EMic EPGN LRHS MDKP
	'Center of Attention' **new**	IBal
	'Challenger'	EMic
	'Change of Tradition' (*lancifolia*) (v)	CBdn EMic
	'Chantilly Lace' (v)	CBdn EGol EMic IBal NMyG SApp WTin
	'Chartreuse Waves'	EGol
	'Chartreuse Wiggles' (*sieboldii*)	EPGN LRHS
	'Cheatin Heart'	EGol IBal
	'Chelsea Babe' (*fortunei*) (v)	EGol
	'Chelsea Ore' (*plantaginea* hybrid) (v)	CHad
	'Cherish' **new**	EMic IBal
	'Cherry Berry' (v)	CBdn CMHG CPen CRez CWin EBee EGol EMic EPGN EVFa IBal MBNS MIDC MWgw NBro NEgg

	NGdn NMyG NPro NRnb SApp SVil WAul WBor
'Cherub' (v)	CBdn EGol
* 'China' (*plantaginea*)	EMic
'Chinese Sunrise' (v)	CBdn EChP EGol EMic EPGN IPot MBNS MHom NMyG
'Chiquita'	EGol
§ 'Chôkô Nishiki' (*montana*) (v)	CBdn CFir EGol EMic EPGN IBal IPot MIDC NGdn SApp SChu
'Christmas Candy' **new**	EPGN IBal NCob
'Christmas Tree' (v)	CBdn CM&M CWin EGol EMic EPGN GBri IBal IPot LRHS MIDC NBPC NEgg NGdn NMyG NRnb SApp SVil WTMC WWye
'Cinnamon Sticks' **new**	IBal
'Citation' (v)	EGol LRHS
'City Lights'	EGol NEgg
clausa var. ***normalis***	CBdn EGol GQui LRHS NBir NGdn NLar NMyG
'Cody' **new**	IBal
'Collector's Choice'	EGol
'Color Glory' (v)	CWin EChP EGol EPGN GAbr GBin GFlt IBal LAst NCGa NEgg NGdn NLar NMyG SApp SPer WAul WBcn WTMC
'Colossal'	EGol EMic
'Columbus Circle' (v)	CBdn EGol
'Coquette' (v)	CBdn EGol EMic
'Cotillion' (v)	CBdn EGol SApp
'County Park'	CBdn EGol EMic
'Cracker Crumbs' **new**	CBdn IBal
'Craig's Temptation'	CBdn
'Cream Cheese' (v)	EGol
'Cream Delight' (*undulata*)	see *H. undulata* var. *undulata*
'Cream Edge'	see *H.* 'Fisher Cream Edge'
'Crepe Soul' (v) **new**	IBal
'Crepe Suzette' (v)	CBdn EGol EPGN LRHS
'Crested Reef'	CBdn EGol EMic NMyG
'Crested Surf' (v)	EGol EMic IBal
§ ***crispula*** (v) ♀H4	CBdn CHad EGol EHon EMic LGro MBar MHom NChi NCob NLon NMyG SChu SHBN WWpP
'Crown Jewel' (v)	EPGN
'Crown Prince' (v)	CBdn EGol EPGN
§ 'Crowned Imperial' (*fortunei*) (v)	CBdn EMic
'Crusader' (v)	CBdn EGol EMic EPGN IBal LRHS NMyG SApp WFar
'Cupboard Love' **new**	SApp
'Cupid's Dart' (v)	EGol
'Curlew' (Tardiana Group)	CBdn EGol
'Dark Star' (v)	CBdn EGol EPGN SApp
'Dartmoor Forest'	CBdn
'Darwin's Standard' (v)	CBdn
'Dawn'	CBdn EGol IBal
'Daybreak'	CBdn CWin EGol EMic EPGN LAst LRHS MBri NBro SApp SVil WTMC WWye
'Day's End' (v)	EGol
'Deane's Dream' **new**	IBal
decorata	CBdn EGol EMic EMil MBar
'Deep Blue Sea' **new**	IBal
'Delia' (v)	EPGN
'Delta Dawn'	IBal
'Devon Blue' (Tardiana Group)	CBdn CPrp EGol
'Devon Desire' (*montana*)	CBdn
'Devon Discovery'	CBdn
'Devon Giant'	CBdn
'Devon Gold'	CBdn
'Devon Green'	CBdn EHan EPGN GBri IBal IPot MHom MIDC MLLN MSte NBro NEgg NGdn NLar NMyG NPro SApp WAul WFar
'Devon Hills'	CBdn
'Devon Mist'	CBdn
'Devon Tor'	CBdn
'Dew Drop' (v)	CAby CBdn EGol EMic IBal NMyG SGSe
'Diamond Tiara' (v)	CBdn EGol EMic EPGN GAbr IBal LAst LRHS MIDC NMyG SChu
'Diana Remembered'	CBdn EMic EPGN IBal WBor
'Dick Ward'	IBal
'Domaine de Courson'	CBdn EMic GBin WFar
'Don Stevens' (v)	CBdn EGol
'Donahue Piecrust'	CBdn EGol
'Dorset Blue' (Tardiana Group)	CBdn EGol EPGN GSki LRHS
'Dorset Charm' (Tardiana Group)	CBdn EGol
'Dorset Flair' (Tardiana Group)	EGol EMic
'Doubloons'	EGol
'Dream Queen' (v) **new**	NMyG
'Dream Weaver' (v)	EBee EGol EMic GFlt IBal NMyG
'Drummer Boy'	CBdn EGol EMic
'Duchess' (*nakaiana*) (v)	EGol
'DuPage Delight' (*sieboldiana*) (v)	CBdn EGol IBal NGdn NLar
'Dust Devil' (*fortunei*) (v)	EGol IBal
'Edge of Night'	CBdn EGol
'Edwin Bibby'	EPGN
'El Capitan' (v)	CBdn EGol EMic EPGN LRHS
'El Niño' (Tardiana Group) (v)	CBdn CWin EBee IBal MIDC MNrw NBro
§ ***elata***	EBee EGol EGra EMic SApp
'Elatior' (*nigrescens*)	CBdn EMic
'Eldorado'	see *H.* 'Frances Williams'
'Eleanor Lachman' (v)	EGol EMic IBal
'Electrum Stater' (v)	CBdn
'Elegans'	see *H. sieboldiana* var. *elegans*
'Elfin Power' (*sieboldii*) (v)	EGol
'Elisabeth'	CBdn NMyG
'Elizabeth Campbell' (*fortunei*) (v)	CBdn EGol EMic MSte SSpi
'Ellen'	EMic
'Ellerbroek' (*fortunei*) (v)	EGol EMic GSki
'Elsley Runner'	EGol
'Elvis Lives'	CBdn EGol EKen GBin IBal IPot LAst LRHS MCCP NGdn NMyG NPro
'Embroidery' (v)	MIDC
'Emerald Carpet'	EGol
'Emerald Necklace' (v)	EGol
'Emerald Skies'	EGol
'Emerald Tiara' (v)	CBdn EGol EMic EPGN GFlt LRHS MIDC NMyG SVil WTin
'Emeralds and Rubies'	EGol EMic
'Emily Dickinson' (v)	CBdn EBee EGol IBal LRHS NEgg SApp
'Eric Smith' (Tardiana Group)	CBdn EGol EMic EPGN LPhx MHom NMyG SChu WFar
'Eternal Flame' **new**	IBal
'Evelyn McCafferty' (*tokudama* hybrid)	EGol
'Evening Magic' (v)	EGol
'Eventide' (v)	EGol
'Everlasting Love' (v)	EGol
'Excitation'	CBdn EGol LPio
'Fair Maiden' (v)	CBdn EGol EPGN IBal
'Fall Bouquet' (*longipes* var. *hypoglauca*)	EGol
'Fall Emerald'	CBdn EMic
'Falling Waters' (v)	EGol IBal
'Fan Dance' (v)	EGol

	Name	Suppliers
	'Fantabulous' (v) **new**	EPGN IBal
	'Fantastic' (*sieboldiana* hybrid)	EGol LRHS
	'Fascination' (v)	EPGN
	'Fatal Attraction' **new**	IBal
	'Feather Boa'	EGol EPGN IBal
	'Fenman's Fascination'	EMic
	'Fire and Ice' (v)	More than 30 suppliers
	'Fire Island' **new**	CBdn
§	'Fisher Cream Edge' (*fortunei*) (v)	CBdn
	'Five O'Clock Shadow' (v) **new**	IBal
	'Flame Stitch' (*ventricosa*) (v)	EGol EMic
	'Floradora'	CBdn EGol EMic IBal NMyG
	'Flower Power'	CBdn EGol
	fluctuans	GBBs GIBF
	'Fond Hope'	CBdn
	'Fool's Gold' (*fortunei*)	CBdn EMic
	'Forest Shadows'	EMic IBal
	'Formal Attire' (*sieboldiana* hybrid) (v)	CBdn EGol EMic IBal LRHS
	'Forncett Frances' (v)	EGol
	'Fortis'	see *H. undulata* var. *erromena*
	fortunei	CBdn CM&M EGol EMic IBal MIDC NLon SChu SPer WCAu WEas WFar WPnP WWye
§	- var. ***albopicta*** 🏆H4	More than 30 suppliers
	- - f. ***aurea*** 🏆H4	CBdn CHad CMHG ECha EGol EHoe ELan EPla GKir LRHS MBar NLar NMyG SChu SPer SPla SRms WFar WWeb
	- - - dwarf	EMic
§	- var. ***aureomarginata*** 🏆H4	More than 30 suppliers
	- var. ***gigantea***	see *H. montana*
§	- var. ***hyacinthina*** 🏆H4	CBdn EGol EMic EPfP GCal LRHS MBar MRav NMyG NOrc NRnb SSpi WFar WPtf WWeb
	- - variegated	see *H.* 'Crowned Imperial'
§	- var. ***obscura***	CBdn ECho EGol EMic WLin
	- var. ***rugosa***	EBee EMic
	'Fourth of July'	EGol
	'Fragrant Blue'	CBdn EBee EGol EMic GBBs IBal LRHS NMyG SMac SPoG
	'Fragrant Bouquet' (v)	CBdn CMHG CWin EBee EGol EMic EPGN IBal LRHS MBri NCGa NEgg NGdn NLar NMyG SChu SVil WPtf
	'Fragrant Dream'	CBdn EMic IBal
	'Fragrant Gold'	EGol
	'Fran Godfrey' **new**	EPGN
	'Francee' (*fortunei*) (v) 🏆H4	More than 30 suppliers
§	'Frances Williams' (*sieboldiana*) (v) 🏆H4	More than 30 suppliers
	'Frances Williams Improved' (*sieboldiana*) (v)	EBee EGol EPfP MWat NEgg
	'Frances Williams' seedlings	NSti
	'Freising' (*fortunei*)	EBee
	'Fresh' (v)	EGol EPGN SApp
	'Fried Bananas'	CBdn EGol EMic
	'Fried Green Tomatoes'	CBdn EGol EMic EPGN LRHS MIDC NLar NMyG NOrc
	'Fringe Benefit' (v)	CWin EGol EMic GAbr GKir SApp
	'Frosted Jade' (v)	CBdn EGol EPGN LRHS NMyG SApp WTin
	'Fulda'	EGol
	'Gaiety' (v)	EGol EPGN
	'Gaijin' (v)	CBdn SApp
	'Gala' (*tardiflora*) (v)	CBdn EPGN NMyG
	'Galaxy' **new**	IBal
	'Gay Blade' (v)	EGol SApp
	'Gay Feather' (v)	IBal LAst NMyG SApp SPoG
	'Gay Search' (v)	EPGN
	'Geisha' (v)	CBdn EGol EPGN GBin IBal MBNS MCCP NMyG NPro WBcn WHal
	'Gene's Joy'	EPGN
	'Ghost Spirit' **new**	IBal
	'Gigantea' (*sieboldiana*)	see *H. elata*
	'Gilt By Association' **new**	IBal
	'Gilt Edge' (*sieboldiana*) (v)	EMic NMyG
	'Ginko Craig' (v)	More than 30 suppliers
	glauca	see *H. sieboldiana* var. *elegans*
	'Glockenspiel'	CBdn EGol
I	'Gloriosa' (*fortunei*) (v)	EGol WFar
	'Glory'	CBdn EGol
	'Goddess of Athena' (*decorata*) (v)	EGol
	'Gold Drop' (*venusta* hybrid)	CBdn ECho EGol EMic IBal LPhx LRHS
	'Gold Edger'	More than 30 suppliers
§	'Gold Haze' (*fortunei*)	CBdn EGol EMic EPGN MHom NBir NCGa NMyG
	'Gold Leaf' (*fortunei*)	EGol
	'Gold Regal'	CBdn CWin EGol EMic EPGN MHom MSte NMyG SMrm WFar WMnd WWpP WWye
	'Gold Rush'[PBR]	CBdn ENot EPGN NMyG
*	'Gold Splash'	WHoo
	'Gold Standard' (*fortunei*) (v)	More than 30 suppliers
	'Goldbrook' (v)	EGol WBcn WTin
	'Goldbrook Genie'	EGol
	'Goldbrook Ghost' (v)	EGol
	'Goldbrook Girl'	EGol
	'Goldbrook Glamour' (v)	EGol
	'Goldbrook Glimmer' (Tardiana Group) (v)	EGol
	'Goldbrook Gold'	EGol
	'Goldbrook Grace'	EGol
	'Goldbrook Gratis' (v)	EGol
	'Goldbrook Grayling'	EGol
	'Goldbrook Grebe'	EGol
	'Golden Age'	see *H.* 'Gold Haze'
	'Golden Anniversary'	CBdn EBee WTMC
	'Golden Ben'	ITim
	'Golden Bullion' (*tokudama*)	CBdn EGol GBri LRHS
	'Golden Decade'	EGol
	'Golden Fascination'	EGol
	'Golden Friendship'	EGol
	'Golden Guernsey' (v)	EMic
	'Golden Isle'	EGol
	'Golden Medallion' (*tokudama*)	CBdn CMHG EGol ELan GKir IBal MBNS NEgg NGdn NMyG WFar WPop
	'Golden Nakaiana'	see *H.* 'Birchwood Parky's Gold'
	'Golden' (*nakaiana*)	see *H.* 'Birchwood Parky's Gold'
	'Golden Oriole'	CBdn
	'Golden Prayers'	EHan WFar
	'Golden Prayers' (*tokudama*)	CBdn ECtt EGol ELan EPGN ERos GSki LPhx LRHS MIDC MRav NBir NBro NGdn NMyG NOrc SChu SPla
	'Golden Scepter'	CBdn CMHG EGol EMic EPGN NMyG SApp WFar
	'Golden Sculpture' (*sieboldiana*)	CBdn EGol LRHS WWye
	'Golden Spider'	EGol EMic
	'Golden Sunburst' (*sieboldiana*)	CBdn CPrp EGol EGra ELan EMic GSki IBal NBid NEgg NGdn WFar
	'Golden Tiara' (v) 🏆H4	More than 30 suppliers
	'Golden Waffles'	CMHG EBee NEgg
	'Goldpfeil'	EMic

'Goldsmith' EGol SApp
'Good as Gold' EMic EPGN NMyG
'Gosan Gold Mist' **new** EMic
'Gosan' (*takahashii*) EGol
gracillima EPGN NRya
'Granary Gold' (*fortunei*) CBdn EGol EPGN LRHS SChu
'Grand Master' EGol IBal MDKP SApp
'Grand Tiara' (v) CBdn EGol EPGN NMyG SApp
'Gray Cole' (*sieboldiana*) CBdn EGol EMic EPGN
'Great Expectations' (*sieboldiana*) (v) CBdn CHid CWin EBee EGol EMic EPGN EPfP EWsh GBri IBal LAst LRHS LSRN MBNS MBri MIDC MNrw NBro NCGa NEgg NGdn NRnb NSti SApp SChu SGSe SPla SVil WAul
'Green Acres' (*montana*) LPhx MSte SChu WFar
'Green Angel' (*sieboldiana*) EGol
'Green Dwarf' **new** NWCA
'Green Eyes' (*sieboldii*) (v) EGol
'Green Fountain' (*kikutii*) CBdn EGol EMic LRHS MIDC MSte WHal
'Green Gold' (*fortunei*) (v) CBdn EMic
'Green Piecrust' CBdn EGol LRHS
'Green Sheen' EGol EPGN NMyG
'Green Summer Fragrance' CBdn
'Green Velveteen' CBdn EGol
'Green with Envy' (v) CBdn EGol
'Grey Ghost' **new** IBal
'Grey Piecrust' EGol IBal
'Ground Cover Trompenburg' **new** SApp
'Ground Master' (v) CBdn CMHG COIW COtt EBrs ECtt EGol ELan ENot EPGN EPfP GAbr GMaP GSki IBal LPBA LRHS MBri MRav MSwo NBro NMyG NSti SGSe SPer WFar WWeb WWye
'Ground Sulphur' EGol EPGN
'Guacamole' (v) CBdn EBee EGol EMic EPGN EUJe IBal IPot MIDC NLar NMyG SApp SUsu SVil WAul WTin WWye
'Guardian Angel' (*sieboldiana*) CBdn EBee EGol EMic EPGN EWTr
'Gum Drop' CBdn EMic
'Gun Metal Blue' EGol
'Hadspen Blue' (Tardiana Group) CBdn CMHG EBee EGol EGra ELan EMic EPGN EPfP GKir GMaP IBal LAst LRHS MBNS MBrN MIDC MRav NBir NBro NMyG NSti SApp SChu SHBN SMrm SPer SPoG WMnd WPop
'Hadspen Hawk' (Tardiana Group) EGol LPhx NMyG SApp
'Hadspen Heron' (Tardiana Group) CBdn EGol MHom NMyG SChu WCot
I 'Hadspen Nymphaea' EGol
'Hadspen Rainbow' CBdn IBal
I 'Hadspen Samphire' EGol EMic EPGN LRHS MHom NBir
'Hadspen White' (*fortunei*) EGol EMic
'Haku-chu-han' (*sieboldii*) (v) CBdn
'Hakujima' (*sieboldii*) EGol LPhx
§ 'Halcyon' (Tardiana Group) ♀[H4] More than 30 suppliers
'Halo' EGol
'Happiness' CBdn CWin EGol EHoe EMic MHom MRav NMyG
'Happy Hearts' EGol EMic
'Harlequin' **new** SApp
'Harmony' (Tardiana Group) CBdn EGol EMic
'Hart's Tongue' **new** IBal
'Harvest Glow' EGol
'Harvest Moon' GKir
'Heart Ache' EGol
'Heart and Soul' (v) EGol
'Heartleaf' EMic
'Heart's Content' (v) CBdn EGol
'Heartsong' (v) EGol NMyG
'Helen Doriot' (*sieboldiana*) EGol EMic
helonioides hort. f. ***albopicta*** see *H. rohdeifolia*
'Herifu' (v) CBdn EGol
'Hidden Cove' (v) EGol IBal
'Hi-ho Silver' (v) **new** ENot EPGN IBal
'Hilda Wassman' (v) EGol
'Hirao Elite' **new** IBal
'Hirao Majesty' CBdn EGol
'Hirao Splendor' EGol NMyG
'Hirao Supreme' CBdn EGol
'Hirao Tetra' CBdn
'Holstein' see *H.* 'Halcyon'
'Honey Moon' CBdn EGol
§ 'Honeybells' ♀[H4] More than 30 suppliers
'Honeysong' (v) CBdn EMic EPGN
'Hoosier Harmony' (v) CBdn EGol EMic LRHS
'Hoosier Homecoming' CBdn SApp
'Hope' (v) EGol EMic IBal
'Hotspur' (v) **new** EGol
§ 'Hyacintha Variegata' (*fortunei*) (v) CMHG GBri IHMH
'Hydon Gleam' EMic
'Hydon Sunset' (*nakaiana*) CBdn CM&M CMHG EGol EMic EPGN GCra GKir IBal LHyd MIDC NMyG NOak NRya NSti SGSe WMnd WPtf WTin
hypoleuca EGol WLin
'Ice Cream' (*cathayana*) (v) EGol
'Iced Lemon' **new** CBdn
'Illicit Affair' **new** EMic IBal
'Ilona' (v) EGol
§ 'Inaho' CBdn EGol EPGN NMyG
'Inca Gold' EGol
'Independence Day' (v) EPGN
'Inniswood' (v) CBdn CWin EGol EPGN EPfP IBal IPot LRHS MBNS NBro NGdn NRnb NSti SApp WMnd WPnP
'Invincible' CBdn EBee EGol EMic EPGN IBal LPhx LRHS MBNS MIDC NLar NMyG NRnb SApp SVil WTin WWye
'Iona' (*fortunei*) CBdn EGol EMic EPGN NMyG SSpi
'Irische see' (Tardiana Group) EGol
'Iron Gate Delight' (v) CBdn
'Iron Gate Glamour' (v) EGol WBcn
'Iron Gate Special' (v) EMic
'Island Charm' (v) CBdn EGol EMic EPGN IBal SApp
'Iwa Soules' EGol
'Jack of Diamonds' **new** IBal
'Jade Beauty' CBdn
'Jade Cascade' CBdn EGol ELan EMic LRHS MSte NBir NEgg NLar NMyG SApp SMrm WCot WLin WOVN
'Jade Scepter' (*nakaiana*) EGol EMic
'Jadette' (v) EGol EPGN SChu
'Janet' (*fortunei*) (v) CBdn EGol GMaP LRHS NGdn WWpP
'Jester' **new** SApp
'Jewel of the Nile' (v) **new** IBal
'Jim Mathews' **new** IBal
'Jimmy Crack Corn' CBdn EGol IBal
'Joker' (*fortunei*) (v) CBdn GKir
'Jolly Green Giant' (*sieboldiana* hybrid) EMic
'Joseph' EGol

'Journeyman'	EBrs EGol EMic LRHS
'Julia' (v)	EGol EMic IBal
'Julie Morss'	CBdn CWin EGol EMic EPGN GMaP MHom SApp WWpP
'Jumbo' (*sieboldiana*)	EMic
'June'PBR (Tardiana Group) (v)	More than 30 suppliers
'June Beauty' (*sieboldiana*)	CTbh EWsh
'Just So' (v)	CBdn EGol EMic EPGN IBal LRHS
'Kabitan'	see *H. sieboldii* var. *sieboldii* f. *kabitan*
'Karin'PBR	CBdn EMic
'Katherine Lewis' (Tardiana Group) (v)	CBdn
'Kelsey'	EGol EMic
§ 'Kifukurin Hyuga' (v)	CBdn
'Kifukurin' (*kikutii*)	see *H.* 'Kifukurin Hyuga'
'Kifukurin Ko Mame' (*gracillima*) (v)	CBdn
I 'Kifukurin' (*pulchella*) (v)	CBdn EGol EMic
'Kifukurin Ubatake' (*pulchella*) (v)	CBdn EPGN IBal
kikutii	EGol EMic WTin
§ - var. ***caput-avis***	EGol EMic
- var. ***polyneuron***	EGol SApp
- var. ***pruinosa***	SApp
- var. ***tosana***	EGol
§ - var. ***yakusimensis***	CBdn EGol EMic ETow GBin SMad
'Kingfisher' (Tardiana Group)	EGol
'King James' **new**	IBal
§ 'Kirishima'	CBdn EPGN
'Kiwi Black Magic'	IBal SSpi
'Kiwi Blue Baby' **new**	IBal
'Kiwi Blue Ruffles' **new**	IBal
'Kiwi Blue Sky' **new**	IBal
'Kiwi Canoe' **new**	IBal
'Kiwi Cream Edge' (v)	EMic
'Kiwi Forest' **new**	IBal
'Kiwi Fruit' **new**	SApp
'Kiwi Full Monty' (v) **new**	EMic IBal
'Kiwi Gold Rush' **new**	IBal
'Kiwi Jordan' **new**	IBal
'Kiwi Leap Frog' **new**	IBal
'Kiwi Minnie Gold' **new**	IBal
'Kiwi Parasol' **new**	IBal
'Kiwi Spearmint'	IBal
'Kiwi Splash' **new**	IBal
'Kiwi Sunlover' **new**	IBal
'Kiwi Sunshine' **new**	IBal
'Kiwi Treasure Trove'	IBal
'Klopping Variegated' (v)	EGol
'Knave's Green'	EPGN
'Knockout' (v)	CBdn CWin EBee EGol EPGN IBal MBNS MNrw NBro NEgg NGdn NLar NMyG NRnb SApp
'Korean Snow' **new**	IBal
'Koriyama' (*sieboldiana*) (v)	CBdn EMic IBal
'Krossa Regal' ♀H4	More than 30 suppliers
* ***laciniata***	WSSM
'Lacy Belle' (v)	CBdn CWin EGol EMic IBal LRHS NBro NGdn NPro NRnb
'Lady Guinevere' **new**	IBal
'Lady Helen'	EMic
'Lady Isobel Barnett' (v)	CBdn EMic NMyG SApp
laevigata	EGol SApp
'Lake Hitchock' **new**	IBal
'Lakeside Accolade' **new**	EPGN NMyG
'Lakeside Black Satin'	CBdn EMic EPGN IBal
'Lakeside Cha Cha' (v)	CBdn EGol EMic
'Lakeside Kaleidoscope'	CBdn EMic IBal
'Lakeside Looking Glass'	CBdn EMic ENot
'Lakeside Neat Petite'	EGol
'Lakeside Ninita' (v)	EGol EMic IBal
'Lakeside Premier'	CBdn EGol EMic
'Lakeside Shoremaster' (v) **new**	IBal
'Lakeside Symphony' (v)	EGol EPGN
§ ***lancifolia*** ♀H4	CBdn CBro CMHG CRow ECha EGol EHrv ELan EMic GFlt GIBF GKir GMaP LGro MRav NGdn NMyG NSti SApp SBod SGSe SRms SSpi WAul WCot WGwG WTin
'Leather Sheen'	EGol EMic EPGN
'Lee Armiger' (*tokudama* hybrid)	EGol
'Lemon Delight'	CBdn EGol EMic EPGN NMyG
'Lemon Frost' **new**	IBal
'Lemon Lime'	CBdn EGol EMic IBal LRHS MHom MNrw NMyG NPro WBrk WIvy WPat WTin WWye
'Lemon Twist'	LRHS
'Leola Fraim' (v)	CBdn EGol EMic EPGN IBal LRHS NMyG WBcn
'Leviathan'	EMic
'Liberty' (v)	CBdn EGol EPGN IBal
* ***lilacina***	WFar
'Lily Pad'	EPGN
'Lime Piecrust'	EGol
'Limey Lisa'	EMic IBal
'Little Aurora' (*tokudama* hybrid)	EGol EMic EPGN IBal
'Little Black Scape'	CPen EBee EGol EMic EPGN EWTr GBin IBal LSRN MBNS MHom NCob NEgg NGdn NLar NMyG NPro SIng SPoG
'Little Blue' (*ventricosa*)	EGol
'Little Bo Beep' (v)	EGol
'Little Caesar' (v)	CBdn EGol EMic EPGN IBal
'Little Doll' (v)	EGol
'Little Razor'	EGol
'Little Sunspot' (v)	CBdn EGol EMic IBal
'Little White Lines' (v)	CBdn EGol EPGN IBal
'Little Wonder' (v)	CBdn EGol SChu
longipes	EGol LPhx SApp
longissima	CMHG EBee EGol WCru
'Louisa' (*sieboldii*) (v)	ECha EGol MSte WIvy
'Love Pat' ♀H4	CBdn CFir CWin EBee EGol EMic EPGN EPfP EWsh GAbr GBin GSki IBal LAst MCCP MIDC MRav NMyG SApp SPla SVil WCAu
'Loyalist'PBR (v)	CBdn EMic EPGN NLar NMyG WCra
'Lucky Charm'	EMic
'Lucy Vitols' (v)	CBdn EGol EMic IBal
'Lunar Eclipse' (v)	CWin EGol LPhx SApp
'Lunar Orbit' (v)	CBdn
'Mack the Knife'	IBal
'Maekawa'	EGol
'Majesty' **new**	EGol GFlt IBal NMyG
'Mama Mia' (v)	EGol EMic EPGN GAbr IBal MBNS NBro
'Maraschino Cherry'	EGol EMic IBal NMyG NRnb
'Margin of Error' (v)	EPGN
'Marginata Alba' misapplied	see *H. crispula*, *H.* 'Albomarginata'
'Marginata Alba' ambig. (*fortunei*) (v)	CBot CHad ECha GKir LPBA
'Marilyn'	EGol LRHS
'Marquis' (*nakaiana* hybrid)	EGol
'Maruba Iwa' (*longipes* var. *latifolia*)	CBdn
'Maruba' (*longipes* var. *latifolia*)	EGol
'Mary Joe'	EMic
'Mary Marie Ann' (*fortunei*) (v)	CBdn EGol EMic EPGN NCGa NMyG

§	'Masquerade' (v)	CBdn EGol EPGN WFar
	'Mediovariegata' (*undulata*)	see *H. undulata* var. *undulata*
	'Medusa' (v)	EGol IBal WCot
	'Mentor Gold'	EGol
	'Mesa Fringe' (*montana*)	CBdn
	'Metallic Sheen'	CBdn LRHS
I	'Metallica'	CBdn
	'Midas Touch'	CBdn NEgg NLar NMyG
§	'Midwest Gold'	MHom SApp
	'Midwest Magic' (v)	CBdn EGol EMic IBal LRHS WBcn
	'Mildred Seaver' (v)	CBdn CWin EGol EMic IBal LRHS MWat NMyG WWye
	'Millie's Memoirs' (v)	EGol
	'Ming Jade'	SApp
	'Minnie Bell' (v) **new**	EGol
	'Minnie Klopping'	EMic
	minor hort. f. ***alba***	see *H. sieboldii* var. *alba*
§	***minor*** Maekawa	CBdn CBro EGol EMic EPGN ERos GEdr GGar GIBF GSki MTho NMyG SSpi WCot WFar
	- from Korea	EGol
	- Goldbrook form	EGol
	'Minor' (*ventricosa*)	see *H. minor*
	'Minuteman' (*fortunei*) (v)	CBdn CWin EBee EMic ENot EPGN EPfP GAbr GBin IBal IPot LAst LRHS MBNS MIDC MSte NCGa NGdn NMyG NOrc NRnb SApp SPla WGor WTMC WTin
	'Moerheim' (*fortunei*) (v)	CBdn EGol EMic EPGN GBin IBal LRHS MBar MBri MIDC SChu WHal WLin WTMC
N	***montana***	CHad EGol EMic
	- B&SWJ 4796	WCru
	- B&SWJ 5585	WCru
	- f. ***macrophylla***	EGol
	'Moon Glow' (v)	EGol NMyG
	'Moon River' (v)	CBdn EGol EMic EPGN LRHS NMyG SApp
	'Moon Shadow' (v)	EGol
	'Moon Waves'	EGol
	'Moonbeam'	CBdn NRnb WTMC
	'Moonlight' (*fortunei*) (v)	CBdn EBee EChP EGol EMic EPGN GMaP LRHS NMyG SApp WBcn WWye
	'Moonlight Sonata'	CBdn EGol
	'Moonstruck'	CBdn EMic EPGN
	'Morning Light'	CBdn EGol EMic EPGN EVFa IBal MBNS MBri NBro NCGa SApp WBor
	'Moscow Blue'	EGol LRHS
	'Mount Everest'	CBdn EMic IBal
	'Mount Fuji' (*montana*)	EGol
	'Mount Hope' (v)	EGol
	'Mount Kirishima' (*sieboldii*)	see *H.* 'Kirishima'
	'Mount Tom' (v) **new**	EGol IBal
	'Mountain Snow' (*montana*) (v)	CBdn CWin EGol EMic LRHS NMyG SApp WTMC
	'Mountain Sunrise' (*montana*)	EGol
	'Mr Big'	MBNS WCot
	'Munchkin' (*sieboldii*)	CBdn
	'Myerscough Magic'	CBdn MSte
	'Naegato'	SApp
	nakaiana	EBee EMic GCal NDlv
	'Nakaimo'	CBdn GBin
	'Nana' (*ventricosa*)	see *H. minor*
§	'Nancy Lindsay' (*fortunei*)	CBdn CTri EGol EMic NGdn SApp SChu WTMC
	'Nancy Minks'	CBdn EMic
	'Neat and Tidy' **new**	IBal
	'Neat Splash' (v)	CBdn EChP NBir
	'New Wave'	EGol

'Niagara Falls'	CBdn EGol
'Nicola'	EGol EMic EPGN MHom NMyG
'Night before Christmas' (v)	CBdn CFir CM&M COtt CWin EGol EPGN GBin IBal IPot LAst MBri MIDC MNrw NBro NCGa NEgg NGdn NMyG NRnb SApp SHBN SPla WSan WTMC WWeb WWye
nigrescens	CBdn CWin EBee EGol EPGN GCal WWye
- 'Cally White' **new**	GCal
'Nokogiryama'	EGol EMic
'North Hills' (*fortunei*) (v)	CBdn EGol EMic LPio LRHS MWgw NBir NCob NGdn SChu SWvt
'Northern Exposure' (*sieboldiana*) (v)	CFir CWin EGol EMic IBal NGdn NMyG NRnb SApp
'Northern Halo' (*sieboldiana*) (v)	EGol EMic
'Northern Lights' (*sieboldiana*)	EGol
'Obscura Marginata' (*fortunei*)	see *H. fortunei* var. *aureomarginata*
'Obsession'	EGol IBal
'Okazuki Special'	CBdn EGol
'Old Faithful'	CBdn EGol
'Old Glory'[PBR] (v) **new**	EGol
'Olga's Shiny Leaf'	EGol EMic
'Olive Bailey Langdon' (*sieboldiana*) (v)	CBdn EMic IBal
'Olive Branch' (v)	EGol
'Olympic Edger'	IBal
'One Man's Treasure' **new**	IBal
'Ophir'	IBal
'Orange Marmalade' **new**	IBal
'Oriana' (*fortunei*)	EGol
'Osprey' (Tardiana Group)	EGol LRHS
'Oxheart'	EMic
pachyscapa	EMic
'Pacific Blue Edger'	CAby CBdn CFir CM&M CWin EGol EMic EPGN LAst MBri SSpe WAul WWye
'Pandora's Box' (v)	CBdn EGol EMic IBal NHar SApp WCot
'Paradigm' (v)	CBdn EBee EBrs EGol EMic EPGN IBal NEgg NMyG
'Paradise Backstage' **new**	CBdn
'Paradise Joyce'[PBR]	CBdn EGol EMic EPGN IBal MIDC NLar NMyG
'Paradise on Fire' **new**	CBdn
'Paradise Power'[PBR]	CBdn EGol EMic IBal
'Paradise Puppet' (*venusta*)	CBdn EPGN
'Paradise Red Delight' (*pycnophylla*)	CBdn EMic
'Paradise Standard' (d)	CBdn
'Pastures Green'	EGol
'Pastures New'	EGol EMic LPhx MHom NMyG SApp
'Pathfinder' (v)	EGol IBal
'Patrician' (v)	EMic EPGN IBal
'Patriot' (v)	More than 30 suppliers
'Paul's Glory' (v)	CBdn CWin EGol EMic EPGN EVFa GBin IBal LAst LRHS MBri NGdn NMyG SApp SUsu SVil WTMC WWye
'Peace' (v)	EGol EMic EPGN
'Pearl Lake'	CBdn EGol EMic IHMH LPhx LRHS MHom MSte MWat NBir NCob NLar NMyG SApp SVil WTin
'Peedee Gold Flash' (v)	CBdn NMyG
'Pelham Blue Tump'	EGol EMic
'Peppermint Ice' (v)	EGol
'Permanent Wave'	EGol

	Name	Suppliers
	'Perry's True Blue'	CBdn
	'Peter Pan'	CBdn EGol EMic
	'Phantom' **new**	SApp
	'Phoenix'	EGol GBin SApp
	'Photo Finish' (v)	EPGN
	'Phyllis Campbell' (*fortunei*)	see *H.* 'Sharmon'
	'Picta' (*fortunei*)	see *H. fortunei* var. *albopicta*
	'Piecrust Power'	CBdn EGol
	'Piedmont Gold'	CBdn EBrs EGol EMic EPGN IBal LPhx MSte WTMC
	'Pilgrim' (v)	CBdn EGol EMic EPGN IBal NBro NMyG SApp SPoG WFar
	'Pineapple Poll'	CBdn EMic EPGN MIDC NMyG WTin
	'Pineapple Upside Down Cake' (v)	EBee EPGN IBal SMrm SPur
	'Pizzazz' (v)	CBdn CWin EBee EGol EMic EPGN GFlt IBal LAst MHom MIDC NGdn NLar NMyG NRnb SApp WHil WTMC WWye
	plantaginea	CBdn EGol EMic EUJe LEdu LPhx MHom MIDC NMyG SSpi WCru WKif WWye
	- var. ***grandiflora***	see *H. plantaginea* var. *japonica*
§	- var. ***japonica*** ♀H4	CBot CDes CHad CStu EBee ECha EHrv EMic EPGN EVFa GSki IBal SApp SChu SGSe WCAu WCFE
	'Platinum Tiara' (v)	CBdn EMic EPGN IBal NBir
	'Pooh Bear' (v)	CBdn EGol
	'Popo'	CBdn EGol IBal
	'Potomac Pride'	CBdn EPGN LRHS NMyG SApp
	'Praying Hands' (v)	CBdn EGol EMic IBal
	'Pretty Flamingo'	EMic
	'Primavera Primrose' **new**	SApp
	'Prince of Wales'	CBdn SApp
	'Puck'	EGol
	'Purple and Gold'	CBdn
	'Purple Dwarf'	CBdn EGol EMic GKir LRHS NGdn NLar WCra WHal WIvy
	'Purple Profusion'	EGol EMic
	pycnophylla	EGol SIgm
	'Queen Josephine' (v)	CBdn COtt CWin EGol EMic EPGN IBal IPot LAst MBNS MBri MHom NCGa NEgg NGdn NMyG NPro SApp WFar WTMC WWye
	'Queen of Islip' (*sieboldiana*) (v)	CBdn
	'Quilting Bee'	EGol
	'Rachel de Thame' **new**	EPGN
	'Radiant Edger' (v)	CBdn CWin EGol EMic EPGN GCra IBal LRHS
	'Raleigh Remembrance'	EGol
	'Rascal' (v)	CBdn EGol EMic LRHS
	'Raspberry Sorbet'	EGol EPGN LRHS
	'Red Neck Heaven' (*kikutii* var. *caput-avis*)	CBdn SApp WTin
	'Red October'	CBdn CMHG EBee EChP EGol EMic EPGN EPfP EVFa GAbr GBin IBal MBri MCCP NEgg NGdn NMyG
	'Red Salamander'	EGol
	'Regal Splendor' (v)	CBdn CWin EGol EMFW EMic EPGN GSki IBal LRHS MHom NBro NCGa NMyG SApp SMrm SPla SVil WAul WMnd WSSM WWpP
	'Remember Me'	CBdn EDAr EGol ELan EMic EPGN GFlt IBal LAst LSRN MCCP MDun NCGa NCob NGdn NLar NMyG NRnb SApp SMac SPoG WGor WWeb
	'Resonance' (v)	EPGN MBri NGdn NLar NPro WTMC
	'Reversed' (v)	CBdn CWin EGol ELan EMic EPGN EPfP EWsh MDKP MIDC MSte NBro NGdn NMyG WTMC
	'Revolution'[PBR] (v)	CBdn CPen CWin EBee EGol EMic EPGN IBal IPot LSRN MBNS MBri MIDC NBro NCGa NCob NLar NMyG NOrc NRnb WPop
	'Rhapsody' (*fortunei*) (v)	EGol
	'Rhapsody in Blue'	EGol
	'Richland Gold' (*fortunei*)	CBdn EBee EGol EMic EPGN LPhx NMyG
	'Rippled Honey'	CBdn CPen EPGN IBal NMyG NPro SApp
	'Rippling Waves'	EGol EMic
	'Riptide'	CBdn
	'Rising Sun'	EGol
	'Risky Business' (v) **new**	IBal
	'Robert Frost' (v)	CBdn EGol EMic IBal WTin
	'Robusta' (*fortunei*)	see *H. sieboldiana* var. *elegans*
§	***rohdeifolia*** (v)	EBrs EGol LBuc LRHS WHal
§	- f. ***albopicta***	CBdn EGol ELan SChu
	'Rosemoor'	CBdn EGol
	'Rough Waters'	SApp
	'Royal Golden Jubilee' **new**	EPGN
§	'Royal Standard' ♀H4	More than 30 suppliers
	'Royalty'	EGol
	rupifraga	EGol
§	'Sagae' (v) ♀H3-4	CBdn CHid CWin EBee EBrs EChP EGol EMic EPGN EPfP EWTr IBal IPot LRHS MBri MHom MIDC MNrw MSte NEgg NGdn NMyG SPla SPoG WAul WFar WTMC
	'Saint Elmo's Fire' (v)	CBdn CHid EGol EMic IBal NCGa NEgg SPla
	'Saint Fiacre'	CBdn
§	'Saishu Jima' (*sieboldii* f. *spathulata*)	EPla SOkd WCru
	'Saishu Yahite Site' (v)	EGol
	'Salute' (Tardiana Group)	CBdn EGol
	'Samurai' (*sieboldiana*) (v)	CBdn CWin EGol IBal IPot LAst MRav NBir NBro NEgg NGdn NRnb SApp WWye
	'Sarah Kennedy' (v)	EPGN
	'Savannah'	EGol LRHS
	'Sazanami' (*crispula*)	see *H. crispula*
	'Scooter' (v)	CBdn EGol EMic EPGN NMyG
	'Sea Bunny'	EGol
	'Sea Dream' (v)	CBdn EGol EMic EPGN NMyG WBcn
	'Sea Drift'	EGol
	'Sea Fire'	EGol LRHS
	'Sea Gold Star'	CBdn EGol EPGN NMyG
	'Sea Gulf Stream'	IBal
	'Sea Hero'	EGol
	'Sea Lotus Leaf'	CBdn EGol EMic EPGN NLar NMyG
	'Sea Mist' (v)	CBdn
	'Sea Monster'	EGol
	'Sea Octopus'	EGol
	'Sea Sapphire'	EGol LRHS
	'Sea Sprite' (v)	LRHS
	'Sea Sunrise'	EPGN
	'Sea Thunder' (v)	CBdn EGol EMic EPGN IBal
	'Sea Yellow Sunrise'	CBdn EGol EMic IBal SApp
	'Second Wind' (*fortunei*) (v)	CBdn EMic EPGN LRHS NMyG
	'see Saw' (*undulata*)	EGol SApp WPnP
	'Semperaurea' (*sieboldiana*)	GFlt GSki
	'September Sun' (v)	CBdn EGol IBal LRHS NMyG
	'Serena' (Tardiana Group)	SApp
	'Serendipity'	CBdn EGol EMic EPGN MHom
	'Shade Beauty' (v)	EGol
	'Shade Fanfare' (v) ♀H4	CBdn EBrs EGol ELan EMic EPGN EPfP GKir IBal LRHS MBNS MBri MIDC MRav MWgw NBir NGdn

		NLar NMyG NSti SApp SPer WCAu WFar WMnd WTin WWye
	'Shade Master'	CBdn EGol GKir LAst SMer
	'Shamoa' **new**	SApp
§	'Sharmon' (*fortunei*) (v)	CBdn CWin EBee EGol EMic EPGN IPot MBNS NMyG SChu
	'Sheila West'	CBdn
	'Shelleys' (v)	EGol
	'Sherborne Profusion' (Tardiana Group)	CBdn EMic
	'Sherborne Swift' (Tardiana Group)	CBdn EGol
	'Shining Tot'	CBdn EGol
	'Shiny Penny' (v) **new**	EGol IBal
	'Shirley Vaughn' (v)	EGol
	'Shogun' (v)	EGol
	'Showboat' (v)	CBdn EGol EPGN IBal NMyG
	'Showtime' **new**	IBal
	sieboldiana	CMHG CSBt CTbh ECha EGol ELan EMic EPfP EUJe GMaP MRav NChi NFor NJOw SPer SPlb SRms WBVN WCru WFar WGwG WTin WWpP
§	- var. ***elegans*** ♀H4	More than 30 suppliers
	- 'George Smith'	IBal
	sieboldii	ECha NEgg
§	- var. ***alba***	CHad EGol SSpi
§	- 'Paxton's Original' (v) ♀H4	CHar EGol EHrv GKir IHMH MBar NLar SRms
§	- var. ***sieboldii*** f. ***kabitan*** (v)	CBdn EBrs EGol EPGN MIDC NBlu NMyG NSti SApp SChu WTin
	- - f. ***shiro-kabitan*** (v)	EGol EMic EPGN
	'Silk Kimono' (v)	EGol
	'Silver Bowl'	EGol
	'Silver Crown'	see *H.* 'Albomarginata'
	'Silver Lance' (v)	CBdn EGol EMic EPGN NMyG
	'Silver Shadow' **new**	CBdn NMyG
	'Silver Spray' (v)	EGol
	'Silvery Slugproof' (Tardiana Group)	CBdn NMyG SApp
	'Sitting Pretty' (v)	EGol EPGN
	'Slick Willie'	EGol
	'Slim Polly'	CBdn
	'Small Sum' **new**	IBal
	'Snow Cap' (v)	CBdn CWin EGol EMic EPGN IBal ITim MBri MIDC NEgg NGdn NLar NMyG NPro SApp WAul WDav
	'Snow Crust' (v)	CBdn EGol EMic LRHS
	'Snow Flakes' (*sieboldii*)	CBdn EGol EPGN EPfP GCal GKir LPio LRHS MBar MBri NBro NGdn NMyG NPro SBod SPer WFar WGwG WSSM WTMC WTin
	'Snow White' (*undulata*) (v)	EGol
	'Snowden'	CBdn CHad CMHG ECha EGol EMic EPGN GMaP NBir NCob NGdn NMyG NPar SApp SSpi WBrk WHoo WPnP
	'Snowstorm' (*sieboldii*)	CBdn
	'So Sweet' (v)	CBdn CWin EBee EGol EHan EMFW EMic EMil EPGN GSki IBal LPBA MBri MHom MIDC MSte MSwo NBPC NBro NEgg NGdn NMyG SMac SMrm SPoG SSpe
	'Solar Flare'	EGol
	'Something Blue'	CBdn
	'Something Different' (*fortunei*) (v)	EGol EPGN
	'Sparkling Burgundy'	CBdn EGol
	'Sparky' (v)	EGol IBal
	'Special Gift'	CBdn EGol EMic LRHS
	'Spilt Milk' (*tokudama*) (v)	CBdn EGol EMic EPGN IBal
§	'Spinners' (*fortunei*) (v)	CBdn ECha EGol EMic SChu SSpi
	'Spinning Wheel' (v)	EGol
	'Spritzer' (v)	CBdn EGol EMic NMyG SApp WBcn
	'Squash Casserole'	EGol
	'Squiggles' (v)	EGol
	'Stained Glass' **new**	EBee
	'Starburst' (v)	EGol
§	'Starker Yellow Leaf'	EMic
	'Stenantha' (*fortunei*)	EMic
	'Stetson' (v)	EGol
	'Stiletto' (v)	CBdn CTbh EGol EMar EMic ENot EPGN IBal IHMH IPot LAst MBNS MHom MIDC NBro NGdn NLar NMyG NPro NRnb NSti SApp SDnm WAul WPtf WWye
	'Striptease' (*fortunei*) (v)	CBdn CWin EBee EGol EMic EPGN EVFa EWTr GBin GKir IBal LAst LPio MBNS MIDC NGdn NLar NOrc NRnb SApp SHBN SVil WTMC WWye
	'Sugar and Cream' (v)	CM&M CWin EBee EGol EMic EPGN GMac LAst LPio LRHS NGdn NRnb SChu WTMC
	'Sugar Plum Fairy' (*gracillima*)	EGol
	'Sultana' (v)	EMic IBal
	'Sum and Substance' ♀H4	More than 30 suppliers
	'Sum of All' **new**	CBdn
	'Summer Breeze' (v)	EGol IBal
	'Summer Fragrance'	CBdn EGol EMic EPGN LRHS NMyG
	'Summer Music' (v)	CBdn CWin EGol EMic EPGN IBal LAst MBNS MBri NMyG SApp
	'Summer Serenade' (v)	CBdn EGol EMic
	'Sun Glow'	EGol
	'Sun Power'	CBdn CPen CWin EGol EMic EPGN EPfP EWTr LRHS MBNS NBro NLar NMyG NSti SApp
	'Sundance' (*fortunei*) (v)	EGol
*	'Sunflower'	NOak
	'Super Bowl'	EGol
	'Super Nova' (v)	CBdn EGol EMic IBal LRHS SApp SPoG
	'Surprised by Joy' (v) **new**	EGol IBal
	'Sweet Bo Beep'	EGol
	'Sweet Home Chicago' (v)	EGol IBal
	'Sweet Marjorie'	EGol
	'Sweet Susan'	EGol EMic LRHS MBNS SApp SPer WWpP
	'Sweet Tater Pie'	CBdn EGol
	'Sweetheart'	EMic
	'Sweetie' (v)	CBdn EGol EMic IBal LRHS SApp
	'Swirling Hearts'	EGol LRHS
	'Tall Boy'	CBdn CSev ECha EGol EPla GCal MWgw NBir SSpi WWye
	'Tamborine' (v)	CBdn EGol EPGN LRHS NMyG SApp
	Tardiana Group	CBdn CBro EGol ELan MHom NGdn
	tardiflora	CBdn CFil EGol ERos SApp WCot WPGP
	tardiva	CBdn LRHS
	'Tattoo' (v)	CBdn EBee EDAr EGol EHan EMic EPGN IBal LSRN MBNS MIDC NCGa NLar NMyG SPoG
	'Tea and Crumpets' (v)	CBdn EPGN
	'Temple Bells'	EGol LRHS
	'Tenryu'	EGol EPGN
	'The Twister'	EGol EMic
	'Thomas Hogg'	see *H. undulata* var. *albomarginata*
	'Thumb Nail'	CBdn ECha EGol GSki SApp
	'Thumbelina'	IBal
	'Thunderbolt' (*sieboldiana*)	CBdn EPGN IBal MBNS NCob

	Name	Suppliers
	'Thunderbolt' (v) **new**	EGol
	tibae	CBdn
	'Timpany's Own' (*sieboldiana*)	ITim
	'Tiny Tears'	CBdn CStu EGol LRHS
	'Titanic'^{PBR}	IBal
	tokudama	CBcs EGol LRHS MHom NBir NGdn NSti SApp SChu WFar
§	- f. ***aureonebulosa*** (v)	CBdn CWin EGol EMic EPGN IBal IPot LPhx LRHS MSte NGdn NMyG NSti WMnd
	- f. ***flavocircinalis*** (v)	CBdn CPrp CWin EGol EMic EPGN GFlt IBal LRHS NBPC NBro NMyG SApp SSpe WFar WHoo WMnd WWye
	'Torchlight' (v)	CBdn EGol EMic LRHS
	'Tot Tot'	EGol
	'Touch of Class'^{PBR} (v) **new**	IBal
	'Touchstone' (v)	CBdn MBri NMyG SWvt
	'Toy Soldier' **new**	IBal
	'Trail's End'	EMic
	'Trill' **new**	SApp
	'True Blue'	CBdn CWin EGol EMic EUJe GAbr IBal LAst NRnb SApp
	'Tutu'	EGol MIDC
	'Twiggy'	SApp
	'Twilight' (*fortunei*) (v)	CBdn CSBt CWin EGol EMic EPGN IBal MBNS NLar NRnb SApp SWvt
	'Twinkle Toes'	EGol
	'Twist of Lime' (v)	CBdn EGol
	'Ultraviolet Light'	EGol
	undulata	CHar ECha MIDC NLon WBrE WFar WWpP
§	- var. ***albomarginata***	More than 30 suppliers
§	- var. ***erromena*** 🏆H4	CBdn EHon EMic EPfP GMaP LPBA MWgw NBid NFla SPer WWpP
§	- var. ***undulata*** (v) 🏆H4	More than 30 suppliers
	- var. ***univittata*** (v) 🏆H4	CBro ECha EGol EPGN EPfP IBal MHom NBir NPro WBrk WFar WKif WMoo
	'Urajiro Hachijo'	EGol WBcn
	'Urajiro' (*hypoleuca*)	EGol
	'Valentine Lace'	CBdn EBee EGol EMic LRHS
	'Van Wade' (v)	CBdn EGol EMic EPGN
	'Vanilla Cream' (*cathayana*)	EGol LRHS NMyG
	'Variegata' (*gracillima*)	see *H.* 'Vera Verde'
	'Variegata' (*tokudama*)	see *H. tokudama* f. *aureonebulosa*
	'Variegata' (*undulata*)	see *H. undulata* var. *undulata*
	'Variegata' (*ventricosa*)	see *H.* 'Aureomarginata' (*ventricosa*)
	'Variegated' (*fluctuans*)	see *H.* 'Sagae'
	ventricosa 🏆H4	CBcs CBdn CBro EGol EGoo EMic EPfP EUJe GAbr GBBs GMaP LPBA MHer MRav SGar WBVN WBrk WCFE WFar WWye
	- var. ***aureomaculata***	CBdn EGol NBir NSti SPer WWye
	- BWJ 8160 from Sichuan	WCru
I	'Venucosa'	EGol EMic WFar
	'Venus Star'	GSki NMyG
	venusta 🏆H4	CBdn CBro CSWP EBee EBrs EDAr EGol EMic EPGN ERos GCra GCrs GEdr GKir LPhx MHer MRav NBir NJOw NMen NMyG NRya NSti SApp SRot WEas WPGP WTMC WTin
	- B&SWJ 4389	WCru
	- dwarf	CSWP LPhx
	- 'Kin Botan' (v) **new**	GEdr
	- ***yakusimensis***	see *H. kikutii* var. *yakusimensis*
§	'Vera Verde' (v)	CBdn EPGN GQui IBal MHom NBir NMyG
	'Verna Jean' (v)	CBdn EGol
	'Veronica Lake' (v)	CBdn EGol EMic IBal LRHS

	Name	Suppliers
	'Vilmoriniana'	EGol EMic
	'Viridis Marginata'	see *H. sieboldii* var. *sieboldii* f. *kabitan*
	'Wagtail' (Tardiana Group)	CBdn EMic
	'Wahoo' (*tokudama*) (v)	EGol
	'Warwick Choice' (v)	CBdn
	'Warwick Curtsey' (v)	EGol IBal
	'Warwick Delight' (v)	EGol IBal
	'Warwick Edge' (v)	CBdn EGol IBal
	'Warwick Essence'	EGol EMic
	'Warwick Sheen'	IBal
	'Waving Winds' (v)	EGol
	'Waving Wuffles'	EMic
	'Wayside Blue'	EMic
	'Wayside Perfection'	see *H.* 'Royal Standard'
	'Weihenstephan' (*sieboldii*)	EGol EMic
	'Weser'	EGol
	'Wheaton Blue'	CBdn EMic LRHS
	'Whirlwind' (*fortunei*) (v)	CBdn CWin EBee EGol EPGN GBBs GBin GFlt IBal IPot MBri MIDC MNrw NBro NEgg NGdn NMyG NRnb SApp SVil WAul WMnd WTMC WWye
	'Whirlwind Tour' (v)	EGol
	'White Christmas' (*undulata*) (v)	EGol EPGN LRHS
	'White Fairy' (*plantaginea*) (d)	CBdn EBee EPGN NMyG
	'White Feather' (*undulata*)	CBdn EMic IBal NBir
	'White Gold'	CBdn EGol EPGN NMyG
	'White Tacchi'	EMon
	'White Triumphator'^{PBR} (*rectifolia*)	CBdn EGol EPGN IBal MBri
	'White Vision'	EGol
	'Whoopee' (v)	EPGN MBNS
	'Wide Brim' (v) 🏆H4	More than 30 suppliers
	'Wind River Gold'	EGol
	'Windsor Gold'	see *H.* 'Nancy Lindsay'
	'Winfield Blue'	CMHG EGol LRHS NEgg
	'Winfield Gold'	CBdn EGol
	'Wogon Giboshi'	see *H.* 'Wogon'
§	'Wogon' (*sieboldii*)	CBdn CM&M EPGN GEdr GMaP NDlv NMen NSti
	'Wogon's Boy'	CBdn EGol EPGN
	'Wolverine' (v)	CBdn EBee EGol EPGN GAbr IBal MBNS MHom MIDC NMyG WCot WLin
	'Wrinkles and Crinkles'	EGol EPGN
	'Wylde Green Cream' **new**	IBal
	'Yakushima-mizu' (*gracillima*)	CBdn EGol
*	***yakushimana***	GCrs NMen
	'Yellow Boa'	EGol
	'Yellow Edge' (*fortunei*)	see *H. fortunei* var. *aureomarginata*
	'Yellow Edge' (*sieboldiana*)	see *H.* 'Frances Williams'
	'Yellow River' (v)	CBdn EGol EMic EPGN IBal LRHS NEgg NGdn NMyG SApp
	'Yellow Splash' (v)	CBdn ECha EPGN LRHS MBNS MHom NMyG SChu
	'Yellow Splash Rim' (v)	EGol MBri NCGa NRnb WBcn
	'Yellow Splashed Edged' (v)	EMic
	'Yellow Waves'	CBdn
	yingeri	EGol SApp
	- B&SWJ 546	WCru
	'Zager Blue'	EMic
	'Zager Green'	EMic
	'Zager White Edge' (*fortunei*) (v)	EGol EMic EPGN NMyG SApp WTin
	'Zounds'	CBdn CBot CMHG EBrs EChP ECtt EGol EHoe ELan EPGN EPfP GFlt

GKir IBal IHMH LRHS MDun MIDC MRav NMyG NOak NOrc NSti SApp SHBN SPla WFar WHil WWye

Hottonia (*Primulaceae*)

palustris	EHon ELan EMFW EMag LPBA NArg NVic WPnP WPop

Houstonia (*Rubiaceae*)

caerulea hort.	see *H. michauxii*
caerulea L.	ECho
- var. ***alba***	IHMH
§ ***michauxii***	SPoG
- 'Fred Mullard'	EWes

Houttuynia (*Saururaceae*)

cordata	GBar IBlr LNCo NArg NEgg SDix WBrE WFar
§ - 'Boo-Boo' (v)	EChP EMan EPfP EPla EWin NBro
§ - 'Chameleon' (v)	More than 30 suppliers
- 'Flame' (v)	MAsh NCGa SMrm
- 'Flore Pleno' (d)	More than 30 suppliers
- 'Joker's Gold'	EMan EPPr EPfP EPla EShb EVFa MBNS MWgw NBro NVic SMrm WWpP
* - 'Pied Piper'	CDoC EBee ENot EWin LRHS SAga
- 'Tequila Sunrise'	CHEx
- 'Terry Clarke' (v)	see *H. cordata* 'Boo-Boo'
- 'Tricolor'	see *H. cordata* 'Chameleon'
- Variegata Group (v)	EBla GBar IBlr LPBA NArg NBro SIng WWpP

Hovenia (*Rhamnaceae*)

acerba	CFil
dulcis	CAgr CBcs CMCN CPle EPfP EUnu IArd ITer LEdu MBlu NLar SMur WBVN

Howea (*Arecaceae*)

forsteriana ♀H1	LRHS MBri NScw WMul

Hoya (*Asclepiadaceae*)

archboldiana	CPLN
§ ***australis***	CPLN
bandaensis	CPLN
bella	see *H. lanceolata* subsp. *bella*
carnosa ♀H1	CBcs CPLN CRHN EBak ELan EOHP ESlt GQui MGol SRms SWal
- 'Compacta'	CHal ESlt
* - 'Hindu Rope'	NPer
* - 'Krinkle'	NPer
- 'Red Princess'	MBri
- 'Tricolor'	NPer
- 'Variegata' (v)	MBri
* ***compacta*** 'Tricolor'	NPer
darwinii hort.	see *H. australis*
gigas **new**	CPLN
imperialis	CPLN ERea
lacunosa	LRHS
§ ***lanceolata*** subsp. ***bella*** ♀H1	CHal EShb GQui SRms
linearis	EShb
motoskei	ERea
multiflora	ESlt

Hugueninia (*Brassicaceae*)

alpina	see *H. tanacetifolia*
§ ***tanacetifolia***	NEgg

Humata (*Davalliaceae*)

tyermannii	WFib

Humea (*Asteraceae*)

elegans	see *Calomeria amaranthoides*

Humulus (*Cannabaceae*)

japonicus	MSal
- 'Variegatus' (v) **new**	EUnu
lupulus	CArn CBcs CDul CPLN CRWN ELau EMag EPfP GBar GPoy ILis MHer MSal NGHP SIde WDin WHer WSel WWye
- (f)	WWFP
- 'Aureus' ♀H4	More than 30 suppliers
- 'Aureus' (f)	CFwr CRHN GBar GGar MAnH MCCP SPla SPoG WCot
- 'Aureus' (m)	MCCP
* - ***compactus***	GPoy
- 'Fuggle'	CAgr GPoy
- 'Golden Tassels' **new**	NGHP SPoG WWeb
- (Goldings Group) 'Mathons'	CAgr
- 'Hip-hop'	EMon EWes
- var. ***neomexicanus*** **new**	EWes
- 'Prima Donna'	CBcs CBct CFwr EBee GBin MBNS NLar SIde SPoG SWvt WWpP
- 'Taff's Variegated' (v)	EMon EWes WBcn WHil WSHC
- 'Wye Challenger'	CAgr GPoy

Hunnemannia (*Papaveraceae*)

fumariifolia 'Sunlite' ♀H4	WCot

Huodendron (*Styracaceae*)

tibeticum	CFil WPGP

Hutchinsia see *Pritzelago*

rotundifolia	see *Thlaspi cepaeifolium* subsp. *rotundifolius*

Hyacinthella (*Hyacinthaceae*)

dalmatica **new**	ERos
dalmatica 'Grandiflora'	ECho WWst
heldreichii	ERos
lazuliria	ERos
leucophaea	ERos
lineata	WWst
millingenii	CMon EHyt ERos

Hyacinthoides (*Hyacinthaceae*)

algeriensis AB&S 4337 from Morocco **new**	CMon
§ ***hispanica***	CBro CHid EBrs EPot IBlr MBri NBir SPer WWye
- 'Alba'	EBrs EPot SPer
- 'Dainty Maid' **new**	WCot
- 'Excelsior'	LRHS
- 'La Grandesse'	CBro
- 'Miss World' **new**	WCot
- 'Queen of the Pinks' **new**	WCot
- 'Rosabella'	CBro
- 'Rose'	CMea EPot SPer
- 'Rosea'	CPom
- 'White City' **new**	WCot
§ ***italica*** ♀H4	CMon WShi
§ ***non-scripta***	CArn CAvo CBro CTri EBrs EPfP EPot GAbr IBlr LAma LRHS MBow MHer NBir NMir SHFr SPer SRms WHer WPop WShi
- 'Alba' **new**	NBir
- 'Bracteata' **new**	CNat
- S&B 194 from Portugal **new**	CMon
reverchonii	WWst

§	***vicentina***	ERos
	- 'Alba'	ERos

Hyacinthus ✿ (*Hyacinthaceae*)

	amethystinus	see *Brimeura amethystina*
	azureus	see *Muscari azureum*
	comosus 'Plumosus'	see *Muscari comosum* 'Plumosum'
	fastigiatus	see *Brimeura fastigiata*
	orientalis	SMeo WShi
	- 'Amethyst'	LAma
	- 'Amsterdam'	LAma
	- 'Anna Marie' ♀H4	CAvo CBro LAma MBri
	- 'Ben Nevis' (d)	LAma MBri
	- 'Bismarck'	LAma
	- 'Blue Giant'	LAma
	- 'Blue Jacket' ♀H4	CBro EBrs LAma
	- 'Blue Magic'	LAma SPer
	- 'Blue Orchid' (d)	LAma
	- 'Blue Star'	LAma
	- 'Borah' ♀H4	LAma
	- 'Carnegie'	CAvo CBro EBrs EPfP LAma SPer
	- 'City of Haarlem' ♀H4	CBro EBrs LAma SPer
	- 'Colosseum'	LAma
	- 'Crystal Palace' (d)	LAma
	- 'Delft Blue' ♀H4	CAvo CBro EBrs EPfP LAma MBri SPer
	- 'Fondant'	LAma SPer
	- 'General Köhler' (d)	LAma
	- 'Gipsy Princess'	LAma
	- 'Gipsy Queen' ♀H4	EBrs LAma LSou MBri SPer
	- 'Hollyhock' (d)	LAma MBri
	- 'Jan Bos'	EBrs EPfP LAma SPer
	- 'King Codro' (d)	LAma MBri SPer
	- 'King of the Blues'	LAma
	- 'La Victoire'	LAma
	- 'Lady Derby'	CBro LAma
	- 'L'Innocence' ♀H4	CBro EPfP LAma SPer
	- 'Marconi' (d)	LAma
	- 'Marie'	LAma
	- 'Mulberry Rose'	LAma
	- 'Myosotis'	LAma
	- 'Odysseus'	LAma
§	- 'Oranje Boven'	LAma
	- 'Ostara' ♀H4	CBro EPfP LAma MBri
	- 'Peter Stuyvesant'	EBrs LAma
	- 'Pink Pearl' ♀H4	CBro EPfP LAma
	- 'Pink Royal' (d)	LAma
	- 'Princess Margaret'	LAma
	- 'Queen of the Pinks'	LAma
	- 'Red Magic'	LAma
	- 'Rosette' (d)	LAma
	- 'Salmonetta'	see *H. orientalis* 'Oranje Boven'
§	- 'Sneeuwwitje'	LAma
	- Snow White	see *H. orientalis* 'Sneeuwwitje'
	- 'Splendid Cornelia'	EBrs SPer
	- 'Violet Pearl'	LAma
	- 'Vuurbaak'	LAma
	- 'White Pearl'	CAvo LAma
	- 'Woodstock'	EBrs LAma LSou MBri SPer WHil

Hydrangea ✿ (*Hydrangeaceae*)

	angustipetala	CFil CSam WPGP
	- B&SWJ 3454	WCru
	- B&SWJ 3814	WCru
	- B&SWJ 7121	WCru
*	- f. ***formosa*** B&SWJ 6038 from Yakushima	WCru
	- B&SWJ 7097	WCru
*	- f. ***macrosepala*** B&SWJ 3476	WCru
*	- f. ***obovatifolia*** B&SWJ 3487b	WCru
	anomala subsp. ***anomala***	SSpi WBcn
	- - B&SWJ 2411	WCru
	- subsp. ***anomala*** 'Winter Glow'	CPLN WCru
	- subsp. ***glabra***	CPLN
	- - B&SWJ 3117	WCru
§	- subsp. ***petiolaris*** ♀H4	More than 30 suppliers
	- - B&SWJ 6081 from Yakushima	WCru
	- - B&SWJ 6337	WCru
	- - B&SWJ 8497	WCru
§	- - var. ***cordifolia***	CFil EBee MBNS NLar
	- - - 'Brookside Littleleaf'	NLar
	- - dwarf	see *H. anomala* subsp. *petiolaris* var. *cordifolia*
	- - 'Furuaziai'	WCru
*	- - var. ***tiliifolia***	EPfP GCal SHyH SNut SPoG WFar
	- - 'Yakushima'	CFil WCru WPGP
*	- subsp. ***quelpartensis*** B&SWJ 8799	WCru
§	***arborescens***	CArn CFil CPLG MRav WFar WPGP
	- 'Annabelle' ♀H4	More than 30 suppliers
	- 'Astrid Lundgren' **new**	MAsh
§	- subsp. ***discolor***	WCru WPat
	- - 'Sterilis'	CFil CMil SPla SSpi WPGP
	- 'Grandiflora' ♀H4	CBcs CBot CFil ELan EPfP LSRN MRav NBro NEgg SPer WCru WDin WHCG WPGP WSHC
	- 'Hills of Snow'	MAsh
	- subsp. ***radiata***	CAbP CFil CMil GIBF LRHS MAsh SSpi WBcn WFar WPGP
	aspera	CFil CHEx CTri GIBF GKir SHyH SLon SSpi SSta WCru WKif
	- 'Anthony Bullivant'	EBee NLar SSpi SWvt WPat
	- Kawakamii Group	CFil CMil CSpe EPla SSpi WCru WPGP
	- - B&SWJ 1420	WCru
	- - B&SWJ 3462	WCru
	- - B&SWJ 6827	WCru
	- - B&SWJ 7025	WCru
	- - B&SWJ 7101	WCru
	- - 'August Abundance'	WCru
	- - 'September Splendour'	WCru
	- 'Kawakamii'	NLar
§	- 'Macrophylla' ♀H3	CFil CMil CWib EPfP LRHS MRav NBlu NEgg NPal SBrw SMad SPer SPoG SSpi WCru WPGP
	- 'Mauvette'	CBcs CFil CMil MBlu NPal SBrw SPer SSpi WBcn WCru WGer WPGP
	- 'Peter Chappell'	NLar SSpi WPGP
§	- subsp. ***robusta***	CFil WCru WPGP
	- 'Rocklon'	CFil CMil NLar SSpi WCru WPGP
	- 'Rosthornii'	see *H. aspera* subsp. *robusta*
	- 'Sam MacDonald'	CFil LRHS NEgg NLar SSpi WBcn WPGP
§	- subsp. ***sargentiana*** ♀H3	CBcs CBot CEnd CFil CHEx CHad COtt EBee ELan ENot EPfP GKir LRHS MAsh MBlu MBri MRav NBea NPal SBrw SHBN SLim SMad SSpi SSta WCru WDin WFar WKif WPGP
	- - large-leaved	WCot
	- 'Spinners'	SSpi
	- subsp. ***strigosa***	CFil CMil CPLG EPfP SBrw WCru WPGP
	- - B&SWJ 8201	WCru
	- 'Taiwan'	LRHS SSpi
	- 'Taiwan Pink'	EPfP NLar
	- 'Velvet and Lace' **new**	LRHS
§	- Villosa Group ♀H3	More than 30 suppliers
	cinerea	see *H. arborescens* subsp. *discolor*
	glandulosa B&SWJ 4031	WCru

	Name	Suppliers
	'Hallasan' (L)	CBcs
§	***heteromalla***	CFai CFil CMHG EPfP SSpi WPGP
	- BWJ 7657 from China	WCru
	- B&SWJ 2142 from India	WCru
	- B&SWJ 2602 from Sikkim	WCru
	- HWJCM 180	WCru
	- HWJK 2127 from Nepal **new**	WCru
	- SF 338	ISea
	- Bretschneideri Group	EPfP GQui MBlu NLar SBrw SHyH WCru WFar
	- 'Fan Si Pan'	WCru
	- 'Krista' **new**	MAsh
	- 'Morrey's Form'	WCru
	- 'Snowcap'	GQui IArd NLar SBrw SHyH SLdr WBcn WCru
	- f. ***xanthoneura***	CFil SSpi
	- - 'Wilsonii'	WCru WKif WSHC
	- 'Yalung Ridge'	WCru
*	***heterophylla***	MGos
	hirta	CFil
	- B&SWJ 5000	WCru
	indochinensis B&SWJ 8307	WCru
	integerrima	see *H. serratifolia*
	integrifolia	CFil CPLN GGGa WCot WPGP
	- B&SWJ 022	WCru
	- B&SWJ 6967	WCru
	involucrata	CFil CPLG EPfP LRHS MMHG SBrw SSpi WBcn WCru WDin
	- dwarf	CFil WCru
	- 'Hortensis' (d) 🏆H3-4	CDul CElw CFil CMil CPLG CPle EPfP MRav SBrw SSpi WAbe WCru WKif WPGP WSHC
*	- 'Plena' (d)	CLAP CMil MBNS MSte WCot WCru WFar WHrl WPGP WTMC
*	- 'Sterilis'	EPfP SSpi
	- 'Viridescens'	SSpi WPGP
	- 'Yokudanka' (d)	CFil
	involucrata x ***aspera*** Kawakamii Group **new**	CFil
	'Korale Red'	WBcn
	lobbii	CFil CPLG
	- B&SWJ 3214	WCru
	longipes	CFil CHEx GQui WCru WPGP
	- BWJ 8188	WCru
	'Love You Kiss' (L)	SPoG WBcn
	luteovenosa	CFil IDee WCru
	- B&SWJ 5602	WCru
*	***macrocephala***	SSpi
	macrophylla	ENot LRHS
	- 'AB Green Shadow'PBR **new**	ENot SPoG
	- 'All Summer Beauty' **new**	MAsh
	- Alpen Glow	see *H. macrophylla* 'Alpenglühen'
§	- 'Alpenglühen' (H)	CBcs CFil CPLG CSBt ELan MAsh SHBN SRms WPGP
	- 'Altona' (H) 🏆H3-4	CBcs CFil CWSG EPfP IArd ISea LRHS MAsh MGos MRav NBir NBlu NPri SBod SPer WPGP
	- 'Amethyst' (H/d)	CFil WPGP
	- 'Ami Pasquier' (H) 🏆H3-4	CBcs CDoC CFil CMac CSBt EBee EPfP GKir LRHS LSRN MRav MSwo SCoo SGar SHyH SLim SPla SSpi SWvt WBcn WGer WWeb
*	- 'Aureomarginata' (v)	EPfP SHyH WCot
	- 'Aureovariegata' (v)	CFil ELan LRHS SNut WBcn
	- 'Ayesha' (H)	More than 30 suppliers
	- 'Ayesha Blue' (H)	CPLG ENot MWgw SWvt
	- 'Bachstelze' (L)	MAsh SSpi
	- 'Beauté Vendômoise' (L)	CFil SSpi WPGP
	- 'Benelux' (H)	CBcs CWSG
§	- 'Blauer Prinz' (H)	CFil CSBt CSam LRHS SHBN SHyH
§	- 'Blauling' (L)	CDoC NEgg SHyH SLdr WBVN WWeb
§	- 'Blaumeise' (L)	CFil ENot MBri MRav NBlu SHyH SLdr SLon SSpi WGer WPGP
	- 'Blue Bonnet' (H)	CFil COtt CSBt EPfP IBal LSRN SPer
	- Blue Butterfly	see *H. macrophylla* 'Blauling'
	- 'Blue Dwarf' **new**	ENot
	- Blue Prince	see *H. macrophylla* 'Blauer Prinz'
	- Blue Sky	see *H. macrophylla* 'Blaumeise'
	- Blue Tit	see *H. macrophylla* 'Blaumeise'
	- 'Blue Wave'	see *H. macrophylla* 'Mariesii Perfecta'
	- Bluebird	see *H. macrophylla* Blauling
	- 'Bluebird' misapplied	see *H. serrata* 'Bluebird'
	- 'Bodensee' (H)	CBcs EGra GKir LRHS SBod SPla WBVN
	- 'Bouquet Rose' (H)	CWib ECtt MAsh MRav NBlu
	- 'Bridal Bouquet' (H)	CDoC
	- 'Brugg' **new**	WPGP
	- 'Brunette' (H)	CFil CMil
	- 'Buchfink' (L)	CFil SSpi WPGP
	- 'Cordata'	see *H. arborescens*
	- 'Deutschland' (H)	CTri
	- 'Domotoi' (H/d)	CFai CFil CMil SNut
	- Dragonfly	see *H. macrophylla* Dragonfly = 'Hobella', *H. macrophylla* 'Libelle'
	- Dragonfly = 'Hobella'PBR (L) **new**	LBuc
*	- 'Dwaag Pink'	MRav
	- 'Early Sensation'	SPoG WHil
	- 'Eldorado' (H)	EHol
§	- 'Enziandom' (H)	CBcs CFil CSBt SHyH SSpi WPGP
	- 'Europa' (H) 🏆H3-4	CBcs CMac CTrw CWSG GKir LRHS MGos NPri SBod SEND WPat
§	- 'Fasan' (L)	CFil WPGP WSPU
	- Firelight	see *H. macrophylla* 'Leuchtfeuer'
	- Fireworks	see *H. macrophylla* 'Hanabi'
	- Fireworks Blue	see *H. macrophylla* 'Jōgasaki'
	- Fireworks Pink	see *H. macrophylla* 'Jōgasaki'
	- Fireworks White	see *H. macrophylla* 'Hanabi'
	- 'Fischer's Silberblau' (H)	CFil
	- 'Forever Pink'	MAsh WGer
§	- 'Frau Fujiyo' (H)	CPLG LRHS
§	- 'Frau Katsuko'	LRHS SPer
§	- 'Frau Mariko' (H)	LRHS
§	- 'Frau Nobuko' (H)	LRHS
	- 'Frillibet' (H)	CAbP CDoC CFil EPfP LRHS WBcn WPGP
	- 'Gartenbaudirektor Kuhnert' (H)	SHyH SMer
§	- 'Générale Vicomtesse de Vibraye' (H) 🏆H3-4	CBcs CDoC CEnd CFil CMHG CTri CWSG EBee EPfP GKir LRHS MBar NCGa SHBN SHyH SLim SNut SPer SSpi WPGP
	- Gentian Dome	see *H. macrophylla* 'Enziandom'
	- 'Geoffrey Chadbund'	see *H. macrophylla* 'Möwe'
	- 'Gerda Steiniger'	CBcs MAsh SHyH SLdr
	- 'Gertrud Glahn' (H)	CBcs MAsh SHyH SLdr WFar
	- 'Glowing Embers'	CFil IArd MAsh MBNS SEND WPGP
	- 'Gold Dust' (v)	CFil
	- 'Goliath' (H)	CFil EPfP LRHS
	- 'Hamburg' (H)	CBcs CEnd CFil CTri CWSG ECtt ENot EPfP LRHS MGos MRav NBlu NEgg SDix SHyH SLdr WBrE WFar WWeb
	- 'Hanabi' (L/d)	CBcs CDoC CFee CFil CMil MAsh MBlu NLar WBcn
	- 'Harlequin'	CFil CMil WCot WPGP
	- 'Harry's Pink Topper' (H)	MAsh
	- 'Hatfield Rose' (H)	CBcs
	- 'Hatsushimo'	CFil NLar

- 'Heinrich Seidel' (H) CBcs CFil WBrE WMoo
- 'Hobergine'[PBR] (H) CBcs
- 'Holstein' (H) CFil MAsh MDun
§ - 'Hörnli' (H) CFil LAst MAsh
- 'Izu-no-hana' (L/d) CBcs CFil CMil MAsh MBlu NLar SSpi SUsu WPGP
- 'Jofloma' **new** CFil NLar
- 'Jōgasaki' CBcs MAsh MBlu NLar WPGP
§ - 'Joseph Banks' (H) CBcs
- 'Kardinal' (L) CFil
- 'King George' (H) CBcs CDoC CFil CSBt CWSG EBee GKir LAst LRHS MBar MGos MRav MWat SHyH SLdr SLim SPer SPoG SWvt WFar WMoo WTel
- 'Kluis Superba' (H) CBcs CFil CTri MAsh MRav SHyH
- 'Komochiana Seruka' **new** CFil
§ - 'Koningin Wilhelmina' (H) CFil WBcn WTel
- 'Kuro-hime' (L) CBcs MAsh
- 'La France' (H) COtt CTri CWSG LRHS MAsh MBar MRav SHyH SLdr WFar
- 'Lady Fujiyo' see *H. macrophylla* 'Frau Fujiyo'
- Lady Katsuko (H) see *H. macrophylla* 'Frau Katsuko'
- 'Lady Mariko' see *H. macrophylla* 'Frau Mariko'
- 'Lady Nobuko' see *H. macrophylla* 'Frau Nobuko'
- 'Lady Taiko Blue' see *H. macrophylla* 'Taiko' blue
- 'Lady Taiko Pink' see *H. macrophylla* 'Taiko' pink
- 'Lanarth White' (L) ♀H3-4 CBcs CDoC CFil CSBt CTri EBee ELan EPfP MAsh MRav MSwo SHBN SHyH SLPl SLdr SLim SPer SReu SRms SSpi WPGP
§ - 'Leuchtfeuer' (H) ENot LRHS SHyH WBcn WGer
- 'Libelle' (L) CBcs CDoC CFil CSBt EPfP MAsh MRav SLim SNut SPer SPoG SSpi WBVN WKif
- 'Lilacina' see *H. macrophylla* 'Mariesii Lilacina'
§ - 'Maculata' (L/v) EHol ELan GQui SGar WGwG
- 'Madame A. Riverain' (H) CFil CWSG LRHS SBod SHyH
§ - 'Madame Emile Mouillère' (H) ♀H3-4 More than 30 suppliers
- 'Madame Faustin Travouillon' **new** MAsh
- 'Maréchal Foch' (H) CFil CTri MAsh
- 'Mariesii' (L) CFil CMHG CSBt CTri EBee ELan ISea LRHS MSwo NEgg SDix SPer WGwG WKif
§ - 'Mariesii Grandiflora' (L) ♀H3-4 CDul CFil ENot EPfP LRHS MAsh MBar NBlu NBro NCGa NPri SBod SEND SHBN SHyH SLdr SNut SPer SRms SSpi WDin WFar WMoo WPGP
§ - 'Mariesii Lilacina' (L) ♀H3-4 CFil EPfP MAsh MWhi SLon SPer SSpi WKif WMoo WPGP
§ - 'Mariesii Perfecta' (L) ♀H3-4 More than 30 suppliers
- 'Mariesii Variegata' (L/v) CWib
- 'Masja' (H) CBcs COtt EBee EGra IArd LRHS MAsh MGos MSwo NBro SHBN SHyH SLdr WWeb
- 'Mathilda Gutges' (H) CDoC CFil CTbh SSpi WPGP WWeb
- 'Max Löbner' **new** SHyH
- 'Merveille Sanguine' CDoC IArd MAsh MRav NLar WBcn WLeb WPGP WPat
- 'Messelina Teller' **new** ENot
- 'Mini Hörnli' see *H. macrophylla* 'Hörnli'
- 'Miss Belgium' (H) CFil CTri
- 'Miss Hepburn' CSBt SHyH SPer
- 'Mousmée' CFil IArd SLPl SSpi
§ - 'Möwe' (L) ♀H3-4 CBcs CDoC CEnd CFil CMil CPLG EBee ECtt MAsh NEgg NPri SChu SCoo SDix SGar SHyH SLdr SNut SPer SRms SSpi SSta WPGP
§ - 'Nachtigall' (L) EBee SNut SSpi
- 'Niedersachsen' (H) CDoC CFil MRav SHyH SMer WPGP
- Nightingale see *H. macrophylla* 'Nachtigall'
- 'Nigra' (H) ♀H3-4 CBcs CChe CFil CPLG CWib ELan EPfP EPla MGos SDix SHBN SHyH SNut SPer WFar WGwG WPGP WPat
- 'Nikko Blue' (H) CBcs CFil CWSG EPfP MBar MDun NBlu NEgg SEND
- var. ***normalis*** NLar
§ - 'Nymphe' (H) LRHS
- 'Oregon Pride' **new** CFil
- 'Otaksa' (H) CFil
- 'Papagei' **new** SPer
- 'Parzifal' (H) ♀H3-4 CBcs CFil CTrw SHyH WPGP
- 'Pax' see *H. macrophylla* 'Nymphe'
- 'Pfau' (L) SSpi
- Pheasant see *H. macrophylla* 'Fasan'
- 'Pia' (H) CBcs CDoC CFil CPLG EHyt ELan GKir IArd MAsh MRav MTho NWCA SBod SLim SMad SPla SPoG SRms WAbe WCru WFar WPat
- Pigeon see *H. macrophylla* 'Taube'
- 'Prinses Beatrix' CBcs CChe CFil SHyH
- 'Quadricolor' (L/v) CAbb CFil CMil CPLG EHoe EPfP LRHS MRav SDix SGar SHBN SHyH SLdr SLim SNut SPer SPla SPlb SRms WCot WHCG WSHC WWeb
- Queen Wilhelmina see *H. macrophylla* 'Koningin Wilhelmina'
- 'R.F. Felton' CBcs MAsh
- 'Ramis Pietis' (L) CBcs
- 'Red Baron' ENot MAsh
- Redbreast see *H. macrophylla* 'Rotkehlchen'
- 'Regula' (H) CTrw
- 'Renate Steiniger' (H) CFai ENot SHyH SLdr WBcn WGwG
- 'Rosita' (H) ENot LRHS MAsh WFar
§ - 'Rotkehlchen' (L) CFai CFil NBlu SSpi
- 'Rotschwanz' (L) CFil CMil MAsh SSpi WPGP
- 'Saint Claire' CBcs
- 'Sandra' **new** ENot MAsh
- 'Schwabenland' NPri
- 'Sea Foam' (L) NBlu WBan WCot
- 'Selina' **new** ENot
- 'Semperflorens' **new** MAsh
- 'Shin Ozaki' **new** CFil
* - 'Shower' ENot LRHS
- 'Sibylla' (H) CBcs CFil
- Sister Therese see *H. macrophylla* 'Soeur Thérèse'
- 'Snow' ENot
- 'Snowball' **new** ENot
§ - 'Soeur Thérèse' (H) CBcs CFil CSBt LRHS MAsh MGos SHyH SWvt WGwG WPGP
- 'Sumida-no-hanabi' **new** CFil
§ - 'Taiko' blue (H) LRHS SPer
§ - 'Taiko' pink (H) LRHS
§ - 'Taube' (L) CBcs CFil CPLG GQui NBlu
N - Teller Blau (L) CDoC COtt CSBt EBee EPfP MAsh MRav NSti SCoo SLim SPoG SWvt WDin WWeb
N - Teller Rosa (L) CDoC CDul EBee EPfP SCoo SWvt WWeb
N - Teller Rot (L) CDoC CSBt EPfP MAsh SCoo SPlb SPoG SWvt WDin WWeb
N - Teller variegated see *H. macrophylla* 'Tricolor'
N - Teller Weiss see *H. macrophylla* 'Libelle'
- 'Tokyo Delight' (L) ♀H3-4 CBrd CChe CDoC CFil CPLG SHyH SLdr SSpi WBcn WPGP

- 'Tovelit' IArd LRHS MAsh
- 'Tricolor' (L/v) CBcs CBot CDoC CFil LAst LRHS MAsh MGos MTis NEgg SBod SHyH SLon SPer SPoG WFar WKif WMoo
- 'Trophee' **new** SPoG
- 'Val de Loire' CWSG
- 'Variegata' see *H. macrophylla* 'Maculata'
- 'Veitchii' (L) ♀H3-4 CBcs CBot CFil CMHG CPLG CSBt ENot EPfP MRav MSwo SBod SDix SGar SHyH SPoG SSpi WPGP
- 'Vicomte de Vibraye' see *H. macrophylla* 'Générale Vicomtesse de Vibraye'
- 'Warabe' **new** CFil MAsh
- 'Westfalen' (H) ♀H3-4 IArd LRHS SDix SPla
- 'White Lace' (L) ELan
- white lacecap (L) **new** SHyH
- 'White Mop' CWib
- 'White Wave' see *H. macrophylla* 'Mariesii Grandiflora'
- 'Zhuni Hito' **new** CFil

'Midori' (L) CBcs
paniculata CFil CMCN CTrw GIBF GKir LAst
- B&SWJ 3556 from Taiwan WCru
- B&SWJ 5413 from Japan WCru
- 'Big Ben' **new** MBri
- 'Brussels Lace' CAbP CFil EBee LRHS MAsh MBri MRav NLar SHyH SNut SPla SPoG SSpi WPat
- 'Burgundy Lace' CBcs MAsh MBlu MBri
- 'Darts Little Dot' **new** MAsh WPat
- 'Dolly' **new** MBri
- 'Everest' CAbP LRHS MAsh SNut
- 'Floribunda' CFil EPfP EWTr LRHS NEgg SSpi WPGP
- 'Grandiflora' ♀H4 More than 30 suppliers
- 'Greenspire' CBcs LRHS MAsh MBlu MBri WBcn
- 'Kyushu' ♀H4 More than 30 suppliers
- 'Limelight'PBR CBcs CMil MAsh MBlu MBri WMoo WOVN
- 'Mega Pearl' **new** MAsh
- 'Mount Aso' CFil CMil NLar WPGP
- 'Mount Everest' SHyH SLdr
- 'October Bride' **new** CFil NLar
- 'Phantom' MBlu MBri WPat
- Pink Diamond = 'Interhydia' ♀H4 CAbP CDoC EBee ENot LAst LRHS MAsh MBlu MBri MRav NPri SHyH SLim SPla SSpi SSta WCru WFar WPat
- 'Pink Jewel' CWib WPat
- 'Pink Lady' **new** MBri
- 'Praecox' SLon SPer WCru WPat
- 'Silver Dollar' **new** MAsh MBri
- 'Tardiva' CBcs CBot CDoC EPfP LRHS MGos MRav NBro SDix SHyH SPer SRms WBan WFar WHCG WKif WPGP WPat WWeb
- 'Unique' ♀H4 CBcs CBrm CDoC CFil CHad CMil EBee EPfP EWTr LRHS MAsh MBri MRav SHyH SMac SNut SPer SPla SSpi WBan WCru WDin WFar WPGP WPat
- 'White Lace' MBlu WWes
- 'White Lady' **new** MAsh
- 'White Moth' CBcs CFil NLar SHyH SLdr SNut

peruviana* x *serratifolia SSpi
petiolaris see *H. anomala* subsp. *petiolaris*
§ 'Preziosa' ♀H3-4 More than 30 suppliers
quelpartensis CBcs CRHN GQui SSpi
- B&SWJ 4400 WCru

quercifolia ♀H3-4 More than 30 suppliers
- 'Alice' **new** CFil EPfP
- 'Burgundy' CFil EPfP MAsh NLar
- 'Flore Pleno' see *H. quercifolia* 'Snow Flake'
- 'Harmony' CEnd CFil EPfP IArd MAsh SSta WHCG WPGP WPat
- 'Lady Anne' **new** CFil
- 'Little Honey' **new** MAsh MBri
- 'Pee Wee' CMil EPfP LRHS MAsh NLar SPoG SReu SSpi SSta WBcn WPGP WPat
- 'Sike's Dwarf' CEnd CFil GCal NLar SSpi WPat
- § 'Snow Flake' (d) CAbP CBcs CDoC CEnd CFil CMil CPMA CPle CSPN ELan EMil EPfP EWTr GKir LRHS MAsh SLon SMur SPer SPla SPoG SSpi SSta WHCG WPGP WPat
- Snow Queen = 'Flemygea' CBcs CDoC CKno CPMA CSBt CWSG EBee ELan EPfP ISea MAsh MGos MRav MSte NLar SLim SPer SPla SWvt WFar WHCG WPGP WPat
- 'Tennessee Clone' CFil

robusta SLPI WBor
'Sabrina'PBR **new** ENot SPoG
sargentiana see *H. aspera* subsp. *sargentiana*
scandens CFil
- B&SWJ 5523 WCru
- B&SWJ 5893 WCru
- § subsp. ***chinensis*** WFar
- - B&SWJ 1488 WCru
- - B&SWJ 3420 WCru
- - B&SWJ 3423 from Taiwan WCru
- - BWJ 8000 from Sichuan WCru
- subsp. ***liukiuensis*** WCru
- - B&SWJ 6022 WCru
- 'Splash' (v) **new** CMil

seemannii More than 30 suppliers
serrata CDul CTrw CWib WDin WKif
- B&SWJ 4817 WCru
- B&SWJ 6241 WCru
- 'Acuminata' see *H. serrata* 'Bluebird'
- 'Aigaku' CFil CLAP CPLG WPGP
- 'Aka Beni-yama' **new** CFil
- 'Amacha' CFil
- 'Amagi-amacha' **new** CMil
- 'Amagyana' CFil CPLG WPGP
- I 'Aurea' **new** SLon
- 'Belle Deckle' see *H. serrata* 'Blue Deckle'
- 'Beni-gaku' CFil CLAP CMil CPLG CTbh NBro NLar WPGP
- 'Beni-yama' CFil CMil WPGP
- 'Blue Billow' **new** MAsh NLar
- 'Blue Deckle' (L) CFil CMHG MAsh MRav SHyH SLdr SNut SPla SSpi WBcn WPGP
- § 'Bluebird' ♀H3-4 CFil CSBt CWSG EBee ELan EPfP GKir GQui LRHS MAsh MBar MBlu MBri MGos MWgw NBlu NCGa NEgg SBod SDix SHBN SLim SNut SPer SSpi SSta SWvt WFar WMoo WWeb
- 'Diadem' ♀H3-4 CFil CMil CPLG SDix WPGP WSHC
- dwarf white WCru
- 'Fuji Snowstorm' CMil
- 'Golden Showers' CFil CMil
- 'Golden Sunlight'PBR EBee LRHS SLon SPoG SWvt
- 'Graciosa' CFil CMil WPGP
- 'Grayswood' ♀H3-4 CBcs CEnd CFil CSBt CWSG GKir GQui LRHS MBri MRav SDix SGar SHyH SPer SSpi WKif WPGP
- 'Hakuchô' **new** MAsh
- 'Hallasan' ambig. **new** CMil
- 'Hime Amacha' **new** CFil
- 'Hime-benigaku' CMil
- 'Impératrice Eugénie' **new** CFil

	- 'Intermedia'	CFil CPLG NBro
	- 'Isuzai Jaku' **new**	CFil
*	- 'Jōgasaki'	CFil
§	- 'Kiyosumi' (L)	CBcs CDoC CEnd CFil CLAP CMil CPLG EBee GQui SSpi WCru WPGP
	- 'Klaveren'	CFil CMil
	- 'Koreana' (L)	CMil MAsh
	- 'Kurenai' (L)	CFil SSpi
	- 'Kurenai-nishiki' (v) **new**	CMil
	- 'Macrosepala'	CFil
	- 'Maiko'	CBcs CFil
	- 'Midori-izu' **new**	MAsh
	- 'Miranda' (L) 🏆H3-4	CBrd CFil CPLG CSam MAsh SSpi WFar
	- 'Miyama-yae-murasaki' (d)	CFil CLAP CMil WPGP
	- 'Ô-amacha' **new**	CMil
	- 'Preziosa'	see *H.* 'Preziosa'
	- 'Professeur Iida'	CFil WPGP
	- f. ***prolifera***	CFil CMil EBee MAsh WPGP
	- 'Ramis Pictis'	CFil MAsh WPGP
	- 'Rosalba' 🏆H3-4	CFil CLAP CPLG EPfP MRav SPer SPla WFar WSHC
	- 'Shichidanka-nishiki' (d/v)	CBcs CFil CPLG MAsh
	- 'Shino-goku' **new**	MAsh
	- 'Shinonome'	CFil CLAP CMil GQui WPGP
	- 'Shirofuji'	CFil CMil EBee WPGP
	- 'Shirotae' (d)	CBcs CFil CMil WPGP
	- 'Shishiva'	CFil
	- 'Spreading Beauty'	CFil CMil WPGP
	- var. ***thunbergii***	CBcs CFil CMHG GQui WFar WPGP
*	- - 'Plena' (d)	WCru
	- 'Tiara' 🏆H3-4	CFil CMil EBee GGGa MAsh SDix SHyH SSpi WBcn WPGP WSHC WWes
	- 'Uzu Azisai'	CFil WPGP
	- 'Woodlander' **new**	MAsh
	- 'Yae-no-amacha'	CFil WPGP
	- subsp. ***yezoensis*** 'Wryneck' (H)	CFil
§	***serratifolia***	CFil CHEx CPLN EPfP EPla SBra SBrw SSpi SSta WCru WFar WGer WPGP
	sikokiana	CLAP
	- B&SWJ 5035	WCru
	- B&SWJ 5855	WCru
	'Sunset' (L)	CBcs
	tiliifolia	see *H. anomala* subsp. *petiolaris*
	villosa	see *H. aspera* Villosa Group
	xanthoneura	see *H. heteromalla*
	'Ya-no-amacha'	CBcs

Hydrastis (*Ranunculaceae*)

	canadensis	CArn GBuc GPoy LEdu WCru

Hydrocharis (*Hydrocharitaceae*)

	morsus-ranae	CDWL CRow EHon EMFW LNCo LPBA NPer WPnP WPop

Hydrocleys (*Limnocharitaceae*)

	nymphoides **new**	XBlo

Hydrocotyle (*Apiaceae*)

	asiatica	see *Centella asiatica*
*	***sibthorpioides***	CPLG EBee EMan EMon EPPr EShb
	'Variegata' (v)	GAbr GCal SIng WCHb WHer WPer
	vulgaris	EMFW NArg WPop

Hydrophyllum (*Hydrophyllaceae*)

	canadense	CLAP EBee EMar WCru
	virginianum	CLAP EBee MSal

Hylomecon (*Papaveraceae*)

*	***hylomecoides*** **new**	WCru
§	***japonica***	CDes CFwr CPom EBee EChP ERos ETow GBBs GCrs GEdr GKev GKir MSte NBir NDov NMen NRya SHGN WAbe WCru WFar WPnP WTin

Hylotelephium see *Sedum*

Hymenanthera see *Melicytus*

Hymenocallis (*Amaryllidaceae*)

	'Advance'	LAma LRHS
§	***caroliniana***	LAma
	x ***festalis*** 🏆H1	ECho EPfP ERea LAma LRHS MBri SPav WCot WFar WWol
	harrisiana	LRHS SSpi WCot
§	***longipetala***	LRHS WCot
	occidentalis	see *H. caroliniana*
	'Sulphur Queen' 🏆H1	CBgR ECho LRHS SPav WCot

Hymenolepis (*Asteraceae*)

	parviflora	see *Athanasia parviflora*

Hymenoxys (*Asteraceae*)

	acaulis var. ***caespitosa***	see *Tetraneuris acaulis* var. *caespitosa*
§	***hoopesii***	EBee

Hyoscyamus (*Solanaceae*)

	albus	CSpe GBar MChe MGol MSal
	niger	CArn EMFP GPoy MChe MGol MSal WWye

Hyparrhenia (*Poaceae*)

	hirta	EPPr XPep

Hypericum ✿ (*Clusiaceae*)

	CC 4134	CPLG
	acmosepalum	CFil GIBF WPGP WPat
§	***addingtonii***	EPla
	aegypticum	CLyd CPBP EDAr EHyt EPot LBee LRHS MHer NJOw NMen NWCA NWoo SBla SIgm SRot WFar WOld WPat WPer XPep
	amblycalyx	SIgm
	androsaemum	CAgr CArn CRWN ECha ELan ELau GKir ISea MHer MRav MSal MSwo NPer SHFr WDin WMoo WWpP
§	- 'Albury Purple'	CElw GBuc GKir LDai MHer MRav WHrl WMoo
	- 'Autumn Blaze'	MGos
§	- 'Dart's Golden Penny'	SPer WBcn
	- 'Excellent Flair'	MGos NLar
	- 'Orange Flair'	WWpP
§	- f. ***variegatum*** 'Mrs Gladis Brabazon' (v)	IFro MWgw NBir NLsd NSti SBod SLon SPoG WBcn WCot WHrl WWpP
§	***annulatum***	EMon
	'Archibald'	EBee
	ascyron	GIBF
	athoum	CLyd EBee EHyt NBir NLAp WPat
	atomarium	EBee WPGP
	attenuatum	GIBF
	balearicum	CFil EHrv IFro MTho SIgm WAbe WPGP XPep
	barbatum	NRya
	bellum	CPle GCal SLon
	- subsp. ***latisepalum***	SLon
	calycinum	CBcs CChe ELan ENot EPfP GKir IHMH LBuc LGro MBar MGos

		MRav MWat NBlu NEgg NLon NWea SHBN SPer SWvt WDin WGwG WMoo WTel WWpP
	- 'Senior' **new**	EWin
§	***cerastioides***	CTri CWib EDAr GKir LBee LRHS SIgm SIng SPoG SRms WAbe WPer
	coris	CLyd EBee EWes LRHS MTho MWat SRms
	crux-andreae **new**	EBee
	cuneatum	see *H. pallens*
	x ***cyathiflorum*** 'Gold Cup'	CDoC CMac
	x ***dummeri*** 'Peter Dummer'	EMil
	elatum	see *H.* x *inodorum*
	elodeoides	EBee
	elodes	EMFW
	empetrifolium	XPep
	- 'Prostatum'	see *H. empetrifolium* subsp. *tortuosum*
§	- subsp. ***tortuosum***	CLyd EWes
§	***forrestii*** ♀H4	CFil EBee EPfP LRHS NWea WFar WPGP
	- B&L 12469	WPGP
	- Hird 54	WPGP
N	***fragile*** hort.	see *H. olympicum* f. *minus*
	frondosum	SOkd
	- 'Buttercup'	NLar
	- 'Sunburst'	EBee EPfP LRHS MGos MWgw WFar
N	'Gemo'	MGos
	'Gold Penny'	see *H. androsaemum* 'Dart's Golden Penny'
	'Golden Beacon'	CElw EBee GBin LAst NEgg NLar SMad SPer SPoG WBcn WCot WWeb
	grandiflorum	see *H. kouytchense*
	henryi	CPle
	- L 753	SRms
	'Hidcote' ♀H4	More than 30 suppliers
	'Hidcote Silver Ghost'	WBcn
	'Hidcote Variegated' (v)	ENot MAsh MCCP SLim SPer SRms WBrE WFar WWeb
	hircinum	EOHP
	- subsp. ***cambessedesii***	LRHS
	hirsutum	NMir
	humifusum	EHyt
§	x ***inodorum***	GGar NBir
	- 'Albury Purple'	see *H. androsaemum* 'Albury Purple'
	- 'Elstead'	EBee ECtt ELan EPfP GKir MBar MGos MMHG MRav MWat NBid NBlu NLRH NLsd SHBN SRms WBan WDin WHCG
	- 'Ysella'	EHoe MRav MSwo
	japonicum	EWes
	kalmianum	CPle EWes
	kelleri	EHyt ITim
§	***kiusianum*** var. ***yakusimense***	GFlt MBar MTho
§	***kouytchense*** ♀H4	CBcs CMCN CPle EPfP EWes GQui IFro LRHS MAsh NLar SPoG WBVN WCFE WPat
	lancasteri	EPfP LRHS SPoG WBcn WPat
	leschenaultii Choisy **new**	CDul CMCN
	leschenaultii misapplied	see *H. addingtonii*, *H.* 'Rowallane'
	linarioides	CLyd EBee GTou
	'Locke'	LAst
	maclarenii	GCal SUsu WPGP
	x ***moserianum*** ♀H4	ENot EPfP MBar MRav NPer SHBN SLon SPer SRms WDin
§	- 'Tricolor' (v)	More than 30 suppliers
	- 'Variegatum'	see *H.* x *moserianum* 'Tricolor'
	'Mrs Brabazon'	see *H. androsaemum* f. *variegatum* 'Mrs Gladis Brabazon'
	nummularium	NBir
	olympicum ♀H4	CAgr CNic CSec CTri ECha ELan EPfP GKir GMaP LRHS MBrN MHer MWat MWgw NFor NLon SBla SHGN SIng SPer SRms WDin XPep
	- 'Grandiflorum'	see *H. olympicum* f. *uniflorum*
§	- f. ***minus***	CNic CTri ECtt EGoo GCal LRHS MWhi NBlu SPlb SRms WPer
§	- - 'Sulphureum'	CBot CPrp ESis EWes GMaP MLLN NBir SPer SRms WCFE WSHC
§	- - 'Variegatum' (v)	EHyt EWes LBee NBir NLAp SIng SPoG WPat
§	- f. ***uniflorum***	EDAr IHMH MBar NBro NPri NVic SEND
	- - 'Citrinum' ♀H4	CLyd CMea ECha ECtt EDAr EHyt LBee LRHS MWat NBro NCGa NDlv NJOw NLAp NLon SBla SIgm SPoG SUsu WAbe WCot WEas WHoo WKif WLin WPGP WPat
	orientale	EWes SHGN
§	***pallens***	ECho NMen
	patulum var. ***forrestii***	see *H. forrestii*
	- var. ***henryi*** Rehder & hort.	see *H. pseudohenryi*
	perforatum	CAgr CArn CHby CWan EBee ELau EOHP EPfP EUnu GBar GPoy MChe MHer NMir SIde WGHP WHer WJek WMoo WSel WWye
	- 'Crusader' (v)	WHer
	- 'Elixir' **new**	EUnu
	- 'Topaz' **new**	MSal
	polyphyllum	see *H. olympicum* f. *minus*
	- 'Citrinum'	see *H. olympicum* f. *minus* 'Sulphureum'
	- 'Grandiflorum'	see *H. olympicum* f. *uniflorum*
	- 'Sulphureum'	see *H. olympicum* f. *minus* 'Sulphureum'
	- 'Variegatum'	see *H. olympicum* f. *minus* 'Variegatum'
	prolificum	CFai ECtt EPla GAbr MMHG WCFE
§	***pseudohenryi***	CPle
	- L 1029	GBuc
	pseudopetiolatum	GTou
	- var. ***yakusimense***	see *H. kiusianum* var. *yakusimense*
	quadrangulum L.	see *H. tetrapterum*
	reptans hort.	see *H. olympicum* f. *minus*
	reptans Dyer	CMea CNic EWes
§	'Rowallane' ♀H3	CPSs CTrC CTrw EPfP EPla ISea SDix SHBN SMrm SSpi SUsu
	stellatum	WBcn WFar
	subsessile	CPle
	'Sungold'	see *H. kouytchense*
	tenuicaule KR 743	ISea
§	***tetrapterum***	CArn MBow MSal
	tomentosum	XPep
	trichocaulon	CLyd EHol EWes NLAp WPat
	uralum HWJ 520	WCru
	xylosteifolium	SLon
	yakusimense	see *H. kiusianum* var. *yakusimense*
	yezoense	WBrE

Hypocalymma (*Myrtaceae*)

angustifolium	ECou
cordifolium 'Golden Veil' (v) **new**	ECou

Hypocalyptus (*Papilionaceae*)

sophoroides	SPlb

Hypochaeris (*Asteraceae*)

maculata	WHer
montana var. ***hookeri*** new	EHyt
radicata	NMir

Hypocyrta see *Nematanthus*

Hypoestes (*Acanthaceae*)

aristata	CPLG ERea EShb
§ ***phyllostachya*** (v) ♀H1	MBri
- 'Bettina' (v)	MBri
- 'Carmina' (v)	MBri
- 'Purpuriana' (v)	MBri
- 'Wit' (v)	MBri
sanguinolenta misapplied	see *H. phyllostachya*

Hypolepis (*Dennstaedtiaceae*)

alpina	EAmu
millefolium	GGar WCot
punctata	EFer

Hypoxis (*Hypoxidaceae*)

hygrometrica	ECou NMen
krebsii	LTwo
parvula	NMen
- var. ***albiflora***	EPot WCot
§ - - 'Hebron Farm Biscuit'	CBro CWrd EWes GEdr SAga SBla WAbe WFar
- pink-flowered	EPot
* ***tasmanica***	EMan
villosa	ERea

Hypoxis x *Rhodohypoxis* see x *Rhodoxis*

H. parvula x ***R. baurii***	see x *Rhodoxis hybrida*

Hypsela (*Campanulaceae*)

sp.	CFee
longiflora	see *H. reniformis*
§ ***reniformis***	EDAr EMan GKir LBee LRHS MRav NJOw NLAp NRya NWCA SIng SPoG WFar
- 'Greencourt White'	GBuc

Hypseocharis (*Oxalidaceae*)

moschata RCB/Arg RA-M-2 new	WCot

Hyssopus (*Lamiaceae*)

ambiguus	XPep
officinalis	More than 30 suppliers
- f. ***albus***	CSev CWan EBee ECha EGoo ELau EPfP EWin GPoy MBow MChe MHer NGHP SHGN SIde SPlb WCHb WGwG WHer WJek WPer WSel WWye
§ - subsp. ***aristatus***	CArn CBod CHrt CWan EBee EDAr ELau GPoy LLWP MChe MHer NChi SIde WCHb WEas WJek WSSM WSel WWye
- - white	WEas
- subsp. ***canescens***	XPep
- 'Roseus'	CBrm CSev CWan EBee ECha EGoo ELau EPPr EPfP EWin GPoy LLWP MBNS MBow MChe MHer NGHP SHGN SIde WCHb WGwG WHer WJek WKif WPer WWye
* ***schugnanicus***	LLWP MHar
seravschanicus	EOHP
tianschanicus	LLWP

Hystrix (*Poaceae*)

patula	CBrm CKno CPLG CWCL EChP EGra EHoe EMon EPPr EPza GCal GFor LLWP LRHS MCCP MMoz MNrw NGdn NOak NSti SHFr SPlb SWal WHal WPer WRos WTin

I

Iberis (*Brassicaceae*)

amara	WBWf
'Betty Swainson'	GBri SMrm
candolleana	see *I. pruitii* Candolleana Group
commutata	see *I. sempervirens*
'Correvoniana'	WEas
'Dick Self'	LRHS
gibraltarica	EWin LRav NFor NPri SECG SRms WBVN WGor
'Golden Candy'	CRez ENot SIng SPoG
§ ***pruitii*** Candolleana Group	EHyt
saxatilis	EDAr XPep
- ***candolleana***	see *I. pruitii* Candolleana Group
semperflorens	WCFE WSPU XPep
§ ***sempervirens*** ♀H4	CBcs CHrt CTri CWib ELan EPfP IFro LAst LGro MHer MWat NArg NBid NBlu NBro NEgg NFor NLon NOrc NVic SEND SRms STre SWal WBrE WCFE WFar WPer
- 'Compacta'	SBod
- 'Little Gem'	see *I. sempervirens* 'Weisser Zwerg'
- 'Pygmaea'	ECtt MWat NMen SBla
- Schneeflocke	see *I. sempervirens* 'Snowflake'
§ - 'Snowflake' ♀H4	ENot EPfP GAbr GKir LRHS LRav NBlu NJOw NLar SBch SIng SPer SPoG SWvt WRHF
§ - 'Weisser Zwerg'	CMea ECha ECtt ELan LAst LBee LRHS MHer MRav NMen SBla SIng SPoG SRms WHoo

Idesia (*Flacourtiaceae*)

polycarpa	CAbP CAgr CBcs CFil CMCN CTho EPfP IDee LRHS NLar SSpi SSta WBVN WDin WFar WPGP WPat

Ilex ✿ (*Aquifoliaceae*)

N x ***altaclerensis***	GKir SHHo
- 'Atkinsonii' (m)	SHHo
- 'Belgica' (f)	SHHo
§ - 'Belgica Aurea' (f/v) ♀H4	CAlb CBcs CDoC CSBt CTho EBee EPfP GKir MBar MBri MGos NWea SEND SHBN SHHo WBcn WFar WWHy
- 'Camelliifolia' (f) ♀H4	CSBt CTho EBee ELan EPfP GKir MBlu MBri MRav MWat NWea SHHo SPer SPla WBcn WFar
- 'Golden King' (f/v) ♀H4	More than 30 suppliers
- 'Hendersonii' (f)	SHHo WBcn
- 'Hodginsii' (m) ♀H4	CTri ECot MBar MRav NWea SEND SHHo WFar WWHy
- 'Howick' (f/v)	SHHo WBcn
- 'James G. Esson' (f)	SBir SHHo
- 'Lady Valerie' (f/v)	IArd SHHo
- 'Lawsoniana' (f/v) ♀H4	CDoC CMHG CSBt CSam ELan EPfP GKir MAsh MBar MBri MRav NBlu NWea SHBN SHHo SLim SLon SPer SPla SPoG SRms SSta WBVN WDin WFar WPat WTel WWHy

	Name	Suppliers
	- 'Maderensis'	NRib
	- 'Maderensis Variegata'	see *I. aquifolium* 'Maderensis Variegata'
	- 'Marnockii' (f)	SHHo WBcn
	- 'Moorei' (m)	SHHo
	- 'Mundyi' (m)	SHHo
	- 'Purple Shaft' (f)	GKir MRav SHHo
	- 'Ripley Gold' (f/v)	GKir MAsh SAga SCoo SHHo WWHy
	- 'Silver Sentinel'	see *I.* x *altaclerensis* 'Belgica Aurea'
	- 'W.J. Bean' (f)	SHHo
	- 'Wilsonii' (f)	EBee NWea SHHo WWHy
	aquifolium ♀H4	More than 30 suppliers
	- 'Alaska' (f)	CAlb CDoC CDul CMCN EBee EMil ENot GKir LAst LBuc NBlu NSti SBir SHHo SWvt WFar WWHy
	- 'Amber' (f) ♀H4	CTri EBee SHHo SMad WBcn
	- 'Angustifolia' (f)	EPla MAsh WFar
	- 'Angustifolia' (m or f)	EPfP MBar MWat SHHo WBVN WBcn WFar
§	- 'Argentea Marginata' (f/v) ♀H4	More than 30 suppliers
§	- 'Argentea Marginata Pendula' (f/v)	CDoC CTri ECrN ELan EPfP GKir LRHS MAsh NWea SHHo SLim SRms WFar WPat WWHy
	- 'Argentea Pendula'	see *I. aquifolium* 'Argentea Marginata Pendula'
	- 'Argentea Variegata'	see *I. aquifolium* 'Argentea Marginata'
	- 'Atlas' (m)	CBcs CDoC LBuc
	- 'Aurea Marginata' (f/v)	CMHG CTho EBee EHoe GKir LBuc MGos NBlu NEgg NWea SBod SCoo SHBN SHHo WCFE WDin WFar WPat
	- 'Aurea Marginata Pendula' (f/v)	CDoC NLar SLim SPer WPat
	- 'Aurea Ovata'	see *I. aquifolium* 'Ovata Aurea'
	- 'Aurea Regina'	see *I. aquifolium* 'Golden Queen'
	- 'Aureovariegata Pendula'	see *I. aquifolium* 'Weeping Golden Milkmaid'
	- 'Aurifodina' (f)	GKir IMGH SHHo WBcn
§	- 'Bacciflava' (f)	More than 30 suppliers
	- 'Bowland' (f/v)	SHHo
	- 'Cookii' (f)	SHHo
	- 'Copper'	WBcn
	- 'Crassifolia' (f)	EPla SHHo SMad WWHy
	- 'Crispa' (m)	CDul EBee MBlu SBir SHHo
	- 'Crispa Aureomaculata'	see *I. aquifolium* 'Crispa Aureopicta'
§	- 'Crispa Aureopicta' (m/v)	SHHo WBcn WPat
	- 'Elegantissima' (m/v)	SCoo SHHo WWHy
	- 'Ferox' (m)	CDul CTbh ELan EPfP GKir LRHS SHHo SPer WBcn WDin WGwG WWHy
	- 'Ferox Argentea' (m/v) ♀H4	More than 30 suppliers
*	- 'Ferox Argentea Picta' (m/v)	LRHS WWHy
	- 'Ferox Aurea' (m/v)	CDoC CSBt CWib EBee ELan EPfP GKir LAst MAsh SHHo SPer SPla WWHy
§	- 'Flavescens' (f)	CBot EBee EPfP SHHo WBcn
*	- 'Forest Weeping'	LRHS
	- 'Foxii' (m)	SHHo
	- 'Fructu Luteo'	see *I. aquifolium* 'Bacciflava'
	- 'Gold Flash' (f/v)	GKir LRHS MBri MGos NBlu SHHo SLim WBcn WDin WWHy
	- 'Golden Hedgehog'	EPfP GKir WWHy
	- 'Golden Milkboy' (m/v)	EBee ELan EMil EPfP GKir MAsh MBlu MGos SHHo SPoG WCFE WDin WPat WWHy
	- 'Golden Milkmaid' (f/v)	EHol
§	- 'Golden Queen' (m/v) ♀H4	CDoC CWSG CWib EBee GKir LRHS MGos NBir NWea SHHo SPer SRms WPat WWHy
	- 'Golden Tears'	SHHo WBcn
	- 'Golden van Tol' (f/v)	CAlb CBcs CDoC CLnd CSBt CTri EBee ECrN ELan ENot EPfP EWTr GKir IMGH LAst LRHS MBar MBlu MGos MSwo NSti SCoo SHBN SHHo SRms WDin WWHy WWeb
	- 'Green Pillar' (f)	EPfP LBuc SHHo WWHy
	- 'Handsworth New Silver' (f/v) ♀H4	More than 30 suppliers
	- 'Harpune' (f)	SHHo WWHy
§	- 'Hascombensis'	EHol GBin MGos NMen WFar WWHy
	- 'Hastata' (m)	CWib IArd WWHy
	- 'Ingramii' (m/v)	SBir SHHo WBcn
	- 'J.C. van Tol' (f/m) ♀H4	More than 30 suppliers
	- 'Latispina' (f)	SHHo
	- 'Laurifolia Aurea' (m/v)	SHHo
	- 'Lichtenthalii' (f)	IArd SHHo
	- 'Madame Briot' (f/v) ♀H4	More than 30 suppliers
§	- 'Maderensis Variegata' (m/v)	SHHo
	- 'Monstrosa' (m)	SHHo
	- moonlight holly	see *I. aquifolium* 'Flavescens'
	- 'Myrtifolia' (m)	CDoC ELan EPfP GKir MBar MBlu MGos MRav NBlu SCoo SPoG WFar WWHy
	- 'Myrtifolia Aurea' (m/v)	SPoG SWvt WBcn WFar
§	- 'Myrtifolia Aurea Maculata' (m/v) ♀H4	CBrm CDoC CSam EBee EHoe ELan EPfP GKir IMGH LAst LRHS MAsh MBri MRav NEgg NWea SHHo SLim SPer SWvt WBVN WFar WPat WWHy
	- 'Myrtifolia Aureovariegata'	see *I. aquifolium* 'Myrtifolia Aurea Maculata'
	- 'Ovata' (m) **new**	WWHy
§	- 'Ovata Aurea' (m/v)	SHHo WWHy
	- 'Pendula' (f)	EPfP SCoo SHHo
	- 'Pendula Mediopicta'	see *I. aquifolium* 'Weeping Golden Milkmaid'
	- 'Purple Lady'	WBcn
	- 'Purple Lord'	WBcn
§	- 'Pyramidalis' (f) ♀H4	CAlb CDoC CDul CEnd CSBt CTho CTri EBee ELan GKir LRHS MAsh MBar MBri MGos MLan MRav NBlu NFor NWea SHHo SRms WDin WFar WMoo WWHy
	- 'Pyramidalis Aureomarginata' (f/v)	CDoC LRHS MGos MLan SHHo WBcn WBor
	- 'Pyramidalis Fructu Luteo' (f) ♀H4	GKir MBar NWea SHHo WBcn
	- 'Rubricaulis Aurea' (f/v)	SHHo WBcn WWHy
	- 'Sharpy' (f)	SBir
	- Siberia = 'Limsi'PBR (f)	EBee SHHo
	- 'Silver King'	see *I. aquifolium* 'Silver Queen'
	- 'Silver Lining' (f/v)	SHHo
	- 'Silver Milkboy' (f/v)	CTho EHoe ELan EMil LRHS MAsh MBNS MBlu MGos WFar WWHy
	- 'Silver Milkmaid' (f/v)	CAlb CDoC CWSG EBee EPfP GKir LAst LRHS MBar MRav NEgg SHBN SHHo SLim SPer SPla SPoG SWvt WMoo WRHF WWHy
§	- 'Silver Queen' (m/v) ♀H4	More than 30 suppliers
	- 'Silver Sentinel'	see *I.* x *altaclerensis* 'Belgica Aurea'
	- 'Silver van Tol' (f/v)	CAlb CDoC ELan IMGH LAst LRHS NPer NWea SHHo SMer SPer SPoG WBcn WFar WWHy WWeb
	- 'Somerset Cream' (f/v) **new**	WWHy
	- 'Victoria' (m)	WBcn

§	- 'Watereriana' (m/v)	EHol LRHS MAsh SMur WBcn
	- 'Waterer's Gold'	see *I. aquifolium* 'Watereriana'
§	- 'Weeping Golden Milkmaid' (f/v)	SHHo WPat
	x ***aquipernyi***	SHHo
	- Dragon Lady = 'Meschick' (f)	GKir SHHo WWHy
	- 'San Jose' (f)	CMCN SHHo
	x ***attenuata***	WFar
	- 'Sunny Foster' (f/v)	CDul CMCN EBee ENot EPla MGos SHHo WBcn WFar
§	***bioritsensis***	CMCN CTri NWea SBir WBcn
	buergeri	CMCN
	cassine	CMCN
	chinensis misapplied	see *I. purpurea*
	ciliospinosa	CFil CMCN WPGP
	colchica	CMCN SHHo
	corallina	CBcs CMCN
	cornuta	ERom LRHS SHHo WBcn WFar
*	- 'Aurea'	SHHo
	- 'Burfordii' (f)	SHHo
§	- 'Dazzler' (f)	SHHo
	- 'Fine Line' (f)	SHHo
	- 'Ira S. Nelson' (f/v)	SHHo
	- 'O. Spring' (f/v)	CMHG SHHo WBcn
	- 'Rotunda' (f)	SHHo
I	- 'Willowleaf' (f)	SHHo
	crenata	CMCN CTri ERom GBin GKir MBar SHHo WDin WFar WNor
	- 'Akagi'	WFar
	- 'Aureovariegata'	see *I. crenata* 'Variegata'
	- 'Braddock Heights' (f)	SHHo
	- 'Cape Fear' (m)	SHHo
	- 'Carolina Upright' (m)	SHHo
	- 'Cole's Hardy' (f)	SHHo
	- 'Convexa' (f) 🏆H4	CBcs EPfP GKir IMGH LRHS MBar MBri NBlu NWea SHHo WFar WPat
	- 'Convexed Gold'	MBri WBcn
	- 'Fastigiata' (f)	CChe CDoC CEnd EBee ECrN EPfP EPla GKir LAst LRHS MAsh MBNS MBar MBri MGos NBlu SCoo SHHo SPer SPoG WFar WWes
	- 'Fructo Luteo'	see *I. crenata* f. ***watanabeana***
	- 'Fukarin'	see *I. crenata* 'Shiro-fukurin'
*	- 'Glory Gem' (f)	SHHo
	- 'Gold Tips'	MGos
	- 'Golden Gem' (f) 🏆H4	More than 30 suppliers
	- 'Green Dragon' (m)	EPla WWes
	- 'Green Hedge'	LBuc
	- 'Green Island' (m)	SHHo
	- 'Green Lustre' (f)	SHHo
	- 'Helleri' (f)	CMCN EPfP EPla MBar SBla SHHo WPat
	- 'Hetzii' (f)	EWTr NLar SHHo
	- 'Ivory Hall' (f)	EPla SHHo
	- 'Ivory Tower' (f)	SHHo
*	- 'Kobold'	SHHo
	- 'Korean Gem'	EPla SHHo
	- var. ***latifolia*** (m)	SHHo
	- 'Luteovariegata'	see *I. crenata* 'Variegata'
	- 'Mariesii' (f)	ESis IMGH MBlu SBla SHHo
	- 'Mount Halla' (f)	CMCN
	- 'Nakada' (m)	SHHo
	- var. ***paludosa***	CFil EBee WPGP
	- 'Pride's Tiny'	SHHo
I	- 'Pyramidalis' (f)	NWea
§	- 'Shiro-fukurin' (f/v)	CMCN CMHG ELan EPfP GKir LAst LRHS MAsh SHHo
	- 'Sky Pencil' (f)	CMCN
	- 'Snowflake'	see *I. crenata* 'Shiro-fukurin'
	- 'Stokes' (m)	LRHS NLar SHHo
§	- 'Variegata' (v)	CMCN EPla GKir LRHS MBar SHHo SPoG
§	- f. ***watanabeana*** (f)	SHHo
	'Dazzler'	see *I. cornuta* 'Dazzler'
	decidua	CMCN CPle
	dimorphophylla	CBcs CDoC CMCN SHHo
	- 'Somerset Pixie'	GKir SHHo
	dipyrena	CFil
	'Doctor Kassab' (f)	CMCN SHHo
	'Drace' (f)	SHHo
	'Elegance' (f)	WFar
	fargesii	CPne CTho
	ficoidea	CMCN
	glabra	SHHo
	'Good Taste' (f)	SHHo WFar
	hascombensis	see *I. aquifolium* 'Hascombensis'
	hookeri	SHHo
	'Indian Chief' (f)	MBlu SMad WFar
	insignis	see *I. kingiana*
	integra	CFil
	'John T. Morris' (m)	SHHo
§	***kingiana***	CFil WFar WPGP
	x ***koehneana***	CBot CDul CFil ELan
	- 'Chestnut Leaf' (f) 🏆H4	CCVT CDoC CFil CLnd CMCN MRav SHHo SMad WBcn WFar WLeb WPGP
	latifolia	CFil CHEx CMCN SHHo SMad WPGP
	'Lydia Morris' (f)	CSam SHHo WFar
	'Mary Nell' (f)	SBir SHHo
	x ***meserveae***	SHHo
	- Blue Angel (f)	CBcs CDoC CDul COtt EBee ELan EMil EPfP GKir IMGH MBar MBri MWat NBlu NEgg NWea SHHo SPer SPoG SRms WDin WFar WPat WWHy
	- Blue Maid = 'Mesid' (f)	EMil
	- Blue Prince (m)	CBcs CBrm CDoC CDul COtt EBee EHol GKir LBuc MBar MBlu NBlu NWea SHBN SHHo SLim SPer SPoG WDin WFar WWHy
	- Blue Princess (f)	CBcs CBrm COtt ECrN ENot EPfP GKir LBuc MBar MBlu MRav NBlu NSti NWea SCoo SHBN SHHo SLim SPoG WWHy
	- Golden Girl = 'Mesgolg' (f)	EMil
*	- 'Red Darling' (f)	CDul
	muchagara	CBcs CMCN
	myrtifolia	CMCN ECot MLan MRav NEgg NPri WCFE
	'Nellie R. Stevens' (f)	CDoC EBee NWea SCoo WBcn WWHy
	nothofagifolia	WAbe
	opaca	CMCN
	pedunculosa	CMCN SHHo
	perado latifolia	see *I. perado* subsp. *platyphylla*
§	- subsp. ***platyphylla***	CBcs CHEx CMCN MBlu SAPC SArc SHHo
	pernyi	CMCN GKir LRHS SHHo SLon WBcn WFar WPic
	- var. ***veitchii***	see *I. bioritsensis*
§	***purpurea***	CMCN SPla
	'Pyramidalis'	see *I. aquifolium* 'Pyramidalis'
	rugosa	CMCN
	'September Gem' (f)	CMCN
	serrata	CMen
	'Sparkleberry' (f)	LRHS
	suaveolens	CMCN
	verticillata	CMCN CPne GKir IMGH NWea WDin WFar
	- (f)	EPfP NWea WFar
	- (m)	CBcs CDoC EPfP
	- 'Christmas Cheer' (f)	WFar
	- 'Maryland Beauty' (f)	CPMA

- 'Southern Gentleman' (m)	CPMA
- 'Winter Red' (f)	CMCN CPMA GKir MMHG
vomitoria	CMCN EShb
x ***wandoensis***	CMCN SHHo
yunnanensis	CMCN

Iliamna see *Sphaeralcea*

Illicium (*Illiciaceae*)

anisatum	CArn CBcs CFil CPle EPfP NLar SBrw SSpi WFar WPGP WPat WSHC
floridanum	CBcs CFil EBee EPfP NLar SBrw SSpi
- 'Halley's Comet'	CFil NLar
- variegated (v)	SSpi
henryi	CFil CMCN CMHG EPfP NLar SSpi WPGP WSHC
aff. ***henryi*** BWJ 8024	WCru
lanceolatum **new**	SSpi
mexicanum **new**	CFil
parviflorum	CFil SSpi
simonsii	CFil
'Woodland Ruby'	SSpi

Ilysanthes see *Lindernia*

Impatiens ✿ (*Balsaminaceae*)

from China	CLAP CPom CSpe EMan GCal MCCP SSpi WCot WPGP
apiculata	GCal
arguta	CDes CFir CPLG CPom CSpe EMan EShb GCal LPhx MDKP WCru WDyG WPGP
auricoma	EBak SHFr
balfourii	EBee EHrv EMan EMon NBir WCot
'Cardinal Red'	CHal
congolensis	EPfP
cristata	CPLG WCot
'Diamond Rose'	CHal
double-flowered (d)	EBak
falcifer	CSpe
flanaganae **new**	CFir
glandulifera 'Candida'	EMon
- 'Mien Ruys' **new**	EMon
(Harmony Series) Harmony Dark Red = 'Danhardkrd' **new**	LAst
- Harmony Lavender **new**	LAst
- Harmony Light Pink = 'Danharltpk'	LAst
- Harmony Salmon = 'Danharsal' **new**	LAst
- Harmony Margenta = 'Danharmgta'	LAst
hawkeri	see *I. schlechteri*
hians	SHFr
kerriae B&SWJ 7219	WCru
kilimanjari x ***pseudoviola***	CFee CSpe GCal
longiloba B&SWJ 6623	WCru
'Madame Pompadour'	CHal
New Guinea Group	see *I. schlechteri*
niamniamensis	CHll EBak ERea EShb WDib
- 'Congo Cockatoo'	CHEx CHal EOHP ESlt LIck SHFr SPoG SRms
- 'Golden Cockatoo' (v)	CHal EBak EShb ESlt IFro MCCP
omeiana	CHEx CLAP CPLG CPom CSpe EBee EMan EPPr EShb GCal ITer MCCP MNrw SBch SSpi WBor WCot WCru WDyG WPGP WSHC
Papete = 'Kipete'PBR (Paradise Series) **new**	NBlu
pseudoviola	SDix SHFr
puberula HWJK 2063 **new**	WCru
'Raspberry Ripple'	CHal
'Salmon' (Fiesta Series)	see *I. walleriana* (Fiesta Series) Fiesta Olé Salmon, 'Sparkler Salmon'
§ ***schlechteri***	CHal EBak MBri
sodenii	CSpe EShb SDys SHFr WCot
stenantha **new**	CFir
sulcata	SHFr
sultani	see *I. walleriana*
tinctoria	CDoC CFil CFir CHEx CHll CPLG CPom CSpe EMon EShb GCal GCra MNrw SIgm SSpi WCot WCru WMul WPGP WPrP
- subsp. ***elegantissima***	CFee
- subsp. ***tinctoria***	IFro
ugandensis	SSpi
uniflora	CFir GCal
violeta B&SWJ 6608	WCru
walkeri	CFee
§ ***walleriana***	EBak MBri
- (Duet Series) 'Dapper Dan' (d/v)	CHal WWol
- (Fiesta Series) 'Burgundy Rose'PBR (d)	LAst WWol
- - Fiesta Appleblossom = 'Balfieplos' (d)	LAst LIck NPri SVil WWol
- - Fiesta Blush = 'Balfieblus' (d)	NPri
- - Fiesta Coral Bells = 'Balfiecobl' (d)	NPri
- - Fiesta Olé Cherry = 'Balolecher' (d)	NPri
- - Fiesta Olé Frost = 'Balolefro' (d)	NPri
- - Fiesta Olé Peppermint = 'Balolepep' (d/v)	SVil
- - Fiesta Olé Salmon = 'Balolesal' (d)	NPri
- - Fiesta Olé Stardust = 'Balolestop' (d)	NPri
- - Fiesta Orange Spice = 'Balfieorce'PBR (d)	LIck WWol
- - Fiesta Sparkler Cherry = 'Balfiespary' (d)	NPri SVil
- - Fiesta Stardust Lavender = 'Balfiesala'PBR	LAst
- - 'Fiesta White'PBR (d)	NPri WWol
- - 'Lavender Orchid'PBR (d)	LIck NPri
- - 'Pink Ruffle'PBR (d)	LAst NPri
- - 'Salsa Red'PBR (d)	LAst NPri WWol
- - Sparkler Hot Pink = 'Balfiesink' (d) **new**	SVil
- - 'Sparkler Rose'PBR (d)	NPri SVil
§ - - 'Sparkler Salmon'PBR (d)	LIck WWol
- (Summer Ice Series) 'Blackberry Ice'PBR (d/v)	WWol
- - 'Cherry Ice'PBR (d/v)	WWol
- - 'Orange Ice'PBR (d/v)	WWol
- - 'Peach Ice' (d/v)	CHal WWol
- - 'Pink Ice'PBR (d/v)	WWol
- (Tempo Series) 'Shocking Pink'	LAst
- - 'Meloblue'	LAst
- - 'Meloda'	LAst
- - 'Melody'	LAst

* - 'Variegata' (v)	CHal
zombensis	SHFr

Imperata (*Poaceae*)

brevifolia	CBrm
cylindrica	CMen MGol MSal SGSe
- 'Red Baron'	see *I. cylindrica* 'Rubra'
§ - 'Rubra'	More than 30 suppliers

Incarvillea (*Bignoniaceae*)

§ ***arguta***	CBot EBrs EShb LPio SBla SHGN WAbe
- var. ***longipedicellata*** BWJ 7875 **new**	WCru
brevipes	see *I. mairei*
compacta	MDKP NSla
- BWJ 7620	WCru
delavayi	More than 30 suppliers
- 'Alba'	see *I. delavayi* 'Snowtop'
- 'Bees' Pink'	EBee EBrs GBuc GCal NArg SHGN
§ - 'Snowtop'	More than 30 suppliers
diffusa	SBla
forrestii	GKev LPio NSla
- KGB 43	EHyt
grandiflora	EHyt ELan GCrs SBla
himalayensis 'Frank Ludlow'	GBuc SIgm
- 'Nyoto Sama'	GBuc
lutea BWJ 7784	WCru
§ ***mairei***	EBee EBrs EGoo EHyt EMan GCrs GSki LRHS MLLN NLar SIgm WPer
- var. ***mairei***	EPot GBuc
- - CLD 101	GCrs
- - f. ***multifoliata***	see *I. zhongdianensis*
- pink	EHyt
§ ***olgae***	CBrm EHyt EMan EShb ESis EWTr GKev GSki MAnH NLar NWCA SHGN
przewalskii	WAbe
§ ***zhongdianensis***	EBee EBrs EPot ERos GBri GBuc GCal GCrs GEdr MDKP MGol NSla SOkd
- BWJ 7692	WCru
- BWJ 7978	WCru
- CLD 233	EHyt

Indigofera (*Papilionaceae*)

amblyantha 🏆 H4	CBcs CHar EPfP GCal IDee IMGH MBlu NLar NLon SBrw SLon SPlb SPoG SSpi WBVN WDin WSHC
australis	EUnu LRav
balfouriana BWJ 7851	WCru
cytisoides	GFai
decora f. ***alba***	EPfP IArd IDee
dielsiana	EPfP SSpi WKif WPGP
frutescens	CPLG
gerardiana	see *I. heterantha*
hebepetala	CPLG WCru WDin WPGP WSHC
§ ***heterantha*** 🏆 H4	More than 30 suppliers
kirilowii	CFil EPfP IArd WPGP WSHC
pendula	EPfP SSpi WPGP WSHC
- B&SWJ 7741	WCru
potaninii	EPfP SHBN SSpi WCru
pseudotinctoria	CPLG EGFP EPfP LRav MGol SRms WFar
subverticillata **new**	WPGP
tinctoria	CArn MSal

Indocalamus (*Poaceae*)

latifolius	EPPr EPla ERod MMoz MWht SEND WJun
- 'Hopei'	EPla
longiauritus	EPla
solidus	see *Bonia solida*
tesselatus f. ***hamadae***	EPla ERod MMoz MWht WJun
§ ***tessellatus*** 🏆 H4	CAbb CDoC CFil CHEx CMCo EAmu EBee EFul ENBC EPfP EPla ERod IFro MCCP MMoz MWht NGdn NMoo SMad WDyG WFar WJun WMoo WMul WPGP WPnP

Inula ✿ (*Asteraceae*)

acaulis	NJOw WCot
barbata	MLLN
britannica	NBre
var. ***chinensis*** **new**	
candida	XPep
crithmoides	WCFE WHer XPep
dysenterica	see *Pulicaria dysenterica*
ensifolia	CBcs CHrt ELan EPfP GBBs GKir MLLN MNFA MRav MSte MTho NBro SLPl WCAu WFar WOld WPnP WWpP
- 'Compacta'	EBee
- 'Gold Star'	EBee EMan EPfP MHer MLLN MNFA MWat NBid NBir NBlu NFor NJOw NLon SBla SPet WFar WGwG WMnd WMow WPer
glandulosa	see *I. orientalis*
helenium	More than 30 suppliers
- 'Goliath'	ELau MLLN
helianthus-aquatilis	MLLN
heterolepis **new**	EBee
hirta	MLLN SLPl WPer
hookeri	More than 30 suppliers
- GWJ 9033	WCru
macrocephala misapplied	see *I. royleana*
macrocephala Boiss. & Kotschy ex Boiss.	MLLN
magnifica	More than 30 suppliers
- 'Sonnenstrahl' 🏆 H4	LPhx
oculus-christi	EBee EWes MLLN
- MESE 437	EPPr
* 'Oriental Star'	GAbr WHil
§ ***orientalis***	CHrt COIW EBee EChP EPPr EPfP EWsh GBBs GIBF IHMH LRHS MBri MNFA MWat NBPC NBre NLon NVic SBri SGSe SHGN SMad SPet SPoG WCAu WFar WMnd WPer WSel WWpP
racemosa	EBee EMon EPla EWes GBin GCal IBlr MGol MNFA MNrw MSte NBid NSti SPlb SRms WFar WTin WWpP
- 'Sonnenspeer'	EMan MNFA NLar SLPl SMad WPer
rhizocephala	CSam EHyt MLLN NJOw WPer
§ ***royleana***	GBuc GCal GFlt GMac MDKP MNrw MRav MSte NBre NChi SBla
salicina	EBee
verbascifolia	ECho

Iochroma (*Solanaceae*)

§ ***australe***	CBcs CHEx CHll CKob CPle CSec CSpe LRav MOak SGar SHFr WCot WKif WPic
§ - 'Andean Snow'	CHll CPLG MOak
§ - 'Bill Evans'	CPLG EWll
cyaneum	CKob CPLG ERea SHFr SYvo
- purple-flowered	CHll
§ - 'Trebah'	ERea MOak SYvo
gesnerioides 'Coccineum'	CHll
§ ***grandiflorum***	CHEx CHll CSev SGar SYvo
violaceum hort.	see *I. cyaneum* 'Trebah'
warscewiczii	see *I. grandiflorum*

Ipheion (*Alliaceae*)

'Alberto Castillo'	CAvo CBro CDes CMea CMon

	CPom EBee EHyt ELan EMan EPot ERos EWes LAma LTwo MAsh MRav MTho SBla SIgm SIng SOkd SUsu WAbe WCot WHoo WIvy WPGP WTin
dialystemon	CMon NMen SBla SOkd WAbe
'Rolf Fiedler' 🏆H2-3	More than 30 suppliers
sellowianum	CMon CPBP NWCA WCot
sessile **new**	SOkd
uniflorum	CAvo CBro CStu CTri EBee ECha GFlt LAma MBri MNrw MRav MWgw NBlu NJOw NMen NWCA SIng SPer SRms WAbb WAul WCot WFar WHoo WPer WPnP WTin
- 'Album'	CBro CMea CPom EBee ECha ELan EPot ERos EWes LPio LRHS MAsh MRav MTho SBla SIng WCot WPnP
- 'Charlotte Bishop'	More than 30 suppliers
- 'Froyle Mill' 🏆H4	CAvo CBro CDes CElw CMea CPom CSWP EBee EBrs ELan EPot ERos EWes LLWP LPio LRHS MRav MTho NJOw NMen SAga SBla SIng SUsu WFar WHoo WPGP WPnP
- 'Wisley Blue' 🏆H4	More than 30 suppliers

Ipomoea (*Convolvulaceae*)

acuminata	see *I. indica*
* ***andersonii***	CPLN
batatas 'Ace of Spades' **new**	EUnu
- 'Blackie'	EShb ESlt EUnu WDyG WFar
- 'Margarita' **new**	EUnu
- 'Pink Frost' (v) **new**	EUnu
brasiliensis	see *I. pes-caprae* subsp. *brasiliensis*
§ ***cairica*** **new**	CPLN CSec
costata	CSec
hederacea **new**	CTbh
§ ***indica*** 🏆H1	CHEx CHal CHll CPLN CTbh EPfP ERea EShb ESlt ISea MJnS SPer SYvo WMul
- 'Betty Mars' **new**	CPLN
- 'Edith Piaf' **new**	CPLN
learii	see *I. indica*
§ ***lobata***	CSpe LRHS LSou SGar SHFr SUsu SYvo
microdactyla **new**	CPLN
muellerii **new**	CSec
x ***multifida*** **new**	CSpe
nil **new**	LRav
ochracea **new**	CSec
§ ***pes-caprae*** subsp. ***brasiliensis***	CSec
purpurea 'Kniola's Purple-black'	CSpe
tricolor **new**	CSec
tuberosa	see *Merremia tuberosa*
versicolor	see *I. lobata*
'Zarah Leander' **new**	CPLN

Ipomopsis (*Polemoniaceae*)

§ ***aggregata***	NPol
rubra	EBee NPol

Iresine (*Amaranthaceae*)

herbstii	CHal EBak ERea SMur
- 'Aureoreticulata'	CHal MOak
- 'Brilliantissima'	CHal MOak SMrm
lindenii 🏆H1	CHal MOak

Iris ✿ (*Iridaceae*)

AC 4623 from Tibet **new**	GIBF
AGSJ 431	EWoo
'Abbey Road' (TB) **new**	WCAu
'Abracadabra' (SDB)	SMrm
'Acoma' (TB)	EWoo WCAu
'Action Front' (TB)	CM&M COtt EBee EChP EHrv ERou LAst MWgw NEgg NGdn SCoo SDnm WCra WWeb
'Actress' (TB)	ECGP EChP EVFa LSRN SPet WCra
'Adobe Rose' (TB)	ESgI
'Adrienne Taylor' (SDB) 🏆H	WCAu WPen
'Afternoon Delight' (TB)	ESgI MRav WCAu
'Agatha Christie' (IB)	WCAu
'Agatha Dawson' (Reticulata/v)	EMon
'Agnes James' (CH) 🏆H3	CBro
'Albatross' (TB)	CKel
albicans 🏆H4	CMon EPot WCAu WHal
§ ***albomarginata***	WWst
'Alcazar' (TB)	EPfP EWTr LSRN NMoo WEas WFar WMnd
'Aldo Ratti' (TB)	ESgI
'Alice Harding' (TB)	ESgI
'Alien Mist' (TB)	CIri
'Alizes' (TB) 🏆H4	CIri ESgI EWoo WCAu
'Allegiance' (TB)	WCAu WEas
'Allendale' (BB) **new**	CIri
'Alpine Journey' (TB)	ESgI
'Alpine Lake' (MDB)	WCAu
'Alsterquelle' (SDB)	WTin
'Amadora' (TB)	CKel
'Amas' (TB)	WCAu
'Ambassadeur' (TB)	EBee ERou EWTr
'Amber Queen' (DB)	EBee ECtt ELan ERos MSte MWgw NBir NEgg NMen SPet SPoG WWeb
'Ambroisie' (TB)	ESgI
'American Patriot' (IB) **new**	WCAu
'America's Cup' (TB)	WCAu
'Amethyst Flame' (TB)	ENot ERou ESgI SRms WCAu
'Amherst Bluebeard' (SDB) **new**	SIri
'Amherst Caper' (SDB) **new**	WCAu
'Amherst Moon' (SDB) **new**	WCAu
'Amherst Purple Ribbon' (SDB) **new**	WCAu
'Amherst Sweetheart' (SDB) **new**	WCAu
'Amigo' (TB)	ESgI
'Amphora' (SDB)	CBro ERos GBuc
'Andalou' (TB)	ESgI
'Andy Dandy' (La) **new**	CWrd
'Angel Unawares' (TB)	WCAu
'Angel's Tears'	see *I. histrioides* 'Angel's Tears'
anglica	see *I. latifolia*
'Anna Belle Babson' (TB)	ESgI
'Annabel Jane' (TB)	CKel WCAu
'Anne Elizabeth' (SDB)	CBro ERos
'Annikins' (IB) 🏆H4	CKel
'Anniversary Celebration' (TB)	CKel
'Antarctique' (IB)	ESgI
'Antigone'	ESgI
'Anvil of Darkness' (TB)	CIri
aphylla	GIBF WCAu
- subsp. ***fieberi*** **new**	WCot
'Apollo' (Dut)	CFwr MBow
'Appledore' (SDB)	CBro ERos
'Appointer'	CRow GBin
'Apricorange' (TB) 🏆H4	CKel
'Apricot Frosty' (BB)	CIri
'Apricot Silk' **new**	EVFa
'Arab Chief' (TB)	CKel
'Arabi Pasha' (TB)	WCAu

*	'Arabic Night' (IB)	WCAu
	'Archie Owen' (Spuria)	WCAu
	'Arctic Fancy' (IB) 🏆H4	CKel
	'Arctic Snow' (TB)	WCAu
	'Arctic Wine' (IB) **new**	WCAu
	arenaria	see *I. humilis*
	'Argus Pheasant' (SDB)	ESgI
	'Armageddon' (TB) **new**	ESgI
	'Art School Angel' (TB)	CIri
	'Ask Alma' (IB)	ESgI WCAu
	'Astrid Cayeux' (TB)	ESgI EWoo
*	'Atlantique' (TB)	CKel
	'Attention Please' (TB)	CKel
§	***attica***	CBro CPBP CStu EHyt EPPr EPot ERos LBee LRHS LTwo NJOw NWCA WAbe WHal WLin
	- lemon	CPBP
§	***aucheri*** 🏆H2	CBro LAma WWst
	'Aunt Martha' (BB)	MBri WCAu
	'Aurean' (IB)	EVFa
	'Austrian Sky' (SDB)	CSam EBee ENot EVFa EWTr NEgg STes WCAu WPGP
	'Autumn Circus' (TB) **new**	WCAu
	'Autumn Leaves' (TB)	WCAu
	'Autumn Tryst' (TB)	WCAu
	'Avalon Sunset' (TB)	ESgI
	'Avanelle' (IB)	ERou
	'Az Ap' (IB)	EBee WCAu
	'Aztec Sun' (TB) **new**	SIri
	'Baboon Bottom' (BB)	CIri WCAu
	'Baby Bengal' (BB)	WCAu
	'Baby Blessed' (SDB)	CBro WCAu
	'Baccarat' (TB)	WCAu
	'Back in Black' (TB)	CKel
	'Back Street Affair' (TB)	CIri
	bakeriana	LAma
	'Bal Masque' (TB)	CIri ESgI
	baldschuanica	WWst
	'Ballerina'	NBir
	'Ballerina Blue' (TB)	ERou
	'Ballet Lesson' (SDB) 🏆H4	CIri
	'Ballyhoo' (TB)	WCAu
	'Banbury Beauty' (CH) 🏆H3	CLAP
	'Banbury Melody' (CH)	CFee GMac
	'Banbury Ruffles' (SDB)	ESgI NMen WCAu
	'Bang' (TB)	CKel
	'Bar de Nuit' (TB)	ESgI
	barnumae	EHyt EPot
	'Baroque Prelude' (TB)	CKel
	'Batik' (BB)	CIri WCAu
	'Batsford' (SDB)	CBro
	'Battle Royal' (TB)	CIri
	'Bayberry Candle' (TB)	CIri ESgI WAul
	'Beachgirl' (TB)	CIri
	'Bedford Lilac' (SDB) 🏆H4	CIri
	'Bedtime Story' (IB)	EBee
	'Bee Wings' (MDB)	WEas
	'Before the Storm' (TB)	CIri CKel ESgI WCAu
	'Beguine' (TB)	ESgI
	'Being Busy' (SDB)	ESgI
	'Bel Azur' (IB)	ESgI
	'Belvi Queen' (TB)	MNrw
*	'Ben Hasel'	ECha
	'Benton Dierdre' (TB)	SRms
	'Benton Evora' (TB)	ENot
	'Benton Nigel' (TB)	WCAu
	'Benton Sheila' (TB)	CFee
	'Berkeley Gold' (TB)	CMea COtt CSBt EBee ECtt ELan EPfP EVFa EWes EWsh GMac NEgg NGdn NOrc NVic SCoo SHBN SPer WCAu
	'Berlin Tiger' 🏆H4	CRow EPPr SApp
	'Best Bet' (TB)	EWoo WCAu
	'Bethany Claire' (TB)	ESgI
	'Betty Cooper' (Spuria)	WCAu
	'Betty my Love' (Spuria)	CIri
	'Betty Simon' (TB)	CKel ESgI EWoo
	'Beverly Sills' (TB)	CIri ESgI WCAu
	'Bewilderbeast' (TB)	CIri WCAu
	'Bianco' (TB) **new**	WCAu
	'Bibury' (SDB) 🏆H4	WCAu
N	'Big Day' (TB)	GFlt
	'Big Dipper' (TB)	EWoo SIri
	'Big Melt' (TB) **new**	CKel
	'Big Money' (CH) 🏆H3	GBuc
	biglumis	see *I. lactea*
	biliottii	CBro
	'Bishop's Robe' (TB)	SSvw
	'Black Beauty' (TB)	SPer
	'Black Dragon' (TB)	WBrE
	'Black Gamecock' (La)	CWrd SSpi
	'Black Hills' (TB)	EBee ENot WCAu
	'Black Ink' (TB)	COIW
	'Black Knight' (TB)	CBrm CSBt EHol EUJe NGdn SPoG
	'Black Night' (IB) **new**	STes
	'Black Swan' (TB)	CHad COtt EChP ECha ECtt EMan ESgI EVFa EWTr LAst LSRN MMil MSte NGdn NLon SDnm SHBN WCAu WCot WCra WEas WWeb
	'Black Taffeta' (TB)	CKel
	'Black Tie Affair' (TB)	ESgI EWoo WCAu
	'Black Watch' (IB)	CKel WAul
	'Blackbeard' (BB) 🏆H4	CKel WCAu
	'Blackout' (TB)	ESgI
	'Blatant' (TB)	ESgI WCAu
	'Blenheim Royal' (TB)	ESgI WCAu
	bloudowii	SOkd
	'Blue Ballerina' (CH) 🏆H3	GBuc WLin
	'Blue Crusader' (TB)	CIri WCAu
	'Blue Denim' (SDB)	CBro CElw ECtt EHyt EPfP GMaP MBNS MRav NBir NBro NCot SMrm WHoo WTin
	'Blue Eyed Blond' (IB)	WCAu
	'Blue Eyed Brunette' (TB)	WCAu
	'Blue Hendred' (SDB)	NBir WCAu
	'Blue Horizon' (TB)	ERos
	'Blue Luster' (TB) 🏆H4	ESgI
	'Blue Note Blues' (TB) **new**	WCAu
	'Blue Pigmy' (SDB)	ERos LBBr MBNS MWgw NEgg NFla NMen NSti SPer SPet WWeb
	'Blue Pools' (SDB)	EHyt MBri NBir WTin
	'Blue Reflection' (TB)	ESgI
	'Blue Rhythm' (TB)	CKel EChP ELan ERou GMaP GMac MRav MSte NMoo SChu SCoo SPer WCAu WMnd
	'Blue Sapphire' (TB)	CHad ESgI SHBN WCAu
	'Blue Shimmer' (TB)	COtt CSBt EBee ELan ENot EPfP ESgI MRav NCGa NFla NGdn SCoo SHBN SPer SPet WCAu WCra WHil
	'Blue Staccato' (TB)	ESgI WCAu
	'Blue Suede Shoes' (TB) **new**	ESgI
	'Blue Velvet' (TB)	WMoo
	'Bluebeard' (TB)	EHyt
	'Bluebird Wine' (TB)	WCAu
	'Bob Nichol' (TB) 🏆H4 **new**	CKel
	'Bodacious' (TB)	ESgI
	'Bohemia Sekt' (TB) **new**	CKel
	'Bohemian' (TB)	ESgI
	'Boisterous' (BB)	CIri
	'Bold Look' (TB)	CIri ESgI
	'Bold Pretender' (La) **new**	CWrd
	'Bold Print' (IB)	WCAu
	'Bollinger'	see *I.* 'Hornpipe'

	Name	Suppliers
	'Bonnie Davenport' (TB)	CIri
	'Bonny' (MDB)	CBro
	'Boo' (SDB)	CKel WAul WCAu WDav
	'Bourne Graceful'	CAby CBct CPLG WCAu
	'Bouzy Bouzy' (TB)	ESgI
	bracteata	CNic GBuc NWoo WPer
	- JCA 13427	CLAP
	'Braggadocio' (TB) **new**	WCAu
	'Braithwaite' (TB)	CKel EBee ELan ENot ERou MSte NGdn SPur SRms WCAu
	'Brandy' (TB)	CIri
	'Brannigan' (SDB)	CBro GKir MBri NBir NSti
	'Brash' (SDB) **new**	SIri
	'Brasilia' (TB)	NBir
	'Brass Tacks' (SDB)	WCAu
	'Brassie' (SDB)	CBro CKel ERos IHMH MBNS NBro SMrm
	'Breakers' (TB) ♀^{H4}	CKel ESgI EWoo WCAu
	brevicaulis	SSpi
§	'Bride' (DB)	EWTr WMnd
	'Bride's Halo' (TB)	EWoo WCAu
	'Brigantino' (BB)	ESgI
	'Bright Button' (SDB)	CKel ESgI EWoo WDav
	'Bright Chic' (SDB)	ESgI
	'Bright Fire' (TB)	EWoo SIri
	'Bright Moment' (SDB)	SIri
	'Bright Vision' (SDB)	ESgI
	'Bright White' (MDB)	CBro EHyt ERos MBNS MBri NMen
	'Bright Yellow' (DB)	MRav
	'Brighteyes' (IB)	GKir SRms
	'Brindisi' (TB)	ESgI
	'Brise de Mer' (TB) **new**	ESgI
	'Broadleigh Ann' (CH)	CBro
	'Broadleigh Carolyn' (CH) ♀^{H3}	CBro
	'Broadleigh Charlotte'	CBro
	'Broadleigh Clare' (CH)	CBro
	'Broadleigh Dorothy' (CH)	CBro GGar
	'Broadleigh Elizabeth' (CH)	CBro
N	'Broadleigh Emily' (CH)	CBro
N	'Broadleigh Florence' (CH)	CBro
	'Broadleigh Jean'	CBro
	'Broadleigh Joan' (CH)	CBro
	'Broadleigh Joyce' (CH)	CBro
	'Broadleigh Lavinia' (CH)	CBro MAvo MRav
	'Broadleigh Mitre' (CH)	CBro
	'Broadleigh Nancy' (CH)	CBro MAvo
	'Broadleigh Peacock' (CH)	CBro CNic EBla IBal IBlr MMil MRav
N	'Broadleigh Rose' (CH)	CBos CBro CElw CHid EBla EBrs EHrv GBuc GKir MBrN MRav SAga SApp SIri SMrm SWal WSHC
	'Broadleigh Sybil' (CH)	CBro GCra GCrs
	'Broadleigh Victoria' (CH)	CBro GBuc
	'Broadway Baby' (IB)	ESgI
	'Broadway Star'	CSBt
	'Bromyard' (SDB) ♀^{H4}	CBro WCAu
	'Bronzaire' (IB) ♀^{H4}	WCAu
	'Bronze Beauty' Werckmeister 1992 (*hoogiana* hybrid)	EPfP GBBs NBir SOkh SPer
	'Bronze Perfection' (Dut)	CRez
	'Bronze Queen' (Dut)	LRHS WRHF
N	'Brown Chocolate'	WCAu
	'Brown Lasso' (BB) ♀^{H4}	CIri WCAu
	'Brown Trout' (TB)	NBir
	'Brummit's Mauve'	WCAu
	bucharica hort.	see *I. orchioides* Carrière
	bucharica ambig.	WBor WHil
§	***bucharica*** Foster ♀$^{H3-4}$	CBro CMdw CPom CSam EBee EPfP EPot GFlt GIBF GKev LAma
	- 'Sanglok' **new**	WWst
	- 'Yellow Dushanbe'	WWst

	Name	Suppliers
	'Buisson de Roses' (TB)	ESgI
	bulleyana	CAby GBBs GBin GCrs GIBF GKev MGol NEgg NWCA NWoo SRms WAbe
	- ACE 1468	GBin
	- ACE 1819	GBin
	- ACE 2296	EBee EHyt GBuc
	- black	GKev
	- - SDR 1792	GKev
	- - SDR 1793	GKev
	- - SDR 2714	GKev
	aff. ***bulleyana***	GBBs
	'Bumblebee Deelite' (MTB) ♀^{H4}	WCAu
	bungei **new**	GKev
	'Burgundy Bubbles' (TB)	CIri
	'Burgundy Party' (TB) **new**	ESgI
	'Burnt Toffee' (TB)	ESgI WAul
	'Butter Pecan' (IB)	WCAu
	'Buttercup Bower' (TB)	WCAu
	'Buttered Popcorn'	SMer
	'Buttermere' (TB)	SRms
	'Butterpat' (IB)	ESgI
	'Butterscotch Carpet' (SDB) **new**	WCAu
	'Butterscotch Kiss' (TB)	EBee EChP ELan ERou MRav MWgw NBir NEgg SCoo SDnm SHBN
	'Cabaret Royale' (TB)	ESgI WCAu
	'Cable Car' (TB)	ESgI EWoo
	'Caliente' (TB)	EPfP MRav WCAu
	'California Style' (IB)	ESgI EWTr
§	Californian hybrids	CAby CElw CPBP CWCL ECGP EPot NBir SSpi WCFE WCot WWhi
	'Cambridge Blue'	see *I.* 'Monspur Cambridge Blue'
	'Camelot Rose' (TB)	WCAu
	'Cameroun' (TB)	ESgI
	'Campbellii'	see *I. lutescens* 'Campbellii'
	canadensis	see *I. hookeri*
	'Candy Clouds' (TB) **new**	WCAu
	'Cannington Bluebird' (TB)	WCAu
	'Cannington Ochre' (SDB)	CBro
	'Cantab' (Reticulata)	CAvo CBro EBrs EPot GBin LAma NJOw
	capnoides	WWst
	'Capricious' (TB)	ESgI
	'Captain Gallant' (TB)	WCAu
	'Caption' (TB)	ESgI
	'Caramba' (TB)	WCAu
	'Carilla' (SDB)	ERos
	'Carnaby' (TB)	ESgI MBri WCAu
	'Carnival Song' (TB) **new**	WCAu
	'Carnival Time' (TB)	EBee ECGP EChP WCra
	'Carnton' (TB)	WEas
	'Carolyn' (CH)	CFir
	'Caronte' (IB)	ESgI
	'Carriwitched' (IB) **new**	CKel
	'Cascade Sprite' (SDB)	SRms
	'Cascadian Skies' (TB)	ERou
	cedretii LB 391 from Lebanon **new**	CMon
*	'Cedric Morris'	EWes
	'Cee Jay' (IB) ♀^{H4}	CIri EWoo
	'Celebration Song' (TB)	ESgI WCAu
	'Celestial Glory' (TB)	WCAu
	chamaeiris	see *I. lutescens*
	'Champagne Elegance' (TB)	ESgI NBir WCAu
	'Champagne Encore' (IB)	ESgI
	'Champagne Music' (TB)	WCAu
	'Champagne Waltz' (TB)	CIri
	'Change of Pace' (TB)	WCAu
	'Chanted' (SDB)	ESgI

	'Chantilly' (TB)	CM&M COtt EBee EChP ELan EPfP MRav MTis NBir NEgg NGdn NOrc SDnm SPer WFoF
	'Chapeau' (TB)	WCAu
	'Chartreuse Ruffles' (TB)	EWoo
	'Char-true' (Spuria) **new**	WCAu
	'Chasing Rainbows' (TB)	CIri WCAu
	'Chaste White' (TB)	ESgI
	'Cherished'	EBee GBin SMer WWol
	'Cherokee Lace' (Spuria)	WTin
	'Cherry Garden' (SDB)	CBro CElw CKel EBee ECtt EGoo EHrv EHyt ELan EPfP EWes GKir IPot MBNS MBri MRav NBir NSti NWCA SMrm WCot WEas WPen
	'Cherry Glen' (TB)	CIri
	'Cherry Orchard' (TB)	NFor NLon
	'Cherry Smoke' (TB)	WCAu
	'Cherub's Smile' (TB)	ESgI
	'Chicken Little' (MDB)	CBro EBee NMoo
	'Chief Moses' (TB)	WCAu
I	'Chieftain' (SDB)	MRav
	'Chivalry' (TB)	WTin
	'Chocolate Vanilla' (TB)	CIri ESgI WCAu
	'Chorus Girl' (TB)	CKel
	'Christmas Angel' (TB)	ERou WCAu
	chrysographes ♀H4	CHid CPrp CWCL EBee EBrs EPfP EWTr GIBF GKir GMac LRHS MBnl MCCP MRav MWrn NMRc NSti SHGN SMac SRms SWal WAul WCAu WCFE WHil WSan WWeb WWhi
	- SDR 2873	GKev
	- ***alba***	NBir
	- black-flowered	More than 30 suppliers
I	- 'Black Beauty'	CFir EPfP GBBs GFlt
I	- 'Black Knight'	CBot CMdw EPfP EWsh GBuc GCal ITim MDun MHer MSte NBid NChi NFor NLar SHGN WMnd
I	- 'Black Velvet'	GAbr
	- crimson-flowered	IBlr NWoo
N	- 'Inshriach'	CFai EHyt GBuc IBlr LEdu WAbe WLin
	- 'Kew Black'	CDes EVFa MBnl NBir NChi NEgg NWCA WHer WHil WPop
	- 'Mandarin Purple'	GBuc GCal GMac SPer WMoo WPtf
§	- 'Rubella'	CRow GCra MMil MSte WFar WPrP
*	- var. ***rubella*** 'Wine'	CHad
	- 'Rubra'	see *I. chrysographes* 'Rubella'
	- 'Tsiri' **new**	NWCA
	chrysographes* x *forrestii	GFlt NBir
	chrysophylla	GBuc
	- JCA 13233	CLAP
	'Chubby Cheeks' (SDB)	CKel WCAu
	'Church Stoke' (SDB)	WCAu
	'Cimarron Rose' (SDB)	ESgI WCAu
	'Cinnabar Red' (Spuria) **new**	WAul
	'Cinnamon Roll' (Spuria) **new**	WCAu
	'Circle Step' (TB)	LBmB
	'City Lights' (TB)	WCAu
	'Clairette' (Reticulata)	CBro LAma
	'Clara Garland' (IB) ♀H4	WCAu
	'Clarence' (TB)	CIri ESgI WCAu
	clarkei	GBin GFlt GIBF WFar
	- B&SWJ 2122	WCru
	- CC 4181	MGol
	- CC 4463	GKev
	- purple-flowered	GFlt
	'Classic Bordeaux' (TB)	CIri
	'Classic Look' (TB)	CIri ESgI
	'Clear Morning Sky' (TB) ♀H4	CIri
N	'Cleo' (TB)	CKel NBir NSti
	'Cleo Murrell' (TB)	ESgI
	'Cliffs of Dover' (TB)	CKel SGar SIri SRms
	'Cloud Mistress' (IB)	ESgI
	'Cloudcap' (TB)	SRms
	'Cloudless Sunrise' (TB)	ERou
	'Coalignition' (TB)	CIri WCAu
	'Cobalt Mesa' (Spuria)	CIri
	'Codicil' (TB)	ESgI EWoo
	'Colette Thurillet' (TB)	ESgI WCAu
	'Colonial Gold' (TB)	WCAu
	'Combo' (SDB)	CKel
	'Coming Up Roses' (TB) **new**	WCAu
	'Confetti' (TB)	CMon
	confusa ♀H3	CAbP CAby CHEx CSev EBee EShb GBin IFro SAPC SArc SBig SEND SGSe SSpi WBor WBrk WDyG WFar WMul WPic WWst
§	- 'Martyn Rix'	More than 30 suppliers
	'Conjuration' (TB)	CIri ESgI EWoo WCAu
	'Conspiracy' (TB)	CIri
	'Constant Wattez' (IB)	CKel EBee ESgI NLar
	'Cool Treat' (BB) ♀H4	CIri
	'Copatonic' (TB)	CIri
	'Copper Classic' (TB)	ESgI SIri
	'Cops' (SDB)	ESgI
	'Coquetterie' (TB)	ESgI
	'Coral Chalice' (TB)	ERou
	'Coral Point' (TB)	WCAu
	'Cordoba' (TB)	CIri WCAu
	'Cozy Calico' (TB)	ESgI WCAu
	'Cradle Days' (MDB) **new**	EBee
	'Cranapple' (BB) ♀H4	CIri WCAu
	'Cranberry Crush' (TB)	WCAu
	'Cranberry Ice' (TB)	EWoo
	'Cream Beauty' (Dut)	SOkh SPer
	'Cream Pixie' (SDP) **new**	WCAu
	'Creme d'Or' (TB)	ESgI
	'Crème Glacée' (TB) **new**	ESgI
	cretensis	see *I. unguicularis* subsp. *cretensis*
	'Crimson Tiger' (TB)	CIri
	'Crinoline' (TB)	CKel
	'Crispette' (TB)	WCAu
	cristata ♀H4	EBla GBuc LEdu NLar NPro SIng SOkd SRms WCru
	- 'Alba'	ERos LRHS NWCA WAbe
	cristata* x *lacustris	ETow GKev NMen
	crocea ♀H4	CPLG GBin GKev
	'Crowned Heads' (TB)	CIri WCAu
	'Crushed Velvet' (TB)	WCAu
	'Crystal Glitters' (TB)	ESgI
	cuniculiformis	MGol
	- ACE 2224	EHyt GBuc
	'Cup Race' (TB)	GFlt WCAu
	'Cupid's Cup' (SDB)	ESgI
	'Curlew' (IB)	WCAu
*	***cuscutiformis*** **new**	WLin
	'Cutie' (IB)	ESgI WAul
	cycloglossa	CFwr EHyt EPot GKev LRHS SSpi WWst
	'Dance Away' (TB)	ESgI WCAu
	'Dancers Veil' (TB)	CHar ECtt ERou ESgI GKir MRav NVic SMer WCAu
	danfordiae	CAvo CBcs CBro EBrs EPfP EPot LAma LRHS NJOw SPet WFar WGwG WLin
	'Danger' (TB)	ESgI
	'Dardanus' (AB)	CFwr CMea EPot MBow
	'Dark Crystal' (SDB)	ESgI

	Name	Suppliers
	'Dark Spark' (SDB)	WCAu
	'Dark Vader' (SDB)	ESgI WCAu
	'Dash Away' (SDB)	ESgI SIri
	'Dauntless' (TB)	ESgI
	'David Guest' (IB) **new**	CKel
	'Dawning' (TB)	CIri ESgI
	'Dazzling Gold' (TB)	ESgI WCAu
§	***decora***	CBro GIBF LEdu NWCA
	'Deep Black' (TB)	CKel COtt EBee EChP EHrv ELan EMan EPfP MBNS MRav MSte MWgw NOrc SChu SDnm SHBN SPer WCAu
	'Deep Caress' (TB)	ESgI
	'Deep Dark Secret' (TB)	CIri
	'Deep Pacific' (TB)	MBri WCAu
	'Deep Purple' (TB)	LAst
	'Deep Space' (TB)	WCAu
	'Deft Touch' (TB)	CKel SIri WCAu
	delavayi ♀H4	CAby EWes GBin GIBF GMaP IBlr MLLN NEgg WCot
	- SDR 50	GKev
	'Delicate Lady' (IB) ♀H4	CKel
	'Delta Blues' (TB)	EWoo
	'Demon' (SDB)	CKel CMil EHyt SMrm WDav
	'Denys Humphry' (TB)	CKel WCAu
	'Deputé Nomblot' (TB)	ESgI
	'Derwentwater' (TB)	SRms WCAu
	'Desert Dream' (AB)	GAbr GGar
	'Desert Echo' (TB)	EVFa
	'Desert Song' (TB)	CKel WCAu
	'Designer Gown' (TB)	ERou
	'Diabolique' (TB)	CIri
	'Die Braut' (DB) **new**	EWTr NBlu
	'Dilly Green' (TB)	CIri
	'Distant Roads' (TB) **new**	WCAu
	'Divine' (TB)	CKel
	'Dixie Darling' (TB)	ESgI
	'Dixie Pixie' (SDB)	WCAu WTin
	dolichosiphon **new**	WLin
	'Doll' (IB)	EWoo
	'Dolly Madison' (TB)	ESgI
	'Don Juan' (TB) **new**	ESgI
	'Don't Be Cruel' (TB)	CIri
	'Double Espoir' (TB)	ESgI
	'Double Lament' (SDB)	CBro ERos
	douglasiana ♀H4	CAvo EChP GBBs GBin GKev IBlr MLLN NEgg SMac SSpi WFar WTin
	- 'Amiguita' (CH)	CFir EBee
*	- Bandon strain	SSpi
	'Dovedale' (TB) ♀H4	WCAu
	'Dover Beach' (TB)	SGar
	'Draco' (TB)	ESgI
	'Dream Indigo' (IB)	WCAu
	'Dreamsicle' (TB)	SIri
	'Dress Circle' (Spuria)	CIri
	'Dualtone' (TB)	CKel
	'Duchess of India' **new**	EWTr
	'Duke of Edinburgh' (TB) **new**	EWTr
	'Dunlin' (MDB)	CBro EHyt ERos NBir NMen
	'Dusky Challenger' (TB)	CIri CKel ESgI EWoo SCoo WCAu
	'Dutch Chocolate' (TB)	ESgI WCAu
	'Dwight Enys' (TB) ♀H4	CKel
	dykesii	CRow
	'Dynamite' (TB)	CIri
	'Earl of Essex' (TB)	WCAu
	'Early Frost' (IB)	CKel WAul
	'Early Light' (TB) ♀H4	CIri WCAu
	'East Indies' (TB)	WCAu
	'Eastertime' (TB)	ESgI
	'Echo de France' (TB)	ESgI EWoo
	'Ecstatic Echo' (TB)	ESgI
	'Ecstatic Night' (TB) **new**	WCAu
	'Edge of Winter' (TB)	CKel SIri
	'Edith Wolford' (TB)	CIri EBee ESgI EWoo GBin WCAu WSan
	'Ed's Blue' (DB)	ELan
	'Edward' (Reticulata)	EPfP EPot LAma SMeo WFar
	'Edward Windsor' (TB)	CBos CHad CMil ELan ERou GMaP NBir NOrc SCoo SDnm WMnd
	'Eileen Louise' (TB) ♀H4	WCAu
	'Elainealope' (TB)	CIri
	'Eleanor Clare' (IB) ♀H4 **new**	CKel
	'Eleanor's Pride' (TB)	CKel ESgI WCAu
	'Electrique' (TB)	WCAu
	elegantissima	see *I. iberica* subsp. *elegantissima*
	'Elizabeth Arden' (TB)	CKel
	'Elizabeth of England' (TB)	LBmB WWol
	'Elizabeth Poldark' (TB)	CIri ESgI WCAu
	'Elsa Sass' (TB) **new**	ESgI
	'Elvinhall'	CBro
	'Empress of India' (TB)	EBee
	'Encircle' (CH)	GBuc GFlt
	'Encre Bleue' (IB)	ESgI
	'English Charm' (TB)	ESgI WCAu
	'English Cottage' (TB)	EBee GCal MWat SMrm SOkd WCAu WCra WIvy
	'Ennerdale' (TB)	SRms
§	***ensata*** ♀H4	CBcs CBen CHEx CMHG COIW ECGP ELan EMFW ENot EPfP GFlt GKev GMac LPBA LRHS MNrw NBro NCob NEgg NGdn NLar SPlb SRms WFar WPer WWpP
	- 'Activity'	CRow CSBt NBro NGby SHar WFar WPrP WSan
	- 'Alba'	ECha GCra
	- 'Aldridge Prelude'	WAul
	- 'Apollo'	CBen CRow
	- 'Artist'	NBro
*	- 'Asahi-no-sora'	LBmB
	- 'Azuma-kagami'	CFir CWrd EBee ELan
I	- 'Azure'	CWrd
	- 'Barnhawk Sybil'	SSpi
	- 'Barr Purple East' ♀H4	CRow
	- 'Beni-Tsubaki'	WAul
I	- 'Blue King'	MBlu NBro
I	- 'Blue Peter'	CBen CRow
	- 'Blush'	NBro
	- 'Butterflies in Flight'	CRow
	- 'Caprician Butterfly' ♀H4	EPfP NLar SMrm WAul WCAu WHil WSan
	- 'Carnival Prince'	CFir NBro SBod WFar WMoo WPnP
	- 'Cascade Crest'	WAul
	- 'Cascade Spice'	WAul
	- 'Cry of Rejoice'	EBee EWTr GBri GFlt NBro WAul WCAu WFar
	- 'Dace'	CWrd EBee
	- 'Dancing Waves'	CRow
	- 'Darling'	CPen CRow CSam EBee EPfP EWTr GFlt IBlr LRHS MBNS NBro NLar SIri WAul WCAu WFar WMoo WPnP WTMC
	- 'Dramatic Moment'	CWrd
	- 'Dresden China'	CRow
	- 'Eden's Blue Pearl'	CHid CM&M EBee EChP GBin IPot NBro
	- 'Eden's Blush'	CMil EBee WAul WPop WSan
	- 'Eden's Charm'	CAby CMil EChP ELan GBin NBro SHar SPet SVil WAul WHil WWye
	- 'Eden's Harmony'	EBee EChP NBro WAul WHil WSan WTMC
	- 'Eden's Paintbrush'	CMil EBee EChP ELan EPfP NBro NGdn SOkh SVil WHil WTMC
	- 'Eden's Picasso'	CFir EBee ELan EPfP IPot NBro NGdn SVil WHil WSan WTMC

	- 'Eden's Purple Glory'	CHid EChP GBin NBro WCot WHil WPop WTin
	- 'Eden's Starship'	CFir EBee NGdn WSan
	- 'Electric Rays'	CWrd WAul
I	- 'Emotion'	EBee EWTr LRHS NBro NGby SMrm WAul WFar WPnP
	- 'Enkaishu'	CWrd
	- 'Fortune'	EHrv GBin SOkh WAul
	- 'Frilled Enchantment'	WAul
	- 'Geisha Gown'	SWal
	- 'Gipsy'	CSpe EBee EWTr LRHS WAul
	- 'Good Omen'	CWrd
	- 'Gracieuse'	CPrp CSev EBee EPPr GBin MBri NBPC NBro NLar SOkh SUsu WAul WFar WHil WMoo WPnP WPop
	- 'Gusto' **new**	CPen WHil WSan
	- 'Hana-aoi'	IBlr
	- 'Hatsu-shimo'	IBlr
	- 'Hercule'	CHad CRow GAbr NBir NGdn WTMC
	- Higo hybrids	IBlr LPBA
	- Higo white	SPer
N	- 'Hokkaido'	CRow IBlr
	- 'Hue and Cry' ♀^{H4}	WAul
*	- 'Innocence'	EHrv LRHS NGby NLar WAul WBor WFar WMoo
	- 'Iso-no-nami'	EBee EWll MBlu NBro WAul WPrP WTMC
	- 'Jodlesong'	EBee WFar
	- 'Kalamazoo'	WFar
	- 'Katy Mendez' ♀^{H4}	WAul
	- 'Kogesho'	EBee EPfP EWTr NBro NLar WAul
	- 'Koh Dom'	SPer
	- 'Kongo San'	CWrd WFar
	- 'Kuma-funjin'	CRow IBlr
	- 'Kumo-no-obi'	EBee EWll NBro WAul
	- 'Laced'	SPer
	- 'Landscape at Dawn'	CRow
	- 'Lasting Pleasure' ♀^{H4}	CWrd
	- 'Laughing Lion'	COtt CRez EBee NBro NOrc WAul WFar WMoo WPnP
	- 'L'Ideal'	CPen
	- 'Light at Dawn'	CPen IPot NBro NLar WAul WFar WHil WMoo WSan
	- 'Lilac Blotch'	SPer
	- 'Loyalty'	CWrd WFar
	- 'Manadzuru'	IBlr
I	- 'Mandarin'	CRow
	- 'Midnight Stars'	WAul
	- 'Midnight Whispers'	WAul
	- 'Midsummer Reverie'	CRow
	- 'Momozomo'	CWrd
§	- 'Moonlight Waves'	CHad CMHG CPrp CRow ELan EMFW EPPr EPfP EShb EWll GBuc GCra GGar GMaP GMac MBri MSte NBro NEgg NGdn NLon SChu SSpi SVil WAul WFar WTMC
	- 'Narihira'	IBlr
	- 'Ocean Mist'	CWrd EBee EVFa NBro
	- 'Oku-banri'	CHEx CPrp IBlr
	- 'Oriental Eyes'	EBee GBin NGdn NLar WAul WCAu
	- pale mauve	NBir SPer
	- 'Peacock'	EBee
	- 'Pin Stripe'	EVFa LBuc MBri NBro SUsu WAul WSan
	- 'Pink Frost'	CRow GKir GMac NBro WAul WFar WTMC WTin
	- 'Pleasant Earlybird'	WAul
	- 'Prairie Frost'	EBee EPfP EWTr SMrm
	- 'Prairie Noble'	EBee NBro NLar WHil
	- 'Purple Glory'	ELan WPop
	- purple-flowered	ITim SPer WWye
	- 'Ranpo'	CRow
	- 'Rebecca Johns'	CRow
	- 'Reign of Glory'	WAul
I	- 'Reveille'	EPPr NBro WAul WPtf
§	- 'Rose Queen' ♀^{H4}	More than 30 suppliers
	- 'Rowden Amir'	CRow
	- 'Rowden Autocrat'	CRow
	- 'Rowden Begum'	CRow
	- 'Rowden Dauphin'	CRow
	- 'Rowden Emperor'	CRow
	- 'Rowden King'	CRow
	- 'Rowden Knave'	CRow
	- 'Rowden Knight'	CRow
	- 'Rowden Mikado'	CRow
	- 'Rowden Nuncio'	CRow
	- 'Rowden Paladin'	CRow
	- 'Rowden Pasha'	CRow
	- 'Rowden Prince'	CRow
	- 'Rowden Queen'	CRow
	- 'Rowden Shah'	CRow
	- 'Rowden Sultana'	CRow
I	- 'Royal Banner'	EBee NBro WAul WFar
I	- 'Ruby King'	GBin WAul
I	- 'Sensation'	CPen GBin MBri NBPC NLar SPoG WAul WCAu WPrP
N	- 'Shihainami'	IBlr
	- 'Signal'	MBri
	- 'Snowy Hills'	WAul
	- var. ***spontanea***	CHVG GIBF
	- - B&SWJ 1103	WCru
	- - B&SWJ 8699	WCru
	- 'Springtime Melody'	WAul
	- 'Strut and Flourish'	WCAu
	- 'Summer Storm' ♀^{H4}	SPer
	- 'Teleyoshi'	SHar
	- 'The Great Mogul' ♀^{H4}	CRow
	- 'Tsumabeni'	CWrd
	- 'Variegata' (v) ♀^{H4}	More than 30 suppliers
	- 'Veinette'	CWrd
	- 'Velvety Queen'	CPrp EPPr WAul
	- 'Waka-murasaki'	EBee EWTr EWll GKir MBNS NBro WAul
	- 'White Ladies'	CSBt CWrd
I	- 'White Pearl'	CRow
	- 'Wine Ruffles'	LSRN SMrm
	- 'Yako-no-tama'	CRow WMoo
	- 'Yamato Hime' **new**	EPfP WSan
	- 'Yedo-yeman'	WFar
	- 'Yezo-nishiki'	GBin MBri NBro SBod SOkh WAul WBor WHil
	- 'Yu Nagi'	SPer
	'Epicenter' (TB) **new**	WCAu
	'Erect' (IB)	CIri
	'Esoteric' (SDB)	ESgI
	'Etched Apricot' (TB) **new**	WCAu
	'Ever After' (TB)	ESgI
	'Everything Plus' (TB)	ERou ESgI WCAu
	'Exclusivity' (TB)	CIri
	'Exotic Gem' (TB)	WCAu
	'Exotic Isle' (TB)	ESgI
	'Eye Shadow' (SDB) **new**	WCAu
	'Eyebright' (SDB) ♀^{H4}	CBro WCAu WPGP
	'Falcon's Crest' (Spuria)	CIri
	'Fall Fiesta' (TB)	ESgI
	'Fancy Woman' (TB)	CIri WCAu
	'Fanfaron' (TB)	ESgI
	'Fantaisie' (TB)	CKel
	'Faraway Places' (TB) **new**	WCAu
	'Fashion Lady' (MDB)	CBro EHyt
	'Fashion Statement' (TB)	CIri
	'Feature Attraction' (TB)	CIri WCAu
	'Feminine Charm' (TB)	WCAu
	'Festive Skirt' (TB)	CKel WCAu

	'Feu du Ciel' (TB)	CIri ESgI
	'Fierce Fire' (IB) ♀H4	CKel
	'Fiesta Time' (TB)	EWoo
	filifolia	CBro CMon
	- var. ***latifolia***	SSpi
	- - MS 437 from Spain **new**	CMon
	- - SF 332 from Morocco **new**	CMon
	'Film Festival' (TB)	ESgI
N	'Fire and Flame' (TB)	NBir
	'Firebug' (IB)	ESgI
	'Firecracker' (TB)	ERou MRav WCAu
	'First Interstate' (TB)	CIri ESgI
	'First Violet' (TB)	WCAu
	'Flareup' (TB)	WCAu
	flavescens	ESgI WCAu
§	'Florentina' (IB/TB) ♀H4	CArn CBro EGoo EMFP ESgI EWoo GPoy IBlr ILis MChe MHer MRav NBid NBir SIde WCAu WPic WWye
	'Flumadiddle' (IB)	CBro CKel
§	***foetidissima*** ♀H4	More than 30 suppliers
	- ***chinensis***	see *I. foetidissima* var. *citrina*
§	- var. ***citrina***	CFir CRow EPla GAbr GCal GKir IBlr LPio MRav SSpi STes SUsu WCot WEas WHoo WSSM WWye
	- 'Fructu Albo'	EBee EChP LPio MBNS NLar NSti WBrk WCot WTin
	- var. ***lutescens***	CHid EPPr IBlr
	- 'Moonshy Seedling'	CSWP EGoI
	- 'Variegata' (v) ♀H4	CBro CElw CFil CRow ECtt EHrv EPfP EPla GMaP MCCP MRav NBir NCob NLar NLon NPar NPer SBch SSpi WBVN WCAu WCot WWhi
	- yellow-seeded	WCot WTin
	'Foggy Dew' (TB)	GKir
	'Folkwang' (TB)	EWTr
	'Fondation Van Gogh' (TB)	CIri ESgI
	'Forest Light' (SDB)	CBro ESgI
	'Forge Fire' (TB)	ESgI
	formosana	CMon
	- B&SWJ 3076	WCru WPrP
	forrestii ♀H4	CHid CRow EChP ENot EPfP EWTr GAbr GBBs GBin GCal GCrs GGar GIBF GKev GKir IBlr LPBA LRHS MBri MHer NBir NBro NCob NGdn SMac SRot SSpi WAbe WHer
	- hybrids	IBlr
	'Fort Apache' (TB)	ESgI EWoo
	'Foxy Lady' (TB)	ESgI
	'Frank Elder' (Reticulata)	CBro CMea EHyt EPot ERos GCrs LAma LPio LRHS MRav MTho NMen
	'Frans Hals' (Dut)	EWTr MMHG MNrw
	'French Fashion' (TB)	CIri
I	'French Rose' (TB) **new**	CKel
	'Fresno Calypso' (TB)	ESgI WCAu
	'Fringe Benefits' (TB) **new**	WCAu
	'Frison-roche' (TB)	ESgI
	'Fritillary Flight' (IB) ♀H4	CKel
	'Frivolité' (TB) **new**	ESgI
	'Frontier Marshall' (TB)	NMoo
	'Frost and Flame' (TB)	CM&M EChP ECtt ELan ENot EPfP ERou EWll GKir MBri MRav MSte NEgg NGdn NMoo NOrc SChu SPer WCra
	'Frosted Angel' (SDB)	WDav
	'Frosty Jewels' (TB)	ESgI
	fulva	CDes CRow EBee GCal GFlt IBlr NBir NBro NSti SSpi WCot WPGP WTin
	- 'Marvell Gold' (La)	CRow
	x ***fulvala*** ♀H4	CAby CDes CFir CPom EBee EMon EPPr EWes GBin IBlr NBir NSti
	- 'Violacea'	EBee
	'Furnaceman' (SDB)	CBro ERos MBri
	'Fuzzy' (MDB)	ERos
	'Gala Gown' (TB)	WCAu
§	***galatica***	EHyt WWst
	'Gallant Moment' (TB)	SIri
	gatesii	EHyt
§	'Gelbe Mantel' (Sino-Sib)	CHid CLAP EBee EBla EChP NBir NBro NGdn NSti STes WFar
	'Gemstar' (SDB) **new**	WCAu
	'Gentius' (TB)	WMnd
	'Gentle Grace' (SDB)	ESgI
	'George' (Reticulata) ♀H4	CAvo CBro EBrs EPot ERos GAbr GCrs GFlt LRHS MAvo MMHG MSte
	'Gerald Darby'	see *I.* x *robusta* 'Gerald Darby'
	germanica ♀H4	EHol NFor WCAu
	- var. ***florentina***	see *I.* 'Florentina'
*	- 'Mel Jope'	NBir
	- 'Nepalensis'	EGoo
*	- 'The King'	WCAu
	'Gibson Girl' (TB)	WCAu
	'Gingerbread Castle' (TB)	WCAu
	'Gingerbread Man' (SDB)	CBro CHad CMea EHrv ERos ESgI LPio MBrN NMen SMrm SWal WCAu WHoo WIvy WLin
	'Glad Rags' (TB)	ESgI
	'Gnu' (TB)	CIri
	'Gnus Flash' (TB)	CIri WCAu
	'Go Between' (TB) **new**	WCAu
	'Godfrey Owen' (TB)	CKel WCAu
	'Godsend' (TB)	CIri CKel WCAu
	'Going My Way' (TB)	ESgI EWoo SIri STes WCAu
	'Gold Country' (TB) **new**	ESgI
	'Gold Mania' (Spuria)	CIri
	'Gold of Autumn' (TB)	CKel SMrm
	'Goldberry' (IB)	WCAu
	'Golden Alps' (TB)	SRms WCAu
	'Golden Child' (SDB)	ESgI
	'Golden Encore' (TB)	CKel WCAu
	'Golden Fair' (SDB)	NBir
	'Golden Forest' (TB)	WCAu
	'Golden Giant' (Dut)	CFwr LRHS
	'Golden Opportunity' (TB)	CIri
	'Golden Planet' (TB)	CKel
N	'Golden Surprise' (TB)	EBee
	'Golden Violet' (SDB)	ESgI
	'Golden Waves' (Cal-Sib) ♀H3	CBro
	'Gondalier' (TB)	LBmB
	'Good Looking' (TB)	CIri WCAu
	'Good Show' (TB)	EWoo WCAu
	'Good Vibrations' (TB) **new**	SIri
	'Goodbye Heart' (TB)	ESgI
	'Gordon' (Reticulata)	EPot GAbr LAma LRHS WFar
	gormanii	see *I. tenax*
	'Gossip' (SDB)	CBro ESgI
	gracilipes	GEdr
	- 'Alba'	GEdr
	gracilipes x ***lacustris***	GEdr WAbe
	graeberiana	EBee EPot
	- white fall	LRHS WWst
	- yellow fall	EPot LRHS WWst
	graminea ♀H4	More than 30 suppliers
	- 'Hort's Variety'	GCal
	- var. ***pseudocyperus***	CRow GKev NSti SDys
	graminifolia	see *I. kerneriana*
	'Granada Gold' (TB)	ENot SRms
	'Grapelet' (MDB)	ERos WCAu
	'Great Lakes'	ESgI
	'Green Prophecy' (TB)	CIri
	'Green Spot' (SDB) ♀H4	CBro CKel EBee ECtt EHrv ELan EPfP EVFa EWTr GKir NBir NEgg

		NMen NWCA SBla SChu SPer SPet WCAu WCFE WEas WHoo
	'Green Streak' (TB)	CIri
	'Gringo' (TB)	WCAu
	'Gypsy Beauty' (Dut)	CFwr EBrs MSph SPer
	'Gypsy Jewels' (TB)	CKel ESgI
	'Gypsy Romance' (TB)	CIri ESgI WCAu
*	'Haizon Bleu'	EWoo
	halophila	see *I. spuria* subsp. *halophila*
	'Handshake' (TB)	CIri
	'Happy Birthday' (TB)	ESgI
*	'Happy Border' (BB)	WCAu
	'Happy Mood' (IB) ♀H4	WCAu
	'Harbor Blue' (TB)	CKel EBee MWat WAul WCAu
	'Harlow Gold' (IB)	ESgI
	'Harmony' (Reticulata)	CAvo CBro EPfP EPot GBBs LAma LRHS MAvo MBri NJOw SPer SPet WFar
	'Harriette Halloway' (TB)	CMil EBee LSRN SMrm
	hartwegii	GFlt
	'Harvest King' (TB)	CIri ESgI
	'Harvest of Memories' (TB) **new**	ESgI
	'Haviland' (TB) **new**	SIri
	'Headlines' (TB)	WCAu
	'Heather Carpet' (SDB) **new**	WCAu
	'Heavenly Days' (TB)	WCAu
	'Helen Boehm' (TB)	ESgI
	'Helen Collingwood' (TB) **new**	ESgI
	'Helen McGregor' (TB)	ESgI
	'Helen Proctor' (IB)	ESgI WCAu
	'Helen Traubel' (TB)	WCAu
	'Helge' (IB)	COIW EPfP
	'Hellcat' (IB)	WAul WCAu
	'Hello Darkness' (TB)	CIri ESgI WCAu
	'Hercules' (Reticulata)	LAma
	'Heure Bleue' (TB)	EWoo
	'High Barbaree' (TB)	WCAu
	'High Blue Sky' (TB) **new**	WCAu
	'High Command' (TB)	CKel SMrm
	'Highline Halo' (Spuria)	WCAu
	'Hildegarde' (Dut)	CFwr
	'Hindu Magic' (TB)	WCAu
	histrio	EHyt EPot LAma
	- subsp. ***aintabensis***	EHyt EPot LAma
	histrioides	WAbe WLin
§	- 'Angel's Tears'	ERos
	- 'Lady Beatrice Stanley'	EPot NMen
N	- 'Major'	CBro CDes GCrs LAma
	- 'Michael Tears' **new**	WWst
	- 'Reine Immaculée'	ERos
	'Hocus Pocus' (SDB)	EWoo
	'Holden Clough' (SpecHybrid) ♀H4	More than 30 suppliers
	'Honey Glazed' (IB)	ESgI WAul WCAu
	'Honeyplic' (IB) ♀H4 **new**	SIri
	'Honington' (SDB)	WCAu
	'Honky Tonk Blues' (TB)	CIri ESgI
	'Honorabile' (MTB)	SMrm WCAu
	hoogiana ♀H3	EBrs EPot LRHS MBow
	- 'Gypsy Beauty'	WFar
	- 'Purpurea'	LRHS
§	***hookeri***	CAby CSam EDAr ELan EPPr EWTr GBBs GEdr GIBF IGor NJOw NWoo SOkd WAbe
	- Brown 0233	CStu
	hookeriana	WCot
§	'Hornpipe' (TB)	WCAu
	'Hot Chocolate' (TB)	CIri
	'Hot Fudge' (IB)	WAul
	'Hot Jazz' (SDB) **new**	WCAu
	'Hot Spice' (IB)	WCAu
	'Howard Weed' (TB)	EBee
	'Hugh Miller' (TB) **new**	WCAu
	'Hula Doll' (MDB)	NMen
§	***humilis***	CGra GKev SOkd
	hyrcana	CBro EHyt LAma LRHS
	'I Seek You' (TB) **new**	ESgI
§	***iberica***	CMea EHyt EPot
	subsp. ***elegantissima***	
	- subsp. ***iberica***	WWst
	'Ice Dancer' (TB) ♀H4	CKel
	'Iced Tea' (TB)	CIri
	'Ida' (Reticulata)	EPot LAma
	'Ila Crawford' (Spuria) ♀H4 **new**	WCAu
	illyrica	see *I. pallida*
	imbricata	CMon
	'Imbue' (SDB)	ESgI
	'Immortal Hour' (TB) **new**	WCAu
	'Immortality' (TB)	CKel ESgI WCAu
	'Imperial Bronze' (Spuria)	NFor WCAu
	'Imprimis' (TB)	CIri ESgI WCAu
	'In Depth' (Spuria)	CIri
	'In Town' (TB)	ESgI EWoo
	'Incoscente' (TB)	ESgI
	'Indian Chief' (TB)	EMil ESgI EVFa GBin SPur WCAu
	'Indian Jewel' (SDB)	EHyt
	'Indian Pow Wow' (SDB)	CSev
N	'Indiana Sunset' (TB)	CKel
	'Indiscreet' (TB)	WCAu
	'Infernal Fire' (TB)	CIri
	'Infinite Grace' (TB)	ESgI
	'Innocent Heart' (IB) ♀H4	WCAu
	innominata	CWCL ECha GFlt GGar GKev IBlr LRHS NBir NBro NEgg NPal SMar SRms SWal WBVN
	- JCA 13225	CLAP SSpi
	- JCA 13227	SSpi
	- apricot	CPrp IBlr
	- Ballyrogan hybrids	IBlr
	- rose	ERos
N	- 'Spinners'	SSpi
	- yellow	CAvo NRya
	'Inscription' (SDB)	EHyt
	'Interpol' (TB)	ESgI EWoo WCAu WWhi
	'Invitation' (TB)	ESgI
	'Irish Doll' (MDB)	WCAu
	'Irish Tune' (TB)	ESgI
	'Isoline' (TB)	ESgI
	'It's Magic' (TB)	CIri
	'J.S. Dijt' (Reticulata)	CAvo CBro EPot LAma LRHS MBow MBri NJOw
	'Jabal' (SDB) **new**	WDay
	'Jane Phillips' (TB) ♀H4	More than 30 suppliers
	'Jane Taylor' (SDB)	CBro
	'Janet Lane' (BB)	CKel
	'Janice Chesnik' (Spuria)	CIri
	japonica ♀H3	CHEx CPLG EHrv LPio NPer WFar
	- 'Aphrodite' (v)	WTin
	- 'Ledger'	CAvo CBro CHll CKel CPLG CPrp CSpe EBee ECha EHrv ELan EPfP IGor MRav SChr SGSe SIri SMad
	- 'Monty' **new**	LPio
	- f. ***pallescens***	CFwr SGSe
N	- 'Rudolph Spring' **new**	GCal
	- 'Variegata' (v) ♀H3	CAvo CBot CHEx CHad CKel CSpe ECha EHrv GGar LRHS NBro NOrc NPer SAPC SAga SArc SMad SPoG SSpi WCFE WEas WFar WHer WHil WPic
	'Jasper Gem' (MDB)	EHyt ERos NBir
	'Jazz Festival' (TB)	WCAu

	Plant	Suppliers
	'Jazzamatazz' (SDB)	ESgI WCAu
	'Jazzed Up' (TB) **new**	WCAu
	'Jean Cayeux' (TB)	ESgI
	'Jean Guymer' (TB)	NBir WCAu
	'Jeanne Price' (TB)	SCoo WCAu
	'Jeannine' (Reticulata)	LAma
	'Jeremy Brian' (SDB) ♀H4	WCAu
	'Jersey Lilli' (SDB)	WCAu
	'Jesse's Song' (TB)	ESgI WCAu
	'Jewel Baby' (SDB)	CBro CKel
	'Jeweler's Art' (SDB)	EWoo
	'Jiansada' (SDB)	CBro
	'Jigsaw' (TB) **new**	ESgI
	'Jitterbug' (TB)	EHrv WCAu
	'Joanna' (TB)	NLar
	'Joanna Taylor' (MDB)	ERos NMen WCAu
	'John' (IB)	CKel
	'Joy Boy' (SDB)	ESgI
	'Joyce' (Reticulata)	CBro EPot GFlt LAma LRHS MBri SPet
	'Joyce Terry' (TB)	ESgI
	'Joyful' (SDB)	ESgI
	'Jubilee Gem' (TB)	CKel
	'Juicy Fruit' (TB) **new**	WCAu
	'Julia Vennor' (TB) **new**	CKel
	'Jungle Fires' (TB)	WCAu
	'Jungle Shadows' (BB)	MRav NBir SMrm WCAu
	'Jurassic Park' (TB)	CIri ESgI WCAu
	'Juris Prudence' (TB)	ESgI
	'Just Dance' (IB)	ESgI
	'Just Jennifer' (BB)	WCAu
	kaempferi	see *I. ensata*
	'Kaibab Trail' (Spuria)	CIri
	'Kangchenjunga' (TB)	ESgI
	kashmiriana	CBcs CMon SGSe
	'Katharine Hodgkin' (Reticulata) ♀H4	CAvo CBro CLAP CMea EBee EBrs EPfP EPot ERos GAbr GBBs GCrs GEdr GFlt GKev LAma LRHS MRav MTho NMen NSla SIng SMrm WAbe WCot WIvy WLin WPnP WSHC
	'Katie-Koo' (IB) ♀H4	CKel WDav
	'Katy Petts' (SDB)	ESgI WCAu
	'Kayleigh-Jayne Louise' (TB)	CKel
	'Kelway Renaissance' (TB)	CKel
	kemaonensis	GIBF
	'Ken's Choice' (TB) ♀H4	CKel
	'Kent Pride' (TB)	CHad CMil EBee ECGP EChP EPPr EPfP ERou GKir MRav MSte MWat SChu SGar SHBN SIri SPer SPoG WBVN WCAu WCra WTin
	'Kentucky Bluegrass' (SDB)	WCAu
§	***kerneriana*** ♀H4	CBro CPom EBrs ERos GBuc LRHS MLLN NBir NEgg SIgm WPen
	'Kevin's Theme' (TB)	CIri WCAu
	'Kildonan' (TB)	WCAu
	'Kilt Lilt' (TB)	WCAu
	'Kirkstone' (TB)	WCAu
	'Kissing Circle' (TB)	ESgI EWoo
	'Kitt Peak' (Spuria) ♀H4	CIri
	'Kiwi Slices' (SDB)	ESgI
	klattii	see *I. spuria* subsp. *musulmanica*
	'Knick Knack' (MDB)	CBro EBee EHyt ERos EVFa GAbr GCrs LBee LPio LRHS MRav MSte NEgg NMen SDnm SOkd WHil
	kolpakowskiana	WWst
	'Kona Nights' (BB)	ESgI
	korolkowii	GIBF
	kuschakewiczii	WWst
	'La Nina Rosa' (BB)	WCAu
	'La Senda' (Spuria)	GFlt WCAu WCot
	'La Vie en Rose' (TB)	ESgI
	'Laced Cotton' (TB)	SCoo WCAu
	'Laced Lemonade' (SDB)	GKir MBri
§	***lactea*** ♀H4	NWCA
	lacustris ♀H4	CBro ERos NBro NMen NWCA WAbe
	'Lady Essex' (TB)	WCAu
	'Lady Friend' (TB)	ERou ESgI EWoo WCAu
	'Lady Ilse' (TB)	WCAu
	'Lady in Red' (SDB)	ESgI
	'Lady Mohr' (AB)	WCAu WTin
	'Lady of Fatima' (TB)	ESgI
§	***laevigata*** ♀H4	CDWL CRow CWat ECha EGol EHon ELan EMFW EPfP GIBF LNCo LPBA MRav NBro NGdn NPer SGar WFar WMoo WPnP WPop WShi WTin WWpP
	- var. ***alba***	CBen CRow ECha EGol EHon ELan EPfP LPBA NArg SSpi WAbe WFar WMoo WPop WWpP
	- 'Albopurpurea'	CDWL CLAP EMFW SGSe WTMC
	- 'Atropurpurea'	CRow EGol IBlr LPBA
	- 'Colchesterensis'	CBen CDWL CLAP CRow CWat EGol EMFW LPBA NPer WCra WHrl WTMC
	- 'Dark Pettale'	CLAP
I	- 'Dorothy'	LPBA NGdn
	- 'Dorothy Robinson'	EMFW LNCo WPnP
	- 'Elegant'	see *I. laevigata* 'Weymouth Elegant'
	- 'Liam Johns'	CRow
	- 'Midnight'	see *I. laevigata* 'Weymouth Midnight'
	- 'Mottled Beauty'	CRow
	- 'Rashomon'	CRow
	- 'Regal'	CDWL
	- 'Richard Greaney'	CRow
	- 'Rose Queen'	see *I. ensata* 'Rose Queen'
	- 'Shirasagi'	CRow
I	- 'Snowdrift'	CBen CLAP CRow CWat EHon EMFW LNCo LPBA NBir NGdn NPer SPer WFar WPnP WTMC WWpP
	- 'Variegata' (v) ♀H4	CBen CDWL CHad CMea CRow CWat ECha EGol EHoe EHon EMFW ENot EPfP EPla GMac LNCo LPBA LRHS NArg NBid NBro NGdn NOrc NPer SPer SSpi WMoo WPop
	- 'Violet Garth'	CRow
	- 'Weymouth'	see *I. laevigata* 'Weymouth Blue'
§	- 'Weymouth Blue'	CRow
§	- 'Weymouth Elegant'	CBen CFir CRow
§	- 'Weymouth Midnight'	CBen CFir CMil CRow ECGP EHon LPBA
N	'Langport Chapter' (IB)	CKel
N	'Langport Chief' (IB)	CKel
N	'Langport Claret' (IB)	CKel
N	'Langport Curlew' (IB)	CKel ESgI
N	'Langport Duchess' (IB)	ESgI WDav
N	'Langport Fairy' (IB)	CKel
N	'Langport Finch' (IB)	NBir WIvy
N	'Langport Flame' (IB)	CKel ESgI WTin
N	'Langport Hope' (IB)	CKel
N	'Langport Lord' (IB)	CKel ESgI
	'Langport Midnight'	SMrm
	'Langport Minstrel' (IB)	CKel
N	'Langport Robe' (IB)	CKel ESgI
N	'Langport Snow' (IB)	CKel
N	'Langport Song' (IB)	ESgI
N	'Langport Star' (IB)	CKel
	'Langport Storm' (IB)	CHad EBee EChP EMil MBri NGdn SChu SHBN WAul WDav WIvy WTin

	Name	Suppliers
N	'Langport Sun' (IB)	CKel SMrm
N	'Langport Swift' (IB)	CKel
	'Langport Sylvia' (IB)	CKel
N	'Langport Tartan' (IB)	CKel
N	'Langport Violet' (IB)	CKel
	'Langport Vista' (IB)	CKel
	'Langport Wren' (IB) ♀H4	CBro CKel CMil ESgI GKir LRHS MBri NBir SMrm WEas WTin
	'Lark Rise' (TB) ♀H4	CKel
	'Larry Gaulter' (TB)	WCAu
	'Las Vegas' (TB) **new**	WCAu
§	***latifolia*** ♀H4	GIBF GKev
	- from the Pyrenees **new**	CMon
	- 'Duchess of York'	EPot
	- 'Isabella'	EBee EPot
	- 'King of the Blues'	EPot WCot
	- 'Mansfield'	EPot
	- 'Montblanc'	CFwr EBee EPot
	- 'Queen of the Blues' (Eng)	CFwr EPot
	'Latin Rock' (TB)	WCAu
	latiphilum	GIBF
	'Laure Louise' (La) **new**	CWrd
§	***lazica*** ♀H4	More than 30 suppliers
	- 'Joy Bishop'	WCot
	- 'Turkish Blue'	CPrp IBlr
	'Leda's Lover' (TB)	ESgI
	'Lemon Brocade' (TB)	ESgI EWoo GKir MBri WCAu
	'Lemon Dilemma' (Spuria)	CIri
	'Lemon Fever' (TB) **new**	ESgI
	'Lemon Flare' (SDB)	ECtt MRav SRms WCAu
	'Lemon Lyric' (TB) **new**	ESgI
	'Lemon Mist' (TB)	ESgI
	'Lemon Pop' (IB) **new**	WCAu
	'Lemon Puff' (MDB)	CBro WCAu
	'Lemon Tree' (TB)	WCAu
	'Lemon Whip' (IB)	EWoo
N	'Lena' (SDB)	CBro
	'Lenna M' (SDB)	CKel
	'Lenora Pearl' (BB)	ESgI WCAu
	'Lent A. Williamson' (TB)	GMaP
	'Lenten Prayer' (TB)	CIri
	'Let's Elope' (IB)	ESgI WCAu
	'Light Cavalry' (IB)	ESgI EWoo
	'Light Laughter' (IB)	WCAu
	'Lilli-white' (SDB)	CKel CStu EBee ELan ENot MBNS MRav MWgw NEgg WCAu
	'Lima Colada' (SDB)	SMrm
	'Limbo' (SpecHybrid)	CRow
	'Limelight' (TB)	SRms
	'Lingering Love' (TB) **new**	WCAu
	linifolia	WWst
	'Lion's Share' (TB)	CIri
	'Liquid Smoke' (TB)	EVFa
N	'Little Amoena'	ERos NMen
	'Little Bill' (SDB)	EHyt
	'Little Black Belt' (SDB)	SIri
	'Little Blackfoot' (SDB)	ESgI WCAu WHoo
	'Little Dandy' (SDB)	WCAu WIvy
	'Little Dogie' (SDB)	EHyt
	'Little Dream' (SDB)	WCAu
	'Little Episode' (SDB)	WCAu
	'Little John' (TB) **new**	WCAu
	'Little Rosy Wings' (SDB)	CBro ERos
	'Little Shadow' (IB)	ENot MRav SRms
	'Little Sheba' (AB)	WCAu
	'Little Tilgates' (CH) ♀H3	CBos WCot
	'Live Coals' (SDB)	CIri
	'Live Jazz' (SDB)	WCAu
	'Llanthony' (SDB)	WCAu
	loczyi	EBee
	'Lodore' (TB)	SRms WCAu
	'Logo' (IB) **new**	WCAu
	'Lois Parrish' (TB)	CIri
	'Lollipop' (SDB)	ESgI SIri
	longipetala	GIBF NBir
	'Loop the Loop' (TB)	CRez EBee EPfP EWoo EWsh
	'Lord Warden' (TB)	ECGP EChP SPet WCAu
	'Loreley' (TB)	ESgI
	'Lorenzaccio de Medecis' (TB)	ESgI
	'Lorilee' (TB)	ESgI
	'Lothario' (TB)	WCAu WFoF
	'Loud Music' (TB)	WCAu
	'Louis d'Or' (TB)	CIri
	'Louvois' (TB)	ESgI
	'Love for Leila' (Spuria) ♀H4	CIri
	'Love Melody' (SDB) **new**	CIri
	'Love the Sun' (TB)	ESgI
	'Lovely Again' (TB)	WCAu
	'Lovely Dawn' (TB)	CIri
	'Lovely Light' (TB)	MBri
	'Lover's Charm' (TB) **new**	WCAu
	'Loveshine' (SDB)	MRav
	'Low Ho Silver' (IB)	WCAu
	'Lugano' (TB)	ESgI
	'Luli-Ann' (SDB) ♀H4	CKel
	'Lullaby of Spring' (TB)	CKel WCAu
	'Lumiere d'Automne' (TB)	ESgI
	'Luna di Miele' (BB) **new**	ESgI
	'Lunar Frost' (IB) **new**	SIri
§	***lutescens*** ♀H4	CMon ERos GEdr GFlt GKev NSla WAbe XPep
§	- 'Campbellii'	CBro EHyt ERos MSte NMen SOkd
	- subsp. ***lutescens***	WLin
§	- 'Nancy Lindsey' **new**	WCAu
	***lutescens* x *gracilipes* new**	SOkd
	***lycotis* new**	EHyt
	'Lyme Tyme' (TB)	CIri
	'Ma Mie' (IB)	ESgI
	***maackii* new**	GIBF
	macrosiphon	GKev
	'Madame Maurice Lassailly' (TB)	ESgI
	'Madeira Belle' (TB)	EWoo WCAu
	'Magharee' (TB)	ESgI
	'Magic Bubbles' (IB) ♀H4	CIri
	'Magic Man' (TB)	EBee
	magnifica ♀H3-4	CBro EPot GKev NWCA WWst
	- 'Agalik'	CMea LRHS
	- 'Alba'	LRHS
	'Maisie Lowe' (TB)	ESgI
	'Making Eyes' (SDB)	ESgI EWoo WCAu
I	'Mandarin' (TB)	ESgI
	'Mandarin Purple' (Sino-Sib)	CDes EBee GGar IBlr NGdn
	mandshurica	GIBF
	'Mango Entree' (TB)	CIri
	'Maple Treat' (TB)	CIri
	'Marcel Turbat' (TB)	ESgI
	'Marche Turque' (TB)	ESgI
	'Marco Polo' (TB)	ESgI
	'Margaret Inez' (TB)	CIri
	'Margarita' (TB)	WCAu
	'Margot Holmes' (Cal-Sib)	GCal IBlr SChu
	'Margrave' (TB)	SIri WCAu
	'Marhaba' (MDB)	CBro ERos
	'Marilyn Holloway' (Spuria)	WCAu
	'Mariposa Skies' (TB)	CIri
	'Marmalade Skies' (BB)	WCAu
	'Martyn Rix'	see *I. confusa* 'Martyn Rix'
	'Mary Constance' (IB) ♀H4	CIri CKel
	'Mary Frances' (TB)	WCAu
	'Mary McIlroy' (SDB) ♀H4	CBro WTin

	Name	Suppliers
	'Mary Randall' (TB)	WCAu
	'Mary Vernon' (TB)	GFlt
	'Matinata' (TB)	CKel
	'Maui Moonlight' (IB) ♀H4	CKel
	'May Melody' (TB)	WCAu
	'Meadow Court' (SDB)	CBro CKel CM&M CRez ERos NBro WCAu WDav
	'Media Luz' (Spuria)	WCAu
	'Medway Valley' (MTB) **new**	WCAu
	'Meg's Mantle' (TB) ♀H4	CKel
	'Melbreak' (TB)	WCAu
	mellita	see *I. suaveolens*
	- var. ***rubromarginata***	see *I. suaveolens*
	'Melon Honey' (SDB)	CKel EHyt WCAu WDav WHal
	'Memphis Blues' (TB)	EWoo
	'Memphis Delight' (TB) **new**	WCAu
	'Mer du Sud' (TB)	ESgI SCoo
	'Mesmerizer' (TB)	CIri WCAu
	'Metaphor' (TB)	WCAu
	'Mezza Cartuccia' (IB)	ESgI
	'Michael Paul' (SDB) ♀H4	ESgI
	'Midnight Fire' (TB)	ERou
	'Midnight Mango' (IB)	CKel
	'Midnight Oil' (TB)	CIri WCAu
	milesii ♀H4	CDes CPou GBuc GIBF IGor MSph NBir NEgg WPer WPic
	'Millennium Sunrise' (TB) **new**	WCAu
	'Mind Reader' (TB)	CIri
	'Mini-Agnes' (SDB)	CBro
	'Miss Carla' (IB)	CKel
	'Miss Nellie' (BB) **new**	CKel
	'Mission Sunset' (TB)	EHrv WCAu
	'Missouri Lakes' (Spuria)	CIri
	'Missouri Rivers' (Spuria)	CIri
	missouriensis ♀H4	IGor NBid SSpi
	'Mister Roberts' (SDB)	ESgI
	'Mme Chereau' (TB)	ESgI WCAu
	'Mme Louis Aureau' (TB)	ESgI
	'Modern Classic' (TB)	EWoo
	'Mogul' (TB)	CIri
	monnieri	GIBF NLar SDix
	Monspur Group	GCal SSpi WCot
§	'Monspur Cambridge Blue' (Spuria) ♀H4	WCAu
	'Moon Sparkle' (IB)	CKel
	'Moonbeam' (TB)	CKel
	'Moonlight' (TB)	NFor WCot
	'Moonlight Waves'	see *I. ensata* 'Moonlight Waves'
	'Moonstruck' (TB)	EWoo
	'Morning's Blush' (SDB) ♀H4	CIri
	'Morwenna' (TB) ♀H4	CKel WCAu
	'Mother Earth' (TB) **new**	ESgI
*	'Mount Stewart Black'	GCal
	'Mrs Horace Darwin' (TB)	CFir WMnd
	'Mrs Nate Rudolph' (SDB)	EBee MBri SMrm
	'Mrs Tait' (Spuria)	GCal NChi
	'Mulberry Rose' (TB)	CFee
	'Mulled Wine' (TB)	ESgI
	'Murmuring Morn' (TB)	WCAu
	'My Honeycomb' (TB)	WCAu
	'My Impulse' (Spuria)	CIri
N	'My Seedling' (MDB)	CBro ERos NMen WIvy
	'Naivasha' (TB)	CKel
	'Nancy' **new**	SApp
	'Nancy Hardy' (MDB)	CBro EHyt ERos NMen
	'Nancy Lindsay'	see *I. lutescens* 'Nancy Lindsay'
	'Nanny' (SDB) **new**	SIri
	narbutii	WWst
	narcissiflora	CFir
	narynensis	WWst
	'Nashborough' (TB)	WCAu
I	'Natascha' (Reticulata)	EPot LAma WLin
	'Natchez Trace' (TB)	WCot
	'Navajo Jewel' (TB)	ESgI EWoo WCAu
	'Nectar' (IB)	ESgI
	nectarifera **new**	EHyt EPot
	'Needlepoint' (TB)	ESgI
	'Neige de Mai' (TB)	ESgI
	nepalensis	see *I. decora*
	nertschinskia	see *I. sanguinea*
	'New Argument' (Juno) **new**	WWst
	'New Centurion' (TB) **new**	WCAu
	'New Idea' (MTB)	ESgI WCAu
	'New Snow' (TB)	WCAu
	'Nibelungen' (TB)	EPfP WFar
	'Nice n' Nifty' (IB)	WTin
	'Nicola Jane' (TB) ♀H4	CKel
	nicolai	WWst
	'Nigerian Raspberry' (TB)	CIri WCAu
	'Night Edition' (TB)	ESgI
	'Night Game' (TB)	CIri WCAu
	'Night Owl' (TB)	CKel WAul
	'Night Ruler' (TB)	ESgI WCAu
	'Nightfall' (TB)	EBee
	'Nights of Gladness' (TB)	ESgI
	'Nineveh' (AB)	WCAu
	'Noces Blanches' (IB)	ESgI
	'Noon Siesta' (TB)	ESgI
	'Nora Eileen' (TB) **new**	CKel
	'Northwest Pride' (TB)	WCAu
	'Northwest Progress' (TB)	CIri
	'Ochraurea' (Spuria)	GCal NGdn NSti
	ochroleuca	see *I. orientalis* Mill.
	odaesanensis	EBee
	'Oklahoma Crude' (TB)	CIri
	'Oktoberfest' (TB)	ESgI
	'Ola Kalá' (TB)	CM&M ECGP ERou ESgI GMaP MSte NEgg SPer SPoG SPur WCAu
	'Old Black Magic' (TB)	CIri
	'Olympiad' (TB)	ESgI
	'Olympic Challenge' (TB)	ESgI WCAu
	'Olympic Torch' (TB)	WCAu
	'One Desire' (TB)	WCAu
	'Open Sky' (SDB)	SIri
	'Orageux' (IB)	ESgI
	'Orange Blaze' (SDB)	CBro
	'Orange Caper' (SDB)	CStu EGoo ESgI GBuc MBri MRav MSte NEgg NLar SPet WIvy WWeb
	'Orange Harvest' (TB)	EWoo
	'Orange Order' (TB)	WCAu
	'Orange Petals' (IB)	CIri
N	'Orange Plaza'	NMen WIvy
	'Orange Tiger' (SDB)	WCAu
	'Orchardist' (TB)	CKel
	'Orchidea Selvaggia' (TB)	ESgI
	orchioides hort.	see *I. bucharica* Foster
§	***orchioides*** Carrière	CMea EBrs EChP EHyt ELan ERos ETow GBBs NWCA WAul WLin
	- 'Urungachsai'	WWst
	'Oregold' (SDB)	WCAu
	'Oregon Skies' (TB)	ESgI EWoo
	'Oriental Argument' (Juno) **new**	WWst
	'Oriental Baby' (IB)	EWoo
I	'Oriental Beauty' (Dut) **new**	NArg SPer
	'Oriental Glory' (TB)	WCAu
	'Oriental Touch' (SpecHybrid)	CRow
	orientalis Thunb.	see *I. sanguinea*

	– 'Alba'	see *I. sanguinea* 'Alba'
§	***orientalis*** Mill. 🏆H4	EPPr GIBF IFro LPBA MSte MWgw SChu SGar SSpi WCAu WDyG
	'Orinoco Flow' (BB) 🏆H4	CHar CIri CKel ESgI WCAu
	'Orloff' (TB) **new**	ESgI
	'Out Yonder' (TB)	WCAu
	'Ovation' (TB)	ESgI
	'Overjoyed' (TB) **new**	WCAu
	'O'What' (SDB)	ESgI
	'Owyhee Desert' (TB)	CIri
	'Ozone Alert' (TB)	CIri
	Pacific Coast hybrids	see *I.* Californian hybrids
	'Pacific Mist' (TB)	WCAu
	'Pacific Panorama' (TB)	ESgI
	'Pagan Princess' (TB)	WCAu
	'Pageant' (TB)	WTin
	'Paint It Black' (TB)	EWoo
	'Pale Primrose' (TB)	WCAu
	'Pale Shades' (IB) 🏆H4	CBro CKel ERos
	'Palissandro' (TB) **new**	ESgI
§	***pallida***	CHad EBee EGoo ESis GKir GMaP MCCP MRav MSte WBrE WCAu WMnd
	– 'Argentea Variegata' (v)	More than 30 suppliers
	– 'Aurea'	see *I. pallida* 'Variegata'
	– 'Aurea Variegata'	see *I. pallida* 'Variegata'
	– var. ***dalmatica***	see *I. pallida* subsp. *pallida*
§	– subsp. ***pallida*** 🏆H4	CBot CKel EChP ECha ELan MBri MWgw SDix SPer
N	– 'Variegata' Hort. (v) 🏆H4	More than 30 suppliers
	'Palomino' (TB)	WCAu
	'Paltec' (IB)	CPou EBee LPhx
	'Pane e Vino' (TB)	ESgI
	'Paradise' (TB)	CKel EPfP
	paradoxa	WWst
	– f. ***choschab***	EHyt EPot SBla SOkd
	'Paricutin' (SDB)	CBro
	'Party Dress' (TB)	EBee EMan ENot ERou LAst LRHS MRav NBir NEgg NFla NGdn NOrc SPer SRms WCFE WCra WWeb
	parvula	WWst
	'Pastel Charm' (SDB)	CM&M CRez GBin SMrm STes WMnd
	'Patches' (TB)	ESgI
	'Path of Gold' (DB)	CBro
	'Patina' (TB)	ESgI EWoo WCAu
	'Patterdale' (TB)	NBir NVic WCAu
	'Pauline' (Reticulata)	CBro EPfP EPot GBBs LAma LRHS SPer SPet WFar
	'Pawnee Princess' (IB) **new**	CIri
	'Peace and Harmony' (TB)	CIri
	'Peaceful Warden' (TB)	EWoo
	'Peach Band' (TB)	ERou
	'Peach Eyes' (SDB)	CBro ERos
	'Peach Float' (TB)	WCAu
	'Peach Melba' (TB)	ESgI
	'Peach Picotee' (TB)	ESgI
	'Peach Spot' (TB)	WCAu
	'Peaches ala Mode' (BB)	WCAu
	'Peacock'	see *I. ensata* 'Peacock'
	'Pearls of Autumn' (TB) **new**	WCAu
	'Pearly Dawn' (TB)	EBee EChP ECha MSte NEgg SChu SCoo SSvw
	'Peggy Chambers' (IB) 🏆H4	SMrm
	'Pele' (SDB)	WCAu
	'Persian Berry' (TB)	WCAu
	persica	EHyt
	'Phaeton' (TB)	CIri
	'Pharaoh's Daughter' (IB)	SIri WAul
	'Pheasant Feathers' (TB)	CIri
	'Phil Keen' (TB) 🏆H4	CKel
	'Picacho Peak' (Spuria)	CIri
	'Picadee'	EPfP GBuc
	'Piero Bargellini' (TB)	CIri ESgI
	'Pigmy Gold' (IB)	EBee ENot ERos
	'Pinewood Amethyst' (CH)	GMac
	'Pink Angel' (TB)	EWoo
	'Pink Attraction' (TB)	ESgI
	'Pink Charm' (TB)	EChP EMan EVFa LRHS SPet
	'Pink Charming' (TB)	CIri
	'Pink Confetti' (TB)	ESgI
	'Pink Fawn' (SDB)	CIri
	'Pink Formal' (TB)	ESgI
	'Pink Horizon' (TB)	EPfP
	'Pink Kitten' (IB)	WCAu
	'Pink Pussycat' (TB)	MBri
	'Pink Ruffles' (IB)	CHar
	'Pink Swan' (TB)	ESgI
	'Pink Taffeta' (TB)	ESgI
	'Pinnacle' (TB)	CKel EWsh WCAu
	'Piper's Tune' (IB)	SMrm
	'Pipes of Pan' (TB)	MRav WCAu
	'Pirate's Patch' (SDB)	ESgI
	'Piroska' (TB)	CIri ESgI
	'Piu Blue' (TB)	ESgI
I	'Pixie' (Reticulata)	EPot SMeo
	'Pixie Flirt' (MDB)	ERos
	planifolia	SSpi WWst
	– PB 449 from Spain **new**	CMon
	'Pledge Allegiance' (TB)	SIri WCAu
	plicata	WCAu
	'Plickadee' (SDB)	CBro EPot
	'Pluie d'Or' (TB)	ESgI
	'Plum Wine' (TB) **new**	CKel
	'Poem of Ecstasy' (TB) **new**	WCAu
	'Pogo' (SDB)	EChP ECtt EHyt ENot EPfP EPot EWoo GBuc GKir GMaP MMHG MRav NBir NWCA SRms
	'Point Made' (TB)	CIri
	'Pond Lily' (TB)	CIri WCAu
	'Pookanilly' (IB) **new**	ESgI
	'Port of Call' (Spuria)	CWrd
	'Power Surge' (TB)	CIri EWoo
	'Precious Heather' (TB) 🏆H4	CKel
	'Pretender' (TB)	LRHS MBri WCAu
	'Pretty Please' (TB)	ESgI
	'Prince Indigo' (TB)	ENot
	'Prince of Burgundy' (IB) 🏆H4	CIri WCAu
	'Princess Beatrice' (TB)	WCAu
	'Princess Sabra' (TB) 🏆H4	CKel
	'Princesse Caroline de Monaco' (TB)	CIri ESgI
	prismatica	CMon GIBF WTin
	– ***alba***	IGor
	'Prodigy' (MDB) **new**	MBri
	'Professor Blaauw' (Dut) 🏆H4	CFwr EBrs LRHS
	'Progressive Attitude' (TB)	CIri WCAu
	'Protocol' (IB) **new**	CKel
	'Proud Tradition' (TB)	WCAu
	'Provencal' (TB)	CKel ESgI WAul WCAu
	'Proverb' (Spuria) **new**	WCAu
	'Prudy' (BB) 🏆H4	CKel
	pseudacorus 🏆H4	More than 30 suppliers
	– B&SWJ 5018 from Japan **new**	WCru
	– from Korea	CRow
	– 'Alba'	CRow EBee GIBF LAst SSpi
	– var. ***bastardii***	CAby CBgR CRow CWat EBee ECha EMFP EMFW IGor LPBA NPer SLon SMHy SPer SSpi WBrk WFar WMoo WTin WWpP

	Plant	Suppliers
	- 'Beuron'	CRow
	- cream	EGol NBir WAul
	- 'Crème de la Crème' **new**	GBin
	- 'Esk'	GBin GCal
N	- 'Flore Pleno' (d)	CBgR CBot CRow EBee EMFW EPPr LPBA MInt NLar NPer WBrk WCot WFar
	- 'Golden Daggers'	CRow
I	- 'Golden Fleece'	SPer
	- 'Golden Queen'	CRow IGor WWpP
	- 'Ilgengold'	CRow
N	- 'Ivory'	CRow
	- 'Lime Sorbet' (v)	WCot
*	- ***nana***	CRow LPBA
	- 'Roccapina' **new**	GBin
	- 'Roy Davidson' ♀H4	CBgR CDWL CKel CLAP CPrp CRow EMFW GBin IBlr LPBA WFar WPtf WTin
*	- 'Sulphur Queen'	WCot
	- 'Sun Cascade'	CRow
	- 'Tiger Brother'	SIri
	- 'Tiggah'	CRow
	- 'Turnipseed'	WTin
	- 'Variegata' (v) ♀H4	More than 30 suppliers
	pseudopumila	ERos
	'Pulse Rate' (SDB)	CBro
	pumila	EPot LRHS MHer NFor NMen NWCA
	- ***atroviolacea***	CKel SMrm WMnd
	- subsp. ***attica***	see *I. attica*
	- 'Aurea'	EWTr
	- blue-flowered	SWal
*	- 'Gelber Mantel'	NBir
	- 'Jackanapes'	WEas
	- 'Lavendel Plicata'	EBee EWTr NBro NGdn STes
	- 'Violacea' (DB)	MBri SRms
	'Pumpin' Iron' (SDB)	CKel ESgI MSte WDav
	purdyi	GBuc
	'Purple Gem' (Reticulata)	CBro EPfP EPot LAma MAvo
	'Purple Sensation' (Dut)	CFwr CRez MSph
	purpurea	see *I. galatica*
	'Quaker Lady' (TB)	ESgI WCAu
	'Quark' (SDB)	CBro CKel
	'Quechee' (TB)	EBee ECGP EChP EMan EPfP ERou GMaP MRav MSte NGdn SChu WCra
	'Queen in Calico' (TB)	ESgI WCAu
	'Queen of May' (TB)	ESgI
	'Queen's Circle' (TB)	CIri
	'Queen's Ivory' (SDB)	WCAu
	'Rabbit's Foot' (SDB) **new**	SIri
	'Radiant Apogee' (TB)	ESgI
	'Rain Dance' (SDB) ♀H4	ESgI WCAu
	'Rajah' (TB)	CSBt EBee EChP EPfP ERou GMaP MRav MSte NGdn NOrc SChu SCoo SPet SPoG SPur WMnd
	'Rameses' (TB)	ESgI
	'Rapture in Blue' (TB)	EWoo
	'Rare Edition' (IB)	CKel EWoo GKir MBri WAul WCAu
	'Rare Treat' (TB)	WCAu
	'Raspberry Acres' (IB)	WCAu
	'Raspberry Blush' (IB) ♀H4	CHad CKel CMil CPar EPfP LAst SHBN WCAu
	'Raspberry Fudge' (TB)	WCAu
	'Raspberry Jam' (SDB)	EHyt
	'Raven Hill' (TB)	WCAu
	'Razoo' (SDB)	CKel
	'Real Coquette' (SDB) **new**	SIri
	'Rebecca Perret' (TB)	EWoo
I	'Red Flash' (TB)	SMrm
	'Red Hawk' (TB)	CIri
	'Red Heart' (SDB)	ESgI GMaP MRav
I	'Red Oak' (Spuria) **new**	WCAu
	'Red Orchid' (IB)	ELan NBlu WCAu
	'Red Revival' (TB)	WCAu
N	'Red Rum' (TB)	CKel
	'Red Tornado' (TB)	ESgI
	'Red Zinger' (IB)	ESgI WAul
	'Redwood Supreme' (Spuria)	CWrd
	'Regal Surprise' (SpecHybrid)	CRow
	'Regards' (SDB)	CBro
§	***reichenbachii***	CPBP ERos LBee LTwo NWCA
	- NS 700	CPou
	'Repartee' (TB)	ESgI EWoo
	'Response' (Spuria)	CWrd
§	***reticulata*** ♀H4	CBcs CBro EBrs LRHS MBNS NJOw SPer SPet WFar WGwG WRHF
*	- 'Violet Queen'	EPot
	'Right Royal' (TB)	ENot
	'Rime Frost' (TB)	WCAu
	'Ringo' (TB)	CIri ESgI WCAu
	'Ripple Chip' (SDB)	WTin
	'Rippling Waters' (TB)	ESgI
	'Rive Gauche' (TB)	ESgI
	'River Avon' (TB) ♀H4	CIri WCAu
	'River Pearl' (TB)	CIri
§	x ***robusta*** 'Gerald Darby' ♀H4	More than 30 suppliers
	- 'Mountain Brook'	CRow
§	'Rocket' (TB)	EChP GMaP IPot MRav NBir NEgg NGdn SCoo
	'Rogue' (TB)	CIri
	'Role Model' (TB)	WCAu
	'Roman Rhythm' (TB)	EWoo WCAu
	'Romance' (TB)	ERou
	'Romano' (Dut)	CFwr CRez EBrs MSph SOkh
	'Ron' (TB)	EWoo
	'Rosalie Figge' (TB)	WCAu
	'Rose Queen'	see *I. ensata* 'Rose Queen'
	'Rose Violet' (TB)	WCAu
	'Rosemary's Dream' (MTB)	SMrm
	rosenbachiana	WWst
	- 'Harangon'	WWst
I	- 'Sina'	WWst
	- 'Varzob'	WWst
	'Roseplic' (TB)	ESgI
	'Rosette Wine' (TB)	CIri ESgI WCAu
	rossii **new**	GIBF
	'Rosy Veil' (TB)	ESgI
	'Rosy Wings' (TB)	EHyt ESgI
	'Roulette' (TB)	MBri
N	'Roy Elliott'	NMen SIng
	'Royal Cadet' (Spuria)	CIri
	'Royal Crusader' (TB) **new**	WCAu
	'Royal Elegance' (TB)	EWoo SIri
	'Royal Intrigue' (TB)	SIri
	'Royal Magician' (SDB)	WTin
	'Royal Satin' (TB)	EWoo
	'Royal Yellow' (Dut)	CFwr
	'Rubacuori' (TB) **new**	ESgI
	'Ruban Bleu' (TB)	ESgI EWoo
	'Rubistar' (TB)	ESgI
	'Ruby Chimes' (IB)	WCAu
	'Ruby Contrast' (TB)	CHad WCAu
	rudskyi	see *I. variegata*
	'Ruffled Canary' (Spuria) **new**	WCAu
	'Ruffled Copper Sunset' (TB)	CIri
	'Ruffled Revel' (SDB)	SIri
	'Rustic Cedar' (TB)	ESgI WCAu
	'Rustic Royalty' (TB)	CIri
	'Rustler' (TB)	CIri ESgI WCAu

	ruthenica	ERos GBin GIBF NMen
	- var. ***nana***	GBin GKev
	- - L 1280	EPot
	'Ryan James' (TB) **new**	CKel
	sabina **new**	GIBF
	'Sable' (TB)	CHad EBee EChP EHrv ELan EMan EPPr ESgI GMaP MBri MRav MSte NGdn NOrc SCoo SHBN WCAu WCra
	'Sable Night' (TB)	CHar CKel ERou
	'Sager Cedric' (TB)	WCAu
	'Saharan Sun' (TB)	CIri
	'Saint Crispin' (TB)	CM&M ERou ESgI GMaP MRav MSte SChu SPer SPoG WWeb
	'Sally Jane' (TB)	WCAu
	'Salonique' (TB)	ESgI EWTr NBlu WCAu WFar
*	'Saltbox' (SDB)	WIvy
	'Saltwood' (SDB)	CBro
	'Sam Carne' (TB)	WCAu
	'San Francisco' (TB)	ESgI
	'San Leandro' (TB)	MBri
	'Sand Princess' (MTB)	SIri SMrm
	'Sandstone Sentinel' (BB)	CIri
	'Sandy Caper' (IB)	WCAu
	'Sangone' (IB)	ESgI
§	***sanguinea*** ♀H4	CHVG GIBF
§	- 'Alba'	IBlr
	- 'Nana Alba'	GBin IBlr SIri
§	- 'Snow Queen'	More than 30 suppliers
	'Sapphire Beauty' (Dut)	NArg
	'Sapphire Gem' (SDB)	CKel WCAu WDav
	'Sapphire Hills' (TB)	WCAu
	'Sarah Taylor' (SDB) ♀H4	CBro EHyt EWoo WCAu
	sari	SBla
	'Sass with Class' (SDB)	WTin
	'Satin Gown' (TB)	GKir WCAu
	'Saturday Night Live' (TB)	CIri
	schachtii purple-flowered	SBla
	'Scribe' (MDB)	CBro GKir NBir WCAu
	'Sea Fret' (SDB)	CBro
	'Sea Monster' (SDB) **new**	WDav
	'Sea Wisp' (La) **new**	CWrd
	'Semola' (SDB)	ESgI
	'Senlac' (TB)	EWTr SMer WMnd
	serbica	see *I. reichenbachii*
	'Serengeti Spaghetti' (TB)	CIri
	'Serenity Prayer' (SDB)	WCAu
	setosa ♀H4	CBro CPne CTri EBee EHyt EKen EMFW EPfP ERos GBBs GCra GFlt GKev IGor LPBA LRHS MNrw MOne NArg NDlv NEgg NGdn NLAp
	- AER 0233	MGol
	- ***alba***	MSte NLar SIng
	- var. ***arctica***	CStr EBee EHyt EMon EPot GBuc LEdu NMen NWCA SBla WHoo WPer
	- subsp. ***canadensis***	see *I. hookeri*
	- dwarf	see *I. hookeri*
§	- 'Hondoensis'	MSte
	- 'Hookeri'	see *I. hookeri*
	- 'Kasho En'	CHad
	- 'Kirigamini'	see *I. setosa* 'Hondoensis'
	- var. ***nana***	see *I. hookeri*
	'Shampoo' (IB)	SIri WAul WCAu
	'Sheer Ecstasy' (TB)	CIri
	'Sheila Ann Germaney' (Reticulata)	EHyt EPot GCrs NMen
	'Shelford Giant' (Spuria) ♀H4	CIri EWTr NBir NEgg
	'Shepherd's Delight' (TB)	GKir WCAu
	'Sherbet Lemon' (IB) ♀H4	CKel WCAu
	'Short Distance' (IB)	EWoo SIri
	'Showman' (TB)	ERou
	shrevei	see *I. virginica* var. *shrevei*
	'Shurton Inn' (TB)	CKel WCAu
	sibirica ♀H4	More than 30 suppliers
	- 'Ann Dasch'	EBee WLin
	- 'Annemarie Troeger' ♀H4	EBee
	- 'Annick'	LPhx
	- 'Anniversary'	CDes CLAP CMdw EBee LRHS MBNS
	- 'Atoll' **new**	SIri
	- 'Baby Sister'	CAby CMHG EBee EBrs GAbr GBin LRHS MBri NBro WAul WWFP
	- 'Berlin Bluebird'	LPhx SMHy
	- 'Bickley Cape'	EBee
	- 'Blaue Milchstrasse' ♀H4 **new**	GBin
	- 'Blue Brilliant'	WLin
	- 'Blue Burgee'	ECha
*	- 'Blue Emperor'	EBee WBrE
	- 'Blue King'	CHid CKel COtt CTbh EBee EChP ELan ENot EPfP GMaP LRHS MBNS MDun MRav NBro NGdn NMoo SMrm SPer SPoG WLin WMnd WMoo
	- 'Blue Meadow Fly'	EBee
	- 'Blue Mere'	WLin
	- 'Blue Moon'	CRez
	- 'Blue Pennant'	CWrd EBee GBin
	- 'Blue Reverie'	CPen EPPr
	- 'Blue Sceptre' **new**	IBlr
	- 'Blue Seraph' **new**	GBin
	- 'Borbeleta'	LPhx
	- 'Bournemouth Beauty' ♀H4	WLin
	- 'Bracknell'	LPhx
	- 'Bridal Jig'	CWrd EBee GBin GFlt
	- 'Butter and Sugar' ♀H4	More than 30 suppliers
	- 'Caesar's Brother'	CHid CPrp EBee EChP ELan EMil IBlr LRHS MBnl MNFA MOne NArg NBro SGSe SPer SWal WCAu WLin WPop WWhi
	- 'Caezar'	CRow GFlt GKir SDys SRms WLin
	- 'Camberley'	WLin
	- 'Cambridge' ♀H4	EBee EBla GFlt MBri MNFA MSte WCAu WFar
	- 'Canonbury Belle'	WLin
	- 'Charming Darlene'	CWrd
	- 'Chartreuse Bounty'	EBee EChP EMan ERou EWes GAbr ITim LAst MAvo MBNS MBnl MLLN NLar SUsu WWeb
	- 'Chateuse Belle'	CWrd
	- 'Circle Round'	CAby EPPr LPhx
	- 'Clee Hills'	WLin
	- 'Cleedownton' ♀H4	WLin
	- 'Clouded Moon'	see *I. sibirica* 'Forncett Moon'
	- 'Colin's Pale Blue'	SMHy
	- 'Cool Spring'	WLin
	- 'Coquet Waters'	WLin
	- 'Coronation Anthem'	NEgg WLin
	- cream	see *I. sibirica* 'Primrose Cream'
	- 'Dance Ballerina Dance'	CRow EBee EChP EMan ERou EWTr GBri GFlt MHar MLLN MNFA NCGa STes SUsu WFar WPtf WSan
	- 'Dancing Moon'	CWrd
	- 'Dancing Nanou'	MMil
	- 'Dark Circle'	CWrd EBee
	- 'Dear Delight'	EPPr
	- 'Dear Dianne'	CKel ECha GMac
	- 'Dewful'	WFar WLin
	- 'Dragonfly'	WWhi
	- 'Dreaming Green'	CWrd GBin

	- 'Dreaming Orange' **new**	CWrd
	- 'Dreaming Spires' 🏆H4	GBin GKir SIri WLin
	- 'Dreaming Yellow' 🏆H4	CBre CFee EBee ECha EMan EPfP GMac MNFA MRav MWgw NArg NBro NChi NGdn NLon SApp SHBN SPer SSpe WCAu WLin WMoo
	- 'Ego'	CHid COtt ECha EWTr GBin GKir GMac LRHS NBro NCGa NGby SGSe WLin WMoo WPrP
	- 'Elinor Hewitt'	EWTr
	- 'Ellesmere'	NGdn
	- 'Emperor'	CRow CWat ERou LPhx MSte MWgw NBur NSti SMrm WLin
	- 'Eric the Red'	IBlr NBur
	- 'Ever Again'	CWrd
	- 'Ewen'	CBos CHid CLAP CMdw CPou CRow CSam EBee GBin GBuc IBlr MNFA MNrw NGdn SGSe WCot WFar WLin WPrP WWlt
	- 'Exuberant Encore' 🏆H4	WLin
	- 'Flight of Butterflies'	More than 30 suppliers
§	- 'Forncett Moon'	GMac WLin
	- 'Fourfold Lavender'	EBee
	- 'Fourfold White'	GMac LPhx LRHS
	- 'Gatineau'	CDes CLAP EBee GBuc
	- 'Gerbel Mantel'	GBin SHBN SPet WFar WHil
	- 'Glaslyn' 🏆H4	WLin
	- grey	SApp
	- 'Gull's Wings'	EBee
	- 'Harpswell Hallelujah'	EBee
	- 'Harpswell Happiness' 🏆H4	CHVG CLAP CPrp EBee EPfP GBin LPio MBnl MBri WAul WMoo
	- 'Harpswell Haze'	ECha WMoo
	- 'Harpswell Velvet'	CWrd
	- 'Heavenly Blue'	EHon SSpe WWpP
	- 'Helen Astor'	CBos CDes CHVG CLAP CMea CRow CSam CTri EBee EWTr LRHS MBNS MHar MRav SApp WTin
	- 'High Standards'	CWrd
	- 'Himmel von Komi'	GBin
	- 'Hoar Edge'	WLin
	- 'Hubbard'	CM&M CPen EShb GBin MNrw NBro
	- 'Illini Charm'	CHid CPen EChP NBro SSvw WFar WMoo
	- 'Indy'	WCot
	- 'Jewelled Crown' **new**	CPen
	- 'Kathleen Mary' 🏆H4 **new**	WLin
	- 'Kingfisher'	WLin
	- 'Lady Vanessa'	CPou CWrd EBee ERou EVFa EWTr GBin LBuc MBnl MRav NBro NSti WAul WHil WSan
	- 'Langthorns Pink'	CMdw ELan MRav SOkh
	- 'Laurenbuhl'	CPLG WLin
	- 'Lavender Bounty'	CHid EBee ENot MBnl NBro SPet WCAu WHil WHoo WRHF
	- 'Lavender Light'	WLin
	- 'Leo Hewitt' **new**	WLin
	- 'Limeheart'	CPou CSev ELan ERou
N	- 'Limelight'	LRHS
	- 'Little Blue'	EBee LRHS
	- 'Little Twinkle Star'	CHid CWrd EBee GBin NPro WFar
	- 'Little White'	SMHy
	- 'Llyn Brianne'	WLin
	- 'Marcus Perry'	CRow MSte
	- 'Marilyn Holmes'	EBee NFor WCot
	- 'Marlene Ahlburg'	WLin
	- 'Marshmallow Frosting'	WFar
§	- 'Melton Red Flare'	CMHG CPen EBee EHon ELan EMan EPPr GBin LRHS MBNS SBch SDys SOkh WCra WFar WWpP
I	- 'Mint Fresh' **new**	SIri
	- 'Moon Moth'	WLin
	- 'Moon Silk' **new**	CWrd
	- 'Mountain Lake'	CPen CSam EMan EPPr GBin LRHS SBch SHel
	- 'Mrs Rowe'	CDes CFee CPou CRow EBee EGra EPPr LLWP MNFA MRav MSte MWat WCAu WFar WLin WTin
	- 'Mrs Saunders'	WLin
	- 'My Love'	WLin
	- 'Navy Brass'	GBuc
	- 'Night Breeze' **new**	SIri
	- 'Nora Distin'	WLin
	- 'Nottingham Lace'	EBee GMac WBcn WLin
	- 'Orville Fay'	EChP GMac WCot WFar
	- 'Ottawa'	CBot CPou CRow ECGP ELan ERou LRHS MBNS WFar
	- 'Outset'	EBee SSvw
I	- 'Pageant' **new**	WCot
	- 'Painted Desert'	EBee
	- 'Papillon'	CTri EBee EChP ECtt ELan EPPr ERou GIBF GKir GMac LRHS MAvo MBnl MNFA NArg NBir NBro NGdn NPri NSti SApp SChu WFar WLin WPer WPnP
N	- 'Pearl Queen'	WFar
	- 'Peg Edwards'	EBee
	- 'Percheron' **new**	SIri
	- 'Perry's Blue'	More than 30 suppliers
I	- 'Perry's Favourite'	CFee CRow
	- 'Perry's Pigmy'	GBuc WLin
	- 'Persimmon'	CFir CHid EBee ECtt EMFW EMan ERou EVFa GKir LRHS MArl MNFA NMoo SHel WFar WMoo
*	- 'Phosphor Flame'	WLin
	- 'Pink Haze'	CHar CRow EBee EMan EWTr GBin MLLN MNFA MTis NBro NSti SPur WHrl
	- 'Pirate Prince'	NPer WCra WHoo
	- Plant World hybrids	CBrm MDKP SWal
	- 'Plissee' 🏆H4 **new**	WLin
	- 'Polly Dodge'	EBrs
	- 'Pounsley Purple'	CPou
§	- 'Primrose Cream'	WCot
	- 'Prussian Blue' 🏆H4 **new**	WLin
	- 'Purple Cloak'	MSte WBcn
	- 'Purple Mere'	WLin
N	- 'Red Flag'	WLin
	- 'Redflare'	see *I. sibirica* 'Melton Red Flare'
	- 'Regality' **new**	EWTr MBnl NBro
	- 'Regency Belle' 🏆H4 **new**	SIri
	- 'Regency Buck'	CWrd
	- 'Rejoice Always'	GMac
	- 'Rikugi-sakura' **new**	EMan NBro WSan
	- 'Roanoke's Choice'	CFwr CWrd EBee GBin NCGa
	- 'Roaring Jelly' **new**	WCAu
N	- 'Roger Perry'	CFee
	- 'Roisin' 🏆H4	WLin
	- 'Rosselline' 🏆H4	WLin
	- 'Rowden Aurelius'	CRow
I	- 'Royal Blue'	ECha GBuc GCra
	- 'Ruby Wine' **new**	CPen
	- 'Ruffled Velvet' 🏆H4	More than 30 suppliers
	- 'Ruffles Plus'	CWrd
	- 'Savoir Faire'	ECha
	- 'Sea Horse'	GBuc WLin
	- 'Sea Shadows'	MBri NBir SHel
	- 'Seren Wib'	WLin
	- 'Shaker's Prayer'	CWrd
	- 'Shall We Dance' 🏆H4	WLin
	- 'Shirley Pope' 🏆H4	CAby CDes EBee EBrs GBin GKir LPhx LRHS MBri MNFA NSti SOkh SSpi SUsu WAul WCot WFar WMoo

- 'Shirley's Choice' **new** SIri
- 'Showdown' EBee ECtt GMaP LRHS SAga WCAu WFar
- 'Silberkante' **new** WLin
- 'Silver Edge' ♀H4 More than 30 suppliers
- 'Siobhan' ♀H4 WLin
- 'Sky Wings' CRow ECha MArl WMoo
- 'Smudger's Gift' ♀H4 **new** WLin
- 'Snow Prince' CWrd
- 'Snow Queen' see *I. sanguinea* 'Snow Queen'
- 'Snowcrest' CBre WLin
- 'Soft Blue' ♀H4 CDes EBee WLin WTin
N - 'Southcombe White' COIW CRow GBin GBuc GCal LPio MHar NGdn SIri SMHy
- 'Sparkling Rosé' More than 30 suppliers
- 'Steve' CHVG CPar EBee EChP EPPr EWTr LPio MBnl MLLN MNFA MTis NBPC NBro NCGa SUsu WAul
- 'Steve Varner' SIri WLin
- 'Summer Sky' CBre EBla SSpi WCAu WCot WLin WTin
- 'Super Ego' WCot WTin
- 'Superba' WLin
- 'Taldra' WLin
- 'Tal-y-Bont' WLin
- 'Tanz Nochmal' **new** GBin
- 'Teal Velvet' ECha SIri WCAu WFar
- 'Tealwood' WLin
- 'Temper Tantrum' CKel CWrd
- 'Trim the Velvet' ♀H4 WLin
- 'Tropic Night' More than 30 suppliers
- 'Tycoon' CHid EBee EShb GBin GBuc IBlr LRHS MNFA NChi SBch SPer WLin
- 'Valda' EBee WLin
- 'Vee One' WLin
- 'Vi Luihn' CBcs ECha EPPr WMoo
- 'Violet Skies' **new** MBnl
- 'Visual Treat' **new** SIri
- 'Walter' **new** EBee
- 'Weisse Etagen' WLin
- 'Welcome Return' CHVG EBee GBin NBro SUsu WFar WMoo
- 'Welfenfurstin' GBin
- white-flowered WOut
I - 'White Swan' LAst
- 'White Swirl' ♀H4 More than 30 suppliers
- 'White Triangles' **new** SIri
- 'Winscombe' CHid
- 'Wisley White' GFlt MWgw SPer WLin
- 'Yankee Consul' CWrd
- 'Yellow Court' CRow
§ 'Sibirica Alba' CBrm CRow ECha EHon EPfP EShb GAbr GBBs GFlt LLWP MHer NChi WBrk WFar WWpP WWye
§ 'Sibirica Baxteri' CFee
sichuanensis EPot
sieboldii see *I. sanguinea*
'Sierra Blue' (TB) ESgI
'Sierra Grande' (TB) EWoo WCAu
sikkimensis GIBF
'Silent Strings' (IB) MBri
'Silicon Prairie' (TB) ESgI
'Silverado' (TB) CKel ESgI WCAu
'Silvery Beauty' (Dut) GBBs NBir SPer WFar
sindjarensis see *I. aucheri*
'Sindpers' (Juno) ♀H3 SBla WWst
sintenisii ♀H4 CBro CHid EHyt
- HH&K 172 CMdw
'Sir Michael' (TB) ESgI
'Sissinghurst' (SDB) WHoo WIvy
'Siva Siva' (TB) ENot ERou MRav WCAu
'Skating Party' (TB) CKel ESgI EWoo
'Skiers' Delight' (TB) CIri WCAu
'Sky Hooks' (TB) CIri
'Skyfire' (TB) ESgI
'Skyline' (Juno) **new** WWst
'Skywalker' (TB) CIri
'Small Sky' (SDB) CBro
N 'Smart Girl' (TB) CKel SMrm
'Smoked Salmon' (TB) CKel
'Smokey Dream' (TB) CKel
'Snow Cloud' (TB) EWoo
'Snow Tracery' (TB) ENot MBri
'Snow Troll' (SDB) WCAu
'Snowbrook' (TB) WCAu
'Snowcone' (IB) ESgI
'Snowmound' (TB) CKel WCAu
'Snowy Owl' (TB) ♀H4 CKel WCAu
'Soaring Kite' (TB) WCAu
'Social Event' (TB) ESgI WCAu
sofarana LB 400 from Lebanon **new** CMon
'Soft Caress' (TB) WCAu
'Solid Mahogany' (TB) MRav WCAu
'Somerset Blue' (TB) ♀H4 CKel WCAu
N 'Somerset Vale' (TB) SMrm
'Somerton Brocade' (SDB) CKel WDav
'Somerton Dance' (SDB) CKel
'Song of Norway' (TB) ESgI SCoo SIri WCAu
'Sonoran Señorita' (Spuria) ♀H4 CIri
'Sopra il Vulcano' (BB) ESgI
'Sostenique' (TB) ESgI WCAu
'Soul Power' (TB) ERou
'Southern Clipper' (SDB) MBri
'Spartan' CKel
'Spellbreaker' (TB) ESgI EWoo
'Spice Lord' (TB) **new** WCAu
'Spiced Custard' (TB) ESgI
'Spiced Tiger' (TB) CIri WCAu
'Spinning Wheel' (TB) **new** SIri
'Spreckles' (TB) ESgI
sprengeri EHyt SOkd
'Spring Festival' (TB) WCAu
'Springtime' (Reticulata) LAma LRHS
'Spun Gold' (TB) ESgI
spuria CPou ELan NEgg
- subsp. ***carthaliniae*** WPer
§ - subsp. ***halophila*** GBin GIBF WCAu
- 'Jubilant Spirit' CWrd EBee EWes
- 'Just Reward' CWrd
- subsp. ***maritima*** EMan SMHy
§ - subsp. ***musulmanica*** ETow GIBF
- subsp. ***notha*** CC 1550 WCot
- subsp. ***ochroleuca*** see *I. orientalis* Mill.
- subsp. ***spuria*** GBuc GIBF
- var. ***subbarbata*** GIBF
x ***squalens*** WCAu
'Stairway to Heaven' (TB) CIri WCAu
'Stapleford' (SDB) CBro
'Star Shine' (TB) WCAu
'Starcrest' (TB) ESgI
'Starship' (TB) ESgI
'Staten Island' (TB) ENot ESgI GFlt GKir MBri SRms WCAu WTin
'Status Seeker' (TB) WCAu
'Stellar Lights' (TB) EWoo WCAu
§ ***stenophylla*** EPot WWst
'Stepping Out' (TB) ♀H4 EBee ESgI GBin LRHS WCAu
'Stinger' (SDB) ♀H4 CIri
'Stitch in Time' (TB) EWoo WCAu
'Stockholm' (SDB) CKel WDav WPen
'Storm Center' (TB) **new** SIri
'Striking' (TB) EWoo
'Study In Black' (TB) WCAu

	Name	Suppliers
	stylosa	see *I. unguicularis*
§	***suaveolens***	CBro CPou EHyt LPio NMen SOkd SRot WDav WIvy
*	- ***rubra nana***	GKev
	- 'Rubromarginata'	ERos NJOw
*	- var. ***violacea***	NMen NWCA WLin
	subbiflora	CMon
	'Sugar' (IB)	NSti WCAu
	'Sultan's Palace' (TB)	CRez ESgI EWsh MBow SMer STes WWol
	'Sumatra' (TB)	ESgI
	'Summer's Smile' (TB)	ESgI
	'Sun Dappled' (TB)	ERou
	'Sundown Red' (IB)	NBir
	'Sunny and Warm' (TB) **new**	CKel
	'Sunny Dawn' (IB) $\mathbb{Y}^{H4}$	CKel WDav
	'Sunny Redwine' (Cal-Sib) **new**	GBin
	'Sunrise in Sonora' (Spuria) $\mathbb{Y}^{H4}$	CIri
	'Sunset Colors' (Spuria) $\mathbb{Y}^{H4}$	CIri
	'Superstition' (TB) $\mathbb{Y}^{H4}$	CRez ESgI GBin SIri SMrm WAul WCAu
	'Supreme Sultan' (TB)	ESgI EWoo WAul WCAu
	'Susan Bliss' (TB)	CKel CRez EBee ELan EPfP ESgI GAbr GMaP MBNS SIri WCAu
	susiana	LAma
	svetlanae **new**	WWst
	'Swain' (TB) **new**	ESgI
	'Swaledale' (TB)	WCAu
	'Swazi Princess' (TB)	CKel ESgI WCAu
	'Sweet Kate' (SDB) $\mathbb{Y}^{H4}$	WCAu
	'Sweet Musette' (TB)	WCAu
	'Sweeter than Wine' (TB)	CIri WCAu
	'Swingtown' (TB)	CIri WCAu
	'Sybil'	GBin
	'Sylvia Murray' (TB)	WCAu
	'Symphony' (Dut)	LRHS NBir
	'Syncopation' (TB)	ESgI WCAu
	'Talish' (Reticulata) **new**	WWst
	'Tall Chief' (TB)	MTis WCAu
	'Tangerine Sky' (TB)	WCAu
	'Tangfu' (IB)	ESgI
	'Tantara' (SDB)	WTin
	'Tanzanian Tangerine' (TB)	CIri WCAu
	'Tarheel Elf' (SDB)	ESgI WTin
	'Tarn Hows' (TB)	SRms WCAu
	tectorum	CSWP EHol ERos GBin GIBF GKev GSki ITer MNrw NWCA WOut
	- 'Alba'	CPBP EPPr ERos
	- 'Variegata' (v)	CPrp EBee EMan EPPr MRav NArg NSti SGSe SPoG
	'Tell Fibs' (SDB)	CBro
	'Temple Gold' (TB)	CKel NPer
	'Temple Meads' (IB)	WCAu
	'Templecloud' (IB) $\mathbb{Y}^{H4}$	CHar CKel
	'Tempting Fate' (TB)	EWoo
	'Temptone' (TB)	CIri
§	***tenax***	CLAP CNic CPBP ECho ETow GBin GBuc GEdr GKir GSki WBVN WLin
	'Tender Years' (IB)	WAul
	'Tennessee Vol' (TB)	CIri
	tenuis	GBin
	tenuissima	GBuc SSpi
	'Terra Rosa' (TB)	CIri
	'Terre de Feu' (TB) **new**	ESgI
	'Thais' (TB)	ESgI
	'The Bride'	see *I.* 'Bride'
	'The Red Douglas' (TB) **new**	ESgI
	'The Rocket'	see *I.* 'Rocket'
	'Theatre' (TB)	ESgI
	'Theseus' (Aril)	EHyt
	'Third Charm' (SDB)	CBro
	'Third World' (SDB)	CBro
	'Thornbird' (TB) $\mathbb{Y}^{H4}$	CIri ESgI WCAu
	'Three Cherries' (MDB)	CBro
	'Thriller' (TB)	ESgI WCAu
	'Throb' (TB)	CIri
	thunbergii	see *I. sanguinea*
	'Thunder Echo' (TB)	ESgI
	'Tickle Me' (MDB) **new**	WCAu
	'Tide's In' (TB)	ERou EWoo
	'Tiffany' (TB)	WTin
	'Tiger Butter' (TB)	ESgI
	'Tiger Honey' (TB)	CIri
	'Tillamook' (TB)	WCAu
	timofejewii x ***subbiflora***	WCot
	tingitana var. ***fontanesii***	CFil SSpi WPGP
	- - AB&S 4452 from Morocco **new**	CMon
	- - AB&S 4521	CMon
	'Tinkerbell' (SDB)	CPBP MSte NBir SChu SPet
	'Tintinara' (TB) $\mathbb{Y}^{H4}$	CKel
	'Titan's Glory' (TB) $\mathbb{Y}^{H4}$	CIri ESgI MRav WAul WCAu WCot
	'To the Point' (TB)	CIri WCAu
	'Tol-long' $\mathbb{Y}^{H4}$	MSte
	'Tom Johnson' (TB)	CIri WCAu
	'Tom Tit' (TB)	WCAu
	'Tomingo' (SDB)	WCAu
	'Tomorrow's Child' (TB)	ESgI
	'Toots' (SDB)	EHyt WTin
	'Top Flight' (TB)	EChP ELan ERou LAst SCoo SHBN SMrm SRms
N	'Topolino' (TB)	CKel SGar SIri SMrm
	'Total Eclipse'	SRms
	'Tracy Tyrene' (TB)	ESgI
	transylvanica	GIBF
	'Trenwith' (TB) **new**	CKel
	'Trillion' (TB)	CIri
	'Triple Whammy' (TB)	ESgI
	trojana	CMon
	tuberosa	see *Hermodactylus tuberosus*
	'Tumultueux' (TB)	ESgI
N	'Tuscan' (TB)	CMil
	'Tut's Gold' (TB)	ESgI WCAu
	typhifolia	NEgg WLin
§	***unguicularis*** $\mathbb{Y}^{H4}$	More than 30 suppliers
	- 'Abington Purple'	CBro WCot
	- 'Alba'	CBro ECha WMnd
N	- 'Bob Thompson'	CBro
	- subsp. ***carica*** var. ***angustifolia***	WCot
§	- subsp. ***cretensis***	CAby EBee EPot NMen SHGN WAbe
	- - MS 860	WCot
	- - white-flowered	CAby SBla
	- 'Diana Clare'	WCot
	- 'Kilndown'	WFar
	- var. ***lazica***	see *I. lazica*
	- 'Marondera'	CAvo
	- 'Mary Barnard' $\mathbb{Y}^{H4}$	CAvo CBro CFee CHar CMea CPou CSam ECGP ECha EHrv ENot IBlr MAvo NBir NMen SBla SIng WCot WMnd
N	- 'Oxford Dwarf'	CBro ECho
	- 'Palette'	ELan
§	- 'Walter Butt'	CAvo ECGP ECha NBir SBla SRot WFar WMnd
	uromovii	GBuc MArl
	'Vague a l'Ame' (TB)	ESgI
	'Valimar' (TB) **new**	WCAu
	'Vamp' (IB)	CKel SIri

	'Vandal Spirit' (TB) **new**	ESgI
	'Vanilla Fluff' **new**	CWrd
	'Vanity' (TB) ♀H4	ESgI WCAu
	'Vanity's Child' (TB)	ERou WCAu
§	***variegata*** ♀H4	CPou EGoo GCal GIBF WCAu WCot
§	- var. ***reginae*** **new**	WCAu
	'Velvet Caper' (SDB)	WTin
	'Velvet Toy' (MDB) **new**	EHyt
	'Veneer' (TB)	CIri
	'Verity Blamey' (TB)	CKel
	verna	ERos
	versicolor ♀H4	CArn CBen CDWL CElw CRow EBee EGol EHon EMFW EPPr GBin GFlt GKev IBlr LNCo LPBA LRHS MNrw MSal NGdn SPlb SRms WAbe WBrk WFar WPop WShi WWpP
	- ***alba*** **new**	GCra
	- 'Between the Lines'	CRow
	- 'Candystriper'	SIri
	- 'China West Lake'	CRow
	- 'Claret Cup'	CPou
	- 'Dottie's Double'	CRow
	- 'Georgia Bay'	CRow
N	- 'Goldbrook'	EGol
	- 'Kermesina'	CDWL CRow CWat EBee ECha EGol EHon ELan EMFW ETow EWTr GBuc GCal GFlt GGar IBlr LPBA NArg NPer NSti SRms WBrk WEas WFar WMoo WPnP WPop WTin WWpP
	- 'Mysterious Monique'	CMdw CRow
	- 'Party Line'	CRow SIri
	- var. ***rosea***	CRow
	- 'Rowden Allegro'	CRow
	- 'Rowden Aria'	CRow
	- 'Rowden Cadenza'	CRow
	- 'Rowden Cantata'	CRow
	- 'Rowden Concerto'	CRow
	- 'Rowden Fugue'	CRow
	- 'Rowden Lyric'	CRow
	- 'Rowden Mazurka'	CRow
	- 'Rowden Nocturne'	CRow
	- 'Rowden Prelude'	CRow
	- 'Rowden Refrain'	CRow
	- 'Rowden Rondo'	CRow
	- 'Rowden Sonata'	CRow
	- 'Rowden Symphony'	CRow
	- 'Rowden Waltz'	CRow
	- 'Silvington'	CRow
	- 'Whodunit'	CRow
	'Vert Gallant' (TB)	ESgI
	'Vibrant' (TB) **new**	WCAu
	'Vibrations' (TB) **new**	ESgI
	vicaria	EPot WWst
I	- 'Sina'	WWst
	'Victoria Falls' (TB)	ESgI WCAu
	'Vigilante' (TB)	CIri
	'Vinho Verde' (IB) ♀H4	CKel
	'Vino Rosso' (SDB)	ESgI
	'Vintage Press' (IB)	WCAu
	'Vintage Year' (Spuria)	WCAu
	violacea	see *I. spuria* subsp. *musulmanica*
	'Violet Beauty' (Reticulata)	EPot LAma LRHS MBow SMeo
	'Violet Classic' (TB)	WCAu
	'Violet Icing' (TB) ♀H4	CKel
	'Violet Rings' (TB)	WCAu
	virginica 'Pond Crown Point'	CRow
	- 'Pond Lilac Dream'	CRow
N	- 'Purple Fan'	CRow
§	- var. ***shrevei***	CRow
	'Vita Fire'	SIri
	'Vitality' (IB)	ESgI
	'Vive la France' (TB)	ESgI EWoo
	'Voltage' (TB)	CIri
	'Volute' (TB)	ESgI
	'Voyage' (SDB)	EWoo
	'Wabash' (TB)	EBee ERou ESgI MBow WCAu WTin
	'Walker Ferguson' (Spuria) **new**	WCAu
	'Walter Butt'	see *I. unguicularis* 'Walter Butt'
	'War Chief' (TB)	ESgI WCAu
	'War Sails' (TB)	SIri WCAu
	warleyensis	WWst
	'Warl-sind' (Juno)	EPot WWst
	'Warrior King' (TB)	WCAu
	wattii	CMon GCal
	'Wedding Candles' (TB)	WCAu
	'Wedding Vow' (TB) **new**	CKel
	'Well Suited' (SDB)	EWoo
	'Westar' (SDB) ♀H4	CKel
	'Westwell' (SDB)	WCAu
	'What Again' (SDB)	SUsu
	'Wheels' (SDB)	WTin
	'White Bridge' (Dut)	MSph
	'White City' (TB)	CHad ECGP EPfP EWTr GMaP MRav MWat NGdn NPer SChu SCoo SDnm SHBN SIri SPoG SRms WAul WCAu WMnd
	'White Cliffs of Dover' **new**	NEgg
	'White Excelsior' (Dut)	LAma LRHS WGHP
	'White Knight' (TB)	EBee ELan ENot EPfP SCoo WMnd
	'White Reprise' (TB) **new**	ESgI
	'White Shimmer' (Spuria)	CIri
	'White Superior' (Dut)	NBir
	'White van Vliet' (Dut)	CFwr
	'White Wedgwood' (Dut)	CFwr
	'White Wine' (MTB) **new**	WCAu
	'Widdershins' (TB)	CIri
	'Widecombe Fair' (SDB)	WIvy
	'Wild Jasmine' (TB) **new**	WCAu
	'Wild Ruby' (SDB) **new**	CKel
	'Wild West' (TB)	CKel
	willmottiana	WWst
	wilsonii ♀H4	CAby GBBs GBin GBuc GIBF NEgg SMHy SSpi
	'Windsor Rose' (TB)	CHar
	'Winemaster' (TB)	EWoo SIri
	winogradowii ♀H4	CAvo CBro EHyt ERos GCrs GKir LAma NMen WAbe
	'Winter Olympics' (TB)	ESgI
	'Wisteria Sachet' (IB)	WCAu
	'Witching' (TB)	WCAu
	'Wizard of Id' (SDB)	WTin
	'Wondrous' (TB)	ESgI
	'Worlds Beyond' (TB) **new**	WCAu
	'Wow' (SDB)	EHyt
	'Wyckhill' (SDB)	WCAu
	'Wyoming Cowboys' (Spuria) ♀H4	CIri
	xiphioides	see *I. latifolia*
	xiphium	GIBF SSpi
	- B&S 411 from Portugal **new**	CMon
	- var. ***lusitanica***	SSpi
	'Yaquina Blue' (TB)	CIri EWoo WCAu
	'Yo-yo' (SDB)	SIri
	'Yvonne Pelletier' (TB)	WCAu
	'Zantha' (TB)	WCAu
	zenaidae **new**	WWst
	'Zinc Pink' (BB)	WCAu
	'Zipper' (MDB)	WCAu

Isatis (*Brassicaceae*)

glauca **new** — NDov
tinctoria — CAgr CArn CBod CHby COld CRWN CSev EOHP EUnu GPoy ILis LRHS MChe MHer MSal NDov NVic SECG SIde SPav WAul WBWf WCHb WGwG WHer WJek WSel WWye

Ischyrolepis (*Restionaceae*)

ocreata — CTrC WNor
§ **subverticillata** — CBig CCtw CHEx CTrC EAmu WMul

Ismene see *Hymenocallis*

Isodon (*Lamiaceae*)

serra 'Korean Zest' — EBee EGoo WCru

Isolepis (*Cyperaceae*)

§ **cernua** — CBrm CHal EMFW EMan EPfP MAvo MBri NArg NOak NPri SCoo WDyG WFar WPrP

Isoloma see *Kohleria*

Isoplexis (*Scrophulariaceae*)

canariensis — CAbb CAby CBcs CBot CCtw CHEx CHll CHrt CRHN CSec CSpe CTbh CTrC ECre EMan EWll SHFr SPlb WCFE WSPU
chalcantha **new** — CSec
isabelliana — EBee EShb LDai MGol WCot
sceptrum — CBcs CBot CCtw CFil CHEx CHVG CHll CHrt CPLG CRHN CSec CSpe ECre EMan SAPC SArc SHFr WGwG
- pink — CDes CSpe WPGP

Isopogon (*Proteaceae*)

anethifolius — SPlb

Isopyrum (*Ranunculaceae*)

biternatum — GBuc NLar
nipponicum — CLAP WCru
thalictroides — EPot WAbe

Isotoma (*Campanulaceae*)

sp. — LAst SWvt
§ **axillaris** — LIck LRHS MOak SBch SCoo SPet SPoG
- 'Fairy Carpet' — EMan MBNS SRms
fluviatilis — CBrm ECou WCru WDyG
- white — ECou

Itea (*Escalloniaceae*)

chinensis **new** — CFil
ilicifolia ♀H3 — More than 30 suppliers
japonica 'Beppu' — MGos SLPl
virginica — CAbP CBcs CMCN CMHG CPle EBee ECrN ELan EPfP EWTr MBlu MRav SLon SPer WBVN WFar WOrn
§ - 'Henry's Garnet' — CDoC CEnd CFai CMCN CPMA CWSG EBee EPfP GAbr LAst MWgw NLar NPri SBra SBrw SLim SPoG SSpi SWvt WDin
- 'Long Spire' — CPMA ECrN NLar
- 'Merlot' — CPMA NLar
- 'Sarah Eve' — CMCN CPMA
- 'Saturnalia' **new** — NLar
- 'Shirley's Compact' — SSpi
- Swarthmore form — see *I. virginica* 'Henry's Garnet'
yunnanensis — CPLG

Itoa (*Flacourtiaceae*)

orientalis SF 92300 — ISea

Ixia (*Iridaceae*)

Bird of Paradise — see *I.* 'Paradijsvogel'
'Blue Bird' — LAma WHil
'Castor' — ECho WHil
conferta var. **ochroleuca** **new** — WCot
dubia — WCot
flexuosa — WCot
'Giant' — ECho WHil
'Hogarth' — LAma WHil
'Holland Glory' — ECho WHil
lutea — WCot
'Mabel' — WCot WHil
maculata — SSpi WCot
monadelpha — WCot
paniculata — WCot
'Panorama' — ECho
§ 'Paradijsvogel' — LAma
pumilio — WCot
purpureorosea — ECho
'Saldanha'
'Rose Emperor' — LAma WHil
'Spotlight' — ECho WHil
thomasiae — WCot
'Venus' — LAma WHil
viridiflora — WCot
'Vulcan' — ECho
'Yellow Emperor' — WCot WHil

Ixiolirion (*Ixioliriaceae*)

pallasii — see *I. tataricum*
§ **tataricum** — EBee EMan GFlt LAma MBow MBri SBch SMeo
- Ledebourii Group — CAvo LAma

J

Jaborosa (*Solanaceae*)

integrifolia — CFir CPLG CSpe CStu ELan GEdr WAul WCot WCru WDyG WPGP WPrP XPep

Jacaranda (*Bignoniaceae*)

acutifolia misapplied — see *J. mimosifolia*
acutifolia Kunth — MBri
§ **mimosifolia** — ELan ERea EShb ESlt GQui LExo MGol SMur SPlb WMul

Jacobinia see *Justicia*

Jamesbrittenia (*Scrophulariaceae*)

§ **jurassica** — EHyt
'Pink Pearl' — COtt

Jamesia (*Hydrangeaceae*)

americana — CBcs CPle NLar

x *Jancaemonda* (*Gesneriaceae*)

vandedemii — SOkd

Jasione (*Campanulaceae*)

§ **crispa** — MDKP
§ **heldreichii** — CSec EBee EBrs GAbr LRHS MWrn SBla SRms

	jankae	see *J. heldreichii*
§	***laevis***	EBrs ECot GAbr IHMH LRHS MDKP SRms WGwG
§	- 'Blaulicht'	CBrm CCge CFis CMHG CWib EBee ECha ECrN EDAr EPfP LRHS MBNS MBow MBri MLan MWat MWrn NBPC NBlu NEgg NJOw NLar SPet SPla SPlb SSvw SUsu WBVN WMoo WWeb
	- Blue Light	see *J. laevis* 'Blaulicht'
	- 'Sangster' **new**	CSec
	montana	EDAr GKir MBow MChe MDKP NLAp SPet WHer WPnn WRHF
	perennis	see *J. laevis*

Jasminum (*Oleaceae*)

	adenophyllum **new**	CPLN
	angulare ♀H1	ERea EShb
	auriculatum **new**	CPLN
	azoricum ♀H1	CPLN CRHN ELan EPfP ERea EShb ESlt LRHS WMul XPep
	beesianum	More than 30 suppliers
	bignoniaceum	CPLN WSHC
	decussatum **new**	CPLN
	dispermum	CPLN CRHN
	floridum	EWes XPep
	fruticans	CMac CPle EPla WBcn WCru XPep
	grandiflorum L.	EBee XPep
	- 'De Grasse' ♀H1	CPLN CRHN ERea EShb
	harmandianum **new**	CPLN
	humile	CPle EHol GSki IMGH MHer SHFr WFar WKif
	- f. ***farreri***	WCru
§	- 'Revolutum' ♀H4	More than 30 suppliers
	- f. ***wallichianum***	CPle
	- - B&SWJ 2559	WCru
§	***laurifolium*** f. ***nitidum***	CPLN ERea EShb
	leratii **new**	CPLN
§	***mesnyi*** ♀H2-3	CMac CPLG CRHN CSBt CTri CWib EBak ELan EPfP ERea IGor SBra SLim SPer STre SYvo WBcn WEas WSHC XPep
	multiflorum **new**	CPLN
	multipartitum	CPLN EShb
	- bushy	CSpe
	nitidum	see *J. laurifolium* f. *nitidum*
§	***nobile*** subsp. ***rex***	CPLN
	nudiflorum ♀H4	More than 30 suppliers
	- 'Argenteum'	see *J. nudiflorum* 'Mystique'
	- 'Aureum'	EBee ELan EPfP EPla LRHS MAsh MCCP MRav NSti SLim SPer SPla SPoG WCot WHCG WPat WTel
§	- 'Mystique' (v)	ELan LRHS MAsh NLar SLon SMur SPer SPoG WCot WPat
	odoratissimum	ERea EShb
	officinale ♀H4	More than 30 suppliers
	- CC 1709	WHCr
§	- f. ***affine***	CBcs CRHN CSPN CSam CTri CWSG CWib ELan ENot EPfP ERea MAsh MRav MWgw NCGa SCoo SDix SLim SPoG SRms WCru WFar
§	- 'Argenteovariegatum' (v) ♀H4	More than 30 suppliers
	- 'Aureovariegatum'	see *J. officinale* 'Aureum'
§	- 'Aureum' (v)	CDoC CMac CWSG CWib EBee ECtt ELan EPfP EPla LRHS MAsh MBri MHer MLan MWgw NBir SCoo SHBN SLim SLon SMad SPer SPoG SRms WHCG WPat WSHC
	- 'Clotted Cream' **new**	LRHS SPoG
	- 'Crûg's Collection'	WCru
	- Fiona Sunrise = 'Frojas'PBR	More than 30 suppliers
	- 'Grandiflorum'	see *J. officinale* f. *affine*
	- 'Inverleith' ♀H4	CDoC CWSG EBee ELan EPfP IArd LRHS MAsh MBNS MBri MCCP MLan MRav NEgg SBra SCoo SLim SMac SMad SPer SPoG WFar
	- 'Variegatum'	see *J. officinale* 'Argenteovariegatum'
	parkeri	CBcs CCVT CFee CMea CTri EBee EHyt EPfP ESis GMaP IMGH MBNS NMen NRya NWCA SBla SIgm SIng SPla SPoG WAbe WCru WFar WPat XPep
	polyanthum ♀H1-2	CArn CBcs CPLG CPLN CRHN CSBt CTri CTrw EBak EBee ELan EPfP ERea ERom EShb LRHS MBri NBlu NPal SBra SLim SRms WCFE XPep
	primulinum	see *J. mesnyi*
	reevesii hort.	see *J. humile* 'Revolutum'
	rex	see *J. nobile* subsp. *rex*
	sambac ♀H1	CHll CPLN CRHN EHol ELan EPfP EShb ESlt WMul XPep
	- 'Grand Duke of Tuscany' (d)	CPLN ERea
	- 'Maid of India' **new**	CPLN
	- 'Thai Beauty' **new**	CPLN
§	***simplicifolium*** subsp. ***australiense*** **new**	CPLN
	x ***stephanense***	More than 30 suppliers
	syringifolium **new**	CPLN
	tortuosum **new**	CPLN
	volubile	see *J. simplicifolium* subsp. *australiense*

Jatropha (*Euphorbiaceae*)

integerrima	ESlt
podagrica ♀H1	ESlt LToo MOak

Jeffersonia (*Berberidaceae*)

diphylla	More than 30 suppliers
dubia	CFir CFwr CLAP EHyt EWes GBuc GCrs GKev GKir IBlr LRHS NBir NMen NSla SBla SIgm SRot WAbe WCot WCru
- B&SWJ 984	WCru
- 'Alba'	SBla

jojoba see *Simmondsia chinensis*

jostaberry see *Ribes* x *culverwellii* Jostaberry

Jovellana (*Scrophulariaceae*)

punctata	CDoC CPLG CPSs CPle IBlr MBlu
repens	CFir EBee IBlr WCru
sinclairii	CHll CPLG ECou EHyt IBlr SSpi WCru
violacea ♀H3	CAbP CAbb CBcs CDoC CHEx CPLG CPSs CPle CSec CTrC CWib EBee EMil ERea GCal GGGa IBlr ISea ITim SAPC SArc SSpi WBor WCru WPic WSHC

Jovibarba ✿ (*Crassulaceae*)

§	***allionii***	CMea CTri CWil EHol EPot GAbr LBee LRHS MHer MOne SBla WAbe WHoo WIvy WPer WTin
	- 'Oki'	CWil MOne
	allionii x ***hirta***	CWil GAbr MOne NJOw NMen SDys
§	***arenaria***	CWil EHol ESis GAbr MDHE NMen SIng
	- from Murtal, Austria	MDHE

- from Passo Monte Crocecar Nico	CWil
'Emerald Spring'	CWil NMen
§ ***heuffelii***	LRHS NJOw NMen NPri WPer
- 'Aga'	WIvy
- 'Angel Wings'	CWil NMen
- 'Apache'	CWil
- 'Aquarius'	CWil
- 'Be Mine'	CWil
- 'Beacon Hill'	CWil WIvy
- 'Belcore'	CWil WIvy
- 'Benjamin'	CWil
- 'Bermuda'	CMea
- 'Blaze' **new**	CWil
- 'Brandaris'	SDys
- 'Brocade'	WIvy
- 'Bronze Ingot'	CWil
- 'Bulgarien' **new**	CWil
- 'Cameo' **new**	WIvy
§ - 'Cherry Glow'	CWil
- 'Chocoleto'	WTin
- 'Copper King'	CWil
- 'Fandango'	CWil MHom WIvy
- 'Giuseppi Spiny'	MHom WIvy WTin
- var. ***glabra***	LBee WHoo
- - from Anabakanak	CWil MHom WTin
- - from Anthoborio	CWil NMen WTin
- - from Haila, Montenegro/Kosovo	CWil NMen
- - from Jakupica, Macedonia	CWil WIvy
- - from Koprovnik, Kosovo	CWil
- - from Ljuboten	CWil NMen WTin
- - from Osljak	CWil
- - from Pasina Glava	CWil
- - from Rhodope	CWil MHom
- - from Treska Gorge, Macedonia	CWil NMen WTin
- 'Grand Slam'	CWil
- 'Green Land'	CWil
- 'Greenstone'	CMea CWil MHom NMen WIvy WTin
- 'Harmony'	CWil
- 'Henry Correvon'	CWil
- var. ***heuffelii*** **new**	CWil
- 'Hot Lips' **new**	CWil
- 'Ikaros'	CWil
- 'Inferno'	MHom
- 'Iuno'	CWil
- 'Jade'	CWil NMen
- var. ***kopaonikensis***	CWil LBee MHom NMen
- 'Mary Ann'	MHom
- 'Miller's Violet'	CWil WTin
- 'Mink' **new**	CWil
- 'Minuta'	CWil NMen WIvy WTin
- 'Mystique'	CMea CWil LBee NMen
- 'Nannette'	CWil
- 'Orion'	CMea CWil NMen
- var. ***patens***	CWil
- 'Pink Skies'	CWil
- 'Prisma'	CWil WIvy WTin
- 'Red Rose'	CWil
- 'Serenade' **new**	CWil
- 'Suntan'	CWil WIvy
- 'Sylvan Memory'	CWil
- 'Tan'	CWil WTin
- 'Torrid Zone'	WIvy WTin
- 'Tuxedo'	CWil
- 'Vesta'	CWil
- 'Violet'	SDys
§ ***hirta***	CHal CWil GAbr GKev MDHE MOne NMen NWCA SBla SIng STre WPer
- subsp. ***borealis***	CWil MOne NDlv
- from Wintergraben	SIng SPlb
- subsp. ***glabrescens***	EPot ESis LRHS
- - from Belianske Tatry	CWil MDHE MOne NDlv
- - from High Tatra	MDHE
- - from Smeryouka	CWil SIng
- 'Lowe's 66'	MOne
- var. ***neilreichii***	LRHS MHom WBVN
- 'Preissiana'	CWil LBee LRHS MOne NDlv NMen SIng WTin
§ ***sobolifera***	CHEx CWil ELau EPot MOne NJOw NMen SIng SPlb WAbe WPer
- 'August Cream'	CWil LBee LRHS
- 'Green Globe'	CWil ELau MDHE SDys WTin
- 'Miss Lorraine'	CWil

Juania (*Arecaceae*)

australis	EAmu EExo WMul

Juanulloa (*Solanaceae*)

aurantiaca	see *J. mexicana*
§ ***mexicana***	ESlt

Jubaea (*Arecaceae*)

§ ***chilensis***	CBrP CDoC CPHo CRoM EAmu EExo LPJP SChr SPoG WMul
spectabilis	see *J. chilensis*

Juglans ✿ (*Juglandaceae*)

§ ***ailanthifolia***	CDul CMCN CTho ECrN
- var. ***cordiformis*** 'Brock' (F)	CAgr
- - 'Campbell CW1' (F)	CAgr
- - 'Fodermaier' seedling	CAgr
- - 'Rhodes' (F) **new**	CAgr
§ x ***bixbyi***	CAgr
cathayensis (F)	WGWT
- B&SWJ 6778	WCru
cinerea (F)	CMCN EGFP
- 'Booth' seedlings (F)	CAgr
- 'Craxezy' (F) **new**	CAgr
- 'Kenworthy' seedling **new**	CAgr
cinerea x ***ailanthifolia***	see *J.* x *bixbyi*
§ ***elaeopyren***	EGFP WGWT
hindsii	CMCN EGFP
x ***intermedia***	WGWT
- 'NG23' **new**	CAgr
- 'NG38' **new**	CAgr
mandschurica	EGFP WGWT
microcarpa	WGWT
- subsp. ***major***	see *J. elaeopyren*
nigra (F) ♀H4	CBcs CCVT CDul CLnd CMCN CTho EBee ECrN ELan EPfP EWTr GKir GTwe ISea LRHS MAsh MBri MGos NBea NWea SEND SHBN SKee SLim SPer WCFE WDin WMou WOrn WPGP
- 'Emma Kay' (F) **new**	CAgr
- 'Laciniata'	CMCN CTho GKir MBlu WGWT
- 'Purpurea'	MBlu
- 'Weschke' (F)	CAgr
'Paradox'	WGWT
'Red Danube' (F)	WGWT
regia (F) ♀H4	More than 30 suppliers
- 'Abbotbad' (F) **new**	WGWT
- 'Axel' (F)	WGWT
- 'Broadview' (F)	CAgr CDoC CDul CEnd CTho ERea GTwe LRHS MBlu MBri MCoo MGos SCoo SKee SPoG WGWT WOrn
- 'Buccaneer' (F)	CAgr CDul CTho ECrN ERea GTwe LRHS SKee WGWT
- 'Coenen' (F)	WGWT

- 'Corne du Périgord' (F) CAgr
- 'Ferjean' (F) CAgr
- 'Fernette'PBR (F) CAgr MCoo
- 'Fernor'PBR (F) CAgr MCoo
- 'Franquette' (F) CAgr CDoC CTho GTwe LRHS MCoo SKee WDin
- 'Hansen' (F) CAgr WGWT
- 'Laciniata' CMCN GKir WGWT
- 'Lara' (F) GTwe MCoo WGWT
- 'Leopold' (F) WGWT
- 'Lu Guang' (F) WGWT
- 'Mayette' (F) CAgr WDin
- 'Metcalfe' (F) WGWT
- 'Meylannaise' (F) CAgr
- number 16 (F) WGWT
- 'Parisienne' (F) CAgr
- 'Pedro' (F) WGWT
- 'Pendula' Pépin WGWT
- 'Plovdivski' (F) CAgr CDul WGWT
- 'Proslavski' (F) CAgr CDul WGWT
- 'Purpurea' CMCN WGWT
- 'Rita' (F) CAgr WGWT
- 'Ronde de Montignac' (F) CAgr
- 'Soleze' (F) CAgr WGWT
- 'Tremlett's Giant' (F) WGWT
- 'Zhong Lin' (F) WGWT

sieboldiana see *J. ailanthifolia*

jujube see *Ziziphus jujuba*

Juncus (*Juncaceae*)

acutus CPen GFor WWye XPep
* ***balticus*** 'Spiralis' CTrC ECho
bulbosus CRWN
conglomeratus EHoe
- 'Spiralis' NGdn

'Curly Gold Strike' (v) new CKno SGSe SPoG
§ ***decipiens*** 'Curly-wurly' More than 30 suppliers
- 'Spiralis' see *J. decipiens* 'Curly-wurly'

effusus CHEx CRWN EMFW GFor LNCo LPBA NArg NPer NSti WPop WWpP
- 'Gold Strike' (v) CKno CWCL EMan EPPr EPla EUJe EWin LIck MAvo SGSe WBcn WWpP
§ - f. ***spiralis*** More than 30 suppliers
- 'Yellow Line'PBR (v) CPen EBee MAvo

ensifolius CDWL CPen CRow CWat EHoe EMFW EPza EWes GFor LIck LNCo LPBA MAvo MMHG NArg NPer WFar WPop WRos WWpP
filiformis 'Spiralis' CBgR CBig CBrm CTbh EWin GFor GIBF MAvo NBre SApp
inflexus CAgr CRWN EHon EPza GFor NArg WWpP
- 'Afro' CBgR CBig CKno CMea EMan EMon EWin LRHS MAvo MBrN MCCP NBro NOak SPlb

membranaceus HLMS 94.0541 NRya
pallidus EPPr GCal GGar LIck NBid
patens 'Carman's Gray' CFee CKno EBrs EMan EPPr EPla GCal LRHS MAvo MCCP MMoz NGdn NOak SApp SGSe WCot WPGP WWpP
- 'Elk Blue' CKno SGSe

'Silver Spears' EMan MCCP SGSe WWpP
'Unicorn'PBR CPen EBee EPPr EWin MWgw SApp SPoG
xiphioides EHoe EPla GCal LRHS NOGN SGSe SWal
- JLS 8609LACA EPPr

Junellia (*Verbenaceae*)

azorelloides F&W 9344 new WAbe
micrantha F&W 9389 new WAbe
odonnellii EBee
sylvestrii F&W 2705 new WAbe
toninii F&W 9332 CPBP
wilczekii WFar
- F&W 7770 NWCA

Juniperus ✿ (*Cupressaceae*)

chinensis CMac CMen SEND
- from Ussuri new GIBF
- 'Aurea' ♀H4 CBcs CKen CMac EHul EOrn LCon MBar MGos SPoG WEve
§ - 'Blaauw' ♀H4 CDoC CMac CMen EHul EOrn GKir LLin MBar MGos SCoo SHBN SLim SPoG STre WFar
- 'Blue Alps' CDoC EHul EOrn GKir IMGH LCon MBar MBri MGos NEgg SCoo SEND SLim SPoG WDin WFar
- 'Blue Point' MBar MGos
- 'Densa Spartan' see *J. chinensis* 'Spartan'
- 'Echiniformis' CKen CMac EOrn
- 'Expansa Aureospicata' (v) CDoC CKen CMac CRob EHul EOrn EPfP LCon LLin MBar MGos SLim SPoG SRms
§ - 'Expansa Variegata' (v) CDoC CMac CRob CWib EGra EHul EOrn EPfP GKir IMGH LCon LLin MAsh MBar MGos SCoo SLim SMer SPoG SRms WDin WFar WMoo WTel
- 'Globosa Cinerea' MBar
- 'Japonica' EOrn MBar SMer
- 'Japonica Variegata' (v) SLim
- 'Kaizuka' ♀H4 CDoC CMac EHul EOrn GKir LBee LCon LRHS MBar SCoo SLim SMad SMer SPoG STre XPep
- 'Kaizuka Variegata' see *J. chinensis* 'Variegated Kaizuka'
- 'Keteleeri' MBar
- 'Kuriwao Gold' see *J.* x *pfitzeriana* 'Kuriwao Gold'
- 'Obelisk' ♀H4 EHul LRHS MBar SBod
- 'Oblonga' CDoC EHul MAsh MBar SMer STre
§ - 'Parsonsii' CMac MBar SHBN STre WCFE
- 'Plumosa' MBar
- 'Plumosa Albovariegata' (v) EOrn MBar
- 'Plumosa Aurea' ♀H4 EHul EOrn LCon MBar WDin WFar
- 'Plumosa Aureovariegata' (v) CKen EOrn MBar SLim
- 'Pyramidalis' ♀H4 CBrm CDoC CRob EBee EHul ENot EPfP GKir IMGH LCon LLin SBod SCoo SPoG SRms WDin WFar
- 'Pyramidalis Variegata' see *J. chinensis* 'Variegata'
- 'Robust Green' CRob EOrn GKir MBar SCoo SLim SPoG
- 'San José' CDoC CMen EHul EOrn LLin MAsh MBar SCoo SLim WDin
§ - var. ***sargentii*** STre
- 'Shimpaku' CKen CMen EOrn MBar NLar
§ - 'Spartan' EHul
- 'Stricta' CKen CSBt EBee EHul ENot GKir LBee LRHS MAsh MBar MGos NBlu SLim SPla WDin
- 'Stricta Variegata' see *J. chinensis* 'Variegata'
- 'Sulphur Spray' see *J.* x *pfitzeriana* 'Sulphur Spray'
- 'Torulosa' see *J. chinensis* L. 'Kaizuka'
§ - 'Variegata' (v) MBar SPoG
§ - 'Variegated Kaizuka' (v) CBrm EHul EOrn GKir LCon MAsh MBar SPoG WEve WFar

	- 'Wilson's Weeping'	WBcn
	communis	CArn CRWN EHul GPoy MBow MHer MSal NWea SIde WBWf
	- (f)	GTSp SIde
	- 'Arnold'	GKir MBar MGos
	- 'Arnold Sentinel'	CKen
	- 'Atholl'	CKen
I	- 'Aureopicta' (v)	MBar WBcn
	- 'Barton'	MBar WBcn
	- 'Berkshire'	CKen CRob
	- 'Brien'	CDoC CKen
	- 'Brynhyfryd Gold'	CKen CRob WBcn
§	- var. ***communis***	ECho MBar NDlv NEgg
	- 'Compressa' ♀H4	More than 30 suppliers
§	- 'Constance Franklin' (v)	ECho EHul GKir LLin MBar STre WBcn
	- 'Corielagan'	CKen CNic MBar NLar
	- 'Cracovia'	CKen EHul
	- var. ***depressa***	GPoy MBar
	- 'Depressa Aurea'	CKen CMac CSBt EHul GKir LBee LCon LLin LRHS MBar MGos NDlv SHBN SMer SPoG WFar WTel
	- 'Depressed Star'	CRob EHul MBar NScw
	- 'Derrynane'	EHul
	- 'Effusa'	CKen
	- 'Gelb'	see *J. communis* 'Schneverdingen Goldmachangel'
§	- 'Gold Cone'	CKen CSli EHul ENot GKir LBee LCon LLin LRHS MAsh MBar MBri MGos NDlv NEgg SLim SMer SPoG WDin WEve WFar
	- 'Golden Showers'	see *J. communis* 'Schneverdingen Goldmachangel'
	- 'Green Carpet' ♀H4	CAgr CDoC CKen CRob EHul EOrn EPfP GKir IMGH LBee LBuc LCon LLin LRHS MAsh MBar NEgg SCoo SLim SMer SPoG WCFE WDin WEve
	- 'Haverbeck'	CKen
	- var. ***hemispherica***	see *J. communis* var. *communis*
	- 'Hibernica' ♀H4	More than 30 suppliers
	- 'Hibernica Variegata'	see *J. communis* 'Constance Franklin'
	- 'Hornibrookii' ♀H4	CMac EHul EOrn LLin MBar MGos SBod SHBN SMer SRms STre WDin
	- 'Horstmann'	MBar SLim SPoG
I	- 'Horstmann's Pendula'	CDoC LCon LLin WBcn
	- 'Kenwith Castle'	CKen
§	- 'Minima'	SBod
	- 'Prostrata'	WFar
	- 'Pyramidalis'	SPlb
	- 'Repanda' ♀H4	CAgr CBcs CDoC CMac CRob CSBt CWib EHul ENot EPfP GKir LCon LLin MAsh MBar MGos NDlv NWea SCoo SLim SMer SPer SPla SPoG SRms WDin WEve WFar
§	- 'Schneverdingen Goldmachangel'	CRob EOrn GKir LLin MAsh MBri SCoo SLim SPoG
	- 'Sentinel'	EHul EPfP LCon LRHS MBar NBlu NEgg SCoo SLim WCFE WDin WEve
	- 'Sieben Steinhauser'	CKen
	- 'Silver Mist'	CKen
	- 'Spotty Spreader' (v)	GKir SCoo SLim SPoG
	- Suecica Group	EHul MBar NLar NWea
	- 'Suecica Aurea'	EHul EOrn
	- 'Zeal'	CKen
	conferta	see *J. rigida* subsp. *conferta*
	- var. ***maritima***	see *J. taxifolia*
	davurica	EHul
	- 'Expansa'	see *J. chinensis* 'Parsonsii'
	- 'Expansa Albopicta'	see *J. chinensis* 'Expansa Variegata'
	- 'Expansa Variegata'	see *J. chinensis* 'Expansa Variegata'
	deppeana 'Silver Spire'	EGra MBar
	foetidissima **new**	GIBF
	x ***gracilis*** 'Blaauw'	see *J. chinensis* 'Blaauw'
	horizontalis	NWea
§	- 'Andorra Compact'	CNic EMil MAsh MBar NLar SCoo
	- 'Bar Harbor'	CKen CMac EHul GKir MBar MGos SBod WGor
§	- 'Blue Chip'	CKen CMac CRob EHul ENot EOrn EPfP GKir LBee LCon LLin LRHS MAsh MBar MGos NBlu NEgg SBod SCoo SLim SPer SPoG WDin XPep
	- 'Blue Moon'	see *J. horizontalis* 'Blue Chip'
	- 'Blue Pygmy'	CKen
	- 'Blue Rug'	see *J. horizontalis* 'Wiltonii'
	- 'Douglasii'	CKen CMac EHol EHul MBar WGor
	- 'Emerald Spreader'	CKen EHul ENot GKir LLin MBar MGos WEve
	- 'Glacier'	CKen WEve
	- Glauca Group	CMac EHul GKir LLin MBar MGos SMer SPer SPoG WDin WEve
	- 'Glomerata'	CKen MBar
	- 'Golden Carpet'	EOrn GKir IMGH LBee LBuc LLin MAsh NBlu NEgg SCoo SLim SPoG WEve
	- 'Golden Spreader'	CDoC GKir
	- 'Grey Pearl'	CKen EHul GKir SBod SLim
	- 'Hughes'	CMac EHul GKir LBee LLin LRHS MAsh MBar MGos NDlv SBod SCoo SLim SPla
	- Icee Blue = 'Monber' **new**	CKen CRob SPoG
	- 'Jade River'	CKen EHul GBin GKir LRHS MGos NLar SCoo SLim SPer SPoG
	- 'Limeglow'	CKen SLim
	- 'Mother Lode'	CKen
	- 'Neumann'	CKen EOrn
	- 'Plumosa'	NDlv
	- 'Plumosa Compacta'	see *J. horizontalis* 'Andorra Compact'
	- 'Prince of Wales'	CRob EHul GKir LLin LRHS MAsh MGos NLar SCoo SLim XPep
	- var. ***saxatalis*** E.Murray	see *J. communis* var. *communis*
	- 'Turquoise Spreader'	CKen CRob CSBt EHul GKir LLin MBar SCoo
	- 'Variegata' (v)	MBar
	- 'Venusta'	see *J. virginiana* 'Venusta'
	- 'Villa Marie'	CKen
	- 'Webber'	MBar
§	- 'Wiltonii' ♀H4	CKen EHul EOrn MGos NBlu
	- 'Winter Blue'	LBee LCon LRHS SLim SPer
	- 'Youngstown'	CMac CRob CSWP GKir LLin MBar MGos SBod WFar WGor
	- 'Yukon Belle'	CKen
N	x ***media***	see *J.* x *pfitzeriana*
§	x ***pfitzeriana***	CDul
	- 'Armstrongii'	EHul
	- 'Blaauw'	see *J. chinensis* 'Blaauw'
	- 'Blue and Gold' (v)	CKen EHul LLin MBar NEgg SHBN SLim
	- 'Blue Cloud'	see *J. virginiana* 'Blue Cloud'
§	- 'Carbery Gold'	CDoC CMac CRob CSBt CSli EGra EHul EOrn GKir LBee LCon LLin LRHS MAsh MBar MGos SCoo SLim SPoG WEve WFar
	- 'Gold Coast'	CDoC CKen CMac CRob CSBt EBee EHul ENot EPfP GKir LBee LRHS MAsh MBar MBri MGos SLim SPer SPla WDin WEve
	- Gold Sovereign = 'Blound'PBR	EOrn GKir LBee LCon MAsh MGos SMer
	- 'Gold Star'	SLim WBcn
*	- 'Golden Joy'	LCon SCoo SLim SPoG

	Name	Suppliers
	- 'Golden Saucer'	MBar SCoo
	- 'Goldkissen'	CRob MBri
§	- 'Kuriwao Gold'	CMac EHul ENot GKir LBee MAsh MBar MGos SBod SCoo SLim SMer STre WEve WFar WOrn
	- 'Milky Way' (v)	SCoo SLim SPoG
	- 'Mint Julep'	CMac CSBt EHul ENot GKir IMGH LBee LLin LRHS MAsh MBar MGos NBlu SCoo SLim SPer WBrE WDin WEve WFar WMoo
	- 'Mordigan Gold'	LBee SPoG
	- 'Old Gold' 🏆H4	CKen CMac EBee EHul EOrn EPfP GKir IMGH LBee LCon LRHS MAsh MBar MGos NBlu NDlv NEgg NWea SBod SCoo SLim SMer SPer SPlb SPoG SRms WDin WEve WFar WTel
	- 'Old Gold Carbery'	see *J.* x *pfitzeriana* 'Carbery Gold'
	- 'Pfitzeriana'	see *J.* x *pfitzeriana* 'Wilhelm Pfitzer'
	- 'Pfitzeriana Aurea'	CBcs CDoC CMac CSBt CTri EHul ENot EPfP GKir LCon LRHS MBar MBri MGos NBlu NEgg NWea SHBN SPoG WCFE WDin WEve WFar WOrn
	- 'Pfitzeriana Compacta' 🏆H4	CMac ECho EHul MBar SCoo SLim
	- 'Pfitzeriana Glauca'	EHul IMGH LRHS MBar SCoo SLim WGor
	- 'Richeson'	MBar
	- 'Silver Cascade'	EHul
§	- 'Sulphur Spray' 🏆H4	CKen CMac CSBt CWib EHul ENot EOrn EPla GKir LBee LCon LLin LRHS MAsh MBar MGos NEgg SLim SPer SPla SPoG SRms WBVN WCFE WDin WEve WFar WMoo WTel
§	- 'Wilhelm Pfitzer'	CMac EHul EPfP MBar NWea
	phoenicea	XPep
§	***pingii*** 'Glassell'	CDoC ECho GKir MBar
§	- 'Pygmaea'	EOrn MBar SPoG
§	- var. ***wilsonii***	CDoC CKen ECho EHul EOrn MBar NEgg NLar SCoo
	procumbens 'Bonin Isles'	GKir LLin SCoo SLim SPoG
	- 'Nana' 🏆H4	CDoC CKen CMac CRob CSBt EHul ENot EOrn EPfP GKir IMGH LBee LCon LLin LRHS MAsh MBar MGos MWat NEgg SCoo SHBN SLim SPla SPoG WCFE WDin WEve WFar
	recurva 'Castlewellan'	EOrn GKir LCon MGos WEve
	- var. ***coxii***	CDoC CMac EHul EOrn GGGa GKir ISea LCon LLin MAsh MBar MGos NEgg SRms WCFE WEve WPic
§	- 'Densa'	CDoC CKen EHul EOrn MBar SHBN
	- 'Embley Park'	EHul MAsh MBar
	- 'Nana'	see *J. recurva* 'Densa'
	rigida	CMen EHul LBee LLin MBar NLar
§	- subsp. ***conferta***	CRob ENot GKir LCon MBar SLim SPer SPoG STre WEve
*	- - 'Blue Ice'	CDul CKen EOrn LLin SPoG
	- - 'Blue Pacific'	CMac COtt CRob EHul GKir MBar SLim SPoG WFar
	- - 'Blue Tosho'	CRob GKir LCon SLim SPoG
	- - 'Emerald Sea'	EHul
	- - 'Silver Mist'	CKen
	sabina	NWea
§	- 'Blaue Donau'	EHul MBar WEve
	- Blue Danube	see *J. sabina* 'Blaue Donau'
	- 'Broadmoor'	EHul
	- 'Buffalo'	EHul
	- Cupressifolia Group	MBar
	- 'Hicksii'	CBcs CMac MBar
	- 'Knap Hill'	see *J.* x *pfitzeriana* 'Wilhelm Pfitzer'
	- 'Mountaineer'	see *J. scopulorum* 'Mountaineer'
	- 'Rockery Gem'	EHul EOrn SLim SPla SPoG WEve WGor
	- 'Skandia'	CKen
	- 'Tamariscifolia'	CBcs CMac CTri CWib ECrN EHul ENot GKir LBee LCon LLin LRHS MAsh MBar MGos NBlu NEgg NWea SBod SHBN SLim SMer SPer SPoG WCFE WDin WEve WFar WTel
	- 'Tripartita'	see *J. virginiana* 'Tripartita'
	- 'Variegata' (v)	CMac EHul MAsh MBar NWea WBcn
	sargentii	see *J. chinensis* var. *sargentii*
	scopulorum	CKen MBar
	- 'Blue Arrow'	CDoC CKen COtt CSBt ECrN ELan ENot EOrn EPfP GKir IMGH LBee LCon LLin LRHS MAsh MBar MBri MGos NBlu NEgg SCoo SLim SPer SPla SPoG WDin WEve WFar WOrn
	- 'Blue Banff'	CKen
	- 'Blue Heaven'	EHul LCon MAsh MBar NLar SRms
	- 'Blue Pyramid'	EHul WEve
	- 'Boothman'	EHul
	- 'Moonglow'	EHul MBar SCoo
§	- 'Mountaineer'	EHul
	- 'Mrs Marriage'	CKen
	- 'Repens'	MBar MGos
	- 'Silver Star' (v)	ECrN EHul MBar MGos WEve
	- 'Skyrocket'	CBcs CDul CMac CSBt CTri ECrN EHul EPfP GKir LBee LCon LRHS MAsh MBar MGos NBlu NEgg NWea SBod SEND SMer SPlb WBVN WCFE WDin WEve WFar WTel
	- 'Springbank'	CMac EHul LBee LRHS MAsh MBar WCFE
	- 'Tabletop'	MBar WBcn
	- 'Tolleson's Blue Weeping'	GKir SIFN
	- 'Wichita Blue'	EHul EPfP LCon SEND WEve WGor
§	***squamata***	WBVN
	- 'Blue Carpet' 🏆H4	More than 30 suppliers
	- 'Blue Spider'	CKen GKir LRHS MBar SCoo SLim SPoG WGor
	- 'Blue Spreader' **new**	NEgg
	- 'Blue Star' 🏆H4	More than 30 suppliers
	- 'Blue Star Variegated'	see *J. squamata* 'Golden Flame'
	- 'Blue Swede'	see *J. squamata* 'Hunnetorp'
	- 'Chinese Silver'	EHul MBar SLim WBcn
	- 'Dream Joy'	CKen SLim
	- var. ***fargesii***	see *J. squamata*
	- 'Filborna'	CKen LBee MBar SLim SMer
	- 'Glassell'	see *J. pingii* 'Glassell'
§	- 'Golden Flame' (v)	CKen
	- 'Holger' 🏆H4	CDoC CKen CMac CRob CSBt EGra EHul EOrn EPfP EPla GKir LBee LCon LLin LRHS MAsh MBar MGos SBod SCoo SLim SPoG WCFE WEve
§	- 'Hunnetorp'	EOrn GKir MBar WEve WGor
	- 'Loderi'	see *J. pingii* var. *wilsonii*
	- 'Meyeri'	CTri EHul ENot EOrn GKir IMGH MBar NWea SBod SCoo SMer SPoG STre WDin WFar WTel
	- 'Pygmaea'	see *J. pingii* 'Pygmaea'
	- 'Wilsonii'	see *J. pingii* var. *wilsonii*
	- 'Yellow Tip'	WBcn
§	***taxifolia***	CDoC EOrn IMGH LBee SPoG
	virginiana	CAgr CPne

§ - 'Blue Cloud' EHul MBar SLim WEve WGor
- 'Burkii' CDoC EHul LCon
- 'Frosty Morn' CKen ECho EHul MBar SCoo WFar
- 'Glauca' CSWP EHul NWea
- 'Golden Spring' CKen
- 'Grey Owl' ♀H4 CMac EHul ELan ENot EPfP GKir LCon MBar NWea SCoo SLim SLon SMer SRms STre WDin WFar WGor WTel
- 'Helle' see *J. chinensis* 'Spartan'
- 'Hetzii' CBcs CMac ECho EHul MBar NLar NWea WDin WFar
- 'Hillii' MBar
- 'Hillspire' EHul
- 'Nana Compacta' MBar
- Silver Spreader = 'Mona' CKen EHul SCoo WBcn WEve
- 'Staver' EHul
- 'Sulphur Spray' see *J.* x *pfitzeriana* 'Sulphur Spray'
§ - 'Tripartita' MBar
§ - 'Venusta' CKen

Jurinea (*Asteraceae*)

cyanoides EShb
dolomiaea CC 4268 MGol
glycacantha EBrs LRHS
mollis GBuc

Jurinella see *Jurinea*

Jussiaea see *Ludwigia*

Justicia (*Acanthaceae*)

sp. CBcs
§ ***brandegeeana*** ♀H1 CHal EShb MBri
- 'Lutea' see *J. brandegeeana* 'Yellow Queen'
§ - 'Yellow Queen' CHal
§ ***carnea*** CHal CSev EBak ERea EShb GCal MBri MTis SMad WMul
guttata see *J. brandegeeana*
'Nørgaard's Favourite' MBri
ovata SMad
'Penrhosiensis' EShb
pohliana see *J. carnea*
rizzinii ♀H1 CHal CHll CPle CSev ERea EShb
spicigera ERea EShb
suberecta see *Dicliptera suberecta*

K

Kadsura (*Schisandraceae*)

sp. CMac
coccinea **new** CPLN
japonica CBcs CMen CPLN EMil EShb WPGP
- B&SWJ 1027 WCru
- 'Shiromi' CPLN EMil EPfP SBra
- 'Variegata' (v) CPLN EPfP EShb SBra SBrw SSpi WSHC
- white fruit **new** NLar

Kaempferia (*Zingiberaceae*)

galanga CKob MOak
linearis CKob
mottled leaf **new** MOak
rotunda CKob LAma MOak

Kageneckia (*Rosaceae*)

oblonga IFro

Kalanchoe (*Crassulaceae*)

alternans **new** EShb
beharensis ♀H1 CAbb CHal EShb LToo MBri SBig
- 'Rusty' CSpe
blossfeldiana EOHP LRHS
- 'Variegata' (v) CHal
daigremontiana CHal EShb SRms
§ ***delagoensis*** CHal EShb STre
fedtschenkoi CHal STre
laciniata **new** EShb
manginii ♀H1 CDoC EOHP
* ***minima glauca*** **new** SBch
pumila ♀H1 CHal EMan ERea EWin EWoo SPet STre WEas
rhombopilosa **new** EShb
sexangularis **new** EShb
'Tessa' ♀H1 MBri MLan SPet SRms STre
tomentosa ♀H1 CHal EShb SHFr SPet WEas
tubiflora see *K. delagoensis*

Kalimeris (*Asteraceae*)

§ ***incisa*** EWll GMac IHMH MRav WBor WFar WMoo WTin
- 'Alba' EBee NLar NRnb SHel SSvw WFar WWpP
- 'Blue Star' EBee EMil NLar NRnb WFar WWpP
- 'Charlotte' EBee EWes NBre NDov NGby
* - 'Variegata' (v) EBee NBre SPoG
integrifolia ECha WMow WTin
intricifolia EBee
§ ***mongolica*** EBee ECha MAnH WFar WPGP WPer
§ ***pinnatifida*** EBee EChP EMan EPPr WCot
- 'Hortensis' CBod NSti WHil
§ ***yomena*** 'Shogun' (v) EBee ECha EGra EHoe ELan EMon ENot EPPr GBri GBuc GEdr GKir MLLN NBir NPri NRnb SAga SPer WBor WCot WFar WSHC
- 'Variegata' see *K. yomena* 'Shogun'

Kalmia ✿ (*Ericaceae*)

angustifolia ♀H4 GKev MBar NLAp SRms WDin WFar
- var. ***angustifolia*** f. ***candida*** WAbe
- var. ***pumila*** SReu WAbe
- f. ***rubra*** ♀H4 CBcs CBrm CDoC CMHG CSBt ELan EPfP GKir ISea LRHS MAsh MGos NBlu NDlv NEgg NVic SBrw SHBN SPer SPoG SReu SSta WFar WHar WPat
latifolia ♀H4 CBcs CEnd CPSs EBee ELan EMil EPfP GIBF MBar MDun MGos MLan NBlu NEgg NWea SPer SPlb SReu SSpi SSta SWvt WBrE WDin WFar WGer WNor
- 'Alpine Pink' CBcs CBrm CRez LRHS MAsh NLar NPen
- 'Carousel' CAbP EBee EPfP GGGa GKir LRHS MGos MLea SBrw WFar
- 'Elf' GEdr LRHS MAsh MGos MLea NLar SBrw WFar
- 'Freckles' ♀H4 CBcs ELan EPfP GEdr GGGa GKir LRHS MAsh MDun MGos MLea NDlv SBrw SPoG WFar
- 'Fresca' CRez LRHS MDun
- 'Galaxy' GGGa
- 'Heart of Fire' CAbP GGGa LRHS NDlv SPoG
- 'Keepsake' GGGa
- 'Little Linda' ♀H4 GEdr GGGa GKir IMGH LRHS MAsh MBri NDlv NLar SBrw

- 'Minuet' — CAbP CDoC CDul CWSG EPfP EPot GEdr GGGa GKir IMGH ISea LRHS MAsh MDun MLan MLea NDlv SPoG SSpi SWvt WBrE WFar
- f. ***myrtifolia*** — GEdr MLea WFar
- 'Nancy' **new** — GEdr SBrw WFar
- 'Olympic Fire' ♀H4 — CEnd ELan EPfP GGGa GKir LRHS MAsh MGos NDlv SSpi
- 'Ostbo Red' — CBcs CDoC CPSs CSBt EBee EMil ENot EPfP EPot GEdr GGGa GKir IMGH ISea MAsh MBri MGos MLea NDlv SBrw SHBN SPer SPoG SReu SSpi SSta SWvt WFar
- 'Peppermint' — GGGa
- 'Pink Charm' ♀H4 — CAbP ELan GGGa GKir GWCH MAsh NDlv SBrw WBan
- 'Pink Frost' — CBcs GEdr GGGa NDlv NLar SBrw WFar
- 'Pristine' — GGGa
- 'Raspberry Glow' — GGGa
- 'Richard Jaynes' — EPot GEdr LRHS WBrE WFar
- 'Sarah' — GGGa MBri NLar SBrw SSpi
- 'Silver Dollar' — GGGa
- 'Snowdrift' — CRez GEdr GGGa LRHS NDlv SBrw SSpi WFar

§ ***microphylla*** — GGGa
polifolia — CBcs MBar NLAp WPat
- var. ***compacta*** — WAbe WSHC
- 'Glauca' — see *K. microphylla*
- f. ***leucantha*** — GGGa NLAp WAbe WPat

Kalmia x *Rhododendron* (*Ericaceae*)

§ ***K. latifolia* x *R. williamsianum***, 'Everlasting' — SReu

Kalmiopsis (*Ericaceae*)

leachiana ♀H4 — EPot GCrs SOkd SSta WAbe
- 'Glendoick' — GGGa LTwo MDun WPat
- 'Hiawatha' — SReu
* - 'Shooting Star' — ITim LTwo WAbe WPat

x *Kalmiothamnus* (*Ericaceae*)

ornithomma 'Cosdon' — WAbe
- 'Haytor' — WAbe
'Sindleberg' — ITim WAbe

Kalopanax (*Araliaceae*)

pictus — see *K. septemlobus*
§ ***septemlobus*** — CBcs CHEx CLnd ELan EPfP EWTr GBin GIBF NEgg NLar WBVN WOVN
- var. ***lutchuensis*** B&SWJ 5947 — WCru
- var. ***maximowiczii*** — CDoC CDul EPfP MBlu NLar WCot

Kelseya (*Rosaceae*)

uniflora — EHyt WAbe

Kennedia (*Papilionaceae*)

coccinea — CBcs CSec
nigricans — CSec ERea EShb ESlt
prostrata — SPlb
rubicunda — CHal CRHN CSec CTbh ERea

Kentranthus see *Centranthus*

Kerria (*Rosaceae*)

***japonica* double-flowered** (d) — see *K. japonica* 'Pleniflora'
- 'Albescens' — CBot CFai WFar
- 'Golden Guinea' ♀H4 — CChe CPLG CPom CWSG EBee ECrN ECtt ELan EPfP GKir LRHS MAsh MGos MNrw MRav MSwo NPro SCoo SPer SPoG SWal SWvt WDin WFar WWeb WWpP
§ - 'Picta' (v) — CDul CWib EBee ECrN EHoe ELan ENot EPfP LAst MBar MBri MGos MRav MSwo SGar SLim SLon SPer SPoG SRms WDin WFar WHil WSHC WTel WWeb WWpP
§ - 'Pleniflora' (d) ♀H4 — More than 30 suppliers
§ - 'Simplex' — CPLG CSBt GKir NWea WDin WFar WTel
- 'Variegata' — see *K. japonica* 'Picta'

Khadia (*Aizoaceae*)

sp. — CStu CTrC

Kickxia (*Scrophulariaceae*)

spuria — MSal

Kigelia (*Bignoniaceae*)

africana **new** — CSec

Kirengeshoma (*Hydrangeaceae*)

palmata ♀H4 — More than 30 suppliers
- dwarf — WCot
§ - Koreana Group — More than 30 suppliers

Kitagawia (*Apiaceae*)

§ ***litoralis*** — GIBF

Kitaibela (*Malvaceae*)

vitifolia — CFee CPLG CSpe EBee ELan EMon EUnu EWTr GCal IFro NBid NEgg SDnm SGar SPav SPlb WHer WPer WPic WRos WTMC
- 'Chalice' — CStr

Kitchingia see *Kalanchoe*

kiwi fruit see *Actinidia deliciosa*

Kleinia (*Asteraceae*)

articulata — see *Senecio articulatus*
grantii — ERea EShb
neriifolia **new** — CSec
repens — see *Senecio serpens*
senecioides — WEas
stapeliiformis ♀H1 — EShb

Knautia (*Dipsacaceae*)

§ ***arvensis*** — CArn CBgR CHll CRWN EMag MBow MChe MHer MLLN MSwo MWgw MWya NLan NLar NMir NPri SGSe WFar WGHP WHer WMoo WPop WSHC WSSM
dipsacifolia — NDov SHar SMHy
§ ***macedonica*** — More than 30 suppliers
§ - 'Crimson Cushion' — CBcs CSpe ECtt GAbr LSou SMHy SOkh SPav WCra WWol
- 'Mars Midget' — More than 30 suppliers
- Melton pastels — CFwr EBee EChP EGoo EMar ENot EPfP EShb EVFa GKir IBal LSRN LSou MAnH MWgw MWrn NArg NCob NPer SMar SPav SPet SRot SWvt WFar WWeb
- pink — CMil CSam WWlt
- red — CWib NCob
- 'Red Dress' — EMon
- short — ECtt EHrv NCob NCot NDov STes WTMC WWlt
- tall, pale — LPhx NDov
sarajevensis — EBee MAvo

Kniphofia ✿ (*Asphodelaceae*)

	Plant	Suppliers
	'Ada'	EBrs ECGP EWTr EWes LRHS MLLN MRav
	'Alcazar'	CDes CPrp CSam EChP ECot ECtt EPfP GAbr GGar GKir LPio LRHS LSRN MRav MSte NCGa NOrc NPri SWvt WCAu WCot WFar WMnd WMul WPGP WWeb WWol
	'Amsterdam'	MWat
	'Apple Court'	NBir
	'Apricot'	CMdw EPla
	'Apricot Souffle'	GBri MLLN WCot WPGP WPrP
	'Atlanta'	CPne EBrs EMon GCal LRHS WCot
	'Barton Fever'	WCot
	baurii	WCot
	'Bee's Gold'	ERou
	'Bees' Lemon'	More than 30 suppliers
	'Bees' Sunset' ♀H4	CDes EBee EPPr EVFa GAbr GBri GBuc MNrw MRav MWgw NBir SHBN SOkh SUsu WCAu WCot WPGP WPrP WTMC
*	***bicolor***	NSti WCot WPrP
	'Border Ballet'	CBrm ERou LRHS MRav NBir NBre NBro NJOw NLar SMar WFar
	brachystachya	CPou EBee GCal SIgm SPlb WCot
	'Bressingham Comet'	EBee EBrs ECtt EMan EPfP GKir LRHS MBri MRav NBir SBla WPGP
	'Bressingham Gleam'	EBrs WCot
	Bressingham hybrids	NBir
	Bressingham Sunbeam = 'Bresun'	CPen EBee EBrs GSki MBri NBir WCot
	Bridgemere hybrids	WFar
	'Brimstone' ♀H4	More than 30 suppliers
	buchananii	EBee
	'Buttercup' ♀H4	CMHG CMdw SOkh WSHC WTin
	'C.M. Prichard' misapplied	see *K. rooperi*
	'C.M. Prichard' Prichard	WCot
	'Candlelight'	CDes CMdw EBee EMan SChu SDys SUsu WPGP
*	'Candlemass'	LPio
	caulescens ♀H3-4	More than 30 suppliers
	- 'Coral Breakers'	EBee WCot WTMC
	- from John May	WCot
	- short	SMrm
	citrina	CFir EMan EPfP EWTr GKev LAst LRHS NBre NChi NLar SMar WCot
	'Cobra'	CDes CStr EBee EBrs LRHS WCot WPGP
	'Comet'	ECtt
	'Corallina'	NHaw WFar
	'Dingaan'	CAbb CPne CPou EBee EChP ECtt EMan EPPr EVFa GBBs GBin GCal GSki MNrw NBir NEgg SAga SDnm SPav WCot WFar WLin
	'Doctor E.M. Mills'	CPrp CSam
	'Dorset Sentry'	CAbP CAbb CHea CMdw CPrp CSam EBee EChP ECtt EMan EMar GBuc GCal GSki LAst MAnH MBnl MBri MEHN MLLN MNrw MSte NBir NEgg NLar NMyG NOrc NSti WCot WFar
	'Dropmore Apricot'	CM&M GSki MBNS SPav
	'Drummore Apricot'	CKno CMHG CSam EBee EChP ECha EGra ELan EMan EVFa EWll GMac LAst MLLN MRav MSte NBir NSti SDnm SMrm WCot WFar WGHP WHoo WHrl WPGP WPrP WTMC WWhi WWye
	'Earliest of All'	COtt EBee EBrs EMan EWll GSki LBmB LRHS MBNS
	'Early Buttercup'	ECot EPfP GBri MRav NHaw WCot WFar
§	***ensifolia***	CPne CPou ECtt EGra GSki NGdn SIgm SRms WBcn
	'Ernest Mitchell'	MRav SMrm WCot
	Express hybrids	EBee NBre NLar
	'Fairyland'	EMan LPio WBrk WTin
	'False Maid'	SMHy
*	'Fat Yellow'	EMar MWgw
	fibrosa	CFir WCot
	'Fiery Fred'	CMil EBee EBrs ELan EMan LRHS MRav NHaw WCot
	'First Sunrise' **new**	ERou
	'Flamenco'	NBre NEgg SPet WSSM WWeb
	'Flaming Torch'	ECha
	foliosa	CPne EMan LRHS SChr SMrm
	'Frances Victoria'	WCot
	galpinii misapplied	see *K. triangularis* subsp. *triangularis*
	galpinii Baker ♀H4	EMar EWTr GBri LRHS MRav SPer SRms WTMC
*	'Géant'	XPep
	'Gilt Bronze'	EBee WCot
	'Gladness'	EBee ECtt GSki MRav NBir NSti SChu WCot WPrP
	'Goldelse'	EBee NBir WCot
	'Goldfinch'	CMdw MRav SMHy SUsu
	gracilis	EBee LEdu
	'Green and Cream'	MNrw
	'Green Jade'	CDes CFir CMdw COtt CRow EBee EChP ECha EPfP ERou GBri GKir MRav NBir SChu SEND SGSe SGar SIgm SMrm SOkh WAul WCot WFar WHoo WPGP WTMC WTin
	'H.E. Beale'	GCal MRav NHaw SMrm WCot
	'Hen and Chickens' **new**	WCot
	hirsuta	CPne CPou CSam ELan EMan EShb ITer LPio MSte WCot
	- JCA 3.461.900	WCot
	- JCA 346 900	SSpi
	- 'Traffic Lights'	EWll LSou MSph MWrn
	'Hollard's Gold'	WCot
	'Ice Queen'	CFir CPar CSam CSev EBee ECGP ERou EVFa GBri GCal LPhx MBri MRav NBro NChi NGdn SMrm SWvt WCot WTin
	ichopensis	CDes CFil EBee GBuc WCot WPGP
	'Ingénue'	EBee EMan LPio WCot
	'Innocence'	EBee EBrs
	'Jane Henry' **new**	CDes
	'Jenny Bloom'	More than 30 suppliers
	'John Benary'	CHar COtt CPou CPrp CSam EBee EChP ECtt EMar GAbr GBin GCal GFlt GMaP GMac GSki IGor LPio LRHS MLLN NCGa NEgg SPer WCAu WCot WFar WHrl WKif WLin WTin
	'Johnathan'	WCot
	laxiflora	CFil CPou LPio SSpi WPGP
	'Lemon Ice'	EBee WCot
	'Light of the World'	see *K. triangularis* subsp. *triangularis* 'Light of the World'
	'Limelight'	EMar
	linearifolia	CFil CPou CTrC GCra GGar MNrw SGSe SPlb WCot
	'Little Elf'	LPio MWat SBla SDys WSHC
	'Little Maid'	More than 30 suppliers
	'Lord Roberts'	CPen EBee ECha EMan ENot GBin GKir LSRN MRav SMad SPav WCot
	'Luna'	WCot
	macowanii	see *K. triangularis* subsp. *triangularis*
	'Maid of Orleans'	CRow GBri NHaw WCot
	'Mermaiden'	CMHG CRow CSam EBee EChP ECtt EMan GFlt GMac GSki LAst MNrw NCob WCot

	'Minister Verschuur'	CRez EBrs EMar GSki LBmB LRHS SAga WFar WMnd WWol
	'Modesta'	GBri SBla WPGP
	'Mount Etna'	WCot WPGP
	multiflora	CPne WCot
	'Nancy's Red'	More than 30 suppliers
	nelsonii Mast.	see *K. triangularis* subsp. *triangularis*
	'Nobilis'	see *K. uvaria* 'Nobilis'
	northiae	CBot CFil CFir CHEx CPou GBin GCal LEdu MNrw SAPC SArc SIgm SPlb SSpi WCru WPGP
I	'Old Court Seedling'	WCot WPrP
	'Orange Torch'	CPou
	'Painted Lady'	CTri GCal MRav WHoo
	parviflora	CPou
	pauciflora	CBro CStr EBee EMan ERos SDys SIgm WCot
	'Percy's Pride'	More than 30 suppliers
	'Perry's White'	SOkh
	'Pfitzeri'	SRms
	porphyrantha	WCot
	x ***praecox***	CFil CPne MAvo WCot
	'Primulina' hort.	CPou EBrs EGra EMan EMar LRHS
	'Prince Igor'	CFir ECha EMan EMar MAvo NBir SChu SIgm SMad WCot
	pumila	CPne EPyc GSki ITer MTis
	'Ralph Idden'	EChP
	'Ranelagh Gardens'	SArc
	ritualis	CFil LSou WCot WLin WPGP
§	***rooperi***	CBot CFil CHEx CMdw CMil CSam EBee EMan GCal GGar GSki IGor LEdu LPio LSRN MHer MMil MNrw NBir SDnm SMac SMrm SPav SPoG SSpi WCot WPnP WPnn WWye
	- 'Torchlight'	CPne CPrp
	'Rougham Beauty'	ERou
	'Royal Caste'	CFwr EBee MMil MRav NBir NEgg NOrc NPri WFar
	'Royal Standard' ♀H4	CBcs COtt EBee ELan EMan ENot EPfP ERou GBri GSki LRHS MNrw MRav NPri SPer SPoG SRms SWvt WCAu WCot WFar WMoo WWeb
	rufa	CPne CPou
	'Safranvogel'	WCot
	'Samuel's Sensation' ♀H4	CFir CSam EBee EBrs EChP EMan GBri GGar GMac GSki LRHS MBnl MBri MNFA MRav NEgg NOrc NSti SHBN WCot WTMC
	sarmentosa	CFil CPne CPou SIgm WCot WPGP XPep
	'September Sunshine'	MRav
	'Shining Sceptre'	CFwr CSam EBee ECha ECtt ERou GKir GSki LIck LPio LRHS MLLN MRav MWat NCGa SGSe SGar SIgm SMad SSvw SWvt WAul WCot WEas WGHP WHil
	'Springtime'	WCot
	'Star of Baden-Baden'	NBir SMad WCot
	'Strawberries and Cream'	CPen EBee ECha EMan EPfP GSki LPio MSte SAga SOkh SUsu WCot
	stricta	CTrC SIgm WCot
	'Sunbeam'	NBir
	'Sunningdale Yellow' ♀H4	CDes CMdw COIW CPou ECha EHrv EMan ERou EVFa GMaP SChu SMHy SOkh SPer SRms WCot WEas WPGP
	'Tawny King'	More than 30 suppliers
	'Tetbury Torch' PBR	LRHS WWeb
	thodei	CPou
	thomsonii	GCal SSpi
	- var. ***snowdenii*** misapplied	see *K. thomsonii* var. *thomsonii*
	- var. ***snowdenii*** ambig.	CPou CSec WPGP WSHC
§	- var. ***thomsonii***	CBot CDes CFir CHVG EBee EMan EMar ETow GBri MNrw SMHy SMrm SSpi SUsu WCot WHal WPrP WWlt WWpP
	- - triploid variety	GSki
	- yellow	GCal
	'Timothy'	More than 30 suppliers
	'Toffee Nosed' ♀H4	More than 30 suppliers
	'Torchbearer'	EBee WCot WFar
	triangularis	CHad CMHG CPne EBee EPfP GCal GSki LRHS SAga SMar WFar
§	- subsp. ***triangularis***	CBro CHad COIW CPrp EBee EChP EMar GBuc ITer LAst LRHS LSRN MRav NBro NHaw SMrm SRms WBrE WCAu WPrP
§	- - 'Light of the World'	More than 30 suppliers
	'Tubergeniana'	WCot
I	'Tuckii'	EMan EWll SRms
	tuckii Baker	see *K. ensifolia*
	typhoides	GCal NBir SPlb SSpi WHal
	tysonii	SPlb
	uvaria	CPne CPou CSBt CTrC EBee EBrs GSki ITer LPio LRHS MHer NBir NPri NVic SECG SRms SSpi WBor WCot WHoo WHrl WMnd WTMC
*	- Fairyland hybrids	LIck WFar
	- 'Flamenco'	CFwr EWll NEgg NGdn SMac WHil WTMC
§	- 'Nobilis' ♀H4	CFir CSam EBee EChP ECha EMan ERou EUJe GAbr GBin GBri GSki LSRN MAvo MLLN MNFA MNrw SAPC SArc SDnm SMad SPav SPoG SSpi SWvt WBVN WCAu WCot WWlt
	'Vanilla'	CFir EBee EChP EMan GSki LAst LPio MBNS MRav NGdn WTMC
	'Wrexham Buttercup'	CDes CKno CPne CSam EBee EChP ECtt EMan ETow GAbr GBri GCal GMac GSki LSRN MAvo MBnl MLLN MNFA MRav SSpi SUsu WBVN WCot WHal WHoo WPrP WTMC WWlt
	'Yellow Cheer'	CPen LRHS
	'Yellowhammer'	EBee ECha EVFa WFar WPrP
	'Zululandiae'	WCot

Knowltonia (*Ranunculaceae*)

	filia **new**	CPLG

Kochia see *Bassia*

Koeleria (*Poaceae*)

	cristata	see *K. macrantha*
	glauca	More than 30 suppliers
§	***macrantha***	CBig EMan GFor NBre NLar NNor NOGN
	vallesiana	EHoe EMon LRHS MNrw

Koelreuteria (*Sapindaceae*)

	bipinnata	CMCN
*	- var. ***integrifoliola***	CFil
*	***orientalis*** **new**	GIBF
	paniculata ♀H4	More than 30 suppliers
	- 'Coral Sun' **new**	MBlu
	- 'Fastigiata'	EPfP GKir LRHS MBlu MBri NPal SPoG
	- 'Rosseels'	CBcs MBlu NEgg NLar NPal

Kohleria (*Gesneriaceae*)

	'Clytie'	MBri
	'Dark Velvet'	CHal WDib
	eriantha ♀H1	CHal EShb MBri WDib

	'Jester' ♀H1	CHal WDib
*	'Linda'	CHal
	'Strawberry Fields' ♀H1	MBri
§	***warscewiczii*** ♀H1	CHal LRHS WDib

Kolkwitzia (*Caprifoliaceae*)

	amabilis	CBcs CElw CPLG CSBt CTrw EBee ELan EMil EPfP GIBF MGos NFor NWea SPlb SRms WCFE WDin WGwG WHCG WHar WMoo WNor WTel
	- 'Maradco'	CPMA EPfP LRHS MAsh MRav NPro SCoo SPoG SSta WPat
	- 'Pink Cloud' ♀H4	More than 30 suppliers

Kosteletzkya (*Malvaceae*)

	virginica	EMan

Krascheninnikovia (*Chenopodiaceae*)

§	***lanata***	XPep

Kunzea (*Myrtaceae*)

	ambigua	CPLG CTrC ECou SPlb
	'Badja Carpet' **new**	WAbe
	baxteri	CTrC ECou EUnu
	ericifolia	SPlb
§	***ericoides***	CTrC ECou GGar
	- 'Auckland'	ECou
	- 'Bemm'	ECou
	parvifolia	CPLG ECou
	pomifera	ECou

L

Lablab (*Papilionaceae*)

§	***purpureus***	SMur
	- 'Ruby Moon'	CSpe

+ *Laburnocytisus* (*Papilionaceae*)

	'Adamii'	CDul CLnd CPMA EBee EPfP GKir LBuc LRHS MBlu MGos SMad SMHT SPer SSpi

Laburnum ✿ (*Papilionaceae*)

	alpinum	CNic EPfP NEgg NWea SPlb SSpi WDin
	- 'Pendulum'	CBcs CDoC CLnd ELan EPfP GKir LRHS MAsh MBar MBri MGos MWat NBee NBlu NEgg SBLw SCrf SLim SPer WDin WOrn
§	***anagyroides***	CDul CWib ISea NWea SBLw SEND SRms WBVN WDin
	- var. ***alschingeri*** **new**	MBlu
	- 'Pendulum'	NEgg
	vulgare	see *L. anagyroides*
I	x ***watereri*** 'Fastigata'	CBcs
	- 'Vossii' ♀H4	More than 30 suppliers

Lachenalia ✿ (*Hyacinthaceae*)

§	***aloides***	CStu EPot EShb MBri
	- var. ***aurea*** ♀H1	CMon ECho LRHS MSte SBch WCot
*	- var. ***bicolor***	WCot
	- 'Nelsonii'	LRHS
	- 'Pearsonii'	LDai LRHS
	- var. ***quadricolor*** ♀H1	ECho LDai LRHS WCot
	bachmanii **new**	CMon
§	***bulbifera*** ♀H1	ECho MBri
	contaminata ♀H1	CMon ECho LRHS WCot
	elegans **new**	ECho
	juncifolia **new**	ECho
	liliiflora	CMon ECho
	mutabilis	LRHS WCot
	neilii	WCot
	orchioides	WCot
	var. ***glaucina***	
	orthopetala	WCot
	pendula	see *L. bulbifera*
	purpureocoerulea	CMon
	pusilla **new**	CMon
	pustulata ♀H1	ECho LRHS WCot
	- blue-flowered **new**	ECho
	reflexa	CMon WCot
	'Robyn' **new**	WCot
	'Rolina'	ECho WCot
	'Romand' **new**	WCot
	'Romelia' PBR	WCot
	'Ronina'	ECho WCot
	'Rosabeth' **new**	WCot
	rosea **new**	WCot
	rubida	ECho WCot
	'Rupert' **new**	WCot
	splendida	WCot
	tricolor	see *L. aloides*
	unicolor	WCot
	unifolia	ECho WCot
	violacea	WCot
	viridiflora ♀H1	ECho LRHS WCot
	zeyheri **new**	WCot

Lactuca (*Asteraceae*)

	alpina	see *Cicerbita alpina*
	intricata **new**	EHyt
	perennis	CWan EBee EMag EMan EVFa GSki MBNS MTho NDov NSti SPla WBor WCFE WCot WHer WHrl
	virosa	CArn MSal

Lagarosiphon (*Hydrocharitaceae*)

§	***major***	CBen CDWL EHon EMFW EPfP LNCo NBlu WFar WPop

Lagarostrobos (*Podocarpaceae*)

§	***franklinii***	CDoC LLin STre WPic

Lagerstroemia (*Lythraceae*)

	indica ♀H1	EShb SEND SPlb
	- 'Rosea'	CBcs SEND

Lagotis (*Scrophulariaceae*)

	glauca **new**	GIBF

Lagunaria (*Malvaceae*)

	patersonii	CHII CPLG WPGP XPep
	- 'Royal Purple'	ERea

Lagurus (*Poaceae*)

	ovatus ♀H3	CFwr CHrt CKno CWCL EGoo EPza MGol SAdn SBch

Lallemantia (*Lamiaceae*)

§	***canescens*** **new**	EMan

Lambertia (*Proteaceae*)

	formosa	ECou
	inermis **new**	SPlb

Lamiastrum see *Lamium*

Lamium ✿ (*Lamiaceae*)

	from Turkey	CStu
	album	CArn GWCH NMir
	- 'Aureovariegatum'	see *L. album* 'Goldflake'

- 'Friday' (v) CBgR EHoe EMan NBir WHer WHil WWye
§ - 'Goldflake' (v) WCHb
armenum WAbe
barbatum EBee
§ ***galeobdolon*** CArn CNat CTri CWib LGro MHar MHer MSal SRms WBrE WWpP
- 'Hermann's Pride' More than 30 suppliers
- 'Kirkcudbright Dwarf' EBee EVFa EWes
- subsp. ***montanum*** 'Canfold Wood' WWpP
§ - - 'Florentinum' CHal CHrt CSBt CWan EChP ECha EHoe ELan EMan EPfP GKir MRav NBlu NLon NVic SHel SPer WBrk WCAu WFar WPer
§ - 'Silberteppich' ECha ELan EMan EMar LRHS MRav MTho
- 'Silver Angel' EMan SBch
- Silver Carpet see *L. galeobdolon* 'Silberteppich'
- 'Variegatum' see *L. galeobdolon* subsp. *montanum* 'Florentinum'
garganicum WTMC
- subsp. ***garganicum*** CDes CPom EWes GBri WPer WWpP
- subsp. ***pictum*** see *L. garganicum* subsp. *striatum*
- subsp. ***reniforme*** see *L. garganicum* subsp. *striatum*
§ - subsp. ***striatum*** SBla
- - DS&T 89011T EPPr
luteum see *L. galeobdolon*
maculatum CArn EGoo IHMH NArg SEND SHFr SRms WSSM
- 'Album' EBee ELan EPfP LGro NLon SAga SHar SPer SRms
- 'Anne Greenaway' (v) CBgR EBee GBri MFOX SChu SPet WCAu WCHb WCot
- 'Annecy' MInt WWye
§ - 'Aureum' CArn EBee ECha EHoe ELan GKir IHMH LAst LGro MTho SPer SPet SUsu SWvt WBVN WCHb WEas WFar WPer
- 'Beacon Silver' CArn EBee EBrs ECha ELan ENot EPfP GGar GKir IHMH LGro LRHS MHer MWgw NCob NFor NSti SBla SPer SPet SPlb SRms SWvt WBVN WCAu WEas WFar WPer WWeb WWpP
- 'Beedham's White' EBee NBir NSti WCot WWpP
- 'Brightstone Pearl' EBee EGoo EWes
- 'Cannon's Gold' ECha ECtt EHoe ELan EWes EWin GBuc IHMH SWvt
- 'Chequers' ambig. CBgR EBee EWin LRHS NBre SPer SPla WCAu WWpP
- 'Dingle Candy' CBgR EVFa
- 'Elaine Franks' CSam
- 'Elisabeth de Haas' (v) EWes NBre WWpP
- 'Forncett Lustre' CBgR EBee EWin
- 'Gold Leaf' see *L. maculatum* 'Aureum'
- Golden Anniversary ='Dellam'[PBR] (v) EBee ECha ELan GAbr LAst LRHS MBow NArg NBro NGdn NOrc SPla SSto WFar
- 'Golden Nuggets' see *L. maculatum* 'Aureum'
- 'Golden Wedding' COtt
- 'Hatfield' EBee GAbr GBuc
- 'Ickwell Beauty' (v) EBee GBri
- 'James Boyd Parselle' CBgR CSam EBee EWin MLLN WCAu WCHb WCot WRHF
- 'Margery Fish' SRms WEas
- 'Pink Nancy' CBot EGoo GKir MTho SWvt WFar
- 'Pink Pearls' CHrt CSBt LRHS NCiC SHar SOkd SPet WFar WMoo
- 'Pink Pewter' CHrt EBee EBrs ECGP ECha ECtt EHoe ELan EWTr GGar GKir GMaP IHMH LGro LRHS NGdn NSti SOkd SPer SPla SPlb SUsu WBrE WCHb
- 'Purple Winter' LRHS
- 'Red Nancy' EBee
§ - 'Roseum' CWib EBee ELan EPfP GAbr GGar GKir GMaP LGro MRav MWat MWgw NArg NFor NLon SGar SPer WCAu WPer WWpP
- 'Shell Pink' see *L. maculatum* 'Roseum'
- 'Silver Shield' EBee EWes
- 'Sterling Silver' EBee WPer
- 'White Nancy' ♀H4 More than 30 suppliers
- 'Wootton Pink' EBee GBuc GCal LRHS MBri MHer NBir NLar NLsd SSvw SWvt WCra WEas
microphyllum EHyt WAbe
orvala More than 30 suppliers
- 'Album' CBot CPle EBee EChP ELan EMon EPPr LRHS MSte NCGa SGar SHar SIng SMrm WCot WHer WTin
- 'Silva' EMan EMon GBin NGby WCot WSHC
sandrasicum CPBP CStu EHyt SBla WAbe WPat
'Silberlicht' EBee

Lampranthus (*Aizoaceae*)

aberdeenensis see *Delosperma aberdeenense*
aurantiacus CBcs CHEx SPet
aureus CTrC
'Bagdad' CHEx
blandus CBcs
'Blousey Pink' **new** CHEx
§ ***brownii*** CBcs CHEx CHal CStu ECho ELan EWin NBir SEND SPet WPnn
coccineus SPet
deltoides see *Oscularia deltoides*
edulis see *Carpobrotus edulis*
glaucus CStu SEND
haworthii CHal
multiradiatus CTrC GGar SEND
oscularis see *Oscularia deltoides*
roseus CHEx EWin SPet
spectabilis CBcs CHal CStu SAPC SArc SMur SPet WBrE
- orange-flowered **new** CDoC
- 'Tresco Apricot' CBcs
- 'Tresco Brilliant' CBcs CHEx SPet
- 'Tresco Fire' CDoC CHal
- 'Tresco Peach' CHal CStu CWCL WAbe
- 'Tresco Red' CBcs CTbh CWCL
- white-flowered **new** CStu
'Sugar Pink' **new** CHEx

Lamprothyrsus (*Poaceae*)

sp. EBee

Lancea (*Scrophulariaceae*)

tibetica **new** NWCA

Lantana (*Verbenaceae*)

'Aloha' (v) CHal SWal WWol
camara CArn ELan EPfP EShb MBri MOak SRms SYvo XPep
- 'Firebrand' SYvo
- 'Kolibri' **new** EWin LAst
- orange-flowered WWol
- pink-flowered WWol
- 'Radiation' SGar
- red-flowered SWal WWol
- 'Snow White' LAst MOak
- 'Sonja' LAst
- variegated **new** EShb
- white-flowered SWal WWol
- yellow-flowered NPri SWal WWol

'Goldsome' **new** EWin
'Ingersheimer' **new** EWin
§ ***montevidensis*** CHal EShb MOak SPet XPep
- RCB/Arg AA-1 WCot
- 'Boston Gold' CHal
'Schneeflocke' **new** EWin
sellowiana see *L. montevidensis*

Lapageria (*Philesiaceae*)

rosea ♀H3 CBcs CHll CPLG CPLN CPne CRHN CSec EBee EPfP GQui MDun NSla SAdn SBrw SHBN WNor
- var. ***albiflora*** CPLN ITim SAdn SBrw
- 'Flesh Pink' CPLG CRHN
- 'Nash Court' EBee ECot EMil

Lapeirousia (*Iridaceae*)

anceps **new** CStu
cruenta see *Anomatheca laxa*
divaricata **new** CStu
laxa see *Anomatheca laxa*
viridis see *Anomatheca viridis*

Lapiedra (*Amaryllidaceae*)

martinezii MS 425 from Spain **new** CMon

Lapsana (*Asteraceae*)

communis 'Inky' CNat EUnu

Lardizabala (*Lardizabalaceae*)

biternata see *L. funaria*
funaria CPLN

Larix (*Pinaceae*)

decidua ♀H4 CAgr CBcs CCVT CDoC CDul CMen CRWN CSBt ECrN ELan ENot EPfP EWTr GKir LCon MBar NBlu NEgg NWea SHBN SPer WDin WEve WFar WHar WMou
- 'Corley' CKen LLin MBlu
- 'Croxby Broom' CKen
- 'Globus' SLim
- 'Horstmann Recurved' LLin NLar SCoo SLim SPoG
- 'Krejci' **new** NLar
- 'Little Bogle' CKen MAsh
- 'Oberförster Karsten' CKen
- 'Pendula' CBcs GFlt GKir WEve
- 'Puli' CEnd COtt GKir LLin MAsh MBlu SCoo SLim SPer SPoG WEve
x ***eurolepis*** see *L.* x *marschlinsii*
europaea Middend. see *L. sibirica*
gmelinii GIBF GKir
- var. ***olgensis*** GKir NLar
- var. ***principis-rupprechtii*** GIBF GKir GTSp
- 'Tharandt' CKen
§ ***kaempferi*** ♀H4 CDoC CDul CLnd CMen CSBt CTri ECrN ELan EMil GKir LBuc LCon MAsh MBar NEgg NScw NWea SCoo SLim SPer STre WDin WEve WFar WMou WNor
- 'Bambino' CKen
- 'Bingman' CKen
- 'Blue Ball' CKen LLin NLar WEve
- 'Blue Dwarf' CKen COtt GKir LCon LLin MAsh MBar MGos NBlu SCoo SLim SPoG WEve WOrn
- 'Blue Haze' CKen
- 'Blue Rabbit' CKen CTho GTSp WEve
- 'Blue Rabbit Weeping' COtt GKir LCon LLin MGos SCoo SLim WDin WEve WOrn
- 'Cruwys Morchard' CKen
- 'Cupido' LLin
- 'Diane' CEnd CKen GKir LCon LLin LRHS MAsh MBar MBlu MGos NLar SBLw SLim SPoG WEve WOrn
- 'Elizabeth Rehder' CKen NLar
- 'Grant Haddow' CKen
- 'Grey Green Dwarf' MAsh
- 'Grey Pearl' CKen LLin NLar
- 'Hanna's Broom' **new** SLim
- 'Hobbit' CKen
- 'Jakobsen' LCon
* - 'Jakobsen's Pyramid' LLin MAsh SCoo SLim SPoG
- 'Nana' CKen GTSp LLin MAsh NLar WWes
I - 'Nana Prostrata' CKen
- 'Pendula' CDul CEnd EBee ECrN EPfP GKir LLin MAsh MBar MBlu MGos SBLw SPer SPoG WEve
- 'Pulii' SBLw
- 'Stiff Weeping' CTri GKir MAsh NLar SLim
- 'Swallow Falls' CKen
- 'Varley' CKen
- 'Walter Pimven' **new** NLar
- 'Wehlen' CKen
- 'Wolterdingen' CKen MBlu NLar SLim
- 'Yanus Olieslagers' CKen
laricina 'Arethusa Bog' CKen MBlu
- 'Bear Swamp' CKen
- 'Bingman' CKen
- 'Hartwig Pine' CKen
- 'Newport Beauty' CKen
leptolepis see *L. kaempferi*
§ x ***marschlinsii*** CSBt GKir NWea WMou
- 'Domino' CKen LLin NLar
- 'Gail' CKen
- 'Julie' CKen SLim
russica see *L. sibirica*
§ ***sibirica*** MBar
'Varied Directions' **new** SLim

Larrea (*Zygophyllaceae*)

tridentata CArn

Laserpitium (*Apiaceae*)

gallicum EBee
halleri EBee
siler CArn EBee GBin MAvo NDov NLar SIgm SMHy SPlb

Lasiagrostis see *Stipa*

Lasiospermum (*Asteraceae*)

bipinnatum **new** SPlb

Lastreopsis (*Dryopteridaceae*)

glabella CTrC WRic
hispida **new** WRic
velutina **new** WRic

Latania (*Arecaceae*)

loddigesii EAmu

Lathyrus ✿ (*Papilionaceae*)

albus CEnd
§ ***articulatus*** ELan SBch WCHb
§ ***aureus*** CBos CDes CHad CPom CSec EBee EBrs EMon GBuc GCal LPhx MAnH MAvo MNFA MTho NBir NChi SBla SUsu WCru WEas WFar WHal WHil WPGP WPat WSan
azureus misapplied see *L. sativus*
chilensis EBee LSou MWat
chloranthus SBch SPav

cirrhosus	CDes EBee EMon WPGP
clymenum articulatus	see *L. articulatus*
cyaneus misapplied	see *L. vernus*
* - 'Alboroseus'	MTho
davidii	CDes EMon WSHC
filiformis	WSHC
fremontii hort.	see *L. laxiflorus*
§ ***gmelinii***	NLar WSan
- 'Aureus'	see *L. aureus*
grandiflorus	CPLN CSev CStr EBee EChP EMon LPhx NLar SBla SMrm WCot
heterophyllus	EMon EWsh MNrw NArg
inermis	see *L. laxiflorus*
laevigatus	NLar
latifolius ♀H4	CAgr CArn CRHN CRWN EChP EPfP GAbr GBar GKir LAst LRav MBow NBid NBlu NLsd NPer SDnm SPoG SRms SWal WBVN WBor WBrk WEas WFar WHer WPer WSSM WWye
§ - 'Albus' ♀H4	CBot CPLN EBee ELan EMan GKir LPhx SPav SRms SSpi WEas
- 'Blushing Bride'	SPav WCot WSel
- deep pink	MHer NSti
- pale pink	NSti
- Pink Pearl	see *L. latifolius* 'Rosa Perle'
- 'Red Pearl'	CBcs EBee EChP ECtt ELan EPfP ERou GAbr MBri MWgw NPri NRnb SMar SPav SPer SPlb SPoG SSvw WFar WPer WWeb
§ - 'Rosa Perle' ♀H4	CBcs CChe CPLN CTri EChP ECtt EMan ERou EWTr GKir MBri MRav MSte NBir NEgg NLar NPer NPri NRnb SBla SBra SPav SPer SSvw WCAu WWeb
- Weisse Perle	see *L. latifolius* 'White Pearl'
- 'White Pearl' misapplied	see *L. latifolius* 'Albus'
§ - 'White Pearl' ♀H4	CBcs EChP ECha EMon EPfP ERou MBri MHer MRav MSte NBir NEgg NLar NPer NPri NRnb NSti SBra SMad SPer SPoG SSvw WCAu WFar WHrl WPer WWFP WWeb WWpP
§ ***laxiflorus***	CDes CPom EMag ETow MCCP MHar MNrw MTho NChi NLar WBVN WPGP
linifolius	CDes EBee EMon NLar WCot WPGP
luteus (L.) Peterm.	see *L. gmelinii*
- 'Aureus'	see *L. aureus*
magellanicus	EBee WSHC
maritimus	CSpe NLar WBWf
montanus	EBee GPoy SSpi WBWf
§ ***nervosus***	CPLN CPou CSpe MTho SBla SRms
neurolobus	CNic CPLG CPom ITer MOne WGwG
niger	CFee CPom EBrs EMon GMac MAnH MHer MLLN MSph NLar NRnb SHFr SMar WFar WHil
nissolia	ELan WBWf
odoratus	CHar EWll
- 'America' ♀H4	WGwG
- 'Bicolor'	ELan
- 'Black Knight'	MSph
- 'Blanche Ferry'	MSph
- 'Captain of the Blues'	WGwG
- 'Cupani'	CHrt SUsu WGwG
- 'Kingsize Navy Blue'	MSph
- 'Matucana'	CSpe MAnH MWat SBch SMrm WGwG
- 'Painted Lady'	MAnH SMrm
- 'Wiltshire Ripple'	MSph
palustris	NLar SMar
polyphyllus	NSti
pratensis	MBow NMir WBWf
pubescens	CRHN GBuc WCot WSPU
'Queen Charlotte' **new**	WGwG
roseus	WSHC
rotundifolius ♀H4	CHad EMag LPhx MNrw MTho SMar WFar WHoo
- hybrids	LPhx
- 'Tillyperone'	EMon WWpP
§ ***sativus***	CSec CSpe ELan SBch WCHb WLFP
- var. ***albus***	WGwG
- var. ***azureus***	see *L. sativus*
sphaericus	WCHb
sylvestris	CAgr CPLG EBee EMon MHer MLLN MNrw MSte MWat SBch SPet SSpi WBWf
- 'Wagneri'	EBee
tingitanus	CRHN CSpe WCHb WWpP
- 'Roseus'	CRHN SBch
tuberosus	CAgr CStr MNrw SMar SSpi WBWf WCot WSHC
'Tubro'	EMon SHar
undulatus	SSpi
venetus	CDes EBee MNrw WSHC
§ ***vernus*** ♀H4	More than 30 suppliers
- 'Alboroseus' ♀H4	More than 30 suppliers
- var. ***albus***	CDes EWes WLFP WPGP
- ***aurantiacus***	see *L. aureus*
- 'Caeruleus'	CBos CDes EBee EMon LPhx SUsu WPGP
* - 'Cyaneus'	SAga SOkh WCot WSan WWpP
- 'Flaccidus'	EBee EChP EMon WCot WKif WSHC WTin
- 'Indigo Eyes'	CDes
- 'Rainbow'	SMad SMar WHil
- 'Rosenelfe'	CBot CDes EBee EMan EWin SMar SOkh WCot WHil WPGP WSan
- f. ***roseus***	CPom ECha ETow MRav NBir SRms WCot WCru
- 'Spring Beauty'	WWpP
- 'Spring Melody'	EBee MRav SOkh WCot WPat
- 'Subtle Hints'	EMon
vestitus var. ***alefeldii***	EBee

Laurelia (*Monimiaceae*)

§ ***sempervirens***	CBcs CFil CTrw WPGP
serrata	see *L. sempervirens*

Laurentia see *Isotoma*

Laurus (*Lauraceae*)

§ ***azorica***	CBcs WFar
canariensis	see *L. azorica*
nobilis ♀H4	More than 30 suppliers
- f. ***angustifolia***	CMCN CSWP EPla GQui MBlu MRav NLar SAPC SArc WBcn WCHb WPGP WSel
- 'Aurea' ♀H4	CBcs CBrm CDul CMHG CSBt EBee ELan ELau EMil ENot EPfP EPla GQui LRHS MBlu MChe SLim SLon SMad SPer SPoG SWvt WCHb WDin WFar WJek WMoo WPat WSel
- 'Crispa'	MRav
- 'Sunspot' (v)	WCot

Lavandula ✿ (*Lamiaceae*)

'Alba'	see *L. angustifolia* 'Alba', *L.* x *intermedia* 'Alba'
'Alba' ambig.	CArn CBcs CBot CSev CWib EGra MHrb SAdn SIde SPer WEas WPer
§ x ***allardii***	CArn CPLG CPrp CSev EShb EWin GBar MChe MHer NGHP NHHG

		NLLv SDow WBad WJek WLav WSel XPep
	- 'African Pride'	GBar SDow XPep
§	***angustifolia***	More than 30 suppliers
	- No. 9	MHrb SDow
	- 'Alba'	CChe CWan EBee EDAr EHoe ELau ENot EPfP GPoy LBuc LSRN MBNS MChe MHer MSwo NGHP NLon NMen SAll SIoW SLon SPlb SSto WDin WFar WSel XPep
	- 'Alba Nana'	see *L. angustifolia* 'Nana Alba'
	- 'Arctic Snow'	CBcs CFai CWan LSRN MHrb NBPC NGHP SAga SDnm SIoW SPer SPoG WBad WLav
	- 'Ashdown Forest'	CSev CWan EBee ELau GBar MChe MHer NGHP SAdn SAga SBch SDow SIde SIoW WBad WHoo WJek WLav
	- 'Beechwood Blue' ♀H4	CWCL MHrb SDow WBad WLav
	- Blue Cushion = 'Lavandula Schola'PBR	ENot EPfP GKir LSRN MBNS NPri SDow WLav
	- 'Blue Ice'	SDow SMer
	- 'Blue Mountain'	CBcs GBar MHer MHrb SDow
	- 'Blue Mountain White'	NLLv SDow
§	- 'Bowles' Early'	CSam CWan GBar MChe NGHP SAdn SAga SMer WBad WFar WLav XPep
	- 'Bowles' Grey'	see *L. angustifolia* 'Bowles' Early'
	- 'Bowles' Variety'	see *L. angustifolia* 'Bowles' Early'
	- 'Cedar Blue'	CSev CWan EGoo ELau EPfP GBar MHer NBur NGHP SDow SHDw SIde SIoW SPla WBad WFar WLav
	- 'Coconut Ice' **new**	ECGP LRHS MHrb NArg NLLv NTHB
	- 'Compacta'	MHrb SDow WBad
	- 'Crystal Lights' **new**	SMrm
	- 'Dwarf Blue'	CRez EBee EWin WBad WFar XPep
I	- 'Eastgrove Nana'	WEas
*	- 'Erbalunga'	XPep
	- 'Folgate'	CArn CBcs CWCL EBee ELau GBar LAst MChe MHer MHrb NBur NGHP NHHG NLon SDow SIde SIoW WBad WFar WHoo WLav WMnd WSel WTel XPep
	- 'Fring Favourite'	SDow
§	- 'Hidcote' ♀H4	More than 30 suppliers
	- 'Hidcote Pink'	CArn CSLe CWib EBee EDAr GBar LSRN MHer MRav MWat NFor NGHP SDow SIoW SPer WBad WFar WGwG WKif WMnd WPer WSel XPep
	- 'Hidcote Superior'	NChi WWeb
	- 'Imperial Gem' ♀H4	More than 30 suppliers
§	- 'Jean Davis'	CWan EBee GBar MAsh MHrb NGHP NHHG NPri SAdn SAga SIde WBad WFar WGwG WLav WSel
	- 'Lady'	MChe SBch SECG SEND SHDw WBad
	- 'Lady Anne'	NTHB SDow SIoW WBad WLav
I	- 'Large White'	SIoW
N	- 'Lavender Lady'	NPer SAdn SSto SWal WPer
	- 'Lavenite Petite'	ENot EPfP LRHS LSRN LTwo MAsh MHrb NCGa NGHP NLar SDow SIoW SPoG SVil WLav WWeb
	- Little Lady = 'Batlad'PBR	CRez MAsh MHer MHrb NGHP NLLv SAll SIoW SSto WBad WLav
	- Little Lottie = 'Clarmo' ♀H4	CWCL EMil ENot EPfP EWin GGar LRHS LSRN MAvo MHer MHrb SCoo SDow SIde SMer SPer SSto SWvt WBad WLav
	- 'Loddon Blue' ♀H4	CBcs CSLe GBar NHHG NLon SAdn SDow SIde SIoW WBad WHoo WLav
§	- 'Loddon Pink' ♀H4	CSLe CWan EBee ELan ENot EPfP GBar GKir GMaP LRHS MAsh MChe MRav NGHP NPri SAdn SIoW SSto WBad WEas WFar WGwG WHoo WLav WPGP
*	- 'Lumière des Alpes'	XPep
	- 'Maillette'	EWin MHrb SDow SIde SIoW XPep
*	- 'Matheronne'	XPep
I	- 'Melissa Lilac'	MHrb SDow
	- 'Middachten'	SAga
	- 'Miss Donnington'	see *L. angustifolia* 'Bowles' Early'
	- 'Miss Katherine'PBR ♀H4	CSBt EBee ELan EPfP LRHS LSRN MAsh MBow MHrb NBPC NCGa NGHP SDow SIoW SPer SPoG SVil WBad WLav
	- Miss Muffet = 'Scholmis' ♀H4	CWCL EMil LTwo NLLv SDow SIoW SPer WBad WLav
	- 'Munstead'	More than 30 suppliers
§	- 'Nana Alba' ♀H4	More than 30 suppliers
	- 'Nana Atropurpurea'	SDow WBad WSel
	- 'Peter Pan'	CBcs CSLe CTbh LSRN MHrb NGHP SDow SIoW SVil WLav
	- 'Princess Blue'	CSBt CSLe ELan GBar LRHS MAsh MBNS NPri SAga SAll SDow SIde SIoW SSto WBad WFar WLav WPer WWeb WWpP XPep
*	- 'Rêve de Jean-Claude'	XPep
§	- 'Rosea'	More than 30 suppliers
	- 'Royal Purple'	CArn CBcs CSLe EBee EWes GBar LRHS MAsh MBNS MHer NGHP NHHG NPri NTHB SAdn SAll SDow SIde SIoW SMur SSto SWvt WBad WLav WSSM WWpP XPep
N	- 'Twickel Purple'	CBcs CSBt CWSG EBee ENot EPfP EWin GKir LRHS LSRN MAsh MChe MRav NBlu NGHP NHHG NPri NTHB SDix SIde SIoW SPer SPla SWvt WBad WFar WLav WSel XPep
	angustifolia* x *latifolia **new**	EWin
	aristibractea	MHer WLav
	'Avonview'	CBcs CWCL GBar MHer SDow WLav
	'Ballerina'	MHrb SDow
	'Blue River'PBR	WFar WLav
	'Blue Star'	EBee MAvo NBlu NGHP WFar WGHP WGwG
	'Bowers Beauty'	WBad WLav
	buchii var. ***buchii***	SDow XPep
	- var. ***gracilis***	CSpe
N	'Cambridge Lady'	WLav
	canariensis	CSev ERea EShb MHer MHrb NHHG SDow WBad WCHb WJek WLav XPep
	x ***christiana***	GBar MAsh MHer MHrb NGHP SDow SHDw WBad WJek WLav XPep
	'Cornard Blue'	see *L.* 'Sawyers'
	dentata	CArn CPrp CSev CTbh GBar MChe MHer NEgg NGHP NHHG SAdn SMer WAbe WBad WHer WPat WPic WWpP WWye XPep
§	- var. ***candicans***	CSev GBar MChe MHer MHrb NHHG NLLv SAga SBch SDow WBad WCHb WLav WWye XPep
	- 'Dusky Maiden'	CWCL MHrb SDow SIoW WLav
	- 'Linda Ligon' (v)	ESis GBar MHrb SDow SIoW WBad WGwG WHer WJek WLav XPep
	- 'Monet' **new**	MHrb NGHP
	- 'Ploughman's Blue'	CWCL MHrb SDow SIoW WBad
	- 'Pure Harmony'	SDow

- f. ***rosea*** SDow
- 'Royal Crown' ♀H2-3 GBar MHer SDow WBad WFar WLav XPep
- 'Royal Standard' SHBN
- silver see *L. dentata* var. *candicans*
- 'Silver Queen' WLav

'Devantville Cuche' WJek WLav XPep

I 'Edelweiss' EWin MRav NBur NGHP NLLv WLav

'Fathead' CElw COtt CPrp CSBt EBee ELan ENot EPfP GBar LAst LRHS LSRN MAsh MHer MHrb MLan NBPC NGHP SAdn SCoo SDow SLim SPoG WBad WBrE WGwG WJek WWpP

'Fragrant Memories' CSLe EBee ELau EWin GBar MAsh MHrb NPri SDow SIde WBad WLav

Goldburg = 'Burgoldeen'PBR (v) CSBt ELan ENot EPfP LAst LBuc LSRN MAsh MBNS MCCP MGos MHer MRav NBur NGHP NLLv NPri SCoo SDnm SLim SPav SPla SPoG SSto WBad WLav WWeb

'Goodwin Creek Grey' GBar MAsh MChe MHrb NLLv SDow WBad WGwG WJek WLav XPep

'Gorgeous' SDow

I 'Hazel' MAsh WLav

'Helmsdale'PBR CEnd CSBt EBee ELan EPfP GKir LAst LRHS LSRN MAsh MBri MHer MLan MRav MSwo MWat NBPC NBlu NGHP SAll SCoo SDow SLim SMad SPer SPla SPoG SVil WBad

heterophylla hort. see *L.* x *allardii*

'Hidcote Blue' see *L. angustifolia* 'Hidcote'

§ x ***intermedia*** SPla WFar
- 'Abrialii' GBar NLLv SDow WLav XPep
- 'Alba' ♀H4 CBcs CPrp CWan GBar NHHG SAga SDow SGar SIoW WBad XPep

* - 'Alexis' XPep

N - 'Arabian Night' ♀H4 CBcs COtt ELau SDow SIoW WBad WGwG WLav WWeb XPep
- 'Badsey Blue' WBad
- 'Bogong' WLav
- 'Chaix' GBar

§ - Dutch Group CArn CSBt CWan CWib EDAr ENot EPfP GBar GKir MAsh MBar MBri MRav MSwo SAga SCoo SDow SGar SLim SPer WBad WFar WJek WPer XPep

§ - - Walberton's Silver Edge = 'Walvera' (v) CRez CWCL ESis LRHS MGos SCoo SDow SIde SIoW SPoG
- 'Dutch White' **new** SDow

* - 'Futura' XPep
- 'Grappenhall' More than 30 suppliers
- 'Grey Hedge' CSLe CWan SAga WBad WLav
- 'Gros Bleu' SDow
- 'Grosso' More than 30 suppliers
- 'Hidcote Giant' ♀H4 CSLe GBar LRHS MHrb NPer SDow SIoW SPer WBad WKif WLav WSel XPep

* - 'Hidcote White' MHer NLLv WBad WLav XPep
- 'Impress Purple' GBar SDow WLav XPep

* - 'Jaubert' XPep

* - 'Julien' XPep
- 'Lullingstone Castle' CBod CPrp CSLe ELau GBar SAga SDow SIoW WBad WGwG WJek WLav WSPU
- 'Old English' CAby CSLe EUnu GBar MHrb SDow SIoW WCFE
- Old English Group CArn CBod ELau MBow SIoW WBad WHoo WJek WLav WSel
- 'Seal' CArn CPrp CSLe EBee ELau GBar MBow MChe MHer MHrb NGHP NHHG SAga SDow SIoW SPoG WBad WFar WHCG WMnd WPer XPep

* - 'Sumian' XPep
- 'Super' SIoW XPep
- 'Sussex' GBar MHrb NGHP SDow WLav

N - 'Twickel Purple' CArn CMHG CSev CWib ECGP ELau ENot EUnu EWes LAst LSRN NHHG SIoW SMrm WHoo WJek WMnd

'Jean Davis' see *L. angustifolia* 'Jean Davis'

lanata ♀H3 CArn CBot ECha EOHP GBar GPoy MChe MHer NHHG NLon NWCA SDow SHFr WBad WEas WLav WWye XPep

lanata x ***angustifolia*** CArn GBar NHHG WBad

§ ***latifolia*** CArn SDow WBad WSSM XPep

'Loddon Pink' see *L. angustifolia* 'Loddon Pink'

mairei XPep

mairei x ***intermedia*** WBad

'Marshwood'PBR CTri EBee EPfP LBuc LRHS LSRN MHrb MRav SCoo SDow SIde SLim SPer SPla WBad

'Midnight' SPoG

minutolii MHer MHrb SDow WBad XPep

multifida CArn CSev EUnu MChe MHer NLLv NLsd SDow WBad WCHb WHer WLav WWFP XPep
- 'Blue Wonder' NGHP WBad

* - 'Tizi-n-Test' XPep

officinalis see *L. angustifolia*

'Passionné' **new** SMrm

§ ***pinnata*** CArn CSev CSpe CTbh EShb GBar MChe MHer MHrb NEgg NHHG NPri SDow SPoG WBad WCHb WPop XPep

'Pippa White' NLLv

pterostoechas pinnata see *L. pinnata*

pubescens XPep

'Quicksilver' SPoG

'Regal Splendour'PBR CAby CWCL ELan EPfP LSRN MAsh MBri MHrb NCGa NGHP NLLv NPri SDow SPoG SVil WLav

'Richard Gray' ♀H3-4 CArn CCge CSLe EBee GBar LRHS LSRN MAsh MHer NCGa NGHP NPri SDnm SDow SSvw SVil WAbe WBad WBcn WLav WMnd XPep

'Rosea' see *L. angustifolia* 'Rosea'

rotundifolia MHer SDow XPep

'Roxlea Park'PBR LSRN MHrb NGHP SIoW WLav

'Saint Brelade' CWCL CWan EPfP EWin GBar MAsh MHrb NLLv SDow WBad WLav

§ 'Sawyers' ♀H4 More than 30 suppliers

'Silver Edge' see *L.* x *intermedia* (Dutch Group) Walberton's Silver Edge = 'Walvera'

'Silver Frost' XPep

N ***spica*** see *L. angustifolia*, *L.* x *intermedia*, *L. latifolia*
- 'Hidcote Purple' see *L. angustifolia* 'Hidcote'

stoechas ♀H3-4 More than 30 suppliers
- var. ***albiflora*** see *L. stoechas* f. *leucantha*
- 'Aphrodite' LRHS MAsh SDow WLav
- subsp. ***atlantica*** WBad
- 'Avenue Bellevue' ITim SIoW
- 'Badsey Starlite' WBad
- dark SAga WBad
- 'Devonshire' CSBt CWCL MHer NTHB SIoW WBad WJek
- 'Evelyn Cadzow' CSec
- 'Kew Red' More than 30 suppliers

I	- 'Lavender Lace' **new**	NGHP
§	- f. ***leucantha***	CArn CBot CCVT CMHG CSBt CSev CWib ECha ELan ELau EPfP GBar LAst MBri MChe MSwo NWoo SChu SDow SPla WAbe WBad WCHb WFar
	- 'Lilac Wings'	LRHS LSRN NGHP
	- subsp. ***luisieri***	GBar
	- subsp. ***lusitanica***	MHer WBad WLav
	- 'Madrid'	CWCL
	- 'Madrid Blue'	CMea CWan NGHP SHGN SIoW SPav WBad WLav
	- 'Madrid Pink' **new**	NGHP WBad
	- 'Madrid Purple'	NGHP SIoW SPav WBad WLav
	- 'Madrid White'	MHrb NGHP NLLv SIoW WBad WLav WPop
	- 'Papillon'	see *L. stoechas* subsp. *pedunculata*
§	- subsp. ***pedunculata*** ♀H3-4	More than 30 suppliers
	- - dark-flowered	WLav
	- - 'James Compton'	CWib EBee ECha LRHS MAsh SLim WBad WLav WTel
	- - 'Purple Ribbon'	WGHP WLav
	- 'Pippa'	WBad
	- 'Provençal' **new**	LRHS
	- 'Pukehou'	EPfP LRHS MAsh MHrb NBPC NLLv SDow SIoW SPav WBad WLav WPat
	- 'Purple Wings' **new**	LRHS
	- 'Rocky Red'	CBcs
	- 'Rocky Road'	LBuc LRHS LSRN MAsh MHrb NGHP SDow SIoW SPav SPer SPoG WLav
	- subsp. ***sampaioana***	WBad WLav
	- - 'Purple Emperor'	SPoG WLav
	- 'Snowman'	CBcs CSBt CWan EBee ENot EPPr EPfP LAst LRHS LSRN MBNS MHer MHrb MWat NGHP NPri SAdn SAga SAll SIoW SLim SPer SPoG SSto SVil SWvt WBad WFar WWeb
	- subsp. ***stoechas***	CSLe
	- - 'Liberty'	LRHS NGHP SDow SIoW
	- 'Sugar Plum'	WBad WLav
	- 'Summerset Mist'	MHrb SIoW WBad WLav
	- 'Victory' **new**	SPoG
	- 'Willow Vale' ♀H3-4	More than 30 suppliers
	- 'Willowbridge Calico'PBR	ECGP NEgg NPro SIoW SMrm WLav
*	- 'Wine Red'	SIoW WBad WLav
	subnuda	WBad
	'Tickled Pink'	CBcs CWCL ELan MAsh MBri MHrb NGHP SDnm SPav SPer SVil WLav
	'Van Gogh'	MHrb SDow
	vera misapplied	see *L.* x *intermedia* Dutch Group
	vera DC.	see *L. angustifolia*
	viridis	CArn CSev ELan ELau EPfP GBar LRHS MChe MHer MSwo NChi NGHP NHHG NLLv NPer SDow SGar SPer SPla SPoG WAbe WBad WCHb WHer WKif WWye XPep

Lavatera (*Malvaceae*)

	arborea	SChr WHer
	- 'Rosea'	see *L.* x *clementii* 'Rosea'
	- 'Variegata' (v)	CBcs ELan EMan LSou MFOX NPer NSti SBod SDix SEND SGar WCHb WCot WEas WHer WHil
	assurgentiflora	EPfP
	bicolor	see *L. maritima*
	cachemiriana	GBuc GCal LSou NBur NPer WPer
	x ***clementii*** 'Barnsley'	More than 30 suppliers
	- 'Barnsley Baby'	LRHS NPri
	- 'Blushing Bride'	CDoC EBee EPfP LRHS MBri NLar NPri SBod SPer SPla SPoG WBcn WHar
	- 'Bredon Springs' ♀H3-4	CAlb CDoC CWSG EBee ECha ECtt EMil ENot EPfP GBri GKir LRHS LSRN MAsh MBri MNrw MSwo NLsd NScw SBod SLim SMer SPer SPla SWvt WFar WWeb
	- 'Burgundy Wine' ♀H3-4	More than 30 suppliers
	- 'Candy Floss' ♀H3-4	EBee EPfP LRHS MAsh MBNS MBar MGos NPer SAdn WDin
	- 'Chedglow' (v)	CNat
	- 'Kew Rose'	CDoC CTri EBee EMil EPfP LRHS MAsh MSwo NPer SDix SLim SPla WWeb
	- 'Lavender Lady'	EBee ECtt NPer
	- 'Lisanne'	EBee LRHS MAsh MCCP MNrw MSwo NPri SMrm
	- 'Mary Hope'	CFai LRHS MAsh
	- Memories = 'Stelav'PBR	CFai CHid EBee ELan EPfP LRHS MAsh NEgg NLar NPer NPri SLim
	- 'Pavlova'	CDoC CPLG EPfP LRHS MAsh SMrm
	- 'Poynton Lady'	MGos
	- 'Rosea' ♀H3-4	More than 30 suppliers
	- 'Shorty'	WFar
	- 'Wembdon Variegated' (v)	NPer
	'Linda'	WBcn
§	***maritima*** ♀H2-3	CBot CDoC CHrt CMHG CPLG CRHN ECtt ELan EPfP NCot NPri SHBN SPer SPoG SUsu SWvt WCFE WEas WFar WHCG WKif XPep
	- ***bicolor***	see *L. maritima*
	- 'Princesse de Lignes'	MBri XPep
	mauritanica	CSec
	oblongifolia	CBot
N	***olbia***	CTri LAst SPlb SRms XPep
	- 'Eye Catcher'	CAlb CFai LRHS MBNS MSwo NEgg NLar SPer SPoG WRHF
	- 'Lilac Lady'	CFai CRez ECha ELan EPfP LRHS LSou MBNS MCCP NBPC NCGa NLar NLon SPer WFar WKif WWeb
	- 'Pink Frills'	CBot EBee LRHS MAsh MBar MBri MNrw NPri SHBN SMrm SPla SPoG WCot WWlt
	'Peppermint Ice'	see *L. thuringiaca* 'Ice Cool'
	'Pink Frills'	see *L. olbia* 'Pink Frills'
	plebeia	EChP
	'Rosea'	see *L.* x *clementii* 'Rosea'
	'Shadyvale Star'	NPro
	'Summer Kisses'PBR	MBri NCGa
	'Sweet Dreams'PBR	LRHS MAsh MBri
	tauricensis	NLar
N	***thuringiaca***	MWhi NPri WFar
§	- 'Ice Cool'	CBot ECha ECtt GCal LRHS MBar MGos NPer NRnb SBla SMrm WCot WFar WWeb
	'Variegata'	see *L.* x *clementii* 'Wembdon Variegated'
	'White Angel'PBR	LAst LRHS MAsh NPri
	'White Satin'PBR	MBri NCGa NPri SMrm SSvw

Ledebouria (*Hyacinthaceae*)

	adlamii	see *L. cooperi*
	concolor **new**	EShb
§	***cooperi***	CHal CStu EBla EHyt ELan EMan ERos ITim NCGa NLAp SIng SRot WPGP WPrP
§	***socialis***	CHEx CHal CSWP CSev CSpe CStu EPem ERos EShb LToo NBir SBch
	violacea	see *L. socialis*

× *Ledodendron* (*Ericaceae*)

§ 'Arctic Tern' ♀H4 — CDoC CSBt ENot GGGa GGar GQui LMil LRHS MAsh MBar MDun MGos MLea NWCA SLdr WBrE WPic

Ledum (*Ericaceae*)

§ × ***columbianum*** — NLar
groenlandicum — MBar MLea SPer WDin WFar WGer WSHC
- 'Compactum' — MAsh NLar SPoG WFar
macrophyllum — CFir
palustre — GGGa GIBF GPoy NLar
- subsp. ***decumbens*** — GCrs GGGa GIBF SOkd
§ - f. ***dilatatum*** — GIBF

Leea (*Leeaceae*)

coccinea — see *L. guineensis*
§ ***guineensis*** — EShb MBri

Leersia (*Poaceae*)

oryzoides — EBee

Leibnitzia (*Asteraceae*)

anandria — EBee NWCA
nepalensis — EBee
pusilla — EBee

Leiophyllum (*Ericaceae*)

buxifolium ♀H4 — EPfP GCrs LRHS NLar SBrw SSpi WPat
- 'Maryfield' **new** — WAbe

Lembotropis see *Cytisus*

Lemna (*Lemnaceae*)

gibba — CWat LPBA NPer
minor — CWat EHon EMFW LPBA NPer
polyrhiza — see *Spirodela polyrhiza*
trisulca — CWat EHon EMFW LPBA NPer

lemon balm see *Melissa officinalis*

lemon grass see *Cymbopogon citratus*

lemon see Citrus limon

lemon verbena see *Aloysia triphylla*

Leonotis (*Lamiaceae*)

leonitis — see *L. ocymifolia*
leonurus — CBcs CHEx CHll CSec CTbh CTrC ENot EShb EWes GGar MGol SMad
- var. ***albiflora*** — CPLG EShb LRav SPav
nepetifolia — MGol
§ ***ocymifolia*** — CFee CPLG CSec EShb WPGP WWye
- var. ***ocymifolia*** — EMan WCot
- var. ***raineriana*** — CHll
'Staircase' — MAnH SDnm SPav WRos

Leontice (*Berberidaceae*)

albertii — see *Gymnospermium albertii*

Leontodon (*Asteraceae*)

autumnalis — NMir
hispidus — NMir
§ ***rigens*** — EBrs EMan GBri GBuc GKir MFOX NBid SBri SDix SMad SMrm WFar WMoo WPrP
- 'Girandole' — CMCo MNrw WRos

Leontopodium (*Asteraceae*)

alpinum — CArn CTri CWan CWib EHyt GAbr GIBF GKev GKir GTou IHMH LRHS NArg NBlu NFor NJOw NWCA SBla SIng SPlb SPoG SRms WPer
- 'Mignon' — CMea ENot EWes GTou WAbe WHoo
- subsp. ***nivale*** — WPat
coreanum — GKev
§ ***discolor*** — WAbe
nanum **new** — GKev
§ ***ochroleucum*** var. ***campestre*** — CBrm EShb MDKP NLar NSla WPer
palibinianum — see *L. ochroleucum* var. *campestre*
pusillum SAQE79 **new** — WAbe

Leonurus (*Lamiaceae*)

artemisia — see *L. japonicus*
cardiaca — CAgr CArn CWan EGoo EMan EMon GBar GPoy MChe MHer MSal SECG SIde WGHP WHer WSel WWye
- 'Crispa' — EMon
§ ***japonicus*** — CSec MSal WOut
macranthus — EFEx
- var. ***alba*** — EFEx
sibiricus L. — MGol MSal SECG SPav

Leopoldia (*Hyacinthaceae*)

comosa — see *Muscari comosum*
spreitzenhoferi — see *Muscari spreitzenhoferi*
tenuiflora — see *Muscari tenuiflorum*

Lepechinia (*Lamiaceae*)

§ ***chamaedryoides*** — CHll CPLG
floribunda — CPle CSev
hastata — CBrd CPom EBee WCot WOut XPep
salviae — CDoC CPne CSec EBee EMan EVFa WBor

Lepidium (*Brassicaceae*)

campestre — CArn
latifolium **new** — MSal
peruvianum — MSal
ruderale — MSal
virginicum — MSal

Lepidothamnus (*Podocarpaceae*)

§ ***laxifolius*** — CMHG

Lepidozamia (*Zamiaceae*)

peroffskyana — CBrP CRoM

Leptecophylla (*Epacridaceae*)

juniperina — ECou
- subsp. ***parvifolia*** — ECou

Leptinella (*Asteraceae*)

§ ***albida*** — CStu LGro
* ***alpina*** — LGro
§ ***atrata*** — IHMH
- subsp. ***luteola*** — NWCA SChu WAbe
'County Park' — ECou
§ ***dendyi*** — ECou EDAr EWes GBin GGar MHer NJOw NLAp NMen NSla
dioica — CTrC GBin
filicula — ECou
hispida — see *Cotula hispida*
§ ***minor*** — ECou WMoo
pectinata var. ***sericea*** — see *L. albida*

- subsp. ***villosa*** CC 475 NWCA
§ ***potentillina*** CTri ECha EHoe ESis GKev MBNS MWgw NJOw NRya SChu SRms WCru WPer WPtf
§ ***pyrethrifolia*** CSec GKev NMen SIng
- 'Macabe' ECou
§ ***rotundata*** ECou WPer
§ ***serrulata*** MBar WCru
§ ***squalida*** ECha ESis GBin GGar IHMH MBar NRya NSti STre WPer
* - ***minima*** **new** NJOw
§ - 'Platt's Black' EBee EDAr EMan EShb ESis EWes GEdr GGar GKev LRHS NSti NWCA SBch SPet WFar WHoo WMoo WPer WPrP WWFP
traillii GGar

Leptocarpus (*Restionaceae*)

similis CTrC
- BR 70 GGar

Leptocodon (*Campanulaceae*)

gracilis HWJK 2155 **new** WCru

Leptodactylon (*Polemoniaceae*)

§ ***californicum*** CPBP EShb NPol
- subsp. ***californicum*** CPBP
pungens GKev
watsonii **new** CPBP

Leptolepia (*Dennstaedtiaceae*)

novae-zelandiae **new** WRic

Leptospermum (*Myrtaceae*)

argenteum **new** CBcs
citratum see *L. petersonii*
* ***compactum*** CPLG
'Confetti' ECou
'County Park Blush' ECou
cunninghamii see *L. myrtifolium*
ericoides see *Kunzea ericoides*
flavescens misapplied see *L. glaucescens*
flavescens Sm. see *L. polygalifolium*
§ ***glaucescens*** CMHG ECou GGar
§ ***grandiflorum*** ELan EPfP GGar ISea LRHS SBrw SSpi WSHC
grandifolium ECou
'Green Eyes' ECou
'Havering Hardy' ECou
humifusum see *L. rupestre*
juniperinum CTrC SPlb
laevigatum 'Yarrum' ECou
§ ***lanigerum*** CMHG CTri ECou EPfP GGar ISea MGol SLim SPoG WBVN
- 'Cunninghamii' see *L. myrtifolium*
- 'Wellington' ECou
liversidgei CChe ECou
luehmannii **new** EUnu
minutifolium ECou
morrisonii ECou
§ ***myrtifolium*** CTri ECou EPla EWes GGar SPer SSta WPat WPic
- 'Newnes Forest' ECou
myrtifolium* x *scoparium ECou
nitidum CTrC ECou GGar SPlb
- 'Cradle' ECou
obovatum CMHG
§ ***petersonii*** CArn ECou EOHP EShb MChe MHer WPic
- 'Chlorinda' ECou
phylicoides see *Kunzea ericoides*
'Pink Falls' ECou
'Pink Surprise' ECou
§ ***polygalifolium*** CTrC ECou GGar MGol SPlb SRms
prostratum see *L. rupestre*
pubescens see *L. lanigerum*
'Red Cascade' SWvt
rodwayanum see *L. grandiflorum*
rotundifolium CTrC ECou
§ ***rupestre*** ♀H4 CDoC CPne CTri ECou EPot GGar GTou MBar SPlb SRms WFar WSHC
rupestre* x *scoparium ECou
scoparium CArn CDul CTrC ECou ELau ERom EUnu MGol SPlb WDin
- 'Adrianne' ELan MAsh
- 'Appleblossom' **new** WCot
- 'Autumn Glory' CAlb CSBt CWSG EBee EHoe SBrw SLim
- 'Avocet' ECou
- 'Black Robin' LRHS
- 'Blossom' (d) CBcs ECou WGer
- 'Boscawenii' SBrw
- 'Burgundy Queen' (d) CBcs CSBt ECou
- 'Chapmanii' CMHG CPen EBee GGar
- 'Coral Candy' CBcs WGer
- 'County Park Pink' ECou
- 'County Park Red' ECou
- 'Crimson Glory' (d) CBrm CRez CTbh WCot
- 'Dove Lake' **new** WAbe
- 'Elizabeth Jane' GGar GQui
- 'Essex' ECou
- 'Fantasia' **new** ECou
- 'Fred's Red' WPat
- 'Gaiety Girl' (d) CBrm CSBt
- 'Grandiflorum' WGer
- var. ***incanum*** 'Keatleyi' ♀H3 ECou
- - 'Wairere' ECou
- 'Jubilee' (d) CBcs CSBt ISea
- 'Kerry' CAbP MAsh
- 'Leonard Wilson' (d) CTri ECou EWes
- 'Lyndon' ECou
- 'Martini' CDoC CRez CSBt LRHS WCot WWeb
- 'McLean' ECou
- (Nanum Group) 'Huia' CBcs
- - 'Kea' CSBt ECou GQui WGer
- - 'Kiwi' ♀H3 CAlb CBcs CBrm CDoC CDul CSBt CTbh CTrC EBee ECou ELan ENot EPfP EWes GQui LRHS MAsh MDun NVic SBrw SLim SPla WFar WGer WPat
- - 'Nanum' ECou EPot NJOw NMen SBod SHBN
- - 'Pipit' EPot EWes ITim WAbe
- - 'Tui' CSBt CTrC
- 'Nichollsii' ♀H3 CTrC CTri GQui SBrw WHar WSHC
- 'Nichollsii Nanum' ♀H2-3 CMea EPot ITim NLAp SRms WPat
- 'Pink Cascade' CBcs CSBt CTri GGar IMGH SBrw SLim
- 'Pink Damask' SWvt
- 'Pink Splash' ECou
- var. ***prostratum*** hort. see *L. rupestre*
- 'Red Damask' (d) ♀H3 More than 30 suppliers
- 'Red Falls' CBcs CPLG ECou
- 'Redpoll' ECou
- 'Roseum' WBrE
- 'Rosy Morn' ISea
- 'Ruby Glow' (d) CTri LRHS
* - 'Ruby Wedding' ELan LRHS SPla SPoG
- var. ***scoparium*** GGar
- 'Snow Flurry' CBcs CTrC EBee ENot SLim SPoG
- 'Sunraysia' CSBt CTrw
- 'Winter Cheer' CBcs WCot WWeb

- 'Wiri Joan' (d)	CBcs
- 'Wiri Linda'	CBcs
- 'Zeehan'	ECou
§ 'Silver Sheen' ♀H3	CEnd ECou ELan EPfP LRHS SBrw SLon SPoG WGer WPGP
'Snow Column'	ECou
sphaerocarpum	ECou
turbinatum **new**	ECou
- 'Thunder Cloud' **new**	ECou
'Wellington Dwarf'	ECou

Leschenaultia (*Goodeniaceae*)

'Angels Kiss'	ECou
biloba	CSec ECou
- 'Sky Blue'	ECou
'Blue Moon'	ECou
'Carnival'	ECou
formosa red-flowered	ECou
- yellow-flowered	ECou
pink-flowered	ECou
'Prima'	ECou

Lespedeza (*Papilionaceae*)

bicolor	CAgr CBcs MGol SEND WDin WFar WHCG
- 'Yakushima'	NEgg NLar
buergeri	NLar SMur WSHC
capitata	MSal SUsu
japonica	CPLG SPlb
thunbergii ♀H4	CBcs CWib EChP ELan EMil EPfP IDee IMGH LRHS MAsh MBlu NBlu SHGC SLon SOkh SPer SSpi SSta WDin WFar WHCG WPat WSHC
- 'Albiflora'	EPfP
- 'Summer Beauty'	CDul EPfP MGos
* - 'Variegata' (v)	LRHS
- 'White Fountain'	WBcn
tiliifolia	see *Desmodium elegans*

Lesquerella (*Brassicaceae*)

arctica var. ***purshii***	WPat

Leucadendron (*Proteaceae*)

argenteum	CDoC CHEx CTbh CTrC
daphnoides	EShb SPlb WSAf
eucalyptifolium	CTrC EShb SPlb
galpinii	CTrC
gandogeri **new**	WSAf
'Inca Gold'	CTrC
'Maui Sunset'	CTrC
'Mrs Stanley'	CTrC
'Safari Sunset'	CAbb CBcs CDoC CTrC EShb SBig WGer
salicifolium	IDee
salignum 'Early Yellow'	CAbb CTrC
- 'Fireglow'	CAbb CDoC CTrC
strobilinum	CDoC CTrC
tinctum	EShb

Leucanthemella (*Asteraceae*)

§ ***serotina*** ♀H4	More than 30 suppliers
- 'Herbststern' **new**	CFir WDyG

Leucanthemopsis (*Asteraceae*)

§ ***alpina***	LRHS
hosmariensis	see *Rhodanthemum hosmariense*
§ ***pectinata***	NSla
radicans	see *L. pectinata*

Leucanthemum ✿ (*Asteraceae*)

* ***angustifolium*** var. ***album***	CHar
atlanticum	see *Rhodanthemum atlanticum*
catananche	see *Rhodanthemum catananche*
graminifolium	NBre WPer
hosmariense	see *Rhodanthemum hosmariense*
mawii	see *Rhodanthemum gayanum*
maximum misapplied	see *L.* x *superbum*
§ ***maximum*** (Ramond) DC.	NBro NLon NPer
* - ***nanus***	WWeb
- ***uliginosum***	see *Leucanthemella serotina*
nipponicum	see *Nipponanthemum nipponicum*
§ x ***superbum***	EHol EWsh MBow MHer MWgw NVic WFar
- 'Aglaia' (d) ♀H4	More than 30 suppliers
- 'Alaska'	CAni EBee EBla EVFa GMac LAst LRHS MAnH NGdn NLRH NOak NPri SPer SPur SWal SWvt WBor WPer WWpP
- 'Amelia'	EBee NBre NLar
- 'Anita Allen' (d)	CAni CElw CFee CPou CStr EBee MAvo WCot WFar WPer WWpP
- 'Anna Camilla' **new**	CAni
- 'Antwerp Star'	NBre NLar WBrk WWpP
- 'Banwell' **new**	CAni
- 'Barbara Bush' (v/d)	More than 30 suppliers
- 'Beauté Nivelloise'	CAni MAvo MHar WCot WFar WPer WRha WWpP
- 'Becky'	CElw EBee EChP ECha EPfP GMac MAvo MBNS NPro WHil
- 'Bishopstone'	CAni CBos ELan EMan ERou NLon SChu WEas WPer WWpP
- 'Christine Hagemann'	CAni CFwr EBee LRHS MAvo MDKP MRav WHoo WWpP
- 'Cobham Gold' (d)	CAni CElw CStr EBee EMan ERea NBre NFla NOrc SOkh SUsu WWpP
- 'Coconut Ice'	WPer
- 'Colwall'	CAni
I - 'Crazy Daisy'	CAni CElw CM&M CTri ECGP GFlt NLar SWal WHrl WWpP
- 'Devon Mist' **new**	CAni
- double cream **new**	EBee
- 'Droitwich Beauty'	CAni CElw EBee MAvo MBct MNrw WBrk WHoo WSPU WTel
- 'Duchess of Abercorn'	CAni CStr
- 'Dwarf Snow Lady' **new**	NBre
- 'Easton Lady' **new**	CAni
- 'Eclipse' **new**	CAni MAvo
- 'Edgebrook Giant'	CAni MAvo
- 'Edward VII' **new**	CAni
- 'Eisstern'	MAvo
- 'Esther Read' (d)	More than 30 suppliers
- 'Etoile d'Anvers'	XPep
- 'Everest'	CAni NOak SRms
- 'Exhibition' **new**	NBre
- 'Fiona Coghill' (d)	CAni CElw CHar CHea CMil CStr EBla ECGP ECtt GBri IBlr MBnl MDKP MHer MLLN NChi WCot WHil WHoo WLin WWpP
- 'Firnglanz'	CAni CFwr GBin MAvo
- 'Gruppenstolz' **new**	CAni
- 'H. Seibert'	CAni CElw CHea EBla MAvo WWpP
- 'Harry' **new**	CAni
- 'Highland White Dream'PBR	WFar WWeb
- 'Horace Read' (d)	CAni CElw CHar CHea CMdw CMea CMil ELan ERea NBir SAga SBch WEas WPer WWpP
- 'Jennifer Read'	CAni ERea WCot
- 'John Murray'	NBir WAbb
- 'Little Miss Muffet'	LRHS NPro
- 'Little Princess'	see *L.* x *superbum* 'Silberprinzesschen'

- 'Manhattan' CAni CFwr CMdw CStr EBla EBrs EWes GBin GBuc LRHS WWpP
- 'Margaretchen' MAvo
- 'Marion Bilsland' **new** CAni MAvo
- 'Mayfield Giant' CAni CTri ERou WPer
- 'Mount Everest' EBee
- 'Northern Lights' SMac
- 'Octopus' CAni EBee MAvo
- 'Old Court' EBee EChP EMan GMac MTis NBre NLar
- 'Phyllis Smith' More than 30 suppliers
- 'Polaris' CFwr GFlt LRHS NBre NOak WMoo
- 'Rags and Tatters' CAni EBee MAvo
- 'Rijnsburg Glory' NBre
* - 'Schneehurken' CAni CElw CFwr EBee EBla MAvo SUsu WLFP
- 'Shaggy' EBee EBla EChP ECtt GMaP MLLN NFla WPrP
§ - 'Silberprinzesschen' CAni COIW CPrp EBla EChP ENot EPfP GKir IFro IHMH LRHS NBlu NMir NOak NPri SPlb SRms WFar WMoo WPer WWpP
- 'Silver Spoon' WHil WPer
- 'Snow Lady' COIW IHMH LRHS NBlu NMir NPer SPet SRms WFar WTel WWeb WWpP
- 'Snowcap' EBla ECha ENot EPfP GSki LRHS MBri MRav NEgg NGdn NLon SBla SPer SPla SWvt WMow WTin WWpP
- 'Snowdrift' CAni CM&M EBee EGoo MAnH MAvo NBre NPri WCot WHil WPer WWeb
§ - 'Sonnenschein' More than 30 suppliers
- 'Starburst' (d) SHel SRms
- 'Stina' CFwr GBin
- 'Summer Snowball' (d) CAni CElw EBee EShb EWes GSki LRHS LSou MAvo SHel SUsu WCot WFar WHrl WTel WWpP
- 'Sunny Killin' WTin
- 'Sunny Side Up'PBR CElw EChP ECtt EWes MBNS MLLN NBre NLar
- Sunshine see *L.* x *superbum* 'Sonnenschein'
- 'T.E. Killin' (d) ♀H4 CElw CHea CKno CPrp CSam EBee EBla EBrs ECha ECtt EMan EMar EPfP GSki LRHS MBnl NChi SUsu WCAu WCot WFar WWpP
- 'White Iceberg' (d) CAni LAst WPer
- 'White Knight' GMac LRHS MAnH NBre WBrk WHil
- 'Wirral Pride' CAni CHar ERou MBnl NPri WCra WMnd WWol WWpP
§ - 'Wirral Supreme' (d) ♀H4 More than 30 suppliers
'Tizi-n-Test' see *Rhodanthemum catananche* 'Tizi-n-Test'
§ ***vulgare*** CArn CHrt CKno CRWN EMag GBar GWCH IHMH MBow MHer NLRH NLan NMir NPri SBch SECG SIde WBVN WBrk WHer WJek WPop WShi WWye
- 'Avondale' (v) NGdn
- 'Filigran' CKno EShb GMac LRHS MAnH NBre SIde
§ - 'Maikönigin' CBgR EBee GAbr GCal IHMH NLRH WHrl WWpP
- May Queen see *L. vulgare* 'Maikönigin'
- 'Sunny' CBre EBla

Leucochrysum (*Asteraceae*)

albicans subsp. ***alpinum*** CStu

Leucocoryne (*Alliaceae*)

alliacea **new** CMon
coquimbensis CMon
ixioides CMon
* - ***alba*** CMon
purpurea ♀H1 CMon ECho LRHS

Leucogenes (*Asteraceae*)

grandiceps CPBP EPot GCrs GTou NSla
leontopodium EPot GCrs GEdr GGar GKev GTou MDKP NLAp NSla WAbe
tarahaoa EPot NSla WAbe

Leucojum (*Amaryllidaceae*)

aestivum CBcs CFee EBee EChP EPfP GAbr GBBs GCrs LAma LRHS MAvo MDun MWgw SRms WBVN WCot WCra WEas WFar WShi WTin WWye
- 'Gravetye Giant' ♀H4 More than 30 suppliers
autumnale ♀H4 More than 30 suppliers
- 'Cobb's Variety' WCot
- var. ***oporanthum*** ERos MSte
* - - SF 352 from Morocco **new** CMon
- var. ***pulchellum*** CBro ERos
longifolium ERos
nicaeense ♀H2-3 CLyd CPBP CStu EBur ECho EHyt EPot ERos MTho SCnR SSpi WCot
roseum CLyd EBur EPot ERos LAma SCnR SIgm SOkd WAbe
tingitanum CBro EHyt EPot SSpi WCot
trichophyllum CBro ERos
valentinum CBro CMon CPBP EPot SCnR SRot SSpi WCot
vernum ♀H4 CAvo CBro CHEx CPLG EBrs EHrv EHyt ELan EPfP EPot GCrs GFlt GKev LAma LPio LRHS MBow MDun MNrw MRav NMen SRms WAbe WCot WFar WHer WPnP WShi
- var. ***carpathicum*** CLAP ECha EHrv GEdr LAma MRav NMen
- var. ***vagneri*** CLAP ECha EHrv EMon GEdr LFox WTin

Leucophyllum (*Scrophulariaceae*)

frutescens XPep
minus XPep

Leucophyta (*Asteraceae*)

§ ***brownii*** CStu ECou EMan EShb EWin MRav SMad XPep

Leucopogon (*Epacridaceae*)

colensoi EPot GCrs MBar MBri MGos NJOw NLar NWCA SBrw SLon SSpi WAbe WPat
ericoides MBar WPat
§ ***fasciculatus*** ECou
§ ***fraseri*** ECou GCrs GEdr
§ ***parviflorus*** ECou

x *Leucoraoulia* (*Asteraceae*)

§ hybrid (***Raoulia hectorii*** x ***Leucogenes grandiceps***) GKev GTou SIng WAbe
§ ***loganii*** CPBP ITim NSla NWCA WAbe

Leucosceptrum (*Lamiaceae*)

canum CPLG
- GWJ 9424 WCru

japonicum B&SWJ 8892 new	WCru
stellipilum var. ***formosanum***	SSpi
- - B&SWJ 1804	WCru

Leucospermum (*Proteaceae*)

cordifolium	WSAf
'Fountain' new	WSAf
'Scarlet Ribbon'	CTrC

Leucothoe (*Ericaceae*)

axillaris 'Curly Red'PBR new	LRHS
Carinella = 'Zebekot'	MBri MGos
davisiae	NLar SBrw
§ ***fontanesiana*** ♀H4	CTbh EPfP LRHS NBea NEgg STre WBrE
- 'Nana'	CRez LRHS MAsh
- 'Rainbow' (v)	More than 30 suppliers
- 'Rollissonii' ♀H4	MBar SRms
keiskei	EPfP LRHS MAsh
- 'Minor'	SSta
- 'Royal Ruby'	CWSG NCGa NLar SPoG WDin WFar
Lovita = 'Zebonard'	CEnd CSam EBee GCal LRHS MBri MRav NCGa NLar SCoo SSta
populifolia	see *Agarista populifolia*
racemosa	NLar
Red Lips = 'Lipsbolwi'PBR	ENot MGos
Scarletta = 'Zeblid'	More than 30 suppliers
walteri	see *L. fontanesiana*

Leuzea (*Asteraceae*)

centaureoides	see *Stemmacantha centaureiodes*
* ***conifera macrocephala***	WAbe

Levisticum (*Apiaceae*)

officinale	CAgr CArn CHby CHrt CSev ELau EUnu GBar GPoy MBar MBow MChe MHer NBid NBlu NGHP SDix SECG SIde SPlb WBrk WGHP WGwG WHer WPer WSel WWye

Lewisia ✿ (*Portulacaceae*)

'Archangel'	NRya
Ashwood Carousel hybrids	EDAr GCrs MAsh MDHE
'Ashwood Pearl'	MAsh
'Ben Chace'	MAsh WAbe
Birch strain	CBcs ECho ELan
brachycalyx ♀H2	EWes GKev GTou MAsh MTho WAbe
cantelovii	MAsh
columbiana	EHyt GTou MAsh MDHE NJOw WAbe
- 'Alba'	MAsh WAbe
- subsp. ***columbiana***	CGra
- 'Rosea'	GCrs MAsh NSla WAbe WGor
- subsp. ***rupicola***	LTwo MAsh MMHG NWCA WGor
- subsp. ***wallowensis***	EHyt MAsh MDHE NMen WGor
congdonii	MAsh
cotyledon ♀H4	GKev LRHS LTwo MNrw MOne NBlu NWCA SPet WBrE WFar WPat
- J&JA 12959	NWCA
- f. ***alba***	GFlt GTou MAsh NWCA
- 'Ashwood Ruby'	MAsh
- Ashwood strain	CNic CTri CWCL ENot EPfP ESis EWes LBee LRHS LSou MAsh MBri MOne NRya SRms WGor
- Crags hybrids	SRms
- 'Fransi'	NLar
- var. ***heckneri*** ♀H4	WGor
- var. ***howellii***	LTwo SRms WGor
- hybrids	CBrm CStu EDAr EHol EPot GTou ITim NMen SIng SPoG WAbe WGor WLin
- 'John's Special'	GCrs
- magenta	GAbr MAsh WGor
§ - 'Regenbogen' mixed	LAst SSto WGor WPer
- 'Rose Splendour'	WGor
- Sunset Group ♀H4	GAbr GKir MBri MHer NJOw NLar NWCA SRms WPer WRHF
- 'White Splendour'	MAsh SIng WGor
'George Henley'	EHyt EPfP EWes MAsh NMen NRya SIng SOkd WAbe
* 'Holly'	MDHE
'Joyce Halley'	GCrs
leeana	EHyt MAsh
'Little Peach' new	SIng
'Little Plum'	CMea CPBP EDAr GEdr GKev ITim MDKP MSte NCGa NDlv NLAp NLar NRya NSla NWCA SIng WGor WLin
§ ***longipetala***	GTou MAsh MOne NSla NWCA
longipetala x ***cotyledon***	GTou
§ ***nevadensis***	ERos ESis GEdr GTou ITim MAsh MBri MNrw MTho NJOw NLAp NMen NRya NWCA SRms SRot WHoo WLin WPer
- ***bernardina***	see *L. nevadensis*
- 'Rosea'	CGra GCrs MAsh NWCA WAbe
oppositifolia	GCrs MAsh
- 'Richeyi'	EHyt
'Phyllellia'	MAsh
'Pinkie'	CPBP EDAr GCrs GEdr IHMH LTwo MAsh MDHE NLAp NMen
pygmaea	CGra EWes GCrs GEdr GTou ITim LAst LRHS MAsh MBri MHer NBir NJOw NLAp NMen NRya NWCA WPer
- from Arizona new	EHyt
- ***alba***	ITim
- subsp. ***longipetala***	see *L. longipetala*
Rainbow mixture	see *L. cotyledon* 'Regenbogen' mixed
'Rawreth'	LTwo WAbe
rediviva	CGra CPBP EWes GCrs GKev GTou ITim MAsh NSla NWCA SIgm SOkd WAbe WLin
- Jolon strain	GKev WGor
- subsp. ***minor***	CGra GKev WAbe
- var. ***rediviva***	EHyt
- white	MAsh
serrata	MAsh
sierrae	MAsh NJOw WPer
'Trevosia'	MDHE
tweedyi ♀H2	EHyt GCrs GKev GTou ITim LRHS MAsh MOne NBir NJOw NWCA SIgm SIng WGor
- 'Alba'	GCrs ITim LRHS MAsh NWCA SOkd
- 'Elliott's Variety'	MAsh WGor
- 'Rosea'	EHyt LRHS MAsh SIng WGor

Leycesteria (*Caprifoliaceae*)

crocothyrsos	CArn CBcs CBrm CHar CPle CWib ELan GQui IFro MMil NBid SLon SMad SPoG WAbe WFar WPic WSHC WWpP
formosa ♀H4	More than 30 suppliers
- Golden Lanterns = 'Notbruce'PBR	CDoC CPLG EBee ENot GTSp MGos NPri SCoo SHGC SPoG
- 'Golden Pheasant' (v)	CPMA
- 'Purple Rain'	NLar WBcn

Leymus (*Poaceae*)

from Falkland Islands	EPPr
§ ***arenarius***	More than 30 suppliers
condensatus 'Canyon Prince'	CKno
hispidus	see *Elymus hispidus*
'Niveus'	EHul
§ ***racemosus***	CHrt MMHG WOut

Lhotzkya see *Calytrix*

Liatris (*Asteraceae*)

aspera	EMan NLar WPer
elegans	EShb NLar SPlb WPer
ligulistylis	EMan GSki WMoo
punctata	EBee
pycnostachya	CRWN EMan MLLN MWrn NLar SRms WMoo WPer
- 'Alexandra'	EBee
scariosa 'Alba'	WPer
- 'Gracious'	CPLG EWll
- 'Magnifica'	CBcs
§ ***spicata***	More than 30 suppliers
- 'Alba'	COlW CPrp CSBt ECha ECtt ELan ENot EPfP GKir GSki IHMH LAma LAst LSRN MNFA MNrw MTis NEgg NRnb SPer SPlb WBrE WGHP WHoo WPer
- ***callilepis***	see *L. spicata*
- 'Floristan Violett'	CBrm CHar EChP EPPr EPfP GMaP LAst LRHS MAnH MHer MTis MWgw MWrn NArg NEgg NLRH NLon SCoo SPlb SPoG SWvt WFar WMnd WMoo WPer WWeb
- 'Floristan Weiss'	CArn CBrm CHar COlW EBee EChP ELau EMar EPPr EPfP GBuc GMaP LRHS MHer MRav MWgw MWrn NArg NBPC NCGa NLRH NPri SPla SPoG SWvt WFar WMnd WMoo WPer WWeb
- Goblin	see *L. spicata* 'Kobold'
§ - 'Kobold'	More than 30 suppliers
squarrosa	EBee

Libertia ✿ (*Iridaceae*)

HCM 98.089	EBee
'Amazing Grace'	CDes CPne EBee EPPr IBlr SBch SUsu WPGP
'Ballyrogan Blue'	CDes IBlr
Ballyrogan hybrid	IBlr
* ***breunioides***	CPLG IBlr
caerulescens	CFil CPLG EBee EChP EMan ERos EVFa GSki IBlr IGor LPio NBir NLar NRnb SBch SMrm WCot WFar WHer WMoo WPGP WSHC WSan
chilensis	see *L. formosa*
elegans	CPLG GBuc IBlr
§ ***formosa***	More than 30 suppliers
- brown-stemmed	IBlr
grandiflora ♀H4	More than 30 suppliers
- Cally strain	GCal
- stoloniferous **new**	GGar
ixioides	CBcs CElw CKno CWil EBee ECou EMan GMac GSki IBlr NSti SGSe WCFE WLeb WPGP WPic WPrP WRHF WWeb
- hybrid	SDix
- 'Tricolor'	GAbr GGar IBlr SIng WMoo
'Nelson Dwarf'	IBlr
paniculata	CPLG
peregrinans	More than 30 suppliers
- East Cape form	IBlr
- 'Gold Leaf'	CBcs CElw CPrp CWil EHrv IBlr LPio SMad SOkh WCot WCru WDyG WPic
* ***procera***	CFil CSpe IBlr WPGP
pulchella	EBrs EMan IBlr
sessiliflora	CFee CFil IBlr NBir WCot WFar WPGP
- RB 94073	MNrw SMad
Shackleton hybrid	IBlr
tricolor	EBee GBuc
* ***umbellata***	IBlr

Libocedrus (*Cupressaceae*)

chilensis	see *Austrocedrus chilensis*
decurrens	see *Calocedrus decurrens*

Libonia see *Justicia*

Licuala (*Arecaceae*)

grandis	MBri

Ligularia ✿ (*Asteraceae*)

B&SWJ 2977	WCru
BWJ 7686 from China	WCru
amplexicaulis	IBlr
- GWJ 9404	WCru
calthifolia	CRow
'Cheju Charmer' **new**	WCru
clivorum	see *L. dentata*
§ ***dentata***	CRow ECtt GFlt GIBF GKir NArg NBro NEgg NGby SMar SRms WFar WWeb
- 'Britt-Marie Crawford'	More than 30 suppliers
- 'Dark Beauty'	EMan ERou GFlt GSki IBal MWhi SMar WMnd
- 'Desdemona' ♀H4	More than 30 suppliers
- 'Dunkellaubig' **new**	MBNS
- 'Enkelrig' **new**	MBNS
- 'Orange Princess'	EBee NPer WPer
- 'Orange Queen' **new**	SMar WWeb
- 'Othello'	More than 30 suppliers
- 'Sommergold'	ECha GSki IBlr SPer WFar
§ ***fischeri***	GSki LEdu MLLN NFor SGSe WCot WPer
- B&SWJ 1158	WFar
- B&SWJ 2570	WCru
- B&SWJ 4478	WCru
- B&SWJ 5540	WCru
- B&SWJ 5841	WCru
glabrescens	CRow
§ 'Gregynog Gold' ♀H4	More than 30 suppliers
x ***hessei***	EBee GKir GMaP GSki NLar WFar WPnP
hodgsonii	CRow EBrs EMan GKir GSki IBlr LEdu MBri MSte WFar WPer
intermedia	WFar
- B&SWJ 4383	WCru
- B&SWJ 606a	WCru
japonica	CHar CRow EBee EBrs ECha GSki ITer LEdu NLar WFar
- B&SWJ 2883	WCru
- 'Rising Sun'	WCru
aff. ***kaialpina*** B&SWJ 5806	WCru
- - B&SWJ 6185	EBee
kanaitzensis ACE 1968	WCru
- BWJ 7758	WCru
macrophylla	CRow MWhi WFar
x ***palmatiloba***	see *L.* x *yoshizoeana* 'Palmatiloba'
§ ***przewalskii*** ♀H4	More than 30 suppliers
sachalinensis	GCal
sibirica	CSam EChP GAbr GSki NLar SMad SMar WCAu WFar WMoo WPer WPnP

	- 'Hietala'	CPne
	- var. ***speciosa***	see *L. fischeri*
	smithii	see *Senecio smithii*
	speciosa	see *L. fischeri*
	stenocephala	EBee EMil GKir IBlr NBro NLar NLsd WFar
	- B&SWJ 283	WCru
	'Sungold'	CBct CSam EBrs WPnP
	tangutica	see *Sinacalia tangutica*
	'The Rocket' ♀H4	More than 30 suppliers
	tsangchanensis	NEgg
	tussilaginea	see *Farfugium japonicum*
	veitchiana	CBct CHEx CRow EBee EMan EPfP EPza GAbr GCal GGar GKev GKir IBlr LAst LEdu MBri MSte NCob NEgg NGdn SDnm SPav WCAu WCot WFar WTMC
	vorobievii	EBee EKen GBin GFlt GIBF GSki MBNS
	'Weihenstephan'	EBee GCal GKir IBlr LRHS MBri
	wilsoniana	CBct CHEx CRow EBee ECtt EMan MLLN MRav SDnm SPav WCAu WFar
§	x ***yoshizoeana*** 'Palmatiloba'	CFai CFir CHEx EBee EBrs ELan EPla EWTr GCal GKir GSki IBlr LPhx LRHS MRav NOak NSti SBla SDnm SPav WAul WCot WCra WFar WPnP
	'Zepter'	EBee GBuc GCal MBri NLar

Ligusticum (*Apiaceae*)

	hultenii **new**	GIBF
	lucidum	CDul CMCN EBee EHol EPfP EWTr LPhx MSal SIgm WFar WPGP
	porteri	MSal
	scoticum	CArn EBee ECrN EOHP EWes GBar GIBF GPoy ILis MSal WBWf WDyG WFar WOut WPtf
	striatum B&SWJ 7259	WCru

Ligustrum ✿ (*Oleaceae*)

	chenaultii	see *L. compactum*
§	***compactum***	CLnd NLar SSpi
§	***delavayanum***	CBcs ERom LRHS MBar SAPC SArc WFar
	ibota **new**	NLar
	ionandrum	see *L. delavayanum*
	japonicum	CCVT CHEx ECrN ENot SEND SMur SPer WDin WFar XPep
I	- 'Aureum'	NBlu
	- 'Coriaceum'	see *L. japonicum* 'Rotundifolium'
	- 'Macrophyllum'	EPfP LRHS MAsh
§	- 'Rotundifolium'	CAbP CDoC CHEx CPLG CPle EBee EMil EPfP EPla LRHS MAsh MRav SBod SCoo SLim SMad SPoG WBcn WFar
	- 'Silver Star' (v) **new**	CPMA SLon
§	- 'Texanum'	LRHS
	lucidum ♀H4	CDoC CSBt CTho EBee ECrN ELan ENot LAst MBar MGos MRav MSwo NLar NWea SAPC SArc SBrw SMad SPer SSpi SWvt WBVN WDin WFar XPep
	- 'Aureovariegatum' (v) **new**	NEgg
	- 'Excelsum Superbum' (v) ♀H4	CAbP CLnd CPMA ELan ENot EPfP LAst LRHS MAsh MBar MGos NBlu SPer SPoG SSpi WBcn
	- 'Golden Wax'	CAbP CPMA ECrN ENot LRHS MRav WBcn
	- 'Latifolium'	CDul
	- 'Tricolor' (v)	CPMA ELan ENot EPfP LRHS SHBN SLim SPla SSpi SSta SWvt WDin WFar
	obtusifolium 'Darts Perfecta'	SLPl
	- var. ***regelianum***	SEND WFar
	ovalifolium	CBcs CCVT CChe CDoC CHll CLnd CSBt CTri ECrN EPfP GKir IHMH LBuc LRHS MAsh MBar MBri MGos MSwo NBlu NWea SLim SPer SWvt WDin WGwG WMou
§	- 'Argenteum' (v)	CBcs CDoC CDul CPLG CTri CWib EBee ECrN EHoe GKir IHMH LBuc LRHS MAsh MBar MBri NBlu NEgg SLim SPer SPla SPoG SWvt WDin WFar WTel
	- 'Aureomarginatum'	see *L. ovalifolium* 'Aureum'
§	- 'Aureum' (v) ♀H4	More than 30 suppliers
*	- 'Lemon and Lime' (v)	EMil SWvt
	- 'Taff's Indecision' (v)	CPMA
	- 'Variegatum'	see *L. ovalifolium* 'Argenteum'
	quihoui ♀H4	ECre ELan EPfP MBri SDix SLon SMad SPer SSpi WBcn WFar WHCG WPat
§	***sempervirens***	EPfP SLon SSta
	sinense	CHEx CMCN EPfP MRav WFar
	- 'Multiflorum'	CWib WFar
	- 'Pendulum'	CFil CLnd EPla
	- 'Variegatum' (v)	CPMA EPla LAst MRav SPer
	- 'Wimbei'	EPla SSpi WBcn WFar
	strongylophyllum	WFar
	texanum	see *L. japonicum* 'Texanum'
	tschonoskii	NLar SLPl
	undulatum 'Lemon Lime and Clippers'	NLar SPoG
	'Vicaryi'	CDul CMHG CPMA EBee ELan ENot EPfP EPla IArd LRHS MAsh MBar MGos NPro SDix SPer SPla WFar
	vulgare	CCVT CDul CRWN CTri CWan ECrN EPfP GKir LAst LBuc MSwo NWea SHFr SWvt WBVN WDin WMou XPep
	- 'Lodense'	MBar SLPl

Lilium ✿ (*Liliaceae*)

	from China (IX)	CLAP
	'Acapulco' (VIId)	LAma LBmB
	African Queen Group (VIa) ♀H4	CAvo EBrs ECot GBuc LAma SCoo SPer SPur WFar
	- 'African Queen' (VIa)	CSut ECri EPfP
	albanicum	see *L. pyrenaicum* subsp. *carniolicum* var. *albanicum*
	amabile (IX)	CLAP EBee LRHS WDav WWst
	- 'Luteum' (IX)	CLAP EBee LRHS WDav
	'Amber Gold' (Ic)	CLAP
	America = 'Holean' (Ia)	IBal WDav
	amoenum (IX)	EPot LAma
	'Angela North' (Ic)	CLAP
	'Apeldoorn' (Ic)	ECri LRHS
	'Aphrodite' (Ia/d)	EPot NBir
	'Apollo' (Ia) ♀H4	CBro EBrs EPot GBuc LAma LRHS MBri
	'Arena' (VIIb)	EBrs LRHS SCoo WFar
	'Ariadne' (Ic)	CLAP
*	Asiatic hybrids (VI/VII)	LAma NGdn SGar
	auratum (IX)	EFEx EPfP GBuc
	- 'Classic' (IX)	CLAP
	- 'Gold Band'	see *L. auratum* var. *platyphyllum*
§	- var. ***platyphyllum*** (IX)	ECri WDav WWst
	- Red Band Group (IX)	WFar
	- var. ***virginale*** (IX)	LAma LRHS WDav
	'Avignon' (Ia)	ECri LAma LRHS
	Backhouse hybrids (II)	CLAP EBee
	bakerianum (IX)	LAma

	- var. ***delavayi*** (IX)	LAma
	- var. ***rubrum***	LAma WDav
	'Barbara North' (Ic)	CLAP
	'Barbaresco' (VII)	SCoo
	'Barcelona' (Ia)	MNrw
	'Batist' (Ia)	ECri LAma
	'Bel Ami'	GFlt
	Bellingham Group (IV)	CLAP GBuc SSpi
	'Bergamo' (VIId)	EPfP SCoo WFar
	'Bianco Uno'	MBri
	'Black Beauty' (VIId)	CAvo CLAP EUJe GBuc LAma LBmB LRHS MSte SSpi
	'Black Bird'	IBal
	'Black Dragon' (VIa)	CHar ECri
	'Black Jack' PBR **new**	IBal
	'Blazing Dwarf' (Ia)	MBri
	bolanderi (IX)	CLAP
	'Bright Pixie'	IBal
	'Bright Star' (VIb)	ECri LAma
	'Brocade' (II)	CLAP
	'Bronwen North' (Ic)	CLAP
	brownii (IX)	EBee LAma
	- var. ***australe*** (IX) B&SWJ 4082	WCru
	'Buff Pixie' PBR (Ia)	LAma
	bulbiferum	CLAP GBuc
	- var. ***croceum*** (IX)	GIBF
	Bullwood hybrids (IV)	CLAP
	'Bums' (Ia/d)	EMon
	buschianum **new**	GIBF
	'Butter Pixie' PBR (Ia)	IBal LAma LBmB NArg WGor
	callosum var. ***luteum***	WWst
	'Cameleon'	IBal
	camtschatcense	GIBF
§	***canadense*** (IX)	EBee GBuc GGGa LAma LPio SSpi
	- var. ***coccineum*** (IX)	CLAP WWst
	- var. ***editorum*** (IX)	LAma
	- var. ***flavum***	see *L. canadense*
	'Cancum'	ECri EPot LRHS
	candidum (IX) ♀H4	CArn CAvo CBcs CBrm CBro CHar CTri EBee EBrs ECha EHrv ELan EPfP EPot EWTr GIBF IBal LAma LRHS MAvo MBri MHer NGHP SIgm SPer WBrE WCot WGwG WPnP
	- 'Plenum' (IX/d)	EMon
	- var. ***salonikae***	GIBF
	carniolicum	see *L. pyrenaicum* subsp. *carniolicum*
	'Casa Blanca' (VIIb) ♀H4	CAvo CBro CSut EBrs ECri EPfP GBuc IBal LAma MLLN SCoo SPur WFar
§	'Casa Rosa' (V)	CSWP MDKP NBir
	'Centrefold' **new**	NArg
	cernuum (IX)	CLAP EBrs GEdr LAma LBmB WCot WPrP
	chalcedonicum (IX) JCA 633.201	SBch
	'Chardonnay'	MBri
	'Chippendale' (Ic)	CLAP
	'Chris North'	CLAP
	'Cinnabar' (Ia)	ECri
	Citronella Group (Ic)	EBrs ECri LAma LRHS WFar
	columbianum (IX)	CLAP EBee GBuc GCrs GEdr NMen SSpi
	- dwarf (IX)	EPot NMen
	'Con Amore' (VIIb)	LRHS SCoo WFar
	concolor (IX)	WDav WWst
	- var. ***coridion***	WWst
	- var. ***stictum***	GIBF
	'Connecticut King' (Ia)	ECri EPfP LAma
	'Coral Butterflies'	CLAP
	'Corina' (Ia)	ECri GBuc SGar WGor
	'Côte d'Azur' (Ia)	CBro EPot GFlt LAma SRms WGor
	'Coulance' (VIId) **new**	EBrs
	'Crimson Pixie' (Ia)	CBro IBal LBmB
	x ***dalhansonii*** (IX)	CLAP WCot
§	- 'Marhan' (II)	CLAP SSpi
	'Dame Blanche' (VII)	LAma
§	***dauricum*** (IX)	GCrs GEdr
	davidii (IX)	CLAP ECri GEdr GIBF LAma LBmB SSpi WCru WDav WWst
	- var. ***unicolor***	CLAP
§	- var. ***willmottiae*** (IX)	CLAP GIBF
	debile	GIBF
	'Denia' (Ib)	IBal
	distichum	GIBF
	- B&SWJ 794	WCru
	'Doeskin' (Ic)	CLAP
	duchartrei (IX)	CLAP GBuc GCrs GEdr GFlt LAma NSla SMac SSpi WAbe WCru WDav
	- white (IX)	WDav
§	'Ed' (VII)	EPot GFlt LAma
	'Eileen North' (Ic)	CLAP
	'Electric' (Ia)	ECri
	'Elfin Sun'	LAma
	'Ellen Willmott' (II)	CLAP
	'Enchantment' (Ia)	ECri IBal LAma MBri
	'Eros'	CLAP
	'Eurydike' (Ic)	CLAP
	'Evelina'	LRHS
	'Everest' (VIId)	WDav
	'Exception' (Ib/d)	LAma
	'Fairest' (Ib-c/d)	CLAP
	'Fancy Joy'	MBri
	fargesii (IX)	LAma
	'Farolito'	MBri
	'Fata Morgana' (Ia/d) ♀H4	EPfP LRHS SCoo
	'Festival' (Ia)	LAma
	'Fire King' (Ib)	CBro CLAP CSut ECGP ECri LAma NBir SCoo WDav WFar
	formosanum (IX)	EBrs EPyc GKir IBal SEND SMac WCot WLFP
	- B&SWJ 1589	WCru
	- var. ***pricei*** (IX)	CBrm CSam EBee EBrs EDAr ELan ENot EPfP EPot ESis GEdr GGar GIBF LBee LRHS MHer MNrw NJOw NLAp NMen NWCA SBla SCoo SRot WBVN WBor WFar WGwG WHer WPer
	- 'Snow Queen' (IX)	EBee EBrs ECri MDKP
	- 'White Swan' (IX)	GBuc
	'Garden Party' (VII) ♀H4	LBmB LRHS WFar WWol
	'George Slate' (Ic/d)	CLAP
§	'Gibraltar' (Ia)	ECri
	'Golden Joy'	MBri
	'Golden Melody' (Ia)	ECri
	Golden Splendor Group (VIa) ♀H4	ECri LAma SCoo SMeo SPer SPur
	'Gran Cru' (Ia) ♀H4	EBrs ECri LAma NArg
	'Gran Paradiso' (Ia)	ECri LAma SRms
	grayi (IX)	CLAP SSpi
	'Green Magic' (VIa)	CAvo ECri
	'Hannah North' (Ic)	CLAP
	hansonii (IX)	CLAP IBlr LAma LBmB WDav
	- B&SWJ 4756	WCru
	henryi (IX) ♀H4	CAvo CLAP CSWP EBee ECho ECri EPfP EPot GIBF LAma LRHS SMeo SPur WCru WDav WPrP
	- 'Carlton Yerex'	WWst
	- var. ***citrinum***	CLAP WWst
	henryi x Pink Perfection Group	CLAP
	'Hit Parade' (VII)	LAma
	x ***hollandicum***	ECri
	'Honeymoon'	WWeb

'Hotlips'	EPfP
Imperial Silver Group (VIIc)	LAma
'Iona' (Ic)	CLAP
'Ivory Pixie' (Ia)	CBro
'Jacqueline'	EBrs WDav
§ 'Jacques S. Dijt' (II)	CLAP
japonicum (IX)	EFEx WCru
- 'Albomarginatum' (IX)	GEdr WWst
'Journey's End' (VIId)	GBuc LAma LRHS SPur
§ 'Joy' (VIIb) ♀H4	ECri LAma
'Karen North' (Ic)	CLAP
§ ***kelleyanum*** (IX)	CLAP GBuc GGGa
- NNS 98-373	WCot
kelloggii (IX)	WCot
'King Pete' (Ib) ♀H4	LBmB
'Kiss Proof' (VIIb)	LRHS
'Kiwi Fanfare'	CBrm
'Kyoto' (VIId)	LAma
'Lady Alice' (VI)	CLAP EBrs
§ ***lancifolium*** (IX)	CArn CHEx EMFP GBin GIBF LAma MOak SSpi WBrk WFar
- B&SWJ 539	WCru
* - ***album***	WBor
- Farrer's form	WCot
- var. ***flaviflorum*** (IX)	CLAP ECri GBuc MSte SSpi
- 'Flore Pleno' (IX/d)	CLAP CMil CSWP CSam EBrs EMFP EMon EPPr EUJe EVFa GAbr GBuc GCal GSki IBlr ITer LRHS NBir NSti SMrm SOkd WCot WCru WDav WFar WTin
- Forrest's form (IX)	CLAP EBrs GKir IBlr
§ - var. ***splendens*** (IX) ♀H4	CBro EBee EBrs ECho ECri EPfP LAma LRHS MWgw SPur WBor
lankongense (IX)	CLAP EBee GEdr GIBF LAma SOkd WDav WWst
'Last Dance' (Ic)	CLAP
'Le Rêve'	see *L.* 'Joy'
leichtlinii	CLAP EBrs ECri WDav
- B&SWJ 4519	WCru
- var. ***maximowiczii***	CLAP WDav WWst
'Lemon Pixie'PBR (Ia)	CSut GKir LAma
leucanthum (IX)	EPot GIBF LAma SSpi
- var. ***centifolium*** (IX)	CLAP WCru WWst
'Liberation' (I)	NBir
lijiangense **new**	GEdr WWst
'Little John'	MBri WWol
'Lollypop' (Ia)	CFwr CSut EBrs EPfP IBal LRHS MLLN MNrw SCoo
longiflorum (IX) ♀H2-3	ECri LAma LRHS SCoo SPur
- B&SWJ 4885	WCru
§ - 'Carmel'	IBal
- 'Memories'	MBri
- 'Mount Carmel'	see *L. longiflorum* 'Carmel'
§ - 'White American' (IX)	CBro CSWP EBrs EPfP LBmB LRHS SPer
- 'White Elegance'	WWol
lophophorum (IX)	EPot GIBF LAma WCru WDav
- var. ***linearifolium***	GIBF
'Lovely Girl' (VIIb)	EBrs LBmB
'Luxor' (Ib)	ECri EPfP LRHS NBir
mackliniae (IX)	CLAP EChP EPot GBuc GCal GCrs GEdr GGGa GKir GTou IBlr ITim SBla SIgm SSpi WAbe WHal
x ***maculatum*** var. ***davuricum***	see *L. dauricum*
- Japanese double (IX)	EMon
'Marco Polo' (Ia)	LAma SCoo WFar
'Marhan'	see *L.* x *dalhansonii* 'Marhan'
'Marie North' (Ic)	CLAP
martagon (IX) ♀H4	More than 30 suppliers
- var. ***album*** (IX) ♀H4	CAvo CBro CLAP CMea CNic CSWP EBrs ECGP EChP ECha EHrv ELan EPfP GBuc GEdr GFlt LAma LPio LRHS MTho NBir NChi SRms WAbe WAul WCot WShi WTin
- pink-flowered (IX)	CBos CLAP
- 'Plenum' (IX/d)	EMon
'Maxwill' (Ic)	CLAP
medeoloides (IX)	CLAP EFEx GBuc GCrs GGGa NMen SSpi WDav
'Mediterrannee' (VIIb/d)	ECri
'Menton'	ECri
michiganense (IX)	CSWP GBuc GCrs
'Milano' (Ia)	ECri
minima	GIBF
'Mirabella'	MBri
'Miss America'	NArg
'Miss Rio' (VII)	LRHS SCoo
'Mona Lisa' (VIIb/d)	EBrs EPfP EPot IBal LAma LAst LRHS MBri MTis WBVN WFar WWol
§ ***monadelphum*** (IX)	CLAP EPot ETow GBuc GCrs LAma SIgm SSpi WDav
'Mont Blanc' (Ia)	LAma NBir
'Montana'	LRHS
'Monte Negro' (Ia)	EBrs ECri IBal WDav
'Montreux' (Ia)	LAma
'Mr Ed'	see *L.* 'Ed'
'Mr Ruud'	see *L.* 'Ruud'
'Mrs R.O. Backhouse' (II)	CLAP
'Muscadet'PBR (VII)	CSut EBrs LRHS MTis WWol
§ ***nanum*** (IX)	EHyt GBuc GCrs GEdr GGGa GKev LAma NMen NSla WCru WHal
- from Bhutan (IX)	GBuc GCrs GEdr WCru
- var. ***flavidum*** (IX)	EHyt GEdr NMen WCru
- 'Len's Lilac' (IX)	WCru
nepalense (IX)	CBcs CBro CLAP CMil CSWP EBee EBla EPot EUJe GCrs GEdr GFlt GIBF GKir LAma LRHS MDun NCob NCot SBla SSpi WCot WCru WFar WLFP WPnP
- B&SWJ 2985	WCru
nobilissimum (IX)	EFEx
'Noblesse' (VII)	LRHS
'Novo Cento' ♀H4	ECri
'Odeon'	ECri
'Olivia' (Ia)	EBrs ECri LAma MLLN
Olympic Group (VIa)	ECri LAma
'Omega' (VII)	LAma
'Orange Pixie' (Ia)	CSut ECri EPfP GKir IBal LAma SCoo WGor
'Orange Triumph' (Ia)	EPfP LAma
'Orestes' (Ib)	CLAP
* Oriental Superb Group	NGdn
§ ***oxypetalum*** (IX)	GCrs GGGa
- var. ***insigne*** (IX)	CLAP EHyt EPot ETow GBin GBuc GCrs GEdr GGGa GIBF LAma NMen NSla SSpi WCru WHal
'Painted Pixie' (Ia)	IBal
'Pan' (Ic)	CLAP
papilliferum	LAma
pardalinum (IX) ♀H4	CAvo CLAP EBee EWTr GKev IBlr IFro LBmB LRHS MSte NSla WCot WCru WDav WHal WPnP WWhi
- var. ***giganteum*** (IX)	CLAP ECri EPfP MNrw WDav WTin
- subsp. ***pardalinum*** (IX) NNS 00-488 **new**	WCot
- subsp. ***shastense*** (IX)	CLAP GCrs NMen SSpi WCot
- subsp. ***shastense*** x ***vollmeri*** NNS 00-490	WCot
parryi (IX)	GBuc
parvum (IX)	GBuc
'Peach Butterflies' (Ic/d)	CLAP

	'Peach Pixie' (Ia)	CSut GFlt LAma NBir SCoo
	'Peggy North' (Ic)	CLAP
	pensylvanicum **new**	GIBF
	'Perugia' (VIId)	LAma
	Petit Pink = 'Hobozi' (Ia)	MBri
	'Petit Pintura'	MBri
	philippinense (IX)	CBrm CFwr EBee EWin SIgm
	- B&SWJ 4000	WCru
	Pink Perfection Group (VIa) ♀H4	CAvo CBro CSut ECri EPfP LAma SBch SCoo SPer SPur WFar
	'Pink Pixie'PBR (Ia)	CSut ECri GFlt IBal SGar
	'Pink Tiger' (Ib)	CLAP ECri LRHS WGor
	pitkinense (IX)	SOkd WWst
	pomponium (IX)	GCal
	primulinum (IX)	WWst
	- var. ***ochraceum***	CLAP LAma WWst
§	***pumilum*** (IX) ♀H4	CBro CLAP EBee EBrs ECri EPot GBuc GCal GEdr GIBF LAma LRHS MLLN MSte MTho WAul WCru WDav WPrP
	- 'Golden Gleam' (IX)	WWst
	pyrenaicum (IX)	CBro CLAP EBee IBlr IFro LPio LTwo WCot WDav WPGP WRha WShi
§	- subsp. ***carniolicum*** (IX)	NSla SSpi
§	- - var. ***albanicum*** (IX)	CLAP EBee SSpi
§	- subsp. ***pyrenaicum*** var. ***pyrenaicum*** (IX)	CLAP
	- - var. ***rubrum*** (IX)	CLAP SSpi WCot
	'Quinta'PBR	MBri
	'Raspberry Butterflies' (Ic/d)	CLAP
	'Red Carpet' (Ia)	ECri LRHS NBir WGor
	'Red Dwarf' (Ia)	CSut IBal
	Red Jewels Group (Ic)	LAma
	'Red Night' (I)	EGoo LRHS
	'Red Rum'	MBri
	'Red Star'	EBrs
	'Red Tiger' (Ib)	CLAP
	'Red Velvet' (Ib)	CLAP
	'Red Wine'	MBri
	regale (IX) ♀H4	More than 30 suppliers
	- 'Album' (IX)	CAvo CSWP EBee EBrs ECri LAma LRHS SCoo SGar SPur WFar
§	- 'Royal Gold' (IX)	ECri EPfP MWgw WDav
	'Reinesse' (Ia)	IBal MBri
	'Rina's Twinkle' **new**	EBrs
	'Roma' (Ia)	LAma LRHS NBir
	'Rosefire' (Ia)	ECri
	'Rosemary North' (I)	CLAP
	Rosepoint Lace Group (Ic)	CLAP
	'Rosita' (Ia)	ECri NArg WFar
	rosthornii	CLAP SSpi WCot WCru
	'Rosy Joy'	MBri
	'Royal Gold'	see *L. regale* 'Royal Gold'
	rubellum (IX)	EFEx GBuc
§	'Ruud' (VII)	EPfP EPot LAma LRHS
	sachalinense	EKen GIBF WWst
	- Brown 0235	CStu
	'Salmon Twinkle' **new**	EBrs
	'Sam' (VII) ♀H4	EPfP EPot GBuc LAma LRHS
	sargentiae (IX)	CLAP ECri GCrs GGGa NMen WCot WCru
	'Scentwood' (IV)	CLAP
	sempervivoideum (IX)	LAma WDav
	'Serrada'PBR	MBri
	shastense	see *L. kelleyanum*
	'Showbiz' (VIII)	LAma
	'Shuksan' (IV)	CLAP
	'Silly Girl' (Ia)	ECri NArg
	'Snow Crystal' (I)	EPfP IBal
	'Snow Princess'	LAma
	'Spark' **new**	NArg
	speciosum (IX)	NSla
	- B&SWJ 4847	WCru
	- var. ***album*** (IX)	ECri GBuc LAma LRHS NBir SBch
	- var. ***gloriosoides*** (IX)	EPot LAma SSpi
	- var. ***roseum*** (IX)	GBuc
	- var. ***rubrum*** (IX)	CAvo CHar CLAP EBee EBrs ECha ECri GBuc GFlt LAma LRHS MLLN NBir SPur WPrP
§	- 'Uchida' (IX)	ECri WDav
	'Staccato' (Ia)	ECri
	'Star Gazer' (VIIc)	CBro CSut EBrs ECot ECri IBal LAma LAst LRHS SCoo SPer WFar WGor
	'Starfighter' (VIId)	EBrs IBal LRHS
	'Sterling Star' (Ia)	CLAP ECri EPfP LAma NArg
	stewartianum (IX)	LAma
	sulphureum	LAma
	'Sun Ray' (Ia)	LRHS
	superbum (IX)	CDes CLAP EBee LAma WCru WDav
	'Sutton Court' (II)	CLAP
	'Sweet Surrender' (I)	ECri LRHS
	szovitsianum	see *L. monadelphum*
	taliense (IX)	GEdr GIBF LAma WCru
	tenuifolium	see *L. pumilum*
	x ***testaceum*** (IX) ♀H4	LAma
	'Theseus' (Ic)	CLAP
	'Tiger White' (Ic)	CLAP
	tigrinum	see *L. lancifolium*
	'Time Out'PBR	WWol
	'Tinkerbell' (Ic)	CLAP
	tsingtauense (IX)	CLAP GIBF WDav
	- B&SWJ 519	WCru
	'Turandot'PBR	MBri
	'Uchida Kanoka'	see *L. speciosum* 'Uchida'
	'Viva' (Ic)	CLAP
	vollmeri (IX)	CLAP EBee GCrs NMen SSpi WCru
	wallichianum (IX)	EBee EPot LAma
	wardii (IX)	WWst
	'White American'	see *L. longiflorum* 'White American'
	'White Butterflies' (Ic/d)	CLAP
	'White Happiness' (Ia)	LAma
	'White Henryi' (VId)	CLAP
	'White Kiss' (Ia/d)	LAma LRHS
I	'White Lace' (Ic/d)	CLAP
	'White Paradise' (V)	SCoo
	'White Pixie'	see *L.* 'Snow Crystal'
	'White Tiger' (Ib)	CLAP
	wigginsii (IX)	CLAP EBee GCrs GGGa SSpi
	willmottiae	see *L. davidii* var. *willmottiae*
	wilsonii **new**	WWst
	xanthellum var. ***luteum***	GEdr WWst
	Yellow Blaze Group (Ia)	EPfP LAma
	'Yellow Bunting' (I)	WWst
	'Yellow Star' (Ib)	LRHS

lime see *Citrus aurantiifolia*

lime, djeruk see *Citrus amblycarpa*

lime, Philippine see x *Citrofortunella microcarpa*

Limnanthes (*Limnanthaceae*)

douglasii ♀H4	CArn CHrt EPfP LRav SIde WWpP
- subsp. ***nivea*** **new**	CSpe

Limnophila (*Scrophulariaceae*)

aromatica	MSal

Limoniastrum (*Plumbaginaceae*)

monopetalum	XPep

Limonium (*Plumbaginaceae*)

bellidifolium	EBee ECha EDAr ESis NJOw SBla SOkd WEas WHoo WPer WTin XPep
- 'Dazzling Blue'	EChP
binervosum	EBee
chilwellii **new**	EBee EMan MSte
cosyrense	CMea CStu MHer NMen WPer
dumosum	see *Goniolimon tataricum* var. *angustifolium*
gmelinii	MLLN SPlb WPer
* - subsp. ***hungaricum***	EWTr NLar
- 'Perestrojka'	EBee
gougetianum	ETow WPer
latifolium	see *L. platyphyllum*
minutum	CNic NJOw SPoG
perezii	EDAr EShb NBre WPer
§ ***platyphyllum***	More than 30 suppliers
- 'Robert Butler'	EBee ECGP EMan GCal LRHS MRav MSte
- 'Violetta'	CTri EBee ECGP ECha ELan EMan EPPr EPfP ERou EVFa GKir LAst LRHS MBri MMHG MRav MTis NCGa NLar SPer WHoo
pruinosum	XPep
speciosum	see *Goniolimon incanum*
'Stardust'	NBre
tataricum	see *Goniolimon tataricum*
vulgare	WBWf WHer XPep

Linanthastrum see *Linanthus*

Linanthus (*Polemoniaceae*)

nuttallii subsp. ***floribundus***	CPBP

Linaria (*Scrophulariaceae*)

aeruginea	CSpe EChP
- subsp. ***nevadensis*** 'Gemstones'	LRHS
alpina	CMea CSpe ECtt GGar GTou MTho SRms WEas WPer
- SDR 3573	GKev
'Anstey'	CElw
anticaria 'Antique Silver'	CHea EBee ECha EMan GBBs GBuc LAst LRHS LSou MGGn MRav NEgg NLar SBch SSvw WPGP WWeb
Blue Lace = 'Yalin'	EBee LAst LSou NPri SMrm SPoG
capraria	CPBP
cymbalaria	see *Cymbalaria muralis*
§ ***dalmatica***	CSpe EBee EChP ECha ELan ERou GBBs GFlt LPhx MFOX MHar MWhi NBid NBro NChi NPri SChu SHGN WCAu WCFE WCot WKif WMoo WPer
x ***dominii*** 'Carnforth'	CPom ECGP EHan LSou NBro SBch WCot WWpP
- 'Yuppie Surprise'	CHid EBee ECGP EChP ECtt EMan EMon LAst LDai NBir NDov NGdn SWvt WCot WCra WPGP
genistifolia	ECtt MDKP SBch
- subsp. ***dalmatica***	see *L. dalmatica*
'Globosa Alba'	see *Cymbalaria muralis* 'Globosa Alba'
hepaticifolia	see *Cymbalaria hepaticifolia*
japonica	GIBF WCot WOut
- Brown 0236	CStu
* ***lobata alba***	SPlb
'Natalie'	SBla
origanifolia	see *Chaenorhinum origanifolium*
pallida	see *Cymbalaria pallida*
pilosa	see *Cymbalaria pilosa*
purpurea	COIW EHrv ELan EPfP MChe MHer MWgw NBPC NBro NLon NPer NPri SRms WCAu WMoo WPer WWye
- 'Alba'	see *L. purpurea* 'Springside White'
- 'Canon Went'	More than 30 suppliers
- 'Charlton White'	CNat
- 'Cotton Candy' **new**	WHil
- pink	MBow
- 'Radcliffe Innocence'	see *L. purpurea* 'Springside White'
§ - 'Springside White'	CElw COIW EBee ECha ECtt EMan GBuc LPhx MAnH MBow MSte NBid NBir NLsd NPri SBla SSvw SUsu WCAu WMoo WPer WRha WWpP
- 'Thurgarton Beauty'	MDKP
- 'Vainglorious'	CNat
repens	CPom MNrw WBWf WCot WHer
reticulata 'Red Velvet' **new**	CSpe
'Toni Aldiss'	CSpe LPhx
triornithophora	CBot CFir CSec CSpe EBee ECha EMan GBuc IGor MFOX MNFA MWrn NJOw NLsd WMoo WPer WRha WWye
- 'Pink Budgies' **new**	LSou
- purple	ELan MHar STes WMoo
vulgaris	CArn EHan ELau GWCH LDai MBow MChe MDKP MHer NMir NPri SECG WHer WJek WLHH
- hemipeloric	CNat
- 'Peloria'	CNat EBee EMon MDKP WCot
'Winifrid's Delight'	CHea EBee EPfP

Lindelofia (*Boraginaceae*)

§ ***anchusoides*** (Lindl.) Lehm.	CStr EPPr GBri NBid
anchusoides misapplied	see *L. longiflora*
§ ***longiflora***	CFir EMan GBin GBuc GCal GCra LRHS MLLN NLar WPGP WPer

Lindera (*Lauraceae*)

aggregata	CBcs
angustifolia	CFil
benzoin	CBcs CMCN CPLG EPfP GIBF MBri MSal NLar SSpi WDin
communis	CFil WPGP
erythrocarpa	CBcs CMCN EPfP NLar SSpi
- B&SWJ 6271	WCru
megaphylla	CBcs CFil CHEx
obtusiloba ♀H4	CAbP CFil CPne EPfP IArd LRHS NLar SBrw SSpi WNor
- var. ***heterophylla*** **new**	ISea
praecox	EPfP WPGP
praetermissa	CFil EPfP
reflexa	CBcs CMCN EPfP NLar WPGP
strychnifolia	CMCN EPfP
umbellata	WCru
var. ***membranaceae*** B&SWJ 6227	

Lindernia (*Scrophulariaceae*)

grandiflora blue	ECou

Linnaea (*Caprifoliaceae*)

borealis	CStu ILis MHar WAbe
- subsp. ***americana***	NWCA

Linum ✿ (*Linaceae*)

alpinum **new**	SHGN
arboreum ♀H4	SBla SIgm WKif WPat
- NS 529	NWCA

Plant	Suppliers
capitatum	EBee NMen NSla WLin
dolomiticum	WPat
flavum	CTri EPfP GTou XPep
- 'Compactum'	GAbr NPri SBla SRms WCot WHrl WRHF
'Gemmell's Hybrid' ♀H4	CLyd CMea EPot EWes LRHS MDKP NBir NMen NRya NWCA SBla WAbe WLin WPat
kingii var. ***sedoides***	LTwo WLin
leonii	LRHS WKif
monogynum	CDes ECou WPGP
§ - var. ***diffusum***	ECou
- dwarf	GTou
- 'Nelson'	see *L. monogynum* var. *diffusum*
mucronatum subsp. ***armenum*** **new**	WLin
narbonense	CSam CSpe ECGP LDai LGro LPhx LRHS NCGa NLar NOak SBch SIgm SMrm SRms WHoo
- 'Heavenly Blue'	ERou
§ ***perenne***	CArn CRWN CTri EBee EChP ECha ELan EPfP ERou GKir GMaP IFro LRHS MChe MHer MWgw NFor NLsd NMir SECG SIde SPer SRms SUsu WCAu WPer XPep
- 'Album'	ECha ELan EPfP ERou MNFA NLar SPer SUsu WCAu WPer
- subsp. ***alpinum*** 'Alice Blue'	CPBP LBee SBla
§ - 'Blau Saphir'	CBgR CBod CTri EBee ECtt EShb LAst LRHS MLLN MRav MWat NCGa NLar NPri SRms WRHF WWeb
- Blue Sapphire	see *L. perenne* 'Blau Saphir'
- 'Diamant'	CBod EBee ECtt EWin LRHS NPri
- 'Himmelszelt'	NLar SMrm
- subsp. ***lewisii***	NBir SMrm
- 'Nanum Diamond'	EShb NLar
- 'White Diamond'	NCob NPri
rubrum	MChe
sibiricum	see *L. perenne*
spathulatum	EHyt
suffruticosum	CPBP
- subsp. ***salsoloides*** 'Nanum'	CStu EHyt NWCA SBla WPat
- - 'Prostratum'	GBuc SIgm
usitatissimum	CRWN MHer SIde

Liparis (*Orchidaceae*)

Plant	Suppliers
coelogynoides	ECou
cordifolia	EFEx
fujisanensis	EFEx
krameri var. ***krameri***	EFEx
kumokiri	EFEx
makinoana	EFEx
nigra	EFEx
sootenzanensis	EFEx

Lippia (*Verbenaceae*)

Plant	Suppliers
alba	MSal
canescens	see *Phyla nodiflora* var. *canescens*
chamaedrifolia	see *Verbena peruviana*
citriodora	see *Aloysia triphylla*
dulcis	CArn CFir EOHP EUnu ILis LRav MSal
nodiflora	see *Phyla nodiflora*
repens	see *Phyla nodiflora*

Liquidambar ✿ (*Hamamelidaceae*)

Plant	Suppliers
acalycina	CPMA EBee EPfP LRHS MBlu MGos NLar SBir SIFN SSpi SSta WNor WPGP WPat
formosana	CEnd CMCN CPle EBee ECrN EPfP IMGH MBlu MGos SBir SPer SSta WNor WPGP
- B&SWJ 6855	WCru
- Monticola Group	CPMA EPfP SBir SIFN SSta
orientalis	CMCN CPMA EPfP SBir SSta
styraciflua	More than 30 suppliers
- 'Andrew Hewson'	CLnd CPMA LRHS MAsh MBri SBir SSpi SSta
- 'Anja'	CPMA MBlu SBir SSta
- 'Anneke'	CPMA LRHS SBir SSta
* - 'Argentea'	CLnd
- 'Aurea'	see *L. styraciflua* 'Variegata'
- 'Aurea Variegata'	see *L. styraciflua* 'Variegata'
- 'Aurora'	CPMA MAsh SBir SCoo SLim
- 'Burgundy'	CLnd CPMA CTho MAsh SBir SSta WPat
- 'Fastigiata'	MBlu
- 'Festeri'	CDul CEnd SBir SSta WPat
- 'Festival'	CPMA MBlu SBLw SSta
- 'Globe'	CPMA
- 'Golden Treasure' (v)	CMCN CPMA LRHS MAsh NLar SMad SSpi WPat
- 'Gum Ball'	CEnd CLnd CMCN CPMA EPfP EWes LTwo MAsh MGos NLar SBir SMad SSta WPat
- 'Happidaze'	CEnd MAsh WPat
- 'Happy Days' **new**	NLar
- 'Jennifer Carol'	CPMA
- 'Kia'	CEnd CPMA MAsh SBir WPat
- 'Kirsten'	CPMA NLar
- 'Lane Roberts' ♀H4	CDoC CDul CLnd CMCN CTho EPfP LRHS MAsh MBlu MBri MGos NEgg NLar SBir SLim SMad SPoG SReu SSta WDin WPGP WPat
- 'Manon' (v)	CDoC CEnd CPMA SBir SLim
- 'Midwest Sunset'	WPGP WPat
- 'Moonbeam' (v)	CEnd CMCN CPMA CTho MAsh NLar SBir SCoo SLim SSta WPat
- 'Moraine'	CMCN CPMA SBLw
- 'Naree'	CMCN CPMA NLar SBir
- 'Oconee'	CEnd MAsh WPat
- 'Paarl'	CMCN CPMA
- 'Palo Alto'	CEnd CPMA LTwo MAsh MBri SBLw SBir SMad SSta WPGP WPat
- 'Parasol'	CEnd CPMA SBir SSta
- 'Pendula'	CLnd CMCN CPMA LRHS SBir SSta
- 'Penwood'	CPMA SSpi SSta
- 'Rotundiloba'	CMCN CPMA EPfP SBir SSpi SSta WPat
- 'Silver King' (v)	CDul CMCN CPMA ECrN EHoe EPfP IMGH LRHS MBlu MGos MWya SCoo SLim SPer SPoG SSta WPat
- 'Stared'	CLnd CPMA SBir WPGP WPat
- 'Stella'	CLnd MAsh WPat
- 'Thea'	CPMA LRHS MBlu SBir SSta
§ - 'Variegata' Overeynder (v)	CBcs CBot CLnd COtt CPMA CTho ELan EPfP LRHS MAsh MBlu MDun MGos NBee NEgg SHBN SLim SPer SSpi SSta WDin WPat
- 'Worplesdon' ♀H4	More than 30 suppliers

Liriodendron ✿ (*Magnoliaceae*)

Plant	Suppliers
chinense	CBcs CDul CMCN CTho EPfP MBlu SSpi WFar WPGP
'T. Jackson'	NLar
tulipifera ♀H4	More than 30 suppliers
- 'Ardis'	CMCN SSpi
- 'Arnold'	CMCN
- 'Aureomarginatum' (v) ♀H4	More than 30 suppliers
- 'Aureum'	CMCN
- 'Crispum'	CMCN

- 'Fastigiatum'	CBcs CDoC CDul CEnd CLnd CMCN COtt CTho EBee ECrN ELan ENot EPfP IArd IMGH LRHS MBlu MBri MGos NPal SBLw SPer SSpi SSta WOrn
- 'Glen Gold'	CEnd CMCN MBlu MGos NLar SMad
- 'Mediopictum' (v)	CMCN CTho
- 'Roodhaan' **new**	NLar

Liriope ✿ (*Convallariaceae*)

'Big Blue'	see *L. muscari* 'Big Blue'
§ ***exiliflora***	CEnd CLAP EBee EMan GCal NLar WCAu WFar
§ - 'Ariaka-janshige' (v)	EMan
§ ***gigantea***	CLAP GSki
graminifolia misapplied	see *L. muscari*
hyacinthifolia	see *Reineckea carnea*
kansuensis	ERos
koreana	EVFa GCal
- B&SWJ 8821	WCru
'Majestic'	CBct EBee ERou GSki MBri SPla WFar
§ ***muscari*** ♀H4	More than 30 suppliers
- B&SWJ 561	WCru
- 'Alba'	see *L. muscari* 'Monroe White'
§ - 'Big Blue'	CBct CBrm CKno CLAP CM&M COIW CPrp EBee EMan ENot EPfP EWll GSki LRHS MRav NArg NLar SGSe SWvt WCAu WCFE WMoo
- 'Christmas Tree'	CBct CPrp SGSe
- 'Evergreen Giant'	see *L. gigantea*
- 'Gold-banded' (v)	CPrp EBee ECrN EMan ENot EPfP GCal LRHS SGSe SHBN WFar
- 'Ingwersen'	CPrp EBee EDAr ENot MSph SMeo
- 'John Burch' (v)	CBct CLAP CPrp EBee EMan EVFa MBNS MCCP NLar
- 'Lilac Beauty'	CPne
- 'Majestic' misapplied	see *L. exiliflora*
§ - 'Monroe White'	CBro CEnd CLAP CPne CPrp EBee EBrs EChP ECha ECtt EHrv ENot EPfP ERou GAbr GCal GSki LAst LEdu LRHS MRav NGdn NLar SGSe SMac SPla WAul WCra WFar
- 'Okina' (v)	EMon WCot
- 'Paul Aden'	CFil EPfP WPGP
- 'Royal Purple'	CBct CBrm CLAP CPrp EBee EMan ENot EPfP GBin GSki NBPC NGdn NLar NOrc SPla WLeb
- 'Silver Ribbon'	CAlb CLAP CPrp EBee EMan EPfP EShb GSki NSti SGSe SMad WPGP
- 'Silver Shadow'	SMad
- 'Silvery Midget' (v)	CPrp SUsu WMoo
- 'Superba'	WCot
§ - 'Variegata' (v)	More than 30 suppliers
* - 'Variegated Alba' (v)	CBcs CFir
- 'Webster Wideleaf'	EBee GSki MSph WCot
'New Wonder'	EHrv
platyphylla	see *L. muscari*
'Samantha'	CBct CPrp ECha LRHS SGSe
§ ***spicata***	CBro EBee ERos LPio SSpi WAul WWeb
- 'Alba'	EBee EBrs GCal MTho WTin
§ - 'Gin-ryu' (v)	CBct CCge CElw CFir CLAP COIW EBee ECrN ENot EPPr EUJe EVFa EWes GSki LEdu LPio LSRN MCCP MRav MSte SLPl WCFE WCot WPGP
- 'Silver Dragon'	see *L. spicata* 'Gin-ryu'
- 'Small Green'	EBee

Lisianthius (*Gentianaceae*)

russelianus	see *Eustoma grandiflorum*

Listera (*Orchidaceae*)

ovata	WHer

Lithocarpus ✿ (*Fagaceae*)

densiflorus	WCot
var. ***echinoides*** NNS 00-504	
edulis	CBcs CHEx SArc WPGP
pachyphyllus	CBcs

Lithodora (*Boraginaceae*)

§ ***diffusa***	SGar SRot
- 'Alba'	EMil EPfP GKir LBee LRHS MGos NLAp NWCA SGar SPer SPoG WFar
- 'Cambridge Blue'	LRHS SLdr SPer
- 'Compacta'	CLyd EWes NWCA WAbe
- 'Grace Ward' ♀H4	GKev MGos MWya SBod WAbe WPat
- 'Heavenly Blue' ♀H4	More than 30 suppliers
- 'Inverleith'	EWes WFar
- 'Pete's Favourite'	WAbe
- 'Picos'	CMea CNic EDAr EPot GCrs GKev GTou NMen SIgm WAbe WPat
- 'Star' PBR	CBcs CLyd CMHG EPfP GKir LRHS NLar SBod SCoo SIng SPer SPoG SRot
fruticosa	CArn XPep
graminifolia	see *Moltkia suffruticosa*
hispidula	SAga WAbe
x ***intermedia***	see *Moltkia* x *intermedia*
§ ***oleifolia*** ♀H4	EPot MWat NBir NMen NSla SBla WPat
rosmarinifolia	CSpe EHyt GKir LRHS
zahnii	CLyd EPot SIgm WPat

Lithophragma (*Saxifragaceae*)

parviflorum	CDes CMea CPom EBee EHyt EMan EMon GFlt MSte MTho NBir NRya NWCA WCru WFar WPnP

Lithospermum (*Boraginaceae*)

diffusum	see *Lithodora diffusa*
doerfleri	see *Moltkia doerfleri*
erythrorhizon	CPLG MSal WWye
officinale	CArn GBar GPoy MSal NMir
oleifolium	see *Lithodora oleifolia*
purpureocaeruleum	see *Buglossoides purpurocaerulea*

Litsea (*Lauraceae*)

glauca	see *Neolitsea sericea*

Littonia (*Colchicaceae*)

modesta	CRHN EShb ITer

Livistona (*Arecaceae*)

australis	CBrP CRoM CTrC EAmu WMul
chinensis ♀H1	CBrP CPHo CRoM CTbh EAmu EExo EUJe LPJP SAin SBig WMul
decipiens	CPHo CRoM CTrC WMul
nitida **new**	CKob

Lloydia (*Liliaceae*)

yunnanensis	EPot GKir

Loasa (*Loasaceae*)

RCB/Arg CC-1 **new**	WCot
triphylla var. ***volcanica***	EMan EWes GCal WSHC

Lobelia (*Campanulaceae*)

B&SWJ 8220 from Vietnam **new**	WCru

	Name	Suppliers
	RCB/Arg S-4	WCot
	'Alice'	MSph WCot WDyG WFar
	anatina	CFir LRHS WDyG
	angulata	see *Pratia angulata*
	'Bees' Flame'	CFir CPrp EBee EMan EMar EPza ERou EShb EVFa MLLN MRav MSte MWgw SChu SVil
	Big Blue = 'Weslobigblue'PBR	EShb LAst LSou
	Blue Star = 'Wesstar'PBR	ECtt LAst
	bridgesii	CFil CPLG CPle CSpe EChP EMan EShb GBin GCal GGar GMac IFro WPGP
	'Butterfly Blue'	CBcs EBee EChP GBuc MTis NEgg SPla
	'Butterfly Rose'	EBee GBuc SRot WCHb
	cardinalis ♀H3	More than 30 suppliers
	- subsp. ***graminea*** var. ***multiflora***	CFir
	'Cherry Ripe'	EBee EMag EMan EPfP LRHS SMrm WCHb WEas WMoo
	'Cinnabar Deep Red'	see *L.* 'Fan Tiefrot'
	'Cinnabar Rose'	see *L.* 'Fan Zinnoberrosa'
	'Complexion'	LRHS
	Compliment Blue	see *L.* 'Kompliment Blau'
	Compliment Deep Red	see *L.* 'Kompliment Tiefrot'
	Compliment Purple	see *L.* 'Kompliment Purpur'
	Compliment Scarlet	see *L.* 'Kompliment Scharlach'
	coronopifolia	EShb
	'Cranberry Crown' **new**	NRnb
	'Cranberry Crush' **new**	NRnb
	'Dark Crusader'	CPrp EBee ECtt ELan EMan EMar EPza LRHS MWgw NGdn SChu SMrm SPla WCHb WEas WMnd WSan
	dortmanna	EMFW
	erinus 'Kathleen Mallard' (d)	ECtt LAst SWvt WBVN
	- 'Richardii'	see *L. richardsonii*
	'Eulalia Berridge'	CSam EBee EChP GBuc IGor SAga SMrm WCru WDyG WFar WMoo WSHC
	excelsa	CPle EShb LSou MAvo NCGa NRnb SIgm SPav SPoG WFar WKif WPic
	'Fan Burgundy' **new**	CBrm
	Fan Deep Red	see *L.* 'Fan Tiefrot'
	'Fan Deep Rose'	see *L.* 'Fan Orchidrosa'
§	'Fan Orchidrosa' ♀H3-4	EShb EVFa NGdn SRot
	'Fan Scharlach' ♀H3-4	EShb IBal NBlu NCGa NLar SBch SGar SRot SWvt WDyG WPop
§	'Fan Tiefrot' ♀H3-4	CBos CBrm CDWL ERou GBuc MWgw NCGa NGdn SBla SHel SMHy SRms SSpi SWvt WCHb WPer
§	'Fan Zinnoberrosa' ♀H3-4	CBcs CBrm CFir CM&M ERou LAst LRHS MFOX MHar NArg SRms SRot SWvt WCHb WMoo WPer WPop WWlt
	'Flamingo'	see *L.* 'Pink Flamingo'
	fulgens	CPne EPfP IHMH LNCo NBlu NPer WEas WFar
§	- 'Elmfeuer'	CAby CFai CMHG EBee EChP ERou EShb EWin MSte NLar SMrm SPlb SWvt WFar
	- 'Illumination'	GBuc
	- Saint Elmo's Fire	see *L. fulgens* 'Elmfeuer'
	x ***gerardii***	CSam EBee EWll SMar WBor WMoo WSHC
	- 'Eastgrove Pink'	WEas
	- 'Hadspen Purple'PBR	CFwr CHad CPen EBee IPot LSRN MBri MCCP NCGa SMeo SPoG
	- 'Rosencavalier'	CBre EBee EMar LRHS MMil WFar
§	- 'Vedrariensis'	More than 30 suppliers
	gibberoa	CHEx
	'Grape Knee-High'	EBee LSRN LSou NCGa NRnb SPoG SRkn
	'Hadspen Purple'PBR	see *L.* x *gerardii* 'Hadspen Purple'
	inflata	CArn GPoy MSal NLsd WCHb
	'Jack McMaster'	SUsu
	kalmii	CFwr WPop
	- 'Blue Shadow' **new**	MNrw WPtf
	'Kimbridge Beet'	CMac
§	'Kompliment Blau'	CFir ERou LRHS NArg SWvt WPer
§	'Kompliment Purpur'	ERou MNrw SWvt
§	'Kompliment Scharlach' ♀H3-4	CBcs CSWP EBee EPfP ERou LRHS MBNS MNrw MWat NPer SSpi SWvt WCHb WFar WMnd WPer
§	'Kompliment Tiefrot'	ERou MNrw MWat NArg SWvt WAul WPer
	laxiflora	CBot EGra MTho SAga SIgm SPet
	- B&SWJ 9064	WCru
	- var. ***angustifolia***	CHEx CPrp CSam CSec EMan ENot ERea EShb GCal MDKP MOak MSte SDnm SHFr SMrm SPav SPoG SRms SUsu WPrP WWye XPep
	lindblomii	CFee CStu GSki WGwG
	linnaeoides	EMan SPlb WEas
	'Lipstick'	WWlt
	longifolia from Chile	CFee
§	***lutea***	LRHS LRav
	'Martha'	EBee
	'Monet Moment'	EBee ERou IPot LSou NCGa NRnb
	'Pauline' **new**	ECtt
	pedunculata	see *Pratia pedunculata*
	perpusilla	see *Pratia perpusilla*
	'Pink Elephant' ♀H4	CHar CSWP EBee GCra IGor MDKP SBla SChu SHar WFar WPGP WRha WWeb
§	'Pink Flamingo'	CM&M EBee EBrs EVFa LRHS MTis SOkh WCHb WFar WSHC WShi WWye
	polyphylla	EKen EShb GBBs GFlt MHar NCGa NRnb SIgm WPic
	preslii	CPBP
	puberula	CFir
	'Purple Towers'	EBee EVFa
	'Queen Victoria' ♀H3	More than 30 suppliers
	'Red Chester'	CWCL
	regalis	WCHb WHal
§	***richardsonii*** ♀H1+3	ECtt LAst LIck SWvt
	'Rosenkavalier'	CFwr CPen
	'Royal Purple'	SUsu
	'Ruby Slippers'	CBcs CFai CWCL EBee ECtt ELan EMan IPot LAst LSRN MTis NCGa NLar SPoG SUsu WCra WFar
N	'Russian Princess' misapplied, purple-flowered	More than 30 suppliers
	seguinii B&SWJ 7065 **new**	WCru
	sessilifolia	CPLG CSec CWat EBee GBuc GCal LPBA MWrn NEgg WBVN WCot WOut WPer WWye
	- B&L 12396	EMon
	siphilitica	More than 30 suppliers
	- 'Alba'	CSam EBee EPfP EWTr LPBA LRHS MLLN NRnb SPav SRms SWvt WCHb WFar WHoo WHrl WMoo WPGP WPer WPop WSan WWpP WWye
	- blue-flowered	NLar NLsd SWvt WSan
	- 'Rosea'	MNrw
	'Sparkle DeVine'	WCot WFar
	x ***speciosa***	GMac WFar
	- dark	CMHG EBee
	- purple-flowered **new**	EWin

- red-flowered **new**	EWin
'Tania'	More than 30 suppliers
tomentosa **new**	EShb
treadwellii	see *Pratia angulata* 'Treadwellii'
Tresahor Series	CHEx
tupa	More than 30 suppliers
- JCA 12527	LAst MBnl WCot
- Archibald's form	CPLG NRnb
- dark orange	SMrm
urens	CFil SSpi WBWf WPGP
valida	CFwr CPBP CSpe EMan EWin NArg SGar SPet SWvt
vedrariensis	see *L.* x *gerardii* 'Vedrariensis'
'Wildwood Splendour'	WFar
'Will Scarlet'	EWin LRHS
'Zinnoberrosa'	see *L.* 'Fan Zinnoberrosa'

Lobularia (*Brassicaceae*)

maritima	XPep

Loeselia (*Polemoniaceae*)

mexicana	CHll

loganberry see *Rubus* x *loganobaccus*

Loiseleuria (*Ericaceae*)

procumbens from Japan	GCrs WAbe

Lomandra (*Lomandraceae*)

confertifolia **new**	ECou
hystrix	EBee WCot
'Little Con' **new**	CBcs
'Little Pal' **new**	CBcs
longifolia	ECou GCal SPlb WCot
- 'Kulnura' **new**	ECou
- 'Orfond' **new**	ECou

Lomaria see *Blechnum*

Lomatia (*Proteaceae*)

ferruginea	CAbb CBcs CDoC CFil CHEx EPfP ISea SAPC SArc SBrw SSpi WCru
fraseri	EPfP SSpi WPGP
hirsuta	CFil
longifolia	see *L. myricoides*
§ ***myricoides***	CAbb CBcs CDoC CFil CHEx CPSs CTrw EPfP LRHS SAPC SArc SLon SPoG SSpi WPGP
silaifolia	CDoC EPfP
§ ***tinctoria***	CDoC CPSs CTrC CTrw EPfP IDee LRHS NLar SArc SSpi

Lomatium (*Apiaceae*)

dissectum	EBee
grayi	EMan SIgm
- NNS 00-522	EPPr
hallii	SIgm
- NNS 00-526	SIgm
utriculatum	MSal

Lonicera ✿ (*Caprifoliaceae*)

B&SWJ 2654 from Sikkim	WCru
from China	WCru
KR 291	EPla
PC&H 17A	SBra
§ ***acuminata***	CPLN GIBF IArd LAst LEdu LRHS SLim WGwG WPnP WSHC
- B&SWJ 3480	WCru
alberti	CFai GBin MBNS MRav SLon WGwG WHCG WSHC
albiflora	WSHC
- var. ***albiflora***	SBra
alpigena	GIBF
alseuosmoides	CFil CPLN CTrC GBin IArd SAga SBra SLon WBcn WCru WPGP WSHC WWeb
x ***americana*** misapplied	see *L.* x *italica*
§ x ***americana*** (Miller) K. Koch	CBcs CHad CRHN EPfP LAst LFol LRHS MAsh MGos NBea NPer NWea SBra SEND SGar SLPl SLim SPla SReu SSta WMoo
x ***brownii***	CMac
§ - 'Dropmore Scarlet'	More than 30 suppliers
- 'Fuchsioides' misapplied	see *L.* x *brownii* 'Dropmore Scarlet'
- 'Fuchsioides' Hort.	ECrN NSti WSHC
caerulea	CMCN MRav STre WHCG
- var. ***edulis***	CAgr GIBF LEdu
- f. ***emphyllocalyx***	WBcn
- subsp. ***kamtschatica***	CAgr CMCN NLar
calcarata **new**	CPLN
§ ***caprifolium*** 🏆H4	CBcs CDoC CRHN ECtt ELan EPfP LBuc LRHS MAsh MBar MLan NBea SBra SHBN WCot
- 'Anna Fletcher'	CRHN CSPN MBNS NHaw SBra SCoo SLim WCFE
- 'Inga'	SBra
- f. ***pauciflora***	see *L.* x *italica*
chaetocarpa	CMHG CPle WBcn WPat
chamissoi	GIBF NLar
§ ***chrysantha***	CMCN GIBF
ciliosa	CBrm
'Clavey's Dwarf'	see *L.* x *xylosteoides* 'Clavey's Dwarf'
deflexicalyx	EPfP GIBF NLar
demissa	GIBF
'Early Cream'	see *L. caprifolium*
elisae	EPfP NLar WPat
etrusca	GIBF LAst MRav SHel WWeb XPep
- 'Donald Waterer' 🏆H4	CBgR CRHN EPfP LRHS MAsh SBra SCoo SPla WFar WGor
- 'Michael Rosse'	ELan IArd LRHS MBNS MSte SBra SRms
- 'Superba' 🏆H4	CPLN CRHN EBee ECrN ECtt ELan EPfP LRHS MAsh MLLN SBra SEND SLim SPla WFar WPen WSHC
ferdinandii	GIBF WWes
flexuosa	see *L. japonica* var. *repens*
fragrantissima	More than 30 suppliers
gibbiflora Maxim.	see *L. chrysantha*
giraldii misapplied	see *L. acuminata*
giraldii Rehder	CBot CPLN EBee EPfP MAsh SBra SLim WCot WCru
glabrata	CPLN EBee LEdu SBra SCoo SLPl SLim
- B&SWJ 2150	SBra WCru
gracilipes	GIBF
gracilis	MBlu
grata	see *L.* x *americana* (Miller) K. Koch
x ***heckrottii***	CDoC CMac CRHN CSBt EBee ECtt LRHS MBar NBea NBlu NSti WDin
- 'Gold Flame'	CChe CSBt EBee ELan ENot EPfP GKir LAst LBuc LRHS MAsh MBar MBri MGos MRav NBea NBlu NEgg SBra SHBN SLim SMer SPer SRms WBVN WDin WFar WMoo WSHC WWeb
§ ***henryi***	More than 30 suppliers
- B&SWJ 8109	WCru
- 'Copper Beauty'	COtt MAsh MBlu
- var. ***subcoriacea***	see *L. henryi*
hildebrandiana	CPLN ERea EShb SBra WPGP XPep
'Hill House'	CHll
'Honey Baby'^{PBR}	ECrN MBlu MGos MRav SPoG WPat WRHF
implexa	EHol MAsh NPro SBra WSHC XPep

	Name	Suppliers
	insularis	see *L. morrowii*
	involucrata	CFee CMCN CMHG CPLG CPMA CPle CWib GQui MBNS MBar MBlu MRav SMac SPoG WCFE WDin WFar
	- var. ***ledebourii***	CBgR CPle EBee ELan EPfP GKir LAst SDys WTel
§	x ***italica*** 🏆[H4]	CMac COlW CRHN CSam CWSG ECrN ECtt ELan LAst LRHS MBri MRav NCGa NPer NSti SBra SDix SLim SPer SSpi WDin WFar WPnn WTel
	- Harlequin = 'Sherlite'[PBR] (v)	CBot CSPN ECtt ELan EMil ENot EPfP GKir LAst LRHS LSRN MGos MWat NBea NCGa NSti SBra SGar SLim SMad SPer SPlb SPoG SWvt WPGP WWeb
*	***jaluana*** **new**	GIBF
	japonica **new**	CCVT
§	- 'Aureoreticulata' (v)	More than 30 suppliers
	- 'Cream Cascade'	CRez LBuc MLLN
	- 'Dart's World'	CAlb SPla WBcn WFar
	- 'Halliana' 🏆[H4]	More than 30 suppliers
	- 'Hall's Prolific'	CDoC CSBt CSam CWSG EBee ECrN ECtt ELan GKir LBuc LRHS MAsh MBar MBlu MBri MGos MRav MWat MWgw NBea SBra SLim SMer SPet SPla SPoG SWvt WFar WWeb
§	- 'Horwood Gem' (v)	EBee ECrN ECtt LFol MGos NPro SBra SCoo WBcn WFar
	- 'Mint Crisp'[PBR] (v)	CFwr CSBt EBee ELan EPfP LAst LRHS LSRN MBri MGos MWgw NLar SHGC SMur SPer SPoG SWvt
	- 'Peter Adams'	see *L. japonica* 'Horwood Gem'
§	- var. ***repens*** 🏆[H4]	More than 30 suppliers
	- 'Variegata'	see *L. japonica* 'Aureoreticulata'
	korolkowii	CBot CPMA EBee EPfP LRHS MBNS MBri NBir SLon SPla WBcn WHCG WLeb WPat WSHC
	- var. ***zabelii*** misapplied	see *L. tatarica* 'Zabelii'
	- var. ***zabelii*** (Rehder) Rehder	ELan
	lanceolata AC 3120	GGar
	maackii	CHll CMCN EPfP GIBF MRav WHCG
*	***macgregorii***	CMCN
	'Mandarin'	CDoC CWSG EBee ELan ENot EPfP GKir LRHS MAsh MBNS MBlu MGos MRav MWgw SBra SCoo SPoG SSta SWvt
	maximowiczii	GIBF
	- var. ***sachalinensis*** **new**	NLar
§	***morrowii***	CMCN GIBF MBlu
	nervosa	GIBF
	nitida	CBcs CCVT CDul CSBt CTri ECrN ENot EPfP MRav NBlu NWea SHBN SPer SPoG STre WBVN WDin WFar WHar
	- 'Baggesen's Gold' 🏆[H4]	More than 30 suppliers
	- 'Cumbrian Calypso' (v)	NPro
	- 'Eden Spring'	NPro
	- Edmée Gold = 'Briloni'	MBri
	- 'Elegant'	LBuc
	- 'Ernest Wilson'	MBar
	- 'Fertilis'	ECrN SPer
	- 'Hohenheimer Findling'	WDin
	- 'Lemon Beauty' (v)	More than 30 suppliers
	- 'Lemon Queen'	CWib ELan MSwo
	- 'Lemon Spreader'	CBcs LBuc
§	- 'Maigrün'	CBcs EBee EGra EMil ENot LBuc LRHS MBri MSwo NPro SPer WDin WFar
	- Maygreen	see *L. nitida* 'Maigrün'
	- 'Red Tips'	CWan EHoe EPfP EPla LRHS MBNS MGos WDin WFar WMoo WWeb
	- 'Silver Beauty' (v)	More than 30 suppliers
	- 'Silver Lining'	see *L. pileata* 'Silver Lining'
	- 'Silver Queen'	WEas
	- 'Twiggy' (v)	CAlb CTbh EMil LBuc LRHS MBri NPro WRHF
	nummulariifolia	XPep
	periclymenum	CArn CDul CRWN CTri GPoy MDun MHer NBea NFor NLon NWea SHFr SPlb WDin WHCG WPnn WWye
	- 'Belgica' misapplied	see *L.* x *italica*
§	- 'Belgica'	More than 30 suppliers
	- 'Cream Cloud'	SBra
	- 'Florida'	see *L. periclymenum* 'Serotina'
	- 'Graham Thomas' 🏆[H4]	More than 30 suppliers
	- 'Heaven Scent'	EMil SBra WPnn
	- 'Honeybush'	CDoC CPMA CPle CSPN EBee MAsh MBlu MTis NPri SLim WWeb
	- 'La Gasnaérie'	SBra SLim WPnn
	- 'Liden'	SBra
	- 'Llyn Brianne'	WBcn
	- 'Munster'	EBee MBri SBra WBcn WPnn WSHC
	- 'Red Gables'	CSam CWan EBee MBNS MBri MGos MRav MSte MWgw SBra SCoo SEND SLim SPla WCot WGor WKif WPat WPnn
N	- 'Serotina' 🏆[H4]	More than 30 suppliers
	- - EM '85	ENot
	- 'Serpentine'	SBra
*	- ***sulphurea***	EWll WFar
	- 'Sweet Sue'	CRHN CSPN EBee ECtt ELan EPfP GCal LAst LRHS MAsh MBNS MGos MLan MSte MTis NCGa NEgg NSti SBra SCoo SPoG SWvt WBcn WFar WPnP WWeb
	- 'Winchester'	EBee
	pileata	CBcs CCVT CDul CSBt CTri EBee ECrN ELan ENot EPfP GKir LBuc LRHS MBar MRav MSwo NBlu NFor NPer SPer SPoG SRms STre WBVN WCFE WDin WFar WHar WTel
	- 'Moss Green'	CDoC EBee ENot WHCG
	- 'Pilot'	SLPl
§	- 'Silver Lining' (v)	EPla GBuc SAga
	- 'Stockholm'	SLPl
	pilosa Willd.	CPLN
	- CD&R 1216	SBra
	praeflorens	CPle
	x ***purpusii***	CDoC CPSs CPle CTri CWSG CWib EBee ECrN EPfP EWTr LAst MBNS MBar MGos MSwo NBea NBlu SLim SPer SPla SRms WFar WHCG WHar WSHC WTel
	- 'Winter Beauty' 🏆[H4]	More than 30 suppliers
	pyrenaica	CPle
	quinquelocularis f. ***translucens***	GIBF MBlu
	ramosissima	NLar
	rupicola var. ***syringantha***	see *L. syringantha*
	saccata	CPMA EPfP
	sempervirens 🏆[H4]	CBot CPLN CRHN CSBt EPfP MBNS MCCP MRav NBea SBra WFar WSHC
	- 'Dropmore Scarlet'	see *L.* x *brownii* 'Dropmore Scarlet'
	- 'Leo'	CSPN
N	- f. ***sulphurea***	EBee EPfP LRHS NBea SBra SPer WSHC

	- - 'John Clayton'	SBra
	setifera	CPle
	- 'Daphnis'	EPfP GKir
	similis var. ***delavayi*** ♀H4	CBot CPLN CRHN CSPN CSam ECrN ELan EPfP IArd LRHS MAsh MLan MRav NBea NSti NVic SBra SDix SEND SLPl SPla SPoG WCru WFar WPGP WPen WSHC
	'Simonet'	SBra
	splendida	SBra WSHC
	standishii	CBcs CTri EBee EHol MGos MRav SPer WDin WFar WHCG WRha
	- 'Budapest'	MBlu MBri MGos NEgg
	stenantha	NLar
	'Stone Green'	MGos NPro SPoG
	subequalis	CFil WPGP
§	***syringantha***	More than 30 suppliers
	- 'Grandiflora'	GQui SLon WAbe
	tatarica	CMCN CWib EBee MRav MWhi SLon WBVN WFar WHCG WTel
	- 'Arnold Red'	CBcs EBee ELan EPfP MBlu MHer NBlu WDin WTel XPep
	- 'Hack's Red'	CBcs CWib EBee EHol EPfP GQui LSRN LSou MRav SPer SWvt WDin WFar WHCG
§	- 'Zabelii'	EPfP MGos
	x ***tellmanniana***	More than 30 suppliers
	- 'Joan Sayer'	EBee MBNS MBri MGos SBra SCoo SLim WBcn WCFE WWeb
	thibetica	GIBF MBlu SPer WBcn WFar
	tianschanica **new**	GIBF
	tragophylla ♀H4	CBcs CDoC CPLG CPLN CSBt ELan EPfP EWTr GCal GIBF LRHS MBNS MBlu MBri MRav NSti SBra SCoo SDnm SLim SPer SPoG SSpi SWvt WDin WSHC
	- 'Maurice Foster'	CMdw SBra
*	- 'Pharoah's Trumpet'	ERea LRHS MAsh SSpi SSta WBcn
	trichosantha var. ***acutiuscula***	GIBF
	vesicaria	CPle
	webbiana	ELan
	x ***xylosteoides***	MRav WFar
	- 'Clavey's Dwarf'	MBlu SLPl
	- 'Miniglobe'	NPro
	xylosteum	CArn WFar

Lopezia (*Onagraceae*)

	racemosa	CSpe SHFr

Lophatherum (*Poaceae*)

	gracile	CPLG EShb GFor SWal WDyG

Lophomyrtus (*Myrtaceae*)

§	***bullata***	CAbP CHEx ECou GQui IDee SPer WCHb WFar
	- 'Matai Bay'	CBcs CTrC EBee
§	***obcordata***	ISea SSpi
§	x ***ralphii***	IDee MHer WCHb WPic
	- 'Gloriosa' (v)	CAbP CDoC CPle SBrw WCHb WGer
§	- 'Kathryn'	CBcs CDoC CPLG CPle EBee ISea NLar SPoG SSpi WCHb
	- 'Little Star' (v)	CBcs CDoC CTrC GBri LRHS SPoG WPat
I	- 'Multicolor' (v)	CBcs CTrC
	- 'Pixie'	CAbP CDoC CTrC SBrw SPoG WPat
	- 'Red Dragon'	CBcs CTrC EBee GBri IDee WPat
	- 'Sundae' (v)	CPLG
§	- 'Traversii' (v)	LRHS SMur SPoG
	- 'Tricolor' (v)	CPle CTrC WCot
	- 'Wild Cherry'	CBcs CTrC

Lophosoria (*Dicksoniaceae*)

	quadripinnata	CFil

Lophospermum (*Scrophulariaceae*)

§	***erubescens*** ♀H2-3	CBot CHEx CHal CRHN EUnu MSte MTis SBch SGar SHFr SMur WPtf
	'Magic Dragon'	MCCP WHil
§	'Red Dragon'	CSpe SBch SGar
§	***scandens***	CBcs CRHN ELan SMur
§	- 'Pink Ice'	LRHS

loquat see *Eriobotrya japonica*

Loropetalum (*Hamamelidaceae*)

	chinense	CFil CMCN CPen CWib SSpi
	- 'Ming Dynasty'	CPen
	- f. ***rubrum***	CFil CPLG CWib WMul
	- - 'Blush'	CFil
	- - 'Burgundy' **new**	WCot
	- - 'Daybreak's Flame'	CPMA CPen SPoG
	- - 'Fire Dance'	CAbP CBcs CDoC CFai CPMA CPen EMil GBin IDee SPoG SSpi SWvt WFar
	- - 'Pipa's Red'	CPen SPoG
I	- - 'Zhuzhou Fuchsia'	CMCN
	- 'Snowdance' **new**	CAbP
	- 'Tang Dynasty'	CPen

Lotus (*Papilionaceae*)

	berthelotii	CFee CHEx ECtt ELan EOHP ERea ESlt EUJe MOak SBrw SChu SPet SPoG
	- deep red ♀H1+3	LIck SWvt
	- 'Gold Fish' **new**	CHEx
	berthelotii x ***maculatus*** 'Fire Vine'	EShb LAst
	corniculatus	CArn GWCH MBow MCoo MHer NLan NMir NTHB SIde SPet WPop XPep
	- 'Plenus' (d)	EPot MTho NLar WPer
	creticus	SHFr
	cytisoides	XPep
§	***hirsutus*** ♀H3-4	More than 30 suppliers
	- 'Brimstone' (v)	CWib EBee ECtt EGoo EPPr EWin LRHS LSou MSph SBrw SOkh SPer SVil SWvt
	- 'Fréjorgues'	XPep
	- 'Lois'	EBee MDKP MWgw WSPU
	maculatus	EOHP ESlt EWin NPri SHFr SPet
	maritimus	EBee EWll LPhx MOne MWgw SHFr SRot
	mascaensis misapplied	see *L. sessilifolius*
	pedunculatus	see *L. uliginosus*
	pentaphyllus	XPep
	- subsp. ***herbaceus***	XPep
§	- subsp. ***pentaphyllus***	EChP
	'Red Flash' **new**	LAst
§	***sessilifolius***	ERea
	suffruticosus	see *L. pentaphyllus* subsp. *pentaphyllus*
	tetragonolobus	SRot WHer
§	***uliginosus***	CAgr NMir

lovage see *Levisticum officinale*

Ludwigia (*Onagraceae*)

	grandiflora	WDyG WWpP
	uruguayensis	LPBA

Luetkea (*Rosaceae*)

	pectinata	NRya

Luma (*Myrtaceae*)

§ ***apiculata*** ♀H3 — More than 30 suppliers
- ICE 100 — WPic
§ - 'Glanleam Gold' (v) ♀H3 — More than 30 suppliers
- 'Penwith' (v) — CTrC
- 'Variegata' (v) — CMHG CTri ISea SAga SLim WCru WWye
§ ***chequen*** — CBcs CFee GGar IDee MHer NLar WCHb WCwm WFar WJek WMoo WPic XPep

Lunaria (*Brassicaceae*)

§ ***annua*** — GAbr GWCH MBow MWgw SIde WHer
- var. ***albiflora*** ♀H4 — MWgw NBir
I - - 'Alba Variegata' (v) — CCge CSpe EBla EMar MHer MWgw WTin
- 'Munstead Purple' — EBla
- 'Variegata' (v) — CHar EBla IBlr MCCP MTho NBir NLsd WEas WHer WSan
- violet — NBir WFar
biennis — see *L. annua*
rediviva — CSpe EBee ECGP ECha EMon EPPr EPla GAbr GCal GCra GGar GKir GLil IBlr IFro LPhx LRHS MBct MRav NBid NPer NSti SSpi SUsu WCot WEas WFar WHer WPGP
- 'Partway White' **new** — CMil

Lupinus ✿ (*Papilionaceae*)

'African Sunset' — CWCL
albifrons — MWgw SIgm XPep
'Amber Glow' — CWCL
'Approaching Storm' — SMrm
'Apricot Spire' — CWCL
arboreus ♀H4 — More than 30 suppliers
- ***albus*** — CSpe CWib NRnb SHGN
- 'Barton-on-Sea' — CNat CSec MAvo NLar NRnb
- blue — CBrm CHar CMea CSec CWCL CWib EBee EBrs ECGP ERou GAbr GBBs MAvo MCCP NLar NLsd SPer SPlb SSth SWvt WBVN WFar WHer
- 'Blue Boy' — CTbh SPla
- cream — ECGP NLon
- 'Mauve Queen' — CHEx CHar CSec EWin NLar NRnb SHGN SSvw SUsu
- mixed — CArn SPet
- prostrate — MDKP MMHG
- 'Snow Queen' — CBrm CFwr CSec CWCL EWin MCCP NBur NLar SPoG
- 'Sulphur Yellow' — ERou SHGN SWvt
- white — CWCL CWib
- yellow and blue **new** — SRkn
arboreus* x *variicolor — CHid WGwG
arcticus — CSpe EBee
'Aston Villa' — CWCL
'Avalon' — CWCL
'Baby Doll' — CWCL
Band of Nobles Series ♀H4 — ECtt SSth WFar
'Beryl, Viscountess Cowdray' — EMon
bicolor — CHar CSec
'Bishop's Tipple' — CWCL EWes
'Blue Moon' — CWCL
'Blue Streak' — CWCL
'Blueberry Pie' — CWCL
breweri — GIBF
'Bruiser' **new** — CWCL
'Bubblegum' — CWCL
'Captain Scarlet' **new** — CWCL
'Casanova' **new** — CWCL
'Cashmere Cream' — CWCL
chamissonis — CSec CSpe CStr CWCL EBee EChP EHrv EMan EWes LRHS MTho MTis SGar SMad SPer SPoG WFar WLin WWpP
'Chandelier' — More than 30 suppliers
'Cherry Belle' — CWCL
'Copperlight' — CWCL
'Desert Sun' — CWCL
'Dolly Mixture' — CWCL
'Dreaming Spires' — CWCL
Dwarf Gallery hybrids — ENot GKir
'Dwarf Lulu' — see *L.* 'Lulu'
elegans 'Dwarf Pink Fairy' — MAnH
Gallery Series — COIW CSBt ENot EVFa LAst NJOw SCoo SPlb WFar
- 'Gallery Blue' — ECtt EPfP GAbr LSRN LSou MBow NCGa NDlv NLar NLon NNor NPri NVic SCoo SPoG SWal WFar
- 'Gallery Pink' — EPfP LRHS LSou NCGa NDlv NLar NPri NVic SCoo SPla SPoG SWal WFar
- 'Gallery Red' — ECtt ENot EPfP GAbr LRHS NCGa NDlv NLar NPri NVic SCoo SPla SPoG SWal WFar
- 'Gallery Rose' — LSRN MBow NLon
- 'Gallery White' — ENot EPfP GAbr LRHS NCGa NDlv NLar NPri NVic SCoo SPla SPoG SWal WFar
- 'Gallery Yellow' — ECtt EPfP GAbr LRHS LSou NCGa NDlv NLar NLon NLsd NPri NVic SCoo SPla SPoG SWal
'Garden Gnome' — LRav WPer
'Heather Glow' **new** — NLar
'Lady Penelope' — CWCL
littoralis — CSec NRnb
'Lollipop' — CWCL
longifolius **new** — EBee
§ 'Lulu' — COtt ECtt LAst LRHS MRav MWat SPer SWvt WFar WMoo
'Manhattan Lights' — CWCL
Minarette Group — CTri ECtt MBri NLsd SGar SPet SRms WFar WGor
'Mrs Perkins' **new** — SMrm
mutabilis — NRnb
'My Castle' — More than 30 suppliers
'Noble Maiden' (Band of Nobles Series) — CBcs CSBt CTri EBee EChP ECtt ELan EPfP ERou GKir LRHS LSRN MBri MRav MWat MWgw MWrn NBPC NEgg NLsd NMir SPer SWal SWvt WCAu WFar WMnd WPer WWeb
nootkatensis — MNFA
'Pagoda Prince' — CWCL
perennis — CAgr EBee
'Pink Cadillac' — CWCL
'Plum Duff' — CWCL
'Plummy Blue' — LSou MCCP
'Polar Princess' — CWCL ERou EWes
polyphyllus — CSec EBee WOut
propinquus — CSec
'Queen of Hearts' — CWCL
'Rainbow Select' **new** — NRnb
'Red Arrow' — CWCL
x ***regalis*** 'Morello Cherry' — CWib MBri MWrn WHil
'Rote Flamme' — EWes
'Ruby Lantern' — CWCL
Russell hybrids — COIW CSBt ELan ENot EPfP GKir LAst MHer NBlu SPet SPlb SRms SWvt WFar WSSM
'Saffron' **new** — CWCL
'Saint George' — CWCL
'Sand Pink' — CWCL EWes
'Sherbert Dip' — CWCL

'Silk Rain'	CWCL
'Snowgoose'	CWCL
'Sparky' **new**	CWCL
'Storm'	CWCL
subcarnosus **new**	SRkn
'Terracotta'	CWCL
texensis	CSpe
'The Chatelaine' (Band of Nobles Series)	More than 30 suppliers
'The Governor' (Band of Nobles Series)	More than 30 suppliers
'The Page' (Band of Nobles Series)	CBcs EBee ELan EPfP ERou LRHS LSRN MBri MRav MWat MWgw NBPC NBlu NEgg NMir SPer SWal SWvt WBVN WFar WMnd WMoo WPer WWeb
'Thor' **new**	CWCL
'Thundercloud'	SMrm
variicolor	CHid CSpe SSpi
versicolor	CSec EMan GBBs LDai LGro MBri MEHN MHer MLLN SMHy WBrk WHoo WPtf WWpP
- 'Dumpty'	LSou

Lutzia (*Brassicaceae*)

cretica	XPep

Luzula ✿ (*Juncaceae*)

from New Guinea	EWes
alpinopilosa	CBig EPPr GBin GFor
x ***borreri***	EPPr
- 'Botany Bay' (v)	ECtt EPla GBin
canariensis	WDyG WWye
forsteri	CBgR EPPr
lactea	EMon EPPr LRHS
luzuloides	CBig GFor NBre WDyG WPer
- 'Schneehäschen'	EBrs EMan EMon EPPr GBin GCal MWgw WWpP
maxima	see *L. sylvatica*
nivalis	EBrs GAbr
nivea	More than 30 suppliers
pilosa	CBgR EPla GCal IBlr
- 'Igel'	GBin SLPl
purpureosplendens	CElw EMon
'Ruby Stiletto'	EBee EPPr MAvo WPtf
rufa	CTrC ECou
§ ***sylvatica***	CHEx CRWN CRow CSWP CTrC ELan EPPr EPfP EPla EPza GKir MBow MLLN MMoz MRav NBro NOrc WDin WFar WHer WPGP WShi
- from Tatra Mountains, Czechoslovakia	EPPr
- 'A. Rutherford'	see *L. sylvatica* 'Taggart's Cream'
- 'Aurea'	More than 30 suppliers
- 'Aureomarginata'	see *L. sylvatica* 'Marginata'
I - 'Auslese'	CBig EPPr GBin GFor GLil LRHS SMar WMoo
- 'Barcode' (v) **new**	CNat
- 'Bromel'	SGSe
- 'Hohe Tatra'	More than 30 suppliers
§ - 'Marginata' (v)	More than 30 suppliers
* - f. ***nova***	EPPr
§ - 'Taggart's Cream' (v)	CElw CRow EBee EBrs EHoe EMar EPla GGar MAvo NBid NLar SApp WDyG WLeb WMoo WPrP
- 'Tatra Gold' **new**	SMad
- 'Tauernpass'	CBgR EHoe EMon EPPr EPla GCal NBid SMac
- 'Wäldler'	EHoe EPPr MBNS
- 'Waulkmill Bay'	SLPl
ulophylla	CBig CFir ECou EMan ESis GBin GEdr GFor NBre NWCA

Luzuriaga (*Philesiaceae*)

radicans	CFee ERos IBlr WCot WCru WFar WSHC
- MK 92	SSpi

Lychnis (*Caryophyllaceae*)

alpina	CMHG EPfP GIBF GKev GKir GTou IHMH NArg NBlu NEgg NJOw NLon NPri NVic WPer
- 'Alba'	GKev GTou NBir
- compact	GTou
- 'Rosea'	NBir
- 'Snow Flurry'	GFlt NCGa NLar
- 'Snowflake' **new**	EWTr
§ x ***arkwrightii***	ECha ELan NNor SIng SRot WFar
- 'Orange Zwerg'	CBct CBrm EBee GKev LAst LSou MAnH NBPC NEgg WWeb
- 'Vesuvius'	CBcs ENot EPfP EUJe GKir LAst LRHS LSRN MNrw MTis NBir NBlu SPav SPer SPoG SRms STes WMnd WPer
* 'Blushing Bride'	ENot WRHF
chalcedonica ♀H4	More than 30 suppliers
- var. ***albiflora***	EBee ECha IBlr LAst LRHS MBri MWgw NArg NBid NBro NLon SHel SPer WFar WMoo WPer WWpP
- - 'Snow White'	SGSe
- apricot	NBid WHrl
- 'Carnea'	EBrs EShb EWsh GCal LRHS NBre SBri WHil
- 'Dusky Pink'	GFlt LSou MWhi NBPC
- 'Dusky Salmon'	ITer MDKP MWrn NBPC NDlv WRHF WWpP
- 'Flore Pleno' (d)	CBot ECha ELan ERou GCal GKir IFro MCCP MLLN MOne NLar NPri WCot WFar
- 'Morgenrot'	EChP MCCP NLar
- 'Pinkie'	EBee ELan NLar SBod SGSe
- 'Rauhreif'	EBee EChP EShb NBre
- 'Rosea'	EBrs EPfP GKir LIck LRHS NBir SMar WFar WHrl WMoo WPer
* - 'Salmonea'	ECtt GBri LPio MBri MTis NBir SRms WCAu
- salmon-pink	COIW WWhi
- 'Summer Sparkle Pink'	SWal
cognata	CDes EBee MDKP MGol
- B&SWJ 4234	WCru
§ ***coronaria*** ♀H4	More than 30 suppliers
- 'Abbotswood Rose'	see *L.* x *walkeri* 'Abbotswood Rose'
- 'Alba' ♀H4	More than 30 suppliers
- 'Angel's Blush'	GAbr LRHS MBnl MDKP MRav NBir SOkh SPav SPer WMow WRha WWpP
- Atrosanguinea Group	CBre EBee EBrs ERou GMaP IBlr LPio LRHS MBnl MRav MTis NCot NEgg NPri
- 'Cerise'	MArl MDKP NBir
- 'Dancing Ladies'	ENot WMnd
- 'Flottbek'	MOne NLar
- 'Hutchinson's Cream' (v)	EMan GFlt NPro WCHb
- Oculata Group	CAby CHrt CSpe EBee ECtt EGoo ERou GKir IBlr MTho NOak NPri NSti SGar SPav SPlb SWal WFar WMoo
§ ***coronata*** var. ***sieboldii***	NBre WSan
dioica	see *Silene dioica*
flos-cuculi	CArn CHrt CNic CRWN CSam EHon EMFW EPfP GKev LNCo LPBA MBow MHer MSal NArg

	NBre NLan NMir NPri SECG SGar WBVN WCAu WHer WMoo WPnP WPop WWpP
- var. ***albiflora***	CBre EMFW EMag LPBA MBow MLLN NBro NLar WCHb WHer WMoo WOut WWpP
- Jenny = 'Lychjen' (d)	SPer
- 'Nana'	CBrm CSpe EDAr NLar NRya WPat WPer
flos-jovis ♀H4	CSec EPfP EWTr IGor ITim NArg NLsd NPri SBch SGSe SMer SRms WMoo WOut WPer
- 'Hort's Variety'	EBrs GKir MRav NSti SBla WRos
- 'Minor'	see *L. flos-jovis* 'Nana'
§ - 'Nana'	IFro MAnH NBid NWCA
- 'Peggy'	CM&M EGoo ESis LRHS MAnH MCCP NBre NCGa NLar WWeb
gracillima	CSec
x ***haageana***	EBee LRHS NBre NWCA SAga SIng SRms
'Hill Grounds' **new**	WCot
lagascae	see *Petrocoptis pyrenaica* subsp. *glaucifolia*
miqueliana	WMoo
- 'Variegated Lacy Red' (v)	EBee
'Molten Lava'	CFir EBee LRHS MHer MRav NArg NBre NOrc SGSe SGar WMoo WPer WWeb
nutans	MSal
preslii minor	EBee
* ***sikkimensis***	EBee
'Terry's Pink'	MLLN NCGa NLar WFar WHil
§ ***viscaria***	CArn ECha GIBF IHMH LDai MSal NCiC NFor SBch SGar SHGN WBVN WFar WHer WMoo WTin
- 'Alba'	CBrm EBee ECha GCal MLLN NBre NBro WRha
- ***alpina***	see *L. viscaria*
§ - subsp. ***atropurpurea***	EBee EChP ECtt NBre NJOw NLRH NLon NLsd SRms WCAu WHrl WOut
- 'Feuer'	CBrm EBee MAnH NCGa NEgg NLar SUsu WCot WMoo
- 'Firebird'	EWes ITim NBre NBur WOut
- 'Plena' (d)	EChP MDun MInt NEgg WBor WSan WTin
- 'Schnee'	CPrp MSte WCAu
- 'Snowbird'	WOut
- 'Splendens'	EPfP IHMH MNFA SPet
- 'Splendens Plena' (d) ♀H4	CHar EBee GMac MArl NBro NLon SBla WEas WFar
- 'White Cloud'	MSph
§ x ***walkeri*** 'Abbotswood Rose' ♀H4	GBuc GFlt IBlr
wilfordii	CFir NEgg SHar
§ ***yunnanensis***	EBee GKev MSte NBid NJOw SGSe SPav WMoo WOut WPer
- ***alba***	see *L. yunnanensis*

Lycianthes (*Solanaceae*)

rantonnetii	see *Solanum rantonnetii*

Lycium (*Solanaceae*)

barbarum	EUnu NBlu SMad
chinense	CArn NLar
cf. ***cinereum*** **new**	EUnu
europaeum	XPep

Lycopodium (*Lycopodiaceae*)

clavatum	GPoy

Lycopsis see *Anchusa*

Lycopus (*Lamiaceae*)

americanus	EBee GPoy MSal
europaeus	CArn ELau GBar GPoy MBow MChe MHer MSal WGwG WHer WWye
lucidus	MSal
virginicus	COld MSal SDys WWye

Lycoris (*Amaryllidaceae*)

albiflora	WCot
aurea	LRHS MOak
chinensis	EBee
haywardii	WCot
radiata	CStu GSki LRHS MOak
sprengeri **new**	WCot
squamigera	EBee ECho WCot
straminea **new**	WCot

Lygodium (*Schizaeaceae*)

japonicum	WFib WRic

Lygos (*Papilionaceae*)

sphaerocarpa	see *Retama sphaerocarpa*

Lyonia (*Ericaceae*)

ligustrina	GIBF LRHS NLar SMur
mariana	NLar

Lyonothamnus (*Rosaceae*)

floribundus subsp. ***aspleniifolius***	CAbb CFil CPSs EBee SAPC SArc SGar SMad SSpi WFar WPGP

Lysichiton (*Araceae*)

americanus ♀H4	More than 30 suppliers
camtschatcensis ♀H4	CBcs CBen CFwr CLAP CRow CWat EBee ECha EHon ELan EMFW EPfP EPza GAbr GIBF LNCo LPBA MDun NArg NEgg NOrc NPer SMad SPer SSpi SWvt WCot WFar WPnP WPop
camtschatcensis x ***americanus***	SSpi

Lysimachia ✿ (*Primulaceae*)

B&SWJ 8632 from Korea **new**	WCru
BWJ 8072 from China **new**	WCru
acroadenia	CPLG
§ ***atropurpurea***	More than 30 suppliers
- 'Beaujolais'	CBod EVFa EWTr EWll LRHS MCCP NBPC SPav SWal WPop WSan WWeb WWlt WWpP
- 'Geronimo'	CSpe
barystachys	CHea CRow EBee EVFa GMac MAnH MGol MRav MWrn SHar SMac SMer WCot WFar WOut
candida	WCot
ciliata	CMHG CPLG CRow ECha EHoe ELan GFlt GMaP GMac MNrw NArg NEgg NFor NGdn NSti SChu WBor WCAu WCot WFar WMnd WPer
§ - 'Firecracker' ♀H4	More than 30 suppliers
- 'Purpurea'	see *L. ciliata* 'Firecracker'
clethroides ♀H4	More than 30 suppliers
- 'Geisha' (v)	EMan MBNS NLar WCot
- 'Lady Jane'	CBrm MWrn NBur SRms
§ ***congestiflora***	NPer SHFr SPet
- 'Golden Falls' **new**	NEgg
- 'Outback Sunset'[PBR] (v)	ECtt EWin LAst LRHS NPri
decurrens	EBee

- JCA 4.542.500	WCot
ephemerum	More than 30 suppliers
fortunei	EBee IHMH SHel SMac WCot
henryi	EWes
hybrida	EBee WCot
japonica var. ***minutissima***	CFee CRow CStu MTho NLar
lichiangensis	CFir EBee EMFP EMan GIBF GKir GSki MBNS MLLN NArg NRnb SHFr WMoo WPer WPnP WWpP
lyssii	see *L. congestiflora*
mauritiana	EMan
- B&SWJ 8815	WCru
melampyroides	WCot
minoricensis	CArn EBee EEls EHrv ELan EMan EVFa EWin IHMH MAnH SGSe WHer WPer
nemorum	WPer
- 'Pale Star'	CBgR CBre WWye
nummularia	CHal COIW CSBt CTri CWat ECtt EHon EPfP GPoy IHMH LNCo LPBA MBar MBow NArg NBlu NFor SHFr WBrk WCot WGwG WWpP WWye
- 'Aurea' ♀H4	More than 30 suppliers
paridiformis	WCot
- var. ***stenophylla***	EBee WCot WPGP
- - DJHC 704	CDes
punctata misapplied	see *L. verticillaris*
punctata L.	More than 30 suppliers
§ - 'Alexander' (v)	More than 30 suppliers
- 'Gaulthier Brousse'	WCot
- 'Golden Alexander' (v)	CBct EChP MBNS MBnl NEgg NLar SGSe SPer
- 'Golden Glory' (v)	WCot WWpP
- 'Ivy Maclean' (v)	EBee EChP EMan EVFa LBBr SSvw SWvt WCot WWpP
- 'Senior'	EMil
- 'Sunspot'	EBee WWpP
- 'Variegata'	see *L. punctata* 'Alexander'
- ***verticillata***	see *L. verticillaris*
serpyllifolia	ECtt
thyrsiflora	EBee EHon EMFW GAbr IHMH LNCo MCCP NBlu NLar NPer WCot WHer WWpP
§ ***verticillaris***	WCot
vulgaris	CArn CRWN LPBA MBow SIde WBWf WCot WFar WMoo WPer WShi WWpP WWye
- subsp. ***davurica***	WCot
yunnanensis	EBee EKen EMan EPPr GIBF GKev LSou MAnH MDKP MGol NBPC NRnb SMad WCot WHil WLin WPer WPtf WWpP

Lysionotus (*Gesneriaceae*)

* ***carniolica*** **new**	CStu
gamosepalus B&SWJ 7241	WCru
aff. ***kwangsiensis*** HWJ 643	WCru
'Lavender Lady' **new**	CSpe
pauciflorus	CDes CStu ETow
- B&SWJ 189	WCru
- B&SWJ 303	WCru
- B&SWJ 335	WCru

Lythrum (*Lythraceae*)

alatum	EShb MGol NBre SMar WWpP
anceps	NBre NLar SMar
salicaria	More than 30 suppliers
- 'Blush' ♀H4	More than 30 suppliers
- 'Brightness'	CDWL NArg
§ - 'Feuerkerze' ♀H4	CDWL CKno CMea CPrp CRow CSam CSec CWCL EBee ECtt ELan EPfP ERou GCal GKir LAst LRHS MRav NBir NDov NEgg NSti NVic SChu SOkh SPer SPla WFar WPer WTel
- Firecandle	see *L. salicaria* 'Feuerkerze'
- 'Happy'	SChu SMrm
- 'Lady Sackville'	CBos CDWL EBee GBuc GMaP LRHS MBNS NDov SSvw SUsu WCAu WTMC WTel
- 'Morden Pink'	CDWL EBee EChP LPhx MBri MDKP MSte NGby WFar
- 'Prichard's Variety'	CKno EBee WPGP
- 'Red Gem'	NEgg
- 'Robert'	More than 30 suppliers
- 'Rose'	ELan MWgw NBir NEgg SWvt
- 'Rosencaule'	EBee
- 'Stichflamme'	NCob
- 'Swirl'	EBee ECtt MDKP WFar WWpP
- 'The Beacon'	CDWL CMHG EBee EMan GCal NPro SRms
- 'Zigeunerblut'	CMHG EBee LPhx MDKP MRav MSte NGby NLar SOkh
virgatum	CBos CMHG LPhx SMHy SUsu WSHC
- 'Dropmore Purple'	CHar CSBt EBee EChP ERou LPhx LRHS MBri MDKP MSte NDov SOkh WCAu WFar WGHP WPtf WWpP
- 'Rose Queen'	EBee ECha EMan MDKP MRav WFar WPer
- 'Rosy Gem'	CM&M CWan EBee ECtt EPfP GKir GMaP GMac MBNS MWgw NBid NBro NLsd NOak SGSe SMer SRms SWvt WFar WGHP WHoo WPer WWeb WWpP
- 'The Rocket'	CKno CM&M CSam CTri EBee EChP EPfP ERou LAst LRHS MRav NBro NDov NEgg SMer SPer SWvt

Lytocaryum (*Arecaceae*)

§ ***weddellianum*** ♀H1	MBri

M

Maackia (*Papilionaceae*)

amurensis	CBcs CMCN CPle ELan EPfP GIBF IDee IMGH LRav MBlu SBrw WBVN WNor
- var. ***buergeri***	CLnd EBee GBin
chinensis	CMCN MBlu
fauriei	CPle

Macbridea (*Lamiaceae*)

caroliniana	CDes EBee WPGP

mace, English see *Achillea ageratum*

Macfadyena (*Bignoniaceae*)

§ ***unguis-cati***	CRHN CSec EShb XPep

Machaeranthera (*Asteraceae*)

§ ***bigelovii***	EBee
shastensis	EBee

Machaerina (*Cyperaceae*)

rubiginosa 'Variegata' (v)	CDWL

Machilus see *Persea*

Mackaya (*Acanthaceae*)

§	***bella*** ♀H1	CHII ERea EShb SYvo

Macleania (*Ericaceae*)

	ericae	WCot

Macleaya (*Papaveraceae*)

	cordata misapplied	see *M.* x *kewensis*
§	***cordata*** (Willd.) R. Br. ♀H4	More than 30 suppliers
	- 'Celadon Ruffles'	GBin
§	x ***kewensis***	EBee ENot GAbr MBri WHoo WPGP
	- 'Flamingo' ♀H4	EBee ECha GCal MRav NEgg SBch SChu SWvt WCAu WWye
§	***microcarpa***	MAnH MFOX MGol SGar WSel
	- 'Kelway's Coral Plume' ♀H4	More than 30 suppliers
	- 'Spetchley Ruby'	EBee EMan GBin LPhx MRav NBir NDov WCot
	'Plum Tassel' **new**	WCot

Maclura (*Moraceae*)

	pomifera	CAgr CFil CMCN IDee MGol NLar SPlb WDin WFar WPGP XPep
	- 'Pretty Woman'	NLar
	tricuspidata	CAgr EGFP

Macrodiervilla see *Weigela*

Macropiper (*Piperaceae*)

§	***excelsum***	CHEx ECou

Macrozamia (*Zamiaceae*)

	communis	CBrP CRoM WNor
	diplomera	CBrP
	dyeri	see *M. riedlei*
	glaucophylla	CBrP
	johnsonii	CBrP
	lucida	CBrP
	miquelii	CBrP
	moorei	CBrP CRoM
	mountperiensis	CBrP
§	***riedlei***	CBrP CRoM
	spiralis	CRoM

Maddenia (*Rosaceae*)

	hypocleuca	NLar

Madia (*Asteraceae*)

	elegans	NBur

Maesa (*Myrsinaceae*)

	japonica **new**	CPLG
	montana	CFil CPLG

Magnolia ✿ (*Magnoliaceae*)

	acuminata	CBcs CDul CLnd CMCN EPfP IDee IMGH NPal
	- 'Golden Glow'	CBcs CMHG
*	- 'Kinju'	CEnd
	- 'Koban Dori'	CBcs CPMA CTho
§	- var. ***subcordata***	CBcs NEgg NLar
§	- - 'Miss Honeybee'	LRHS SSpi
	'Advance'	CBcs CPMA
	'Albatross'	CBcs CDoC CEnd CTho LRHS SSpi
	amoena	CBcs CSdC CTho WNor
	- 'Multiogeca'	CBcs
	'Ann' ♀H4	CPLG CSdC CTrh SSpi
	'Anticipation' **new**	CEnd
	'Apollo'	CBcs CEnd CPMA SSpi
	ashei	see *M. macrophylla* subsp. *ashei*
	'Athene'	CBcs CDoC CMHG COtt CPMA LRHS MBri SSpi
	'Atlas'	CBcs CEnd CMHG CPMA CTho EMil LMil LRHS SSpi
	'Betty' ♀H4	CBcs CDoC CDul CSdC IDee MGos NLar NScw SBrw SSta WDin WFar WOrn
	'Big Dude'	CEnd IArd SSpi
	biondii	CBcs CFil CTho NLar SSpi WNor WPGP
I	'Black Tulip'	ENot LRHS MGos NPri SCoo SPoG SSpi
	x ***brooklynensis***	CTho
	'Evamaria'	
	- 'Hattie Carthan'	WPGP
	- 'Woodsman'	NLar SSta WBcn
	- 'Yellow Bird'	CEnd CMCN COtt CPMA CTho EBee ENot EPfP IDee LRHS MAsh MBlu MDun MGos NLar SLim SSpi WGer
	'Butterflies'	CBcs CDoC CEnd CFai CFil CMHG CPMA CTho ELan EPfP ISea LHyd LRHS MAsh MDun NLar SHBN SSpi SSta WBVN WFar WPGP
	'Caerhays Belle'	CBcs CPMA SSpi
	'Caerhays New Purple' **new**	COtt
	'Caerhays Surprise'	CBcs CPMA SSpi
	campbellii	CBcs CFil CMCN CTho ELan EPfP ISea LRHS MDun SHBN SSpi SSta WFar WPic
	- Alba Group	CBcs CEnd CTho MGos WFar WPGP
	- - 'Strybing White'	CBcs
I	- - 'Trelissick Alba'	CTho
	- 'Betty Jessel'	CBcs CPMA CTho
	- 'Darjeeling'	CBcs EMil
	- 'Lamellan Pink'	CTho
	- 'Lamellan White'	CTho
	- subsp. ***mollicomata***	CBcs CEnd CHEx CSam CTrw EPfP ISea SSpi WFar
	- - 'Lanarth'	CBcs CEnd SSpi
	- - 'Maharanee'	CBcs
	- - 'Peter Borlase'	CDoC CTho LRHS
	- (Raffillii Group)	CAbP CBcs CDul CLnd ELan EMil
	'Charles Raffill'	EPfP IMGH MDun MGos MLan SHBN SLim SPer SPoG WDin
	- - 'Kew's Surprise'	CBcs CPMA
	'Candy Cane'	SSpi WPGP
	Chameleon	see *M.* 'Chang Hua'
§	'Chang Hua'	MDun NLar
	'Charles Coates'	MDun NLar
	China Town = 'Jing Ning'	MDun
*	***chingii***	CBcs
	'Columbus'	CFil CPMA SSpi WPGP
	'Coral Lake'	MDun
	cordata	see *M. acuminata* var. *subcordata*
	- 'Miss Honeybee'	see *M. acuminata* var. *subcordata* 'Miss Honeybee'
	cylindrica misapplied	see *M.* 'Pegasus'
	cylindrica Wilson	CMCN CPMA EPfP IArd LRHS SPoG SSpi SSta
§	'Darrell Dean'	CTho WPGP
	'David Clulow'	CBcs CPMA CTho LRHS SSpi
	dawsoniana	CBcs CMCN EPfP IMGH NLar SSpi
	- 'Chyverton Red'	SSpi
	'Daybreak'	SSpi
	delavayi	CBcs CBrP CFil CHEx EPfP GGGa LRHS SAPC SArc SSpi WMul
§	***denudata*** ♀H3-4	CBcs CMCN CPMA CTho CTrw EMil EPfP ISea LMil LRHS SBrw SMur SReu SSpi SSta WDin WFar WMul WNor
	- 'Dubbel'	CBcs MDun

- 'Forrest's Pink' CBcs
- Fragrant Cloud = 'Dan Xin' CWib MDun NLar
- Yellow River = 'Fei Huang' CDoC CEnd CTbh CWib EBee IDee MBri MDun NLar SPoG WMul WOrn
'Editor Hopkins' **new** SSpi
'Elisa Odenwald' SSpi
'Elizabeth' ♀H4 CDoC CDul CMCN CPMA CTho EBee ELan ENot EPfP GGGa IMGH ISea LAst LMil LRHS MAsh MDun MGos SHBN SPer SPoG SSpi SSta WPGP
'Eskimo' **new** SSpi
'Felix Jury' **new** MAsh
'Fireglow' CTho
'Flamingo' **new** ENot
'Frank Gladney' CPMA CTho
'Frank's Masterpiece' MDun
fraseri AM form SSpi
'Full Eclipse' CFil WPGP
'Galaxy' ♀H4 CBcs CDoC CEnd CFil CMCN CSdC CTho EPfP IArd IMGH ISea LBuc LRHS MBar MBri MGos MSte NVic SBrw SLdr SLim SSpi SSta WBVN WBcn WBrE WDin WPGP
'George Henry Kern' CBcs CDoC COtt EBee IArd ISea LBuc LRHS MBri MSte NBlu NLar SSpi SSta WCFE WDin WFar
globosa CFil CPLG EBee GGGa WFar WPGP
- from India SSpi
'Gold Crown' SSpi
'Gold Star' CBcs CEnd CFil CMCN CPMA CTho EBee LBuc LRHS MBlu MGos NLar SHBN SSpi WBcn WOrn
'Golden Endeavour' MDun
'Golden Gift' SSpi
grandiflora CMCN CPLG EPfP EUJe LAst LRHS LSRN MRav MWya NBlu NLar SAPC SArc SHBN WBVN WDin WFar WGwG WMul WNor WOrn
- 'Bracken's Brown Beauty' **new** SSpi
- 'Edith Bogue' CPMA MAsh MGos MRav NLar WBVN
- 'Exmouth' ♀H3-4 More than 30 suppliers
- 'Ferruginea' CBcs NBea SLim
- 'Francois Treyve' IDee WGer
- 'Galissonnière' CBcs COtt CWib ECrN IMGH LRHS MGos MRav NBlu SBrw SLim SSpi SWvt WDin WFar WPGP
- 'Goliath' CBcs CEnd CFil CHEx CPSs ELan EPfP SBra SBrw SPoG SSpi WPGP
- 'Harold Poole' CBcs
- 'Little Gem' CBcs CDoC CPMA EBee EPfP LRHS SPoG SSpi WBcn WGer
- 'Mainstreet' CBcs
- 'Nannetensis' CPMA
- 'Overton' CBcs
- 'Russet' CBcs CPMA
- 'Saint Mary' CPMA
- 'Samuel Sommer' CPMA SAPC SArc
- 'Symmes Select' CBcs
- 'Undulata' WGer
- 'Victoria' ♀H3-4 CDoC CDul CPMA CTho EBee ELan EPfP LAst LHyd LRHS MAsh MBlu SBrw SLim SPoG SReu SSpi SSta WFar WPGP
'Heaven Scent' ♀H4 More than 30 suppliers
heptapeta see *M. denudata*
'Honey Liz' SSpi
§ 'Hong Yur' CEnd CPMA MDun WMul
'Hot Flash' **new** CEnd
hypoleuca see *M. obovata* Thunb.
'Iolanthe' CBcs CEnd CFil CMCN CMHG CPMA CSdC CTho ELan GKir LRHS MGos SPer SSpi SSta WFar WPGP
'J.C. Williams' CDoC CTho LRHS
'Jane' ♀H4 CDoC COtt CSdC ELan EPfP EWTr LMil LRHS MAsh MBri MGos SBrw SHBN SLdr SPer
'Jersey Belle' CBcs CPMA
§ 'Joe McDaniel' CDoC MBri SSpi WGer
'Jon Jon' CPMA
'Judy' COtt NEgg
'Kay Paris' **new** SSpi
kobus CBcs CLnd CMCN CSBt CTho EWTr IMGH MDun MWya NMoo SBLw SHBN SPer SPoG WDin WFar WNor
- var. ***borealis*** CPMA CTho
- 'Norman Gould' see *M. stellata* 'Norman Gould'
'Lamellan Surprise' CTho LRHS
'Leda' CMCN SSpi
§ ***liliiflora*** CTrw MBar WMul
§ - 'Nigra' ♀H4 More than 30 suppliers
- 'Oldfield' WPGP
* 'Limelight' SSpi
x ***loebneri*** CBcs GTSp LRHS WNor
- 'Ballerina' CDoC COtt MBri SBrw SSta
- 'Donna' NLar SSpi WGer
- 'Leonard Messel' ♀H4 More than 30 suppliers
- 'Merrill' ♀H4 CBcs CMCN CMHG CTho CTrh EBee ELan EPfP ISea LRHS MAsh MBri MGos SBrw SPer SReu SSpi SSta WBVN WDin WFar WPGP
- 'Snowdrift' NLar SSta
lotungensis NLar SSpi
macrophylla CBrP CFil CHEx CMCN EPfP IDee MBlu SAPC SArc SSpi WNor
§ - subsp. ***ashei*** SSpi WNor
macrophylla x ***macrophylla*** subsp. ***ashei*** **new** SSpi
'Manchu Fan' CBcs CDoC CMCN CPMA CSdC EMil IArd MDun NLar SMur SSpi SSta
'Margaret Helen' CBcs CPMA
'Marj Gossler' SSpi
'Mark Jury' CBcs
'Maryland' CFil CPMA CWib SBrw SSpi SSta
'Maxine Merrill' **new** IDee
'Milky Way' ♀H4 CBcs CMHG CPMA CTho LRHS MGos SMur SSpi
'Nimbus' CPMA SSpi
obovata Diels see *M. officinalis*
§ ***obovata*** Thunb. ♀H4 CFil CHEx CMCN CPMA CTho EPfP IDee IMGH MDun MLan NLar SHBN SPer SSpi SSta WDin WPGP
§ ***officinalis*** CFil CMCN EPfP NLar WBVN WFar WPGP
- var. ***biloba*** EPfP NLar SSpi
§ 'Pegasus' CEnd ISea SSpi SSta
'Peppermint Stick' CBcs CSdC SSta
'Peter Smithers' CPMA CTho WFar
'Phillip Tregunna' CBcs CTho LRHS
'Pickard's Opal' WBcn
'Pickard's Sundew' see *M.* 'Sundew'
'Pinkie' ♀H4 LRHS MBri NLar SSpi SSta WGer
'Pirouette' SSpi
'Princess Margaret' CPMA MBri SSpi
x ***proctoriana*** CAbP CDoC CFil CPLG EBee EPfP LRHS WPGP
- 'Proctoriana' LMil
- 'Slavin's Snowy' LRHS

	quinquepeta	see *M. liliiflora*
	'Randy'	EPfP
	'Raspberry Ice'	CDoC CMHG COtt CPLG CSam CSdC CTho CTrw EBee EPfP ISea LRHS MAsh NLar WFar
	'Ricki'	COtt CSdC EMil EPfP LBuc MBlu MGos NBlu NLar SPoG WFar
	rostrata	CFil SSpi WPGP
	'Rouged Alabaster'	LRHS
	'Royal Crown'	CBcs CDoC CSdC EMil MRav SLim WGer
	'Ruby'	CBcs CPMA MGos
	'Ruth'	CBcs
	salicifolia ♀H3-4	CBcs CFil CMCN EPfP ISea LRHS SBrw SSpi SSta
	- 'Jermyns'	SSpi
	- 'Wada's Memory' ♀H4	CDoC CFil CMCN CMHG CPMA CTho EBee ELan ENot EPfP GKir ISea LRHS MAsh MBri MSte NBea NVic SPer SSpi SSta WBVN WDin WFar
	- 'Windsor Beauty'	SSpi
	sargentiana var. ***robusta***	CBcs CBrd CEnd CMCN CTho ELan EPfP IMGH ISea MDun MGos SPer SSpi SSta WDin WFar
	- - 'Blood Moon'	SSpi
	- - 'Multipetal'	CBrd
	'Sayonara' ♀H4	CPMA EPfP MBri SBrw SSpi WDin WPGP
	'Schmetterling'	see *M.* x *soulangeana* 'Pickard's Schmetterling'
	'Serene'	CBcs CMHG CPMA LMil MBri SSpi SSta
	'Shirazz'	CBcs CPMA
	sieboldii	More than 30 suppliers
	- B&SWJ 4127	WCru
	- from Korea, hardy	GGGa
	- 'Colossus'	SSpi
	- 'Genesis'	SSpi
	- 'Michiko Renge'	NLar
	- subsp. ***sinensis***	CBcs CDoC CMCN CPMA CSam CTho ELan EPfP GGGa GGar IMGH LRHS MBlu MDun MWya SBrw SSpi SSta WCwm WDin WGer
	x ***soulangeana***	More than 30 suppliers
§	- 'Alba'	CBcs CDoC CEnd CSBt ECrN ENot EPfP LRHS MGos NBlu SLim SPer SSpi WBVN WFar
	- 'Alba Superba'	see *M.* x *soulangeana* 'Alba'
	- 'Alexandrina'	CBcs EPfP LRHS NLar SBrw
	- 'Amabilis'	COtt
	- 'Brozzonii' ♀H3-4	CDoC EPfP LRHS NLar SBrw SSpi
	- 'Burgundy' Clarke	CBcs CBot CDoC CTbh LRHS MBri WFar
	- 'Lennei' ♀H3-4	CBcs CDoC CEnd CMCN CMHG CSBt EPfP IMGH LRHS MAsh MGos MSwo NBea NPri SBrw SHBN SLim SRms WBVN WFar WNor WOrn
	- 'Lennei Alba' ♀H3-4	CDoC CMCN CSdC LRHS SBrw SLdr SPer WFar
	- 'Nigra'	see *M. liliiflora* 'Nigra'
	- 'Pickard's Ruby'	CBcs CRez MBri MDun
§	- 'Pickard's Schmetterling'	CDoC CSdC LMil MAsh SSta
	- 'Pickard's Snow Queen'	WGer
	- 'Pickard's Sundew'	see *M.* 'Sundew'
	- 'Picture'	CBcs CDoC WDin
	- Red Lucky	see *M.* 'Hong Yur'
	- 'Rubra' misapplied	see *M.* x *soulangeana* 'Rustica Rubra'
§	- 'Rustica Rubra' ♀H3-4	CBcs CDoC CMCN CSBt CTri EBee ELan ENot EPfP IMGH LAst LMil LRHS LSRN MAsh MBri MDun NVic SBrw SHBN SPer SPoG SReu SSpi SSta WBVN WDin WFar WPGP
	- 'San José'	CBcs LMil LRHS MAsh MDun NLar SSpi SSta WFar
	- 'Verbanica'	LMil LRHS MAsh NLar SPoG SSpi
	'Spectrum'	CBcs CEnd CFil CPMA CSdC IArd IDee LMil MGos NLar SSpi WPGP
	sprengeri	WNor WWes
	- 'Copeland Court'	CBcs CTho LRHS
	- var. ***diva***	CBcs CEnd CFil SSpi WPGP
	- - 'Burncoose'	CBcs CDoC
	- - 'Claret Cup'	SSpi
	- - 'Lanhydrock'	CFil CTho LRHS SSpi
	- var. ***elongata***	COtt
	- 'Eric Savill'	CTho LRHS SSpi
	- 'Marwood Spring'	CMHG CTho LRHS
	'Star Wars' ♀H4	CBcs CDoC CEnd CFil CPMA CSdC CTho EMil ENot EPfP LMil MAsh MBri NLar SBrw SMur SSpi SSta WGer WPGP
	'Stellar Acclaim'	MDun
§	***stellata*** ♀H4	More than 30 suppliers
	- 'Centennial'	CBcs CDoC MBri NLar SBrw WFar
	- 'Chrysanthemiflora'	LMil SSpi
	- 'Jane Platt'	MDun SSpi
	- f. ***keiskei***	CEnd COtt CSdC
	- 'King Rose'	CBcs CDoC COtt CSdC EPfP ISea LAst LRHS MAsh MBri MSte SPla
§	- 'Norman Gould'	CDoC EPfP MBri NLar SBrw SSta WDin WGer
	- 'Pink Perfection'	MDun
	- 'Rosea'	CMCN COtt ECrN ELan LRHS MBri MDun MGos MSwo NBlu NLar SHBN WDin
I	- 'Rosea Massey'	WFar
	- 'Royal Star'	More than 30 suppliers
	- 'Waterlily' ♀H4	CBcs CMCN CTbh EBee ELan EMil EPfP GKir IMGH LAst LRHS LSRN MAsh NLar NVic SLim SPla SPoG SSpi SSta WDin WFar
	'Summer Solstice'	CPMA SSpi
	'Sunburst'	MDun SSpi
	'Sundance'	CBcs CFil CPMA EMil MDun MGos NLar
I	'Sundew'	CBcs CDoC CMCN EPfP IArd MGos NLar SBrw SHBN WBVN
	'Susan' ♀H4	More than 30 suppliers
	'Susanna van Veen'	CBcs
	x ***thompsoniana***	CMCN EPfP IDee SSpi
	- 'Olmenhof'	SSpi
	'Thousand Butterflies'	CPMA
	'Tina Durio'	CDoC
	'Todd Gresham'	CPMA WPGP
	'Tranquility'	MDun SSpi
	'Trewidden Belle'	CEnd
	tripetala	CBcs CHEx CLnd CMCN CPne CTho EPfP IMGH MBlu MDun MLan NWea SHBN SSpi SSta WDin WMul WOrn WPGP
	x ***veitchii***	CDoC CDul CSBt EPfP SSpi SSta
	- 'Isca'	CTho
	- 'Peter Veitch'	CTho SSta
	virginiana	CMCN CPMA CPne CTho EBee EPfP LRHS SBig SPoG SSpi WDin WPGP
	- 'Havener'	IArd IDee
	- 'Henry Hicks'	SSpi
	- 'Moonglow'	CPMA
	'Vulcan'	CBcs CEnd CMCN CMHG CPMA CTho MAsh MBlu MDun
	x ***watsonii***	see *M.* x *wieseneri*
§	x ***wieseneri***	CBcs CFil CMCN CPMA CTho

	ELan EPfP GKir IDee LRHS MAsh MBlu SPer SSpi SSta WFar WPGP
- 'Aashild Kalleberg'	SSpi
wilsonii ♀H4	More than 30 suppliers
- 'Gwen Baker'	CEnd
'Yellow Fever'	CBcs CMCN CMHG CPMA CTho EMil MDun SMur SSta
'Yellow Lantern'	CAbP CBcs CEnd CMCN EPfP IDee LRHS MAsh MBlu NBea NLar SPoG SSpi SSta
zenii	CMCN CSdC

x *Mahoberberis* (*Berberidaceae*)

aquisargentii	ECrN EPfP GKir MRav SLon SPoG WDin WFar WPat
'Dart's Treasure'	EPla WFar
'Magic'	MGos
miethkeana	MBar SRms

Mahonia ✿ (*Berberidaceae*)

§ ***aquifolium***	CAgr CBcs CDul EBee ECrN ENot GKir LAst MBar MGos MRav NBlu NWea SHBN SPer SPlb SReu WCFE WDin WFar
- 'Apollo' ♀H4	More than 30 suppliers
- 'Atropurpurea'	CBcs ELan ENot EPfP EPla GKir LRHS MAsh NEgg NLar SHBN SPer SPla WDin
* - 'Cosmo Crawl'	MGos
- 'Fascicularis'	see *M.* x *wagneri* 'Pinnacle'
- 'Green Ripple'	EPfP MBri MGos NLar WBcn WFar
- 'Orange Flame'	EPfP MBlu NLar
- 'Smaragd'	CBcs CDoC CMac EBee ELan ENot EPfP EWTr LRHS LSRN MAsh MBlu MGos MRav WHCG
- 'Versicolor'	MBlu
bealei	see *M. japonica* Bealei Group
confusa	CDoC CFil NLar SSpi WBcn WCru WFar WPGP
eutriphylla	see *M. trifolia*
fortunei	EPla IDee NLar WBcn
fremontii	GCal SIgm
gracilipes	CFil EBee MBlu MDun NLar WBcn WCot WSPU
haematocarpa	SIgm
japonica ♀H4	More than 30 suppliers
§ - Bealei Group	CBcs CDul CSBt EBee ELan EPfP EPla EWTr GKir LAst LRHS MAsh MBar MGos MRav MSwo NBlu NEgg NPer SCoo SLim SMer SPoG SWvt WBor WDin WFar WWeb
- 'Gold Dust' **new**	IDee
- 'Hiemalis'	see *M. japonica* 'Hivernant'
§ - 'Hivernant'	EPla MGos NBlu WOrn
leschenaultii B&SWJ 9535 **new**	WCru
lomariifolia ♀H3	CBcs CBot EPfP LRHS SAPC SArc SBrw SSpi SSta
x ***media*** 'Buckland' ♀H4	CAbP CBcs CDul CMac CSBt CSam CTrw CWSG EBee EPfP ISea LAst LRHS MDun MRav NPen SPer SRms WPat
- 'Charity'	More than 30 suppliers
- 'Charity's Sister'	EBee EPla
- 'Faith'	EPla
- 'Lionel Fortescue' ♀H4	CBcs CBrm CEnd CMac CPSs CSBt CTrw CWSG EBee ELan EPfP EPla ISea LRHS MAsh MRav NCGa SMad SPer SPoG SReu SSpi SSta WFar WHCG
- 'Underway' ♀H4	EPfP EPla LRHS MAsh NLar SMur WWes
- 'Winter Sun' ♀H4	More than 30 suppliers
nervosa	CBcs COtt EPfP EPla IDee MBlu SBrw SPer WBcn WCru WPat
pallida	CFil EBee SIgm WCot
pinnata misapplied	see *M.* x *wagneri* 'Pinnacle'
pinnata ambig.	EBee ENot EPfP EPla MBar
pumila	SSpi WCru
repens	EPla MWhi NLar
- 'Rotundifolia'	EPla
russellii	CFil
x ***savilliana***	CFil EPla MBlu WCru WPGP
- 'Commissioner'	CWib
§ ***trifolia***	EPla
trifoliolata	EPfP
- var. ***glauca***	CEnd NLar
x ***wagneri*** 'Fireflame'	EPla
- 'Hastings Elegant'	NLar
- 'Moseri'	EMil NLar SSpi WPat
§ - 'Pinnacle' ♀H4	ELan EPfP EPla EWTr LRHS MGos MLan NFor SMur SPer
- 'Sunset'	MBlu NLar
- 'Undulata'	EPfP MBlu NEgg NLar SDix SPer SRms SWvt WHCG

Maianthemum (*Convallariaceae*)

bifolium	CAvo CBct CHid CPLG CRow EMan EPot GBuc GCra GFlt GKir LEdu MDun MNrw MTho NBro NMen SRms WCru WPGP WPnP WTin WWye
- from Yakushima	SOkd
§ - subsp. ***kamtschaticum***	CAvo CCol CLAP CRow EBee EHrv GIBF GKir LBuc SMac WCot WTin
- - B&SWJ 4360	WCru WPrP
* - - var. ***minimum***	WCru
canadense	EBee GKir NBid NMen WCru
* ***chasmanthum***	EBrs GKir LRHS
dilatatum	see *M. bifolium* subsp. *kamtschaticum*
racemosum	see *Smilacina racemosa*

Maihuenia (*Cactaceae*)

patagonica F&W 10241 **new**	WCot
poeppigii	EHyt SIgm SPlb
- JCA 2.575.600	WCot

Maireana (*Chenopodiaceae*)

georgei	SPlb

Malacothamnus (*Malvaceae*)

fremontii	EMan MDKP

Malcolmia (*Brassicaceae*)

littorea	XPep

Malephora (*Aizoaceae*)

crocea var. ***purpureocrocea***	XPep

Mallotus (*Euphorbiaceae*)

japonicus	CPLG
- B&SWJ 6852	WCru

Malpighia (*Malpighiaceae*)

coccigera	ESlt

Malus ✿ (*Rosaceae*)

§ 'Adirondack'	CDoC EPfP GKir LRHS MAsh MBri MGos SCoo SPoG
'Admiration'	see *M.* 'Adirondack'
x ***adstringens*** 'Almey'	ECrN
- 'Hopa'	CDul CLnd CTho SCrf
- 'Simcoe'	CLnd CTho EBee

Plant	Suppliers
'Aldenhamensis'	see *M.* x *purpurea* 'Aldenhamensis'
'Amberina'	CLnd
* ***arborescens***	CLnd CTho
x ***atrosanguinea***	CTho
§ - 'Gorgeous'	CCAT CDul CLnd COtt CTho CWSG ECrN GKir GTwe LRHS MAsh MGos MSwo NBlu SCoo SCrf SKee SLim SPer SPoG WDin WJas WOrn
baccata	CLnd CMCN CTho GTwe NWea SEND WNor
- W 264	GIBF
- 'Dolgo'	CCAT CDoC CTho LRHS SKee
- 'Gracilis'	SBLw
- 'Jackii' **new**	CTho
- 'Lady Northcliffe'	CLnd CTho SFam
- var. ***mandshurica***	CTho EPfP GIBF
- var. ***sibirica*** **new**	GIBF
aff. ***baccata***	MAsh NWea
-MF 96038	SSpi
§ ***bhutanica***	CDul CTho EPfP GIBF NLar SPer WNor
brevipes	CLnd CTho GKir SCoo
'Butterball'	CLnd CTho ECrN EPfP GKir LRHS MAsh MBlu SCoo SKee SPoG WDin WJas
* 'Cheal's Weeping'	ECrN LAst NBea
Coccinella = 'Courtarou'PBR	WDin
'Coralburst'	MBri SCoo
coronaria var. ***dasycaly*** x 'Charlottae' (d)	CDul CLnd EBee EPfP GKir LRHS MBri SCrf SFam SPer SPur
- 'Elk River'	LRHS MAsh
- 'Nieuwlandiana'	GIBF
'Crimson Brilliant'	CLnd
'Crittenden'	ECrN GKir MRav SMHT
denticulata	GIBF
* 'Directeur Moerlands'	CCVT CDoC EBee ECrN EGra EMil EPfP GKir LRHS MBri SPur WDin WJas
domestica (F)	MGos WMou
- 'Acme' (D)	SKee
- 'Adams's Pearmain' (D)	CCAT CTho GBut GKir GTwe LRHS MBri SFam SKee WJas
- 'Akerö' (D)	SKee
- 'Alfriston' (C)	CAgr SKee
- 'Alkmene' (D) ♀H4	GTwe SKee
- 'All Doer' (D/C/Cider)	CTho
- 'Allen's Everlasting' (D)	GTwe SKee
- 'Allington Pippin' (D)	CSBt CTho CTri ECrN LRHS SKee WJas
- 'American Golden Russet' (D)	CTho
- 'American Mother'	see *M. domestica* 'Mother'
- 'Annie Elizabeth' (C)	CAgr CCAT CTho CWib ECrN GKir GTwe LAst LBuc LRHS MBri SFam SKee WJas
- 'Api Rose' (D)	WJas
- 'Ard Cairn Russet' (D)	GBut GTwe SKee
- 'Aromatic Russet' (D)	SKee
- 'Arthur Turner' (C) ♀H4	CCVT CDoC CTri ECrN GBut GKir GTwe LBuc LRHS MGos SCrf SFam SKee WJas
- 'Ashmead's Kernel' (D) ♀H4	CAgr CCAT CSBt CTho CTri CWib ECrN EPfP ERea GKir GTwe LBuc LRHS MRav MWat NWea SCrf SFam SKee WHar WJas WOrn
- 'Ashton Bitter' (Cider)	CCAT CTho GTwe
- 'Ashton Brown Jersey' (Cider)	CCAT CTho
- 'Autumn Pearmain' (D)	CTho WJas
- 'Backwell Red' (Cider)	CCAT
- 'Baker's Delicious' (D)	ECrN SKee
- 'Ball's Bittersweet' (Cider)	CCAT CTho
- 'Ballyfatten' (C)	CTho
- 'Balsam'	see *M. domestica* 'Green Balsam'
- 'Barnack Beauty' (D)	CTho SKee
- 'Barnack Orange' (D)	SKee
- 'Barnhill Beauty'	CTho
- 'Baumann's Reinette' (D)	SKee
- 'Baxter's Pearmain' (D)	SKee
- 'Beauty of Bath' (D)	CAgr CCAT CCVT CDoC CTho CTri CWib ECrN GBut GKir GTwe LBuc LRHS SCrf SFam SKee WJas
- 'Beauty of Bedford' (D)	SKee
- 'Beauty of Hants' (D)	ECrN SKee
- 'Beauty of Moray' (C)	GBut GQui SKee
- 'Bedwyn Beauty' (C)	CTho
- 'Beeley Pippin' (D)	GTwe SKee
- 'Belfleur Kitaika' (D)	SKee
- 'Belfleur Krasnyi' (D) **new**	SKee
- 'Bell Apple' (Cider/C)	CCAT CTho
- 'Belle de Boskoop' (C/D) ♀H4	CCAT GTwe MCoo
- 'Belvoir Seedling' (D/C) **new**	SKee
- 'Ben's Red' (D)	CAgr CCAT CEnd CTho
- 'Bess Pool' (D)	SFam WJas
- 'Bewley Down Pippin'	see *M. domestica* 'Crimson King'
- 'Bickington Grey' (Cider)	CTho
- 'Billy Down Pippin' (F)	CTho
- 'Bismarck' (C)	CCAT SKee
- 'Black Dabinett' (Cider)	CCAT CTho
- 'Black Tom Putt' (C/D)	CTho
- 'Blackamore Red' (C)	CTho
- 'Blenheim Orange' (C/D) ♀H4	CCAT CCVT CDoC CSBt CTho CTri CWib ECrN ENot EPfP GKir GTwe LBuc LRHS MBri MCoo MRav MWat SCrf SFam SKee SPer WJas WOrn
- 'Blenheim Red' (C/D)	see *M. domestica* 'Red Blenheim'
- 'Bloody Butcher' (C)	CTho
- 'Bloody Ploughman' (D)	GKir GTwe SKee
- 'Blue Pearmain' (D)	SKee
- 'Blue Sweet' (Cider)	CTho
- Bolero = 'Tuscan'PBR (D/Ball)	ENot LRHS MGos SKee
- 'Bonum' (D/C)	CTho
- 'Boston Russet'	see *M. domestica* 'Roxbury Russet'
- 'Bountiful' (C)	CAgr CDoC COtt CSBt CTri CWib ECrN GKir GTwe LBuc LRHS MBri MGos SKee SPoG WBVN WHar
- 'Bow Hill Pippin' (D)	SKee
- 'Box Apple' (D)	SKee
- 'Braddick Nonpareil' (D)	SKee
- 'Braeburn' (D)	ECrN SKee
- 'Braintree Seedling' (D) **new**	SKee
- 'Bramley's Seedling' (C) ♀H4	More than 30 suppliers
- 'Bramley's Seedling' clone 20	CDoC MBri SCoo SPoG
- 'Bread Fruit' (C/D)	CEnd CTho
- 'Breakwell's Seedling' (Cider)	CCAT CTho
- 'Breitling' (D)	SKee
- 'Bridgwater Pippin' (C)	CCAT CTho WJas
- 'Broad-eyed Pippin' (C)	SKee
- 'Broadholm Beauty' **new**	MBri
- 'Brown Snout' (Cider)	CCAT CTho
- 'Brownlees Russet' (D)	CAgr CCAT CTho GTwe NWea SFam

- 'Brown's Apple' (Cider) CCAT GTwe
- 'Broxwood Foxwhelp' (Cider) CCAT CTho
- 'Bulmer's Norman' (Cider) CCAT
- 'Burn's Seedling' (D) CTho
- 'Burr Knot' (C) SKee
- 'Burrowhill Early' (Cider) CTho
- 'Bushey Grove' (C) SKee
- 'Buttery Do' CTho
- 'Byfleet Seedling' (C) **new** SKee
- 'Caledon' CTho
- 'Calville Blanc d'Hiver' (D) SKee
- 'Cambusnethan Pippin' (D) GBut GQui SKee
- 'Camelot' (Cider/C) CCAT CTho
- 'Cap of Liberty' (Cider) CCAT
- 'Captain Broad' (D/Cider) CCAT CEnd CTho
- 'Captain Kidd' (D) SKee
- 'Captain Smith' (F) CEnd
- 'Carlisle Codlin' (C) GKir GTwe
- 'Carswell's Honeydew' (D) **new** SKee
- 'Carswell's Orange' (D) **new** SKee
- 'Catshead' (C) CAgr CCAT CCVT GKir GQui SKee WJas
- 'Cellini' (C/D) SKee
- 'Charles Ross' (C/D) ♀H4 CAgr CCAT CDoC CMac CSBt CTho CTri ECrN GBon GBut GKir GTwe LAst LBuc LRHS MBri MCoo MRav MWat NBlu NWea SFam SKee WHar WJas WOrn
- 'Charlotte'PBR (C/Ball) ENot LRHS MGos SKee
- 'Chaxhill Red' (Cider/D) CCAT CTho
- 'Cheddar Cross' (D) CAgr CTri SKee
- 'Chelmsford Wonder' (C) SKee
- 'Chisel Jersey' (Cider) CCAT CTri
- 'Chivers Delight' (D) CAgr CCAT CSBt ECrN GTwe LBuc LRHS MCoo SCrf SKee WJas
- 'Chorister Boy' (D) CTho
- 'Christmas Pearmain' (D) CTho GTwe SFam SKee
- 'Cider Lady's Finger' (Cider) CCAT CTho
- 'Claygate Pearmain' (D) ♀H4 CCAT CTho GTwe MCoo SFam SKee WJas
- 'Cleeve' (D) **new** SKee
- 'Clopton Red' (D) SKee
- 'Clydeside' **new** GQui
- 'Coat Jersey' (Cider) CCAT
- 'Cockle Pippin' (D) CAgr CTho
- 'Cockpit' (C) **new** SKee
- 'Coeur de Boeuf' (C/D) SKee
- 'Coleman's Seedling' (Cider) CTho
- 'Collogett Pippin' (C/Cider) CCAT CEnd CTho
- 'Colonel Vaughan' (C/D) CTho SKee
- 'Colonel Yate' (D) **new** SKee
- 'Comrade' (D) **new** SKee
- 'Cooper's Seedling' (C) SCrf
- 'Cornish Aromatic' (D) CAgr CCAT CTho GTwe SCrf SFam SKee WJas
- 'Cornish Gilliflower' (D) CCAT CTho ECrN MCoo SFam SKee WJas WOrn
- 'Cornish Honeypin' (D) CTho SKee
- 'Cornish Longstem' (D) CAgr CEnd CTho
- 'Cornish Mother' (D) CEnd CTho
- 'Cornish Pine' (D) CEnd CTho SKee
- 'Coronation' (D) SKee
- 'Corse Hill' (D) CTho
- 'Cortland' (D) SKee
- 'Costard' (C) GTwe SKee
- 'Cottenham Seedling' (C) SKee
- 'Coul Blush' (D) GBut SKee
- 'Court of Wick' (D) CAgr CCAT CTho GKir SKee
- 'Court Pendu Plat' (D) CCAT CTho GKir LBuc MWat NWea SFam SKee WJas WOrn

§ - 'Court Royal' (Cider) CCAT CTho
- 'Cow Apple' (C) CTho
- 'Cox's Orange Pippin' (D) CBcs CCAT CCVT CMac CSBt CTri CWib ECrN ENot GTwe LBuc LRHS MWat NBlu NEgg NPri NWea SCrf SFam SKee SPer WJas WOrn
- 'Cox's Pomona' (C/D) CTho SKee WJas
- 'Cox's Rouge de Flandres' (D) SKee
- 'Cox's Selfing' (D) CDoC CWSG CWib EPfP ERea GTwe LBuc MBri MGos NBlu SCrf SKee SPoG WHar WJas
- 'Crawley Beauty' (C) CAgr CCAT GTwe SFam SKee WJas
- 'Crawley Reinette' (D) **new** SKee
- 'Crimson Beauty of Bath' (D) **new** CAgr
- 'Crimson Bramley' (C) CCAT

§ - 'Crimson King' (Cider/C) CAgr CCAT CTho
- 'Crimson King' (D) **new** CAgr
- 'Crimson Peasgood' (C) GKir
- 'Crimson Queening' (D) SKee WJas
- 'Crimson Victoria' (Cider) CTho
- Crispin see *M. domestica* 'Mutsu'

§ - 'Crowngold' (D) GTwe
- 'Curl Tail' (D) SKee
- 'Dabinett' (Cider) CCAT CTho CTri GTwe LBuc SCrf SKee WOrn
- 'D'Arcy Spice' (D) CCAT CLnd ECrN EMil EPfP SFam SKee
- 'Dawn' (D) SKee
- 'De Boutteville' (Cider) CTho
- 'Decio' (D) SKee
- 'Delprim' (D) SKee
- 'Devon Crimson Queen' (D) CTho
- 'Devonshire Buckland' (C) CEnd CTho
- 'Devonshire Quarrenden' (D) CCAT CEnd CTho GBut GKir SFam SKee WJas
- 'Devonshire Red' (D/C) CTho
- 'Discovery' (D) ♀H4 CAgr CBcs CCAT CDoC CSBt CTri CWib ECrN ENot EPfP GBon GBut GKir GTwe LBuc LRHS MBri MRav MWat NBlu NWea SFam SKee SPer SPoG WJas WOrn
- 'Doctor Hare's' (C) MCoo WJas
- 'Doctor Harvey' (C) ECrN SFam
- 'Doctor Kidd's Orange Red' see *M. domestica* 'Kidd's Orange Red'
- 'Doll's Eye' CTho
- 'Domino' (C) SKee
- 'Don's Delight' (C) CTho
- 'Dove' (Cider) CTho
- 'Downton Pippin' (D) WJas
- 'Dredge's Fame' (D) CTho
- 'Duchess of Oldenburg' (C/D) SKee
- 'Duchess's Favourite' (D) SKee
- 'Duck's Bill' (D) SKee
- 'Dufflin' (Cider) CCAT CTho
- 'Duke of Cornwall' (C) CTho
- 'Duke of Devonshire' (D) CTho GBut SFam SKee WJas
- 'Duke of Gloucester' (C) WJas

N - 'Dumeller's Seedling' (C) see *M. domestica* 'Dummellor's Seedling'

	Name	Suppliers
§	- 'Dummellor's Seedling' (C) 🏆H4	CCAT CTho SKee
	- 'Dunkerton Late Sweet' (Cider)	CCAT CTho
§	- 'Dutch Mignonne' (D)	SKee
	- 'Dymock Red' (Cider)	CCAT
	- 'Eady's Magnum' (C)	SKee
	- 'Early Blenheim' (D/C)	CEnd CTho
	- 'Early Bower' (D)	CEnd
	- 'Early Julyan' (C)	GBut GQui SKee WJas
	- 'Early Victoria'	see *M. domestica* 'Emneth Early'
	- 'Early Worcester'	see *M. domestica* 'Tydeman's Early Worcester'
	- 'East Lothian Pippin' (C) **new**	GBut GQui
	- 'Easter Orange' (D)	GTwe SCrf SKee
	- 'Ecklinville' (C)	SKee WJas
	- 'Edith Hopwood' (D) **new**	SKee
	- 'Edward VII' (C) 🏆H4	CDoC GBut GKir GTwe SCrf SFam SKee WJas
	- 'Egremont Russet' (D) 🏆H4	More than 30 suppliers
	- 'Ellis' Bitter' (Cider)	CCAT CTho GTwe
	- 'Ellison's Orange' (D) 🏆H4	CCAT CSBt CTri CWib ECrN GBon GBut GKir GTwe LBuc LRHS NEgg NWea SFam SKee WHar WJas
	- 'Elstar' (D) 🏆H4	CWib ECrN GTwe MRav NBlu SKee
	- 'Elton Beauty' (D)	SKee
§	- 'Emneth Early' (C) 🏆H4	CAgr ECrN GBut GTwe SFam SKee WJas WOrn
	- 'Empire' (D)	SKee
	- 'English Codling' (C)	CTho
	- 'Epicure' (D)	see *M. domestica* 'Laxton's Epicure'
	- 'Excelsior' (C) **new**	SKee
	- 'Exeter Cross' (D)	CCAT SFam
	- 'Fair Maid of Devon' (Cider)	CCAT CTho
	- 'Fairfield' (D)	CTho
	- 'Fall Russet' (D)	GTwe
	- 'Falstaff'PBR (D) 🏆H4	CAgr CCAT CDoC ECrN EPfP GKir GTwe MGos SCoo SKee WBVN WJas
	- 'Farmer's Glory' (D) **new**	CAgr CTho
	- 'Fiesta'PBR (D) 🏆H4	CAgr CCAT CDoC CSBt CTri CWSG CWib ECrN ENot EPfP GBon GTwe LBuc LRHS MBri MGos NBlu NPri SCoo SFam SKee SPoG WBVN WHar WJas WOrn
	- 'Fillbarrel' (Cider)	CCAT CTho
	- 'Five Crowns' (D)	SKee
	- 'Flame' (D) **new**	SKee
	- 'Flamenco'	see *M. domestica* 'Obelisk'
§	- 'Flower of Kent' (C)	CCAT SCrf SKee
	- 'Flower of the Town' (D)	SKee
	- 'Forfar'	see *M. domestica* 'Dutch Mignonne'
	- 'Forge' (D)	CAgr SKee
	- 'Fortune'	see *M. domestica* 'Laxton's Fortune'
	- 'Forty Shilling' (D) **new**	GBut
	- 'Foster's Seedling' (D)	SKee
	- 'Francis' (D)	SKee
	- 'Frederick' (Cider)	CCAT CTho
	- 'French Crab' (C)	CTho
	- 'Freyberg' (D)	SKee
	- 'Fuji' (D)	SKee
	- 'Gala' (D)	CSBt GBon GTwe NEgg NPri SCoo SCrf SFam SKee
§	- 'Gala Mondial' (D)	WJas
I	- 'Gala Royal'	see *M. domestica* 'Royal Gala'

	Name	Suppliers
	- 'Galloway Pippin' (C)	GBut GKir GQui GTwe SKee
	- 'Garnet' (D) **new**	SKee
	- 'Gascoyne's Scarlet' (D)	CCAT SFam SKee
	- 'Gavin' (D)	GBut SKee
	- 'Genet Moyle' (C/Cider)	CCAT CTho WJas
	- 'George Carpenter' (D)	CTho SKee
	- 'George Cave' (D)	CTho ECrN GBut GTwe MCoo SCrf SFam SKee WJas
	- 'George Neal' (C) 🏆H4	CAgr CTho SFam
	- 'Gilliflower of Gloucester' (D)	CTho
	- 'Ginny Lin' (D)	CTho
	- 'Gladstone' (D)	CAgr CTho SKee WJas
§	- 'Glass Apple' (C/D)	CEnd CTho
	- 'Gloria Mundi' (C)	SKee
	- 'Gloster '69' (D)	GTwe NBlu
	- 'Gloucester Cross' (D)	SKee
	- 'Gloucester Royal' (D)	CTho
	- 'Gloucester Underleaf'	CTho
	- 'Golden Ball'	CTho
	- 'Golden Bittersweet' (D)	CTho
	- 'Golden Delicious' (D) 🏆H4	CSBt CWib ECrN ENot GBon NBlu NWea SCrf SKee SPer WHar WOrn
	- 'Golden Harvey' (D)	CAgr CCAT CTho
	- 'Golden Knob' (D)	CCAT CTho SKee
	- 'Golden Monday' (D) **new**	GBut
	- 'Golden Noble' (C) 🏆H4	CCAT CDoC CTho ECrN GKir GTwe MCoo SFam SKee WOrn
	- 'Golden Nugget' (D)	CAgr
	- 'Golden Pippin' (C)	CAgr CCAT CTho GBut SKee
	- 'Golden Reinette' (D)	GTwe SKee
	- 'Golden Russet' (D)	CAgr GTwe SKee
	- 'Golden Spire' (C)	GBut MCoo SKee
	- 'Gooseberry' (C)	SKee
	- 'Goring' (Cider)	CTho
	- 'Grand Sultan' (D)	CCAT CTho
	- 'Granny Smith' (D)	CLnd CWib ECrN GTwe NPri SCrf SKee SPer
	- 'Gravenstein' (D)	CCAT GQui SFam SKee
	- 'Greasy Butcher'	CTho
	- 'Greasy Pippin' (D/C)	CTho
§	- 'Green Balsam' (C)	CTri
	- 'Green Kilpandy Pippin' (C) **new**	GQui
	- 'Greensleeves'PBR (D) 🏆H4	CAgr CCAT CDoC CSBt CTri CWSG CWib ECrN GKir GTwe LRHS MGos NEgg NWea SKee SPoG WBVN WHar WJas WOrn
	- 'Greenup's Pippin' (D)	GBut
	- 'Grenadier' (C) 🏆H4	CAgr CDoC CSBt CTri ECrN GBut GKir GTwe LRHS MGos NEgg SCrf SKee WBVN WJas WOrn
	- 'Halstow Natural' (Cider)	CAgr CTho
	- 'Hambledon Deux Ans' (C)	SKee
	- 'Hangy Down' (Cider)	CCAT CTho
	- 'Hannan Seedling' (D) **new**	SKee
	- 'Harragan Payne' (D)	CTho
§	- 'Harry Master's Jersey' (Cider)	CCAT CTho CTri
	- 'Harry Pring' (D) **new**	SKee
	- 'Harvester' (D)	CTho
	- 'Harvey' (C)	SKee
	- 'Hawthornden' (C)	GBut GQui GTwe SKee
	- 'Hereford Cross' (D)	SKee
	- 'Herefordshire Beefing' (C)	SKee WJas WOrn
	- 'Herefordshire Pippin' (D)	CTho
	- 'Herring's Pippin' (D)	CTri GTwe SKee

- 'Heusgen's Golden Reinette' (D) — CCAT SKee
- 'Hibernal' (C) — SKee
- 'High View Pippin' (D) — SKee
- 'Hoary Morning' (C) — CCAT CTho SKee
- 'Hocking's Green' (C/D) — CAgr CCAT CEnd CTho
- 'Holland Pippin' (C) — SKee
- 'Hollow Core' (C) — CAgr CTho
- 'Holstein' (D) — COtt CTho GTwe SKee
- 'Hood's Supreme' (D) **new** — GBut
- 'Horneburger Pfannkuchen' (C) — SKee
- 'Howgate Wonder' (C) — CAgr CCAT CCVT CDoC CSBt CWib ECrN GBon GBut GKir GTwe LBuc LRHS NPri SCrf SFam SKee SPer WBVN WJas
- 'Hubbard's Pearmain' (D) — SKee
- 'Hunt's Duke of Gloucester' (D) — CTho
- 'Idared' (D) 🏆^{H4} — CWib ECrN GBon GKir MGos SKee
- 'Improved Dove' (Cider) — CCAT
- 'Improved Keswick' (C/D) — CEnd CTho
- 'Improved Lambrook Pippin' (Cider) — CCAT CTho CTri
- 'Improved Redstreak' (Cider) — CTho
- 'Ingrid Marie' (D) — SCrf SKee WJas
- 'Irish Johnnies' — CTho
- 'Irish Peach' (D) — CAgr CCAT ECrN GBut GKir GTwe LBuc LRHS MCoo SFam SKee WJas
- 'Isaac Newton's Tree' — see *M. domestica* 'Flower of Kent'
- 'Jackson's' (Cider) — see *M. domestica* 'Crimson King'
- 'James Grieve' (D) 🏆^{H4} — More than 30 suppliers
- 'Jester' (D) — ECrN GTwe SKee
- 'John Apple' (C) — SKee
- 'John Standish' (D) — CAgr CCAT CTri GTwe SCrf
- 'John Toucher's' — see *M. domestica* 'Crimson King'
- 'Johnny Andrews' (Cider) — CAgr CCAT CTho
- 'Johnny Voun' (D) — CEnd CTho
- 'Jonagold' (D) 🏆^{H4} — CTri CWib ECrN GTwe NWea SCrf SFam SKee SPer WJas
- 'Jonagold Crowngold' — see *M. domestica* 'Crowngold'
- § 'Jonagored'^{PBR} (D) — ECrN SKee
- 'Jonared' (D) — GTwe
- 'Jonathan' (D) — SKee
- 'Jordan's Weeping' (C) — GTwe WJas
- 'Joybells' (D) — GKir SKee
- 'Jubilee' — see *M. domestica* 'Royal Jubilee'
- 'Jupiter'^{PBR} (D) 🏆^{H4} — CCAT CSBt CTri CWib ECrN GBon GKir GTwe MGos NPri SCoo SKee WJas WOrn
- 'Karmijn de Sonnaville' (D) — SKee
- § 'Katja' (D) — CAgr CCAT CCVT CDoC CTri CWib ECrN EPfP GBon GBut GKir GTwe LBuc LRHS SCoo SCrf SKee SPer WHar WJas WOrn
- Katy — see *M. domestica* 'Katja'
- 'Keegan' — CTho
- 'Kent' (D) — GTwe MCoo SCrf SKee
- 'Kentish Fillbasket' (C) — SKee
- 'Kentish Pippin' (C/Cider/D) — SKee
- 'Kerry Pippin' (D) — GBut SKee
- 'Keswick Codlin' (C) — CTho ECrN GBut GKir GTwe MCoo NWea SKee WJas
- § 'Kidd's Orange Red' (D) 🏆^{H4} — CCAT CTri ECrN GQui GTwe LBuc LRHS SCrf SFam SKee WJas
- 'Kill Boy' — CTho
- 'Killerton Sharp' (Cider) — CTho
- 'Killerton Sweet' (Cider) — CTho
- 'King Byerd' (C/D) — CEnd CTho
- 'King Charles' Pearmain' (D) — CTho SKee
- 'King George V' (D) — SKee
- § 'King of the Pippins' (D) 🏆^{H4} — CCAT CTho CTri ECrN GBut GTwe LBuc MCoo SCrf SFam SKee WOrn
- 'King's Acre Bountiful' (C) — WJas
- 'King's Acre Pippin' (D) — CCAT SFam WJas
- 'Kingston Bitter' (Cider) — CTho
- 'Kingston Black' (Cider/C) — CCAT CTho CTri GTwe SKee
- 'Kirton Fair' (D) — CTho
- 'Knobby Russet' (D) — GTwe SKee
- 'Lady Henniker' (D) — CCAT CTho ECrN GTwe SKee WJas
- 'Lady Isabel' (D) **new** — SKee
- 'Lady of the Wemyss' (C) — GBut GQui SKee
- 'Lady Sudeley' (D) — CTho GBut SKee
- 'Lady's Finger' (C/D) — CEnd GKir
- 'Lady's Finger of Lancaster' (C/D) — SKee
- 'Lakeland' (D) — SKee
- 'Lake's Kernel' (D) — CTho
- 'Lamb Abbey Pearmain' (D) — SKee
- 'Lamb's Seedling' (D) **new** — SKee
- 'Lane's Prince Albert' (C) 🏆^{H4} — CCAT CSBt ECrN GBon GBut GKir GTwe LRHS MGos MRav MWat NWea SCoo SCrf SFam SKee WJas WOrn
- § 'Langworthy' (Cider) — CCAT CTho
- 'Lass o' Gowrie' (C) — GBut GQui SKee
- § 'Laxton's Epicure' (D) 🏆^{H4} — CAgr ECrN GBon GTwe LAst SFam SKee WJas
- § 'Laxton's Fortune' (D) 🏆^{H4} — CCAT CMac CSBt CTri CWib ECrN GBut GKir GTwe MGos NWea SCrf SFam SKee WHar WJas
- 'Laxton's Rearguard' (D) — SKee WJas
- § 'Laxton's Superb' (D) — CBcs CCAT CCVT CDoC CSBt CTri CWib ECrN ENot GBon GKir GTwe LAst LBuc LRHS MBri MCoo NEgg NPri SCrf SKee SPer WHar WJas WOrn
- 'Leathercoat Russet' (D) — CAgr CTho SKee
- 'Leatherjacket' (C) **new** — SKee
- 'Lemon Pippin' (C) — CCAT CTho SKee WJas
- 'Lemon Pippin of Gloucestershire' (D) — CTho
- 'Lewis's Incomparable' (C) — SKee
- 'Liberty' (D) — GBut
- 'Limberland' (C) — CTho
- 'Limelight' (D) — MBri SCoo SKee
- 'Linda' (D) — SKee
- 'Listener' (Cider/D) — CTho
- 'Lobo' (D) — SCrf
- § 'Loddington' (C) — SKee
- 'London Pippin' (C) — CAgr CTho SKee
- 'Longkeeper' (D) — CAgr CEnd CTho
- 'Longstem' (Cider) — CTho
- 'Lord Burghley' (D) — GTwe SKee
- 'Lord Derby' (C) — CCAT CMac CTho CWib ECrN GBut GKir GTwe MBri SCrf SFam SKee
- 'Lord Grosvenor' (C) — GTwe
- 'Lord Hindlip' (D) — GTwe SFam WJas
- 'Lord Lambourne' (D) 🏆^{H4} — CAgr CCAT CCVT CDoC CSBt CTri CWib ECrN EPfP GKir GTwe LRHS

MCoo MWat SCoo SCrf SFam SKee SPer WBVN WHar WJas WOrn
- 'Lord of the Isles' (F) CCAT
- 'Lord Stradbroke' (C) SKee
- 'Lord Suffield' (C) CTri
- 'Love Beauty' (D) **new** GBut
- 'Lucombe's Pine' (D) CAgr CEnd CTho
- 'Lucombe's Seedling' (D) CTho
- 'Lynn's Pippin' (D) SKee
- 'Maclean's Favourite' (D) SKee
- 'Madresfield Court' (D) SKee WJas
- 'Maggie Sinclair' (D) **new** GBut GQui
- 'Major' (Cider) CCAT CTho
- 'Maldon Wonder' (D) **new** SKee
- 'Malling Kent' (D) SFam
- 'Maltster' (D) SKee WJas
- 'Manaccan Primrose' (C/D) CEnd CLnd
- 'Manks Codlin' (C) GBut
- 'Margil' (D) CCAT GTwe SFam SKee
- 'Mary Golds' CTho
- 'May Beauty' (D) **new** SKee
- 'May Queen' (D) SFam WJas
- 'Maypole'[PBR] (D/Ball) LRHS MGos WJas
- 'Maypole 2000' (C/Ball) ENot
- 'McIntosh' (D) SKee
- 'Melba' (D) SKee
- 'Melcombe Russet' (D) CTho
- 'Melrose' (D) ECrN GTwe SKee
- 'Merchant Apple' (D) CTho
- 'Mère de Ménage' (C) SFam
- 'Meridian'[PBR] (D) CDoC ECrN MBri SKee
- 'Merton Knave' (D) GTwe MGos SFam
- 'Merton Worcester' (D) ECrN SKee
- 'Michaelmas Red' (D) GTwe SKee WJas
- 'Michelin' (Cider) CCAT CTri GTwe SKee WOrn
- 'Miller's Seedling' (D) GTwe SKee WJas
- 'Mollie's Delicious' (D) SKee
- 'Monarch' (C) CCAT CTri ECrN GBut GTwe SFam SKee WJas

I - 'Mondial Gala' see *M. domestica* 'Gala Mondial'
- 'Monidel'[PBR] ECrN SKee
- 'Montfort' (D) **new** SKee
- 'Morgan's Sweet' (C/Cider) CCAT CTho CTri SKee

§ - 'Mother' (D) ♀H4 CCAT CDoC CSBt CTri GTwe SCrf SFam SKee WJas
- 'Munster Tulip' (D/C) CTho

§ - 'Mutsu' (D) CCAT CTri ECrN GTwe SCrf SKee
- 'Nanny' (D) **new** SKee
- 'Nemes Szercsika Alma' (C) SKee
- 'Newton Wonder' (D/C) ♀H4 CAgr CCAT CDoC CMac CSBt CTho CTri CWib ECrN GTwe LBuc LRHS SCrf SFam SKee WJas
- 'Nine Square' (D) CTho
- 'No Pip' (C) CTho
- 'Nolan Pippin' (D) **new** SKee
- 'Nonpareil' (D) SKee
- 'Norfolk Beauty' (C) SKee
- 'Norfolk Beefing' (C) ECrN SFam SKee
- 'Norfolk Royal' (D) CDoC ECrN GTwe SKee
- 'Norfolk Royal Russet' (D) **new** GBut
- 'Norfolk Summer Broadend' (C) SKee
- 'Norfolk Winter Coleman' (C) SKee
- 'Northcott Superb' (D) CTho
- 'Northern Greening' (C) GTwe SKee

§ - 'Northwood' (Cider) CCAT CTho
- 'Nutmeg Pippin' (D) ECrN
- 'Oaken Pin' (C) CCAT CTho

§ - 'Obelisk' (D) ENot MGos SKee
- 'Old Pearmain' (D) CTho
- 'Old Somerset Russet' (D) CTho
- 'Opal' (D) **new** SKee
- 'Opalescent' (D) SKee
- 'Orange Goff' (D) SKee
- 'Orkney Apple' (F) SKee
- 'Orleans Reinette' (D) CAgr CCAT CTho CTri CWib ECrN GBut GTwe LBuc LRHS MWat SCrf SFam SKee WJas
- 'Oslin' (D) GBut SKee
- 'Owen Thomas' (D) CTri SKee
- 'Paignton Marigold' (Cider) CTho
- 'Palmer's Rosey' (D) SKee
- 'Park Farm Pippin' **new** SKee
- 'Pascoe's Pippin' (D/C) CTho
- 'Paulared' (D) SKee
- 'Payhembury' (C/Cider) CTho
- 'Peacemaker' (D) SKee
- 'Pear Apple' (D) CAgr CEnd CTho
- 'Peasgood's Nonsuch' (C) ♀H4 CCAT CDoC ECrN GKir GTwe LRHS SCrf SFam SKee WJas WOrn
- 'Peck's Pleasant' (D) SKee
- 'Pendragon' (D) CTho
- 'Penhallow Pippin' (D) CTho
- 'Peter Lock' (C/D) CAgr CEnd CTho
- 'Pickering's Seedling' (D) SKee
- 'Pig's Nose Pippin' (D) CEnd
- 'Pig's Nose Pippin' Type III (D) CAgr CTho
- 'Pig's Snout' (Cider/C/D) CCAT CEnd CTho
- 'Pine Golden Pippin' (D) SKee
- 'Pinova' (D) **new** SKee
- 'Pitmaston Pine Apple' (D) CCAT CTho CTri ECrN LAst LRHS MCoo SCrf SFam SKee WJas WOrn
- 'Pitmaston Russet Nonpareil' (D) SKee
- 'Pixie' (D) ♀H4 CCAT CSam CWib GTwe SFam SKee WJas
- 'Plum Vite' (D) CAgr CTho CTri
- 'Plympton Pippin' (C) CEnd CTho
- Polka = 'Trajan'[PBR] (D/Ball) ENot LRHS MGos SKee
- 'Polly' (C/D) CEnd
- 'Polly Whitehair' (C/D) CTho
- 'Pomeroy of Somerset' (D) CCAT CTho SKee
- 'Ponsford' (C) CAgr CCAT CTho
- 'Pónyik Alma' (c) SKee
- 'Port Allen Russet' (C/D) **new** GQui
- 'Port Wine' see *M. domestica* 'Harry Master's Jersey'
- 'Porter's Perfection' (Cider) CCAT CTho
- 'Pott's Seedling' (C) SKee
- 'Princesse' GKir SKee WBVN
- 'Quarry Apple' (C) CTho
- 'Queen' (C) CAgr CCAT CTho SKee
- 'Queen Caroline' (C) **new** SKee
- 'Queen Cox' (D) ECrN GBon SKee
- 'Queen Cox' self-fertile CWib
- 'Queens' (D) CTho
- 'Quench' (D/Cider) CTho
- 'Radford Beauty' MCoo
- 'Rajka' (D) **new** SKee
- 'Red Alkmene' (D) MBri
- 'Red Belle de Boskoop' (D) **new** CAgr

§ - 'Red Blenheim' (C/D) SKee
- 'Red Bramley' (C) CWib

	Cultivar	Suppliers
	- 'Red Delicious' (D)	SCrf SKee
	- 'Red Devil' (D)	CAgr COtt CTri CWSG ECrN GKir GTwe LRHS MBri SCoo SKee SPoG WJas
	- 'Red Ellison' (D)	CCAT CTho CTri GTwe SCrf
	- 'Red Elstar' (D)	SCrf
	- 'Red Falstaff'PBR (D)	CAgr CDoC ECrN GKir LBuc LRHS MBri MCoo NBlu NLar SKee SPoG WBVN
	- 'Red James Grieve' **new**	SKee
	- 'Red Jersey' (Cider)	CCAT
	- 'Red Joaneting' (D)	SKee
	- 'Red Jonagold'PBR	see *M. domestica* 'Jonagored'
	- 'Red Miller's Seedling' (D)	SCrf
	- 'Red Rattler' (D)	CTho
	- 'Red Robin' (F)	CEnd
	- 'Red Roller' (D)	CTho
	- 'Red Ruby' (F)	CTho
	- 'Red Victoria' (C)	GTwe
	- 'Red Windsor'	GKir SCoo SKee SPoG
	- 'Redsleeves' (D)	CAgr ECrN GTwe SKee
	- 'Redstrake' (Cider)	CCAT
	- 'Reine des Reinettes'	see *M. domestica* 'King of the Pippins'
	- 'Reinette d'Obry' (Cider)	CCAT
	- 'Reinette du Canada' (D)	SKee
	- 'Reinette Rouge Etoilée' (D)	CCAT
	- 'Reverend W. Wilks' (C)	CAgr CCAT CDoC COtt CTri ECrN GKir LRHS MWat SCrf SFam SKee WJas
	- 'Ribston Pippin' (D) 🏆H4	CCAT CTho CWib ECrN GBut GTwe LBuc LRHS MCoo MWat SCrf SFam SKee WJas
	- 'Rival' (D)	CAgr WJas
	- 'Robin Pippin' (D)	GTwe
	- 'Rosemary Russet' (D) 🏆H4	CAgr CCAT CTho GBut GTwe MCoo SCrf SFam SKee
	- 'Ross Nonpareil' (D)	CAgr GTwe SKee
	- 'Rosy Blenheim' (D) **new**	SKee
	- 'Roter Ananas' (D)	SKee
	- 'Roter Eiserapfel' (D)	SKee
	- 'Rough Pippin' (D)	CEnd CTho
	- 'Roundway Magnum Bonum' (D)	CAgr CCAT CTho
§	- 'Roxbury Russet' (D)	SKee
§	- 'Royal Gala' (D) 🏆H4	ECrN LRHS
§	- 'Royal Jubilee' (C)	CCAT
	- 'Royal Russet' (C)	ECrN
	- 'Royal Snow' (D)	SKee
	- 'Royal Somerset' (C/Cider)	CCAT CTho
	- 'Rubens' (D)	SKee
	- 'Rubinette' (D)	COtt ECrN GTwe MGos SKee WBVN
	- 'Saint Cecilia' (D)	WJas
§	- 'Saint Edmund's Pippin' (D) 🏆H4	CTho ECrN GTwe SCrf SFam SKee
	- 'Saint Edmund's Russet'	see *M. domestica* 'Saint Edmund's Pippin'
	- 'Saint Everard' (D)	SKee
	- 'Saltcote Pippin' (D)	SKee
	- 'Sam Young' (D)	CAgr SKee
	- 'Sandringham' (C)	ECrN SKee
	- 'Sanspareil' (D)	CAgr SKee
	- 'Santana' (D) **new**	SKee
	- 'Saturn'PBR	CTri GBut GTwe SKee SPoG
	- 'Saw Pits' (F)	CAgr CEnd
	- 'Scarlet Crofton' (D)	SKee
	- 'Scarlet Nonpareil' (D)	SKee
	- 'Scarlet Pimpernel' (D)	SCrf
	- 'Scilly Pearl' (C)	WJas
	- 'Scotch Bridget' (C)	GBut GKir NBid SCoo SKee WJas WOrn
	- 'Scotch Dumpling' (C)	GBut GKir GTwe LRHS MCoo
	- 'Scrumptious'PBR (D)	CAgr CDoC GKir MBri NBlu NLar SCoo SKee SPer SPoG WBVN
	- 'Seabrook's Red' (D) **new**	SKee
	- 'Sercombe's Natural' (Cider)	CTho
	- 'Severn Bank' (C)	CCAT CTho
	- 'Shakespeare' (D)	WJas
	- 'Sheep's Nose' (C)	CCAT SKee
	- 'Shenandoah' (C)	SKee
	- 'Shoesmith' (C)	SKee
	- 'Sidney Strake' (C)	CAgr CEnd
	- 'Sikulai Alma' (D)	SKee
	- 'Sir Isaac Newton's'	see *M. domestica* 'Flower of Kent'
	- 'Sisson's Worksop Newtown' (D)	SKee
	- 'Slack Ma Girdle' (Cider)	CCAT CTho
	- 'Snell's Glass Apple'	see *M. domestica* 'Glass Apple'
	- 'Somerset Lasting' (C)	CTho
	- 'Somerset Redstreak' (Cider)	CCAT CTho GTwe
	- 'Sops in Wine' (C/Cider)	CCAT CTho
	- 'Sour Bay' (Cider)	CAgr CTho
	- 'Sour Natural'	see *M. domestica* 'Langworthy'
	- 'Spartan' (D)	CCAT CDoC CSBt CTri CWib ECrN GBon GKir GTwe LRHS MGos NBlu NEgg NPri SCoo SCrf SFam SKee SPer SPoG WJas WOrn
	- 'Spencer' (D)	CTri ECrN SKee
	- 'Spotted Dick' (Cider)	CTho
	- 'Stable Jersey' (Cider)	CCAT
	- 'Stanway Seedling' (C) **new**	SKee
	- 'Star of Devon' (D)	CCAT
	- 'Starking' (D)	ECrN
	- 'Starkrimson' (D)	SKee
	- 'Stembridge Cluster' (Cider)	CCAT
	- 'Stembridge Jersey' (Cider)	CCAT
	- 'Stirling Castle' (C)	CAgr GBut GKir GQui GTwe SKee
	- 'Stobo Castle' (C)	GQui SKee
	- 'Stockbearer' (C)	CTho
	- 'Stoke Edith Pippin' (D)	WOrn
	- 'Stoke Red' (Cider)	CCAT CTho
	- 'Stone's'	see *M. domestica* 'Loddington'
	- 'Stoup Leadington' (C)	SKee
	- 'Strawberry Pippin' (D)	CTho WJas
	- 'Striped Beefing' (C)	SKee
	- 'Strippy' (C)	CTho
	- 'Stub Nose' (F)	SKee
	- 'Sturmer Pippin' (D)	CSBt ECrN GTwe LRHS MWat SCrf SFam SKee WJas
*	- 'Sugar Apple'	CTho
	- 'Sugar Bush' (C/D)	CTho
	- 'Summer Golden Pippin' (D)	SKee
	- 'Summerred' (D)	ECrN EMil
	- 'Sunburn' (D)	SKee
I	- 'Sunrise' (D)	LRHS SKee
	- 'Sunset' (D) 🏆H4	CCAT CCVT CDoC CSBt CSam CTho CTri CWib ECrN EPfP GBut GKir GTwe LBuc LRHS MBri MRav NBlu NPri NWea SCoo SCrf SFam SKee SPer SPoG WHar WJas WOrn
	- 'Suntan' (D) 🏆H4	CCAT CWib ECrN GBon GTwe MWat SKee
	- 'Superb'	see *M. domestica* 'Laxton's Superb'
	- 'Surprise' (D)	GTwe
	- 'Sweet Alford' (Cider)	CCAT CTho
	- 'Sweet Bay' (Cider)	CTho

Name	Suppliers
- 'Sweet Caroline' (D) **new**	ECrN
- 'Sweet Cleave' (Cider)	CCAT CTho
- 'Sweet Coppin' (Cider)	CTho CTri
- 'Sweet Ermgaard' (D) **new**	ECrN
- 'Sweet Society' (D) **new**	MBri
- 'Tale Sweet' (Cider)	CCAT CTho
- 'Tamar Beauty' (F)	CEnd
- 'Tan Harvey' (Cider)	CCAT CEnd CTho
- 'Taunton Cross' (D)	CAgr
- 'Taunton Fair Maid' (Cider)	CCAT CTho
- 'Taylor's' (Cider)	CCAT
- 'Ten Commandments' (D/Cider)	CCAT WJas
- 'Téton de Demoiselle' (D)	SKee
- 'Tewkesbury Baron' (D)	CTho
- 'The Rattler' (F)	CEnd
- 'Thorle Pippin' (D)	GBut SKee
- 'Tidicombe Seedling' (D)	CTho
- 'Tom Putt' (C)	CCAT CCVT CTho CTri CWib ECrN GKir GTwe LBuc LRHS SKee WJas WOrn
- 'Tommy Knight' (D)	CAgr CCAT CEnd CTho
- 'Topaz' (D) **new**	SKee
- 'Totnes Apple' (D)	CTho
- 'Tower of Glamis' (C)	GQui GTwe SKee
- Town Farm Number 59 (Cider)	CTho
- 'Transparente de Croncels' (C)	CTho
- 'Tregonna King' (C/D)	CCAT CEnd CTho
- 'Tremlett's Bitter' (Cider)	CCAT CTho
- 'Twenty Ounce' (C)	CCAT GTwe WJas
§ - 'Tydeman's Early Worcester' (D)	CAgr CLnd CWib ECrN GTwe LRHS SKee WJas
- 'Tydeman's Late Orange' (D)	CTri ECrN GTwe LAst MCoo SFam SKee
- 'Upton Pyne' (D)	CCAT CTho SCrf SKee
- 'Vallis Apple' (Cider) **new**	CTho
- 'Veitch's Perfection' (C/D)	CTho
- 'Venus Pippin' (C/D)	CEnd
- 'Vileberie' (Cider)	CCAT
- 'Vista-bella' (D)	ECrN GTwe SKee WJas
- 'Wagener' (D)	SKee
- Waltz = 'Telamon'PBR (D/Ball)	LRHS MGos SKee
- 'Wanstall Pippin' (D)	SKee
- 'Warner's King' (C) ♀H4	CTho CTri SCrf SKee WJas
- 'Warrior'	CTho
- 'Wealthy' (D)	SKee
- 'Wellington' (C)	see *M. domestica* 'Dummellor's Seedling'
- 'Wellington' (Cider)	CTho
§ - 'Wellspur' (D)	GTwe
- 'Wellspur Red Delicious'	see *M. domestica* 'Wellspur'
- 'West View Seedling' (D) **new**	SKee
- 'White Alphington' (Cider)	CTho
- 'White Astrachan' (D)	CTho
- 'White Close Pippin' (Cider)	CTho
- 'White Jersey' (Cider)	CCAT
- 'White Joaneting' (D)	GTwe
- 'White Melrose' (C)	GBut GKir GTwe MCoo SKee
- 'White Paradise' (C)	SKee
- 'White Transparent' (C/D)	SKee
- 'Wick White Styre' (Cider) **new**	CTho
- 'William Crump' (D)	CCAT CTho ECrN SFam WJas
- 'Winston' (D) ♀H4	CAgr CCAT CCVT CSBt CTri ECrN GTwe NWea SCrf SFam
- 'Winter Banana' (D)	ECrN SKee
- 'Winter Gem' (D)	CDoC COtt ECrN GKir LBuc LRHS MBri MGos SKee SPoG WBVN
- 'Winter Lawrence' **new**	CTho
- 'Winter Lemon' (C/D) **new**	GQui
- 'Winter Peach' (D/C)	CEnd CTho
- 'Winter Pearmain' (D)	SKee
- 'Winter Stubbard' (C)	CTho
- 'Wolf River' (D/C) **new**	SKee
- 'Woodbine'	see *M. domestica* 'Northwood'
- 'Woodford' (C) **new**	SKee
- 'Woolbrook Pippin' (D)	CAgr CCAT CTho
- 'Woolbrook Russet' (C)	CCAT CTho SKee
- 'Worcester Pearmain' (D) ♀H4	CBcs CCAT CCVT CDoC CSBt CTho CTri CWib ECrN ENot GBon GBut GKir GTwe LBuc LRHS MWat NPri NWea SCoo SFam SKee SPer SPoG WHar WJas WOrn
- 'Wormsley Pippin' (D)	ECrN SKee
- 'Wyatt's Seedling'	see *M. domestica* 'Langworthy'
- 'Wyken Pippin' (D)	CCAT ECrN GBut GTwe SFam SKee WJas
- 'Yarlington Mill' (Cider)	CCAT CTho CTri SKee
- 'Yellow Ingestrie' (D)	SFam SKee WJas
- 'Yellow Styre' (Cider)	CTho
- 'Yorkshire Aromatic' (C) **new**	GBut
- 'Zabergäu Renette' (D)	SKee
'Donald Wyman'	SCoo
'Echtermeyer'	see *M.* x *gloriosa* 'Oekonomierat Echtermeyer'
'Evelyn' **new**	MBri
§ 'Evereste' ♀H4	More than 30 suppliers
florentina	CMCN CTho EPfP GIBF LTwo SCoo
floribunda ♀H4	CCAT CDoC CDul CEnd CLnd CSBt CSam CWSG EBee ELan ENot EPfP GKir GTwe LBuc LRHS MBri MGos MRav MSwo NWea SCrf SHBN SKee SPer WDin WHar WJas WNor WOrn
'Gardener's Gold'	CEnd CTho
§ x ***gloriosa*** 'Oekonomierat Echtermeyer'	CCAT GKir MAsh SCrf WDin WJas
'Golden Gem'	CCAT EPfP GBut GTwe LRHS MAsh MDun SKee
'Golden Hornet'	see *M.* x *zumi* 'Golden Hornet'
'Goldsworth Red'	CCAT
'Harry Baker'	ERea LRHS MAsh MBlu SCoo
'Hillieri'	see *M.* x *schiedeckeri* 'Hillieri'
hupehensis ♀H4	CCAT CCVT CDul CEnd CLnd CMCN CSBt CTho EBee ENot EPfP GKir GTwe LRHS MBlu MRav SCrf SFam SHBN SLPl SPer WMou
'Hyde Hall Spire' **new**	MBri SCoo
'John Downie' (C) ♀H4	More than 30 suppliers
'Kaido'	see *M.* x *micromalus*
kansuensis	CLnd GIBF WCwm WMou
'Laura'PBR	COtt EPfP GKir LRHS MAsh MBlu MGos SCoo SKee SPoG
x ***magdeburgensis***	CCVT CLnd CSBt
'Mandarin'	LRHS MAsh
'Marshal Ôyama'	CTho MBlu
'Mary Potter' **new**	CTho
§ x ***micromalus***	CLnd
x ***moerlandsii***	CLnd
- 'Liset'	CCVT CEnd CLnd CWib EBee ECrN MAsh MRav NEgg SCoo SFam SPer SPoG WFar WJas

§	- 'Profusion'	CBcs CDul CLnd CTri ECrN ELan ENot GKir LRHS MBri MGos MRav MSwo NEgg NWea SCrf SHBN SPer WBVN WDin WJas
	- 'Profusion Improved'	CCAT CEnd COtt CSBt CWSG GKir MAsh MWat SCoo SKee SLim WOrn
	- 'Red Profusion' **new**	CTho
	niedzwetzkyana	see *M. pumila* 'Niedzwetzkyana'
	orthocarpa	CLnd
	Perpetu	see *M.* 'Evereste'
	'Pink Glow'	LRHS MAsh MBlu SCoo SLim SPoG
	'Pink Mushroom' **new**	SCoo
	'Pink Perfection'	CDoC CEnd CLnd ENot LRHS MDun SHBN SKee SPer
	Pom'Zaï = 'Courtabri'	CDoC
	'Prairie Fire'	EBee MAsh MBri SCoo
	prattii	CLnd CTho
	'Profusion'	see *M.* x *moerlandsii* 'Profusion'
	prunifolia 'Fastigiata'	GIBF
	- 'Fructu Coccinea' **new**	CTho
	- var. ***prunifolia***	GIBF
	- var. ***rinkii***	GIBF
	pumila 'Cowichan'	LRHS
	- 'Dartmouth'	CCAT CDul CLnd CSBt CSam CTho CTri ECrN NEgg SFam
	- 'Montreal Beauty'	GKir LRHS SCoo WJas WOrn
§	- 'Niedzwetzkyana'	CLnd
§	x ***purpurea*** 'Aldenhamensis'	CCAT CLnd SCrf WDin WOrn
	- 'Eleyi'	CLnd ECrN MRav NWea SCrf WDin
	- 'Lemoinei'	CLnd ECrN
	- 'Neville Copeman'	CDoC CDul CLnd CTri ECrN EWTr LRHS MBlu MGos SMHT SPur WJas
	- 'Pendula'	see *M.* x *gloriosa* 'Oekonomierat Echtermeyer'
	'R.J. Fulcher'	CLnd CTho
	'Ralph Shay'	CLnd
	'Red Barron'	CLnd
	'Red Glow'	CLnd COtt ECrN MAsh SCrf WJas
	'Red Jade'	see *M.* x *schiedeckeri* 'Red Jade'
	'Red Obelisk' **new**	GKir
	'Robinson' **new**	MAsh SPoG
§	x ***robusta***	CLnd CTri GTwe LRHS NWea SCrf SLon
	- 'Red Sentinel' ♀H4	More than 30 suppliers
	- 'Red Siberian'	ECrN SHBN SPer
	- 'Yellow Siberian'	CLnd SPer
	rockii	GIBF
	'Royal Beauty' ♀H4	CDoC CLnd CWib EGra ENot EPfP GKir GTwe LRHS MAsh MBri MGos MRav MSwo SCoo SCrf SMHT SPer WDin WHar WOrn
	'Royalty'	More than 30 suppliers
	'Rudolph'	CAlb CCAT CCVT CDul CLnd EBee ECrN EWTr LRHS MAsh MRav SCoo SLim SPoG WJas
	'Ruth Ann'	CLnd
	sargentii	see *M. toringo* subsp. *sargentii*
	'Satin Cloud'	CLnd
§	x ***scheideckeri*** 'Hillieri'	CCAT CDul CLnd CTho ECrN MAsh SCrf SFam
§	- 'Red Jade'	More than 30 suppliers
	Siberian crab	see *M.* x *robusta*
	sieboldii	see *M. toringo*
	sikkimensis	GIBF WHCr
	- B&SWJ 2431	WCru
	'Silver Drift'	CLnd
	'Snowcloud'	CCAT CDul CEnd CLnd EBee ECrN ENot LRHS MAsh MBlu MBri SHBN SPer WOrn
	spectabilis	CLnd
	'Street Parade'	CLnd
	'Striped Beauty' **new**	CTho
	x ***sublobata*** **new**	CTho
	'Sun Rival'	CCAT CDoC CDul CEnd COtt CSBt CWSG EPfP GKir GTwe LRHS MAsh MBri MDun MGos SCoo SFam SLim SPoG WHar WJas
	sylvestris	CArn CCVT CDul CLnd CRWN CTri ECrN EPfP GKir LBuc MRav NBee NWea WDin WMou
§	***toringo***	CLnd CTho ECrN GIBF SCoo SSpi WSHC
	- var. ***arborescens***	CTho GIBF
§	- subsp. ***sargentii***	CDul CLnd CMCN CTho ECrN EWTr GKir LRHS MBri MGos MRav NWea SFam SPer SPoG WNor
	- - 'Tina'	CLnd
	toringoides	see *M. bhutanica*
	- 'Mandarin' **new**	SCoo
	transitoria ♀H4	CCAT CDoC CDul CEnd CFil CLnd CTho EBee ECrN EMil EPfP GIBF GKir LRHS MAsh MBlu NWea SCoo SPer SSpi WPGP
	- 'Thornhayes Tansy'	CTho LRHS MBri
	trilobata	CCAT CFil CLnd CTho EPfP MAsh MBlu MBri MGos NLar SCoo SPoG WMou WPGP
	- 'Guardsman'	EBee GKir MBri
	tschonoskii ♀H4	More than 30 suppliers
	'Van Eseltine'	CAlb CCAT CDul CLnd CSBt CWSG CWib GKir GTwe LRHS MAsh MBri MWat NEgg SFam SKee SPer SPoG WJas
	'Veitch's Scarlet'	CDul CLnd CSBt CTho GTwe SFam
§	'White Star'	CDoC CDul CSBt CWSG ECrN LRHS SCoo SKee SLim
	'Winter Gold'	CDoC CDul CLnd CSam SCrf SPoG
	'Wisley Crab'	CLnd EMil GTwe SFam SKee
	yunnanensis	GIBF
	- var. ***veitchii***	CTho GIBF
	x ***zumi*** var. ***calocarpa***	CLnd CTho
§	- 'Golden Hornet' ♀H4	More than 30 suppliers
	- 'Professor Sprenger'	CLnd CSam

Malva (Malvaceae)

	alcea	CAgr EPfP
	- var. ***fastigiata***	CArn EMan ERou LRHS MBow NBid NBro NBur SPer SRms WPer
	bicolor	see *Lavatera maritima*
	fastigiata **new**	SMar
	'Gibbortello'	CCge NBur
	moschata	CAgr CArn CBcs CElw CPrp CRWN CSev EBee EChP ECtt ELan EPfP ERou GKev MBow MChe MHer NBlu NLsd NMir SECG SIde SMad SPer SPlb WGwG WHer WMoo WWye
	- f. ***alba*** ♀H4	More than 30 suppliers
	- 'Romney Marsh'	see *Althaea officinalis* 'Romney Marsh'
	- ***rosea***	EPfP GMaP LAst NBlu NCot NEgg NPer SWvt WPnP WWeb
	'Park Allee'	EBee EChP ECtt GBin LDai MAvo MCCP MMHG SUsu
	'Park Rondell' **new**	EBee
	sylvestris	CAgr CArn GWCH MBow MChe NBro NMir SMad WHer WJek WMoo WWye
	- 'Alba'	CArn EMon
	- 'Brave Heart'	CM&M GBri NBur NLar NLsd SPav SRkn SWvt WGwG
I	- 'Magic Hollyhock' (d)	SGar

- Marina = 'Dema'PBR ELan NLar
- subsp. ***mauritiana*** CHea EPfP GBri NPer WMoo
- - 'Bibor Fehlo' CSpe EWin MAnH NArg NBur NGdn WCFE WHil
- 'Mystic Merlin' CBgR CM&M EBee SPav WCAu WGwG
- 'Perry's Blue' EBee NPer
- 'Primley Blue' CBot CElw EBee EChP ECha ECtt ELan EMan EPfP GBri GMaP MRav MTho NBPC NBlu NCot NGdn NPer NSti SMad SPer WFar WGwG
- 'Richard Perry' CBcs NPer
- 'Windsor Castle' NLsd
- 'Zebrina' CM&M EBee GBri LDai NBur NGdn NLsd NPri SWvt WHil WHlf WMoo WRha

verticillata 'Crispa' CAgr MChe

Malvastrum (*Malvaceae*)

I x ***hypomadarum*** see *Anisodontea* x *hypomadara* (Sprague) D.M. Bates
lateritium More than 30 suppliers
* ***latifolium*** SOkh

Malvaviscus (*Malvaceae*)

arboreus CHll CKob XPep
- var. ***mexicanus*** CPLG ERea SYvo
- pink CKob

mandarin see *Citrus reticulata*

Mandevilla (*Apocynaceae*)

x ***amabilis*** 'Alice du Pont' ♀H1 CBcs CPLN CRHN CSpe CTbh ELan EMil ERea ESlt
boliviensis ♀H1 CPLN ELan ESlt
hirsuta new CPLN
§ ***laxa*** ♀H2 CHEx CHll CPLN EBee ELan ERea EShb ESlt SBrw SHFr WCot WCru WHrl WSHC
sanderi EShb MBri
- 'Rosea' CSpe ERea
splendens ♀H1 CPLN EBak LRHS
suaveolens see *M. laxa*

Mandragora (*Solanaceae*)

autumnalis EEls GCal ITer LEdu MGol MSal NJOw NLar
caulescens CFir CFwr GAbr
§ ***officinarum*** CFwr EEls GCal GPoy LEdu MGol MHer MSal SMad

Manettia (*Rubiaceae*)

inflata see *M. luteorubra*
§ ***luteorubra*** ELan

Manfreda see *Agave*

Manglietia (*Magnoliaceae*)

chevalieri HWJ 533 new WCru
conifera CBcs CFil SSpi WPGP
fordiana new CBcs
insignis CBcs CFil CHEx SSpi WPGP

Manihot (*Euphorbiaceae*)

esculenta CKob
- 'Variegata' CKob EAmu

Mansoa (*Bignoniaceae*)

hymenaea new CPLN

Manulea (*Crassulaceae*)

altissima 'Lemon Haze' new NLsd

Maranta (*Marantaceae*)

leuconeura EShb XBlo
var. ***erythroneura*** ♀H1
- var. ***kerchoveana*** ♀H1 CHal LRHS MBri XBlo

Margyricarpus (*Rosaceae*)

§ ***pinnatus*** CFee CPLG CPle GEdr GGar NWCA WPer
setosus see *M. pinnatus*

Mariscus see *Cyperus*

marjoram, pot see *Origanum onites*

marjoram, sweet see *Origanum majorana*

marjoram, wild, or oregano see *Origanum vulgare*

Marrubium (*Lamiaceae*)

candidissimum see *M. incanum*
catariifolium MGGn
cylleneum ECha MGGn
* - 'Velvetissimum' CStr SBla WCHb
friwaldskyanum XPep
'Gold Leaf' ECha
§ ***incanum*** CBot EChP EGoo EMan IFro MBri MGGn NCGa WEas
libanoticum ECha MGGn WPer
pestalloziae EBee WCot
supinum CArn CStr XPep
vulgare CArn CWan ELau GBar GPoy GWCH MChe MGGn MHer SECG SIde WCHb WGHP WHer WPer WSel WWye
- 'Green Pompon' ELau NLar

Marshallia (*Asteraceae*)

grandiflora CDes NLar SIgm SUsu
trinerva EBee SUsu WCot

Marsilea (*Marsileaceae*)

quadrifolia IHMH WWpP

Massonia (*Hyacinthaceae*)

depressa CStu
echinata CMon CStu
aff. ***echinata*** new CStu
pustulata CMon CStu

Mathiasella (*Apiaceae*)

bupleuroides WCot
from Mexico SIgm

Matricaria (*Asteraceae*)

chamomilla see *M. recutita*
parthenium see *Tanacetum parthenium*
maritima see *Tripleurosperma maritimum*
§ ***recutita*** GPoy MChe
tchihatchewii XPep

Matteuccia (*Woodsiaceae*)

intermedia see *Onoclea intermedia*
orientalis CAby CLAP ERod GCal NGby NLar NOrc WFar WRic
pensylvanica CLAP EMon WRic
struthiopteris ♀H4 More than 30 suppliers
- 'Bedraggled Feathers' EMon
* - 'Depauperata' CLAP
- 'Jumbo' new CLAP

Matthiola (*Brassicaceae*)

§	***fruticulosa***	EWin
	- 'Alba'	CDes EBee EWin WPGP
	- subsp. ***perennis***	EBee NWCA WHal
	incana	CBgR CBos MArl NSti SSth WMnd WPer WRHF
	- ***alba***	CBot CHrt ELan GBBs LSou NBir SPav WBVN WCot
	- purple **new**	LSou
	thessala	see *M. fruticulosa*
	white perennial	CArn CHad CMea CMil CSev CSpe ECGP ERou ETow EVFa LPhx LRav MBct MSte MWgw NBrk NPer SEND SSth SWal WCAu WEas

Maurandella (*Scrophulariaceae*)

§	***antirrhiniflora***	CSec LRHS

Maurandya (*Scrophulariaceae*)

§	***barclayana***	CBot CHII CRHN CSpe MBri SGar WRos
	- ***alba***	CBot CSpe
	erubescens	see *Lophospermum erubescens*
	lophantha	see *Lophospermum scandens*
	lophospermum	see *Lophospermum scandens*
	'Pink Ice'	see *Lophospermum scandens* 'Pink Ice'
	'Red Dragon'	see *Lophospermum* 'Red Dragon'
§	'Victoria Falls'	LSou

Maytenus (*Celastraceae*)

	boaria	CMCN EPfP LEdu NLar SAPC SArc SLon WFar WPGP
	- 'Worplesdon Fastigiate'	CFil
	chubutensis	LEdu
	disticha **new**	LEdu
	magellanica	CFil WFar

Mazus (*Scrophulariaceae*)

	radicans	CStu WCru
	reptans	CTbh EBee EDAr EMan EPfP ESis GEdr NFla NWCA SIng WOut WPer
	- 'Albus'	EBee EDAr EMFW NJOw SIng SPlb WPer

Meconopsis ✿ (*Papaveraceae*)

	aculeata	GGGa GTou
	baileyi	see *M. betonicifolia*
	Ballyrogan form	GEdr IBlr
	x ***beamishii***	GBuc GFle NLon
§	***betonicifolia*** ♀H4	More than 30 suppliers
	- var. ***alba***	EBee EDAr ELan EPfP GBuc GCra GGGa GGar GKev GMaP ITim MBri NChi NEgg NLar SPer SRms WCAu WPnP
	- 'Glacier Blue'	GAbr GGar
	- 'Hensol Violet'	CAby EBee EChP GBuc GCal GCra GCrs GFle GGGa GGar GKev ITim NLar
	- purple	ITim
	cambrica	CHrt CTri EBee EHrv ELan EMar GGar GTou MBow NCot NLsd NPri SChu SGar SIng WAbe WBrk WFar WGwG WHer WPnP WWye
	- 'Anne Greenaway' (d)	ELan WCot
	- var. ***aurantiaca***	EBee LSou SBch
	- ***flore-pleno*** (d)	CHar GBuc MTho NBid
	- - orange (d)	NBid NBir NPol WAbe WCot
	- - yellow (d)	WCot
§	- 'Frances Perry'	CBgR ETow GBuc GCal IBlr WCot WFar WRos
	- 'Muriel Brown' (d)	GKev NCot
	- 'Rubra'	see *M. cambrica* 'Frances Perry'
	chelidoniifolia	GCal GCra GKir IBlr IGor NBid SSpi WCru WFar
	delavayi	GGGa
	dhwojii	GBri GKev LRHS NEgg
	- GWJ 9264	WCru
	discigera HWJK 2282 **new**	WCru
	(Fertile Blue Group) 'Blue Ice'	see *M.* (Fertile Blue Group) 'Lingholm'
N	- 'Lingholm'	CAby CLAP CPne CSam EBee EPza GBBs GBuc GCal GCra GCrs GEdr GFle GFlt GGar GKev GMaP GTou IPot ITer ITim MDun NCGa NChi NEgg NGdn SSpi WBVN WPGP
	forrestii **new**	GFle WHil
N	George Sherriff Group	EBee GAbr GBuc GCal GCra GEdr IBlr NBir
N	- 'Ascreavie'	GCrs GMaP
N	- 'Branklyn' ambig.	CFil EBee GAbr GBri IBlr WFar WPGP
N	- 'Huntfield'	GCrs GMaP
N	- 'Jimmy Bayne'	GAbr GBuc GCrs GEdr GGGa GMaP
	- 'Spring Hill'	GBuc IBlr
	grandis misapplied	see *M.* George Sherriff Group
N	***grandis*** ambig.	CHar CPLG CSam ENot EWTr GEdr GGGa GIBF ITim LRHS MNrw NEgg NSla SBla SPoG SRms WAbe WBVN WHlf WPnP
	grandis Prain **new**	GFle GKev
	- from Sikkim **new**	GCrs
	- GS 600	see *M.* George Sherriff Group
	- GWJ 9275	WCru
	- HWJK 2304	WCru
	- 'Alba' **new**	GAbr
	- Balruddery form	GGGa
	henrici	GGGa
	horridula	CAby GFle GGGa GKev LRHS MTho NEgg NLar
	- BWJ 7983	WCru
	- HWJK 2293	WCru
*	- ***alba*** **new**	GFle
	- var. ***racemosa***	see *M. racemosa* var. *racemosa*
N	(Infertile Blue Group) 'Bobby Masterton'	GBuc GCrs
N	- 'Crewdson Hybrid'	EBee EChP GBuc GCrs GMaP NLar
N	- 'Cruickshank'	GCrs
N	- 'Dawyck'	GCra GCrs
N	- 'Mrs Jebb'	GBuc GCra GCrs GMaP
	- 'Mrs McMurtrie'	IBlr
N	- 'Slieve Donard' ♀H4	GAbr GBri GBuc GCra GCrs GMaP GMac IBlr
	integrifolia	EBee GFle GGGa GKev LRHS
	- ACE 1798	GTou
§	- subsp. ***integrifolia*** 'Wolong'	GCrs
	'Keillour'	GKev
	Kingsbarns hybrids	GCrs GGGa
	lancifolia	GGGa
	latifolia	GGGa NEgg
	napaulensis	CFil CPLG CSam EBee EDAr ENot GAbr GCrs GEdr GFlt GGGa GGar GKev GKir GMaP IBlr LRHS MBri MDun NChi NEgg NLar SPoG WHil WLin WMoo
	- pink-flowered	CBcs EBee GKev NEgg NGdn WPGP
	- red-flowered	CBcs GBuc GKev ITim MDun WCru
	nudicaulis	see *Papaver nudicaule*
	'Ormswell' ambig.	GBuc IBlr

paniculata	GGGa GIBF GKev IBlr ITer ITim LRHS MDun NBir NEgg WAbe WLin
- CC&McK 296	GTou
- GWJ 9312	WCru
- HWJK 2167	WCru
- HWJK 2315	WCru
- from Ghunsa, Nepal	CDes CLAP
- ginger foliage	MDun
- pink/yellow stripes **new**	GKev
pseudointegrifolia	GCra GGGa GKev GKir NEgg
- B&SWJ 7595	WCru
punicea	GCrs GGGa GIBF GKev GMac
quintuplinervia ♀H4	CBos CLAP GBri GCra GCrs GEdr GFle GFlt GGGa GKev GMaP GTou IBlr IGor NBid NBir NRya NSla
- 'Kaye's Compact'	GBuc GEdr IBlr
***racemosa* new**	GFle
§ - var. ***racemosa***	GFle
regia	EBee GAbr GIBF GKev LRHS NBPC NLar WMoo
regia* x *grandis	GBuc
robusta	CPne EBee
x ***sarsonsii***	GKev
x ***sheldonii*** misapplied (sterile)	see *M.* Infertile Blue Group
N x ***sheldonii*** ambig.	CBcs CWCL EBee ENot EPfP EWTr GAbr GBin GBuc GGGa GKir LAst MBri MDun NBPC NBir NBlu NLon SMac SPoG SRms WCru WFar WHlf WPnP
simplicifolia	GGGa GKev NEgg
superba	GBuc GGGa GKev NEgg
villosa	CPLG GBuc GFle GGGa GKev GTou IBlr WBVN WCru
wallichii	EBee GGGa GIBF GKev NEgg
- GWJ 9400	WCru
- white-flowered	GKev
'Willie Duncan'	GMaP

Medeola (*Convallariaceae*)

virginica	LAma WCru

Medicago (*Papilionaceae*)

arborea	CArn IBlr SEND SPlb XPep
sativa	WHer WMoo
- subsp. ***sativa***	IBlr

Medinilla (*Melastomataceae*)

magnifica ♀H1	LRHS MBri

medlar see *Mespilus germanica*

Meehania (*Lamiaceae*)

cordata	CDes EBee IFro NLar
urticifolia	CDes EBee EPPr MHar MSte WSHC WTMC
- B&SWJ 1210	WCru
- 'Wandering Minstrel' (v)	CDes EBee EMan EMon WCot

Megacodon (*Gentianaceae*)

stylophorus	GKev

Melaleuca (*Myrtaceae*)

acuminata	SPlb
alternifolia	CArn ECou ELau EOHP EShb GBar GPoy IDee MGol MHer MSal NTHB WHer
armillaris	CDoC CHEx CTrC SGar SPlb
bracteata	CTrC ECou
cuticularis	SPlb
decussata	ECou EUnu SPlb
§ ***diosmatifolia***	EUnu
ericifolia	CTri SPlb
erubescens	see *M. diosmatifolia*
fulgens	EShb SPlb
gibbosa	CChe CFwr CPLG CRez EBee ECou IArd IDee WSHC
hypericifolia	CPLG CTrC ECou SPlb
incana	CTrC
lateritia	ECou EShb
leucadendra	MSal
linariifolia	CTrC ECou SPlb
nesophila	ECou EShb IDee SPlb
pulchella	EShb
pungens	SPlb
pustulata	ECou
radula	EShb
***scabra* new**	EShb
squamea	CTrC EBee
squarrosa	CPLG CTrC ECou GKir SPlb
thymifolia	ECou SPlb
viridiflora	GQui
wilsonii	ECou

Melandrium see *Vaccaria*

rubrum	see *Silene dioica*

Melanoselinum (*Apiaceae*)

§ ***decipiens***	CArn CHEx CSpe GCal ITer LPhx SIgm WPGP

Melasphaerula (*Iridaceae*)

graminea	see *M. ramosa*
§ ***ramosa***	CBre CStu ERos WPrP

Melia (*Meliaceae*)

§ ***azedarach***	CArn CBcs CHEx ELau EShb LRav WPGP
- B&SWJ 7039	WCru
- var. ***japonica***	see *M. azedarach*

Melianthus (*Melianthaceae*)

comosus	EShb EUnu EWes GGar LPio SPlb WGwG
elongatus	CPne CSec CTrC EShb
major ♀H3	More than 30 suppliers
minor	CFir LPio SIgm
villosus	CFir CPle CSec CTrC EShb EUnu GFlt LPio MCCP SGar SIgm SPlb WOut

Melica (*Poaceae*)

altissima 'Alba'	EHoe
- 'Atropurpurea'	More than 30 suppliers
ciliata	CBig COIW EHoe GBin GFor MMoz NNor SMar SSvw WMnd WRos WWpP
- subsp. ***taurica***	EPPr
macra	EBee EHoe EPPr SApp
nutans	CBig CBrm CWCL EHoe EPPr EPla EPza EWsh GBin GFor GWCH NWCA SBch SHel SYvo WHal WHil WRos WWye
penicillaris	EPPr WPer
persica	EPPr
torreyana	EPPr
transsilvanica	GFor NBre NNor
- 'Atropurpurea'	EBee EChP EWll SPer
- 'Red Spire'	CBig EShb IBal LRav MWhi SGSe WWpP
uniflora	GFor NBre
- f. ***albida***	CFil ECha EHoe EMan MBct SLPl WCot

	- 'Variegata' (v)	CBre CFil EBee ECha EHoe EMan EPPr EPla EShb GCal MBrN MBri MMoz NGdn WCot WTin

Melicope (*Rutaceae*)

	ternata	ECou

Melicytus (*Violaceae*)

	alpinus	ECou
	angustifolius	ECou
	crassifolius	CPle ECou EPla WFar WHCG
	obovatus	ECou
	ramiflorus	ECou

Melilotus (*Papilionaceae*)

	officinalis	CArn CWCL GPoy MChe MGol SIde WHer WSel WWye

Melinis (*Poaceae*)

	repens	SUsu WCot WHrl WWpP
	roseus	EHul

Meliosma (*Meliosmaceae*)

	cuneifolia **new**	NLar
	parviflora B&SWJ 8408	WCru
	pinnata var. ***oldhamii*** **new**	CBcs

Melissa (*Lamiaceae*)

	officinalis	More than 30 suppliers
	- 'All Gold'	CArn CBre CHal CPrp CSev ECha EDAr EHoe ELan ELau EUnu GBar MBri MChe NBid NPri NSti NVic SPer SPoG WMoo WSSM WWye
§	- 'Aurea' (v)	More than 30 suppliers
*	- 'Compacta'	GPoy MHer
	- 'Quedlinburger Niederliegende'	CArn
N	- 'Variegata' misapplied	see *M. officinalis* 'Aurea'

Melittis (*Lamiaceae*)

	melissophyllum	CBrm CFir CPom EBee EMan EMon EShb GBBs LPio LSou MGol MHar MRav MSte MTis NMen SIgm SIng SRms SSpi SSvw WAbb WCAu WWye
	- subsp. ***albida***	EBee SSpi
	- pink EMon SOkh	
	- 'Royal Velvet Distinction'PBR	CPen MBri MRav

Melliodendron (*Styracaceae*)

	xylocarpum	IArd

Menispermum (*Menispermaceae*)

	canadense	CPLN CTri GPoy MGol MSal SHBN
	davuricum	MGol MSal NLar

Menstruocalamus (*Poaceae*)

	sichuanensis	CFil WPGP

Mentha ✿ (*Lamiaceae*)

	angustifolia Corb.	see *M.* x *villosa*
	angustifolia Host	see *M. arvensis*
	angustifolia ambig.	EOHP SIde
	aquatica	CArn CBen CPrp CRow CWat EHon ELau EMFW EMag EPfP GPoy IHMH LNCo LPBA MBow MChe MHer NArg NPer SIde SPlb SWal WFar WHer WMoo WPnP WWpP
§	- var. ***crispa***	IHMH SIde
	- krause minze	see *M. aquatica* var. *crispa*
	- 'Mandeliensis'	EOHP EUnu IHMH
§	***arvensis***	CArn ELau GIBF IHMH MHer MSal SIde WHer WJek
	- 'Banana'	EOHP EUnu LSou MHer NGHP
	- var. ***piperascens***	MSal SIde
§	- - 'Sayakaze'	CArn ELau
	asiatica	ELau MHer SIde WHer
	Bowles' mint	see *M.* x *villosa* var. *alopecuroides* Bowles' mint
*	***brevifolia***	EOHP IHMH SIde WHer
§	***cervina***	CBen CDWL CWat EMFW EOHP IHMH LPBA MHer NArg SIde WJek WPop WWpP
*	- ***alba***	CDWL IHMH LPBA MHer WWpP
I	'Chocolate Peppermint' **new**	SECG
	citrata	see *M.* x *piperita* f. *citrata*
	'Clarissa's Millennium'	SIde
	cordifolia	see *M.* x *villosa*
	corsica	see *M. requienii*
	crispa L. (1753)	see *M. spicata* var. *crispa*
	crispa L. (1763)	see *M. aquatica* var. *crispa*
	crispa x ***piperita***	EDAr GBar
	'Dionysus'	EOHP IHMH SIde
	x ***dumetorum***	IHMH
	'Eau de Cologne'	see *M.* x *piperita* f. *citrata*
	eucalyptus mint	ELau EOHP GBar MHer NGHP WGwG WRha
	gattefossei	CArn ELau
	x ***gentilis***	see *M.* x *gracilis*
§	x ***gracilis***	CArn CHby ELau EOHP GBar GWCH IHMH MBow MChe NGHP NPri SECG SIde WJek WWye
	- 'Aurea'	see *M.* x *gracilis* 'Variegata'
§	- 'Variegata' (v)	CAgr CBrm CHrt CPrp CSev CWan ECha EHoe ELau EMar EUnu GGar GPoy ILis MBar MHer NArg NPri NVic SPlb WFar WGHP WHer WPer WSel
	haplocalyx	CArn ELau EOHP MSal SIde
*	'Hillary's Sweet Lemon'	ELau EOHP MHer SIde
	'Julia's Sweet Citrus'	EOHP MHer SIde
*	***lacerata***	IHMH SIde
	lavender mint	CBod CPrp CWan ELau EMan ESis GBar GPoy MHer MRav NGHP NTHB SECG WGHP WJek WRha
§	***longifolia***	CAgr CPrp CWan ELau EMag GBar MBow MRav NSti SBch SIde SPlb WEas WHer WJek WPer WSel WWye
	- Buddleia Mint Group	CArn EBee ELau EMan ESis EUnu GAbr GGar GKir IHMH MHer MRav NGHP NLsd SIde WRha WSel
	- subsp. ***capensis***	GGar
	- subsp. ***schimperi***	SIde WJek
	- silver	CAgr CArn ELau ESis GWCH MHer
*	- 'Variegata' (v)	CBod CPrp ELau EMar NSti WJek
*	***micromeria*** **new**	SECG
	'Mountain' **new**	SECG
	Nile Valley mint	CArn CBod CPrp ELau EOHP EUnu SHDw SIde WCHb
	x ***piperita***	CArn CHby CHrt COkL CSev CWan ECha EDAr EHoe ELau GBar GGar GPoy ILis MBow MBri MChe MHer NArg NBlu NFor NGHP NPri NVic SPlb WGHP WPer WWye
	- 'After Eight'	IHMH
*	- alba	CArn EUnu GBar MHer WGwG
	- 'Black Mitcham'	CArn EOHP GBar
	- black peppermint	CAgr CHby EPfP ESis EUnu GWCH IHMH MWat NGHP NTHB SWal WGHP WGwG WSSM

§	- f. ***citrata***	More than 30 suppliers
*	- - 'Basil'	CBod CHrt CPrp CWan ELau EOHP EUnu GBar IHMH LLWP MHer MRav NGHP NTHB SHDw SIde WGHP WGwG WJek WRha
	- - 'Bergamot'	EOHP EUnu IHMH
	- - 'Chocolate'	CAgr CArn CPrp CWan ELau EMan EOHP EPfP ESis EUnu GBar GGar GKir IHMH ILis MHer NArg NGHP NPri SHDw SIde WGHP WGwG WJek WMoo WPer WPop WWpP
	- - 'Grapefruit'	CWan EOHP EVFa GBar ILis LFol LSou NGHP SWal WGwG WJek
	- - 'Lemon'	CPrp CWan ELau EMan EOHP GAbr GBar IHMH MBow MBri MHer NGHP SHDw SIde WCHb WGHP WGwG WJek WPer WRha WSel
	- - 'Lime'	CHrt COkL CPrp CWan EMan EOHP GBar ILis LSou MBow MHer NGHP NPri SECG SHDw SIde SPlb WCHb WGHP WGwG WJek WSSM
	- - orange	EOHP EUnu GBar MHer MWat
	- - 'Swiss Ricola'	EOHP EUnu MHer SIde
*	- 'Extra Strong'	IHMH
	- 'Logee's' (v)	CWan EBee EMan EOHP EUnu EVFa EWes GBar MHer NBlu NGHP NPri NTHB SIde WCHb WCot WHer WJek WRha
§	- 'Multimentha'	EOHP
	- f. ***officinalis***	ELau IHMH SIde
	- var. ***ouweneellii*** Belgian mint	IHMH SIde
	- 'Reine Rouge'	EOHP IHMH SIde
	- 'Reverchonii'	IHMH SIde
	- 'Swiss' **new**	WGHP
I	- Swiss mint	CArn CPrp NGHP WGwG
	pulegium	CAgr CArn CHby CPrp CRWN CSev CTri CWan EDAr ELau GBar GPoy IHMH MChe MHer NArg NVic SECG SIde SPlb SRms SWal WCHb WHer WJek WPer WWpP WWye
	- 'Upright'	CArn CBod CPrp GBar GPoy MHer NTHB SHDw SIde WCHb WJek WPer WSel WWpP
§	***requienii***	More than 30 suppliers
	rotundifolia misapplied	see *M. suaveolens*
	rotundifolia (L.) Hudson	see *M.* x *villosa*
	rubra var. ***raripila***	see *M.* x *smithiana*
	'Sayakarze'	see *M. arvensis* var. *piperascens* 'Sayakaze'
§	x ***smithiana***	CAgr CArn CPrp CWan ELau EOHP GAbr GBar GPoy IHMH ILis MChe MHer NBir NGHP NPri WHer WPer WRha WWye
	- 'Capel Ulo' (v)	ELau WHer
§	***spicata***	More than 30 suppliers
	- Algerian fruity	EOHP EUnu IHMH SIde
*	- 'Brundall'	ELau EOHP EUnu ILis SIde
	- 'Canaries'	EOHP EUnu IHMH
*	- var. ***crispa***	CArn CPrp CWan ECha EDAr ELau EOHP EUnu GAbr GBar GGar IHMH MHer NArg NGHP NPri SIde SPlb WCHb WCot WPer WRha WSel WWye
	- - large-leaved	IHMH
	- - 'Moroccan'	CArn COkL CPrp CSev EDAr ELau EOHP ESis EUnu GAbr GBar GGar GKir GPoy IHMH MHer NArg NGHP NPri NVic SHDw SIde STre WCHb WGHP WHer WJek WSel WWye
	- - 'Persian'	IHMH
	- 'Guernsey'	EOHP SHDw SIde
	- 'Mexican'	CArn
	- 'Newbourne'	ELau ESis EUnu SIde
I	- 'Pharaoh Mint' **new**	CArn
	- 'Rhodos'	EOHP IHMH
	- 'Russian'	EWin NGHP NTHB SIde
	- 'Small Dole' (v)	SHDw
	- 'Spanish Furry'	EOHP MHer SIde
	- 'Spanish Pointed'	ELau EOHP SIde
	- 'Tashkent'	CArn CHby ELau EOHP GWCH MHer SHDw SIde WCHb WGwG WJek WWpP
	- subsp. ***tomentosa***	EOHP IHMH
*	- 'Variegata' (v)	SHDw WGwG WHer
	- 'Verte Blanche'	EUnu IHMH
§	***suaveolens***	CAgr CArn CHby CWan ELau EUnu GBar GMaP GPoy GWCH IHMH ILis MBow MBri MHer NGHP NLRH NPri SECG SIde SPlb SWal WBrk WGHP WLHH WPer WSSM
*	- 'Grapefruit'	CPrp ESis IHMH NPri
	- 'Jokka'	EBee
*	- 'Mobillei'	EOHP SIde WJek
*	- 'Pineapple'	COkL ESis NArg NLRH WGwG
	- subsp. ***timija***	ELau SIde WJek
§	- 'Variegata' (v)	More than 30 suppliers
I	'Sweet Pear'	EOHP EUnu LSou
	sylvestris L.	see *M. longifolia*
	Thüringer minze	see *M.* x *piperita* 'Multimentha'
*	***verona*** **new**	MHer
§	x ***villosa***	CArn EOHP IHMH SIde
§	- var. ***alopecuroides*** Bowles' mint	CAgr CBre CHrt CPrp ELau EMan GBar GGar GPoy IHMH ILis MChe MHer NGHP NSti SIde STre WGwG WHer WJek WWye
	viridis	see *M. spicata*

Menyanthes (*Menyanthaceae*)

	trifoliata	CBen CRow CWat EHon ELau EMFW EMag GBar GPoy LNCo LPBA MCCP NPer NVic WBVN WFar WPnP WWpP

Menziesia (*Ericaceae*)

	alba	see *Daboecia cantabrica* f. *alba*
	ciliicalyx	SSpi
	- 'Glendoick Glaucous'	GGGa
	- ***lasiophylla***	see *M. ciliicalyx* var. *purpurea*
	- var. ***multiflora***	CPLG CStu GGGa MDun
§	- var. ***purpurea***	CPLG GGGa
	ferruginea	SReu SSta
	'Spring Morning'	WAbe

Mercurialis (*Euphorbiaceae*)

	perennis	GPoy MGol WHer WShi

Merendera (*Colchicaceae*)

	attica **new**	EPot
	filifolia	ECho
	- PB 422 from Menorca **new**	CMon
	- AB&S 4665 from Morocco **new**	CMon
§	***montana***	ERos WIvy
	pyrenaica	see *M. montana*
	sobolifera	CMon EHyt EPot WCot WFar

Merremia (*Convolvulaceae*)

	pinnata	MSal
§	***tuberosa***	EShb MGol

Mertensia (*Boraginaceae*)

ciliata	CAbP CMdw CPom GKir LRHS MArl MBri MNrw
franciscana	GCal
maritima	CAby EWll GIBF GPoy MSal NGby
- subsp. ***asiatica***	see *M. simplicissima*
primuloides	GEdr
pterocarpa	see *M. sibirica*
pulmonarioides	see *M. virginica*
§ ***sibirica***	CLAP CSpe EBee ETow GKir LPhx NDlv NLAp NLar NPri SMrm SPlb
§ ***simplicissima***	CBot CFir CMea CSpe EBee EBrs ECho EHyt EMan ETow GIBF GKev GKir LPhx MNrw NBir NWCA SBla SGar SMad SOkd SPlb SUsu WFar WHoo
virginica ♀H4	CBot CBro CLAP EBee EBrs ELan EPfP EPot EVFa EWTr GBBs GFlt GGar GKir LAma NBPC NBid NBir NLar NPri NWCA SMac SMrm SRms STes SUsu WCru WFar WSan
viridis	LPhx

Merxmuellera see *Rytidosperma*

Meryta (*Araliaceae*)

sinclairii	CHEx WMul

Mesembryanthemum (*Aizoaceae*)

'Basutoland'	see *Delosperma nubigenum*
brownii	see *Lampranthus brownii*

Mespilus (*Rosaceae*)

germanica (F)	CBcs CDul CLnd CTri EBee ECrN ELan EWTr IDee MWat NFor SDnm SHBN SPoG WDin WFar WMou WOrn
- 'Bredase Reus' (F)	SKee
- 'Dutch' (F)	SFam SKee
- 'Large Russian' (F)	ERea GTwe
- 'Macrocarpa'	SKee
- 'Nottingham' (F)	CAgr CCVT CEnd CTho CWib EBee ECrN ENot EPfP ERea GKir GTwe LBuc LRHS MAsh MBlu MGos MLan MWya NBee NPri SCoo SCrf SFam SKee SPer WJas WMou
- 'Royal' (F)	CAgr SKee
- 'Westerveld' (F)	SKee

Metapanax see *Pseudopanax*

Metaplexis (*Asclepiadaceae*)

japonica B&SWJ 8459	WCru

Metasequoia (*Cupressaceae*)

glyptostroboides ♀H4	More than 30 suppliers
- 'Emerald Feathers' **new**	ECho
- 'Gold Rush'	CBcs CDoC CDul CEnd CMCN CTho CTri CWSG EBee EPfP GKir LCon LLin LRHS MAsh MBlu MBri MGos MWya NLar NPal SCoo SLim SPer SPoG SWvt WEve WFar
- 'Green Mantle'	EHul
- 'Sheridan Spire'	CEnd CTho WPGP
- 'Spring Cream'	SLim SPoG
- 'White Spot' (v)	LLin SLim SPoG

Metrosideros (*Myrtaceae*)

carminea	CTrC EShb
- 'Carousel' (v)	ERea
- 'Ferris Wheel'	ERea
excelsa	CHEx CTrC EBak ECou EShb SHFr
- 'Aureus'	ECou
- 'Fire Mountain'	CTrC
- 'Parnell'	CBcs
- 'Scarlet Pimpernel'	ERea
- 'Spring Fire'	CBcs
- 'Vibrance'	CTrC
'Goldfinger' (v)	ERea
kermadecensis	ECou
- 'Radiant' (v)	CPLG
- 'Variegatus' (v)	CBcs CDoC CTrC ECou ERea
lucida	see *M. umbellata*
'Mistral'	ECou
'Pink Lady'	CTrC
robusta	EShb
'Thomasii'	EShb ESlt
tomentosa	see *M. excelsa*
§ ***umbellata***	CBcs CHEx CPne CTrC ECou EShb GGar IDee SBrw
villosa 'Tahiti'	CBcs

Meum (*Apiaceae*)

athamanticum	CBos CSev EBee EHrv EMan GBri GCal GPoy LRHS MAvo MRav MSal MTho NBid NCGa NSti SBla SGar SIgm WFar WHil WPer WPrP WTin

Michauxia (*Campanulaceae*)

campanuloides	WLin
tchihatchewii	CSpe GKev

Michelia (*Magnoliaceae*)

cavalerieri	CBcs CFil WPGP
champaca **new**	ERea
chapensis	CBcs SSpi WPGP
- HWJ 621	WCru
compressa	EPfP
doltsopa	CBcs CFil CHEx ECre EMil GQui SBrw SSpi WPGP
- 'Silver Cloud'	CBcs SSpi
figo	CDoC CFil EPfP ERea GQui SBrw SSpi WPGP
- var. ***crassipes***	SSpi
- var. ***figo*** **new**	SSpi
foveolata	CBcs CFil SSpi WPGP
macclurei	CBcs CFil SSpi
martinii	SSpi
maudiae	CBcs CDoC CFil EBee EPfP ISea SSpi WPGP
sinensis	see *M. wilsonii*
§ ***wilsonii***	CFil SSpi WHCr
yunnanensis	CFil SSpi

Microbiota (*Cupressaceae*)

decussata ♀H4	CBcs CDoC CKen CMac CRob CSBt EHul ENot EOrn EPla GKir LBee LCon LLin LRHS MBar MBri MGos MWat SLim SPoG WCFE WEve WFar
- 'Gold Spot'	NLar
- 'Jakobsen'	CDoC CKen
- 'Trompenburg'	CKen

Microcachrys (*Podocarpaceae*)

tetragona	CDoC ECho ECou EHul EOrn LCon LLin MAsh MBri SCoo SIng SPoG

Microcoelum see *Lytocaryum*

Microglossa (*Asteraceae*)

albescens	see *Aster albescens*

Microlaena see *Ehrharta*

Microlepia (*Dennstaedtiaceae*)

speluncae	MBri
***strigosa* new**	CLAP

Micromeria (*Lamiaceae*)

corsica	see *Acinos corsicus*
croatica	EHyt ETow
dalmatica	XPep
fruticosa	EWin XPep
graeca	XPep
rupestris	see *M. thymifolia*
§ ***thymifolia***	EMan GPoy NMen SPlb

Microseris (*Asteraceae*)

ringens hort.	see *Leontodon rigens*

Microsorum (*Polypodiaceae*)

diversifolium	see *Phymatosorus diversifolius*

Microstrobos (*Podocarpaceae*)

fitzgeraldii	CKen
niphophilus	CDoC ECou

Microtropis (*Celastraceae*)

petelotii HWJ 719	WCru

Miersia (*Alliaceae*)

***chilensis* new**	CMon

Mikania (*Asteraceae*)

§ ***dentata***	MBri
ternata	see *M. dentata*

Milium (*Poaceae*)

effusum	COld
- 'Aureum' ♀H4	More than 30 suppliers
- var. ***esthonicum***	EBee EPPr WWpP
- 'Yaffle' (v)	CBgR CBre CFir CKno CNat CRez EBee ECha EMan EPPr EUJe GCal LEdu MCCP SPoG SSvw SUsu WCot WLeb WWpP

Millettia (*Papilionaceae*)

japonica 'Hime Fuji' **new**	NLar

Milligania (*Asteliaceae*)

densiflora	IBlr

Mimosa (*Mimosaceae*)

pudica	LExo LRHS SMur

Mimulus (*Scrophulariaceae*)

'A.T. Johnson'	NVic
'Andean Nymph'	see *M. naiandinus*
§ ***aurantiacus*** ♀H2-3	CElw CFee CHal CPle CSpe EBak ECtt EPot ERea MHar MOak NBir NPer SAga SDnm SGar SHFr SMrm SPlb SPoG SUsu SWal WAbe
§ - var. ***puniceus***	CHal CPle CSpe CTri EMan LAst LRHS LSou MHar MOak SAga SMrm SUsu
'Aztec Trumpet'	EDAr
x ***bartonianus***	see *M.* x *harrisonii*
bifidus	MHar
- 'Tapestry'	CSpe
- 'Tawny'	SAga
- 'Trish'	CSpe
§ - 'Verity Buff'	CSpe LIck MOak
- Verity hybrids	ERea
§ - 'Verity Purple'	CSpe LIck SAga SUsu
- 'Wine'	see *M. bifidus* 'Verity Purple'
x ***burnetii***	LPBA SRms
cardinalis ♀H3	CDWL CSec EChP EHon ELan GKev IHMH LPBA MAnH MNrw MTho NWCA SHFr SPer SPoG WBor WCot WFar WMoo WPer WPnP WWpP
- NNS 95-344	EMan
- 'Dark Throat'	SGar
cupreus	GKev
- 'Minor'	ECho
- 'Whitecroft Scarlet' ♀H4	ECtt EDAr ELan EPfP LPBA LRHS LSou MHer SRms WPer
DK hybrid	MDKP
'Eleanor'	EMan LSou SAga SMrm SPet SUsu SWal
glutinosus	see *M. aurantiacus*
- ***atrosanguineus***	see *M. aurantiacus* var. *puniceus*
- ***luteus***	see *M. aurantiacus*
§ ***guttatus***	GPoy NPer SECG SRms WMoo WPer WPnP WWpP
§ - 'Richard Bish' (v)	CWat EMan GKev MCCP
x ***harrisonii***	EBee EMan EPfP EWes GFlt GMac SAga
'Highland Orange'	EDAr EPfP EPot GGar GKir IHMH MHer NJOw SPlb SPoG WGor WPer
'Highland Pink'	EDAr EPfP EPot GGar GKir NBlu NJOw SIng SPlb SPoG WGor WPer
I 'Highland Pink Rose'	EPot
'Highland Red' ♀H4	ECtt EDAr EPfP EPot GAbr GGar GKev GKir IHMH LPBA NArg NBlu NJOw NPri SIng SPlb SPoG SRms WPer
'Highland Yellow'	ECtt EDAr EPot GGar GKev GKir LPBA MHer NBlu SIng SPlb SPoG WPer
hose-in-hose (d)	CDWL EMFW NPer
'Inca Sunset'	EDAr EWes
langsdorffii	see *M. guttatus*
lewisii ♀H3	CHll CSec EBee EMan EShb GFlt GGar GTou MTho SPav SPer SRms WPer WRha
longiflorus 'Santa Barbara'	LIck
luteus	CWat EHon EPfP GAbr IHMH LNCo LPBA MHer NPer SHFr SPlb SWal WBrk WFar WPnP WWpP
- 'Gaby' (v)	LPBA MTho WPop
- 'Variegatus' misapplied	see *M. guttatus* 'Richard Bish'
- 'Variegatus'	see *M. luteus* 'Gaby'
- 'Variegatus' ambig. (v)	NPer
* 'Major Bees'	EPfP LSou
'Malibu Ivory'	MDKP
'Malibu Orange' **new**	EPfP
'Malibu Red'	MDKP
moschatus	CRow EBee
naiandinus ♀H3	CM&M CPBP EBee GKev GKir LRHS SPlb SRms WFar
- C&W 5257	SRot WRos
'Orange Glow'	EPfP IHMH WHal
orange hose-in-hose (d)	NBir
§ 'Orkney Gold' (d)	EBee
'Orkney Lemon'	NSti
'Popacatapetl'	CHal CHll CSpe EMan LIck LSou MHar MOak MSte SAga SChu SMrm SUsu
primuloides	EPot NWCA SIng SPlb
- var. ***linearifolius***	GKev
'Puck'	ECtt GMac LRHS
'Purple Mazz'	SAga
'Quetzalcoatl'	LSou MOak SAga SMrm

ringens	CWat EHon EMFW EPfP GBri LNCo LPBA NBir NBlu NPer SPer SPlb SRms WFar WMoo WPer WPop WWpP
'Threave Variegated' (v)	EBee EMan EWin GBuc GCal MBri MRav NBir WFar
tilingii	ECho EShb GTou SMar
'Western Hills'	MLLN
'Wine Red'	see *M. bifidus* 'Verity Purple'
'Wisley Red'	ECot ELan SRms
yellow hose-in-hose (d)	see *M.* 'Orkney Gold'

Mina see *Ipomoea*

mint, Bowles' see *Mentha* x *villosa* var. *alopecuroides*

mint, curly see *Mentha spicata* var. *crispa*

mint, eau-de-Cologne see *Mentha* x *piperita* f. *citrata*

mint, ginger see *Mentha* x *gracilis*

mint, horse or long-leaved see *Mentha longifolia*

mint, pennyroyal see *Mentha pulegium*

mint, peppermint see *Mentha* x *piperita*

mint, round-leaved see *Mentha suaveolens*

mint, spearmint see *Mentha spicata*

Minuartia (*Caryophyllaceae*)

caucasica	see *M. circassica*
§ ***circassica***	CLyd ETow NWCA WPer
juniperina	ESis
laricifolia	CLyd LRHS
parnassica	see *M. stellata*
§ ***stellata***	EPot ESis ETow NDlv NJOw NMen SIng
- NS 758	NWCA
§ ***verna***	NMen
- subsp. ***caespitosa*** 'Aurea'	see *Sagina subulata* var. *glabrata*

Mirabilis (*Nyctaginaceae*)

jalapa	CArn CHrt CPLG CStu ELan EPfP EUJe LAma LRHS MBri MGol MSal SEND SHFr SRms SYvo
- white **new**	CSpe
multiflora	EShb MGol

Miscanthus ✿ (*Poaceae*)

***capensis* new**	CBig
flavidus B&SWJ 3697	WCru
floridulus misapplied	see *M.* x *giganteus*
floridulus ambig.	MAvo MBrN NOak WFar WPrP
- HWJ 522	WCru
x ***giganteus***	CFir CFwr CHEx CKno CSev EBee EHoe EPPr EUJe EWsh GAbr GCal LRHS MCCP MMoz NBea NVic SApp SDix SEND SMad SPlb WCot WFar
- 'Gilt Edge' **new**	EWsh SApp
- 'Gotemba' **new**	EWes EWsh
'Golden Bar' **new**	NCob
'Gotemba Gold' **new**	SApp
'Mount Washington' **new**	SApp
nepalensis	CAbb CBig CBrm CHrt CKno CMil CPLG ECre EHoe EWes LEdu MAnH MAvo SGSe SMrm WGHP
oligostachyus	CBig GCal NGdn
§ - 'Afrika'	CBig CFwr CPen EBrs LPhx
I - 'Nanus Variegatus' (v)	CBrm CKno CRow EBee EBrs EHoe EMan EWes MMoz WCot WPGP
'Pos' **new**	SApp
§ 'Purpurascens'	CBrm CFwr CKno CPrp EBrs ECha EHoe EHrv EHul EPla EUJe EWTr EWsh GSki LAst LRHS MAvo MBnl MBrN MMoz MWgw NGdn NOak SGSe SPer SWal WCot WGHP WTin
sacchariflorus	More than 30 suppliers
sinensis	CAgr CBig CHEx CHrt EBla EUJe GBin GFor GKir MGol MMoz MWrn NOak WDin WMoo WRos XPep
- B&SWJ 6749	WCru
- from Yakushima	CTbh
- 'Adagio'	CAbb CBig CFwr CKno CPen EBee EMan EPPr GBin LEdu LPhx SMHy WCot
- 'Afrika'	see *M. oligostachyus* 'Afrika'
- 'Arabesque'	CBig CBrm CFwr EPPr IPot MMoz NLar SApp
- 'Augustfeder'	CFwr EBee EBrs LRHS
- 'Autumn Light'	CFwr CKno EPPr IPot SGSe
- 'Ballerina' **new**	CFwr
- 'Blütenwunder'	CKno IPot
- 'China'	More than 30 suppliers
- var. ***condensatus***	CBig EPPr
- - 'Cabaret' (v)	CBrm CFwr CHEx CKno CPen CRez CWCL EBee EHoe EMan EPPr EPyc EUJe IPot LEdu LSRN MBri NGdn SMad SPoG SRos WCot WHal
- - 'Central Park'	see *M. sinensis* var. *condensatus* 'Cosmo Revert'
- - 'Cosmo Revert'	CBig CKno CPen EBee EMil MMoz WDyG
- - 'Cosmopolitan' (v) ♀H4	More than 30 suppliers
- - 'Emerald Giant'	see *M. sinensis* var. *condensatus* 'Cosmo Revert'
- 'David' **new**	CPen
- 'Dixieland' (v)	CBig CBrm CKno EHoe EPPr IPot LEdu MMoz MRav SApp
- dwarf	SMad
- 'Emmanuel Lepage' **new**	EPPr
- 'Etincelle' **new**	EPPr
- 'Federriese'	EBrs
- 'Ferner Osten'	More than 30 suppliers
- 'Feuergold'	MSte
- 'Flamingo' ♀H4	More than 30 suppliers
- 'Flammenmeer'	EBee
* - 'Gaa' **new**	SApp
- 'Gearmella'	CBig CFwr EBee EBrs EPPr EWsh GKir LEdu LRHS
- 'Gewitterwolke' ♀H4	CBig CFwr CKno IPot LPhx SMHy
- 'Ghana' ♀H4	CFwr EBee GBin LPhx SMHy
- 'Giraffe'	CDes CFwr CKno CPen EBrs WPGP
- 'Gnome' **new**	CPen
- 'Gold Bar' (v) **new**	EPPr LBuc MBNS SPer SPoG WCot
- 'Goldfeder' (v)	CFwr EHoe WBcn
- 'Goliath'	CBig CFwr CPen EBrs EHoe EPPr GBin IPot
- 'Gracillimus'	More than 30 suppliers
- 'Graziella'	CDul CEnd CFwr CHar CKno CWib EBla EBrs EHoe EHrv EPPr EPza LEdu LPhx LRHS MBow MBri MMoz MSte NBPC NDov NGdn NOak NOrc SLPl SPer SUsu WPGP WPrP WTMC

- 'Grosse Fontäne' ♀H4 CBig CBrm CKno EBla EBrs EHoe EPGN EPPr EPla EWsh GKir LEdu LRHS SGSe SMHy WAul WMoo
- 'Haiku' CFwr CKno CPen GBin LPhx
- 'Helga Reich' CBig EBee SApp
- 'Hercules' CBig EPPr MAvo MMoz SApp
- 'Hermann Müssel' CFwr CPen EBee EPPr GBin LPhx NDov SMHy
- 'Hinjo' (v) CDes CKno CSpe EBee EPPr GBin SApp WCot WHrl WPGP
I - 'Jubilaris' (v) **new** EWes
- 'Juli' CBig GBin IPot
- 'Kaskade' ♀H4 CBig CBrm CFwr CKno CWCL EBrs EHoe EPGN EPPr EPla EUJe GKir IPot LPhx LRHS MAvo MMoz MSte NOGN SApp SMrm WBcn WFar WMoo
- 'Kirk Alexander' (v) SApp
- 'Kleine Fontäne' ♀H4 More than 30 suppliers
- 'Kleine Silberspinne' ♀H4 More than 30 suppliers
- 'Krater' EBee EBrs EPPr LEdu MBrN SGSe
- 'Kupferberg' CFwr
§ - 'Little Kitten' CDes CFwr CKno CPen EBee EPPr EPla EWsh LEdu MBar MGol SGSe SMad SPoG WPGP
- 'Malepartus' More than 30 suppliers
- 'Morning Light' (v) ♀H4 More than 30 suppliers
- new hybrids CBcs CPen EChP EHul LRav
- 'Nippon' CAbb CBig CElw CHad CKno CPrp EBee EBla EBrs EHoe EPPr EPla EPza LEdu LRHS MAvo MCCP MMoz NDov NGdn NOrc SChu SDys SGSe SPer WCAu WPGP
- 'Nishidake' CFwr CPen EBee
- 'November Sunset' EBee EPPr EWes IPot MMoz
- 'Poseidon' EBrs EPPr SDys
- 'Positano' CBig CKno EBee EBrs MMoz WPGP
- 'Professor Richard Hansen' CFwr CPen GBin
- var. ***purpurascens*** misapplied see *M.* 'Purpurascens'
- 'Pünktchen' (v) CBig CBrm CElw CFwr CKno CPen EBee EBrs ECha EPPr EPla GBin LBBr LEdu LPhx MAvo MWgw SApp SGSe SMHy SMad SMrm WTin
- 'Rigoletto' (v) EPPr SApp
- 'Roland' CBig CFwr CKno CPen EBee GBin LPhx SAga
- 'Roterpfeil' LPhx
- 'Rotfuchs' CFwr EBee EPPr GKir LPhx MGos SAga WFar
- 'Rotsilber' More than 30 suppliers
- 'Samurai' CFwr EBrs GMaP
- 'Sarabande' CBig CBrm CFwr CKno EBee EBrs EHoe EHul EPPr EWsh GBin GKir IPot LRHS SApp SMHy WFar WMoo
- 'Septemberfuchs' **new** LEdu
- 'Septemberrot' ♀H4 CFwr CKno COIW CPrp SPoG
§ - 'Silberfeder' ♀H4 More than 30 suppliers
- 'Silberpfeil' zur Linden (v) MSte
- 'Silberspinne' CBig CMdw EBla EBrs ENot EPla GKir LEdu LPhx LRHS MCCP NGdn SAga SApp SDix SGSe SMHy SPlb WAul WDin
- 'Silberturm' CFwr CKno SPoG
- Silver Feather see *M. sinensis* 'Silberfeder'
- 'Sioux' CBig CFwr CKno EBee EBrs EHoe EPPr EPla EPza EShb EWsh GBin GKir LEdu LRHS MMoz SGSe SPer WBcn WTin
- 'Sirene' CBig CFwr CKno EBee EBrs ECGP EHoe EMan EPGN EPPr EPla GKir LRHS MBNS MBlu SGSe WCAu WFar WPrP
- 'Slavopour' EPla
- 'Spätgrün' EPla
- 'Strictus' (v) ♀H4 More than 30 suppliers
- 'Tiger Cub' (v) CBig CWCL EBee SApp
- 'Undine' ♀H4 CFwr CKno CMea CPrp EBla EBrs ECha EHoe EHrv ELan EPGN EPla EPza EWsh LEdu LPhx LRHS MLLN MMoz NDov SChu SDix SHFr SPla WCAu WGHP
- 'Variegatus' (v) ♀H4 More than 30 suppliers
- 'Vorläufer' CBrm CFwr CKno EBrs EHoe EPPr EWsh GKir LPhx SAga
- 'Wetterfahne' CFwr EBrs
§ - 'Yaku-jima' CFwr CRez ECha SPoG XPep
- 'Yakushima Dwarf' More than 30 suppliers
- 'Zebrinus' (v) ♀H4 More than 30 suppliers
- 'Zwergelefant' CBig CFwr EBrs MMoz SMHy
I 'Spartina' **new** SApp
tinctorius 'Nanus Variegatus' misapplied see *M. oligostachyus* 'Nanus Variegatus'
transmorrisonensis CBig CBod CFwr CHid CHrt CKno EBee EHoe EMan EPPr EWsh GBin GFor LEdu LRav MMoz NOak SAdn SApp SWal WSSM WWpP
yakushimensis see *M. sinensis* 'Yaku-jima', *M. sinensis* 'Little Kitten'

Mitchella (*Rubiaceae*)

repens CBcs WCru
undulata B&SWJ 4402 WCru

Mitella (*Saxifragaceae*)

breweri CHal CNic CSam EBee GBin GGar MAvo MRav MSte NSti SHFr SMac SRms SSpi WEas WFar WMoo WTin WWye
caulescens EBee ECha NBro WMoo WPnP
diphylla EBee EPPr
formosana B&SWJ 125 EBee WCru
japonica B&SWJ 4971 WCru
kiusiana CLAP
- B&SWJ 5888 GEdr WCru
makinoi CLAP
- B&SWJ 4992 WCru
ovalis EBee
pauciflora B&SWJ 6361 WCru
pentandra **new** WMoo
stauropetala NWoo
stylosa B&SWJ 5669 WCru
yoshinagae GEdr SBch WMoo
- B&SWJ 4893 WCru WPnP WPrP WPtf

Mitraria (*Gesneriaceae*)

coccinea CBcs CMac CPLG CPLN CPle CSec CTrw CWib ELan ERea EShb GGGa IDee MBlu MDun MMil SArc SLon SPer SSpi WCot WPat WPic
- Clark's form CSam CTrC GGar LAst MDun WBor
- from Lake Puyehue CAby CBcs CDoC CFee ERea GQui LRHS MAsh MGos SBra SPoG SSta SWvt WAbe WCru WCwm WFar WPGP WSHC
- 'Lake Caburgua' GCal GGar IArd NSti

Moehringia (*Caryophyllaceae*)

lateriflora **new** GIBF

Molinia (Poaceae)

altissima	see *M. caerulea* subsp. *arundinacea*
caerulea	CBig COtt CRWN EHul EPPr GFor LAst LPhx MBlu WGHP WWpP
§ - subsp. ***arundinacea***	CBig CBrm CWCL ECha EPPr GBin GFor GKir MBNS MTis NChi SApp SLPl WPer
- - 'Bergfreund'	CSam EHoe EPPr EVFa EWsh GCal LPhx MAvo SApp SDys SHel SMHy SUsu WDyG WGHP WMoo WPrP WTin WWye
- - 'Cordoba'	CBig LPhx
- - 'Fontäne'	CBig CPen CSam EBee EHoe EPPr LPhx MSte NDov SApp SGSe SMHy
- - 'Karl Foerster'	CHar CKno CSpe EHoe EHul EPPr EPfP GBin GMaP LEdu LPhx MAvo MMil MMoz NBid NDov SApp SGSe SUsu SVil SYvo WCot WFar WGHP WMoo WPnP
- - 'Skyracer'	CBig CFwr CKno COIW CPrp EBee EBrs EHoe EPPr GBri LIck LPhx MAnH MAvo MBri MMoz SMHy SMad SPoG WCot WFar WGHP WMoo WWpP
- - 'Staefa'	EHoe
- - 'Transparent'	More than 30 suppliers
- - 'Windsaule'	CBig EPPr LPhx
- - 'Windspiel'	CKno CRow CSam CWCL EBee EBrs ECha EHoe EMil EMon EPGN EPPr EWsh GCal LEdu LPhx MAnH MWgw NDov SApp SWal WCot WGHP WMoo WPGP
- - 'Zuneigung'	CBig CKno CSam EBee EBrs EHoe EPPr LPhx NDov SApp
- subsp. ***caerulea***	CMdw
- - 'Carmarthen' (v)	CElw CNat EBee EPPr IPot MAvo SApp SMHy SUsu WGHP WHal WPrP
- - 'Claerwen' (v)	ECha EMan EPPr GBuc GCal SMHy WMoo
- - 'Dauerstrahl'	EPPr GBin GCal MAvo WGHP
- - 'Edith Dudszus'	CEnd CFwr CHar CKno CM&M CWCL ECha EHoe EPPr EVFa EWsh LEdu LPhx LRHS MAvo MBrN MMoz NGdn NOGN SApp SMHy SVil WGHP WMoo WPGP WWeb
- - 'Heidebraut'	CBig CFwr ECGP ECha EHoe EHul EPPr GBin LPhx LRHS MBri MWgw NBro NCGa NDov SApp SVil WFar WMoo WPnP
- - 'Moorflamme'	CBig CBrm CKno EPPr LPhx
zur Linden	
- - 'Moorhexe'	More than 30 suppliers
- - 'Strahlenquelle'	CElw CKno CSam EBee ELan EMan EMon EPGN EPPr EPla GBin GCal LRHS MAvo MMoz NBro NCGa NDov NOGN WPGP
- - 'Variegata' (v) ♀H4	More than 30 suppliers
- 'Winterfreude'	GBin
litoralis	see *M. caerulea* subsp. *arundinacea*

Molopospermum (Apiaceae)

peloponnesiacum	CAby EBee EMan GCal ITer LEdu LPhx MLLN NChi NLar SIgm WCot WCru

Moltkia (Boraginaceae)

§ ***doerfleri***	CPle NChi
graminifolia	see *M. suffruticosa*
§ x ***intermedia*** ♀H4	CMea SLon SOkd SPet WAbe
petraea	SIgm WLin WPat
§ ***suffruticosa***	NBir

Momordica (Cucurbitaceae)

balsamina	MSal
charantia	MSal

Monadenium (Euphorbiaceae)

lugardae	MBri
'Variegatum' (v)	MBri

Monarda ✿ (Lamiaceae)

'Adam'	EBee GAbr GCal LRHS MLLN MSte WCAu WSHC
'Amethyst'	EBee EWes SIde
'Aquarius'	CElw CWCL EBee EChP EMar EPza ERou EVFa GAbr GKir LAst LRHS MSte NCob NGHP NPro NSti SChu SPla WAul WCAu WCHb WFar WMnd
austromontana	see *M. citriodora* subsp. *austromontana*
'Baby Spice'	EBee ENot LRHS NCob WRHF
§ 'Balance'	CSam CWCL EBee EChP ECtt EMan EPPr LRHS MRav NBro NCob NDov NGHP NSti SChu SMeo SPla WCHb WFar WPGP WSHC
'Beauty of Cobham' ♀H4	CPrp ECha ELan EPfP ERou GAbr GBBs GKir GMaP LPhx LRHS MAnH MBow MBri MHer MSte NGHP NLar NRnb SChu SMad SPer WBor WCHb WGHP WSan
'Blaukranz'	SChu
§ 'Blaustrumpf'	CElw ECtt EMan GBri MSte NCob NLar NOrc SPer WLin
Blue Stocking	see *M.* 'Blaustrumpf'
Bowman	see *M.* 'Sagittarius'
bradburyana	EShb MWrn NBre WCHb WHal
'Cambridge Scarlet' ♀H4	More than 30 suppliers
'Capricorn'	CStr EBee EHol EMan EMar ERou GBuc LRHS MSte SChu WCHb
'Cherokee'	EBee GBri NCob WCHb WFar
citriodora	CArn ECtt EUnu GPoy LRHS MChe MSal NSti SIde SPlb SRms WGwG WJek WLHH WSel
§ - subsp. ***austromontana***	CArn EBee EMag EMan MDKP MSte MWrn NArg NBir NJOw SGar SIde WCot WFar WPer
'Comanche'	CStr EHrv EPfP EWes NCob NDov SBri WCHb WFar
'Croftway Pink' ♀H4	CBcs COIW CPLG CPrp CSBt CWCL EBee ECha ECtt ELan ELau EPfP ERou EWTr GKir GMaP LRHS MHer NDov NGHP NOrc SIde SPer SRms SWvt WCAu WCHb WFar WGHP WSHC
didyma	CAgr CArn CHar EDAr EPfP GKir MChe MSal NArg NBro NGHP NLon SECG WBrE WJek
- 'Alba'	MGol SMar
- 'Duddiscombe'	CSam CWCL
- 'Goldmelise'	CFwr NGHP SMar WMoo
'Donnerwolke'	SChu
'Elsie's Lavender'	CAby CStr GBri GBuc LPhx MAnH NBro NDov SAga WAul WCHb WGHP
'Fireball'[PBR]	CWCL EBee ERou LTwo MBnl WHil
§ 'Fishes'	CHVG CSam EBee EChP ECtt EHrv ELan EMar EPPr EVFa EWes MRav MSte NCob NDov NGHP NLar

	NRnb SAga SChu SPla WCAu WCHb WFar WMnd WSHC
fistulosa	CArn CWan EBee EUnu EWTr GPoy MBow MChe MSal MWrn SMar WHer WJek WLHH WMoo WPer
- f. ***albescens*** **new**	EBee
'Gardenview'	CMdw EWes GCal GCra MAnH NSti SMrm WBrk WRHF
'Gardenview Scarlet' ♀H4	EBee EBrs ECtt EGra GBri GKir LPhx LRHS MBri MDKP MWat NCGa NChi NGHP NGby SPoG WCHb WPer WSan
Gemini	see *M.* 'Twins'
'Hartswood Wine'	SMad
'Kardinal'	EBee GBin
'Lambada'	CFwr LRHS SPav
Libra	see *M.* 'Balance'
'Lilac Queen' **new**	NCob
'Loddon Crown'	CBos CHar CHea EBee ECtt EMar EVFa LRHS MBri MDKP NCob NGHP SIde WCHb WFar WRha
I 'Mahogany'	CHar EBee EChP ERou EVFa GAbr GBBs GBri GKir GMaP LRHS MAnH MBow MHer MRav MTis NCGa NChi NCob NGHP SMad SPer WCHb WSHC WSan
'Marshall's Delight' ♀H4	CElw EBee EChP GKir LSou NCob NGHP NRnb SMrm WCAu WHil
'Melissa'	WSan
menthifolia	CArn EBee GCal LRHS LSou MCCP SMrm
'Mohawk'	CMea CWCL EBee EChP ECtt EHrv EMan EPPr ERou EVFa LRHS MAnH MWat MWgw NChi NDov NOrc WCAu WCHb
'Mrs Perry'	EWes MHer NGHP
'Neon' **new**	NDov
'On Parade' **new**	ENot
'Ou Charm'	CElw EBee EChP EPPr ERou EWes GBri LRHS MLLN MWat MWrn NCGa NCiC NDov NGHP SMad STes WAul WCHb WCot WFar WSan
'Panorama'	ECtt MSal SGar SPlb WMoo WPer
'Panorama Red Shades'	CFwr CWib MAnH MWrn NBlu NGHP NLsd
'Pawnee'	SChu WCHb
Petite Delight = 'Acpetdel'PBR	CAbP CRez EBee ECtt ENot EPfP EShb GBin LRHS MBnl MDun MSph NCob NDov NEgg NGby NGdn NLar SPla SUsu WAul WCot WFar WWeb WWlt
'Petite Pink Supreme'	EBee EPfP MBnl WHil
'Pink Supreme'PBR **new**	EMar
'Pink Tourmaline'	CFwr EBee EChP LPhx NDov NGby SMad SMrm WCAu WCHb WFar
Pisces	see *M.* 'Fishes'
'Poyntzfield Pink'	GPoy
Prairie Night	see *M.* 'Prärienacht'
§ 'Prärienacht'	More than 30 suppliers
punctata	CArn ELan EMan EPza EUnu EWTr GFlt GSki LRHS MLLN MMHG MNFA MSal MWgw MWrn NGdn NJOw SDnm SMrm SPav WCHb WJek WMoo WPtf
- 'Fantasy' **new**	CFwr EMar LBuc MBri NArg NGHP NSti
'Purple Ann'	MAnH NCGa NDov
'Raspberry Wine'	GBri MAnH
'Ruby Glow'	CAby CHad CWCL EBee EChP EHrv EMan EMar EPPr LPhx LRHS MArl MBri MTis NCGa NChi NDov SAga SChu SMad WCHb WFar
§ 'Sagittarius'	EBee EChP EMan GKir LRHS MMil NCob SChu SPla WCAu WCHb
'Sahin's Mildew-free'	WCHb
'Saxon Purple' **new**	NDov
§ 'Schneewittchen'	CPrp EChP ECha ECtt EHrv ELan ERou GKir GMaP LRHS MAnH MBow MLLN MRav NBro NGHP NLar NOrc NRnb NSti SChu SIde SPer SWvt WAul WCAu WGHP WMnd WSHC
§ 'Scorpion'	CSam EBee EChP ECtt EHrv ELan EPPr GAbr GKir LPhx LRHS MAnH MRav MSte NBir NCob NDov NOrc NPro SChu SPet SWvt WAul WCAu WCHb WMnd WPGP
'Sioux'	EHrv EWes GBuc GKir LRHS WCHb WFar WRha
'Snow Maiden'	see *M.* 'Schneewittchen'
'Snow Queen'	CSam ECtt EMar EPPr EVFa GKir LRHS MWat MWgw NCob NPro SHar SPla STes WMnd
Snow White	see *M.* 'Schneewittchen'
'Squaw' ♀H4	More than 30 suppliers
§ 'Twins'	CMil CPrp EBee EChP EMar EPPr ERou EWTr LRHS MLLN NGHP NRnb SWvt WCAu WCHb WLin WSan
'Velvet Queen'	LSou SMrm
'Vintage Wine'	CAby ECtt GBri NCob NDov SMrm WCHb WCot WFar
'Violacea'	WCHb WWpP
'Violet Queen' ♀H4	EBee EBrs EChP EMan EMar EPza EVFa EWes LRHS NCob NPro SHel WCAu

Monardella (*Lamiaceae*)

macrantha	CPBP SBla
nana subsp. ***arida***	CPBP
odoratissima	CArn EMag EMan LRav MSal SBla WJek WPtf

Monochoria (*Pontederiaceae*)

hastata	CDWL WPop

Monopsis (*Campanulaceae*)

lutea	see *Lobelia lutea*
Midnight = 'Yagemon'PBR	LAst
unidentata	EMan

Monsonia ✿ (*Geraniaceae*)

crassicaulis **new**	LToo
speciosa	CMon
vanderietiae **new**	LToo

Monstera (*Araceae*)

deliciosa (F) ♀H1	MBri SRms XBlo
- 'Variegata' (v) ♀H1	MBri SRms

Montbretia see *Crocosmia*

x ***crocosmiiflora***	see *Crocosmia* x *crocosmiiflora*
pottsii	see *Crocosmia pottsii*

Montia (*Portulacaceae*)

australasica	see *Neopaxia australasica*
californica	see *Claytonia nevadensis*
parvifolia	see *Naiocrene parvifolia*
perfoliata	see *Claytonia perfoliata*
sibirica	see *Claytonia sibirica*

Moraea (*Iridaceae*)

alpina	GCrs

alticola CFil CPne EBee GCrs SSpi
- CDL 181 CStu
§ ***aristata*** CMon WCot
atropunctata **new** WCot
§ ***bellendenii*** WCot
bipartita WCot
comptonii **new** WCot
elegans CPBP WCot
§ ***fugax*** CMon IBlr WCot
gawleri CMon WCot
glaucopsis see *M. aristata*
huttonii CDes CFir EBee GSki SBla SGSe SMad WBVN WCot WCru WLin WPic WSHC
iridioides see *Dietes iridioides*
* ***lankenensis*** **new** CDes
longifolia Sweet see *M. fugax*
loubseri CMon WCot
lurida WCot
moggii CStu
natalensis SBla
papilionacea CStu EBee
pavonia var. ***lutea*** see *M. bellendenii*
polyanthos CMon
polystachya EBee LRHS
spathacea see *M. spathulata*
§ ***spathulata*** CBro CPLG CStu EBee EMan ERos GCal GMac LPio WCot
thomsonii LPio
tripetala WCot
vegeta CPBP WCot
versicolor CStu
villosa CMon WCot

Moricandia (*Brassicaceae*)

moricandioides CSpe

Morina (*Morinaceae*)

* ***afghanica*** GAbr
alba GCra NChi
betonicoides **new** GKev
longifolia More than 30 suppliers
- GWJ 9240 WCru
nepalensis WLin
persica EChP GBBs GBuc LPio SIgm WHoo
polyphylla GPoy
- CC 3397 GKev

Morisia (*Brassicaceae*)

hypogaea see *M. monanthos*
§ ***monanthos*** IHMH MBar NLAp NWCA SRot
- 'Fred Hemingway' EHyt GCrs ITim LRHS NMen NSla SIng WAbe WPat

Morus ✿ (*Moraceae*)

§ ***alba*** CAgr CArn CBcs CDul CLnd CMCN CMen CTho ECrN ELan EPfP ERea GKir GTwe LBuc MGos SBLw SHBN WBVN WDin WFar
- 'Macrophylla' CMCN SMad
- var. ***multicaulis*** ERea
- 'Pendula' CBcs CDoC CEnd CLnd CTho CTri ECrN ELan EPfP ERea GTwe LRHS MAsh MBlu MBri MLan SBLw SCoo SHBN SLim WDin WOrn
- 'Platanifolia' MBlu SBLw
- var. ***tatarica*** CAgr LEdu
§ ***bombycis*** SBLw
'Illinois Everbearing' (F) CAgr ECrN
kagayamae see *M. bombycis*
latifolia 'Spirata' NLar
nigra (F) ♀H4 More than 30 suppliers
§ - 'Chelsea' (F) CEnd COtt CTho CTri ECrN EPfP ERea GTwe MBri MGos MLan MWya NWea SCoo SKee SLim SPer SPoG
- 'King James' see *M. nigra* 'Chelsea'
- 'Wellington' (F) CEnd
rubra **new** NLar

Mosla (*Lamiaceae*)

dianthera CPom EMan GCal

Mucuna (*Papilionaceae*)

macrocarpa **new** CPLN
sempervirens **new** CPLN
sloanei **new** CPLN

Muehlenbeckia (*Polygonaceae*)

astonii CBcs ECou
axillaris misapplied see *M. complexa*
§ ***axillaris*** Walp. CBcs CTri ECou GCal GGar
- 'Mount Cook' (f) ECou
- 'Ohau' (m) ECou
§ ***complexa*** CBcs CDoC CHEx CHal CPLG CPLN CTrC CTri CWib EBee ECou EPla EShb ESlt GQui IBlr LRHS MCCP NSti SAPC SArc SBra SLim SLon SMac SWvt WCFE WSHC XPep
- (f) ECou
- 'Nana' see *M. axillaris* Walp.
- var. ***trilobata*** CPLN EPla IBlr WCru WDyG XPep
- 'Ward' (m) ECou
ephedroides ECou
- 'Clarence Pass' ECou
- var. ***muricatula*** ECou
gunnii ECou
platyclados see *Homalocladium platycladum*

Muhlenbergia (*Poaceae*)

capillaris CBrm CKno
japonica 'Cream Delight' (v) CPen EBee EHoe EMan MCCP WWpP
mexicana CBig CPen EBee EPPr EPza GFor NBre WPGP WWpP
rigens CBig CKno SApp XPep

Mukdenia (*Saxifragaceae*)

acanthifolia LEdu WCru
§ ***rossii*** EMan EMon EPla GCal LEdu MSte NLar NMyG SMac SMad SSpi WCru WTMC WTin
- dwarf GCal
- 'Ôgon' WCru
- variegated EMon

mulberry see *Morus*

Murraya (*Rutaceae*)

exotica see *M. paniculata*
koenigii EOHP GPoy
§ ***paniculata*** CArn ERea SMur

Musa ✿ (*Musaceae*)

from Yunnan, China see *M. itinerans* 'Yunnan'
§ ***acuminata*** MBri
- 'Bordelon' CKob
- 'Buitenzorg' CKob
- 'Double' (AAA+ Group) (F) CKob
§ - 'Dwarf Cavendish' (AAA Group) (F) ♀H1 CKob EAmu EExo ELan EPfP ESlt EUJe LExo MJnS NGHP NScw SPoG WMul XBlo
- 'Dwarf Red' (AAA Group) (F) CKob XBlo

- 'Dwarf Red Jamaican' (AAA Group) (F)	CKob
- 'Igitsiri' (AAA Group) (F)	CKob
- 'Iholena Ula'ula' (AAA Group) (F)	CKob
- 'Kru' (AA Group) (F)	CKob
- 'Mai'a oa'	CKob
- 'Malaysian Blood' (AA Group) (F)	CKob
- 'Monyet'	CKob
- 'Pink Striped' (AA Group) (F)	CKob
- 'Pisang Berlin' (AA Group) (F)	CKob
- 'Pisang Jari Buaya' (AA Group) (F)	CKob
- 'Pisang Lidi' (AA Group) (F)	CKob
- 'Red Iholena' (AAA Group) (F)	CKob XBlo
* - 'Rose' (AA Group) (F)	CKob
- 'Tapo' (AA Group) (F)	CKob
- 'Tuu Ghia' (AA Group) (F)	CKob
- 'White Iholena' (AAA Group) (F)	CKob
- 'Williams' (AAA Group) (F)	EAmu
- 'Zebrina' ♀$^{H1+3}$	CKob EAmu LRHS MJnS XBlo
- 'Zebrina' x ***acuminata*** 'Grand Nain'	EAmu
balbisiana	CKob EAmu EUJe LExo WMul XBlo
- 'Cardaba' (BBB Group) (F)	CKob
- 'Tani' (BB Group) (F)	CKob
basjoo ♀$^{H3-4}$	More than 30 suppliers
- 'Sakhalin'	CKob WMul
beccarii	CKob
'Burmese Blue'	CKob
'Butuhan' (*balbisiana* x *textilis*)	CKob
'Cavendish Super Dwarf'	MJnS
'Cavendish Zan Moreno'	MJnS
cavendishii	see *M. acuminata* 'Dwarf Cavendish'
§ ***coccinea*** ♀^{H1}	CKob LExo XBlo
ensete	see *Ensete ventricosum*
(Fe'i Group) 'Utafan' (F)	CKob
hookeri	see *M. sikkimensis*
itinerans 'Yunnan'	CKob EAmu ITer LExo MJnS WMul WPGP XBlo
* 'Kru' (F)	XBlo
§ ***lasiocarpa***	CAbb CDWL CDoC CHEx CHll CKob CTrC EAmu ESlt EUJe LRHS MBri MJnS SBig WGwG WMul WPGP
laterita	CKob EUJe
mannii	CKob WMul
nana auct.	see *M. acuminata* 'Dwarf Cavendish'
nana Lour.	see *M. acuminata*
ornata ♀^{H1}	ERea LExo WMul XBlo
- 'African Red'	CKob
- 'Macro'	CKob
- 'Purple'	CKob
x ***paradisiaca*** AAB Group	XBlo
- 'Belle' (AAB Group) (F)	CKob
- 'Dwarf Orinoco' (ABB Group) (F)	CKob
- 'Ele-ele' (AAB Group) (F)	CKob
- Goldfinger = 'FHIA-01' (AAAB Group) (F)	CKob
- 'Hajaré' (ABB Group) (F)	CKob
- 'Hua Moa' (AAB Group) (F)	CKob
- 'Malbhog' (AAB Group) (F)	CKob
- 'Monthan' (ABB Group) (F)	CKob
- 'Mysore' (AAB Group) (F)	CKob
- 'Ney Mannan' (AAB Group) (F)	CKob
- 'Ney Poovan' (AB Group) (F)	CKob EAmu
- 'Orinoco' (ABB Group) (F)	CKob EAmu WMul
- 'Pisang Awak' (AAB Group) (F)	CKob
- 'Pisang Seribu' (AAB Group) (F)	CKob
- 'Popoulu' (AAB Group) (F)	CKob
- 'Rajapuri' (AAB Group) (F)	CKob EAmu MJnS
- 'Safet Velchi' (AB Group) (F)	CKob
- 'Silk' (AAB Group) (F)	CKob
- 'Yawa Dwarf' (ABB Group) (F)	CKob
'Royal Pink' (*ornata* hybrid)	CKob
'Royal Purple' (*ornata* hybrid)	CKob
'Royal Red' (*ornata* hybrid)	CKob
'Saba' ambig. (F)	CKob
sanguinea	CKob
§ ***sikkimensis***	CDoC CKob EAmu ELan EShb ESlt EUJe EWes LPJP LRHS MJnS SBig SChr WGwG WMul WPGP XBlo
textilis	CKob
'Tropicana'	SMer SSto XBlo
uranoscopus misapplied	see *M. coccinea*
velutina ♀$^{H1+3}$	CKob EAmu EUJe LExo MJnS SBig WMul WPGP XBlo
* 'Violacea' (*ornata* hybrid)	LExo
'Wompa' (AS Group) (F)	CKob

Muscari ✿ (*Hyacinthaceae*)

ambrosiacum	see *M. muscarimi*
armeniacum ♀^{H4}	CBro EBrs ENot EPfP ERos IHMH LRHS MBri NJOw SChr SRms WCot WShi
- 'Argaei Album'	EPot LAma
- 'Babies Breath'	see *M. neglectum* 'Baby's Breath'
- 'Blue Eyes' **new**	WCot
- 'Blue Pearl'	LRHS
- 'Blue Spike' (d)	CBro ENot EPfP LAma LRHS MBri NBir NBlu SChr SPer WCot WGwG
- 'Christmas Pearl' ♀^{H4}	CStu WCot
- 'Early Giant'	LAma
- 'Fantasy Creation'	CRez EBrs EChP EPot LRHS WCot
- 'Heavenly Blue'	LAma
- 'Saffier' ♀^{H4}	LAma LRHS WCot
- 'Valerie Finnis'	CAvo CBos CBre CBro CFwr CMea EPPr EPfP EPot GCrs ITim LPhx LRHS MNrw MSte SAga SPer WAbe WAul WCot WPen
§ ***aucheri*** ♀^{H4}	ECho LAma MSte NRya
* - var. ***bicolor*** **new**	WCot
- 'Blue Magic'	EPot
- 'Tubergenianum' **new**	EBrs
§ ***azureum*** ♀^{H4}	CAvo CBgR CBro CNic EBrs EHyt EPfP ERos LAma LRHS NJOw NMen WCot
- 'Album'	CBro CRez CStu EBrs ERos LAma LRHS NJOw WCot
botryoides	CStu LAma
- 'Album'	CAvo CBro CMea CStu EChP ENot EPfP GFlt LAma LRHS MBri SPer SRms WBor WShi

	chalusicum	see *M. pseudomuscari*
§	***comosum***	CBro EPfP LRHS NWCA
	- 'Monstrosum'	see *M. comosum* 'Plumosum'
	- 'Pinard'	ERos
§	- 'Plumosum'	CAvo CBro EMan EMon EPot GFlt ITim LAma LRHS MBri SBch WAul WCot
	'Dark Eyes' **new**	SOkh
	dionysicum	EBee
	- HOA 8965	WCot
	grandifolium JCA 689.450	WCot
	latifolium ♀H4	CAvo CBro CMea EHyt ENot EUJe GFlt GGar ITim LAma LPhx LRHS MLLN NChi SPer WCot WHoo WTin
*	- 'Blue Angels'	NBir
§	***macrocarpum***	CAvo CBro CMea EBee ECha EHyt EPot ERos LAma SOkh SSpi WAbe WCot
	- 'Golden Fragrance' **new**	ENot
	moschatum	see *M. muscarimi*
§	***muscarimi***	CBro LAma NWCA WCot WWFP
	- var. ***flavum***	see *M. macrocarpum*
§	***neglectum***	CBgR CFil CMea CSWP ECho ERos EUJe LAma SEND SOkh WShi WWst
§	- 'Baby's Breath'	CMil EHrv SAga SCnR SMad SMrm WCot
	pallens	EHyt NWCA
	paradoxum	see *Bellevalia paradoxa*
	parviflorum	ECho ERos
§	***pseudomuscari*** ♀H4	ERos
	- BSBE 842	EHyt
	racemosum	see *M. neglectum*
§	***spreitzenhoferi***	ERos
	- MS 712 from Crete **new**	CMon
§	***tenuiflorum***	WCot
	tubergenianum	see *M. aucheri* 'Tubergenianum'
	weissii	ERos
	'White Beauty'	LRHS

Muscarimia (*Hyacinthaceae*)

ambrosiacum	see *Muscari muscarimi*
macrocarpum	see *Muscari macrocarpum*

Musella (*Musaceae*)

lasiocarpa	see *Musa lasiocarpa*

Mussaenda (*Rubiaceae*)

incana **new**	EShb
philippica **new**	CPLN

Musschia (*Campanulaceae*)

wollastonii	CAby CHEx CPLG MGol

Mutisia (*Asteraceae*)

	clematis	CRHN
	coccinea	CBcs
	decurrens	CPLN WCot
	'Glendoick'	GGGa
	ilicifolia	IBlr LRHS SBrw WSHC
	latifolia	CBcs
*	***longifolia*** **new**	CSec
	oligodon	CPLN IBlr SBrw
	retrorsa	WCot
	retusa	see *M. spinosa* var. *pulchella*
§	***spinosa*** var. ***pulchella***	SSpi
	subulata f. ***rosea***	CFil

Myoporum (*Myoporaceae*)

debile	see *Eremophila debilis*
laetum	CDoC CHEx CPLG CTrC IDee XPep
parvifolium	XPep

Myosotidium (*Boraginaceae*)

§	***hortensia***	More than 30 suppliers
	- white	ITer ITim NCot NLar WNor
	nobile	see *M. hortensia*

Myosotis (*Boraginaceae*)

§	***alpestris***	EHyt
	- 'Ruth Fischer'	NBir NMen
	arvensis	GWCH MBow
	australis	NWCA
	'Bill Baker'	CPLG EMon
	capitata	GCrs
	colensoi	ECou EDAr NMen NWCA
	explanata	NMen
	palustris	see *M. scorpioides*
	pulvinaris	CPBP GEdr ITim SIng WAbe
	rakiura	GTou ITim MAvo NLAp SBch
	rupicola	see *M. alpestris*
§	***scorpioides***	CBen CRow CWat EHon EMFW EPfP LNCo LPBA MBow NGdn SCoo SPlb SRms WEas WMoo WPnP WPop WWpP
	- 'Alba'	LPBA
	- Maytime = 'Blaqua' (v)	CDWL EMon NBir NGdn
	- 'Mermaid'	CBen CRow CWat ECha EHon EPfP GAbr GMac LPBA LRHS NDov SDix WFar WPer WPtf WWpP
	- 'Pinkie'	CDWL CRow CWat EMFW GMac LPBA NGdn WPop
	- 'Snowflakes'	CRow CWat EMFW WWpP
	sylvatica	CRWN NMir
	- 'Pompadour' **new**	NBlu
	- 'Ultramarine' ♀H4 **new**	NBlu

Myrcia (*Myrtaceae*)

tomentosa	GIBF

Myrica (*Myricaceae*)

californica	CFil CPle LEdu WPGP
cerifera	CAgr CArn LEdu
gale	CAgr CRWN GPoy MGos WDin WFar WWye
pensylvanica	GIBF GTSp IFro NBlu

Myricaria (*Tamaricaceae*)

§	***germanica*** **new**	NLar

Myriophyllum (*Haloragaceae*)

	propinquum	EMFW NArg
*	'Red Stem'	LPBA
	spicatum	EHon EMFW WPop
	verticillatum	EHon SCoo

Myrrhidendron (*Apiaceae*)

donnellsmithii B&SWJ 9099	WCru

Myrrhis (*Apiaceae*)

odorata	More than 30 suppliers

Myrsine (*Myrsinaceae*)

africana	CPLG CPle XPep
divaricata	CTrC IDee
nummularia	GGar

Myrteola (*Myrtaceae*)

§	sp.	GAbr ISea

Myrtus (*Myrtaceae*)

apiculata	see *Luma apiculata*

	bullata	see *Lophomyrtus bullata*
	chequen	see *Luma chequen*
	communis 🏆H3	More than 30 suppliers
*	- 'Alhambra'	XPep
	- 'Baetica'	XPep
*	- 'Cascade'	XPep
	- 'Flore Pleno' (d)	GQui SBrw XPep
	- 'Jenny Reitenbach'	see *M. communis* subsp. *tarentina*
*	- 'La Clape'	XPep
*	- 'La Clape Blanc'	XPep
	- 'Merion'	WJek
	- 'Microphylla'	see *M. communis* subsp. *tarentina*
	- 'Nana'	see *M. communis* subsp. *tarentina*
§	- subsp. ***tarentina*** 🏆H3	More than 30 suppliers
	- - 'Compacta'	CStu WSel
*	- - 'Granada'	XPep
§	- - 'Microphylla Variegata' (v)	CBcs CPle GBar GQui MHer NGHP SAga SPer STre WBrE WJek WSHC WSel
	- - pink-flowered	XPep
I	- - 'Variegata'	EHol XPep
*	- - 'Vieussan'	XPep
	- 'Tricolor'	see *M. communis* 'Variegata'
§	- 'Variegata' (v)	More than 30 suppliers
	dulcis	see *Austromyrtus dulcis*
	'Glanleam Gold'	see *Luma apiculata* 'Glanleam Gold'
	lechleriana	see *Amomyrtus luma*
	luma	see *Luma apiculata*
	nummularia	see *Myrteola nummularia*
	obcordata	see *Lophomyrtus obcordata*
*	***paraguayensis***	CTrC
	x ***ralphii***	see *Lophomyrtus* x *ralphii*
	'Traversii'	see *Lophomyrtus* x *ralphii* 'Traversii'
	ugni	see *Ugni molinae*

N

Naiocrene (*Portulacaceae*)

§	***parvifolia***	CNic

Nananthus (*Aizoaceae*)

	vittatus **new**	WAbe

Nandina (*Berberidaceae*)

	domestica 🏆H3	More than 30 suppliers
	- B&SWJ 4923	WCru
	- 'Fire Power' 🏆H3	More than 30 suppliers
	- 'Harbor Dwarf'	LRHS WFar
	- var. ***leucocarpa***	EPla MBlu
	- 'Nana'	see *N. domestica* 'Pygmaea'
	- 'Nana Purpurea'	CDul EPla
§	- 'Pygmaea'	CMen WDin
	- 'Richmond'	CBcs CPMA CSBt ECrN ELan EPfP EPza LRHS MAsh MGos NLar NVic SBod SHBN SPer SPla SPoG SRkn WBrE WFar

Nannorrhops (*Arecaceae*)

	ritchieana	WMul

Napaea (*Malvaceae*)

	dioica	EBee EMan

Narcissus ✿ (*Amaryllidaceae*)

	'Abba' (4) **new**	CQua
	'Aberfoyle' (2) 🏆H4	GEve
	'Abstract' (11a)	CQua
	'Accent' (2) 🏆H4	CQua
	'Achduart' (3)	CQua GEve
	'Achentoul' (4)	CQua
	'Achnasheen' (3)	CQua GEve
	'Acropolis' (4)	CQua LAma LRHS
	'Actaea' (9) 🏆H4	CFen CQua LBmB LRHS MBri
	'Adele Thomson' (3) **new**	GEve
	'Admiration' (8)	CQua
*	'Adrem' **new**	CFen
	'Advocat' (3)	CQua
	'Aflame' (3)	CFen LAma
	'African Sunset' (3) **new**	IRhd
	'After All' **new**	CFen
	'Ahwahnee' (2)	CQua IRhd
	'Aintree' (3)	CQua
	'Aircastle' (3)	CQua
	'Akepa' (5)	CQua
	'Albatross' (3) **new**	CQua
I	***albidus*** subsp. ***occidentalis*** (13)	ERos
I	- - SF 15 from Morocco **new**	CMon
	- - SF 270	CMon
	'Albus Plenus Odoratus'	see *N. poeticus* 'Plenus'
	'Alpine Winter' (1) **new**	IRhd
	'Alston' (2)	IRhd
	'Alto' (2)	IRhd
	'Altruist' (3)	CQua
	'Altun Ha' (2)	CQua IRhd
	'Amazing Grace' (2)	IRhd
	'Amber Castle' (2)	CQua
	'Ambergate' (2)	GEve LAma
	'American Heritage' (1)	CQua IRhd
	'American Robin' (6)	CQua
	'American Shores' (1)	CQua IRhd
	'Amstel' (4)	CQua
	'Andalusia' (6)	ERos
	'Angel Face' (3)	IRhd
	'Angelito' (2)	IRhd
	'Angel's Wings' (2) **new**	CQua
	'Angkor' (4)	CQua
	'An-gof' (7)	CQua
	'Annalong' (3)	IRhd
	'Apotheose' (4)	CFen CQua MBri
	'Applins' (2)	IRhd
	'Apricot' (1)	CBro
	'April Love' (1)	CQua
	'April Snow' (2)	CBro CQua
	'Aranjuez' (2)	CFen CQua
	'Arctic Gold' (1) 🏆H4	CQua LAma LBmB
	'Ardglass' (3)	GEve IRhd
	'Ardress' (2)	CQua
	'Ardview' (3)	IRhd
	'Areley Kings' (2)	CQua
	'Arid Plains' (3)	IRhd
	'Arish Mell' (5)	CQua
	'Arkle' (1) 🏆H4	CQua GEve LBmB
	'Arleston' (2)	IRhd
	'Armada' (2) 🏆H4 **new**	CFen
	'Armidale' (3)	IRhd
	'Armoury' (4) **new**	CQua
	'Arndilly' (2)	CQua
	'Arpege' (2)	CQua
	'Arran Isle' (2)	IRhd
	'Arthurian' (1)	IRhd
	'Arwenack' (11a)	CQua
	'Ashmore' (2)	CQua IRhd
	'Asila' (2)	IRhd
	'Assertion' (2)	IRhd
§	***assoanus*** (13)	CBro CQua ECho EPot ERos GKir LAma
	'Astropink' (11a) **new**	CQua
§	***asturiensis*** (13) 🏆H3-4	CBro CSam ECho EHyt IBlr LPhx MNrw

'Atricilla' (11a)	IRhd
'Audubon' (2)	CQua
'Auntie Eileen' (2)	CQua
'Auspicious' (2)	IRhd
'Avalanche' (8) ♀H3	CQua LRHS
'Avalanche of Gold' (8) **new**	CQua
'Avalon' (2)	CQua
'Azocor' (1)	IRhd
'Baby Moon' (7)	CQua EPot GFlt LAma LRHS LSou MBri NJOw SPer
'Badanloch' (3)	CQua
'Badbury Rings' (3) ♀H4	CQua
'Balalaika' (2)	CQua
'Baldock' (4)	CQua
'Ballinamallard' (3)	IRhd
'Ballygarvey' (1)	CQua
'Ballygowan' (3)	IRhd
'Ballykinler' (3)	IRhd
'Ballymorran' (1)	IRhd
'Ballynahinch' (3)	IRhd
'Ballynichol' (3)	IRhd
'Ballyrobert' (1)	CQua
'Baltic Shore' (3)	IRhd
'Balvenie' (2)	CQua
'Bambi' (1)	ERos
'Bandesara' (3)	CQua IRhd
'Bandit' (2)	CQua
'Banstead Village' (2)	CQua
'Bantam' (2) ♀H4	CBro CQua ERos MBri
'Barleywine' (2)	IRhd
'Barlow' (6)	CQua
'Barnesgold' (1)	IRhd
'Barnsdale Wood' (2)	CQua
'Barnum' (1) ♀H4	IRhd
'Barrett Browning' (3)	LBmB MBri
'Bartley' (6)	CQua
'Bath's Flame' (3)	CQua
'Bear Springs' (4)	IRhd
'Bebop' (7)	CBro
'Bedruthan' (2)	CQua
'Beersheba' (1) **new**	CQua
'Belbroughton' (2)	CQua
'Belcanto' (11a)	CQua
'Belfast Lough' (1) **new**	IRhd
'Belisana' (2)	LAma
'Bell Rock' (1)	CQua
'Bell Song' (7)	CAvo CBro CQua EPfP ERos GFlt LRHS LSou MBri SPer
'Ben Aligin' (1)	CQua
'Ben Armine' (2)	GEve
'Ben Hee' (2) ♀H4	CQua
'Ben Loyal' (2)	GEve
'Ben Vorlich' (2)	GEve
'Berceuse' (2)	CQua IRhd
'Bere Ferrers' (4)	CQua
'Bergerac' (11a)	CQua
'Berlin' (2)	ERos LBmB
'Bernardino' (2) **new**	CQua
bertolonii from Algeria **new**	CMon
'Beryl' (6)	CBro CQua ERos LAma LRHS
'Best of Luck' (3)	IRhd
'Bethal' (3)	CQua
'Betsy MacDonald' (6)	CQua
'Biffo' (4)	CQua
'Big John' (1)	GEve
'Bikini Beach' (2) **new**	IRhd
'Bilbo' (6)	CBro CQua
'Binkie' (2)	CBro CQua LAma SPer
'Birdsong' (3)	CQua
'Birkdale' (2)	GEve
'Birma' (3)	LAma
'Birthday Girl' (2)	IRhd
'Bishops Light' (2)	CQua
'Blair Athol' (2) **new**	CQua
'Blarney' (3)	CQua
'Blisland' (9)	CQua
'Blossom' (4)	CQua
'Blue Danube' (1)	IRhd
'Blushing Maiden' (4)	CQua
'Bobbysoxer' (7)	CBro CQua ERos LAma MTho
'Bobolink' (2)	CQua
'Bodelva' (2) **new**	CQua
'Bodwannick' (2)	CQua
'Bold Prospect' (1) **new**	CQua
'Bolton' (7)	CBro
'Bon Viveur' (11a)	IRhd
'Bosbigal' (11a)	CQua
'Boscastle' (7)	CQua
'Boscoppa' (11a)	CQua
'Boslowick' (11a) ♀H4	CQua
'Bosmeor' (2)	CQua
'Bossa Nova' (3)	CQua
'Bossiney' (11a)	CQua
'Bosvale' (11a)	CQua
'Bouzouki' (2)	IRhd
'Bowles' Early Sulphur' (1)	CRow
'Boyne Bridge' (1)	IRhd
'Brandaris' (11a)	CQua GEve
'Bravoure' (1) ♀H4	CQua LBmB
'Brentswood' (8)	CQua
'Bridal Crown' (4) ♀H4	CFen EBrs EPfP LAma LRHS SPer
'Bright Flame' (2)	CQua
'Brindaleena' (2) **new**	IRhd
'Brindle Pink' (2)	IRhd
'Broadland' (2)	CQua
'Broadway Star' (11b)	EBrs LAma LRHS
'Brodick' (3)	CQua GEve IRhd
'Brookdale' (1)	CQua
'Broomhill' (2) ♀H4	CQua
broussonetii (13)	CFil
- EKB from Morocco **new**	CMon
- SF 269 from Morocco	CMon
'Brunswick' (2)	CFen
'Budock Bells' (5)	CQua
'Budock Water' (2) **new**	CQua
'Bugle Major' (2)	CQua
bulbocodium (13) ♀H3-4	CBro CFil CNic EHyt LBee LPhx LRHS NRya NWCA SBch SMeo SPer SRms WLin WPGP
§ - subsp. ***bulbocodium*** (13)	CBro
- - var. ***bulbocodium*** x 'Jessamy'	EHyt
§ - - var. ***citrinus*** (13)	EHyt SSpi
- - var. ***conspicuus*** (13)	CArn CBro CNic CPMA CQua CSam EHyt EPot ERos GCrs GEdr IFro ITim LAma MS&S NJOw NRya SBch SGar WCot
* - - ***filifolius*** (13)	CBro
§ - - var. ***graellsii*** (13)	NSla
- - var. ***nivalis*** (13)	ECho ERos
- - var. ***pallidus*** (13) **new**	ERos
§ - - var. ***tenuifolius*** (13)	CNic CStu EPot MNrw
- - var. ***tenuifolius*** x ***triandrus*** (13)	EHyt
§ - 'Golden Bells' (10)	CAvo CBro CMea CPom CQua EBrs EPot GFlt LBmB LRHS MBri NJOw SPer
- var. ***mesatlanticus***	see *N. romieuxii* subsp. *romieuxii* var. *mesatlanticus*
- subsp. ***praecox*** (13) **new**	ECho
- - var. ***paucinervis*** (13)	CAvo
- subsp. ***romieuxii***	see *N. romieuxii*

I	- subsp. ***viriditubus*** (13)	EHyt ERos
	- subsp. ***vulgaris***	see *N. bulbocodium* subsp. *bulbocodium*
	'Bunchie' (5)	CQua
	'Bunclody' (2)	CQua
	'Bunillidh Beauty' (2) **new**	GEve
	'Bunting' (7) Υ^{H4}	CQua
	'Burning Bush' (3)	IRhd
	'Burntollet' (1)	CQua
	'Busselton' (3)	IRhd
	'Buttercup' (7)	CBro
	'Butterscotch' (2)	CQua
	'Cabernet' (2)	IRhd
	'Cacatua' (11a)	IRhd
	'Cadgwith' (2)	CQua
	'Cairntoul' (3)	CQua
	'Calamansack' (2)	CQua
	calcicola (13)	CWoo ERos
	- B&S 413 from Spain **new**	CMon
	'California Rose' (4)	CQua IRhd
	'Camelot' (2) Υ^{H4}	CQua EPfP LBmB
	'Cameo Angel' (2) **new**	CQua
	'Cameo King' (2)	CQua
	'Camoro' (10) **new**	ITim
	'Campernelli Plenus'	see *N.* x *odorus* 'Double Campernelle'
	'Campion' (9)	CQua IRhd
	'Canaliculatus' (8)	CArn CBro CQua ERos LAma LRHS MBri SPer WGwG
	canaliculatus Gussone	see *N. tazetta* subsp. *lacticolor*
	'Canary' (7)	CQua
	'Canarybird' (8)	CBro
	'Canasta' (11a)	CQua
	'Canisp' (2)	CQua
	'Cantabile' (9) Υ^{H4}	CBro CQua
	cantabricus (13)	CFil EPot LBmB LPhx SSpi WPGP
	- SF 348 from Morocco **new**	CMon
	- subsp. ***cantabricus*** (13)	EHyt ERos
	- - var. ***foliosus*** (13) Υ^{H2}	EPot SCnR
	- - - SF 172 from Morocco **new**	CMon
	- - var. ***petunioides*** (13)	LAma SOkd
	cantabricus x ***romieuxii*** (13)	ITim
	'Capax Plenus'	see *N.* 'Eystettensis'
	'Cape Cornwall' (2)	CQua
	'Cape Helles' (3)	IRhd
	'Cape Point' (2)	IRhd
	'Capisco' (3)	CQua IRhd
	'Caramba' (2)	CQua
	'Carbineer' (2)	CQua LAma
	'Carclew' (6)	CQua
	'Cardinham' (3) **new**	CQua
	'Cargreen' (9)	CQua
	'Carib Gipsy' (2) Υ^{H4}	CQua IRhd
	'Carlton' (2) Υ^{H4}	CQua LAma LBmB MBri
	'Carnearny' (3)	CQua
	'Carnkeeran' (2)	CQua
	'Carnkief' (2)	CQua
	'Carnyorth' (11a)	CQua
	'Carole Lombard' (3)	CQua IRhd
	'Cassata' (11)	EBrs EPfP LAma LBmB LRHS NBir
	'Castanets' (8)	IRhd
	'Casterbridge' (2)	CQua IRhd
	'Castlehill' (3)	IRhd
	'Castlerock' **new**	CFen
	'Catalyst' (2)	IRhd
	'Catherine MacKenzie' (3)	GEve
	'Catistock' (2)	CQua
	'Causeway Sunset' (2)	IRhd
	'Cavalryman' (3)	IRhd
	cavanillesii SF 239 from Morocco **new**	CMon
	- MS&CL 450 from Spain **new**	CMon
*	- ***mauretanicus*** SF 260 from Morocco **new**	CMon
	'Cavendish' (4)	IRhd
	'Cazique' (6)	CQua
	'Ceasefire' (2)	IRhd
	'Cedar Hills' (3)	CQua
	'Cedric Morris' (1)	CBro CDes CElw CHid CLAP ECha EHrv GFlt NDov SMrm SSpi WCot
	'Celtic Gold' (2)	CQua
	'Centannées' (11b)	EBrs
	'Centrefold' (3)	CQua
	'Cha-cha' (6)	CBro CQua
	'Chanson' (1)	IRhd
	'Chanterelle' (11a)	LAma
	'Chapman's Peak' (2)	IRhd
	'Charity May' (6) Υ^{H4}	CBro CQua LAma MBri
	'Charleston' (2)	CQua
	'Chasseur' (2) **new**	IRhd
	'Chaste' (1)	CQua IRhd
	'Chat' (7)	CQua
	'Cheer Leader' (3)	CQua GEve
	'Cheerfulness' (4) Υ^{H4}	CAvo CQua ITim LAma LBmB LRHS MBri
	'Cheesewring' (3)	CQua
	'Cheetah' (1)	IRhd
	'Chelsea Girl' (2)	CQua
	'Cheltenham' (2)	CQua
	'Chenoweth' (2) **new**	CQua
	'Chérie' (7)	CBro CQua
	'Cherrygardens' (2)	CQua IRhd
	'Chesterton' (9) Υ^{H4}	CQua
	'Chickadee' (6)	CBro CQua
	'Chickerell' (3)	CQua
	'Chief Inspector' (1)	IRhd
	'Chiffon' **new**	CFen
	'Chiloquin' (1)	CQua
	'China Doll' (2)	CQua
	'Chinchilla' (2)	CQua IRhd
	'Chingah' (1)	IRhd
	'Chinita' (8)	CBro CQua
	'Chit Chat' (7) Υ^{H4}	CBgR CBro CQua EPot ERos LAma LBmB
	'Chobe River' (1)	IRhd
	'Chorus Line' (8)	IRhd
	'Churchman' (2)	IRhd
	'Churston Ferrers' (4)	CQua
	'Cisticola' (3)	IRhd
	citrinus	see *N. bulbocodium* subsp. *bulbocodium* var. *citrinus*
	'Citron' (3)	CQua
	'Citronita' (3)	CQua
	'Clare' (7)	CBro CQua
	'Clashmore' (2)	GEve
	'Claverley' (2)	CQua
	'Clearbrook' (2)	CQua
	'Close Harmony' (4)	IRhd
	'Cloud Nine' (2)	CBro
	'Clouded Yellow' (2)	IRhd
	'Clouds Hill'	CQua
	'Clouds Rest' (2)	IRhd
	'Codlins and Cream'	see *N.* 'Sulphur Phoenix'
	'Colin's Joy' (2)	CQua
	'Colleen Bawn'	CAvo
	'Colley Gate' (3)	CQua
	'Colliford' (2)	CQua
	'Colorama' (11a)	CQua
	'Colour Sergeant' (2)	IRhd
	'Colourful' (2)	IRhd
	'Columbus' (2)	CQua

'Colville' (9)	CQua
'Comal' (1)	CQua
'Compressus'	see *N.* x *intermedius* 'Compressus' (8)
'Compton Court' (3)	IRhd
concolor (Haworth) Link	see *N. triandrus* subsp. *triandrus* var. *concolor*
'Conestoga' (2)	IRhd
'Congress' (11a)	CQua
* 'Connie Number 2'	EHyt
'Conowingo' (11a) **new**	CQua
'Conspicuus' ambig. **new**	LAma
'Cool Autumn' (2) **new**	CQua
'Cool Crystal' (3)	CQua IRhd
'Cool Evening' (11a)	CQua IRhd
'Cool Pink' (2)	CQua
'Coombe Creek' (6)	CQua
'Copper Nob' (2)	IRhd
'Cora Ann' (7)	CBro
'Corbiere' (1)	CQua IRhd
cordubensis (13)	ECho EHyt EPot SSpi
- MS 434 from Spain **new**	CMon
'Cornet' (6)	CQua
'Cornish Chuckles' (12)	CFen CQua
'Cornish Vanguard' (2) **new**	CQua
'Corofin' (3)	CQua
'Coromandel' (2)	IRhd
'Cosmic Dance' (3)	IRhd
'Cotinga' (6)	CQua EBrs
'Countdown' (2)	CQua
'Court Martial' (2) **new**	CFen
'Crackington' (4) ♀H4	CQua IRhd
'Cragford' (8)	LAma
'Craig Stiel' (2)	CQua GEve
'Creag Dubh' (2)	CQua GEve
'Crenver' (3)	CQua
'Crevenagh' (2)	IRhd
'Crewenna' (1) **new**	CQua
'Crill' (7) **new**	CQua
'Crimson Chalice' (3)	CQua IRhd
'Cristobal' (1)	CQua
'Crock of Gold' (1)	CFen CQua
'Croesus' (2)	CQua
'Crofty' (6)	CQua
'Croila' (2)	CQua
'Crowndale' (4)	CQua IRhd
'Cryptic' (1)	CQua IRhd
'Crystal Star' (2)	CQua
'Cuan Gold' (4)	IRhd
cuatrecasasii (13)	ERos
'Cudden Point' (2) **new**	CQua
'Cul Beag' (3)	CQua
'Culmination' (2)	CQua
'Cultured Pearl' (2)	CQua
'Cupid's Eye' (3)	CQua IRhd
'Curlew' (7)	CQua
cyclamineus (13) ♀H4	CBro CDes CFil CPom CStu CWoo LAma MS&S SBla SCnR SIgm SRms SSpi WAbe WCru WLFP WPGP
'Cyclope' (1)	CQua
cypri (8)	CQua
'Cyros' (1)	CQua
'Dailmanach' (2)	CQua IRhd
'Dailmystic' (2)	IRhd
'Dallas' (3)	CQua
'Damson' (2)	CQua
'Dan du Plessis' (8)	CQua
'Dancing Queen' (2)	IRhd
'Dardanelles' (2)	IRhd
'Dateline' (3)	CQua
'David Alexander' (1)	CQua
'David Mills' (2) **new**	CQua
'Davochfin Lass' (1)	GEve
'Dawn Call' (2) **new**	IRhd
'Dawn Run' (2)	IRhd
'Daydream' (2) ♀H3	CQua LAma
'Daymark' (8) **new**	CQua
'Dayton Lake' (2) **new**	CQua
'Debutante' (2)	CQua
'December Bride' (11a)	CQua
'Delia' (6)	IRhd
'Délibes' (2)	LAma LBmB
'Dell Chapel' (3)	CQua
'Delnashaugh' (4)	CQua LAma
'Delos' (3)	CQua
'Delphin Hill' (4)	IRhd
'Delta Flight' (6)	IRhd
'Demand' (2)	CQua
'Denali' (1)	IRhd
'Derryboy' (3)	IRhd
'Descant' (1)	IRhd
'Desdemona' (2) ♀H4	CQua
'Desert Bells' (7)	CQua
'Desert Orchid' (2)	CQua
'Diatone' (4)	GEve
'Dick Wilden' (4)	LAma
'Dickcissel' (7) ♀H4	CBro CQua ERos
'Dimity' (3)	CQua
'Dimple' (9)	CQua
'Dinkie' (3)	CBro
'Diversity' (11a)	IRhd
'Doctor Hugh' (3) ♀H4	CQua GEve IRhd
'Doombar' (1)	CQua
'Dora Allum' (2)	CQua
'Dorchester' (4)	CQua IRhd
'Double Campernelle'	see *N.* x *odorus* 'Double Campernelle'
double pheasant eye	see *N. poeticus* 'Plenus'
double Roman	see *N.* 'Romanus'
'Double White' (4)	CQua
'Doubleday' (4)	IRhd
'Doublet' (4)	CQua
'Doubtful' (3)	CQua
'Dove Wings' (6) ♀H4	CQua LAma
'Dover Cliffs' (2)	CQua
'Downpatrick' (1)	CQua
'Dragon Run' (2)	CQua
'Drama Queen' (11a)	IRhd
'Drumbeg' (2)	IRhd
'Drumlin' (1) ♀H4	IRhd
dubius (13)	CBro ECho
- MS 512 from Spain **new**	CMon
'Duiker' (6)	IRhd
'Dulcimer' (9)	CQua
'Dunadry Inn' (4)	IRhd
'Dunkeld' (2)	CQua
'Dunkery' (4)	CQua IRhd
'Dunley Hall' (3)	CQua IRhd
'Dunmurry' (1)	CQua
'Dunskey' (3)	CQua
'Dupli Kate' (4) **new**	IRhd
'Dusky Lad' (2)	IRhd
'Dusky Maiden' (2)	IRhd
'Dutch Delight' (2)	IRhd
'Dutch Master' (1) ♀H4	CQua EBrs LAma LBmB MBri
'Early Bride' (2)	CFen CQua
'Early Splendour' (8)	CQua LAma
'Earthlight' (3)	CQua
'Easter Bonnet' (2)	LAma MBri
'Eastern Dawn' (2)	CQua
'Eaton Song' (12) ♀H4	CBro CQua
'Eddy Canzony' (2)	CFen CQua
'Edenderry' (1)	IRhd
'Edgbaston' (2)	CQua
'Edge Grove' (2)	CQua
'Edward Buxton' (3)	CFen CQua MBri

Name	Suppliers
'Egard' (11a)	CQua
'Eiko' **new**	CQua
'Eland' (7)	CQua
'Elburton' (2) **new**	CQua
'Electrus' (11a)	IRhd
elegans (13) **new**	ECho
- var. ***fallax*** from Tunisia **new**	EShb
- - MS&CL 324	CMon
- AB&S 4301 from Morocco **new**	CMon
'Elf' (2)	CBro CQua
'Elfin Gold' (6)	CQua IRhd
'Elizabeth Ann' (6)	CQua
'Elka' (1)	CBro CQua
'Ella D' (2) **new**	CQua
'Elphin' (4)	CQua GEve
'Elrond' (2)	CQua
'Elven Lady' (2)	CQua
'Elvira' (8)	CBro CQua
'Embo' (2)	GEve
'Emerald Pink' (3) **new**	CQua
'Emily' (2)	CQua
'Eminent' (3)	CQua
'Emperor's Waltz' (6)	CQua IRhd
'Empress of Ireland' (1) ♀H4	CQua IRhd LBmB
'Englander' (6)	EPot
'Ensemble' (4)	CQua
'Epona' (3) **new**	CQua
'Eribol' (2)	GEve
'Eriskay' (4)	GEve
'Erlicheer' (4)	CQua
'Escapee' (2)	IRhd
'Estrella' (3) **new**	CQua
'Ethereal Beauty' (2)	IRhd
'Ethos' (1)	IRhd
'Euryalus' (1)	CQua
'Evelix' (2)	GEve
'Evening' (2)	CQua
'Evesham' (3)	IRhd
'Eyeglass' (3)	IRhd
'Eyelet' (3)	IRhd
'Eype' (4)	IRhd
'Eyrie' (3)	IRhd
§ 'Eystettensis' (4)	CBro ECha ERos GCrs IBlr
'Fair Head' (9)	CQua
'Fair Prospect' (2)	CQua
'Fair William' (2)	CQua
'Fairgreen' (3)	CFen CQua
'Fairlawns' (3)	CQua
'Fairmile' (3) **new**	CQua
'Fairy Chimes' (5)	CBro CQua
'Fairy Footsteps' (3)	IRhd
'Fairy Island' (3)	CQua
'Fairy Spell' (3)	IRhd
'Falconet' (8) ♀H4	CBro CQua ERos
'Falmouth Bay' (3)	CQua
'Falstaff' (2)	CQua
'Fanad Head' (9)	IRhd
'Far Country' (2)	CQua GEve
'Faro' (1)	IRhd
'Farranfad' (2)	IRhd
I 'Fashion' (11b) **new**	CQua
'Fastidious' (2)	CQua
'February Gold' (6) ♀H4	CAvo CBro EBrs EPfP EPot ERos LAma LBmB LRHS MBri NBir SPer SRms WShi
'February Silver' (6)	CBro EPot LAma LRHS SMeo
'Felindre' (9)	CQua
'Feline Queen' (1)	IRhd
'Fellowship' (2)	GEve
'Feock' (3)	CQua
fernandesii (13)	CBro ECho ERos SCnR
- B&S 467 from Spain **new**	CMon
'Ferndown' (3)	CQua IRhd
'Ffitch's Ffolly' (2)	CQua
'Filoli' (1)	CQua IRhd
'Fine Gold' (1)	CQua
'Fine Romance' (2)	CQua
'Finland' (2) **new**	CFen
'Finlandia' (1) **new**	CQua
'Fiona MacKillop' (2)	IRhd
'Fionn' (2)	GEve
'Firebrand' (2)	CQua
'First Formal' (3)	CQua
'Flambards Village' (4) **new**	CQua
'Flirt' (6)	CQua
'Flomay' (7)	CBro
'Florida Manor' (3)	IRhd
'Flower Drift' (4)	LAma
'Flower Record' (2)	LAma SPer
'Flycatcher' (7)	CQua IRhd
'Flying Colours' (4)	IRhd
'Flying High' (3) **new**	CQua
'Foresight' (1)	LBmB
'Forge Mill' (2)	CQua
'Fortune' (2)	CQua LAma MBri
'Foundling' (6) ♀H4	CBro CQua GEve
'Fragrant Breeze' (2)	EBrs
'Fragrant Rose' (2)	CQua IRhd
'Francolin' (1)	IRhd
'Freedom Rings' (2)	CQua
'Fresco' (11a)	IRhd
'Fresno' (3)	IRhd
'Frogmore' (6)	CQua
'Front Royal' (2)	CQua
'Frosted Pink' (2)	IRhd
'Frostkist' (6)	CBro CQua
'Frou-frou' (4)	CQua
'Fruit Cup' (7)	CQua
'Fulwell' (4)	CQua
'Furnace Creek' (2)	IRhd
'Fynbos' (3)	IRhd
gaditanus (13)	CBro ERos SSpi
'Garden News' (3)	IRhd
'Garden Princess' (6)	CBro
'Gay Cavalier' (4)	CQua
'Gay Kybo' (4) ♀H4	CQua LBmB
'Gay Song' (4)	CQua
'Gay Time' (4)	CFen
§ ***gayi*** (13)	CBro CQua
'Geevor' (4)	CQua
'Gemini Girl' (2)	CQua
'George Leak' (2)	CFen CQua
'Georgia Moon' **new**	CFen
'Georgie Girl' (6)	CQua
'Geranium' (8) ♀H4	CBro CQua EPfP LAma LBmB LRHS MBri SPer
'Gettysburg' (2)	CQua
'Gigantic Star' (2)	LAma MBri
'Gillan' (11a)	CQua
'Gin and Lime' (1) ♀H4	CQua
'Gipsy Queen' (1)	CQua EHyt
'Gironde' (11)	CQua
'Glacier' (1) **new**	CQua
'Glen Cassley' (3)	CQua GEve
'Glen Clova' (2)	CQua GEve LBmB
'Glen Lorne' (2)	GEve
'Glencalvie' (2)	GEve
'Glenfarclas' (1) ♀H4	GEve LBmB
'Glenmorangie' (2)	GEve
'Glenside' (2)	CQua
'Glissando' (2)	CQua
'Gloriosus' (8)	CQua
'Glowing Pheonix' (4)	CQua

'Glowing Red' (4)	CQua
'Goff's Caye' (2)	CQua IRhd
'Gold Bond' (2)	CQua IRhd
'Gold Charm' (2)	CQua
'Gold Convention' (2) ♀H4	CQua IRhd
'Gold Ingot' (2)	IRhd
'Gold Medal' (1)	LAma
'Gold Medallion' (1)	CQua
'Gold Mine' (2)	IRhd
'Gold Strike' (1)	GEve
'Golden Amber' (2)	CQua
'Golden Anniversary' **new**	CFen
'Golden Aura' (2) ♀H4	CQua
'Golden Bear' (4)	CQua
'Golden Bells'	see *N. bulbocodium* 'Golden Bells'
'Golden Cheer' (2)	CQua
'Golden Cycle' (6)	CQua
'Golden Dawn' (8) ♀H3	CQua EBrs
'Golden Ducat' (4)	CQua LAma MBri NBir
'Golden Halo' (2)	CQua
'Golden Harvest' (1)	CQua LAma LRHS MBri SPer
'Golden Incense' (7)	CQua
'Golden Jewel' (2) ♀H4	CQua GEve
'Golden Joy' (2)	CQua
'Golden Marvel' (1) **new**	CQua
'Golden Orbit' (4)	CQua
'Golden Phoenix' (4) **new**	WShi
'Golden Quince' (12)	CBro CQua
'Golden Rain' (4)	CQua
'Golden Rapture' (1) ♀H4	CQua LBmB
'Golden Sceptre' (7)	CBro
'Golden Sheen' (2)	CQua
'Golden Spur' (1)	CQua LAma
'Golden Strand' (2)	IRhd
'Golden Topaz' (2)	IRhd
'Golden Torch' (2) **new**	CQua
'Golden Vale' (1) ♀H4	CQua
'Goldfinger' (1) ♀H4	CQua IRhd
'Goldhanger' (2)	CQua
'Goldsithney' (2)	CBro
'Golitha Falls' (2)	CQua
'Good Measure' (2)	CQua
'Goonbell' (2) **new**	CQua
'Goose Green' (3)	IRhd
'Gorran' (3)	CQua
'Gossmoor' (4)	CQua
graellsii	see *N. bulbocodium* subsp. *bulbocodium* var. *graellsii*
'Grand Monarque'	see *N. tazetta* subsp. *lacticolor* 'Grand Monarque'
'Grand Opening' (4)	IRhd
'Grand Primo Citronière' (8)	CQua
'Grand Prospect' (2)	CQua
'Grand Soleil d'Or' (8)	CQua LAma
'Grapillon' (11a)	GEve
'Grasmere' (1) ♀H4	GEve
'Great Expectations' (2)	CQua
'Greatwood' (1)	CQua
'Green Howard' (3) **new**	LAma
'Green Island' (2)	CFen
'Green Lodge' (9)	IRhd
'Greenlet' (6)	CBro CQua LRHS MSte
'Greenodd' (3)	CQua
'Greenpark' (9)	IRhd
'Grenoble' (2) **new**	CQua
'Gresham' (4)	CQua IRhd
'Gribben Head' (4)	CQua
'Groundkeeper' (3)	IRhd
'Gulliver' (3)	CQua
'Gunwalloe' (11a)	CQua
'Gwennap' (1)	CQua
'Gwinear' (2)	CQua

'Halley's Comet' (3)	CQua IRhd
'Halvose' (8)	CBro
'Hambledon' (2) ♀H4	CQua
'Happy Dreams' (2)	IRhd
'Happy Fellow' (2)	CQua
'Harbour View' (2)	IRhd
'Harmony Bells' (5)	CQua
'Harp Music' (2)	IRhd
'Harpers Ferry' (1)	CQua
'Hartlebury' (3)	CQua
* 'Hat' (10)	EHyt
'Hawangi' (3)	IRhd
'Hawera' (5) ♀H4	CAvo CBro CQua EBrs ECGP EPfP EPot GFlt LAma LBmB LRHS LSou MBri NJOw SPer WLin WPen
'Hazel Rutherford' (2)	GEve
'Heamoor' (4)	CQua
hedraeanthus (13) SG 13	WCot
'Helford Dawn' (2)	CQua
'Helford Sunset' (2) **new**	CQua
'Helios' (2)	CQua
hellenicus	see *N. poeticus* var. *hellenicus*
henriquesii	see *N. jonquilla* var. *henriquesii*
'Henry Irving' (1) **new**	CQua
'Hero' (1)	CQua
'Hesla' (7)	CBro
'Heslington' (3)	CQua
'Hexameter' (9)	CQua
'Hexworthy' (3) **new**	CQua
'Hicks Mill' (1) **new**	CQua
'High Life' **new**	CFen
'High Society' (2) ♀H4	CQua IRhd
'Highfield Beauty' (8) ♀H4	CQua
'Highlite' (2)	CQua
'Hilda's Pink' (2) **new**	CQua
'Hilford' (2)	IRhd
'Hill Head' (9)	IRhd
'Hillstar' (7)	CQua IRhd
'Hocus Pocus' (3)	IRhd
'Holland Sensation' (1)	LAma
'Holly Berry' (2)	CFen CQua
'Hollypark' (3)	IRhd
'Holme Fen' (2)	CQua
'Homestead' (2) ♀H4 **new**	IRhd
'Honey Pink' (2)	CQua
'Honeybird' (1)	CQua
'Honeyorange' (2)	IRhd
'Honolulu' (4)	CQua
'Hoopoe' (8) ♀H4	CBro CQua
'Horace' (9)	CQua
'Horn of Plenty' (5)	CBro CQua
'Hornpipe' (1)	IRhd
'Hors d'Oeuvre' (8)	CBro
'Hospodar' (2)	CQua
'Hot Gossip' (2)	CQua
'Hotspur' (2)	CQua
'Hugh Town' (8)	CAvo CQua
'Hullabaloo' (2)	IRhd
'Hunting Caye' (2)	CQua
'Huntley Down' (1)	CQua
'Ice Chimes' (5) **new**	CQua
'Ice Diamond' (4)	CQua
'Ice Follies' (2) ♀H4	CQua LAma LBmB MBri NBir NBlu SPer
'Ice King' (4)	NBir
'Ice Wings' (5) ♀H4	CAvo CBro CPBP CQua EPot ERos LBmB LRHS MSte WShi
'Idless' (1)	CQua
'Immaculate' (2)	CQua
'Inara' (4)	CQua
'Inca' (6)	CQua
x ***incomparabilis***	GIBF
'Independence Day' (4)	CQua

	Name	Suppliers
	'Indian Maid' (7) ♀H4	CQua IRhd
	'Indora' (4)	CQua
	'Inner Glow' (2)	IRhd
	'Innisidgen' (8) **new**	CQua
	'Innovator' (4)	IRhd
	'Inny River' (1)	IRhd
	'Interim' (2)	CFen CQua
§	x ***intermedius*** (13)	CBro CQua ERos
§	- 'Compressus' (8)	CQua
	'Intrigue' (7) ♀H4	CQua IRhd
	'Invercassley' (3)	GEve
	'Inverpolly' (2)	GEve
	'Ipi Tombi' (2)	ERos
	'Ireland's Eye' (9)	CQua
	'Irish Light' (2)	CQua
	'Irish Linen' (3)	CQua
	'Irish Luck' (1)	CQua
	'Irish Minstrel' (2) ♀H4 **new**	CQua
	'Irish Wedding' (2) **new**	CQua
	'Isambard' (4)	CQua
	'Islander' (4)	CQua
	'Islandhill' (3)	IRhd
	'Ita' (2)	IRhd
	'Itzim' (6) ♀H4	CBro CQua EBrs ERos
	'Jack Snipe' (6) ♀H4	CAvo CBro CNic CQua EBrs ECGP EPfP EPot ERos LAma LBmB LRHS MBri MSte WShi
	'Jack Wood' (11a)	CQua
	'Jackadee' (2)	IRhd
	'Jake' (3)	IRhd
	'Jamage' (8)	CQua
	'Jamaica Inn' (4)	CQua
	'Jambo' (2)	IRhd
	'Jamboree' (2)	CQua
	'Jamestown' (3)	IRhd
	'Jane Frances' (1)	GEve
	'Jane MacLennan' (4)	GEve
	'Jane van Kralingen' (3)	GEve
	'Janelle' (2)	CQua
	'Jantje' (11a)	CQua
	'January Moon'	MBri
	'Javelin' (2) **new**	IRhd
	jeanmonodii (13) JCA 701.870	WCot
	'Jeanne Bicknell' (4) **new**	CQua
	'Jedna' (2) **new**	CQua
	'Jenny' (6) ♀H4	CAvo CBro CFen CQua EBrs EPot ERos LAma LBmB LRHS NBir WShi
	'Jersey Pride'	MBri
	'Jetage' (6)	CBro
	'Jetfire' (6) ♀H4	CBro CQua EBrs EPfP EPot ERos GEve GKir LAma LBmB LRHS LSou SPer
	'Jezebel' (3)	CBro
	'Jim's Gold' (2) **new**	CQua
	'Jodi's Sister' (11a) **new**	IRhd
	'Johanna' (5)	CBro
	'John Ballance' (1)	IRhd
	'John Daniel' (4)	CQua
	'John's Delight' (3)	CQua
	x ***johnstonii*** **new**	CBro EPot
	- 'Queen of Spain' (10) **new**	CBgR
	'Joke Fulmer' **new**	CFen
	jonquilla (13) ♀H4	CAvo CBro CPBP CQua EPot ERos LAma LPhx LRHS NJOw WLin WPGP WShi
	- B&S 459 from Spain **new**	CMon
§	- var. ***henriquesii*** (13)	CBro CFil CQua ECho LAma SCnR WPGP
	- - MS 419 from Spain **new**	CMon
	'Joppa' (7)	CQua
	'Joy Bishop'	see *N. romieuxii* 'Joy Bishop'
	'Joybell' (6)	CQua
	'Juanita' (2)	CFen EPfP
	'Jules Verne' (2)	CQua
	'Julia Jane'	see *N. romieuxii* 'Julia Jane'
	'Jumblie' (12) ♀H4	CBro CQua EPfP EPot ERos GGar LAma LRHS MBri NJOw SPer
	juncifolius	see *N. assoanus*
	'June Allyson' **new**	CFen
	'June Lake' (2)	CQua IRhd
	'Kabani' (9)	CQua
	'Kalimna' (1)	CQua
	'Kamau' (9)	GEve IRhd
	'Kamms' (1)	CQua
	'Kamura' (2)	CQua
	'Kate Fraser' (2) **new**	GEve
	'Kathleen Munro' (2)	GEve
	'Kathy's Clown' (6)	CQua
	'Kaydee' (6) ♀H4	CQua IRhd
	'Kea' (6)	CQua
	'Keats' (4)	CBro LAma
	'Kebaya' (2)	CQua
	'Kehelland' (4)	CBro
	'Kenellis' (10)	CBgR CBro CQua EPot GEdr MSte
	'Kernow' (2)	CQua
	'Kidling' (7)	CQua
	'Killara' (8)	CQua
	'Killearnan' (9)	CQua
	'Killeen' (2)	IRhd
	'Killigrew' (2)	CQua
	'Killivose' (3) **new**	CQua
	'Killyleagh' (3)	IRhd
	'Kilmood' (2)	IRhd
	'Kiltonga' (2)	IRhd
	'Kilworth' (2)	CQua LAma
	'Kimmeridge' (3)	CQua
	'King Alfred' (1)	CQua EPfP SPer
	'King Size' (11a)	GEve
	'Kinglet' (7)	CQua
	'King's Grove' (1) ♀H4	CQua IRhd
	'Kings Pipe' (2)	CQua
	'Kingscourt' (1) ♀H4	CQua
	'Kirkcubbin' (3)	IRhd
	'Kit Hill' (7)	CQua
	'Kitten' (6)	CQua
	'Kitty' (6)	CBro ERos
	'Kiwi Magic' (4)	CQua IRhd
	'Kiwi Solstice' (4)	CQua
	'Kiwi Sunset' (4)	CQua
	'Knight of Saint John' **new**	CFen
	'Knocklayde' (3)	CQua
	'Kokopelli' (7)	CBro
	'Korora Bay' (1)	IRhd
	'La Riante' (3)	CQua
	'Ladies' Choice' (7)	IRhd
	'Ladies' Favorite' (7) **new**	IRhd
	'Lady Ann' (2)	IRhd
	'Lady Emily' (2)	IRhd
	'Lady Eve' (11a)	IRhd
	'Lady Margaret Boscawen' (2)	CQua
	'Lady Serena' (9)	CQua
	'Lake Tahoe' (2)	IRhd
	'Lalique' (3)	CQua
	'Lamanva' (2)	CQua
	'Lamlash' (2)	IRhd
	'Lanarth' (7)	CBro
	'Lancaster' (3)	CQua IRhd
	'Langarth' (11a) **new**	CQua
	'Lapwing' (5)	CBro ERos IRhd
	'Larkelly' (6)	CBro ERos
	'Larkhill' (2)	CQua
	'Larkwhistle' (6) ♀H4	CBro ERos LAma

'Latchley' (2) **new**	CQua
'Lauren' (3)	IRhd
'Lavender Lass' (6)	CQua
'Leading Light' (2)	CQua
'Lee Moor' (1)	CQua
'Lemon Beauty' (11b)	CQua LBmB LRHS
'Lemon Drops' (5) ♀H4	CBro CQua EPot ERos LBmB MSte
'Lemon Grey' (3)	IRhd
'Lemon Heart' (5)	CBro
'Lemon Silk' (6)	CBro CMea CQua
'Lemon Snow' (2)	IRhd
'Lemonade' (3)	CQua
'Lennymore' (2)	CQua IRhd
'Lewis George' (1)	CQua
'Libby' (2)	IRhd
'Liberty Bells' (5)	CBro CQua EPot LAma LRHS MBri
'Life' (7)	CQua
'Lighthouse' (3)	CQua GEve
'Lighthouse Reef' (1)	CQua IRhd
'Lilac Charm' (6)	CQua IRhd
'Lilac Hue' (6)	CBro
'Limbo' (2)	CQua IRhd
'Limehurst' (2)	CQua
'Limpopo' (3)	IRhd
'Lindsay Joy' (2)	CQua
'Lintie' (7)	CBro CQua ERos LRHS MBri
'Lisbarnett' (3)	IRhd
'Lisnamulligan' (3)	IRhd
'Lisnaruddy' (3)	IRhd
'Little Beauty' (1) ♀H4	CAvo CBgR CBro CQua EPot ERos GFlt LAma
'Little Dancer' (1)	CBro CQua
'Little Gem' (1) ♀H4	CAvo CBro CMea CQua EPot LAma SPer
'Little Jewel' (3) **new**	CQua
'Little Karoo' (3)	IRhd
'Little Rosie' (2)	IRhd
'Little Sentry' (7)	CBro CQua
'Little Soldier' (10)	CQua
'Little Spell' (1)	CBro LAma
'Little Witch' (6)	CAvo CBro CQua EPot ERos LAma LRHS MBri NJOw WShi
'Littlefield' (7) **new**	CQua
'Liverpool Festival' (2)	CQua
'Lobularis'	see *N. pseudonarcissus* 'Lobularis'
lobularis Schultes	see *N. obvallaris*
'Loch Alsh' (3)	CQua IRhd
'Loch Assynt' (3)	CQua GEve
'Loch Brora' (2)	CQua GEve
'Loch Coire' (3)	CQua
'Loch Fada' (2)	CQua
'Loch Hope' (2)	CQua GEve
'Loch Leven' (2)	CQua
'Loch Lundie' (2)	CQua
'Loch Maberry' (2)	CQua
'Loch Naver' (2)	CQua GEve
'Loch Stac' (2)	CQua
'Logan Rock' (7)	CQua
longispathus (13) MS 546	SSpi
'Lordship' (1) **new**	CQua
'Lorikeet' (1)	CQua
'Lothario' (2)	LAma MBri
'Lough Bawn' (2)	GEve
'Lough Gowna' (1)	IRhd
'Lough Ryan' (1)	IRhd
'Loveny' (2)	CQua
'Lowin' **new**	CFen
'Lucifer' (2)	CQua WShi
'Lucky Chance' (11a)	IRhd
'Lundy Light' (2)	CQua
'Lyrebird' (3)	CQua
'Lyric' (9)	CQua
'Lysander' (2)	CQua
x ***macleayi*** (13)	CQua
'Madam Speaker' (4)	CQua
'Magician' (2)	IRhd
'Magna Carta' (2)	CQua
'Magnet' (1)	LAma MBri
'Magnificence' (1)	LAma
'Majestic Star' (1)	CQua
'Malin Head' (5)	IRhd
'Mallee' (11a)	IRhd
'Manaccan' (1)	CQua
'Mangaweka' (6)	CQua
'Manly' (4) ♀H4	CQua LBmB
'Mantle' (2)	CQua
'March Sunshine' (6)	CBro LAma
'Marilyn Anne' (2)	CQua
'Marjorie Hine' (2) **new**	CQua
'Marjorie Treveal' (4)	CQua
'Marlborough' (2)	CQua
'Marlborough Freya' (2)	CQua
'Martha Washington' (8)	CBro CQua
'Martinette' (8)	CFen CQua LRHS MBri
'Martinsville' (8) **new**	CQua
marvieri	see *N. rupicola* subsp. *marvieri*
'Mary Copeland' (4)	LAma MMHG
'Mary Kate' (2)	CQua IRhd
'Mary Lou' (6)	IRhd
'Mary Schouten' (2)	GEve
'Marzo' (7)	CQua IRhd
'Matador' (8)	CQua IRhd
'Max' (11a)	CQua LAma
'Maya Dynasty' (2)	CQua
'Mayan Gold' (1)	IRhd
'Mazzard' (4)	CQua
'Media Girl' (2)	IRhd
x ***medioluteus*** (13)	CBro CQua
'Medusa' (8)	CBro
'Melancholy' (1)	CQua
'Melbury' (2)	CQua
'Meldrum' (1)	CQua
'Melen' **new**	CFen
'Memento' (1)	CQua
'Menabilly' (4)	CQua
'Men-an-Tol' (2)	CQua
'Menehay' (11a) ♀H4	CQua IRhd
'Mentor' (2)	GEve
'Mercato' (2)	LAma
'Merida' (2)	IRhd
'Merlin' (3) ♀H4	CQua GEve LAma LBmB
'Merry Bells' (5)	CQua
'Merrymeet' (4)	CQua
'Mexico City' (2)	IRhd
'Midas Touch' (1)	CQua
'Midget'	CAvo CBro CMea EBrs EPot ERos GEdr LAma
'Mike Pollock' (8)	CQua
'Millennium' (1)	CBro
'Millennium Sunrise' (2)	CQua
'Millennium Sunset' (2)	CQua
'Minicycla' (6)	CAvo CBro
minimus hort.	see *N. asturiensis*
'Minnow' (8) ♀H3	CAvo CBro CQua EBrs EPot ERos GFlt ITim LAma LBmB LRHS MBri NJOw SBch SPer
§ ***minor*** (13) ♀H4	CBro CQua ECha EHyt LAma WShi
- 'Douglasbank' (1)	CBro
- var. ***pumilus*** 'Plenus'	see *N.* 'Rip van Winkle'
- Ulster form	IBlr
'Minute Waltz' (6)	CQua
'Miss Muffitt' (1) **new**	CQua
'Mission Bells' (5) ♀H4	CQua IRhd
'Mission Impossible' (11a) **new**	CQua
'Misty Dawn' (3)	IRhd

	Name	Suppliers
	'Misty Glen' (2) 🏆H4	CQua GEve
	'Mite' (6) 🏆H4	CBro CMea CQua EPot ERos GEdr LAma
	'Mitylene' (2)	CQua
	'Mitzy' **new**	SCnR
	'Mockingbird' (7)	IRhd
	'Mondragon' (11a)	CQua MBri
	'Mongleath' (2)	CQua
	'Monksilver' (3)	CQua
	'Montclair' (2)	CQua
	'Montego' (3)	CQua
	'Moon Dream' (1)	CQua
	'Moon Ranger' (3)	CQua IRhd
	'Moon Rhythm' (4)	IRhd
	'Moon Shadow' (3)	CQua
	'Moon Tide' (3)	IRhd
	'Moon Valley' (2)	GEve IRhd
	'Moonspell' (2)	IRhd
	'Moralee' (4)	IRhd
§	***moschatus*** (13) 🏆H4	CBgR CBro CQua ECho EPot LAma WCot
	- 'Cernuus Plenus' (4)	CAvo
	'Motmot' **new**	CQua
	'Mount Fuji' (2)	CQua
	'Mount Hood' (1) 🏆H4	EBrs EPfP LAma LBmB MBri NBir SPer
	'Mount Rainier' (1) **new**	CQua
	'Mount Royal' (2)	IRhd
	'Movie Star' (2)	IRhd
	'Mowser' (7)	CQua
	'Mrs Langtry' (3)	CQua WShi
	'Mrs R.O. Backhouse' (2)	CQua LAma MBri WShi
	'Muirfield' (1)	GEve
	'Mullion' (3)	CQua
	'Mulroy Bay' (1)	CQua IRhd
	'Murlough' (9)	CQua IRhd
	'Muscadet' (2)	CQua
	'Naivasha' (2)	IRhd
	'Namraj' (2)	CQua
	'Nancegollan' (7)	CBro CQua
	'Nangiles' (4)	CQua
	'Nanpee' (7)	CQua
	'Nansidwell' (2)	CQua
	'Nanstallon' (1)	CQua
	'Nederburg' (1)	IRhd
	'Nether Barr' (2)	IRhd
§	***nevadensis*** (13)	SBla SSpi
	'New Hope' (3)	CQua
	'New Life' (3)	CQua
	'New Penny' (3)	CQua IRhd
	'New-baby' (7)	CQua
	'Newcastle' (1)	CQua
	'Night Music' (4)	CQua
	'Nightcap' (1)	CQua
	'Nirvana' (7)	CBro
	'Niveth' (5)	CFen CQua
	nobilis var. ***nobilis*** (13)	EPot
	'Nonchalant' (3)	CQua IRhd
	'Norma Jean' (2)	CQua
	'Nor-nor' (2)	CBro ERos
	'Northern Sceptre' (2)	IRhd
	'Noss Mayo' (6)	CBro CQua
	'Notre Dame' (2) 🏆H4	CQua IRhd
	'Nouvelle' (3)	IRhd
	'Numen Rose' (2)	IRhd
	Nylon Group (10)	CBro CNic EPot SSpi
	'Oadby' (1)	CQua
	'Obelisk' (11a)	CQua
	obesus (13)	EHyt ERos
	'Obsession' (2)	CQua
	obvallaris (13) 🏆H4	CArn CAvo CBro CQua EPot ERos NJOw SGar SPer WBWf WHer WShi
	'Ocarino' (4)	CQua
	'Ocean Blue' (2)	IRhd
	'Odd Job' **new**	CQua
	x ***odorus*** (13)	WShi
§	- 'Double Campernelle' (4)	CQua ECho LAma SBch SPer WCot WShi
	- 'Rugulosus'	see *N.* 'Rugulosus'
	'Odyssey' (4)	IRhd
	'Oecumene' (11a)	CQua
	old pheasant's eye	see *N. poeticus* var. *recurvus*
	'Orange Walk' (3)	CQua IRhd
	'Orangery' (11a)	LAma LRHS MBri
	'Orchard Place' (3) **new**	CQua
	'Oregon Pioneer' (2)	IRhd
	'Ormeau' (2) 🏆H4	CQua
	'Oryx' (7) 🏆H4	CQua IRhd
	'Osmington' (2)	CQua
	'Ottoman Gold' (2)	IRhd
	'Ouma' (1)	CQua
	'Outline' (2)	IRhd
	'Ouzel' (6)	CQua
	'Oykel' (3)	CQua GEve
	'Oz' (12)	CBro CQua ERos
	'Pacific Coast' (8) **new**	LAma
	'Pacific Mist' (11a) **new**	CQua
	'Pacific Rim' (2)	IRhd
	'Painted Desert' (3)	CQua
	'Pale Sunlight' (2)	CQua
§	***pallidiflorus*** (13)	ECha
	- var. ***intermedius*** from France **new**	CMon
	'Palmares' (11a)	CQua
	'Pamela Hubble' (2)	CQua
	'Pampaluna' (11a) **new**	CQua
	'Panache' (1)	CQua
	panizzianus (13)	SIgm SSpi
	'Paper White'	see *N. papyraceus*
	'Paper White Grandiflorus' (8)	CQua SPer
	'Papillon Blanc' (11b)	LAma
	'Papua' (4) 🏆H4	CQua
	papyraceus (13)	CQua CStu LAma MBri WCot
	- subsp. ***panizzianus*** **new**	CQua
	- subsp. ***papyraceus*** AB&S 4399 from Morocco **new**	CMon
	- - PB 442 from Spain **new**	CMon
	- subsp. ***polyanthus*** SF 116 from Morocco **new**	CMon
	'Paradigm' (4)	IRhd
	'Parcpat' (7)	CBro
	'Parisienne' (11a)	LAma SPer
	'Park Springs' (3)	CQua
	'Parkdene' (2)	CQua
	'Party Time' (2)	IRhd
	'Passionale' (2) 🏆H4	CQua LAma NBir SPer
	'Pastiche' (2)	CQua
	'Patabundy' (2)	CQua
	'Patois' (9)	CQua IRhd
	'Paula Cottell' (3)	CBro
	'Pay Day' (1)	CQua
	'Peach Prince' (4)	CQua
	'Peacock' (2)	IRhd
	'Pearlshell' (11a)	CQua GEve
	'Peeping Tom' (6) 🏆H4	CBgR CBro ERos LAma LBmB MBri SRms
	'Peggy's Gift' (3)	IRhd
	'Pemboa' **new**	CQua
	'Pencrebar' (4)	CBro CQua EPot ERos LAma LRHS MBri NMyG WShi
	'Pend Oreille' (3)	CQua
	'Pengarth' (2)	CQua

	'Penjerrick' (9)	CQua
	'Penkivel' (2)	CQua
	'Pennance Mill' (2)	CQua
	'Pennine Way' (1)	CQua
	'Pennyfield' (2) **new**	CQua
	'Pennyghael' (2)	GEve
	'Penpol' (7)	CBro CFen CQua
	'Penril' (6)	CQua ERos
	'Penstraze' (7) **new**	CQua
	'Pentille' (1)	CQua
	'Pentire' (11a) **new**	CQua
	'Penvale' **new**	CQua
	'Pepper' (2)	CBro
	'Peppercorn' (6) **new**	CQua
	'Pequenita' (7)	CBro
	'Percuil' (6)	CQua
	'Perdredda' (3)	CQua
	'Perimeter' (3)	CQua
	'Peripheral Pink' (2)	CQua
§	'Perlax' (11a)	CQua
	'Permissive' (2)	IRhd
	'Perseus' (1)	GEve
	'Petit Four' (4)	LAma LBmB
	'Petrel' (5)	CBro CQua EBrs EPot GFlt LRHS MSte NJOw
	'Phalarope' (6)	CQua
	'Phantom' (11a)	CQua
	'Phil's Gift' (1)	CQua
	'Phinda' (2)	IRhd
	'Picoblanco' (2)	CBro CQua
	'Pineapple Prince' (2) **new**	CQua
	'Pink Angel' (7)	CQua
	'Pink Champagne' (4)	CQua
	'Pink Formal' (11a) **new**	CQua
	'Pink Gilt' (2) **new**	IRhd
	'Pink Glacier' (11a) **new**	CQua
	'Pink Holly' (11a)	CQua
	'Pink Ice' (2) **new**	CQua
	'Pink Pageant' (4)	CQua IRhd
	'Pink Paradise' (4)	CQua IRhd LBmB
	'Pink Perry' (2)	IRhd
	'Pink Sapphire' (2) **new**	CQua
	'Pink Silk' (1)	CQua IRhd
	'Pink Smiles' (2) **new**	CFen
	'Pink Surprise' (2) **new**	CQua
	'Pink Tango' (11a)	CQua
	'Pipe Major' (2)	CQua
	'Pipers Barn' (7)	CBro CQua
	'Pipestone' (2)	CQua
	'Pipit' (7) ♀H4	CAvo CBro CMea CQua EPfP EPot ERos ITim LAma LRHS MNrw NBir NJOw SPer WShi
	'Piraeus' (4)	IRhd
	'Pismo Beach' (2)	CQua GEve
	'Pitchroy' (2)	CQua
	'Pixie's Sister' (7) ♀H4	CQua
	poeticus (13)	CAvo LAma LRHS WBWf WHer
§	- var. ***hellenicus*** (13)	CBro CQua
	- old pheasant's eye	see *N. poeticus* var. *recurvus*
	- var. ***physaloides*** (13)	CQua ECho SMHy
	- 'Plenus' ambig. (4)	CBro CQua EBrs EPot GQui WCot WShi
	- 'Praecox' (3)	CBro CQua
§	- var. ***recurvus*** (13) ♀H4	CArn CBro CFen CQua EBrs ECGP ECho EPfP EPot LAma LBmB NBir WShi
	'Poet's Way' (9)	CQua
	'Pol Crocan' (2)	CQua IRhd
	'Pol Dornie' (2)	CQua
	'Pol Voulin' (2)	CQua IRhd
	'Polar Ice' (3) **new**	LAma
	'Polglase' (8)	CBro
	'Polly's Pearl' (8)	CQua
	'Polnesk' (7)	CBro
	'Polruan' **new**	CQua
	'Poltreen' **new**	CQua
	'Polwheveral' (2)	CQua
	'Pontresina' (2)	LBmB
	'Pooka' (3)	IRhd
	'Poppy's Choice' (4)	CQua
	'Pops Legacy' (1)	CQua IRhd
	'Port Patrick' (3)	IRhd
	'Port William' (3)	IRhd
	'Porthchapel' (7)	CQua
	'Portrush' (3)	CQua
	'Portstewart' (3)	IRhd
	'Potential' (1)	CQua
	'Powerstock' (2)	IRhd
	'Prairie Fire' (3)	CQua IRhd
	'Preamble' (1)	CQua
I	'Precocious' G.E. Mitsch (2) ♀H4	CQua
	'Premiere' (2)	CQua
	'Presidential Pink' (2)	CQua
	'Pride of Cornwall' (8)	CBro
	'Primrose Beauty' (4)	CFen CQua
	'Princeps' (1)	CQua
	'Princess Zaide' (3)	CQua
	'Princeton' (3)	CQua
	'Prism' (2)	CQua
	'Probus' (1)	CQua
	'Professor Einstein' (2)	LAma LBmB
	'Prologue' (1)	CQua
	'Prototype' (6)	IRhd
	pseudonarcissus (13) ♀H4	CBro CQua CRow EBrs LAma MBow SSpi WBWf WHer WPop WShi
	- subsp. ***gayi***	see *N. gayi*
§	- 'Lobularis'	CAvo CBro CQua EPot ERos LRHS NJOw SPer
	- subsp. ***moschatus***	see *N. moschatus*
	- subsp. ***nevadensis***	see *N. nevadensis*
	- subsp. ***pallidiflorus***	see *N. pallidiflorus*
	'Ptolemy' (1)	LRHS
	'Pueblo' (7)	CAvo EBrs ERos LRHS WShi
	pulchellus	see *N. triandrus* subsp. *triandrus* var. *pulchellus*
	'Pulsar' (2)	IRhd
	pumilus (13)	ECho EPot ERos LRHS
	'Punchline' (7)	CQua
	'Puppet' (5)	CQua
	'Purbeck' (3) ♀H4	CQua IRhd
	'Quail' (7) ♀H4	CBro CQua EBrs EPot ERos LAma LBmB LRHS LSou MBri SPer WHil
	'Quasar' (2)	CQua GEve
	Queen Anne's double daffodil	see *N.* 'Eystettensis'
	'Queen's Guard' (1)	IRhd
	'Queensland' (2) **new**	CFen
	'Quick Step' (7)	CQua IRhd
	'Quiet Hero' (3)	IRhd
	'Quiet Man' (1) **new**	IRhd
	'Quiet Waters' (1)	CQua
	'Quince' (12)	CBro CQua EPot ITim LSou MSte SPer
	'Quirinus' (2)	LAma
	'Radiant Gem' (8) **new**	CQua
	radiiflorus var. ***poetarum*** (13)	CBro
	'Radjel' (4)	CQua
	'Rainbow' (2) ♀H4	CQua SPer
	'Rame Head' (1)	CQua
	'Rameses' (2)	CQua
	'Rapture' (6) ♀H4	CQua IRhd
	'Raspberry Ring' (2)	CQua
	'Ravenhill' (3)	CQua
	'Rebekah' (4) **new**	CQua

	'Recital' (2)	CQua
I	'Red Coat' **new**	CQua
	'Red Devon' (2) ♀H4	MBri
	'Red Era' (3) **new**	CQua
	'Red Goblet' (2)	LAma
	'Red Reed' (1) **new**	IRhd
	'Red Socks' (6)	CQua
	'Reference Point' (2)	GEve
	'Refrain' (2)	CQua
	'Regal Bliss' (2)	CQua
	'Reggae' (6) ♀H4	CBro CQua GEve IRhd
	'Rembrandt' (1)	CFen LAma MBri
	'Replete' (4)	CQua EBrs
	requienii	see *N. assoanus*
	'Ribald' (2)	IRhd
	'Ridgecrest' (3)	IRhd
	rifanus	see *N. romieuxii* subsp. *romieuxii* var. *rifanus*
	'Rijnveld's Early Sensation' (1) ♀H4	CAvo CBro CFen CMea CQua EBrs ECha ERos LBmB MBri WCot
	'Rikki' (7)	CBro CQua ERos
	'Rima' (1)	CQua
	'Rimmon' (3)	CQua
	'Ring Fence' (3)	IRhd
	'Ringhaddy' (3)	IRhd
	'Ringing Bells' (5)	CQua
	'Ringleader' (2)	CQua
	'Ringmaster' (2)	CQua
	'Rio Bravo' (2)	IRhd
	'Rio Gusto' (2)	IRhd
	'Rio Lobo' (2)	IRhd
	'Rio Rondo' (2)	IRhd
	'Rio Rouge' (2)	IRhd
§	'Rip van Winkle' (4)	CBro CQua CSWP EBrs EPot ERos ITim LAma LRHS MBri WHil WShi
	'Rippling Waters' (5) ♀H4	CBro CQua EBrs ECGP EPot ERos LAma LBmB LRHS
	'Ristin' (1)	CQua
	'Rival' (6)	CQua
	'River Dance' (2)	IRhd
	'River Queen' (2)	CQua IRhd
	'Roberta' **new**	CFen
	'Rockall' (3)	CQua
	'Roger' (6)	CBro CQua
	'Romance' (2) ♀H4	LAma LBmB
§	'Romanus' (4)	CQua
§	***romieuxii*** (13) ♀H2-3	CAvo CBro CFil EPot ERos ITim LRHS SBch SCnR SSpi WCot WPGP
	- JCA 805	EPot
	- subsp. ***albidus*** (13)	EPot
	- - SF 110	EHyt
§	- - var. ***zaianicus*** (13)	ECho
	- - - SB&L 82	WCot
	- - - SF 379 from Morocco	CMon
§	- - - f. ***lutescens*** (13) **new**	EHyt
	- 'Atlas Gold'	EHyt
§	- 'Joy Bishop' ex JCA 805 (10)	EPot ERos SCnR
§	- 'Julia Jane' ex JCA 805 (10)	EPot ERos GEdr SCnR SOkd
	- subsp. ***romieuxii*** **new**	ECho WCot
	- - SF 126/1 from Morocco **new**	CMon
§	- - var. ***mesatlanticus*** (13)	CStu EHyt ERos ITim
§	- - var. ***rifanus*** (13)	SSpi
	- 'Treble Chance' (10)	EPot
	romiexii subsp. ***albidus*** var. ***albidus*** SF 110 from Morocco **new**	CMon
	'Rosannor Gold' (11a)	CQua
	'Roscarrick' (6)	CQua
	'Rose Gold' (1)	IRhd
	'Rose Royale' (2)	CQua
	'Rose Umber' (2)	IRhd
	'Rosedown' (5)	CBro
	'Rosemerryn' (2)	CQua
	'Rosemoor Gold' ♀H4 **new**	CFen CQua
	'Roseworthy' (2)	ERos
	'Rossferry' (2)	IRhd
	'Rosy Trumpet' (1)	CBro
	'Roxton' (4)	IRhd
	'Royal Armour' (1) **new**	CFen
	'Royal Ballet' (2)	CQua
	'Royal Connection' (8)	CQua
	'Royal Dornoch' (1)	GEve
	'Royal Marine' (2)	CQua
	'Royal Princess' (3)	CQua
	'Royal Regiment' (2)	CQua
	'Rubh Mor' (2)	CQua
	'Ruby Rose' (4)	IRhd
	'Ruby Wedding' (2)	IRhd
	'Rubythroat' (2)	CQua
	'Ruddy Rascal' (2) **new**	IRhd
	'Rugulosus' (7) ♀H4	CBro CQua ECho ERos LAma
*	'Rugulosus Flore Pleno' (d)	EBrs
	rupicola (13)	CAvo CBro CQua CWoo ERos GCrs MS&S NSla NWCA SSpi
§	- subsp. ***marvieri*** (13) ♀H2	ERos SSpi
§	- subsp. ***watieri*** (13)	CBro ERos GCrs IFro LPhx SCnR
	- - AB&S 4518	SSpi
	'Rustom Pasha' (2)	CQua
	'Rytha' (2)	CQua
	'Saberwing' (5)	CQua
	'Sabine Hay' (3)	CQua IRhd LBmB
	'Sacajawea' (2)	CFen
	'Saint Agnes' (8)	CQua
	'Saint Budock' (1)	CQua
	'Saint Day' (5)	CQua
	'Saint Dilpe' (2)	CQua
	'Saint Duthus' (1)	GEve
	'Saint Keverne' (2) ♀H4	CQua LAma
	'Saint Keyne' (8)	CQua
	'Saint Magnus' (1)	GEve
	'Saint Patrick's Day' (2)	CFen CQua LAma SPer
	'Saint Piran' (7)	CQua MBri
	'Salakee' (2)	CQua
	'Salmon Trout' (2)	CQua
	'Salome' (2) ♀H4	CQua EPfP LAma LRHS MBri NBir
	'Salute' (2)	CQua
	'Samantha' (4)	CQua
	'Samaria' (3)	CBro
	'Samba' (5)	ERos
	'Sancerre' (11a)	CQua
	'Sandycove' (2)	IRhd
	'Sandymount' (2)	IRhd
	'Sarah' (2)	MBri
	'Satin Pink' (2)	MBri
	'Satsuma' (1) **new**	CQua
	'Saturn' (3)	CQua
	'Savoir Faire' (2)	IRhd
	scaberulus (13)	CBro CStu ERos
	'Scarlet Chord' (2)	CQua
	'Scarlet Elegance' (2)	LAma
	'Scarlet Gem' (8)	LAma
	'Scarlett O'Hara' (2)	CQua LAma
	'Scented Breeze' (2)	IRhd
	'Scilly White' (8) **new**	CQua
	'Sea Dream' (3)	CQua
	'Sea Gift' (7)	CBro
	'Sea Green' (9)	CQua
	'Sea Shanty' (2)	IRhd
	'Seagull' (3)	CQua LAma WShi
	'Sealing Wax' (2)	CFen CQua

	Name	Suppliers
	'Segovia' (3) 🏆H4	CBro CQua EPot ERos LAma LBmB SCnR SPer
	'Sempre Avanti' (2)	LAma LBmB MBri
	'Sennocke' (5)	CBro SOkd
	'Seraglio' (3)	CQua
	'Serena Beach' (4)	IRhd
	'Serena Lodge' (4) 🏆H4	CQua IRhd
	serotinus (13)	ECho EPot GIBF
	- var. ***deficiens*** SF 169 from Morocco **new**	CMon
*	- subsp. ***orientalis*** PB 141 from Crete **new**	CMon
	'Sextant' (6)	CQua
	'Shangani' (2)	IRhd
	'Sheelagh Rowan' (2)	CQua IRhd
	'Sheer Joy' (6)	IRhd
	'Shepherd's Hey' (7)	CQua
	'Sherborne' (4)	CQua
	'Sherpa' (1)	IRhd
	'Sheviock' (2)	CQua
	'Shin Falls' (1)	GEve
	'Shindig' (2)	IRhd
	'Shining Light' (2)	CQua
	'Sidley' (3)	CQua IRhd
	'Signorina' (2)	IRhd
	'Silent Valley' (1) 🏆H4	CQua
	'Silk Cut' (2)	CQua
	'Silkwood' (3)	CQua
	'Silver Bells' (5)	CQua IRhd
	'Silver Chimes' (8)	CAvo CBro CFen CQua EPfP ERos LAma NBir
	'Silver Crystal' (3)	IRhd
	'Silver Kiwi' (2) **new**	CQua
	'Silver Moon' (2) **new**	CFen
	'Silver Plate' (11a)	CQua
	'Silver Shell' (11a)	CQua
	'Silver Standard' (2)	CQua
	'Silver Surf' (2)	CQua IRhd
	'Silversmith' (2)	CQua
	'Silverthorne' (3)	CQua
	'Silverwood' (3)	CQua IRhd
	'Singing Pub' (3)	IRhd
	'Sinopel' (3)	LAma
	'Sir Samuel' (2) **new**	CQua
	'Sir Watkin' (2)	CQua
	'Sir Winston Churchill' (4) 🏆H4	CQua EPfP LAma LBmB LRHS SPer
	'Skerry' (2)	CQua
	'Skibo' (2)	GEve
	'Skilliwidden' (2)	CQua
	'Skywalker' (2)	IRhd
	'Slieveboy' (1)	CQua
	'Sligachan' (1)	GEve
	'Slipstream' (6)	IRhd
	'Small Fry' (1)	CQua
	'Small Talk' (1)	CAvo CQua MBri
	'Smokey Bear' (4)	CQua
	'Smooth Sails' (3) **new**	CQua
	'Snoopie' (6)	CQua
	'Snow Bunting' (7)	CBro
	'Snowcrest' (3)	CQua
	'Snowshill' (2)	CQua
	'Soft Focus' (2)	IRhd
	'Solar System' (3)	IRhd
	'Solar Tan' (3)	CQua IRhd
	'Soleil d'Or' (8)	MBri
	'Solferique' (2) **new**	CQua
	'Soloist' (2)	IRhd
	'Solveig's Song'	EHyt EPot
	'Sonata' (9)	CQua
	'Songket' (2)	CQua
	'Soprano' (2)	CQua IRhd
	'Sorcerer' (3)	CQua
	'South Street' (2)	CQua
	'Sovereign' (11a)	IRhd
	'Spaniards Inn' (4)	CQua
	'Sparkling Tarts' (8) **new**	CQua
	'Sparnon' (11a)	CQua
	'Sparrow' (6)	CQua
	'Special Envoy' (2) 🏆H4	CQua IRhd
	'Speenogue' (1)	IRhd
	'Spellbinder' (1) 🏆H4	LAma LBmB MBri
	'Spencer Tracy' **new**	CFen
	'Sperrin Gold' (1)	IRhd
	'Spindletop' (3) 🏆H4 **new**	IRhd
	'Spirit of Rame' (3)	CQua
	'Split Image' (2)	IRhd
	'Split Vote' (11a)	IRhd
	'Sportsman' (2)	CQua
	'Spring Dawn' (2)	LSou SPer
	'Spring Joy'	ERos
	'Spring Morn' (2)	IRhd
	'Stainless' (2) **new**	EBrs MSte
	'Stanway' (3)	CQua IRhd
	'Star Glow' (2)	CQua
	'Star Quality' (3) **new**	IRhd
	'Starfire' (7)	CQua
	'State Express' (2)	CQua
	'Steenbok' (3)	IRhd
	'Stella' (2) **new**	WShi
	'Step Forward' (7)	ERos
	'Stilton' (9)	CQua
	'Stinger' (2)	CQua
	'Stint' (5) 🏆H4	CBro CQua
	'Stocken' (7)	CBro CQua ERos
*	'Stockens Gib' **new**	EHyt
	'Stoke Charity' (2)	CQua
	'Stormy Weather' (1)	CQua
	'Strathkanaird' (1)	GEve
	'Stratosphere' (7) 🏆H4	CQua
	'Strines' (2)	CQua
	'Suave' (3)	CQua
	'Sugar Bird' (2)	IRhd
	'Sugar Cups' (8) **new**	CQua
	'Sugar Loaf' (4)	CQua
	'Sugarbush' (7)	CBro MBri
	'Suilven' (3)	GEve
	'Suisgill' (4)	CQua
	'Sulphur Phoenix' (4)	CQua WShi
	'Summer Solstice' (3)	IRhd
	'Sun Disc' (7) 🏆H4	CBro CQua EBrs EPot ERos LAma LRHS LSou MBri NJOw SPer
	'Sun 'n' Snow' (1)	GEve
	'Sunday Chimes' (5)	CQua
	'Sundial' (7)	CBro CQua EPot ERos LAma LRHS
	'Sunrise' (3) **new**	CQua
	'Sunstroke' (2) **new**	CQua
	'Suntory' (3)	CQua
	'Suntrap' (2)	IRhd
	'Surfside' (6) 🏆H4	CBro CQua ERos LRHS
	'Surrey' (2)	CQua
	'Suzie Dee' (6)	IRhd
	'Suzie's Sister' (6)	IRhd
	'Suzy' (7) 🏆H4	CBro CMea LAma MBri
	'Swaledale' (2)	CQua
	'Swallow Wing' (6)	IRhd
	'Swanpool' **new**	CQua
	'Swanvale' (1)	CQua
	'Swedish Fjord' (2)	CQua
	'Sweet Blanche' (7)	CQua
	'Sweet Pepper' (7)	CBro GEve
	'Sweetness' (7) 🏆H4	CAvo CBro CFen CMea CQua LAma SPer WShi
	'Swing Wing' (6)	CQua
	'Sydling' (5)	CQua
I	'Sylph' G.E. Mitsch (1)	CQua

'Taffeta' (10) CBro EHyt
'Tahiti' (4) ♀H4 CFen CQua EBrs EPfP LAma LBmB LRHS MBri
'Tain' (1) GEve
'Tamar Fire' (4) ♀H4 CQua
'Tamar Lad' (2) CQua
'Tamar Lass' (3) CQua
'Tamar Snow' (2) CQua
'Tamara' (2) CFen CQua
'Tangent' (2) CQua
'Tarlatan' (10) CBro ERos
'Tasgem' (4) CQua
'Taslass' (4) CQua
'Tater-Du' (5) CQua
tazetta subsp. ***italicus*** MS 520 from France **new** CMon
§ - subsp. ***lacticolor*** (13) CQua NJOw WPGP
§ - - 'Grand Monarque' (8) CQua
* - var. ***odoratus*** **new** CQua
- subsp. ***papyraceus*** see *N. papyraceus*
* - subsp. ***syriacus*** **new** CMon
- subsp. ***tazetta*** LB 328 from Lebanon **new** CMon
- - MS 752 CMon
- - MS 719 from Crete **new** CMon
'Tehidy' (3) CQua
§ 'Telamonius Plenus' (4) CBro IGor LAma WShi
'Temple Cloud' (4) IRhd
tenuifolius see *N. bulbocodium* subsp. *bulbocodium* var. *tenuifolius*
'Terracotta' (2) CQua IRhd
'Terrapin' (3) IRhd
'Tête-à-tête' (12) ♀H4 CAvo CBro CMea CQua EBrs EPfP EPot ERos GKir LAma LBmB LRHS LSou MBri NJOw SPer
'Texas' (4) LAma MBri
'Thalia' (5) CAvo CBro EBrs EPfP ERos GFlt LAma LRHS LSou MBri MSte NBir SPer WPen WShi
'The Alliance' (6) CQua
'The Grange' (1) CQua
'The Knave' (6) CQua
'Thistin' (1) IRhd
'Thoughtful' (5) CBro CQua
'Tibet' (2) LRHS
'Tideford' (2) **new** CQua
'Tiercel' (1) CQua
'Tiffany Jade' (3) CQua
'Tiger Moth' (6) CQua
'Timolin' (3) CQua
'Tinderbox' (2) IRhd
'Tiritomba' (11a) CQua
'Tittle-tattle' (7) CBro CFen CQua
'Toby' (2) CBro ERos
'Toby the First' (6) CMea CQua
'Top Hit' (11a) CQua
'Topkapi' (2) IRhd
'Topolino' (1) ♀H4 CAvo CBro CQua EPot LAma LBmB SBch
'Toreador' (3) **new** CFen
'Torianne' (2) CQua
'Torridon' (2) CQua GEve
'Toto' (12) ♀H4 CAvo CBro CQua MBri
'Tracey' (6) ♀H4 CBro CQua LAma
'Trebah' (2) CQua
'Treble Two' (7) CQua
'Trecara' (3) CQua
'Trefusis' (1) CQua
'Trehane' (6) CQua
'Trelissick' **new** CQua
'Trena' (6) ♀H4 CBro CQua
'Tresamble' (5) CBro CQua LAma
'Treverva' (6) CQua
'Treviddo' (2) CQua
'Trevithian' (7) ♀H4 CBro CQua GFlt LAma LBmB LRHS WLin
'Trewarvas' (2) CQua
'Trewirgie' (6) CBro CQua
triandrus (13) ♀H3 NSla WPGP
§ - subsp. ***triandrus*** var. ***concolor*** (13) CBro ECho
§ - - var. ***pulchellus*** (13) LAma
'Trident' (3) CQua
'Tripartite' (11a) ♀H4 CQua GEve LBmB
'Triple Crown' (3) ♀H4 CQua IRhd
'Tropic Isle' (4) CQua
'Tropical Heat' (2) IRhd
'Trousseau' (1) CFen CQua
'Troutbeck' (3) CQua
'Trueblood' (3) IRhd
'Trumpet Warrior' (1) CQua IRhd
'Tudor Minstrel' (2) CQua
'Tuesday's Child' (5) ♀H4 CQua ERos
'Tullynagee' (3) IRhd
'Turncoat' (6) CQua
'Tutankhamun' (2) CQua
'Twink' (4) CQua
'Tyee' (2) CQua
'Tyrian Rose' (2) IRhd
'Tyrone Gold' (1) ♀H4 CQua IRhd
'Tyrree' (1) IRhd
'Ulster Bank' (3) CQua
'Ulster Bride' (4) CQua
'Ulster Bullion' (2) IRhd
'Una Bremner' (2) GEve
'Uncle Duncan' (1) CQua IRhd
'Unique' (4) ♀H4 CFen CQua LAma
'Unsurpassable' (1) LAma LBmB
'Upalong' (12) **new** CQua
'Urchin' (2) IRhd
'Utiku' (6) CQua
'Val d'Incles' (3) CQua IRhd
'Valdrome' (11a) CQua MBri
'Valinor' (2) CQua
'Van Sion' see *N.* 'Telamonius Plenus'
'Vanellus' (11a) IRhd
'Veneration' (1) CQua
'Verdin' (7) CQua
'Verger' (3) LAma MBri
'Vernal Prince' (3) ♀H4 CQua GEve
'Verona' (3) ♀H4 CQua LBmB
'Verran Rose' (2) IRhd
'Vers Libre' (9) CQua GEve
'Vice-President' (2) CQua
'Vickie Linn' (6) IRhd
'Victorious' (2) CQua
'Vigil' (1) ♀H4 CQua
'Viking' (1) ♀H4 CQua GEve
'Violetta' (2) CQua
'Virginia Waters' (3) **new** CQua
viridiflorus (13) SSpi
- MS 500 SSpi
'Vulcan' (2) ♀H4 CQua
'W.P. Milner' (1) CAvo CBos CBro CMea CQua EBrs EPot LAma LRHS MBri WCot WLin WShi
'Wadavers' (2) CQua
'Waif' (6) CQua
'Waldon Pond' (3) **new** CQua
'Waldorf Astoria' (4) CQua IRhd
'Walton' (7) CQua
'War Dance' (3) IRhd
'Warbler' (6) CQua LAma
'Warleggan' **new** CFen
'Warmington' (3) **new** CQua
'Watamu' (3) IRhd

'Waterperry' (7) CBro GFlt LAma NJOw SPer
'Watership Down' (2) **new** CQua
watieri see *N. rupicola* subsp. *watieri*
'Wavelength' (3) IRhd
'Waxwing' (5) CQua
'Wee Bee' (1) CQua
'Weena' (2) **new** CQua
'Welcome' (2) CQua
'Westward' (4) CQua
'Whang-hi' (6) CQua ERos
'Wheal Bush' (4) CQua
'Wheal Coates' (7) ♀H4 CQua
'Wheal Honey' (1) CQua
'Wheal Jane' (2) CQua
'Wheal Kitty' (7) CQua ERos
'Wheatear' (6) CQua IRhd
'Whetstone' (1) CQua
'White Emperor' (1) CQua
'White Empress' (1) **new** CQua
'White Hill' (2) IRhd
'White Lady' (3) CAvo CQua LAma NMyG WShi
'White Lion' (4) ♀H4 CQua LAma
'White Majesty' (1) **new** CQua
'White Marvel' (4) CQua LRHS
'White Nile' (2) CQua
'White Star' (1) CQua IRhd
'Wicklow Hills' (3) CQua
willkommii (13) CBro ERos
'Winged Victory' (6) CQua
'Winholm Jenni' (3) CQua
'Winifred van Graven' (3) CFen CQua
'Winter Waltz' (6) CQua
'Witch Doctor' (3) IRhd
'Witch Hunt' (4) IRhd
'Woodcock' (6) CBro CQua
'Woodland Prince' (3) CQua
'Woodland Star' (3) CQua
'Woodley Vale' (2) CQua
'Woolsthorpe' (2) CQua
'Xit' (3) CAvo CBro CQua GCrs SCnR
'Xunantunich' (2) IRhd
'Yellow Belles' (5) **new** IRhd
'Yellow Cheerfulness' (4) ♀H4 EPfP LAma LBmB LRHS MBri
'Yellow Minnow' (8) CQua
'Yellow River' (1) **new** LAma
'Yellow Xit' (3) CQua
'York Minster' (1) CQua IRhd
'Young American' (1) CQua
'Young Blood' (2) CQua IRhd
'Yum-Yum' (3) IRhd
zaianicus see *N. romieuxii* subsp. *albidus* var. *zaianicus*
- *lutescens* see *N. romieuxii* subsp. *albidus* var. *zaianicus* f. *lutescens*
'Zekiah' (1) CQua
'Zion Canyon' (2) CQua

Nardophyllum (*Asteraceae*)

bryoides GTou

Nardostachys (*Valerianaceae*)

grandiflora CArn GPoy

Nardus (*Poaceae*)

stricta CRWN

Narthecium (*Melanthiaceae*)

ossifragum ERea WShi

Nassella (*Poaceae*)

cernua CBig EPPr SWal WRos
lepida CBig
pulchra CBig
tenuissima see *Stipa tenuissima*
trichotoma CMea EHoe EMan EMon EPPr EPla EWsh GFlt LRHS MBNS MCCP SLim SPoG WPGP WRos

Nastanthus (*Calyceraceae*)

patagonicus **new** WCot

Nasturtium (*Brassicaceae*)

officinale CPrp EMFW WHer

Natal plum see *Carissa macrocarpa*

Nautilocalyx (*Gesneriaceae*)

pemphidius WDib

nectarine see *Prunus persica* var. *nectarina*

Nectaroscordum (*Alliaceae*)

bivalve ERos
§ ***siculum*** More than 30 suppliers
§ - subsp. ***bulgaricum*** CBro CHad EBee ECha EMar EPfP EPot ERos GSki IBlr LPhx LPio LRHS MAvo MDun MNrw MWgw NArg NBid NGHP SAga SSpi WAbb WBrE WCot WCra WGHP WTin WWhi
tripedale CMea

Neillia (*Rosaceae*)

affinis CPle EBee LAst LTwo MTis NBid NLar NPro SBrw SCoo SSpi WBVN WDin WHCG
longiracemosa see *N. thibetica*
sinensis CMCN CPle MRav
§ ***thibetica*** More than 30 suppliers
thyrsiflora WCru
var. ***tunkinensis*** HWJ 505 **new**

Nelumbo (*Nelumbonaceae*)

'Baby Doll' CDWL
'Chawan Basu' CDWL
'Debbie Gibson' CDWL
'Momo Botan' CDWL
'Mrs Perry D. Slocum' CDWL
nucifera XBlo
- 'Shiroman' CDWL

Nematanthus (*Gesneriaceae*)

'Apres' WDib
'Black Magic' CHal WDib
'Christmas Holly' WDib
'Freckles' WDib
§ ***gregarius*** ♀H1 CHal EBak WDib
§ - 'Golden West' (v) CHal WDib
- 'Variegatus' see *N. gregarius* 'Golden West'
radicans see *N. gregarius*
'Tropicana' ♀H1 CHal WDib

Nemesia (*Scrophulariaceae*)

'Amélie' COtt SPer SPoG
Blue Lagoon = 'Pengoon'PBR (Maritana Series) LAst LSRN SCoo SMrm SPoG
Bluebird = 'Hubbird'PBR CHll
§ ***caerulea*** ECtt MWgw WPer
- 'Joan Wilder' (clonal) ECtt EMan WEas WSPU
N - 'Joan Wilder' (seed-raised) see *N. caerulea* lilac/blue
§ - lilac/blue WPer

Candy Girl = 'Pencand'PBR (Maritana Series)	LIck SCoo
§ ***denticulata*** 🏆H3-4	CHal CHar ECtt EPfP IHMH LAst LRHS MArl MBNS MTis NBlu SAga SCoo SGar SPoG SRms WBrE WFar WFoF WWeb
- 'Celebration' **new**	LRHS WWeb
- 'Confetti'	see *N. denticulata*
foetens	see *N. caerulea*
'Fragrant Cloud'PBR	EBee EChP ELan ENot EPfP LBBr LRHS LSou MCCP MNrw NEgg SMac SPla
'Fragrant Gem' **new**	LIck
fruticans misapplied	see *N. caerulea*
fruticans Benth.	ETow
Honey Girl = 'Penhon'PBR (Maritana Series)	LAst SCoo WGor
'Innocence' 🏆H3	CHal EBee EMan LAst MArl MHar
Karoo Blue = 'Innkablue'	LSou SCoo
Karoo Pink = 'Innkapink'	LSou NPri
Melanie = 'Fleuron'PBR 🏆H3	EPfP LRHS
'Morning Haze'	LIck
'Orchard Blue'	EBee EPfP EWin LIck
'Pippa Manby'	ECtt LAst
'Rose Wings'	EPfP
Sugar Girl = 'Pensug'PBR (Maritana Series)	LAst LIck LSou NPri SMrm
(Sunsatia Series) Sunsatia Blackberry = 'Inuppink' **new**	LSou
- Sunsatia Coconut = 'Intraiwhi' **new**	NPri
- Sunsatia Cranberry = 'Intraired' **new**	LAst LSou NPri
- Sunsatia Lemon = 'Intraigold' **new**	LSou
- Sunsatia Peach = 'Inupcream' **new**	LAst LSou NPri
sylvatica	CSpe
'Tanith's Treasure'	EMan
umbonata hort.	see *N. caerulea* lilac/blue
Vanilla Mist = 'Grega'PBR	EPfP
'White Wings'PBR	EPfP
'Wisley Vanilla' **new**	LRHS

Nemopanthus (*Aquifoliaceae*)

mucronatus	CPle

Nemophila (*Hydrophyllaceae*)

menziesii 'Penny Black'	CSpe

Neodypsis (*Arecaceae*)

decaryi	see *Dypsis decaryi*

Neolitsea (*Lauraceae*)

glauca	see *N. sericea*
§ ***sericea***	CBcs CHEx SSpi

Neomarica (*Iridaceae*)

caerulea	CDes SSpi WCot
gracilis	CFil WCot WPGP

Neopanax see *Pseudopanax*

Neopaxia (*Portulacaceae*)

§ ***australasica***	ECou
- blue-leaved	see *N. australasica* 'Kosciusko'
- bronze-leaved	see *N. australasica* 'Ohau'
- grey	see *N. australasica* 'Kosciusko'
§ - 'Kosciusko'	GAbr GGar
- 'Lyndon'	ECou
§ - 'Ohau'	ECou

Neoregelia (*Bromeliaceae*)

carolinae	MBri
§ - (Meyendorffii Group) 'Flandria' (v)	MBri
- - 'Meyendorffii'	MBri XBlo
- f. ***tricolor*** (v) 🏆H1	CHal MBri
Claret Group	MBri
'Hojo Rojo' **new**	XBlo
'Marconfos' **new**	XBlo
marmorata 🏆H1	ESlt

Neottianthe (*Orchidaceae*)

cucullata	EFEx

Nepenthes (*Nepenthaceae*)

alata	CSWC
alata x ***ventricosa***	SHmp
ampullaria	CSWC
x ***coccinea***	MBri
fusca	CSWC
fusca x ***maxima***	SHmp
§ x ***hookeriana***	CSWC
khasiana	SHmp
maxima x ***mixta***	SHmp
rafflesiana	CSWC
sanguinea	SHmp
spectabilis	SHmp
stenophylla	SHmp

Nepeta (*Lamiaceae*)

CC 3766	WCot
RCB/TQ H-6	WCot
'Blue Beauty'	see *N. sibirica* 'Souvenir d'André Chaudron'
bucharica	GBuc GFlt WOut
* ***buddlejifolium***	NLar
camphorata	GBar GTou MLLN MSte NBre NLsd SAga SIde
cataria	CArn CPrp CSev ELau EUnu GBar GPoy MBow MChe MHer MSal MWrn NBro NGHP NPri NTHB SECG SIde WHer WMoo WPer WSel WWye XPep
§ - 'Citriodora'	CArn CHar CPrp ELan ELau EUnu EWTr GBar GPoy MBow MHer MSal NVic SChu SECG SHGN SIde SPoG WCHb WGHP WHer WSSM WSel
citriodora Dum.	see *N. cataria* 'Citriodora'
clarkei	CStr EBee EMan EPPr GIBF LEdu LPhx MAnH MDKP MMHG MSte MWrn NBPC NCGa SBla SBod SHGN SIde WCot WMoo WPer WSSM WWhi
curviflora	EUnu
'Dropmore'	EBee XPep
§ x ***faassenii*** 🏆H4	More than 30 suppliers
- 'Alba'	CBrm COIW CStr EBee ECtt EPfP MAnH NBre NGHP NLar SHGN SMar WMnd WWpP
- 'Kit Cat' **new**	WHil
glechoma 'Variegata'	see *Glechoma hederacea* 'Variegata'
govaniana	More than 30 suppliers
grandiflora	EBee EWsh MRav SBla SIde WFar WHer WOut
- 'Blue Danube'	NDov
- 'Bramdean'	CMea CPrp CSam CStr EBee EMan EWin LPhx MBri MHar MRav NCGa NDov NLsd SAga WKif WOut
- 'Dawn to Dusk'	More than 30 suppliers

- 'Pool Bank'	CStr EBee ECtt EGoo EMan LSou NCGa NGby SAga SChu SGar SIde SUsu
- 'Wild Cat' **new**	LPhx
hederacea 'Variegata'	see *Glechoma hederacea* 'Variegata'
italica	EBee MAnH SBla SHar SIde
kubanica	CStr EMan LPhx
laevigata	EBee
lanceolata	see *N. nepetella*
latifolia	LPhx SIde
'Lilac Cloud'	NBir
* ***longipes*** hort.	CPrp CSam CStr EBee EWTr GMaP LAst MAnH MLLN MNFA MRav MSte NCGa NGdn NSti SBla SChu SMrm SPoG SSvw WCAu WFar WHal WMnd WOut WPer WTMC XPep
macrantha	see *N. sibirica*
melissifolia	EBee MHer SBch WCHb WPer WWye XPep
mussinii hort.	see *N.* x *faassenii*
mussinii Spreng.	see *N. racemosa*
§ ***nepetella***	EBee GBri MGol NBir NChi NLar WFar WOut WPer
nervosa	More than 30 suppliers
- 'Blue Carpet'	GCal
- 'Blue Moon' **new**	CStr
- 'Forncett Select'	CSam EMan SDys SMrm
§ ***nuda***	CPom CSam EBee EChP ECha ECtt EMan LDai MDKP MFOX MLLN SIde WCAu WFar WMnd XPep
- subsp. ***albiflora***	ECha
* - 'Anne's Choice'	MSte
* - 'Grandiflora'	NLar WMoo
- 'Isis'	EBee
- subsp. ***nuda***	CStr
- 'Snow Cat' **new**	LPhx
pannonica	see *N. nuda*
parnassica	More than 30 suppliers
phyllochlamys	CPBP EBee
'Porzellan'	CPrp CStr EBee EChP EMan EVFa EWin LAst MAnH MMil MSte NCGa SMrm
§ ***prattii***	CM&M EBee EChP EMag ERou MWat NBPC NCGa NLar SBod SIde SMrm SPla SPoG STes WPer WSHC
§ ***racemosa*** ♀H4	CArn CBot COlW CSev ELau EPfP GBar GKir LRHS MChe MRav SIde WGHP WMoo WWye XPep
- ***alba***	EVFa WFar
- 'Blue Ice'	GBuc SIde
- 'Grog'	EBee SIde
- 'Leporello' (v)	EPPr
- 'Little Titch'	CBod CPrp EMan EPPr EVFa EWTr GBar GCal LAst LRHS MSte NLar SAga SChu SIde SMrm SPla SPoG WFar WOut WSHC WWeb
- 'Snowflake'	CBcs CMea COlW CPrp EBee ELan EPfP GCal GKir GMaP LRHS MHer MSte NBir SAga SChu SIde SPer SPet SPla SPoG STes SUsu SWvt WCAu WFar WSel XPep
§ - 'Superba'	EMon GBuc WHoo
- 'Walker's Low'	More than 30 suppliers
reichenbachiana	see *N. racemosa*
§ ***sibirica***	EBee ECha ELan ELau EPfP EWTr GBBs GKir LEdu LRHS MAnH MHer MRav MWrn NBid NBro NCGa NDov NPri SChu WCot WFar WHal WPer WWhi
§ - 'Souvenir d'André Chaudron'	More than 30 suppliers
sintenisii	CSWP IFro
'Six Hills Giant'	More than 30 suppliers
stewartiana	CStr EChP EWTr GBuc GFlt LDai MAnH MLLN NEgg NLar STes WHoo WMoo WOut WSan
- ACE 1611	GBuc
- BWJ 7999	WCru
- CLD 551	EMan
subsessilis	More than 30 suppliers
- 'Candy Cat' **new**	EBee EHrv WHil
- 'Cool Cat' **new**	LPhx NLar SMrm WHil
- pink	ECha EVFa GBuc MAnH MAvo MLLN MSte SAga SBla
- 'Sweet Dreams'	CFwr CHar EBee ECGP EChP ECtt EMil EWin GBri LAst LPhx MAnH MBri MDKP MGol NGby NLar NLsd NSti SHar SSvw WFar WHil WOut WRHF WWeb
tenuifolia	MSal
transcaucasica	CArn CStr WOut
- 'Blue Infinity'	EKen EWTr MAnH NArg WMnd
troodii	EKen SIde
tuberosa	CHVG CSam CSpe CStr EBrs EChP ECha EKen EMag EMan GBri LPhx LRHS MAnH MAvo MHer MRav NBPC SBch SBla SChu SIde SPav SPoG STes WCot WMoo WWye XPep
yunnanensis	EBee EMan MAnH SOkh

Nephrolepis (*Oleandraceae*)

cordifolia	ERea MBri
exaltata ♀H2	EFtx ERea LRHS
- 'Bostoniensis'	MBri
- 'Smithii'	MBri
- 'Smithii Linda'	MBri
- 'Teddy Junior'	MBri

Nephrophyllidium (*Menyanthaceae*)

crista-galli	IBlr

Nerine ✿ (*Amaryllidaceae*)

'Afterglow'	ECho LAma
'Albivetta'	EBee ECho EPot
alta **new**	CMon
angustifolia	CMon
'Audrey'	WCot
'Bennett Poe' **new**	CMon
'Berlioz'	CMon
bowdenii ♀H3-4	More than 30 suppliers
- 'Alba'	CBro CStu EBrs ECho ELan LRHS SCoo SMHy
- 'Codora'	ECho LSou
- 'E.B. Anderson'	CMon EBee WCot
- 'Kinn McIntosh' **new**	WCot
- 'Manina'	CMdw CMon MSte WCot
- 'Mark Fenwick'	CAvo CBcs CBro EBee ECha MSte SOkd WCot WOld
- 'Marnie Rogerson'	CBro MBri MSte WCot
§ - 'Mollie Cowie' (v)	EBee EBrs EMon EVFa GCal IBlr WCot WCru
- pale pink striped darker **new**	CDes
- 'Pink Triumph'	CAbP CBcs CLyd EBee EBla EBrs EMan GBuc GQui IBlr LAma LRHS MSte SChr SPer SPla WCot WDav WHoo
- 'Porlock' **new**	EBee
- 'Quinton Wells'	LPhx
- 'Variegata'	see *N. bowdenii* 'Mollie Cowie'
- Washfield form **new**	SMHy
- 'Wellsii'	CDes CMil CMon EBee EMan WCot WLFP

	'Brocade'	CMon
	'Celestial' **new**	CMon
	'Coralina' **new**	CMon
	corusca 'Major'	see *N. sarniensis* var. *corusca*
	crispa	see *N. undulata*
	filamentosa	CBro CMon
	filifolia	CMon CPen ECho EHyt EPot ERos GCal ITim MNrw MTho WCot
	flexuosa	CMon CPne GSki MRav
	- 'Alba'	CBro CMon CStu EBee ECha EPot EWTr GSki LAma LPhx LPio LRHS MRav MSte WCot WWhi
	'Fucine'	CDes
	'Gaby Deslys'	CMon
	'Grilse'	CMon
	'Hera'	CBro EMon LPhx MBri MSte WCot
	humilis	CMon CStu EBee
	- Breachiae Group	CMon CStu SBch
	- Tulbaghensis Group	CMon
	'King of the Belgians'	ECho LAma WCot
	'Kodora' **new**	CFwr
	krigei	EBee
	'Lady Eleanor Keane'	CMon
	'Lord Grenfell'	IBlr
	'Mansellii'	CBro CMon
	'Maria'	WCot
	'Mars' **new**	CMon
	masoniorum	CBro CMon CStu EHyt ERos MTho NMen SBch SChr WCot
	'Miss Cator'	WCot
	'Nikita' **new**	CFwr MSte
	peersii	WCot
	'Plymouth'	CMon SChr
	pudica	CMon SBch
	- pink flowered **new**	WCot
	'Red Pimpernel'	LAma
	'Rose Camellia'	CMon
	'Rushmere Star'	CMon SChr
	sarniensis ♀H2-3	CBro CFwr ECha EPot LRHS MSte WCot WDav
§	- var. ***corusca***	CStu LAma
	- - 'Major'	SChr WCot
	- var. ***curvifolia*** f. ***fothergillii***	WCot
	- very late dull red **new**	CDes
	'Sidney Smee' **new**	CMon
	'Stephanie'	CBro CMon EShb LAma LRHS LSou SPer WDav
§	***undulata***	CBgR CBro CFwr CMon CPne CSut EBee ECha EPot ERos LAma LRHS LSou MSte WCot WHil
	'White Swan'	LAma
	'Zeal Candy Stripe'	CFir
	'Zeal Giant' ♀H3-4	CAvo CBro CFir CMon CPne GCal NGby
	'Zeal Grilse' **new**	CDes CPne
	'Zeal Silver Stripe'	CFir

Nerium ✿ (*Apocynaceae*)

	oleander	CAbb CArn CMdw CTri EBak EBee EEls ELan EShb LRHS MJnS MTis SArc SPoG SRms WMul
	- 'Agnes Campbell'	XPep
*	- 'Alassio'	XPep
	- 'Album'	EEls
	- 'Album Maximum'	XPep
	- 'Album Plenum' (d)	EEls SGar XPep
*	- 'Almodovar'	XPep
	- 'Alsace'	EEls XPep
	- 'Altini'	EEls XPep
	- 'Angiolo Pucci'	EEls XPep
*	- 'Apache'	XPep
*	- 'Aquarelle'	XPep
*	- 'Arad'	XPep
*	- 'Aramis' (d)	XPep
*	- 'Argunista'	XPep
*	- 'Arizona'	XPep
*	- 'Art Déco'	XPep
*	- 'Atlas'	XPep
*	- 'Barcelona'	XPep
	- 'Belle Hélène'	XPep
	- 'Bousquet d'Orb'	EEls
	- 'Calypso'	XPep
*	- 'Campane'	XPep
	- 'Cap Saint Vincent'	XPep
§	- 'Carneum Plenum' (d)	EEls XPep
*	- 'Caro'	XPep
	- 'Cavalaire' (d)	EEls XPep
*	- 'Cheyenne'	XPep
*	- 'Christine'	XPep
*	- 'Claudia'	XPep
	- 'Commandant Barthélemy'	XPep
	- 'Cornouailles'	EEls XPep
*	- 'Dimona'	XPep
	- 'Docteur Golfin'	EEls
	- 'Dottore Attilio Ragionieri'	XPep
	- 'East End Pink'	XPep
	- 'Ed Barr'	XPep
*	- 'Elat'	XPep
	- 'Emile Sahut'	EEls XPep
	- 'Emilie'	EEls
*	- 'Eole'	XPep
	- 'Eugenia Fowler' (d)	XPep
*	- 'Feuille d'Eucalyptus'	XPep
*	- 'Fiesta Pienk'	XPep
*	- 'Fiesta Rodi'	XPep
	- 'Flavescens Plenum' (d)	EEls XPep
	- 'Framboise'	XPep
*	- 'Galipette' (d)	XPep
*	- 'Garlaban'	XPep
	- 'Géant des Batailles' (d)	EEls
	- 'General Pershing' (d)	XPep
	- 'Grandiflorum'	XPep
*	- 'Haïfa'	XPep
	- 'Hardy Red'	EEls XPep
*	- 'Harriet Newding'	XPep
	- 'Hawaii'	EEls XPep
*	- 'Icare'	XPep
*	- subsp. ***indicum***	XPep
*	- 'Isabelle'	EEls
	- 'Isle of Capri'	EEls XPep
	- 'Italia'	XPep
	- 'J.R.'	EEls XPep
*	- 'Jack'line'	XPep
	- 'Jannoch'	EEls XPep
*	- 'Jardin du Luxembourg'	XPep
*	- 'Jordan Valley'	XPep
*	- 'La Fontaine'	XPep
	- 'Lady Kate'	XPep
	- 'Lane Taylor Sealy'	XPep
*	- 'Lisou'	XPep
	- 'Louis Pouget' (d)	EEls XPep
	- 'Madame Allen' (d)	EEls XPep
*	- 'Madame de Billy'	XPep
	- 'Magaly'	XPep
	- 'Maguelone'	XPep
*	- 'Mainate'	XPep
	- 'Maresciallo Graziani'	EEls XPep
	- 'Margaritha'	EEls XPep
	- 'Marie Gambetta'	EEls XPep
	- 'Marie Mauron'	XPep
	- subsp. ***mascatense***	XPep
*	- 'Massif de l'Etoile'	XPep
*	- 'Maurin des Maures'	XPep

*	- 'Mer Egée'	XPep
	- 'Minouche'	XPep
*	- 'Mishna'	XPep
	- 'Mont Blanc'	EEls XPep
*	- 'Mont Rose'	XPep
*	- 'Monts Saint Cyr'	XPep
	- 'Moshav'	XPep
	- 'Mrs Burton' (d)	XPep
	- 'Mrs Magnolia Willis Sealy' (d)	XPep
	- 'Mrs Roeding'	see *N. oleander* 'Carneum Plenum'
	- 'Mrs Swanson' (d)	XPep
	- 'Mrs Trueheart'	XPep
	- 'Mrs Willard Cooke'	XPep
	- 'Nana Rosso'	EEls XPep
*	- 'Natou'	XPep
	- 'Navajo'	XPep
*	- 'Neguev'	XPep
*	- 'Nomade'	XPep
	- 'Oasis'	EEls XPep
	- subsp. ***oleander***	EEls XPep
*	- 'Osiris'	XPep
	- 'Papa Gambetta'	EEls XPep
*	- 'Pasadena'	XPep
	- 'Petite Pink'	EEls XPep
	- 'Petite Red'	EEls XPep
	- 'Petite Salmon'	EEls XPep
*	- 'Petite White'	XPep
	- 'Pietra Ligure'	XPep
	- 'Pink Beauty'	XPep
*	- 'Pirate Des Caraïbes'	XPep
	- 'Porto'	XPep
	- 'Professeur Granel' (d)	EEls XPep
	- 'Professeur Parlatore'	XPep
	- 'Provence' (d)	EEls XPep
*	- 'Rivage'	XPep
	- 'Rosa Bartolini'	XPep
	- 'Rosario' (d)	XPep
	- 'Rose des Borrels'	EEls XPep
*	- 'Rose des Vents' (d)	XPep
	- 'Rosée du Ventoux' (d)	EEls
	- 'Roseum'	EEls
	- 'Roseum Plenum' (d)	CRHN EEls XPep
	- 'Rosita'	EEls XPep
*	- 'Rossignol'	XPep
*	- 'Rubis' (d)	XPep
*	- 'Sabra'	XPep
*	- 'Sainte Beaume'	XPep
*	- 'Sainte Victoire'	XPep
*	- 'Santa Fe'	XPep
*	- 'Sausalito'	XPep
	- 'Scarlet Beauty'	XPep
	- 'Sealy Pink'	EEls XPep
*	- 'Simie'	XPep
	- 'Soeur Agnès' (d)	EEls XPep
*	- 'Soeur Elisabeth' (d)	XPep
	- 'Soleil Levant'	EEls XPep
*	- 'Solfège'	XPep
*	- 'Sophie'	XPep
	- 'Souvenir d'Emma Schneider'	EEls XPep
	- 'Souvenir des Iles Canaries'	EEls XPep
	- 'Splendens Foliis Variegatis' (d)	XPep
	- 'Splendens Giganteum' (d)	EEls XPep
	- 'Splendens Giganteum Variegatum' (d/v)	EEls
*	- 'Tamouré' (d)	XPep
*	- 'Tavira'	XPep
	- 'Tiberias'	XPep
	- 'Tito Poggi'	EEls XPep
*	- 'Toulouse'	XPep
	- 'Vanilla Cream' **new**	CBcs
	- 'Variegatum' (v) ♀H1+3	CBot
	- 'Variegatum Plenum' (d/v)	WCot
*	- 'Vénus'	XPep
	- 'Villa Romaine'	EEls XPep
*	- 'Ville d'Aubagne'	XPep
	- 'Ville de Carpentras' (d)	EEls XPep
	- 'Virginie'	XPep
*	- 'Zoulou'	XPep

Nertera (*Rubiaceae*)

	balfouriana	ECou
	depressa	WCot
	granadensis	MBri

Neviusia (*Rosaceae*)

	alabamensis	CBcs NLar WWes

Nicandra (*Solanaceae*)

	physalodes	CArn CHby EUnu EWll ILis MGol MSal NVic SUsu SYvo WRos
	- 'Splash of Cream' (v)	EMan EUnu EWll LSou NLsd
	- 'Violacea'	CSpe GGar SRms SWvt

Nicotiana (*Solanaceae*)

	alata 'Grandiflora'	LRav
	glauca	CHll CPLG CSec CSpe EShb LRav MGol MOak MSte NLar SDnm SPav
	knightiana	CSec CSpe EBee
	langsdorffii ♀H3	CBcs CHad CSpe EBee EBla EMan EMon EWin GBri LRav MGol SDnm SMrm SPav SPet SUsu WEas
	- 'Cream Splash' (v)	EChP
	'Lime Green' ♀H3	CSpe
	longiflora	CStr
*	***mutabilis***	CHll CSpe CStr EBee SBch WPGP
	mutabilis* x *alata **new**	CSec
	quadrivalvis var. ***bigelovii***	MGol
	rustica	MGol
	suaveolens	CBre
	sylvestris ♀H3	CHEx CHad CSpe CStr CWSG EBee ELan EMan EPfP EWTr MAnH MGol MOak SBch SDnm SEND SMrm SPav SWvt WEas WWhi WWye
	tabacum	CArn MGol SPav

Nidularium (*Bromeliaceae*)

	billbergioides **new**	EOas
	flandria	see *Neoregelia carolinae* (Meyendorffii Group) 'Flandria'
	fulgens ♀H1 **new**	EOas

x *Niduregelia* (*Bromeliaceae*)

§	'Surprise'	MBri

Nierembergia (*Solanaceae*)

	caerulea	see *N. linariifolia*
	frutescens	see *N. scoparia*
	hippomanica	see *N. linariifolia*
§	***linariifolia*** ♀H1	CAbP ECha EHrv EMan
§	***repens***	CFee ECGP EDAr EPot ESis GKir LRHS NLar
	rivularis	see *N. repens*
§	***scoparia***	LPhx XPep
	- 'Mont Blanc'	LRHS
	- 'Purple Robe'	LRHS

Nigella (*Ranunculaceae*)

papillosa 'Midnight' **new**	CSpe
sativa	WJek

Nigritella see *Gymnadenia*

Nipponanthemum (*Asteraceae*)

§ ***nipponicum***	CDes CNic CWan EBee EWin GCal GMac LAst LPio MNrw NJOw NSti SRms WBrk WCot WTin

Noccaea see *Thlaspi*

Nolina (*Dracaenaceae*)

beldingii	SIgm
bigelovii	CBrP
greenii	SIgm
longifolia	EOas
microcarpa	XPep
recurvata	see *Beaucarnea recurvata*
stricta	see *Beaucarnea stricta*
texana	CTrC NWCA SIgm WCot

Nomocharis (*Liliaceae*)

aperta	CPLG EHyt EPot GBuc GCrs GEdr GFlt GGar GKir ITim LAma MLul SSpi WCru
- ACE 2271	GCrs
- CLD 229	GBuc GKir
farreri	EPot GCrs GEdr GFlt GKir WCru
x ***finlayorum***	ITim
mairei	see *N. pardanthina*
meleagrina	EPot GBuc GEdr GFlt GIBF LAma WAbe
nana	see *Lilium nanum*
oxypetala	see *Lilium oxypetalum*
§ ***pardanthina***	GBuc GGGa GMac LAma NSla WAbe WCru
- CLD 1490	GCrs
- f. ***punctulata***	GBuc GGGa GKir WCru
saluenensis	GCrs GGGa GTou WAbe WCru

Nonea (*Boraginaceae*)

lutea	EChP ECtt GFlt MLLN NOrc NSti WCHb WHal WRos WSSM WWye

Nothochelone see *Penstemon*

Nothofagus ✿ (*Fagaceae*)

§ x ***alpina***	CDul CFil CLnd CMCN GKir NWea WMou WNor WPGP
antarctica	More than 30 suppliers
cunninghamii	GGGa IArd IDee STre WNor
dombeyi	CDoC CDul CFil CLnd CTho EPfP LHyd LRHS SAPC SArc SSpi STre WNor WPGP
fusca	CBcs CDoC CTrC MGos
menziesii	CAbb CBcs CDul CTrC
§ ***nervosa***	LRHS WDin
obliqua	CDoC CDul CLnd CMCN ECrN NWea WDin WMou WNor
procera misapplied	see *N.* x *alpina*
procera Oerst.	see *N. nervosa*
solanderi	CAbb CTrC
- var. ***cliffortioides***	CBcs WCwm

Notholaena see *Cheilanthes*

Notholirion (*Liliaceae*)

bulbuliferum	EBee GKir WAbe WCot
macrophyllum	EBee GBuc GCrs GEdr NLar
thomsonianum	GCrs

Nothopanax see *Polyscias*

Nothoscordum (*Alliaceae*)

bivalve	CStu
gracile	CFir CPLG EBee WPrP
inodorum	EBee GBuc
neriniflorum	see *Caloscordum neriniflorum*

Notospartium (*Papilionaceae*)

carmichaeliae	ECou
- 'Hodder'	ECou
- 'Seymour'	ECou
glabrescens	ECou
- 'Ben More'	ECou
- 'Woodside'	ECou
'Joy'	ECou
torulosum	ECou
- 'Blue Butterfly'	ECou
- 'Malvern Hills'	ECou
torulosum x ***glabrescens***	ECou

Nuphar (*Nymphaeaceae*)

advenum	LPBA
japonica	CDWL WPop
- var. ***variegata*** (v)	CRow
lutea	CDWL CRow EHon EMFW LNCo LPBA NArg SCoo WFar WPnP WPop
- subsp. ***advena***	EMFW

Nuxia (*Buddlejaceae*)

congesta	EShb
floribunda	EShb

Nylandtia (*Polygalaceae*)

spinosa	SPlb

Nymphaea ✿ (*Nymphaeaceae*)

'Afterglow' (T/D)	CDWL
alba (H)	CBen CRWN CRow CWat EHon EMFW EPfP LNCo LPBA NArg SCoo WFar WPop
'Albatros' misapplied	see *N.* 'Hermine'
'Albatros' Latour-Marliac (H)	CDWL LNCo LPBA WBcn WPnP
* 'Albida'	CDWL XBlo
'Amabilis' (H)	CBen CDWL CRow EMFW LPBA WBcn
'American Star' (H)	CWat EMFW
'Andreana' (H)	CDWL CWat LPBA
'Arabian Nights' (T/D)	CDWL
'Arc-en-ciel' (H)	CDWL LPBA SCoo WPop
'Arethusa' (H)	LPBA
'Atropurpurea' (H)	CBen CDWL EMFW LPBA WBcn
'Attraction' (H)	CBen CDWL CRow EHon EMFW LNCo LPBA MCCP NPer SCoo WPop XBlo
'Aurora' (H)	CDWL EMFW LPBA WPnP
'Barbara Dobbins' (H)	CDWL LPBA WPop
'Berit Strawn' (H)	CDWL EMFW
'Berthold' (H)	CBen
'Blue Beauty' (T/D)	CBen
'Blue Horizon' (T/D)	CDWL
'Brakeleyi Rosea' (H)	LPBA
'Burgundy Princess' (H)	CDWL
candida (H)	CBen EHon EMFW
'Candidissima' (H)	CDWL
§ ***capensis*** (T/D)	XBlo
'Caroliniana' (H)	CDWL CWat
'Caroliniana Nivea' (H)	CBen CDWL EMFW
'Caroliniana Perfecta' (H)	CBen LPBA
§ 'Charlene Strawn' (H)	CWat EMFW LPBA WBcn

'Charles de Meurville' (H)	CBen CDWL CRow EMFW LNCo LPBA NArg NPer WPop
'Chubby' (H)	EMFW
'Colonel A.J. Welch' (H)	CBen CDWL CRow EHon EMFW LNCo LPBA NArg NPer SCoo WFar WPnP WPop
'Colorado' (H)	CDWL
colorata	see *N. capensis*
'Colossea' (H)	CBen CWat EHon EMFW LNCo LPBA WPnP WPop
'Comanche' (H)	CBen EMFW NPer
'Conqueror' (H)	EMFW IArd LNCo LPBA SCoo WFar
§ 'Darwin' (H)	CBen CDWL CWat EMFW LPBA WPop
'David' (H)	CWat
'Director George T. Moore' (T/D)	CDWL
'Ellisiana' (H)	CBen CDWL CWat EMFW LPBA
'Escarboucle' (H) ♀H4	CBen CDWL CRow CWat EHon EMFW LNCo LPBA NPer SCoo WBcn WPnP WPop XBlo
'Evelyn Randig' (T/D)	CDWL
'Excalibur'	CDWL
§ 'Fabiola' (H)	CBen CDWL CRow EHon EMFW EPfP LPBA NArg SCoo WBcn WFar
'Fire Crest' (H)	CBen EHon EMFW LNCo LPBA MCCP NBlu SCoo WBcn WFar
'Froebelii' (H)	CBen CDWL CRow CWat EHon EMFW LNCo LPBA NArg WBcn WFar WPop
'Galatée' (H)	CDWL
'Geisha Girl'	CDWL
'General Pershing' (T/D)	CDWL
'Georgia Peach' (H)	CDWL
'Gladstoneana' (H) ♀H4	CBen CRow CWat EHon EMFW LNCo LPBA NArg NPer SCoo WPop
'Gloire du Temple-sur-Lot' (H)	CBen CDWL EMFW WPop
'Gloriosa' (H)	CBen CDWL LPBA SCoo WFar
'Gold Medal' (H)	CBen
'Golden West' (T/D)	CDWL
'Gonnère' (H) ♀H4	CBen CDWL CRow CWat EHon EMFW EPfP LNCo LPBA NArg WBcn WPnP WPop
'Graziella' (H)	LPBA NArg WBcn WPnP WPop
'Green Smoke' (T/D)	CDWL
'H.C. Haarstick' (T/N)	CDWL
'Helen Fowler' (H)	CDWL EMFW
x ***helvola***	see *N.* 'Pygmaea Helvola'
§ 'Hermine' (H)	CBen CDWL EMFW WPop
'Hollandia' misapplied	see *N.* 'Darwin'
'Indiana' (H)	CBen CDWL EMFW LPBA
'Irene Heritage' (H)	CBen
'James Brydon' (H) ♀H4	CBen CDWL CRow CWat EHon EMFW EPfP LNCo LPBA NArg NPer SCoo WBcn WFar WPnP WPop
'Joey Tomocik' (H)	CBen CDWL CWat LNCo LPBA SCoo WPop
'June Alison' (T/D)	CDWL
'Lactea' (H)	CDWL
'Laydekeri Alba'	CDWL
'Laydekeri Fulgens' (H)	CBen CDWL EMFW LPBA
'Laydekeri Lilacea' (H)	CBen CDWL CRow EMFW LNCo LPBA WPop
'Laydekeri Purpurata' (H)	CDWL EMFW LPBA WBcn
'Laydekeri Rosea' misapplied	see *N.* 'Laydekeri Rosea Prolifera'
§ 'Laydekeri Rosea Prolifera' (H)	CBen EMFW LPBA
'Lemon Chiffon' (H)	CDWL
'Little Sue' (H)	CDWL
'Livingstone' (H)	CWat
'Luciana'	see *N.* 'Odorata Luciana'
'Lucidia' (H)	CBen CDWL CWat EMFW LPBA WPop
'Madame de Bonseigneur' (H)	CDWL
'Madame Ganna Walska' (T/D)	CDWL
'Madame Wilfon Gonnère' (H)	CBen CDWL CWat EHon EMFW LNCo LPBA WBcn WPnP WPop
'Marliacea Albida' (H)	CBen CWat EHon EMFW LNCo LPBA MCCP WFar WPnP WPop XBlo
'Marliacea Carnea' (H)	CBen CDWL CRow EHon EMFW EPfP LNCo LPBA NArg NPer SCoo WBcn WFar WPop
§ 'Marliacea Chromatella' (H) ♀H4	CBen CDWL CRow CWat EHon EMFW EPfP LNCo LPBA NArg SCoo WBcn WFar WPnP WPop XBlo
'Marliacea Rosea' (H)	EMFW NArg XBlo
'Marliacea Rubra Punctata' (H)	LPBA
'Martin E. Randig'	CDWL
'Masaniello' (H)	CBen CDWL CRow EHon EMFW LPBA NArg WBcn
'Maurice Laydeker' (H)	CDWL
'Mayla'	LPBA
§ 'Météor' (H)	CBen CWat EMFW WBcn
mexicana	NArg
'Millennium Pink'	CDWL
'Moorei' (H)	CBen CDWL EHon EMFW LPBA WPop
'Mrs George C. Hitchcock' (TN)	CDWL
'Mrs Richmond' Latour-Marliac (H)	XBlo
'Mrs Richmond' misapplied	see *N.* 'Fabiola'
'Newton' (H)	CDWL
'Norma Gedye' (H)	CBen LPBA WPop
'Odalisque' (H)	CWat EMFW
§ ***odorata*** (H)	CBen CRow EHon LPBA NArg SCoo WBcn
'Odorata Alba'	see *N. odorata*
§ 'Odorata Luciana' (H)	EMFW
§ ***odorata*** var. ***minor*** (H)	CBen CDWL CRow EMFW LPBA WFar
- 'Pumila'	see *N. odorata* var. *minor*
'Odorata Sulphurea' (H)	CDWL LNCo NArg NBlu WBcn WFar WPnP
§ 'Odorata Sulphurea Grandiflora' (H)	CBen CDWL CRow CWat EMFW LPBA SCoo WBcn WPop XBlo
odorata subsp. ***tuberosa*** (H)	CBen LPBA
§ 'Odorata Turicensis' (H)	LPBA
'Odorata William B. Shaw'	see *N.* 'W.B. Shaw'
'Orange Commanche'	CDWL
'Pam Bennett' (H)	CBen
'Pamela' (T/D)	CBen
'Panama Pacific' (T/D) **new**	XBlo
'Patio Joe'	CDWL
'Paul Hariot' (H)	CDWL CWat EHon EMFW LPBA WBcn WPop
'Peaches and Cream' (H)	CDWL
'Perry's Baby Red' (H)	CBen CDWL CWat SCoo
'Perry's Double White' (H)	CBen
'Perry's Fire Opal' (H)	CDWL
'Perry's Viviparous Pink' (H)	CBen
'Perry's Yellow Sensation'	see *N.* 'Yellow Sensation'
'Peter Slocum' (H)	CDWL EMFW
'Phoebus' (H)	CDWL WBcn
pink hybrid	CDWL

'Pink Opal' (H)	CBen CDWL CWat EMFW LPBA
'Pink Sensation' (H)	CBen CDWL EMFW NArg WPop
'Pöstlingberg' (H)	LPBA WPop
'Princess Elizabeth' (H)	EHon LPBA
'Pygmaea Alba'	see *N. tetragona*
§ 'Pygmaea Helvola' (H) ♀H4	CBen CDWL CRow CWat EHon EMFW LNCo LPBA NBlu NPer SCoo WPnP WPop
'Pygmaea Rubis' (H)	CRow EHon LPBA
'Pygmaea Rubra' (H)	CBen CDWL CWat EMFW LNCo NPer SCoo WPnP WPop
'Ray Davies' (H)	EMFW
'Red Spider' (H)	LPBA
'Rembrandt' misapplied	see *N.* 'Météor'
'Rembrandt' Koster (H)	CDWL LPBA
'René Gérard' (H)	CBen CDWL CWat EHon EMFW LNCo LPBA NArg WBcn WFar WPnP WPop
'Rose Arey' (H)	CBen CDWL CRow CWat EMFW LPBA NArg SCoo WBcn
'Rose Magnolia' (H)	CDWL
§ 'Rosea' (H)	CBen LPBA
'Rosennymphe' (H)	CBen LPBA WFar
'Saint Louis Gold' (T/D)	CDWL
'Seignouretti' (H)	EMFW WBcn
'Sioux' (H)	CBen CDWL EHon EMFW LPBA NArg NBlu NPer WBcn WPop XBlo
'Sir Galahad' (T/N)	CDWL
'Sirius' (H)	CBen CDWL EMFW LPBA
'Snow Princess'	LPBA WPnP WPop
'Sunny Pink'	CDWL
'Sunrise'	see *N.* 'Odorata Sulphurea Grandiflora'
§ ***tetragona*** (H)	CBen CDWL CRow CWat EHon LNCo LPBA NArg WFar WPop
- 'Alba'	see *N. tetragona*
'Texas Dawn' (H)	CDWL WPop
'Tina' (T/D)	CDWL
'Tuberosa Flavescens'	see *N.* 'Marliacea Chromatella'
'Tuberosa Richardsonii' (H)	EHon EMFW LNCo WFar WPop
tuberosa 'Rosea'	see *N.* 'Rosea'
'Turicensis'	see *N.* 'Odorata Turicensis'
'Vésuve' (H)	CDWL EMFW
'Virginalis' (H)	LPBA WPop
§ 'W.B. Shaw' (H)	CBen EHon EMFW LNCo LPBA NArg WPnP WPop
'Walter Pagels' (H)	CDWL EMFW WPop
'Weymouth Red' (H)	CBen
'White Delight' (TD)	CDWL
'William Doogue' (H)	WBcn
'William Falconer' (H)	CBen CDWL CWat EMFW LPBA WPop
'Wow' (H)	CDWL
'Yellow Commanche'	CDWL
'Yellow Dazzler' (T/D)	CDWL
'Yellow Princess' (H)	CDWL
§ 'Yellow Sensation' (H)	CBen
'Zeus'	CDWL

Nymphoides (*Menyanthaceae*)

peltata	CWat EMFW EPfP LNCo NArg NPer SCoo WFar WPnP WWpP
§ - 'Bennettii'	EHon LPBA

Nyssa (*Cornaceae*)

aquatica	CTho IArd LRHS SSpi SSta
sinensis ♀H4	CAbP CBcs CDoC CEnd CLnd CMCN CPMA CTho ELan EPfP GKir IDee LRHS MBlu MBri SBrw SPer SReu SSpi SSta WCwm WNor
- Nymans form	EPfP LRHS SSpi
- Savill form **new**	SIFN
sylvatica ♀H4	More than 30 suppliers
- 'Autumn Cascades'	EPfP IArd MBlu NLar
- var. ***biflora***	CMCN
- 'Jermyns Flame'	CAbP EPfP LRHS SSpi
- 'Red Red Wine'	EPfP MBlu
- 'Sheffield Park'	CAbP CMCN EPfP LRHS SSpi
- 'Windsor'	EPfP LRHS SSpi
- 'Wisley Bonfire'	CAbP ECrN EPfP LRHS NLar SPoG SSpi

O

Oakesiella see *Uvularia*

Ochagavia (*Bromeliaceae*)

sp.	SAPC SArc
carnea	EOas
elegans **new**	CFil WPGP
* ***rosea***	CHEx

Ochna (*Ochnaceae*)

serrulata	CSec

Ocimum (*Lamiaceae*)

'African Blue'	CArn CBod ELau EMan EOHP GPoy LSou MHer NBlu SPoG
americanum 'Spice'	see *Ocimum* 'Spice'
basilicum	CArn CHrt CSev GPoy LRHS MBow MBri MChe NBlu NPri SECG SIde WPer WSel
- 'Anise'	see *O. basilicum* 'Horapha'
* - 'Cinnamon'	CHrt EMan LRHS MBow MChe MSal NGHP SHDw WJek WSel
- 'Genovese'	CHrt ELau MHer NGHP NVic
- 'Glycyrrhiza'	see *O. basilicum* 'Horapha'
- 'Green Globe'	MChe
- 'Green Ruffles'	EPfP LRHS MChe WJek WSel
- 'Holy'	see *O. tenuiflorum*
§ - 'Horapha'	CArn CSev MBow MChe MHer MSal NGHP SIde WJek
* - 'Horapha Nanum'	NGHP WJek
- 'Napolitano'	CBod MChe MHer NGHP SIde WJek
- var. ***purpurascens***	CArn CSev MBri MChe NBlu SIde
- - 'Dark Opal'	CBod NGHP SHDw WJek WSel
- - 'Purple Ruffles'	EPfP MBow MChe SIde WJek WSel
- - 'Red Rubin'	MChe MHer WJek
- 'Thai'	see *O. basilicum* 'Horapha'
x ***citriodorum***	CArn GPoy LRHS MBow MChe MSal NGHP SHDw SIde WJek WSel
- 'Lime'	CHrt LSou NGHP WJek
- 'Siam Queen'	CHrt LRHS MHer WJek
gratissimum	ELau MHer
§ ***kilimandscharicum***	GPoy
kilimandscharicum x ***basilicum*** var. ***purpurascens***	GPoy
minimum	CArn CBod CHrt CSev ELau LRHS MBri MChe MHer NBlu SIde WJek WPer WSel
sanctum	see *O. tenuiflorum*
'Spice'	MChe
'Spicy Globe'	WJek
§ ***tenuiflorum***	CArn GPoy LRHS MChe MSal NGHP SHDw SIde WJek

Odontites (*Scrophulariaceae*)

vernus **new**	WBWf

Odontonema (*Acanthaceae*)

strictum	WMul

Oemleria (*Rosaceae*)

§	***cerasiformis***	CBcs CPLG CPle EPfP EPla SHel SSpi WCot WEas WHCG WSHC

Oenanthe (*Apiaceae*)

	aquatica	IHMH WPop
	- 'Variegata' (v)	EMFW
*	***javanica*** 'Atropurpurea'	EHoe
	- 'Flamingo' (v)	CRow EChP EGra ELan EMan EMon EPfP GGar IHMH LPBA LRHS MBNS NArg NBro NJOw SGar WFar WPer WSHC WWpP

Oenothera ✿ (*Onagraceae*)

	from South America	MTho
§	***acaulis***	CBot CSpe EBee ECrN GCal MNrw NArg SBch SBri SGar WRos
	- ***alba***	MDKP
§	- 'Aurea'	SRot WGwG WPer
	- 'Lutea'	see *O. acaulis* 'Aurea'
	'Apricot Delight'	EBee EChP ECrN EMag EMan ENot GBBs LRHS MBrN MCCP MGol MWrn NBur STes WMnd WMoo WPen
§	***biennis***	CArn CSev CWan EHoe ELan EUnu EWTr GPoy MBow MChe MDun MHer NBro NGHP SECG SGar SIde WBrk WEas WFar WHer WJek WPer
	caespitosa	CHrt NRib
	- subsp. ***caespitosa*** NNS 93-505	NWCA
*	***campylocalyx***	EChP EMag EUnu LDai NBur WMoo WWpP
	childsii	see *O. speciosa*
	cinaeus	see *O. fruticosa* subsp. *glauca*
	'Colin Porter'	CCge EBur EDAr NArg NBur NWCA SGar WMoo WPer
	'Crown Imperial'	EBee GKir MCCP SHar SIng SPoG SSpi SSto
	drummondii	XPep
§	***elata*** subsp. ***hookeri***	WPer
	erythrosepala	see *O. glazioviana*
	'Finlay's Fancy'	LEdu WCru
§	***fruticosa***	CSam EChP IFro NLar SPlb WWpP
	- 'African Sun'^PBR^	EBee ECtt EMan EWes SBod SRot
	- 'Camel' (v)	CBct EMan LDai MDKP MFOX NEgg NPro SMrm SUsu WHil WHrl
	- Fireworks	see *O. fruticosa* 'Fyrverkeri'
§	- 'Fyrverkeri' ♀H4	More than 30 suppliers
§	- subsp. ***glauca*** ♀H4	CElw CHrt COIW EBee EPfP ERou GBBs GSki MDKP MNrw MTho MWgw MWhi NBlu NEgg NGHP NPro SPet SRms SYvo WEas WHil WPer
	- - 'Erica Robin' (v)	CElw CMea CPrp EBee EChP ECtt EGra EHoe EMon EPla GBuc LAst LRHS MArl MRav NEgg NGdn SAga SMad SMrm SPla SPoG SRot SSpe SUsu WCAu WCot WHoo WLin WPGP
	- - 'Frühlingsgold' (v)	CBct SUsu
	- - narrow grey-leaved	SUsu
	- - Solstice	see *O. fruticosa* subsp. *glauca* 'Sonnenwende'
§	- - 'Sonnenwende'	CBre CElw EBrs EMon LRHS MLLN NGHP NLar NPro WMoo WTel
	- - 'Sunspot' (v)	GBuc GFlt
	- 'Lady Brookeborough'	MRav
	- 'Michelle Ploeger'	EBee EMan NCGa
	- 'Silberblatt'	EMan EPPr WAul
	- 'Yellow River'	CElw LRHS WBrk WWeb
	- 'Youngii'	EHan EPfP ERou GCrs LIck MCCP MLLN SSto WPer
	glabra Miller	see *O. biennis*
	glabra misapplied	ECha NSti SIng SUsu
	glazioviana	CWan EBee EChP EMag EUnu NBir WFar WHrl WPer WWye
	grandis **new**	WGwG
	hookeri	see *O. elata* subsp. *hookeri*
	howardii	GKev
	kunthiana	EDAr EMag EMan ERou EShb IFro MDKP NArg NWCA SPet WMnd WMoo WPer
	- 'Glowing Magenta' **new**	LSou
	lamarckiana	see *O. glazioviana*
	'Lemon Sunset'	CSim CWan EMag LSou MCCP NArg NBur NGHP SSvw WMoo
	linearis	see *O. fruticosa*
	'Longest Day'	LRHS MArl MBrN WWeb
§	***macrocarpa*** ♀H4	More than 30 suppliers
	- 'Greencourt Lemon'	LPhx
	- subsp. ***incana***	CMea CSpe EMan EShb NBre NGHP SAga SMad
*	***minima***	MDKP WLin
	missouriensis	see *O. macrocarpa*
	muricata	EBee
	nana **new**	NJOw
	oakesiana	CSec EBee
	odorata misapplied	see *O. stricta*
	odorata Hook. & Arn.	see *O. biennis*
	odorata Jacquin	CArn CStr GCal IBlr NOrc
	- cream	WPen
	- 'Sulphurea'	see *O. stricta* 'Sulphurea'
	organensis	EBee MLLN WPGP
	pallida	EBee EWTr NGHP
	- 'Innocence'	CBot ECtt LRHS MBNS MGol WPer
	- 'Wedding Bells'	NPer
	parviflora **new**	CSec
	'Penelope Hobhouse'	CBct GBuc LSou SUsu
§	***perennis***	CNic CStr GKir NBre NPro SRms WBVN WEas WPer
	pumila	see *O. perennis*
	rosea	NBur
	speciosa	CMHG CRWN CSim EBee EWin MRav NBre SAga SEND SMar SPer WCot WPer XPep
*	- 'Alba'	EBee XPep
	- 'Ballerina'	EMan WCFE
	- var. ***childsii***	see *O. speciosa*
	- 'Pink Petticoats'	ECha ECtt EKen EMag EShb MArl MCCP NGHP NPer WSan
§	- 'Rosea'	CBot CFir CNic EBee ECrN EMag LRHS MNrw SGar SPlb WPer
	- 'Siskiyou'	CFis CHrt COtt CSpe ECrN ENot EPfP GBuc LRHS MArl NPri SBod SCoo SGar SHar SIng SMad SMrm SPoG SRot SUsu WHer
	- 'Woodside White'	SMrm
§	***stricta***	CHar CHrt CMea CSam ECGP EGoo MBri NPro SIng SMar WBrk WPer WWye
*	- 'Moonlight'	SGar
§	- 'Sulphurea'	CHad CHar CMHG CMil EChP EGoo ELan EMag EMan GCal IBlr IFro MNFA MWgw NPer SChu SGar SMrm SUsu WAbb WCot WPer
	'Summer Sun'	EBee LRHS MSph MSte NBre SPoG SSpe
	syrticola **new**	NBre
	taraxacifolia	see *O. acaulis*
	tetragona	see *O. fruticosa* subsp. *glauca*
	- var. ***fraseri***	see *O. fruticosa* subsp. *glauca*

- 'Sonnenwende'	see *O. fruticosa* subsp. *glauca* 'Sonnenwende'
versicolor 'Sunset Boulevard'	CHad CHrt CM&M CMea CSpe EChP ECtt GBuc LDai MBri MHer MWrn NGHP SBod SECG SGar SMrm SPer SPoG WHer WMnd WMoo WPer WSan WWeb

Olea (*Oleaceae*)

europaea (F)	More than 30 suppliers
- subsp. ***africana***	CFil CTrC WPGP XPep
- 'Aglandau' (F)	CAgr ERea
- 'Amygdalolia' (F)	ERea
- 'Bouteillan' (F)	CAgr ERea
- 'Cailletier' (F)	CAgr ERea
- 'Chelsea Physic Garden'	WPGP
§ - 'Cipressino' (F)	ERea SBLw XPep
- 'El Greco' (F)	CBcs ERea
- subsp. ***europaea*** var. ***sylvestris***	XPep
- 'Frantoio' (F) **new**	CAgr
- 'Manzanillo' (F)	ERea
- 'Picholine' (F)	ERea
- 'Pyramidalis'	see *O. europaea* 'Cipressino'

Olearia ✿ (*Asteraceae*)

albida misapplied	see *O.* 'Talbot de Malahide'
albida Hook. f.	GGar
- var. ***angulata***	CBcs CTrC
algida	ECou GGar
arborescens	GGar GSki
argophylla	ECou GGar
avicenniifolia	CBcs CTrC ECou GGar WBcn WSHC
canescens	CPne
capillaris	CDoC CPle ECou GAbr GGar WCwm
chathamica	CPLG GGar IDee
§ ***cheesemanii***	CBcs CDoC CMHG CPLG CPle GGar SPer
coriacea	ECou GGar
'County Park'	ECou
erubescens	CDoC CPLG CPle
floribunda	CPle GGar
furfuracea	CPle
glandulosa	ECou GGar
gunniana	see *O. phlogopappa*
x ***haastii***	More than 30 suppliers
- 'McKenzie'	ECou
hectorii	ECou
§ 'Henry Travers'	CDoC CPLG CPle EPfP GGar GQui IBlr IDee MDun NLar
§ ***ilicifolia***	CDoC CFil CPle EBee GGar GSki IDee LRHS MDun SSpi
§ ***ilicifolia*** x ***moschata***	CPle GGar IDee LRHS NLar WKif
insignis	see *Pachystegia insignis*
lacunosa	MDun
ledifolia	GGar
lepidophylla	ECou
- silver	ECou
lirata	ECou GGar
macrodonta ♀H3	More than 30 suppliers
- 'Intermedia'	GGar
- 'Major'	GGar SHBN
- 'Minor'	CBcs CDoC CTrC ELan EPfP GGar GQui NLar SPlb WBcn WFar
minor **new**	CBcs
x ***mollis*** hort.	see *O. ilicifolia* x *O. moschata*
x ***mollis*** (Kirk) Cockayne	CPle GQui SSpi WBcn WSHC
- 'Zennorensis' ♀H3	CBcs CDoC CPLG CPle GGar IArd IDee ISea MDun WBcn WCru WDin WEas WGer WPGP
moschata	CPle GGar NLar
myrsinoides	CFai CPle WGer
nummularifolia	CDoC CPle CTrC CTri ECou EPfP EPla GGar ISea NLon SEND SPer SSto WDin WFar WKif WSHC WTel
- var. ***cymbifolia***	ECou WGer
- hybrids	ECou
- 'Little Lou'	ECou
odorata	CPle ECou GGar ISea NLar WFar WHCG
oleifolia	see *O.* 'Waikariensis'
paniculata	CDoC CMHG CPLG CPle CTrC CTri EPfP GGar GSki IDee ISea SLon WGer
§ ***phlogopappa***	CSBt CTri ECou GGar WBrE
- 'Comber's Blue'	CBcs EPfP GGar IBlr LRHS NCGa SCoo
§ - 'Comber's Pink'	CBcs CDoC CPLG EPfP GGar IBlr ISea LRHS NCGa NPer SBrw SCoo SPer WEas WHil WKif WWeb
- pink	CBrm
- 'Rosea'	see *O. phlogopappa* 'Comber's Pink'
- Splendens Group	CAbb CDul WFar
- var. ***subrepanda***	CPle CTrC GGar LEdu SEND WAbe
§ ***ramulosa***	CDoC CPLG CPle CTrC WKif
- 'Blue Stars'	ECou GGar LRHS
- var. ***ramulosa***	ECou
- 'White Stars'	ECou
rani hort.	see *O. cheesemanii*
rani Druce	ISea
x ***scilloniensis*** hort.	see *O. stellulata* DC.
x ***scilloniensis*** Dorrien-Smith ♀H3	CAlb CBcs CBrm CWCL GGar NBlu NLon XPep
- 'Compacta' **new**	CBcs
- 'Master Michael'	CBot CDoC CTbh EHol EPfP NLar SBrw SPer SPoG WAbe WEas WKif WSHC WWeb
semidentata misapplied	see *O.* 'Henry Travers'
solandri	CDoC CHEx CPle CSam CTrC ECou EPla GGar SDix SHFr SPer STre XPep
- 'Aurea'	CBcs GQui
stellulata hort.	see *O. phlogopappa*
§ ***stellulata*** DC.	CBot CChe CPLG CSBt CSLe CWSG CWib ECou ECrN ELan EPfP ISea SAga SCoo SDix SPer SPla WBrE WDin WEas WFar WHCG WKif WPic WSHC
- 'Michael's Pride'	CPLG
§ 'Talbot de Malahide'	CDoC EHol GGar
traversii	CAbb CBcs CDoC CMHG CSBt CTrC GGar NBlu SBrw SEND WGer WHer XPep
§ - 'Tweedledum' (v)	CAlb CDoC CTrC CWib ECou EHoe GGar MOak SSto
virgata	CHEx ECou GGar GQui GSki GTSp WCot XPep
- var. ***laxiflora***	WHer
- var. ***lineata***	CDoC CPle ECou ECrN GGar NLar SEND SMur WDin WPic WSHC
- - 'Dartonii'	CBcs ECou EHol GGar MBlu SLPl WSHC
viscosa	CPle GGar
§ 'Waikariensis'	CBot CMHG CPLG CPle CTrC ECou GGar IDee LRHS SBrw SChu SEND SLon WCFE WDin WGer WPat

Oligoneuron see *Solidago*

Oligostachyum (*Poaceae*)

lubricum	see *Semiarundinaria lubrica*

olive see *Olea europaea*

Olsynium (*Iridaceae*)

§	***biflorum***	WCot
§	***douglasii*** ♀H4	CBro CMea EBee EDAr EHyt ELan EPot ETow GCrs GEdr LTwo NMen NRya SIng WAbe WCot
	- 'Album'	CMea EHyt EPot GCrs GEdr NMen NRya NSla WCot
	- var. ***inflatum***	EWes
§	***filifolium***	NWCA
§	***junceum***	CFil MDKP SBla WCot WPGP
	- JCA 12289	MTho
	- JCA 14211	CFir
	lyckolmii **new**	WCot

Omphalodes (*Boraginaceae*)

	cappadocica ♀H4	CBos CElw EBee EBrs ECha EPot ESis GKir LLWP LPio LRHS NBro NCGa NCob NFor NLon NPer SGar SPer SRms SSpi WBrk WPat WSSM
	- 'Alba'	GKir LLWP
	- 'Anthea Bloom'	GBuc IBlr NEgg
	- 'Blue Rug'	IHMH
	- 'Cherry Ingram' ♀H4	More than 30 suppliers
	- 'Cherry Ingram' variegated (v) **new**	CFir
	- 'Lilac Mist'	CElw CLAP CPom EBee EMan LLWP MRav NCob SBch SRms SSvw SWvt WPnP WTin
	- 'Parisian Skies'	CElw CLAP
	- 'Starry Eyes'	More than 30 suppliers
	kuzinskyanae **new**	WGwG
§	***linifolia*** ♀H4	CMea CSpe EMag NMen SBch
	- alba	see *O. linifolia*
	lojkae	NSla SBla SOkd WLin
	luciliae	CLAP WHoo
	nitida	EMon GGar NRya SSpi
	verna	More than 30 suppliers
	- 'Alba'	CBot CBre CDes EBee EChP ECha ELan EMon ENot EPfP GAbr GBBs LAst LRHS MHar MTho NCGa NChi NCot NLar SPer SRms SSvw SWvt WBor WFar WWpP
	- 'Elfenauge'	CMil EBee EMon EPPr NBir NCot NRya
	- grandiflora	WCot

Omphalogramma (*Primulaceae*)

delavayi	GCrs GFle

Oncostema see *Scilla*

onion see *Allium cepa*

Onixotis (*Colchicaceae*)

stricta	CPLG
triquetra	WCot

Onobrychis (*Papilionaceae*)

cornuta **new**	EBee
tournefortii	EBee
viciifolia	EBee EMan MGol MSal SECG WBWf

Onoclea (*Woodsiaceae*)

§	***intermedia***	EMon
	sensibilis ♀H4	More than 30 suppliers
	- copper	CFil CHEx CRow SBla WPGP

Ononis (*Papilionaceae*)

repens	CArn MBow MSal NMir
rotundifolia	CWCL MSal
spinosa	CPom EBee EWin EWll LRav MHer MSal NMir WFar WPer XPep

Onopordum (*Asteraceae*)

	acanthium	More than 30 suppliers
	arabicum	see *O. nervosum*
	bracteatum	WPer
	illyricum **new**	WCot
§	***nervosum*** ♀H4	CArn CSpe EBee NBur SRms WFar

Onosma (*Boraginaceae*)

alborosea	CMdw CPom CSev ECha EGoo EVFa GBri GCal GEdr NLAp NMRc SAga SChu WEas WKif WPGP WPat
conferta BWJ 7735	WCru
helvetica	EMan WPat
taurica ♀H4	MOne NBir

Onychium (*Adiantaceae*)

contiguum	WAbe
japonicum	CFil EFer EFtx GQui SBla SChu SRms WAbe
- 'Dali'	SBla

Ophiopogon ✿ (*Convallariaceae*)

	BWJ 8244 from Vietnam	WCru
	from Vietnam	CFil
	'Black Dragon'	see *O. planiscapus* 'Nigrescens'
	bodinieri	CBct ERos EWes LEdu SMac WRHF
	- B&L 12505	CLAP EBee EPPr EPla
	aff. ***caulescens*** HWJ 590	WCru
	chingii	EMon EPla GCal LEdu SCnR
	- 'Chinese Whisper'	EMon
	formosanus	CFil CPrp GBin
	- B&SWJ 3659	WCru
	'Gin-ryu'	see *Liriope spicata* 'Gin-ryu'
	graminifolius	see *Liriope muscari*
	intermedius	CBct EBee EPla ERos ESis MSte WCot WPGP
	- GWJ 9387	WCru
	- HWJK 2093	WCru
§	- 'Argenteomarginatus'	ERos EWes WPGP
	- parviflorus	NSti
	- 'Variegatus'	see *O. intermedius* 'Argenteomarginatus'
§	***jaburan***	EBee EShb LAma LEdu MSte WPnP
	- 'Variegatus'	see *O. jaburan* 'Vittatus'
§	- 'Vittatus' (v)	CMHG CPrp CSBt EBee EHoe ELan EMan EPfP EShb EWes GSki ITer LEdu LRHS MCCP MGos NBlu SAga SPer SYvo WCot WFar
	japonicus	CBro EPPr EPfP EPla EShb GSki LEdu NSti XPep
	- B&SWJ 1842	WCru
	- 'Albus'	CLAP
	- 'Compactus'	CDoC CFil CStu EBee LRHS SMac SPla SSpi WPGP WWye
	- 'Kigimafukiduma'	CBgR CBrm EBee MRav NLar SGSe
	- 'Kyoto'	GSki
	- 'Minor'	CBct CEnd CSBt EPfP EPla NLar SMac WPGP
	- 'Nanus Variegatus' (v)	CDes EBee EMon
	- 'Nippon'	CM&M CPrp EBee EHoe EPPr EPza LAst LPio LRHS MSph MWgw
	- 'Tama-ryu'	EHyt
*	- 'Tama-ryu Number Two'	ECho EPPr SIng
	- 'Torafu' (v)	EPPr

*	- 'Variegatus' (v)	CPrp LEdu SIng SLPl
	longifolius 'Takashi-shimomura' (v) **new**	WCot
	malcolmsonii B&SWJ 5264	WCru
	planiscapus	CEnd CFee CKno CMHG CPLG CSWP CSev CStu EBee EPla GAbr GCal MSte MTho NBro NLon SPla STre WBVN WMoo
*	- 'Albovariegatus'	SPoG
	- 'Green Dragon'	ELan
	- ***leucanthus***	EPPr WCot
	- 'Little Tabby' (v)	CDes CFil CLAP CSpe EBee EPla MDKP MMoz NPro SAga WCot WDyG WGwG WPGP WTin
*	- ***minimus***	ERos
§	- 'Nigrescens' ♀H4	More than 30 suppliers
	- 'Silver Ribbon'	MDKP SGar
	scaber B&SWJ 1871	WCru
	'Spring Gold'	EMon
	'Tama-hime-nishiki' (v)	EMon
	wallichianus	EMar EPPr EPla EVFa GIBF GKev NLar SGar SSpi WCot WPGP

Ophrys (*Orchidaceae*)

	apifera	CHdy WHer

Oplismenus (*Poaceae*)

§	***africanus*** 'Variegatus' (v) ♀H1	CHal
	undulatifolius	NBro

Opuntia ✿ (*Cactaceae*)

	compressa	see *O. humifusa*
	erinacea var. ***utahensis*** x ***polycantha*** NNS 99-263	WCot
§	***humifusa***	EBee NPal SChr SMad WMul
	microdasys **new**	SWal
	- var. ***albospina*** **new**	SWal
	polyacantha	EOas SChr SPlb
	rhodantha	see *O. polyacantha*

orange, sour or Seville see *Citrus aurantium*

orange, sweet see *Citrus sinensis*

Orbea (*Asclepiadaceae*)

	variegata ♀H1	EShb

Orchis (*Orchidaceae*)

	anthropophora	EFEx
	elata	see *Dactylorhiza elata*
	foliosa	see *Dactylorhiza foliosa*
	fuchsii	see *Dactylorhiza fuchsii*
	laxiflora	see *Anacamptis laxiflora*
	maculata	see *Dactylorhiza maculata*
	maderensis	see *Dactylorhiza foliosa*
	majalis	see *Dactylorhiza majalis*
§	***mascula***	CHdy WHer
	morio	see *Anacamptis morio*

oregano see *Origanum vulgare*

Oreopanax (*Araliaceae*)

	dactylifolius	LEdu

Oreopteris (*Thelypteridaceae*)

§	***limbosperma***	SRms WRic

Oresitrophe (*Saxifragaceae*)

	rupifraga	WCru

Origanum ✿ (*Lamiaceae*)

	from Santa Cruz	CArn
	from Yunnan, China	NWoo
	acutidens	EHyt WCHb XPep
	amanum ♀H2-3	CPBP CStu EBee EHyt ETow EWes LRHS NBir NMen SBla SChu SIgm WAbe WHoo WLin WPat WWye
	- var. ***album***	ECho SBla WAbe WPat
	x ***applii***	EDAr ELau
	'Barbara Tingey'	CBot CSpe CWCL EBee EChP EHyt ELan ETow EWes ITim LBee LPhx LRHS MHer MNrw MSte MTho NWCA SAga SBla SChu SUsu WAbe WCFE WCru WHoo WPat
I	'Bristol Cross'	CStr EBee ECha GBar WPat
	'Buckland'	CHea EBee EDAr EHyt EPot LPhx LRHS MHer MSte NWCA SBla WLin WPat
	caespitosum	see *O. vulgare* 'Nanum'
§	***calcaratum***	EMan ETow LRHS MTho SBla SMrm WAbe WPat
	creticum	see *O. vulgare* subsp. *hirtum*
	dictamnus	CArn EEls EHyt GPoy LRHS LTwo MDKP SBla SHDw WAbe WJek WLin XPep
	'Dingle Fairy'	CM&M EBee EGoo ELan EMan EPot EVFa EWes GBar MHer MLLN MMHG MNrw MTho NBir NWCA SBch SIde SIng WGwG WMoo WWye
	'Emma Stanley' **new**	WAbe
	'Erntedank'	EBee
	'Frank Tingey'	ECho EHyt ELan LTwo SUsu WAbe
	'Fritz Kummert' **new**	NCGa
	'Gold Splash'	EDAr EPfP GBar SIde
	'Goudgeel'	CStr
	heracleoticum L.	see *O. vulgare* subsp. *hirtum*
	'Hot and Spicy' **new**	EOHP EWin NPri
§	x ***hybridinum***	SBla WLin WPat
	'Ingolstadt'	SAga WWye
	'Kent Beauty'	More than 30 suppliers
	kopetdaghense	XPep
	laevigatum ♀H3	CArn CLyd CMHG CStr ELan EPfP EPot MHar MHer NBro NMir NPer NWCA SAga SGar SIde SMer SUsu WMoo WPer WSHC WWhi XPep
	- 'Herrenhausen' ♀H4	More than 30 suppliers
	- 'Hopleys'	More than 30 suppliers
	- 'Purple Charm'	EBee ELau
	- 'Springwood'	WWye
	majorana	CArn CHrt CSev ELan ELau GWCH MBow MChe MHer MSal SECG SIde WJek WPer WSel WWye XPep
I	- 'Aureum'	SWal
	- Pagoda Bells = 'Lizbell'PBR	EDAr SIng
	'Marchants Seedling' **new**	SMHy
	microphyllum	CArn CFee CMHG EDAr EHyt GBar LRHS MTho NMen SBla SChu SIng SOkd WAbe WCru WPat WWye XPep
	minutiflorum	ECho LTwo
	'Norton Gold'	CBre EBee EBrs ECha EPot GBar GBuc LRHS MBow NPer SIde
	'Nymphenburg'	CFee CSam EBee EChP EMan LSou MSte NCob SChu SIde SMrm SOkd WCru WHer WWhi
	onites	CArn CHby CWan ELau EUnu GBar GPoy IHMH ILis MChe MHer MSal MWat SIde SPlb WBrk WGwG WHer WJek WPer WSel WWye XPep

- 'Noa' **new** — EWin
'Pilgrim' — SIde
'Pink Cloud' — EDAr
* ***prismaticum*** — GBar
pulchellum — see *O.* x *hybridinum*
'Purple Cloud' — EDAr NBir
'Rosenkuppel' — CMea CPrp EBee EBrs EChP ECha ELan EPot ETow GCal IHMH LPhx MHer MRav MSte NCGa NGHP SBla SChu SMad SMrm SOkh SPla SPlb WGHP WMnd WMoo WTel WWye XPep
'Rotkugel' — CPrp EBee EBrs EChP EMan EWin LPhx LSou MBow MSte WCru
rotundifolium ♀H4 — CArn CDes CMea EBee EDAr ELan LEdu MDKP MHer NBir SBch SBla SChu WAbe
- hybrid — MDKP
scabrum — CArn WWye
- subsp. ***pulchrum*** — CStu XPep
- - 'Newleaze' — SBch WHoo
sipyleum — EBee EHyt NWCA SBla WAbe
syriacum — XPep
'Tinpenny Pink' — WTin
tournefortii — see *O. calcaratum*
tytthanthum — XPep
villosum — see *Thymus villosus*
virens — CArn GBar ILis MCCP
vulgare — CAgr CArn CHrt CRWN CSev CWan EDAr EMag GBar GKir GMaP GPoy IHMH MBar MBow MChe MHer NBlu NBro NLan NMir NPri SGar SIde SPlb SWal WHer WPer WWye XPep
- from Israel — ELau
- 'Acorn Bank' — CArn CBod CPrp CWan EBee EGoo EGra ELau EShb EUnu EWes EWin MHer SAga SIde WCHb WGwG WHer WJek
- var. ***album*** — CElw CStr MHer WHer WJek
- - 'Aureum Album' — WHer
- 'Aureum' ♀H4 — More than 30 suppliers
- 'Aureum Crispum' — CPrp CWan ECha EDAr EGoo ELau GAbr GBar GPoy IHMH ILis NBid NBlu NGHP SBch SIde WGwG WJek WRha WSel WWpP WWye
- 'Compactum' — More than 30 suppliers
- 'Corinne Tremaine' (v) — NBir WHer
- 'Country Cream' (v) — More than 30 suppliers
- 'Curly Gold' — MBow MWat
- ***formosanum*** B&SWJ 3180 — WCru
§ - 'Gold Tip' (v) — CMea CSev CStr EBee EDAr EHoe ELau EUnu GBar IHMH ILis MHer NArg NGHP NPri SIde SPlb WCAu WCHb WFar WHer WWpP WWye
- 'Golden Shine' — CM&M EOHP EWes NGHP WRha
§ - subsp. ***hirtum*** — CArn CHby EOHP GPoy LEdu MSal NWoo SPlb WJek WPer WWpP XPep
- - 'Greek' — CAgr CBod CPrp CWan ELau EUnu GWCH MBow MHer NGHP NPri SECG WGwG
§ - 'Nanum' — CStr GBar LRHS WJek
- 'Nyamba' — GPoy
- 'Polyphant' (v) — CMHG CSev EBee EChP EDAr EMan EOHP GBar LPio MLLN NBir WBrE WCHb WHer WJek WMoo WSel WWye
- 'Thumble's Variety' — CBod CElw CMea CPrp EBee ECha EGoo EHoe EMag GBar GKir IHMH LPhx LRHS MBri MHer MRav NCob SIde SSvw WEas WMnd WMoo WWpP XPep
- 'Tomintoul' — GPoy
- 'Variegatum' — see *O. vulgare* 'Gold Tip'
- 'Webb's White' — GBar
- 'White Charm' **new** — EOHP
- yellow, long-leaved — ECha
'White Cloud' — EDAr
'Z'Attar' — MHer SIde

Orites (*Proteaceae*)

myrtoidea — CFil

Orixa (*Rutaceae*)

japonica — CBot EBee EPfP SSpi WFar WPGP
- 'Variegata' (v) — EPfP LRHS

Orlaya (*Apiaceae*)

grandiflora — CHrt CSpe MNrw SBch SUsu WCot WFar

Ornithogalum (*Hyacinthaceae*)

arabicum — CBro EChP EPfP EUJe LAma LRHS MBri MLLN SPet WCot WDav
arcuatum — CMon WCot
balansae — see *O. oligophyllum*
caudatum — see *O. longibracteatum*
chionophilum — CFwr EBee
ciliiferum — CMon
collinum — WWst
dubium ♀H1 — CBgR EBrs NBlu WCot
fimbriatum — EBee WCot
lanceolatum — CAvo EHyt WCot
§ ***longibracteatum*** — CHEx CStu EBee EPem SChr SYvo WGwG
magnum — CAvo CMea EBee EChP WPnP
- 'Saguramo' — WCot
montanum — WWst
'Mount Everest' — CFwr
'Mount Fuji' **new** — CFwr
nanum — see *O. sigmoideum*
narbonense — CFwr EBee GBuc GFlt LPhx LRHS SBch WCot WDav
nutans ♀H4 — CAvo CBro CFwr CMea EBee EBrs EChP EMan EMon EPfP EPot GFlt LAma LPhx MAvo MEHN MLLN MNrw NMen WAul WBrk WCot WGHP WPer
§ ***oligophyllum*** — CBgR CMea CStu EBee EPot MNrw NWCA SMeo WCot WDav
oreoides — WWst
orthophyllum — CStu WCot
- subsp. ***kochii*** — WWst
ponticum — ERos
pyramidale — CDes CFwr CSpe EBee EChP EPot MNrw WCot
- AB&S 4600 from Morocco **new** — CMon
pyrenaicum — CAvo CPLG CStu ECha ERos WCot WShi
reverchonii — CDes EBee
- AB&S 4400 from Morocco **new** — CMon
- AB&S 4600 from Morocco — CMon
saundersiae — EBee
schmalhausenii — WWst
sessiliflorum AB&S 4400 from Morocco **new** — CMon
-AB&S 4619 from Morocco — CMon
sibthorpii — see *O. sigmoideum*
§ ***sigmoideum*** — CStu WAbe
sintenisii — EBee WWst
sphaerocarpum **new** — WCot

tenuifolium — see *O. orthophyllum*
- subsp. ***aridum*** **new** — WWst
thyrsoides ♀H1 — EPfP LAma LRHS MBri SPet WWol
umbellatum — CBro CNic CPLG EBrs ELan EMon EPfP GFlt GPoy LAma LRHS MBri MNrw NBlu NMen SPer SRms WBVN WCot WFar WPer WShi WWye

Orontium (*Araceae*)

aquaticum — CBen CDWL CWat EHon EMFW GAbr LNCo LPBA NArg NLar WPnP WWpP

Orostachys (*Crassulaceae*)

furusei — EMan GGar WCot WFar
iwarenge — CStu
§ ***spinosa*** — CStu EMan ETow NMen WCot WFar WRos

Oroxylum (*Bignoniaceae*)

indicum **new** — CArn

Orphium (*Gentianaceae*)

frutescens — CPLG EShb

Orthrosanthus (*Iridaceae*)

chimboracensis — CDes CFir EBee EMan WCot WFar WPGP WPer WPic
- JCA 13743 — CPou
laxus — CFir CPle EBee ERos EWsh GBuc GFlt GMac MAvo NEgg SMad WPic
multiflorus — CDes CElw CWCL EBee WPGP
polystachyus — CAby CPle CPom CRez CSpe EBee EChP EMan ERos MAvo SGSe WPic WSHC

Oryzopsis (*Poaceae*)

lessoniana — see *Anemanthele lessoniana*
miliacea — CBig CHrt ECha EHoe EMan EPPr GFor WCot WPGP
paradoxa — EBee EPPr EShb

Oscularia (*Aizoaceae*)

§ ***deltoides*** ♀H1-2 — CStu EUJe MRav WCot WEas

Osmanthus (*Oleaceae*)

americanus — WBcn
armatus — CAbP CFil CTri EPfP MWya WFar
§ x ***burkwoodii*** ♀H4 — More than 30 suppliers
§ ***decorus*** — CBcs CSBt CTri ELan EPfP GKir MGos MRav NWea SPer SPla SSta WBcn WDin WFar
- 'Angustifolius' — WBcn
delavayi ♀H4 — More than 30 suppliers
- 'Latifolius' — EPfP GKir LRHS SLon WBcn WFar
forrestii — see *O. yunnanensis*
x ***fortunei*** — CPle EPfP LRHS SLPl WFar
fragrans — EShb
- f. ***thunbergii*** — SSpi
§ ***heterophyllus*** — CBcs CDul EMil ENot EPfP MBar MRav MWya NFor SPer SReu SRms SSpi SSta WDin WFar XPep
§ - all gold — CAbP CDoC EGra LAst MBlu SMer SPer SPla SPoG WSHC
- 'Argenteomarginatus' — see *O. heterophyllus* 'Variegatus'
§ - 'Aureomarginatus' (v) — CBcs CDoC CFil CHar CMHG CSBt EBee EHoe EMil EPfP LRHS MWya SHBN SLon SPer SPoG
- 'Aureus' misapplied — see *O. heterophyllus* all gold
- 'Aureus' Rehder — see *O. heterophyllus* 'Aureomarginatus'
§ - 'Goshiki' (v) — More than 30 suppliers
N - 'Gulftide' ♀H4 — CDoC EBee ECrN EMil EPfP LRHS MGos MWht NLar SCoo WFar
- 'Purple Shaft' — CAbP ELan EPfP LRHS MAsh
- 'Purpureus' — CAbP CBcs CBot CDoC CMHG CSam CWib ECrN EGra EHoe EPfP LRHS MBri MDun MGos MRav MSph NDlv SCoo SLim SLon SPoG SSpi SWal WDin WRHF WWeb
- 'Rotundifolius' — CBcs CFil
- Tricolor — see *O. heterophyllus* 'Goshiki'
§ - 'Variegatus' (v) ♀H4 — CBcs CBot CBrm CSBt CWib EBee ECrN EGra ELan EMil ENot EPfP LAst LRHS LSRN MAsh MBar MGos MRav SLim SPer SPla SPoG SReu SSta WBVN WDin WFar WHar WPat
ilicifolius — see *O. heterophyllus*
serrulatus — CAbP CBot CFil NLar WPGP
suavis — CFil EPfP GKir LRHS NLar SPoG SSpi
§ ***yunnanensis*** — EPfP LRHS MBlu SAPC SArc SSpi WBcn WFar WPGP

x *Osmarea* (*Oleaceae*)

burkwoodii — see *Osmanthus* x *burkwoodii*

Osmaronia see *Oemleria*

Osmorhiza (*Apiaceae*)

aristata B&SWJ 1607 — WCru

Osmunda ✿ (*Osmundaceae*)

cinnamomea ♀H4 — CFil CFwr CLAP CPLG EBee EFtx EWes GBin NBPC SSpi WPGP WRic
claytoniana ♀H4 — CAby CFil CLAP CPLG CRez EBee EPfP GCal MAsh NBid NLar NOGN NVic WCru WMoo WRic
japonica — EBee
lancea — NLar
regalis ♀H4 — More than 30 suppliers
§ - 'Cristata' ♀H4 — CFil CFwr CLAP CPLG EBee ELan GBin GCal LPBA MRav NBid WFib WMoo WPGP WRic
- 'Purpurascens' — More than 30 suppliers
- var. ***spectabilis*** — CLAP WRic
§ - 'Undulata' — ELan GBin LPBA WFib

Osteomeles (*Rosaceae*)

schweriniae — EMan
- B&L 12360 — CPle SAga
subrotunda — CFil

Osteospermum ✿ (*Asteraceae*)

'African Queen' — see *O.* 'Nairobi Purple'
'Almach' (Springstar Series) **new** — LAst
'Antares'PBR (Springstar Series) — LAst
'Arctur'PBR — CBcs
barberae hort. — see *O. jucundum*
'Blackthorn Seedling' — see *O. jucundum* 'Blackthorn Seedling'
'Blue Streak' — NBur
'Brickell's Hybrid' — see *O.* 'Chris Brickell'
'Brightside'PBR (Side Series) — WWol
'Buttermilk' ♀H1+3 — CHal ELan LRHS MBri SMrm WWlt
'Cannington Katrina' — MOak
'Cannington Roy' — CMHG CSam CTbh ECtt EPfP MBri NBur NLon WAbe
caulescens hort. — see *O.* 'White Pim'
§ 'Chris Brickell' — CHal GCal MOak MSte NBur
'Countryside' (Side Series) — WWol
'Darkside' (Side Series) — WWol

	ecklonis	CHll CTbh EChP GGar GMaP IBlr ISea MHer NBro NGdn WFar WPer
	- var. ***prostratum***	see *O.* 'White Pim'
	'Edna Bond'	WEas
	fruticosum	XPep
I	- 'Album'	XPep
	'Gemma'PBR (Springstar Series)	MBNS SMrm WGor
	'Giles Gilbey' (v)	CHal CPLG CTbh MBNS MOak NBur
	'Gold Sparkler' (v)	LRHS SMrm
	'Helen Dimond'	COtt WWeb
	'Hopleys' ♀H3-4	MBNS MHer MWrn SEND
	'Irish'	EPot IGor LSou MWrn
	'James Elliman'	MOak
	'Jewel' (v)	COtt
§	***jucundum*** ♀H3-4	CMHG CMea CPLG CWCL EChP ECha EPfP EWTr LRHS MBow MNrw MRav MTis MWgw NBir NChi NEgg NGdn NPer SEND SIng SPlb SRms WPat WWeb WWpP
§	- 'Blackthorn Seedling' ♀H3-4	CMea ECha MBri NFla NGdn NLon SAga SBla
	- var. ***compactum***	CHEx CLyd CPBP MBri MHar NPer SMrm SPur WAbe WHoo
	- 'Elliott's Form'	MBri
	- 'Jackarandum'	MDKP
§	- 'Killerton Pink'	CMHG WPer
§	- 'Langtrees' ♀H3-4	SMrm
	'Keia' (Springstar Series) **new**	LAst
	'Killerton Pink'	see *O. jucundum* 'Killerton Pink'
§	'Lady Leitrim' ♀H3-4	CHEx CHrt ECha EPfP GBri GCra GGar IBlr MArl MBNS MBnl MBow MOak MWrn NPer SAga SChu SSvw WAbe WCAu WWeb WWpP
	'Langtrees'	see *O. jucundum* 'Langtrees'
§	'Nairobi Purple'	CDoC CFee CHEx CHal CPLG ELan GGar MOak NBur
	Nasinga Purple = 'Aksullo'PBR **new**	NBlu
	Nasinga Series	CElw
	Orania Terracotta = 'Akterra'	SGar
	'Pale Face'	see *O.* 'Lady Leitrim'
	'Peggyi'	see *O.* 'Nairobi Purple'
I	'Pink Superbum' **new**	CHEx
	'Pink Whirls' ♀H1+3	CBot CHal LRHS MBri NBur
	'Pollux'PBR (Springstar Series)	MBNS
	'Port Wine'	see *O.* 'Nairobi Purple'
	'Seaside'PBR (Side Series)	WWol
	'Seaspray'	COtt
	'Silver Sparkler' (v) ♀H1+3	CSLe ELan EShb EWin LRHS MBNS MHer MOak NBur SChu SSto WBrE
	'Snow White'	CHal
	'Sparkler'	CHEx MSte
	'Stardust'PBR	COtt LRHS NPer SCoo SPoG
	'Stringston Gemma'	CHal
	'Sunny Alex'PBR	LRHS
	'Sunny Amelia'PBR	LAst
	'Sunny Dark Martha'PBR	LAst
	'Sunny Martha'PBR	LAst LRHS
	'Sunny Nathalie'PBR **new**	LAst
	'Sunny Serena'PBR	LAst
*	'Superbum'	CHEx
I	'Superbum' x 'Lady Leitrim' **new**	CHEx
	'Svelte'	MSte
	(Symphony Series)	CHVG EShb LIck LSou SCoo
	Banana Symphony = 'Sekiin47' **new**	
	- Cream Symphony = 'Seidacre'PBR	CBcs LAst LSou
	- 'Lemon Symphony'PBR	LAst LIck MBNS SCoo
	- Milk Symphony = 'Seremi' **new**	SCoo
	- Orange Symphony = 'Seimora'PBR	CBcs CTbh EShb LAst LIck LSou MBNS SMrm
	- Peach Symphony = 'Seitope'PBR	CBcs LAst LIck LSou MBNS
	'Tauranga'	see *O.* 'Whirlygig'
	'Tresco Peggy'	see *O.* 'Nairobi Purple'
	'Tresco Pink'	IBlr
	'Tresco Purple'	see *O.* 'Nairobi Purple'
	'Vega'	LAst WGor
	'Weetwood' ♀H3-4	CMHG CPLG ECtt EPot EShb EWin MBNS MBri MHer MSte SAga SBla SMrm WAbe WEas WWeb
	'Westside' (Side Series)	WWol
§	'Whirlygig' ♀H1+3	CHal MBri MHer MOak
§	'White Pim' ♀H3-4	CHll CMHG ELan LRHS NPer SChu SDix SPer SUsu XPep
	'Wildside'PBR (Side Series)	EShb WWol
	'Wine Purple'	see *O.* 'Nairobi Purple'
	Wisley hybrids	WEas
	'Wisley Pink'	CStr EPyc
	'Zaire'PBR **new**	NBlu
	'Zambesi'	LRHS
	'Zaurak' (Springstar Series) **new**	LAst
	'Zimba'PBR	ELan LRHS
	'Zulu'PBR	LRHS MHer

Ostrowskia (*Campanulaceae*)

	magnifica	MTho

Ostrya (*Corylaceae*)

	carpinifolia	CAgr CBcs CDul CLnd CMCN CTho IMGH LRHS MBar MBlu NLar SBLw WDin WNor WOrn
	japonica	CFil CMCN NLar
	virginiana	CFil CMCN ECrN EPfP IMGH WNor

Otanthus (*Asteraceae*)

	maritimus	XPep

Otatea (*Poaceae*)

	aztecorum	CFil

Othonna (*Asteraceae*)

	capensis	CHal
§	***cheirifolia***	CBot CMea CSam CSev EGoo ELan EMan EVFa MFOX NBir NFor SIgm SPer WBrk WCot WEas WPer XPep

Othonnopsis see *Othonna*

Ourisia (*Scrophulariaceae*)

	caespitosa	GCrs GKev IBlr NMen NRya
	- var. ***gracilis***	GEdr GGar GTou IBlr NMen
§	***coccinea***	EMan GAbr GBuc GCra GEdr GGar GKev GMac IBlr LRHS NBir NGby NRya SSpi WAbe
	crosbyi	GEdr GGar IBlr
	crosbyi x ***macrocarpa***	IBlr
	elegans	see *O. coccinea*
	lactea	IBlr
	'Loch Ewe'	CPLG GAbr GBuc GCrs GEdr GGar IBlr MDun NCGa WCru WPGP
	macrocarpa	IBlr
	macrophylla	EBee GBin GBuc GCra GGar GKev IBlr IGor WAbe
	macrophylla x ***modesta***	IBlr

	microphylla	CGra NWCA WAbe
*	- f. ***alba***	EHyt WAbe
	modesta	IBlr
	polyantha F&W 8487	CPBP WAbe
	- 'Cliftonville Scarlet' **new**	CPBP EHyt WAbe
	sessilifolia **new**	GKev
	'Snowflake' 🏆H4	EPot GAbr GBin GCrs GEdr GFlt GKev IBlr MDun MOne NBir NMen WAbe

Oxalis ✿ (*Oxalidaceae*)

	F&W 8673	CPBP
	acetosella	CHid CMea CNat CRWN MBow MHer WHer WShi
	- var. ***subpurpurascens***	WCot
	adenophylla 🏆H4	More than 30 suppliers
	- 'Brenda Anderson'	SBla
	- dark	MTho
	anomala	CMon EMan ERos WCot
	arborescens	CHEx
§	***articulata***	EMan ETow MTho NPer SEND
	- 'Alba'	ETow LRHS
	- 'Aureoreticulata'	MTho
	- 'Festival'	EBee WCot
	'Beatrice Anderson'	EHyt GCrs MTho NJOw NMen SBla WAbe
	bowiei	CMon CPBP CStu EPot
	'Bowles' White'	MTho
	brasiliensis	CPBP CStu EPot MTho NJOw NMen
	brick-orange	WCot
	chrysantha	IHMH SIng WAbe
	compacta F&W 8011	CPBP
	corniculata var. ***atropurpurea***	MTho
	'Dark Eye'	GCrs
	debilis 'Aureoreticulata'	WCot
	deppei	see *O. tetraphylla*
§	***depressa***	CMon CStu CTri EBee EPot EWes GEdr GSki LTwo MTho NBir NEgg NJOw NMen NRya NSla SIng SRms WBrE WCot WFar
	- 'Irish Mist'	EBee
	ecklonianа **new**	CMon
*	- var. ***sonderi***	WCot
	enneaphylla 🏆H4	CElw EMan EPot GAbr GCrs GGar LRHS MTho NMen NRya
	- 'Alba'	CGra EBrs EHyt ERos ETow GBuc GGar ITim NMen NSla WAbe WIvy WLin
I	- 'Hythe Seedling'	EHyt
	- 'Lady Elizabeth'	SBla
	- 'Minutifolia'	ERos GCrs LRHS LTwo MTho NMen NRya NSla WIvy
*	- 'Minutifolia Rosea'	CGra
	- 'Rosea'	EHyt EPot ERos MTho NRya NSla SBla
	- 'Ruth Tweedie'	NSla
	- 'Sheffield Swan'	CGra EHyt NMen SBla SOkd WAbe
	enneaphylla x ***adenophylla***	see *O.* 'Matthew Forrest'
	europaea	GWCH
	falcatula	WCot
	'Fanny'	EBee
	flava	CMon LAma NJOw
	floribunda hort.	see *O. articulata*
	fourcadii	WCot
	geminata	NBir
	glabra	CMon CPBP
	'Gwen McBride'	GCrs SBla WAbe
	'Hemswell Knight'	NMen WAbe
	hirta	CDes CMon CPBP MTho NJOw
	- 'Gothenburg'	CPBP EMan ERos MTho NMen
	imbricata	CMon EPot LTwo
	inops	see *O. depressa*
	'Ione Hecker' 🏆H4	CGra CLyd EHyt EPot ERos GCrs GEdr GGar GTou ITim MTho NMen NRya NSla NWCA NWoo SBla SIgm WAbe WIvy WLin WPnP
*	***karroica***	CMon WCot
§	***laciniata***	CGra EHyt ERos GCrs MTho NMen NSla SBla WAbe
	- dark	EHyt
	- 'Seven Bells'	CGra SBla WAbe
	lactea double	see *O. magellanica* 'Nelson'
	lasiandra	EPot ERos
	loricata **new**	EHyt
	magellanica	CMHG CPom CRow CSpe CTri EBla ESis GGar LBee MTho SIng SPlb WFar WPer
	- 'Flore Pleno'	see *O. magellanica* 'Nelson'
§	- 'Nelson' (d)	CNic CPLG CRow CSpe CStu EBee EMan EWes GCal GGar GMac IFro LBee LRHS MTho NBir NBro NJOw NPer NWoo SSvw WCru WMoo WPer WPnP WPrP
	massoniana	CMon SIng
§	'Matthew Forrest'	CPBP WAbe
	megalorrhiza	SChr
	melanosticta	CMon
	monophylla **new**	CMon
	nahuelhuapiensis F&W 8469	CPBP
	namaquana	WCot
	obtusa	CLyd CMon CNic CStu EBee EMan EPot ESis ETow MTho SCnR WCot
	- apricot	WCot
	oregana	CDes CNic CRez CRow EBee GBuc GGar GMac WBor WCot WCru WPGP WPrP WSHC
	- f. ***smalliana***	EBee EWes WCru
	palmifrons	CMon CPBP EPot LTwo MTho NJOw
	patagonica	EPot ERos GCrs NMen WPnP
	perdicaria	CBro CMon CNic CStu EHyt EMan ERos ETow EWes LRHS MTho NJOw SBch WAbe
	pes-caprae	CMon
	- 'Flore Pleno' (d) **new**	CMon
	polyphylla **new**	CMon
§	***purpurea***	IHMH WAbe
	- 'Ken Aslet'	CBro CFee CLyd CNic CPBP CStu EHyt EMan EPot GCrs GFlt LTwo NJOw NLar SIng WAbe
	regnellii	see *O. triangularis* subsp. *papilionacea*
	rosea hort.	see *O. rubra*
§	***rubra***	EBee
	semiloba	CMon EBee EMan GCal WCot
	speciosa	see *O. purpurea*
	squamata	NLAp WPat
	squamosoradicosa	see *O. laciniata*
	stipularis	CMon CNic
	succulenta Barnéoud	CHII CSpe
	'Sunset Velvet' **new**	LAst
	'Superstar'	WAbe
§	***tetraphylla***	CAgr CM&M CMon EBee EPot GSki LAma LRHS MBri MTho NEgg NOrc NPer WRha
	- ***alba***	EBee
	- 'Iron Cross'	CFwr CHEx EBee EMan EPot ESis GSki LAma MMHG NBir NJOw WBVN WBrE WHil
	triangularis	CAgr CHEx CStu EOHP EShb LAma NBir NEgg NPer WBrE WFar
	- 'Cupido'	EBee GGar WPer
	- 'Mijke'	EBee

§	- subsp. ***papilionacea*** ♀H1	CMon EBee EMan EUJe GSki LAma LRHS MMHG NEgg NJOw
	- - 'Atropurpurea'	CSpe EBee WBVN WCot
*	- - ***rosea***	EBee EMan WCot
	- subsp. ***triangularis***	EBee EUJe NJOw
	tuberosa	EUnu GPoy ILis LEdu
	- 'Fat Red'	EOHP
	- 'Fat White'	EOHP EUnu
	- pink	EUnu
	- red	EUnu
	'Ute'	CGra GEdr SOkd
	valdiviensis	EMan MDKP NBur
	versicolor ♀H1	CFwr CPBP CSpe CStu EHyt EMan EPot ERos MTho NMen SBla SCnR SOkd SUsu WAbe WCot
	- 'Clove Ball' **new**	WPtf
	vulcanicola	CStu LSou SDix WDyG
	zeekoevleyensis	WCot

Oxera (Verbenaceae)

pulchella **new**	CPLN

Oxycoccus see *Vaccinium*

Oxydendrum (Ericaceae)

arboreum	CAbP CBcs CDoC CEnd CMCN ECrN EPfP GKir IDee IMGH LEdu MAsh MBri MGos NLar SBrw SPer SPoG SSpi SSta WCru WDin WFar WNor
- 'Chameleon'	EPfP LRHS SSpi SSta

Oxylobium (Papilionaceae)

ellipticum	ECou

Oxypetalum (Asclepiadaceae)

caeruleum	see *Tweedia caerulea*

Oxyria (Polygonaceae)

digyna	CAgr EMan GGar NBro NLar WCot WHer

Oxytropis (Papilionaceae)

deflexa var. ***deflexa***	LTwo
exscerta **new**	GIBF
lambertii	LTwo
maydelliana **new**	GIBF
megalantha	EMan NWCA
ochotensis **new**	GIBF
popoviana **new**	GIBF
pumilio **new**	GIBF
purpurea	EMan LTwo WSHC
shokanbetsuensis	EMan LTwo SOkd
uralensis	LTwo

Ozothamnus (Asteraceae)

	antennaria	WSHC
§	***coralloides*** ♀H2-3	EPot GCrs GGar NDlv NJOw NWCA SIng
§	'County Park Silver'	EWes GEdr GKev ITim MDKP NDlv NLAp NWCA WPat
§	***hookeri***	CAbb CDoC CMdw ECou GGar MBrN NLar NWCA SBrw SChu SPer WJek WPat
§	***ledifolius*** ♀H4	CBcs CDoC CMHG CPle ELan EPfP GGar GTou LRHS MBri NBir NBlu NLon NScw SBrw SChu SLon SPer SSpi WDin WHCG WHar WPat WSHC
§	***rosmarinifolius***	CBcs CDoC CMHG EBee ELan EPfP GGar IFro LRHS MSwo NLon SBrw SChu SPer WBrE WDin WEas WFar WHCG XPep
	- 'Kiandra'	ECou
	- 'Silver Jubilee' ♀H3	CBcs CDoC CEnd CHEx CSBt CSam CTrC EBee ECrN ELan EPfP LRHS MAsh MSwo NEgg NLon SBrw SHBN SLon SPer SPlb SPoG SRkn SSpi WDin WFar WHCG WKif XPep
	scutellifolius	ECou
§	***selago***	ECou EPot NRya WCot
	- var. ***intermedium***	GGar
	- 'Minor'	NWCA
§	- var. ***tumidus***	SIng
	'Sussex Silver'	SBrw
	'Threave Seedling'	CDoC CSam LRHS SBrw SPer SSpi
§	***thyrsoideus***	CPLG WFar

P

Pachyphragma (Brassicaceae)

§	***macrophyllum***	CPom CSev EBrs ECGP ECha EHrv ELan EWTr GCal IBlr LRHS MNFA MRav NCiC NLar NMRc NSti SSpi WCot WCru WEas WPGP WSHC

Pachyphytum (Crassulaceae)

oviferum **new**	SChr

Pachypodium (Apocynaceae)

bispinosum	CRoM
geayi ♀H1	CRoM SBig
horombense	CRoM
lamerei ♀H1	CRoM LToo MBri SBig
lealii subsp. ***saundersii***	CRoM LToo
namaquanum **new**	LToo
rosulatum var. ***gracilius***	CRoM LToo
succulentum	CRoM LToo

Pachysandra (Buxaceae)

axillaris	CLAP GCal SSpi
procumbens	CLAP EHrv EPla NLar SSpi WCot WCru
stylosa	CBct EPla MRav NLar SMad
terminalis	More than 30 suppliers
- 'Green Carpet' ♀H4	CAlb CBcs CDoC CSam CWib EBee ECot EGol ELan EPfP EWTr GKir IHMH LAst LRHS LSRN MAsh MBar MBri MGos MSwo NBlu NPro SMac SPer SPla SPoG SWvt WCAu
- 'Variegata' (v) ♀H4	More than 30 suppliers

Pachystachys (Acanthaceae)

lutea ♀H1	CHal ERea EShb LRHS MBri

Pachystegia (Asteraceae)

insignis	GGar
minor	WCru

Pachystima see *Paxistima*

Packera (Asteraceae)

§	***aurea***	ECha EMan MSal SSpi

Paederia (Rubiaceae)

scandens	CPLG CPLN WCru WSHC
- HWJ 656	WCru
- var. ***mairei*** B&SWJ 989	WCru

Paederota (Scrophulariaceae)

§	***bonarota***	CLyd

lutea	NWCA

Paeonia ✿ (*Paeoniaceae*)

albiflora	see *P. lactiflora*
'Alice Roberts' **new**	LRHS
'Alley Cat' **new**	WAul
'America'	MBri
'Angelet'	CKel
'Angelo Cobb Freeborn'	WCAu
anomala	CFir MHom MPhe NPar NSla SSpi WCot
- var. ***intermedia***	GCal
- subsp. ***veitchii***	see *P. veitchii*
arietina	see *P. mascula* subsp. *arietina*
'Avant Garde'	WCAu WKif
bakeri	MBri
banatica	see *P. officinalis* subsp. *banatica*
'Black Monarch' **new**	WCAu
'Black Pirate' (S)	CKel WCAu
'Blaze'	WCAu
Blue and Purple Giant	see *P. suffruticosa* 'Zi Lan Kui'
'Bridal Icing'	WCAu
broteroi	SSpi
'Buckeye Belle'	CKel GBin GKir LPio MBri MPhe MSte WAul WCAu WHil
'Burma Ruby'	WCAu
cambessedesii ♀H2-3	CBrd CBro CFil EHyt EPot ETow GCrs LRHS MTho NBir NMen NSla SBla SIgm SRot SSpi WCot
'Carol'	WCAu
caucasica	see *P. mascula* subsp. *mascula*
'Cheddar Royal' **new**	LRHS
'China Pink'	MBri
'Chinese Dragon' (S)	CKel WCAu
'Claire de Lune'	GBin MBri WCAu WCot
'Claudia'	WCAu
'Coral Charm'	MBri WCot
'Coral Fay'	MSte WCAu
'Coral 'n' Gold' **new**	MBri WCAu
'Coral Supreme' **new**	WCot
corallina	see *P. mascula* subsp. *mascula*
coriacea var. ***atlantica***	CBro
Crimson Red	see *P. suffruticosa* 'Hu Hong'
'Crusader' **new**	WCAu
'Cytherea'	WCAu
'Dancing Butterflies'	EBee LRHS LSRN WCAu WHil
daurica	see *P. mascula* subsp. *triternata*
decomposita	MPhe
decora	see *P. peregrina*
'Defender'	WCAu
delavayi (S) ♀H4	CBcs CHad CKel EBee EChP EPfP EPla GAbr GCal GKir IBlr LRHS MAsh MDun MTis MWat NBir NCGa NSti SBrw SLPl SMad SPer SRms SSpi WBrE WCAu WFar
- BWJ 7775	WCru
- from China (S)	MPhe
§ - var. ***angustiloba*** f. ***angustiloba***	SSpi
- - - ACE 1047	EPot
- var. ***atropurpurea***	NEgg NFor
- hybrid (S)	ENot NEgg
§ - var. ***ludlowii*** (S) ♀H4	More than 30 suppliers
§ - var. ***lutea*** (S)	CDul CHad EBee ENot EPfP IFro LRHS MAsh MLan SAga SHBN SLon SPoG SRms STre WAul WBrE WFar WHar WHoo WTin
- 'Mrs Sarson'	GBin MCCP
- Potaninii Group (S)	see *P. delavayi* var. *angustiloba* f. *angustiloba*
- Trollioides Group (S)	WCAu
delavayi x ***delavayi*** var. ***lutea***	ELan GKir
Drizzling Rain Cloud	see *P. suffruticosa* 'Shiguregumo'
'Early Scout'	WAul WCAu
'Early Windflower' **new**	WCAu
'Eastgrove Ruby Lace'	WEas
'Eden's Perfume' **new**	NLar
'Ellen Cowley'	WCAu
emodi	CDes LPio WCot
'Fairy Princess'	MBri WAul WCAu
'Firelight' **new**	WCAu
'Flame'	EBee EWTr GBin MNrw MSte NLar SPer WAul WCAu WCot WHil
Fragrance and Beauty	see *P. suffruticosa* 'Lan Tian Yu'
§ Gansu Mudan Group (S)	CKel MPhe
- 'Bai Bi Fen Xia' (S)	MPhe
- 'Bai Bi Lan Xia' (S)	MPhe
- 'Cheng Xin' (S)	MPhe
- 'Fen He' (S)	MPhe
- 'Feng Xian' (S)	MPhe
- 'Hei Xuan Feng' (S)	MPhe
- 'Huang He' (S)	MPhe
- 'Lan Hai Yiu Bo' (S)	MPhe
- 'Lan He' (S)	MPhe
- 'Li Xiang' (S)	MPhe
- 'Lian Chun' (S)	MPhe
- 'Xue Lian' (S)	MPhe
- 'Zie Pie' (S)	MPhe
'Gold Standard' **new**	LRHS WAul
'Golden Bowl'	CKel
'Golden Glow' **new**	WCAu
'Golden Isles'	CKel
Green Dragon Lying on a Chinese Inkstone	see *P. suffruticosa* 'Qing Long Wo Mo Chi'
'Hei Hua Kui'	see *P. suffruticosa* 'Hei Hua Kui'
'High Noon' (S)	CKel MPhe WCAu
'Ho-gioku' **new**	GBin
'Hoki'	CKel
'Honor'	WCAu
§ 'Huang Hua Kui' (S)	MPhe
humilis	see *P. officinalis* subsp. *microcarpa*
'Illini Warrior'	WAul WCAu
'Isani Gidui'	see *P. lactiflora* 'Isami-jishi'
'Jack Frost' **new**	LRHS
japonica misapplied	see *P. lactiflora*
'Jean E. Bockstoce'	WCAu
jishanensis	MPhe
'Joseph Rock'	see *P. rockii*
'Joyce Ellen'	WCAu
kavachensis	EBee GCal GIBF
kevachensis	see *P. mascula* subsp. *mascula*
'Kinkaku'	see *P.* x *lemoinei* 'Souvenir de Maxime Cornu'
'Kinko'	see *P.* x *lemoinei* 'Alice Harding'
'Kinshi'	see *P.* x *lemoinei* 'Chromatella'
'Kintei'	see *P.* x *lemoinei* 'L'Espérance'
'Kokkou-Tsukasa'	CKel
'Kun Shan Ye Guang'	CKel
§ ***lactiflora***	EHrv MPhe SSpi WBor
- 'A.F.W. Hayward'	CKel
- 'Adolphe Rousseau'	CBcs NBlu WCAu
* - 'Afterglow'	CKel
- 'Agida'	EBee
- 'Agnes Mary Kelway'	CKel
- 'Albert Crousse'	CBcs CKel GBin GKir NBir NBlu WCAu
- 'Alexander Fleming'	EChP ECot GKir NBir WCAu WHoo
- 'Algae Adamson'	CKel
- 'Alice Balfour'	CKel
- 'Amibilis'	WCAu
- 'Amo-no-sode' **new**	WCAu
- 'Angel Cheeks'	WCAu
- 'Anna Pavlova'	CKel

Cultivar	Suppliers
- 'Antwerpen'	ERou MBri WCAu
- 'Arabian Prince'	CKel
- 'Argentine'	WCAu
- 'Artist'	CKel
- 'Asa Gray'	CKel WCAu
- 'Auguste Dessert'	CKel EBee WCAu
§ - 'Augustin d'Hour'	CKel ERou
- 'Aureole'	CKel
- 'Avalanche'	EBee MAvo NLar SMrm SPur
- 'Ballerina'	CKel
- 'Barbara'	CKel WCAu
- 'Baroness Schröder'	ELan
- 'Barrington Belle'	EPfP GKir MBri MSte WAul WCAu
- 'Barrymore'	CKel
- 'Beacon'	CKel
- 'Beatrice Kelway'	CKel
- 'Belle Center'	WCAu
- 'Best Man'	WCAu
- 'Bethcar'	CKel
- 'Better Times'	WCAu
- 'Big Ben'	WCAu
- 'Blaze of Beauty'	CKel
- 'Blenheim'	CKel
- 'Blush Queen'	ELan WCAu
- 'Border Gem'	WCAu
- 'Boulanger'	WHil
- 'Bower of Roses'	CKel
- 'Bowl of Beauty' 🏆H4	More than 30 suppliers
- 'Bowl of Cream'	NLar SWvt WCAu
- 'Bracken'	CKel
- 'Break o' Day'	WCAu
- 'Bridal Gown'	WCAu
- 'Bridal Veil'	CKel
- 'Bridesmaid'	CKel
- 'British Beauty'	CKel
- 'British Empire'	NPar
- 'Bunker Hill'	CKel EWTr GKir SMur SPer SWvt WCAu
- 'Butter Bowl'	MBri WCAu
- 'Calypso'	CKel
- 'Canarie'	CKel MBri
- 'Candeur'	CKel
- 'Cang Long'	CKel
- 'Captivation'	CKel
- 'Carnival'	CKel EBee
- 'Caroline Allain'	CKel
- 'Cascade'	CKel
- 'Catherine Fontijn'	CKel WCAu WHil
- 'Challenger'	CKel
- 'Charlemagne'	CKel
- 'Charles' White'	EBee LPio LRHS WCAu
- 'Charm'	WCAu
- 'Cheddar Charm'	WAul WCAu
- 'Cheddar Cheese'	MBri
- 'Cheddar Gold' 🏆H4	MBri
- 'Cherry Hill'	WCAu
- 'Chestine Gowdy'	CKel
- 'Christine Kelway'	CKel
- 'Chun Xiao'	CKel
- 'Claire Dubois'	CKel ERou GBin WCAu
- 'Colonel Heneage'	CKel
- 'Cornelia Shaylor'	WCAu
- 'Coronation'	CKel
- 'Country Girl'	CKel
- 'Couronne d'Or'	WCAu
- 'Crimson Glory'	CKel
- 'Crimson Velvet'	CKel
- 'Cringley White'	SBod
- 'Da Fu Gui'	CKel
- 'Dandy Dan'	WCAu
- 'Dark Lantern'	MBri
- 'Dark Vintage'	CKel
- 'Dawn Crest'	CKel EBee
- 'Dayspring'	CKel
- 'Delachei'	CKel
- 'Desire'	CKel
- 'Diana Drinkwater'	CKel
- 'Dinner Plate'	EBee MBri SPer WCAu WCot
- 'Display'	CKel
- 'Do Tell'	SPer WCAu
- 'Docteur H. Barnsby'	CKel
- 'Doctor Alexander Fleming'	CKel SWvt
- 'Dominion'	CKel
- 'Doreen'	CFir WCAu
- 'Doris Cooper' **new**	WCAu
- 'Dorothy Welsh'	CKel
- 'Dresden'	CKel WCAu
- 'Duchess of Bedford'	CKel
- 'Duchess of Somerset'	CKel
- 'Duchesse de Nemours' 🏆H4	CKel COtt EChP ELan EPfP GKir GMaP LAst MBri MSte MWgw NBir NCGa NEgg NLar SGSe SMrm SPer SPoG SRms SWvt WAul WCAu WCot WHil WHoo
- 'Duchesse d'Orléans'	WCAu
- 'Duke of Devonshire'	CKel
- 'Eden's Temptation'	SPer SVil
- 'Edmund Spencer'	CKel
- 'Edouard Doriat'	WCAu
- 'Edulis Superba'	CKel EChP ELan ENot GKir LRHS MBNS NPer SMer SPur WCAu
- 'Elaine'	CKel
- 'Elizabeth Stone'	CKel
- 'Ella Christine Kelway'	CKel
- 'Elma'	CKel
- 'Elsa Sass'	WCAu
- 'Emma Klehm'	WCAu
- 'Emperor of India'	CKel
- 'Empire State'	WCAu
- 'Enchantment'	CKel
- 'English Princess'	CKel
- 'Ethelreda'	CKel
- 'Ethereal'	CKel
- 'Evening Glow'	CKel
- 'Evening World'	CKel
- 'Faire Rosamond'	CKel
- 'Fairy's Petticoat'	WCAu
- 'Fashion Show'	CKel
- 'Felicity'	CKel
- 'Félix Crousse' 🏆H4	CKel CTri ELan EMil ENot EPfP ERou GKir GMaP LAst MBNS MSte MWgw NBir SPer SPoG SPur SRms WCAu WHil
- 'Fen Chi Jin Yu'	CKel
- 'Fen Mian Tao Hua'	CKel
- 'Festiva Maxima' 🏆H4	CKel CSBt CTri EChP ECot ELan EPfP ERou GKir LRHS MBri MSte MWgw NEgg NLar SPer SPla SRms SWvt WAul WCAu WHil WHoo
- 'Florence Ellis'	WCAu
- 'France'	CKel
- 'Fuji-no-mine' **new**	GBin
- 'Gainsborough'	CKel
- 'Gardenia'	EBee
- 'Gay Ladye'	WCAu
- 'Gay Paree'	GBin NLar SPer WCAu
- 'Gayborder June'	CKel EMil MBri WCAu
- 'Gene Wild' **new**	WCAu
- 'Général MacMahon'	see *P. lactiflora* 'Augustin d'Hour'
- 'General Wolfe'	CKel
- 'Germaine Bigot'	CKel WCAu
- 'Gilbert Barthelot'	WCAu
- 'Gleam of Light'	CKel MBri
- 'Globe of Light'	GBin
- 'Gloriana'	WCAu

- 'Glory Hallelujah' WCAu
- 'Glowing Candles' WCAu
- 'Gold Mine' CKel
- 'Golden Fleece' WCAu
- 'Goodform' CKel
- 'Grover Cleveland' CKel
- 'Guidon' WCAu
- 'Gypsy Girl' CKel
- 'Hakodate' CKel
- 'Heartbeat' CKel
- 'Helen Hayes' WCAu
- 'Henri Potin' CKel
- 'Henry Woodward' CKel
- 'Her Grace' CKel
- 'Her Majesty' NBir
- 'Herbert Oliver' CKel
- 'Hiawatha' WCAu
- 'Hit Parade' WCAu
- 'Honey Gold' ELan NBPC SHBN SPoG WAul WCAu
- 'Huang Jin Lun' CKel
- 'Hyperion' CKel
- 'Immaculée' EBee ENot NLar SPoG WHil
- 'Ingenieur Doriat' CKel
- 'Inspecteur Lavergne' CKel CM&M LRHS SPer WAul WCAu WCot
- 'Instituteur Doriat' CKel GBin MPhe WCAu

§ - 'Isami-jishi' GBin WCAu
- 'Israel' CKel
- 'Jacorma' **new** CFir WHoo
- 'Jacques Doriat' CKel
- 'James Pillow' WCAu
- 'James William Kelway' CKel
- 'Jan van Leeuwen' CPen EBee EPfP ERou GBin GKir WCAu
- 'Jeanne d'Arc' CKel
- 'Jewel' CKel
- 'Jin Chi Yu' CKel
- 'Jin Dai Wei' CKel
- 'Joan Kelway' CKel
- 'John Howard Wigell' WCAu
- 'Joseph Plagne' CKel
- 'Joy of Life' CKel
- 'June Morning' CKel
- 'June Rose' WCAu
- 'Kansas' CKel EBee ELan ERou GKir MPhe WCAu WFar
- 'Karen Gray' WCAu
- 'Karl Rosenfield' CKel CSBt EChP ECot ENot EPfP GKir LAst LRHS MSte NEgg SPer SPla SPoG SRms SWvt WFar WHil WHoo
- 'Kathleen Mavoureen' CKel EBee
- 'Kelway's Betty' CKel
- 'Kelway's Brilliant' CKel
- 'Kelway's Circe' CKel
- 'Kelway's Daystar' CKel
- 'Kelway's Exquisite' CKel
- 'Kelway's Fairy Queen' CKel
- 'Kelway's Glorious' EBee EChP EPfP ERou EWTr GKir NLar SPoG WCAu
- 'Kelway's Gorgeous' GBin
- 'Kelway's Lovely' CKel
- 'Kelway's Lovely Lady' CKel
- 'Kelway's Majestic' CKel
- 'Kelway's Queen' CKel
- 'Kelway's Scented Rose' CKel
- 'Kelway's Silvo' CKel
- 'Kelway's Supreme' CKel
- 'King of England' CKel
- 'Knighthood' CKel
- 'Kocho-jishi' CKel
- 'Krinkled White' EBee GBin LPio MBri MHom MPhe NCGa NLar NSti SMeo SUsu WAul WCAu WCot
- 'La Belle Hélène' CKel
- 'La France' GBin
- 'La Lorraine' CKel WCAu
- 'La Perle' CKel
- 'Lady Alexandra Duff' ♀H4 EChP EPfP EWTr GKir MRav NFla SCoo SRms SWvt WCAu WHil
- 'Lady Kate' WCAu
- 'Lady Ley' CKel
- 'Lady Mayoress' CKel
- 'Lady Orchid' WCAu

I - 'Langport Cross' CKel
- 'Langport Triumph' CKel
- 'Largo' WCAu
- 'Laura Dessert' ♀H4 EBee EPfP ERou EWTr EWll GBin GKir MWgw SHBN WCAu
- 'Le Cygne' MBri
- 'Le Jour' WCAu
- 'Leading Lady' CKel
- 'L'Eclatante' CKel
- 'Legion of Honor' CKel
- 'Lemon Ice' CKel
- 'Lemon Queen' CKel
- 'Letitia' CKel EBee
- 'Lillian Wild' WCAu
- 'Lois Kelsey' WCAu
- 'Longfellow' CKel
- 'Lora Dexheimer' WCAu
- 'Lord Calvin' WCAu
- 'Lord Derby' CKel
- 'Lord Kitchener' CKel GBin MBri
- 'Lorna Doone' CKel
- 'Lotus Queen' WCAu
- 'Louis Barthelot' WCAu
- 'Louis Joliet' EChP ELan MSte
- 'Lowell Thomas' WCAu
- 'Lyric' CKel
- 'M. Millet' CKel
- 'Madame Calot' MSph SRms WCAu WHil
- 'Madame Claude Tain' WCot
- 'Madame de Verneville' CKel WCAu
- 'Madame Ducel' CKel WCAu
- 'Madame Edouard Doriat' CKel
- 'Madame Emile Debatène' CKel EBee LBuc MAvo SPoG WCAu
- 'Madame Jules Dessert' WCAu
- 'Madelon' CKel WCAu
- 'Magic Melody' CKel
- 'Magic Orb' CKel
- 'Margaret Truman' CKel NLar WCAu
- 'Marguérite Gerard' WCAu
- 'Marie Clutton' CKel
- 'Marie Crousse' WCAu
- 'Marie Lemoine' CKel EBee SMur WCAu WCot
- 'Marietta Sisson' WCAu
- 'Marquisite' CKel
- 'Mary Brand' WCAu
- 'Masterpiece' CKel
- 'Meteor Flag' CKel
- 'Midnight Sun' MBri WCAu
- 'Minnie Shaylor' WCAu
- 'Mischief' CKel WCAu
- 'Miss America' WCAu
- 'Miss Eckhart' CKel EBee ERou WCAu
- 'Mister Ed' WCAu
- 'Mistral' MBri
- 'Mo Zi Ling' WCAu
- 'Monsieur Jules Elie' ♀H4 CKel EChP EPfP ERou GKir LAst MBri MHom MPhe SMer SPer SPla SVil WAul WCAu
- 'Monsieur Martin Cahuzac' CFir WCAu

	- 'Moon of Nippon'	EBee MPhe
	- 'Moonglow'	WCAu
	- 'Mother's Choice'	EBee WCAu
	- 'Mr G.F. Hemerik'	CKel EBee GKir MBri MPhe WCAu WHil
	- 'Mr Thim' **new**	WCAu
	- 'Mrs Edward Harding'	WCAu
	- 'Mrs F. J. Hemerik'	WCAu
	- 'Mrs Franklin D. Roosevelt'	WCAu
	- 'Mrs J.V. Edlund'	WCAu
	- 'Mrs Livingston Farrand'	WCAu
	- 'My Pal Rudy'	WCAu
	- 'Myrtle Gentry'	GBin
	- 'Nancy Nicholls'	WCAu
	- 'Nancy Nora'	NLar
I	- 'Nellie'	CKel
	- 'Newfoundland'	CKel
	- 'Nice Gal'	WCAu
	- 'Nick Shaylor'	GKir WCAu
	- 'Nippon Beauty'	CPen SPoG
	'Nobility'	CKel
	- 'Ornament'	CKel
	- 'Orpen'	CKel
	- 'Othello'	CKel
	- 'Paola'	CKel
	- 'Paul M. Wild'	EChP WCAu
	- 'Peche'	CPen EBee WHil
*	- 'Pecher'	NPer SMrm SPoG
	- 'Peregrine'	CKel
	- 'Peter Brand'	CKel NLar
	- 'Philippe Rivoire'	WCAu
	- 'Philomèle'	WCAu
	- 'Pico'	WCAu
	- 'Pillow Talk'	WCAu
	- 'Pink Cameo'	EBee NLar SHBN SPoG WCAu WCot
	- 'Pink Giant'	WCAu
	- 'Pink Lemonade'	WCAu
	- 'Pink Parfait'	CKel WCAu
	- 'Pink Princess'	MBri WCAu
	- 'Polar King'	WCAu
	- 'Port Royale'	CKel
	- 'President Franklin D. Roosevelt'	GKir WCAu
	- 'Président Poincaré'	CKel GKir SMur
	- 'President Taft'	see *P. lactiflora* 'Reine Hortense'
	- 'Primevere'	EPfP EWll GBin MBNS MSte SMrm SPer SPoG SPur WCAu
	- 'Princess Beatrice'	CKel
	- 'Qi Hua Lu Shuang'	CKel
	- 'Qing Wen'	CKel
	- 'Queen of Sheba'	WCAu
	- 'Raoul Dessert'	WCAu
	- 'Raspberry Sundae'	ERou NLar SPer WCAu
	- 'Red Champion' **new**	MBri
	- 'Red Dwarf'	CKel
	- 'Red Emperor'	WCAu
	- 'Red King'	CKel
	- 'Red Sarah Bernhardt'	MBri
§	- 'Reine Hortense'	CKel GBin WCAu
	- 'Renato'	LRHS
	- 'Richard Carvel' **new**	WCAu
	- 'Rose of Delight'	CKel
	- 'Ruth Cobb'	WCAu
	- 'Sante Fe'	WCAu
	- 'Santorb'	CKel
	- 'Sarah Bernhardt' ♀H4	More than 30 suppliers
	- 'Sea Shell' **new**	NLar
	- 'Shawnee Chief'	WCAu
	- 'Shen Tao Hua'	CKel
	- 'Shimmering Velvet'	CKel
	- 'Shirley Temple'	CKel EBee ELan EWTr GBin GKir MRav MSte MWgw SGSe SPoG WCAu WCot WHil
	- 'Silver Flare'	CKel
	- 'Sir Edward Elgar'	CKel
	- 'Snow Swan'	CKel
	- 'Solange'	CKel EBee EChP LPio NCGa SPoG WCAu
	- 'Sorbet'	CPen EChP EPfP LRHS NArg NPer SMrm SPoG WCAu WHil
	- 'Spearmint'	CKel
	- 'Starlight' **new**	WCAu
	- 'Strephon'	CKel
	- 'Surugu'	MBri
	- 'Suzanne Dessert'	CKel
	- 'Sweet Sixteen'	WCAu
	- 'Sword Dance'	EBee GBin MPhe SPoG WHil
	- 'Taff'	SPur
	- 'Tamate-boko'	WCAu
	- 'The Nymph'	CPen
	- 'Thérèse'	WCAu
	- 'Top Brass'	MRav NLar WCAu
	- 'Toro-no-maki'	WCAu
	- 'Victoire de la Marne'	EWTr SMur WHil
	- 'Vogue'	SMur SWvt WCAu
	- 'Westerner'	WCAu
	- 'White Angel'	EBee SPoG
	- 'White Ivory'	WCAu
	- 'White Rose of Sharon'	CKel
	- 'White Wings'	CBcs CKel CPen EBee ELan EPfP GBin GKir MBri MSte SPer SSpi SWvt WAul WCAu WCot WWye
	- 'Whitleyi Major' ♀H4	GKir WCot
	- 'Wiesbaden'	WCAu
	- 'Wilbur Wright'	GBin WCAu
	- 'Wladyslawa'	NLar WCot
	- 'Xuan Li Duo Cai'	CKel
	- 'Xue Feng'	CKel
	- 'Yan Fei Chu Yu'	CKel
	- 'Yan Zi Dian Yu'	CKel
	- 'Zhu Sha Dian Yu'	CKel
	- 'Zus Braun'	EBee
	- 'Zuzu'	WAul WCAu
	'Late Windflower'	MHom
§	x ***lemoinei*** 'Alice Harding' (S)	CKel ENot WCAu
§	- 'Chromatella' (S)	CKel LAma
§	- 'L'Espérance' (S)	LAma SPer
§	- 'Souvenir de Maxime Cornu' (S)	CKel LAma LRHS MGos MPhe WCAu
	'L'Etincelante' **new**	GBin
	lithophila	see *P. tenuifolia* subsp. *lithophila*
	'Little Joe' **new**	LRHS
	lobata 'Fire King'	see *P. peregrina*
	'Lois Arleen'	WCAu
	ludlowii	see *P. delavayi* var. *ludlowii*
	lutea	see *P. delavayi* var. *lutea*
	- var. ***ludlowii***	see *P. delavayi* var. *ludlowii*
	macrophylla	MPhe
	'Magenta Gem' **new**	WAul
	'Mai Fleuri'	GKir WCAu
	mairei	CFir MPhe
	'Marchioness' **new**	WCAu
§	***mascula***	CAvo CBro EPfP GIBF LRHS NBir WBWf
§	- subsp. ***arietina***	ECha MWat SIgm WEas WKif
	- - 'Northern Glory'	GKir LSpr MBri WCAu
	- from Samos **new**	SSpi
	- from Sicily	MPhe
	- subsp. ***hellenica***	EBee GCrs MHom
	- - from Sicily	MPhe
§	- subsp. ***mascula***	CBro EBee EPot GIBF GKir MAvo NLar
	- - from Georgia	MPhe WPGP

	Plant	Suppliers
§	- subsp. ***russoi***	GIBF SIgm SSpi WCot
	- - from Sardinia	MPhe
§	- subsp. ***triternata***	CLAP EBee MPhe SSpi
	- - from Crimea	WPGP
	'Mikuhino Akebono'	CKel
	mlokosewitschii ♀H4	CAvo CBct CBot CBro CFil CKel EBrs ECha EHyt ETow GCrs GKir LRHS MNrw MPhe MWat MWgw NBir NChi NMen SBla SChu SUsu WCot WEas WHoo WPGP WTin
	mollis	see *P. officinalis* subsp. *villosa*
	'Montezuma'	MBri WCAu
	'Moonrise'	WCAu
	'Nymphe'	CKel EBee EChP EPfP LRHS MBNS MRav SPoG WAul WCAu WHil
	obovata ♀H4	CFir GIBF GKir MPhe MSal SSpi WCot
	- var. ***alba*** ♀H4	EWTr GBin GCrs GKev NSla WEas
	- 'Grandiflora'	EBrs GKir
	- var. ***willmottiae***	MPhe
	officinalis	CMil EWsh NEgg SBla
	- 'Alba Plena'	CKel CPou EWTr GKir GMaP MBri MRav MSte NEgg SWvt WAul WCAu
	- 'Anemoniflora Rosea' ♀H4	CKel EBee EChP EPfP GBin GKir LRHS MBri MHom SWvt WCAu
§	- subsp. ***banatica***	EBee LAst MHom MPhe SSpi WCAu
	- 'China Rose'	GBin WCAu
	- WM 9821 from Slovenia	MPhe
	- subsp. ***humilis***	see *P. officinalis* subsp. *microcarpa*
	- 'Lize van Veen'	WCAu
§	- subsp. ***microcarpa***	GIBF SBla SSpi WCAu
	- 'Mutabilis Plena'	EBee IBlr WCAu
	- 'Rosea Plena' ♀H4	CKel EBee ECtt EPfP GBin GKir GMaP LAst MRav NEgg SGSe SPer SWvt WCAu
	- 'Rosea Superba Plena'	EBee EWTr NEgg SPoG WCAu
	- 'Rubra Plena' ♀H4	CKel CPou EBee ECtt EMil EPfP GAbr GBin GKir GMaP LAst MHom NEgg NGdn SPer SPoG SRms SWvt WAul WCAu WCot WFar WHil
§	- subsp. ***villosa***	CKel EBee ELan GAbr LPio MTis WAul WCAu
	'Oriental Gold'	CKel
	ostii (S)	CFwr CKel MPhe SSpi
	papaveracea	see *P. suffruticosa*
	paradoxa	see *P. officinalis* subsp. *microcarpa*
	'Paula Fay'	EChP MBri MPhe MRav NLar WCAu
	Peony with the Purple Roots	see *P. suffruticosa* 'Shou An Hong'
§	***peregrina***	ECho GBin GCal MHom MPhe NSla SBla SIgm SSpi WCAu WCot
	- 'Fire King' **new**	GBin
§	- 'Otto Froebel' ♀H4	MBri WCAu WCot
	- 'Sunshine'	see *P. peregrina* 'Otto Froebel'
	'Phoenix White' (S)	MBlu
	'Pink Haiwaiian Coral' **new**	WCot
	'Postilion'	MBri WCAu
	potaninii	see *P. delavayi* var. *angustiloba* f. *angustiloba*
	'Red Charm'	EBee MBri MPhe SPoG WCAu
	'Red Magic'	NLar SMrm SPoG WHil
	'Red Red Rose' **new**	WCAu
	'Requiem'	GBin WCAu
	'Robert W. Auten'	WCAu
§	***rockii*** (S)	EPfP MPhe SSpi
	- 'Bing Shan Xue Lian' (S)	MPhe
	- 'He Ping Lian' (S)	MPhe
	- 'Hong Lian' (S)	MPhe
	- 'Hui He' (S)	MPhe
	- hybrid	see *P.* Gansu Mudan Group
	- subsp. ***linyanshani***	MPhe
	- 'Shu Sheng Peng Mo' (S)	MPhe
	- 'Zi Die Ying Feng' (S)	MPhe
	'Roman Gold'	CKel
	romanica	see *P. peregrina*
	'Rose Garland'	WCAu
	'Roselette'	WCAu
	Rouge Red	see *P. suffruticosa* 'Zhi Hong'
	ruprechtiana	WCot
	russoi	see *P. mascula* subsp. *russoi*
	'Scarlett O'Hara'	SPer SPoG WCAu
	'Shaggy Dog' **new**	LRHS
	Shandong Red Lotus	see *P. suffruticosa* 'Lu He Hong'
	sinensis	see *P. lactiflora*
	'Smouthii'	GKir MBri
	'Stardust' **new**	WCAu
	steveniana	GBin MHom MPhe
§	***suffruticosa*** (S)	CWib EBee ELan MGos MPhe SBrw SSpi
	- 'Akashigata' (S)	CKel
	- 'Alice Palmer' (S)	CKel
	- 'Bai Yu' (S)	CBcs
	- 'Bai Yuan Hong Xia'	WCAu
	- 'Bai Yulan'	MWgw NBlu
	- Best-shaped Red	see *P. suffruticosa* 'Zhuan Yuan Hong'
	- Bird of Rimpo	see *P. suffruticosa* 'Rimpo'
	- Black Dragon Brocade	see *P. suffruticosa* 'Kokuryû-nishiki'
	- Black Flower Chief	see *P. suffruticosa* 'Hei Hua Kui'
	- 'Cardinal Vaughan' (S)	CKel
	- Charming Age	see *P. suffruticosa* 'Howki'
	- 'Da Hong Ye'	MPhe
	- 'Da Hu Hong'	MPhe
	- 'Dou Lu' (S)	CBcs CKel MPhe
	- Double Cherry	see *P. suffruticosa* 'Yae-zakura'
	- 'Duchess of Kent' (S)	CKel
	- 'Duchess of Marlborough' (S)	CKel
	- 'Er Qiao' (S)	CBcs CKel MPhe
	- Eternal Camellias	see *P. suffruticosa* 'Yachiyo-tsubaki'
§	- 'Fei Yan Hong Zhuang' (S) **new**	WCAu
	- 'Fen Qiao' (S)	CBcs
§	- 'Feng Dan Bai' (S)	CFwr CKel MPhe NBlu WCAu
	- Flight of Cranes	see *P. suffruticosa* 'Renkaku'
	- Floral Rivalry	see *P. suffruticosa* 'Hana-kisoi'
	- Flying Swallow Lady in Red	see *P. suffruticosa* 'Fei Yan Hong Zhuang'
	- 'Fuji Zome Goromo'	CKel
*	- 'Glory of Huish' (S)	CKel
	- 'Godaishu' (S)	CKel LAma LRHS MPhe
	- 'Guan Qun Fang'	MPhe
	- 'Guan Shi Mo Yu' (S)	MPhe
§	- 'Hakuojisi' (S)	CKel EBee ENot WCAu
§	- 'Hana-daijin' (S)	LAma LRHS WCAu
§	- 'Hana-kisoi' (S)	CKel LAma MPhe WCAu
	- 'Haru-no-akebono' (S)	CKel
§	- 'He Hua Lu' (S)	WAul
§	- 'Hei Hua Kui' (S)	CKel MPhe WCAu
§	- 'Higurashi' (S)	EBee ENot
§	- 'Howki' (S)	WCAu
§	- 'Hu Hong' (S)	CFwr NBlu WBrE WCAu
	- Jewel in the Lotus	see *P. suffruticosa* 'Tama-fuyo'
	- Jewelled Screen	see *P. suffruticosa* 'Tama-sudare'
	- 'Jia Ge Jin Zi' (S)	CKel
	- 'Jin Xing Xiu Lang'	MPhe
	- 'Jitsugetsu-nishiki' (S)	CKel
	- 'Joseph Rock'	see *P. rockii*

	- Kamada Brocade	see *P. suffruticosa* 'Kamada-nishiki'
§	- 'Kamada-fuji' (S)	CKel LAma WCAu
§	- 'Kamada-nishiki' (S)	CKel
§	- 'Kaow' (S)	CKel WCAu
	- King of Flowers	see *P. suffruticosa* 'Kaow'
	- King of White Lions	see *P. suffruticosa* 'Hakuojisi'
*	- 'Kingdom of the Moon' (S)	LRHS
	- 'Kinkaku'	see *P.* x *lemoinei* 'Souvenir de Maxime Cornu'
	- 'Kinshi'	see *P.* x *lemoinei* 'Alice Harding'
§	- 'Kokuryû-nishiki' (S)	CKel LAma SPoG
	- 'Koshi-no-yuki' (S)	CKel
	- 'Lan Fu Rong'	CBcs MPhe
§	- 'Lan Tian Yu' (S)	MPhe
	- Lotus Green	see *P. suffruticosa* 'He Hua Lu'
§	- 'Lu He Hong' (S)	WCAu
	- Magnificent Flower	see *P. suffruticosa* 'Hana-daijin'
	- 'Mikasayama'	MPhe
	- 'Montrose' (S)	CKel
*	- 'Mrs Shirley Fry' (S)	CKel
	- 'Mrs William Kelway' (S)	CKel
	- 'Muramatsu-zakura' **new**	ENot
	- 'Nigata Akashigata' (S)	CKel
	- Pride of Taisho	see *P. suffruticosa* 'Taisho-no-hokori'
	- 'Qie Lan Dan Sha'	MPhe
§	- 'Qing Long Wo Mo Chi' (S)	CKel WCAu
	- 'Reine Elisabeth' (S)	CKel
§	- 'Renkaku' (S)	CKel LRHS WCAu
§	- 'Rimpo' (S)	CKel EBee ENot LAma MPhe
	- subsp. ***rockii*** (S)	see *P. rockii*
	- 'Rou Fu Rong' (S)	MPhe WCAu
	- 'Ruan Zhi Lan' (S)	MPhe
	- 'Sheng Hei Zi'	CBcs
§	- 'Shiguregumo' (S)	CKel
	- 'Shimadaigin'	CKel MPhe
	- 'Shimane-chojuraku' (S)	CKel
	- 'Shimane-hakugan' (S)	CKel
	- 'Shimane-seidai' (S)	CKel
	- 'Shintoyen' (S)	CKel
	- 'Shirotae' (S)	CKel
§	- 'Shou An Hong' (S)	MPhe
	- 'Si He Lian' (S)	MPhe
	- 'Sumi-no-ichi' (S)	CKel
	- 'Superb' (S)	CKel
§	- 'Taisho-no-hokori' (S)	LRHS WCAu
§	- 'Taiyo' (S)	CKel ENot LAma LRHS MPhe SPer
§	- 'Tama-fuyo' (S)	CKel LAma
§	- 'Tama-sudare' (S)	CKel SPer WCAu
	- The Sun	see *P. suffruticosa* 'Taiyo'
	- 'Tian Xiang'	MPhe
	- Twilight	see *P. suffruticosa* 'Higurashi'
	- Wisteria at Kamada	see *P. suffruticosa* 'Kamada-fuji'
	- 'Wu Jin Yao Hui' (S)	CBcs MPhe WCAu
	- 'Wu Long Peng Sheng'	CFwr CKel MPhe WCAu
	- 'Xiao Tao Hong'	CBcs
	- 'Xue Ta' (S)	CKel
	- 'Xue Ying Tao Hua'	MPhe
§	- 'Yachiyo-tsubaki' (S)	CKel ENot LAma WCAu
§	- 'Yae-zakura' (S)	LAma SPer WCAu
	- 'Yakumo' **new**	SPer
	- 'Yan Long Zi Zhu Pan' (S)	CKel
	- 'Yin Hong Qiao Dui' (S)	CKel
	- 'Yomo-zakura' (S)	LRHS
	- 'Yoshinogawa' (S)	CKel EBee ENot LRHS
	- 'Yu Xi Ying Xue' (S)	MPhe
	- 'Zhao Fen' (S)	MPhe NPer
§	- 'Zhi Hong' (S)	CKel
	- 'Zhu Sha Lei' (S)	CKel MPhe NBlu
*	- 'Zhuan Yuan Hong' (S)	NBlu
	- 'Zi Er Qiao' (S)	CKel MPhe
§	- 'Zi Lan Kui' (S)	CKel
	'Sunshine'	see *P. peregrina* 'Otto Froebel'
	tenuifolia	CBot CDes CLAP GCal GIBF LPio MDun MHom NCGa NMen NSla SBla SIgm SPoG SSpi WCAu WCot
	- subsp. ***carthalinica***	MHom MPhe
§	- subsp. ***lithophila***	GBin GKir MHom MPhe
	- 'Plena'	GKir LPio MPhe
	tomentosa	CMil MPhe WWst
	'Vanilla Twist' **new**	WAul
	veitchii	GBin GIBF GKev MTho MWgw NDlv NMen SIgm SSpi WCAu WCot WHil
	- from China	MPhe
	- 'Alba' **new**	SMHy
	- dwarf	MPhe
	- var. ***woodwardii***	CLyd CMil ERos GCra GCrs GKev MTho NSla NWCA SIgm SOkd SSpi WCAu WCot WHoo
	'Vesuvian'	CKel WCAu
	'Walter Mains' **new**	WCAu
	White Phoenix	see *P. suffruticosa* 'Feng Dan Bai'
	wittmanniana	CBro GBin GKir MDun WCAu WCot
§	'Yao Huang' (S)	CBcs MPhe WCAu
	Yao's Yellow	see *P.* 'Yao Huang'
	'Yellow Crown'	WCAu
	'Yellow Dream'	WCAu WCot
	'Yellow Emperor'	WCot
	Yellow Flower of Summer	see *P.* 'Huang Hua Kui'

Paesia (*Dennstaedtiaceae*)

	scaberula	CDes CLAP CWil NBir SSpi WAbe

Paliurus (*Rhamnaceae*)

	spina-christi	CArn CBcs CPle EGFP IDee NLar SLon SMad XPep

Pallenis (*Asteraceae*)

	maritima	LIck XPep
	- 'Golden Dollar'	NPri

Panax (*Araliaceae*)

	ginseng	GPoy
	japonicus	GPoy WCru
	- BWJ 7932	WCru
	quinquefolius	EBee GPoy MSal
	sambucifolius	CPLG

Pancratium (*Amaryllidaceae*)

	canariense MS 924 from Tenerife **new**	CMon
	maritimum	EBee LRHS MLul WCot
	- from Spain **new**	CMon
	zeylanicum **new**	WMul

Pandanus (*Pandanaceae*)

	furcatus	CBrP

Pandorea (*Bignoniaceae*)

	'Charisma' **new**	CHll LSou
	jasminoides	CFwr CHal CHll CPLN CRHN EBak ECot EPfP EShb LRHS MRav
	- 'Alba' **new**	EShb
§	- 'Charisma' (v)	CBcs CPLN EHol EMil EPfP EShb WCot
§	- 'Lady Di'	ERea SYvo WCot
	- 'Rosea'	MCCP MJnS
	- 'Rosea Superba' ♀H1	CBcs CFwr CHEx CPLN CRHN EBee EMil ERea LRHS
	- 'Southern Sunset' **new**	CPLN
	- 'Variegata'	see *P. jasminoides* 'Charisma'
	lindleyana	see *Clytostoma calystegioides*

	pandorana	CPLN CRHN ERea IDee SAdn SLim SYvo WCot
	- 'Golden Showers'	CBcs CMdw CPLN CRHN EBee ERea EShb SLim
	- 'Ruby Heart' **new**	CPLN
	- 'Snowbells'	CPLN

Panicum (*Poaceae*)

	bulbosum	EHoe EPPr EPla
	clandestinum	CFwr EBee EHoe EPPr EPla EWes LEdu MCCP NPro WHil
	miliaceum	EBrs
	- 'Violaceum'	CBig CSpe EMan GFlt GKev MAvo WWpP
	'Squaw'	EBrs LRHS NOrc WTin
	virgatum	CBig CHrt CRWN CTri EPza GFor LRav NBre WPer XPep
	- 'Blue Tower'	LPhx MAnH SApp SGSe SUsu
	- 'Cloud Nine'	CBig CKno CPen EBee EPPr LPhx MAnH MAvo SApp SGSe SMHy SUsu
	- 'Dallas Blues'	CKno CPen EMan EPPr EWes SApp SMHy WFar
	- 'Hänse Herms'	CBig CKno CRez EHoe EPPr IPot LPhx SApp SHel SPla SPoG WFar WGHP WWpP
	- 'Heavy Metal'	More than 30 suppliers
	- 'Heiliger Hain' **new**	CFwr
I	- 'Kupferhirse' **new**	CBig
	- 'Northwind'	CKno CPen EPPr MAvo SApp SMHy WFar
	- 'Pathfinder'	SApp SGSe
	- 'Prairie Sky'	CAby CKno CStr EMan EPPr GBin LPhx MAnH MAvo MWgw SApp SGSe SMHy SUsu WPGP
	- 'Red Cloud'	CKno
	- 'Rehbraun'	CSBt EBrs EHoe EPPr EWTr IPot LEdu LPhx NGdn NOak SApp WCAu WFar WGHP WTin
	- 'Rotstrahlbusch'	CBig CKno CPrp EBee EHoe EMan EPPr EShb GKev MAvo MSte MWhi NBea NOrc SMad SPer STes SWal WCot WGHP WPGP
	- 'Rubrum'	CKno COIW CSBt EBrs EChP ECha ECot EHoe ELan ENot EPPr EPfP EPza EVFa LRHS MRav NBPC SApp SChu SDix SHBN SPer SPla WGHP WMoo WPrP
	- 'Shenandoah'	CAbb CBig CBrm CKno CPen CStr EBee EPPr EShb GBin IPot MAvo MBNS MBri NPro SApp SGSe
	- 'Squaw'	More than 30 suppliers
	- 'Strictum'	CBig EBee EHoe EHul EMan EMil EPPr EWes LPhx NLar SApp SHel SMHy
I	- 'Strictum Compactum' **new**	SGSe
	- 'Warrior'	More than 30 suppliers
	- 'Wood's Variegated' (v)	LEdu

Papaver ✿ (*Papaveraceae*)

	alboroseum	EDAr GIBF GTou
§	***alpinum***	CSpe EDAr GKev GKir GTou LRHS MMHG SIng SRms WCot WFar
	- 'Flore Pleno' (d)	NBir
	amurense	CHVG GCal GIBF MFOX NLar
	anomalum album	CSpe NArg
	apokrinomenon	ELan
	argemone	WBWf
§	***atlanticum***	EBee EMag EMar GBuc GKev GMac LDai MLan MWgw NBro SPlb
	- 'Flore Pleno' (d)	CSam CSpe MCCP NBro WBrk WFar
	bracteatum	see *P. orientale* var. *bracteatum*
	burseri	SRot
	commutatum ♀H4	CSpe ELan WEas
	fauriei	GKev
	heldreichii	see *P. spicatum*
	involucratum **new**	EHyt
	lateritium	CPou MLLN SRms
	- 'Fireball' (d)	EChP ECha ETow GCal IGor MLLN MTis NBre NBro NLar SHGN WMnd WRHF
	'Lauffeuer'	EMon
	'Medallion' (Super Poppy Series)	WHoo
§	***miyabeanum***	CSec CSpe EDAr ELan GAbr GKir GTou LRHS WEas WFar WPer WTMC
	- album	ECho
	- tatewakii	see *P. miyabeanum*
	nanum 'Flore Pleno'	see *P. lateritium* 'Fireball'
§	***nudicaule***	CSec ELan NBlu NEgg WPer
	- Champagne Bubbles Group	EWll GWCH LRHS NPri WFar
	- Constance Finnis Group	EMon GBuc LRHS
	- var. ***croceum*** 'Flamenco'	ERou LRHS
	- Garden Gnome Group	see *P. nudicaule* Gartenzwerg Series
§	- Gartenzwerg Series	COIW CSpe EMil GAbr MBri NBlu NEgg NJOw NLar NPri SPlb WGor
	- 'Kelmscott Giant'	MWgw
	- 'Matador' **new**	NEgg
	- 'Meadow Pastels'	CSim
	- 'Pacino'	EChP EDAr EMil EWin EWll GBuc LRHS NLar SPet SPoG SRms WFar WWeb
	- 'Solar Fire Orange'	EWll
	- 'Summer Breeze Orange'	NPri
	- 'Summer Breeze Yellow'	NPri
	- Wonderland Series	EHrv
	- - 'Wonderland Orange'	NPri
	- - 'Wonderland Pink Shades'	NPri
	- - 'Wonderland White'	NPri
	- - 'Wonderland Yellow'	NPri
	oreophilum	CSec
	orientale	CBcs CHrt EPfP IHMH LAst MBow NBlu SRms WBor WBrE WFar WPer
	- 'Aglaja' ♀H4	CMil EBee EChP EMil EVFa GBin LAst LPhx LPio MAnH MNFA MSph MSte NDov NEgg NGdn NRnb NSti SPoG SUsu WCot WHoo WWhi
	- 'Aladin'	NRnb
	- 'Ali Baba'	NBre
	- 'Allegro'	CMea CPrp CSBt CSam ECtt GAbr GKir GMaP IBal LAst LRHS MBNS MBct MBri MHer MRav NCGa NVic SPer SPlb SWvt WCAu
	- 'Arwide'	CMil
	- 'Aslahan'	ECha NBre
	- 'Avebury Crimson'	LPhx MBct MWat
	- 'Ballkleid'	ECha
	- 'Beauty Queen'	EBee ECha ECot EMan GKir GMac LRHS MAnH MNFA MRav MWgw NGdn SDix
	- 'Big Jim'	EBee SPla
	- 'Black and White' ♀H4	CElw CFwr CHad CSpe EChP ECha EHrv ELan EMar EPfP ERou GKir GMaP LRHS MAnH MAvo MBow MBri MRav SApp SPer SPla WCAu WCra WPGP WSan
	- 'Blackberry Queen'	EMan LPio MBow
	- 'Bloomsbury'	EChP

	Name	Suppliers
	- 'Blue Moon'	NCGa WHal
	- 'Bonfire'	CAby CSam EHrv MBri NCob NLsd NRnb SOkh
	- 'Bonfire Red'	EBee LRHS WCAu
§	- var. ***bracteatum*** 🏆H4	EChP ECha EWll NBir NBur SMHy
	- 'Brilliant'	LRHS NBur NLar SMar WFar WMoo
	- 'Brooklyn'	CWCL EBee EMan ERou LPio
*	- 'Carneum'	CSim EChP LRHS NBre NLar WHil
	- 'Carnival'	CMil EBee NBre NLar
	- 'Catherina'	NRnb
	- 'Cedar Hill'	EBee EMar EWes GMac LRHS MRav NRnb
	- 'Cedric Morris' 🏆H4	CMil CSpe EBee ECha ELan EPPr ERou GCal GMac LAst LPhx MAnH MRav MSte MWgw NSti SChu SMrm WCAu WCot WEas WMnd WWhi
	- 'Charming'	CAby CHad CPar EBee EChP EMan EMar GBin LPhx LRHS MBri MNFA NGdn
	- 'Checkers'	LRav SBch SPur WRHF
	- 'China Boy'	CMil NBre WWeb
	- 'Choir Boy'	CM&M CMdw ECtt ENot NBur NLar NRnb SGar SMar SPoG STes WHrl WRHF
	- 'Coral Reef'	EMar EWll GBBs MHer MWhi NBur NEgg SAga SBch SSth WCra WHer WHrl WPen
	- 'Coralie'	CMil
	- 'Curlilocks'	CPar EChP ECtt ELan EPfP ERou IBal LAst LRHS MAnH MBow MRav NRnb SAga SPer SPoG SRms SWvt WCot WHoo WSan
*	- 'Diana'	SMrm
	- 'Distinction'	CHad
	- double orange (d)	IBal
	- 'Double Pleasure' (d)	EBee IBal WHrl
	- 'Doubloon'	ERou GKir NGdn NRnb WFar
	- 'Dwarf Allegro'	GBuc NFor NLon WMnd
	- 'Effendi' 🏆H4	CHea CMil IPot LPhx MAvo MBct NBre SDys SMHy SUsu
	- 'Elam Pink'	CMil LPhx MLLN MTis WCot
	- 'Erste Zuneigung'	ECha EVFa LPhx
	- 'Fatima'	CDes CHad CMil MAnH WWeb
	- 'Feuerzwerg'	IBal
	- 'Fiesta'	CMil NBre
	- 'Flamenco'	ECtt NBre
	- 'Forncett Summer'	CAby CHea EBee EChP EMan EMar ERou EVFa GBin GFlt GMac LAst LPio MWgw NBre NGdn SChu STes WCAu WCot
	- 'Garden Glory'	CAby CPar EBee EChP ECtt EMan LAst LRHS LSRN MBri NBre NBro NRnb SMrm WCAu WTMC WWol
	- 'Garden Gnome'	ENot EPfP SPet
	- 'Glowing Embers'	ERou GKir LRHS
	- 'Glowing Rose'	NBre
	- Goliath Group	CElw CMil ECha ELan EMan GKir GMac IBal LRHS MAvo MBri MRav NBro NPri NVic SAga SDix SPer SRms WCra WEas WFar WMnd
	- - 'Beauty of Livermere'	More than 30 suppliers
	- 'Graue Witwe'	CAby CMil GBuc MBow SApp SMHy WPGP WTin
	- 'Harvest Moon'	CAby EBee EChP ERou GKir IBal LPio LRHS MBow NEgg NLsd NPer NPri WHil
	- 'Helen Elisabeth'	CMHG CSpe EBee EBrs EChP ECtt EMan EMar EPPr ERou GCal GKir IBal LAst LPio MBow MLLN MNFA MSte MTis NBPC NGdn NLsd NPri NRnb SMer STes WCAu WFar WTMC
	- 'Hewitt's Old Rose' **new**	WCot
	- 'Hula Hula'	ECha NBre
	- 'Indian Chief'	CMHG CPrp EChP EMan EPfP ERou GBin GMac IPot LPio LRHS MAnH MRav MSte NBro NGdn NPer SAga SPoG WCAu WFar WHil WMnd WWhi
	- 'Joanne'	NLar
	- 'John III' 🏆H4	EBee LPhx LPio MSph SMHy
	- 'John Metcalf'	CMil EBee EMan EPPr LPio LRHS MLLN NBre NSti SChu SMrm WCAu WCot
	- 'Juliane'	CAby ECha EVFa GMac LPhx MBct MNFA MSte MWgw NSti SAga WCot WTin WWhi
	- 'Karine' 🏆H4	More than 30 suppliers
	- 'King George'	GBuc
	- 'Kleine Tänzerin'	CMil CSam EBee EChP EMan EMar ERou GBin GBri LBmB LPhx LRHS MLLN MWgw NGdn NSti SPoG SUsu WCAu WCot WHil WWeb
	- 'Lady Frederick Moore'	GMac LPio LRHS MBow MLLN
	- 'Lady Roscoe'	NBre
	- 'Ladybird'	EBee ENot ERou LRHS MBow MRav MSte NBre
I	- 'Lauren's Lilac'	CMil LPhx MAnH NBre SMeo
	- 'Lavender Girl'	CFir EVFa
	- 'Leuchtfeuer' 🏆H4	ECha LPhx MSph SMHy
	- 'Lilac Girl'	CElw CMil CSpe EBee EChP ECha ECtt EVFa EWTr EWll LPhx LPio MBow MRav MSph MSte NLar NSti SApp STes WCAu WCot WHoo WHrl WWhi
	- 'Little Dancer'	EMan GMac WWol
	- 'Maiden's Blush'	CMil EBee NBre NSti
	- 'Manhattan' **new**	EMan ERou GFlt MBnl NCob NCot SPer SPla STes WCot WCra
	- 'Marcus Perry'	EBee ENot EPfP ERou EWes GMaP LRHS MRav NEgg NPri NRnb SPer SPoG WCAu WFar
	- 'Mary Finnan'	LPio NBre
	- 'May Queen' (d)	EChP EWes IBlr LAst LRHS MRav NBre NBro NCGa NSti WCot WPen WPnn
	- 'May Sadler'	COIW ENot NBre NLsd NRnb
	- 'Midnight'	ERou
	- 'Mrs H.G. Stobart'	MBow
	- 'Mrs Marrow's Plum'	see *P. orientale* 'Patty's Plum'
	- 'Mrs Perry'	More than 30 suppliers
	- 'Nanum Flore Pleno'	see *P. lateritium* 'Fireball'
	- 'Orange Glow'	NCot NPri NRnb SMrm WMoo
	- 'Orangeade Maison'	LPio
	- 'Oriana'	EHol LRHS MMil NBre NGdn NLar
	- 'Pale Face'	ERou
	- 'Papillion' **new**	NSti
§	- 'Patty's Plum'	More than 30 suppliers
	- 'Perry's White'	More than 30 suppliers
	- 'Peter Pan'	CAby GBin MLLN NBre
	- 'Petticoat'	EChP ECtt ELan EMan IPot LAst
	- 'Picotée'	More than 30 suppliers
	- 'Pink Ruffles' [PBR]	EBee EMan ERou MBri NCot SPoG
	- 'Pinnacle'	CMil CSWP EBee ERou LRHS MBri NGdn NPri SGSe WFar WSan
	- 'Pizzicato'	CMea CPar CWib EChP EHrv ERou EShb GBBs LRHS MBri NArg NPer SGar SPet WFar WMoo
	- 'Pizzicato White'	NRnb
	- Princess Victoria Louise	see *P. orientale* 'Prinzessin Victoria Louise'
	- 'Prinz Eugen'	CMil EBee ECGP MAnH NBre
§	- 'Prinzessin Victoria Louise'	CBot CSWP EChP EPfP EWTr GAbr GBBs GFlt GKir GMaP IBal LAst LRHS MDun MLLN MMil

	NBro NCGa NLsd NPri SSvw WBVN WCAu WFar WPer WPop
- 'Queen Alexandra'	CBot CSim EHrv NLar WPop
- 'Raspberry Queen'	More than 30 suppliers
- 'Raspberry Ruffles'	LPhx
- 'Rembrandt'	ECot EHrv ERou LRHS MMil NBre NLsd NMoo NPri WPer
- 'Rose Queen' **new**	NBre WCot
- 'Rosenpokal'	CMil EBee EChP LRHS NGdn NRnb
- 'Roter Zwerg'	ECha
- 'Royal Chocolate Distinction'	CWCL EBee EChP EMan EPfP ERou GBri IPot MAnH MAvo MTis NSti SMrm STes WCAu
- 'Royal Wedding'	CBot EBee EChP ERou EWTr GKir IBal LAst LPio LRHS MBri MDun MHer MMil NGdn NLar NPri NRnb SChu SGSe SMad SMrm SPer SPla SSvw WCot WMoo WPop WWeb WWhi
* - 'Saffron'	CAby CHad CMil EVFa MAnH
- 'Salmon Glow'	CBcs CRez EChP GKir GLil IBal LAst MHer NRnb SSvw WFar WPer
- scarlet	MWgw NCot
- 'Scarlet King'	EMan EWll LRHS MMil NEgg
- 'Showgirl'	EBee MBow MLLN SOkh
* - 'Silberosa'	ECha
- 'Sindbad'	GMac LPhx LRHS MAvo MRav NLar NRnb
- 'Snow Goose'	CMil LPhx MAnH WHoo
- 'Spätzünder'	NBre
- 'Springtime'	CSpe EBee EChP EMan EWes GMac LAst LRHS MRav NGdn NLar WCAu WHoo WSan WTMC WTin WWhi
- 'Stokesby Belle'	MWgw
- Stormtorch	see *P. orientale* 'Sturmfackel'
§ - 'Sturmfackel'	EBee ERou IBal
- 'Sultana'	ECha ERou GMac LPhx MAnH MWat WCAu
- 'Tiffany' **new**	EBee LBuc MBnl NCot SPer SPla STes WCot
- 'Turkish Delight'	CAby CElw EPfP ERou EVFa GKir LRHS MBow MMil MRav MTis NBid NBir NBro NPri SMer SPer SWvt WCAu WFar
- 'Tutu'	EBee IBal
- 'Türkenlouis'	CHar CMHG COlW CWCL EBrs ECtt ENot EPfP ERou GAbr GFlt GKir GLil GMaP GMac IBal LAst LRHS MAnH NBPC SPoG STes WCAu WFar WHoo WTin WWlt
- 'Walking Fire' **new**	MNrw
- 'Watermelon'	CMil COtt EChP ECtt EMan ERou GKir IPot LAst LRHS MAnH MBri MLLN MRav NGdn NPri NSti WCAu WFar WHoo WPop WTMC WWhi
- 'Wild Salmon'	WRHF
- 'Wunderkind'	EBee EChP ECtt EMan IBal LAst MNrw WCAu
'Party Fun'	CSpe NEgg WWeb
pilosum	CHrt EBee EMan GBuc SGSe SRms WCot WTin
radicatum subsp. ***hyperboreum*** **new**	CSec
rhaeticum	EHyt NBre
rhoeas	CArn GPoy MBow WJek
- Angels' Choir Group (d)	ERou
- Mother of Pearl Group	CSpe
- Shirley Group	MBow NLsd
rupifragum	CFir CHar CHrt CMCo CSec EBee EChP ECha ECtt GAbr LPio MLLN NPol SGar SOkd SWal WCot WEas WFar WHrl WPer WPnn WRha WTMC
- 'Double Tangerine Gem'	see *P. rupifragum* 'Flore Pleno'
- 'Flore Pleno' (d)	CSWP CSpe EMan EMar ENot LAst LPio LRHS LSou MBri NChi WCFE WMoo WWhi
- 'Tangerine Dream'	IBal MCCP MDun NEgg
sendtneri	CSec MHer
somniferum	CArn GPoy MSal
- 'Black Beauty' (d)	CBot CSpe NLsd
I - 'Black Paeony' **new**	SBch
- 'Flemish Antique'	SBch
- 'Pink Chiffon'	WEas
- 'Swansdown' (d)	CSpe
§ ***spicatum***	CMea ECGP ECha EGoo EHyt EMan GCal GIBF MSte NBir SIgm WCot WMoo
'The Cardinal'	WRHF
triniifolium	CSec CSpe SIgm
'Water Melon' **new**	WSan

papaya (paw paw) see *Carica papaya*

Parabenzoin see *Lindera*

Parachampionella see *Strobilanthes*

Paradisea (*Asphodelaceae*)

liliastrum ♀H4	CHid EBee EBrs EMan EPPr ERos GIBF GKev IGor LPio MTis NWoo SRms WBVN WHoo
- 'Major'	GSki
lusitanica	CBrm CDes CHid CMHG EBee EChP ERos EVFa GFlt GMac LPio MWgw MWrn SGSe SMHy SSpi WLin WPGP WThu WTin WWeb

Parafestuca (*Gramineae*)

albida **new**	EPPr

Parahebe (*Scrophulariaceae*)

'Arabella'	LRHS
'Betty'	GGar
x ***bidwillii***	MHer NDlv NWCA SRms SRot
- 'Kea'	CFee ECou ECtt GEdr MDKP SBla SRot WPer
canescens	ECou
§ ***catarractae***	CHar CMHG CPLG CTri ECou ENot GCra GGar GKir MNrw MTis MWat NBee NBro NLAp NPri SAga SPoG SUsu WBrE WCru WFar WKif WPer WWhi
- from Chatham Island	EWes
- 'Baby Blue'	CAbP EPfP SPoG
- blue	CHar EPfP NBee SPer
- 'County Park'	ECou
- 'Cuckoo'	ECou
§ - 'Delight' ♀H3	CNic ECou EWes GGar GMaP LRHS MHer NEgg NPer SDix SHFr SIgm SRot STre WEas WFar
- subsp. ***diffusa***	ECou LRHS MHer NPer NVic
- - 'Annie'	ECou NJOw
- - 'Pinkie'	ECou
- garden form	ECha LLWP NLAp SBla
- subsp. ***martinii***	ECou NJOw
- 'Miss Willmott'	ENot NLAp NPri NVic SBch SPer SPlb WBVN WPer
- 'Porlock Purple'	see *P. catarractae* 'Delight'
- 'Rosea'	COkL ESis SSto WBrE
- white	CPom ECha IBlr NChi SUsu WBVN WEas WPer WWhi

densifolia	see *Chionohebe densifolia*
§ ***formosa***	CPle ECou WHCG
- erect	ECou GGar
'Gillian'	WPer
'Greencourt'	see *P. catarractae* 'Delight'
§ ***hookeriana***	GGar ITim
§ - var. ***olsenii***	ECou GGar
'Joy'	ECou EWes
'Julia'	GGar
'June'	GGar
'Lesley'	GGar
linifolia	CTri
- 'Blue Skies'	EDAr
§ ***lyallii***	CHar COkL ECou EDAr ESis GMaP LAst MBar MHer MSwo MWat NChi NDlv NEgg NJOw NPol NWCA SBla SPlb SRms WKif
- 'Baby Pink'	EPfP SPoG
- 'Clarence'	CLyd ECou EHol
- 'Glacier'	ECou
- 'Julie-Anne' ♀H3	CAbP COkL ECou EPfP ESis GCal GMaP LRHS MAsh SPoG
- 'Rosea'	CTri GGar WPer
- 'Summer Snow'	ECou
'Mervyn'	CNic CTri ECtt EDAr MDKP NDlv NLRH NLon WPer
olsenii	see *P. hookeriana* var. *olsenii*
§ ***perfoliata*** ♀H3-4	More than 30 suppliers
- dark blue	GBuc GCal SMad
- 'Pringle'	CAbP EPfP LRHS MAsh SPoG
'Snowcap'	CDoC EPfP LRHS SPlb SPoG

Parajubaea (*Arecaceae*)

cocoides	LPJP

Parakmeria see *Magnolia*

Paranomus (*Proteaceae*)

reflexus **new**	EShb

Paraquilegia (*Ranunculaceae*)

adoxoides	see *Semiaquilegia adoxoides*
§ ***anemonoides***	GCrs GGGa GTou SBla WAbe WLin
grandiflora	see *P. anemonoides*

Paraserianthes (*Mimosaceae*)

distachya	see *P. lophantha*
§ ***lophantha*** ♀H1	CHEx CRHN CTrC EBak ERea IDee SAPC SArc

Parasyringa see *Ligustrum*

x *Pardancanda* (*Iridaceae*)

norrisii	CFir EBee EChP EMan EWes GSki LIck LRHS MBNS WAul WFoF
- 'Dazzler'	EShb MBNS

Pardanthopsis (*Iridaceae*)

dichotoma	EBee WHrl

Parietaria (*Urticaceae*)

§ ***judaica***	GPoy MSal WHer

Paris ✿ (*Trilliaceae*)

bashanensis	SSpi WCru
chinensis	WCru
- B&SWJ 265 from Taiwan	WCru
cronquistii	CLAP
delavayi	EMar WCru
fargesii	LAma WCru
- var. ***brevipetalata***	WCru
- var. ***petiolata***	SSpi WCru
forrestii	WCru
incompleta	CAvo CLAP EPot GCrs SBla SOkd SSpi WCot WCru
japonica	SBla SOkd WCru
lancifolia B&SWJ 3044 from Taiwan	WCru
mairei	LAma WCru
marmorata	EMar WCru
§ ***polyphylla***	CBro CFir CLAP EMar EUJe GFlt GKev LAma SSpi WAbe WCot WCru WFar WPnP
- B&SWJ 2125	WCru
- F 5947	ITim
- Forrest 5945	GCal
- HWJCM 475	WCru
- var. ***alba*** **new**	CFir GFlt
- var. ***stenophylla***	CFir CLAP GEdr LAma WCru
purple-leaved **new**	GFlt
quadrifolia	CArn CFil CFir CLAP EBee EMar EUJe GPoy LPhx MDun NMen SSpi WBWf WCot WCru WHer WShi WTin
tetraphylla	WCru
thibetica	CFir CLAP WCru
- var. ***apetala***	WCru
- var. ***thibetica***	GEdr SSpi
verticillata	CLAP GEdr GFlt LAma WCru
violacea **new**	WWst

Parnassia (*Parnassiaceae*)

palustris	GKev WHer

Parochetus (*Papilionaceae*)

§ ***africanus*** ♀H2	CHid EWes GBuc
communis misapplied	see *P. africanus*
communis ambig.	CBcs CFee CPLG GKev NPer WRha WWhi
- B&SWJ 7215 Golden Triangle	WCru
- from Himalaya	IBlr
- HWJCM 526 from Himalaya	WCru
* - 'Blue Gem'	EWin IHMH
- dark	GCal

Paronychia (*Illecebraceae*)

argentea	CLyd NLAp WPat WPer
§ ***capitata***	CHal CLyd CNic CTri IFro SRms WPer
§ ***kapela***	EMan ETow SPlb WPer
- 'Binsted Gold' (v)	EMan LRHS WPer
§ - subsp. ***serpyllifolia***	ESis GBin NRya XPep
nivea	see *P. capitata*
serpyllifolia	see *P. kapela* subsp. *serpyllifolia*

Parrotia (*Hamamelidaceae*)

persica ♀H4	More than 30 suppliers
- 'Burgundy'	CPMA
- 'Jodrell Bank'	MBlu NLar
§ - 'Lamplighter' (v)	CPMA
- 'Pendula'	CMCN CPMA EPfP
- 'Vanessa'	CDoC CMCN CPMA EWes GKir IArd LBuc MBlu MBri NLar SBrw WFar WMou WOrn
- 'Variegata'	see *P. persica* 'Lamplighter'

Parrotiopsis (*Hamamelidaceae*)

jacquemontiana	CBcs CPMA MBlu NLar NPal SBrw

Parrya (*Brassicaceae*)

albida	EBee
nudicaulis **new**	GIBF

parsley see *Petroselinum crispum*

Parsonsia (*Apocynaceae*)

	capsularis	CPLG ECou
	heterophylla	ECou

Parthenium (*Asteraceae*)

	integrifolium	CArn GPoy MSal

Parthenocissus (*Vitaceae*)

§	***henryana*** 🏆H4	More than 30 suppliers
	heptaphylla	WWes
	himalayana	WCot
	- 'Purpurea'	see *P. himalayana* var. *rubrifolia*
§	- var. ***rubrifolia***	CPLN EBee ELan LRHS MAsh MRav MWgw NEgg SLim SLon SPoG WCru WFar
§	***quinquefolia*** 🏆H4	More than 30 suppliers
	- var. ***engelmannii***	EBee LAst LBuc MGos NBlu WCFE
	- 'Guy's Garnet'	WCru
	semicordata	CPLN
	- B&SWJ 6551	WCru
	striata	see *Cissus striata*
§	***tricuspidata*** 🏆H4	CAgr CWib EBee ECtt EHoe EPfP GKir LAst MGos NFor NLon SMer SPer SReu WDin WFar WWeb
	- 'Beverley Brook'	CMac EBee LBuc MBri SBra SPer SPla SRms
	- 'Crûg Compact'	CPLN WCru
	- 'Fenway Park'	LBuc MAsh MBlu SPoG
	- 'Green Spring'	CPLN IArd MBri MGos NEgg
	- 'Lowii'	CMac EBee ECot EPfP EPla LBuc LRHS MBlu MGos MRav SBra SLon SPer SPoG WBcn
	- 'Minutifolia'	SPer
	- 'Purpurea'	MBlu
	- 'Robusta'	CHEx CPLN EBee MBNS XPep
§	- 'Veitchii'	More than 30 suppliers

Pasithea (*Anthericaceae*)

	caerulea	CMon WCot

Paspalum (*Poaceae*)

	glaucifolium	CElw LEdu WDyG
	quadrifarium	EMan EPPr WCot

Passerina (*Thymelaeaceae*)

	montana **new**	NWCA

Passiflora ✿ (*Passifloraceae*)

	RCB/Arg P-12	WCot
	RCB/Arg R-7	WCot
	actinia	CRHN SLim
	alata (F) 🏆H1	CAbb EBak LExo MJnS
	x ***alatocaerulea***	see *P.* x *belotii*
	'Allardii'	CPLN
§	'Amethyst' 🏆H1	CPLN CRHN CSPN EMil EShb LRHS MJnS SBra SHGC SPet SPoG WFar WPGP WPat WWeb
	amethystina misapplied	see *P.* 'Amethyst'
§	***amethystina*** Mikan	CBcs CDoC CPLN ECre EHol ERea LRHS
	ampullacea (F)	EShb
	antioquiensis misapplied	see *P.* x *exoniensis*
	antioquiensis ambig.	CBcs CPLN CRHN EHol ERea GQui LRHS MTis SMur
§	***aurantia***	CPLN
	banksii	see *P. aurantia*
§	x ***belotii***	ECre EHol EShb LRHS
	- 'Impératrice Eugénie'	see *P.* x *belotii*
	'Blue Bird'	EShb
	x ***caeruleoracemosa***	see *P.* x *violacea*
§	***caerulea*** 🏆H3	More than 30 suppliers
	- 'Clear Sky' **new**	NBlu
	- 'Constance Elliott'	CBcs CBot CBrm CDoC CMac CPLN CRHN CSBt CSPN CWSG EBee ELan EMil EPfP EShb LRHS MAsh NBlu SAga SBra SHGC SLim SPer SPla SPoG SWvt WFar WGwG WWeb
	- ***rubra***	CPLN CSBt LRHS WFar
	x ***caponii***	ERea
	chinensis	see *P. caerulea*
	cinnabarina	CPLN
	citrina	ERea ESlt
	coccinea (F)	CTbh LRHS
	x ***colvillii***	CHII
§	***coriacea***	LRHS
	'Eden'	COtt EAmu LRHS MBri SCoo
	edulis (F)	CAgr IDee LRHS MJnS
	- 'Crackerjack' (F)	ERea
	- f. ***flavicarpa*** (F)	ESlt
	'Empress Eugenie'	see *P.* x *belotii*
§	x ***exoniensis*** 🏆H1	CHII CRHN ECre
	gibertii	EShb
	gilbertiana	WFar
	herbertiana (F)	CPLN ITer
	incarnata (F)	CAgr CArn EShb ITer MSal SPlb
	'Incense' (F) 🏆H1	LRHS SLim SPlb
	'Lady Margaret' **new**	EShb NBlu
	laurifolia (F)	SLim
§	***ligularis*** (F)	LRHS
	'Lilac Lady'	see *P.* x *violacea* 'Tresederi'
	lowei	see *P. ligularis*
	maliformis (F)	CHII
	manicata (F)	EShb
	'Mavis Mastics'	see *P.* x *violacea* 'Tresederi'
	mayana	see *P. caerulea*
	mixta (F)	CPLN
	mixta x ***antioquiensis***	CDoC CTrC
	mixta x ***manicata*** **new**	EShb
	mollissima (F) 🏆H1	CBcs CPLN CRHN CSec EBak EPfP ERea EShb IDee LExo SMrm SPlb
	'New Incense'	EShb
	obtusifolia	see *P. coriacea*
	onychina	see *P. amethystina* Mikan
	phoenicea	CPLN
	pinnatistipula (F)	EUnu
	'Purple Haze'	CRHN EShb NScw WWeb
	'Purple Rain'	NScw
	quadrangularis L. (F) 🏆H1	CHII CPLN CTbh CWSG EBak ERea EShb LRHS MJnS SMur WGwG WMul
	racemosa 🏆H2	CPLN ERea IBlr LAst LRHS
	rovirosae	LRHS
	rubra	SLim
	sanguinolenta	CPLN LRHS
	sexflora	LRHS
	standleyi	CPLN
	'Star of Bristol' 🏆H2	SBra SLim
	'Sunburst'	CHEx CPLN
§	***tetrandra***	ECou
	x ***tresederi***	see *P.* x *violacea* 'Tresederi'
	trifasciata	EShb
	umbilicata	WCru
§	x ***violacea*** 🏆H1	CBrm CRHN CTbh ERea EShb ESlt MBri MJnS WFar
	- 'Lilac Lady'	see *P.* x *violacea* 'Tresederi'
§	- 'Tresederi'	CPLN ELan MAsh SAga WFar
	- 'Victoria'	CSBt EBee SLim
	vitifolia (F)	CPLN ERea EShb ESlt LRHS

passion fruit see *Passiflora*

passion fruit, banana see *Passiflora mollissima*

Patersonia (*Iridaceae*)

occidentalis	WCot

Patrinia (*Valerianaceae*)

gibbosa	CLyd CSec EBee EMan IFro LRHS MGol NLAp SMac WCru WFar WMoo WPat WPnP WWye
intermedia **new**	WLin
rupestris	GIBF
scabiosifolia	CDes CHll CMea CSec EBee EChP ECha EWsh GAbr GBuc GFlt GIBF GSki IFro LPio MLLN NBir NCGa NLar NSti SEND SIgm SMac SSvw SUsu WBVN WFar WHer WHoo WMoo
- 'Nagoya'	MNrw
triloba	CLyd EBrs EDAr GBuc GCrs GKir LRHS LSou MGol MRav MWrn NWoo SMac SSpi SUsu WBVN WMoo
* - 'Minor'	ECho
- var. ***palmata***	WDyG WFar WMoo
- var. ***triloba***	ETow GCal
villosa	EBee NDov NGdn NLar SSvw

Paulownia (*Scrophulariaceae*)

catalpifolia	CBcs CFil EBee EPla WPGP
elongata	CBcs NLar WPGP
fargesii Osborn	see *P. tomentosa* 'Lilacina'
fargesii Franch.	SLPl
fortunei	EBee MBlu NPal SPlb WBVN WNor
kawakamii	CFil WPGP
- B&SWJ 6784	WCru
taiwaniana B&SWJ 7134 **new**	WCru
tomentosa ♀H3	More than 30 suppliers
- 'Coreana'	CHll
- 'Coreana' B&SWJ 8503 from Ullüngdo	WCru
§ - 'Lilacina'	CBcs CFil

Pavonia (*Malvaceae*)

hastata **new**	EShb
missionum	EShb
multiflora ♀H1	ERea
praemorsa	CBot

paw paw (false banana) see *Asimina triloba*

Paxistima (*Celastraceae*)

canbyi	EHyt NLar WWes
myrsinites	see *P. myrtifolia*
§ ***myrtifolia***	EPla

peach see *Prunus persica*

pear see *Pyrus communis*

pear, Asian see *Pyrus pyrifolia*

pecan see *Carya illinoinensis*

Pecteilis (*Orchidaceae*)

* ***dentata***	EFEx
§ ***radiata***	EBee EFEx
* - 'Albomarginata' (v)	EFEx
* - 'Aureomarginata' (v)	EFEx

Pedicularis (*Scrophulariaceae*)

albolabiata **new**	GIBF
alopecuroides **new**	GIBF
amoena **new**	GIBF
axillaris SDR 1745 **new**	GKev
longiflora	GKev
var. ***tubiformis***	
rhinanthoides	GKev
subsp. ***tibetica***	

Peganum (*Zygophyllaceae*)

harmala	CArn EMan MGol MHer MSal WWye

Pelargonium ✿ (*Geraniaceae*)

'A Happy Thought'	see *P.* 'Happy Thought'
'A.M. Mayne' (Z/d)	CWDa WFib
'Abba' (Z/d)	CWDa WFib
'Abel Carrière' (I/d)	SKen SPet
abrotanifolium (Sc)	CRHN CSev EWoo MBPg MHer SSea WFib XPep
'Abundance' (Sc)	LDea
'Acapulco' (I)	WWol
acerifolium hort.	see *P. vitifolium*
acetosum	GCal LPio MSte SHFr SMrm
* - 'Variegatum' (v)	LPio MSte
'Acushla by Brian' (Sc)	MBPg MWhe
'Ada Green' (R)	LDea
'Ada Sutterby' (Dw/d)	SKen
'Adagio' (Dw)	ESul
'Adam's Quilt' (Z/C)	SKen WEas
'Adele' (Min/d)	ESul
'Ade's Elf' (Z/St)	NFir SSea
'Aerosol' (Min)	ESul
'Aida' (R) **new**	WGor
'Ailsa' (Min/d)	ESul SKen
'Ainsdale Angel' (A)	LDea
'Ainsdale Eyeful' (Z)	WFib
'Akela' (Min)	ESul
'Alberta' (Z)	SKen
album	CWDa
'Alcantra' **new**	WGor
alchemilloides	CRHN NCiC
'Alcyone' (Dw/d)	ESul SKen WFib
'Alde' (Min)	ESul MWhe NFir SKen WFib
'Aldenham' (Z)	WFib
'Aldham' (Min)	ESul WFib
'Aldwyck' (R)	ESul LDea WFib
'Alex' (Z)	CWDa SKen
'Alex Kitson' (Z)	WFib
'Alex Mary' (R)	SSea
'Algenon' (Min/d)	ESul WFib
I 'Alice' (Min)	WFib
'Alice Greenfield' (Z)	NFir
'Alison' (Dw)	ESul
'Alison Jill' (Z/d)	CWDa
'Alison Wheeler' (Min/d)	MWhe
'All My Love' (R)	LDea
'Alma' (Dw/C)	ESul
'Almond' (Sc)	MBPg
'Almost Heaven' (Dw/Z/v)	MWhe
'Alpine Glow' (Z/d)	MWhe
'Alpine Orange' (Z/d)	CWDa
'Altair' (Min/d)	ESul
I 'Amalfi' (R) **new**	EWoo
'Amari' (R)	LDea WFib
'Ambrose' (Min/d)	ESul WFib
'American Prince of Orange' (Sc)	MBPg
'Amethyst' (R)	LDea SCoo SPet WFib
§ Amethyst = 'Fisdel'PBR (I/d) ♀H1+3	ECtt LDea LVER MWhe NPri SKen
I 'Amy' (Dw)	WFib
'Andersonii' (Sc)	MBPg MHer
'Andrew Salvidge' (R)	LDea
'Angel Josie' (A) **new**	LAst
'Angela' (R)	LDea

Name	Suppliers
'Angela Brook'	CWDa
'Angela Read' (Dw)	ESul
'Angela Tandy'	LPio
'Angela Woodberry' (I/d)	CWDa
'Angela Woodberry' (Z)	WFib
Angeleyes Series	CTbh LAst
- Angeleyes Burgundy = 'Pacburg' **new**	LSou
- Angeleyes Light = 'Paceyes' **new**	LSou
- Angeleyes Randy (A) **new**	LSou
'Angelique' (Dw/d)	ESul LVER NFir WFib
'Angel's Wings'	NWoo
'Anglia' (Dw)	ESul
'Ann Field' (Dw/d)	ESul
'Ann Hoystead' (R) ♀H1+3	ESul WFib
'Ann Redington' (R)	LDea
'Anna' (Min)	ESul
'Anna Scheen' (Min)	ESul
'Anne' (I/d)	WFib
'Annsbrook Aquarius' (St)	ESul NFir
'Annsbrook Beauty' (A/C)	ESul LDea MBPg NFir WFib
'Annsbrook Capricorn' (St/d)	ESul
'Annsbrook Fruit Sundae' (A) **new**	LDea
'Annsbrook Jupitor' (Z/St)	ESul NFir SMrm
'Annsbrook Mars' (St/C)	ESul
'Annsbrook Peaches' (Min)	ESul
'Annsbrook Pluto' (Z/St)	ESul
'Annsbrook Rowan' (Min)	ESul
'Annsbrook Squirrel' (Min)	ESul
'Annsbrook Venus' (Z/St)	ESul
'Antigua' (R)	LDea
'Antoine Crozy' (ZxI/d)	WFib
'Antoinette' (Min)	ESul
'Apache' (Z/d) ♀H1+3	CHal CWDa WFib
'Aphrodite' (Z)	CWDa ECtt
'Apollo' (R)	CWDa
'Apple Betty' (Sc)	EWoo LDea MBPg MHer WFib
'Apple Blossom Rosebud' (Z/d) ♀H1+3	CAby ECtt EShb ESul LAst LRHS LVER MBri MWhe SKen SMrm SSea WBrk WFib WWol
'Appledram' (R)	LDea
'Apri Parmer' (Min)	ESul
'Aprica' **new**	WGor
'Apricot' (Z/St)	ESul LAst SAga SKen WGor
'Apricot Queen' (I/d)	LDea
'Apricot Star'	CSpe MSte MWhe
'April Hamilton' (I)	EWoo LDea WFib
'April Showers' (A)	LDea WFib
Arcona 2000 = 'Klecona'PBR	LAst LSou
'Arctic Frost'	WFib
§ 'Arctic Star' (Z/St)	CSpe ESul LRHS LVER NFir SKen SSea WBrk WFib
'Ardens'	CSpe EBee ESul EWoo IBal LPio MSte NFir SAga SMrm SSea SUsu SWvt WCot WEas WFib
'Ardwick Cinnamon' (Sc)	ESul EWoo LDea LVER MBPg NFir WFib
'Aries' (Min)	MWhe
'Arizona' (Min/d)	SKen
'Arnside Fringed Aztec' (R)	LDea WFib
'Aroma' (Sc)	EWoo LIck MBPg
'Arron Dixon' (A)	NFir
'Arthington Slam' (R)	LDea
'Arthur Biggin' (Z)	MWhe SKen
'Ashby' (U/Sc)	EWoo LVER MBPg NFir SSea
'Ashfield Blaze' (Z/d)	LVER
'Ashfield Jubilee' (Z/C)	NFir SKen
'Ashfield Monarch' (Z/d) ♀H1+3	LVER MWhe NFir
'Ashfield Serenade' (Z) ♀H1+3	SKen WFib
'Ashley Stephenson' (R)	WFib
'Askham Fringed Aztec' (R) ♀H1+3	ESul LDea LVER WFib
'Askham Slam' (R)	LDea
asperum Ehr. ex Willd.	see *P.* 'Graveolens'
'Asperum'	MBPg
'Athabasca' (Min)	ESul
§ 'Atomic Snowflake' (Sc/v)	CArn CHal CTbh ESul GBar LDea LVER MBPg MHer MSte MWhe SDnm SIde SKen SPet SSea WBrk WFib
'Atrium' (U)	WFib
'Attar of Roses' (Sc) ♀H1+3	CArn CHal CHby CRHN ESul GBar LAst LDea LVER MBPg MHer MSte MWhe NFir NHHG SDnm SECG SIde SKen SSea WFib WGwG
'Attraction' (Z/Ca/d)	SSea
'Audrey Baghurst' (I)	CWDa
'Audrey Clifton' (I/d)	SKen
'Augusta'	SAga SMrm
'Auntie Billie' (A) **new**	LDea
auritum subsp. ***auritum***	NFir
'Aurora' (Z/d)	MWhe SKen
'Aurore' (U)	see *P.* 'Unique Aurore'
australe	CFir CMon CRHN EWoo LPio SBch SSpi WFib
'Australian Bute' (R)	ESul LVER
'Australian Mystery' (R/Dec)	CSpe ESul MSte NFir SAga WFib
'Autumn' (Z/d)	MWhe
'Autumn Colours' (Min)	ESul
'Avril'	ESul
'Aztec' (R) ♀H1+3	ESul LDea LVER MSte NFir WFib
'Baby Bird's Egg' (Min)	CSpe ESul WFib
'Baby Brocade' (Min/d)	ESul WFib
'Baby Face' (R)	EWoo
'Baby Harry' (Dw/v)	WFib
'Baby Helen' (Min)	ESul
'Baby James' (Min)	ESul
'Baby Snooks' (A)	ESul LDea MWhe
'Babylon' (R)	EWoo NFir SSea
'Badley' (Dw)	ESul
Balcon Imperial	see *P.* 'Roi des Balcons Impérial'
'Balcon Lilas'	see *P.* 'Roi des Balcons Lilas'
'Balcon Rose'	see *P.* 'Hederinum'
'Balcon Rouge'	see *P.* 'Roi des Balcons Impérial'
'Balcon Royale'	see *P.* 'Roi des Balcons Impérial'
I 'Ballerina' (Min)	WFib
'Ballerina' (Z/d)	MWhe
'Ballerina' (R)	see *P.* 'Carisbrooke'
'Bandit' (Min)	ESul
'Banstead Beacon' **new**	LVER
'Banstead Village' (Z)	LVER
'Bantam' (Min/d)	ESul WFib
§ 'Barbe Bleu' (I/d)	ECtt EWoo LDea LVER MWhe NFir SKen SSea WFib
'Barham' (Min/d)	ESul
'Barking' (Min)	ESul NFir
barklyi	CMon
'Barnston Dale' (Dw/d)	ESul NFir
'Barock '96'	NPri
'Bath Beauty' (Dw)	SKen WEas
'Baylham' (Min)	ESul
Beach = 'Fisbea' (I/d)	NPri
'Beacon Hill' (Min)	ESul
'Beatrice Cottington' (I/d)	SKen WFib
'Beatrix' (Z/d)	LVER SKen
'Beauty of Diane' (I/d)	LDea

	Name	Suppliers
	'Beauty of Eastbourne' misapplied	see *P.* 'Lachskönigin'
	'Beauty of El Segundo' (Z/d)	SKen
	'Beckwith's Pink' (Z)	SKen
	'Belinda Adams' (Min/d) ♀H1+3	MWhe NFir
§	Belladonna = 'Fisopa' (I/d)	ECtt NPri SCoo
	'Belvedere' (R)	ESul
	'Bembridge' (Z/St/d)	SSea WFib
	'Ben Franklin' (Z/d/v) ♀H1+3	ESul LVER MWhe NFir SPet
	'Ben Matt' (R)	LDea WFib
	'Ben Nevis' (Dw/d)	ESul LVER
	'Ben Picton' (Z/d)	WFib
	'Bentley' (Dw)	ESul
	'Berkswell Dainty' (A)	LDea
	'Berkswell Lace' (A) **new**	LDea
	'Berliner Balkon' (I)	SKen
	Bernardo = 'Guiber'PBR (I/d)	LAst WGor
	'Bernice Ladroot' **new**	LDea
	'Beromünster' (Dec)	CSpe ESul EWoo LDea MSte NFir SSea WFib
	'Bert Pearce' (R)	LDea WFib
	'Beryl Gibbons' (Z/d)	LVER MWhe
	'Beryl Read' (Dw)	ESul
	'Beryl Reid' (R)	ESul LDea WFib
	'Berylette' (Min/d)	ESul SKen
	'Bess' (Z/d)	ESul SKen
	'Bette Shellard' (Z/d/v)	MWhe NFir
	'Betty' (Z/d)	LVER
	'Betty Hulsman' (A)	LDea NFir
	'Betty Merry' (R)	LDea
	'Betty Read' (Dw)	ESul
	'Betty West' (Min/d)	ESul
	betulinum	EWoo WFib
	'Betwixt' (Z/v)	SKen SSea
	'Bianca' (Min/d)	ESul WGor
	'Bi-coloured Startel' (Z/St/d)	MWhe
I	'Big Apple' (Sc)	MBPg
	'Bildeston' (Dw/C)	ESul NFir WFib
	'Bill Holdaway' (Z)	LVER
	'Bill West' (I)	WFib
	'Billie Read' (Dw/d)	ESul
	'Bingo' (Min)	ESul
	'Bird Dancer' (Dw/St) ♀H1+3	CHal CSpe ESul LVER MSte MWhe NFir SAga SHFr SKen SSea WBrk
	'Birdbush Blush' (Sc)	MBPg
	'Birdbush Bold and Beautiful' (Sc)	MBPg
	'Birdbush Bramley' (Sc)	MBPg
	'Birdbush Chloe' (St)	MBPg
	'Birdbush Eleanor' (Z)	MBPg
	'Birdbush Lemon and Lime' (Sc)	MBPg
	'Birdbush Matty'	MBPg
	'Birdbush Nutty' (Sc)	MBPg
	'Birdbush Sweetness' (Sc)	MBPg
	'Birdbush Velvet' (Sc)	MBPg
	'Birthday Girl' (R)	WFib
	'Bitter Lemon' (Sc)	ESul MBPg
	'Black Butterfly'	see *P.* 'Brown's Butterfly'
	'Black Country Bugle' (Z/d)	CWDa
	'Black Knight' (R)	CSpe EWoo LDea LVER MSte SAga
	'Black Knight' Lea (Dw/d/c)	ESul MSte NFir
	'Black Magic' (R)	NPri WWol
	'Black Night' (A)	ESul MBPg
	'Black Pearl' (Z/d)	LVER
	'Black Prince' (R)	EWoo NFir WFib
	'Black Velvet' (R)	LDea
	'Black Vesuvius'	see *P.* 'Red Black Vesuvius'
	'Blackdown Delight' (Dw) **new**	NFir
	'Blakesdorf' (Dw)	ESul MWhe
	Blanca = 'Penwei'PBR (Dark Line Series)(Z/d)	LAst LSou LVER
	Blanche Roche = 'Guitoblanc' (I/d)	EWoo LAst LSou SCoo
§	'Blandfordianum' (Sc)	EWoo LDea MHer MSte
	'Blandfordianum Roseum' (Sc)	LDea
§	'Blauer Frühling' (I x Z/d)	LVER
	'Blaze Away'	SSea
	'Blazonry' (Z/v)	MWhe SKen SSea WFib
	'Blendworth' (R)	LDea
	'Blooming Gem' (Min/I/d)	LDea
	'Blue Beard'	see *P.* 'Barbe Bleu'
	'Blue Fox' (Z)	CWDa
	'Blue Peter' (I/d)	SKen
	Blue Spring	see *P.* 'Blauer Frühling'
	Blue Sybil = 'Pacblusy' (I/d)	LAst LSou LVER
	'Blue Wine' **new**	LAst
	Blue Wonder (Z) **new**	LSou
	'Bluebeard'	see *P.* 'Barbe Bleu'
	Blue-Blizzard = 'Fisrain'PBR (I)	SCoo WWol
§	Blues = 'Fisblu'PBR (Z/d)	CWDa
	'Blush Petit Pierre' (Min)	ESul
	'Blushing Bride' (I/d)	LDea SKen
	'Blushing Emma' (Dw/d)	ESul
	'Bob Hall' (St) **new**	ESul
	'Bobberstone' (Z/St)	LVER WFib
	'Bode's Trina' (I)	CWDa
	'Bold Candy' (R)	LDea
	'Bold Carmine' (Z/d)	NFir
	'Bold Dawn' (Z)	NFir
	'Bold Flame' (Z/d)	WFib
	'Bold Gypsy' (R)	LDea
	'Bold Sunrise' (Z/d)	LVER NFir
	'Bold Sunset' (Z/d)	LVER NFir WFib
	'Bold White' (Z)	NFir
	'Bolero' (U) ♀H1+3	EWoo LVER MSte NFir SKen SSea WFib
	'Bon Bon' (Min/St)	WFib
	'Bonito' (I/d)	LVER
	'Bosham' (R)	ESul LDea WFib
	'Both's Snowflake' (Sc/v)	EWoo MBPg
	'Botley Beauty' (R)	LDea
	bowkeri	WFib
	'Brackenwood' (Dw/d) ♀H1+3	ESul LVER NFir
	'Bramford' (Dw)	ESul
	'Braque' (R)	LDea
	Bravo = 'Fisbravo'PBR (Z/d)	LAst MWhe WFib
	'Break o' Day' (R)	LDea WEas
	'Bredon' (R) ♀H1+3	ESul
	'Brenda' (Min/d)	ESul WFib
	'Brenda Hyatt' (Dw/d)	ESul WFib
	'Brenda Kitson' (Z/d)	LVER MWhe
	'Brettenham' (Min)	ESul
	'Briarlyn Beauty' (A)	LDea MBPg MWhe NFir
	'Briarlyn Moonglow' (A)	ESul LDea LVER SSea
	'Bridesmaid' (Dw/d)	ESul NFir SKen WFib
	'Bright Eyes' (Dw)	WFib
	'Brightstone' (Z/d)	WFib
	'Brightwell' (Min/d)	ESul
	'Brilliant' (Dec)	MBPg MHer WFib
	'Brilliantine' (Sc)	ESul EWoo MBPg MHer WFib
	'Bristol' (Z/v)	SKen SSea

Name	Suppliers
'Britannia' (R)	LDea
'Brixworth Boquet' (Min/C/d)	MWhe
'Brixworth Charmer' (Z/v)	MWhe
'Brixworth Melody' (Z/v)	MWhe
'Brixworth Pearl' (Z)	MWhe WFib
'Brixworth Rhapsody' (Z/v)	MWhe
'Brixworth Starlight' (I/v)	MWhe
'Brockbury Scarlet' (Ca)	WFib
'Bronze Corinne' (Z/C/d)	SKen SPet
'Bronze Nuhulumby' (R)	ESul
'Bronze Queen' (Z/C)	MWhe
'Bronze Velvet' (R)	LDea
'Brook's Purple'	see *P.* 'Royal Purple'
'Brookside Betty' (Dw/C/d)	ESul
'Brookside Bolero' (Z)	ESul
'Brookside Candy' (Dw/d)	ESul
'Brookside Champagne' (Min/d)	ESul
'Brookside Fiesta' (Min/d) **new**	ESul
'Brookside Flamenco' (Dw/d)	ESul MWhe WFib
'Brookside Primrose' (Min/C/d)	ESul MWhe NFir WFib
'Brookside Rosita' (Min)	ESul
'Brookside Serenade' (Dw)	ESul WFib
'Brookside Spitfire' (Dw/d)	ESul
§ 'Brown's Butterfly' (R)	ECtt EShb LDea NFir SMrm SSea WFib
§ 'Bruni' (Z/d)	CHal MWhe
'Brunswick' (Sc)	ESul EWoo LDea LPio LVER MBPg MHer MSte SSea WFib
'Brutus' (Z)	CWDa
'Bucklesham' (Dw)	ESul
'Bumblebee' (Dw)	ESul
'Burgenlandmädel' (Z/d)	LVER SKen
'Burstall' (Min/d)	ESul
'Bushfire' (R) ♀H1+3	ESul EWoo LDea WFib
'Butley' (Min)	ESul
'Butterfly' (Min/v)	ECtt NPri
§ Butterfly = 'Fisam'PBR (I)	SCoo
'Button 'n' Bows' (I/d)	WFib
'Cal'	see *P.* 'Salmon Irene'
'Caledonia' (Z)	SKen
'California Brilliant' (U)	MBPg
'Cameo' (Dw/d)	MWhe
'Camisole' (Dw/d)	LVER
'Camphor Rose' (Sc)	ESul EWoo LDea MBPg MHer NFir SSea
'Can-can' (I/d)	WFib
candicans	LPio
'Candy' (Min/d)	ESul
'Candy Kisses' (D)	ESul
canescens	see *P.* 'Blandfordianum'
'Capel' (Dw/d)	ESul
capitatum	EWoo MBPg MHer WFib
'Capri' (Sc)	MBPg WFib
'Caprice' (R)	EWoo
'Capricorn' (Min/d)	ESul
'Captain Starlight' (A)	CRHN ESul EWoo LDea LVER MBPg MHer NFir NWoo SKen SSea WFib
'Caravan' (A)	LDea
'Cardinal'	see *P.* 'Kardinal'
'Cardinal Pink' (Z/d)	CWDa
'Cardington' (St/Dw) **new**	ESul
'Carefree' (U)	EWoo LPio MSte NFir WFib
'Cariboo Gold' (Min/C) ♀H1+3	ESul
§ 'Carisbrooke' (R) ♀H1+3	LDea SKen SSea WEas WFib
'Carl Gaffney'	LDea
'Carmel' (Z)	WFib
'Carnival' (R)	see *P.* 'Marie Vogel'
carnosum	CMon
'Carol' (R)	ESul
'Carol Gibbons' (Z/d)	MWhe NFir WFib
'Carol Helyar' (Z/d)	WFib
'Carole Munroe' (Z/d)	LVER
'Caroline Plumridge' (Dw)	ESul
'Caroline Schmidt' (Z/d/v)	CHal ESul LAst LRHS LVER MSte MWhe NFir NWoo SKen SPet SSea WBrk WFib
'Carolyn' (Dw)	ESul
'Carolyn Hardy' (Z/d)	WFib
'Carousel' (Z/d)	CWDa
Cascade Lilac	see *P.* 'Roi des Balcons Lilas'
Cascade Pink	see *P.* 'Hederinum'
Cascade Red	see *P.* 'Red Cascade'
'Catford Belle' (A) ♀H1+3	CHal CSpe ESul LDea MWhe SAga SSea WFib
'Cathay' (Z/St)	ESul MWhe NFir SSea
'Catherine Wheels' (Z/St)	LVER
'Cathy' (R)	NFir
caucalifolium subsp. ***convolvulifolium***	WFib
'Cayucas' (I/d)	SKen
'Celebration' (Z/d)	ESul
'Celsia' **new**	WGor
'Cézanne' (R)	GGar LDea LVER WFib
§ Champagne (Z)	CWDa
'Chantilly Claret' (R)	LDea
'Chantilly Lace' (R)	ESul LDea
'Charity' (Sc) ♀H1+3	CHal ESul EWoo LDea LIck LVER MBPg MHer MSte MWhe NFir SSea WBrk WFib
'Charlie Boy' (R)	LDea
'Charlotte Amy' (R)	LDea
'Charlotte Bidwell' (Min)	ESul
'Charlotte Bronte' (Dw/v)	WFib
'Charm' (Min)	ESul
'Charmant'	CWDa
'Charmay Alf' (A)	LDea
'Charmay Aria' (A) **new**	LDea
'Charmay Bagatelle' (A) **new**	LDea
'Charmay Marjorie' (A)	LDea
'Charmay Snowflake' (Sc/v)	ESul MBPg
'Charmer' (R)	LDea
'Chattisham' (Dw/C)	ESul
'Chelmondiston' (Min/d)	ESul MWhe
'Chelsea Diane' (Min)	LVER
§ 'Chelsea Gem' (Z/d/v) ♀H1+3	LRHS LVER NFir SKen SSea WFib
'Chelsea Morning' (Z/d)	WFib
'Chelsworth' (Min/d)	ESul
'Chelvey' (R)	LDea
'Cherie' (R)	LDea
'Cherie Bidwell' (Dw/d/v)	ESul
'Cherie Maid' (Z/v)	ESul SSea
'Cherry' (Min)	LVER WFib
'Cherry Baby' (Dec)	LPio NFir
'Cherry Cocktail' (Z/d/v)	MWhe NFir
'Cherry Hazel Ruffled' (R)	LDea
'Cherry Orchard' (R)	LDea LVER SSea
'Cherry Sundae' (Z/d/v)	ESul
'Cheryldene' (R)	LDea
'Chew Magna' (R)	WFib
'Chi-Chi' (Min)	ESul
'Chieko' (Min/d)	ESul MWhe WFib
'Chime' (Min/d)	ESul
'China Doll' (Dw/d)	WFib
'Chinz' (R)	CSpe NFir SAga
'Chocolate Drops' (Z)	LVER

	Name	Suppliers
§	'Chocolate Peppermint' (Sc)	CHal CHrt CSev CTbh ESul LDea LVER MBPg MHer MWhe NBur NFir NHHG SIde SSea SYvo WBrk WFib
	'Chocolate Tomentosum'	see *P.* 'Chocolate Peppermint'
	'Chrissie' (R)	ESul WFib
	'Christina Beere' (R)	LDea
	'Christopher Ley' (Z)	LVER SKen
	'Cindy' (Dw/d)	ESul WFib
	'Circus Day' (R)	LDea
	'Citriodorum' (Sc) 🏆$^{H1+3}$	LDea MBPg MHer NHHG SSea WFib
	'Citronella' (Sc)	CRHN CTbh LDea MBPg MHer MSte WFib
	citronellum (Sc)	MBPg
	'Clara Read' (Dw)	ESul LVER
	'Claret Cruz' (I)	CWDa
	'Claret Rock Unique' (U)	EWoo LDea MBPg MHer MSte SKen WFib
	'Clarissa' (Min)	ESul
	'Clatterbridge' (Dw/d)	ESul LVER NFir
	'Claude Read' (Dw)	ESul
	'Claudette' (Min)	ESul
	'Claudius' (Min)	ESul
	'Claydon' (Dw/d)	ESul
	'Claydon Firebird' (R)	ESul
	'Clorinda' (U/Sc)	CHal CHrt CRHN EShb ESul EWoo GBar LVER MBPg MHer MSte NBur SIde SKen SSea WFib
	'Clorinda Variegated'	see *P.* 'Variegated Clorinda'
	'Coconut Ice' (Dw)	ESul
	Coconut Ice **new**	LVER
§	Coco-Rico (I)	SKen
	'Coddenham' (Dw/d)	WFib
§	'Colonel Baden-Powell' (I/d)	LDea WFib
	'Conner' (Min)	ESul
	'Constance Spry' (Z)	WEas
	'Contrast' (Z/d/C/v)	ESul LAst LRHS MBri MWhe NEgg SCoo SKen SPoG SSea WFib
	'Cook's Peachblossom'	WFib
	'Copdock' (Min/d)	ESul
	'Copthorne' (U/Sc) 🏆$^{H1+3}$	CRHN ESul EWoo LDea LVER MBPg MHer MSte SKen SSea WBrk WFib
	'Coral Frills' (Min/d)	ESul
	'Coral Reef' (Z/d)	LVER
	'Coral Sunset' (d)	CWDa
	cordifolium	CRHN EWoo WFib
	coriandrifolium	see *P. myrrhifolium* var. *coriandrifolium*
	'Cornell' (I/d)	ECtt WFib
	'Coronia' (Z/Ca)	CWDa
	'Corsair' (Z/d) 🏆$^{H1+3}$	MWhe
	'Corvina' (R)	WFib
	'Cotta Lilac Queen' (I/d)	LVER
	'Cottenham Beauty' (A)	ESul EWoo LDea NFir
	'Cottenham Charm' (A)	ESul
	'Cottenham Delight' (A)	ESul LDea NFir
	'Cottenham Gem' (A)	ESul
	'Cottenham Glamour' (A)	ESul
	'Cottenham Harmony' (A)	ESul
	'Cottenham Jubilee' (A)	ESul
	'Cottenham Surprise' (A)	ESul LDea MBPg MSte MWhe NFir
	'Cottenham Treasure' (A)	ESul
	'Cotton Candy' (Min/d)	ESul
	'Cottontail' (Min)	ESul WFib
	cotyledonis	WFib
	'Countess Mariza'	see *P.* 'Gräfin Mariza'
	'Countess of Scarborough'	see *P.* 'Lady Scarborough'
	'Country Girl' (R)	SPet
	'Cover Girl' (Z/d)	WFib
	'Cramdon Red' (Dw)	SKen WFib
	'Crampel's Master' (Z)	LVER SKen
	'Cransley Blends' (R)	ESul LDea
	'Cransley Star' (A)	LDea MWhe WFib
	'Cream 'n' Green' (R/v)	NFir
	'Creamery' (d)	MWhe WFib
§	'Creamy Nutmeg' (Sc/v)	CArn CHal CHrt ESul EWoo GBar LDea LVER MHer MWhe NBur NFir SRob SSea
	'Creeting Saint Mary' (Min)	ESul
	'Creeting Saint Peter' (Min)	ESul
	'Crescendo' (I/d)	ECtt
	'Crimson Crampel' (Z)	CWDa
	'Crimson Fire' (Z/d)	MBri MWhe SKen
	'Crimson Unique' (U) 🏆$^{H1+3}$	CRHN CSpe EWoo MBPg MHer SAga SKen SSea WFib
§	***crispum*** (Sc)	CHrt EUnu GBar GPoy LDea MBPg NHHG WRha
	- 'Golden Well Sweep' (Sc/v)	MBPg NFir WFib
	- 'Major' (Sc)	ESul MBPg SKen WFib
	- 'Minor' (Sc)	MBPg MHer
	- 'Peach Cream' (Sc/v)	CHal ESul MBPg MWhe WFib
	- 'Prince Rupert' (Sc) **new**	MBPg
	- 'Variegatum' (Sc/v) 🏆$^{H1+3}$	CHal CRHN CSev GBar GGar GPoy LDea LVER MBPg MHer MWhe NFir SIde SPet SSea WFib
	crithmifolium	MHer
	'Crock O Day' (I/d)	LVER
	'Crocketta' (I/d/v)	LVER NFir SSea
	'Crocodile' (I/C/d)	ECtt EShb LDea LVER MWhe NFir SKen SSea WFib
	'Crowfield' (Min/d)	ESul WFib
I	'Crowfoot Rose' (Sc) **new**	EWoo MBPg
	'Crown Jewels' (R)	LDea
	'Crystal Palace Gem' (Z/v)	LAst LRHS LVER MWhe SKen SMrm SSea WFib
	cucullatum	ESul EWoo MHer SSea WFib
	- 'Flore Pleno'	WFib
	'Culpho' (Min/C/d)	ESul
	'Cupid' (Min/Dw/d)	ESul WFib
	'Cyril Read' (Dw)	ESul
§	'Czar' (Z/C)	SCoo
	'Dainty Lassie' (Dw/v)	ESul
	'Dainty Maid' (Sc)	ESul EWoo GGar LVER MBPg NFir SAga SSea
	'Dale Queen' (Z)	WFib
	'Dallimore' (Dw)	ESul
	'Dandee' (Z/d)	SAga
	'Danielle Marie' (A)	LDea
I	'Daphne' (A)	LAst
	'Dark Ascot' (Dec)	ESul
	'Dark Lady' (Sc)	MBPg
	'Dark Red Irene' (Z/d)	LVER MWhe SKen WFib
	'Dark Secret' (R)	CSpe ESul EWoo LDea MSte SKen SMrm WFib
	'Dark Venus' (R)	EWoo LDea WFib
	Dark-Red-Blizzard = 'Fisblizdark' (I)	NPri WWol
	'Darmsden' (A) 🏆$^{H1+3}$	ESul EWoo LDea NFir
	'David John' (Dw/d)	ESul
	'David Mitchell' (Min/Ca/d)	ESul
	'Davina' (Min/d)	ESul MWhe WFib
	'Dawn Star' (Z/St)	ESul NFir
	'Deacon Arlon' (Dw/d)	ESul LVER MWhe SKen
	'Deacon Avalon' (Dw/d)	WFib
	'Deacon Barbecue' (Z/d)	ESul LVER MWhe SKen WFib
	'Deacon Birthday' (Z/d)	ESul LVER MWhe WFib
	'Deacon Bonanza' (Z/d)	ESul LVER MWhe SKen WFib
	'Deacon Clarion' (Z/d)	ESul SKen WFib
	'Deacon Constancy' (Z/d)	ESul LVER MWhe
	'Deacon Coral Reef' (Z/d)	ESul MWhe SKen WFib
	'Deacon Delight' (Sc)	EWoo

	Name	Suppliers
	'Deacon Finale' (Z/d)	ESul LVER
	'Deacon Fireball' (Z/d)	ESul LVER MWhe SKen WFib
	'Deacon Flamingo' (Z/d)	ESul MWhe WBrk
	'Deacon Gala' (Z/d)	ESul LVER MWhe WFib
	'Deacon Golden Bonanza' (Z/C/d)	ESul WFib
	'Deacon Golden Gala' (Z/C/d)	ESul SKen
	'Deacon Golden Lilac Mist' (Z/C/d)	ESul SKen WFib
	'Deacon Golden Mist'	see *P.* 'Golden Mist'
	'Deacon Jubilant' (Z/d)	ESul LVER MWhe SKen
	'Deacon Lilac Mist' (Z/d)	ESul LVER MWhe SKen WFib
	'Deacon Mandarin' (Z/d)	ESul MWhe SKen WFib
	'Deacon Minuet' (Z/d)	ESul MWhe NFir SKen WFib
	'Deacon Moonlight' (Z/d)	ESul MWhe
	'Deacon Peacock' (Z/C/d)	ESul LVER MWhe WFib
	'Deacon Picotee' (Z/d)	ESul MWhe WFib
	'Deacon Regalia' (Z/d)	ESul LVER MWhe SKen WFib
	'Deacon Romance' (Z/d)	ESul LVER MWhe SKen
§	'Deacon Summertime' (Z/d)	ESul MWhe WFib
	'Deacon Sunburst' (Z/d)	ESul LVER MWhe SKen
	'Deacon Suntan' (Z/d)	ESul MWhe SKen
	'Deacon Trousseau' (Z/d)	ESul MWhe WFib
	'Dean's Delight' (Sc)	LDea MBPg
	'Debbie' (A)	MBPg
	'Debbie Parmer' (Dw/d)	ESul
	'Debbie Thrower' (Dw)	ESul
	'Decora Impérial' (I)	LAst LVER
	'Decora Lavender'	see *P.* 'Decora Lilas'
§	'Decora Lilas' (I)	ECtt LAst LVER SPet
	'Decora Mauve'	see *P.* 'Decora Lilas'
I	'Decora Pink'	LAst
I	'Decora Red'	LAst
§	'Decora Rose' (I)	CWDa ECtt LAst SPet
	'Decora Rouge' (I)	ECtt SPet
	'Deerwood Darling' (Min/v/d)	WFib
	'Deerwood Don Quixote' (A)	MWhe
	'Deerwood Lavender Lad' (Sc)	ESul EWoo LDea MBPg MHer SSea WFib
	'Deerwood Lavender Lass'	ESul LDea MBPg MHer
	'Deerwood Pink Puff' (St/d)	WFib
	'Delightful' (R)	WFib
	'Delilah' (R)	LDea
	'Delli' (R)	EWoo NPer SMrm WFib
	'Delta' (Min/d)	ESul
	'Denebola' (Min/d)	ESul
	denticulatum	EWoo GBar MHer NHHG SKen SSea
§	- 'Filicifolium' (Sc)	CHal CRHN EShb ESul EWoo MBPg MHer NHHG SSea WFib
	'Diana Hull'	MBPg
	'Diana Palmer' (Z/d)	SKen
	'Diane' (Min/d)	ESul
	'Dibbinsdale' (Z)	ESul NFir
	dichondrifolium (Sc)	EWoo LVER MBPg MHer NCiC NFir WFib
	dichondrifolium x ***reniforme*** (Sc)	ESul NFir
	'Diddi-Di' (Min/d)	ESul
	'Didi' (Min)	ESul SKen
	'Dingley Bell' **new**	MWhe
	'Dinky' (Min/d)	ESul
§	Disco = 'Fisdis' (Z/d)	CWDa
	'Display' (Dw/v)	WFib
	'Distinction' (Z)	LAst MWhe NFir SAga SKen SPoG SSea WFib
	'Doctor A. Chipault' (I/d)	LDea
	'Doctor A. Vialettes' (Z/d)	CWDa

	Name	Suppliers
	'Dodd's Super Double' (Z/d)	CHal SMrm
	'Dollar Bute' (R)	ESul LDea
	'Dollar Princess' (Z/C)	SKen
	'Dolly Read' (Dw)	ESul
	'Dolly Varden' (Z/v) ♀H1+3	ESul LDea MWhe NFir SKen SSea WFib
	'Don Quixote' (A)	LDea
	'Don's Barbra Leonard' (Dw/B)	NFir
	'Don's Helen Bainbridge' (Z/C)	NFir
	'Don's Judith Ann' (Z/v)	LVER
	'Don's Mona Noble' (Z/C/v)	NFir SKen
	'Don's Richard A. Costain' (Z/C)	NFir
	'Don's Seagold'	NFir
	'Don's Shiela Jane' (Z/C/d)	NFir
	'Don's Silva Perle' (Dw/v)	SKen
	'Don's Southport' (Z/v)	NFir
	'Don's Stokesley Gem' (Z/C)	NFir
	'Don's Swanland Girl' (Min)	ESul
	'Don's Whirlygig' (Z/C)	NFir
	'Dorcas Brigham Lime' (Sc)	CSpe EWoo SAga
	'Dorcus Bingham' (Sc)	MBPg
	'Doreen' (Z/d)	LVER
	'Doris Frith' (R)	LDea
	'Dorothy May' (A)	LDea
	'Double Bird's Egg' (Z/d)	CWDa SKen
	'Double Grace Wells' (Min/d)	ESul
	'Double Lilac White' (I/d)	SKen
	'Double New Life' (Z/d)	CHal CWDa
	'Double Orange' (Z/d)	SKen
	'Dovedale' (Dw/C)	ESul NFir WFib
	'Downlands' (Z/d)	WFib
	'Dragon's Breath' (Z/St)	LVER
	'Dream' (Z)	CWDa
	'Dresden China' (R)	LDea
	'Dresden Pippa Rosa' (Z)	SKen
	'Dresden White' (Dw)	WFib
	'Dresdner Amethyst' (I/d)	LAst
	Dresdner Apricot = 'Pacbriap'[PBR] (I/d) **new**	LVER
	Dresdner Coralit = 'Coralit' (I/d)	LVER
	Dresdner Rosalit = 'Rosalit'[PBR] (I/d)	LVER
	'Drummer Boy' (Z)	CWDa SKen
	'Dryden' (Z)	SKen
	'Dubonnet' (R)	LDea
	'Duchess of Devonshire' (U)	EWoo WFib
	'Duke of Devonshire' (Z/d)	LVER
	'Duke of Edinburgh'	see *P.* 'Hederinum Variegatum'
	'Dulcie' (Min)	ESul
	'Dunkery Beacon' (R)	WFib
	'Dusty Rose' (Min)	ESul
§	'Dwarf Miriam Baisey' (Min)	LVER
	'Dwarf Miriam Read'	see *P.* 'Dwarf Miriam Baisey'
	'E. Dabner' (Z/d)	CWDa SKen WFib
	'Earl of Chester' (Min/d) ♀H1+3	WFib
	'Earliana' (Dec)	ESul LDea SKen
	'Earlsfour' (R)	LDea MSte
	'Easter Morn' (Z/St)	SSea

	Ecco Extra = 'Klesectra'PBR **new**	WGor
	echinatum	CSpe EWoo MBPg MHer SAga
	- 'Album'	WFib
	- 'Miss Stapleton'	see *P.* 'Miss Stapleton'
	'Eclipse' (I/d)	MWhe SKen
	'Eden Gem' (Min/d)	WFib
	'Edith Stern' (Dw/d)	ESul LVER
	'Edmond Lachenal' (Z/d)	WFib
	'Edward Humphris' (Z)	EWoo SKen
	'Eileen' (Min/d)	ESul NFir
	'Eileen Postle' (R) 🏆H1+3	WFib
	'Eileen Stanley' (R)	LDea
	'Elaine' (R)	LDea
	Elbe Silver = 'Pensil'PBR (I)	LAst NFir SCoo
	'Electra' (Z/d)	CWDa LVER
	'Elizabeth Angus' (Z)	SKen WFib
	'Elizabeth Read' (Dw)	ESul
	'Elmsett' (Dw/C/d)	ESul LVER NFir WFib
	'Elna' (Min)	ESul
	elongatum	CMon
	'Els' (Dw/St)	ESul LVER SKen WBrk
	'Elsi' (I x Z/d/v)	LVER WFib
	'Elsie Gillam' (St) **new**	LVER
	'Elsie Hickman' (R)	LDea
	'Elsie Portas' (Z/C/d)	ESul SKen
	'Embassy' (Min)	ESul WFib
	'Emerald' (I)	SKen
	'Emilia Joy' (A)	MHer
	'Emma Hössle'	see *P.* 'Frau Emma Hössle'
	'Emma Jane Read' (Dw/d)	ESul MWhe NFir WFib
	'Emma Louise' (Z)	SKen
	'Emmy Sensation' (R)	LDea
	'Emperor Nicholas' (Z/d)	MWhe SKen
	'Empress' (Z)	SKen
	'Ena' (Min)	ESul
	'Enchantress' (I)	SKen
	'Encore' (Z/d/v)	LRHS LVER MWhe
	endlicherianum	CMon NWCA SIgm WCot WWFP
	'Endsleigh' (Sc)	MBPg MHer
*	'Eric Lee'	CWDa
	'Eroica 2000'	LAst
	'Erwarton' (Min/d)	ESul NFir
	'Escapade' (Min/d)	ESul
	'Evelyn' (Min)	ESul
	Evening Glow = 'Bergpalais'PBR	LAst
	'Evka'PBR (I/v)	LAst LVER NFir SCoo SSea
	'Excalibur' (Z/Min/v)	LVER
	'Explosive' (I)	NPri
	exstipulatum	EShb EWoo WEas XPep
	'Eyes Randy' (A)	LAst
	'Fair Dinkum' (Z/v)	ESul MWhe NFir
§	'Fair Ellen' (Sc)	ESul EWoo LDea MBPg MHer SKen WFib
	'Fairlee' (DwI)	WFib
	'Fairy Lights' (Dw/St)	ESul NFir
	'Fairy Orchid' (A)	ESul LDea LVER SSea WFib
	'Fairy Princess' (R)	LDea
	'Fairy Queen'	LDea MHer
	'Falkenham' (Min)	ESul
	'Falkland Brother' (Z/C/v)	ESul WFib
	'Falkland Hero' (Z/v)	NFir
	'Fandango' (Z/St)	ESul MWhe NFir WFib
*	'Fanfare'	CWDa
	'Fanny Eden' (R)	WFib
	'Fantasia' white (Dw/d) 🏆H1+3	ESul MWhe WFib
	'Fareham' (R) 🏆H1+3	LDea MSte WFib
	'Faye Brawner' (Z/St)	LVER
	'Feneela' (Dw/d)	ESul
	'Fenton Farm' (Dw/C)	ESul NFir WFib
I	'Fern Mint' (Sc)	MBPg
	'Festal' (Min/d)	ESul
	'Feuerriese' (Z)	LVER SKen
	'Fiat' (Z/d)	CWDa SKen
	'Fiat Queen' (Z/d)	SKen WFib
	'Fiat Supreme' (Z/d)	SKen
	'Fiery Sunrise' (R)	ESul EWoo LDea
	'Fiesta' (I/d)	LDea
	'Fifth Avenue' (R)	CSpe EWoo MSte WFib
	'Filicifolium'	see *P. denticulatum* 'Filicifolium'
	'Fir Trees Audrey B' (St)	NFir
	'Fir Trees Big Show' (I/v)	NFir
	'Fir Trees Echoes of Pink' (A)	EWoo NFir
	'Fir Trees Eileen' (St)	NFir SMrm
	'Fir Trees Ele' (A/v)	NFir
	'Fir Trees Flamingo' (Dw)	NFir
	'Fir Trees Jack' (Z/Dw)	NFir
	'Fir Trees John Grainger' (Z/v)	NFir
	'Fir Trees Nan' (Dec) **new**	NFir
	'Fir Trees Roseberry Topping' (Dw)	NFir
	'Fir Trees Ruby Wedding' (C)	NFir
	'Fir Trees Silver Wedding' (Z/C/d)	NFir
	'Fir Trees Sparkler' (Min/C)	NFir
	'Fire Dragon' (Z/St/d)	SKen SSea
	'Fireball'PBR **new**	LSou WGor
	'Firebrand' (Z/d)	LVER
	'Firefly' (Min/d)	ESul
	'Firestone' (Dw)	ESul
	(Fireworks Series)	LSou
	Fireworks Cherry-white = 'Fiwocher'PBR (Z) **new**	
	- Fireworks Light Pink = 'Fiwopink'PBR (Z)	LAst
	- Fireworks Salmon = 'Fiwosal'PBR (Z) **new**	LSou
	- Fireworks White = 'Fiwowit'PBR (Z)	LAst
	'First Blush' (R)	WFib
	'First Love' (Z)	LVER NFir
	'Flakey' (I/d/v) 🏆H1+3	CSpe ESul LDea NFir SKen
	'Flarepath' (Z/C/v)	NFir
	'Flash' (Min) **new**	ESul
	'Flesh Pink' (Z/d)	CWDa
	'Fleur-de-lys' (A) **new**	LDea
	'Fleurette' (Min/d)	CHal ESul MWhe SKen SPet
	'Fleurisse' (Z)	WFib
	'Flirt' (Min)	ESul
§	Flirt (Min)	WFib
	'Floria Moore' (Dec)	ESul EWoo NFir SAga
	'Flower Basket' (R/d)	EWoo LDea NFir
	'Flower of Spring' (Z/v) 🏆H1+3	CHal LVER MWhe SKen SSea
	'Flowton' (Dw/d)	ESul
*	'Forever' (d)	CWDa
	'Foxhall' (Dw)	ESul
	Fragrans Group (Sc)	CHal CRHN CSev CTbh ESul EWoo GBar GPoy LPio LVER MBPg MHer MWhe NHHG SDnm SKen SPet WFib XPep
§	- 'Fragrans Variegatum' (Sc/v)	CSev ESul LIck MBPg MWhe NFir SKen WBrk WFib
	- 'Snowy Nutmeg'	see *P.* (Fragrans Group) 'Fragrans Variegatum'
	'Fraiche Beauté' (Z/d)	CWDa WFib
	'Francis Gibbon' (Z/d)	WFib
	'Francis James' (Z)	WFib

'Francis Parrett' (Min/d) ♀H1+3 ESul MWhe SKen WFib
'Francis Read' (Dw/d) ESul
'Frank Headley' (Z/v) ♀H1+3 CHal CSpe EShb ESul LAst LRHS LVER MSte MWhe NPer NVic SCoo SDnm SIde SKen SMrm SSea WBrk WFib
§ 'Frau Emma Hössle' (Dw/d) ESul MWhe WFib
'Frau Käthe Neubronner' (Z/d) CWDa
'Freak of Nature' (Z/v) ESul MWhe NFir SKen SSea WFib
'Frensham' (Sc) ESul EWoo MBPg MHer SSea WFib
'Freshfields Suki' (Dw) NFir
'Freshwater' (St/C) ESul MWhe
'Freston' (Dw) ESul
'Friary Wood' (Z/C/d) ESul NFir WFib
'Friesdorf' (Dw/Fr) ESul LVER MHer MWhe NFir SKen WBrk WFib
'Frills' (Min/d) ESul MWhe NFir
'Fringed Angel' (A) CFee LDea
'Fringed Apple' (Sc) LDea MBPg NBur
§ 'Fringed Aztec' (R) ♀H1+3 ESul LDea NFir SPet SSea WFib
'Fringed Jer'Ray' (A) LDea
'Fringed Petit Pierre' (Min) **new** MWhe
'Fringed Rouletta' (I) LDea
'Frosty' misapplied see *P.* 'Variegated Kleine Liebling'
'Frosty Petit Pierre' see *P.* 'Variegated Kleine Liebling'
'Fruity' (Sc) MBPg
frutetorum MBPg MHer
fruticosum EShb EWoo LPio WFib
'Frühlingszauber Lila' (R) ESul
'Fuji' (R) NFir
fulgidum CSpe EWoo MHer WFib
'Fynn' (Dw) ESul
'Gabriel' (A) ESul EWoo LDea LVER MBPg NFir
'Galilee' (I/d) ♀H1+3 LDea LVER SKen
Galleria Sunrise = 'Sunrise' (R) ESul LDea SKen WEas
'Galway Girl' (Sc) MBPg
'Galway Star' (Sc/v) ♀H1+3 MBPg MHer SKen WBrk WFib
'Garibaldi' (Z/d) CWDa
'Garland' (Dw/d) ESul LVER
'Garnet' (Z/d) ESul LVER
'Garnet Rosebud' (Min/d) ESul WFib
'Gartendirektor Herman' (Dec) ESul EWoo NFir WFib
'Gary Salvidge' (R) LDea
'Gaudy' (Z) WFib
'Gay Baby' (DwI) ESul LDea MWhe
'Gay Baby Supreme' (DwI) ESul
§ 'Gemini' (Z/St/d) ESul MWhe NFir SSea WFib
'Gemma' (R) LVER NFir SAga
'Gemma Finito' (R) LDea
'Gemma Jewel' (R) ♀H1+3 ESul
'Gemma Rose' (R) LDea
'Gemma Sweetheart' (R) LDea
I 'Gemstone' (Min) ESul
'Gemstone' (Sc) ♀H1+3 EWoo LDea MBPg MHer NFir WBrk
'Genie' (Z/d) LVER MWhe WFib
'Gentle Georgia' (R) WFib
'Geoff May' (Min) ESul
'Georgia' (R) WFib
'Georgia Mai Read' ERea
'Georgia Peach' (R) ESul WFib
'Georgie' (R) LDea
'Georgina Blythe' (R) ♀H1+3 WFib
'Geo's Pink' (Z/v) MWhe
'Geosta' LAst
'Gerald Portas' (Dw/C) ESul
'Gerald Wells' (Min) ESul
'Geraldine' (Min) ESul
'Gess Portas' (Z/v) ESul
'Ghost Storey' (Z/C) NFir
'Giant Butterfly' (R) LDea
'Giant Oak' (Sc) ESul MBPg MHer MSte
gibbosum EWoo MHer WFib
'Gilbert West' (Z) SKen
'Gilda' (R/v) LDea NFir
'Gill' (Min/Ca) ESul
'Ginger Frost' (Sc/v) WFib
'Ginger Rogers' (Z) NFir
'Glacier Claret' (Z) WFib
'Glacier Crimson' (Z) SKen
'Glacis'PBR (Quality Series) (Z/d) LAst
'Gladys Evelyn' (Z/d) WFib
'Gladys Stevens' (Min/d) ESul
'Gleam' (Z/d) LVER
'Gloria Pearce' (R) LDea
'Glowing Embers' (R) LDea
§ ***glutinosum*** MBPg MHer WFib
'Goblin' (Min/d) ESul SKen WFib
'Godfreys Pride' (Sc) **new** MBPg
'Godshill' (R) LDea
'Goesta' (Z/d) **new** LSou
'Gold Star' (Z/St/C) ESul
'Golden Baby' (DwI/C) ESul LDea NFir WFib
'Golden Brilliantissimum' (Z/v) ESul LRHS MWhe SKen SSea WFib
'Golden Butterfly' (Z/C) ESul
'Golden Chalice' (Min/v) ESul MWhe WFib
'Golden Clorinda' (U/Sc/C) CRHN EWoo LDea MBPg MHer NFir WEas
'Golden Crest' (Z/C) SKen SMrm
'Golden Ears' (Dw/St/C) ESul MWhe NFir NPer WFib
'Golden Edinburgh' (I/v) WFib
'Golden Everaarts' (Dw/C) ESul
'Golden Fleece' (Dw/C/d) ESul
'Golden Gates' (Z/C) ESul SKen
'Golden Harry Hieover' (Z/C) ♀H1+3 ESul MBri MHer
'Golden Lilac Gem' (I/d) WFib
§ 'Golden Mist' (Dw/C/d) LVER
'Golden Petit Pierre' (Min/C) ESul
'Golden Princess' (Min/C) WFib
'Golden Roc' (Min/C) ESul
'Golden Staphs' (Z/St/C) ESul LVER NFir SSea WFib
'Golden Stardust' (Z/St) ESul LVER
'Golden Wedding' (Z/d/v) LRHS LVER MWhe NFir
'Golden Well Sweep' see *P. crispum* 'Golden Well Sweep'
'Goldilocks' (A) ESul LDea
'Gooseberry Leaf' see *P. grossularioides*
'Gordano Midnight' (R) EWoo LDea
'Gosbeck' (A) LDea SSea WFib
'Gossamer Carnival' (Z/d) NFir
'Gothenburg' (R) ESul
'Grace' (A) LDea
'Grace Thomas' (Sc) ♀H1+3 EWoo LDea MBPg MHer WFib
'Grace Wells' (Min) ESul WFib
§ 'Gräfin Mariza' (Z/d) SKen
'Grand Duchess' (R) LDea
'Grand Slam' (R) ESul LDea LVER NFir WFib
'Grandad Mac' (Dw/St) ESul NFir
grandiflorum EWoo WFib
'Grandma Fischer' see *P.* 'Grossmutter Fischer'
'Grandma Ross' (R) ESul LDea
'Granny Hewitt' (Min/d) ESul
graveolens EWoo SBch

	Name	Suppliers
§	'Graveolens' (Sc)	CHal ESul GBar GPoy LVER MBPg MHer MWhe SSea WFib
	'Great Bricett' (Dw/d)	ESul LVER
	'Green Ears' (Z/St)	ESul
	'Green Eyes' (I/d)	SKen
	'Green Goddess' (I/d)	LDea SKen
	'Green Gold Petit Pierre' (Min)	ESul
	'Green Lady' (Sc)	MBPg
	'Green Woodpecker' (R)	LDea LVER SSea
§	'Greengold Kleine Liebling' (Min/C/v)	ESul SKen
	'Greengold Petit Pierre'	see *P.* 'Greengold Kleine Liebling'
	'Greetings' (Min/v)	ESul LVER MBri WFib
§	'Grenadier' (Z)	CWDa
	'Grey Lady Plymouth' (Sc/v)	ESul EWoo LDea MBPg MHer NFir WFib
	'Grey Sprite' (Min/v)	ESul WFib
*	'Groombridge Success' (d)	CWDa
§	'Grossmutter Fischer' (R)	LDea
§	***grossularioides***	EOHP IFro MBPg MHer
	- B&SWJ 6497	WCru
I	- 'Coconut'	MBPg
	'Grozser Garten' (Dw)	ESul
	'Grozser Garten Weiss' (Dw)	ESul
	'Guardsman' (Dw)	ESul
	Guido = 'Kleugudo' (Z/d)	LAst LRHS
	'Gustav Emich' (Z/d)	SKen
	'Gwen' (Min/v)	MWhe NFir
	'H. Rigler' (Z)	SKen
	'Hadleigh' (Min)	ESul
	'Hamble Lass' (R)	LDea
§	'Hannaford Star' (Z/St)	ESul NFir WFib
	'Hansen's Pinkie' (R)	LDea
	'Hansen's Wild Spice' (Sc)	EWoo MBPg SAga
	'Happy Appleblossom' (Z/v/d)	NFir SKen
	Happy Face Mex **new**	LVER
§	'Happy Thought' (Z/v) ♀H1+3	CHal ESul LAst LVER MBri MOak MWhe NFir NVic SCoo SKen SSea WFib
	'Happy Valley' (R)	ESul
	'Harbour Lights' (R)	LDea WFib
	'Harewood Slam' (R)	ESul EWoo LDea MSte WFib
	'Harkstead' (Dw)	ESul
	'Harlequin' (Dw)	ESul
	'Harlequin Alpine Glow' (I/d)	LVER MWhe
	'Harlequin Candy Floss' (I/d)	CWDa
	'Harlequin Mahogany' (I/d)	LDea LVER MWhe SKen
§	'Harlequin Miss Liver Bird' (I)	SKen
	'Harlequin Picotee' (I/d)	LDea LVER SKen
	'Harlequin Pretty Girl' (I x Z/d)	LVER MWhe WFib
	'Harlequin Rosie O'Day' (I)	LDea MWhe SKen WFib
	'Harlequin Ted Day' (I/d)	LDea LVER
	Harmony (Z/Dw)	LVER
	'Harriet Le Hair' (Z)	SKen
	'Harvard' (I/d)	LVER WFib
	'Harvey' (Z)	MWhe
	'Havenstreet' (Dw/St)	ESul
	'Hayley Charlotte' (Z/v)	MWhe
	'Hazel' (R)	LVER WFib
	'Hazel Anson' (R)	LDea
	'Hazel Barolo' (R)	LDea
	'Hazel Birkby' (R)	LDea
	'Hazel Burtoff' (R)	ESul LDea
	'Hazel Carey' (R)	LDea
	'Hazel Cerise' (R)	LDea
	'Hazel Cherry' (R)	LDea MSte WFib
	'Hazel Choice' (R)	ESul LDea NFir
	'Hazel Dean' (R)	NFir
	'Hazel Glory' (R)	LDea
	'Hazel Gowland' (R)	LDea
	'Hazel Gypsy' (R)	ESul LDea
	'Hazel Harmony' (R)	LDea
	'Hazel Henderson' (R)	LDea
	'Hazel Herald' (R)	LDea
	'Hazel Perfection' (R)	LDea NFir
	'Hazel Rose' (R)	LDea
	'Hazel Saga' (R)	ESul
	'Hazel Satin' (R)	LDea
	'Hazel Shiraz' (R)	LDea
	'Hazel Star' (R)	ESul
	'Hazel Stardust' (R)	NFir
	'Hazel Wright' (R)	LDea
§	'Hederinum' (I)	LSou LVER
§	'Hederinum Variegatum' (I/v)	CHal SPet WFib
	'Heidi' (Min/d)	ESul
*	'Helen Bowie'	CWDa
	'Helen Christine' (Z/St)	ESul MWhe NFir WFib
	'Helena' (I/d)	LDea MWhe SKen
	'Hemingstone' (A)	LDea
	'Hemley' (Sc)	LDea MBPg
	'Henhurst Gleam' (Dw/d)	ESul
	'Henley' (Min/d)	ESul
	'Henry Weller' (A)	ESul MBPg MWhe NFir
	'Hermanus Show' (Sc)	MBPg
	'Hermione' (Z/d)	CHal MWhe WFib
	'High Tor' (Dw/C/d)	LVER SKen
	'Highfields Always' (Z/d)	LVER
	'Highfields Appleblossom' (Z)	LVER SKen
	'Highfields Attracta' (Z/d)	LVER SKen WFib
	'Highfields Ballerina' (Z/d)	LVER
	'Highfields Candy Floss' (Z/d)	LVER NFir
	'Highfields Charisma' (Z/d)	LVER
	'Highfields Choice' (Z)	LVER SKen
	'Highfields Comet' (Z)	SKen
	'Highfields Contessa' (Z/d)	LVER SKen WFib
	'Highfields Dazzler' (Z)	LVER
	'Highfields Delight' (Z)	LVER
	'Highfields Fancy' (Z/d)	LVER NFir SKen
	'Highfields Festival' (Z/d)	LVER MWhe NFir SKen WFib
	'Highfields Flair' (Z/d)	LVER
	'Highfields Melody' (Z/d)	WFib
	'Highfields Orange' (Z)	MWhe
	'Highfields Paramount' (Z)	SKen
	'Highfields Perfecta' (Z)	CWDa
	'Highfields Pride' (Z)	SKen WFib
	'Highfields Prima Donna' (Z/d)	LVER MWhe SKen
	'Highfields Promise' (Z)	SKen
	'Highfields Snowdrift' (Z)	LVER SKen
	'Highfields Sugar Candy' (Z/d)	SKen WFib
	'Highfields Supreme' (Z)	LVER
	'Highfields Symphony' (Z)	LVER
	'Hilbre Island' (Z/C/d)	NFir
	'Hildegard' (Z/d)	CHal SKen
	'Hills of Snow' (Z/v)	CHal LVER MBri MHer SKen SSea WFib
	'Hillscheider Amethyst'PBR	see *P.* Amethyst = 'Fisdel'
	'Hindoo' (RxU)	CSpe EWoo LVER NFir SSea WFib
I	'Hindoo Rose' (U)	NFir
	'Hintlesham' (Min)	ESul
	hispidum	MBPg MHer
	'Hitcham' (Min/d)	ESul WFib

'Holbrook' (Dw/C/d) ESul NFir WFib
'Honeywood Lindy' (R) ESul
'Honeywood Margaret' (R) ESul
'Honeywood Suzanne' (Min/Fr) ESul LVER NFir SKen
'Honne Frühling' (Z) SKen
'Honneas' (Dw) ESul
'Honnestolz' (Dw) ESul SKen
'Hope Valley' (Dw/C/d) ♀H1+3 ESul MWhe NFir SKen
'Horace Parsons' (R) WFib
'Horace Read' (Dw) ESul
'Horning Ferry' (Dw) ESul
'House and Garden' (R) NFir
'Howard's Orange' (R) LDea
'Hugo de Vries' (Dw/d) CWDa
'Hula' (U x R) EWoo MHer
'Hulda Conn' (Z/Ca/d) WFib
'Hulverstone' (Dw/St) ESul
'Hunter's Moon' (Z/C) NFir
'Hurdy-gurdy' (Z/d/v) ESul MWhe
'Ian Read' (Min/d) ESul
'Icecrystal'PBR (Sweetheart Series) (Z/d) CWDa LAst
'Icing Sugar' (I/d) ESul LDea SSea WFib
ignescens MBPg
* 'Ilse Fisher' CWDa
'Immaculatum' (Z) WFib
'Imperial'PBR (R) LAst
'Imperial Butterfly' (A/Sc) CRHN ESul GGar LDea LVER MBPg MSte MWhe NFir SKen WFib
incrassatum NBur
Ingres = 'Guicerdan'PBR (I/d) ♀H1+3 LAst
ionidiflorum CSpe EShb EWoo LPio MBPg MHer SAga XPep
'Ipswich Town' (Dw/d) ESul
'Irene' (Z/d) ♀H1+3 SKen WFib
'Irene Cal' (Z/d) ♀H1+3 SKen
'Irene Collet' (R) LDea
'Irene Picardy' (Z/d) SKen
'Irene Toyon' (Z) ♀H1+3 SKen WFib
* 'Iris Monroe' CWDa
§ 'Isabell' (Quality Series) (Z/d) LAst LSou
'Isidel' (I/d) ♀H1+3 SKen WFib
I 'Islington Peppermint' (Sc) MBPg SSea WFib
'Isobel Eden' (Sc) LDea MBPg
'Italian Gem' (I) SKen
'Ivalo' (Z/d) MWhe SKen WFib
'Ivory Snow' (Z/d/v) ESul LVER MWhe NFir SKen WFib
'Jacey' (Z/d) LVER SKen
'Jack of Hearts' (I x Z/d) WFib
'Jack Wood' (Z/d) NFir WFib
§ 'Jackie' (I/d) EShb EWoo LVER MBri WFib
'Jackie Davies' (R) LDea
'Jackie Gall' see *P.* 'Jackie'
'Jackie's Gem' (I/d) MWhe
'Jacko' (I/d) EWoo
I 'Jackpot Wild Rose' (Z/d) WFib
'Jacqueline' (Z/d) SKen
'Jane Biggin' (Dw/C/d) ESul MWhe SKen
'Janet Dean' (R) LDea
'Janet Hofman' (Z/d) WFib
'Janet Kerrigan' (Min/d) ESul MWhe WEas
'Janet Scott' (Z) CWDa
'Jasmin' (R) ESul LDea
'Jaunty' (Min/d) ESul
'Jayne' (Min/d) ESul
'Jayne Eyre' (Min/d) CHal ESul MWhe NFir SKen WFib
§ 'Jazz' CWDa WWol
'Jean Bart' (I) CWDa LVER
'Jean Beatty' (Dw/d) LVER
'Jean Oberle' (Z/d) SKen
'Jeanetta' (R) LDea
§ 'Jeanne d'Arc' (I/d) SKen WFib
'Jenifer Read' (Dw) ESul
'Jennifer' (Min) ESul
'Jer'Ray' (A) ESul EWoo LDea MBPg MWhe NFir WFib
'Jessel's Unique' (U) LDea MHer MSte SPet SSea
'Jessica' **new** LVER
* 'Jetfire' (d) CWDa
'Jewel' (Z/d) LAst
'Jewel' (R) ESul
'Jinny Reeves' (R) ESul LDea
'Joan Cashmere' (Z/d) ESul
'Joan Fontaine' (Z) WFib
'Joan Hayward' (Min) ESul
'Joan Morf' (R) ESul EWoo LDea LVER NFir SSea WFib
'Joan of Arc' see *P.* 'Jeanne d'Arc'
'Joan Sharman' (Min) ESul
'Joanna Pearce' (R) LDea SKen
'John Thorp' (R) LDea
'John's Angela' LVER
'John's Pride' MBri NFir
'Joseph Haydn' (R) ESul LDea MSte
'Joseph Wheeler' (A) ESul LDea MWhe
'Joy' (R) ♀H1+3 ESul EWoo LDea LRHS LVER NFir WFib
'Joy' (I) SPet
I 'Joy' (Z/d) SKen
'Joy Lucille' (Sc) CSev ESul EWoo LDea MBPg MHer
'Joyden' CWDa
'Joyful' (Min) ESul
'Jubel Parr' (Z/d) CWDa
'Judy Read' (Dw) ESul
'Julia' (R) ♀H1+3 LDea
'Juliana' (R) LDea
'Julie Bannister' (R) ESul
'Julie Smith' (R) LDea WFib
'June Filbey' (R) **new** LDea
'Jungle Night' (R) ESul EWoo
'Juniper' (Sc) EWoo MBPg MHer WFib
'Jupiter' (Min/d) SKen
'Jupiter' (R) ESul NFir
'Just Rita' (A) SSea
'Just William' (Min/C/d) ESul WFib
'Kamahl' (R) WFib
§ 'Kardinal' (Z/d) SPet
'Karl Hagele' (Z/d) LVER SKen SYvo WFib
'Karmin Ball' CWDa WFib
karrooense Knuth MHer
'Karrooense' see *P. quercifolium*
'Kathleen' (Min) ESul
'Kathleen Gamble' (Z) WFib
'Kathryn' (Min) ESul
'Kathryn Portas' (Z/v) ESul SKen
'Katie' (R) EWoo
'Kayleigh Aitken' (R) **new** NFir
'Kayleigh West' (Min) ESul
'Keepsake' (Min/d) ESul WFib
'Keith Vernon' (Z) NFir
'Kelly Brougham' (St/dw) **new** ESul
'Kelvedon Beauty' (Min) WEas
'Ken Lea' (Z/v) LVER
'Ken Salmon' (Dw/d) ESul
'Kennard Castle' (Z) CWDa
'Kenny's Double' (Z/d) WFib
'Kensington' (A) LDea
'Kerensa' (Min/d) ESul SKen WFib
'Kershy' (Min) ESul
'Kesgrave' (Min/d) ESul LVER WFib
'Kettlebaston' (A) ♀H1+3 LDea WFib

	Name	Suppliers
	'Kewense' (Z)	EShb
	'Key's Unique' (U)	EWoo
	'Kimono' (R)	ESul LDea NFir
	'Kinder Gaisha' (R)	NFir
	'King Edmund' (R)	LDea
	'King of Balcon'	see *P.* 'Hederinum'
	'King of Denmark' (Z/d)	LVER WFib
	'King Solomon' (R)	LDea
	'King's Ransom' (R)	LDea
	'Kirton' (Min/d)	ESul
§	'Kleine Liebling' (Min)	ESul MWhe WFib
I	'Korcicum' (Sc)	MBPg
	'Krista' (Min/d)	ESul WBrk WFib
	'Kyoto' (R)	NFir
	'Kyra' (Min/d)	ESul WFib
	'L.E. Wharton' (Z)	SKen
	'La France' (I/d) 🏆H1+3	LDea LVER MWhe SKen WFib
	'La Paloma' (R)	WFib
	'Laced Mini Rose Cascade' (I)	NFir
	Laced Red Mini Cascade = 'Achspen' (I)	NFir
	Lachsball (Z/d)	SKen
§	'Lachskönigin' (I/d)	LVER SKen SPet WFib
	'Lady Alice of Valencia'	see *P.* 'Grenadier'
	'Lady Cullum' (Z/C/v)	MWhe
	'Lady Ilchester' (Z/d)	SKen WFib
	'Lady Love Song' (R)	ESul LVER NFir SSea
	'Lady Mary' (Sc)	ESul EWoo LVER MBPg MHer
	'Lady Mavis Pilkington' (Z/d)	WFib
	'Lady Plymouth' (Sc/v) 🏆H1+3	CHal CHrt CRHN CSpe ESul GBar LDea LPio LRHS LVER MBPg MHer MSte MWhe NFir NHHG NScw SKen SMrm SPet SSea WBrk WFib
	Lady Ramona = 'KLEP01007'	LAst
§	'Lady Scarborough' (Sc)	ESul EWoo LDea LPio MBPg WFib
	'Lady Scott' (Sc)	MBPg
	'Lady Woods' (Z)	SSea
	'Lakeland' (I)	ESul
	'Lakis' (R)	LDea
	'Lamorna' (R)	LDea SKen
	'Langley' (R)	LDea
	'Lanham Lane' (I)	LDea
	'Lanham Royal' (Dw/d)	ESul
	'Lara Aladin' (A)	LDea MBPg
	'Lara Ballerina'	NFir
	'Lara Candy Dancer' (Sc) 🏆H1+3	CRHN ESul LDea MBPg MHer WFib
	'Lara Jester' (Sc)	EWoo MBPg MHer WFib
	'Lara Maid' (A) 🏆H1+3	CHrt MWhe WFib
	'Lara Nomad' (Sc)	EWoo LDea MBPg
	'Lara Starshine' (Sc) 🏆H1+3	CHal ESul EWoo LPio MBPg MHer NFir SSea WFib
	'Lara Susan' (Dec)	EWoo NFir
	'Lara Waltz' (R/d)	WFib
	'Lark' (Min/d)	ESul
	'Larkfield' (Z/v)	SSea
N	'Lass o' Gowrie' (Z/v)	ESul LRHS LVER MSte MWhe NFir SKen
	'Lateripes' (I)	SKen
	'Laura Parmer' (Dw/St)	ESul
	'Laura Wheeler' (A)	ESul LDea MWhe
	'Laurel Hayward' (R)	WFib
	Lauretta = 'Pacamla'PBR (Quality Series)(Z/d)	LAst LSou
	Lavenda = 'Penlava'PBR (Dark Line Series)(Z/d)	LAst LSou
	'Lavender Grand Slam' (R) 🏆H1+3	ESul LDea LVER NFir
	'Lavender Harewood Slam' (R)	ESul LDea
	'Lavender Mini Cascade'PBR	see *P.* Lilac Mini Cascade = 'Lilamica'
	'Lavender Sensation' (R)	WFib
	'Lavender Wings' (I)	LDea
	'Lawrenceanum'	ESul NFir WFib
	'Layham' (Dw/d)	ESul
	'Layton's White' (Z/d)	CWDa
	'Le Lutin' (Z/d)	CWDa
	'L'Elégante' (I/v) 🏆H1+3	CHal EWoo LAst LDea LVER MWhe NFir SKen SSea WEas WFib
	'Lemon Air' (Sc)	ESul EWoo MBPg
	'Lemon Crisp'	see *P. crispum*
	'Lemon Fancy' (Sc)	EWoo LDea LVER MBPg MHer MWhe NFir WFib
	'Lemon Kiss' (Sc)	EWoo MBPg
	'Lemon Meringue' (Sc) **new**	MBPg
	'Lemon Toby' (Sc)	MBPg
	'Len Chandler' (Min)	ESul
	'Lenore' (Min/d)	ESul
	'Leo' (Min)	ESul
	'Leonie Holbrow' (Min)	ESul
	'Leopard' (I/d)	CWDa
	'Leslie Salmon' (Dw/C)	ESul MWhe
	'Lesmona' **new**	LAst LSou
	'Lessland' **new**	LVER
	Lila Compakt-Cascade	see *P.* 'Decora Lilas'
	Lilac Cascade	see *P.* 'Roi des Balcons Lilas'
	'Lilac Domaine de Courson' (Sc) **new**	MBPg
	'Lilac Domino'	see *P.* 'Telston's Prima'
	'Lilac Elaine' (R)	LDea
	'Lilac Gem' (Min/I/d)	LDea LVER MWhe NFir SKen
	'Lilac Jewel' (R)	ESul
	'Lilac Joy' (R)	LVER
§	Lilac Mini Cascade = 'Lilamica'PBR (I)	ESul LDea LVER NFir
	'Lili Marlene' (I)	LVER SPet
	'Lilian' (Min)	ESul LAst LSou
	'Lilian Pottinger' (Sc)	CArn CHal CRHN ESul GBar LDea MBPg MHer MWhe NFir SKen SSea
	'Lilo Cascade'	MBPg
	'Limelight' (Z/v)	SSea
	'Limoneum' (Sc)	CSev LDea MBPg MHer NBur SKen
	'Linda' (R)	ESul LDea
	'Lindsey' (Min)	ESul
	'Lindy Portas' (I/d)	SKen
	'Lipstick' (St)	WFib
	'Lisa' (Min/C)	ESul WFib
	'Lisa Jo' (St/v/Dw/d)	WFib
	'Little Alice' (Dw/d) 🏆H1+3	ESul MWhe NFir WFib
	'Little Blakenham' (A)	ESul LDea
	'Little Fi-fine' (Dw/C)	ESul NFir
	'Little Gem' (Sc)	EWoo LDea LVER MBPg MHer SSea WFib
	'Little Jim' (Min) **new**	NFir
	'Little Jip' (Z/d/v)	LVER NFir WFib
	'Little Margaret' (Min/v)	ESul
	'Little Perky' (MinI)	ESul
	'Little Primular' (Min)	ESul
	'Little Rascal' (A) **new**	LDea
	'Lively Lady' (Dw/C)	ESul
	'Liverbird'	see *P.* 'Harlequin Miss Liver Bird'
	longicaule	MBPg
	'Lord Baden-Powell'	see *P.* 'Colonel Baden-Powell'
	'Lord Bute' (R) 🏆H1+3	CSpe CTbh ECtt EShb ESul EWoo GGar LAst LDea LIck LPio LRHS LVER MHer MSte NCiC NFir NPer NWoo SDnm SIde SKen SMer SMrm SPet SUsu WEas WFib WPen
	'Lord Constantine' (R)	LDea
	'Lord de Ramsey'	see *P.* 'Tip Top Duet'

	Name	Suppliers
	'Lord Roberts' (Z)	WFib
	'Lorelei' (Z/d)	CWDa
	Lorena = 'Pacdala'PBR (Dark Line Series)(Z/d)	LAst
	'Loretta' (Dw)	ESul
	'Lorna' (Dw/d)	ESul
	'Lorraine' (Dw)	ESul
	'Lotusland' (Dw/St/C)	ESul LAst LVER NFir WFib
	'Louise' (Min)	ESul
I	'Louise' (R)	ESul NFir
	'Love Song' (R/v)	ESul LDea NFir SSea WFib
	'Love Story' (Z/v)	ESul
	'Loveliness' (Z)	WFib
*	'Loverly' (Min/d)	ESul
	'Lovesdown' (Dw/St)	ESul
	'Lucilla' (Min)	ESul
	'Lucinda' (Min)	ESul
	'Lucy' (Min)	ESul
	'Lucy Gunnett' (Z/d/v)	ESul MWhe NFir
	'Lucy Jane' (R)	LDea
	'Lulu' (I/d)	NPri
	Luna = 'Fisuna' (I/d)	NPri
	'Lustre' (R)	ESul
	'Lyewood Bonanza' (R)	ESul LDea
	'Lynne Valerie' (A)	LDea
	'Lyric' (Min/d)	ESul WFib
	'Mabel Grey' (Sc) 🏆H1+3	CHal CRHN CSev CSpe EShb ESul EWoo LIck LVER MBPg MHer MSte MWhe NBur NFir NHHG NPer SBch SIde SKen SSea WFib
§	'Madame Auguste Nonin' (U/Sc)	CHal CHrt ESul EWoo LVER MBPg MHer NFir NWoo SKen WFib
	'Madame Butterfly' (Z/d/v)	ESul MWhe NFir SKen
	'Madame Crousse' (I/d) 🏆H1+3	WFib
	'Madame Fournier' (Dw/C)	ESul
	'Madame Hibbault' (Z)	SKen
	'Madame Layal' (A)	EWoo LDea LIck MHer MSte NFir SAga SKen WFib
	'Madame Margot'	see *P.* 'Hederinum Variegatum'
	'Madame Salleron' (Min/v) 🏆H1+3	LDea LRHS LVER MSte SKen
	'Madame Thibaut' (R)	LDea MSte
	'Madge Taylor' (R)	NFir
	'Magaluf' (I/C/d)	SSea
	'Magda' (Z/d)	ESul LVER
	magenteum	EWoo
	'Magic Lantern' (Z/C)	NFir
	'Magnum' (R)	WFib
	'Maid of Honour' (Min)	ESul
	'Maiden Petticoat'	LAst SAga
	'Maiden Rosepink' (R)	LAst WGor
	'Maiden Sunrise'	LAst
	'Mairi' (A)	EWoo LDea WFib
	'Mamie' (Z/d)	SKen
	'Mandarin' (R)	ESul
	'Mangles' Variegated' (Z/v)	SPet SSea WFib
	'Mantilla' (Min)	ESul SKen
	'Manx Maid' (A)	ESul LDea NFir SKen
	'Maple Leaf' (Sc)	EWoo MBPg
	'Marble Sunset'	see *P.* 'Wood's Surprise'
	'Marchioness of Bute' (R)	EMan LDea LVER MSte NFir NPer SSea WFib
	'Maréchal MacMahon' (Z/C)	SKen SPet
	'Margaret Parmenter' (I/C)	ESul
	'Margaret Pearce' (R)	LDea
	'Margaret Salvidge' (R)	LDea
	'Margaret Soley' (R) 🏆H1+3	LDea
	'Margaret Stimpson' (R)	LDea
	'Margaret Thorp'	LVER
	'Margaret Waite' (R)	WFib
	'Margery Stimpson' (Min/d)	ESul WFib
	'Maria Thomas' (Sc)	MBPg
	'Maria Wilkes' (Z/d)	WFib
	'Marie Rober' (R)	SKen
	'Marie Rudlin' (R)	LVER
	'Marie Thomas' (Sc)	LDea MHer SBch SSea
§	'Marie Vogel' (R)	MSte
	'Marilyn' (Dw/d)	ESul
	Marimba = 'Fisrimba'PBR	NPri SCoo
	'Marion' (Min)	ESul
	'Mariquita' (R)	WFib
	'Marja' (R)	LDea
	'Marmalade' (Min/d)	ESul MWhe WFib
	'Marquis of Bute' (R/v)	ESul LVER NFir
	'Martha Parmer' (Min)	ESul
	'Martin Parrett' (Min/d)	WFib
	'Martin's Splendour' (Min)	ESul
	'Martlesham' (Dw)	ESul
	'Mary Ellen Tanner' (Min/d)	ESul
	'Mary Read' (Min)	ESul
	'Mary Rose' (R)	LDea
	'Mary Webster' (Min)	ESul
	'Masquerade' (R)	SPet
	'Masquerade' (Min)	ESul
	'Master Paul' (Z/v)	ESul
	'Matthew Salvidge' (R)	ESul
	'Maureen' (Min)	ESul NFir
	'Mauve Beauty' (I/d)	SKen WFib
	'Maxime Kovalevski' (Z)	WFib
	'Maxine' (Z/C)	NFir
	'Maxine Colley' (Z/d/v)	LVER
	'May Day' (R)	LDea
	'May Magic' (R)	NFir WFib
	'Mayor of Seville' (Z/d)	WFib
I	'Meadowside Dark and Dainty' (St)	WFib
	'Meadowside Fancy' (Z/d/C)	LVER
	'Meadowside Harvest' (Z/St/C)	NFir WFib
	'Meadowside Julie Colley' (Dw)	NFir
I	'Meadowside Mahogany' (Z/C)	LVER
	'Meadowside Mardi Gras' (Dw/d)	NFir
	'Meadowside Midnight' (St/C)	CSpe MHer MWhe SHFr WFib
	'Meadowside Orange' (Z/d)	LVER
	'Medallion' (Z/C)	MHer SSea
	'Meditation' (Min)	ESul
	'Medley' (Min/d)	MWhe WFib
	'Melanie' (R)	LDea
	'Melanie' (Min)	ESul
*	'Melissa' (Min)	ESul
	Melosilver = 'Penber' (Tempo Series) (Z/d/v)	LAst SPoG
	'Memento' (Min/d)	ESul SKen WFib
	'Mendip' (R)	WFib
	'Mendip Anne' (R)	NFir
	'Mendip Barbie' (R)	NFir
	'Mendip Blanche' (R)	NFir
	'Mendip Candy Floss' (R)	ESul
	'Mendip Sentire' (R)	NFir
	'Meon Maid' (R)	ESul LDea WFib
	'Mere Caribbean' (R)	NFir
	'Mere Casino' (Z)	LVER WFib
	'Mere Greeting' (Z/d)	MWhe WFib
	'Mere Sunglow' (R)	LDea
	'Merle Seville' (Z/d)	SKen

'Merlin' (Sc)	MBPg
'Merry-go-round' (Z/C/v)	LVER MWhe
'Mexica Katrine'	LAst
Mexica Tomcat (I/d)	LAst LSou WGor
'Mexican Beauty' (I)	CHal WFib
'Mexicana'	LAst
'Mexicanerin'	see *P.* 'Rouletta'
'Michael' (A)	ESul LDea MHer
'Michelle' (Min/C)	LDea
'Michelle West' (Min)	ESul WFib
'Midas Touch' (Dw/C/d)	ESul
'Milden' (Dw/Z/C)	ESul NFir
'Millbern Choice' (Z)	MWhe
'Millbern Clover' (Min/d)	ESul MWhe
'Millbern Engagement' (Min/d)	MWhe
'Millbern Peach' (Z)	MWhe
'Millbern Serenade'	MWhe
'Millbern Sharna' (Min/d)	ESul MWhe
'Millbern Skye' (A)	MWhe
Millennium Dawn (Dw)	LVER
'Miller's Valentine' (Z/v)	ESul WFib
'Millfield Gem' (I/d)	LVER SKen WFib
'Millfield Rose' (I/d)	LVER MWhe
'Millie' (Z/d)	CWDa
'Mimi' (Dw/C/d)	ESul SSea
'Mini-Czech' (Min/St)	ESul LVER
'Minnie' (Z/d/St)	ESul LVER WBrk
'Minstrel Boy' (R)	CSpe ESul EWoo LDea NFir WFib
'Minx' (Min/d)	WFib
* 'Mirage'	CWDa
'Miranda' (Dw)	ESul
'Miriam Basey'	see *P.* 'Dwarf Miriam Baisey'
'Miss Australia' (R/v)	LDea MBPg
'Miss Burdett Coutts' (Z/v)	ESul LVER MWhe SKen SSea WFib
'Miss Flora' (I)	CWDa MWhe
'Miss Liverbird' (I/d)	ECtt
'Miss McKinsey' (Z/St/d)	LVER NFir
§ 'Miss Stapleton'	EWoo LPio MHer WFib
'Miss Wackles' (Min/d)	ESul
'Mistress' (Z/C)	NFir
'Misty' (Z)	ESul
'Modesty' (Z/d)	WFib
'Mohawk' (R)	ESul LVER NFir WFib
Molina = 'Fismoli'PBR (I/d)	NPri
'Mollie' (R)	CSpe
'Molly' (A)	NFir
'Mona Lisa'PBR	ESul
'Monarch' (Dw/v)	ESul
'Monica Bennett' (Dw)	ESul SKen WEas
'Monkwood Charm' (R)	LDea
'Monkwood Rose' (A)	LDea NFir
'Monkwood Sprite' (R)	LDea SMrm
'Monsal Dale' (Dw/C/d)	ESul SKen
'Monsieur Ninon' hort.	see *P.* 'Madame Auguste Nonin'
§ 'Monsieur Ninon' (U)	CRHN EWoo MSte WFib
'Mont Blanc' (Z/v)	ESul LVER MWhe SKen WFib
'Montague Garabaldi Smith' (R)	WFib
'Moon Maiden' (A)	CSpe ESul EWoo LDea WFib
'Moor' (Min/d)	ESul
'Moppet' (Min/d)	ESul
'Morella' (Z) **new**	WGor
'Morning Cloud' (Min/d)	ESul
'Morse' (Z)	SKen
'Morval' (Dw/C/d) ♀H1+3	ESul LVER MWhe SKen WFib
'Morwenna' (R)	ESul EWoo LDea LPio LVER MSte NFir SKen WFib
'Mosaic Gay Baby' (I/v/d)	WFib
'Mosaic Silky' (Z/C/d/v)	LVER
'Mountie' (Dw)	ESul
'Mr Everaarts' (Dw/d)	ESul MWhe
'Mr Henry Apps' (Dw/C/d)	MWhe
'Mr Henry Cox' (Z/v) ♀H1+3	ESul MHer MWhe NFir SKen WFib
'Mr Wren' (Z)	CHal LVER MWhe SKen WFib
'Mrs A.M. Mayne' (Z)	SKen
'Mrs Cannell' (Z)	SKen WFib
'Mrs Dumbrill' (A)	ESul LDea LIck
'Mrs E.G. Hill' (Z)	CWDa
'Mrs Farren' (Z/v)	MWhe SKen SSea
'Mrs G.H. Smith' (A)	ESul LDea MBPg MSte MWhe NFir WFib
'Mrs G. Morf' (R)	ESul SSea
'Mrs J.C. Mappin' (Z/v) ♀H1+3	SAga SKen SSea
'Mrs Kingsbury' (U)	WEas WFib
'Mrs Langtry' (R)	LDea
'Mrs Lawrence' (Z/d)	SKen
'Mrs Martin' (I/d)	WFib
'Mrs McKenzie' (Z/St)	WFib
'Mrs Morf' (R)	LDea NFir
'Mrs Parker' (Z/d/v)	ESul LRHS LVER MWhe NFir SKen WFib
'Mrs Pat' (Dw/St/C)	MWhe NFir
'Mrs Pollock' (Z/v)	LAst LRHS LVER MWhe NEgg NVic SCoo SKen SSea WBrk WFib
'Mrs Quilter' (Z/C) ♀H1+3	LVER MBri MHer MWhe NVic SAga SKen SMrm SSea WFib
'Mrs Salter Bevis' (Z/Ca/d)	ESul LVER WFib
'Mrs Strang' (Z/d/v)	LVER MWhe SKen SSea
'Mrs Tarrant' (Z/d)	CHal
'Mrs Taylor' (Sc)	MBPg
'Mrs W.A.R. Clifton' (I/d)	LDea SKen WFib
multicaule	EWoo
- subsp. ***multicaule***	EShb
mutans	WFib
§ 'Mutzel' (I/v)	LVER NFir
'My Chance'	EWoo NFir
'My Choice' (R)	LDea
§ ***myrrhifolium*** var. ***coriandrifolium***	CSpe SAga
'Mystery' (U) ♀H1+3	EWoo LVER MBPg NFir SAga SSea WFib
'Müttertag' (R)	LDea MSte
'Nacton' (Min)	ESul
'Nancy Grey' (Min)	ESul NFir
'Nançy Mac' (St) **new**	ESul
'Naomi' (R)	LDea
'Narina' (I)	NPri SCoo
'Natalie' (Dw)	ESul
'Naughton' (Min)	ESul
'Needham Market' (A)	ESul LDea MSte WFib
'Neene' (Dw)	ESul
'Neil Clemenson' (Sc)	MBPg WFib
'Neil Jameson' (Z/v)	LVER SKen
'Nell Smith' (Z/d)	WFib
'Nellie' (R)	LDea
'Nellie Nuttall' (Z)	WFib
'Nervosum' (Sc)	ESul MBPg MOak
'Nervous Mabel' (Sc) ♀H1+3	ESul EWoo LDea MBPg MHer NFir WBrk WFib
'Nettlecombe' (Min/St)	ESul
'Nettlestead' (Dw/d)	ESul LVER
'Neville West' (Z)	SSea
'New Day' (A)	LDea
'New Life' (Z)	ESul MWhe
'Newton Rigg' (Sc) **new**	MBPg
'Nicola Buck' (R)	LDea NFir
'Nicor Star' (Min)	ESul WFib
'Nikki' (A)	LDea
'Nimrod' (R)	LDea
'Noche' (R)	LDea SKen SMrm
'Noel' (Z/Ca/d)	WFib
'Noele Gordon' (Z/d)	LVER WFib
'Nomad' (R)	EWoo NFir

'Nomad's Sweetheart' (A) LVER
'Nono' (I) WFib
'Norrland' (Z/d) LVER
* 'Norvic' (d) CWDa
'Nostra' LAst LSou
'Notting Hill Beauty' (Z) SKen
oblongatum **new** CMon NFir
'Occold Embers' (Dw/C/d) ESul LVER NFir
'Occold Lagoon' (Dw/d) ESul
'Occold Orange Tip' (Min/d) ESul
'Occold Profusion' (Dw/d) ESul NFir
'Occold Ruby' (Dw/C) CWDa
'Occold Shield' (Dw/C/d) ESul LAst LRHS SDnm SMrm WBrk WFib
'Occold Tangerine' (Z) WFib
'Occold Volcano' (Dw/C/d) WFib
odoratissimum (Sc) CHal ESul EWoo GBar GPoy LDea LVER MBPg MHer NFir NHHG SKen SSea WFib
'Offton' (Dw) ESul
'Old Orchard' (A) LDea SSea
'Old Rose' (Z/d) WFib
'Old Spice' (Sc/v) ESul GBar LVER MBPg MHer NFir SWal WFib
'Oldbury Duet' (A/v) LDea LVER MBPg MWhe NFir SSea
'Olga Shipstone' (Sc) EWoo MBPg
'Olympia' (Z/d) CWDa
'Onalee' (Dw) ESul WFib
'Opera House' (R) WFib
'Orange' (Z/St) MBPg
'Orange Fizz' (Sc) ESul EWoo SDnm
'Orange Fizz' (Z/d) LDea
'Orange Imp' (Dw/d) ESul
'Orange Parfait' (R) WFib
I 'Orange Princeanum' (Sc) MBPg
'Orange Ricard' (Z/d) MWhe SKen
'Orange Ruffy' (Min) ESul
'Orange Splash' (Z) LVER SKen
'Orangeade' (Dw/d) ESul LVER SKen WFib
'Orangesonne' (Z/d) LVER
'Orchid Clorinda' (Sc) MBPg WFib
'Orchid Paloma' (Dw/d) ESul SKen
'Oregon Hostess' (Dw) ESul
'Orion' (Min/d) ESul LVER MWhe SKen WFib
'Orsett' (Sc) ♀H1+3 EWoo LDea LVER MBPg
'Oscar' (Z/d) CWDa
'Osna' (Z) LAst SKen
'Otto's Red' (R) EWoo NFir
'Our Gynette' (Dec) EWoo NFir
ovale subsp. ***ovale*** EShb
'Oyster' (Dw) ESul
'Paddie' (Min) ESul
'Pagoda' (Z/St/d) ESul LVER MSte MWhe SKen WFib
'Paisley Red' (Z/d) NFir WFib
'Palais' (Z/d) LRHS SKen
'Pam Craigie' (R) LDea
'Pampered Lady' (A) LDea
panduriforme EWoo MBPg WFib
papilionaceum CHEx CRHN CTbh EWoo MHer MOak WEas WFib
'Parisienne' (R) ESul EWoo LDea WFib
'Parmenter Pink' (Min) ESul
'Party Dress' (Z/d) MWhe WFib
'Pascal' (Z) SKen
'Pat Hannam' (St) WFib
'Paton's Unique' (U/Sc) ♀H1+3 CHal CRHN CTbh EShb EWoo LIck LVER MBPg MHer MSte NFir SPet WFib
* 'Patricia' (I) CWDa
'Patricia Andrea' (T) ESul LVER NFir NPer WFib
'Patricia Read' (Min) ESul
'Patsy 'Q'' (Z/C) SKen
'Paul Crampel' (Z) CHal LVER MHer WFib
'Paul Gotz' (Z) SKen
'Paul Gunnett' (Min) MWhe
'Paul West' (Min/d) ESul
'Paula Scott' (R) EWoo LDea
'Pauline' (Min/d) ESul MWhe
'Pauline Harris' (R) LDea
'Pax' (R) LDea
'Pazzaz' **new** LVER
'Peace' (Min/C) ESul WFib
'Peace Palace' (Dw) ESul
'Peach Blossom' **new** LVER
'Peach Princess' (R) ESul NFir SAga SSea
'Peaches' (Z) LAst LSou WGor
'Peaches and Cream' (R) MBPg
'Peacock' LDea
'Pearly Queen' (Min/d) ESul
'Pebbles' (Z/Min) LVER
'Peggy Clare' (Dw/St) ESul
'Peggy Sue' (R) ESul LDea LVER
PELFI cultivars see under cultivar name
peltatum WFib
'Penny' (Z/d) MWhe WFib
'Penny Dixon' (R) NFir
'Penny Lane' (Z) WFib
'Penny Serenade' (Dw/C) ESul SKen
'Pensby' (Dw) ESul
'Peppermint Lace' (Sc) EWoo LDea MBPg
I 'Peppermint Scented Rose' (Sc) MBPg
'Peppermint Star' (Z/St) ESul LVER
'Perchance' (R) SSea
'Percival' (Dw/d) MWhe
'Perfect' (Z) SKen WFib
* 'Perle Blanche' (I) CWDa
§ Perlenkette Orange = 'Orangepen'[PBR] (Quality Series)(Z/d) LAst LSou
'Perlenkette Sabine' (Quality Series) (Z/d) LAst
'Pershore Princess' WBrk
'Persian King' (R) LDea
'Persian Ruler' (Min) ESul
'Persimmon' (Z/St) WFib
'Petals' (Z/v) MSte SKen
'Peter Godwin' (R) ESul LDea WFib
'Peter Read' (Dw/d) ESul
'Peter's Choice' (R) ESul LDea WFib
'Peter's Luck' (Sc) ♀H1+3 ESul MBPg
'Petit Pierre' see *P.* 'Kleine Liebling'
'Petite Blanche' (Dw/d) WFib
'Petronella' (Z/d) ESul
'Phil Rose' (I) CWDa
'Philomel' (I/d) SPet
'Phlox New Life' (Z) ESul
'Phyllis' (Z) LDea
'Phyllis' (U/v) ESul EWoo LVER MBPg NFir SSea
'Phyllis Read' (Min) ESul
'Phyllis Richardson' (R/d) LDea LVER
'Picotee Kleiner Leibling' (Min) LVER
'Pin Mill' (Min/d) ESul
'Pink Aura' (Min/St) ESul
'Pink Aurore' (U) MHer MSte WFib
'Pink Bonanza' (R) ESul LDea WFib
'Pink Bouquet' (R) ESul
'Pink Capitatum' see *P.* 'Pink Capricorn'
§ 'Pink Capricorn' (Sc) CRHN ESul EWoo MBPg MHer SDnm WFib
'Pink Carnation' (I/d) LDea
'Pink Cascade' see *P.* 'Hederinum'
'Pink Champagne' (Sc) CRHN ESul EWoo MBPg MHer
'Pink Countess Mariza' (Z) SKen

	Name	Suppliers
	'Pink Crampel' (Z)	CWDa
	'Pink Dolly Varden' (Z/v)	LVER SSea WFib
	'Pink Domaine de Courson' (Sc) **new**	MBPg
	'Pink Flamingo' (R)	LDea
	'Pink Fondant' (Min/d)	ESul WFib
	'Pink Gay Baby'	see *P.* 'Sugar Baby'
	'Pink Golden Ears' (Dw/St/C)	ESul SKen
	'Pink Golden Harry Hieover' (Z/C)	ESul
	'Pink Happy Thought' (Z/v)	LAst LRHS LVER MWhe SDnm SPet SSea WFib
	'Pink Hindoo' (Dec) **new**	EWoo
	'Pink Ice' (Min/d)	ESul NFir
	'Pink Mini Cascade'	see *P.* 'Rosa Mini-cascade'
	'Pink Needles' (Min/St)	ESul
	'Pink Paradox'	LDea MBPg
	'Pink Rambler' (Z/d)	MWhe SKen WFib
	'Pink Rosebud' (I/d)	SKen
	'Pink Rosebud' (Z/d)	WFib
	'Pink Snow' (Min/d)	ESul
	'Pink Splash' (Min/d)	ESul
	'Pink Tiny Tim' (Min)	ESul
	Pink-Blizzard = 'Fispink' (I)	NPri WWol
	'Pippa' (Min/Dw) **new**	ESul
	'Pixie' (Min)	ESul
	'Playmate' (Min/St)	ESul SKen WFib
	'Plenty' (Z/d)	CWDa
	'Plum Rambler' (Z/d)	EShb SKen WFib
	'Poetesse' (A)	LDea
	'Polka' (U)	ESul EWoo LVER MBPg MHer NFir SSea WFib
	'Pompeii' (R)	ESul LDea NFir WFib
	'Poquita' (Sc)	MBPg
	'Porchfield' (Min/St)	ESul
	'Potpourri' (Min)	SKen
	'Potter Heigham' (Dw)	ESul
	'Powder Puff' (Dw/d)	ESul WFib
	'Presto' (Dw/St)	ESul MWhe
	'Preston Park' (Z/C)	SKen SPet WFib
	'Pretty Girl' (I)	LDea
	'Pretty Petticoat' (Z/d)	WFib
	'Pretty Polly' (Sc)	LDea MBPg WFib
	'Pride of Exmouth'	CStu
	'Prim' (Dw/St/d)	ESul WFib
	'Primavera' (R)	LDea
	'Prince' (R)	SKen
	'Prince Consort' (R)	LDea
	'Prince of Orange' (Sc)	CArn CRHN CSev CTbh EOHP ESul EWoo GBar GPoy LDea LIck LVER MBPg MHer MSte MWhe NFir NHHG SIde WFib
	'Princeanum' (Sc) ♀H1+3	MBPg MHer WFib
	'Princess Alexandra' (R)	LVER SSea
	'Princess Alexandra' (Z/d/v)	ESul MWhe NFir
	'Princess Anne' (Z)	MSte
	'Princess Josephine' (R)	LDea WFib
	'Princess of Balcon'	see *P.* 'Roi des Balcons Lilas'
	'Princess of Wales' (R)	LVER WFib
	'Princess Virginia' (R/v)	LDea LIck LVER WFib
	'Priory Salmon' (St/d) **new**	ESul
	'Prospect' (Z/d)	MWhe
	'Prosperity'	LDea MBPg
	pseudoglutinosum	EWoo WFib
	'Pungent Peppermint' (Sc) **new**	MBPg
	'Purple Ball'	see *P.* Purpurball
	Purple Blizzard04 = 'Fisblipur' (I) **new**	WWol
	'Purple Emperor' (R)	ESul LDea WFib
	'Purple Heart' (Dw/St/C)	ESul NFir
	'Purple Muttertag' (R)	ESul
	'Purple Orchard' (R)	LDea
	'Purple Pride' (I/d)	CWDa
I	'Purple Radula Rosea' (Sc)	MBPg
	'Purple Rambler' (Z/d)	ESul MWhe
	'Purple Unique' (U/Sc)	CTbh EShb ESul EWoo LDea MHer MOak MSte NFir SKen WFib
§	Purpurball (Z/d)	LAst SKen
	Purpurball 2 = 'Penbalu' [PBR] (Quality Series)(Z/d)	LAst LSou
	'Pygmalion' (Z/d/v)	SSea WFib
	'Quakermaid' (Min)	ESul
	'Quantock' (R)	WFib
	'Quantock Beauty' (A)	ESul LDea MWhe NFir
	'Quantock Blonde' (A)	LDea NFir
	'Quantock Butterfly' (A)	NFir
	'Quantock Candy' (A)	NFir
	'Quantock Chloe' (A) **new**	NFir
	'Quantock Dragonfly' (A) **new**	NFir
	'Quantock Kendy' (A)	ESul NFir
	'Quantock Kirsty' (A)	LDea NFir
	'Quantock Marjorie' (A)	ESul MBPg MWhe NFir
	'Quantock Matty' (A)	ESul EWoo LDea MWhe NFir
	'Quantock Maureen Ward' (A)	NFir
	'Quantock May' (A)	EWoo LDea NFir
	'Quantock Medoc' (A)	ESul LDea MBPg NFir
	'Quantock Millennium' (A)	ESul LDea MBPg NFir
	'Quantock Mr Nunn' (A) **new**	NFir
	'Quantock Philip' (A)	ESul MBPg
	'Quantock Piksi' (A) **new**	NFir
	'Quantock Plume' (A)	MBPg NFir
	'Quantock Rita' (A)	MWhe
	'Quantock Rory' (A)	LDea
	'Quantock Rose' (A)	ESul EWoo LDea MBPg NFir
	'Quantock Sapphire' (A)	LDea
	'Quantock Sarah' (A)	ESul NFir
	'Quantock Shirley' (A)	ESul NFir
	'Quantock Star' (A)	LDea MBPg MWhe NFir
	'Quantock Star Gazer' (A) **new**	NFir
	'Quantock Ultimate' (A)	ESul MBPg NFir
	'Quantock Victoria' (A)	ESul MBPg NFir
	'Queen of Denmark' (Z/d)	LVER WFib
	'Queen of Hearts' (I x Z/d)	LVER WFib
	'Queen of Sheba' (R)	LDea
I	'Queen of the Lemons'	CTbh EWoo
N	***quercifolium*** (Sc)	CHal CRHN CSev EWoo GPoy MBPg MHer NFir NHHG SKen SYvo WFib
	- variegated (v)	MBPg MHer
	quinquelobatum	CSpe
	'R.A. Turner' (Z/d)	WFib
	'Rachel' (Min)	ESul
	radens (Sc)	EPfP WFib
	'Rads Star' (Z/St)	ESul NFir SSea WFib
	'Radula' (Sc) ♀H1+3	CSev ESul EWoo GBar LDea LIck MBPg MHer MOak MWhe SKen WFib
	'Radula Roseum' (Sc)	EWoo MBPg SSea WFib
	radulifolium	CMon
	'Ragamuffin' (Dw/d)	ESul MWhe
	'Rager's Pink' (Dw/d)	ESul
	'Rager's Star' (Dw)	ESul
	'Rager's Veri-Star' (Min/C)	ESul
	'Ragtime' (St)	NPri
	'Rakastani' (Z)	SKen
	'Raphael' (A)	LDea
	'Raspberry Parfait' (R)	LDea
	'Raspberry Ripple' (A)	ESul LDea MWhe NFir SAga WFib

	Name	Suppliers
	'Raspberry Surprise' (R)	LVER
	'Ray Bidwell' (Min)	ESul LVER MWhe NFir
	'Raydon' (Min)	ESul
	'Rebecca' (Min/d)	ESul WFib
	'Red Admiral' (Min/d/v)	ESul SKen
§	'Red Black Vesuvius' (Min/C)	CHal ESul MWhe SKen WEas WFib
	'Red Cactus' (St)	NFir
	'Red Capri' (Sc)	MBPg
§	'Red Cascade' (I) 🏆H1+3	MWhe WFib
	'Red Galilee' (I/d)	MWhe
	'Red Glow' (Min)	ESul
	'Red Ice' (Min/d)	ESul MWhe NFir
*	'Red Irene' (Z/d)	CWDa
	'Red Magic Lantern' (Z/C)	SKen
	'Red Pandora' (T)	LVER NFir WFib
	'Red Rambler' (Z/d)	CHal ESul LVER MWhe SKen WBrk WFib
	Red Satisfaction = 'Usredsat'[PBR] (Z/d)	LAst
	'Red Silver Cascade'	see *P.* 'Mutzel'
	'Red Spider' (Min/Ca)	ESul WFib
	'Red Startel' (Z/St/d)	MWhe SKen WFib
	'Red Susan Pearce' (R)	ESul LDea WFib
	'Red Sybil Holmes' (I)	LSou LVER
	Red Sybil = 'Pensyb'[PBR] (I/d)	LAst
	'Red Unique' (U) **new**	CTbh
	'Red Witch' (Dw/St/d)	ESul LVER WFib
	Red-Blizzard = 'Fizzard'[PBR] (I)	NPri SCoo WWol
§	Red-Mini-Cascade = 'Rotemica' (I)	ESul LAst LDea LVER MWhe SKen WFib
	'Redondo' (Min/d)	ESul LVER MWhe SPet
	'Reflections' (Z/d)	WFib
	'Reg 'Q'' (Z/C) **new**	NFir
	'Regina' (Z/d)	LVER NFir SKen WFib
	'Rembrandt' (R)	LDea LVER SKen SSea WFib
	'Renate Parsley'	EShb ESul MBPg NFir WFib
	'Rene Roué' (Dw/d/v)	ESul NFir
	'Renee Ross' (I/d) 🏆H1+3	CWDa
	reniforme	EWoo GBar MBPg MHer SAga SSea SUsu WEas WFib
	'Retah's Crystal' (Z/v)	ESul LRHS LVER MWhe
	'Rhian Harris' (A) **new**	LDea
	Rhodonit = 'Paccherry'[PBR] (I/d)	LAst
	'Richard Gibbs' (Sc)	EWoo LDea MBPg MHer
	'Richard Key' (Z/d/C)	WFib
	'Richard West' (I/d)	CWDa
	'Ricky Promise' (A)	LDea
	'Ricky Ruby' (A)	LDea
	'Rietje van der Lee' (A)	ESul WFib
	'Rigel' (Min/d)	ESul MWhe NFir SKen
	'Rigi' (I/d)	MBri SKen
	'Rigoletto' (I)	LDea NFir
	'Rimey' (St)	NFir
	'Rimfire' (R)	ESul EWoo LDea LVER NFir WFib
	'Rio Grande' (I/d)	LDea LVER MWhe NFir NWoo SKen SPet WFib
	'Rising Sun'	NFir
	'Rita Scheen' (A/v)	ESul LDea MWhe SSea
	'Ritchie' (R)	ESul
	'Robe'[PBR] (Quality Series) (Z/d)	LAst LRHS LVER WGor
I	'Rober's Lemon Rose' (Sc)	CRHN ESul EWoo GBar LDea MBPg MHer SIde SKen SSea
	'Rober's Salmon Coral' (Dw/d)	ESul
	'Robert Fish' (Z/C)	ESul LRHS SCoo
	'Robert McElwain'	WFib
	'Robin' (R)	LDea
	'Robin' (Sc)	LDea LVER MBPg
	'Robin's Unique' (U)	EWoo NFir WFib
	rodneyanum	WAbe
	'Roger's Delight' (R/Sc)	EWoo LDea MBPg
	'Rogue' (R)	ESul EWoo LDea MSte WFib
	'Roi des Balcons'	see *P.* 'Hederinum'
§	'Roi des Balcons Impérial' (I) 🏆H1+3	MWhe
§	'Roi des Balcons Lilas' (I) 🏆H1+3	LSou MWhe SKen WFib
	'Roi des Balcons Rose'	see *P.* 'Hederinum'
§	Rokoko = 'Fisfid'[PBR] (Z)	CWDa
	'Roller's David' (I/d)	CWDa
	'Roller's Echo' (A)	ESul LDea LIck MWhe WFib
	'Roller's Gabriella' (A)	LDea
	'Roller's Pathfinder' (I/d/v)	LDea LVER
	'Roller's Pioneer' (I/v)	EWoo LDea LVER SAga SKen
	'Roller's Satinique' (U) 🏆H1+3	EWoo LIck MBPg MHer SSea
	'Roller's Shadow' (A)	LDea
	'Rollisson's Unique' (U)	MBPg MHer MSte NBur SSea WFib
	'Romeo' (R)	EWoo LVER
§	Romy (I)	LDea
§	'Rosa Mini-cascade' (I)	ESul LAst LVER MWhe NFir
	'Rosaleen' (Min)	ESul
	'Rosalie' (R)	ESul
	'Rose Bengal' (A)	CRHN ESul LDea MWhe WFib
	'Rose Crystal' **new**	WGor
	Rose Evka = 'Penevro'[PBR] (Dw/I/v)	LAst NFir
	'Rose Irene' (Z/d)	MWhe
	'Rose Jewel' (R)	ESul
	'Rose of Amsterdam' (Min/d)	ESul
	'Rose Paton's Unique' (U/Sc)	LDea
	'Rose Silver Cascade' (I)	LDea LVER
	'Rosebud Supreme' (Z/d)	ESul WFib
	'Rosecrystal'[PBR] (Sweetheart Series)(Z/d)	LVER
*	'Roselo'	CWDa
	'Rosemarie' (Z/d)	MWhe
	'Rosemary Reville' (R) **new**	EWoo
	'Rosina Read' (Dw/d)	ESul LVER
	'Rosmaroy' (R)	ESul LDea LVER NFir WFib
§	'Rospen' (Z/d)	SKen
	'Rosy Dawn' (Min/d)	WFib
	'Rosy Morn' (R)	NFir
	'Rote Mini-cascade'	see *P.* Red-Mini-Cascade = 'Rotemica'
§	'Rouletta' (I/d)	CHrt ECtt LDea LVER MWhe NPri SKen WFib
I	'Round Leaf Rose' (U) **new**	MBPg
	'Rousillon' (R)	LDea
	'Royal Ascot' (R)	CHal CSpe ESul EWoo LDea MSte NFir SAga SMrm SPet
	'Royal Carpet' (Min/d)	ESul
	'Royal Court' (R)	LDea
	'Royal Decree' (R)	LDea
	'Royal Guernsey' (R) **new**	EWoo
	'Royal Norfolk' (Min/d)	ESul LVER MWhe NFir SKen
	'Royal Oak' (Sc) 🏆H1+3	CSev CTbh ESul EWoo GBar LDea MBPg MHer MWhe NBur SGar SPet SSea WFib WRha
	'Royal Opera' (R)	LDea
	'Royal Pride' (R) **new**	LDea
§	'Royal Purple' (Z/d)	CHal LVER WFib
	Royal Salmon = 'KLEP03109'	CWDa
	'Royal Sovereign' (Z/C/d)	LDea
	'Royal Star' (R)	LDea
	'Royal Surprise' (R)	ESul EWoo LDea NFir

	Name	Suppliers
	'Royal Wedding' (R)	LDea
	'Royal Winner' (R) **new**	LDea
	'Rubi Lee' (A)	MWhe
*	'Rubican'	CWDa
	'Rubin Improved' (Z/d)	SKen
	'Ruby' (Min/d)	ESul WFib
	'Ruby Orchid' (A)	LDea NFir
	'Ruffled Velvet' (R)	EWoo SSea
	'Rushmere' (Dw/d)	ESul WFib
	'Rusty' (Dw/C/d)	ESul
	'Sabine'[PBR] (Z/d)	LVER
	'Saint Elmo's Fire' (St/Min/d)	WFib
	'Saint Helen's Favourite' (Min)	ESul
	Saint Malo = 'Guisaint'[PBR] (I)	LAst
	'Sally Munro' (R)	LDea SSea
	'Sally Read' (Dw/d)	ESul
	'Salmon Beauty' (Dw/d)	WFib
	'Salmon Black Vesuvius' (Min/C)	ESul
§	'Salmon Irene' (Z/d)	WFib
	'Salmon Queen'	see *P.* 'Lachskönigin'
	'Salmon Startel' (Z/St/d)	ESul MWhe
	salmoneum	SSea
	'Samantha' (R)	ESul WFib
	'Samantha Stamp' (Dw/d/C)	SAga WFib
	Samelia = 'Pensam'[PBR] (Dark Line Series)(Z/d)	LAst
	'Sancho Panza' (Dec) Y[H1+3]	CSpe ESul EWoo LDea LVER MBPg MHer MSte SAga SKen SSea WFib
	'Sandford' (Dw/St)	ESul
	'Sandown' (Dw/d)	ESul
	'Sandra Lorraine' (I/d)	WFib
	'Sanguineum'	CSpe SAga
	'Santa Fé' (Z)	LVER
	'Santa Maria' (Z/d)	SKen
	'Santa Marie' (R)	LDea
	'Santa Paula' (I/d)	ECtt LDea SKen
	'Sarah Don'[PBR] (A/v) **new**	WFib
	'Sarah Jane' (Sc)	MBPg
	'Sassa'[PBR] (Quality Series) (Z/d)	CWDa LAst LSou WGor
	'Satsuki' (R)	ESul LDea NFir
§	***scabrum***	MBPg
	'Scarlet Gem' (Z/St)	WFib
*	'Scarlet Kewense' (Dw)	ESul
	'Scarlet Nosegay'	CHal
I	'Scarlet O'Hara' (Z) **new**	LVER
	'Scarlet Pet' (U)	CFee CRHN ESul MBPg NFir
	'Scarlet Pimpernel' (Z/C/d)	ESul
	'Scarlet Rambler' (Z/d)	EShb EWoo LVER SKen SMrm WFib
	'Scarlet Unique' (U)	CHrt CRHN CTbh EWoo LDea MHer MSte NFir SKen SSea WFib
	'Scatterbrain' (Z)	CWDa
	schizopetalum	WFib
§	'Schneekönigin' (I/d)	ECtt LDea LVER MSte SKen
§	'Schöne Helena'[PBR] (Z/d)	CWDa
	x ***schottii***	see *P.* 'Schottii'
	'Schottii'	NFir WFib
	'Secret Love' (Sc)	LDea MBPg
	'Seeley's Pansy' (A)	CSpe EWoo LDea MHer SAga WFib
	'Sefton' (R) Y[H1+3]	ESul LDea WFib
	'Selecta Royal Blue' (I) **new**	LSou
	'Selena' (Min)	LDea
	'Semer' (Min)	ESul SKen
*	'Serre de la Madone' (Sc)	WEas
	'Shalimar' (St)	MSte NFir SAga
	'Shanks' (Z)	NFir
	'Shannon'	WFib
	'Sharon' (Min/d)	ESul
	'Sheila' (Dw)	ESul
	'Shelley' (Dw)	ESul SKen
	'Sheraton' (Min/d)	MWhe
	'Shimmer' (Z/d)	MWhe
	'Shirley Ash' (A)	LDea WFib
	'Shirley Maureen' (R)	LDea
	Shocking Pink = 'Pensho'[PBR](Quality Series) (Z/d)	LAst WGor
	Shocking Violet = 'Pacshovi' (Quality Series) (Z/d) **new**	LSou
	'Shogan' (R)	NFir
	'Shottesham Pet' (Sc)	ESul EWoo MBPg MHer
	'Shrubland Pet' (U/Sc)	EWoo MHer
	'Sid' (R)	LDea
	sidoides	CSpe CTrC EBee EPyc EShb ESul EWoo IFro LPhx LPio MBPg MHer NFir SAga SMrm SSea WCot WEas WFib
	- black	CSpe SUsu
	- 'Sloe Gin Fizz'	CSpe SAga
	'Sienna' (R)	LDea NFir
*	'Sils'	CWDa
	'Silver Anne' (R/v)	ESul NFir
	'Silver Delight' (v/d)	WFib
	'Silver Kewense' (Dw/v)	ESul WFib
I	'Silver Leaf Rose' (Sc)	MBPg
*	'Silver Lights'	CWDa
	'Silver Wings' (Z/v)	ESul LRHS MWhe NFir SSea
	'Silvia' (R)	ESul
	'Simon Portas' (I/d)	SKen
	'Simon Read' (Dw)	ESul
	'Simplicity' (Z)	LVER
	'Single New Life' (Z)	LVER
	'Sir Colin' (Z)	SSea
	'Skelly's Pride' (Z)	LVER SKen WEas WFib
	'Skies of Italy' (Z/C/d)	CHal MBri MHer SKen SSea WFib
	'Small Fortune' (Min/d)	ESul SKen
	'Smuggler' (R)	LDea
	'Snape' (Min)	ESul
	'Sneezy' (Min)	ESul NFir
	'Snow Cap' (MinI)	NFir
	'Snow Flurry' (Sc) **new**	MBPg
	Snow Queen	see *P.* 'Schneekönigin'
	'Snow White' (Min)	ESul
	'Snowbaby' (Min/d)	ESul
	'Snowberry' (R)	ESul
	'Snowdrift' (I/d)	LVER WFib
	'Snowflake' (Min)	see *P.* 'Atomic Snowflake'
	'Snowmass' (Z/d)	CHal MWhe
	'Snowstorm' (Z)	WFib
	'Snowy Baby' (Min/d)	WFib
	'Sofie'	see *P.* 'Decora Rose'
	'Solent Waves' (R)	ESul LDea
	'Solferino' (A)	ESul LDea
§	Solidor (I/d) Y[H1+3]	LDea NFir
	Solo = 'Guillio' (Z/I)	LVER
	'Somersham' (Min)	ESul WFib
	'Something Special' (Z/d)	LVER MWhe NFir WFib
	'Sonata' (Dw/d)	ESul
	Sophie Casade	see *P.* 'Decora Rose'
	'Sophie Dumaresque' (Z/v)	MBri MWhe NFir SKen SSea WFib
	'Sorcery' (Dw/C)	ESul MWhe SKen
	'Sound Appeal' (A)	ESul LDea MBPg
	'South African Sun' (Z/d)	LVER
	'South American Bronze' (R) Y[H1+3]	LDea SKen SMrm WFib
	'South American Delight' (R)	LVER

'South Walsham Broad' (Dw) ESul
'Southern Belle' (A) LDea
'Southern Belle' (Z/d) WFib
'Southern Cherub' (A) LDea
'Southern Gem' (Min/d) ESul
'Southern Peach' (Min/d) ESul
'Souvenir' (R) CHal LDea SSea
I 'Sowoma Lavender' (Sc) **new** MBPg
'Spanish Angel' (A) ♀H1+3 ESul LDea NFir NWoo SSea WFib
'Sparkler' (Z) LVER
'Spellbound' (R) WFib
'Spital Dam' (Dw/d) ESul
'Spitfire' (Z/Ca/d/v) ESul LVER WFib
'Spithead Cherry' (R) LDea
§ 'Splendide' CSpe EShb ESul LPio MBPg MHer NFir SAga SSea SWvt WCot WEas WFib WPen
'Splendide' white-flowered MBPg
'Spotlite Hotline' (I) LDea
'Spotlite Winner' (I) LDea
'Spot-on-bonanza' (R) ESul LDea NFir WFib
'Spring Bride' (R) LDea
'Spring Park' (A) ESul LVER WFib
'Springfield Ann' (R) ESul
'Springfield Black' (R) ESul EWoo LDea LVER SSea
'Springfield Charm' (R) ESul
'Springfield Pearl' (R) LDea
'Springfield Purple' (R) ESul
'Springfield Unique' (R) LDea
'Springtime' (Z/d) MWhe WFib
'Sprite' (Min/v) MWhe
'Sproughton' (Dw) ESul
'Stacey' (R) LDea
'Stadt Bern' (Z/C) LAst LRHS LVER MBri MSte MWhe NFir SKen
'Staplegrove Fancy' (Z) SKen
x ***stapletoniae*** see *P.* 'Miss Stapleton'
'Star Flecks' NFir
'Star of Persia' (Z/Ca/d) WFib
'Starflecks' (St) LVER
'Starlet' (Ca) WFib
'Starlight' (R) WFib
'Starlight Magic' (A) ♀H1+3 ESul LDea
'Starry Eyes' (Dw) ESul
'Stella Read' (Dw/d) ESul
'Stellar Arctic Star' see *P.* 'Arctic Star'
'Stellar Cathay' (Z/St/d) LRHS
'Stellar Hannaford Star' see *P.* 'Hannaford Star'
* 'Stellar Orange Pixie' (St/d) CWDa
'Stephen Read' (Min) ESul
'Stewart Meehan' (R) LDea
'Stirling Stent' (Z) CWDa
'Strawberries and Cream' (Z/St) NFir
'Strawberry Fayre' (Dw/St) LVER
'Strawberry Sundae' (R) ESul LDea LVER MSte WFib
'Stringer's Delight' (Dw/v) ESul LVER
'Stringer's Souvenir' (Dw/d/v) LVER
'Stuart Mark' (R) LDea
'Stutton' (Min) ESul
'Suffolk Agate' (R) ESul
'Suffolk Amethyst' (A) ESul
'Suffolk Coral' (R) ESul
'Suffolk Emerald' (A) ESul
'Suffolk Garnet' (A) ESul MWhe
'Suffolk Jade' (Min) ESul
'Suffolk Jet' (Min) ESul
§ 'Sugar Baby' (DwI) ECtt ESul LDea MBri SKen WFib
'Summer Cloud' (Z/d) SKen WFib
Summer Rose Lilac = 'Fisbilly'[PBR] (I) NPri
'Summertime' (Z/d) see *P.* 'Deacon Summertime'
'Sun Rocket' (Dw/d) MWhe WFib
'Sundridge Moonlight' (Z/C) WFib
'Sunraysia' (Z/St) WFib
'Sunridge Moonlight' (Dw) NFir
'Sunset Snow' (R) ESul LVER NFir WFib
'Sunspot' (Min/C) NFir
'Sunspot Kleine Liebling' (Min) WFib
'Sunspot Petit Pierre' (Min/v) WFib
'Sunstar' (Min/d) ESul WFib
'Super Rose' (I) SKen SPet
'Super Rupert' (Sc) **new** MBPg
'Super Spot-on-bonanza' (R) LVER
'Supernova' (Z/St/d) CWDa ESul MWhe SKen WFib
'Surcouf' (I) WFib
'Susan Hillier' (R) LDea
'Susan Payne' (Dw/d) ESul MHer
'Susan Pearce' (R) LDea LVER SKen
'Susan Read' (Dw) ESul
* 'Susan Screen' CWDa
'Susie 'Q'' (Z/C) MWhe SKen SSea
'Sussex Beauty' (Dw/d/v) CWDa
'Sussex Delight' (Min) CWDa SKen SPet
'Sussex Gem' (Min/d) ESul SKen WFib
'Sussex Lace' see *P.* 'White Mesh'
'Swan Lake' (Min) ESul
'Swanland Lace' (I/d/v) WFib
'Swedish Angel' (A) ESul EWoo LDea LVER MWhe NFir SSea WFib
'Sweet Lady Mary' (Sc) LDea MBPg
'Sweet Mimosa' (Sc) ♀H1+3 CHal CRHN ESul EWoo LIck LVER MBPg MHer MSte NFir SDnm SKen SSea WFib
'Sweet Miriam' (Sc) LDea MBPg
'Sweet Rosina' (Sc) MBPg
'Sweet Sixteen' **new** WFib
'Sweet Sue' (Min) ESul
I 'Sweet William' (St) ESul LVER
'Swilland' (A) LDea LVER MWhe WFib
'Sybil Bradshaw' (R) LDea
'Sybil Holmes' (I/d) ECtt LAst LVER MBri MWhe SKen SPet WFib
'Sylvia Marie' (Dw/d) MWhe NFir SKen
'Taffety' (Min) ESul WFib
Tamara = 'Genor'[PBR] (Z/d) CWDa
'Tamie' (Dw/d) ESul MWhe NFir
'Tammy' (Dw/d) ESul LVER MWhe
'Tangerine' (Min/Ca/d) ESul LVER SSea WFib
'Tangerine Elf' (St) WFib
Tango Neon Purple = 'Fistaneon'[PBR] (Z/d) LAst
Tango Pink = 'Fisgopi'[PBR] LAst
'Tanzy' (Min) ESul
'Tapestry' (R) WEas
'Taspo' (R) ESul
'Tattingstone' (Min) ESul
'Tattoo' (Min) ESul
'Tavira' (I/d) LVER SPet
'Tazi' (Dw) ESul
'Telstar' (Min/d) ESul SKen
§ 'Telston's Prima' (R) LDea
'Tenderly' (Dw/d) ESul
'Tenerife Magic' (MinI/d) ESul
tetragonum CRHN EShb MBPg MHer SHFr SSea WFib
'The Axe' (A) LDea MWhe

	Name	Suppliers
	'The Barle' (A) ♀H1+3	LDea MWhe WFib
	'The Boar' (Fr) ♀H1+3	CTbh EShb EWoo LDea MSte SRms WFib
	'The Bray' (A)	LDea
	'The Creedy' (A)	LDea
	'The Culm' (A)	ESul EWoo LDea MSte WFib
	'The Czar'	see *P.* 'Czar'
	'The Dart' (A)	LDea
	'The Heddon' (A)	LDea
	'The Joker' (I/d)	WFib
	'The Kenn-Lad' (A)	LDea NFir
	'The Lowman' (A)	LDea
	'The Lyn' (A)	ESul EWoo LDea MWhe
	'The Mole' (A)	ESul LDea LVER MBPg MHer MSte WFib
	'The Okement' (A)	EWoo LDea MSte NFir
	'The Otter' (A)	ESul LDea MWhe
	'The Speaker' (Z/d)	SKen
	'The Tamar' (A)	CFee EWoo LDea
	'The Tone' (A) ♀H1+3	EWoo LDea MWhe
	'Thomas Gerald' (Dw/C)	ESul SKen
	'Tilly' (Min)	CHal NFir SAga
	'Tim' (Min)	ESul LVER
	'Timothy Clifford' (Min/d)	ESul MWhe
	'Tinkerbell' (A)	LDea
§	'Tip Top Duet' (A) ♀H1+3	CAby CHal ESul EWoo LAst LDea LIck LRHS LSou LVER MHer MWhe NFir NWoo SMrm SSea WFib
	'Tom Portas' (Dw/d)	ESul
	'Tom Tit' (Z)	SPet
	'Tomcat'[PBR] (I/d)	LAst LSou LVER SSea WGor
	tomentosum (Sc) ♀H1+3	CArn CHEx CHal CRHN CSev CSpe CTbh EShb ESul EWoo GBar GPoy IFro LDea LPio MBPg MHer MOak MWhe NFir NHHG SSea WFib
	- 'Chocolate'	see *P.* 'Chocolate Peppermint'
	Tomgirl = 'Pactomgi' (IxZ/d)	LAst LSou LVER
	'Tommay's Delight' (R)	LDea
	'Tony' (Min)	ESul
	'Topan' (R)	ESul
	'Topcliffe' (Dw/St)	ESul
	'Topscore' (Z/d)	WFib
	'Tornado' (R)	ESul NFir SAga WFib
	'Torrento' (Sc)	ESul EWoo LDea MBPg MHer SKen WFib
	'Tortoiseshell' (R)	WFib
	'Tracy' (Min/d)	ESul NFir
	transvaalense	NFir
	'Traute Hausler' (A)	LDea
	'Trautlieb' (Z/d)	CWDa
	'Trésor' (Z/d)	CWDa
	tricolor hort.	see *P.* 'Splendide'
	trifidum	EWoo MBPg SSea WFib
	'Trimley' (Dw/d)	ESul
	'Trinket' (Min/d)	SKen WFib
	'Triomphe de Nancy' (Z/d)	WFib
	triste	CMon EWoo WFib
	'Trixie' (R)	LDea
	'Trudie' (Dw/Fr)	ESul LVER MHer SHFr SKen WBrk WFib
	'Trulls Hatch' (Z/d)	MWhe SKen
	'Tu Tone' (Dw/d)	ESul
	'Tuddenham' (Min/d)	ESul
	'Tuesday's Child' (Dw/C)	ESul SKen
	'Turkish Coffee' (R)	ESul LVER NFir WFib
	'Turkish Delight' (Dw/C)	ESul MWhe NFir WFib
	'Turtle's Surprise' (Z/d/v)	SKen
	'Turtle's White' (R)	LDea
	'Tuyo' (R)	WFib
	'Tweedle-Dum' (Dw)	ESul MWhe
	'Twinkle' (Min/d)	ESul WFib
	'Tyabb Princess' (R)	LDea
	'Ullswater' (Dw/C)	ESul
§	'Unique Aurore' (U)	LPio LVER MBPg MHer MSte SKen
	'Unique Mons Ninon'	see *P.* 'Monsieur Ninon'
	'Unity' (Dw)	LVER
	urbanum **new**	EShb
	'Urchin' (Min)	ESul MWhe NFir SHFr WFib
	'Ursula Key' (Z/c)	SKen WFib
	'Valentina' (Min/d)	ESul
	'Valentine' (R)	ESul
	'Vancouver Centennial' (Dw/St/C) ♀H1+3	CSpe CTbh ESul LAst LRHS LVER MBri MHer MWhe NFir SAga SCoo SDnm SHFr SKen SMad SPoG SSea WFib
	'Vandersea'	EWoo
I	'Variegated Attar of Roses' (Sc/v)	MBPg
§	'Variegated Clorinda' (Sc/v)	EWoo WFib
	'Variegated Fragrans'	see *P.* (Fragrans Group) 'Fragrans Variegatum'
	'Variegated Joy Lucille' (Sc/v)	MBPg
§	'Variegated Kleine Liebling' (Min/v)	ESul LVER SSea WFib
	'Variegated Madame Layal' (A/v) ♀H1+3	WFib
	'Variegated Petit Pierre' (Min/v)	WFib
	'Vasco da Gama' (Dw/d)	ESul
	'Vectis Allure' (Z/St)	LVER
	'Vectis Blaze' (I)	EWoo
	'Vectis Cascade'	EWoo
	'Vectis Glitter' (Z/St)	CSpe ESul LVER MWhe NFir SSea WFib
	'Vectis Sparkler' (Dw/St)	ESul
	'Vectis Spider' (St/dw) **new**	ESul
	'Velvet' (Z)	CWDa LVER
	'Velvet Duet' (A) ♀H1+3	CHal EWoo LAst LDea LIck LPio LRHS LVER MBPg MWhe NFir SKen SSea WGor
	'Venus' (Min/d)	ESul LRHS
	'Vera Dillon' (Z)	SKen
	'Verdale' (A)	GGar LDea WFib
	'Verity Palace' (R)	EWoo LDea WFib
	'Verona' (Z/C)	CHal MBri SKen
	'Verona Contreras' (A)	ESul LDea MWhe NFir WFib
I	'Veronica' (Z/d)	MWhe SKen
	'Vic Claws' (Dw/St) **new**	ESul
	'Vicki Town' (R)	WFib
	'Vicky Claire' (R)	CSpe ESul LDea NFir SKen SMrm WFib
	Victor = 'Pacvi' (Quality Series) (Z/d)	LAst
	'Victoria' (Z/d)	LAst SKen
	'Victoria Regina' (R)	LDea
	'Viking' (Min/d)	SKen
	'Viking Red' (Z)	MWhe
	'Village Hill Oak' (Sc)	ESul LDea LVER MBPg MHer
	Ville de Dresden = 'Pendresd'[PBR] (I)	WWol
	'Ville de Paris'	see *P.* 'Hederinum'
	'Vina' (Dw/C/d)	ESul MWhe SKen WFib
	'Vincent Gerris' (A)	ESul LDea MWhe
	Vinco = 'Guivin'[PBR] (I/d)	CWDa LSou WGor
	violareum hort.	see *P.* 'Splendide'
	'Violet Lambton' (Z/v)	WFib
	'Violet Unique' (U)	MHer
I	'Violetta' (R) **new**	EWoo
I	'Violetta' (R)	LDea WFib
	'Virginia' (R)	LDea SPet

	'Viscossisimum' (Sc)	MHer SKen
	viscosum	see *P. glutinosum*
§	***vitifolium***	MBPg
	'Viva' (R)	ESul
	'Vivat Regina' (Z/d)	WFib
	'Voo Doo' (Dec)	ESul LPio
	'Voodoo' (U) ♀H1+3	CBrm CSpe EShb EWoo LSou MBPg MHer MSte NCiC NFir SAga SKen SSea SUsu WCot WFib
	'Wallace Fairman' (R)	LDea
	'Wallis Friesdorf' (Dw/C/d)	ESul MWhe
	'Wantirna' (Z/v)	ECtt LIck LVER MHer NFir
	'Warrenorth Coral' (Z/C/d)	LVER NFir WFib
	'Warrenorth Rubellite' (Z/v)	LVER
	'Warrion' (Z/d)	LVER
	'Washbrook' (Min/d)	ESul NFir
	'Watersmeet' (R)	LDea
	'Wattisham' (Dec)	LDea
	'Waveney' (Min)	ESul
	'Wayward Angel' (A) ♀H1+3	ESul LDea LVER MWhe WFib
	'Wedding Royale' (Dw/d)	ESul LVER WFib
	'Welcome' (Z/d)	WFib
	'Welling' (Sc)	ESul GBar LDea LVER MBPg NFir
	'Wellington' (R)	LDea
	'Wendy' (Min)	LAst
	'Wendy Anne'	SKen
	'Wendy Jane' (Dw/d)	WFib
	'Wendy Read' (Dw/d)	ESul LVER MWhe WFib
	'Wendy-O' (R) **new**	LDea
	'Wensum' (Min/d)	ESul
	'Westdale Appleblossom' (Z/d/C)	ESul LVER WBrk WFib
*	'Westdale Beauty' (d)	CWDa
	'Wherstead' (Min) **new**	ESul
	'Whisper' (R)	WFib
	'White Bird's Egg' (Z)	WFib
	'White Boar' (Fr)	EShb EWoo MSte WFib
	'White Bonanza' (R)	ESul WFib
	'White Charm' (R)	ESul LDea
	'White Chiffon' (R)	LVER
	'White Duet' (A)	LDea MWhe
	'White Eggshell' (Min)	ESul LVER WFib
	'White Feather' (Z/St)	MHer
	'White Glory' (R) ♀H1+3	ESul LDea NFir
	'White Lively Lady' (Dw/C)	ESul
§	'White Mesh' (I/v)	ECtt MBri SKen
	'White Prince of Orange' (Sc)	MBPg
	'White Queen' (Z/d)	CWDa
	'White Roc' (Min/d)	ESul
	'White Truffle'	LAst
	'White Unique' (U)	CHal EWoo LDea MBPg MHer MSte NBur SPet SSea WFib
	'White Velvet Duet' (A)	ESul
	White-Blizzard = 'Fisbliz'PBR	NPri SCoo WWol
	'Wickham Lad' (R)	LDea
	Wico = 'Guimongol'PBR (I/d)	LAst LSou WGor
	'Wild Spice' (Sc)	LDea LPio LVER
	'Wildmalva' (Sc)	MBPg
	'Wilf Vernon' (Min/d)	ESul
	'Wilhelm Kolle' (Z)	WFib
	'Wilhelm Langath'	SCoo SDnm
	'Winnie Read' (Dw/d)	ESul
	'Winston Churchill' (R)	LDea
	'Wirral Target' (Z/d/v)	ESul MWhe
	'Wishing Star' (Min/St)	ESul
	'Wispy' (Dw/St/C)	ESul
	'Witnesham' (Min/d)	ESul
§	'Wood's Surprise' (MinI/d/v)	EShb ESul LDea MWhe NFir SAga SKen SWal
	'Wookey' (R)	GGar
	'Wooton's Unique'	CSpe
	'Wordsworth'	MBPg
	'Wroxham' (Dw)	ESul
	'Wychwood' (A/Sc)	EWoo LDea MBPg
	'Wyck Beacon' (I/d)	SKen
	'Yale' (I/d) ♀H1+3	CHal LDea LVER MBri MSte MWhe SKen WFib
	'Yhu' (R)	ESul LDea NFir SAga SMrm WFib
	'Yolanda' (Dw/C)	ESul
	'York Florist' (Z/d/v)	LVER
	'York Minster' (Dw/v)	SKen
	'Yvonne' (Z)	WFib
	'Zama' (R)	ESul NFir
	'Zemmies' (MinI)	ESul
	'Zena' (Dw)	ESul
	'Zinc' (Z/d)	WFib
	'Zoe' (A)	LDea
	zonale	EWoo SSea WFib
	'Zulu King' (R)	WFib
	'Zulu Warrior' (R)	WFib

Peliosanthes (*Convallariaceae*)

	monticola B&SWJ 5183	WCru

Pellaea (*Adiantaceae*)

	atropurpurea	CLAP WFib
	cordifolia	WRic
	falcata	CLAP MBri WRic
	rotundifolia ♀H2	CHal CLAP CTrC MBri SMur WBor WRic
	viridis **new**	WRic

Pellionia see *Elatostema*

Peltandra (*Araceae*)

	alba	see *P. sagittifolia*
§	***sagittifolia***	CRow WDyG
	undulata	see *P. virginica*
	virginica	CDWL CRow EMFW LPBA NPer
	- 'Snow Splash' (v)	CRow

Peltaria (*Brassicaceae*)

	alliacea	CSpe EBee EPPr GBin LEdu SAga

Peltiphyllum see *Darmera*

Peltoboykinia (*Saxifragaceae*)

§	***tellimoides***	CCol CLAP EBee EVFa GCal GKev NBir SMac WBVN WFar WMoo
	watanabei	CDes CLAP CSec EBee EPPr GEdr GIBF GTou LEdu SMac WCru WFar WMoo WPGP

Pennantia (*Icacinaceae*)

	baylisiana	ECou
	corymbosa	ECou
	- 'Akoroa'	ECou
	- 'Woodside'	ECou

Pennellianthus see *Penstemon*

Pennisetum (*Poaceae*)

	B&SWJ 3854	WCru
§	***alopecuroides***	More than 30 suppliers
	- Autumn Wizard	see *P. alopecuroides* 'Herbstzauber'
	- 'Bruno Ears'	EHoe
	- 'Cassian's Choice'	CBig CBrm CKno EHoe NCGa SMrm SUsu
	- 'Caudatum'	CBig CKno CPen SApp

	- f. ***erythrochaetum*** 'Ferris'	WCru
	- 'Hameln'	More than 30 suppliers
§	- 'Herbstzauber'	CFir CFwr CPen CPrp EBee EHoe EPfP GCal SMHy
	- 'Little Bunny'	CHar CKno COIW CPen EBrs EChP EHoe EMan EPfP EPla GCal GKir LAst LRHS NGdn NPro SApp SGSe SWvt WDin WPGP
	- 'Little Honey' (v)	CBrm CKno CPrp EBee EMan EPPr MAvo NLar SGSe SPla WCot WPGP
	- 'Magic' **new**	CFwr
	- 'Moudry'	CBig CBrm CKno CPen CStr EHoe EPPr WFar
	- 'National Arboretum'	CFwr CPen EHoe IPot SApp
	- var. ***purpurascens***	CAby CBig CWCL
	- - B&SWJ 5822	WCru
	- f. ***viridescens***	CBrm CFwr CKno CStr ECha EHoe ELan EMan EPfP EPza GFor LRHS MLLN MMoz MWgw SApp SMHy SWal
	- 'Weserbergland'	CBig CFir CKno CStr EBee EHoe EPPr SApp
	- 'Woodside'	CBig CBrm CKno CMea CPen CSam CWCL EBee EBrs EHoe EMan EPPr LBBr MBNS SApp SHel SPla
	compressum	see *P. alopecuroides*
	flaccidum	CSam EBee EHul EMan EMon EPPr SGSe SHel
	glaucum 'Purple Majesty' **new**	CKno CSpe NPri SGSe SUsu WPrP
	incomptum	CSam EHoe GKir LRHS XPep
	- purple	CBig CBrm CKno CStr MMoz
	longistylum hort.	see *P. villosum*
	macrostachyum 'Burgundy Giant'	CBig CKno CPen SMad
	macrourum	CBrm CFil CFwr CHea CHrt CKno CMea CSam ECha EHoe EPGN EPla EWsh MAnH MWhi SMHy SMad SMrm SUsu SWal WPGP
	massaicum 'Red Buttons'	CBig CKno CPen IPot
	orientale ♀H3	More than 30 suppliers
	- 'Karley Rose'PBR	CBig CFwr CKno CPen CRez EBee EHrv IPot LPhx LRHS MAvo MBNS MWgw SUsu
I	- 'Robusta'	SApp
	- 'Shenandoah' **new**	SApp
*	- 'Shogun'	CPen LPhx MAvo WCot
	- 'Tall Tails'	CBig CFwr CKno CPen EBee EHoe EMan EPPr GFor IPot MAvo NSti WCot
	'Paul's Giant' **new**	SApp
	rueppellii	see *P. setaceum*
§	***setaceum*** ♀H3	CBig CKno CPen CWCL EMan EPPr MAnH MNrw SIde SMar SWal XPep
	- 'Eaton Canyon'	CKno CPen SGSe
	- 'Rubrum'	CAbb CBig CKno CPen EBee EPfP MAnH SCoo SDix SGSe SMad SPoG SUsu SWal SWvt
	spatheolatum 'Malibu'	CKno
§	***villosum*** ♀H3	More than 30 suppliers

pennyroyal see *Mentha pulegium*

Penstemon ✿ (*Scrophulariaceae*)

	P&C 150	CFee
	RCB/Arg V-1	WCot
	'Abberley'	WEll WPer
	'Abbotsmerry'	CElw EBee LPhx SAga SGar WEll WSPU
	'Agnes Laing'	LPen LRHS MBNS SPlb
	albertinus	see *P. humilis*
	albidus	NLAp
§	'Alice Hindley' ♀H3	More than 30 suppliers
	alpinus	CLyd CNic CSec GAbr GTou NEgg NLAp NOak WEll
	ambiguus	WLin
§	'Andenken an Friedrich Hahn' ♀H4	More than 30 suppliers
§	***angustifolius***	MNrw SRms
	- var. ***caudatus*** NNS 99-281 **new**	NWCA
	'Apple Blossom' misapplied	see *P.* 'Thorn'
	'Apple Blossom' ♀H3-4	More than 30 suppliers
	aridus	CNic NWCA
	arizonicus	see *P. whippleanus*
	arkansanus	NLAp
	'Ashton'	CElw CStr LPen SLon WEll WSPU
	attenuatus NNS 96-176	WCot
	'Audrey Cooper'	CChe WEll
	'Axe Valley Penny Mitchell'	CStr
	'Axe Valley Suzie'	CStr WEll
	azureus	CFir CPBP NWCA
	- var. ***azureus*** **new**	GKev
	'Barbara Barker'	see *P.* 'Beech Park'
§	***barbatus***	CBot CFee ECha EHrv ELan EPfP LPhx MLan MWat NLAp SChu SECG SRms WHCG XPep
§	- 'Blue Spring'	ECtt
	- 'Cambridge Mixed'	EDAr EWll LRHS LRav
	- subsp. ***coccineus***	ENot LPen LPhx LRHS MBNS MBri MCCP NBPC NChi NDlv NLar WCAu WMow
	- 'Jingle Bells'	LPen MWgw SMar SPav
	- 'Navigator' **new**	SECG
	- orange-flowered	SAga SMrm SPlb
	- 'Peter Catt'	LSou SAga SMrm
	- var. ***praecox***	CFwr MBNS NJOw NLAp WPer
	- - f. ***nanus***	CBot EMan LRHS MSte SRms
	- - - 'Rondo'	NLar NWCA WWeb
	barrettiae	NLAp
	'Beckford'	CPrp CStr WCFE WEll WSPU
§	'Beech Park' ♀H3	ECtt ELan ERou EWes IGor LPen LRHS MBNS NBir SAga WHCG WSPU
§	***berryi***	EPot
	'Bisham Seedling'	see *P.* 'White Bedder'
	'Blackbird'	More than 30 suppliers
	'Bodnant'	LSou WBan WPer
	bradburii	see *P. grandiflorus*
	'Bredon'	CElw CHea CStr WEll WSPU
	breviculus	CNic
	bridgesii	see *P. rostriflorus*
	'Burford Purple'	see *P.* 'Burgundy'
	'Burford Seedling'	see *P.* 'Burgundy'
	'Burford White'	see *P.* 'White Bedder'
§	'Burgundy'	CBcs CElw CHar CHrt CMHG CSam CWCL ECtt ENot GKir GMaP GMac LLWP LPen LRHS MBow MWgw MWhi NBir NPer SChu SGar SWal WFar WHCG WHil WPer WSHC
	caeruleus	see *P. angustifolius*
	caespitosus	CSec NRnb
	- 'Claude Barr' misapplied (purple-flowered)	see *P. procumbens* 'Claude Barr'
	- subsp. ***suffruticosus***	see *P. tusharensis*
§	***californicus***	CPBP WAbe WLin
	calycosus	EBee WLin
§	***campanulatus***	CMHG ECtt EHyt EPfP EPot EWes GBBs GEdr LPen MLLN NMen NRnb SIng SRms WEll WHCG WPer WSPU
*	- PC&H 148	EMan GBri NOak SGar WEll WLin

	- ***pulchellus***	see *P. campanulatus*
	- ***roseus*** misapplied	see *P. kunthii*
	'Candy Pink'	see *P.* 'Old Candy Pink'
	cardwellii	EWes GTou ITim MDKP SRms
	cardwellii x ***davidsonii***	WAbe
	'Carolyn Orr' (v)	EBee EMan WCot
	'Castle Forbes'	EPyc GMac LAst LPen MBNS MLLN NBur WBan WEll WHCG WPer WSSM
	'Catherine de la Mare'	see *P. heterophyllus* 'Catherine de la Mare'
*	'Centra'	LPen MLLN MWgw WEll
	'Charles Rudd'	CWCL ECtt EMar ERou GMac LLWP LPen LRHS MBNS MLLN NCob SAga SBai SChu SPav SUsu SWvt SYvo WCot WEll WHCG WLin WSSM
§	'Cherry' ♀H3	GMac LPen MBNS MHer NBur SPla SPlb WHCG WPer WSPU WWhi
	'Cherry Ripe' misapplied	see *P.* 'Cherry'
§	'Chester Scarlet' ♀H3	CElw CMCo CWCL ENot GBri GMac LPen MNrw MOak MRav MSte SDix SGar SLon WEll WHCG WPer WSPU
	clevelandii subsp. ***connatus***	WCot
	cobaea	CNic CSec EBee GKev SUsu
	'Comberton'	CHea EBee WEll WSPU
	confertus	CMHG CSec CTri EBee EGra EHyt EPot LPen LPio MBNS MHer NChi NLAp NMen NWCA SECG SGar SRms WBVN WGwG WHCG WLin WPer WSPU
	'Connie's Pink' ♀H3	ENot LPen MBNS MSte NBur WEll WHCG WSPU
*	'Coral Pink'	SLon
	'Cottage Garden Red'	see *P.* 'Windsor Red'
§	'Countess of Dalkeith'	CBcs CHea COlW EBee ECtt EGra ELan EMar ERou EVFa EWes LLWP LPen LRHS MLLN MNrw MOak MRav SBai SGar SPer SPlb SUsu SWvt WCAu WCot WFar WHCG WSPU
	'Craigieburn Taffeta' **new**	GCra
	crandallii	CPBP
	- subsp. ***glabrescens***	WHCG WLin
§	- subsp. ***taosensis***	NWCA SMrm
	cristatus	see *P. eriantherus*
	davidsonii	EWes NLAp SRms WAbe WPat
	- var. ***davidsonii***	CPBP WLin
§	- var. ***menziesii*** ♀H4	EBee GTou MDun NWCA SRms
	- - 'Broken Top Mountain'	CLyd
	- - 'Microphyllus'	EPot LTwo NSla WAbe WLin
	- var. ***praeteritus***	CNic EPot GKev MDKP
	'Dazzler'	CM&M CWCL ERou LPen NChi SWal SWvt WEll WPer WSPU
§	***deaveri***	WSPU
	'Devonshire Cream'	CElw CStr CWCL LPen LRHS MBNS SAga WHCG
	diffusus	see *P. serrulatus*
	digitalis	CRWN ECha EMan LPen LPhx MBNS NLAp NWCA WFar WHCG WMow WPer
§	- 'Husker Red'	More than 30 suppliers
	- 'Purpureus'	see *P. digitalis* 'Husker Red'
	- 'Ruby Tuesday'	CDes EWes
	- white-flowered	GBBs LPhx SRms
	discolor pale lavender-flowered	NBir WFar
	dissectus	NLAp SGar
§	'Drinkstone'	EGoo EHol LPen LRHS NChi SAga SDix WEll WHCG WPer WSPU
	'Drinkwater Red'	see *P.* 'Drinkstone'
	eatonii subsp. ***undosus*** NNS 95-381	WCot
	'Edithae'	LPen NLon SChu SRms WEas WHCG WIvy WKif
	'Electric Blue' **new**	NPri
	'Elmley'	CStr MLLN SAga WEll WSPU
§	***eriantherus***	CGra GKev WHCG
	'Etna'	CStr CWCL ECtt ENot GKev GKir LRHS MBri MMil NCob NEgg SGar WEll
	euglaucus	EBee EHyt LTwo SGar
§	'Evelyn' ♀H4	More than 30 suppliers
	'Firebird'	see *P.* 'Schoenholzeri'
	'Flame'	EMan LPen LRHS NBur SLon WEll WHCG WPer WSPU
	'Flamingo'	CWCL EChP ECtt EPfP ERou EWes LAst LPen LRHS MAsh MAvo MBNS MSte NBir NCGa NEgg SAga SBai SWvt WCFE WEll WFar WHil WSPU WWol
	fremontii	WLin
	frutescens	GIBF GTou WSPU
	fruticosus	CSec EBee MNrw NWCA WAbe
§	- var. ***scouleri*** ♀H4	MOne NLAp SRms WBVN WCFE WSPU
	- - f. ***albus*** ♀H4	LPen NWCA SChu WAbe WIvy WKif
	- - 'Amethyst'	NLAp WAbe WLin
	- - f. ***ruber*** **new**	NWCA
	- var. ***serratus***	LPen NLAp
	- - 'Holly'	NMen SAga SBla SHGN
	Fujiyama = 'Yayama'PBR	ECtt LRHS LSou MBow MBri MMil NEgg SGar WFar
	'Gaff's Pink'	SChu
	'Gaiety'	CM&M
	'Garden Red'	see *P.* 'Windsor Red'
	'Garnet'	see *P.* 'Andenken an Friedrich Hahn'
	gentianoides	MNrw NBro
	'Geoff Hamilton'	CElw LPen MBNS SAga
	'George Elrick'	LPen MBNS
§	'George Home' ♀H3	CWCL ECGP ECtt EWes LPen LRHS MBNS MLLN MSte NBur SChu SMrm SSvw WBVN WHCG
	'Ghent Purple'	CFee
	'Gilchrist'	LPhx LRHS SGar SLon WEll WLin WWeb
	glaber	CMHG CMea GMac LLWP LPen LRHS LSRN MBNS MBri MEHN NBro NGdn NLAp SBai SECG SHFr SMrm SPlb WBVN WEll WHCG WKif WPer WSPU
	- 'Roundway Snowflake'	CMea CStr LPhx
	- white-flowered	SGar
	globosus	WLin
	'Gloire des Quatre Rues'	LPen
	gormanii	CSec CStr EBee SGar
	gracilis	GCal WPer
§	***grandiflorus***	CSec EBee EMan EShb NLAp WCAu
	- 'Prairie Snow'	EBee
	hallii	CGra CNic EPot EWes GTou LRHS NWCA WPat
	hartwegii ♀H3-4	CBrm EPyc GMac LPen SChu WBan WHCG WPer WSPU
	- 'Albus'	EVFa LPen LRHS MSte SAga SGar WEll WHCG WSPU
I	- 'Tubular Bells Rose'	NPri SPet
	heterodoxus	EHyt SGar
§	***heterophyllus***	CWCL ETow LPen MNrw NBir SChu SECG SGar SMer SRms WAbe WEas WEll WHCG WPer WSPU
	- 'Blue Eye'	WSPU

	Name	Suppliers
	- 'Blue Fountain'	LPen WEll WSPU
	- 'Blue Gem'	CElw CTri ECtt LRHS NChi SIng SPla WPGP WSPU
	- 'Blue Spring'	CBot CBrm ECtt LPen LRHS MAnH MSte NBir NLAp SAga SBla WAbe
§	- 'Catherine de la Mare' 🏆H4	CHar CStr ELan GKir LPen LRHS LSRN MBow MBri MHer MWat NBir NBro NLAp SChu SMrm SPla SWal SWvt WEas WFar WKif WSPU
	- 'Heavenly Blue'	CSBt CWCL ECtt EPfP ERou LAst LPen LRHS MAvo MBNS MDun NLAp NLon SBai SOkh SPav SPoG SWal SWvt WCra WEll WHil WMnd WWhi WWol
	- 'Hergest Croft'	CElw SChu WEll
	- 'Jeanette'	WCot WHoo
	- subsp. ***purdyi***	EPyc WEll WHCG
	- 'Roehrslev'	LPen
	- 'True Blue'	see *P. heterophyllus*
	- 'Züriblau'	CFai CMdw LPen WWFP
	'Hewell Pink Bedder' 🏆H3	CBcs CElw CHar COIW ECtt ENot EPfP ERou GBri LPen LRHS MBNS MOak MSte NBPC NBlu NEgg SBai SChu SWal SWvt WCra WFar WHCG WHil WMnd WPer WSPU WWeb WWol
	'Hewitt's Pink'	ECtt NEgg SAga WEll
§	'Hidcote Pink' 🏆H3-4	More than 30 suppliers
	'Hidcote Purple'	CElw CM&M NGdn SAga SChu SHar
*	'Hidcote White'	CM&M GBri MHer SWvt WEll
	'Hillview Pink'	WHil
	'Hillview Red'	WHil
§	***hirsutus***	CNic CSec LPen MNrw NLAp SGar SIng SUsu WBVN WPer WSan
	- f. ***albiflorus***	ECtt LPen NLAp NWCA
	- var. ***minimus***	NLAp
	- var. ***pygmaeus***	CLyd CMea CNic EDAr GTou LBee LPen MHer NArg NJOw NMen NWCA SBla SGar SPlb SRms SRot SWal WGwG WHoo WPer
	- - f. ***albus***	EHyt SHGN WPer
	- - 'Purpureus'	WLin
	'Hopleys Variegated' (v)	EMan MHer NBir SAga SBai SPav SWvt WCot WSPU WWeb
§	***humilis***	CNic EBee LEdu MLLN NLAp SRms WLin
	- 'Pulchellus'	NLAp NWCA
	idahoensis	NWCA
	immanifestus	NWCA
	isophyllus 🏆H3-4	CAby CTri EChP EPfP LPen LRHS MAsh MMil SChu WEll WFar WHCG WPer WSPU
	jamesii	CGra CSec EChP EHyt WHrl
	janishiae	CGra NWCA
	Jean Grace = 'Penbow'	CHar GKir LRHS NLar
	'John Booth'	MSte WEas
	'John Nash'	MHer SAga SChu WEll
	'John Nash' misapplied	see *P.* 'Alice Hindley'
	'John Spedan Lewis'	SLon
	'Joy'	EPyc LPen MLLN MSte WCFE WPer
	'June'	see *P.* 'Pennington Gem'
	Kilimanjaro = 'Yajaro'	ENot LSou WEll
	'King George V'	More than 30 suppliers
	'Knight's Purple'	CElw LPen WEll WHCG
	'Knightwick' **new**	WEll
	'Knightwick' ambig.	CElw LPen SGar WEll WPer WSPU
§	***kunthii***	CStr EBee EPPr GEdr LLWP LPen MDKP NBur NLAp WEll WHrl WSPU
	- upright	SGar WLin
§	***laetus*** subsp. ***roezlii***	EHyt EPot GCrs GEdr GGar LRHS MBar MDun NLAp NLon NSla NWCA SRms WBVN
	laricifolius	CNic
§	'Le Phare'	LPen LRHS MBNS MHar WEll WHCG WPer WSPU
	leiophyllus	EHyt WLin
	leonensis	CSec NArg WLin
	'Lilac and Burgundy'	CHar CHea EChP EMar ERou EWTr LPen LRHS MBNS SBai SWvt WEll WFar WLin WWol
	linarioides	CStr LPen NLAp WPat
	- subsp. ***sileri***	WLin
	'Little Witley'	LPen SAga WEll WHCG WPer
	'Lord Home'	see *P.* 'George Home'
	lyallii	EBee EHrv ELan EMan GKev LPen MCCP MLLN MNrw NLAp NMRc SRms WPtf WSPU WSan
	'Lynette'	LPen LRHS MBNS SAga SPlb WEll WHCG WPer
	'Macpenny's Pink'	EBee EPyc LPen MBNS SChu WEll
§	'Madame Golding'	CWCL GMac LPen LRHS MBNS MNrw SGar WEll WHCG WPer WSPU
	'Malvern Springs' **new**	WEll
	'Margery Fish' 🏆H3	CElw CStr EMar ERou EWes LPen LRHS MMil MNrw MSte SBai WEll WPer WSPU
	'Maurice Gibbs' 🏆H3	More than 30 suppliers
	menziesii	see *P. davidsonii* var. *menziesii*
	Mexicali hybrids	CPBP EBee LPen MLLN
	mexicanus	WLin
	'Midnight'	CHar CPLG EBee EChP ELan EPfP EVFa GBri LLWP LPen MOak MRav MSte SGar SIgm SWvt WBVN WCFE WCot WHCG WHoo WMnd WPer WSPU WWeb
	'Mint Pink'	SGar
	'Modesty'	EGra LPen LRHS MBNS NBur SMar WEll WHCG WPer WSPU
	montanus	CNic NLAp SAga
	'Mother of Pearl'	More than 30 suppliers
	'Mrs Miller'	LPen MBNS NBur
	'Mrs Morse'	see *P.* 'Chester Scarlet'
	mucronatus **new**	NArg
	multiflorus	CStr LPen
§	'Myddelton Gem'	CHar LPen LRHS MBNS MNrw WCot WEll WFoF WHCG WSPU
	'Myddelton Red'	see *P.* 'Myddelton Gem'
	nanus	CGra
	nemorosus NNS 00-572	EPPr
	neotericus	NWCA
	newberryi 🏆H4	CBrm CMea CNic CSec GKev GKir NRnb SRot WBVN WKif WPat
	- subsp. ***berryi***	see *P. berryi*
	- f. ***humilior***	EPot WLin
§	- subsp. ***sonomensis***	EPot NWCA WAbe WLin
*	'Newbury Gem'	EWin MBNS NBur SBai SWvt WEll WFar WWol
§	***nitidus***	MNrw
	'Oaklea Red'	ECtt EPyc ERou LPen
§	'Old Candy Pink'	CFee LLWP LPen MSte SBai SWvt WEll WPer WSPU
	'Old Silk'	WCot
	oliganthus	LRav
	'Osprey' 🏆H3	More than 30 suppliers
	ovatus	CSec EBee EVFa GBBs LPen LPhx LPio MBow MLLN NDlv NLAp SBla SGar SIgm SRms WCot WHCG WKif WLin WSan WWeb
	'Overbury'	EBee LPen WSPU
	pallidus	EBee
	palmeri	EMan SECG
	'Papal Purple'	CChe CMHG CMea CWCL ERou LLWP LPen LRHS MBNS MSte NBir

		NChi SAga SBai SChu SLon SRms SWal WEll WFar WHCG WSPU WWhi
	'Papal Purple' x 'Evelyn'	CMHG LPen
	'Patio Bells Pink'	ERou LPen MLLN WEll
	Patio Bells Red = 'Yapbred'	CWCL
	'Patio Bells Shell'	GKir LRHS WRHF
	'Patio Wine'	WEll
	payettensis	LTwo
	'Peace'	LPen LRHS MBNS SLon WEll WHCG WSPU
	'Pearl'	EPyc
§	'Pennington Gem' ♀H3	CElw ECtt EGra ELan GBri GKir GMac LLWP LPen LRHS MHer MNrw MSte NBir NGdn SBai SIng SPer SWvt WHCG WPer WSPU WWlt
	'Pensham Arctic Fox'	EBee MBri WCot
	'Pensham Arctic Sunset'	WEll
	'Pensham Avonbelle'	MBnl WEll
	'Pensham Bilberry Ice'	CHar EBee MLLN SPav WEll WWol
	'Pensham Blackberry Ice'	CFir CRez MBnl SPav WEll WWol
	'Pensham Blueberry Ice'	CHar CRez EBee MAnH MBnl MBri MLLN SPav WCra WFar WWol
	'Pensham Bow Bells'	SAga
	'Pensham Capricorn Moon'	EBee SAga WEll
	'Pensham Cassis Royale'	CStr MLLN WEll
	'Pensham Charles Romer'	WEll
	'Pensham Choir Boy'	CStr
	'Pensham Claret'	WEll
	'Pensham Daybreak'	WEll
	'Pensham Dorothy Wilson'	WEll
	'Pensham Edith Biggs'	CWCL EBee WEll WFar
	'Pensham Freshwater Pearl'	CElw CStr SAga WEll
	'Pensham Great Expectations'	EBee MLLN SAga SOkh SPoG WEll
	'Pensham Just Jayne'	CElw EBee MBnl MLLN NPro SLon WEll WWol
	'Pensham Kay Burton' **new**	WEll
	'Pensham Marjorie Lewis'	WEll
	'Pensham Miss Wilson'	CStr WEll
	'Pensham Petticoat'	EBee MBnl MBri SOkh WEll
	'Pensham Plum Dandy'	CStr WEll
	'Pensham Plum Jerkum'	EBee MBnl MBri MLLN SPav WCra WEll
	'Pensham Prolific'	WEll
	'Pensham Raspberry Ice'	EBee MBnl MLLN SPav WWol
	'Pensham Saint James's'	WEll
	'Pensham Son of Raven'	CStr WEll
	'Pensham Tayberry Ice'	CRez EBee MBnl MLLN SPav WEll WWol
	'Pensham The Dean's Damson'	WEll
	'Pensham Tiger Belle Coral'	MBnl WEll WWol
I	'Pensham Tiger Belle Rose'	SAga WEll
	'Pensham Twilight'	CStr
	'Pensham Victoria Plum'	CStr WEll
	'Pensham Wedding Bells'	CStr EBee MBri SPoG SUsu WFar
	perfoliatus	EBee
	'Pershore Carnival'	NPro WSPU WSSM
	'Pershore Fanfare'	CElw CStr LPen WEll WHrl WSPU
	'Pershore Pink Necklace'	EMar LPen MLLN SAga SBai SMrm SWvt WCot WEll WHCG WSPU WSan WWeb
	'Phare'	see *P.* 'Le Phare'
	'Phyllis'	see *P.* 'Evelyn'
	pinifolius ♀H4	CBrm CMHG CMea CWCL ECtt EDAr EHyt EPot GAbr GCrs GKir GMaP LRHS NEgg NFor NJOw NLAp NLon NWCA SBla SPoG SRms WBVN WFar WHoo WPat WSPU
	- 'Mersea Yellow'	CMea EBee ECtt EDAr EHyt EPfP EPot GAbr GCrs GEdr GKir LPen LRHS NChi NDlv NJOw NLAp NWCA SAga SBla SECG SPlb SPoG SWal WBVN WFar WLin WPat WPer WSPU
	- 'Wisley Flame' ♀H4	EPfP GEdr GKev NJOw NRya NWCA SIgm
	'Pink Bedder'	see *P.* 'Hewell Pink Bedder', 'Sutton's Pink Bedder'
	'Pink Dragon'	CLyd WHCG
	'Pink Endurance'	CMea EBee ERou LPen MSte SWal WEll WHCG WHal WPer WSPU
	'Pink Ice'	WHil
	'Pink Profusion'	MRav SIgm
	'Pixie' **new**	CPen
	'Port Wine' ♀H3	CHar CSam CTri CWCL EMar GMaP LLWP LPen LRHS LSRN MBow MLLN NBir NChi SAga SBai SPla SPoG SWal WCot WHCG WHoo WMnd WPer WSPU
	'Powis Castle'	EWes MHar WBan WEll WPer WWlt
	'Prairie Dusk'	LPen
	'Prairie Fire'	EBee ERou LPen WSPU
*	'Prairie Pride'	LPen
	'Priory Purple'	WEll WHCG WPer
	procerus	EChP GBri GCal LPen MDHE MLLN NEgg SRms WEll WLin WPer
	- var. ***brachyanthus***	CNic
§	- var. ***formosus***	EHyt EPot NWCA WAbe WLin
	- var. ***procerus***	EHyt
§	- 'Roy Davidson' ♀H4	CAby CMea CPBP EHyt ETow LBee LRHS NLAp SBla WAbe WEll WFar WLin
	- var. ***tolmiei***	EPot GCal GEdr LBee LPen NChi NSla WLin
	- - white	WLin
§	***procumbens*** 'Claude Barr'	CPBP
	pubescens	see *P. hirsutus*
	pulchellus Greene	see *P. procerus* var. *formosus*
	pulchellus Lindl.	see *P. campanulatus*
*	***pulcherrimus***	NBro
	pumilus	SRms
	'Purple and White'	see *P.* 'Countess of Dalkeith'
	'Purple Bedder'	CElw CHea CHrt COIW EBee EGra EPfP ERou LAst LPen LRHS LSRN MAsh MLLN MNrw MWat NBir NGdn SAga SBai SPav SPoG SWvt WCFE WEll WFar WGor WHCG WHil WSPU
	'Purple Passion'	CElw EBrs EChP EHrv EPfP EWes GBBs LPen LRHS WEll
	'Purpureus Albus'	see *P.* 'Countess of Dalkeith'
	purpusii	NWCA SIgm WCot WLin
	'Rajah'	LPen
	'Raven' ♀H3	More than 30 suppliers
	'Razzle Dazzle'	LPen LRHS MBNS SPlb WCot WEll WHil WPer
	'Red Ace'	MNrw WEll
	'Red Emperor'	CStr ECtt LPen MBNS MHar SPlb WEll WHCG WPer WSPU
	'Red Knight'	CWCL GCra LPen LRHS MBNS
	'Red Rocks' **new**	WCot
	'Red Sea'	CStr
	'Rich Purple'	EPyc LLWP LRHS MBNS SPlb
	'Rich Ruby'	More than 30 suppliers
	richardsonii	CStu EBee EHyt EShb MDKP MNrw NWCA SIgm SRms WEll

	– var. ***dentata*** **new**	WLin
	'Ridgeway Red'	WSPU
	roezlii Regel	see *P. laetus* subsp. *roezlii*
§	***rostriflorus*** NNS 95-407	WCot
	– 'Rosy Gem'	WSSM
	'Rosy Blush'	LPen LRHS MBNS SPlb WHCG
	'Roundhay'	CFee
	'Roy Davidson'	see *P. procerus* 'Roy Davidson'
	'Royal White'	see *P.* 'White Bedder'
	'Rubicundus' ♀H3	CWCL EBee EBrs ECtt EHrv ELan EPfP ERou LPen LRHS MAsh MBNS SAga SBai SMrm SPla SWvt WCot WCra WEll WFar WHCG WMnd WSPU WWeb WWol
	'Ruby'	see *P.* 'Schoenholzeri'
	'Ruby Field'	EPyc WCFE WEll WHCG
	'Ruby Gem'	LPen LRHS MBNS
	rupicola ♀H4	EHyt GCrs GKev GTou LRHS NSla SIgm WAbe WLin
	– 'Albus'	NSla WAbe
	– 'Conwy Lilac'	WAbe
	– 'Conwy Rose'	WAbe
	– 'Diamond Lake'	CMea NLAp WPat
	'Russian River'	ECtt EPfP EWes LLWP LPen LRHS NBur SGar SMrm SOkh SPlb SWal WHCG WPer WSPU
	rydbergii	CSec NLAp
	– var. ***oreocharis*** **new**	WLin
§	'Schoenholzeri' ♀H4	More than 30 suppliers
	scouleri	see *P. fruticosus* var. *scouleri*
§	***serrulatus***	CNic CSec EPot EWes GTou ITim LPen MSte MWgw NArg NLAp SGar SHFr SMad WBVN WHrl WKif WSPU
	– 'Albus'	EShb LPen MSte WSPU
	'Shell Pink'	CTbh LPen NChi WEll WPer
*	'Sherbourne Blue'	GBuc SLon WCot WEll WPer
	'Shock Wave' **new**	MSte
*	'Shrawley'	WPer
	'Sissinghurst Pink'	see *P.* 'Evelyn'
	'Six Hills'	NLAp SRms WAbe WHCG WLin WPat WSPU
	'Skyline'	COkL EPfP
	smallii	CMHG CTbh EBee EDAr EMan EShb EWTr EWes LPen LPhx LSRN MCCP NLAp NWCA SGar SIgm SIng SMrm SPoG WHoo
	'Snow Storm'	see *P.* 'White Bedder'
	'Snowflake'	see *P.* 'White Bedder'
	'Son of Raven'	WEll
	sonomensis	see *P. newberryi* subsp. *sonomensis*
	'Sour Grapes' misapplied	see *P.* 'Stapleford Gem'
§	'Sour Grapes' M. Fish ♀H3-4	More than 30 suppliers
	'Southcombe Pink'	LPen MLLN WEll WHCG
	'Southgate Gem'	GKir LPen LRHS MNrw SWvt WEll WHCG
	'Souvenir d'Adrian Regnier'	LPen
	'Souvenir d'André Torres' misapplied	see *P.* 'Chester Scarlet'
	'Souvenir d'André Torres'	LLWP LPen WEll
	spatulatus **new**	WLin
§	'Stapleford Gem' ♀H3	More than 30 suppliers
	'Strawberry Fizz'	LPen MBNS
	strictus	EGoo EMan LBBr LPen LPio LRHS MBNS MCCP MHar MLLN NLAp SGar SRms WPer WSPU WWeb
	Stromboli = 'Yaboli'	MBri SGar SIng WEll
	superbus **new**	GKev
	'Sutton's Pink Bedder'	LRHS MBNS SPlb WEll WSPU
	'Sylvia Buss'	LPen
	tall pink	see *P.* 'Welsh Dawn'
N	'Taoensis'	EWes SGar WEll
	taosensis	see *P. crandallii* subsp. *taosensis*
	teucrioides	EPot GEdr NLAp NWCA WLin
	– JCA 1717050	CPBP
	'The Juggler'PBR	EBee EPfP EWin LPen LRHS MBNS SPav WFar WWol
	thompsoniae	WLin
§	'Thorn'	CBcs CSpe EBee ECtt EGra ELan ERou GBBs LPen LRHS MBow MLLN MNrw MSte MTis NBPC NBir SAga SBai SMrm SPer SPla SWal SWvt WHCG WLin WSPU WWeb
	'Threave Pink'	CPrp CWCL ERou EVFa LBBr LLWP MRav SMrm SPer SPoG SWvt WEll WLin WMoo
*	'Threave White'	WPen
	'Torquay Gem'	GBuc LPen SDys WCot WHCG WPer
	'True Sour Grapes'	see *P.* 'Sour Grapes' M.Fish
	'Tubular Bells Red'	NPri
§	***tusharensis***	SBla
	utahensis	CBot GBri
	venustus	CFir EBee GBuc MHar MNrw NCob SGar SRms SRot WHCG WRos WWye
	Vesuvius = 'Yasius'	CStr ENot EPyc GKev GKir LPen LSou MBri NEgg SGar SWal WEll WFar
	'Violet Dusk' **new**	WPtf
	virens	CNic CPBP NLAp WPat WPer
	virgatus subsp. ***arizonicus***	see *P. deaveri*
	– 'Blue Buckle'	CBrm CPBP EBee EShb EWTr MBri NBir NMyG
	– subsp. ***virgatus***	CMHG NLAp
	washingtonensis	CNic
	watsonii	CSec CStr EBee EMan MLLN SRms WHCG WHoo
§	'Welsh Dawn'	CStr LPen WEll WSPU
§	***whippleanus***	LPen MSte NRnb SAga WAbb WLin
	– 'Chocolate Drop'	CBgR CDes EBee WPtf
§	'White Bedder' ♀H3	More than 30 suppliers
	'Whitethroat' Sidwell	LLWP LPen LRHS MBNS SAga SLon WEll WHCG WSPU
I	'Whitethroat' purple-flowered	WPer
	wilcoxii	EBee NEgg
	'Willy's Purple'	SLon WEll
§	'Windsor Red'	CTri ECtt EMar EPfP ERou LPen LRHS MAsh MBNS MSte SBai SGar SPav SPoG SUsu SWvt WCot WGor WHCG WHil WSPU WSSM WWol
	wislizeni	CSec EPfP MLan MNrw MOne SRms
	'Woodpecker' **new**	WHil

Pentachondra (*Epacridaceae*)

	pumila **new**	IBlr

Pentaglottis (*Boraginaceae*)

§	***sempervirens***	CArn EPfP MHer MSal WWye
	– 'Ballydowling'	CNat

Pentapanax (*Araliaceae*)

	leschenaultii HWJK 2385 **new**	WCru

Pentapterygium see *Agapetes*

Pentas (*Rubiaceae*)

	lanceolata	CHal ELan LRHS MBri

Peperomia (*Piperaceae*)

§	***argyreia*** ♀H1	MBri
	arifolia	CHal
	caperata	LRHS MBri
	clusiifolia	CHal
	- 'Variegata' (v)	CHal
	glabella	CHal
	- 'Variegata' (v)	CHal
	obtusifolia 'Jamaica'	MBri
	- (Magnoliifolia Group) 'Golden Gate' (v)	MBri
	- - 'Greengold'	CHal MBri
	- - 'USA' ♀H1	MBri
	- 'Tricolor' (v)	MBri
	orba 'Pixie'	MBri
I	- 'Pixie Variegata' (v)	MBri
	pulchella	see *P. verticillata*
	sandersii	see *P. argyreia*
	scandens ♀H1	MBri
	- 'Variegata' (v)	CHal MBri
§	***verticillata***	CHal

pepino see *Solanum muricatum*

peppermint see *Mentha piperita*

Perezia (*Asteraceae*)

	linearis	GBuc MAvo NLar
	recurvata	GTou

Pericallis (*Asteraceae*)

§	***lanata***	CHII ELan MBlu SAga SBch WDyG WPic
	- Kew form	CRHN CSpe SAga SMrm
	multiflora	SAga

Perilla (*Lamiaceae*)

§	***frutescens*** var. ***crispa*** ♀H2	CArn EUnu MChe WJek
	- green-leaved	EOHP EUnu
	- var. ***nankinensis***	see *P. frutescens* var. *crispa*
	- var. ***purpurascens***	CArn CSpe EOHP EShb EUnu MChe WJek

Periploca (*Asclepiadaceae*)

	graeca	CArn CBcs CMac CPLN CRHN GQui ITer SLon SPoG SYvo WSHC
	purpurea B&SWJ 7235	WCru
	sepium	CPLG

Peristrophe (*Acanthaceae*)

	speciosa	ECre ERea

Pernettya see *Gaultheria*

Perovskia (*Lamiaceae*)

	abrotanoides	XPep
	atriplicifolia	CArn CBot CMea GPoy MHer WHCG WPer
	- 'Little Spire'PBR	MBri NPro SPer
	'Blue Haze'	GCal SMHy
	'Blue Spire' ♀H4	More than 30 suppliers
	'Filigran'	EBee ECGP EVFa GBuc LAst LRHS NSti SChu SMHy SPoG WPat XPep
	'Longin'	XPep

Persea (*Lauraceae*)

	ichangensis	CPLG
	indica	CFil CPLG WPGP
	lingue	LEdu
	thunbergii	CFil CHEx WPGP

Persicaria (*Polygonaceae*)

§	***affinis***	CBcs CSBt EBee ENot GAbr GKir MBar MTho MWhi NBro NVic SMer WBVN WBor WBrE WCFE WFar WMoo
	- 'Darjeeling Red' ♀H4	More than 30 suppliers
	- 'Dimity'	see *P. affinis* 'Superba'
	- 'Donald Lowndes' ♀H4	More than 30 suppliers
	- 'Kabouter'	LBuc
	- 'Ron McBeath'	CRow
§	- 'Superba' ♀H4	More than 30 suppliers
	alata	see *P. nepalensis*
	alpina	CRow SBch
	amphibia	CRow
§	***amplexicaulis***	CBre COld CPrp CRow ELan EMar EWes GCra GMaP LGro MHer MSte NChi NFor NLon NOrc SChu SEND WBor WFar WMoo WRHF WTel WTin WWpP
	- 'Alba'	CElw CHar CRow EBee ECha EMan EPla ERou EVFa GMaP LPhx MLLN NDov SHar SMrm WCAu WCot WFar WGHP WMoo WPnP WTin WWhi
	- 'Atrosanguinea'	CNic CRow CTri EBee EBrs ECha EGra EMFW EMan EPla ERou GGar LPhx LRHS MNFA MRav MWgw NBir NDov NEgg NVic SPer SRms SWvt WFar WOld WWpP
	- 'Baron'	CRow
*	- 'Blush Clent'	EBee WSPU WTin
	- 'Border Beauty'	EBee
	- 'Clent Charm'	WGHP WSPU
	- 'Cottesbrooke Gold'	CRow EMan
	- 'Dikke Floskes'	CRow
	- 'Firedance'	LPhx NDov SMHy SMrm SUsu WCot
	- 'Firetail' ♀H4	More than 30 suppliers
	- 'High Society'	EBee
	- 'Inverleith'	CBre CHar CKno CRow EBee EBrs ECha ECtt EPla WMoo WPGP
*	- var. ***pendula***	CRow EBrs NBir SBla WFar WMoo
	- 'Pink Lady'	CRow
	- 'Rosea'	CBos CRow CSam EBee ECha ELan EMan EPPr EPla EWTr LPhx MRav MSte NBro NDov NSti SDys WCAu WFar WGHP WMoo WPGP
	- 'Rowden Gem'	CRow EPla WMoo
	- 'Rowden Jewel'	CRow EPla
	- 'Rowden Rose Quartz'	CRow
	- 'Summer Dance'	EBee EMon
	- Taurus = 'Blotau'	CElw CKno CRow EBee EBrs EPla ERou MLLN MWgw SMHy WFar WPGP WTin
§	***bistorta***	CArn CHar CRow ELau GBar GPoy MChe MHer MSal MWhi NBir NGHP SRms WCra WGwG WSel WWpP WWye
	- subsp. ***carnea***	CRow EBee EBla EBrs ECha EMan EWsh GGar LRHS MNFA NBir NDov WFar WMoo
	- 'Hohe Tatra'	CRow EBee EBrs EMan GBin GKir LPhx WFar WTMC
	- 'Superba' ♀H4	More than 30 suppliers
	bistortoides	MSal
	campanulata	CElw CRow EChP ECha ECtt GAbr GBuc GCal GGar MHar NBid NBro NDov NFor NGdn NLon SPer WBcn WFar WMoo WOld WWpP WWye
	- Alba Group	CElw CRow EBee GCal GGar GKir NBro NGdn WHer WMoo WWye

	- 'Madame Figard'	CRow
	- 'Rosenrot'	CBre CKno CRow EMan EPPr GBuc GCal NBir NGdn NLar SSpi WCot WFar WWpP
	- 'Southcombe White'	CRow EPPr EPla GBri
§	***capitata***	CHal CPLG CRow EMan SHFr SIng SRms WEas WMoo XPep
	- CC 3693	WCot
	- 'Pink Bubbles'	ECtt SPet SWvt
	conspicua	EBee
	coriacea	CRow
	elata	EMan GBuc GGar NBur
	emodi	CRow
§	***longiseta***	MSal
§	***macrophylla***	CRow EBee EBrs LDai NLar WFar WGHP
	microcephala	CRow EWes MHer SMac
	- 'Red Dragon'PBR	More than 30 suppliers
	- var. ***wallichii***	CRow
*	***milletii***	CDes CRow EBrs EWes GAbr GBuc GKir MBri MTho SMac WCAu WCru WFar
§	***mollis***	CRow WPGP
*	- var. ***frondosa***	EBee
	neofiliformis	EBee
§	***nepalensis***	CRow EPPr SMad
§	***odorata***	CArn ELau EOHP EPza EUnu GPoy ILis LRav MChe MHer MSal NGHP SHDw SIde WJek
	orientalis	MSal
*	***polymorpha***	CBct CDes CFwr CKno CRow EBee EBrs ECha EHrv ELan EMan EMon EPPr GMaP LPhx MRav NCGa NDov SMad SSpe WCot WFar WMoo WTin WWhi
	polystachya	see *P. wallichii*
*	***regeliana***	LRHS
§	***runcinata***	CPLG CRow EBee ECtt EMar GGar NBid NBir NCob NLar WFar WHer WMoo WPer WPtf
	- Needham's form	CRow NBid
	scoparia	see *Polygonum scoparium*
	sphaerostachya	see *P. macrophylla*
	tenuicaulis	CBre CLyd CRow EBee EHrv EMon EPPr EPla GGar WAbe WCot WCru WFar WMoo
§	***tinctoria***	EBee EOHP
	vacciniifolia ♀H4	More than 30 suppliers
	- 'Ron McBeath'	CRow
§	***virginiana***	CRow EBrs ECtt EMan MSal NLar WMoo WTMC
	- Compton's form	CBct CRow EBee EBrs ECha EMan EMar EPPr EVFa EWin LDai NCob WCot WMoo WTMC WWpP
	- 'Filiformis'	EBee ECtt MAvo WCot
	- 'Lance Corporal'	CRow EPla NCob WMnd WMoo
	- Variegata Group	CBot CM&M CRow EBee EChP ECha EMan ERou EShb GCal MBNS NLar WAul WCot WMoo WOld
§	- 'Painter's Palette' (v)	More than 30 suppliers
	- white-flowered	EPPr GCal NCob
	vivipara	CRow NLar
§	***wallichii***	CRow EBee ECha GBri NLar NSti SDix WCot WMoo
§	***weyrichii***	EBee EMan EMon EPPr GCal GIBF NBir NBro NLar WCot WFar WMoo

persimmon see *Diospyros virginiana*

persimmon, Japanese see *Diospyros kaki*

Petalostemon see *Dalea*

Petamenes see *Gladiolus*

Petasites (*Asteraceae*)

	albus	EBee EMon GGar GPoy GSki NLar
	formosanus	LEdu
	- B&SWJ 3025	WCru
	fragrans	CNat ELan EMon MHer NLar WFar WHer
§	***frigidus*** var. ***palmatus***	CRow EBee EPla LEdu MWgw NLar NSti WCru WPGP
	- - JLS 86317CLOR	SMad WCot
	- var. ***palmatus*** 'Golden Palms'	EHrv NSti SPur SSpi
	hybridus	EMFW LEdu SMad WHer
	japonicus	CBcs
	- var. ***giganteus***	CArn CHEx CRow ECha ELan EMon EPfP EUJe LEdu NVic SGSe WCru WMoo WTMC
§	- - 'Nishiki-buki' (v)	CHEx CMCo CRow EBee EMag EMan EMon EPPr EPla EUJe IBlr ITer MFOX NSti SGSe SMad WBor WCHb WCot WCru WFar WPGP WPnP WTMC WWpP
	- - 'Variegatus'	see *P. japonicus* var. *giganteus* 'Nishiki-buki'
	- f. ***purpureus***	EBee EMan EPPr EUJe SGSe WCot WCru WPGP WPnP
	palmatus	see *P. frigidus* var. *palmatus*
	paradoxus	CLAP EBee LEdu MRav NLar SMad WCot

Petrea (*Verbenaceae*)

	volubilis	CHII CPLN

Petrocallis (*Brassicaceae*)

	lagascae	see *P. pyrenaica*
§	***pyrenaica***	GKev NWCA WLin

Petrocoptis (*Caryophyllaceae*)

	pseudoviscosa	WAbe
	pyrenaica	EBur SBla SRms
§	- subsp. ***glaucifolia***	EDAr EMan GTou NBir NJOw NLar

Petrocosmea (*Gesneriaceae*)

	sp.	LAma
	- B&SWJ 7249 from Thailand	WCru
	kerrii B&SWJ 6634	WCru

Petrophytum (*Rosaceae*)

	caespitosum	CMea GTou NSla
	cinerascens	NWCA SIng
§	***hendersonii***	GGar NWCA WAbe

Petrorhagia (*Caryophyllaceae*)

	illyrica subsp. ***haynaldiana***	SPet
	'Pink Starlets'	LRav SHGN
§	***saxifraga*** ♀H4	CNic EBur EShb MBow NJOw NPri SRms SWal WMoo WPer WPnn WPtf
§	- 'Rosette'	MTho

Petroselinum (*Apiaceae*)

§	***crispum***	CArn CHrt CSev EDAr GPoy GWCH ILis LRHS MBar MChe MDun MWat NBlu NGHP SECG SIde SWal WLHH WPer WSel WWye
	- 'Bravour' ♀H4	ELau MBow MHer
	- 'Darki'	CSev NGHP NPri

- French — CArn EDAr ELau MBow MHer NBlu NPri NVic WJek WLHH WWye
- 'Italian' — see *P. crispum* var. *neapolitanum*
§ - var. ***neapolitanum*** — ELau GWCH MHer SIde WLHH
- 'Super Moss Curled' — NVic
§ - var. ***tuberosum*** — MHer SIde WHer
hortense — see *P. crispum*
tuberosum — see *P. crispum* var. *tuberosum*

Petteria (*Papilionaceae*)

ramentacea — EGFP EPfP NLar SLPl WBVN

Petunia (*Solanaceae*)

* 'Angels Blue' — LAst
Candyfloss = 'Kercan'PBR (Tumbelina Series) — LAst NPri
(Cascadias Series) Blue Spark = 'Dancasblue'PBR — LAst
- Cascadias Yellow Eye = 'Dancasye'PBR ♥H3 — LAst WWol
'Charlie's Angels Pink' (Charlie's Angel Series) — LAst
(Conchita Series) Conchita Blossom White = 'Conbloss'PBR **new** — LSou
- Conchita Blueberry Frost = 'Conblue'PBR ♥H3 **new** — LSou
- Conchita Cranberry Frost = 'Concran'PBR ♥H3 **new** — LSou
- Conchita Strawberry Frost = 'Constraw'PBR ♥H3 **new** — LSou
(Conchita Doble Series) Conchita Doble Dark Blue = 'Conblue'PBR (d) — LAst
- Conchita Doble Lavender = 'Condolavender' (d) — LAst
- Conchita Doble Orchid Lace = 'USTUNI131' (d) — LAst
- Conchita Doble Pink = 'Condopink' (d) — LAst
- Conchita Doble Velvet = 'USTUNI140' (d) — LAst
- Conchita Doble White = 'Condowhite (d)' — LAst
(Doubloon Series) Doubloon Blue Star = 'Dandbblst' (d) — LAst
- Doubloon Pink Star = 'Dandbpkst' (d) — LAst
Julia = 'Kerjul'PBR (Tumbelina Series) — LAst NPri
Million Bells Series — see *Calibrachoa* Million Bells Series
patagonica **new** — CPBP
Pink Spark = 'Dancaspink'PBR — LAst
Priscilla = 'Kerpril'PBR (Tumbelina Series) — LAst LSou NPri
* 'Purple Surprise' — LAst
Rosella = 'Kerros' (Tumbelina Series) — LAst
Rosella Improved = 'Kerrosim' (Tumbelina Series) — LAst
Superbells Series — see *Calibrachoa* Superbells Series
(Supertunia Series) Supertunia Blushing Princess = 'Kakegawa S38' **new** — LAst
- Supertunia Lavender Morn = 'Kakegawa S29' **new** — LAst
- Supertunia Lavender Pink = 'Kakegawa S37' **new** — LAst
- Supertunia Mystic Pink = 'KakeS29' **new** — LAst
- Supertunia Royal Magenta = 'KakeS36' **new** — LAst
- Supertunia Royal Velvet = 'Kakegawa S28' **new** — LAst
- Supertunia White = 'Kakegawa S30' **new** — LAst
Surfinia Baby Pinkmorn = 'Sunpimo' — LAst
Surfinia Blue = 'Sunblu' — LAst LSou NPri
Surfinia Blue Vein = 'Sunsolos'PBR — LAst NPri
Surfinia Crazy Pink **new** — WWol
Surfinia Double Purple = 'Keidopuel'PBR (d) — LAst WWol
Surfinia Double White **new** — WWol
Surfinia Hot Pink = 'Marrose'PBR — LAst LSou NPri
Surfinia Lime = 'Keiyeul'PBR — LAst NPri
Surfinia Pastel 2000 = 'Sunpapi'PBR — NPri
Surfinia Patio Blue = 'Keipabukas'PBR — LAst WWol
Surfinia Pink Ice = 'Hakice'PBR (v) — LAst NPri
Surfinia Pink Vein = 'Suntosol'PBR ♥H3 — GKir NPri
Surfinia Purple = 'Shihi Brilliant' ♥H3 — LSou NPri
* Surfinia Purple Sunrise — LAst
Surfinia Red = 'Keirekul' — LAst LSou NPri WWol
Surfinia Rose Vein = 'Sunrove' — LAst
Surfinia Sky Blue = 'Keilavbu'PBR ♥H3 — LAst LSou NPri
Surfinia Vanilla **new** — LSou WWol
Surfinia White = 'Kesupite' — GKir LAst

Peucedanum (*Apiaceae*)

formosanum B&SWJ 3647 — WCru
japonicum — CSpe
litorale — see *Kitagawia litoralis*
ostruthium — GPoy MSal
- 'Daphnis' (v) — CElw CSpe EMan EMar EMon EPPr EVFa LEdu NChi NGby NPro WCot WEas WHrl WPGP
siamicum B&SWJ 264 — WCru
verticillare — CArn CSec CSpe EBee EBrs EMan LPhx MDun MWgw NBid NChi NDov NLar SDix SIgm SMad SSpi WCot WMoo

Phacelia (*Hydrophyllaceae*)

bolanderi — SPet
sericea — EMan WLin
tanacetifolia — EWTr

Phaedranassa (*Amaryllidaceae*)

carmiolii	CMon WCot
cloracra **new**	CMon
dubia	CMon WCot
* ***haurii*** **new**	CMon
* ***montana***	LRHS
viridiflora	CMon WCot

Phaedranthus see *Distictis*

Phaenocoma (*Asteraceae*)

prolifera	SPlb

Phaenosperma (*Poaceae*)

globosa	CAby CHar CHrt CSec EBee EHoe EPPr EPla EPza EShb EWes EWsh LEdu LRHS WBor WDyG WPGP WPrP

Phaiophleps see *Sisyrinchium*

nigricans	see *Sisyrinchium striatum*

Phaius (*Orchidaceae*)

minor	EFEx

Phalaris (*Poaceae*)

§ ***aquatica***	MGol MRav
arundinacea	CWCL EGra EMFW EWTr GFor MBNS MGol MLan SPlb WBan WTin
- 'Elegantissima'	see *P. arundinacea* var. *picta* 'Picta'
- var. ***picta***	CDul CHEx CHrt CWib EMFW GKir LRHS NArg NBid NBur NPer SApp SHel SPoG SYvo WDin WFar
- - 'Aureovariegata' (v)	CBcs CSWP MRav NGdn NPer WMoo
- - 'Feesey' (v)	More than 30 suppliers
- - 'Luteopicta' (v)	EHoe EMan EPPr EPfP EPla MMoz WLeb WTin WWpP
- - 'Luteovariegata' (v)	EMon NGdn
§ - - 'Picta' (v) ♀H4	COlW EBee EHon ELan EPfP EPla GFor GWCH IHMH LEdu LGro LPBA LRHS MBar MWgw NFor NLon NScw SPer SWal WMoo WWpP WWye
- - 'Streamlined' (v)	EMon EPla EWsh SLPl WFar
- - 'Tricolor' (v)	CPen EHoe EMon EPla MBar
tuberosa var. ***stenoptera***	see *P. aquatica*

Phanerophlebia (*Dryopteridaceae*)

caryotidea	see *Cyrtomium caryotideum*
falcata	see *Cyrtomium falcatum*
fortunei	see *Cyrtomium fortunei*

Pharbitis see *Ipomoea*

Phaseolus (*Papilionaceae*)

caracalla	see *Vigna caracalla*

Phegopteris (*Thelypteridaceae*)

§ ***connectilis***	EFer EFtx EMon NVic SRms WRic
decursive-pinnata	CFwr CLAP EFtx EMon GBri NBlu SPoG WOut WRic

Phellodendron (*Rutaceae*)

amurense	CBcs CDul CFil CMCN EPfP GIBF LEdu NLar SBLw SPer SSpi WBor WDin WNor WPGP WPic
- var. ***sachalinense***	CBcs GIBF LRHS
chinense	CMCN
lavalleei	EPfP

Phenakospermum (*Strelitziaceae*)

guianense	XBlo

Philadelphus ✿ (*Hydrangeaceae*)

'Albâtre' (d)	LRHS
argyrocalyx **new**	CPLN
'Avalanche'	CMHG CPLG EBee GKir LRHS NLar NPro SRms WDin WFar WHCG
'Beauclerk' ♀H4	CDoC CMHG CSBt CTri EBee ECrN ENot EPfP EWTr GKir GQui LRHS MGos MRav NEgg NWea SLim SPer SPoG SReu SRms SSpi SWvt WHCG WKif
'Belle Etoile' ♀H4	More than 30 suppliers
'Bicolore'	MWya
'Boule d'Argent' (d)	CMHG
'Bouquet Blanc'	GKir GQui MRav NLar SPer SPoG SRms WPat
brachybotrys	EPfP MRav WHCG
'Buckley's Quill' (d)	EBee EPfP MRav MWya WBcn
'Burfordensis'	CFil EBee EPfP GKir WPGP
'Burkwoodii'	LRHS
aff. ***calvescens*** BWJ 8005	WCru
caucasicus L 317	CFil
coronarius	EBee EPfP LBuc LRHS MWhi NFor NLon SGar SHBN SHel SMer SPer WBVN WDin XPep
- 'Aureus' ♀H4	More than 30 suppliers
- 'Bowles' Variety'	see *P. coronarius* 'Variegatus'
§ - 'Variegatus' (v) ♀H4	More than 30 suppliers
'Cotswold'	WBcn
'Coupe d'Argent'	CPLG MRav
'Dame Blanche' (d)	EBee EWTr GKir LRHS MAsh MRav
'Debureaux' (v) **new**	EVFa
delavayi	CFil CPSs CPle EPfP GKir NWea SGar SSpi WCru WCwm WHCG WPGP
- AC 1648	GGar
- EDHCH 97170	EPPr
- var. ***calvescens***	see *P. purpurascens*
'Enchantement' (d)	MRav SDix
§ 'Erectus'	CSBt CWib EBee EHol ENot EPfP GKir ISea MRav SMac SPla SPoG WDin WHCG WPat WTel
'Etoile Rose'	GKir
fragrans	CFil WPGP
'Frosty Morn' (d)	CBcs GKir LBuc LRHS MGos MRav NBlu NEgg SMac SPer SPla WGwG
incanus	GKir
- B&SWJ 8616	WCru
§ 'Innocence' (v)	More than 30 suppliers
'Innocence Variegatus'	see *P.* 'Innocence'
§ ***insignis***	MRav
intectus	GKir
x ***lemoinei***	CDul CTri EBee EWTr GKir MGos NFor SHBN SMer WDin WFar
- 'Erectus'	see *P.* 'Erectus'
- 'Lemoinei'	NWea
'Lemon Hill'	NEgg WBcn
lewisii	CFil GKir LPhx
- L 1896	WPGP
- 'Waterton'	LBuc
madrensis	CFil CPLN
- CD&R 1226	WPGP
'Manteau d'Hermine' (d) ♀H4	More than 30 suppliers
'Marjorie'	CHar
mexicanus	GCal MWya
- 'Rose Syringa'	CFil WPGP
microphyllus	CBot CDul CFil CMHG CPSs ELan EPfP GKir LAst LRHS MRav MWhi

		SLon SPer SReu SSpi WBVN WBor WHCG WPat WSHC
	- var. ***occidentalis***	CFil NLar
	'Miniature Snowflake' (d)	WPat
	'Minnesota Snowflake' (d)	CBcs CMac EBee ECtt EWes GKir LBuc LRHS MRav NLar NPro SPur WFar
	'Mont Blanc'	CBcs WFar
	'Mrs E.L. Robinson' (d)	CMac EBee ECtt GKir LAst LRHS
	'Natchez' (d)	CMac ECtt MBNS WBcn WTel
	'Norma'	WBcn
	'Oeil de Pourpre'	MRav WBcn
	palmeri	CFil
	pekinensis	CPLG
	'Perryhill'	MRav
§	***purpurascens***	CFil EWes GIBF GKir GQui MRav NEgg SLon SSpi WBcn WCwm WPat
	- BWJ 7540	WCru
	x ***purpureomaculatus***	WPat
	'Russalka'	MWya
	schrenkii	CFil NLar WPGP
	- B&SWJ 8465	WCru
§	'Silberregen'	CDul CMac EBee ECtt EPfP GKir LAst LRHS MBar MGos MRav NCGa NPro SHBN SPoG SRms SWvt WFar WPat
	Silver Showers	see *P.* 'Silberregen'
	'Snow Velvet'	LRHS
	'Snowflake'	CWSG EMil GKir NMoo
	'Souvenir de Billiard'	see *P. insignis*
	subcanus	GKir MRav
	- L 524	CFil
	'Sybille' ♀H4	CMHG EBee ECrN ENot EPfP GKir LRHS MBri MRav SDix SPoG SRms SSpi WBcn WHCG WKif WPat WSHC
	tenuifolius	CMCN GIBF NLar
	tomentosus	CFil CPLG EBee GKir WHCG WPGP WPat
	- B&SWJ 2707	WCru
	- GWJ 9215	WCru
	'Velléda'	CFil
	'Virginal' (d)	More than 30 suppliers
	'Voie Lactée'	CFil MRav
	White Icicle = 'Bialy Sopel'	MBri
	White Rock = 'Pekphil'	CDoC CMac CWSG EBee GKir LAst LRHS LTwo NMoo SPer SPoG WPat
	'Yellow Cab' **new**	SPoG

Philesia (*Philesiaceae*)

	buxifolia	see *P. magellanica*
§	***magellanica***	EMil GGGa GSki ITim SOkd SSpi WCru WSHC

Phillyrea (*Oleaceae*)

	angustifolia	CBcs CDul CFil CMCN EBee EHol ELan EPfP ERom MGos SEND SLPl SPer SSpi WBVN WBcn WDin WFar WSHC XPep
	- from Mallorca	SSpi
	- f. ***rosmarinifolia***	CFil EPla LAst WFar WPGP XPep
	decora	see *Osmanthus decorus*
§	***latifolia***	CFil CHEx CPLG EBee ELan EPfP LRHS SAPC SArc SLPl SSpi WBcn WDin WFar XPep
	media	see *P. latifolia*
I	- 'Rodrigueziensis'	WCFE

Philodendron (*Araceae*)

	epipremnum	see *Epipremnum pinnatum*
	erubescens 'Burgundy' ♀H1	LRHS
	- 'Red Emerald'	CHal
	scandens ♀H1	CHal XBlo
	selloum	EAmu MOak WMul
	xanadu	XBlo

Phlebodium see *Polypodium*

Phleum (*Poaceae*)

	bertolonii	CRWN
	pratense	CBig EHoe

Phlomis ✿ (*Lamiaceae*)

*	***anatolica***	XPep
*	- 'Lloyd's Variety'	CAbP CSam ELan GCal LRHS MAsh MBri MSte SPer SPoG SSvw WCot WPen
	atropurpurea	EBee GBin WPGP
	betonicoides B&L 12600	EPPr
	bovei subsp. ***maroccana***	CBot CStr GCal IFro LPio WHal WOut XPep
	bracteosa **new**	MGol
	cashmeriana	CBot ECha LDai MGol MNFA NLar WCFE WLin
	chrysophylla ♀H3	CAbP CBot CStr ECha ELan EMan EPfP LRHS SBla SDix SPer SPoG WCFE WCot XPep
*	***cristata***	CCge
	cypria	XPep
§	'Edward Bowles'	CBot EBee NBid SIgm SLPl SLon SWvt WCot XPep
*	'Elliot's Variety'	CPLG
	fruticosa ♀H4	More than 30 suppliers
	- 'Butterfly'	XPep
	grandiflora	CBot SEND XPep
	herba-venti	XPep
	italica	More than 30 suppliers
	lanata ♀H3-4	CAbP CCge CStr EBee ELan EMan EPfP LRHS LSRN MSte NCGa NPro SBla SPer SPoG SSpi WEas WKif WWye XPep
	- 'Pygmy'	NPro SLon XPep
	'Le Sud'	XPep
	leucophracta	XPep
	- 'Golden Janissary'	CFil EBee WPGP XPep
	longifolia	CBgR CBot CHad EBee EPfP LRHS SIgm SPer WGer XPep
	- var. ***bailanica***	LRHS WFar WSPU
	lunariifolia	XPep
	lychnitis	MWrn SIgm XPep
	lycia	CStr LRHS SIgm XPep
	monocephala	XPep
	purpurea	CAbP CPLG CSam ELan EPfP GFlt LRHS MAsh MGol MHer NBir SBrw SPoG WCot WOVN WSHC XPep
	- ***alba***	CBot EPfP WSHC XPep
	- subsp. ***almeriensis***	CPom CStr XPep
	- subsp. ***caballeroi***	XPep
	rigida	WCru
§	***russeliana*** ♀H4	More than 30 suppliers
	samia Boiss.	see *P. russeliana*
	samia L.	EWTr LDai MGol NChi NGdn NLar SMar WCot WFar XPep
	- JMT 285	LRHS
	tuberosa	More than 30 suppliers
	- 'Amazone'	CFir CKno EBee EChP ECha EHrv EMan EPfP EVFa LAst MBri MTis NBid NEgg NFla NSti SAga SMad SMrm SUsu WCAu WCot WFar WGHP WTMC
	- 'Bronze Flamingo' **new**	EWin NDov WPer
	viscosa misapplied	see *P. russeliana*

viscosa Poiret — XPep

Phlox ✿ (*Polemoniaceae*)

adsurgens ♀H4 — EDAr ITim NCob SBch
- 'Alba' — NSla SBla
- 'Red Buttes' — CLyd EPot SBla
- 'Wagon Wheel' — CLyd CWCL EBee ECtt EDAr EHyt EPot EWes GBBs GGar ITim LRHS NLAp NRya NSla SIng SMrm SPlb SRms SRot WCFE WFar WPat WSHC

alyssifolia — CPBP
amplifolia **new** — EBee
x ***arendsii*** 'Anja' — WCot
- 'Early Star' — EBee
- 'Eyecatcher' **new** — CM&M NBro NGdn
- 'Hilda' — CStr
- 'Lilac Star' — CFir LAst WHil
- 'Lisbeth' — SUsu
§ - 'Luc's Lilac' — CBos CMHG CPrp EMan EMar GBin LPhx LRHS LTwo NBro NDov NGdn NVic SMeo STes
§ - (Spring Pearl Series) 'Miss Jill' — CBos CHea CM&M EBee EChP ENot NCob SBla WCot WTin
§ - - 'Miss Jo-Ellen' — GBri
§ - - 'Miss Karen' — EChP ENot ERou NBro
§ - - 'Miss Margie' — EChP ERou GBri GMaP LAst NBir WHil
§ - - 'Miss Mary' — EChP ENot GBri GMaP MDKP NPro STes
§ - - 'Miss Wilma' — CBos ENot GMaP
- 'Ping Pong' — EBee LDai MBnl MTis NBro NPro STes WSan
- 'Pink Attraction' **new** — CFwr MNrw NBro
- 'Purple Star' — EBee MBnl
- 'Rosa Star' — CFir EBee LAst
- 'Sabine' — CFir EBee
- 'Suzanne' — EBee

austromontana — EPot ITim NWCA WLin
bifida 'Alba' — EHyt LSou LTwo WLin
- blue — LRHS LSou SBla SUsu
- 'Colvin's White' — CLyd EDAr SAga SBla
- 'Minima Colvin' — ECtt EPot GKev
- 'Petticoat' — CLyd CMea CPBP EPot GEdr LRHS SAga SBla SUsu WLin
- 'Ralph Haywood' — CLyd EPot GBuc ITim NLAp WLin
- 'Starbrite' — CLyd CRez GBBs LRHS NLar WFar
- 'Thefi' — EWes LTwo MNrw

borealis — see *P. sibirica* subsp. *borealis*
* - ***arctica*** — EPot
caespitosa — EWes NDlv NWCA
- subsp. ***condensata*** — see *P. condensata*
- subsp. ***pulvinata*** — see *P. pulvinata*
canadensis — see *P. divaricata*
carolina 'Bill Baker' ♀H4 — More than 30 suppliers
- 'Magnificence' — CBos CPrp EBee EChP EMan EWes GBuc GMac LAst MDKP MSte NFla SOkh STes WCot WSHC WTin
- 'Miss Lingard' ♀H4 — More than 30 suppliers

'Charles Ricardo' — CElw ETow EWes GBuc LSou SMrm SUsu WHoo
'Chattahoochee' — see *P. divaricata* subsp. *laphamii* 'Chattahoochee'
§ ***condensata*** — CNic NLAp NWCA WPat
covillei — see *P. condensata*
'Daniel's Cushion' — see *P. subulata* 'McDaniel's Cushion'

§ ***divaricata*** ♀H4 — EHol GKir MRav MSte SBod SHBN SPlb WPer
- f. ***albiflora*** — ELan
- 'Blue Dreams' — CFir CHea CMHG EBee EBrs EChP EHrv EPPr GBuc GKir LRHS MNrw MSte NCob NGdn SChu SPla SUsu WCAu WFar WHal WPGP WSHC WSan WWlt
- 'Blue Perfume' — CM&M CMHG EChP LSou NBid NBro NCGa NGdn NLar NMyG NSti SHGN
- 'Clouds of Perfume' — CHea CM&M CPrp EBee EBrs EChP EMan GBri GMaP LAst LRHS LSRN MTis MWgw NCGa NCob NSti SBla SBod SMer SMrm STes WAul WFar
- 'Dirigo Ice' — CElw CLyd EBee EHrv EMan GBri NLar SAga SBla WFar WSHC
- 'Eco Texas Purple' — EChP EMan MHar NCob NPro SIgm SMrm WFar WPGP
- 'Fuller's White' — CLyd CWCL
§ - subsp. ***laphamii*** — EWes NSti SOkh SUsu WFar WFoF
§ - - 'Chattahoochee' ♀H4 — CBot CPBP CSpe CWCL EBee EChP ECtt EDAr EHyt ELan EPfP EWes GBuc GMac LRHS MWgw NCob NEgg SBla SIng SMer SMrm SOkh SPoG SRot WAbe WCFE WHoo WSHC
- - 'Chattahoochee Variegated' (v) — EDAr LRHS
§ - 'Louisiana Purple' — WSHC
- 'May Breeze' — CLyd EBee EHrv GKir GMaP LAst LRHS MNrw MSte MWgw NCGa NCob NGdn SPla WCAu WFar WPGP WSHC WWlt
- 'Plum Perfect' — NLar SHar WPtf
* - 'White Perfume' — CM&M CMHG EBee EChP EMil EWes GBri LAst LSou MBrN MDKP NBro NCob NLar NSti SChu SHGN SMrm STes

douglasii — NPol NWCA SRms
- 'Apollo' — CLyd CTri EDAr LRHS LTwo NMen SBla
- 'Boothman's Variety' ♀H4 — CLyd CMea ECha EDAr ELan EPfP EPot GKir LRHS MWat NMen SPoG SRms WEas WLin
- 'Crackerjack' ♀H4 — CLyd CMea ECtt EDAr ELan ENot EPfP EPot GAbr GKev GKir GMaP ITim LRHS MBow MHer NBir NEgg NLon NMen NPro SIng SPoG WAbe WFar WLin
- 'Eva' — CLyd CM&M CPBP EDAr ELan EPot GAbr GKir GMaP GTou ITim LRHS NBir NMen NWCA SPoG WLin
- 'Galaxy' — CLyd EWes
- 'Ice Mountain' — CRez ECho EDAr ELan EPot ITim NEgg NWCA SPoG SRot WLin
- 'Iceberg' ♀H4 — CLyd EPot GKev NMen WLin
- 'Lilac Cloud' — NPro SHGN
- Lilac Queen — see *P. douglasii* 'Lilakönigin'
§ - 'Lilakönigin' — EDAr WRHF
- 'Napoleon' — CPBP EPot ITim LTwo NMen
- 'Ochsenblut' — EHyt EPot GEdr LTwo MDHE MHer SIng
- 'Red Admiral' ♀H4 — CNic EWes GKev GKir GMaP LRHS NLon NMen WCFE WFar WGwG
- 'Rose Cushion' — EDAr EWes ITim LRHS MDHE MHer NMen
- 'Rose Queen' — CLyd
- 'Rosea' — EDAr ELan GMaP LRHS NMen NPol WFar WRHF
- 'Silver Rose' — EPot GTou NWCA
- 'Sprite' — SRms
- 'Tycoon' — see *P. subulata* 'Tamaongalei'
- 'Violet Queen' — EWes GKev WFar WPat
- 'Waterloo' — CLyd EPot ITim LRHS NMen SChu
I - 'White Admiral' — EPot LSRN NPro SIng WBVN

'Fancy Feelings' **new** — NBro NCob SPoG STes WHil

Plant	Suppliers
'Geddington Cross'	MWgw
hendersonii	CGra
hoodii	CLyd CPBP ECho
***idahoensis* new**	SOkd
'Junior Dance' **new**	WWeb
'Junior Dream' **new**	WWeb
'Junior Surprise' **new**	WWeb
'Kelly's Eye' ♀H4	CLyd CM&M CPBP ELan EPot LRHS NBir NMen SPoG WFar WLin
kelseyi	NWCA
- 'Lemhi Purple'	SOkd
- 'Rosette'	CLyd EPot LRHS MDKP NMen WLin WPer
Light Pink Flame = 'Bareleven'PBR **new**	CPen
longifolia subsp. ***brevifolia***	CPBP SOkd
'Louisiana'	see *P. divaricata* 'Louisiana Purple'
maculata	NOrc WBVN WPer
- 'Alba'	CMea WTin
- 'Alpha' ♀H4	More than 30 suppliers
- Avalanche	see *P. maculata* 'Schneelawine'
- 'Delta'	CHea CWCL EBee EBrs EChP EMan EPfP GBuc LRHS LSou NBPC NEgg NLon NSti SMad SOkh SPer SWvt WCAu WFar WPnP
- 'Natascha'	More than 30 suppliers
- 'Omega' ♀H4	CHea CMHG COIW EBrs EPfP GBuc GGar GKir GMaP LRHS MRav MSte NBPC NBid NEgg NGdn NLar SChu SMad SOkh SPer SPla SSpi SWvt WCAu WFar WSHC
'Princess Sturdza' ♀H4	SDix
- 'Reine du Jour'	GMac LPhx LSou MSte NDov SAga SMrm SOkh SUsu WSHC
- 'Rosalinde'	COIW EBee EBrs EChP EMan EMar GBuc LPhx LRHS MRav MSte NBPC NCob NEgg NLar SBla SChu SPla SPoG SWvt WCAu WFar WHil WSHC
§ - 'Schneelawine'	NCob SChu
'Matineus'	LPhx
'Millstream'	see *P.* x *procumbens* 'Millstream'
nivalis	CPBP NMen
- 'Camlaensis'	CLyd
- 'Jill Alexander'	CMea SAga
- 'Nivea'	EPot LRHS LSou WAbe WLin
paniculata	CHad EWTr GFlt LPhx NBid NDov NFor SDix SMeo WCot WOld WTin
- 'A.E. Amos'	ERou
- 'Aida'	CBcs
- var. ***alba***	GCal NDov SDix WCot WTin
- 'Alba Grandiflora' ♀H4	EHrv GMaP NCob SBla WEas
- 'Amethyst' misapplied	see *P. paniculata* 'Lilac Time'
- 'Amethyst' Foerster	CFir CFwr CSam EHrv EPfP ERou GKir MTis NBir NBlu NEgg NOrc SMer WCAu WFar WWye
- 'Ann'	CFwr
- 'Antoinette Six'	CFwr EBee MDKP
I - 'Aureovariegata Undulata' (v) **new**	WCot
- 'Babyface' **new**	CFwr
- 'Balmoral'	CFwr EBrs ECtt EPfP GKir LLWP LRHS MRav MSte NCob NPri NSti SMer SWvt
- 'Barnwell'	GMac
- 'Becky Towe'PBR (v)	CFwr COtt EBee EMan EVFa LRHS LTwo SGSe SPoG
- 'Betty Symons-Jeune'	CFwr
- 'Bill Green'	EBee LRHS
- 'Blue Boy'	CElw CFwr EBee ERou GMaP LAst LRHS MDKP NBir NBro NChi NGby NRnb WFar
- 'Blue Evening'	LPhx LSou NCob
- 'Blue Ice' ♀H4	EBee ELan EMar LPhx LRHS MMHG MRav NBro NEgg SChu SPla
- 'Blue Paradise'	More than 30 suppliers
- 'Blushing Bride'	SRms
- 'Border Gem'	CBcs CFwr EBee ECtt ERou GKir MSte MWgw NChi NCob NEgg NLRH NLar SDix SMer SPur SWvt WCot
- 'Branklyn'	EBee GKir LRHS SMer WFar
- 'Brigadier' ♀H4	CBla CSam EBrs ECtt ELan EWTr GBin GKir GMaP LRHS MDKP MWat NCob NEgg NVic SPer SPla SRms WCAu WFar
- 'Bright Eyes' ♀H4	CBcs CBla CFwr COtt CSBt EBee ECtt ERou GKir LRHS LSRN MArl MDKP NCGa NCob NEgg NLsd SMer SPoG STes SUsu SWvt WCAu WFar WTel
- 'Burgi'	CBos SDix
- 'Caroline van den Berg'	GKir SRms
- 'Cecil Hanbury'	ERou NBlu NLar SBri SRms
- 'Chintz'	MRav SRms
- 'Cinderella'	CFwr CSBt ERou
§ - 'Cool of the Evening'	CFwr LPhx
- Count Zeppelin	see *P. paniculata* 'Graf Zeppelin'
- 'Daisy Field'	NCob
- 'Danielle'	CFwr
- 'Darwin's Choice'	see *P. paniculata* 'Norah Leigh'
- 'David'	CBos EBee EChP ECha ERou IPot LAst LPhx LRHS MBnl NBid NBro NCGa NChi NCob NGby NOrc NRnb STes SUsu WAul WBor WCAu WCot WHil WWol
- 'Delilah' **new**	NCob WHil
- 'Discovery'	ECGP EMar EWes NCob SPla STes
- 'Dodo Hanbury-Forbes' ♀H4	EHol
- 'Doghouse Pink'	NCob
- 'Düsterlohe'	CBrm CElw CSam EBee ERou GBuc GMac LSou NBir NLar NRnb NSti SMrm STes WCAu WFar WHil WHoo
- 'Early Flower'	CFwr
- 'Eclaireur' misapplied	see *P. paniculata* 'Duesterlohe'
- 'Eclaireur' Lemoine	CFwr EBee NCob
- 'Eden's Crush'	CM&M EChP NRnb NVic WWpP
- 'Eden's Flash'	ERou NRnb
- 'Eden's Glory'	EChP NRnb
- 'Eden's Glow'	EChP NRnb WHil
- 'Eden's Smile'	EBee EChP ERou NRnb SHar
- 'Elizabeth' (v) **new**	LAst NRnb STes
- 'Elizabeth Arden'	CFwr ERou MSte NLar
- 'Empty Feelings'PBR	EBee EChP GBin NBro NCob WHil
- 'Ending Blue' **new**	CFwr NRnb
- 'Etoile de Paris'	see *P. paniculata* 'Toits de Paris'
- 'Europa'	CBcs EBee ELan EPfP ERou GFlt LRHS MBri NBir NCob NEgg NGdn NLar SChu SPer SPla WCAu WFar
- 'Eva Cullum'	EBrs ECtt GCra GFlt GKir LRHS MArl MBnl MRav MTis NBPC SMer SPer SPet WCot
- 'Eventide' ♀H4	CWCL EBee ECtt EPfP GKir LAst LRHS MArl MWgw NCob NLar SChu SMer SPer SPet WCAu WCot
- 'Excelsior'	MRav
- 'Fairy's Petticoat'	MWat
- 'Flamingo'	CFwr EBee EBrs ERou LRHS MBrN NGby NLar SWvt
- 'Franz Schubert'	CHrt EBee EBrs ECtt GCra GKir GMac LRHS MRav NBir NChi NLar NSti SChu STes SWvt WCot WTel

§ - 'Frau Alfred von Mauthner' CFwr MBri
- 'Frosted Elegance' (v) EChP EMan EPPr WHil
- 'Fujiyama' see *P. paniculata* 'Mount Fuji'
- 'Glamis' MWat
- 'Gnoom' CFwr
- 'Goldmine'[PBR] (v) CFai CWCL MBnl MCCP MLLN NBro NCob SPoG WCot
§ - 'Graf Zeppelin' CBla CFwr ELan EWll LRHS NGby SRms
- 'Harlequin' (v) More than 30 suppliers
I - 'Hesperis' CFwr LPhx MAnH NDov NFla SMHy SMeo SMrm SUsu WHil
I - 'Hogg Rose' **new** NCob
- 'Iceberg' GKev NCob
- 'Iris' CDes GBuc LPio SRms
- 'Jubilee' CFwr CM&M NRnb WHil
- 'Judy' CFwr NBro
- 'Jules Sandeau' CFwr EBrs LRHS MBri NCob
§ - 'Juliglut' EChP ERou NCGa WCot
- July Glow see *P. paniculata* 'Juliglut'
- 'Katarina' CElw CHea EChP ECtt EMar EPfP NCGa NLar SUsu WBor WHil
- 'Katherine' CFwr
- 'Kelway's Cherub' **new** NCob
- 'Kirchenfürst' CFwr MBri NBir SMrm
- 'Kirmesländler' CBcs CFwr EBee ERou LRHS MLLN NCob NLar SVil
- 'Lady Clare' SRms
- 'Landhochzeit' EBee LRHS NCob
* - 'Laura' CM&M COtt EBee ERou IPot NBPC NBro NRnb NVic SGSe SMrm SPoG STes WFar WHil WHoo WWeb WWol
§ - 'Lavendelwolke' CFwr CSam GCal NBir NCob NLar WAul
- Lavender Cloud see *P. paniculata* 'Lavendelwolke'
- 'Le Mahdi' ♀H4 CFwr ELan GBin MBrN MRav MWat SMeo SRms
- 'Lichtspel' CAby LPhx NDov SMeo
§ - 'Lilac Time' CBla CFwr EHrv EWll MDKP MSte NCob SWvt
- 'Little Boy' CElw EChP ECtt ERou LRHS LSou MDKP NLar SPoG STes WFar WHil WWeb
- 'Little Laura' CElw CHea CMHG MBnl MCCP NCGa NLar
- 'Little Princess' CFwr NCGa NFla NLar SPoG WHil
- 'Lizzy'[PBR] CFwr ERou MBri NCGa NLar
- 'Look Again' CFwr
- 'Manoir d'Hézèques' WCot
- 'Mary Christine' (v) EBee
- 'Mary Fox' CSam EBrs
- 'Mia Ruys' ERou GMac MArl MBri MLLN SMrm
- 'Midnight Feelings' **new** LBuc LTwo NBro NCob WAul WCot
- 'Mies Copijn' CFwr GMaP WFar
- 'Milly van Hoboken' CBos WKif
- 'Miss Elie' CM&M ERou GFlt LAst SGSe SPoG WFar WHoo
- 'Miss Holland' CHea EChP GFlt NRnb WHil WHoo WSan
- 'Miss Jessica' ERou LAst
- 'Miss Jill' see *P.* x *arendsii* 'Miss Jill'
- 'Miss Jo-Ellen' see *P.* x *arendsii* 'Miss Jo-Ellen'
- 'Miss Karen' see *P.* x *arendsii* 'Miss Karen'
- 'Miss Kelly' CFwr CM&M COtt WHoo
- 'Miss Margie' see *P.* x *arendsii* 'Miss Margie'
- 'Miss Mary' see *P.* x *arendsii* 'Miss Mary'
- 'Miss Pepper' CBos CWCL EMil ERou EWll IPot LRHS NLar SMrm WCAu WFar WHil
- 'Miss Universe' CM&M MCCP NRnb SGSe WHoo WSan
- 'Miss Wilma' see *P.* x *arendsii* 'Miss Wilma'
- 'Monica Lynden-Bell' CBos CDes CFai CSam EBee EChP GBri LAst MAvo MBnl MEHN MMil MNrw NBPC NChi NCob NDov NEgg NLar SMrm SPla STes SUsu WAul WCot WFar WPGP WWlt
- 'Mother of Pearl' ♀H4 EBee ELan EMar GMac LRHS MWat NCob NVic SBla SPet
§ - 'Mount Fuji' ♀H4 More than 30 suppliers
- 'Mount Fujiyama' see *P. paniculata* 'Mount Fuji'
- 'Mrs A.E. Jeans' SRms
- 'Natural Feelings'[PBR] CSpe GBin MCCP NBro NCob NLar SPoG STes WCot WSan WTMC
- 'Newbird' CFwr CSBt SRms
- 'Nicky' see *P. paniculata* 'Duesterlohe'
§ - 'Norah Leigh' (v) More than 30 suppliers
- 'Orange Perfection' see *P. paniculata* 'Prince of Orange'
- 'Othello' EBee EBrs EMar EWll LRHS NChi NCob NSti
- 'Otley Choice' LAst LRHS MRav MSte MWat NLar NSti SChu SCoo
- 'P.D. Williams' WCot
- 'Pastorale' WCot WTel
- 'Pax' EBee EMon ERou LPhx SMeo
- 'Petite Chérie' WCot
- 'Pink Posie'[PBR] (v) MBri WFar
- 'Pinky Hill' **new** CFwr
- 'Pinwheel' **new** CFwr
- 'Popeye' ECtt MBri NLar
§ - 'Prince of Orange' ♀H4 CBcs CSam EBee EChP ECtt ELan EPfP ERou GKir LAst LRHS LSRN MHer MOne MRav MWat MWgw NBlu NCob NLon NPri NRnb SAga SPer SPet SPoG SWvt WCot WHil
- 'Prospero' ♀H4 CHar CSam EBee ECGP EHrv GFlt NBid NEgg SChu SMer SUsu WCAu WTel
- 'Rainbow' CFwr
- 'Red Feelings'[PBR] EBee NBro NCob SPoG WHil WSan
- 'Red Indian' MWat SMer
- 'Red Riding Hood' CFwr CWCL LAst
I - 'Reddish Hesperis' SMHy
- 'Rembrandt' EBrs ERou GBri LRHS NBlu SBla
- 'Rijnstroom' CBcs CFwr CSBt EBee ECot ERou LRHS MBow WFar WTel
- 'Robert Poore' NCob
- 'Rosa Pastell' CBos CFwr EHrv EMon IPot LPhx LSou NCob SAga SUsu
- 'Rosa Spier' CFwr
- 'Rosy Veil' CFwr
- 'Rowie' **new** MBnl NBid NCob WBor WHil
- 'Rubymine'[PBR] (v) CFai EChP EMan ERou NCob
- 'San Antonio' CFwr EBrs WFar
- 'Sandringham' EBee EHrv EPfP GKir LRHS MArl MNrw MRav MSte NBir SBla SMer SWvt WCAu
§ - 'Schneerausch' GKir LPhx
- 'Septemberglut' CFwr NLar
- 'Silvermine' (v) EChP EMan MCCP NBro NLar SDnm WCot
- 'Sir Malcolm Campbell' CFwr EBee
- 'Skylight' LRHS LSRN NBro NVic SDix WLin
- 'Snow White' NVic
- Snowdrift see *P. paniculata* 'Schneerausch'
- 'Speed Limit' CFwr
- 'Speed Limit 45' WCot
- 'Spitfire' see *P. paniculata* 'Frau Alfred von Mauthner'
- 'Starburst' EBee NGdn STes WHil

	Plant	Suppliers
	- 'Starfire' 🏆[H4]	More than 30 suppliers
	- 'Steeple Bumpstead'	EBee WCot
	- 'Sweetheart'	GFlt
	- 'Tenor'	CFir CWCL EChP ERou GKir LRHS MDKP MSte NCob NGdn NPri NRnb SBla SChu SMer SPet SPla SPoG SWvt WBor WCAu WCot WFar
	- 'The King'	EBee EBrs EChP EWll GBri LRHS MAvo MDKP MSte NBro NGby SUsu WBor WCot WHil WMow WTel
	- 'Toits de Paris' misapplied	see *P. paniculata* 'Cool of the Evening'
	- 'Toits de Paris' ambig.	CBos SMHy
§	- 'Toits de Paris' Symons-Jeune	LPhx WSHC
	- 'Uspekh'	CFwr EBee ECGP EMar EPPr EVFa EWes MDKP MSte MTis NBro NCob SChu SPer SUsu SVil WFar
	- 'Utopia'	LPhx NFla NRnb SMHy SUsu
	- 'Van Gogh'	CFwr EBee EHrv
	- 'Victorian Lilac' **new**	NCob
	- 'Vintage Wine'	MSte
	- 'Violetta Gloriosa'	LPhx
	- 'Visions'	EBee WHil
	- 'Wenn Schon Denn Schon'	GBin
	- 'White Admiral' 🏆[H4]	CBcs CBla CHrt CSBt EBee ECtt EHrv ELan EPfP ERou GAbr GKir GMaP GMac LRHS MHer MRav MWat MWgw MWrn NVic SMer SPer SPla SRms STes SWvt WTel WWpP
	- 'White Sparr' **new**	CFwr
	- 'Wilhelm Kesselring'	CFai CFwr CHrt EBee GBin WBor
	- 'Windsor' 🏆[H4]	CBla EBrs ECtt EPfP ERou GBBs GBri GKir LRHS MLLN NDov NEgg SCoo SMer SPoG SRms SWvt WCAu WFar
I	- 'Zurstock Rose'	CFwr
	pilosa	ECha EMan NPro WFar
	- subsp. ***ozarkana***	SSpi
	Pink Flame = 'Bartwelve'[PBR] **new**	CPen
§	x ***procumbens*** 'Millstream' 🏆[H4]	EDAr GAbr SBla
	- 'Variegata' (v)	CBrm ECha EDAr EPot LRHS MDKP NWCA SBla SPlb SRot WFar WLin WPat
§	***pulvinata***	CPBP
	Purple Flame = 'Barfourteen'[PBR] **new**	CPen
	'Sandra'	LRHS
	'Scented Pillow'	LRHS
§	***sibirica*** subsp. ***borealis***	EDAr
	'Sileniflora'	EPot
	stansburyi	EHyt
	stolonifera	CBcs MNrw
I	- 'Alba'	SPur
	- 'Ariane'	EBee EBrs ECha EDAr MBri MNrw SBch SBla WCFE WFar
I	- 'Atropurpurea'	CBcs
	- 'Blue Ridge' 🏆[H4]	CFir CWCL ECha EDAr EMan ENot EPfP GBuc GKir LAst MBri MRav SMer SRms WFar WSan
	- 'Bob's Motley' (v)	EMan WCot
	- compact	EPot
	- 'Compact Pink'	WFar
	- 'Fran's Purple'	CLyd EMan MWhi NBro WCFE WFar WPGP WSPU
	- 'Home Fires'	CAby CFwr EBee EDAr EWin GAbr MDKP MNrw NBro NLar SAga SBla SMrm SPlb
	- 'Mary Belle Frey'	EMan MSte WFar
	- 'Montrose Tricolor' (v)	EBee NBro
	- 'Pink Ridge'	EWll MBri MNrw NBir WDyG WRos
	- 'Purpurea'	LSou MDKP
	- variegated (v)	WCot
	- 'Violet Vere'	CLyd EDAr GBuc MNrw WFar
	subulata	CBrm GKir NWCA SBch WBrE
	- 'Alexander's Surprise'	CMea ECtt EDAr EPfP EPot LBee LRHS MDKP NBir SChu SPlb SPoG
	- 'Amazing Grace'	CWCL EDAr ELan EPfP EWes GKir LBee LRHS MHer NSla NWCA SChu SIng SPoG WBVN
	- 'Apple Blossom'	EDAr NEgg NPro SPoG SRms
	- 'Atropurpurea'	LRHS NFor NJOw NLon NPro
	- Beauty of Ronsdorf	see *P. subulata* 'Ronsdorfer Schöne'
	- 'Betty'	ECtt MBNS MDHE NJOw
	- 'Blue Eyes'	see *P. subulata* 'Oakington Blue Eyes'
	- 'Blue Saucer'	MDHE
	- 'Bonita'	CPBP CWCL EHyt EWin GKir LBee LRHS SMer
	- 'Bressingham Blue Eyes'	see *P. subulata* 'Oakington Blue Eyes'
	- 'Brightness'	CNic GKir GTou LRHS
	- subsp. ***brittonii*** 'Rosea'	GEdr
	- 'Candy Stripe'	see *P. subulata* 'Tamaongalei'
	- 'Cavaldes White'	MDKP
	- 'Christine Bishop'	LRHS
	- 'Coral Eye'	EPfP
	- 'Drumm'	see *P. subulata* 'Tamaongalei'
	- 'Emerald Cushion'	CSam CTri ECtt EDAr GKev MDKP MHer NFor NLon WCFE WRHF
	- 'Emerald Cushion Blue'	CBrm CNic EPfP GKir GTou MBow NMen NPri NPro SBla SGar SPlb WLin WPer
	- 'Fairy'	WPer
	- 'Fort Hill' **new**	NHar
	- 'G.F. Wilson'	see *P. subulata* 'Lilacina'
	- 'Greencourt Purple'	EDAr NBur
*	- 'Holly'	EPot ITim MDHE NMen
	- 'Jupiter'	SChu
	- 'Kimono'	see *P. subulata* 'Tamaongalei'
§	- 'Lilacina'	CLyd CMea ECha EDAr ELan GEdr GMaP GTou LGro LRHS MWat NFor NJOw SBla SChu SPoG
§	- 'Maischnee'	CLyd CMea ECtt EDAr EPfP EPot GAbr GKir LGro LRHS MHer MWat NFor SIng SPlb WEas
	- 'Marjorie'	CLyd ECtt LBee MDKP MHer NBir NPri NWCA SMer SPoG
	- May Snow	see *P. subulata* 'Maischnee'
§	- 'McDaniel's Cushion' 🏆[H4]	CLyd CNic ECha EDAr ELan EPfP EPot GAbr GKev GKir GMaP GTou ITim LBee LRHS NFor NJOw NLon NMen NWCA SPlb SPoG WBVN WCFE WFar WRHF WTel
	- 'Mikado'	see *P. subulata* 'Tamaongalei'
	- 'Model'	LGro
	- 'Moonlight'	CLyd ECtt
	- 'Nettleton Variation' (v)	EDAr EPot EWes GKir LBee LRHS MDKP MHer NPri SIng SPlb SPoG WPat
§	- 'Oakington Blue Eyes'	CNic GKir LRHS SRms
	- 'Pink Pearl'	EWes
	- 'Purple Beauty'	NBlu NHar SBla WSHC
	- 'Red Wings' 🏆[H4]	ECtt EHyt EPfP GKir LRHS NMen SPoG SRms WFar
§	- 'Ronsdorfer Schöne'	EPot ITim LBee LRHS NJOw
	- 'Rose Mabel'	EDAr

- 'Samson' GTou LRHS SMer
- 'Scarlet Flame' CMea CSam ECha ECtt EDAr ELan EPfP EPot LGro MHer MWat NEgg NPri
- 'Schneewittchen' CLyd
- 'Sensation' GTou SBla
- 'Snow Queen' see *P. subulata* 'Maischnee'
- 'Starglow' GTou
§ - 'Tamaongalei' CLyd CMea CPBP EBrs EDAr EHyt EPfP EPot EWes GKev GKir LRHS MHer NArg NEgg SAga SBla SChu SCoo SIng SPet SPoG SRms WBVN WCFE WFar
- 'Temiskaming' ECha EDAr ELan ENot EWes GEdr LBee LGro LRHS NMen SBla SChu SPoG SRms WSHC
- violet seedling CLyd
- 'White Delight' CLyd ECtt ELan GTou LBee NMen SHel SPoG WRHF
- 'Woodside' CNic
'Tiny Bugles' SBla
'Vivid' EDAr MDHE

Phoebe (*Lauraceae*)

sheareri CFil WPGP

Phoenix (*Arecaceae*)

canariensis ♀H1+3 More than 30 suppliers
dactylifera (F) CRoM EAmu EExo SBig WMul
reclinata CKob CRoM EAmu EExo LPJP NPal WMul
roebelenii ♀H1+3 CBrP CDoC CRoM EExo EPfP ESlt EUJe MBri NPal SAin WMul
rupicola CRoM
sylvestris EAmu WMul
theophrasti CFil CPHo EAmu LEdu LPJP WMul

Phormium ✿ (*Phormiaceae*)

'Alison Blackman' CBcs CPen CTrC CWil ENot IBal IBlr ISea LSRN SCoo SPoG
'Amazing Red' CWil IBlr
'Apricot Queen' (v) CAbb CBcs CBrm CDoC CSBt CTrC CWil EPfP GQui IBlr LRHS MBri MCCP MDun NMoo NPal NPri SLim SPer SPoG SSto WBcn WFar WPat
Ballyrogan variegated (v) IBlr
* 'Black Edge' CWil IBlr MRav NPri
'Bronze Baby' More than 30 suppliers
'Buckland Ruby' CDoC CWil MAsh
'Candy Stripe' **new** CPen
colensoi see *P. cookianum*
§ ***cookianum*** CTrC CWil ECre EMil EPfP IBlr MGos SAPC SArc SCoo SEND SMad WFar WMul
- 'Alpinum Purpureum' see *P. tenax* 'Nanum Purpureum'
- dwarf IBlr SLPl
- 'Flamingo' CTrC CWil ECre EPfP MBri MWgw SLim SSto
- 'Golden Wonder' IBlr
- subsp. ***hookeri*** 'Cream Delight' (v) ♀H3-4 CAbb CBcs CBrm CDoC CElw CEnd CKno CSBt CTbh CTrC CWil EBee ECrN EHoe ENot EPfP LRHS MBlu MCCP MGos MRav MSwo SAga SHBN SPer SSto SWvt WCFE WCot WLeb
- - 'Tricolor' ♀H3-4 More than 30 suppliers
* 'Copper Beauty' COtt CWil NMoo SMer WDyG
'Crimson Devil' CBcs CPen EBee
'Dark Delight' CBcs IBlr
'Dazzler' (v) EBee EWsh IBlr MGos WCot
'Duet' (v) ♀H3 CBcs CDoC COtt CSBt CWil EBee EHoe EPfP IBlr LRHS MAsh NLar SPla SWvt WBcn WFar
'Dusky Chief' CPen CSBt CWil EBee LRHS MAsh WPat
'Dusky Princess' MAsh
'Emerald Isle' CDoC CWil MAsh
* 'Emerald Pink' COtt
'Evening Glow' (v) CPen CTrC CWil EBee ELan EPfP IBal IBlr LRHS MAsh MBri SAga SPla SWvt WCot WGer WPat
'Firebird' IBlr LSRN SAga SLon SWvt
'Flamingo' (v) CBcs CMHG CSBt CTbh CWil LRHS LSou SLim SPer SPoG WCot WPat
'Fortescue's Bronze' CWil
'Glowing Embers' CBrm CPen CTrC
'Gold Ray' CBcs CTrC IBlr
'Gold Sword' (v) CBcs CMHG COtt CSBt CTrC CWil EBee IBlr LRHS MAsh MBri SSto
'Guardsman' (v) IBlr
'Jack Spratt' (v) CBcs CBrm CChe CFwr CMHG COtt CPen CWil EBee ECou EHoe IBlr LRHS MAsh MSwo SWvt WLeb WPrP
'Jester' (v) More than 30 suppliers
'Limelight' CBcs CWil SWvt
'Mahogany' CWil
§ 'Maori Chief' CFil CSBt CWil EBee EPfP GQui IBlr LRHS NMoo SHBN SWvt WLeb WPat
'Maori Eclipse' CPen CWil
'Maori Elegance' CWil
§ 'Maori Maiden' (v) CBcs CBrm CDoC CMHG CSBt CTrC CTri EBee ECre EHoe GKir GQui IBal LRHS MAsh MGos MRav SWvt WCot WFar WLeb
§ 'Maori Queen' (v) CBcs CDoC CDul CMHG CSBt CTbh CTrC CWil EPfP GQui IBal IBlr LRHS MAsh MGos MRav MSwo NMoo SPer SSto SWvt WCot WFar
§ 'Maori Sunrise' (v) CBcs CBrm CDoC CKno CSam CTrC EBee ENot EPfP IArd IBal IBlr LRHS LSRN MAsh MBrN MCCP MGos MRav NBlu NPri NScw SLim SPer SSto SWvt WCot WFar WLeb
'Margaret Jones' CPen CWil EBee
'Merlot' CPen CWil EKen NLar
'Pink Panther' (v) More than 30 suppliers
'Pink Stripe' (v) CSBt CWil ECrN ENot IBlr LRHS MAsh MBri NPal SPoG SWvt WCot WGer WPat
'Platt's Black' More than 30 suppliers
'Rainbow Chief' see *P.* 'Maori Chief'
Rainbow hybrids CSpe
'Rainbow Maiden' see *P.* 'Maori Maiden'
'Rainbow Queen' see *P.* 'Maori Queen'
'Rainbow Sunrise' see *P.* 'Maori Sunrise'
'Red Sensation' **new** CPen
I 'Rubrum' CWil NBlu
'Sea Jade' CWil IBlr
'Stormy Dawn' WCot
'Sundowner' (v) ♀H3 CBcs CCVT CDoC CFwr CSBt CTrC CWil EBee EMil ENot EPfP GQui IBal IBlr LRHS MAsh MGos MRav SHBN SLdr SLim SPer SPla SPlb SWvt WCot WFar WLeb WMul WPat
'Sunset' (v) CBcs CSBt IBlr SWvt
'Surfer' (v) COtt CTrC CWil EHoe IBlr MCCP WBcn WLeb WPat WWhi
'Surfer Boy' CSBt CWil SMer
'Surfer Bronze' CPen CSBt CWil EAmu LSou MGos SHGC WGer

	'Surfer Green'	CDoC MGos WHer
	tenax 🏆H4	More than 30 suppliers
	- 'Atropurpureum' **new**	CHEx
	- 'Bronze'	CHEx CWil ECrN SWal SWvt
	- 'Co-ordination'	CWil EPfP IBal IBlr LRHS SCoo WBcn
*	- dwarf	IBlr SLPl
I	- 'Giganteum' **new**	CHEx
*	- ***lineatum***	SEND WMul
§	- 'Nanum Purpureum'	CPLG IBlr MSte SEND SMad
	- 'Platinum'	IBlr
	- Purpureum Group 🏆H3-4	More than 30 suppliers
	- 'Radiance' (v)	CWil IBlr
	- 'Rainbow Queen'	see *P.* 'Maori Queen'
	- 'Rainbow Sunrise'	see *P.* 'Maori Sunrise'
	- 'Variegatum' (v) 🏆H3-4	CBrm CFil CSBt EPfP IBlr LRHS NBlu NMoo SAPC SArc SEND SRms WBrE WFar WMul WPat
	- 'Veitchianum' (v)	CWil IBlr LRHS SPer
	'Thumbelina'	CBcs CTri EBee EHoe IBal LRHS MSte SSto WPat
	'Tom Thumb'	CBrm CWil GGar WDin WDyG WPrP WRos
	'Wings of Gold' **new**	CPen
	'Yellow Wave' (v) 🏆H3	More than 30 suppliers

Photinia ✿ (*Rosaceae*)

	'Allyn Sprite'[PBR] **new**	ENot
	arbutifolia	see *Heteromeles salicifolia*
	beauverdiana	CSam CTho SRms WFar
	- var. ***notabilis***	EPfP NLar
§	***davidiana***	CDul CSam EBee ELan EPfP GIBF ISea MBar MRav NLar SPer SRms WDin WFar WNor
	- 'Palette' (v)	More than 30 suppliers
	- var. ***undulata***	CMHG LRHS WBcn
	- - 'Fructu Luteo'	CMHG CSam EPfP EPla LRHS MBri MRav NLar SPer SPoG WFar
	- - 'Prostrata'	ELan EPfP MBar MRav SPer WDin WFar
	x ***fraseri***	CMCN
	- 'Birmingham'	EBee EHoe GKir LRHS MAsh SLim SRms WDin WWeb
	- 'Canivily' **new**	NLar
	- 'Purple Peter'	LRHS
	- 'Red Robin' 🏆H4	More than 30 suppliers
	- 'Red Select' **new**	WWeb
	- 'Robusta'	CTrC EPfP LRHS SLim SWvt
	- 'Super Hedger'	LBuc
	glabra	SArc
	- B&SWJ 8903	WCru
§	- 'Parfait' (v)	CAbP ELan LRHS MRav SHBN SPla SPoG WFar
	- 'Pink Lady'	see *P. glabra* 'Parfait'
	- 'Rubens'	ELan EPfP LRHS MAsh SPer SPla SSta WPat
	- 'Variegata'	see *P. glabra* 'Parfait'
	glomerata misapplied	see *P. prionophylla*
	lasiogyna	CMCN WWes
	niitakayamensis	GIBF
	nussia	CDoC
	parvifolia	EPfP
	prionophylla	CHEx
§	'Redstart'	CBrm CSam EPfP LRHS MGos NEgg NPro SLon SPer SSta SWvt WMoo
§	***serratifolia***	CBcs CBot CDul CHEx CMHG EPfP LRHS SAPC SArc SPer SPoG SSpi SSta WBcn WFar WPGP WSHC XPep
	serrulata	see *P. serratifolia*
	villosa 🏆H4	CAbP CTho GIBF GKir MBar NPal
	- B&SWJ 8877	WCru
	- var. ***laevis***	EPfP EWTr LBuc
	- f. ***maximowicziana***	EPfP GIBF
*	- var. ***zollingeri*** **new**	SLon

Phragmites (*Poaceae*)

	from Sichuan, China	EPPr
§	***australis***	CRWN EBee EMFW GFor LPBA MGol NArg NMir WDyG WFar XPep
	- subsp. ***australis*** var. ***striatopictus***	EMon EPPr
	- - 'Variegatus' (v)	More than 30 suppliers
	- subsp. ***pseudodonax***	EMon EPPr
	communis	see *P. australis*
	karka	EPPr
	- 'Candy Stripe' (v)	CDWL EPPr
	- 'Variegatus' (v)	LRav NLar

Phrynium (*Marantaceae*)

	pubinerve	CKob

Phuopsis (*Rubiaceae*)

§	***stylosa***	More than 30 suppliers
	- 'Purpurea'	CElw CWCL ELan MNrw MRav NChi SChu WHal

Phygelius ✿ (*Scrophulariaceae*)

	aequalis	CFee CSev MNrw SChu SHom SPla WMoo WPer WSHC WSan
	- ***albus***	see *P. aequalis* 'Yellow Trumpet'
	- 'Aureus'	see *P. aequalis* 'Yellow Trumpet'
	- Cedric Morris form	SHom
	- 'Cream Trumpet'	see *P. aequalis* 'Yellow Trumpet'
	- 'Indian Chief'	see *P.* x *rectus* 'African Queen'
*	- 'Pink Trumpet'	CDoC CHEx CWCL GCal LRHS NLon SCoo SMrm SPer
	- Sensation = 'Sani Pass'[PBR]	CBcs CPom CSpe EChP ECtt EGra EPfP GBri LRHS LSRN MCCP MDun MOak NCGa NPri SCoo SPet SPoG SWvt
	- 'Trewidden Pink' 🏆H4	More than 30 suppliers
§	- 'Yellow Trumpet' 🏆H3-4	More than 30 suppliers
	aequalis x ***capensis***	see *P.* x *rectus*
§	***capensis*** 🏆H3-4	CChe CWib EBee EChP ELan ENot EPfP LSpr MAsh MBNS MHer NLar SBch SGar SHom SPer SPet SRms SSth WFar WHil WMnd WMoo WPer WWye
	- CD&R	EWes
	- ***coccineus***	see *P. capensis*
	- 'Janet's Jewel' (v)	SHom
	- orange-flowered	SHom
	'Golden Gate'	see *P. aequalis* 'Yellow Trumpet'
	Logan form	EBee MCCP WWpP
	New Sensation = 'Blaphy'[PBR]	COtt MAsh NArg SBla SPer
§	x ***rectus***	MDKP SYvo
§	- 'African Queen' 🏆H3-4	More than 30 suppliers
	- 'Aylesham's Pride'	SHom
	- 'Bridgetown Beauty'	SHom
	- 'Devil's Tears' 🏆H4	More than 30 suppliers
	- 'Ivory Twist' **new**	SHom
	- 'Jodie Southon' **new**	LSou
	- Logan form	SHom
*	- 'Logan's Pink'	LSRN NGdn
	- 'Moonraker'	More than 30 suppliers
	- 'Pink Elf'	ELan SHom SLon
	- 'Raspberry Swirl'	EPfP MAsh NArg SHom SSta
	- 'Salmon Leap' 🏆H4	More than 30 suppliers
	- 'Sunshine'	COtt EBee EGra EHoe ELan EMan EPza EWes LAst LRHS MAsh MDKP SPoG SWal WWpP

- 'Sweet Dreams' **new** SHom
§ - 'Winchester Fanfare' More than 30 suppliers
- 'Winton Fanfare' see *P.* x *rectus* 'Winchester Fanfare'
Somerford Funfair Coral = 'Yapcor' **new** LRHS LSou MAsh MBri SPav SRkn
Somerford Funfair Cream = 'Yapcre' **new** EPfP LRHS LSou MAsh MBri SGSe SPav SRkn
Somerford Funfair Orange = 'Yapor' **new** CBcs LRHS LSou MAsh MBri SGSe SPav SPoG
Somerford Funfair Wine = 'Yapwin' **new** CBcs LSou MAsh MBri SGSe SPav SPoG SRkn
Somerford Funfair Yellow = 'Yapyel' **new** LRHS MAsh

Phyla (*Verbenaceae*)

§ ***nodiflora*** CNic CStu ECha EEls EWin GKir NWCA SBch SBla SEND SIng WPer XPep
- 'Alba' CNic
- var. ***canescens*** GMac WCru

Phylica (*Rhamnaceae*)

arborea 'Superba' CBcs CPLG
ericoides CPLG

x *Phylliopsis* (*Ericaceae*)

'Coppelia' ♀H4 EPot GCrs GEdr GGGa ITim LTwo SBrw SReu SSta WAbe WPat
hillieri 'Askival' GCrs GGGa LSou WAbe
- 'Pinocchio' GCrs GTou ITim LRHS MDun NLAp NLar WAbe WPat
'Hobgoblin' WAbe WPat
'Mermaid' GGGa ITim WAbe
'Puck' WAbe
'Sprite' GCrs WAbe WPat
'Sugar Plum' CWSG IDee ITim MDun NLar SBrw SSpi SSta SWvt WAbe WPat

Phyllitis see *Asplenium*

Phyllocladus (*Phyllocladaceae*)

trichomanoides var. ***alpinus*** CDoC CTrC GKir LCon LLin NLar WEve

Phyllodoce (*Ericaceae*)

aleutica GCrs GGGa GKir MBar NDlv NMen SRms WAbe
aleutica x ***caerulea*** GCrs
breweri GIBF WAbe
caerulea ♀H4 GEdr NDlv
- ***japonica*** see *P. nipponica*
* - var. ***japonica*** **new** WThu
- 'Viking' GCrs
empetriformis MBar SRms
§ ***nipponica*** ♀H4 GCrs NMen WAbe
- var. ***oblongo-ovata*** GCrs
tsugifolia GCrs

Phyllostachys ✿ (*Poaceae*)

angusta CFil EPla SBig WJun
arcana ENBC EPla GKir WJun
- 'Luteosulcata' CBcs CFil EPla GKir MMoz MWht NLar NPal WJun WNor WPGP
§ ***atrovaginata*** EPla ERod WJun
aurea ♀H4 More than 30 suppliers
- 'Albovariegata' (v) EFul
- 'Flavescens Inversa' EPla ERod EUJe WJun
- 'Holochrysa' CBrP EFul EPla ERod MWht WJun
- 'Koi' CFil EFul EPla ERod MMoz MWht NMoo SBig
aureocaulis see *P. aureosulcata* f. *aureocaulis*, *P. vivax* f. *aureocaulis*
aureosulcata CBcs CWib EExo EFul EPfP EPla EPza ERod GKir LRHS MAsh MMoz NMoo WBVN WJun WMoo
- f. ***alata*** see *P. aureosulcata* f. *pekinensis*
- 'Argus' EPla
- f. ***aureocaulis*** ♀H4 More than 30 suppliers
- 'Harbin' EPla ERod
- 'Harbin Inversa' EPla ERod
- 'Lama Temple' CFil EPla
§ - f. ***pekinensis*** CFil EBee EPla NLar SBig WPGP
- f. ***spectabilis*** ♀H4 More than 30 suppliers
bambusoides CBcs EPla GKir SBig SDix WJun
- 'Allgold' see *P. bambusoides* 'Holochrysa'
- 'Castilloni' CAbb CAlb CBcs CFil EAmu EExo EFul ENBC EPla EPza ERod EWes GKir LEdu MMoz MWht NBea NMoo NPal SBig SDix SEND WJun WMul WPGP
- 'Castilloni Inversa' CFil ENBC EPla EPza ERod MMoz MWht WJun WMul WPGP
§ - 'Holochrysa' CDoC CFil CPen EPla ERod GKir MMoz NMoo NPal SEND WJun WMul WPGP
- 'Katashibo' EPla
- 'Kawadana' EPla ERod
- f. ***lacrima-deae*** CFil CTrC EPfP EPla WMul
- 'Marliacea' EPla ERod LPJP SBig WJun
- 'Subvariegata' CFil EPla WPGP
- 'Sulphurea' see *P. bambusoides* 'Holochrysa'
- 'Tanakae' ENBC MMoz MSwo NLar NMoo SBig WPGP
- 'Violascens' NMoo SBig
bissetii More than 30 suppliers
circumpilis EPla
congesta hort. see *P. atrovaginata*
decora CAbb EAmu EPla ERod MBri MMoz MWht NLar NMoo NPal SEND WJun WPGP
dulcis EPfP EPla ERod LEdu LPJP SBig WJun
§ ***edulis*** CBcs CTrC EFul EHoe EPla EPza ERod IFro MMoz SBig WJun WMul WPGP
- 'Bicolor' WMul
- f. ***pubescens*** see *P. edulis*
flexuosa CBcs CFil CPen EFul EPfP EPla IMGH MWht WJun WMul WPGP
glauca CAbb EPla ERod MMoz MWht NLar NMoo NPal SBig WMul
- f. ***yunzhu*** EPla ERod MWht WJun
heteroclada NMoo WJun
- 'Solid Stem' misapplied see *P. purpurata* 'Straight Stem'
heterocycla f. ***pubescens*** see *P. edulis*
humilis CBcs CDul ENBC EPla ERod LAst MCCP MGos MMoz MWht NLar NMoo NPal SBig WJun
iridescens EPla MSwo NLar SBig WJun
lofushanensis CFil EPla
makinoi ERod
mannii CPen EPla
meyeri CPen EPla
nidularia EBee EPla ERod MMoz SBig WJun
- f. ***farcta*** CFil EPla
§ - f. ***glabrovagina*** EPla
- smooth sheath see *P. nidularia* f. *glabrovagina*
nigella EPla
nigra ♀H4 More than 30 suppliers
- 'Boryana' CAbb CBig CBrm CDoC CFil EAmu EFul ENBC EPfP EPla GKir LAst MAsh MGos MMoz MWht NMoo SArc SBig SWvt WFar WJun WMoo WMul WPGP

- 'Fulva' EPla
- 'Hale' EPla
- f. ***henonis*** ♀H4 CAbb CBcs CFil EAmu EFul EMil ENBC EPla ERod MMoz MWht NBea NLar NMoo SBig WDyG WJun WMul WPGP
- 'Megurochiku' EPla ERod WJun
- f. ***nigra*** EPla SPer
- f. ***punctata*** CBrm CDoC CFil ENBC EPfP EPla ERod MAvo MWht NGdn SEND WDyG WJun WPGP
- 'Tosaensis' EPla
- 'Wisley' EPla

nuda EAmu ENBC EPla ERod GKir MGos MMoz MWht NLar NPal WJun
- f? ***localis*** MWht

parvifolia EPla ERod WJun
platyglossa CFil EPla ERod WPGP
praecox EPla NMoo WJun
propinqua CBig CDoC CDul ENBC EPla ERod MCCP MMoz MWht WJun WMul
* - 'Bicolor' WJun
- 'Li Yu Gan' CFil EPla

* ***pubescens*** 'Mazel' NMoo
§ ***purpurata*** 'Straight Stem' EPla MWht
rubicunda CFil EPla WJun
rubromarginata CFil CPen EPla ERod MWht NLar WJun
stimulosa EPla ERod WJun
§ ***sulphurea*** NMoo
- 'Houzeau' EPla ERod
- 'Robert Young' EPla
- 'Sulphurea' see *P. sulphurea*
- f. ***viridis*** EPla ERod GKir MAsh MWht NMoo SBig

violascens CBcs CFil EFul EPla ERod MMoz SBig WJun WPGP
virella CFil EPla
viridiglaucescens CAbb CBcs CFil CHEx EAmu EFul EPfP EPla GKir MBrN MMoz MWht SArc SBig SEND SPla WJun WMul
viridis see *P. sulphurea* f. *viridis*
vivax EExo EFul EPfP EPla ERod GQui LEdu MMoz MWht SBig WJun WMul WNor
- f. ***aureocaulis*** ♀H4 More than 30 suppliers

* - f. ***huanvenzhu*** CFil CTrC EFul ENBC EPla ERod MMoz NMoo WJun WMul
- 'Katrin' LEdu

x *Phyllothamnus* (*Ericaceae*)

erectus GCrs GGGa SOkd SReu SSta WAbe WPat

Phymatosorus (*Polypodiaceae*)

§ ***diversifolius*** CFil SSpi

Phymosia (*Malvaceae*)

§ ***umbellata*** CBot CRHN ERea

Phyodina see *Callisia*

Physalis (*Solanaceae*)

SDR 2501 **new** GKev
alkekengi ♀H4 EBee EPfP GKir MLan NBir NLRH SWvt WFar
- var. ***franchetii*** More than 30 suppliers
- - dwarf NLar NRnb WHil
- - 'Gigantea' ECGP GBuc NLar NRnb SPlb
- - 'Gnome' EBee NEgg
- - 'Variegata' (v) ECha ECtt EMan EPla EWes IBlr MAvo NPro WOld

angulata B&SWJ 7016 WCru
edulis (F) see *P. peruviana*
§ ***peruviana*** (F) LRav SHDw

Physocarpus (*Rosaceae*)

malvaceus EWes
monogynus **new** NLar
opulifolius CDul GIBF IFro MSal
- 'Dart's Gold' ♀H4 More than 30 suppliers
- 'Diabolo'PBR ♀H4 More than 30 suppliers

§ - 'Luteus' CBot CDoC CMHG CSam CWib EBee EPfP GKir IMGH ISea MBar MDun MRav MWhi NEgg NLon SPer SRms WDin WFar WMoo
ribesifolius 'Aureus' see *P. opulifolius* 'Luteus'

Physochlaina (*Solanaceae*)

orientalis CPom EMan MSal NChi WAul

Physoplexis (*Campanulaceae*)

§ ***comosa*** ♀H2-3 CStu EPot EWes GKev LRHS NSla SBla WHoo

Physostegia (*Lamiaceae*)

angustifolia CSam
§ ***virginiana*** CHrt CKno CSBt EBee EGra EWTr GBar GKir GMaP LAst MBNS NBlu SGar WBrk WFar WRHF
- 'Alba' CBot CSBt EBee EChP EGra EPfP EShb GBar GBri GKir GMaP LRHS MSte MTis NLar NOrc NRnb SPet SPlb WEas WHrl WRha

§ - 'Crown of Snow' CDWL CFir CM&M EBee ECtt ERou GKir MBNS MBow MHer MRav MWhi MWrn NArg NLon NLsd STes SWal SWvt WFar WHil WPer WWpP
- 'Grandiflora' CFir
- 'Grandiflora Rose' NArg NBre NPri SWvt
- 'Miss Manners' EBee MSte SUsu WCot WHil
- 'Olympic Gold' (v) EBee EMan ENot EPPr EPfP MDKP WRHF
- 'Red Beauty' CFir EBee ERou LRHS MDKP NLRH SPla
- 'Rose Queen' MFOX NArg NBre NLRH SMar WTin
- 'Rosea' CBcs CBot EBee EChP ERou GKir IGor MBow MDKP NBPC NRnb WFar WGHP WHrl WPer
- Schneekrone see *P. virginiana* 'Crown of Snow'
- 'Snow Queen' see *P. virginiana* 'Summer Snow'
- var. ***speciosa*** EMon WFar

§ - - 'Bouquet Rose' CDWL CPrp CTbh EBee EBrs ECha EMan EPfP LRHS MHer MNFA MRav MSte NBir NOak SChu SMac SPer SWvt WAul WCAu WFar WMoo WRos WSan WTel WWeb
- - Rose Bouquet see *P. virginiana* subsp. *speciosa* 'Bouquet Rose'

§ - - 'Variegata' (v) More than 30 suppliers
§ - 'Summer Snow' ♀H4 CBcs CPrp ECha ELan ENot EPfP IBal LRHS MBri MNFA MWgw NCGa SChu SPer SPla SRms WBrk WCAu WCot WFar WHoo WMnd
- 'Summer Spire' EBee ECha EHrv ELan EMan LSou MSte SPer WFar
- 'Vivid' ♀H4 More than 30 suppliers
- 'Wassenhove' EBee EMon

Phyteuma (*Campanulaceae*)

comosum see *Physoplexis comosa*
hemisphaericum GKev WPat
humile EDAr WAbe

	nigrum	CDes GCal LRHS MNrw NBid WCot WPGP
	orbiculare	WAbe
	scheuchzeri	CNic EBee EMan EPfP GEdr GTou MHer NChi NEgg NJOw NOrc NPri NWCA SBla SPet SRms SRot WAbe WHoo
	sieberi	NBir WAbe
	spicatum	CDes NBro

Phytolacca (*Phytolaccaceae*)

	acinosa	GPoy MGol MSal NLar
	- HWJ 647	WCru
§	***americana***	CAgr CArn CHEx CSev EBee ECha ELan ELau EMar EPfP GPoy ITer MBNS MChe MHer MSal NEgg NLar SEND SIde SRms WCru WEas WFar WHil WJek WMnd WMoo WSHC WWye
	- 'Silberstein' (v)	CBct EBee ITer LBuc NEgg WCot
	clavigera	see *P. polyandra*
	decandra	see *P. americana*
	dioica	CHEx CPLG SBig
	esculenta	LEdu
	icosandra B&SWJ 8988	WCru
	japonica B&SWJ 4897	WCru
	octandra	CPLG
	- B&SWJ 9514	WCru
§	***polyandra***	CPLG ECha NBid NBro SGar SRms WBan WBor WWye

Picea ✿ (*Pinaceae*)

§	***abies***	CCVT CDul CLnd CSBt CTri CWib EHul ENot EPfP GKir LBuc LRHS MBar MBri MGos NBlu NWea SCoo SLim SPoG WBVN WDin WEve WMou
	- 'Acrocona'	ECho EHul EOrn GKir LCon LLin LRHS MAsh MBar MBlu MBri MGos SCoo WEve
	- 'Archer'	CKen
	- 'Argenteospica' (v)	WEve
	- 'Aurea'	ECho EOrn IMGH LLin WEve
	- 'Capitata'	CKen GTSp MBar NLar
	- 'Cinderella'	MBri
	- 'Clanbrassiliana'	CDoC CKen IMGH LCon MAsh MBar WEve
	- Compacta Group	LBee LRHS NEgg
I	- 'Congesta'	CKen
	- 'Crippsii'	CKen
I	- 'Cruenta'	CKen
	- 'Cupressina'	CKen EBrs
	- 'Diffusa'	CKen LCon MBar
	- 'Dumpy'	LCon NLar
	- 'Elegans'	MBar
	- 'Ellwangeriana'	NLar
	- 'Excelsa'	see *P. abies*
	- 'Fahndrich'	CKen
	- 'Finedonensis'	LCon NLar WEve
	- 'Formanek'	CDoC CKen CMen LCon LLin NLar
	- 'Four Winds'	CAbP CKen
	- 'Frohburg'	CDoC COtt EBrs GKir LRHS MBar MGos
	- 'Globosa'	MBar
	- 'Globosa Nana'	MGos
	- 'Goblin' **new**	NLar
	- 'Gregoryana'	CKen CMac GKir IMGH MBar NDlv
	- 'Heartland Gem'	CKen
	- 'Himfa' **new**	NLar
	- 'Horace Wilson'	CKen
	- 'Humilis'	CKen MGos
	- 'Hystrix'	CRob LCon NLar
	- 'Inversa'	EHul EOrn LCon LLin MBar MBlu MGos SLim WEve
	- 'J.W. Daisy's White'	see *P. glauca* 'J.W. Daisy's White'
	- 'Jana'	CKen
	- 'Kral'	CKen
	- 'Little Gem' ℽH4	CDoC CFee CKen CMac CMen CRob EHul EOrn GBin GKir IMGH LBee LCon LLin LRHS MAsh MBar SLim SPer SPoG WEve
	- 'Maxwellii'	EHul GKir MBar
	- 'Mikulasovice'	NLar
	- 'Nana'	MBar NEgg
	- 'Nana Compacta'	CKen CRob EHul IMGH LBee MAsh MBar WFar
	- 'Nidiformis' ℽH4	CDoC CKen CMac CRob CSBt CTri EHul ENot EOrn GBin GKir LCon LLin LRHS MAsh MBar NBlu NWea SLim SPoG SRms WDin WEve WFar
	- 'Norrkoping'	CKen
	- 'Ohlendorffii'	CKen EHul LCon MBar MGos NLar
	- 'Pachyphylla'	CKen
	- 'Pendula Major'	SHBN
	- 'Procumbens'	MBar
	- 'Pumila'	EOrn
	- 'Pumila Nigra'	CMac EHul LCon LLin MBar MGos SCoo SLim SPoG
	- 'Pusch'	CKen
	- 'Pygmaea'	CKen GTSp MBar MGos
	- 'Reflexa'	EHul GBin IMGH LCon MAsh WEve
	- 'Repens'	LRHS MBar MBlu
	- 'Rydal'	EBrs LCon MAsh NLar
	- 'Saint James'	CKen
	- 'Tabuliformis'	MBar
	- 'Tufty'	EOrn
	- 'Vermont Gold'	CKen NLar SLim
	- 'Waldbrunn'	LLin MAsh WEve
	- 'Walter Bron'	CKen
	- 'Waugh'	MBar
	- Will's Dwarf	see *P. abies* 'Wills Zwerg'
§	- 'Wills Zwerg'	LRHS MAsh
	ajanensis	GIBF
I	***alcoquiana*** 'Prostrata'	LCon MBar
	- var. ***reflexa***	MPkF
	breweriana ℽH4	More than 30 suppliers
	engelmanii 'Compact' **new**	EBrs
	engelmannii	GKir GTSp MBar
	- subsp. ***engelmannii***	MBar
	glauca	CDul CTri WEve
	- 'Alberta Blue'	CDoC CKen CRob CSBt EOrn GKir LCon LLin LRHS MAsh SCoo SLim WEve WFar
	- var. ***albertiana*** 'Alberta Globe'	CDoC CRob CSBt EHul EOrn GKir IMGH LBee LCon LLin MAsh MBar MBri MGos NDlv NEgg SAga SCoo SLim SPoG WEve WFar
	- - 'Conica'	More than 30 suppliers
	- - 'Gnome'	CKen WEve
	- - 'Laurin'	CDoC CKen CRob EOrn GKir LBee LCon LLin LRHS MAsh MBar MGos SCoo WEve
	- - 'Tiny'	CKen EOrn LCon LLin MBar
	- 'Arneson's Blue Variegated' (v)	CKen LLin MAsh MBri SLim SPoG WEve WFar
	- 'Blue Planet'	CKen NLar
	- 'Coerulea'	LCon MBar
I	- 'Coerulea Nana'	NLar
	- 'Cy's Wonder'	CKen
	- 'Densata'	CDul
	- 'Echiniformis' ℽH4	CKen ECho GKir LBee LRHS MBar MBri
	- var. ***glauca***	GIBF

	- 'Goldilocks'	CKen
§	- 'J.W. Daisy's White'	CKen CRob EBrs EOrn GKir LCon LLin LRHS MAsh MGos SCoo SLim SMur SPer SPoG WEve WFar WGor
	- 'Lilliput'	CKen EHul EOrn LCon MBar MGos NLar WEve
	- 'Nana'	CKen
	- 'Piccolo'	CKen LRHS MAsh SLim
	- 'Pixie'	CKen
	- 'Rainbow's End' (v)	CKen SCoo SLim WFar
	- 'Sander's Blue'	CKen CRob EOrn LBee SCoo SLim SPoG WEve
	- 'Zucherhut'	LRHS MBar MBri
	glehnii	LCon
	- 'Sasanosei'	CKen
	- 'Shimezusei'	CKen
	jezoensis	CMen GKir MGos
	- subsp. ***hondoensis***	WNor
	- 'Yatsabusa'	CKen CMen
	koraiensis	CDul GIBF GKir
	kosteri 'Glauca'	see *P. pungens* 'Koster'
	likiangensis	CMCN EPfP GTSp ISea LCon
	- var. ***balfouriana***	see *P. likiangensis* var. *rubescens*
	- var. ***purpurea***	see *P. purpurea*
§	- var. ***rubescens***	CDoC GKir IDee LCon WWes
	mariana	GKir GTSp NWea
	- 'Aureovariegata' (v)	WFar
I	- 'Austria Broom' **new**	CKen
	- 'Doumetii'	EOrn
	- 'Fastigiata'	CKen EOrn
	- 'Nana' ♀H4	CDoC CKen CMac CMen CRob EHul EPfP GKir IMGH LCon LLin LRHS MAsh MBar MNrw MWat NBlu NDlv NWea SCoo SLim SPoG WBrE WDin WEve WFar
I	- 'Pygmaea'	CKen
	x ***mariorika***	MBar
§	- 'Gnom'	MGos
	meyeri **new**	GKir
	obovata	GIBF
	- var. ***coerulea***	GIBF NLar
	omorika ♀H4	CBcs CDul CMCN ENot GKir LBuc LCon LRav MBar MGos NWea SPer SPoG WBrE WCFE WDin WEve WFar WMou
	- 'Frohnleiten'	CKen
	- 'Frondenberg'	CKen
	- 'Karel'	CKen NLar
	- 'Minimax' **new**	CKen
	- 'Nana' ♀H4	CMac EHul LBee LCon MAsh MBar SCoo SLim WEve
	- 'Pendula' ♀H4	CDoC EBrs GKir GTSp LCon LRHS MBar MBlu NLar SCoo SHBN SLim SPoG SSta
	- 'Pimoko'	CKen GKir LCon LLin LRHS MAsh MGos NLar
	- 'Pygmy' **new**	CKen
	- 'Schneverdingen'	CKen
	- 'Tijn'	CKen
	- 'Treblitsch'	CDoC CKen MGos
	orientalis ♀H4	CDul GKir LCon LRav NWea WMou
§	- 'Aurea' (v) ♀H4	CMac ECho ECrN EHul ELan ENot GKir LCon LLin MBar MBri MLan SCoo SHBN SLim WDin
	- 'Aureospicata'	CDoC CTho ECho MAsh MBlu WEve
	- 'Bergman's Gem'	CKen
	- 'Early Gold' (v)	IArd
	- 'Golden Start' **new**	NLar
	- 'Gowdy'	MBar NLar
	- 'Jewel'	CKen
	- 'Kenwith'	CKen

	- 'Mount Vernon'	CKen
	- Pendula Group	MGos
	- 'Professor Langner'	CKen
	- 'Skylands'	CDoC CKen EBrs GKir LCon LLin MAsh MBri MGos SCoo SLim SPoG WEve
	- 'Tom Thumb' **new**	CKen
*	- 'Wittbold Compact'	LBee
	pungens	GKir MBar NWea WDin WNor
	- 'Baby Blueeyes'	MPkF
	- 'Blaukissen'	CKen
	- 'Blue Mountain'	MPkF
	- 'Drayer'	MPkF
	- 'Edith'	MPkF SLim WFar
	- 'Endtz'	MPkF
	- 'Erich Frahm'	CTri GKir LCon LRHS MAsh MBar MBri MGos MPkF MWya NBlu SCoo SLim WFar
	- 'Fat Albert'	CDul CRob CWib GKir LBee MGos SLim SPoG WFar
	- 'Frieda' **new**	SLim
	- Glauca Group	CBrm CDul CLnd EWTr GKir GWCH LBee MBar NWea SCoo SPoG WBVN WDin WEve WFar WMou WOrn
N	- 'Glauca Pendula'	EBrs
	- 'Glauca Procumbens'	CMen NLar
§	- 'Glauca Prostrata'	EHul GKir MBar WEve
	- 'Globe'	CKen CMen
I	- 'Globosa' ♀H4	CBcs CDoC CKen CRob EHul EOrn GKir LBee LCon LLin MAsh MBar MBri MGos MWat SCoo SHBN SLim SPoG SRms WEve WFar
	- 'Gloria'	CKen EBrs
	- 'Hoopsii' ♀H4	CBcs CDoC CDul CMac CRob CSBt ECrN EHul ENot EOrn EPfP GKir LCon LRHS MAsh MBar MGos MWya NBee NBlu NWea SCoo SHBN SLim SWvt WDin WEve WFar
	- 'Hoto'	EBrs EHul EOrn LCon MBar
	- 'Hunnewelliana'	EOrn
	- 'Iseli Fastigiate'	CDoC COtt CRob EBrs GKir LCon LLin MAsh MBri MGos SCoo SLim SPoG WEve
§	- 'Koster' ♀H4	CDoC CMac CRob CSBt EHul EOrn EPfP GKir LCon LLin MAsh MBar MGos NWea SCoo SLim SPoG SRms WDin WEve WFar
	- 'Lucky Strike'	CDoC CKen LCon LLin MGos NLar
	- 'Maigold' (v)	CKen NLar SLim
	- 'Moerheimii'	EHul EOrn LCon MBar MGos NLar WEve
	- 'Montgomery'	CKen GKir LCon LLin MBar NLar WEve
	- 'Mrs Cesarini'	CKen
	- 'Nimety'	CKen NLar
	- 'Oldenburg'	MBar NBee NLar
	- 'Omega'	GKir
	- 'Procumbens'	CKen
	- 'Prostrata'	see *P. pungens* 'Glauca Prostrata'
	- 'Prostrate Blue Mist'	WEve
	- 'Rovelli's Monument'	EBrs NLar
	- 'Saint Mary's Broom'	CKen
	- 'Schovenhorst'	EHul EOrn WFar
	- 'Snowkiss'	MPkF WFar
	- 'Spek'	MPkF
	- 'Thomsen'	EHul EOrn LCon MAsh
	- 'Thuem'	EHul EOrn GKir LLin MGos NDlv NLar WEve WFar
	- 'Wendy'	CKen
§	***purpurea***	GKir LCon WEve

	retroflexa	GIBF
	rubens	GKir LCon NLar WEve
	schrenkiana	GKir LCon
	sitchensis	CDul GKir LCon NWea WMou
	- 'Nana'	CDoC LLin NLar
	- 'Papoose'	see *P. sitchensis* 'Tenas'
	- 'Silberzwerg'	CKen NLar SLim
	- 'Strypemonde'	CKen
§	- 'Tenas'	CDoC CKen CRob EBrs EOrn LCon MAsh MGos NLar SLim WEve
	- 'Trinket'	NLar
	smithiana	CDoC CTho EPfP GKir GTSp ISea LCon NLar WMou
I	- 'Aurea' **new**	MGos
	- 'Sunray'	LCon
	wilsonii	GIBF GKir LCon NLar

Picrasma (*Simaroubaceae*)

	ailanthoides	see *P. quassioides*
§	***quassioides***	CFil CMCN EPfP

Picris (*Asteraceae*)

	echioides	CArn WHer

Picrorhiza (*Scrophulariaceae*)

	kurrooa	GPoy

Pieris ✿ (*Ericaceae*)

	'Bert Chandler'	GKir LRHS SPer SSpi
	'Brouwer's Beauty'	MGos SLim
	'Firecrest' ♀H4	CAlb CBcs CMHG CTrh SBrw SSpi
	'Flaming Silver' (v) ♀H4	More than 30 suppliers
	floribunda	MBar SPer
	'Forest Flame' ♀H4	More than 30 suppliers
	formosa B&SWJ 2257	WCru
	- var. ***forrestii***	CDoC CTrw CWib ISea NWea
	- - 'Ball of Fire'	SSpi
	- - 'Fota Pink'	WHar
	- - 'Jermyns'	SBrw SHBN
	- - 'Wakehurst' ♀H3	CAbP CBcs CDul CSBt CWSG ENot EPfP LHyd LRHS MRav NWea SBrw SPer SPoG SReu SSpi SSta WFar
	Havila = 'Mouwsvila' (v)	MBri MGos NLar SBrw WFar
	japonica	CBcs CTrw GIBF MBar MGos NWea SArc SReu WDin
	- 'Bisbee Dwarf'	ITim MBar SSta
	- 'Blush' ♀H4	GKir LRHS MBri SBod SBrw SHBN
	- 'Bonfire'	CEnd CFwr LBuc LRHS MBri MGos NLar SPoG
	- 'Carnaval' (v)	CAlb CEnd CFwr CSBt CWib EBee EGra ELan ENot EPfP LBuc LRHS LSRN MAsh MGos NLar NPri SPoG SWvt WFar
	- 'Cavatine' ♀H4	CMHG LRHS SBod
§	- 'Christmas Cheer'	MGos NLar SSto WMoo
	- 'Compacta'	WAbe
	- 'Cupido'	CDoC EMil LRHS MAsh MBar MBri MGos SPoG WFar
	- 'Daisen'	CTrw
§	- 'Debutante' ♀H4	CBcs CWSG CWib ELan ENot EPfP GKir LRHS MAsh MBri MDun SBrw SPoG SSpi SWvt WFar
	- 'Don'	see *P. japonica* 'Pygmaea'
	- 'Dorothy Wyckoff'	CBcs CMHG CSBt CWSG GKir LRHS MBri MDun NDlv SBrw SHBN SSta WCwm
	- 'Flaming Star'	ECot SWvt WBrE
	- 'Flamingo'	CTrw GKev LRHS MBar MGos NDlv WPat
	- 'Geisha'	WPat
	- 'Grayswood' ♀H4	EPfP LRHS MBri SBrw WFar
	- 'Katsura'	EPfP LBuc LRHS MAsh SPer SPoG SSpi SSta
	- 'Little Heath' (v) ♀H4	More than 30 suppliers
	- 'Little Heath Green' ♀H4	CChe CDoC CMHG CSBt GKir LHyd LRHS MAsh MBar MGos NDlv NEgg SPoG SSta SSto SWvt WBrE WFar WMoo WPic
	- 'Minor'	ITim MBar
	- 'Mountain Fire' ♀H4	More than 30 suppliers
	- 'Pink Delight' ♀H4	CAbP CBcs CDoC GKir LRHS LSRN MAsh MBar MGos MRav NEgg SBrw SHBN SPer SPoG SRms SSto WGwG WPat
	- 'Prelude' ♀H4	CSBt CWSG GKir LRHS MAsh MBri SPoG WAbe WFar WPat
	- 'Purity' ♀H4	CBcs CDoC CMHG CWSG EPfP LRHS MBar MGos MLan NBlu SBrw SMer SPoG SReu SSta SSto SWvt WDin WFar
§	- 'Pygmaea'	CMHG SSta WAbe
	- 'Red Mill'	CEnd CSBt CWSG ENot EPfP GKir LRHS MAsh NEgg SPer SSpi WFar
	- 'Robinswood'	WBcn
	- 'Rosalinda'	NBlu NLar WFar
	- 'Rosea'	LHyd WBVN
	- 'Sarabande' ♀H4	COtt LRHS MBar MBri MGos NLar SBrw SPoG SSta WPat
	- 'Scarlett O'Hara'	CSBt MGos NLar
	- 'Select'	CFwr MGos
	- 'Silver Mills'	MGos
	- 'Snowdrift'	LRHS
	- 'Spring Candy'	MGos
	- 'Spring Snow'	LRHS
	- Taiwanensis Group	CMHG EPfP LRHS MBar MDun NWea SRms SSta WFar WPat
	- 'Temple Bells'	CSBt ENot SMer
	- 'Valley Rose'	COtt CSBt ELan ENot EPfP GKir MGos NBlu SPer SPoG SSpi WFar
	- 'Valley Valentine' ♀H4	CBcs CBrm CDoC CDul CEnd COtt CSBt CTrh CWSG CWib ENot EPfP GAbr GKir LRHS LSRN MBri MGos NDlv SBrw SLim SPer SPoG SReu SSta SSto SWvt WCwm WFar WPat
	- 'Variegata' misapplied	see *P. japonica* 'White Rim'
§	- 'Variegata' (Carrière) Bean (v)	CMHG EPfP EPot GKir LHyd MAsh MBar MGos NDlv SHBN SPer SPoG SReu SSta WDin WFar WHar WPat WSHC
	- 'Wada's Pink'	see *P. japonica* 'Christmas Cheer'
	- 'White Cascade'	SBrw
	- 'White Pearl'	CAbP CBcs MAsh MGos SBrw
§	- 'White Rim' (v) ♀H4	CDul EPfP GKev GKir MAsh MGos NEgg SBrw SPlb WFar
	- 'William Buchanan'	GCrs MBar WAbe
	koidzumiana	SSta
	nana	MBar
	- 'Redshank'	SOkd
	'Tilford'	LRHS MBri

Pilea (*Urticaceae*)

*	'Anette'	MBri
	cadierei ♀H1	CHal MBri
	depressa	CHal
	involucrata 'Norfolk' ♀H1	CHal
§	***microphylla***	CHal EBak EShb
	muscosa	see *P. microphylla*
	nummulariifolia	CHal
	peperomioides ♀H1	CHal CSev EPem
	repens	MBri

Pileostegia (*Hydrangeaceae*)

	viburnoides ♀H4	More than 30 suppliers
	- B&SWJ 3565	WCru

Pilosella (*Asteraceae*)

§	***aurantiaca***	CArn CHrt CMCo CNic CRWN ELan MBow MHer MWgw NArg NBid NBlu NOrc NPri NSti SGSe SIde SIng SPet WCAu WHer WMoo WPop WWye
§	- subsp. ***carpathicola***	GGar
§	***officinarum***	NRya

Pilularia (*Marsileaceae*)

	globulifera	CBgR EFer

Pimelea (*Thymelaeaceae*)

	coarctata	see *P. prostrata*
	drupacea	ECou
	ferruginea **new**	EShb
	filiformis	ECou
	ligustrina	GGar
§	***prostrata***	CBcs CLyd CTri ECou EPot ESis MBar NJOw SRot WPat WPer
	- f. ***parvifolia***	ECou
	- Tennyson's form	EHyt ETow SBla
	tomentosa	ECou

Pimpinella (*Apiaceae*)

	anisum	CArn MSal SIde WSel
	bicknellii	CDes SIgm WCot WPGP
	flahaultii	NChi
	major 'Rosea'	CAby CBos CDes CHad CPLG EMon IFro LPhx MAvo SBla SMrm WCot WEas WFar WHal WPGP
	niitakayamensis B&SWJ 6942	WCru
	saxifraga	CAgr

pineapple see *Ananas comosus*

pineapple guava see *Acca sellowiana*

Pinellia (*Araceae*)

	cordata	CPom EMan LEdu MDKP MSte NMen SBla SOkd WCot WCru
	pedatisecta	CDes CRow EBee EMan ERos LPio WCot WPnP
	pinnatisecta	see *P. tripartita*
	ternata	CRow CStu ERos MSal NMen WCot WWye
	- B&SWJ 3532	WCru
§	***tripartita***	CPom CStu MDKP WBVN WCot WCru WPnP WPrP
	- B&SWJ 1102	WCru
	- 'Purple Face'	ITer WCru
	- - B&SWJ 4850	

Pinguicula (*Lentibulariaceae*)

	acuminata	SHmp
	crassifolia	LHew
	crassifolia* x *emarginata	SHmp
	cyclosecta	LHew SHmp
	ehlersiae	EFEx
	esseriana	EFEx
	gracilis	LHew
	grandiflora	CSWC EFEx GCrs GEdr IFro LRHS MCCP NMen NRya WAbe WHer WPGP
	hemiepiphytica	LHew
	heterophylla	SHmp
	jaumavensis	LHew
	lauana	LHew
	leptoceras **new**	CFir
	longifolia subsp. ***longifolia***	EFEx WPGP
	macrophylla	LHew SHmp
	moctezumae	SHmp
	moranensis var. ***caudata***	EFEx
	- ***moreana***	EFEx
	- ***superba***	EFEx
*	***pilosa***	SHmp
	primuliflora	CSWC
	rotundiflora	LHew SHmp
	'Sethos'	SIng
	vallisneriifolia small	LHew
	vulgaris	EFEx
	'Weser'	CSWC SIng
	zecheri* x *macrophylla	SHmp

pinkcurrant see *Ribes rubrum* (P)

Pinus ✿ (*Pinaceae*)

	albicaulis	WNor
	- 'Flinck'	CKen
	- 'Nana'	see *P. albicaulis* 'Noble's Dwarf'
§	- 'Noble's Dwarf'	CKen
	aristata	CDul CFil CLnd CMCN EHul EOrn GKir LCon LLin MAsh MBar MBlu MGos SIng SSpi STre WDin WEve
	- 'Cecilia'	CKen
	- 'Sherwood Compact'	CKen
	armandii	CDoC CDul GKir GTSp IDee LCon WEve
	- 'Gold Tip'	CKen
	attenuata	GKir
	austriaca	see *P. nigra* subsp. *nigra*
N	***ayacahuite***	LCon
	balfouriana dwarf **new**	CKen
	banksiana	CDul CLnd GKir GTSp LCon
	- 'Arctis'	NLar
	- 'Chippewa'	CKen LLin
I	- 'Compacta'	CKen
	- 'H.J. Welch'	CKen
	- 'Manomet'	CKen
	- 'Neponset'	CKen
	- 'Schneverdingen'	CKen
	- 'Schoodic'	LLin SLim
	- 'Uncle Fogy'	NLar WEve
	- 'Wisconsin'	CKen
	bungeana	CDoC CLnd CMCN CTho EPfP GKir LCon LLin MBlu SLPl SSpi WEve WNor
	- 'Diamant'	CKen
	canariensis	EHul IDee ISea
	cembra	CDul CLnd EHul GIBF GKir LCon MBar NLar NWea STre WEve
	- 'Aurea'	see *P. cembra* 'Aureovariegata'
§	- 'Aureovariegata' (v)	CKen EBrs GKir LLin LRHS NDlv SPoG WEve
	- 'Barnhourie'	CKen
	- 'Blue Mound'	CKen
	- 'Chalet'	CKen
	- 'Compacta Glauca'	CDoC MBri
	- Glauca Group	EBrs
*	- 'Griffithii'	WDin
	- 'Inverleith'	CKen
	- 'Jermyns'	CKen
	- 'King's Dwarf'	CKen
	- 'Roughills'	CKen
	- 'Stricta'	CKen
	- witches' broom	CKen

	Name	Suppliers
	contorta	CBcs CDoC CDul CTrC GKir LCon MBar MGos NWea WDin WMou
	- 'Asher'	CKen
	- 'Frisian Gold'	CKen EBrs LLin SLim
	- var. ***latifolia***	CDul CLnd GKir LCon LRav WDin
	- 'Spaan's Dwarf'	CDoC CKen GKir LCon LLin MAsh MBar MGos NLar SCoo SLim SPoG WEve
	coulteri ♀H4	CDul CMCN EPfP GKir GTSp LCon LLin SBig SSpi WNor
	densiflora	CDul CMCN GKir GTSp LEdu WNor
	- SF 99088	ISea
	- 'Alice Verkade'	CDoC CRob EHul GKir LBee LCon LLin LRHS MAsh MBri NDlv SCoo SLim WEve WFar
	- 'Aurea'	MBar MGos SLim
	- 'Jane Kluis'	CKen COtt EHul GKir LBee LLin LRHS MAsh MBri NDlv NLar SCoo SLim WEve
I	- 'Jim Cross'	CKen
	- 'Low Glow'	CKen
	- 'Oculus-draconis' (v)	GKir LLin MBar MGos SCoo SLim SPoG WEve
	- 'Pendula'	CKen EOrn GKir LLin MBri NEgg SLim WEve WFar
*	- 'Pyramidalis'	ECho
	- 'Umbraculifera'	CDoC GKir IMGH LCon LLin MAsh MBar MGos NLar SSta WEve WFar
I	- 'Umbraculifera Nana'	LLin
§	***devoniana***	CBrP LCon LRHS MAsh SLim
	edulis	CAgr
	- 'Juno'	CKen
	elliottii	SBig
	flexilis	CDul GKir LCon
	- 'Firmament'	LLin SLim
	- 'Glenmore Dwarf'	CKen
	- 'Nana'	CKen
	- 'Pendula'	LLin
I	- 'Pygmaea'	NLar
	- 'Vanderwolf's Pyramid'	CRob GKir MAsh MBri NLar
	- WB No. 1	CKen
	- WB No. 2	CKen
	gerardiana	GKir
	greggii	CTho EPfP
	griffithii	see *P. wallichiana*
	halepensis	ECrN
§	***heldreichii*** ♀H4	CDoC GKir LCon LRav MBar SCoo WNor
	- 'Aureospicata'	LCon LLin MBar NLar WEve
	- 'Dolce Dorme' **new**	CKen
	- 'Groen'	CKen
	- var. ***leucodermis***	see *P. heldreichii*
	- - 'Compact Gem'	CDoC CKen EBrs GKir LBee LCon LLin LRHS MAsh MBar MBri MGos SCoo SLim SSta WEve
	- 'Malink'	CKen
	- 'Ottocek'	CKen
	- 'Pygmy'	CKen
	- 'Satellit'	CDoC CTri EHul EOrn GKir LCon LLin LRHS MAsh NLar SCoo SLim SPoG WEve
§	- 'Smidtii' ♀H4	CDoC CKen CRob EBrs LCon LLin MAsh MBar MGos NLar SLim
	- 'Zwerg Schneverdingen'	CKen
	jeffreyi ♀H4	CLnd CMCN CTrC GKir GTSp ISea LCon LRav MBar NWea WEve
	- 'Joppi'	CKen CRob
	koraiensis	GKir SLim WNor
	- 'Bergman'	CKen
	- 'Dragon Eye'	CKen
	- 'Jack Corbit'	CKen
	- 'Shibamichi' (v)	CKen
	- 'Silver Lining'	MAsh
	- 'Silveray'	GKir MAsh
	- 'Silvergrey'	CKen
	- 'Winton'	CKen EBrs
	leucodermis	see *P. heldreichii*
	longaeva	EPfP
	magnifica	see *P. devoniana*
	massoniana	ISea WNor
	monophylla	LLin
	montezumae ambig.	SAPC SArc WNor
	montezumae Lamb. **new**	SBig
	monticola	CDul
	- 'Pendula'	CKen MBar
	- 'Pygmy'	see *P. monticola* 'Raraflora'
§	- 'Raraflora'	CKen
	- 'Skyline'	MBar NLar WEve
	- 'Strobicola'	LCon
	- 'Windsor Dwarf'	CKen
	mugo	CBcs CDul CSBt CTri EHul ENot GKir MBar MGos NWea WBor WBrE WDin WEve WFar
	- 'Allgau' **new**	CKen
	- 'Benjamin'	CKen
	- 'Bisley Green'	LLin WEve
	- 'Brownie'	CKen
	- 'Carsten'	CKen EBrs LLin SLim SPoG WEve
	- 'Carsten's Wintergold'	LCon MAsh MBri SCoo WEve
	- 'Corley's Mat'	CKen GKir LLin MAsh SCoo SLim WEve
	- 'Devon Gem' **new**	SPoG
	- 'Dezember Gold' **new**	NLar SLim
	- 'Flanders Belle' **new**	SLim
	- 'Frohlings Gold' **new**	NLar
	- 'Gnom'	CDoC CMac EHul EOrn GKir IMGH LCon LLin LRHS MBar MBri MGos SCoo WDin WEve WFar
	- 'Golden Glow'	CKen LLin MBri SLim
	- 'Hoersholm'	CKen
	- 'Humpy'	CDoC CKen CMen CRob EOrn GKir IMGH LBee LCon LLin LRHS MAsh MBar MGos SCoo SLim WEve WFar
	- 'Jacobsen'	CKen NLar
	- 'Janovsky'	CKen
	- 'Kissen'	CKen LCon LLin MGos NLar WEve
	- 'Klosterkotter'	MGos NLar
	- 'Kobold'	NDlv WFar
	- 'Krauskopf'	CKen
	- 'Laarheide'	CRob MGos NLar WEve
	- 'Laurin'	CKen
	- 'Marand'	LLin
	- 'March'	CKen EHul LLin
	- 'Mini Mops'	CKen CMen NLar
	- 'Minikin'	CKen MAsh
	- 'Mops' ♀H4	CDoC CDul CRob EHul EPfP EPla GKir LBee LCon LLin LRHS MAsh MBar MBlu MGos SCoo SLim SPer SPoG SSta WDin WEve WFar
	- 'Mops Midget'	CRob GKir LBee LCon LLin MAsh MBri WEve
	- var. ***mughus***	see *P. mugo* subsp. *mugo*
§	- subsp. ***mugo***	EOrn GKir LBuc MAsh MBar NBlu NWea WEve WFar
	- 'Mumpitz'	CKen
	- 'Ophir'	CDoC CDul CKen CRob EBrs EHul EOrn EPfP EPla GKir IMGH LBee LCon LLin LRHS MAsh MBar MBri MGos SCoo SLim SPer SPla SSta WDin WEve WFar
	- 'Pal Maleter' (v)	CRob GKir LCon LLin MAsh NLar SCoo SLim SPoG WEve
	- 'Paul's Dwarf' **new**	CKen

	Name	Suppliers
	- 'Piggelmee'	CKen
	- Pumilio Group ♀H4	CDoC CLnd CMac EHul ENot EOrn GBin GKir LBee LCon LLin MBar MGos MLan NBlu NPal NWea SCoo SHBN STre WBVN WDin WFar WMoo WNor
	- 'Pygmy'	NDlv
	- var. ***rostrata***	see *P. mugo* subsp. *uncinata*
	- 'Rushmore'	CKen
	- 'Spaan'	CKen WEve
	- 'Sunshine' (v)	CKen GKir NLar
	- 'Suzi' **new**	CKen
	- 'Tuffet' **new**	LLin MGos NLar
§	- subsp. ***uncinata***	GIBF GKir NWea SLim WFar
	- - 'Grüne Welle'	CKen
	- - 'Paradekissen'	CKen NLar
	- 'Varella' **new**	CKen
	- 'White Tip'	CKen
	- 'Winter Gold'	CKen EBrs EHul EOrn EPfP GKir LCon LLin MAsh MGos NLar SCoo SPoG SSta WEve WFar
	- 'Winter Sun'	CRob GKir MAsh
	- 'Winzig'	CKen
	- 'Zundert'	CDoC CKen EHul GKir LLin MAsh MBar MGos NLar WEve
	- 'Zwergkugel'	CKen
	muricata ♀H4	CDoC CLnd GKir GTSp LCon LRav MGos NWea
	nigra ♀H4	CBcs CDoC CDul CLnd CSBt CTri ECrN GKir LCon MBar MGos SAPC SArc SHBN WBrE WDin WEve WMou
	- var. ***austriaca***	see *P. nigra* subsp. *nigra*
	- 'Bambino' **new**	CKen
	- 'Black Prince'	CDul CFee CKen EBrs EOrn GKir IMGH LBee LCon LLin LRHS MAsh MGos NLar SCoo SLim SPoG WEve WGor
N	- 'Cebennensis Nana'	CKen
	- var. ***corsicana***	see *P. nigra* subsp. *laricio*
*	- 'Fastigiata' **new**	EBrs
	- 'Frank'	CKen NLar
	- 'Hornibrookiana'	CKen GBin LLin SCoo
§	- subsp. ***laricio*** ♀H4	CAgr CDoC CDul CKen CSBt EMil ENot GKir GWCH LAst LBuc LCon LRav MBar NWea SBLw WMou
	- - 'Aurea' **new**	EBrs
	- - 'Bobby McGregor'	CKen GKir LLin SLim
	- - 'Globosa Viridis'	GKir IMGH LLin SLim WEve
	- - 'Goldfingers'	CKen LLin NLar WEve
§	- - 'Moseri'	CKen EOrn LLin SLim SSta
	- - 'Pygmaea'	CKen ECho EOrn NDlv WEve WFar
	- - 'Spingarn'	CKen
	- - 'Talland Bay'	CKen
	- - 'Wurstle'	CKen
	- subsp. ***maritima***	see *P. nigra* subsp. *laricio*
	- 'Nana'	CDoC LBee
§	- subsp. ***nigra***	CAgr CCVT CDoC CLnd ENot GKir LBuc MGos NWea SPer WEve WFar
	- - 'Birte' **new**	CKen
	- - 'Bright Eyes'	CFee CKen CRob ECho EOrn GKir IMGH LBee LCon LLin LRHS MAsh NLar SCoo SHGC SLim SPoG WEve
	- - 'Helga'	CKen
	- - 'Schovenhorst'	CKen
	- - 'Strypemonde'	CKen
	- - 'Yaffle Hill'	CKen
	- 'Obelisk'	CKen NLar
	- subsp. ***pallasiana***	CDul LCon NLar WPGP
	- 'Richard'	CKen
	- subsp. ***salzmannii***	GIBF

	Name	Suppliers
	- 'Uelzen'	CKen
	palustris	CDoC LCon LLin LRHS MAsh SBig SLim SSpi
	parviflora	CDul CTri GKir STre WDin WNor
	- 'Adcock's Dwarf' ♀H4	CDoC CKen GKir LCon LLin MBar MGos NLar SLim SPoG
	- Aizu-goyo Group	LLin
	- 'Al Fordham'	CKen
	- 'Aoi'	CKen CMen
	- 'Ara-kawa'	CKen CMen
	- Azuma-goyo Group	CKen
I	- 'Baasch's Form'	CKen MGos
	- 'Bergman'	LCon MAsh MBar NLar
	- 'Blauer Engel' **new**	MGos
	- 'Blue Giant'	ECho NLar
	- 'Bonnie Bergman'	CKen LLin WEve
	- 'Dai-ho'	CKen
	- 'Daisetsusan'	CKen
	- 'Doctor Landis Gold'	CKen
	- 'Fatsumo' **new**	CKen
	- 'Fukai' (v)	CKen MGos NLar
	- 'Fukiju'	CKen
	- Fukushima-goyo Group	CKen CMen WEve
	- 'Fuku-zu-mi'	CKen LLin WEve
	- 'Fu-shiro'	CKen
	- 'Gin-sho-chuba'	CKen
	- Glauca Group	CDoC CMac CRob EHul LCon LLin MAsh MBar MBlu MBri MGos NPal SPoG WEve WFar
I	- 'Glauca Nana'	CKen
I	- 'Goldilocks'	CKen
	- 'Gyok-ke-sen'	CKen
	- 'Gyo-ko-haku'	CKen
	- 'Gyokuei'	CKen
	- 'Gyokusen Sämling'	CKen NLar
	- 'Gyo-ku-sui'	CKen LLin
	- 'Hagaromo Seedling'	CKen LLin MAsh NLar
	- 'Hakko'	CKen
	- 'Hatchichi'	CKen
	- 'Ibo-can'	CKen CMen
	- 'Ichi-no-se'	CKen
	- 'Iri-fune'	CKen
	- Ishizuchi-goyo Group	CKen
	- 'Ka-ho'	CKen LLin
	- 'Kanzan'	CKen
	- 'Kiyomatsu'	CKen
	- 'Kobe'	CKen LLin WEve
	- 'Kokonoe'	CKen CMen LLin
	- 'Kokuho'	CKen
	- 'Koraku'	CKen
	- 'Kusu-dama'	CKen
	- 'Meiko'	CKen
	- 'Michinoku'	CKen
	- 'Momo-yama'	CKen
	- 'Myo-jo'	CKen
	- Nasu-goyo Group	CKen
	- 'Negishi'	CDoC CKen CMen CRob LCon LLin LRHS MAsh MBri NLar SLim WEve
	- 'Ogon-janome'	CKen
	- 'Ossorio Dwarf'	CKen
	- 'Regenhold'	CKen
	- 'Richard Lee'	CKen
	- 'Ryo-ku-ho'	CKen
	- 'Ryu-ju'	CKen
	- 'Sa-dai-jin' **new**	CKen
	- 'San-bo'	CKen MBar MGos
§	- 'Saphir'	CKen ECho
	- 'Setsugekka'	CKen
	- 'Shika-shima'	CKen
	- Shiobara-goyo Group	CKen
	- 'Shizukagoten'	CKen
	- 'Shu-re'	CKen
	- 'Sieryoden'	CKen

	- 'Tani-mano-uki'	CKen
	- 'Tempelhof'	COtt CTho GKir LRHS MAsh MBar NBlu SLim
	- 'Templeflora'	MLan
	- 'Tenysu-kazu'	CKen
I	- 'Torulosa'	LLin
	- 'Tribune' **new**	NLar
	- 'Venus'	NDlv
	- 'Watnong' **new**	CKen
I	- 'Zelkova'	CMen LLin
	- 'Zui-sho'	CKen
	patula ♀H2-3	CAbb CBcs CDoC CDul CFwr CLnd CTrC ECre EGra GKir LAst LCon LRav SAPC SArc SBig SBir SCoo SIFN SLim SPlb SPoG WEve
	peuce	CDoC EHoe GKir LCon LRav MBar NWea STre
	- 'Arnold Dwarf'	CKen
	- 'Cesarini'	CKen
	pinaster ♀H4	CAgr CBcs CDoC CLnd EHul GKir LCon WBVN
	pinea ♀H4	CAgr CDoC CFil CKen CLnd CMac CTho ECrN EPfP GIBF GKir LCon LEdu LRHS LRav MGos SAPC SArc SBLw SCoo SEND WEve WNor WPGP
	- 'Queensway'	CKen
	ponderosa ♀H4	CDul CLnd CMCN GTSp LCon LRav WEve WPGP
	pumila	CRob NEgg
	- from Kamchatka **new**	GIBF
	- 'Buchanan'	CKen
	- 'Draijer's Dwarf'	CDoC EOrn GKir LLin SCoo SLim
	- 'Dwarf Blue'	CRob MAsh NDlv
§	- 'Glauca' ♀H4	CKen LLin LRHS MAsh MBar
	- 'Globe'	GKir LBee LCon LLin MAsh MBri
	- 'Jeddeloh'	CKen
	- 'Knightshayes'	CKen
	- 'Säntis'	CKen
	- 'Saphir'	see *P. parviflora* 'Saphir'
	radiata ♀H3-4	CAgr CBcs CDoC CDul CSBt CTrC CTri CTrw ECrN ELan ENot GBin GKir LCon LRHS LRav NWea SAPC SArc SHBN STre WDin WEve
	- Aurea Group	CDoC CDul CKen CTho EOrn GKir LBee LCon LLin LRHS MAsh MBri SBir SCoo SLim SMur WEve WFar
	- 'Bodnant'	CKen
	- 'Isca'	CKen
	- 'Marshwood' (v)	CKen LCon SLim
	- var. ***radiata***	NPal
	resinosa	GIBF
	- 'Don Smith'	CKen
	- 'Joel's Broom'	CKen
	- 'Quinobequin'	CKen
	rigida	LCon
	roxburghii	GKir ISea LCon SSpi
	x ***schwerinii***	CDoC GKir LCon LRHS MAsh
	- 'Wiethorst'	CKen
	sibirica	GIBF
	strobiformis	ISea LCon
	strobus	CDul CMen CTho EMil GKir ISea LCon MBar NWea SLim STre WDin WEve WNor
§	- 'Alba'	MGos SLim
	- 'Amelia's Dwarf'	CKen
	- 'Anna Fiele'	CKen
	- 'Bergman's Mini'	CKen NLar
	- 'Bergman's Pendula Broom'	CKen
I	- 'Bergman's Sport of Prostrata'	CKen
	- 'Bloomer's Dark Globe'	CKen
	- 'Blue Shag'	CKen COtt EMil EOrn GKir LLin MGos NLar SLim SPoG WEve
	- 'Cesarini'	CKen
	- 'Densa'	CKen LCon MAsh
	- 'Dove's Dwarf'	CKen
	- 'Ed's Broom'	CKen
	- 'Elkins Dwarf'	CKen
	- 'Fastigiata'	CKen GBin GKir IMGH LLin MBri SPoG
	- 'Greg'	CKen
	- 'Hershey' **new**	CKen
	- 'Hillside Gem'	CKen
	- 'Himmelblau'	NLar SLim
	- 'Horsford'	CKen LLin MBlu
	- 'Jericho'	CKen EOrn
	- 'Krügers Lilliput'	GKir LCon LLin LRHS MBri NLar SCoo SLim
	- 'Louie'	CKen NLar SLim
	- 'Macopin'	MGos NLar
	- 'Mary Butler'	CKen
	- 'Merrimack'	CKen
	- 'Minima'	CKen EOrn LBee LCon LLin LRHS MAsh MBar MBlu MBri MGos SCoo SLim SPoG WEve WGor
	- 'Minuta'	CKen
	- 'Nana'	see *P. strobus* Nana Group
	- Nana Group	LLin
	- 'Nivea'	see *P. strobus* 'Alba'
	- 'Northway Broom'	CKen LCon LLin SLim
	- 'Ontario'	MBlu
	- 'Pendula'	CKen
I	- 'Pendula Broom' **new**	CKen
§	- 'Radiata'	CTri EHul EPla GKir LCon MBar NLar SLim SPoG
I	- 'Radiata Aurea'	WEve
	- 'Reinshaus'	CKen LLin
	- 'Sayville'	CKen
	- 'Sea Urchin'	CKen SLim
	- 'Uncatena'	CKen
	- 'Verkade's Broom'	CKen
	sylvestris ♀H4	More than 30 suppliers
	- 'Abergeldie'	CKen
	- 'Alderly Edge'	CMen WEve WFar
	- 'Andorra'	CKen MAsh
§	- 'Argentea'	SLim
§	- Aurea Group ♀H4	CDul CKen CMac CMen EBrs EHul EPfP GBin GKir IMGH LBee LCon LLin LRHS MAsh MBar SCoo SHBN SLim SPer SSta WEve
	- 'Aurea'	see *P. sylvestris* Aurea Group
	- 'Avondene'	CKen
	- 'Bergfield'	NLar WEve
	- 'Beuvronensis' ♀H4	CKen CLnd CMac CMen EOrn GKir IMGH LBee LLin LRHS MAsh MGos SCoo SLim WEve
	- 'Bonna'	GKir LCon SCoo SIFN SLim
	- 'Brevifolia'	MBar
	- 'Buchanan's Gold'	CKen
	- 'Burghfield'	CKen LLin WEve
	- 'Chantry Blue'	CDoC CMen CRob EHul EOrn GKir IMGH LBee LCon LLin LRHS MAsh MBar MGos NLar SCoo SLim WEve WFar
	- 'Clumber Blue'	CKen
	- 'Compressa'	LLin SLim
	- 'Corley'	GKir LLin
	- 'Dereham'	CKen LLin
	- 'Doone Valley'	CKen GKir LLin MGos NLar WEve
	- 'Edwin Hillier'	see *P. sylvestris* 'Argentea'
	- Fastigiata Group	CDoC CEnd CKen CMen CRob EOrn GKir IMGH LBee LCon LLin

	LRHS MAsh MBar MGos SCoo SLim SPoG WEve WFar
- 'Frensham'	CDoC CKen EOrn IMGH LCon LLin MAsh MGos WEve WFar
- 'Globosa'	GKir LRHS WEve
- 'Gold Coin'	CDoC CKen EOrn EPfP GKir LBee LCon LLin MAsh MGos NLar SCoo SLim SPoG WFar
- 'Gold Medal'	CKen GKir LLin SIFN SLim WEve
- 'Grand Rapids'	CKen
- 'Gwydyr Castle'	CKen
- 'Hibernia'	CRob
- 'Hillside Creeper'	CKen GKir LCon LLin NLar SCoo SLim WEve
- 'Inverleith' (v)	EHul GKir LBuc LCon LLin MBar MGos SCoo SLim SPoG WEve
- 'Jeremy'	CKen EBrs LCon LLin SCoo SLim SPoG WEve
- 'John Boy'	CMen LLin NLar
- 'Kelpie'	LLin SLim
- 'Kenwith'	CKen
- 'Lakeside Dwarf'	LLin WEve
- 'Lodge Hill'	CMen CRob EBrs EOrn GKir IMGH LCon LLin LRHS MAsh SCoo SLim WEve
- 'Longmoor'	CKen NLar
- 'Martham'	CKen LLin WEve
- var. ***mongolica***	GIBF
* - 'Moseri'	ECho GKir LBee LRHS MAsh SPoG WEve
- 'Munches Blue'	CKen
- 'Nana' misapplied	see *P. sylvestris* 'Watereri'
- 'Nana Compacta'	CMen GKir LLin
§ - 'Nisbet's Gem'	CKen LLin NLar
- 'Padworth'	CKen CMen LLin NLar
- 'Pixie'	CKen LLin NLar
I - 'Prostrata'	GKir SCoo
- 'Pulham'	LLin WEve
- 'Pygmaea'	GKir SCoo SLim
- 'Reedham'	LLin WEve
- 'Repens'	CKen
- 'Saint George'	CKen
- 'Sandringham'	LLin WEve
- 'Saxatilis'	CKen EOrn GKir LBee LCon LLin MAsh WEve
- subsp. ***scotica***	GIBF
- 'Scott's Dwarf'	see *P. sylvestris* 'Nisbet's Gem'
- 'Scrubby'	LLin NLar
- 'Sentinel'	CKen SLim
- 'Skjak I'	CKen
- 'Skjak II'	CKen LLin
- 'Spaan's Slow Column'	CKen SLim
- 'Tabuliformis'	LLin
- 'Tage'	CKen LLin WEve
- 'Tanya'	CKen MAsh
- 'Tilhead'	CKen
- 'Treasure'	CKen LLin
- 'Variegata' (v)	WEve
§ - 'Watereri'	CMac EHul GKir IMGH LBee LCon LLin LRHS MAsh MBar SCoo SLim SPer WDin WEve WFar
- 'Westonbirt'	CKen CMen EHul LLin MAsh WEve
- 'Wishmoor'	LLin WEve
- 'Wolf Gold'	CKen
tabuliformis	CDul CMCN GIBF GKir IDee ISea LCon MBlu
thunbergii	CDul CLnd EHul GKir GTSp LCon LLin MGos STre WNor
- 'Akame'	CKen CMen
- 'Akame Yatsabusa'	CMen
- 'Aocha-matsu' (v)	CKen CMen NLar
- 'Arakawa-sho'	CKen CMen
- 'Banshosho'	CKen CMen NLar
- 'Beni-kujaku'	CKen CMen
- 'Compacta'	CKen CMen
- 'Dainagon'	CKen CMen
- 'Iwai'	CMen
- 'Katsuga'	CMen
- 'Kotobuki'	CKen CMen CRob GKir NLar
- 'Koyosho'	CMen GKir
- 'Kujaku'	CKen CMen
- 'Kyushu'	CKen CMen
- 'Miyajuna'	CKen CMen
- 'Nishiki-ne'	CKen CMen
- 'Nishiki-tsusaka'	CMen
- 'Oculus-draconis' (v)	CMen GKir LBuc LLin
- 'Ogon'	CKen CMen EBrs NLar
- 'Porky'	CKen CMen
§ - 'Sayonara'	CKen CMen GKir LLin MAsh NLar SLim
- 'Senryu'	CKen CMen
- 'Shinsho'	CKen CMen
- 'Shio-guro'	CKen CMen
- 'Suchiro Yatabusa'	CKen CMen
- 'Sunsho'	CKen CMen
- 'Taihei'	CKen CMen
I - 'Thunderhead'	CKen CMen NLar
- 'Yatsubusa'	see *P. thunbergii* 'Sayonara'
- 'Ye-i-kan' **new**	CKen
- 'Yumaki'	CKen CMen
uncinata	see *P. mugo* subsp. *uncinata*
- 'Jezek'	CKen NLar
- 'Kostelnicek' **new**	NLar
- 'Leuco-like' **new**	CKen
- 'Offenpass' **new**	CKen
- 'Susse Perle'	CKen
virginiana 'Wate's Golden'	CKen
§ ***wallichiana*** ♀H4	CDoC CDul CKen CMCN CRob CTho EHul EPfP EPla GKir LCon LLin MAsh MBar MBlu MGos NEgg NWea SBir SLim SSpi STre WDin WEve WFar WGer WNor WOrn WPGP
- SF 00001	ISea
- 'Nana'	CKen EHul LCon LLin MBar NLar SCoo SLim WEve
- 'Umbraculifera'	LRHS MBri
- 'Zebrina' (v)	LBee MAsh MBar MGos NLar SMad WEve
yunnanensis	GIBF GKir SSpi WBor WEve WNor

Piper (*Piperaceae*)

betle	MSal
excelsum	see *Macropiper excelsum*
nigrum	MSal

Piptanthus (*Papilionaceae*)

forrestii	see *P. nepalensis*
laburnifolius	see *P. nepalensis*
§ ***nepalensis***	More than 30 suppliers
- B&SWJ 2241	WCru
aff. ***nepalensis***	GIBF
tomentosus	CFil WPGP

Pistacia (*Anacardiaceae*)

atlantica	EGFP
chinensis	CBcs CBrd CMCN CPMA EPfP SSpi WPic XPep
lentiscus	CBcs XPep
terebinthus	XPep

Pistia (*Araceae*)

stratiotes	LPBA NArg NPer SCoo

Pitcairnia (*Bromeliaceae*)

heterophylla **new**	WCot

Pithecoctenium (*Bignoniaceae*)

***cynanchiodes* new**	CPLN

Pittosporum ✿ (*Pittosporaceae*)

anomalum	ECou
- (f)	ECou
- (m)	ECou
- 'Falcon'	ECou
- 'Raven' (f)	ECou
- 'Starling' (m)	ECou
'Arundel Green'	CDoC CWSG EPfP LRHS SLim SPoG SWvt
bicolor	CFil CPle ECou EShb GQui SAPC SArc WBor WPGP
- 'Cradle' (f)	ECou
- 'Mount Field' (f)	ECou
buchananii	SGar WCwm
colensoi	CTrC ECou
- 'Cobb' (f)	ECou
- 'Wanaka' (m)	ECou
crassifolium	CFil CHEx CPle ECou ERea IDee WPGP XPep
- 'Compactum'	XPep
- 'Havering Dwarf' (f)	ECou
- 'Napier' (f)	ECou
- 'Variegatum' (v)	CPne WSPU
crassifolium* x *tenuifolium	CWib ECou SWvt
'Craxten' (f)	ECou EJRN
'Crinkles' (f)	ECou
daphniphylloides B&SWJ 6789	WCru
- var. ***adaphniphylloides***	CFil
'Dark Delight' (m)	ECou
divaricatum	ECou
'Essex' (f/v)	ECou EJRN
eugenioides	CBcs CHEx CMHG CPen CTrC GGar IDee SLon
- 'Mini Green' **new**	CAlb CPen LSou NLar
- 'Platinum' (v)	CBcs MGos
- 'Tens Gold' **new**	CPen
- 'Variegatum' (v) ♀H3	CAbb CAlb CBcs CBrm CDoC CHEx EMil EPfP GGar GQui IArd LRHS SAga SLim SPer SSpi SSto WGer WPGP WSHC WSPU
'Garnettii' (v) ♀H3	More than 30 suppliers
heterophyllum	CPen ECou XPep
- 'Ga Blanca' **new**	CPen
- variegated (v)	ECou SLim SSpi WSHC
'Humpty Dumpty'	ECou
illicioides* var. *illicioides B&SWJ 6712	WCru
'Limelight' (v)	CBcs CPen CSBt CSPN CTrC EMil LRHS SPoG WWes
lineare	ECou
§ 'Margaret Turnbull' (v)	CBcs CMHG CPen CTrC ECou EMil EWes IArd LRHS LSRN MGos WBcn
michiei	ECou
- (f)	ECou
- (m)	ECou
- 'Jack' (m)	ECou
- 'Jill' (f)	ECou
'Nanum Variegatum'	see *P. tobira* 'Variegatum'
obcordatum	ECou
- var. ***kaitaiaense***	ECou
omeiense	CFil ECou ECre EWes
phillyreoides	CFil XPep
pimeleoides* var. *reflexum (m)	ECou
'Purple Princess'	ECou EJRN
ralphii	ECou WPic
- 'Green Globe'	ECou XPep
- 'Variegatum' (v)	SSpi WPGP
* ***robustum***	EWes
'Saundersii' (v)	CBcs ECrN
tenuifolium ♀H3	More than 30 suppliers
- 'Abbotsbury Gold' (f/v)	CAbb CBcs CChe CDoC CMac CSam CTri EBee ECou ECrN ELan EMil EWes GBri LRHS SAga SEND SHBN SLim SPer SSto WSHC
- 'Atropurpureum'	CBcs WBcn
- 'County Park Dwarf'	CPen EBee ECou EJRN WCru
- 'Deborah' (v)	ECou EHol EJRN LRHS LSou WBcn
- 'Dixie'	CPen ECou
§ - 'Eila Keightley' (v)	CMHG SAga
- 'Elizabeth' (m/v)	CDoC CMac CPen CTrC EBee ECou LRHS WBcn
- 'French Lace'	CBcs CPen EBee ECou NLar WFar WWeb
- 'Gold Star'	CBcs CDoC CPen CTrC ECou EMil ENot LAst LRHS NPal SCoo SLim SPoG
- 'Golden Cut' **new**	NLar
- 'Golden King'	CDoC CMHG CMac CSBt LRHS LSou NScw SLim SPoG SRms SSto WWeb
- 'Golden Princess' (f)	ECou EJRN
- 'Green Elf'	CTrC ECou EJRN
- 'Green Thumb'	CWSG LRHS
- 'Irene Paterson' (m/v) ♀H3	More than 30 suppliers
- 'James Stirling'	CPMA ECou EPfP LRHS SSto
- 'John Flanagan'	see *P.* 'Margaret Turnbull'
- 'Loxhill Gold'	CPen EBee LRHS LSou NScw SSto
- 'Marjory Channon' (v)	CBcs LRHS SSpi
- 'Mellow Yellow'	CAbP LRHS WBcn
- 'Moonlight' (v)	CTrC
- 'Mountain Green' **new**	LSou
- 'Nutty's Leprechaun' **new**	SPoG
- 'Pompom' **new**	SPoG
- 'Purpureum' (m)	CBrm CMac CPle CSBt CSam CTri CTrw ECou EPfP LAst LRHS LSRN LSpr MWgw SAga SCoo SHBN SPer SPla SPoG SRms SSto WGer WSHC
- 'Silver Magic' (v)	CBcs CPen CSBt EJRN EMil MGos
- 'Silver 'n' Gold'	LRHS
- 'Silver Princess' (f)	ECou EJRN
- 'Silver Queen' (f/v) ♀H3	More than 30 suppliers
- 'Silver Sheen' (m)	CBcs CPen ECou LRHS
- 'Stirling Gold' (f/v)	ECou EPfP EWes
- 'Sunburst'	see *P. tenuifolium* 'Eila Keightley'
- 'Tandara Gold' (v)	CAbb CAlb CBrm CDoC CTrC ECou EJRN EMil ENot EPfP LSRN SLim SPla SPoG WFar WGer WWeb
- 'Tiki' (m)	CBcs CTrC ECou
- 'Tom Thumb' ♀H3	More than 30 suppliers
- 'Tresederi' (f/m)	CBrm CMac CTrC CTrw ECou LRHS
- 'Variegatum' (m/v)	CBcs CDoC CSBt ECou EMil GBri LAst LRHS SPoG SWvt
- 'Victoria' (v)	CDoC CPen CTrC EBee EMil SPoG
- 'Warnham Gold' (m) ♀H3	CMac COtt CSBt CTrw CWib EBee ECou ECrN ELan EPfP GBri LAst LRHS MCCP SCoo SLim SPoG SSpi WAbe WDin
- 'Wendle Channon' (m/v)	CBcs CMHG CMac CSBt CSam CTrC ECot ECou EPfP LRHS NCGa SLim SPer SSto WBcn
- 'Winter Sunshine'	LRHS SSta
tobira ♀H3	More than 30 suppliers
- B&SWJ 4362	WCru
* - 'Cuneatum'	SAga
* - 'Nanum'	CBcs CDoC EBee ECou ELan EPfP ERea MGos MWya SAPC SArc SLim SPoG WBcn WDin WGer XPep

§	- 'Variegatum' (v) ♀H2-3	CBcs CBot CMac CPle CSam EBee ECou ECrN ELan EPfP EUJe GQui LRHS MWya NPal SAga SDnm SLim SLon SPer SPla SPoG SSta SSto WBcn WCru WDin WGer WSHC XPep
	truncatum	ECre EWes XPep
*	- 'Variegatum'	XPep
	undulatum	CHEx CPen ECou
	viridiflorum	ECou EShb

Plagianthus (*Malvaceae*)

	betulinus	see *P. regius*
	divaricatus	CBcs CFil CTrC ECou ECre WPGP
	lyallii	see *Hoberia lyallii*
§	***regius***	CBcs CTrC ECou GGar GQui LRHS SBig

Plagiobothrys (*Boraginaceae*)

	figuratus **new**	LRav

Plagiorhegma see *Jeffersonia*

Plantago (*Plantaginaceae*)

	asiatica	MSal
	- 'Ki Fu' (v)	ITer MAvo
	- 'Variegata' (v)	CRow EMan GBuc MBNS NBro NLar WGwG WWye
	camtschatica **new**	EPPr
	cynops	MTho XPep
	holosteum	GKev
	lanceolata	NMir
	- 'Ballydowling Variegated' (v)	EBee EChP
	- 'Blond Bomi-noka'	CNat
	- 'Bomi-noka'	CNat
	- 'Burren Rose'	CBgR CRow
	- 'Dent's Downs Link' (v) **new**	WCot
	- 'Golden Spears'	CBgR CBre EBee EChP NSti SBch
	- 'Keer's Pride' (v)	WCot
	- 'Pink Bomi-noka'	CNat
	- 'Streaker' (v)	CRow EBee WCot WHal
	major 'Atropurpurea'	see *P. major* 'Rubrifolia'
	- 'Bowles' Variety'	see *P. major* 'Rosularis'
	- 'Frills'	CBre CNat CRow EBee WHer
*	- 'Karmozijn'	EMan
§	- 'Rosularis'	CArn CNat CRow CSpe EChP ILis ITer LEdu MAnH MHer MTho MWgw NBid NBro NChi NEgg NLsd NWCA SBch SPav WEas WHer WPer WWye
§	- 'Rubrifolia'	CArn CHid CPom CRow CSpe EBee EChP EMag IHMH ITer LDai MHer MWgw NBid NBro NChi NEgg NLsd NSti WBVN WCAu WHer WMoo WPer WRos WWye
	- 'Tony Lewis'	CNat
	maritima	WHer
	media	CBgR MHer WBWf
	nivalis	EBee SMad
	psyllium L.	CArn MSal
	raoulii	NChi WCot
	rosea	see *P. major* 'Rosularis'
	uniflora Hook. f.	WCot

Platanthera (*Orchidaceae*)

	hologlottis	EFEx
	metabifolia	EFEx

Platanus ✿ (*Platanaceae*)

	x ***acerifolia***	see *P.* x *hispanica*
§	x ***hispanica*** ♀H4	CBcs CCVT CDul CLnd CMCN CTho EBee ECrN EMil ENot EPfP GKir LBuc LRHS MGos NWea SBLw SEND SHBN SPer STre WDin WFar WMou
	- 'Bloodgood'	SBLw
	- 'Dakvorm'	SBLw
	- 'Dortmund'	SBLw
	- 'Pyramidalis'	CTho SBLw WOrn
	- 'Suttneri' (v)	CEnd CLnd CTho SBLw SMad WBcn WMou
	- 'Tremonia'	LRHS
	occidentalis	NEgg
	orientalis ♀H4	CCVT CDul CLnd CMCN CTho EBee ECrN EPfP LEdu NLar NWea SBLw SDix SLPl WDin WMou
	- MSF 0028 from Sfendili, Crete	WPGP
	- 'Cuneata'	GKir LRHS MBri
§	- f. ***digitata*** ♀H4	CDoC CDul CLnd CMCN CTho ENot EPfP ERod MBlu SBLw SLPl SMad WMou
	- var. ***insularis***	CEnd
	- 'Laciniata'	see *P. orientalis* f. *digitata*
	- 'Minaret'	EMil WMou
	- 'Mirkovec'	CDoC LRHS MBri SMad SPer WMou

Platycarya (*Juglandaceae*)

	strobilacea	CBcs EPfP

Platycerium (*Polypodiaceae*)

	alcicorne hort.	see *P. bifurcatum*
§	***bifurcatum*** ♀H1	LRHS MBri

Platycladus (*Cupressaceae*)

	orientalis 'Aurea Nana' ♀H4	CDoC CKen CMac CSBt CWib EHul ENot EPfP GKir IMGH ISea LBee LCon LLin LRHS MAsh MBar MBri NBlu NWea SLim SMer SPla SPoG WCFE WDin WEas WEve WFar WTel
	- 'Autumn Glow'	CKen CRob LBee LRHS MAsh SCoo SPoG WGor
	- 'Beverleyensis'	LLin NLar WEve
	- 'Blue Cone'	MBar WEve
	- 'Caribbean Holiday'	MAsh
	- 'Collen's Gold'	CTri EHul EOrn MAsh MBar WBcn
	- 'Conspicua'	CKen CWib EHul LBee LRHS MAsh MBar
	- 'Elegantissima' ♀H4	CMac EHul EOrn LBee LRHS MAsh MBar SCoo
	- 'Golden Minaret'	WBcn
	- 'Golden Pillar'	EOrn
	- 'Golden Pygmy'	CKen EOrn MAsh WBcn
	- 'Juniperoides'	EHul MBar
	- 'Kenwith'	CKen
	- 'Lemon 'n' Lime'	SPoG WEve
	- 'Little Susie' **new**	CRob
	- 'Madurodam'	LLin MBar
	- 'Magnifica'	EHul
	- 'Meldensis'	CDoC CTri EHul MBar WTel
	- 'Minima'	CRob EHul WGor
	- 'Minima Glauca'	CKen MBar
	- 'Mint Chocolate'	LLin
	- 'Purple King'	LRHS SCoo SLim SPoG
I	- 'Pyramidalis Aurea'	LBee LCon LRHS NBlu WEve
	- 'Rosedalis'	CKen CMac CSBt EHul ENot EOrn EPfP LBee LCon LLin LRHS MAsh MBar MBri SCoo SLim SMer SPla SPoG WEve WFar WTel
	- 'Sanderi'	MBar WCFE
	- 'Semperaurea'	CMac IMGH
	- 'Shirley Chilcott'	MAsh

- 'Sieboldii'	EHul
- 'Southport'	LBee LCon LLin LRHS MAsh
- 'Summer Cream'	CKen EHul MBar
- 'Westmont' (v)	CKen CSBt EOrn WBcn

Platycodon ✿ (*Campanulaceae*)

grandiflorus ♀H4	CArn CBot CMea COlW CTri EBrs ECha ELau EPot GKev LEdu MAnH MBow MHer MNrw MSal NEgg SGar SGSe SRms WBrE WHoo WWye
- 'Albus'	CBro CSec EBee EChP EPfP GKev LAst MBri SPer SPla SWvt WHoo WPer
- 'Apoyama' ♀H4	CLyd CStu EBee GKev GMac LBee LRHS NMen WHoo WPer
- ***apoyama albus***	CStu GKev WEas WHoo
- - 'Fairy Snow'	EBee ELan EMar EShb WHoo WSel
- (Astra Series) 'Astra Blue'	NEgg WHil WHoo
- - 'Astra Double Blue' (d)	NEgg
- - 'Astra Pink' **new**	WHoo
- - 'Astra White' **new**	WHoo
- 'Blue Haze'	EBee
- 'Blue Pearl'	WHoo
- 'Florist Rose'	SGSe WWye
- 'Florist Snow'	SGSe WWye
- 'Fuji Blue'	EBee ITim LAst LIck NBro NLar SPet SPur WGwG WSel
- 'Fuji Pink'	CBro EBee ELan EMar EPfP ERou LAst MRav MTis NBro NEgg NLar SMrm SPer SPet SPoG SPur SWvt WCAu WSel
- 'Fuji White'	ELan ERou LAst NBro NLar SMrm SPet SPur WSel
- 'Hakone'	EMan MRav SMrm WHoo
- 'Hakone Blue'	ITim NLar
* - 'Hakone Double Blue' (d)	EBee ECGP ECrN ELan EMar LRHS MTis SBch SPoG SRms WCAu
- 'Hakone White'	CBot CBrm CMdw EBee ECGP GKev ITim NGby NLar NMen SBch SChu SGSe SMad SPet SPoG WCAu WHoo
- 'Mariesii' ♀H4	CBro CPLG CSBt EBee EChP ECtt EMar EPfP ERou GKir LRHS MRav MWgw NBir NEgg NMen SMrm SPer SPet SPla SRms SWvt WCAu WEas WHoo WPer
- ***mariesii albus***	WHoo
- 'Misato Purple'	WSel
- Mother of Pearl	see *P. grandiflorus* 'Perlmutterschale'
* - 'Nanus' **new**	GKev
- 'Park's Double Blue' (d)	WHoo
§ - 'Perlmutterschale'	CBot CBrm CM&M EBee EChP EMar EPPr EPfP EWTr MBNS MBri NEgg SPet WAul WCAu WHoo
- ***pumilus***	CStu EBee NChi NWCA WHoo
- ***roseus***	CNic MNrw NEgg
- 'Sentimental Blue'	CWib NJOw NLar
- 'Shell Pink'	see *P. grandiflorus* 'Perlmutterschale'
- white-flowered, double	CBro
- 'Zwerg'	GMac

Platycrater (*Hydrangeaceae*)

arguta	NLar WCru
- B&SWJ 6266	WCru

Plecostachys (*Asteraceae*)

§ ***serpyllifolia***	CHal MOak SPet

Plectranthus (*Lamiaceae*)

CC 4071	ITer
from Puerto Rico	CArn
ambiguus	EOHP
- 'Manguzuku'	EOHP
- 'Umigoye'	EOHP
amboinicus	CArn CHal EOHP MOak NHor
* - 'Variegatus' (v)	EOHP EUnu
- 'Well Sweep Wedgewood'	EOHP EUnu
argentatus ♀H2	CDoC CHad CHal CHrt CMdw CPLG CSev CSpe EMan EOHP EShb GGar MOak MSte MTis SAga SBch SDix SGar SHFr SUsu WDyG WKif WWlt
- 'Hill House' (v)	CHll CHrt CPne EMan EOHP EShb LDai MOak
australis misapplied	see *P. verticillatus*
behrii	see *P. fruticosus*
Blue Angel = 'Edelblau' **new**	EOHP
ciliatus	CPne EOHP LPhx MOak SGar WWlt
- 'All Gold'	CPne
- 'Easy Gold'	EOHP MOak
- 'Sasha'	CDoC CHal CHll EOHP EShb LAst LSou NPri
coleoides 'Marginatus'	see *P. forsteri* 'Marginatus'
- 'Variegatus'	see *P. madagascariensis* 'Variegated Mintleaf'
crassus	EOHP
Cuban oregano	EOHP WJek
cylindraceus **new**	EOHP LToo
ecklonii	EOHP
- 'Medley-Wood'	EOHP
ernstii	EOHP MOak
excisus	EMon
§ ***forsteri*** 'Marginatus'	CHal ERea MOak SGar
§ ***fruticosus***	CHal CPne EOHP GBri MOak
- 'Frills'	CPne EOHP
- 'James'	CPne EOHP
hadiensis var. ***tomentosus***	EOHP MOak
- - 'Carnegie'	EOHP
- - green-leaved	EOHP
I - 'Variegata'	CPne
hilliardiae	CPne
hirtellus gold	EOHP MOak
- variegated (v)	EOHP MOak
'Lavender Moment' **new**	CCtw
madagascariensis	CPne EOHP
- gold-leaved	EOHP
§ - 'Variegated Mintleaf' (v) ♀H1	CHal EOHP SHFr SPet SRms
menthol-scented, large-leaved	EOHP
menthol-scented, small-leaved	EOHP
neochilus **new**	LPhx
'Nico'	CSpe EOHP
§ ***oertendahlii*** ♀H1	CHal CPne EBak EOHP MOak SMur
- silver-leaved	EOHP
- 'Uvongo'	CPne
ornatus	EOHP MOak NHor NScw
- 'Pee Off' **new**	EOHP
purpuratus	EOHP
rehmannii	EOHP
saccatus	CPne EOHP GFai
spicatus	EOHP
- 'Nelspruit'	EOHP
- 'Ubombo'	EOHP
Swedish ivy	see *P. verticillatus*, *P. oertendahlii*
§ ***thyrsoideus***	CHal ECre EOHP SBch

§ ***verticillatus*** CHal EOHP
Vick's plant EOHP EUnu LSou
zatarhendii CPne EMan EOHP
zuluensis CDoC CFee CHal CMdw CPne CSpe EOHP EShb MOak SUsu WBor WHal
- dark-leaved EOHP
- 'Symphony' **new** CFee

Pleioblastus ✿ (*Poaceae*)

argenteostriatus **new** CTrC
§ - f. ***glaber*** (v) MAsh
§ - 'Okinadake' (v) EPla
§ - f. ***pumilus*** CDoC CSam EHoe ENot EPfP GKir LAst LRHS MBlu MMoz SPla SPlb WFar WJun WNor WPat WPer
auricomus see *P. viridistriatus*
- 'Vagans' see *Sasaella ramosa*
§ ***chino*** EPla
- var. ***argenteostriatus*** see *P. argenteostriatus* 'Okinadake'
- f. ***aureostriatus*** (v) EPla MMoz
- f. ***elegantissimus*** CDoC CEnd CFir EBee ENBC EPla EPza ERod LAst MGos MMoz MWhi NMoo SBig SEND SPoG WJun WMoo WPGP
fortunei see *P. variegatus*
* ***funghomii*** SEND
'Gauntlettii' see *P. argenteostriatus* f. *pumilus*
glaber 'Albostriatus' see *Sasaella masamuneana* f. 'Albostriata'
gramineus EPla WJun
§ ***hindsii*** EPla ERod MMoz NMoo SArc SEND
§ ***humilis*** ELan ENBC EPza SSto
- var. ***pumilus*** see *P. argenteostriatus* f. *pumilus*
kongosanensis 'Aureostriatus' (v) EPla
linearis CAbb CBcs CMCo EAmu EFul EPla ERod EShb LAst MMoz NMoo SBig WJun WMoo
longifimbriatus see *Sinobambusa intermedia*
oleosus EPla WJun
§ ***pygmaeus*** More than 30 suppliers
- 'Distichus' EFul EHul ENBC EPPr EPla LAst LRHS MGos MMoz MWht NDlv NGdn NMoo SSto WJun WMoo
§ - 'Mirrezuzume' CPLG WFar
* - var. ***pygmaeus*** 'Mini' WCot WWpP
§ ***simonii*** CBcs EFul GBin GCal LAst LRHS MBNS MMoz MWhi SArc SPoG
- var. ***heterophyllus*** see *P. simonii* 'Variegatus'
§ - 'Variegatus' (v) CFil EPla MBar NGdn SPer WJun WPGP
§ ***variegatus*** (v) ♀H4 More than 30 suppliers
- 'Tsuboii' (v) CAbb CBig CDoC CKno CTrC ENBC EPPr EPla ERod GQui IFro LAst LPJP LRHS MBNS MBrN MBri MMoz MWhi MWht NMoo WFar WJun WMoo WMul WPGP WPnP
- var. ***viridis*** see *P. argenteostriatus* f. *glaber*
viridistriatus ♀H4 More than 30 suppliers
- 'Chrysophyllus' EPla MMoz SMad WJun
- f. ***variegatus*** (v) CHEx CHar EPza SAga SWvt WMoo

Pleione ✿ (*Orchidaceae*)

albiflora CHdy
Alishan g. CHdy CNic GCrs
- 'Foxhill' NSpr
- 'Merlin' LBut NSpr
- 'Mount Fuji' LBut
- 'Soldier Blue' LBut
Asama g. CHdy
- 'Bittern' LBut
- 'Red Grouse' LBut
aurita EPot LBut NSpr
Bandai-san g. LBut
- 'Sand Grouse' **new** LBut
x ***barbarae*** LBut NSpr
Barcena g. CHdy LBut
Berapi g. CHdy LBut
- 'Purple Sandpiper' **new** LBut
Brigadoon g. CHdy EPot GCrs LBut NSpr NWCA
- 'Stonechat' LBut
Britannia g. CHdy LBut
- 'Doreen' EPot LBut NSpr
§ ***bulbocodioides*** EPot ERos LBut NSpr
- Limprichtii Group see *P. limprichtii*
- Pricei Group see *P. formosana* Pricei Group
§ - 'Yunnan' EPot NSpr
Burnsall g. NSpr
Captain Hook g. LBut NSpr
Chinese Dragon g. NSpr
§ ***chunii*** EFEx LAma
x ***confusa*** CHdy EPot LBut
Danan g. LBut
Deriba g. EPot LBut
Eiger g. CHdy EPot ERos LBut NSpr
- cream ERos LBut
- 'Pinchbeck Diamond' GCrs
El Pico g. GCrs
- 'Goldcrest' EPot NSpr
- 'Kestrel' EPot
- 'Pheasant' LBut NSpr
- 'Starling' LBut
Erebus g. CHdy
- 'Quail' LBut
Erh Hai g. NSpr
Etna g. CHdy EPot GCrs LBut
Follifoot g. 'Princess Tiger' NSpr
formosana ♀H2 CKob CStu EFEx EPot ETow GBuc GCrs LAma NCGa SAga WFar WPGP WPnP
- 'Achievement' LBut
- Alba Group CHdy GCrs WFar
- - 'Claire' CHdy EPot ERos GCrs LBut NSpr
- - 'Roydon' EPot
- - 'Snow Bunting' LBut
- 'Avalanche' LBut NSpr
- 'Blush of Dawn' CHdy GCrs LBut NSpr NWCA
- 'Cairngorm' NSpr
- 'Chen' CHdy
- 'Christine Anne' CHdy NSpr
- 'Eugenie' CHdy
- 'Greenhill' LBut
I - 'Iris' CHdy EPot
- 'Lilac Jubilee' CHdy
- 'Little Winnie' EPot
- 'Lucy Diamond' EPot NSpr
- 'Lulu' CHdy
- 'Pitlochry' LBut
- 'Polar Sun' CHdy NSpr
§ - Pricei Group EPot ERos ETow
- - 'Oriental Grace' CHdy LBut
- - 'Oriental Splendour' CHdy LBut
- 'Red Spot' EPot
- 'Snow White' EPot GCrs LBut
forrestii EFEx EPot LAma
Fu Manchu g. NSpr
Fuego g. CHdy NSpr
Gerry Mundey g. LBut NSpr
Giacomo Leopardi g. NSpr
§ ***grandiflora*** LBut
Heathfield g. NSpr
Hekla g. CHdy EPot ERos GCrs NSpr

- 'Partridge' LBut
Helgafell g. LBut
hookeriana GCrs
humilis LBut NSpr
Irazu g. GCrs NSpr
Jorullo g. CHdy LBut NSpr
- 'Long-tailed Tit' LBut
Katla g. CHdy
Katmai g. LBut
Keith Rattray g. 'Kelty' LBut
Kenya g. LBut
Kilauea g. EPot LBut
- 'Curlew' LBut
Kituro g. LBut
Kohala g. LBut
x ***kohlsii*** **new** NSpr
Krakatoa g. NSpr
Kublai Khan g. **new** NSpr
§ ***limprichtii*** ♀H2 EFEx EPot ETow LBut NSpr WPnP
maculata EFEx
Marco Polo g. LBut NSpr
Marion Johnson g. **new** LBut
Masaya g. LBut
Matupi g. NSpr
Mawenzi g. **new** LBut
Mazama g. LBut
Myojin g. CHdy LBut NSpr
Novarupta g. LBut
Orinoco g. CHdy LBut
- 'Gemini' LBut
Orizaba g. LBut
Paricutin g. LBut NSpr
Pavlof g. LBut
pinkepankii see *P. grandiflora*
Piton g. CHdy EPot LAma LBut
pleionoides LBut
- 'Blakeway-Phillips' CHdy
pogonioides misapplied see *P. pleionoides*
pogonioides (Rolfe) Rolfe see *P. bulbocodioides*
Quizapu g. 'Peregrine' **new** LBut
Rainier g. LBut
Rakata g. CHdy EPot LBut
- 'Blackbird' LBut
- 'Redwing' LBut
- 'Shot Silk' LBut NSpr
- 'Skylark' LBut
Ruby Wedding g. LBut
San Salvador g. LBut
Sangay g. **new** LBut
Santorini g. LBut
scopulorum EFEx
Shantung g. CFir EPot GCrs LAma LBut NSpr
- R6.7 NSpr
- R6.48 **new** NSpr
- 'Candyfloss' NSpr
- 'Christine' **new** NSpr
- 'Ducat' EPot GCrs LAma LBut NSpr
- 'Gerry Mundey' LBut NSpr
- 'Golden Jubilee' NSpr
- 'Golden Plover' LBut
- 'Gwen' EPot
- 'Mikki' NSpr
- 'Muriel Harberd' ♀H2 NSpr
- 'Pixie' **new** NSpr
- 'Ridgeway' CHdy EPot LBut NSpr
- 'Silver Anniversary' LBut
- 'Top Score' **new** EPot
Shepherd's Warning g. 'Gillian Clare' NSpr
- 'Mary Buchanan' NSpr
Sorea g. LBut
Soufrière g. EPot LBut NSpr
- 'Sunrise' NSpr
speciosa Ames & Schltr. see *P. pleionoides*
Starbotton g. NSpr
Stromboli g. CHdy GCrs NSpr
- 'Fireball' EPot GCrs LBut NSpr
- 'Robin' LBut
Surtsey g. EPot
- 'Stephanie Rose' NSpr
Swaledale g. **new** NSpr
x ***taliensis*** LBut
Tarawera g. LBut
Tolima g. CHdy CNic LBut NSpr
- 'Moorhen' EPot
Tongariro g. CHdy CPBP EPot ERos GCrs LBut NSpr
- 'Jackdaw' CHdy EPot LBut NSpr
Versailles g. CHdy EPot ERos NWCA
- 'Bucklebury' ♀H2 CNic EPot LBut NSpr
- 'Heron' CHdy LBut
- 'Muriel Turner' EPot NSpr
Vesuvius g. CHdy EPot LBut
- 'Aphrodite' EPot
- 'Grey Wagtail' LBut
- 'Leopard' LBut NSpr
* - 'Phoenix' EPot LBut NSpr
- 'Tawny Owl' LBut
Vicky g. **new** NSpr
Volcanello g. CHdy EPot GCrs LBut NSpr
- 'Honey Buzzard' LBut
- 'Song Thrush' LBut
Wunzen g. LBut
yunnanensis misapplied see *P. bulbocodioides* 'Yunnan'
yunnanensis (Rolfe) Rolfe CHdy LAma
Zeus Weinstein g. EPot LBut NSpr
- 'Desert Sands' LBut

Pleomele see *Dracaena*

Pleurospermum (*Apiaceae*)

from Nepal HWJK 2329 **new** WCru
aff. ***amabile*** BWJ 7886 WCru
benthamii SIgm
- B&SWJ 2988 WCru
brunonis EBee
calcareum B&SWJ 8008 WCru
gmelinii **new** GIBF

plum see *Prunus domestica*

Plumbago (*Plumbaginaceae*)

§ ***auriculata*** ♀H1-2 CBcs CEnd CHEx CRHN CSBt CTri CWSG EBak EBee ELan EPfP ERea EShb EUJe ISea MBri MLan MOak MRav MTis NPal SPer SRms SYvo XPep
- var. ***alba*** ♀H1-2 CBcs CHEx CHal CRHN CSev EBak EBee EMil EPfP ERea EShb LRHS MLan MOak SEND SPer SYvo XPep
* - ***aurea*** LIck
- 'Crystal Waters' CDoC CTbh ELan
- dark blue-flowered CSpe MJnS XPep
- 'Escapade Blue' (Escapade Series) EShb
- 'Tobago Blue' **new** CPLN
capensis see *P. auriculata*
§ ***indica*** ♀H1 CHal LRHS MJnS
- ***rosea*** see *P. indica*
larpentiae see *Ceratostigma plumbaginoides*

Plumeria (*Apocynaceae*)

rubra ♀H1 ESlt

Pneumatopteris see *Cyclosorus*

Poa (Poaceae)

alpina	CBig GFor NBre NGdn NJOw NLar
- nodosa	CBig EMan GFor SWal
chaixii	CBig EHoe EMan EPPr EPla EPza GFor GKir NNor SLPl WFoF WWpP
cita	CBig GFor LRav
colensoi	CBrm CKno CRez EBee EHoe EPPr MAvo NFor WGHP WPnP
eminens from Magadan, Siberia	EMan EPPr
x ***jemtlandica***	EHoe EPPr
labillardierei	CBrm CKno CMea CWCL EBee EBrs ECha EHoe EMan EPPr EPza GGar GKir MAvo NBid SPoG SUsu WDyG WGHP WMoo WPrP XPep
rodwayi **new**	CBig
trivialis	CRWN
I 'Variegata' **new**	SApp

Podalyria (Papilionaceae)

calyptrata	SPlb
sericea	SPlb

Podocarpus (Podocarpaceae)

acutifolius	CBcs CDoC ECou EPla GGar MBar STre
- (f)	ECou
- (m)	ECou
andinus	see *Prumnopitys andina*
'Autumn Shades' (m)	ECou
'Blaze' (f)	CBcs CDoC CRob ECou EPla LBuc LCon LLin MBrN NLar SCoo SLim SPoG WEve
chilinus	see *P. salignus*
'Chocolate Box' (f)	ECou
'County Park Fire'PBR (f)	CBcs CDoC CKen CRob CWSG ECou ENot EOrn EPfP LCon LLin MGos NPal SCoo SLim SPoG SWvt WEve WFar WGor
cunninghamii	CBcs ECou WCwm
- 'Kiwi' (f)	CBcs ECou
- 'Roro' (m)	CBcs ECou LLin
cunninghamii x ***nivalis*** (f)	ECou
dacrydioides	see *Dacrycarpus dacrydioides*
elongatus	CTrC IDee
'Flame'	CDoC ECou EPla NEgg WEve
'Havering' (f)	ECou
henkelii	CTrC EShb GGar
'Jill' (f)	ECou
latifolius	ECou EShb
lawrencei	ECho EHul GGar
- (f)	ECou MBar
- 'Alpine Lass' (f)	ECou
- 'Blue Gem' (f)	CDoC CRob ECou EOrn EPla IArd IDee LCon LLin LRHS MAsh MBar MGos MOne NDlv SCoo SLim SPoG WBcn WFar
- 'Kiandra'	ECou
- 'Red Tip'	CDoC GBin LLin MAsh SCoo SLim
'Macho' (m)	ECou
macrophyllus	CBcs CHEx CTrC EOrn NLar SAPC SArc SMad STre WFar
- (m)	ECou
- 'Aureus' **new**	CBcs
'Maori Prince' (m)	CDoC ECou EPla LLin
nivalis	CBcs CMac CTrC ECou EOrn EPla GGar LLin MBar SCoo SRms
- 'Arthur' (m)	ECou
- 'Bronze'	EPla WEve
- 'Christmas Lights' (f)	ECou
- 'Clarence' (m)	ECou LLin
- 'Cover Girl' **new**	CRob
- 'Green Queen' (f)	ECou
- 'Hikurangi' **new**	CDoC
- 'Jack's Pass' (m)	ECou
- 'Kaweka' (m)	ECou
- 'Kilworth Cream' (v)	CBcs CDoC CRob ECou EPla GTSp LBuc LCon LLin MAsh MGos NLar SCoo SLim SWvt WEve
- 'Little Lady' (f)	ECou
- 'Livingstone' (f)	ECou
- 'Lodestone' (m)	ECou
- 'Moffatt' (f)	CBcs CDoC ECou LLin
- 'Otari' (m)	CBcs ECou LLin NLar WEve
- 'Park Cover'	ECou
- 'Princess' (f)	ECou MBrN
- 'Ruapehu' (m)	CDoC ECou EPla
- 'Trompenburg'	NLar
nubigenus **new**	CBcs
'Orangeade' (f)	CBcs NLar
'Red Embers' **new**	NEgg
* 'Redtip'	LBuc SLim
'Rough Creek'	LLin
§ ***salignus*** ♀H3	CAbb CBcs CBrd CDoC CDul CHEx EPla IDee ISea SAPC SArc SLim WFar WPic WSHC
- (f)	ECou
- (m)	ECou
spicatus	see *Prumnopitys taxifolia*
'Spring Sunshine' (f)	CBcs CDoC ECou EPla LLin NLar WEve
totara	CBcs CTrC ECou GGar LEdu STre WFar
- 'Albany Gold'	CTrC IDee
- 'Aureus'	CBcs CDoC ECou EPla MBar SCoo SHBN WBcn WEve WFar
- 'Pendulus'	CDoC ECou
'Young Rusty' (f)	CBcs CDoC ECou EPla GTSp LLin MGos WEve

Podophyllum (Berberidaceae)

aurantiocaule **new**	WCot
§ ***delavayi***	CBct CLAP EBla GFlt MDun NLar WCru
difforme	CLAP GFlt MGol SSpi WCot WCru
emodi	see *P. hexandrum*
- var. ***chinense***	see *P. hexandrum* 'Chinense'
§ ***hexandrum***	More than 30 suppliers
- 'Chinense'	CBro CLAP CRow EBla EMan GBuc GEdr GKev IBlr LEdu SMad WCru WPnP
- - BWJ 7908	WCru
- 'Chinese White' CT 232	CFwr WCot
- 'Majus'	CFir CLAP SMad WCot WHal
peltatum	CArn CBct CBro CLAP CRow EBee EBla EUJe GBBs GEdr GFlt GPoy IBlr LAma LPhx MLul NMyG NSti SSpi WCru WFar WPGP WPnP
pleianthum	CBct CLAP EBee MMil SSpi WCot WCru
- short	WCru
veitchii	see *P. delavayi*
versipelle	CLAP SSpi WCot WCru

Podranea (Bignoniaceae)

brycei	CRHN EShb
§ ***ricasoliana***	CHEx CPLN CRHN ERea EShb XPep
- 'Comtesse Sarah'	XPep

Pogonatherum (Poaceae)

§ ***paniceum***	LRHS MBri
saccharoideum	see *P. paniceum*

Pogonia (*Orchidaceae*)

	ophioglossoides	SSpi

Pogostemon (*Lamiaceae*)

	from An Veleniki Herb Farm, Pennsylvania	CArn
§	***cablin***	GPoy MGol MSal
	patchouly	see *P. cablin*

Polemonium (*Polemoniaceae*)

	acutiflorum	see *P. caeruleum* subsp. *villosum*
	acutifolium var. ***nipponicum***	see *P. caeruleum* var. *nipponicum*
	ambervicsii	see *P. pauciflorum* subsp. *hinckleyi*
	'Apricot Beauty'	see *P. carneum* 'Apricot Delight'
N	***archibaldiae*** ♀H4	NBir SRms
§	***boreale***	EBee EMan GKir IGor MBow NArg NLRH NPol SBch SBla SPet SWvt WFar WMoo
*	- ***album***	WBrE
	- 'Heavenly Habit'	NPro NRnb NVic SHGN SMar SPet WRHF WWeb
§	***brandegeei*** Greene	NArg NBro SAga SHGN SHop WPer
	- subsp. ***mellitum***	see *P. brandegeei* Greene
	Bressingham Purple = 'Polbress'	EBrs MMHG SPer WFar
	caeruleum misapplied, Himalayan	see *P. cashmerianum*
§	***caeruleum***	More than 30 suppliers
	- subsp. ***amygdalinum***	see *P. occidentale*
	- 'Bambino Blue'	IBal LRHS SUsu SWvt WHil WPer WPop
	- 'Blue Bell'	ELau
	- Brise d'Anjou = 'Blanjou'PBR (v)	More than 30 suppliers
	- subsp. ***caeruleum*** **new**	GKev
	- - f. ***album***	More than 30 suppliers
I	- f. ***dissectum***	NPol
	- 'Everton White' **new**	MWrn
	- 'Golden Showers' (v)	CCge NPro
	- var. ***grandiflorum***	see *P. caeruleum* subsp. *himalayanum*
	- f. ***hidakanum***	CStr GIBF NPol
§	- subsp. ***himalayanum***	NChi WPer
	- 'Humile'	see *P.* 'Northern Lights'
	- 'Idylle'	EMan EMon MAnH MAvo NPol
	- 'Larch Cottage' (v)	NLar NPol
	- 'Newark Park'	NPol
§	- var. ***nipponicum***	EBee GBin GIBF NPol WPer
	- 'Sky Blue'	NRnb
	- 'Snow and Sapphires' (v)	CBct CSBt EBee EPfP EVFa GBin LAst LRHS MBNS MBri MCCP MSte NCGa NLar NPer NPri NTHB SPav SPoG SRkn STes SVil WCot WPop WSan WWeb
	- 'Southern Skies'	CStr
§	- subsp. ***villosum***	CStr NPol
	- subsp. ***vulgare***	NPol
	californicum	NPol
	carneum	CTri CWan ECha EMan GFlt GKir GMaP LAst MCCP MNFA MNrw MTho NJOw NPol SECG SSpi STes WAul WCAu WFar WMoo WPer WSan
§	- 'Apricot Delight'	CBot EChP EMag EMar EWTr GBri LAst LRHS MAnH MCCP MNrw MTis NBir NGHP NGdn NJOw NLon NPol NPri NSti SGar SIde SPoG STes WBVN WHer WPer WPnP WWeb
	- 'Rachael'	NPol
§	***cashmerianum***	EBee EPPr LRHS MHar NBur SPet WFar WHoo WSan
	- ***album***	WBor
	chartaceum	LTwo
	'Churchills'	CBre CLAP EBee EChP NPol WPGP WPrP
	confertum	NPol
§	'Dawn Flight'	NPol WFar
	delicatum	see *P. pulcherrimum* subsp. *delicatum*
	'Eastbury Purple'	CElw CStr MAnH MBct NPol
	'Elworthy Amethyst'	CElw EBee EMan NCot NPol SBch WPGP
	eximium	EWTr
	flavum	see *P. foliosissimum* var. *flavum*
	foliosissimum misapplied	see *P. archibaldiae*
	foliosissimum A. Gray	CSec IGor MBct MNrw WPer
	- var. ***albiflorum***	see *P. foliosissimum* var. *alpinum*
§	- var. ***alpinum***	EBee NBir NPol
	- 'Bressingham'	NPol
	- 'Cottage Cream'	CBre CStr EBee NPol
§	- var. ***flavum***	NPol
	- var. ***foliosissimum***	EWes NPol
	- - NNS 99-422	EPPr
	- 'Scottish Garden'	NPol
	- 'White Spirit'	EBee NPol
	'Glebe Cottage Lilac'	CCge CElw CHar CMil CStr EBee MAvo NBir SBch WPGP
	'Glebe Cottage Violet'	NPol
	grandiflorum	NPol
	'Hannah Billcliffe'	CDes CElw MAnH NCot NPol
§	'Hopleys'	CStr EChP EMan GBar GBri GCal IFro NCot NGdn NLsd NPol WFar
	x ***jacobaea***	CDes EBee EMan EPPr NPol WCot WTin
	'Katie Daley'	see *P.* 'Hopleys'
	kiushianum	EBee
	'Lace Towers'	NSti
§	'Lambrook Mauve' ♀H4	More than 30 suppliers
	'Mary Mottram'	NPol
	mellitum	see *P. brandegeei* Greene
	'North Tyne'	EBee NBid NChi NPol
§	'Northern Lights'	CDes CSev CStr EBee EMan EMon EPPr EWes GBri GMac MAnH MBnl MBri MNFA MNrw NCot NDov NPol NSti SAga SBch STes SUsu WFar WMoo WPGP
	'Norwell Mauve'	MNrw NPol
§	***occidentale***	EBee
	- subsp. ***occidentale***	NPol
	'Pam' (v)	EBee NPol
§	***pauciflorum***	CHrt ECtt EHrv GKir GTou IFro LAst LPio LRHS MAnH MNFA MNrw MTho NBid NBir NLsd SHFr SYvo WAbe WFar WMoo WPer WWeb WWhi WWlt
§	- subsp. ***hinckleyi***	EPPr NCot NPol SBch SGar WOut
	- subsp. ***pauciflorum***	LRHS NPol SGar SPav WSan
	- silver-leaved	see *P. pauciflorum* subsp. *pauciflorum*
	- 'Sulphur Trumpets'	LSou MAnH SPav SWvt WGwG
	- subsp. ***typicum***	see *P. pauciflorum* subsp. *pauciflorum*
§	'Pink Beauty'	CBre ELan EMar EPPr EPfP EVFa LRHS NCot NPol SUsu WWhi
	pulchellum Salisb.	see *P. reptans*
	pulchellum Turcz.	see *P. caeruleum*
	pulcherrimum misapplied	see *P. boreale*
	- 'Tricolor'	see *P. boreale*
	pulcherrimum Hook.	GTou NBro SPoG WLin WPer WWeb

- ***album*** CGra
§ - subsp. ***delicatum*** MTho NPol
- subsp. ***pulcherrimum*** GKev LTwo NPol
§ ***reptans*** CAgr CArn CHea EMag GBar GBri GPoy MHer MSal NBro NPol SIng WFar WMoo WPer WWeb WWye
- 'Album' see *P. reptans* 'Virginia White'
- 'Blue Ice' NPol
- 'Blue Pearl' CElw CMea COIW EBee EChP EMan EPfP LRHS MLLN MNrw NBro NChi NCob NFor NGdn NLon NPol SGar SPla SWal WFar WSan WWeb
- 'Firmament' EBee WPGP
- 'Pink Dawn' EBee EChP EMil EPfP MLLN MNFA MWgw NCob NGdn SPla STes
* - 'Sky Blue' NBro
§ - 'Virginia White' CBcs CBre CDes CElw CMea CSev CStr EBee LRHS MBnl NChi NPol SUsu WFar
- 'White Pearl' COIW IGor WBVN
'Ribby' NPol
richardsonii misapplied see *P.* 'Northern Lights'
richardsonii Graham see *P. boreale*
'Sapphire' CBre CStr ELan EMan EMon MBrN NPol
scopulinum see *P. pulcherrimum* subsp. *delicatum*
I 'Sonia's Bluebell' CDes CElw CMil CStr EBee ECGP EMan EPPr EVFa EWes MBnl MDKP MNrw MSte NCot NDov NPol SBch SUsu WOut WPGP
'Theddingworth' NPol WFar
vanbruntiae EBee NPol
viscosum GBuc GKev NPol SGar SYvo
- 'Blue Whirl' MGol NLsd
- f. ***leucanthum*** NPol
yezoense CBre CStr GBri MNrw NPol WFar WPnP
- 'Purple Rain' CHar CSpe CStr EBee EHrv EMan ENot EPfP EWes GBuc GFlt GMaP MAnH MBnl MCCP MLLN MNrw MTis NLon NPol SPoG SSpi STes WFar WWhi

Polianthes (*Agavaceae*)

nelsonii CFir
tuberosa ♀H1-2 CBcs CSpe LRHS
- 'The Pearl' (d) LAma

Poliomintha (*Lamiaceae*)

bustamanta EBee NBir SAga
incana **new** EBee

Poliothyrsis (*Flacourtiaceae*)

sinensis ♀H4 CAbP CFil CPne EPfP GIBF LAst LRHS MBri NLar WPGP WWes

Pollia (*Commelinaceae*)

japonica CMCN EMan IFro
- B&SWJ 8884 WCru

Polygala (*Polygalaceae*)

alpicola SOkd
alpina **new** WLin
amoenissima SOkd
calcarea LTwo NLAp WAbe WBWf WPat
- Bulley's form EPot LRHS
- 'Lillet' ♀H4 EHyt EPot LRHS LTwo NLAp NLar NMen NSla SOkd WFar WPat
- 'Susan's Blush' **new** NLAp
chamaebuxus ♀H4 CBcs GCrs LSou MDKP MGos NLAp NLar NSla SRms WBVN WTin
- ***alba*** GKir LBee LRHS LSou NLar WAbe
§ - var. ***grandiflora*** ♀H4 CBcs CFir CWCL EPot GAbr GEdr GGar GKev GKir LBee MAsh MBar MDun MGos NLAp NMen NSla SBla SChu WAbe WBVN WFar WPat WSHC
- 'Kamniski' CMHG EPot LBuc
- 'Loibl' EPot
- 'Purpurea' see *P. chamaebuxus* var. *grandiflora*
- var. ***rhodoptera*** **new** SBla
§ x ***dalmaisiana*** ♀H1 CAbb CHEx CHII CRHN CSpe EBee ERea GQui SBla SBrw SMur WAbe WBor WCFE
'Domino' **new** NLAp
myrtifolia CPLG CSec CTrC IDee SGar SHFr SIgm SMrm SPlb WWye XPep
- 'Grandiflora' see *P.* x *dalmaisiana*
pauciflora SOkd
'Rosengarten' SBla
tenuifolia **new** CArn
vayredae GEdr NLar
virgata CSec ERea EShb ESlt

Polygonatum ✿ (*Convallariaceae*)

acuminatifolium EBla
altelobatum EBla
- B&SWJ 286 WCru
§ ***biflorum*** CArn CBro CHEx CHid CPou EBla EBrs EGol EHrv ELan EPla EPot ERou GBBs GKir GMaP GSki IBlr MSal NLar SHar SMad SMer SSpi SWvt WAul WCot WCru WFar WPnP
- dwarf EBla EPla IBlr
canaliculatum see *P. biflorum*
cirrhifolium CDes CFir CLAP CPom EBee EBla ELan GBin GKir MDun WCot WCru WHil WPGP
commutatum see *P. biflorum*
'Corsley' **new** CPou
cryptanthum EBla WCru
curvistylum CAvo CBct CLAP CPom CStu EBla ECha EHrv GFlt IBlr LPhx NLar NRya WAbe WCru WFar
- CLD 761 GEdr
cyrtonema misapplied see *Disporopsis pernyi*
cyrtonema Hua CLAP LEdu
- B&SWJ 271 WCru
falcatum misapplied see *P. humile*
§ ***falcatum*** A. Gray CLyd EBla EPla EPot IBlr NOak WHer
- B&SWJ 1077 WCru
- silver-striped **new** GEdr
- 'Variegatum' see *P. odoratum* var. *pluriflorum* 'Variegatum'
'Falcon' see *P. humile*
filipes WCru
fuscum WCru
geminiflorum CLAP EBee EBla IBlr SOkd WFar
- McB 2448 GEdr
giganteum see *P. biflorum*
glaberrimum EBla WCot
§ ***graminifolium*** CBct CLAP EBee EBla EPot ERos GEdr MSte NCGa NMen SCnR WCot WCru
- G-W&P 803 IPot
§ ***hirtum*** CBct CLAP CPom EBla EMon EPla IBlr WCru WFar
- dwarf **new** WCot
hookeri More than 30 suppliers
- McB 1413 GEdr
§ ***humile*** CBct CLAP EBee EBla EHrv EHyt ELan EMan ERos GBri GCal IBlr

		NJOw NMen SMac SSpi SUsu WAbe WAul WCot WCru WFar
§	× ***hybridum*** ♀H4	More than 30 suppliers
	- 'Betberg'	CBct CLAP CRow EBla ECha EHrv NBPC NBir WCot
	- 'Flore Pleno' (d)	EBla WHer
	- 'Nanum'	CHid EBla
§	- 'Striatum' (v)	More than 30 suppliers
	- 'Variegatum'	see *P.* × *hybridum* 'Striatum'
	- 'Wakehurst'	EBla EHrv
	inflatum	EBla WCru
	- B&SWJ 922	WCru
	involucratum	WCru
	japonicum	see *P. odoratum*
	kingianum	WCru
	yellow-flowered B&SWJ 6562	
	'Langthorns Variegated' (v)	ELan
	lasianthum	WCru
	latifolium	see *P. hirtum*
	maximowiczii	GCal GIBF GSki
	multiflorum misapplied	see *P.* × *hybridum*
	multiflorum L.	CBcs CDes CElw CRow CSBt EBee ECha EPla EPza EWsh GAbr GKir LRHS MAvo NEgg NVic SAga SMer SPlb SRms
	- ***giganteum*** hort.	see *P. biflorum*
*	***nanum*** 'Variegatum' (v)	CBcs
	nodosum	EBla WCru
	obtusifolium	EBee EBla
§	***odoratum*** ♀H4	CAby CAvo CBct CBro CRow CSWP EBla EHrv ELau EPfP EPla GEdr GIBF GMaP IBlr MSal NBid NLar NRya SAga SSpi WCru WFar WHil WPnP
§	- dwarf	IBlr LEdu
	- 'Flore Pleno' (d) ♀H4	CDes CLAP CRow EBee EBla ECha EHrv EPla ERou IBlr SBla SCnR SMHy WCot WHoo WPGP WPnP
	- 'Grace Barker'	see *P.* × *hybridum* 'Striatum'
	- var. ***pluriflorum***	GBuc IBlr SSpi
§	- - 'Variegatum' (v) ♀H4	More than 30 suppliers
	- 'Red Stem'	WCru
	- 'Silver Wings' (v)	CLAP EBla ECha EHrv ERou NBid NBir
	officinale	see *P. odoratum*
	oppositifolium	EBla WFar
	- B&SWJ 2537	WCru
§	***orientale***	CHid CLAP EBla WCot
	pluriflorum	see *P. graminifolium*
	polyanthemum	see *P. orientale*
	prattii	EBla SOkd
	pubescens	WCru
	pumilum	see *P. odoratum* dwarf
	punctatum	LEdu WFar
	- B&SWJ 2395	CBct EBla WCru
	racemosum	SIng
	roseum	CDes WHer WPGP WPnP
	sewerzowii	EBee EBla EPla
	sibiricum	CAvo EBla GEdr IBlr WCru
	- DJHC 600	CDes
	stenophyllum	CAvo EBla
	stewartianum	CLAP EBee EPPr IBlr NPar
	tonkinense HWJ 551	WCru
	verticillatum	CAvo CBct CBro CHid CLyd CRow EBla EBrs ECha EPfP EPla GKir GLil IBlr MNrw MTho SMad WCot WCru WFar WPGP
	- CC 1324	CPLG
	- 'Himalayan Giant'	CHid EBee EBla IPot
*	- ***rubrum***	CArn CBct CLAP CRow EBla EHrv EPPr IBlr IPot LPhx MSte MTho NBid NGby WCot WPrP
	- 'Serbian Dwarf'	CHid EBee EBla IPot
	aff. ***verticillatum***	EMon
	zanlanscianense	CBct EBla WCru

Polygonum ✿ (*Polygonaceae*)

	affine	see *Persicaria affinis*
	amplexicaule	see *Persicaria amplexicaulis*
	aubertii	see *Fallopia baldschuanica*
	aviculare	CArn
	baldschuanicum	see *Fallopia baldschuanica*
	bistorta	see *Persicaria bistorta*
	capitatum	see *Persicaria capitata*
	compactum	see *Fallopia japonica* var. *compacta*
	equisetiforme hort.	see *P. scoparium*
	filiforme	see *Persicaria virginiana*
	hydropiper 'Fastigiatum' **new**	CArn EUnu
	longisetum	see *Persicaria longiseta*
	molle	see *Persicaria mollis*
	multiflorum	see *Fallopia multiflora*
	odoratum	see *Persicaria odorata*
	polystachyum	see *Persicaria wallichii*
	runciforme	see *Persicaria runcinata*
§	***scoparium***	CBcs CBrm CRow EMan EPPr EPla SDys SIng SMad WCot WDyG WFar WTin
	tinctorium	see *Persicaria tinctoria*
	weyrichii	see *Persicaria weyrichii*

Polylepis (*Rosaceae*)

	australis	CFil LEdu SMad SSpi WBcn WCru WPGP
	pauta **new**	CFil WPGP

Polymnia (*Asteraceae*)

	sonchifolia	EUnu LEdu MSal
	uvedalia	see *Smallanthus uvedalius*

Polypodium ✿ (*Polypodiaceae*)

	australe	see *P. cambricum*
§	***cambricum***	EFer SGSe WCot WFib WRic
§	- 'Barrowii'	CLAP WAbe WFib
	- 'Cambricum' ♀H4	CLAP WAbe WRic WWye
	- 'Cristatum'	CLAP NBid WFib
	- (Cristatum Group) 'Grandiceps Forster'	CLAP
	- - 'Grandiceps Fox' ♀H4	WFib
	- 'Hornet'	WFib
	- 'Macrostachyon'	CLAP EFer WFib
	- 'Oakleyae'	SMHy WPGP
	- 'Omnilacerum Oxford'	CLAP WRic WWye
	- 'Prestonii'	WAbe WFib
	- Pulcherrimum Group	CLAP WAbe
	- - 'Pulchritudine' **new**	CLAP WAbe
	- 'Pulcherrimum Addison'	WAbe WWye
	- 'Richard Kayse'	CDes CLAP WAbe WFib WPGP WWye
	- Semilacerum Group	WRic
	- - 'Carew Lane'	WFib
	- - 'Robustum'	WFib
	- 'Whilharris' ♀H4	CLAP SMHy WAbe WPGP
I	× ***coughlinii*** bifid **new**	WFib
	glycyrrhiza	CLAP GPoy WFib
	- bifid	see *Polypodium* × *coughlinii* bifid
	- 'Longicaudatum' ♀H4	CLAP EMon WAbe WCot WFib WSPU WWye
	- 'Malahatense'	CLAP
	- 'Malahatense' (sterile)	WAbe
	interjectum	CLAP CWCL EFer MMoz NOrc NVic WAbe WRic
	- 'Cornubiense' ♀H4	CFil CLAP EFer EMon GCal MMoz

		NBir NBro NVic SSpi WAbe WPGP WTin
	- 'Glomeratum Mullins' **new**	WFib
	x ***mantoniae***	WFib WIvy
	- 'Bifidograndiceps'	NBid WFib WPGP
	scouleri	CLAP NBro
	vulgare	More than 30 suppliers
	- 'Bifidocristatum'	see *P. vulgare* 'Bifidomultifidum'
	- 'Bifidomultifidum'	CLAP EMon GBin GEdr MAsh MCCP SPla SSpi WCot WOut
*	- 'Congestum Cristatum'	SRms
	- 'Cornubiense Grandiceps'	SRms WIvy WRic
*	- 'Cornubiense Multifidum'	EBee WCot
	- 'Elegantissimum' **new**	WFib
	- 'Ramosum Hillman' **new**	WFib
	- 'Trichomanoides Backhouse'	CLAP WAbe WFib

Polypompholyx see *Utricularia*

Polyscias (*Araliaceae*)

	'Elegans'	MBri
	fruticosa	MBri
	scutellaria 'Pennockii' (v)	MBri

Polystichum ✿ (*Dryopteridaceae*)

	BWJ 8182 from China **new**	WCru
	acrostichoides	CFwr CLAP CMHG CPrp EPPr ERod EWTr GCal GEdr GQui IBal NGby NLar SNut SSpi WRic
	aculeatum ♀H4	More than 30 suppliers
I	- Densum Group	EFer
	- Grandiceps Group	EFer
	- 'Portia' **new**	WFib
	andersonii	CLAP CWCL
	braunii	CBcs CMHG CPrp CWCL EGol GBin GMaP MLan MMoz NOGN WFib WPnP WRic
	caryotideum	see *Cyrtomium caryotideum*
	falcatum	see *Cyrtomium falcatum*
	fortunei	see *Cyrtomium fortunei*
	imbricans	CLAP SArc
	lonchitis	NWoo
	makinoi	CLAP WFib
	mohrioides	CLAP
	munitum ♀H4	More than 30 suppliers
	- 'Incisum'	GCal
	neolobatum	WFib
	polyblepharum ♀H4	More than 30 suppliers
	proliferum	CFwr CLAP EAmu GCal LAst SBig WFib WRic
*	- ***plumosum***	CFwr NEgg NOak
	richardii	SBig WAbe WRic
	rigens	CElw CFwr CLAP CPrp EFer GCal LSou NDlv NOGN SGSe SNut SRms SRot WCru WFib WRic
§	***setiferum*** ♀H4	More than 30 suppliers
§	- Acutilobum Group	CBcs CFil CFwr CLAP CMHG CPrp CWCL ECha ENot GMaP MBow SDix SMac SMad SPer SSpi STes WCru WMoo WPGP WPnP WPrP
	- Congestum Group	CPrp GBin MBri MMoz NCGa SChu SRms WFib WRic
	- 'Congestum'	CFwr CLAP ELan ENot EPfP ERod GCal LRHS MAsh MBct MDun NBir NFor NSti SMac SNut SPla SPoG SSto WGor WMoo WPrP
	- 'Cristatopinnulum'	CFil CLAP GBin WPGP
	- Cristatum Group	CLAP EHrv SRms
	- Cruciatum Group	CLAP
	- 'Cruciatum Kaye' **new**	CLAP
	- Divisilobum Group	CBcs CElw CFee CFil CLAP CMHG CRow EFer ELan EMon ENot LPBA MBct MGos MMoz NVic SBla SPla SRms STre WAbe WAul WFar WFib WHoo WIvy WPGP WRic WTin WWhi
	- - 'Dahlem'	CDoC CFwr CLAP ECha EFer ELan EMon GKir GMaP MDun MMoz MSte NFor SNut SPoG SSto WAbe WFib WMoo WPnP WRic
	- - 'Herrenhausen'	More than 30 suppliers
	- - 'Madame Patti'	GBin
	- - 'Mrs Goffey'	WFib
	- 'Divisilobum Densum' ♀H4	CLAP EHrv ENot EPfP NBir NOrc SNut SSpi
	- 'Divisilobum Iveryanum' ♀H4	CLAP GBin SRms WFib
	- 'Divisilobum Laxum'	CLAP SChu
	- Foliosum Group	EFer
	- 'Foliosum'	CLAP GBin
	- 'Gracile'	NBir
	- 'Grandiceps'	CLAP EFer ELan
	- Green Lace = 'Gracillimum'	GBin
	- 'Hamlet'	GBin WFib
	- 'Helena'	GBin WFib
	- 'Hirondelle'	SRms
	- Lineare Group	CFil CLAP NEgg WFib
	- Multilobum Group	CLAP SRms WFib
	- 'Nantes'	GBin
	- 'Othello' **new**	WFib
	- Perserratum Group	NBid WFib
	- 'Plumosodensum'	see *P. setiferum* 'Plumosomultilobum'
	- Plumosodivisilobum Group	CLAP CMil CRow ECha EGol LSou NBid SPla WAbe WCru WFib
	- - 'Baldwinii'	CLAP WFib
	- - 'Bland' **new**	WFib
§	- 'Plumosomultilobum'	CFwr CLAP CPrp CWCL ENot EPPr EPfP GBin LAst LRHS MAsh MBnl MMoz MWgw NBir NCGa NEgg NSti SGSe SMer SNut SPla WBVN WCot WFib WMoo WPnP WPrP WRic
	- Plumosum Group	CLAP CMHG CSam CSpe EChP EFer NEgg NOrc SAPC SArc SBla SChu SRot WBor
	- - dwarf	CSBt
*	- ***plumosum grande*** 'Moly'	CLAP SRms
	- Proliferum Group	see *P. setiferum* Acutilobum Group
*	- 'Proliferum Wollaston'	CFwr CPrp ENot MMoz NRib SNut SSto WWeb
	- 'Pulcherrimum Bevis' ♀H4	CLAP GBin NBid SHFr WFib WPGP
*	- 'Ramopinnatum'	CLAP
	- Revolvens Group	EFer
	- - 'Revolvens Lowe' **new**	CLAP
	- Rotundatum Group	CLAP
	- - 'Cristatum'	CLAP
	- 'Rotundatum Ramosum' **new**	CLAP
	- 'Smith's Cruciate'	CLAP GBin WFib
	- 'Wakeleyanum'	SRms
N	- 'Wollaston'	CFwr CLAP GBin MAsh NEgg WAbe
	tsussimense ♀H4	More than 30 suppliers
	vestitum	CLAP CTrC SBig WRic

Polyxena (*Hyacinthaceae*)

	corymbosa	CStu WCot
§	***ensifolia***	CMon ERos

odorata | CLyd CStu WCot
pygmaea | see *P. ensifolia*

Pomaderris (*Rhamnaceae*)

elliptica | ECou

pomegranate see *Punica granatum*

Poncirus (*Rutaceae*)

§ ***trifoliata*** | CArn CBcs CDoC CFil EBee ELan ENot EPfP ERea IDee IMGH LRHS MBlu MJnS MRav NEgg NWea SLon SMad SPer SPoG WBVN WDin WFar WPGP WPat WSHC WTel

Pontederia (*Pontederiaceae*)

cordata ♀H4 | CBen CDWL CHEx CRow CWat ECha EHon ELan EMFW EPfP LNCo LPBA MCCP NArg NPer SCoo SPlb WFar WPnP WPop WWpP
- f. ***albiflora*** | CDWL CRow CWat EMFW EPfP LPBA MCCP NLar WPop WWpP
- 'Blue Spires' | CDWL
§ - var. ***lancifolia*** | CRow ECha EMFW EPfP LPBA MCCP NBlu NPer WTin WWpP
- 'Pink Pons' | CRow NLar
lanceolata | see *P. cordata* var. *lancifolia*

Populus ✿ (*Salicaceae*)

x ***acuminata*** | WMou
alba | CCVT CDoC CDul CLnd CSBt CTri CWib ECrN ENot GKir LBuc MBar NBee NWea SBLw SHBN SPer WBVN WDin WMou WOrn
- 'Bolleana' | see *P. alba* f. *pyramidalis*
- 'Nivea' | SBLw
§ - f. ***pyramidalis*** | CBcs SRms WMou
§ - 'Raket' | CCVT CLnd CTho ECrN ELan MGos NWea SBLw SPer
- 'Richardii' | CDul CLnd CTho EBee ECtt GKir MBar SPer WCot WFar WMou
- Rocket | see *P. alba* 'Raket'
alba x ***grandidentata*** | WMou
§ 'Balsam Spire' (f) ♀H4 | CDoC CDul CLnd CTho GKir NWea WDin WMou
§ ***balsamifera*** | CCVT CDoC CTho CTri ECrN ENot GKir MGos NWea SBLw SHBN SPer SRms WCot WDin WFar
x ***berolinensis*** | CDoC
x ***canadensis*** | ECrN SBLw
- 'Aurea' ♀H4 | CDoC CDul CLnd CTho CWib EBee ENot MDun MRav SPer WDin WFar WMou
- 'Aurea' x ***jackii*** 'Aurora' | MRav WBVN WDin
- 'Eugenei' (m) | CTho
- 'Robusta' (m) | CDoC CDul CLnd CTri EBee EMil ENot LBuc NWea WDin WMou
- 'Serotina' (m) | CDoC ECrN WDin WMou
x ***candicans*** misapplied | see *P.* x *jackii*
x ***canescens*** | CDoC ECrN GKir MBri SBLw WDin WMou
- 'De Moffart' (m) | SBLw
- 'Tower' | WMou
x ***generosa*** 'Beaupré' | CTho GKir LBuc WDin WMou
§ x ***jackii*** (f) | NEgg WDin
- 'Aurora' (f/v) | CBcs CCVT CDul CLnd CSBt CTrw ELan GKir LBuc LRHS MBar MBri MGos MRav MWat NBee NBlu NLon NWea SBLw SHBN SPer SRms WDin WFar WHar WJas
lasiocarpa ♀H4 | CDoC CEnd CFil CPLG CSdC CTho EBee EPfP EPla MBlu MRav SBLw SLPl SMad WMou WPGP
* - var. ***tibetica*** | WMou
maximowiczii | WMou
nigra | CDul CLnd EPfP NWea WDin
- (f) | ECrN SLPl
- (m) | SLPl
- subsp. ***betulifolia*** | CCVT CDul CTho CWan LBuc MDun NWea WDin WMou
- - (f) | WMou
- - (m) | WMou
N - 'Italica' (m) ♀H4 | CCVT CDoC CDul CLnd CSBt CTho CTri CWib ECrN ELan ENot GKir LBuc LRHS MBri MGos NBee NWea SBLw SHBN SPer SRms WDin WOrn
- 'Italica Aurea' | see *P. nigra* 'Lombardy Gold'
§ - 'Lombardy Gold' (m) | CEnd CTho MBlu
- 'Pyramidalis' | see *P. nigra* 'Italica'
simonii 'Fastigiata' | WMou
- 'Obtusata' | WMou
szechuanica | WMou
- var. ***tibetica*** | CFil
tacamahaca | see *P. balsamifera*
'Tacatricho 32' | see *P.* 'Balsam Spire'
tomentosa | WMou
tremula ♀H4 | CCVT CDoC CDul CLnd CRWN CSBt CTho CWib ECrN ELan ENot GKir LBuc LRHS NBee NWea SBLw SHBN SKee SPer SPoG WDin WMou WOrn
§ - 'Erecta' | CDul CEnd CLnd CTho EBee GKir LRHS MBlu MBri SMad WFar WMou
- 'Fastigiata' | see *P. tremula* 'Erecta'
- 'Pendula' (m) | CEnd CLnd CTho ECrN GKir SBLw WCFE WDin WMou
trichocarpa | CDul CTho ECrN SPer
- 'Columbia River' | GKir
- 'Fritzi Pauley' (f) | CDul CTho WMou
violascens | see *P. lasiocarpa* var. *tibetica*
yunnanensis | CFil CLnd CMHG WMou

Porophyllum (*Asteraceae*)

coloratum **new** | EUnu
ruderale | EUnu MSal

Portulaca (*Portulacaceae*)

grandiflora | MBri
oleracea | CArn MChe MHer SIde WJek WLHH
- var. ***aurea*** | MChe WJek WLHH

Potamogeton (*Potamogetonaceae*)

crispus | EHon EMFW NArg WPop

Potentilla ✿ (*Rosaceae*)

alba | CPLG CSev CTri EBee ECha ELan GBuc GGar LGro NChi NFla NSti SPer SUsu WAul WPer
alchemilloides | MNrw SMer WPer
alpicola | WPer
ambigua | see *P. cuneata*
andicola | EBee
anserina | CArn GBar MHer WHer XPep
- 'Golden Treasure' (v) | EPPr EVFa ITer MLLN NBre NEgg WCot WHer
- 'Shine' | WCot
anserinoides | EGoo EMan GCal WCot WDyG WMoo WPer
arbuscula hort. | see *P. fruticosa* 'Elizabeth'
'Arc-en-ciel' | CFwr CHid CKno CRez EChP EMan EMar GSki LSRN MBNS MBri

	NLar NPro SHar SUsu WBor WCAu WFar WHil WMoo WSan WWye
argentea	CRWN CSWP CSev LIck MBNS SPlb WFar WPer WPop
argyrophylla	see *P. atrosanguinea* var. *argyrophylla*
* - ***insignis rubra***	NChi NRnb
astracanica	CStr EBee
atrosanguinea	More than 30 suppliers
§ - var. ***argyrophylla***	EBee EChP ECha ELan EPfP GCal GTou LRHS MRav MWat MWgw NBir NBro NCGa NCot NJOw NMir NOak SBri SOkh SRms WFar WHil WMoo WPer WWhi
- - SS&W 7768	MSte
- var. ***leucochroa***	see *P. atrosanguinea* var. *argyrophylla*
aucheriana	EHyt
aurea	ECtt EDAr EPfP GAbr IHMH MTho NArg NBlu NEgg NLAp NMen NMir NWCA WBVN WBrk WPat
- 'Aurantiaca'	EDAr EWes NLar SRot
§ - subsp. ***chrysocraspeda***	GCrs NMen
§ - 'Goldklumpen'	ECtt MRav NPro
- 'Plena' (d)	GTou NSla SRot
'Blazeaway'	EBee EChP EMan EVFa LRHS MBNS MNFA MWgw NGdn WCAu WFar
* ***boraea*** **new**	CSec
burmiensis	SBri
calabra	ECha EDAr EMan SHGN SMer SSvw WHer
§ ***cinerea***	CTri LBee
clusiana	WLin
collina	SBri
concinna var. ***concinna*** **new**	GKev
§ ***crantzii***	CMea EBee GCrs GTou MBar MSte SRms
- 'Nana'	see *P. crantzii* 'Pygmaea'
§ - 'Pygmaea'	ECtt EPfP MOne NBir NJOw NMen
§ ***cuneata*** ♀H4	CLyd CNic EDAr GAbr GTou IHMH MTho NLAp NRya NWCA SIng WPer
aff. ***cuneata***	MDun
'Custard and Cream'	EChP
delavayi	GIBF MNrw
detommasii	MHar WPer
- MESE 400	EBee
dickinsii	CNic CSec GKev NMen SOkd
'Emilie'	CMea CSpe EChP EMan EMar GCal GLil MBNS NLar NPro NRnb SUsu SWvt WFar WHil
§ ***erecta***	CArn CRWN CWan EOHP GBar GPoy GWCH MChe MHer MSal WWye
eriocarpa	CLyd CNic ECtt EHol EHyt GEdr IMGH MWat NJOw NLAp NMen SBri SOkd WAbe WPat
'Etna'	More than 30 suppliers
'Everest'	see *P. fruticosa* 'Mount Everest'
'Fireflame'	ECha NLar SBri WMoo
fissa	CSec EBee EMag MNrw MSte NBir WMoo
'Flambeau' (d)	CBos CFwr CHad EBee EChP EMan EPPr MNFA MRav NCob NGdn NLar WCra
'Flamenco'	CSam CTri EBee EChP ECtt EMil ERou GKir GMac MArl MBri MNrw MRav NBir NFor SAga SUsu WAbb WFar WPGP WSan
fragariiformis	see *P. megalantha*
fruticosa	LBuc NWea
- CC 3929	CPLG
- 'Abbotswood' ♀H4	More than 30 suppliers
- 'Abbotswood Silver' (v)	ECtt LAst MBNS MSwo SLim SPoG WFar WMoo
- 'Alice'	WWeb
- 'Annette'	LRHS NPro WWeb
- 'Apple Blossom'	CWib
- var. ***arbuscula*** hort.	see *P. fruticosa* 'Elizabeth'
- 'Argentea Nana'	see *P. fruticosa* 'Beesii'
- 'Barnbarroch'	WWeb
§ - 'Beesii'	ELan EPfP LRHS MBNS MBar SIgm SPla SPoG WTel
- 'Bewerley Surprise'	EHol NBir WHCG WWeb
- 'Cascade'	WBcn
- 'Charlotte'	WBcn
* - 'Chelsea Star' ♀H4	WWeb
- 'Chilo' (v)	MGos NEgg WBcn WMoo WWeb
- 'Clotted Cream'	MBar
- var. ***dahurica*** 'Farrer's White'	WFar
- - 'Hersii'	see *P. fruticosa* 'Snowflake'
- - 'Rhodocalyx'	CPle WFar
- 'Dart's Cream'	LRHS
- 'Dart's Golddigger'	CRez CTri ECtt
- 'Daydawn'	More than 30 suppliers
§ - 'Elizabeth'	CBcs CDoC CSam CTri CWib ENot EPfP GKir LGro LRHS MBar MGos MRav NBlu NEgg NLon NWea SCoo SHBN SPer SPoG SRms SWvt WBVN WCFE WDin WFar WMoo WTel
- 'Farreri'	see *P. fruticosa* 'Gold Drop'
- 'Floppy Disc'	EPfP LRHS MAsh MGos NWoo SHBN SPer SPla
- 'Frances, Lady Daresbury'	GKir WWeb
- 'Glenroy Pinkie'	CSam EBee EPfP LRHS MTis SCoo SLon WWeb
§ - 'Gold Drop'	WHCG WTel
- 'Gold Parade'	WWeb
- 'Golden Dwarf'	LRHS MGos
- 'Golden Spreader'	WWeb
- 'Goldfinger'	CChe CDoC CSBt EBee ELan EPfP GKir LRHS MGos MRav MSwo MWat NEgg SCoo SLim SMer SPer SPlb SPoG WDin WHar WTel WWeb
- Goldkugel	see *P. fruticosa* 'Gold Drop'
- 'Goldstar'	GKir IArd LRHS MBNS MBri SCoo SLon SPoG WFar WHCG WWeb
- 'Goldteppich'	LBuc MBar NBlu NCGa SHBN
- 'Goscote'	MGos
- 'Grace Darling'	CAbP ELan EPfP EWes GGar NBir NEgg SPoG SWvt WBVN WHCG WMoo
- 'Groneland' ♀H4	WWeb
- 'Haytor's Orange'	CWib
- 'Honey'	WWeb
- 'Hopleys Orange' ♀H4	CChe ENot EPfP EWes GKir LRHS MAsh MBri MWat NCGa NEgg NPri SCoo WFar WGor WHCG WMoo WWeb
- 'Hopleys Pink'	WWeb
- 'Hunter's Moon'	WWeb
- 'Hurstbourne'	NPro
- 'Jackman's Variety' ♀H4	CSam CWib ECtt ENot SRms WWeb
- 'Janet'	WWeb
- 'Jolina'	WWeb
- 'Katherine Dykes'	CChe CDoC CDul CSBt CWib EBee EPfP GKir LRHS LSRN MBar MDun MRav NWea SCoo SLim SLon SPer SRms WBVN WDin WFar WHar WMoo WTel WWeb

*	- 'King Cup' 🏆H4	WWeb
	- 'Klondike'	CBcs CSBt EBee EMil EPfP GKir NWea
§	- 'Knap Hill'	WWeb
	- 'Knap Hill Buttercup'	see *P. fruticosa* 'Knap Hill'
	- 'Kobold'	MBar
*	- 'Lemon and Lime'	MBlu NBir NPro WWeb
	- 'Limelight' 🏆H4	CSBt EBee ELan EPfP GKir LRHS LSou MAsh MBri MRav MSwo NPri SPla SPoG WBcn WFar WHCG WWeb
	- 'Longacre Variety'	CTri MBar MSwo NWea WFar WTel
	- 'Lovely Pink'PBR	see *P. fruticosa* 'Pink Beauty'
§	- 'Maanelys'	CTrw EBee ECtt ELan MWat NWea SPer SRms WDin WFar WHCG WMoo
§	- 'Manchu'	CDoC CTri MBar MRav MWat NLon NPro SChu SHBN SPer SRms WCFE WTel
	- Marian Red Robin = 'Marrob'PBR 🏆H4	CDoC CSBt CWib EBee ELan ENot EPfP GKir LAst LRHS MAsh MBri MRav MSwo MWat NCGa NWea SCoo SLim SLon SPer SPoG SWvt WDin
	- 'Maybe'	WWeb
	- 'McKay's White'	WWeb
	- 'Medicine Wheel Mountain' 🏆H4	ELan ENot EWes LRHS MAsh MBri MRav NLar NPro SCoo SLim SPer WHCG WWeb
	- Moonlight	see *P. fruticosa* 'Maanelys'
§	- 'Mount Everest'	EHol NWea SLon SRms WWeb
	- 'Nana Argentea'	see *P. fruticosa* 'Beesii'
	- 'New Dawn'	CDoC GKir LRHS MAsh MBNS MBri NCGa WBcn WFar WWeb
	- 'Orange Star'	WHCG WWeb
	- 'Orangeade'	LRHS MAsh SMur WWeb
	- 'Peaches and Cream'	WEas WWeb
*	- 'Peachy Proud'	NPro
	- 'Pink Beauty'PBR 🏆H4	CDoC COtt CSBt ENot EPfP LRHS LSRN MAsh MBNS MRav NBlu NEgg NPri SCoo SPer SPoG SWvt WMoo WWeb
	- 'Pink Pearl'	WBcn WMoo
	- 'Pink Queen'	CBcs EMil MBri
	- 'Pink Whisper'	WWeb
	- 'Pretty Polly'	CSBt CTri CWSG EBee EPfP GKir LAst LRHS MAsh MBar MGos MSwo NBlu SHBN SPer SPla SSta WDin WFar WHCG WHar WMoo WWeb
	- 'Primrose Beauty' 🏆H4	CDoC CDul EBee EGra ELan ENot EPfP GKir LAst LRHS MAsh MBar MRav MSwo MWgw NBlu NCGa NJOw NLon SCoo SLim SMer SPlb WDin WFar WHar WMoo WWeb
	- Princess = 'Blink'PBR	CDul CSBt CTri CWSG ELan GKir LRHS MAsh MBNS MBar MRav MSwo NBlu NEgg SCoo SLim SPer SReu SRms WDin WFar WHar WWeb
	- 'Prostrate Copper'	NJOw
	- var. ***pumila***	WPat
	- 'Red Ace'	More than 30 suppliers
	- var. ***rigida***	WBcn
	- 'Royal Flush'	MBar
	- 'Snowbird'	EPfP LRHS MBNS MGos NPro SLim SPoG WFar WWeb
§	- 'Snowflake'	CBcs WGwG WMoo
	- 'Sommerflor' 🏆H4	EBee ENot EPfP MRav NCGa
	- 'Sophie's Blush'	CChe EBee MRav NWea WDin WHCG WSHC WWeb
	- 'Summer Sorbet'	MAsh
	- 'Sunset'	CBcs CBrm CSBt CSam CWSG CWib EBee ELan EPfP GKir LRHS MBar MGos MRav NBir NEgg NLon NWea SAga SCoo SLim SReu SRms SSta WBVN WFar WMoo WWeb
	- 'Tangerine'	CBcs CDoC CDul CTrw CWSG CWib EPfP GKir LRHS MBar MGos MRav MSwo NBir NEgg NJOw NWea SLim SPer SPlb SPoG SRms SWvt WBVN WDin WFar WHar WMoo WTel WWeb
	- 'Tilford Cream'	CDoC CSBt CSam EBee ELan EPfP LAst LRHS LSRN MAsh MBar MRav MSwo MWgw NBir NBlu NCGa NEgg SHBN SPer SPoG SReu SRms WBVN WCFE WDin WFar WHCG WMoo WWeb
	- 'Tom Conway'	WHCG
	- 'Tropicana'	WBcn
§	- var. ***veitchii***	CSBt SHBN
	- 'Vilmoriniana'	CBot CTri ELan EPfP LRHS MAsh MRav NLon NPro SIgm SLon SPer SPoG SSpi WAbe WCFE WHCG WSHC WTel WWeb
	- 'Wessex Silver'	CFai WHCG
	- 'Whirligig'	CFai WHCG
	- 'White Rain'	GKir NLon WWeb
	- 'Wickwar Beauty'	CWib
	- 'Wickwar Trailer'	CLyd WHoo
	- 'William Purdom'	WHCG
	- 'Wychbold White'	WWeb
	- 'Yellow Bird' 🏆H4	LRHS MGos
	- 'Yellow Carpet'	WWeb
	- 'Yellow Giant'	WWeb
	gelida	EHyt
	'Gibson's Scarlet' 🏆H4	More than 30 suppliers
	glandulosa	GAbr MNrw NOak WBrk WHil
	'Gloire de Nancy' (d)	CKno GCal IGor LRHS MRav NBir WCot WPGP WPrP WWhi
	'Gold Clogs'	see *P. aurea* 'Goldklumpen'
	gracilis	CSec EBee NEgg SBri
	grandiflora new	CSec
	'Harlow Cream'	NBid
	'Helen Jane'	GBuc GKir LPio LRHS MBri MHer NBir NGdn NJOw NLar NPro STes WFar WMnd WPer
	heptaphylla	GSki NBre
	'Herzblut'	EBee EPfP GBuc MNrw NLar
	x ***hopwoodiana***	More than 30 suppliers
*	x ***hybrida*** 'Jean Jabber'	EBee EWll GBuc GMac MRav NBur NLar
	hyparctica	MDKP
	- ***nana***	CLyd LBee LRHS WPat
	'Jack Elliot'	WWeb
	'Mandshurica'	see *P. fruticosa* 'Manchu'
§	***megalantha*** 🏆H4	More than 30 suppliers
	- 'Gold Sovereign'	ENot EPfP NGdn NPro SPoG
	'Melton'	EBee EMag MNrw NBir NOak
*	'Melton Fire'	CWan ECtt EGra GFlt GKir MBri MWrn NArg NBir NBur NCot NJOw SBri SGar SUsu WMnd WMoo
	'Monarch's Velvet'	see *P. thurberi* 'Monarch's Velvet'
	'Monsieur Rouillard' (d)	CSam EBee EMar EVFa GCra GKir MHer MNrw MRav MWat NCob NCot NDov NFor NGdn NLon NLsd SHop SWal WHoo WMnd WSan WWhi
	'Mont d'Or'	MBri MRav
	montana	WHer WPer
	nepalensis	CSec EDAr EPPr GKir IMGH LAst NBro NChi NFor NLon NPro SBri SHFr SHel WBrk WGwG

	- 'Flammenspiel'	WFar
	- 'Master Floris'	SAga WFar WHer
§	- 'Miss Willmott' ♀H4	More than 30 suppliers
	- 'Ron McBeath'	CBrm CHea EBee EChP ECtt EMan EMar GBin GBuc GCra GKir GSki LRav MBNS MBri NRnb NSti SBri SIng SPer SWvt WCra WHil WHoo WMoo WWeb
	- 'Roxana'	EBee ECGP ELan ERou GBuc GKir GSki MBNS MDKP MRav NBro WAbb WFar WHoo WMoo WPer WRos
	- 'Shogran'	CBgR EBee EChP EPza ESis GAbr GBuc GMac MWrn NCGa NGby NLar SBri SMar WHil WWeb
§	***neumanniana***	NBir NPri WFar XPep
	- 'Goldrausch'	ECha MRav SBla
§	- 'Nana'	EPot LBee LRHS MHer NEgg NJOw NLAp NLar NMen SPlb SPoG SRms WEas WFar WMoo
	nevadensis	CLyd CTri ECho GEdr SRms WPer
	nitida	GEdr GKev NMen SRms WAbe WLin
	- 'Alba'	EPot NLAp NMen WAbe
	- 'Lissadell'	CPBP
	- 'Rubra'	CFir CMea EDAr GCrs GTou IMGH NBir NLAp NWCA SAga SBla SRms WAbe WPat
	nivea	GTou SRot
*	'Olympic Mountains'	WPer
	ovina	WPer
	palustris	MBow NLar WMoo
	pamiroalaica	EHyt
	pedata	LLWP
	pensylvanica **new**	NEgg
	'Pink Orleans'	WWeb
	aff. ***polyphylla*** CHP&W 314	GKev
	recta	CStr ELau EMan ERou GTou NPri SMar WRos
	- 'Alba'	EBee EGoo GMaP NBur NEgg WPer
	- 'Citrina'	see *P. recta* var. *sulphurea*
	- 'Macrantha'	see *P. recta* 'Warrenii'
§	- var. ***sulphurea***	CHad CMea CSam EBee EChP EGoo EVFa GCal GSki IGor MNrw MTis NBir NBre NLsd SIng SUsu WCAu WCra WFar WHal WHer WHoo WLin WMoo WPer WTin WWhi
§	- 'Warrenii'	CHea CSBt EBee EChP EPla GMaP LAst LRHS MBNS MRav MTis MWat NBir NDov NEgg NJOw NMir NOrc SIng SPer SRms WCAu WFar WHal WMoo WPer
	reptans	CRWN XPep
	- 'Pleniflora' (d)	MInt
	'Roxanne' (d)	EBrs MHer
	rupestris	EBee EChP ECha EPPr EWTr LAst MLLN MNrw NChi NDlv NEgg NSti SBri SGar WBWf WCAu WFar WHal WMoo WPer WWye
	sibbaldiopsis tridentata 'Nuuk'	CStu GSki LRHS MBar MWgw
	speciosa	EWes IGor SMar WMoo
	sterilis	CHid IHMH
	'Sungold'	ECho WHCG
	tabernaemontani	see *P. neumanniana*
	ternata	see *P. aurea* subsp. *chrysocraspeda*
	thurberi	CHid CStr EBee EGra EMan GCal GMac LPhx LPio MMHG MNrw NLar SHGN WLin WMoo
§	- 'Monarch's Velvet'	More than 30 suppliers
	tommasiniana	see *P. cinerea*
	x ***tonguei*** ♀H4	More than 30 suppliers
	tormentilla	see *P. erecta*
	tridentata	see *Sibbaldiopsis tridentata*
	uniflora **new**	GCrs
	verna	see *P. neumanniana*
	- 'Pygmaea'	see *P. neumanniana* 'Nana'
	'Versicolor Plena' (d)	CMea
	villosa	see *P. crantzii*
	'Volcan'	CKno CMea CMil EVFa EWes GCal IGor LPhx MBNS MBri NChi NPro SOkh SUsu WAbb WCra WFar WPGP
§	'White Queen'	EWll GKir MNrw NBur NCob NJOw NPri SHar SPoG SRot
	'William Rollison' ♀H4	More than 30 suppliers
	willmottiae	see *P. nepalensis* 'Miss Willmott'
	'Yellow Queen'	CBcs CTri EMil ENot EPfP ERou GMaP GSki MBNS MNrw MRav SPer WCAu WFar

Poterium see *Sanguisorba*

	sanguisorba	see *Sanguisorba minor*

Prasium (*Lamiaceae*)

	majus	XPep

Pratia (*Campanulaceae*)

§	***angulata***	EWll GGar
	- 'Tim Rees'	IHMH
§	- 'Treadwellii'	ECha EDAr EMan ESis EWin GMac LBee LRHS MBNS SPlb WHal
	- 'Woodside'	ECou
	'Celestial Spice'	ECou
	angulata x ***pedunculata***	GGar
	macrodon	WCru
§	***pedunculata***	More than 30 suppliers
	- 'County Park'	CElw CMea CSpe CTri ECha ECou EDAr ELan EPfP EPot ESis GAbr GGar IHMH ITim MBar NJOw NWCA SAga SBla SIng SPet SPlb SPoG SRms WFar WHoo WPat WPer WWhi
	- 'Kiandra'	ECou
	- 'Tom Stone'	MBNS MWgw
	- 'White Stars'	WLFP
§	***perpusilla***	ECou
	- 'Fragrant Carpet'	ECou
	- 'Summer Meadows'	ECou WPer

Preslia see *Mentha*

Prestonia (*Apocynaceae*)

	quinquangularis **new**	CPLN

Primula ✿ (*Primulaceae*)

	AC 4777 from Tibet **new**	GIBF
	Lismore 79-26	EHyt
	acaulis	see *P. vulgaris*
	'Adrian Jones' (2)	ITim WAbe
	'Aire Mist' (*allionii* hybrid) (2)	CGra CPBP CStu EPot GCai GKev ITim MFie MOne NLAp NRya WAbe WLin
	'Alan Robb' (dPrim)(30)	EPfP NCGa NGHP WFar
	'Alexina' (*allionii* hybrid) (2)	ITim MFie WLin
	algida (11)	ECho GFle GKev
§	***allionii*** (2) ♀H2	EHyt GTou ITim MFie NLAp NWCA WAbe
	- KRW 56/380	EPot
	- KRW 56/392	EPot

	Plant	Suppliers
	- KRW 60/394	EPot
	- KRW 67/412	EPot
	- KRW 74/481	EPot
	- KRW 75/504	CNic
	- KRW 76/504	EPot
	- 'A.K. Wells' (2)	EPot WAbe
	- 'Agnes' (2)	EHyt
	- 'Aire Waves'	see *P.* x *loiseleurii* 'Aire Waves'
	- var. ***alba*** (2)	EHyt
*	- 'Alexander' (2)	CGra
	- 'Amy'	ITim
	- 'Andrew' **new**	CGra EHyt
	- 'Anna Griffith' (2)	EHyt GKev ITim LRHS MFie NRya NWCA WAbe WLin
	- 'Anne' (2)	EHyt EPot ITim NDlv NLAp
§	- 'Apple Blossom' (2)	GAbr GKev MDHE NLAp
	- 'Archer' (2)	EHyt ITim NDlv NLAp WLin
	- 'Austen' (2)	ITim NDlv
	- 'Avalanche' (2)	ITim WAbe
	- 'Beryl'	EHyt
	- 'Bill Martin' (2)	EPot ITim
	- 'Brilliant' (2)	NLAp WAbe
	- 'Chivalry' (2)	CGra
	- 'Claude Flight' (2)	WLin
	- 'Crowsley Variety' (2)	LRHS NLAp NSla NWCA WAbe
	- 'Crusader' (2)	EHyt ITim NLAp
	- 'Crystal' (2)	EHyt
	- 'Duncan' (2)	CNic ITim
§	- 'Edinburgh' (2)	CNic GKir ITim MFie NJOw
	- 'Edrom' (2)	ITim
	- 'Elizabeth Baker' (2)	ITim MFie WAbe
	- 'Elizabeth Burrow' (2)	EHyt
	- 'Elizabeth Earle' (2)	EHyt EPot ITim WAbe
	- 'Elliott's Large'	see *P. allionii* 'Edinburgh'
	- 'Elliott's Variety'	see *P. allionii* 'Edinburgh'
	- 'Eureka'	CGra
	- 'Fanfare' (2)	EPot ITim LRHS WGwG WLin
	- 'Flute' (2)	EHyt
	- 'Frank Barker' (2)	EPot
	- GFS 1984 (2)	CGra
§	- 'Gilderdale Glow' (2)	CGra GKev NRya
	- 'Giuseppi's Form'	see *P. allionii* 'Mrs Dyas'
	- 'Grandiflora' (2)	ITim
	- 'Hocker Edge' (2)	ITim
	- 'Huntsman' (2)	MFie
	- 'Imp'	EHyt
	- Ingwersen's form (2)	GTou
	- 'James' **new**	EHyt
	- 'Jan' (2) **new**	EHyt
	- 'Jenny' (2)	CGra EPot
	- 'Joseph Collins'	CGra
	- K R W	see *P. allionii* 'Ken's Seedling'
§	- 'Kath Dryden' (2)	EHyt
§	- 'Ken's Seedling' (2)	CNic EPot NJOw
	- 'Little O' **new**	WAbe
	- 'Louise' (2)	EHyt
	- 'Malcolm' (2)	EHyt
	- 'Margaret Earle' (2)	EHyt WAbe
	- 'Marion' (2)	ITim
	- 'Marjorie Wooster' (2)	EHyt ITim MFie NWCA SBla WAbe
	- 'Martin' (2)	ITim
	- 'Mary Berry' (2)	EHyt MFie NRya WAbe
	- 'Maurice Dryden' (2)	EHyt
§	- 'Mrs Dyas' (2)	EHyt WAbe
	- 'New Dawn' (2)	EHyt
I	- 'Norma' (2) **new**	EHyt
	- pale (2) **new**	WLin
I	- 'Paula' (2)	EHyt
	- 'Peace' (2)	EPot
	- 'Peggy Wilson' (2)	EPot GKev
	- 'Pennine Pink' (2)	ITim
	- 'Pennine Pink' x ***allionii*** 'Stephen' (2) **new**	EHyt
	- 'Perkie' (2)	EHyt
	- 'Picton's Variety' (2)	NDlv
	- 'Pink Ice' (2) **new**	GCai
	- 'Pinkie' (2)	CGra NLAp WLin
	- 'Pippa' **new**	EHyt
	- 'Praecox' (2)	CGra NSla
	- 'Raymond Wooster' (2)	EHyt ITim LRHS
	- 'Robert' (2)	CGra
I	- 'Roy' (2)	NLAp
	- 'Snowflake' (2)	CGra EHyt GKev ITim LRHS NWCA WAbe
	- 'Stanton House' (2)	MFie NDlv
	- 'Stephen' (2)	EHyt ITim
	- 'Sue'	EHyt
	- 'Superba'	EHyt
	- 'Tranquillity' (2)	EHyt ITim MFie NJOw NLAp WAbe
§	- 'Travellers' (2)	EHyt
	- 'Val' **new**	EHyt
	- 'Viscountess Byng' (2)	ITim WLin
	- 'William Earle' (2)	EHyt GCrs ITim LRHS MFie NDlv NWCA WAbe
	allionii x ***auricula*** 'Blairside Yellow' (2)	CPBP
	- x - 'Old Red Dusty Miller' (2)	GCrs MFie NJOw WLin
	allionii x ***hirsuta*** (2)	ITim MFie
	allionii x 'Lismore Treasure' (2)	CPBP NWCA WLin
	allionii x ***pubescens*** 'Harlow Car' (2)	CLyd GMac ITim
	allionii x ***rubra*** (2)	ITim
	allionii x 'Snow Ruffles' (2)	ITim
	allionii x ***pedemontana***	see *P.* x *sendtneri*
	allionii x 'White Linda Pope' (2)	ITim MFie
	alpicola (26) ♀H4	CFee CRow CSWP EPfP EPot GCra GCrs GEdr GFle GGar GIBF GKir LPBA LRHS MAnH MFOX MFie NBid NBro NDlv NLAp NRnb SPer SPoG WAbe WBVN WLin
	- var. ***alba*** (26)	CRow CSWP GBuc GEdr GGar ITim MBow MNrw
§	- var. ***alpicola*** (26)	CLAP CSWP EBee GBuc GEdr GFle GKev MNrw WAbe
	- hybrids (26)	GMac NEgg NRnb
	- var. ***luna***	see *P. alpicola* var. *alpicola*
	- var. ***violacea*** (26)	CAby CDWL CLAP CRow CSWP EWTr GGar GKev LRHS MBow MFie MNrw NBid WAbe WWhi
	'Altaica'	see *P. elatior* subsp. *meyeri*
	altaica grandiflora	see *P. elatior* subsp. *meyeri*
	'Amanda Gabrielle' **new**	CGra
	amoena	see *P. elatior* subsp. *meyeri*
	anisodora	see *P. wilsonii* var. *anisodora*
	'Annemijne'	EMon
	apoclita (17) **new**	WAbe
	'April Rose' (dPrim)(30)	ENot MRav NBid
	x ***arctotis***	see *P.* x *pubescens*
	aurantiaca (4)	CFir GBar GCai GEdr GFle GIBF SRms WHil
	aureata (21)	GGGa GKev NLAp WAbe
	- subsp. ***fimbriata*** (21)	ITim
	auricula ambig. (2)	WRHF
§	***auricula*** L. (2) ♀H4	EDAr ELan GKir GTou LRHS MFie MHer NBro NJOw NSla SPer SPet SPlb WAbe
	- var. ***albocincta*** (2)	EBee NWCA
	- subsp. ***auricula*** (2)	GTou
	- subsp. ***balbisii***	see *P. auricula* subsp. *ciliata*
§	- subsp. ***ciliata*** (2)	GFle NLAp
	auricula hort. '2nd Vic'	SPop
	- A74 (A)	NCob WBrE

- 'Abundance' (A)	MAln
- 'Achates' (A)	MAln
- 'Admiral' (A)	MAln MCre
- 'Adrian' (A)	GAbr MCre MFie NBro NLAp SPop WHil WLin
- 'Adrienne Ruan' (A)	MAln MOne
- 'Aga Khan' (A)	MAln
- 'Agamemnon' (A)	MAln MCre
- 'Alamo' (A)	MCre SPop
- 'Alan Ravenscroft' (A)	MAln MFie
- 'Alansford' (A)	MAln
- 'Albert Bailey' (S/d)	GCai ITim MAln MCre SPop
- 'Alexandra Georgina' (A)	MAln
- 'Alf' (A)	MAln
- 'Alfred Charles' (A)	MAln
- 'Alfred Niblett' (S)	NLAp WLin
- 'Alice Haysom' (S)	CNic ELan ENot GCai MCre MFie NJOw NLAp SDnm SPav SPop WHil WLin
- 'Alicia' (A)	ENot MCre MFie SDnm SPop
- 'Alison Jane' (A)	CLyd MCre MFie NOak SUsu
- 'Alison Telford' (A) **new**	WHil
- 'Allensford' (A)	MCre
- alpine mixed (A)	CNic MBow SRms
- 'Amber Light' (S)	MAln
- 'Amicable' (A)	MCre MFie SPop WHil
- 'Ancient Order' (A)	MAln
- 'Ancient Society' (A)	SPop
- 'Andrea Julie' (A)	GAbr ITim MCre MFie MOne NRya SPop WHil WLin
- 'Andrew Hunter' (A)	MAln MFie SPop
- 'Andy Cole' (A)	MAln
- 'Angelo' (A)	MAln
- 'Angie' (d)	MAln
- 'Ann Taylor' (A)	MAln
- 'Anne Hyatt' (d)	MAln WLin
- 'Anne Swithinbank' (d)	MAln
- 'Antoc' (S)	SPop
- 'Anwar Sadat' (A)	GAbr MCre MFie SPop
- 'Applecross' (A)	ITim MCre MFie WHil WLin
- 'April Moon' (S)	MAln SPop
- 'April Tiger' (S)	MAln
- 'Arabian Night' (A)	MAln
- 'Arapaho' (A)	MAln
- 'Arctic Fox'	MAln
- 'Argus' (A)	CLyd GAbr MCre MFie NBir SPop SUsu WHil WLin
- 'Arlene' (A)	MAln
- 'Arthur Delbridge' (A)	MCre MFie
- 'Arundel Star'	NLAp
- 'Arundell' (S/St)	GAbr GCai ITim MCre MFie NJOw NLAp SPop WHil WLin
- 'Ashcliffe Gem' (A)	MAln
- 'Ashcliffe Gold' (A)	MAln
- 'Astolat' (S)	CWCL ITim MCre NJOw NLAp NOak NRya SDnm SPav SPop SUsu WHil WLin
- 'Athene' (S)	MAln MOne
- 'Audacity' (d) **new**	MAln
- 'Aurora' (A)	MFie
- 'Austin' (A)	MAln
- 'Avril' (A)	MAln
- 'Avril Hunter' (A)	MCre MFie SPop WLin
- 'Aztec' (d)	MAln
- 'Bacchante' (d)	MAln
- 'Bacchus' (A)	MCre MFie
- 'Balbithan' (B)	GAbr
- 'Barbara Mason'	MAln
- 'Barbarella' (S)	MCre MFie SPop WLin
- Barnhaven doubles (d)	CSWP GAbr MAnH WLin
- 'Basilio' (S)	MAln
- 'Basuto' (A)	MCre MFie SPop WHil
- 'Beatrice' (A)	EShb GAbr GCai MCre MFie SPop WHil WLin
- 'Beauty of Bath' (S)	MAln NLAp
- 'Beckminster' (A)	MAln
- 'Bedford Lad' (A)	MCre
- 'Beechen Green' (S)	GAbr GCai MCre NJOw NLAp SPop WLin
- 'Belle Zana' (S)	MAln SPop
- 'Bellezana'	MFie
- 'Ben Lawers' (S)	WLin
- 'Ben Wyves' (S)	MCre
- 'Bendigo' (S)	MAln
- 'Bewitched' (A)	MAln
- 'Bilbao' (A)	MAln
- 'Bilbo Baggins' (A)	MAln
- 'Bill Bailey'	MOne
- 'Bilton' (S)	NLAp
- 'Black Ice' (S)	MAln
- 'Black Jack'[PBR]	COtt MAln
- 'Black Knight' (d)	MAln
- 'Blackfield' (S)	MFie
- 'Blackhill' (S)	NLAp
- 'Blackpool Rock' (St)	MAln
- 'Blairside Yellow' (B)	EHyt EWes NLAp NSla
- 'Blakeney' (d)	GCai MAln MFie NLAp
- 'Blossom' (A)	MFie WLin
- 'Blue Bonnet' (d)	MAln
- 'Blue Bonnet' (A/d)	GAbr NLAp SPop
- 'Blue Chips' (S)	MAln
- 'Blue Cliffs' (S)	MAln
- 'Blue Denim' (S)	MAln
- 'Blue Frills'	MAln
- 'Blue Heaven'	GAbr MOne
- 'Blue Jean' (S)	MFie NLAp SPop
- 'Blue Miller' (B)	GAbr
- 'Blue Mist' (B)	GAbr
- 'Blue Moon' (S)	MAln
- 'Blue Nile' (S)	MCre NLAp SPop
- 'Blue Steel' (S)	MAln
- 'Blue Velvet' (B)	MFie NBro SPop WHil WLin
- 'Bob Lancashire' (S)	ITim MCre MFie NLAp SPop SUsu WCot WHil
- 'Bold Tartan' (St)	MAln
- 'Bolero' (A)	SPop
- 'Bollin Tiger' (St)	MAln
- 'Bonanza' (S)	MAln
- 'Bookham Firefly' (A)	ITim MCre MFie NRya SPop WHil WLin
- 'Boromir' (A)	MAln
- 'Boy Blue' (S)	MAln WHil
- 'Bradford City' (A)	MAln SDnm SPav
- 'Branno' (S)	MAln
- 'Brasso'	MAln
- 'Brazil' (S)	GAbr ITim LRHS MCre MFie MOne NLAp NOak SPav SPop WHil WLin
- 'Brazos River' (A)	MAln
- 'Brenda's Choice' (A)	MCre MFie
- 'Brentford Bees' (St)	MAln
- 'Bright Eyes' (A)	MCre MFie
- 'Broad Gold' (A)	MAln MCre MOne SPop
- 'Broadwell Gold' (B)	CLyd GAbr WLin
- 'Brocade' (St)	MAln
- 'Brompton' (S)	MAln
- 'Brookfield' (S)	ITim MCre MFie NLAp SPop WHil WLin
- 'Brookgood' **new**	WHil
- 'Broughton' (S)	MFie WLin
- 'Brown Ben'	MFie
- 'Brown Bess' (A)	GCai ITim MCre MFie MOne SPop WLin
- 'Brownie' (B)	NBir SDnm SPav
- 'Buccaneer'	MAln
- 'Bucks Green' (S)	SPop

- 'Bunty' (A) MFie
- 'Butterwick' (A) ENot GAbr LRHS MBNS MCre MFie SPav SPop WLin
- 'C.F. Hill' (A) MAln
- 'C.G. Haysom' (S) GAbr MCre MFie SPop
- 'C.W. Needham' (A) MCre MFie NLAp WLin
I - 'Calypso' (A) MAln
- 'Cambodunum' (A) MCre MFie SPop
- 'Camelot' (d) CLyd ELan GCai MCre MFie MOne NBro NPri SPop SUsu WFar WHil
- 'Cameo' (A) MCre
- 'Camilla' (A) MAln
I - 'Candida' (d) MAln MCre SPop
- 'Caramel' (A) MAln
- 'Carioca' (A) MAln
- 'Carole' (A) MFie WLin
- 'Catherine Redding' (d) MAln
- 'Catherine Wheel' (St) MAln
- 'Chaffinch' (S) GAbr MOne NLAp
- 'Chamois' (B) GAbr
- 'Channel' (S) MAln
- 'Chantilly Cream' (d) MAln MCre
- 'Charles Bronson' (d) MAln
- 'Charles Rennie' (B) MAln
- 'Charlie's Aunt' (A) MAln
- 'Checkmate' MAln
- 'Chelsea Bridge' (A) ITim MCre MFie NLAp SPop
- 'Chelsea Girl' (d) MOne
- 'Cheops' **new** WHil
- 'Cherry' (S) ITim MFie NLAp
- 'Cherry Picker' (A) MCre MFie
- 'Cheyenne' (S) GAbr MCre MFie WLin
- 'Chiffon' (S) MAln SPop
- 'Chirichua' (S) MAln
- 'Chloë' (S) MOne
- 'Chloris' (S) MAln NBir
- 'Chocolate Soldier' (A) MAln
- 'Chorister' (S) ELan ENot GAbr GCai ITim MCre MFie MOne NBir NLAp NOak NPri SUsu WHil WLin
- 'Cicero' (A) MAln
I - 'Cinnamon' (d) ITim MCre MFie SPop WLin
- 'Ciribiribin' (A) MAln
- 'Clare' (S) MCre MFie NRya
- 'Clatter-Ha' (d) GCrs
- 'Claudia Taylor' WLin
- 'Clouded Yellow' (S) MAln
- 'Clunie' (S) ITim MCre
- 'Clunie II' (S) ITim NLAp WLin
- 'Cobden Meadows' (A) MAln
I - 'Coffee' (S) CWCL MCre MFie NLAp SUsu
- 'Colbury' (S) MCre SPop
- 'Colonel Champney' (S) ITim MCre MFie NJOw NLAp SPop WLin
- 'Comet' (S) WHil
- 'Confederate' (S) MAln
- 'Connaught Court' (A) MAln
- 'Conservative' (S) GAbr MFie SUsu WLin
- 'Consett' (S) MFie NLAp WHil
- 'Coppi' (A) MAln SPop
- 'Coral' (S) MFie
- 'Coral Sea' (S) MAln
- 'Cornmeal' (S) MAln MFie
- 'Corntime' (S) MAln
- 'Corporal Kate' (St) MAln
- 'Corrie Files' (d) MAln
- 'Cortez Silver' (S) MAln
- 'Cortina' (S) EBee ECGP GCai ITim MCre MOne NLAp NOak NRya SDnm SPav SPop SUsu WHil WLin
- 'County Park Red' (B) ECou
- 'Craig Vaughan' (A) MFie WHil WLin
- 'Cranbourne' (A) MAln
- 'Crecy' (A) MAln
- 'Crimple' (S) MAln
- 'Crimson Glow' (d) MAln NLAp SPop
- 'Cuckoo Fair' SPop
- 'Cuckoo Fare' (S) MAln
- 'Cuddles' (A) MAln
- 'Curry Blend' (B) GAbr
- 'D.S.J.' (S) WLin
- 'Daftie Green' (S) GAbr ITim MCre NLAp WHil
- 'Dakota' (S) NLAp
- 'Dales Red' (B) MAln MFie SDnm WHil WLin
- 'Dan Tiger' (St) MAln NLAp
- 'Daniel' (A) MAln
- 'Daphnis' (S) MAln MCre
- 'Dark Eyes' (d) MAln NLAp
- 'Dark Lady' (A) MAln
- 'David Beckham' (d) MAln
- 'Decaff' (St) MAln
- 'Delilah' (d) GAbr MCre MFie MOne WLin
- 'Denise' (S) MAln
- 'Denna Snuffer' (d) GAbr ITim NLAp
- 'Devon Cream' (d) MCre MFie WFar
- 'Diamond' (d) MAln
- 'Diane' (A) MFie
- 'Digit' (d) MAln
- 'Digsby' (d) MAln
* - 'Dill' (A) MAln
- 'Dilly Dilly' (A) MAln
- 'Divint Dunch' (A) MCre MFie SPop
- 'Doctor Duthie' (S) MAln
- 'Doctor Jones' (d) MAln
- 'Doctor Lennon's White' (B) MCre MFie SPop
- 'Dolly Viney' (d) MAln
- 'Donhead' (A) MCre MFie SPop
- 'Donna Clancy' (S) ITim MFie
- 'Dorado' (d) MAln
- 'Doreen Stevens' (A) MAln MFie
- 'Doris Jean' (A) MFie
- 'Dorothy' (S) MAln
- 'Doublet' (d) GAbr GCai ITim MCre MFie NLAp NOak NRya SPop WHil WLin
- 'Doublure' (d) GAbr ITim MCre
- 'Douglas Bader' (A) MCre MFie
- 'Douglas Black' (S) GAbr MCre NLAp SPop WLin
- 'Douglas Blue' (S) MAln
- 'Douglas Gold' WLin
- 'Douglas Green' (S) MFie SPop
- 'Douglas Red' (A) WLin
- 'Douglas White' (S) MFie
- 'Dovedale' (S) MAln
- 'Dowager' (A) MFie
- 'Doyen' (d) MAln MFie
- 'Drax' (A) MAln
- 'Dubarii' (A) MAln
- 'Duchess of Malfi' (S) SPop
- 'Duchess of York' (2) GBuc
* - 'Dusky' WLin
- 'Dusky Girl' (A) MAln
- 'Dusky Maiden' (A) GCai MCre MFie SPop WHil WLin
- 'Dusty Miller' (B) MRav NBid NBir
- 'Eastern Promise' (A) GCai MAln MFie NLAp SPop
- 'Ed Spivey' (A) MCre
- 'Eddy Gordon' (A) MAln
- 'Eden Carmine' (B) MFie
- 'Eden David' (B) MFie
- 'Edith Allen' (A) MAln
- 'Edith Major' (D) **new** MFie
- 'Edward Sweeney' (S) MAln
- 'Eli Jenkins' MAln
- 'Elizabeth Ann' (A) GAbr MCre
- 'Ellen Thompson' (A) MCre MFie WLin
- 'Elsie' (A) MCre

	Name	Suppliers
	- 'Elsie May' (A)	ITim MCre MFie MOne NLAp SPop WHil WLin
	- 'Elsinore' (S)	MCre
	- 'Emberglow' (d)	MAln
	- 'Embley' (S)	ITim NLAp SPop
	- 'Emery Down' (S)	NLAp SPop
	- 'Emma Louise'	MFie
	- 'Emmett Smith' (A)	MAln
	- 'Enigma' (S)	MAln
	- 'Envy' (S)	MAln
I	- 'Erica' (A)	MCre MFie SUsu WHil WLin
	- 'Erjon' (S)	MAln MFie
	- 'Error' (S)	MAln
	- 'Ethel'	WHil
	- 'Etna' (S)	MAln
	- 'Ettrick' (S)	MAln
	- 'Eventide' (S)	NLAp SPop
	- 'Everest Blue' (S)	SPop SUsu
	- 'Excalibur' (d)	MAln WLin
	- (Exhibition Series) 'Exhibition Blau' (B)	MFie
	- - 'Exhibition Gelb' (B)	MFie
	- - 'Exhibition Rot' (B)	MFie
	- 'Eyeopener' (A)	MAln MCre SPop
	- 'Fairy' (A)	MAln
	- 'Fairy Moon' (S)	MAln
	- 'Falaraki' (A)	MAln
	- 'Falstaff' (d)	MAln
	- 'Fanciful' (S)	MFie WLin
	- 'Fandancer' (A)	MAln
	- 'Fanfare' (S)	MAln SPop WGwG
	- 'Fanny Meerbeck' (S)	GAbr GCai GFlt ITim MFie NLAp NOak SPop WLin
	- 'Faro' (S)	MAln
	- 'Favorite'	ITim WLin
	- 'Favourite' (S)	MCre MFie MOne NJOw NLAp SPop WHil
	- 'Fen Tiger' (St)	MAln
	- 'Fennay' (S)	MAln
	- 'Figaro' (S)	MAln MFie SPop WLin
	- 'Finavon'	GCrs
	- 'Finchfield' (A)	MCre SUsu
	- 'Firecracker'	MAln
	- 'Firenze' (A)	SPop
	- 'Firsby' (d)	MAln
	- 'First Lady' (A) **new**	MAln
	- 'Fishtoft' (d)	MAln
	- 'Flame' (A)	ITim
	- 'Florence Brown' (S)	ITim
	- 'Forest Pines' (S)	MAln
	- 'Fradley' (A)	MAln
	- 'Frank Bailey' (d)	MAln
	- 'Frank Crosland' (A)	MFie WHil
	- 'Frank Faulkner' (A)	MAln
	- 'Frank Jenning' (A)	MAln
	- 'Fred Booley' (d)	SPop WHil WLin
	- 'Fred Livesley' (A)	MAln
	- 'Friskney' (d)	MAln
	- 'Frittenden Yellow' (B)	GAbr WLin
	- 'Fuller's Red' (S)	CLyd MFie NLAp SPop
	- 'Fuzzy' (St)	MAln
	- 'Gaia' (d)	MAln
	- 'Galatea' (S)	MAln
	- 'Galen' (A)	MCre MFie WLin
	- 'Ganymede' (d)	MAln
	- 'Gary Pallister' (A)	MAln
	- 'Gavin Ward' (S)	MAln
	- 'Gay Crusader' (A)	ITim MCre MFie SPop
	- 'Gazza' (A)	MAln
	- 'Gee Cross' (A)	MCre MFie SPop
§	- 'Geldersome Green' (S)	GCai MCre MFie SPop WLin
	- 'Generosity' (A)	MCre SPop
	- 'Geordie' (A)	MAln
	- 'George Harrison' (B)	GAbr
	- 'George Jennings' (A)	MAln
	- 'George Stephens' (A)	MAln
	- 'Geronimo' (S)	MFie NLAp SPop
	- 'Girl Guide' (S)	MAln
	- 'Gizabroon' (S)	CLyd CWCL GCai MCre MFie NLAp SDnm SPav WLin
	- 'Glasnost' (S)	MAln
	- 'Gleam' (S)	CWCL ENot GCai GCrs LTwo MCre MFie NJOw NLAp SPop WHil WLin
	- 'Gleneagles' (S)	EShb GCai ITim MAln MCre NLAp SPop
	- 'Glenelg' (S)	GAbr GCrs ITim MCre MFie NLAp SPop WHil WLin
	- 'Glenna Goodwin' (d)	MAln
	- 'Gold Seam' (A)	MAln
	- 'Golden Boy' (A)	MAln
	- 'Golden Chartreuse' (d)	GAbr MCre
	- 'Golden Eagle' (A)	MAln
	- 'Golden Eye' (S)	MAln
	- 'Golden Fleece' (S)	GAbr GCai MFie NLAp SPop WHil
	- 'Golden Girl' (A)	MAln
	- 'Golden Glory' (A)	MAln
	- 'Golden Hill' (S) **new**	NLAp
	- 'Golden Hind' (d)	SPop WLin
	- 'Golden Splendour' (d)	MCre MFie NLAp SPop
	- 'Golden Wedding' (A)	MAln SPop
	- 'Goldthorn' (A)	MCre
	- 'Goldwin' (A)	MAln MCre
	- 'Gollum' (A)	MAln
	- 'Good Report' (A)	MFie SPop
	- 'Gordon Douglas' (A)	MCre MFie
	- 'Grabley' (S)	MAln
	- 'Grandad's Favourite' (B)	SPop
	- 'Green Finger' (S)	SPop
	- 'Green Frill'	ITim
	- 'Green Goddess' (St)	MAln
	- 'Green Isle' (S)	GAbr MCre MFie MOne NBir NLAp SPop WLin
	- 'Green Jacket' (S)	MCre
	- 'Green Magic' (S)	MAln
	- 'Green Meadows' (S)	MAln SPop
	- 'Green Parrot' (S)	CLyd ITim MCre SPop WHil
	- 'Green Shank' (S)	ITim MFie NLAp SPop WHil WLin
	- 'Greenfinger' (S)	MAln
	- 'Greenpeace' (S)	LRHS SPop
	- 'Greensleeves' (S)	SPop
	- 'Greenways' (S)	MAln
	- 'Greta' (S)	ELan ITim MCre NLAp NOak SPop WHil WLin
	'Gretna Green' (S)	MFie NLAp SPop
	- 'Grey Dawn' (S)	MAln
	- 'Grey Edge'	ITim SUsu
	- 'Grey Friar' (S)	MAln
	- 'Grey Hawk' (S)	MFie WLin
	- 'Grey Lady' (S)	MAln
	- 'Grey Lag' (S)	MFie WHil
	- 'Grey Monarch' (S)	GCai ITim MCre MFie WLin
	- 'Grey Owl' (S)	MAln
	- 'Grey Shrike' (S)	MAln
	- 'Grizedale' (S)	MAln
	- 'Guildersome Green'	see *P. auricula* 'Geldersome Green'
	- 'Guinea' (S)	GAbr MFie NLAp SPop WHil WLin
	- 'Gwen' (A)	MAln MCre NLAp SPop
	- 'Gwen Gaulthiers' (S)	MAln
	- 'Gwenda' (A)	MAln WHil
	- 'Gypsy Rose Lee' (A)	MAln
	- 'Habanera' (A)	MCre MFie SPop
	- 'Hadrian's Shooting Star' (d)	MAln

- 'Haffner' (S)	MAln
- 'Hallmark' (A)	MAln
- 'Hardley' (S)	MAln
- 'Harmony' (B)	MFie NBro
- 'Harry Hotspur' (A)	MFie SPop
- 'Harry 'O'' (S)	MCre NLAp SPop
- 'Harvest Glow' (S) **new**	WHil
- 'Haughmond' (A)	MCre
- 'Hawkwood' (S)	CWCL ITim MCre NJOw NLAp SDnm SPav SPop SUsu WHil
- 'Hawkwood Fancy' (S)	MFie WLin
* - 'Hazel' (A)	MCre MFie MOne
- 'Headdress' (S)	GAbr MCre MFie SPop
- 'Heady' (A)	SPop
- 'Heart of Gold' (A)	MAln SPop
- 'Hebers'	MAln
- 'Helen' (S)	MFie SPop WHil
- 'Helen Barter' (S)	NLAp SPop
- 'Helen Ruane' (d)	MAln SPop WLin
- 'Helena' (S)	ITim MCre MFie NLAp NOak
- 'Helena Dean' (d)	MAln
- 'Helmswell Blush'	MOne
- 'Helmswell Ember'	GAbr MOne
- 'Henry Hall'	MOne
- 'Hetty Woolf' (S)	GAbr ITim MCre
- 'High Hopes'	MAln
- 'Hillhouse' (A)	MCre
- 'Hinton Admiral' (S)	ITim MAln NLAp
- 'Hinton Fields' (S)	EBee ECGP GCai MCre MFie NLAp SDnm SPav SPop WHil WLin
- 'Hinton Green Fields'	ENot EShb GAbr
- 'Hobby Horse'	WLin
- 'Hogton Gem' (d)	MAln
- 'Holyrood' (S)	GAbr
- 'Honey' (d)	MAln SPop
- 'Honeymoon' (S)	MAln
- 'Hopleys Coffee' (d)	GAbr GCai MAln SPop
- 'Howard Telford' (A)	MCre
- 'Hurstwood Midnight'	MFie
* - 'Hyacinth' (S)	LRHS
- 'Iago' (S)	MAln
- 'Ian Greville' (A)	MAln
- 'Ibis' (S)	MAln MCre
- 'Ice Maiden'	MAln SPop
- 'Idmiston' (S)	MCre SPop WLin
- 'Immaculate' (A)	MAln SPop WHil
- 'Impassioned' (A)	MAln MFie SPop
- 'Impeccable' (A)	MAln
- 'Imperturbable' (A)	MAln
- 'Indian Love Call' (A)	ITim MCre MFie SPop WHil
- 'Isabel' (S)	MAln
- 'Isabella'	MAln
- 'Jack Dean' (A)	MAln MCre MFie SPop WHil
- 'James Arnot' (S)	GAbr MFie NOak NRya SPop
- 'Jane' (S)	MAln
- 'Jane Myers' (d)	MAln MFie WHil
- 'Janet'	GEdr
- 'Janie Hill' (A)	MCre MFie MOne
- 'Jean Fielder' (A)	MAln
- 'Jean Jacques' (A)	MAln
- 'Jeanne' (A)	MFie
- 'Jeannie Telford' (A)	MCre MFie SPop
- 'Jenny' (A)	EBee ENot GEdr ITim MBNS MCre MFie NLAp SPop WHil
- 'Jersey Bounce' (A)	MAln
- 'Jesmond' (S)	MAln
- 'Jessie' (d)	MAln
- 'Joan Elliott' (A)	GAbr
- 'Joanne' (A)	MCre
- 'Joe Perks' (A)	MAln MFie NLAp NRya WHil
- 'Joel' (S)	MAln MCre MFie NLAp SPop WLin
- 'Johann Bach' (B)	MFie
- 'John Gledhill' (A)	MCre
- 'John Millard' **new**	MOne
- 'John Stewart' (A)	MCre MFie
- 'John Wayne' (A)	MCre MFie
- 'Jonathon' (A)	MAln
- 'Joy' (A)	CLyd ITim LTwo MCre MFie NLAp SPop WHil
- 'Joyce' (A)	GAbr MCre MFie NBir SPop WLin
- 'Julia' (S)	MAln
- 'July Sky' (A)	MCre
- 'June' (A)	MAln
- 'Jungfrau' (d)	MAln
- 'Jupiter' (S)	MAln
- 'Jura' (A)	MAln
- 'Just Steven' (A)	MAln
- 'Karen Cordrey' (S)	GAbr ITim MCre MFie NLAp SDnm SPav SPop WHil WLin
- 'Karen McDonald' (A)	SPop
- 'Kath Dryden'	see *P. allionii* 'Kath Dryden'
- 'Kelso' (A)	MFie
- 'Ken Chilton' (A)	MAln MFie WHil
- 'Kens Green' (S)	NLAp
- 'Kercup' (A)	MFie SPop
- 'Kevin Keegan' (A)	SPop
- 'Key West' (A)	MAln
- 'Khachaturian' (A)	MAln
- 'Kim' (A)	MCre MFie MOne WLin
- 'Kingcup' (A)	MCre MFie SPop
- 'Kingfisher' (A)	SPop WHil
- 'Kiowa' (S)	SPop
- 'Kirklands' (d)	MFie SPop WHil
- 'Klondyke' (A)	MAln
- 'Königin der Nacht' (St)	MAln
- 'Lady Daresbury' (A)	MCre MFie SPop
- 'Lady Diana' (S)	MAln
- 'Lady Emma Monson' (S)	CHad NLAp
- 'Lady Joyful' (S)	MCre
- 'Lady of the Vale' (A)	MAln
- 'Lady Penelope' (S)	MAln
- 'Lady Zoë' (S)	MAln MCre MFie SPop
- 'Lamplugh'	MOne WHil
- 'Lancelot' (d)	MAln SPop
- 'Landy' (A)	GCrs MCre MFie SPop
- 'Langley Park' (A)	EShb ITim MCre MFie SPop WHil
- 'Lara' (A)	MAln
- 'Laredo' (A)	MAln
- 'Larry' (A)	MAln MCre MFie SPop
- 'Lavender Lady' (B)	SPav
- 'Lavenham' (S)	MAln
- 'Laverock' (S)	MCre NBir NBro
- 'Laverock Fancy' (S)	GCai ITim MFie SUsu WLin
- 'Lazy River' (A)	MAln
- 'Leather Jacket'	GAbr
- 'Lechistan' (S)	ITim MCre MFie SPop WHil WLin
- 'Lee' (A)	MAln MCre
- 'Lee Clark' (A)	MAln
- 'Lee Paul' (A)	GCai ITim MCre MFie NLAp NRya SPop WHil WLin
- 'Lee Sharpe' (A)	MAln SPop
- 'Lemon Drop' (S)	MCre NBro NLAp SPop
- 'Lemon Sherbet' (B)	MFie
- 'Lemon Sorbet' **new**	NRya
- 'Lepton Jubilee' (S)	MAln
- 'Leroy Brown' (A)	MAln
- 'Letty' (S)	MAln
- 'Leverton' (d)	MAln
- 'Lewis Telford' (A)	MAln
- 'Lich' (S)	NLAp
- 'Lichfield' (A/d)	MAln MCre
- 'Light Hearted'	MFie NLAp
- 'Lila' (A)	MAln
- 'Lilac Domino' (S)	MCre MFie NLAp SPop WHil WLin
- 'Lilac Domino' (A)	ITim MAln SPop
- 'Lillian Hill' (A)	MAln

- 'Lima' (d) MAln
- 'Limelight' (A) MAln SPop
- 'Limelight' (S) MAln
- 'Lindsey Moreno' (S) MAln
- 'Ling' (A) ITim MCre MFie SPop
- 'Liptons Jubilee' **new** GAbr
- 'Lisa' (A) CLyd MCre MFie SPop WLin
- 'Lisa Clara' (S) GCai ITim MFie WLin
- 'Lisa's Red' (S) **new** NLAp
- 'Lisa's Smile' (S) GCai MFie MOne NLAp WHil
- 'Little Rosetta' (d) MAln MFie NJOw WHil
- 'Lord Saye and Sele' (St) GAbr GCai ITim MCre MFie NLAp SPop WLin
- 'Lothlorien' (A) MAln
- 'Louisa Woolhead' (d) SPop
- 'Lovebird' (S) GAbr MCre MFie SPop SUsu WHil WLin
- 'Lucky Strike' MAln
- 'Lucy Locket' (B) NBir
- 'Ludlow' (S) GAbr MAln NLAp
- 'Lupy Minstrel' (S) MAln
- 'Lynn' (A) MAln
- 'Lynn Cooper' WLin
- 'Maggie' (S) GAbr ITim MCre NLAp WLin
- 'Magnolia' (B) MFie
- 'Maid Marion' (d) MCre
- 'Maizie' (S) MAln
- 'Mandarin' (A) MCre MFie SPop
- 'Mansell's Green' (S) MAln NJOw NLAp
- 'Mara Cordrey' **new** MOne
- 'Margaret Dee' (d) MAln
- 'Margaret Faulkner' (A) GCai ITim MCre MFie WLin
- 'Margaret Irene' (A) MAln SPop WHil
- 'Margaret Martin' (S) MAln NLAp WLin
- 'Margot Fonteyn' (A) GAbr MAln SPop WHil
- 'Marie Crousse' (d) CPBP MFie SPop
- 'Marigold' (d) CLyd WFar
- 'Marion Howard Spring' (A) MAln MFie
- 'Marion Tiger' (St) MAln
- 'Mark' (A) ITim MCre MFie NBro SPop
- 'Marmion' (S) MAln MFie NLAp SPop WHil
- 'Martha Livesley' (A) MAln
- 'Martha's Choice' (A) MAln
- 'Martin Luther King' (S) MFie
- 'Mary' (d) GAbr MCre
- 'Mary Taylor' (S) MAln NLAp
- 'Mary Zach' (S) NLAp WHil
- 'Matthew Yates' (d) CHad GAbr GCai ITim MCre MFie MOne NPri SDnm SPav SPop SUsu WCot WHil WLin WRha
- 'Maureen Millward' (A) MCre MFie SPop WHil
- 'May' (A) MAln MCre
- 'Mazetta Stripe' (S/St) GAbr ITim NLAp NLar SPop WLin
- 'McWatt's Blue' (B) GAbr IGor WLin
- 'Meadowlark' (A) MAln MCre MFie
- 'Mease Tiger' (St) GAbr MAln
- 'Megan' (d) MAln
- 'Mehta' (A) MAln
- 'Mellifluous' MAln MFie
- 'Mere Green' (S) MAln
- 'Merlin' (A) WLin
- 'Merlin' (S) MAln NLAp
- 'Merlin Stripe' (St) MCre MFie MOne SPop WHil
- 'Mermaid' (d) GAbr MCre
- 'Merridale' (A) MCre MFie
- 'Mersey Tiger' (S) GAbr ITim MFie NLAp SPop
- 'Mesquite' (A) MAln
- 'Mexicano' (A) MAln
- 'Michael' (S) MAln
- 'Michael Watham' (S) MAln
- 'Michael Wattam' (S) MAln
- 'Mick' (A) MAln
- 'Midnight' (A) MAln
- 'Mikado' (S) MCre MFie SPop
- 'Milkmaid' (A) MAln
- 'Millicent' (A) MAln MFie
- 'Mink' (A) MFie WHil
- 'Minley' (S) GCai ITim MCre MFie NBir NBro NLAp SPop WHil WLin
- 'Minsmere' (S) MAln
- 'Mirabella Bay' (A) MAln
- 'Mirandinha' (A) MAln MCre
- 'Miriam' (A) MAln
- 'Mish Mish' (d) WHil
- 'Miss Bluey' (d) MAln
- 'Miss Newman' (A) MAln SPop
- 'Mohawk' (S) MCre
- 'Mojave' (S) CWCL ITim MCre MFie NLAp NRya SPop WHil WLin
- 'Mollie Langford' (A) MAln MCre SPop
- 'Monet' (S) MAln
- 'Moneymoon' (S) MFie NLAp
- 'Monica' (A) MFie
- 'Monk' (S) MCre MFie WHil
- 'Monk's Eleigh' (A) MAln
- 'Moonglow' (S) MFie NLAp
- 'Moonlight' (S) GAbr MAln
- 'Moonrise' (S) MFie
- 'Moonriver' (A) MAln MCre MFie SPop WHil
- 'Moonshadow' (d) MAln
- 'Moonstone' (d) MFie WLin
- 'Moselle' (S) MAln
- 'Mr 'A'' (S) CLyd MCre SPop WHil WLin
- 'Mrs L. Hearn' (A) MCre MFie SPop
- 'Murray Lanes' (A) MAln
- 'My Fair Lady' (A) MAln
- 'Myrtle Park' (A) MAln
- 'Nankenan' (S) MAln MFie WHil
- 'Neat and Tidy' (S) LRHS MCre MFie NLAp NOak NRya SPop WFar WHil WLin
- 'Nefertiti' (A) MAln SPop WHil
- 'Nessundorma' (A) MAln
- 'Neville Telford' (S) ITim MCre MFie NLAp WLin
- 'Nickity' (A) GAbr MCre MFie SPop WLin
- 'Nicola Jane' (A) MAln
- 'Nigel' (d) GAbr ITim NLAp WLin
- 'Night and Day' (S) MFie NLAp
- 'Nightwink' (S) MAln
- 'Nina' (A) MAln
- 'Nita' (d) MAln
- 'Nitelford' **new** MOne
- 'Nocturne' (S) MCre MFie NBro NLAp SPop WLin
- 'Noelle' (S) ITim
- 'Nona' (d) **new** SPop
- 'Nonchalance' (A) MCre MFie
- 'Norma' (A) MFie WLin
- 'Notability' (A) MAln
- 'Notable' (A) MAln
- 'Nureyev' (A) MAln
- 'Oakie' (S) MAln
- 'Ol' Blue Eyes' (St) MAln
- 'Old Clove' **new** MOne
- 'Old Clove Red' **new** GAbr
- 'Old England' (S) MFie SPop
- 'Old Gold' (S) GAbr SUsu WLin
- 'Old Irish Blue' (B) IGor NLAp
- 'Old Irish Scented' (B) GAbr IGor NBro WHil WLin
- 'Old Mustard' (B) SMHy WLin
- 'Old Pink Dusty Miller' **new** GAbr
- 'Old Red Dusty Miller' (B) ECha LTwo NBir NLAp WHil WLin
- 'Old Red Elvet' (S) MAln NLAp SPop
- 'Old Smokey' (A) MAln MFie SPop
- 'Old Suffolk Bronze' (B) GAbr

- 'Old Wine' (A) CLyd
- 'Old Yellow Dusty Miller' (B) CLyd EWes GAbr GCai MFie MSte NBro NLAp NRya WHil WLin
- 'Olton' (A) MFie
- 'Opus One' (A) MAln
- 'Orb' (S) CLyd GAbr ITim MCre MFie NLAp SPop WHil
- 'Ordvic' (S) MAln NRya WLin
- 'Orlando' (S) MAln
- 'Orwell Tiger' (St) SPop
- 'Osbourne Green' (B) GAbr GCai MCre MFie NJOw NLAp SPop SUsu WHil
- 'Otto Dix' (A) MAln
- 'Overdale' (A) MAln MCre
- 'Paddlin Madeleine' (A) MAln
- 'Pagoda Belle' (A) MAln
- 'Paleface' (A) MAln MCre WHil
- 'Pam Tiger' (St) MAln
- 'Panache' (S) MAln
- 'Papageno' (St) MAln
- 'Paradise Yellow' (B) GEdr SPop
- 'Paragon' (A) MAln MCre WHil
- 'Paris' (S) MAln
- 'Party Time' (S) MAln
- 'Pastiche' (A) MCre MFie
- 'Pat' (S) MFie NLAp SPop
- 'Pat Barnard' NJOw
- 'Patience' (S) NJOw SPop WHil
- 'Patricia Barras' (S) MAln
- 'Pauline' (A) MFie
- 'Pauline Taylor' (d) MAln
- 'Pear Drops' GAbr
- 'Pegasus' (d) MAln SPop
- 'Peggy' (A) WHil WLin
- 'Peggy's Lad' (A) MAln
- 'Pequod' (A) MAln
- 'Peter Beardsley' (A) MAln
- 'Peter Hall' (d) MAln
- 'Phantom' MAln
- 'Pharaoh' (A) EShb MAln MFie NLAp SPop
- 'Phate' **new** MOne
- 'Phyllis Douglas' (A) ITim MCre MFie NLAp SPop
- 'Pierot' (A) MCre MFie SPop
- 'Piers Telford' CWCL GCai MCre MFie NLAp SBch SDnm SPav SPop WHil WLin
- 'Pink Fondant' (d) MAln
- 'Pink Lady' (A) MFie NBro SPop
- I - 'Pink Lilac' NLAp
- 'Pink Panther' (S) MAln
- 'Pinkie' (A) MAln
- 'Pinstripe' MOne SPop WHil
- 'Pioneer Stripe' (S) NJOw WHil
- 'Pippin' (A) MCre MFie NBro SPop WLin
- 'Pixie' (A) MAln
- 'Playboy' (A) MAln
- 'Plush Royal' (S) MAln MFie
- 'Polestar' (A) MCre MFie SPop WLin
- 'Pop's Blue' (S/d) SPop
- 'Portree' (S) GAbr
- 'Pot o' Gold' (S) ITim MCre MFie NLAp NOak SPop WHil
- 'Prague' (S) GAbr MCre MFie NBir SPop SUsu WLin
- 'Pretender' (A) MAln SPop
- 'Prince Bishop' (S) MAln
- 'Prince Charming' (S) ITim MFie MOne SPop SUsu WLin
- 'Prince Igor' (A) MAln
- 'Prince John' (A) ITim MCre MFie NBro SPop WHil WLin
- 'Prince Regent' (B) NBro
- 'Prometheus' (d) MAln
- 'Purple Glow' (d) MAln WLin
- 'Purple Sage' (S) GCai NLAp
- 'Purple Velvet' (S) SPop
- 'Quality Chase' (A) MCre
- 'Quatro' (d) MAln
- 'Queen Alexander' GAbr
- 'Queen Bee' (S) GAbr ITim MFie NLAp WHil
- 'Queen of Sheba' (S) MAln NLAp
- 'Quintessence' (A) MAln MCre MFie
- 'Rab C. Nesbitt' (A) MAln
- 'Rabley Heath' (A) CLyd GCai MCre MFie SPop
- 'Rachel' (A) GAbr MAln
- 'Rajah' (S) CWCL ELan ITim MFie NLAp NRya SPop WHil
- 'Raleigh Stripe' (S) MAln NLAp SPop
- 'Ralenzano' (A) MAln
- 'Rameses' (A) MAln MCre
- 'Rebecca Hyatt' (d) MAln
- 'Red Admiral' MAln
- 'Red Arrows' MAln
- 'Red Beret' (S) MFie NLAp
- 'Red Denna' (d) MAln
- 'Red Embers' (S) MAln
- 'Red Gauntlet' (S) EDAr GCai ITim LBBr MBri MFie MRav MSte NLAp SPop WHil WLin
- 'Red Mark' (A) MCre MFie
- 'Red Rum' (S) GAbr ITim MFie NLAp
- 'Redcar' (A) MAln MCre
- 'Redstart' (B) ITim WHil
- 'Regency' (A) MAln
- 'Remus' (S) ELan GAbr GCai LTwo MCre MFie NLAp SPop SUsu WHil
- 'Renata' (S) NLAp
- 'Rene' (A) GAbr MFie NLAp
- 'Respectable' (A) MAln
- 'Reverie' (d) MAln
- 'Riatty' (d) GAbr MAln MFie
- 'Richard Shaw' (A) MFie MOne WHil WLin
- 'Ring of Bells' (S) MAln
- 'Rita' (S) MAln
- 'Robert Lee' (A) MAln
- 'Roberto' (S) MAln
- 'Robin Hood' (A) MAln
- 'Rock Sand' (S) GCai MFie NLAp WHil WLin
- 'Rodeo' (A) GAbr MCre MFie NLAp WPat
- 'Rolts' (S) CLyd ELan EShb GAbr ITim MCre MFie NBir NBro NLAp NOak SDnm SPav SPop WHil WLin
- 'Rondy' (S) MAln NLAp
- 'Ronnie Johnson' MAln
- 'Ronny Simpson' MCre
- 'Rosalie' SPop
- 'Rosalie Edwards' (S) ITim MFie
- 'Rose Conjou' (d) GAbr MAln
- 'Rose Kaye' (A) MAln SPop
- 'Rosebud' (S) GAbr
- 'Rosemary' (S) ITim MCre MFie NLAp SUsu WHil
- 'Rothesay Robin' (A) MAln
- 'Rover Stripe' (St) **new** NLAp
- 'Rowena' (A) GCai MCre MFie NBro SDnm SPav SPop
- 'Roxborough' (A) MAln
- 'Roxburgh' (A) MCre MFie SPop
- 'Roy Keane' (A) MAln MFie SPop
- 'Royal Mail' (S) MAln
- 'Royal Marine' (S) MAln
- 'Royal Purple' (S) NBir
- 'Royal Velvet' (S) GAbr WHil
- 'Ruby Hyde' (B) GAbr
- 'Rusty Dusty' GAbr IGor
- 'Ryecroft' (A) MAln
- 'Sabrina' (A) **new** MAln
- 'Saginaw' (A) MAln
- 'Sailor Boy' (S) MFie NLAp
- 'Saint Boswells' (S) GAbr MAln MCre MFie NLAp SPop

	- 'Saint Elmo' (A)	MFie
	- 'Saint Quentin' (S)	MAln
	- 'Salad' (S)	GCrs
	- 'Sale Green' (S)	MFie
	- 'Sally' (A)	MAln MCre
	- 'Sam Gamgee' (A)	MAln
	- 'Sam Hunter' (A)	MAln SPop
	- 'Samantha' (A) **new**	MAln
	- 'San Antonio' (A)	MAln
	- 'Sandhills' (A)	MAln MCre MFie
	- 'Sandmartin' (S)	MFie NLAp
	- 'Sandra' (A)	ELan GAbr MCre MFie SPop WLin
	- 'Sandra's Lass' (A)	MAln
	- 'Sandwood Bay' (A)	CLyd EShb GAbr GCai LRHS MCre MFie MOne NBro SPop WHil
	- 'Sarah Humphries' (d)	MAln
	- 'Sarah Lodge' (d)	GAbr MFie WLin
	- 'Satchmo' (S)	NLAp
	- 'Scipio' (S)	MAln
	- 'Scorcher' (S)	MAln
	- 'Sea Mist' (d)	MAln
	- 'Serenity' (S)	MCre MFie NLAp
	- 'Sergeant Wilson'	MAln
	- 'Shako' (A)	MAln
	- 'Shalford' (d)	MFie SPop WLin
	- 'Sharman's Cross' (S)	MAln MFie
	- 'Sharon Louise' (S)	MCre NLAp WLin
	- 'Sheila' (S)	MCre MFie NJOw NLAp SPop WHil WLin
	- 'Shere' (S)	MCre MFie NLAp SPop WLin
	- 'Shergold' (A)	MCre MFie
	- 'Sherwood' (S)	GCai ITim MCre MFie SPop WHil WLin
	- 'Shirley' (S)	MAln
	- 'Shotley' (A)	MCre
	- 'Showman' (S)	MAln
	- 'Sibsey' (d)	MAln SPop
	- 'Sidney' (A)	MAln
	- 'Silas' (B)	SPav
	- 'Silmaril'	MAln
	- 'Silverway' (S)	MCre NLAp SPop WHil WLin
	- 'Simply Red'	MAln
	- 'Sir John' (A)	MAln MFie
	- 'Sir John Hall'	MAln
	- 'Sir Robert' (d)	MAln
	- 'Sirbol' (A)	MCre MFie NLAp
	- 'Sirius' (A)	CLyd GAbr LRHS MCre MFie MOne NLAp SPop WCot WHil WLin
	- 'Sister Josephine' (d)	MAln
	- 'Skipper' (d)	SPop
	- 'Skylark' (A)	MAln MCre SPop WHil
	- 'Slioch' (S)	GAbr ITim MCre MFie NLAp SPop WLin
	- 'Slip Anchor' (A)	MAln
	- 'Smart Tar' (S)	MAln
	- 'Snooty Fox' (A)	GAbr MFie MOne NJOw
	- 'Snooty Fox II' (A)	MCre SPop
	- 'Snowy Owl' (S)	MCre MFie NLAp SPop
	- 'Somersby' (d)	MAln SPop
	- 'Soncy Face' (A)	MAln
	- 'Sonny Boy' (A)	MAln
	- 'Sonya' (A)	ITim WLin
	- 'Sophie' (d)	MAln
	- 'South Barrow' (d)	GAbr MCre SPop SUsu WHil
	- 'Sparky' (A)	MAln
	- 'Spartan'	MAln
	- 'Spring Meadows' (S)	CWCL GAbr MCre MFie MOne NLAp NPri SPop SUsu WHil
	- 'Springtime' (A)	MAln SPop
	- 'Standish' (d)	GAbr
	- 'Stant's Blue' (S)	EShb GCai ITim MCre MFie NBro
	- 'Star Wars' (S)	GAbr ITim MAln MFie NLAp SPop WLin
	- 'Starburst' (S)	MAln
	- 'Starling' **new**	GAbr
	- 'Starry' (S)	MOne
	- 'Stella Coop' (d)	MAln
	- 'Stetson' (A)	MAln
	- 'Stoke Poges' (A)	MAln
	- 'Stoney Cross' (S)	NLAp
	- 'Stonnal' (A)	MCre MFie SPop
	- 'Stormin Norman' (A)	MAln
	- 'Stripey' (d)	MAln
	- 'Stuart West' (A)	MCre
	- 'Stubb's Tartan' (S)	NLAp WLin
	- 'Subliminal' (A)	MAln MCre
	- 'Sue' (A)	MCre MFie
	- 'Sugar Plum Fairy' (S)	GAbr
	- 'Sultan' (A)	MAln
	- 'Summer Sky' (A)	MCre SPop
	- 'Summer Wine' (A)	MAln
	- 'Sumo' (A)	MAln MCre MFie SPop WHil WLin
I	- 'Sunflower' (S)	EShb GAbr MCre MFie NLAp SPop WLin
	- 'Sunstar' (S)	MFie
	- 'Super Para' (S)	GAbr MCre MFie NLAp SPop WLin
	- 'Superb' (A)	MAln
	- 'Susan' (A)	ITim MCre MFie
	- 'Susannah' (d)	GAbr GCai ITim LRHS MFie MOne NPri SDnm SPav SPop
	- 'Suzanne' **new**	ENot
*	- 'Sweet Chestnut' (S)	MAln
	- 'Sweet Georgia Brown' (A)	MAln
	- 'Sweet Pastures' (S)	GAbr ITim MCre MFie NLAp SPop
	- 'Swift' (S)	MFie
	- 'Sword' (d)	GAbr GCrs MAln MCre MFie MOne NLAp SPop WHil WLin
	- 'Symphony' (A)	MFie MOne SUsu WHil
	- 'T.A. Hadfield' (A) **new**	MFie
	- 'Taffeta' (S)	MAln SDnm SPav
	- 'Tall Purple Dusty Miller' (B)	SPop
	- 'Tally-ho' (A)	MAln
	- 'Tamino' (S)	MAln
	- 'Tandem' (St)	MAln
	- 'Tarantella' (A)	GAbr MCre MFie WLin
	- 'Tawny Owl' (B)	GAbr NBro
	- 'Tay Tiger' (St)	SPop
	- 'Teawell Pride' (d) **new**	WHil
	- 'Ted Gibbs' (A)	MAln MCre MFie
	- 'Ted Roberts' (A)	EShb MCre MFie NLAp SPop SUsu WHil WLin
	- 'Teem' (S)	MCre MFie NRya SPop WLin
	- 'Temeraire' (A)	MAln
	- 'Tenby Grey' (S)	MCre MFie WLin
	- 'Tender Trap' (A)	MAln
	- 'Terpo' (A)	MAln
	- 'Tess' (A)	MAln
	- 'The Baron' (S)	GCai ITim MCre MFie MOne SPop WLin
	- 'The Bishop' (S)	MFie SPop WHil
	- 'The Bride' (S)	NLAp
	- 'The Cardinal' (d)	MAln SUsu
	- 'The Egyptian' (A)	MAln SPop WHil
	- 'The Hobbit' (A)	MAln
	- 'The Raven' (S)	ITim MFie NLAp SPop
	- 'The Sneep' (A)	MCre SPop WHil
	- 'The Snods' (S)	MFie NLAp
	- 'The Wrekin' (S)	MAln
	- 'Thebes' (A)	MAln
	- 'Thetis' (A)	MCre MFie SPop
	- 'Thirlmere' (d)	MAln
	- 'Three Way Stripe' (St)	MCre WHil
	- 'Thutmoses' (A)	MAln
	- 'Tiger Tim'	MAln

Name	Suppliers
- 'Tinker' (S)	MAln
- 'Tinkerbell' (S)	MCre MFie SPop
- 'Toddington Green' (S)	MAln
- 'Toffee Crisp' (A)	MAln
- 'Tomboy' (S)	MFie SDnm SPop
- 'Toolyn' (S)	MAln
- 'Top Affair' (d)	MAln
- 'Tosca' (S)	GCai GCrs ITim MCre NLAp NRya SPop WHil WLin
- 'Trish'	GAbr
- 'Trouble' (d)	GAbr LPio LRHS MBNS MCre MFie MOne SPop WLin
- 'Troy Aykman' (A)	MAln
- 'Trudy' (S)	GAbr GCai ITim MCre MFie MOne NLAp SPop WHil
- 'True Briton' (S)	MCre MFie SPop
- 'Trumpet Blue' (S)	MFie
- 'Tumbledown' (A)	MFie
- 'Tummel'	MAln SPop
- 'Twiggy' (S)	MAln
- 'Tye Lea' (S)	MAln
- 'Typhoon' (A)	MCre MFie SPop
- 'Uncle Arthur' (A)	MAln
- 'Unforgettable' (A)	MAln MCre
- 'Upton Belle' (S)	MAln
- 'Valerie' (A)	ITim MCre NLAp SPop
- 'Valerie Clare'	MAln
- 'Vee Too' (A)	MCre MFie SPop
- 'Vega' (A)	MAln
- 'Vein' (St)	MAln
- 'Velvet Moon' (A)	MAln MFie
- 'Venetian' (A)	MAln MFie SPop
- 'Venus' (A)	MAln
- 'Vera Hill' (A)	MAln
- 'Verdi' (A)	ITim MAln MCre
- 'Victoria' (S)	MAln
- 'Victoria de Wemyss' (A)	MCre MFie
- 'Victoria Park' (A)	MAln
- 'Virginia Belle' (St)	MAln NLAp
- 'Vivian' (S)	MAln
- 'Vulcan' (A)	MFie NBro SPop WLin
- 'Waincliffe Red' (S)	MFie
- 'Walhampton' (S)	NLAp
- 'Walter Lomas' (S)	MAln
- 'Walton' (A)	CWCL MCre MFie SPop WHil
- 'Walton Heath' (d)	MCre MFie SPop WLin
- 'Waltz Time' (A)	MAln
- 'Watchett' (S)	MAln
- 'Waterfall' (A)	MAln
- 'Wayward' (S)	MAln
- 'Wedding Day' (S)	MAln MFie NLAp
- 'Wentworth' (A)	MAln
- 'Whistle Jacket' (S)	MAln
- 'White Ensign' (S)	GAbr ITim MCre MFie NLAp NOak SPop WHil WLin
- 'White Water' (A)	MAln SPop
- 'White Wings' (S)	GCai MCre MFie NLAp SPop
- 'Whitecap' (S)	MAln
- 'Whoopee' (A)	MAln
- 'Wichita Falls' (A)	MAln
- 'Wide Awake' (A)	MCre MFie
- 'Wilf Booth' (A)	MAln SPop
- 'William Telford' **new**	MOne
- 'Wincha' (S)	EShb GCai MFie NLAp SPop
- 'Windways Pisces' (d)	MAln
- 'Winifrid' (A)	CLyd EShb GAbr LRHS MCre MFie SPop WHil
- 'Winnifred' (B)	MFie NLAp SPop
- 'Woodmill' (A)	MAln SPop
- 'Wookey Hole' (A)	MAln
- 'Wor Jackie' (S)	NLAp
- 'Wycliffe Midnight'	GAbr
- 'Wye Hen' (St)	MAln

	Name	Suppliers
	- 'Y.I. Hinney' (A)	MCre MFie
	- 'Yellow Hammer' (S)	MAln
	- 'Yellow Isle' (S)	MAln
	- 'Yitzhak Rabin' (A)	MAln
	- 'Yorkshire Grey' (S)	MFie NBro
	- 'Zambia' (d)	CLyd GAbr MCre MFie SPop SUsu
	- 'Zircon' (S)	MAln
	- 'Zodiac' (S)	MAln
	- 'Zoe' (A)	MAln
	- 'Zoe Ann' (S)	MAln
I	- 'Zona' (A)	MAln
	- 'Zorro' (St)	MAln
	auriculata (11)	GKev SBla
	- 'Cloudy Bay' (11) **new**	WCot
	'Barbara Barker' (2) **new**	GEdr
	'Barbara Midwinter' (6x30)	CMea WAbe
	Barnhaven Blues Group (Prim)(30) ♀H4	CSWP GAbr MAnH
	Barnhaven doubles (dPoly)(30)	CSWP
	Barnhaven Gold-laced Group	see *P.* Gold-laced Group Barnhaven
	Barnhaven hybrids	MAnH
	Barnhaven Traditional Group	CSWP MAnH
	'Beatrice Wooster' (2)	CLyd CNic GAbr GKev ITim LRHS MFie NDlv NJOw NLAp NWCA
	'Bee' x 'Jo-Jo'	EHyt GCrs
	'Beeches' Pink'	GAbr
	beesiana (4)	More than 30 suppliers
	bella	GKev ITim
	'Bellamy's Pride'	CLyd GAbr WAbe
	bellidifolia (17)	GEdr GFle GIBF
	aff. ***bellidifolia***	GKev
	beluensis	see *P.* x *pubescens* 'Freedom'
	Bergfrühling Julianas Group (Prim)(30)	MFie
§	x ***berninae*** 'Windrush' (2)	WAbe
	'Bewerley White'	see *P.* x *pubescens* 'Bewerley White'
	bhutanica	see *P. whitei* 'Sherriff's Variety'
	x ***biflora*** (2)	WAbe
	'Big Red Giant' (dPrim)(30)	MOne NGHP WCot
	bileckii	see *P.* x *forsteri* 'Bileckii'
	'Blue Riband' (Prim)(30)	EDAr ENot EPfP SBla WFar
	'Blue Sapphire' (dPrim)(30)	EPfP GAbr LRHS MBNS MBow MFie MOne NCGa NGHP NWCA WWol
	'Blutenkissen' (Prim)(30)	GAbr
	'Bon Accord Cerise' (dPoly)(30) **new**	GAbr
	'Bon Accord Purple' (dPoly)(30)	WFar
	'Bonfire' (Poly)(30) **new**	NCob
	'Bootheosa' (21)	NCob
	boothii (21)	CBos
	- EN 382	WThu
	- ***alba*** (21)	GCrs GFle GFlt GGGa LTwo
	- subsp. ***autumnalis*** (21)	GGGa
	- subsp. ***repens*** (21)	MNrw
	'Boothman's Ruby'	see *P.* x *pubescens* 'Boothman's Variety'
	boveana (12)	MFie
§	***bracteosa*** (21)	GCrs GFle ITim NLAp
	Bressingham (4)	WFar
	brevicaula	see *P. chionantha* subsp. *brevicaula*
	brevicula x ***chionantha*** subsp. ***sinopurpurea***	NEgg
	brigantia	GIBF

'Broadwell Chameleon' **new** EHyt
'Broadwell Pink' (2) EHyt ITim
'Broadwell Ruby' (2) EHyt WAbe
'Bronwyn' (Prim)(30) NBir
'Broxbourne' CLyd ITim NLAp
'Buckland Wine' (Prim) (30) CElw
x ***bulleesiana*** (4) CM&M EBee EChP EMFW EMar EWTr GFlt LRHS MBri MTis NBro NLAp NLar NRnb NScw SMrm SPer SRms STes WFar WMnd WMoo WPer
- Moerheim hybrids (4) WFar
bulleyana (4) ♀H4 More than 30 suppliers
- ACE 2484 WAbe
burmanica (4) GBuc GEdr GGar GIBF ITim MDun NEgg NLsd SIng SRms WBVN WFar WGwG WMoo
'Butter's Bronze' (Prim) WOut
'Butterscotch' (Prim)(30) CSWP
'Caerulea Plena' (dPrim) (30) GCal
calderiana (21) GFle GKev
Candelabra hybrids (4) CBre CBro CHar COIW CTbh EChP ENot EPot GFlt GGar ITim LSou MDun NBir NCob NRnb SGSe SPet SWal WRos
Candy Pinks Group (Prim)(30) CSWP
capitata (5) CAby CM&M CSWP EBee EDAr GCrs GFle GIBF GTou IFro ITim MFie NLAp NWCA WAbe WFar WGwG
- subsp. ***crispata*** (5) WLin
- subsp. ***mooreana*** (5) CFir CSec EChP GFle GIBF GKev MHar NDlv NLsd SPlb SRot WBVN
- subsp. ***sphaerocephala*** (5) GKev
'Captain Blood' (dPrim)(30) EPfP MBNS MBow MFie MSte NLar NWCA WFar WRha
'Carmen' (Prim)(30) CLyd ITim
Carnation Victorians Group (Poly)(30) MFie
carniolica (2) GFle MFie
Casquet mixture (Prim) (30) CSWP
cawdoriana (8) GIBF
AC 4345 **new**
cernua (17) GFle GIBF GKev NArg WLin
Chartreuse Group (Poly)(30) CSWP MFie WRha
§ ***chionantha*** (18) ♀H4 CLAP CMil EDAr GCrs GFle GGar GKev GKir GTou LRHS MDun MFie MNrw NBir NCob NEgg NLAp SPer WAbe WFar WGwG
- subsp. ***brevicaula*** GKev
- subsp. ***chionantha*** (18) **new** GIBF
- - SDR 1865 GKev
§ - subsp. ***melanops*** (18) GFle GIBF GMac LRHS
§ - subsp. ***sinopurpurea*** (18) CLAP EChP GFle GGar GIBF GKev GTou NLar WAbe WFar WHil WPer
chungensis (4) CBcs CLAP CMil EBee EDAr EWTr GCra GEdr GFle GGar GIBF GKev GKir GTou ITim MLLN NDlv NEgg NRnb NSti SRms SWvt WAbe WMoo
§ ***chungensis*** x ***pulverulenta*** (4) CLAP EChP GBuc GCai GEdr MFie NEgg NGdn NLar NMyG NRnb SMrm WAbe WFar WMnd
x ***chunglenta*** see *P. chungensis* x *pulverulenta*
§ 'Clarence Elliott' (2) CGra CLyd EHyt GCrs GKev ITim SBch WAbe WLin
clarkei (11) CLyd EHyt GEdr GFle GTou NWCA WAbe
clusiana (2) GFle GKev MFie NSla
- 'Murray-Lyon' (2) GCrs NMen NSla
cockburniana (4) ♀H4 CBcs CRow CSec EBee EChP GBBs GEdr GFle GGar GIBF GKev GQui GTou MDKP MFie NEgg NGdn NSti SRms WAbe WFar WHil WRos
- yellow-flowered GGar GKev
concholoba (17) GFle GFlt GKev GTou MFie NLAp
'Corporal Baxter' (dPrim)(30) ENot EPfP MBNS MNrw MOne NCGa NGHP SPer WRha
cortusoides (7) CLAP CSec GFle GIBF LSou NLar NRnb SRms
Cowichan (Poly)(30) GAbr
Cowichan Amethyst Group (Poly)(30) CSWP GAbr MAnH
Cowichan Blue Group (Poly)(30) CSWP GAbr MAnH
Cowichan Garnet Group (Poly)(30) CSWP EWoo GAbr GBuc MAnH MFie WCot WPGP
Cowichan Red Group (Poly)(30) MAnH WFar
Cowichan Venetian Group (Poly)(30) CSWP GAbr MAnH WFar
Cowichan Yellow Group (Poly)(30) GAbr WCot
'Coy' CGra EHyt WAbe
'Craven Gem' (Poly)(30) GBuc
Crescendo Series (Poly)(30) GAbr
'Crimson Beauty' (dPrim)(30) **new** NCob
'Crimson Velvet' (2) GAbr ITim NLAp
crispa see *P. glomerata*
* ***cuneata*** GTou
cuneifolia (8) CSec GFle GFlt GKev
daonensis (2) GFle GKev
darialica (11) CNic
'Dark Rosaleen' (Poly) GAbr
'David Valentine' (30) GAbr WAbe
'Dawn Ansell' (dPrim)(30) CHad CPLG CRow EPfP GAbr ITer LRHS MBNS MFie MOne MSte NBir NGHP NWCA SPer SUsu WCot WHer
Daybreak Group (Poly)(30) CSWP MFie
deflexa (17) GCrs GFle LRHS
- BWJ 7877 WCru
denticulata (9) ♀H4 More than 30 suppliers
- var. ***alba*** (9) CSam CTri CWat EBee ECha EPfP EWTr GCra GGar GKir GTou IHMH LRHS MBri MFie MWgw NBid NCob NJOw NLAp NOrc SPer WCAu WMoo WPer WWeb WWpP
- blue (9) GAbr GKir NLar
- 'Bressingham Beauty' (9) EBrs
- var. ***cachemiriana*** hort. (9) NCot
- 'Glenroy Crimson' (9) CLAP SRms SWvt
- 'Karryann' (9/v) EBee EMon MBNS MBnl NEgg WCot
- lilac (9) EHon GKir GTou MFie NCob NCot NLAp NPri WWeb
- 'Prichard's Ruby' (9) **new** NCob
- purple (9) GKir IBlr WMoo
- red (9) EPfP GGar GKir MWgw NLAp NOrc WMoo
- 'Robinson's Red' (9) GBuc
- 'Ronsdorf' (9) LRHS
- 'Rubin' CWat EHon EPfP GAbr GTou IHMH MBrN MBri MFie NBlu NBro

	NCob NOak SRms WHil WPer WWpP
- 'Rubin Auslese'	CSam
- 'Rubinball' (9)	GCrs GKir WCot
- 'Snowball' (9)	NOak
deorum (2)	GKev
x ***deschmannii***	see *P.* x *vochinensis*
'Desert Sunset' (Poly)(30)	CSWP MFie
deuteronana (21)	GKev
'Devon Cream' (Prim)(30)	GBuc WFar
'Dianne'	see *P.* x *forsteri* 'Dianne'
'Dorothy' (Poly)(30)	MRav
'Double Lilac'	see *P. vulgaris* 'Lilacina Plena'
'Duckyls Red' (Prim)(30)	GBuc
'Dusky Lady'	MBri WFar
'Easter Bonnet' (dPrim)(30)	ENot LRHS MOne NBid
edelbergii (12)	CNic
edgeworthii	see *P. nana*
§ ***elatior*** (30) ♀H4	More than 30 suppliers
- hose-in-hose (30)(d)	MAnH NBid
- subsp. ***intricata*** (30)	GFle
I - 'Jessica' **new**	WHil
- subsp. ***leucophylla*** (30)	EBee ECho
§ - subsp. ***meyeri*** (30)	GCrs GFle GKev NEgg
- subsp. ***pallasii*** (30)	GCrs GFle
'Elizabeth Killelay'PBR (dPoly)(30)	More than 30 suppliers
'Ellen Page' (2)	MFie
ellisiae (21)	CGra GFle NSla SOkd
'Ethel Barker' (2)	CGra ITim LRHS NDlv
'Eugénie' (dPrim)(30)	CHid GAbr MBNS MDun MFie MOne NGHP
'Fairy Rose' KRW 180/48 (2)	ITim WAbe
farinosa (11)	CLyd EBee GFle MFie NEgg NRya SPoG WAbe WBWf
fasciculata (11)	EHyt GCai GEdr GKev NLAp NWCA SBla
- CLD 345	WAbe
- ex CLD 345	GFle
'Fife Yellow' (dPoly)(30)	GBuc
'Fire Dance' (Poly)(30)	MFie
firmipes (26)	EWes GCrs GIBF WCot
§ ***flaccida*** (28)	GFle GGGa GIBF ITim MHar WAbe
Flamingo Group (Poly)(30)	CSWP MFie
§ x ***floerkeana*** (2)	GCrs
- f. ***biflora*** 'Alba' (2)	SBla
florida (29)	NCob WAbe
- SDR 2820	GKev
I - 'Pectinata'	GCrs
florida x ***souliei*** (28) **new**	GKev
florindae (26) ♀H4	More than 30 suppliers
- bronze (26)	GQui MFie NBir WWhi
I - 'Butterscotch' (26)	WHrl
- hybrids (26)	CDWL CPne EChP EHrv GAbr GEdr GGar ITim MFie MWrn NCob NEgg WHil
- Keilour hybrids **new**	NChi WPtf
- magenta (26) **new**	MDKP
- orange (26)	CSam EBee GMac IBlr MDKP MNrw NRnb WCru WFar WMoo WWpP
- peach (26) **new**	MDKP
- 'Ray's Ruby' (26)	CHar CLAP EBee GBBs GBuc GMac MDKP MFOX MNrw NBir NLsd WHrl WWFP WWhi WWpP
- red (26)	GBuc GCal GFlt GGar GKev MFie NBid NEgg NLar NRnb WBVN WFar
- terracotta (26)	CSWP
Footlight Parade Group (Prim)(30)	CSWP
forbesii CC 4084 **new**	CPLG
forrestii (3)	EHyt GGGa GIBF GKev MFie NLAp SSpi WAbe
- ACE 2474	GFle
- ACE 2480	EPot
§ x ***forsteri*** (2)	GFle MFie WAbe
§ - 'Bileckii' (2)	CStu EHyt GCrs GFle ITim LRHS NBir NLAp NWCA SRms WAbe
- 'Bileckii' white-flowered **new**	GCrs
§ - 'Dianne' (2)	GAbr GBuc NBro NJOw NLAp NRya WAbe
- 'Dianne' hybrids (2)	MFie
'Francisca' (Poly)	CBct CElw CSpe EBee MBNS MBnl NGdn WCot
'Freckles' (dPrim)(30)	ENot MBNS MDun SPer
'Freedom'	see *P.* x *pubescens* 'Freedom'
frondosa (11) ♀H4	CLyd GFle GIBF LRHS MDKP MFie NLAp NMen NWCA SOkd WAbe WBVN
Fuchsia Victorians Group (Poly)(30)	MFie
'Garnet' (*allionii* hybrid) (2)	MFie WLin
'Garryard Guinevere'	see *P.* 'Guinevere'
'Garryarde Crimson'	WCot
gemmifera (11)	GFle GGGa
- var. ***zambalensis*** (11)	GCrs GFle GKev WAbe
geraniifolia (7)	SOkd
§ 'Gigha' (Prim)(30)	CSWP GCrs GKev
glabra	GKev WAbe
glaucescens (2)	CGra CLyd CNic EHyt GCrs GFle MFie NSla
§ ***glomerata*** (5)	GBuc GFle GGGa WLin
- GWJ 9213	WCru
- GWJ 9280	WCru
'Glowing Embers' (4)	CSpe LRHS MFie NBir WHil
glutinosa All.	see *P. allionii*
glutinosa Wulfen (2) **new**	GKev
Gold-laced Group (Poly)(30)	CBot CBre CM&M CMea CSWP CWCL EBee EChP EPfP EWoo IHMH ITer MAnH MBri MHer NChi NJOw NRya NWCA SPer SPet SUsu WCot WFar WHer WHil WWeb WWhi
§ - Barnhaven (Poly)(30)	CDes GAbr LPio MAnH MFie NBir NEgg
- Beeches strain (Poly)(30)	MAnH NCob SSth
- red (Poly)(30) **new**	MAvo
'Gordon'	MOne
gracilipes (21)	CDes CLAP GCrs GFle GGGa GGar ITim SRms WAbe
- L&S 1166	WAbe
- early-flowering (21)	WAbe
- 'Major'	see *P. bracteosa*
- 'Minor'	see *P. petiolaris*
graminifolia	see *P. chionantha*
Grand Canyon Group (Poly)(30)	MFie
grandis	GFle GKev
griffithii (21)	GGGa
'Groenekan's Glorie' (Prim)(30)	GAbr GEdr LRHS MBri MRav NBir NBro WFar
§ 'Guinevere' (Poly)(30) ♀H4	More than 30 suppliers
'Hall Barn Blue'	GAbr
§ ***halleri*** (11)	CAby GFle GKev GTou MFie NDlv NMen NRnb WAbe WLin
- 'Longiflora'	see *P. halleri*
Harbinger Group (Prim)(30)	CSWP GAbr LLWP

	Harbour Lights mixture (Poly)(30)	CSWP MFie
	Harlow Carr hybrids (4)	CSWP GCai GQui LRHS MLLN NDlv NEgg NSla NWCA WEas WMoo
	Harvest Yellows Group (Poly)(30)	MFie
	'Helen Evans' **new**	EHyt
	helodoxa	see *P. prolifera*
§	'Hemswell Blush' (2)	GCai GKev ITim NLAp
§	'Hemswell Ember' (2)	CNic EPot GCai GCrs NDlv NLAp NRya WLin
	heucherifolia (7)	GFle
	hidakana (24)	EHyt GEdr NMen SOkd
	'High Point' (2)	CGra
	hirsuta (2)	CNic EHyt GCrs GEdr GFle GIBF GTou ITim MFie
	- var. ***exscapa*** (2)	GFle
	- 'Lismore Snow' (2)	NLAp SOkd WAbe
	- ***nivea*** (2)	CStu
	- red-flowered **new**	GKev
	hongshanensis	GKev
	hose-in-hose (Poly)(30)(d)	CSWP GFlt ITer MAnH MHer MNrw
§	'Hyacinthia' (2)	CLyd GIBF MFie
	ianthina	see *P. prolifera*
	iljinskyi	WLin
	incana	GFle NEgg
	Indian Reds Group (Poly)(30)	CSWP MFie
	'Ingram's Blue' (Poly)(30)	LRHS WPen
	Inshriach hybrids (4)	CMHG CSWP EBrs MBri MFie NLar WFar
	integrifolia (2)	GEdr GFle WAbe
	integrifolia x ***minima*** 'Kilchuimin' **new**	GEdr
§	'Inverewe' (4) ♀H4	GBin GCal GCra GKev GQui NBir SUsu
	involucrata (11)	see *P. munroi*
	ioessa (26)	EWes GCra GFle GGGa GQui WAbe
	- hybrids (26)	NLAp
	'Iris Mainwaring' (Prim)(30)	GAbr GCra GEdr MDHE NWCA
	irregularis (21)	GCrs GGGa
	issiori	GIBF
	Jack in the Green Group (Poly)(30)	CSWP ITer MCre MNrw MRav MWgw WBor WFar WRha
	'Jackie Richards' (2)	EHyt GCrs MFie WLin
	japonica (4)	More than 30 suppliers
	- 'Alba' (4)	EBee EHrv GIBF MAvo NArg NDlv NMyG NPri NRnb WAbe WCAu WFar WHil WMnd
	- 'Apple Blossom' (4)	CFir GBri GCai GKev SWvt
*	- 'Carminea' (4)	CMil EBee EWTr GBuc NBro NLar WFar
	- 'Fromfield Pink' (4)	WHil
	- 'Fuji' (4)	CSWP NBro
	- 'Fuji' hybrids (4)	NLar
	- 'Merve's Red' (4)	CDes WPGP
	- 'Miller's Crimson' (4) ♀H4	More than 30 suppliers
	- 'Oriental Sunrise' (4)	CMil CSWP MAnH MFie NEgg
	- 'Postford White' (4) ♀H4	More than 30 suppliers
	- red (4)	WAbe
	- 'Valley Red' (4)	GBuc GCai
	jesoana (7)	CStu EHyt GGar GKev LTwo
	- B&SWJ 618	WCru
	'Joan Hughes' (*allionii* hybrid) (2)	CLyd SBla WAbe WLin
	'Joanna'	ECou GCrs
	'Johanna' (11)	GAbr GBuc GEdr GFle GKev NPro NSla NWCA SOkd WAbe WLin
	'John Fielding' (6x30)	CBgR CBro CElw GAbr GEdr
	'Jo-Jo' (2)	CLyd WAbe WLin
	juliae (30)	EHyt ETow GFle GIBF GKev LLWP LRHS NWCA SPlb WAbe WCot WEas
I	- 'Millicent' (30)	WCot
	'Kate Haywood'	CLyd WLin
	'Ken Dearman' (dPrim)(30)	ENot EPfP MBNS MBow MFie MOne MRav MSte NBir NGHP NWCA SPer WFar WWol
	kewensis (12) ♀H2	EShb GGar GKev
	'Kinlough Beauty' (Poly)(30)	EMon GAbr GEdr GFle LRHS NRya NSti NWCA WEas
§	***kisoana*** (7)	CLAP EBee GCai MTho NLAp SBla WCru
	- var. ***alba*** (7)	CLAP GGGa
	- var. ***shikokiana***	see *P. kisoana*
	kitaibeliana **new**	GKev
	'Lady Greer' (Poly)(30) ♀H4	CSam CStu EBee EDAr EPfP ETow GAbr GBuc GKev LLWP MFie MRav NBir NChi NLAp NRya NSti NWCA SMac SUsu
	'Lambrook Yellow' (Poly)(30) **new**	GAbr
§	***latifolia*** (2)	GFle GIBF SOkd
	latisecta (7)	GFle SOkd
§	***laurentiana*** (11)	CSec GFle GIBF NMen WAbe
	'Lea Gardens' (*allionii* hybrid) (2)	EHyt ITim MFie
	'Lee Myers' (*allionii* hybrid) (2)	EPot ITim MFie NDlv
	leucophylla	see *P. elatior*
	'Lilac Domino' (2)	ITim
	'Lilac Fairy'	CNic ITim WLin
	'Lilian Harvey' (dPrim)(30)	CElw EPfP LRHS MFie MOne MRav NBir
	'Lindum Moonlight'	EHyt
	'Lingwood Beauty' (Prim)(30)	GAbr
	'Linnet' (21)	ITim
	'Lismore' (2)	EHyt WLin
	'Lismore Jewel' (2)	GCrs
	'Lismore Treasure' (2) **new**	WAbe
	'Lismore Yellow' (2)	EPot GTou NLAp WAbe WLin
	Lissadel hybrids (4)	GFle
	littoniana	see *P. vialii*
§	x ***loiseleurii*** 'Air Waves' (2)	EHyt GCai ITim NLAp WLin
	longiflora	see *P. halleri*
	luteola (11)	GFle GGar LTwo NEgg NLar WFar
	macrophylla (18)	GFle GKev GTou NEgg WAbe
	magellanica (11)	WAbe
	- subsp. ***magellanica*** J&JA 2.749.900	NWCA
	malacoides (3)	CTbh MBri
	mandarin red (4)	CSWP
	marginata (2) ♀H4	CPne EPot GAbr GCrs GFle LFox LRHS NDlv NJOw NLAp SBch SIng WAbe WFar
	- from the Dolomites (2)	NLAp
	- 'Adrian Evans' (2)	EHyt ITim
	- ***alba*** (2)	LRHS NBro NDlv NLAp
	- 'Barbara Clough' (2)	CLyd GEdr ITim MFie NSla
	- 'Beamish' (2) ♀H4	CLyd NBro NRya NSla SOkd
	- 'Beatrice Lascaris' (2)	GCrs ITim MFie MOne WAbe
	- 'Beverley Reid' (2)	ITim
	- 'Boothman's Variety' (2)	CTri GCrs ITim NLAp
	- 'Caerulea' (2)	CLyd GKev ITim MOne NLAp WAbe
	- 'Casterino' **new**	GCrs
	- 'Clear's Variety' (2)	ITim NJOw
	- 'Correvon's Variety' (2)	CLyd

	Name	Suppliers
	- cut-leaved (2)	ITim
	- 'Doctor Jenkins' (2)	ITim NLar
	- 'Drake's Form' (2)	ITim NLAp NLar SOkd
	- dwarf (2)	LRHS MFie
I	- 'Earl L. Bolton'	see *P. marginata* 'El Bolton'
	- 'El Bolton' (2)	WAbe
	- 'Elizabeth Fry' (2)	CLyd LFox
	- 'Highland Twilight' (2)	NSla
	- 'Holden Clough' (2)	NJOw NRya
	- 'Holden Variety' (2)	CStu EPot ITim NDlv WAbe
	- 'Ivy Agee' (2)	CLyd GCrs ITim NLAp NRya
	- 'Janet' (2)	CLyd NLAp
	- 'Jenkins Variety' (2)	CLyd
	- 'Kesselring's Variety' (2)	CLyd CM&M CMea ELan GCai MOne NDlv NJOw NLAp WAbe WTin
	- 'Laciniata'	SBla
	- lilac-flowered	LFox
	- 'Linda Pope' (2) ♀H4	CLyd GCai ITim NBir NDlv NSla SUsu WAbe
	- 'Manfield' **new**	WThu
	- maritime form (2)	NJOw
	- 'Millard's Variety' (2)	CLyd ITim
	- 'Nancy Lucy' (2)	WAbe
	- 'Napoleon' (2)	EHyt GEdr ITim NLAp
	- 'Prichard's Variety' (2) ♀H4	CLyd ELan GAbr ITim LBee LFox MFie NCob NDlv NJOw NLAp NMyG NRya NWCA SBla WAbe WFar
	- 'Sheila Denby' (2)	ITim NLAp
	- 'Stradbrook Dream' **new**	ITim
	- 'Stradbrook Lucy' **new**	ITim
	- 'The President' (2)	ITim
	- 'Waithman's Variety' (2)	GCrs GTou ITim NLAp NRya
	- wild-collected (2)	ITim MFie
	'Maria Talbot' (*allionii* hybrid) (2)	EHyt NJOw
	'Marianne Davey' (dPrim)(30)	MRav NBir
	'Marie Crousse' (dPrim)(30)	CBgR ENot EPfP LRHS MBNS MDun MFie MOne MWgw WCot WFar WRha
	Marine Blues Group (Poly)(30)	CSWP MAnH MFie
	'Maris Tabbard'	EHyt WAbe
	'Marlene' **new**	NBir
	'Mars' (*allionii* hybrid) (2)	ITim NDlv NLAp NRya WLin
	'Marven' (2)	CLyd GCai GEdr NJOw
	'Mary Anne'	GAbr
	Mauve Victorians Group (Poly)(30)	CSWP MFie
	maximowiczii **new**	GKev
	'McWatt's Claret' (Poly)(30)	GAbr LLWP NPar
	'McWatt's Cream' (Poly)(30)	CSWP EBee EBla EDAr GCra GCrs GEdr GFle GGar NChi NMen WCot
	megalocarpa **new**	GKev
	- HWJK 2265	WCru
	melanops	see *P. chionantha* subsp. *melanops*
	x ***meridiana*** (2)	MFie
§	- 'Miniera' (2)	CLyd ITim WAbe
	'Mexico'	MFie
	Midnight Group	CSWP MAnH MFie
	'Miniera'	see *P.* x *meridiana* 'Miniera'
	minima (2)	CLyd GFle GKev GTou NBro NLar NSla SIng WAbe
	- var. ***alba*** (2)	CStu GCrs GFle GGGa MFie NRya NSla
	minima x ***hirsuta*** (2)	see *P.* x *forsteri*
	minima x ***wulfeniana*** (2)	see *P.* x *vochinensis*
	minor **new**	GCrs

	Name	Suppliers
	'Miss Indigo' (dPrim)(30)	ENot EPfP GAbr LRHS MBNS MDun MFie MOne MRav MSte MWgw NCGa NGHP NWCA SPer WCAu WCot WFar
	mistassinica alba (11)	NEgg
	- var. ***macropoda***	see *P. laurentiana*
	miyabeana (4)	GFle
	- B&SWJ 3407	WCru
	modesta alba (11)	GFle
	- var. ***faurieae*** (11)	GKev MFie NWCA
	- var. ***matsumurae*** (11)	GFle
	- - 'Alba' **new**	GKev
	mollis (7)	GIBF
	'Mother's Day'	CElw
	moupinensis (21)	CDes CLAP CStu GCrs GGGa GKev ITim
	- C&H 7038	GFle GGGa
*	'Mrs Eagland'	GAbr
	'Mrs McGillivray' (Prim)(30)	GAbr
§	***munroi*** (11)	GFle NSla WAbe
§	- subsp. ***yargongensis*** (11)	GAbr GCrs GFle GGar GKev GTou LRHS NLAp NPen WAbe WDyG WFar
	muscarioides (17)	GFle GKev GTou WAbe
	Muted Victorians Group (Poly)(30)	CSWP MFie
§	***nana*** (21)	GKev ITim WAbe
	- blue-flowered **new**	GKev
	nanobella **new**	SOkd
	'Netta Dennis'	ITim
	nevadensis	GFle
	New Pinks Group (Poly)(30)	CSWP MFie
	'Nightingale'	ITim
	nivalis Pallas	see *P. chionantha*
	- subsp. ***xanthobasis*** **new**	GKev
	nutans Delavay ex Franch.	see *P. flaccida*
§	***nutans*** Georgi (25)	GKev NEgg
	obconica (19)	LRHS MBri WGwG
	'Old Port' (Poly)(30)	CElw LLWP NLAp WCot WPat
	Old Rose Victorians Group (Poly)(30)	CSWP MFie
	'Olive Wyatt' (dPrim)(30)	NBir
	orbicularis	WAbe
	'Oriental Sunset' **new**	MDKP
	Osiered Amber Group (Prim)(30)	CSWP
	'Our Pat' (dPoly)(30)	GAbr
	Pagoda hybrids (4)	NEgg
	palinuri (2)	GIBF
	palmata (7)	GCrs GEdr GFle GFlt GGGa NSla WAbe
	'Paris '90' (Poly)(30)	CSWP GAbr MFie
	parryi (20)	CGra GCrs GFle GIBF GKev WFar
	'Pat Cottle' (d) (Poly) (30)	CBos
	'Peardrop' (2)	CGra GAbr NLAp
	pedemontana (2)	GFle MSte NWCA WAbe
	- 'Alba' (2)	EHyt
	'Peggy Fell' **new**	WHil
	'Perle von Bottrop' (Prim)(30)	GAbr
	'Peter Klein' (11)	CBos CElw GBuc GEdr GFle GKev LTwo NLAp NLar NWCA WAbe WTin
	petiolaris misapplied	see *P.* 'Redpoll'
§	***petiolaris*** (21)	EHyt GCra GCrs GFle GGGa GKev ITim MDun NWCA WAbe
	- L&S 19856	GFle
	- Sherriff's form	see *P.* 'Redpoll'
	'Petticoat'	NCGa NLar
	phuhonica 'Groenekan's Glory' **new**	EWTr

§	'Pink Aire' (2)	EHyt ITim MFie
	'Pink Fairy'	ITim
	'Pink Ice' (*allionii* hybrid) (2)	CGra CLyd CPBP GCrs ITim MFie NRya WLin
	pinnatifida (17)	GGGa
	poissonii (4)	More than 30 suppliers
	- ACE 1946	NWCA
	- ACE 2030	EPot
	- B&SWJ 7525	WCru
*	- f. ***alba*** **new**	GIBF
	polyanthus (30)	WFar
	polyneura (7)	ECha EDAr GFle GGar GIBF IGor ITim MFie NBid NEgg NPen NVic SPoG SRms WAbe
	'Port Wine' (30)	GAbr GCra MBct
	prenantha (4)	GGGa GKev WAbe
	'Prince Silverwings' (dPoly)(30)	WEas
§	***prolifera*** (4) ♀H4	More than 30 suppliers
	- double-flowered (d)	CFir
§	x ***pubescens*** (2) ♀H4	LFox NEgg NJOw NLAp WPer
	- 'Alba' (2)	WAbe
	- 'Alison Gibbs' (2)	MOne
	- 'Apple Blossom' (2)	CLyd ITim MFie
	- 'Balfouriana' (2)	CNic LFox
§	- 'Bewerley White' (2)	CStu EBee EDAr MOne NDlv NJOw NLAp
	- 'Blue Wave' (2)	NJOw
§	- 'Boothman's Variety' (2)	CLyd CRez EPfP EWTr GKev ITim LRHS MFie MSte NDlv NLAp NMyG NRnb NWCA WFar WHoo WTin
	- 'Carmen'	see *P.* x *pubescens* 'Boothman's Variety'
	- 'Christine' (2)	CLyd CMea MFie NBir NDlv NLAp WCot
	- 'Cream Viscosa' (2)	ITim MFie NDlv NLAp
	- 'Deep Mrs Wilson' (2)	SUsu
	- 'Faldonside' (2)	CLyd CNic NDlv
§	- 'Freedom' (2)	CLyd CTri GAbr GKev GTou ITim LRHS MFie NBir NDlv NJOw NLAp SRms WEas
	- 'Harlow Car' (2)	CLyd GMac ITim MFie NDlv NLAp WFar WTin
	- 'Henry Hall' (2)	CLyd EWes
	- 'Herbert Beresford' (2)	GCrs
	- 'Joan Danger' (2)	CLyd CNic ITim
	- 'Joan Gibbs' (2)	CLyd GCai ITim MFie MOne NLAp
	- 'Kath Dryden' (2)	ITim
	- 'Lilac Fairy' (2)	ITim NDlv NJOw
	- 'Mrs J.H. Wilson' (2)	CGra CLyd EHyt GEdr ITim LRHS MFie NDlv NRya WPat
	- 'Pat Barwick' (2)	CNic GCrs ITim LFox MFie NDlv NLAp
	- 'Peggy' (2)	MFie
	- 'Peggy Fell' (2)	MDHE
	- 'Rufus' (2)	CLyd ETow GAbr GCrs WTin
	- 'Snowcap'	EHyt GCrs WLin
	- 'Sonya' (2)	ITim
	- 'The General' (2)	CLyd ITim MOne SPop
§	- 'Wedgwood' (2)	GCai ITim NRya
	x ***pubescens*** x 'White Linda Pope' (2)	ITim
	pulchella (11)	WAbe
	pulchra (21)	GCrs GEdr GKir
	pulverulenta (4) ♀H4	More than 30 suppliers
	- Bartley hybrids (4) ♀H4	CBot CDes GBuc GGar SMur SSpi
	- 'Bartley Pink' (4)	CHar GBuc SSpi SUsu WEas
	'Quaker's Bonnet'	see *P. vulgaris* 'Lilacina Plena'
	'Rachel Kinnen' (2)	EHyt ITim MFie SIng SOkd WLin
	'Ramona' (Poly)(30)	MAnH MFie
	'Ravenglass Vermilion'	see *P.* 'Inverewe'
	'Red Velvet' (dPrim)(30)	ECGP ENot MDun MOne MSte NGHP
§	'Redpoll' (21)	CLAP GCrs WAbe
	reidii (28)	GFle
	- var. ***williamsii*** (28)	GGGa GTou ITim
	- - ***alba*** (28)	GFle
	reptans (16)	GCrs
	'Reverie' (Poly)(30)	CSWP MAnH MFie
	'Rheniana' (2)	EPot ITim
	'Rose O'Day' (dPrim)(30)	MNrw MOne NBir
	rosea (11) ♀H4	CAby CRow EBee EDAr EPfP GEdr GFle GGGa GKir GTou MFie MWgw NBid NBir NLAp NRya NSti NVic SSpi WFar
	- 'Delight'	see *P. rosea* 'Micia Visser-de Geer'
	- 'Gigas' (11)	CRez GAbr
	- 'Grandiflora' (11)	EHon EPfP GBar GFle GGar GKev IHMH LPBA MBow MBri MRav NDlv NEgg NWCA SIng SPoG SRms WFar WPer WWpP
§	- 'Micia Visser-de Geer' (11)	LRHS
	rotundifolia	see *P. roxburghii*
	'Rowallane Rose' (4)	CBro GBuc GFlt WWFP
I	'Rowena' **new**	GCrs WCot
§	***roxburghii*** (25)	GKev
	'Roy Cope' (dPrim)(30)	MFie NBir NWCA WBor WFar WWol
	'Roydon Ruby'	WCot
	rusbyi (20)	GFle GIBF GKev NWCA
	Rustic Reds Group (Poly)(30)	CSWP
	saxatilis (7)	GCrs GKev MFie
	scandinavica (11)	GCrs GIBF GKev MFie
	x ***scapeosa*** (21)	GFle GGGa
	scapigera (21)	GGGa
§	'Schneekissen' (Prim)(30)	CBre MBri MHer NBir NBro NChi NGHP NMyG NPro SBla WHil
	scotica (11)	CSec GCrs GFle GIBF GKev GPoy GTou LFox MFie NLAp NSla NWCA SOkd WAbe WBWf WGwG
	secundiflora (26)	More than 30 suppliers
	- B&SWJ 7547	WCru
§	x ***sendtneri*** (2)	MFie
	septemloba (7)	GFle
	x ***serrata***	see *P.* x *vochinensis*
	serratifolia (4)	GGGa GGar GIBF
	sibthorpii	see *P. vulgaris* subsp. *sibthorpii*
	sieboldii (7) ♀H4	CRow EHyt GCai GFle GKev ITim LFox MNrw NEgg NMen NRya NWCA SIng SMac SRms SSpi SUsu WAbe WFar
	- ***alba*** (7)	CDes CLAP EBee GMac NBro NMen SRot WCru WFar WPGP WTin
	- blue-flowered (7)	CLAP NMen
	- 'Blush'	CLAP
	- 'Carefree' (7)	CLAP GMac LTwo NBro NLar NMen
	- 'Cherubim' (7)	EBee EBrs WCra
	- 'Dancing Ladies' (7)	CLAP CMil CSWP MFie NBro
	- 'Galaxy' (7)	NBro
	- 'Geisha Girl' (7)	CFir CLAP EBrs MRav NLar WAbe WFar
	- 'Lilac Sunbonnet' (7)	ENot EPfP LRHS LTwo
	- 'Manakoora' (7)	CLAP CSWP MFie NBro
	- 'Mikado' (7)	CFir CLAP EBee EBrs MFie MRav
	- 'Pago-Pago' (7)	CLAP MFie NBro
	- 'Purple Back' (7)	EBee
	- 'Seraphim' (7)	CLAP EBee EBrs WCra
	- 'Snowflake' (7)	CLAP EBrs NLar NSla SBla WAbe WCra
	- 'Tah-ni' (7)	NBro
	- 'Winter Dreams' (7)	CLAP CSWP MFie NBid NBro

	Name	Suppliers
§	***sikkimensis*** (26) 𝕐H4	CAby CMil CRow EBrs EPot EWTr GCrs GEdr GFle GGGa GGar GIBF GKev GKir ITim LPBA MNrw NPen SOkd SPoG WAbe WBVN WHil WLin WRos
	- ACE 1422	GBuc WCru
	- B&SWJ 4808	WCru
	- CC 3409	WRos
	- CC&McK 1022	GQui GTou
	- DJHC 01051	WCru
	- var. ***hopeana*** (26)	GCrs GFle
	- var. ***pudibunda*** (26)	GEdr
	- 'Tilman Number 2' (26)	GAbr SPer
	aff. ***sikkimensis*** (26)	ITim NArg NEgg
	-ACE 2176	GBuc
	Silver-laced Group (Poly)(30)	SWvt
	- 'Silver Lining' (Poly)(30)	LRHS
	'Silverwells' (4)	GEdr
	sinopurpurea	see *P. chionantha* subsp. *sinopurpurea*
	'Sir Bedivere' (Prim)(30)	GBuc NLar
	smithiana	see *P. prolifera*
	'Snow Carpet'	see *P.* 'Schneekissen'
	'Snow Cushion'	see *P.* 'Schneekissen'
	'Snow White' (Poly)(30)	EHyt GEdr MRav
	Snowcushion	see *P.* 'Schneekissen'
	'Snowruffles'	ITim
	sonchifolia (21)	CFir CLAP GGGa GKev ITim MDun
	- from Tibet (21)	MDun
	sorachiana	see *P. yuparensis*
	souliei (29) **new**	GKev ITim
	spathulifolia (16) **new**	WAbe
	spectabilis (2)	EHyt GEdr GFle
	specuicola (11)	GIBF
	Spice Shades Group (Poly)(30)	CSWP MFie WCot
	x ***steinii***	see *P.* x *forsteri*
	stenocalyx **new**	WAbe
	'Stradbrook Charm' (2)	EHyt EPot WLin
	'Stradbrook Dainty' (2)	EHyt ITim MFie WLin
	'Stradbrook Dream' (2)	CNic EHyt EPot ITim MFie NLAp
	'Stradbrook Gem' (2)	SOkd WAbe WLin WPat
	'Stradbrook Lilac Lustre' (2)	CGra MFie
	'Stradbrook Lucy' (2)	EHyt ITim NLAp WAbe WLin
	'Stradbrook Mauve Magic' (2)	MFie
	stricta (11)	GFle
	Striped Victorians Group (Poly)(30)	CSWP MFie
	'Sue Jervis' (dPrim)(30)	MBow NBir NCGa NGHP NLar SPer WCAu WGwG WHal WRha WWol
	suffrutescens (8)	GKev NSla WAbe WLin
	'Sunrise' (2)	WLin
	'Sunshine Susie' (dPrim)(30)	ENot EPfP GAbr LRHS MBNS MFie MOne MRav MSte NCGa NGHP WCAu WCot WWol
	takedana (24)	GGGa
	tanneri (21)	GFle
	'Tantallon' (21)	GGGa GGar ITim NLAp
§	Tartan Reds Group (Prim)(30)	CSWP MAnH
	'Tawny Port' (Poly)(30)	GAbr NBro SRms
	tibetica (11)	GFle GGGa ITim
	'Tie Dye' (Prim)(30)	ENot LRHS NLar WCot
	'Tipperary Purple' (Prim)(30)	GAbr GEdr
	'Tomato Red' (Prim)(30)	WCot
	'Tony' (2)	CPBP WAbe WLin
	tosaensis var. ***brachycarpa*** (24)	GFle
	'Tournaig Pink' (4)	GGar
	tournefortii	GFle
	'Tye Dye'	GBri
*	***urumiensis*** **new**	GKev
	vaginata (7) **new**	WAbe
	'Val Horncastle' (dPrim)(30)	LRHS MBNS MDKP MNrw MOne MSte MWgw NCGa NGHP NLar NWCA SPer WCot
	Valentine Victorians Group (Poly)(30)	MFie
	veris (30) 𝕐H4	More than 30 suppliers
	- subsp. ***columnae*** (30) **new**	EBee
	- hybrids (30)	NEgg SGar WLin
	- 'Katy McSparron' (30/d)	CMea EBee WCot
§	- subsp. ***macrocalyx*** (30)	EBee NWCA
	- orange-flowered	WMoo
	- red-flowered (30)	CM&M NBid
	- 'Sunset Shades' (30)	NEgg NGHP NJOw NLar
	vernalis	see *P. vulgaris*
	verticillata (12)	GKev
§	***vialii*** (17) 𝕐H4	More than 30 suppliers
§	***villosa*** (2)	GFle GKev GTou
	- var. ***cottica***	see *P. villosa*
	violacea (17) **new**	WAbe
	Violet Victorians Group (Poly)(30)	CSWP MFie
	viscosa All.	see *P. latifolia*
§	x ***vochinensis*** (2)	CFee CLyd ITim NWCA
§	***vulgaris*** (Prim)(30) 𝕐H4	More than 30 suppliers
	- ***alba*** (30)	CRow NSla WBrk
	- 'Alba Plena' (Prim)(30)	CRow GBuc GGar IBlr IGor ITer
	- green-flowered	see *P. vulgaris* 'Viridis'
	- 'Greyshot'	NBir
§	- 'Lilacina Plena' (dPrim)(30)	ECGP ENot EPfP IBlr MBNS MBow MNrw MRav NCGa NCot NGHP SPer WCAu WCot WGwG
§	- subsp. ***sibthorpii*** (Prim)(30) 𝕐H4	CMHG CSam EBee EBrs ETow GAbr GKev GTou ITim LFox LLWP LRHS MHer MRav MWgw NBro NChi NGHP NMyG NWCA SBla SRms WEas WHil WOut
	- - HH&K 337	GFle
§	- 'Viridis' (Prim)(30)	CDes CRow IBlr
	walshii	WLin
	waltonii (26)	EBee GAbr GCai GCrs GEdr GFle GMac MAnH MDKP MNrw NChi
	- hybrids (26)	NEgg
	'Wanda' (Prim)(30) 𝕐H4	CBcs CStu CTri ENot GAbr GCra LLWP LRHS NBid NSti NVic SBla SRms WBrk WCFE WCot WEas WFar WTin
	Wanda Group (Prim)(30)	CBcs CNic NEgg
	'Wanda Hose-in-hose' (Prim)(30)(d)	EMon GAbr MMHG NBir NChi WCot WHer
	'Wanda Jack in the Green' (Prim)(30)	CBgR CRow MLLN WCot WFar
	wardii	see *P. munroi*
	warshenewskiana (11)	CNic GEdr GKev MDKP MNrw NCob NLAp NMen NRya NWCA SIng WAbe WFar WGwG WPat
	watsonii (17)	GCrs GGGa GKev GTou ITim NLAp
	'Wedgwood'	see *P.* x *pubescens* 'Wedgwood'
	'Wharfedale Ballerina' (2)	EHyt
	'Wharfedale Bluebell' (2)	CLyd EHyt NBir
	'Wharfedale Buttercup' (2)	NHar
	'Wharfedale Butterfly' (2)	EHyt ITim
	'Wharfedale Crusader' (2)	ITim
	'Wharfedale Gem' (*allionii* hybrid) (2)	GCai ITim MFie NLAp NRya WAbe

'Wharfedale Ling' (*allionii* hybrid) (2) CGra CPBP CStu GCai GCrs MFie NRya SOkd WLin
'Wharfedale Sunshine' (2) EHyt MFie NLAp
'Wharfedale Superb' (*allionii* hybrid) (2) EHyt ITim MFie NLAp WLin
'Wharfedale Village' (2) CLyd GKev ITim WGwG WLin
'White Linda Pope' (2) CLyd WLin
'White Wanda' (Prim) (30) CRow GAbr NCGa NDov
'White Waves' (*allionii* hybrid) (2) EHyt ITim
whitei (21) MDun
§ - 'Sherriff's Variety' (21) CLAP GCrs IBlr
'Whitewaves' ITim
wigramiana (28) WAbe
'William Genders' (Poly)(30) GAbr
wilsonii (4) CMHG CTri EChP EPot GBBs GBuc GGar GMac LDai MAnH MOne NDlv NEgg NRnb NWCA WBVN WFar WGwG WHer WLin
§ - var. ***anisodora*** (4) EBee GCrs GFle GGar GKev MFie NEgg NLAp
'Windrush' see *P.* x *berninae* 'Windrush'
'Windward Blue' SBla
'Winter White' see *P.* 'Gigha'
'Wisley Crimson' see *P.* 'Wisley Red'
§ 'Wisley Red' (Prim)(30) CElw
wollastonii (28) GCrs GKev
'Woodland Blue' NWoo
wulfeniana (2) CGra GCrs GEdr GFle GKev MFie WAbe
- subsp. ***baumgarteniana*** (2) **new** WLin
xanthobasis (18) GIBF
yargongensis see *P. munroi* subsp. *yargongensis*
You and Me Series (poly) **new** CSpe
aff. ***yunnanensis*** **new** GIBF
§ ***yuparensis*** (11) CSec EBee GFle NEgg WAbe

Prinsepia (*Rosaceae*)

sinensis CArn CBcs CFee CMCN GBin MBlu WBcn WPic WSHC

Pritzelago (*Brassicaceae*)

alpina CNic NJOw

Prostanthera (*Lamiaceae*)

aspalathoides EBee ECou EWes WCot
'Badja Peak' CPom WAbe WSHC
baxteri ECou
cuneata ♀H4 More than 30 suppliers
- 'Alpine Gold' CMHG CRez CWSG WFar
- Kew form CFil CPLG WPGP
§ ***incisa*** CPLG CTrw SHDw SPla
lasianthos CBcs CDoC CHll ECou EShb EWes SAga SBrw SHDw
- var. ***subcoriacea*** CPLG CPle CRHN
'Mauve Mantle' ECou
melissifolia CArn CPLG ECre EShb ESlt SBrw WSel
§ - var. ***parvifolia*** CTbh CTrw EBee ECre WAbe
nivea ECou
ovalifolia ♀H2 CPle EBee ECou
I - 'Variegata' **new** ECou
'Poorinda Ballerina' CDoC CPLG CTbh CWSG ECou EMan EShb ESlt MCCP MDun MGos SMur SPer SPoG WFar WLeb
rotundifolia ♀H2 CAbb CBcs CBrm CFwr CHEx CPle CSBt CSev CTri CWSG EBee EOHP ERea MWgw NGHP SBrw SEND SMad SPer WLeb
- 'Chelsea Girl' see *P. rotundifolia* 'Rosea'
§ - 'Rosea' ♀H2 CSBt CTbh CTrC ECou ERea GGar NGHP SPoG
scutellarioides 'Lavender Lady' ECou
sieberi misapplied see *P. melissifolia* var. *parvifolia*
sieberi Benth. **new** WPen
walteri CBrm CDoC ECou

Protea ✿ (*Proteaceae*)

aurea EShb
burchellii SPlb WSAf
coronata SPlb
cynaroides CBcs CCtw CHEx CTbh CTrC IDee SBig SPlb WSAf
dracomontana SPlb
effusa SPlb
eximia CDoC EShb WSAf
grandiceps SPlb
lacticolor SPlb
laurifolia CDoC SPlb
magnifica WSAf
mundii **new** WSAf
nana WSAf
neriifolia WSAf
obtusifolia SPlb
'Pink Ice' WSAf
subvestita SIgm
susannae CBcs CDoC SPlb

Prumnopitys (*Podocarpaceae*)

§ ***andina*** WFar
elegans see *P. andina*
§ ***taxifolia*** CTrC ECou

Prunella (*Lamiaceae*)

§ ***grandiflora*** CArn ECha GBar GKir MWat NLon NLsd SMac SPet WBrE WCHb WFar WMoo WMow WPGP WWpP WWye
- 'Alba' CSBt EBee ECha EPfP EPyc GKir GMaP LPio LSpr MFOX MRav MWgw NBid NGHP NGdn NLar NLsd NOrc SPer SPla SPoG WCAu WCHb WFar WMnd WWpP
- 'Blue Loveliness' EMan GTou WCHb
- 'Carminea' EBee MNrw SPer
- light blue-flowered CSim NLar WMoo
- 'Little Red Riding Hood' see *P. grandiflora* 'Rotkäppchen'
- 'Loveliness' ♀H4 CDoC EBee ECha ECtt GGar GKir GMaP LAst LSpr MFOX MRav MTis MWgw NBro NGdn NSti NVic SOkh SPer SPla SPlb SPoG WCAu WFar WMnd WTin
- 'Pagoda' CSpe GGar LIck NLar SMac SWal WCHb WMoo WSSM
- 'Pink Loveliness' CMCo CSBt ENot GTou LRHS NArg SRms WCHb WFar WWpP
- ***rosea*** CSBt EBee EPfP MWat WOut
§ - 'Rotkäppchen' ECtt MNrw
- 'Rubra' CSim EBee NGHP NLar SBch WMoo WPer
- 'White Loveliness' CElw CTri EBee LRHS WFar WMow WPer WWye
hispida WOut
hyssopifolia XPep
incisa see *P. vulgaris*
* 'Inshriach Ruby' NBir WCHb
laciniata CMCo EShb WCHb WMoo
§ ***vulgaris*** CAgr CArn CRWN GBar GPoy MBow MChe MGol MHer MSal NLan NMir NPri SECG WCHb WHer WWye

- 'Gleam' (v)	EBee EPPr EVFa WCot
- var. ***leucantha***	GBar WHer
- var. ***rubrifolia***	WRha
- 'Ruth Wainwright' (v)	WCHb
x ***webbiana***	see *P. grandiflora*

Prunus ✿ (*Rosaceae*)

'Accolade' 🏆H4	More than 30 suppliers
§ 'Amanogawa' 🏆H4	More than 30 suppliers
x ***amygdalopersica*** 'Pollardii'	ENot MAsh WJas
- 'Robijn' (F)	LBuc
- 'Spring Glow'	CDoC LRHS MBri WJas
amygdalus	see *P. dulcis*
armeniaca 'Alfred' (F)	CTho ERea GTwe SKee SPer
- var. ***ansu*** 'Flore Pleno' (d) **new**	NEgg
- 'Blenheim' (F)	ERea
- 'Early Moorpark' (F)	CAgr CTri EPfP ERea GBon GTwe LRHS MBri WOrn
- 'Farmingdale' (F)	ERea
- 'Garden Aprigold' (F)	ENot NPri
- 'Goldcot' (F)	EPfP ERea
- 'Golden Glow' (F)	CTri GTwe LRHS MCoo SKee
- 'Goldrich' (F) **new**	CAgr
- 'Harglow' (F)	ERea
- 'Hargrand' (F) **new**	CAgr
- 'Harogem' (F) **new**	CAgr
- 'Hemskirke' (F)	ERea SKee
- 'Isabella' (F)	MBri SPoG
- 'Moorpark' (F) 🏆H3	CEnd CSBt CWib ENot ERea GKir GTwe LBuc MGos SHBN SKee SPer
- 'New Large Early' (F)	ERea GTwe SEND SKee WBVN
- 'Tom Cott' (F) **new**	MCoo SFam
- 'Tomcot' (F)	MBri SPoG
'Asano'	see *P.* 'Geraldinae'
avium 🏆H4	CBcs CCVT CDul CLnd CRWN CSBt CWib ECrN ENot EPfP GIBF GKir LBuc MBar MGos MRav MSwo NBee NWea SFam SHBN SKee SPer WDin WHar WMoo WMou WOrn
- 'Amber Heart' (F)	SKee
- 'August Heart' (F) **new**	SKee
- 'Bigarreau de Schrecken' **new**	SKee
- 'Bigarreau Gaucher' (F)	SHBN SKee
§ - 'Bigarreau Napoléon' (F)	GTwe MGos SHBN SKee
- 'Birchenhayes'	see *P. avium* 'Early Birchenhayes'
- 'Black Eagle' (F)	CTho SKee
- 'Black Elton' (F) **new**	SKee
- 'Black Glory' (F)	SKee
- 'Black Heart' (F)	CWib
- 'Black Tartarian' (F)	SKee
- 'Bottlers'	see *P. avium* 'Preserving'
- 'Bradbourne Black' (F)	SCrf SKee
- 'Bullion' (F)	CEnd CTho
- 'Burcombe' (F)	CEnd CTho
- Celeste = 'Sumpaca'PBR (D)	GTwe LRHS MBri SFam SKee SPoG
- 'Cherokee'	see *P. avium* 'Lapins'
- 'Colney' (F) 🏆H4	GTwe SFam SKee WJas
- 'Dun' (F)	CTho
§ - 'Early Birchenhayes' (F)	CEnd CTho
- 'Early Rivers' (F)	CSBt CWib ENot GTwe LRHS SHBN SKee
- 'Elton Heart' (F)	CTho SKee
- 'Emperor Francis' (F) **new**	SKee
- 'Fice' (F)	CEnd CTho
- 'Florence' (F)	SKee
- 'Governor Wood' (F)	CWib GTwe SKee
- 'Grandiflora'	see *P. avium* 'Plena'
- 'Greenstem Black' (F)	CTho
- 'Hannaford' (D/C)	CTho
- 'Hertford' (F)	SFam SKee
- 'Inga' (F)	SFam SKee
- 'Ironsides' (F)	SKee
- 'Kassins Frühe Herz' (F)	SKee
- 'Kentish Red' (F)	CTho SKee
§ - 'Lapins' (F)	CAgr CTho ECrN GTwe LRHS SFam SKee WHar WJas WOrn
- 'May Duke'	see *P.* x *gondouinii* 'May Duke'
- 'Merchant' (F) 🏆H4	GTwe SKee
- 'Merpet' (F)	GTwe
- 'Merton Crane' (F)	SKee
- 'Merton Favourite' (F)	SKee
- 'Merton Glory' (F)	CSBt ENot GTwe MGos SCrf SFam SKee WOrn
- 'Merton Late' (F)	SKee
- 'Merton Marvel' (F)	SKee
- 'Merton Premier' (F)	SKee
- 'Nabella' (F)	WJas
- 'Napoléon'	see *P. avium* 'Bigarreau Napoléon'
- 'Noble' (F)	SKee
- 'Noir de Guben' (F)	GTwe SKee
- 'Noir de Meched' (D)	SKee
- 'Nutberry Black' (F)	SKee
- 'Old Black Heart' (F)	SKee
§ - 'Plena' (d) 🏆H4	CBcs CCVT CDul CLnd CSBt CTho CWSG EBee ECrN ELan ENot EPfP GKir LBuc LRHS MGos MRav MSwo NWea SCrf SFam SPer WDin WFar WHar WJas WOrn
§ - 'Preserving' (F)	CTho
- 'Ronald's Heart' (F)	SKee
- 'Roundel Heart' (F)	SKee
- 'Sasha' (F)	GTwe
- 'Small Black' (F)	CTho
- 'Starkrimson' (F)	GTwe
- 'Stella' (F) 🏆H4	CAgr CEnd CMac CTri CWSG CWib EPfP ERea GBon GKir GTwe LBuc LRHS MBri MGos MRav SCoo SCrf SFam SHBN SKee SPer SPoG WHar WJas WOrn
- 'Stella Compact' (F)	CWib ENot MBri WHar
- 'Summer Sun' (D)	CTho CTri GTwe MBri MCoo SCoo SFam SKee SPoG
- 'Summit' (F)	SHBN SKee
- 'Sunburst' (F)	CAgr CCVT CEnd CTho CTri CWib GTwe LBuc LRHS MBri SCoo SFam SKee SPoG WJas WOrn
- 'Sweetheart' (F) **new**	ENot SPoG
- 'Sylvia' (F)	SFam SKee
- 'Turkish Black' (F)	SKee
- 'Van' (F)	ECrN ENot GTwe SKee
- 'Vega' (F)	CAgr GTwe SFam SKee WJas
- 'Waterloo' (F)	CTho SKee
- 'White Heart' (F)	CTho CWib SKee
- 'Wildstar'	CEnd
* 'Beni-no-dora'	SMur
* 'Beni-yutaka'	CEnd GKir LBuc LRHS MAsh SCoo SLim
'Blaze'	see *P. cerasifera* 'Nigra'
x ***blireana*** (d) 🏆H4	CDoC CDul CEnd CTri EBee ENot EPfP EWTr LRHS MBar MBri MDun MRav MWat SBLw SCoo SPer SPoG WFar WHar
- 'Moseri' (d)	SBLw
'Blushing Bride'	see *P.* 'Shôgetsu'
'Candy Floss' **new**	GKir
cerasifera	CAgr CRWN CTri ECrN GKir LBuc NWea SKee SPer WDin WMou
- 'Cherry Plum' (F)	CTri SKee
- 'Crimson Dwarf'	GKir SCoo
- 'First' (F) **new**	CAgr

	Name	Suppliers
	- 'Hessei' (v)	CEnd EBee LRHS MAsh MBri MDun MGos MRav SCoo SLim SPoG
§	- Myrobalan Group (F)	GKir MRav SKee
§	- 'Nigra' Υ^{H4}	More than 30 suppliers
	- 'Pendula'	CTho ECrN
§	- 'Pissardii'	CWib ECrN GKir MAsh MBar MRav NBea NEgg NFor NWea SCoo SFam SLim WFar WJas
*	- 'Princess'	CEnd CWSG SLim
	- 'Rosea'	LRHS MBri
	- 'Spring Glow'	CDul CEnd EGra EPfP LRHS MAsh SCoo SLim SPoG WOrn
§	- 'Woodii'	SBLw
	cerasus 'Montmorency' (F)	SKee
	- 'Morello' (C) Υ^{H4}	CAgr CCVT CMac CSBt CTho CTri CWSG CWib ENot EPfP GBon GKir GTwe LBuc LRHS MBri MGos SCrf SFam SHBN SKee SPer SPoG WJas WOrn
	- 'Nabella' (F)	SKee
	- 'Rhexii' (d)	CDul ECrN GKir MAsh MGos SPer
	- 'Wye Morello' (F)	SKee
	'Champagne Dream' **new**	SCoo
	'Cheal's Weeping'	see *P.* 'Kiku-shidare-zakura'
	'Chocolate Ice'	GKir LRHS
§	'Chôshû-hizakura'	GKir
§	x ***cistena*** Υ^{H4}	CBcs CCVT CSBt CWSG EBee ELan ENot EPfP GKir LAst LRHS MBri MDun MGos NBee NBlu NLon SBLw SCoo SHBN SLim SPer SPla SPoG WBVN WCFE WDin
	- 'Crimson Dwarf'	see *P.* x *cistena*
	'Collingwood Ingram'	GKir LRHS
	conradinae	see *P. hirtipes*
	'Daikoku' **new**	GKir
	davidiana	CTho SPlb
	domestica 'Allgroves Superb' (D)	ERea
	- 'Angelina Burdett' (D)	ERea GTwe SKee
	- 'Anna Späth' (C/D)	SKee
	- 'Ariel' (C/D)	SKee
	- 'Autumn Compote' (C)	SKee
	- 'Avalon' (D)	CAgr CCVT ECrN GTwe SKee
	- 'Belgian Purple' (C)	SKee
	- 'Belle de Louvain' (C)	CTho CTri ECrN ERea GTwe SKee
	- 'Birchenhayes' (F)	CEnd
	- 'Blaisdon Red' (C)	CTho
	- 'Blue Tit' (C/D) Υ^{H4}	CAgr CTho ERea GTwe SKee
	- 'Bonne de Bry' (D)	SKee
§	- 'Bountiful' (C)	ERea
	- 'Brandy Gage' (C/D)	SKee
	- 'Bryanston Gage' (D)	CTho SKee
	- 'Burbank's Giant'	see *P. domestica* 'Giant Prune'
	- 'Burcombe'	CEnd
	- 'Bush' (C)	SKee
	- 'Cambridge Gage' (D) Υ^{H4}	CAgr CDoC CTho CTri CWib ECrN EPfP ERea GBon GKir GTwe LRHS MBri MGos MWat SCoo SCrf SFam SHBN SKee SPer SPoG WJas WOrn
	- 'Chrislin' (F)	CAgr CTho
	- 'Coe's Golden Drop' (D)	CDoC ECrN ERea GKir GTwe LRHS MGos MRav SCoo SFam SKee
	- 'Count Althann's Gage' (D)	ERea GTwe SFam SKee
	- 'Cox's Emperor' (C)	SKee
	- 'Crimson Drop' (D)	ERea SKee
	- 'Cropper'	see *P. domestica* 'Laxton's Cropper'
	- 'Czar' (C) Υ^{H4}	CAgr CDoC CSBt CTri CWib ECrN EPfP GBut GKir GTwe LBuc LRHS MGos NPri NWea SFam SKee SPer SPoG WOrn
	- 'Delicious'	see *P. domestica* 'Laxton's Delicious'
	- 'Denniston's Superb'	see *P. domestica* 'Imperial Gage'
	- 'Diamond' (C)	SKee
	- 'Dittisham Black' (C)	CAgr CTho
	- 'Dittisham Ploughman' (C)	CTho SKee
	- 'Dunster Plum' (F)	CAgr CTho CTri CWSG CWib
	- 'Early Laxton' (C/D) Υ^{H4}	ECrN ERea GTwe SFam SKee
	- 'Early Prolific'	see *P. domestica* 'Rivers's Early Prolific'
	- 'Early Rivers'	see *P. domestica* 'Rivers's Early Prolific'
	- 'Early Transparent Gage' (C/D)	CSBt CTho CTri ECrN ERea GTwe LBuc MCoo SFam SKee SPer
	- 'Edwards' (C/D) Υ^{H4}	CTri CWib ECrN GTwe SFam SKee
	- 'Excalibur' (D)	ECrN GTwe SKee
§	- German Prune Group (C)	CTho SKee
§	- 'Giant Prune' (C)	CWib ECrN GTwe SKee
	- 'Golden Transparent' (D)	CTho ERea GTwe MCoo SFam SKee
	- 'Goldfinch' (D)	GTwe MCoo SKee
	- Green Gage Group	see *P. domestica* Reine-Claude Group
	- - 'Old Green Gage'	see *P. domestica* (Reine-Claude Group) 'Reine-Claude Vraie'
	- 'Grey Plum' (F)	CAgr CTho
	- 'Grove's Late Victoria' (C/D)	SKee
	- 'Guthrie's Late Green' (D)	SKee
	- 'Herman' (C/D)	CAgr ECrN GTwe LBuc LRHS MBri SKee SPoG
	- 'Heron' (F)	ECrN GTwe SKee
	- 'Impérial Epineuse' (D)	SKee
§	- 'Imperial Gage' (C/D) Υ^{H4}	CSBt CTho CTri CWib ECrN ERea GTwe SFam SKee SPoG WOrn
	- 'Jan James' (F)	CEnd
	- 'Jefferson' (D) Υ^{H4}	CAgr ECrN ERea GTwe SFam SKee
*	- 'Jubilaeum' (D)	GTwe MBri SKee
	- 'Kea' (C)	CAgr CTho SKee
	- 'Kirke's' (D)	CTho CTri ECrN ERea GTwe SFam SKee WOrn
	- 'Landkey Yellow' (F)	CAgr CTho
	- 'Late Muscatelle' (D)	ERea SKee
	- 'Laxton's Bountiful'	see *P. domestica* 'Bountiful'
§	- 'Laxton's Cropper' (C)	CTri GTwe MCoo SKee
§	- 'Laxton's Delicious' (D)	GTwe SKee
	- 'Laxton's Delight' (D) Υ^{H4}	GTwe
	- 'Mallard' (D) Υ^{H4} **new**	SKee
	- 'Manaccan' (C)	CAgr CTho
	- 'Marjorie's Seedling' (C) Υ^{H4}	CAgr CDoC CSBt CTho CTri CWib ECrN ERea GBon GTwe LBuc LRHS MGos MWat NPri SCoo SEND SFam SKee SPer SPoG WJas WOrn
	- 'McLaughlin' (D)	SKee
	- 'Merton Gem' (C/D)	GTwe SFam SKee
	- 'Monarch' (C)	GTwe SKee
	- 'Olympia' (C/D)	SKee
	- 'Ontario' (C/D)	SKee
	- 'Opal' (D) Υ^{H4}	CAgr CDoC CWSG CWib ECrN ERea GBut GKir GTwe LBuc MBri MGos MLan MWat NWea SCrf SEND SFam SKee SPoG WOrn
	- 'Orleans' (C)	SKee
	- 'Oullins Gage' (C/D) Υ^{H4}	CAgr CDoC CSBt CTri CWib ECrN ENot EPfP ERea GBon GKir GTwe

		LBuc MBri MRav SFam SKee SPer SPoG WJas WOrn
	- 'Pershore' (C) 🏆H4	CTho CWib ECrN ERea GTwe MBri SFam SKee WOrn
	- 'Pond's Seedling' (C)	CSBt SKee
	- 'President' (C/D)	GTwe
	'Prince Englebert' (C)	SKee
	- 'Purple Pershore' (C)	CAgr CTri CWib ECrN ERea GTwe SFam SKee
	- 'Quetsche d'Alsace'	see *P. domestica* German Prune Group
	- 'Reeves' (C) 🏆H4	GTwe MCoo SFam SKee
§	- Reine-Claude Group (C/D)	ECrN GTwe SFam SKee SPer
	- - 'Reine-Claude de Bavais' (D)	CTho CTri ERea GTwe SFam SKee
§	- - 'Reine-Claude Vraie' (C/D)	CCVT CSBt CWib EPfP ERea LBuc SCrf SKee WJas WOrn
§	- - 'Willingham Gage' (C/D)	ERea GTwe LRHS MLan
	- 'Reine-Claude Dorée'	see *P. domestica* Reine-Claude Group
	- 'Reine-Claude Violette' (D)	ERea SKee
§	- 'Rivers's Early Prolific' (C)	CSBt CTho CTri ECrN ENot EPfP ERea GBut GTwe MCoo NWea SCoo SHBN SKee
	- 'Royale de Vilvoorde' (D)	ERea SKee
	- 'Sanctus Hubertus' (D) 🏆H4	CDoC CRez ECrN EPfP GTwe SKee
	- 'Severn Cross' (D)	GTwe SKee
	- 'Stella'	CCVT
	- 'Stint' (C/D)	SKee
	- 'Swan' (C)	ECrN GTwe SKee
	- 'Syston'	CTho
	- 'Thames Cross' (D)	SKee
	- 'Transparent Gage' (D)	ERea
	- 'Upright' (F)	CEnd
	- 'Utility' (D)	SKee
	- 'Valor' (C/D) 🏆H4	ECrN MCoo
	- 'Victoria' (C/D) 🏆H4	More than 30 suppliers
I	- 'Violetta' (C/D)	ERea GTwe SKee SPoG
	- 'Warwickshire Drooper' (C)	CTho CWib ERea GBon GTwe SFam SKee SPoG WBVN
	- 'Washington' (D)	ERea SKee
	- 'White Magnum Bonum' (C)	CTho
	- 'Willingham'	see *P. domestica* (Reine-Claude Group) 'Willingham Gage'
	- 'Wyedale' (C)	ECrN GTwe
§	***dulcis***	CDul CTri CWib ECrN EWTr LRHS MWat NBea NWea SBLw SCoo SCrf SFam SKee WDin WOrn
	- 'Ai' (F) **new**	CAgr
	- 'Ardechoise' (F) **new**	CAgr
	- 'Balatoni' (F)	LRHS
	- 'Ferraduel' (F) **new**	CAgr
	- 'Ferragnes' (F) **new**	CAgr
	- 'Lauranne' (F) **new**	CAgr
	- 'Macrocarpa' (F)	ECrN
	- 'Mandaline' (F) **new**	CAgr
	- 'Titan' (F)	ECrN
	Easter Bonnet = 'Comet'PBR	LRHS
	x ***eminens*** 'Umbraculifera'	SBLw
	Fragrant Cloud = 'Shizuka'	CEnd CWSG GKir LRHS MAsh MBri SCoo SLim SPer SPoG
	fruticosa 'Globosa'	CWSG LRHS MAsh
	'Fugenzô'	CSBt
	'Fuki'	GKir MAsh MBri
§	'Geraldinae'	LRHS
	glandulosa 'Alba Plena' (d)	CEnd CPLG CPle CSBt EBee ECrN LRHS MBow MDun NBea SBLw SHBN SPer SPlb SPoG SRms SWvt WAul WCFE WDin WSHC
	- 'Rosea Plena'	see *P. glandulosa* 'Sinensis'
§	- 'Sinensis' (d)	CEnd CPLG CPle CSBt EBee LRHS SBLw SHBN SPer SPoG SRms WDin WSHC
§	x ***gondouinii*** 'May Duke' (F)	CTho
	- 'Schnee'	SBLw
	'Gyoikô'	CEnd CTho GKir
	'Hally Jolivette'	CEnd COtt CPle ELan GKir LRHS MAsh SBLw WDin
	'Hanagasa'	EBee LRHS MAsh MBri SCoo
	'Hillieri'	ECrN MBar MGos
	'Hillieri Spire'	see *P.* 'Spire'
	'Hilling's Weeping'	EBee GKir LRHS SPoG
§	***hirtipes***	CTho SPoG
	'Hisakura'	see *P.* 'Chôshû-hizakura'
	'Hokusai'	GKir
	Hollywood	see *P.* 'Trailblazer'
	'Horinji'	GKir MBri
	'Ichiyo' (d) 🏆H4	CLnd ECrN GKir MBri SCoo SCrf SPoG SPur
	incisa	CTri NBea SPer SSpi
	- 'Beniomi'	MRav
	- 'February Pink'	CAbP CPMA LRHS MRav NPro SBLw WDin
	- 'Fujima'	SMur
	- 'Kojo-no-mai'	More than 30 suppliers
	- 'Mikinori'	GKir MBri MGos NLar SCoo SPoG WFar
	- 'Oshidori'	GKir LRHS MBri MGos NLar SCoo SLim WFar
*	- 'Otome'	MBri WFar
	- 'Paean'	NLar WSPU
	- 'Pendula'	CPMA GKir LRHS MBri SCoo
	- 'Praecox' 🏆H4	CTho EPfP LRHS SCoo SPoG
	- 'The Bride'	CDul CEnd GKir LRHS MAsh MBri SCoo
§	- f. ***yamadae***	CBcs CEnd CPMA EBee LRHS NLar SLim WBcn
§	***insititia*** (F)	CAgr CRWN
§	- 'Bradley's King Damson' (C)	CWib ECrN GTwe SKee
	- 'Dittisham Damson' (C)	CTho
	- 'Farleigh Damson' (C) 🏆H4	CAgr CWib ECrN ERea GBut GKir GTwe LBuc SFam SKee SPer SPoG WJas
	- 'Golden Bullace'	see *P. insititia* 'White Bullace'
	- 'King of Damsons'	see *P. insititia* 'Bradley's King Damson'
	- 'Langley Bullace' (C)	CTho ECrN ERea GTwe SKee
	- 'Merryweather Damson' (C)	CAgr CCAT CCVT CDoC CMac CSBt CTho CTri CWib ECrN ENot ERea GBon GKir GTwe LBuc MBri SFam SKee SPer SPoG WHar WJas WOrn
	- 'Mirabelle de Nancy' (C)	CTho CTri GTwe MBri SFam SKee
§	- 'Prune Damson' (C) 🏆H4	CDoC CTho CTri CWSG CWib ECrN EPfP ERea GBon GTwe LBuc MBri MGos SCrf SFam SKee SPer WHar WJas WOrn
	- 'Shepherd's Bullace' (C)	CTho ERea SKee
	- 'Shropshire Damson'	see *P. insititia* 'Prune Damson'
	- 'Small Bullace' (C)	CAgr SKee
§	- 'White Bullace' (C)	ERea SKee
	- 'Yellow Apricot' (C)	ERea SKee
§	***jamasakura***	CTho
	japonica	GIBF
	'Jô-nioi'	CEnd CLnd CTho SBLw
§	'Kanzan' 🏆H4	More than 30 suppliers
§	'Kiku-shidare-zakura' 🏆H4	More than 30 suppliers
	Korean hill cherry	see *P. verecunda*

	kurilensis	see *P. nipponica* var. ***kurilensis***
	'Kursar' 🏆H4	CDul CLnd CSBt CTho CTri EPfP GKir LRHS MAsh MBri NWea SCoo SCrf SFam SLim SPoG WOrn
	laurocerasus 🏆H4	CBcs CBrm CCVT CChe CDul CPMA CWSG EBee ECrN ELan EPfP GKir MRav MWat NBea NEgg NFor NWea SEND SPer SPoG SReu WFar WMoo WMou
I	- 'Albomaculata'	WBcn
	- 'Angustifolia'	WDin
	- 'Aureovariegata'	see *P. laurocerasus* 'Taff's Golden Gleam'
	- 'Camelliifolia'	CTri EPla MBlu WBcn WCFE WDin WHCG
§	- 'Castlewellan' (v)	CBot CDoC CPLG CTri CTrw CWib EBee EGra EPfP EPla ISea LAst MBar MGos MSwo NBea NEgg NPro SDix SEND SPer SPoG SSta WDin WFar WHar WLeb WMoo
	- 'Caucasica'	MGos
	- 'Cherry Brandy'	ENot MRav SPer WBcn WCot WDin
	- Etna = 'Anbri'^{PBR}	EBee ENot EPfP LRHS MBri MGos MRav NPri SCoo
	- 'Golden Splash'	WBcn
	- 'Green Marble' (v)	CTri EBee WSHC
	- 'Herbergii'	ECrN
§	- 'Latifolia'	CHEx EPla GKir SArc SLPl
§	- Low 'n' Green = 'Interlo'	EBee ENot MRav
	- 'Magnoliifolia'	see *P. laurocerasus* 'Latifolia'
	- 'Mano'	MGos NBlu NLar
	- 'Marbled White'	see *P. laurocerasus* 'Castlewellan'
	- 'Mischeana'	SLPl
	- 'Mount Vernon'	EBee MBar MBlu MGos WBcn WDin
	- 'Novita'	EMil
	- 'Otinii'	CHEx
	- 'Otto Luyken' 🏆H4	CBcs CCVT CDul CPLG CSBt CTri EBee ECrN EGra ELan ENot EPfP GKir LBuc LRHS MBar MDun MGos MRav MSwo NBir NBlu NWea SHBN SPer SPla WCot WDin WFar WTel
	- Renault Ace = 'Renlau'	EBee MGos MRav
	- 'Reynvaanii'	LRHS MBri WBcn
	- 'Rotundifolia'	CDoC CSBt CTri CWib ELan EMil ENot GKir LBuc LRHS LSRN MBNS MBar MBri MGos MSwo NBea NBlu NEgg NWea SLim SPoG SRms SWvt WDin WHar WMoo WTel
	- 'Schipkaensis'	SLPl SPer
§	- 'Taff's Golden Gleam' (v)	SMad WBcn
	- 'Van Nes'	EMil WDin
	- 'Variegata' misapplied	see *P. laurocerasus* 'Castlewellan'
	- 'Variegata' ambig. (v)	CWib EPla MBNS MGos SRms
	- 'Zabeliana'	CDul CTri EBee ECrN ENot EPfP GKir MBar MGos MSwo NWea SHBN SPer SRms WDin WFar WTel
	litigiosa	GKir LRHS LSRN MBri SCoo
*	***longipedunculata***	LRHS
	lusitanica 🏆H4	More than 30 suppliers
	- subsp. ***azorica***	CDoC EPla MRav WFar WPGP
	- 'Myrtifolia'	EBee EPfP EPla GKir LAst LRHS MBri MLLN MRav SLon SMad SWvt WCFE WDin WGer
	- 'Variegata' (v)	More than 30 suppliers
	maackii	CTho ECrN EPfP GIBF GKir MDun SBLw SEND SSpi WDin
	- 'Amber Beauty'	CDoC CDul CEnd EBee EPfP GKir LRHS MRav SBLw SCoo WDin
	mahaleb	CTho
	mandshurica	GIBF
	'Matsumae-beni-murasaki'	GKir MAsh SCoo
	'Matsumae-beni-tamanishiki'	GKir MAsh
	'Matsumae-hana-gasa'	MBri
	maximowiczii	GIBF
	'Mount Fuji'	see *P.* 'Shirotae'
	mume	CMCN WDin WNor
§	- 'Beni-chidori'	CWib ECrN EPfP LBuc LRHS MAsh MBlu MBri MGos NBea SHBN SLim SPoG SSpi SSta WJas WPGP
I	- 'Beni-shidori'	see *P. mume* 'Beni-chidori'
*	- 'Ken Kyo'	LRHS
*	- 'Kyo Koh'	LRHS
§	- 'Omoi-no-mama' (d)	CEnd LRHS
	- 'Omoi-no-wac'	see *P. mume* 'Omoi-no-mama'
	- 'Pendula'	LRHS
	- 'Yae-kankobane' (d)	LRHS
	myrobalana	see *P. cerasifera* Myrobalan Group
§	***nipponica***	CBcs
	var. ***kurilensis***	
	- - 'Brilliant'	CBcs GKir MAsh MBri MGos NLar SCrf WOrn
	- - 'Ruby'	CBcs CEnd GKir LRHS MBri MGos NBlu NEgg SMur WFar
	- - 'Spring Joy'	LRHS
	'Okame' 🏆H4	CDul CLnd CTho ENot EPfP GKir LRHS MAsh MBri MGos MRav NBlu NEgg NWea SCoo SCrf SLim SPer WBVN WFar WOrn WWeb
*	'Okame Harlequin' (v)	SLim SPoG
	'Okumiyako' misapplied	see *P.* 'Shôgetsu'
	padus	CCVT CDul CLnd CRWN CSBt CTri ECrN ENot GIBF GKir LBuc MDun MGos MSwo NBea NBee NBlu NWea SBLw SHGC SSpi WDin WMou WOrn
	- 'Albertii'	CTho GKir MDun WJas
	- 'Colorata' 🏆H4	CDoC CDul CEnd CMHG CSam CTho ECrN ELan GKir LBuc MBri MDun MGos NBee SBLw SCoo SHBN SPer SSpi WDin WFar WJas
	- 'Grandiflora'	see *P. padus* 'Watereri'
	- 'Plena' (d)	CTho
	- 'Purple Queen'	CEnd CTho ECrN ENot
§	- 'Watereri' 🏆H4	CBcs CCVT CDoC CDul CLnd CMCN CTho CWib EBee ECrN ELan ENot EPfP EWTr GKir LRHS MBri MDun NWea SBLw SCoo SHBN SLim SPer WDin WJas WOrn
	'Pandora' 🏆H4	CBcs CLnd CRez EBee ECrN ENot EPfP GKir LAst LRHS MAsh MBri MDun MGos MRav MSwo NBea NBee NWea SBLw SCoo SCrf SEND SHBN SPer SPoG WFar WOrn
	pendula **new**	SCrf
§	- 'Pendula Rosea' 🏆H4	CDoC CDul CEnd CSBt CTri CWib EPfP GKir LRHS MAsh SBLw SCrf SPer WFar WJas WOrn
§	- 'Pendula Rubra' 🏆H4	CDoC CEnd CLnd CSBt CWib EBee ECrN ENot EPfP GKir LAst LRHS MBri MGos MSwo SCoo SFam SHBN SLim SPer SPoG
§	- 'Stellata'	LRHS MBri SPer
	persica 'Amsden June' (F)	ERea GTwe SFam SKee
	- 'Bellegarde' (F)	ERea GTwe SFam SKee
	- 'Bonanza' (F)	EMil ERea
	- 'Clara Meyer' **new**	MDun
	- 'Duke of York' (F) 🏆H3	CTri ERea GTwe LRHS SFam SKee WOrn
	- 'Dymond' (F)	ERea

- 'Flat China' (F) — ERea
- 'Foliis Rubris' (F) — CDul WPGP
- 'Francis' (F) — SKee
- 'Garden Anny' (F) — EMil ERea LRHS
- 'Garden Lady' (F) — ERea GTwe SKee SPoG
- 'Hale's Early' (F) — ERea GTwe SEND SFam SKee SPer SPoG WOrn
- 'Melred' — MGos
- 'Melred Weeping' — SBLw
- var. ***nectarina*** 'Early Gem' (F) — ERea
- - 'Early Rivers' (F) ♀H3 — ERea GTwe
- - 'Elruge' (F) — ERea GTwe SEND SFam
- - 'Fantasia' (F) — ERea
- - 'Garden Beauty' (F/d) — ENot
- - 'Humboldt' (F) — ERea GTwe SKee
- - 'John Rivers' (F) — ERea GTwe SFam
- - 'Lord Napier' (F) ♀H3 — CAgr CDoC CSBt CWSG CWib EPfP ERea GKir LBuc LRHS MGos SEND SFam SKee SPer WBVN WOrn
- - 'Nectared' (F) — CWib GTwe
- - 'Nectarella' (F) — CRez ERea GTwe LRHS SKee
- - 'Pineapple' (F) — CTri ERea GTwe LRHS SFam SKee
- - 'Ruby Gold' (F) — GKir
- - 'Terrace Ruby' (F) — ENot GKir
- 'Peregrine' (F) ♀H3 — CAgr CMac CSBt CTri CWSG CWib ENot EPfP ERea GBon GKir GTwe LBuc LRHS MBri MGos SFam SHBN SKee SPer WJas
- 'Red Haven' (F) — CAgr GTwe SKee
- 'Rochester' (F) ♀H3 — CAgr CWSG ENot ERea GBon GKir GTwe LRHS MBri SFam SKee SPer SPoG WOrn
- 'Royal George' (F) — GTwe SFam
- 'Sagami-shidare' — LRHS
- 'Saturne' (F) — LRHS SKee SPoG
- 'Springtime' (F) — ERea
- 'Terrace Amber' — ENot
- 'Terrace Diamond' — ENot
- 'Terrace Garnet' — ENot NPri
- 'Terrace Pearl' — NPri
- 'Weeping Flame' (F) — LRHS
- 'White Cascade' — LRHS

'Pink Perfection' ♀H4 — CBcs CDul CLnd CSBt CWSG CWib EBee ECrN ENot EPfP LRHS MBri NBee SCrf SHBN SPer WDin WFar WJas WOrn
'Pink Shell' ♀H4 — CLnd CTho EPfP GKir LRHS MAsh MBri SFam SPur WOrn
pissardii — see *P. cerasifera* 'Pissardii'
'Pissardii Nigra' — see *P. cerasifera* 'Nigra'
prostrata — WPat
* - 'Anita Kistler' — ECho
* - var. ***discolor*** — NLar WNor
pseudocerasus 'Cantabrigiensis' — ECrN
pumila var. ***depressa*** — EMil MBar MBlu MRav NLar NPro
'Rebecca' **new** — SCoo
'Rosie's Dream' **new** — SCoo
'Royal Burgundy' — CEnd CWSG EBee EMil ENot GKir LRHS MAsh MBri MDun MGos MWat NBee SCoo SKee SLim SPer SPoG SPur WGer WOrn
rufa — CLnd CPMA CTho GKir MDun SSpi
sachalinensis — GIBF
salicina — GIBF
- 'Beauty' — ERea
- 'Methley' (D) — ECrN ERea
- 'Satsuma' (F) — ERea
- 'Shiro' (D) — ERea
sargentii ♀H4 — More than 30 suppliers
- 'Charles Sargent' — GKir
- 'Columnaris' — GKir LRHS
- 'Rancho' — CLnd SLPl WOrn
x ***schmittii*** — CLnd ECrN ENot MAsh SCoo SPer WJas
'Sekiyama' — see *P.* 'Kanzan'
serotina — CDul NLar SBLw
§ ***serrula*** ♀H4 — More than 30 suppliers
- Branklyn form — GKir MBri
- Dorothy Clive form — GKir LRHS MDun SCoo
§ - 'Mahogany Lustre' — CLnd
- var. ***tibetica*** — see *P. serrula*
serrula x ***serrulata*** — CBcs CTho
serrulata 'Erecta' — see *P.* 'Amanogawa'
- 'Grandiflora' — see *P.* 'Ukon'
- 'Longipes' — see *P.* 'Shôgetsu'
- 'Miyako' misapplied — see *P.* 'Shôgetsu'
N - var. ***pubescens*** — see *P. verecunda*
- 'Rosea' — see *P.* 'Kiku-shidare-zakura'
- var. ***spontanea*** — see *P. jamasakura*
'Shidare-zakura' — see *P.* 'Kiku-shidare-zakura'
'Shimizu-zakura' — see *P.* 'Shôgetsu'
'Shirofugen' ♀H4 — CBcs CDoC CDul CLnd CMCN CSBt CTho CWib EBee ECrN EMil ENot EPfP GKir LBuc LRHS MAsh MBri MRav NBee NEgg SCrf SFam SPer SPoG WDin WJas WOrn
§ 'Shirotae' ♀H4 — More than 30 suppliers
§ 'Shôgetsu' ♀H4 — CBcs CDul CEnd CLnd CSBt CTho ECrN ELan ENot EPfP GKir LAst LRHS MBri NBlu SCrf SFam SHBN SLim SPer WDin
'Shosar' — CEnd CLnd CWib ECrN GKir LAst LRHS MAsh MBri SCoo SPer SPoG
'Snow Goose' — CDoC EBee GKir LAst LRHS MBri NEgg SCoo
'Snow Showers' — CEnd CWSG GKir LRHS MAsh MBri MDun NWea SPer WGer WGor
spinosa — CCVT CDoC CDul CRWN CTri ECrN EPfP LBuc LRHS MBar MBlu MBri NWea SPer WDin WFar WMou WNor XPep
- 'Plena' (d) — CEnd CTho MBlu
- 'Purpurea' — MBlu WBcn WDin WHCG WMou WPat
§ 'Spire' ♀H4 — CCVT CDoC CDul CLnd CMCN CSBt CTho CWib ECrN EPfP GKir LBuc LRHS MAsh MGos MRav MSwo NBlu NWea SCoo SHBN SPer SPoG WDin WFar WJas WOrn
ssiori **new** — GIBF
x ***subhirtella*** — WNor
- 'Autumnalis' ♀H4 — More than 30 suppliers
- 'Autumnalis Rosea' ♀H4 — More than 30 suppliers
§ - 'Dahlem' — LRHS
- 'Fukubana' — CLnd CTho EBee GKir LRHS MAsh MBri SBLw
- 'Pendula' hort. — see *P. pendula* 'Pendula Rosea'
- 'Pendula Plena Rosea' (d) — SBLw
- 'Pendula Rubra' — see *P. pendula* 'Pendula Rubra'
- 'Plena' — see *P.* x *subhirtella* 'Dahlem'
N - 'Rosea' — CLnd ENot GKir MRav WBVN
- 'Stellata' — see *P. pendula* 'Stellata'
'Sunset Boulevard' — GKir LRHS
'Taihaku' ♀H4 — More than 30 suppliers
'Taki-nioi' — ECrN NWea
'Taoyame' — CLnd LRHS
tenella — CAgr CBcs ECrN ELan WCot
- 'Fire Hill' — CBcs CPMA CRez CSBt CWib ELan ENot EPfP GKir LRHS MBri MGos

	SBLw SCrf SHBN SPer SSpi WCot WDin WJas WOrn WPat
tibetica	see *P. serrula*
tomentosa	CRez ECrN WBVN
§ 'Trailblazer' (C/D)	CEnd CLnd CSBt CTho ECrN LAst MGos NWea SBLw SKee
triloba	CBcs CSBt CTri ECrN EMil ENot GIBF LBuc LRHS LSRN MDun NBee NBlu NWea SBLw SHBN SPoG WDin
- 'Multiplex' (d)	ENot LRHS MGos MRav NPri SPer SRms WJas
- Rosemund = 'Korros'	LRHS
§ 'Ukon' ♀H4	CBcs CDoC CDul CLnd CMCN CTho CTri EBee ECrN ENot EPfP EWTr GKir LBuc LRHS MAsh MBar MBri MGos MRav NBee NWea SCrf SFam SHBN SPer WDin WFar WOrn
'Umineko'	CCVT CDoC CLnd ECrN ENot GKir MGos SCoo SPer SPur WDin WMoo
ussuriensis **new**	GIBF
§ ***verecunda***	CDoC CLnd NWea SPur WJas
- 'Autumn Glory'	CTho NBea
virginiana 'Schubert'	CDul CLnd ECrN SBLw WFar WJas WOrn
'White Cloud'	CTho
yamadae	see *P. incisa* f. *yamadae*
§ x ***yedoensis*** ♀H4	CCVT CDul CLnd CMCN CSBt CSam CTho CTri ECrN ENot EPfP GKir LAst NWea SBLw SFam SLim SPer WDin WJas WOrn
- 'Ivensii'	CBcs CDul CSBt CTri CWib EBee GKir LRHS MAsh MDun NBee NEgg SCoo SFam SHBN SPer WDin
- 'Pendula'	see *P.* x *yedoensis* 'Shidare-yoshino'
- 'Perpendens'	see *P.* x *yedoensis* 'Shidare-yoshino'
§ - 'Shidare-yoshino'	CCVT CEnd CLnd EBee ECrN EPfP GKir LRHS MAsh MBar MBri MGos MRav MSwo NWea SBLw SLim SPer SPoG WOrn
- 'Tsubame'	LRHS
'Yoshino'	see *P.* x *yedoensis*
'Yoshino Pendula'	see *P.* x *yedoensis* 'Shidare-yoshino'

Pseuderanthemum (*Acanthaceae*)

seticalyx	ESlt

Pseudocydonia (*Rosaceae*)

§ ***sinensis***	CAgr CBcs

Pseudofumaria see *Corydalis*

Pseudogynoxys (*Asteraceae*)

chenopodioides	CPLN ELan ERea ESlt

Pseudolarix (*Pinaceae*)

§ ***amabilis*** ♀H4	CDoC CEnd CFil CMCN CTho ECrN EHul EPfP GBin GKir LCon MBar MBlu MBri NBlu SCoo SLim SPoG STre WNor WPGP
kaempferi	see *P. amabilis*

Pseudomuscari see *Muscari*

Pseudopanax (*Araliaceae*)

(Adiantifolius Group) 'Adiantifolius'	CBcs CHEx CTrC GQui IDee SMad
- 'Cyril Watson' ♀H1	CBcs CDoC CHEx SBig
arboreus	CAbb CBcs CDoC CHEx CTrC LEdu
'Black Ruby'	CBcs
chathamicus	CDoC CHEx SAPC SArc
crassifolius	CAbb CBcs CBot CBrP CTrC EAmu SAPC SArc SBig SMad WCot
- var. ***trifoliolatus***	CHEx
davidii	SLon
discolor	ECou LEdu
ferox	CAbb CBcs CBrP EAmu EUJe IDee ITer LEdu SAPC SArc SBig SMad WCot
laetus	CAbb CHEx CTrC ECou IDee LEdu SAPC SArc SBig
lessonii	CBcs CHEx ECou
- 'Gold Splash' (v) ♀H1	CBcs CHEx SBig SEND
- 'Rangitira' **new**	SBig
'Linearifolius'	CHEx CTbh CTrC IDee LEdu
'Purpureus' ♀H1	CHEx
'Sabre'	CBcs CHEx SMad
'Trident'	CDoC CHEx CTrC IDee LEdu

Pseudophegopteris (*Thelypteridaceae*)

levingei	EMon

Pseudophoenix (*Arecaceae*)

* ***nativo***	MBri

Pseudosasa (*Poaceae*)

amabilis misapplied	see *Arundinaria gigantea*
§ ***amabilis*** (McClure) Keng f.	WFar
§ ***japonica*** ♀H4	More than 30 suppliers
§ - 'Akebonosuji' (v)	EFul EPla MMoz MWht NMoo WJun WNor WPGP
I - var. ***pleioblastoides***	EPla MWht
- 'Tsutsumiana'	CHEx CPen CRez ENot EPla EPza ERod MMoz MWht NLar NMoo SBig WJun
- 'Variegata'	see *P. japonica* 'Akebonosuji'
orthotropa	see *Sinobambusa orthotropa*
usawai	EPla WJun
viridula	NMoo

Pseudotsuga (*Pinaceae*)

§ ***menziesii*** ♀H4	CAgr CBcs CDoC CDul CLnd ECrN EPfP GKir LBuc LCon LLin LRHS LRav MBar MBlu NWea SPoG WDin WFar WMou
- 'Bhiela Lhota'	CKen MAsh
- 'Blue Wonder'	CKen
- 'Densa'	CKen
- 'Fastigiata'	CKen LCon
- 'Fletcheri'	CKen MBar
- var. ***glauca***	LCon MBar
- 'Glauca Pendula'	LCon MBar MGos
I - 'Gotelli's Pendula'	CKen
- 'Graceful Grace'	CKen
- 'Idaho Gem'	CKen
- 'Julie'	CKen
- 'Knaphill'	NLar WEve
- 'Little Jamie'	CKen MBar
- 'Lohbrunner'	CKen
- 'McKenzie'	CKen
- 'Nana'	CKen
- 'Stairii'	CKen
taxifolia	see *P. menziesii*

Pseudowintera (*Winteraceae*)

§ ***colorata***	CBcs CDoC CPLG CTrw GCal GGar GKir IDee IMGH ISea MDun NRib SLon WCru WFar WFoF
- 'Mount Congreve'	LRHS SSpi WGer

Psidium (*Myrtaceae*)

cattleyanum	see *P. littorale* var. *longipes*
guajava (F)	XBlo
littorale (F)	ERea
§ - var. ***longipes*** (F)	XBlo

Psilotum (*Psilotaceae*)

nudum	ECou

Psoralea (*Papilionaceae*)

aphylla **new**	EShb
bituminosa	WSHC XPep
- HH&K 174	CStr
glabra	SPlb
glandulosa	CArn CFil LRav WSHC
oligophylla	SPlb
pinnata	CHEx CPLG CTrC GGar IDee

Psychotria (*Rubiaceae*)

capensis	CPLG EShb
carthagenensis	MGol
viridis	MGol

Ptelea (*Rutaceae*)

trifoliata	CBcs CDul CFil CLnd CMCN CTho CWib EBee ECrN EPfP IMGH MBlu SBLw SPer SPoG SRms SSpi WDin WFar WHCG WNor WOrn WPGP
- 'Aurea' ♀H4	CAbP CBcs CBot CEnd CLnd CMCN CPMA CTho EBee ELan ENot EPfP EWTr GBin GKir LRHS MAsh MBlu MBri MGos SBLw SBrw SHBN SMur SPer SPoG SSpi WDin WHCG WPat

Pteracanthus see *Strobilanthes*

Pteridophyllum (*Papaveraceae*)

racemosum	EFEx GCrs WCru

Pteris (*Pteridaceae*)

from Yunnan **new**	CLAP
angustipinna B&SWJ 6738	WCru
argyraea	MBri WRic
cretica ♀H1+3	CHEx MBri SAPC SArc
- var. ***albolineata*** ♀H1	GQui MBri SRms
- 'Cristata'	MBri
- 'Gautheri'	MBri
- 'Parkeri'	MBri
- 'Rivertoniana'	MBri
- 'Rowei'	MBri
- 'Wimsettii'	MBri
dentata **new**	WRic
ensiformis	MBri
* - 'Arguta'	MBri
- 'Victoriae'	MBri
gallinopes	WAbe
quadriaurita **new**	WRic
tremula	CHEx GQui MBri SRms WRic
umbrosa	MBri WRic
vittata	SRms
wallichiana	CFil CHEx CLAP

Pterocarya (*Juglandaceae*)

fraxinifolia ♀H4	CBcs CDul CLnd CMCN ECrN EPfP EWTr MBlu NBee SBLw WDin
x ***rehderiana***	CTho MBlu WMou
stenoptera	CBcs CFil CLnd CMCN CTho SLPl
- 'Fern Leaf'	CFil MBlu SMad WMou WPGP

Pteroceltis (*Ulmaceae*)

tatarinowii	CMCN WHCr

Pterocephalus (*Dipsacaceae*)

dumetorum **new**	CSec
parnassi	see *P. perennis*
§ ***perennis***	CMea EDAr LRHS MHer NBir NJOw NLar NLon NMen NRya NWCA SBla SPet SRms WAbe WEas WHoo XPep
- subsp. ***perennis***	EGoo WHrl
pinardii	NWCA

Pterodiscus (*Pedaliaceae*)

ngamicus **new**	LToo
speciosus **new**	LToo

Pterostylis (*Orchidaceae*)

acuminata var. ***ingens***	EPot
coccinea	SSpi
curta	CStu SCnR
Nodding Grace g.	CDes
revoluta **new**	EPot
truncata	SSpi

Pterostyrax (*Styracaceae*)

corymbosa	CBcs CMCN CPMA IArd IDee MBlu NLar SSpi WFar
hispida ♀H4	CBcs CDul CEnd CFil CHEx CLnd CMCN CPMA CPne CSam EBee EPfP EPla GKir IArd IDee LAst LRHS MBlu MRav NLar SSpi SSta WBVN WDin WFar WMul WPGP
psilophylla	CMCN

Pteryxia (*Umbelliferae*)

§ ***hendersonii*** **new**	GKev

Ptilostemon (*Asteraceae*)

afer	CPom EHrv EMan MWgw
§ ***diacantha***	CSam EVFa LSRN NLar NVic SPoG WHil WMnd
echinocephalus **new**	GBri NBre

Ptilotrichum see *Alyssum*

Puccinellia (*Poaceae*)

distans	CRWN

Pueraria (*Papilionaceae*)

montana var. ***lobata***	CAgr CArn CBcs LRav MSal WBcn

Pulicaria (*Asteraceae*)

§ ***dysenterica***	CAgr CArn IHMH MChe MHer MSal NMir SIde WCHb WDyG WLHH WWye

Pulmonaria ✿ (*Boraginaceae*)

'Abbey Dore Pink'	EBee WAbb
affinis	CLAP EMon LRHS
- 'Margaret'	NCob
* ***altaica***	GBin
angustifolia ♀H4	EPfP EWTr GKev GKir GMaP LRHS MDun MSal NOrc SChu SRms WCru WEas WFar WTin
- subsp. ***azurea***	More than 30 suppliers
- 'Blaues Meer'	CFir CSBt CSam EBee EPfP GBuc GKir LPio MBNS MNFA NFla NLsd SBod WCru
- 'Munstead Blue'	CElw CHea CLAP ECha EHrv ENot IBlr LPio LRHS LSpr MNFA MRav MTho MWgw NCob NLon NRya NSti SRms WCru
- 'Rubra'	see *P. rubra*
'Apple Frost'	EBrs ECtt MBnl NSti WCra WWol

	Name	Suppliers
	'Barfield Regalia'	CMHG EBee EMon IGor MBct NSti SDys WCru
	'Benediction'	CAby LPhx NSti SAga
	'Berries and Cream'	NSti
§	'Beth's Blue'	ECha EMon WCAu WCru
	'Beth's Pink'	ECha GAbr WCru WFar WWpP
	'Blauer Hügel'	CBct CElw EMon GKir NSti
§	'Blauhimmel'	EMon LRHS
	'Blue Buttons'	CFir CHea EBee GBin NSti
	'Blue Crown'	CElw CLAP CSev EBee EHrv EMon EWes LRHS MBri SAga SChu SSpe WCAu WCru WEas WHal
	'Blue Ensign'	More than 30 suppliers
	'Blue Moon'	see *P. officinalis* 'Blue Mist'
	'Blue Pearl'	EBee EMon NSti
	'Blueberry Muffin'	CSpe
	'Bonnie'	CMea
	'Botanic Hybrid'	WCru
	'British Sterling'	EBee
	Cally hybrid	CElw CLAP EBee EMon GBin GCal NSti WCot WCru
	'Cedric Morris'	CElw
	'Chintz'	CLAP CSam EBee GBin GBuc MAvo WCru WHal
	'Cleeton Red'	NSti WCru
	'Coral Springs'	EBrs GKir NSti
	'Corsage'	EBee ECtt
	'Cotton Cool'	CElw CFil CLAP CPrp EBee ECGP ECtt EMan EMon EPla MAvo MBNS MBnl MBri MMHG MNFA NCGa NDov NEgg NSti SSpi SUsu WCAu WCot WCru WMoo WPGP
	'Crawshay Chance'	WCru
	'Dark Vader'[PBR]	NSti
	'De Vroomen's Pride' (v)	CHid CSam EChP EMan LAst MSte WMnd WSan
	'Diana Clare'	More than 30 suppliers
	'Duke's Silver'	CLAP
	'Elworthy Rubies'	CElw MAvo
	'Emerald Isles'	NSti
	'Esther'	GSki NSti WCru
	'Excalibur'	CBct CHid EBrs EHrv EMan ENot GBin GBuc GKir MBct MBri NSti SHar WWol
	'Fiona'	CBct GFlt WCAu
	'Glacier'	CBro CElw CStr EBee ECGP EMon EWTr LPio LRHS MArl MMil MSte NSti SAga SMHy WHal WWhi
	'Hazel Kaye's Red'	CElw LPio NSti WCru
	'High Contrast'[PBR]	NSti
	'Highdown'	see *P.* 'Lewis Palmer'
	'Ice Ballet' (Classic Series)	EBee LRHS MBri
	'Joan's Red'	CElw WTin
§	'Lewis Palmer' 🏆[H4]	More than 30 suppliers
	'Lime Close'	LPhx SAga
	'Linford Blue' **new**	WCru
	'Little Blue'	NSti
	'Little Star'	EBee EGoo EMon GBuc NSti SChu SUsu WCru
	longifolia	More than 30 suppliers
§	- 'Ankum'	CBct CBos CElw CLAP CSam EBee EPfP EPla GBuc GKir IBlr ITer LPio LRHS MBrN MRav MSte NBir NSti SMrm SPoG SSpe SVil WCot WMoo WSHC WWlt
	- 'Ballyrogan Blue'	IBlr
	- 'Bertram Anderson'	COIW EChP ECtt GKir GMaP LAst LRHS MBow MLLN NBir NCGa NOrc NVic SBla SGSe SIng SPer SWvt WBrk WCAu WCot WCra WCru WFar WGHP WMnd WWol
	- subsp. ***cevennensis***	CAby CBgR CLAP CSam EBrs EChP EMan ENot EPfP GKir LAst MBnl MBri MLLN MSte NCGa NSti SHar SSpe SSpi
	- 'Coen Jansen'	see *P. longifolia* 'Ankum'
	- 'Coral Spring'	EMan MBNS SHGN WCAu
	- 'Dordogne'	CLAP EBee EBrs EMan GBuc GKir LRHS MLLN MRav NBir NEgg NOrc SBla WCAu WCru
	- 'Howard Eggins'	EBee WSPU
	'Lovell Blue'	CElw NCot
	'Majesté'	More than 30 suppliers
§	'Margery Fish' 🏆[H4]	CBro CLAP CSam EBee EChP EMar EPfP EPla GKir IBlr LAst LPio LRHS MBct MBow MLLN MNFA NBro NPri SGSe SPer WCru WMnd WMoo WTel WWye
	'Mary Mottram'	CElw CMea EChP ECtt ELan EMan GMac LAst MLLN MNFA NBir NLon NPol NSti SAga SBla SMrm SSpe WCru WHal WMnd WMoo WWhi
	'Matese Blue'	SBla
	'Mawson's Blue'	CLAP ECha EMon GKir LPio LRHS MRav MWat NBir SWvt WCru WEas WMoo WRHF WSHC WWhi WWye
	'May Bouquet'[PBR]	NRnb NSti
	'Melancholia'	IBlr
	'Merlin'	CLAP EMon LRHS NSti SSpi
	'Middleton Red'	CElw
§	'Milchstrasse'	CLAP
	Milky Way	see *P.* 'Milchstrasse'
	mollis	CLAP CSWP EBee ECGP EGoo EMon GCal IBlr LRHS NSti SBch SSpi WCru
	- WM 9206	SBla
	- 'Royal Blue'	MRav
	- 'Samobor'	CLAP
	'Monksilver'	EMon
	'Moonshine'	NSti
	'Moonstone'	CElw CLAP CPom LAst LPhx LPio WCru
	'Mountain Magic'	NSti
	'Mournful Purple'	CElw EHrv EMag WCru
	'Mrs Kittle'	CBct CElw CM&M EBee EChP EMan EPPr GBri MLLN MNFA MRav NBir NSti SDys SSpi WBrk WCru WFar WHal WLin WMnd
	'Netta Statham'	ECha
	'Northern Lights'[PBR]	SHar
	'Nürnberg'	EMon LRHS MAvo WHal
	obscura	LRHS
	officinalis	CAgr CArn CBro CHby EHon GBBs GBar GPoy LLWP LRHS MChe MDun MHer NVic SIde WBrk WCru WFar WHal WSSM WWpP WWye
	- 'Alba'	ELan GBBs NLon WBrk WCru
§	- 'Blue Mist'	CBro CElw CLAP ECha ELan EMon GBri GBuc GMac NBir NPar SSpi WAbb WBrk WCot WCru WHal WHoo WMnd WMoo WTin
	- 'Bowles' Blue'	see *P. officinalis* 'Blue Mist'
	- Cambridge Blue Group	CPrp EBee EChP EMar EMon GMaP LAst LRHS MBNS MNFA MRav NBir NLar WCAu WCot WCru WEas WHal WPtf
	- 'Marjorie Lawley'	NPar
	- 'Plas Merdyn'	IBlr
	- ***rubra***	see *P. rubra*
	- 'Stillingfleet Gran'	LPio NSti
	- 'White Wings'	CElw CHea CLAP EBrs EPla GKir LPio LRHS MBNS NPri NSti SIde SPoG WEas WFar WMoo

'Oliver Wyatt's White'	CLAP EBee
Opal = 'Ocupol'	More than 30 suppliers
'Pewter'	LPio WCru
'Pippa's Pink' **new**	SBla
'Polar Splash'	CAby CBct EBee GBin MBnl NSti SIde SPoG SRot WCra WFar
'Purple Haze'	NSti SHar
'Raspberry Ice'	NSti
'Raspberry Splash'PBR	CBct CLAP CPom CRez EBee EMan NEgg NLar NSti SHar SIde SPoG SRot
* 'Rowlatt Choules'	SSpi
'Roy Davidson'	CElw CLAP CSam EBee EChP ECtt EHrv EMon EPPr GKir LRHS MBow MNFA NBir NCGa NDov NSti SAga SBla WCra WCru WHal WPnP WWol
§ ***rubra*** ♀H4	CElw CSWP CStr ECha ELan EMar EWTr GKir IBlr LLWP NBid NCob NOrc NSti SBla SChu SRms WCAu WFar WTin
- var. ***alba***	see *P. rubra* var. *albocorollata*
§ - var. ***albocorollata***	CBct CBre CElw CMHG EBee ECha EHrv EMon GAbr GKir LRHS MSte WCAu WCru WFar
- 'Ann'	CBct CElw CLAP EBee EChP IBlr LRHS MBNS MBct NSti WCru WFar WTin
- 'Barfield Pink'	CBro CElw CPom EBee EChP ECtt ELan EWTr GBar GCal GKir LAst LRHS MAvo MLLN NBir NLar SChu SHGN WBrk WCru WHal
- 'Barfield Ruby'	EMon GBuc LRHS MAvo
- 'Bowles' Red'	ECtt EHrv EPfP GKir LRHS MRav MWgw NBir NCGa NGdn SBch SIde SPer WFar WHal WMnd
- 'David Ward' (v)	More than 30 suppliers
- 'Prestbury Pink'	LRHS
- 'Rachel Vernie' (v)	CLAP CPou EBee EMon WCot
- 'Redstart'	More than 30 suppliers
§ ***saccharata***	ECha EHrv ELan EWTr GFlt GMaP IHMH LGro NEgg SChu SIde SPet SRms WCAu WCru WFar
- 'Alba'	CBro CElw ECha GBuc SRms
- Argentea Group ♀H4	CBro CSev EBee ECha ELan EMag EPfP EWTr GMaP LAst LRHS MRav MTho NBro NGdn NLon SBla SPet SSpi SWvt WCAu WCot WSan
- blue-flowered **new**	WCru
- 'Brentor'	EBee WCru WWpP
- 'Clent Skysilver'	EBee WSPU
- 'Dora Bielefeld'	More than 30 suppliers
- 'Frühlingshimmel'	CBro CElw CMea CSam EBee EBrs ECtt GBBs GKir LPhx LPio MRav SChu WFar WHal WLin
- 'Glebe Cottage Blue'	CElw ECGP LPio MAvo NSti WCru WWpP
- 'Jill Richardson'	ELan
- 'Lady Lou's Pink'	WCru
- 'Leopard'	CBct CElw CLAP CMea CSam EBee EChP ECtt GBuc GKir GMaP GSki LAst LRHS MLLN NBir NBre NSti SApp SBla SGSe SUsu WBrk WCot WCru WFar WGHP WHoo WMnd
- 'Mrs Moon'	CSam EBee ECtt EMar ENot EPfP GKir GMaP LRHS MBNS MHer MWgw NBlu NOrc NPri SChu SIng SMer SPer SWvt WMnd WPnP
- 'Old Rectory Silver'	CLAP NBir
- 'Picta'	see *P. saccharata*
- 'Pink Dawn'	CMHG EMan LRHS WCru WMnd
- pink-flowered	WCru
- 'Reginald Kaye'	CElw ECha EWes SHBN
- 'Silverado'PBR	CHid EBee EBrs ENot MBNS NLar NOrc NSti
- 'Stanhoe'	EBee EWes
- 'White Barn'	see *P.* 'Beth's Blue'
'Saint Ann's'	CBct CElw EMon LRHS NBre NSti WCru
'Samurai' **new**	EBee
'Silver Maid'	WCAu
'Silver Mist'	MAvo
'Silver Sabre'	IBlr
'Silver Shimmers'	SHar
'Silver Streamers'PBR	MAvo
'Silver Surprise'	WCot
'Sissinghurst White' ♀H4	More than 30 suppliers
'Skylight'	CElw
'Smoky Blue'	CHid CLAP CRez EBee ECtt EMon EPfP LRHS MRav MWgw NSti SMar WCru WFar WHal WMnd WMoo
'Spilled Milk'	EBee EMan NLar NSti
'Stillingfleet Meg' **new**	CBct CSam EMar EPPr LBuc LRHS MAvo MBNS NCob NSti SPla SVil WCra
'Tim's Silver'	NPar WBcn
'Trevi Fountain'	CBct CLAP CRez EMan EShb NEgg NSti SHar SMac SPoG SRot
'Ultramarine'	EBee
'Vera May'	EBee MAvo
'Victorian Brooch'PBR	CBct CLAP EBee GAbr GCai LRHS LSou NEgg NLar NSti SIde WFar WPtf
'Weetwood Blue'	CBre CLAP EBee EPfP EPla MSte WCru
'Wendy Perry'	CElw
'Wisley White'	CElw

Pulsatilla (*Ranunculaceae*)

alba	CBro NSla NWCA WCra WWol
albana	EHyt LRHS SBla
- 'Lutea'	GKev SOkd WAbe
alpina	CBot EChP SRms WPat
- subsp. ***alpina*** **new**	GKev
§ - subsp. ***apiifolia*** ♀H4	ELan GFlt GKev GTou MFOX NRya
- subsp. ***sulphurea***	see *P. alpina* subsp. *apiifolia*
ambigua	SIgm
aurea	WLin
bungeana	EHyt
- subsp. ***astragalifolia*** **new**	GKev
campanella	GAbr
caucasica	LRHS
cernua	CBrm CBro EBrs GBuc LRHS SIgm
dahurica	CSec
x ***gayeri***	NBir
georgica	EHyt NSla SIgm WLin
halleri ♀H4	GKev GKir NSla SIgm
- from Moran Hills **new**	SOkd
* - ***alba***	SMHy
- pale blue-flowered **new**	SOkd
- subsp. ***slavica*** ♀H4	CLyd GCrs LRHS NSla NWCA
- subsp. ***taurica***	MSte WCot
lutea	see *P. alpina* subsp. *apiifolia*
montana	GBuc SPlb
multifida	GIBF
patens var. ***multifida***	GBuc
pratensis	GPoy GTou SRms
- subsp. ***nigricans***	CBro CSec EHyt LRHS WGwG
rubra	GKev GKir NEgg NGHP WWol
turczaninovii	GBuc GKev SIgm
§ ***vernalis*** ♀H2	EPot GAbr GBuc GCrs GTou NSla NWCA SBla WLin
§ ***vulgaris*** ♀H4	More than 30 suppliers
- 'Alba' ♀H4	More than 30 suppliers
- 'Barton's Pink'	CBro EWes EWll GKir LRHS SBla

	- 'Blaue Glocke'	CBrm GSki MAnH NLar SWvt WHil WWeb
	- Czech fringed hybrids	CNic
	- 'Eva Constance'	CBro EBee EHyt ENot GKir LRHS NBir SIng
	- 'Flore Pleno' (d)	CNic
	- 'Gotlandica'	CLyd SIgm
	- subsp. ***grandis***	NMen WCot
	- - 'Budapest Seedling'	GCrs
	- - 'Papageno'	CAby CBot CSpe EBee ECGP EChP EDAr EMar GKev GMaP LRHS MAvo NChi NLar NWCA SIgm SMrm SPoG STes WHil
	- Heiler hybrids	EBee ECGP EMar EVFa MWgw NChi NEgg NGdn
	- Red Clock	see *P. vulgaris* 'Röde Klokke'
§	- 'Röde Klokke'	CAby CBrm COIW EBee EChP ENot EWTr GEdr GKev IBal LRHS MAnH MNFA NBPC NChi NJOw NLar NPri NWCA SWvt WCot WHil WSel WWeb
	- ***rosea***	EHyt GAbr
	- Rote Glocke	see *P. vulgaris* 'Röde Klokke'
	- var. ***rubra***	More than 30 suppliers
	- violet blue-flowered	ITim
§	- 'Weisse Schwan'	GEdr GMaP NMen
	- White Swan	see *P. vulgaris* 'Weisse Schwan'

pummelo see *Citrus maxima*

Punica (*Lythraceae*)

	granatum	CHEx ERea ERom ESlt SBLw SDnm SLim STre WSHC XPep
	- 'Chico'	XPep
	- 'Fina Tendral'	ERea
	- 'Fruits Violets'	XPep
	- 'Legrelleae' (d)	XPep
	- 'Maxima Rubra'	XPep
	- 'Mollar de Elche'	XPep
	- var. ***nana*** ♀H3	CArn CHal CPle EPfP ERea EShb ESlt SBrw SMrm SPoG SRms WPat
	- 'Nana Racemosa'	CBcs
	- f. ***plena*** (d)	CBcs MRav WCFE
	- - 'Flore Pleno Luteo' (d)	XPep
	- 'Provence'	XPep

Purshia (*Rosaceae*)

	aff. ***mexicana*** B&SWJ 9040	WCru

Puschkinia (*Hyacinthaceae*)

	scilloides	EBrs LRHS NBir
§	- var. ***libanotica***	CBro EPfP EPot GAbr LAma LPhx LRHS WPer WShi
	- - 'Alba'	EPot LAma LPhx LRHS

Putoria (*Rubiaceae*)

	calabrica	CLyd NWCA

Puya (*Bromeliaceae*)

	RCB/Arg L-3	WCot
	RCB/Arg L-5	WCot
	RCB/Arg S-2	WCot
	alpestris	CBrP CHEx CTrC EOas EShb SAPC SSpi WMul
	berteroana	SPlb WMul
	chilensis	CAbb CBcs CBrd CCtw CDoC CHEx CKob CPne EBee EOas SAPC SArc SChr SPlb WMul
	coerulea	CFir EAmu EOas LEdu MGol SIgm SMad SPlb WMul
§	- var. ***violacea***	EPyc
	ferruginea	EOas
	gilmartiniae	CHEx CTrC IDee WCot
	laxa	SChr
	laxa x ***mirabilis***	CFir
	mirabilis	CAbb CHEx CKob CTrC EBee EOas MFOX WMul WSPU
	venusta	WMul
	violacea	see *P. coerulea* var. *violacea*
	weberbaueri **new**	CHEx

Pycnanthemum (*Lamiaceae*)

	pilosum	CAgr CArn EBee ELau EMan EUnu GPoy MHer MSal NLar NPri SBch SIde WPer WPic WWye
	tenuifolium	EMan NLar

Pycnostachys (*Lamiaceae*)

	reticulata	EShb WOut
	urticifolia	ECre EOHP EWes

Pygmea see *Chionohebe*

Pyracantha ✿ (*Rosaceae*)

	Alexander Pendula = 'Renolex'	EHol MRav MSwo SRms WFar WHar
	angustifolia	WCFE
§	***atalantioides***	CMac SPlb WCFE
	'Brilliant'	EPfP
	'Buttercup'	EPla SPoG
§	***coccinea*** 'Lalandei'	LAst SMer SPer XPep
	- 'Red Column'	CBcs CCVT CChe CMac EBee ECtt EGra ELan EPfP EWTr GKir LAst LBuc LRHS MBNS MBar MGos MRav MSwo MWat NBlu NEgg NWea SCoo SPoG SWvt WDin WFar WHar WWeb
	- 'Red Cushion'	CAlb ENot LRHS MGos MRav SPoG SRms
	crenulata	WCFE
	Dart's Red = 'Interrada'	CSBt LRHS SPoG
	'Fiery Cascade' **new**	SPoG
	gibbsii	see *P. atalantioides*
	'Golden Charmer' ♀H4	EBee ECtt ENot EPfP GKir LRHS MAsh MGos MRav MSwo NBlu NEgg NLon NWea SHBN SPer SPoG SRms SWvt WDin WFar WHar
	'Golden Dome'	LRHS
	'Golden Glow'	LRHS
	'Golden Sun'	see *P.* 'Soleil d'Or'
	'Harlequin' (v)	ECtt EHoe EHol NPro SHBN
	'John Stedman'	see *P.* 'Stedman's'
	'Knap Hill Lemon'	CChe MBlu
	'Mohave'	CBrm CChe CMac EBee ECrN ELan GKir LRHS MBar MGos MWat NEgg NWea SHBN SPer SRms SWvt WDin
	'Mohave Silver' (v)	CCVT CWSG EBee ECrN EHoe LAst LRHS MBNS MGos MWat
	'Molten Lava'	MBri
	'Monrovia'	see *P. coccinea* 'Lalandei'
	'Mozart'	WWeb
	'Navaho'	EPfP SPoG WBcn WBrE
	'Orange Charmer'	CBrm CTri EBee ELan ENot EPfP GKir MGos MRav MWat NBlu NEgg NWea SHBN SMer SPer SPlb WFar WTel
	'Orange Glow' ♀H4	More than 30 suppliers
	'Orangeade'	MBri
*	'Red Pillar'	GKir
	'Renault d'Or'	SLPl
	rogersiana ♀H4	EBee ECrN ENot EPfP GKir MRav WFar WTel

- 'Flava' ♀H4 — CBrm CSBt CTri ECrN EHol EPfP LAst MAsh MBar MRav MWhi NLon NWea SMer SPoG WTel
'Rosedale' — EBee WSPU
Saphyr Jaune = 'Cadaune'PBR — CAlb CBcs CDoC CEnd CSBt CWSG EBee ENot EPfP GKir MBNS MGos MRav SBra SMer SPer SPoG WWeb
Saphyr Orange = 'Cadange'PBR ♀H4 — CAlb CBcs CDoC CEnd COtt CSBt CWSG EBee EMil ENot EPfP EPla GKir LRHS MBri MGos MRav NCGa NPri SBra SPer WRHF WWeb
Saphyr Panache = 'Cadvar' (v) **new** — SPoG
Saphyr Rouge = 'Cadrou'PBR ♀H4 — CAlb CBcs CCVT CDoC CEnd COtt CSBt CWSG EBee ENot EPfP GKir LRHS MBri MGos MRav NCGa SBra SPer SPoG WWeb
'Shawnee' — CMac CSBt ECot EPfP MSwo MWat WWeb
§ 'Soleil d'Or' — More than 30 suppliers
'Sparkler' (v) — CMac EHoe LAst LRHS MGos WFar WHar
§ 'Stedman's' — NLar
'Teton' ♀H4 — CMac CWSG EBee ECrN ELan EPfP EPla GKir LAst LRHS MAsh MBar MBri MRav MSwo NBlu SMac SPoG SRms WDin WFar WWeb
'Watereri' — ECrN SLPl SPer WTel
'Yellow Sun' — see *P.* 'Soleil d'Or'

Pyrenaria (*Theaceae*)

spectabilis — see *Tutcheria spectabilis*

Pyrethropsis see *Rhodanthemum*

Pyrethrum see *Tanacetum*

Pyrola (*Ericaceae*)

minor **new** — WBWf
rotundifolia — GKev SSpi WHer

Pyrostegia (*Bignoniaceae*)

venusta — CPLN ESlt

Pyrrhopappus (*Asteraceae*)

carolinianus — SSpi

Pyrrocoma (*Asteraceae*)

clementis — EBee

Pyrrosia (*Polypodiaceae*)

lingua **new** — WRic

Pyrus ✿ (*Rosaceae*)

amygdaliformis — CTho
- var. ***cuneifolia*** — CLnd CTho
betulifolia — WJas
calleryana 'Bradford' — CLnd
- 'Chanticleer' ♀H4 — More than 30 suppliers
- 'Chanticleer' variegated **new** — CLnd
x ***canescens*** — CTho
communis (F) — CCVT CDul CTri GIBF LBuc SBLw SKee SPer STre WMou
- 'Autumn Bergamot' (D) — SKee
- 'Barnet' (Perry) — CTho
- 'Baronne de Mello' (D) — CTho SFam
- 'Beech Hill' (F) — CDul CLnd EBee ECrN EMil EPfP SBLw SPer
- 'Belle Guérandaise' (D) — SKee
- 'Belle Julie' (D) — SKee
- 'Bergamotte Esperen' (D) — SKee
- 'Beth' (D) ♀H4 — CAgr CDoC CSBt CTri CWib ECrN EPfP GBon GTwe LBuc LRHS MBri MGos NBlu NPri SFam SKee SPer WHar WOrn
- 'Beurré Alexandre Lucas' (D) — SKee
- 'Beurré Bedford' (D) — SKee
- 'Beurré Clairgeau' (C/D) — SKee
- 'Beurré d'Amanlis' (D) — SKee
- 'Beurré de Beugny' (D) — SKee
- 'Beurré de Naghin' (C/D) — SKee
- 'Beurré Diel' (D) — SKee
- 'Beurré Dumont' (D) — SFam
- 'Beurré Hardy' (D) ♀H4 — CAgr CCAT CDoC CSBt CTho CTri CWib ECrN ERea GKir GTwe LRHS MRav MWat SFam SKee SPer WOrn
- 'Beurré Mortillet' (D) — SKee
- 'Beurré Six' (D) — SKee
- 'Beurré Superfin' (D) — ECrN GTwe MCoo SFam SKee
- 'Bianchettone' (D) — SKee
- 'Black Worcester' (C) — ECrN GTwe SFam SKee WJas WOrn WSPU
- 'Blakeney Red' (Perry) — CTho
- 'Blickling' (D) — SKee
- 'Brandy' (Perry) — CTho SKee
- 'Bristol Cross' (D) — GTwe SKee
- 'Catillac' (C) ♀H4 — CAgr CTho GTwe SFam SKee
- 'Chalk' — see *P. communis* 'Crawford'
- 'Chaumontel' (D) — SKee
- 'Clapp's Favourite' (D) — CTho ECrN GTwe SKee
- 'Colmar d'Eté' (D) — CTho
- 'Comte de Lamy' (D) — SKee
- 'Concorde'PBR (D) ♀H4 — CAgr CCVT CDoC CSBt CTho CTri CWib ECrN ENot EPfP ERea GTwe LBuc LRHS MBri MGos MLan NBlu NWea SFam SKee SPer SPoG WBVN WHar WJas WOrn
- 'Conference' (D) ♀H4 — More than 30 suppliers
- 'Crassane' — CTho
§ - 'Crawford' (D) — SKee
- 'Docteur Jules Guyot' (D) — ECrN SKee
- 'Double de Guerre' (C/D) — SKee
- 'Doyenné Blanc' (F) — SKee
- 'Doyenné Boussoch' (D) — SKee
- 'Doyenné d'Eté' (D) — ERea SFam SKee
- 'Doyenné du Comice' (D) ♀H4 — CAgr CCVT CDoC CMac CSBt CTho CTri CWSG CWib ECrN ENot EPfP ERea GBon LBuc LRHS MBri MRav MWat NBlu NWea SCrf SFam SKee SPer SPoG WHar WJas WOrn
- 'Doyenné Georges Boucher' (D) — SKee
- 'Duchesse d'Angoulême' (D) — SKee
- 'Durondeau' (D) — CTho GTwe SFam SKee
- 'Emile d'Heyst' (D) — CTho GTwe MCoo
- 'Fertility' (D) — CLnd SKee
- 'Fertility Improved' — see *P. communis* 'Improved Fertility'
- 'Fondante d'Automne' (D) — CTho
- 'Forelle' (D) — ERea SKee
- 'Gin' (Perry) — CTho
- 'Glou Morceau' (D) — CAgr CTho ECrN GTwe LRHS MCoo MWat SFam SKee
- 'Glow Red Williams' (D) — SFam
- 'Gorham' (D) — CAgr CTho ECrN GTwe MCoo SFam SKee

- 'Gratiole de Jersey' (D)	CTho
- 'Green Horse' (Perry)	CTho
- 'Green Pear of Yair' (D)	SKee
- 'Hacon's Imcomparable' (D)	SKee
§ - 'Hellen's Early' (Perry)	SKee
- 'Hessle' (D)	GTwe MCoo SFam SKee
- 'Highland' (D)	SKee
§ - 'Improved Fertility' (D)	CAgr CDoC GBon GTwe SKee SPoG
- 'Jargonelle' (D)	CAgr CTho ECrN GTwe SFam SKee
- 'Joséphine de Malines' (D) ♀H4	CTho GTwe LRHS SFam SKee
- 'Laxton's Foremost' (D)	SKee
- 'Laxton's Satisfaction' (D)	SFam
- 'Louise Bonne of Jersey' (D) ♀H4	CAgr CDoC CTho CTri ECrN GTwe LRHS MGos SFam SKee
- 'Max Red Bartlett'	MCoo
- 'Merton Pride' (D)	CTho ECrN GTwe MWat SFam SKee
- 'Moonglow' (D/C)	CAgr MCoo SKee
- 'Nouveau Poiteau' (C/D)	CAgr CTho ECrN GTwe LRHS SKee
- 'Onward' (D) ♀H4	CAgr CLnd CTri CWib ECrN GTwe MBri MGos NWea SFam SKee WHar WOrn
§ - 'Packham's Triumph' (D)	CAgr CDoC CTri CWib ECrN GTwe SKee
- 'Passe Colmar' (D)	CTho
- 'Passe Crassane' (D)	SKee
- 'Pitmaston Duchess' (C/D) ♀H4	ECrN GTwe SKee
- 'Red Comice' (D/C)	GTwe SKee
- 'Red Sensation Bartlett' (D/C)	GTwe MBri SKee
- 'Robin' (C/D)	ERea SKee
- 'Roosevelt' (D)	SKee
- 'Santa Claus' (D)	SFam SKee
- 'Seckel' (D)	SFam SKee
- 'Soleil d'Automne' (F)	SKee
- 'Swan's Egg' (D)	CTho
- 'Terrace Pearl'	ENot
- 'Thompson's' (D)	GTwe SFam
- 'Thorn' (Perry)	CTho SKee
- 'Triomphe de Vienne' (D)	SFam
- 'Triumph'	see *P. communis* 'Packham's Triumph'
- 'Uvedale's St Germain' (C)	CTho SKee
- 'Verbelu'	SKee
- 'Vicar of Winkfield' (C/D)	GTwe SKee
- 'Williams' Bon Chrétien' (D/C) ♀H4	CAgr CCVT CMac CSBt CTho CTri CWSG CWib ECrN ENot ERea GBon GKir LBuc LRHS MBri MGos MWat NBlu SCrf SFam SKee SPer SPoG WHar WJas WOrn
- 'Williams Red' (D/C)	GTwe SKee
- 'Winnal's Longdon' (Perry)	CTho
- 'Winter Nelis' (D)	CTho CTri CWib ECrN GTwe MBri SFam SKee
cordata	CDul CTho SKee
cossonii	CTho
elaeagnifolia	CTho CWSG LRHS
- var. ***kotschyana***	CDul CEnd CLnd GIBF GKir LRHS SLim WOrn
- 'Silver Sails'	CLnd LRHS MAsh MBlu MGos SCoo
korshinskyi	GIBF
nivalis	CDul CLnd CTho EBee ECrN ENot EPfP GIBF SBLw SCoo SHBN SPer
- 'Catalia'	LRHS MBri SCoo SPoG
pashia	NLar
pyraster	CDul
pyrifolia '20th Century'	see *P. pyrifolia* 'Nijisseiki'
- 'Chojuro' (F)	ERea
§ - 'Nijisseiki' (F)	ERea
- 'Shinseiki' (F)	CLnd ERea LRHS SKee
- 'Shinsui' (F)	SKee
salicifolia 'Pendula' ♀H4	More than 30 suppliers
ussuriensis	GIBF

Qiongzhuea see *Chimonobambusa*

Quercus ✿ (*Fagaceae*)

§ ***acuta***	CBcs
§ ***acutissima***	CLnd CMCN ECrN EPfP MBlu SBir WDin WNor
aegilops	see *Q. ithaburensis* subsp. *macrolepis*
affinis	CMCN
agrifolia	CDul CMCN SBir
alba	CDul CMCN CTho ECrN WDin
- f. ***elongata***	EPfP LRHS
aliena	CMCN SBir
- var. ***acutiserrata***	CMCN
alnifolia	CDul
arkansana	CMCN SBir
austrina	CMCN
x ***beadlei***	see *Q.* x *saulii*
bicolor	CDul CMCN ECrN IArd LRHS SBir WDin WNor
borealis	see *Q. rubra*
breweri	see *Q. garryana* var. *breweri*
buckleyi	SBir
x ***bushii***	CMCN EPfP MBlu
canariensis ♀H4	CLnd CMCN CTho EPfP IArd LRHS
castaneifolia	CMCN EPfP SBLw WDin
- 'Green Spire' ♀H4	CDoC CMCN CTho EPfP GKir IArd LRHS MBlu MBri SMad SPer
cerris	CBcs CCVT CDoC CDul CLnd CMCN EBee ECrN EMil ENot EPfP GKir IArd LAst LRHS MGos MLan NWea SBLw SBir SEND SPer WDin WMou
§ - 'Argenteovariegata' (v)	CDul CEnd CMCN CTho EBee ELan EPfP GKir IArd LRHS MAsh MBlu MBri MGos SBir SIFN SMad SPoG WPGP
* - 'Marmorata'	SBir
- 'Variegata'	see *Q. cerris* 'Argenteovariegata'
- 'Wodan'	CMCN EPfP GKir LRHS MBlu
chapmanii	CMCN
chrysolepis	CMCN
coccifera	CFil CMCN SSpi WDin WPGP WWes
- subsp. ***calliprinos***	CMCN
coccinea	CBcs CDul CLnd CMCN CWSG ECrN EPfP EWTr GIBF GKir LRHS MWht NBea NWea SBLw SBir SPer SSta STre WDin WNor WOrn
- 'Splendens' ♀H4	CDoC CDul CEnd CMCN CTho CTri EBee ELan EPfP GKir LRHS MBlu MBri NEgg SBLw SHBN SMad SPer SPoG WDin WPat
dentata	CBcs CMCN EPfP LRHS WDin
- 'Carl Ferris Miller'	CMCN EPfP IArd IDee LRHS MBlu SBir SMad WPat

	Name	Suppliers
	- 'Pinnatifida'	CMCN EPfP GKir IArd LRHS MBlu SMad
	- subsp. ***yunnanensis***	CMCN
	douglasii	CLnd CMCN
	dumosa	CMCN SBir WNor
	ellipsoidalis	CDul CMCN GKir LRHS SBir WNor
	- 'Hemelrijk'	CDoC EPfP GKir LRHS MBlu
	emoryi	SBir
	fabrei	SBir
	faginea	CBcs CMCN
	falcata	CMCN EPfP
	- var. ***pagodifolia***	see *Q. pagoda*
	x ***fernaldii***	CMCN
	frainetto	CCVT CDoC CDul CLnd CMCN CTho ECrN ENot EPfP EWTr GKir ISea LRHS MAsh MBri SBLw SEND SPer WDin WMou WNor
	- 'Hungarian Crown' ♀H4	CMCN EPfP GKir LRHS MBlu SMad
	- 'Trotworth' **new**	SMad
	- 'Trump'	CMCN MBlu
	fruticosa	see *Q. lusitanica*
	gambelii	CMCN
	garryana	CMCN
§	- var. ***breweri***	SBir
	- var. ***fruticosa***	see *Q. garryana* var. *breweri*
	georgiana	CMCN SBir
	glandulifera	see *Q. serrata*
§	***glauca***	CFai CMCN EPfP SAPC SArc SBir WNor
	gravesii	SBir
	grisea	CMCN SBir
	x ***hastingsii***	CMCN EPfP
	hemisphaerica	CMCN EPfP SBir
	x ***heterophylla***	CDul CMCN EPfP SBir
	x ***hickelii***	CMCN LRHS
	- 'Gieszelhorst'	MBlu
	hinckleyi	WDin
§	x ***hispanica***	CLnd WPic
	- 'Ambrozyana'	CDul CMCN EPfP LRHS SBir SMad WDin
	- 'Diversifolia'	CMCN EPfP GKir MBlu
	- 'Fulhamensis'	CMCN MBlu SEND
§	- 'Lucombeana' ♀H4	CBcs CDul CMCN CSBt CTho EPfP IArd MBlu SBir SPer
§	- 'Pseudoturneri'	CBcs CDul EPfP GKir MBlu SIFN
	- 'Suberosa'	CTho
	- 'Wageningen'	CMCN EPfP IArd SBir
	ilex ♀H4	More than 30 suppliers
	- 'Fordii'	CTho
	ilicifolia	CDul CMCN LRHS SBir WNor
	imbricaria	CDul CMCN ECrN LRHS MBlu SBir WDin
	incana Roxb.	see *Q. leucotrichophora*
§	***incana*** Bartram	CMCN
	infectoria	CDul
	ithaburensis	CMCN EPfP
§	- subsp. ***macrolepis***	CMCN LEdu SBir
	kelloggii	CMCN LRHS
	x ***kewensis***	CMCN
	laevigata	see *Q. acuta*
	laevis	CMCN EPfP SBir
§	***laurifolia***	CDul CMCN MBlu SBir
§	***leucotrichophora***	CMCN
	liaotungensis	see *Q. wutaishanica*
	x ***libanerris***	CDul IArd SBir
	- 'Rotterdam'	CMCN
	libani	CMCN EPfP WDin
	lobata	CMCN LEdu
	x ***lucombeana***	see *Q.* x *hispanica*
	- 'William Lucombe'	see *Q.* x *hispanica* 'Lucombeana'
	x ***ludoviciana***	CMCN EPfP GKir SBir
§	***lusitanica*** Lamarck	CMCN
	lyrata	CMCN
	'Macon'	LRHS
	macranthera	CLnd CMCN EPfP GKir
	macrocarpa	CLnd CMCN EPfP LRHS SBir WDin WNor
	macrocarpa x ***turbinella***	CMCN
	macrolepis	see *Q. ithaburensis* subsp. *macrolepis*
	margarettiae	CMCN
	marilandica	CDul CEnd CMCN EPfP IArd IDee LRHS SBir
	mexicana	CMCN SBir
	michauxii	CMCN LRHS
	mongolica subsp. ***crispula*** var. ***grosseserrata***	CMCN
§	***montana***	CMCN
	muehlenbergii	CDul CMCN EPfP LRHS MBlu SBir
	myrsinifolia	see *Q. glauca*
	myrtifolia	CMCN EPfP
	nigra	CMCN CMHG SBir WNor
	nuttallii	see *Q. texana*
	obtusa	see *Q. laurifolia*
§	***pagoda***	CMCN MBlu SBir
	palustris ♀H4	CCVT CDoC CDul CLnd CMCN CTho ECrN ENot EPfP EWTr GKir LRHS MAsh MBlu MBri MLan NEgg NWea SBLw SBir SPer WDin WNor WOrn
*	- 'Compacta'	EPfP
	- 'Green Dwarf'	CMCN
	- 'Pendula'	CEnd CMCN
	- 'Swamp Pygmy'	CMCN MBlu
	pedunculata	see *Q. robur*
	pedunculiflora	see *Q. robur* subsp. *pedunculiflora*
§	***petraea*** ♀H4	CDoC CDul CLnd CSBt ECrN EPfP GKir IMGH LBuc MBlu NBee NWea SBLw SPer WDin WMou
	- 'Acutiloba' **new**	GKir
§	- 'Insecata'	CDoC CDul CEnd CMCN LRHS
	- 'Laciniata'	see *Q. petraea* 'Insecata'
	- 'Mespilifolia'	CTho
§	- 'Purpurea'	CDul CLnd CMCN GKir LRHS MBlu
	- 'Rubicunda'	see *Q. petraea* 'Purpurea'
	- 'Westcolumn'	IArd
§	***phellos***	CLnd CMCN CTho ECrN EPfP LRHS MBlu SLPl SPoG WDin WNor
	- var. ***latifolia***	see *Q. incana* Bartram
	phillyreoides	CBcs CDul CMCN EPfP IDee SBir SLPl WDin WNor
	polymorpha	CMCN
	'Pondaim'	CMCN LRHS SBir
	pontica	CMCN EPfP LRHS MBlu NWea
	prinoides	CMCN
	prinus Engelm.	see *Q. montana*
*	***prinus*** L.	CLnd CMCN SBir
	pubescens	CFil CMCN GKir SBir
	pumila Michx.	see *Q. montana*
	pumila Walt.	see *Q. phellos*
	pyrenaica	CMCN CTho
	- 'Pendula'	CMCN GKir WDin
	rhysophylla	EPfP GKir MBlu
§	***robur*** ♀H4	More than 30 suppliers
	- 'Argenteomarginata' (v)	CDul CMCN MBlu SMad SSta
	- 'Atropurpurea'	CDul GTSp MGos WDin
*	- 'Compacta'	GKir MBlu
	- 'Concordia'	CBcs CDoC CEnd CFil CLnd CMCN EBee EPfP GKir LRHS MBlu MBri NLar SIFN WDin
	- 'Contorta'	CMCN LRHS

- 'Cristata' CDul CMCN MBlu
- 'Cucullata' CMCN
* - ***dissecta*** CMCN
- 'Facrist' CDul CEnd
- f. ***fastigiata*** CAlb CDoC CDul CLnd CTho EBee ECrN ENot EPfP GKir IMGH LBuc LRHS MBar MGos NBee NWea SBLw SCoo SLPl SLim SPer WDin WFar WOrn
- 'Fennesseyi' CMCN LRHS
- 'Filicifolia' misapplied see *Q. robur* 'Pectinata'
- 'Filicifolia' see *Q.* x *rosacea* 'Filicifolia'
- 'Hentzei' CMCN
- 'Hungaria' LRHS
- 'Irtha' EPfP
§ - 'Pectinata' CTho EPfP MBlu WDin
§ - subsp. ***pedunculiflora*** CDul CMCN
- 'Pendula' CDul CEnd CMCN CTho MBlu MGos
- 'Purpurascens' CEnd CMCN GKir MBlu
- 'Raba' CMCN
§ - 'Salfast' MBlu
- 'Salicifolia' **new** MBlu
- 'Salicifolia Fastigiata' see *Q. robur* 'Salfast'
- 'Strypemonde' CMCN
- 'Totem' MBlu SMad
- f. ***variegata*** (v) LRHS MGos
- - 'Fürst Schwarzenburg' (v) CMCN
robur x ***turbinella*** CMCN
robusta f. ***fastigiata*** 'Koster' ♀^{H4} CDoC CDul CMCN EPfP GKir MBlu NBee SIFN SSta
§ x ***rosacea*** 'Filicifolia' CEnd CLnd GTSp NBea NEgg NLar WPat WWes
§ ***rubra*** ♀^{H4} More than 30 suppliers
- 'Aurea' CEnd CFil CMCN CPMA EPfP GKir LRHS MBlu SPer SSpi
- 'Boltes Gold' MBlu
- 'Magic Fire' MBlu SMad
* - 'Sunshine' CMCN LRHS MBlu SMad
rugosa CMCN SBir
sadleriana CMCN
§ x ***saulii*** CMCN SBir
x ***schochiana*** EPfP
x ***schuettei*** SBir
§ ***serrata*** CDoC CMCN
sessiliflora see *Q. petraea*
shumardii CMCN EPfP LRHS MBlu SBir WDin WNor
stellata CMCN SBir
suber CBcs CDoC CDul CFil CLnd CMCN CTho ECrN EPfP IArd IDee ISea LEdu LRHS SAPC SArc SEND SSpi WDin WPGP
- 'Cambridge' EPfP
§ ***texana*** CMCN EPfP SBir
trojana CMCN
turbinella CMCN
x ***turneri*** CDoC CLnd CMCN CTho EPfP WDin WMou
- 'Pseudoturneri' see *Q.* x *hispanica* 'Pseudoturneri'
vacciniifolia CMCN
variabilis CMCN EPfP SBir
velutina CDul CLnd CMCN CPMA CTho EPfP LRHS SBir
- 'Albertsii' MBlu
- 'Rubrifolia' CMCN EPfP
'Vilmoriana' CMCN
virginiana CMCN
'Warburgii' EPfP
x ***warei*** SBir
wislizeni CBcs CMCN SBir
§ ***wutaishanica*** CMCN SBir

Quillaja (*Rosaceae*)

saponaria CPle

quince see *Cydonia oblonga*

Quisqualis (*Combretaceae*)

indica CPLN
- double-flowered (d) **new** CPLN

R

Rabdosia (*Lamiaceae*)

calycina **new** SPlb

Racosperma see *Acacia*

Ramonda (*Gesneriaceae*)

§ ***myconi*** ♀^{H4} CLAP CPBP CStu EHyt GKev ITim LTwo NLar NMen NSla NWCA NWoo SBla SRms
- var. ***alba*** CLAP MTho WKif
- 'Jim's Shadow' WAbe
- 'Rosea' CLAP SBla
nathaliae ♀^{H4} CLAP CPBP WAbe
- JCA 686 SOkd
- 'Alba' CLAP NSla SBla SOkd WAbe
pyrenaica see *R. myconi*
serbica SBla

Ranunculus ✿ (*Ranunculaceae*)

abnormis GCrs NRya
aconitifolius EBee EChP ECha NEgg NGby NLar SHar WMnd
- 'Flore Pleno' (d) ♀^{H4} More than 30 suppliers
acris EWTr NBir NLan NPer
* - ***citrinus*** CBgR CElw EBrs EChP ECtt EMag EWoo GFlt LRHS MFOX MHar MSte NCGa NRya WBVN WCAu WMoo WRha
- 'Farrer's Yellow' CRow
- 'Flore Pleno' (d) ♀^{H4} CDes CElw CFee CFir CRez CRow EBee EChP ECha EHrv ELan EPPr GBuc GKir LPio MInt MSte NBid NBro NDov NPri NRya SRms STes WCAu WHal WHil WMoo
- 'Hedgehog' EPPr EVFa NDov
- 'Stevenii' CFee CRow EPPr IGor SDix
- 'Sulphureus' CBre ECha WEas WFar WHal
alpestris GEdr NMen NRya
amplexicaulis EBee ERos GCrs GTou MRav NLar NMen NSla SBla WAbe
aquatilis EHon EMFW NArg WPop
x ***arendsii*** 'Moonlight' SBla SRot
asiaticus EPot
- var. ***albus*** SBla
- var. ***flavus*** SBla
- Tecolote hybrids LAma
buchananii GKev
buchananii x ***lyallii*** **new** GKev
bulbosus NMir WBWf
§ - 'F. M. Burton' CBos ECtt EHrv ETow GCal NRya WCot WTMC
- ***farreri*** see *R. bulbosus* 'F. M. Burton'
- 'Speciosus Plenus' see *R. constantinopolitanus* 'Plenus'
calandrinioides ♀$^{H2-3}$ EWes GIBF NBir SBla SIng SVal WAbe WCot
- SF 137 WCot

	Name	Suppliers
§	***constantinopolitanus*** 'Plenus' (d)	CElw CRow EBee ECha GCal GKir GMac MBri MInt MLLN MRav NBid NBro NRya WCot WEas WFar WMoo
	cortusifolius	CFir CMHG EBee SBla SHar WCot WCru
	crenatus	EBee GCrs GEdr GIBF GTou NMen NRya NSla SOkd WAbe WHal
	ficaria	CArn CNat CRow ELau GBar MBow MChe MHer MSal NMir WFar WHer WShi WWye
	- 'Aglow in the Dark'	CHid CNat
	- var. ***albus***	CHid CRow EMon ERos LRHS NRya SIng WOut
	- anemone-centred	see *R. ficaria* 'Collarette'
	- 'Art Nouveau'	CNat
	- 'Ashen Primrose'	CRow EBee
§	- var. ***aurantiacus***	CNic CRow ECha EMon ERos EWsh LPhx LRHS MRav NJOw NRya SIng SRms WAbe WFar
	- 'Bantam Egg'	CRow
	- 'Blackadder'	CRow
	- 'Bowles' Double'	see *R. ficaria* 'Double Bronze', 'Picton's Double'
	- 'Brambling'	CBre CHea CLAP CNic CRow ECGP EMon LRHS MRav SIgm SSvw
	- 'Brazen Child'	CRow EBee
	- 'Brazen Daughter'	CRow
	- 'Brazen Hussy'	More than 30 suppliers
	- 'Bregover White'	CRow
	- 'Broadleas Black'	CNat
	- 'Budgerigar'	CRow
	- subsp. ***bulbilifer*** 'Chedglow'	CRow MDKP
	- 'Bunch' (d)	CRow
	- 'Camouflage' (v)	CNat
	- 'Cartwheel' (d)	CRow
	- 'Champernowne Giant'	CRow
	- 'Chocolate Cream'	CRow
§	- subsp. ***chrysocephalus***	CRow ECha EMon NRya SIng WCot WFar
	- 'Clouded Yellow' (v)	CRow
	- 'Coffee Cream'	CRow EBee
	- 'Coker Cream'	CRow
§	- 'Collarette' (d)	CHid CRow CStu EBee EHyt EMon EPot ERos GBar GBuc GGar LRHS MAvo MRav MTho NBir NJOw NMen NRya SBla SIng SMac WAbe WFar
	- 'Coppernob'	CBre CElw CHid CRow EBee ECGP ECha GAbr LPio MAvo SBla WCot WFar WPnP WWpP
	- 'Corinne Tremaine'	WHer
	- 'Coy Hussy' (v)	CNat
	- 'Crawshay Cream'	CDes CElw CRow EBee LPhx
	- 'Cupreus'	see *R. ficaria* var. *aurantiacus*
	- 'Damerham' (d)	CHid CRow EMon LRHS
	- 'Deborah Jope'	CRow
	- 'Diane Rowe'	EMon
	- 'Dimpsey'	CRow
§	- 'Double Bronze' (d)	CHid CRow CStu ECGP EMon ERos LRHS MDKP MTho NBir NLar NRya SIng
	- double cream (d)	see *R. ficaria* 'Double Mud'
	- double green eye (d)	CHid CRow
§	- 'Double Mud' (d)	CHid CLAP CRow CStu ECGP EMon ERos EWsh GAbr GBuc LRHS MTho NJOw NRya SBla SIng WAbe WFar WHal WWpP
	- double yellow (d)	see *R. ficaria flore-pleno*
	- 'Dusky Maiden'	CRow EMon LRHS NLar SBch SIng WFar
	- 'E.A. Bowles'	see *R. ficaria* 'Collarette'
	- 'Elan' (d)	CDes CRow EBee
	- subsp. ***ficariiformis***	EMon
§	- ***flore-pleno*** (d)	CFee CHid CRow CStu ECha ELan EMar EMon EPPr EPfP ERos GGar LRHS NJOw NRya NSti SIng SRms WAbe WCot WFar
	- 'Fried Egg'	CRow
	- 'Green Petal'	CHid CRow CStu EMon LPhx MDKP MRav MTho NBir NJOw NLar NRya SIng SSvw WHal WHer WWpP
	- 'Greencourt Gold' (d)	CRow
	- 'Holly'	see *R. ficaria* 'Holly Green'
	- 'Holly Bronze'	CRow
§	- 'Holly Green'	CRow
	- 'Hoskin's Miniature'	CRow
	- 'Hoskin's Variegated' (v)	CRow
	- 'Hyde Hall'	EMon LRHS NLar SIng WFar
	- 'Inky'	CNat
	- 'Jake Perry'	CDes EBee
	- 'Jane's Dress'	CHid CNat CRow
	- 'Ken Aslet Double' (d)	CDes CRow EBee EMon LRHS WHal WOut
	- 'Lambrook Black'	WHer
	- 'Laysh On' (d)	CRow
	- 'Lemon Queen'	CHid
	- 'Leo'	EMon
	- 'Limelight'	CRow
	- 'Little Southey'	CRow EBee
	- subsp. ***major***	see *R. ficaria* subsp. *chrysocephalus*
	- 'Mimsey' (d)	CRow
	- 'Mobled Jade'	CHid CNat CRow EBee
	- 'Newton Abbot'	CBre CRow
	- 'Oakenden Cream'	CRow
	- 'Old Master'	EBee MAvo WCot
	- 'Orange Sorbet'	CRow EMon NLar
§	- 'Picton's Double' (d)	CRow CStu ECGP EHyt GBar MTho NJOw NRya WAbe
	- 'Primrose'	CHid CRow EMon GGar LRHS MRav MTho NLar NRya WCot
	- 'Primrose Elf'	CRow
	- 'Quantock Brown'	CBgR
	- 'Quillet' (d)	CRow EMon
	- 'Ragamuffin' (d)	CDes CRow EBee EMon
	- 'Randall's White'	CRow CSWP CStu LPhx MRav MTho SHar SIgm WCot WFar WSHC WWpP
	- 'Rowden Magna'	CRow
	- 'Salad Bowl' (d)	CRow
	- 'Salmon's White'	CBre CFee CRow ELan EMar EPPr EPot LPhx MRav NBir NCGa NJOw NRya SIng SSvw WAbe WFar WHal WHer WHrl WLin
	- 'Samidor'	CRow
	- 'Sheldon'	CRow
	- 'Sheldon Silver'	CHid CNat CRow
	- 'Silver Collar'	EMon
	- single cream	EMon
	- 'South Downs'	CNat
	- 'Suffusion'	CNat CRow
	- 'Sutherland's Double' (d)	CRow
	- 'Sweet Chocolate'	CRow
	- 'Torquay Elf'	CRow
	- 'Tortoiseshell'	CHid CRow EBee MAvo MRav WFar
	- 'Trenwheal' (d)	CRow
	- 'Winkworth'	EMon
	- 'Wisley White'	NSti
	- 'Yaffle'	CBre CHid CRow EBee EChP EMon LRHS MDKP MRav SIng
	flammula	CRow EHon EMFW LNCo LPBA WPop WWpP

- subsp. ***minimus***	CRow WWpP
gouanii	ETow NRya
gramineus ♀H4	CMea CSam EBee EHyt EPot ERos GBuc GCrs LBee LPhx LRHS MNrw MRav MTho NMen NRya SIgm SMad SRms WCAu WFar WLin WPer
- 'Pardal'	SBla WFar
* ***guttatus*** new	NMen
illyricus	ECha NRya WHal
lanuginosus	EPPr EVFa SUsu
lapponicus	GIBF
lingua	CFir COld EMFW EMag MCCP SPlb
- 'Grandiflorus'	CBen CRow EHon LNCo LPBA NPer WHal WPop WWpP WWye
lyallii	CBos GGar GKev SBla WAbe
macauleyi	GCrs
millefoliatus	EHyt ERos GBuc MTho NMen NRya WPGP
montanus double (d)	EBee EBrs SBla WCot
- 'Molten Gold' ♀H4	CStu ECtt GAbr GCrs MRav MTho NRya SBla SRot WAbe
parnassiifolius	ETow GAbr GCrs GTou NMen NSla SBla WAbe
platanifolius	EBrs LPhx SMHy
pyrenaeus	NMen
repens 'Boraston O.S.' (v)	WCHb
* - 'Buttered Popcorn'	CRow EBee EPPr NLar WMoo
- 'Cat's Eyes' (v)	EBee EMan WCot
- 'Gloria Spale'	CBre CRow
- 'Joe's Golden'	EHoe
- var. ***pleniflorus*** (d)	CBgR CBre CRow EBee EChP ECha GAbr GGar GKir NSti WEas WFar
- 'Snowdrift' (v)	WCot
- 'Timothy Clark' (d)	CBre EMon MInt WSHC
sceleratus	WHer
seguieri new	GKev
serbicus	EBee EPPr GCal
sericophyllus new	GKev
speciosus 'Flore Pleno'	see *R. constantinopolitanus* 'Plenus'

Ranzania (*Berberidaceae*)

japonica	WCru

Raoulia (*Asteraceae*)

australis misapplied	see *R. hookeri*
australis Hook.	EDAr EPot GEdr GGar ITim MBar MWat NRya NWCA SIng WHoo
§ - Lutescens Group	ECha EPot ESis ITim
glabra	GAbr
haastii	ECou WBrE
§ ***hookeri***	ECha ECou EDAr EPot GAbr GEdr GKir ITim NWCA SIng SPlb SRms WAbe WBrE WFar WLin WPat
- var. ***laxa***	EPot EWes
x ***loganii***	see x *Leucoraoulia loganii*
lutescens	see *R. australis* Lutescens Group
x ***petrimia*** 'Margaret Pringle'	EPot ITim WAbe
subsericea	CLyd ECou EWes GCrs NMen NWCA WBrE
tenuicaulis	ECha ECou SPlb

Raoulia x *Leucogenes* see x *Leucoraoulia*

raspberry see *Rubus idaeus*

Ratibida (*Asteraceae*)

columnifera	CRWN EBee EHan EMan EPfP LRHS MGol SPav SPet
- f. ***pulcherrima***	CFai CMea CSpe EGoo EMan MBNS MNFA NJOw SMad SPav SPet WHal
- red	LRav SPav
- 'Red Midget'	MDKP SPav
pinnata	CFwr CRWN CSam EBee EBrs LRHS MWgw SPav SPet SUsu WCAu WLin
tagetes	SPav

Rauvolfia (*Apocynaceae*)

serpentina	MGol

Ravenala (*Strelitziaceae*)

madagascariensis	EAmu WMul XBlo

Ravenea (*Arecaceae*)

rivularis	EAmu WMul

Rechsteineria see *Sinningia*

redcurrant see *Ribes rubrum* (R)

Rehderodendron (*Styracaceae*)

indochinense	CFil
macrocarpum	CBcs

Rehmannia (*Scrophulariaceae*)

angulata misapplied	see *R. elata*
§ ***elata*** ♀H2	More than 30 suppliers
- 'White Dragon'	CSpe
glutinosa ♀H3	WWye

Reichardia (*Asteraceae*)

picroides	CAgr

Reineckea (*Convallariaceae*)

§ ***carnea***	CDes CFee CHid CPLG CPom CStu EBee EChP ECha EGra ELan EMar EPla ERos EWTr GCal GEdr LRHS MRav NJOw NSti SDys SHel SPlb SUsu WCot WCru WPGP WTin
- B&SWJ 4808	WCru
- SDR 330	GKev
- 'Alba'	SSpi
- 'Variegata' (v)	WCot WCru

Reinwardtia (*Linaceae*)

elata	SMrm
§ ***indica***	CHII CPLG EShb SUsu
trigyna	see *R. indica*

Remusatia (*Araceae*)

hookeriana	CKob EAmu EUJe MOak
pumila	CKob EAmu EUJe MOak
vivipara	CKob EUJe MJnS MOak WMul

Reseda (*Resedaceae*)

alba	MHer
lutea	MBow MSal SIde
luteola	CHby GBar GPoy MChe MHer MSal WCHb WHer WWye

Restio (*Restionaceae*)

bifarius	CTrC
brunneus new	EBee
festuciformis	EAmu
quadratus	WMul WNor
subverticillatus	see *Ischyrolepis subverticillata*
tetraphyllus	CAbb CBct CBig CBod CBrm CFir CPen CTrC EBee EMan EPPr EUJe GGar LAst MBNS NVic SSpi WCot WDyG WPrP

Retama (Papilionaceae)

§ ***monosperma***	CBcs EShb XPep
raetam	XPep
§ ***sphaerocarpa***	SSpi

Reynoutria see *Fallopia*

Rhagodia (Chenopodiaceae)

triandra	ECou

Rhamnus (Rhamnaceae)

alaternus	XPep
- var. ***angustifolia***	CFil WFar WPGP
§ - 'Argenteovariegata' (v) ♀H4	More than 30 suppliers
- 'Variegata'	see *R. alaternus* 'Argenteovariegata'
californica	SSpi
var. ***occidentalis*** **new**	
caroliniana **new**	NLar
cathartica	CAgr CCVT CDul CLnd CTri ECrN GIBF LBuc NWea WDin WMou WTel
dahurica	GIBF
frangula	CArn CBgR CCVT CDul CLnd CRWN ECrN LBuc MBlu MBow NWea STre WDin WFar WMou
- 'Aspleniifolia'	CFai CTho EBee ENot EPfP LBuc MBlu MBri MRav NLar SMur WBcn WDin WFar WPat
- 'Columnaris'	EMil SLPl
imeretina **new**	WPat
prinoides	CFil
pumila	NLar
purshiana	MSal

Rhaphiolepis (Rosaceae)

x ***delacourii***	CMHG CWSG CWib EPfP GQui LRHS SBrw SMur WBcn WHCG
- 'Coates' Crimson'	CDoC EMil EPfP GQui IArd SBra SBrw SHBN SLon WDin WPat WSHC
- Enchantress = 'Moness'	CBrm CMHG EBee ELan SMur SPoG
- 'Spring Song'	EBee SLon
indica	ERom
- B&SWJ 8405	WCru
- 'Coppertone' **new**	SBra
- Springtime = 'Monme'	SPer WDin XPep
umbellata ♀H2-3	CBcs CBot CHEx CPLG CTri CWib EBee EPfP GQui IDee LAst LRHS MRav SBra SBrw SEND SLon WFar WHCG WSHC
- f. ***ovata***	CRez
- - B&SWJ 4706	WCru

Rhaphithamnus (Verbenaceae)

cyanocarpus	see *R. spinosus*
§ ***spinosus***	CPle ERea

Rhapidophyllum (Arecaceae)

hystrix	CBrP CRoM NPal

Rhapis (Arecaceae)

§ ***excelsa*** ♀H1	CBrP CRoM CTrC EAmu EExo NPal WMul

Rhazya (Apocynaceae)

orientalis	see *Amsonia orientalis*

Rheum ✿ (Polygonaceae)

GWJ 9329 from Sikkim **new**	WCru
§ 'Ace of Hearts'	More than 30 suppliers
'Ace of Spades'	see *R.* 'Ace of Hearts'
acuminatum	CFil CRow EBee GBin GIBF SBla WPGP
- HWJCM 252	WCru
alexandrae	CAgr CFir GCal GIBF GKir IBlr WCot
- BWJ 7670	WCru
- SDR 2924	GKev
'Andrew's Red'	GTwe
§ ***australe***	CAgr CArn CFir CRow GCal GIBF LEdu LPBA LRHS MLLN NBro NLar SMad WCot WFar WHoo WMnd
delavayi	EBee GIBF
- BWJ 7592	WCru
- SDR 1668	GKev
emodi	see *R. australe*
forrestii	CAgr GIBF
x ***hybridum*** 'Appleton's Forcing'	GTwe
- 'Baker's All Season'	GTwe
- 'Brandy Carr Scarlet' **new**	NGHP
- 'Canada Red'	GTwe
- 'Cawood Delight'	GTwe NGHP SEND
- 'Champagne'	GTwe
- 'Daw's Champion'	GTwe
- 'Early Cherry'	GTwe
- 'Fenton's Special'	GTwe MCoo NGHP
- 'Glaskin's Perpetual'	LBuc MAsh
- 'Goliath'	GTwe
- 'Grandad's Favorite' ♀H4	EBrs LRHS
- 'Greengage'	GTwe
- 'Hammond's Early'	GTwe SEND
- 'Harbinger'	GTwe
- 'Hawke's Champagne' ♀H4	GTwe
- 'Holsteiner Blut'	EBee
- 'Livingstone'PBR (F) **new**	ENot LRHS NPri
- 'Mac Red' ♀H4	GTwe
- 'Prince Albert'	GTwe
- 'Red Champagne' **new**	NGHP
- 'Red Prolific'	GTwe
- 'Reed's Early Superb' ♀H4	GTwe
- 'Stein's Champagne' ♀H4	GTwe
- 'Stockbridge Arrow'	CSut GTwe NGHP
- 'Stockbridge Bingo'	GTwe SPoG
- 'Stockbridge Emerald'	GTwe
- 'Stockbridge Guardsman'	GTwe
- 'Strawberry'	GTwe
- 'Strawberry Surprise' **new**	GTwe
- 'Sutton's Cherry Red'	GTwe
- 'The Sutton'	GTwe
- 'Timperley Early' ♀H4	CAgr CDoC CMac CTri ENot EPfP GTwe LRHS MAsh NBlu NGHP NPri SCoo SKee SPer
- 'Tingley Cherry'	GTwe
- 'Victoria'	GKir GTwe LBuc LRHS MAsh MCoo MHer NGHP WTel
- 'Zwolle Seedling'	GTwe
kialense	CBct CDes GCal NBid NMRc NSti
moorcroftianum	GCal
nobile HWJK 2290	WCru
- SDR 2783	GKev
officinale	CAgr CBct CHEx GCal GKir LRHS MBri SIde
palmatum	CArn CBcs CDWL COIW ECha ELan EMFW ENot EPfP EPza EUnu

EWTr GIBF GKir GMaP LAst LPBA LRHS MRav MSal MWat NEgg NGdn SPer SSpi WCAu WFar WMul WWeb
- 'Atropurpureum' — see *R. palmatum* 'Atrosanguineum'
§ - 'Atrosanguineum' ♀H4 — CBct CBot CMea CRow EChP ECha ELan EPla GBuc GKev GKir LPBA LRHS LRav MBri MRav MWgw NBid NBro NFor NLon SMad SPer SPlb WCot WCru
- 'Bowles' Crimson' — CBct CHad GKir LRHS MBri
- 'Hadspen Crimson' — CBct CDes CHad WCot
- 'Red Herald' — CBct SBla WCot
- ***rubrum*** — COtt GKir LRHS MCCP NArg NBir WFar
- 'Saville' — GKir LRHS MBri MRav
- var. ***tanguticum*** — More than 30 suppliers
I - - 'Rosa Auslese' — LPhx WHil
rhaponticum — NLar
ribes — GBin WCot
subacaule — GKev NLar
tataricum — LEdu

Rhigozum (*Bignoniaceae*)

obovatum — CSec

Rhodanthe (*Asteraceae*)

§ ***anthemoides*** — ECou
- 'Paper Cascade'PBR — LRHS

Rhodanthemum (*Asteraceae*)

from High Atlas, Morocco — SIng
'African Eyes' — EBee EMan EPfP GGar SRot
§ ***atlanticum*** — ECho EWes
§ ***catananche*** — EBee ECho EPot ETow EWes MBNS SRot XPep
- 'Tizi-n-Test' — LRHS SBla WKif
- 'Tizi-n-Tichka' — CPBP EWes LRHS NBir SBla SUsu WLin
§ ***gayanum*** — ECtt EShb EWes LRHS WCot XPep
- 'Flamingo' — see *R. gayanum*
§ ***hosmariense*** ♀H4 — CHrt CMHG CMea EBee ECha EDAr ELan EPfP GGar LRHS NPri SBla SCoo SPer SPoG SRms SRot WAbe WCot WEas XPep

Rhodiola (*Crassulaceae*)

atuntsuensis — EHyt
bupleuroides CLD 1196 — EMon
coccinea — GCal
crassipes — see *R. wallichiana*
cretinii HWJK 2283 **new** — WCru
§ ***fastigiata*** — EMon NMen
§ ***heterodonta*** — ECha ELan EMon LPio MRav WCot
himalensis (D. Don) Fu — EMon
- HWJK 2258 — WCru
§ ***ishidae*** — CTri
§ ***kirilovii*** — EMon GBin GTou
- var. ***rubra*** — EBrs WFar
linearifolia — EMon
pachyclados — CLyd CNic CSLe EBur EDAr EGoo EHoe EPot ESis GKir GTou LBee LRHS MBar MDHE MHer MOne NBir NRya SChu SIng SPlb SPoG SRot WAbe WEas WFar WHoo WPer
aff. ***purpureoviridis*** BWJ 7544 — WCru
§ ***rosea*** — CPrp EBee EBrs ECha EHoe ELan EMan EPfP EPla GCal MHer MNFA NBid NBir NFor NGdn NSti SRms STre WAbb WCAu WCFE WCot WDyG WEas WFar WTin WWhi
semenovii — MHar NLar
sinuata HWJK 2318 **new** — WCru
- HWJK 2326 — WCru
§ ***trollii*** — CNic CStu GCrs
§ ***wallichiana*** — GCrs NBid WCot WDyG
- GWJ 9263 — WCru
- HWJK 2352 — WCru

Rhodochiton (*Scrophulariaceae*)

§ ***atrosanguineus*** ♀H1-2 — CArn CBcs CEnd CHEx CRHN CSec CSpe ELan EPfP ERea GFlt GGar IDee LRHS MAsh NEgg SGar SHFr SPoG WBVN WBor WGwG
volubilis — see *R. atrosanguineus*

Rhodocoma (*Restionaceae*)

arida — CBct CCtw WMul
capensis — CAbb CBct CBig CCtw CFir CPen CSpe CTrC IDee WMul
foliosa — WMul
fruticosa — CTrC
gigantea — CAbb CBig CCtw CFwr CTrC ITer WMul WNor
* ***ovida*** **new** — CBig

Rhododendron ✿ (*Ericaceae*)

FH134 **new** — SLdr
'A.J. Ivens' — see *R.* 'Arthur J. Ivens'
'Abegail' — MGos SLdr
aberconwayi — CWri LMil NLar NPen SLdr SReu
- 'His Lordship' — GGGa LHyd
acrophilum (V) Argent 2768 — GGGa
'Actress' — WCwm
'Ada Brunieres' (K) — CSdC
'Addy Wery' (EA) ♀H3-4 — CDoC LKna MBar MGos NPen SCam SLdr SPoG
adenogynum — GGGa LMil NPen SLdr
- CLD 795 — LMil
- Cox 6502 — GGGa
§ - Adenophorum Group F 20444 — SLdr
- - R 11471 — NPen
- - 'Kirsty' — NPen
- white — NPen
adenophorum — see *R. adenogynum* Adenophorum Group
adenopodum — GGGa LMil NPen SLdr
adenosum — NPen
- R 18228 — GGGa
'Admiral Piet Hein' — SReu
'Adonis' (EA/d) — CMac MBar NEgg NLar SCam SLdr
'Adriaan Koster' (M) — SLdr
adroserum — see *R. lukiangense*
'Advance' (O) — LRHS SLdr
aeruginosum — see *R. campanulatum* subsp. *aeruginosum*
aganniphum — GGGa ISea LMil NPen
- CN&W 1174 — LMil
- EGM 284 — LMil
§ - var. ***aganniphum*** Doshongense Group — GGGa
- - - KR 4979 — LMil
- - Glaucopeplum Group — GGGa
- - Schizopeplum Group — GGGa
- var. ***flavorufum*** — GGGa MDun NPen
- - EGM 160 — LMil
- pink, KR 3528 from Pe, Doshang La — LMil
- 'Rusty' — NPen
x ***agastum*** PW 98 — LMil
'Aida' (R/d) — CSBt SReu

	Name	Suppliers
	'Aksel Olsen'	CTri ECho GEdr GKir MAsh MBar MDun
	'Aladdin' (EA)	CDoC ECho SLdr WFar
	Aladdin Group	SReu
	'Aladdin' (*auriculatum* hybrid)	GGGa
	Albatross Group	IDee LKna LMil SLdr SReu
	'Albatross Townhill Pink'	LMil
	'Albert Schweitzer' ♀H4	CWri EMil GGGa LMil MBar MDun NBlu SLdr SPoG WFar
	albiflorum (A)	GGGa
	albrechtii (A)	GGGa LHyd LMil SReu SSpi
	- Whitney form (A)	LMil
	'Alena'	GGGa LMil
	'Alexander' (EA) ♀H4	CDoC LMil MGos SHBN SReu
	'Alfred'	LMil LRHS
	'Alice' (EA)	LHyd LKna
	'Alice' (hybrid) ♀H4	CSBt ENot LHyd LKna LMil SBrw SLdr SReu
	'Alice de Stuers' (M)	SLdr
	Alison Johnstone Group	GGGa ISea MDun NPen SLdr SReu WPic
	'Alix'	LHyd
	'Aloha'	MBar NDlv SHBN
	Alpine Gem Group	GQui SLdr
	'Alpine Gem' **new**	LHyd
	alutaceum var. ***alutaceum***	GGGa LMil
§	- - Globigerum Group	LMil
	- - - R 11100	GGGa NPen
§	- var. ***iodes***	GGGa LMil NPen
§	- var. ***russotinctum***	GGGa MDun
	- - R 158	SLdr
§	- - Triplonaevium Group USDAPI 59442/R10923	GGGa
	amagianum (A)	GGGa LMil
	Amaura Group	WCwm
	ambiguum	LMil NPen SLdr SReu
	- KR 185 select*	GGGa
I	- 'Crosswater'	LMil
	- 'Jane Banks'	LMil
	'Ambrosia' (EA)	CSBt
	'America'	CBcs MAsh MBar MDun SLdr WFar
	amesiae	GGGa NPen
§	'Amethystinum' (EA)	LKna
	'Amity'	CWri ECho ISea LMil MAsh MLea NPen SLdr WFar WOrn
§	'Amoenum' (EA/d)	CDoC CMac CSBt CTrw LHyd LKna LRHS MBar MGos NBlu NPen SCam SLdr SPer WAbe WFar WPic
	'Amoenum Coccineum' (EA/d)	GKev SCam SReu WPat
	Amor Group	LHyd
	'Anah Kruschke'	ENot SLdr
	'Analin'	see *R.* 'Anuschka'
	'Anchorite' (EA)	LMil SLdr
*	'Andrae' **new**	SReu
	'Andre'	SLdr
	'Angelo'	LHyd LMil
	Angelo Group	CWri LHyd LMil SLdr SReu
	'Ann Callingham' (K)	CSdC
	'Ann Lindsay'	SReu
	'Anna Baldsiefen'	ENot LMil SReu
	'Anna H. Hall'	MAsh
	'Anna Rose Whitney'	CBcs CWri GGGa GKir LHyd LKna LMil LRHS MAsh MBar MDun MGos NPen NPri SHBN WBVN WMoo
	'Annabella' (K) ♀H4	CSdC MAsh MBri SLdr
	annae	GGGa LMil NPen
§	- Hardingii Group	NPen

	Name	Suppliers
	aff. ***annae*** C&H 7185	LMil
	'Anne Frank' (EA)	COtt EBee MGos SReu WFar
	'Anne George'	LHyd
	'Anne Rothwell' (EA)	LHyd
	'Anne Teese'	IDee LMil
	'Annegret Hansmann'	GGGa
	'Anneke' (A)	ENot LMil MBar MDun NDlv SLdr SReu SSta WFar
	'Anny' (EA)	LKna SLdr
	anthopogon	GCrs LMil
	- from Marpha Meadow, Nepal	WAbe
	- 'Betty Graham'	GGGa LMil
I	- 'Crosswater'	LMil
§	- subsp. ***hypenanthum***	LMil MDun
	- - 'Annapurna'	GGGa LMil WAbe
§	***anthosphaerum***	GGGa NPen SLdr SReu
	- Gymnogynum Group	NPen
§	'Antilope' (Vs)	CWri LMil MDun MLea SLdr SReu SSta WBVN
	'Antje'	MAsh
	'Antonio'	LMil WGer
	Antonio Group	ELan
§	'Anuschka'	GKir LRHS MAsh
§	***anwheiense***	CWri LHyd LMil NPen
	aperantum	GGGa
	- F 27022	GGGa
	- JN 498	GGGa
	apodectum	see *R. dichroanthum* subsp. *apodectum*
	'Apotrophia'	SLdr
	'Apple Blossom' Wezelenburg (M)	NBlu SLdr
N	'Appleblossom'	see *R.* 'Ho-o'
	'Apple Blossom' ambig.	CMac CTrh
	'Apricot Fantasy'	LMil
	'Apricot Surprise'	GKir LRHS MAsh
	'Apricot Top Garden'	SLdr
	'April Dawn'	GGGa
§	'April Glow'	LHyd
	'April Showers' (A)	LMil
	'Arabesk' (EA)	SLdr WFar
	araiophyllum	GGGa
	- BASEX 9698	GGGa
	- KR 4029	LMil
§	***arborescens*** (A)	GGGa LHyd LKna LMil NPen SLdr
	- pink (A)	LMil
	arboreum	CBcs CDoC CHEx GGGa IDee ISea LMil MDun NPen SReu WPic
	- B&SWJ 2244	WCru
	- C&S 1651	NPen
	- C&S 1695	NPen
	- 'Blood Red'	NPen SLdr
	- subsp. ***cinnamomeum***	GGGa LMil NPen SLdr SReu
	- - var. ***album***	LHyd SLdr SReu
	- - var. ***cinnamomeum*** Campbelliae Group	NLar NPen SLdr
	- - var. ***roseum***	GGGa NPen
*	- - - ***crispum***	SLdr
	- - - 'Tony Schilling'	CDoC LHyd LMil SLdr SReu
§	- subsp. ***delavayi***	GGGa ISea LMil NPen SLdr
	- - C&H 7178	GGGa
	- - CN&W 994	LMil
	- - EGM 360	LMil
	- 'Heligan'	CWri SReu
	- mid-pink	SLdr
§	- subsp. ***nilagiricum***	GGGa SLdr
	- var. ***roseum***	SLdr
§	- subsp. ***zeylanicum***	SLdr
	'Arcadia' (EA)	LKna
	'Arctic Fox' (EA)	GGGa
	'Arctic Regent' (K)	CSdC GQui MAsh SLdr
	'Arctic Tern'	see x *Ledodendron* 'Arctic Tern'

	Plant	Suppliers
§	***argipeplum***	GGGa LMil NPen SLdr
	'Argosy' ♀H4	LMil SLdr SReu
	argyrophyllum	CWri NPen SLdr
	- subsp. ***argyrophyllum***	SLdr
	- - W/A 1210	SLdr
§	- subsp. ***hypoglaucum***	NPen
§	- - 'Heane Wood'	GGGa
	- subsp. ***nankingense***	GGGa LMil NPen
	- - 'Chinese Silver' ♀H4	CDoC IDee LHyd LMil LRHS MDun NPen SReu WGer
§	***arizelum***	GGGa LMil LRHS MDun NPen SLdr
	- BASEX 9580	GGGa
	- R 25	GGGa
	- subsp. ***arizelum*** Rubicosum Group	LMil LRHS MDun NPen
	'Armantine'	LKna
	armitii (V) Woods 2518	GGGa
	'Arneson Gem' (M)	CDoC CSam GGGa LMil NDlv NLar SLdr
§	'Arpege' (Vs)	LMil MDun NLar SReu
	'Arthur Bedford'	CSBt LHyd LKna SLdr SReu
§	'Arthur J. Ivens'	SLdr
	'Arthur Osborn'	GGGa
	'Arthur Stevens'	SLdr
	'Arthur Warren'	LKna
	'Asa-gasumi' (EA)	LHyd SCam SLdr
	'Ascot Brilliant'	SBrw
	asterochnoum	LMil
	- C&H 7051	GGGa
	- EGM 314	LMil
	Asteroid Group	SLdr
	'Astrid'	ENot
	atlanticum (A)	GGGa GKev LMil NPen SSpi
	- 'Rosa' x ***flammeum*** **new**	GKev
	- 'Seaboard' (A)	LMil SLdr
	Augfast Group	CTrw ISea SLdr
	'August Lamken'	MBri MDun
	augustinii	CTrw CWri GGGa ISea LHyd LMil LRHS MLea NPen SLdr SPer SSpi SSta
	- subsp. ***augustinii*** C&H 7048	GGGa
§	- subsp. ***chasmanthum***	GGGa LMil MDun SLdr
	- - white-flowered C&Cu 9407	GGGa
	- compact EGM 293	LMil
§	- Electra Group	CDoC GGGa IDee LHyd LMil MDun NPen SLdr
	- Exbury best form	LHyd LMil SReu
§	- subsp. ***hardyi***	GGGa SLdr
	- pale lilac	SLdr
§	- subsp. ***rubrum***	GGGa
*	- 'Trewithen'	LMil
I	- 'Werrington'	SReu
§	***aureum***	GGGa LMil NPen SLdr
	- from Kamchatka **new**	GIBF
	auriculatum	GGGa IDee LHyd LMil LRHS MDun NLar NPen SLdr SReu SSpi SSta WGer
	- PW 50	GGGa
	- Reuthe's form	SReu
	auriculatum x ***hemsleyanum***	GGGa
	auritum	GGGa NPen SLdr WPic
	'Aurora' (K)	SLdr WPic
	'Aurore de Rooighem' (A)	SLdr
§	***austrinum*** (A)	LMil SPoG
	- yellow (A)	LMil
	'Autumn Gold'	SBrw SLdr
	'Avalanche' ♀H4	LMil SLdr SReu
	Avocet Group	LMil SLdr
	'Award'	LMil
	'Ayah'	SBrw
	'Aya-kammuri' (EA)	LHyd SLdr
	Azamia Group	LHyd
	Azor Group	LHyd NPen SBrw SReu
	Azrie Group	SLdr
§	'Azuma-kagami' (EA)	CDoC LHyd LKna LMil
	'Azurro'	GGGa MBri
	'Azurwolke'	LMil
$	'Babette'	see *R.* (Volker Group) 'Babette'
	'Babuschka'	LMil
	'Baden-Baden'	CDoC ENot GCrs GEdr LHyd LKna MAsh MBar MDun MGos NEgg NPen NWea SHBN SLdr WBrE WFar
	'Bagshot Ruby'	LKna NWea SBrw SLdr SReu
	baileyi	GGGa NPen SLdr WAbe
	bainbridgeanum	LMil
	'Balalaika'	MDun
	balangense EN 3530	GGGa
	balfourianum	GGGa LMil NPen SLdr
	- SSNY 224	GGGa
	- var. ***aganniphoides***	NPen
	'Balsaminiflorum'	see *R. indicum* 'Balsaminiflorum'
	'Baltic Amber' (A)	GGGa
	'Balzac' (K)	LHyd LMil MGos MLea NEgg SLdr SPur WBVN
	'Bambi'	CWri SLdr SReu
	'Bandoola'	SReu
	'Barbara Coates' (EA)	SLdr
	barbatum	GGGa GGar GTSp IDee LHyd LMil MDun NPen SLdr
	- B&SWJ 2237	WCru
	'Barbecue' (K)	LMil
	Barclayi Group	SLdr
	'Barclayi Helen Fox'	NPen
	'Bariton'	LMil
	barkamense **new**	LMil
	'Barmstedt'	CWri
	'Barnaby Sunset'	GGGa GKir LMil LRHS MAsh
	'Bashful' ♀H4	CSBt ENot EPfP GKir LHyd LRHS MGos NPen SLdr SReu
§	***basilicum***	GGGa IDee LMil LRHS NPen SLdr
	- AC 616	NPen
	- AC 3009	WCwm
	x ***bathyphyllum*** Cox 6542	GGGa
	bauhiniiflorum	see *R. triflorum* var. *bauhiniiflorum*
	beanianum	GGGa NPen SLdr
	- KC 122	GGGa
	- KW 6805	NPen
	- compact	see *R. piercei*
	'Beatrice Keir'	LMil SReu
	Beau Brummel Group	ELan LMil SPoG
	'Beaulieu Manor'	GQui
	'Beauty of Littleworth'	LHyd LKna SPer SReu
	beesianum	GGGa LMil NPen
	- CN&W 1316	ISea
	- JN 300	GGGa
	- KR 4114	LMil
	- KR 4150	LMil
	'Beethoven' (EA) ♀H3-4	LHyd NPen SCam SLdr SReu WGor WMoo WPic
	'Belkanto'	LMil MAsh NBlu SPoG
	'Belle Heller'	SBrw SLdr
	'Ben Morrison' (EA)	SReu
	'Bengal'	GEdr GKir MAsh MBar MDun NDlv SReu
	'Bengal Beauty' (EA)	GQui SLdr
	'Bengal Fire' (EA)	CMac SLdr
§	'Benifude' (EA)	LHyd
	'Bergie Larson'	CBcs CDoC LMil MBri MDun MLea SLdr
	bergii	see *R. augustinii* subsp. *rubrum*

'Berg's Yellow'	CWri MBri MDun MLea WBVN WFar
'Bernard Shaw'	SReu
'Bernstein'	EMil NBlu SPoG WFar
'Berryrose' (K) ♀H4	CBcs CSBt CWri ENot EPfP GKir LHyd LKna LMil MAsh MBar MGos MLea NBlu SLdr WBVN WFar
Berryrose Group	CDoC MDun
'Bert's Own'	CBcs SLdr
§ 'Beryl Taylor'	GGGa
'Betty' (EA)	LHyd SLdr
'Betty Anne Voss' (EA)	ENot GKir LHyd LMil LRHS MAsh NPri SCam SCoo SLdr SReu
* 'Betty Robinson' **new**	ISea
'Betty Wormald'	CSBt GKir LHyd LKna LMil MBri MGos MLea NPen SHBN SLdr WBVN WOrn
bhutanense	LMil
- AC 119	NPen
- AC 124	NPen
- CH&M	GGGa
Bibiani Group	SLdr
'Big Punkin'	LMil
'Bijinsui' (EA) **new**	LHyd
'Billy Budd'	SLdr
'Birthday Girl'	CBcs COtt ENot LMil MDun MLea
Biskra Group	GGGa LMil
'Blaauw's Pink' (EA) ♀H3-4	CDoC CMac CSBt CTbh CTrh EBee EGra ENot EPfP GKir GQui LHyd LKna LMil LRHS MAsh MBar MBri MGos NPen SCam SLdr SPer SPlb SReu SRms WFar
'Black Hawk' (EA)	CBcs
'Black Knight' (A)	SLdr
'Black Magic'	CWri LMil
'Black Satin'	LMil
'Black Sport'	MLea
Blaue Donau	see *R.* 'Blue Danube'
'Blazecheck'	LRHS MGos SCoo
'Blewbury' ♀H4	LHyd LMil LRHS MDun SLdr SPoG SReu SSta
'Blue Beard'	SLdr
'Blue Bell'	LKna SBrw
'Blue Boy'	ENot LMil
'Blue Chip'	LHyd SLdr
§ 'Blue Danube' (EA) ♀H3-4	CDoC CMac CSBt CTrh CTri EBee ENot GKir LHyd LKna LMil LRHS MAsh MBar MBri MDun MGos NBlu NPen NPri SCam SLdr SPer SReu SSta WFar WPic
Blue Diamond Group	CBcs CBrm CMHG CTrh ENot EPfP LKna LRHS MBar MDun MGos NPen NWea SHBN SLdr SReu SRms WPic
'Blue Diamond'	CSBt WMoo
'Blue Gown'	LKna
'Blue Moon'	MBar
'Blue Mountain'	NWea
'Blue Peter' ♀H4	CDoC CSBt CWri EMil ENot EPfP GGGa LHyd LKna LMil MAsh MBar MBri MDun MGos SBrw SHBN SLdr SReu SSta
'Blue Pool'	LMil MBar
Blue Ribbon Group	CMHG CTrw ISea SLdr
'Blue Silver'	GGGa LMil MAsh SPoG
'Blue Star'	GGar GKir LHyd LRHS MDun MLea NMen
'Blue Steel'	see *R. fastigiatum* 'Blue Steel'
Blue Tit Group	CBcs CSBt GKir LHyd LKna LRHS MBar NEgg NPen SHBN SLdr SReu SSta WPic
Bluebird Group	CSBt ECho ENot LKna MBar MDun MGos NDlv NWCA SLdr SRms WMoo
'Bluette'	MDun NDlv
'Blurettia'	CWri LMil NLar
'Blutopia'	LMil
'Bob Bovee'	NLar
'Bobbie'	SReu
'Bob's Blue'	MDun
'Boddaertianum'	LHyd SLdr SReu
bodinieri USDAPI 59585/R11281	NPen
'Bodnant Yellow'	LMil
'Bonfire'	SLdr SReu
boothii	GGGa
'Bo-peep'	GQui LMil LRHS SReu
Bo-peep Group	CBcs LMil NPen SLdr
'Boskoop Ostara'	LMil
'Boule de Neige'	MDun
'Bouquet de Flore' (G) ♀H4	CDoC CSdC LMil MBar SLdr SPer SReu
Bow Bells Group	CSam ISea LHyd LKna LMil MAsh MBar MDun MGos MLea SHBN
'Bow Bells' ♀H4	EPfP GEdr GKir LMil LRHS NBlu NLar NPri SLdr WFar
'Bow Street'	LHyd
brachyanthum	GGGa
- subsp. ***hypolepidotum***	GGGa LMil
brachycarpum	GGGa GIBF NPen SLdr
- subsp. ***brachycarpum*** Tigerstedtii Group	LMil SReu
- 'Roseum Dwarf'	GGGa
brachysiphon	see *R. maddenii* subsp. *maddenii*
'Brambling' **new**	GGGa
'Brazier' (EA)	CTrh LHyd LRHS MAsh NPen SCam SLdr SPoG
'Brazil' (K)	CSBt LKna SBrw SReu
'Bremen'	LMil
Bric-à-brac Group	CBcs CTrw SLdr
'Bric-à-brac'	MDun
'Bride's Bouquet' (EA/d)	SReu
'Bridesmaid' (O)	ENot EPfP SLdr
'Brigadoon'	LMil MBri
'Bright Forecast' (K)	CWri MAsh SLdr WGor
'Brigitte'	CDoC CWri GGGa LMil LRHS MAsh SLdr
'Brilliant' (EA)	MGos
'Brilliant' (hybrid)	MGos WFar
'Brilliant Blue'	MAsh
'Brilliant Crimson' (EA)	SLdr
'Britannia'	CSBt CSam CWri ENot EPfP GKir ISea LHyd LKna MAsh MBar NPen NWea SHBN SLdr SPer SReu WFar
'Britannia' x ***griersonianum***	SLdr
'Brocade'	CSam LKna LMil MDun NPen SLdr
'Bronze Fire' (A)	SLdr SReu
'Brown Eyes'	ISea MDun MLea SLdr WFar
'Bruce Brechtbill' ♀H4	CDoC CWri GGGa GKir ISea LMil LRHS MAsh MBri MDun MGos NPri SLdr SReu SSta WOrn
§ 'Bruns Elfenbein'	NLar
'Bruns Gloria'	LMil
'Buccaneer' (EA)	LHyd SLdr
'Bud Flanagan'	ENot LMil MDun SBrw
'Buketta'	GGGa MDun
bullatum	see *R. edgeworthii*
bulu C&V 9503	GGGa
'Bungo-nishiki' (EA/d)	CMac
bureavii ♀H4	CAbP CWri GGGa IDee LHyd LMil MDun NPen SLdr SReu SSta
- C&H 7158	GGGa
- F 15609	NPen
- R 25439	NPen
- SEH 211	LMil
- SF 517	ISea

	Name	Suppliers
	- 'Ardrishaig'	GGGa
*	- ***cruentum***	LMil
I	- 'Lem's Variety'	NLar
	bureavii x Elizabeth Group	SReu
	bureavioides	LMil MDun NPen SReu
	- Cox 5076	GGGa
	'Burletta'	GGGa
	burmanicum	GGGa LMil MDun NPen SLdr
	'Burning Love'	NLar
	'Butter Brickle'	LMil MDun MLea WBVN
	'Butter Yellow'	ECho MDun
	'Buttercup' (K)	MBar
	'Butterfly'	LKna MDun SLdr
	'Buttermilk' (V)	ISea
	'Buttermint'	GQui MBri MDun MGos MLea NPen SBod SHBN WBVN WGwG
	'Buttons and Bows' (K)	GGGa
	'Buzzard' (K)	CSdC LKna LMil
	'Byron' (A/d) **new**	SLdr
	'Caerhays Lavender'	CBcs
	caesium	GGGa SLdr
	calendulaceum (A)	GKev LMil SReu
	- red (A)	LMil
	- yellow	LMil
	Calfort Group	SLdr
	'Calico' (K)	CSdC
	caliginis (V)	GGGa
	callimorphum	GGGa LMil NPen
	- var. ***myiagrum*** F 21821a	NPen SLdr
	- - KW 6962	NPen
	calophytum 🏆H4	GGGa IDee LHyd LMil LRHS NPen SLdr
	- EGM 343	LMil
	- var. ***openshawianum***	C&H 7055 GGGa
	- - EGM 318	LMil
	calophytum x ***praevernum***	WCwm
	calostrotum	CWri WAbe
	- SF 357	ISea
	- 'Gigha' 🏆H4	CDoC GGGa GKir LMil LRHS LTwo MDun MGos SLdr SSpi WAbe WGer
§	- subsp. ***keleticum*** 🏆H4	CDoC GEdr LMil MBar MDun MGos WAbe
	- - R 58	LMil
§	- - Radicans Group	GCrs GEdr LMil MBar MDun MLea WAbe WPat
	- - - USDAPI 59182/ R11188	MLea
	- subsp. ***riparium***	LMil
	- - SF 95089	ISea
	- - Calciphilum Group	GGGa MDun
§	- - Nitens Group	CDoC GGGa IDee LMil MAsh NDlv NMen WAbe WPGP
§	- - Rock's form R178	GGGa WAbe
	caloxanthum	see *R. campylocarpum* subsp. *caloxanthum*
	'Calsap'	GGGa
	Calstocker Group	LMil
	camelliiflorum	GGGa MDun
	'Cameronian' (Ad)	LKna
	campanulatum	LHyd LKna MDun NPen SLdr SReu WAbe
	- HWJCM 195	WCru
§	- subsp. ***aeruginosum***	GGGa LMil MDun NLar NPen SLdr SReu
	- - Airth 10	GGGa
	- ***album***	NPen SLdr
	- subsp. ***campanulatum*** 'Roland Cooper'	NPen
	- 'Knap Hill'	LHyd NPen
	- 'Waxen Bell'	LHyd
§	'Campfire' (EA)	SLdr
	Campirr Group	LHyd
	campylocarpum	GGGa LHyd LMil MDun NPen SLdr SReu
§	- subsp. ***caloxanthum***	GGGa LMil MDun NPen SLdr
	- - KR 3516 from Pe, Doshang La	LMil
	- - KR 6152	LMil
	- - Telopeum Group	NPen
	- - - KW 5718B	NPen
	- East Nepal	MDun
	campylogynum 🏆H4	GCrs LMil MLea NMen SSpi WAbe
	- Cox 6051	GGGa
	- Cox 6096	GGGa
	- SF 95181	ISea
	- 'Album'	see *R.* 'Leucanthum'
I	- 'Bramble'	MDun
	- Castle Hill form	LMil
	- Charopoeum Group	GCrs GGGa LMil MBar MDun
	- - 'Patricia'	ECho GBin MDun WAbe
	- claret	ECho GGGa MDun
§	- Cremastum Group	GGGa LHyd NPen
	- - 'Bodnant Red'	GGGa LHyd MDun NPen WAbe
	- var. ***leucanthum***	see *R.* 'Leucanthum'
	- Myrtilloides Group	CDoC CTbh CTrw GGGa GQui IDee LHyd LMil LRHS MAsh MDun NLAp NMen NPen SLdr SReu WAbe
	- - Farrer 1046	GGGa
	- pink	MBar WAbe
	- salmon pink	ECho EPot GEdr MDun
	camtschaticum	GGGa LMil WAbe
	- from Hokkaido, Japan	GCrs NMen
	- var. ***albiflorum***	GGGa NMen
	- red	GGGa
	canadense (A)	GGGa SLdr SReu
	- f. ***albiflorum*** (A)	GGGa LMil
	- dark-flowered (A)	LMil
	- 'Deer Lake' (A)	SReu
	'Canary'	LKna SReu
	canescens (A)	LMil
	'Cannon's Double' (K/d) 🏆H4	CWri GGGa LHyd LMil MAsh MBri MDun MGos MLea NLar NPen SLdr
	'Canzonetta' (EA) 🏆H4	GGGa LMil MGos
	'Capistrano'	GGGa
	capitatum	GGGa
	'Caprice' (EA)	SReu
	'Captain Jack'	GGGa SLdr
	'Caractacus'	EMil MBar WFar
	'Carat'	SLdr SReu
	cardiobasis	see *R. orbiculare* subsp. *cardiobasis*
	Carita Group	LKna SReu
	'Carita Charm' **new**	SLdr
	'Carita Golden Dream'	LKna LMil
	'Carita Inchmery'	LHyd LKna SLdr
	'Carmen'	CBrm CWri GGGa GKir ISea LHyd LKna LMil LRHS MBar MDun MGos MLea NMen NPen NWea SHBN SLdr SReu SRms
	carneum	GGGa LMil
	'Caroline Allbrook' 🏆H4	CDoC CWri ENot GGGa ISea LHyd LMil MAsh MDun MGos MLea NDlv NPen SLdr SPoG WBVN
	'Caroline de Zoete'	LHyd
	carolinianum	see *R. minus* var. *minus*
	'Cary Ann'	CBcs CWri ENot GKir LRHS SLdr SReu WFar
	'Casablanca' (EA)	SLdr
	'Cassley' (Vs)	LMil SLdr
	'Castle of Mey'	SLdr

catacosmum	GGGa
§ 'Catalode'	GGGa
catawbiense	GGGa LHyd NPen SLdr
'Catawbiense Album'	CWri GGGa GKir LRHS MAsh NWea WFar
'Catawbiense Boursault'	SLdr WFar
'Catawbiense Grandiflorum'	GKir LRHS MAsh WFar
'Catherine Hopwood'	SLdr
§ ***caucasicum*** 'Cunningham's Sulphur'	MDun
'Caucasicum Pictum'	GGGa LHyd LMil MBar SLdr
'Cecile' (K) ♀H4	CBcs CWri GKir LHyd LKna LMil MAsh MBar MBri MDun MGos MLea NBlu NPen SBod SLdr SReu
'Celestial' (EA)	CMac
'Centennial'	see *R.* 'Washington State Centennial'
cephalanthum	GGGa LMil
- subsp. ***cephalanthum*** SBEC 0751	GGGa WAbe
- - Crebreflorum Group	GGGa LMil LRHS WAbe
- - Nmaiense Group C&V 9513	GGGa
- subsp. ***platyphyllum***	GGGa LMil
- - CN&W 835	LMil
cerasinum	GGGa ISea LMil NPen
- C&V 9504	GGGa
- KR 3460	LMil
- KR 3490 from Pe, Doshang La	LMil
- KW 11011	NPen
- SF 95067	ISea
- 'Cherry Brandy'	LHyd NPen
- 'Coals of Fire'	NPen
- deep pink-flowered	NPen
'Cetewayo' ♀H4	CWri SReu
chaetomallum	see *R. haematodes* subsp. *chaetomallum*
'Chaffinch' (K)	LKna
chamaethomsonii	GGGa LMil
- CCH&H 8195	GGGa
- SF 95084	ISea
- var. ***chamaethauma*** KW 5847	LMil
- - KR 3506 from Pe, Doshang La	LMil
- var. ***chamaethomsonii*** F 21723	NPen
chameunum	see *R. saluenense* subsp. *chameunum*
§ 'Champagne' ♀H3-4	CSBt GKir LHyd LKna LMil LRHS MDun MLea NLar NPen SLdr SReu
championiae	GGGa
'Chanel' (Vs)	MDun SReu SSta
'Chanticleer' (EA)	CTrh SCam SLdr SReu
chapaense	see *R. maddenii* subsp. *crassum*
'Chapeau'	LMil
charitopes	GGGa LMil
- subsp. ***charitopes*** F 25570	SReu
§ - subsp. ***tsangpoense***	GGGa GQui LMil WPic
- - C&V 9575*	GGGa
'Charlemagne' (G)	SLdr
* 'Charles Puddle'	WPic
'Charlotte de Rothschild' (hybrid)	LMil NPen SLdr
Charmaine Group	GGGa SReu
'Charme La'	GGGa
chasmanthum	see *R. augustinii* subsp. *chasmanthum*
'Cheer'	COtt CWri ENot MAsh MBar SLdr SReu WFar WGor WMoo
'Cheerful Giant' (K)	GKir LMil LRHS MGos
'Chelsea Reach' (K/d)	CSdC LKna
'Chelsea Seventy'	COtt GKir LRHS MAsh NLar SLdr
'Chenille' (K/d)	LKna
'Cherokee'	SCam SLdr
'Cherries and Cream'	LMil
'Cherry Drop' (EA)	MAsh
'Chetco' (K)	LMil
'Chevalier Félix de Sauvage' ♀H4	EMil LMil SReu
'Cheyenne'	SLdr
'Chicago' (M)	LKna
'Chiffchaff'	LHyd NMen WAbe
'Chikor'	CSBt GGGa GKir LKna MBar MBri MDun MGos MLea NPen SLdr SReu WBVN WFar
China Group	LKna SBrw SReu
'China A'	LKna SBrw SLdr
'Chinchilla' (EA)	GQui WGor
'Chink'	CBcs ENot MBar MDun SLdr
'Chionoides'	GGGa LKna SLdr
'Chipmunk' (EA/d)	LMil LRHS MAsh
'Chippewa' (EA)	GGGa GKir LMil LRHS
'Chocolate Ice' (K/d)	LKna LMil SLdr
'Choremia' ♀H3	LHyd LMil SReu
'Chorister' (K)	LKna
'Chris' (EA)	SLdr
'Chris Bagley' **new**	SBrw
christi (V)	GGGa
'Christina' (EA/d)	CMac SLdr SReu WGor
'Christmas Cheer' (EA/d)	see *R.* 'Ima-shojo'
'Christmas Cheer' (hybrid)	CMac CSBt CWri GGGa ISea LHyd LKna LMil MAsh MGos MLea NPen SHBN SLdr SPer SPoG SReu WPic
§ 'Christopher Wren' (K)	SLdr
chrysanthum	see *R. aureum*
chryseum	see *R. rupicola* var. *chryseum*
chrysodoron	GGGa LMil
ciliatum	CBcs CWri GGGa LHyd NPen SLdr
ciliicalyx subsp. ***lyi***	see *R. lyi*
- 'Walter Maynard'	LMil
Cilpinense Group	CBcs ENot GKir LKna LMil LRHS MBar MDun NPen SLdr WFar
'Cilpinense' ♀H3-4	CSBt EMil EPfP GGGa LHyd LMil LRHS NPri SReu WBrE WPic
cinnabarinum	LMil MDun NPen SLdr
- 'Caerhays Lawrence'	SLdr
- subsp. ***cinnabarinum***	MDun SLdr
- - BL&M 234	LMil
- - from Ghunsa, Nepal	MDun
- - 'Aestivale'	LMil
- - Blandfordiiflorum Group	GGGa LMil NPen SLdr
§ - - 'Conroy'	GGGa LMil LRHS MDun MLea SReu SSpi
- - 'Nepal'	LHyd LMil
- - ex LS&M 21283	LMil
- - Roylei Group	GGGa LMil MDun MLea NPen SLdr SReu WPic
- - - 'Magnificum' **new**	MDun
- - - 'Vin Rosé'	LMil MDun
§ - subsp. ***tamaense***	GGGa
- - KW 21021	GGGa
§ - subsp. ***xanthocodon***	IDee LMil MDun MLea NPen SLdr
- - KW 8239	NPen
§ - - Concatenans Group	CBcs GGGa LMil MDun MLea NPen SLdr WPic
- - - C&V 9523	GGGa
- - - KW 5874	LMil
- - - 'Amber'	LMil MDun MLea
- - - 'Copper'	SLdr
- - Purpurellum Group	GGGa MDun NPen SLdr
Cinnkeys Group	GGGa MDun

Cinzan Group	LMil SReu
citriniflorum	LMil NPen
- R 108	GGGa LMil
- Brodick form **new**	LMil
- var. ***citriniflorum***	LMil
- var. ***horaeum***	NPen
- - F 21850*	GGGa
'Citronella'	SLdr
'Claydian Variegated' (v)	GGGa
clementinae	GGGa LMil MDun NPen SLdr SReu
- F 25705	LMil NPen
- JN 352	GGGa
- JN 722	GGGa
- JN 723	GGGa
- JN 729	GGGa
clementinae x ***pronum***	GGGa
'Cliff Garland'	GQui LMil
'Coccineum Speciosum' (G) ♀H4	CSBt CSdC GGGa LMil MBar SReu
'Cockade' (EA)	LKna
'Cockatoo' (K)	LKna
§ ***coelicum*** F 25625	GGGa
coeloneuron	CBcs GGGa LMil MDun
- EGM 334	LMil
'Colin Kenrick' (K/d)	LKna SLdr
collettianum H&W 8975	GGGa
'Colonel Coen'	CDoC CWri GGGa LRHS MBri MGos MLea NPen NPri SHBN
Colonel Rogers Group	LHyd SLdr SReu
x ***columbianum***	see *Ledum* x *columbianum*
Comely Group	LHyd
- 'Golden Orfe'	SLdr
complexum F 15392	GGGa
'Comte de Gomer' (hybrid)	CBcs
concatenans	see *R. cinnabarinum* subsp. *xanthocodon* Concatenans Group
concinnum	CTrw CWri LHyd MDun MLea NPen
- Pseudoyanthinum Group	GGGa GQui LMil MDun NPen SLdr SReu WPic
'Concorde'	NBlu
'Conroy'	see *R. cinnabarinum* subsp. *cinnabarinum* 'Conroy'
'Constable'	LHyd
'Constant Nymph'	LKna
'Contina'	GGGa
Conyan Group	LHyd
cookeanum	see *R. sikangense* var. *sikangense* Cookeanum Group
'Coral Mist'	GGGa LMil MDun
'Coral Reef'	SLdr SReu
'Coral Sea' (EA)	MDun SLdr SReu
'Coralie' (EA/d)	SLdr
coriaceum	GGGa LMil LRHS NPen WCwm
- R 120	NPen
'Corneille' (G/d) ♀H4	CSBt LKna LMil SLdr SPer SReu
'Cornish Cracker'	SLdr
Cornish Cross Group	LHyd NPen SLdr SReu
Cornish Early Red Group	see *R.* Smithii Group
'Cornish Red'	see *R.* Smithii Group
Cornubia Group	SLdr
'Corona'	LKna
'Coronation Day'	SLdr SReu
'Coronation Lady' (K)	ENot LKna
'Corringe' (K)	LMil
'Corry Koster'	LKna
coryanum	GGGa NPen
- KR 5775	LMil
- KR 6315	LMil
- 'Chelsea Chimes' ex KW 6311	LMil SLdr
'Cosmopolitan'	CWri ENot GGGa LMil MBar MDun MGos SLdr SPoG WFar

'Costa del Sol'	NPen
Cote Group (A)	SLdr
'Cotton Candy'	LMil
'Countess of Athlone'	LKna SBrw SLdr
'Countess of Derby'	SReu
'Countess of Haddington' ♀H2	CBcs ISea LMil MDun SLdr
'Countess of Stair'	WFar WPic
'County of York'	see *R.* 'Catalode'
cowanianum	GGGa
Cowslip Group	CSam CTri CWri GKir LHyd LKna LMil LRHS MBar MDun MGos MLea NPen NPri SHBN SLdr SReu
coxianum C&H 475B	GGGa
'Cranbourne'	LHyd SReu
'Crane' ♀H4	GGGa GKir GQui LMil LRHS MAsh MDun NPri WAbe WGer
crassum	see *R. maddenii* subsp. *crassum*
'Cream Crest'	GQui MDun SHBN WFar
'Cream Glory'	LHyd SReu
'Creamy Chiffon'	CWri GGGa MDun MGos MLea
§ 'Creeping Jenny'	GGGa GGar LHyd MBar MDun SLdr
cremastum	see *R. campylogynum* Cremastum Group
§ 'Crest' ♀H3-4	CWri GGGa LHyd LKna LMil MDun MGos SHBN SLdr SPer SReu
'Crete'	COtt GKir LMil MDun SReu
'Crimson Pippin'	LMil
crinigerum	GGGa LHyd LMil MDun NPen
- JN 756	GGGa
- var. ***crinigerum*** KW 7123	NPen
- - KW 8164	NPen
'Crinoline' (EA)	SCam
'Crinoline' (K)	LRHS SLdr SReu
'Croceum Tricolor' (G)	CSdC
Crossbill Group	CBcs WPic
* ***crossium***	SReu
'Crosswater Belle'	LMil
'Crosswater Red' (K)	LMil
cubittii	see *R. veitchianum* Cubittii Group
cucullatum	see *R. roxieanum* var. *cucullatum*
§ ***cumberlandense*** (A)	GGGa LMil LRHS
- 'Sunlight' (A)	LMil LRHS
cuneatum	GGGa
'Cunningham's Blush'	GGGa GKir LRHS MAsh SHBN
'Cunningham's Sulphur'	see *R. caucasicum* 'Cunningham's Sulphur'
'Cunningham's White'	CBcs CSBt CSam CTbh CWri ELan ENot EPfP GGGa GKir LKna LMil LRHS MAsh MBar MDun MGos NPen NWea SLdr SPer SPoG SReu WFar
'Cupcake'	see *R.* 'Delp's Cupcake'
'Cupreum Ardens'	CSdC
'Curlew' ♀H4	CBrm CDoC CSBt EPfP EPot GEdr GGGa GGar GKir LMil LRHS MAsh MBar MBri MDun MGos NMen NPen SHBN SLdr SPoG SReu SSpi WBVN WFar WOrn
cyanocarpum	GGGa LMil NPen
- AC 676	NPen
- Bu 294	GGGa
'Cynthia' ♀H4	CSBt CWri EPfP GGGa LHyd LKna LMil MBar MBri MGos NPen NWea SBrw SHBN SLdr SPer SReu SSta WBVN WFar
'Daimio' (EA)	LHyd
'Dairymaid'	LKna SReu
dalhousieae	GGGa SLdr
§ - var. ***rhabdotum***	GGGa ISea LMil SLdr
Damaris Group	NPen SLdr
'Damaris Logan'	see *R.* 'Logan Damaris'

	Name	Suppliers
	'Damozel'	SLdr
	'Dandy' (hybrid)	LKna
	'Dartmoor Blush'	SReu
	'Dartmoor Pixie'	SReu
*	'Dartmoor Rose'	SReu
	dasycladum	see *R. selense* subsp. *dasycladum*
	dasypetalum	ECho MBar MDun NDlv
	dauricum	SLdr
	- 'Arctic Pearl'	GGGa SLdr
	- 'Hokkaido' x ***leucaspis***	GGGa
	- 'Midwinter' ♀^{H4}	GGGa LHyd LMil SLdr
	'David' ♀^{H4}	LHyd LKna SLdr SReu
	davidii AC 4100	LMil
	davidsonianum ♀$^{H3-4}$	CTrw GGGa ISea LHyd LMil NPen SLdr SSpi WPic
	- EGM 351	LMil
	- Bodnant form	LMil
	- 'Caerhays Blotched'	SLdr
	- 'Caerhays Pink'	GGGa SLdr
	- 'Ruth Lyons'	LMil
	'Daviesii' (G) ♀^{H4}	CBcs CDoC CSBt CSdC CTri CWri ENot EPfP GGGa GKir GQui IDee LHyd LKna LMil MAsh MBri MDun MLea SBod SLdr SPer SReu SSpi WBVN WBrE WFar
	'Dawn's Delight'	SLdr
*	'Day Dawn'	SReu
	'Day Dream'	SReu
	Day Dream Group	LKna
	'Daybreak' (K)	GQui
N	'Daybreak' (EA/d)	see *R.* 'Kirin'
	'Dear Grandad' (EA)	CTri LMil LRHS MAsh NPri SCoo
	decorum ♀^{H4}	GGGa IDee LHyd LMil LRHS MDun NPen SLdr SReu WPic
	- AC 757	NPen
	- C&H 7023	GGGa
	- SF 252	ISea
	- 'Cox's Uranium Green'	SReu
	- subsp. ***decorum*** SBEC 1060	NPen
	- - SBEC 181	NPen
§	- subsp. ***diaprepes***	LMil
	- - 'Gargantua'	LMil SReu
	- pink-flowered	SLdr
	degronianum	GGGa NPen
§	- subsp. ***degronianum***	LMil NPen SLdr
	- - 'Gerald Loder'	LHyd
§	- subsp. ***heptamerum***	GGGa MDun NPen
	- - 'Ho Emma'	LMil MDun
	- - var. ***kyomaruense***	LMil
	- - 'Oki Island'	LMil
	- 'Rae's Delight'	LMil
	dekatanum	GGGa
	deleiense	see *R. tephropeplum*
	'Delicatissimum' (O)	CWri GGGa GQui MLea NLar SLdr WBVN
	'Delp's Cupcake'	NLar
	'Delta'	NBlu
	dendricola	SLdr
	- KW 20981	GGGa
	dendrocharis	GGGa
	- CC&H 4012	GGGa
	- Cox 5016	GGGa WAbe
	- 'Glendoick Gem'	GGGa
	- 'Glendoick Jewel'	GGGa
*	'Denny's Rose' (A)	LMil SLdr SReu
	'Denny's Scarlet'	SReu
	'Denny's White'	LMil SLdr SReu
	denudatum C&H 70102	GGGa
	- C&H 7118	GGGa
	- EGM 294	LMil
	- SEH 334	LMil
	'Desert Orchid'	LHyd
	'Desert Pink' (K)	LKna
	desquamatum	see *R. rubiginosum* Desquamatum Group
	x ***detonsum*** F13784	SLdr
	'Devisiperbile' (EA)	SLdr
	'Diabolo' (K)	LKna
	Diamant Group (EA)	GGGa
	- 'Diamant Enzianblau' (EA) **new**	LMil
	- lilac (EA)	GGGa LMil MLea
	- pink (EA)	ECho LMil MDun MGos MLea SLdr SReu
§	- purple (EA)	ECho LMil MDun MGos MLea NBlu NEgg SLdr
§	- red (EA)	LMil MDun MLea SLdr
	- rosy red (EA)	ECho
	- salmon pink (EA) **new**	LMil
	- white (EA)	ECho LRHS MDun MLea NBlu SLdr
	'Diamant Rot'	see *R.* Diamant Group red
	'Diamant Purpur'	see *R.* Diamant Group purple
	'Diana Pearson'	LHyd
	'Diane'	LKna
	diaprepes	see *R. decorum* subsp. *diaprepes*
	dichroanthum	GGGa LHyd LMil MDun NPen SLdr SReu
	- CCH&H 8198	GGGa
§	- subsp. ***apodectum***	GGGa LMil NPen
	- subsp. ***dichroanthum***	LMil
	- - F 6781	NPen
	- - SBEC 545	GGGa
§	- subsp. ***scyphocalyx***	GGGa LMil NPen SLdr
	- - F 24546	GGGa
	- - F 27115	GGGa
	- - Farrer 1024	GGGa
	- subsp. ***septentroniale***	GGGa
	- - JN 575	GGGa
	dictyotum	see *R. traillianum* var. *dictyotum*
	didymum	see *R. sanguineum* subsp. *didymum*
	'Dietrich'	WFar
	dignabile C&V 9569	GGGa
	- KR 5385	LMil
	dilatatum	LMil
	- 'Satsumense' **new**	NPen
	dimitrum	MDun
	'Diny Dee'	MGos
	'Diorama' (Vs)	SReu SSta WFar
§	'Directeur Moerlands' (M)	SLdr
	discolor	see *R. fortunei* subsp. *discolor*
	'Doc'	ENot EPfP GKir LMil LRHS MAsh MBar MDun MGos NBlu NDlv SLdr SReu WFar
	'Doctor A. Blok'	SLdr
	'Doctor Chas Baumann' (G)	SLdr
	'Doctor Ernst Schäle'	GGGa
	'Doctor H.C. Dresselhuys'	MBar SHBN
	'Doctor Herman Sleumer' (V)	GGGa
	'Doctor M. Oosthoek' (M) ♀^{H4}	CSBt SLdr SReu
	'Doctor V.H. Rutgers'	MBar WFar
	'Don Giovanni'	NLar
	'Don Quixote' (K)	CSdC MAsh
	'Doncaster'	ENot GKir LKna MBar MGos NWea SHBN WFar
	'Dopey' ♀^{H4}	CBcs CDoC CSBt CWri ENot EPfP GGGa GKir LHyd LMil LRHS MAsh MBar MDun MGos MLea NDlv NPen SHBN SLdr SPoG SReu
	'Dora Amateis' ♀^{H4}	COtt GGGa GKir ISea LHyd LMil LRHS MBar MGos NPen NPri SLdr SPer SReu WPic

	Name	Suppliers
	Dormouse Group	GGGa LMil SLdr SReu WBVN
	'Dorothea'	SLdr
	'Dorothy Corston' (K)	LKna
	'Dorothy Hayden' (EA)	SLdr
	'Dorset Sandy' (EA)	LMil
	'Dörte Reich'	GGGa
	doshongense	see *R. aganniphum* var. *aganniphum* Doshongense Group
	'Double Beauty' (EA/d)	LKna MAsh SPoG SReu SSta
	'Double Damask' (K/d) 🏆H4	LKna SBrw SLdr SReu
	'Double Date' (d)	CDoC SLdr
	'Douglas McEwan'	MDun SLdr
	'Dracula' (K)	GGGa
	Dragonfly Group	SReu
	Dragonfly Group x ***serotinum***	SLdr
	'Drake's Mountain'	ECho MBar MDun MLea
	'Dreamland' 🏆H4	COtt CSBt CWri ENot LMil MAsh MDun MGos MLea NPri SLdr SReu WFar WOrn
	'Driven Snow' (EA)	SLdr
	drumonium	see *R. telmateium*
	'Drury Lane' (K)	GQui LMil LRHS
	dryophyllum hort.	see *R. phaeochrysum* var. *levistratum*
	'Duchess of Teck'	SBrw SReu
	'Dusky Dawn'	SLdr
	'Dusky Orange'	SReu
	'Dusty'	MDun
	'Dusty Miller'	COtt ENot GKir ISea LRHS MAsh MBar MDun MGos NDlv SHBN SLdr
	'Earl of Athlone'	LHyd SReu
	'Earl of Donoughmore'	LHyd LKna SReu SSta
	'Early Beni' (EA)	LHyd
	Early Brilliant Group	LKna
	'Ebony Pearl'	CWri GGGa MGos MLea WBVN
	eclecteum	LMil MDun SLdr
	- Cox 6054	GGGa
	- 'Rowallane Yellow'	SLdr
	'Eddy' (EA)	LKna
§	***edgeworthii*** 🏆H2-3	CTbh GGGa ISea LMil SLdr WAbe
	- KC 0106	GGGa
	edgeworthii x ***leucaspis***	CBcs
	'Edith Bosley'	GGGa
	'Edith Mackworth Praed'	SReu
	Edmondii Group	LHyd
	'Edna Bee' (EA)	LMil SLdr
	'Effner'	LMil
	'Egret' 🏆H4	EPot GGGa GKir MAsh MBar MDun MGos MLea NLar SLdr WAbe WBVN
	'Eider'	GGGa ISea SLdr SReu WFar
	'Eileen'	LMil SBrw SReu
	'El Camino'	COtt MBri NPen SHBN SLdr
	'El Greco'	SLdr
	Eldorado Group	GQui
	'Eleanor Habgood'	SLdr
	Electra Group	see *R. augustinii* Electra Group
	elegantulum	GGGa LMil MDun NPen
	'Elfenbein'	see *R.* 'Bruns Elfenbein'
	'Elfin Gold'	SReu
	'Elisabeth Hobbie' 🏆H4	GGGa LKna LMil MBar MDun WMoo
	Elizabeth Group	CBcs CDoC CTrh CTrw CWri GGGa LHyd LKna LMil LRHS MAsh MBar NPen NWea SHBN SLdr SPer SReu WFar
N	'Elizabeth' (EA)	CSBt EPfP GKir MGos NWCA
	'Elizabeth'	MGos NPri WOrn
	'Elizabeth de Rothschild'	MDun NPen SLdr

	Name	Suppliers
	'Elizabeth Jenny'	see *R.* 'Creeping Jenny'
	'Elizabeth Lockhart'	GEdr GGGa GKir GQui MBar MDun MGos MLea
	'Elizabeth of Glamis'	GGGa
	'Elizabeth Red Foliage'	CDoC CTri GGGa GKir LHyd LMil LRHS MAsh MDun SPer SReu
	elliottii	GGGa SReu
	Elsae Group	SLdr SReu
	'Else Frye'	GGGa
	'Elsie Lee' (EA/d) 🏆H3-4	CTrh GGGa LMil SLdr
	'Elsie Pratt' (A)	MBar
	'Elsie Straver'	SHBN SLdr SReu
	'Elsie Watson'	GGGa LMil
	'Elspeth'	LHyd LKna
§	'Emasculum'	COtt LKna SLdr SReu
	Emerald Isle Group	SReu
	'Empire Day'	LKna
	'Endsleigh Pink'	LMil
	'English Roseum'	NBlu SLdr
	'Erato'	GGGa
	eriocarpum 'Jitsugetsuse'	LHyd
	eriogynum	see *R. facetum*
	eritimum	see *R. anthosphaerum*
	'Ernest Inman'	LHyd SLdr
	erosum	GGGa NPen SLdr
N	'Esmeralda'	CMac
	Ethel Group	SLdr
	'Etna' (EA)	SCam SLdr
	'Etta Burrows'	CWri GGGa MDun
	'Euan Cox'	GGGa NMen
	euchroum	NPen
	eudoxum	GGGa NPen
	- KW 5879*	NPen
	'Eunice Updike' (EA)	LHyd
	'Europa'	SReu
	eurysiphon	NPen
	- Arduaine form	GGGa
	'Eva Goude' (K)	LKna
	'Evelyn Hyde' (EA)	SLdr
	'Evening Fragrance' (A)	SReu
	'Evensong' (EA)	LKna
	'Everbloom' (EA)	SLdr
	'Everest' (EA)	ENot LHyd LMil MAsh SLdr
	'Everestianum'	GGGa LKna MBar
	'Everitt Hershey' (A)	SLdr
	'Everlasting'	see *Kalmia latifolia* x *R. williamsianum*, 'Everlasting'
	'Everred' **new**	GGGa
	exasperatum KC 0116	GGGa
	- KC 0126	GGGa
	- KW 8250	GGGa
	'Exbury Albatross'	LKna
	'Exbury Calstocker'	LMil
	'Exbury Naomi'	LHyd LKna LMil NPen SLdr
	'Exbury White' (K)	EPfP GQui
	'Excalibur'	GGGa
	excellens	LMil WCwm
	- AC 146	GGGa
	- SF 92074	ISea
	- SF 92079	ISea
	- SF 92303	ISea
	eximium	see *R. falconeri* subsp. *eximium*
	'Exquisitum' (O) 🏆H4	CDoC CWri EPfP GGGa LMil MBri MLea NLar SLdr SSpi WBVN
	exquisitum	see *R. oreotrephes* Exquisitum Group
§	***faberi***	GGGa LMil NPen SLdr
	- subsp. ***prattii***	see *R. prattii*
	'Fabia' 🏆H3	GGGa LHyd LMil MDun WPic
	Fabia Group	LKna MDun NPen SLdr
	'Fabia Roman Pottery'	MDun
§	'Fabia Tangerine'	LHyd MDun MLea SReu

'Fabia Waterer'	LMil SLdr
§ ***facetum***	GGGa LMil MDun NPen
- AC 3049	LMil
'Faggetter's Favourite' ♀H4	LKna LMil MDun SPoG SReu SSta
Fairy Light Group	LMil SLdr
'Falcon'	see *R.* (Hawk Group) 'Hawk Falcon'
falconeri ♀H3-4	CHEx GGGa IDee ISea LHyd LMil LRHS MDun NPen SLdr WGer
- from East Nepal **new**	MDun
§ - subsp. ***eximium***	GGGa LMil MDun
- subsp. ***falconeri***	CWri
'Fanal' (K)	CDul SLdr
'Fanny'	see *R.* 'Pucella'
'Fantastica' ♀H4	CDoC ELan GGGa LHyd LMil LRHS MAsh MBri MDun NLar SPoG SReu
fargesii	see *R. oreodoxa* var. *fargesii*
'Fashion'	SLdr
fastigiatum	GCrs LMil MBar NLAp NPen
- C&H 7159	GGGa
- SBEC 804/4869	GGGa MDun
§ - 'Blue Steel' ♀H4	CBcs CDoC COtt CWri GKir LMil LRHS MAsh MDun MGos NPen SPlb SPoG SReu WPat
'Fastuosum Flore Pleno' (d) ♀H4	CSBt CWri ENot GBin GGGa GKir ISea LHyd LKna LMil MBar MBri MDun MGos MLea NPen NWea SLdr SPoG SReu SSta WFar
§ ***faucium***	GGGa LMil NPen
- C&V 9508	GGGa
- KR 3465 from Pe, Doshang La	LMil
- KR 3771	LMil
- KR 5024	GGGa
- KR 5040	LMil
- KR 6229	LMil
- KW 6401	NPen
- SF 95098	ISea
aff. ***faucium*** KW 5732	NPen
'Favorite' (EA)	CTrw LHyd LKna LRHS NPen SCam SLdr
'Fedora' (EA)	CBcs LHyd LKna SLdr
'Fernanda Sarmento' (A)	SReu
ferrugineum	GGGa LKna LMil MBar MGos NPen SReu
* - ***compactum***	ECho
- 'Plenum' (d)	MDun
'Festive'	LHyd
'Feuerwerk' (K)	NEgg SLdr
fictolacteum	see *R. rex* subsp. *fictolacteum*
Fire Bird Group	LHyd SLdr
'Fire Rim'	GGGa
'Fireball' (K) ♀H4	CBcs CDoC CTri CWri GGGa LHyd LMil LRHS MAsh MLea NDlv SBrw SLdr
'Fireball' (hybrid)	GKir LRHS NPri SLdr
Firedrake Group	SReu
'Fireglow'	CSBt CSdC SLdr WFar
'Flaming Bronze'	SReu
'Flaming June' (K)	LKna
Flamingo Group	SLdr
§ ***flammeum*** (A)	LMil
'Flanagan's Daughter'	LMil LRHS MAsh
I Flava Group	see *R.* Volker Group
flavidum	CBcs GGGa LMil SLdr WAbe
- Cox 6143	GGGa
- 'Album'	LMil LRHS SLdr
§ 'Flavour'	LKna
fletcherianum	NPen
- 'Yellow Bunting'	GGGa
fleuryi KR 3286	GGGa
§ ***flinckii***	GGGa LHyd LMil LRHS MDun
- CH&M 3080	GGGa
floccigerum	GGGa LMil NPen SLdr
- bicolored	NPen
'Floradora' (M)	SReu
'Floriade'	LKna
floribundum	LMil LRHS NPen SLdr WCwm
- EGM 294	LMil
- 'Swinhoe'	SLdr
'Florida' (EA/d) ♀H3-4	CMac LKna LMil NBlu SBrw SLdr SReu WFar WMoo
'Flower Arranger' (EA)	LMil MAsh NPri SCoo
formosanum	GGGa
formosum	CBcs GGGa GQui NPen SLdr
§ - var. ***formosum*** Iteaphyllum Group	GGGa LMil
- - 'Khasia' C&H 320	GGGa
- var. ***inaequale*** C&H 301	GGGa
forrestii	GGGa NPen
- subsp. ***forrestii***	LMil
- - LS&T 5582	NPen
- - Repens Group	GGGa LMil SLdr
- - - 'Seinghku'	GGGa
- Tumescens Group	GGGa SLdr
- - C&V 9517	GGGa
Fortune Group	SLdr
fortunei	CBcs GGGa ISea LHyd LKna LMil MDun NPen SLdr SReu
§ - subsp. ***discolor*** ♀H4	GGGa LMil MDun NPen SLdr WGer
- - PW 34	GGGa
§ - - Houlstonii Group	LMil NPen SLdr
- - - 'John R. Elcock'	LMil
- subsp. ***discolor*** x 'Lodauric Iceberg'	SLdr
- 'Foxy'	SLdr
- 'Lu-Shan'	MDun
- 'Mrs Butler'	see *R. fortunei* 'Sir Charles Butler'
§ - 'Sir Charles Butler'	LMil LRHS MDun SLdr
'Fox Hunter'	LKna SLdr
fragariiflorum	ISea
- C&V 9519	GGGa
- LS&E 15828	GGGa
'Fragrans' **new**	SLdr
'Fragrant Star' (A)	GGGa
'Fragrantissimum' ♀H2-3	CBcs CDoC CTrw CWri GGGa ISea LHyd LMil MDun MRav NLar NPen SLdr WGer WPic
'Francesca'	GGGa
Francis Hanger (Reuthe's) Group	NPen SLdr SReu
'Frank Baum'	SReu
'Frank Galsworthy' ♀H4	LKna LMil NLar SReu
'Frans van der Bom' (M)	SLdr
'Fraseri' (M)	GGGa SLdr
'Fred Hamilton'	CWri
'Fred Nutbeam' (EA)	LMil
'Fred Peste'	GKir LMil MAsh MDun MGos MLea NPen SReu WBVN
'Fred Wynniatt'	CWri LHyd NPen SLdr
'Fred Wynniatt Stanway'	see *R.* 'Stanway'
'Frere Organ' (G)	SLdr
'Freya' (R/d)	LMil SLdr
'Fridoline' (EA)	GGGa
'Frieda' (EA) **new**	SLdr
'Frigate'	SLdr
'Frilled Petticoats'	SReu
'Frilly Lemon' (K/d)	CDoC MAsh MDun NLar SLdr
'Frome' (K)	LKna
'Frosted Orange' (EA)	LMil MAsh SLdr
'Frosthexe'	GGGa WAbe
§ 'Frühlingstraum'	LHyd
'Fudesute-yama' (EA) **new**	LHyd
'Fuko-hiko' (EA)	NPen

	Name	Suppliers
	'Fulbrook'	LHyd
	fulgens	GGGa LHyd LMil MDun NPen
	fulvum 🏆H4	CDoC GGGa IDee LHyd LMil LRHS MDun NPen SLdr SReu SSta
	- AC 3083	LMil
	- subsp. ***fulvoides***	LMil
	- - Cox 6532	GGGa
	'Fumiko' (EA)	SLdr
	'Furnivall's Daughter' 🏆H4	CSBt CWri ENot EPfP GGGa LHyd LKna LMil LRHS MBar MDun MGos NPen SLdr SReu SSta WFar
	'Fusilier'	LHyd SReu
	'Gabrielle Hill' (EA)	CDoC COtt ENot LMil MAsh SLdr
	'Gaiety' (EA)	LMil SReu
	'Galactic'	NPen SLdr
	galactinum	LMil MDun
	- EN 3537	GGGa
	'Galathea' (EA)	CDoC
	'Gandy Dancer'	CWri MBri MDun NPen SLdr WBVN
	'Garden State Glow' (EA/d)	SLdr
	'Gartendirektor Glocker'	CWri GGGa MDun MLea NPen SLdr
	'Gartendirektor Rieger' 🏆H4	CWri GGGa LMil MDun SReu
	'Gauche' (A)	GQui SLdr
	'Gaugin'	GQui
	Gaul Group	SLdr
	'Gauntlettii' x ***thomsonii***	SLdr
	'Gay Lady'	SLdr
	'Geisha' (EA)	MBar
	'Geisha Lilac' (EA)	COtt ECho GKir LMil LRHS MBar MDun MLea NDlv
§	'Geisha Orange' (EA) 🏆H4	COtt CTbh CTrh EGra GGGa GKir LMil LRHS MAsh MBar MDun MGos MLea NBlu NDlv NPri SLdr
	'Geisha Purple' (EA)	COtt CSBt CTbh ENot LMil MBar MDun MLea NBlu WFar
	'Geisha Red' (EA)	COtt ENot EPfP LMil MAsh MBar MDun MLea NBlu NDlv WFar
	Geisha White = 'Hisako' (EA)	MDun MLea NDlv
	'Gekkeikan' (EA)	CBcs
	'Gena Mae' (A/d)	GGGa LMil SLdr
	'General Eisenhower'	CSBt SReu
	'General Eric Harrison'	LHyd SLdr
	'General Practitioner'	NPen SLdr
	'General Sir John du Cane'	NPen
	'General Wavell' (EA)	CMac LKna SLdr
	'Gene's Favourite'	SReu
	genestierianum CC&H 8080	GGGa
	'Genghis Khan'	NPen
	'Genoveva' **new**	LMil
	'Geoffroy Millais'	LMil
	'Georg Arends' (EA)	NPri
	'Georg Arends'	SLdr
	'George Haslam'	SLdr
	'George Hyde' (EA)	ENot LMil MAsh NPri SCoo
	'George Reynolds' (K)	LHyd SLdr
	'George's Delight'	CWri GGGa MLea WMoo
	'Georgette'	LHyd SLdr
§	x ***geraldii***	SLdr
	'Germania'	LMil MAsh MBar
	Gertrud Schäle Group	CTri GEdr MBar MDun SReu
	Gibraltar Group	CTri
	'Gibraltar' (K) 🏆H4	CBcs CDoC CSBt CWri ENot EPfP GGGa GKir LKna LMil LRHS MAsh MBar MBri MGos NBlu NPri SBrw SLdr SReu SSta WFar
	giganteum	see *R. protistum* var. *giganteum*
	'Gilbert Mullie' (EA)	MBri NBlu
I	'Gill's Arboreum' **new**	SLdr
	'Gill's Crimson' **new**	SLdr
	'Ginger' (K)	CSBt CWri EPfP LMil LRHS MAsh SLdr
	'Ginny Gee' 🏆H4	CDoC COtt CSBt CTrh CWri ENot EPfP GGGa GGar GKir LHyd LMil LRHS MAsh MBar MBri MDun MGos MLea NMen NPen NPri SLdr SPoG SReu SSta WAbe WFar WOrn
§	'Girard's Hot Shot' (EA)	CTrh ECho ENot GQui MGos SLdr SReu WFar
	'Girard's Hot Shot' variegated (EA/v)	GGGa MAsh NMyG
	'Glacier' (EA)	MGos SLdr
	'Glamora' (EA)	SLdr
	glanduliferum	LRHS
	- C&H 7131	GGGa
	- EGM 347	LMil
	- PW 044 from Miao Miao Shan	LMil
	glaucophyllum	GGGa LHyd LMil MDun NPen SLdr WAbe
	- B&SWJ 2638	WCru
	- var. ***album***	GGGa
	- Borde Hill form	LMil
§	- subsp. ***tubiforme***	NPen
	'Glendoick Butterscotch'	GGGa
	'Glendoick Crimson' (EA)	GGGa
	'Glendoick Dream' (EA)	GGGa
	'Glendoick Ermine' (EA)	GGGa
	'Glendoick Garnet' (EA)	GGGa
	'Glendoick Glacier'	GGGa
	'Glendoick Goblin' (EA)	GGGa
	'Glendoick Gold'	GGGa
	'Glendoick Honeydew' **new**	GGGa
	'Glendoick Mystique' **new**	GGGa
	'Glendoick Ruby'	GGGa
	'Glendoick Vanilla'	GGGa
	'Glendoick Velvet'	GGGa
	'Glen's Orange'	CWri
	'Gletschernacht'	CWri LMil
	glischrum	GGGa NPen
	- subsp. ***glischroides***	GGGa LMil NPen
	- subsp. ***glischrum***	GGGa LMil
§	- subsp. ***rude***	GGGa LMil NPen
	- - C&V 9524	GGGa
	globigerum	see *R. alutaceum* var. *alutaceum* Globigerum Group
	'Glockenspiel' (K/d)	LKna SLdr
	'Gloria'	see *R.* 'Bruns Gloria'
	'Gloria Mundi' (G)	WFar
	'Glory of Littleworth' (Ad)	LMil
	'Glowing Embers' (K)	CDoC CTri CWri ENot GKir LMil LRHS MAsh MBri MDun MLea NPri SLdr SPur SReu WBVN WFar WOrn
	Goblin Group	SLdr
	'Gog' (K)	CSBt LKna
	'Gold Crest' (K)	LKna
	'Gold Dust' (K)	SBrw SLdr
	'Gold Mohur'	SLdr SReu
	'Gold Tee' **new**	LHyd
	'Goldball'	see *R.* 'Christopher Wren'
§	'Goldbukett'	GGGa LHyd LMil LRHS MGos
	'Golden Bee'	GGGa
	'Golden Belle'	CWri
	Golden Bouquet	see *R.* 'Goldbukett'
	'Golden Clipper'	LHyd
	'Golden Coach'	COtt CWri ISea MDun MGos MLea SLdr WBVN

	Name	Suppliers
	'Golden Eagle' (K)	CDoC CDul COtt GKir LHyd LMil MAsh MDun MGos NEgg SBrw SCoo SLdr WBVN WOrn
	'Golden Eye' (K)	LKna SLdr
	'Golden Flare' (K)	CBcs CDoC MAsh MLea NBlu SLdr SPer WBrE WMoo
	'Golden Fleece'	LKna SReu
	'Golden Gate'	CDoC MDun NPen WGor WOrn
	'Golden Horn' (K)	GQui MAsh SLdr WGor
	'Golden Horn Persimmon'	see *R.* 'Persimmon'
	'Golden Lights' (A)	CDoC CWri GKir LMil LRHS MBri MDun MGos NPri SBod WBVN
	'Golden Orfe'	LHyd
	Golden Oriole Group	CBcs
§	- 'Talavera'	CBcs
	'Golden Oriole'	LKna
	'Golden Princess'	COtt LMil MDun
	'Golden Ruby'	MBri
	'Golden Splendour'	LMil
	'Golden Sunset' (K)	COtt CSdC LHyd MBar MBri MDun MLea NEgg SBrw SLdr SPur WFar
	'Golden Torch' ♀H4	CAbP CBcs CMHG COtt CSBt CTbh CWri ENot EPfP GGGa GKir LHyd LMil LRHS MAsh MDun MGos MLea NDlv NPen SHBN SLdr SPer SPoG SReu SSta WBVN WOrn
	'Golden Wedding'	CBcs CSBt CWri ENot LHyd LMil MDun MGos MLea NLar SLdr WBVN
	'Golden Wit'	ECho MDun SLdr
	'Goldfinch' (K)	LKna
	'Goldfinger'	MDun
	'Goldflimmer' (v)	CAlb EMil ENot GGGa GKir LMil LRHS MAsh MGos MLan MLea NBlu NPri SLdr SPoG SReu WFar
	'Goldfort'	CWri LKna SBrw SReu
	'Goldika'	LMil
	'Goldkrone' ♀H4	CDoC CWri ENot EPfP GGGa LHyd LMil MBri MDun MGos MLea NLar NPen SBod SLdr SPoG SReu WBVN WOrn
	Goldschatz = 'Goldprinz'	GGGa
	'Goldstrike'	LMil SLdr
	'Goldsworth Crimson'	LHyd
	'Goldsworth Orange'	CSBt GGGa LKna MGos NPen SBrw SLdr SReu
	'Goldsworth Pink'	LKna SReu
	'Goldsworth Yellow'	CSBt LKna MGos SBrw SLdr SReu
	'Golfer'	GGGa LMil
	'Gomer Waterer' ♀H4	CDoC CSBt CSam CWri ENot EPfP GGGa GKir LHyd LKna LMil MBar MBri MDun MGos MLea NPen NWea SLdr SPer SReu SSta WBVN WFar
	'Good News'	SLdr
	'Gorbella'	WFar
	'Gordon Jones'	GGGa
	'Govenianum' (Ad)	LKna SLdr
	'Grace Seabrook'	CDoC COtt CSam CTri CWri ENot GGGa GKir LHyd LRHS MAsh MDun MGos NPri SLdr SPer SReu WBVN WOrn
	gracilentum (V)	GGGa
	'Graciosum' (O)	LKna SReu
	'Graf Lennart'	LMil
	'Graham Thomas'	LMil SReu
	'Grand Slam'	MDun NPen WBVN
	grande	GGGa NPen SLdr
	- KC 0105	GGGa
	- pink	NPen
	'Grandeur Triomphante' (G)	CSdC SReu

	Name	Suppliers
	gratum	see *R. basilicum*
	'Graziella'	GGGa
	'Greensleeves'	LKna LMil
	'Greenway' (EA)	CBcs SLdr
	'Gretia'	LHyd
	'Gretzel'	NLar SReu
	griersonianum	CBcs GGGa LHyd LMil MDun WPic
	griffithianum	CWri GGGa SLdr
	'Grilse'	LHyd
	'Gristede' ♀H4	CDoC GGGa LMil MDun SLdr SReu
	groenlandicum	see *Ledum groenlandicum*
	'Grosclaude'	NPen
	'Grouse' x ***keiskei*** var. ***ozawae*** 'Yaku Fairy'	ECho
	'Grumpy'	CBrm CDoC CSBt CWri ENot GGGa GKir LHyd LMil LRHS MBar MGos NDlv NPen SHBN SLdr SReu
	'Guelder Rose'	SLdr
§	'Gumpo' (EA)	CMac EPot SLdr
	'Gumpo Pink' (EA)	SLdr
	'Gumpo White' (EA)	ENot MAsh
	'Gwenda' (EA)	SLdr
	'Gwillt-king'	WCwm
	'H.H. Hume' (EA)	SLdr
	habrotrichum	GGGa LMil NPen
	'Hachmann's Brasilia'	MAsh MBri
	'Hachmann's Charmant'	GGGa LMil MBri
	'Hachmann's Constanze' **new**	LMil
	'Hachmann's Diadem'	LMil
	'Hachmann's Feuerschein'	LMil
	'Hachmann's Kabarett'	LMil
	'Hachmann's Marlis' ♀H4	ENot LHyd LMil SReu
§	'Hachmann's Polaris' ♀H4	LHyd LMil MDun
	'Hachmann's Porzellan'	LMil
§	'Hachmann's Rokoko' (EA)	ECho GGGa LMil
	haematodes	GGGa LHyd LMil MDun NPen SRms
	- AC 710	NPen
	- CLD 1283	LMil
	- 'Blood Red'	SLdr
§	- subsp. ***chaetomallum***	GGGa LMil NPen SLdr
	- - JN 493	GGGa
	- subsp. ***haemotodes***	LMil
	- - SBEC 585	GGGa
	'Haida Gold'	MLea SLdr SReu
	'Halfdan Lem'	CBcs CDoC GGGa MBri MDun MGos MLea NPen SHBN SLdr SPer SReu SSta WOrn
	'Hamlet' (M)	LMil
	'Hammondii' (Ad)	LKna
	'Hana-asobi' (EA)	LHyd LRHS SCam SLdr
	hanceanum	SLdr
	- 'Canton Consul'	GGGa LHyd
	- Nanum Group	GGGa
	'Hanger's Flame' (A) **new**	SLdr
	'Hansel'	CDoC CWri LMil MAsh MDun NLar SLdr
§	***haofui*** Guiz 75	GGGa
	Happy Group	SHBN
§	'Hardijzer Beauty' (Ad)	LKna LRHS SLdr SReu
	hardingii	see *R. annae* Hardingii Group
	hardyi	see *R. augustinii* subsp. *hardyi*
	'Harkwood Premiere'	GGGa
	'Harkwood Red' (EA)	CTrh LHyd SCam SLdr
	Harmony Group	SLdr
	'Harry Tagg'	SLdr WPic
	'Harumiji' (EA)	SLdr
	'Harvest Moon' (K)	MDun SCoo SReu

	'Harvest Moon' (hybrid)	MBar SBrw SReu
	'Hatsugiri' (EA)	CMac ENot EPfP LHyd LKna LMil MBar SCam SLdr SReu
	(Hawk Group) 'Hawk Buzzard'	SLdr
§	- 'Hawk Falcon'	SReu
	'Heather Macleod' (EA)	LHyd SLdr
	heatheriae KR 6150	GGGa
	- KR 6158	GGGa
	- SF 99068	ISea
	heftii	NPen SLdr
	'Helen Close' (EA)	CTrh SCam SLdr
	'Helen Curtis' (EA)	SReu
	'Helen Martin'	NLar
	'Helena Pratt' (Vs)	LMil
	'Helene Schiffner' ♀H4	GGGa LMil SReu
	heliolepis	GGGa LMil
	- AC 759	NPen
	- SF 489	ISea
	- SF 516	ISea
	- var. ***fumidum***	see *R. heliolepis* var. *heliolepis*
§	- var. ***heliolepis***	LMil
	- - CN&W 1038	ISea
	x ***hemigynum***	NPen
	hemsleyanum	GGGa GTSp LMil MDun NPen SLdr
	hemsleyanum x ***ungernii***	GGGa
	heptamerum	see *R. degronianum* subsp. *heptamerum*
	'Herbert' (EA)	CMac
	'Heureuse Surprise' (G)	SLdr
	'High Summer'	LMil WGer
	'Hilda Margaret'	SReu
	'Hilda Niblett' (EA) **new**	ENot
	'Hille'PBR	LMil
	'Hino-crimson' (EA) ♀H3-4	CDoC CMac CSBt CTrh CTri ENot LKna LMil LRHS MAsh MBar MBri MGos SCam SLdr SPer SReu SSta WFar
	'Hinode-giri' (EA)	CBcs CMac CSBt CTrw LHyd LKna SCam SLdr SReu WFar WPic
	'Hinode-no-kumo' (EA)	SLdr
	'Hinode-no-taka' (EA) **new**	LHyd
N	'Hinomayo' (EA) ♀H3-4	CMac CSBt EPfP GQui LHyd LKna LMil LRHS MAsh MBar NPen SCam SLdr SReu SSta WPic
	'Hino-scarlet'	see *R.* 'Campfire'
	'Hino-tsukasa' (EA)	SLdr
	hippophaeoides	CDoC EPfP LMil MDun NMen NPen SLdr WAbe WFar
	- F 22197a	SLdr
	- Yu 13845	GGGa LMil MDun
	- 'Bei-ma-shan'	see *R. hippophaeoides* 'Haba Shan'
	- 'Glendoick Iceberg'	GGGa
§	- 'Haba Shan' ♀H4	GGGa LMil MDun
§	- var. ***hippophaeoides*** Fimbriatum Group	WThu
	hirsutum	GGGa LHyd LMil SReu WPat
	- f. ***albiflorum***	GGGa SReu
	- 'Flore Pleno' (d)	ECho EPot GCrs GGGa MBar MDun MLea
	hirtipes	GGGa LMil
	- C&V 9546	GGGa
	- KR 5059	LMil
	- KR 5219	LMil
	- KW 6223	NPen
	- LS&T 3624	NPen
	hodgsonii	GGGa IDee LHyd LMil LRHS MDun NPen SLdr SReu WGer
	- B&SWJ 2656	WCru
	- LS&H 21296	NPen

	- TSS 9	SLdr
	- TSS 42A	SLdr
	- 'Poet's Lawn'	NPen
	'Holden'	WFar
	'Hollandia' (hybrid)	SHBN
	'Homebush' (K/d) ♀H4	CBcs CDoC CDul CTri CWri ENot EPfP GGGa GKir LHyd LKna LMil MAsh MBar MBri MDun MLea SBrw SLdr SReu SSta WBVN
	'Honey'	LKna SBrw
	'Honeysuckle' (K)	MBar SLdr SReu
	'Hong Kong'	MAsh
	hongkongense	GGGa NPen
§	'Ho-o' (EA)	CBcs NEgg NLar SLdr
	hookeri	LHyd LMil NPen SReu
	- Tigh-na-Rudha form	GGGa
	'Hope Findlay'	LHyd
	'Hoppy'	CDoC CSBt CWri ENot GKir GWCH LMil LRHS MDun MGos MLea NBlu NPen SLdr SPoG SReu WBVN WCwm WOrn
	'Horizon Lakeside'	GGGa LMil
	'Horizon Monarch' ♀H3-4	CWri GGGa LMil LRHS MDun
	horlickianum	GGGa
	'Hortulanus H. Witte' (M)	CSBt SLdr SReu WFar
	'Hot Shot'	see *R.* 'Girard's Hot Shot'
	'Hotei' ♀H4	CBcs CDoC CSBt CSam CTri CWri GEdr GGGa GKir LHyd LMil LRHS MAsh MBar MDun MGos NPen NPri SHBN SReu SSta WFar
	Hotspur Group (K)	GGGa LHyd SCoo
	'Hotspur' (K)	CSBt CTri CWri GKir MGos SLdr
	'Hotspur Red' (K) ♀H4	CDoC GKir LKna LMil SBrw SReu WOrn
	'Hotspur Yellow' (K)	SReu
	houlstonii	see *R. fortunei* subsp. *discolor* Houlstonii Group
	huanum	LMil
	- C&H 7073	GGGa
	- EGM 316	LMil
	'Hugh Koster'	CSBt LKna MGos SLdr
	'Humboldt'	WFar
	Humming Bird Group	CMHG CSam GGGa ISea LHyd LKna MBar MDun MLea SHBN SLdr SReu SRms
	hunnewellianum **new**	NPen
	- 'Crane'	GGGa
	'Hurricane'	COtt MDun SLdr
	'Hussar'	CWri
	'Hyde and Seek'	GQui
	'Hydie' (EA/d)	ENot LMil MAsh MGos NPri SCoo
	'Hydon Amethyst'	LHyd
	'Hydon Ball'	LHyd
	'Hydon Ben'	LHyd
	'Hydon Comet'	LHyd
	'Hydon Dawn' ♀H4	CDoC COtt CWri GGGa GKir LHyd LMil LRHS MAsh MDun MGos MLea NDlv NLar NPen SLdr SReu SSta
	'Hydon Glow'	LHyd
	'Hydon Gold'	LHyd
	'Hydon Haley'	LHyd
	'Hydon Hunter' ♀H4	COtt ISea LHyd LMil MAsh MLea NDlv NPen SLdr SPer SReu SSta
	'Hydon Juliet'	LHyd
	'Hydon Mist'	LHyd
	'Hydon Pearl'	LHyd
	'Hydon Primrose'	LHyd
	'Hydon Rodney'	LHyd
	'Hydon Salmon'	LHyd
	'Hydon Velvet'	LHyd SReu
	hylaeum	NPen
	- BASEX 9659	GGGa

	Name	Suppliers
	- KW 6833	NPen
	Hyperion Group	LKna LMil SReu SSta WFar
	hyperythrum	GGGa LHyd LMil MDun SLdr SSpi
	- ETOT 196	MDun
	hypoglaucum	see *R. argyrophyllum* subsp. *hypoglaucum*
	- 'Heane Wood'	see *R. argyrophyllum* subsp. *hypoglaucum* 'Heane Wood'
	'Ice Cream'	LKna
	'Ice Cube'	ISea MDun MLea NLar WBVN WOrn
	'Ice Maiden'	SReu
	'Iceberg'	see *R.* 'Lodauric Iceberg'
	'Icecream Flavour'	see *R.* 'Flavour'
	'Icecream Vanilla'	see *R.* 'Vanilla'
	'Idealist'	SReu
	'Ightham Gold'	SReu
	'Ightham Peach'	SReu
	'Ightham Purple'	SReu
	'Ightham Yellow'	NPen SLdr SReu
	'Igneum Novum' (G)	SReu
	'Il Tasso' (R/d)	SLdr
§	'Ilam Melford Lemon' (A)	LMil
§	'Ilam Ming' (A)	LMil
	'Ilam Violet'	LHyd LKna LMil
	'Imago' (K/d)	CSdC LKna MBri SLdr
§	'Ima-shojo' (EA/d)	CSBt LHyd LMil SCam SLdr
	'Impala' (K)	LKna
	impeditum	CBcs CDoC CSBt CWib ENot GGGa GQui ISea LHyd LKna MAsh MBar MDun MGos MLea NLAp NMen NPen NWea SLdr SPer SReu SSta WBVN WFar
	- F 29268	GGGa
	- 'Blue Steel'	see *R. fastigiatum* 'Blue Steel'
	- dark, compact	LKna
	- 'Indigo'	CMHG MAsh MDun WAbe
	- 'Johnston's Impeditum'	LKna
	- 'Pygmaeum'	WAbe
	- Reuthe's form	SReu
	- 'Williams'	SLdr
	imperator	see *R. uniflorum* var. *imperator*
	'Impi'	SReu
	Impi Group	LKna MDun NLar NPen
	'Inamorata'	SLdr
§	***indicum*** (EA)	GIBF WBVN
§	- 'Balsaminiflorum' (EA/d)	CMac SLdr WAbe
	- 'Macranthum' (EA) **new**	LHyd
	- orange (EA)	SLdr
	x ***inopinum***	GGGa
	insigne ♀H4	GGGa GTSp IDee LHyd LMil MDun NPen WGer
	- Reuthe's form	SReu
	insigne x ***yakushimanum***	SReu
	x ***intermedium*** white	GGGa
	Intrepid Group	SReu
	intricatum	GGGa WAbe
	Intrifast Group	GGGa LHyd NMen SLdr
	iodes	see *R. alutaceum* var. *iodes*
	'Irene Koster' (O) ♀H4	CSBt CWri EPfP GGGa LHyd LKna LMil MBri MDun MLea NLar SLdr SReu
	'Irohayama' (EA) ♀H3-4	CMac CTrw GQui LHyd LKna LMil SCam SLdr SReu
	irroratum	LMil NPen SLdr
	- C&H 7185	GGGa
	- CN&W 392	WCwm
	- CN&W 395	WCwm
	- SF 384	ISea
	- SF 92304	ISea
	- subsp. ***irroratum*** C&H 7100	GGGa
*	- subsp. ***kontumense*** var. ***ningyuenense*** EGM 339	LMil
	- 'Langbianense' KR 3295	LMil
	- pale pink	NPen
	- 'Polka Dot'	GGGa LHyd LMil NPen SLdr
	'Isabel Pierce'	CWri LMil
	Isabella Group **new**	WFar
	'Isabella Mangles'	LHyd
	'Isola Bella'	GGGa
	iteaphyllum	see *R. formosum* var. *formosum* Iteaphyllum Group
	'Ivette' (EA)	CMac LHyd LKna
	Iviza Group	SReu
	'Ivory Coast'	LMil
	'J.C. Williams'	CBcs
	'J.G. Millais'	SLdr
	'J.M. de Montague'	see *R.* 'The Hon. Jean Marie de Montague'
	'J.R.R. Tolkien'	SLdr
	'Jabberwocky'	LHyd
	'Jack Skilton'	LHyd SLdr
	'Jacksonii'	ISea LKna MBar NPen SLdr SReu
	Jacquetta Group **new**	WPic
	Jalisco Group	NPen SLdr
	'Jalisco Eclipse'	LKna
	'Jalisco Elect'	CDoC CWri LKna LMil NPen SLdr SPer WCwm
	'Jalisco Goshawk'	SLdr
	'Jalisco Janet'	NPen SLdr
	'James Barto'	LHyd SLdr
	'James Burchett' ♀H4	LKna LMil NLar SLdr SPoG SReu
	'James Gable' (EA)	SLdr
	'Jan Bee'	SLdr
	'Jan Dekens'	SReu
	'Jan Steen' (M)	SLdr
	'Jane Abbott' (A)	GGGa
	'Janet Blair'	CDoC CWri ISea MDun SLdr WBVN
	'Janet Ward'	LHyd LKna SReu
	'Janine Alexandre Debray'	SLdr
	japonicum (A. Gray) Valcken	see *R. molle* subsp. *japonicum*
	japonicum Schneider var. ***japonicum***	see *R. degronianum* subsp. *heptamerum*
	- var. ***pentamerum***	see *R. degronianum* subsp. *degronianum*
	'Jason'	SLdr
	javanicum (V)	GGGa
	'Jazz Band' (V)	GGGa
	'Jean Marie Montague'	see *R.* 'The Hon. Jean Marie de Montague'
	'Jeanette' (EA)	LKna
	'Jeff Hill' (EA)	ECho LRHS SLdr SReu
	'Jennie Dosser'	LMil
	'Jenny'	see *R.* 'Creeping Jenny'
	'Jeremy Davies'	SReu
§	'Jervis Bay'	SReu
	'Jingle Bells'	GGGa NLar
	'Joan Paton' (A)	SLdr
	Jock Group	CBcs CMHG CTrw
	'Jock Brydon' (O)	GGGa LMil SLdr
	'Jock Coutts' (K)	CSdC LKna
	'Johanna' (EA) ♀H4	CDoC CTri EBee GGGa GKir LMil LRHS MAsh MBar NPri SLdr SPer SReu
	'John Barr Stevenson'	LHyd
	'John Cairns' (EA)	CMac LHyd LKna MBar SCam SLdr WPic
	'John Walter'	MBar SLdr
	'John Waterer'	CSBt LKna WFar
	'Johnny Bender'	SLdr
	johnstoneanum	CBcs GGGa LMil NPen SLdr

	- 'Double Diamond' (d)	CBcs LMil
	'Jolie Madame' (Vs)	CWri LMil SLdr SPur SReu
	'Jonathan Shaw'	GGGa LMil SPoG
	'Josefa Blue'	GGGa
	'Joseph Baumann' (G)	CSdC SLdr
	'Joseph Hill' (EA)	ECho SReu WPat
	'Josephine Klinger' (G)	CSdC SReu
	'Joy's Delight' (Ad)	LKna
	'Jubilant'	SLdr
	'Jubilee'	LKna SLdr
	Jubilee Queen Group	SLdr
	'June Bee'	GGGa
	'June Fire' (A)	SReu
	'June Yellow'	GGGa
	'Jungfrau'	CWri
	kaempferi (EA)	GGGa LMil SLdr
	- 'Damio'	see *R. kaempferi* 'Mikado'
§	- 'Mikado' (EA)	LMil SReu
	'Kalinka'	ENot GKir LHyd LMil LRHS MAsh MDun MGos SPoG
	'Kaponga'	MGos
	'Karen Triplett'	LMil
	'Karin'	COtt MDun SHBN SLdr
	'Karin Seleger'	GGGa
	'Kasane-kagaribi' (EA)	LHyd
	'Kate Waterer' ♀H4	CWri LKna MBar MGos MLan SReu WFar
N	'Kathleen' (A)	SLdr
	'Kathleen' van Nes (EA) **new**	LHyd
	'Kathleen' rosy red (EA)	LKna
	'Katisha' (EA)	LHyd SLdr
	'Katy Watson'	SReu
	kawakamii (V)	GGGa
	'Keija'	SReu
	keiskei	LHyd
	- compact	SLdr
	- Cordifolium Group	WAbe
	- 'Ebino'	WAbe
	- var. ***ozawae*** 'Yaku Fairy' ♀H4	GGGa ITim LMil LRHS MDun SOkd WAbe
	keleticum	see *R. calostrotum* subsp. *keleticum*
§	'Ken Janeck'	GGGa NLar
§	***kendrickii***	GGGa MDun
	- MH 62	GGGa
	'Kentucky Colonel'	SLdr
	'Kentucky Minstrel' (K)	SLdr
	'Kermesinum' (EA)	COtt CTri GGGa LMil MBar SLdr SPlb SReu WPat
I	'Kermesinum Album' (EA)	LMil MBar MGos SLdr SReu
I	'Kermesinum Rosé' (EA)	CSBt GGGa LMil MBar MDun NBlu SLdr SReu
	kesangiae	MDun
	- AC 110	NPen SLdr
	- CH&M 3058	GGGa
	- CH&M 3099	GGGa
	- var. ***kesangiae*** KR 1136	NPen
	aff. ***kesangiae*** KR 1640	MDun NPen
	Kewense Group	LHyd
	keysii	CBcs GGGa LHyd LMil MDun SLdr
	- CER 9906	GGGa
	- EGM 064	LMil
	- KC 0112	GGGa
	- KC 0115	GGGa
	'Kilimanjaro'	GGGa LHyd LMil SReu
	Kilimanjaro Group	LMil SSta
	'Kimberly'	GGGa
	'Kimbeth'	GGGa
	'Kimigayo' (EA)	LHyd
	'King George' Loder	see *R.* 'Loderi King George'
	'King George' van Nes	SReu
	'King of Shrubs'	NLar
	kingianum	see *R. arboreum* subsp. *zeylanicum*
	'Kings Ride'	LHyd
	'Kingston'	MDun
§	'Kirin' (EA/d)	CMac CSBt CTbh CTrw LHyd LKna LRHS SLdr WPat
	'Kirishima' (EA)	LKna SRms
	'Kiritsubo' (EA)	LHyd
	'Kitty Cole'	SLdr
	kiusianum (EA) ♀H4	GGGa LHyd NPen SReu SRms WAbe
	- 'Album' (EA)	LHyd LMil SReu WAbe
	- 'Hillier's Pink' (EA)	LMil
	- var. ***kiusianum*** 'Mountain Gem' (EA)	LRHS
	'Kiwi Majic'	LMil MBri MDun
	'Klondyke' (K) ♀H4	CBcs CSBt CTri ENot EPfP GGGa GKir LMil LRHS MAsh MBri MDun MGos NPri SBrw SLdr SReu
	'Kluis Sensation' ♀H4	CBcs CSBt LKna MDun NPen NWea SHBN SLdr SReu
	'Kluis Triumph'	LKna SReu
	'Knap Hill Apricot' (K)	LKna LMil
	'Knap Hill Red' (K)	CDoC LKna LMil WMoo
	'Knap Hill White' (K)	CSdC
	'Kobold' (EA)	SLdr
	'Koichiro Wada'	see *R. yakushimanum* 'Koichiro Wada'
	'Kokardia'	CDoC LMil SLdr
	kongboense	GGGa LMil
	- C&V 9540	GGGa
	- KR 5689	LMil
	aff. ***kongboense*** KR 3725	LMil
	'Königstein' (EA) **new**	LMil
§	'Koningin Emma' (M)	LMil NLar SLdr
§	'Koningin Wilhelmina' (M)	SLdr
	konori var. ***phaeopeplum*** (V)	GGGa
	'Koster's Brilliant Red' (M)	CSBt ENot EPfP LMil SReu
	kotschyi	see *R. myrtifolium*
	'Kralingen'	NLar
	'Kupferberg'	GGGa
§	'Kure-no-yuki' (EA/d)	CSBt EPfP LHyd LKna LMil MAsh SCam SLdr
$	'Lackblatt'	see *R.* (Volker Group) 'Lackblatt'
	lacteum	LMil MDun NPen SLdr
	- AC 928	LMil
	- CN&W 936	LMil
	- EGM 356 from Wumenshan	LMil
	- KR 2760	GGGa
	- SBEC 345	GGGa
	- SF 374	ISea
	- bright yellow-flowered	NPen
	'Lady Adam Gordon'	SLdr
	'Lady Alice Fitzwilliam' ♀H2-3	CBcs CDoC CEnd CMHG GGGa IDee ISea LHyd LMil WGer
	'Lady Annette de Trafford'	LKna
	'Lady Armstrong'	CSBt
	Lady Bessborough Group	SLdr
	'Lady Bowes Lyon'	LHyd SLdr
	Lady Chamberlain Group	GGGa NPen SLdr
	'Lady Chamberlain Salmon Trout'	see *R.* 'Salmon Trout'
	'Lady Clementine Mitford' ♀H4	CDoC CSBt CWri ENot EPfP GGGa LHyd LKna LMil MBri MGos MLea NPen NWea SHBN SLdr SPoG SReu
	'Lady Decies'	SReu
	'Lady Digby'	CWri
	'Lady Eleanor Cathcart'	EPfP LKna NPen SLdr
	'Lady Elphinstone' (EA)	SLdr
	'Lady Grey Egerton'	LKna
	'Lady Longman'	LHyd

	Name	Suppliers
	'Lady Louise' (EA)	SLdr
	'Lady Primrose'	SReu
	'Lady Robin' (EA)	SLdr
	'Lady Romsey'	LMil NPen
	'Lady Rosebery' (K)	CSdC MDun
	Lady Rosebery Group	MLea
	Ladybird Group	LMil SReu
	laetum (V)	GGGa
	Lamellen Group	LHyd SLdr
	'Lampion'	GGGa
	'Lamplighter'	SLdr SReu
	lanatoides	LMil
	- C&C 7548	GGGa
	- C&C 7574	GGGa
	- C&C 7577	GGGa
	- KR 6385	LMil
	lanatum	LMil NPen
	- dwarf, cream-flowered	GGGa
	- Flinckii Group	see *R. flinckii*
	'Langmans' (EA)	LKna
	'Langworth'	CWri ECho LKna LMil MDun MLea SLdr SReu
	lanigerum	LMil MDun NPen SReu
	- C&V 9530	GGGa
	- KW 8251	GGGa
	- pink-flowered	NPen
	- red-flowered	NPen
	- 'Round Wood'	LHyd
	lapidosum	GGGa
	lapponicum Confertissimum Group	GGGa
	- Parvifolium Group from Kamchatka **new**	GIBF
	- - from Siberia	GGGa WAbe
	'Lapwing' (K)	LKna SLdr
	'Lascaux'	SReu
	'Late Love' (EA)	CDoC MGos
	late pink from Inverewe	WBVN WMoo
*	***laterifolium***	GGGa
§	***latoucheae*** (EA)	SSpi
	- PW 86	GGGa
	laudandum var. ***temoense***	GGGa
	Laura Aberconway Group	SLdr
	'Laura Morland' (EA)	LHyd
	'Lava Flow'	LHyd
	'Lavender Girl' ♀H4	GGGa LHyd LKna LMil NLar NPen SLdr SPoG SReu SSta
	'Lavender Queen'	CWri ENot SLdr
	'Lavendula'	GGGa LMil
	'Le Progrès'	LMil MAsh SReu WGer
	'Lea Rainbow'	MLea
	'Ledifolium'	see *R.* x *mucronatum*
	'Ledifolium Album'	see *R.* x *mucronatum*
	'Lee's Dark Purple'	CDoC CSBt CWri LMil MBar NPri NWea WFar
	'Lee's Scarlet'	LKna LMil SLdr
*	'Lemon Drop' (A)	GGGa
	'Lemon Lights' (A)	MAsh
	'Lemonora' (M)	LMil SLdr
	'Lem's 45'	CWri MDun SLdr
	'Lem's Cameo' ♀H3	GGGa LHyd LMil NPen SPoG SReu SSta
	'Lem's Monarch' ♀H4	CBcs CDoC CWri GGGa LHyd LMil MBri MDun MGos MLea SLdr SReu SSta WBVN
	'Lem's Tangerine'	LMil SPoG
	'Lemur' (EA)	GGGa MAsh MDun MLea NLar SReu WPat
	'Leni'	GKir LRHS MAsh
	'Leo' (EA)	GQui LHyd LKna LRHS NPen SCam SLdr
	'Leo' (hybrid)	EPfP LRHS
	'Leonardslee Giles'	SLdr
	'Leonardslee Primrose'	SLdr
	Leonore Group	SReu
	lepidostylum	CBcs CDoC CWri GGGa LHyd LMil LRHS MBar MDun NLAp NPen SLdr SReu WFar
	lepidotum	GGGa MDun WAbe
	- Elaeagnoides Group	GGGa
	- purple-flowered EN 6280	LMil
	- yellow-flowered	ITim
	- - McB 110	WThu
§	***leptocarpum***	GGGa LMil
	leptothrium	GGGa NPen WAbe
	Letty Edwards Group	CSBt LKna SLdr SReu
§	'Leucanthum'	GGGa
	leucaspis	GGGa LHyd MDun NPen SLdr SReu
	'Leverett Richards'	SReu
	levinei	GGGa
	'Lila Pedigo'	COtt CWri GGGa ISea MAsh MDun MLea SLdr WBVN WFar
	'Lilac Time' (EA)	MBar SLdr
	'Lilacinum' (EA)	WPic
	liliiflorum Guiz 163	GGGa
	'Lilliput' (EA)	MAsh
	'Lily Marleen' (EA)	CTri LRHS SCoo SReu
	'Linda' ♀H4	CDoC CSam CTri GGGa LMil LRHS MAsh MBar MDun MGos NBlu SLdr
	lindleyi	CBcs GQui LHyd LMil
	- L&S	GGGa
	- 'Dame Edith Sitwell'	LMil
	'Linearifolium'	see *R. stenopetalum* 'Linearifolium'
	'Linnet' (K/d)	LKna
	Lionel's Triumph Group	LMil NPen SLdr
	'Little Beauty' (EA)	SCam SLdr
	'Little Ben'	ECho MBar MDun NDlv
	'Loch Earn'	GGGa
	'Loch Leven'	GGGa
	'Loch Lomond' **new**	GGGa
	'Loch o' the Lowes'	GGGa LHyd LMil MBri MDun MGos MLea NPen SLdr
	'Loch Rannoch'	GGGa GKir LMil MGos NPri WOrn
	'Loch Tummel'	GGGa
	lochiae misapplied (V)	see *R. viriosum*
	'Lochinch Spinbur'	GQui
	x ***lochmium***	GGGa
	Lodauric Group	SLdr SReu
§	'Lodauric Iceberg' ♀H3-4	LKna LMil SLdr SReu
	'Lodbrit'	SReu
§	Loderi Group	SLdr
	'Loderi Fairy Queen'	SLdr
	'Loderi Fairyland'	LHyd
§	'Loderi Game Chick' ♀H3-4	LHyd MDun MLea SLdr SReu
	'Loderi Georgette'	SLdr
	'Loderi Helen'	NPen SLdr
§	'Loderi King George' ♀H3-4	CBcs CWri GGGa IDee LHyd LKna LMil MDun MGos MLea NPen SHBN SLdr SReu SSta WBVN
	'Loderi Patience'	SLdr
	'Loderi Pink Coral'	SLdr
	'Loderi Pink Diamond' ♀H3-4	CWri LMil MDun SLdr WGer
	'Loderi Pink Topaz' ♀H3-4	LHyd LMil SLdr
	'Loderi Pretty Polly'	CWri
	'Loderi Princess Marina'	SLdr
	'Loderi Sir Edmund'	LHyd SLdr
	'Loderi Sir Joseph Hooker'	LHyd SLdr
	'Loderi Titan'	SReu
§	'Loderi Venus' ♀H3-4	CDoC CWri GGGa LHyd LKna LMil LRHS MDun MLea SHBN SLdr SReu SSta WBVN

	Name	Suppliers
	'Loderi White Diamond'	LHyd SLdr
	'Loder's White' 🏆H3-4	CWri ENot GGGa LHyd LKna LMil LRHS MDun NPen SLdr SReu SSta
§	'Logan Damaris'	LHyd SLdr SReu
	longesquamatum	GGGa LMil NPen SLdr
	longipes	SLdr
	- EGM 336	LMil
	- EGM 337	LMil
	- var. ***chienianum***	LMil
	- var. ***longipes*** C&H 7072	GGGa
	- - C&H 7113	GGGa
	longistylum	GGGa
	'Longworth'	NPen
	'Looking Glass'	LRHS MDun SHBN
	lopsangianum LS&T 5651	NPen
	'Lord Roberts' 🏆H4	CBcs CTri CWri ENot EPfP GGGa GKir LKna LMil MAsh MBar MGos MLea NEgg NPen SHBN SLdr SReu WBVN WFar WMoo WOrn
	'Lord Swaythling'	LHyd SLdr
	'Lori Eichelser'	MDun MLea NDlv
	'Lorna' (EA)	ENot GQui LMil
	'Louis Aimée van Houtte' (G) **new**	SLdr
	'Louis Hellebuyck' (G)	SLdr
	'Louis Pasteur'	SReu
	'Louisa Hill' (EA) **new**	ENot
	'Louise' (EA)	SLdr
	'Louise Dowdle' (EA)	LMil SCam SLdr
	'Love Song' (EA)	LRHS
	'Lovely William'	LMil NPen SLdr
	lowndesii	WAbe
	luciferum CER 9935	GGGa
	- PIC 8535	GGGa
	'Lucy Lou'	GGGa
	ludlowii	GGGa
	ludwigianum	GGGa
§	***lukiangense***	NPen
	'Lullaby' (EA)	LKna SLdr
	'Lunar Queen'	LHyd NPen SLdr
	Luscombei Group	LHyd SLdr
	luteiflorum	LMil
	- KW 21556	GGGa
	lutescens	CBcs CWri ISea LMil MDun NPen SLdr SLon SReu SSta WAbe
	- C&H 7124	GGGa
	- 'Bagshot Sands' 🏆H3-4	GGGa LHyd LMil LRHS SReu
§	***luteum*** (A) 🏆H4	CBrm CDoC CMHG CTri CWri ENot EPfP GGGa GGar ISea LHyd LKna LMil LRHS MAsh MBar MBri MDun MGos MLea NBlu NEgg NPen SLdr SReu SRms SSta WBVN WPic
§	***lyi*** KR 2962	GGGa
	maccabeanum 🏆H3-4	CBcs CDoC EPfP GGGa GTSp IDee LHyd LMil LRHS MDun NPen SLdr SReu SSpi SSta WFar WHer
	- KW 7724	NPen
	- deep cream-flowered	CWri SLdr
	- Reuthe's form	SReu
	maccabeanum x ***sinogrande***	SReu
	macgregoriae (V) Woods 2646	GGGa
	macranthum	see *R. indicum*
	'Macranthum Roseum' (EA)	SReu
	macrophyllum	GGGa
	macrosmithii	see *R. argipeplum*
	maculiferum	GGGa NPen SLdr
	- subsp. ***anwheiense***	see *R. anwheiense*
	'Madame Albert Moser'	LKna
	'Madame de Bruin'	LKna
	'Madame Galle' **new**	NBlu
	'Madame Knutz' (A)	SLdr
	'Madame Masson'	CTri CWri GGGa GKir GWCH LMil LRHS MAsh MBri MDun MGos MLea NBlu NPen NPri SHBN SLdr SReu SSta WBVN WFar
	'Madame van Hecke' (EA)	COtt CTri EPfP GKir LMil LRHS MAsh MBri NBlu SLdr SReu WFar WGor
	maddenii	IDee LMil SLdr WPic
§	- subsp. ***crassum***	CTrw GGGa LMil SLdr WPic
§	- subsp. ***maddenii*** KR 2978	LMil
§	- - Polyandrum Group	CBcs CTbh GQui ISea SLdr
	'Madeline's Yellow'	SLdr
	'Mademoiselle Masson'	ENot WFar
	'Magic Flute' (EA)	ENot MAsh
I	'Magic Flute' (V)	LMil NPri SCoo
	'Magnificum' (O)	LMil SLdr
	magnificum	SReu
	'Maharani'	GGGa LRHS MAsh SBrw
	'Maja' (G)	SLdr
§	***makinoi*** 🏆H4	GGGa LHyd LMil LRHS MDun NLar NMen NPen SLdr SReu SSpi SSta
	- 'Fuju-kaku-no-matsu'	MGos NLar
	mallotum	CWri GGGa IDee LHyd LMil MDun NPen SLdr SReu
	- BASEX 9672	GGGa
	- Farrer 815	GGGa
	'Manda Sue'	WGor
	Mandalay Group	LHyd
	'Mandarin Lights' (A)	LMil LRHS MBri NPri
	'Manderley'	LMil
	maoerense **new**	GGGa
	'Marcel Ménard'	LMil MAsh NLar SReu WFar
	'Marchioness of Lansdowne'	CSBt
	'Marcia'	SLdr
	'Mardi Gras'	GGGa LMil MBri
	Margaret Dunn Group	CWri
	'Margaret Falmouth'	SReu
	'Margaret George' (EA)	LHyd
	'Maria Derby' (EA)	ENot
	'Maricee'	GGGa SLdr
	'Marie Curie'	SReu
	'Marie Verschaffelt' (G)	SLdr
	'Marietta' **new**	LHyd
	'Marilee' (EA)	CDoC GKir LRHS MGos NLar SLdr
	Mariloo Group	SLdr
	'Marinus Koster'	LKna SLdr
	'Marion Merriman' (K)	LKna
	'Marion Street' 🏆H4	LHyd LMil SLdr SReu
	'Mark Turner'	SReu
	'Markeeta's Flame'	MDun
	'Markeeta's Prize' 🏆H4	CDoC CWri GGGa LMil LRHS MAsh MBri MDun MGos MLea SBod SLdr SPoG WBVN
	'Marley Hedges'	GGGa LMil MAsh
	'Marlies' (A)	SLdr
	'Marmot' (EA)	MBar MDun MLea
	'Mars'	GGGa SLdr SReu
	'Martha Hitchcock' (EA)	LKna SRms
	'Martha Isaacson' (Ad) 🏆H4	MGos SReu WCwm
	'Martine' (Ad)	LKna MGos
	martinianum	LMil SLdr
	aff. ***martinianum*** KW 21557	GGGa
	'Maruschka' (EA)	LMil
	'Mary Drennen'	LMil SPoG
	'Mary Fleming'	MDun SLdr

	Name	Suppliers
	'Mary Helen' (EA)	GKir LHyd LRHS MAsh SCoo SReu WPat
	'Mary Hoffman' (EA) **new**	SPoG
	'Mary Meredith' (EA)	LHyd
	'Mary Poppins' (K)	ENot GKir LMil LRHS MBri NPri SCoo
	'Maryke'	LMil
	Matador Group	NPen SLdr SReu
	'Matador'	LHyd
	'Mauna Loa' (K)	LKna
	'Maurice Skipworth'	CBcs
	maximum	GGGa SLdr
	- 'Weeldon's Red'	SLdr
	'Maxine Childers'	LMil
§	'Maxwellii' (EA)	CMac
	'May Day' ♀H3-4	CDoC LHyd
	May Day Group	CBcs CTrw CWri ISea LKna MDun MGos NPen SHBN SLdr
	'May Glow'	MGos
	May Morn Group	SReu
	'Mayor Johnstone'	CTri GKir LRHS MAsh NPri
	'Mazurka' (K)	LKna
	meddianum	GGGa
	- var. ***atrokermesinum*** KW 2100a	GGGa
	Medea Group	SLdr
	Medusa Group	GGGa SReu
	megacalyx	CBcs GGGa ISea
	'Megan' (EA)	GGGa MAsh NLar WGwG
	megaphyllum	see *R. basilicum*
	megeratum	GGGa SLdr SReu
	- 'Bodnant'	WAbe
	mekongense	GGGa
	- KR 5044	LMil
	- var. ***mekongense***	SReu
	- - Rubroluteum Group	see *R. viridescens* Rubroluteum Group
§	- var. ***melinanthum***	SReu
	- var. ***rubrolineatum***	LMil
	'Melford Lemon'	see *R.* 'Ilam Melford Lemon'
	'Melidioso'	LMil
	'Melina' (EA/d)	GGGa LMil
	melinanthum	see *R. mekongense* var. *melinanthum*
	'Merganser' ♀H4	GGGa LMil MDun MLea NDlv SReu WAbe
	'Merlin' (EA)	SLdr
	metternichii	see *R. degronianum* subsp. *heptamerum*
	- var. ***pentamerum***	see *R. degronianum* subsp. *degronianum*
	'Mi Amor'	LMil
	'Miami' (A)	SLdr
	'Michael Hill' (EA)	CBcs CDoC COtt LHyd MAsh SLdr
	'Michael Waterer'	MDun NPen
	'Michael's Pride'	CBcs GQui
	micranthum	GGGa MDun SLdr
	microgynum	LMil NPen
	- F 14242	GGGa NPen
	microleucum	see *R. orthocladum* var. *microleucum*
	micromeres	see *R. leptocarpum*
	microphyton	ISea
	'Midnight Mystique'	GGGa
	'Midori' (EA)	SLdr
	'Midsummer'	SLdr
	'Mikado' (EA)	see *R. kaempferi* 'Mikado'
	'Milton' (R)	SLdr
	mimetes	LMil NPen
§	- var. ***simulans*** F 20428	GGGa
	'Mimi' (EA)	CMac LHyd
	'Mimra'	SLdr
	'Mina van Houtte' (G) **new**	SLdr
	'Mindy's Love'	LMil
	'Ming'	see *R.* 'Ilam Ming'
	'Minterne Cinnkeys'	MDun
	minus	GQui
	- var. ***chapmanii***	SSpi
§	- var. ***minus***	SLdr
§	- - Carolinianum Group	LMil
	- - - 'Epoch'	LMil
§	- - Punctatum Group	MBar
	'Miss Muffet' (EA)	SLdr
§	'Moerheim' ♀H4	CWri EMil GKir LRHS MAsh MBar MGos NPri SReu WBVN WOrn
§	'Moerheim's Pink'	LHyd LKna LMil MDun SPer
	'Moerheim's Scarlet'	LKna
	'Moffat'	SReu
	'Moidart' (Vs)	LMil
	'Moira Salmon' (EA)	LHyd
	'Molalla Red' (K)	LMil
§	***molle*** subsp. ***japonicum*** (A)	GGGa SLdr
	- - JR 871	GGGa
	- subsp. ***molle*** (A) C&H 7181	GGGa
	mollicomum	NPen
	- F 30940	SLdr
	'Mollie Coker'	CWri SLdr
	Mollis orange (M)	MBar SRms
	Mollis pink (M)	GGGa MBar NBlu SRms
	Mollis red (M)	MBar NBlu SRms
	Mollis salmon (M)	GGGa GQui
	Mollis yellow (M)	GQui MBar NBlu SRms
	'Molly Ann'	GGGa LRHS MDun SLdr SReu WGor
	'Molten Gold' (v)	ENot LRHS MAsh
	monanthum CCH&H 8133	GGGa
	monosematum	see *R. pachytrichum* var. *monosematum*
	montiganum AC 2060	LMil
	montroseanum	ISea LMil LRHS MDun SLdr WCru
*	- 'Baravalla'	GGGa
	'Moon Maiden' (EA)	GQui NLar SLdr WOrn
	Moonbeam Group	LKna
	Moonshine Group	SLdr
	'Moonshine'	SReu
	'Moonshine Bright'	LHyd MDun
	'Moonshine Supreme'	LKna
	Moonstone Group	MBar MDun MLea NPen SLdr
	- pink-tipped	GEdr
	'Moonstone Yellow'	GGGa
	'Moonwax'	CWri SLdr
§	'Morgenrot'	GGGa LMil LRHS MAsh MGos NBlu SReu WFar
	morii	GGGa LHyd LMil MDun NPen
	'Morning Cloud' ♀H4	CAbP GKir LHyd LMil LRHS MBar NDlv SReu
	'Morning Magic'	CWri LHyd SLdr
	Morning Red	see *R.* 'Morgenrot'
	'Moser's Maroon'	CWri ENot LKna MGos MLea NLar NPen SLdr WBVN
	'Moser's Strawberry'	LKna
	'Motet' (K/d)	CSdC LKna SLdr
	'Mother Greer'	GGGa
	'Mother of Pearl'	LKna SLdr SReu
	'Mother Theresa'	LKna
	'Mother's Day' (EA) ♀H4	CDoC CMac CSBt CTrh CTri ENot EPfP GKir GQui LHyd LKna LMil LRHS MBar MBri MDun MGos MLea NBlu NMen NPen SCam SLdr SPer SPoG SReu SSta WFar
	Moulten Gold = 'Blattgold'	GGGa
	'Mount Everest'	GGGa LHyd LMil SReu SSta
	'Mount Rainier' (K)	LMil MBri SLdr SReu

Name	Suppliers
'Mount Saint Helens'	GGGa LMil MLea SLdr
'Mount Seven Star'	see *R. nakaharae* 'Mount Seven Star'
'Mountain Star'	SLdr
moupinense	CBcs GGGa IDee LHyd LMil NPen SLdr SReu
- pink-flowered	LMil
'Mr A.C. Kenrick' **new**	SLdr
'Mrs A.T. de la Mare' ♀H4	CSBt CWri GGGa LHyd LKna LMil MDun NPen SReu SSta
'Mrs Anthony Waterer' (O)	LKna
'Mrs Anthony Waterer' (hybrid)	LKna
'Mrs Betty Robertson'	GWCH MDun MGos MLea SLdr SReu
'Mrs C.B. van Nes'	SReu
Mrs C. Whitner Group	SLdr
'Mrs Charles E. Pearson' ♀H4	CBcs CSBt CWri ENot LHyd LKna LMil NPen SHBN SLdr SReu
'Mrs Davies Evans' ♀H4	CWri LHyd LKna MBar SReu SSta
'Mrs Dick Thompson'	SReu
'Mrs Donald Graham'	SBrw SReu
'Mrs E.C. Stirling'	ENot LHyd LKna SRms
'Mrs Emil Hager' (EA)	LHyd SLdr
'Mrs Furnivall' ♀H4	CBcs CWri EPfP GBin GGGa LHyd LKna LMil MDun MGos MLea SLdr SReu WOrn
'Mrs G.W. Leak'	CSBt CSam CWri EPfP GGGa ISea LHyd LKna LMil MDun MLea SHBN SLdr SPer SReu
'Mrs Helen Koster'	LKna
'Mrs J.C. Williams' ♀H4	LKna LMil
'Mrs J.G. Millais'	LKna LMil MDun
'Mrs John Kelk'	LMil
'Mrs Kingsmill'	SLdr
'Mrs Lindsay Smith'	LKna
'Mrs Lionel de Rothschild' ♀H4	MDun SReu
Mrs Lionel de Rothschild Group	CWri LKna
'Mrs P.D. Williams'	LKna SReu
'Mrs Peter Koster' (M)	SLdr WFar
'Mrs Philip Martineau'	LKna
'Mrs R.S. Holford' ♀H4	LKna SLdr
'Mrs T.H. Lowinsky' ♀H4	CSBt EPfP GGGa LKna LMil MAsh MDun MGos MLea NPen NWea SLdr SPer SReu SSta WBVN
'Mrs W.C. Slocock'	LHyd LKna MDun SLdr SReu
'Mrs William Agnew'	LKna
'Mucronatum'	see *R.* x *mucronatum*
§ x ***mucronatum*** (EA)	LHyd SRms WPic
'Mucronatum Amethystinum'	see *R.* 'Amethystinum'
mucronulatum	GGGa NPen
- pink-flowered	WPGP
- var. ***chejuense***	see *R. mucronulatum* var. *taquetii*
- 'Cornell Pink' ♀H4	GGGa LHyd LMil WFar
§ - var. ***taquetii***	GGGa
§ 'Multiflorum'	SReu
'Muncaster Bells'	NPen
'Muncaster Mist'	LHyd NPen
§ ***myrtifolium***	LMil
nakaharae (EA)	NPen SLdr SReu
§ - 'Mariko' (EA)	EPot GGGa LHyd MBar MGos NLAp SLdr WPat
§ - 'Mount Seven Star' (EA) ♀H4	ECho GGGa LHyd LMil LRHS MAsh MGos NLAp SLdr SReu WAbe WPat
§ - orange-flowered (EA)	GKir LMil LRHS MGos NPen NPri SHBN SReu SSta
- pink-flowered (EA)	GKir LMil LRHS MGos NPen NPri SLdr SPer SReu SSta
- red-flowered (EA)	MGos SLdr
- 'Scree' (EA)	SReu

Name	Suppliers
'Nakahari Orange'	see *R. nakaharae* orange-flowered
'Nakahari-mariko'	see *R. nakaharae* 'Mariko'
nakotiltum	NPen
'Nancy Evans' ♀H3-4	CDoC COtt CSBt CWri GGGa GKir LHyd LMil LRHS MAsh MDun MLea NPri SLdr SPoG SReu SSpi WFar WGer WOrn
'Nancy of Robinhill' (EA)	ENot
'Nancy Waterer' (G) ♀H4	NLar SBrw SLdr SReu
'Nanki Poo' (EA)	LHyd SLdr
Naomi Group	CWri LHyd LKna NPen SLdr
'Naomi' (EA)	GQui LKna LMil NPen SCam SHBN SLdr WPic
'Naomi Astarte'	LKna MDun NPen SLdr
'Naomi Hope'	SLdr
'Naomi Stella Maris'	LHyd SLdr
'Narcissiflorum' (G/d) ♀H4	CDoC CSBt ENot EPfP IDee LHyd LKna LMil LRHS NLar SPer SPoG SReu
'Naselle'	GGGa LMil
neriiflorum	GGGa LMil MDun NPen SReu
- Bu 287	GGGa
- subsp. ***neriiflorum*** L&S 1352	GGGa
§ - subsp. ***phaedropum***	MDun NPen
- - C&H 422	NPen
- - CCH&H 8125	GGGa
- - KR 5593	LMil
- - KW 6845*	NPen
nervulosum Sleumer (V)	GGGa
'Nestor'	SReu
'New Comet'	LHyd NPen SLdr
'New Moon'	SReu
'Newcomb's Sweetheart'	LMil MDun
'Niagara' (EA) ♀H3-4	CTrh ENot EPfP GQui LHyd LMil NMen SLdr
'Nichola' (EA)	MAsh SReu
'Nico' (EA)	CMac GKir LRHS MAsh WPat
'Nicoletta'	ENot LMil MBri
'Night Sky'	CDoC COtt GGGa LHyd LMil LRHS MAsh MDun MGos MLea SLdr WBVN
'Nightingale'	SBrw SReu
nigroglandulosum	GGGa
nilagiricum	see *R. arboreum* subsp. *nilagiricum*
'Nimbus'	LKna LMil SLdr
Nimrod Group	SLdr
'Nippon'	SLdr
nipponicum	SReu
'Nishiki' (EA)	CMac
nitens	see *R. calostrotum* subsp. *riparium* Nitens Group
nitidulum	NPen
- var. ***omeiense***	NPen
- - KR 185	GGGa LMil
nivale subsp. ***boreale*** **new**	LMil WPic
- - Ramosissimum Group	GGGa
§ - - Stictophyllum Group	GGGa WAbe
niveum ♀H4	CDoC GGGa IDee LMil LRHS MDun NPen SLdr SReu WGer
- B&SWJ 2675	WCru
- 'Nepal'	LHyd
§ Nobleanum Group	GGGa LHyd LKna LMil NPen SLdr SSta
'Nobleanum Album'	GGGa LHyd LKna LMil NPen SLdr SReu SSta
'Nobleanum Coccineum'	NPen SLdr SReu
'Nobleanum Lamellen'	SLdr
'Nobleanum Venustum'	CSBt CWri IDee LHyd LKna LMil SLdr SReu SSta
'Nofretete'	GGGa

	'Nora'	WPic
	'Nordlicht' (EA)	SLdr
N	'Norma' (R/d) 🏆^{H4}	LMil SReu
	Norman Shaw Group	LHyd
	'Northern Hi-Lights' (A)	GKir LMil LRHS SLdr
	'Northern Star'	LHyd
	'Northern Starburst'	LMil
	'Nova Zembla'	EPfP GGGa LMil MAsh MBar MGos NBlu NPri NWea SBrw SHBN SLdr SPer SPoG SReu SSta WBVN
	nudiflorum	see *R. periclymenoides*
	nudipes	LMil
	nuttallii	CBrd GGGa LMil SLdr
	'Oban'	GGGa LMil LRHS MDun MLea NLAp NMen WAbe
	Obtusum Group (EA)	LHyd SLdr
	obtusum f. ***amoenum***	see *R.* 'Amoenum'
	occidentale (A) 🏆^{H4}	GGGa LMil LRHS MDun SLdr SSpi
	- 'Crescent City Double' SM 28-2	GGGa
	ochraceum	LMil
	- C&H 7052	GGGa
	- EGM 312	LMil
	'Odee Wright'	CDoC CTri CWri GGGa LRHS MAsh MLea NLar SLdr SPer SReu
	'Odoratum' (Ad)	MLea
	'Oi-no-mezame' (EA)	LHyd
	'Old Copper'	CWri SLdr
	'Old Gold' (K)	MLea SLdr SReu
	'Old Port' 🏆^{H4}	CWri LHyd LMil SHBN SReu
	oldhamii (EA) B&SWJ 3742	WCru
	- ETOT 601	GGGa
	'Olga' 🏆^{H4}	LHyd LKna LMil SLdr SPoG SReu SSta
	'Olga Mezitt'	LHyd
	'Olga Niblett' (EA)	LMil SLdr
	oligocarpum	GGGa
	- Guiz 148*	GGGa
	'Olive'	LHyd LKna LMil
	'Oliver Cromwell'	SReu
	Olympic Lady Group	LHyd MLea SLdr
	Omar Group	MBar
§	'One Thousand Butterflies'	COtt GGGa MDun MLea NPen SLdr
N	'Ophelia'	SCam SLdr
	'Oporto'	SLdr
	'Orange Beauty' (EA) 🏆$^{H3-4}$	CDoC CMac CSBt CTrh GGGa LHyd LKna LMil MAsh MBar MGos NPen SCam SLdr SReu WBVN WFar WOrn WPic
	'Orange King' (EA)	ENot
	'Orange Scout'	SLdr WGor WMoo
	'Orange Splendour' (A)	LRHS
	'Orange Sunset'	MDun
	'Orangengold'	MDun
	orbiculare 🏆$^{H3-4}$	GGGa LHyd LMil MDun NPen SLdr SSta
	- C&K 230	GGGa
§	- subsp. ***cardiobasis***	LMil MDun SLdr
	- Sandling Park form	SReu
	'Orchid Lights'	GKir LRHS MAsh SLdr
	'Oregon' (EA)	SLdr
	oreodoxa	LMil NPen WPic
§	- var. ***fargesii*** 🏆^{H4}	GGGa LHyd LMil SLdr
	- var. ***oreodoxa***	LMil
	- - EN 4212	GGGa
	- var. ***shensiense***	GGGa
	oreotrephes	CBcs LHyd LMil LRHS MDun MLea NPen SLdr SReu
	- 'Bluecalyptus' **new**	GGGa
§	- Exquisitum Group	SLdr SReu
	- 'Pentland'	LMil
	- Timeteum Group	SReu
	Orestes Group	SLdr
	orthocladum	LMil MDun
§	- var. ***microleucum***	GGGa LMil WAbe
	- var. ***orthocladum*** F 20488	GGGa
	- - JN 819	GGGa
	'Oryx' (O)	CSdC LKna
	'Osmar' 🏆^{H4}	CBcs GGGa MGos SReu
	'Ostara'	CBcs COtt MGos
	'Ouchiyama'	LKna
	'Oudijk's Sensation'	CBcs CWri LKna MAsh MDun MGos NBlu SLdr
	ovatum (EA)	CBcs NPen
	- CN&W 548	ISea
	'Oxydol' (K)	SLdr
§	***pachypodum***	GGGa
	pachysanthum 🏆^{H4}	CDoC GTSp IDee LHyd LMil MDun NPen SLdr SReu SSpi
	- RV 72/001	GGGa SLdr
	- 'Crosswater'	LMil LRHS MDun
	pachytrichum	GGGa NPen SLdr
§	- var. ***monosematum***	SLdr SReu
	- - CN&W 953	LMil
	- - W/V 1522	NPen
	- var. ***pachytrichum*** 'Sesame'	LMil
	'Palestrina' (EA) 🏆$^{H3-4}$	CBcs CMac CSBt CTrh EPfP LHyd LKna LMil LRHS MGos NPen SCam SLdr SPer SReu SSta WFar WMoo
	'Pallas' (G)	SLdr SReu
	'Pamela Miles' (EA)	LHyd
	'Pamela Robinson'	LHyd
	'Pamela-Louise'	LHyd
	'Pancake'	CMac
	'Panda' (EA) 🏆^{H4}	CDoC CTri GGGa LHyd LMil LRHS MAsh MBar MDun MLea NDlv NPri SCoo SLdr SPoG SReu
	'Papageno'	NLar
	'Papaya Punch'	LMil MDun
	'Paprika Spiced'	CDoC COtt CWri LMil MDun MGos MLea SBod SLdr WBVN WOrn
	'Paradise Pink' (EA)	LMil
	paradoxum	GGGa
	'Paramount' (K/d)	LKna
§	'Paris'	LHyd
	'Parkfeuer' (A)	SLdr
	parmulatum	LMil MDun NPen
	- C&C 7538	GGGa
	- mauve-flowered	NPen
	- 'Ocelot'	GGGa LHyd MDun NPen SLdr
	- pink-flowered	GGGa NPen
	parryae	GGGa
	'Patty Bee' 🏆^{H4}	More than 30 suppliers
	patulum	see *R. pemakoense* Patulum Group
	'Pavane' (K)	LKna
	'Peace'	GGGa
	'Peach Blossom'	see *R.* 'Saotome'
	'Peach Lady'	SLdr
	'Peep-bo' (EA)	LHyd SLdr
	'Peeping Tom'	CDoC GKir LMil MDun SHBN SReu
	pemakoense	CDoC CSBt CTbh ENot GGGa IDee MBar NPen SLdr SReu
§	- Patulum Group	MBar NPen SLdr
	'Pemakofairy'	WAbe
	pendulum LS&T 6660	GGGa
	Penelope Group	SReu
	'Penheale Blue' 🏆^{H4}	CDoC CTrh GBin GGGa LMil NDlv NPen
	'Penjerrick Cream'	NPen SLdr
	'Penjerrick Pink'	LHyd NPen

	pennivenium	see *R. tanastylum* var. *pennivenium*
	pentaphyllum (A)	LMil
	'Percy Wiseman' 🏆^{H4}	More than 30 suppliers
	'Perfect Lady'	LMil
§	***periclymenoides*** (A)	GGGa LMil LRHS SLdr
	'Persil' (K) 🏆^{H4}	CBcs CSBt CWri ENot EPfP GGGa LHyd LKna LMil MAsh MBar MBri MDun MGos MLea NBlu SCoo SLdr SPer SReu WBVN WBrE WMoo WOrn
§	'Persimmon'	LKna
	'Peter Alan'	CWri
	'Peter Berg'	MGos
	'Peter John Mezitt'	see *R.* (PJM Group) 'Peter John Mezitt'
	'Peter Koster' (hybrid)	CWri SHBN WFar
	petrocharis Guiz 120	GGGa
	'Petrouchka' (K)	LKna MBri MDun
	phaedropum	see *R. neriiflorum* subsp. *phaedropum*
	phaeochrysum	GGGa LMil NPen SLdr
	- var. ***agglutinatum***	GGGa LMil NPen
§	- var. ***levistratum***	LMil NPen SLdr SReu
	- - AC 1757	WCwm
	'Phalarope'	GGGa MBar SReu
	'Phoebe' (R/d)	SLdr SReu
	'Phyllis Korn'	CDoC CWri LHyd MDun NLar SLdr SPer WBVN
	'Piccolo' (K/d)	CSdC LKna
§	***piercei***	LMil MDun NPen
	- KW 11040	GGGa
	Pilgrim Group	LKna LMil
	pingianum	NPen SLdr
	- EGM 304	LMil
	- KR 150	NPen
	- KR 184	GGGa
	'Pink and Sweet' (A)	LMil
	'Pink Bountiful'	LKna
	'Pink Bride'	SLdr
	'Pink Cameo'	CWri
	'Pink Cherub' 🏆^{H4}	ENot LRHS MBar MDun NBlu SBod SLdr SReu WOrn
	'Pink Delight'	LHyd LKna
I	'Pink Delight' (A)	MAsh
	'Pink Drift'	CSBt ENot LKna LMil MAsh MBar MDun MGos NWea SHBN SLdr SPer
	'Pink Gin'	LMil
	'Pink Glory'	SLdr
	'Pink Leopard'	LMil MLea SLdr
	'Pink Mimosa' (Vs)	SLdr
	'Pink Pancake' (EA) 🏆^{H4}	CBcs GQui LMil LRHS MGos SLdr SSpi WGer
	'Pink Pearl' (EA)	see *R.* 'Azuma-kagami'
	'Pink Pearl' (hybrid)	CBcs CSBt CTri ENot EPfP GGGa GKir LKna LMil LRHS MAsh MBar MDun MGos NPen NPri NWea SLdr SPer SPoG SReu SSta WBVN WFar WMoo
	'Pink Pebble' 🏆$^{H3-4}$	CTrw LHyd MAsh MDun WBVN WOrn
	'Pink Perfection'	MBar MGos NPen SLdr SReu WFar
	'Pink Photo'	SLdr
	'Pink Polar Bear' **new**	LMil
	'Pink Rosette'	LKna
	'Pink Sensation'	MDun
	'Pinkerton'	LKna
	'Pintail'	GGGa IDee LMil WAbe
	'Pipit'	GGGa WAbe
	'Pippa' (EA)	CMac
	PJM Group	MDun
§	- 'Peter John Mezitt' 🏆^{H4}	LHyd LMil MAsh SLdr SReu
	'PJM Elite'	GGGa LHyd LMil
	planetum	LMil
	pocophorum	GGGa NPen SLdr
	- 'Cecil Nice' **new**	LHyd
§	- var. ***hemidartum***	GGGa NPen
	- var. ***pocophorum***	SLdr
	'Point Defiance'	CWri GGGa LMil MDun NLar NPen SLdr SPer WBVN
	'Polar Bear' (EA)	LRHS MBar MDun SLdr
	'Polar Bear' 🏆$^{H3-4}$	IDee LHyd LMil LRHS MGos MLan SReu WBVN
	Polar Bear Group	CWri GGGa GKir LMil MLea NPen SLdr
	'Polar Haven' (EA)	LKna
	'Polaris'	see *R.* 'Hachmann's Polaris'
	'Polaris' (EA)	ENot SReu
§	***poluninii***	GGGa
	polyandrum	see *R. maddenii* subsp. *maddenii* Polyandrum Group
§	***polycladum***	LMil
§	- Scintillans Group	LHyd MBar MDun MLea NPen SLdr WPic
	- - 'Policy' 🏆^{H4}	GGGa SReu
	polylepis	GGGa LMil NPen
	- C&K 284	GGGa
§	***ponticum***	CSBt CTri IDee MBar MGos NWea SPer WFar
	- AC&H 205	GGGa
	- 'Foliis Purpureis'	SReu
§	- 'Silver Edge' (v)	CSBt LMil SMur
	- 'Variegatum' (v)	CBcs CTri ENot EPfP GGGa GKir LRHS MAsh MBar MDun MGos NBlu NPen NPri SPer SPoG SReu SRms SSta WFar
	'Pooh-Bah' (EA)	LHyd
	'Pook'	LHyd
	'Popcorn' (V)	GGGa
	'Popocatapetl'	SReu
	'Port Knap' (EA)	LKna
	'Port Wine' (EA)	LKna
	'Potlatch'	GGGa
	poukhanense	see *R. yedoense* var. *poukhanense*
§	'Praecox' 🏆^{H4}	CBcs CSBt CTrw ENot EPfP GGGa ISea LHyd LKna LMil LRHS MAsh MBar MDun MGos NBlu NPri SHBN SLdr SPer SPoG SReu SSta WFar WPic
	praestans	GGGa LMil MDun NPen SLdr
	- KW 13369	NPen
	praevernum	GGGa LMil
§	***prattii***	NPen SLdr
	- 'Perry Wood'	LMil
	'Prawn'	LKna SReu
	Prelude Group	SLdr
	preptum	GGGa SLdr
	'President Roosevelt' (v)	CSBt GKir LKna LMil LRHS MAsh MDun MGos MLea NPri SHBN SPoG SReu WFar
	'Pretty Girl'	LKna
	'Pretty Woman'	GGGa LMil
	'Pride of Leonardslee'	SLdr
	'Pridenjoy'	LMil
	'Prima Donna'	ENot LMil
	primuliflorum	GGGa WAbe
	- CN&W 1237	ISea
	- 'Doker-La'	LMil LRHS WAbe
	- white-flowered	WAbe
	'Prince Camille de Rohan'	LMil
	'Prince Henri de Pays Bas' (G)	CSdC LMil SLdr
	'Princess Alice'	CBcs LHyd WGer WPic
	'Princess Anne' 🏆^{H4}	CMHG CSam EPfP GGGa GKir LHyd LMil LRHS MAsh MBar

Name	Suppliers
	MDun MGos MLea NPen SHBN SLdr SPer SReu SSta WMoo
'Princess Galadriel'	SLdr
'Princess Ida' (EA)	LHyd
'Princess Juliana'	LMil WGor WMoo
'Princess Margaret of Windsor' (K)	GQui LMil MAsh
'Princess Margaret Toth'	CSdC
principis	LMil SLdr
- C&V 9547	GGGa
- SF 95085	ISea
- Tzo KR 3844 from Pasum	LMil
- 'Lost Horizon'	LMil MDun
§ ***prinophyllum*** (A)	LMil LRHS
'Prins Bernhard' (EA)	LKna SCam SLdr
'Prinses Juliana' (EA)	SLdr SReu WFar
'Professor Hugo de Vries' 🏆H4	LKna SLdr SReu
'Professor J.H. Zaayer'	MGos
pronum	GGGa
- R.B. Cooke form	GGGa
- Towercourt form	GGGa
§ 'Prostigiatum'	SLdr
prostigiatum	see *R.* 'Prostigiatum'
prostratum	see *R. saluenense* subsp. *chameunum* Prostratum Group
proteoides	GGGa
- EGM 281	LMil
- R 151	NPen
* - 'Ascreavie'	GGGa
protistum	SLdr
- KR 1986	GGGa
§ - var. ***giganteum***	SReu
pruniflorum	GGGa
prunifolium (A)	GGGa LMil LRHS SLdr SSpi
przewalskii	GGGa LHyd
- subsp. ***dabanshanense***	GGGa
pseudochrysanthum 🏆H4	CDoC CStu GGGa LHyd LMil LRHS NLar NPen SLdr SReu SSta
- dwarf	WAbe
pseudociliipes **new**	GGGa
Psyche Group	see *R.* Wega Group
'Psyche' (EA)	MDun
'Ptarmigan' 🏆H3-4	CBcs CDoC ENot EPfP GGGa IDee LHyd LMil MAsh MBar MGos MLea NEgg NLAp NMen NPen SLdr SReu SSta WBVN WFar
pubescens	LMil
- KW 3953	GGGa
pubicostatum	LMil
- AC 2051	LMil
- CN&W 906	ISea
§ 'Pucella' (G) 🏆H4	CWri NLar SLdr SReu
pudorosum L&S 2752	GGGa
'Pulchrum Maxwellii'	see *R.* 'Maxwellii'
pumilum	GGGa MDun NPen WAbe
'Puncta'	GGGa
punctatum	see *R. minus* var. *minus* Punctatum Group
purdomii	GGGa
'Purple Diamond'	see *R.* Diamant Group purple
'Purple Emperor'	LKna
purple Glenn Dale (EA)	SLdr
'Purple Heart'	ENot LMil
'Purple Queen' (EA/d)	MAsh
'Purple Splendor' (EA)	CMac LKna SCam SLdr
'Purple Splendour' 🏆H4	CBcs CSBt CWri ENot EPfP IDee LHyd LKna LMil LRHS MAsh MBar MBri MDun MGos MLea NEgg NPen NWea SHBN SLdr SPer SReu SSta WBVN WFar WMoo
'Purple Triumph' (EA) 🏆H3	CBcs LKna LMil SCam SLdr SReu SSta
'Purpurkissen' (EA) **new**	LMil
'Purpurtraum' (EA) 🏆H4	GGGa
'Quail'	GGGa
Quaver Group	SRms
'Queen Alice'	LRHS MAsh MDun
'Queen Elizabeth II' 🏆H4	LHyd
Queen Emma	see *R.* 'Koningin Emma'
'Queen Mary'	MBar MDun
'Queen Mother'	see *R.* 'The Queen Mother'
'Queen of England' (G)	CSdC
Queen of Hearts Group	CWri
'Queen of Hearts'	LHyd SLdr
'Queen Souriya'	SLdr SReu
Queen Wilhelmina	see *R.* 'Königin Wilhelmina'
'Queens Wood' **new**	LHyd
'Queenswood Centenary'	LMil
'Quentin Metsys' (R)	LMil SLdr
quinquefolium (A)	GGGa LMil NPen SLdr
racemosum 🏆H4	LMil MBar MDun NPen SLdr SSpi WAbe WPic
- AC 719	NPen
- ACE 1367	WAbe
- SF 365	ISea
- SSNY 47	GGGa
- Yu 10993	GIBF
- 'Glendoick'	GGGa
- 'Rock Rose' ex R 11265 🏆H3-4	EPfP GGGa LHyd LMil WGer
- 'White Lace'	LHyd
racemosum x ***tephropeplum***	MBar
'Racil'	LKna MBar MDun MGos
'Racine' (G)	SLdr
'Racoon' (EA) 🏆H4	GGGa
'Radiant' (M)	SLdr
radicans	see *R. calostrotum* subsp. *keleticum* Radicans Group
'Rainbow'	LKna SLdr
'Ramapo' 🏆H4	ENot GGGa GKir LMil LRHS MAsh MBar MDun MGos NMen NPri SPer SPoG SReu
* 'Rambo' **new**	ISea
ramsdenianum	GGGa LMil SLdr
- KR 5619	LMil
- KR 6033	LMil
'Rangoon'	MBri
'Raphael de Smet' (G/d)	SReu
'Rashomon' (EA)	LHyd SLdr SReu
'Raspberry Ripple'	LKna SReu
'Rasputin' **new**	LMil
'Razorbill' 🏆H4	CDoC GGGa LHyd LMil LRHS MGos
recurvoides	GGGa LHyd LMil MDun NPen SLdr SReu SSpi
- Keillour form	GGGa
recurvum	see *R. roxieanum* var. *roxieanum*
'Red Arrow'	LHyd
'Red Carpet'	LMil SLdr
'Red Delicious'	CWri GGGa LMil
'Red Diamond'	see *R.* Diamant Group red
'Red Fountain' (EA)	ENot LMil MAsh SLdr WPat
'Red Glow'	LHyd
'Red Glow' x ***yakushimanum*** **new**	SLdr
'Red Jack'	LMil MAsh
'Red Pimpernel' (EA) **new**	SLdr
'Red Riding Hood'	LKna
'Red Sunset' (EA/d)	LRHS
'Red Wood'	GGGa
'Redpoll'	LHyd
'Redwing' (EA)	CDoC MAsh SLdr

Name	Suppliers
Remo Group	SLdr
'Rendezvous' ♀H4	LMil SLdr SReu
'Rennie' (A)	MAsh MGos
'Renoir' ♀H4	CSBt LHyd LMil SLdr SReu
'Replique' (Vs)	SLdr
reticulatum (A)	CBcs GGGa LMil NPen SLdr SReu
* - ***leucanthum*** (A)	GGGa
retusum (V)	GGGa
§ 'Reuthe's Purple'	GGGa LHyd SReu WAbe
'Rêve d'Amour' (Vs)	MDun SLdr SReu SSta
Review Order Group	WPic
'Rex' (EA)	CTbh ENot MAsh SLdr WFar
rex	CDoC GGGa IDee LHyd LMil LRHS MDun NPen SLdr
- EGM 295	LMil
- subsp. ***arizelum***	see *R. arizelum*
§ - subsp. ***fictolacteum*** ♀H3-4	CDoC GGGa LHyd LMil MDun NPen SLdr SReu
- - SF 649	ISea
- - Miniforme Group	LMil MDun
- subsp. ***gratum***	LMil
- - AC 3009 from Zibenshan	LMil
- yellow-flowered AC 2079	LMil
- - AC 901	MDun
rhabdotum	see *R. dalhousieae* var. *rhabdotum*
'Ria Hardijzer'	LKna
'Ribera' (R)	SLdr
rigidum	ISea WAbe
'Ring of Fire'	CWri LMil MBri MDun MGos MLea NEgg SLdr SReu
'Ripe Corn'	LHyd LKna NPen SLdr SReu
ripense (EA)	LHyd
'Riplet'	GEdr MDun NDlv
'Ripples' (EA)	CTrh
ririei	CBcs GGGa LHyd LMil NPen SLdr SReu WCwm
- AC 2036	LMil
- W/V 1808	NPen
- W/V 5139	NPen
'Robert Croux'	SLdr
'Robert Keir'	SLdr
'Robert Korn'	LMil MDun
'Robert Seleger'	GGGa LMil LRHS MAsh SReu WAbe
'Robert Whelan' (A)	MDun NLar SReu
'Robin Hill Frosty' (EA)	SLdr
'Robinette'	CBcs CWri ISea MBri SLdr
'Rocket'	CTri ENot GKir MAsh MDun MLea NPen SLdr WBVN
'Rokoko'	see *R.* 'Hachmann's Rokoko'
Romany Chai Group	LHyd
'Romany Chal'	LHyd
'Romy'	WPic
'Rosa Mundi'	CSBt ENot
Rosalind Group	LHyd
'Rosata' (Vs) ♀H4	MBri MDun SReu SSta
'Rose Bud'	CSBt CTri MDun
'Rose de Flandre' (G)	SLdr
'Rose Elf'	ECho MDun NDlv
'Rose Glow' (A)	MDun SReu
'Rose Gown'	SReu
'Rose Greeley' (EA)	CDoC CTrh GQui LRHS SCam SLdr SReu WFar
'Rose Haze' (A)	SReu
'Rose Torch' (A)	MDun SReu
roseatum F 17227	GGGa
'Rosebud' (EA/d) ♀H3-4	CBcs CMac CTrh CTrw ECho LHyd LKna MAsh MBar MGos NPen SCam SLdr SReu
'Rosemary Hyde' (EA)	SCoo SLdr
'Rosenkavalier'	LHyd
roseotinctum	see *R. sanguineum* subsp. *sanguineum* var. *didymoides* Roseotinctum Group
roseum	see *R. prinophyllum*
'Roseum Elegans'	CTri ECho LRHS MAsh MBar NPri WFar
'Rosiflorum'	see *R. indicum* 'Balsaminiflorum'
'Rosy Bell'	LKna
'Rosy Dream'	CAbP COtt CWri LMil MAsh MDun NPen
'Rosy Fire' (A)	SReu
'Rosy Lea'	MLea
'Rosy Lights' (A)	CTri MAsh MBri
'Rothenburg'	CSam CWri LHyd MDun SBrw SLdr
rothschildii	GGGa LMil LRHS
- AC 1868 from Dapo Shan	LMil
- C&Cu 9312	GGGa
rousei (V)	GGGa
roxieanum	LHyd LMil NPen SReu
- R 25422	NPen
§ - var. ***cucullatum***	ISea LRHS MDun NPen
- - CN&W 680	GGGa
- - CN&W 690	LMil
- - CN&W 695	LMil
- - SBEC 350	GGGa
- var. ***oreonastes*** ♀H4	CDoC GGGa LHyd LMil LRHS MDun NPen SSta WGer
- - USDAPI 59222/R11312	GGGa
- - Nymans form	SReu
- var. ***parvum***	GGGa
- var. ***recurvum***	LMil
§ - var. ***roxieanum***	NPen
'Royal Blood'	LHyd SLdr
'Royal Command' (K)	COtt CWri GKir MAsh MBar NEgg SBrw SLdr
Royal Flush Group	ISea
'Royal Lodge' (K)	SLdr
'Royal Ruby' (K)	CWri MBri MGos MLea SLdr WOrn
'Roza Stevenson'	LHyd NPen SLdr
'Rozanne Waterer' (K)/d	LKna
'Rubicon'	CDoC CWri LHyd MAsh MLea SLdr
rubiginosum	CBcs GGGa GTSp LHyd LMil NPen SReu
- SF 368	ISea
§ - Desquamatum Group	CBcs LHyd SLdr
- pink-flowered	LMil
- white-flowered	LMil
rubineiflorum	GGGa
'Rubinetta' (EA)	LMil LRHS WFar
rubroluteum	see *R. viridescens* Rubroluteum Group
'Ruby F. Bowman'	SReu
'Ruby Hart'	CBcs GGGa MAsh MDun SReu
Ruddigore Group	LHyd
rude	see *R. glischrum* subsp. *rude*
'Ruffles and Frills'	ECho MDun
rufum	GGGa SLdr
- AC 4110	LMil
- Sich 155	GGGa
'Rumba' (K)	LKna
rupicola	LMil NMen SLdr
§ - var. ***chryseum***	GGGa LHyd
- var. ***muliense*** Yu 14042	GGGa
russatum ♀H4	CBcs ENot EPfP GGGa LHyd LMil MDun NPen SLdr WAbe WFar WPic
- blue-black-flowered	LMil LRHS
- 'Purple Pillow'	CSBt
russotinctum	see *R. alutaceum* var. *russotinctum*
'Sacko'	CWri ECho GGGa LMil LTwo MAsh MDun NLar WBVN

	'Saffrano'	NLar
	'Saffron Queen'	CBcs CTrw ISea WPic
	'Sahara' (K)	CSdC LKna SLdr
	'Saint Breward'	GGGa GQui LHyd MDun MLea SLdr
	'Saint Keverne'	SLdr
	'Saint Kew'	SLdr
	'Saint Merryn' ♀H4	CDoC ENot GGGa LHyd MDun SLdr
	'Saint Michael'	SReu
	'Saint Minver'	LHyd SLdr
	'Saint Tudy'	EPfP LHyd LKna MDun SLdr WAbe
	'Sakon' (EA)	SLdr
	'Salmon Bedspread'	SReu
	'Salmon King' (EA) **new**	CTbh
	'Salmon Queen' (M) **new**	WFar
	'Salmon Sander' (EA)	SLdr
§	'Salmon Trout'	LMil SPoG
	'Salmon's Leap' (EA/v)	CBcs COtt CSBt ENot GQui LMil LRHS NPri SHBN SLdr SReu WAbe WFar
	saluenense	GGGa LHyd LMil NPen SLdr
	- JN 260	GGGa
§	- subsp. ***chameunum***	GGGa LMil SLdr
	- - ACE 2143	WAbe
§	- - Prostratum Group	GGGa LMil WAbe
	- subsp. ***riparioides***	see *R. calostrotum* subsp. *riparium* Rock's form
	- subsp. ***saluenense*** Exbury form R 11005	LMil
	'Sammetglut'	CWri SReu
	'Samuel Taylor Coleridge' (M)	NLar
	'Sang de Gentbrugge' (G)	CSdC GGGa SReu
	sanguineum	GGGa LMil MDun NPen SLdr
§	- subsp. ***didymum***	GGGa MDun NPen
	- subsp. ***sanguineum*** var. ***cloiophorum*** R 10899	NPen
	- - var. ***didymoides*** Consanguineum Group	NPen
§	- - - Roseotinctum Group USDAPI 59038/R10903	GGGa
	- - var. ***haemaleum***	GGGa LMil NPen
	- - - F 21732	NPen
	- - - F 21735	GGGa NPen
	- - var. ***sanguineum*** F 25521	LMil
	'Santa Maria'	COtt LRHS NBlu SLdr SReu SSta
§	'Saotome' (EA)	LHyd SLdr
	'Sapphire'	CSBt LKna MAsh MBar MDun NDlv SLdr SRms
	'Sappho'	CBcs CSBt CWri ENot EPfP GBin GGGa LHyd LKna LMil LRHS MBar MDun MGos MLea NPen SBrw SHBN SLdr SPer SReu SSta WBVN WFar WGer WOrn
	'Sapporo'	GGGa LMil MBri
	'Sarah Boscawen'	SReu
	sargentianum	GGGa LMil MLea NMen NPen WAbe
	- 'Whitebait'	GGGa WAbe
	'Sarita Loder'	LHyd
	'Sarled' ♀H4	GGGa LMil NLAp NMen SReu
	Sarled Group	SRms WAbe
	'Saroi' (EA)	SLdr
	'Sarsen' (K)	CSdC
	'Saskia' (K)	LKna
	'Satan' (K) ♀H4	CSBt LKna SReu
	'Satschiko'	see *R.* 'Geisha Orange'
	'Satsop Surprise'	GGGa
	'Satsuki' (EA)	ECho
	'Saturnus' (M)	MAsh
§	***scabrifolium*** var. ***spiciferum***	GGGa SLdr
	- - SF 502	ISea
	'Scandinavia'	LHyd
	'Scarlet Romance'	MBri
	'Scarlet Wonder' ♀H4	CDoC CMHG CSBt CTrh CWri ENot EPfP GGGa GKir IDee LKna LMil LRHS MAsh MBar MBri MDun MGos MLea NBlu NPen NPri NWea SLdr SPer SReu SSta WBVN WFar WMoo
	'Schlaraffia'	NLar
	schlippenbachii (A)	GGGa GIBF LMil NPen SLdr SPer SReu SSpi
	- 'Sid's Royal Pink' (A)	LMil MDun
	'Schneebukett' **new**	LMil
	'Schneeflöckchen'	GGGa
	'Schneekrone'	GGGa LMil MAsh MBri MDun NBlu
	'Schneeperle' (EA)	LMil
	'Schneewolke'	LMil
	'Schubert' (EA)	MBar SLdr
	scintillans	see *R. polycladum* Scintillans Group
	'Scintillation'	CWri GGGa LMil MAsh MBar MDun MLea NPen SBrw SHBN SLdr
	scopulorum	SLdr
	- C&C 7571	GGGa
	- KR 5770	LMil
	- KW 6354	GGGa
	scottianum	see *R. pachypodum*
	scyphocalyx	see *R. dichroanthum* subsp. *scyphocalyx*
	Seagull Group	NPen SLdr
	searsiae	LMil SLdr
	'Seb'	SLdr
	'Second Honeymoon'	CDoC CWri ISea MLea NPen SLdr SReu
	seinghkuense CCH&H 8106	GGGa
	- KW 9254	GGGa
	selense	GGGa LMil
§	- subsp. ***dasycladum***	LMil NPen
	- subsp. ***jucundum***	GGGa LMil MDun NPen
	- - SF 660	ISea
	semnoides	GGGa SLdr
	'Senator Henry Jackson'	GGGa
	'Sennocke'	LHyd
	'September Song'	COtt CWri GGGa LHyd LMil MBri MDun MGos MLea NLar SLdr WBVN WPic
	'Serendipity'	GGGa
	serotinum	LMil NPen SLdr SReu
	- C&H 7189	GGGa
	- KR 4653	LMil
	- SEH 242	LMil
	serpyllifolium (A)	CBcs GGGa SLdr
	'Sesostris' (G)	CSdC
	'Sesterianum'	CMHG SLdr
	Seta Group	CBcs SLdr SReu
	'Seta'	WPic
	setosum	GGGa LMil MDun
	'Seven Stars'	CSBt SReu
	'Seville'	SLdr
	'Shamrock'	CDoC ENot EPfP GCrs GKir ISea LRHS MAsh MBar MDun MGos MLea SLdr SPoG SReu WFar
	'Shanty' (K/d)	LKna
	'Sheiko' **new**	SPoG
	'Sheila' (EA)	CSBt MAsh NPri
	shepherdii	see *R. kendrickii*
	sherriffii	GGGa LMil MDun NPen
	'Shiko' (EA)	MAsh

	Name	Suppliers
I	'Shiko Lavender' (A)	ENot LMil
	Shilsonii Group	LHyd NPen SLdr SReu
	'Shintoki-no-hagasane' (EA)	LHyd
	'Shira-fuji' (EA/v)	SLdr
	Shot Silk Group	SLdr
	'Shrimp Girl'	LHyd LRHS MAsh MDun NPen SLdr SReu
	shweliense	GGGa SReu
	sichotense	GGGa GIBF GKir
	sidereum	GGGa LMil NPen SLdr
	- AC 3056	WCwm
	- KW 6792	NPen
	- SF 314	ISea
	- SF 318	ISea
	siderophyllum	LMil SLdr
	sikangense	NPen SLdr
	- EGM 108	LMil
	- R 18142	NPen
	- var. ***exquisitum***	GGGa MDun
	- - EGM 349 from Wumenshan	LMil
	- var. ***sikangense***	LMil
§	- - Cookeanum Group	LHyd
§	'Silberwolke'	COtt ENot LMil SReu
	'Silver Anniversary'	MGos
	Silver Cloud	see *R.* 'Silberwolke'
	'Silver Edge'	see *R. ponticum* 'Silver Edge'
	'Silver Fountain' (EA)	LMil LRHS
	'Silver Glow' (EA)	CMac
	'Silver Jubilee'	LHyd LMil LRHS WGer
	'Silver Moon' (EA)	SCam SLdr
	'Silver Queen' (A)	ECho MGos
	'Silver Sixpence'	ENot EPfP GKir LRHS MAsh MBar MDun MGos NPen NWea SHBN SLdr SReu WOrn
	'Silver Skies'	LMil
	'Silver Slipper' (K) ♀H4	ENot GKir LHyd LKna LMil LRHS MBar MBri MDun MLea SLdr SPer SReu SSta WFar WGor
	'Silver Thimbles' (V)	GGGa
	'Silverwood' (K)	LMil
	'Silvester' (EA)	COtt MBri SCam SLdr
	'Simona'	CWri LRHS SReu
	simsii (EA)	CMac SLdr
	- SF 431	ISea
	simulans	see *R. mimetes* var. *simulans*
	sinofalconeri	IDee LMil SLdr
	- C&H 7183	GGGa
	- SEH 229	LMil
	sinogrande ♀H3	CBcs CDoC CHEx EPfP GGGa IDee LHyd LMil LRHS MDun NPen SLdr SPer SSpi WFar WGer WPic
	- AC 1888	WCwm
	- KR 4027	LMil
	- SF 350	ISea
	'Sir Charles Lemon' ♀H3-4	CDoC CWri LMil LRHS MDun NLar NPen SLdr SReu SSpi
	'Sir William Lawrence' (EA)	LKna SReu
	'Skookum'	ECho LMil MGos WBVN WOrn
	'Sleeping Beauty'	WAbe
	'Sleepy'	MGos NDlv NPen WOrn
	smirnowii	GGGa GTSp LMil LRHS NPen SReu
	smithii	see *R. argipeplum*
	- Argipeplum Group	see *R. argipeplum*
§	Smithii Group	CBcs CWri SReu
	'Sneezy'	CBcs CSBt CWri ENot EPfP GGGa GKir LHyd LMil LRHS MBar MGos NPen SLdr SPoG WFar
	'Snipe'	CBcs CDoC ENot GGGa GKir ISea LHyd LMil LRHS MBar MDun MGos NPri NWea SReu WOrn

Name	Suppliers
'Snow' (EA)	CSBt LRHS MBar SCam SLdr
'Snow Crown' (*lindleyi* hybrid)	MAsh
'Snow Hill' (EA)	GQui LHyd LMil
'Snow Lady'	CBcs ENot EPfP GEdr GQui LMil MAsh MBar MDun MGos NLAp SLdr SReu
Snow Queen Group	LKna LMil SReu
'Snowbird' (A)	GGGa LMil LRHS NLar NPri
'Snowdrift'	GGGa
'Snowflake' (EA/d)	see *R.* 'Kure-no-yuki'
'Snowhite' (EA)	NPri
'Snowstorm'	ECho WBVN
'Soho' (EA)	CSdC GQui
'Soir de Paris' (Vs)	GGGa LHyd MBar MBri MDun MLea NPen SBod SLdr SReu SSta WBVN WFar
'Soldier Sam'	SBrw SReu
'Solidarity'	ECho MDun MLea SLdr WBVN
'Solway' (Vs)	CSdC LMil
'Sonata'	CWri GGGa MDun SReu
'Songbird'	LHyd LKna LMil LRHS MBar MDun NPen SLdr SReu
'Sophie Hedges' (K/d)	LKna
sororium (V) KR 3080	GGGa
- KR 3085	LMil
- var. ***wumengense*** CN&W 990	LMil
Souldis Group	LMil MDun SLdr
souliei	LMil MDun SLdr
- deep pink-flowered	GGGa
- white-flowered	GGGa
'Southern Cross'	MLea SLdr
'Souvenir de D.A. Koster'	SLdr
'Souvenir de Doctor S. Endtz' ♀H4	CSBt LKna MBar SLdr
'Souvenir du Président Carnot' (G/d)	LKna
'Souvenir of Anthony Waterer' ♀H4	LKna MDun SReu
'Souvenir of W.C. Slocock'	LKna SHBN SLdr SReu
'Sparkler' (Vs)	GGGa
'Sparkler' (hybrid)	LRHS
speciosum	see *R. flammeum*
'Spek's Orange' (M) ♀H4	MGos
sperabile	NPen
- var. ***weihsiense***	GGGa LMil NPen SLdr
- - AC 1915	LMil
sperabiloides	GGGa NPen
sphaeranthum	see *R. trichostomum*
sphaeroblastum	GGGa LMil SLdr
- KR 1481*	NPen
- var. ***wumengense***	MDun
- - CN&W 510	ISea
- - CN&W 962	LMil
- - CN&W 968	GGGa
- - CN&W 1051	LMil
- - EGM 350	LMil
- - EGM 359	LMil
spiciferum	see *R. scabrifolium* var. *spiciferum*
spilotum	GGGa LMil NPen SLdr
spinuliferum	GGGa NPen
- SF 247	ISea
'Spitfire'	SBrw SReu
'Splendens' (G)	CSdC
'Spoonbill' (K)	LKna
'Spring Beauty' (EA)	CMac SCam SLdr SReu
'Spring Magic'	LMil NPen SLdr
'Spring Pearl'	see *R.* 'Moerheim's Pink'
'Spring Rose'	SLdr
'Spring Sunshine'	LMil

	Name	Suppliers
	'Springbok'	LHyd
	'Squirrel' (EA) ♀H4	CDoC COtt GGGa GKir LHyd LMil LRHS MAsh MDun MGos MLea NDlv NPen SLdr SReu WGer
	'Squirrel' tall (EA)	SLdr
	'Staccato'	GGGa
	Stadt Essen Group	LMil SLdr
	stamineum	GGGa LMil NPen
	- SF 417	ISea
	'Stanley Rivlin'	LHyd
§	'Stanway'	LMil SLdr
	'Star of Woking' **new**	LKna
	'Starbright Champagne'	LMil
	'Starcross'	LHyd
	'Starfish'	SReu
§	***stenopetalum*** 'Linearifolium' (A)	CMac ISea LHyd LMil SLdr WAbe
	stenophyllum	see *R. makinoi*
	stewartianum	GGGa LMil MDun SLdr
	- SF 370	ISea
	'Stewartstonian' (EA)	CMac LHyd MBar MBri SReu SSta WFar WPic
	stictophyllum	see *R. nivale* subsp. *boreale* Stictophyllum Group
	'Stoat' (EA)	GQui MDun
	'Stopham Girl' (A)	LMil
	'Stopham Lad' (A)	LMil
	'Stranraer'	MDun
	'Strategist'	SLdr
	'Strawberry Cream'	GGGa
	'Strawberry Ice' (K) ♀H4	CBcs CDoC CSBt CTri CWri EPfP GGGa GKir LKna LMil LRHS MBar MBri MDun MGos MLea MMHG SLdr SPer SReu WMoo WOrn
	strigillosum	GGGa LHyd MDun NPen SLdr
	- C&H 7035	GGGa
	- EGM 305	LMil
	- EGM 338	LMil
	- Reuthe's form	SReu
	subansiriense C&H 418	GGGa
	suberosum	see *R. yunnanense* Suberosum Group
	succothii	LHyd MDun
	- EGM 086	LMil
	- LS&H 21295	SLdr
	'Suede'	MDun
	'Sugared Almond' (K)	LMil
	'Sui-yohi' (EA) **new**	LHyd
	sulfureum SBEC 249	GGGa
	'Sulphamer'	SLdr
	'Summer Blaze' (A)	SReu
	'Summer Flame'	SReu
	'Summer Fragrance' (O) ♀H4	LMil MDun SReu SSta
	'Sun Chariot' (K)	CBcs LKna MAsh NEgg SLdr SReu
	'Sunbeam' (EA)	see *R.* 'Benifude'
	'Sunbeam' (hybrid)	LKna SReu
	'Sunny' (V)	GGGa
	(Sunrise Group) 'Sunrise'	NPen SLdr
	'Sunset Pink' (K)	SLdr
	'Sunspray' **new**	NPen
	'Sunte Nectarine' (K) ♀H4	GQui LHyd LMil MDun SCoo
	superbum (V)	GGGa
	'Superbum' (O)	SBrw SLdr
	'Surprise' (EA)	CDoC CTrh CTri LRHS SCam SCoo SLdr SPoG
	'Surrey Heath'	CBcs COtt CWri ENot EPfP GKir ISea LMil LRHS MAsh MBar MDun MGos MLea NBlu NDlv NPen SLdr SReu WOrn
	'Susan' ♀H4	CDoC CSBt CWri GGGa LHyd LKna LMil MDun MLea SLdr SPoG SReu
	'Susannah Hill' (EA)	CDoC ENot MGos SLdr
	'Sussex Bonfire'	SLdr
	sutchuenense	GGGa IDee LMil MDun NPen SLdr WCwm
	- var. ***geraldii***	see *R.* x *geraldii*
	'Swamp Beauty'	CWri LMil MDun NLar NPen
	'Swansong' (EA)	CMac
	'Sweet Simplicity'	CSBt CWri LKna
	'Sweet Sue'	NBlu NPen SLdr SReu
	'Swift'	CDoC GGGa GQui LMil LRHS LTwo MAsh SReu WGer
	'Sword of State' (K)	MAsh
	'Sylphides' (K)	LKna
	'Sylvester'	MGos NMen SReu
	'T.S. Black' (EA)	SLdr
	taggianum 'Cliff Hanger' ex KW 8546	LMil
	'Taka' (A)	SLdr
	'Taka-no-tsukasa' (EA)	SLdr
	'Takasago' (EA/d)	LHyd LMil
	'Talavera'	see *R.* (Golden Oriole Group) 'Talavera'
	taliense	GGGa LHyd LMil MDun NPen
	- F 6772	NPen
	- JN 782	GGGa
	- KR 2765	GGGa
	- KR 4056 from Cangshan	LMil
	- SSNY 352	GGGa
	'Tally Ho'	LHyd SLdr
	Tally Ho Group	SLdr
	tamaense	see *R. cinnabarinum* subsp. *tamaense*
	'Tama-no-utena' (EA)	LHyd SLdr
	'Tamarindos'	LMil SPoG
	'Tan Crossing'	SBrw
	'Tanager' (EA)	CTrh LKna
§	***tanastylum*** var. ***pennivenium*** SF 593	ISea
	'Tangerine'	see *R.* 'Fabia Tangerine'
	tapetiforme	GGGa WAbe
	'Tarantella'	LMil NEgg
	tashiroi (EA)	SLdr
	'Tatjana' ♀H4	LRHS
	tatsienense	GGGa
	'Taurus' ♀H4	CDoC COtt CWri GGGa LMil MAsh MDun MGos MLea NPen SBod WBVN
	taxifolium (v)	GGGa
	'Tay' (K)	SLdr
	'Teal'	MBar MDun MGos MLea
	'Teddy Bear'	CWri GGGa LMil LRHS MDun SLdr
§	***telmateium***	SLdr
	temenium	MDun
	- var. ***dealbatum***	LMil
	- var. ***gilvum*** 'Cruachan'	GGGa LMil
	'Temple Belle'	MDun
	Temple Belle Group	CSam LHyd LKna MLea NDlv SLdr
	'Tender Heart' (K)	SLdr
	'Tensing'	SLdr
§	***tephropeplum***	GGGa LHyd MDun
	- SF 92069	ISea
	- USDAPQ 3914/R18408	GGGa
	- Deleiense Group	see *R. tephropeplum*
	'Tequila Sunrise'	LHyd LMil
	'Terra-cotta'	LKna LMil
	'Terra-cotta Beauty' (EA)	WPat
	'Tessa'	CBcs MAsh SLdr
	Tessa Group	LKna LMil LRHS MGos
	'Tessa Bianca'	GGGa
	'Tessa Roza' ♀H4	GGGa GQui LHyd NBlu
	thayerianum	GGGa LMil SLdr
	'The Dowager'	SLdr
	'The Freak'	SLdr

§	'The Hon. Jean Marie de Montague' ♀H4	CAbP CWri EPfP LKna LMil MBri MDun MGos MLea NPen SLdr SPer SPoG SReu WBVN
	'The Master' ♀H4	LHyd LKna LMil SLdr SReu WGer
§	'The Queen Mother'	LHyd
	thomsonii	GGGa IDee LHyd LMil LRHS MDun SLdr SReu
	- AC 113	NPen
	- B&SWJ 2638	WCru
§	- subsp. ***lopsangianum***	GGGa
	- - LS&T 6561	NPen
	- subsp. ***thomsonii*** L&S 2847	GGGa
	Thor Group	GGGa SBrw SReu
	'Thousand Butterflies'	see *R.* 'One Thousand Butterflies'
	'Thunderstorm'	LHyd LKna SReu
	thymifolium	GGGa
	'Tibet' ♀H3-4	GQui LMil MBar MDun SHBN SLdr
	'Tidbit' ♀H4	GGGa LKna LMil MGos NPen SLdr
	'Tilford Seedling'	LKna
I	'Tilgates Peach'	CWri
	'Timothy James'	ENot LRHS MAsh
	'Tinkerbird'	GGGa
	'Tinsmith' (K)	SLdr
	'Tit Willow' (EA)	GKir LHyd LMil LRHS MAsh NPri SCoo SLdr
	'Titian Beauty'	CBcs COtt CSBt CWri ENot EPfP GBin GGGa GKir ISea LHyd LMil LRHS MAsh MDun MGos NBlu NDlv NPen NPri SBod SLdr SPer WBVN WBrE WFar WOrn
	'Titipu' (EA)	LHyd SLdr
	'Titness Park'	LHyd
	'Tolkien'	SReu
	'Tom Hyde' (EA)	LMil
	'Top Banana'	LRHS MDun SLdr
	'Topsvoort Pearl'	SReu
	'Torch'	LKna
	'Toreador' (EA)	SCam SLdr
	'Torero'	GGGa LMil
	'Torridon' (Vs)	LMil
	'Tortoiseshell Champagne'	see *R.* 'Champagne'
	'Tortoiseshell Orange' ♀H3-4	CDoC CSBt LHyd LKna LMil MBri MDun NBlu SHBN SLdr SPoG SReu SSta
	'Tortoiseshell Salome'	LKna SReu
	'Tortoiseshell Scarlet'	MDun SReu
	'Tortoiseshell Wonder' ♀H3-4	LKna LMil MAsh NPri SLdr SReu
	'Totally Awesome' (K)	MBri
	'Toucan' (K)	CSBt MDun SLdr
	'Tower Beauty' (A)	LHyd
	'Tower Dainty' (A)	LHyd
	'Tower Daring' (A)	LHyd SLdr
	'Tower Dexter' (A)	LHyd
	'Tower Dragon' (A)	LHyd LMil SLdr
	'Trail Blazer'	GGGa
	traillianum	GGGa LMil NPen SLdr
	- CN&W 746	ISea
	- F 5881	NPen
§	- var. ***dictyotum***	NPen
	- - 'Kathmandu'	SLdr
	Treasure Group	LHyd SLdr
	'Trebah Gem'	SLdr
	'Treecreeper' **new**	GGGa
	'Tregedna'	SLdr
	'Tregedna Red'	SReu
	'Trelawny' **new**	SLdr
	'Trewithen Orange'	MBar MDun NPen SHBN SLdr
	'Trewithen Purple'	CTrw
	trichanthum	CPne GGGa LMil NPen
	- 'Honey Wood'	LHyd LMil SLdr
	- white-flowered	LMil
	trichocladum	NPen
	- CN&W 880	ISea
	- SF 661	ISea
	- SF 96179	ISea
§	***trichostomum***	GGGa LRHS WAbe
	- Ledoides Group	MLea SReu
	- - 'Collingwood Ingram' ♀H4	LMil SLdr SReu
	triflorum	GGGa ISea LMil MDun NPen
	- C&V 9573	GGGa
	- SF 95149	ISea
§	- var. ***bauhiniiflorum***	CBcs NPen
	- var. ***triflorum*** Mahogani Group	NPen
	'Trilby'	SReu
	trilectorum	GGGa
	'Trill' (EA) **new**	SLdr
	'Trinidad'	MDun
	triplonaevium	see *R. alutaceum* var. *russotinctum* Triplonaevium Group
	'Tromba'	GGGa LMil
	'Troupial' (K)	LKna
	'Trude Webster'	GGGa SReu
	tsangpoense	see *R. charitopes* subsp. *tsangpoense*
	tsariense	GGGa LMil NPen SOkd
	- Poluninii Group	see *R. poluninii*
	- var. ***trimoense***	CDoC GGGa LMil MDun NPen
	- 'Yum Yum'	GGGa SLdr
	tsariense* x *proteoides	GGGa
§	***tsusiophyllum***	GGGa
	'Tsuta-momiji' (EA)	LHyd SLdr
	tubiforme	see *R. glaucophyllum* subsp. *tubiforme*
	'Tuffet'	SLdr SReu
	'Tulyar'	LKna
	'Tunis' (K)	ECho
	'Turacao' **new**	GGGa
	'Twilight Pink'	ENot SLdr
	'Twilight Sky' (A)	SBrw SLdr
	'Tyermannii'	LMil
	'Ukamuse' (EA/d)	LHyd SLdr
	'Umpqua Queen' (K)	MBri
	ungernii	GGGa LMil NPen SLdr
§	***uniflorum*** var. ***imperator***	LMil
	- - KW 6884	GGGa
	'Unique' (G)	EPfP ISea LKna LRHS NEgg SLdr SPer
	'Unique' (*campylocarpum* hybrid) ♀H4	CBcs CDoC CSam GGGa GKir LHyd LKna LMil LRHS MAsh MBri MDun MGos NPen NPri SHBN SLdr SReu SSta WMoo
	'Unique Marmalade'	LMil NPen SLdr WBVN WOrn
	uvariifolium	GGGa NPen SLdr
	- CN&W 127	ISea
	- CN&W 1275	ISea
	- Cox 6519	GGGa
	- KR 4158 from Zhongdian, Napa Hai	LMil
	- var. ***griseum***	IDee SLdr
	- - C&C 7506	GGGa
	- - KR 3423	LMil
	- - KR 3428	LMil
	- - KR 3774	LMil
	- - KR 3782	LMil
	- - SF 95184	ISea
	- 'Reginald Childs'	LMil LRHS SLdr
	- 'Yangtze Bend'	GGGa
	vaccinioides (V) CCH&H 8051	GGGa
	'Valentine' (EA)	GGGa

valentinianum	CBcs GGGa NPen SLdr
- F 24347	NPen
- var. ***oblongilobatum*** C&H 7186	LMil
'Van'	LMil
'Van Houttei Flore Pleno' (d)	SLdr
'Van Nes Sensation'	LMil
'Van Weerden Poelman'	EMil
Vanessa Group	LMil SReu
'Vanessa Pastel' ♀H3-4	GGGa LHyd LMil MDun MLea SReu WGer
§ 'Vanilla'	LKna
vaseyi (A) ♀H3-4	GGGa LMil SLdr
- 'White Find'	GGGa
- white-flowered (A)	LMil
'Vayo' (A) **new**	SLdr
veitchianum	GGGa
§ - Cubittii Group	GGGa SLdr
- - 'Ashcombe'	LHyd
- KNE Cox 9001	GGGa
'Veldtstar'	LHyd
'Velvet Gown' (EA)	ENot
venator	GGGa MDun WPic
'Venetian Chimes'	ENot ISea MDun NLar NPen SLdr SReu
vernicosum	GGGa LMil NPen
- F 5881	NPen
- JN 180	GGGa
- SF 416	ISea
'Veryan Bay'	CBcs
'Vespers' (EA)	MAsh
vialii (A)	GGGa
'Victoria Hallett'	SLdr SReu
'Victory' x 'Idealist'	SLdr
'Vida Brown' (EA/d)	CMac LKna SLdr SReu WPat
'Viennese Waltz'	GGGa
'Viking' (EA)	LHyd
'Viking Silver' **new**	GGGa
'Vincent van Gogh'	GGGa NPen
'Vinecourt Duke' (R/d)	CWri ECho MDun SLdr
'Vinecourt Troubador' (K/d)	CDoC CWri ECho LMil MDun SBod SLdr
'Vineland Dream' (K/d)	CWri ECho LRHS SLdr
'Vineland Fragrance'	MDun SLdr
'Vintage Rosé' ♀H4	ENot LMil MLea SLdr SReu
'Violet Longhurst' (EA)	LHyd
'Violetta' (EA)	LRHS NMen SLdr
Virginia Richards Group	CWri GKir LRHS MAsh MGos SLdr SReu SSta
viridescens 'Doshong La'	GGGa LMil
§ - Rubroluteum Group	LMil
viriosum (V)	GGGa
viscidifolium	GGGa NPen
'Viscosepalum' (G)	CSdC
viscosum (A) ♀H4	GGGa GIBF GQui IDee LHyd LKna LMil LRHS MAsh MDun SLdr SPer SReu SSpi WBVN WBrE WMoo WPic
- 'Grey Leaf' (Vs)	LMil
- var. ***montanum*** (A)	IBlr
- f. ***rhodanthum*** (A)	LMil
- 'Roseum' (Vs)	LMil
'Viscount Powerscourt'	ENot LMil SLdr
'Viscy' ♀H4	CDoC CWri ECho GGGa GQui ISea LHyd LMil MDun MGos MLea NLar NPen WBVN WOrn
§ Volker Group	CWri LMil LRHS MBar MDun NDlv SReu SSta WFar
- 'Babette'	ENot LMil NLar
- 'Lackblatt'	CDoC LMil MBri MGos MLea SLdr
'Vulcan' ♀H4	CBcs EPfP GGGa LMil MLea SHBN
'Vulcan' x ***yakushimanum***	SReu

'Vuyk's Rosyred' (EA) ♀H4	CDoC CDul CMac CSBt CTri ENot GQui LHyd LKna LMil LRHS MAsh MBar MGos NPri SCam SLdr SPer SReu WFar
'Vuyk's Scarlet' (EA) ♀H4	CBcs CBrm CDoC CMac CSBt CTrh EBee EGra EPfP GGGa GKir GQui LHyd LKna LMil LRHS MAsh MBar MDun MGos NPen SCam SLdr SPer SPlb SReu SSta WFar WMoo
'W.E. Gumbleton' (M)	SReu
'W.F. H.' ♀H4	CWri LMil NPen SLdr WGer
'W. Leith'	SLdr
wallichii	GGGa LHyd MDun SLdr
- B&SWJ 2633	WCru
- DM 21	LMil
- LS&H 17527	NPen
Walloper Group	NPen SReu
'Wallowa Red' (K)	ECho MAsh MBri MLea SLdr
'Wally Miller'	ISea LMil MAsh MDun SReu SSta WBVN
aff. ***walongense*** C&H 373	GGGa
wardii	GGGa IDee ISea LHyd LMil LRHS MDun NPen SLdr SSpi
- C&V 9558	GGGa
- C&V 9606	GGGa
- KR 3684	LMil
- KR 4913	LMil
- KR 5268	LMil
- L&S	SReu
- var. ***puralbum***	GGGa NPen
- var. ***wardii***	LMil
- - C&V 9548	GGGa
- - CN&W 1079	ISea
- - LS&T 5679	NPen
§ - - Litiense Group	SLdr
'Ward's Ruby' (EA)	CTrh CTrw
§ 'Washington State Centennial' (A)	GGGa MBri SLdr
wasonii	GGGa LHyd LMil NPen
- f. ***rhododactylum***	NPen
- - KW 1876	GGGa
- var. ***wenchuanense***	GGGa
- - C 5046	GGGa
watsonii	GGGa SLdr
- Cox 5075	GGGa
'Waxbill'	GGGa
'Waxwing'	LKna MBri
websterianum	SLdr
- Cox 5123	GGGa
- EGM 146	LMil
'Wee Bee' ♀H4	CBcs CDoC GCrs GGGa GGar GKir LMil LTwo MAsh MDun MLea NDlv SPoG SReu WAbe
§ Wega Group	LHyd
'Western Lights' (A) **new**	MAsh
'Westminster' (O)	LKna LMil
'Weston's Pink Diamond' (d)	GGGa LMil
'Weybridge'	SLdr
weyrichii (A)	GGGa
'Wheatear'	GGGa
'Whidbey Island'	LMil
'Whisperingrose'	LMil MDun MGos MLea NDlv
White Glory Group	SLdr
'White Gold'	GGGa MDun
'White Grandeur' (EA)	CTrh
'White Jade' (EA)	SLdr
'White Lady' (EA)	LKna MBar SCam SLdr WGor
'White Lights' (A) ♀H4	LMil LRHS MBri SLdr
'White Olympic Lady'	LKna
'White Perfume'	MDun SReu

	'White Peter'	GGGa
	'White Rosebud' (EA) **new**	WFar
	'White Swan' (hybrid)	LKna SBrw SReu
	'White Wings'	GQui LHyd SLdr WPic
	'Whitethroat' (K/d) ♀H4	CSdC CWri EPfP GKir GQui LKna LMil MAsh MBri MDun MMHG SLdr SPer WBVN
	'Whitney's Dwarf Red'	SLdr
	'Wigeon'	GGGa GKir LMil LRHS MAsh
	wightii	GGGa MDun NPen SLdr
	'Wild Affair'	MDun
	'Wilgen's Ruby'	CDoC CSBt LKna LMil MBar MGos NBlu NPen NWea SHBN SLdr SPoG WFar
	'Willbrit'	CDoC CWri ECho LHyd MAsh MGos SLdr WGor
	'William III' (G)	SLdr
	williamsianum ♀H4	CBcs CDoC CTbh CWri EPot GBin GGGa LHyd LMil LRHS MAsh MBar MDun MLea NPen NWea SLdr SReu SRms SSpi WFar WPic
	- Caerhays form	LMil MDun SLdr
	- 'Special'	GGGa
	'Willy' (EA)	CTrh SCam SLdr
	wilsoniae	see *R. latoucheae*
	Wilsonii Group	LKna
	wiltonii ♀H4	GGGa LHyd LMil MDun SLdr
	- CC&H 3906	GGGa
	'Windlesham Scarlet'	ENot LHyd SLdr
	'Windsor Lad'	LKna SBrw SReu
	'Windsor Peach Glow' (K)	LMil
	'Windsor Sunbeam' (K)	CWri
	'Winsome' (hybrid) ♀H3	CBcs CDoC GGGa LHyd LMil NPri SReu
	Winsome Group	CBcs CTrw CWri GKir LKna LRHS MAsh MBar MDun NPen SLdr SSta
	'Winston Churchill' (M)	MBar SReu
I	'Wintergreen' (EA)	COtt
	'Wishmoor'	SLdr SReu
	'Wisley Blush' **new**	LMil
	'Witch Doctor'	ECho LMil MDun MLea WBVN
	'Witchery'	GGGa
	'Wojnar's Purple'	MBri
	'Wombat' (EA) ♀H4	COtt CTri EPot GGGa GKir LHyd LMil LRHS MAsh MGos SLdr SReu
	'Wonderland'	LKna
	wongii	GGGa GQui LMil NPen SLdr
	'Woodcock'	LHyd
*	'Woodstock' **new**	SLdr
	'Wren'	GCrs GEdr GGGa LRHS MAsh MBar MDun MLea SLdr SReu WAbe
	'Wryneck' (K)	CSdC LHyd LMil SLdr SReu
	'Wye' (K)	SLdr
	x ***xanthanthum***	MLea
	xanthocodon	see *R. cinnabarinum* subsp. *xanthocodon*
	xanthostephanum CCH&H 8070	GGGa
	- KR 3095	LMil
	- KR 4462	LMil
	'Yaku Angel'	MDun
	'Yaku Duke'	LHyd
	'Yaku Incense'	MAsh MDun NPen WBVN
	'Yaku Prince'	MDun MGos SLdr
	yakushimanum	CBcs CDoC CMHG CSam CWri ENot EPfP GGGa GIBF IDee LHyd LKna LMil LRHS MAsh MBar MBri MDun MGos MLea NPen NWea SLdr SPer SPlb SReu SSta WGer WOrn
I	- 'Beefeater'	SLdr

	- 'Berg'	MDun
	- 'Edelweiss'	ENot
	- Exbury form	SReu
	- Exbury form x ***roxieanum*** var. ***oreonastes***	SReu
	- FCC form	see *R. yakushimanum* 'Koichiro Wada'
§	- 'Koichiro Wada' ♀H4	ENot EPfP GGGa GGar LHyd LMil LRHS MAsh MDun MGos SLdr SPoG SReu WGer
	- subsp. ***makinoi***	see *R. makinoi*
	- 'Snow Mountain'	SReu
I	- 'Torch'	WBrE
	yakushimanum x ***bureavii***	SReu
	- x ***decorum***	SLdr SReu
	- x 'Elizabeth'	GGGa
	- x 'Floriade'	SLdr
	- x ***griersonianum***	SLdr
	- x ***lanatum***	GGGa
	- x ***pachysanthum***	GGGa SLdr SReu
	- x ***proteoides***	GGGa
	- x ***rex***	SReu
	- x 'Kilimanjaro' **new**	SLdr
	- x ***tsariense***	GGGa
	'Yaye' (EA)	CDoC SLdr
	'Yaye-hiryu' (EA) **new**	LHyd
§	***yedoense*** var. ***poukhanense***	SLdr SReu
	'Yellow Cloud' (K)	ECho LMil MBri MDun
	'Yellow Hammer' ♀H4	CBcs EPfP ISea MDun NWea WBVN WBrE WFar WPic
	Yellow Hammer Group	CBcs CWri GGGa LKna LMil MBar MGos NPen SHBN SLdr SPer SReu SSta
	'Yellow Petticoats'	MLea
	'Yellow Rolls Royce'	MDun
	'Yoga' (K)	LKna
	'Yol'	SLdr
I	'Yolanta'	WAbe
	'Yorozuyo' (EA) **new**	LHyd
	'Youthful Sin'	ISea
	yuefengense **new**	GGGa
	yungningense	LMil MDun
§	- Glomerulatum Group **new**	SLdr
	yunnanense	GGGa ISea LHyd LMil MDun NPen SLdr SSpi WPic
	- AC 751	MDun NPen
	- C&H 7145	GGGa
	- KGB 551	SReu
	- KGB 559	SReu
	- SF 379	ISea
	- SF 400	ISea
	- SF 96102	ISea
	- 'Openwood' ♀H3-4	GGGa LMil
	- pink-flowered	GGGa
	- 'Red Throat'	SLdr
	- red-blotched	LMil
§	- Suberosum Group	SLdr
	- white-flowered	GGGa LMil
	zaleucum	LMil MDun
	- AC 685	MDun
	- F 15688	GGGa
	- KR 2687	GGGa
	- KR 3979	LMil
	- SF 347	ISea
	- SF 578	ISea
	Zelia Plumecocq Group	SLdr SReu
	zeylanicum	see *R. arboreum* subsp. *zeylanicum*
	Zuiderzee Group	SLdr

Rhodohypoxis (*Hypoxidaceae*)

	Name	Suppliers
	'Albrighton'	EPot ERos EWes GEdr IBal ITim LAma NMen SAga SBla SIng WAbe WPat
I	'Andromeda'	EWes
	'Appleblossom'	CWrd EPot ERos EWes IBal ITim LBee MSte NLAp NMen SCnR SIng WAbe
	baurii ♀H4	CElw CMea CNic CPBP GCrs GEdr IBal ITim LRHS MTho NMen NSla SAga SPoG SRms WAbe WFar
	- 'Alba'	CMea EDAr IBal ITim NMen
	- var. ***baurii***	CWrd EWes LBee NJOw SIng
	- 'Bridal Bouquet' (d) **new**	EWes
	- 'Coconut Ice'	EPot IBal
	- var. ***confecta***	EWes ITim SAga SBla SIng
	- 'Daphne Mary'	EWes
	- 'Dulcie'	EWes GBin ITim SCnR SIng SOkd SUsu
	- 'Lily Jean' (d)	CFwr CStu CWrd ENot EPfP EWes GEdr IBal LRHS NCGa NLAp SIng
	- 'Mars'	EWes
	- 'Pearl'	ITim
	- 'Perle'	EPot ERos EWes GEdr NJOw NMen SCnR SIng WAbe
	- 'Pictus'	IBal ITim
	- 'Pink Pearl'	EPot EWes IBal ITim
	- pink-flowered	ITim NLAp WCru
	- var. ***platypetala***	CFwr CStu CWrd ENot EPfP EPot EWes IBal ITim NLAp NMen SIng WAbe
	- var. ***platypetala*** x ***milloides***	IBal LTwo
	- - Burtt 6981	EWes
	- 'Rebecca'	EWes
	- 'Red King'	EWes IBal
	- red-flowered	NLAp SPlb
	- 'Susan Garnett-Botfield'	CWrd EPot EWes GEdr IBal ITim NMen SIng WAbe
	- white-flowered	EPot ITim NLAp NMen WCru
	'Betsy Carmine'	GEdr IBal
	'Burgundy'	SIng
	'Candy' **new**	IBal
	'Candy Stripe'	EWes GEdr SIng
	'Carina'	EWes
	'Confusion'	CWrd EWes WAbe WFar
	'Dawn'	CWrd EPot EWes IBal ITim LAma NLAp NMen SAga SBla SIng WAbe
	deflexa	CGra CLyd CWrd EWes GCrs IBal ITim MSte NLAp SAga SBla SCnR SIng WAbe WFar
	'Donald Mann'	EWes ITim NMen
	double, red-flowered (d)	CStu
	'Douglas'	CWrd ENot EPfP EPot EWes IBal ITim LAma NMen SAga SBla SIng WAbe WPat
	'Dusky'	CWrd
	'E.A. Bowles'	EWes GCrs IBal ITim NMen SIng WAbe
	'Ellicks' **new**	IBal
	'Emily Peel'	CWrd EWes WAbe
	'Eva-Kate'	CWrd ERos EWes ITim LAma SBla SIng WPat
	'Fred Broome'	CNic CWrd EPot EWes ITim LAma NMen SAga SBla SIng WAbe WPat
	'Garnett'	CWrd EDAr EWes IBal ITim NMen SBla WAbe WPat
	'Great Scott'	CWrd ECho ERos EWes IBal ITim SCnR SIng
	'Harlequin'	CWrd EPot EWes IBal ITim LAma NMen SIng WAbe
	'Hebron Farm Biscuit'	see *Hypoxis parvula* var. *albiflora* 'Hebron Farm Biscuit'
	'Hebron Farm Cerise'	see x *Rhodoxis* 'Hebron Farm Cerise'
	'Hebron Farm Pink'	see x *Rhodoxis hybrida* 'Hebron Farm Pink'
§	'Helen'	EPot EWes IBal ITim SBla SIng WAbe
	'Hinky Pinky' **new**	CFwr
	hybrids	CAvo ELan
	'Kiwi Joy' (d)	CStu
	'Margaret Rose'	CWrd EPot EWes IBal NMen SIng WAbe
	milloides	CNic EPot EWes GEdr GGar IBal ITim LBee LRHS NLAp NMen NWCA SAga SBla SCnR SIng SSpi WAbe WFar
	- 'Claret'	CSam CStu CWrd EWes IBal LTwo SAga SBla SIng SUsu WAbe WFar WPat
	- 'Damask'	CNic CStu EWes SAga SBla
	- 'Drakensberg Snow'	EWes
	- giant	IBal
	'Monty'	EPot EWes GEdr IBal SIng
	'Mystery' **new**	EWes
	'Naomi' **new**	EWes
	'New Look'	ERos EWes IBal ITim LTwo NMen SIng WAbe
	'Pearl White' **new**	IBal
	'Picta' (v)	CWrd EPot EWes GCrs GEdr IBal LAma SAga SBla SSpi WAbe WPat
	'Pink Ice'	GEdr IBal
	'Pinkeen'	EPot EWes GEdr IBal ITim LTwo SIng WAbe WFar
	'Pinkie' **new**	IBal
	'Pintado'	EWes SBla
	'Rosie Lee' **new**	EWes
	'Ruth'	EWes IBal LAma MSte SBla SIng WAbe
	'Shell Pink'	EWes IBal ITim
	'Snow White' **new**	EWes
	'Starlett'	EWes
	'Starry Eyes' (d)	CStu EWes
	'Stella'	EPot ERos EWes GEdr IBal ITim MSte NMen SAga SBla SIng WAbe
	tetra	ITim
	'Tetra Pink'	EWes IBal SIng WAbe
	'Tetra Red'	CFwr CWrd EPot EWes IBal ITim NMen SIng WAbe
	'Tetra White'	see *R.* 'Helen'
	thodiana	CStu CWrd ERos EWes GEdr NLAp NMen SBla SCnR SIng SSpi WAbe
	'Venetia'	CMea IBal SIng
	'Westacre Picotee' **new**	EWes
	'White Prince' **new**	IBal
	'Wild Cherry Blossom' **new**	CFwr EWes

Rhodophiala (*Amaryllidaceae*)

	Name	Suppliers
§	***advena***	CFil WCot
	andicola **new**	WCot
	bagnoldii F&W 8695	WCot
§	***bifida***	CFil CMon WCot
	- ***spathacea***	CMon
	chilensis	CFil WCot
	elwesii	WCot
	fulgens **new**	WCot
	mendocina **new**	SOkd WCot
	- BC&W 5028	CStu
	rhodolirion **new**	WCot

Rhodora see *Rhododendron*

Rhodothamnus (*Ericaceae*)

	chamaecistus	GCrs WAbe

Rhodotypos (*Rosaceae*)

	kerrioides	see *R. scandens*
§	***scandens***	CBcs CBot CPle CTri EBee EPfP EWTr IMGH MMHG SLon SMac SSpi WCru WSHC WSPU

Rhoeo see *Tradescantia*

x *Rhodoxis* (*Hypoxidaceae*)

	'Aurora'	EWes
	'Hebron Farm Biscuit'	see *Hypoxis parvula* var. *albiflora* 'Hebron Farm Biscuit'
§	'Hebron Farm Cerise'	CWrd ERos EWes GEdr NMen SUsu
§	***hybrida***	CPne EWes IBal NMen SIng WAbe
	- 'Aya San'	EWes
§	- 'Hebron Farm Pink'	CBro CNic CWrd ERos EWes GEdr IBal NMen SAga SBla SCnR SIng WAbe WFar
	- 'Hebron Farm Red Eye'	CWrd EWes GEdr SBla SCnR SIng WAbe WFar

Rhopalostylis (*Arecaceae*)

	baueri	CBrP WMul
	sapida	CBrP CKob CTrC WMul
	- 'Chatham Island'	CBrP
	- 'East Cape' **new**	SBig

rhubarb see *Rheum* x *hybridum*

Rhus (*Anacardiaceae*)

	ambigua	CPLN EPfP
	- B&SWJ 3656	WCru
§	***aromatica***	CAgr CArn EPfP IArd NEgg NLar
	chinensis	CDoC CMCN EGFP EPfP
	copallina	ELan EPfP LRHS
	- red-leaved	WPat
	coriaria	CArn EPfP NLar
	cotinus	see *Cotinus coggygria*
	glabra	CAgr CArn CBcs CDoC EPfP MGos SPer WDin
	- 'Laciniata' misapplied	see *R.* x *pulvinata* Autumn Lace Group
	- 'Laciniata' Carrière	NLar
	glauca	EShb
N	***hirta***	see *R. typhina*
	incisa	SPlb
	integrifolia	CArn LRav
	magalismontana	EShb
	potaninii	EPfP LRHS SSpi
§	x ***pulvinata*** Autumn Lace Group	CDoC ENot EPfP GKir MGos SDix SHBN WPat
	- - 'Red Autumn Lace' ♀H4	GKir LRHS MBlu MBri SPer
	punjabensis var. ***sinica***	WPic
§	***radicans***	CArn COld GPoy
	sylvestris	EPfP
	toxicodendron	see *R. radicans*
	trichocarpa	EPfP SSpi
	trilobata	see *R. aromatica*
N	***typhina*** ♀H4	CBcs CDoC CDul CHEx CLnd ECrN ELan ENot EPfP GKir LRHS MAsh MBar MGos NBea NBlu NFor NLon NWea SHBN SPer SPoG SSta WBrE WDin WFar WTel
§	- 'Dissecta' ♀H4	CBcs CDoC CLnd CSBt EBee ECrN ELan ENot EPfP GKev GKir MAsh MBar MBri MGos MWat NBea NBlu NEgg SEND SPer SPoG WDin WFar WMul WOrn WTel
	- 'Laciniata' hort.	see *R. typhina* 'Dissecta'
§	***verniciflua***	CLnd CMCN EPfP IArd SSpi

Rhynchelytrum see *Melinis*

Rhynchospora (*Cyperaceae*)

§	***colorata***	CRow CStu NOak NPer WHal
	latifolia	WCot

Ribes ✿ (*Grossulariaceae*)

	alpinum	CAgr CPLG ECrN LBuc MRav MWht NSti NWea SPer SRms WDin WGwG
	- 'Aureum'	CMHG EHoe EPla NFor NLon WCot WDin WSHC
	- 'Schmidt'	EBee LBuc MBar
	americanum	WBcn
	- 'Variegatum' (v)	CRez EHoe ELan EPla MRav SPer WPat
	aureum hort.	see *R. odoratum*
*	- 'Roxby Red'	MCoo
	'Ben Hope'PBR (B) **new**	MAsh
	'Black Velvet' (D)	LRHS MCoo
	x ***culverwellii***	CAgr GTwe LBuc LEdu LRHS
	Jostaberry (F)	MAsh
	diacanthum	CFil
	divaricatum	CAgr LEdu
	- 'Worcesterberry'	see *R.* 'Worcesterberry'
	fasciculatum var. ***chinense***	SSpi
	gayanum	CBcs CPMA CPle ECrN NLar SLPl
	x ***gordonianum***	CDoC CMHG CPLG CPMA EBee ELan EPfP EPla GBin GKir LAst LRHS MAsh MRav NVic SEND SLim SLon SPer SPoG SSpi WCot WFar WHCG
	latifolium **new**	CPLG
	laurifolium	CBcs CBot CFil CPLG ELan SBrw SLim SPer WBor WCru WDin WHCG WSHC
	- (f)	CPMA EPfP GKir
	- (m)	CHar CPMA EPfP GKir WCFE WPat
	- 'Mrs Amy Doncaster'	EPla
	- Rosemoor form	CSam EPfP SBrw SPoG SSpi WCot WHCG
	lobbii	EWes
	nigrum 'Baldwin' (B)	CDoC CMac CTri CWSG EPfP GBon LRHS SKee SPoG
	- 'Barchatnaja' (B) **new**	CAgr
	- 'Ben Alder'PBR (B)	LRHS MAsh
	- 'Ben Connan'PBR (B) ♀H4	CAgr CCVT CDoC COtt EPfP GTwe LRHS MAsh MBri MGos NBlu SCoo SKee SPoG
	- 'Ben Lomond'PBR (B) ♀H4	CAgr CSBt CTri ENot GBon GKir GTwe LBuc LRHS MAsh MGos MRav SPer
	- 'Ben Loyal' (B)	GTwe
	- 'Ben More' (B)	CAgr CSBt GKir GTwe LRHS MBri
	- 'Ben Nevis' (B)	CAgr CSBt CTri GTwe MAsh SKee
	- 'Ben Sarek'PBR (B) ♀H4	CAgr CDoC CSBt CSut CTri CWSG ENot GKir GTwe LBuc LRHS MAsh MGos MRav SKee SPer SPoG WOrn
	- 'Ben Tirran'PBR (B)	CAgr CDoC LBuc LRHS MAsh MBri MGos SKee SPoG WOrn
	- 'Black Reward' (B)	CAgr LRHS
	- 'Blacksmith' (B)	MCoo
	- 'Boskoop Giant' (B)	CAgr GTwe LRHS SPer
*	- 'Byelorussian Sweet' (B) **new**	CAgr
	- 'Consort' (B) **new**	CAgr
	- 'Daniel's September' (B)	GTwe MCoo
*	- 'Hystawneznaya' (B) **new**	CAgr
	- 'Jet' (B)	CAgr ENot GTwe LRHS SPer

* - 'Kosmicheskaya' (B) **new** CAgr
- 'Laciniatum' EMon
- 'Laxton's Giant' (B) GTwe
- 'Mendip Cross' (B) GTwe
- 'Pilot Alexander Mamkin' (B) **new** CAgr
- 'Seabrook's' (B) CAgr
- 'Wellington XXX' (B) CAgr CSBt CTri GTwe LBuc LRHS NBlu SPer
- 'Westwick Choice' (B) GTwe

§ ***odoratum*** More than 30 suppliers
- 'Crandall' CAgr

praecox CBcs SEND

rubrum 'Blanka' (W) CSut
- 'Cascade' (R) **new** CAgr
- 'Cherry' (R) CAgr
- 'Fay's New Prolific' (R) GTwe
- 'Hollande Rose' (P) GTwe
- 'Jonkheer van Tets' (R) ♀H4 CAgr CCVT CSBt CWSG EPfP GKir GTwe IArd LRHS MAsh MCoo SKee
- 'Junifer' (R) CAgr GTwe SKee
- 'Laxton's Number One' (R) CAgr CTri ENot GBon GTwe LRHS MRav SPer
- 'Laxton's Perfection' (R) MCoo
- 'October Currant' (P) GTwe
- 'Raby Castle' (R) GTwe
- 'Red Lake' (R) ♀H4 CAgr CMac CWSG EPfP ERea GBon GTwe LBuc LRHS MGos NBlu SKee SPer SPoG WOrn
- 'Redstart'PBR (R) CAgr COtt CSBt GTwe LBuc LRHS MAsh MBri SKee SPoG
- 'Rondom' (R) CAgr
- 'Rovada' (R) CAgr CSut GTwe MAsh SKee
- 'Stanza' (R) ♀H4 CAgr GTwe
- 'Transparent' (W) GTwe

§ - 'Versailles Blanche' (W) CAgr CMac CSBt CTri ENot EPfP GKir GTwe LBuc MAsh MBri MGos SKee SPer SPoG WOrn
- 'White Dutch' (W) MCoo
- 'White Grape' (W) ♀H4 GTwe
- 'White Pearl' (W) CBcs
- White Versailles see *R. rubrum* 'Versailles Blanche'
- 'Wilson's Long Bunch' (R) GTwe

sanguineum GKir MBar NEgg NLon WFar WMoo
- 'Albescens' SPer WBcn

I - 'Atrorubens Select' MBri
- 'Brocklebankii' CAbP CPLG EBee ELan EPfP EPla GKir LRHS MGos MRav MWat NLon NPri NSti SHBN SLim SLon SPer SPla WEas WPen WSHC
- double see *R. sanguineum* 'Plenum'
- 'Elk River Red' LRHS
- 'Elkington's White' **new** SLon
- 'Flore Pleno' see *R. sanguineum* 'Plenum'
- var. ***glutinosum*** 'Albidum' SChu
- 'King Edward VII' More than 30 suppliers
- 'Koja' GBin LAst LRHS MAsh SPoG WBcn WPat
- 'Lombartsii' MRav

§ - 'Plenum' (d) CBot
- 'Poky's Pink' GSki MGos MRav SPoG WOVN
- 'Pulborough Scarlet' ♀H4 CBcs CChe CDoC CTri CWSG ECrN ELan ENot EPfP GKir LRHS MAsh MGos MRav MWat NBir NEgg SLim SMer SPer SPla SPlb SPoG SRms SWvt WCFE WFar WMoo WWeb
- 'Red Pimpernel' CDoC CSBt LAst LSRN MAsh MBNS MBri NCGa SCoo SWvt WBcn WFar
- 'Taff's Kim' (v) EPla SLon SMad
- 'Tydeman's White' CChe CDul CPLG CSBt ELan EPfP LAst MAsh MBar NLar NPri SDnm SSpi WPat
- var. ***variegata*** **new** WFar
- White Icicle = 'Ubric' ♀H4 More than 30 suppliers

speciosum ♀H3 More than 30 suppliers

trilobum LEdu

uva-crispa 'Admiral Beattie' (F) GTwe
- 'Annelii' CAgr
- 'Aston Red' see *R. uva-crispa* 'Warrington'
- 'Bedford Red' (D) GTwe
- 'Bedford Yellow' (D) GTwe
- 'Beech Tree Nestling' (F) GTwe
- 'Blucher' (D) GTwe
- 'Bright Venus' (D) GTwe
- 'Broom Girl' (D) GTwe
- 'Captivator' (F) GTwe
- 'Careless' (C) ♀H4 CMac CSBt ENot GBon GKir GTwe LRHS MAsh MBri MGos MRav SPer
- 'Champagne Red' (F) GTwe
- 'Cook's Eagle' (C) GTwe
- 'Crown Bob' (C/D) GTwe LRHS
- 'Dan's Mistake' (D) GTwe LRHS
- 'Drill' (F) GTwe
- 'Early Sulphur' (D/C) GTwe LRHS
- 'Firbob' (D) GTwe
- 'Forester' (D) GTwe
- 'Gipsey Queen' (F) GTwe
- 'Glenton Green' (D) GTwe
- 'Golden Drop' (D) GTwe LRHS
- 'Green Gem' (C/D) GTwe
- 'Green Ocean' (F) GTwe
- 'Greenfinch'PBR (F) ♀H4 CAgr GTwe LRHS SPoG
- 'Gretna Green' (F) GTwe
- 'Guido' (F) GTwe
- 'Gunner' (D) GTwe
- 'Heart of Oak' (F) GTwe
- 'Hedgehog' (D) GTwe
- 'Hero of the Nile' (C) GTwe
- 'High Sheriff' (D) GTwe
- 'Hinnonmäki' (F) **new** CAgr
- 'Hinnonmäki Gul' CAgr ENot
- 'Hinnonmäki Röd' (F) CAgr ENot GTwe MCoo
- 'Howard's Lancer' (C/D) GTwe
- 'Invicta'PBR (C) ♀H4 CAgr CCVT CDoC CMac CSBt CSut CTri CWSG ENot EPfP GBon GKir LBuc LRHS MAsh MBri MGos SCoo SKee SPer SPoG WBVN WOrn
- 'Ironmonger' (D) GTwe LRHS
- 'Jubilee' (C/D) COtt LBuc MBri MGos
- 'Keepsake' (C/D) GTwe LRHS MRav
- 'King of Trumps' (F) GTwe LRHS
- 'Lancashire Lad' (C/D) GTwe LRHS
- 'Langley Gage' (D) GTwe LRHS MCoo
- 'Laxton's Amber' (D) GTwe
- 'Leveller' (D) ♀H4 CMac CSBt CSut CTri ENot GBon GKir GTwe LBuc LRHS MAsh MGos MRav SKee SPer
- 'London' (C/D) GTwe LRHS
- 'Lord Derby' (C/D) GTwe
- 'Martlet' (F) CAgr GTwe
- 'May Duke' (C/D) LRHS
- 'Mitre' (C) GTwe
- 'Pax'PBR (F) CAgr CDoC CSBt EPfP GTwe LBuc MAsh MBri SKee SPoG WOrn
- 'Peru' (F) GTwe
- 'Pitmaston Green Gage' (D) GTwe
- 'Plunder' (F) GTwe

- 'Prince Charles' (F)	GTwe
- 'Queen of Trumps' (D)	GTwe
- 'Rokula'PBR (D)	CDoC GTwe SKee
- 'Rosebery' (D)	GTwe
- 'Scotch Red Rough'	GTwe
- 'Scottish Chieftan' (D)	GTwe
- 'Snow' (F)	EBee EPfP ERob ESCh NBrk NHaw NTay SCoo SLim SLon WBGC
- 'Snowdrop' (D)	GTwe
- 'Surprise' (C)	GTwe
- 'Telegraph' (F)	GTwe
- 'Tom Joiner' (F)	GTwe
- 'Victoria' (C/D)	GTwe
- 'Warrington' (D)	GTwe
- 'Whinham's Industry' (C/D) ♀H4	CCVT CMac CSBt CSut CTri ENot GBon GKir GTwe LBuc MAsh MBri MGos MRav SPer
- 'White Lion' (C/D)	GTwe
- 'White Transparent' (C)	GTwe
- 'Whitesmith' (C/D)	GTwe LRHS NBlu
- 'Woodpecker' (D)	GTwe LRHS
- 'Yellow Champagne' (D)	GTwe LRHS
viburnifolium	CBcs CPle CSam LEdu
§ 'Worcesterberry' (F)	LRHS MBri MGos SPer

Richea (*Epacridaceae*)

dracophylla	GGar SAPC
sprengelioides	SSpi

Ricinocarpos (*Euphorbiaceae*)

pinifolius	ECou

Ricinus (*Euphorbiaceae*)

communis	SWal SYvo
- 'Carmencita' ♀H3	CHEx EUJe LRav SGar
- 'Gibsonii'	WMul
- 'Impala'	CSpe SYvo
- 'Zanzibariensis'	EShb EUJe WMul

Riocreuxia (*Asclepiadaceae*)

torulosa	CPLG EShb SPlb

Robinia (*Papilionaceae*)

x ***ambigua***	SSpi WPGP
- 'Decaisneana'	EWTr
fertilis	EBee SIgm SSpi
§ ***hispida***	CDul CEnd CLnd CWib ECrN ELan EPfP EWTr MAsh MBlu SBLw SHBN SPer SPoG SSpi WDin WJas WOrn WSHC WSPU
- 'Macrophylla'	CEnd SSpi
- 'Rosea' misapplied	see *R. hispida*
- 'Rosea' ambig.	CBcs CBot EBee ENot SBLw
kelseyi	CDul MAsh SPer
x ***margaretta*** Casque Rouge	see *R.* x *margaretta* 'Pink Cascade'
§ - 'Pink Cascade'	CAlb CDoC CDul CEnd CLnd EBee ECrN EPfP EWTr LRHS MBlu MBri SBLw SCoo SCrf SHBN SLim SPer SSpi WDin
neomexicana	CLnd
pseudoacacia	CAgr CCVT CDul CLnd EBee ECrN ELan EPfP EWTr LBuc MCoo SBLw SPlb WBVN WDin WFar WNor
- 'Bessoniana'	EBee ECrN SBLw WDin
- 'Fastigiata'	see *R. pseudoacacia* 'Pyramidalis'
- 'Frisia' ♀H4	More than 30 suppliers
- 'Inermis' hort.	see *R. pseudoacacia* 'Umbraculifera'
§ - 'Lace Lady'PBR	EBee ELan ENot EPfP LRHS MAsh MBri MGos MRav NLar SCoo SLim SPoG WWes
* - 'Mimosifolia'	MBri
- 'Myrtifolia'	SBLw
§ - 'Pyramidalis'	SBLw
- 'Red Cascade'	SBLw
- 'Rozynskiana'	CDul LRHS SFam
- 'Tortuosa'	CDul CEnd CLnd EBee ECrN ELan EMil EPfP LRHS MBlu MBri SBLw SPer WPGP
- Twisty Baby PBR	see *R. pseudoacacia* 'Lace Lady'
§ - 'Umbraculifera'	CDul CLnd ECrN EMil LRHS MGos SBLw SFam
- 'Unifoliola'	SBLw
x ***slavinii*** 'Hillieri' ♀H4	CDoC CDul CEnd CLnd EBee ECrN ELan EPfP EWTr LRHS MAsh MBlu MGos SCoo SCrf SPer SPoG SSpi WOrn WPGP

Rochea see *Crassula*

Rodgersia ✿ (*Saxifragaceae*)

ACE 2303	GBuc
aesculifolia ♀H4	More than 30 suppliers
- green bud	IBlr
- pink-flowered	IBlr SSpi
- 'Red Dawn'	IBlr
aff. ***aesculifolia*** petaloid	IBlr
'Blickfang'	IBlr
'Die Anmutige'	CRow
'Die Schöne'	CLAP
'Elfenbeinturm'	EBee IBlr
'Fireworks' **new**	CFir
henrici	CBct CLAP CRow EBrs GKir IBlr LBuc MBri NBro NMyG WMoo WTin
- 'Buckshaw White'	IBlr
- 'Castlewellan'	IBlr
- hybrid	CAby EBee EMan EWTr GBuc ITim NLar WAul WHil
'Herkules'	CBct EBee EMan GCal GLil MBNS NLar SSpi WMul
'Irish Bronze' ♀H4	CLAP EBrs EMan EPla GBin GKir IBlr LPio LRHS SSpi WCAu WFar WMoo WPnP
'Koriata'	IBlr
'Kupfermond'	CRow IBlr
'Maigrün'	IBlr
nepalensis	CFil CLAP IBlr MDun
'Panache'	IBlr
'Parasol'	CBct CFil CHad CLAP GBuc IBlr SSpi WPnP
pinnata	More than 30 suppliers
- B&SWJ 7741A	WCru
- from SW China	GIBF
- L 1670	CLAP SSpi
- SDR 3301	GKev
- 'Alba'	EBee GKir IBlr MLLN WPnP
- 'Buckland Beauty'	CLAP IBlr SBla SSpi
- 'Cally Salmon'	EWes GCal
- 'Crûg Cardinal'	WCru
- 'Elegans'	CBct CHad EBee EBrs EChP ELan EMan ENot EPfP EPla GKir IBlr LAst LRHS MRav NEgg NMyG NOrc SMad SWvt WAul WCot WHil WPnP WPop
- 'Maurice Mason'	SDix SMHy
- 'Mont Blanc'	IBlr
- Mount Stewart form	IBlr
- 'Perthshire Bronze'	IBlr
- 'Rosea'	IBlr
- 'Superba' ♀H4	More than 30 suppliers
- white-flowered	GAbr GCal
podophylla ♀H4	More than 30 suppliers
- 'Braunlaub' **new**	NBro
- 'Bronceblad'	IBlr

- Donard form CFil GBin IBlr MBri WPGP
- 'Rotlaub' CDes CLAP CRow EBee GCal IBlr LRHS WCot WMoo WPGP
- 'Smaragd' CDes CLAP CRow EBrs GCal IBlr LRHS NLar
purdomii hort. CDes CLAP EBee GCal GKir LRHS SSpi WCot WPGP
§ 'Reinecke Fuchs' IBlr
'Rosenlicht' CRow
'Rosenzipfel' IBlr
sambucifolia CBcs CLAP COlW CRow EBee EBrs EUJe EWTr GBBs GFlt GKir ITim LEdu NEgg NLar NSti SMac SPer SSpi WCAu WCru WFar WMoo WPnP WTin
- B&SWJ 7899 WCru
- dwarf pink-flowered GKir IBlr
- dwarf white-flowered IBlr
- large green-stemmed IBlr
- large red-stemmed IBlr
- 'Mountain Select' WFar
- white-flowered ITim
sambucifolia x ***pinnata*** IBlr
tabularis see *Astilboides tabularis*

Rohdea (*Convallariaceae*)

japonica CFil WCot WPGP
- B&SWJ 4853 WCru
- 'Godaishu' (v) WCot
- 'Gunjaku' (v) EMon WCot
- 'Lance Leaf' EPla
- long-leaved WCru WFar
- 'Miyakonojo' (v) **new** EBee WCot
- 'Talbot Manor' (v) CFil EBee EBla EPla WCot
- 'Tama-jishi' (v) WCot
- 'Tuneshige Rokujo' (v) WCot
watanabei B&SWJ 1911 WCru

Romanzoffia (*Hydrophyllaceae*)

§ ***californica*** **new** CPom NJOw
§ ***sitchensis*** CTri EBee MAvo NJOw
suksdorfii see *R. sitchensis*
tracyi CLAP CPom CStu EBee GGar NRya WBor WCru
unalaschcensis CLAP CPom GKev GTou NJOw NWCA SGar SRms WBVN WPer

Romneya (*Papaveraceae*)

coulteri ♀H4 More than 30 suppliers
§ - var. ***trichocalyx*** CFil CFir CLAP CPLG GMac SBrw SSpi WPGP
§ - 'White Cloud' ♀H4 CFil EHol ENot ERea SBrw WPGP
x ***hybrida*** see *R. coulteri* 'White Cloud'
trichocalyx see *R. coulteri* var. *trichocalyx*

Romulea (*Iridaceae*)

amoena 'Niewoodlville' ECho
atrandra CStu
autumnalis CStu ECho
barkerae 'Paternoster' ECho
battandieri AB&S 4659 from Morocco **new** CMon
bifrons AB&S 4359 from Morocco **new** CMon
bulbocodium CBro CNic ESis
- var. ***clusiana*** CNic
- - MS 239 EHyt
- - from Morocco **new** CMon
* - 'Knightshayes' EHyt
- var. ***leichtliniana*** CNic
- - from Crete **new** CMon
camerooniana **new** CPLG
columnae CNic
- var. ***melitensis*** from Malta **new** CMon
dichotoma ECho
engleri CStu
- SF 3 from Morocco **new** CMon
gigantea CStu
hirta CMon
kamisensis ECho
leipoldtii ECho
ligustica var. ***rouyana*** SF 360 from Morocco **new** CMon
linaresii CNic EHyt
- CE&H 620 from Greece **new** CMon
* ***luteoflora*** var. ***sanguinea*** **new** GCrs
macowanii var. ***alticola*** CNic WAbe
monticola CMon
namaquensis ECho
nivalis EHyt
obscura var. ***blanda*** ECho
- var. ***obscura*** ECho
- var. ***subtestacea*** ECho
pearsonii **new** EHyt
ramiflora CPBP
- subsp. ***gaditana*** EHyt
requienii CNic NMen
- L 65 EHyt
* ***zahnii*** CNic

Rorippa (*Brassicaceae*)

nasturtium-aquaticum EMFW NArg WPop WWpP

Rosa ✿ (*Rosaceae*)

ACE 241 CFee
A Shropshire Lad = 'Ausled'PBR (S) CSam ESty LRHS MAus MBri MJon NEgg SPoc SWCr
Abbeyfield Rose = 'Cocbrose'PBR (HT) ♀H4 ENot GCoc GGre MGan MRav SPer SWCr
§ 'Abbotswood' (*canina* hybrid) EBls MAus
Abigaile = 'Tanelaigib'PBR (F) MJon NBat
Abraham Darby = 'Auscot'PBR (S) CGro CTri EBee EPfP ESty GGre LRHS LStr MAsh MAus MFry MJon MRav MWgw NEgg SMad SPer SPoG SPoc SSea SWCr WHCG
Acapulco = 'Dicblender'PBR (HT) IDic
acicularis GIBF
- var. ***nipponensis*** EBls
'Adam' (ClT) EBls
'Adam Messerich' (Bb) EBee EBls MAus SWCr WHCG
'Adélaïde d'Orléans' (Ra) ♀H4 CRHN EBls LRHS MAsh MAus MRav SFam SPer SPoc SWCr WAct WHCG
Admirable = 'Searodney' (Min) MJon
'Admiral Rodney' (HT) MGan MJon
Adriana = 'Frydesire' (HT) MBri MFry
'Agatha' see *R.* x *francofurtana* 'Agatha'
Agatha Christie = 'Kormeita'PBR (ClF) ENot MBri MRav SPoc SWCr
'Aglaia' (Ra) MAus WHCG
'Agnes' (Ru) ♀H4 EBee EBls ECnt EMFP ENot EPfP EWTr GCoc IArd LRHS MAus MRav NBPC SPer SPoc SSea SWCr WAct WHCG WOVN
agrestis **new** WBWf

	Name	Suppliers
	'Aimée Vibert' (Ra)	CSam EBee EBls MAus MRav SPer SPoc SWCr WAct WHCG
	'Alain Blanchard' (G)	EBls MAus SWCr WHCG
	x ***alba*** (A)	EBls
§	- 'Alba Maxima' (A)	EBls EMFP ENot GCoc GGre LRHS MAus MRav NBPC NEgg SFam SPer SSea SWCr WAct WHCG
§	- 'Alba Semiplena' (A) 🏆H4	CHad EBls EMFP LRHS MAus SPer SWCr WAct WHCG
	- Celestial	see *R.* 'Céleste'
	- 'Maxima'	see *R.* x *alba* 'Alba Maxima'
	Alba Meidiland = 'Meiflopan'[PBR] (S/GC)	WOVN
	'Albéric Barbier' (Ra) 🏆H4	More than 30 suppliers
	'Albertine' (Ra) 🏆H4	More than 30 suppliers
	'Alchymist' (S/Cl)	CHad CPou EBee EBls ENot EPfP LRHS MAus MBNS MBri MGan MJon MRav SPer SPoc SWCr WAct WHCG WKif
	Alec's Red = 'Cored' (HT)	CBcs CGro CSBt CTri CWSG EBls ENot GCoc GGre GKir LStr MAsh MAus MGan MJon MRav NPri SPer SPoG SWCr
	Alexander = 'Harlex' (HT) 🏆H4	CGro CSBt EBls ENot GCoc GGre LGod LStr MAus MFry MGan MJon MRav SPer SPoc SSea SWCr
	'Alexander Hill Gray' (T)	EBls
	'Alexander von Humboldt' (Cl)	MGan
	'Alexandre Girault' (Ra)	CRHN EBee EBls EMFP LRHS MAus SPer SWCr WHCG
§	'Alfred Colomb' (HP)	EBls
	'Alfred de Dalmas' misapplied	see *R.* 'Mousseline'
	'Alfresco'[PBR] (ClHT)	CSBt LGod MJon SPoc SSea SWCr
	'Alida Lovett' (Ra)	EBls MAus
	Alison = 'Coclibee'[PBR] (F)	GCoc SPoc SWCr
	'Alison Wheatcroft' (F)	EBls
§	'Alister Stella Gray' (N)	EBee EBls LRHS MAus MRav NEgg SPer SSea SWCr WAct WHCG
	'Allen Chandler' (ClHT)	EBls MAus
	'Allgold' (F)	CBcs CGro EBls GKir MGan MJon SSea SWCr
	Alnwick Castle = 'Ausgrab' (S)	MAus
	'Aloha' (ClHT) 🏆H4	CBcs CGro CSam EBee EBls EPfP ESty GKir LAst LRHS LStr MAus MBri MFry MGan MJon MRav SChu SPer SPoG SSea SWCr WAct WHCG
	alpina	see *R. pendulina*
	'Alpine Sunset' (HT)	CTri EBls ESty GGre MAsh MRav SPer SPoG SWCr
	altaica hort.	see *R. pimpinellifolia* 'Grandiflora'
	Altissimo = 'Delmur' (Cl)	CHad EBee EBls EMFP LRHS MAus MGan MJon SPer SSea SWCr WAct
	'Amadis' (Bs)	EBls MAus WHCG
	Amanda = 'Beesian' (F)	MBri
	'Amazing Grace' (HT)	GCoc GGre SWCr
	Amber Abundance = 'Harfizz'[PBR] (S)	MAsh SPoc SWCr
	Amber Cover = 'Poulbambe'[PBR] (GC)	ECnt ESty MAsh SWCr
	Amber Hit = 'Poultrav'[PBR] (Patio)	SPoc SWCr
	Amber Nectar = 'Mehamber'[PBR] (F)	MJon
	Amber Queen = 'Harroony'[PBR] (F) 🏆H4	CGro CSBt CTri EBee EBls EPfP ESty GCoc GGre IArd LGod LStr MAsh MAus MBri MFry MGan MJon MRav NPri SPer SPoG SPoc SWCr
	Amber Star = 'Manstar' (Min)	MJon NBat
	Amber Sunset = 'Manamsun' (Min)	MJon NBat
	amblyotis **new**	GIBF
§	'Ambossfunken' (HT)	MGan
	Ambridge Rose = 'Auswonder' (S)	LRHS MAus MJon NEgg SPer SWCr
	'Amélia'	see *R.* 'Celsiana'
	Amelia = 'Poulen011' (S)	ECnt
	'American Pillar' (Ra)	CGro CRHN CSBt CSam CTri CWSG EBls ECnt ELan ENot GKir LRHS LStr MAsh MAus MRav SPer SPoG SPoc SSea SWCr WAct WHCG
	'Amy Robsart' (RH)	EBls EMFP MAus SWCr
	Anabell = 'Korbell' (F)	NBat
	'Anaïs Ségalas' (G)	MAus
§	'Andersonii' (*canina* hybrid)	EBls ISea MAus SWCr
	'Andrea' (ClMin) **new**	MJon
§	'Anemone' (Cl)	EBls MAus
	anemoniflora	see *R.* x *beanii*
	anemonoides	see *R.* 'Anemone'
	- 'Ramona'	see *R.* 'Ramona'
	'Angel Gates'	WAct
	Angela Rippon = 'Ocaru' (Min)	CSBt MFry MJon SPer SWCr
	'Angela's Choice' (F)	MGan
	'Angèle Pernet' (HT)	EBls
	'Angelina' (S)	EBls
	Anisley Dickson = 'Dickimono'[PBR] (F) 🏆H4	IDic LGod MGan NBat SPer
	'Ann Aberconway' (F)	MJon
	Ann = 'Ausfete'[PBR]	LRHS MAus
	Ann Henderson = 'Fryhoncho' (F) **new**	MFry
	'Anna de Diesbach' (HP)	EBls
	Anna Ford = 'Harpiccolo'[PBR] (Min/Patio) 🏆H4	CWSG LStr MAus MJon SPer SWCr
	Anna Livia = 'Kormetter'[PBR] (F) 🏆H4	ECnt ENot MBri MGan MJon MRav
	'Anna Olivier' (T)	EBls
	'Anna Pavlova' (HT)	EBls
	Anne Boleyn = 'Ausecret'[PBR] (S)	LRHS MAsh MAus MJon NEgg SPoc SWCr
	'Anne Cocker' (F)	GCoc
	'Anne Dakin' (ClHT)	MAus
	Anne Harkness = 'Harkaramel' (F)	MAus MGan MJon SPer
	Anne Marie Laing = 'Jospink' (F)	EBls
	'Anne of Geierstein' (RH)	EBls MAus SWCr
	'Anne Watkins' (HT)	EBls
	Annick = 'Fryfrenzy' (F)	MFry
	'Anthony' (S)	EBls
	Antique '89 = 'Kordalen'[PBR] (ClF)	EBee EBls ENot MJon MRav WGer
	'Antoine Rivoire' (HT)	EBls
	'Antonine d'Ormois' (G)	EBls
	Anvil Sparks	see *R.* 'Ambossfunken'
	Aperitif = 'Macwaira'[PBR] (HT)	ECnt GCoc MJon
	apothecary's rose	see *R. gallica* var. *officinalis*
	'Apple Blossom' (Ra)	EBls SWCr WHCG
	'Applejack' (S)	EBls
	Apricot Ice = 'Diceyti'[PBR] (Poly/F)	ESty IDic
	'Apricot Nectar' (F)	MAus MGan SPer
	'Apricot Silk' (HT)	CBcs CTri EBls MAus MGan MRav SPer SWCr
	Apricot Summer = 'Korpapiro'[PBR] (Patio)	ENot MAsh MBri MJon SPoG SWCr

Name	Suppliers
Apricot Sunblaze = 'Savamark'PBR (Min)	CSBt EBls
Arc Angel = 'Fryorst' (HT)	MFry
Arcadian = 'Macnewye' (F)	MJon
'Archiduc Joseph' misapplied	see *R.* 'Général Schablikine'
'Archiduchesse Elisabeth d'Autriche' (HP)	EBls
'Ardoisée de Lyon' (HP)	EBls
Ards Beauty = 'Dicjoy' (F)	MGan SPer
'Ards Rover' (ClHP)	EBls
'Arethusa' (Ch)	EBls SPla SWCr
'Aristide Briand' (Ra)	EBls
'Arizona Sunset' (Min)	MJon NBat
§ ***arkansana*** var. ***suffulta***	EBls WHCG
Armada = 'Haruseful' (S)	SSea SWCr
'Arrillaga' (HP)	MAus
'Arthur Bell' (F) ♀H4	CSBt CWSG EBls ENot EPfP ESty GGre IArd LAst LRHS LStr MAsh MAus MGan MRav NPri SPer SPoG SPoc SSea SWCr WBVN
'Arthur de Sansal' (DPo)	EBls MAus SWCr WHCG
Arthur Merril = 'Hormerry' (F)	NBat
arvensis	CCVT CRWN EBls LBuc MAus NHaw NWea WAct
§ 'Aschermittwoch' (Cl)	EBls
Ash Wednesday	see *R.* 'Aschermittwoch'
'Assemblage des Beautés' (G)	EBls MAus
'Astra Desmond'	see *R.* 'White Flight'
'Astrid Späth Striped' (F)	EBls
Atco Royale = 'Frywinner'PBR (F)	MFry
Atlantic Star = 'Fryworld'PBR (F)	MFry
Atlantis Palace = 'Poulsiana'PBR (F)	MAsh SWCr
Audrey Wilcox = 'Frywilrey' (HT)	CSBt MFry
'August Seebauer' (F)	EBls
'Auguste Gervais' (Ra)	EBls LRHS MAus SPer WHCG
'Augustine Guinoisseau' (HT)	EBls
'Augustine Halem' (HT)	EBls
Austrian copper rose	see *R. foetida* 'Bicolor'
Austrian yellow	see *R. foetida*
'Autumn Delight' (HM)	EBls MAus WHCG
Autumn Fire	see *R.* 'Herbstfeuer'
'Autumn Sunlight' (ClF)	MGan SPer SPoc SWCr
'Autumn Sunset' (S)	EBls MJon
'Autumnalis'	see *R.* 'Princesse de Nassau'
'Aviateur Blériot' (Ra)	EBls MAus
'Avignon' (F)	ECnt
Avon = 'Poulmulti'PBR (GC) ♀H4	EBee ECnt ELan GCoc LGod MJon MRav NPri SPer SSea SWCr WHCG
Awakening	see *R.* 'Probuzení'
Awareness = 'Frybingo'PBR (HT)	MFry
'Ayrshire Splendens'	see *R.* 'Splendens'
'Baby Bio' (F/Patio)	CBcs ESty MGan
'Baby Faurax' (Poly)	MAus
Baby Gold Star (Min)	see *R.* 'Estrellita de Oro'
'Baby Katie' (Min)	NBat
Baby Love = 'Scrivluv'PBR (yellow) (Min/Patio) ♀H4	MAsh MAus MJon SPoG SWCr
Baby Masquerade = 'Tanba' (Min)	ENot MJon SPer
Baby Sunrise = 'Macparlez' (Min)	MJon
Babyface = 'Rawril'PBR (Min) **new**	ESty SWCr
'Bad Neuenahr' (Cl)	MGan
'Ballerina' (HM/Poly) ♀H4	More than 30 suppliers
Ballindalloch Castle = 'Cocneel'PBR (F)	GCoc
'Baltimore Belle' (Ra)	CRHN EBls MAus SWCr WHCG
banksiae (Ra)	CPLN CPou GQui SRms
- SF 96051	ISea
- ***alba***	see *R. banksiae* var. *banksiae*
§ - var. ***banksiae*** (Ra/d)	CBot CPou CSBt CTri EBee ELan EPfP ERea LStr MAus SBra SSea WBcn WGer XPep
- 'Lutea' (Ra/d) ♀H3	More than 30 suppliers
- 'Lutescens' (Ra)	XPep
- var. ***normalis*** (Ra)	CBot CSBt LRHS MAus NSti SLon SWCr WHer WOut XPep
'Bantry Bay' (ClHT)	CSBt EBee EBls ELan ENot LStr MGan MRav NBlu SPer SPla SPoc SSea SWCr
Barbara Austin = 'Austop'PBR (S)	LRHS MAus SWCr
'Barbara Carrera' (F)	EBls
Barkarole = 'Tanelorak'PBR (HT)	CSBt LStr MJon
'Baron de Bonstetten' (HP)	EBls
'Baron de Wassenaer' (CeMo)	EBls
'Baron Girod de l'Ain' (HP)	EBee EBls MAsh MAus MRav NEgg SPla SPoc SSea SWCr WGer WHCG
'Baroness Rothschild' (HP)	see *R.* 'Baronne Adolph de Rothschild'
§ 'Baronne Adolph de Rothschild' (HP)	EBee EMFP MRav SPoc SWCr WHCG
Baronne Edmond de Rothschild = 'Meigriso' (HT)	MAus MGan WAct
Baronne Edmond de Rothschild, Climbing = 'Meigrisosar' (Cl/HT)	CSBt
'Baronne Henriette de Snoy' (T)	EBls
'Baronne Prévost' (HP)	EBls MAus SFam WAct WHCG
Baroque = 'Harbaroque'PBR (GC/F/S)	GGre SWCr
§ x ***beanii*** (Ra)	EPla SMad
'Beau Narcisse' (G)	MAus
'Beauté' (HT)	EBls MGan
Beautiful Britain = 'Dicfire'PBR (F)	CWSG EBls IDic LStr MGan MRav SWCr
Beautiful Sunrise = 'Bostimebide'PBR (Cl/Patio)	ESty MBri MJon SPoc SWCr
'Beauty of Rosemawr' (ClT)	EBls
Beauty Star = 'Frystar'PBR	see *R.* Liverpool Remembers = 'Frystar'
Behold = 'Savahold' (Min)	MJon NBat
'Bel Ange' (HT)	MGan
bella	LRHS
Bella = 'Pouljill'PBR (S)	CPou EBee SWCr
'Belle Amour' (AxD)	EBls MAus SWCr WAct WHCG
'Belle Blonde' (HT)	MGan SPer
'Belle de Crécy' (G) ♀H4	CPou CSam EBee EBls GKir LRHS LStr MAsh MAus SFam SPer SWCr WAct WHCG
'Belle des Jardins' misapplied	see *R.* x *centifolia* 'Unique Panachée'
Belle Epoque = 'Fryyaboo'PBR (HT)	GCoc LStr MAus MFry MGan MJon SPoc SWCr
'Belle Isis' (G)	EBls MAus MRav SPer SWCr

'Belle Lyonnaise' (ClT)	EBls
'Belle Poitevine' (Ru)	EBls MAus
'Belle Portugaise' (ClT)	EBls MAus
§ 'Belvedere' (Ra)	EBls MAus MBri SPer SWCr WHCG
Benita = 'Dicquarrel'[PBR] (HT)	IDic
Benjamin Britten = 'Ausencart'[PBR] (S)	CSBt ECnt EPfP MAus MBri MJon NEgg SWCr
§ 'Bennett's Seedling' (Ra)	EBls
Benson and Hedges Gold = 'Macgem' (HT)	CWSG
Benson and Hedges Special = 'Macshana'[PBR] (Min)	ELan ENot ESty MJon
Berkshire = 'Korpinka'[PBR] (GC) ♀H4	ENot LStr MJon MRav SSea SWCr
Best of Friends = 'Pouldunk' (HT)	EBee ECnt
Best Wishes = 'Chessnut'[PBR] (Cl/v)	COtt GGre SPoc SSea SWCr
Bettina = 'Mepal' (HT)	MGan
Betty Boop = 'Wekplapic'[PBR] (F)	GCoc MJon SPoc SWCr
Betty Driver = 'Gandri'[PBR] (F)	MGan SPer
Betty Harkness = 'Harette'[PBR] (F)	GCoc GGre LStr MJon SWCr
'Betty Prior' (F)	GCoc MGan
'Betty Uprichard' (HT)	EBls
Bewitched = 'Poulbella'[PBR] (F)	ECnt SPoc SWCr
Bianco = 'Cocblanco'[PBR] (Patio/Min)	ENot GCoc GGre MAus SWCr
Biddulph Grange = 'Frydarkeye' (S)	MFry
§ ***biebersteinii***	EBls
'Big Chief' (HT)	MJon
Big Purple = 'Stebigpu'[PBR] (HT)	ECnt GGre MJon
Birthday Girl = 'Meilasso'[PBR] (F)	LAst MJon MRav SPoc SSea SWCr
Birthday Wishes = 'Guesdelay' (HT)	SWCr
Bishop Elphinstone = 'Cocjolly' (F)	GCoc
'Black Beauty' (HT)	MAus MJon
'Black Ice' (F)	CGro MGan
'Black Jack' (Ce)	see *R.* 'Tour de Malakoff'
Black Jack = 'Minkco' (Min/Patio)	NBat
Black Jade = 'Benblack' (Min/Patio)	MJon
'Black Prince' (HP)	EBls
'Blairii Number One' (Bb)	EBls
'Blairii Number Two' (ClBb) ♀H4	EBls LRHS MAus MRav NEgg SFam SPer SPoc SWCr WAct WHCG
'Blanche de Vibert' (DPo)	EBee EBls MAus SWCr
'Blanche Double de Coubert' (Ru) ♀H4	CDul CSam EBee EBls ECnt ELan ENot EPfP GCoc LBuc LRHS LSRN LStr MAus MFry MJon MWgw NLon SFam SPer SSea SWCr WAct WHCG WOVN
'Blanche Moreau' (CeMo)	EBls EWTr GGre MAus SPer SWCr WAct
'Blanchefleur' (CexG)	EBls MAus MRav SWCr WAct
blanda	EBls
'Blessings' (HT) ♀H4	CBcs CGro CSBt EBls ENot GGre LAst LStr MAsh MAus MFry MGan MJon MRav NBlu SPer SPoc SWCr
'Bleu Magenta' (Ra) ♀H4	EBee EBls EWTr IArd MAus MRav SPoc SWCr WAct WHCG WKif
'Bliss' (S)	EBls
'Blonde Bombshell' (F)	ESty
'Bloomfield Abundance' (Poly)	CPou EBls MAus MRav SPer SWCr WHCG WHer
'Bloomfield Dainty' (HM)	EBls
Blooming Marvellous (Patio)	GGre SWCr
'Blossomtime' (Cl)	SMad SPer
'Blue Diamond' (HT)	MGan SWCr
Blue Moon = 'Tannacht' (HT)	CGro CTri EBls ELan EPfP GCoc GGre LAst LGod MAsh MGan MJon NPri SPer SPoG SSea SWCr
Blue Peter = 'Ruiblun'[PBR] (Min)	ESty MFry MJon
'Blush Boursault' (Bs)	EBls
'Blush Damask' (D)	EBls SWCr WHCG
'Blush Hip' (A)	MAus
'Blush Noisette'	see *R.* 'Noisette Carnée'
'Blush Rambler' (Ra)	CSBt EBee EBls EWTr MAus SPer SPla SWCr WHCG
'Blushing Lucy' (Ra)	LRHS SMrm WAct WHCG
Blythe Spirit = 'Auschool'[PBR] (S)	LRHS MAus MBNS NEgg SWCr
Bob Greaves = 'Fryzippy' (F)	MFry
'Bob Woolley' (HT)	NBat
'Bobbie James' (Ra) ♀H4	CHad EBee EBls LRHS LStr MAus MFry MJon MRav NEgg SPer SPoG SPoc SSea SWCr WAct WBVN WHCG
'Bobby Charlton' (HT)	MFry MGan SSea
'Bon Silène' (T)	EBls
Bonbon Hit = 'Poulbon'[PBR] (Patio)	SPoc SWCr
'Bonfire Night' (F)	ENot
Bonica = 'Meidomonac'[PBR] (GC) ♀H4	CSam CTri EBee EBls ECnt ELan ENot EPfP ESty GCoc LGod LRHS LStr MAsh MAus MFry MJon MRav MWgw NBlu SPer SPoG SSea SWCr WAct WBor WHCG WOVN
'Bonn' (HM/S)	CBcs
'Bonnie Scotland' (HT)	MGan
Boogie-Woogie = 'Poulyc006' (Cl)	ECnt
'Bottanix' (F) **new**	MGan
'Botzaris' (D)	EBls SFam
'Boula de Nanteuil' (G)	EBls
'Boule de Neige' (Bb)	EBee EBls ECnt ELan ENot EPfP GCoc LRHS LStr MAus MRav SFam SPer SPla SPoG SWCr WAct WHCG WOVN
'Bouquet d'Or' (N)	EBee EBls MAus SWCr
'Bouquet Tout Fait' misapplied	see *R.* 'Nastarana'
'Bouquet Tout Fait' (N)	WHCG
'Bourbon Queen' (Bb)	EBls EMFP MAus SWCr WHCG
'Bournville' (Cl)	GGre LRHS MAsh
Bow Bells = 'Ausbells' (S)	MAus
Bowled Over = 'Tandolgnil'[PBR] (F)	ESty SCoo SPoc SWCr
Boy O Boy = 'Dicuniform'[PBR] (GC)	IDic
Boys' Brigade = 'Cocdinkum' (Patio)	GCoc
§ ***bracteata***	CHII CRHN EHol GQui MAus WHCG
Brass Ring[PBR]	see *R.* Peek-a-boo = 'Dicgrow'
Brave Heart = 'Horbondsmile' (F)	ENot GGre MAsh MAus MBri MRav NBat SCoo SPoG SWCr
Breath of Life = 'Harquanne'[PBR] (ClHT)	CGro CSBt CTri CWSG EBls ELan EPfP ESty GGre GKir LGod LRHS LStr MAsh MAus MBri MFry MGan MJon MRav SPer SPoG SPoc SSea SWCr

Breathtaking = 'Hargalore'PBR (HT) — ESty SPoc SWCr
Bredon = 'Ausbred' (S) — MAus MBri
'Breeze Hill' (Ra) — EBls
§ 'Brenda Colvin' (Ra) — ISea MAus
'Brennus' (China hybrid) — EBls
Brian Rix = 'Harflipper'PBR (S) — SWCr
'Briarcliff' (HT) — EBls
Bridal Pink = 'Jacbri' (F) — MJon
Bride = 'Fryyearn'PBR (HT) — GCoc LStr MFry MJon SWCr
Bridge of Sighs = 'Harglowing'PBR (Cl) — EBee ECnt GGre LStr MAsh MBri MJon SPoG SPoc SWCr
Bright Cover **new** — ECnt
Bright Day = 'Chewvermillion' (Min) (Cl) — ESty SPoc SWCr
Bright Fire = 'Peaxi'PBR (Cl) — MJon SSea SWCr
Bright Ideas = 'Horcoffdrop' — EBls
Bright Smile = 'Dicdance'PBR (F/Patio) — IDic MAus MFry MGan MRav SPer SSea SWCr
Brilliant Pink Iceberg = 'Probril' (F) **new** — ECnt LStr MFry
'Brindis' (ClF) — MGan
Britannia = 'Frycalm'PBR (HT) — ECnt ESty MFry MJon SPoG SPoc SWCr
Broadlands = 'Tanmirsch'PBR (GC) — CTri LGod MRav SChu SPoc SWCr
Brother Cadfael = 'Ausglobe'PBR (S) — EBee LRHS MAsh MAus MBri MJon SPer SSea SWCr
Brown Velvet = 'Maccultra'PBR (F) — MJon SPoc SWCr
§ ***brunonii*** (Ra) — CDoC CPLN EBls EWes MAus
- 'Betty Sherriff' (Ra) — CDoC SSpi
§ - 'La Mortola' (Ra) — EBee EHol MAus MRav SPer SPoc SWCr
Bubbles = 'Frybubbly'PBR (GC) — MFry
Buck's Fizz = 'Poulgav'PBR (F) — MGan
'Buff Beauty' (HM) ♀H4 — More than 30 suppliers
'Bullata' — see *R.* x *centifolia* 'Bullata'
§ 'Burgundiaca' (G) — EBls LRHS MAus SWCr WAct
Burgundian rose — see *R.* 'Burgundiaca'
'Burma Star' (F) — MGan
burnet, double pink — see *R. pimpinellifolia* double pink
burnet, double white — see *R. pimpinellifolia* double white
Bush Baby = 'Peanob'PBR (Min) — LGod LStr SPer SPoc SWCr
Buttercup = 'Ausband'PBR (S) — LRHS MAus
Buxom Beauty = 'Korbilant'PBR (HT) — EBee ECnt ENot ESty GCoc MBri MJon NBat
'C.F. Meyer' — see *R.* 'Conrad Ferdinand Meyer'
§ ***caesia*** subsp. ***glauca*** — SPoc
'Café' (F) — WBcn
'Caledonian' (HT) — NBat
californica (S) — GIBF MAus
- 'Plena' — see *R. nutkana* 'Plena'
Calliope = 'Harfracas'PBR (F) — SWCr
'Callisto' (HM) — EBee EMFP MAus SWCr WHCG
Calypso = 'Poulclimb'PBR (Cl) — ECnt MBri SPoc SSea SWCr
'Camayeux' (G) — CPou EBls EWTr MAus SPer SSea SWCr WAct WHCG
Cambridgeshire = 'Korhaugen'PBR (GC) — LGod LStr MAus MRav NPri SPer SSea SWCr
'Camélia Rose' (Ch) — EBls WHCG
'Cameo' (Poly) — EBls MAus
Camille Pisarro = 'Destricol' (F) — ESty SPoc SWCr
'Canary Bird' — see *R. xanthina* 'Canary Bird'
Candle in the Wind = 'Mackincat'PBR (S) — MJon SWCr
Candy Rose = 'Meiranovi' (S) — GGre
canina (S) — CArn CCVT CDul CGro CLnd CRWN CTri EPfP GIBF GKir LBuc MAus MRav NPri NWea WMou XPep
- 'Abbotswood' — see *R.* 'Abbotswood'
- 'Andersonii' — see *R.* 'Andersonii'
'Cantabrigiensis' (S) ♀H4 — CSam EBee EBls MAus SFam SPer SPoc SSea SWCr WAct WFar WHCG
Canterbury = 'Ausbury' (S) — MAus
'Capitaine Basroger' (CeMo) — EBls MAus
'Capitaine John Ingram' (CeMo) ♀H4 — EBls MAus SPer SSea WHCG
'Captain Christy' (ClHT) — see *R.* 'Climbing Captain Christy'
'Captain Hayward' (HP) — EBls
'Cardinal de Richelieu' (G) ♀H4 — CPou CSam EBee EBls EPfP EWTr GCoc LRHS LStr MAsh MAus MDun MRav NEgg SFam SPer SPoG SPoc SWCr WAct WHCG
Cardinal Hume = 'Harregale' (S) — EBls SPer SWCr
'Care 2000' (S) — EBls
Carefree Days = 'Meirivouri' (Patio) — ENot MAsh SPoG SWCr
§ Carefree Wonder = 'Meipitac' (S) — SWCr
Caribbean Dawn = 'Korfeining'PBR (Patio) **new** — ENot
'Caring' (Patio) — SWCr
Caring for You = 'Coclust'PBR (HT) — GCoc GGre SWCr
'Carmen' (Ru) — EBls
§ 'Carmenetta' (S) — EBls MAus SWCr WAct
'Carnival' (HT) **new** — ECnt
'Carol' (Gn) — see *R.* 'Carol Amling'
§ 'Carol Amling' (Gn) — MJon SWCr
carolina — SLPl WHCG
Caroline de Monaco = 'Meipierar' (HT) — MJon
'Caroline Testout' — see *R.* 'Madame Caroline Testout'
Casino = 'Macca' (ClHT) — CTri EBls ESty GCoc MAsh MFry MGan MJon MRav SPer SPoG SWCr
Castle apricot (F) — EPfP MAsh
Castle cream (F) **new** — MAsh
Castle fuchsia pink (F) — EPfP MAsh
§ Castle Howard Tercentenary = 'Tantasch'PBR (F) — NBlu
Castle lilac (F) **new** — MAsh
Castle of Mey = 'Coclucid' (F) — GCoc GGre SWCr
Castle peach (F) — MAsh
Castle red (F) — EPfP MAsh
Castle white (F) **new** — MAsh
Castle yellow (F) — EPfP MAsh
Catherine Cookson = 'Noscook' (HT) — MJon
'Catherine Mermet' (T) — EBls MAus
'Catherine Seyton' (RH) — EBls
§ 'Cécile Brünner' (Poly) ♀H4 — CTri EBee EBls ECnt ELan EMFP ENot GCoc LStr MAus MRav SPer SPla SPoc SSea SWCr WAct WHCG
'Cécile Brünner, White' — see *R.* 'White Cécile Brünner'

	Name	Suppliers
	Cecily Gibson = 'Evebright' (F)	MJon
	Celebration 2000 = 'Horcoffitup'[PBR] (S)	MAus
§	'Céleste' (A) 🏆[H4]	EBls EMFP GCoc LGod LStr MFry MRav SFam SPer SWCr WAct WHCG WOVN
	'Célina' (CeMo)	EBls
	'Céline Forestier' (N) 🏆[H3]	CPou EBls EMFP EWTr MAus MRav SFam SPer SWCr WHCG
§	'Celsiana' (D)	CSam EBls LRHS MAus NEgg SFam SPer SWCr WAct WHCG
	Centenaire de Lourdes = 'Delge' (F)	EBls ESty SPoc SWCr
	Centenary = 'Koreledas'[PBR] (F) 🏆[H4]	ENot SPer
§	x ***centifolia*** (Ce)	EBls MAus MRav SSea SWCr WAct WHCG
§	- 'Bullata' (Ce)	EBls MAus
§	- 'Cristata' (Ce) 🏆[H4]	CSam EBee EBls ECnt EMFP EPfP EWTr LRHS LStr MAsh MRav SFam SPer SSea SWCr WAct WHCG
§	- 'De Meaux' (Ce)	EBls MAus MRav SPer SPla SPoc SWCr WAct WHCG
§	- 'Muscosa' (CeMo)	EBls GCoc LRHS MAus MRav MWgw NEgg SFam SPoc SSea SWCr WAct
	- 'Muscosa Alba'	WAct
	- 'Parvifolia'	see *R.* 'Burgundiaca'
§	- 'Shailer's White Moss' (CeMo)	EBee EBls LRHS MAus SFam SSea SWCr WHCG
§	- 'Spong' (G)	EBls MAus SWCr WAct
§	- 'Unique' (Ce)	EBls MAus SSea SWCr
§	- 'Unique Panachée' (Ce)	EBls MAus
	'Centifolia Variegata'	see *R.* x *centifolia* 'Unique Panachée'
	Centre Stage = 'Chewcreepy' (S/GC)	MJon
	Century Sunset = 'Tansaras'[PBR] (HT)	SPoc SWCr
	'Cerise Bouquet' (S) 🏆[H4]	EBls LRHS MAus MRav SPer SWCr WAct WHCG
	Champagne Cocktail = 'Horflash'[PBR] (F) 🏆[H4]	GGre MJon SPer SPoG SWCr
	'Champagne Dream' (Patio) **new**	MAsh
	Champagne = 'Korampa' (F)	MJon
	'Champneys' Pink Cluster' (China hybrid)	EBls MAus SFam
	Champs Elysées = 'Meicarl' (HT)	MGan
	'Chanelle' (F)	EBls GCoc MAus MGan SPer
	Chapeau de Napoléon	see *R.* x *centifolia* 'Cristata'
	'Chaplin's Pink Climber' (Cl)	EBls SWCr
	Charity = 'Auschar' (S)	LRHS MAus SWCr
	Charles Austin = 'Ausles' (S)	MAus MRav WHCG
	Charles Darwin = 'Auspeet' (S) **new**	MAus
	'Charles de Mills' (G) 🏆[H4]	CHad EBee EBls ECnt ELan EMFP ENot EPfP LGod LRHS LStr MAus MDun MFry MRav NBPC NEgg SFam SPer SPoc SSea SWCr WAct WHCG
	'Charles Gater' (HP)	EBls
	'Charles Lefèbvre' (HP)	EBls
	'Charles Mallerin' (HT)	EBls
	Charles Notcutt = 'Korhassi' (S)	ENot
	Charles Rennie Mackintosh = 'Ausren'[PBR] (S)	CSBt LRHS MAus MBNS MJon NEgg SPoc SWCr
	Charleston = 'Meiridge' (F)	MGan
	Charlie's Rose = 'Tanellepa' (HT)	MBri SPoc SWCr
	Charlotte = 'Auspoly'[PBR] (S) 🏆[H4]	CAbP EPfP ESty LRHS MAsh MAus MJon SPer SPoc SSea SWCr WAct
	Charmant = 'Korpeligo'[PBR] **new**	ENot
	Charmian = 'Ausmian' (S)	MAus
	Charming Cover = 'Poulharmu'[PBR] (GC/S)	MAsh SWCr
	'Charter 700' (F)	MFry
	Chartreuse de Parme = 'Delviola' (S)	SPoc SWCr
	'Château de Clos-Vougeot' (HT)	IArd
	Chatsworth = 'Tanotax'[PBR] (Patio/F)	MJon MRav SPer SPoc SSea SWCr
§	Chaucer = 'Auscer' (S)	MAus
	Cheerful Charlie = 'Cocquimmer' (F) **new**	GCoc
	Chelsea Belle = 'Talchelsea' (Min)	MJon NBat
§	Cherry Brandy '85 = 'Tanryrandy'[PBR] (HT)	CSBt MGan MJon
	Cheshire = 'Fryelise'[PBR] (HT)	GCoc MFry MJon SPoc SWCr
	Cheshire = 'Korkonopi'[PBR] (County Rose Series)(S)	ENot MAus NPri
	'Cheshire Life' (HT)	MAus MFry MGan MJon MRav NPri SWCr
	Chester Cathedral = 'Franshine' (HT)	MJon
	'Chevy Chase' (Ra) **new**	WAct
	Chianti = 'Auswine' (S)	EBls MAus SWCr WAct WHCG
	Chicago Peace = 'Johnago' (HT)	EBls MGan MJon NBlu SWCr
	Childhood Memories = 'Ferho' (HM/Cl)	SPla
	Child's Play = 'Savachild' (Min)	NBat
	Chilterns = 'Kortemma'[PBR] (GC)	ENot MRav SPoc SWCr
	'Chinatown' (F/S) 🏆[H4]	CBcs CGro CSBt CTri EBls ENot EPfP GGre LStr MAsh MAus MGan MJon MRav SPer SPoG SWCr
	chinensis misapplied	see *R.* x *odorata*
	chinensis Jacq.	EBls
I	- 'Angel Rose' (Min)	NJOw
	- 'Minima' *sensu stricto* hort.	see *R.* 'Pompon de Paris'
	- 'Mutabilis'	see *R.* x *odorata* 'Mutabilis'
	- 'Old Blush'	see *R.* x *odorata* 'Pallida'
	Chivalry = 'Macpow' (HT)	SWCr
	Chloe = 'Poulen003'[PBR] (S)	CHad CPou ECnt SPoc SWCr
	'Chloris' (A)	CPou EBls SWCr
	'Chorus Girl' (F)	MGan
	Chris = 'Kirsan'[PBR] (Cl)	EBee ECnt ESty LStr MJon SPoc SWCr WGor
	Christian Dior = 'Meilie' (HT)	EBls SWCr
	'Christine Gandy' (F)	MGan

Name	Suppliers
Christopher = 'Cocopher' (HT)	GCoc
Christopher Columbus = 'Meinronsse' (HT)	IArd
Christopher Marlowe = 'Ausjump' (S)	MAsh MAus SWCr
§ 'Chromatella' (N)	EBls
'Chrysler Imperial' (HT)	EBls
Cider Cup = 'Dicladida' PBR (Min/Patio) 🏆H4	ENot EPfP ESty IDic LStr MAus MFry NBat SWCr
'Cinderella' (Min)	CSBt
cinnamomea	see *R. majalis*
'Circus' (F)	MGan SWCr
Citron-Fraise = 'Delcifra' (S) **new**	SPoc SWCr
City Lights = 'Poulgan' PBR (Patio)	CSBt ENot
City Livery = 'Harhero 2000' (F) **new**	GGre SWCr
City of Belfast = 'Macci' (F)	EBls MAus
'City of Leeds' (F)	CWSG GGre MAsh MGan SWCr
City of London = 'Harukfore' PBR (F)	CSBt EBls GGre LStr MJon SPer SWCr
'City of Oelde' (S)	EBls
'City of Portsmouth' (F)	CBcs
City of York = 'Direktör Benschop' (Cl)	EBls
Clair Matin = 'Meimont' (ClS)	CPou EBls MAus SPer SWCr WAct
'Claire Jacquier' (N)	EBee EBls MAus SFam SPer SWCr WHCG
Claire Rayner = 'Macpandem' PBR (F/Patio)	MJon
Claire Rose = 'Auslight' PBR (S)	CGro ESty GGre LRHS MAus MJon MRav SPer SWCr
Clara = 'Poulen004' (S)	ECnt SPoc
'Clarence House' (Cl)	EBls
Clarinda = 'Cocsummery' PBR (F)	GCoc
Claude Monet = 'Jacdesa' (HT) **new**	SPoc SWCr
'Clementina Carbonieri' (T)	EBls
Cleo = 'Beebop' (HT)	MJon
§ Cleopatra = 'Korverpea' PBR (HT)	ENot
'Cliff Richard' (F)	ESty SWCr
'Climbing Alec's Red' (ClHT)	SPer
'Climbing Allgold' (ClF)	EBls SSea SWCr
'Climbing Arthur Bell' PBR (ClF) 🏆H4	CSBt CTri ESty GGre LGod MAsh SPer SPoG SPoc SSea SWCr
'Climbing Ballerina' (Ra)	CSBt MGan SPoc SWCr
Climbing Bettina = 'Mepalsar' (ClHT)	EBls SWCr
'Climbing Blessings' (ClHT)	EBls
'Climbing Blue Moon' (ClHT)	CFee MGan SWCr
§ 'Climbing Captain Christy' (ClHT)	EBls MAus
'Climbing Cécile Brünner' (ClPoly) 🏆H4	CSBt EBee EBls ECnt EPfP LRHS LStr MAsh MAus MGan MRav MWgw NBPC SPer SPoc SSea SWCr WAct WHCG
'Climbing Château de Clos-Vougeot' (ClHT)	EBls MAus
'Climbing Christine' (ClHT)	MAus
§ 'Climbing Columbia' (ClHT)	ERea SPer WHCG
'Climbing Comtesse Vandal' (ClHT)	EBls
'Climbing Crimson Glory' (ClHT)	CPou EBls EMFP MAus MGan SWCr
§ 'Climbing Devoniensis' (ClT)	CPou EBls
'Climbing Ena Harkness' (ClHT)	CBcs EBls GCoc GGre LRHS MAus MGan MRav SPer SPla SPoG SWCr
'Climbing Ernest H. Morse' (ClHT)	MGan
'Climbing Etoile de Hollande' (ClHT) 🏆H4	CSBt CSam CTri CWSG EBls EMFP EPfP GCoc GGre GKir LRHS LStr MAus MGan MJon MRav MWgw NBPC SFam SMad SPer SPoG SPoc SSea SWCr
'Climbing Fashion' (ClF)	EBls
Climbing Fragrant Cloud = 'Colfragrasar' (ClHT)	CBcs ELan MGan
§ 'Climbing Frau Karl Druschki' (ClHP)	EBls
'Climbing General MacArthur' (ClHT)	EBls
§ Climbing Gold Bunny = 'Meigro-Nurisar' PBR (ClF)	MJon
'Climbing Grand-mère Jenny' (ClHT)	EBls
'Climbing Iceberg' (ClF) 🏆H4	CGro CSBt EBee EBls ELan ENot EPfP ESty GGre GKir IArd LRHS LStr MAsh MAus MGan MJon MRav SPer SPla SPoG SPoc SSea SWCr WHCG
'Climbing Josephine Bruce' (ClHT)	LRHS MGan
'Climbing la France' (ClHT)	MAus MRav
§ 'Climbing Lady Hillingdon' (ClT) 🏆H3	EBls EMFP EPfP EWTr LRHS MAus MGan MRav MWgw NEgg SFam SPer SPoc SSea SWCr WAct WHCG
'Climbing Lady Sylvia' (ClHT)	CSBt EBee EBls EPfP LRHS MAus MGan SPer SWCr
'Climbing Little White Pet'	see *R.* 'Félicité Perpétue'
'Climbing Madame Abel Chatenay' (ClHT)	EBls MAus
'Climbing Madame Butterfly' (ClHT)	CPou EBls LRHS MAus MGan SPer SWCr
'Climbing Madame Caroline Testout' (ClHT)	CPou EBls MAsh MAus SPer SWCr WBcn
§ 'Climbing Madame Edouard Herriot' (ClHT)	EBls MAus MGan SWCr
'Climbing Madame Henri Guillot' (ClHT)	EBls MAus
'Climbing Maman Cochet' (ClT)	EBls MAus
'Climbing Masquerade' (ClF)	EBls GGre MAus MGan MJon MRav SPer SPoc SSea SWCr
'Climbing McGredy's Yellow' (ClHT)	MGan
§ 'Climbing Mevrouw G.A. van Rossem' (ClHT)	EBls MAus
'Climbing Mrs Aaron Ward' (ClHT)	EBls MAus
'Climbing Mrs G.A. van Rossem'	see *R.* 'Climbing Mevrouw G.A. van Rossem'
'Climbing Mrs Herbert Stevens' (ClHT)	CPou EBee EBls LRHS MAus MRav SPer SWCr WHCG

	'Climbing Mrs Sam McGredy' (ClHT) 🏆[H4]	CGro CSBt CSam EBls MAus MGan MJon SWCr
	'Climbing Niphetos' (ClT)	EBls MAus
	'Climbing Ophelia' (ClHT)	CPou EBls MAus SPer
	Climbing Orange Sunblaze = 'Meiji Katarsar'[PBR] (ClMin)	ENot MJon SPer SWCr
	'Climbing Pascali' (ClHT)	MGan
§	'Climbing Paul Lédé' (ClT)	EBee EBls LRHS MAus NEgg SPoc SWCr
	'Climbing Peace' (ClHT)	CSBt SWCr
	'Climbing Picture' (ClHT)	EBls MAus MGan
§	'Climbing Pompon de Paris' (ClMinCh)	CBot CTri EBls EMFP LRHS MAus MGan MRav SPer SWCr WHCG
	'Climbing Richmond' (ClHT)	EBls
	'Climbing Roundelay' (Cl)	EBls
	'Climbing Ruby Wedding'	GGre SPoG SWCr
	'Climbing Shot Silk' (ClHT) 🏆[H4]	CSBt EBee EBls EMFP EWTr MGan SPer SWCr
§	'Climbing Souvenir de la Malmaison' (ClBb)	CPou EBls MAus SPer SPoc SWCr WAct WHCG
	Climbing Super Star = 'Tangostar' (ClHT)	MAus
	'Climbing Sutter's Gold' (ClHT)	MGan
	'Climbing Talisman' (ClHT)	EBls
	'Climbing The Doctor' (ClHT) **new**	MGan
	'Climbing The Queen Elizabeth' (ClF)	EBls SWCr
	Clodagh McGredy (F) = 'Macswanle'[PBR]	ESty MJon
	'Cloth of Gold'	see *R.* 'Chromatella'
	Cloud Nine = 'Fryextra' (HT) **new**	ECnt ESty LGod MFry
	Cocktail = 'Meimick' (S)	EBls
	Colchester Beauty = 'Cansend' (F)	ECnt
§	Colibri = 'Meimal' (Min)	SPer
§	'Colonel Fabvier'	EBls MAus XPep
	colonial white	see *R.* 'Sombreuil'
	'Columbian' (ClHT)	see *R.* 'Climbing Columbia'
§	Colwyn Bay (F)	MJon
	'Commandant Beaurepaire' (Bb)	EBee EBls LRHS MAus SWCr
	common moss	see *R.* x *centifolia* 'Muscosa'
	Commonwealth Glory = 'Harclue'[PBR] (HT)	ESty GGre SPoc SWCr
	'Compassion' (ClHT) 🏆[H4]	More than 30 suppliers
§	'Complicata' (G) 🏆[H4]	CAbP EBls EPfP LRHS LStr MAsh MAus MRav MWgw SFam SPer SPoc SSea SSpi SWCr WAct WHCG WOVN
N	'Comte de Chambord' misapplied	see *R.* 'Madame Knorr'
	Comtes de Champagne = 'Ausufo'[PBR] (S)	MAsh MAus SCoo
	'Comtesse Cécile de Chabrillant' (HP)	EBls MAus
	'Comtesse de Lacépède' misapplied	see *R.* 'Du Maître d'Ecole'
§	'Comtesse de Murinais' (DMo)	EBls MAus SFam
	Comtesse de Ségur = 'Deltendre' (S)	SPoc SWCr
§	'Comtesse du Caÿla' (Ch)	MAus SSea
	'Condesa de Sástago' (HT)	EBls
§	'Conditorum' (G)	EBls SFam WAct
	Congratulations = 'Korlift'[PBR] (HT)	CSBt CTri EBee ECnt ENot GCoc IArd LGod LStr MAus MFry MGan MJon MRav NPri SPer SPoG SPoc SSea SWCr
	Connie = 'Boselftay'[PBR] (F) **new**	GGre SWCr
	Conquest = 'Harbrill'[PBR] (F)	MRav
§	'Conrad Ferdinand Meyer' (Ru)	CSBt EBls MAus MDun SPer
	Conservation = 'Cocdimple'[PBR] (Min/Patio)	GCoc GGre LAst MBri SSea SWCr
	Constance Finn = 'Hareden'[PBR] (F)	GGre SPoG SWCr
	Constance Spry = 'Austance' (Cl/S) 🏆[H4]	CGro EBee EBls ECnt ELan ENot EPfP LRHS LStr MAsh MAus MJon MRav NEgg NPri SFam SPer SPoc SSea SWCr WAct WGer WHCG
§	'Cooperi' (Ra)	EBls EMFP MAus SLon SPer SPoc SSea SWCr WAct WHCG
	Cooper's Burmese	see *R.* 'Cooperi'
	'Copenhagen' (ClHT)	EBee EBls LRHS MAus
	Copper Pot = 'Dicpe' (F)	MGan SPer
	'Coral Cluster' (Poly)	EBls MAus
	'Coral Creeper' (ClHT)	EBls
	'Coral Dawn' (ClHT)	EBls MFry MJon
	Coral Reef = 'Cocdarlee'[PBR] (Min/Patio)	ESty GGre SWCr
	'Coral Satin' (Cl)	MGan
	'Coralie' (D)	EBls
	Cordelia = 'Ausbottle'[PBR] (S)	LRHS MAus MBri
	'Cornelia' (HM) 🏆[H4]	CBcs CSBt CSam EBee EBls ECnt ENot EPfP GBin GCoc GGre IArd LRHS LStr MAsh MAus MFry MJon MRav SFam SPer SPoc SSea SWCr WAct WHCG WOVN
	'Coronet' (F)	WHCG
	Corvedale = 'Ausnetting'[PBR] (S)	MAus SWCr
	'Coryana'	EBls
	corymbifera	EBls
	corymbulosa	EBls
	'Cosimo Ridolfi' (G)	EBls
	cottage maid	see *R.* x *centifolia* 'Unique Panachée'
	Cottage Rose = 'Ausglisten'[PBR] (S)	MAus MJon MRav NEgg SPoc SWCr
	Country Living = 'Auscountry' (S)	LRHS
	'Coupe d'Hébé' (Bb)	EBls MAus
§	Courage = 'Poulduf'[PBR] (HT)	EBee ECnt
	Courvoisier = 'Macsee'	CSBt
	'Cramoisi Picotée' (G)	EBls MAus
	'Cramoisi Supérieur' (Ch)	EBls MAus WHCG
	Crathes Castle = 'Cocathes'	GCoc
	Crazy for You = 'Wekroalt'[PBR] (F)	ESty LGod MJon SPoc SSea SWCr
	Cream Abundance = 'Harflax'[PBR] (F)	LStr MAsh SPoc SWCr
	'Crème Anglaise' (Cl) **new**	CGro ECnt MGan
	Creme Brulee (Cl) **new**	MGan
	Crème de la Crème = 'Gancre'[PBR] (Cl)	CGro CSBt EBee ECnt ESty GCoc MBri MGan MJon SPoc SSea SWCr
	'Crépuscule' (N)	EBls SSea WHCG
	Cressida = 'Auscress' (S)	MAus
	crested moss	see *R.* x *centifolia* 'Cristata'
	Cricri = 'Meicri' (Min)	MAus

Name	Suppliers
Crimson Cascade = 'Fryclimbdown'^{PBR} (Cl)	CSam ESty GKir LRHS MAsh MAus MBri MFry MRav NBat SPoG SPoc SSea SWCr WHCG
'Crimson Conquest' (ClHT)	EBls
crimson damask	see *R. gallica* var. *officinalis*
'Crimson Descant' (Cl)	EBee ECnt
Crimson Floorshow = 'Harglamour'^{PBR} (GC)	MBri
'Crimson Glory' (HT)	EBls MGan
'Crimson Rambler' (Ra)	WBcn
'Crimson Shower' (Ra) $\mathbb{Y}^{H4}$	EBls EMFP LRHS MAus MJon MRav NEgg SPer SWCr WGer WHCG WHer
'Cristata'	see *R.* x *centifolia* 'Cristata'
Crocus Rose = 'Ausquest'^{PBR} (S)	EBee ECnt EPfP LRHS MAsh MAus NEgg SWCr
Crown Princess Margareta = 'Auswinter'^{PBR} (S)	ECnt LRHS MAus MBNS MJon NEgg SCoo SPer SPoc SWCr
Crowning Glory = 'Dicyardstick'^{PBR} (S)	IDic SWCr
Crystal Palace = 'Poulrek'^{PBR} (F/Patio)	ENot SPoc SWCr
cuisse de nymphe	see *R.* 'Great Maiden's Blush'
'Cupid' (ClHT)	EBls MAus SPer SPoc SWCr
§ Cymbeline = 'Auslean' (S)	SPer
'Cynthia Brooke' (HT)	EBls
'D'Aguesseau' (G)	EBee EBls MAus SWCr
'Daily Mail'	see *R.* 'Climbing Madame Edouard Herriot'
Daily Sketch = 'Macai' (F)	SWCr
'Dainty Bess' (HT)	EBee EBls MAus SSea
'Dainty Maid' (F)	EBls MAus
'Daisy Hill' ('Macrantha' hybrid)	EBls MJon
x ***damascena*** var. ***bifera***	see *R.* x *damascena* var. *semperflorens*
§ - var. ***semperflorens*** (D)	CBgR EBls EMFP EWTr MAus MRav SPoc SSea SWCr WAct WHCG
N - 'Trigintipetala' misapplied	see *R.* 'Professeur Emile Perrot'
§ - var. ***versicolor*** (D)	EBls SFam SPer SSea SWCr WAct WHCG
§ 'Dame de Coeur' (HT)	NBlu SWCr
'Dame Edith Helen' (HT)	EBls
Dame Wendy = 'Canson' (F)	MAus MGan
Dames de Chenonceau = 'Delpabra' (S) **new**	SPoc SWCr
'Danaë' (HM)	CHad EBee EBls EMFP MAus SWCr WHCG
Dancing Pink = 'Hendan' (F)	MJon
Danny Boy = 'Dicxcon'^{PBR} (Patio)	IDic MJon WGor
§ Danse des Sylphes = 'Malcair' (Cl)	EBls SWCr
'Danse du Feu' (Cl)	CBcs CGro CSBt CTri CWSG EBee EBls ELan GCoc GGre GKir LGod LRHS LStr MAsh MAus MGan MJon MRav NPri SPer SPoG SPoc SSea SWCr
'Daphne Gandy' (F)	MGan
Dapple Dawn = 'Ausapple' (S)	MAus SPer
Darling Flame = 'Meilucca' (Min)	MRav SWCr
'Dart's Defender'	SLPl
David Whitfield = 'Gana'^{PBR} (F)	MGan
davidii	EBls MAus SWCr

Name	Suppliers
Dawn Chorus = 'Dicquasar'^{PBR} (HT) $\mathbb{Y}^{H4}$	CGro CSBt CWSG ECnt ENot EPfP ESty GCoc GGre IDic LGod LStr MAsh MAus MBri MGan MRav SPer SPoG SPoc SSea SWCr
'Daybreak' (HM)	EBls MAus SWCr WAct WHCG
Dazzling Delight = 'Cocuseful' (F) **new**	GCoc
'De Meaux' (Ce)	see *R.* x *centifolia* 'De Meaux'
'De Meaux, White'	see *R.* 'White de Meaux'
§ 'De Rescht' (DPo) $\mathbb{Y}^{H4}$	CPou EBls ENot EPfP ESty LRHS MAsh MAus MJon MRav MWgw SPer SPla SPoc SWCr WAct WGer WHCG
'Dearest' (F)	CBcs CSBt MGan MRav SPer SWCr
'Debbie Thomas' (HT)	MJon
§ Deborah Devonshire = 'Boscherrydrift'^{PBR} (F)	GGre SWCr
Deb's Delight = 'Legsweet'^{PBR} (F)	ELan MJon
'Debutante' (Ra)	CHad CSam EBee EBls LRHS MAus WHCG
'Deep Secret' (HT) $\mathbb{Y}^{H4}$	CGro CTri CWSG ECnt EPfP ESty GCoc GGre MAsh MFry MGan MJon MRav SPer SPoG SPoc SSea SWCr
'Delambre' (DPo)	EBls MAus MRav
'Delicata' (Ru)	MAus
Della Balfour = 'Harblend'^{PBR} (Cl)	GGre SWCr
'Dembrowski' (HP)	EBls
'Dentelle de Malines' (S)	EBls LRHS MAus WAct
'Deschamps' (N)	EBls
'Desprez à Fleurs Jaunes' (N)	CPou EBee EBls IArd LRHS MAus MRav NEgg SFam SPer SPoc SWCr WHCG
'Deuil de Paul Fontaine' (Mo)	EBls
'Devon Maid' (Cl)	SWCr
'Devoniensis' (ClT)	see *R.* 'Climbing Devoniensis'
Devotion = 'Interfluco' (HT)	IDic
Diamond Border = 'Pouldiram'^{PBR} (S)	ECnt
'Diamond Jubilee' (HT)	EBls MGan
Diamond = 'Korgazell'^{PBR} (Patio) **new**	ENot ESty GCoc
'Diana Armstrong' (HT)	NBat
'Dicelope' (F) **new**	IDic
Dick's Delight = 'Dicwhistle'^{PBR} (GC)	IDic SPoc SWCr
'Dickson's Flame' (F)	MGan
Die Welt = 'Diekor' (HT)	MBri MJon NBat
'Diorama' (HT)	MAus MGan SWCr
'Directeur Alphand' (HP)	EBls WHCG
Disco Dancer = 'Dicinfra'^{PBR} (F)	IDic
Dixieland Linda = 'Beadix' (ClHT)	EBls MJon SSea
Dizzy Heights = 'Fryblissful'^{PBR} (Cl)	ECnt ESty GCoc MAsh MBri MFry MGan MJon SPoc SWCr
'Docteur Andry' (HP)	EBls
'Docteur Grill' (T)	EBls MAus
'Doctor A.J. Verhage' (HT)	MGan
Doctor Dick = 'Cocbaden' (HT)	MBri MJon NBat
'Doctor Edward Deacon' (HT)	EBls
§ Doctor Goldberg = 'Gandol' (HT)	MGan SWCr
Doctor Jackson = 'Ausdoctor' (S)	MAus

	Name	Suppliers
§	Doctor Jo = 'Fryatlanta'^{PBR} (F)	MFry SPoc SWCr
	'Doctor John Snow' (HT)	MGan
	Doctor McAlpine = 'Peafirst' (F/Patio)	MBri
	'Doctor W. Van Fleet' (Ra/Cl)	EBls MAus
	'Doktor Eckener' (Ru)	EBls
	'Don Charlton' (HT)	NBat
	'Don Juan' (Cl)	MGan
§	'Doncasteri'	EBls
	'Doris Tysterman' (HT)	CGro CTri EBls GGre LStr MAus MGan MJon NBlu SPer SSea SWCr
	Dorothy = 'Cocrocket' (F) **new**	GCoc
	'Dorothy Perkins' (Ra)	CGro CRHN CSBt CTri EBls GCoc GGre LRHS MAus MJon MRav NPer SPer SSea SWCr WHCG
	'Dorothy Wheatcroft' (F)	MGan
	'Dorothy Wilson' (F)	EBls
	'Dortmund' (ClHScB) ♀^{H4}	CPLG EBls LGod LRHS MAus MGan SPer SWCr WAct WHCG
	Double Delight = 'Andeli' (HT)	CGro ESty GCoc GGre MGan MJon MRav SPer SPoG SPoc SSea SWCr
	'Dream Girl' (Cl)	MAus SFam
	Dream Lover = 'Peayetti'^{PBR} (Patio)	MAsh MJon MRav SPoG SPoc SWCr
	'Dreaming Spires' (Cl)	CSBt ENot ESty MBri MJon SPer SSea SWCr
	Dreamland = 'Träumland' (F)	MGan
	'Dresden Doll' (MinMo)	EBls MAus
	Drummer Boy = 'Harvacity'^{PBR} (F/Patio)	GGre MGan SWCr
	'Du Maître d'Ecole' (G)	EBls MAus MRav SWCr WHCG
	Dublin Bay = 'Macdub' (Cl) ♀^{H4}	CHad CSBt CSam CTri EBee EBls ECnt ELan ENot EPfP ESty GGre GKir IArd LGod LRHS LStr MAsh MFry MGan MJon MRav SPer SPoG SPoc SSea SWCr WGer
	'Duc de Fitzjames' (G)	EBls
	'Duc de Guiche' (G) ♀^{H4}	CSam EBls MAus SFam SPer SWCr WAct WHCG
	'Duchess of Portland'	see *R.* 'Portlandica'
	'Duchesse d'Albe' (T)	EBls
	'Duchesse d'Angoulême' (G)	EBls MAus SFam
	'Duchesse d'Auerstädt' (N)	EBls
	'Duchesse de Buccleugh' (G)	EBls MAus MRav NBPC SWCr WAct
§	'Duchesse de Montebello' (G) ♀^{H4}	EBee EBls EWTr LRHS MAus SFam SPer SWCr WAct WHCG
	'Duchesse de Rohan' (CexHP)	EBls
	'Duchesse de Verneuil' (CeMo)	EBls MAus SFam
	'Duke of Edinburgh' (HP)	EBls MAsh MAus
	Duke of Edinburgh = 'Poulac008' **new**	SWCr
	'Duke of Wellington' (HP)	EBls SWCr WHCG
	'Duke of Windsor' (HT)	MGan SPer
	'Duke of York' (Ch)	EBls
	'Dundee Rambler' (Ra)	EBls MAus
§	'Duplex' (S)	EBls LRHS MAus MRav WAct
	'Dupontii' (S)	EBls LRHS MAus MRav SFam SPer SWCr WAct WOVN XPep
	'Dupuy Jamain' (HP)	EBls WHCG
	'Dusky Maiden' (F)	CHad EBls MAus MJon SWCr WHCG
	'Dutch Gold' (HT)	CGro CWSG MAus MGan MRav SPer SSea SWCr
	'E.H. Morse'	see *R.* 'Ernest H. Morse'
	'Easlea's Golden Rambler' (Ra) ♀^{H4}	CSBt EBee EBls EWTr LRHS MAus MRav SWCr WAct WHCG
	'Easter Morning' (Min)	SWCr
	Easy Cover = 'Pouleas'^{PBR} (GC)	MAsh SWCr
	Easy Going = 'Harflow'^{PBR} (F)	GCoc GGre IArd MAsh MJon SWCr
	ecae	EBls LRHS MAus
	'Eclair' (HP)	EBls WHCG
	'Eddie's Jewel' (*moyesii* hybrid)	EBls MAus
	'Eden Rose' (HT)	EBls MGan
	Eden Rose '88 = 'Meiviolin'^{PBR} (ClHT)	MJon SPer SPoc SWCr
	'Edith Bellenden' (RH)	EBls
	Edith Holden = 'Chewlegacy'^{PBR} (F)	MJon
	'Edward Hyams'	MAus
	eglanteria	see *R. rubiginosa*
	Eglantyne = 'Ausmak'^{PBR} (S) ♀^{H4}	CAbP CSBt EPfP GCoc LRHS LStr MAsh MAus MBri MJon MRav SPer SPoc SSea SWCr
	Eleanor Annelise = 'Cocslightly' (HT)	GCoc
	Eleanor = 'Poulberin'^{PBR} (S)	ECnt
	'Elegance' (ClHT)	EBls MAus MGan SWCr
§	***elegantula*** 'Persetosa' (S)	EBls MAus SPer SPoc SWCr WAct WHCG
§	Elina = 'Dicjana'^{PBR} (HT) ♀^{H4}	CSBt EBee ECnt ENot ESty GGre IDic LGod LStr MAus MFry MGan MJon MRav NBat NBlu SPer SPoG SPoc SWCr
	'Eliza Boëlle' (HP)	WHCG
	Elizabeth = 'Coctail' (F) **new**	GCoc
	'Elizabeth Harkness' (HT)	CWSG EBls MAus MGan SPer SWCr
	Elizabeth of Glamis = 'Macel' (F)	CGro CTri CWSG EBls GCoc GGre MGan SPer SWCr
	Elle = 'Meibderos'^{PBR} (HT)	SPoc SWCr
	Ellen = 'Auscup' (S)	MAus
	'Ellen Willmott' (HT)	EBee EBls EMFP MAus SWCr
	'Elmshorn' (S)	CBcs SWCr WHCG
	'Else Poulsen' (Poly)	WHCG
	Emanuel = 'Ausuel' (S)	MAus
	'Emily Gray' (Ra)	CGro CSBt EBee EBls ECnt ENot ESty GKir LRHS LStr MAsh MAus MRav NPri SPer SSea SWCr WAct WHCG
	'Emma Wright' (HT)	MAus
	'Emotion' (F) **new**	GGre SWCr
	'Empereur du Maroc' (HP)	EBls EMFP MAus MRav SWCr WHCG
	Empress Josephine	see *R.* 'Impératrice Joséphine'
	Empress Michiko = 'Dicnifty'^{PBR} (HT)	IDic
	'Ena Harkness' (HT)	CTri EBls ELan GGre MGan SWCr
§	'Enfant de France' (HP)	EBls
	x ***engelmannii***	EBls
§	England's Rose = 'Ausrace'^{PBR} (S)	MAus SCoo SWCr
	English Elegance = 'Ausleaf' (S)	MAus
	English Garden = 'Ausbuff'^{PBR} (S)	CGro EBee EMFP ENot EPfP GGre LRHS LStr MAus MRav SPer SSea
	'English Miss' (F) ♀^{H4}	CSBt CTri EBee EBls ECnt EPfP ESty LAst LStr MAsh MAus MGan MJon MRav SPer SPoG SPoc SSea SWCr
	'Eos' (*moyesii* hybrid)	EBls

	Name	Suppliers
	'Erfurt' (HM)	EBls EMFP MAus SPer SWCr WHCG
§	'Erinnerung an Brod' (S)	WHCG
§	'Ernest H. Morse' (HT)	CSBt CTri CWSG EBls GCoc LAst MGan MJon MRav SPer SSea SWCr
	'Ernest May' (HT)	SSea
	Escapade = 'Harpade' (F) ♀H4	EBls MAus MGan SWCr
	Especially for You = 'Fryworthy'PBR (HT)	CSBt CTri ESty GCoc GGre LGod LStr MAsh MFry SCoo SPoG SPoc SSea SWCr
	Essex = 'Poulnoz'PBR (GC)	MRav SPer SWCr WHCG
§	'Estrellita de Oro' (Min)	SPer
	'Etain' (Ra)	EBee ECnt
§	'Etendard'	SPla SPoc WAct
	Eternal Flame = 'Korassenet'PBR (F)	ENot SPoc SWCr
§	Eternally Yours = 'Macspeego'PBR (HT)	MJon
	'Ethel' (Ra)	EBee EMFP SWCr
	'Etoile de Hollande' (HT)	CHad EBee ELan ENot GKir MAsh MJon NEgg NPri SSea
	'Etoile de Lyon' (T)	EBls
	'Etude' (Cl)	WBVN
	'Eugène Fürst' (HP)	EBls
	'Eugénie Guinoisseau' (Mo)	EBls WHCG
	Euphoria = 'Intereup'PBR (GC/S)	GCoc IDic SPoc SWCr
	Euphrates = 'Harunique' (*persica* hybrid)	MAus WAct
	'Europeana' (F)	MGan
	'Eva' (HM)	EBls
	'Evangeline' (Ra)	EBls MAus
	Evelyn = 'Aussaucer'PBR (S) ♀H4	CSBt EBee EMFP ENot EPfP ESty GCoc GGre LGod LRHS LStr MAsh MAus MFry MJon MRav NEgg NPri SChu SPer SPla SPoc SWCr
§	Evelyn Fison = 'Macev' (F)	CSBt ELan ENot GGre MAus MGan MJon MRav SPer SPoc SWCr
	Evening Light = 'Chewpechette' **new**	MJon
	Evening Light = 'Tarde Gris' (Min) (Cl)	ESty SWCr
	'Everest Double Fragrance' (F)	EBls
	'Excelsa' (Ra)	CSBt CTri EBls EPfP GGre GKir IArd LGod MAsh MRav NWea SSea SWCr WAct
	'Expectations'	CSBt
§	Eye Paint = 'Maceye' (F)	MAus MJon SMrm
	'Eyecatcher' (F)	ECnt
	Eyeopener = 'Interop'PBR (S/GC)	EBls IDic
	'F. E. Lester'	see *R.* 'Francis E. Lester'
§	'F. J. Grootendorst' (Ru)	EBee EBls LRHS MAus MJon SSea SWCr WAct
	Fab = 'Bosconpea'PBR (F)	GGre SWCr
	'Fabvier'	see *R.* 'Colonel Fabvier'
	Fairhope = 'Talfairhope' (Min)	MJon NBat
§	Fairy Damsel = 'Harneatly' (Poly/GC)	EBls
§	Fairy Prince = 'Harnougette' (GC)	MAsh
	Fairy Queen = 'Sperien' (Poly/GC)	IDic MAsh SPoG
	'Fairy Rose'	see *R.* 'The Fairy'
	'Fairy Shell' (Patio)	MAsh
§	Fairy Snow = 'Holfairy' (S)	SPoc
§	Fairygold = 'Frygoldie'PBR (Patio)	MFry
	Fairyland = 'Harlayalong' (Poly)	EBls MAsh SWCr
	Faithful = 'Haressay'PBR (F) **new**	GGre SPoG SWCr
	Falstaff = 'Ausverse'PBR (S)	CSBt EBee ECnt EPfP ESty LRHS MAsh MAus MBNS MJon NEgg SPoc SWCr
	'Fantin-Latour' (*centifolia* hybrid) ♀H4	CSam CTri EBee EBls ECnt ELan ENot EPfP EWTr GCoc LGod LRHS LStr MAus MBri MDun MRav MWgw NEgg SFam SPer SPoc SSea SWCr WAct WHCG
	fargesii hort.	see *R. moyesii* var. *fargesii*
	farreri var. ***persetosa***	see *R. elegantula* 'Persetosa'
	Fascination = 'Jacoyel' (HT)	LStr MBri SCoo
§	Fascination = 'Poulmax'PBR (F) ♀H4§	CSBt ECnt ENot EPfP ESty GCoc LGod MAsh MAus MFry MGan MJon MRav SPer SPoG SPoc SSea SWCr
	Favourite Hit = 'Poululv' (Patio)	ECnt
	fedtschenkoana hort.	EBls LRHS MAus SPer WAct WHCG
	fedtschenkoana Regel	SLPl
	'Felicia' (HM) ♀H4	CHad CSBt CSam EBee EBls ECnt ELan ENot EPfP GCoc GGre LGod LRHS LStr MAsh MAus MDun MFry MJon MRav SFam SPer SPoG SPoc SSea SWCr WAct WHCG WKif WOVN
	'Félicité Parmentier' (AxD) ♀H4	CSam EBls EMFP EWTr LRHS MAus MRav NEgg SFam SPer SWCr WAct WHCG
§	'Félicité Perpétue' (Ra) ♀H4	CBcs CBrm EBee EBls ELan ENot EPfP GCoc GGre GKir ISea LRHS LStr MAsh MAus MBri MRav MWgw NEgg SFam SPer SPoc SSea SWCr WAct WHCG XPep
	Felicity Kendal = 'Lanken' (HT)	MJon
	'Fellemberg' (ClCh)	EBls MAus SWCr WHCG XPep
	Fellowship = 'Harwelcome'PBR (F) ♀H4	ECnt ENot ESty GCoc GGre LGod LStr MAsh MAus MFry MGan MJon MRav SCoo SPoG SPoc SSea SWCr
	'Femina' (HT)	MGan
	'Ferdinand Pichard' (Bb) ♀H4	CPou EBee EBls ECnt EMFP ENot EPfP LRHS MAus MBri MDun MJon MRav MWgw NBPC NEgg SPer SPoc SSea SWCr WAct WFoF WGer WHCG WKif WOVN
§	Ferdy = 'Keitoli'PBR (GC)	EBls MRav SPer SWCr
	Fergie = 'Ganfer'PBR (F/Patio)	MGan
	Festival = 'Kordialo'PBR (Patio)	ENot ESty LGod LStr MAus MRav NBlu SPer SWCr
	'Festive Jewel' (S) **new**	EBls
§	'Feuermeer' (F)	MJon
	Fiery Hit = 'Poulfiry'PBR (Min)	ECnt
	Fiery Sunblaze = 'Meineyta'PBR (Min)	SPoc SWCr
	Fiesta = 'Macfirinlin' (Patio)	MBri MJon
	Fifi = 'Hanfif' (F)	NBat
	filipes	GIBF
	- 'Brenda Colvin'	see *R.* 'Brenda Colvin'
§	- 'Kiftsgate' (Ra) ♀H4	More than 30 suppliers
§	'Fimbriata' (Ru)	CPou EBee EBls EWTr MAus MBri SPer SWCr WAct WHCG
	Financial Times Centenary = 'Ausfin' (S)	MAus

	Fiona = 'Meibeluxen'PBR (S/GC)	EBls GGre SWCr
	'Fire Princess' (Min)	SWCr
	'Firecracker' (F)	EBls
	Firefly = 'Macfrabro' (Min)	MJon
	Firestorm = 'Peazoe' (Patio)	SPoc
	'First Class' (HT) **new**	GGre
	'First Love' (HT)	EBls MGan
	'Fisher and Holmes' (HP)	EBls MAus WAct WHCG
	Fisherman's Friend = 'Auschild'PBR (S)	MAus SPer
	Flamenco = 'Poultika'PBR (Cl)	ECnt SSea
	Flash Dance = 'Poulyc004' (Cl)	ECnt GGre LRHS MAsh SWCr
	Flirt = 'Korkopapp'PBR **new**	ENot
	'Flora McIvor' (RH)	EBls MAus
	'Flore' (Ra)	CRHN EBls MAus SFam
	'Florence Mary Morse' (S)	SDix
	Florence Nightingale = 'Ganflor'PBR (F)	MGan SPer
	Flower CarpetPBR	see *R.* Pink Flower Carpet
	'Flower Carpet Coral'PBR (GC)	CGro ENot LRHS MAsh SCoo SPoG SWCr
	Flower Carpet Red Velvet = 'Noare'PBR (GC)	CGro ELan ENot GGre MAsh MRav SCoo SPoG
§	Flower Carpet Sunshine = 'Noason'PBR (GC)	CGro ELan ENot EPfP GCoc GGre LRHS LStr MAsh MRav SCoo SPoG SWCr
§	Flower Carpet Twilight = 'Noatwi'PBR (GC)	GGre LRHS SPoG
	Flower Carpet Velvet (GC/S)	CGro EPfP GGre LRHS SWCr
	Flower Carpet White = 'Noaschnee'PBR (GC) ♀H4	CGro CTri EBee ELan ENot EPfP GCoc GGre LRHS LStr MAsh MFry MRav SCoo SPer SPoG SWCr
	Flower Power = 'Frycassia'PBR (Patio)	CSBt ECnt ESty GCoc GGre LStr MAsh MAus MFry MJon MRav SPoG SPoc SWCr
	'Flying High' (CL) **new**	GGre
§	***foetida*** (S)	EBls MAus
§	- 'Bicolor' (S)	EBee EBls LRHS MAus NHaw SPer WAct
§	- 'Persiana' (S)	EBls MAus NHaw
	foliolosa	EBls SLPl WHCG
	Fond Memories = 'Kirfelix'PBR (Patio)	GCoc LStr MJon SPoc SWCr
	Forever Royal = 'Franmite' (F)	ESty
	Forever Young = 'Jacimgol'PBR (F)	IDic MJon
	forrestiana	EBls MAus WHCG
	x ***fortuneana*** (Ra)	EBls WFar
	Fortune's double yellow	see *R.* x *odorata* 'Pseudindica'
	'Fountain' (HT/S)	EBls MAus SPer SWCr
	Fragrant Cloud = 'Tanellis' (HT)	CGro CTri CWSG EBee EBls ECnt ENot EPfP ESty GCoc GGre LStr MAsh MAus MBri MFry MGan MJon MRav NBat SPer SPoc SSea SWCr
	'Fragrant Delight' (F) ♀H4	CSBt ECnt GCoc LAst LStr MAus MGan MJon MRav SPer SWCr
	Fragrant Dream = 'Dicodour'PBR (HT)	CGro ESty IDic LStr MGan SWCr
	Fragrant Gold = 'Tandugoft'PBR (HT)	SPoG
	Fragrant Memories = 'Korpastato'PBR (HT/S)	ENot GCoc MAsh SCoo SPoG SPoc SWCr WOVN
	France Info = 'Delcril' (S) **new**	SPoc SWCr
	Frances Perry = 'Bosrexcity'PBR (F)	GGre SPoG SWCr
	'Francesca' (HM)	CPou EBee EBls LRHS MAus SFam SPer SWCr WAct WHCG
	Francine Austin = 'Ausram'PBR (S/GC)	LRHS MAus MJon NEgg SPer SWCr WAct
	'Francis Dubreuil' (T)	EBls
§	'Francis E. Lester' (HM/Ra)	CHad CRHN CSam EBee EBls EWTr LRHS MAus MBri MJon SPer SPoc SSea SWCr WAct WHCG
	x ***francofurtana*** misapplied	see *R.* 'Impératrice Joséphine'
§	- 'Agatha'	EBls
	'François Juranville' (Ra) ♀H4	CHad CPou CRHN CSBt EBee EBls GGre LRHS LStr MAus MBri MGan MRav SPer SPoc SWCr WAct
§	'Frau Karl Druschki' (HP)	EBls MAus WAct
	'Fräulein Octavia Hesse' (Ra)	EBls
	'Fred Loads' (F/S) ♀H4	EBls MAus MJon MRav
	Freddie Mercury = 'Batmercury' (HT)	MJon NBat
	Free as Air = 'Mehbronze'PBR (Patio)	MBri
	Freedom = 'Dicjem'PBR (HT) ♀H4	ECnt ENot GCoc GGre IDic LGod LStr MAus MFry MGan MJon MRav NBat NPri SPer SPoc SWCr
	'Freiherr von Marschall' (T)	EBls
	'Frensham' (F)	CBcs EBls LStr MGan SSea SWCr
	Fresco = 'Ruico' (F) **new**	NBlu
	Friend for Life = 'Cocnanne'PBR (F) ♀H4	GCoc GGre MAsh MJon MRav SWCr
	'Friendship' (P) **new**	GGre SWCr
	'Fritz Nobis' (S) ♀H4	CAbP CHad EBls EMil ENot LRHS LStr MAus MRav SPer SPoc SWCr WAct WHCG
	Frothy = 'Macfrothy'PBR (Patio)	ECnt MJon
	'Fru Dagmar Hastrup' (Ru) ♀H4	CAlb CDul CSBt CSam EBee EBls ECnt ELan ENot EPfP GCoc LBuc LStr MAus MDun MFry MJon SPer SPoG SPoc SWCr WAct WHCG WOVN
	'Frühlingsanfang' (PiH)	EBls MAus SWCr WAct
	'Frühlingsduft' (PiH)	EBls SWCr
	'Frühlingsgold' (PiH) ♀H4	CBcs CGro EBls ELan ENot EPfP GCoc GKir LRHS LStr MAus MDun MFry MRav NWea SPer SWCr WAct WHCG WOVN
	'Frühlingsmorgen' (PiH)	EBls ENot GCoc GKir LStr MAus MBri MRav NPri SPer SSea SWCr WAct WHCG WOVN
	'Frühlingsschnee' (PiH)	EBls
	'Frühlingszauber' (PiH)	EBls
	fuchianus	GIBF
	'Fulgens'	see *R.* 'Malton'
	Fulton Mackay = 'Cocdana'PBR (HT)	GCoc GGre MGan SWCr
	Fyvie Castle = 'Cocbamber' (HT)	GCoc MGan
	'Gail Borden' (HT)	MGan
§	***gallica*** (G)	EBls
§	- var. ***officinalis*** (G) ♀H4	CAbP CSam EBls EMFP GCoc GPoy LRHS MAsh MAus MJon MRav SFam SPer SPoc SSea SWCr WAct WHCG
	- ***rubus***	WAct
	- 'Velutiniflora' (G)	EBls SSea
§	- 'Versicolor' (G) ♀H4	More than 30 suppliers

	Galway Bay = 'Macba' (ClHT)	GGre GKir LRHS MAsh MGan MRav SPer SWCr
§	Garden News = 'Poulrim'PBR (HT)	ECnt ESty MAsh SCoo SWCr
	'Gardenia' (Ra)	CPou EBee MAus SPoc SWCr WHCG
	'Gardiner's Pink' (Ra)	WHCG
	'Garnette Carol'	see *R.* 'Carol Amling'
	'Garnette Pink'	see *R.* 'Carol Amling'
	'Gavotte' (HT)	MJon
	'Général Galliéni' (T)	EBls
	'Général Jacqueminot' (HP)	EBls MAus
	'Général Kléber' (CeMo)	EBls MAus MRav SFam SPer SSea SWCr WAct WHCG
§	'Général Schablikine' (T)	EBls EMFP EWTr MAus SWCr
	gentiliana H.Lév. & Vaniot	see *R. multiflora* var. *cathayensis*
N	***gentiliana*** ambig. (Ra)	EBls LRHS MAus SWCr WBor WHCG XPep
	Gentle Touch = 'Diclulu'PBR (Min/Patio)	CSBt CWSG EBls ENot IDic MFry MJon MRav SMad SPer SPla SWCr
	Geoff Hamilton = 'Ausham'PBR (S)	CSBt EBls ENot ESty LRHS LStr MAsh MAus MBNS MJon NEgg SCoo SPer SPoG SPoc SWCr
	'Georg Arends' (HP)	EBls MAus
	'George Dickson' (HT)	EBls MAus
	'George R. Hill' (HT)	NBat
	'George Vancouver' (S)	EBls
	'Georges Vibert' (G)	EBee EBls MAus SWCr WHCG
	Geraldine = 'Peahaze' (F)	MGan SWCr
§	'Geranium' (*moyesii* hybrid) ♀H4	CBcs CGro CHad EBee ELan ENot EPfP GCoc GGre GKir IArd LGod LRHS LStr MAsh MAus MBri MJon MRav NBlu NEgg NScw SPer SPoc SSea SWCr WAct WHCG WOVN
	'Gerbe Rose' (Ra)	EBls MAus
	Gertrude Jekyll = 'Ausbord'PBR (S) ♀H4	More than 30 suppliers
	'Ghislaine de Féligonde' (Ra/S)	CHad CPou EBee EBls EMFP LStr SPer SSea SWCr WHCG WPen
	gigantea	EBls ISea
	- 'Cooperi'	see *R.* 'Cooperi'
	Giggles = 'Kingig' (Min)	MJon
	Ginger Syllabub = 'Harjolly' (Cl)	ESty GCoc GGre LStr MJon SPoG SPoc SWCr
§	Gingernut = 'Coccrazy'PBR (Patio)	GGre SPoG SWCr
	Gipsy Boy	see *R.* 'Zigeunerknabe'
	giraldii	EBls
	Glad Tidings = 'Tantide'PBR (F)	CSBt CWSG LAst MBri MGan MRav SPer SWCr
	Glamis Castle = 'Auslevel'PBR (S)	CBcs CSam CTri EBls ESty LRHS LStr MAsh MAus MBNS MBri MJon MWgw NEgg SPer SPoc SWCr
§	***glauca*** Pourr. (S) ♀H4	More than 30 suppliers
	'Glenfiddich' (F)	CGro CSBt CTri CWSG GCoc GGre LStr MAus MBri MJon MRav NPri NWea SPer SSea SWCr
	Glenshane = 'Dicvood'PBR (GC/S)	ESty IDic SPoc SWCr
	Global Beauty = 'Tan94448' (HT)	ESty SPoc SWCr
	'Gloire de Bruxelles' (HP)	EBls
	'Gloire de Dijon' (ClT)	More than 30 suppliers
	'Gloire de Ducher' (HP)	MAus MRav SWCr WAct WHCG
	'Gloire de France' (G)	EBls EWTr MAus MRav SWCr
	'Gloire de Guilan' (D)	EBls MAus SPoc SWCr WAct
	'Gloire des Mousseuses' (CeMo)	EBee EBls EWTr SFam SWCr WAct WHCG
	'Gloire du Midi' (Poly)	MAus
	'Gloire Lyonnaise' (HP)	EBee EBls EWTr SWCr WHCG
	'Gloria Mundi' (Poly)	EBls SWCr
	Gloriana = 'Chewpope'PBR (ClMin)	ESty GGre LRHS MAsh MAus MBri MJon SCoo SPer SPoc SSea SWCr
	Glorious = 'Interictira'PBR (HT)	GCoc IDic MBri MJon SPoc SWCr
	Glorious = 'Leoglo' (HT)	NBat
	Glowing Amber = 'Manglow' (Min)	MJon NBat
	glutinosa	see *R. pulverulenta*
	'Goethe' (CeMo)	EBls
	Gold Reef = 'Pouldom'PBR **new**	ECnt
	Gold Symphonie = 'Macfraba' (Min) **new**	SPoc
	'Goldbusch' (RH)	EBls WAct
	'Golden Anniversary' (Patio)	GCoc GGre LStr MAsh SPer SWCr
	Golden Beauty = 'Korberbeni' (F)	ENot ESty
	Golden Beryl = 'Manberyl' (Min)	MJon
	Golden Celebration = 'Ausgold'PBR (S) ♀H4	CSBt CWSG EBee ECnt ENot EPfP ESty GCoc GGre GKir LGod LRHS LStr MAsh MAus MBri MJon MRav NPri SMad SPer SPoc SWCr WGer
	'Golden Chersonese' (S)	EBls MAus
	Golden Future = 'Horanymoll'PBR (Cl)	GGre MJon SPoc SWCr
	'Golden Glow' (Cl)	EBls
§	Golden Jewel = 'Tanledolg'PBR (Patio)	ESty MAsh NBlu SPoG SWCr
	Golden Jubilee = 'Cocagold' (HT)	CGro CTri GCoc GGre MRav SWCr
	Golden Kiss = 'Dicalways'PBR (HT)	ECnt ESty GCoc IDic MJon NBat SPoc SWCr
	Golden Melody = 'Irene Churruca' (HT)	EBls
	Golden Memories = 'Koreholesea' (F)	CGro ESty GCoc LGod LRHS LStr MFry MJon NPri SCoo SPoG SPoc SSea SWCr
	Golden Moments = 'Frytranquil'PBR (HT)	MFry
	'Golden Moss' (Mo)	EBls
	Golden Oldie = 'Fryescape'PBR (HT)	GCoc MFry
	'Golden Ophelia' (HT)	EBls
§	Golden Penny = 'Rugul' (Min)	MFry
	'Golden Rambler'	see *R.* 'Alister Stella Gray'
	'Golden Salmon Supérieur' (Poly)	EBls
	'Golden Shot' (F)	MGan
	'Golden Showers' (Cl) ♀H4	More than 30 suppliers
	'Golden Slippers' (F)	CBcs MGan
	'Golden Sunblaze'	see *R.* 'Rise 'n' Shine'
	Golden Topas = 'Mantopas' (Min) **new**	ECnt
	Golden Tribute = 'Horannfree' (F) **new**	MGan
	Golden Trust = 'Hardish'PBR (Patio)	GGre LStr SWCr
	Golden Wedding = 'Arokris'PBR (F/HT)	More than 30 suppliers
	'Golden Wedding Celebration' **new**	GGre
	'Golden Wings' (S) ♀H4	CHad CTri EBls ECnt ELan ENot EPfP EWTr GCoc LRHS LStr MAsh MAus MFry MJon MRav SPer SPoc SSea SWCr WAct WHCG
	Golden Years = 'Harween'PBR (F)	MAus

	Name	Suppliers
	'Goldfinch' (Ra)	CHad EBee EBls ELan EMFP LRHS LStr MAus MBri MRav NEgg SPer SPoc SWCr WAct WHCG
§	Goldstar = 'Candide' (HT)	ECnt MGan SWCr
	Good as Gold = 'Chewsunbeam'[PBR] (ClMin)	CSBt ESty LStr MBri MFry MJon NPri SPer SPoc SSea SWCr WGer
	Good Life = 'Cococircus'[PBR] (HT)	GCoc GGre SCoo SPoG SWCr
	Good Luck = 'Burspec'[PBR] (F/Patio)	GCoc SPer
	Good News 95 = 'Chespink'[PBR] **new**	SWCr
§	Gordon Snell = 'Dicwriter' (F)	IDic
	Gordon's College = 'Cocjabby'[PBR] (F) ♀H4	ESty GCoc MJon
	'Grace Abounding' (F)	MJon
	Grace = 'Auskeppy'[PBR] (S)	CSBt ECnt EPfP LGod MAus MBri MJon NEgg SWCr
	'Grace Darling' (T)	EBls
	Grace de Monaco = 'Meimit' (HT)	EBls MGan
	Gracious Queen = 'Bedqueen' (HT)	GCoc SWCr
	Graham Thomas = 'Ausmas'[PBR] (S) ♀H4	More than 30 suppliers
	'Granada' (HT) Lindquist 1963	EBls
	Grand Hotel = 'Mactel' (ClHT)	MJon SPer
	Grand Palace = 'Poulgrad'[PBR] (F) **new**	MAsh SPoG SWCr
	Grand-mère Jenny = 'Grem' (HT)	EBls MGan
	'Grandpa Dickson' (HT)	CSBt CWSG EBls GGre LGod MAsh MAus MGan MJon MRav NPri SPer SWCr
	Granny's Favourite (F)	GGre SWCr
	Great Expectations = 'Jacdal' (F)	ENot
	Great Expectations = 'Lanican' (HT)	CBcs
	Great Expectations = 'Mackalves'[PBR] (F)	CSBt ECnt EPfP ESty GCoc GGre IArd LGod LStr MAsh MFry MJon SCoo SPer SPoc SWCr
§	'Great Maiden's Blush' (A)	EBls GCoc GGre MRav NBPC SFam SPoc WAct
	'Great News' (F)	MAus
	'Great Ormond Street' (F)	EBls
	'Great Western' (Bb)	EBls
	'Green Diamond' (Min)	MJon
	Greenall's Glory = 'Kirmac'[PBR] (F/Patio)	MAus MJon
	'Greenmantle' (RH)	EBls MAus
	Greensleeves = 'Harlenten' (F)	EBls SPer SPoc SWCr
	Greetings = 'Jacdreco'[PBR] (F)	GGre IDic MAsh MRav SWCr
	Grenadine = 'Poulgrena'[PBR] (HT)	ECnt SPoc SWCr
	Grimaldi = 'Delstror' (F) **new**	SPoc SWCr
	'Grimpant Cramoisi Supérieur' (ClCh)	EBls WHCG
	'Grootendorst'	see *R.* 'F.J. Grootendorst'
	'Grootendorst Supreme' (Ru)	MAus SPer SWCr
N	'Gros Choux de Hollande' hort. (Bb)	EBls WHCG
§	Grouse 2000 = 'Korteilhab'[PBR] (GC)	ENot
	Grouse = 'Korimro'[PBR] (S/GC) ♀H4	CTri EBls GCoc LRHS MAus MJon MRav SPer SWCr WAct WOVN
	'Gruss an Aachen' (Poly)	EBls EMFP EPfP LStr MAus SPer SWCr WAct WHCG
	'Gruss an Teplitz' (China hybrid)	EBls MAus SPer SWCr WHCG
	'Guinée' (ClHT)	CHad CSBt EBee EBls ECnt ELan ENot EPfP ESty EWTr GKir LRHS LStr MAus MGan MRav NPri SChu SPer SPla SPoG SPoc SSea SWCr WHCG
	'Gustav Grünerwald' (HT)	EBls MAus
	Guy Savoy = 'Delstrimen' (F) **new**	SPoc SWCr
	Gwen Mayor = 'Cocover'[PBR] (HT)	GCoc GGre
	Gwent = 'Poulurt'[PBR] (GC)	CSBt ELan GCoc LSRN LStr MAus MRav SPer SPoG SSea SWCr WAct WOVN
§	***gymnocarpa*** var. ***willmottiae***	EBls SPer SSea SWCr WAct WHCG
	Gypsy Boy	see *R.* 'Zigeunerknabe'
	'Hadangel'	see *R.* 'Smooth Angel'
	'Hadvelvet'	see *R.* 'Smooth Velvet'
	'Hakuun' (F/Patio) ♀H4	MAus MGan SWCr
	Hallé = 'Fryelectric' (HT)	ECnt GGre MFry
	'Hamburger Phönix' (Ra)	CGro EBls SPer SWCr WAct
	Hampshire = 'Korhamp'[PBR] (GC)	MAus MRav
	Hampton Palace = 'Poulgret'[PBR] (F)	ECnt
	Hand in Hand = 'Haraztec'[PBR] (Patio/Min)	GGre MAsh SPoG SPoc SWCr
	Handel = 'Macha' (Cl) ♀H4	CGro CSBt CTri CWSG EBls ELan ENot EPfP ESty GGre GKir LAst LRHS LStr MAsh MBri MFry MGan MJon MRav SPer SPoc SSea SWCr
	Hanky Panky = 'Wektorcent' **new**	MJon
	Hannah Gordon = 'Korweiso'[PBR] (F)	ECnt ENot MGan MJon NBat SSea
	'Hannah Hauxwell' (Patio/F)	NBat SWCr
	'Hansa' (Ru)	CDul EBee EBls GCoc LBuc MAus SPer SWCr WHCG WOVN
	Happy Anniversary = 'Bedfranc'[PBR]	MJon NBPC
	Happy Anniversary = 'Delpre' (F)	CGro GGre GKir LStr MAsh MRav SPoG SSea
	'Happy Birthday' (Min/Patio)	CWSG ENot ESty GGre LStr SPoG SSea SWCr
	Happy Child = 'Auscomp'[PBR] (S)	CWSG LRHS MAus MJon SCoo SPer SPoc SWCr
	Happy Ever After = 'Dicvanilla'[PBR] (F)	IDic MJon
	'Happy Memories' (F)	EBls
	Happy Retirement = 'Tantoras'[PBR] (F)	ESty GCoc GGre LStr MAsh SCoo SPoc SSea SWCr
	'Happy Thought' (Min)	CWSG
	Happy Times = 'Bedone'[PBR] (Patio/Min)	ENot GGre MAsh SPoG SWCr
	Harewood = 'Taninaso'[PBR] (Patio/F)	MRav
§	x ***harisonii*** 'Harison's Yellow' (PiH)	EBls ENot MAus SPer SWCr
§	- 'Lutea Maxima' (PiH)	EBls
§	- 'Williams' Double Yellow' (PiH)	EBls GCoc MAus SWCr WAct
	Harper Adams = 'Fryflash' (F)	MFry
	'Harry Edland' (F)	GGre SPoG SSea SWCr

'Harry Maasz' (GC/Cl) EBls
'Harry Wheatcroft' (HT) CBcs CGro EBls ESty GGre MAus MGan MJon SPer
Harvest Fayre = 'Dicnorth'PBR (F) CGro CTri ENot IDic MGan SPer
'Headleyensis' EBee EBls MAus WHCG
Heart of Gold = 'Coctarlotte' (HT) GCoc
§ Heartbeat '97 = 'Cocorona'PBR (F) GCoc GGre LGod SWCr
Heartbreaker = 'Weksibyl' (Min) NBat
Heather Austin = 'Auscook'PBR (S) LRHS MAus
§ 'Heather Muir' (*sericea* hybrid) (S) EBls MAus
'Heaven Scent' (F) MJon
Heavenly Rosalind = 'Ausmash'PBR (S) LRHS MAus
§ 'Hebe's Lip' (DxSwB) EBls MAus SWCr WAct
'Hector Deane' (HT) EBls
'Heinrich Schultheis' (HP) EBls
§ 'Helen Knight' (*ecae* hybrid) (S) EBls MAsh MAus MBri SSea SWCr WHCG
'Helen Traubel' (HT) EBls MGan
Helena = 'Poulna'PBR (S) ECnt LRHS MAsh SPoG SPoc SWCr
helenae CTri EBee EBls GCal MAus SPer SWCr
- hybrid WHCG
hemisphaerica (S) EBls MAus SWCr WAct
hemsleyana CHid
'Henri Fouquier' (G) EBls
§ 'Henri Martin' (CeMo) EBee EBls MAus SPer SPoc SWCr WAct WHCG
Henri Matisse = 'Delstrobla' (HT) ESty SWCr
'Henry Nevard' (HP) EBls MAus
'Her Majesty' (HP) EBls MAsh
Her Majesty = 'Dicxotic'PBR (F) IDic SWCr
§ 'Herbstfeuer' (RH) EBls MAus SPer
Heritage = 'Ausblush'PBR (S) CGro EBee EBls ECnt ELan EMFP ENot EPfP GCoc GGre LGod LRHS LStr MAsh MAus MFry MJon MRav MWgw NEgg NPri SMad SPer SPla SPoG SPoc SSea SWCr WHCG WOVN
'Hermosa' (Ch) EBee EBls EMFP LRHS MAsh MAus MRav SPla SPoc SWCr WAct WHCG XPep
Hero = 'Aushero' (S) MAus
Hertfordshire = 'Kortenay'PBR (GC) ♀H4 ELan ENot MAus MRav NPri SPer SWCr
Hi Society = 'Cocquation'PBR (Patio) GCoc
'Hiawatha' (Ra) EBls SWCr
'Hidcote Gold' (S) EBls MAus
'Hide and Seek' (F) GCoc
Hide and Seek = 'Diczodiac'PBR (F) IDic
High Flier = 'Fryfandango' (Cl) **new** MFry
High Hopes = 'Haryup'PBR (Cl) ♀H4 CSBt EBee ECnt GGre LGod LRHS LStr MAsh MAus MGan MJon SPer SPla SPoG SPoc SSea SWCr WHCG
'High Society' (HT) **new** GGre
§ 'Highdownensis' (*moyesii* hybrid) (S) EBls ELan MAus SPer
Highfield = 'Harcomp'PBR (Cl) CSBt LGod MAus MJon MRav SPer SPoc SWCr

Hilda Murrell = 'Ausmurr' (S) MAus
Hilde = 'Benhile' (Min) NBat
§ 'Hillieri' (S) EBls MAus
'Hippolyte' (G) EBls MAus
holodonta see *R. moyesii* f. *rosea*
holy rose see *R.* x *richardii*
Home of Time = 'Cocquamber'PBR (HT) ESty GCoc
'Home Sweet Home' (HT) EBls
Home Sweet Home = 'Mailoeur' (Cl/G) SPoc SSea SWCr
'Homère' (T) EBls MAus
Honey Bunch = 'Cocglen'PBR (F) ESty GCoc GGre LGod LStr SPer SWCr
Honeymoon see *R.* 'Honigmond'
Honeywood = 'Fryfixit' (F) GCoc MFry
§ 'Honigmond' (F) CWSG SWCr
'Honorine de Brabant' (Bb) CHad CPou EBls LRHS MAus SPer SPla SPoc SWCr WAct WHCG
'Horace Vernet' (HP) EBls
horrida see *R. biebersteinii*
'Horstmanns Rosenresli' (F) EBls
Hospitality = 'Horcoff'PBR (F) MJon
Hot Gossip = 'Jacati' (Patio/Min) GGre SPoG SWCr
Hot Stuff = 'Maclarayspo' (Min) **new** MJon
Hot Tamale = 'Jacpoy' (Min) MJon NBat
House Beautiful = 'Harbingo'PBR (Patio) GGre MRav SWCr
'Hugh Dickson' (HP) EBls MAus SPoc SWCr
hugonis see *R. xanthina* f. *hugonis*
- 'Plenissima' see *R. xanthina* f. *hugonis*
'Hula Girl' (Min) LGod
Humanity = 'Harcross'PBR (F) MRav
Hume's blush see *R.* x *odorata* 'Odorata'
'Hunslet Moss' (Mo) EBls
'Hunter' (Ru) WAct
Hyde Hall = 'Ausbosky' **new** LRHS SCoo
I Love You = 'Geelove' (HT) ESty
Ice Cream = 'Korzuri'PBR (HT) ♀H4 CWSG ENot LStr MAus MGan MJon MRav SPoc SSea SWCr
§ Iceberg = 'Korbin' (F) ♀H4 CBcs CGro CSBt CWSG EBee EBls ECnt ENot EPfP ESty GCoc GGre LAst LGod LStr MAsh MAus MFry MGan MJon MRav NBlu SPer SPoG SPoc SSea SWCr
'Iced Ginger' (F) MGan SPer
'Illusion' (Cl/F) MGan SPoc SWCr
'Ilse Krohn Superior' (Cl) EBls
Imagination = 'Pouldrom' (F) EBee ECnt
§ 'Impératrice Joséphine' ♀H4 CSam EBee EBls MAus MRav NEgg SFam SSea SWCr WAct WHCG
In the Pink = 'Peaverity'PBR (F) SPoc SWCr
Incognito = 'Briincog' (Min) **new** MJon
Indian Summer = 'Peaperfume'PBR (HT) ♀H4 CSBt CWSG GCoc GGre LAst LGod MBri MFry MRav SPoc SWCr
'Indica Major' XPep
'Indigo' (DPo) CPou EBls MAus SWCr WHCG
Ingrid Bergman = 'Poulman'PBR (HT) ♀H4 CSBt ECnt ENot ESty GCoc LGod LStr MAus MFry MGan MJon MRav SPoc SWCr

	Name	Suppliers
§	Innocence = 'Cocoray'[PBR] (Patio)	GCoc GGre SWCr
	Intense Cover = 'Poultwoo1' (GC/S)	MAsh SWCr
	'Intermezzo' (HT)	MGan
§	Intrigue = 'Korlech'[PBR] (F)	CSBt ENot LStr MJon SSea
	Invincible = 'Runatru'[PBR] (F)	EBee ECnt MAus MFry MGan
	'Ipsilanté' (G)	EBls MAus WAct WHCG
	'Irene Av Danmark' (F)	EBls
	'Irène Watts' (Ch)	CPou EBee EBls ECre EMFP EPfP EWTr MAus SPla SPoc SWCr WAct WHCG
	'Irish Elegance' (HT)	EBls
	Irish Eyes = 'Dicwitness'[PBR] (F)	CWSG ECnt EPfP ESty GCoc GGre IArd IDic LGod LStr MAsh MBri MFry MGan MJon MRav NPri SCoo SPer SPoc SSea SWCr
	'Irish Fireflame' (HT)	EBls
	Irish Hope = 'Harexclaim'[PBR] (F)	GGre MAsh SCoo SPoG SPoc SWCr
	Irresistible = 'Tinresist' (Min/Patio)	MJon NBat
	Isabella = 'Poulisab'[PBR] (S)	CPou CTri ECnt GGre LRHS MAsh SPoG SWCr
	Isobel Derby = 'Horethel'[PBR] (HT)	MJon SPoc SWCr
	'Ispahan' (D) 🏆[H4]	CFee CHad EBls EPfP EWTr LRHS MAsh MAus NEgg SFam SPer SPoc SWCr WAct WHCG
	'Ivor' (S) **new**	EBls
	'Ivory Fashion' (F)	EBls
	Jack Wood = 'Frydabble'[PBR] (F)	MFry
	Jack's Wish = 'Kirsil' (HT)	MJon
§	x *jacksonii* 'Max Graf' (GC/Ru)	EBls ENot GGre LRHS MAus MRav WAct WFar
§	- White Max Graf = 'Korgram'[PBR] (GC/Ru)	ENot MRav WAct
	Jacobite rose	see *R.* x *alba* 'Alba Maxima'
	'Jacpico'[PBR]	see *R.* 'Pristine'
	Jacqueline du Pré = 'Harwanna'[PBR] (S) 🏆[H4]	CSBt EBee ECnt EPfP GCoc LRHS MAsh MAus MJon MRav SChu SPer SPoc SWCr WAct WHCG
	Jacquenetta = 'Ausjac' (S)	MAus
N	'Jacques Cartier' hort.	see *R.* 'Marchesa Boccella'
	'James Bourgault' (HP)	EBls
	James Galway = 'Auscrystal'[PBR] (S)	CSBt CWSG LGod MAus MBri MJon NEgg SCoo SWCr
	'James Mason' (G)	CSam EBls MAus
	'James Mitchell' (CeMo)	EBls MAus SSea SWCr WHCG
	'James Veitch' (DPoMo)	EBls MAus WHCG
	Jane Asher = 'Peapet'[PBR] (Min/Patio)	MJon SWCr
	Jane Eyre = 'Mehpark'[PBR] (Cl)	COtt MGan
	Janet = 'Auspishus' (S) **new**	MAus
	'Janet's Pride' (RH)	EBls MAus
§	'Japonica' (CeMo)	MAus
§	Jardins de Bagatelle = 'Meimafris'[PBR] (HT)	MJon
	Jayne Austin = 'Ausbreak'[PBR] (S)	CSBt CWSG LRHS MAus MJon SMad SPer SWCr
	Jazz[PBR] (Cl)	see *R.* That's Jazz = 'Poulnorm'
	'Jean Armour' (F) **new**	GGre
	Jean = 'Cocupland' (Patio) **new**	GCoc
	Jean Kenneally = 'Tineally' (Min)	MJon NBat
	'Jean Mermoz' (Poly)	MAus SWCr
	'Jean Rosenkrantz' (HP)	EBls
	'Jean Sisley' (HT)	EBls
	'Jeanie Deans' (RH)	MAus
	'Jeanne de Montfort' (CeMo)	EBls MAus
§	Jemma Giblin = 'Horjemma' (Patio/F)	NBat
	'Jenny Duval' misapplied	see *R.* 'Président de Sèze'
	'Jenny Wren' (F)	EBls MAus
	'Jenny's Dream' (HT)	LGod
	Jenny's Rose = 'Cansit' (F)	EBee ECnt
	'Jens Munk' (Ru)	WAct
	'Jersey Beauty' (Ra)	EBls
	'Jill Dando' (S)	EBls
	Jillian McGredy = 'Macarnhe'[PBR] (F)	MJon
	Jill's Rose = 'Ganjil'[PBR] (F)	MGan SPoc SWCr
	Jilly Jewel = 'Benmfig' (Min)	NBat
	'Jiminy Cricket' (F)	EBls
	'Jimmy Greaves' (HT)	MGan
	'Joanna Hill' (HT)	EBls
	'Joanne' (HT)	MJon
	'Jocelyn' (F)	EBls
	Joey's Palace = 'Pouljoey'[PBR] (Patio)	MAsh SWCr
	'John Cabot' (S)	SSea
	John Clare = 'Auscent'[PBR] (S)	LRHS MAus SWCr
	'John Hopper' (HP)	EBls MAus SWCr
	John Willan = 'Fryeager' (HT) **new**	MFry
	Johnnie Walker = 'Frygran'[PBR] (HT)	ESty MFry
	Jose Carreras = 'Pouljose'[PBR] (HT)	EBee ECnt
	'Josephine Bruce' (HT)	CBcs CSBt EBls LGod MGan MRav
	'Joseph's Coat' (S/Cl)	IArd LGod LStr MFry SSea SWCr
	'Journey's End' (HT)	MGan
I	'Joy' (F) **new**	SWCr
	'Jubilee Celebration' (F)	EPfP MAsh
	Jubilee Celebration = 'Aushunter' (S)	MAus SWCr
	Jude the Obscure = 'Ausjo'[PBR] (S)	CAbP ESty LRHS MAus MJon NEgg SWCr
§	Judi Dench = 'Peahunder' (F)	EPfP
	'Judy Fischer' (Min)	LGod SWCr
	'Julia's Rose'[PBR] (HT)	CGro LStr MAus MGan MJon SPer SPoc SSea SWCr
	'Juliet' (HP)	EBls
	jundzillii	CFee
	'Juno' (Ce)	EBls MAus WAct WHCG
	'Just for You' (F)	GGre SWCr
	'Just Jenny' (Min)	MJon NBat
	'Just Joey' (HT) 🏆[H4]	CGro CSBt CWSG EBee EBls ECnt ELan ENot EPfP ESty GCoc GGre IArd LAst LGod LStr MAus MBri MFry MGan MJon MRav NPri SPer SPoG SPoc SSea SWCr
	'Karl Foerster' (PiH)	EBls MAus
	'Kassel' (S/Cl)	EBls
	'Katharina Zeimet' (Poly)	CPou EBls MAus SWCr WAct WHCG
	Katherine Mansfield = 'Meilanein' (HT)	CSBt
	'Kathleen' (HM)	EBls
	'Kathleen Ferrier' (F)	EBls MGan SWCr
	'Kathleen Harrop' (Bb)	EBee EBls LRHS LStr MAus SFam SPer SPoc SSea SWCr WAct WHCG
	Kathleen's Rose = 'Kirkitt' (F)	MJon

	Name	Suppliers
	Kathryn McGredy = 'Macauclad'[PBR] (HT)	MJon
§	Kathryn Morley = 'Ausclub'[PBR] (F)	CAbP LRHS MAus MJon MWgw SWCr
	'Katie' (ClF)	MGan SWCr
	'Kazanlik' misapplied	see *R.* 'Professeur Emile Perrot'
	Keep in Touch = 'Hardrama'[PBR] (F)	GGre SPoc SWCr
	Keep Smiling = 'Fryflorida' (HT) **new**	MFry
	Keepsake = 'Kormalda' (HT)	MGan MJon
	'Ken 'n' Norma Bright' (HT)	NBat
§	Kent = 'Poulcov'[PBR] (S/GC) 🏆[H4]	CSBt ECnt ELan ENot EPfP ESty EWTr GCoc LStr MAsh MFry MJon MRav NPri SPer SPla SPoG SPoc SSea SWCr WAct WHCG
	'Kew Rambler' (Ra)	CRHN CSam EBee EBls MAus MRav SFam SPer SPoc SWCr WHCG
	'Kiftsgate'	see *R. filipes* 'Kiftsgate'
	'Kilworth Gold' (HT)	MGan
	Kind Regards = 'Peatiger' (F)	LAst SWCr
	King's Macc = 'Frydisco' (HT)	ESty LGod MFry
	'King's Ransom' (HT)	CBcs CSBt EBls ENot MGan MJon MRav SPer SSea SWCr
	'Kirsten Poulsen' (Poly)	EBls
	'Kitty Hawk' (Min)	NBat
*	'Kitty's Rose' (S)	EBls
	Knock Out = 'Dadler' (F)	GCoc MJon
	x ***kochiana***	EBls
	'Köln am Rhein' (Cl)	MGan
§	'Königin von Dänemark' (A) 🏆[H4]	CHad EBee EBls EMFP ENot EPfP GCoc MAus MBri MJon MRav MWgw NEgg SPer SPoc SSea SWCr WAct WHCG
	Korona = 'Kornita' (F)	MGan SPer
	'Korresia' (F)	CSBt CTri EBee EBls ECnt ENot EPfP ESty GCoc GGre LGod LStr MAsh MAus MBri MFry MGan MJon MRav SPer SPoG SPoc SWCr
§	Kristin = 'Benmagic' (Min)	MJon NBat
	Kronenbourg = 'Macbo' (HT)	EBls
	'Kronprinzessin Viktoria' (Bb)	EBls MAus WHCG
	L.D. Braithwaite = 'Auscrim'[PBR] (S) 🏆[H4]	CGro CTri ELan EPfP ESty GCoc GGre LGod LRHS LStr MAsh MAus MFry MJon MRav NEgg NPri SPer SPoc SWCr WAct WHCG
	La Bamba = 'Diczoom'[PBR] (GC)	IDic
	'La Belle Distinguée' (RH)	EBls MAus WHCG
	'La Belle Sultane'	see *R.* 'Violacea'
	'La Follette' (Cl)	EBls
	'La France' (HT)	EBls MAus
	'La Mortola'	see *R. brunonii* 'La Mortola'
	'La Noblesse' (Ce)	EBls
	'La Perle' (Ra)	CRHN MAus
	'La Reine' (HP)	EBls
	'La Reine Victoria'	see *R.* 'Reine Victoria'
	'La Rubanée'	see *R.* x *centifolia* 'Unique Panachée'
	La Sévillana = 'Meigekanu'[PBR] (F/GC)	EBls SPer SWCr WOVN
	'La Ville de Bruxelles' (D) 🏆[H4]	EBls MAus MRav SFam SPer SWCr WAct WHCG
	'Lady Alice Stanley' (HT)	EBls
	'Lady Barnby' (HT)	EBls
	'Lady Belper' (HT)	EBls
	'Lady Curzon' (Ru)	EBls MAus SWCr
	'Lady Forteviot' (HT)	EBls
	'Lady Gay' (Ra)	SWCr WHCG
	'Lady Godiva' (Ra)	MAus
	'Lady Hillingdon' (T)	MAus
	'Lady Hillingdon' (ClT)	see *R.* 'Climbing Lady Hillingdon'
	'Lady Iliffe' (HT)	MGan
	Lady in Red = 'Sealady' (Min)	MJon
	'Lady Love '95' (Patio)	ENot GGre SWCr
	Lady MacRobert = 'Coclent' (F)	GCoc
	'Lady Mary Fitzwilliam' (HT)	EBls
§	Lady Meillandina = 'Meilarco' (Min)	CSBt
	Lady Penelope = 'Chewdor'[PBR] (ClHT)	CSBt GGre MAsh MJon SSea SWCr
§	'Lady Penzance' (RH) 🏆[H4]	CBcs EBls MAus SPer SPoc SWCr
§	Lady Rachel = 'Candoodle' (F)	EBee ECnt
	'Lady Romsey' (F)	EBls
	Lady Rose = 'Korlady' (HT)	MAsh SPoG SWCr
	'Lady Sylvia' (HT)	CSBt CTri EBls MAus MGan NEgg SPer
	'Lady Waterlow' (ClHT)	EBee EBls MAus SPer SWCr WHCG
	laevigata (Ra)	CArn EBls MAus SWCr XPep
	- 'Anemonoides'	see *R.* 'Anemone'
	'Lafter' (S)	EBls
	'Lagoon' (F)	EBls
	L'Aimant = 'Harzola'[PBR] (F) 🏆[H4]	CSBt ESty GCoc GGre LGod LStr MAus MFry MGan MJon SPoc SWCr
	'Lamarque' (N)	EBee MAus
	'Laminuette' (F) **new**	MJon
§	Lancashire = 'Korstesgli'[PBR] (GC) 🏆[H4]	ECnt ENot ESty GCoc LSRN LStr MAus MRav SSea SWCr
§	'Lanei' (CeMo)	EBls
	Laura Anne = 'Cocclarion' (HT)	GCoc
§	Laura Ashley = 'Chewharla' (GC/ClMin)	MAus SWCr
	Laura Ford = 'Chewarvel'[PBR] (ClMin) 🏆[H4]	CSBt CTri ENot ESty GGre LRHS LStr MAsh MAus MBri MJon MRav NBat NPri SPer SSea SWCr
	'Laura Jane' (HT)	MGan
	'Laura Louisa' (Cl)	EBls SWCr
§	'Laure Davoust' (Ra)	CPou EBee SWCr
I	'Lavender Jewel' (Min)	MAus
	'Lavender Lassie' (HM) 🏆[H4]	EBee EMFP MAus MGan SPer SPoc SSea SWCr WHCG
	'Lavender Pinocchio' (F)	MAus
§	Lawinia = 'Tanklewi'[PBR] (ClHT) 🏆[H4]	CSBt GKir LRHS LStr MJon MRav NPri SPer SSea SWCr
	'Lawrence Johnston' (Cl)	EBls LRHS MAus MJon SPer SWCr WAct
	Lazy Days (F)	EBee ECnt
	'Le Havre' (HP)	EBls
	'Le Rêve' (Cl)	EBls MAus SWCr
	'Le Vésuve' (Ch)	EBls MAus
	Leander = 'Auslea' (S)	MAus
	Leaping Salmon = 'Peamight'[PBR] (ClHT)	CGro CSBt EBee ELan GCoc LAst LGod LStr MAus MGan MJon MRav SChu SPer SPoc SSea SWCr
	'Leda' (D)	EBls MAus SFam SPer SSea SWCr WAct
	'Lemon Pillar'	see *R.* 'Paul's Lemon Pillar'
	Léonardo de Vinci = 'Meideauri'[PBR] (F)	CSBt
	'Léonie Lamesch' (Poly)	EBls

'Léontine Gervais' (Ra) CAbP CRHN LRHS MAsh MAus SPoc SWCr WAct
'Leo's Eye' SLon
Leslie's Dream = 'Dicjoon'PBR (HT) IDic MJon
'Leverkusen' (Cl) ♀H4 CHad EBee EBls LRHS MAsh MAus MJon MRav NEgg SPer SPla SPoc SSea SWCr WAct WHCG
'Leveson-Gower' (Bb) EBls
'Ley's Perpetual' (ClT) EBee EBls
x ***lheritieriana*** (Bs) SWCr
§ Lichtkönigin Lucia = 'Korlillub' (S) SSea
Life Begins at 40! = 'Horhohoho' (F) GGre SPoG SWCr
'Lilac Charm' (F) EBls
'Lilac Dream' (F) **new** GGre SPoG SWCr
§ Lilac Rose = 'Auslilac' (S) MAus
Lilian Austin = 'Ausli' (S) MAus MBri
Lilian Baylis = 'Hardeluxe'PBR (F) GGre SWCr
Liliana = 'Poulsyng'PBR (S) ECnt LRHS MAsh SPla SPoG SPoc SWCr
§ Lilli Marlene = 'Korlima' (F) CSBt CWSG EBls GCoc MGan SPer SWCr
Lincoln Cathedral = 'Glanlin'PBR (HT) GGre MJon SPer SWCr
Lincolnshire Poacher = 'Glareabit' (HT) NBat
'Lionheart' (F) **new** GGre
Lions International = 'Frycharm'PBR (HT) MFry
Little Amy = 'Battamy' (Min) **new** NBat
Little Artist = 'Macmanly' (Min) MJon
Little Bo-peep = 'Poullen'PBR (Min/Patio) ♀H4 ENot MJon
'Little Buckaroo' (Min) LGod SPer SWCr
'Little Flirt' (Min) MAus SWCr
'Little Gem' (DPMo) EBls MAus
Little Jackie = 'Savor' (Min) MJon NBat
Little Muff = 'Horluisbond' (Min) MJon NBat
Little Rambler = 'Chewramb'PBR (MinRa) ♀H4 CBrm CSBt ECnt ELan ENot LRHS LStr MAsh MAus MJon SCoo SPer SPoG SPoc SWCr WGer
'Little White Pet' see *R.* 'White Pet'
Little Woman = 'Diclittle'PBR (Patio) IDic LStr SWCr
'Liverpool Echo' (F) MJon
§ Liverpool Remembers = 'Frystar'PBR (HT) LGod MFry
Lochinvar = 'Ausbilda' (S) MAus
Lolita Lempicka = 'Meizincaro' **new** SPoc SWCr
'Long John Silver' (Cl) EBls MAus SSea
longicuspis misapplied see *R. mulliganii*
longicuspis Bertoloni (Ra) EBls SPla
- AC 2097 GGar
§ - var. ***sinowilsonii*** (Ra) EBls GCal MAus
aff. ***longicuspis*** AC 1808 GGar
§ Lord Byron = 'Meitosier'PBR (ClHT) MBri MJon SWCr
'Lord Penzance' (RH) CBgR EBls EMFP EWTr MRav SPer SPoc SWCr
L'Oréal Trophy = 'Harlexis' (HT) MJon
'Lorraine Lee' (T) EBls
'Los Angeles' (HT) EBls
'L'Ouche' misapplied see *R.* 'Louise Odier'
'Louis Gimard' (CeMo) EBls MAus SPer WAct
'Louis Philippe' (Ch) EBls
'Louis XIV' (Ch) CHad EBls WHCG
Louisa Stone = 'Harbadge' (S) GGre SWCr
Louise Clements = 'Clelou' (S) EBls
§ 'Louise Odier' (Bb) EBee EBls ECnt EMFP EPfP IArd LRHS LStr MAsh MAus MBri MJon MRav MWgw SFam SPer SPla SPoc SSea SWCr WAct WHCG WOVN
Love & Peace = 'Baipeace' (HT) **new** ELan ESty SPoc SWCr
Love Knot = 'Chewglorious'PBR (ClMin) CSBt ECnt ESty MJon SPoc SWCr WGor
Lovely Fairy = 'Spevu'PBR (Poly/GC) IDic MAsh SWCr WAct
Lovely Lady = 'Dicjubell'PBR (HT) ♀H4 CTri EBee ECnt ESty IDic LStr MAus MGan MJon MRav NBlu SPoc SSea SWCr
Lovely Meidiland = 'Meiratcan'PBR (Patio) MAsh SWCr
'Lovers' Meeting'PBR (HT) MGan MRav SPer SSea SWCr
Loving Memory = 'Korgund'PBR (HT) CGro CSBt CWSG EBee ECnt ENot GCoc GGre IArd LStr MFry MGan MJon MRav NPri SPer SPoG SPoc SWCr
Lucetta = 'Ausemi' (S) MAus SPer
luciae EBls
- var. ***onoei*** CLyd EPot NLar
Lucky Duck = 'Diczest'PBR (Patio) IDic MJon
'Lucy Ashton' (RH) MAus
Lucy = 'Kirlis' (F) **new** MJon
Ludlow CastlePBR see *R.* England's Rose = 'Ausrace'
Luis Desamero = 'Tinluis' (Min) NBat
'Lutea Maxima' see *R.* x *harisonii* 'Lutea Maxima'
'Lykkefund' (Ra) EBls MAus
'Lyon Rose' (HT) EBls
'Ma Perkins' (F) EBls
'Ma Ponctuée' (DPMo) EBls
'Mabel Morrison' (HP) EBls MAus
Macartney rose see *R. bracteata*
Macmillan Nurse = 'Beamac' (S) EBls ESty
'Macrantha' (Gallica hybrid) EBls LRHS MAsh MAus SPer WAct
macrophylla MAus SWCr
- B&SWJ 2603 WCru
§ - 'Master Hugh' ♀H4 ex SS&W 7822 EBls MAus
'Madame Abel Chatenay' (HT) EBls MAus
'Madame Alfred Carrière' (N) ♀H4 More than 30 suppliers
'Madame Alice Garnier' (Ra) CPou EBee EBls SPer SWCr
'Madame Antoine Mari' (T) EBls
'Madame Berkeley' (T) EBls
Madame Bovary = 'Deljam' (S) **new** SPoc SWCr
'Madame Bravy' (T) EBls MAus
'Madame Butterfly' (HT) EBls MAus MGan SFam SSea
§ 'Madame Caroline Testout' (HT) EBee LRHS MRav SFam SPoG
'Madame Charles' (T) EBls
'Madame d'Arblay' (Ra) EBls
'Madame de Sancy de Parabère' (Bs) EBee EBls IArd MAus SFam SWCr WHCG
'Madame de Watteville' (T) EBls
'Madame Delaroche-Lambert' (DPMo) CPou EBee EBls MAus SWCr WAct WHCG

	Name	Suppliers
	'Madame Driout' (ClT)	EBls WHCG
	'Madame Eliza de Vilmorin' (HT)	EBls
	'Madame Ernest Calvat' (Bb)	CPou EBee EBls MAus
	'Madame Eugène Résal' misapplied	see *R.* 'Comtesse du Caÿla'
	Madame Figaro = 'Delrona' (S) **new**	SPoc
	'Madame Gabriel Luizet' (HP)	EBls
	'Madame Georges Bruant' (Ru)	EBls MAus
§	'Madame Grégoire Staechelin' (ClHT) 🏆H4	CWSG EBee EBls ECnt ELan EMFP ENot EPfP LRHS LStr MAus MBri MGan MJon MRav NEgg SChu SFam SPer SPoG SPoc SWCr WAct WHCG
	'Madame Hardy' (ClD) 🏆H4	CPou CSBt CSam EBls EMFP ENot EPfP EWTr GCoc LGod LRHS LStr MAus MJon MRav NEgg SFam SPer SPoc SSea SWCr WAct WHCG WOVN
	'Madame Isaac Pereire' (ClBb) 🏆H4	CHad CTri EBee EBls ECnt ENot EPfP GCoc LGod LRHS LStr MAus MDun MFry MGan MJon MRav NBPC NEgg SFam SMad SPer SPoG SPoc SSea SWCr WAct WHCG
	'Madame Jules Gravereaux' (ClT)	EBls MAus
	'Madame Jules Thibaud' (Poly)	MAus
§	'Madame Knorr' (DPo) 🏆H4	CPou EBee EBls EMFP EPfP LRHS MAsh MWgw SPer SPoc SSea SWCr WAct WOVN
	'Madame Laurette Messimy' (Ch)	EBee EBls MAus SWCr WHCG
	'Madame Lauriol de Barny' (Bb)	EBls MAus MRav SFam SWCr WHCG
	'Madame Legras de Saint Germain' (AxN)	CPou EBls LRHS MAus SFam SPer SWCr WAct WHCG
	'Madame Lombard' (T)	EBls
	'Madame Louis Laperrière' (HT)	EBls MAus MGan SPer
	'Madame Louis Lévêque' (DPMo)	EBls SWCr WHCG
	'Madame Pierre Oger' (Bb)	EBee EBls ECnt EWTr LRHS LStr MAus MRav SPer SPoc SSea SWCr WAct
	'Madame Plantier' (AxN)	CPou EBee EBls LRHS MAsh MAus MRav SPer SWCr WHCG WOVN
	'Madame Scipion Cochet' (T)	EBls WHCG
	'Madame Victor Verdier' (HP)	EBls
	'Madame Wagram, Comtesse de Turenne' (T)	EBls
	'Madame William Paul' (PoMo)	EBls
	'Madame Zöetmans' (D)	EBls MAus
	'Madeleine Selzer' (Ra)	EBls MGan
	'Madge' (HM)	SDix
	Madrigal = 'Harextra'[PBR] (S/F)	GGre SPoc SWCr
	'Magenta' (S/HT)	EBls MAus SPer
	Magenta Floorshow = 'Harfloorshow'[PBR] (GC)	SWCr
	Magic Carpet = 'Jaclover'[PBR] (S/GC) 🏆H4	CWSG ECnt GCoc IDic LGod LRHS MAus MFry MRav NPri SPer SPoc SSea SWCr
§	Magic Carrousel = 'Moorcar' (Min)	MAus
	'Magic Fire' (Patio) **new**	ESty
	Magic Fire = 'Lapjaminal' (F)	GGre SWCr
	Magic Hit = 'Poulhi004'[PBR] (Min)	SWCr
	'Magna Charta' (HP)	EBls
	'Magnifica' (RH)	EBls MAus
	'Maid of Kent'[PBR] (Cl)	CSBt MJon SCoo SPer SWCr
	'Maiden's Blush' Hort. (A) 🏆H4	CSam CTri EBls ELan EMFP EWTr GGre LRHS MAus MRav SChu SFam SPer SPoc SSea SWCr WHCG
	'Maiden's Blush, Great'	see *R.* 'Great Maiden's Blush'
	'Maigold' (ClPiH) 🏆H4	More than 30 suppliers
§	***majalis***	EBls
	Majestic = 'Poulpm001' (HT)	EBee ECnt
	Make a Wish = 'Mehpat'[PBR] (Min/Patio)	LStr
	Maltese rose	see *R.* 'Cécile Brünner'
§	'Malton' (China hybrid)	EBls
	Malvern Hills = 'Auscanary'[PBR] (Ra)	CSBt LRHS MAus MJon
	Mandarin = 'Korcelin'[PBR] (Min)	ENot ESty LStr MJon SSea
	'Manettii' (N)	EBls
	'Manning's Blush' (RH)	CBgR EBls MAus MRav WAct
	'Mannington Cascade' (Ra)	EBls
	'Mannington Mauve Rambler' (Ra)	EBls
	'Manx Queen' (F)	MGan MJon
	Many Happy Returns = 'Harwanted'[PBR] (S/F) 🏆H4	CGro CSBt CWSG EBee ECnt ELan ENot EPfP GCoc GGre GKir LAst LGod LStr MAsh MFry MGan MJon MRav SPer SPoG SPoc SSea SWCr
	'Marbrée' (DPo)	EBls MAus
	'Marcel Bourgouin' (G)	EBls
	'Märchenland' (F/S)	EBls MAus
§	'Marchesa Boccella' (DPo) 🏆H4	CPou CSam CTri EBee EBls EMFP ENot EPfP LRHS MAsh MAus MDun SPer SPla SPoc SSea SWCr WAct
	'Marcie Gandy' (HT)	MGan
	'Maréchal Davoust' (CeMo)	EBls MAus MRav SFam
	'Maréchal Niel' (N)	CRHN EBls ERea EShb MAus MGan SPer SWCr WHCG
	'Margaret' (HT)	MGan
	Margaret Chessum = 'Bossexpaint' (F)	GGre SWCr
	'Margaret Hall' (HT)	NBat
	Margaret Merril = 'Harkuly' (F/HT) 🏆H4	CSBt CWSG EBee EBls ECnt ELan ENot EPfP ESty GCoc GGre IArd LGod LStr MAsh MAus MBri MFry MGan MJon MRav SPer SPoG SPoc SSea SWCr
§	Margaret Thatcher = 'Korflüg'[PBR] (HT)	MJon
	Margaret's World = 'Kirbill' (F)	MJon
	'Margo Koster' (Poly)	EBls MAus
	Marguerite Anne = 'Cocredward'[PBR] (F)	GCoc SWCr
	'Marguérite Guillard' (HP)	EBls
	'Marguerite Hilling' (S) 🏆H4	CAbP CTri EBee EBls ENot EPfP GCoc MAus MJon MRav SPer SSea SWCr WAct WHCG WOVN
	Maria McGredy = 'Macturangu'[PBR] (HT)	MBri MJon SPoG
	'Maria Theresa' (HT)	MJon
	x ***mariae-graebnerae***	MAus SLPI WHCG
	'Marie de Blois' (CeMo)	EBls

'Marie Louise' (D)	EBee EBls MAus SFam SWCr WAct WHCG
'Marie Pavič' (Poly)	CHad EBls MAus WHCG
'Marie van Houtte' (T)	EBls MAus
'Marie-Jeanne' (Poly)	EBls MAus
'Marijke Koopman' (HT)	MFry
Marinette = 'Auscam'PBR (S)	MAus MJon
Mario Lanza = 'Horaardvark' (HT) **new**	MJon
Marjorie Fair = 'Harhero' (Poly/S) ♀H4	EBls ECnt GGre MAsh MAus MRav SPoG SPoc SWCr
Marjorie Marshall = 'Hardenier'PBR	GGre SPoc SWCr
Marjorie May = 'Horsunpegy' (HT)	MJon
'Marlena' (F/Patio)	GCoc MAus MGan
Marry Me = 'Dicwonder'PBR (Patio) ♀H4	ESty IDic MBri MJon
'Martha' (Bb)	EBls MAus
'Martin Frobisher' (Ru)	EBls MAus SSea
'Mary' (Poly)	LStr
Mary Donaldson = 'Canana' (HT)	MGan
§ Mary Gammon = 'Frysweetie' (Min/Patio)	MFry
Mary Magdalene = 'Ausjolly'PBR (S)	LRHS MAus NEgg SWCr
'Mary Manners' (Ru)	EBls SPer SWCr
Mary Rose = 'Ausmary'PBR (S) ♀H4	CGro CHad CSBt CTri CWSG EBee EBls ELan ENot EPfP ESty EWTr GCoc GGre LGod LRHS LStr MAsh MAus MBri MFry MJon MRav NPri SPer SPoG SPoc SSea SWCr
'Mary Wallace' (Cl)	EBls MAus
Mary Webb = 'Auswebb' (S)	MAus MBri
'Masquerade' (F)	CBcs CGro CSBt CWSG EBls ELan ENot LStr MGan MJon MRav SPer SSea SWCr
'Master Hugh'	see *R. macrophylla* 'Master Hugh'
Matangi = 'Macman' (F) ♀H4	MGan
Matawhero MagicPBR	see *R.* Simply the Best = 'Macamster'
'Maude Elizabeth' (GC)	EBls
'Maurice Bernardin' (HP)	EBls
'Max Graf'	see *R.* x *jacksonii* 'Max Graf'
'Maxima'	see *R.* x *alba* 'Alba Maxima'
maximowicziana	GIBF
'May Queen' (Ra)	CPou CRHN EBls EMFP LRHS MAus MRav NLar SFam SPer SPoc SWCr WHCG
Mayor of Casterbridge = 'Ausbrid'PBR (S)	LRHS MAus MJon
'McGredy's Yellow' (HT)	EBls MGan
'Meg' (ClHT)	EBee EBls EWTr LRHS MAus MGan SPer SPoc SSea SWCr WAct WHCG
'Meg Merrilies' (RH)	EBls MAus SSea SWCr WAct
'Megiddo' (F)	MGan
'Meicobius'PBR	see *R.* Terracotta = 'Meicobuis'
Mellow Yellow = 'Wekosomit' (HT) **new**	GCoc
Melody Maker = 'Dicqueen'PBR (F)	CWSG IDic
Memento = 'Dicbar' (F) ♀H4	MGan SWCr
'Memoriam' (HT)	MGan
Memory Lane = 'Peavoodoo'PBR (F)	SPoc SWCr
Mercedes = 'Merkor' (F)	MJon
'Merlot' (Min) **new**	NBat
'Mermaid' (Cl) ♀H3-4	CBcs CBrm CGro CRHN CSBt CWSG EBee EBls ECnt ENot EPfP GCoc GKir LRHS LStr MAus MGan MJon MRav SBra SMad SPer SPla SPoG SSea SWCr WAct WBVN WHCG XPep
'Merveille de Lyon' (HP)	EBls
§ Message = 'Meban' (HT)	MGan SWCr
'Meteor' (F/Patio)	MGan
§ 'Mevrouw Nathalie Nypels' (Poly) ♀H4	EBee EBls EWTr LRHS LStr MAus MRav SPer SPoc SWCr WKif WOVN
§ Michael Crawford = 'Poulvue'PBR (HT)	ECnt MJon
Michel Bras = 'Deltil' (F) **new**	SPoc SWCr
'Michèle Meilland' (HT)	EBls MAus MJon
'Michelle Cholet' (Min) **new**	NBat
micrantha	WBWf
x ***micrugosa***	EBls MAus
- 'Alba'	EBls MAus
Middlesborough Football Club = 'Horflame' (HT)	NBat
Midsummer Night's Dream = 'Rawroyal' **new**	SWCr
Mike Thompson = 'Sherired' (HT)	NBat
'Millennium Rose 2000'PBR	see *R.* Rose 2000 = 'Cocquetrum'
'Mills and Boon' (F) **new**	MGan
Mini Metro = 'Rufin' (Min)	MFry
'Minnehaha' (Ra)	EBls EMFP LGod MAus SSea SWCr
Minnie Pearl = 'Savahowdy' (Min)	MJon
mirifica stellata	see *R. stellata* var. *mirifica*
Mischief = 'Macmi' (HT)	EBls MGan SPer SWCr
Miss Alice = 'Ausjake'PBR (S)	LRHS MAus
'Miss Edith Cavell' (Poly)	EBls MAus
Miss Flippins = 'Tuckflip' (Min)	MJon NBat
'Miss Lowe' (Ch)	EBls
§ 'Mister Lincoln' (HT)	EBls ESty LGod MGan SPer SSea SWCr
Mistress Quickly = 'Ausky'PBR (S)	CTri LRHS MAus MJon NEgg
Misty Hit = 'Poulhi011' (Patio)	ECnt
'Moersdag' (Poly/F)	GGre LAst LStr MJon NPri SPoG SWCr
'Mojave' (HT)	MGan
'Moje Hammarberg' (Ru)	MJon SWCr WAct
§ Molineux = 'Ausmol'PBR (S) ♀H4	CGro CSBt CTri ENot EPfP ESty GCoc LRHS MAsh MAus MBri NEgg NPri SWCr
§ ***mollis***	MJon
'Monique' (HT)	EBls MGan
'Monsieur Tillier' (T)	EBls
Moonbeam = 'Ausbeam' (S)	MAus
'Moonlight' (HM)	CHad CTri EBee EBls ECnt LRHS MAus MRav SPer SPoc SWCr WAct WHCG
'Morgengruss' (Cl)	MGan SWCr
Moriah = 'Ganhol'PBR (HT)	MGan
'Morlettii' (Bs)	EBee EBls EHol MRav SWCr WHCG

	Name	Suppliers
	'Morning Jewel' (ClF) ♀H4	GCoc MFry MGan SPer SPoc SWCr
	Morning Mist = 'Ausfire' (S)	LRHS MAus
	Mortimer Sackler = 'Ausorts' (S)	MAus MJon
	moschata (Ra)	EBls MAus MRav SSea SWCr WAct
	- 'Autumnalis'	see *R.* 'Princesse de Nassau'
	- var. ***nepalensis***	see *R. brunonii*
	Mother's Day	see *R.* 'Moersdag'
	Mother's Joy = 'Horsiltrop' **new**	GGre SWCr
	Mountain Snow = 'Aussnow' (Ra)	LRHS MAus
	Mountbatten = 'Harmantelle'[PBR] (F) ♀H4	CBcs CGro CWSG EBls ELan EPfP GGre LGod LStr MAus MFry MGan MJon MRav SPer SPoG SPoc SSea SWCr
§	'Mousseline' (DPoMo)	CPou EBls EMFP MAus NBPC SPer SSea SWCr WAct WHCG
	'Mousseuse du Japon'	see *R.* 'Japonica'
	moyesii (S)	CDul CTri EBls ELan GCra ISea MAus MDun MFry MJon NWea SPer WAct WOVN
	- 'Evesbatch' (S)	WAct
§	- var. ***fargesii*** (S)	EBls
	- ***holodonta***	see *R. moyesii* f. *rosea*
§	- f. ***rosea*** (S)	EBls GCal
	'Mozart' (HM)	MJon SWCr WHCG
	'Mr Bluebird' (MinCh)	MAus SWCr
	'Mrs Anthony Waterer' (Ru)	EBls MAsh MAus SPer SWCr WAct WHCG
	'Mrs Arthur Curtiss James' (ClHT)	EBee SWCr
	'Mrs B.R. Cant' (T)	EBls
	Mrs Doreen Pike = 'Ausdor'[PBR] (Ru)	LRHS MAus WAct
	'Mrs Eveline Gandy' (HT) **new**	MGan
	'Mrs Foley Hobbs' (T)	EBls
	'Mrs Honey Dyson' (Ra)	CHad
	'Mrs John Laing' (HP)	EBls EPfP LRHS MAus MRav NBPC SPoc SWCr WHCG
	'Mrs Oakley Fisher' (HT)	CHad EBls EMFP EWTr MAus MBri SPer SWCr WAct
	'Mrs Paul' (Bb)	EBls MAus
	'Mrs Pierre S. duPont' (HT)	EBls
	'Mrs Sam McGredy' (HT)	CSBt MAus MGan SSea
	'Mrs Walter Burns' (F/Patio)	MGan
	'Muff's Pet' (Min) **new**	NBat
	'Mullard Jubilee' (HT)	MGan NBlu
§	***mulliganii*** (Ra) ♀H4	EBee EBls EPfP MAus SWCr WHCG
	multibracteata (S)	EBls MAus WHCG
	multiflora (Ra)	EBls GIBF IFro LBuc MAus NHaw NWea WPic
	- 'Carnea' (Ra)	EBls
§	- var. ***cathayensis*** (Ra)	EBls
§	- 'Grevillei' (Ra)	EBee EBls MAus SPer SWCr
	- 'Platyphylla'	see *R. multiflora* 'Grevillei'
	- var. ***watsoniana***	see *R. watsoniana*
	Mummy[PBR]	see *R.* Newly Wed = 'Dicwhynot'
	mundi	see *R. gallica* 'Versicolor'
	- 'Versicolor'	see *R. gallica* 'Versicolor'
	'Mutabilis'	see *R.* x *odorata* 'Mutabilis'
	'My Choice' (HT)	MGan
	'My Joy' (HT)	NBat
	My Love = 'Cogamo' (HT)	MJon
	Myra = 'Battoo' (HT)	NBat
	Myriam = 'Cocgrand' (HT)	GCoc MJon
	Mystique = 'Kirmyst' (F)	MJon
	'München' (HM)	EBls MAus
	Nahéma = 'Deléri' (Cl) **new**	SPoc SWCr
	'Nan of Painswick'	WAct
	'Nancy's Keepsake' (HT)	NBat
	nanothamnus	CPom
	'Narrow Water' (Ra)	CPou EBee EBls SPoc SWCr WAct WHCG
§	'Nastarana' (N)	EBee EBls
	'Nathalie Nypels'	see *R.* 'Mevrouw Nathalie Nypels'
	'National Trust' (HT)	EBls ENot GGre IArd MAsh MGan MJon SPer SWCr
*	'Navie Viaud'	WAct
	'Nestor' (G)	EBls MAus
	'Nevada' (S) ♀H4	CGro CSBt EBee ECnt ELan ENot EPfP GCoc GKir IArd LGod LStr MAus MFry MRav NLon SPer SSea SWCr WAct WHCG WOVN
	New Age = 'Wekbipuhit'[PBR] (F)	ESty GCoc MJon SPoc SWCr
	New Arrival[PBR]	see *R.* 'Red Patio'
	'New Arrival' (Patio/Min)	GCoc GGre SWCr
§	'New Dawn' (Cl) ♀H4	More than 30 suppliers
	'New Look' (F)	MGan
	'New Penny' (Min)	MRav
	New Zealand = 'Macgenev'[PBR] (HT)	MJon NBat SPoc SWCr
§	Newly Wed = 'Dicwhynot'[PBR] (Patio)	IDic MJon SSea
	News = 'Legnews' (F)	MAus MGan
	Nice Day = 'Chewsea'[PBR] (ClMin) ♀H4	CGro CSBt CWSG ECnt ENot EPfP ESty GGre LGod LStr MAsh MFry MJon MRav SPer SPoG SPoc SSea SWCr
	'Nice 'n' Easy' (Patio) **new**	GGre
	'Nicola' (F)	MGan
	Nigel Hawthorne = 'Harquibbler' (S)	WAct
	Night Light = 'Poullight'[PBR] (Cl)	ECnt MFry MGan MJon SPoc SWCr
	Night Sky = 'Dicetch' (F) **new**	IDic
	Nina = 'Mehnina'[PBR] (S)	SPoc SWCr
	Nina Nadine = 'Kirhand' (F) **new**	MJon
	'Nina Weibull' (F)	NBlu
	nitida	EBls LRHS MAus NHaw NWea SPer SSea SWCr WAct WHCG WHer WOVN
	Noble Antony = 'Ausway'[PBR] (S)	ENot LRHS MAus MJon MWgw SPoc SWCr
§	'Noisette Carnée' (N)	CHad CSam EBee EBls EMFP EPfP LStr MAus MBNS MJon MRav MWgw SLPl SPer SPoc SSea SWCr WAct WHCG
	'Nordini' (CL) **new**	GGre
	Norfolk = 'Poulfolk'[PBR] (GC)	EBls SPer SPla SWCr
	'Norma Major' (HT)	MJon
	Northamptonshire = 'Mattdor'[PBR] (GC)	EBls MRav
	'Northern Lights' (HT)	GCoc
	'Norwich Castle' (F)	EBls
	Norwich Cathedral = 'Beacath' (HT)	EBls
	'Norwich Pink' (Cl)	MAus
	'Norwich Salmon' (Cl)	MAus
	'Norwich Union' (F)	EBls MBri
	Nostalgia = 'Savarita' (Min)	ESty
	Nostalgie = 'Taneiglat'[PBR] (HT)	GGre LStr MBri MJon SCoo SPoc SSea SWCr
	'Nottingham Millennium' (F)	MGan
	'Nova Zembla' (Ru)	EBls MAus

'Nozomi' (ClMin/GC) ♀H4 CGro CLyd EBls ECnt ELan ENot ESty GCoc GGre MAus MJon MRav MWgw NWCA SMad SPer SSea SWCr WAct WHCG WOVN
'Nuits de Young' (CeMo) ♀H4 EBls GCoc MAus SFam SPoc SSea SWCr WHCG
'Nur Mahal' (HM) EBee EBls MAus SWCr WHCG
nutkana (S) EBls MAus
§ - var. ***hispida*** (S) EBls
§ - 'Plena' (S) ♀H4 EBls EPfP MAus SFam SWCr WAct WGer WHCG
'Nymphenburg' (HM) EBls MAus SPer SWCr
'Nypels' Perfection' (Poly) MAus
'Nyveldt's White' (Ru) EBls MAus
Octavia Hill = 'Harzeal'[PBR] (F/S) CSBt MRav NPri SPer SWCr
x ***odorata*** ENot GIBF XPep
* - 'Burmese Crimson' SLon
- 'Fortune's Double Yellow' see *R.* x *odorata* 'Pseudindica'
§ - 'Mutabilis' (Ch) ♀H3-4 CHad CRHN EBls ECre EHol EMFP ENot EPfP GCoc MAus NBPC SMrm SPer SPoG SPoc SSea SWCr WAct WBcn WBor WCFE WCot WHCG WOVN XPep
§ - 'Ochroleuca' (Ch) EBee EBls
§ - 'Odorata' (Ch) EBls
- old crimson China (Ch) EBls WAct
§ - 'Pallida' (Ch) CBgR CHad EBls EMFP EPfP GCoc LRHS MAus MRav SPer SPla SPoc SSea SWCr WAct WHCG
§ - 'Pseudindica' (ClCh) EBls MAus
§ - Sanguinea Group (Ch) EBls WHCG XPep
§ - 'Viridiflora' (Ch) EBls LFol LRHS MAus SPer SPoc SSea SWCr WAct WHCG
Odyssey = 'Franski' (F) **new** ESty SWCr
'Oeillet Flamand' see *R.* 'Oeillet Parfait'
'Oeillet Panaché' (Mo) WAct
§ 'Oeillet Parfait' (G) EBls MAus
officinalis see *R. gallica* var. *officinalis*
'Ohl' (G) EBls
'Oklahoma' (HT) MGan
old blush China see *R.* x *odorata* 'Pallida'
old cabbage see *R.* x *centifolia*
Old John = 'Dicwillynilly'[PBR] (F) IDic MJon
old pink moss rose see *R.* x *centifolia* 'Muscosa'
Old Port = 'Mackati'[PBR] (F) IArd MJon
old red moss see *R.* 'Henri Martin', *R.* 'Lanei'
old velvet moss see *R.* 'William Lobb'
old yellow Scotch (PiH) see *R.* x *harisonii* 'Williams' Double Yellow'
Oliver Roellinger = 'Delkal' (F) **new** SPoc SWCr
Olympic Palace = 'Poulymp'[PBR] (Min) ECnt MAsh SWCr
'Omar Khayyám' (D) EBls MAus MRav SWCr
§ 'Ombrée Parfaite' (G) EBls
omeiensis see *R. sericea* subsp. *omeiensis*
Open Arms = 'Chewpixcel'[PBR] (ClMin) ♀H4 ENot ESty MAsh MAus MFry MJon SPer SPoc SSea SWCr WGer
'Ophelia' (HT) EBls MAsh MAus MGan NEgg
§ 'Orange Sensation' (F) CTri CWSG EBls ENot MAus MGan
§ Orange Sunblaze = 'Meijikatar'[PBR] (Min) CSBt SPer SWCr
'Orange Triumph' (Poly) EBls
Orangeade (F) MGan SWCr
§ Oranges and Lemons = 'Macoranlem'[PBR] (S/F) CGro ECnt ELan ENot ESty GCoc GGre LGod LStr MAus MFry MGan MJon SCoo SPoG SPoc SSea SWCr

'Oriana' (HT) SWCr
'Orient Express' (HT) CWSG MJon
'Orpheline de Juillet' see *R.* 'Ombrée Parfaite'
Othello = 'Auslo'[PBR] (S) ESty MAus SPer WAct
Our George = 'Kirrush' (Patio) MJon WGor
§ Our Jubilee = 'Coccages' (HT) ESty
Our Love = 'Andour' (HT) CWSG
Our Molly = 'Dicreason'[PBR] (GC/S) IDic MJon
Oxfordshire = 'Korfullwind'[PBR] (GC) ♀H4 ENot LStr MRav NPri SSea SWCr
Paddy McGredy = 'Macpa' (F) CGro MGan
Paddy Stephens = 'Macclack'[PBR] (HT) GGre MFry MGan MJon SPoc SWCr
Painted Moon = 'Dicpaint'[PBR] (HT) ESty IDic
Panache = 'Poultop'[PBR] (Patio) ECnt LStr SPoG SWCr
'Papa Gontier' (T) EBls MAus
'Papa Hémeray' (Ch) EBls
Papa Meilland = 'Meisar' (HT) CGro CSBt EBls MAus MGan MJon SPer
Paper Anniversary (Patio) SWCr
Papi Delbard = 'Delaby' (Cl) **new** SPoc SWCr
'Papillon' (ClT) EBls
'Pâquerette' (Poly) EBls
'Parade' (Cl) ♀H4 MAus MFry MRav SWCr WHCG
'Paradise' (Patio) **new** GGre
Paradise = 'Weizeip' (HT) MGan
'Parkdirektor Riggers' (Cl) CHad CRHN CSam EBee EBls LStr MAus MBri MGan MJon SPer SWCr WHCG
Parks's yellow China see *R.* x *odorata* 'Ochroleuca'
'Parkzierde' (Bb) EBls
Parson's pink China see *R.* x *odorata* 'Pallida'
Partridge = 'Korweirim'[PBR] (GC) EBls ENot MAus MJon SPer SWCr WAct WOVN
'Party Girl' (Min) MJon NBat
Party Trick = 'Dicparty'[PBR] (F) IDic MBri
parvifolia see *R.* 'Burgundiaca'
Pas de Deux = 'Poulhult'[PBR] (Cl) ECnt GGre MAsh MGan SWCr
Pascali = 'Lenip' (HT) CTri EBls EPfP GCoc GGre MAus MGan MJon MRav NBlu SPer SSea SWCr
§ Pat Austin = 'Ausmum'[PBR] (S) ♀H4 CSBt ECnt ENot ESty GGre LRHS LStr MAsh MAus MBNS MBri MJon NEgg SPoc SWCr
Pathfinder = 'Chewpobey'[PBR] (GC) MDun MJon
Paul Cézanne = 'Jacdeli' (S) **new** SPoc SWCr
'Paul Crampel' (Poly) EBls MAus WAct
'Paul Lédé' (ClT) see *R.* 'Climbing Paul Lédé'
'Paul Neyron' (HP) EBls EMFP MAus SPer SWCr WHCG
'Paul Ricault' (CexHP) EBls MAus
Paul Shirville = 'Harqueterwife'[PBR] (HT) ♀H4 ELan ENot ESty MAus MGan MRav SPer SSea
'Paul Transon' (Ra) ♀H4 CPou CRHN EBee EBls EMFP LRHS MAus NEgg SPer SPoc SWCr
'Paul Verdier' (Bb) EBls
§ 'Paulii' (Ru) CArn EBls MAus SWCr WAct WOVN

'Paulii Alba' see *R.* 'Paulii'
'Paulii Rosea' (Ru/Cl) EBls MAus SWCr WAct
'Paul's Early Blush' (HP) EBls
'Paul's Himalayan Musk' (Ra) ♀H3-4 More than 30 suppliers
§ 'Paul's Lemon Pillar' (ClHT) EBls LRHS MAus MBNS SPer SSea SWCr
'Paul's Perpetual White' (Ra) EBls WHCG
'Paul's Scarlet Climber' (Cl/Ra) CGro CSBt EBls ECnt ELan EPfP GGre GKir LGod LRHS LStr MAsh MAus MJon MRav NBPC NBlu NEgg NPri SPer SSea SWCr
Paws = 'Beapaw' (S) EBls
'Pax' (HM) CPou EBee EBls EMFP MAus SWCr WHCG WKif
Peace = 'Madame A. Meilland' (HT) ♀H4 CGro CSBt EBls ECnt ELan ENot EPfP ESty GCoc GGre LAst LGod LStr MAsh MAus MBri MFry MGan MJon MRav NBlu SPer SPoG SPoc SSea SWCr
Peace Sunblaze (Min) see *R.* Lady Meillandina = 'Meilarco'
Peacekeeper = 'Harbella'PBR (F) CSBt GGre MAsh MRav SWCr
Peach Blossom = 'Ausblossom'PBR (S) LRHS MAus
'Peach Dream' (Patio) ESty
§ Peach Sunblaze = 'Meixerul'PBR (Min) SPoc SWCr
Peach Surprise = 'Poulrise'PBR (HT) EBee ECnt
'Pearl Abundance' **new** MAsh SCoo SWCr
§ Pearl Anniversary = 'Whitston'PBR (Min/Patio) GCoc GGre LStr MRav SPoG SSea SWCr
Pearl Drift = 'Leggab' (S) EBls MAus MJon SPer SPoc SWCr WHCG
Pearly King = 'Gendee'PBR (S) SWCr
§ Peek-a-boo = 'Dicgrow'PBR (Min/Patio) IDic MFry SPer SWCr
§ Peer Gynt = 'Korol' (HT) MGan NBlu SWCr
Pegasus = 'Ausmoon'PBR (S) LRHS LStr MAus MJon NEgg SPoc SSea SWCr
'Pélisson' (CeMo) EBls
§ ***pendulina*** EBls GIBF MAus NHaw WHCG
'Penelope' (HM) ♀H4 CHad CSBt CSam EBee EBls ECnt ELan ENot EPfP GCoc GGre LRHS LStr MAsh MAus MBri MFry MJon MRav MWgw SFam SPer SPoc SSea SWCr WAct WHCG WKif WOVN XPep
Penelope Keith = 'Macfreego' (Min/Patio) MJon
'Penelope Plummer' (F) EBls
Penny Lane = 'Hardwell'PBR (Cl) ♀H4 CGro CSBt EBee ECnt ENot EPfP GCoc GGre LAst LGod LRHS LStr MAsh MAus MBri MFry MGan MJon MRav MWgw NBat NPri SCoo SPer SPoG SPoc SSea SWCr
Pensioner's Voice = 'Fryrelax'PBR (F) MFry MGan SWCr
x ***penzanceana*** see *R.* 'Lady Penzance'
Perception = 'Harzippee'PBR (HT) NBat SPoc SWCr
Perdita = 'Ausperd' (S) CGro LRHS MAus MJon MRav SPer SWCr
Perennial Blue = 'Mehblue' **new** ESty SPoc SWCr
§ Perestroika = 'Korhitom'PBR (F/Min) ENot MJon
Perfect Day = 'Poulrem' (F) ECnt
§ Perfecta = 'Koralu' (HT) EBls MGan SWCr
'Perle des Jardins' (T) EBls MAus
'Perle des Panachées' (G) EBls
§ 'Perle d'Or' (Poly) ♀H4 CHad ECnt EMFP ENot EPfP GCoc LRHS MAus SChu SPer SWCr WAct WHCG
'Perle von Hohenstein' (Poly) EBls
'Pernille Poulsen' (F) EBls
Perpetually Yours = 'Harfable'PBR (Cl) CGro GCoc GGre LGod LStr MJon MRav SCoo SPoc SWCr
Persian yellow see *R. foetida* 'Persiana'
Peter Beales = 'Cleexpert' (S) EBls
'Peter Frankenfeld' (HT) **new** MJon
Peter Pan = 'Chewpan'PBR (Min) MAsh MAus MJon SWCr
Peter Pan = 'Sunpete' (Patio) ENot SPoG
'Petite de Hollande' (Ce) EBls EMFP MAus SWCr WAct WHCG
Petite Folie = 'Meiherode' (Min) SWCr
'Petite Lisette' (CexD) EBls MAus
'Petite Orléannaise' (Ce) EBls
Phab Gold = 'Frybountiful'PBR (F) GCoc MFry
'Pharisäer' (HT) EBls
§ Pheasant = 'Kordapt'PBR (GC) ENot GCoc MAus MJon SPer SWCr WAct WHCG WOVN
Phillipa = 'Poulheart'PBR (S) ECnt SWCr
Phoebe (Ru) see *R.* 'Fimbriata'
phoenicia EBls
'Phyllis Bide' (Ra) ♀H4 CAbP CSam EBee EBls EMFP EPfP IArd LRHS LStr MAsh MAus MJon SPer SPoc SSea SWCr WHCG
'Piano' **new** ECnt
Picasso = 'Macpic' (F) EBls MGan
Piccadilly = 'Macar' (HT) CGro CSBt CTri EBls ENot GGre MGan MJon MRav NBlu SPer SSea SWCr
Piccolo = 'Tanolokip'PBR (F/Patio) CGro ESty LStr MBri MFry MJon SSea SWCr
'Picture' (HT) EBls MGan SPer
Pierre Gagnaire = 'Delroli' (F) **new** SPoc SWCr
'Pierre Notting' (HP) EBls
Pigalle '84 = 'Meicloux' (F) SWCr
'Pilgrim'PBR see *R.* The Pilgrim = 'Auswalker'
Pimpernelle = 'Deldog' (S) **new** SPoc SWCr
§ ***pimpinellifolia*** CDul EBee EBls ENot LBuc MAus NHaw NLon NWea SPer SSea WAct WBWf WHCG WOVN
- 'Altaica' see *R. pimpinellifolia* 'Grandiflora'
§ - 'Andrewsii' ♀H4 MAus MRav WAct
§ - double pink EBls WBor
§ - double white CNat EBls ECha GCoc IGor MAus SWCr WAct WBcn
- double yellow see *R.* x *harisonii* 'Williams' Double Yellow'
§ - 'Dunwich Rose' EBee EBls ENot EPfP LRHS MAsh MAus MJon NEgg SPer SWCr WAct WHCG
- 'Falkland' EBls ECha GCra MAus
§ - 'Glory of Edzell' EBls MAus
§ - 'Grandiflora' EBls MAus SWCr
- 'Harisonii' see *R.* x *harisonii* 'Harison's Yellow'

	Name	Suppliers
	- 'Irish Marbled'	EBls
	- 'Lutea'	see *R.* x *harisonii* 'Lutea Maxima'
	- 'Marbled Pink'	EBls MAus
	- 'Mary, Queen of Scots'	EBls MAus SRms SWCr WAct
	- 'Mrs Colville'	EBls MAus
	- 'Ormiston Roy'	MAus
§	- 'Robbie'	WAct
	- 'Single Cherry'	EBls MAus SSea
	- 'Variegata' (v)	CArn
	- 'William III'	EBls EWes GCra MAus SLPl
	Pink Abundance = 'Harfrothy'[PBR] (F)	LStr MAsh SPoc SWCr
	Pink Bells = 'Poulbells'[PBR] (GC)	CGro EBls ENot GCoc MAus SPer SWCr WHCG
	'Pink Bouquet' (Ra)	CRHN
	'Pink Favorite' (HT)	CSBt MGan SPer SWCr
	Pink Fizz= 'Polycool'	SWCr
§	Pink Flower Carpet = 'Noatraum'[PBR] (GC) 🏆H4	CGro CSBt CTri EBee ELan ENot EPfP GCoc GGre GKir LRHS LStr MAsh MAus MFry MRav SCoo SPer SWCr
	'Pink Garnette'	see *R.* 'Carol Amling'
	'Pink Grootendorst' (Ru) 🏆H4	EBee EBls EPfP EWTr LRHS LStr MAus MJon SPer SSea SWCr WAct WHCG
§	Pink Hit = 'Poutipe'[PBR] (Min/Patio)	ECnt ENot SWCr
	Pink La Sevillana = 'Meigeroka'[PBR] (F/GC)	SWCr
	pink moss	see *R.* x *centifolia* 'Muscosa'
	'Pink Parfait' (F)	EBls MAus MGan SPer SWCr
	'Pink Patio'[PBR] (Patio)	GGre
	Pink Peace = 'Meibil' (HT)	ESty GGre MRav SWCr
	'Pink Perpétué' (Cl)	CGro CSBt CTri EBls ECnt ELan ENot EPfP GCoc GGre GKir LAst LRHS MAus MBri MGan MJon MRav SPer SPoG SSea SWCr
	'Pink Petticoat' (Min)	SWCr
	'Pink Prosperity' (HM)	EBls MAus
	'Pink Showers' (ClHT)	WAct
	Pink Skyliner = 'Franwekpink' (ClS) **new**	MJon
§	Pink Sunblaze = 'Meijidiro' (Min/Patio)	SWCr
	Pink Surprise = 'Lenbrac' (Ru)	MAus
	Pinocchio = 'Rosenmärchen' (F)	EBls
	'Pinta' (HT)	EBls
	Pirouette = 'Poulyc003' (Cl) **new**	ECnt MGan
	pisocarpa	EBls
	Playtime = 'Morplati' (F)	ENot MAsh MAus
	Pleine de Grâce = 'Lengra' (S)	EBls LRHS MAus WAct
	'Plentiful' (F)	EBls MBri
	Poetry in Motion = 'Harelan'[PBR] (HT)	ESty GGre MJon NBat SPoG SPoc SWCr
	Polar Star = 'Tanlarpost'[PBR] (HT)	CSBt EBee EBls ECnt LGod LStr MFry MGan MRav SPer SWCr
	x ***polliniana***	SLPl
	'Polly' (HT)	EBls MGan
	pomifera	see *R. villosa*
	- 'Duplex'	see *R.* 'Wolley-Dod'
	Pomona = 'Fryyeh'[PBR] (F)	MFry
	'Pompon Blanc Parfait' (A)	EBls MAus
	'Pompon de Bourgogne'	see *R.* 'Burgundiaca'
	'Pompon de Paris' (ClMinCh)	see *R.* 'Climbing Pompon de Paris'
§	'Pompon de Paris' (MinCh)	EBls
	'Pompon Panaché' (G)	EBls MAus
	Portland rose	see *R.* 'Portlandica'
§	'Portlandica'	EBls LRHS MAsh MAus SPer SPoc SWCr WAct WHCG
	Portmeirion = 'Ausguard'[PBR] (S)	MAus SCoo
	Pot o' Gold = 'Dicdivine'[PBR] (HT)	IDic MAus MFry MGan MRav SPer
	Pour Toi = 'Para Ti' (Min)	ENot MAus MJon NPri SPer SWCr
	prairie rose	see *R. setigera*
	Precious Moments = 'Lyopr'	ESty GGre SWCr
	'Precious Platinum' (HT)	LGod MJon MRav SPer SWCr
	Preservation = 'Bosiljurika'[PBR] (S/F)	GGre SWCr
§	'Président de Sèze' (G) 🏆H4	EBls MAus SFam SPer SWCr WAct WHCG
	President Heidar Aliyev = 'Cocosimber'[PBR] (HT)	GCoc MJon
	'President Herbert Hoover' (HT)	EBls
	Pretty in Pink = 'Dicumpteen'[PBR] (GC)	ECnt IDic MJon SPoc SWCr
	Pretty Jessica = 'Ausjess' (S)	CTri LRHS MAus MJon MRav SPer
	Pretty Lady = 'Scrivo'[PBR] (F) 🏆H4	LStr MAus MJon SPoc SSea SWCr
	Pretty Polly = 'Meitonje'[PBR] (Min) 🏆H4	CGro CTri EPfP ESty GGre GKir LStr MAsh MBri MFry MGan MJon MRav SPoG SPoc SWCr
	Pride of England = 'Harencore'[PBR] (HT)	GCoc GGre MJon SPoG SWCr
	Pride of Scotland = 'Macwhitba' (HT) **new**	GCoc MJon
	'Prima Ballerina' (HT)	CGro CSBt CTri CWSG EBls ENot GCoc GKir LAst LStr MAsh MGan MJon SPer SSea SWCr
	primula (S) 🏆H3-4	EBls EMFP EWTr MAus MJon SPer SPoc SSea SWCr WAct WHCG
	'Prince Camille de Rohan' (HP)	EBls MAus WHCG
	'Prince Charles' (Bb)	EBls MAus SPoc SSea SWCr WHCG
	Prince Palace = 'Poulzin'[PBR] (F)	ECnt SWCr
	Prince Regent = 'Genpen' (S)	SSea
	Princess Alexandra = 'Pouldra'[PBR] (S)	CTri ECnt MAsh SPoc SWCr
	Princess Alice = 'Hartanna' (F)	LGod MGan MJon
	Princess Nobuko = 'Coclistine' (HT)	GCoc
	'Princess of Wales' (HP)	EPfP
	Princess of Wales = 'Hardinkum'[PBR] (F) 🏆H4	CGro CSBt ECnt ENot GCoc GGre LStr MAsh MBri MFry MGan MJon MRav NPri SCoo SPer SPoG SPoc SWCr
	Princess Royal = 'Dicroyal'[PBR] (HT)	GCoc IDic MBri
§	'Princesse de Nassau' (Ra)	EBls MAus WAct WHCG
	'Princesse Louise' (Ra)	CRHN MAus SFam
	'Princesse Marie' misapplied	see *R.* 'Belvedere'
§	'Pristine'[PBR] (HT)	IDic MAus MGan MJon SPer
§	'Probuzení' (Cl)	CHad EBee EBls SWCr WHCG
N	'Professeur Emile Perrot' (D)	EBls WAct
	'Prolifera de Redouté' misapplied	see *R.* 'Duchesse de Montebello'
	'Prosperity' (HM) 🏆H4	CBcs CTri EBls EMFP ENot EPfP GCoc LRHS MAus MFry MJon

Name	Suppliers
	MRav MWgw SPer SWCr WAct WHCG WOVN
Prospero = 'Auspero' (S)	CSam MAus MBri
pulverulenta	EBls
Pur Caprice = 'Deljavert' (S) **new**	SWCr
Pure & Simple = 'Horcogwheel' (GC) **new**	GGre
Pure Bliss = 'Dictator'PBR (HT)	EBee ECnt GCoc IDic MGan MJon
Pure Magic = 'Mattgrex' (Patio)	MAsh SPoG SWCr
'Purity' (Cl)	EBee SWCr
'Purple Beauty' (HT)	MGan SWCr
Purple Skyliner = 'Franwekpurp' (ClS) **new**	MJon
Purple Tiger = 'Jacpurr'PBR (F)	ESty IDic MJon SPoc SSea SWCr
'Purpurtraum' (Ru)	WHCG
Quaker Star = 'Dicperhaps' (F)	IDic
quatre saisons	see *R.* x *damascena* var. *semperflorens*
'Quatre Saisons Blanche Mousseuse' (DMo)	EBee EBls SWCr
Queen Elizabeth	see *R.* 'The Queen Elizabeth'
Queen Margarethe = 'Poulskov'PBR (F)	ECnt
Queen Mother = 'Korquemu'PBR (Patio) 🏆H4	CSBt EBls ELan ENot EPfP GCoc GGre LGod LRHS LStr MAsh MAus MFry MGan MRav NPri SPer SPoG SPoc SSea SWCr
'Queen of Bedders' (Bb)	EBls
Queen of Denmark	see *R.* 'Königin von Dänemark'
Queen of the Belgians	see *R.* 'Reine des Belges'
Queen's Palace = 'Poulelap'PBR (F)	ECnt
'Rachel' ambig.	GCoc SCoo
Rachel = 'Tangust'PBR (HT)	ESty MJon SPoG SPoc SWCr
Racy Lady = 'Dicwaffle'PBR (HT)	IDic MJon NBat
Radio Times = 'Aussal'PBR (S)	ESty MAus
Rainbow Magic = 'Dicxplosion'PBR (Patio)	ESty IDic MJon SWCr
'Ralph Tizzard' (F)	SSea
'Rambling Rector' (Ra) 🏆H4	More than 30 suppliers
§ 'Ramona' (Ra)	EBls MAus SWCr
§ 'Raubritter' ('Macrantha' hybrid)	CAbP EBls MAus SPer SPoc SSea SWCr WAct WHCG
Ray of Hope = 'Cocnilly'PBR (F)	GCoc LGod MAsh SWCr
Ray of Sunshine = 'Cocclare'PBR (Patio)	GCoc MFry
'Raymond Carver' (S)	EBls
'Raymond Chenault' (Cl)	MGan
Razzle Dazzle = 'Frybright'PBR (F)	MFry
Real Hit = 'Poulra007'PBR (Patio)	ECnt
Rebecca (Patio)	ESty
'Rebecca Claire' (HT)	MJon SPoc SWCr
Reconciliation = 'Hartillery'PBR (HT)	ESty SPoc SWCr
Red Bells = 'Poulred'PBR (Min/GC)	CGro EBls ENot MAus MRav SPer SWCr WHCG WOVN
Red Blanket = 'Intercell'PBR (S/GC)	CGro EBls GCoc IDic MAus MRav SPer SWCr WAct WOVN
§ Red Coat = 'Auscoat' (F)	MAus
Red Devil = 'Dicam' (HT)	GGre MGan MJon MRav NBat SWCr
Red Eden Rose = 'Meidrason' (Cl) **new**	SPoc SWCr
Red Finesse = 'Korvillade'PBR **new**	ENot
'Red Grootendorst'	see *R.* 'F.J. Grootendorst'
Red Haze = 'Tanzahde'PBR (GC)	SWCr
Red Meidiland = 'Meineble'PBR (GC)	MDun
red moss	see *R.* 'Henri Martin'
Red New Dawn	see *R.* 'Etendard'
§ 'Red Patio'PBR (FPatio)	MGan
Red Rascal = 'Jacbed'PBR (S/Patio)	CSBt ECnt IDic MFry
red rose of Lancaster	see *R. gallica* var. *officinalis*
§ Red Sunblaze = 'Meirutral'PBR (Min)	MJon
Red Trail = 'Interim'PBR (S/GC)	ESty MJon
§ 'Red Wing' (S)	EBls MAus
§ Redgold = 'Dicor' (F)	MGan
Redouté = 'Auspale'PBR (S)	CAbP LRHS MAus SPer SWCr
Regensberg = 'Macyoumis'PBR (F/Patio)	MAus MFry MGan MJon MRav SPer SSea SWCr
§ 'Reine des Belges' (Cl)	EBls
'Reine des Centifeuilles' (Ce)	EBls SFam
'Reine des Violettes' (HP)	CHad CPou EBls EPfP IArd LRHS LStr MAus MRav SChu SPer SPoc SWCr WAct WHCG
'Reine Marie Henriette' (ClHT)	EBls
'Reine Olga de Wurtemberg' (N)	EBls
§ 'Reine Victoria' (Bb)	EBls EMFP EPfP LRHS LStr MAsh MAus MRav SPer SPla SPoc SWCr WAct
Remember Me = 'Cocdestin'PBR (HT) 🏆H4	CWSG EBls ECnt ENot EPfP ESty GCoc GGre IArd LGod LStr MAus MBri MFry MGan MJon MRav NBat NPri SPer SPoG SPoc SSea SWCr
Remembrance = 'Harxampton'PBR (F) 🏆H4	CTri ESty LGod LStr MAsh MFry MGan MJon MRav SPer SPoG SWCr
Renaissance = 'Harzart'PBR (HT)	CSBt ESty GCoc GGre LStr MFry MRav SPoc SSea SWCr
'René André' (Ra)	CPou CRHN EBls EMFP MAus SWCr
'René d'Anjou' (CeMo)	EBls MAus
'Rescht'	see *R.* 'De Rescht'
Rest in Peace = 'Bedswap' (Patio/F)	GGre SWCr
'Rêve d'Or' (N)	CSam EBee EBls MAus SPer SWCr
'Réveil Dijonnais' (ClHT)	EBls MAus
'Reverend F. Page-Roberts' (HT)	EBls
Rhapsody in Blue = 'Frantasia'PBR (S)	CGro CSBt CTri EBee ECnt ELan ENot ESty GGre LGod LRHS LStr MAsh MAus MBri MFry MGan MJon NPri SCoo SPer SPoG SPoc SSea SWCr
§ x ***richardii***	EBls MAus MRav SWCr WAct WHCG
Ring of Fire = 'Morfire' (Patio)	MAsh SPoG SWCr

§	'Rise 'n' Shine' (Min)	LGod
	'Ritter von Barmstede' (Cl)	MGan
	'Rival de Paestum' (T)	EBls MAus
	'River Gardens'	NPer
	'Rivers's George IV' (Ch)	EBls
	Rob Roy = 'Cocrob' (F)	GCoc MGan SPer SWCr
	Robbie Burns = 'Ausburn' (PiH)	MAus SWCr
	'Robert Burns' (HT) **new**	GGre SWCr
	'Robert le Diable' (Ce)	CPou EBls MAus SPer SWCr WAct WHCG
	'Robert Léopold' (Mo)	EBls
	'Robin Hood' (HM)	EBls SWCr
	Robin Redbreast = 'Interrob'PBR (Min/GC)	EBls IDic WGor
§	Robusta = 'Korgosa' (Ru)	EBls ECnt MAus MJon SSea SWCr
	'Roger Lambelin' (HP)	EBls MAus
	Romance = 'Tanezamor'PBR (S)	MJon MRav SWCr
	'Romantic Heritage' (F) **new**	GGre
	Romantic Palace = 'Poulmanti'PBR (F)	ECnt MAsh SWCr
§	Rosabell = 'Cocceleste'PBR (F/Patio)	ESty GCoc MFry
	Rosalie Coral = 'Chewallop'PBR (ClMin)	ESty MJon
	Rosarium Uetersen = 'Kortersen' (ClHT)	MJon
§	Rose 2000 = 'Cocquetrum'PBR (F)	SWCr
	'Rose à Parfum de l'Haÿ' (Ru)	EBls
	'Rose Ball'	EBls
§	'Rose d'Amour' (S) ♀H4	CFee EBls MAus WHCG
	'Rose de Meaux'	see *R.* x *centifolia* 'De Meaux'
	'Rose de Meaux White'	see *R.* 'White de Meaux'
	'Rose de Rescht'	see *R.* 'De Rescht'
	'Rose des Maures' misapplied	see *R.* 'Sissinghurst Castle'
	'Rose d'Hivers' (D)	EBls
	'Rose d'Orsay' (S)	EBls
	'Rose du Maître d'Ecole'	see *R.* 'Du Maître d'Ecole'
	'Rose du Roi' (HP/DPo)	EBls EWTr MAus SWCr WAct WHCG
	'Rose du Roi à Fleurs Pourpres' (HP)	EBls MAus
	'Rose Edouard' (Bb)	EBls
§	Rose Gaujard = 'Gaumo' (HT)	EBls GGre LGod MAsh MGan NBlu SWCr
	'Rose of Yunnan' **new**	WAct
	Rose Pearl = 'Korterschi'PBR	ENot MGan SWCr
	Rose-Marie = 'Ausome' (S) **new**	MAus
§	'Rose-Marie Viaud' (Ra)	CFee CPou CSam MAus SWCr WHCG
	'Rosemary Foster'	SSpi
	'Rosemary Gandy' (F)	MGan
	Rosemary Harkness = 'Harrowbond'PBR (HT)	ESty LStr MJon MRav SPer SPoc SWCr
	'Rosemary Rose' (F)	EBls SPer
	Rosemoor = 'Austough' **new**	LRHS
	Rosenprofessor SieberPBR	see *R.* The Halcyon Days Rose = 'Korparesni'
	'Roseraie de l'Haÿ' (Ru) ♀H4	More than 30 suppliers
	Roses des Cisterciens = 'Deltisse' **new**	SPoc SWCr
	'Rosette Delizy' (T)	EBls
	'Rosy Cheeks' (HT)	MGan
	Rosy Cushion = 'Interall'PBR (S/GC) ♀H4	CSam IDic MAus MRav SPer SWCr WAct WHCG WOVN
	Rosy Future = 'Harwaderox'PBR (F/Patio)	CSBt SPoc SWCr
	'Rosy Mantle' (Cl)	CBcs CSBt MGan SPer SWCr
§	Rote Max Graf = 'Kormax'PBR (GC/Ru)	EBls ENot MRav WAct
	'Roundelay' (HT)	EBls MAus SWCr
§	Roxburghe Rose = 'Cocember' (HT)	GCoc
	roxburghii (S)	CArn LEdu MBri SWCr WAct WHCG
	- var. ***hirtula*** (S)	CPLG
	- f. ***normalis*** (S)	CFee EBls
	- 'Plena'	see *R. roxburghii* f. *roxburghii*
§	- f. ***roxburghii*** (d/S)	MAus
	'Royal Albert Hall' (HT)	EBls GCoc
	Royal Copenhagen = 'Poulht001' (HT)	ECnt
	'Royal Gold' (ClHT)	EBls LAst MBri MFry MGan SSea SWCr
	'Royal Highness' (HT)	EBls
	'Royal Occasion' (F)	MRav SPer SWCr
	Royal Salute = 'Macros' (Min)	ENot
	'Royal Smile' (HT)	EBls
	Royal Star and Garter = 'Frybizzy' (Cl)	MFry
	Royal William = 'Korzaun'PBR (HT) ♀H4	CSBt ECnt ELan ENot ESty GGre LGod LStr MAsh MAus MBri MGan MJon MRav NBlu NPri SPer SPoG SPoc SWCr
	'Rubens' (HP)	EBls
§	***rubiginosa***	CArn CCVT CGro CRWN EBls ENot EPfP GPoy IFro ILis LBuc MAus MHer MJon MRav SFam SPer SWCr WAct WMou
	rubra	see *R. gallica*
	rubrifolia	see *R. glauca*
	'Rubrotincta'	see *R.* 'Hebe's Lip'
	rubus (Ra)	MAus MBNS
	- SF 96062	ISea
	- ***velutescens***	WAct
	Ruby Anniversary = 'Harbonny'PBR (Patio)	CSBt CWSG ESty LStr MAsh MFry MRav SSea SWCr
	'Ruby Baby' (Min) **new**	NBat
	Ruby Celebration = 'Peawinner'PBR (F)	CWSG ESty MJon SPoc SWCr
	'Ruby Pendant' (Min)	MJon
	'Ruby Wedding' (HT)	More than 30 suppliers
	'Ruby Wedding Anniversary' (F) **new**	GGre
	'Ruga' (Ra)	EBls
	rugosa (Ru)	CAgr CDul CLnd CTri EPfP GKir LBuc MAus MBri MHer MRav NBlu NWea SPlb SWCr WBVN
	- 'Alba' (Ru) ♀H4	CAlb CBcs CCVT CDul EBee EBls ECGP ECnt ELan ENot EPfP GBin LAst LBuc LRHS LStr MAus MJon MRav NWea SPer SSea SWCr WAct WOVN
	- 'Rubra' (Ru) ♀H4	CAlb CBcs CCVT CTri CWib ENot EPfP LAst LBuc MFry SPer WAct
	- Sakhalin form **new**	GIBF MCCP
	- 'Scabrosa'	see *R.* 'Scabrosa'
	'Rugspin' (Ru)	SWCr WAct
	'Ruhm von Steinfurth' (HP)	EBls

'Rumba' (F)	NBlu SWCr
Running Maid = 'Lenramp' (S/GC)	MAus
Rush = 'Lenmobri' (S)	MAus
Rushing Stream = 'Austream'PBR (GC)	MAus MBNS
'Ruskin' (HPxRu)	EBls MAus SWCr
'Russelliana' (Ra)	EBee EBls MAus SFam SSea SWCr WAct WHCG WRha
Rutland = 'Poulshine'PBR (Min/GC)	SWCr
'Sadler's Wells' (S)	EBls
'Safrano' (T)	EBls
Saint Alban = 'Auschesnut' (S) **new**	MAus
Saint Boniface = 'Kormatt' (F/Patio)	CSBt ENot
'Saint Catherine' (Ra)	CFee
Saint Cecilia = 'Ausmit'PBR (S)	LRHS MAus MJon MWgw SWCr
Saint Dunstan's Rose = 'Kirshru' (S)	MJon
Saint Edmunds Rose **new**	ECnt
'Saint Ethelburga' (S)	EBls
Saint John = 'Harbilbo'PBR (F)	CSBt MRav
Saint John's rose	see *R.* x *richardii*
Saint Mark's rose	see *R.* 'Rose d'Amour'
'Saint Nicholas' (D)	CAbP EBls MAus
'Saint Prist de Breuze' (Ch)	EBls
Saint Swithun = 'Auswith'PBR (S)	GQui LRHS MAus MJon SPoc SWCr
'Salet' (DPMo)	EBls MAus SWCr WHCG
Salita = 'Kormorlet' (Cl)	MJon
'Sally Holmes'PBR (S) ♀H4	CHad EBls ENot GCoc MAus MFry MJon MRav MWgw SPer SPoc SSea SWCr WAct WHCG
Sally's Rose = 'Canrem' (HT)	ECnt SPoc SWCr
Salmo = 'Poulnoev'PBR (Patio)	ENot MBri MJon
Salsa = 'Poulslas'PBR (Cl)	ECnt
§ Samaritan = 'Harverag'PBR (HT)	CSBt ESty GGre MAsh SPoc SWCr
sancta	see *R.* x *richardii*
'Sander's White Rambler' (Ra) ♀H4	CRHN CSam CTri EBee EBls EMFP EPfP ESty EWTr LRHS LStr MAus MJon MRav NEgg NPri SMad SPer SPoc SSea SWCr WAct WHCG
'Sandringham Centenary' (HT)	EBls
'Sanguinea'	see *R.* x *odorata* Sanguinea Group
§ Sarabande = 'Meihand' (F)	MGan
'Sarah van Fleet' (Ru)	CGro CTri EBls EPfP GCoc IArd LBuc LRHS LStr MAus MDun MFry MRav SFam SPer SPla SWCr WAct WOVN
Savoy Hotel = 'Harvintage'PBR (HT) ♀H4	CGro CSBt ECnt EPfP GGre LGod LStr MAus MGan MRav SPer SPoG SWCr
§ 'Scabrosa' (Ru) ♀H4	EBls ECnt EMFP EWTr GCoc LRHS MAus MJon SPer SSea SWCr WAct WHCG WOVN
Scarborough Fair = 'Ausoran' (S) **new**	MAus
Scarlet Fire	see *R.* 'Scharlachglut'
Scarlet Glow	see *R.* 'Scharlachglut'
Scarlet Hit = 'Poulmo'PBR (F) **new**	ECnt SWCr
Scarlet Patio = 'Kortingle'PBR (Patio)	ENot MAsh SWCr
Scarlet Queen Elizabeth = 'Dicel' (F)	CBcs EBls GGre MRav SWCr
'Scarlet Showers' (Cl)	MGan SWCr
'Scented Air' (F)	MGan SPer
Scentimental = 'Wekplapep'PBR (F)	ESty GGre MAsh MBri SCoo SPoG SPoc SWCr
'Scentsation' (Min) **new**	NBat
§ Scent-sation = 'Fryromeo'PBR (HT)	CWSG ESty GCoc GGre LGod MAsh MFry MRav NPri SCoo SPoG SPoc
Scepter'd Isle = 'Ausland'PBR (S) ♀H4	CAbP CSBt ENot LRHS MAsh MAus MJon NPri SCoo SPer SPoc SWCr
§ 'Scharlachglut' (ClS) ♀H4	CPou EBls ENot LRHS MAus MRav SPer SWCr WAct WHCG WOVN
* ***schmidtiana***	CFee
'Schneelicht' (Ru)	EBls MAus
§ 'Schneezwerg' (Ru) ♀H4	EBee EBls GCoc MAus MJon MRav SPer SPla SPoc SSea SWCr WAct WHCG WOVN
'Schoolgirl' (Cl)	CBcs CGro CSBt CTri EBee EBls ELan ENot EPfP ESty GGre GKir LAst LStr MAsh MBri MFry MGan MJon MRav SPer SPoG SPoc SSea SWCr
'Scintillation' (S/GC)	MAus
'Scotch Pink' **new**	WAct
Scotch rose	see *R. pimpinellifolia*
Scotch yellow	see *R.* x *harisonii* 'Williams' Double Yellow'
'Scotch Yellow' (HT)	MJon SSea
'Scottish Celebration' (F) **new**	GGre SWCr
Sea of Fire	see *R.* 'Feuermeer'
'Seagull' (Ra) ♀H4	CGro CTri CWSG EBee EBls ECnt EMFP EPfP ESty GGre LGod LRHS LStr MAsh MAus MGan MJon MRav NPri NWea SMad SPer SPla SPoG SPoc SSea SWCr WHCG WHer
'Seale Peach' (Patio) **new**	SSea
§ 'Sealing Wax' (*moyesii* hybrid)	EBls LRHS MBri MJon WAct
Selfridges = 'Korpriwa' (HT)	MJon NBat
'Semiplena'	see *R.* x *alba* 'Alba Semiplena'
sempervirens (Ra)	XPep
'Sénateur Amic' (Cl)	EBls
sericea (S)	CFee MAus WHCG
- CC 3306	WRos
* - var. ***morrisonensis*** B&SWJ 7139	WCru
§ - subsp. ***omeiensis*** BWJ 7550	WCru
- - f. ***pteracantha*** (S)	EBee EBls ELan ENot EPfP GGar MAus MRav NWea SMad SPer SSea SWCr WAct WOVN
- - - 'Atrosanguinea' (S)	CArn
sertata	GIBF
§ ***setigera***	EBls GIBF MAus
setipoda	EBls MAus SWCr WAct WFar WHCG
seven sisters rose	see *R. multiflora* 'Grevillei'
Seventh Heaven = 'Fryfantasy' (HT) **new**	MFry
Sexy Rexy = 'Macrexy'PBR (F) ♀H4	CGro EPfP ESty GCoc GGre LStr MAsh MAus MBri MFry MGan MJon MRav NBat SPer SPoc SSea SWCr
'Shailer's White Moss'	see *R.* x *centifolia* 'Shailer's White Moss'

Sharifa Asma = 'Ausreef'PBR (S) — CSBt EBee ELan ENot LRHS LStr MAsh MAus MBNS MJon MRav NEgg SPer SPoc SWCr
'Sheelagh Baird' (S/Poly) — SWCr
Sheila's Perfume = 'Harsherry'PBR (HT/F) — CGro ECnt ESty GCoc GGre LStr MGan MJon MRav SPer SPoG SPoc SSea SWCr
'Shepherd's Delight' (F) — MGan
sherardii — WBWf
Shine On = 'Dictalent'PBR (Patio) ♀H4 — CSBt ECnt ESty IDic MAsh MBri MFry MJon MRav SPoG SPoc SWCr
Shining Light = 'Cocshimmer'PBR (Patio) — ENot GCoc GGre MAsh SCoo SWCr
Shirley Spain = 'Cocharod' (F) — GCoc
Shocking Blue = 'Korblue'PBR (F) — CSBt ECnt ENot MAus MGan MJon SPer SPoc SWCr
Shona = 'Dicdrum' (F) — IDic
'Shot Silk' (HT) — CSBt EBls MGan
Shrimp Hit = 'Poulshrimp'PBR (Patio) — ECnt SWCr
'Shropshire Lass' (S) — LRHS MAus SPer
Sightsaver = 'Fryaffair'PBR (HT) — ESty MFry
§ Silver Anniversary = 'Poulari'PBR (HT) ♀H4 — CGro CSBt CTri ECnt ELan ENot GCoc GGre LAst LGod LRHS LStr MAsh MAus MBri MFry MGan MJon MRav NPri SCoo SPer SPoG SPoc SSea SWCr
'Silver Jubilee' (HT) ♀H4 — CBcs CGro CSBt EBls ECnt ENot EPfP ESty GCoc GGre IArd LGod LRHS LStr MAsh MAus MFry MGan MJon MRav NBat SPer SPoG SPoc SWCr
'Silver Lining' (HT) — EBls SWCr
'Silver Moon' (Cl) — CRHN EBls
'Silver Wedding' (HT) — CSBt CWSG EBls GCoc GGre IArd LAst LRHS MAus MFry MRav NBlu SPer SPoc SWCr
Silver Wedding Celebration (F) — CTri ESty GGre SPoG SWCr
Silver Wishes = 'Poulhipe' **new** — SWCr
§ Simba = 'Korbelma'PBR (HT) — ENot MGan
Simon Robinson = 'Trobwich' (Min/GC) — SWCr
Simply Heaven = 'Diczombie'PBR (HT) — ESty GCoc IDic LGod MJon SPoc SWCr
§ Simply the Best = 'Macamster'PBR (HT) — CGro CSBt ECnt ELan ENot ESty GCoc GGre LGod LRHS LStr MAsh MAus MBri MFry MJon SCoo SPer SPoG SPoc SWCr
§ Singin' in the Rain = 'Macivy'PBR (F) — MJon SPoc SWCr
sinowilsonii — see *R. longicuspis* var. *sinowilsonii*
'Sir Cedric Morris' (Ra) — CRHN EBls SSea WAct
Sir Clough = 'Ausclough' (S) — MAus
Sir Edward Elgar = 'Ausprima'PBR (S) — EBls LStr MAus
'Sir Frederick Ashton' (HT) — EBls
'Sir Joseph Paxton' (Bb) — CAbP MAus
Sir Neville Marriner = 'Glanmusic' (F) — NBat
§ Sir Walter Raleigh = 'Ausspry' (S) — MAus MRav
§ 'Sissinghurst Castle' (G) — EBls
Smarty = 'Intersmart'PBR (S/GC) — CAbP IDic MAus SPer SWCr WAct
§ 'Smooth Angel' (HT) — LGod MGan
Smooth Lady = 'Hadlady' (HT) — LGod MGan
Smooth Prince = 'Hadprince' (HT) — LGod MGan SPoc
Smooth Romance = 'Hadromance' (HT) — MGan
§ 'Smooth Velvet' (HT) — MGan SPer
Snow Carpet = 'Maccarpe'PBR (Min/GC) — EBls ENot GCoc MAus MFry MJon
'Snow Dwarf' — see *R.* 'Schneezwerg'
Snow Goose = 'Auspom'PBR (Cl/S) — CSBt MAus MJon SWCr
Snow Hit = 'Poulsnows'PBR (Min/Patio) — ECnt SPoc SWCr
'Snow Queen' — see *R.* 'Frau Karl Druschki'
§ Snow Sunblaze = 'Meigovin'PBR (Min) — CSBt MRav SPer SWCr
Snow White = 'Landisney' (HT) — MJon
Snowball = 'Macangeli' (Min/GC) — MJon
Snowcap = 'Harfleet'PBR (Patio) — ESty GGre SPoG SSea
'Snowdon' (Ru) — EBls MAus SWCr
'Snowdrift' (Ra) — WHCG
§ Snowdrop = 'Amoru' (Min/Patio) — MFry
'Snowflake' (Ra) — WHCG
'Soldier Boy' (Cl) — SWCr WHCG
§ Solitaire = 'Macyefre'PBR (HT) — MJon
Solo Mio = 'Poulen002'PBR (S) — CTri ECnt EWTr MAsh SPla SWCr
§ 'Sombreuil' (ClT) — CHad EBls EMFP EPfP EWTr IArd LRHS MAus MRav NEgg SChu SFam SPer SPla SPoc SSea SWCr WAct WHCG
Someday Soon = 'Seasoon' (Min) — NBat
Something Special = 'Macwyo'PBR (HT) — ECnt GCoc MJon
'Sophie's Perpetual' (ClCh) — EBls EMFP ENot LRHS MAus SPer SPoc SWCr WAct WHCG XPep
Sophy's Rose = 'Auslot'PBR (S) — MAus MBri MJon NEgg SPoc SWCr
soulieana (Ra/S) ♀H3-4 — EBls MAus SWCr WAct WKif
'Soupert et Notting' (DPoMo) — LRHS MAus MRav SPer WAct
'Southampton' (F) ♀H4 — EBls ENot GGre LStr MAus MGan MRav SPer SPoc SSea SWCr
'Souvenir d'Alphonse Lavallée' (ClHP) — EBls WHCG
'Souvenir de Brod' — see *R.* 'Erinnerung an Brod'
'Souvenir de Claudius Denoyel' (ClHT) — CSam EBee EBls MAus SPer
'Souvenir de François Gaulain' (T) — EBls
'Souvenir de Jeanne Balandreau' (HP) — EBls WHCG
'Souvenir de la Malmaison' (ClBb) — see *R.* 'Climbing Souvenir de la Malmaison'
'Souvenir de la Malmaison' (Bb) — EBls ENot GCoc LRHS MAus MRav SPer SWCr WAct
Souvenir de Louis Amade = 'Delalac' (S) **new** — SPoc SWCr
'Souvenir de Madame Léonie Viennot' (ClT) — CPou EBls EHol MAus MRav

	Name	Suppliers
	Souvenir de Marcel Proust = 'Delpapy' (S) **new**	SPoc SWCr
	'Souvenir de Philémon Cochet' (Ru)	EBls
	'Souvenir de Pierre Vibert' (DPMo)	EBls
	'Souvenir de Saint Anne's' (Bb)	CHad EBls MAus SWCr WAct WHCG
	'Souvenir d'Elise Vardon' (T)	EBls
	'Souvenir di Castagneto' (HP)	MRav
	'Souvenir du Docteur Jamain' (ClHP)	CHad CPou EBls EHol LRHS LStr MAus SFam SMrm SPer SPoc SSea SWCr WAct WHCG WKif
	'Souvenir du Président Carnot' (HT)	EBls
	'Souvenir d'un Ami' (T)	EBls
	spaldingii	see *R. nutkana* var. *hispida*
	Spangles = 'Ganspa'[PBR] (F)	MGan SPoc
	'Spanish Beauty'	see *R.* 'Madame Grégoire Staechelin'
	Sparkling Scarlet = 'Meihati' (ClF)	ELan GGre MAsh MGan SWCr
	Sparkling Yellow = 'Poulgode'[PBR] (GC/S)	ECnt MAsh
	'Special Anniversary'	MAsh SCoo SPoG SWCr
	Special Child = 'Tanaripsa'	GGre SPoc SWCr
	Special Friend = 'Kirspec'[PBR] (Patio)	GCoc LStr MJon
	Special Occasion = 'Fryyoung'[PBR] (HT)	ENot ESty GCoc GGre MFry MRav SPoc SWCr
	'Spectabilis' (Ra)	EBls WHCG
	'Spek's Yellow' (HT)	EBls
	'Spencer' misapplied	see *R.* 'Enfant de France'
	Spice of Life = 'Diccheeky' (F) **new**	GCoc IDic
	spinosissima	see *R. pimpinellifolia*
	Spirit of Freedom = 'Ausbite' (S)	MAsh MAus NEgg SWCr
§	'Splendens' (Ra)	CHad EBee EBls SLPl SPoc SWCr WAct
	'Spong'	see *R.* x *centifolia* 'Spong'
	'Spring Bride' (Ra)	GGre
§	St Tiggywinkle = 'Korbasren'[PBR] (GC)	ENot LGod SWCr
§	'Stanwell Perpetual' (PiH)	CTri EBls EMFP ENot GCoc LStr MRav SPer SPoc SSea SWCr WAct WHCG WOVN
	'Star of Waltham' (HP)	WHCG
	'Star Performer'[PBR] (ClPatio)	CSBt ESty GGre MAsh MJon SPoc SWCr
	Stardust = 'Peavandyke'[PBR] (Patio/F)	ESty MJon
	Starlight Express = 'Trobstar'[PBR] (Cl)	SCoo SPer SPoG SPoc SWCr
	Starry Eyed = 'Horcoexist' (Patio) **new**	MGan
	'Stars 'n' Stripes' (Min)	LGod MAus MFry
	Stella (HT)	EBls MGan SWCr
	stellata	MAus
§	- var. ***mirifica***	EBee EBls MAus SSea SWCr
	'Stephanie Diane' (HT)	MJon
	'Sterling Silver' (HT)	EBls LStr MGan SPoG
	Sting = 'Meimater'[PBR] **new**	SWCr
	Strawberries and Cream = 'Geestraw' (Min/Patio)	ELan ESty
	Strawberry Fayre = 'Arowillip'[PBR] (Min/Patio)	CTri LAst MAsh MFry MRav SPoG SWCr
	Strawberry Fields = 'Rawbus' (GC) **new**	SPoc SWCr
§	Sue Hipkin = 'Harzazz'[PBR] (HT)	ESty SPoc SWCr
	Sue Lawley = 'Macspash' (F)	MGan MJon
§	Suffolk = 'Kormixal'[PBR] (S/GC)	CBrm CGro CSBt ELan ENot GCoc LStr MAus MRav NPri SPer SSea SWCr WAct
	suffulta	see *R. arkansana* var. *suffulta*
	Sugar and Spice = 'Peallure' (Patio)	MBri SPoG SWCr
	Sugar Baby = 'Tanabagus'[PBR] (Patio)	MAsh SPoG SWCr
	Sugar 'n' Spice = 'Tinspice' (Min)	MAsh MRav SWCr
	Suma = 'Harsuma'[PBR] (GC)	EPfP ESty GCoc MJon SWCr WAct
	Summer Breeze = 'Korelasting'[PBR] (Cl)	ENot
	Summer Dream = 'Frymaxicot'[PBR] (F)	CSBt LStr MFry
§	Summer Dream = 'Jacshe' (HT)	LAst
§	Summer Fragrance = 'Tanfudermos'[PBR] (HT)	CSBt GCoc SWCr
	Summer Gold = 'Poulreb'[PBR] (F)	ECnt ENot SPoc SWCr
	'Summer Holiday' (HT)	SPer SWCr
	Summer Lady = 'Tanydal' (HT)	MJon
	Summer Love = 'Franluv' (F)	MJon
	'Summer Magic' (Patio)	GGre
	Summer Palace = 'Poulcape'[PBR] (F/Patio)	ECnt MAsh SPoc SWCr
	Summer Snow = 'Weopop' (Patio)	MJon
	'Summer Sunrise' (GC)	EBls
	'Summer Sunset' (GC)	EBls
	Summer Wine = 'Korizont'[PBR] (Cl) ♀H4	CSBt EBee ECnt ENot ESty MGan MJon SPer SPoc SSea SWCr
	Summertime = 'Chewlarmoll' (Patio/Cl) **new**	ECnt ESty MFry
§	Sun Hit = 'Poulsun'[PBR] (Patio)	CGro CSBt ECnt ENot ESty LGod MRav SPoc SWCr
	Sunblest = 'Landora' (HT)	CGro GGre MAsh MFry MRav NBlu SPoG SWCr
	Sunderland Supreme = 'Nossun' (HT)	MJon
	Sunrise = 'Kormarter'[PBR] (Cl)	ENot ESty MFry MJon SPoc SWCr WGer
§	Sunseeker = 'Dicracer'[PBR] (F/Patio)	ENot EPfP ESty GGre IDic LGod MAsh MRav SPoG SWCr
§	Sunset Boulevard = 'Harbabble'[PBR] (F) ♀H4	CSBt ECnt ENot GGre LGod LStr MAsh MAus MGan MRav SCoo SPer SPoc SSea SWCr
	Sunset Strip = 'Arocore' (Min)	NBat
	'Sunshine' (Poly)	SPer
	'Sunshine Abundance' (F) **new**	MAsh SPoG SWCr
	'Sunsilk' (F)	SWCr

Sunsplash = 'Cocweaver' (F) GCoc GGre SPoG SWCr
Super Dorothy = 'Heldoro' (Ra) MAus MJon SPoc SWCr
Super Elfin = 'Helkleger'PBR (Ra) ♀H4 ECnt ENot LStr MFry MJon MRav SPer SPoc SSea SWCr
Super Excelsa = 'Helexa' (Ra) ESty GGre LStr MAus MJon MRav SPoG SSea SWCr
Super Fairy = 'Helsufair'PBR (Ra) ECnt ENot ESty LStr MAus MFry MJon MRav SPer SPoc SSea SWCr
§ Super Sparkle = 'Helfels'PBR (Ra) ECnt LStr MJon SSea
§ Super Star = 'Tanorstar' (HT) CTri EBls GGre LStr MGan MJon MRav SPoc SWCr
'Surpasse Tout' (G) EBls MAus SWCr WHCG
§ 'Surpassing Beauty of Woolverstone' (ClHP) EBls WHCG
§ Surrey = 'Korlanum'PBR (GC) ♀H4 CSBt CTri ECnt ELan ENot ESty LGod LStr MAus MFry MRav NPri SPer SPla SPoc SSea SWCr WAct
Susan Hampshire = 'Meinatac' (HT) EBls MGan
Susan = 'Poulsue' (S) ECnt MAsh SPoG SPoc SWCr
Sussex = 'Poulave'PBR (GC) CSBt ECnt GCoc LStr MFry MRav NPri SPer SPoG SPoc SSea SWCr
'Sutter's Gold' (HT) EBls MAus MGan
Swan = 'Auswhite' (S) MAus
Swan Lake = 'Macmed' (Cl) EBee EBls ECnt ELan ENot EPfP ESty GGre LGod LRHS MFry MGan MRav NBlu NPri SPer SWCr
Swany = 'Meiburenac' (Min/GC) ♀H4 CGro EBls ESty LSRN MAus SPer SWCr WHCG
Sweet Caroline = 'Micaroline' (Min) NBat
Sweet Cover = 'Poulweeto'PBR MAsh SWCr
Sweet Dream = 'Fryminicot'PBR (Patio) ♀H4 CGro CSBt ECnt ELan ENot EPfP ESty GCoc GGre LAst LGod LStr MAsh MAus MBri MFry MGan MJon MRav NBat NBlu NPri SPer SPla SPoG SPoc SSea SWCr
'Sweet Fairy' (Min) CSBt
Sweet Juliet = 'Ausleap'PBR (S) CAbP CHad CSBt CWSG EBls ESty LGod LRHS MAus MJon NEgg NPri SPer SPoc SWCr
* 'Sweet Lemon Dream' (Patio) MAsh
Sweet Magic = 'Dicmagic'PBR (Min/Patio) ♀H4 CGro CSBt CTri ENot EPfP GGre IDic LGod LStr MAsh MBri MFry MJon MRav NPri SPla SWCr
Sweet Memories = 'Whamemo' (Patio) COtt CTri ECnt EPfP ESty GCoc LGod LStr MAsh MJon MRav SCoo SPer SPla SPoG SPoc SSea SWCr WGer
§ Sweet Promise = 'Meihelvet' (GC) MGan
'Sweet Remembrance' (HT) **new** LStr MJon
'Sweet Repose' (F) MGan
§ Sweet Symphonie = 'Meibarke'PBR (Patio) SWCr
'Sweet Velvet' (F) MGan
'Sweet Wonder' (Patio) COtt ENot EPfP ESty GGre MAsh SWCr
N Sweetheart = 'Cocapeer'PBR (HT) GCoc MGan
sweginzowii GCal MAus
- 'Macrocarpa' EBls
'Sydonie' (HP) EBls WHCG
'Sympathie' (ClHT) ENot MFry MGan SPer SSea SWCr
Symphony = 'Auslett' (S) MJon
'Talisman' (HT) EBls
Tall Story = 'Dickooky'PBR (F) ♀H4 EBls IDic MJon SPoc SWCr WHCG WOVN
'Tallyho' (HT) EBls
Tamora = 'Austamora' (S) MAus
§ Tango = 'Macfirwal' (F) MJon
Tango = 'Poulyc005' (Cl) ECnt
Tapis Jaune see *R.* Golden Penny = 'Rugul'
Tatton = 'Fryentice'PBR (F) GGre MBri MFry MJon
Tattoo = 'Poulyc0005' (Cl) ECnt GGre
§ 'Tausendschön' (Ra) EBls
Tawny Tiger = 'Frygolly' (F) **new** MFry
'Tea Rambler' (Ra) EBls
§ Tear Drop = 'Dicomo'PBR (Min/Patio) IDic LStr MFry MJon SPoG
§ Teasing Georgia = 'Ausbaker'PBR (S) ECnt EPfP LRHS MAus MBri MJon NEgg SPoc SWCr
'Telstar' (F) MGan
Temptress = 'Korramal' (Cl) **new** ENot ESty
Tequila Sunrise = 'Dicobey'PBR (HT) ♀H4 CTri ECnt ELan EPfP ESty GGre IDic LStr MAsh MAus MBri MGan MJon MRav SMrm SPer SPoG SPoc SSea SWCr
§ Terracotta = 'Meicobuis'PBR (HT) MJon SWCr
Tess of the D'Urbervilles = 'Ausmove'PBR (S) MAsh MAus MBNS MJon NEgg SWCr
'Tessa' (F) **new** MGan
'Texas Centennial' (HT) EBls
§ Thaïs = 'Memaj' (HT) EBls
Thank You = 'Chesdeep'PBR (Patio) GCoc GGre LStr SPoG SWCr
§ That's Jazz = 'Poulnorm'PBR (ClF) EBee ECnt MJon SWCr
§ The Alexandra Rose = 'Ausday'PBR (S) LRHS MAus
'The Bishop' (CexG) EBls MAus
'The Bride' (T) EBls
The Care Rose = 'Horapsunmolbabe' (Patio) **new** MGan
The Cheshire Regiment = 'Fryzebedee' (HT) MFry
'The Colwyn Rose' see *R.* Colwyn Bay
The Compass Rose = 'Korwisco'PBR (S) ENot SPer
The Compassionate Friends = 'Harzodiac'PBR (F) GGre SWCr
§ The Countryman = 'Ausman'PBR (S) LRHS MAus MBri MFry
§ The Daily Telegraph = 'Peahigh' (F) SPoc SWCr
The Dark Lady = 'Ausbloom'PBR (S) LRHS MAus MJon NEgg SPer SPoc SWCr
'The Doctor' (HT) EBls MGan SSea SWCr
§ The Dove = 'Tanamola'PBR (F) MGan
'The Ednaston Rose' (Cl) WHCG
§ 'The Fairy' (Poly) ♀H4 CSBt CSam EBee EBls ECnt ELan ENot EPfP ESty GGre LGod LStr MAsh MAus MFry MJon MRav SMad SPer SPla SPoc SSea SWCr WAct WCFE WCot WHCG WOVN
The Flower Arranger = 'Fryjam' (F) LRHS
'The Garland' (Ra) ♀H4 CRHN EBee EBls EMFP LRHS MAsh MAus SFam SPer SPoc SWCr WAct WHCG XPep
The Generous Gardener = 'Ausdrawn' (S) MAsh MAus NEgg SCoo SWCr

Entry	Suppliers
§ The Halcyon Days Rose = 'Korparesni'PBR (F)	ENot
The Herbalist = 'Aussemi' (S)	LRHS MAus
The Ingenious Mr Fairchild = 'Austijus' (S) **new**	MAus SCoo SWCr
The Jubilee Rose = 'Poulbrido'PBR (F)	ECnt MAsh SCoo SWCr
The Lady = 'Fryjingo'PBR (S) ♀H4	MAus MFry MJon SWCr
The Maidstone Rose = 'Kordauerpa'PBR	SCoo SWCr
The Mayflower = 'Austilly'PBR (S)	CSBt MAus MJon SSea SWCr
§ The McCartney Rose = 'Meizeli'PBR (HT)	LStr MJon SPer SPoG SPoc SWCr
'The New Dawn'	see *R.* 'New Dawn'
The Nun = 'Ausnun' (S)	MAus
The Painter = 'Mactemaik'PBR (F)	LStr MJon SSea
The People's Princess = 'Geepeop' (F)	MAsh
§ The Pilgrim = 'Auswalker'PBR (S)	CAbP CHad CSBt CSam EMFP ENot EPfP ESty EWTr LRHS MAus MBri MJon NEgg SChu SPer SPla SPoc SWCr WHCG
The Prince = 'Ausvelvet'PBR (S)	LRHS LStr MAsh MAus MBNS MBri MJon NEgg SPer SSea SWCr
The Prince's Trust = 'Harholding'PBR (Cl)	GGre LStr SPoG SWCr
'The Prioress' (S)	MAus
§ 'The Queen Elizabeth' (F)	CBcs CGro CSBt CWSG EBls ECnt ENot GCoc GGre LGod LStr MAsh MBri MFry MGan MJon MRav SPer SPoG SPoc SSea SWCr
The Reeve = 'Ausreeve' (S)	MAus
The Rotarian = 'Fryglitzy' (HT) **new**	MFry
I 'The Royal Society of Organists' Rose' (HT) **new**	SPoc
I 'The Rugby Rose' (HT) **new**	MGan
The Scotsman = 'Poulscots'PBR (HT)	ECnt GCoc
The Seckford Rose = 'Korpinrob' (S)	ENot MJon
The Soroptimist Rose = 'Benstar' (Patio) **new**	MJon
§ The Squire = 'Ausquire' (S)	MAus
§ The Times Rose = 'Korpeahn'PBR (F) ♀H4	EBee ECnt ENot LGod LStr MAus MGan MJon MRav SPer SPoc SWCr
'Thelma' (Ra)	EBls MAus
Thelma Barlow = 'Fryforce' (HT)	MFry
'Thérèse Bugnet' (Ru)	EBls MAus
Thinking of You = 'Frydandy'PBR (HT)	ESty GCoc GGre LGod LStr MAsh MFry MJon SPoc SWCr
'Thisbe' (HM)	EBls MAus SWCr WAct WHCG XPep
§ Thomas Barton = 'Meihirvin' (HT)	LStr SPoG SWCr
'Thoresbyana'	see *R.* 'Bennett's Seedling'
'Thoughts of You' (Patio) **new**	SWCr
'Thoughts of You' (HT)	GGre
Thousand Beauties	see *R.* 'Tausendschön'
threepenny bit rose	see *R. elegantula* 'Persetosa'
Tiger Cub = 'Poulcub'PBR (Patio)	ENot
Tigris = 'Harprier' (*persica* hybrid) (S)	WAct
'Till Uhlenspiegel' (RH)	EBls
Times Past = 'Harhilt' (Cl)	ESty GCoc LStr MJon SPoc SWCr
'Tina Turner' (HT)	MJon NBat
Tintinara = 'Dicuptight'PBR (HT)	EBee ECnt IDic MGan
Tip Top = 'Tanope' (F/Patio)	CBcs MGan SPer
'Tipo Ideale'	see *R.* x *odorata* 'Mutabilis'
'Tipsy Imperial Concubine' (T)	EBls
Titanic = 'Macdako'PBR (F)	MJon SPoc SWCr
Tivoli = 'Poulduce'PBR (HT)	ECnt MAus
'Toby Tristam' (Ra)	CRHN
'Tom Foster' (HT)	MJon NBat
tomentosa	WBWf
Too Hot to Handle = 'Macloupri'PBR (S/Cl)	MJon SSea
Top Marks = 'Fryministar'PBR (Min/Patio)	CGro CSBt CTri EPfP GCoc LAst LGod LStr MBri MFry MJon MRav NPri SCoo SPer SWCr
'Top of the Bill' (Patio)	SWCr
Topkapi Palace = 'Poulthe'PBR (F)	ECnt MAsh SWCr
§ Toprose = 'Cocgold'PBR (F)	GCoc GGre MAsh SWCr
'Topsi' (F/Patio)	SPer
§ 'Tour de Malakoff' (Ce)	CPou CSBt EBls EHol LRHS MAus MRav NBPC SFam SPer SWCr WAct WHCG
Tournament of Roses = 'Jacient' (HT)	MAus MJon
Tower Bridge = 'Haravis' (HT)	GGre SWCr
'Trade Winds' (HT)	MGan
Tradescant = 'Ausdir'PBR (S)	LRHS MAus MBNS SPoc SWCr
§ Tradition '95 = 'Korkeltin'PBR (Cl) ♀H4	ENot
'Treasure Trove' (Ra)	CRHN EBls EMFP LRHS MAus MJon SPoc SWCr WAct
Trevor Griffiths = 'Ausold'PBR (S)	LRHS MAus
'Tricolore de Flandre' (G)	EBls MAus
'Trier' (Ra)	CPou EBee EBls MAus SWCr WHCG
'Trigintipetala' misapplied	see *R.* 'Professeur Emile Perrot'
'Triomphe de l'Exposition' (HP)	MAus
'Triomphe du Luxembourg' (T)	EBls MAus
triphylla	see *R.* x *beanii*
Troika = 'Poumidor' (HT) ♀H4	CSBt ENot ESty GGre LStr MAsh MAus MFry MGan MJon MRav NBlu SPer SPoG SPoc SWCr
Troilus = 'Ausoil' (S)	MAus
Trumpeter = 'Mactru' (F) ♀H4	CSBt ECnt ENot ESty GGre IArd LGod LStr MAsh MAus MFry MGan MJon MRav NBat SPer SPoG SSea SWCr
Tumbling Waters = 'Poultumb'PBR (F/S)	ENot MRav
'Tuscany' (G)	GCoc MAus WAct WHCG
'Tuscany Superb' (G) ♀H4	CHad CPou CSam EBls EMFP ENot EPfP ISea LAst LRHS MAsh MAus MRav SPer SPoc SSea SWCr WAct WHCG WKif
Twenty-fifth = 'Beatwe' (F)	EBls
§ Twenty-one Again! = 'Meinimo'PBR (HT)	MJon SPoc SWCr

Name	Suppliers
Twice in a Blue Moon = 'Tan96138' **new**	ESty LGod SPoc
Twist = 'Poulstri'PBR (Cl)	CGro ECnt ESty GGre MAsh MGan SWCr
Tynwald = 'Mattwyt'PBR (HT)	ENot LStr MJon SPer
'Ulrich Brünner Fils' (HP)	EBls MAus
'Uncle Bill' (HT)	EBls
Uncle Walter = 'Macon' (HT)	EBls SWCr
UNICEF = 'Cocjojo'PBR (F)	GCoc
'Unique Blanche'	see *R.* x *centifolia* 'Unique'
Valencia = 'Koreklia'PBR (HT) ♀H4	CSBt ECnt ENot ESty LGod MAus MJon NBat
§ Valentine Heart = 'Dicogle'PBR (F) ♀H4	CSBt ESty IArd IDic LGod MAsh MAus MFry MJon MRav SPoG SPoc SWCr
Valiant Heart = 'Poulberg' (F)	ECnt
'Vanguard' (Ru)	EBls
'Vanity' (HM)	EBls MAus
'Variegata di Bologna' (Bb)	EBee EBls EMFP EPfP LRHS MAus MRav SPoc SSea SWCr WAct
Variety Club = 'Haredge'PBR (Patio)	LGod
'Veilchenblau' (Ra) ♀H4	CHad CRHN EBee EBls ECnt ELan EPfP EWTr LGod LRHS LStr MAus MBri MJon MRav MWgw NEgg NPri SPer SPoc SSea SWCr WAct WHCG
Velvet Fragrance = 'Fryperdee'PBR (HT)	CSBt ECnt ESty GCoc GGre MAsh MAus MFry MJon MRav SPoG SWCr
'Venusta Pendula' (Ra)	EBls MAus
'Vermilion Patio'	MAsh SWCr
Versailles Palace = 'Poulsail'PBR (F)	SPoc SWCr
'Verschuren' (HT/v)	MJon
versicolor	see *R. gallica* 'Versicolor'
'Vick's Caprice' (HP)	EBee EBls MAus SWCr
'Vicomtesse Pierre du Fou' (ClHT)	EBls MAus
Vidal Sassoon = 'Macjuliat'PBR (HT)	MGan MJon SPoc SWCr
'Village Maid'	see *R.* x *centifolia* 'Unique Panachée'
villosa misapplied	see *R. mollis*
§ ***villosa*** L.	EBls MAus WAct WBWf
- 'Duplex'	see *R.* 'Wolley-Dod'
§ 'Violacea' (G)	EBls MAus SWCr WHCG
'Violette' (Ra)	CPou CRHN EBee EBls MAus SWCr WAct WHCG WHer
'Violinista Costa' (HT)	EBls
virginiana ♀H4	CFee EBls GCal GIBF MAus MSte NHaw NWea SPer SWCr WAct WHCG WOVN
- 'Harvest Song' **new**	NHaw
- 'Plena'	see *R.* 'Rose d'Amour'
'Virgo' (HT)	EBls
'Viridiflora'	see *R.* x *odorata* 'Viridiflora'
'Vivid' (Bourbon hybrid)	EBls
vosagiaca	see *R. caesia* subsp. *glauca*
'W.E. Lippiat' (HT)	EBls
Waltz = 'Poulkrid'PBR (Cl)	ECnt GGre MAsh SWCr
Wandering Minstrel = 'Harquince' (F)	GGre SPoG SWCr
wardii var. ***culta***	MAus
Warm Welcome = 'Chewizz'PBR (ClMin) ♀H4	CBrm CGro ECnt ENot EPfP ESty GGre LGod LStr MAsh MAus MBri MFry MJon MRav MWgw NBat NEgg SMad SPer SPoG SPoc SSea SWCr
§ Warm Wishes = 'Fryxotic'PBR (HT) ♀H4	CSBt ECnt ENot ESty GCoc GGre LAst LGod LStr MAsh MAus MBri MFry MGan MJon NBlu SPoG SPoc SWCr
'Warrior' (F)	MGan SPer
Warwick Castle = 'Auslian'PBR (S)	MAus SPer
Warwickshire = 'Korkandel'PBR (GC)	MRav SPer SWCr WOVN
§ ***watsoniana*** (Ra)	EBls
webbiana	EBls MAus SPer SPoc WHCG
'Wedding Day' (Ra)	CRHN CSBt CSam EBee EBls ECnt ELan ENot EPfP ESty GGre LRHS LStr MAsh MAus MBNS MBri MFry MJon MRav MWgw NPri SPer SPoc SSea SWCr WAct WHCG
Wee Cracker = 'Cocmarris'PBR (Patio)	ENot ESty GCoc GGre LGod SWCr
Wee Jock = 'Cocabest'PBR (F/Patio)	GCoc GGre SPoG SSea SWCr
'Weetwood' (Ra)	CRHN SPer
Welcome Home = 'Koraubala'PBR (F) **new**	ENot
'Well Done' (Patio)	GGre SPoG SWCr
'Well-Being' **new**	ESty
Welwyn Garden Glory = 'Harzumber'PBR (HT)	ESty SPoc SWCr
'Wendy Cussons' (HT)	CBcs CGro CTri CWSG EBls GCoc MGan MJon MRav SPer SSea SWCr
Wenlock = 'Auswen' (S)	ESty GGre MAus SPer SPoG SWCr
'West Country Millennium' (F)	MGan
§ Westerland = 'Korwest' (F/S) ♀H4	MJon NBPC SPoc SWCr
§ Westminster Pink = 'Fryamour'PBR (HT)	ECnt MFry
Where the Heart Is = 'Cocoplan'PBR (HT)	GCoc
'Whisky Gill' (HT)	MGan
Whisky Mac = 'Tanky' (HT)	CBcs CGro CSBt CTri CWSG EBls ELan GCoc GGre MFry MGan MJon MRav NPri SPer
'White Bath'	see *R.* x *centifolia* 'Shailer's White Moss'
White Bells = 'Poulwhite'PBR (Min/GC)	EBls ENot MRav SPer SWCr WHCG WOVN
§ 'White Cécile Brünner' (Poly)	EBls MAus WHCG
'White Christmas' (HT)	MGan
§ White Cloud = 'Korstacha'PBR (S/ClHT) ♀H4	CSBt EBee ECnt ENot ESty LGod MJon SPoc SWCr WHCG
White Cloud = 'Savacloud' (Min)	MBri MFry
'White Cockade' (Cl)	EBee EBls GCoc MGan SPer SWCr
White CoverPBR	see *R.* Kent = 'Poulcov'
§ 'White de Meaux' (Ce)	EBls MAus
White Diamond = 'Interamon'PBR (S)	IDic MJon
§ 'White Flight' (Ra)	WTin
§ White Gold = 'Cocquiriam'PBR (F)	ENot GCoc GGre MJon SPoG SWCr
'White Grootendorst' (Ru)	EBls MAus SSea WAct
White Knight (HT)	see *R.* Message = 'Meban'
White Knight = 'Poullaps' (ClHT/S)	SPoc SWCr
white moss	see *R.* 'Comtesse de Murinais', *R.* x *centifolia* 'Shailer's White Moss'

§ 'White Pet' (Poly) ♀H4 CHad CSBt CSam ECnt EMFP ENot EPfP ESty EWTr GCoc LGod LRHS LStr MAus MBri MGan MJon MRav NEgg SPer SPla SPoc SWCr WAct
white Provence see *R.* x *centifolia* 'Unique'
'White Queen Elizabeth' (F) EBls
white rose of York see *R.* x *alba* 'Alba Semiplena'
White Skyliner = 'Franwekwhit' (ClS) **new** MJon
'White Tausendschön' (Ra) MAus
'White Wings' (HT) CHad EBls MAus MGan SPer SWCr WAct WHCG
N ***wichurana*** (Ra) EBls MAus SWCr WHCG XPep
- 'Variegata' (Ra/v) CSWP MCCP
* - 'Variegata Nana' (Ra/v) MRav
'Wickwar' (Ra) CSWP EBls EHol EPla GCal MSte SSpi SWCr WAct WHCG
§ Wife of Bath = 'Ausbath' (S) MAus MBri
Wildeve = 'Ausbonny' (S) **new** MAus
Wildfire = 'Fryessex' (Patio) **new** MFry
'Wilhelm' (HM) EBls MAus MRav SPer SWCr WHCG
'Will Scarlet' (HM) MAus SWCr
'Willhire Country' (F) EBls
'William Allen Richardson' (N) EBls MAus SWCr WHCG
'William and Mary' (S) EBls
'William Cobbett' (F) SSea
§ 'William Lobb' (CeMo) ♀H4 CHad CPou CRHN CSBt EBls ENot EPfP LGod LRHS LStr MAsh MAus MBri MWgw NEgg SChu SPer SPoc SSea SWCr WAct WHCG WKif
William Morris = 'Auswill'PBR (S) CSBt ECnt MAsh MAus MJon NEgg SPoc SWCr
William Quarrier = 'Coclager' (F) GCoc
'William R. Smith' (T) EBls
William Shakespeare 2000 = 'Ausromeo'PBR (S) CSBt ECnt LGod MAsh MAus MJon SPoc SWCr
William Shakespeare = 'Ausroyal'PBR (S) ENot EPfP GCoc MBNS NEgg SPer SSea
'William Tyndale' (Ra) MJon SWCr WHCG
'Williams' Double Yellow' see *R.* x *harisonii* 'Williams' Double Yellow'
willmottiae see *R. gymnocarpa* var. *willmottiae*
Wilton = 'Eurosa' SPoc SWCr
Wiltshire = 'Kormuse'PBR (S/GC) ♀H4 CSBt ECnt ENot ESty LSRN LStr MFry MJon MRav NPri SPoc SSea SWCr WOVN
Winchester Cathedral = 'Auscat'PBR (S) CGro CSBt EBee EBls ECnt EMFP EPfP ESty GGre LGod LRHS LStr MAsh MAus MBri MJon MRav MWgw NEgg NPri SChu SPer SPoG SPoc SWCr
Windflower = 'Auscross' (S) LRHS MAus
Windrush = 'Ausrush' (S) MAus MJon SWCr WAct WHCG
Wine and Dine = 'Dicuncle'PBR (GC) IDic
x ***wintoniensis*** WAct WHCG
Wise Portia = 'Ausport' (S) MAus
Wishing = 'Dickerfuffle'PBR (F/Patio) IDic MAus MGan MJon
Wisley = 'Ausintense' **new** LRHS SCoo
With Love = 'Andwit' (HT) GGre MJon SPoG SWCr
With Thanks = 'Fransmoov'PBR (HT) ESty LAst MBri SWCr
'Woburn Abbey' (F) CWSG EBls SSea
'Wolley-Dod' see *R.* 'Duplex'
§ Woman o'th' North = 'Kirlon' (F/Patio) MJon
'Woman's Hour' (F/Patio) EBls
Wonderful News = 'Jonone'PBR (Patio) **new** ESty GCoc MJon
§ ***woodsii*** EBls IFro MAus WHCG
- var. ***fendleri*** see *R. woodsii*
'Woolverstone Church Rose' see *R.* 'Surpassing Beauty of Woolverstone'
Worcestershire = 'Korlalon'PBR (GC) CSBt ENot ESty GCoc MAus MRav SPer SPoc SWCr
World Peace 2000 = 'Peayellow'PBR (HT) SPoc SWCr
§ ***xanthina*** 'Canary Bird' (S) ♀H4 More than 30 suppliers
§ - f. ***hugonis*** ♀H4 EBls MAus NHaw SPer SPoc WAct
- f. ***spontanea*** CArn EBls
'Xavier Olibo' (HP) EBls
X-rated = 'Tinx' (Min) MJon NBat
Yellow Button = 'Auslow' (S) WAct
'Yellow Cécile Brünner' see *R.* 'Perle d'Or'
Yellow Charles Austin = 'Ausyel' (S) MAus
§ Yellow Dagmar Hastrup = 'Moryelrug'PBR (Ru) CBrm EBee ENot EPfP MAus MJon SPer SPla SWCr WAct WOVN
'Yellow Doll' (Min) MAus
'Yellow Dream' (Patio) GGre SPoG
'Yellow Patio' (Min/Patio) LStr MAsh SSea SWCr
yellow Scotch see *R.* x *harisonii* 'Williams' Double Yellow'
Yellow Sunblaze = 'Meitrisical' (Min) CSBt
Yellow Sweet Magic = 'Dicyellmag'PBR (Patio) IDic
'Yesterday' (Poly/F/S) ♀H4 EBls MAsh MAus MGan MRav SPoG SWCr
'Yolande d'Aragon' (HP) EBls
York and Lancaster see *R.* x *damascena* var. *versicolor*
Yorkshire Bank = 'Rutrulo'PBR (HT) MFry
Yorkshire = 'Korbarkeit'PBR (GC) ENot GCoc LStr MRav SSea
'Yorkshire Lady' (HT) MJon NBat
'Yvonne Rabier' (Poly) ♀H4 EBls LStr MAus MRav SPer SSea SWCr WAct WHCG
Zambra = 'Meicurbos' (F) CBcs
'Zéphirine Drouhin' (Bb) More than 30 suppliers
§ 'Zigeunerknabe' (S) EBee EBls ECnt EMFP EWTr MAus MRav SPer SSea SWCr WAct WHCG
'Zitronenfalter' (S) **new** MGan
Zorba **new** ECnt
'Zweibrücken' (Cl) MGan

Roscoea ✿ (*Zingiberaceae*)

ACE 2539 GEdr
alpina CBct CBro CLAP CPLG EBee EBrs EChP EHrv EHyt ERos EUJe GEdr GFlt GKev GKir IBlr ITim MTho MTis NLAp NMen NWCA SOkd SRms WCot WCru WLin WSan
- CC 3667 GEdr WRos
- pink-flowered EBrs ITer
auriculata More than 30 suppliers
- early-flowering WCru
- 'Floriade' CLAP IBlr

- late-flowering	WCru
- 'Special'	CLAP
australis	CFir GEdr IBlr MNrw SOkd WCru
'Beesiana'	CBct CBro CDWL CFir CFwr CHEx CLAP CMea EBee EChP EMar ERos GBuc GEdr GSki IBlr LAma LPhx MRav MTho NBid NMyG WAbe WCru WFar WHil
'Beesiana' dark-flowered **new**	ERos
'Beesiana' pale-flowered	ERos IBlr LEdu WCru
'Beesiana' white-flowered	CBct CDes CFwr CLAP EBee EHrv EPfP EPot GEdr GSki IBlr LAst LPhx MBNS MMHG NBir SMeo WAbe WPGP
bhutanica	IBlr
brandisii **new**	CBct
capitata **new**	SOkd
cautleyoides ♀H4	More than 30 suppliers
- CLD 687	GEdr
I - 'Alba' **new**	GFlt
- Blackthorn strain	SBla
- var. ***cautleyoides***	CDWL CFir GFlt
- 'Early Purple'	CLAP EBee
- hybrid	GSki MLLN
- 'Jeffrey Thomas'	CBct CFwr CLAP CSam EPot GEdr GSki IBlr SMeo WCot
- 'Kew Beauty' ♀H4	CDes CFir CLAP EBee EBrs ETow GKir MTho SRms WCot WPGP
- 'Kew Beauty' seedlings	EMan GCal
- 'Purple Giant'	CLAP WCot
- purple-flowered	IBlr NHar
- 'Reinier'	CLAP WCot
cautleyoides* x *humeana	CLAP IBlr
'Gestreept'	CLAP
'Himalaya'	CLAP
humeana ♀H4	CBct CBro CFee CLAP CSam EBrs EHyt ERos GBin GCrs GEdr GMac LAma LRHS SBla WCot WCru WPrP
- f. ***lutea***	IBlr
- 'Purple Streaker'	CBct CDes CLAP EBee WPGP
- 'Rosemoor Plum'	CLAP
- 'Snowy Owl' **new**	CLAP
- f. ***tyria***	IBlr
kunmingensis var. ***elongatobractea***	IBlr
- var. ***kunmingensis***	IBlr
'Monique'	CDes CLAP IBlr
procera	see *R. purpurea*
§ ***purpurea***	More than 30 suppliers
- CC 3628	WCot
- HWJK 2400	WCru
- L&S 20845	IBlr
- 'Brown Peacock'	CDes CLAP WCot
- var. ***gigantea***	CFir CLAP IBlr
- - CC 1757	MNrw
- lilac-flowered	CDWL GSki SOkd
- 'Nico'	CLAP WCot
- 'Niedrig'	EBee
- pale-flowered	EBla
- 'Peacock'	CLAP WFar
- 'Peacock Eye'	CLAP WCot
- var. ***procera***	see *R. purpurea*
- 'Red Gurkha'	SBla
- short	CLAP
- tall	CLAP
§ ***scillifolia***	CBro CDes CFir CPBP EBee EBrs EPot ERos GBuc GCal GEdr GKev GKir GSki IBlr LAma LRHS MAvo MTho NBir NMen WCot WCru WLin WPrP
- dark-flowered	CPom CStu EHrv WCru WPGP
- pink-flowered	CBct CPne EChP EHrv EMar ERos GEdr IBlr NMen WAbe WCot
tibetica	CFir CLAP GEdr GKev IBlr NLAp SOkd WCot WCru
tumjensis	CLAP EBee IBlr
'Vincent'	WCot
wardii **new**	EHyt
'Yeti'	CLAP

rosemary see *Rosmarinus officinalis*

Rosmarinus ✿ (*Lamiaceae*)

corsicus 'Prostratus'	see *R. officinalis* Prostratus Group
eriocalyx	XPep
lavandulaceus misapplied	see *R. officinalis* Prostratus Group
lavandulaceus Noë	see *R. eriocalyx*
officinalis	More than 30 suppliers
- var. ***albiflorus***	CArn CPrp CSev ELau EPfP ESis GBar GPoy LRHS MBar MBow MChe MHer MSwo NHHG NLon SChu SDow SHDw SLim SPer SPlb STre WCHb WGwG WWpP WWye XPep
- - 'Lady in White'	CRez CSBt ELan EPfP LAst LRHS NGHP SDow SPer WGwG WJek
- 'Alderney'	GBar MHer SDow
- var. ***angustissimus***	XPep
§ - - 'Benenden Blue' ♀H4	CMHG CSBt CSev CWan CWib EBee EGoo ELau GBar GPoy LRHS MChe MHer MWgw NHHG SChu SDix SDow SMHy SMer SPer SPlb STre WWye
§ - - 'Corsican Blue'	CArn EBee ELan EPfP GBar GPoy MHer NGHP SDow SHDw SIde SLon WBrE WPer XPep
- - 'Corsicus Prostratus'	CBcs ELau
- 'Aureovariegatus'	see *R. officinalis* 'Aureus'
§ - 'Aureus' (v)	GBar IBlr NHHG WCHb WEas
- 'Baie d'Audierne'	XPep
- 'Baie de Douarnenez'	XPep
- 'Barbecue'PBR	MHer NGHP SIde
- 'Barcelona'	XPep
- 'Blue Boy'	MHer
- 'Blue Lagoon'	EBee EOHP EWin MHer NGHP WCHb WGwG WJek
- 'Blue Rain'	MHer NGHP
* - 'Boule'	CPrp MHer WCHb XPep
- 'Cap Béar'	XPep
- 'Capercaillie'	SDow
- 'Cisampo'	XPep
- 'Collingwood Ingram'	see *R. officinalis* var. *angustissimus* 'Benenden Blue'
- dwarf, blue-flowered	ELau GBar
- dwarf, white-flowered	WCHb
- 'Eve'	XPep
- 'Farinole'	CPrp XPep
- 'Fastigiatus'	see *R. officinalis* 'Miss Jessopp's Upright'
- 'Fota Blue'	CArn CBod CPrp CSev CWib ELau EOHP GBar IArd MHer NGHP NHHG SAga SDow SHDw SIde WCHb WJek WWye
- 'Golden Rain'	see *R. officinalis* 'Joyce DeBaggio'
- 'Gorizia'	GBar SDow XPep
- 'Green Ginger'	CBod CPrp CSpe EChP EOHP EUnu GBin MChe MHer NCot NPer SDow SPoG WBcn WCHb WGwG WMnd
- 'Guilded'	see *R. officinalis* 'Aureus'
- 'Gunnel's Upright'	GBar WRha
- 'Haifa'	CBgR CBod EBee EWin NGHP SIde WCHb
- 'Heavenly Blue'	GBar WGwG

	- 'Henfield Blue'	SHDw
	- 'Iden Blue'	SIde
	- 'Iden Blue Boy'	SIde
	- 'Iden Pillar'	SIde
§	- 'Joyce DeBaggio' (v)	LSou MHer SDow
	- 'Ken Taylor'	LPhx
	- 'Lady in Blue'	WGwG
	- ***lavandulaceus***	see *R. officinalis* Prostratus Group
	- 'Lérida'	XPep
	- 'Lilies Blue'	GPoy
	- 'Lockwood Variety'	see *R. officinalis* (Prostratus Group) 'Lockwood de Forest'
	- 'Loupian'	XPep
	- 'Majorca Pink'	CBcs CChe CPrp CSBt CSam CWan EGoo ELau ENot GBar MBow MHer MRav SDow SIde SLon SPer SRms SSto WCHb WGwG WSSM WWye XPep
	- 'Maltese White'	CStr WCot
	- 'Marenca'	WCHb XPep
	- 'Marinka' **new**	CWan
	- 'Mason's Finest'	SDow
	- 'McConnell's Blue' ♀H4	CArn CDoC CPrp EBee ELan ELau ENot GBar LRHS MAsh MGos MRav MWgw SDow SHDw SPla WCHb WFar WHoo WPGP WTel WWye
	- 'Minerve'	XPep
§	- 'Miss Jessopp's Upright' ♀H4	More than 30 suppliers
	- 'Montagnette'	XPep
	- 'Mrs Harding'	CBod CPrp MHer
	- 'Pat Vlasto'	CStr
	- 'Pointe du Raz'	EBee ELan MRav SPoG
§	- 'Primley Blue'	CArn CPrp CSam CSev CWSG EBee ECtt ELau GBar LRHS MChe MHer MRav NGHP NHHG NJOw SChu SIde SMer WCHb WPer
§	- Prostratus Group	More than 30 suppliers
	- - 'Capri'	CSBt EBee ENot EOHP LRHS MHer MRav NGHP
	- - 'Gethsemane'	SIde
	- - 'Deben Blue' **new**	ENot
	- - 'Jackman's Prostrate'	CBcs ECtt
§	- - 'Lockwood de Forest'	GBar
	- 'Punta di Canelle'	XPep
	- f. ***pyramidalis***	see *R. officinalis* 'Miss Jessopp's Upright'
	- 'Rampant Boule'	GBar SDow
	- ***repens***	see *R. officinalis* Prostratus Group
	- 'Roman Beauty'	LAst SVil
	- 'Rosemarey'	XPep
	- 'Roseus'	CArn CMHG CPrp CSBt CWib EBee EChP ELan ELau EMil EPfP GPoy LRHS MBct MChe MHer NHHG NLon SChu SDow SLim SPoG WAbe WHer WMnd WPer WWeb WWye
	- 'Russell's Blue'	WFar
	- 'Saint Florent'	XPep
	- 'Salem' **new**	MHer
	- 'Santa Barbara Blue'	XPep
	- 'Sawyer's Select'	MHer
	- 'Sea Level'	CBod MBow WCHb
	- 'Severn Sea' ♀H4	CArn CBcs CChe CMHG CPrp CSBt CSev CWSG EBee ECtt ELan EPfP GBar GPoy LRHS MGos MHer MRav MSwo NFor SDow SIde SLon SMer SPer WCFE WCHb WEas WPer WWeb
	- 'Silver Sparkler'	WPat
	- Silver Spires = 'Wolros'	LRav
	- 'Sissinghurst Blue' ♀H4	CArn CBcs CSev CWan EBee ELan ELau EMil EPfP GAbr GBar LAst LRHS MBow MRav NGHP SDow SIde SLim SPer SPlb SRms WCHb WGwG WSel WWye XPep
	- 'Sissinghurst White'	WGwG
	- 'South Downs Blue'	SHDw
	- 'Sudbury Blue'	CRez EBee ELau EPfP GBar MChe MHer NGHP NHHG NLon SDow SHDw WEas WJek XPep
	- 'Trusty'	CWan EBee GBar LRHS WBcn XPep
	- 'Tuscan Blue'	More than 30 suppliers
	- 'Ulysse'	XPep
	- 'Variegatus'	see *R. officinalis* 'Aureus'
	- 'Vicomte de Noailles'	ERea XPep
	repens	see *R. officinalis* Prostratus Group

Rostrinucula (*Lamiaceae*)

	dependens	EMan
	- Guiz 18	CBot
	sinensis **new**	CPLG

Rosularia ✿ (*Crassulaceae*)

	from Sandras Dag	CWil LBee LRHS
	alba	see *R. sedoides*
	alpestris from Rhotang Pass **new**	WThu
§	***chrysantha***	EBur EPot MHer NJOw NMen SIng SPlb
	- number 1	CWil LRHS
	crassipes	see *Rhodiola wallichiana*
§	***muratdaghensis***	EBur SIng
	pallida	see *R. chrysantha*
	platyphylla hort.	see *R. muratdaghensis*
§	***sedoides***	CWil LRHS MBar NBlu SChu SIng
§	- var. ***alba***	EDAr EHol EPot GGar MBar NLAp SChu WTin
	sempervivum	CWil EWes NMen WCot
§	- subsp. ***glaucophylla***	CWil NSla WAbe
	spatulata hort.	see *R. sempervivum* subsp. *glaucophylla*

Rothmannia (*Rubiaceae*)

	capensis	EShb
§	***globosa***	ERea

Rubia (*Rubiaceae*)

	cordifolia **new**	MSal
	manjith	GPoy
	peregrina	CArn GPoy MSal
	tinctorum	CArn CHby ELau EOHP EUnu GBar GPoy GWCH MSal WCHb WHer WWye

Rubus (*Rosaceae*)

	RCB/Eq C-1	WCot
	alceifolius	CFee CStr SDys SMac
	arcticus	EBee EPPr GGar GIBF MCCP NLAp NLar SRms SRot WCot WCru WGHP WPat
	- subsp. ***stellarcticus*** 'Sofia' (F)	SCoo
	x ***barkeri***	ECou
§	'Benenden' ♀H4	More than 30 suppliers
	'Betty Ashburner'	CAgr CBcs CDoC ECrN ENot EPfP EWTr GQui LAst LBuc MGos MRav MWgw MWhi NArg SPer SPoG WBVN WDin WGHP WTin
	biflorus ♀H4	CBcs CFil CPle EBee EMon EPfP EWes LRHS MBlu SMac WPGP
	'Boysenberry, Thornless' (F)	GTwe LBuc LRHS SPer

	calophyllus	CFil WBor WPGP
	calycinoides	see *R. pentalobus*
	chamaemorus	GIBF GPoy
	cissoides	WCot
	cockburnianus (F)	CArn CBcs CPle CTri EBee ELan ENot EPfP GCra GKir LBuc LRHS MBlu MRav MSwo NBea NLRH NLon NSti NWea SPer SPlb SRms WDin WEas WFar
	- 'Goldenvale' ♀H4	More than 30 suppliers
	coreanus	CFil EPla
	crataegifolius	CBrd CWan SMac WPat
§	***discolor*** (F)	ENot
	'Emerald Spreader'	GKir LRHS MBri SBod
	flagelliflorus	MBar
	fockeanus hort.	see *R. pentalobus*
	formosensis B&SWJ 1798	WCru
	fruticosus 'Adrienne' (F)	CAgr
	- 'Ashton Cross' (F)	GTwe LBuc
	- 'Bedford Giant' (F)	CSBt ENot GTwe LBuc LRHS MAsh MGos MRav SKee SPoG
	- 'Black Satin' (F)	CAgr LRHS NLar
	- 'Cottenham Green'	EMon
	- 'Fantasia'PBR (F) ♀H4	NEgg
	- 'Helen'	CAgr CSut LRHS SKee
	- 'Himalayan Berry'	see *R. discolor*
	- 'Himalayan Giant' (F)	GTwe LRHS MRav NEgg SPer
	- 'Loch Ness'PBR (F) ♀H4	COtt CSBt ENot GKir GTwe IArd LBuc LRHS MAsh MBri MGos NEgg SCoo SKee SPer SPoG
	- 'Merton Thornless' (F)	CSBt GTwe LRHS MAsh MGos
	- 'Oregon Thornless' (F)	CAgr CCVT CSBt ENot GTwe MAsh MBri MRav NEgg SCoo SKee SPer SPoG SRms
	- 'Parsley Leaved' (F)	MRav
*	- 'Sylvan' (F)	LRHS MCoo MGos SKee
	- 'Thornfree' (F)	CAgr
	- 'Variegatus' (v)	CBot IFro MBlu SMad WPat
	- 'Waldo'	CAgr COtt CSBt LBuc LRHS MAsh MGos
	'Golden Showers'	CWib
	hakonensis B&SWJ 5555	WCru
	henryi	CBot EPla LRHS MRav NLar NSti SLon SMac SPoG WCot WFar
	- var. ***bambusarum***	CFil CMCN CPLN EMan EPfP EPla MCCP NVic WCru WPat WTin
	hupehensis	SLPl
	ichangensis	CBot CPLN CStr EPla LEdu
I	***idaeus*** 'Allgold'	see *R. idaeus* 'Fallgold'
	- 'Aureus' (F)	ECha ELan EPla MRav NBid NBre SMac WCot WFar
	- 'Autumn Bliss'PBR (F) ♀H4	CAgr CSBt CSut CTri CWSG ENot EPfP GKir GTwe LBuc LRHS MAsh MBri MGos MRav NEgg SCoo SKee SPer SPoG WOrn
§	- 'Fallgold' (F)	CAgr EPfP LRHS MAsh MCoo SKee SPer SPoG WOrn
	- 'Glen Ample'PBR (F) ♀H4	CAgr CSBt CSut CWSG EPfP GTwe LBuc LRHS MAsh MBri MCoo SCoo SKee SPer SPoG
	- 'Glen Clova' (F)	CAgr CSBt CTri ENot GKir GTwe LRHS MAsh MRav NBlu NEgg SKee SPer SPoG WOrn
	- 'Glen Lyon'PBR (F)	GTwe LBuc LRHS MAsh MBri SCoo
	- 'Glen Magna'PBR (F)	CAgr CSBt CSut CWSG GTwe LBuc LRHS MAsh MBri SCoo SKee SPoG
	- 'Glen Moy'PBR (F) ♀H4	CSBt EPfP GTwe LRHS MAsh MBri MGos MRav SCoo SKee
	- 'Glen Prosen'PBR (F) ♀H4	CAgr CSBt GKir GTwe LRHS MAsh MBri MRav SCoo SKee SPer
	- 'Glen Rosa'PBR (F)	GTwe LRHS
	- 'Glen Shee'PBR (F)	GTwe
	- 'Heritage' (F)	ENot LRHS MAsh MRav SCoo
	- 'Julia' (F)	CAgr GTwe MCoo
	- 'Leo'PBR (F) ♀H4	CAgr CSBt GTwe MAsh MGos NEgg SCoo SKee
	- 'Malling Admiral' (F) ♀H4	CTri ENot GKir GTwe LRHS MAsh SCoo SPer
	- 'Malling Delight' (F)	CSBt GKir LRHS MAsh MRav SCoo
	- 'Malling Jewel' (F) ♀H4	COtt CSBt CTri ENot GKir GTwe LBuc LRHS MAsh NEgg SKee SPer
	- 'Summer Gold' (F)	GTwe
	- 'Tulameen' (F)	LBuc MAsh MBri SCoo SKee SPoG
	- 'Zeva Herbsternte' (F)	MAsh
	illecebrosus (F)	GIBF ITer LEdu NLar
	irenaeus	CFil CPLN SSpi
	Japanese wineberry	see *R. phoenicolasius*
	'Kenneth Ashburner'	CDoC NLar SLPl WFar WTin
	laciniatus	EHol EPla
	lambertianus	CFil
	leucodermis NNS 00-663	EPPr
	lineatus	CBot CDoC CMCo CPLG CPle EPfP GKir LRHS NSti SDix SMad SSpi WCru WDin WPGP WPat
	- HWJK 2045	WCru
	x ***loganobaccus*** 'LY 59' (F) ♀H4	ENot EPfP GTwe MRav NEgg SKee SRms
	- 'LY 654' (F) ♀H4	GKir GTwe LBuc LRHS MBri MGos SPer
	- thornless (F)	CAgr CTri CWSG ECot ENot GKir GTwe MAsh
	'Margaret Gordon'	MRav WHCG
	microphyllus 'Variegatus' (v)	CRez EMan MGos WPat
§	***nepalensis***	CAgr CDoC CEnd GKir LEdu NLAp
	niveus	EPla
	nutans	see *R. nepalensis*
	odoratus	CPle CPom CStr CTri ELan EPfP EWTr MRav NPal SPer WBor WCot WHCG WTin
	parviflorus	CArn
	- double (d)	EMon WCru
	- 'Sunshine Spreader'	NPro WPat
	parvus	ECou
	pectinellus	WBcn
	- var. ***trilobus***	CFee NLar SMac
	- - B&SWJ 1669B	GSki LPio NPro WCru WDyG
	peltatus	CFil NLar
§	***pentalobus***	CRez CTri ELan EMan EPla MBar MWhi NFor SMac WFar
	- B&SWJ 3878	WCru
	- 'Emerald Carpet'	CAgr ECrN NLar SBod
§	***phoenicolasius***	CAgr EPfP EWTr GKir GTwe LEdu LRHS MBlu MBri MRav MWhi NSti SPer WAbb WCru WHCG
	rolfei	EPPr
	- B&SWJ 3546	WCru
	rosifolius	CBcs CSpe
	- 'Coronarius' (d)	CFee CHar CPom CSpe ECrN ELan EMan GAbr LRHS LSou MBow MRav NPro NSti WCot WFar WHil WOVN
	sachalinensis	GIBF
	saxatilis	GIBF
	setchuenensis	CMCN CSWP
	'Silvan' (F) ♀H4	GTwe
	spectabilis	CBcs CPle CPom CSev CWib ELan EPPr EPla MRav WFar WRha WSHC
	- 'Flore Pleno'	see *R. spectabilis* 'Olympic Double'
§	- 'Olympic Double' (d)	More than 30 suppliers
	splendidissimus B&SWJ 2361	WCru
	squarrosus	CPle ECou EHol

'Sunberry' (F)	GTwe
swinhoei B&SWJ 1735	WCru
taiwanicola	GEdr NLar WWhi
- B&SWJ 317	GBin MHar NPro WCru
Tayberry Group (F) 🏆H4	CTri ENot GKir GTwe MAsh MBri MGos NLar SPer SRms
- 'Buckingham' (F)	CSut GTwe LBuc LRHS MBri
- 'Medana Tayberry' (F)	CAgr LRHS SKee SPoG
§ ***thibetanus*** 🏆H4	More than 30 suppliers
- 'Silver Fern'	see *R. thibetanus*
tricolor	CAgr CBcs CDul CHEx CSBt CTri CWib ECrN ENot EPfP GBri GIBF GKir LGro MRav MSwo MTis MWhi NEgg NFor SDix SHBN SLon SMac SPer WDin WGHP WHCG
- 'Dart's Evergreen'	SLPl
- 'Ness'	SLPl
tridel 'Benenden'	see *R.* 'Benenden'
trilobus	GAbr
- B&SWJ 9096	WCru
'Tummelberry' (F)	GTwe
ulmifolius 'Bellidiflorus' (d)	CBot EBee MBlu MRav MSwo NFor NLon NSti SChu SDix SMac SPer WAbb WHal
ursinus	LEdu
'Veitchberry' (F)	GTwe
xanthocarpus	NLar

Rudbeckia ✿ (*Asteraceae*)

Autumn Sun	see *R.* 'Herbstsonne'
californica	CRez CSam MAnH MNrw WPer
deamii	see *R. fulgida* var. *deamii*
echinacea purpurea	see *Echinacea purpurea*
§ ***fulgida*** var. ***deamii*** 🏆H4	More than 30 suppliers
- var. ***fulgida***	NLsd NRnb WHil WRHF
§ - var. ***speciosa*** 🏆H4	CKno CM&M CSam CWCL EBee ECha ECtt ELan EPfP ERou GAbr LRHS MHar NGdn SBch SDix SGSe SMac SPer SPlb SRms WEas WFar WMoo WPer WTel WTin WWpP
- var. ***sullivantii*** 'Goldsturm' 🏆H4	More than 30 suppliers
- Viette's Little Suzy = 'Blovi'	EBee EBrs EMan LRHS WCra
gloriosa	see *R. hirta*
'Golden Jubilee'	LRHS NLRH WWeb
§ ***hirta***	CHar EBrs NBir
- 'Goldilocks'	GWCH SHGN
- 'Indian Summer' 🏆H3	SPav
- 'Irish Eyes'	LRHS LRav SPav
- 'Marmalade' **new**	NEgg NJOw
- var. ***pulcherrima***	EPPr SBch
- 'Sonora'	COtt
- 'Toto' 🏆H3	SPav SWvt WSan WWpP
July Gold	see *R. laciniata* 'Juligold'
laciniata	CBrm CElw CStr EBee EBrs EChP ELan EMan EMon EPPr EPfP GCal MDKP MWrn NLar NOrc NRnb NSti WCot WMoo
- var. ***ampla***	MDKP
- 'Golden Glow'	see *R. laciniata* 'Hortensia'
- 'Goldquelle' (d) 🏆H4	More than 30 suppliers
- 'Herbstsonne' 🏆H4	More than 30 suppliers
§ - 'Hortensia' (d)	EMon
- 'Juligold'	CPrp EBee EMan ETow EVFa LRHS MAvo MWgw NEgg NGdn SHel SMrm SPla SPoG SSpe WCAu WFar WWhi
maxima	CBot CDes EBee EChP ECha EMan EMon EWsh LEdu LPhx LRHS MAnH MBri MCCP MNFA NCGa NDov NEgg NLar NSti SChu SDix SMad SMrm SPlb SUsu WAul WCot WFar WWpP
missouriensis	EBee SUsu
mollis	EBee
newmannii	see *R. fulgida* var. *speciosa*
nitida	IHMH
occidentalis	EBrs MLLN NBre NRnb NVic WFar WPer
- 'Black Beauty'PBR	EBee EChP EMan EPfP MBNS MMHG MTis NLar NSti SHop WGwG WMnd
- 'Green Wizard'	More than 30 suppliers
* ***paniculata***	WCot
purpurea	see *Echinacea purpurea*
speciosa	see *R. fulgida* var. *speciosa*
subtomentosa	EBee EBrs EMan EMon GCal LRHS MDKP MNFA NSti WCAu WOld
'Takao'	EBee GMac MDKP MLLN MSph NLar SPoG SUsu
triloba	CMea CSam EBee EBrs EMan EPPr EPfP GBri LRHS MNrw NFla NRnb SMad SMar WCAu WFar WHoo WMoo WSan WTin

rue see *Ruta graveolens*

Ruellia (*Acanthaceae*)

amoena	see *R. graecizans*
brittoniana **new**	MJnS
§ ***graecizans***	ECre
humilis	EBee EMan EShb NLar
macrantha	MJnS
makoyana 🏆H1	CHal CSev IBlr MBri
'Mr Foster'	CHal
* ***muralis***	MAvo

Rumex (*Polygonaceae*)

§ ***acetosa***	CArn CHby CSev CWan ELau GBar GPoy GWCH IHMH LRHS MBow MChe MHer NBir NGHP NPri SIde SWal WHer WLHH WSel WWye
- 'Abundance'	ELau
- subsp. ***acetosa*** 'Saucy' (v)	WCot
- 'De Belleville'	CPrp
- 'Profusion'	GPoy
- subsp. ***vinealis***	EBee EMan WCot
acetosella	CArn MSal NMir WSel
alpinus	EUnu LEdu WCot
- HWJK 2354	WCru
flexuosus	EHoe EShb EUnu ITer NLar WJek
hydrolapathum	CArn CHEx EMFW LPBA SPlb WWpP
obtusifolius 'Golden My Foot'	CNat
patientia	CAgr
sanguineus	CAgr CTri EMan EPza EShb EUnu GBBs GGar IHMH LPBA MWgw NCob NLar SWal WBrk WFar WMnd WPop WWeb WWpP
- var. ***sanguineus***	CArn CBgR CElw CPrp CRow CSev EDAr EHoe ELan EPla LRHS MHer MNrw MTho NBro SGSe WHer WLHH WPer WSel WWye
'Schavel'	CAgr
scutatus	CAgr CArn CHby CSev ELau EUnu GPoy MChe MHer MWat SIde SPlb WGHP WHer WJek WLHH WWye
- 'Silver Shield'	CBod CRow ELau EMar EPPr SIde WCHb WCot WJek WLHH
venosus	MSal

Rumohra (*Davalliaceae*)

adiantiformis ♀H1 SEND WFib
- RCB/Arg D-2 WCot

Ruschia (*Aizoaceae*)

karrooica SChr
uncinata SChr

Ruscus ✿ (*Ruscaceae*)

aculeatus CArn CBcs CRWN EBee ELan ENot EPfP GKir GPoy IDee MGos MRav MWat NWea SAPC SArc SCoo SPlb SPoG SRms SSta WDin WHer WPGP WRHF WWye
- (f) WFar WMou
- (m) WMou
- hermaphrodite EPfP EPla EWes GCal SMad SPer WGer
- var. **aculeatus** 'Lanceolatus' (f) GCal
- var. **angustifolius** Boiss. EPla
- - (f) EPla
* - 'Wheeler's Variety' (f/m) CPMA EBee
hypoglossum EPla SEND SLon WRHF
racemosus see *Danae racemosa*

Russelia (*Scrophulariaceae*)

§ **equisetiformis** ♀H1 CHll EShb SIgm XPep
- yellow-flowered **new** EShb
juncea see *R. equisetiformis*

Ruta (*Rutaceae*)

chalepensis CArn XPep
corsica CArn
graveolens CArn CDul CWan EChP EPfP EWin GBar GPoy GWCH MChe NBlu NPri SIde SPet WGHP WJek WPer WWye XPep
- 'Jackman's Blue' CBcs CBot CSev CTri CWCL EBee ECrN EHoe ELan ENot EPfP GKir GMaP GPoy LAst LGro MGos MHer MRav MSwo MWgw NFor SMer SPer SRms WBrE WEas WMnd WTel
- 'Variegata' (v) CBot CWan ELan EMan GBar MChe MFOX NFor NPer SPer WJek

Ruttya (*Acanthaceae*)

fruticosa 'Scholesii' ERea

x *Ruttyruspolia* (*Acanthaceae*)

'Phyllis van Heerden' GFai

Rytidosperma (*Poaceae*)

arundinaceum EShb

S

Sabal (*Arecaceae*)

§ **bermudana** CRoM EAmu WMul
causiarum CRoM
domingensis CRoM EAmu
mauritiiformis WMul
§ **mexicana** CRoM CTrC EAmu WMul
minor CBrP CHEx CPHo CRoM CTrC EAmu EExo NPal SBig WMul
palmetto CArn CDoC CRoM CTrC EAmu WMul WNor
princeps see *S. bermudana*
'Riverside' CRoM
rosei WMul
texana see *S. mexicana*

Saccharum (*Poaceae*)

arundinaceum EPPr
§ **baldwinii** CBig GFor
brevibarbe var. **contortum** CBig EBee GFor
officinarum MJnS
ravennae CBig CPLG CPen EBee EHoe EMan EMon EPza GFor LRav MSte NBid SApp SMad SPlb WFar
strictum (Ell.) Ell. ex Nutt. see *S. baldwinii*
strictum (Host) Spreng. **new** NBre

sage see *Salvia officinalis*

sage, annual clary see *Salvia viridis*

sage, biennial clary see *Salvia sclarea*

sage, pineapple see *Salvia elegans* 'Scarlet Pineapple'

Sageretia (*Rhamnaceae*)

§ **thea** STre
theezans see *S. thea*

Sagina (*Caryophyllaceae*)

boydii EWes
subulata IHMH
§ - var. **glabrata** 'Aurea' CTri ECha ECtt EDAr GKir LGro MBNS MWhi SIng SPoG SRms WEas WHal WPer WWpP

Sagittaria (*Alismataceae*)

'Bloomin Babe' CRow
graminea 'Crushed Ice' (v) CRow
japonica see *S. sagittifolia*
latifolia COld EMFW LPBA NPer
§ **sagittifolia** CBen CDWL CRow CWat EHon EMFW EPfP LNCo LPBA NArg NBlu WFar WPnP WPop WWpP
- 'Flore Pleno' (d) ambig. CDWL CRow CWat EMFW LPBA WPnP WPop
- var. **leucopetala** 'Flore Pleno' (d) NArg NLar NPer

Saintpaulia (*Gesneriaceae*)

'Beatrice Trail' **new** WDib
'Blue Dragon' WDib
'Bob Serbin' (d) WDib
'Bohemian Sunset' **new** WDib
'Buffalo Hunt' WDib
'Centenary' WDib
'Cherries 'n' Cream' WDib
'Chiffon Fiesta' WDib
'Chiffon Mist' (d) WDib
'Chiffon Moonmoth' WDib
'Chiffon Stardust' WDib
'Chiffon Vesper' WDib
'Coroloir' WDib
'Delft' (d) WDib
'Golden Glow' (d) WDib
'Halo' (Ultra Violet Series) WDib
'Halo's Aglitter' WDib
'Irish Flirt' (d) WDib
'Lemon Drop' (d) WDib
'Lemon Whip' (d) WDib

'Love Spots'	WDib
'Lucky Lee Ann' (d)	WDib
'Marching Band'	WDib
'Mermaid' (d)	WDib
'Midget Lillian' (d)	WDib
'Midnight Flame'	WDib
'Midnight Waltz' **new**	WDib
'Nubian Winter'	WDib
'Otoe'	WDib
'Powder Keg' (d)	WDib
'Powwow' (d/v)	WDib
'Ramblin' Magic' (d)	WDib
'Rapid Transit' (d)	WDib
'Rob's Bamboozle'	WDib
'Rob's Denim Demon' **new**	WDib
'Rob's Dust Storm' (d)	WDib
'Rob's Firebrand'	WDib
'Rob's Gundaroo' (d)	WDib
'Rob's Heat Wave' (d)	WDib
'Rob's Hopscotch'	WDib
'Rob's Ice Ripples' (d)	WDib
'Rob's Mad Cat' (d)	WDib
'Rob's Rinky Dink' (d)	WDib
'Rob's Sarsparilla' (d)	WDib
'Rob's Seduction' **new**	WDib
'Rob's Shadow Magic' (d)	WDib
'Rob's Sticky Wicket'	WDib
'Rob's Tippy Toe' (d)	WDib
'Rob's Toorooka' (d)	WDib
shumensis	WDib
'Sky Bandit' (d)	WDib

Salix ✿ (*Salicaceae*)

	acutifolia	ELan GIBF SPla WDin WGHP
	- 'Blue Streak' (m) ♡H4	CDul CEnd CWiW EPfP EPla EWes MAsh MBlu MRav NBir NLon SLon SMHy WFar WGHP
	- 'Pendulifolia' (m)	SBLw WPat
	aegyptiaca	CDoC CLnd ECrN MBlu NWea WMou
	alba	CAgr CCVT CDul CLnd CWiW ECrN GKir LBuc NWea SBLw WDin WMou WOrn
	- f. ***argentea***	see *S. alba* var. *sericea*
	- 'Aurea'	CLnd CTho MRav WGHP WIvy WMou
	- 'Belders' (m)	SBLw
	- var. ***caerulea***	CAgr CDul CLnd MRav NWea WMou
	- - 'Wantage Hall' (f)	CWiW
	- 'Cardinalis' (f)	CWiW WGHP
	- 'Chermesina' hort.	see *S. alba* subsp. *vitellina* 'Britzensis'
	- 'Dart's Snake'	CEnd CTho EBee ELan ENot EPfP LRHS MRav SCoo SPer WBcn
	- 'Hutchinson's Yellow'	CDoC CTho MGos NWea WDin
	- 'Liempde' (m)	MRav SBLw
	- 'Raesfeld' (m)	CWiW
§	- var. ***sericea*** ♡H4	CBcs CDoC CLnd CTho ECrN EPfP GKir MBlu MRav NFor NLon NWea SBLw SHBN SPer WDin WGHP WGer WIvy WMou
	- 'Splendens'	see *S. alba* var. *sericea*
	- 'Tristis' misapplied	see *S.* x *sepulcralis* var. *chrysocoma*, *S. humilis*
	- 'Tristis' ambig.	CCVT CLnd CTri ECrN ELan GKir LRHS MBri MGos MSwo NBee NLar NWea SBLw SLim SRms WDin WFar WHar
	- subsp. ***vitellina*** ♡H4	CDul EPfP GKir LBuc MBNS MBrN NWea SLon WDin WGHP WIvy WJas WMoo
§	- - 'Britzensis' (m) ♡H4	More than 30 suppliers
	- 'Vitellina Pendula'	see *S. alba* 'Tristis'
	- 'Vitellina Tristis'	see *S. alba* 'Tristis'
	- subsp. ***vitellina*** 'Yelverton'	LRHS MRav WGHP WWes
§	***alpina***	CLyd GIBF NBir
	'Americana'	CWiW
	amplexicaulis 'Pescara' (m)	CWiW
	amygdaloides	CWiW WGHP
	apoda (m)	EWes GIBF NBir NWCA WPer
	'Aquatica Gigantea' **new**	NWea
§	***arbuscula***	CBcs GIBF NWCA WDin
	arctica var. ***petraea***	NLAp WPat
	arenaria	see *S. repens* var. *argentea*
	aurita	LRav NLar NWea
	babylonica	CEnd NBee SBLw SHBN WMou
	- 'Annularis'	see *S. babylonica* 'Crispa'
§	- 'Crispa'	CDul CFai CFwr CRez ELan EPla NPro SMad SPla SPoG WBcn WFar
	- 'Pan Chih-kang'	CWiW
§	- var. ***pekinensis*** 'Tortuosa' ♡H4	More than 30 suppliers
*	- 'Tortuosa Aurea'	MCCP SWvt WBrE
	x ***basaltica*** (m)	GIBF
	bicolor (f)	GIBF
	- (m)	GIBF
	'Blackskin' (f)	CWiW
	bockii	LRHS LTwo MBar SSpi WCFE WFar
§	'Bowles' Hybrid'	CAgr MRav WMou
	'Boydii' (f) ♡H4	CBrm CFee EPfP EPot GAbr GCrs GKir GTou ITim MDun MGos NBir NFor NLon NMen NRya NSla SBla SIng SPoG SRms WAbe WFar WPat
§	'Boyd's Pendulous' (m)	CFee CLyd CWib EHyt MBar
	breviserrata	CLyd GIBF
	caesia	GIBF NWCA
	candida	GIBF
	caprea	CAgr CBcs CCVT CDul CLnd CRWN CTri ECrN ENot EPfP GKir LBuc NWea SBLw SPer WDin WMou
	- 'Black Stem'	CNat
	- 'Curlilocks'	COtt MBar MSwo NEgg
§	- 'Kilmarnock' (m)	More than 30 suppliers
	- var. ***pendula*** (m)	see *S. caprea* 'Kilmarnock' (m)
	cascadensis	GIBF
	cashmiriana	CFai CLyd GEdr NWCA WPat
	x ***cepusiensis*** (f)	GIBF
	x ***cernua***	NWCA
	'Chrysocoma'	see *S.* x *sepulcralis* var. *chrysocoma*
	cinerea	CAgr CBcs CDoC ECrN ENot GKir LBuc NWea SBLw WDin
	- 'Tricolor' (v)	CArn NPro SLim
	commutata	GIBF
§	***cordata***	ECrN SLPl WDin
	x ***cottetii***	GIBF IArd MBar WDin
	daphnoides	CCVT CDoC CDul CLnd EBee EPfP GKir LRHS MBrN MSwo NWea SBLw SPer SPla SRms STre WDin WFar WGHP WJas WMou
	- 'Aglaia' (m)	CBcs CTri ECrN WIvy
	- 'Meikle' (f)	CAgr CWiW WGHP
	- 'Netta Statham' (m)	CWiW
	- 'Ovaro Udine' (m)	CWiW
	- 'Oxford Violet' (m)	ECrN WIvy
	- 'Sinker'	WIvy
	- 'Stewartstown' (m)	CWiW
	- 'Wynter Bloom' **new**	WGHP
	'E.A. Bowles'	see *S.* 'Bowles' Hybrid'
	x ***doniana*** 'Kumeti'	CWiW
	x ***ehrhartiana***	CNat

	Name	Suppliers
§	***elaeagnos***	CAgr CCVT CDoC CLnd CTho CTri EBee ECrN ENot EPfP GKir LRHS MBlu MBrN MRav SLon WDin WFar WGHP WIvy WMou
§	- subsp. ***angustifolia*** 🏆H4	CDul EBee ELan EMil MBar MRav MTis NLar NWea SRms STre WGHP
	'Elegantissima'	see *S.* x *pendulina* var. *elegantissima*
	eriocephala 'American Mackay' (m)	CWiW WGHP
	- 'Kerksii' (m)	CWiW
	- 'Mawdesley' (m)	CWiW
	- 'Russelliana' (f)	CWiW
§	'Erythroflexuosa'	CBcs CDoC CEnd EBee ELan ENot EPfP EPla GKir LAst LRHS MAsh MBar MGos MRav MWya NBea NBlu NWea SLim SPer SPla SPoG WDin WFar WHer WIvy WPat
	exigua	More than 30 suppliers
	fargesii	CBot CDoC CEnd CFee CFil EBee ELan EPfP GIBF GKir LEdu LRHS MBlu MDun MGos MRav SBrw SDix SMad SPoG SSpi WCru WFar WPGP WPat
§	x ***finnmarchica***	GEdr GIBF NWCA
	foetida (f)	GIBF
	formosa	see *S. arbuscula*
	fragilis	CCVT CDul CLnd ECrN GKir MRav NWea SBLw WDin WMou
	- 'Legomey'	WIvy
	x ***fruticosa*** 'McElroy' (f)	CWiW
§	***fruticulosa***	CBcs CTri GKev GTou NWCA SBla WPat
	'Fuiri-koriyanagi'	see *S. integra* 'Hakuro-nishiki'
	furcata	see *S. fruticulosa*
	glauca	CNat
	- subsp. ***callicarpaea*** (f)	GIBF
	'Golden Curls'	see *S.* 'Erythroflexuosa'
	gracilistyla	CTho ECrN SLPl WMou
§	- 'Melanostachys' (m)	More than 30 suppliers
	x ***grahamii*** (f)	GIBF
	x ***greyi***	NPro
	hastata (f)	GIBF
	- 'Wehrhahnii' (m) 🏆H4	More than 30 suppliers
	helvetica 🏆H4	CBcs EBee ELan EPfP GAbr GGar GKir LRHS LRav MAsh MBar MBlu MBri MDun MGos MRav NBir NEgg NFor NLon NWCA NWea SHBN SPer WDin WFar WHar WPat
	herbacea	EPot GEdr GIBF GTou NMen
	hibernica	see *S. phylicifolia*
	hookeriana	CFil CLnd CMHG CTho ELan EPla MBlu MBrN MRav SLPl SSpi WCFE WIvy WMou WPGP WTin
	incana	see *S. elaeagnos*
	integra 'Albomaculata'	see *S. integra* 'Hakuro-nishiki'
	- 'Flamingo' PBR	WOrn
§	- 'Hakuro-nishiki' (v)	More than 30 suppliers
	- 'Pendula' (f)	CEnd LRHS
	irrorata	CDul CLnd ECrN MBlu WGHP
	'Jacquinii'	see *S. alpina*
	kinuyanagi (m)	ELan EPla WGHP WIvy
§	***koriyanagi***	CWiW
	'Kuro-me'	see *S. gracilistyla* 'Melanostachys'
	x ***laestadiana***	GIBF
	lanata 🏆H4	More than 30 suppliers
	- 'Drake's Hybrid'	NMen
	lapponum	GIBF GKir NWea SRms
	- (m)	GIBF
	- var. ***daphneola*** (f)	GIBF
	- - (m)	GIBF
	liliputa	see *S. turczaninowii*
§	***lindleyana***	NBir
	lucida	ECrN
	'Maerd Brno' (f)	MBlu
	magnifica 🏆H4	CDul CEnd CFil CLnd CMCN EBee ELan EMil EPfP EPla GIBF GKir IDee LEdu LRHS MSte NWea SMad SPoG SSpi WCru WDin WFar WMou WPGP
§	'Mark Postill' (f)	CBgR CDoC EMil GBin LRHS MBNS SPla SPoG SPur WPen
	matsudana 'Tortuosa'	see *S. babylonica* var. *pekinensis* 'Tortuosa'
	- 'Tortuosa Aureopendula'	see *S.* 'Erythroflexuosa'
	'Melanostachys'	see *S. gracilistyla* 'Melanostachys'
	x ***meyeriana***	WIvy
	- 'Lumley' (f)	CWiW
	x ***mollissima*** var. ***hippophaifolia*** 'Jefferies' (m)	CWiW
	- - 'Notts Spaniard' (m)	CWiW
	- - 'Stinchcombe'	WIvy
	- - 'Trustworthy' (m)	CWiW
	- var. ***undulata*** 'Kottenheider Weide' (f)	CWiW
	moupinensis	EPfP
§	***myrsinifolia***	EPla MBlu NSti WGHP
§	***myrsinites***	GIBF
	- var. ***jacquiniana***	see *S. alpina*
	myrtilloides	CLyd
	- 'Pink Tassels' (m)	EHyt MBrN NWCA SIng
	myrtilloides x ***repens***	see *S.* x *finnmarchica*
	nakamurana var. ***yezoalpina***	CEnd CFai CFee EPot GEdr GIBF GKir LRHS MRav NLAp NLRH NPro WFar WIvy WPat
	nepalensis	see *S. lindleyana*
	nigricans	see *S. myrsinifolia*
	nivalis	see *S. reticulata* subsp. *nivalis*
	x ***obtusifolia***	GIBF
	'Onusta' (m)	EWTr
	onychiophylla (f)	GIBF
	x ***ovata***	CLyd NMen
§	x ***pendulina*** var. ***elegantissima***	CTho ECrN
	pentandra	CAgr CBot CDul CLnd ECrN LRav NWea WDin WFar WMou
	- 'Patent Lumley'	CWiW
	'Philip's Fancy'	NWCA
§	***phylicifolia***	ECrN WGHP WMou
	- 'Malham' (m)	CWiW
	polaris	CLyd GIBF
	x ***punctata***	GIBF
§	***purpurea***	CBcs CCVT CDul GIBF MBrN NWea SRms WDin WMou
	- 'Abbeys'	WIvy
	- 'Brittany Green' (f)	CWiW
	- 'Continental Reeks' (f)	CWiW WIvy
	- 'Dark Dicks' (f)	CWiW WGHP WIvy
	- 'Dicky Meadows' (m)	CAgr CWiW WGHP WIvy
*	- 'Elegantissima'	WGHP
	- 'Goldstones' (m)	CAgr CWiW WIvy
	- f. ***gracilis***	see *S. purpurea* 'Nana'
	- 'Green Dicks' (m)	CAgr CWiW WIvy
	- 'Helix'	see *S. purpurea*
	- 'Howki' (m)	WMou
	- 'Irette' (m)	CWiW
	- 'Jagiellonka' (f)	CWiW WIvy
	- var. ***japonica***	see *S. koriyanagi*
	- subsp. ***lambertiana***	CWiW WIvy
	- 'Lancashire Dicks' (m)	CWiW
	- 'Leicestershire Dicks' (m)	CWiW
	- 'Light Dicks'	CWiW
	- 'Lincolnshire Dutch' (f)	CWiW

§ - 'Nana' CLyd EPfP EWTr MWhi NLar SLPl SLon SPer SPur STre WFar WGHP WMoo
- 'Nancy Saunders' (f) CHad CTho CWiW EHoe EPPr EPla GBuc MBNS MBlu MBrN MBri MRav MSte NPro NSti SCoo SMHy SUsu WCot WGHP WIvy WPen
- 'Pendula' ♀H4 CEnd CWib ECrN ENot LRHS MAsh MBar MRav MSwo NBlu NWea SPer SPoG WDin
- 'Read' (f) CWiW WGHP
- 'Reeks' (f) CWiW
- 'Richartii' (f) CWiW WGHP
- 'Uralensis' (f) CWiW
- 'Welsh Dicks' **new** WGHP
pyrenaica CLyd EHyt GIBF NWCA
repens ECrN GIBF GKir MBar SRms STre WDin
§ - var. ***argentea*** ENot EPfP GIBF MBar MRav MWhi NWCA NWea SLim SPer WDin WFar
- 'Armando'PBR MGos NLar
- 'Iona' (m) CLyd MBar
- ***pendula*** see *S.* 'Boyd's Pendulous'
- 'Voorthuizen' (f) CWib EHol EHyt MBar MGos WDin WGer
reticulata ♀H4 EPot GCrs GIBF GKir GTou NBir NLAp NMen NRya NSla NWoo WPat
§ - subsp. ***nivalis*** GIBF
retusa CTri GIBF GKir GTou NBir NLAp WPat
retusa x ***pyrenaica*** ECho
rosmarinifolia hort. see *S. elaeagnos* subsp. *angustifolia*
x ***rubens*** 'Basfordiana' (m) CDoC CDul CLnd CRez CTho CWiW EPla EWes MBNS MRav NEgg NWea WGHP WMou
- 'Bouton Aigu' CWiW
- 'Farndon' CWiW
- 'Flanders Red' (f) CWiW WGHP
- 'Fransgeel Rood' (m) CWiW
- 'Glaucescens' (m) CWiW WGHP
- 'Golden Willow' CWiW
- 'Jaune de Falaise' CWiW
- 'Jaune Hâtive' CWiW
- 'Laurina' CWiW
- 'Natural Red' (f) CWiW
- 'Parsons' CWiW
- 'Rouge Ardennais' CWiW
- 'Rouge Folle' CWiW
- 'Russet' (f) CWiW
x ***rubra*** CWiW
- 'Abbey's Harrison' (f) CWiW
- 'Continental Osier' (f) CWiW
- 'Eugenei' (m) CDul CTho ECrN EPla GQui MBlu WBcn WIvy WMou
- 'Fidkin' (f) CWiW
- 'Harrison's' (f) CWiW
- 'Harrison's Seedling A' (f) CWiW
- 'Mawdesley' (f) CWiW
- 'Mawdesley Seedling A' (f) CWiW
- 'Pyramidalis' CWiW
Scarlet Curls = 'Scarcuzam' WPat
x ***sepulcralis*** NWea
- 'Aokautere' CWiW
- 'Caradoc' CWiW
§ - var. ***chrysocoma*** CBcs CDoC CDul CSBt CWib ECrN ENot EPfP EWTr GKir LAst LBuc LRHS MBar MGos MWat NBea NBee NBlu NEgg SBLw SCoo SHBN SLim SPer SPoG WDin WOrn
serpyllifolia CLyd CTri EHyt GIBF NLAp NMen WPat
serpyllifolia x ***retusa*** EPot NWCA
serpyllum see *S. fruticulosa*
'Setsuka' see *S. udensis* 'Sekka'
x ***simulatrix*** CLyd EHyt EPot GIBF MBar NWCA
x ***sobrina*** GIBF
x ***stipularis*** (f) CMHG NWea
§ 'Stuartii' GAbr GIBF MBar NMen NWCA SRms
subopposita CDul EBee ELan EWes MBNS MBar NPro SLon STre
x ***tetrapla*** GIBF
thomasii GIBF
'Tora'PBR LRav
triandra LRav WMou
- 'Black German' (m) CWiW
- 'Black Hollander' (m) CAgr CWiW WIvy
- 'Black Maul' CAgr CWiW WGHP
- 'Grisette de Falaise' CWiW
- 'Grisette Droda' (f) CWiW
- 'Long Bud' CWiW
- 'Noir de Challans' CWiW
- 'Noir de Touraine' CWiW
- 'Noir de Villaines' (m) CWiW WGHP WIvy
- 'Rouge d'Orléans' ECrN
- 'Sarda d'Anjou' CWiW
- 'Semperflorens' (m) CNat
- 'Whissender' (m) CAgr CWiW WIvy
x ***tsugaluensis*** 'Ginme' (f) CMHG SLPl WPat
§ ***turczaninowii*** (m) GIBF
§ ***udensis*** 'Sekka' (m) CMHG CTho EBee ECtt ELan NBir NWea STre WFar WGHP WIvy WMou
uva-ursi CLyd GIBF
viminalis CCVT CDul CLnd ECrN LBuc NWea WDin WGHP WMou
- 'Brown Merrin' CAgr WIvy
- 'Green Gotz' CWiW WIvy
- 'Reader's Red' (m) CAgr WIvy
- 'Riefenweide' WIvy
- 'Yellow Osier' CAgr WIvy
vitellina 'Pendula' see *S. alba* 'Tristis'
§ ***waldsteiniana*** GIBF MBar NWCA
x ***wimmeriana*** SRms
'Yelverton' see *S. alba* subsp. *vitellina* 'Yelverton'

Salsola (*Chenopodiaceae*)

soda **new** EUnu

Salvia ✿ (*Lamiaceae*)

ACE 2172 SPin
B&SWJ 9032 blue, from Guatemala WCru
BWJ 9062 pale blue, from Guatamala WCru
CC&McK 77 GTou
CD&R 1148 WHil
CD&R 1162 CAby SPin
CD&R 1495 SPin
CD&R 3071 CStr SPin
acetabulosa see *S. multicaulis*
aethiopis CPle CSev CStr LPhx SDnm SGar SPav SPin WWye XPep
§ ***africana*** CPle CStr GGar LPio SPin WDyG WWye XPep
africana-caerulea see *S. africana*
africana-lutea see *S. aurea*
agnes CStr LIck MRod SPin
albimaculata SBla SPin
algeriensis CSpe LPhx SPin

	'Allen Chickering'	XPep
	amarissima	CPle CStr MRod SPin
	'Amber'	SPin SUsu
	ambigens	see *S. guaranitica* 'Blue Enigma'
§	***amplexicaulis***	CPle EPPr MGol NBPC NLar SPin WCAu WPer WWye XPep
	angustifolia Cav.	see *S. reptans*
	angustifolia Mich.	see *S. azurea*
	'Anthony Parker'	CPle CStr MRod SDys SPin
	apiana	CArn EPyc EUnu GPoy MDKP MGol MHer MSal SGar SPin WCot XPep
	argentea ♀H3	More than 30 suppliers
	arizonica	CPle CPom CStr CWCL LIck MLLN MRod SDys SPin XPep
	atrocyanea	CAby CPle CSpe CStr EPyc LIck MAsh MLLN SDys SGar SPin SUsu WDyG WWlt WWye
	aucheri	CPle GBar GCal
§	***aurea***	CBot CHal CHll CPle CSev CStr EKen ELan EShb GGar LPio MOak MSte SAga SGar SPin WDyG WPer XPep
	- 'Kirstenbosch'	CPle CSev CStr EBee ECtt EMan MAsh MLLN NCGa SDys SPin WCot WHer WHil WOut WPer WRos WWye
	aurita	LIck SPin
	- var. ***galpinii*** **new**	SPin
	austriaca	CPle CStr SHFr SPin WPer
§	***azurea***	CPle CRWN EBee EUnu LPhx LPio MRod MSte SAga SBod SMrm SPin XPep
	- var. ***grandiflora***	CStr EBee SPin
	bacheriana	see *S. buchananii*
§	***barrelieri***	CPle SHFr SPin WOut XPep
	'Bee's Bliss'	XPep
	'Belhaven'	WDyG
	bertolonii	see *S. pratensis* Bertolonii Group
	bicolor	see *S. barrelieri*
	'Black Knight' **new**	MRod SPin
	blancoana	CArn CMea CPle CSLe CStr ECha ELau GBar LEdu MAsh MHer MLLN MOak MSte SAga SDys SPin
	blepharophylla	CPle CPrp CSpe CStr EBee ECtt EShb LAst LIck MAsh MHar MHer MRod MSte NCGa SAga SDnm SPav SPin SRot WPen WWye
	- 'Diablo'	ECtt SDys SPin
	- 'Painted Lady' **new**	MRod SPin
	'Blue Chiquita'	CStr LIck MRod SDys SPin
	'Blue Sky' **new**	MRod
	'Blue Vein' **new**	NPri
§	***buchananii*** ♀H1+3	CDoC CHal CHll CPle CPom CSWP CSam CStr EBee ELan EPfP GQui IFro LIck MAsh MHar MHer MLLN MRod SAga SChu SPav SPin SPoG SRkn SWal WFar WWol
	bulleyana misapplied	see *S. flava* var. *megalantha*
	bulleyana	CBgR EChP EMFP EWes GBar LEdu LIck MDKP MHer MLLN NLar SDnm SHFr SPav SWal WCru WFar WLin
	cacaliifolia ♀H1+3	CPle CPne CRHN CSpe CStr CWCL ECtt GBar LIck MEHN MHer MLLN MNrw MRod MSte SGar SHFr SPin SRkn SUsu WOut WSHC WWye
	cadmica	SPin
	caerulea misapplied	see *S. guaranitica* 'Black and Blue'
	caerulea L.	see *S. africana*
	caespitosa	EHyt GEdr NWCA SBla SPin
	campanulata	CPle CPom LPhx MGol SPin WCot
	- CC 4038	ITer
	- CC 4193	MGol
	- CC&McK 1071	CFir
	- GWJ 9294	WCru
	canariensis	CFil CPle CStr EShb IGor MLLN MSte SHFr SPin WWye XPep
	- f. ***albiflora***	WOut
	- f. ***candidissima***	XPep
	candelabrum ♀H3-4	CArn CDes CMea CPle CSpe ECtt LPhx MHer MLLN MRod MSte SAga SHFr SPav SPin WCHb WCot WEas WKif WSHC WWlt WWye XPep
	candidissima	SPin
	canescens	XPep
	cardinalis	see *S. fulgens*
	carduacea	MRod SPin
	castanea	CAby CPle CPom MHar
	cedrosensis **new**	SDys
§	***chamaedryoides***	CPle CPom CSev CStr CWCL LPhx MAsh MRod NDov SBla SChu SDys SGar SPin SSpi WSHC XPep
	- var. ***isochroma***	MAsh SBch SDys SPin
	- 'Marine Blue'	MAsh MRod
	- silver-leaved	CAby CBgR CStr LPhx MSte SAga SPin XPep
	chamaedryoides* x *microphylla	XPep
	chamelaeagnea	CStr SDys SPin XPep
	chapalensis	CStr SAga SPin
	chiapensis	CPle CStr MAsh MRod SPin
	chinensis	see *S. japonica*
	'Christine Yeo'	CDes CDoC CPle EChP ECtt EPPr EPyc GAbr GGar LIck MAsh MDKP MRod MSte SBch SDys SGar SPav SPin SUsu SWal WDyG WHil WMnd WPGP WPtf WSHC WWye
	cinnabarina	MRod
	cleistogama misapplied	see *S. glutinosa*
	cleistogama DeBary & Paul	MHer
	clevelandii	CPle MGol MHer SPav XPep
	- 'Winnifred Gilman'	SDys SPin
	clinopodioides	SPin
	coahuilensis misapplied	see *S. greggii* x *S. serpyllifolia*
	coahuilensis	CAby CMdw EBla LIck LPhx LSou MAsh NDov SAga SGar SHFr SMeo SMrm SPin SUsu WSHC WWye
	coccinea	MGol MHer MRod MSte SHFr SPin WWye
	- 'Bicolor' **new**	MRod
	- 'Brenthurst'	CStr MRod SDys SPin
	- 'Coral Nymph' (Nymph Series)	ECtt LDai LIck LRHS MGol MRod SChu SDnm SDys SMrm SPav SPin SUsu
	- 'Indigo'	see *S. guaranitica* 'Indigo Blue'
	- 'Lady in Red' (Nymph Series) ♀H3	CBre CStr ECtt LIck MRod SDys SPav
*	- 'Snow Nymph' (Nymph Series)	LIck
	columbariae	MRod SPin
	concolor misapplied	see *S. guaranitica*
	concolor Lamb.	CDes CPle CPne CStr GCal MRod SPin WDyG WOut WSHC WWye
	confertiflora	More than 30 suppliers
	corrugata	More than 30 suppliers
	'Crème Caramel' **new**	SDys
	cristata	see *S. officinalis* 'Crispa'
	cryptantha	WLin
	cyanescens	CPle CStu EPot SPin XPep
	daghestanica **new**	SDys
	darcyi misapplied	see *S. roemeriana*

darcyi J. Compton	CFil CHll CPle CPom CStr EChP EPyc LIck LPhx MAsh SAga SDys SHFr SPin SSpi WEas WSHC XPep
'Darky' **new**	SPin
davidsonii	SPin
'Dear Anja'	see *S.* x *superba* 'Dear Anja'
dentata	CStr EUnu SDys SPin WCot WOut XPep
desoleana	XPep
digitaloides BWJ 7777	SPin WCru
discolor 🏆H1	More than 30 suppliers
* - ***nigra***	CMdw WDin
disermas	CPle EUnu MRod SPin SPlb XPep
disjuncta	CStr MAsh MRod SPin
- 'Strybing' **new**	MRod
divinorum	EOHP GPoy MGol MRod MSal WWye
dolichantha	EBee EMFP EPyc EShb GFlt MDKP MGol MHar MWrn NBPC SBch SBod SPin WHil WLin WWye
dolomitica	CStr SPav SPin XPep
dombeyi	CPne CStr SDys SPin
dominica	SPin XPep
dorisiana	CFee CPle CPne CSpe CStr ELan EOHP EUnu LPhx MAsh MLLN MRod MSte SAga SDys SPin WGHP WOut WWye
dorrii	CStr SPin
eigii	SPin
§ ***elegans***	CPle CSev CStr ELau EWes LIck MAsh MSte NVic SOkd WFar WGHP WOut WWye
- 'Honey Melon'	EOHP EUnu MAsh MRod
§ - 'Scarlet Pineapple'	More than 30 suppliers
- 'Sonoran Red'	SDys
* - 'Tangerine'	CArn CDoC CPrp CWan EDAr ELau EOHP GBar GGar LAst LFol LSou MBow MGol MHer MRod NGHP SBch SDnm SPet SPin SWal WGwG
evansiana	SPin
- BWJ 8013	SPin WCru
fallax	CStr MRod SPin
farinacea	SPin
- 'Rhea'	LIck LRHS
- 'Strata'	ECtt LRHS MRod SDys
- 'Victoria' 🏆H3	CStr ELau MHer MRod NArg SDys
flava	SPin
§ - var. ***megalantha***	CHea CPle ELan GBin LRHS NChi NGdn WBor WFar WPer WWye
forreri	CDes EBee MAsh MRod SAga SDys SPin SSpi WPGP WSPU
- CD&R 1269	CPle CStr
§ ***forsskaolii***	More than 30 suppliers
'Frieda Dixon'	EBee EOHP LSou
§ ***fruticosa***	CArn CPle CPrp CStr ELau EOHP LRHS SIde WGHP XPep
§ ***fulgens*** 🏆H3	CAby CPle CPne CSec CStr GBar IFro ILis MAsh MHer MRod SBch SGar SHFr SPer SPin SRkn WFar WOut WRha WWeb WWlt WWye
gesneriiflora	CAby CPle CPne CStr ECtt MHom MRod MSte SPin WWye
- 'Tequila' **new**	MAsh MRod
gilliesii	CStr MRod SPin XPep
glechomifolia **new**	MRod SPin
§ ***glutinosa***	CArn CHad CPle EBee ECtt EPPr EPyc GCal LDai MGol MNrw MRod NBro SAga SMar SPav SPin SSpi WCAu WGwG WOut WPer WWye
gracilis **new**	SPin
grahamii	see *S. microphylla* var. *microphylla*
greggii	CBot CPle EBee ECtt EWes LPio MHer MRod MSte MTis SUsu WKif WPer XPep
- CD&R	MRod
- CD&R 1148	CPle LIck LSou SDys WSPU
- 'Alba'	CBgR CHal CPle CSev EBee ENot EOHP LIck MAsh MHer MRod NBur NGHP SDys SPin WSHC WWol XPep
- 'Blush Pink'	see *S. microphylla* 'Pink Blush'
- 'Caramba' (v)	CBrm CStr EBee EOHP EPyc EShb EWin MAsh MLLN MRod NGHP SAga SDnm SHGN SPav SPoG WCra WWol
- 'Dark Dancer'	see *S.* x *jamensis* 'Dark Dancer'
- 'Desert Blaze'	see *S.* x *jamensis* 'Desert Blaze
- 'Devon Cream'	see *S. greggii* 'Sungold'
- 'Furman's Red'	XPep
- 'Keter's Red'	CPle MRod
- ***lycioides***	see *S. greggii* x *S. serpyllifolia*
- 'Magenta'	MDKP
* - 'Navajo Cream'	EPyc WFar
* - 'Navajo Dark Purple'	EPyc LSou WFar
* - 'Navajo Salmon Red'	EPyc WFar
* - 'Navajo White'	EPyc LSou WFar
- 'Peach' misapplied	see *S.* x *jamensis* 'Pat Vlasto'
I - 'Peach'	CDes CDoC CPle CSpe EBee ELau EPfP LPhx LPio LRHS MAsh MDKP MHer MLLN MRod MSte NCGa NDov NGHP SAga SDnm SGar SPav SPin SUsu WMnd WWeb WWol
- 'Plum Wine'	see *S.* x *jamensis* 'Plum Wine'
- 'San Isidro Moon'	see *S.* x *jamensis* 'San Isidro Moon'
- 'Sierra San Antonio'	see *S.* x *jamensis* 'Sierra San Antonio'
- 'Sparkler' (v)	CPle MAsh MRod SBch SBri
- 'Stormy Pink'	CDes CSpe CStr MAsh MRod WPGP
§ - 'Sungold'	CDes CPle CStr EPfP LIck LPhx LRHS MAsh MLLN MRod NGHP SAga SBch SDys SHGN SPin SUsu SWal WMnd WPGP WSan WWeb WWol
- variegated	CBot XPep
- yellow-flowered	LPio LRHS XPep
greggii x ***serpyllifolia***	CAbP CFil CPle EBee EMFP EPyc LPhx LPio MAsh NGHP SDys SGar SPin WPGP WWye XPep
§ ***guaranitica***	CBcs CBot CFil CHEx CHrt CPle CPne CTbh ECtt EShb GCra LPio MHer SAga SDnm SPav SPer SPin SRkn WCHb WPGP WSan WWlt WWye
- 'Argentine Skies'	CPle CStr EPyc EVFa LIck LPhx LPio MRod SAga SChu SDys SMrm SPin WDyG WPGP WWlt WWye
§ - 'Black and Blue'	CFil CPLG CPle CPne CPrp CRHN CSWP CSev CStr EBee EPPr EVFa ITim LIck LPhx MAsh MAvo MFOX MRod MSte SDnm SGar SPav SPin SUsu WPGP WPer WPrP WWye
§ - 'Blue Enigma' 🏆H3-4	More than 30 suppliers
§ - 'Indigo Blue'	EPfP MLLN MRod NEgg WSan WWlt
- 'Purple Splendor' **new**	CPne
- purple-flowered **new**	CSam
haematodes	see *S. pratensis* Haematodes Group
haenkei	CStr MRod SPin SUsu
heldreichiana	CSec CSev CStr SPin
henryi	SPin

Plant	Suppliers
hians	CFir CPle EBee EWTr EWin GBBs GBar LAst LPhx MDKP MLLN MNrw SBla SDnm SGar SPav SPin SRms WCot WHoo WPer WWye
- CC 1787	SPin
- GWJ 9261	WCru
hierosolymitana	CPle
hispanica misapplied	see *S. lavandulifolia*
hispanica L.	SPin
holwayi **new**	SPin
horminum	see *S. viridis* var. *comata*
huberi	CStr SPin
hypargeia	CPle
indica	SPin XPep
'Indigo Spires'	CHll CHrt CPle CSpe CStr ECha ECtt EGra EShb EVFa GCra GMaP LPhx MAsh MHar MHom MLLN MRod NCGa SBla SMrm SPin SUsu WDyG WOut WPen WSHC WWye
interrupta	CPle CStr EHol EOHP EWes LIck MAsh SChu SHFr SPin WPen XPep
involucrata ♀H3	CFir CPLG CPle CPom CSev CStr GCal GCra GQui MAsh MHar MRod NBro NBur SDys SMrm SPet SPin WOut WSHC
- 'Bethellii' ♀H3-4	More than 30 suppliers
- 'Boutin' ♀H3	CPle CStr GBri MAJR MAsh MLLN MRod SAga SBri SDys
§ - 'Hadspen'	CHad CHll CSam CStr LIck MSte SPin WKif WWye
- 'Mrs Pope'	see *S. involucrata* 'Hadspen'
I - var. ***puberula***	CPle CStr SDys SPin
I - - from Hidalgo **new**	MAsh MRod
I - - 'Cyaccado' **new**	MRod
- - 'El Butano'	MRod
- var. ***puberula*** x ***karwinskii*** **new**	MAsh
- 'Smith's College' **new**	MAsh MRod
iodantha	CPle CStr LIck MRod SAga SPin WWye
- 'Louis Saso' **new**	MRod
x ***jamensis***	CStr MDKP SDys XPep
- - CPN 5096	SAga
- 'Cherry Queen'	CPle CSpe CStr EBee LSou MAsh MRod SAga SDys WFar WWol WWye
- 'Devantville'	CAby CPle LPhx SAga
§ - 'Dark Dancer'	CPle MRod
§ - 'Desert Blaze' (v)	CBgR CDes CDoC CPle CStr EBee EChP ECtt EMan EVFa LIck MAsh MDKP MHar MRod NCGa NDov NGHP SDys SPin SWal WCot WHer WSPU WWeb
- 'Dyson's Orangy Pink' **new**	MRod
- 'El Durazno'	CPle LPio
- 'James Compton'	LIck LPio LSou MSte SDys SGar SIgm WHoo
- 'La Luna'	CPle CPom CPrp CSam CSev CTri ECtt EPfP EVFa LPhx LPio MAsh MHar MHer MRod MSte NDov SAga SBri SDys SGar SHGN SPin SWal WFar WMnd WPGP WSHC WWol WWye
- 'La Siesta'	CPle CWCL EBee LPio MAsh MRod SDys WWeb
- 'La Tarde'	CAby CPle CStr CTri LPio MAsh MRod MSte SAga SBch SDys
- 'Lemon Sorbet'	SDys
- 'Los Lirios' ♀H3-4	CBgR CPle CPom CStr CTri EVFa LIck MRod MSte SAga SBri SDys SMrm SPin WSPU
§ - 'Maraschino'	CAbP CStr MRod SDys SMrm WCot WMnd
* - 'Mauve'	SDys
- 'Moonlight Over Ashwood' (v)	CPle MAsh MRod SDys SPin SUsu
- 'Moonlight Serenade'	CAby CPle CSev CStr EBee EWin LPhx MAsh MRod SAga SBch SDys SHGN WHil WHoo WSPU WWeb
§ - 'Pat Vlasto'	CAby CPle CStr EBee EPyc LIck MRod SDys SMrm SPin WHoo WPen WWye
- 'Pleasant Pink'	CPle CSev EBee LIck MAsh MRod SAga SPin WPGP
§ - 'Plum Wine'	CPle MRod
§ - 'Raspberry Royale' ♀H3-4	More than 30 suppliers
§ - 'Red Velvet'	CPle MAsh MHom MRod SUsu WEas
§ - 'San Isidro Moon'	CPle MAsh MRod
- 'Señorita Leah' **new**	MRod
§ - 'Sierra San Antonio'	CPle CSpe ECtt MAsh MRod SDys SMrm SUsu
§ - 'Trebah'	CAby CDes CPle CPom CTbh ECre EPyc LSou MAsh MRod MSte SDys SGar SPav SPin SRot WWye
§ - 'Trenance'	CPle CTbh ECre EPyc LRHS LSou MAsh MRod MSte SDys SGar SPav SPin SRot
- white-flowered **new**	SPin
§ ***japonica***	CArn CPle CStr SPin WWye
judaica	CPle EBee EChP NChi SPin XPep
jurisicii	CArn CFir CPle CStr CWib EPyc EShb GKev MGol NLar SGar SPav SPin WJek WOut WWye
- pink-flowered	CStr SPin
karwinskyi	CStr MRod SPin
lanceolata	CStr SPin XPep
lanigera	SPin
§ ***lavandulifolia***	More than 30 suppliers
- white-flowered **new**	MAsh
lavanduloides **new**	CStr
lemmonii	see *S. microphylla* var. *wislizenii*
leptophylla	see *S. reptans*
leucantha ♀H1	More than 30 suppliers
- 'Eder' **new**	MAsh MRod
- 'Midnight'	LIck
- 'Purple Velvet'	CPle CStr MAsh MHar MRod SDys SPin
I - 'San Marcos Lavender' **new**	SPin
- 'Santa Barbara'	MAsh MRod SDys
leucophylla	CBot CStr MRod SPin XPep
- NNS 01-375	SPin
- NNS 95-445	WCot
littae **new**	MRod SPin
longispicata	MRod SPin
longistyla **new**	SPin
lycioides misapplied	see *S. greggii* x *S. serpyllifolia*
lycioides A. Gray	CAbP CHll CPle CStr MRod SDys SPin SRkn WDyG XPep
lyrata	CBgR CPle EBee EMan EOHP ITim MDKP MGol MRod MSal MSph SGar SHFr SPin SUsu WOut WWye
- 'Burgundy Bliss'	SHar
- 'Purple Knockout'	EChP EMFP EMan EPyc GKev GSki LAst LPhx MBri MRod NGHP SGar SPav SPin SPoG WHrl WWeb
- 'Purple Vulcano' **new**	EMag
macellaria misapplied	see *S. microphylla*
macellaria Epling	CSam
madrensis	CStr LIck MOak MRod SPin
- 'Dunham'	MAsh
'Maraschino'	see *S.* x *jamensis* 'Maraschino'
melissodora	CStr MAsh MRod SDys
mellifera	CArn CPle CStr SPin XPep

	merjamie	CPle SPin XPep
	- 'Mint-sauce'	CElw CPen ELan EMar GBar SHFr WHer WPer
	mexicana	CPle CPrp LIck SBch SPin SSpi WWye
	- T&K 550	CArn CBot
	- 'La Placita' **new**	MRod
	- 'Limelight'	CStr MRod
	- 'Lollie Jackson' **new**	MRod
	- var. ***major***	MRod
	- var. ***mexicana*** **new**	MRod
	- var. ***minor***	CPle CStr MRod
	- - CD&R 1438	MRod
	- 'Puerto de la Zorra' **new**	MRod
	- 'Snowflake' **new**	MRod
	- 'Tula'	MRod SDys
	meyeri	CStr MRod SPin SUsu
§	***microphylla***	CArn CHrt CMHG CPle CPom CPrp CWan ELau EOHP EWes GBar GGar LFol MBow MChe MHer NSti SBri SHFr SPet SSpi SYvo WCru WHCG WPer XPep
	- CD&R 1142	MRod
	- CD&R 1495	MRod
	- ***alba***	SUsu
	- 'Cerro Potosi'	CBgR CMdw CPle CPom CSev CSpe CStr EBee MAsh MLLN MRod MSte SAga SBch SDys SGar SHFr SMrm SPin WDyG WHil WPen WWye
	- 'Dieciocho de Marzo'	CPle MAsh MRod
	- 'Hot Lips' **new**	MRod SPin
	- 'Huntington'	CPle EOHP
	- hybrid, purple-flowered	EBee GCal
	- 'Kew Red' ♀H3-4	CDoC CFir CPle CSpe CStr EBee MAsh MNrw MRod SAga SBch SPin WHoo WPen WWeb
	- 'La Trinidad'	CPle MAsh MRod
§	- var. ***microphylla***	More than 30 suppliers
	- - 'La Foux'	CAby CHea CPle ECtt LPhx LSou MDKP MRod SAga SBch SDys SMeo SMrm WSPU
	- - 'Newby Hall' ♀H3-4	CAby CBrm CPle CStr EBee ECtt EWes LIck LPhx MRod MSte SChu SMeo WPGP
	- var. ***neurepia***	see *S. microphylla* var. *microphylla*
	- 'Orange Door'	CPle MAsh MRod
	- 'Oregon Peach'	LRHS
	- 'Oxford'	CPle CStr MRod SAga SDys SPin
§	- 'Pink Blush' ♀H3-4	CPle CPne CPom EBee ECtt ELan ENot EPfP EVFa GBri LRHS MAsh MHer MLLN MMil MRod MSte NGHP SMrm SPin SSpi WKif WPGP WSHC
	- 'Pleasant View' ♀H3-4	CPle EWin MAsh MRod
	- 'Red Velvet'	see *S.* x *jamensis* 'Red Velvet'
§	- 'Ruth Stungo' (v)	CPle EOHP
	- 'San Carlos Festival'	CDes EBee ECtt MAsh MRod SBch SDys SPin
	- 'Trebah Lilac White'	see *S.* x *jamensis* 'Trebah'
	- 'Trelawny Rose Pink'	see *S.* 'Trelawny'
	- 'Trelissick Creamy Yellow'	see *S.* 'Trelissick'
	- 'Trenance Lilac Pink'	see *S.* x *jamensis* 'Trenance'
	- 'Trewithen Cerise'	see *S.* 'Trewithen'
	- 'Variegata' splashed	see *S. microphylla* 'Ruth Stungo'
	- 'Wild Watermelon'	CPle EBee MAsh MRod SDys SPoG WWeb
§	- var. ***wislizeni***	CPle CStr MAsh MRod SDys SPin WPer
	- 'Zaragoza'	CPle MRod
	microstegia	WLin
	miltiorhiza	CArn MGol MSal SPin
	miniata	CPle CStr LIck MAsh MRod SDys SPin
	misella	CSpe CWCL SPin
	mohavensis **new**	SPin
	'Monrovia' **new**	EWin
	moorcroftiana	MGol SDnm SPin
	'Mrs Beard'	XPep
	muelleri misapplied	see *S. greggii* x *S. serpyllifolia*
	muirii **new**	SPin
	'Mulberry Wine'	CDes CHII CPle EBee ECtt MAJR MAsh MRod SAga SDys SPin SUsu WKif WWeb
§	***multicaulis*** ♀H4	CPle ECha EMan ETow GBri MAsh MSte SHFr SPin WEas WSHC
	munzii	CFir XPep
*	***murrayi***	CAbP MAsh SPin WCot
	namaensis	CSpe CStr LIck SDys SPin XPep
	napifolia	CStr EBee EKen GBBs GSki LPhx MGol SAga SBod SDnm SPav SPin WGwG WSPU
	'Nel' **new**	EMon
	nemorosa	NLar SHFr SPin SRms XPep
	- 'Amethyst' ♀H4	More than 30 suppliers
	- 'Blue Mound' **new**	ENot
	- 'Caradonna'	CPom EBee ECGP EChP EMan EMon EPPr EPfP ERou EWTr IBal LDai MLLN MNrw NDov NGby NLar NMyG NPro SDys SMHy SMer SPoG SSpe SUsu WAul WCot WPtf
	- East Friesland	see *S. nemorosa* 'Ostfriesland'
	- 'Lubecca' ♀H4	CPrp EBee EBrs ECGP ECtt EHrv EMan EPfP EPla LRHS MLLN MWgw NCGa NDov SPer WCAu WMnd
	- Marcus = 'Haeumanarc'	CElw CFir EBee EBrs ELan EMan ENot EPfP EPyc LAst LRHS LSRN MBNS MBri MLLN MTis NDov NLar SDys SMer SPla SPoG SUsu WCot WHil
	- 'Midsummer'	MGol
§	- 'Ostfriesland' ♀H4	More than 30 suppliers
	- 'Phoenix Pink'	LPhx
	- 'Plumosa'	see *S. nemorosa* 'Pusztaflamme'
	- 'Porzellan' ♀H4	ECtt
§	- 'Pusztaflamme' ♀H4	CPrp CStr EBee EChP ECha ECtt EMan EPfP EVFa LRHS MMHG NPro NSti SBla SPin SUsu WAul WCAu
	- 'Rose Queen'	CAby CStr ECtt EMFP EPPr GKir GSki LAst NBir NDlv SDys SPer SPin SPla WFar
	- 'Rosenwein'	CBrm CElw CSam EBee EMan EPyc GBuc LDai LPhx MDKP SMrm
	- 'Royal Distinction'	ECtt EMan MSph
	- 'Schwellenburg'	EBee EMan EVFa IPot LBuc MSph SMrm SPoG SPur SUsu WCot WHil
§	- subsp. ***tesquicola***	EBee ECha EGoo LPhx MNFA NLar SMrm WGHP
	- 'Wesuwe'	CPle EBee NDov NGby WGHP
	neurepia	see *S. microphylla* var. *microphylla*
	nilotica	CArn CPle EBrs EKen MGol SHFr SPin WHer XPep
	nipponica	CPle
	- B&SWJ 5829	SPin WCru
	- 'Fuji Snow' (v)	EMan EWes MLLN WCot
	nubicola	CBgR CPle CStr EPPr GPoy LDai MGol MHer SPin WOut WWye XPep
	officinalis	More than 30 suppliers

	Name	Suppliers
	- 'Alba'	see *S. officinalis* 'Albiflora'
§	- 'Albiflora'	ECtt EGoo EOHP GBar MLLN NGHP NWoo SBch SPin WCHb WJek WPer XPep
N	- 'Aurea' ambig.	CWib GPoy MBar NPri
	- 'Berggarten'	CArn CBot CPrp ECha ELau EMan EOHP EPfP EUnu GBar GCal GKir LPhx LPio MHer MRav NSti SChu SDix SPin SSvw WCFE WCot WHer WMnd XPep
I	- 'Blackcurrant'	CHal EUnu LSou SPin WGwG
§	- broad-leaved	CBot CSWP CWan ELau MHer SBch WGHP WJek WWye
	- 'Crispa'	SPin WCHb XPep
	- 'Extrakta'	EOHP EUnu
	- 'Herrenhausen'	EVFa MSte
§	- 'Icterina' (v) 🏆H4	More than 30 suppliers
	- 'Kew Gold'	ELau MRav WJek
	- ***latifolia***	see *S. officinalis* broad-leaved
	- 'Minor'	EGoo
	- narrow-leaved	see *S. lavandulifolia*
*	- 'Pink Splash' (v)	WCHb
	- ***prostrata***	see *S. lavandulifolia*
	- 'Purpurascens' 🏆H4	More than 30 suppliers
	- 'Purpurascens Variegata' (v)	CStr GBar MAsh SPet WEas
	- 'Robin Hill'	GBar
	- 'Rosea'	SECG WBcn WCHb
	- tangerine	see *S. elegans* 'Tangerine'
	- Tomentosa Group	CArn
	- 'Tricolor' (v)	More than 30 suppliers
	- 'Variegata'	see *S. officinalis* 'Icterina'
	- 'Würzburg'	CSam
	oppositiflora ambig.	CBgR CPle CStr EMan LIck MHer SDys SPin
	pachyphylla	SPin XPep
	pachystachya	SPin
	palaestina	XPep
§	***patens*** 🏆H3	More than 30 suppliers
	- 'Alba' misapplied	see *S. patens* 'White Trophy'
*	- 'Blue Trophy'	LIck
	- 'Cambridge Blue' 🏆H3	More than 30 suppliers
	- 'Chilcombe'	CMdw CPle CSam CStr CWCL ECtt EPyc EWin LIck LSou MAsh MHar MLLN MRod SAga SChu SDys SHFr SPin SSvw WCra WOut WSHC WWlt WWye
	- 'Guanajuato'	More than 30 suppliers
	- 'Oxford Blue'	see *S. patens*
	- 'Royal Blue'	see *S. patens*
§	- 'White Trophy'	CHal CPle CStr CTbh CWCL EBee EChP ECtt ENot ERou EShb LDai LIck LRHS MHer MRod MSte NGHP NPri SDnm SDys SGar SPer SPin SWal WFar WSHC WWeb WWol WWye
	pauciserrata **new**	SPin
	penstemonoides	SPin XPep
	phlomoides	MGol
	pinguifolia	SPin
	pisidica **new**	SPin
	plectranthoides **new**	SPin
	polystachya	CPle CStr MRod SPin WWye
	pratensis	CArn CPle CStr EBee ELan LPio MSal MWgw NLsd SECG SGar SMar SPin WGHP WOut WPer WWye XPep
	- 'Albiflora'	LRHS
§	- Bertolonii Group	SEND
§	- Haematodes Group 🏆H4	CBot CPle EBee EChP ECha ELan LDai MGol MNrw NLar SBch SBla SDnm SPav SRms WPer WWye XPep
	- 'Indigo' 🏆H4	CDes CPrp CStr EBee ECGP EMan EPPr EPfP EWll LRHS MRav MWgw NDov NLar WAul WMnd
	- 'Lapis Lazuli'	CDes CPle EMon EVFa LPhx
	- 'Pink Delight'	EBee ERou
	- 'Rhapsody in Blue'	see *S.* x *sylvestris* 'Rhapsody in Blue'
	- 'Rosea'	CBgR CPle EBee EBrs ECha LPhx LRHS SPin WGHP WWye
	prunelloides	CStr MRod SPin
	przewalskii	CDes CHar CPle CPom CStr EWsh GIBF GKev GSki IFro LPhx MCCP MGol MSal MWgw NBid NEgg NLsd NMRc SDnm SGar SHFr SPin WBVN WOut WPer WWye
	- ACE 1157	EBee WCot WCru
	- BWJ 7920	SPin WCru
	- DJH 210524	EPPr
	'Purple Majesty'	CHea CHll CPle CPne CSev CSpe CStr EBee EMan LIck LPhx LPio MLLN MRod MSte NCGa SDys SMrm SPin SSpi SUsu WKif WSan WWeb WWlt WWye
	'Purple Queen' **new**	CPle
	purpurea	CM&M CPle CStr LSRN MRod SPin
	recognita	CBot CPle CPom CStr WKif WSHC XPep
§	***reflexa***	CStr
	regeliana misapplied	see *S. virgata* Jacq.
	regeliana Trautv.	CPle EBee MLLN NBir SPin
	regla	CPle CStr MAsh MRod SDys SPin WOut XPep
	- 'Jame'	WCot
	- 'Mount Emory' **new**	MRod SPin
	repens	CPle CSec CStr IGor SDys SPin WDyG WWye
	- var. ***repens***	SGar XPep
§	***reptans***	CPle CSam CSpe CStr CWCL LIck MHar MRod SAga SPin WDyG WOut WPer XPep
	- from Mexico **new**	SDys
	- from Western Texas **new**	SDys
	ringens	CPom CStr GFlt SDys SPin WOut XPep
	riparia misapplied	see *S. rypara*
	roborowskii	SPin
	roemeriana 🏆H3	CPle CStr EPyc LIck MAsh MHom MRod NWCA SDnm SDys SPin WPGP XPep
	'Royal Crimson Distinction' PBR	EBee
	rubescens	CStr LIck MRod SDys SPin
	rubiginosa	MRod SDys SPin
	runcinata	XPep
	rutilans	see *S. elegans* 'Scarlet Pineapple'
	rypara	CPle CPom MRod SDys SPin
	sagittata	CSpe CStr MRod SDys SPin WOut
*	***sauntia***	SPin
	scabiosifolia	CPom SPin
	scabra	CFir CPle CStr EBee EChP MGol MSte SDys SPin WCAu WOut WWye XPep
	sclarea	CArn CBot CHby CPle CWan EBee EBrs ECtt EGoo ELau GPoy LRHS MChe MHer NGHP NGdn SECG SIde SPin WCHb WHer WHoo WPer WWye XPep
§	- var. ***sclarea***	CKno EBee EWTr MAnH NSti
	- var. ***turkestanica*** hort.	More than 30 suppliers
§	- 'Vatican White'	CPle EMar EWTr GKir LDai NCGa NLar SBch SDnm SMad SPav WHil WWeb

	Plant	Suppliers
	– white-bracted	CWib EMag EOHP MAnH MRod NDlv NGHP NLar SBod SPin SWal SWvt WGwG XPep
*	***scordifolia*** **new**	SPin
	scutellarioides	CStr MRod
	semiatrata misapplied	see *S. chamaedryoides*
	semiatrata Zucc.	CDes CPle CPom CSpe EBee LIck LSou MRod SAga SDys SPin SRkn SUsu WWye
	serpyllifolia **new**	SDys SPin
	sessei	CStr SPin
	'Shirley's Creeper'	XPep
	'Silke's Dream'	CPle ECtt SDys SPin SUsu WSHC
	sinaloensis	CBgR CPle CSpe CStr EBee EMan EPyc EShb LSou MHar MRod MSte SBch SDys SPin SUsu WFar
	– 'Blue Eyes'	SPer
	somalensis	CDoC CPle CStr MRod SDys SHar SPin WOut WPen XPep
	sonomensis	XPep
	spathacea ♀H3-4	CAby CPle CStr EMan EShb LPhx MRod SDys SIgm SPin WSHC WWye XPep
	splendens	CStr SPin
I	– 'Peach'	CStr SPin
§	– 'Van-Houttei' ♀H3	CDoC CPle CStr ECre LIck MLLN MRod SDys SPin WWye
	sprucei	CStr MRod SPin WBor
§	***staminea***	CPle CStr MGol SHFr SPin WSan WWye XPep
	stenophylla	CPle CSec CStr EBee EChP MGol SPin WOut WPer
	stepposa	SPin XPep
	x ***superba*** ♀H4	CBot CPrp CSBt EBee ECtt ELan EPfP EWTr LAst LEdu LRHS MBri MHer MMil MWat NEgg SDix SPer SRms SSpe SSvw WHoo WMnd WWhi WWye
	– 'Adrian'	SChu
	– 'Dear Anja'	LPhx NDov
	– 'Forncett Dawn'	EBee SChu
	– 'Merleau' **new**	EMar
*	– 'Rosea' **new**	NEgg
	– 'Rubin' ♀H4	EBee NDov SChu SMrm
	– 'Superba'	CSev ECha ECtt EHrv LPhx MRav WCAu
§	x ***sylvestris***	LAst XPep
	– 'Blauhügel' ♀H4	CPrp CSev EBee EBrs EChP ECha ECtt ELan EPfP EVFa GCal LPhx LRHS MArl MAvo MLLN MSte MWgw NDov NPri SBla SChu SLon SMrm WCAu WGwG WPer WPtf
§	– 'Blaukönigin'	EBee EPfP ERou EWTr GKir GMaP IBal IHMH LRHS LSRN MWat NArg NBPC NDlv NEgg NGHP NJOw NLar NMir NVic SIgm SPet SPlb SPoG SWvt WBrk WFar WPer WWeb
	– Blue Queen	see *S.* x *sylvestris* 'Blaukönigin'
	– 'Lye End'	CBos ECtt ERou MRav NCGa NDov
§	– 'Mainacht' ♀H4	More than 30 suppliers
	– May Night	see *S.* x *sylvestris* 'Mainacht'
	– 'Negrito'	EBee GBin NDov
§	– 'Rhapsody in Blue'	EBee NLar WCot
	– 'Rose Queen'	More than 30 suppliers
	– 'Rügen'	CBgR EBee EChP EMan IBal LRHS MBri NDov SOkh WHil
	– 'Schneehügel'	EBee EChP ECha ELan EMan EPPr EPfP GKir GMaP LAst LRHS MBNS MBri MMil MWgw NBPC NCGa NPri NPro SBla WCAu WGHP WHil WMnd
	– 'Tänzerin' ♀H4	EBee LPhx NDov SChu SDys WCot WGHP
	– 'Viola Klose'	CStr EBee EBrs EMan EVFa GCal GKir LPhx LRHS MAvo NCGa NFla NLar SMrm SSvw WCAu
	tachiei hort.	see *S. forsskaolii*
	'Tammy' **new**	SPin
	taraxacifolia	CPle CStr MRod SPin
	tesquicola	see *S. nemorosa* subsp. *tesquicola*
	tiliifolia	CArn EUnu MGol MRod SHFr SPav SPin SRms
	tomentosa	CPle EMag EUnu MGol SPin
	transcaucasica	see *S. staminea*
	transsylvanica	CArn CHea CPle EChP EPPr LRHS MRod MWgw SChu SDnm SPav SPin WCAu WPer XPep
	– 'Blue Spire'	CPrp MBri MWhi MWrn SPav SPur SSvw
	'Trebah'	see *S.* x *jamensis* 'Trebah'
§	'Trelawny'	CTbh EPyc LRHS MAsh MHar MRod MSte SDys SPav SRot
§	'Trelissick'	CTbh ECre ECtt EPyc LAst LRHS MAsh MRod MSte SDys SPav SPin SRot
	'Trenance'	see *S.* x *jamensis* 'Trenance'
§	'Trewithen'	CPle CTbh ECre ECtt EPyc LAst LRHS MRod MSte SPav SPin SRot
	trijuga	MRod SPin WOut
	triloba	see *S. fruticosa*
	tubifera	SAga SPin
	uliginosa ♀H3-4	More than 30 suppliers
	– 'African Skies'	CChe MNrw SPin WDyG
	urica	CSpe MAsh MRod SDys SPav SPin
	– 'Blue Ribbon' **new**	MRod
	– short **new**	MRod
	'Van-Houttei'	see *S. splendens* 'Van-Houttei'
	'Vatican City'	see *S. sclarea* 'Vatican White'
	verbenaca	CArn ITim MBow MHer MSal NMir SPin WGHP WHil WOut WPer WWye XPep
	– pink	WOut
	verticillata	CArn CPle CStr EBee ECha EGoo EHrv ITim LRHS MGol MHer MRod MWgw NSti SDys SPer SPin WCAu WGwG WOut WPer WWye XPep
§	– 'Alba'	CAbP CPle CSec EBee EChP ECtt EPfP EPPr ERou EShb LBBr LRHS LSRN MRav MTis NGdn NSti SBla SPer SPet SPin WCAu WGHP WHer WMnd WPer XPep
	– subsp. ***amasiaca***	SGar
	– 'Purple Rain'	More than 30 suppliers
	– 'Smouldering Torches'	LPhx NDov SMHy
	– 'White Rain'	see *S. verticillata* 'Alba'
	villicaulis	see *S. amplexicaulis*
	villosa **new**	MRod SPin
§	***virgata***	CPle EBee SGar SPin WCAu WWye
	viridis	EWsh SPin
§	– var. ***comata***	CArn EMar GSki MChe NGHP SECG SIde WJek
	– var. ***viridis***	SBod WHrl
	viscosa Jacquin	CPle CStr MRod SPin WWye XPep
	wagneriana	CStr MRod SPin
	'Waverly'	CDes CPle CStr MAsh MRod
	xalapensis	SPin
	yunnanensis	EBee
	– BWJ 7874	WCru

Salvinia (*Salviniaceae*)

	Plant	Suppliers
	sp. **new**	LPBA
	auriculata	WDyG
	natans **new**	EFtx

Sambucus ✿ (*Caprifoliaceae*)

	adnata	EBee WFar
	- B&SWJ 2252	WCru
	caerulea	see *S. nigra* subsp. *cerulea*
	callicarpa	NLar SSpi
	chinensis	EBee
	- B&SWJ 6542	WCru
	coraensis	see *S. williamsii* subsp. *coreana*
	ebulus	GKir LEdu NLar NSti SMad WDyG
	- DJHC 0107	WCru
	formosana	LEdu
	- B&SWJ 1543	WCru
*	***himalayensis***	EWes
§	***javanica*** B&SWJ 4047	WCru
	kamtschatica	GIBF
	miquelii	GIBF SPoG
	nigra	CCVT CDul CElw CRWN ENot GKir GPoy GWCH IHMH LBuc MHer MSwo NWea SHFr SIde WDin WMou XPep
	- 'Albomarginata'	see *S. nigra* 'Marginata'
	- 'Albovariegata' (v)	CDoC CDul GKir LSou WMoo
*	- 'Ardwall'	GCal
N	- 'Aurea' 🏆H4	CBcs CCVT CDul CLnd CSBt CWan ECrN ELan ENot EPfP EWTr GKir MBar MRav NLon NWea SPer WDin WFar WMoo WSHC
	- 'Aureomarginata' (v)	EBee ECrN ELan ENot EPfP EVFa GKir ISea MRav NFor NLar NLon NPen NSti SHBN WCFE WFar
	- 'Black Beauty'	see *S. nigra* f. *porphyrophylla* 'Gerda'
	- 'Black Lace'	see *S. nigra* f. *porphyrophylla* 'Eva'
	- 'Bradet' **new**	CAgr
	- 'Cae Rhos Lligwy'	WHer
	- subsp. ***canadensis***	NWea
	- - 'Aurea'	CWib MBar MBlu NWea WHar
	- - 'John's' **new**	CAgr
	- - 'Maxima'	EPfP SMad WBcn WCot
	- - 'York' (F)	CAgr
§	- subsp. ***cerulea***	CAgr EPfP NLar SMad
	- 'Frances' (v)	WBcn WCot
	- 'Fructu Luteo' **new**	EPla
	- 'Godshill' (F)	CAgr
	- 'Golden Locks'	EVFa MWgw
	- 'Heterophylla'	see *S. nigra* 'Linearis'
	- 'Ina'	CAgr
	- f. ***laciniata*** 🏆H4	CBcs CMHG ELan EPfP EPla EVFa GKir MBlu MLLN MRav NBea NEgg NFor NGHP NLon NSti SChu SDix SLon SSpi SSta WCFE WCot WDin WFar WPGP WSHC
§	- 'Linearis'	CFai CPMA ELan EPla MRav NLar
	- 'Long Tooth'	CNat
	- 'Luteovariegata' (v)	EVFa WBcn
	- 'Madonna' (v)	CBcs CMHG EBee EPla EVFa EWTr LRHS LSou MBri MGos MLLN MRav NLar SPer SPla SPoG SPur WCot
§	- 'Marginata' (v)	CDul CMHG CPLG CWan CWib EHoe GAbr ISea LRHS MBar MHer MLLN MRav SDix SLon SPer WCot WDin WFar WHar
	- 'Marion Bull' (v)	CNat
I	- 'Monstrosa' **new**	SMad
	- 'Nana'	EMon
	- 'Plaque' (v)	CNat
	- 'Plena' (d)	EPla MInt WCot
	- 'Pulverulenta' (v)	CBgR CDoC CHar EPfP EPla EVFa GCal GKir LRHS MLLN MRav SPer WBcn WCot WSHC
	- 'Purpurea'	see *S. nigra* f. *porphyrophylla* 'Guincho Purple'
	- 'Pyramidalis'	CPMA EPla MBlu NLar SMad
	- 'Sambu' (F) **new**	CAgr
	- 'Samdal' (F)	CAgr
	- 'Samidan' (F)	CAgr
	- 'Samnor' (F)	CAgr
	- 'Sampo' (F) **new**	CAgr
	- 'Samyl' (F) **new**	CAgr
*	- 'Tenuifolia'	MRav
	- 'Variegata'	see *S. nigra* 'Marginata'
§	- f. ***porphyrophylla*** 'Eva'	More than 30 suppliers
§	- - 'Gerda'[PBR] 🏆H4	More than 30 suppliers
§	- - 'Guincho Purple'	CBcs CDoC CDul CWib EBee ECrN EHoe ELan EPfP GAbr GCal GKir IHMH ISea LRHS MBar MBlu MCCP MDun MHer MRav MSwo NFor NLon WBor WCot WDin WFar WMoo WSHC
	- - 'Purple Pete'	CNat
	- - 'Thundercloud'	CElw CMHG EVFa GKir LRHS MBri MTis NChi NPro WBcn WCot WFar WPat WPen
	- f. ***viridis***	CAgr CBgR CNat EMon
	racemosa	CAgr EPfP GIBF GWCH NWea WRha
	- 'Aurea'	EHoe GKir NEgg
	- 'Chedglow' **new**	CNat
	- 'Crûg Lace'	WCru
	- 'Goldenlocks'	CBgR CRez EVFa EWes GKir MGos MSwo NLar SPer WBcn
	- 'Plumosa Aurea'	More than 30 suppliers
	- 'Sutherland Gold' 🏆H4	More than 30 suppliers
	- 'Tenuifolia'	CMHG CPMA CSWP ELan EPfP LRHS NLar WPGP WPat
	wightiana	see *S. javanica*
§	***williamsii*** subsp. ***coreana***	CMCN WFar

Samolus (*Primulaceae*)

	repens	CPBP ECou

Sanchezia (*Acanthaceae*)

	nobilis hort.	see *S. speciosa*
§	***speciosa***	CHal

Sandersonia (*Colchicaceae*)

	aurantiaca	CPne EPot LAma LRHS

Sanguinaria (*Papaveraceae*)

	canadensis	More than 30 suppliers
	- f. ***multiplex*** (d)	CDes CFil CLAP EMan EMon EPPr EPot ERos GEdr GKir LRHS SOkd
	- - 'Paint Creek Double' (d)	SSpi
	- - 'Plena' (d) 🏆H4	CAvo CBct CBro CLyd CMea EBee GBBs GCrs IMGH LAma NCGa NDov NLar NMen NRya SBla SIgm SIng SMac SRot SSpi WBVN WEas WHil WLin WPGP WSHC WSan WTin WWhi
	- 'Peter Harrison'	LPhx

Sanguisorba (*Rosaceae*)

	DJHC 535 from Korea **new**	SMHy
§	***albiflora***	CDes CFwr CRow EBee EBla EBrs ELan EMon EPPr ERou GBuc MRav NLar NPro SChu SHop WFar WPGP WTin WWpP
	armena	EBee EBla EWes MNrw MSph SSvw WTin
	benthamiana	CHEx EBla
	canadensis	More than 30 suppliers

* ***caucasica*** CAby EWes LPhx SMeo WGHP WWye
hakusanensis CDes CHar EBee EBla ECha IFro MNrw NBir NBro NDov NPro WCot WFar WPGP
- B&SWJ 8709 WCru
magnifica CBot CDes CFir
- ***alba*** see *S. albiflora*
menziesii More than 30 suppliers
§ ***minor*** More than 30 suppliers
- subsp. ***muricata*** GWCH
obtusa More than 30 suppliers
- var. ***albiflora*** see *S. albiflora*
officinalis CArn CBrm CHar CKno CSam CWan EBee EBla EHrv EPfP EWTr GBar GBin IHMH MBow MHer NDov NEgg NMir NPro WCAu WGHP WMoo WWpP WWye
- CDC 282 LPhx
- 'Arnhem' CKno CMdw EBee EBla EPPr LPhx NDov SMHy SOkh SUsu
- late-flowering **new** NDov
- 'Lemon Splash' (v) WCot
I - 'Martin's Mulberry' EBee EWes
- 'Pink Tanna' CFwr EBee EBla EMan EMon EPPr LPhx MBri MDKP NSti SMHy SOkh SUsu WCAu WCot WHil
- 'Shiro-fukurin' (v) **new** WCot
parviflora see *S. tenuifolia* var. *parviflora*
pimpinella see *S. minor*
'Pink Brushes' EBla LPhx
'Red Thunder' **new** CFir
sitchensis see *S. stipulata*
§ ***stipulata*** EBee EBrs GCal IBlr MNrw NDov NGby
'Tanna' More than 30 suppliers
'Tanna' seedling **new** EPPr
tenuifolia CBrm CKno EBee EBla LPhx LRHS MGol MSph NChi NDov NLar NPro WAul WCAu WGHP WMoo
- 'Alba' CDes CKno EBee EBla GBuc GGar LPhx MBri MDun NDov NPro SAga SBla SMHy SMad SOkh WCot WFar WPGP
- - CDC LPhx NDov
§ - var. ***parviflora*** CBot EBee MNrw NLar
- - white-flowered EBla WTin
- 'Pink Elephant' CDes CFwr CKno EBee EBla GBin NLar WPGP
- 'Purpurea' CDes CKno EBla NLar WFar WPGP
- 'Stand Up Comedian' EBee NLar

Sanicula (*Apiaceae*)

europaea EBee GBar GPoy SECG WHer WTin WWye
odorata EBee

Sansevieria ✿ (*Dracaenaceae*)

trifasciata 'Golden Hahnii' (v) 🏆H1 MBri
- var. ***laurentii*** (v) 🏆H1 MBri

Santolina (*Asteraceae*)

benthamiana XPep
§ ***chamaecyparissus*** 🏆H4 More than 30 suppliers
- var. ***corsica*** see *S. chamaecyparissus* var. *nana*
- 'Double Lemon' EPfP EWin SPla SPoG WCot
- 'Lambrook Silver' CDoC CHar EBee EGoo ENot EPfP GKir LRHS MAsh SCoo SLim SPla SPoG
- 'Lemon Queen' CArn CBcs CBot CDoC CSLe EBee EGoo ELau EPfP GBar GKir LAst LRHS MAsh MBow MGos MHer MSwo NBir NPri SIde SPla WCHb WFar WGwG WPer XPep
§ - var. ***nana*** 🏆H4 CBcs CBot EBee ECha ENot EPfP GKir LRHS MAsh MBar MDun MHer MRav MSwo NFor NWoo SPer SPoG SRms WPer XPep
- 'Pretty Carol' CAbP CBot EBee ELan EMil EPfP GBar GGar GKir LRHS MAsh NGHP NLRH SCoo SIde SLim SPla WFar WWeb XPep
- 'Small-Ness' CBot CDoC CLyd EBee EGoo ELan EPfP EWes GBar GEdr GKir LRHS LSRN MAsh MHer MSte SLim SMrm SPer STre SWvt WFar WPat
- subsp. ***squarrosa*** XPep
elegans WAbe
incana see *S. chamaecyparissus*
* ***lindavica*** XPep
'Oldfield Hybrid' EChP MLan WCot XPep
pectinata see *S. rosmarinifolia* subsp. *canescens*
§ ***pinnata*** CArn CSLe CSev CTri MHer WPer
§ - subsp. ***neapolitana*** 🏆H4 CArn CSBt CSev EBee ECha ECrN ELan ENot EPfP GBar LRHS MBri MWat NCob NFor NPri SDix SIde WEas WHCG WMnd WSel WTin WWye XPep
- - cream see *S. pinnata* subsp. *neapolitana* 'Edward Bowles'
§ - - 'Edward Bowles' More than 30 suppliers
- - 'Sulphurea' CHar CMea EBee ECrN EGoo EPfP LPhx LRHS MAsh NCob NGHP SPer WKif WPer WWhi WWpP XPep
rosmarinifolia CArn CBrm CDoC CWan EBee ECrN ELau GWCH MRav MWhi NGHP SLon SPlb SRms WCHb WSel WWye XPep
I - 'Caerulea' XPep
§ - subsp. ***canescens*** EPfP LRHS MBri WPer WWye
§ - subsp. ***rosmarinifolia*** More than 30 suppliers
- - 'Primrose Gem' 🏆H4 CBcs CBot CDoC CHar CSBt CTri EBee EChP ECha ECrN ELau EMil EPfP GBar GKir LRHS MAsh MSwo MWat NCob NPri SBod SPer SPla SWvt WCot WPer WWye XPep
- - white-flowered **new** LPhx
tomentosa see *S. pinnata* subsp. *neapolitana*
virens see *S. rosmarinifolia* subsp. *rosmarinifolia*
viridis see *S. rosmarinifolia* subsp. *rosmarinifolia*

Sanvitalia (*Asteraceae*)

sp. LAst
'Aztekengold' **new** EWin
'Little Sun' LRHS NPri SPet
'Sunbini'PBR CSpe NPri SPoG WGor

Sapindus (*Sapindaceae*)

mukorossi **new** CBcs
saponaria var. ***drummondii*** EGFP

Sapium (*Euphorbiaceae*)

japonicum CFil CMCN EGFP WPGP
- B&SWJ 8744 WCru

Saponaria (*Caryophyllaceae*)

'Bressingham' 🏆H4 CNic CPBP ECGP ECtt EDAr EPfP LBee LRHS NMen SBla SBod SIng SPoG WAbe WPat
caespitosa EWes GTou NJOw WAbe

x ***lempergii*** 'Max Frei'	CAbP CSam EBee EMan EPPr GBuc LPhx LRHS MSte NDov SAga SBla SDix SHar WCot WGHP WOVN WSHC XPep
lutea	NWCA
ocymoides ♀H4	More than 30 suppliers
- 'Alba'	ECha GAbr WFar
- 'Rubra Compacta' ♀H4	LRHS NSla
- 'Snow Tip'	CBrm EDAr EPfP EShb ESis NLar SBch SMar WGor
- 'Splendens'	XPep
officinalis	CAgr CArn CBre CHby CWan ELau EUnu GBar GPoy LEdu MChe MHer MSal NGHP NPri SECG SIde SPlb WBrk WFar WHer WMoo WPer WWpP WWye
- 'Alba Plena' (d)	CAby EBee ECha EMag GBar GKir NLar NSti WCHb WFar WHer WPer WPtf WRha WTin
- 'Betty Arnold' (d)	CDes EBee WCot WFar WTin WWpP
§ - 'Dazzler' (v)	EMan EPPr EUnu GBar NBir WCHb WHer
- 'Rosea Plena' (d)	More than 30 suppliers
- 'Rubra Plena' (d)	CBre CHad EBee ELan MWhi NBre NGHP NSti SHar WCHb WHer WRha WTin
- 'Variegata'	see *S. officinalis* 'Dazzler'
x ***olivana*** ♀H4	CNic EDAr GAbr MTho NMen SBla SPoG WAbe WPat
pamphylica	MNrw
pulvinaris	see *S. pumilio*
§ ***pumilio***	GTou
'Rosenteppich'	SBla WPat
zawadskii	see *Silene zawadskii*

Saposhnikovia (*Apiaceae*)

divaricata	CArn MSal

Sarcocapnos (*Papaveraceae*)

enneaphylla	LSRN

Sarcococca ✿ (*Buxaceae*)

confusa ♀H4	More than 30 suppliers
hookeriana ♀H4	CFil ECot EPfP GSki LAst LSRN WBrE WFar WPGP
- B&SWJ 2585	WCru
- HWJK 2393	WCru
- Sch 2396	EPla
- var. ***digyna*** ♀H4	More than 30 suppliers
- - 'Purple Stem'	CBrm CTri EHol EPfP EPla MGos MRav NLar SPoG WCru WDin
I - - 'Schillingii'	MAsh
- var. ***hookeriana***	CPMA
- - GWJ 9369	WCru
- var. ***humilis***	More than 30 suppliers
orientalis	CAbP CFil CMCN CPMA ELan EPfP EPla LBuc LRHS MAsh MGos SLon SPla SPoG SSpi WFar WPGP
'Roy Lancaster'	see *S. ruscifolia* 'Dragon Gate'
ruscifolia	CBcs CMCN CPMA CSBt EBee ECrN ELan ENot EPfP EPla GKir LRHS LSRN MAsh MGos MRav MSwo NCGa SLim SLon SMac SPer SPoG SRms SSpi WCru WFar
- var. ***chinensis*** ♀H4	CFil CPMA CSam EPfP EPla MRav SLon WCru WFar WPGP
- - L 713	EPla
§ - 'Dragon Gate'	CFil CPMA ELan EPfP EPla LRHS LTwo MAsh SReu SSta WBcn WPGP
saligna	CBcs CFil CPMA EPfP NLar WBcn WCru
vagans B&SWJ 7285 **new**	WCru
wallichii	CFil SSpi
- B&SWJ 2291	WCru
- GWJ 9427	WCru

Sarcopoterium (*Rosaceae*)

spinosum	XPep

Sarcostemma (*Asclepiadaceae*)

viminale **new**	EShb

Sarmienta (*Gesneriaceae*)

repens ♀H2	NMen WAbe WCru

Sarothamnus see *Cytisus*

Sarracenia ✿ (*Sarraceniaceae*)

alata	CFwr CSWC MCCP SHmp WSSs
- 'Black Tube'	WSSs
- heavily-veined	SHmp WSSs
- pubescent	CSWC WSSs
- 'Red Lid'	CSWC WSSs
- wavy lid	SHmp WSSs
- white-flowered	WSSs
alata x ***flava*** var. ***maxima***	CSWC
alata x ***purpurea***	see *S.* x *exornata*
x ***areolata***	CSWC WSSs
x ***catesbyi*** ♀H1	CFil CSWC WHlf WSSs
'Dixie Lace'	CSWC
x ***excellens*** ♀H1	CSWC WSSs
x ***exornata***	CSWC
flava ♀H1	CFil CFwr CSWC EBla MCCP WSSs
- all green giant	see *S. flava* var. *maxima*
- var. ***atropurpurea***	WSSs
- 'Burgundy'	WSSs
- var. ***cuprea***	WSSs
- var. ***flava***	WSSs
§ - var. ***maxima***	CSWC WNor WSSs
- var. ***ornata***	CSWC SHmp WSSs
- var. ***rubricorpora***	WSSs
- var. ***rugelii***	SHmp WSSs
- veinless	CSWC
x ***harperi***	CSWC
'Ladies in Waiting'	CSWC
leucophylla ♀H1	CFwr CSWC EBla SHmp WHlf WSSs
- pubescent	WSSs
- 'Schnell's Ghost'	WSSs
'Lynda Butt'	SHmp WSSs
x ***miniata***	SHmp
minor	CSWC SHmp WSSs
- 'Okee Giant'	CSWC EBla LHew WSSs
- 'Okefenokee Giant'	see *S. minor* 'Okee Giant'
minor x ***oreophila***	CSWC
x ***mitchelliana*** ♀H1	CFwr WSSs
x ***moorei***	WSSs
- 'Brook's Hybrid'	CSWC LHew WSSs
oreophila	CSWC SHmp WSSs
oreophila x ***leucophylla***	CSWC
oreophila x ***minor***	CSWC
x ***popei***	CSWC
psittacina	CSWC SHmp WSSs
purpurea	CFil EBla NWCA WHlf
- subsp. ***purpurea***	CFwr CSWC MCCP WSSs
- - f. ***heterophylla***	CSWC WSSs
- subsp. ***venosa***	CSWC SHmp WSSs
- - var. ***burkii***	CSWC WSSs
- subsp. ***venosa*** x ***oreophila***	CSWC
x ***readii***	SHmp WSSs
- 'Farnhamii'	CSWC
x ***rehderi***	SHmp

rubra	CSWC WSSs
- subsp. ***alabamensis***	CSWC SHmp WSSs
- subsp. ***gulfensis***	CSWC SHmp WSSs
* - - f. ***heterophylla***	CSWC WSSs
- subsp. ***jonesii***	CSWC WSSs
* - - f. ***heterophylla***	CSWC WSSs
- subsp. ***rubra***	CSWC WSSs
- subsp. ***wherryi***	CSWC WSSs
- - giant	WSSs
- - yellow-flowered	CSWC WSSs

Saruma (*Aristolochiaceae*)

henryi	CAby CLAP SBla WCot WSHC

Sasa ✿ (*Poaceae*)

chrysantha hort.	see *Pleioblastus chino*
disticha 'Mirrezuzume'	see *Pleioblastus pygmaeus* 'Mirrezuzume'
glabra f. ***albostriata***	see *Sasaella masamuneana* 'Albostriata'
kagamiana	NLar
kurilensis	EPla MWht NMoo WFar WJun
§ - 'Shima-shimofuri' (v)	EPfP EPla ERod WJun
- 'Shimofuri'	see *S. kurilensis* 'Shima-shimofuri'
- short	EPla
nana	see *S. veitchii* f. *minor*
nipponica	WJun
oshidensis	EPla
§ ***palmata***	CAbb CBcs CDul CHad COld CWib EHoe ENot GFlt MCCP MWhi SEND WDin WFar WHer WPnP
- f. ***nebulosa***	CBcs CBct CDoC CFir CHEx EBee EFul EHul ENBC ENot EPfP EPla EPza EWes MBrN MMoz MWht NMoo SAPC SArc SSto WDyG WFar WJun WMoo WMul
quelpaertensis	EPla
tessellata	see *Indocalamus tessellatus*
tsuboiana	CBcs CDoC EBee ENBC EPla EPza GQui MAsh MMoz MWht NGdn NLar SBig WDyG WFar WMoo
§ ***veitchii***	CAbb CBcs CKno CPLG CTrC ECha EHoe ENBC ENot EPfP EPla GKir LEdu MAsh MBri MDun MMoz MWhi NMoo SPer SPla WBor WDin WFar WJun WMoo WMul WWye
§ - f. ***minor***	EBee EPza MCCP MMoz WMoo

Sasaella (*Poaceae*)

glabra	see *S. masamuneana*
§ ***masamuneana***	CDul ENBC EPla EUJe LAst
§ - 'Albostriata' (v)	CDoC CFil CMCo COtt CWib EBee ENBC EPPr EPla ERod GAbr LEdu MBar MCCP MMoz MWgw MWht NGdn NMoo SBig SSto WDyG WFar WJun WMoo WMul WPGP
- f. ***aureostriata*** (v)	COtt EPla GCal MMoz NPal
§ ***ramosa***	CFwr CHEx EBee ENot EPla LAst LEdu MCCP MMoz MWht NMoo NRya WDin WMul

Sassafras (*Lauraceae*)

albidum	CArn CFil CTho EPfP LRHS SSpi WPGP
tzumu	CFil EBee WPGP

satsuma see *Citrus unshiu*

Satureja ✿ (*Lamiaceae*)

amani	XPep
§ ***coerulea*** ♀H4	CWan EWes NBir NLAp
douglasii	CArn EOHP SHDw WGHP WJek
- 'Indian Mint'	EDAr NGHP WLHH
georgiana	SSpi
hortensis	CBod GPoy ILis MChe MHer MLan SIde WJek WLHH WSel
montana	CArn CHby CWan ELau EUnu GPoy ILis LLWP MBri MChe MHer NMen SDix SHGN SIde SRms SRob WCHb WGHP WHer WPer XPep
* - ***citriodora***	GPoy MHer XPep
- 'Coerulea'	see *S. coerulea*
§ - subsp. ***illyrica***	LLWP WJek
- 'Purple Mountain'	GPoy LLWP MHer
- ***subspicata***	see *S. montana* subsp. *illyrica*
parnassica	LLWP WPer
repanda	see *S. spicigera*
§ ***spicigera***	CArn CBod CLyd CNic CPBP EDAr ELau EPot GBar GEdr LEdu LFol LLWP MHer NBir NMen NPri SHGN SIde WCHb WJek WLHH WSel WWye
thymbra	CArn EOHP LLWP SHDw WJek XPep

Satyrium (*Orchidaceae*)

nepalense	GGGa
princeps **new**	WCot

Saurauia (*Actinidiaceae*)

subspinosa	CHEx

Sauromatum (*Araceae*)

guttatum	see *S. venosum*
§ ***venosum***	CHEx CKob CMea EAmu EBee EBrs EMan EShb EUJe ITer LAma LEdu LRHS MBri MOak MSph WCot WCru WRos

Saururus (*Saururaceae*)

cernuus	CHEx CRow CWat EHon ELan EMFW EPfP LNCo LPBA SRms WPnP WPop WWpP
chinensis	CRow WCru

Saussurea (*Asteraceae*)

albescens	EBee EMan WCot
auriculata HWJCM 490	WCru
obvallata CC 4447	GKev
- HWJK 2272	WCru
uniflora GWJ 9269 **new**	WCru

savory, summer see *Satureja hortensis*

Saxegothaea (*Podocarpaceae*)

conspicua	CBcs CDoC CMCN ECou EPla WCwm

Saxifraga ✿ (*Saxifragaceae*)

McB 1377	CLyd
McB 1397 from Nepal	CLyd
SEP 22	CLyd EHyt
SEP 45	CLyd
'Ada' (x *petraschii*) (7)	NMen
'Aemula' (x *borisii*) (7)	NMen
§ 'Afrodite' (*sempervivum*) (7)	CLyd
aizoides (9)	GKev
- var. ***atrorubens*** (9)	SIng
aizoon	see *S. paniculata*
'Aladdin' (x *borisii*) (7)	NMen
* 'Alan Hayhurst' (8)	MDHE WAbe
'Alan Martin' (x *boydilacina*) (7)	CLyd EPot ITim NMen

'Alba' (x *apiculata*) (7)	ELan EPot GTou LFox LRHS MHer NLAp NMen NRya SBla SChu SPlb WPat
'Alba' (x *arco-valleyi*)	see *Saxifraga* 'Ophelia'
'Alba' (*oppositifolia*) (7)	CLyd EHyt ELan EWes GKev GKir GTou NDlv NLAp NWCA WAbe
'Albert Einstein' (x *apiculata*) (7)	NMen
'Albertii' (*callosa*) (8)	see *S.* 'Albida'
§ 'Albida' (*callosa*) (8)	GTou LRHS NLar WAbe
'Aldebaran' (x *borisii*) (7)	NMen
'Alfons Mucha' (7)	CLyd EPot NMen
'Allendale Acclaim' (x *lismorensis*) (7)	NDlv NMen
'Allendale Accord' (*diapensioides* x *lilacina*) (7)	NDlv NMen
'Allendale Allure' (7)	NMen
'Allendale Amber' (7) **new**	NMen
'Allendale Andante' (x *arco-valleyi*) (7)	NMen
'Allendale Angel' (x *kepleri*) (7)	NMen
'Allendale Argonaut' (7)	NDlv NMen
'Allendale Ballad' (7)	NMen
'Allendale Ballet' (7)	CLyd EHyt NMen
'Allendale Bamby' (x *lismorensis*) (7)	NMen
'Allendale Banshee' (7)	NMen
'Allendale Beau' (x *lismorensis*) (7)	CPBP NMen
'Allendale Beauty' (7)	CPBP NMen
'Allendale Betty' (x *lismorensis*) (7)	CLyd EHyt NMen SOkd
'Allendale Billows' (7)	NMen
'Allendale Bonny' (7)	GCrs NMen
'Allendale Bounty' (7)	NMen
'Allendale Bravo' (x *lismorensis*) (7)	CLyd EHyt NMen WAbe
'Allendale Cabal' (7)	CLyd NMen
'Allendale Celt' (x *novacastelensis*) (7)	EHyt NMen
'Allendale Charm' (Swing Group) (7)	CLyd NMen SOkd WAbe
'Allendale Chick' (7)	GCrs NMen
'Allendale Comet' (7)	GCrs NMen
'Allendale Dance' (7)	NMen
'Allendale Dream' (7)	EHyt EPot NMen
'Allendale Duo' (7)	NMen
'Allendale Elegance' (7)	NMen
'Allendale Elf' (7)	GCrs NMen
'Allendale Elite' (7)	CLyd NMen
'Allendale Enchantment' (7)	NMen
'Allendale Envoy' (7)	NMen
'Allendale Epic' (7)	NMen
'Allendale Fairy' (7)	NMen
'Allendale Fame' (7)	NMen
'Allendale Frost' (7)	NMen
'Allendale Garnet' (7)	CLyd NDlv NMen
'Allendale Ghost' (7)	NMen
'Allendale Goblin' (7)	NMen
'Allendale Grace' (7)	NMen
'Allendale Gremlin' (7)	NMen
'Allendale Joy' (x *wendelacina*) (7)	NMen
'Allendale Pearl' (x *novacastelensis*) (7)	CLyd EHyt NMen
'Allendale Ruby' (7)	CLyd EHyt NDlv NMen
'Allendale Snow' (x *rayei*) (7)	NDlv NMen
'Alpenglow' (7)	NMen
alpigena (7)	CLyd NSla WAbe
'Amitie' (x *gloriana*) (7)	CFee NMen
andersonii (7)	CLyd NDlv NMen NRya
x ***andrewsii*** (8x11)	MDHE MTho WAbe
angustifolia	see *S. hypnoides*
'Anna' (x *fontanae*) (7)	NMen
'Anne Beddall' (x *goringiana*) (7)	CLyd NMen WAbe
'Antonio Vivaldi' (7) **new**	WAbe
'Aphrodite' (*sempervivum*) (7)	see *S.* 'Afrodite'
x ***apiculata*** *sensu stricto* hort.	see *S.* 'Gregor Mendel'
'Apple Blossom' (15)	ECtt GTou MDHE NRya SPoG WGor
aquatica (15)	NLAp
§ 'Arco' (x *arco-valleyi*) (7)	NJOw
x ***arco-valleyi*** *sensu stricto* hort.	see *S.* 'Arco'
x ***arendsii*** (15)	WEas
- pink (15) **new**	NBlu
- purple (15)	NBlu
- red (15) **new**	NBlu
§ 'Aretiastrum' (x *boydii*) (7)	CLyd EPot ITim LFox NDlv NMen
aretioides (7)	NMen
'Ariel' (x *hornibrookii*) (7)	CLyd LFox NMen
'Arthur' (x *anglica*) (7)	NMen
'Assimilis' (x *petraschii*) (7)	CLyd NMen WAbe
'August Hayek' (x *leyboldii*) (7)	ITim NMen
'Aurea Maculata' (*cuneifolia*)	see *S.* 'Aureopunctata'
§ 'Aureopunctata' (x *urbium*) (11/v)	COkL ECha EMan GAbr GBuc GCal MHer MWgw SPer SPlb SPoG SRms WMoo WPtf WWpP
'Autumn Tribute' (*fortunei*) (5) **new**	WAbe
'Balcana' (*paniculata*) (8) **new**	EPot
'Baldensis'	see *S. paniculata* var. *baldensis*
'Ballawley Guardsman' (15)	ECho LFox MBNS MDHE
§ 'Beatrix Stanley' (x *anglica*) (7)	CLyd ITim LFox MHer NDlv NLAp NMen NRya WGor
'Becky Foster' (x *borisii*) (7)	NMen
'Beechcroft White' (15)	LRHS MDHE
'Bellisant' (x *hornibrookii*) (7)	CLyd NMen
'Berenika' (x *bertolonii*) (7)	NMen
'Beryl' (x *anglica*) (7)	NMen
'Bettina' (x *paulinae*) (7)	NMen
x ***biasolettoi*** *sensu stricto* hort.	see *S.* 'Phoenix'
x ***bilekii*** (7)	CLyd
'Black Beauty' (15)	CMea ECho LRHS MDHE MHer
'Black Ruby' (*fortunei*) (5)	More than 30 suppliers
'Blackberry and Apple Pie' (*fortunei*) (5)	CBct CBod CElw CLAP EBee EChP EMar GBin GEdr GFlt IBal MBrN MNrw MSte MWgw NBro NEgg NMen NMyG NPri SSpi SWvt WBor WCot WFar WOld WWeb WWhi
'Blaník' (x *borisii*) (7)	CLyd NMen
'Blanka' (x *borisii*) (7)	NMen
'Blütenteppich' (15)	WPer
'Bob Hawkins' (15/v)	CLyd ELan LFox LRHS MDHE MHer
§ 'Bodensee' (x *hofmannii*) (7)	NDlv WPat
'Bohdalec' (x *megaseiflora*) (7)	NMen
'Bohemia' (7)	CLyd EPot NMen NSla SBla WAbe
x ***borisii*** *sensu stricto* hort.	see *S.* 'Sofia'

'Bornmuelleri' (7) NMen
'Boston Spa' (x *elisabethae*) (7) CLyd LRHS MHer NDlv NJOw NLAp NMen SChu SPlb WPat
'Brailes' (x *poluanglica*) (7) CLyd ITim NMen
'Bridget' (x *edithae*) (7) CLyd CMea GKir LFox LRHS NDlv NMen SIng
'Brno' (x *elisabethae*) (7) EPot NMen
bronchialis (10) CLyd CNic
- var. ***vespertina*** see *S. vespertina*
'Brookside' (*burseriana*) (7) ITim NMen
brunoniana see *S. brunonis*
§ ***brunonis*** (1) LFox WCru
- CC&McK 108 NWCA
bryoides (10) CLyd GCrs GTou NRya NWCA
x ***burnatii*** Sünd (8) CLyd LFox LRHS NDlv NLar NMen NPro WGor
burseriana (7) GKir NLAp NRya WAbe WGor
'Buster' (x *hardingii*) (7) NMen
'Buttercup' (x *kayei*) (7) CLyd GTou NJOw NLAp NMen NWCA WHoo WPat
x ***byam-groundsii*** (7) CLyd
caesia hort. (x *fritschiana*) see *S.* 'Krain'
caesia L. (8) SRms
§ ***callosa*** (8) ♀H4 ECGP GTou MWat NLAp SBla WEas WPat WTin
- var. ***bellardii*** see *S. callosa*
- subsp. ***callosa*** (8) SOkd
§ - - var. ***australis*** (8) EPot GCrs GKev MDHE NBro NMen WAbe
- - var. ***callosa*** (8) MDHE
§ - subsp. ***catalaunica*** (8) SOkd
- var. ***lantoscana*** see *S. callosa* subsp. *callosa* var. *australis*
- ***lingulata*** see *S. callosa*
callosa x ***cochlearis*** (8) see *S.* Silver Farreri Group
'Cambridge Seedling' (7) NDlv NMen
§ 'Carmen' (x *elisabethae*) (7) GKir LRHS NDlv NLAp NMen NRya WAbe
§ 'Carniolica' (*paniculata*) (8) CLyd EPot LFox LRHS MBar MDHE NBro NMen NWCA SBla
'Carniolica' (x *pectinata*) (8) MDHE WAbe
'Carnival' (15) COkL
carolinica see *S.* 'Carniolica'
'Castor' (x *bilekii*) (7) NMen
catalaunica see *S. callosa* subsp. *catalaunica*
'Caterhamensis' (*cotyledon*) (8) NHar
'Cathy Reed' (x *polulacina*) (7) NMen
caucasica var. ***desoulavyi*** see *S. desoulavyi*
cebennensis (15) ♀H2 CLyd EPot LFox NMen NRya
- dwarf (15) WAbe
'Cecil Davies' (8) MDHE
cespitosa (15) MDHE WAbe
'Chambers' Pink Pride' see *S.* 'Miss Chambers'
'Charlecote' (x *poluanglica*) (7) CLyd ITim
'Charles Chaplin' (7) CPBP NHar WAbe
'Cheap Confections' (*fortunei*) (4) More than 30 suppliers
'Chelsea Pink' (x *urbium*) (11) **new** GCra
§ ***cherlerioides*** (10) ECtt MBNS NEgg NRya NVic WEas
'Cherry Pie' (*fortunei*) (5) CBct CHea CLAP EBee EMan GAbr LTwo MBNS MNrw NBir NEgg NMyG WCot
'Cherrytrees' (x *boydii*) (7) NMen NSla
'Chetwynd' (*marginata*) (7) NMen WAbe
'Chez Nous' (x *gloriana*) (7/v) CLyd NJOw NMen
'Chodov' (7) NMen
'Christine' (x *anglica*) (7) CLyd LFox NDlv NLAp NMen
cinerea (7) GCrs NMen WAbe
'Citronella' (7) WAbe
'Claire Felstead' (*cinerea* x *poluniniana*) (7) GCrs NMen
'Clare' (x *anglica*) (7) NMen
'Clare Island' (15) MDHE
§ 'Clarence Elliott' (*umbrosa*) (11) ♀H4 CLyd CMea CTri EHyt EWes GCal GKev GKir LRHS MDKP MHar MHer NFla NRya NVic WAbe WHoo WPat
'Claudia' (x *borisii*) (7) NMen
'Cleo' (x *boydii*) (7) NMen
§ x ***clibranii*** (15) MDHE
§ 'Cloth of Gold' (*exarata* subsp. *moschata*) (15) CLyd ECha ECtt ELan GTou LAst LRHS MBar MHer NJOw NMen NRya SIng SPlb SPoG SRms WAbe WBVN WFar
cochlearis (8) COkL CTri EHyt ESis GEdr GKir LBee LRHS MWat NBro NDlv NMen WAbe WPer
'Cockscomb' (*paniculata*) (8) EPot MDHE NJOw NLAp NMen NRya WAbe
columnaris (7) EHyt NMen NSla
columnaris x ***dinnikii*** **new** NSla
'Combrook' (x *poluanglica*) (7) **new** CLyd
continentalis (15) NWCA
'Conwy Snow' (*fortunei*) (5) WAbe
'Conwy Star' (*fortunei*) (5) WAbe
'Coolock Gem' (7) EHyt NMen
'Coolock Kate' EHyt NMen
'Cordata' (*burseriana*) (7) NMen
'Corona' (x *boydii*) (7) LFox NMen
'Correnie Claret' (15) EWes GTou
I 'Correvoniana' hort. (*brevifolia*) (8) ECtt EPot GKir LRHS MHer MOne NDlv NJOw NRya WGor
§ 'Corrie Fee' (*oppositifolia*) (7) GCrs GFlt GTou
§ ***cortusifolia*** (5) CHid CLAP SSpi
- B&SWJ 5879 WCru
- var. ***fortunei*** see *S. fortunei*
- var. ***stolonifera*** (5) B&SWJ 6205 WCru
'Cotton Crochet' (*fortunei*) (5/d) CBct EBee EChP EMan GSki LAst MBNS MLLN NMyG WCot WFar WOld
cotyledon (8) GCrs LBee LRHS MDHE NFor WEas WPer
§ 'Cranbourne' (x *anglica*) (7) ♀H4 CLyd EPot GCrs LFox LRHS NLAp NMen SBla WPat
'Cream Seedling' (x *elisabethae*) (7) NDlv NJOw NLAp NMen
'Crenata' (*burseriana*) (7) CLyd EPot GCrs LFox LRHS NDlv NMen WAbe WHoo
'Crimson Rose' (*paniculata*) (8) see *S.* 'Rosea'
§ ***crustata*** (8) EHyt MDHE MDKP NMen WAbe
- var. ***vochinensis*** see *S. crustata*
'Crystal Pink' (*fortunei*) (5/v) CBct CFai CMil EBee EChP EHrv EMil EVFa GAbr GEdr GFlt LAst MBri MNrw NBro NMen NMyG SGSe WCot WFar WGor WOld
'Crystalie' (x *biasolettoi*) (7) EPot LRHS NRya WPat
'Cultrata' (*paniculata*) (8) NBro
'Cumulus' (*iranica* hybrid) (7) ♀H4 CLyd CPBP EHyt GCrs ITim NLAp NMen SBla WAbe
§ ***cuneifolia*** (11) CNic GGar IHMH LBee LRHS MHer MWat NDlv NFla NSti NWCA WPer WRos
- var. ***capillipes*** see *S. cuneifolia* subsp. *cuneifolia*

§ - subsp. ***cuneifolia*** (11) ECtt
* - var. ***subintegra*** (11) ECho
cuscutiformis (5) see *S.* 'Cuscutiformis'
§ 'Cuscutiformis' (*stolonifera*) (5) CElw CHid CPLG EBee EBla ETow GCal MMil SBch SBla SRms WAbe WCru
cymbalaria (2) EBur SIng
- var. ***huetiana*** (2) CNic
'Cyril Mortimor Prichard' (X *hardingii*) (7) CLyd
dahurica see *S. cuneifolia*
'Dainty Dame' (X *arco-valleyi*) (7) CLyd LFox LRHS NDlv NMen
'Dana' (X *megaseiflora*) (7) CLyd NMen
'Dartington Double' (15/d) EWes GKir GTou LRHS MDHE NLAp
'Dartington Double White' (15/d) MDHE NJOw
'Dawn Frost' (7) CLyd EPot ITim NDlv NLAp NMen SBla WAbe
'Delia' (X *hornibrookii*) (7) CLyd EPot ITim NMen
§ 'Denisa' (X *pseudokotschyi*) (7) NMen
densa see *S. cherlerioides*
'Dentata' (X *geum*) see *S.* 'Dentata' (X *polita*)
§ 'Dentata' (X polita) (11) CMea CNic CStr ECha EPla GGar NVic SUsu WMoo
'Dentata' (X *urbium*) see *S.* 'Dentata' (X *polita*)
§ ***desoulavyi*** (7) GTou NMen
diapensioides (7) CLyd WAbe
dinnikii **new** WAbe
'Doctor Clay' (*paniculata*) (8) EPot GKev LBee MDHE NLAp NMen NRya WAbe
'Doctor Ramsey' Irving (8) EHyt EWes GEdr GTou LBee LRHS NBro NDlv NJOw NLar NMen WAbe WGor WPnn
'Don Giovanni' (7) **new** WAbe
'Donald Mann' (15) EWes
'Dorothy Milne' (7) NMen
aff. ***doyalana*** (7) CPBP NDlv
- - SEP 45 EHyt
drabiformis (1) **new** GKev
'Drakula' (*ferdinandi-coburgi*) (7) CLyd LRHS NDlv NMen SIng
'Dubarry' (15) ECho EWes MDHE NRya WPnn
'Dulcimer' (X *petraschii*) (7) NMen
'Duncan Lowe' (*andersonii*) (7) ♀H4 CLyd GCrs
'Dwight Ripley' (7) LFox NMen
'Edgar Irmscher' (7) CLyd LFox NMen NWCA
'Edie Campbell' (15) MDHE
'Edith' (X *edithae*) (7) LRHS NJOw SIng
X ***elegantissima*** (15) see *S.* X *clibranii*
'Elf' (7) see *S.* 'Beatrix Stanley'
'Elf' (15) ECtt EPfP LRHS NMen SPoG SRms WGor
'Eliot Hodgkin' (X *millstreamiana*) (7) LFox
X ***elisabethae*** *sensu stricto* hort. see *S.* 'Carmen'
'Elizabeth Sinclair' (X *elisabethae*) (7) CLyd EPot ITim NJOw NMen
'Ellie Brinckerhoff' (X *hornibrookii*) (7) NMen
X ***engleri*** (8) CLyd
epiphylla BWJ 7750 **new** WCru
§ 'Ernst Heinrich' (X *heinrichii*) (7) CLyd NMen NRya
'Esther' (X *burnatii*) (8) CMea COkL EPot GCrs GKev GKir LBee LRHS NMen NWCA SBla SMer WAbe WHoo WPnn
§ 'Eulenspiegel' (X *geuderi*) (7) CLyd EPot NMen
'Eva Hanzliková' (X *izari*) (7) CLyd CPBP WAbe
exarata (15) LFox LRHS NMen
§ - subsp. ***moschata*** (15) MDHE
fair maids of France see *S.* 'Flore Pleno'
'Fairy' (*exarata* subsp. *moschata*) (15) ECtt ELan EPot
'Faldonside' (X *boydii*) (7) ♀H4 CLyd CPBP LFox NDlv NLAp NMen NRya SBla WAbe WHoo WPat
'Falstaff' (*burseriana*) (7) CLyd LFox NDlv
X ***farreri*** hort. (8) see *S.* Silver Farreri Group
§ 'Faust' (X *borisii*) (7) NMen WAbe
§ ***federici-augusti*** (7) GCrs
§ - subsp. ***grisebachii*** (7) ♀H2-3 CLyd GKev GTou NSla WAbe WLin
'Ferdinand' (X *hofmannii*) (7) NMen
ferdinandi-coburgi (7) ♀H4 CLyd ECtt LFox LRHS NDlv NRya NWCA WAbe WBrE
§ - var. ***rhodopea*** (7) CLyd EPot GCrs LRHS NDlv NMen SBla SIng
'Findling' (15) EPot IHMH LRHS NJOw NMen SPoG WAbe
'Five Color' (*fortunei*) (5) EBee LTwo MBnl NBPC NGdn SPer WGor
§ ***flagellaris*** (1) NMen WAbe
'Flavescens' misapplied see *S.* 'Lutea'
'Flavescens' Farrer (*paniculata*) NDlv
'Flavescens' (*paniculata*) (8) NBro
X ***fleischeri*** (7) NMen
§ 'Flore Pleno' (*granulata*) (15/d) CFir EWes LFox MAvo NBir NLar SIng WFar
'Florissa' (*oppositifolia*) (7) CLyd
florulenta see *S. callosa*
'Flowers of Sulphur' see *S.* 'Schwefelblüte'
§ ***fortunei*** (5) ♀H4 CHEx EBee EWTr GMaP ITim MRav NBir NLAp SPer SRms SSpi WAbe WCru WMoo
- f. ***alpina*** (5) CLAP
- - from Hokkaido WCru
- var. ***incisolobata*** (5) SSpi
- var. ***koraiensis*** (5) B&SWJ 8688 WCru
- var. ***obtusocuneata*** (5) CLAP EBee ECho EHyt LTwo NMen WAbe
- f. ***partita*** CLAP WCru
- var. ***pilosissima*** (5) B&SWJ 8557 WCru
- pink (5) CLAP WAbe WFar WTMC
- var. ***suwoensis*** (5) CLAP
'Foster's Gold' (X *elisabethae*) (7) CLyd NMen
'Four Winds' (15) EWes LRHS WMoo
'Francesco Redi' (7) NMen WAbe
'Francis Cade' (8) GAbr WAbe
'Frank Sinatra' (X *poluanglica*) (7) CLyd NMen
'Franz Liszt' (7) **new** WAbe
'Franzii' (X *paulinae*) (7) NMen
'Frederik Chopin' (7) **new** WAbe
'Friar Tuck' (X *boydii*) (7) NMen
'Friesei' (X *salmonica*) (7) CLyd EPot NLAp NMen
X ***fritschiana*** *sensu stricto* hort. (8) see *S.* 'Krain'
'Fumiko' (*fortunei*) (5) B&SWJ 6124 WCru
'Funkii' (X *petraschii*) (7) NMen
funstonii (10) CGra
'Gaertneri' (*mariae-theresiae*) (7) NMen

'Gaiety' (15) COkL ECho MDHE SPoG
'Galaxie' (x *megaseiflora*) (7) CLyd EPot LFox NDlv NMen
'Ganymede' (*burseriana*) (7) NJOw NMen
§ x ***gaudinii*** (8) CLyd ECtt EGoo GGar GTou LRHS NDlv NMen NWCA SPoG WGor WPer
'Gelber Findling' (7) EPot LRHS MDHE WAbe
'Gem' (x *irvingii*) (7) CLyd NDlv NLAp NMen WAbe
'General Joffre' (15) see *S.* 'Maréchal Joffre'
'Geoff Wilson' (x *biasolettoi*) **new** EPot
georgei (7) CLyd EPot GCrs NDlv NLAp NMen
- hybrid (7) GCrs
georgei x 'Winifred' CLyd
'Gertie Pritchard' (x *megaseiflora*) see *S.* 'Mrs Gertie Prichard'
x ***geuderi*** *sensu stricto* hort. see *S.* 'Eulenspiegel'
§ x ***geum*** (11) CHid MRav NWoo SIng WFar WMoo
- Dixter form (11) ECha SMHy SUsu WFar WWpP
'Glauca' (*paniculata* var. *brevifolia*) see *S.* 'Labradorica'
'Gleborg' (15) EWes MDHE SPoG
'Gloria' (*burseriana*) (7) ♀H4 CLyd EHyt LFox LRHS NMen NSla SBla SIng WPat
x ***gloriana*** (7) see *S.* 'Godiva'
'Gloriana' see *S.* 'Godiva'
'Gloriosa' (x *gloriana*) (7) see *S.* 'Godiva'
§ 'Godiva' (x *gloriana*) (7) CLyd NMen WAbe
'Goeblii' (7) NDlv
'Gold Dust' (x *eudoxiana*) (7) CLyd GCrs GTou LFox NJOw NLAp NMen NRya
'Golden Falls' (15/v) EWes GKir GTou LRHS MBNS NEgg SPlb SPoG WPat
Golden Prague (x *pragensis*) see *S.* 'Zlatá Praha'
'Goring White' (7) NMen
'Gothenburg' (7) CLyd NMen WAbe
'Grace' (x *arendsii*) (15/v) see *S.* 'Seaspray'
'Grace Farwell' (x *anglica*) (7) EPot LRHS MBar NDlv NMen NRya NWCA SBla WHoo
granulata (15) CNic CRWN EDAr NLar
granulata 'Flore Pleno' see 'Flore Pleno'
'Gratoides' (x *grata*) (7) NMen
§ 'Gregor Mendel' (x *apiculata*) (7) ♀H4 CLyd CMea EPot GTou ITim LRHS NDlv NJOw NLAp NMen SBla SRms WAbe WHoo WTel
grisebachii see *S. federici-augusti* subsp. *grisebachii*
- subsp. ***montenegrina*** see *S. federici-augusti*
'Haagii' (x *eudoxiana*) (7) ELan GTou NDlv NMen WTel
'Harbinger' (7) CLyd WAbe
'Hareknoll Beauty' EPot GCrs MDHE NHar NMen NRya SOkd WAbe
'Harlow Car' (7) CLyd LFox NMen NSla
'Harlow Car' x ***poluniniana*** (7) CPBP
'Harold Bevington' (*paniculata*) (8) MDHE
'Harry Marshall' (x *irvingii*) (7) CLyd NDlv NMen
'Hartside Pink' (*umbrosa*) (11) CLyd NWoo
'Hartswood White' (15) MDHE MWat
'Harvest Moon' (*stolonifera*) (5) CBct CHEx EBee EMan GAbr MBnl NCGa NMyG NPri
'Hedwig' (x *malbyana*) (7) NMen
x ***heinreichii*** *sensu stricto* hort. see *S.* 'Ernst Heinrich'
'Hi-Ace' (15/v) CLyd ECtt GTou LFox MHer NLAp SPlb SPoG WFar
'Highdownensis' (8) MDHE NDlv
'Hime' (*stolonifera*) (5) SIng WCru
'Hindhead Seedling' (x *boydii*) (7) CLyd LRHS NDlv NJOw NMen SIng WAbe
hirsuta (11) EBla EBrs EMar GGar IFro MDHE NFla WCru WHal
'Hirsuta' (x *geum*) see *S.* x *geum*
'Hirtella' Ingwersen (*paniculata*) (8) EPot MDHE
'His Majesty' (x *irvingii*) (7) LFox NMen WAbe
'Hocker Edge' (x *arco-valleyi*) (7) CLyd ITim LFox NDlv NMen WAbe
'Holden Seedling' (15) ECtt EWes MDHE
'Honington' (x *poluanglica*) (7) ITim
x ***hornibrookii*** (7) NLAp WPat
hostii (8) CLyd GKev GTou LBee LRHS NJOw WTin
§ - subsp. ***hostii*** (8) MDHE
- - var. ***altissima*** (8) STre
- subsp. ***rhaetica*** (8) MDHE NBro NDlv NMen WAbe
'Hsitou Silver' (*stolonifera*) (5) CFee GCal
- - B&SWJ 1980 EVFa WCru
'Hunscote' ITim NMen
hybrid JB 11 NMen
§ ***hypnoides*** (15) MOne WAbe
hypostoma (7) CLyd
'Icicle' (x *elisabethae*) (7) NMen WAbe
'Ignaz Dörfler' (7) WAbe
imparilis (5) WCru
'Ingeborg' (15) ECha LRHS MDHE
iranica (7) CLyd CStu EHyt ITim NLAp NMen NSla
- pink (7) EHyt
'Irene Bacci' (x *baccii*) (7) CLyd NMen
'Iris Prichard' (x *hardingii*) (7) CLyd ITim WAbe WHoo
'Irish' (15) MDHE
x ***irvingii*** (7) NDlv
x ***irvingii*** *sensu stricto* hort. see *S.* 'Walter Irving'
'Ivana' (x *caroliquarti*) (7) WAbe
jacquemontiana (1) WAbe
'James Bremner' (15) LRHS MDHE NBur
'Jan Palach' (x *krausii*) (7) NMen
'Jason' (x *elisabethae*) (7) NMen
'Jenkinsiae' (x *irvingii*) (7) ♀H4 CFee CLyd EPot ESis GKir GTou ITim LRHS NDlv NLAp NMen NRya NWCA SChu SIng SMer WAbe WHoo WPat
§ 'Johann Kellerer' (x *kellereri*) (7) CFee EPot LFox NDlv NSla SBla
'John Tomlinson' (*burseriana*) (7) CLyd NMen
'Jorg' (x *biasolettoi*) **new** EPot
'Josef Capek' (x *megaseiflora*) (7) CLyd EPot NMen
'Josef Mánes' (x *borisii*) (7) NMen
'Joy' see *S.* 'Kaspar Maria Sternberg'
'Joy Bishop' (7) WAbe
'Judith Shackleton' (x *abingdonensis*) (7) CLyd NDlv NMen WAbe
'Juliet' see *S.* 'Riverslea'
§ ***juniperifolia*** (7) CMea GAbr GKir GTou LRHS MHer NDlv NJOw NLAp NWCA SChu SMer SRms
- subsp. ***sancta*** see *S. sancta*
'Jupiter' (x *megaseiflora*) (7) CLyd LRHS NDlv NLAp NMen
'Kampa' (7) CLyd NMen

§ ***karadzicensis*** (7)	NMen
'Karasin' (7)	CLyd NMen
'Karel Capek' (x *megaseiflora*) (7)	CLyd CMea EPot NDlv NJOw NRya NSla WAbe
'Karel Stivín' (x *edithae*) (7)	CLyd NMen
'Karlstejn' (x *borisii*) (7)	NDlv
§ 'Kaspar Maria Sternberg' (x *petraschii*) (7)	CLyd LFox NJOw NMen WPat
'Kath Dryden' (x *anglica*) (7)	GKev ITim NLAp
'Kathleen Pinsent' (8) ♀H4	CLyd EPot GCrs MDHE NDlv NWCA WAbe
'Kathleen' (x *polulacina*) (7)	CLyd NLAp
'Katrin' (x *borisii*) (7) **new**	WAbe
x ***kellereri*** *sensu stricto* hort.	see *S.* 'Johann Kellerer'
'Kew Gem' (x *petraschii*) (7)	NMen
'Kewensis' (x *kellereri*) (7)	NDlv NMen WAbe
'Kineton' (x *poluanglica*) (7)	ITim NMen
'King Lear' (x bursiculata) (7)	CLyd EPot LFox LRHS NMen SBla
'Kingscote White' (15)	ITim MDHE
'Kinki Purple' (*stolonifera*) (5)	GCal WCru
'Knapton Pink' (15)	MDHE NBlu NPri NRya WAbe WFar
'Knapton White' (15)	MDHE
§ x ***kochii*** (7)	EHyt
§ 'Kolbiana' (x *paulinae*) (7)	CLyd
§ 'Krain' (x *fritschiana*) (8)	EPot SOkd
'Krákatit' (x *megaseiflora*) (7)	NMen WAbe
'Krasava' (x *megaseiflora*) (7)	CLyd CPBP EPot ITim NMen
'Kyrillii' (x *borisii*) (7)	CLyd NMen
'Labe' (x *arco-valleyi*) (7)	CLyd CNic CPBP EPot LRHS NMen SBla WAbe
§ 'Labradorica' (*paniculata*) (8)	MDHE
'Lady Beatrix Stanley'	see *S.* 'Beatrix Stanley'
'Lagraveana' (*paniculata*) (8)	NDlv
x ***landaueri*** *sensu stricto* hort.	see *S.* 'Leonore'
'Latonica' (*callosa*) (8)	EPot SOkd
'Lemon Hybrid' (x *boydii*) (7)	NMen
'Lemon Spires' (7)	NMen
'Lenka' (x *byam-groundsii*) (7)	NJOw NMen NSla WAbe
'Leo Gordon Godseff' (x *elisabethae*) (7)	LRHS NMen
§ 'Leonore' (x *landaueri*) (7)	LRHS
'Letchworth Gem' (x *urbium*) (11)	GCal NWCA
x ***leyboldii*** (7)	GTou
'Lidice' (7)	CLyd NDlv NLAp NMen WAbe WHoo
'Lilac Time' (x *youngiana*) (7)	NMen
lilacina (7)	CLyd NMen WAbe WPat
'Limelight' (*callosa*) (8)	MDHE WAbe
'Lindau' (7)	NMen
lingulata	see *S. callosa*
'Lismore Carmine' (x *lismorensis*) (7)	CLyd GCrs NDlv NLAp NMen NWCA
'Lismore Cherry' (7)	CLyd
'Lismore Gem' (x *lismorensis*) (7)	NLAp NMen
'Lismore Mist' (x *lismorensis*) (7)	CLyd EHyt NMen
'Lismore Pink' (x *lismorensis*) (7)	CLyd EPot NDlv NLAp NMen NWCA
'Little Piggy' (*epiphylla*) (5)	WCru
'Lohengrin' (x *hoerhammeri*) (7)	EPot
longifolia (8)	GKev NSla WAbe WGor WLin
'Louis Armstrong' (Blues Group)	EPot WAbe
Love Me	see *S.* 'Miluj Mne'
lowndesii (7)	EHyt
'Ludmila Subrová' (x *bertolonii*) (7)	CLyd NMen
'Lusanna' (x *irvingii*) (7)	CLyd
'Luschtinetz' (15)	MDHE
'Lutea' (*diapensioides*)	see *S.* 'Wilhelm Tell', 'Primulina'
'Lutea' (*marginata*)	see *S.* 'Faust'
§ 'Lutea' (*paniculata*) (8) ♀H4	EPot GTou LBee LRHS NBro NDlv NJOw SChu
'Luzníce' (x *poluluteopurpurea*) (7)	NDlv NMen
macedonica	see *S. juniperifolia*
'Magdalena' (x *thomasiana*) (7)	NMen
'Major' (*cochlearis*) (8) ♀H4	EPot LRHS WGor
§ 'Maréchal Joffre' (15)	MDHE NEgg NPri
'Margarete' (x *borisii*) (7)	CLyd NMen
marginata (7)	CLyd LFox WAbe
- var. ***balcanica***	see *S. marginata* var. *rocheliana*
- var. ***boryi*** (7)	CLyd LRHS NMen
- var. ***coriophylla*** (7)	EPot NMen NWCA WAbe
- var. ***karadzicensis***	see *S. karadzicensis*
§ - var. ***rocheliana*** (7)	CLyd EPot LRHS NMen
- - 'Balkan' (7)	CLyd
'Maria Callas' (x *poluanglica*) (7)	CLyd
'Maria Luisa' (x *salmonica*) (7)	GCrs LFox NDlv NMen NWCA WAbe
'Marianna' (x *borisii*) (7)	CLyd ITim NDlv NMen NRya
'Marie Louise' **new**	CFee
'Maroon Beauty' (*stolonifera*) (5)	EBee ECtt EMan EMar MDKP WCot
'Mars' (x *elisabethae*) (7)	NMen
'Marshal Joffre' (15)	see *S.* 'Maréchal Joffre' (15)
§ 'Martha' (x *semmleri*) (7)	CLyd NMen
'Mary Golds' (Swing Group) (7)	CLyd
matta-florida (7)	NMen
'May Queen' (7)	NMen
x ***megaseiflora*** *sensu stricto* hort.	see *S.* 'Robin Hood'
'Melrose' (x *salmonica*) (7)	NMen
mertensiana (6)	CLyd GTou NBir WCru
'Meteor' (7)	NDlv NJOw NRya
micranthidifolia (4)	CLAP EBee WPGP
(Milford Group) 'Aldo Bacci' (7)	NMen
'Millstream Cream' (x *elisabethae*) (7)	CLyd ITim NJOw NMen
§ 'Miluj Mne' (x *poluanglica*) (7)	EHyt ITim LFox NDlv NLAp
'Minnehaha' (x *elisabethae*) (7)	ITim WAbe
'Minor' (*cochlearis*) (8) ♀H4	EHyt GTou LFox LRHS NMen NWCA SChu SIng WPat
'Minor Glauca' (*paniculata*)	see *S.* 'Labradorica'
'Minutifolia' (*paniculata*) (8)	CPBP LFox LRHS MDHE NDlv NWCA
§ 'Miss Chambers' (x *urbium*) (11)	EMan MWgw SMHy SUsu WCot WMoo WPen WSHC

	Plant	Suppliers
	'Mona Lisa' (x *borisii*) (7)	CLyd NLAp NMen WAbe WPat
	'Monarch' (8) **new**	WAbe
	'Moonlight'	see *S.* 'Sulphurea'
	moschata	see *S. exarata* subsp. *moschata*
	'Mossy Red' **new**	COkL
	'Mossy Triumph' **new**	GAbr NEgg
	'Mother of Pearl' (x *irvingii*) (7)	CLyd EPot ITim NDlv NLAp NMen
	'Mother Queen' (x *irvingii*) (7)	CLyd NLAp NMen WPat
	'Mount Nachi' (*fortunei*) (5)	CBct CDes CLyd EBee EBrs EMar EPfP EWes GAbr GCal GEdr GMaP IBal IPot LRHS MSte NBro NMen NMyG SChu SPla SPoG SSpi WAbe WCot WFar WOld WPGP WPer
	'Mrs E. Piper' (15)	COkL MDHE
§	'Mrs Gertie Prichard' (x *megaseiflora*) (7)	LFox NMen WAbe
	'Mrs Helen Terry' (x *salmonica*) (7)	CLyd EPot LRHS NDlv NMen
	'Mrs Leng' (x *elisabethae*) (7)	MDKP NMen
	mutata (8)	CLyd GKev
	'Myra' (x *anglica*) (7)	CLyd LFox LRHS NMen NWCA WHoo WPat
	'Myra Cambria' (x *anglica*) (7)	NDlv NMen WAbe
	'Myriad' (7)	CLyd NMen
	'Nancye' (x *goringiana*) (7)	CLyd EHyt EPot NDlv NLAp NMen WAbe
§	***nelsoniana*** (4)	NJOw
	'Nimbus' (*iranica*) (7)	CLyd NMen WAbe
	'Niobe' (x *pulvilacina*) (7)	CLyd EHyt NMen
	'Norvegica' (*cotyledon*) (8)	GTou MDHE
	'Notata' (*paniculata*) (8)	NLAp
	'Nottingham Gold' (x *boydii*) (7)	CLyd EPot ITim NJOw NMen
	'Obristii' (x *salmonica*) (7)	NDlv NMen NRya
§	***obtusa*** (7)	EPot NMen
	'Ochroleuca' (x *elisabethae*) (7)	NMen
	'Odysseus' (*sancta*) (7)	NMen
	'Olymp' (*scardica*) (7)	NMen
	'Opalescent' (7)	CLyd LFox NJOw NMen
§	'Ophelia' (x *arco-valleyi*) (7)	NMen
	oppositifolia (7)	GIBF GKir GTou MBNS MHer MOne NLAp NSla SPlb SPoG SRms WAbe
	- from Iceland (7)	WAbe
	- 'Le Bourg d'Oisans' **new**	EHyt
*	- subsp. ***oppositifolia*** var. ***latina*** (7)	CLyd EPot GCrs GKev GTou NLAp
	oppositifolia x ***biflora***	see *S.* x *kochii*
	'Oriole' (x *boydii*) (7)	NMen
	'Ottone Rosai' (7) **new**	SOkd
	'Oxhill' (7)	ITim NMen
§	***paniculata*** (8)	CNic EPot ESis GGar GKev GKir GTou LRHS MDKP MHer MWat NDlv NLAp NSla SAga SPlb SRms WFar WHoo
§	- var. ***baldensis*** (8)	CLyd CTri EHyt GKir GTou LRHS MBar MWat NBro NDlv NLAp NMen NRya SBla SIng SPlb WAbe
§	- var. ***brevifolia*** (8)	COkL
§	- subsp. ***cartilaginea*** (8)	SBla WAbe
	- subsp. ***kolenatiana***	see *S. paniculata* subsp. *cartilaginea*
	- subsp. ***neogaea*** (8)	see *S.* 'Labradorica'
	paradoxa (15)	COkL EPot LRHS SBla WGor
	'Parcevalis' (x *finnisiae*) (7x9)	CLyd
	'Parsee' (x *margoxiana*) (7)	NDlv NJOw NMen NRya
	x ***patens*** (8x9)	NJOw
§	'Paula' (x *paulinae*) (7)	NMen
	'Peach Blossom' (7)	CLyd EPot ITim LRHS NDlv NMen NRya
	'Peach Melba' (7)	CLyd CPBP CStu EPot NMen WAbe
	'Pearl Rose' (x *anglica*) (7)	LFox
	'Pearly Gates' (x *irvingii*) (7)	CLyd NDlv NMen
	'Pearly Gold' (15)	CMea LRHS NRya
	'Pearly King' (15)	ECho LRHS MHer NPri WAbe WFar
	'Pearly King' variegated (v) (15)	COkL
	x ***pectinata*** (8)	see *S.* 'Krain'
	pedemontana subsp. ***cervicornis*** (15)	MDHE
*	- from Mount Kasbak (15)	CLyd MDHE
	'Penelope' (x *boydilacina*) (7)	CLyd CMea EPot LRHS NMen WAbe WHoo WPat
	pensylvanica (4)	GCal
	'Perikles' (7)	NMen
	'Peter Burrow' (x *poluanglica*) (7) ♀H4	CLyd CPBP EHyt ITim NLAp NMen NWCA
	'Peter Pan' (15)	EPfP EPot GKir GTou LFox MHer NMen NPri NPro NRya SIng SPoG WPat WPnn
	'Petra' (7)	CLyd EPot ITim NJOw NMen WAbe
	x ***petraschii*** (7)	CLyd ITim
§	'Phoenix' (x *biasolettoi*) (7)	EHyt LRHS
	'Pilatus' (x *boydii*) (7)	NMen
	'Pink Cloud' (*fortunei*) (5) **new**	WAbe
	'Pink Haze' (*fortunei*) (5) **new**	WAbe
	'Pink Mist' (*fortunei*) (5) **new**	WAbe
	'Pink Pagoda' (*rufescens*) (5)	CLAP GEdr WCru
	'Pink Pearl' (7)	CMea NMen
	'Pixie' (15)	COkL CTri ECtt GKir LRHS NArg NLAp NMen NPri SIng SPoG SRms
	'Pixie Alba'	see *S.* 'White Pixie'
	'Plena' (*granulata*)	see *S.* 'Flore Pleno'
	'Pollux' (x *boydii*) (7)	EPot NMen
	x ***poluanglica*** (7)	NLAp
	poluniniana (7)	CLyd LFox NWCA WAbe
	poluniniana x 'Winifred'	CLyd
	'Pompadour' (15)	LRHS MDHE
	'Popelka' (*marginata*) (7)	CLyd
	porophylla (7)	GCrs NMen
	- var. ***thessalica***	see *S. sempervivum* f. *stenophylla*
	aff. ***porophylla*** (7)	NWCA
	'Portae' (x *fritschiana*) (8)	NJOw
	'Primrose Bee' (x *apiculata*) (7)	EPot
	'Primrose Dame' (x *elisabethae*) (7)	ITim MDKP NMen WAbe
	'Primulaize' (9x11)	CLyd MHer NLar NMen
	'Primulaize Salmon' (9x11)	NDlv NWoo WHoo WPer
§	'Primulina' (x *malbyana*) (7)	LFox NDlv NMen
	primuloides	see *S.* 'Primuloides'
§	'Primuloides' (*umbrosa*) (11) ♀H4	LFox NPri SPoG SRms SWvt WEas
	'Prince Hal' (*burseriana*) (7)	CLyd EPot LRHS NDlv NJOw NLAp NMen
	'Princess' (*burseriana*) (7)	CLyd EHyt LRHS NJOw NMen
	'Probynii' (*cochlearis*) (8)	EPot MDHE MWat NDlv NMen WAbe
	'Prometheus' (x *prossenii*) (7)	CLyd
	'Prospero' (x *petraschii*) (7)	NMen

	Name	Suppliers
	x ***prossenii*** *sensu stricto* hort.	see *S.* 'Regina'
	'Pseudofranzii' (x *paulinae*) (7)	NWCA
	x ***pseudokotschyi*** *sensu stricto* hort.	see *S.* 'Denisa'
	'Pseudopungens' (x *apiculata*) (7)	EPot
	'Pseudoscardica' (x wehrhahnii) (7)	NMen
	'Pseudovaldensis' (*cochlearis*) (8)	CNic MDHE NHar WAbe
	pubescens (15)	WAbe
	- subsp. ***iratiana*** (15)	EPot NLAp
	punctata (4)	see *S. nelsoniana*
	'Pungens' (x *apiculata*) (7)	NDlv NJOw NMen
	'Purple Piggy' (*epiphylla*)	CLAP WCru
	'Purple Piggy' (*stolonifera*) (5)	CFee CLAP
	'Purpurea' (*fortunei*)	see *S.* 'Rubrifolia'
	'Purpurteppich' (15)	MDHE WPer
§	'Pygmalion' (x *webrii*) (7)	CLyd WGor WPat
	'Pyramidalis' (*cotyledon*) (8)	EPfP EWTr SRms
	'Pyrenaica' (*oppositifolia*) (7)	NMen
	'Quarry Wood' (x *anglica*) (7)	CLyd NMen
	'Rainsley Seedling' (8)	EPot GKev MDHE NBro NMen
	ramulosa (7)	NMen
	'Red Poll' (x *poluanglica*) (7)	CLyd CPBP EHyt EPot ITim NDlv NMen NRya WAbe
§	'Regina' (x *prossenii*) (7)	CLyd MHer NMen
	retusa (7)	CLyd NLAp NMen NSla NWCA
	'Rex' (*paniculata*) (8)	EHyt EPot
§	'Riverslea' (x *hornibrookii*) (7)	LFox LRHS NMen
§	'Robin Hood' (x *megaseiflora*) (7)	CFee CLyd LFox LRHS NMen SBla WHoo WPat
	'Rokujô' (*fortunei*) (5)	CLAP EBrs GKir NLar NLon NPro WFar WTMC
	'Romeo' (x *hornibrookii*) (7)	CLyd
	'Rosea' (*cortusifolia*) (5)	CLAP
§	'Rosea' (*paniculata*) (8) 🏆H4	GKir GTou LBee NBro NDlv NSla SBla SRms WTel
	'Rosea' (x *stuartii*) (7)	NDlv NMen
	'Rosemarie' (x *anglica*) (7)	CLyd NMen
	'Rosenzwerg' (15)	LRHS WFar
	'Rosina Sündermann' (x *rosinae*) (7)	NDlv
	rotundifolia (12)	CLyd EBee GBin MDKP SSpi
§	- subsp. ***chrysospleniifolia*** var. ***rhodopea*** (12)	WCru
	'Roy Clutterbuck' (7)	NMen
	'Rubella' (x *irvingii*) (7)	CLyd
§	'Rubrifolia' (*fortunei*) (5)	More than 30 suppliers
*	'Ruby Red'	NPro
	'Ruby Wedding' (*cortusifolia*) (5)	WCru
	rufescens (5)	GEdr SOkd
	- BWJ 7510	WCru
	- BWJ 7684	WCru
	'Rusalka' (x *borisii*) (7)	CLyd NMen
	'Russell Vincent Prichard' (x *irvingii*) (7)	NMen
	'Ruth Draper' (*oppositifolia*) (7)	NLAp NWCA WAbe
	'Ruth McConnell' (15)	CMea LRHS MDHE
	'Sabrina' (x *fallsvillagensis*) (7)	CLyd
	'Saint John's' (x *fritschiana*) (8)	COkL EBur MDHE NJOw WAbe
	'Saint Kilda' (*oppositifolia*) (7)	GCrs GTou
	x ***salmonica*** *sensu stricto* hort.	see *S.* 'Salomonii'
§	'Salomonii' (x *salmonica*) (7)	CLyd NDlv NMen SRms
	'Samo' (x *bertolonii*) (7)	CLyd NMen
	sancta (7)	CLyd EPot LFox LRHS NMen SRms
	- subsp. ***pseudosancta*** (7)	see *S. juniperifolia*
	- - var. ***macedonica***	see *S. juniperifolia*
	'Sandpiper' (7)	NMen
	sanguinea (1)	MDHE
	'Sanguinea Superba' (x *arendsii*) (15) 🏆H4	MDHE SIng
	'Sara Sinclair' (x *arco-valleyi*) (7)	CMea
	sarmentosa	see *S. stolonifera*
	'Sartorii'	see *S.* 'Pygmalion'
	'Saturn' (x *megaseiflora*) (7)	NMen
	'Sázava' (x *poluluteopurpurea*) (7)	CLyd NMen WAbe
	scardica (7)	NBro NMen
	- var. ***dalmatica***	see *S. obtusa*
	- f. ***erythrantha*** (7)	CLyd
	- subsp. ***korabensis*** (7)	GCrs
	- var. ***obtusa***	see *S. obtusa*
§	'Schelleri' (x *petraschii*) (7)	EHyt NJOw NMen
	'Schneeteppich' (15)	WPer
§	'Schwefelblüte' (15)	GTou LRHS NJOw NPri NWCA SPoG WPat
	scleropoda (7)	NMen
§	'Seaspray' (x *arendsii*) (15/v)	EWes
	'Seissera' (*burseriana*) (7)	EPot ITim NMen
	x ***semmleri*** *sensu stricto* hort.	see *S.* 'Martha'
	sempervivum (7)	CLyd LFox NMen NSla NWCA WTin
§	- f. ***stenophylla*** (7)	GTou MHer
	sendaica (5)	WCru
	- B&SWJ 7448	GEdr
	'Sendtneri' (8)	WAbe
	sibirica (14)	GTou
§	'Silver Cushion' (15/v)	CMea COkL CTri CWan ELan EPfP GAbr GTou LAst LRHS MBar MDHE NJOw SMer SPlb SPoG WAbe WMoo
	'Silver Edge' (x *arco-valleyi*) (7)	NMen WAbe
	Silver Farreri Group (8)	NDlv
	- 'Snowflake' (8) 🏆H4	CNic MDHE NDlv
	'Silver Maid' (x *fritschiana*) (8)	NMen SOkd WAbe
	'Silver Mound'	see *S.* 'Silver Cushion'
	'Sir Douglas Haig' (15)	MDHE
	'Snowcap' (*pubescens*) (15)	EHyt EPot NDlv NWCA
	'Snowdon' (*burseriana*) (7)	NMen
§	'Sofia' (x *borisii*) (7)	EPot LFox
	'Somerset Seedling' (8)	MDHE
	'Sorrento' (*marginata*) (7)	NMen
§	'Southside Seedling' (8) 🏆H4	CLyd COkL EPot GEdr GGar GKev GKir GMaP GTou IHMH LRHS MAvo MBar NBro NJOw NMen NPri NRya NSla NWCA SIng SPet SPoG SRms WAbe WFar WHoo WPat WTin
	'Spartakus' (x *apiculata*) (7)	NDlv
	spathularis (11)	EBee MHar WCot WEas
	'Speciosa' (*burseriana*) (7)	NDlv

	'Splendens' (*oppositifolia*) (7) 🏆H4	EHyt ELan EPfP GKev LFox NDlv NLAp SBla SMer SRms WAbe WPat
	'Spotted Dog'	GEdr
	'Sprite' (15)	LRHS MDHE NPri SPoG
	spruneri (7)	LRHS NMen SIng
	- var. ***deorum*** (7)	NMen
	'Stansfieldii' (*rosacea*) (15)	GKir LRHS MDHE NJOw NMen SPlb
§	'Stella' (x *stormonthii*) (7)	SBla
	stellaris (4)	GTou
	stenophylla	see *S. flagellaris* subsp. ***stenophylla***
	stolitzkae (7)	NLAp NMen NWCA WAbe
§	***stolonifera*** (5) 🏆H2	CArn CHEx CHal CSpe ECho EWTr GBin LDai MHar NBro SBri SDix SIng SWvt WEas WFar WMoo WPnn
	'Stormonth's Variety'	see *S.* 'Stella'
	stribrnyi (7)	NMen SOkd
	- JCA 861-400	NWCA
	'Sturmiana' (*paniculata*) (8)	NMen SRms
	aff. ***subsessiliflora*** (7)	NWCA
	'Suendermannii' (x *kellereri*) (7)	NDlv SIng
	'Suendermannii Major' (x *kellereri*) (7)	CLyd LRHS NRya
	'Sugar Plum Fairy' (*fortunei*) (5)	CBcs CBct CLAP EBee EChP EHrv GSki LAst MBNS NBro SPer SPoG WCot WTMC
§	'Sulphurea' (x *boydii*) (7)	CMea CNic LFox LRHS NMen SChu SIng WAbe WHoo WPat
	'Sunset' (*anglica*) (7) **new**	WThu
	'Superba' (*callosa* var. *australis*) (8)	GCrs GTou MDHE
	'Swan' (x *fallsvillagensis*) (7)	NMen
	'Sylva' (x *elisabethae*) (7)	NMen
	'Symons-Jeunei' (8)	MDHE WAbe
	'Tábor' (x *schottii*) (7)	NMen
	'Tamayura' (*fortunei*) (5)	EBee MBNS
	taygetea (12)	ETow
	'Theoden' (*oppositifolia*) (7) 🏆H4	CLyd CMea EHyt EWes GCrs GTou NJOw NLAp NWCA SBla
	'Theresia' (x *mariae-theresiae*) (7)	NDlv NMen
	'Thorpei' (7)	NMen
	'Timmy Foster' (x *irvingii*) (7)	CLyd NMen
	tombeanensis (7)	CLyd NMen
	'Tricolor' (*stolonifera*) (5) 🏆H2	EBak LRHS SPer WFar
	trifurcata (15)	GGar
	'Triumph' (x *arendsii*) (15)	ECtt GTou LRHS NEgg NPri SBla WBVN
	'Tully' (x *elisabethae*) (7)	WPat
	'Tumbling Waters' (8) 🏆H4	EBee EPot GAbr LRHS NLAp NMen NSla SHel SIng WAbe WGor WPat
§	'Tvůj Den' (x *poluanglica*) (7)	NDlv NMen WAbe
§	'Tvůj Písen' (x *poluanglica*) (7)	CLyd NDlv NLAp
§	'Tvůj Polibek' (x *poluanglica*) (7)	EHyt EPot MDKP NDlv NLAp NMen SBla WAbe
§	'Tvůj Prítel' (x *poluanglica*) (7)	NDlv NLAp
§	'Tvůj Úsmev' (x *poluanglica*) (7)	CLyd NDlv NLAp NMen
§	'Tvůj Úspech' (x *poluanglica*) (7)	CLyd EHyt NDlv NLAp NMen SBla SOkd WAbe
	'Tycho Brahe' (x *doerfleri*) (7)	CLyd NDlv NMen WAbe
	'Tysoe' (7)	CLyd ITim NMen
	umbrosa (11)	CBrm EBee ENot LRHS MRav SPer SPlb SRms SWvt WCAu WMoo
	- 'Aurea'	see *S.* 'Aureopunctata'
	- var. ***primuloides***	see *S.* 'Primuloides'
	'Unique'	see *S.* 'Bodensee'
	x ***urbium*** (11) 🏆H4	CHEx EBee ELan EPfP EPza GKir LAst LEdu LGro MWgw NLon NSti SPet SRms WBVN WBor WBrk WCFE WFar WPer
	- ***primuloides*** 'Elliott's Variety'	see *S.* 'Clarence Elliott'
	'Vaccariana' (*oppositifolia*) (7)	ECho
	'Václav Hollar' (x *gusmusii*) (7)	NMen
	'Vahlii' (x *smithii*) (7)	NMen
	'Valborg'	see *S.* 'Cranbourne'
	'Valentine'	see *S.* 'Cranbourne'
	'Valerie Finnis'	see *S.* 'Aretiastrum'
	(Vanessa Group) 'Cio-Cio-San' (7)	NMen
I	'Variegata' (*cuneifolia*) (11/v)	ECho ECtt EPfP GGar IHMH MBar NBlu NEgg NVic SHFr SIng SPet SPlb SPoG WFar WMoo WPer WTel
	'Variegata' (*umbrosa*)	see *S.* 'Aureopunctata'
I	'Variegata' (x *urbium*) (11/v)	EBee EPfP GGar GKir LAst LGro LRHS MRav NFor NLar NSti NVic SRms SSto WBrk WEas WFar
	vayredana (15)	GCrs NWCA WAbe
	veitchiana (5)	GEdr NBro WCru
	'Venetia' (*paniculata*) (8)	MDHE
	'Vesna' (x *borisii*) (7)	CLyd NJOw NLAp NMen
§	***vespertina*** (10)	CGra
	'Vincent van Gogh' (x *borisii*) (7)	CLyd NMen
	'Vladana' (x *megaseiflora*) (7)	CLyd EPot NJOw NMen NRya SIng
	'Vlasta' (7)	CLyd NMen
	'Vltava' (7)	CLyd NMen
	'Volgeri' (x *hofmannii*) (7)	CLyd
	'Vreny' (8) **new**	GKev
	'W.A. Clark' (*oppositifolia*) (7)	WAbe
	'Wada' (*fortunei*) (5)	CAbP CBcs CBct CDes CElw CHar CLAP EBee EChP ECtt LAst MBri MDun MSte NBir NMyG NPri SGSe SPer SSpi WAul WCot WFar WOld WPGP WPop WTMC WWeb
§	'Wallacei' (15)	ECho MDHE NMen
	'Walpole's Variety' (8)	CBrm WPer
	'Walter Ingwersen' (*umbrosa*) (11)	SIng SRms
§	'Walter Irving' (x *irvingii*) (7)	CLyd EPot ITim LRHS NLAp NMen
	'Walton' (7)	ITim
	'Wasperton' (x *poluanglica*) (7) **new**	ITim
	'Weisser Zwerg' (15)	MDHE WAbe
	'Wellesbourne' (x *abingdonensis*) (7)	CLyd ITim
	'Welsh Dragon' (15)	MDHE WAbe
	'Welsh Red' (15)	WAbe
	'Welsh Rose' (15)	WAbe
	wendelboi (7)	CLyd EHyt LFox NMen
	'Wendrush' (x *wendelacina*) (7)	CLyd NMen
	'Wendy' (x *wendelacina*) (7)	NMen WAbe
	'Wetterhorn' (*oppositifolia*) (7)	CLyd
	'Wheatley Lion' (x *borisii*) (7)	NMen
	'Wheatley Rose' (7)	CLyd ITim LRHS

	'White Cap' (x *boydii*) (7)	NMen
§	'White Pixie' (15)	CLyd ECtt EPfP GKir LFox LRHS MHer NArg NJOw NLAp NPri NPro NRya SBla SIng SPlb SPoG SRms
	'White Star' (x *petraschii*)	see *S.* 'Schelleri'
	'Whitehill' (8) ♀H4	CLyd CMea ELan ESis GEdr GKir GMaP GTou LBee LFox LRHS NBro NLAp NMen SPet WHoo WPat WPer WTin
§	'Wilhelm Tell' (x *malbyana*) (7)	NMen
	'William Boyd' (x *boydii*) (7)	NSla WAbe
	'Winifred' (x *anglica*) (7)	CLyd EPot GCrs LFox NLAp NMen WAbe
	'Winifred Bevington' (8x11) ♀H4	CLyd EPot ESis GKev GTou LBee LRHS NBro NDlv NJOw NLAp NMen NRya SOkd WAbe WHoo WLin WPer WPnn
	'Winston Churchill' (15)	EPfP LRHS MBNS MDHE NPri
I	'Winston Churchill Alba' **new**	NPri
	'Winton' (x *paulinae*) (7)	CLyd NMen
	'Wisley' (*federici-augusti* subsp. *grisebachii*) (7) ♀H2-3	CNic NLAp NMen WHoo WPat
	'Wisley Primrose'	see *S.* 'Kolbiana'
	'Yellow Rock' (7)	NDlv NRya
	Your Day	see *S.* 'Tvůj Den'
	Your Friend	see *S.* 'Tvůj Prítel'
	Your Good Fortune	see *S.* 'Tvůj Uspech'
	Your Kiss	see *S.* 'Tvůj Polibek'
	Your Smile	see *S.* 'Tvůj Usmev'
	Your Song	see *S.* 'Tvůj Písen'
	Your Success	see *S.* 'Tvůj Uspech'
	x ***zimmeteri*** (8x11)	CLyd NMen
§	'Zlatá Praha' (x *pragensis*) (7)	CLyd CPBP NDlv NMen WAbe
	'Zlin' (x *leyboldii*) (7)	NMen

Scabiosa (*Dipsacaceae*)

	africana	CElw
	'Agnes Whitfield'	EChP EWin
	alpina	see *Cephalaria alpina*
	argentea	EWes
	atropurpurea	EGoo NArg SPav
	- 'Ace of Spades'	CDes CHad CSpe CWCL EChP LPio LRHS MDun SMad SPav SPoG WPGP WSan
§	- 'Chile Black'	More than 30 suppliers
§	- 'Chilli Pepper'PBR	CHar EBee EMan EWll LBmB LIck NCGa NPri SAga SPoG SUsu WWol
	- 'Chilli Red'	EBee SAga
§	- 'Chilli Sauce'PBR	CBcs CHar EBee EMan EPfP LBmB LIck NCGa NPri SUsu WWol
	- dark-flowered	LEdu SPav
§	- subsp. ***maritima***	EBee
	- 'Mixed Chile'	SUsu
	- 'Peter Ray'	CElw ECtt MSph SOkh SPav WWlt
	banatica	see *S. columbaria*
	'Betsy Trotwood'	LPio
	'Burgundy Bonnets'	CWCL LRHS
§	'Butterfly Blue'	EBee ENot EPfP GKir IHMH LRHS LSRN MBNS MBri NLar NRnb SCoo SHBN SMrm SPer SPla SPoG SWvt WAul WCAu WFar WWhi
	caucasica	CWCL EPfP GFlt GKev LAst NBlu NChi WBVN WFar WHoo
	- var. ***alba***	CKno EHrv EPfP MBow WFar WHoo
	- 'Blausiegel'	CFir CSam EBee EChP LAst LRHS MBNS MTis NFla NGdn SPet SPla SPoG WCAu
	- 'Clive Greaves' ♀H4	More than 30 suppliers
	- 'Crimson Cushion'	see *Knautia macedonica* 'Crimson Cushion'
	- 'Fama'	CFai CMdw CSim CSpe EBee EKen EMan EShb EVFa EWTr MBNS MWgw MWrn NArg NBir NLar SPlb SPoG SRms WFar WHil
	- 'Goldingensis'	CWCL GKir GMac GWCH MBNS MHer NBPC NGdn NPri SGSe WPer
	- House's hybrids	CSBt MMHG NGdn NVic SRms
	- 'Isaac House'	NEgg NLar
	- 'Kompliment'	CSim ENot LRHS MWgw NChi NEgg NLar SSvw WHoo
	- 'Lavender Blue'	CHar NBPC WFar
	- 'Miss Willmott' ♀H4	CHad CM&M CSam CWCL EBee EChP ECha ELan EPfP ERou GKir GSki LAst LRHS MBri MHer MWat MWgw SPer SPet SPla SPoG SWvt WAul WCAu WFar WMnd
	- 'Moerheim Blue'	EBee ERou NGby
	- 'Nachtfalter'	EBee
	- Perfecta Series	CSpe EBee EChP LAst LPio LRHS MMHG MWgw NGdn NLar SMrm
	- - 'Perfecta Alba'	COIW CSpe EBee EChP EMan GKir GMaP LAst LPio MWat NChi NLar NOrc NPri NRnb SMrm STes WHil WPop
	- - 'Perfecta Lilac Blue'	CWCL CWib GMaP GMac NRnb SGSe STes WCot
	- 'Stäfa'	CKno CM&M EBee ERou GSki LRHS MBri MMHG NLar SBla SPet SPla SUsu WAul WFar WMnd
	'Chile Black'	see *S. atropurpurea* 'Chile Black'
	'Chile Pepper'PBR	see *S. atropurpurea* 'Chilli Pepper'
	'Chile Red'	see *S. atropurpurea* 'Chilli Red'
	'Chile Sauce'PBR	see *S. atropurpurea* 'Chilli Sauce'
	cinerea	CSec
§	***columbaria***	CBgR EBee EBrs ECGP ENot MChe MLLN NLan NMir NWCA SMrm WHer WJek
*	- ***alpina***	CSec
	- 'Flower Power'	EBee
	- 'Misty Butterflies' **new**	CSam EShb GBri GSki NJOw SBch SHBN SPoG
	- 'Nana'	CBrm CMdw ECGP EGoo EShb GEdr GSki IBal NBir NCGa NGdn NLar NLsd NMen NPri SGSe SMar WCFE WMow WSan
§	- subsp. ***ochroleuca***	More than 30 suppliers
	- - var. ***webbiana***	SUsu
	cretica	XPep
	drakensbergensis	CHar EBee EKen EMan GGar LPhx LPio MDKP SHar SPav WHrl
	farinosa	CDes EBee LSou MHar MHer SGar WPer
	gigantea	see *Cephalaria gigantea*
	graminifolia	EBrs EDAr EGoo EHol EMan GBuc LPio LRHS MDKP NBir NMen NRnb NWCA SBch SRms
	- 'Pinkushion'	CStr
	- ***rosea***	EWes
	'Helen Dillon'	CBgR CFir CSam EBee EMan NLar NPro SHBN SOkh WWhi
	hymnettia	XPep
	incisa	EShb
	'Irish Perpetual Flowering'	EMan NDov WCot
	japonica	NEgg WHil WPer
	- var. ***acutiloba***	NChi NDov WHil
	- var. ***alpina***	CHar CSec CSpe EBee EChP EMag ESis GAbr GBuc GSki GTou IBal MLLN NArg NBlu NGdn NLon SHGN SPet SRot WHoo WSan WTin

- 'Blue Diamonds'	IBal
lucida	CDes CHea EBee EBrs EChP EMan EPfP GTou LRHS MRav MWrn NJOw NLAp NPri SAga SBla SPet WCAu WMnd WPGP WPat WPer
maritima	see *S. atropurpurea* subsp. *maritima*
'Midnight'	CMea CSpe SBch
'Miss Havisham'	CElw EBee ECtt EMan LPio WPGP
montana	see *Knautia arvensis*
ochroleuca	see *S. columbaria* subsp. *ochroleuca*
parnassi	see *Pterocephalus perennis*
'Peggotty'	EChP
'Pink Buttons'	CFir EVFa LAst LRHS MBNS MMHG NEgg NFla SPet SPla
'Pink Mist'PBR	EBee EMan EPfP GKir LRHS MBri NBir NEgg NLar SCoo SHBN SPer SPoG SRms WCAu
prolifera	LPhx WGwG
pterocephala	see *Pterocephalus perennis*
'Rosie's Pink'	ECtt EMan SMrm
rumelica	see *Knautia macedonica*
'Satchmo'	see *S. atropurpurea* 'Chile Black'
songarica JJ&JH 90/216	EBee
succisa	see *Succisa pratensis*
tatarica	see *Cephalaria gigantea*
tenuis	EMan LPhx NDov SHar
triandra	EBee SUsu
ucranica	EShb WOut XPep
'Ultra Violet'	SHar

Scadoxus (*Amaryllidaceae*)

multiflorus	CFwr LAma LRHS MBri MOak WCot
§ - subsp. ***katherinae*** ♀H1	ERea
natalensis	see *S. puniceus*
§ ***puniceus***	CDes ERea SYvo

Scaevola (*Goodeniaceae*)

aemula 'Blue Fan'PBR	see *S. aemula* 'Blue Wonder'
§ - 'Blue Wonder'PBR	EMan LAst LSou MOak NPer SHFr SWvt
- 'Petite'	CHal
- 'Zig Zag'PBR	LAst LSou WWol
Blauer Facher = 'Saphira'PBR	EWin WWol
Blue Ice = 'Danscaice'	LAst
crassifolia	SPlb
'Diamond' **new**	LSou SPoG

Scandix (*Apiaceae*)

pecten-veneris	MSal

Sceletium (*Aizoaceae*)

tortuosum **new**	MGol

Schefflera (*Araliaceae*)

actinophylla ♀H1	EBak SRms WMul
arboricola ♀H1	SEND WMul XBlo
- B&SWJ 7040	WCru
- 'Compacta'	MBri WMul
- 'Gold Capella' ♀H1	LRHS MBri SEND XBlo
- 'Trinetta'	MBri
delavayi	CHEx WMul
digitata	CTrC
elegantissima ♀H1	EShb
gracilis HWJ 622	WCru
hoi var. ***fantsipanensis*** B&SWJ 8228	WCru
impressa	CHEx
microphylla B&SWJ 3872	WCru
pueckleri	WMul
taiwaniana **new**	CHEx
- B&SWJ 7096	WCru

Schima (*Theaceae*)

argentea	see *S. wallichii* subsp. *noronhae* var. *superba*
wallichii	CFil
subsp. ***liukiuensis***	
§ - subsp. ***noronhae*** var. ***superba***	EPfP SSpi
- subsp. ***wallichii*** var. ***khasiana***	ISea
* ***yunnanensis***	GGGa

Schinus (*Anacardiaceae*)

molle	IDee XPep
polygamus	CBcs

Schisandra (*Schisandraceae*)

arisanensis	NLar
- B&SWJ 3050	WCru
aff. ***bicolor*** BWJ 8151	WCru
chinensis	CAgr CArn CPLN EBee LEdu MSwo WBVN WNor WSHC
- B&SWJ 4204	WCru
grandiflora	CDoC CPLN EBee ECot ELan EPfP LRHS MBlu NLar SBrw SCoo
- B&SWJ 2245	WCru
henryi	WCru
subsp. ***yunnanensis*** B&SWJ 6546	
nigra B&SWJ 5897	WCru
propinqua var. ***sinensis***	CBot CPLN CSPN LEdu MBlu NLar SBrw WCru WSHC
- - BWJ 8148	WCru
rubriflora	CBrm CHEx CPLN CRHN CSPN CTri CWSG EPfP LRHS MBlu MDun MGos NRib NSti SBrw SHBN SSpi
- (f)	CBcs ELan MGos SBra WSHC
- (m)	EMil
- BWJ 7898	WCru
rubriflora x ***grandiflora***	CPLN WCru
sphenanthera	ELan EMil EPfP GBin IMGH LRHS MDun NLar WSHC
verrucosa HWJ 664	WCru

Schivereckia (*Brassicaceae*)

doerfleri	CNic CSec

Schizachyrium (*Poaceae*)

§ ***scoparium***	CBig CBrm CKno CSpe EBee EHoe EMan EPPr EPza GFor GSki LRHS LRav MWhi NSti SGSe SUsu WDyG WGHP WMnd WWeb
- blue **new**	LRav
- 'The Blues'	CBig

Schizocodon see *Shortia*

Schizolobium (*Caesalpiniaceae*)

excelsum **new**	SBig

Schizophragma (*Hydrangeaceae*)

corylifolium	CPLN NLar
hydrangeoides	CBcs CDoC CFil CHEx CPLN EBee ELan EMil EPfP EWTr GKir LRHS MBlu MDun MGos NPal SBra SBrw SLim SLon SMur SPer SPoG SSpi SSta SWvt WDin
- B&SWJ 5954	WCru
- B&SWJ 6119	WCru

- 'Brookside Littleleaf'	see *Hydrangea anomala* subsp. *petiolaris* var. *cordifolia* 'Brookside Littleleaf'
- B&SWJ 6119 from Yakushima, Japan **new**	WCru
- 'Iwa Garami' **new**	NLar
- 'Moonlight' (v)	More than 30 suppliers
* - f. ***quelpartensis*** B&SWJ 1160	WCru
- 'Roseum' ♀H4	More than 30 suppliers
integrifolium ♀H4	CBcs CFil CMac CPLN ELan EPfP LRHS NEgg SBrw SDix SHBN SSpi WPGP
- var. ***fauriei***	WSHC
- - B&SWJ 1701	WCru
- var. ***molle*** **new**	CPLN
aff. ***megalocarpum***	CPLN
- BWJ 8150	WCru

Schizostachyum (*Poaceae*)

§ ***funghomii***	EPla MMoz WJun WPGP

Schizostylis ✿ (*Iridaceae*)

§ ***coccinea***	More than 30 suppliers
- f. ***alba***	More than 30 suppliers
- 'Anne'	WHoo
- 'Ballyrogan Giant'	CFir EBee IBlr MAvo WPGP
- 'Cardinal'	MAvo WFar
- 'Cindy Towe'	EBee
- 'Countesse de Vere' **new**	EBee
- 'Elburton Glow'	WFar WHoo
- 'Fenland Daybreak'	CHar EBrs EChP ELan ENot EVFa GKir IBal LIck LRHS MAvo MLan NGdn NLar SGSe SGar SPet SSpe WCAu WFar WHoo
- 'Gigantea'	see *S. coccinea* 'Major'
- 'Grandiflora'	see *S. coccinea* 'Major'
- 'Hilary Gould'	GBuc MAvo NCGa SChr WFar WHal
- 'Hint of Pink'	MAvo MDKP
- 'Jennifer' ♀H4	More than 30 suppliers
- late-flowering	NBPC
- 'Maiden's Blush'	CSpe EBee EBrs ECGP EChP ECtt EHrv GKir LPio LRHS MAvo MBnl MDKP MSte NFla NLar WFar
§ - 'Major' ♀H4	More than 30 suppliers
* - 'Marietta'	CHid MAvo
- 'Mollie Gould'	CStu EBee EHrv EMar EShb LAst MAvo MBNS NBre NLar SCoo WOut WTin
- 'Mrs Hegarty'	More than 30 suppliers
- 'November Cheer'	EBrs ECot GKir IBlr LRHS MAvo MSte NBir NLar NLon SSpe WFar
- 'Oregon Sunset'	EBee
- 'Pallida'	CAby CMil CPom CSam ECha EGra EHrv ELan EMan GBuc MRav NBir WFar WMoo
- 'Professor Barnard'	CFee CFwr CPrp CSpe GCal GMac IBlr LAst MSte NBir SApp SPla WFar WOld WPnn
- 'Red Dragon'	EBee MAvo WFar
- 'Salmon Charm'	EBee EBrs LRHS MAvo WFar
- 'Silver Pink'	IBlr
- 'Snow Maiden'	CAbP CElw CFai GBuc IBal LRHS MBNS SPav WLFP
I - 'Strawberry'	SPav
- 'Strawberry Fair' **new**	SMrm
§ - 'Sunrise' ♀H4	More than 30 suppliers
- 'Sunset'	see *S. coccinea* 'Sunrise'
- 'Tambara'	CMHG CMdw CPou EBee EHrv EMan GMac NGdn SApp WFar
- 'Viscountess Byng'	CBro CFwr CHea CPrp CTri CWCL EBee ERou GAbr GCal IBlr IGor LAst LRHS SPav SPer WFar WPer WWye
- 'Wilfred H. Bryant'	CBro CPen EMar IBal LAst LRHS MAvo NSti
- 'Zeal Salmon'	CBro CFee CFir CPou CPrp EBee ECha GAbr IBlr NBir SApp SMHy SSpi WFar WMoo

Schoenoplectus (*Cyperaceae*)

§ ***lacustris***	EMFW EPza GFor IHMH NArg WPop
- subsp. ***tabernaemontani***	EPza GFor LNCo
- - 'Albescens' (v)	CDWL CKno CWat EHon EMFW EPza GIBF LNCo LPBA NArg SWal WCot WDyG WHal WPop WPrP WWpP
- - 'Zebrinus' (v)	CBen CBot CDWL CFwr CKno CMea CWat EHon ELan EMFW EPfP EPza EUJe LPBA NArg SPlb SWal WCot WDyG WFar WHal WMoo WPnP WPop WPrP WWpP
pungens	GFor NBre

Schoenus (*Cyperaceae*)

pauciflorus	CFil CWCL EBee ECou EHoe EMan EWes NBro NChi SPoG WDyG WHal WMoo WPGP WPrP

Schotia (*Caesalpiniaceae*)

afra	CKob
brachypetala	CKob

Schrebera (*Oleaceae*)

alata	CKob

Sciadopitys (*Sciadopityaceae*)

verticillata ♀H4	CBcs CDoC CKen CTho EHul GKir IDee LBee LCon LLin LRHS MAsh MBar MBlu MBri MDun MGos SCoo SLim SPoG SSpi SWvt WDin WEve WFar WNor WOrn
- 'Firework'	CKen
- 'Globe'	CKen
- 'Gold Star'	CKen
- 'Golden Rush'	CKen LLin MGos NLar
- 'Goldmahne' **new**	CKen
- 'Grüne Kugel'	CKen
- 'Jeddeloh Compact'	CKen
- 'Kupferschirm' **new**	CKen
- 'Mecki'	CKen LLin
- 'Megaschirm' **new**	CKen
- 'Ossorio Gold' **new**	CKen
- 'Picola'	CKen
- 'Pygmy'	CKen
- 'Richie's Cushion' **new**	CKen
- 'Shorty'	CKen
- 'Speerspitze' **new**	CKen
- 'Starburst' **new**	CKen
- 'Sternschnuppe'	CKen LLin NLar

Scilla (*Hyacinthaceae*)

adlamii	see *Ledebouria cooperi*
amethystina	see *S. litardierei*
x ***allenii***	see x *Chionoscilla allenii*
amoena	WCot WShi
aristidis from Algeria **new**	CMon
autumnalis	CAvo CNic CStu EPot LAma LRHS WShi
- AB&S 4305 from Morocco **new**	CMon
- MS 771 from Crete **new**	CMon
bifolia ♀H4	CAvo CBro CPom EPot LAma LLWP LPhx LRHS WShi

- 'Alba'	CMea LPhx LRHS
- 'Rosea'	EPot LAma LLWP LRHS
bithynica ♀H4	SSpi WShi
campanulata	see *Hyacinthoides hispanica*
chinensis	see *S. scilloides*
cilicica	CMon CStu LAma
greilhuberi	CStu ERos WAbe WCot
haemorrhoidalis	CMon
MS 923 from Tenerife **new**	
hohenackeri	ERos
- BSBE 811	CMon WCot
hyacinthoides	CMon EBrs WBVN WCot
ingridiae	WWst
italica	see *Hyacinthoides italica*
japonica	see *S. scilloides*
kraussii	GIBF
latifolia SF 25 from Morocco **new**	CMon
libanotica	see *Puschkinia scilloides* var. *libanotica*
liliohyacinthus	CAby CAvo CBro CRow EHyt IBlr MMHG SBch SSpi
- 'Alba'	ERos
lingulata	CStu
- var. ***ciliolata***	CBro EPot ERos
- - SF 288 from Morocco **new**	CMon
§ ***litardierei*** ♀H4	CAvo CPom CStu EPot ERos GIBF LAma LPhx LRHS MBri NMen WCot
- from Yugoslavia **new**	CMon
madeirensis from Madeira **new**	CMon
mauretanica alba	CMon
- SF 65 from Morocco **new**	CMon
melaina **new**	WCot
messeniaca	CPom GIBF SHel
- MS 38 from Greece	CMon WCot
- 'Grecian Sky'	SIgm SUsu
§ ***mischtschenkoana*** ♀H4	CAvo CBro EHyt EPot LAma LRHS MBri WDav
- 'Tubergeniana' ♀H4	CMea GKev LPhx WCot
monophyllos	CFil
- S&B 184 from Portugal **new**	CMon
- var. ***tingitana***	ERos
morrisii	ERos
natalensis	CMon WCot WHil
non-scripta	see *Hyacinthoides non-scripta*
nutans	see *Hyacinthoides non-scripta*
obtusifolia AB&S 4410 from Morocco **new**	CMon
persica ♀H4	CPom ERos WCot
- BSBE 1054 from Iran **new**	CMon
- JCA 0.876.501	WCot
peruviana	More than 30 suppliers
- from Spain **new**	CMon
- S&L 285	WCot
- SB&L 20/1	WCot
- 'Alba'	CBcs CBro CFwr CMon CSWP CSpe CStu EBee ECha LAma LPio MTho SMrm WCot
- var. ***elegans*** from Morocco **new**	CMon
- var. ***gattefossei*** from Morocco **new**	CMon
- 'Grand Bleu' **new**	CFwr
* - var. ***ifniensis***	WCot
- - from Morocco **new**	CMon
- var. ***venusta*** S&L 311/2	WCot
- - from Morocco **new**	CMon
pratensis	see *S. litardierei*
puschkinioides	LAma
reverchonii	CFil EHyt ERos
- MS 418 from Spain **new**	CMon
rosenii	EHyt
- 'Bakuriani'	WWst
§ ***scilloides***	CBro EPot ERos GIBF SCnR SRot WCot
- MSF 782	SSpi
siberica ♀H4	CAvo EBrs EPfP GKev LAma LRHS NBlu NJOw SBch SPer WPer WShi
- 'Alba'	CBro EPfP EPot LAma LRHS SBch WShi
- subsp. ***armena***	CHEx
- 'Spring Beauty'	CBro CMea EPot LAma LPhx LRHS MBri SRms
- var. ***taurica***	ERos
'Tubergeniana'	see *S. mischtschenkoana*
verna	CDes CNic ERos WHer WShi
vicentina	see *Hyacinthoides vicentina*
violacea	see *Ledebouria socialis*

Scindapsus (*Araceae*)

aureus	see *Epipremnum aureum*
pictus (v)	LRHS MBri

Scirpoides (*Cyperaceae*)

§ ***holoschoenus***	CBig CRWN GFor

Scirpus (*Cyperaceae*)

angustifolius	LNCo
cernuus	see *Isolepis cernua*
cyperinus	CBrm CFwr GFor WWpP
holoschoenus	see *Scirpoides holoschoenus*
lacustris	see *Schoenoplectus lacustris*
- 'Spiralis'	see *Juncus effusus* f. *spiralis*
maritimus	see *Bolboschoenus maritimus*
sylvaticus	GFor
tabernaemontani	see *Schoenoplectus lacustris* subsp. *tabernaemontani*

Scleranthus (*Illecebraceae*)

biflorus	CTrC CWil EDAr ESis EWes NDlv NWCA SPlb WPer
uniflorus	CLyd CTrC EDAr EShb ESis GAbr GEdr NWCA SPlb WPrP

Scoliopus (*Trilliaceae*)

bigelowii	CStu SBla SCnR SOkd WFar
hallii	NMen SCnR SOkd WCru

Scolopendrium see *Asplenium*

Scopolia (*Solanaceae*)

anomala	CArn
carniolica	CArn CFir COld EBee EBrs EChP ELan EMon GCal GFlt GPoy IBlr LEdu LPhx MBlu MSal MSte NChi NLar NSti SPlb WAul WCru WPGP WSHC
§ - var. ***brevifolia***	CAvo EHrv EPPr LSpr SDys WBcn WTin
- - WM 9811	MPhe
- subsp. ***hladnikiana***	see *S. carniolica* var. *brevifolia*
- 'Zwanenburg'	EBee EHrv EPPr
lurida	see *Anisodus luridus*
physaloides	MSal
sinensis	see *Atropanthe sinensis*
stramoniifolia **new**	CElw

Scorzonera (*Asteraceae*)

suberosa subsp. ***cariensis***	EBee EHyt

Scrophularia (*Scrophulariaceae*)

	aquatica	see *S. auriculata*
§	***auriculata***	ELau LPBA MHer MSal NMir NPer WHer WWpP WWye
§	- 'Variegata' (v)	More than 30 suppliers
	buergeriana	MSal
	- 'Lemon and Lime' misapplied	see *Teucrium viscidum* 'Lemon and Lime'
	calliantha **new**	NJOw
	chrysantha **new**	NJOw
	grandiflora	WDyG WFar WSan
	nodosa	CArn CRWN EBee ELau GPoy MChe MSal NMir WCAu WHer WSel
	- ***tracheliodes***	CNat
	- ***variegata***	see *S. auriculata* 'Variegata'
	scopolii	EBee
	vernalis	EBee

Scutellaria ✿ (*Lamiaceae*)

	albida	EBee EPPr
§	***alpina***	CLyd CPBP EBee EMan GCrs GEdr GKev LBee LRHS NJOw SBla SPlb SRms SRot WBVN WGor WPer
	- 'Arcobaleno'	EPPr NLar SPet
	- 'Moonbeam' **new**	SHGN
	altissima	CArn EBee EBrs ELan EMan EMar GBuc MSal MWrn NBro NCGa NJOw SHel SPlb STes SYvo WCHb WPer
	'Amazing Grace'	EChP EMan EWes
	baicalensis	CArn EPPr EWll GPoy IBlr MSal SBla SIgm SPet SSvw WPer
	barbata	MSal
	californica NNS 98-511	WCot
	canescens	see *S. incana*
	columnae	EBee IFro
	diffusa	CPBP ECtt WPer
	formosana 'China Blue'	CAbP EPfP SBch
	galericulata	GPoy GWCH MHer MSal NVic WCHb WHer WJek WWye
	hastata	see *S. hastifolia*
§	***hastifolia***	CTri ECot ECtt EDAr EHyt NFor NSti WPer
*	***heldreichii*** **new**	EWTr
§	***incana***	CPom CSam EBee EBrs ECGP EHrv ELan EMan EMon EWTr LPhx LRHS NCGa NDov NSti SMrm SOkh SSvw SUsu WCAu WCot WWye
	indica	MSph WCFE
	- var. ***japonica***	see *S. indica* var. *parvifolia*
§	- var. ***parvifolia***	CLyd CPBP CStu EBee EBur EHyt EMan EWes LBee LRHS NWCA SBla SRot WPat
	- - 'Alba'	CLyd CPBP EHyt EMan ETow LBee LRHS LTwo SBla WPat
	lateriflora	CArn CBod CSec EBee ELau EOHP GBar GPoy MChe MGol MSal WCHb WHer WJek WPer WSel WWye
	maekawae B&SWJ 557a **new**	WCru
	nana var. ***sapphirina***	GKev NWCA
	novae-zelandiae	ECou EHyt LRHS NWCA
	orientalis	CPBP EBee ECtt GEdr LRHS NLAp SBch SBla WLin WPat
	- subsp. ***bicolor***	ECtt NWCA
	- subsp. ***carica***	WWye
	- 'Eastern Star'	NArg SPet
	- 'Eastern Sun'	GFlt SOkh
	- subsp. ***pinnatifida***	EHyt NLar NWCA
	pontica	CSec EWTr EWll MAvo NJOw NLar SBch WLin
	prostrata	CMHG EMan LTwo NLAp WPat
	scordiifolia	CLyd CMea CMil CNic CSam EBee ECha GKir IHMH NRya NWCA SBla SRms SUsu WFar WHal WHoo WTin WWye
	- 'Seoul Sapphire'	EMan GBin GCrs SOkd SOkh WBVN WCot WPtf
	serrata	EBee
	suffrutescens	XPep
	supina	see *S. alpina*
	tournefortii	EChP ECtt LLWP

seakale see *Crambe maritima*

Sebaea (*Gentianaceae*)

thomasii	GCrs WAbe

Securigera see *Coronilla*

Sedastrum see *Sedum*

Sedum ✿ (*Crassulaceae*)

	B&SWJ 737	EGoo
	NS 622	NWCA
§	'Abbeydore'	CKno EBee EBrs ECGP EChP EDAr EGoo EMan EMon EVFa MAnH NGby NSti WPGP WWeb
	acre	CTri ECot GPoy LAst MBar MHer NBlu SPlb XPep
	- 'Aureum'	EDAr EPfP ESis IHMH MBar MOne NBlu NLar SIng SPoG WFar WPat
	- 'Elegans'	ECtt EDAr GTou NJOw
§	- var. ***majus***	CChe CNic
	- 'Minus'	EDAr WFar
	adolphi **new**	EPfP
§	***aizoon***	EBee SChu SIde SPlb
	- 'Aurantiacum'	see *S. aizoon* 'Euphorbioides'
§	- 'Euphorbioides'	CMea CWCL EBee ECha ECtt EGoo ELan EWTr LDai LRHS MBNS MHer MRav MWgw NLar SGar SPer SPlb WFar WTin
	albescens	see *S. rupestre* f. *purpureum*
	alboroseum	see *S. erythrostictum*
§	***album***	CHal IHMH MBNS NBro WPer
§	- 'Chloroticum'	EDAr
	- 'Coral Carpet'	CBrm CNic EDAr EPfP ESis EWTr GAbr IHMH MBar MWat NJOw NRya SChu SPoG XPep
	- var. ***micranthum***	see *S. album* 'Chloroticum'
§	- subsp. ***teretifolium*** 'Murale'	CTri MBar
	altissimum	see *S. sediforme*
	altum	EMon LPhx WCot WFar WMoo
	amplexicaule	see *S. tenuifolium*
§	***anacampseros***	CNic EGoo SUsu WPer
	anglicum	MBow SChr
	athoum	see *S. album*
	atlanticum	see *S. dasyphyllum* subsp. *dasyphyllum* var. *mesatlanticum*
	Autumn Joy	see *S.* 'Herbstfreude'
§	'Bertram Anderson' ♀H4	More than 30 suppliers
	bithynicum 'Aureum'	see *S. hispanicum* var. *minus* 'Aureum'
	'Black Emperor'	EBee
*	***brachyphyllum*** **new**	EWTr
	brevifolium	GGar IHMH
	caeruleum	WGwG
	'Carl'	CKno COIW CPrp EBee EBrs EChP ECha EGoo EMan EMon GMaP LRHS MNFA MRav MSte MWgw

NBro NCGa NSti SUsu WCot WMnd WMoo WWeb
caucasicum WAbb WEas
cauticola 🏆H4 CLyd CNic COkL COlW CSpe EDAr EMan GCal MBrN MHer MRav SMrm SPoG SRms SRot WAbe
- from Lida ECho
- 'Coca-Cola' **new** CBct EPPr EWin
§ - 'Lidakense' CHEx CMea CStu CTri ECtt EMan GKir LRHS MBar MBri MTis NSla SBla SChu SIng SRot WFar
- 'Purpurine' GCal
- 'Robustum' EBee EWll
cauticola x **tatarinowii** EWes
'Citrus Twist' EBee EMan MBnl NPro
confusum EOas SChr SEND
crassipes see *Rhodiola wallichiana*
crassularia see *Crassula milfordiae*
cryptomerioides B&SWJ 054 WCru
cyaneum WAbe
dasyphyllum CNic GTou MBar MHer MOne MWat NRya NWCA SRms XPep
- subsp. **dasyphyllum** var. **glanduliferum** CHal
- - 'Lilac Mound' MDHE
§ - - var. **mesatlanticum** CNic MDHE NBir
- **mucronatis** see *S. dasyphyllum* subsp. *dasyphyllum* var. *mesatlanticum*
divergens XPep
douglasii see *S. stenopetalum* 'Douglasii'
drymarioides EBee
'Dudley Field' MHer SBch
'Eleanor Fisher' see *S. telephium* subsp. *ruprechtii*
ellacombeanum see *S. kamtschaticum* var. *ellacombeanum*
§ **erythrostictum** EBrs MTho
- 'Frosty Morn' (v) More than 30 suppliers
§ - 'Mediovariegatum' (v) CChe COlW EBee EChP EGoo ELan EMon EPfP ERou EVFa EWTr IFro LRHS MHer MNrw MRav NBPC NEgg SAga SHBN SWvt WBrE WFar WMnd WMoo WPer
§ **ewersii** CHEx CSLe EDAr GMaP GTou LRHS MHer NBro NLar SPlb WAbe
§ - var. **homophyllum** IHMH
§ **fabaria** EChP EMan WAbb WCot WFar
fastigiatum see *Rhodiola fastigiata*
floriferum see *S. kamtschaticum*
forsterianum subsp. **elegans** LGro SPlb
frutescens STre
furfuraceum NMen
'Gold Mound' CStu CTbh ENot LAst MGos NLar
* 'Green Expectations' EBee EChP MSph MSte
gypsicola EBee WPer
'Harvest Moon' CStr EBur
§ 'Herbstfreude' 🏆H4 More than 30 suppliers
heterodontum see *Rhodiola heterodonta*
hidakanum CAby CLyd ECtt EMFP GGar GMaP GTou NBro NMen SUsu WGHP WHoo WPat WTin
§ **hispanicum** ECho IHMH SPlb
- 'Albescens' CNic
- **glaucum** see *S. hispanicum* var. *minus*
§ - var. **minus** ECtt GTou MBar NPri NRya SChu SIng SPlb SPoG WMoo
§ - - 'Aureum' ECha EDAr ESis MBar NJOw SPoG WMoo
humifusum CPBP EBur EHyt EPot ETow NWCA SIng
hybridum WEas
- 'Immergrünchen' COkL
ishidae see *Rhodiola ishidae*
'Joyce Henderson' COlW CPrp CStr EBee EBrs EChP ECtt EMan EWTr LPio MRav NCGa NEgg NLar SBla SPer SUsu WBrk WCot WEas WMoo WOld WRHF WTin
§ **kamtschaticum** 🏆H4 ESis MBar MHer NJOw WFar
§ - var. **ellacombeanum** 🏆H4 CNic EDAr EGoo MHer NMen WCot
- - B&SWJ 8853 WCru
§ - var. **floriferum** 'Weihenstephaner Gold' More than 30 suppliers
- var. **kamtschaticum** 'Variegatum' (v) 🏆H4 CBrm CLyd CMea COkL ECtt EDAr EPPr EPfP LBee MHer MWat SBla SIng SPoG SRms SRot SWvt WEas WFar
- var. **middendorffianum** see *S. middendorffianum*
'Karfunkelstein' GBin
kirilovii see *Rhodiola kirilovii*
laxum subsp. **heckneri** SSpi
lineare CHEx LAst SSto
- 'Variegatum' (v) SChr
§ **lydium** GTou MBar MHer MOne SPlb
- 'Aureum' see *S. hispanicum* var. *minus* 'Aureum'
- 'Bronze Queen' see *S. lydium*
'Lynda Windsor'PBR CWCL EBee EChP EMan EPfP MBNS MBri MCCP NBro NLar NSti SPer SSpi
makinoi 'Ogon' CStu EBee
maweanum see *S. acre* var. *majus*
maximowiczii see *S. aizoon*
§ **middendorffianum** CLyd ECho EDAr EGoo EPPr GTou MBrN MDHE MHer MWat NMen SRms SRot WHoo
monregalense EDAr
'Moonglow' ECtt NMen
moranense CHal CNic ETow
morganianum 🏆H1 CHal EBak
murale see *S. album* subsp. *teretifolium* 'Murale'
'Neon' **new** LRHS
N **nevii** hort. SPlb
nicaeense see *S. sediforme*
obcordatum NMen
§ **obtusatum** COkL ECtt EDAr GGar NBlu NBro NJOw NSla
§ **ochroleucum** XPep
oppositifolium see *S. spurium* var. *album*
§ **oreganum** ECha EDAr ESis GAbr GMaP GTou IHMH MBar MWat NMen SPlb SRms SRot WPer
- 'Procumbens' see *S. oreganum* subsp. *tenue*
§ - subsp. **tenue** NRya WPat
§ **oregonense** CLyd EBur GTou NJOw NMen
oryzifolium 'Minor' EBur
oxypetalum STre
pachyclados see *Rhodiola pachyclados*
pachyphyllum **new** EPfP
palmeri CHEx CNic CSpe EMan EOas ETow NBir SChr SDix XPep
pilosum NMen
'Pink Chablis'PBR EBee EChP EMan MBnl NLar WHil
§ **pluricaule** CStu EHyt SChu SPlb SRms SRot WAbe
populifolium CMHG ECha GCal MHer STre WPer
praealtum EOas GGar SChr STre
pruinosum see *S. spathulifolium* subsp. *pruinosum*
pulchellum EWTr
§ 'Purple Emperor' More than 30 suppliers

'Red Cauli' **new** SMHy SUsu
'Red Rum' LRHS
reflexum L. see *S. rupestre*
reptans NRya
rhodiola see *Rhodiola rosea*
'Ringmore Ruby' WCot
'Rose Carpet' MBrN SWvt WWeb
rosea see *Rhodiola rosea*
rubroglaucum misapplied see *S. oregonense*
rubroglaucum Praeger see *S. obtusatum*
x ***rubrotinctum*** CHEx CHal SChr XPep
- 'Aurora' SChr
§ 'Ruby Glow' ♀H4 More than 30 suppliers
'Ruby Port' CSpe
§ ***rupestre*** CNic EPfP GGar MBNS MBar MHer MWhi NBlu SChu SPlb SPoG WHer XPep
- 'Angelina' EBee EPPr EWes MAvo NBir SBri SIng SUsu WCot
- 'Minus' CNic
- 'Monstrosum Cristatum' ITer NBir SMad
§ - f. ***purpureum*** NRya
ruprechtii see *S. telephium* subsp. *ruprechtii*
sarcocaule hort. see *Crassula sarcocaulis*
§ ***sediforme*** CArn EBrs EDAr XPep
- ***nicaeense*** see *S. sediforme*
selskianum COkL CRez EBee EWin GGar GTou IHMH MOne WFar
sexangulare EDAr ESis GAbr GGar IHMH MBar MHer MOne NRya SPlb SRms WFar XPep
sibiricum see *S. hybridum*
§ ***sieboldii*** CStu SIng
- 'Mediovariegatum' (v) ♀H2-3 CHEx EMan SPlb WFar WPer
'Silver Moon' EBur MDHE
spathulifolium ECha EPot ESis GTou MDKP MOne SChu WEas
- 'Aureum' EBur ECtt GKir GTou MBar NRya
- 'Cape Blanco' ♀H4 More than 30 suppliers
§ - subsp. ***pruinosum*** MDHE
- 'Purpureum' ♀H4 CBrm COIW EDAr EPfP GAbr GGar GKev GKir GMaP GTou IHMH LBee LRHS MBar MBri MHer MWat NBlu NJOw NMen NRya SBla SMer SPlb SPoG WAbe WBVN WFar WPer
§ ***spectabile*** ♀H4 CArn CHEx CHrt CPrp EBee ELan EPfP GKev GMaP LRHS MHer MRav NLsd SHFr SPer SPlb SRms WBor WBrk WCAu WFar WHil WTel WTin WWpP XPep
- 'Abendrot' EMon
- 'Album' CHEx
- 'Brilliant' ♀H4 More than 30 suppliers
- 'Carmen' EBee NEgg WMoo
- 'Iceberg' More than 30 suppliers
- 'Indian Chief' CM&M COIW CPrp EBee EBrs EChP ENot GCra GKir GMaP LAst LRHS MBrN MSte SPoG SVil WFar WMnd WMoo
- 'Lisa' EMon NLar
- 'Meteor' CStr MBNS MLLN MSte MWat NLar WAbe WCAu WPer
* - 'Mini' ELan MRav
- 'Rosenteller' EBee EMon
- September Glow see *S. spectabile* 'Septemberglut'
§ - 'Septemberglut' EBrs EGoo EMan EMon GKir NSti WCAu WCot
- 'Stardust' COIW CPrp CTbh EBee EBrs EMil ENot EPfP ERou GBBs GLil GMaP LPio LRHS MBNS MHer NCGa SPer SPet SPoG WAbe WCAu WFar WGor WWeb
- 'Steve Ward' EBee EWes
- 'Variegatum' see *S. erythrostictum* 'Mediovariegatum'
spinosum see *Orostachys spinosa*
spurium CHEx EGoo LGro MBNS NBlu SEND SRms WWpP
§ - var. ***album*** EGoo NRya
* - 'Atropurpureum' ECha NFor NLon
- 'Coccineum' MBar MHer SSto WBVN WGHP
- Dragon's Blood see *S. spurium* 'Schorbuser Blut'
- 'Erdblut' GKir LRHS NFla NJOw NMen
- 'Fuldaglut' CHal CNic COkL EDAr EHoe EMan ESis GBuc GMaP IHMH MBNS MWat NRya SChu SIng SMrm WMoo WPer
- 'Green Mantle' EBee ECha ESis EWin MWgw SMer SSto WWpP
- Purple Carpet see *S. spurium* 'Purpurteppich'
- 'Purpureum' EGoo NBlu SIng SRms WGHP
§ - 'Purpurteppich' COkL ESis GKir LGro LRHS MRav NBro NLar SRms
- 'Roseum' EWll SRms
- 'Ruby Mantle' NPro WBVN
§ - 'Schorbuser Blut' ♀H4 CMea ECtt EDAr EPfP ESis GKir IHMH MBNS MWat NBir NJOw NRya NVic SMar SPlb SRms WEas WFar WGHP WHoo WPat WRHF WTin WWeb
I - 'Splendens Roseum' LGro
- 'Summer Glory' NLar
- 'Tricolor' see *S. spurium* 'Variegatum'
I - 'Variegatum' (v) CBrm CHEx CNic CTri EBee ECha EDAr EGoo EHoe ESis GGar LAst MBar MHer MRav NFla NJOw NRya SBod SIng SPlb SPoG WEas WFar WMoo WPat
stenopetalum IHMH SPlb
§ - 'Douglasii' CNic MOne SRms
'Stewed Rhubarb Mountain' CFwr CPrp EBee ECGP EChP ECtt EMan EVFa EWTr LDai LSRN MBNS MRav MStc MWgw NBro NDov SChu WCot WHil WMoo WPGP
stoloniferum 'Variegata' WWeb
'Strawberries and Cream' More than 30 suppliers
stribrnyi see *S. urvillei* Stribrnyi Group
'Sunset Cloud' CHEx CMHG CSam EBee ECtt EMon EPPr EWes GCal LRHS MRav
takesimense B&SWJ 8518 WCru
§ ***tatarinowii*** CLyd EDAr
§ ***telephium*** CAgr CArn CHrt CMca MBNS MFOX NBir SRms WGwG WWye
- 'Abbeydore' see *S.* 'Abbeydore'
- 'Arthur Branch' EPPr GBuc MNrw MSte MTho
- var. ***borderei*** CElw EMan EMon LRHS SBch SUsu
- 'El Cid' EBee EWes
- subsp. ***fabaria*** see *S. fabaria*
* - 'Hester' EBee EChP WWpP
- 'Jennifer' EMan WCot
- 'Matrona' More than 30 suppliers
§ - subsp. ***maximum*** CBrm SChu
- - 'Atropurpureum' ♀H4 CBot CBrm CHad CHrt CMea EBee ECha ELan EMag EMan EPfP GCra MRav NLon SChu SWvt WCot WEas WMoo
- - 'Gooseberry Fool' CFwr EBee ECtt EGoo EMan EMon ERou EVFa GMaP LPhx LPio MAnH NSti SBch SHar WCot WFar WWeb
- 'Mohrchen' CPrp EBee EChP ECha EHrv GMaP LPio LRHS MLLN MRav NGdn NSti

	SBla SChu SMrm SPla SPoG WCAu WFar WGHP WMnd WMoo WOld
- 'Munstead Red'	More than 30 suppliers
§ - subsp. ***ruprechtii***	More than 30 suppliers
- - 'Hab Gray'	CSpe EBee EChP EWes LAst MSte WCot WWhi
- subsp. ***telephium*** 'Lynda et Rodney'	CKno EGoo EMan EMon MSph MSte WCot
- - var. ***purpureum*** B&SWJ 8480	WCru
- 'Variegatum' (v)	COtt EMag LRHS MDKP WHal
§ ***tenuifolium***	EBur
- subsp. ***tenuifolium***	EBur
ternatum	EWTr
trollii	see *Rhodiola trollii*
urvillei **new**	NRya
§ - Stribrnyi Group	CLyd
ussuriense	EMon SUsu WOut
§ 'Vera Jameson' ♀H4	CPrp CSLe EChP ECha EDAr EHoe EPfP EWTr LRHS LSRN MBrN MRav MTis MWat NSti SBla SChu SHBN SPer WEas WFar WMoo WWhi
viviparum B&SWJ 8662 **new**	WCru
'Washfield Purple'	see *S.* 'Purple Emperor'
'Weihenstephaner Gold'	see *S. kamtschaticum* var. *floriferum* 'Weihenstephaner Gold'
weinbergii	see *Graptopetalum paraguayense*
yezoense	see *S. pluricaule*

Seemannia see *Gloxinia*

Selaginella ✿ (*Selaginellaceae*)

apoda	MBri
braunii	WCot
helvetica	CStu
kraussiana ♀H1	CHal CLAP MBri NRya WRic
- 'Aurea'	CHal CLAP GGar MBri SMad
- 'Brownii' ♀H1	CLAP MBri
- 'Gold Tips' **new**	CLAP
- 'Variegata' (v) ♀H1	MBri
lepidophylla **new**	EUJe
plana **new**	WRic
sanguinolenta	CStu SIng
uncinata ♀H1	WRic

Selinum (*Apiaceae*)

carvifolium	CSpe EBee EMan MLLN MWgw NLar WTin
tenuifolium	see *S. wallichianum*
§ ***wallichianum***	CHad CMil CRow CSec CSpe EChP EGoo EMan EWTr GBuc GGar GIBF LPhx MLLN NBid NCGa SIgm SMHy SMeo SSpi WHer WMoo WPGP WPrP WWhi
- EMAK 886	GPoy MBri NSti SDix
- HWJK 2224	WCru
- HWJK 2347	WCru

Selliera (*Goodeniaceae*)

radicans	ECou GGar

Semele (*Ruscaceae*)

androgyna	CHEx CRHN EShb

Semiaquilegia (*Ranunculaceae*)

§ ***adoxoides***	CPom
- B&SWJ 1190	WCru
'Early Dwarf'	NLar
§ ***ecalcarata***	CPom CSec EDAr EMan GBin GGar GIBF LDai MNrw NLar SBch SMrm SRms WCru WFar WPGP WPer WSan WWFP WWhi
* - f. ***bicolor***	CPom WCru
- 'Flore Pleno' (d)	EChP
simulatrix	see *S. ecalcarata*

Semiarundinaria (*Poaceae*)

from Korea	EPla
§ ***fastuosa*** ♀H4	CAbb CBig CDoC CHEx EAmu EFul EPfP EPla ERod MBri MMoz MWht NMoo NVic SAPC SArc SDix SPlb WJun WMul
- var. ***viridis***	EPla ERod LPJP WCru WJun
kagamiana	CDoC CPen EBee ENBC EPla MBri MMoz MWht NMoo SEND WJun
§ ***lubrica***	CFil
makinoi	EPla MWht WJun WPGP
nitida	see *Fargesia nitida*
§ ***okuboi***	EPla ERod MMoz MWht SEND WJun
villosa	see *S. okuboi*
yamadorii	EPla ERod MMoz MWht WJun
- 'Brimscombe'	EPla
yashadake	EPla ERod WJun
- f. ***kimmei***	CAbb CAlb CDoC CDul CFil CPen EPla ERod MAsh MMoz MWht NMoo SBLw SBig SEND WDyG WFar WJun WMoo WMul WPGP

Semnanthe see *Erepsia*

Sempervivella see *Rosularia*

Sempervivum ✿ (*Crassulaceae*)

from Sierra del Cadi	MOne
from Sierra Nova	NDlv
'Abba'	MOne WHal WPer
acuminatum	see *S. tectorum* var. *glaucum*
'Adelaar'	CWil NMen
'Adelmoed'	CWil
'Aglow'	MHom MOne NMen
'Aladdin'	CWil NMen SRms
'Alchimist'	MOne
'Alcithoë'	MOne
'Aldo Moro'	CWil ESis GAbr LBee LRHS MHom MOne NMen
'Alidae'	MOne
allionii	see *Jovibarba allionii*
'Alpha'	ESis LBee LRHS MOne NMen SIng SRms STre WHal WPer WTin
altum	CWil MHom NMen
'Amanda'	CWil NMen SIng SRms WHoo WPer WTin
'Ambergreen'	NMen
andreanum	ESis MHom NBro NMen SIng
'Apache'	CWil NMen
'Apple Blossom'	CMea GCrs NMen
arachnoideum ♀H4	More than 30 suppliers
- from Ararat	SDys
- from Cascade Piste 7	MOne
- from Gorges du Valais	EPem
- 'Abruzzii'	GCrs SIng
- 'Boria'	MOne
- var. ***bryoides***	CWil ESis NMen WAbe WIvy WPer
- 'Clairchen'	NMen NSla
- cristate	CWil
* - ***densum***	EHyt ESis NRya WAbe
- subsp. ***doellianum***	see *S. arachnoideum* var. *glabrescens*
§ - var. ***glabrescens***	EHyt NMen SDys
- 'Laggeri'	see *S. arachnoideum* subsp. *tomentosum*
- 'Mole Harbord'	LRHS

- red	NMen
- 'Rubrum'	CHEx COlW LRHS MCCP MOne NEgg
- 'Sultan'	MOne
- subsp. ***tomentosum*** misapplied	see *S.* x *barbulatum* 'Hookeri'
§ - subsp. ***tomentosum*** (C.B. Lehm. & Schittsp.) Schinz & Thell ♀H4	CHEx CHal CWil EPot GKir LRHS MHer NMen NPer NRya SChu SIng SRms WAbe WBIE WPer
- - GDJ 92.04	CWil
- - 'Minor'	NJOw NMen SIng
§ - - 'Stansfieldii'	GAbr NMen SDys SIng STre WHal
§ - 'White Christmas'	CWil
- 'Yukon Snow' **new**	ESis
arachnoideum* x *calcareum	CWil NMen WIvy WTin
arachnoideum* x *montanum	SIng
arachnoideum* x *nevadense	CWil SDys
arachnoideum* x *pittonii	CWil NJOw NMen WAbe
arenarium	see *Jovibarba arenaria*
armenum	MOne NMen
'Arondina' **new**	CWil
'Aross'	CLyd CMea NMen
'Arrowheads Red'	MOne
'Artist'	CWil NMen
arvernense	see *S. tectorum*
'Ashes of Roses'	EGoo EPot ESis MHom MOne NMen WAbe WPer
'Asteroid'	CWil NMen
'Astrid' **new**	CWil
atlanticum	GEdr MHom NDlv NJOw NMen NSla WOut
- from Atlas Mountains, Morocco	CWil
- from Oukaimaden	CWil MOne NMen WTin
- 'Edward Balls'	CWil EPem MOne SDys
'Atropurpureum'	CHEx CWil GAbr MOne NMen SRms WGor WIvy WPer
'Atropurpureum' Hemlich form	MOne
'Aureum'	see *Greenovia aurea*
'Averil' **new**	CWil
§ 'Aymon Correvon'	MOne
balcanicum	CWil EDAr NMen WIvy
ballsii	NMen
- from Kambeecho	MHom
- from Smólikas	CWil MHom MOne NMen
- from Tschumba Petzi	CWil MHom SDys SIng
'Banderi'	CWil MOne
'Banjo'	MOne
'Banyan' **new**	CWil
'Barbarosa'	MOne
§ x ***barbulatum***	NMen SDys WPer
§ - 'Hookeri'	CWil MOne NLar NMen SIng WAbe WPer
'Bascour Zilver'	CWil LBee SIng WHal
'Beaute'	CWil
'Bedivere'	CLyd CPBP CWil LBee LRHS MOne NMen SRms
'Bedivere Crested'	CWil
'Bedley Hi'	MHom
'Bella Donna'	ESis MDHE MHom NMen WPer
'Bella Meade'	CWil EPem NMen SRms WPer
'Bellotts Pourpre'	CWil
'Bennerbroek'	MDHE
'Bernstein'	MHer WHal
'Beta'	MHom NMen WAbe WPer WTin
'Bethany'	CWil ESis NMen WHal
'Bicolor'	EPfP
'Big Slipper'	EPem
'Birchmaier'	EDAr MOne NMen
'Black Cap'	MOne
'Black Knight'	CStu ESis LBee LRHS SBla SRms WHal
'Black Mini'	CWil MDKP NBir NMen SRms
'Black Mountain'	CHEx CWil LBee LRHS MOne
'Black Prince'	CLyd GCrs
'Black Velvet'	CWil WIvy WPer
'Bladon'	WPer
'Blari'	MOne
'Blood Tip'	CHEx CHal CLyd CWil EHyt ESis GAbr LBee LRHS MHer NJOw NMen SChu SPoG SRms WGor WHal
'Blue Boy'	CWil ESis GAbr LBee LRHS MOne MSte NMen SIng SRms WHoo WPer
'Blue Moon'	CLyd MOne NMen
'Blue Time'	CWil MOne SChu WTin
'Boissieri'	see *S. tectorum* subsp. *tectorum* 'Boissieri'
'Bold Chick'	MOne
'Booth's Red'	CHEx CLyd EPem MOne NMen SIng WGor
'Boreale'	MOne
borisii	see *S. ciliosum* var. *borisii*
borissovae	CWil EDAr MHom NMen SDys
'Boromir'	CWil MOne SChu
'Boule de Niege' **new**	NMen
'Bowles' Variety'	WPer
'Britta'	MOne SDys
'Brock'	CWil MHer MHom WPer
'Bronco'	CWil EBee ESis LBee MHom MOne NMen SChu SRms SUsu
'Bronze Pastel'	CLyd CNic CWil MHom MOne NMen NSla SRms WTin
'Brown Owl'	CWil ESis MOne SRms
'Brownii'	GAbr MOne NMen SBla WPer WTin
'Brunette'	GAbr
'Burgundy'	MOne
'Burgundy Velvet'	MOne
'Burnatii'	MOne NMen
'Butterbur'	CWil
'Butterfly'	MOne
'Café'	CWil EGoo ESis NMen SIng SRms WIvy WPer
x ***calcaratum***	EDAr SIng SRms
calcareum	CNic COlW CWil EHyt EPot MOne NBro NEgg NMen SPlb SRms WBVN WHoo WPer
- from Alps, France	CWil MOne
- from Calde la Vanoise, France	CWil NMen
- from Ceuze	CWil WIvy
- from Col Bayard, France	CWil NMen
- from Colle St Michael	CWil MOne NMen
- from Gleize	CWil MOne NMen
- from Gorges du Cains	CWil MOne NMen
- from Guillaumes, Mont Ventoux, France	CWil MOne NMen WHoo
- from Mont Ventoux, France	CWil MOne
- from Queyras	CWil MOne NMen
- from Route d'Annôt	CWil MOne NMen
- from Triora	CWil MOne NMen
- 'Atropurpureum'	SChu
- 'Benz'	SDys
- 'Extra'	CHEx CWil SBch
- GDJ 92.15 from Petite Ceuse **new**	CWil
- GDJ 92.16 from Petite Ceuse	CWil

	- 'Greenii'	CWil ESis MOne NDlv NMen SPlb
§	- 'Grigg's Surprise'	CWil ESis MHer MOne NMen
	- 'Limelight'	CMea CWil ESis NMen SChu WHal WTin
	- 'Monstrosum'	see *S. calcareum* 'Grigg's Surprise'
	- 'Mrs Giuseppi'	CWil ESis GAbr LBee LRHS MOne MSte NMen NOak SBla SChu SRms STre WAbe WPer
	- 'Pink Pearl'	CWil EGoo MOne NMen SDys WTin
	- 'Sir William Lawrence'	CMea CPBP CWil EPem ESis NMen SChu WAbe WHal WHoo WIvy WPer WTin
*	***callosum barnesii***	GAbr
	'Canada Kate'	WPer
	'Cancer'	MOne
	'Candy Floss'	CWil MOne NMen
	cantabricum	CWil MDHE NMen
	- subsp. ***cantabricum*** from Leitariegos	CWil ETow GAbr MHom MOne NMen
	- - GDJ 93.13 from Peña de Llesba **new**	CWil
	- - from Pico del Lobo **new**	CWil
	- from Cue Vas de Sol **new**	CWil
	- from Lago de Enol	MOne
	- from Peña Prieta	NMen
	- from Piedrafita, Spain	MOne
	- from Riaño, Spain	CWil GAbr
	- from San Glorio	CWil GAbr MOne NMen
	- from Sierra del Cadi, Spain	CLyd
	- from Ticeros	EPem MOne NMen
	- from Tizneros **new**	CWil
	- from Valvernera	NMen
	- subsp. ***guadarramense***	see *S. vicentei* subsp. *paui*
	- - from Lobo No. 1	MOne
	- - from Lobo No. 2	EPem MOne
	- - from Navafria No. 1	CWil WTin
	- - from Valvanera No. 1	CWil NMen
	- subsp. ***urbionense***	CLyd CWil SIng
	- - from El Gaton **new**	CWil
	- - from Picos de Urbión, Spain	CWil MOne NMen
	- - GDJ 94.09 from Sierra de la Demanda **new**	CWil
	- - GDJ 94.10	CWil
	- - GDJ 94.12 from Sierra de Urbion **new**	CWil
	- - GDJ 95.01 from Sierra de Pineda **new**	CWil
	cantabricum x ***montanum*** subsp. ***stiriacum***	WEas WTin
	cantabricum x ***giuseppii*** GDJ 93.10 from Picos de Europa **new**	CWil
	cantabricum x ***montanum*** subsp. ***stiriacum*** 'Lloyd Praeger' **new**	CWil
	'Caramel'	MOne
*	'Carinal'	NBir
*	x ***carlsii***	MOne
	'Carluke'	MOne
	'Carmen'	CHal GAbr MOne
	'Carneus'	MOne
	'Carnival'	CHal NMen WPer
	caucasicum	CWil EHol MHom MOne NMen
	'Cauticolum'	MOne
	'Cavo Doro'	CWil MDHE
	'Celon'	MOne
	'Centennial'	MOne
	'Chalon'	MOne
	charadzeae	CWil LBee LRHS
	'Cherry Frost'	CLyd ITim MOne NJOw NMen
	'Cherry Glow'	see *Jovibarba heuffelii* 'Cherry Glow'
	'Chocolate'	WAbe
	x ***christii***	MOne NMen
	ciliosum ♀H4	CMea CPBP CWil ESis NMen NRya SChu SIng
	- from Alí Butús, Bulgaria	GCrs SDys
*	- from Gallica	CLyd
§	- var. ***borisii***	CWil EPfP ESis GCal GKev GTou NDlv NMen NRya SChr WAbe WHal
	- var. ***galicicum*** 'Mali Hat'	GCrs NMen
	ciliosum x ***ciliosum*** var. ***borisii***	CHal GEdr ITim NMen
	ciliosum x ***marmoreum***	NMen
	'Cindy'	CWil SRms
	'Circlet'	CWil NMen
*	***cistaceum***	WEas
	'Clara Noyes'	SMer WPer
	'Clare'	CLyd EPem MHer MOne
	'Clemanum'	MOne
	'Cleveland Morgan'	EPem LRHS MHom NBro NMen
	'Climax'	EPem EWll MHom NMen SMer SSto
	'Clipper' **new**	CWil
	'Cobweb Capers'	MHom MOne
	'Cobweb Centre'	MOne NMen
	'Collecteur Anchisi'	CWil MOne SDys
	'Commander Hay' ♀H4	CHEx CLyd CMea CWil EPfP EWes GKev MHom NMen NPer SBch SRms WEas WHal WPer
	'Comte de Congae'	ESis MOne NMen
	'Congo'	MOne NMen
	'Corio'	MOne
	'Corona'	CWil ESis MOne SRms WPer
	'Corsair'	CWil ESis MBrN MOne NMen WGor WIvy WOut WPer WTin
	'Cranberry'	MOne
	'Cresta'	MOne
	crested	MOne
	'Crimson Velvet'	CHEx CMea EDAr LBee LRHS MDHE MOne WPer
§	'Crispyn'	CBrm CLyd CWil EHyt EPot ESis LBee MHom MOne NMen SIng WEas WPer
	'Croky'	MOne
	'Croton'	SIng WPer
	'Cupream'	CWil MDHE NDlv SRms WPer
	'Dakota'	CWil NMen
	'Dallas'	CLyd CWil MOne NMen SRms
	'Damask'	CWil LBee MDHE NMen WPer
	'Dame Arsac'	MOne
	'Darjeeling' **new**	CWil
	'Dark Beauty'	CLyd CMea CWil EHyt MOne NMen WAbe WGor WHal WHoo WPer
	'Dark Cloud'	CWil ESis GAbr LBee LRHS WIvy WPer
	'Dark Point'	CWil MHom MOne NMen
	'Darkie'	CWil WPer
	davisii	CWil
	'Deebra'	CWil
	'Deep Fire'	CWil MOne NMen SRms WTin
	x ***degenianum***	GAbr NMen WPer
	'Delta'	NMen WHoo WTin
	densum	see *S. tectorum*
	'Diamant'	MOne
	'Diane'	CWil
	'Director Jacobs'	CWil EDAr GAbr MOne NMen WEas WPer WTin

dolomiticum	NMen
dolomiticum* x *montanum	CWil MOne NBro NMen WTin
'Downland Queen'	CWil
'Duke of Windsor'	MOne NMen
'Dyke'	CTri CWil GAbr NMen WHal
dzhavachischvilii	MOne NMen
'Edge of Night'	CWil SRms
'Eefje' CWil	
'El Greco'	MOne
'El Toro'	MHom
'Elene'	MOne
'Elgar'	MOne WIvy WPer
'Elizabeth'	WPer
'Elvis'	CLyd CWil GAbr NMen
'Emerald Giant'	CWil ESis MOne SRms WPer WTin
'Emerson's Giant'	CWil MOne NMen
'Emma Jane'	MOne
'Emmchen'	CWil
'Engle's'	CLyd EWin GKev LRHS MHer MOne NMen SChu SRms WHal WPer
'Engle's 13-2'	MOne NBro NMen SChu
'Engle's Rubrum'	CPBP GAbr GTou LBee NMen
erythraeum	CLyd ESis MHom NMen WAbe WHal
- from Pirin, Bulgaria	NMen
- from Rila, Bulgaria	NMen
- 'Red Velvet'	MOne
'Excalibur'	CLyd NMen WIvy
'Exhibita'	CWil SDys SRms
'Exorna'	CWil MHom MOne NMen SIng WEas WIvy WPer
'Fair Lady'	CWil MHom MOne NMen
'Fame'	EPem MDHE MOne
'Fat Jack' **new**	CWil
x ***fauconnettii***	CWil NMen SIng
- 'Thompsonii'	CWil MOne NMen SIng
'Feldmaier'	MOne
'Festival'	NMen
'Feu de Printemps'	MOne
'Fiery Furness'	MOne
'Fiesta'	WHal
fimbriatum	see *S.* x *barbulatum*
'Finerpointe'	MOne
'Fire Glint'	CWil MOne SIng SRms
'Firebird'	ESis NMen
'Firefly'	MOne
'First Try'	MOne
'Flaming Heart'	CWil MBrN MOne NMen WPer
'Flamingo'	NMen
'Flamme'	MOne
'Flander's Passion'	EPot LBee LRHS NMen SRms WPer
'Flasher'	WEas WPer
'Fluweel'	MOne
'Fontanae'	MOne
'Forden'	CHEx MOne WGor
'Ford's Amability'	SDys
'Ford's Shadows'	SDys
'Ford's Spring'	CLyd CWil MOne NJOw NMen WIvy WPer
'Freckles'	MOne
'Freeland'	WPer
'Frigidum'	NDlv
'Frolic'	SIng
'Fronika' **new**	CWil
'Frosty'	CWil MOne SRms
'Fuego'	CWil ESis MHom MOne
x ***funckii***	CHEx CWil EDAr ESis IHMH MBrN NMen SDys SIng WOut WPer WTin
- var. ***aqualiense*** **new**	CWil
'Furryness'	MOne
'Fuzzy Wuzzy'	MOne
'Galahad'	ESis GAbr
'Gallivarda'	CWil
'Gamma'	CHEx CWil ESis LBee LRHS NMen SChu SDys SIng SRms WEas WTin
'Garnet'	WPer
'Gay Jester'	CTri CWil MOne WHoo WTin
'Gazelle'	WIvy WPer
'Genevione'	CWil ESis
'Georgette'	CWil NMen WPer
'Ginger'	MOne
'Ginnie's Delight'	CWil ESis NMen
'Gipsy'	CWil
giuseppii	MHer NMen SIng WPer
- GDJ 93.04 from Cumbre de Cebolleda **new**	CWil
- GDJ 93.17 from Coriscao **new**	CWil
- from Peña Espigüete, Spain	CWil GAbr MOne NMen SDys
- from Peña Prieta, Spain	CWil MOne NMen
- from Vega de Liordes-W **new**	CWil
'Gizmo'	CWil
I 'Glaucum'	MOne
'Gleam'	MOne
'Gloriosum'	GAbr WPer
'Glowing Embers'	CWil ESis MHom MOne NMen WHal WPer
'Goldie'	MOne
'Gollum'	MOne
'Graceum' **new**	CWil
'Granada'	GAbr NMen
'Granat'	CLyd EDAr IGor MHer MOne NMen SRms WPer
'Granby'	CWil LBee MOne NMen SDys
grandiflorum	CBrm CWil NMen SIng WBrE WPer
- from Valpine	MOne NMen
- 'Fasciatum'	CWil MOne NMen
- 'Keston'	MOne
grandiflorum* x *ciliosum	CWil MOne NMen
grandiflorum* x *montanum	NMen
grandiflorum* x *tectorum GDJ 96B.11 from Valtournenche **new**	CWil
'Grannie's Favourite'	MOne
'Grapetone'	MHom NMen SDys WHal
'Graupurpur'	CWil
'Gray Dawn'	MHom
'Green Apple'	GAbr MHom NMen SDys
'Green Disk'	CWil
'Green Dragon' **new**	CWil
'Green Gables'	WPer
'Greenwich Time'	NMen
* ***greigii***	GEdr
'Grenadier'	MOne
'Grey Ghost'	NMen WIvy WPer
'Grey Green'	CWil
'Grey Lady'	CMea CWil
'Grey Owl' **new**	LRHS
'Greyfriars'	CLyd CMea EPot EWll LBee LRHS NMen WGor WOut WPer
'Greyolla'	CLyd CWil WPer
'Grünrand'	MOne
'Grünschnabel'	MOne
'Grünspecht'	MOne
'Gulle Dame'	CWil ESis
'Gypsy'	MOne
'Halemaumau'	CWil MOne
'Hall's Hybrid'	CWil ESis GAbr NBro SRms
'Happy'	CWil MOne NMen SRms WIvy WPer

	'Hart'	CWil EPem SRms WTin
	'Hartside'	MOne
	'Haullauer's Seedling'	MOne
I	'Hausmanni'	MOne
	'Havana'	CWil NMen
	'Hayling'	LRHS MOne NMen SRms WPer
	'Heigham Red'	CWil ESis GCrs LBee LRHS MCCP MOne NMen WPer
	'Heike' **new**	CWil
I	'Heliotroop'	MOne SDys
	helveticum	see *S. montanum*
	'Hester'	CHEx CLyd CWil EPyc ESis GAbr MDHE NBro NMen SRms WFar
	'Hey-Hey'	CLyd COkL EPot ESis GCrs LBee LRHS MBrN NMen SIng SPlb SRms WAbe WPer
	'Hidde'	CWil ESis WPer
	'Hiddes Roosje'	MOne NMen
	hirtum	see *Jovibarba hirta*
	'Hispidulum'	MOne
	'Hookeri'	see *S.* x *barbulatum* 'Hookeri'
	'Hopi'	CWil MOne SRms
	'Hortulanus Smit'	NMen
	'Hot Shot'	CLyd
	'Hullabaloo'	MOne
	'Hurricane'	MOne WPer
	'Icicle'	CHEx CMea LRHS NBro NLAp NMen SIng SRms WAbe WGor
	imbricatum	see *S.* x *barbulatum*
	'Imperial'	CLyd CWil MHom
	ingwersenii	MHom MOne SIng
	'Interlace'	MOne
	'Iophon'	LBee MOne
	'Irazu'	CWil GAbr MOne NMen SDys SRms WPer
	'Isaac Dyson'	SDys
	ispartae	CWil
	italicum	NMen MHom
	'Itchen'	MOne NMen SIng
	'IWO'	CHEx NMen
	'Jack Frost'	CMea CWil MOne NBro NMen SChu
	'Jade' ambig.	MOne
	'Jane'	MOne
	'Jelly Bean'	CWil ESis MOne NMen
	'Jet Stream'	CWil NMen SDys
	'Jewel Case'	CWil LRHS MOne NMen SIng SRms
	'John T.'	MOne WEas
	'Jolly Green Giant'	MHom MOne
	'Jo's Spark'	NSla
	'Jubilee'	CLyd CMea CWil EHyt ELan EPem EPyc NMen SRms WGor WPer
	'Jubilee Tricolor'	CSLe GFlt NMen
	'Jungle Fires'	CWil EPot ESis SDys SRms WHoo
	'Jupiter'	ESis
	'Justine's Choice'	CWil ESis SRms
	'Kalinda'	CLyd CWil MHom NMen
§	'Kappa'	CTri CWil MOne NBro NMen SDys WPer
	'Katmai'	CWil
	'Kelly Jo'	CLyd CWil ESis EWll NBro NMen WCot WTin
	'Kelut'	MOne
	'Kermit'	MHom NMen
	'Kibo'	MOne
	'Kimble'	WPer
	kindingeri	CLyd CWil GTou MHom NMen NWCA
	'King George'	CHal CLyd CTri CWil EPem ESis ITim LBee LRHS MOne NMen SChu SIng SRms WBVN WGor WHal WHoo WPer WTin
	'Kip'	CMea NMen WIvy WPer
	'Kismet'	NMen
	'Koko Flanel'	CWil
	'Kolagas Mayfair'	MOne
	'Kolibri'	MDHE
	'Korspel Glory' **new**	CWil
	'Korspel Glory 4'	CWil
	'Korspelsegietje'	CWil ESis
	kosaninii	ESis LRHS MOne NMen SIng WPer WTin
	- from Koprivnik	CLyd MOne NMen SDys WAbe
*	- from Visitor	CWil MOne
	'Krakeling'	MOne
	'Kramers Purpur'	NMen
	'Kramers Spinrad'	CHEx CLyd CMea CWil EPyc ESis LBee LEdu LRHS MOne NMen SChu SDys WEas WHoo WTin
	'La Serenissima'	MOne
	'Lady Kelly'	CLyd CMea CNic MOne NMen SIng WIvy
	'Launcelot'	WPer
	'Lavender and Old Lace'	CHEx CLyd CWil ESis GAbr GCrs LRHS MCCP NLAp NMen SChu WPer
	'Laysan'	CWil
	Le Clair's hybrid No. 4	NMen
	'Lennik's Glory'	see *S.* 'Crispyn'
	'Lentevur'	CWil ESis
	'Lentezon'	CWil
	'Leocadia's Nephew'	MOne NMen
	'Leon Smits'	CWil ESis
	'Les Yielding'	MOne
	'Lilac Time'	CLyd CWil ESis GAbr GEdr LRHS MHer MOne NMen SChu SIng SRms WHal WIvy WPer
	'Limbo' **new**	CWil
	'Lipari'	EWll NMen SRms
	'Lipstick'	CLyd ESis NMen
	'Little Bo Bo' **new**	ESis
	'Lively Bug'	CWil ESis LBee LRHS SDys WPer
	'Lloyd Praeger'	see *S. montanum* subsp. *stiriacum* 'Lloyd Praeger'
	'Lonzo'	CWil SRms
	'Lustrous'	MOne
	'Lynne's Choice'	GAbr MOne SIng WHal WIvy
	'Lynn's Choice' **new**	CWil
	macedonicum	EDAr NDlv NMen WTin
	- from Ljuboten	CWil MOne NMen
	'Madeleine'	CWil ESis
	'Magic Spell'	CWil MOne NMen
	'Magical'	CWil
	'Magnificum'	CWil NMen WGor
I	'Mahogany'	CHEx CLyd CTri CWil ESis EWll LBee LRHS MOne NBlu NMen SBla SChu SRms SWal WEas WGor WHal
	'Maigret'	CWil SIng WPer
	'Majestic'	CWil ESis LBee NMen
	'Major White' **new**	CHEx
	'Malby's Hybrid'	see *S.* 'Reginald Malby'
	'Marella'	CWil WPer
	'Maria Laach'	CWil ESis
	'Marijntje'	CWil NMen
	'Marion' **new**	CWil
	'Marjorie Newton'	CWil ESis
§	***marmoreum***	CLyd EPot ESis GKev LBee LRHS NMen SChu SRms STre WHal WPer
	- from Kanzas Gorge	EPot MOne NMen
	- from Monte Tirone	CWil SDys
	- from Okol	MOne NMen
	- 'Brunneifolium'	CLyd CWil EGoo GAbr LBee LRHS MOne NMen SChu SIng WPer
	- subsp. ***marmoreum*** var. ***dinaricum***	CWil EDAr NMen

§ - 'Ornatum' SRms
'Matador' MOne
'Mate' NMen
'Maubi' CHEx COkL CWil
'Mauvine' MOne
'Mayfair Imp' MOne
'Maytime' **new** ESis
'Medallion' MOne
'Meisse' MOne
'Melanie' CWil MBrN NMen WIvy
'Mercury' CWil GAbr LRHS MDHE NBro NMen SRms
'Merkur' MOne
'Merlin' ESis
'Metallicum' **new** ESis
'Midas' CWil ESis
'Mila' CLyd
'Minaret' ESis MOne
'Mini Frost' CLyd CWil GAbr NMen SIng WPer
'Minima Nana' **new** CWil
'Mixed Spice' CMea CWil
'Moerkerk's Merit' CWil GAbr NMen
'Monasses' **new** ESis
'Mondstein' CWil MOne SRms WIvy
'Montage' CWil
§ ***montanum*** CLyd ESis GCrs LEdu LRHS NMen WPer
- from Anchisis MOne
- from Arbizion CWil MOne
- from Mt. Tonale **new** CWil
- from Windachtal CWil NMen
- subsp. ***burnatii*** CWil MHom SIng
- subsp. ***carpaticum*** CWil
- - 'Cmiral's Yellow' EPot NMen WIvy
* - Fragell form SChr
- subsp. ***montanum*** CWil
- - var. ***braunii*** NLAp
- 'Rubrum' see *S.* 'Red Mountain'
§ - subsp. ***stiriacum*** CWil MOne NMen SIng
§ - - 'Lloyd Praeger' CWil LBee LRHS MOne NMen SDys WIvy
montanum x ***tectorum*** var. ***boutignyanum*** GDJ 94.15 **new** CWil
'More Honey' CWil NMen SRms
'Morning Glow' WGor WHal
'Mount Hood' LRHS SRms WHal
'Mrs Elliott' MOne
'Mulberry Wine' CLyd CWil LBee LRHS
'Mystic' CLyd CWil MBrN NMen WPer
nevadense CWil EPot MOne NMen SRms
- GDJ 96A-07 from Calar de Santa Barbara **new** CWil
- from Puerto de San Francisco CWil MOne
- var. ***hirtellum*** CWil NMen SIng
* ***nevadense*** x ***calopticum*** WTin
'Nico' SRms
'Night Raven' CLyd CMea WIvy
'Nigrum' see *S. tectorum* 'Nigrum'
'Niobe' MOne
'Noir' CWil EMFP EWll IHMH NBro NMen SChu
'Norbert' CWil SRms
'Norne' MOne
'Nortofts Beauty' MOne
'Nouveau Pastel' CMea CWil MOne NMen WHal
'Novak' **new** CWil
'Octet' CWil EPem MOne NMen SIng
octopodes CLyd MDHE NBir SIde
- var. ***apetalum*** CWil GAbr MOne NMen SIng SRms
'Oddity' CPBP CWil MHer NMen WCot WPer
'Ohio Burgundy' MDHE MOne NDlv NMen WAbe WPer WTin
'Old Rose' MOne
'Olga' ESis
'Olivette' MDHE NMen WPer WTin
'Omega' MOne WPer
'Opitz' CLyd WPer
'Ornatum' EPot ESis MHer MOne NMen WAbe WEas WHal WIvy
ossetiense CWil GAbr MOne NMen SIng
'Othello' CHEx CHal CTri EMFP EPfP ESis GAbr GKev MBNS NBir STre WCot WTin
'Pacific Feather Power' **new** NMen
'Packardian' CWil MOne NMen WIvy
'Painted Lady' CWil
'Palissander' GAbr MOne NMen
'Pam Wain' MHom NMen
'Parade' MOne
'Paricutin' SDys
'Passionata' **new** CWil
'Pastel' CWil NMen SIng
patens see *Jovibarba heuffelii*
'Patrician' CWil ESis LBee LRHS SRms
'Pekinese' CLyd CWil EPem EPot ESis GEdr MSte NBro NMen SIng SRms WCot WEas WGor WPer
'Peterson's Ornatum' MOne SDys
'Petsy' CWil SRms
'Pilatus' LBuc MBNS SRms
'Pink Astrid' CWil ESis
'Pink Cloud' CWil NMen SBla SRms
'Pink Dawn' MOne
'Pink Delight' MOne
'Pink Flamingoes' MOne
'Pink Lemonade' MHom
'Pink Mist' WPer
'Pink Puff' CLyd CWil MHom MOne NMen SRms
'Pippin' CWil ESis SRms WPer
'Piran' CWil MOne
pittonii CHal CMea CWil GAbr GCrs NMen WHal
'Pixie' CLyd CNic CWil GCrs MOne NDlv NMen
'Plumb Rose' CWil MOne NMen SChu WIvy
'Pluto' CWil
'Polaris' CLyd MHom
'Poldark' MOne
'Pompeon' MOne
'Ponderosa' CWil
'Pottsii' CWil MHer MOne
I 'Powellii' MOne
'Prairie Sunset' CWil ESis GCrs
'Prince Charles' **new** CWil
'Procton' MOne
'Proud Zelda' CWil ESis GAbr MOne NMen
'Pruhonice' CWil MOne SRms
'Pseudo-ornatum' EPfP LBee LRHS SChu SRms
'Pumaros' NMen SDys
pumilum CWil MBar NMen
- from Adyl Su no. 1 CWil
- from Armchi SDys
- from Armchi x *ingwersenii* MOne NMen
- from El'brus no. 1 CWil
- from Techensis CWil NMen
pumilum x ***arachnoideum*** GAbr

	pumilum* x *ingwersenii	CWil
	'Purdy'	MHom WAbe
	'Purdy's 50-6'	CWil
	'Purdy's 70-40'	MOne
	'Purple Beauty'	CLyd CWil GKev MOne
	'Purple King'	CMea MHom SDys
	'Purple Queen' **new**	CWil
	'Purple Ruby' **new**	ESis
	'Purpurriese'	CWil EDAr
	'Pygmalion'	CWil GCrs
	'Queen Amalia'	see *S. reginae-amaliae*
	'Queen Amealia' **new**	CWil
	'Quintessence'	CWil GCrs SRms
	'Racy'	CWil
	'Ragtime'	MOne
	'Ramses'	MOne SDys
	'Raspberry Ice'	CLyd CMea LBee NBro NMen WPer
	'Rauer Kulm'	CWil
	'Rauheit'	MOne
	'Red Ace'	CWil EWll NBro NMen SRms
	'Red Beam'	CWil MDHE MOne
	'Red Chips'	MHom
	'Red Cross'	MOne
	'Red Delta'	CWil MOne NBir NMen
	'Red Devil'	CLyd CWil EHyt MOne NMen WMow WTin
	'Red King'	MOne
	'Red Lion'	CWil
	'Red Lynn'	CWil
§	'Red Mountain'	CHal CWil EWll LBee LRHS MOne NJOw SRms
	'Red Pink'	CWil MOne
	'Red Robin'	MOne
	'Red Rum'	SIng WPer
	'Red Shadows'	CWil LBee WPer WTin
	'Red Spider'	CWil MHom NBro NMen
	'Red Summer'	MOne
	'Red Wings'	MOne NMen SRms
	'Regal'	MOne NMen
	'Reggy'	CWil WGor
	'Regina'	NMen
	reginae	see *S. reginae-amaliae*
§	***reginae-amaliae***	NMen
	- from Kambeecho No. 2	MDHE NMen SDys
	- from Mavri Petri	CLyd CWil MOne SDys SIng
	- from Sarpun	CWil NMen SDys WTin
	- from Vardusa	CWil SDys
§	'Reginald Malby'	CTri LRHS MDHE NMen SRms
	'Reinhard'	CBrm CMea CWil EPot ESis GEdr MBrN MCCP MDHE MHer MOne NJOw NMen SIng SRms WHal WHoo WPer
	'Remus'	CWil MOne NMen SDys SIng SRms WGor
	'Rex'	NMen
	'Rhone'	CWil LBee MOne
*	***richardii***	MBar
	'Risque'	CWil WPer
	'Rita Jane'	CLyd CWil ESis MHom MOne NMen WTin
	'Robin'	CLyd EPot ITim LBee LRHS NBro NLar SRms WTin
	'Ronny'	CWil
	'Rose Queen' **new**	ESis
	x ***roseum***	MOne
	- 'Fimbriatum'	CWil GAbr LBee LRHS NDlv WEas
	'Rosie'	CLyd CMea CNic CPBP CWil EPot ESis GAbr LBee LRHS MCCP MOne NMen SIng SPoG SRms WHal WHoo WPer WTin
	'Rotkopf'	CWil MOne NMen SChu SRms
	'Rotmantel'	SDys WTin
	'Rotsandsteinriese'	MOne
	'Rotund'	CWil
	'Rouge'	CWil NMen
	'Royal Mail'	MOne
	'Royal Opera'	CWil MOne NMen
	'Royal Ruby'	GAbr LBee LRHS MBrN NMen SChu SRms
	'Rubellum'	CWil MOne
	'Rubikon Improved'	ESis MOne
	'Rubin'	CTri CWCL ECGP EGoo EPfP EPyc ESis GAbr GEdr IHMH MCCP MSte NBir NEgg NLAp NMen NPri SPoG SRms WAbe WEas WHoo WPer
	'Rubrum Ash'	CWil EHyt EPem GAbr MOne NMen WAbe WTin
	'Rubrum Ornatum'	MHom
	'Rubrum Ray'	CWil MOne SRms
*	'Ruby Glow'	ESis
	'Russian River'	WHoo WTin
	'Rusty'	CWil WFar
	ruthenicum	LRHS MHom
	'Sabanum'	CLyd
	'Safara'	CWil
	'Saffron'	MOne NMen
	'Saga'	EPem ESis MHom MOne
	'Sanford's Hybrid'	MOne
	'Sarah'	MOne NMen
	'Sassy Frass'	CLyd NMen
	'Saturn'	MOne NMen
	schlehanii	see *S. marmoreum*
	schnittspahnii	MOne
	x ***schottii***	MOne
	'Seminole'	CWil MOne
	'Serena'	MOne
	'Sharon's Pencil'	CWil ESis
	'Sheila'	GAbr
	'Shirley Moore'	CWil MOne WTin
	'Shirley's Joy'	CHal ESis GAbr NMen WTin
	'Sideshow'	CWil MOne
	'Sigma'	MOne
	'Silberkarneol' misapplied	see *S.* 'Silver Jubilee'
	'Silberspitz'	CWil ESis MHer MHom NBro NMen WPer
	'Silver Cup'	CWil
§	'Silver Jubilee'	CMea CWil EDAr ESis MDHE NBro NDlv SPlb SRms
	'Silver Queen'	CWil
	'Silver Thaw'	CWil NMen SIng WCot
	'Silverine'	CWil ESis
	'Silvertone'	CWil
	'Simonkaianum'	see *Jovibarba hirta*
	'Sioux'	CLyd CPBP CWil ESis EWll GAbr LBee LRHS MBrN NMen SIng WIvy WPer WTin
	'Skrocki's Bronze'	CWil GAbr SChu WPer
	'Skrocki's Purple Rose'	CWil
	'Slabber's Seedling'	CWil
	'Small Wonder' **new**	CWil
	'Smaragd' **new**	LBee
	'Sněhová Koule' **new**	SIng
	'Snowberger'	CLyd CMea CWil EPem EPot ESis LRHS MOne NMen SRms WHal WPer
	'Soarte'	MOne
	soboliferum	see *Jovibarba sobolifera*
	'Somerwise' **new**	ESis
	'Soothsayer'	CWil MOne NMen
	'Sopa'	CWil MOne NMen
	sosnowskyi	CWil MOne NMen
	'Soul Sister'	CWil
	'Spanish Dancer'	NMen
	'Speciosum'	ESis MOne
	'Spherette'	CMea CWil NMen WPer
	'Spice'	MOne

	'Spider's Lair'	SIng
	'Spinnelli'	MOne WTin
	'Spiver's Velvet'	MOne
	'Sponnier'	MOne
	'Spring Mist'	CMea CWil MOne NLar SPoG SRms WGor WPer WTin
	'Sprite'	CWil MOne NMen SDys WTin
	stansfieldii	see *S. arachnoideum* subsp. *tomentosum* 'Stansfieldii'
	'Starion'	CWil MOne
	'Starshine'	MHer NMen
	'State Fair'	CWil NMen SIng WIvy WPer
*	***stolonifera***	GAbr
	'Strawberry Fields'	MOne
	'Strider'	GAbr WTin
	'Stuffed Olive'	CWil ESis MOne SDys
I	'Subanum'	MOne
	'Sun Waves'	CWil MOne SDys
	'Sunrise'	MOne
	'Super Dome'	CWil
	'Superama'	CWil
	'Supernova'	MOne
	'Syston Flame'	CWil NMen
	'Tamberlane'	CWil
	'Tambimuttu'	CWil MOne
	'Tarita'	CWil
	'Tarn Hows'	MOne
	'Teck'	CWil
§	***tectorum*** ♀H4	CArn CHby CLyd COkL CPrp CSam CWil ELan EPfP GKev GPoy GTou LBee LRHS MBar MDHE MHer NLon NMen SIde SIng SPlb STre WJek WWye
	- from Eporn	CWil MOne NMen
	- subsp. ***alpinum***	CWil NMen SIng
	- var. ***andreanum*** **new**	CWil
	- 'Atropurpureum'	ELan NMen WTin
	- 'Atrorubens'	EPem
	- 'Atroviolaceum'	EDAr GCal NLar NMen WIvy WTin
	- var. ***boutignyanum*** GDJ 94.02 from Sant Joan de Caselles **new**	CWil
	- - GDJ 94.03	CWil
	- - GDJ 94.04 from Route de Tuixèn **new**	CWil
	- var. ***calcareum***	MOne
	- subsp. ***cantalicum***	SRms
§	- var. ***glaucum***	NDlv
§	- 'Nigrum'	EHyt ESis LBee LRHS MHer MOne NBro NMen SDys SRms WGor WTin
	- 'Red Flush'	CWil ESis MBrN NMen SDys SPoG
	- 'Royanum'	ESis GAbr
*	- subsp. ***sanguineum***	EDAr
	- 'Sunset'	CWil NMen SDys WHal
	- subsp. ***tectorum***	MOne
§	- - 'Boissieri'	CWil NMen SRms WIvy
	- - 'Triste'	CHEx CWil EBee LBee LRHS MOne NMen SRms WAbe
	- 'Violaceum'	CLyd MHom SIng SRms STre WAbe
	tectorum x ***ciliosum***	WTin
	tectorum x ***grandiflorum***	MOne
	tectorum x ***zeleborii***	WTin
	'Tederheid'	MBNS MOne
	'Telfan'	MOne NMen
	'Tenburg'	MOne
	'Terracotta Baby'	CWil
	'Thayne'	NMen
	'The Platters' **new**	CWil
	'The Rocket'	CWil
	thompsonianum	CWil NDlv NMen
	'Thunder'	CWil
	'Tiffany'	CBrm WPer
	'Tina'	WPer
	'Tip Top'	CNic CWil
	'Titania'	CWil EPem ESis NBro NMen WHal WTin
	'Tombago'	CWil MOne
	'Topaz'	CWil EBee ESis LBee LRHS MOne NMen SBla SChu SRms
	'Tordeur's Memory'	CWil LBee LRHS MOne NMen
	'Trail Walker'	CWil ESis LBee LRHS MOne SRms
	transcaucasicum	CWil
	'Tree Beard'	CWil
	triste **new**	CWil
	'Tristesse'	CLyd CWil MOne NMen WGor WGwG
	'Truva'	CWil MOne NMen
	'Twilight Blues'	CWil
	'Undine' **new**	CWil
	x ***vaccarii***	CWil NMen
	'Van Baelen' **new**	CWil
	'Van der Steen' **new**	CWil
	'Vanbaelen'	GAbr NMen SDys
	'Vanessa'	CWil ESis
*	***verschaffii***	EPem
	'Veuchelen'	MOne
	vicentei	MHom NDlv NMen WTin
	- from Gaton	LBee LRHS MOne NMen
§	- subsp. ***paui***	NSla
	'Victorian'	MOne
	'Video'	CWil ESis MHom NMen
	'Viking' **new**	ESis
	'Virgil'	CWil ESis GAbr MBrN NMen SDys SIng WGor WPer WTin
	'Virginus'	CLyd CWil
	'Warners Pink'	MDKP
	'Watermelon Rind'	MOne
	webbianum	see *S. arachnoideum* subsp. *tomentosum*
	'Webby Flame'	CWil
	'Webby Ola'	NMen
	'Wega' **new**	NMen
	'Weirdo'	CWil
	'Wendy'	CLyd MOne NMen
	'Westerlin'	CLyd CWil MOne NMen
	'White Christmas'	see *S. arachnoideum* 'White Christmas'
	'White Eyes'	NMen SOkd
	'Whitening'	GAbr NMen
	'Witchery' **new**	ESis
	'Wollcott's Variety'	CWil EPem ESis EWin GAbr LRHS MDKP MOne NBir NMen WPer WTin
	wulfenii	CWil NMen
*	- ***roseum***	EDAr
	'Xaviera' **new**	CWil
	'Zaza'	CWil
	zeleborii	CHal SDys WHal
	'Zenith'	CWil ESis GAbr SRms
I	'Zenobia'	MHom
	'Zenocrate'	CWil WHal
	'Zepherin'	CWil
	'Zeppelin No. 3' **new**	CWil
	'Zilver Moon'	CWil NMen
	'Zircon'	NMen
	'Zone'	CHEx NMen
	'Zorba'	NMen
	'Zulu'	ESis

Senecio (*Asteraceae*)

B&SWJ 9115 from Guatemala **new**	WCru
HWJK 2118 from Nepal **new**	WCru

§ ***articulatus*** CHal EShb
aureus see *Packera aurea*
bicolor subsp. ***cineraria*** see *S. cineraria*
bidwillii see *Brachyglottis bidwillii*
buchananii see *Brachyglottis buchananii*
candicans see *S. cineraria*
cannabifolius GCal GIBF
chrysanthemoides see *Euryops chrysanthemoides*
chrysocoma **new** CSec
§ ***cineraria*** XPep
- 'Silver Dust' ♀H3 CSLe ENot EPfP LRHS
- 'White Diamond' ECha LGro SBch

* ***coccinilifera*** **new** SBch
compactus see *Brachyglottis compacta*
cyaneus SSpi
doria LRHS WCot WFar
doronicum EBee
fistulosus **new** LEdu
glastifolius ERea GGar
'Goldplate' WCot
'Gregynog Gold' see *Ligularia* 'Gregynog Gold'
greyi misapplied see *Brachyglottis* (Dunedin Group) 'Sunshine'
greyi Hook. see *Brachyglottis greyi*
heritieri DC. see *Pericallis lanata*
hoffmannii CPLN EShb
integrifolius subsp. ***capitatus*** NChi
kleiniiformis **new** EShb
laxifolius hort. see *Brachyglottis* (Dunedin Group) 'Sunshine'
leucophyllus SOkd
leucostachys see *S. viravira*
macroglossus CHll
- 'Variegatus' (v) ♀H1 CHal ERea EShb LAst SMur

macrospermus WWhi
maritimus see *S. cineraria*
monroi see *Brachyglottis monroi*
nemorensis **new** NBre
ovatus NBre
petasitis CHEx
polyodon CSpe EBla EShb GBri MCCP MNrw NCGa SBch SUsu
- S&SH 29 CFir
- subsp. ***subglaber*** EMan EMon IFro SSpi

przewalskii see *Ligularia przewalskii*
pulcher CDes CFil CFwr CSam EBee ETow GBri LEdu LSou MNrw MTho SMrm SUsu WCot WPGP
reinholdii see *Brachyglottis rotundifolia*
rowleyanus EBak EShb
scandens CMac ELan ERea EShb MNrw MTho WCwm WHer WPGP
seminiveus EBee
§ ***serpens*** CHal CStu CTbh EShb
§ ***smithii*** CRow EBee ELan EMan GFlt NBid NChi WBcn WCot WCru WFar
speciosus NBir
spedenii see *Brachyglottis spedenii*
squalidus WHer
'Sunshine' see *Brachyglottis* (Dunedin Group) 'Sunshine'
tamoides **new** CPLN
- 'Variegatus' (v) ERea

tanguticus see *Sinacalia tangutica*
§ ***viravira*** ♀H3-4 CSLe EGoo EHol EPfP ERea EShb LIck MWgw SMad SMrm SPer WCot WEas WGHP WSHC XPep

Senna (*Caesalpiniaceae*)

alexandrina WPGP
artemisioides ♀H1 CTrC XPep
§ ***corymbosa*** CBcs CHEx CRHN CTbh ERea LRHS LRav SYvo XPep
x ***floribunda*** XPep
hebecarpa EMan
§ ***marilandica*** CArn EBee ELan ELau SIgm
§ ***obtusifolia*** MSal
retusa CHEx
roemeriana **new** EBee
septemtrionalis WPGP
spectabilis **new** CSec

Sequoia (*Cupressaceae*)

sempervirens ♀H4 CBcs CDoC CDul CLnd CMCN CTho ECrN EHul EPfP ERom GKir LCon MBar MLan SCoo SLon SPoG WDin WEve WMou WNor
- 'Adpressa' CDoC CDul CMac CRob CSli CTho EHul EOrn EPla GKir LCon LLin MAsh MBar MGos NWea SCoo SLim SPoG WEve WFar
- 'Cantab' CDul
- 'Prostrata' CDoC CSli EOrn GBin LLin MAsh MBar SLim WFar

Sequoiadendron (*Cupressaceae*)

giganteum ♀H4 More than 30 suppliers
- 'Argentea Spicata' **new** NLar
- 'Barabits Requiem' MBlu NLar SLim
- 'Blauer Eichzwerg' **new** NLar
- 'Blue Iceberg' CKen
- 'Bultinck Yellow' **new** NLar SMad
- 'Cannibal' MBri
- 'French Beauty' **new** NLar
- 'Glaucum' CDoC CTho EMil LCon MAsh MBlu MBri NLar SMad WEve
- 'Greenpeace' MBri
- 'Little Stan' **new** NLar
- 'Pendulum' CDoC CKen ERod GKir GTSp LCon MBlu MGos NLar SLim SWvt WEve
- 'Peve Bonsai' NLar
- 'Pygmaeum' NLar
- 'Variegatum' (v) CDoC GKir WBcn WEve
- 'Von Martin' **new** NLar

Serapias (*Orchidaceae*)

lingua EHyt LAma SBla SCnR SSpi WHil
- peach-flowered SSpi

parviflora WHer

Serenoa (*Arecaceae*)

repens CBrP CRoM

Seriphidium (*Asteraceae*)

caerulescens var. ***gallicum*** EEls XPep
§ ***canum*** EEls MHer
§ ***ferganense*** EEls
§ ***fragrans*** EEls
§ ***maritimum*** CArn GGar ILis MHer NSti XPep
- subsp. ***humifusum*** WCot
- var. ***maritimum*** EEls

§ ***nutans*** CSLe EBee EEls MWat
§ ***tridentatum*** CArn EUnu
- subsp. ***tridentatum*** EEls
- subsp. ***wyomingense*** EEls

tripartitum var. ***rupicola*** EEls
§ ***vallesiacum*** ♀H4 EBee ECGP EEls WEas XPep
vaseyanaum EEls

Serissa (*Rubiaceae*)

foetida see *S. japonica*

§ ***japonica*** STre
- ***rosea*** STre
- 'Sapporo' SSpi
- 'Variegata' (v) CHal STre

Serratula (*Asteraceae*)

coronata EBrs
§ ***seoanei*** CMea CPom CStu CTri EBee ECha EDAr EMan EMon LPhx MHer MWat NJOw SAga SDix SIng SRms WCot WFar WPGP WPat WPrP WTin WWhi
shawii see *S. seoanei*
tinctoria CArn CBgR EBee ELau EMan GBar MSal NLar NMir
- subsp. ***macrocephala*** EBrs LRHS

Sesamum (*Pedaliaceae*)

indicum CArn

Sesbania (*Papilionaceae*)

punicea SGar XPep

Seseli (*Apiaceae*)

elatum CSpe
- subsp. ***osseum*** CFil LPio SIgm
globiferum LPhx LPio SIgm
gummiferum CAby CArn CBot CFwr CSpe EBee EMan EMar EWin LEdu LPhx LPio MCCP NLar NSti
hippomarathrum SIgm WCot WHoo WPGP
libanotis CSpe LPhx LPio NDov
montanum CDes WPGP
varium LPio

Sesleria (*Poaceae*)

§ ***albicans*** EPPr
§ ***argentea*** GIBF
autumnalis EMon EPPr LBBr LPhx WGHP
caerulea CAby CHrt CSam EChP EHoe ELan EPza EUJe GFor LAst LBuc LPhx MBar MBri MLLN MMoz MWhi SWal WGHP XPep
- subsp. ***calcarea*** see *S. albicans*
- 'Malvern Mop' CBrm EBee WPGP
* ***candida*** EPPr
cylindrica see *S. argentea*
glauca CRez EHoe NLar NOak NPro SChu WPer
heufleriana CElw EChP EHoe EMan EPPr EPla NLar SLPl SPlb WCot WGHP
insularis CSWP EMon LRHS
'Morning Dew' GCal
nitida CBig CKno EBee EHoe EMan EMon GFor LPhx LRHS MMoz SApp SWal WGHP WPGP
rigida EHoe
sadleriana EBee EPPr EWes GFor WPrP

Setaria (*Poaceae*)

RCB/Arg BB-2 **new** WCot
macrostachya ♀H3 CHrt CKno LLWP LPhx SBch
palmifolia CAby CHEx CHll CKno EPPr SGSe WCot WDyG WHal
viridis CHrt NChi NSti WCot WTin

Setcreasea see *Tradescantia*

shaddock see *Citrus maxima*

Shepherdia (*Elaeagnaceae*)

argentea CAgr CBcs CPle NLar

Sherardia (*Rubiaceae*)

arvensis MSal

Shibataea (*Poaceae*)

kumasaca CAbb CBcs CBig CBrm CDoC CHEx EHoe ENBC ENot EPfP EPla EPza ERod GCal GKir IBal LEdu MBrN MCCP MGos MMoz MWhi MWht NMoo NVic SBig SLPl WJun WMul WNor
- f. ***aureostriata*** EPla
lancifolia EPla WJun

Shortia (*Diapensiaceae*)

galacifolia IBlr
- var. ***brevistyla*** IBlr
x ***intertexta*** 'Ahlfeld' IBlr
- 'Leona' IBlr
soldanelloides GKev IBlr SSpi
- f. ***alpina*** IBlr
- var. ***ilicifolia*** IBlr SSpi
- var. ***magna*** IBlr
uniflora IBlr
* - var. ***kamtchatica*** WCru
- var. ***kantoensis*** IBlr
* - var. ***nana*** WCru
- var. ***orbicularis*** 'Grandiflora' GCrs IBlr SSpi

Sibbaldia (*Rosaceae*)

procumbens GFlt GKir

Sibbaldiopsis (*Rosaceae*)

§ ***tridentata*** CBgR EMar GMac
- 'Lemon Mac' SIng SMac
- 'Nuuk' CNic NBlu NLon SMac

Sibiraea (*Rosaceae*)

altaiensis see *S. laevigata*
§ ***laevigata*** CFil

Sibthorpia (*Scrophulariaceae*)

europaea CHEx CPLG

Sida (*Malvaceae*)

acuta MGol
hermaphrodita EBee EMan WCot

Sidalcea (*Malvaceae*)

'Brilliant' CDWL EBee EChP EMan EPfP LRHS MBnl MDKP NFla NPri NRnb NSti SPer WBor WFar WMoo
candida More than 30 suppliers
- 'Bianca' CBot CMdw EHrv ERou LAst MFOX MSte NLar NPri SMar WFar WMoo WMow WPer WWhi WWpP
- 'Shining Heart' CFwr
'Crimson King' WFar
'Croftway Red' CBcs CFir EBee ELan EMan EPfP GCra GGar GKir LRHS MRav NBro NCob NEgg NRnb SChu SHel SPet SPoG SWvt WCAu WMoo WSan
cusickii WOut
'Elsie Heugh' ♀H4 More than 30 suppliers
* ***grandiflora*** **new** WMow
hendersonii EBee WMow
hickmanii subsp. ***anomala*** EBee
hirtipes EBee
'Interlaken' NOrc WMow
'Jimmy Whittet' WBrE

'Little Princess'[PBR]	CFai CFir EMan GBri MBri NLar SPoG
'Loveliness'	CM&M EBee EChP ELan EMan EVFa LSou MRav NBro NCob NGdn NLar SAga SOkh SVil
malviflora	MGol NSti SChu SRms SYvo WWpP
- 'Alba'	WFar
- dark-flowered	WMow
'Mary Martin'	EMan
'Monarch'	MDKP WFar WHil WPnP
'Moorland Rose Coronet'	WMoo
'Mr Lindbergh'	EMan EPfP ERou LRHS SOkh WFar
'Mrs Borrodaile'	CM&M ECtt EMan EMar GBuc LAst LRHS MBNS MBnl MMil MRav MTis MWgw NBro NCob NEgg NGdn NPro SChu SHel SPoG WCAu WFar WMoo WMow
'Mrs Galloway'	WFar
'Mrs T. Alderson'	EMan WFar WMoo WMow
'My Love'	NDov
neomexicana	EMan GCal NChi
'Oberon'	EBee EBrs GBuc WFar WMow
oregana	NBid NGdn
- subsp. ***spicata***	EPPr WFar WMoo
'Party Girl'	More than 30 suppliers
'Präriebrand'	LSou SAga
'Purpetta'	CBrm EChP MAnH MDKP MFOX NChi NLar NPro NRnb STes
'Reverend Page Roberts'	EBee MMHG MRav WCot WFar WMow
'Rosaly'	CBrm EChP MAnH MWrn NChi NLar NVic SMar WGor
'Rosanna'	EChP GMaP LPhx LRHS MAnH MDKP NLar WHil WMow WWeb WWpP
'Rose Queen'	EBee ECha EPPr LRHS MFOX MRav MTis NBro NCob SChu SPer SRms WCAu WFar WMoo WMow
'Rosy Gem'	ECtt LRHS MBNS WFar
Stark's hybrids	LRHS SRms
'Sussex Beauty'	CFwr CMCo CSam EBee EMan LRHS MArl MLLN MRav MSte NCiC NDov NEgg NGdn SChu SRkn WAul WCot WFar WMoo WMow WWeb
'Sweet Joy'	SMrm
'The Duchess'	WFar
'William Smith' ♀H4	COtt CSam CWCL EBee ECtt EGra EPfP EVFa EWTr EWes LAst LRHS MLLN MRav NChi NCiC NCob NGdn NLon NOrc SGar SOkh SPer SPla WCAu WFar
'Wine Red'	CFir CM&M EBee EMan ERou EVFa MBnl MDKP MSte SWvt WCra WHil

Sideritis (*Lamiaceae*)

cypria	XPep
hyssopifolia	EBee
scordioides	EBee XPep
syriaca	CArn EBee EMan EOHP EWll IFro SGar SHFr SIgm SSvw

Sieversia (*Rosaceae*)

pentapetala	see *Geum pentapetalum*

Silaum (*Apiaceae*)

silaus	NMir WBWf

Silene (*Caryophyllaceae*)

acaulis	EDAr EHyt GTou LBee LRHS MTho NLar NMen SBla SRms WAbe
§ - subsp. ***acaulis***	CGra SPlb SRms
- 'Alba'	CGra EPot EWes LRHS NLan SOkd WAbe
- 'Blush' **new**	NMen WAbe
§ - subsp. ***bryoides***	NWCA
- subsp. ***elongata***	see *S. acaulis* subsp. *acaulis*
- subsp. ***exscapa***	see *S. acaulis* subsp. *bryoides*
- 'Frances'	EPot GCrs GEdr GMaP GTou NMen NRya NSla NWCA WAbe
- 'Francis Copeland'	ECho NMen
* - ***minima***	CLyd
- 'Mount Snowdon'	EDAr ELan EPfP EWes GMaP LBee LRHS NEgg NLar NMen NRya NWCA SPoG SRms WPat
- 'Pedunculata'	see *S. acaulis* subsp. *acaulis*
alba	see *S. latifolia*
alpestris	CSec EPfP GKev MBar MHer MTho NLon SRms SRot WFar WMoo
- 'Flore Pleno' (d) ♀H4	EWes LBee LRHS NFor NLon NSla
andicola F&W 8174	NWCA
argaea	EHyt
x ***arkwrightii***	see *Lychnis* x *arkwrightii*
armeria	EBee WHer
asterias	GBuc GCal GCra IFro IGor MBNS MHar MNrw NBid NBre NBro NSti WPer
- MESE 429	GBin
atropurpurea	see *Lychnis viscaria* subsp. *atropurpurea*
bellidioides	WPGP
brahuica **new**	CSec
californica	NWCA
caroliniana subsp. ***wherryi***	NGdn
chlorifolia	NWCA
chungtienensis	EBee
§ ***compacta***	CSec EWTr MAnH NLar
delavayi	GKev
dinarica	WAbe
§ ***dioica***	CArn CHrt CRWN EGoo EPfP MBow MChe MHer NLan NLar NMir NVic SECG SGar WFar WMoo WRos WShi
- 'Clifford Moor'[PBR] (v)	ECtt EHoe LRHS NSti SCoo WCHb
- 'Compacta'	see *S. dioica* 'Minikin'
§ - 'Flore Pleno' (d)	CBgR ECha GCra GMac LLWP MNrw MRav MTho NBid NBro NGdn NWoo SBch SMrm WEas WFar WHoo WPer WTin
§ - 'Graham's Delight' (v)	EMag EMon SBch WCHb WMoo
- 'Inane'	CBgR CNat MAvo SBch SHar
- f. ***lactea***	MHer
§ - 'Minikin'	CBgR ECha EMon LRHS MAvo SPer WTin
- 'Pat Clissold' (v)	WCHb
- 'Pembrokeshire Pastel' (v)	MAvo
- 'Richmond' (d)	EBee GBuc MAvo MInt SBch
§ - 'Rosea Plena' (d)	CBre EMan EMon MAnH MTho NCob SChu WHer WPer WWFP
- 'Rubra Plena'	see *S. dioica* 'Flore Pleno'
- 'Thelma Kay' (d/v)	CBgR CDes CFee CMil CSev EBee ECtt EWes GBuc MDun NBid NBre NLar WMoo WPGP
- 'Underdine'	EBee EWes
- 'Variegata'	see *S. dioica* 'Graham's Delight'
elisabethae	NEgg
§ ***fimbriata***	CBot CBre CSec CSpe EHrv ELan EMag EPyc GCal MAnH MMHG MNFA MRav MWat NSti SBla SBri SChu SHel SMrm WAbb WCot WKif WPen WRHF WSHC WTin WWye

	Name	Suppliers
	- 'Marianne'	MNrw
	gallica	CSec NLar
	var. ***quinquevulnera***	
	gonosperma HWJK 2287 **new**	WCru
	gracilicaulis **new**	GKev
	hookeri	MTho WBVN WLin
	- Ingramii Group	CGra CPBP
	'Ice Clips' **new**	WPtf
	inflata	see *S. vulgaris* Garcke
	italica	WCot
	'Jack Flash' **new**	EMag WSan
	keiskei	ECha EMag WBVN
	- var. ***minor***	EWes LRHS MTho WAbe
	laciniata **new**	WOut
	latifolia	CArn MBow NMir
	- subsp. ***alba***	CHrt GWCH SECG
	maritima	see *S. uniflora*
	maroccana	CRWN
	morrisonmontana B&SWJ 3149	WCru
	multifida	see *S. fimbriata*
	nigrescens	GKev NChi NWCA
	nutans	CArn MNrw SMar SRms SSth WHer
	- subsp. ***smithiana***	WBWf
	- - var. ***salmoniana***	WBWf
	orientalis	see *S. compacta*
	parishii var. ***latifolia***	CPBP WLin
	petersonii	NWCA
	pusilla	CHal NLar
	regia	CDes LRav MNrw SSpi WPGP
	rubra	see *S. dioica*
	saxifraga	XPep
	schafta ♀H4	CHal CHrt ECha ECtt EDAr EPfP GKev GKir LRHS MWat NArg NBid NBlu NCob NJOw NWCA SHGN SIng SPet SRms WAbe WFar WHoo WPer
	- 'Abbotswood'	see *Lychnis* x *walkeri* 'Abbotswood Rose'
	- 'Robusta'	GKev LRHS SBla
§	- 'Shell Pink'	EWes LBee LRHS LSou NBid NCob NWCA WHoo
	sieboldii	see *Lychnis coronata* var. *sieboldii*
	'Snowflake'	COkL
	suksdorfii	CLyd CSec EPot WHoo
	tartarica **new**	SHGN
*	***tenuis***	GBuc
	- ACE 2429	GBuc
	thessalonica	MCCP
§	***uniflora***	ECtt EGoo EMar EPfP GGar IHMH MWat NBid NBlu NBro NJOw NLon NWoo SPlb SRms WFar WHer WMoo
	- 'Alba Plena'	see *S. uniflora* 'Robin Whitebreast'
I	- 'Compacta'	EPPr ESis EWTr NDlv SHGN WMoo
§	- 'Druett's Variegated' (v)	CMHG CMea COkL ECha ECtt EDAr EPfP EPot ESis EWes GBuc GKir LAst LBee LRHS MBar MHer NBid NJOw NMen NPri NVic SIng SPet SPlb SPoG SRms WBVN WCot WPat
	- 'Flore Pleno'	see *S. uniflora* 'Robin Whitebreast'
	- pink-flowered	LBee
§	- 'Robin Whitebreast' (d)	CHar CNic CSLe ECha ECtt GCal GKir GMaP MBar MTho MWat NBid NBro NOak SRms SRot WMoo WPer
	- 'Rosea'	CNic EBee ECtt EMar GGar IHMH LRHS MRav NFor NJOw SPlb SRot SUsu WPer
	- 'Silver Lining' (v)	GBuc
	- 'Swan Lake' (d)	IHMH
	- 'Variegata'	see *S. uniflora* 'Druett's Variegated'
	- Weisskehlchen	see *S. uniflora* 'Robin Whitebreast'
	- 'White Bells'	CTri ECtt EPfP SPet WHoo WKif WSHC
	vallesia	WPer
	virginica	CDes GIBF
§	***vulgaris***	CRWN MChe MHer NLan NMir SECG
	- subsp. ***maritima***	see *S. uniflora*
	wallichiana	see *S. vulgaris*
	'Wisley Pink'	CHal ECtt
	yunnanensis	LPhx
§	***zawadskii***	GBuc GKev MDKP NJOw WPer WTin

Silphium (*Asteraceae*)

	Name	Suppliers
	integrifolium	EBee NBre SAga WCot
	laciniatum	CArn EMan LPhx NBre SMad SMrm WCot
	perfoliatum ♀H4	CArn EBee GPoy LPhx NBre NLar NRnb NSti SMad SMrm WCot WFar
	terebinthinaceum	LPhx MSal SMad WCot

Silybum (*Asteraceae*)

	Name	Suppliers
	marianum	CArn CSec CSpe ELan EMag EMan EPfP GAbr GPoy MSal MWgw NArg NGHP NLsd SECG SIde SPav WFar WHer WWye
	- 'Adriana'	EMag EUnu EWll NArg SPav

Simmondsia (*Simmondsiaceae*)

	Name	Suppliers
	chinensis	EShb MSal

Sinacalia (*Asteraceae*)

	Name	Suppliers
§	***tangutica***	CRow CSam EBee ECha EPPr GGar MBNS MFOX NBid NBro NSti SDix WAbb WCru WDyG WFar WMoo

Sinarundinaria (*Poaceae*)

	Name	Suppliers
	anceps	see *Yushania anceps*
	jaunsarensis	see *Yushania anceps*
	maling	see *Yushania maling*
	murielae	see *Fargesia murielae*
	nitida	see *Fargesia nitida*

Sinningia (*Gesneriaceae*)

	Name	Suppliers
	'Blue Wonder'	MBri
*	***caerulea***	WDib
	canescens ♀H1	CHal ERea WDib
§	***cardinalis***	CHal EBak WDib
	- 'Innocent'	WDib
§	x ***cardosa***	MBri
	'Diego Rose'	MBri
	douglasii	CSpe
	'Duchess of York'	CSut
	'Duke of York'	CSut
	'Kaiser Wilhelm'	LAma MBri
	nivalis	WDib
	speciosa 'Etoile de Feu'	LAma MBri
	- 'Hollywood'	LAma
	- 'Kaiser Friedrich'	LAma MBri
	- 'Mont Blanc'	LAma MBri
	- 'Violacea'	MBri
	tubiflora	CMon

Sinobambusa (*Poaceae*)

	Name	Suppliers
§	***intermedia***	EPla WJun
*	***orthotropa***	CFil EPla WPGP
	rubroligula	CFil EPla NMoo WPGP
	tootsik	EPla WJun
	- 'Albostriata' (v)	LPJP
	- 'Variegata'	see *S. tootsik* 'Albostriata'

Sinocalycanthus (*Calycanthaceae*)

chinensis CBcs CMCN CPMA CPle EBee EPfP EWTr IDee IMGH MBlu NPal SBrw SMad SSpi WBVN WFar WPGP

Sinofranchetia (*Lardizabalaceae*)

sp. CPLG CPLN GCal WCru

Sinojackia (*Styracaceae*)

xylocarpa EPfP MBlu NLar SSpi WFar

Sinowilsonia (*Hamamelidaceae*)

henryi CBcs NLar SBrw

Siphocampylus (*Campanulaceae*)

foliosus CFil EBee
- CDPR 3240 WPGP

Siphocranion (*Labiatae*)

macranthum CDes CPom CPne EBee WPGP

Sisymbrium (*Brassicaceae*)

§ **luteum** SHar WHer

Sisyrinchium ✿ (*Iridaceae*)

from Andes Mountains EWes
x **anceps** see *S. angustifolium*
§ **angustifolium** CMHG CNic EBur ECha GKir LPBA MBNS MBar MSal MWat NBir NChi NLAp SPlb SPur SRms WPer
- **album** GKir NChi NLar
§ **arenarium** CPBP EBur EPot GEdr NRya
atlanticum NBro SUsu WPer
bellum hort. see *S. idahoense* var. *bellum*
bermudianum see *S. angustifolium*
- 'Album' see *S. graminoides* 'Album'
'Biscutella' CHad CKno CLyd CPrp CTri EBee EBur ECtt EDAr GMaP ITer ITim NEgg NMen NRya SChu SIng SPla SPlb SPoG SSth SWal SWvt WFar WHal WHoo WKif WMoo WTin
'Blue Ice' CBrm CMea CPBP CWCL EBur EDAr MAvo SBch WAbe WFar WHoo WMoo WPat WPer
boreale see *S. californicum*
brachypus see *S. californicum* Brachypus Group
'Californian Skies' More than 30 suppliers
§ **californicum** CBen CBrm EBur EGra EHon EMFW EPfP EShb ESis LPBA MBar MWat NBid NBlu NBro NLsd SSth WBVN WFar WPer WWpP WWye
§ - Brachypus Group CBro CHar ECtt EDAr EPot GAbr GGar GTou IHMH MBNS MOne MWgw NBir NBlu NJOw NLAp NLar NPri NVic SGar SPet SPlb SPoG SWvt WBrE WMoo
* **capsicum** CPLG
§ **chilense** ERos
coeleste EBur
coeruleum see *Gelasine coerulea*
commutatum CHar EDAr GBuc MNrw SGar
convolutum EChP LRHS NDov WCot
cuspidatum see *S. arenarium*
'Deep Seas' NLar SUsu
demissum CLyd EBur
depauperatum CLyd EBur MNrw WHer WPer
'Devon Blue' WFar
'Devon Skies' CHid CMCo CMHG CRez CWCL EBur MDKP SBch SIng SWvt WAbe WFar
douglasii see *Olsynium douglasii*
'Dragon's Eye' CElw CMea CPBP EBur MBrN MSph SIng SMHy SOkd SRot SSth SSvw SUsu WKif
'E.K. Balls' CBrm CLyd EBur ECtt EPfP GMaP LAst LBee LRHS MTho MWgw NBro NJOw NMen NRya SBla SIng SPoG SRms SSvw SUsu SWvt WAbe WBrE WMoo WPat
elmeri EBur
'Emmeline' EBur
filifolium see *Olsynium filifolium*
graminoides EBur NBro SYvo WPer
§ - 'Album' EBur GGar LRHS NBro WPer
grandiflorum see *Olsynium douglasii*
'Hemswell Sky' CLyd EBur EHoe LAst MDHE NRya
'Iceberg' EBur EShb MWgw SSth SUsu WKif
idahoense ECha EDAr ESis GAbr GEdr GGar GKev LRHS LSou MHer NJOw NRya SPlb SRms
§ - 'Album' ♀H4 CMea CTri EBur EDAr EGra EHyt ELan ERos GAbr GFlt GTou LPhx LRHS MTho MWat NJOw NLAp NLon SAga SHBN SUsu WAbe WFar WPat WPer WWpP WWye
§ - var. **bellum** CBro CTri EBur ELan EPfP GTou IFro IHMH LRHS MBNS MWhi NEgg NLsd NMen NPri NWCA SPet SRms SSto WPat WPer WSSM WWpP XPep
- - pale-flowered SMHy
- - 'Rocky Point' CElw CLyd CMCo CSpe EBee EBur NLAp SPoG SRot WHoo WPat
- blue EGra
- var. **macounii** WFar
iridifolium see *S. micranthum*
junceum see *Olsynium junceum*
littorale CPLG EBur NLar WPer
macrocarpon ♀H2-3 CFee CLyd CPBP EBur ERos GTou LBee LRHS MDKP NJOw NMen SBch SBla SBri SChr SWal WPer
'Marie' EBur
'Marion' CMea CPBP MAvo NLar SBch SMHy SPet SRot SSth SSvw SUsu WWye
'May Snow' see *S. idahoense* 'Album'
'Miami' EBur
§ **micranthum** CBro EBur
montanum ERos IHMH
'Mrs Spivey' EBur ECtt MBar MHer NBir NOak WRHF
'North Star' see *S.* 'Pole Star'
nudicaule x **montanum** CFee EBur GAbr MDHE MNrw NJOw NRya SRot WPer
palmifolium CDes CFil EBee MAvo MDKP SMad SSpi
- JCA 2.880.010 WPGP
patagonicum CPLG EBur EDAr ERos GBuc GFlt WCot WPer
§ 'Pole Star' CFee CLyd CNic CSpe EBur EChP GTou IBlr LRHS LSou WFar WMoo WPer
'Quaint and Queer' CHea CMil CPLG CWCL EBur EChP ECha ECtt EGra EMar ERou EVFa MBrN MTho NBir NBro NChi NJOw SHBN SWvt WMnd WMoo WPer WPnP WWhi WWpP WWye
I 'Raspberry' CMea EBur NJOw WAbe
scabrum see *S. chilense*
'Sisland Blue' EBur EWes
§ **striatum** More than 30 suppliers
§ - 'Aunt May' (v) More than 30 suppliers
- 'Variegatum' see *S. striatum* 'Aunt May'

Sium (*Apiaceae*)

	sisarum	ELau EOHP EUnu GBar GPoy MHer MSal

Skimmia ✿ (*Rutaceae*)

	anquetilia	CMac MBar WBcn
	arborescens GWJ 9374 **new**	WCru
	- subsp. ***nitida*** B&SWJ 8239 **new**	WCru
	arisanensis B&SWJ 7114	WCru
	x ***confusa***	EHol SBch WFar
	- 'Isabella'	SPer
	- 'Kew Green' (m) 🏆^{H4}	More than 30 suppliers
§	***japonica***	CDul CMHG CMac CTrw CWib EMil GKir GQui MGos NScw SReu SSta WDin WFar WHCG
	- (f)	CMac CTri ELan ENot EPfP SPer SRms
	- B&SWJ 5053	WCru
	- 'Alba'	see *S. japonica* 'Wakehurst White'
	- 'Bowles' Dwarf Female' (f)	CMHG EPla LRHS MBar MBri MGos MRav MWht SLim SLon
	- 'Bowles' Dwarf Male' (m)	CMHG EPla LRHS MBar MBri MHar SLim
	- 'Bronze Knight' (m)	CMac ENot LRHS MBar MRav SLim WFar
	- 'Cecilia Brown' (f)	WFar
	- 'Chameleon'	LAst
	- 'Claries Repens'	EPla LRHS SPer
	- 'Emerald King' (m)	EBee LRHS MBar MBri WBcn WFar
N	- 'Foremanii'	see *S. japonica* 'Veitchii'
§	- 'Fragrans' (m) 🏆^{H4}	CDoC CMac CSBt CSam CTri CTrw CWib EBee ECrN ENot EPfP GKir LRHS MBar MGos MRav MWgw NCGa SHBN SLim SPer SWvt WFar WGwG
	- 'Fragrant Cloud'	see *S. japonica* 'Fragrans'
	- 'Fragrantissima' (m)	LRHS MBri WFar
	- 'Fructu Albo'	see *S. japonica* 'Wakehurst White'
	- 'Godrie's Dwarf' (m) **new**	SPoG
	- 'Highgrove Redbud' (f)	EBee LRHS MBar MGos SLim WBcn
	- var. ***intermedia*** f. ***repens***	WFar
	- - B&SWJ 5560	WCru
	- 'Keessen' (f)	WFar
	- 'Kew White' (f)	CAbP CBcs CDoC CWib EBee ECrN EPfP GKir IArd MBri MGos MLan MWat SLon SSta SWvt WCFE WFar WHCG
	- Luwian = 'Wanto'^{PBR}	EBee LRHS WFar
	- 'Marlot' (m)	EPfP MGos SPoG WBcn
	- 'Nymans' (f) 🏆^{H4}	CDoC CEnd CSam EBee ELan EPfP GKir LRHS MAsh MBar MBri MRav MWht NDlv SHBN SLim SMer SPer SPla SPoG SReu SSpi SSta WFar
	- 'Oblata'	SMer
	- 'Obovata' (f)	EPla
	- 'Red Dragon'	CMac
	- 'Red Princess' (f)	EPla LAst MAsh MBri WBcn WFar
*	- 'Red Riding Hood'	SLon
	- 'Redruth' (f)	CBcs CDoC CMac CSBt CSam EBee GKir LAst LRHS MAsh MBar MGos MWat MWgw MWht SLim SSta WBcn WFar
§	- subsp. ***reevesiana***	More than 30 suppliers
	- - B&SWJ 3763	WCru
	- - 'Chilan Choice'	EPfP GKir LRHS MAsh SLim SPla SPoG SSta
	- - 'Fata Morgana' (m)	MGos
	- - var. ***reevesiana*** B&SWJ 3544	WCru
	- - 'Robert Fortune'	MBar
§	- Rogersii Group	CMac CTri MBar
	- - 'Dunwood'	MBar
	- - 'George Gardner'	MBar
	- - 'Helen Goodall' (f)	MBar
§	- - 'Nana Mascula' (m)	CTri
	- - 'Rockyfield Green'	MBar
	- - 'Snow Dwarf' (m)	LRHS MBar MBri WFar
	- 'Rubella' (m) 🏆^{H4}	More than 30 suppliers
	- 'Rubinetta' (m)	EBee EPfP GKir IArd LSRN MAsh MBar MGos NCGa SLim WFar
	- 'Ruby Dome' (m)	LRHS MBar WBcn WFar
	- 'Ruby King' (m)	CDoC CSBt ECrN GKir IArd LRHS LSRN MAsh MBar
	- 'Scarlet Dwarf' (f)	MBar
	- 'Scarlet Queen' (f)	CWib
	- 'Stoneham Red'	EPla MBri
	- 'Tansley Gem' (f)	EPfP GKir LRHS MAsh MBar MBri MWht SPoG SSta WFar
	- 'Thelma King'	GKir LRHS WFar
§	- 'Veitchii' (f)	CBcs CDul CMac CSBt CTri EBee ECrN ELan ENot EPfP GKir IArd IMGH MAsh MBar MDun MGos MRav MSwo SEND SHBN SLim SMer SPer SWvt WDin WTel
§	- 'Wakehurst White' (f)	CBcs CMHG CMac CPle CSBt CTrw EPfP GKir MBar MRav SLim SLon SReu SSpi SSta WFar
	- 'White Gerpa'	MGos WBcn
	- 'Winifred Crook' (f)	EPla GKir MBar MBri WFar
	- 'Winnie's Dwarf'	MGos
	- 'Wisley Female' (f)	CTri ECtt EPla SAga WFar
	laureola	CBcs CDoC CSam EBee ECot MRav SRms WFar WSHC
	- GWJ 9364	WCru
	- 'Borde Hill' (f)	NPri
	- subsp. ***multinervia*** B&SWJ 8259	WCru
	'Olympic Flame'	EPfP EWTr GKir LRHS MGos SLim WFar
	reevesiana	see *S. japonica* subsp. *reevesiana*
	rogersii	see *S. japonica* Rogersii Group

Smallanthus (*Asteraceae*)

	uvedalius	MSal

Smilacina (*Convallariaceae*)

	atropurpurea	CBct WCru
	bicolor **new**	CDes
	flexuosa B&SWJ 9069 **new**	WCru
	formosana	CBct WCot
	- B&SWJ 349	WCru
	forrestii	WCru
	fusca	GBin WCru
	henryi	WCru
	japonica	CBct WCru
	- B&SWJ 1179	WCru
	oleracea	GBin GEdr GFlt WCot WCru
	- B&SWJ 2148	WCru
§	***racemosa*** 🏆^{H4}	More than 30 suppliers
	- var. ***amplexicaulis***	GCal
	- - 'Emily Moody'	CFil CPou ELan SSpi WPGP
	salvinii	LEdu
	- B&SWJ 9000	WCru
	stellata	CAvo CBct CHEx CRow EBee ECha EPPr EPla EPot EWTr GBBs GKir MDun MLLN MRav NChi NFla SMac WAul WCru WPnP WTin
	szechuanica	WCru
	tatsiensis	WCru

Smilax (*Smilacaceae*)

B&SWJ 6628 from Thailand	WCru
asparagoides 'Nanus'	see *Asparagus asparagoides* 'Myrtifolius'
aspera	CFil CPLN EPla EShb LEdu WCru WPGP
- 'Silver Shield'	SSpi
china B&SWJ 4427	WCru
discotis	CBcs SEND
glaucophylla B&SWJ 2971	WCru
nipponica B&SWJ 4331	WCru
rotundifolia	LEdu
sagittifolia	NArg
sieboldii	MRav
- B&SWJ 744	WCru

Smithiantha (*Gesneriaceae*)

'Little One'	WDib

Smyrnium (*Apiaceae*)

olusatrum	CAgr CArn CHrt CSev CSpe GBar IHMH MChe MHer MSal SIde WHer WWye
perfoliatum	CPom CSpe EHrv ELan EMar EWes GBuc SDix WEas WSHC
rotundifolium	WCot

Solandra (*Solanaceae*)

grandiflora misapplied	see *S. maxima*
grandiflora Swartz	CPLN ERea WMul
hartwegii	see *S. maxima*
longiflora	CPLN ERea
§ ***maxima***	CPLN ERea EShb SBig

Solanum (*Solanaceae*)

aculeatissimum **new**	EUnu
atropurpureum	CSpe
aviculare G.Forst.	EUnu XPep
bonariense	XPep
crispum	EHol SGar WDin
- 'Autumnale'	see *S. crispum* 'Glasnevin'
- 'Elizabeth Jane Dunn' (v) **new**	WCot
§ - 'Glasnevin' ♀H3	More than 30 suppliers
- 'Variegatum' (v)	WGwG
dulcamara	CArn GPoy MGol
- 'Hullavington' (v)	CNat
- 'Variegatum' (v)	CBcs CMac CWan EBee ECrN EHoe EPfP IBlr LRHS MBNS MBri NSti SBra SPet WBVN WFar WSHC
giganteum **new**	EUnu
hispidum	CHEx
jasminoides	see *S. laxum*
laciniatum	CArn CBrm CHEx CPLG CSec CSev CSpe EMan EWes GGar IBlr SAPC SArc SBig SGar SHFr SNew SPav WWlt
§ ***laxum***	CDul CPLN EBee ECrN EPfP EShb LRHS MSwo NSti SBra SCoo SPer SPet SPoG SRms SWvt WDin WFar WSHC XPep
- 'Album' ♀H3	More than 30 suppliers
- 'Album Variegatum' (v)	CWib ELan GQui LAst LRHS MBNS NSti SBra WCot WSHC
* - 'Aureovariegatum' (v)	CBcs CSBt EBee EPfP LRHS MGos NBlu NEgg SCoo SLim SPer SPla SPlb SPoG WRHF WWeb
linearifolium	CHea WCot WPat WSPU
muricatum (F)	EShb ESlt EUnu EWin
- 'Lima' (F)	ECrN EUnu
- 'Otavalo' (F)	EUnu
- 'Quito' (F)	ECrN EUnu
pseudocapsicum	EUnu MBri SWal
- 'Ballon'	MBri
- variegated	EShb WCot
quitoense (F)	CHEx EUnu MGol WMul
§ ***rantonnetii***	CHll ELan ERea EShb IDee MOak SYvo WCot XPep
- 'Royal Robe'	CBcs CRHN GQui
* - 'Variegatum' (v)	ERea EShb ESlt MOak
salicifolium	EShb
seaforthianum	CPLN
§ ***sessiliflorum*** (F)	EUnu
sinaicum 'Burbankii' **new**	EUnu
sisymbriifolium	CSec EUnu WWlt
* ***spontaneum*** **new**	EUnu
tomentosum **new**	EUnu
topiro	see *S. sessiliflorum*
valdiviense 'Variegatum' (v)	WDin
vespertilio **new**	CSec
wendlandii	CPLN ERea

Solaria (*Alliaceae*)

sp. **new**	GCal

Soldanella (*Primulaceae*)

alpina	GCra GCrs GKev GTou ITim MTho NMen SBla SIng SRms WAbe WBVN WLin
I - 'Alba'	WAbe
austriaca	WAbe
carpatica	EDAr EHyt ETow GTou LTwo NRya NWCA SIng WAbe
- 'Alba'	EDAr GKev MDKP NLAp NSla SBla WAbe
carpatica x ***pusilla***	CPBP NRya NSla SBla
carpatica x ***villosa***	MDKP
cyanaster	EHyt GEdr GKev NRya NSla SBla WAbe WLin
dimoniei	CFee GKev ITim NMen NSla NWCA SBla WAbe
§ ***hungarica***	CLyd ITim MTho WAbe
minima	CLyd EHyt GCrs GGar ITim NBro NDlv NMen NRya NSla NWCA SBla WAbe
- 'Alba'	WAbe
montana	CLAP CLyd CMea GCrs GFlt GKev GTou LTwo MTho NJOw NLar NMen SIng WAbe WRha
- subsp. ***hungarica***	see *S. hungarica*
pindicola	EBee EHyt EMan EWes GKev MOne NDlv NJOw NMen NWCA WAbe WFar
pusilla	GFlt GKev ITim NSla WAbe
villosa	CDes CLAP GCrs GGar GKev LRHS MTho NJOw NRya NSla SAga SBla WAbe WFar WSHC

Soleirolia (*Urticaceae*)

soleirolii	CHEx CHal CTri EPot LPBA LRHS MBri MCCP MWhi SHFr SIng STre WDyG WHer XPep
- 'Argentea'	see *S. soleirolii* 'Variegata'
§ - 'Aurea'	CHal CTri EPot ESis EWin SIng STre
- 'Golden Queen'	see *S. soleirolii* 'Aurea'
- 'Silver Queen'	see *S. soleirolii* 'Variegata'
§ - 'Variegata' (v)	CHal LPBA WHer

Solenomelus (*Iridaceae*)

chilensis	see *S. pedunculatus*
§ ***pedunculatus***	CFee CFil EHyt WPGP
sisyrinchium	CPBP ERos

Solenopsis (*Campanulaceae*)

axillaris	see *Isotoma axillaris*

Solenostemon ✿ (*Lamiaceae*)

'Angel of the North' **new**	NHor
'Anne Boleyn' (v)	CHal
'Autumn'	MOak
'Autumn Gold'	CHal NHor
'Autumn Rainbow' **new**	WDib
'Beauty' (v)	CHal MOak WDib
'Beauty of Lyons'	CHal NHor
'Beckwith's Gem'	CHal
'Billy Elliot' **new**	NHor
'Bizarre Croton' (v)	CHal NHor
'Black Dragon'	CHal
'Black Heart' **new**	NHor WDib
'Black Prince'	CHal MOak WDib
'Blackheart'	MOak
'Brilliant' (v)	NHor WDib
'Buttercup'	CHal NHor WDib
'Buttermilk' (v) ♀H1	CHal MOak NHor
'Carnival' (v)	CHal WDib
'Carousel' (v)	NHor
'Catherine Cookson' **new**	NHor
'Chamaeleon' (v)	WDib
'City of Durham' (v) **new**	NHor
'City of Liverpool'	CHal NHor
'City of Newcastle' **new**	NHor
'City of Sunderland' **new**	NHor
'Combat' (v)	CHal WDib
'Copper Sprite'	CHal
'Coppersmith'	NHor
'Crimson Ruffles' (v) ♀H1	CHal MOak NHor WDib
'Crimson Velvet'	CHal MOak
'Crinkly Bottom'	NHor
'Dairy Maid' (v)	CHal NHor
'Dazzler' (v)	CHal MOak
'Display'	CHal MOak NHor
'Dracula'	CHal NHor
'Durham Gala' **new**	NHor
'Ellas Fire' **new**	NHor
'Etna' (v)	CHal NHor
'Fire Fingers'	MOak
'Firebrand' (v) ♀H1	CHal
'Firedance' (v)	NHor
'Firefly'	CHal
'Flamenco Dancer' **new**	NHor
'Freckles' (v)	CHal NHor WDib
'Funfair' (v)	CHal NHor
'Gloriosus'	CHal
'Glory of Luxembourg' (v) ♀H1	CHal MOak NHor
'Goldie' (v)	CHal NHor
'Grace Darling' **new**	NHor
'Hanna Hauxwell' **new**	NHor
'Hannay Harding' **new**	NHor
'Holly' (v)	NHor
'Inky Fingers' (v)	CHal MOak WDib
'Jean' (v)	NHor
'Juliet Quartermain'	CHal LAst MOak NHor WDib
'Jupiter'	CHal MOak
'Kentish Fire' (v)	CHal NHor
'Kiwi Fern' (v)	CHal MOak WDib
'Klondike'	CHal NHor
'Laing's Croton' (v)	CHal
'Lemon Dash'	MOak NHor
'Lemondrop'	CHal
'Leopard' (v)	NHor
'Lord Falmouth' ♀H1	CHal MOak NHor WDib
'Luminous' **new**	NHor
'Melody' (v)	CHal WDib
'Midas'	CHal NHor
'Midnight'	MOak
'Mission Gem' (v)	CHal NHor WWol
'Mrs Pilkington' (v)	NHor
'Muriel Pedley' (v)	CHal MOak
'Nettie' (v)	NHor
'Ottoman'	CHal
'Paisley Shawl' (v) ♀H1	CHal NHor WDib
'Palisandra'	CSpe
pentheri	CHal
'Percy Roots'	NHor
'Peter Wonder' (v)	CHal WDib
'Phantom'	NHor
'Picturatus' (v) ♀H1	CHal NHor WDib
'Pineapple Beauty' (v) ♀H1	CHal MOak NHor WDib
'Pineapplette' ♀H1	CHal MOak NHor WDib WWol
'Pink Devil' (v)	NHor
'Primrose Cloud' (v)	NHor
'Purple Oak'	CHal NHor
'Raspberry Ripple'	CHal
'Red Croton' (v)	NHor
'Red Mars'	MOak WDib
'Red Nettie' (v)	CHal NHor WDib
'Red Rosie'	CHal NHor WDib
'Red Stinger'	CHal WWol
'Red Velvet'	CHal NHor WWol
'Rob Roy'	MOak
'Rose Blush' (v)	CHal MOak WDib WWol
'Rosie'	NHor
'Roy Pedley'	CHal
'Royal Scot' (v) ♀H1	CHal NHor WDib
'Salmon Plumes' (v)	CHal NHor
'Scarlet Poncho' **new**	NHor
'Scarlet Ribbons'	CHal MOak NHor
'Speckles' (v)	CHal
'Spire' (v)	NHor
'Strawberry Jam'	CHal MOak
'Sunbeam' (v)	NHor
thyrsoideus	see *Plectranthus thyrsoideus*
'Tom Cooke'	NHor
'Treales' (v)	CHal WDib
'Vesuvius'	CHal
'Walter Turner' (v) ♀H1	CHal MOak NHor WDib WWol
'White Gem' (v)	CHal NHor
'White Pheasant' (v)	CHal
'Winsome' (v)	CHal MOak WDib
'Winter Sun' (v)	CHal MOak NHor
'Wisley Flame'	WDib
'Wisley Tapestry' (v) ♀H1	CHal MOak NHor WDib

Solidago (*Asteraceae*)

	Babygold	see *S.* 'Goldkind'
	brachystachys	see *S. cutleri*
	caesia	EBee ECha EMon ERou EWes MFOX MSte NBir WCot WFar WMoo WOld
	canadensis	CAgr CTri ELan NBre SPlb WFar WHer WSSM
§	- var. ***scabra***	WOld WTin
I	'Citronella' **new**	NFla
	'Cloth of Gold'	CBcs COtt EBee GKir LRHS NPro SWvt WMnd WOld
§	'Crown of Rays'	CLyd CPrp EBee ECtt ERou LRHS MRav NArg WFar WLin WMnd
§	***cutleri***	CLyd EBee ELan ESis EWsh MBar MTho MWat NJOw NLar SBla SPlb SRms WFar WPat WPer
	- ***nana***	EWes WBor
	'Early Bird'	WFar
	'Featherbush'	EBrs LRHS
§	***flexicaulis***	GMaP NLon
	- 'All Gold' (v) **new**	WCot

§	- 'Variegata' (v)	CWan EBee EChP ELan EMag EMan EMar EMon EPfP GBin GMaP LRHS MHar NLar NSti SBch WCAu WCot WFar WHer WOld WPer
	'Gardone' ♀H4	WFar
	gigantea	EMon NBid WPer
	glomerata	EMon NBre NLar WPer
	Golden Baby	see *S.* 'Goldkind'
§	'Golden Dwarf'	LRHS
	'Golden Falls'	EBrs
	'Golden Fleece'	see *S. sphacelata* 'Golden Fleece'
	'Golden Rays'	see *S.* 'Goldstrahl'
	'Golden Shower'	CSam CWCL MWat
	'Golden Thumb'	see *S.* 'Queenie'
	'Golden Wings'	CBre ERou MWat
	'Goldenmosa' ♀H4	CRez CSBt CSam EMan EPfP ERou GMaP LRHS MRav MWat NLon SChu SPer SPoG WCot WFar WOld
	'Goldilocks'	LRHS NPri SRms
§	'Goldkind'	CHrt CM&M COIW CSBt EBee ECtt EPfP EPza ERou GAbr GKir IHMH MBow NArg NBPC NChi NEgg NLsd NOrc SPet SPoG SWal SWvt WFar WMoo WRHF WSSM WWeb WWpP
§	'Goldstrahl'	LRHS
	Goldzwerg	see *S.* 'Golden Dwarf'
	'Harvest Gold'	CElw ERou
	hispida	EMon
	hybrida	see x *Solidaster luteus*
	latifolia	see *S. flexicaulis*
	'Laurin'	EBrs EMil EPfP LRHS NLar WTin
	'Ledsham'	EMFP EVFa LRHS SPoG WMnd
	'Lemore'	see x *Solidaster luteus* 'Lemore'
	'Leraft'	EBee
*	***leuvalis***	CStr
	multiradiata	ESis
	odora	MGol MSal
	ohioensis	EBee
*	'Peter Pan'	ERou WFar
§	'Queenie'	ECha MHer NPro NVic SPer SRms
	rigida	LRHS MRav NBre WCot WPer WWpP
	- JLS 88002WI	EMon
	- subsp. ***humilis***	EBee
	roanensis **new**	NBre
	rugosa	ECha LPhx MWgw WCot
	- subsp. ***aspera***	EMon
	- 'Fireworks'	CBre CSam CStr EBrs EChP EMan EPPr ERou LRHS MHar MNFA NBPC NDov SUsu WCot WHil WHoo WOld WTin WWpP
	sciaphila **new**	EBee
	sempervirens	EMon WCot
	simplex subsp. ***simplex*** var. ***nana***	WPer
	spathulata var. ***nana***	NWCA
	speciosa	EUnu NBre WPer
§	***sphacelata*** 'Golden Fleece'	EBee LRHS NBre SPoG WHoo WMnd
	Strahlenkrone	see *S.* 'Crown of Rays'
	'Summer Sunshine'	ERou
	Sweety = 'Barseven'PBR	MBri
	'Tom Thumb'	MRav SRms WEas
	uliginosa	EShb
	ulmifolia	EBee LRHS
	virgaurea	CArn EBee GPoy GWCH MHer NBre NLar WHer WPer WSel WWye
	- subsp. ***alpestris*** var. ***minutissima***	CLyd CStu NBre
§	- 'Variegata' (v)	EHoe NPro
	vulgaris 'Variegata'	see *S. virgaurea* 'Variegata'

Sollya (*Pittosporaceae*)

	fusiformis	see *S. heterophylla*
§	***heterophylla*** ♀H1	More than 30 suppliers
	- 'Alba'	CBcs CRez ELan SPoG SWvt
	- mauve	ECou
	- pink	CBcs CRez CSPN EPfP SAdn SWvt
	- 'Pink Charmer'	ELan ERea LRHS MWgw SBra SMur SPoG WSHC

x *Solidaster* (*Asteraceae*)

	hybridus	see x *S. luteus*
§	***luteus***	CTri EBee EWTr GBri GKir MBri MHar SRms WEas WFar
§	- 'Lemore' ♀H4	CElw CHea CHrt CMea COIW CPrp EBee EBrs ELan EMan ENot EPfP ERou EWsh GLil GMac LRHS MWat NCGa NPri NVic SPer WCot WFar WLin
	'Super'	CStr WCot WFar

Sonchus (*Asteraceae*)

	fruticosus **new**	CSec
	palustris	EMon

Sophora (*Papilionaceae*)

§	***davidii***	CPle CWib ECou EPfP IDee MBlu MGos NPal SIgm WDin WPGP WSHC
	flavescens	NLar
	japonica ♀H4	CAbP CBcs CDul CLnd CTho EMil EPfP EWTr LRHS MDun MGos MWhi SBLw SBrw SHBN SMHT SPer SPlb WBVN WDin WNor WOrn
	- 'Pendula'	CDul GKir LRHS MBlu SBLw
	- 'Red Dragon' **new**	SBrw
§	'Little Baby'	CBcs CRez CWib EPfP ERea LAst MCCP MGos SBrw SHFr SMur SPoG SWvt WPGP WPat
	macrocarpa	CFil GQui SBra
	microphylla	CBcs CHEx CPle CWCL EBee ECou EPfP IFro SEND SIgm WHer WPGP
	- 'Dragon's Gold'	CBcs ECou ELan EPfP ERea LRHS SPoG SSta WDin
	- 'Early Gold'	ERea GQui SPoG
	- var. ***fulvida***	ECou
	- var. ***longicarinata***	ECou
	mollis	CPle
	prostrata Buch.	CBcs CBot ECou
	prostrata misapplied	see *S.* 'Little Baby'
	- Pukaki form	ECou
	secundiflora	MGol SIgm
	Sun King = 'Hilsop'PBR ♀H4	EMil LRHS MBlu MGos SCoo SPoG
	tetraptera ♀H3	CAbP CBcs CDul CMac CPne EBee ECou EPfP GQui ISea MLan SEND SPer SRms
	- 'Grandiflora' **new**	CBrm
	viciifolia	see *S. davidii*

Sorbaria (*Rosaceae*)

	SF 95205	ISea
	aitchisonii	see *S. tomentosa* var. *angustifolia*
	arborea	see *S. kirilowii*
	aff. ***assurgens*** BWJ 8185	WCru
§	***kirilowii***	GIBF IFro NLon SLon WDyG
	lindleyana	see *S. tomentosa*
	rhoifolia	EPfP
	sorbifolia	CAbP CBcs CMCo EBee ECrN EMil EWTr GIBF GKir LRHS MBar

	MDun MTis MWhi NPro SEND SLPl SPer SPoG WCot WDin WFar WHil
- var. ***stellipila***	CFil SLPl
- - B&SWJ 776	WCru
§ ***tomentosa***	CAbP SHBN WHCG
§ - var. ***angustifolia*** ♀H4	CBcs CDul CTri CWan EBee ELan EPfP GKir IMGH LRHS MDun MRav NPro SEND SLon SPer SPoG WCru WEas WFar WHer

Sorbus ✿ (*Rosaceae*)

CLD 310	GIBF
Harry Smith 12732	GKir LRHS MDun
Harry Smith 12799	GIBF
§ ***alnifolia***	CLnd CMCN CTho EPfP GFlt GIBF MBlu SLPl
amabilis **new**	NLar
americana	CLnd GIBF NWea
- 'Belmonte'	GKir LRHS SBLw
- ***erecta***	see *S. decora*
aff. ***amurensis*** B&SWJ 8665	WCru
anglica	CDul CNat
'Apricot'	CEnd GKir
'Apricot Lady'	GKir LRHS MAsh WJas
'Apricot Queen'	CLnd ECrN EMil GKir MDun NEgg SBLw
aria	CCVT CDul CLnd CSBt CTri ECrN EPfP GKir LBuc MBar NBee NEgg NWea WDin WMou WOrn
- 'Aurea'	CLnd MBlu WFar
- 'Chrysophylla'	CDul CSBt ECrN GKir IMGH LRHS MBri MGos NWea SLim SPer SPoG
- 'Decaisneana'	see *S. aria* 'Majestica'
- 'Gigantea'	CDul EWTr
- 'Lutescens' ♀H4	More than 30 suppliers
- 'Magnifica'	CDoC CDul CTho ECrN ELan EWTr NEgg SBLw WDin WJas
§ - 'Majestica' ♀H4	CCVT CDoC CDul CLnd CTho ECrN GIBF GKir LRHS NWea SBLw SPer SPoG WDin WJas WOrn
- 'Mitchellii'	see *S. thibetica* 'John Mitchell'
- 'Orange Parade'	SBLw
- var. ***salicifolia***	see *S. rupicola*
x ***arnoldiana*** 'Cerise Queen'	GKir
- 'Golden Wonder'	CDul SBLw
- 'Maidenblush'	SBLw
- 'Schouten'	GKir SBLw
aronioides misapplied	see *S. caloneura*
arranensis	CDul CNat GIBF
§ ***aucuparia***	More than 30 suppliers
- 'Aspleniifolia'	CBcs CCVT CDul CLnd CMCN CSBt CTho CWSG EBee ECrN ENot GKir LRHS MAsh MBri MDun MGos NWea SBLw SLim SPer SPoG WDin WFar WJas WOrn
I - 'Aurea'	SBLw
§ - 'Beissneri'	CDul CLnd EMil GKir MBri MGos SCoo
- Cardinal Royal = 'Michred'	CDoC ECrN ENot GKir GQui LRHS NEgg SCoo WJas
- 'Crème Lace'	CDul CRez GKir SCoo
- 'Dirkenii'	CDul CLnd CWSG GKir IMGH LRHS MAsh MDun SLim SPoG WDin WJas
- var. ***edulis*** (F)	CDul CLnd CTho LBuc MGos SBLw SCoo WDin
- - 'Rossica Major'	CDul CTho ECrN GQui SBLw SCoo WFar
- 'Ember Glow' **new**	GKir MBri
§ - 'Fastigiata'	CDul CEnd CLnd CSBt CTri ECrN EPfP GKir LRHS MGos NBee NWea SBLw SHBN WDin WFar
- 'Hilling's Spire'	CTho GKir LRHS MAsh MLan SLPl
- 'Pendula'	EBee SBLw
- ***pluripinnata***	see *S. scalaris*
- var. ***rossica*** Koehne	see *S. aucuparia* var. *edulis*
- 'Rossica Major'	see *S. aucuparia* var. *edulis* 'Rossica Major'
- 'Sheerwater Seedling' ♀H4	CBcs CCVT CDoC CDul CLnd CMCN CTho EBee ECrN ELan ENot EPfP EWTr GKir LRHS MLan MRav MSwo NBee NBlu NEgg SCrf SLim SPer SSta WDin WFar WOrn
- 'Wettra'	SBLw
- 'Winterdown'	CNat
- 'Xanthocarpa'	see *S. aucuparia* var. *xanthocarpa*
- var. ***xanthocarpa*** ♀H4	CLnd EPfP MGos SBLw WDin
Autumn Spires = 'Flanrock'	CDoC CRez CWSG GKir LRHS MBri SCoo
'Bellona'	WPat
§ ***caloneura***	CFil EPla SSpi WPGP
'Carpet of Gold'	CLnd
cashmiriana hort. pink-fruited	CDul GKir LRHS SSpi
cashmiriana Hedl. ♀H4	More than 30 suppliers
- 'Rosiness'	CLnd GKir LRHS MAsh MBri MDun SCoo SLim
chamaemespilus	GIBF WPat
'Chamois Glow'	MAsh WJas
'Chinese Lace'	More than 30 suppliers
§ ***commixta***	CBcs CDul CEnd CLnd CMCN CTho EBee ECrN EGra EPfP EPla GIBF GKir LAst LRHS MBar MBlu MBri MGos MLan MRav MSwo NBea NBee SBLw SLim SPer WDin WJas WOrn
- 'Embley' ♀H4	CAlb CBcs CCVT CDul CLnd CMCN CSBt CSam CTho CTri ECrN ELan ENot EPfP GKir LRHS MBar MDun MGos MRav SLim SPoG SSpi SSta WDin WOrn
- 'Jermyns'	GKir
- var. ***rufoferruginea***	GQui
- - B&SWJ 6078	WCru
conradinae misapplied	see *S. pohuashanensis* (Hance) Hedlund
conradinae Koehne	see *S. esserteauana*
'Copper Kettle'	GKir MBri SCoo
'Coral Beauty'	CLnd
'Covert Gold'	CEnd CLnd
croceocarpa	CDul CNat
cuspidata	see *S. vestita*
§ ***decora*** (Sarg.) C.K. Schneid.	CTho GIBF NBlu SBLw
* - 'Grootendorst'	CDul
- var. ***nana***	see *S. aucuparia* 'Fastigiata'
devoniensis	CAgr CDul CNat CTho WMou
discolor misapplied	see *S. commixta*
discolor (Maxim.) Maxim.	CLnd CMCN EBee GKir MAsh MBlu MSwo NLar NWea WJas
domestica	CDul CLnd CMCN CTho ENot EPfP NWea SLPl SPer WDin
- 'Maliformis'	see *S. domestica* f. *pomifera*
§ - f. ***pomifera***	EHol
dumosa	GIBF
'Eastern Promise'	CWSG ECrN EMil GKir LRHS MAsh MBlu MBri MGos MWat NLar SCoo SLim SMHT SPoG SSta WDin WJas
eminens	CDul CNat
§ ***esserteauana***	CDoC CLnd CTho
- 'Flava'	CTho GKir LRHS

	'Fastigiata'	see *S. aucuparia* 'Fastigiata', *S.* x *thuringiaca* 'Fastigiata'
	folgneri	CDoC CEnd
	- 'Emiel'	MBlu
	- 'Lemon Drop'	CDul CEnd CLnd EPfP GKir LRHS MAsh MBlu NLar SCoo SMad SSpi
§	***foliolosa***	CDul CRez EPfP GIBF NWea WKif
	- 'Lowndes'	CLnd
	forrestii	EPfP GKir NBea NLar SLPl SMHT SSpi
*	***fortunei***	CLnd
I	***fruticosa*** McAllister	CEnd CLnd EBee EPfP GIBF GKev GKir NWea SSpi SSta WJas
	- 'Koehneana'	see *S. koehneana*
	'Ghose'	CEnd CLnd CTho GKir IMGH LRHS MBlu SCoo SPer SSpi
	'Golden Wonder'	see *S.* 'Lombarts Golden Wonder'
N	***gonggashanica***	CLnd EGFP GKir
*	***gorrodini***	CLnd
§	***graeca***	CMCN GIBF SEND
	'Harvest Moon'	GKir GQui LRHS
	hedlundii	GTSp IBlr NLar WPGP WWes
	hemsleyi	CLnd GIBF GKir MBri MDun
	x ***hostii***	CLnd LRHS MRav SPer
§	***hupehensis*** C.K. Schneid. ♀H4	More than 30 suppliers
	- SF 96268	ISea
	- 'November Pink'	see *S. hupehensis* 'Pink Pagoda'
§	- var. ***obtusa*** ♀H4	CCVT CDoC CDul CMCN EPfP GIBF GKir MBlu MDun SSpi SSta WDin
§	- 'Pink Pagoda'	CDoC CDul CLnd CWSG CWib EPfP GKev GKir IArd IMGH LAst LRHS MAsh MBlu MDun MGos MLan MSwo MWat NWea SCoo SLim SLon SPer SPoG WDin
	- 'Rosea'	see *S. hupehensis* var. *obtusa*
*	- ***roseoalba***	GKir
	hybrida misapplied	see *S.* x *thuringiaca*
	hybrida L.	ECrN NWea
	- 'Gibbsii' ♀H4	CDoC CLnd EBee ELan EPfP GKir LRHS MAsh MBri SPur
	insignis	CDoC EPfP GIBF
	intermedia	CBcs CCVT CDul CLnd CSBt CTho CTri CWib ECrN GIBF GKir LRHS MGos NBee NBlu NWea SBLw WDin WMou
	- 'Brouwers'	ELan SBLw WMoo
	'Joseph Rock'	More than 30 suppliers
§	x ***kewensis***	CDul CLnd EBee GKir SMHT SPer SPlb WBrE
	'Kirsten Pink'	CLnd CWib EBee ECrN GKir MDun SMHT WFar
§	***koehneana*** C.K. Schneid. ♀H4	CBcs CLnd CMCN ECrN EGra GBin GCrs GGGa GKev GKir GQui LRHS MAsh MBri MDun NBlu NMen NSla SHFr WPat WTin
	aff. ***koehneana*** Schneider	GKir WCwm
	- Harry Smith 12799	GKir GQui
	'Kukula'	GKir MDun
	kurzii	GIBF
	lanata hort.	see *S. vestita*
	lancastriensis	CNat CTho GIBF
	latifolia	CLnd ECrN GIBF NWea SBLw WDin
	'Leonard Messel'	CTho GKir LRHS MBri NBea
	'Leonard Springer'	ECrN EPfP GKir GQui SSta
	leptophylla **new**	CDul
	leyana	WMou
§	'Lombarts Golden Wonder'	CBcs CDoC CLnd GKir MAsh MBlu MDun NWea WJas
	matsumurana misapplied	see *S. commixta*
	matsumurana (Makino) Koehne	GKir
	megalocarpa	CDoC CFil CPMA EPfP GKir SSpi WCwm WNor WPGP WPat
	microphylla GWJ 9252	WCru
	minima	WMou
	'Molly Sanderson'	IBlr SSta
	monbeigii (Card.) Yü	CLnd GIBF
	moravica 'Laciniata'	see *S. aucuparia* 'Beissneri'
	mougeotii	GIBF GKir
	multijuga	GIBF
§	***munda***	CMCN GBin GKir SCoo
N	***parva***	GIBF
	'Peachi-Ness'	CLnd
	'Pearly King'	CBcs CSam CTho GKir LRHS MAsh NBea WJas
	pekinensis	see *S. reticulata* subsp. *pekinensis*
§	'Pink Pearl'	CDul GKir LRHS MDun
	'Pink Veil'	NBlu
	'Pink-Ness'	EBee GKir LRHS MBri SCoo SLim
	pogonopetala Koehne	GIBF
	pohuashanensis misapplied	see *S.* x *kewensis*
§	***pohuashanensis*** (Hance) Hedlund	CTho
	porrigentiformis	CDul CNat CTho
	poteriifolia	GCrs
	prattii misapplied	see *S. munda*
	prattii Koehne	CLnd GKev GKir WCwm
	- var. ***subarachnoidea***	see *S. munda*
	pseudofennica	GIBF
N	***pseudovilmorinii***	EMon GBin GIBF GKir NLar
	- MF 93044	SSpi
	randaiensis	GIBF GQui SPlb
	- B&SWJ 3202	SSpi WCru
	'Ravensbill'	CTho GKir MBlu
	'Red Robin'	NBlu
	'Red Tip'	CDul CLnd MBar
	reducta ♀H4	CBcs CEnd CMCN CSWP CSec EPfP GBin GIBF GKev GKir GQui ISea ITim LRHS MBlu NBlu NWea SBrw SCoo SOkd SPer SPoG SSpi SSta WDin WFar WNor
	reflexipetala misapplied	see *S. commixta*
	rehderiana misapplied	see *S. aucuparia*
	rehderiana Koehne	CLnd GIBF GKir WNor
§	***reticulata*** subsp. ***pekinensis***	GIBF
	rhamnoides GWJ 9363	WCru
	'Rose Queen'	MBri
	'Rowancroft Coral Pink'	CTho EWTr MBar MGos
§	***rupicola***	CTho GIBF
	'Salmon Queen'	CLnd
	sambucifolia	GBin GIBF
	sargentiana ♀H4	CDul CEnd CLnd CMCN CTho CTri EBee ECrN EGra ELan EPfP GKir IMGH LBuc LRHS MBlu MBri MGos MRav MSwo NWea SLim SMad SPer SSpi WDin WJas WOrn
§	***scalaris*** Koehne	CBcs CEnd CTho CTri EBee EPfP GKir LAst LRHS MBlu MBri SCoo SPer SPoG SSpi WDin WJas WOrn
	'Schouten'	ECrN ENot LRHS
	scopulina misapplied.	see *S. aucuparia* 'Fastigiata'
	setschwanensis	GGGa GKir
	sibirica	GIBF
	'Signalman'	GKir LRHS
	'Sunshine'	CDoC GKir LRHS MAsh MBri NBlu WDin WJas
	thibetica	WPGP
§	- 'John Mitchell' ♀H4	CAgr CDul CEnd CLnd CMCN CTho CWib ECrN ENot EPfP GKir GQui LRHS MAsh MBlu MBri

	MGos MRav MWya NBea NWea SBir SLim SPer WJas WOrn WPat
aff. ***thibetica*** BWJ 7757a	WCru
§ x ***thuringiaca***	CSBt NBea WMou
§ - 'Fastigiata'	CAlb CBcs CDul CLnd GIBF GKir MGos NBee SBLw WDin WJas
torminalis	CCVT CDul CLnd CTho CTri EBee ECrN EPfP GKir LBuc LRHS MBri MRav MWya NWea SBLw SCoo SPer WDin WFar WMou WOrn
umbellata	CMCN
- var. ***cretica***	see *S. graeca*
ursina	see *S. foliolosa*
x ***vagensis***	CLnd GIBF WMou
verrucosa var. ***subulata*** HWJ 579	WCru
§ ***vestita***	CLnd CMCN CTho MBlu
vexans	CDul CNat GBin GIBF
vilmorinii ♀H4	More than 30 suppliers
- 'Robusta'	see *S.* 'Pink Pearl'
aff. ***vilmorinii*** **new**	GIBF
wardii	CBcs CTho LRHS MBlu
'White Swan'	NBlu
'White Wax'	CDul CRez CWSG EPfP GKir GTSp LAst MAsh MDun MGos MLan SBLw SCoo SPer WDin
'Wilfrid Fox'	CLnd SHBN SLPl
willmottiana	CDul
wilsoniana	CLnd GQui
'Wisley Gold'	GKir LRHS MBri SCoo

Sorghastrum (*Poaceae*)

avenaceum	see *S. nutans*
§ ***nutans***	CBig CKno CRWN EBee ECha EMan GFor NBre SMad
- 'Indian Steel'	CAby CBig CBrm CPen EBee EChP EGoo EMan EPPr EPza EUJe GFor MSte MWrn NBre SMad SMar WMnd

Sorghum (*Poaceae*)

halepense	MSte

Soroseris (*Asteraceae*)

rosularis **new**	GKev
umbrella **new**	GKev

sorrel, common see *Rumex acetosa*

sorrel, French see *Rumex scutatus*

Souliea see *Actaea*

soursop see *Annona muricata*

Sparaxis (*Iridaceae*)

elegans	EPot
grandiflora subsp. ***grandiflora***	WCot
hybrids	LAma
tricolor	MDun

Sparganium (*Sparganiaceae*)

§ ***erectum***	CRow EHon EMFW EMag GFor LNCo LPBA NArg NPer WFar WHer WWpP
ramosum	see *S. erectum*

Sparrmannia (*Tiliaceae*)

africana ♀H1	CBcs CHEx CHll CKob CPLG CPle EAmu ERea EShb GQui MBri SAPC SArc SDnm SMur SPav SYvo
- 'Variegata' (v)	ERea
palmata	see *S. ricinocarpa*
§ ***ricinocarpa***	CKob

Spartina (*Poaceae*)

patens	EHoe EPPr
pectinata	CHEx EChP GBin GFor GKir WFar
- 'Aureomarginata' (v)	More than 30 suppliers

Spartium (*Papilionaceae*)

junceum ♀H4	More than 30 suppliers
- 'Brockhill Compact'	LRHS SPoG

Spartocytisus see *Cytisus*

Spathantheum (*Araceae*)

orbignyanum	EBee WCot

Spathipappus see *Tanacetum*

Spathiphyllum (*Araceae*)

'Viscount'	MBri
wallisii	CHal EOHP LRHS MBri

spearmint see *Mentha spicata*

Speirantha (*Convallariaceae*)

§ ***convallarioides***	CDes CFil CLAP CPom CStu EBee EHrv ERos SOkd SSpi WCot WCru WPGP
gardenii	see *S. convallarioides*

Spergularia (*Caryophyllaceae*)

rupicola	SECG WGwG

Sphacele see *Lepechinia*

Sphaeralcea (*Malvaceae*)

ambigua	EBee ELan XPep
'Childerley'	CSpe EMan SAga
coccinea	SPlb
fendleri	CBcs CBot CHll CSam WWye
- subsp. ***venusta***	CBrm GFlt XPep
grossulariifolia	LRav
'Hopleys Lavender'	EBee EChP EMan EWin NLar SAga SVil
'Hyde Hall'	EChP EPPr MAvo MCCP MMil WBor
incana	CBrm SPet
malviflora	WPer
miniata	CBot CHll ELan MLLN MOak SAga
munroana	CBot CPom CSLe CSev CWCL EBee ELan EPPr MOak SSth WCFE WSHC XPep
- 'Dixieland Pink'	EBee
- 'Manor Nursery' (v)	EMan EWes
- pale pink	CBot CSpe ECtt EMan EWin LPhx SAga
* - 'Shell Pink'	ECGP
'Newleaze Coral'	EBee EMan EPPr LLWP NLar SAga SPoG
'Newleaze Pink'	SAga
remota	EMan EShb GFlt MGol SPlb
rivularis	EMan MGol
umbellata	see *Phymosia umbellata*

Sphaeromeria (*Asteraceae*)

§ ***capitata***	EPot NWCA

Spigelia (*Loganiaceae*)

marilandica 'Wisley Jester' **new**	LRHS MBri

Spilanthes (*Asteraceae*)

acmella	see *Acmella oleracea*
oleracea	see *Acmella oleracea*

Spiraea ✿ (*Rosaceae*)

	'Abigail'	CDoC
	albiflora	see *S. japonica* var. *albiflora*
	arborea	see *Sorbaria kirilowii*
§	'Arguta' ♀H4	More than 30 suppliers
	x ***arguta*** 'Bridal Wreath'	see *S.* 'Arguta'
	- 'Compacta'	see *S.* x *cinerea*
	- 'Nana'	see *S.* x *cinerea*
	bella	SLon WHCG WTin
	betulifolia	EBee MRav NLon SMac WHCG
	- var. ***aemiliana***	CBot CWSG EBee ECtt GKir MAsh MGos SLPl WFar
	x ***billardii*** 'Triumphans'	see *S.* x *pseudosalicifolia* 'Triumphans'
	x ***bumalda***	see *S. japonica* 'Bumalda'
	- 'Wulfenii'	see *S. japonica* 'Walluf'
	callosa 'Alba'	see *S. japonica* var. *albiflora*
§	***cantoniensis*** 'Flore Pleno' (d)	CPle SLon
	- 'Lanceata'	see *S. cantoniensis* 'Flore Pleno'
§	x ***cinerea***	CMac SSta
	- 'Grefsheim' ♀H4	CBcs CDoC COtt CSBt EBee ECtt EMil ENot GKir LRHS MBri MGos NEgg SLim SPer SSta WCFE WDin WFar WRHF
	crispifolia	see *S. japonica* 'Bullata'
	decumbens	CPle
	douglasii	MBar
	- subsp. ***menziesii***	NLon
	formosana B&SWJ 1597	CPLG
§	x ***foxii***	SLPl
	fritschiana	CMac SLPl SLon
	hayatana	SLon
	hendersonii	see *Petrophytum hendersonii*
§	***japonica***	SBod SMer WFar
	- 'Alba'	see *S. japonica* var. *albiflora*
§	- var. ***albiflora***	More than 30 suppliers
	- 'Alpina'	see *S. japonica* 'Nana'
	- 'Alpine Gold'	CFai GBin NPro WWeb
	- 'Anthony Waterer' (v)	More than 30 suppliers
	- 'Barkby Gold' **new**	MGos
	- 'Blenheim'	SRms
§	- 'Bullata'	CFee CMHG CMac EPfP GEdr MBar NWCA SRms WAbe WHCG
§	- 'Bumalda'	GKir WFar
	- 'Candlelight' ♀H4	CAbP CBcs CSBt CWSG EBee EGra EPfP GKir LAst LRHS MAsh MBri MGos NCGa NEgg SCoo SLim SPer SPla SPoG SWvt WMoo
§	- 'Crispa'	CRez EPfP LRHS MBar NPro WFar WWeb
	- 'Dart's Red' ♀H4	GKir LRHS SSta WFar
	- 'Firelight'	CAbP CBcs CChe CSBt EBee ECrN EGra ELan ENot EPfP GKir LRHS MAsh MBri MGos MSwo SCoo SLim SPer SPla SPoG SSta SWvt WBrE
	- 'Glenroy Gold'	SLon
	- 'Gold Mound'	CMHG CMac CWSG CWib EBee ECrN ELan ENot EPfP GKir LRHS MBar MHer MRav MSwo MWhi NFor NLon SCoo SHBN SHFr SPer SPlb SRms WDin WFar WHar WWeb
	- 'Gold Rush'	CMHG MBNS
	- Golden Princess = 'Lisp'PBR ♀H4	CMac CTri CWSG EPfP GKir LAst LBuc LRHS MAsh MBar MGos SCoo SMer SPer SReu SRms SSta WCFE WDin WFar WWeb
	- 'Goldflame'	More than 30 suppliers
	- 'Little Princess'	CBcs CMac CWSG CWib EBee ECrN EMil ENot GKir LRHS MAsh MBar MBri MRav MSwo MWat MWhi NBlu NEgg SCoo SLim SPer SRms SSta SWvt WBVN WDin WFar WHar
	- Magic Carpet = 'Walbuma'PBR ♀H4	CBcs LRHS MAsh SCoo SPoG
	- 'Magnifica'	WHCG WPat
§	- 'Nana' ♀H4	CMac CSBt EHyt MAsh MBar MRav MTho NLon SRms WEas WPat WPer
	- 'Nyewoods'	see *S. japonica* 'Nana'
	- 'Shirobana'	see *S. japonica* var. *albiflora*
	- 'Snow Cap'	CWib
§	- 'Walluf'	CFai CMac CPle CTri CWib NFor NLon WBcn WHCG
	- 'White Cloud'	ELan
	- 'White Gold'PBR	CAbP ELan EPfP LAst LBuc LRHS MAsh NPro SCoo SPer SPoG WMoo
	'Margaritae'	NPro SHBN SPer SWvt
	micrantha	CPLG
	nipponica	CBcs MBar
	- 'Halward's Silver'	CFai LBuc LRHS MRav NPro SLPl SPoG WBcn
	- 'June Bride'	NBlu
§	- 'Snowmound' ♀H4	More than 30 suppliers
	- var. ***tosaensis*** misapplied	see *S. nipponica* 'Snowmound'
	- var. ***tosaensis*** (Yatabe) Makino	SReu
	palmata 'Elegans'	see *Filipendula purpurea* 'Elegans'
§	***prunifolia*** (d)	CFai CMac EBee ECrN ELan MBlu MRav SLon SPer SPoG WHCG WTel
	- 'Plena'	see *S. prunifolia*
§	x ***pseudosalicifolia*** 'Triumphans'	SHFr
	salicifolia	WFar
	stevenii	SPer
	'Summersnow'	SLPl
	'Superba'	see *S.* x *foxii*
	tarokoensis ETE 212	GIBF
	thunbergii ♀H4	CDul CSBt CTri CWib EBee ENot EPfP MRav NLon NWea SCoo SLim SMer SRms WDin WGwG WHCG
	- 'Fujino Pink'	WDin
	- 'Mellow Yellow'	see *S. thunbergii* 'Ôgon'
	- 'Mount Fuji' (v)	CAbP CMac CWib EHoe GSki LRHS MGos NPro WBcn WFar
§	- 'Ôgon'	WFar WPen
*	- ***rosea***	WBcn
	- 'Tickled Pink'	CAbP LRHS
	ulmaria	see *Filipendula ulmaria*
	x ***vanhouttei***	CBcs CSBt CTri EBee ENot EPfP MBar MRav MSwo NEgg NLRH NLon SHBN SHFr SPer SPla SRms WDin WFar WTel
	- 'Gold Fountain'	WBcn WFar
	- 'Pink Ice' (v)	CAbP CBcs CDoC CMHG COtt CPMA CSLe CWib EBee EHoe EMil EPfP LAst LRHS MAsh MGos MTis SHBN SPer SPlb SPoG SWvt WDin WFar WHar WTel
	veitchii	MRav WBcn
	venusta 'Magnifica'	see *Filipendula rubra* 'Venusta'

Spiranthes (*Orchidaceae*)

aestivalis	SSpi
cernua	MS&S
- var. ***odorata***	CPom

- - 'Chadd's Ford'	CBcs CBro CDes CFwr EBee EBla EChP ECtt EHrv EVFa EWll GAbr GBri LAst LRHS MCCP MDun NBir NCob NMen NMyG NSti SAga SBla SUsu WCot WFar WPGP WWhi

Spirodela (*Lemnaceae*)

§ ***polyrhiza***	EMFW

Spodiopogon (*Poaceae*)

sibiricus	CAby CBig CKno CWCL EBee EChP ECha EHoe EMan EMon EPPr EPza GFor LBBr LEdu MSte NFor SMad

Sporobolus (*Poaceae*)

airoides	CBig EBee EPPr
cryptandrus	EBee EPPr
heterolepis	CBig EHoe EShb GFor LPhx SMad WPrP
indicus **new**	EPPr
wrightii	EBee WGHP WSPU

Spraguea (*Portulacaceae*)

'Powder Puff'	LRHS
umbellata	WLin
var. ***caudicifera*** **new**	

Sprekelia (*Amaryllidaceae*)

formosissima	CSpe CStu LAma LRHS SPav

Staberoha (*Restionaceae*)

aemula **new**	CBig

Stachys ✿ (*Lamiaceae*)

aethiopica 'Danielle'	see *S. thunbergii* 'Danielle'
§ ***affinis***	CAgr CArn CFir ELau GPoy LEdu MGGn
albens	IFro MGGn NLsd
§ ***albotomentosa***	EBee EMan EShb GBri LPhx MDKP MGGn NBir SAga SSvw WCHb WCot WOut
alpina	CNat EBee MGGn
x ***ambigua***	MGGn NSti
atherocalyx	MGGn
bacanica **new**	MGGn
- MESE	WPGP
balansae	MGGn NSti
betonica	see *S. officinalis*
§ ***byzantina***	More than 30 suppliers
§ - 'Big Ears'	CAby EBee ECha EMan ENot EWTr GMaP MAnH MBri MGGn MWat NDov SBch SGSe SMrm SPoG WBor WCAu WCot WFar WMnd WMoo
§ - 'Cotton Boll'	COIW EBee ECha GCal GMac LRHS MBct MGGn MHar SBch SPer WCot WFar
- 'Countess Helen von Stein'	see *S. byzantina* 'Big Ears'
- gold-leaved	see *S. byzantina* 'Primrose Heron'
- large-leaved	see *S. byzantina* 'Big Ears'
- 'Limelight'	MGGn WCot
- 'Margery Fish' **new**	NJOw
§ - 'Primrose Heron'	COtt EBee ECha ECot EMan EPfP LAst LRHS MGGn MWgw NLar NOrc SMer SPer SPoG SWvt WCAu
- 'Sheila McQueen'	see *S. byzantina* 'Cotton Boll'
- 'Silver Carpet'	More than 30 suppliers
§ - 'Striped Phantom' (v)	EMan MGGn WCAu WCHb WCot WEas
- 'Variegata'	see *S. byzantina* 'Striped Phantom'
candida	EHyt MGGn WPat
chrysantha	EHyt LPhx MGGn SAga
citrina	CMea GCal LRHS MGGn SBla SPoG
coccinea	CBot CPom EBee EChP ECtt EHrv EMan EVFa EWsh GBBs LRHS MHer MTis NBir SDnm SHFr SPav SPet SRkn WCHb WHil WMoo WOut WRos WSSM
corsica	EBee MGGn WPGP
cretica	EMan WWlt XPep
- subsp. ***cretica*** **new**	MGGn
- subsp. ***salviifolia***	MGGn XPep
densiflora	see *S. monieri*
§ ***discolor***	CMea EBee EChP EPPr GBri IFro MLLN NLar SBch WAbe WCot WOut WPer
dregeana	SAga SSvw SUsu
germanica	CPom EMan MGGn NArg NLar
- subsp. ***bithynica***	EBee MGGn
glutinosa	XPep
grandiflora	see *S. macrantha*
heraclea	MGGn XPep
'Hidalgo'	CSpe
iva	LPhx
lanata	see *S. byzantina*
lavandulifolia	EHyt
§ ***macrantha***	More than 30 suppliers
* - 'Alba'	ECha WMoo
- 'Hummelo'	see *S. monieri* 'Hummelo'
* - 'Nivea'	EBee EHrv ELan EMan GCal MMHG WCot WPat
§ - 'Robusta' ♀H4	CDes CStr EBee ELan GKir MGGn NBro NGdn SHel SVal WCAu WCot WRHF WWye
- 'Rosea'	CElw CMHG EBee EGra ELan GMaP LLWP MArl MGGn NLon SHel SPlb WEas WPer WRha WWye
- 'Superba'	CFwr EBee EChP ECtt EGra EPfP EVFa GKir GMaP IBal LAst LRHS MBri MDun MGGn MMHG MRav NEgg NScw SBla SMrm SPer SWvt WBor WCAu WCHb WCot WFar WMoo
- 'Violacea'	CStr EBee GFlt MAvo MGGn NChi WCot WPGP
marrubiifolia	EBee
mexicana misapplied	see *S. thunbergii*
monieri misapplied	see *S. officinalis*
§ ***monieri*** ambig.	CAbP CM&M EBee EChP LRHS NLar WOut WPer
monieri (Gouan) P.W. Ball	GBin MGGn SBch WOut
- 'Hummelo'	see *S. officinalis* 'Hummelo'
* - 'Rosea'	EBee GBin NBre SBla
- 'Saharan Pink'	see *S. officinalis* 'Saharan Pink'
- 'Spitzweg'	SUsu
nivea	see *S. discolor*
obliqua **new**	WOut
§ ***officinalis***	CArn CRWN CSev CStr CWan EBee EUnu GBar GPoy IHMH MChe MHer MSal NEgg NLan NMir NPri SOkh WGHP WGwG WHer WWye
- 'Alba'	CArn CBot EBee MGGn NBro NRya STes WCAu WCHb WFar WHer WOut WRha WTin WWye
- dwarf **new**	MGGn
- dwarf, white **new**	MGGn
- 'Hummelo'	EBee EBrs ENot EPfP EVFa LPhx LSou MDKP MGGn NDov NLar SAga SHop SUsu WCAu WFar WWeb
- mauve-flowered	WTin
- 'Rosea'	CMea MGGn NBro SHop STes SUsu WCAu WCot WFar WGHP WTin

- 'Rosea Superba'	CBgR ECha MDKP MGGn SIng WCAu WCot WFar WMoo
- 'Saharan Pink'	CBgR EBee EPfP EWll LSou MGGn MHer NJOw SSvw WOut
- 'Wisley White'	EBee WCot
olympica	see *S. byzantina*
ossetica **new**	MGGn
palustris	LPBA MGGn NLan NMir WFar WOut
'Pinkie' **new**	LRHS WWeb
plumosa	EBee XPep
rigida **new**	MGGn
saxicola	MDKP MGGn
setifera	EBee MGGn
spicata	see *S. macrantha*
swainsonii	MGGn XPep
sylvatica	CArn MGol NLan NMir SECG WHer
- 'Hoskin's Variegated' (v)	WCHb WWpP
- 'Huskers' (v)	EBee EPPr ITer MCCP MGGn
- 'Shade of Pale'	MGGn
thirkei	EBee MGGn SBch XPep
thunbergii	CDes EShb LLWP LPhx MDKP MGGn MMHG MSte MWrn SMeo WHil WOut WPGP WPrP
- 'Danielle'	EBee ECtt MGGn MHer NBre SPoG SRkn SVil WCot WOVN
tournefortii **new**	MGGn
tuberifera	see *S. affinis*

Stachyurus (*Stachyuraceae*)

chinensis	CBcs CMCN CPMA CPle IArd IDee IMGH LRHS MGos NLar SBrw SPoG
- 'Celina'	EBee MBlu MGos NLar
- 'Joy Forever' (v)	CBcs CEnd CMCN EBee EPfP IDee LTwo MBlu MGos NLar SPoG SSpi SSta SWvt
himalaicus	CBcs IArd IDee NLar
- HWJCM 009	WCru
- HWJK 2035	WCru
leucotrichus	CPMA
'Magpie' (v)	CPMA ENot EPfP LRHS NLar SLon SPer SSpi WCru
praecox ♀H4	More than 30 suppliers
- B&SWJ 8898	WCru
§ - var. ***matsuzakii***	CBcs CFil
- - B&SWJ 2817	WCru
- - 'Scherzo' (v)	WCru
* - 'Rubriflora'	CBcs CPMA ELan EPfP LRHS MAsh NLar SSpi WFar
salicifolius	CFil CMCN CPMA IDee SLon WPGP
sigeyosii B&SWJ 6915	WCru
szechuanensis	CBcs
aff. ***szechuanensis*** BWJ 8153	WCru
yunnanensis	CFil CPMA

Staehelina (*Asteraceae*)

dubia	EMan XPep

Stapelia (*Asclepiadaceae*)

gettliffei **new**	EShb

Staphylea (*Staphyleaceae*)

bolanderi **new**	NLar
bumalda	CBcs CPMA EPfP NLar
colchica	CBcs EBee ELan EPfP EWTr NPal SBrw WDin WSHC
- 'Rosea'	CBcs
holocarpa	CBcs CDul CPMA CPle EPfP MRav SSpi WBVN WFar
N - var. ***rosea***	CPMA ENot EPfP SMad
N - 'Rosea'	CBcs CMCN MBlu NLar SBrw SSpi
pinnata	CBcs CPMA EPfP LEdu NLar SBrw WHCr WNor WPat
trifolia	CAgr CBcs

Statice see *Limonium*

Stauntonia (*Lardizabalaceae*)

hexaphylla	CBcs CBrm CDoC CHEx CPLN CSam CTri EBee EHol EPfP GQui LRHS MAsh MDun SAdn SBra SBrw SPer SPoG SReu SRkn SSpi SSta WBrE WSHC
- B&SWJ 4858	WCru
purpurea	CPLN EBee NLar
- B&SWJ 3690	WCru

Stegnogramma (*Thelypteridaceae*)

pozoi	EFer

Stellaria (*Caryophyllaceae*)

graminea	NBid
holostea	CRWN MBow MChe NMir NPri WShi

Stemmacantha (*Asteraceae*)

carthamoides	MSal NLar
centaureiodes	EBee ECGP EVFa GAbr GBin GCal LPhx MAvo NBid SAga SUsu WHil

Stenanthium (*Melanthiaceae*)

robustum	WPGP

Stenocarpus (*Proteaceae*)

sinuatus	EShb

Stenochlaena (*Blechnaceae*)

palustris	MBri
tenuifolia **new**	WRic

Stenomesson (*Amaryllidaceae*)

aurantiacum **new**	CMon
coccineum **new**	CMon
§ ***miniatum***	CStu WCot
pearcei **new**	CMon
variegatum (v)	CMon

Stenotaphrum (*Poaceae*)

secundatum	XPep
- 'Variegatum' (v) ♀H1	CHal EShb LAst WDyG

Stephanandra (*Rosaceae*)

chinensis **new**	SLon
incisa	CBcs CPLG WHCG
§ - 'Crispa'	CDoC CDul CPle CTri EBee ECrN ELan EMil ENot EPfP GKir LAst LRHS MBar MBlu MRav MWgw MWhi NEgg NFor SHBN SPer SPla SPoG WCFE WDin WFar WHCG WMoo WTel
- 'Dart's Horizon'	SLPl
- 'Prostrata'	see *S. incisa* 'Crispa'
tanakae	CBcs CDoC CPLG CPle CTri ELan EPfP GKir IMGH LAst MBar MBlu MRav NEgg NFor NLon SHBN SLPl SLon SPer SPla WDin WFar WHCG WPat

Stephania (*Menispermaceae*)

japonica B&SWJ 2396	WCru
rotunda	EUJe

Stephanotis (*Asclepiadaceae*)

floribunda 🏆H1 — CBcs EBak GQui LRHS MBri SMur

Sterculia (*Sterculiaceae*)

rupestris — EShb

Sternbergia (*Amaryllidaceae*)

'Autumn Gold' **new** — GKev
candida — CBro EHyt LAma
- JCA 933000 — SSpi
§ **clusiana** — LAma
colchiciflora — EHyt
fischeriana — CBro
greuteriana — EHyt SOkd
lutea — CAvo CBro CFwr CNic CStu EHyt EPot EWes LAma LPhx LRHS MRav NMen NWCA SDix SSpi WEas WLin WTin
- Angustifolia Group — CBro CDes CMea EHyt EMon WCot
- var. **lutea** MS 971 — CMon
- - B&S from Italy **new** — CMon
macrantha — see *S. clusiana*
sicula — CBro CStu EHyt EPot XPep
- MS 956 from Italy **new** — CMon
- var. **graeca** — EHyt
- - MS 802 from Crete **new** — CMon
- 'John Marr' — CDes

Stevia (*Asteraceae*)

rebaudiana — CPLG EOHP EUnu GPoy MSal

Stewartia ✿ (*Theaceae*)

gemmata — MDun NLar SSpi WNor
'Korean Splendor' — see *S. pseudocamellia* Koreana Group
koreana — see *S. pseudocamellia* Koreana Group
malacodendron 🏆H4 — EPfP LRHS SBrw SSpi
monadelpha — CMen EPfP SSpi WNor
ovata — CMen SSpi
N - var. **grandiflora** — CMen GKir LRHS SBrw
pseudocamellia 🏆H4 — More than 30 suppliers
- var. **koreana** — see *S. pseudocamellia* Koreana Group
§ - Koreana Group 🏆H4 — CBcs CEnd CFil CMCN CMen CTho ECrN EPfP LRHS MDun NLar SBrw SSpi WDin WFar WNor WPGP
pteropetiolata — CBcs
- var. **koreana** — LRHS
rostrata — CBcs CMCN GIBF MBlu NLar SSpi WNor
serrata — CMen SSpi
sinensis 🏆H4 — CFil CMen CPMA EPfP MBlu MDun SBrw SSpi SSta WNor
yunnanense **new** — SSpi

Stictocardia (*Convolvulaceae*)

beraviensis **new** — CPLN
campanulata **new** — CPLN

Stigmaphyllon (*Malpighiaceae*)

ciliatum — CPLN ERea

Stilbocarpa (*Araliaceae*)

polaris — SSpi

Stipa (*Poaceae*)

RBS 0227 **new** — MAvo
B&SWJ 2302 from Sikkim — EBee
arundinacea — see *Anemanthele lessoniana*
- 'Autumn Tints' — EHoe EPPr EPza
- 'Golden Hue' — EHoe EVFa SMac
barbata — CBig CBrm CDes CKno CSpe EBee EBrs EHoe EMan EVFa EWes GFor LPhx LRHS MAvo NDov NOGN SApp SMad SPer SUsu WCot WHal WPGP WRos XPep
- 'Silver Feather' — CBig CHrt EPza LIck MAnH MWhi NBPC
boysterica — CFee
brachytricha — see *Calamagrostis brachytricha*
§ **calamagrostis** — More than 30 suppliers
- 'Lemperg' — EPPr
capillata — CKno COIW EBee EBrs EChP EHoe EPPr GBin GFor GKir LRHS MWhi NBea NCGa NChi SMad SWal SYvo WCot WHal WOVN WPGP WPnP WWye XPep
- 'Brautschleier' — CHrt CWib EPza GCal LIck SWal WPtf
* - 'Lace Veil' — CBig LRav
chrysophylla — CFil
- F&W 9321 — WPGP
columbiana — MLLN
comata — EBee IFro NFor
elegantissima — CKno EHoe EVFa
extremiorientalis — CAby CBig CKno ECha EPPr EPza GSki LAst NOGN SLPl SMad WHal WWpP
* **gerardi** **new** — SApp
gigantea 🏆H4 — More than 30 suppliers
- 'Gold Fontaene' — CBig CDes CFir CKno EPPr EWes LPhx MMoz MNrw NDov SBch SMad WPGP
- 'Pixie' **new** — EWsh SApp
grandis — CBig CKno ECha EPPr GBin GFor WHal WMoo WPer
joannis — GCal
krylovii **new** — EWsh
lasiagrostis — see *S. calamagrostis*
lessingiana — CFil CHrt CM&M CPLG CSam EBee EHul GBin ITim WPGP WPnP WWpP
offneri — CKno CStr EBee EPPr EWes LPhx SBla
pennata — CBcs CBig CKno EHoe EMan GBin GCal GFor GKir LRav NCGa NOak SMer
pulcherrima — CKno EMan EVFa GCal GFor XPep
- 'Windfeder' — CFir SLPl SMad SMrm
ramosissima — CKno
robusta — EBee EPPr XPep
spartea — CBrm
splendens misapplied — see *S. calamagrostis*
§ **splendens** Trin. — CBig EHoe EMag EMan EPPr LEdu WFoF
stenophylla — see *S. tirsa*
stipoides — GGar
tenacissima — CKno ECha EHoe EHul EUJe GSki NCob WDin WMoo XPep
tenuifolia misapplied — see *S. tenuissima*
tenuifolia Steud. — CHar CMea CMil EHul EPfP EUJe GKir LRHS MAnH MBri MMil MRav NBea NBir NBro NSti NVic SIng SPer WCAu WHal WMoo XPep
§ **tenuissima** — More than 30 suppliers
- 'Pony Tails' — CBig COIW ECtt EDAr EPfP IBal LAst LRav MBNS MBar MFOX MLan MWgw NCGa NJOw NLar SMar SWvt WMnd

§ ***tirsa***	EBrs GBin
turkestanica	CAby CStr EBee EVFa GBin MMoz NDov SUsu
ucrainica	CBig GAbr GFor
verticillata	CAby CKno CRez

Stoebe (*Asteraceae*)

alopecuroides	CSLe

Stokesia (*Asteraceae*)

cyanea	see *S. laevis*
§ ***laevis***	CFwr CHea EBee ECGP ECha EPfP EWTr GKir LAst LEdu LRHS NBro NFor NLar NLon NWCA SHGN SMrm SPet WBrE WCAu WFar WPer WSan WWeb
- 'Alba'	CHea CM&M COIW EBee ECha EHrv ELan EMan EPfP ERou GKir GMac LAst LPhx LRHS MRav SChu SPer SSpi STes
- 'Blue Star'	CBcs CElw CMHG COIW CSam EBee EChP EGra ELan EMar EPfP GKir GMac LPhx LRHS MAvo MBri MNFA MWgw NDov NOak SAga SChu SPer SPet SPoG SWvt WMnd WSan WWeb
- 'Klaus Jelitto' **new**	CFwr SHBN
- 'Mary Gregory'	More than 30 suppliers
- mixed	CPou MLan
- 'Omega Skyrocket'	CBre CBrm CFai CFwr CMHG COIW CPou EBee EChP EMan EMar ERou LRHS MLLN NBPC NOak SMrm SOkh SPoG SSpi SUsu WBor WCAu WCot WFar
- 'Peach Melba' **new**	SPoG
- 'Purple Parasols'	CElw CFai CM&M COIW COtt EBee EChP EMar ERou EWll MBow MSph NCGa NEgg NOak NSti SHar SOkh SPoG STes SUsu SWvt WAul WBVN WBor WCot WCra WFar WWeb WWhi
- 'Silver Moon'	CFai CMHG EBee EChP EMan EMar EMil LAst LBuc NBir NCot NEgg NPri SAga SHar SOkh SPoG SVil WCot WFar WTMC
- 'Träumerei'	EBee EChP EMan EMar LAst LRHS SPet WCAu WMnd WMoo

Stranvaesia see *Photinia*

x *Stranvinia* see *Photinia*

Stratiotes (*Hydrocharitaceae*)

aloides	CDWL CWat EHon EMFW EMag LNCo LPBA NArg WPop WWpP

strawberry see *Fragaria*

Strelitzia (*Strelitziaceae*)

alba	EAmu
juncea **new**	XBlo
nicolai	CAbb CHEx CRoM EAmu EShb EUJe ITer LExo SBig WMul XBlo
reginae 🏆H1	CAbb CBcs CBrP CTbh ELan ERea EShb ESlt EUJe GQui LExo LRHS MJnS MOak NPal SAPC SArc SBig SPlb SRms WMul XBlo
- var. ***citrina*** **new**	ERea
- 'Humilis'	XBlo
- 'Kirstenbosch Gold'	XBlo

Streptocarpella see *Streptocarpus*

Streptocarpus ✿ (*Gesneriaceae*)

'Albatross' 🏆H1	SBrm SDnm SPav WDib
'Alice' **new**	WDib
'Amanda' Dibley 🏆H1	WDib
'Anne'	CSpe SBrm WDib
'Athena'	WDib
baudertii	WDib
'Beryl'	WDib
'Bethan' 🏆H1	SBrm WDib
'Beverley Ruth'	MOak
I 'Black Gardenia'	WDib
'Black Panther'	SBrm WDib
'Blue Bird'	MOak
'Blue Gem'	WDib
'Blue Heaven'	SBrm WDib
'Blue Ice'	MOak
'Blue Moon'	CHal WDib
'Blue Nymph'	WDib
'Blue Pencil'	SBrm
§ 'Blue Upstart'	MOak
'Blushing Bride' (d)	SDnm SPav WDib
'Blushing Pink'	MOak SBrm
'Border Line'	MOak
* 'Boysenberry Delight'	WDib
'Branwen'	SBrm SDnm SPav WDib
'Brimstone'	MOak SBrm
'Bristol's Black Bird'	SBrm WDib
'Bristol's Ice Castle'	WDib
'Bristol's Very Best'	WDib
'Buttons'	SBrm
caeruleus	WDib
candidus	WDib
'Carol'	WDib
'Carolyn Ann'	MOak
'Carys' 🏆H1	WDib
'Catrin' 🏆H1	SBrm WDib
caulescens	CHal WDib
* - 'Compactus'	CHal
- var. ***pallescens***	WDib
'Charlotte'	MOak WDib
'Chorus Line' 🏆H1	SDnm SPav WDib
'Clare' **new**	WDib
'Clouds'	CSpe
'Concord Blue'	WDib
'Constant Nymph'	SBrm WDib
'Copper Knob'	MOak
'Crystal Beauty'PBR	WDib
'Crystal Blush'PBR	WDib
'Crystal Charm' **new**	WDib
'Crystal Dawn' **new**	WDib
'Crystal Ice'PBR 🏆H1	WDib
'Crystal Snow'	WDib
'Crystal Wonder' **new**	WDib
cyaneus	WDib
- subsp. ***polackii***	WDib
'Cynthia' 🏆H1	SBrm WDib
'Dainty Lady' **new**	MOak
I 'Daphne' 🏆H1	WDib
'Dark Eyes Mary'	SBrm
'Dark Secret'	SBrm
'Demeter'	SBrm
'Diana'	SBrm WDib
dunnii	SGar WDib
'Elegance'	MOak SBrm
'Ella'	MOak SBrm
'Elsi'	SBrm SDnm SPav WDib
'Emily'	WDib
'Emma'	SBrm WDib
'Falling Stars' 🏆H1	CSpe ERea SBrm WDib
'Festival Wales'	SBrm WDib

'Fiona'	SBrm WDib
floribundus	WDib
'Frances' **new**	SBrm
gardenii	WDib
'Gillian'	MOak
glandulosissimus ♀H1	CHal WDib
'Gloria' ♀H1	CSpe SBrm WDib
'Good Hope'	ERea
'Gower Daybreak'	SBrm
'Gower Garnet'	MOak
'Gower Midnight'	MOak SBrm
'Grape Slush'	WDib
'Gwen'	SBrm WDib
'Hannah Ellis'	MOak SBrm
'Happy Snappy' ♀H1	SBrm SDnm SPav WDib
'Heidi' ♀H1	SBrm SDnm SPav WDib
'Helen' ♀H1	SBrm WDib
'Huge White'	CSpe
'Ida'	MOak SBrm
'Inky Fingers'	MOak SBrm
'Izzy'	MOak SBrm
'Jane Elizabeth'	MOak SBrm
'Jennifer' ♀H1	SBrm SDnm SPav WDib
'Joanna'	SBrm WDib
johannis	WDib
'Josie' **new**	SBrm
'Judith'	MOak
'Julie'	WDib
'Karen'	SBrm SDnm SPav WDib
kentaniensis	WDib
'Kerry's Gold'	MOak
'Kim' ♀H1	CSpe SBrm SDnm SPav WDib
kirkii	WDib
'Kisie'	MOak SBrm
'Largesse'	SBrm
'Laura' ♀H1	SBrm WDib
'Lemon Ice' **new**	SBrm
'Lisa' ♀H1	SBrm
'Little Gem'	CSpe SBrm
'Louise'	SBrm WDib
'Lynette'	SBrm
'Lynne'	SBrm WDib
'Maassen's White' ♀H1	ERea SBrm WDib
'Magpie'	MOak
'Mandy'	SDnm SPav WDib
'Margaret' Gavin Brown	SBrm WDib
'Marie'	WDib
'Mary'	MOak SBrm
'Megan'	SBrm WDib
'Melanie' ♀H1	SBrm WDib
meyeri	WDib
'Midnight Flame'	ERea SBrm WDib
'Mini Nymph'	WDib
'Modbury Lady'	MOak
modestus	WDib
'Molly' **new**	SBrm
'Moonlight'	SBrm WDib
'Muse'	MOak SBrm
'Neptune'	SBrm WDib
'Nerys' **new**	WDib
'Nia'	WDib
'Nicola'	SBrm WDib
'Nita'	MOak
'Olga'	SBrm WDib
'Olwen'	WDib
'Party Doll'	SBrm WDib
'Passion Pink'	SBrm WDib
'Patricia'	MOak SBrm
'Paula' ♀H1	SBrm WDib
pentherianus	WDib
'Pink Fondant'	CSpe
'Pink Souffle'	SBrm SDnm SPav WDib
'Plum Crazy'	SBrm
polyanthus subsp. ***dracomontanus***	WDib
primulifolius	WDib
- subsp. ***formosus***	WDib
prolixus	WDib
'Purple Haze'	MOak
* 'Purple Passion'	SBrm
'Raspberry Dream'	MOak
rexii	WDib
'Rhiannon'	SBrm SDnm SPav WDib
'Rose Gower'	MOak
'Rosebud'	SBrm WDib
'Rosemary' (d)	SPav WDib
'Ruby' ♀H1	SBrm WDib
'Ruby Anniversary'	MOak
'Ruffled Lilac'	CSpe SBrm
'Ruffles' **new**	SBrm
'Sally'	SBrm WDib
'Samantha'	MOak
'Sandra'	SBrm SDnm SPav WDib
'Sarah'	SBrm SPav WDib
saxorum ♀H1	CHal EMan EOHP EShb EWin LIck LSou MBri MOak SRms WDib WFar
- compact	EOHP WDib
'Sian'	SBrm SDnm SPav WDib
silvaticus	WDib
'Snow White' ♀H1	CSpe SDnm SPav WDib
'Something Special'	SBrm SDnm WDib
'Sophie'	WDib
'Southshore'	WDib
'Spider'	MOak
'Stacey'	MOak SBrm
'Stella' ♀H1	SBrm WDib
'Stephanie'	WDib
stomandrus	WDib
'Strawberry Fondant'	MOak SBrm
'Sugar Almond'	CSpe SBrm
'Susan' ♀H1	WDib
'Swaybelle'	SBrm
'Tanga' **new**	SBrm
'Terracotta'	MOak SBrm
'Texas Hot Chili'	SBrm WDib
'Texas Sunrise'	MOak
thompsonii **new**	WDib
'Tina' ♀H1	SBrm SDnm SPav WDib
'Tracey'	SBrm WDib
'Turbulent Tide'	SBrm
'Upstart'	see 'Blue Upstart'
variabilis	WDib
'Velvet Underground'	SBrm
'Vera'	SBrm
'Violet Lace'	CSpe SBrm
wendlandii	WDib
'Wendy'	SBrm SPav WDib
'White Wings'	MOak SBrm
'Wiesmoor Red'	WDib
'Winifred'	SBrm WDib

Streptolirion (*Commelinaceae*)

volubile B&SWJ 8569	WCru

Streptopus (*Convallariaceae*)

amplexifolius	GBuc GIBF WCru
- M&PS 98/022	GCrs NLar
roseus	GCrs GFlt LAma SOkd

Streptosolen (*Solanaceae*)

jamesonii ♀H1	CHal CHll CPle CSev CTbh EBak ELan ERea EShb MOak
- 'Fire Gold'	ERea

Strobilanthes (*Acanthaceae*)

CC 4071	CPLG

anisophylla	WCot
atropurpurea misapplied	see *S. attenuata*
atropurpurea Nees	see *S. wallichii*
attenuata	More than 30 suppliers
- subsp. ***nepalensis***	CLAP EMar WOut WPrP WWye
- 'Out of the Ocean'	WOut
dyeriana (v) ♀H1	CHal EBak EMan EShb WCot WRha
flexicaulis	WCot WPen
- B&SWJ 354	WCru
nutans	CDes CLAP CPom CPou CStr WCot WPGP WPrP
rankanensis	CDes CLAP EBee EDAr
- B&SWJ 1771	CPom WCru
violacea	CPrp CStu ERea WPer
wallichii	CDes CLAP EBee EPPr LRHS NMRc SMHy WCAu WCot WCru WFar WPGP WPrP

Stromanthe (*Marantaceae*)

amabilis	see *Ctenanthe amabilis*
sanguinea	CHal MBri
- 'Triostar'PBR (v) **new**	XBlo
'Stripestar'	MBri

Strongylodon (*Papilionaceae*)

macrobotrys	CPLN

Strophanthus (*Apocynaceae*)

caudatus **new**	CPLN
gratus **new**	CPLN
speciosus	CPLN CSec EShb

Stuartia see *Stewartia*

Stylidium (*Stylidiaceae*)

affine	SPlb
graminifolium	GGar
soboliferum	ECou

Stylophorum (*Papaveraceae*)

diphyllum	CFwr CPom CPou ECha EMar GBri GEdr GKir LAma MRav MSal NMen SBch WAul WCru WFar WPnP
lasiocarpum	CPBP CPLG CPom EMan EMar MGol NDlv SBri SGar WCot WCru WPrP WRos

Styphelia (*Epacridaceae*)

colensoi	see *Leucopogon colensoi*

Styrax (*Styracaceae*)

americanus	CBcs
confusus	CMCN
faberi **new**	CFil
formosanus	EBee
- var. ***formosanus***	CFil WPGP
- - B&SWJ 3803	WCru
hemsleyanus ♀H4	CAbP CBcs CEnd CFil CTho EPfP IDee IMGH LRHS MBlu MDun SPer SSpi WBor WFar WNor WPGP
japonicus ♀H4	More than 30 suppliers
- B&SWJ 4405	WCru
§ - Benibana Group ♀H4	CFil SReu SSta
- - 'Pink Chimes'	CAbP CBcs CMCN CPLG CPMA ELan EPfP IDee LRHS MBlu MBri MDun NLar SCoo SPer SSpi SSta
- 'Carillon'	CFil LRHS
- 'Fargesii'	CDoC CFil CTho EPfP GKir IMGH LRHS MAsh MBri MDun SCoo SPoG SSpi WFar
- 'Roseus'	see *S. japonicus* Benibana Group
- 'Sohuksan'	CFil WPGP
obassia ♀H4	CArn CBcs CMCN CPne CTho EPfP IMGH LRHS MBlu MDun MWya NLar SSpi WNor
- B&SWJ 6023	WCru
odoratissimus	CFil WPGP
serrulatus	CFil

Suaeda (*Chenopodiaceae*)

vera	XPep

Succisa (*Dipsacaceae*)

§ ***pratensis***	CArn EBee EMag MAnH MBow MChe MHer NLan NLar NMen NWCA SBch SMHy SSpi WHer WPrP
- ***alba***	EBee MDKP
- 'Buttermilk'	SSpi
- 'Corinne Tremaine' (v)	WHer
- dwarf	NGby NRya
- 'Forest Pearls'	SSpi
- 'Forest Pink'	SSpi
- 'Peddar's Pink'	EBee EMan EVFa EWes MAnH

sunberry see *Rubus* 'Sunberry'

Sutera (*Scrophulariaceae*)

African Sunset = 'Rarosil'	CSpe
'Blizzard'PBR	LAst LSou WGor WWol
Candy Floss = 'Yasflos'	EShb LAst LSou
cordata Blue Showers = 'Bacoble'PBR	LAst
- 'Bridal Showers'	NPri
- 'Giant Cloud' **new**	LAst
- Lavender Showers = 'Sunlav'PBR	NPri
- pale pink	LAst
- 'Pink Domino'	ECtt EWin LAst WGor
§ - 'Snowflake'	CTbh ECtt LAst MLan MOak NBlu SCoo SPet SPoG
- 'Typhoon White P.'	LAst
'Giant Cloud' **new**	EWin
jurassica	see *Jamesbrittenia jurassica*
neglecta	WPGP
Olympic Gold = 'Prosutv' (v)	ECtt LAst SCoo SPoG
Sea Mist = 'Yagemil'PBR	NPri
Suteranova Pink = 'Mogoto'PBR **new**	LAst

Sutherlandia (*Papilionaceae*)

frutescens	CArn GGar SPlb WCot XPep
* - var. ***alba***	WCot
- 'Prostrata'	EMan
montana	WPic

Swainsona (*Papilionaceae*)

galegifolia	CHll
- 'Albiflora'	CSpe LPhx SBla

sweet cicely see *Myrrhis odorata*

Swertia (*Gentianaceae*)

bimaculata	WGwG

Syagrus (*Arecaceae*)

§ ***romanzoffiana***	CBrP CRoM EAmu LPJP

x *Sycoparrotia* (*Hamamelidaceae*)

semidecidua	CBcs CFil CPMA GKir LRHS MBlu NLar SBrw WPGP

Sycopsis (*Hamamelidaceae*)

heterophylla **new**	EBee

sinensis	CMCN EPfP LRHS MBlu NLar SBrw SDnm SMur SSpi WBcn WDin WFar WSHC

Symphoricarpos (*Caprifoliaceae*)

albus	CDul ECrN MSwo NWea SPoG WDin
- 'Constance Spry'	SRms
§ - var. ***laevigatus***	EPfP LBuc MBar
§ - 'Taff's White' (v)	WMoo
- 'Variegatus'	see *S. albus* 'Taff's White'
x ***chenaultii*** 'Hancock'	CSBt ECrN ELan ENot EPfP MBar MRav MSwo NLon NPro SHBN SPer WDin WFar
x ***doorenbosii*** 'Magic Berry'	EBee GKir LRHS MBar MRav NWea
- 'Mother of Pearl'	EBee ELan ENot EPfP GKir LRHS MBar MGos MRav NBlu NWea SPoG
- 'White Hedge'	CSBt ELan ENot LBuc LRHS MRav NWea SPer SPlb SPoG WTel
orbiculatus	IMGH LRHS SLon
- 'Albovariegatus'	see *S. orbiculatus* 'Taff's Silver Edge'
- 'Argenteovariegatus'	see *S. orbiculatus* 'Taff's Silver Edge'
- 'Bowles' Golden Variegated'	see *S. orbiculatus* 'Foliis Variegatis'
§ - 'Foliis Variegatis' (v)	CTri ECrN EGra EHoe ELan EPfP LRHS MGos MRav NPro NSti SHBN SPer WDin WEas WFar WHCG WSHC
§ - 'Taff's Silver Edge' (v)	EBee EHoe LRHS MBar NSti
- 'Variegatus'	see *S. orbiculatus* 'Foliis Variegatis'
rivularis	see *S. albus* var. *laevigatus*

Symphyandra see *Campanula*

asiatica	see *Hanabusaya asiatica*

Symphyotrichum see *Aster*

Symphytum (*Boraginaceae*)

asperum	CPom ECha ELan EMon GAbr MSal NLar WCHb WMoo WTMC
* ***azureum***	MBri MSte NLar WCAu WCHb WFar WMnd WTMC
'Belsay'	CSam GBuc GFlt
'Belsay Gold'	SDix
caucasicum ♀H4	CElw CMHG ECha ELau GBar GFlt GPoy IFro IHMH LEdu LRHS MAnH MBri MHar MWat NSti SBch SIde SSvw WCHb WHer WMoo WRha WWpP WWye
- 'Eminence'	CMdw EGoo WCHb
- 'Norwich Sky'	CKno EBee EChP MMil NMir WCHb
cordatum	EMon
'Denford Variegated' (v)	CBgR ITer MInt
§ 'Goldsmith' (v)	More than 30 suppliers
grandiflorum	CTri CWan GKev GPoy WGwG
* - 'Sky-blue-pink'	EBee NCot
'Hidcote Blue'	CBre CPrp CTri EBee EChP ECha ECtt EPfP EPla GBar ILis LRHS MBri MSte MWgw NArg NBro NEgg NGHP NMRc SIng SLPl SPer SPoG WCAu WCru WMnd WMoo WTMC
§ 'Hidcote Pink'	CBct CPrp EBee EChP ECha ENot EPla EPza EWsh LRHS MBow MSte MWgw NBir NEgg SLPl SPoG WCAu WFar WMnd WMoo WPnP WTMC
'Hidcote Variegated' (v)	WCHb
ibericum	CAgr CArn CMHG CSam EBee ECha EHrv ELau EPfP EPla GBar GMaP GPoy IHMH LGro LRHS MTis MWgw NBlu NSti SGar SIng SRms WBor WCAu WCHb WMoo WTMC WWpP WWye
- 'All Gold'	EBee ECha ECtt ELau EWsh GSki WCAu WMoo WTMC
- 'Blaueglocken'	CSev EChP ECha WMoo WPrP WSan
- dwarf	NPri WMoo
- 'Gold in Spring'	EBee EGoo NLar WCHb WFar
- 'Jubilee'	see *S.* 'Goldsmith'
- 'Lilacinum'	EBee WHer
- 'Pink Robins'	WCHb
- 'Variegatum'	see *S.* 'Goldsmith'
- 'Wisley Blue'	EBee EPfP EWTr IHMH NLar WBan WFar WMnd WMoo
'Lambrook Sunrise'	CFis CLAP CPrp EBee LAst LRHS MMil NBro NSti SChu SPla WCot WMoo WTMC WWpP
'Langthorns Pink'	CPom ELan EMar GBar GBri GBuc WCHb
'Mereworth'	see *S.* x *uplandicum* 'Mereworth'
officinale	CAgr CArn COld CSev CWan GBar GPoy MChe MHer MNrw MSal NGHP NMir NPer NSti SIde SRms WBrk WHer WWye
- 'Bohemicum' **new**	SIng
- 'Boraston White'	MHer WCHb
- var. ***ochroleucum***	WHer WTMC
orientale	CAgr CPom EMon GCal STes WCHb
peregrinum	see *S.* x *uplandicum*
'Roseum'	see *S.* 'Hidcote Pink'
'Rubrum'	CDes CPrp EBee ECot EHrv ELan ELau EPPr EPfP EWes GSki LAst LRHS MHer MSte NEgg NGHP NOrc SPer WCAu WCot WFar WGwG WPGP WSan WTMC WWpP
tuberosum	CArn CBre CElw COld CPom CSam ELau EOHP EPPr GPoy IHMH MBow MDun MHer MSte NSti SMac WBor WCHb WCot WFar WHer WRha WTMC WWye
§ x ***uplandicum***	CSev CTri ELan ELau EMar GBar GPoy GWCH IHMH MHer MSal SIde WCHb WJek WWye
- 'Axminster Gold' (v)	CBct CLAP CMea EBee EMan IBlr ITer LPhx NBid SAga SSpi WPGP
- 'Axminster' (v) **new**	NPar
- 'Bocking 14'	CAgr CBod CHby CPrp GAbr GBar IHMH SIde
- 'Droitwich' (v)	WCot
§ - 'Mereworth' (v)	CBct SMad SUsu WCHb
- 'Moorland Heather'	MAvo WMoo
- 'Variegatum' (v) ♀H4	CBot CLAP EBee ECtt EMar EPfP EWTr EWes GCal GKir GMaP GPoy ITer MTho MWgw NBir NGHP NGdn NSti SDix WCAu WCHb WCot WFar WMoo WTMC

Symplocarpus (*Araceae*)

foetidus	EBee GIBF ITer SSpi WCot

Symplocos (*Symplocaceae*)

paniculata	CBcs CDul NLar WWes
pyrifolia	CFil

Syncarpha (*Asteraceae*)

eximia	SPlb

Syneilesis (*Asteraceae*)

aconitifolia CFwr CLAP GEdr
- B&SWJ 879 WCru
palmata CLAP GEdr WCot
- B&SWJ 1003 WCru
subglabrata CLAP
- B&SWJ 298 WCru

Syngonium (*Araceae*)

'Maya Red' MBri
podophyllum ♀H1 XBlo
- 'Emerald Gem' CHal
- 'Silver Knight' MBri
- 'Variegatum' (v) MBri
'White Butterfly' CHal MBri

Synnotia see *Sparaxis*

Synthyris (*Scrophulariaceae*)

missurica CDes CLAP EBrs ETow GBuc SSpi WLin
- var. **stellata** CLAP EBee EBrs EHrv GGar SBla SSpi WFar WPGP
pinnatifida GBuc NWCA
reniformis CLAP GBuc IBlr

Syringa ✿ (*Oleaceae*)

afghanica misapplied see *S. protolaciniata*
amurensis see *S. reticulata* subsp. *amurensis*
x **chinensis** CTho EWTr WDin WFar
- 'Alba' **new** SLon
- 'Saugeana' IDee NLar SLPl SPer
x **diversifolia** 'William H. Judd' WBcn
emodi WHCG
- 'Aurea' IArd NLar
- 'Aureovariegata' (v) CBcs CEnd EPfP LRHS MAsh MDun NEgg SSpi WBcn WDin
x **henryi** 'Alba' WBcn
x **hyacinthiflora** 'Clarke's Giant' IArd IDee
- 'Esther Staley' ♀H4 EBee ENot EPfP MRav SBLw
'Josee' EBee SPoG SWvt WFar WPat WWeb
x **josiflexa** **new** CPLG
- 'Anna Amhoff' **new** NLar
- 'Bellicent' ♀H4 CDul CEnd CLnd CTho EBee ELan ENot EPfP GKir MBar MRav NEgg NPri NSti SHBN SMur SPer SPlb SPoG SRms SSpi WDin WHCG WPat WPen WTel
- 'James MacFarlane' NLar
- 'Lynette' EPla NPro WBcn
§ - 'Royalty' LBuc NBlu
josikaea CSBt CTho EBee GIBF LBuc MBar NLar SPer WHCG
komarovii GIBF NLar
- L 490 GGGa
§ - subsp. **reflexa** CDul CTho EPfP MBar MGos SSpi WDin WFar
§ x **laciniata** CBot CPMA EBee EHol EHyt EPfP GKir LRHS MBri MRav NLar SCoo SMur SPer SSpi WGor WHCG WKif WPGP
meyeri 'Palibin' ♀H4 More than 30 suppliers
microphylla see *S. pubescens* subsp. *microphylla*
- 'Superba' see *S. pubescens* subsp. *microphylla* 'Superba'
'Minuet' MGos NBlu
'Miss Canada' MBri
palibiniana see *S. meyeri* 'Palibin'
patula misapplied see *S. meyeri* 'Palibin'
patula (Palibin) Nakai see *S. pubescens* subsp. *patula*
pekinensis see *S. reticulata* subsp. *pekinensis*
x **persica** ♀H4 CPLG CPMA CSam CTri EPfP EWTr GKir MGos NLar SLon SPoG WTel XPep
- 'Alba' ♀H4 CBot CMil CPMA GQui SMad WBcn WFar WHCG WPat
- var. **laciniata** see *S.* x *laciniata*
pinnatifolia IArd NLar WHCG WPat
x **prestoniae** 'Agnes Smith' LRHS MGos NLar WBcn
- 'Coral' WFar
- 'Desdemona' SSpi SSta
- 'Elinor' ♀H4 CMHG CPle EBee ENot EPfP MRav NSti SPer
- 'Hiawatha' MGos WBcn
- 'Isabella' MGos SCoo
- 'Kim' CTho NLar WRHF WWeb
- 'Miss USA' **new** EBee
- 'Nocturne' LRHS MGos WFar
- 'Redwine' LRHS MGos NBlu
- 'Royalty' see *S.* x *josiflexa* 'Royalty'
§ **protolaciniata** CPle EPla IDee WAbe WFar
- 'Kabul' EPfP NLar
§ **pubescens** subsp. **microphylla** CBrm EWTr SRkn
§ - - 'Superba' ♀H4 More than 30 suppliers
§ - subsp. **patula** CMac EGra EPfP GIBF LAst MRav NEgg NWea SLon SPla SSta WFar
§ - - 'Miss Kim' ♀H4 CDoC CSBt CWSG EBee ENot GKir IArd LRHS LSRN MBri MGos MRav MSwo NBlu NEgg NLon SCoo SHBN SLim SPoG SSta WDin WFar WHCG WPat
'Red Pixie' LRHS MBri SCoo WBcn
reflexa see *S. komarovii* subsp. *reflexa*
§ **reticulata** subsp. **amurensis** CPle GIBF
- 'City of Toronto' **new** EBee
- 'Ivory Silk' CTho CWSG EPfP MBri NLar
- var. **mandschurica** see *S. reticulata* subsp. *amurensis*
§ - subsp. **pekinensis** CMCN CPle CTho
- - 'Pendula' IArd IDee
x **swegiflexa** CDul CPLG NLar SPoG
sweginzowii CTho EWTr GIBF LBuc NLar SPer WFar
- 'Lark Song' **new** NLar
tomentella CTho LBuc NWea SRms
velutina see *S. pubescens* subsp. *patula*
villosa MWhi SPlb WBVN WDin
vulgaris CLnd GIBF LBuc MBar NWea WBVN WBrE XPep
- var. **alba** MBar
- 'Albert F. Holden' WBcn
§ - 'Andenken an Ludwig Späth' ♀H4 CBot CDoC CLnd CMac CSBt CTho CTri EBee ECrN ELan ENot EPfP GKir IArd LRHS MAsh MBar MBri MGos MRav MSwo NWea SBLw SHBN SLim SLon SPer WBVN WFar WGwG
- 'Aurea' CNat EPla MRav NPro WBcn WFar
- Beauty of Moscow see *S. vulgaris* 'Krasavitsa Moskvy'
- 'Belle de Nancy' (d) EBee ELan GKir MRav SBLw SHBN SLim WDin
- 'Calvin Coolidge' **new** WBcn
- 'Charles Joly' (d) ♀H4 More than 30 suppliers
- 'Congo' CRez ENot GKir LSRN MRav NMoo SPer
- 'Edward J. Gardner' (d) ECrN LRHS SCoo SPer
- 'Firmament' ♀H4 CTho ELan ENot EPfP GKir LSRN MRav NEgg NLar SCoo SHBN SPer

- 'G. J. Baardse'	SBLw
- 'Général Pershing'	SBLw
- 'Katherine Havemeyer' (d) ♀H4	More than 30 suppliers
§ - 'Krasavitsa Moskvy'	GKir LRHS MBri
- 'La Tour d'Auvergne'	SBLw
- 'Madame Antoine Buchner' (d)	ECrN ENot GKir MRav SPer
- 'Madame Florent Stepman'	CMac
- 'Madame Lemoine' (d) ♀H4	More than 30 suppliers
- 'Masséna'	MRav
- 'Maud Notcutt'	ECrN ENot GBin SPer
- 'Michel Buchner' (d)	CBcs EBee ELan GKir MAsh MBar MRav NBlu SBLw SCoo SLim SPer
- 'Miss Ellen Willmott' (d)	MRav SBLw
- 'Mont Blanc'	SBLw
- 'Mrs Edward Harding' (d) ♀H4	EBee ECrN ENot EPfP GKir LBuc MGos NPri NWea SCoo
- 'Olivier de Serres'	SBLw
- 'Président Grévy' (d)	CDoC CLnd CMac NEgg SBLw SPer
- 'President Lincoln'	SBLw
- 'Primrose'	CBcs CDoC CMac CSBt CTho EBee ECrN ELan ENot EPfP GBin GKir IArd LAst LRHS MBri MDun MGos MRav NEgg SCoo SPer SPoG SSta WBVN WDin WFar
- 'Sensation'	CDoC CPle CSBt CWSG EBee ECrN ENot EPfP GBin GKir IArd IMGH LAst LBuc LRHS LSRN MAsh MBri MDun MRav MSwo NEgg SCoo SHBN SLim SPer SPoG SSta
- 'Souvenir d'Alice Harding' (d)	GKir LRHS
- 'Souvenir de Louis Spaeth'	see *S. vulgaris* 'Andenken an Ludwig Späth'
- 'Sweetheart'	GKir MBri
- variegated (v)	SLim SPoG
- variegated double (d/v)	EVFa WBcn
- 'Vestale' ♀H4	ENot MRav SCoo
- 'Znamya Lenina' **new**	MBri
wolfii	CArn GIBF NLon WBVN
yunnanensis	CPLG CTho GIBF LTwo WDin

Syringodea (*Iridaceae*)

luteonigra	CStu

Syzygium (*Myrtaceae*)

australe	EShb
jambos **new**	EShb

T

Tabernaemontana (*Apocynaceae*)

coronaria	see *T. divaricata*
§ ***divaricata***	ESlt

Tacca (*Taccaceae*)

chantrieri	EAmu
integrifolia	CKob EAmu

Tacitus see *Graptopetalum*

Tagetes (*Asteraceae*)

lemmonii	SHDw XPep
lucida	CArn EOHP MSal NTHB WJek
tenuifolia	CArn

Talbotia (*Velloziaceae*)

elegans	CSpe SOkd WCot WFar

Talinum (*Portulacaceae*)

caffrum **new**	LToo
calycinum	WDyG
okanoganense	CGra
'Zoe'	CGra

tamarillo see *Cyphomandra betacea*

tamarind see *Tamarindus indica*

Tamarindus (*Caesalpiniaceae*)

indica (F)	SPlb XBlo

Tamarix (*Tamaricaceae*)

gallica	CSBt EBee ENot NWea SAPC SArc WSHC XPep
§ ***parviflora***	EMil LRHS MGos
pentandra	see *T. ramosissima*
§ ***ramosissima***	CTri ECrN ELan EPfP MBar MBrN SEND SMrm SRms SSta WDin WSHC
- 'Pink Cascade'	CBcs CSBt EBee ECrN EMil ENot EPfP GKir LRHS MBri MGos MRav NBlu SPer SPoG SWvt WDin XPep
- 'Rosea' **new**	SLon
§ - 'Rubra' ♀H4	CChe CDoC EBee EMil EPfP LRHS MBlu MGos SLon WDin
- 'Summer Glow'	see *T. ramosissima* 'Rubra'
tetrandra ♀H4	More than 30 suppliers
- var. ***purpurea***	see *T. parviflora*

Tamus (*Dioscoreaceae*)

communis	CArn MSal

Tanacetum ✿ (*Asteraceae*)

CC&McK 460	GTou
§ ***argenteum***	MRav MTho SIde
- subsp. ***canum***	EWes LRHS
armenum **new**	WLin
§ ***balsamita***	CAgr CArn CCge COld CPrp EBee ELan ELau EOHP GPoy MBri MHer MSal NTHB SHGN WGHP WJek WLHH WPer WSel WTin WWye XPep
§ - subsp. ***balsamita***	CBod CWan GPoy MSal SIde
§ - subsp. ***balsamitoides***	CBod CHby CPrp ELau GBar GWCH MChe MHer NPri WJek WLHH WWye
- var. ***tanacetoides***	see *T. balsamita* subsp. *balsamita*
- ***tomentosum***	see *T. balsamita* subsp. *balsamitoides*
capitatum	see *Sphaeromeria capitata*
§ ***cinerariifolium***	CArn CBod CPrp CWan EChP EOHP GBar GPoy WPer XPep
§ ***coccineum***	EWTr GPoy MSal NBPC SGar SRms WFar WSSM
- 'Aphrodite' (d)	CPrp EBee ECtt LRHS NEgg SBch WCAu
- 'Beauty of Stapleford'	CPrp EBee LRHS NEgg WCAu
- 'Bees' Pink Delight'	CPrp EBee LRHS MWgw NEgg
- 'Brenda'	CPrp EBee EHan EPfP LRHS NEgg NLRH SBch SPoG
- 'Duro'	CFir EChP GBuc WHrl
- 'Eileen May Robinson' ♀H4	CBcs CPrp EBee ECot EHol ENot EPfP LRHS MWgw NEgg SUsu
- 'Evenglow'	CPrp EBee ECtt EPfP LRHS NEgg WCAu
- 'H.M. Pike'	CPrp EBee SPur SUsu
- 'James Kelway' ♀H4	CPrp EBee ECot ECtt EHan EHol

		EPfP EWll LRHS MWgw NBir NEgg SRms WCAu WHer
	- 'King Size'	NArg SGar WFar
	- 'Laurin'	EBee EBrs
	- 'Madeleine' (d)	CPrp EBee
	- 'Robinson's'	ENot
	- Robinson's giant-flowered	GFlt SRms WMoo
	- 'Robinson's Pink'	CMdw CPrp EBee EChP ELan ENot EPfP GKir GMaP LAst LRHS MWgw NBre NOrc SRms
	- 'Robinson's Red'	CSBt EChP GKir GMaP IBal IHMH LAst LIck MBNS NOrc NPri NVic SGSe SPur SRms SWvt
I	- 'Robinson's Rose'	MBNS
*	- ***rubrum***	GWCH
	- 'Snow Cloud'	CPrp EBee ELan LRHS MWgw WCAu WHil
	- 'Vanessa'	CPrp EBee NEgg NSti
§	***corymbosum***	EBee GMac SMHy WCot
	densum	ECho EPot WCFE
	- subsp. ***amani***	ECha EMFP GBar GMaP GTou LGro LRHS MHer MWat NWCA SEND SPer SRms XPep
	'H.M. Pike' **new**	LRHS
§	***haradjanii***	CMea ECtt ELan NFor NLAp NLon SBch SBla SChu SUsu WHer WSHC
	herderi	see *Hippolytia herderi*
	karelinianum	WLin
	macrophyllum misapplied	see *Achillea grandifolia*
§	***macrophyllum*** (Waldst. & Kit.) Sch.Bip.	EChP ECtt EMon EPPr GCal GKir LPhx WCot WPer
	niveum	CArn EOHP MSal SBch WCot
	- 'Jackpot'	CWib EBee EWes LRHS MBri NLsd SBch SHar SPoG SSvw
§	***parthenium***	CArn CBod CHby CWan ELau GBar GPoy IHMH MBow MChe MHer NPer SECG SIde SRms WGwG WHer WSSM WWye
	- 'Aureum'	CHid CRow ECha ELan ELau EOHP EWes GBar GPoy IHMH LGro MBow MBri MChe MHer NGHP NLsd SECG SIng SPer SPlb SRms WCot WEas WGwG WHer WMoo WPer WSSM WWpP
	- double white (d)	CSWP EUnu GBar NPer SEND SRms WWpP
	- 'Golden Ball'	ETow WWpP
	- 'Golden Moss'	NVic
	- 'Malmesbury'	CNat
	- 'Minety'	CNat
	- 'Plenum' (d)	EHrv SIng
§	- 'Rowallane' (d)	CHea EHol ELan GBuc GMac MAvo SUsu WCot
	- 'Sissinghurst White'	see *T. parthenium* 'Rowallane'
	- 'White Bonnet' (d)	EChP WEas
	poteriifolium	EBee EBrs
	ptarmiciflorum	EChP ECha MFOX SECG WJek
	'Silver Feather'	WWpP
	tatsiense **new**	WLin
	vulgare	CAgr CArn CBod CHby CPrp CSev ECtt ELau GMaP GPoy IHMH MBow MChe MHar MHer MSal SIde WGHP WMoo WWpP WWye
	- 'All Gold'	EMar WCAu
	- var. ***crispum***	CBod CHby CPrp CWan EBee EHol ELau EOHP GAbr GBar GPoy MBri MHer NLon SIde SMad WCot WFar WHer WJek WRha WSel
	- 'Isla Gold' (v)	CBos CElw EBee EPPr EWes GBar GCal MHar NBid NSti SUsu WCHb WCot WFar WGHP WMoo WRha WWpP WWye
	- 'Silver Lace' (v)	CElw EBee GBar GBri ITer NGHP NLsd NSti SEND WBVN WCHb WFar WHer WMoo

Tanakaea (*Saxifragaceae*)

radicans	WCru

tangelo see *Citrus* x *tangelo*

tangerine see *Citrus reticulata*

tangor see *Citrus* x *nobilis* Tangor Group

Tapeinochilos (*Costaceae*)

ananassae	MOak

Taraxacum (*Asteraceae*)

albidum	CNat EBee WCot
- DJH 452	CHid
coreanum	CNat
faeroense	WCot
officinale agg. variegated (v)	WCot
pamiricum	EHyt
rubrifolium	CSpe NChi WHrl

Tarchonanthus (*Asteraceae*)

camphoratus	CTrC

tarragon see *Artemisia dracunculus*

Tasmannia see *Drimys*

Taxodium (*Cupressaceae*)

§	***distichum*** ♀H4	More than 30 suppliers
	- 'Cascade Falls'PBR **new**	MBlu NLar
§	- var. ***imbricatum***	CFil CMCN EPfP WPGP
	- - 'Nutans' ♀H4	CBcs CEnd CTho ECrN LCon LRHS MAsh MBlu MBri SCoo SLim SMad
	- 'Minaret'	MBlu
	- 'Peve Minaret'	NLar SLim
	- 'Peve Yellow'	NLar SLim
	- 'Secrest'	CBcs LRHS MBlu MBri SLim
	- Shawnee Brave = 'Mickelson' **new**	MBlu
	mucronatum	CDoC CFil

Taxus ✿ (*Taxaceae*)

	baccata ♀H4	More than 30 suppliers
	- 'Adpressa' (f) **new**	NEgg
	- 'Adpressa Aurea' (v)	CKen EPla GKir
	- 'Adpressa Variegata' (m/v) ♀H4	CDoC EHul LCon MAsh SLim
	- 'Aldenham Gold'	CKen
	- 'Amersfoort'	CDoC EOrn EPla LCon MDun NLar SCoo SLim SPoG WBcn
	- 'Argentea Minor'	see *T. baccata* 'Dwarf White'
§	- Aurea Group	SRms
I	- 'Aurea Pendula'	EOrn
I	- 'Aureomarginata' (v)	CBcs CSBt EOrn GKir LEar MAsh NEgg SWvt
	- 'Autumn Shades'	CBcs
	- 'Cavendishii' (f)	ECho
	- 'Compacta'	EOrn EPla
	- 'Corleys Coppertip'	CKen CRob EHul GKir LCon MAsh MBar NEgg NLar SCoo SLim WEve WFar
	- 'Cristata'	CKen
	- 'David'	IArd NLar SPoG WEve
	- 'Dovastoniana' (f) ♀H4	CMac GKir MBar NLar NWea WMou

- 'Dovastonii Aurea' (m/v) ♀H4	CMac EHul EOrn EPfP EPla GKir LBee LCon LRHS MBar MBlu MBri NEgg NLar NWea SCoo SLim WCFE WDin WFar
- 'Drinkstone Gold' (v)	EHul WBcn
§ - 'Dwarf White' (v)	EOrn EPla MAsh SCoo SPoG WGor
- 'Elegantissima' (f/v)	ECrN EHul EPfP MTis SPoG WEve WFar
- 'Erecta' (f)	EHul SHBN
§ - 'Fastigiata' (f) ♀H4	More than 30 suppliers
- Fastigiata Aurea Group	CLnd CWib ECrN EHul ENot EPfP IArd LBuc LEar LLin MAsh MGos NGHP NRar SRms WBrE WEve WFar WHar
- 'Fastigiata Aureomarginata' (m/v) ♀H4	More than 30 suppliers
- 'Fastigiata Robusta' (f)	CDoC CRob EPfP EPla GKir LCon LRHS MBar MBri SPoG WEve WFar WGer
- 'Goud Elsje'	CKen EOrn
- 'Green Column'	CKen
- 'Green Diamond'	CKen NLar WBcn
- 'Hibernica'	see *T. baccata* 'Fastigiata'
- 'Icicle'	CBcs EPla LCon LLin MAsh MGos NLar
- 'Itsy Bitsy' **new**	CKen
- 'Ivory Tower'	CBcs CDoC CKen LCon LLin MAsh MGos NLar SPoG WEve WFar WGor
- 'Klitzeklein'	CKen
- 'Laurie'	SPoG
- 'Lutea' (f)	ECrN
- 'Melfard'	CDoC EHul
- 'Nutans'	CDoC CKen CNic CRob CSBt EHul EOrn IMGH LLin MBar NDlv SCoo SPoG
- 'Overeynderi'	EHul
- 'Pendula'	MRav
- 'Prostrata'	CMac WFar
- 'Pygmaea'	CKen
- 'Repandens' (f) ♀H4	CDoC EHul IArd LCon MBar SHBN WCFE WDin WFar
I - 'Repens Aurea' (v) ♀H4	CDoC CKen CRob ECrN EHul EOrn EPfP LCon LLin LRHS MAsh MBar MGos NEgg SCoo WFar
- 'Semperaurea' (m) ♀H4	CBcs CDoC CMac EHul EOrn GKir LBuc LCon LRHS MAsh MBar MGos NEgg NWea SCoo SLim SPla SPoG WCFE WDin WFar
- 'Silver Spire' (v)	CKen MDKP WBcn
- 'Standishii' (f) ♀H4	More than 30 suppliers
- 'Stove Pipe' **new**	CKen
- 'Summergold' (v)	CRob EHul ELan ENot EPfP GKir LCon MAsh MBar MGos NBlu NEgg SCoo SLim SPoG WDin WEve WFar
- 'Washingtonii' (v)	IArd MBar SHBN
- 'White Icicle'	EOrn WGor
brevifolia	EPla
cuspidata	CMen
- 'Aurescens' (v)	CKen EPla SRms
- var. ***nana***	CNic EHul EOrn LCon MBar
- 'Robusta'	EHul LLin
- 'Straight Hedge'	CDoC EHul IMGH SLim WGor
x ***media*** 'Brownii'	EHul LBuc
- 'Hicksii' (f) ♀H4	CDul EHul GKir IMGH LBuc LRHS MBar NBlu NWea SLim WFar
- 'Hillii'	MBar
- 'Lodi'	LBee

tayberry see *Rubus* Tayberry Group

Tecoma (*Bignoniaceae*)

capensis ♀H1	CHEx CPLG CPLN CSec CSev EBak EShb LRHS SHFr SYvo
- 'Aurea'	CSev
- 'Lutea'	LRHS
garrocha	EShb
ricasoliana	see *Podranea ricasoliana*

Tecomanthe (*Bignoniaceae*)

dendrophila **new**	CPLN
speciosa	CPLN ECou

Tecomaria see *Tecoma*

Tecophilaea (*Tecophilaeaceae*)

cyanocrocus ♀H2	CAvo CBro EHyt EPot GCrs LAma LRHS SBla SOkd WCot
- 'Leichtlinii' ♀H2	CBro EHyt EPot LAma LRHS SCnR SSpi
- 'Purpurea'	see *T. cyanocrocus* 'Violacea'
- Storm Cloud Group	GCrs
§ - 'Violacea'	CAvo CBro EPot GCrs LRHS
violiflora	LAma

Tectaria (*Dryopteridaceae*)

gemmifera	GQui

Telanthophora (*Asteraceae*)

grandifolia	CHEx SAPC SArc

Telekia (*Asteraceae*)

§ ***speciosa***	More than 30 suppliers

Telesonix see *Boykinia*

Teline see *Genista*

Tellima (*Saxifragaceae*)

grandiflora	More than 30 suppliers
- 'Delphine' (v)	EBee EMan EPPr EVFa SAga SUsu WCot
- 'Forest Frost'	EBee EMan GCai LAst MDun NGdn NLar NSti SPoG WCot WGor WMoo
- Odorata Group	CBre EChP ECha EGoo MRav NSti WMoo WWpP WWye
- 'Purpurea'	see *T. grandiflora* Rubra Group
- 'Purpurteppich'	EBee EBrs ECha EGoo EHrv EMan GAbr GKir LRHS MRav NGdn SChu WCot WMnd WMoo WTMC
§ - Rubra Group	More than 30 suppliers
- 'Silver Select' **new**	EPPr

Telopea (*Proteaceae*)

oreades	CTrC
speciosissima	CBcs CTrC SPlb SSpi
truncata	CDoC CFil SSpi

Templetonia (*Papilionaceae*)

retusa	ECou

Temu see *Blepharocalyx*

Tephroseris (*Asteraceae*)

integrifolia	WHer

Tephrosia (*Papilionaceae*)

virginiana	SUsu
vogelii	CArn

Tetracentron (*Tetracentraceae*)

sinense	CBcs CMCN EPfP GQui IArd LRHS NLar

Tetradenia (*Lamiaceae*)

riparia EOHP EShb

Tetradium (*Rutaceae*)

B&SWJ 6882 **new** WPGP
§ ***daniellii*** CBcs CFil CMCN EPfP GKir IArd IDee NLar SSpi WPGP
§ - Hupehense Group CBcs CMCN CPle GKir MBri SSpi WDin
glabrifolium CFil EBee
- B&SWJ 3541 WCru
ruticarpum B&SWJ 6882 **new** WCru
I ***velutinum*** CMCN

Tetragonia (*Tetragoniaceae*)

tetragonoides **new** CArn

Tetragonolobus see *Lotus*

Tetraneuris (*Asteraceae*)

§ ***acaulis*** var. ***caespitosa*** WLin
scaposa EPot LRHS

Tetrapanax (*Araliaceae*)

§ ***papyrifer*** ♀H2-3 CHEx EUJe NLar SAPC SArc SBig WBan WMul XBlo
- B&SWJ 7135 WCru
- 'Empress' WCru
- 'Rex' CPLG WCru WMul

Tetrapathaea see *Passiflora*

Tetrastigma (*Vitaceae*)

obtectum CPLN ECre
voinierianum ♀H1 ESlt MBri SAPC SArc WCot

Tetratheca (*Tremandraceae*)

thymifolia ECou

Teucrium (*Lamiaceae*)

* ***ackermannii*** CLyd EGoo LBee LRHS NMen SBla SMac SUsu WAbe WEas WHoo WPat WTin XPep
arduinoi XPep
aroanium CLyd EPot LBee LRHS MWat NMen NWCA SBla WAbe
asiaticum CPom EGoo XPep
bicolor CPle
botrys EGoo MHer MSal
brevifolium XPep
canadense MSal
chamaedrys misapplied see *T.* x *lucidrys*
chamaedrys L. CHal CPom CSam CWan CWib EGoo EHyt GAbr GBar IHMH LRHS LSRN NBlu NGHP NJOw NWCA SLim SRms STre WBrk WCAu WJek WSel WTin WWeb XPep
- 'Nanum' CLyd NLAp WPat WWye
I - 'Rose' WMoo
- 'Rose Carpet' EChP ECrN EGoo
- 'Variegatum' (v) EMan EVFa GBar WCHb WPer WRha
§ ***cossonii*** XPep
§ ***creticum*** WLin
divaricatum XPep
dunense XPep
flavum EChP EGoo NBre SGar SHFr WCHb WJek WOut XPep
- subsp. ***grandiflorum*** XPep
fruticans More than 30 suppliers
- 'Azureum' ♀H3 CBcs CBot CHar CM&M CPle CWSG EChP EPfP EWin LRHS LSou SBra SIgm SLim SPer WEas XPep
- 'Collingwood Ingram' EBee
- 'Compactum' CDoC EMan ENot EWTr LRHS LSou MCCP SLon SPer SPla WAbe WBcn
- dark SPoG
- 'Drysdale' CDoC
gnaphalodes XPep
hircanicum More than 30 suppliers
- 'Paradise Delight' **new** NBid WCra WSan
- 'Purple Tails' CPrp CWib LBBr LSou NCob
laciniatum XPep
§ x ***lucidrys*** More than 30 suppliers
lucidum XPep
marum CArn EOHP MSal NMen SBla SIgm WJek XPep
- 'Feuilles Vertes' XPep
'Massif Central' LRHS
massiliense misapplied see *T.* x *lucidrys*
massiliense L. EBee EGoo EMan WHer XPep
microphyllum XPep
micropodioides XPep
montanum EGoo EShb GBar NJOw SHGN XPep
musimonum EPot
orientale XPep
polium CArn CPLG MWat NLAp SIgm WJek WPat XPep
- subsp. ***aureum*** EHyt NWCA SBla XPep
- subsp. ***capitatum*** XPep
pyrenaicum CHal CMea CPom EBee EHyt EMan EPot GCrs GEdr MHer NSla NWCA SBla WPat WWye
rosmarinifolium see *T. creticum*
rotundifolium EBee
scordium CNat
scorodonia CArn COld CRWN CSev EGoo ELau GBar GPoy MChe MHer MSal NMir WHer WJek WLHH WSSM WSel XPep
- 'Binsted Gold' EBee EGoo EMan EMon EPPr LDai LSou MHar WOut
- 'Crispum' CHby CWan ELau EMar EUnu GBar MHar MHer MLLN MWat MWgw NBid NBro NCob NJOw SOkh WBrE WCHb WGwG WHoo WKif WMoo WPer WPtf WSel WTin
* - 'Crispum Aureomarginatum' EBee EChP
§ - 'Crispum Marginatum' (v) CBot COlW EChP ECha EGoo EHoe EHrv EMag EMar EPPr EPfP EVFa GBar IBlr ILis LRHS MDun MNrw MRav MTis NOak NSti SAga SOkh WCot WCra WEas WFar WTin WWeb
- 'Winterdown' (v) CMea EBee EGoo EMan EPPr NPro SAga SBch WCHb WCot WHoo WLin WWeb
subspinosum CLyd CMea LBee LRHS NLAp NMen NWCA SBch WHoo WPat XPep
§ ***viscidum*** 'Lemon and Lime' (v) EBee ECtt EMan NSti SDnm WCot WPGP
webbianum CSec ECho
'Winterdown' GBri

Thalia (*Marantaceae*)

dealbata CDWL CHEx EAmu EMFW EShb EUJe LPBA MJnS NArg NLar SDix SSpi WMul WPop WWpP

	geniculata	CDWL EShb WMul

Thalictrum (*Ranunculaceae*)

	ACE 1141	WCot
	CC 3691	ITer
	CC 4051	WCot
	from Afghanistan	see *T. isopyroides*
	actaeifolium	CLAP EBee
	- B&SWJ 4664	WCru
	- var. ***brevistylum*** B&SWJ 8819	WCru
	adiantifolium	see *T. minus* 'Adiantifolium'
	alpinum	EPPr NRya SBch
	angustifolium	see *T. lucidum*
	aquilegiifolium	More than 30 suppliers
	- var. ***album***	CBos CFwr CMil COIW ECha ELan EPfP LPhx MBri MDun MNrw MWgw NBid NChi SBla SPla SSpi WCAu WCru WMnd WPer WSHC
	- dwarf	CMea
*	- 'Hybridum'	CHad GBBs NArg WFar WMoo WPer
	- Purple Cloud	see *T. aquilegiifolium* 'Thundercloud'
	- 'Purpureum'	CPom CSev LPio MDun NLar SPla WCAu WCru WHoo
	- 'Roseum'	WCot
	- 'Sparkler' **new**	GCai
§	- 'Thundercloud' ♀H4	CBct CFir CKno CMil CWan EBee ECtt ENot EPfP GCal GKir LRHS MBri NLar NRnb NSti SWvt WBrE WCra WWeb
	baicalense	CPom EBee
	'Braveheart' **new**	NRnb
§	***chelidonii***	EBee EBrs GKir GMaP MGol
	- GWJ 9349	WCru
	- HWJK 2216	WCru
	clavatum	CDes CLAP WPGP
	contortum	EBee SDys
	coreanum	see *T. ichangense*
	cultratum	CDes CWCL EChP NSti
	- HWJCM 367	CAby EBee NLar SSpi WCru
	dasycarpum	EBee EMan MLLN NLar
*	***decorum***	CBos CFwr CLAP CWCL EVFa GBin GMac LPhx LPio NCGa NCob NDov SMHy WCru WLFP WSHC
	- CD&R 2135	CAby
§	***delavayi*** ♀H4	More than 30 suppliers
	- BWJ 7903	WCru
	- var. ***acuminatum*** BWJ 7535	WCru
	- - BWJ 7971	WCru
	- 'Album'	CFwr CLAP CPom CSpe CWCL EBee EBrs ECha GKev GKir LPhx LPio LRHS NCGa NDov NLar NOak SPer SPoG WMoo WPrP
	- 'Hewitt's Double' (d) ♀H4	More than 30 suppliers
	- var. ***mucronatum*** **new**	WCru
	- purple-stemmed BWJ 7748 **new**	WCru
	diffusiflorum	CDes CLAP EVFa GBri GBuc GEdr GKir SBla SUsu WSHC
	dipterocarpum misapplied	see *T. delavayi*
	dipterocarpum Franch.	GCra MDun WMnd
	- ACE 4.878.280	CMil
	elegans	EBee
	- from China **new**	CFwr
	- HWJK 2271	WCru
	'Elin'	CElw CFir CLAP CSpe EBee EMan ERou GMac IPot MAnH MBri NBir NCob NCot NDov NEgg SBla SMHy SPoG SUsu WKif WWhi
	fendleri	GBin GBuc
	filamentosum	EMon
	- B&SWJ 777	WCru
	- var. ***tenerum*** Heronswood form	CKno MBnl
	- var. ***yakusimense*** B&SWJ 6094 **new**	WCru
	finetii	CLAP SMHy
	- DJHC 473	CDes CPom
	aff. ***finetii***	CLAP
	flavum	EBee EBrs ECtt EDAr GBBs GBin GFlt GKir LPhx MBow NBro SSpi WBrE WShi
§	- subsp. ***glaucum*** ♀H4	More than 30 suppliers
	- 'Illuminator'	CBot CHad CKno CPar EBee EPPr GBri GFlt GKir LPio LRHS MArl MBow MOne MRav MWgw NEgg NPri SMrm SPlb SPoG SUsu WCAu WCot WCra WPnP WPrP WWhi
	flexuosum	see *T. minus* subsp. *minus*
	foetidum	EBee NBre
	- BWJ 7558	WCru
	aff. ***foetidum*** BWJ 7558	WCru
	foliolosum B&SWJ 2705	WCru
	- HWJK 2181	WCru
	- S&SH 382	GBri
	grandiflorum	EBee NCob
	- from Gansu, China **new**	CFwr
	honanense **new**	CFwr
§	***ichangense***	EBee GBri GKir SAga
*	- var. ***minus*** **new**	WCru
§	***isopyroides***	More than 30 suppliers
	javanicum	EBee LEdu
	- var. ***puberulum*** B&SWJ 6770	WCru
	johnstonii B&SWJ **new**	WCru
	kiusianum	More than 30 suppliers
	- Kew form	EBee SAga SRot WSHC
	- white-flowered	CFir
	koreanum	see *T. ichangense*
§	***lucidum***	CAby CPou EBee ELan EMan IHMH LPhx MAnH MRav MWrn NBre NDov NLar NSti SBla SHar SMHy WCot WFar WPrP
	minus	CAgr CBos CMHG EBrs ECGP ELan EMan EMon GBuc MLLN NOak SECG WWye
§	- 'Adiantifolium'	EBee GBin LPio MLLN MRav MWgw NBre NCob NLar NOak SHar SRms WFar WPer
	- var. ***hypoleucum*** B&SWJ 8634 **new**	WCru
§	- subsp. ***minus***	NBre
§	- subsp. ***olympicum***	WPer
	- subsp. ***saxatile***	see *T. minus* subsp. *olympicum*
	- var. ***sipellatum*** B&SWJ 5051	WCru
	occidentale	EBee
	- JLS 86255	MNrw
	omeiense BWJ 8049	WCru
	orientale	SBla
	polygamum	see *T. pubescens*
	przewalskii **new**	WCru
§	***pubescens***	CAby EBrs ECha GBin GBri GMaP LPhx MSal NDov SHar SUsu WPrP
	punctatum	CBos CLAP MDun NEgg
	- B&SWJ 1272	EMan GBin LPhx WCru
	reniforme	CBos CFir EVFa GKev LPio
	- B&SWJ 2159	EMan
	- B&SWJ 2610	WCru
	- HWJK 2152	WCru

reticulatum WCru
rochebruneanum More than 30 suppliers
sachalinense EPPr GIBF MCCP SOkd
- AER 0279 EKen MGol
- RBS 0279 MHar
simplex LPio
- var. **brevipes** B&SWJ 4794 WCru
speciosissimum see *T. flavum* subsp. *glaucum*
sphaerostachyum CDes GKir IFro LRHS MBri SMrm WGer
squarrosum EBrs LPio LRHS
tenuisubulatum BWJ 7929 new WCru
tuberosum CBos CDes CElw CMea EHyt GKir MLLN NDov NLAp SBla SSpi WAbe WPGP WPat
uchiyamae EBee EBrs EPPr GBin GBri
virgatum B&SWJ 2964 WCru

Thamnocalamus (*Poaceae*)

aristatus EPfP EPla
crassinodus SBig
- dwarf EPla
- 'Gosainkund' EPla
- 'Kew Beauty' CAbb CDoC CPen EFul EPfP EPla ERod MBrN MMoz MWht SBig WJun WMul WPGP
- 'Lang Tang' EFul EPla ERod WJun WPGP
- 'Merlyn' CDoC CPen EPla ERod MMoz MWht WJun WPGP
falcatus see *Drepanostachyum falcatum*
falconeri see *Himalayacalamus falconeri*
funghomii see *Schizostachyum funghomii*
khasianus see *Drepanostachyum khasianum*
maling see *Yushania maling*
spathaceus misapplied see *Fargesia murielae*
§ **spathiflorus** CFil EFul EPla WJun
- subsp. **nepalensis** EPla SBig
§ **tessellatus** CAbb EFul EPla MMoz WDyG WJun

Thamnochortus (*Restionaceae*)

bachmannii CBcs
cinereus CBcs CBct CBig CCtw CTrC EAmu
insignis CBig CCtw CHEx CTrC WMul WNor WPrP
spicigerus CBig

Thapsia (*Apiaceae*)

decipiens see *Melanoselinum decipiens*
garganica CArn EMan SIgm
maxima SIgm
villosa SIgm

Thea see *Camellia*

Thelypteris (*Thelypteridaceae*)

* **dentata** new SGSe
kunthii WRic
limbosperma see *Oreopteris limbosperma*
nevadensis NNS 00-725 new WCot
palustris CAby CPLG CRWN EBee EFer EMon EPza LPBA NVic NWoo SRms WFib WRic
phegopteris see *Phegopteris connectilis*

Themeda (*Poaceae*)

japonica EHoe EPPr GFor GIBF WDyG
triandra EPza GIBF SMad

Thermopsis (*Papilionaceae*)

caroliniana see *T. villosa*
fabacea see *T. lupinoides*
lanceolata CHad CTri EBee ECGP EChP EMan GBin LRHS LSpr MBri MEHN MLLN MMil MNFA MWgw NBPC NCGa NPri NSti SAga SOkh SPoG WAul WCAu WFar WHrl WPer WWye
§ **lupinoides** CPne ECha EHrv EVFa GIBF GLil LPio MFOX MGol NEgg NOrc SUsu WCot WFar WPer
- AER 0280 MGol
mollis NBid
montana see *T. rhombifolia* var. *montana*
§ **rhombifolia** var. **montana** CRez EBee ELan EPfP GGar GMaP MNrw MSte MWat MWgw NEgg NOrc NPol NSti SPer WAbb WBVN WPer
§ **villosa** EMan GIBF MGol MLLN MRav MSte MWrn NDov SBla SMHy SMar WCot WPGP

Thevetia (*Apocynaceae*)

neriifolia new CSec
peruviana LRHS MSal

Thladiantha (*Cucurbitaceae*)

dubia CPLN SDix

Thlaspi (*Brassicaceae*)

alpinum EPot NJOw
bellidifolium NBir
biebersteinii see *Pachyphragma macrophyllum*
bulbosum GTou
§ **cepaeifolium** subsp. **rotundifolium** GTou
diacicum new NJOw
fendleri MNrw
praecox new NJOw
rotundifolium see *T. cepaeifolium* subsp. *rotundifolium*

Thrinax (*Arecaceae*)

radiata EAmu

Thryptomene (*Myrtaceae*)

saxicola ECou
- 'F. C. Payne' CBcs

Thuja ✿ (*Cupressaceae*)

'Extra Gold' see *T. plicata* 'Irish Gold'
'Gnome' IBal
§ **koraiensis** IDee LCon MBar SLim SPoG WCwm
occidentalis 'Amber Glow' CDoC CKen CRob GBin LCon LLin MAsh MGos NLar SCoo SLim SPoG WBor WEve
- Aurea Group MBar
- 'Aureospicata' EHul
- 'Bateman Broom' CKen
- 'Beaufort' (v) CKen EHul MBar
- 'Brabant' SLim
- 'Brobecks Tower' new CKen
- 'Caespitosa' CFee CKen ESis LLin LRHS NEgg NLar SCoo SPoG WEve WGor
- 'Cristata Aurea' CKen
- 'Danica' ♀H4 CMac CRob EHul ENot EOrn GKir LCon LLin MAsh MBar NEgg NWea SBod SCoo SLim SMer SPoG SRms WCFE WEve WFar

	- 'Dicksonii'	EHul
	- 'Douglasii Aurea' (v)	CKen
	- 'Ellwangeriana Aurea'	MGos
	- Emerald	see *T. occidentalis* 'Smaragd'
	- 'Ericoides'	CDoC CTri EHul LRHS MBar SRms
	- 'Europa Gold'	CDoC EHul GKir LBee MAsh MBar MGos NLar SLim
	- 'Fastigiata'	MBar
	- 'Filiformis'	CKen EPla
	- 'Globosa'	CMac MBar SBod WGor
I	- 'Globosa Variegata' (v)	CKen MBar WEve
	- 'Gold Drop'	CKen
	- 'Golden Globe'	CDoC EHul EOrn LLin MBar MGos NEgg SBod SCoo SLim SPla SPoG WDin
	- 'Golden Minaret'	EHul
	- 'Hetz Midget'	CKen EHul EOrn ESis IMGH LLin MBar NEgg NLar SCoo SLim SMer SPlb SPoG WDin WFar
	- 'Holmstrup' ♀H4	CDoC CMac CRob CSBt CTri CWib EHul EOrn GKir LLin LRHS MAsh MBar SCoo SLim SPoG SRms WDin WEve WFar WTel
	- 'Holmstrup's Yellow'	CKen EGra EHul GKir LCon SCoo SLim SPoG WBVN WCFE WEve
	- 'Hoveyi'	CMac CTri EHul WEve
	- 'Linesville'	CKen
	- 'Little Champion'	EHul
	- 'Little Gem'	EHul GKir MGos NPro SRms WDin WGor
	- 'Lutea Nana' ♀H4	CMac EHul EOrn MBar NDlv WCFE
	- 'Marrisen's Sulphur'	CSli EHul EOrn NLar SCoo SLim SPla WBcn WEve
	- 'Meineke's Zwerg' (v)	CKen NLar
	- 'Miky'	CKen WBcn
	- 'Ohlendorffii'	CDoC CKen EHul EOrn LLin MBar
	- 'Orientalis Semperaurescens'	see *Platycladus orientalis* 'Semperaurea'
I	- 'Pygmaea'	CKen MBar SLon
	- 'Pyramidalis Aurea'	WEve
	- 'Pyramidalis Compacta'	EHul WGor
	- 'Recurva Nana'	EHul MBar
	- 'Rheingold' ♀H4	More than 30 suppliers
§	- 'Smaragd' ♀H4	More than 30 suppliers
*	- 'Smaragd Variegated' (v)	CKen
	- 'Southport'	CKen WEve
	- 'Spaethii'	EHul EOrn
	- 'Spiralis'	EHul IMGH MBar NLar WCFE
§	- 'Stolwijk' (v)	EHul EOrn LLin MBar MGos WBcn
	- 'Sunkist'	CKen CMac CRob CSBt CSli CTri CWib ECrN EHul ENot EOrn GKir MAsh MBar MGos NEgg SBod SCoo SLim SMer SPla SPoG WEve WFar
	- 'Suzie'	LLin
	- 'Teddy'	CFee CRob LCon LLin MAsh NLar SCoo SLim SPoG WEve WFar
	- 'Tiny Tim'	CDoC CMac CNic CRob CSBt CWib EHul ESis IMGH LLin MBar MGos SCoo WEve WFar WGor
	- 'Trompenburg'	CRob ECho EHul EOrn MAsh SCoo WBcn
	- 'Wansdyke Silver' (v)	CMac EHul EOrn MBar SCoo SLim SPoG
	- 'Wareana'	CMac
	- 'Wareana Aurea'	see *T. occidentalis* 'Wareana Lutescens'
§	- 'Wareana Lutescens'	CWib EHul EOrn MBar WEve
	- 'Woodwardii'	EHul MBar SMer
	- 'Yellow Ribbon'	CSBt CSli EHul GKir LCon LRHS MBar SCoo SLim SMer SPla SPoG WEve WFar
	orientalis	see *Platycladus orientalis*
	plicata	CDul CTho EHul EPfP GIBF MBar MGos NBlu NWea SLim SPer SPoG WDin WMou
	- 'Atrovirens' ♀H4	CTri ECrN ENot GKir LBee LBuc LCon LRHS MAsh MBar MBri MGos SBLw SCoo SLim SMer SPoG SRms WDin WEve WHar
*	- 'Atrovirens Aurea'	SLim WBcn WEve
	- 'Aurea' ♀H4	EHul LBee LRHS MAsh SLim SPoG SRms
	- 'Barabits'	EBrs
	- 'Brooks Gold'	CKen
	- 'Can-can' (v)	CRob GKir NLar SCoo
I	- 'Cole's Variety'	CWib MBar SLim
	- 'Collyer's Gold'	CBrm CTri EHul MAsh NLar SRms WEve
	- 'Compacta' **new**	CDul
	- 'Copper Kettle'	CBrm CKen CSli ECrN EHul GKir LCon MAsh MBar NDlv NEgg NPro SCoo SLim WEve WGor
	- 'Cuprea'	CKen EHul MBar
	- 'Doone Valley'	CKen CSli EHul EOrn MBar NDlv
	- 'Emerald' PBR	WEve
	- 'Fastigiata' ♀H4	CMac LRHS WTel
	- 'Gelderland'	EHul NBlu NLar SCoo SLim WEve WFar
	- 'Gracilis Aurea'	ECho EHul WBcn
	- 'Grüne Kugel'	CDoC
	- 'Hillieri'	MBar
§	- 'Irish Gold' (v) ♀H4	CAbP CDul CMac LCon LLin LRHS NLar SAga WBcn
	- 'Rogersii'	CDoC CKen CMac CSli CTri EHul EOrn EPfP GKir LCon LLin LRHS MAsh MBar MGos SCoo SPoG SRms WFar WTel
	- 'Stolwijk's Gold'	see *T. occidentalis* 'Stolwijk'
	- 'Stoneham Gold' ♀H4	CDoC CKen CMac EGra EHul EOrn GKir LBee LCon LRHS MAsh MBar MGos SBod SLim SMer SPoG SRms WCFE WEve WTel
	- 'Sunshine'	CKen
*	- 'Windsor Gold'	EHul
	- 'Winter Pink' (v)	CKen NLar
	- 'Zebrina' (v)	More than 30 suppliers
	plicata* x *standishii	WCwm
	standishii	WCwm

Thujopsis (*Cupressaceae*)

	dolabrata ♀H4	CBcs CTho ECrN EHul GKir LBee MBar MMHG NDlv NEgg NLar NWea SHBN SPer WBrE WDin WFar
	- 'Aurea' (v)	CDoC CKen EHul EOrn LCon MBar MGos NLar SCoo SHBN SLim WBcn WEve
	- 'Laetevirens'	see *T. dolabrata* 'Nana'
§	- 'Nana'	CDoC CKen CMac EHul EOrn IArd LBee LCon LLin MBar SCoo SLim SPoG SRms STre WEve WFar
	- 'Variegata' (v)	CDoC CDul CFee EHul EOrn LCon LLin MBar NDlv SCoo SHFr SLim SPoG WDin WEve WFar
	koraiensis	see *Thuja koraiensis*

Thunbergia (*Acanthaceae*)

	'Alamain Glory' **new**	CPLN
	alata	MBri SYvo
	- 'African Sunset'	CSpe EShb
	battiscombeii **new**	CPLN MJnS
	coccinea	CPLN EShb MJnS
I	- 'Lutea' **new**	CPLN
	erecta	CKob CPLN ELan ERea ESlt

	fragrans	ERea EShb
	gibsonii **new**	CPLN
	grandiflora ♀H1	CHII CPLN ELan EPfP ERea EShb ESlt MJnS WMul
	- 'Alba'	CHII CPLN WMul
	gregorii ♀H1+3	CHII CPLN CSpe ERea
	laevis **new**	CPLN
	'Molly' **new**	CPLN
	mysorensis ♀H1	CPLN ERea
	natalensis	CSpe ERea

Thymbra (*Lamiaceae*)

	spicata	XPep

thyme, caraway see *Thymus herba-barona*

thyme, garden see *Thymus vulgaris*

thyme, lemon see *Thymus* x *citriodorus*

thyme, wild see *Thymus serpyllum*

Thymus ✿ (*Lamiaceae*)

	from Turkey	EWes LLWP SHDw
	'Alan Bloom' **new**	LLWP
	'Anderson's Gold'	see *T. pulegioides* 'Bertram Anderson'
	azoricus	see *T. caespititius*
	'Blush' **new**	SHDw
	'Caborn Lilac Gem'	LLWP SHDw
	'Caborn Purple Haze'	LLWP
§	***caespititius***	CArn CLyd ELau EPot EUnu GBar GMaP GPoy LLWP MHer NLRH NMen NRya SPlb SRot WCHb WPer
	caespitosus	CTri GKir LLWP
	camphoratus	CArn CBod ELau EOHP EUnu EWes GBar LLWP LPhx MHer NGHP SHDw WJek XPep
	- 'A Touch of Frost'	SHDw
	- 'Derry'	CSpe LLWP
	capitatus	CArn XPep
	carnosus misapplied	see *T. vulgaris* 'Erectus'
	carnosus Boiss.	GBar XPep
	'Carol Ann' (v)	CBod ELau EWes GBar LLWP MBNS
	'Caroline' **new**	SHDw
	'Carshalton' **new**	CWan
	cephalotos	EHyt WAbe
	ciliatus	CArn LLWP MWat WPer XPep
	cilicicus Boiss. & Bail.	EHyt ETow EWes GBar MChe NMen SBla WAbe WCHb WJek WWye
	x ***citriodorus***	CArn CHby CHrt CWan EDAr ELau GAbr GBar GPoy LGro LLWP MBow MBrN MChe MHer NBlu NGHP SWal WBrE WFar WGwG WJek WPer WSSM WWye XPep
	- 'Archer's Gold'	see *T. pulegioides* 'Archer's Gold'
	- 'Argenteus' (v)	LLWP
	- 'Aureus'	see *T. pulegioides* 'Aureus'
	- 'Bertram Anderson'	see *T. pulegioides* 'Bertram Anderson'
§	- 'Golden King' (v)	CBrm CLyd ECha EDAr ELan GBar LLWP LRHS MBar MBri MChe MHer NArg NGHP NSti WCHb WHoo WPer WSel
	- 'Golden Lemon' misapplied	see *T. pulegioides* 'Aureus'
§	- 'Golden Lemon' (v)	CArn GPoy LLWP WJek WWye
	- 'Golden Queen' (v)	CMea COIW EDAr GBar LBBr MBow MHer MWat NBlu NPri SHDw SPer SPet SRms WFar
	- 'Lemon Supreme'	LLWP
	- 'Lime'	LLWP
	- 'Nyewoods' (v)	GAbr
	- ***repandus***	see *T.* 'Rosemary's Lemon Carpet'
	- 'Silver King' (v)	LLWP
	- 'Silver Posie'	see *T. vulgaris* 'Silver Posie'
	- 'Silver Queen' (v) ♀H4	CAgr CBcs CLyd CSam ECha EDAr ELan ENot EOHP EPfP GBar GGar GKir IBal LRHS MBar MChe MHer NBlu NGHP NLon SPlb WFar WGHP
	- 'Variegatus' misapplied	see *T.* x *citriodorus* 'Golden King'
*	- 'Variegatus' (v)	CMea GBar LSRN MBri MChe NGHP WFar
	- 'Villa Nova' (v)	LLWP
	'Coccineus'	see *T.* Coccineus Group
N	Coccineus Group ♀H4	CArn CHby CTri ECha ECtt EDAr EHyt ELan ELau GKir GMaP GTou IHMH LGro LLWP LRHS MBar MBri MChe MHer NCGa SBla SIng SRms SRot WHoo WPat WTel
§	- 'Atropurpureus' misapplied	LLWP SHDw
	- 'Hardstoft Red' (v)	GBar LLWP MChe
	- 'Purple Beauty'	LLWP MHer
	- 'Purpurteppich'	LLWP
	- 'Red Elf'	GBar SHDw WJek
	'Coccineus Major'	CMea CWan EDAr GAbr GKir LRHS MHer SIde WAbe WJek WSSM XPep
	'Coconut' **new**	LSou
	comosus	EDAr GBar LLWP MChe MHer SHDw WEas WPer
	'Cow Green'	LLWP SHDw
	'Creeping Lemon'	ELau EUnu GBar LLWP MHer SHDw WGwG WJek
	'Creeping Mauve'	LLWP
	'Creeping Orange'	LLWP
	'Dark Eyes' **new**	SHDw
	'Dartmoor'	GBar GCal LLWP SHDw
	'Desboro'	GBar LLWP MBNS MHer
	doerfleri	CLyd ECha LLWP WSel XPep
	- 'Bressingham'	CArn CMea CWan ECtt EDAr ELau GBar GKir LBee LGro LLWP LRHS MChe MHer NGHP SBla SIng SPlb SRms SWal WPat WPer WTel WWye
	'Doone Valley' (v)	More than 30 suppliers
	drucei	see *T. polytrichus*
	'E.B. Anderson'	see *T. pulegioides* 'Bertram Anderson'
	'Eastgrove Pink'	LLWP SHDw
	'Emma's Pink'	LLWP
	erectus	see *T. vulgaris* 'Erectus'
*	***ericoides***	EPot MHer
	'Fragrantissimus'	CArn ELau EOHP EUnu GBar GPoy GWCH LLWP MChe MHer MWat NGHP SIde SPlb WJek WPer WWye
	'Gibson's Cave'	LLWP
	'Glenridding'	LLWP
	'Goldie' **new**	SHDw
	'Gowbarrow'	LLWP
	'Grattan'	SHDw
	'Hans Stam'	LLWP
	'Hardstoft Red'	see *T.* (Coccineus Group) 'Hardstoft Red'
§	'Hartington Silver' (v)	More than 30 suppliers
	herba-barona	CAgr CArn CHrt CMea CTri CWan ECha EDAr ELau EOHP EUnu GBar GPoy LEdu LLWP MBow MHer NFor NGHP NRya SIde SRms STre WGwG WPer WWye XPep
	- 'Bob Flowerdew'	LLWP

	- ***citrata***	see *T. herba-barona* 'Lemon-scented'
§	- 'Lemon-scented'	CArn ECha ELau GBar GPoy LLWP MHer NLon SHDw SIde WCHb
	'Highdown'	ECtt SHDw
	'Highdown Adus' **new**	SHDw
	'Highdown Lemon'	SBch SHDw
	'Highdown Red'	SHDw
	'Highdown Stretham' **new**	SHDw
	'Highland Cream'	see *T.* 'Hartington Silver'
	hirsutus	NBir XPep
	hyemalis	LLWP
	integer	SBla
	'Kurt'	LLWP SHDw
	'Lake District'	LLWP
I	'Lantanii' **new**	LLWP SHDw
	lanuginosus misapplied	see *T. pseudolanuginosus*
§	'Lavender Sea'	ELau EOHP EWes LLWP
	'Lemon Caraway'	see *T. herba-barona* 'Lemon-scented'
*	'Lemon Variegated' (v)	EDAr ELau EPfP GBar
	leucotrichus	WPat XPep
	'Lilac Time'	COkL EWes GBar LLWP MHer SHDw SIde SPlb WCHb WGwG WJek
	longicaulis	CArn CLyd ECha ELau EWin GBar LLWP MBNS WJek XPep
	'Low Force'	LLWP
	marschallianus	see *T. pannonicus*
	mastichina	CAgr CArn CBrm GBar MChe SBla SChu WGwG WWye XPep
	- 'Didi'	CArn LLWP MHer
	membranaceus	WAbe
	micans	see *T. caespititius*
	minus	see *Calamintha nepeta*
	montanus Waldst. & Kit.	see *T. pulegioides*
	neiceffii	CArn CLyd ECha ELau GBar LLWP NWCA XPep
	'New Hall' **new**	SHDw
*	***nummularius***	ELau
	odoratissimus	see *T. pallasianus* subsp. *pallasianus*
	'Orange Balsam' **new**	LLWP
	'Orange Spice'	EUnu LLWP SHDw
	pallasianus	ELau LLWP SHDw
§	- subsp. ***pallasianus***	CBod GBar MHer
§	***pannonicus***	EOHP LLWP MHer WPer
	parnassicus	XPep
	'Pat Milne' **new**	LGro
	'Peter Davis'	CArn CPBP EDAr EOHP GBar LLWP MBNS MBow MChe MHer NBir NCGa NGHP SBla SChu SIde WAbe WJek WRHF
§	'Pink Ripple'	CBod CMea ELau EOHP EWes GBar LLWP MChe MHer SHDw SIde SIng WCHb WGwG WHoo WJek
	polytrichus misapplied	see *T. praecox*
§	***polytrichus*** A. Kern. ex Borbás	XPep
§	- subsp. ***britannicus***	EPot GPoy LLWP NSti SHDw SPlb WAbe WJek WPer
	- - 'Minor'	EPot LLWP WPer
§	- - 'Thomas's White' ♀H4	LLWP MHer
	pongicaulis **new**	EOHP
	'Porlock'	CMea CSev CWan EDAr ELau EPfP ESis ETow GBar GPoy LLWP MChe MHer NArg NGHP NRya SIde SRms STre WGHP WGwG WHoo WJek WPer
	praecox	GBar LLWP MHer NLan
	- subsp. ***arcticus***	see *T. polytrichus* subsp. *britannicus*
	'Provence'	LLWP
§	***pseudolanuginosus***	CArn CMea ECha EDAr ELau EPot GAbr GBar GGar GMaP GTou LBee LGro LLWP LRHS MBNS MBar MBri MHer MWgw NChi NGHP NSti NWCA SPlb SRms WGwG WHoo WPer XPep
	- 'Hall's Variety'	ELau GBar
	- 'Mountain Select'	LLWP SHDw
§	***pulegioides***	CArn CBod CHby CHrt ELau ESis GBar GGar GPoy LLWP MBow MBri MHer NPri NRya SHDw SIde WGwG WJek WPer WWye
§	- 'Archer's Gold'	More than 30 suppliers
§	- 'Aureus' ♀H4	CRez EDAr ESis GAbr GBar GKir GMaP GTou LLWP LRHS MBar MBow MBri NBlu NWCA SBla SPer SPla WFar WHoo
§	- 'Bertram Anderson' ♀H4	More than 30 suppliers
	- 'Foxley' (v)	CBod CWan EHoe ELau EOHP EPfP EUnu LLWP LSou MChe MHer NGHP NPro NTHB SHDw SIde SPlb WCHb WJek WWpP
	- 'Golden Dwarf'	LLWP
§	- 'Goldentime'	GBar GKir LGro LLWP LRHS MChe NGHP WJek WSel
	- 'Sir John Lawes'	LLWP MHer SHDw
	- 'Sundon Hills' **new**	LLWP
	- 'Tabor'	EUnu GMaP NGHP NTHB SHDw WJek
	- variegated	GBar
	'Redstart'	CBod CLyd ECha ELau EOHP EPot GBar LBee LLWP LRHS MChe SBch SHDw SIde SIng WCHb
*	***richardii*** subsp. ***nitidus***	STre WWye
	- - 'Compactus Albus'	see *T. vulgaris* 'Snow White'
	'Rosa Creeping' **new**	SHDw
	'Rosalicht'	LLWP
	'Rosalind' **new**	SHDw
	'Rosedrift'	LLWP SHDw
	'Rosemary's Lemon Carpet'	LLWP
	rotundifolius	ELau LLWP MHer SHDw XPep
§	'Ruby Glow'	ELau EWes LLWP MChe MHer SHDw SMHy WJek
	serpyllum ambig.	CArn ELau GKir LLWP MBri MChe NGHP SIde SPet SPlb SRms WJek WPer
	serpyllum L.	WBVN XPep
	- var. ***albus***	ECha ELau GKir GPoy GTou LLWP MBow NGHP SBla SChu SIde SPer SRms SWal WHoo WWye XPep
	- 'Albus Variegatus'	see *T.* 'Hartington Silver'
N	- 'Annie Hall'	CMea CWan EDAr ELau EPfP EPot GAbr GBar GGar LGro LLWP LRHS MChe MHer NFor NGHP SIde SIng WCFE WGwG WPer WWye
	- 'Atropurpureus'	see *T.* (Coccineus Group) 'Atropurpureus' misapplied
	- 'Barwinnock Snowdrift' (v)	GBar
	- ***coccineus*** 'Minor' misapplied	see *T.* Coccineus Group
	- ***coccineus*** 'Minor' Bloom	see *T.* 'Alan Bloom'
	- 'Conwy Rose'	WAbe
N	- 'East Lodge'	LLWP WWpP
	- 'Elfin'	CArn CLyd EDAr EWes GTou LBee LRHS MBri NLAp SBla SHDw SPlb WAbe XPep

	- 'Flossy'	LLWP
N	- 'Fulney Red'	EWes LLWP
	- 'Goldstream' (v)	CBrm CLyd CMea ELau EPfP ESis GBar IHMH LLWP LRHS MBar MBri MChe MHer NGHP NRya NSti SPlb SRms WCHb WGwG WPer
	- subsp. ***lanuginosus***	see *T. pseudolanuginosus*
	- 'Lemon Curd'	CBod CBrm CWan ELau EOHP EUnu GBar LLWP MChe MHer NGHP NSti SHDw SIde SMer SPlb WCHb WFar WGHP WGwG WJek WRHF WRha WSel WWye XPep
	- 'Minimalist'	CArn CBrm CLyd CMea ECha ELau ESis GBar LLWP LRHS MBow MBri MChe MHer NGHP NLAp NRya NSti SIde SPet SPlb SRot WBVN WCHb WHoo WPat WPer WSel WWye
	- 'Minimus'	see *T. serpyllum* 'Minimalist'
	- 'Minor'	CArn ECtt GBar GWCH LLWP MChe NMen NSla SBla SHDw WAbe WGwG WLin WTin XPep
N	- 'Minor Albus'	GAbr GBar
	- 'Minus'	see *T. serpyllum* 'Minor'
	- 'Petite'	EWes LLWP
N	- 'Pink Chintz' ♀H4	CBrm CHar CLyd CMea ECha ECtt EDAr ELau EPfP GBar GBuc GKir GPoy GTou LGro LLWP LRHS MBar MBri MHer NBlu NGHP NRya SBla SIng SPer SPlb WHoo WPer WWye
	- subsp. ***pulchellus***	LLWP
	- 'Purple Beauty'	see *T.* (Coccineus Group) 'Purple Beauty'
	- 'Purpurteppich'	see *T.* (Coccineus Group) 'Purpurteppich'
	- 'Pygmaeus'	LLWP
	- 'Rainbow Falls' (v)	CBod EOHP EPfP GBar LLWP MBow MChe MHer NGHP SHDw SIde WGHP WGwG
	- 'Red Carpet' **new**	NOrc
	- 'Red Elf'	see *T.* (Coccineus Group) 'Red Elf'
	- 'Roger's Snowdrift'	LLWP
N	- 'Roseus'	EOHP GBar SIde
N	- 'Russetings'	CBrm CLyd COkL ECtt EDAr ELau EPfP EPot EUnu GBar LLWP MBar MChe MHer NEgg NMen SIde SIng SRms WWpP WWye
N	- 'September'	LLWP MHer
	- 'Snowcarpet' **new**	LLWP
N	- 'Snowdrift'	CArn CMea CWan ECtt EDAr ELau EPfP EPot GBar GKev LEdu MBar MChe MHer NRya NSti SIde SPlb WAbe WCFE WGwG WJek WLin WPat WPer WWpP
N	- 'Splendens'	LLWP
	- 'Variegatus'	see *T.* 'Hartington Silver'
	- 'Vey'	EWes GBar GMaP LLWP MChe MHer SHDw SIng WCHb
	sibthorpii	CArn
N	'Silver Posie'	see *T. vulgaris* 'Silver Posie'
	'Snowdonia Ifor' **new**	LLWP
	'Snowdonia Imperial Beauty'	LLWP
	'Snowdonia Isolde' **new**	LLWP
	'Snowdonia Lass'	LLWP SHDw
	'Snowdonia Pearl' **new**	LLWP
	'Snowdonia Pedr' **new**	LLWP
	'Snowdonia Pink Gem'	LLWP
	'Snowdonia Rosie'	LLWP
	'Snowdonia Rowena'	LLWP
	'Snowman' **new**	SHDw
	'Swaledale'	LLWP
*	***taeniensis***	CArn
*	***valesiacus***	LLWP SHDw
§	***villosus***	ESis
	vulgaris	CArn CHby CSam CSev ECha EDAr ELau GPoy LAst LLWP MBar MBow MBri MChe MHer MWat NBlu NGHP NVic SDix SPer SPlb SWal WGHP WGwG WJek WPer XPep
	- ***albus***	GBar LLWP
	- 'Aureus' hort.	see *T. pulegioides* 'Goldentime'
	- 'Boule'	XPep
*	- 'Compactus'	IBal LLWP
	- 'Diamantis'	LLWP
	- 'Dorcas White'	LLWP MHer WPer
	- 'English Winter'	GBar SIde
§	- 'Erectus'	CArn CLyd CStu ETow GBar LLWP MHer WPer WWye
	- French	ELau LLWP MHer SHDw SPlb
	- 'French Summer'	SIde
	- 'Golden Pins'	CArn GBar
	- 'Haute Vallée de l'Aude'	XPep
	- 'Lemon Queen'	ELau
	- 'Lucy'	CPrp EOHP EUnu GBar LLWP
	- 'Pinewood'	LLWP MHer SIde SMHy
	- pink	LLWP
	- 'Saint Chinian Blanc'	XPep
	- 'Saint Chinian Rose'	XPep
§	- 'Silver Posie'	More than 30 suppliers
§	- 'Snow White'	ELau EWes LLWP SHDw SWal WJek
	'Widecombe' (v)	LLWP MHer SHDw
	zygis	CArn XPep

Tiarella (*Saxifragaceae*)

	'Black Ruby'	CHid
	'Black Snowflake'	GCai LBuc
	'Black Velvet' PBR	CBct EPyc GCai MLLN NCGa NLar SPer SRot
	'Bronze Baby'	NEgg
	'Butterfly Wings' **new**	MBnl NRnb
	collina	see *T. wherryi*
	cordifolia ♀H4	More than 30 suppliers
	- 'Eco Red Heart'	SSpi
	- 'Glossy'	CBct EBee GBuc GKir SSpi WPGP
	- 'Oakleaf'	CLAP EChP EMan MWgw NBro NEgg NSti SOkh WCAu
	- 'Rosalie'	see x *Heucherella alba* 'Rosalie'
	- 'Running Tapestry'	CFwr CLAP WMoo
	- 'Slick Rock'	ECha EPPr
	'Cygnet' PBR	CBct CLAP CRez EBee EMan EPPr EShb GCai LAst MLLN NCGa NEgg SHar SPer SPoG SRot WFar
	'Dark Star'	ECtt
	'Dunvegan'	EBee MLLN NRnb WFar WGHP WMoo WWeb
	'Elizabeth Oliver'	CLAP
	'Freckles'	MRav
	'Inkblot'	EBee EChP ELan MLLN NBro NRnb SHar SMac WCAu WFar WMoo WPnP
	'Iron Butterfly' PBR	More than 30 suppliers
	'Jeepers Creepers' PBR	GCai MHar NCob SHar
*	'Laciniate Runner'	CLAP
	'Martha Oliver'	CLAP EBee GBuc SBch WHal WPGP WTin
	'Mint Chocolate' PBR	More than 30 suppliers
	'Neon Lights'	CHar EBee MBnl NBro NCGa NCob NGdn SHar SPer SPoG SWvt WHlf
§	'Ninja' PBR	More than 30 suppliers
	'Petite Pink Bouquet'	GSki NGdn

'Pink Bouquet' CAbP CLAP EBee EBrs EChP ECtt EHrv EMan GSki LRHS MBNS MBnl MLLN MSph MWgw NDov NEgg NMyG SOkh SPla SVil WBVN WCot WFar WGor WMoo WPnP WWlt
'Pink Brushes' **new** NRnb
'Pink Skyrocket' GCai NCob SHar
'Pinwheel' EBee ECha LRHS MRav WTMC
'Pirate's Patch' **new** GCai
polyphylla ELan GAbr GBBs GBin LGro MGol MLLN MWat SBri SMac SWal WCru WFar WMoo
- 'Filigran' MWrn NLar
- 'Moorgrün' EBrs GCal WFar
- pink CLAP EHrv WGwG
- - BWJ 8088 WCru
'Running Tiger' **new** NRnb
'Skeleton Key' CLAP EBrs LRHS
'Skid's Variegated' (v) CBct EBee EChP ECtt EMan EShb GFlt LAst MBNS MSph NPro SGSe STes SWvt WCot
'Skyrocket' **new** EKen
'Spring Symphony'PBR CHar CLAP CWCL EBee EShb GBin GCai LSou MBri NBir NCGa NEgg NLar NMyG SHar SIng SPoG WFar
'Starfish' EBee MLLN NCob SHar WPrP
'Tiger Stripe' CLAP COtt EBee ECha ELan EMan ENot EPfP LRHS MRav MWrn NBro NEgg NRnb SPer SPur WFar WMoo WPnP WPop
trifoliata ELan MRav SBla WFar
unifoliata CHrt CMCo MSal
'Viking Ship'PBR see x *Heucherella* 'Viking Ship'
§ ***wherryi*** ♀H4 More than 30 suppliers
- 'Bronze Beauty' CBct CLAP CMea COtt EBee EChP EPPr EWTr GBuc GSki LAst MAvo MRav NDov NPro SAga SPla SSpi WAbe WBrk WCot WFar WGHP WHlf WMoo WPGP WPnP WWhi
- 'Green Velvet' ECha
- 'Heronswood Mist' (v) CAbP CBct CFir CHar EBee EChP GBri MBNS MLLN NBPC NBro NCGa NSti SWvt WCot WCra WHlf WWhi
- 'Montrose' CLAP WPGP

Tibouchina (*Melastomataceae*)

grandifolia CRHN
graveolens ERea
'Jules' CBcs ERea ESlt
organensis CBcs ERea GQui WPGP
paratropica CPle CRHN SSpi
semidecandra hort. see *T. urvilleana*
§ ***urvilleana*** ♀H1 CBcs CDoC CHEx CKno CRHN CSpe CTbh EBak ECre ELan ERea ESlt ISea MTis NCGa SAPC SArc SDnm SPer SRkn SRms SYvo WCot WGwG WMul
- 'Edwardsii' CSev EMan LSou MLan SMrm SUsu
- 'Rich Blue Sun' CSpe
- variegated (v) WCot

Tigridia ✿ (*Iridaceae*)

multiflora CFir
pavonia CAby CPLG CSpe ERea EUJe IGor LAma MBri SPet
- 'Lilacea' EBee

Tilia ✿ (*Tiliaceae*)

americana CLnd CMCN EBee NWea
- 'Dentata' CDul
- 'Nova' CDoC SBLw
amurensis CMCN GIBF
argentea see *T. tomentosa*
begoniifolia see *T. dasystyla*
chenmoui MBlu
chinensis CMCN
chingiana CDul CMCN GKir LRHS MBlu SBir SPoG
cordata ♀H4 CAgr CBcs CCVT CDul CLnd CSBt EBee ECrN ELan ENot EPfP GKir IMGH LBuc MSwo NBee NWea SBLw SHBN SPer WDin WMou WOrn
§ - 'Böhlje' CDul ECrN SBLw SLPl WMoo
- 'Dainty Leaf' CDul
- 'Erecta' see *T. cordata* 'Böhlje'
- 'Greenspire' ♀H4 CCVT CDoC CDul CLnd CTho CWib EBee ECrN ENot LRHS NBee SBLw WOrn
- 'Lico' WMou
- 'Morden' WMou
- 'Plymtree Gold' CDul
- 'Swedish Upright' CDul CLnd CTho
- 'Winter Orange' CDul CEnd CRez EBee GKir LRHS MBlu SBir SCoo WMou
§ ***dasystyla*** CLnd CMCN
x ***euchlora*** ♀H4 CAlb CBcs CCVT CDul CLnd CMCN EBee ECrN ENot EPfP GKir LAst MBri MWat NBee NWea SBLw SPer SSta WDin WFar WMou WOrn
x ***europaea*** CBcs CDul CLnd CRWN ECrN ELan NWea SBLw WMou
- 'Pallida' CDul CLnd CTho SBLw WMou
- 'Wratislaviensis' ♀H4 CDoC CDul CLnd CTho EPfP LRHS MAsh MBlu MBri NWea SMad WMou
x ***flavescens*** 'Glenleven' CDul SBLw
henryana CDoC CDul CEnd CMCN CTho CWib EBee EPfP ERod GKir IArd LRHS MBlu SBir WDin WMou WPGP
- var. ***subglabra*** WMou
§ ***heterophylla*** CLnd CMCN CTho LRHS
- var. ***michauxii*** CLnd
insularis CMCN MBlu WMou
japonica CDul CMCN WMou
kiusiana CMCN GKir WMou
mandshurica CMCN
maximowicziana CDul WPGP
mexicana WMou
miqueliana CMCN WMou
'Moltkei' CLnd CMCN WPGP
mongolica CDoC CDul CLnd CMCN CTho EBee ENot EPfP GKir SMHT WMou
monticola see *T. heterophylla*
oliveri CDul CMCN GKir MBlu NWea SBir WMou WPGP
paucicostata CMCN
'Petiolaris' ♀H4 CCVT CDoC CDul CEnd CLnd CMCN ELan EPfP EWTr GKir LRHS MBri MSwo NWea SBLw SHBN SPer SSta WDin WMou
platyphyllos CAlb CCVT CDul CLnd CMCN CSBt ECrN EPfP EWTr GKir LBuc NBee NWea SBLw SCoo SPer WDin WMou
- 'Aurea' CDul CLnd CTho ECrN MBlu WMou
- 'Corallina' see *T. platyphyllos* 'Rubra'
- 'Dakvorm' SBLw
- 'Delft' SBLw
- 'Erecta' see *T. platyphyllos* 'Fastigiata'
§ - 'Fastigiata' CDul CTho ECrN ENot SBLw SLPl

- 'Laciniata'	CDul CEnd CMCN CTho EBee GKir WMou
- 'Örebro'	SLPl
* - 'Pendula'	CTho
§ - 'Rubra' 🏆H4	CDoC CLnd CTho ECrN ENot EPfP GKir LBuc LRHS MBri MGos NWea SBLw SLPl WDin WFar WMou
- 'Tortuosa'	CDoC CTho
§ ***tomentosa***	CAlb CDul CLnd CMCN CTho ECrN ELan GKir IMGH NWea SBLw SEND WDin WMou
- 'Brabant' 🏆H4	CDoC ENot EPfP SBLw
tuan	CMCN WMou
x ***vulgaris***	see *T.* x *europaea*

Tillaea see *Crassula*

Tillandsia (*Bromeliaceae*)

aeranthos	EOas SChr
argentea 🏆H1	MBri
cyanea 🏆H1	LRHS MBri SMur
usneoides	CHal SHmp

Tinantia (*Commelinaceae*)

pringlei **new**	SSpi
- AIM 77	WCot

Titanopsis (*Aizoaceae*)

calcarea 🏆H1	EPfP EShb

Tithonia (*Asteraceae*)

rotundifolia 'Torch'	SMrm

Todea (*Osmundaceae*)

barbara	WRic

Tofieldia (*Melanthiaceae*)

pusilla	ERos

Tolmiea (*Saxifragaceae*)

menziesii	ECha EWTr LGro MBNS MBri MWgw SPer WBrE WMoo WWpP
- 'Goldsplash'	see *T. menziesii* 'Taff's Gold'
- 'Maculata'	see *T. menziesii* 'Taff's Gold'
§ - 'Taff's Gold' (v) 🏆H4	CRow CWan EBee ECha EHoe EMar EOHP GAbr GMaP IHMH MBri MHer NBid NGdn NMRc NVic SPlb WEas WHoo WMoo WTin WWpP WWye
- 'Variegata'	see *T. menziesii* 'Taff's Gold'

Tolpis (*Asteraceae*)

barbata	SUsu

Tonestus (*Asteraceae*)

§ ***lyallii***	NLAp WPer
§ ***pygmaeus***	CStu NLAp

Toona (*Meliaceae*)

§ ***sinensis***	CDul CEnd CMCN CPle CTho CWib EPfP EPla EWTr IDee SBrw WBVN WFar WMul WPGP
- 'Flamingo' (v)	CBcs EPfP IDee LRHS SBig SMad

Torenia (*Scrophulariaceae*)

concolor var. ***formosana*** B&SWJ 124	MOak WCru
Pink Moon = 'Dantopkmn'	LAst
Purple Moon = 'Dantopur' (Summer Wave Series)	LAst
Summer Wave Series	SCoo

Torreya (*Taxaceae*)

californica	CDul
grandis	CBcs EGFP

Townsendia (*Asteraceae*)

alpigena var. ***alpigena***	CGra EHyt
condensata	CPBP
exscapa	EHyt
formosa	NBir
hirsuta **new**	GKev
hookeri	CGra EHyt
incana	CPBP EHyt
leptotes	CGra CPBP EHyt
mensana	GKev
montana	see *T. alpigena* var. *alpigena*
nuttallii	CGra
§ ***rothrockii***	CGra CPBP EHyt NMen
spathulata	CGra CPBP EHyt
wilcoxiana misapplied	see *T. rothrockii*

Toxicodendron (*Anacardiaceae*)

vernicifluum	see *Rhus verniciflua*

Trachelium (*Campanulaceae*)

§ ***asperuloides***	EHyt WAbe
caeruleum 🏆H1	ERea SGar WBrE
- 'Purple Umbrella'	CHby CPLG EMan
- 'White Umbrella'	EMan
jacquinii subsp. ***rumelianum***	CPBP NWCA SBch WPat

Trachelospermum ✿ (*Apocynaceae*)

from Nanking, China	SLon
§ ***asiaticum*** 🏆H2-3	More than 30 suppliers
- B&SWJ 4814	WCru
* - 'Aureum'	ERea LRHS
- 'Golden Memories'	EPfP SMur SPoG SSpi SSta
- 'Goshiki' (v)	ERea GQui MGos SBrw SSpi
- var. ***intermedium***	WPGP
- - B&SWJ 8733	WCru
- 'Nagaba' (v)	SSpi
- 'Theta'	SSpi
jasminoides 🏆H2-3	More than 30 suppliers
- B&SWJ 5117	WCru
§ - 'Japonicum'	CRHN CSPN EBee GCal IArd LRHS SBra SBrw SLPl SLon SPla SSpi
- 'Major'	CSPN SSpi WBcn
* - 'Oblanceolatum'	GCal
- 'Tricolor' (v)	CBcs CRHN EBee IArd SBrw SSpi SSta SWvt
- 'Variegatum' (v) 🏆H2-3	More than 30 suppliers
- 'Waterwheel'	SBra SPoG SSpi WBcn WPGP WSHC
- 'Wilsonii'	More than 30 suppliers
majus misapplied	see *T. jasminoides* 'Japonicum'
majus Nakai	see *T. asiaticum*

Trachycarpus (*Arecaceae*)

§ ***fortunei*** 🏆H3-4	More than 30 suppliers
- 'Nanus'	MGos
latisectus	CBrP CKob EAmu LPJP NPal SBig WMul
martianus	CKob CTrC EAmu EExo LPJP SBig SChr WMul
nanus	CKob
oreophilus	WMul
takil	CBrP CKob EAmu EExo LPJP NPal SBig WMul
wagnerianus	CBrP CPHo CTrC EAmu EBee EPla LPJP NPal WMul WPGP

Trachymene (*Apiaceae*)

***coerulea* new**	CSpe

Trachystemon (*Boraginaceae*)

orientalis	CBre CHEx CHid CPLG CSev ECha EGol ELan EPfP EWTr MHar MRav NBid SDnm SLon WBor WCAu WCot WCru WDyG WFar WHer WMoo WPnP WWye

Tradescantia ✿ (*Commelinaceae*)

	albiflora	see *T. fluminensis*
	x *andersoniana* W. Ludwig & Rohw. nom. inval.	see *T.* Andersoniana Group
§	Andersoniana Group	IHMH MSal NFor NJOw SPet SWal WPer WWeb WWpP
	- 'Baby Doll'	EBrs GKir
	- 'Bilberry Ice'	More than 30 suppliers
	- 'Blanca'	MWrn NChi SMar
	- 'Blue and Gold'	CBcs CBct CFwr EBee ECtt EHoe EMFW EMon ENot EPPr EPfP EVFa GBuc LAst LRHS MBNS NEgg NPri NSti SGSe SPla SPoG SWvt WCAu WCot
	- 'Blue Stone'	CMdw CMea CRez ECha ECtt ERou LBBr MBNS NCGa NPri SOkh SRms WFar WMoo WTin
	- 'Bridal Veil'	CHll
	- 'Caerulea Plena'	see *T. virginiana* 'Caerulea Plena'
	- Carmine Glow	see *T.* (Andersoniana Group) 'Karminglut'
	- 'Charlotte'	CElw CStr EBrs ECGP EChP ECha EMFW GSki LRHS MOne MWgw NBro NEgg NGdn NMyG SBch SChu SOkh WCAu WMnd WTMC
	- 'Concord Grape'	More than 30 suppliers
	- 'Danielle'	EChP ENot EPfP GMac NGdn NMyG NRnb WTMC
	- 'Domaine de Courson'	LPio
	- 'In the Navy'	EBee ERou WCot WDyG
	- 'Innocence'	More than 30 suppliers
	- 'Iris Prichard'	CM&M CPrp EBee EChP ELan EPfP EPla ERou GMaP LRHS NCGa NLar WFar
	- 'Isis' 🏆H4	CBcs CHar CMHG CPrp CSBt EBee EBrs EChP ECtt ELan EPfP EPla GKir LRHS MRav MWgw NBir NCGa NGdn NOrc SBod SChu SPer SPla SWvt WMnd WTin
	- 'J.C. Weguelin' 🏆H4	EMil EPfP GKir LRHS NBir NDlv SRms WMnd
§	- 'Karminglut'	CHar EBee ECtt ELan EMan EPfP ERou GKir GMaP IHMH LRHS MBri MNrw NBir NGdn NOrc NVic SGSe WHoo WWye
	- 'Leonora'	COIW EBrs ENot EPfP ERou LRHS NLar
	- 'Little Doll'	CElw ECtt EMan ERou GBri GKir GSki LAst LRHS MBri MDKP MHar MLLN MNFA MSph MWrn NBPC NBro NCGa NPri NRnb SOkh WCot WFar WHil WTMC WWhi
	- 'Little White Doll'	CM&M CPrp CStr EBee ERou GMac GSki LAst MDKP MNFA MSph MSte NBPC SHGN SOkh SPoG SWvt WCot WFar WLin
	- 'Mariella'	EBee GMac
	- 'Mrs Loewer'	EMon
	- 'Osprey' 🏆H4	More than 30 suppliers
	- 'Pauline'	CHar ECtt EMan EPla ERou GKir GSki LAst LRHS MNrw MRav NBir NLar SChu SPoG SWvt WFar WHoo WTel WTin
	- 'Perinne's Pink' **new**	EMan EPfP EWTr LBuc NSti SUsu WHil
	- 'Pink Chablis'	EBee ERou NBro WHil
	- 'Purewell Giant'	EBee ECot EMil ERou NBro NDlv NEgg NLar SChu SPer SWvt WGor WKif WMnd
	- 'Purple Dome'	CHar EBee ECtt EMFW EPla GKir GMaP LAst LRHS MHar MRav MWgw NBir NBro NCGa NGdn SMac SPla SPoG STes WMnd WTin WWye
	- 'Red Grape'	EBee EBrs ECtt ENot ERou GKir GSki LRHS MBNS NCGa NPro NSti WBor WCAu
	- 'Rubra'	CPrp EBee EChP EPfP ERou GSki MOne MWgw NDlv NOrc NPri SBod SChu SRms WMoo
	- 'Satin Doll'	EBee EMan ENot SPoG
	- 'Sweet Kate'	EMan ERou MCCP MDKP MSph NBro SAga SHop WBor
	- 'Sylvana'	CM&M EBee GMac SApp WCAu WHil
	- 'Valour'	CSBt CWat EBee LRHS WFar
	- 'Zwanenburg Blue'	CM&M EBee EChP ECha ECtt ELan EMan ENot ERou GKir GMac LRHS MWgw NCGa NRnb SBch SGSe SPlb WMnd WTel
	'Angel Eyes'	GSki MDKP
	'Baerbel'	CSBt EBee GSki SBod
	bracteata	ETow
	brevicaulis	ECha EMFP EPla ERos GBuc LRHS MTho NBro
	'Bridesmaid'	MOak
	canaliculata	see *T. ohiensis*
	cerinthoides	CHal
	fluminensis	SChr
	- 'Albovittata'	CHal
	- 'Aurea' 🏆H1	CHal MBri
	- 'Laekenensis' (v)	CHal MBri
	- 'Maiden's Blush' (v)	CHal CSpe EShb EWin MOak SGar SRms WFoF
	- 'Quicksilver' (v) 🏆H1	CHal MBri
	- 'Tricolor Minima' 🏆H1	CHal
	multiflora	see *Tripogandra multiflora*
	navicularis	see *Callisia navicularis*
§	***ohiensis***	CFee EBee EMan LPBA MAvo
§	***pallida*** 🏆H2-3	CHal IBlr
§	- 'Purpurea' 🏆H2-3	EShb MOak
	pendula	see *T. zebrina*
	'Purple Sabre'	CBcs LAst
	purpurea	see *T. pallida* 'Purpurea'
	sillamontana 🏆H1	CHal EOHP MBri
	spathacea	EShb
	- 'Vittata' 🏆H1	CHal
	tricolor	see *T. zebrina*
	virginiana	CM&M MWhi SGar
	- 'Alba'	GCal WPer
§	- 'Caerulea Plena' (d)	CM&M CMHG EBee EChP ELan EMan EPfP EPla ERou GSki LRHS MRav NCGa NChi NLRH SChu SPoG SRms WCra WFar WHil
	- 'Rubra'	CM&M SPet SPlb
§	***zebrina*** 🏆H1	CHal SChr
	- ***discolor***	CHal
	- ***pendula***	see *T. zebrina*
	- 'Purpusii' 🏆H1	CHal SRms
	- 'Quadricolor' (v) 🏆H1	CHal

Tragopogon (*Asteraceae*)

crocifolius	CSpe EMan WCot
porrifolius	ILis SECG

pratensis CArn NMir

Trapa (*Trapaceae*)

natans NArg WFar

Trautvetteria (*Ranunculaceae*)

carolinensis GEdr WCru
var. ***japonica***
- var. ***occidentalis*** GEdr GKir IFro WCru

Trevesia (*Araliaceae*)

palmata CKob WMul

Trichopetalum (*Anthericaceae*)

§ **plumosum** CBro CMon

Trichosanthes (*Cucurbitaceae*)

kirilowii new MSal

Tricuspidaria see *Crinodendron*

Tricyrtis ✿ (*Convallariaceae*)

B&SWJ 6705 MSph
CC 3454 WCot
'Adbane' CBct CLAP EBla ELan EMan EWes GBuc GKir LRHS MMHG NLar SGSe WCot WFar WRha
affinis CLAP EBla GAbr GBuc GGar NLar
- B&SWJ 2804 WCru
- B&SWJ 5640 WCru
- B&SWJ 5847 WCru
- B&SWJ 6182 WCru
- 'Variegata' see *T.* 'Variegata'
'Amanagowa' CLAP WFar
bakeri see *T. latifolia*
dilatata see *T. macropoda*
'Eco Gold Spangles' SSpi
'Empress' CBct CPLG EBee EBla EMan EPfP ERou EWTr EWes GCai LBuc LSou MAvo MBnl MCCP NArg NCob NEgg SGSe SMrm SPoG WPop
flava EBrs WCru
formosana ♀H4 More than 30 suppliers
- B&SWJ 306 CLAP EBla MNrw WCot WCru WFar WRos
- B&SWJ 355 WCru WFar
- B&SWJ 3073 WCru
- B&SWJ 3616 WCru
- B&SWJ 3635 WFar
- B&SWJ 3712 WCru WFar
- B&SWJ 6705 CLAP WCru WPrP
- B&SWJ 6741 WCru
- B&SWJ 6905 WCru
- B&SWJ 6970 WCru
- dark GAbr GBBs GKir WFar
- 'Dark Beauty' CDes CLAP EBee EHrv EMan EMar ERou EWTr GFlt GSki LRHS MBnl MBri MCCP MTis SPur SUsu WFar WPrP
- 'Gilt Edge' (v) CBct CPLG CRez EBee EBla EChP EMar EPfP EPyc ERou EWTr GCai LAst LSou MAvo MBNS MBnl MCCP MDKP MDun NBid NBro NEgg NGdn NMyG NPri NSti SGSe WPop WPrP
- f. ***glandosa*** B&SWJ 7084 new WCru
- 'Lodge Farm' EBla
- pale CBct GBBs LRHS WFar
- 'Purple Beauty' CBct CFwr EBee MDKP
- 'Samurai' (v) CLAP CMil EBee EBla EMan EPPr ERou EVFa EWes NCGa WCot
- 'Shelley's' CBct CLAP CPLG GCal NBro WPrP
- 'Small Wonder' WCru
§ - Stolonifera Group CBcs CBro CM&M CMHG EBee EBrs EHrv ELan EMar EPfP LEdu LRHS MRav MWgw NEgg NGdn NSti SDix SPoG WFar WMnd WPnP WWeb
- 'Variegata' (v) CBct CBro CLAP EBla GBBs LEdu NBir WBor WCru WFar
'Harlequin' NLar WFar
§ **hirta** More than 30 suppliers
- B&SWJ 2827 WCru
§ - 'Alba' CSam EHrv ELan GEdr SGSe WFar
* - 'Albomarginata' (v) CPrp EBee EBla EChP EMar EPPr EPfP EVFa LBuc MCCP MNFA MTis NCGa SBch SPoG SSpi SWvt WCAu WMnd WPGP
- 'Golden Gleam' CHea EBee EBla WCot WFar
- hybrids CM&M WFar
- 'Kinkazan' EBla WFar
- 'Makinoi Gold' WFar
- var. ***masamunei*** WCru
- 'Matsukaze' CLAP CPom WFar
- 'Miyazaki' CBct CFir CHea CHid CLAP CPom EBee EBla ELan EMan GBuc LRHS MHer MNrw NCGa NLar SMac SMrm WFar
* - 'Nana' WFar
- 'Silver Blue' WFar
- 'Taiwan Atrianne' CSam EBla GAbr MAvo MBri MDKP
- 'Variegata' (v) CBct CLAP EBrs EMan EWes GBuc SBla SMad SUsu WCot WCru WFar WPnP WPrP
- 'White Flame' (v) WCot
N Hototogisu CBro CLAP CMea CPom EBla ELan EMar EPPr EPza GAbr GMac LRHS MCCP MNFA MTho NBir NCGa NEgg SDnm SPav SUsu WCAu WFar WHil WMnd WPnP
ishiiana CDes CLAP EBee EBla EMar WCru WFar WPGP
- var. ***surugensis*** EBla WCru WFar
'Ivory Queen' WFar
japonica see *T. hirta*
'Kohaku' CBct CLAP CPom EBee EBla ELan ENot NPro SPav WCot WCru WFar WPGP
lasiocarpa CBct CLAP LEdu
- B&SWJ 3635 CLAP CMil CPom EBla WCru WFar
- B&SWJ 6861 WCru
- B&SWJ 7013 WCru WPrP
- B&SWJ 7014 WCru
- B&SWJ 7104 WCru
§ **latifolia** CBct EBrs EChP ELan EPPr EPot GAbr GBBs GEdr GFlt GGar GKev GMaP MNrw NGdn NLar WAul WCot WCru WFar
'Lemon Lime' (v) CBct CBro CLAP EBla EMan ENot LRHS MDKP MSph NPro SBla SGSe SPav SUsu WFar
'Lightning Strike' (v) EBee LBuc MDKP MDun NCob NMyG WCot
'Lilac Towers' CBct ELan GBBs GKir NLar SBri WCru WFar WPnP
macrantha GAbr GBBs GFlt GGar
§ - subsp. ***macranthopsis*** CBct CLAP EBla EPot GEdr SSpi WCru WDyG WFar
macranthopsis see *T. macrantha* subsp. *macranthopsis*
* **macrocarpa** CFwr EChP WFar
N **macropoda** CBct CFwr CHid CSam EBee EBla EDAr ELan EMan EPfP GAbr GBuc GMaP ITim LAst LEdu MAvo MCCP

	NGdn NWCA SGSe SMac SMad WBor WFar WMnd
- B&SWJ 1271	CBct EBla WCru
- B&SWJ 5013	WCru
- B&SWJ 5556	WCru
- B&SWJ 5847	WCru
- B&SWJ 6209	WCru
- B&SWJ 8700	WCru
- B&SWJ 8829	WCru
- from Yungi Temple, China	CLAP EBee EBla EPPr WCot
- variegated (v)	WCru
maculata	CPLG
- HWJCM 470	WCru
- HWJK 2010	WCru
- HWJK 2411	WCru
nana	CLAP GKev LEdu WCru
- 'Raven's Back'	WCru
ohsumiensis	CBct CDes CLAP CPom EBee EBla ECha EMan EPot GBuc GEdr LEdu MTho NGby SBch SUsu WCru WFar WPGP
perfoliata	CLAP EBla LEdu WCru WFar
setouchiensis **new**	WCru
'Shimone'	CHid CLAP CPLG CStu EBla ECha ELan GBuc SGSe WFar WKif WPrP
stolonifera	see *T. formosana* Stolonifera Group
'Tojen'	More than 30 suppliers
'Toki-no-mai'	EBla
'Tresahor White'	CBct
§ 'Variegata' (*affinis* hybrid) (v)	WCot WCru WFar WPnP
'Washfields'	CBct WPGP
'White Towers'	More than 30 suppliers

Trientalis (*Primulaceae*)

europaea	SOkd
- rosea	CNat

Trifolium (*Papilionaceae*)

alpinum	WSan
badium	GBri MMHG
incarnatum	MHer SUsu
ochroleucon	CElw CFwr CHea EBee EChP EHrv EMar EShb EWTr GBri GFlt GLil GMaP LPhx MCCP MWgw MWrn NCGa NGHP NSti SSvw STes WCot WHil WMoo WSan
pannonicum	CFir CMea EBee EChP EHrv EMon EVFa GCal MLLN MSte NCot SEND SOkh SUsu WFar WPGP WPen WSHC WTin
pratense	MHer SECG
- 'Dolly North'	see *T. pratense* 'Susan Smith'
- 'Ice Cool'	see *T. repens* 'Green Ice'
- 'Nina'	CBgR CNat EBee EMan WWye
§ - 'Susan Smith' (v)	CElw CRow EBee EChP EHoe EMan EMon EShb EVFa EWes EWin LRHS MLLN MNrw MOak NGHP WCHb WFar WWpP
repens	COld EHrv WCAu
- 'Cherhill'	CNat
- 'Douglas Dawson'	EMan LDai
- 'Dragon's Blood'	MBNS NEgg NPro
- 'Gold Net'	see *T. pratense* 'Susan Smith'
- 'Good Luck'	CNat CRow MTho WWye
§ - 'Green Ice'	CBre CRow EBee EChP EMan EWin GMac MRav MTho NBir NSti WCHb WDyG WFar WHer WWye
- 'Harlequin' (v)	CBre EBee EWin GMac MAvo MFOX MHer MTho WCot WFar WPer WWpP WWye
- pale pink	CBgR
- 'Pentaphyllum'	see *T. repens* 'Quinquefolium'
- 'Purple Velvet'	MFOX
- 'Purpurascens'	CArn CBre GGar GMac ILis LRHS MAvo MBNS MHer MWgw NLsd NSti SPoG WKif WWhi
§ - 'Purpurascens Quadrifolium'	CMea CNic CStu CWan EBee EChP ECha EDAr EGra EUJe EVFa EWes NBid NEgg NGHP NMir NPer SIde SIng SPer SPlb WCHb WFar WRHF WWpP WWye
- 'Quadrifolium'	EHoe
§ - 'Quinquefolium'	EBee IHMH
- 'Tetraphyllum Purpureum'	see *T. repens* 'Purpurascens Quadrifolium'
* - 'Velvet and Baize' (v)	CNat
- 'Wheatfen'	CBre CRow EBee EMan EWin GMac MRav MTho NDov NGHP NPer WCHb WCot WDyG
- 'William'	CBre EBee EMan EWin MAvo MRav WCot WWye
rubens	More than 30 suppliers
- 'Peach Pink'	EBee EChP EMan EMon EShb LPhx LSou MHar MMHG STes SUsu WCot
- 'Red Feathers'	CFwr EWin MAvo SGSe
'White Bunnies' **new**	NDov

Triglochin (*Juncaginaceae*)

maritimum	CRWN
palustre	CRWN

Trigonella (*Papilionaceae*)

foenum-graecum	CArn MSal SIde WLHH

Trigonotis (*Boraginaceae*)

rotundifolia	EMan

Trillidium see *Trillium*

Trillium ✿ (*Trilliaceae*)

albidum	CLAP EHyt EPot GBuc GCrs GFlt GKir GMaP ITim NMen SSpi WCru
angustipetalum	CLAP GEdr
- hybrid	SSpi
apetalon	LAma WCru
camschatcense	CLAP GEdr GIBF GKir LAma SSpi WCru
- from China **new**	CFwr WWst
- from Japan **new**	WWst
§ ***catesbyi***	CBro CLAP EBee EHrv EPot GCrs GEdr GKir IBal LAma MNFA NMyG SSpi WCru
cernuum	CLAP GKir IBal LAma WCru
chloropetalum	CBro ETow GKir ITim SBla SOkd SSpi WCru WKif WPGP
§ - var. ***giganteum*** ♀H4	CLAP GBuc GEdr GKev NDov NMen NWoo SSpi WAbe WCru
- 'Ice Creme'	SSpi
- var. ***rubrum***	see *T. chloropetalum* var. *giganteum*
- 'Volcano'	SSpi
- white	CLAP ECha GFlt IBal SSpi
cuneatum	More than 30 suppliers
- red	GCrs
cuneatum x ***luteum***	EMar EPot
decipiens	SSpi
erectum ♀H4	More than 30 suppliers
§ - f. ***albiflorum***	CBro CFir CLAP EBrs EPot GBuc GEdr GKir LAma SSpi WCru
- 'Beige'	CLAP ETow GBBs GCrs GEdr GSki IBal
- f. ***luteum***	CBct CLAP EPfP LAma SSpi WCru

- purple-flowered **new** IBal
- red-flowered **new** IBal
flexipes CBro CLAP EPot GCrs GEdr GFlt GKir IBal LAma WCru
flexipes* x *erectum CLAP GBuc GKir NMen SSpi WCru
govanianum GFlt LAma SOkd WCru
grandiflorum ♀H4 More than 30 suppliers
- dwarf **new** NHar
- 'Flore Pleno' (d) ♀H4 CLAP ECha ETow GBuc GKir MTho SBla SCnR SOkd
- 'Jenny Rhodes' IBlr
- f. ***roseum*** CLAP GKir
- 'Snowbunting' (d) EBrs GCrs SOkd
kurabayashii CFil CFir CLAP GFlt ITim SSpi WPGP
ludovicianum SSpi
§ ***luteum*** ♀H4 More than 30 suppliers
ovatum CLAP GCrs GGar GKev GKir LAma NMen WHal
- from Oregon CLAP
- var. ***hibbersonii*** CBro CStu EHyt ETow GBuc GCrs GEdr NMen SBla WHal
- 'Roy Elliott' EPot NBir
***ovatum* x *rivale* new** ITim
parviflorum CLAP GEdr NMen SSpi
pusillum CLAP ELan EPot GBBs GEdr GKev IBal ITim SSpi
- var. ***pusillum*** GCrs SBla
- var. ***virginianum*** CBro CLAP LAma WAbe WCru
recurvatum CBcs CLAP CPen EHrv EMar EPot EUJe GAbr GEdr GKir GSki IBal LAma MDun NMen SHBN SPer WCru WFar WPnP
rivale ♀H3 CBos CBro CElw CLAP CStu EHrv EPot GBuc GCrs GKev ITim LAma NMen SBla SOkd SSpi WAbe WFar
- pink **new** GEdr NMen
- 'Purple Heart' CLAP EPot GCrs GEdr
rugelii CBro CLAP GBuc GCrs GEdr GKir GMaP LAma NMen SSpi WCru
- Askival hybrids CLAP GBuc GCrs GFlt GKir NMen SSpi
rugelii* x *vaseyi GKir SSpi
sessile CFwr CLAP CMea EPot EUJe EWTr GAbr GBBs GBuc GEdr GFlt GKev GKir GSki IBal LAma MAvo NBir NCGa NMyG SSpi WCAu WCru WFar WHlf WKif WPnP WSHC WSan WShi
- var. ***luteum*** see *T. luteum*
- purple GKir
- 'Rubrum' see *T. chloropetalum* var. *giganteum*
simile CLAP GCrs GKir SSpi
smallii GEdr LAma WCru
stamineum CLAP EBee EMar EPot GEdr GFlt GKir IBal MDun SSpi
stylosum see *T. catesbyi*
sulcatum CBro CLAP EBee EPot GBBs GBuc GCrs GEdr GGar GKir GMaP IBal NMen SSpi WCru WFar
tschonoskii CLAP GEdr LAma SSpi WCot WCru
- var. ***himalaicum*** WCru
underwoodii SSpi
undulatum CLAP EBee EPot GEdr GFlt GGar GKir IBal LAma WCru
vaseyi CBro CLAP EBee EMar EPot GBBs GBuc GCrs GEdr GFlt GKir LAma NMen SSpi WCru
viride CLAP GBBs IBal NGby WCru WFar WPnP
viridescens CLAP GEdr LAma SSpi WFar

Trinia (*Apiaceae*)
glauca EBee

Triosteum (*Caprifoliaceae*)
himalayanum GKev
- BWJ 7907 WCru
pinnatifidum CDes CLAP GCal GKev

Tripetaleia (*Ericaceae*)
§ ***bracteata*** GKir

Tripleurospermum (*Asteraceae*)
§ ***maritimum*** XPep

Tripogandra (*Commelinaceae*)
§ ***multiflora*** CHal

Tripsacum (*Poaceae*)
dactyloides EPPr

Tripterospermum (*Gentianaceae*)
* aff. ***chevalieri*** B&SWJ 8359 WCru
cordifolium B&SWJ 081 WCru
fasciculatum B&SWJ 7197 WCru
aff. ***hirticalyx*** B&SWJ 8264 WCru
japonicum WAbe WBor
- B&SWJ 1168 WCru
lanceolatum B&SWJ 085 WCru
taiwanense B&SWJ 1205 WCru

Tripterygium (*Celastraceae*)
regelii CBcs CFil CPLN NLar WPGP
- B&SWJ 5453 WCru
***wilfordii* new** CPLN WCru

Trisetum (*Poaceae*)
distichophyllum EHoe
flavescens CBig GFor NBre

Tristagma (*Alliaceae*)
* ***nivale*** f. ***nivale*** F&W 9612 **new** WCot

Tristellateia (*Malpighiaceae*)
australasiae CPLN

Triteleia (*Alliaceae*)
***bridgesii* new** CMon WCot
californica see *Brodiaea californica*
§ 'Corrina' CAvo EBee MNrw SBch SMeo
grandiflora WCot
hendersonii NNS 00-738 **new** WCot
hyacinthina EBee ERos LAma LRHS WCot
ixioides EBee EBrs ERos
- var. ***scabra*** ETow
- 'Splendens' EBee
- 'Starlight' CAvo CFwr EBee EPPr EPot GBBs GFlt SBch WCot WHil
§ ***laxa*** CAvo CMea LAma
- NNS 95-495 WCot
- 'Allure' EBee
§ - 'Koningin Fabiola' CMea CTri EBee EBrs EMan GFlt LAma MBri NBir SBch SMeo WBrE WCot WLin
* - var. ***nimia*** NNS 00-743 **new** WCot
- Queen Fabiola see *T. laxa* 'Koningin Fabiola'
§ ***peduncularis*** EBee GKir LAma WCot

- NNS 95-499	WCot
x ***tubergenii***	EBee LAma
uniflora	see *Ipheion uniflorum*

Trithrinax (*Arecaceae*)

acanthocoma	CBrP LPJP SBig
campestris	CBrP CTrC EAmu SBig WMul

Tritoma see *Kniphofia*

Tritonia (*Iridaceae*)

bakeri subsp. ***lilacina*** NNS 00-745 **new**	WCot
crocata ♀H2-3	CPou LPio NMen WHer WHil
- 'Baby Doll'	CDes EBee
- 'Bridal Veil'	EPot
- 'Pink Sensation'	CDes EBee EPot WCot WHil
- 'Prince of Orange'	CDes CPou
- 'Princess Beatrix'	CDes WCot
- 'Serendipity'	CDes EBee
§ ***disticha*** subsp. ***rubrolucens***	More than 30 suppliers
laxifolia	CPne EBee EPot
lineata	CDes CPou EBee WPGP WPrP
pallida	SPlb
rosea	see *T. disticha* subsp. *rubrolucens*
securigera	GGar

Tritoniopsis (*Iridaceae*)

pulchra	CDes

Trochetiopsis (*Sterculiaceae*)

§ ***ebenus***	CFil WPGP
melanoxylon misapplied	see *T. ebenus*
melanoxylon (Sol. ex Sims) Marais	CFil EShb

Trochocarpa (*Epacridaceae*)

thymifolia	SOkd WAbe
- white-flowered	SOkd WAbe

Trochodendron (*Trochodendraceae*)

aralioides	CBcs CDoC CFil CHEx CTho CWib EBee EPfP GKir IMGH LRHS MGos SAPC SArc SBrw SHGC SLPl SLon SMad SReu SSpi SSta WCot WDin WPGP
- B&SWJ 6727 from Taiwan	WCru

Trollius (*Ranunculaceae*)

ACE 1187	GEdr
acaulis	EBee EWes GAbr MTho NLAp NRya WFar WPat
asiaticus	GBuc GKir
aff. ***buddae*** BWJ 7958	WCru
§ ***chinensis***	EBee ECha GCal GKev IHMH NChi SBla SRms
- 'Golden Queen' ♀H4	More than 30 suppliers
x ***cultorum*** 'Alabaster'	More than 30 suppliers
- - seedlings	SSpi
- 'Baudirektor Linne'	MRav NGdn WFar
- Bressingham hybrids	WFar
- 'Byrne's Giant'	WFar WPnP
- 'Canary Bird'	ELan EMil EPfP GBri NGdn SMur SRms WCot
- 'Cheddar'	COtt ENot ERou MBri MCCP MRav MTis NBro NGdn NLar NPro SMHy SOkh SUsu WCot WCra WFar WPnP
- 'Commander-in-chief'	CDes WFar WPGP WPnP
- 'Earliest of All'	CDWL CSBt CSam GKir LRHS MBri MSte NGby NGdn SPer SRms WCra WFar
- 'Etna'	CDWL EBee EChP ERou GKir SPet WFar WLin WPnP WSan
§ - 'Feuertroll'	CDWL ECha EMar EPPr MBNS NCGa NCob NGby NPro SHar SMur WCra WFar WHoo
- Fireglobe	see *T.* x *cultorum* 'Feuertroll'
- 'Glory of Leiden'	EBee
- 'Golden Cup'	ECot NBir NGdn
- 'Golden Monarch'	WFar
- 'Goldquelle' ♀H4	EHon SMur WWpP
- 'Goliath'	NCob WFar
- 'Helios'	CSam ECha SBla
- 'Lemon Queen'	CDWL CWat EChP EMan EPfP ERou GCal GKir GMaP LPBA LRHS MBri MNFA MRav MTis NBlu NFor NRnb SPer SPoG WCAu WFar WPnP WSan
- 'Meteor'	WFar
- 'Orange Crest'	EBee GCal WFar
- 'Orange Globe'	GAbr NCob NGby SMrm SOkh WFar WWeb
- 'Orange Princess' ♀H4	CDWL CSBt CWat EBee EMFW ENot EPfP ERou GBin GKir GMaP LRHS MCCP MSte NBro NLar NPri SPer SRms WAul WPnP
- 'Orange Queen'	SWvt
- 'Prichard's Giant'	CDWL CM&M CRez EBee EChP ELan EMan EMar NBro NGby NRnb SPoG WFar
- 'Salamander'	SMur
§ - 'Superbus' ♀H4	CDes CFwr CM&M CPSs EBee EChP EHol ELan EPfP GKir GMaP LAst MBNS NGdn NRnb SPer SSpi WFar WLin WMoo
- 'T. Smith'	NBro NGby WCot WFar
* - 'Taleggio'	EMon NLar
- 'Yellow Beauty'	SMer WFar
europaeus	More than 30 suppliers
- 'Superbus'	see *T.* x *cultorum* 'Superbus'
hondoensis	EBrs EPPr GBin GIBF GKir NBur NLar NPro
laxus	EWes NLar
- 'Albiflorus' **new**	NWCA
ledebourii misapplied	see *T. chinensis*
* ***orientalis*** **new**	GIBF
pumilus	EBee EBrs ECha ELan GCrs GMaP LBee LRHS MHer NChi NJOw NRya NWCA SPer SUsu WFar WPer WWeb
- ACE 1818	EPot GBuc WCot
- 'Wargrave'	NMen
riederianus	EBrs GKir
stenopetalus	EChP ECha EWes GCal GKir MBri MRav NRnb SHar WFar WPnP
yunnanensis	EBrs GBuc GIBF GKev GKir LRHS NBid NGby WFar WPnP WWpP
- CD&R 2097	WCru
- f. ***eupetalus*** BWJ 7614	WCru

Tropaeolum ✿ (*Tropaeolaceae*)

azureum	GKev LSou
beuthii F&W 8990 **new**	WCot
brachyceras	CSec NLar WCot
ciliatum ♀H1	CBro CFil CFir CPLN CSam CStu ELan EPot GCal MTho NSti WBor WCot WCru WFar WHer WNor WPGP
hookerianum subsp. ***austropurpureum***	CFil ERos
- subsp. ***hookerianum***	CFil
- - F&W 8630	WCot
- - F&W 9467	WPGP
incisum	CFil SOkd WCot

	lepidum	GFlt WCot
	majus	WSel
	– Alaska Series (v) ♀H3	CPrp SIde WJek WSel
*	– 'Clive Innes'	ERea
	– 'Crimson Beauty'	CSpe
§	– 'Darjeeling Double' (d) ♀H4	EShb EWin LRHS WCot WCru
	– 'Darjeeling Gold' (d)	see *T. majus* 'Darjeeling Double'
	– 'Empress of India'	CPrp LRHS WBor WEas WJek
	– 'Forest Flame'	LRHS
	– 'Hermine Grashoff' (d) ♀H2-3	CSWP CSpe ERea EWin LRHS NPer
	– 'Margaret Long' (d)	CSpe EWin GCal LRHS SBch WCot
	– 'Melba Yellow' **new**	LSou
	– 'Peach Melba' **new**	LSou
*	– 'Peaches and Cream'	CPrp WJek
	– 'Red Wonder'	CSWP CSpe EWin LRHS LSou NPri SMrm
	– 'Ruffled Apricot'	CSpe
	– 'Sunset Pink' **new**	LSou
	– Tom Thumb mixed	WJek
	– 'Wina'	WJek
	moritzianum **new**	CFil
	pentaphyllum	CFil CPLN CSpe EBee ECha ELan ETow GCal GCrs IBlr LTwo MTho WBor WCot
	polyphyllum	CDes CFil EBee ECha EHyt GBuc GCrs SBla SMHy SSpi WBGC WCot WPGP
	sessilifolium	CFil CSec
	speciosum ♀H4	More than 30 suppliers
	sylvestre	CPLN EBee NVic WCru
	tricolor ♀H1	CFil CPLN EHyt ELan EPot ETow GFlt LSou MTho WBor
	tuberosum	CEnd GPoy LRHS WBrE WPrP
	– var. ***lineamaculatum*** 'Ken Aslet' ♀H3	More than 30 suppliers
	– var. ***piliferum*** 'Sidney'	CFil EBee IBlr WCru

Tsuga (*Pinaceae*)

	canadensis	EHul GTSp LCon MBar NBlu NWea SHBN WDin WMou
	– 'Abbott's Dwarf'	CKen EOrn LCon MGos
§	– 'Abbott's Pygmy'	CKen
	– 'Albospica' (v)	EOrn LRHS WFar WGor
	– 'Arnold Gold Weeper'	CKen
	– 'Aurea' (v)	LCon MBar WBcn WEve
	– 'Bacon Cristate' **new**	CKen
	– 'Baldwin Dwarf Pyramid'	MBar
	– 'Beehive'	WGor
	– 'Bennett'	EHul MBar
	– 'Betty Rose' (v)	CKen
	– 'Brandley'	CKen
§	– 'Branklyn'	CKen WBcn
	– 'Cappy's Choice'	CKen
	– 'Cinnamonea'	CKen
	– 'Coffin'	CKen
	– 'Cole's Prostrate'	CDoC CKen EOrn GKir LLin MAsh MBar NLar SHBN
	– 'Coryhill'	MAsh
	– 'Creamey' (v)	CKen
	– 'Curley'	CKen
	– 'Curtis Ideal'	CKen
	– 'Essex' **new**	NLar
*	– 'Everitt's Dense Leaf'	CKen
	– 'Everitt's Golden'	CKen
	– 'Fantana'	CDoC CRob EHul LBee LLin LRHS MAsh MBar NLar SCoo SLim
	– 'Gentsch White' (v)	LCon LLin MGos
	– 'Golden Splendor'	LLin
	– 'Horsford'	CKen NLar
	– 'Horstmann' No. 1 **new**	CKen
	– 'Hussii'	CKen LCon NLar
	– 'Jacqueline Verkade'	CKen
	– 'Jeddeloh' ♀H4	CDoC CMac CNic CRob EHul EOrn EPot GKir IMGH LCon LLin LRHS MAsh MBar MBri MGos SCoo SLim SPoG WDin WEve
	– 'Jervis'	CDoC CKen LCon MAsh NLar
	– 'Julianne'	CKen
	– 'Kingsville Spreader'	CKen
	– 'Little Joe'	CKen
	– 'Little Snow' **new**	CKen
I	– 'Lutea'	CKen
	– 'Many Cones'	CKen
	– 'Minima'	CKen
	– 'Minuta'	CDoC CKen EHul EOrn LBee LCon LLin LRHS MBar MGos SCoo SLon SPoG WGor
	– 'Nana'	CMac EHul WDin
	– 'Palomino'	CKen MBar
	– 'Pendula' ♀H4	CBrm CDoC CKen EHul EOrn LCon LRHS MAsh MBar MBri SLim SPoG WDin WEve WFar WMou
	– 'Pincushion'	CKen
	– 'Prostrata'	see *T. canadensis* 'Branklyn'
	– 'Pygmaea'	see *T. canadensis* 'Abbott's Pygmy'
	– 'Rugg's Washington Dwarf'	CKen SCoo
	– 'Snowflake'	CKen LCon
	– 'Stewart's Gem'	CKen
	– 'Verkade Petite'	CKen
	– 'Verkade Recurved'	CDoC CKen LCon MBar NLar WBcn
	– 'Von Helms' Dwarf'	CKen
	– 'Warnham'	CKen ECho EOrn LBee LRHS MAsh MBri SCoo
	caroliniana 'La Bar Weeping'	CKen
	chinensis	GIBF
	diversifolia 'Gotelli'	CKen
	heterophylla ♀H4	CDoC CDul CLnd EPfP GKir LBuc LCon LRHS MBar NWea SCoo SHBN SMad SPer SPoG STre WDin WEve WFar
	– 'Iron Springs'	CKen EOrn
	– 'Laursen's Column'	CKen
	– 'Thorsens Weeping' **new**	CKen
	menziesii	see *Pseudotsuga menziesii*
	mertensiana	LCon
	– 'Blue Star'	CKen MAsh
	– 'Elizabeth'	CDoC CKen
	– 'Glauca' **new**	CKen
I	– 'Glauca Nana'	CKen
	– 'Quartz Mountain'	CKen
	sieboldii 'Baldwin'	CKen
	– 'Honeywell Estate'	CKen
	– 'Nana'	CKen

Tsusiophyllum (*Ericaceae*)

	tanakae	see *Rhododendron tsusiophyllum*

Tuberaria (*Cistaceae*)

	lignosa	CMea CStu EMan MWrn SGar WAbe

Tulbaghia ✿ (*Alliaceae*)

	acutiloba	CAvo ERos
	alliacea	CFee EBla ERos EShb WCot WPrP
	alliacea* x *violacea	EBee
	capensis	CFee LPio MHom
	cepacea	CStu ERos NBir WSPU
§	– var. ***maritima***	CAvo CDes EMar ERos EShb MHom WCot

	cepacea x ***natalensis*** **new**	ERos
	coddii	CAvo CFee EBla MHom WCot WPrP
	coddii x ***violacea***	CPne EBee
	cominsii	CFil CStu SBch SCnR
	cominsii x ***violacea***	CAvo CDes CFil ERos MHom WPrP
	dregeana	ERos
	'Fairy Star'	CDes ERos WCot WPrP
	fragrans	see *T. simmleri*
	galpinii	CFil CPen ERos SChr
	'John May's Special'	CDes CKno EBee EGra EMan EMar MSph MSte SSpi WCot WPGP
	leucantha	CAvo CStu EBee EBla ERos SBla WCot
	maritima	see *T. cepacea* var. *maritima*
	montana	CDes EBee WPrP
	natalensis	CPou SUsu
	- pink	ERos MHom SOkh WCot WPrP
§	***simmleri***	CPou CSec EBla ERos EShb ESis EWes GSki LAma LPio MSph NArg WCot
	- pink-flowered	CPen
	- white	CPen CPou
	verdoorniae	ERos WCot
	violacea	More than 30 suppliers
*	- 'Alba'	EBla ERos GSki LPio NLAp WFar WHoo
	- deep mauve-flowered **new**	EMar
I	- 'Fine Form'	SMHy
	- 'John Rider'	WPer
*	- ***pallida***	CAvo CBro CDes CMdw CPne CPou WPrP
	- 'Pearl' **new**	CPou
	- var. ***robustior*** **new**	CPou
§	- 'Silver Lace' (v)	More than 30 suppliers
	- 'Variegata'	see *T. violacea* 'Silver Lace'

Tulipa ✿ (*Liliaceae*)

	'Abba' (2)	LBmB MBri
	'Abu Hassan' (3)	CAvo LAma MBri
	acuminata (15)	CBro LAma LRHS
	'Ad Rem' (4)	LAma
	'Addis' (14) 🏆H4	LAma
	'African Queen' (3)	LAma
	aitchisonii	see *T. clusiana*
	'Aladdin' (6)	EBrs LAma LRHS
	albertii (15)	LAma NJOw WWst
	'Albino' (3)	LAma
	aleppensis (15)	LAma
	'Alfred Cortot' (12) 🏆H4	LAma
	'Ali Baba' (14) 🏆H4	MBri
	'Allegretto' (11)	LAma MBri
	altaica (15) 🏆H4	EPot LAma WWst
	amabilis	see *T. hoogiana*
	'Ancilla' (12) 🏆H4	CBro LAma SGar
	'Angélique' (11) 🏆H4	CAvo CMea EBrs EPfP LAma LBmB LRHS MBri NBir SPer WHal
	'Anne Claire' (3)	LAma
	'Apeldoorn' (4)	LAma LRHS MBri
	'Apeldoorn's Elite' (4) 🏆H4	LAma LRHS
	'Apricot Beauty' (1) 🏆H4	CHid EBrs EPfP LAma LBmB LRHS MBri NBir SPer
	'Apricot Jewel'	see *T. linifolia* (Batalinii Group) 'Apricot Jewel'
	'Apricot Parrot' (10) 🏆H4	EPfP LAma LBmB MBri SPer
	'Arabian Mystery' (3)	CAvo CMea LAma NBir WHal
	'Aristocrat' (5) 🏆H4	LAma
	armena var. ***lycica*** **new**	WWst
	'Artist' (8) 🏆H4	EChP LAma NBir
	'Athleet' (3)	LAma LRHS
	'Attila' (3)	EBrs LAma LRHS
	aucheriana (15) 🏆H4	CBro EHyt EPot ERos LAma LRHS LTwo
	aximensis (15)	WWst
	bakeri	see *T. saxatilis* Bakeri Group
	'Ballade' (6) 🏆H4	LAma MBri MSte SPer
	'Ballerina' (6) 🏆H4	CAvo CBro CMea EBrs LAma LPhx MBri MWgw SMeo SPer WGHP WHal
	'Banja Luka' (4) **new**	EBrs
	batalinii	see *T. linifolia* Batalinii Group
	'Beauty of Apeldoorn' (4)	LAma
	'Bellflower' (7)	LAma
	'Bellona' (3)	LAma
	'Berlioz' (12)	LAma
	biebersteiniana (15)	LAma
§	***biflora*** (15)	CBro EPot LAma LRHS LTwo
	bifloriformis (15)	LRHS WWst
	'Big Chief' (4) 🏆H4	LAma MBri
	'Bing Crosby' (3)	EBrs LAma
	'Bird of Paradise' (10) **new**	EBrs
	'Black Hero'	LAma SPer
	'Black Horse'	LAma
	'Black Parrot' (10) 🏆H4	CAvo EBrs EPfP EUJe LAma LBmB LPhx LRHS MBri MSte SMeo
	'Black Swan' (5)	LBmB
	'Blenda' (3) **new**	EBrs
	'Bleu Aimable' (5)	CAvo EBrs LAma LRHS WGHP
	'Blue Heron' (7) 🏆H4	LAma
	'Blue Parrot' (10)	EBrs LAma LRHS MSte
	'Blushing Beauty' (5)	LBmB
	'Blushing Bride' (5)	LBmB
	'Blushing Lady' (5)	LAma
	'Bonanza' (11)	LAma LRHS
	'Boule de Neige' (2)	LAma
	'Boutade'	NPer
	'Bravissimo' (2)	MBri
	'Brilliant Star' (1)	LAma MBri
	'Burgundy' (6)	EBrs LAma SMeo
	'Burgundy Lace' (7)	LAma LRHS
	'Burns' (7)	LAma
	butkovii (15)	LAma
I	'Calypso' (14) 🏆H4 **new**	EBrs
	'Candela' (13) 🏆H4	LAma
	'Candy Club' (5)	LAma LBmB SPer
	'Cantata' (13)	CBro LAma
	'Cape Cod' (14)	EPfP LAma
	carinata (15)	LAma
	'Carlton' (2)	LAma
	'Carnaval de Nice' (11/v) 🏆H4	CAvo EBrs LAma MBri
	'Cassini' (3)	LAma SPer
§	***celsiana*** (15)	LAma LRHS
	'César Franck' (12)	LAma
	'China Pink' (6) 🏆H4	CAvo CMea EBrs EPfP LAma MBri WHal
	'China Town' (8) 🏆H4 **new**	LAma
	'Chopin' (12)	LAma
	'Christmas Marvel' (1)	LAma LRHS
	chrysantha Boiss. ex Baker	see *T. montana*
	'Cloud Nine' **new**	LAma
§	***clusiana*** (15)	CAvo CBro CMea LAma WWst
§	- var. ***chrysantha*** (15) 🏆H4	CAvo CMea EBrs LAma LRHS
	- - 'Tubergen's Gem' (15)	CBro LAma LRHS MBri
	- 'Cynthia' (15) 🏆H4	CSWP ECGP EPot LAma LPhx LRHS MSte
§	- var. ***stellata*** (15)	LAma
	'Colour Spectacle'[PBR] (5)	LBmB LSou SPer
	'Concerto' (13)	CBro LAma MBri NPer
	'Corsage' (14) 🏆H4	LAma
	'Couleur Cardinal' (3)	CBro EBrs LAma

'Czaar Peter' ♀H4	GFlt NPer
'Dancing Show' (8)	EBrs LAma
dasystemon (15)	EPot LAma LTwo
'Daydream' (4) ♀H4	LBmB
'Diana' (1)	CAvo
didieri	see *T. passeriniana*
'Dillenburg' (5)	LAma
'Doll's Minuet' (8)	LAma SPer
'Don Quichotte' (3) ♀H4	LAma
'Donna Bella' (14) ♀H4	EPfP LAma
'Douglas Bader' (5)	CAvo LAma LRHS
'Dreaming Maid' (3)	LAma
'Duc de Berlin'	LAma
'Duc van Tol Rose'	LAma
'Duc van Tol Salmon'	LAma
'Easter Parade' (13)	LAma
'Easter Surprise' (14) ♀H4	LAma
§ ***edulis*** (15)	LAma
eichleri	see *T. undulatifolia*
'Electra' (5)	LAma MBri
'Elegant Lady' (6)	EBrs LAma SPer
'Erfurt' (11)	LBmB
'Esperanto' (8/v) ♀H4	EChP LAma
'Estella Rijnveld' (10)	EBrs LAma LRHS MSte NBir SPer
'Eye Catcher' (8) **new**	EBrs
'Fancy Frills' (7) ♀H4	LAma LBmB MBri
'Fantasy' (10) ♀H4	LAma LRHS
'Fashion' (12)	EPfP LAma
ferganica (15)	EPot LAma WWst
'Fire Queen' (3) ♀H4	LAma
'Fireside'	see *T.* 'Vlammenspel'
'Flair' (1)	LAma MBri
'Flaming Parrot' (10)	LAma LBmB
* 'Flowerdale'	CAvo
fosteriana (13)	MBri WWst
'Franz Léhar' (12)	LAma
'Fresco' (14)	LAma
'Fringed Beauty' (7) ♀H4	MBri
'Fringed Elegance' (7) ♀H4	LAma
'Fritz Kreisler' (12)	LAma LRHS
'Fulgens' (6)	LAma
'Gaiety' (12)	LAma LRHS
'Galata' (13)	LAma
galatica (15)	LAma
'Garden Party' (3) ♀H4	LAma
'Gavota' (3)	LAma LBmB SPer
'Generaal de Wet' (1)	LAma MBri
'Georgette' (5)	LAma LSou MBri
'Giuseppe Verdi' (12)	LAma LRHS MBri
'Glück' (12) ♀H4	LAma
'Gold Medal' (11)	LAma MBri
'Golden Apeldoorn' (4)	LAma LRHS MBri
'Golden Artist' (8)	LAma MBri
'Golden Emperor' (13)	EPfP LAma LRHS SPer
'Golden Melody' (3)	CMea LAma WHal
'Golden Oxford' (4)	LAma
'Golden Parade' (4)	LAma
'Golden Springtime' (4)	LAma
'Gordon Cooper' (4)	LAma
'Goudstuk' (12)	LAma
'Grand Prix' (13)	LAma
'Green Eyes' (8)	LAma
'Green Spot' (8)	LRHS
'Green Wave' (10)	LAma LBmB
greigii (14)	CBro
grengiolensis (15)	LAma LRHS WWst
'Greuze' (5)	LAma
'Groenland' (8)	EBrs LAma MBri SPer
'Gudoshnik' (4)	LAma
'H. D. Genscher' **new**	EBrs
hageri (15)	EBrs LAma MBri
- 'Splendens' (15)	EChP LAma LRHS
'Halcro' (5) ♀H4	LAma
'Hamilton' (7) ♀H4	EPfP LAma MBNS
'Happy Family' (3)	LAma
'Happy Generation' (3)	LAma LBmB
'Havran'	LAma
'Heart's Delight' (12)	CBro EBrs LAma LRHS
'Hermitage' (3) **new**	LAma
'Hit Parade' (13)	LAma
'Hoangho' (2)	LAma
'Hocus Pocus' (5)	LBmB
'Hollands Glorie' (4) ♀H4	LAma
'Hollywood' (8)	LAma
§ ***hoogiana*** (15)	LAma
§ ***humilis*** (15)	CBro EWTr LAma MBri
- 'Eastern Star' (15)	CMea LAma LRHS MBri
§ - 'Lilliput' (15)	CBro CMea EPot LRHS
- 'Odalisque' (15)	LAma LRHS
- 'Persian Pearl' (15)	EPfP EPot GFlt LAma LRHS MBri SBch SPer WBor
§ - var. ***pulchella*** Albocaerulea Oculata Group (15)	CMea EBrs EPot LAma LTwo MSte WWst
§ - Violacea Group (15)	CMea EChP LAma MBri SPer WBor
§ - - black base (15)	CBro EBrs EPot LRHS MBri NJOw
- - yellow base (15)	EPot LAma LRHS
'Humming Bird' (8)	CAvo LAma
'Hytuna' (11)	LAma
'Ibis' (1)	LAma
'Ice Follies' (3)	LBmB
'Ile de France' (5)	LAma
iliensis (15)	EPot
ingens (15)	LAma WWst
'Insulinde'	LAma
'Inzell' (3)	EBrs EPfP LAma
'Ivory Floradale' (4) ♀H4	LAma LBmB
'Jacqueline' (6)	EBrs
'Jan Reus'	LAma
'Jeantine' (12) ♀H4	EPfP
'Jewel of Spring' (4) ♀H4	LAma
'Jockey Cap' (14)	LAma
'Joffre' (1)	LAma MBri
'Johann Strauss' (12)	CBro LAma MBri
'Juan' (13) ♀H4	LAma MBri
'Kansas' (3)	LAma
'Karel Doorman' (10)	LAma
kaufmanniana (12)	CAvo EPot
- 'Ugam' **new**	WWst
§ 'Kees Nelis' (3)	LAma MBri
'Keizerskroon' (1) ♀H4	LAma
kolpakowskiana (15) ♀H4	EChP EPfP ITim LAma LRHS MBri NJOw
kurdica (15)	CPBP LAma LRHS WWst
* 'Lady Diana' (14)	MBri
'Leen van der Mark' (3)	LAma
'Lefeber's Favourite' (4)	LAma
'Libretto Parrot' (10)	LAma
'Lilac Perfection' (11)	LBmB
'Lilac Time' (6)	LAma
'Lilac Wonder'	see *T. saxatilis* (Bakeri Group) 'Lilac Wonder'
'Lilliput'	see *T. humilis* 'Lilliput'
linifolia (15) ♀H4	CAvo CPBP EChP EHyt EPfP EPot GIBF ITim LAma LRHS NJOw NWCA SSpi
§ - Batalinii Group (15) ♀H4	CBro LAma MBri
§ - - 'Apricot Jewel' (15)	CBro EPot MSte
- - 'Bright Gem' (15) ♀H4	CAvo CBro EPot GCrs LAma LRHS MBri WCra WHoo
- - 'Bronze Charm' (15)	CAvo CBro CMea ECGP EPot LAma LPhx MBri MSte NMen
- - 'Red Gem' (15)	LAma
- - 'Red Jewel' (15)	GFlt MSte SBch

- - 'Yellow Jewel' (15)	EPot LAma
§ - Maximowiczii Group	CBro EPot LAma NJOw SMeo
'Little Beauty' (15) ♀H4	CMea EBrs LAma SOkd
'Little Princess'	EPfP LAma
'London' (4)	LAma
'Lucky Strike' (3)	LAma
§ 'Lustige Witwe' (3)	LAma
'Lydia' (3)	LAma
§ 'Madame Lefeber' (13)	CBro MBri
'Magier' (5)	LAma
'Maja' (7)	LAma
'Mamasa' (5)	LAma
'March of Time' (14)	MBri
'Maréchal Niel' (2)	LAma
'Mariette' (6)	CBro LAma LBmB LRHS MBri SPer
'Marilyn' (6)	CAvo EBrs LAma LBmB LRHS
marjolletii (15)	CAvo CBro LAma
'Mary Ann' (14)	LAma
'Maureen' (5) ♀H4	EBrs LAma
mauritiana (15)	LAma
maximowiczii	see *T. linifolia* Maximowiczii Group
'Maytime' (6)	LAma MBri MWgw SPer
'Maywonder' (11) ♀H4	LAma MBri
'Meissner Porzellan' (3)	LBmB
'Menton' (5)	LAma
Merry Widow	see *T.* 'Lustige Witwe'
'Miss Holland' (3)	MBri
'Mona Lisa' (6)	LAma LBmB
'Monsella' (2)	EBrs LBmB
§ ***montana*** (15)	EPot GIBF LAma NBid SMeo
'Monte Carlo' (2) ♀H4	LAma LRHS MBri
'Montreux'	LAma
'Mount Tacoma' (11)	EBrs LAma MBri SPer
'Mr Van der Hoef' (2)	LAma MBri
'Mrs John T. Scheepers' (5) ♀H4	LAma WGHP
'Murillo' (2)	LAma
'My Lady' (4) ♀H4	LAma
'Negrita' (3)	LAma
neustruevae (15)	CBro CMea EPot NJOw
'New Design' (3/v)	EBrs LAma MBri SPer
'Ollioules' (4) ♀H4	LBmB SPer
'Orange Bouquet' (3) ♀H4	LAma
'Orange Elite' (14)	LAma MBri
'Orange Emperor' (13) ♀H4	LAma LRHS MBri SPer
'Orange Favourite' (10)	LAma LRHS
'Orange Princess' (11) ♀H4	EBrs LBmB
'Orange Triumph' (11)	MBri
'Oranje Nassau' (2) ♀H4	LAma MBri
'Oratorio' (14) ♀H4	LAma LRHS MBri
'Oriental Beauty' (14) ♀H4	LAma LRHS
'Oriental Splendour' (14) ♀H4	EPfP LAma
orphanidea (15)	LAma LRHS SCnR
- 'Flava' (15)	ECGP EPot LAma WWst
§ - Whittallii Group (15) ♀H4	CAvo CMea LAma SMeo
'Oscar' (3)	LBmB
ostrowskiana (15)	LAma WWst
'Oxford' (4) ♀H4	LAma
'Oxford's Elite' (4)	LAma
'Page Polka' (3)	EBrs LAma
'Palestrina' (3)	LAma
'Pandour' (14)	LAma MBri
'Parade' (4) ♀H4	LAma MBri
§ ***passeriniana*** (15)	LAma
patens	WWst
'Paul Richter' (3)	LAma
'Pax' (3)	LAma
'Peach Blossom' (2)	EBrs LAma LRHS MBri SPer
'Perestroyka' (5)	LBmB
'Perlina' (14)	LAma
persica	see *T. celsiana*
'Philippe de Comines' (5)	LAma
'Picture' (5) ♀H4	LAma
'Pieter de Leur'	EPfP LAma SPer
'Pimpernel' (8/v)	LAma
'Pink Beauty' (1)	LAma
'Pink Impression' (4) ♀H4	LAma SPer
'Pinkeen' (13)	LAma
'Pinocchio' (14)	SGar
'Plaisir' (14) ♀H4	LAma MBri
platystigma (15)	LAma
polychroma	see *T. biflora*
praestans (15)	CNic EPfP LAma
- 'Fusilier' (15) ♀H4	CBro CMea EPot LAma LRHS MBri NBir NJOw SBch SGar
- 'Unicum' (15/v)	LAma LRHS MBri
- 'Van Tubergen's Variety' (15)	LAma LRHS NJOw
'Preludium' (3)	LAma
'President Kennedy' (4) ♀H4	LAma
'Prince of Austria' (1)	LAma
'Princeps' (13)	CBro LAma MBri
'Prinses Irene' (3) ♀H4	CMea EPfP LAma MBri NBir SPer WHal
'Professor Röntgen' (10)	LAma
pulchella humilis	see *T. humilis*
§ 'Purissima' (13) ♀H4	CAvo CBro LAma LRHS SPer
'Purple Prince' (5)	EPfP
'Quebec' (14) **new**	SBch
'Queen Ingrid' (14)	LAma LRHS
'Queen of Bartigons' (5) ♀H4	LAma
'Queen of Night' (5)	CAvo CBro CMea EBrs EPfP EUJe LAma LRHS MBri MWgw SBch SPer WGHP WHal
'Queen of Sheba' (6) ♀H4	CAvo LAma
'Rajka' (6)	LAma
'Red Emperor'	see *T.* 'Madame Lefeber'
'Red Georgette' (5) ♀H4	LAma LRHS LSou MBri NBir
'Red Parrot' (10)	LAma
'Red Riding Hood' (14) ♀H4	CAvo CBro CMea ENot EPfP EUJe LAma LRHS MBri NBir NJOw SPer
'Red Shine' (6) ♀H4	CBro LAma MBri
'Red Springgreen' (8) **new**	LAma
'Red Wing' (7) ♀H4	LAma LBmB
Rembrandt mix	MBri
'Renown Unique' (11) **new**	LAma
rhodopea	see *T. urumoffii*
'Ringo'	see *T.* 'Kees Nelis'
'Rococo' (10)	LBmB MBri
'Rosy Wings' (3)	LAma
'Sapporro' (6)	CAvo LAma
saxatilis (15)	CBro CNic EPfP LAma LRHS MBri MWgw NJOw SMeo
§ - Bakeri Group (15)	CPou LAma WWst
§ - - 'Lilac Wonder' (15) ♀H4	CAvo CBro EBrs EChP EPot GGar LAma MBri MWgw SBch SPer WBor
'Scarlet Baby' (12)	EPfP LRHS
'Schoonoord' (2)	LAma MBri
schrenkii (15)	EPot LAma WWst
'Scotch Lassie' (5)	LAma
'Shakespeare' (12)	CBro LAma
'Shirley' (3)	CAvo EBrs EPfP LAma LRHS MBri
'Showwinner' (12) ♀H4	CBro LAma MBri
'Sigrid Undset' (5)	LAma
'Silentia' (3)	LAma
'Silverstream' (4) **new**	LAma

'Snow Parrot' (10)	CAvo LBmB
'Snowflake' (3)	LAma
'Snowpeak' (5)	LAma
sogdiana (15)	LAma
'Sorbet' (5) ♀H4	LAma
'Sparkling Fire' (14)	LAma
sprengeri (15) ♀H4	CAvo CBro CFil CLAP CNic ECGP ECha EHyt LAma SCnR SOkd SSpi WIvy
- Trotter's form (15)	WCot
'Spring Green' (8) ♀H4	CAvo EBrs EPfP EUJe LAma LBmB LRHS MBri MSte SPer WHal
'Spring Pearl' (13)	LAma
'Spring Song' (4)	LAma
stellata	see *T. clusiana* var. *stellata*
'Stockholm' (2) ♀H4	LAma
'Stresa' (12) ♀H4	CBro LAma LRHS
'Striped Apeldoorn' (4)	LAma
subpraestans (15)	EPot LAma
'Sunray' (3)	LAma
'Super Parrot' **new**	LAma
'Susan Oliver' (8)	LAma
'Swan Wings' (7)	LAma SPer
'Sweet Harmony' (5) ♀H4	LAma LRHS MBri
'Sweet Lady' (14)	LAma
'Sweetheart' (13)	CBro LAma MBri SPer
sylvestris (15)	CAvo CBro EBrs LAma LRHS MBow SSpi WBWf WCot WHer WShi WTin
tarda (15) ♀H4	CAvo CBro EBla EPfP EPot GFlt GGar GIBF LAma LRHS MBri MWgw NJOw SBch
tetraphylla (15)	LAma WWst
'Texas Flame' (10)	LAma LRHS MBri
'Texas Gold' (10)	LAma
'The First' (12)	CBro LAma
'Tinka' (15)	LBmB
'Toronto' (14) ♀H4	EPfP LAma LRHS LSou MBri
'Toulon' (13) ♀H4	MBri
'Towa' (14)	LAma
'Toyota' (5)	LBmB SPer
'Trinket' (14) ♀H4	LAma
'Triumphator' (2)	LAma
tschimganica (15)	LAma WWst
tubergeniana (15)	LAma
- 'Keukenhof' (15)	LAma
turkestanica (15) ♀H4	CAvo CBro CSWP EChP EPfP EPot EWTr GFlt LAma LPhx MBri MWgw NJOw NSla SBch WBrE WGHP WHoo
'Turkish Delight'	NPer
'Uncle Tom' (11)	EPfP LAma MBri
§ ***undulatifolia*** (15)	LAma WWst
'Union Jack' (5) ♀H4	LAma
'United States' (14)	NPer
urumiensis (15) ♀H4	CAvo CBro EPot LAma MBri NJOw SBch WHoo
§ ***urumoffii*** (15)	LAma
'Valentine' (3) ♀H4	LAma
'Van der Neer' (1)	LAma
'Varinas' (3)	LAma
'Verona' (2) **new**	EBrs
'Veronique Sanson' **new**	EBrs
violacea	see *T. humilis* Violacea Group
'Viridiflora' (8)	EBrs
'Vivaldi' (12)	LAma
'Vivex' (4) ♀H4	LAma
§ 'Vlammenspel' (1)	LAma
'Vuurbaak' (2)	LAma
vvedenskyi (15)	EPot LAma
- 'Tangerine Beauty' (15) ♀H4	EBrs LRHS MBri
'Weber's Parrot' (10)	LBmB MBri
'Weisse Berliner' (3) **new**	LAma
'West Point' (6) ♀H4	CAvo CBro EBrs LAma MBNS MBri
'White Dream' (3)	EBrs LAma LRHS
'White Elegance' (6)	CAvo LBmB SPer
'White Emperor'	see *T.* 'Purissima'
'White Parrot' (10)	LAma LRHS MSte
'White Triumphator' (6) ♀H4	CAvo CBro CMea EBrs GFlt LAma LPhx LRHS MWgw NBir SMeo WHal
'White Virgin' (3)	LAma
whittallii	see *T. orphanidea* Whittallii Group
'Willem van Oranje' (2)	EBrs LAma
'Willemsoord' (2)	LAma LRHS MBri
wilsoniana	see *T. montana*
'World Expression' (5) ♀H4	LBmB
'Yellow Dawn' (14)	LAma LRHS
'Yellow Emperor' (5)	MBri
'Yellow Empress' (13)	LAma
'Yellow Flight' (3)	LAma
'Yellow Present' (3)	LAma
'Yellow Purissima' (13) ♀H4	EPfP
'Yokohama' (3)	LAma
'Zampa' (14) ♀H4	LAma
'Zombie' (13)	LAma
'Zomerschoon' (5)	LAma
'Zurel' (3) **new**	LAma

tummelberry see *Rubus* 'Tummelberry'

Tunica see *Petrorhagia*

Tupistra (*Convallariaceae*)

aurantiaca	WCot
- B&SWJ 2267	WCru
chinensis 'Eco China Ruffles'	WCot
nutans	CKob

Turbina (*Convolvulaceae*)

corymbosa	MGol

Turnera (*Turneraceae*)

ulmifolia	MSal

Turraea (*Meliaceae*)

obtusifolia	EShb

Tussilago (*Asteraceae*)

farfara	CArn CNat ELau GBar GPoy GWCH MHer MSal NMir WHer

Tutcheria (*Theaceae*)

§ ***spectabilis***	EPfP

Tweedia (*Asclepiadaceae*)

§ ***caerulea*** ♀H2	CBcs CSpe EMan ERea LPhx LPio SBch SHFr SPer SWal WRos
- pink	LPio

Tylecodon (*Crassulaceae*)

* ***luteosquamata*** **new**	LToo
paniculatus **new**	LToo
reticulatus **new**	LToo
wallichii **new**	LToo

Typha (*Typhaceae*)

angustifolia	CAgr CBen CKno CRow CWat EHon EMFW EPza GFor LNCo LPBA NArg NPer SPlb WFar WPnP WPop WWpP WWye
gracilis	ENot

latifolia	CAgr CBen CRow CWat EHon EMFW EPza GFor LPBA NBlu NPer WDyG WFar WHer WPop WWpP WWye
- 'Variegata' (v)	CBen CDWL CKno CRow CWat ELan EMFW EPza LPBA NArg WCot
§ ***laxmannii***	CBen CDWL CRow CStu EHon EMFW EPza GFor LPBA NArg WPnP WPop WWpP
minima	CBen CDWL CFwr CMHG CRow CStu CWat EHoe EHon EMFW EPfP EPza EUJe GBin LEdu LNCo LPBA NArg NBlu NPer SCoo SGSe SMad SWal WFar WPnP WPop WRos WWpP
- var. ***gracilis***	ENot
shuttleworthii	CRow
stenophylla	see *T. laxmannii*

Typhonium (*Araceae*)

***giganteum* new**	WCot
***trilobatum* new**	EUJe

Typhonodorum (*Araceae*)

***lindleyanum* new**	XBlo

U

Ugni (*Myrtaceae*)

§ ***molinae***	CBcs CDul CFir CPLG CPle CSBt CTrC IDee LEdu MCCP MDun SAdn SHFr SLPl SWvt WCHb WDin WFar WJek WMoo WPic WSHC WWye XPep
- 'Flambeau'	MGos SWvt

Ulex (*Papilionaceae*)

europaeus	CArn CCVT CDoC CDul CRWN ECrN ELan ENot EPfP GPoy GWCH LBuc MCoo MWat NWea SCoo SPer WDin WHar WMou
§ - 'Flore Pleno' (d) ♀H4	CBcs CBgR CDoC CSBt EMon ENot EPfP EPla GAbr GGar IArd MBlu MGos NEgg NLar NWea SHBN SPer SPoG WBcn WCot WFar
- 'Plenus'	see *U. europaeus* 'Flore Pleno'
- 'Prostratus'	MBar
gallii	WDin
- 'Mizen Head'	GCal GGGa GSki MBlu MWhi SLon WBcn
§ ***minor***	EPla
nanus	see *U. minor*

Ulmus ✿ (*Ulmaceae*)

americana 'Princeton' **new**	CKno
'Dodoens'	EWTr IArd LBuc MGos SBLw
§ ***glabra***	CDul CRWN ECrN GKir NWea SBLw WDin
- 'Camperdownii'	CDoC CTho EBee ECrN ELan LRHS NBee NEgg SBLw SCoo SPer
- 'Exoniensis'	CDul CTho SBLw
- 'Gittisham'	CTho
- 'Horizontalis'	see *U. glabra* 'Pendula'
- 'Lutescens'	CDoC CEnd CTho CTri LRHS SBLw SCoo SLim
- 'Nana'	WPat
§ - 'Pendula'	CDul SBLw SLim
x ***hollandica*** 'Commelin'	SBLw
- 'Dampieri'	SBLw
- 'Dampieri Aurea'	CBot CDul CEnd CLnd CTho EBee ELan EPfP GKir LBuc LRHS MAsh MBar MBlu MGos NBee NBlu SBLw SHBN SLim SPer WDin WOrn WPat
- 'Groeneveld'	SBLw
- 'Jacqueline Hillier'	EBee ELan EPfP EPla EWTr IMGH LAst MBar MGos NBlu NLAp NWea SBLw SLon SPer SPoG SSto STre WCFE WDin WFar WOld WPat
- 'Lobel'	CDul MGos SBLw
- 'Wredei'	see *U. hollandica* 'Dampieri Aurea'
laevis	CDul CTho ECrN
minor	NEgg SBLw
- 'Dampieri Aurea'	see *U.* x *hollandica* 'Dampieri Aurea'
- subsp. ***sarniensis***	SBLw
- 'Variegata' (v)	EPot ESis SCoo
montana	see *U. glabra*
parvifolia	CMCN CMen CTho ECrN NWea SFam SMad STre WNor
- 'Frosty' (v)	ECho
- 'Geisha' (v)	EBee ELan EMil MAsh MGos NLAp SPoG WBcn WPat
§ - 'Hokkaido'	CMen LBee LTwo NLAp NLar SBla WAbe WPat
- 'Pygmaea'	see *U. parvifolia* 'Hokkaido'
- 'Yatsubusa'	CLyd EPot ESis EWes LTwo NLAp NLar STre WBcn WPat
'Plantijn'	SBLw
procera	CDul CTho LBuc MDun WDin
- 'Argenteovariegata' (v)	CDul CTho MGos SMad WBcn
pumila	CAgr CDul EPot ESis WNor
rubra	CArn MSal
'Sapporo Autumn Gold'PBR	WDin
x ***vegeta***	SBLw

Umbellularia (*Lauraceae*)

californica	CArn CPne EPfP IArd SAPC SArc SSpi WSHC

Umbilicus (*Crassulaceae*)

rupestris	CArn CRWN EChP GEdr NWCA SChr WCru WHer WShi WWye

Uncinia (*Cyperaceae*)

from Chile	GCal
* ***cyparissias*** from Chile **new**	NBir
egmontiana	CMea EBee EBla EChP EHoe EKen EMan EPPr EPyc GFlt GFor GSki LPhx MAnH MNrw MWrn NChi NLon SHGN SMac WFoF WHrl WLeb WWpP
***lechleriana* new**	GBin
N ***rubra***	More than 30 suppliers
uncinata	CFil CM&M ECha EMan GGar GSki MFOX NCob SDix WCot
* - ***rubra***	CBrm CFir CKno COlW CTri CWCL ECot EHol EHrv EPza EUJe GSki IFro LAst LRHS MAsh MMHG MNrw MWgw NBPC NCGa NCob NGdn SLim SMer STes SWvt WGwG WWeb

Uniola (*Poaceae*)

latifolia	see *Chasmanthium latifolium*
***paniculata* new**	SApp

Urceolina (*Amaryllidaceae*)

miniata	see *Stenomesson miniatum*

peruviana	see *Stenomesson miniatum*

Urechites see *Pentalinon*

Urginea (*Hyacinthaceae*)

maritima	CArn EBee GCal LAma MNrw MSal

Urospermum (*Asteraceae*)

dalechampii	COtt CSam CSec EBee EBrs ECha EMan GKir LLWP

Ursinia (*Asteraceae*)

alpina	CPBP
montana	NWCA

Urtica (*Urticaceae*)

dioica 'Dog Trap Lane' **new**	CNat
- 'Good as Gold'	CNat
- subsp. ***gracilis*** var. ***procera***	CNat
galeopsifolia	CNat

Utricularia (*Lentibulariaceae*)

alpina	CSWC
australis	EFEx
bisquamata	CSWC SHmp
blancheti	CSWC
calycifida	CSWC SHmp
dichotoma	CSWC EFEx
exoleta R. Brown	see *U. gibba*
§ ***gibba***	EFEx
heterosepala **new**	LHew
intermedia	EFEx
lateriflora	EFEx LHew
livida	CSWC EFEx
longifolia	CSWC
macrorhiza	CSWC
menziesii	EFEx
monanthos	CSWC EFEx LHew
- Queenstown, Tasmania	MCCP
nephrophylla	SHmp
novae-zelandiae	CSWC
ochroleuca	EFEx
paulineae **new**	LHew
praelonga	CSWC SHmp
pubescens	CSWC LHew SHmp
reniformis	CSWC EFEx SHmp
- ***nana***	CSWC EFEx
sandersonii	CSWC SHmp
- blue	CSWC
subulata	EFEx
tricolor	CSWC SHmp
uniflora	LHew
vulgaris	CDWL CSWC EFEx LHew

Uvularia (*Convallariaceae*)

§ ***caroliniana***	EBee IBlr
disporum	LAma
grandiflora ♀H4	More than 30 suppliers
- dwarf	IBlr
- var. ***pallida***	CAvo CBct CBos CLAP CPom CStu EBee ECha EHrv EMan EPot GBri GBuc GCal GEdr IBlr LPhx MRav SBla SMHy SOkh SUsu WAbe WCru WFar WPGP WPnP
- 'Susie Lewis'	WCru
grandiflora x ***perfoliata***	IBlr
perfoliata	CBct CLAP EBee ECha EDAr EHyt EMan EPfP EVFa GBri GCrs GGar IBlr IPot LAma LEdu MRav SIng SOkd SSpi WAbe WBrE WCru WHil WPGP WPnP
pudica	see *U. caroliniana*
sessilifolia	CBct CLAP EBee EPPr EPot GBBs IBlr LAma NLar NMen SCnR SSvw WCru

V

Vaccaria (*Caryophyllaceae*)

§ ***hispanica***	MSal
segetalis	see *V. hispanica*

Vaccinium ✿ (*Ericaceae*)

from Bolivia	EWes
arctostaphylos	NLar SReu SSta SWvt
caespitosum	SOkd
'Cinderella'	SSta
consanguineum	SReu
corymbosum (F) ♀H4	CBcs CRez EPfP MBar MGos SCoo SReu SSta WBVN WDin
- 'Berkeley' (F)	CTrh GTwe LBuc LRHS
- 'Blue Ray' (F)	CWib SCoo
- 'Bluecrop' (F)	CAgr CTrh CWib EPfP GKir GTwe LBuc LRHS MBri MGos SCoo SKee SPer SPoG SWvt WFar
- 'Bluegold' (F)	LRHS SCoo
- 'Bluejay' (F)	CTrh LRHS MAsh SCoo
- 'Bluetta' (F)	CWib GTwe LRHS SCoo WFar
- 'Brigitta Blue' (F) **new**	GTwe
- 'Concord' (F)	ENot SCoo
- 'Darrow' (F)	LRHS SPoG
- 'Duke' (F) ♀H4	CTrh ELan EPfP GKir LRHS
- 'Earliblue' (F)	LRHS MGos
- 'Goldtraube' (F)	CTri CWSG CWib GKir MBlu MBri MGos SKee SPoG
- 'Herbert' (F)	CTrh GTwe LBuc MGos SCoo
- 'Ivanhoe' (F)	SCoo
- 'Jersey' (F)	GKir LRHS MAsh MGos SCoo
- 'Misty' (F) **new**	SPoG
- 'Nelson' (F)	CTrh SCoo
- 'Northland' (F)	CWib GTwe SCoo
- 'Patriot' (F)	CTrh CWib GTwe LRHS MGos SCoo
- 'Pioneer' (F)	MBar
- 'Spartan' (F) ♀H4	GTwe LRHS SCoo
- 'Stanley'	ELan LRHS MAsh
- 'Sunrise' (F)	GTwe LRHS
- 'Top Hat' (F)	LRHS
- 'Toro' (F)	GTwe LRHS MAsh
crassifolium subsp. ***sempervirens*** 'Well's Delight' (F)	GKir LRHS
cylindraceum ♀H4	EPfP NLar SSta WAbe WFar WPat
- 'Tinkerbelle'	ITim NLAp WAbe
delavayi	GGar GKir LRHS MAsh MBar MDun SReu SSpi SSta WAbe WFar
donianum	see *V. sprengelii*
dunalianum	CBcs
- var. ***caudatifolium*** B&SWJ 1716	WCru
floribundum	CBcs CDoC CFil CMHG GKir GTou IDee LRHS MAsh MDun NLar SBrw SPoG SSpi WPGP WPic
glaucoalbum ♀H3-4	CAbP CDoC CPLG EPfP GGGa GKir LRHS MAsh MBar MRav SBrw SMad SPer SPoG SSpi WDin
griffithianum	SReu SSta
§ ***macrocarpon*** (F)	ELan GKir GTwe LRHS MAsh MBar MBri NWCA SRms

- 'CN' (F)	MGos
- 'Early Black' (F)	CBcs MGos
- 'Franklin' (F)	EPot
- 'Hamilton' (F)	CStu GCrs GEdr LTwo NLAp WPat
mortinia	NMen
moupinense	CDoC GKir IMGH LRHS MAsh WAbe
- 'Variegatum' (v)	LTwo
myrtillus	GPoy MBar WDin
'Nimo Pink'	MBar
nummularia	EHyt GEdr GKir NLAp SReu SSpi WAbe WPic
ovalifolium	GIBF
ovatum	CBcs CMHG GBin IDee LRHS MBar MDun SPer SSta
- 'Thundercloud'	CAbP LRHS MAsh
§ ***oxycoccos*** (F)	CArn GPoy WWes
* - ***rubrum***	NLar
padifolium	CFil WCwm WPGP
pallidum	IBlr
palustre	see *V. oxycoccos*
praestans	GIBF NLar
- Brown 0285	CStu
retusum	CTrw WDin WPic
sikkimense	GGGa
§ ***sprengelii***	CBcs
uliginosum	GIBF WGwG
vitis-idaea	CNic GBin GGar GPoy MBar MGos NLAp SPoG SRot WFar
- Brown 0287	CStu
- 'Autumn Beauty'	NLar
- 'Betsy Sinclair'	CStu
- 'Compactum'	EWes LSou NLAp
- Koralle Group ♀H4	EPfP MBar MBri SBrw WPat
- var. ***minus***	GCrs GKir MAsh NLar NMen SOkd WAbe
- 'Red Pearl'	CSBt EPfP LRHS MAsh MGos MSwo SPer
* - 'Variegatum' (v)	EWes NLAp WPat

Vagaria (*Amaryllidaceae*)

olivieri SF 266 from Morocco **new**	CMon
parviflora from Israel **new**	CMon

Valeriana (*Valerianaceae*)

'Alba'	see *Centranthus ruber* 'Albus'
alliariifolia	EBee EMon GCal NBro NSti WCot
arizonica	CLyd CStu EDAr MSte
'Coccinea'	see *Centranthus ruber*
coreana	CFee WMoo
hardwickii	EBee GPoy WCot
jatamansii	CArn GPoy
montana	GTou NBro NRya SRms
moyanoi	CFil
officinalis	More than 30 suppliers
- subsp. ***sambucifolia***	CFee CPom NDov SHar WCAu
* - 'Variegata' (v)	WCHb
phu 'Aurea'	More than 30 suppliers
pyrenaica	CAby ECha EHrv EPPr EVFa LPhx SHar WCot WMoo
saxatilis	NLar NRya
supina	NWCA
wallrothii	WCot

Valerianella (*Valerianaceae*)

§ ***locusta***	CArn GPoy
olitoria	see *V. locusta*

Vallea (*Elaeocarpaceae*)

stipularis	CDoC
- var. ***pyrifolia***	CPLG CPle

Vallota see *Cyrtanthus*

Vancouveria (*Berberidaceae*)

chrysantha	CDes CElw CFil CLAP CPom EBee ECha EMan ERos GBuc IBlr MNrw MRav NLar NRya NWCA SSpi WCru WMoo WSHC
hexandra	CDes CFil CLAP CPom EBee EBrs EHrv EMan EMon ERos GBuc GCal GFlt GKir IBlr NRya NSti SMad SSpi WCru
planipetala	CLAP IBlr SSpi WCru

Vania see *Thlaspi*

veitchberry see *Rubus* 'Veitchberry'

Vellozia (*Velloziaceae*)

elegans	see *Talbotia elegans*

Veltheimia (*Hyacinthaceae*)

§ ***bracteata*** ♀H1	CFil CHal EBak IBlr LToo SYvo WCot WDav
§ ***capensis*** ♀H1	CSev
viridifolia misapplied	see *V. capensis*
viridifolia Jacq.	see *V. bracteata*

Venidium see *Arctotis*

x *Venidioarctotis* see *Arctotis*

Veratrum ✿ (*Melanthiaceae*)

album	EBee ECha GBuc GIBF LRHS MRav NEgg SBla SChu SSpi WBrE WCot WCru WFar
- var. ***flavum***	IPot LPhx WCru
- var. ***oxysepalum***	WCru
californicum	CFil EBee GCal IBlr WSHC
dolichopetalum B&SWJ 4416	WCru
formosanum	MMil MNrw
- B&SWJ 1575	WCru
maackii var. ***maackii*** B&SWJ 5831	WCru
mengtzeanum F&W 8990 **new**	WCot
nigrum ♀H4	More than 30 suppliers
stamineum	WCru
viride	EBee GFlt IBlr SBla SSpi

Verbascum ✿ (*Scrophulariaceae*)

acaule x ***phoeniceum*** **new**	NWCA
adzharicum	IFro MAnH NBur WHoo
Allestree hybrids	CFee EHrv
'Annie May'	EBee EMag EMan EPfP LAst LPhx LRHS LSRN MMHG NCob NGdn NSti SUsu SVil WCra
'Apricot Sunset'	EBee EMag EMan LAst LPhx LRHS LSRN MAnH MAvo NCob NGdn NSti SUsu SVil WCra WPGP
'Arctic Summer'	see *V. bombyciferum* 'Polarsommer'
arcturus	WPer
'Aurora'	LPhx LPio SJoh
'Aztec Gold'	LPhx SJoh
* ***bakerianum***	EBla ECtt EMan MAnH WWFP
'Banana Custard'	EBee EMan ENot EWin MAnH MBct SPet SPoG WPop
'Bill Bishop'	NHar SIng

	blattaria	CHrt EBee EHrv GKev LIck LRHS MBow MWgw NBir NLsd NRnb SPav WFar WHer WPer WWhi
	- f. ***albiflorum***	CBot CNic CSpe EBee EChP EMar ERou IFro LLWP LPhx LRHS NSti SBch SGar SPlb WHer WPer WTin
	- pink-flowered	EGoo SPav STes
	- yellow-flowered	NRnb SPav
*	***boerhavii*** bicolor	MAnH WRos
§	***bombyciferum***	CBre CSev EBee EChP ECha GMaP MFOX NGdn NLsd NSti SPur SRms WCot WSSM WWpP XPep
	- BSSS 232	WCru
*	- 'Arctic Snow'	EMar SPav
	- 'Caribbean Crush' **new**	CCge
§	- 'Polarsommer'	CBot CHrt CSam CSpe EBee ENot EPfP ERou EWTr GGar GKir LRHS MBri MDun NBir NBlu NScw NVic SPav SPer SPet SPoG SRms WWeb
	- 'Silver Lining'	NBur NPer SDnm SPav
	'Brookside'	EMag LPhx MSte
	'Broussa'	see *V. bombyciferum*
I	'Buttercup'	CFai EMan
	'Butterscotch'	MAnH MSph
	'Caribbean Crush'	CFai CHar CPen CSpe CWCL EBee ELan EMan EPfP EShb LAst LSou MBNS MMil NCGa NEgg NLar NPri SPav WPop WSan WWlt
	- 'Mango'	EMan ENot EPfP
	chaixii	CHea CHrt CSam EBee ECha ECtt EHrv EUnu GAbr GBuc GFlt LRHS MMHG MWat MWgw NBir NEgg SBla WAul WFar WMoo WPer
	- 'Album' $\mathbb{Y}^{H4}$	More than 30 suppliers
	- 'Helene Bowles'	CHar LPhx
	chaixii x 'Wendy's Choice'	MAvo MDKP
	'Charles Harper'	EMag LPhx MSph MSte
	'Cherokee' **new**	LPhx
	'Cherry Helen' **new**	CFwr CPen CWCL EBee EMar EPfP LRHS MBNS NLar NRnb SPoG WHlf WOVN WSan WWeb
	'Claire'	LPhx SJoh
	'Clementine'	LPhx LPio SJoh
	(Cotswold Group) 'Cotswold Beauty' $\mathbb{Y}^{H4}$	CHad COtt CPar CSam EBee EChP ECtt EMar EPfP ERou GKir LAst LPhx LRHS MAnH MAvo MRav MTis MWat MWgw NDov NGdn NLar SBla SChu SPla SUsu WCAu WMnd WPGP
	- 'Cotswold Queen'	More than 30 suppliers
	- 'Gainsborough' $\mathbb{Y}^{H4}$	More than 30 suppliers
	- 'Mont Blanc'	EBee EChP ECot EHrv EMan GMaP LAst LPhx LPio LRHS MLLN SChu
	- 'Pink Domino' $\mathbb{Y}^{H4}$	More than 30 suppliers
	- 'Royal Highland'	COIW EBee EChP ECot ECtt EHrv ELan EMar EPfP ERou GAbr GKir LAst LPhx LPio LRHS MAnH MAvo MTis NGdn NLar SChu SDnm SPav SWvt WFar WMnd WWeb
	- 'White Domino'	EBee EMar ERou LBmB LRHS MBNS NGby SPla WCAu WWol
	'Cotswold King'	CSpe LPio MBri MSph NDov NEgg SBch SDnm SPav SPla WCot WPGP WSan
	creticum	EBee LPhx SUsu WPer
	- 'Allomnis' **new**	MAnH
	'Daisy Alice'	EMag LPhx LPio MAnH MAvo MSte SBla
§	***densiflorum***	CArn EBee EMag ERou SMar WFar WPer
	'Dijon'	EBee ECtt EMan EWes
	dumulosum $\mathbb{Y}^{H2-3}$	EDAr EHyt NWCA WLin
	'Ebenezer Howard' **new**	LPhx LPio
	epixanthinum	CHar EBrs EMag EMan GMac ITer MAnH MCCP MDKP NCGa NLar NRnb
	'Golden Wings' $\mathbb{Y}^{H2-3}$	ECtt ITim NMen WAbe
	'Helen Johnson'	More than 30 suppliers
	'Hiawatha'	LPhx SJoh
	'High Noon'	LPhx SJoh
I	x ***hybridum*** 'Copper Rose'	CWan ECGP EMan ENot EPfP MAnH MHer NRnb SPet WHil WPer WSan
	- 'Snow Maiden'	CWan EBee EMan ENot MAnH MHer NRnb SDnm WHil
	- 'Wega'	CBot
	'Hyde Hall Sunrise' **new**	ENot LBuc LRHS
	'Innocence'	MAvo MDKP
	'Jackie'	More than 30 suppliers
	'Jackie in Pink' **new**	MCCP
	'Jolly Eyes'	EBee EChP EMan EMar NCGa NRnb SOkh WHil WSan
	'June Johnson'	MAnH SHar
	'Kalypso'	LPhx SJoh
	'Klondike'	LPhx LPio SJoh
	'Kynaston'	EMar MAnH SHar
	'Letitia' $\mathbb{Y}^{H3}$	CBcs EBee ECtt EHyt ELan EWes GCal IMGH LAst LRHS MAvo MBnl MTho NJOw NMen NPri NWCA SBla SIng SPav SPoG SRot SWvt WAbe WKif WPop
	longifolium	LRHS WFar
	- var. ***pannosum***	see *V. olympicum*
*	***luridifolium***	WPGP
	lychnitis	CArn LPhx WHer
	'Megan's Mauve'	EBee ECot EMan EWll NEgg SWvt
	'Monster'	EMag LPhx MAnH MSph MSte
	'Moonshadow'	LPhx SJoh
	'Mystery Blonde'	LPhx SJoh
	nigrum	CArn CHrt EBee ECtt EPfP GAbr LRHS MAnH MBNS MBow MChe MWrn NChi NGHP SBri SECG SEND SRob WBVN WCAu WFar WMoo WPer WWpP
	- var. ***album***	GMac LPio MAnH NChi NGHP NLar WCAu WMoo WWpP
	'Nimrod'	LPhx SJoh
	'Norfolk Dawn'	EBee EMag EMan EMar EPfP LAst LPhx LPio LSRN MAnH MAvo MSte MWgw NCob NGdn NSti SUsu SVil WCra WPGP
§	***olympicum***	CHrt CSam EBee ECtt EGoo ELan ENot EPfP EUJe GKir LRHS MBNS MWat MWgw NBPC NLRH NOak SDix SEND SPoG SRob WCAu WCot WFar WGHP WPer XPep
	oreophilum	EBee
	'Patricia'	EMag LPhx MAvo MSph MSte WPGP
	'Petra' **new**	LPhx
	phlomoides	EMan WOut
	phoeniceum	CArn ELan EPfP ITim LRHS MWgw NBlu NBro NEgg NOak SBri SGar SPet SPlb WAul WBVN WEas WPer WSSM
*	- 'Album'	CSpe EBee LIck NJOw WBrE
	- 'Flush of Pink'	ECtt
	- 'Flush of White'	CBot CBrm ECtt EGoo EMan ERou EWTr GMac LAst LPhx LRHS MWat NChi SDnm SPav SRob STes WGor WHil WMoo WRHF
	- hybrids	CBot CSpe ECtt EGoo EMan GMaP MHer NBid NChi NEgg NGdn NJOw NLsd NVic SRms WFar WGor WPer

	- 'Rosetta' **new**	CBrm EMar EPPr GBri
	- 'Violetta'	More than 30 suppliers
I	'Phoenix'	LPhx SJoh
	'Pink Glow' **new**	LRHS
	'Pink Ice'	EPPr MAvo MDKP
	'Pink Kisses' **new**	LRHS
	'Pink Petticoats' **new**	ENot LBuc NLar
	'Primrose Cottage'	CPen EMag LPhx MAnH
	'Purple Prince' **new**	ECtt
	pyramidatum	CBot EBee LPhx WHer
	'Raspberry Ripple'	EBee ELan EMan EMar EPfP IHMH MAnH MAvo SPav WHlf
	'Raspberry Sorbet'	EMan
	rorippifolium	CFwr CHea EWll LPhx NCGa NRnb WCot WHil
	'Southern Charm'	EChP ECtt EMan ERou EWTr EWll GMaP GMac LRHS MAnH MAvo MBct MBri MCCP NArg NChi NGHP NVic SPav SPoG STes WFar WHil WPtf WSan
*	'Spica'	CBot EBee NLar
	spicatum	CBot WFar
	spinosum	SBla
	'Summer Sorbet'	CPen EBee ELan EMan ENot EPfP LSRN SPer SRkn WHlf
*	Sunset shades	MSph WWpP
	thapsiforme	see *V. densiflorum*
	thapsus	COld CSev EBee GPoy GWCH MBow MChe MHer NMir NRnb WSel WWye
	'Tilney Moonbeam'	ECtt EMar
	undulatum	CArn
	'Valerie Grace'	EMag LPhx MAnH MSte
	'Vernale'	CBot
	'Virginia'	LPhx SJoh
	wiedemannianum	EBee LPhx SIgm
	'Yellow Johnson'	EMan

Verbena (*Verbenaceae*)

	'Adonis Light Blue' (G)	LRHS
	'Aphrodite'	LAst
	'Apple Blossom' (G)	LRHS
	'Aveyron' (G)	GBri SChu
	(Aztec Series) Aztec Magic Pink = 'Balazpima'PBR (G)	LIck
	- Aztec Magic Plum = 'Balazplum'PBR (G)	NPri
	- Aztec Magic Silver = 'Balazsilma' (G)	LIck NPri SCoo
	- Aztec Pearl (G) **new**	SCoo
	- Aztec Red = 'Balazred'PBR (G)	LIck NPri SCoo
	- Aztec White = 'Balazwhit' (G)	LIck
	'Betty Lee'	ECtt
	'Blue Cascade' (G)	LAst SAga
	'Blue Lagoon'	NPri
	'Blue Prince' (G)	CSpe
§	***bonariensis*** ♀H3-4	More than 30 suppliers
	- variegated (v)	ITer
	'Boon' (G)	ECtt LSou
	'Booty' (G)	ECtt LSou SAga
	'Boughton House' (G)	MSte
	brasiliensis Vell. **new**	MDKP
	canadensis (G)	EBee
	- 'Perfecta' (G)	MGol WWhi
	'Candy Carousel' (G)	SPet
	'Carousel' (G)	LAst SPoG
	chamaedrifolia	see *V. peruviana*
§	'Claret' (G)	CAby CElw CSam ECtt EMan EPfP EWin GBri SAga SMHy SMrm SUsu WPen
	'Corsage Peach' **new**	LAst WWol
	'Corsage Red' **new**	LAst WWol
	corymbosa	CHea CHll CM&M CWCL EBee EChP ECha EGra EPPr GBBs GSki LLWP MDKP NBPC NLar SAga SBla SBod WLin WPer WPtf WWpP
	- 'Gravetye'	CHad CHrt CStr GBuc NChi NCiC NCob WFar
	'Diamond Butterfly' (G)	EWin SAga
	'Diamond Carouselle' (G)	EWin
	'Diamond Merci' (G)	SAga
	Donalena Dark Red **new**	WWol
	Donalena Pink **new**	WWol
	Donalena Purple Red **new**	WWol
	Donalena Violet Blue **new**	WWol
	'Edith Eddleman' (G)	EBee EChP ECtt EWin LRHS MNrw
	'Freefall'	GBri
	hastata	More than 30 suppliers
	- 'Alba'	CHar EBee EChP EMan EMon EPyc GBar GBuc GSki LDai MCCP MDKP MLLN NBPC NDov NRnb SHGN SPoG STes WCAu WMoo WPer WWhi WWpP
	- 'Rosea'	More than 30 suppliers
	'Hidcote Purple' (G)	MSte
	'Homestead Purple' (G)	CHrt CSev EBee ECGP EChP ECtt EMan EPfP GSki LDai LIck LSRN MAsh NRnb SAga SGSe SGar SMrm SPoG SUsu SWvt WGwG
	'Huntsman' (G)	GBuc
	'Imagination' (G)	LRHS
	incompta	EBee
	'Jenny's Wine'	see *V.* 'Claret'
	'La France' (G)	CAby CHea CSam ECha ECtt EMan EPfP EShb EWin GBri LPhx LSou MAnH SAga SChu SDix SMHy SMrm SOkh SUsu WHoo
	(Lanai Series) Lanai Blue = 'Lan Bule' **new**	LIck
	- Lanai Burgundy = 'Lan Burg' **new**	LAst
	- Lanai Lavender Star = 'Lan Lav Star'	NPri
	- Lanai Peach = 'Lan Peachy' **new**	LAst LIck
	- Lanai Royal Purple = 'Lan Roypur'PBR **new**	LIck
	'Lawrence Johnston' (G) ♀H3	MAJR
	litoralis	EBee
	'Lois' Ruby'	see *V.* 'Claret'
	'Loveliness' (G)	SMer
	macdougalii	CBos EChP EGoo EMan MDKP MGol NEgg NRnb WWpP
	officinalis	CArn CRWN CWan EDAr GBar GPoy MChe MGol MHer MSal SECG SIde SMar WGHP WHer WJek WLHH WPer WSel WWye XPep
	patagonica	see *V. bonariensis*
	'Peaches and Cream' (G) ♀H3	LRHS LSou NPri
§	***peruviana*** (G)	CAby EPfP EWin MAsh SBla SChu SDix SIng SRms
	'Pink Bouquet'	see *V.* 'Silver Anne'
	'Pink Parfait' (G)	CHal CHrt EMan EPfP EWin LAst SPet SPoG WWol
	'Pink Pearl' (G)	ECtt
	platensis (G)	EBee
	- RCB/Arg P-2	WCot

	‘Raspberry Crush’ (G)	LRHS
	‘Red Cascade’	SPet
§	***rigida*** ♀H3	More than 30 suppliers
	- ‘Lilacina’	WCot XPep
	- ‘Polaris’	CHar EBee EMan EShb IBal LRHS SMHy SMrm SUsu WCAu WRos WWpP
§	‘Silver Anne’ (G) ♀H3	CHrt CSam ECtt EMan EWin LDai LSou SAga SChu SDix SMer SUsu
§	‘Sissinghurst’ (G) ♀H2-3	CSam ECtt EMan EWin NPri SAga SIng SMrm SPoG SRms
	‘Sissinghurst Pink’ **new**	LAst
*	‘Snow Flurry’	CFir
	(Superbena Series)	LSou
	Superbena Burgundy = ‘USBENAL5’ **new**	
	- Superbena Ruby Red = ‘USBENA5122’ **new**	LSou
	- Superbena Violet Blue = ‘USBENAS10’ **new**	NPri
	Tapien Pink = ‘Sunver’[PBR] (G)	LAst WWol
	Tapien Salmon = ‘Sunmaref’ (G)	LAst LSou
	Tapien Violet = ‘Sunvop’[PBR] (G)	LAst LSou WWol
	Tapien White = ‘Suntapipurew’ (G)	LAst
	Temari Blue = ‘Sunmariribu’[PBR] (G)	LAst
	Temari Coral Pink = ‘Sunmariripi’[PBR] (G)	LAst
	Temari Scarlet = ‘Sunmarisu’[PBR] (G)	LAst
	Temari Vanilla (G) **new**	WWol
	Temari White = ‘Sunmaririho’[PBR] (G)	LAst WWol
	‘Tenerife’	see *V.* ‘Sissinghurst’
	tenuisecta (G)	MGol SMar WPer XPep
	venosa	see *V. rigida*
	‘White Sissinghurst’ (G)	LAst

Verbesina (*Asteraceae*)

alternifolia	CArn EMan MGol
- ‘Goldstrahl’	WCAu WPer
encelioides **new**	CSec
helianthoides	CSec EWll MGol NRnb WHil

Vernonia (*Asteraceae*)

crinita	CAby ECha MWat NLar SIgm SMad SSvw WBor WCAu
- ‘Mammuth’	CFwr EBee EMan LBuc LPhx MBNS NCob SAga SPoG WCot
fasciculata	EBee EBrs EChP EMan EVFa LRHS NLar SSvw WCAu WCot
gigantea	NLar
noveboracensis	MGol MHar NLar WPer WWpP
- ‘Albiflora’	NLar WPer

Veronica (*Scrophulariaceae*)

	amethystina	see *V. spuria*
	‘Anna’[PBR] **new**	NDov
	armena	CLyd EWes MDKP MHer MSte MWat NJOw NLRH NMen NWCA SBla SHel SPoG SRot WFar
§	***austriaca***	GSki MLLN NChi WFar WMoo
	- var. ***dubia***	see *V. prostrata*
	- ‘Ionian Skies’	CLyd CMea CPBP CTri EBee EGoo EWes GBuc LBee LPhx LRHS MHar MNrw NCGa NDov SBla SChu SGar SHel SIgm SOkh SPer WCru WFar WKif WPat WPer WSHC
§	- subsp. ***teucrium***	CArn CSam GBin GSki MFOX MWgw NDlv NEgg NLon SMac SRms WFar WPer
	- - ‘Blue Fountain’	LLWP
	- - ‘Crater Lake Blue’ ♀H4	EBee ECha ECtt ENot ERou EVFa LPhx LRHS MAvo MRav NBid NCGa NFor NLon NVic SMrm SPla SPlb SRms WCot WEas WFar WMnd WPat WPer
	- - ‘Kapitän’	ECha GBuc MNrw NCGa NPro WFar WPer
	- - ‘Knallblau’	EBee EMil LRHS MBri NCGa SSvw
	- - ‘Royal Blue’ ♀H4	EBee ECot EMan EPfP EWin GBuc GSki LPio LRHS MArl MNFA NOak NSti SRms WFar WMnd WWeb
	bachofenii	WTin
	beccabunga	CArn CBen CWat EHon ELan EMFW EPfP GPoy LNCo LPBA MBow NArg NBlu NMir NPer WFar WHer WPop WWpP
	- var. ***limosa***	WWye
	bellidioides	GTou
	‘Bergen’s Blue’	EChP EPfP NLar
	Blue Bouquet	see *V. longifolia* ‘Blaubündel’
	‘Blue Indigo’	CHar EBee ELan IBal
	‘Blue Spire’	WPer
	bombycina	CStu EHyt NWCA
	- subsp. ***bolkardaghensis***	EHyt NMen SBla
	bonarota	see *Paederota bonarota*
	caespitosa	CPBP MDHE
	- subsp. ***caespitosa***	CLyd EHyt NMen WAbe
	candida	see *V. spicata* subsp. *incana*
	x ***cantiana*** ‘Kentish Pink’	CStr EGoo GBuc MHer SHel SPla WDyG WMoo WPer
	caucasica	LPhx SAga WCru
	chamaedrys	NMir XPep
§	- ‘Miffy Brute’ (v)	EBee NBir NPro
	- ‘Pam’ (v)	CBre EMan EPPr WCHb
	- ‘Variegata’	see *V. chamaedrys* ‘Miffy Brute’
	- ‘Waterrow’	EMon
	cinerea ♀H4	CLyd SAga SBch WEas WHoo WSHC
	dabneyi	CDes
	‘Darwin’s Blue’[PBR]	CMHG EChP GAbr MBNS MBri MSph NLar SPoG SPur WCot
	‘Ellen Mae’	EBee WCAu
	‘Eveline’	EBee EMan EPfP ERou MBNS MBnl MSph SUsu WCot
	exaltata	EChP EMan GBuc LPhx MSte NBur NChi SAga WCot WPer
	‘Fantasy’	SMHy
	filiformis	GWCH
	- ‘Fairyland’ (v)	CBgR EMan EWes WCHb
	formosa	see *Parahebe formosa*
§	***fruticans***	GTou NMen
	fruticulosa	NEgg NWCA
	- HZ 2000-036	EHyt
	gentianoides ♀H4	More than 30 suppliers
	- ‘Alba’	CMea GCal NBid NBre NChi NSti SAga
	- ‘Barbara Sherwood’	EBee EBrs GKir GMac MLLN MNFA WCot
	- ‘Blue Streak’	GSki NDlv WHil
	- ‘Lilacina’	EBee LRHS
	- ‘Nana’	CAby EBee MMil WBrE
	- ‘Pallida’	EBee EMan ENot EPfP IHMH LRHS MBrN MRav MSph NPri SPlb WFar
	- ‘Robusta’	EBee ECGP GMac GSki LRHS MSph NCGa NFla SBch SPet WMnd
	- ‘Tissington White’	CHar CMea EBee EBla EMar EWTr GMaP GMac LAst LPhx LRHS MLLN MTis NBir NLsd NPri SAga

	SBla SHar SOkh SPoG WAbb WCAu WFar WGHP WLin WMoo WWeb
- 'Variegata' (v)	More than 30 suppliers
gigantea **new**	MGol
'Goodness Grows'	EMan LAst LRHS SChu
grandis	EBee EChP EMan EPPr EWll GAbr MAnH MDKP MGol MTis MWhi MWrn NBur NChi NLar SHGN SPoG WBVN WBrk WHoo WMoo WOut
x ***guthrieana***	CAbP CNic ELan MAsh MBNS NMen SOkd SRms SRot WFar WPer
'Heraud'	WCAu
incana	see *V. spicata* subsp. *incana*
* - 'Candidissima'	GCal
'Inspiration'	EBee LPhx NDov
kellereri	see *V. spicata*
kiusiana	CStr EBee EKen EMan MAnH MDKP MTis MWrn NBPC NLar SPoG
* - var. ***maxima***	CSec
kotschyana	CPBP
liwanensis	EDAr NMen XPep
- Mac&W 5936	EPot MDKP
longifolia	CMea CSBt EBrs ECha ELan EPfP EShb EWTr GCra GSki GWCH MWgw NEgg SHGN STes WBVN WEas WFar WGHP WMoo WWye
- 'Alba'	CHea EBee EChP ELan EMan EPfP STes WCAu WMoo
§ - 'Blaubündel'	EBee ERou NDlv NGdn
- 'Blauer Sommer'	EBee EChP EHan EMan LRHS MWgw NGdn SPur WMnd
§ - 'Blauriesin'	CM&M COIW CTri EBee EBrs ECGP EMil ERou GLil GMaP MBnl MBow MBri NSti SPer SSvw WFar
- Blue Giantess	see *V. longifolia* 'Blauriesin'
- 'Blue John'	EBee WCAu
- 'Fascination'	NGdn NPro SMrm WSan
- 'Foerster's Blue'	see *V. longifolia* 'Blauriesin'
- 'Joseph's Coat' (v)	EBee
- 'Lila Karina'	WPer
- 'Lilac Fantasy'	CM&M EBee NArg WCAu
- 'Oxford Blue'	EBee LRHS WRHF
- 'Rose Tone'	ECha ERou EWTr GSki MDKP MFOX MGol NEgg NLsd WHrl WMoo WSSM
- 'Rosea'	EChP ERou EVFa MGol STes WBrE WPer
- 'Schneeriesin'	CPrp EBee ECGP ECha EHrv GMaP LRHS MBnl MBri NBir NLar SChu SPer SPur
lyallii	see *Parahebe lyallii*
montana 'Corinne Tremaine' (v)	CBgR EBee EMan EMar EMon EWin IFro IHMH LSou MBct MHar NBir NCGa NLar SRms WCot WHer WRHF WWye
- golden variegated **new**	EWin
nipponica	WPer
nummularia	NBur WPer
oenei	CPBP WLin
officinalis	CArn
oltensis	CLyd CPBP EHyt EPot EWes LTwo MHer NMen WPat
orchidea	EBee SRms
orientalis subsp. ***orientalis***	EPot ESis NMen
ornata	EBee EMan MGol WCot WPer
'Pacific Ocean' **new**	CBgR
pectinata	ECtt ESis
- 'Rosea'	ECtt EWes GKir NJOw WPer XPep
peduncularis	LRHS WEas
- 'Alba'	WPer
§ - 'Georgia Blue'	More than 30 suppliers
- 'Oxford Blue'	see *V. peduncularis* 'Georgia Blue'
perfoliata	see *Parahebe perfoliata*
petraea 'Madame Mercier'	EWin SRot
'Pink Damask'	CFwr CHar CSpe EBee EChP ECtt ELan ERou EVFa GLil LRHS MBri NCob NDov NLar NSti SMrm SUsu WFar WHoo WMnd WTin WWlt
pinnata 'Blue Eyes'	LBee
prenja	see *V. austriaca*
'Prince of Wales Feathers' **new**	NCGa
§ ***prostrata*** ♀H4	CLyd CMea CSam CTri ECtt EPfP EWTr GEdr GKir IHMH LBee LRHS MWat NJOw SHFr SIng SRms WAbe WCru WEas WFar WHoo WLin WMoo
- 'Alba'	MWat WHoo WLin
- 'Aztec Gold'	EBee LBuc MBNS NBro NLar NPro WCot
§ - 'Blauspiegel'	CPBP SBla SIgm WCru
- Blue Mirror	see *V. prostrata* 'Blauspiegel'
- 'Blue Sheen'	CBrm ECtt EHyt GEdr GKir LRHS MBNS NBir SAga SChu SIng WAbe WFar WPer
- 'Lilac Time'	NBir NLar SIng SRms
- 'Loddon Blue'	GKir LRHS NVic SBla SRms WCot WPer
- 'Mrs Holt'	CLyd CPBP CSam ECtt EHyt GEdr GKir LRHS NBir NFor NMen SBla SRms WAbe WBVN WCru
- 'Nana'	ECtt EPot EWes MWat NMen WAbe
- 'Nestor' **new**	NDlv
- 'Rosea'	MWat SIgm WLin WPer
- 'Spode Blue' ♀H4	CHar CMea COIW ECtt EPot GAbr LRHS MOne NWCA SBla SPoG SRms WBVN WLin
- 'Trehane'	COIW CRez ECtt EDAr LBee LGro LRHS MHer MWat NOak NRya SIng SPlb SPoG SRms SRot WAbe WBVN WLin WMoo
* ***pseudolysimachion***	WCot WMoo
* ***pyrolifolia***	NWoo
repens	ESis EWTr IHMH NBlu NJOw NNor SPlb WGwG WPer
'Rosalinde'	CBot GBuc WPer
'Royal Pink'	CM&M EChP
rupestris	see *V. prostrata*
saturejoides	CPBP SRms WPer
saxatilis	see *V. fruticans*
schmidtiana	GSki GTou NArg WPer
- 'Nana'	CPBP
selleri	see *V. wormskjoldii*
§ 'Shirley Blue' ♀H4	CPrp EBee EBrs ECGP EGra ELan EPfP GKir IHMH MBNS MHer MWat NCGa SMer SPer SPoG SRms WBVN WCFE WGHP WHil WPer WTel WWhi
§ ***spicata***	EBee ELan EPfP LEdu LRHS MBNS MDun MWgw NBid NBlu NFor NLon SECG SHel SPet SRms WBrk WCAu WFar WPer WWye
- 'Alba'	EBee EMan EMil MBNS MRav SMar WFar WPer WTin
- 'Barcarolle'	ELan EPfP MLLN NBro NGby
§ - 'Blaufuchs'	CSam ECtt MWrn WTel
- 'Blue Bouquet'	IBal NBre NLar WWeb
- Blue Fox	see *V. spicata* 'Blaufuchs'
§ - 'Erika'	ECha ECtt GBuc IHMH MLLN NArg NBir NOak SAga SMar
§ - 'Glory'PBR	EHan ELan ENot EPfP GBri GMac LBuc MAvo MWgw NCot SPer SPoG SUsu WCFE WCot WCra

	- 'Heidekind'	More than 30 suppliers
	- subsp. ***hybrida***	WCot WHer
§	- 'Icicle'	CM&M CStr LRHS MBrN MSte NBro SAga SSvw SUsu
§	- subsp. ***incana***	CMea CSBt CSpe EHoe ELan ENot EPfP ERou EWTr GEdr GKir GSki IFro MWat NFor NLon SAga SBla SPlb SRms WBVN WFar WMoo WPat WPer WTin WWeb XPep
	- - 'Nana'	ECha ESis NBir SRms
	- - 'Saraband'	WPer
	- - 'Silbersee'	EWTr
	- - 'Silver Carpet'	EBee EMan LAst LBBr LRHS MNFA MRav MWgw NSti SChu SPer SPla WMnd
	- - 'Wendy'	CStr GCal
	- 'Nana Blauteppich'	EMan MBNS MWhi NBre NLar WWeb
	- 'Noah Williams' (v)	EBee EChP EMan GBuc MBNS MBnl MFOX NPro NSti SPur SUsu
	- 'Pink Goblin'	NBre WPer
	- Red Fox	see *V. spicata* 'Rotfuchs'
	- 'Romiley Purple'	ECGP ERou MLLN MSte MTis SChu SHel WAul WFar
	- 'Rosalind'	NLar
	- ***rosea***	see *V. spicata* 'Erika'
	- 'Rosenrot'	CRez EMan MHar WRHF
§	- 'Rotfuchs'	CFwr CPrp CStr EBee ECtt EHoe ELan ENot ERou EWsh GKir GLil IHMH MBow MRav MWgw NBir NBro NEgg NPri NSti SPer SRms WBVN WCot WFar WHil WPer WSHC WTel
	- 'Royal Candles'PBR	see *V. spicata* 'Glory'
	- 'Sightseeing'	EHan ERou GFlt MGol MMHG NArg NBir NBre SPet SRms
	- ***variegata*** (v)	CStr MLLN NBir
§	***spuria*** L.	CStr EVFa GGar NBur WPer
	stelleri	see *V. wormskjoldii*
	subsessilis **new**	WPer
	- 'Blaue Pyramide'	NBre NMyG
	'Sunny Border Blue'	EBee EMan EMar EPfP GBuc GMac MBNS MSph NLar SUsu WCot WFar
	tauricola	MDHE
	- JJH 92101536	SAga
	telephiifolia	ECtt EMan EWes MDKP NJOw NMen NWCA
	teucrium	see *V. austriaca* subsp. *teucrium*
	thessalica	EDAr EPot
	thessalonica	EDAr
	thymoides subsp. ***pseudocinerea***	NWCA
	urticifolia **new**	EWTr
	virginica	see *Veronicastrum virginicum*
	'Waterperry Blue'	LRHS NWoo WPer
	wherryi	WPer
	'White Icicle'	see *V. spicata* 'Icicle'
	'White Jolanda'	EBee EChP ENot EPfP LRHS MBnl NLar NPro
	'White Spire'	CBot
	whitleyi	CLyd CNic NWoo
§	***wormskjoldii***	EDAr ESis IHMH MBrN NCGa NEgg NJOw NMen NWCA SBla SHel SRms WLin WPer
	- 'Alba'	MDHE MDKP WPer

Veronicastrum (*Scrophulariaceae*)

	brunonianum **new**	GCal
	japonicum	CSec SGar
	latifolium	CPLN WSHC
	- BWJ 8158	WCru
	sibiricum	CStr ECha EMar EPyc EWTr GCal NBid NBre SBla SMar SVal WCot WHoo WMoo
	- BWJ 6352	WCru
	- var. ***yezoense*** **new**	GIBF
	- - AER 0290	MGol
	- - RBS 0209	MAvo
	- - RBS 0290	NPro
	villosulum	CPLN CPom CSpe EBee LBuc NBid NBro WCot WCru
§	***virginicum***	CArn CHea CKno EChP ECha ECtt EHrv EPyc EVFa GKir MGol NBir NSti SRms WGwG WMoo WPer WWhi WWlt WWpP
	- 'Alboroseum'	EMan WTin
	- 'Album'	More than 30 suppliers
	- 'Apollo'	CBre EBee EChP ECtt EMan EPfP ERou GAbr LAst LPhx LRHS MBri MLLN MWgw NBro NLar NSti SMHy WAul WCAu WTMC
	- 'Diane'	CElw EBee LPhx NDov
	- 'Fascination'	More than 30 suppliers
§	- var. ***incarnatum***	CKno CMea EBee ELan EMan GKir GMaP LPhx LRHS MBow MRav MWgw NBro NChi NDov NFla SMHy SPoG STes WBor WFar WHoo WMoo
	- - 'Pink Glow'	CHar COIW EBee EBrs ECtt EHoe EHrv ELan EMan EMil EPfP GAbr GKir LPhx MBnl MTis NBPC NCGa NGdn NSti SAga SMrm SOkh SPla STes WCAu WFar WMnd
	- 'Lavendelturm'	EBee ECha EMil IPot LPhx LRHS MLLN NCGa NDov SOkh WAul WCot WTMC
	- 'Pointed Finger'	SMHy SMrm SOkh SUsu WWlt
	- ***roseum***	see *V. virginicum* var. *incarnatum*
	- 'Spring Dew'	CBre CElw EBee EChP EMan ERou LPhx MLLN MWgw NBid NBro NDov NLar WCAu WMnd
	- 'Temptation'	EBee EChP EMan ERou EWTr LPhx MLLN NBro NDov NLar SMHy SPur SUsu WAul WCAu
	'White Jolan'	CFir CHar

Verschaffeltia (*Arecaceae*)

splendida	XBlo

Vestia (*Solanaceae*)

§	***foetida*** ♀H1	CBcs CPom CSec CSpe CWib EChP EMan EPfP ERea MNrw NArg SBrw SDnm SGar SHFr WHil WKif WPGP WPer WPic WSHC WWye
	lycioides	see *V. foetida*

Vetiveria (*Poaceae*)

zizanioides	MSal

Viburnum ✿ (*Caprifoliaceae*)

acerifolium	CBcs CFil CPle GIBF WFar WHCG WPat
alnifolium	see *V. lantanoides*
atrocyaneum	CFil CPle EBee WBcn WFar WHCG WPGP WPat
- B&SWJ 7272	WCru
awabuki	CFil CHEx EPfP MBlu NLar WPGP
- B&SWJ 8404	WCru
- 'Emerald Lustre'	CDoC CHEx CSam
betulifolium	CAbP CBcs CBrd CFil CMCN CPLG CPMA CPle CTrw EPfP EPla GIBF NLar SBrw SLon SMad WHCG WPat

- B&SWJ 1619	WCru
- B&SWJ 3200	WCru
bitchiuense	CPMA CPle ELan WWes
x ***bodnantense***	CBot CMac CTri CTrw CWSG MDun MRav MWat NFor NLon WHar WTel
- 'Charles Lamont' ♀H4	More than 30 suppliers
- 'Dawn' ♀H4	More than 30 suppliers
- 'Deben' ♀H4	CDoC CMac EBee ENot EPfP GKir LRHS MBri MRav MWya NLar SPer WCru WDin WFar
bracteatum	CFil CPle EPfP
buddlejifolium	CMac EPfP GKir SSpi WBcn WCru WFar WHCG WPGP
burejaeticum	GIBF
x ***burkwoodii***	More than 30 suppliers
- 'Anne Russell' ♀H4	CAbP CBcs CMac CPMA CTri EBee ECrN ELan ENot EPfP EWes GKir IArd LRHS MAsh MGos MRav MSwo NSti SHBN SLon SPer SPla SPlb SSta WDin WFar
- 'Chenaultii'	EPfP WCru WDin
- 'Compact Beauty'	CPMA EPfP WPat
- 'Conoy'	CPMA
- 'Fulbrook' ♀H4	CAbP CMHG EPfP LRHS MAsh MBri WDin WFar
- 'Mohawk'	CAbP CDoC CEnd CPMA ELan EPfP GKir LRHS MAsh MBri NLar SCoo SMur SPla SSpi SWvt WBcn WFar WPGP WPat
- 'Park Farm Hybrid' ♀H4	CAbP CDoC CMac CPLG CPMA CPSs CSam CTri CWSG EBee ECrN ELan ENot EPfP GKir LRHS MAsh MRav MSwo NBea NSti SLPl SPer SRms WPat
x ***carlcephalum*** ♀H4	More than 30 suppliers
- 'Cayuga'	NLar WPat
* - 'Variegatum' (v)	CPMA
carlesii	CBcs CMac CWib ENot EPfP GIBF GKir LRHS MBlu MRav NPri SBLw SCoo SLim SMer SPer SReu WTel
- B&SWJ 8838	WCru
- 'Aurora' ♀H4	More than 30 suppliers
- 'Charis'	CMHG CMac CPLG CPMA CSBt GKir LRHS NLar WBcn
- 'Compactum'	CPMA
- 'Diana'	CEnd CMHG CMac CPMA EPfP GKir LRHS MAsh MWya NLar SPer SSpi WPGP WPat WPen
- 'Marlou'	CPMA NLar
cassinoides	CPle CRez EPfP GBin GKir WFar WPat
'Chesapeake'	CBrm CDoC CMHG CPMA EWes LRHS NLar NPro SEND WBcn WDin WWes
chingii	CFil CPMA CPle GGGa SLon WBcn WCru WPGP
'Chippewa'	NLar
cinnamomifolium ♀H3	CAbP CBcs CBot CFil CHEx CMac CPle ECre EPfP GKir ISea LRHS MAsh SAPC SArc SLon SPer SPoG SSpi WFar WHCG WPGP WSHC
cotinifolium	CPle GKir
cylindricum	CBot CFil CMCN CPle EPfP GIBF SSpi WBcn WCru WPGP
- B&SWJ 6479 from Thailand **new**	WCru
- B&SWJ 7239	WCru
- HWJCM 434 from Nepal **new**	WCru
dasyanthum	CPle EPfP GIBF GKir IArd NLar
davidii ♀H4	More than 30 suppliers
- (f)	CBcs CBot CDoC CSBt ELan EPfP GIBF GKir MAsh MDun MGos SHBN SPer SPla SPoG SReu SRms SSta WPat
- (m)	CBcs CBot CDoC CSBt CWSG ELan EPfP GIBF GKir MAsh MDun MGos MRav SPer SPla SPoG SReu SRms SSta WPat
dentatum	EPfP
- var. ***deamii***	GIBF
- 'Moon Glo' **new**	NLar
dilatatum	CPne GIBF SPoG SSpi
- B&SWJ 4456	WCru
- 'Erie'	EBee EPfP NLar
- 'Iroquois'	EPfP
erosum B&SWJ 3585	WCru
erubescens	CPMA GKir WFar WWes
- B&SWJ 8281	WCru
- var. ***gracilipes***	CPMA CPle EPfP WPat
'Eskimo'	CAbP CMac CPMA CWSG EBee ECrN ENot EPfP GKir LAst LRHS LSRN MAsh MBNS MBlu MGos MRav NBlu NMoo SLim SMur SPoG SReu SSpi SWvt WDin WFar WHCG WPat WWes
§ ***farreri*** ♀H4	More than 30 suppliers
- 'Album'	see *V. farreri* 'Candidissimum'
§ - 'Candidissimum'	CBot CMac ELan EPfP GKir IArd LPio LRHS MMHG NLar SPer SPoG SSpi WBcn WPat
- 'December Dwarf'	NLar
- 'Farrer's Pink'	CAbP CPMA NLar
- 'Fioretta'	NLar
- 'Nanum'	CMac CPMA EBee EPfP MBar MBrN MRav MWat NLar SChu WFar WHCG WPat
foetens	see *V. grandiflorum* f. *foetens*
foetidum	CPle
- var. ***rectangulatum*** B&SWJ 3637	WCru
fragrans Bunge	see *V. farreri*
'Fragrant Cloud'	ECrN ENot
furcatum ♀H4	EPfP GIBF IArd IDee NLar SBrw SSpi WHCG
- B&SWJ 5939	WCru
x ***globosum*** 'Jermyns Globe'	CAbP CBcs CDoC CEnd CFil CMHG EBee GKir MBar MGos MSte MTis SLon SMur SPoG WCru WDin WFar WHCG WPGP
grandiflorum	CPMA CSBt NLar
- HWJK 2163	WCru
§ - f. ***foetens***	EPfP NLar
- 'Snow White'	ERea
harryanum	CFil CMHG CPle CPne EPfP GKir IDee LRHS MBNS WCru WFar
henryi	CAbP CFil CPMA CPle ECrN EPfP GKir LRHS NLar WBcn WDin WHCG WPat
x ***hillieri***	CAbP CFil CPle GBin MWhi WBcn WFar WHCG WKif
- 'Winton' ♀H4	CAbP CDoC CPMA EPfP EPla GKir LRHS LSRN MBri MTis SBrw SHBN SLim SLon SPoG SSpi WCru WDin WFar WPGP
'Huron' **new**	NEgg
ichangense	NLar
japonicum	CFil CHEx CMac CPLG CPle EPfP GKir NLar SBrw SHBN SLon
- B&SWJ 5968	WCru
x ***juddii*** ♀H4	More than 30 suppliers
koreanum B&SWJ 4231	WCru
lantana	CBgR CCVT CDul CLnd CRWN CTri ECrN ENot GKir GWCH LBuc

	Name	Suppliers
		MBow NWea SPer SPoG WDin WFar WMou
	- 'Aureum'	CBot EBee ECtt EHoe MAsh MBlu NLar WBcn
	- 'Mohican'	NLar WWes
	- 'Variefolium' (v)	CPMA
	- 'Xanthocarpum'	CMac GKir
§	***lantanoides***	EPfP GKir NLar SSpi
	lentago	CAbP CBot CMac CPle NLar
	lobophyllum	CPle EPfP GIBF NLar
	luzonicum B&SWJ 3930	WCru
*	- var. ***floribundum*** B&SWJ 8281 **new**	WCru
	- var. ***oblongum*** B&SWJ 3549	WCru
	macrocephalum	CPMA WDin
	- f. ***keteleeri***	CEnd CPMA CPle SSpi
	mariesii	see *V. plicatum* f. *tomentosum* 'Mariesii'
	mongolicum **new**	NLar
	nervosum B&SWJ 2251a	WCru
	nudum	CPle EBee EPfP GIBF NLar WWes
	- var. ***angustifolium***	GIBF
	- 'Pink Beauty'	CPMA CWSG LRHS LSRN WFar WPGP
	- 'Winterthur' **new**	NLar
	odoratissimum misapplied	CBcs CFil CPle EPfP IArd SHBN SSpi WSHC
	odoratissimum	CHEx CPLG CSam IDee SBrw SMad SMur XPep
	- B&SWJ 6913	WCru
	- 'Emerald Lustre'	see *V. awabuki* 'Emerald Lustre'
	'Oneida'	NLar WDin
	opulus	More than 30 suppliers
§	- var. ***americanum***	GIBF NLar
	- 'Apricot' **new**	NLar
	- 'Aureum'	More than 30 suppliers
	- 'Compactum' 𝕐H4	More than 30 suppliers
N	- 'Fructu Luteo'	ENot GKir
*	- 'Harvest Gold'	GKir SCoo SLim SPoG
	- 'Nanum'	CAbP CPle EBee ELan EPfP EPla EPot ESis GKir MBar MRav NLar NMen NPro WDin WHCG WPat
	- 'Notcutt's Variety' 𝕐H4	EBee ENot EPfP MBlu MGos NLar SHBN SHFr SMur SRms WBcn WPat
	- 'Park Harvest'	EBee GKir LRHS MBri NLar NSti SLPl WPat
§	- 'Roseum' 𝕐H4	More than 30 suppliers
	- 'Sterile'	see *V. opulus* 'Roseum'
*	- 'Sterile Compactum'	IMGH
N	- 'Xanthocarpum' 𝕐H4	CBcs CDoC CDul CMHG CMac CSam EBee EGra ELan EPfP GKir LAst LRHS MBar MBlu MGos MRav MSwo MWat NGHP SLPl SLon SPer SPoG SRms SWvt WDin WFar WTel
	- 'Xanthocarpum Compactum'	EMon
	parvifolium	NLar
N	***plicatum***	CBot CTri CWib GKir IArd MBar WDin
	- 'Janny' **new**	MBlu
	- 'Mary Milton' **new**	NLar
	- 'Nanum'	see *V. plicatum* f. *tomentosum* 'Nanum Semperflorens'
	- f. ***plicatum***	CBot
	- 'Popcorn'	CAbP GKir LRHS MAsh SLon SPoG SReu SSpi SSta WHCG WPat
	- 'Rosace'	MBlu
	- 'Roseum' **new**	CPle
N	- 'Sterile'	see *V. plicatum* f. *plicatum*
	- f. ***tomentosum***	EWTr WDin
	- - 'Cascade'	NEgg NLar SHBN SSpi
	- - 'Dart's Red Robin'	ECtt GKir LRHS NLar WBcn WPat
	- - 'Grandiflorum'	CDoC CPle EBee EPfP GKir LRHS MBar MBri SPer WBcn WHCG WMoo
	- - 'Lanarth'	CBcs CDoC CMac CSBt CSam CWSG CWib EBee ECrN ECtt EMil EPfP GKir LRHS MBlu MGos MRav MWhi NSti SPer SPla SWal SWvt WDin WFar WHCG WPat
§	- - 'Mariesii' 𝕐H4	More than 30 suppliers
	- - 'Molly Schroeder' **new**	NLar
§	- - 'Nanum Semperflorens'	CDoC CMac CWSG EBee ECtt EGra IArd MBlu MDun MGos NBlu SHBN SPer SPoG WFar WHCG WPat WSHC
	- - 'Pink Beauty' 𝕐H4	More than 30 suppliers
	- - 'Rotundifolium'	IArd NLar SHBN WPat
	- - 'Rowallane'	EPfP WPat
	- - 'Saint Keverne'	IArd SHBN
	- - 'Shasta'	CMCN COtt EPfP LRHS MBri NLar SSpi WDin
	- - 'Summer Snowflake'	CBrm CDoC CEnd CMHG CWSG EBee ECrN ENot EPfP GKir LRHS MRav NEgg SHBN SPer SPoG WDin WFar WHCG
	- 'Watanabe'	see *V. plicatum* f. *tomentosum* 'Nanum Semperflorens'
	'Pragense' 𝕐H4	CAbP CBcs CDul CMCN EBee EPfP GKir MBar MGos MRav NBlu NRib SLon SPer WDin WFar WHCG WPat
	propinquum	CAbP NLar WFar
	- B&SWJ 4009	WCru
	prunifolium **new**	NLar
	punctatum B&SWJ 9532 **new**	WCru
	x ***rhytidophylloides***	GKir WFar
	- 'Alleghany'	NLar
	- Dart's Duke = 'Interduke'	GKir LRHS MBri SLPl
	- 'Willowwood'	EBee LRHS NLar SMad WPat
	rhytidophyllum	More than 30 suppliers
	- 'Roseum'	CBot CPLG MRav SLPl SWvt
	- 'Variegatum' (v)	CPMA NLar WBcn
§	***rigidum***	CFil
	'Royal Guard' **new**	WPat
	rufidulum	NLar
	sargentii	EPfP GBin GIBF
	- f. ***flavum***	NLar
	- 'Onondaga' 𝕐H4	More than 30 suppliers
	- 'Susquehanna'	EPfP
	semperflorens	see *V. plicatum* f. *tomentosum* 'Nanum Semperflorens'
§	***setigerum***	CPle EPfP GIBF IArd IDee NLar SBrw SLPl SSpi WPat
	- 'Aurantiacum'	EPfP
	sieboldii	CBcs CPle GIBF
	- B&SWJ 2837	WCru
	- 'Seneca'	EPfP NLar
	subalpinum	NLar
	suspensum	CBcs
	taiwanianum B&SWJ 3009	WCru
	theiferum	see *V. setigerum*
	tinus	More than 30 suppliers
	- 'Bewley's Variegated' (v)	CBcs CDoC ECrN EMil ENot GKir MGos MRav SPer
I	- 'Compactum'	LSou NLar SWvt
	- 'Eve Price' 𝕐H4	More than 30 suppliers
	- 'French White' 𝕐H4	CBot CDoC CMac CRez CWSG EBee ECrN ENot EPfP EPla LRHS MAsh MBri MGos MRav MSwo SCoo SPoG SWvt WFar
	- 'Gwenllian' 𝕐H4	More than 30 suppliers

	- 'Israel'	EMil SPer SPla WFar
	- 'Little Bognor'	EBee LRHS NLar
	- 'Lucidum'	CBcs CPMA CSam SHBN SHGC WCFE WDin WFar
	- 'Lucidum Variegatum' (v)	CFil CMac CPMA EHol SLim
*	- 'Macrophyllum'	SWvt WBcn WFar WWeb XPep
	- 'Pink Prelude'	MWya
	- 'Purpureum'	CBcs CSBt EBee ECrN EHoe EPfP EPla GKir LRHS MAsh MGos MRav MSwo NEgg SCoo SHBN SLPl SLim SPer SPoG WDin WFar WMoo WPat WWeb
	- subsp. ***rigidum***	see *V. rigidum*
	- Spirit = 'Anvi'	NLar SPoG
	- 'Spring Bouquet'	MGos MWya NLar
	- 'Variegatum' (v)	CBot CBrm CDul CMac CSBt CWib EBee ELan EPfP LRHS MAsh MBar MSwo NSti SHBN SLim SPla SPlb SPoG SReu SSta WCFE WCru WDin WFar WPat WTel XPep
	- 'Villa Noailles'	XPep
	tomentosum	see *V. plicatum*
	trilobum	see *V. opulus* var. *americanum*
	- 'Bailey's Compact'	WPat
	- 'Phillips' **new**	CAgr
	- 'Wentworth' **new**	CAgr
	urceolatum B&SWJ 6988	WCru
	utile	CBot EPfP WFar WHCG WWes
	wrightii	CPle EPfP WHCG WPat
	- 'Hessei'	EPfP LRHS NLar
	- var. ***stipellatum*** B&SWJ 5844 **new**	WCru

Vicia (*Papilionaceae*)

	cracca	GWCH MBow NLan NMir
	sylvatica	CBgR EWes WBWf

Vigna (*Papilionaceae*)

	adenantha **new**	CPLN
§	***caracalla***	CPLN CSpe MJnS

Viguiera (*Asteraceae*)

	multiflora	WCot

Villarsia (*Menyanthaceae*)

	bennettii	see *Nymphoides peltata* 'Bennettii'

Vinca (*Apocynaceae*)

	difformis 🏆H3-4	CHad CHar COIW CStr CTri EBee ECha EMan LLWP LRHS NCGa SBri SDix WHer WPic WWye
*	- 'Alba'	CPom SBch
	- subsp. ***difformis***	CHid EMon
	- Greystone form	CHid EPPr EPfP EPla MBNS SEND WCAu WGwG WPnP WRHF
	- 'Jenny Pym'	CBgR CFwr CHid CPom EBee EPPr MSte SBch SMad SPoG WFar WOut WWeb
	- 'Oxford'	SLPl
	- 'Snowmound'	CBgR MRav SPoG
	'Hidcote Purple'	see *V. major* var. *oxyloba*
	major	CAgr CBcs CDul CSBt CWib EBee ELan ENot EPfP GKir GPoy LBuc LRHS MBri MGos MHer MSwo NCGa NPri NWea SHBN SPer SPoG SRms WDin WFar WGwG WMoo XPep
	- 'Alba'	GBuc WEas
	- 'Caucasian Blue'	CFil EBee WPGP
	- 'Elegantissima'	see *V. major* 'Variegata'
§	- subsp. ***hirsuta*** (Boiss.) Stearn	EMon MWgw WWye
	- var. ***hirsuta*** hort.	see *V. major* var. *oxyloba*
	- 'Honeydew' (v)	EMon
	- 'Jason Hill'	EMon
§	- 'Maculata' (v)	CBcs CDoC CSBt EBee EMar EMon LRHS MBar MSwo NBPC NEgg SLim SPer SPoG WCru WDin WMoo WWeb
§	- var. ***oxyloba***	CFis CNic COld CPLG CTri CWCL EBee ECtt ELan EMon EPla GSki MRav MWat SLPl SLim SMac SRms WFar WHer WPic
	- var. ***pubescens***	see *V. major* subsp. *hirsuta*
	- 'Reticulata' (v)	ELan EMon
	- 'Surrey Marble'	see *V. major* 'Maculata'
§	- 'Variegata' (v) 🏆H4	More than 30 suppliers
	minor	CAgr CDoC CDul CSBt ELan ENot EPfP GAbr GKir GPoy MAsh MBar MHer NBlu NPri NWea SHFr SPoG WBrE WDin WFar WWye XPep
	- f. ***alba*** 🏆H4	CBcs CBot CDoC EBee ECha EGoo EPfP LRHS MAsh MBar MGos MHer MWat MWgw NBlu NPri SHBN SMac SPer STre WCot WCru WFar WWpP WWye
	- - 'Gertrude Jekyll' 🏆H4	CBrm CDoC CSBt EBee ELan ENot EPfP EWTr GKir ILis LRHS LSRN MAsh MBri MGos MRav NCGa NPri SChu SCoo SEND SLim SPer SPla SPoG SVil WDin WMoo
	- 'Alba Aureavariegata'	see *V. minor* 'Alba Variegata'
§	- 'Alba Variegata' (v)	CPLG EHoe ENot EPla GAbr GGar GKir MBar MGos MHer NChi NGHP NPri NPro SPer SRms STre WBVN WEas WFar WTel
§	- 'Argenteovariegata' (v) 🏆H4	More than 30 suppliers
§	- 'Atropurpurea' 🏆H4	More than 30 suppliers
	- 'Aurea'	LBBr SPla WFar
§	- 'Aureovariegata' (v)	CBcs CBot CChe EBee GAbr GKir IHMH LRHS MAsh MBar MGos MRav NBlu NCGa NFor NPri SPlb WFar WTel WWye
	- 'Azurea'	CHid
§	- 'Azurea Flore Pleno' (d) 🏆H4	More than 30 suppliers
*	- 'Blue and Gold'	EGoo EMon
	- 'Blue Drift'	EMon EWes MBNS MSwo
	- 'Blue Moon'	ECtt SPer SPla
	- 'Bowles' Blue'	see *V. minor* 'La Grave'
	- 'Bowles' Variety'	see *V. minor* 'La Grave'
	- 'Burgundy'	SRms WWye
	- 'Caerulea Plena'	see *V. minor* 'Azurea Flore Pleno'
	- 'Dartington Star'	see *V. major* var. *oxyloba*
	- 'Double Burgundy'	see *V. minor* 'Multiplex'
	- Green Carpet	see *V. minor* 'Grüner Teppich'
§	- 'Grüner Teppich'	EMon WFar
	- 'Illumination' (v)	More than 30 suppliers
§	- 'La Grave' 🏆H4	CBcs CChe CDoC CSBt CSev EBee ECGP ECha ELan ENot EPfP EPla GKir LSRN MAsh MRav MWgw NBlu NCGa SLim SMac SPer SPla SRms SSvw STre SWvt WFar WWpP XPep
	- 'Maculata' (v)	EGoo ELan WBcn
	- 'Marie'	LBuc MGos
	- 'Marion Cran'	GSki
§	- 'Multiplex' (d)	CBgR EBee ECtt EMan EPPr EPla LBuc MAsh MBar MInt NChi NLon NPri SRms WCFE WCru WHrl
	- 'Persian Carpet' (v)	EMon
	- 'Purpurea'	see *V. minor* 'Atropurpurea'
	- 'Ralph Shugert' **new**	EPPr
	- 'Rubra'	see *V. minor* 'Atropurpurea'

- 'Sabinka'	CHid EGoo EMon EPla
- 'Silver Service' (d/v)	CHid CWan EMan EMon GBuc MInt MRav WBcn WCot WHoo
- 'Variegata'	see *V. minor* 'Argenteovariegata'
- 'Variegata Aurea'	see *V. minor* 'Aureovariegata'
- 'White Gold'	EBee NPri NPro
sardoa	EMon EPPr

Vincetoxicum (*Asclepiadaceae*)

§ ***hirundinaria***	EBee GPoy LEdu WWye
nigrum	EMon MGol MSal NBur NChi WCot WTin
officinale	see *V. hirundinaria*

Viola ✿ (*Violaceae*)

B&SWJ 8301 from Vietnam **new**	WCru
'Ada Jackson' (ExVa)	WOFF
'Admiral' (Va)	GMac WWhi
'Admiration' (Va)	GMac WBou
adunca	NWCA
- var. ***minor***	see *V. labradorica* ambig.
aetolica	CSec ESis WOut
'Agnes Cochrane' (ExVa)	WOFF
'Alanta' (Va)	WWhi
§ ***alba***	EWes NMen WBWf WBrE
'Alethia' (Va)	GMac
'Alex Blackwood' (SP)	WOFF
'Alice' (Vt)	CDev
'Alice Witter' (Vt)	CBre CDev ECha NChi SHar
'Alice Wood' (ExVa)	WOFF
* 'Alison' (Va)	GMac WBou WWhi
'Alma' (Va)	WOFF
'Amelia' (Va)	WBou
'Amiral Avellan' (Vt)	CDev CGro
'Ann' (SP)	WOFF
I 'Annie' (Vt)	CGro
'Annie Roberts' (FP)	WOFF
'Antique Lace' (Va)	MHer
'Arabella' (Va)	LRHS SChu WBou
arborescens	SSpi
'Ardross Gem' (Va)	CSam EBee EChP ECtt EDAr GAbr GKir GMaP GMac LRHS NChi SMeo WBou WEas WFar WPer WWhi
arenaria	see *V. rupestris*
'Arkwright's Ruby' (Va)	LRHS SRms
'Ashvale Blue' (PVt)	CGro
'Aspasia' (Va) ♀H4	GMac LRHS WBou WWhi
'Atalanta' (Vtta)	LRHS
'Avril Lawson' (Va)	CElw SHar WBou
'Azurella'	LRHS
'Baby Lucia' (Va)	CElw SBch SRms
'Barbara' (Va)	WBou WOFF
'Barnsdale Gem'	MBNS
'Baroness de Rothschild' (Vt)	CGro WHer
'Baronne Alice de Rothschild' (Vt)	CDev
'Beatrice' (Vtta)	WBou
'Becky Groves' (Vt)	CGro
* ***bella***	WEas
I 'Bella' (C)	EBee
§ 'Belmont Blue' (C)	ECtt EWes GAbr GMaP GMac LRHS MBow MHer MRav MWat MWgw NBir NCGa NChi NLsd SBla SChu SPer SRkn SRms WBou WFar WSHC WWhi
'Bernard Cox' (FP)	WOFF
§ ***bertolonii***	WBou
'Beshlie' (Va) ♀H4	ECtt GMac MBNS SChu WBou WEas WTin
'Betty' (Va)	WOFF
'Betty Dale' (ExVa)	WOFF
biflora	CMHG EBee MTho NChi
'Bishop's Belle' (FP)	WOFF
'Blackfaulds Gem' (SP)	WOFF
'Blue Bird' (Va)	GMac
'Blue Butterfly' (C)	GMac WSHC
'Blue Carpet' (Va)	GMac
'Blue Horns' (C) **new**	SUsu
'Blue Moon' (C)	SChu WBou WTin
'Blue Moonlight' (C)	CElw GBuc GMac LRHS NChi
'Blue Perfection' (Va)	LRHS
'Blue Tit' (Va)	SChu
'Boughton Blue'	see *V.* 'Belmont Blue'
'Bournemouth Gem' (Vt)	CBre CDev CGro
§ 'Bowles' Black' (T)	CArn CDev CSWP CSpe EDAr EPfP ESis GKev LRHS MAnH MHer MWat NBro NGHP NVic SBla SPla SRms WBou WCAu WEas WGwG
'Boy Blue' (Vtta)	ECtt
* 'Bryony' (Vtta)	WBou
'Bullion' (Va)	EBee WCot
'Burncoose Yellow'	WBou
'Buttercup' (Vtta)	COIW EBee EWin GMac NEgg SChu SPoG WBou WWhi
'Butterpat' (C)	GMac
'California' (Vt)	CDev
Can Can Series	WHer
canadensis	NWCA
'Candy'	CDev
canina	NBro NMir
* - ***alba***	CBre
'Catforth Blue Ribbon'	CElw
* 'Catforth Gold'	NCob
'Catforth Suzanne'	NCob
'Catherine Williams' (ExVa)	WOFF
'Cat's Whiskers'	CElw NChi
cazorlensis	CGra SBla
§ ***chaerophylloides*** var. ***sieboldiana***	CPMA
'Chantreyland' (Va)	NBir
'Charles William Groves' (Vt)	CGro
'Charlotte'	WBou
'Cherub'	GMac
'Christmas' (Vt)	CDev CGro
'Cinders' (Vtta)	GMac
'Citron' (Va) **new**	GMac
'Cleeway Crimson' (FP)	WOFF
'Clementina' (Va) ♀H4	CElw MRav
'Cleo' (Va)	EBee GMac WBou
'Clive Groves' (Vt)	CBre CDev CGro CHid
'Coconut Sorbet'	LRHS
'Coeur d'Alsace' (Vt)	CBre CDev CNic CPBP EBee NLar WCot WEas WWhi
'Columbine' (Va)	CDev CElw CGro EBee EChP GKir GMaP GMac LAst LRHS MHer NBir NEgg NWoo SChu SIng SMrm SPer SPoG SSto WBou WCot WEas WFar WKif WPop WWhi
'Comte de Chambord' (dVt)	CGro SHar WFar WRha
§ 'Conte di Brazza' (dPVt)	CDev EShb GMac SHar WHer WRha
'Connigar'	CSam
'Connor Glendinning' (ExVa)	WOFF
'Cordelia' (Va)	EBee SBla WFar
'Cornetto'	EBee MBow MHer
* 'Cornish White'	CDev
cornuta ♀H4	CElw CMea EBee EPot EVFa GCra GGar GKev MWat NBir NBro NChi

	Name	Suppliers
		NCob SBch SRms WBou WFar WGHP WHoo WRos WWpP
	- Alba Group ♀[H4]	More than 30 suppliers
§	- 'Alba Minor'	EPfP EWes GMac IGor MAnH MBNS NBro NChi SChu SHGN WAbe WFar
	- blue	MHer NCob SHGN WMoo WWhi
	- 'Cleopatra' (C)	GMac
	- 'Clouded Yellow'	GMac SMeo
	- 'Gypsy Moth' (C)	GMac
	- Lilacina Group (C)	ECha MRav MSte NChi SChu WFar WMnd
	- 'Maiden's Blush'	EMan GMac NChi
	- 'Minor' ♀[H4]	GMac LRHS NBro SBla WBou
	- 'Minor Alba'	see *V. cornuta* 'Alba Minor'
	- 'Pale Apollo' (C) **new**	GMac
	- pale blue	LRHS
*	- 'Paris White'	EBee EPfP
	- 'Purple Gem'	GAbr GMac
	- Purpurea Group	CBos CMea ECha GBuc NCob WMnd
	- 'Spider'	CRez GMac WWhi
	- 'Victoria's Blush' (C)	CBos CSpe ECtt GBuc GMaP GMac MHer MSte NBir NChi NDov SMrm SPoG WBou WWhi
	- 'Violacea'	CBos GMac LRHS
	- 'Yellow King'	EHrv WCot
	corsica	EMan SHGN WOut XPep
*	'Cottage Garden' (Va)	LRHS
	'Countess of Shaftesbury' (dVt)	CDev
	'Cox's Moseley' (ExVa)	WOFF
	'Crepuscle' (Vt)	CGro
§	***cucullata*** ♀[H4]	EVFa SChu SRms WFar WPrP
§	- 'Alba' (Vt)	CBro CGro ECGP LLWP NBir NChi SRms WEas
	- ***rosea***	EWes
*	- 'Striata Alba'	LRHS MWgw NBro
	curtisii	see *V. tricolor* subsp. *curtisii*
	'Cuty' (Va)	LRHS
I	'Czar'	see *V.* 'The Czar'
§	'Czar Bleu' (Vt)	CDev
	'Daisy Smith' (Va)	GMac SChu WBou
	'Dancing Geisha' (Vt)	EBee EHrv EMan ENot EPfP GCai IBal LRHS MBNS NBPC WAul WCot
	'David Rhodes' (FP)	WOFF
	'David Wheldon' (Va)	WOFF
	'Davina' (Va)	SChu
	'Dawn' (Vtta)	EWin GMaP LSou WBou
	'Delicia' (Vtta)	NChi WBou
	'Delmonden' (Va)	SBla
	delphinantha	GKev WAbe
	'Delphine' (Va)	MLLN MSte NChi SChu
	'Desdemona' (Va)	GMac WBou
	'Desmonda' (Va)	SChu
	'Devon Cream' (Va)	GMac WBou
	'Diana Groves'	CGro
	dissecta	WCot WPer
	- var. ***chaerophylloides*** f. ***eizanensis***	see *V. eizanensis*
	- var. ***sieboldiana***	see *V. chaerophylloides* var. *sieboldiana*
	doerfleri	WLin
	'Donau' (Vt)	CBre CDev CGro
	'Double White' (dVt)	CGro NWCA
	dubyana	GBuc
	'Duchesse de Parme' (dPVt)	CDev CGro EShb GBar GMac IFro NWCA SHar SRms WHer
	'D'Udine' (dPVt)	CDev CGro GMac
	'Dusk'	WBou
	'E.A. Bowles'	see *V.* 'Bowles' Black'
	'Eastgrove Blue Scented' (C)	EMan GMac NCob WBou WCot WEas WPtf WWFP
	'Eastgrove Elizabeth Booth'	WEas WSHC
	'Eastgrove Ice Blue' (C)	WBou WEas
	'Eastgrove Twinkle' (C)	NCob WEas
§	***eizanensis***	CGro MTho
	'Elaine Quin'	CElw NChi SChu SPoG WBou
§	***elatior***	CNic CPom CSWP EBee EBla EMon EPPr EWTr GBri GBuc LRHS MNrw NChi SChu WCot WLin WPer WSHC WWye
	'Elizabeth' (Va)	ECtt NCGa SChu WBou
	'Elizabeth McCallum' (FP)	WOFF
	'Elliot Adam' (Va)	WBou
	'Elsie Coombs' (Vt)	CDev WPer
	'Emma' (Va)	CMea
	'Emperor Blue Vein' **new**	LSou
	'Emperor Magenta Red' **new**	LSou
	'Emperor White' **new**	LSou
	erecta	see *V. elatior*
	'Eris' (Va)	NChi WBou
	'Etain' (Va)	CHar COlW EBee ECha ELan EWes GBuc GMaP GMac LAst LPhx MSte NCGa NDov NEgg SPoG WBou WEas WPop WWhi
	'Evelyn Jackson' (Va)	WOFF
	'Fabiola' (Vtta)	GMac NBir
	'Famecheck Apricot'	LSou NChi
*	'Fantasy'	WBou
	'Farewell' (ExVa)	WOFF
	'Fiona' (Va)	CAby EBee GMaP GMac MSte NChi NCob SChu WBou
	flettii	CSec GFlt NChi
	'Florence' (Va)	WBou
	'Foxbrook Cream' (C)	EMan GBuc GMac WBou WWhi
	'Frances Perry'	WWhi
	'Freckles'	see *V. sororia* 'Freckles'
	'Frederica'	CDev
I	'Gazania' (Va)	WBou
	'George Carter' (FP)	WOFF
	'George Hughes' (FP)	WOFF
	'George Lee' (Vt)	CGro
	'Gladys Findlay' (Va)	GMac WBou WOFF
	'Gladys Hughes' (FP)	WOFF
*	'Glenda'	WBou
	'Glenholme'	GMac SMeo
	'Gloire de Verdun' (PVt)	NWCA
	'Gloriole' (Vt)	CGro
	'Governor Herrick' (Vt)	CDev CGro NLsd WPer
§	***gracilis***	NBir WFar
	- 'Lutea'	CSam
	- 'Major'	WBou
	'Graziella' **new**	CBos
	'Green Goddess'[PBR]	CSpe EBee EWin LAst MBNS NCGa NEgg
	'Green Jade' (v)	EMan MBNS NBir
	'Grey Owl' (Va)	EBee LRHS SChu WBou WCot WEas WKif WPGP
	grisebachiana	GKev
	'Grovemount Blue' (C)	CMea
§	***grypoceras*** var. ***exilis***	CNic EHoe EMan GBri LRHS SChu SGSe
	- 'Variegata' (v)	NBir
	'Gustav Wermig' (C)	GAbr WBou
	'H.H. Hodge' (ExVa)	WOFF
	'Hansa' (C)	NChi
	'Haslemere'	see *V.* 'Nellie Britton'
*	'Heaselands'	SMHy SSth SUsu
§	***hederacea***	CDev CMHG CStu ECou GQui MBNS NBro SAga SRms WPop WWye
	- blue	CFee WPer
	'Helen' (Va)	EChP ECtt

§	'Helen Mount' (T)	LRHS
	'Helen W. Cochrane' (ExVa)	WOFF
	'Helena' (Va)	SChu WBou
	heterophylla subsp. ***epirota***	see *V. bertolonii*
*	'Hetty Gatenby'	WBou WOFF
	hirsutula	EBla EHrv EMon
I	- 'Alba' **new**	EBla
I	- 'Purpurea' **new**	EBla
	'Hudsons Blue'	CElw WEas
	'Hugh Campbell' (ExVa)	WOFF
	'Huntercombe Purple' (Va) Υ^{H4}	CBos LRHS MWat NBir SBch SBla SChu SRms SUsu WBou WKif
	'I.G. Sherwood' (FP)	WOFF
	'Icy but Spicy' (C)	EBee EHrv GKir WCot SSvw
	'Iden Gem' (Va)	WBou
	'Inverurie Beauty' (Va) Υ^{H4}	GKir GMaP GMac NDov SChu WBou WKif WPen
	'Irene Hastings' (ExVa)	WOFF
	'Irish Elegance'	see *V.* 'Sulfurea'
	'Irish Mary' (Va)	SChu
	'Irish Molly' (Va)	More than 30 suppliers
	'Ivory Queen' (Va)	EBee GMac MWgw WBou
	'Ivory White' (Va)	CDev
	'Jack Frost' (FP)	WOFF
	'Jack Sampson' (Vt)	CDev CGro
	'Jackanapes' (Va) Υ^{H4}	CElw EBee ECha ECtt ELan EPPr EPfP GKir LRHS NChi NEgg SChu SIng SPoG SRms WBou WFar WWhi
	'Jacqueline Snocken' (ExVa)	WOFF
	'Janet' (Va)	EWin NCGa
	japonica	GGar
	'Jean Arnot' (Vt)	WHer
	'Jeannie Bellew' (Va)	ECtt GMac IHMH SChu SPer SPoG SRms WBou WFar WKif
	'Jennifer Andrews' (Va)	WOFF
	'Jersey Gem' (Va)	GMac
	'Jessie' (SP)	WOFF
	'Jessie East'	WEas
	'Jessie Taylor' (FP)	WOFF
	'Jimmy's Dark' (ExVa)	WOFF
	'Joanna' (Va)	WBou
	'John Goddard' (FP)	WOFF
	'John Powell' (FP)	WOFF
	'John Raddenbury' (Vt)	CDev CGro SHar
	'John Rodger' (SP)	WOFF
	'Johnny Jump Up'	see *V.* 'Helen Mount'
	jooi	CPBP EBee EShb EVFa GTou NBir NBro NChi NMen SBla SRms WPat WRha
	'Jordieland Gem' (c)	EMan GMac
	'Josephine' (Vt) **new**	CGro
	'Joyce Gray' (Va)	GMac WBou
	'Julian' (Va)	CAby CElw EBee GMac SBla SRms WBou
	'Juno' (Va)	GMac
	'Jupiter' (Va)	EBee
	'Kathleen Hoyle' (ExVa)	WOFF
	keiskei	NEgg
	'Kerry Girl' (Vt)	CDev
	'Kiki McDonough' (C)	SChu
	'Kim'	CDev
	'King of Violets' (dVt)	SHar WCot
	'Kitten'	EBee GMac LRHS MSte NChi SAga SChu WBou WPtf
I	'Kitty'	CCge
§	'Königin Charlotte' (Vt)	CDev CGro GMac MHer MWgw NChi NJOw NWCA SSto WCot WHil WMoo
	koreana	see *V. grypoceras* var. *exilis*
	- 'Sylettas'	CStu GBin LSou MCCP MHer NJOw NSti WPtf
	kunawurensis **new**	CSec
	'La France' (Vt)	CGro SBla
N	***labradorica*** hort.	see *V. riviniana* Purpurea Group
§	***labradorica*** ambig.	CHar EMil LRHS MRav NBlu NPri SHFr SMer WCra WFar
N	- ***purpurea*** misapplied	see *V. riviniana* Purpurea Group
	'Lady Finnyoon' (Va)	WOFF
	'Lady Hume Campbell' (PVt)	CBre CGro EShb NWCA WHer
	'Lady Jane' (Vt)	CGro
	'Lady Saville'	see *V.* 'Sissinghurst'
	'Lady Tennyson' (Va)	GMac WOFF
	lanceolata	SSpi
	'Laura' (C)	EVFa GBuc IHMH NCob
	'Laura Cawthorne'	EBee NDov
	'Lavender Lady' (Vt)	CBre CGro
	'Lavinia' (Va)	LRHS WBou
*	'Lee's Victoria Regina' (Vt) **new**	CGro
	'Lemon Sorbet'	GBuc
	'Lesley Keay' (ExVa)	WOFF
	'Letitia' (Va)	GMac NEgg SRms SSvw WBou WCot WFar
	'Lianne' (Vt)	CDev WPer
	'Lilac Rose' (Va)	WBou
	'Lilac Time' **new**	CBos
	'Little David' (Vtta) Υ^{H4}	CSam CTri GMac SRms WBou WPGP WWhi
	'Lord Plunket' (Va)	WBou WOFF
	'Lorna' (Va) Υ^{H4}	WOFF
	'Lorna Cawthorne' (C)	CAby MSte WBou
	'Lorna Moakes' (Va)	SAga
	'Louisa' (Va)	GMac SChu
	'Louise'	WBou
	'Louise Gemmell' (Va)	SChu
	'Love Duet'	NBir
§	***lutea***	NChi WBou
	- subsp. ***elegans***	see *V. lutea*
	'Luxonne' (Vt)	CBre CGro
	'Lydia' (Va)	SChu
	'Lydia Groves' (Vt)	CDev CGro
	'Lydia's Legacy' (Vt) **new**	CGro
	'Madame Armandine Pagès' (Vt)	CBre CDev EBee
	'Maggie Mott' (Va) Υ^{H4}	CElw EBee ECha ECtt EDAr GAbr GBuc GKir GMaP GMac LRHS MBri NChi NDov SBla SPer WBou WFar WWFP WWhi
	'Magic'	CAby GMaP GMac SChu WBou
	'Magnifico'	LRHS
	mandshurica	CDev NWCA
	- 'Fuji Dawn' (v)	EBee EHoe EMan ITer LRHS MFOX SGSe WCot
	- f. ***hasegawae*** **new**	EPPr
	'Margaret' (Va)	WBou
	'Marie-Louise' (dPVt)	CDev CGro CTri EBee EShb SHar
I	'Mars'	ENot LSRN MWgw NCGa SGSe WCot
	'Mars' (Va)	EBee ECtt MCCP NEgg SBch
	'Martin' (Va) Υ^{H4}	COIW EBee ECha EWin GMac MRav NDov SAga SChu SSto WBou WFar
	'Mauve Haze' (Va)	GMac MSte WBou WEas
	'Mauve Radiance' (Va)	GMac NVic WBou
	'May Mott' (Va)	EBee GMac WBou
	'Mayfly' (Va)	MSte WBou
	'Melinda' (Vtta)	WBou
*	'Melissa' (Va)	SChu
	'Mercury' (Va)	WBou
	'Merry Cheer' (C)	SUsu
	'Milkmaid' (Va)	EWll NBir WWhi

	'Mina Walker' (ExVa)	WOFF
	'Miss Brookes' (Va)	WBou WOFF
	'Misty Guy' (Vtta)	NChi WBou
	'Molly Sanderson' (Va) ♀H4	More than 30 suppliers
	'Monica' (Va)	SChu
	'Moonbeam' **new**	WPtf
	'Moonlight' (Va) ♀H4	ECha EDAr ELan EVFa GMac MHer SBla SChu WBou WWhi
	'Moonraker'	NBir
	'Morwenna' (Va)	WWhi
	'Mrs C.M. Snocken' (FP)	WOFF
	'Mrs Chichester' (Va)	WBou WOFF
	'Mrs Cotterell'	EBee GBuc
	'Mrs David Lloyd George' (dVt)	CDev
	'Mrs G. Robb' (ExVa)	WOFF
	'Mrs Lancaster' (Va)	CHid EBee EWin GMaP GMac MBNS NBir NChi SChu SPoG SRms WBou
	'Mrs R. Barton' (Vt)	CDev CGro SHar
	'Myfawnny' (Va)	CElw CMea ECtt EDAr ELan EVFa EWes GMac LRHS MWat NChi NPri SBch SChu SPoG SRms WBou WFar WWhi
	'Neapolitan'	see *V.* 'Pallida Plena'
§	'Nellie Britton' (Va) ♀H4	ECtt GMac SChu SRms WWhi
	'Netta Statham'	see *V.* 'Belmont Blue'
	'Noni' (Vt)	CGro
	'Nora'	WBou
	'Norah Church' (Vt)	CDev SBla SHar
	'Norah Leigh' (Va)	EOHP WBou
	obliqua	see *V. cucullata*
	odorata (Vt)	More than 30 suppliers
	- 'Alba' (Vt)	CBre CDev CPom CSWP EBee ELan EMan EWTr GBar GGar ILis LAst MAnH MHer MWgw NCob NPri SRms WMoo WWhi WWye
	- 'Alba Plena' (dVt)	NChi SBla WHer
	- apricot	see *V.* 'Sulfurea'
	- 'Double Foncée de Madame Dumas' (d)	EVFa
	- var. ***dumetorum***	see *V. alba*
	- pink	see *V. odorata* Rosea Group
	- 'Red Devil' **new**	WFar
	- ***rosea***	see *V. odorata* Rosea Group
§	- Rosea Group (Vt)	CDes CGro EBee EVFa GBar GMac MRav SIde WCot WWhi
*	- subsp. ***subcarnea*** (Vt)	WBWf
	- 'Sulphurea'	see *V.* 'Sulfurea'
	'Orchid Pink' (Vt)	CGro SHar
	'Painted Lady' (Va)	GMac
§	'Pallida Plena' (dPVt)	CBre CDev CGro
	palmata	NPro
	'Palmer's White' (Va)	WBou
	palustris	CRWN MBow WHer WShi
	'Pamela Zambra' (Vt)	CDev SHar WPrP
	papilionacea	see *V. sororia*
*	'Paradise Blue' (Vt)	CGro
	'Parme de Toulouse' (dPVt)	CBre CDev CGro EBee NLar
	'Pasha' (Va) **new**	GMac
	'Pat Creasy' (Va)	GMac WBou
	'Pat Kavanagh' (C)	CBos GMac WBou
	pedata	CBro CFai EMan EPot GFlt LRHS MWrn NCGa SOkd SSpi WAbe WCot WHil WPer
	- 'Bicolor'	SOkd WAbe
	pedatifida	CFai EMan MBNS MTho NJOw
	- white-flowered	CFai
	'Peggy Brookes' (FP)	WOFF
	pensylvanica	see *V. pubescens* var. *eriocarpa*
	'Peppered-palms'	EBee EHrv LRHS SGSe
	'Perle Rose' (Vt)	CDev CGro EShb SBla
	'Pete'	SChu
	'Phyl Dove' (Vt)	CGro
	'Pickering Blue' (Va)	WBou
	'Pilar' (Va)	SChu
	pilosa B&SWJ 7204 **new**	WCru
	'Primrose Dame' (Va)	WBou
	'Primrose Pixie' (Va)	WBou
	'Prince John' (T)	LRHS
	'Princess Mab' (Vtta)	WBou
	'Princess of Prussia' (Vt)	CBre CDev WHer
	'Princess of Wales'	see *V.* 'Princesse de Galles'
§	'Princesse de Galles' (Vt)	CDev CGro CTri NSti SHar
§	***pubescens*** var. ***eriocarpa***	SRms
	pumila	MHer
	'Purity' (Vtta)	GMac
	'Purple Wings' (Va)	WBou
	'Putty'	ECou WCru
	Queen Charlotte	see *V.* 'Königin Charlotte'
	'Queen Victoria'	see *V.* 'Victoria Regina'
	'R.N. Denby' (ExVa)	WOFF
	'Raven'	GMac LPhx NChi SChu WBou
	'Rawson's White' (Vt)	CDev CGro SHar
	'Rebecca' (Vtta)	CBos CSam CSpe EBee ECtt ELan EPfP EPot GKir GMaP GMac LAst MBNS MBow MHer NBir NCGa NChi NEgg NPri SChu SPer SPoG SRms WBou WFar WPop WWhi
	'Red Charm' (Vt)	EBee
	'Red Giant' (Vt)	CGro SHar
	'Red Lion' (Vt)	CDev
	'Red Queen' (Vt)	CDev NSti
	reichei	CRWN
	'Reid's Crimson Carpet' (Vt) **new**	CGro
	reniforme	see *V. hederacea*
	riviniana	CArn CRWN GWCH MBow MHer SECG WHer WJek WShi
	- 'Ed's Variegated' (v)	EBee EMan EPPr EVFa WCot
§	- Purpurea Group	More than 30 suppliers
	- white	EWes NWoo
	'Rodney Davey' (Vt/v)	EMan NBir NBro
	'Rodney Fuller' (FP)	WOFF
	'Rodney Marsh'	NBir
*	'Rosanna' (Vt)	CDev NCob
	'Roscastle Black'	CElw CMea EBee GMac LRHS MAnH MBNS SBch SMrm WBou WCot WPGP WPop WWhi
*	'Royal Elk' (Vt)	CDev CGro
	'Royal Robe' (Vt)	CDev
	'Rubra' (Vt)	EGoo MAnH WPer
§	***rupestris***	SHar
*	- ***rosea***	CDev CNic CPom EBee EDAr GAbr IFro LLWP MHer MWgw NWCA SBch STre WEas
	'Russian Superb' (Vt)	CDev
*	'Ruth Elkins' (Va)	GMac WOFF
	'Saint Helena' (Vt)	CBre CDev
	'Sarah Binnie' (ExVa)	WOFF
	schariensis	EWes
	selkirkii	CDev CNic EHyt ITer NBro NWCA
	- 'Variegata' (v)	CGro GBri GBuc NBir
	septentrionalis	see *V. sororia*
	- ***alba***	see *V. sororia* 'Albiflora'
	- 'Rubra' **new**	EVFa
	'Serena' (Va)	WBou
	'Sheila' (Va)	WBou
	'Sherbet Dip'	WBou
	'Shirobana'	NBir WCru
	'Sidborough Poppet'	EGoo EWes
§	'Sissinghurst' (Va)	GMac MHer NBir
	'Sisters' (Vt)	CGro

	'Smugglers' Moon'	MSte SChu WBou
	'Snow Queen' (Va)	WWhi
	'Sophie' (Vtta)	SChu WBou
§	***sororia***	EBee ECha EMan EPPr GSki LRHS MFOX MNrw MOne MRav MWgw NBir NBro NRya WEas WPen
*	- 'Albiflora' ♀H4	CBre CHid CM&M CSWP EBee EChP EDAr EMil EPfP GEdr GSki IHMH LRHS MBNS MRav MSph NJOw NPro NWCA SOkd WCAu WCFE WFar WPer
§	- 'Freckles'	More than 30 suppliers
	- 'Freckles' dark	EBee NWCA
	- 'Priceana'	CBre CCge CDes CDev CElw CM&M EBee ECGP ECha EMan NBir NChi WPGP
	- 'Speckles' (v)	CDev CGro EMon
*	'Spencer's Cottage'	WBou
	stojanowii	CGro SBla WEas WGwG
§	'Sulfurea' (Vt)	CDev CPBP CPMA CSWP EShb EVFa MAnH MHar MHer MMHG NCGa NWCA SChu WCot WEas WPer WWhi
	-lemon form (Vt)	CGro
	'Susie' (Va)	WBou
	'Swanley White'	see *V.* 'Conte di Brazza'
	'Sybil' (SP)	WBou
	'Sylvia Hart'	MTho WPnP
	'Talitha' (Va)	GMac
	'Tanith' (Vt)	CBre CDev EBee
	'Thalia' (Vtta)	WBou
§	'The Czar' (Vt)	CBre CGro ILis NChi
	'Tiger Eyes'	CSpe EBee EBla LSou MAnH MBNS NCGa NEgg WPop
	'Tina' (Va)	WOFF
	'Tinpenny Purple'	WCot WTin
	'Tom' (SP)	WOFF
	'Tom Tit' (Va)	WBou
	'Tony Venison' (C/v)	CElw EBee EDAr EHoe EMan EPPr EWin MBNS MTho NEgg SPoG WBou WFar WHer
	tricolor	CPrp GBar GPoy GWCH MHer NGHP NLsd NPri SBch SIde WGHP WHer WJek WSel
§	- subsp. ***curtisii***	WBWf
	- 'Sawyer's Blue'	WPer
	'Vanessa' (Va) **new**	GMac
	velutina	see *V. gracilis*
	verecunda	CLAP GFlt NCGa
	- B&SWJ 604a	WCru
§	- var. ***yakusimana***	CStu SIng
	'Victoria'	see *V.* 'Czar Bleu'
	'Victoria Cawthorne' (C)	CAby CBos CElw EBee EMan GBuc GMaP GMac MAnH MHer MOne MSte MWat NDov SBla SChu WBou WEas WWhi
§	'Victoria Regina' (Vt)	CBre CDev CGro
	'Virginia' (Va)	GMac SChu WBou
	'Vita' (Va)	GBuc GMac MBNS NDov SBla SChu SRms WBou WWhi
	'Wasp' (Va)	GMac
	'White Ladies'	see *V. cucullata* 'Alba'
	'White Pearl' (Va)	CBos GMac LPhx WBou
	'White Perfection' (C)	CWib EWTr LRHS MBNS
	'White Swan' (Va)	GMac
	'William' (Va)	NDov
	'William Fife' (ExVa)	WOFF
	'William Snocken' (FP)	WOFF
	'Winifred Jones' (Va)	WBou
	'Winifred Warden' (Va)	MBNS
	'Winona Cawthorne' (C)	EBee GMac NChi NDov NLsd SChu WWhi
	'Wisley White'	EBee EWes LBmB WFar
	'Woodlands Cream' (Va)	GMac MHer WBou WOFF
	'Woodlands Lilac' (Va)	SChu WBou
	'Woodlands White' (Va)	WBou WOFF
	yakusimana	see *V. verecunda* var. *yakusimana*
	'Zara' (Va)	WBou
	'Zoe' (Vtta)	EBee EWin GMac NCGa NPri WBou WFar WWol

Viscaria (*Caryophyllaceae*)

	vulgaris	see *Lychnis viscaria*

Vitaliana (*Primulaceae*)

§	***primuliflora***	CLyd GCrs GKev GKir GTou NLAp NMen NRya NSla
	- subsp. ***assoana*** **new**	GKev
	- subsp. ***praetutiana***	EHyt EPot NMen NWCA SBla WAbe WFar WLin WPat
	- subsp. ***tridentata***	NMen

Vitex (*Verbenaceae*)

	agnus-castus	CAgr CArn CBcs CDul EBee EDAr ELau EShb EUnu GPoy LEdu LRHS MCCP MHer SIgm SLon SMad SPer WDin WFar WHer WSHC WWye XPep
	- 'Alba'	CWib XPep
	- 'Blushing Bride'	WCot
	- var. ***latifolia***	CWib ENot EPfP LRHS LSRN SBrw SPoG WDin WPGP XPep
I	- 'Rosea'	NLar XPep
	- 'Silver Spire'	ELan SPoG WPGP
	incisa	see *V. negundo* var. *heterophylla*
	lucens	CHEx
	negundo	CArn
§	- var. ***heterophylla***	CPle

Vitis ✿ (*Vitaceae*)

	'Abundante' (F)	WSuV
	'Alden' (O/B)	WSuV
	'Amandin' (G/W) **new**	WSuV
	amurensis	CPLN EBee EPfP GIBF LAst LRHS NLar
	- B&SWJ 4138	WCru
	'Aurore' Seibel 5279 (W)	WSuV
	'Baco Noir' (O/B)	GTwe WSuV
	'Bianca' (O/W) **new**	WSuV
	Black Hamburgh	see *V. vinifera* 'Schiava Grossa'
*	'Black Strawberry' (B)	WSuV
§	'Boskoop Glory' (F)	CMac EMil LBuc MAsh NBlu NPal SCoo SEND WSuV
	'Brant' (O/B) ♀H4	More than 30 suppliers
	'Brilliant' (B)	WSuV
	'Buffalo' (B)	WSuV
	'Canadice' (O/R/S)	WSuV
	'Cascade' (O/B)	see *V.* Seibel 13053
	Castel 19-637 (B)	WSuV
	'Chambourcin' (B)	WSuV
	coignetiae ♀H4	More than 30 suppliers
	- B&SWJ 4550 from Korea	WCru
	- B&SWJ 4744	WCru
	- from Korea	CBot
	- Claret Cloak = 'Frovit'[PBR]	EBee ELan EPfP GKir LRHS MAsh MRav SBra SMur SPer SPoG SSpi WPGP WPat
	- cut-leaved	LAst
	- 'Purple Cloak' **new**	CHEx
*	- 'Rubescens' **new**	CPLN
	'Dalkauer' (W)	WSuV
I	'Diamond' (B)	WSuV
	'Dutch Black' (O/B) **new**	WSuV
	'Edwards No. 1' (O/W) **new**	WSuV
	'Eger Csillaga' (O/W) **new**	WSuV

	'Einset' (B/S)	WSuV
	ficifolia	see *V. thunbergii*
	flexuosa B&SWJ 5568	WCru
	- var. ***choii*** B&SWJ 4101	WCru
§	'Fragola' (O/R)	CAgr CMac EBee ENot EPfP EPla ERea GTwe MAsh MRav SEND SRms WSuV
	'Gagarin Blue' (O/B)	CAgr ERea GTwe NPer WSuV
	'Glenora' (F/B/S)	ERea WSuV
	'Hecker' (O/W) **new**	WSuV
	henryana	see *Parthenocissus henryana*
	'Himrod' (O/W/S)	ERea GTwe WSuV
	inconstans	see *Parthenocissus tricuspidata*
	'Interlaken' (O/W/S)	ERea WSuV
	'Kempsey Black' (O/B)	WSuV
	'Kozmapalme Muscatoly' (O/W) **new**	WSuV
	'Kuibishevski' (O/R)	WSuV
	labrusca **new**	CPLN
	- 'Concord' (O/B)	ERea
	Landot 244 (O/B)	WSuV
	'Léon Millot' (O/G/B)	CAgr CSBt ERea WSuV
	'Maréchal Foch' (O/B)	WSuV
	'Maréchal Joffre' (O/B)	GTwe WSuV
	'Muscat Bleu' (O/B)	ERea WSuV
	'New York Muscat' (O/B)	ERea WSuV
	Oberlin 595 (O/B)	WSuV
	'Orion' (O/W)	WSuV
	'Paletina' (O/W) **new**	WSuV
	parsley-leaved	see *V. vinifera* 'Ciotat'
	parvifolia	WPat
	'Perdin' (O/W) **new**	WSuV
	'Phönix' (O/W)	GKir GTwe MBri MGos SKee SLim WSuV
	piasezkii	WCru
	- B&SWJ 5236	WCru
*	'Pink Strawberry' (O)	WSuV
	'Pirovano 14' (O/B)	ERea GTwe WSuV
§	'Plantet' (O/B)	WSuV
*	'Poloske Muscat' (W)	WSuV
	pseudoreticulata	WPGP
	'Pulchra'	CPLN
	purpurea 'Spetchley Park' (O/B) **new**	WSuV
	quinquefolia	see *Parthenocissus quinquefolia*
	Ravat 51 (O/W)	WSuV
	'Rayon d'Or' (O/W) **new**	WSuV
	'Regent'[PBR]	CWSG GTwe MBri MCoo MGos SKee SLim SPoG WOrn WSuV
	'Reliance' (O/R/S)	ERea WSuV
	'Rembrant' (R)	WSuV
	riparia	NLar WCru
	'Rondo' (O/B) EM 6494-5	WSuV
	'Schuyler' (O/B)	WSuV
	Seibel (F)	GTwe SPoG
§	Seibel 13053 (O/B)	ERea LRHS MAsh WSuV
	Seibel 138315 (R)	WSuV
	Seibel 5409 (W)	WSuV
	Seibel 5455	see *V.* 'Plantet'
	Seibel 7053	WSuV
	Seibel 9549	WSuV
	'Seneca' (W)	WSuV
	'Serena' (O/W) **new**	WSuV
§	'Seyval Blanc' (O/W)	CAgr ERea GTwe WSuV
	Seyve Villard 12.375	see *V.* 'Villard Blanc'
	Seyve Villard 20.473 (F)	MAsh WSuV
	Seyve Villard 5276	see *V.* 'Seyval Blanc'
	'Suffolk Seedless' (B/S)	WSuV
	'Tereshkova' (O/B)	CAgr ERea WSuV
	'Thornton' (O/S)	WSuV
§	***thunbergii*** B&SWJ 4702	WCru
	'Triomphe d'Alsace' (O/B)	CAgr CSBt LRHS NPer WSuV
	'Trollinger'	see *V. vinifera* 'Schiava Grossa'
	'Vanessa' (O/R/S)	ERea WSuV
§	'Villard Blanc' (O/W)	WSuV
	vinifera EM 323158B	WSuV
	- 'Abouriou' (O/B)	WSuV
	- 'Adelheidtraube' (O/W)	WSuV
	- 'Albalonga' (W)	WSuV
§	- 'Alicante' (G/B)	ERea GTwe NPal WSuV
	- 'Apiifolia'	see *V. vinifera* 'Ciotat'
	- 'Appley Towers' (G/B)	ERea
	- 'Augusta Louise' (O/W)	WSuV
	- 'Auxerrois' (O/W)	WSuV
	- 'Bacchus' (O/W)	WSuV
	- 'Baresana' (G/W)	MAsh WSuV
	- 'Black Alicante'	see *V. vinifera* 'Alicante'
	- 'Black Corinth' (G/B/S)	ERea
	- 'Black Frontignan' (G/O/B)	ERea WSuV
	- Black Hamburgh	see *V. vinifera* 'Schiava Grossa'
	- 'Black Monukka' (G/B/S)	ERea WSuV
	- 'Black Prince' (G/B)	WSuV
	- 'Blauburger' (O/B)	WCru
	- 'Blue Portuguese'	see *V. vinifera* 'Portugieser'
§	- 'Bouvier' (W)	WSuV
	- 'Bouviertraube'	see *V. vinifera* 'Bouvier'
	- 'Buckland Sweetwater' (G/W)	ERea GTwe MGos WSuV
	- 'Cabernet Sauvignon' (O/B)	MAsh WSuV
	- 'Canners' (F/S)	ERea
	- 'Canon Hall Muscat' (G/W)	ERea
	- 'Cardinal' (O/R)	ERea WSuV
	- 'Chaouch' (G/W)	ERea
	- 'Chardonnay' (O/W)	MAsh NPer WSuV
§	- 'Chasselas' (G/O/W)	ERea LRHS MAsh WSuV
	- 'Chasselas de Fontainebleau' (F)	EMil
	- 'Chasselas de Tramontaner' (F)	EMil
	- 'Chasselas d'Or'	see *V. vinifera* 'Chasselas'
	- 'Chasselas Rosé' (G/R)	ERea WSuV
	- 'Chasselas Vibert' (G/W)	ERea WSuV
	- 'Chenin Blanc' (O/W)	WSuV
§	- 'Ciotat' (F)	CPLN EPla ERea WBcn WSuV
	- 'Crimson Seedless' (R/S)	ERea
	- 'Csabyongye' (O/W)	WSuV
	- 'Dattier de Beyrouth' (G/W)	WSuV
	- 'Dattier Saint Vallier' (O/W) **new**	WSuV
	- 'Dolcetto' (O/B) **new**	WSuV
	- 'Dornfelder' (O/R)	SPoG WSuV
	- 'Dunkelfelder' (O/R)	WSuV
	- 'Early Van der Laan' (F)	EMil NBlu
	- 'Ehrenfelser' (O/W)	WSuV
	- 'Elbling' (O/W)	WSuV
	- 'Excelsior' (W)	WSuV
	- 'Faber' (O/W)	WSuV
	- 'Ferdinand de Lesseps'	ERea
	- 'Fiesta' (W/S)	WSuV
	- 'Findling' (W)	WSuV
	- 'Flame Seedless' (G/O/R/S)	WSuV
	- 'Forta' (O/W)	WSuV
	- 'Foster's Seedling' (G/W)	ERea GTwe SPoG WSuV
	- 'Frühburgunder' (O/B) **new**	WSuV
	- 'Gamay Hâtif' (O/B)	ERea
	- 'Gamay Hâtif des Vosges'	WSuV
	- 'Gamay Noir' (O/B)	WSuV
	- Gamay Teinturier Group (O/B)	WSuV
	- 'Gewürztraminer' (O/R)	LRHS MAsh WSuV

- 'Glory of Boskoop'	see *V.* 'Boskoop Glory'
- 'Golden Chasselas'	see *V. vinifera* 'Chasselas'
- 'Golden Queen' (G/W)	ERea
- 'Goldriesling' (O/W)	WSuV
- 'Gros Colmar' (G/B)	ERea
- 'Gros Maroc' (G/B)	ERea
- 'Grüner Veltliner' (O/W)	WSuV
- 'Gutenborner' (O/W)	WSuV
- 'Helfensteiner' (O/R)	WSuV
- 'Huxelrebe' (O/W)	WSuV
- 'Incana' (O/B)	CPLN EPfP EPla MRav WCFE WCot WSHC
- 'Juliaumsrebe' (O/W)	WSuV
- 'Kanzler' (O/W)	WSuV
- 'Kerner' (O/W)	WSuV
- 'Kernling' (F)	WSuV
- 'King's Ruby' (F/S)	ERea
- 'Lady Downe's Seedling' (G/B)	ERea
- 'Lady Hastings' (G/B)	ERea
- 'Lady Hutt' (G/W)	ERea
- 'Lakemont' (O/W/S)	ERea SKee SPoG WSuV
- 'Lival' (O/B) **new**	WSuV
- 'Madeleine Angevine' (O/W)	CAgr CDul CSBt ERea GTwe LRHS MAsh MGos WSuV
- 'Madeleine Celine' (B)	WSuV
- 'Madeleine Royale' (G/W)	ERea WSuV
- 'Madeleine Silvaner' (O/W)	CSBt ERea GTwe LRHS MGos NPer SPer WBVN WSuV
- 'Madresfield Court' (G/B)	ERea GTwe WSuV
- 'Merlot' (G/B)	WSuV
§ - 'Meunier' (B)	WSuV
- 'Mireille' (F)	GTwe WSuV
- 'Morio Muscat' (O/W)	WSuV
- 'Mrs Pearson' (G/W)	ERea
- 'Mrs Pince's Black Muscat' (G/B)	ERea
- 'Muscat Blanc à Petits Grains' (O/W)	SWvt WSuV
- 'Muscat Champion' (G/R)	ERea
- 'Muscat de Lierval' (O/B) **new**	WSuV
- 'Muscat de Saumur' (O/W)	WSuV
- 'Muscat Hamburg' (G/B)	EMil ERea MAsh MGos SWvt WSuV
- 'Muscat of Alexandria' (G/W)	CBcs CMac EHol ERea NPal SPoG
- 'Muscat of Hungary' (G/W)	ERea
- 'Muscat Ottonel' (O/W)	WSuV
- 'Muscat Saint Laurent' (W)	WSuV
§ - 'Müller-Thurgau' (O/W)	ENot ERea GKir GTwe LRHS MAsh MGos SPer WSuV
- 'No. 69' (W)	WSuV
- 'Noir Hâtif de Marseille' (O/B)	ERea WSuV
- 'Oliver Irsay' (O/W)	ERea WSuV
- 'Optima' (O/W)	WSuV
- 'Ora' (O/W/S) **new**	WSuV
- 'Ortega' (O/W)	WSuV
- 'Perle' (O/W)	WSuV
- 'Perle de Czaba' (G/O/W)	EMil ERea WSuV
- 'Perlette' (O/W/S)	ERea WSuV
- 'Petit Rouge' (R)	WSuV
- 'Pinot Blanc' (O/W)	LRHS MAsh WSuV
- 'Pinot Gris' (O/B)	WSuV
- 'Pinot Noir' (O/B)	WSuV
§ - 'Portugieser' (O/B)	WSuV
- 'Précoce de Bousquet' (O/W)	WSuV
- 'Précoce de Malingre' (O/W)	ERea
- 'Prima' (O/B) **new**	WSuV
- 'Primavis Frontignan' (G/W)	WSuV
- 'Prince of Wales' (G/B)	ERea
- 'Purpurea' (O/B) ♀H4	More than 30 suppliers
- 'Queen of Esther' (B)	GTwe MBri SKee SLim SPoG WSuV
- 'Reichensteiner' (O/G/W)	WSuV
- 'Reine Olga' (O/R)	ERea
- 'Riesling' (O/W)	LRHS MAsh WSuV
- Riesling-Silvaner	see *V. vinifera* 'Müller-Thurgau'
- 'Rish Baba'	ERea
- 'Royal Muscadine' (G/O/W)	WSuV
- 'Saint Laurent' (G/O/W)	ERea WSuV
- 'Sauvignon Blanc' (O/W)	WSuV
- 'Scheurebe' (O/W)	WSuV
§ - 'Schiava Grossa' (G/B/D)	CBcs CMac CSBt CSam CTri ECrN ELan ENot EPfP ERea GKir GTwe LBuc LRHS LSRN MAsh MBlu MBri NBea NPer SKee SLim SPer SPoG SWvt WDin WFar WSuV
- 'Schönburger' (O/W)	WSuV
- 'Schwarzriesling'	see *V. vinifera* 'Meunier'
- 'Sémillon'	MAsh
- 'Septimer' (O/W)	WSuV
- 'Shiraz' (B)	WSuV
- 'Siegerrebe' (O/W/D)	ERea GTwe LRHS WSuV
- 'Silvaner' (O/W)	WSuV
- 'Spetchley Red'	CPLN WCru WPGP WPat WSPU
- strawberry grape	see *V.* 'Fragola'
- 'Suffolk Red' (G/R/S)	ERea
§ - 'Sultana' (W/S)	ERea GTwe WSuV
- 'Syrian' (G/W)	ERea
- Teinturier Group (F)	ERea
- 'Theresa'	MBri SPoG WOrn WSuV
- 'Thompson Seedless'	see *V. vinifera* 'Sultana'
- 'Trebbiano' (G/W)	ERea
- 'Triomphrebe' (W)	WSuV
- 'Wrotham Pinot' (O/B)	WSuV
- 'Würzer' (O/W)	WSuV
- 'Zweigeltrebe' (O/B)	WSuV
* 'White Strawberry' (O/W)	WSuV
'Zalagyöngye' (W)	WSuV

Vriesea (*Bromeliaceae*)

carinata	MBri
hieroglyphica	MBri
philippo-coburgii **new**	EOas
x ***poelmanii***	MBri
x ***polonia***	MBri
saundersii ♀H1	MBri
splendens ♀H1	MBri
'Vulkana'	MBri

W

Wachendorfia (*Haemodoraceae*)

brachyandra	EMan GCal WCot
thyrsiflora	CAbb CAby CDes CFir CHEx CMCo CPLG CPne EShb GGar IGor SAga WCFE WCot WDyG WFar WPGP WPic WPrP

Wahlenbergia (*Campanulaceae*)

sp.	ECou
albomarginata	ECou EMan GKev GTou LRHS NJOw NLAp NLar NWCA WLin

	- 'Blue Mist'	ECou
	ceracea	GKev NJOw
	congesta	CNic EHyt LRHS MDKP WBVN
	gloriosa	GCrs GEdr GKev LRHS NJOw NLAp WAbe WFar
	pumilio	see *Edraianthus pumilio*
	rivularis **new**	CSec GGar
§	***saxicola***	CRow EHyt EMan GTou NDlv NWCA
	serpyllifolia	see *Edraianthus serpyllifolius*
	simpsonii	GTou
	tasmanica	see *W. saxicola*
	undulata	CSec CSpe GGar

Waldsteinia (*Rosaceae*)

	fragarioides	WPer WPtf
	geoides	EBee EMan EPPr EPfP IHMH LRHS NPro SPer
	ternata	More than 30 suppliers
§	- 'Mozaick' (v)	EBee GKir NBir NPro
	- 'Variegata'	see *W. ternata* 'Mozaick'

Wallichia (*Arecaceae*)

densiflora	CBrP

walnut, black see *Juglans nigra*

walnut, common see *Juglans regia*

Wasabia (*Brassicaceae*)

japonica	CArn GPoy LEdu

Washingtonia (*Arecaceae*)

filifera ♀H1	CAbb CBrP CDoC CPHo CRoM EAmu EExo EShb EUJe LExo MBri SAPC SAin SArc SBig SEND SPlb SWal WMul
robusta	CRoM CTrC EAmu EExo LExo NPal SChr SMad SPlb WMul

Watsonia (*Iridaceae*)

	aletroides	CCtw CDes CFil EBee LPio LRHS SIgm WCot WPGP
	amatolae **new**	CPLG
	angusta	CDes CFil CPne CPrp EBee IBlr ITer WPGP
	- JCA 3.950.409	WCot
	ardernei	see *W. borbonica* subsp. *ardernei* 'Arderne's White'
	beatricis	see *W. pillansii*
I	'Best Red'	GCal LPio
§	***borbonica***	CAbb CCtw CPne CPou EShb IBlr LPio WCot
	- subsp. ***ardernei*** misapplied	see *W. borbonica* subsp. *ardernei* 'Arderne's White'
	- subsp. ***ardernei*** (Sander) Goldblatt **new**	EShb
§	- - 'Arderne's White'	CAby CBre CDes CFil CPne ERos EShb GCal GGar IBlr LPio MSte SBla WPGP
	- subsp. ***borbonica***	CAby CDes EBee WPGP
	brevifolia	see *W. laccata*
	coccinea	CDes CFil CMon WCot WPGP
	densiflora	CFil CPou EShb GFlt IBlr IDee LPio MSte WCot
	'Flame'	NCGa
	fourcadei	CAby CPne CPrp EBee EShb WPGP
	- S&SH 89	CDes
	fulgens	CPne LEdu MSte
	galpinii	CFil CFir IBlr
	gladioloides	CFil CPLG
§	***humilis***	CDes CFil CMon CPou EBee SSpi WPGP
	'Ida Edwards' **new**	EBee
	knysnana	CFil CPou EShb IBlr
§	***laccata***	CFil CFir CPou EShb SChr WCot
	lepida	CFil CPou
	x ***longifolia***	CAbb
	marginata	CFil CPou WCot
	- 'Star Spike'	WCot
	marlothii	CFil
	meriania	CFil CPou GGar GSki IBlr WCot WHil
	- var. ***bulbillifera***	CAby CFwr EBee GAbr GMac IBlr LPio LRHS
§	***pillansii***	CCtw CFil CHEx CPen CPne CPou CPrp CTrC EMan ERos EShb GMac GSki IBlr LRHS SIgm SMrm WCot WFar
	- JCA 3.953.609	SSpi
	- pink-flowered	CPen CPrp
	- salmon-flowered	CPen
	pink	CDes
	pyramidata	see *W. borbonica*
	roseoalba	see *W. humilis*
	schlechteri **new**	CFil
	spectabilis	CFil CPne WFar
	'Stanford Scarlet'	CAby CDes CPne CPou EBee IBlr SBla WPGP WSHC
	stenosiphon	IBlr
	strubeniae	IBlr
	tabularis	CAbb CCtw GGar IBlr
	'Tresco Dwarf Pink'	CDes CPLG CPrp EMan IBlr LPio NGby WCot WPGP
	Tresco hybrids	CAbb CPne CTbh WCFE
	vanderspuyae	CCtw CFil CPou GGar IBlr WCot
	versfeldii	EBee
	watsonioides	WCot
	'White Dazzler'	SApp
	wilmaniae	CFil CPou CPrp EBee IBlr
	- JCA 3.955.200	SSpi

Wattakaka see *Dregea*

Wedelia (*Asteraceae*)

§	***texana***	EBee

Weigela ✿ (*Caprifoliaceae*)

	CC 1231	CPLG
	'Abel Carrière'	CDul CMac CRez CTri ECtt EPfP NWea SEND WCFE WFar WTel
	'Avalanche' hort.	see *W.* 'Candida'
	'Avalanche' Lemoine	see *W. praecox* 'Avalanche'
	'Boskoop Glory'	GQui SPer
	Briant Rubidor = 'Olympiade' (v)	More than 30 suppliers
	'Brigela'PBR	CBcs CDoC ENot EPfP MBri
	'Bristol Ruby'	More than 30 suppliers
§	'Candida'	CTri EBee ELan EWes GSki LRHS MBar MRav NBlu SPer WTel
	Carnaval = 'Courtalor'PBR	CBcs COtt CWib EBee GKir LRHS
	'Conquête'	GKir SLon
	coraeensis	CHll IArd MBlu MMHG MWgw
	decora	GQui
	'Emerald Edge'	WBcn
	'Eva Rathke'	CBot CTri GKir NWea SCoo WFar WTel
	'Evita'	MBar MGos NLar WFar
	Feline = 'Courtamon'	MBri
	florida	CDul CTrw EPfP MBar SMer
	- B&SWJ 8439	WCru
	- f. ***alba***	CBcs WFar
*	- 'Albovariegata' (v)	CPLG WBVN WBrE
	- 'Bicolor'	CMac ELan

- 'Bristol Snowflake' CBot EPfP GKir LSou MBNS MBar MGos MHer MSwo NEgg NLar SLon SPoG
- 'Foliis Purpureis' ♀H4 More than 30 suppliers
- 'Java Red' LRHS
- 'Langtrees Variegated' (v) **new** EVFa
- 'Pink Princess' MSwo WWeb
- 'Samabor' WFar
- 'Suzanne' (v) CDul EVFa LRHS MGos NPro
- 'Tango' CPMA ECtt LRHS MAsh MWya NPro WBcn WWeb

'Florida Variegata' (v) ♀H4 More than 30 suppliers

florida 'Versicolor' CBot CMHG CMac CPLG CWib GQui SLon SMrm WFar WGor
- Wine and Roses = 'Alexandra' CAbP CBcs CDoC EBee EGra ELan ENot EPfP EVFa LAst LSRN MAsh MBNS NPri SMac SPoG SWvt WLeb WOVN WWeb

'Gold Rush' NLar
'Golden Candy' NPro
'Gustave Malet' CMCN GQui
hortensis CPLG GIBF
- 'Nivea' CPle MBri NPro
japonica 'Dart's Colourdream' EBee ECtt EWes GKir LSou MRav SCoo SLPl SLim SMer WBVN
- var. ***sinica*** **new** CFil
- 'Variegated Dart's Colourdream' (v) **new** EVFa

'Jean's Gold' EBee ELan MGos MRav
'Kosteriana Variegata' (v) CSLe LRHS MAsh SLon WFar
lonicera **new** WHil
'Looymansii Aurea' CBot CMHG CPLG CRez CTri ELan EPfP GKir LAst LRHS MRav SBch SLon WDin WFar WHar WPen
Lucifer = 'Courtared'PBR CDoC NLar
maximowiczii CPLG CPle GQui GSki
§ ***middendorffiana*** More than 30 suppliers
'Minuet' EPfP GSki MBar MGos MRav MSwo NPro WWeb
'Mont Blanc' CBot MMHG
Nain Rouge = 'Courtanin'PBR CBcs LRHS MBri
'Nana Variegata' (v) CPLG EPfP LRHS MBar MBri NBlu
Naomi Campbell = 'Bokrashine'PBR WMoo
'Newport Red' ENot GKir LRHS MBNS MRav MWat NWea SMer WFar
'Pink Poppet' CSBt GTSp LAst LRHS LSRN LSou MAsh NCGa SCoo SPoG SWvt WOVN
praecox GIBF
§ - 'Avalanche' ECtt MRav
'Praecox Variegata' (v) ♀H4 CChe CTri ELan EPfP GKir LAst LRHS MAsh MRav SMac SPer SPla SPoG SReu SRms WCFE WCru WFar WHCG WSHC
'Red Prince' ♀H4 EBee ELan GWCH LAst LRHS MGos MSwo NBlu NCGa NEgg SPoG
'Red Trumpet' **new** SLon
'Ruby Queen'PBR EPfP LRHS
'Rumba' EMil EWTr GSki MMHG MRav NPro
'Samba' LRHS
sessilifolia see *Diervilla sessilifolia*
'Snowflake' EBee ECtt NLon NPri NPro SRms WDin WFar
subsessilis B&SWJ 1056 WCru
'Victoria' CDoC CHar CMHG CWib ECtt ELan EPfP LAst LRHS MAsh MSwo NEgg SCoo SPer SPla SPoG WBrE WGor WHar
'Wessex Gold' (v) CFai WHCG

Weinmannia (*Cunoniaceae*)

racemosa 'Kamahi' CTrC
trichosperma ISea SAPC SArc

Weldenia (*Commelinaceae*)

candida EBla EHyt LTwo NMen SIng SOkd WAbe

Westringia (*Lamiaceae*)

angustifolia ECou
brevifolia ECou
- Raleighii Group ECou
§ ***fruticosa*** ♀H1 CArn CBcs CPLG CPle ECou EShb WJek XPep
- 'Morning Light' (v) EMan WCot
- 'Variegata' (v) CPle GQui WJek
- 'Wynyabbie Gem' EMan
longifolia ECou
rosmariniformis see *W. fruticosa*

whitecurrant see *Ribes rubrum* (W)

Whitfieldia (*Acanthaceae*)

elongata **new** EShb

Widdringtonia (*Cupressaceae*)

cedarbergensis CPLG CPne GGar
cupressoides see *W. nodiflora*
§ ***nodiflora*** GGar
schwarzii CPLG GGar

Wigandia (*Hydrophyllaceae*)

caracasana CHII CKob

Wikstroemia (*Thymelaeaceae*)

gemmata SCoo SSta
kudoi WCru

Willdenowia (*Restionaceae*)

incurvata **new** CBig

wineberry see *Rubus phoenicolasius*

Wisteria ✿ (*Papilionaceae*)

§ ***brachybotrys*** CMCN SLim
§ - Murasaki-kapitan CEnd SIFN
- 'Okayama' SIFN
- 'Pink Chiffon' **new** MAsh
§ - 'Shiro-kapitan' CBcs CEnd CHad CPMA CSPN CTri ENot EPfP LRHS MBri MDun SBra SHBN SIFN SLim SLon SPer WPGP
* - 'White Silk' CEnd CPMA LAst LSRN MGos NCGa
§ 'Burford' CEnd CSPN LRHS MAsh MBri MDun NBea NRib SCoo SLim SPoG WHar WPGP
'Caroline' CBcs CDoC CEnd CMen CPLN CSBt CSPN CSam EPfP ERea GKir LRHS MBlu MGos NBea SBLw SPer SPur SSpi WPGP
floribunda CBcs CRHN CWib ELan LRHS SBLw SBra SHBN WDin WFar WNor
§ - 'Alba' ♀H4 More than 30 suppliers
§ - 'Asagi' EBee
- 'Black Dragon' see *W.* x *formosa* 'Yae-kokuryû' (d)
- 'Burford' see *W.* 'Burford'
- 'Cannington' SCoo SLim
* - 'Cascade' CBcs CPMA MGos NCGa

§	- 'Domino'	CBcs CEnd CTri EBee EPfP GKir LRHS MBar NBea SBLw SBra SLim SPer SSta WFar WSHC
	- 'Fragrantissima'	see *W. sinensis* 'Jako'
	- 'Geisha'	CEnd SBLw SIFN
*	- 'Harlequin'	CBcs CHad CSPN EBee LRHS MGos SPoG
	- 'Hichirimen'	see *W. floribunda* 'Asagi'
	- 'Hon-beni'	see *W. floribunda* 'Rosea'
	- 'Honey Bee Pink'	see *W. floribunda* 'Rosea'
	- 'Honko'	see *W. floribunda* 'Rosea'
	- 'Issai Perfect'	LSRN
	- 'Jakohn-fuji'	see *W. sinensis* 'Jako'
§	- 'Kuchi-beni'	CBcs CEnd CSBt CSPN EBee ECrN ELan ENot GKir LAst LRHS MAsh MGos NCGa SBra SLim SPer SPoG
	- 'Lawrence'	CEnd CSPN LRHS MBri SIFN
	- 'Lipstick'	see *W. floribunda* 'Kuchi-beni'
	- 'Longissima'	see *W. floribunda* 'Multijuga'
	- 'Longissima Alba'	see *W. floribunda* 'Alba'
	- 'Macrobotrys'	see *W. floribunda* 'Multijuga'
	- 'Magenta'	CBcs ECrN LRHS
§	- 'Multijuga' ♀H4	More than 30 suppliers
	- Murasaki-naga	see *W. floribunda* 'Purple Patches'
	- 'Nana Richin's Purple'	CDul CEnd LRHS
	- 'Peaches and Cream'	see *W. floribunda* 'Kuchi-beni'
	- 'Pink Ice'	see *W. floribunda* 'Rosea'
§	- 'Purple Patches'	GKir LRHS MGos NPri SLim
	- Reindeer	see *W. sinensis* 'Jako'
§	- 'Rosea' ♀H4	CBcs CEnd CMen CSPN CWib EBee ECrN ELan ENot EPfP IMGH LBuc LRHS LSRN MAsh MBar MBri MDun MGos MWgw NBea SBLw SBra SHBN SIFN SLim SPer SWvt WDin WFar
	- 'Royal Purple'	ERea LAst LRHS MBri WGor
	- 'Russelliana'	SLim
	- 'Shiro-naga'	see *W. floribunda* 'Alba'
	- 'Shiro-noda'	see *W. floribunda* 'Alba'
	- 'Snow Showers'	see *W. floribunda* 'Alba'
	- 'Violacea Plena' (d)	CAlb CBcs CDoC EBee EPfP LRHS LSRN MGos MRav NBlu NPri SEND SHBN SPer SPur SWvt WDin WFar
	x ***formosa***	SLim
	- 'Black Dragon' (d)	see *W.* x *formosa* 'Yae-kokuryû' (d)
	- 'Domino'	see *W. floribunda* 'Domino'
	- 'Issai' Wada pro parte	see *W. floribunda* 'Domino'
	- 'Kokuryû' (d)	see *W.* x *formosa* 'Yae-kokuryû' (d)
§	- 'Yae-kokuryû' (d)	CBcs CEnd CMen CSBt CSPN EBee ECrN ELan ENot EPfP GKir LAst LRHS MBri MGos SBra SHBN SLim SMad SPer SReu SSpi SSta SWvt WFar WGor
	frutescens	SBLw WNor
	- 'Alba'	see *W. frutescens* 'Nivea'
	- 'Amethyst Falls'	SIFN
	- 'Magnifica'	see *W. macrostachya* 'Magnifica'
§	- 'Nivea'	SIFN
	Kapitan-fuji	see *W. brachybotrys*
§	'Lavender Lace'	CBcs CEnd EPfP LRHS MAsh NCGa SPoG WFar
	macrostachya 'Bayou Two o'Clock'	SIFN
	- 'Clara Mack'	SIFN
§	- 'Magnifica'	EBee MAsh
	- 'Pondside Blue'	SIFN
	multijuga 'Alba'	see *W. floribunda* 'Alba'
	'Showa-beni'	CEnd LRHS SCoo SIFN SLim SPoG WPGP
	sinensis ♀H4	More than 30 suppliers
	- 'Alba' ♀H4	CBcs CDoC CDul CHad CMen CWib EBee ECrN ELan EPfP ISea LBuc LRHS LSRN MBar NBlu SBra SEND SLim SPer SPla SPoG WDin WFar WOrn
	- 'Amethyst'	CBcs CEnd CSBt CSPN EBee EPfP ERea LRHS MAsh MDun MGos MRav NSti SBLw SBra SIFN SPla SPoG SReu
	- 'Blue Sapphire'	CBcs CMen CSPN EBee LAst LRHS SBra SPur
	- 'Consequa'	see *W. sinensis* 'Prolific'
	- 'Cooke's Special'	SIFN
§	- 'Jako'	CEnd SBra SIFN
	- 'Oosthoek's Variety'	see *W. sinensis* 'Prolific'
I	- 'Pink Ice' **new**	ISea
	- 'Prematura'	see *W. floribunda* 'Domino'
	- 'Prematura Alba'	see *W. brachybotrys* 'Shiro-kapitan'
§	- 'Prolific'	CPLN CSBt CSam CTri CWib EBee ELan EPfP LBuc LRHS MBri MDun MGos NBlu SBLw SBra SEND SPer SPla SSpi SWvt WFar WOrn WPat
	- 'Rosea'	CMen LSRN SKee SPur SWvt
	venusta	see *W. brachybotrys* 'Shiro-kapitan'
	- var. ***violacea*** hort.	see *W. brachybotrys* Murasaki-kapitan
	- var. ***violacea*** Rehder	see *W. brachybotrys* Murasaki-kapitan
	villosa	WNor

Withania (*Solanaceae*)

somnifera	CArn EOHP EUnu GPoy MGol MSal SHDw

Wittsteinia (*Alseuosmiaceae*)

vacciniacea	EBee WCru WWes

Wodyetia (*Arecaceae*)

bifurcata	EAmu

Woodsia (*Woodsiaceae*)

intermedia	NBro
obtusa	CLAP EFer EUJe GCal GMaP LAst LRHS SRot WRic
polystichoides ♀H4	GQui SRms WAbe

Woodwardia (*Blechnaceae*)

from Emei Shan, China	CLAP
areolata	SSpi
fimbriata	CFwr CHid CLAP CTbh ERod GBin GCal MAsh MAvo NWCA SSpi WCot WFib WMoo WPGP WPtf WRic
orientalis	SSpi WPic WRic
- var. ***formosana***	CLAP
- - B&SWJ 6865	WCru
radicans ♀H3	CAbb CFil CHEx CLAP CPLG EWes GQui ISea SAPC SArc WAbe WCot WFib WPic
unigemmata	CHEx CLAP EDAr EFer SAPC SArc SSpi WAbe WFib WHal
virginica	CLAP

Worcesterberry see *Ribes divaricatum*

Wulfenia (*Scrophulariaceae*)

amherstiana	GCed SOkd
blechicii subsp. ***rohlenae***	GIBF
carinthiaca	GAbr GEdr GIBF MOne NBir NLar
x ***schwarzii***	EBee

Wyethia (*Asteraceae*)

arizonica **new**	LRav
helianthoides	EMan
scabra	LRav

Xanthium (*Asteraceae*)

sibiricum	CArn

Xanthoceras (*Sapindaceae*)

sorbifolium ♀H3-4	CBcs CBot CFil CLnd CMCN CWib EBee ECrN ELan EPfP GKir IArd IDee LBuc LEdu MBlu SBrw SCoo SPoG SSpi WDin WFar WNor WPat XPep

Xanthorhiza (*Ranunculaceae*)

simplicissima	CBcs CFil CRow EBee EPfP GCal LEdu NLar SBrw SDys SSpi WPGP

Xanthorrhoea (*Xanthorrhoeaceae*)

australis	EShb SPlb WGer
johnsonii	WMul
preisii	WMul

Xanthosoma (*Araceae*)

sagittifolium	CKob EAmu EUJe MJnS MOak WMul
violaceum	CDWL CKob EAmu EUJe MJnS MOak WMul

Xerochrysum (*Asteraceae*)

bracteatum 'Coco'	CMHG EMan GMac WCot WWlt
- 'Dargan Hill Monarch'	CHll CMHG CSev CSpe SRms WWlt
- 'Skynet'	CSev GCal GMac
- (Sundaze Series) Sundaze Magenta = 'Redbramag'	LAst
- - Sundaze Orange = 'Flobraora' **new**	CHVG
- 'Wollerton' **new**	WWlt

Xeronema (*Phormiaceae*)

callistemon	CTrC

Xerophyllum (*Melanthiaceae*)

tenax	CFir EPot GBin GIBF NMen WLin

Xylorhiza see *Machaeranthera*

Xyris (*Xyridaceae*)

juncea	ECou
torta **new**	CFil WPGP

Y

Ypsilandra (*Melanthiaceae*)

cavaleriei **new**	GEdr
thibetica	EBla GEdr LAma SIgm SSpi WCot WCru WSHC

Yucca ✿ (*Agavaceae*)

aloifolia	CHEx ISea LRHS MGos SAPC SArc SBig SChr SNew SPlb WMul
- 'Purpurea'	SPlb
I - 'Spanish Bayonet'	SEND
- 'Variegata' (v)	SAPC SArc
angustifolia	see *Y. glauca*
angustissima	GCal
- NNS 99-509	WCot
arizonica	CBrP GCal
baccata	CTrC GCal WMul XPep
- NNS 99-510	WCot
brevifolia	CHEx WMul
carnerosana	CTrC WMul
§ ***elata***	CTrC SChr WMul
§ ***elephantipes*** ♀H1	EAmu EExo LRHS MBri SEND SMur WMul
- 'Jewel' (v)	EAmu SEND WMul
filamentosa ♀H4	More than 30 suppliers
- 'Bright Edge' (v) ♀H3	More than 30 suppliers
- 'Color Guard' (v)	CDul CTrC EUJe MBri WBrk WCot WFar
- 'Garland's Gold' (v)	CBcs CBrm CDoC ENot GQui LRHS MDun MGos MSph WCot WFar WPat
- 'Variegata' (v) ♀H3	CBcs CBot CDul EBee EPfP LRHS MGos SAga SRms WDin WFar WGer
flaccida	CBcs NBlu NEgg SDix SEND SPoG
- 'Golden Sword' (v) ♀H3	More than 30 suppliers
- 'Ivory' ♀H3-4	More than 30 suppliers
x ***floribunda***	SAPC SArc
§ ***glauca***	CAbb CBcs CBrP CMHG EPfP GCal LRHS MBri NPal SAPC SEND SPoG WMul XPep
- var. ***radiosa***	CTrC
gloriosa ♀H4	CBcs CDoC CDul CHEx CTri EBee EExo EGra EPfP EPla EWTr LAst LRHS LRav NPal NScw SAPC SArc SEND SHBN SMad SPoG SSpi SWvt WBrE WBrk WMul
- 'Aureovariegata'	see *Y. gloriosa* 'Variegata'
- 'Moon Frost'	SPoG
§ - 'Variegata' (v) ♀H4	More than 30 suppliers
guatemalensis	see *Y. elephantipes*
harrimaniae	GCal SIgm
kanabensis	GCal
navajoa	GCal
'Nobilis'	SDix
radiosa	see *Y. elata*
recurvifolia ♀H4	CHEx EPfP MGos NPal SAPC SArc WPic
- 'Variegata' (v)	WCot
rigida	CBrP CTrC WMul
rostrata	CAbb CBrP CTrC EAmu SAPC SArc SChr WMul XPep
schidigera	GCal WCot WMul
schottii	CAbb CBrP CTrC GCal
thompsoniana	CTrC GCal
torreyi	CTrC GCal SChr WCot XPep
whipplei	CAbb CBot CBrP CCtw CDoC CFil CRoM LEdu LRHS NPal SAPC SBig SEND SSpi WBrE XPep
- subsp. ***parishii***	SIgm

Yushania (*Poaceae*)

§ ***anceps***	CAbb CBcs CDoC CFil CHEx CHad EBee EFul ENBC EPfP EPla EPza GBin MBar MGos MMoz MWht NVic SAPC SArc SBig SPer WBrE WDin WFar WMoo WMul WPGP
- 'Pitt White'	CFil EPla WJun WPGP
- 'Pitt White Rejuvenated'	ERod
chungii	CFil EPla
maculata	EPla ERod MMoz MWht SBig WJun
§ ***maling***	EPfP EPla ERod MMoz WJun

Z

Zaluzianskya (*Scrophulariaceae*)

JCA 15665	WAbe
capensis	CPLG
'Katherine'	EMan LPhx SIng SRot
'Orange Eye'	CPBP CStu EBee SBla WAbe
ovata	CPBP CPLG CPom EBee EHyt EPot GBri LPio LSpr MTho NBir NBur NJOw NSla NWCA SAga SBla SIng SUsu WAbe
pulvinata **new**	CPBP SPlb
'Semonkong'	CMdw CPom EMan GCal LPio MAvo MNrw MSte

Zamia (*Zamiaceae*)

fischeri	WMul
floridana	CRoM
furfuracea	CBrP EAmu WMul
neurophyllidia	CBrP
pumila	CBrP WMul
roezlii	CBrP
standleyi	CBrP
vazquezii	CBrP

Zamioculcas (*Araceae*)

zamiifolia	ESlt

Zantedeschia (*Araceae*)

§ ***aethiopica*** ♀H3	More than 30 suppliers
- B&SWJ 3959	WCru
- 'Apple Court Babe'	CAby CElw CRow CStu GCal MNrw WDyG
- 'Caerwent' **new**	CPen
- 'Childsiana'	EBee SApp
- 'Crowborough' ♀H3	More than 30 suppliers
- 'Gigantea'	CHEx
- 'Glow'	ITer MNrw WCot
- 'Green Goddess' ♀H3	More than 30 suppliers
- 'Little Gem'	LPio SMad WFar
* - 'Marshmallow'	EBla LRHS
- 'Mr Martin'	EBee EMan MNrw WCot WPGP
- 'Pershore Fantasia' (v)	EBee EBla EVFa MAvo MNrw WCot WFar WSPU
- pink	CHEx
- 'Tiny Tim'	SChr
- 'Whipped Cream'	MNrw
- 'White Gnome'	EBee WCot WFar
- 'White Mischief'	EBee
- 'White Pixie'	COtt EBee EMan ENot EPfP SAga
- 'White Sail'	CBct EBee EBla EMan EMar EPza GCal LAst LRHS MNrw MRav SPoG WFib
albomaculata	CPLG EPfP EVFa LAma MNrw SGar
'Anneke'	EPfP EPot WBrE WFar
'Apricot Glow'	CHll
'Best Gold'	see *Z.* 'Florex Gold'
black	CSut
'Black Eyed Beauty'	CStu IHMH LAma WPnP
'Black Magic'	EPfP LAma WFar
'Black Pearl'	LAma
'Bridal Blush'	LAma
'Cameo'	CSut EPfP LAma MNrw WFar
'Carmine Red'	MNrw WBrE
'Chianti'	MNrw
'Crystal Blush'	EPot LAma
'Dominique'	MNrw
elliottiana ♀H1	CBcs CFir CHEx CHal CPou EPfP EUJe GQui ITer LAma MNrw WPnn
§ 'Florex Gold'	LAma
'Harvest Moon'	LAma
'Kiwi Blush'	CAbP CBot CDWL CFir CHEx CRow CSpe EBee EBla ELan EMan ERou IBal LPBA LRHS MAvo MCCP NPal SApp SPla SSpi WFar WSan
'Lavender Petite'	LAma
'Lime Lady'	ECha
'Majestic Red'	EPfP EPot
'Mango'	EPfP IHMH LAma MNrw WCot WPnP
'Maroon Dainty'	LAma
'Pink Mist'	EBee EMar EVFa LAma WPnP
'Pink Persuasion'	LAma MNrw WFar WPnP
red	IHMH
rehmannii ♀H1	CPou CStu EPfP EPot GQui IHMH LAma MNrw NLar SRms WSPU
rose-flowered **new**	CSut
salmon-orange	IHMH
'Schwarzwalder'PBR	EUJe
'Sensation'	IHMH
'Silver Lining'	LAma MNrw
'Solfatare'	LAma MNrw WPnP
'Treasure'	EPot WCot

Zanthorhiza see *Xanthorhiza*

Zanthoxylum (*Rutaceae*)

acanthopodium B&SWJ 7237	WCru
ailanthoides	CFil EPfP
- B&SWJ 8535	WCru
americanum	CAgr CBcs ELan
armatum	CAgr CFil WPGP
bungeanum	CAgr CFil
- HWJK 2131	WCru
coreanum	CFil
molle	CFil
oxyphyllum	CFil WPGP
piasezkii	CBcs
piperitum	CFil SMad WPGP
- B&SWJ 8593	WCru
- purple-leaved	CFil
planispinum	LEdu
* ***rhetsoides***	CFil
schinifolium	CAgr CBcs LEdu SSpi
- B&SWJ 1245	WCru
simulans	CBcs CFil CLnd CPLG EBee MBlu WBcn WPGP
stenophyllum	CBcs

Zauschneria (*Onagraceae*)

arizonica	see *Z. californica* subsp. *latifolia*
§ ***californica***	CBrm CHll CSam EBee EPfP GQui MBrN NMen SGar SLon WHrl
- 'Albiflora'	EPot WAbe
§ - subsp. ***cana***	ECGP ECha MHar SChu SIgm XPep
- - 'Sir Cedric Morris'	EPfP LRHS MAsh SMur
- 'Catalina'	XPep
- 'Clover Dale'	EWes
§ - 'Dublin' ♀H3	More than 30 suppliers
- 'Ed Carman'	ECtt EMan
§ - subsp. ***garrettii***	NWCA SDys SIgm XPep
- 'Glasnevin'	see *Z. californica* 'Dublin'
§ - subsp. ***latifolia***	EPot SIgm XPep
- - 'Sally Walker'	EWes
§ - subsp. ***mexicana***	CWib EPot MHer SRms
- 'Olbrich Silver'	CWCL EBee ECha EMan EShb EWes NWCA SUsu WAbe WCot WHoo WPat
- 'Schieffelin's Choice'	XPep
- 'Sierra Salmon'	XPep

- 'Solidarity Pink' MTho NWCA WKif WPat WSHC XPep
- 'Western Hills' ♀H4 CFir CLyd CSpe EBee ECtt LPhx LSou MRav NWCA SAga SBch SBla SIgm SIng WAbe WHoo XPep

cana villosa see *Z. californica* subsp. *mexicana*

I 'Pumilio' NMen

§ ***septentrionalis*** ETow SBla

Zebrina see *Tradescantia*

Zelkova ✿ (*Ulmaceae*)

carpinifolia CDoC CDul CMCN CMen CTho LRHS SBLw STre WDin WMou WNor

'Kiwi Sunset' **new** ENot

schneideriana CMen

serrata ♀H4 CBcs CDul CLnd CMCN CMen CTho EBee ECrN ELan EPfP EWTr GKir IArd LRHS MBar NBea NPal NWea SBLw SPer STre WCru WDin WFar WMou WNor WOrn

- B&SWJ 8491 from Korea WCru
- 'Goblin' CLnd WPat
- 'Green Vase' CLnd LRHS SCoo SLim
- 'Variegata' (v) CPMA MBlu MGos WBcn
- 'Yatsubusa' STre
- 'Yrban Ruby' MGos

sinica CLnd CMCN CMen WNor

x ***verschaffeltii*** GKir

Zenobia (*Ericaceae*)

pulverulenta More than 30 suppliers

- 'Blue Sky' CMCN EPfP MBlu NLar SSpi WPGP
- 'Raspberry Ripple' **new** MBlu NLar

Zephyranthes ✿ (*Amaryllidaceae*)

atamasca CStu ERos

candida CAvo CBro CStu EBee EMan EMon EPot EPyc ERea ERos ITim LAma LRHS SDix WCot

citrina EBee EHyt EPot ERos LAma WCot

drummondii CMon CStu EBee WCot

flavissima CBro CMon WCot WPGP WPrP

'Grandjax' WCot

x ***lancasterae*** CMon

lindleyana EBee WCot

macrosiphon CMon EBee

'Mary' **new** CMon

mexicana ERos

minima CMon CStu EBee

robusta see *Habranthus robustus*

rosea EBee EPot LAma

smallii CMon

sulphurea LAma

verecunda CStu

Zexmenia (*Asteraceae*)

hispida see *Wedelia texana*

Zieria (*Rutaceae*)

cytisoides **new** ECou

Zigadenus (*Melanthiaceae*)

elegans EBrs ECha EHyt EMan ERos GAbr LRHS SMad SSpi SUsu WBVN

fremontii EBee EBla MDKP WCot WLin

glaberrimus SSpi

muscitoxicus **new** EBrs

nuttallii EBee EMan ERos MDKP WCot WLin

Zingiber (*Zingiberaceae*)

chrysanthum CKob EUJe

clarkei CKob EUJe MOak WMul

gracile CKob

'Midnight' CKob MOak

mioga CKob GPoy LEdu MSal WDyG

- 'Dancing Crane' (v) **new** CKob

officinale CKob GPoy MOak MSal

purpureum CKob EUJe MOak

'Red Dwarf' CKob

rubens CKob EUJe MOak

spectabile CKob

'Yellow Delight' CKob

zerumbet CKob EUJe MOak WMul

- 'Darceyi' (v) CKob EUJe MOak

Zinnia (*Asteraceae*)

'Red Spider' **new** CSpe

Zizia (*Apiaceae*)

aptera CDes EBee EMan EMar LPhx WPGP

aurea EBee LPhx WSHC WTin

Ziziphus (*Rhamnaceae*)

§ ***jujuba*** (F) CAgr LEdu

- 'Lang' (F) ERea
- var. ***spinosa*** CArn

sativa see *Z. jujuba*

Zoysia (*Poaceae*)

matrella XPep

tenuifolia XPep

BIBLIOGRAPHY

This is by no means exhaustive but lists some of the more useful works used in the preparation of the *RHS Plant Finder.* Included are websites, all of which were available on line in February/March 2003. The websites of raisers of new plants (not listed here) are also an invaluable source of information. The PBR grant holder will be found in the appropriate PBR source listed below.

GENERAL

Allan, H.H., et al. 2000. *Flora of New Zealand.* Wellington. (5 vols).

Bailey, L.H. & Bailey, E.Z. et al. 1976. *Hortus Third.* New York: Macmillan.

Bean, W.J. 1988. *Trees and Shrubs Hardy in the British Isles.* (8th ed. edited by Sir George Taylor & D.L. Clarke & Supp. ed. D.L. Clarke). London: John Murray.

Beckett, K. (ed.). 1994. *Alpine Garden Society Encyclopaedia of Alpines.* Pershore, Worcs: Alpine Garden Society (2 vols).

Brickell, C. (ed.). 1996. *The Royal Horticultural Society A-Z Encyclopedia of Garden Plants.* London: Dorling Kindersley.

Brickell, C. (ed.). 2003. *The RHS New Encyclopedia of Plants and Flowers.* London: Dorling Kindersley.

Brummitt, R.K. & Powell, C.E. (eds). 1992. *Authors of Plant Names.* Kew: Royal Botanic Gardens.

Brummitt, R.K. (comp.). 1992. *Vascular Plant Families and Genera.* Kew: Royal Botanic Gardens.

Bond, P. & Goldblatt, P. 1984. *Plants of the Cape Flora: A Descriptive Catalogue.* Journal of South African Botany Supplementary Vol. No. 13. Kirstenbosch, South Africa: National Botanic Gardens.

Bramwell, D. & Bramwell, Z.I. 2001. *Wild Flowers of the Canary Islands.* (2nd ed.). Madrid: Editorial Rueda, S.L.

Castroviejo, S., Laínz, M., López González, G., Montserrat, P., Munoz Garmendia, F., Paiva, J. & Villar, L. (eds). *Flora Iberica.* 1987-2001. (Vols 1-8, 14). Madrid: Real Jardín Botánico, C.S.I.C.

Cave, Y. & Paddison, V. 1999. *The Gardener's Encyclopaedia of New Zealand Native Plants.* Auckland: Godwit.

Chittenden, F.J. & Synge, P.M. (eds). 1956. *The Royal Horticultural Society Dictionary of Gardening.* (2nd ed.). Oxford: Clarendon Press. (4 vols).

Clement, E.J. & Foster, M.C. 1994. *Alien Plants of the British Isles.* London: Botanical Society of the British Isles.

Cooke, I. 1998. *The Plantfinder's Guide to Tender Perennials.* Newton Abbot, Devon: David & Charles.

Cronquist, A., Holmgren, A.H., Holmgren, N.H., Reveal, J.L. & Holmgren, P.H. et al. (eds). *Intermountain Flora: Vascular Plants of the Intermountain West, USA.* (1986-97). (Vols 1, 3-6). New York: New York Botanical Garden.

Cullen, J. (ed.). 2001. *Handbook of North European Garden Plants.* Cambridge University Press.

Davis, P.H., Mill, R.R. & Tan, K. (eds). 1965. *Flora of Turkey and the East Aegean Islands* (1965-1988) (Vols 1-10). Edinburgh University Press.

Forrest, M. (comp.) & Nelson, E.C. (ed.). 1985. *Trees and Shrubs Cultivated in Ireland.* Dublin: Boethius Press for An Taisce.

Goldblatt, P. & Manning, J. 2000. *Cape Plants. A Conspectus of the Cape Flora of South Africa.* South Africa / USA: National Botanical Institute of South Africa / Missouri Botanical Garden.

Graf, A.B. 1963. *Exotica 3. Pictorial Cyclopedia of Exotic Plants.* (3rd ed.). New Jersey, USA: Roehrs

Graf, A.B. 1986. *Tropica.* Color Cyclopedia of Exotic Plants and Trees. (3rd ed.). New Jersey, USA: Roehrs

Greuter, W., et al. (eds). 2000. *International Code of Botanical Nomenclature (Saint Louis Code).* Königstein, Germany: Koeltz Scientific Books.

Greuter, W., Brummitt, R.K., Farr, E., Kilian, N., Kirk, P.M. & Silva, P.C. (comps). 1993. *NCU-3. Names in Current Use for Extant Plant Genera.* Konigstein, Germany: Koeltz Scientific Books.

Grierson, A.J.C., Long, D.G. & Noltie, H.J. et al. (eds). 2001. *Flora of Bhutan.* Edinburgh: Royal Botanic Garden.

Griffiths, M. (ed.). 1994. *The New RHS Dictionary Index of Garden Plants.* London: Macmillan

Güner, A., Özhatay, N., Ekîm, T., Baser, K.H.C. & Hedge, I.C. 2000. *Flora of Turkey and the East Aegean Islands.* Supplement 2. Vol. 11. Edinburgh: Edinburgh University Press.

Harkness, M.G. 1993. *The Bernard E. Harkness Seedlist Handbook.* (2nd ed.). London: Batsford.

Hickman, J.C. (ed.). 1993. *The Jepson Manual. Higher Plants of California.* Berkeley & Los Angeles: University of California Press. Newton Abbot, Devon: David & Charles.

Hillier, J. & Coombes, A. (eds). 2002. *The Hillier Manual of Trees & Shrubs.* (7th ed.).

Hirose, Y. & Yokoi, M. 1998. *Variegated Plants in Colour.* Iwakuni, Japan: Varie Nine

Hirose, Y. & Yokoi, M. 2001. *Variegated Plants in Colour.* Vol. 2. Iwakuni, Japan: Varie Nine

Hoffman, M.H.A., van de Laar, H.J., de Jong, P.C. & Geers, F. (eds). 2000. *Naamlijst van Houtige Gewassen.* (List of Names of Woody Plants). Boskoop, Netherlands: Boomteelt Praktijkonderzoek.

Hoffman, M.H.A., van de Laar, H.J., de Jong, P.C. & Geers, F. (eds). 2000. *Naamlijst van Vaste Plantem. (List of Names of Perennials).* Boskoop, Netherlands: Boomteelt Praktijkonderzoek.

Huxley, A., Griffiths, M. & Levy, M. (eds). 1992. *The New RHS Dictionary of Gardening.* London: Macmillan.

Jacobsen, H. 1973. *Lexicon of Succulent Plants.* London: Blandford.

Jellitto, L. & Schacht, W. 1990. *Hardy Herbaceous Perennials.* Portland, Oregon: Timber Press. (2 vols).

Kelly, J. (ed.). 1995. *The Hiller Gardener's Guide to Trees and Shrubs.* Newton Abbot, Devon: David & Charles.

Krüssmann, G. & Epp, M.E. (trans.). 1986. *Manual of Cultivated Broad-leaved Trees and Shrubs.* London: Batsford (3 vols).

Leslie, A.C. (trans.). *New Cultivars of Herbaceous Perennial Plants 1985-1990.* Hardy Plant Society.

Mabberley, D.J. 1997. *The Plant-Book. A Portable Dictionary of the Vascular Plants.* (2nd ed.). Cambridge: Cambridge University Press.

McGregor, R.L., Barkley, T.M., Brooks, R.E. & Schofield, E.K. et al. (eds). 1987. *Flora of the Great Plains.* Lawrence, Kansas: University Press of Kansas.

Metcalf, L.J. 1987. *The Cultivation of New Zealand Trees and Shrubs.* Auckland: Reed Methuen.

Munz, P. 1973. *A Californian Flora and Supplement.* London: University of California Press.

Nelson, E.C. 2000. *A Heritage of Beauty: The Garden Plants of Ireland: An Illustrated Encyclopaedia.* Dublin: Irish Garden Plant Society.

Ohwi, J. 1965. *Flora of Japan.* Washington DC: Smithsonian Institution.

Phillips, R. & Rix, M. 1989. *Shrubs.* London: Pan

Phillips, R. & Rix, M. 1993. *Perennials.* London: Pan (2 vols).

Phillips, R. & Rix, M. 1997. *Conservatory and Indoor Plants.* London: Macmillan. (2 vols).

Platt, K. (comp.). 2002. *The Seed Search.* (5th ed.). Sheffield: Karen Platt

Polunin, O. & Stainton, A. 1984. *Flowers of the Himalaya.* Oxford: Oxford University Press.

Press, J.R. & Short, M.J. (eds). 1994. *Flora of Madeira.* London: Natural History Museum/HMSO.

Rehder, A. 1940. *Manual of Cultivated Trees and Shrubs Hardy in North America.* (2nd ed.). New York: Macmillan.

Stace, C. 1997. *New Flora of the British Isles.* (2nd ed.). Cambridge: Cambridge University Press.

Stainton, A. 1988. *Flowers of the Himalaya. A Supplement.* Oxford University Press.

Stearn, W.T. 1992. *Botanical Latin.* (4th ed.). Newton Abbot, Devon: David & Charles.

Stearn, W.T. 1996. *Stearn's Dictionary of Plant Names for Gardeners.* London: Cassell

Thomas, G.S. 1990. *Perennial Garden Plants. A Modern Florilegium.* (3rd ed.). London: Dent.

Thomas, G.S. 1992. *Ornamental Shrubs, Climbers & Bamboos.* London: John Murray

Trehane, P. (comp.). 1989. *Index Hortensis. Volume 1: Perennials.* Wimborne: Quarterjack

Trehane, P., et al. 1995. *International Code of Nomenclature for Cultivated Plants.* Wimborne, UK: Quarterjack

Tutin, T.G., et al. (ed.). 1993. *Flora Europaea. Volume 1. Psilotaceae to Platanaceae.* (2nd ed.). Cambridge University Press.

Tutin, T.G., et al. 1964. *Flora Europaea.* Cambridge University Press. Vols 1-5.

Walter, K.S. & Gillett, H.J. (eds). 1998. *1997 IUCN Red List of Threatened Plants.* Gland, Switzerland and Cambridge, UK: IUCN.

Walters, S.M. & Cullen, J. et al. (eds). 2000. *The European Garden Flora.* Cambridge: Cambridge University Press. (6 vols).

Willis, J.C. & Airy-Shaw, H.K. (eds). 1973. *A Dictionary of the Flowering Plants and Ferns.* (8th ed.). Cambridge University Press.

General Periodicals

New, Rare and Unusual Plants.

The Hardy Plant Society. *The Hardy Plant.*

The Hardy Plant Society. *The Sport.*

Internationale Stauden-Union. *ISU Yearbook.*

Royal Horticultural Society. *The Garden.*

Royal Horticultural Society. *The Plantsman.*

Royal Horticultural Society. *The New Plantsman.*

General Websites

Australian Cultivar Registration Authority. Jan 2004. www.anbg.gov.au/acra

Australian Plant Breeders Rights – Database Search. Jan 2004. http://cber.bio.waikato.ac.nz

Australian Plant Names Index. Australian National Botanic Gardens (comp.). May 2003. www.anbg.gov.au/anbg/names.html

Canadian Plant Breeders' Rights Office: Canadian Food Inspection Agency. Dec 2003. www.inspection.gc.ca/english/plaveg/pbrpov/pbrpove.shtml

Community Plant Variety Office List of Grants and Applications for Plant Variety Rights. Jan 2004. www.cpvo.fr/en/default.html

DEFRA Plant Varieties and Seeds Gazette. Dec 2003. www.defra.gov.uk/planth/pvs/gaz.htm

Flora Europaea Search Form. http://rbg-web2.rbge.org.uk/FE/fe.html

Flora Mesoamericana Internet Version (W3FM). Apr 2003 Missouri Botanical Garden. www.mobot.org/fm/intro.html

Flora of China Checklist. Jan 2004. http://flora.huh.harvard.edu/china
Flora of Korea. http://user.Ksucc.ac.kr/~ecolab/flora.html
Flora of North America Website. 2002. Morin, N.R., et al. http://hua.huh.harvard.edu/fna/index.html
GRIN (Germplasm Resources Information Network) Taxonomy. Aug 2000. www.ars-grin.gov/npgs/tax/index.html
International Perennial Plant Register. 2003. Internationale Stauden-Union. www.isu-perennials.org/e/indexe.htm
International Plant Names Index. Aug 2002. www.ipni.org
IOPI Provisional Global Plant Checklist. Sept 2003. www.bgbm.fu-berlin.de/iopi/gpc/query.asp
List of Plant Species of the Waikito. University of Waikato. Dec 2003. http://cber.bio.waikato.ac.nz
Manual de plantas de Costa Rica. www.mobot.org/manual.plantas/lista.html
New Ornamentals Database. Oct 2003. Hatch, L.C. (comp.). http://members.tripod.com.~Hatch_L/nos.html
Plants Database. Version 3.5. Jan 2004. USDA, NRCS. http://plants.usda.gov/
Synonymized Checklist of the Vascular Flora of the United States, Puerto Rico and the Virgin Isles. July 1998. BIOTA of North America Program. www.csdl.tamu.edu/FLORA/b98/check98.htm
US Patent Full-Text Database. US Patent and Trademark Office, (comp.). Jan 2004. www.uspto.gov/patft/index.html
VAST TROPICOS. Jan 2004. Missouri Botanical Garden. http://mobot.mobot.org/W3T/Search/vast.html

GENERA

Acacia
Beckett, K.A. 1993. Some Australian Wattles in Cultivation. *The Plantsman* 15(3):131-47.
Simmons, M.H. 1987. *Acacias of Australia.* (2nd ed.). Melbourne: Nelson.
Acer
Harris, J.G.S. 2000. *The Gardener's Guide to Growing Maples.* Newton Abbot, Devon: David & Charles.
Van Gelderen, C.J. & Van Gelderen, D.M. 1999. *Maples for Gardens.* A Color Encyclopedia. Portland, Oregon: Timber Press.
Vertrees, J.D. 2001. *Japanese Maples.* Momiji and Kaede. (3rd ed.). Portland, Oregon: Timber Press.
Actaea
Compton, J. 1992. *Cimicifuga* L. *Ranunculaceae. The Plantsman* 14(2):99-115.
Compton, J. 1992. *Cimicifuga.* A Bane of a Name for a Fine Plant. *The Garden* (RHS) 117(11):504-506.
Compton, J.A. & Culham, A. 2000. The Name is the Game. *The Garden* (RHS) 125(1):48-52.
Compton, J.A., Culham, A. & Jury, S.L. 1998. Reclassification of *Actaea* to Include *Cimicifuga* and *Souliea* (*Ranunculaceae*). *Taxon* 47:593-634.
Adiantum
Goudey, C.J. 1985. *Maidenhair Ferns in Cultivation.* Melbourne: Lothian.
Agapanthus
Snoeijer, W. 1998. *Agapanthus.* A Review. Gouda: Wim Snoeijer.
Agavaceae
Irish, M. & Irish, G. 2000. *Agaves, Yuccas and Related Plants.* A Gardener's Guide. Portland, Oregon: Timber Press.
Aizoaceae
Burgoyne, P., Hartmann, H., Hammer, S., Chesselet, P., van Jaarsveld, E., Klak, C., Smith, G., van Wyk & H. Kurzweil, B. 1998. *Mesembs of the World. Illustrated Guide to a Remarkable Succulent Group.* South Africa: Briza Publications.
Allium
Dadd, R. 1997. RHS Trials: Grand Alliums. *The Garden* (RHS) 122(9) p658-661.
Davies, D. 1992. *Alliums. The Ornamental Onions.* London: Batsford .
Gregory, M., et al. 1998. *Nomenclator Alliorum.* London: RBG, Kew.
Mathew, B. 1996. *A Review of Allium Section Allium.* Kew: Royal Botanic Gardens.
Androsace
Smith, G. & Lowe, D. 1997. *The Genus Androsace.* Pershore, Worcs: Alpine Garden Society Publications Limited.
***Anemone*, Japanese**
McKendrick, M. 1990. Autumn Flowering Anemones. *The Plantsman* 12(3):140-151.
McKendrick, M. 1998. Japanese Anemones. *The Garden* (RHS) 123(9):628-633.
Anthemis
Leslie, A. 1997. Focus on Plants: *Anthemis tinctoria. The Garden* (RHS) 122(8):552-555.
Apiaceae
Ingram, T. 1993. *Umbellifers.* Pershore, Worcs: Hardy Plant Society.
Pimenov, M.G. & Leonov, M.V. 1993. *The Genera of the Umbelliferae.* Kew: Royal Botanic Gardens.
Aquilegia
Munz, P.A. 1946. *Aquilegia:* the Cultivated and Wild Columbines. *Gentes Herb.* 7(1):1-150.
***Arecaceae* (*Palmae*, palms)**
Jones, D.L. 1995. *Palms Throughout the World.* Chatswood, NSW: Reed Books.
Uhl, N.W. & Dransfield, J. 1987. *Genera Palmarum.* A Classification of Palms Based on the Work of Harold E. Moore Jr. Lawrence, Kansas: Allen Press.

Argyranthemum

Cheek, R. 1993. La Belle Marguerite. *The Garden* (RHS) 118(8):350-355.

Humphries, C.J. 1976. A Revision of the Macaronesian Genus *Argyranthemum. Bull. Brit. Mus. (Nat. Hist.) Bot.* 5(4):145-240.

Arisaema

Gusman, G. & Gusman, L. 2002. *The Genus Arisaema: A Monograph for Botanists and Nature Lovers.* Ruggell, Leichtenstein: A.R. Gantner Verlag Kommanditgesellschaft.

Pradhan, U.C. 1997. *Himalayan Cobra Lilies* (Arisaema). Their Botany and Culture. (2nd ed.). Kalimpong, West Bengal, India: Primulaceae Books.

Arum

Bown, D. 2000. *Plants of the Arum Family.* (2nd ed.). Portland, Oregon: Timber Press.

Boyce, P. 1993. *The Genus Arum.* London: HMSO.

Aster

Picton, P. 1999. *The Gardener's Guide to Growing Asters.* Newton Abbot: David & Charles.

Ranson, E.R. 1946. *Michaelmas Daisies and Other Garden Asters.* London: John Gifford Ltd.

Astilbe

Noblett, H. 2001. *Astilbe.* A Guide to the Identification of Cultivars and Common Species. Cumbria: Henry Noblett.

Aubrieta

1975. *International Registration Authority Checklist.* Weihenstephan, Germany: (Unpublished).

Bamboos

Bell, M. 2000. *The Gardener's Guide to Growing Bamboos.* Newton Abbot: David & Charles.

Chao, C.S. 1989. *A Guide to Bamboos Grown in Britain.* RBG, Kew.

Ohrnberger, D. 1999. *The Bamboos of the World.* Amsterdam: Elsevier.

Begonia

American Begonia Society Astro Branch Begonia Data Base. Jan 2000. http://absastro.tripod.com/data.htm.

Ingles, J. 1990. *American Begonia Society Listing of Begonia Cultivars.* Revised Edition Buxton Checklist. American Begonia Society.

Thompson, M.L. & Thompson, E.J. 1981. *Begonias.* The Complete Reference Guide. New York: Times Books.

Berberidaceae

Stearn, W.T. & Shaw, J.M.H. 2002. *The Genus Epimedium and Other Herbaceous Berberidaceae including the Genus Podophyllum.* Kew: Royal Botanic Gardens.

Betula

Ashburner, K. & Schilling. T. 1985. *Betula utilis* and its Varieties. *The Plantsman* 7(2):116-125.

Ashburner, K.B. 1980. *Betula* – a Survey. *The Plantsman* 2(1):31-53.

Hunt, D. (ed.). 1993. *Betula: Proceedings of the IDS Betula Symposium 1992.* Richmond, Surrey: International Dendrology Society.

Boraginaceae

Bennett, M. 2003. *Pulmonarias and the Borage Family.* London: Batsford.

Bougainvillea

Bor, N.L. & Raizada, M.B. 1982. *Some Beautiful Indian Climbers and Shrubs.* (2nd ed.). Bombay Nat. Hist. Soc.

Gillis, W.T. 1976. Bougainvilleas of Cultivation (*Nyctaginaceae). Baileya* 20(1):34-41.

Iredell, J. 1990. *The Bougainvillea Grower's Handbook.* Brookvale, Australia: Simon & Schuster.

Iredell, J. 1994. *Growing Bougainvilleas.* London: Cassell.

MacDaniels, L.H. 1981. A Study of Cultivars in *Bougainvillea* (*Nyctaginaceae). Baileya* 21(2):77-100.

Singh, B., Panwar, R.S., Voleti, S.R., Sharma, V.K. & Thakur, S. 1999. *The New International Bougainvillea Check List.* (2nd ed.). New Delhi: Indian Agricultural Research Institute.

Bromeliaceae

Beadle, D.A. (comp.) 1998. *The Bromeliad Cultivar Registry* (with 2001 updates). Torrance, California: Bromeliad Society International.

Beadle, D.A. 1991. *A Preliminary Listing of all the Known Cultivar and Grex Names for the Bromeliaceae.* Corpus Christi, Texas: Bromeliad Society.

Bromeliad Cultivar Registry Online Databases. Jan 2004. Bromeliad Society International http://fcbs.org

Luther, H.E. 2002. *An Alphabetical List of Bromeliad Binomials.* (8th ed.) Orlando, Florida: Bromeliad Society International.

Rauh, W. 1979. *Bromeliads for Home, Garden and Greenhouse.* Blandford, Dorset: Blandford Press.

Brugmansia

Haik, M. (comp.). Dec 2003. Brugmansia Database. American Brugmansia and Datura Society. http://abads-database.org.

Bulbs

Bryan, J.E. 1989. *Bulbs.* Vols 1 & 2. Bromley, Kent: Christopher Helm.

Du Plessis, N. & Duncan, G. 1989. *Bulbous Plants of Southern Africa.* Cape Town: Tafelberg.

Grey-Wilson, C. & Mathew, B. 1981. *Bulbs.* London: Collins.

Leeds, R. 2000. *The Plantfinder's Guide to Early Bulbs.* Newton Abbot, Devon: David & Charles.

Phillips, R., Rix, M. & Mathew. B. (ed.). 1981. *The Bulb Book. A Photographic Guide to Over 800 Hardy Bulbs.* London: Ward Lock Ltd.

Van Scheepen, J. (ed.). 1991. *International Checklist for Hyacinths and Miscellaneous Bulbs.* Hillegom, Netherlands: Royal General Bulbgrowers' Association (KAVB).

Buxus

Batdorf, L.R. 1995. *Boxwood Handbook. A Practical Guide to Knowing and Growing Boxwood.* Boyce, VA, USA: The American Boxwood Society.

Camellia

Trujillo, D. J. (ed.). 2002. *Camellia Nomenclature.* (24th revd ed.). Southern California Camellia Society.

Savige, T.J. (comp.). 1993. *The International Camellia Register.* The International Camellia Society. (2 vols).

Savige, T.J. (comp.). 1997. *The International Camellia Register.* Suppl. to vols 1 and 2. The International Camellia Society.

Campanula

Lewis, P. & Lynch, M. 1998. *Campanulas. A Gardeners Guide.* (2nd ed.). London: Batsford.

Lewis, P 2002. *Campanulas in the Garden.* Pershore, Worcs.: Hardy Plant Society.

Canna

Cooke, I. 2001. *The Gardener's Guide to Growing Cannas.* Newton Abbot, Devon: David & Charles.

Hayward, K. 2000. *Canna Handbook.* (Edition 1.01). Farnborough, Hants: Hart Canna.

Carnivorous Plants

D'Amato, P. 1998. *The Savage Garden.* Berkeley, USA: Ten Speed Press.

Pietropaulo, J. & Pietropaulo, P. 1986. *Carnivorous Plants of the World.* Oregon, USA: Timber Press.

Schlauer, J. (comp.). Aug 2003. Carnivorous Plant Database. www2.labs.agilent.com/bot/cp_home

Slack, A. 1988. *Carnivorous Plants.* (Revd ed). Sherborne, Dorset: Alphabooks.

Cercidiphyllum

Dosmann, M.S. 1999. Katsura: a Review of *Cercidiphyllum* in Cultivation and in the Wild. *The New Plantsman* 6(1):52-62.

Dosmann, M., Andrews, S., Del Tredici, P. & Li, J. 2003. Classification and Nomenclature of Weeping Katsuras. *The Plantsman* 2(1): 21-27.

Chaenomeles

Weber, C. 1963. Cultivars in the Genus *Chaenomeles. Arnoldia (Jamaica Plain)* 23(3):17-75.

***Chrysanthemum* (*Dendranthema*)**

Brummitt, D. 1997. *Chrysanthemum* Once Again. *The Garden* (RHS) 122(9):662-663.

Gosling, S.G. (ed.). 1964. *British National Register of Chrysanthemums.* Whetstone, London: National Chrysanthemum Society.

National Chrysanthemum Society. 2000. *British National Register of Names of Chrysanthemums Amalgamated Edition 1964-1999.* Tamworth, Staffordshire: The National Chrysanthemum Society.

Cistus

Bygrave, P. & Page, R.G. 2002. *Cistus – a Guide to the Collection at Chelsea Physic Garden.* Wisley: NCCPG.

Page, R.G. July 2003. National Collection of Cistus and Halimium Website. www.cistuspage.org.uk

Citrus

Davies, F.S. & Albrigo, L.G. 1994. *Citrus.* Wallingford, Oxon: Cab International.

Saunt, J. 1990. *Citrus Varieties of the World.* An Illustrated Guide. Norwich: Sinclair

Clematis

Grey-Wilson, C. 2000. *Clematis: the Genus.* London: Batsford

HelpMeFind Clematis. Nov 2003. www.helpmefind.com/clematis

Johnson, M. 2001. *The Genus Clematis.* Södertälje, Sweden: Magnus Johnsons Plantskola AB & Bengt Sundström.

Matthews, V. (comp.). 2002. *The International Clematis Register and Checklist 2002.* London: Royal Horticultural Society.

Toomey, M. & Leeds, E. 2001. *An Illustrated Encyclopedia of Clematis.* Portland, Oregon: Timber Press.

Conifers

den Ouden, P. & Boom, B.K. 1965. *Manual of Cultivated Conifers.* The Hague: Martinus Nijhof.

Farjon, A. 1998. *World Checklist and Bibliography of Conifers.* Kew: Royal Botanic Gardens.

Krüssmann, G. & Epp, M.E. (trans.). 1985. *Manual of Cultivated Conifers.* London: Batsford.

Lewis, J. & Leslie, A.C. 1987. *The International Conifer Register. Part 1. Abies* to *Austrotaxus.* London: Royal Horticultural Society.

Lewis, J. & Leslie, A.C. 1989. *The International Conifer Register. Part 2. Belis* to *Pherosphaera,* excluding the Cypresses. London: Royal Horticultural Society.

Lewis, J. & Leslie, A.C. 1992. *The International Conifer Register. Part 3. The Cypresses.* London: Royal Horticultural Society.

Lewis, J. & Leslie, A.C. 1998. *The International Conifer Register. Part 4. Juniperus.* London: Royal Horticultural Society.

Trehane, P. Mar 2000. Complete List of Conifer Taxa Accepted for Registration. Royal Horticultural Society. www.rhs.org.uk/research/registration_conifers_accepted.asp

Welch, H.J. 1979. *Manual of Dwarf Conifers.* New York: Theophrastus.

Welch, H.J. 1991. *The Conifer Manual.* Vol. 1. Dordrecht, Netherlands: Kluwer Academic Publishers.

Welch, H.J. 1993. *The World Checklist of Conifers.* Bromyard, Herefordshire: Landsman's Bookshops Ltd.

Cornus

Howard, R.A. 1961. Registration Lists of Cultivar Names in *Cornus L. Arnoldia (Jamaica Plain)* 21(2):9-18.

Corydalis
Lidén, M. & Zetterlund, H. 1997. *Corydalis. A Gardener's Guide and a Monograph of the Tuberous Species.* Pershore, Worcs.: Alpine Garden Society Publications Limited.
Mathew, B. 2001. Earning their Spurs (*Corydalis*). *The Garden* (RHS) 126(3):184-187.
Corylus
Crawford, M. 1995. *Hazelnuts: Production and Culture.* Dartington, Devon: Agroforestry Research Trust.
Game, M. 1995. Champion of the Cobnut. *The Garden* (RHS) 120(11):674-677.
Cotoneaster
Fryer, J. & Hylmö, B. 1998. Seven New Species of *Cotoneaster* in Cultivation. *The New Plantsman* 5(3):132-144.
Fryer, J. & Hylmö, B. 2001. Captivating Cotoneasters. *The New Plantsman* 8(4):227-238.
Fryer, J. 1996. Undervalued Versatility. *Cotoneaster. The Garden* (RHS) 121(11):709-715.
Crassulaceae
Eggli, U. & Hart, H. 1995. *Evolution and Systematics of the Crassulaceae.* Leiden, Netherlands: Backhuys Publishers.
Rowley, G. 2003. *Crassula: A Grower's Guide.* Venegono superiore, Italy: Cactus & Co.
Crocosmia
Dunlop, G. 1999. Bright Sparks. *The Garden* (RHS) 124(8):599-605.
Kostelijk, P.J. 1984. *Crocosmia* in Gardens. *The Plantsman* 5(4):246-253.
Crocus
Jacobsen, N., van Scheepen, J. & Ørgaard, M. 1997. The *Crocus chrysanthus – biflorus* Cultivars. *The New Plantsman* 4(1):6-38.
Mathew, B. 1982. *The Crocus. A Review of the Genus Crocus (Iridaceae).* London: Batsford.
Mathew, B. 2002. *Crocus* Up-date. *The Plantsman* 1(1): 44-56
Cyclamen
Clennett, C. Jan. 2003. Register of Cultivar Names. www.cyclamen.org/registrar_set.html
Grey-Wilson, C. 2003. *Cyclamen. A Guide for Gardeners, Horticulturists & Botanists.* London: Batsford.
Grey-Wilson, C. 2002 Sprenger's Alpine Cyclamen. *The Plantsman* 1(3): 173-177
Cypripedium
Cribb, P. 1997. *The Genus Cypripedium.* Portland, Oregon: Timber Press.
Dahlia
American Dahlia Society website. Oct 2003. www.dahlia.org
National Dahlia Society. 2003. *Classified Directory and Judging Rules.* (27th ed.) Aldershot, Hants: National Dahlia Society.
RHS & Hedge, R. (comps). 1969. *Tentative Classified List and International Register of Dahlia Names 1969.* (& Supplements 1-13). London: Royal Horticultural Society.
Daphne
Brickell, C. & White, R. 2000. A Quartet of New Daphnes. *The New Plantsman* 7(1):6-18.
Brickell, C. 2000. *Daphne.* Part 2: Henderson's Daphne. *The New Plantsman* 7(2):114-122.
Brickell, C.D. & Mathew, B. 1976. *Daphne. The Genus in the Wild and in Cultivation.* Woking, Surrey: Alpine Garden Society.
Grey-Wilson, C. (ed.). 2001. *The Smaller Daphnes. The Proceedings of 'Daphne 2000', a Conference held at the Royal Horticultural Society.* Pershore, Worcs: Alpine Garden Society Publications Ltd.
Delphinium
1949. *A Tentative Check-list of Delphinium Names.* London: Royal Horticultural Society.
1970. *A Tentative Check-list of Delphinium Names.* Addendum to the 1949 tentative check-list of *Delphinium* names. London: Royal Horticultural Society.
Leslie, A.C. 1995. The International Delphinium Register Supplement 1993-94. *The Delphinium Society Year Book 1995.*
Leslie, A.C. 1996. *The International Delphinium Register Cumulative Supplement 1970-1995.* London: Royal Horticultural Society.
Leslie, A.C. 1996-2000. The International Delphinium Register Supplement 1994-99. *The Delphinium Society Year Book 1996-98.* London: Royal Horticultural Society.
Dianthus
Bird, R. 1994. *Border Pinks.* London: Batsford.
Galbally, J. & Galbally, E. 1997. *Carnations and Pinks for Garden and Greenhouse.* Portland, Oregon: Timber Press.
Leslie, A.C. *The International Dianthus Register.* 1983-2002. (2nd ed & Supps 1-19). London: Royal Horticultural Society.
Diascia
Benham, S. 1987. *Diascia:* A Survey of the Species in Cultivation. *The Plantsman* 9(1):1-17.
Harrison, H. 1996. *Diascia (Scrophulariaceae). Hardy Plant* 18(1):41-47.
Lord, T. 1996. *Diascia* on Trial. *The Garden* (RHS) 121(4):192-194.
Dierama
Hilliard, O.M. & Burtt, B.L. 1991. *Dierama. The Harebells of Africa.* Johannesburg; London: Acorn Books.
Dionysia
Grey-Wilson, C. 1989. *The Genus Dionysia.* Woking, Surrey: Alpine Garden Society.

Douglasia

Mitchell, B. 1999. Celebrating the Bicentenary of David Douglas: a Review of *Douglasia* in Cultivation. *The New Plantsman* 6(2):101-108.

Dracaena

Bos, J.J., Graven, P., Hetterscheid, W.L.A. & van de Wege, J.J. 1992. Wild and cultivated *Dracaena fragrans. Edinburgh J. Bot.* 49(3):311-331.

Echinacea

Vernon, J. 1999. Power Flowers. *The Garden* (RHS) 124(8):588-593.

Epimedium

Barker, D.G. 1996. *Epimediums and other herbaceous Berberidaceae.* Pershore, Worcs.: The Hardy Plant Society.

White, R. 1996. *Epimedium:* Dawning of a New Area. *The Garden* (RHS) 121(4):208-214.

Episcia

Dates, J.D. 1993. *The Gesneriad Register 1993.* Check List of Names with Descriptions of Cultivated Plants in the Genera *Episcia* & *Alsobia.* Galesburg, Illinois: American Gloxinia & Gesneriad Society, Inc.

Erica

Baker, H.A. & Oliver, E.G.H. 1967. *Heathers in Southern Africa.* Cape Town: Purnell.

Schumann, D., Kirsten, G. & Oliver, E.G.H. 1992. *Ericas of South Africa.* Vlaeberg, South Africa: Fernwood Press.

Erodium

Clifton, R. 1994. *Geranium Family Species Checklist. Part 1 Erodium.* (4th ed.). The Geraniaceae Group.

Leslie, A.C. 1980. The Hybrid of *Erodium corsicum* With *Erodium reichardii. The Plantsman* 2:117-126.

Toomey, N., Cubey, J. & Culham, A. 2002. *Erodium* x *variabile. The Plantsman* 1(3): 166-172

Victor, D.X. (comp.). 2000. *Erodium: Register of Cultivar Names.* The Geraniaceae Group.

Erythronium

Mathew, B. 1992. A Taxonomic and Horticultural Review of *Erythronium* L. (*Liliaceae*). *J. Linn. Soc., Bot.* 109:453-471.

Mathew, B. 1998. The Genus *Erythronium. Bull. Alpine Gard. Soc. Gr. Brit.* 66(3):308-321.

Euonymus

Brown, N. 1996. Notes on Cultivated Species of *Euonymus. The New Plantsman* 3(4):238-243.

Lancaster, C.R. 1982. *Euonymus* in Cultivation – Addendum. *The Plantsman* 4:61-64, 253-254.

Lancaster, C.R. 1981. An Account of *Euonymus* in Cultivation and its Availability in Commerce. *The Plantsman* 3(3):133-166.

Euphorbia

Turner, R. 1995. *Euphorbias. A Gardeners Guide.* London: Batsford.

Witton, D. 2000. *Euphorbias.* Pershore, Worcs: Hardy Plant Society.

Fagales:

Govaerts, R. & Frodin, D.G. 1998. *World Checklist and Bibliography of Fagales.* Royal Botanic Gardens, Kew.

Fagus

Dönig, G. 1994. *Die Park-und Gartenformen der Rotbuche Fagus sylvatica L.* Erlangen, Germany: Verlag Gartenbild Heinz Hansmann.

Wyman, D. 1964. Registration List of Cultivar Names of *Fagus* L. *J. Arnold Arbor.* 24(1):1-8.

Fascicularia

Nelson, E.C. & Zizka, G. 1997. *Fascicularia* (*Bromeliaceae*): Which Species are Cultivated and Naturalized in Northwestern Europe. *The New Plantsman* 4(4):232-239.

Nelson, E.C., Zizka, G., Horres, R. & Weising, K. 1999. Revision of the Genus *Fascicularia* Mez (*Bromeliaceae*). *Botanical Journal of the Linnean Society* 129(4):315-332.

Ferns

Checklist of World Ferns. Oct 2001. http://homepages.caverock.net.nz/~bj/fern/

Johns, R.J. 1996. *Index Filicum.* Supplementum Sextum pro annis 1976-1990. RBG, Kew.

Johns, R.J. 1997. *Index Filicum.* Supplementum Septimum pro annis 1991-1995. RBG, Kew.

Jones, D.L. 1987. *Encyclopaedia of Ferns.* Melbourne, Australia: Lothian.

Kaye, R. 1968. *Hardy Ferns.* London: Faber & Faber

Rickard, M.H. 2000. *The Plantfinder's Guide to Garden Ferns.* Newton Abbot, Devon: David & Charles.

Rush, R. 1984. *A Guide to Hardy Ferns.* London: British Pteridological Society.

Forsythia

INRA Forsythia website. Dec 2000. www.angers.inra.fr/forsy/indexeng.html

Fragaria

Day, D. (ed.). 1993. *Grower Digest 3: Strawberries.* (Revd ed.). London: Nexus Business Communications.

Fritillaria

Clark, T. & Grey-Wilson, C. 2003. Crown Imperials. *The Plantsman* 2(1):33-47.

Mathew, B., et al. 2000. *Fritillaria* Issue. *Bot. Mag.* 17(3):145-185.

Pratt, K. & Jefferson-Brown, M. 1997. *The Gardener's Guide to Growing Fritillaries.* Newton Abbot: David & Charles.

Turrill, W.B. & Sealy, J.R. 1980. *Studies in the Genus Fritillaria (Liliaceae).* Hooker's Icones Plantarum Vol. 39 (1 & 2). Royal Botanic Gardens, Kew.

Fruit

Anon. 1997. *Catalogue of Cultivars in the United Kingdom National Fruit Collection.* Kent, UK: Brogdale Horticultural Trust.

Bowling, B.L. 2000. *The Berry Grower's Companion.* Portland, Oregon: Timber Press.

Hogg, R. 1884. *The Fruit Manual.* (5th Ed.). London: Journal of Horticulture Office.

Index of the Bush Fruit Collection at the National Fruit Trials 1987. 1987. Faversham, Kent: MAFF.

Fuchsia

Bartlett, G. 1996. *Fuchsias – A Colour Guide.* Marlborough, Wilts: Crowood Press.

Boullemier, Leo.B. (comp.). 1991. *The Checklist of Species, Hybrids and Cultivars of the Genus Fuchsia.* London, New York, Sydney: Blandford Press.

Boullemier, Leo.B. (comp.). 1995. *Addendum No. 1 to the 1991 Checklist of Species, Hybrids and Cultivars of the Genus Fuchsia.* Dyfed, Wales: The British Fuchsia Society.

Goulding, E. 1995. *Fuchsias: The Complete Guide.* London: Batsford.

Johns, E.A. 1997. *Fuchsias of the 19th and Early 20th Century.* An Historical Checklist of Fuchsia Species & Cultivars, pre-1939. Kidderminster, Worcs: The British Fuchsia Society

Nijhuis, M. 1994. *1000 Fuchsias.* London: Batsford.

Nijhuis, M. 1996. *500 More Fuchsias.* London: Batsford.

Stevens, R. Jan 2004. Find That Fuchsia. www.findthatfuchsia.info

Van Veen, G. Dec 2003. Gelderse Fuchsia Info-site. http://home.tiscali.nl/veenvang

Galanthus

Bishop, M., Davis, A. & Grimshaw, J. 2001. *Snowdrops. A monograph of cultivated Galanthus.* Maidenhead: Griffin Press.

Davis, A.P., Mathew, B. (ed.) & King, C. (ill.). 1999. *The Genus Galanthus. A Botanical Magazine Monograph.* Oregon: Timber Press.

Gentiana

Bartlett, M. 1975. *Gentians.* Dorset: Blandford Press.

Halda, J.J. 1996. *The Genus Gentiana.* Dobré, Czech Republic: Sen.

Wilkie, D. 1950. *Gentians.* (2nd ed. revised). London: Country Life.

Geranium

Bath, T. & Jones, J. 1994. *The Gardener's Guide to Growing Hardy Geraniums.* Newton Abbot, Devon: David & Charles.

Clifton, R.T.F. 1995. *Geranium Family Species Check List Part 2.* Geranium. (4th ed. issue 2). Dover: The Geraniaceae Group.

Jones, J., et al. 2001. *Hardy Geraniums for the Garden.* (3rd ed., revised and enlarged). Pershore, Worcs: Hardy Plant Society.

Victor, D.X. 2001. *Geranium.* Register of Cultivar Names. The Geraniaceae Group. www.hardy geraniums.com/register_of_cultivar_names.htm

Yeo, P.F. 2002. *Hardy Geraniums.* (3rd ed.). Kent: Croom Helm.

Gesneriaceae

American Gloxinia and Gesneriad Society. Listing of registered gesneriads. Sept 2003. www.aggs.org/ir_ges

Dates, J.D. 1986-1990. *The Gesneriad Register 1986-1987 & 1990.* Galesburg, Illinois: American Gloxinia & Gesneriad Society, Inc.

Gladiolus

British Gladiolus Society List of Cultivars Classified for Show Purposes 1994. Mayfield, Derbyshire: British Gladiolus Society.

1997-1998. British Gladiolus Society List of European Cultivars Classified for Exhibition Purposes 1997 & 1998. Mayfield, Derbyshire: British Gladiolus Society.

1997-1998. British Gladiolus Society List of New Zealand Cultivars Classified for Exhibition Purposes 1997 & 1998. Mayfield, Derbyshire: British Gladiolus Society.

1997-1998. British Gladiolus Society List of North American Cultivars Classified for Exhibition Purposes 1997 & 1998. Mayfield, Derbyshire: British Gladiolus Society.

Goldblatt, P. & Manning, J. 1998. *Gladiolus in Southern Africa.* Vlaeberg, South Africa: Fernwood Press.

Goldblatt, P. 1996. *Gladiolus in Tropical Africa.* Systematics Biology and Evolution. Oregon: Timber Press.

Lewis, G.J., Obermeyer, A.A. & Barnard, T.T. 1972. A Revision of the South African Species of *Gladiolus. J. S. African Bot.* (Supp. Vol.)

Gleditsia

Santamour, F.S. & McArdle, A.J. 1983. Checklist of Cultivars of Honeylocust (*Gleditsia triacanthos* L.). *J. Arboric.* 9:271-276.

Grevillea

Olde, P. & Marriott, N. 1995. *The Grevillea Book.* (3). Kenthurst, NSW: Kangaroo Press.

Haemanthus

Snijman, D. 1984. A Revision of the Genus *Haemanthus. J. S. African Bot.* (Supp.) 12.

Hamamelis

Coombes, A.J. 1996. Winter Magic. Introduction to Witch Hazels. *The Garden* (RHS) 121(1):28-33.

Lane, C. 1998. *Hamamelis* in Small Spaces. *The Garden* (RHS) 123(1):38-41.

Strand, C. 1998. Asian Witch Hazels and their Hybrids: a History of *Hamamelis* in cultivation. *The New Plantsman* 5(4):231-245.

Heathers

Nelson, E.C. Feb 2002. International Cultivar Registration Authority for Heathers. www.heathersociety.org.uk/registration.html

Nelson, E.C. & Small, D.J. (eds). 2000. *International Register of Heather Names.* Volume 1: Hardy Cultivars & European Species. Part 1-4. The Heather Society.

Small, D. & Small, A. (comps). 2001. *Handy Guide to Heathers.* (3rd ed.) Creeting St Mary, Suffolk: The Heather Society.

Underhill, T. 1990. *Heaths & Heathers.* The Grower's Encyclopedia. Newton Abbot: David & Charles.

Hebe

Chalk, D. 1988. *Hebes and Parahebes.* Bromley, Kent: Christopher Helm (Publishers) Ltd.

Hutchins, G. 1997. *Hebes: Here and There.* A Monograph on the Genus *Hebe.* Caversham, Berks: Hutchins & Davies.

Metcalf, L.J. 2001. *International Register of Hebe Cultivars.* Canterbury, New Zealand: Royal New Zealand Institute of Horticulture (Inc.).

Hedera

McAllister, H. 1988. Canary and Algerian Ivies. *The Plantsman* 10(1):27-29.

McAllister, H.A. & Rutherford, A. 1990. *Hedera helix and H. hibernica* in the British Isles. *Watsonia* 18:7-15.

Rose, P.Q. 1996. *The Gardener's Guide to Growing Ivies.* David & Charles.

Rutherford, A., McAllister, H. & Mill, R.R. 1993. New Ivies from the Mediterranean Area and Macaronesia. *The Plantsman* 15(2): 115-128.

Hedychium

Schilling, T. 1982. A Survey of Cultivated Himalayan and Sino-Himalayan *Hedychium* Species. *The Plantsman* 4:129-149.

Spencer-Mills, L. 1996. Glorious *Hedychium. The Garden* (RHS) 121(12):754-759.

Heliconia

Berry, F. & Kress, W.J. 1991. *Heliconia.* An Identification Guide. Washington: Smithsonian Institution Press.

Helleborus

Mathew, B. 1989. *Hellebores.* Woking: Alpine Garden Society.

Rice, G. & Strangman, E. 1993. *The Gardener's Guide to Growing Hellebores.* Newton Abbot, Devon: David & Charles.

Hemerocallis

AHS – Registered Daylily Database. May 2003. http://database.tinkersgardens.com

Baxter, G.J. (comp.) 2003. *Hemerocallis Cultivar Registrations 1890-2002.* (CD-ROM Version 2003a.) Jackson, Tennessess: American Hemerocallis Society.

Erhardt, W. 1988. *Hemerocallis Daylilies.* London: Batsford.

Grenfell, D. 1998. *The Gardener's Guide to Growing Daylilies.* Newton Abbott: David & Charles.

Kitchingman, R.M. 1985. Some Species and Cultivars of *Hemerocallis. The Plantsman* 7(2):68-89.

Herbs

Page, M. & Stearn, W. *Culinary Herbs: A Wisley Handbook.* London: Royal Horticultural Society.

Phillips, R. & Foy, N. 1990. *Herbs.* London: Pan Books Ltd.

Hibiscus

Beers, L. & Howie, J. 1990. *Growing Hibiscus.* (2nd ed.). Kenthurst, Australia: Kangaroo Press.

Chin, H.F. 1986. *The Hibiscus: Queen of Tropical Flowers.* Kuala Lumpur: Tropical Press Sdn. Bhd.

Noble, C. July 2003. Official International Hibiscus Cross Check List and Register Database. Australian Hibiscus Society. www.geocities.com/auhibsoc/ira/boot.htm

Walker, J. 1999. *Hibiscus.* London: Casell.

Hippeastrum

Alfabetische Lijst van de in Nederland in Cultuur Zijnde Amaryllis (*Hippeastrum*) *Cultivars.* 1980. Hillegom, Netherlands: Koninklijke Algemeene Vereeniging Voor Bloembollencultur (KAVB).

Read, V.M. 1998. Blooming Bold. *The Garden* (RHS) 123(10):734-737.

Hosta

Hammelman, T. Mar 2001. Giboshi.com Hosta Database. www.giboshi.com

Hosta Library. Jan. 2003. www.hostalibrary.org

Grenfell, D. 1990. *Hosta.* London: Batsford.

Grenfell, D. 1993. *Hostas.* Pershore, Worcs: Hardy Plant Society.

Grenfell, D. 1996. *The Gardener's Guide to Growing Hostas.* Newton Abbot: David & Charles.

Schmid, W.G. 1991. *The Genus Hosta.* London: Batsford.

Hyacinthus

Clark, T. 2000. Focus on Plants: Treasures of the East (Hyacinths). *The Garden* (RHS) 125(9):672-675.

Stebbings, G. 1996. Heaven Scent. *The Garden* (RHS) 121(2):68-72.

Hydrangea

Church, G. 1999. *Hydrangeas.* London: Cassell.

Haworth-Booth, M. 1975. *The Hydrangeas.* London: Garden Book Club.

Lawson-Hall, T. & Brian, R. 1995. *Hydrangeas.* A Gardener's Guide. London: B.T. Batsford.

Mallet, C. 1992. *Hydrangeas. Species and Cultivars.* Vol. 1. Varengeville Sur Mer: Centre d'Art Floral.

Mallet, C. 1994. *Hydrangeas. Species and Cultivars.* Vol. 2. Varengeville Sur Mer: Editions Robert Mallet.

Hypericum

Lancaster, R. & Robson, N. 1997. Focus on Plants: Bowls of Beauty. *The Garden* (RHS) 122(8):566-571.

Ilex

Andrews, S. 1983. Notes on Some *Ilex* x *altaclerensis* Clones. *The Plantsman* 5(2):65-81.

Andrews, S. 1984. More Notes on Clones of *Ilex* x *altaclerensis. The Plantsman* 6(3):157-166. Erratum vol.6 p.256.

Andrews, S. 1985. Holly Berries of a Varied Hue. *The Garden* (RHS) 110(11):518-522.

Andrews, S. 1994. Hollies with a Difference. *The Garden* (RHS) 119(12):580-583,].

Dudley, T.R. & Eisenbeiss, G.K. 1992. *International Checklist of Cultivated Ilex.* Part 1 *Ilex opaca.* Washington USA: United States Department of Agriculture.

Dudley, T.R. & Eisenbeiss, G.K. 1992. *International Checklist of Cultivated Ilex.* Part 2 *Ilex crenata.* United States National Arboretum: United States Department of Agriculture.

Galle, F.C. 1997. *Hollies: the Genus Ilex.* Portland, Oregon: Timber Press.

Iridaceae

Innes, C. 1985. *The World of Iridaceae. A Comprehensive Record.* Ashington, Sussex: Holly Gate International Ltd.

Iris

American Iris Society Database. 2000. www.irisregister.com/

Hoog, M.H. 1980. Bulbous Irises . *The Plantsman* 2(3):141-64.

Mathew, B. 1981. *The Iris.* London: Batsford.

Mathew, B. 1993. The Spuria Irises. *The Plantsman* 15(1):14-25.

Service, N. 1990. *Iris unguicularis. The Plantsman* 12(1):1-9.

Stebbings, G. 1997. *The Gardener's Guide to Growing Iris.* Newton Abbot: David & Charles.

The Species Group of the British Iris Society, (ed.). 1997. *A Guide to Species Irises.* Their Identification and Cultivation. Cambridge, UK: Cambridge University Press.

Jovibarba* see under *Sempervivum

Kalmia

Jaynes, R.A. 1997. *Kalmia. Mountain Laurel and Related Species.* Oregon: Timber Press.

Pullen, A. 1997. *Kalmia latifolia. The Garden* (RHS) 122(6):400-403.

Kniphofia

Grant-Downton, R. 1997. Notes on *Kniphofia thomsonii* in Cultivation and in the Wild. *The New Plantsman* 4(3):148-156.

Taylor, J. 1985. *Kniphofia* – a Survey. *The Plantsman* 7(3):129-160.

Kohleria

Dates, J.D. (ed.) & Batcheller, F.N. (comp.). 1985. *The Gesneriad Register 1985. Check List of Names with Descriptions of Cultivated Plants in the Genus Kohleria.* Lincoln Acres, California: American Gloxinia and Gesneriad Society, Inc.

Lachenalia

Duncan, G.D. 1988. *The Lachenalia Hand Book.*

Lantana

Howard, R.A. 1969. A Check List of Names Used in the Genus *Lantana. J. Arnold Arbor.* 29(11):73-109.

Lathyrus

Norton, S. 1996. *Lathyrus. Cousins of Sweet Pea.* Surrey: NCCPG

Lavandula

McNaughton, V. 2000. *Lavender. The Grower's Guide.* Woodbridge, Suffolk: Garden Art Press

Tucker, A.O. & Hensen, K.J.W. 1985. The Cultivars of Lavender and Lavandin (*Labiatae*). *Baileya* 22(4):168-177.

Upson, T. 1999. Deep Purple. *The Garden* (RHS) 124(7):524-529.

Legumes

ILDIS. International Legume Database and Information Service. Aug 2003. V6.06. www.biodiversity.soton.ac.uk/LegumeWeb

Lewis, G.P. 1987. *Legumes of Bahia.* London: Royal Botanic Gardens, Kew.

Lock, J.M. & Heald, J. 1994. *Legumes of Indo-China.* Kew: Royal Botanic Gardens.

Lock, J.M. & Simpson, K. 1991. *Legumes of West Asia.* Kew: Royal Botanic Gardens.

Lock, J.M. 1989. *Legumes of Africa: A Checklist.* Kew: Royal Botanic Gardens.

Roskov, Yu, R., Sytin, A.K. & Yakovlev, G.P. 1996. *Legumes of Northern Eurasia.* Kew: Royal Botanic Gardens.

Leptospermum

Check List of *Leptospermum* Cultivars. 1963. *J. Roy. New Zealand Inst. Hort.* 5(5):224-30.

Dawson, M. 1997. A History of *Leptospermum scoparium* in Cultivation – Discoveries from the Wild. *The New Plantsman* 4(1):51-59.

Dawson, M. 1997. A History of *Leptospermum scoparium* in Cultivation – Garden Selections. *The New Plantsman* 4(2):67-78.

Lewisia

Davidson, B.L.R. 2000. *Lewisias.* Portland, Oregon: Timber Press.

Elliott, R. 1978. *Lewisias.* Woking: Alpine Garden Society.

Mathew, B. 1989. *The Genus Lewisia.* Bromley, Kent: Christopher Helm.

Liliaceae sensu lato

Mathew, B. 1989. Splitting the *Liliaceae. The Plantsman* 11(2):89-105.

Lilium

Leslie, A.C. *The International Lily Register 1982-2002.* (3rd ed. & suppls 1-20). London: Royal Horticultural Society.

Lonicera

Bradshaw, D. 1996. *Climbing Honeysuckles.* Surrey: NCCPG

Magnolia

Callaway, D.J. Sept 2001. Magnolia Cultivar Checklist. www.magnoliasociety.org/index.html

Callaway, D.J. 1994. *Magnolias.* London: Batsford .

Frodin, D.G. & Govaerts, R. 1996. *World Checklist and Bibliography of Magnoliaceae.* Kew: Royal Botanic Garden.

Gardiner, J. 2000. *Magnolias.* A Gardeners' Guide. Portland, Oregon: Timber Press.

Hunt, D. (ed.). 1998. *Magnolias and their Allies.* Proceedings of an International Symposium, Royal Holloway, University of London, Egham, Surrey. 1996. International Dendrology Society/ The Magnolia Society.

Malus

Crawford, M. 1994. *Directory of Apple Cultivars.* Devon: Agroforestry Research Trust.

Fiala, J.L. 1994. *Flowering Crabapples.* The genus *Malus.* Portland, Oregon: Timber Press.

Morgan, J. & Richards, A. 1993. *The Book of Apples.* London: Ebury Press.

Parfitt, B. 1965. *Index of the Apple Collection at the National Fruit Trials.* Faversham, Kent: MAFF.

Rouèche, A. Sept 2003. Les Crets Fruits et Pomologie. http://perso.club_internet.fr/lescrets/

Spiers, V. 1996. *Burcombes, Queenies and Colloggetts.* St Dominic, Cornwall: West Brendon.

Taylor, H.V. 1948. *The Apples of England.* London: Crosby Lockwood.

Meconopsis

Brickell, C. & Stevens, E. 2002. *Meconopsis* 'Lingholm'. *The New Plantsman* 1(2): 88-92

Cobb, J.L.S. 1989. *Meconopsis.* Bromley, Kent: Christopher Helm.

Grey-Wilson, C. 1992. A Survey of the Genus *Meconopsis* in Cultivation. The Plantsman 14(1):1-33

Stevens, E. & Brickell, C. 2001. Problems with the Big Perennial Poppies. *The New Plantsman* 8(1):48-61.

Stevens, E. 2001. Further Observations on the Big Perennial Blue Poppies. *The New Plantsman* 8(2):105-111.

Moraea

Goldblatt, P. 1986. *The Moraeas of Southern Africa.* Kirstenbosch: National Botanic Gardens

Musa

Germplasm available from INIBAP (list of accessions with genome groups). Jan 2003. International Network for the Improvement of Banana and Plantain. www.inibap.org/research/itctable2_eng.htm

Rimmington, G. July 2002. Sorting Musa Names. http://gmr.landfood.unimelb.edu.au/Plantnames/Sorting/Musa.html

Narcissus

Blanchard, J.W. 1990. *Narcissus – a guide to wild daffodils.* Lye End Link, St John's, Woking, Surrey GU21 1SW: Alpine Garden Society.

Kington, S. (comp.). 1998. *The International Daffodil Register and Classified List 1998* (3rd ed. & Supps 1-5, 1998-2002). London: Royal Horticultural Society. www.rhs.org.uk/research/registerpages/intro.asp

Nematanthus

Arnold, P. 1978. *The Gesneriad Register 1978.* Check List of *Nematanthus.* American Gloxinia and Gesneriad Society, Inc.

Nerium

Pagen, F.J.J. 1987. Oleanders. *Nerium* L. and the Oleander Cultivars. Agricultural University Wageningen Papers.

Toogood, A. 1997. *Nerium oleander. The Garden* (RHS) 122(7):488-491.

Nymphaea

International Water Lily Society. 1993. *Identification of Hardy Nymphaea.* Stapeley Water Gardens Ltd. Includes nomenclaturally adjusted contents page (1995) with Erratum & Addendum.

Knotts, K. & Sacher, R. (comps). 2000. *Provisional Check List of Names/Epithets of Nymphaea L.* International Waterlily & Water Gardening Society. Cocoa Beach, Florida.

Swindells, P. 1983. *Waterlilies.* London: Croom Helm.

Orchidaceae

Cribb, P. & Bailes, C. 1989. *Hardy Orchids.* Bromley, Kent: Christopher Helm.

Hunt, P.F. & Hunt, D.B. 1996. *Sander's List of Orchid Hybrids: Addendum 1991-1995.* London: Royal Horticultural Society.

Hunt, P.F. 2000. New Orchid Hybrids. *Orchid Rev.* 108(1233): Supplement.

Shaw, J.M.H. 2003. The International Orchid Register. www.rhs.org.uk/research/registration_orchids.asp

Origanum

Paton, A. 1994. Three Membranous-bracted Species of *Origanum. Kew Mag.* 11(3):109-117.

White, S. 1998. *Origanum. The Herb Marjoram and its Relatives.* Surrey: NCCPG.

Paeonia

Harding, A. & Klehm, R.G. 1993. *The Peony.* London: Batsford.

Haworth-Booth, M. 1963. *The Moutan or Tree Peony.* London: Garden Book Club.

Help Me Find Peonies. Nov 2003. www.helpmefind.com/peony/index.html

Kessenich, G.M. 1976. *Peonies.* (Variety Check List Pts 1-3). American Peony Society.

Osti, G.L. 1999. *The Book of Tree Peonies.* Turin: Umberto Allemandi

Page, M. 1997. *The Gardener's Guide to Growing Peonies.* Newton Abbott: David & Charles

Rogers, A. 1995. *Peonies.* Portland, Oregon: Timber Press

Wang, L., et al. 1998. *Chinese Tree Peony.* Beijing: China Forestry Publishing House.

Papaver

Grey-Wilson, C. 1998. Oriental Glories. *The Garden* (RHS) 123(5):320-325.

Grey-Wilson, C. 2000. *Poppies. The Poppy Family in the Wild and in Cultivation.* London: Batsford.

Passiflora

Vanderplank, J. 2002. *Passion Flowers.* (3rd ed.). London, England: Cassell.

Pelargonium

Abbott, P.G. 1994. *A Guide to Scented Geraniaceae.* Angmering, West Sussex: Hill Publicity Services.

Anon. 1985. *A Checklist and Register of Pelargonium Cultivar Names.* Pt 2: C-F. Australian Pelargonium Society.

Anon. 1978. *A Checklist and Register of Pelargonium Cultivar Names.* Pt 1 A-B. Australian Pelargonium Society.

Bagust, H. 1988. *Miniature and Dwarf Geraniums.* London: Christopher Helm.

Clifford, D. 1958. *Pelargoniums.* London: Blandford Press.

Clifton, R. 1999. *Geranium Family Species Checklist, Part 4: Pelargonium.* The Geraniaceae Group.

Complete Copy of the Spalding Pelargonium Checklist. (Unpublished). USA.

Key, H. 2000. *1001 Pelargoniums.* London: Batsford.

Miller, D. 1996. *Pelargonium.* A Gardener's Guide to the Species and Cultivars and Hybrids. London: B. T. Batsford.

Pelargonium Palette: The Geranium and Pelargonium Society of Sydney Incorporated. Varieties – Alphabetical List. July 2000. www.elj.com/geranium/var/alphaind.htm

Van der Walt, J.J.A., et al. 1977. *Pelargoniums of South Africa.* (1-3). Kirstenbosch, South Africa: National Botanic Gardens.

Penstemon

Lindgren, D.T. & Davenport, B. 1992. List and description of named cultivars in the genus *Penstemon* (1992). University of Nebraska.

Lord, T. 1994. Peerless Penstemons. *The Garden* (RHS) 119(7):304-309.

Nold, R. 1999. *Penstemons.* Portland, Oregon: Timber Press.

Way, D. & James, P. 1998. *The Gardener's Guide to Growing Penstemons.* Newton Abbott: David & Charles.

Phlomis

Mann Taylor, J. 1998. *Phlomis: The Neglected Genus.* Wisley: NCCPG.

Phlox

Harmer, J. & Elliott, J. 2001. *Phlox.* Pershore, Worcs: Hardy Plant Society

Stebbings, G. 1999. Simply Charming. *The Garden* (RHS) 124(7):518-521.

Wherry, E.T. 1955. The Genus *Phlox.* Morris Arboretum Monographs III.

Phormium

Heenan, P.B. 1991. *Checklist of Phormium Cultivars.* Royal New Zealand Institute of Horticulture.

McBride-Whitehead, V. 1998. Phormiums of the Future. *The Garden* (RHS) 123(1):42-45.

Pieris

Bond, J. 1982. *Pieris* – a Survey. *The Plantsman* 4(2):65-75.

Wagenknecht, B.L. 1961. Registration Lists of Cultivar Names in the Genus *Pieris* D. Don. *Arnoldia (Jamaica Plain)* 21(8):47-50.

Plectranthus

Miller, D. & Morgan, N. 2000. Focus on Plants: A New Leaf. *The Garden* (RHS) 125(11):842-845.

Shaw, J.M.H. 1999. Notes on the Identity of Swedish Ivy and Other Cultivated *Plectranthus. The New Plantsman* 6(2):71-74.

Pleione

Cribb, P. & Butterfield, I. 1999. *The Genus Pleione.* (2nd ed.). Kew: Royal Botanic Gardens.

Shaw, J.M.H. (comp.). Oct 2002. Provisional List of *Pleione* Cultivars. Royal Horticultural Society. www.rhs.org.co.uk/research/registerpages/Pleione_cv.PDF

Poaceae (Gramineae,* grasses*)

Clayton, W.D. & Renvoize, S.A. 1986. *Genera Graminum.* Grasses of the World. London: HMSO.

Darke, R. 1999. *The Colour Encyclopedia of Ornamental Grasses.* Sedges, Rushes, Restios, Cattails and Selected Bamboos. London: Weidenfeld & Nicolson.

Grounds, R. 1998. *The Plantfinder's Guide to Ornamental Grasses.* Newton Abott, Devon: David & Charles.

Ryves, T.B., Clement, E.J. & Foster, M.C. 1996. *Alien Grasses of the British Isles.* London: Botanical Society of the British Isles.

Wood, T. 2002. *Garden Grasses, Rushes and Sedges.* (3rd ed.). Abingdon: John Wood.

Polemonium

Nichol-Brown, D. 1997. *Polemonium.* Teeside: Trimdon.

Potentilla

Davidson, C.G., Enns, R.J. & Gobin, S. 1994. *A Checklist of Potentilla fruticosa: the Shrubby Potentillas.* Morden, Manitoba: Agriculture & Agri-Food Canada Research Centre. Data also on Plant Finder Reference Library professional version CD-ROM 1999/2000.

Miller, D.M. 2002. *RHS Plant and Trials Awards. Shrubby Potentilla.* London: Royal Horticultural Society.

Primula

Fenderson, G.K. 1986. *A Synoptic Guide to the Genus Primula.* Lawrence, Kansas: Allen Press.

Green, R. 1976. *Asiatic Primulas.* Woking: The Alpine Garden Society.

Halda, J.J. 1992. *The Genus Primula in Cultivation and the Wild.* Denver, Colorado: Tethys Books.

Hecker, W.R. 1971. *Auriculas & Primroses.* London: Batsford.

Kohlein, F. 1984. *Primeln.* Stuttgart, Germany: Ulmer.

Richards, J. 2002 (2nd ed.). *Primula.* London: Batsford.

Smith, G.F., Burrow, B. & Lowe, D.B. 1984. *Primulas of Europe and America.* Woking: Alpine Garden Society.

Wemyss-Cooke, T.J. 1986. *Primulas Old and New.* Newton Abbot: David & Charles.

Primula allionii

Archdale, B. & Richards, D. 1997. *Primula allionii Forms and Hybrids.* National Auricula & Primula Society, Midland & West Section.

***Primula auricula* hort.**

Baker, G. *Double Auriculas.* National Auricula & Primula Society, Midland & West Section.

Baker, G. & Ward, P. 1995. *Auriculas.* London: Batsford.

Hawkes, A. 1995. Striped Auriculas. National Auricula & Primula Society, Midland & West Section.

Nicholle, G. 1996. *Border Auriculas.* National Auricula & Primula Society, Midland & West Section.

Robinson, M.A. 2000. *Auriculas for Everyone.* How to Grow and Show Perfect Plants. Lewes: Guild of Master Craftsmen Publications.

Telford, D. 1993. *Alpine Auriculas.* National Auricula & Primula Society, Midland & West Section.

Ward, P. 1991. *Show Auriculas.* National Auricula & Primula Society, Midland & West Section.

Proteaceae

Rebelo, T. 1995. *Proteas.* A Field Guide to the Proteas of Southern Africa. Vlaeberg: Fernwood Press / National Botanical Institute.

Prunus

1986. *Index of the Cherry Collection at the National Fruit Trials 1986.* Faversham, Kent: MAFF.

Bultitude, J. *Index of the Plum Collection at the National Fruit Trials.* Faversham, Kent: MAFF.

Crawford, M. 1996. *Plums.* Dartington, Devon: Agroforestry Research Trust.

Crawford, M. 1997. *Cherries: Production and Culture.* Dartington, Devon: Agroforestry Research Trust.

Grubb, N.H. 1949. *Cherries.* London: Crosby Lockwood.

Jacobsen, A.L. 1992. *Purpleleaf Plums.* Portland, Oregon: Timber Press.

Jefferson, R.M. & Wain, K.K. 1984. *The Nomenclature of Cultivated Flowering Cherries (Prunus).* The Satu-Zakura Group. Washington: USDA.

Kuitert, W. 1999. *Japanese Flowering Cherries.* Oregon: Timber Press.

Smith, M.W.G. 1978. *Catalogue of the Plums at the National Fruit Trials.* Faversham, Kent: MAFF.

Taylor, H.V. 1949. *The Plums of England.* London: Crosby Lockwood.

Pulmonaria

Hewitt, J. 1994. *Pulmonarias.* Pershore, Worcs.: The Hardy Plant Society.

Hewitt, J. 1999. Well Spotted. *The Garden* (RHS) 124(2):98 – 103.

Pyracantha

Egolf, D.R. & Andrick, A.O. 1995. *A Checklist of Pyracantha Cultivars.* Agricultural Research Service.

Pyrus

Crawford, M. 1996. *Directory of Pear Cultivars.* Totnes, Devon: Agroforestry Research Institute.

Parfitt, B. 1981. *Index of the Pear Collection at the National Fruit Trials.* Faversham, Kent: MAFF.

Smith, M.W.G. 1976. *Catalogue of the British Pear.* Faversham, Kent: MAFF.

Quercus

Avalos, S.V. 1995. *Contribución al Concimiento del Género Quercus (Fagaceae) en el Estado de Guerrero, Mexico.* Mexico City: Facultad de Ciencias, UNAM.

Miller, H.A. & Lamb, S.H. 1985. *Oaks of North America.* Happy Camp, California: Naturegraph Publishers.

Mitchell, A. 1994. The Lucombe Oaks. *The Plantsman* 15(4):216-224.

Rhododendron

Argent, G., Fairweather, C. & Walter, K. 1996. *Accepted Names in Rhododendron section Vireya.* Royal Botanic Garden, Edinburgh.

Argent, G., Bond, J., Chamberlain, D., Cox, P. & Hardy, A. 1997. *The Rhododendron Handbook 1998.* Rhododendron Species in Cultivation. London: The Royal Horticultural Society.

Chamberlain, D.F. & Rae, S.J. 1990. A Revision of *Rhododendron* IV. Subgenus *Tsutsusi. Edinburgh J. Bot.* 47(2).

Chamberlain, D.F. 1982. A Revision of *Rhododendron* II. Subgenus *Hymenanthes. Notes Roy. Bot. Gard. Edinburgh* 39(2).

Cox, P. & Cox, K. 1988. *Encyclopedia of Rhododendron Hybrids.* London: Batsford.

Cullen, J. 1980. A Revision of *Rhododendron* I. Subgenus *Rhododendron* sections *Rhododendron* and *Pogonanthum. Notes Roy. Bot. Gard. Edinburgh* 39(1).

Davidian, H.H. 1982-1992 *The Rhododendron Species Volume I-IV.* Batsford.

Galle, F.C. 1985. *Azaleas.* Portland, Oregon: Timber Press.

Lee, F.P. 1958. *The Azalea Book.* New York: D. Van Nostrand Co. Ltd.

Leslie, A. C. (comp.). 1980. *The Rhododendron Handbook 1980.* London: The Royal Horticultural Society.

Leslie, A. C. *The International Rhododendron Register.* Checklist of Rhododendron Names Registered 1987-2001. (& Supps 28-40). London: Royal Horticultural Society.

Salley, H.E. & Greer, H.E. 1986. *Rhododendron Hybrids.* A Guide to their Origins. London: Batsford.

Tamura, T. (ed.). 1989. *Azaleas in Kurume.* Kurume, Japan: International Azalea Festival '89.

Ribes

Crawford, M. 1997. *Currants and Gooseberries: Production and Culture.* Dartington, Devon: Agroforestry Research Trust.

Rosa

Austin, D. 1988. *The Heritage of the Rose.* Woodbridge, Suffolk: Antique Collectors' Club.

Beales, P. 1992. *Roses.* London: Harvill.

Beales, P., Cairns, T., Duncan, W., Fagan, G., Grant, W., Grapes, K., Harkness, P., Hughes, K., Mattock, J. & Ruston, D. 1998. *Botanica's Roses.* The Encyclopedia of Roses. UK: Grange Books PLC.

Cairns, T. (ed.). 2000. *Modern Roses XI.* The World Encyclopedia of Roses. London: Academic Press.

Dickerson, B.C. 1992. *The Old Rose Advisor.* Portland, Oregon: Timber Press.

Dobson, B.R. & Schneider, P. (comps). 1996. *Combined Rose List.*

Haw, S.G. 1996. Notes on Some Chinese and Himalayan Rose Species of Section *Pimpinellifoliae. The New Plantsman* 3(3):143-146.

Help Me Find Roses. Jan 2004. www.helpmefind.com/sites/rose/index.html

McCann, S. 1985. *Miniature Roses.* Newton Abbot: David & Charles.

Phillips, R. & Rix, M. 1988. *Roses.* London: Macmillan.

Phillips, R. & Rix, M. 1993. *The Quest for the Rose.* London: BBC Books.

Quest-Ritson, C. 2003. *Climbing Roses of the World.* Portland, Oregon: Timber Press.

Quest-Ritson, C. & Quest-Ritson, B. 2003. *The Royal Horticultural Society Encyclopedia of Roses: The Definitive A-Z Guide.* London: Dorling Kindersley.

Thomas, G.S. 1995. *The Graham Stuart Thomas Rose Book.* London: John Murray.

Verrier, S. 1996. *Rosa Gallica.* Balmain, Australia: Florilegium.

Rosularia

Eggli, U. 1988. A Monographic Study of the Genus *Rosularia. Bradleya* (Suppl.) 6:1-118.

Saintpaulia

Moore, H.E. 1957. *African Violets, Gloxinias and Their Relatives.* A Guide to the Cultivated Gesneriads. New York: Macmillan

Salix

Newsholme, C. 1992. *Willows.* The Genus *Salix.* London: Batsford

Salvia

Clebsch, B. 2003. *A Book of Salvias.* (2nd ed.). Oregon: Timber Press.

Compton, J. 1994. Mexican Salvias in Cultivation. *The Plantsman* 15(4):193-215.

Saxifraga

Bland, B. 2000. *Silver Saxifrages.* Pershore, Worcs: Alpine Garden Society Publications.

Horn?, R., Webr, K.M., Byam-Grounds, J. & Zoulova, E. (ill.). 1986. *Porophyllum Saxifrages.* Stamford, Lincolnshire: Byam-Grounds Publications.

Kohlein, F. 1984. *Saxifrages and Related Genera.* London: Batsford.

McGregor, M. Feb 2003. Saxbase. The Saxifrage Society. www.saxifraga.org/plants/saxbase/default.asp

McGregor, M. (ed.). 2000. *Saxifrage 2000.* Driffield, E. Yorks: Saxifrage Society.

McGregor, M. 1995. *Saxifrages: The Complete Cultivars & Hybrids.* First Edition of the International Register of Saxifrages. (1st ed.).

Stocks, A. 1995. *Saxifragaceae.* Hardy Plant Society.

Webb, D.A. & Gornall, R.J. 1989. *Saxifrages of Europe.* Bromley, Kent: Christopher Helm.

Sedum

Evans, R.L. 1983. *Handbook of Cultivated Sedums.* Motcombe, Dorset: Ivory Head Press.

Stephenson, R. 1994. *Sedum.* The Cultivated Stonecrops. Portland, Oregon: Timber Press.

Sempervivum

Miklánek, M. 2000. *List of Cultivars: Sempervivum and Jovibarba* v. 15.1. http://miklanek.tripod.com~miklanek/MCS/cv.html

Mitchell, P.J. (comp.). 1985. *International Cultivar Register for Jovibarba, Rosularia, Sempervivum.* Vol. 1. Burgess Hill: The Sempervivum Society.

Sinningia

Dates, J.D. 1988. *The Gesneriad Register 1988. Check List of Names with Descriptions of Cultivated Plants in the Genus Sinningia.* Galesburg, Illinois: American Gloxinia and Gesneriad Society, Inc.

Solenostemon

Pedley, W.K. & Pedley, R. 1974. *Coleus – A Guide to Cultivation and Identification.* Edinburgh: Bartholemew.

Sorbus

McAllister, H. 1984. The Aucuparia Section of *Sorbus. The Plantsman* 6(4):248-255.

McAllister, H. 1996. *Sorbus:* Mountain Ash and its Relatives. *The Garden* (RHS) 121(9):561-567.

Snyers d'Attenhoven, C. 1999. *Sorbus* Lombarts hybrids *Belgische Dendrologie*: 76-81. Belgium.

Wright, D. 1981. Sorbus – a Gardener's Evaluation. *The Plantsman* 3(2):65-98.

Streptocarpus

Arnold, P. 1979. *The Gesneriad Register 1979: Check List of Streptocarpus.* Binghamton, New York: American Gloxinia & Gesneriad.

Succulents

Eggli, U. (ed.). 2001. *Illustrated Handbook of Succulent Plants. Monocotyledons.* Heidelberg, Germany: Springer-Verlag.

Eggli, U. & Taylor, N. 1994. *List of Names of Succulent Plants other than Cacti Published 1950-92.* Kew: Royal Botanic Gardens.

Grantham, K. & Klaassen, P. 1999. *The Plantfinder's Guide to Cacti and Other Succulents.* Newton Abbot, Devon: David & Charles.

Syringa

Fiala, J.L. 1988. *Lilacs. The Genus Syringa.* London: Christopher Helm.

Rogers, O.M. 1976. *Tentative International Register of Cultivar Names in the Genus Syringa.* Research Report no. 49.

Vrugtman, F. 2000. *International Register of Cultivar Names in the Genus Syringa L. (Oleaceae).* (Contribution No. 91). Hamilton, Canada: Royal Botanic Gardens.

Tillandsia

Kiff, L.F. 1991. *A Distributional Checklist of the Genus Tillandsia.* Encino, California: Botanical Diversions.

Trillium

Case, F.W.J. & Case, R.B. 1997. *Trilliums.* Portland, Oregon: Timber Press.

Jacobs, D.L. & Jacobs, R.L. 1997. *American Treasures.* Trilliums in Woodland Garden. Decatur, Georgia: Eco-Gardens.

Tulipa

Informatie over de KAVB registratie van bol-, knol- en wortelstok gewassen. Jan 2004. www.bulbgrowing.nl/registraties.cfm

van Scheepen, J. (ed.). 1996. *Classified List and International Register of Tulip Names.* Hillegom, The Netherlands: Koninklijke Algemeene Vereeniging Voor Bloembollencultuur.

Ulmus

Green, P.S. 1964. Registratration of Cultivar Names in *Ulmus. Arnoldia (Jamaica Plain)* 24:41-80.

Vegetables

Official Journal of the European Communities. Common catalogue of varieties of vegetable species C167A. 1999. (21st ed.). Luxembourg: Office for Official Publications of the European Communities. http://europa.eu.int/eur_lex/en/archive/1999/ca16719990615en.html

Phillips, R. & Rix, M. 1993. *Vegetables.* London: Pan.

Viola

Coombes, R.E. 2003. *Violets.* (2nd ed.). London: Batsford

Farrar, R. 1989. *Pansies, Violas & Sweet Violets.* Reading: Hurst Village Publishing.

Fuller, R. 1990. *Pansies, Violas & Violettas.* The Complete Guide. Marlborough: The Crowood Press.

Perfect, E.J. 1996. *Armand Millet and his Violets.* High Wycombe: Park Farm Press.

Silvers, T.E. 2003. Checklist of the Cultivated Forms of the Genus *Viola* including the Register of Cultivars. American Violet Society. www.americanvioletsociety.org/Registry

Zambra, G.L. 1950. *Violets for Garden and Market.* (2nd ed.). London: Collingridge.

Vitis

Pearkes, G. 1989. *Vine Growing in Britain.* London: Dent.

Robinson, J. 1989. *Vines, Grapes and Wines.* London: Mitchell Beazley.

Watsonia

Goldblatt, P. 1989. *The Genus Watsonia.* A Systematic Monograph. South Africa: National Botanic Gardens.

Weigela

Howard, R.A. 1965. A Checklist of Cultivar Names in *Weigela. Arnoldia (Jamaica Plain)* 25:49-69.

Wisteria

Valder, P. 1995. *Wisterias.* A Comprehensive Guide. Australia: Florilegium.

Zauschneria

Raven, P.H. 1977. Generic and Sectional Delimitation in *Onagraceae,* Tribe *Epilobieae. Ann. Missouri Bot. Gard.* 63(2):326-340.

Robinson, A. 2000. Focus on Plants: Piping Hot (*Zauschneria* Cultivars). *The Garden* (RHS) 125(9):698-699.

INTERNATIONAL PLANT FINDERS

NETHERLANDS

Terra/Lannoo (5th edition) *Plantenvinder voor de lage landen.* ISBN 90-5897-056-6. Approx. 50,000 plants and 150 nurseries. Orders: Terra/Lannoo Publishing, PO box 1080, 7230 AB Warnsveld, Netherlands. T +31 (575) 581310, F +31 (575) 525242. E-mail: info@terralannoo.nl; website: www.terralannoo.com Price €14.95.

UNITED KINGDOM

Pawsey, Angela (ed.). (22nd ed.) 2004-2005. *Find that Rose!* Published May 2004. Lists approximately 3,300 varieties available in the U.K. with basic type, colour and fragrance. New varieties are highlighted and cross-referenced where applicable to alternative selling names. Includes standard roses. Details of around 60 growers/outlets, many offering mail order. How to find a rose with a particular Christian name or to celebrate a special event and where to see roses in bloom. For further information send S.A.E. to: 303 Mile End Road, Colchester, Essex CO4 5EA. To order send a cheque for £3.25 made out to *Find That Rose!* to the above address.

USA

Hill, Susan & Narizny, Susan (comp.) (2004), *The Plant Locator®: Western Region.* ISBN 0-88192-633-7. Directory of sources for plants (not seeds) available at retail and mail-order nurseries in 13 western states of the USA (California, Oregon, Washington, Idaho, Montana, Colorado, Wyoming, Utah, New Mexico, Arizona, Neveda, Alaska, and Hawaii) and British Columbia, Canada. Information on how to contact nurseries and purchase plants. Includes a common name/botanical name index. Co-published by Black-Eyed Susans Press. E-mail: susans@blackeyedsusanspress.com; website: www.blackeyedsusanspress.com and Timber Press. Price: UK £14.99, Europe €22.95, elsewhere US$19.95, plus postage. Order Online only from: www.timberpress.com

Nurseries

The following nurseries between them stock an unrivalled choice of plants. Before making a visit, please remember to check with the nursery that the plant you seek is currently available.

Nursery Codes and Symbols

The first letter of each nursery code represents the area of the country in which the nursery is situated.

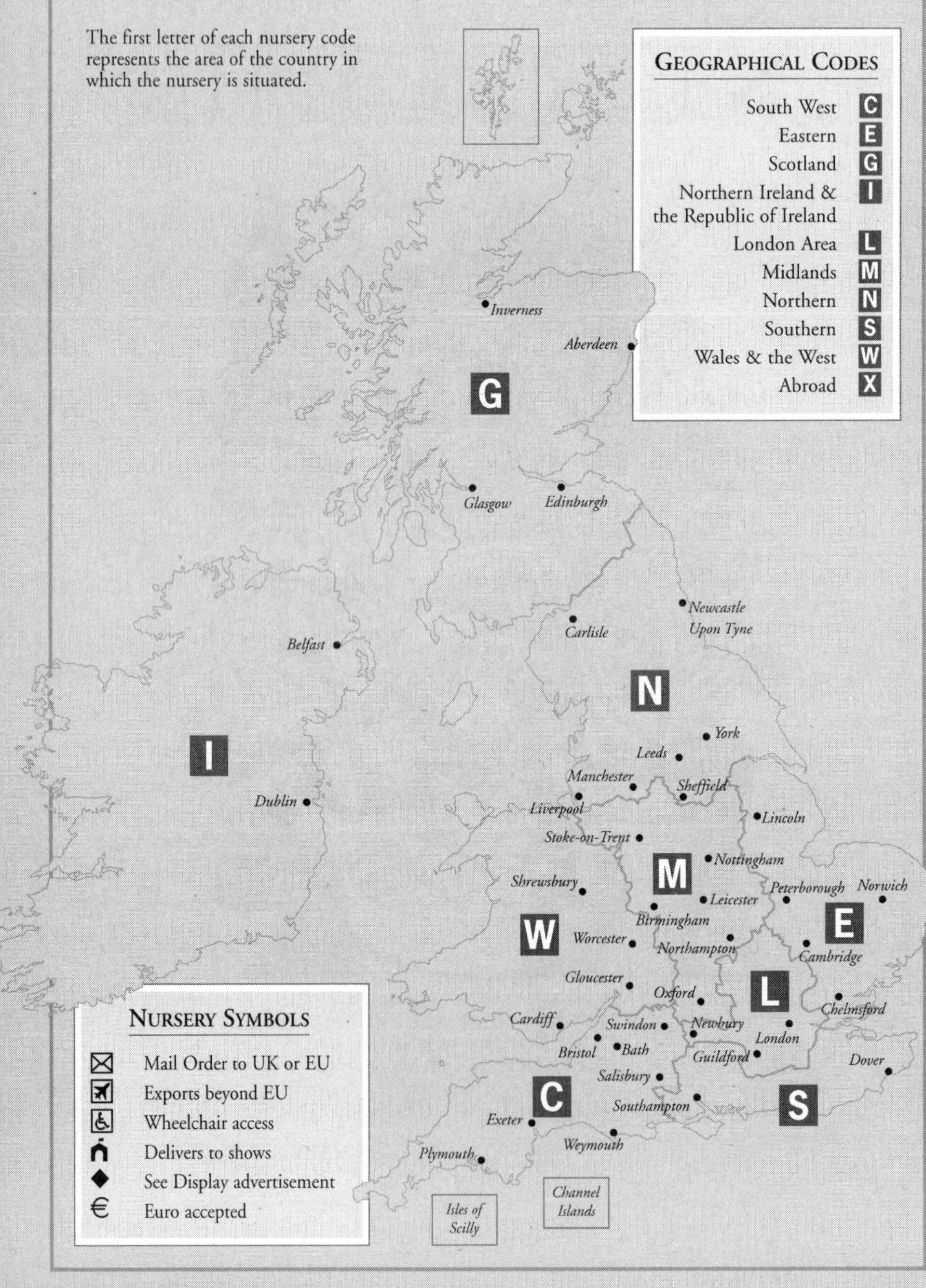

Geographical Codes

South West	C
Eastern	E
Scotland	G
Northern Ireland & the Republic of Ireland	I
London Area	L
Midlands	M
Northern	N
Southern	S
Wales & the West	W
Abroad	X

Nursery Symbols

- ⊠ Mail Order to UK or EU
- Exports beyond EU
- Wheelchair access
- Delivers to shows
- ◆ See Display advertisement
- € Euro accepted

USING THE THREE NURSERY LISTINGS

Your main reference from the Plant Directory is the Nursery Details by Code listing, which includes all relevant information for each nursery in order of nursery code. The Nursery Index by Name is an alphabetical list for those who know a nursery's name but not its code and wish to check its details in the main list. The Specialist Nurseries index is to aid those searching for a particular plant group.

1 NURSERY DETAILS BY CODE

Once you have found your plant in the Plant Directory, turn to this list to find out the name, address, opening times and other details of the nurseries whose codes accompany the plant.

KEY
- ⊠ Mail order to UK or EU
- ✈ Exports beyond EU
- ♿ Wheelchair access
- Delivers to shows
- € Euro accepted
- ◆ See Display advertisement

LLin — *A geographical code is followed by three letters reflecting the nursery's name*

LINCLUDEN NURSERY ⊠ ✈ € ♿ ◆ — *Refer to the box at the base of each right-hand page for a key to the symbols*

Bisley Green, Bisley, Woking, Surrey, GU24 9EN
Ⓣ (01483) 797005
Ⓕ (01483) 474015
Ⓔ sales@lincludennursery.co.uk
Ⓦ www.lincludennursery.co.uk
Also sells wholesale
Contact: Mr & Mrs J A Tilbury
Opening Times: 0930-1630 Tue-Sat all year excl. B/hols. Closed Chelsea week & Xmas.
Min Mail Order UK: Nmc
Min Mail Order EU: Nmc
Cat. Cost: 3 x 1st class
Credit Cards: Visa MasterCard Solo Switch
Specialities: Dwarf, slow-growing & unusual conifers. — *A brief summary of the plants available plus any other special characteristics of the nursery*
Map Ref: L, C3 — *The map letter is followed by the map square in which the nursery is located*
OS Grid Ref: SU947596 — *The Ordnance Survey national grid reference for use with OS maps*

2 NURSERY INDEX BY NAME

If you seek a particular nursery, look it up in this alphabetical index. Note its code and turn to the Nursery Details by Code list for full information.

Brian Lewington	SBLw
Lilliesleaf Nursery	GLil
Lime Cross Nursery	SLim
Lincluden Nursery	LLin
Lingen Nursery and Garden	WLin
Linnett Farm Plants	WLFP
Liscahane Nursery	ILsc
Lisdoonan Herbs	ILis

3 SPECIALIST NURSERIES

A list of 32 categories under which nurseries have classified themselves if they exclusively, or predominantly, supply this range of plants.

CONIFERS

CKen, CLnd, CMen, CRob, CTho, ECho, EOrn, ERom, GTre, LCon, LLin, MBar, MGos, MPkF, SLim, WEve, WGor, WMou, WThu

How to Use the Nursery Listings

The details given for each nursery have been compiled from information supplied to us in answer to a questionnaire. In some cases, because of constraints of space, the entries have been slightly abbreviated.

Nurseries are not charged for their entries, and inclusion in no way implies a value judgement.

Nursery Details by Code (*page 788*)

Each nursery is allocated a code, for example GKir. The first letter of each code indicates the main area of the country in which the nursery is situated. In this example, G=Scotland. The remaining three letters reflect the nursery's name, in this case Kirkdale Nursery in Aberdeenshire.

In this main listing the nurseries are given in alphabetical order of codes for quick reference from the Plant Directory. All of the nurseries' details, such as address, opening times, mail order service etc., will be found here.

Opening Times

Although opening times have been published as submitted and where applicable, it is always advisable, especially if travelling a long distance, to check with the nursery first. The initials NGS indicate that the nursery is open under the National Gardens Scheme.

Mail Order - ⊠

Many nurseries provide a mail order service, which, in some cases, extends to all members of the European Union. Where such a service is offered, the minimum charge to the EU will be noted in the Nursery entry.

Where **'No minimum charge' (Nmc)** is shown please note that to send even one plant may involve the nursery in substantial postage and packing costs. Even so, some nurseries may not be prepared to send tender or bulky plants.

Export ✈

Export refers to mail order beyond the European Union. Nurseries that are prepared to consider exporting are indicated. However, there is usually a substantial minimum charge and, in addition, all the costs of Phytosanitary Certificates and Customs have to be met by the purchaser.

Catalogue Cost

Some nurseries offer their catalogue free, or for a few stamps (the odd value quoted can usually be made up from a combination of first or second class stamps), but a large (at least A5) stamped addressed envelope is always appreciated as well. Overseas customers should use an equivalent number of International Reply Coupons (IRCs) in place of stamps.

Wheelchair Access ♿

Nurseries are asked to indicate if their premises are suitable for wheelchair users. Where only partial access is indicated, this is noted in the Specialities field and the nursery is not marked with the symbol.

The assessment of ease-of-access is entirely the responsibility of the individual nursery.

Specialities

Nurseries list here the plants or genera that they supply, together with other information on the services they offer. In this section you will find notes on any restrictions to mail order or export, on limited wheelchair access, or the site address if this is different to the office address. Some nurseries hold National Collections of plants to which they may charge an entry fee. Always enquire before visiting.

Delivery to Shows

Many nurseries will deliver pre-ordered plants to flower shows for collection by customers. These are indicated by a marquee symbol. Contact the nursery for details of shows they attend.

Payment in Euros €

A number of UK nurseries have indicated that they will accept payment in Euros. You should, however, check with the nursery concerned before making such a payment, as some will only accept cash and some only cheques, whilst others will expect the purchaser to pay bank charges.

MAPS

If you wish to visit any of the nurseries you can find its approximate location on the relevant map (following p.916), unless the nursery has requested this is not shown. Nurseries are also encouraged to provide their Ordnance Survey national grid reference for use with OS publications such as the Land Ranger series.

NURSERY INDEX BY NAME (*page 907*)

For convenience, an alphabetical index of nurseries is included on p.907. This gives the names of all nurseries listed in the book in alphabetical order of nursery name together with their code.

SPECIALIST NURSERIES (*page 914*)

This list of nurseries is intended to help those with an interest in finding specialist categories of plant. Nurseries have been asked to classify themselves under one or more headings where this represents the type of plant they *predominantly* or *exclusively* have in stock. For example, if you wish to find a nursery specialising in ornamental grasses, look up 'Grasses' in the listing where you will find a list of nursery codes. Then turn to the Nursery Details by Code, for details of the nurseries.

Please note that not all nurseries shown here will have plants listed in the Plant Directory. This may be their choice or because the *RHS Plant Finder* does not list seeds or annuals and only terrestrial orchids and hardy cacti. For space reasons, it is rare to find a nursery's full catalogue listed in the Plant Directory.

In all cases, please ensure you ring to confirm the range available before embarking on a journey to the nursery.

The specialist plant groups listed in this edition are:

Acid-loving
Alpines/rock
Aquatics/marginals
Bamboos
British wild flowers
Bulbous plants
Cacti & succulents
Carnivorous
Chalk-loving
Climbers
Coastal
Conifers
Conservatory
Drought-tolerant
Ferns
Fruit
Grasses
Hedging
Herbs
Marginal/bog plants
Orchids
Organic
Ornamental trees
Peat-free
Period plants
Propagate to order
Roses
Seeds
Specimen-sized plants
Topiary
Tropical plants

Perennials and shrubs have been omitted as these are considered to be too general and serviced by a great proportion of the nurseries.

DELETED NURSERIES

Every year some nurseries ask to be removed from the book. This may be a temporary measure because they are moving, or it may be permanent due to closure, sale, retirement, or a change in the way in they trade. Occasionally, nurseries are unable to meet the closing date and will re-enter the book in the following edition. Some nurseries simply do not reply and, as we have no current information on them, they are deleted.

Please, never use an old edition

Nursery Details by Code

Please note that all these nurseries are listed in alphabetical order by their code. All nurseries are listed in alphabetical order by their name in the **Nursery Index by Name** on page 907.

South West

CAbb ABBOTSBURY SUB-TROPICAL GARDENS ⊠ ♿
Abbotsbury, Nr. Weymouth, Dorset, DT3 4LA
Ⓣ (01305) 871344
Ⓕ (01305) 871344
Ⓔ info@abbotsburygardens.co.uk
Ⓦ www.abbotsburyplantsales.co.uk
Contact: David Sutton
Opening Times: 1000-1800 daily mid Mar-1st Nov. 1000-1500 Nov-mid Mar.
Min Mail Order UK: £10.00 + p&p
Cat. Cost: £2.00 + A4 Sae + 42p stamp
Credit Cards: Access Visa MasterCard Switch
Specialities: Less common & tender shrubs incl. palms, tree ferns, bamboos & plants from Australia, New Zealand & S. Africa.
Map Ref: C, C5

CAbP ABBEY PLANTS ⊠ ♿
Chaffeymoor, Bourton, Gillingham, Dorset, SP8 5BY
Ⓣ (01747) 840841
Contact: K Potts
Opening Times: 1000-1300 & 1400-1700 Tue-Sat Mar-Nov. Dec-Feb by appt.
Cat. Cost: 2 x 2nd class
Credit Cards: None
Specialities: Flowering trees & shrubs. Shrub roses incl. many unusual varieties. Limited stock.
Map Ref: C, B4 **OS Grid Ref:** ST762304

CAby THE ABBEY NURSERY ♿
Forde Abbey, Chard, Somerset, TA20 4LU
Ⓣ (01460) 220088
Ⓕ (01460) 220088
Ⓔ TheAbbeyNursery@o2.co.uk
Contact: Paul Bygrave and Peter Sims
Opening Times: 1000-1700 7 days, 1st Mar-31st Oct. Please phone first to check opening times in Mar.
Cat. Cost: None issued.
Credit Cards: All major credit/debit cards.
Specialities: Hardy herbaceous perennials & grasses.
Map Ref: C, C4 **OS Grid Ref:** ST359052

CAgr AGROFORESTRY RESEARCH TRUST ⊠
46 Hunters Moon, Dartington,
Totnes, Devon,
TQ9 6JT
Ⓣ (01803) 840776
Ⓕ (01803) 840776
Ⓔ mail@agroforestry.co.uk
Ⓦ www.agroforestry.co.uk
Contact: Martin Crawford
Opening Times: Not open, mail order only.
Min Mail Order UK: Nmc
Min Mail Order EU: Nmc
Cat. Cost: 4 x 1st class
Credit Cards: MasterCard Visa
Specialities: Top & soft fruit & nut trees. Mostly trees, shrubs & perennials. *Alnus, Berberis, Amelanchier, Carya, Elaeagnus, Juglans, Pinus, Quercus* & *Salix*. Also seeds. Some plants in small quantities only.

CAlb ALBION PLANTS ⊠
Cliston Barton, Roborough, Winkleigh, Devon, EX19 8TP
Ⓣ (01805) 603502
Ⓕ (01805) 603502
Ⓔ huggons@albion-plants.co.uk
Ⓦ www.albion-plants.co.uk
Also sells wholesale.
Contact: Neil & Brenda Huggons
Opening Times: Mail order only at present.
Min Mail Order UK: Nmc
Cat. Cost: Available by email on request.
Credit Cards: None.
Specialities: *Vinca, Cornus, Viburnum, Salix, Ceanothus.* Specimen-sized shrubs & container-grown trees.
Map Ref: C, B3 **OS Grid Ref:** SS584173

CAni **ANITA ALLEN** ⊠ ♿
Shapcott Barton Estate, East Knowstone, South Molton, North Devon, EX36 4EE
Ⓣ (01398) 341664
Ⓕ (01389) 341664
Contact: Anita Allen
Opening Times: By appt. only.
Min Mail Order UK: £10.00
Cat. Cost: 5 x 1st class
Credit Cards: None.
Specialities: National Collection of *Leucanthemum superbum*. 70+ accurately named Shata daisies, a few in very short supply. Also some hardy perennials & *Anthemis tinctoria* cultivars.
Map Ref: C, B3 **OS Grid Ref:** SS846235

CArn **ARNE HERBS** ⊠ ✈ € ♿
Limeburn Nurseries, Limeburn Hill, Chew Magna, Bristol, BS40 8QW
Ⓣ (01275) 333399
Ⓕ (01275) 333399
Ⓔ lyman@lyman-dixon.freeserve.co.uk
Ⓦ www.arneherbs.co.uk
Also sells wholesale.
Contact: A Lyman-Dixon & Jenny Thomas
Opening Times: Most times, please check first.
Min Mail Order UK: Nmc
Min Mail Order EU: Nmc
Cat. Cost: £3.75 UK, 10 x IRC refundable on first order. Or Online.
Credit Cards: None.
Specialities: Herbs, wild flowers & cottage flowers. A few plants ltd., please see catalogue for details. Will deliver to Farmers' Markets.
Map Ref: C, A5 **OS Grid Ref:** ST563638

CAvo **AVON BULBS** ⊠
Burnt House Farm, Mid-Lambrook, South Petherton, Somerset, TA13 5HE
Ⓣ (01460) 242177
Ⓕ (01460) 242177
Ⓔ info@avonbulbs.co.uk
Ⓦ www.avonbulbs.co.uk
Contact: C Ireland-Jones
Opening Times: Thu, Fri, Sat mid Sep-end Oct & mid Feb-end Mar for collection of pre-booked orders.
Min Mail Order UK: £10.00 + p&p
Min Mail Order EU: £20.00 + p&p
Cat. Cost: 4 x 2nd class
Credit Cards: Visa Access Switch
Specialities: Mail order supply of a very wide range of smaller, often unusual bulbs.
Map Ref: C, B5

CBcs **BURNCOOSE NURSERIES** ⊠ ✈ ⌂ ♿
Gwennap, Redruth, Cornwall, TR16 6BJ
Ⓣ (01209) 860316
Ⓕ (01209) 860011
Ⓔ burncoose@eclipse.co.uk
Ⓦ www.burncoose.co.uk
Also sells wholesale.
Contact: C H Williams
Opening Times: 0830-1700 Mon-Sat & 1100-1700 Sun.
Min Mail Order UK: Nmc
Min Mail Order EU: Nmc*
Cat. Cost: £1.50 incl. p&p
Credit Cards: Visa Access Switch
Specialities: Extensive range of over 3500 ornamental trees & shrubs and herbaceous. Rare & unusual Magnolia, Rhododendron. Conservatory plants. 30 acre garden. Note: individual quotations for EU sales.
Map Ref: C, D1 **OS Grid Ref:** SW742395

CBct **BARRACOTT PLANTS** ⊠ ⌂ € ◆
Old Orchard, Calstock Road, Gunnislake, Cornwall, PL18 9AA
Ⓣ (01822) 832234
Ⓔ GEOFF@geoff63.freeserve.co.uk
Also sells wholesale.
Contact: Geoff Turner, Thelma Watson
Opening Times: 0900-1700 Thu-Sat, Mar-end Sep. Other times by appt.
Min Mail Order UK: £10.00
Cat. Cost: 2 x 1st class
Credit Cards: None.
Specialities: Herbaceous plants: shade-loving, foliage & form. *Acanthus, Astrantia, Bergenia, Convallaria, Ligularia, Liriope, Roscoea, Smilacina, Symphytum & Tricyrtis.*
Map Ref: C, C3 **OS Grid Ref:** SX436702

CBdn **BOWDEN HOSTAS** ⊠ ✈ ♿ ◆
Sticklepath, Okehampton, Devon, EX20 2NL
Ⓣ (01837) 840989
Ⓕ (01837) 851549
Ⓔ info@bowdenhostas.com
Ⓦ www.bowdenhostas.com
Also sells wholesale.
Contact: Tim Penrose
Opening Times: By appt. only.
Min Mail Order UK: Nmc
Min Mail Order EU: Nmc
Cat. Cost: 3 x 1st class

KEY
⊠ Mail order to UK or EU ⌂ Delivers to shows
✈ Exports beyond EU € Euro accepted
♿ Accessible by wheelchair ◆ See Display advertisement

C

Credit Cards: Visa Access Eurocard Switch
Specialities: Hosta only. Nat. Coll. of modern hybrid Hosta.
Map Ref: C, C3 **OS Grid Ref:** SX640940

CBdw **BODWEN NURSERY** ⊠
Pothole, St Austell, Cornwall, PL26 7DW
Ⓣ No phone
Ⓦ www.bodwen.com
Also sells wholesale.
Contact: John Geraghty
Opening Times: Not open.
Min Mail Order UK: Nmc
Cat. Cost: 4 x 2nd class
Credit Cards: None.
Specialities: Japanese maples. Some rarer cultivars available in limited quantities only.

CBen **BENNETT'S WATER LILY FARM** ⊠ ♿
Putton Lane, Chickerell, Weymouth, Dorset, DT3 4AF
Ⓣ (01305) 785150
Ⓕ (01305) 781619
Ⓔ JB@waterlily.co.uk
Ⓦ www.waterlily.co.uk
Contact: J Bennett
Opening Times: Tue-Sun Apr-Aug, Tue-Sat Sept & Mar.
Min Mail Order UK: £25.00 + p&p
Min Mail Order EU: £25.00 + p&p
Cat. Cost: Sae for price list
Credit Cards: Visa Access MasterCard Switch
Specialities: Aquatic plants. Nat. Coll. of Water Lilies. Note: mail order Apr-Sep only.
Map Ref: C, C5 **OS Grid Ref:** SY651797

CBgR **BEGGAR'S ROOST PLANTS** ⌂ ♿
Lilstock, Bridgwater, Somerset, TA5 1SU
Ⓣ (01278) 741519
Ⓕ (01278) 741519
Ⓔ nunnington@aol.com
Contact: Rosemary FitzGerald, Kate Harris
Opening Times: By appt. only.
Credit Cards: None.
Specialities: British native plants & their garden-worthy varieties. Hardy ferns. Classic perennials, incl. Salvia & winter interest plants. Available in small quantities only.
Map Ref: C, B4 **OS Grid Ref:** ST168450

CBig **THE BIG GRASS CO.** ⊠ ☒ ⌂ €
Hookhill Plantation,
Woolfardisworthy East, Black Dog,
Nr. Crediton, Devon, EX17 4RX
Ⓣ (01363) 866146
Ⓕ (01363) 866146
Ⓔ alison@big-grass-co.co.uk
Ⓦ www.big-grass.com
Also sells wholesale.
Contact: Alison & Scott Evans
Opening Times: By appt. only.
Min Mail Order UK: Nmc
Min Mail Order EU: Nmc
Cat. Cost: £2.50 cheque or stamps
Credit Cards: None.
Specialities: Grasses.
Map Ref: C, B3

CBla **BLACKMORE & LANGDON LTD** ⊠ ☒
Pensford, Bristol, BS39 4JL
Ⓣ (01275) 332300
Ⓕ (01275) 332300/(01275) 331207
Ⓔ plants@blackmore-langdon.com
Ⓦ www.blackmore-langdon.com
Contact: J S Langdon
Opening Times: 0900-1700 Mon-Fri, 1000-1600 Sat & Sun.
Min Mail Order UK: Nmc
Min Mail Order EU: Nmc
Cat. Cost: Sae 2 x 2nd class
Credit Cards: MasterCard Visa Switch
Specialities: Phlox, Delphinium & Begonia. Also seeds.
Map Ref: C, A5

CBod **BODMIN PLANT AND HERB NURSERY** ⊠ ♿
Laveddon Mill, Laninval Hill, Bodmin, Cornwall, PL30 5JU
Ⓣ (01208) 72837
Ⓕ (01208) 76491
Ⓔ bodminnursery@aol.com
Contact: Mark Lawlor
Opening Times: 0900-1800 (or dusk) Mon-Sat, 1000-1600 Sun.
Min Mail Order UK: Nmc
Cat. Cost: 2 x 1st class
Credit Cards: All major credit/debit cards.
Specialities: Herbs, herbaceous & grasses, aquatic, marginal & bog plants, plus interesting range of shrubs. Wide range of fruit & ornamental trees. New range of coastal, patio & conservatory plants. Note: mail order herbs only.
Map Ref: C, C2 **OS Grid Ref:** SX053659

CBos **BOSVIGO PLANTS**
Bosvigo House, Bosvigo Lane, Truro, Cornwall, TR1 3NH
Ⓣ (01872) 275774
Ⓕ (01872) 275774
Ⓔ bosvigo.plants@virgin.net
Ⓦ www.bosvigo.com
Contact: Wendy Perry
Opening Times: 1100-1800 Thu & Fri Mar-end Sep.

Cat. Cost: 4 x 1st class
Credit Cards: None.
Specialities: Rare & unusual herbaceous.
Map Ref: C, D2 **OS Grid Ref:** SW815452

CBot THE BOTANIC NURSERY ⊠ ♠ €
(Office) Bath Road, Atworth,
Nr. Melksham, Wiltshire,
SN12 8NU
Ⓜ 07850 328756
Ⓕ (01225) 700953
Ⓔ enquiries@thebotanicnursery.com
Ⓦ www.TheBotanicNursery.com
Contact: T & M Baker
Opening Times: 1000-1700 Tue-Sat + themed openings – send for details.Sun by appt. only. Closed Nov-Feb.
Min Mail Order UK: £11.00 for 24hr carriage service.
Cat. Cost: Online & mail order list only.
Credit Cards: Visa Access
Specialities: Rare hardy shrubs & perennials for lime soils. *Eryngium, Papaver orientale* cultivars, *Delphinium*. National Collection of *Digitalis*. Note: nursery & plant sales at Cottles Lane, Nr. Stonar School, Atworth, Nr. Melksham.
Map Ref: C, A5

CBow BOWLEY PLANTS ♿ ◆
Church Farm, North End, Ashton Keynes, Nr. Swindon, Wiltshire, SN6 6QR
Ⓣ (01285) 640352
Ⓜ 07855 524929
Also sells wholesale.
Contact: G P Bowley
Opening Times: 1000-1600 Tue & Sat, 1300-1600 Sun, Mar-Oct incl.
Cat. Cost: 2 x 1st class
Credit Cards: None.
Specialities: Variegated plants & coloured foliage. Alpines, perennials. shrubs, ferns, grasses, conifers & herbs.
Map Ref: C, A6 **OS Grid Ref:** SU043945

CBrd BROADLEAS GARDENS LTD
Broadleas, Devizes, Wiltshire,
SN10 5JQ
Ⓣ (01380) 722035
Ⓕ (01380) 722035
Ⓔ broadleasgardens@btinternet.com
Contact: Lady Anne Cowdray
Opening Times: 1400-1800 Wed, Thu & Sun Apr-Oct.
Cat. Cost: 1 x 1st class
Credit Cards: None.
Specialities: General range.
Map Ref: C, A6

CBre BREGOVER PLANTS ⊠ ♠
Hillbrooke, Middlewood, North Hill,
Nr. Launceston, Cornwall, PL15 7NN
Ⓣ (01566) 782661
Contact: Jennifer Bousfield
Opening Times: 1100-1700 Wed, Mar-mid Oct and by appt.
Min Mail Order UK: Nmc
Min Mail Order EU: Nmc
Cat. Cost: 3 x 1st class
Credit Cards: None.
Specialities: Unusual hardy perennials grown in small garden nursery. Note: ltd. stocks, mail order Oct-Mar only.
Map Ref: C, C2 **OS Grid Ref:** SX273752

CBrm BRAMLEY LODGE GARDEN NURSERY € ♿
Beech Tree Lane, Ipplepen, Newton Abbot, Devon, TQ12 5TW
Ⓣ (01803) 813265
Ⓔ blnursery@btopenworld.com
Ⓦ www.bramleylodge-nursery.co.uk
Contact: Susan Young
Opening Times: 1000-1600 Thu-Sun Mar-Oct, 1000-1600 Sun Nov-Feb.
Cat. Cost: 3 x 1st class
Credit Cards: None.
Specialities: Grasses. Also trees, shrubs, perennials & rock plants. Several small model themed gardens.
Map Ref: C, C3 **OS Grid Ref:** SX828673

CBro BROADLEIGH GARDENS ⊠ ♠ ♿
Bishops Hull, Taunton, Somerset, TA4 1AE
Ⓣ (01823) 286231
Ⓕ (01823) 323646
Ⓔ info@broadleighbulbs.co.uk
Ⓦ www.broadleighbulbs.co.uk
Contact: Lady Skelmersdale
Opening Times: 0900-1600 Mon-Fri for viewing only. Orders collected if notice given.
Min Mail Order UK: Nmc
Min Mail Order EU: Nmc
Cat. Cost: 2 x 1st class
Credit Cards: Visa MasterCard
Specialities: Jan catalogue: bulbs in growth (*Galanthus, Cyclamen* etc.) & herbaceous woodland plants (trilliums, hellebores etc). Extensive list of *Agapanthus*. June catalogue: dwarf & unusual bulbs, *Iris* (DB & PC). Nat. Coll. of Alec Grey hybrid daffodils.
Map Ref: C, B4

KEY
⊠ Mail order to UK or EU ♠ Delivers to shows
✈ Exports beyond EU € Euro accepted
♿ Accessible by wheelchair ◆ See Display advertisement

CBrP **BROOKLANDS PLANTS** ⊠
25 Treves Road, Dorchester, Dorset, DT1 2HE
Ⓣ (01305) 265846
Ⓔ IanWatt@quicklink.freeserve.co.uk
Contact: Ian Watt
Opening Times: By appt. for collection of plants only.
Min Mail Order UK: £25.00 + p&p
Min Mail Order EU: £25.00 + p&p
Cat. Cost: 2 x 2nd class
Credit Cards: None.
Specialities: Cycad nursery specialising in the more cold tolerant species. Also hardy palms, *Agave, Yucca, Dasylirion, Restio* & bamboos. Note: some species available in small quantities only.
Map Ref: C, C5

CBur **BURNHAM NURSERIES** ⊠ ⊠ ♿
Forches Cross, Newton Abbot, Devon, TQ12 6PZ
Ⓣ (01626) 352233
Ⓕ (01626) 362167
Ⓔ mail@burnhamnurseries.co.uk
Ⓦ www.orchids.uk.com
Also sells wholesale
Contact: Any member of staff
Opening Times: 1000-1600 Mon-Sun.
Min Mail Order UK: Nmc
Min Mail Order EU: £100.00 + p&p
Cat. Cost: A4 Sae + 44p stamp
Credit Cards: Visa Switch Amex MasterCard
Specialities: All types of orchid except British native types. Note: please ask for details on export beyond EU.
Map Ref: C, C4

CCAT **CIDER APPLE TREES** ⊠ €
Kerian, Corkscrew Lane, Woolston, Nr. North Cadbury, Somerset, BA22 7BP
Ⓣ (01963) 441101
Also sells wholesale
Contact: Mr J Dennis
Opening Times: By appt. only.
Min Mail Order UK: £7.50
Min Mail Order EU: £7.50
Cat. Cost: Free
Credit Cards: None.
Specialities: *Malus* (speciality standard trees).
Map Ref: C, B5

CCge **COTTAGE GARDEN PLANTS AND HERBS** ♿
North Lodge, Canonteign, Christow, Exeter, Devon, EX6 7NS
Ⓣ (01647) 252950
Contact: Shirley Bennett
Opening Times: 1000-1700 w/ends & B/hols Mar-Sep. Ring for private visit at other times. Lectures given on 'Hardy Geraniums' & 'Cottage Garden Plants'.
Credit Cards: None.
Specialities: Cottage garden plants, herbs and esp. hardy geraniums (over 200 kinds available).
Map Ref: C, C3 **OS Grid Ref:** SX836829

CCha **CHAPEL FARM HOUSE NURSERY** € ♿
Halwill Junction, Beaworthy, Devon, EX21 5UF
Ⓣ (01409) 221594
Ⓕ (01409) 221594
Contact: Robin or Toshie Hull
Opening Times: 0900-1700 Tue-Sat, 1000-1600 Sun & B/hol Mons.
Cat. Cost: None issued.
Credit Cards: None.
Specialities: Plants from Japan. Also herbaceous. Japanese garden design service offered.
Map Ref: C, C3

CChe **CHERRY TREE NURSERY** ♿
(Sheltered Work Opportunities), off New Road Roundabout, Northbourne, Bournemouth, Dorset, BH10 7DA
Ⓣ (01202) 593537 (01202) 590840
Ⓕ (01202) 590626
Also sells wholesale
Contact: Stephen Jailler
Opening Times: 0830-1530 Mon-Fri, 0900-1200 most Sats.
Cat. Cost: A4 sae + 66p stamps
Credit Cards: None.
Specialities: Hardy shrubs, perennials, climbers, grasses.
Map Ref: C, C6

CCol **COLD HARBOUR NURSERY** ⊠
(Office) 28 Moor Road, Swanage, Dorset, BH19 1RG
Ⓣ (01929) 423520 evenings
Ⓔ coldharbournursery@hotmail.com
Ⓦ www.dorset-perennials.co.uk
Contact: Steve Saunders
Opening Times: 1000-1700 Tue-Fri & most w/ends 1st Mar-end Oct. Other times by appt.
Min Mail Order UK: £6.00 + p&p
Cat. Cost: 3 x 2nd class
Credit Cards: None.
Specialities: Unusual herbaceous perennials incl. hardy *Geranium*, daylilies & grasses. Note: nursery is at Bere Road (opp. Silent Woman Inn), Wareham.
Map Ref: C, C5

CCtw CHURCHTOWN NURSERIES ⊠ ⌂
Gulval, Penzance,
Cornwall,
TR18 3BE
Ⓣ (01736) 362626
Ⓕ (01736) 362626
Ⓔ Churchtownnurseries@Hotmail.com
Contact: Chris or Fay Osborne
Opening Times: 1000-1700 Apr-Sep, 1000-1600 Oct-Mar or by appt.
Min Mail Order UK: £25.00 + p&p
Cat. Cost: 1 x 1st class Sae for list.
Credit Cards: None.
Specialities: Good, ever-increasing, range of shrubs, herbaceous & tender perennials & ornamental grasses incl. some more unusual.
Map Ref: C, D1 **OS Grid Ref:** SW486317

CCVT CHEW VALLEY TREES ⊠
Winford Road, Chew Magna,
Bristol, BS40 8QE
Ⓣ (01275) 333752
Ⓕ (01275) 333746
Ⓔ info@chewvalleytrees.co.uk
Ⓦ www.chewvalleytrees.co.uk
Also sells wholesale
Contact: J Scarth
Opening Times: 0800-1700 Mon-Fri all year. 0900-1600 Sat beginning Sep-mid May. Closed Sun & B/hols.
Min Mail Order UK: Nmc
Cat. Cost: Free
Credit Cards: Visa MasterCard Switch
Specialities: Native British & ornamental trees, shrubs, apple trees & hedging. Partial wheelchair access. Note: max. plant height for mail order 2.7m.
Map Ref: C, A5 **OS Grid Ref:** ST558635

CDes DESIRABLE PLANTS ⊠ ⌂
Pentamar, Crosspark,
Totnes, Devon,
TQ9 5BQ*
Ⓣ (01803) 864489 evenings
Ⓔ sutton.totnes@lineone.net
Ⓦ www.desirableplants.com
Contact: Dr J J & Mrs S A Sutton
Opening Times: Not open, mail order only.
Min Mail Order UK: £15.00
Cat. Cost: 4 x 2nd class for concise list or free full list on web.
Credit Cards: None.
Specialities: Eclectic range of choice & interesting herbaceous plants by mail order. Monthly retail event in Totnes, phone or see web for details. *Note: nursery not at this address.

CDev DEVON VIOLET NURSERY ⊠ € ♿
Rattery, South Brent, Devon, TQ10 9LG
Ⓣ (01364) 643033
Ⓕ (01364) 643033
Ⓔ virgin.violets@virgin.net
Ⓦ www.sweetviolets.co.uk
Contact: Robert Sidol, Sarah Bunting
Opening Times: All year round. Please ring first.
Min Mail Order UK: £4.50
Min Mail Order EU: £5.50
Cat. Cost: 1 x 1st class
Credit Cards: None.
Specialities: Violets & Parma violets. Nat. Coll. of *Viola odorata*.
Map Ref: C, C3 **OS Grid Ref:** SX747620

CDob SAMUEL DOBIE & SON ⊠
Long Road, Paignton, Devon, TQ4 7SX
Ⓣ 0870 112 3623
Ⓕ 0870 112 3624
Ⓦ www.dobies.co.uk
Contact: Customer Services
Opening Times: 0830-1700 Mon-Fri (office). Also answerphone.
Min Mail Order UK: Nmc*
Cat. Cost: Free
Credit Cards: Visa MasterCard Switch Delta
Specialities: Wide selection of popular flower & vegetable seeds. Also includes young plants, summer flowering bulbs & garden sundries. Note: mail order to UK & Rep. of Ireland only.

CDoC DUCHY OF CORNWALL ⊠ ◆
Cott Road, Lostwithiel, Cornwall,
PL22 0HW
Ⓣ (01208) 872668
Ⓕ (01208) 872835
Ⓔ sales@duchynursery.co.uk
Ⓦ www.duchyofcornwallnursery.co.uk
Contact: Tracy Wilson
Opening Times: 0900-1700 Mon-Sat, 1000-1700 Sun & B/hols.
Min Mail Order UK: Nmc
Cat. Cost: 8 x 1st class, CD catalogue 12 x 1st class.
Credit Cards: Visa Amex Access Switch Delta
Specialities: Very wide range of garden plants incl. trees, shrubs, conifers, roses, perennials, fruit & half-hardy exotics. Nursery partially available for wheelchair users.
Map Ref: C, C2 **OS Grid Ref:** SX112614

KEY
⊠ Mail order to UK or EU ⌂ Delivers to shows
✈ Exports beyond EU € Euro accepted
♿ Accessible by wheelchair ◆ See Display advertisement

C

CDul **DULFORD NURSERIES** ⊠ ♿
Cullompton, Devon,
EX15 2DG
Ⓣ (01884) 266361
Ⓕ (01884) 266663
Ⓔ dulford.nurseries@virgin.net
Ⓦ www.dulford-nurseries.co.uk
Also sells wholesale
Contact: Paul & Mary Ann Rawlings
Opening Times: 0730-1630 Mon-Fri.
Min Mail Order UK: Nmc
Min Mail Order EU: Nmc
Cat. Cost: Free
Credit Cards: None.
Specialities: Native, ornamental & unusual trees & shrubs incl. oaks, maples, beech, birch, chestnut, ash, lime, *Sorbus* & pines.
Map Ref: C, C4 **OS Grid Ref:** SY062062

CDWL **DORSET WATER LILIES** ⌂ ♿
Yeovil Road, Halstock,
Yeovil, Somerset,
BA22 9RR
Ⓣ (01935) 891668
Ⓕ (01935) 891946
Ⓔ dorsetwaterlily@tiscali.co.uk
Website: www.dorsetwaterlily.co.uk
Also sells wholesale
Contact: Richard Gallehawk
Opening Times: 0900-1600 Mon & Fri only, plus Sat in summer.
Cat. Cost: Free
Credit Cards: None.
Specialities: Hardy & tropical water lilies, lotus, marginal & bogside plants.
Map Ref: C, C5 **OS Grid Ref:** ST543083

CElm **ELM TREE NURSERY** ⊠
Sidbury, Sidmouth, Devon,
EX10 0QG
Ⓣ (01395) 597790
Ⓔ elmtreecyclamen@btopenworld.com
Contact: M Saunders
Opening Times: Not open, mail order only.
Min Mail Order UK: Nmc
Min Mail Order EU:
Cat. Cost: 1 x 1st class
Specialities: Hardy *Cyclamen*. Rarest cultivars only available in small quantities.

CElw **ELWORTHY COTTAGE PLANTS** ⌂ ♿
Elworthy Cottage, Elworthy Nr. Lydeard
St Lawrence, Taunton, Somerset,
TA4 3PX
Ⓣ (01984) 656427
Ⓔ mike@elworthy-cottage.co.uk
Ⓦ www.elworthy-cottage.co.uk
Contact: Mrs J M Spiller
Opening Times: 1000-1600 Wed, Thu & Fri mid Mar-end Jun & Thu only Jul-Sep. Also by appt.
Cat. Cost: 3 x 2nd class
Credit Cards: None.
Specialities: *Clematis* & unusual herbaceous plants esp. hardy *Geranium, Geum*, grasses, *Campanula, Crocosmia, Pulmonaria, Astrantia* & *Viola*. Note: nursery on B3188, 5 miles north of Wiveliscombe, in centre of Elworthy village.
Map Ref: C, B4 **OS Grid Ref:** ST084349

CEnd **ENDSLEIGH GARDENS** ⊠ ♿ ◆
Milton Abbot, Tavistock, Devon, PL19 0PG
Ⓣ (01822) 870235
Ⓕ (01822) 870513
Ⓔ Treemail@endsleigh-gardens.com
Ⓦ www.endsleigh-gardens.com
Contact: Michael Taylor
Opening Times: 0800-1700 Mon-Sat. 1000-1700 Sun (closed Sun Jan).
Min Mail Order UK: £12.00 + p&p
Cat. Cost: 2 x 1st class
Credit Cards: Visa Access Switch MasterCard
Specialities: Choice & unusual trees & shrubs incl. *Acer* & *Cornus* cvs. Old apples & cherries. *Wisteria*. Grafting service.
Map Ref: C, C3

CFai **FAIRHAVEN NURSERY** ⊠ ⌂
Clapworthy Cross, Chittlehampton,
Umberleigh, Devon, EX37 9QT
Ⓣ (01769) 540528
Ⓔ fairhavennursery@hotmail.com
Contact: Derek & Pauline Burdett
Opening Times: 1000-1600 all year, but please check first.
Min Mail Order UK: £10.00 + p&p
Cat. Cost: 2 x 1st class
Credit Cards: None.
Specialities: Propagate & grow wide selection of more unusual varieties of hardy trees, shrubs & perennials. Many grown in small batches that may not be ready for despatch on request. Orders taken for delivery when available.
Map Ref: C, B3

CFee **FEEBERS HARDY PLANTS** ⊠ ♿ ◆
1 Feeber Cottage, Westwood, Broadclyst,
Nr. Exeter, Devon, EX5 3DQ
Ⓣ (01404) 822118
Ⓔ Feebers@onetel.net.uk
Contact: Mrs E Squires
Opening Times: 1000-1700 Wed Mar-Jul & Sep-Oct. Sat & Sun by prior appt.
Min Mail Order UK: Nmc

Min Mail Order EU: Nmc
Cat. Cost: Sae + 36p stamp
Credit Cards: None.
Specialities: Plants for wet clay soils, alpines & hardy perennials incl. those raised by Amos Perry. Notes: mail order ltd. Plants held in small quantities unless grown from seed. Accessible for wheelchairs in dry weather only.
Map Ref: C, C4

CFen FENTONGOLLON FARM ⊠ ♿
Tresillian, Truro, Cornwall, TR2 4AQ
Ⓣ (01872) 520209
Ⓕ (01872) 520606
Ⓔ james@flowerfarm.co.uk
Ⓦ www.flowerfarm.co.uk
Also sells wholesale
Contact: James Hosking
Opening Times: 0900-1800 7 days, Aug-end Oct.
Min Mail Order UK: Nmc
Min Mail Order EU: Nmc
Cat. Cost: 2 x 1st class
Credit Cards: MasterCard Switch
Specialities: Daffodils. Stock available in small quantities.
Map Ref: C, D2

CFil FILLAN'S PLANTS ⊠
Tuckermarsh Gardens, Tamar Lane, Bere Alston, Devon, PL20 7HN
Ⓣ (01822) 840721
Ⓕ (01822) 841551
Ⓔ fillansplants@yahoo.co.uk
Ⓦ www.fillan.com
Also sells wholesale
Contact: Mark Fillan
Opening Times: 1000-1700 Sat Mar-Sep & by appt. any other time.
Min Mail Order UK: £20.00 + p&p
Cat. Cost: 3 x 1st class
Credit Cards: All major credit/debit cards.
Specialities: Bamboos, *Hydrangea* & unusual woody plants. Many plants available in small quanitities only.
Map Ref: C, C3 **OS Grid Ref:** SX444678

CFir FIR TREE FARM NURSERY ⊠ €
Tresahor, Constantine, Falmouth, Cornwall, TR11 5PL
Ⓣ (01326) 340593
Ⓔ jimcave@cornwallgardens.com or ftfnur@aol.com
Ⓦ www.cornwallgardens.com
Contact: Jim Cave
Opening Times: 1000-1700 Thu-Sun 1st Mar-30th Sep.
Min Mail Order UK: £25.00 + p&p
Min Mail Order EU: £40.00 + p&p
Cat. Cost: 6 x 1st class
Credit Cards: Visa Access Delta Switch
Specialities: Over 4000 varieties of cottage garden & rare perennials with many specialities. Also 80 varieties of *Clematis*.
Map Ref: C, D1

CFis MARGERY FISH GARDENS €
East Lambrook Manor, East Lambrook, South Petherton, Somerset, TA13 5HL
Ⓣ (01460) 240328
Ⓕ (01460) 242344
Ⓔ enquiries@eastlambrook.com
Ⓦ www.eastlambrook.com
Contact: Mark Stainer
Opening Times: 1000-1700 1st Feb-31st Oct 7 days.
Credit Cards: Visa Switch MasterCard
Specialities: Hardy *Geranium, Euphorbia, Helleborus* & herbaceous. National Collection of hardy *Geranium* on site. All stock in small quantities.
Map Ref: C, B5

CFul THE RODNEY FULLER HELIANTHEMUM COLLECTION ⊠
Coachman's Cottage, Higher Bratton Seymour, Wincanton, Somerset, BA9 8DA
Ⓣ (01963) 34480
Ⓔ coachmans@tinyworld.co.uk
Contact: Rodney Fuller
Opening Times: By appt. only.
Min Mail Order UK: £18.00
Cat. Cost: 2 x 1st class
Credit Cards: None.
Specialities: *Helianthemum*. Available in small quanitites.
Map Ref: C, B5

CFwr THE FLOWER BOWER ⊠
Woodlands, Shurton, Stogursey, Nr. Bridgwater, Somerset, TA5 1QE
Ⓣ (01278) 732134
Ⓕ (01278) 732134
Ⓔ flower.bower@virgin.net
Contact: Sheila Tucker
Opening Times: 1000-1700, open most days mid-Mar-31st Oct, please phone first.
Min Mail Order UK: £10.00 + p&p
Min Mail Order EU: £20.00 + p&p
Cat. Cost: 4 x 1st class
Credit Cards: None.

C

Specialities: Unusual perennials. *Anemone, Epimedium, Euphorbia,* hardy geraniums, *Phlox,* grasses & ferns. Note: mail order Mar onwards.
Map Ref: C, B4 **OS Grid Ref:** ST203442

CGOG GLOBAL ORANGE GROVES UK ⊠ ♿
Horton Road, Horton Heath, Wimborne, Dorset, BH21 7JN
Ⓣ (01202) 826244
Ⓕ (01202) 814651
Ⓦ www.globalorange.co.uk
Also sells wholesale
Contact: P K Oliver
Opening Times: 1030-1700 7 days, unless exhibiting.
Min Mail Order UK: Nmc
Min Mail Order EU: Nmc
Cat. Cost: Sae
Credit Cards: None.
Specialities: *Citrus* trees, citrus fertiliser & book "Success with *Citrus*". Peaches, apricots, nectarines, mangoes, avocados, pomegranates, figs, persimmon, *Ziziphus jujube.*
Map Ref: C, B6

CGra GRAHAM'S HARDY PLANTS ⊠ ⌂
Southcroft, North Road, Timsbury, Bath, BA2 0JN
Ⓣ (01761) 472187
Ⓔ graplant@aol.com
Ⓦ www.members.aol.com/graplant
Contact: Graham Nicholls
Opening Times: Not open to the public. Mail order and show sales only.
Min Mail Order UK: £2.00 + p&p
Min Mail Order EU: £2.00 + p&p
Cat. Cost: 2 x 1st class or 2 x IRC
Credit Cards: None.
Specialities: North American alpines esp. *Lewisia, Eriogonum, Penstemon, Campanula, Kelseya, Phlox.*
Map Ref: C, B5

CGro C W GROVES & SON ⊠ ♿
West Bay Road, Bridport, Dorset, DT6 4BA
Ⓣ (01308) 422654
Ⓕ (01308) 420888
Ⓔ c.w.grovesandson@zetnet.co.uk
Ⓦ www.users.zetnet.co.uk/c.w.grovesandson/ or www.violet-uk.com
Contact: C W Groves
Opening Times: 0830-1700 Mon-Sat, 1030-1630 Sun.
Min Mail Order UK: Nmc
Min Mail Order EU: £15.00 + p&p
Cat. Cost: 2 x 1st class
Credit Cards: All major credit/debit cards.
Specialities: Nursery & garden centre specialising in Parma & hardy *Viola*. Note: mainly violets by mail order.
Map Ref: C, C5 **OS Grid Ref:** 466918

CHad HADSPEN GARDEN & NURSERY € ♿
Hadspen House, Castle Cary, Somerset, BA7 7NG
Ⓣ (01749) 813707
Ⓕ (01749) 813707
Ⓔ pope@hadspengarden.co.uk
Ⓦ www.hadspengarden.co.uk
Contact: N & S Pope
Opening Times: 1000-1700 Thu-Sun & B/hols. 1st Mar-1st Oct. Garden open at the same time.
Cat. Cost: 4 x 1st class
Credit Cards: All major credit/debit cards.
Specialities: Large-leaved herbaceous. Old fashioned and shrub roses.
Map Ref: C, B5

CHal HALSWAY NURSERY ⊠
Halsway, Nr. Crowcombe, Taunton, Somerset, TA4 4BB
Ⓣ (01984) 618243
Contact: T A & D J Bushen
Opening Times: Most days, please phone first.
Min Mail Order UK: £2.00 + p&p
Cat. Cost: 2 x 1st class*
Credit Cards: None.
Specialities: *Coleus* & *Begonia* (excl. tuberous & winter flowering). Good range of greenhouse & garden plants. *Note: list for *Coleus* & *Begonia* only, no nursery list.
Map Ref: C, B4

CHar WEST HARPTREE NURSERY ⊠ ⌂ €
Bristol Road, West Harptree, Bath, Somerset, BS40 6HG
Ⓣ (01761) 221370
Ⓕ (01761) 221989
Ⓔ bryn@herbaceousperennials.co.uk
Ⓦ www.herbaceousperennials.co.uk
Also sells wholesale
Contact: Bryn & Helene Bowles
Opening Times: From 1000 Tue-Sun 1st Mar-30th Nov.
Min Mail Order UK: £50.00*
Cat. Cost: Large SAE for free names list.
Credit Cards: MasterCard Switch Visa
Specialities: Unusual herbaceous perennials & shrubs. Bulbs & grasses. *Note: mail order Oct-Mar only.
Map Ref: C, B5

CHby **The Herbary** ⊠ ✈
161 Chapel Street, Horningsham, Warminster, Wiltshire, BA12 7LU
Ⓣ (01985) 844442
Ⓜ 07773 661547
Ⓔ info@beansandherbs.co.uk
Ⓦ www.beansandherbs.co.uk
Contact: Pippa Rosen
Opening Times: Apr-Oct by appt. only.
Min Mail Order UK: Nmc
Min Mail Order EU: Nmc
Cat. Cost: 4 x 1st class
Credit Cards: None.
Specialities: Culinary, medicinal & aromatic herbs organically grown. Note: mail order all year for organic herb seed & large variety of organic bean seed.
Map Ref: C, B5 **OS Grid Ref:** ST812414

CHdy **Hardy Orchids** ⊠ ✈
New Gate Farm, Scotchey Lane, Stour Provost, Gillingham, Dorset, SP8 5LT
Ⓣ (01747) 838368
Ⓕ (01747) 838308
Ⓔ hardyorchids@supanet.com
Ⓦ www.hardyorchids.supanet.com
Contact: N J Heywood
Opening Times: By appt. only.
Min Mail Order UK: £10.00 + p&p
Min Mail Order EU: £10.00 + p&p
Cat. Cost: 2 x 1st class
Credit Cards: None.
Specialities: Hardy orchids. *Cypripedium, Dactylorhiza, Pleione, Anacamptis, Orchis, Ophrys* & *Epipactis.*
Map Ref: C, B5 **OS Grid Ref:** ST778217

CHea **Heather Bank Nursery** ⊠ ∩
Woodlands,1 High Street, Littleton Panell, Devizes, Wiltshire, SN10 4EL
Ⓣ (01380) 812739
Ⓔ mullanhbn.fsnet.co.uk
Ⓦ www.heatherbanknursery.co.uk
Contact: Mrs B Mullan
Opening Times: 0900-1800 Mon, Tue, Thu & Fri & w/ends. Please check by phone first if coming a long distance.
Min Mail Order UK: £10.00 + p&p
Cat. Cost: 3 x 1st class
Credit Cards: None.
Specialities: *Campanula* & cottage garden plants.
Map Ref: C, B6

CHEx **Hardy Exotics** ⊠ ♿
Gilly Lane, Whitecross, Penzance, Cornwall, TR20 8BZ
Ⓣ (01736) 740660
Ⓕ (01736) 741101
Ⓔ contact@hardyexotics.co.uk
Ⓦ www.hardyexotics.co.uk
Also sells wholesale
Contact: C Shilton/J Smith
Opening Times: 1000-1700 7 days Mar-Oct, 1000-1700 Mon-Sat Nov-Feb. Please phone first in winter months if travelling a long way.
Min Mail Order UK: 4 plants+ carriage
Cat. Cost: £1.00 postal order or 4 x 1st class (no cheques)
Credit Cards: Visa Access MasterCard Connect Delta
Specialities: Largest collection in the UK of trees, shrubs & herbaceous plants for tropical & desert effects. Hardy & half-hardy plants for gardens, patios & conservatories.
Map Ref: C, D1 **OS Grid Ref:** SW524345

CHid **Hidden Valley Nursery** ⊠ ∩ €
Umberleigh, Devon, EX37 9BU
Ⓣ (01769) 560567
Ⓔ lindleypla@tiscali.co.uk
Contact: Linda & Peter Lindley
Opening Times: Daylight hours, but please phone first.
Min Mail Order UK: Nmc
Cat. Cost: 2 x 1st class
Credit Cards: None.
Specialities: Hardy perennials esp. shade lovers. Note: mail order during Mar only.
Map Ref: C B3 **OS Grid Ref:** SS567205

CHII **Hill House Nursery & Gardens** € ♿
Landscove, Nr. Ashburton, Devon, TQ13 7LY
Ⓣ (01803) 762273
Ⓕ (01803) 762273
Ⓔ sacha@garden.demon.co.uk
Ⓦ www.garden.demon.co.uk
Contact: Raymond, Sacha & Matthew Hubbard
Opening Times: 1100-1700 7 days, all year. Open all B/hols incl. Easter Sun. Tearoom open 1st Mar-30th Sep.
Cat. Cost: None issued.
Credit Cards: Delta MasterCard Switch Visa
Specialities: 3000+ varieties of plants, most propagated on premises, many rare or unusual. The garden, open to the public, was laid out by Edward Hyams. Pioneers of glasshouse pests control by beneficial insects.
Map Ref: C, C3

KEY
⊠ Mail order to UK or EU ∩ Delivers to shows
✈ Exports beyond EU € Euro accepted
♿ Accessible by wheelchair ◆ See Display advertisement

C

CHrt HORTUS NURSERY ⊠ ♿
Shrubbery Bungalow, School Lane, Rousdon, Lyme Regis, Dorset, DT7 3XW
Ⓣ (01297) 444019
Ⓜ 07747 043997
Ⓕ (01297) 444019
Ⓔ plants@hortusnursery.com
Ⓦ www.hortusnursery.com
Contact: Marie-Elaine Houghton
Opening Times: 1000-1700 Wed-Sat, Mar-Oct. Other times by appt.
Min Mail Order UK: Nmc
Cat. Cost: 2 x 1st class
Credit Cards: None.
Specialities: Ornamental grasses & perennials, particularly *Carex, Aster, Digitalis, Euphorbia, Geranium & Penstemon.* Garden Open as nursery. Garden design & planting service.
Map Ref: C, C4 **OS Grid Ref:** SY296914

CHVG HIDDEN VALLEY GARDENS ♿
Treesmill, Nr. Par, Cornwall, PL24 2TU
Ⓣ (01208) 873225
Ⓦ www.hiddenvalleygardens.co.uk
Contact: Mrs P Howard
Opening Times: 1000-1800 beginning Mar-end Oct 7 days. Please phone for directions.
Cat. Cost: None issued
Credit Cards: None.
Specialities: Cottage garden plants, *Crocosmia, Iris sibirica* & many unusual perennials which can be seen growing in the garden. Note: some stock available in small quantities.
Map Ref: C, D2 **OS Grid Ref:** SX094567

CIri THE IRIS GARDEN ⊠ € ◆
Lufton Byre, Lufton, Yeovil, Somerset, BA22 8SY
Ⓣ (01935) 425636
Ⓕ (01935) 425636
Ⓔ theirisgarden@aol.com
Ⓦ www.theirisgarden.co.uk
Contact: Clive Russell
Opening Times: Nursery not open. Visit our iris exhibits at shows. Please phone for show details.
Min Mail Order UK: £15.00 + p&p
Min Mail Order EU: £25.00 + p&p
Cat. Cost: 8 x 1st class.
Credit Cards: All major credit/debit cards.
Specialities: Modern bearded & spuria *Iris* from breeders in UK, USA, France, Italy & Australia. Note: orders for bearded iris must be received by end Jun & by end Aug for spurias.

CJas JASMINE COTTAGE GARDENS ⊠ ♿
26 Channel Road, Walton St Mary, Clevedon, Somerset, BS21 7BY
Ⓣ (01275) 871850
Ⓔ margaret@bologrew.demon.co.uk
Ⓦ www.bologrew.pwp.blueyonder.co.uk
Contact: Mr & Mrs M Redgrave
Opening Times: May to Sep, daily by appt. Garden open at the same times.
Min Mail Order UK: Nmc*
Cat. Cost: None issued
Credit Cards: None.
Specialities: *Rhodochiton, Asarina, Maurandya, Dicentra macrocapnos, Salvia, Solenopsis, Isotoma,* half-hardy geraniums. *Note: mail order seed only.
Map Ref: C, A4 **OS Grid Ref:** ST405725

CKel KELWAYS LTD ⊠ ☒ ⌂ €
Langport, Somerset, TA10 9EZ
Ⓣ (01458) 250521
Ⓕ (01458) 253351
Ⓔ sales@kelways.co.uk
Ⓦ www.kelways.co.uk
Also sells wholesale
Contact: Mr David Root
Opening Times: 0900-1700 Mon-Fri, 1000-1700 Sat, 1000-1600 Sun.
Min Mail Order UK: £4.00 + p&p*
Min Mail Order EU: £8.00 + p&p
Cat. Cost: Free
Credit Cards: Visa Access
Specialities: *Paeonia, Iris, Hemerocallis* & herbaceous perennials. Nat. Coll. *Paeonia lactiflora*. *Note: mail order for *Paeonia* & *Iris* only.
Map Ref: C, B5:

CKen KENWITH NURSERY (GORDON HADDOW) ⊠ ☒ € ♿ ◆
Blinsham, Nr. Torrington, Beaford, Winkleigh, Devon, EX19 8NT
Ⓣ (01805) 603274
Ⓕ (01805) 603663
Ⓔ conifers@kenwith63.freeserve.co.uk
Ⓦ www.kenwithnursery.co.uk
Contact: Gordon Haddow
Opening Times: 1000-1630 Wed-Sat Nov-Feb & by appt. 1000-1630 Tue-Sat, Mar-Oct.
Min Mail Order UK: £10.00 + p&p
Min Mail Order EU: £50.00 + p&p
Cat. Cost: 3 x 1st class
Credit Cards: Visa MasterCard Eurocard
Specialities: All conifer genera. Grafting a speciality. Many new introductions to UK. Nat. Coll. of Dwarf Conifers.
Map Ref: C, B3

CKno KNOLL GARDENS ⊠ ♘ ♿
Hampreston, Stapehill, Nr. Wimborne, Dorset, BH21 7ND
Ⓣ (01202) 873931
Ⓕ (01202) 870842
Ⓔ enquiries@knollgardens.co.uk
Ⓦ www.knollgardens.co.uk
Also sells wholesale
Contact: N R Lucas
Opening Times: 1000-1700 (or dusk if earlier) Wed-Sun. Closed Xmas period.
Min Mail Order UK: Nmc
Cat. Cost: 9 x 2nd class or order Online
Credit Cards: Visa MasterCard
Specialities: Grasses (main specialism). Select perennials. Nat. Collections of *Pennisetum, Phygelius* & deciduous *Ceanothus.*
Map Ref: C, C6

CKob KOBAKOBA ⊠ ✈ ♘
2 High Street, Ashcott, Bridgwater, Somerset, TA7 9PL
Ⓣ (01458) 210700
Ⓜ 07870 624969
Ⓕ (01458) 210650
Ⓔ plants@kobakoba.co.uk
Ⓦ www.kobakoba.co.uk
Contact: Christine Smithee & David Constantine
Opening Times: Please phone for opening times.
Min Mail Order UK: Nmc
Min Mail Order EU: Nmc
Cat. Cost: Plantlist 1 x 1st class or catalogue £2.00
Credit Cards: Visa MasterCard Delta
Specialities: Plants for tropical effect incl. *Ensete, Musa, Hedychium, Curcuma* & other *Zingiberaceae.* Conservatory & greenhouse plants.
Map Ref: C, B5 **OS Grid Ref:** ST4237

CLAP LONG ACRE PLANTS ⊠ ♘ ♿
South Marsh, Charlton Musgrove, Nr. Wincanton, Somerset, BA9 8EX
Ⓣ (01963) 32802
Ⓕ (01963) 32802
Ⓔ info@longacreplants.co.uk
Ⓦ www.longacreplants.co.uk
Contact: Nigel & Michelle Rowland
Opening Times: 1000-1700 Fri-Sat Feb-Jun & Sept.
Min Mail Order UK: £15.00 + p&p
Min Mail Order EU: £30.00 + p&p
Cat. Cost: 4 x 1st class
Credit Cards: Switch MasterCard Visa
Specialities: Ferns, lilies, woodland bulbs & perennials. Nat. Coll. of *Asarum.*
Map Ref: C, B5

CLCN LITTLE CREEK NURSERY ⊠ ♿
39 Moor Road, Banwell, Weston-super-Mare, Somerset, BS29 6EF
Ⓣ (01934) 823739
Ⓕ (01934) 823739
Ⓦ www.littlecreeknursery.co.uk
Contact: Julie Adams
Opening Times: By appt only.
Min Mail Order UK: Nmc
Min Mail Order EU: Nmc
Cat. Cost: 3 x 1st class
Credit Cards: None.
Specialities: Species *Cyclamen* (from seed), *Helleborus, Agapanthus* & *Schizostylis.*
Map Ref: C, B4

CLnd LANDFORD TREES ⊠ €
Landford Lodge, Landford, Salisbury, Wiltshire, SP5 2EH
Ⓣ (01794) 390808
Ⓕ (01794) 390037
Ⓔ sales@landfordtrees.co.uk
Ⓦ www.landfordtrees.co.uk
Also sells wholesale
Contact: C D Pilkington
Opening Times: 0800-1700 Mon-Fri.
Min Mail Order UK: Please enquire
Min Mail Order EU: Please enquire
Cat. Cost: Free
Credit Cards: None.
Specialities: Deciduous ornamental trees.
Map Ref: C, B6 **OS Grid Ref:** SU247201

CLoc C S LOCKYER ⊠ ✈ ♘ € ◆
Lansbury, 70 Henfield Road, Coalpit Heath, Bristol, BS36 2UZ
Ⓣ (01454) 772219
Ⓕ (01454) 772219
Ⓔ sales@lockyerfuchsias.co.uk
Ⓦ www.lockyerfuchsias.co.uk
Also sells wholesale
Contact: C S Lockyer
Opening Times: 1000-1300, 1430-1700 most days, please ring. Many open days & coach parties. Limited wheelchair access.
Min Mail Order UK: 6 plants + p&p
Min Mail Order EU: £12.00 + p&p
Cat. Cost: 4 x 1st class
Credit Cards: None.
Specialities: *Fuchsia.*
Map Ref: C, A5

KEY
⊠ Mail order to UK or EU ♘ Delivers to shows
✈ Exports beyond EU € Euro accepted
♿ Accessible by wheelchair ◆ See Display advertisement

C

CLyd **Lydford Alpine Nursery** ⊠ ♿
2 Southern Cottages, Lydford,
Okehampton, Devon,
EX20 4BL
Ⓣ (01822) 820398
Contact: Julie & David Hatchett
Opening Times: By appt. only. Please ring for directions.
Min Mail Order UK: £10.00 + p&p*
Cat. Cost: Sae for saxifrage list.
Credit Cards: None.
Specialities: *Saxifraga*. Very wide range of choice & unusual alpines in small quantities. *Note: mail order *Saxifraga* only.
Map Ref: C, C3 **OS Grid Ref:** SX504830

CM&M **M & M Plants** ♿
Lloret, Chittlehamholt,
Umberleigh, Devon,
EX37 9PD
Ⓣ (01769) 540448
Ⓕ (01769) 540448
Ⓔ MMPlants@Chittlehamholt.freeserve.co.uk
Contact: Mr M Thorne
Opening Times: 0930-1730 Tue-Sat, Apr-Oct & 1000-1600 Tue-Fri, Nov-Mar. Sat by appt. Aug.
Cat. Cost: 3 x 1st class
Credit Cards: None.
Specialities: Perennials. We also carry a good range of alpines, shrubs, trees & roses.
Map Ref: C, B3

CMac **Macpennys Nurseries** ⊠
154 Burley Road, Bransgore, Christchurch,
Dorset, BH23 8DB
Ⓣ (01425) 672348
Ⓕ (01425) 673945
Ⓔ office@macpennys.co.uk
Ⓦ www.macpennys.co.uk
Contact: T & V Lowndes
Opening Times: 0900-1700 Mon-Sat, 1100-1700 Sun. Closed Xmas & New Year.
Min Mail Order UK: Nmc
Cat. Cost: A4 Sae with 4 x 1st class
Credit Cards: Access Delta Access Eurocard MasterCard Visa Switch Solo
Specialities: General. Nursery partially accessible for wheelchairs.
Map Ref: C, C6

CMCN **Mallet Court Nursery** ⊠ ⊠ ♿ € ♿
Curry Mallet, Taunton,
Somerset, TA3 6SY
Ⓣ (01823) 481493
Ⓕ (01823) 481493
Ⓔ harris@malletcourt.freeserve.co.uk
Ⓦ www.malletcourt.co.uk
Also sells wholesale
Contact: J G S & P M E Harris F.L.S.
Opening Times: 0930-1700 Mon-Fri summer, 0930-1600 winter. Sat & Sun by appt.
Min Mail Order UK: Nmc
Min Mail Order EU: Nmc
Cat. Cost: £1.50
Credit Cards: All major credit/debit cards.
Specialities: Maples, oaks, *Magnolia,* hollies & other rare and unusual plants including those from China & South Korea. Note: mail order Oct-Mar only.
Map Ref: C, B4

CMCo **Meadow Cottage Plants** ♿ € ♿
Pitt Hill, Ivybridge,
Devon, PL21 0JJ
Ⓣ (01752) 894532
Also sells wholesale
Contact: Mrs L P Hunt
Opening Times: By appt. only.
Cat. Cost: 2 x 2nd class
Credit Cards: None.
Specialities: Hardy geranium, other hardy perennials, ornamental grasses and bamboos.
Map Ref: C, D3

CMdw **Meadows Nursery** ♿
5 Rectory Cottages, Mells,
Frome, Somerset,
BA11 3PA
Ⓣ (01373) 813025
Ⓕ (01373) 812268
Also sells wholesale
Contact: Sue Lees & Eddie Wheatley
Opening Times: 1000-1800 Wed-Sun 1st Feb-31st Oct & B/hols.
Cat. Cost: 4 x 1st class
Credit Cards: None.
Specialities: Hardy perennials, shrubs & some conservatory plants. *Kniphofia*.
Map Ref: C, B5 **OS Grid Ref:** ST729492

CMea **The Mead Nursery** ♿
Brokerswood, Nr. Westbury,
Wiltshire,
BA13 4EG
Ⓣ (01373) 859990
Contact: Steve & Emma Lewis-Dale
Opening Times: 0900-1700 Wed-Sat & B/hols, 1200-1700 Sun, 1st Feb-10th Oct. Closed Easter Sun.
Cat. Cost: 5 x 1st class
Credit Cards: None.
Specialities: Perennials, alpines, pot grown bulbs and grasses.
Map Ref: C, B5 **OS Grid Ref:** ST833517

CMen MENDIP BONSAI STUDIO ♠
Byways, Back Lane, Downside,
Shepton Mallet, Somerset, BA4 4JR
Ⓣ (01749) 344274
Ⓕ (01749) 344274
Ⓔ jr.trott@ukonline.co.uk
Ⓦ www.mendipbonsai.co.uk
Contact: John Trott
Opening Times: By appt. only.
Cat. Cost: large sae for plant & workshop lists
Credit Cards: MasterCard Visa
Specialities: Bonsai & garden stock. Acers, conifers, *Stewartia*. Operates education classes in bonsai.
Map Ref: C, B5

CMHG MARWOOD HILL GARDENS ♿
Barnstaple, Devon, EX31 4EB
Ⓣ (01271) 342528
Ⓔ malcolmpharoah@supanet.com
Ⓦ www.marwoodhillgarden.co.uk
Contact: Malcolm Pharoah
Opening Times: 1100-1630, 7 days.
Cat. Cost: 3 x 1st class
Credit Cards: Visa Delta MasterCard Switch Solo
Specialities: Large range of unusual trees & shrubs. *Eucalyptus*, alpines, *Camellia*, *Astilbe*, bog plants & perennials. Nat. Colls. of *Astilbe*, *Tulbaghia* & *Iris ensata*.
Map Ref: C, B3

CMil MILL COTTAGE PLANTS ⊠ ♠ ♿
The Mill, Henley Lane, Wookey,
Somerset BA5 1AP
Ⓣ (01749) 676966
Ⓔ mcp@tinyworld.co.uk
Ⓦ www.millcottageplants.co.uk
Contact: Sally Gregson
Opening Times: 1000-1800 Wed Mar-Sep or by appt. Phone for directions.
Min Mail Order UK: £5.00 + p&p
Min Mail Order EU: £10.00 + p&p
Cat. Cost: 4 x 1st class
Credit Cards: None.
Specialities: Rare *Hydrangea serrata* cvs, *H. aspera* cvs. Also *Papaver orientale*, *Dierama*, hardy *Geranium*, ferns, & grasses.
Map Ref: C, B5

CMon MONOCOT NURSERY ⊠ ✈
St Michaels, Littleton, Somerton,
Somerset, TA11 6NT
Ⓣ (01458) 272356
Ⓕ (01458) 272065
Contact: M R Salmon
Opening Times: 1000-1800 Wed-Sun, Feb-Nov, or by appt.
Min Mail Order UK: Nmc
Min Mail Order EU: Nmc
Cat. Cost: Free to UK & EU. Overseas $2.00 or equivalent.
Credit Cards: None.
Specialities: Bulbs, corms, tubers, rhizomes. Hardy to tropical.

CNat NATURAL SELECTION ⊠ €
1 Station Cottages,
Hullavington, Chippenham,
Wiltshire,
SN14 6ET
Ⓣ (01666) 837369
Ⓔ martin@worldmutation.demon.co.uk
Ⓦ www.worldmutation.demon.co.uk
Contact: Martin Cragg-Barber
Opening Times: Please phone first.
Min Mail Order UK: £9.00 + p&p
Cat. Cost: £1.00 or 5 x 2nd class
Credit Cards: None.
Specialities: Unusual British natives & others. Also seed. Only available in small quantities.
Map Ref: C, A5 **OS Grid Ref:** ST898828

CNCN NAKED CROSS NURSERIES ⊠ ♿
Waterloo Road, Corfe Mullen,
Wimborne, Dorset,
BH21 3SR
Ⓣ (01202) 693256
Ⓕ (01202) 693259
Also sells wholesale
Contact: Peter French
Opening Times: 0900-1700 7 days.
Min Mail Order UK: 10 heathers
Cat. Cost: 2 x 1st class
Credit Cards: Visa Amex Switch MasterCard
Specialities: Heathers.
Map Ref: C, C6

CNic NICKY'S ROCK GARDEN NURSERY ♠ ♿
Broadhayes, Stockland, Honiton,
Devon, EX14 9EH
Ⓣ (01404) 881213
Ⓔ Dianabob.Dark@nickys.sagehost.co.uk
Contact: Diana & Bob Dark
Opening Times: 0900-dusk 7 days. Please phone first to check & for directions.
Cat. Cost: 3 x 1st class
Credit Cards: None.
Specialities: Plants for rock gardens, scree, troughs, banks, walls & front of border & dwarf shrubs. Many unusual. Plants

propagated in small numbers. Ring to check availability before travelling.
Map Ref: C, C4 **OS Grid Ref:** ST236027

CNMi NEWPORT MILLS NURSERY ⊠
Wrantage, Taunton, Somerset, TA3 6DJ
Ⓣ (01823) 490231
Ⓜ 07950 035668
Ⓕ (01823) 490231
Contact: John Barrington, Rachel Pettitt
Opening Times: By appt. only.
Min Mail Order UK: Nmc
Min Mail Order EU: Nmc
Cat. Cost: Free
Credit Cards: None.
Specialities: *Delphinium.* Mail order Apr-Sep for young delphiniums in 7cm pots. Dormant plants can be sent out in autumn/winter if requested. Some varieties only available in small quantities & propagated to order.
Map Ref: C, B4

COkL OAK LEAF NURSERIES ⊠
24 Crantock Drive, Almondsbury, Bristol, BS32 4HG
Ⓣ (01454) 620180
Ⓜ 07718 667940
Also sells wholesale.
Contact: David Price
Opening Times: Not open, mail order only.
Min Mail Order UK: Nmc
Cat. Cost: 2 x 1st class
Credit Cards: None.
Specialities: Wide range of rock & herbaceous plants, some unusual, incl. *Dianthus, Helianthemum, Lavandula, Hebe* & *Saxifraga.* Shrubs also a speciality.
Map Ref: C, A5

COld THE OLD MILL HERBARY
Helland Bridge, Bodmin, Cornwall, PL30 4QR
Ⓣ (01208) 841206
Ⓕ (01208) 841206
Ⓔ enquiries@oldmillherbary.co.uk
Ⓦ www.oldmillherbary.co.uk
Contact: Mrs B Whurr
Opening Times: 1000-1700 Thu-Tue 25th Apr-30th Oct.
Cat. Cost: 6 x 1st class
Credit Cards: None.
Specialities: Culinary, medicinal & aromatic herbs, shrubs, climbing & herbaceous plants.
Map Ref: C, C2 **OS Grid Ref:** SX065717

COlW THE OLD WITHY GARDEN NURSERY ⊠
The Grange Fruit Farm, Gweek, Helston, Cornwall, TR12 6BE
Ⓣ (01326) 221171
Ⓔ WithyNursery@fsbdial.co.uk
Also sells wholesale
Contact: Sheila Chandler or Nick Chandler
Opening Times: 1000-1700 Wed-Mon, mid Feb-end Oct. 1000-1730 7 days, Apr-Sep.
Min Mail Order UK: £15.00
Cat. Cost: 4 x 1st class
Credit Cards: MasterCard Visa Delta Switch
Specialities: Cottage garden plants, perennials, some biennials & grasses. Good selection of *Achillea, Eryngium, Euphorbia,* hardy geraniums, *Penstemon* & *Sedum.*
Map Ref: C, D1 **OS Grid Ref:** SW688255

COtt OTTER NURSERIES LTD ♿
Gosford Road, Ottery St. Mary, Devon, EX11 1LZ
Ⓣ (01404) 815815
Ⓕ (01404) 815816
Ⓔ otter@otternurseries.co.uk
Contact: Mrs Pam Poole
Opening Times: 0800-1730 Mon-Sat, 1030-1630 Sun. Closed Xmas, Boxing Day & Easter Sun.
Cat. Cost: None issued
Credit Cards: Visa Access Amex Diners Switch
Specialities: Large garden centre & nursery with extensive range of trees, shrubs, conifers, climbers, roses, fruit & hardy perennials.
Map Ref: C, C4

CPar PARKS PERENNIALS
242 Wallisdown Road, Wallisdown, Bournemouth, Dorset, BH10 4HZ
Ⓣ (01202) 524464
Contact: S Parks
Opening Times: Apr-Oct most days, please phone first.
Cat. Cost: None issued.
Credit Cards: None.
Specialities: Hardy herbaceous perennials.
Map Ref: C, C6

CPBP PARHAM BUNGALOW PLANTS ⊠ ♿ €
Parham Lane, Market Lavington, Devizes, Wiltshire, SN10 4QA
Ⓣ (01380) 812605
Ⓔ jjs@pbplants.freeserve.co.uk
Contact: Mrs D E Sample
Opening Times: Please ring first.
Min Mail Order UK: Nmc
Min Mail Order EU: Nmc
Cat. Cost: Sae
Credit Cards: None.
Specialities: Alpines & dwarf shrubs.
Map Ref: C, B6

C

CPen **PENNARD PLANTS** ⊠ ✈ ♠ €
3 The Gardens, East Pennard, Shepton Mallet, Somerset, BA4 6TU
Ⓣ (01749) 860039
Ⓕ (01749) 860232
Ⓔ sales@pennardplants.com
Ⓦ pennardplants.com
Contact: Chris Smith
Opening Times: By appt. only.
Min Mail Order UK: Nmc
Min Mail Order EU: Nmc
Cat. Cost: 3 x 1st class
Credit Cards: All major credit/debit cards.
Specialities: Ornamental grasses, *Agapanthus, Crocosmia, Dierama, Kniphofia* phormiums & South African bulbous plants. Note: nursery at The Walled Garden at East Pennard.
Map Ref: C, B5

CPev **PEVERIL CLEMATIS NURSERY** ♿
Christow, Exeter, Devon, EX6 7NG
Ⓣ (01647) 252937
Contact: Barry Fretwell
Opening Times: 1000-1300 & 1400-1730 Fri-Wed, 1000-1300 Sun. Nov-1st Mar closed.
Cat. Cost: 2 x 1st class
Credit Cards: None.
Specialities: *Clematis.*
Map Ref: C, C3

CPhi **ALAN PHIPPS CACTI** ⊠ €
62 Samuel White Road, Hanham, Bristol, BS15 3LX
Ⓣ (0117) 9607591
Ⓦ www.cactus-mall.com/alan-phipps/index.html
Contact: A Phipps
Opening Times: 10.00-1700 but prior phone call essential to ensure a greeting.
Min Mail Order UK: £5.00 + p&p
Min Mail Order EU: £20.00 + p&p
Cat. Cost: Sae or 2 x IRC (EC only)
Credit Cards: None.
Specialities: *Mammillaria, Astrophytum* & *Ariocarpus*. Species & varieties will change with times. Ample quantities exist in spring. Ltd. range of *Agave*. Note: Euro accepted as cash only.
Map Ref: C, A5 **OS Grid Ref:** ST644717

CPHo **THE PALM HOUSE** ⊠
8 North Street, Ottery St Mary, Devon, EX11 1DR
Ⓣ (01404) 815450
Ⓔ george@thepalmhouse.co.uk
Ⓦ www.thepalmhouse.co.uk
Also sells wholesale
Contact: George Gregory
Opening Times: By appt. only.
Min Mail Order UK: £15.00
Cat. Cost: 2 x 1st class
Credit Cards: None.
Specialities: Palms.
Map Ref: C, C4 **OS Grid Ref:** SY098955

CPin **PINSLA GARDEN AND NURSERY** ♿ ◆
Pinsla Lodge, Glynn, Bodmin, Cornwall, PL30 4AY
Ⓣ (01208) 821339
Ⓕ (01208) 821339
Ⓔ info@pinslagarden.co.uk
Ⓦ www.pinslagarden.co.uk
Contact: Mark and Claire Woodbine
Opening Times: 1000-1800, 7 days, 1st Mar-31st Oct. Winter, w/ends only.
Cat. Cost: None issued.
Credit Cards: All major credit/debit cards.
Specialities: Plant-lovers paradise, overflowing with perennials, ferns, acers, bamboos, grasses, succulents, alpines, climbers & shrubs.
Map Ref: C, C2 **OS Grid Ref:** SX665117

CPle **PLEASANT VIEW NURSERY** ⊠ ♿
Two Mile Oak, Nr. Denbury, Newton Abbot, Devon, TQ12 6DG
Ⓣ (01803) 813388 answerphone
Contact: Mrs B D Yeo
Opening Times: Nursery open 1000-1700 Wed-Fri mid Mar-end Sep (closed for lunch 1245-1330).
Min Mail Order UK: £20.00 + p&p
Min Mail Order EU: £20.00 + p&p (Salvias only)
Cat. Cost: 3 x 2nd class or 2 x IRC
Credit Cards: None.
Specialities: *Salvia* & unusual shrubs for garden & conservatory. Nat. Colls. of *Salvia* & *Abelia*. Note: nursery off A381 at T.M. Oak Cross towards Denbury.
Map Ref: C, C3 **OS Grid Ref:** SX8368

CPLG **PINE LODGE GARDENS & NURSERY** ♿
Cuddra, Holmbush,
St Austell, Cornwall,
PL25 3RQ
Ⓣ (01726) 73500
Ⓕ (01726) 77370
Ⓔ garden@pine-lodge.co.uk
Ⓦ www.pine-lodge.co.uk
Contact: Ray & Shirley Clemo

KEY
⊠ Mail order to UK or EU ♠ Delivers to shows
✈ Exports beyond EU € Euro accepted
♿ Accessible by wheelchair ◆ See Display advertisement

C

Opening Times: 1000-1700 7 days 1st Mar-31st Oct.
Cat. Cost: 5 x 2nd class
Credit Cards: None.
Specialities: Rare & unusual shrubs & herbaceous, some from seed collected on plant expeditions each year. Nat. Coll. of *Grevillea*. Ltd. stocks of all plants.
Map Ref: C, D2 **OS Grid Ref:** SX045527

CPLN THE PLANTSMAN NURSERY ⊠ ⊠
North Wonson Farm, Throwleigh, Okehampton, Devon, EX20 2JA
Ⓣ (01647) 231699 office/(01647) 231618 nursery
Ⓕ (01647) 231157
Ⓔ pnursery@aol.com
Ⓦ www.plantsman.com
Contact: Guy & Emma Sisson
Opening Times: Mail order only.
Min Mail Order UK: £40.00 + p&p
Min Mail Order EU: £50.00 + p&p
Cat. Cost: £2.50 for full colour catalogue.
Credit Cards: All major credit/debit cards.
Specialities: Unusual hardy & tender climbers and wall shrubs.

CPMA P M A PLANT SPECIALITIES ⊠ ⊠
Junker's Nursery Ltd., Lower Mead, West Hatch, Taunton, Somerset, TA3 5RN
Ⓣ (01823) 480774
Ⓕ (01823) 481046
Ⓔ karan@junker.net
Ⓦ www.junker.net
Also sells wholesale
Contact: Karan or Nick Junker
Opening Times: Strictly by appt. only.
Min Mail Order UK: Nmc
Min Mail Order EU: Nmc
Cat. Cost: 6 x 2nd class
Credit Cards: None.
Specialities: Choice & unusual shrubs incl. grafted *Acer palmatum, Cornus, Magnolia* & a wide range of *Daphne*. Ltd. numbers of some hard to propagate plants, esp. daphnes. Reserve orders accepted.
Map Ref: C, B4

CPne PINE COTTAGE PLANTS ⊠ ⊠ €
Pine Cottage, Fourways, Eggesford, Chulmleigh, Devon, EX18 7QZ
Ⓣ (01769) 580076
Ⓕ (01769) 581427
Ⓔ pcplants@supanet.com
Ⓦ www.pcplants.co.uk
Also sells wholesale
Contact: Dick Fulcher
Opening Times: By appt. only. Special open weeks for *Agapanthus*, 1000-1800 daily excl. Sun mornings Jul & Aug 2004.
Min Mail Order UK: £15.00 + p&p
Min Mail Order EU: £20.00 + p&p
Cat. Cost: 4 x 1st class
Credit Cards: None.
Specialities: Nat. Coll. of *Agapanthus*. Note: mail order *Agapanthus* from Oct-Jun. Some cvs available in small quantities only.
Map Ref: C, B3 **OS Grid Ref:** SS6171

CPom POMEROY PLANTS
Tower House, Pomeroy Lane, Wingfield, Trowbridge, Wiltshire, BA14 9LJ
Ⓣ (01225) 769551
Contact: Simon Young
Opening Times: Mar-Nov. Please phone first.
Cat. Cost: 2 x 1st class
Credit Cards: None.
Specialities: Hardy, mainly species, herbaceous perennials. Many unusual and often small numbers. Specialities *Allium, Salvia* & shade-lovers, esp. *Epimedium*.
Map Ref: C, B5 **OS Grid Ref:** ST817569

CPou POUNSLEY PLANTS ⊠ ń € ♿
Pounsley Combe, Spriddlestone, Brixton, Plymouth, Devon, PL9 0DW
Ⓣ (01752) 402873
Ⓕ (01752) 402873
Ⓔ pou599@aol.com
Ⓦ www.pounsleyplants.com
Also sells wholesale
Contact: Mrs Jane Hollow
Opening Times: Normally 1000-1700 Mon-Sat but please phone first.
Min Mail Order UK: £10.00 + p&p
Min Mail Order EU: £20.00 + p&p
Cat. Cost: 2 x 1st class
Credit Cards: None.
Specialities: Unusual herbaceous perennials & cottage plants. Selection of *Clematis* & old roses. Large selection of South African monocots. Note: mail order Nov-Feb only.
Map Ref: C, D3 **OS Grid Ref:** SX521538

CPrp PROPERPLANTS.COM ⊠ ń
Penknight, Edgcumbe Road, Lostwithiel, Cornwall, PF22 0JD
Ⓣ (01208) 872291
Ⓕ (01208) 872291
Ⓔ info@Properplants.com
Ⓦ www.ProperPlants.com
Contact: Sarah Wilks
Opening Times: 1000-1800 or dusk if earlier, Tue & B/hols mid-Mar to end-Sep & by appt.

Min Mail Order UK: Nmc
Min Mail Order EU: Nmc
Cat. Cost: 4 x 1st class
Credit Cards: All major credit/debit cards.
Specialities: Wide range of unusual & easy herbaceous perennials, ferns & grasses. Less common herbs. Partially accessible for wheelchair users.
Map Ref: C, C2 **OS Grid Ref:** SX093596

CPSs PLANTS FOR THE SENSES ⊠
Corner Cottage, North Street,
Dolton, Winkleigh,
Devon, EX19 8QQ
Ⓣ (01805) 804467
Ⓔ michaelross@freenetname.co.uk
Contact: Michael Ross
Opening Times: Not open.
Min Mail Order UK: Nmc
Cat. Cost: 1 x 1st class
Credit Cards: None.
Specialities: Some emphasis on scented plants. Some stock in small quantities. Note: nursery is 5 miles away from above address.

CQua QUALITY DAFFODILS ⊠ ✈ € ◆
14 Roscarrack Close, Falmouth,
Cornwall, TR11 4PJ
Ⓣ (01326) 317959
Ⓕ (01326) 317959
Ⓔ rascamp@daffodils.uk.com or info.@.qualitydaffodils.co.uk
Ⓦ www.qualitydaffodils.co.uk
Also sells wholesale
Contact: R A Scamp
Opening Times: Not open, mail order only.
Min Mail Order UK: Nmc
Min Mail Order EU: Nmc
Cat. Cost: 3 x 1st class
Credit Cards: All major credit/debit cards.
Specialities: *Narcissus* hybrids & species. Some stocks are less than 100 bulbs.
Map Ref: C, D1

CRde ROWDE MILL NURSERY € ♿
Rowde, Devizes, Wiltshire,SN10 1SZ
Ⓣ (01380) 723016
Ⓕ (01380) 723016
Ⓔ cholmeley@supanet.com
Contact: Mrs J Cholmeley
Opening Times: 1000-1700 Thu-Sun & B/hol Mon Apr-Sep.
Cat. Cost: None issued
Credit Cards: None.
Specialities: Wide range of hardy perennials, all grown on the nursery. Plants offered in pots or lifted from stockbeds.
Map Ref: C, A6 **OS Grid Ref:** ST973628

CRea REALLY WILD FLOWERS ⊠ €
H V Horticulture Ltd,
Spring Mead, Bedchester,
Shaftesbury, Dorset, SP7 0JU
Ⓣ (01747) 811778
Ⓕ (01747) 811499
Ⓔ rwflowers@aol.com
Ⓦ www.reallywildflowers.co.uk
Also sells wholesale
Contact: Grahame Dixie
Opening Times: Not open to public.
Min Mail Order UK: £40.00 + p&p
Min Mail Order EU: £100.00 + p&p
Cat. Cost: 3 x 1st class
Credit Cards: None.
Specialities: Wild flowers for grasslands, woodlands, wetlands & heaths. Seeds, orchids. Advisory & soil analysis services.

CRez REZARE NURSERIES ⊠
Rezare, Nr. Treburley, Launceston,
Cornwall, PL15 9NX
Ⓣ (01579) 370969
Ⓔ REZARENURSERIES@aol.com
Contact: Kym & Rick Finney/Mel & Jim Gearing
Opening Times: 1000-1730, 7 days 1st Feb-end Nov. Other times by appt.
Min Mail Order UK: £10.00
Cat. Cost: 4 x 1st class
Credit Cards: MasterCard Visa
Specialities: Growers of a full & varied range of choice & unusual plants of the highest quality, incl. a good selection of herbaceous perennials, shrubs & trees. Notes: mainly perennials, grasses & ferns by mail order. Credit cards not accepted for mail order.
Map Ref: C, C2

CRHN ROSELAND HOUSE NURSERY ⊠ ⛺
Chacewater, Truro, Cornwall, TR4 8QB
Ⓣ (01872) 560451
Ⓔ clematis@roselandhouse.co.uk
Ⓦ www.roselandhouse.co.uk
Contact: C R Pridham
Opening Times: 1300-1800 Tue & Wed, Apr-Sep.
Min Mail Order UK: Nmc
Cat. Cost: 2 x 1st class
Credit Cards: None.
Specialities: Climbing & conservatory plants. National Collection of *Clematis viticella* cvs.
Map Ref: C, D1

KEY
⊠ Mail order to UK or EU ⛺ Delivers to shows
✈ Exports beyond EU € Euro accepted
♿ Accessible by wheelchair ◆ See Display advertisement

C

CRob **ROBERTS NURSERIES** ⊠
East Allington, Totnes, Devon, TQ9 7QE
Ⓣ (01548) 521412,
Ⓜ 07940 858778
Ⓕ (01548) 521533
Ⓔ info@conifersdirect.com
Ⓦ www.conifersdirect.com
Also sells wholesale
Contact: W R Bartoszyn
Opening Times: By appt. only.
Min Mail Order UK: Nmc
Cat. Cost: 2 x 1st class stamps
Credit Cards: None.
Specialities: Extensive range of hardy dwarf, ornamental conifers incl. old favourites, choice varieties & new introductions. A selected range of specimen shrubs & conifers in patio planters.
Map Ref: C, D3 **OS Grid Ref:** SX763495

CRoM **ROSEDOWN MILL PALMS AND EXOTICS** ⊠
Hartland, Bideford, Devon, EX39 6AH
Ⓣ (01237) 441527
Ⓔ sales@rosedownmill.co.uk
Ⓦ www.rosedownmill.co.uk
Contact: Huw Collingbourne
Opening Times: By appt. only.
Min Mail Order UK: £25.00
Min Mail Order EU: £25.00
Cat. Cost: Sae for list
Credit Cards: None.
Specialities: Palms, cycads, pachypodiums.
Map Ref: C, B2 **OS Grid Ref:** SS276248

CRow **ROWDEN GARDENS** ⊠ ✈ ♿
Brentor, Nr. Tavistock, Devon, PL19 0NG
Ⓣ (01822) 810275
Ⓕ (01822) 810275
Ⓔ rowdengardens@btopenworld.com
Also sells wholesale
Contact: John R L Carter
Opening Times: By appt only.
Min Mail Order UK: Nmc
Min Mail Order EU: Nmc
Cat. Cost: 6 x 1st class
Credit Cards: None.
Specialities: Aquatics, damp loving & associated plants incl. rare & unusual varieties. Nat. Coll. of *Polygonum, Ranunculus ficaria, Caltha* & Water *Iris*. Note: some stock available in small quantities only.
Map Ref: C, C3

CRWN **THE REALLY WILD NURSERY** ⊠ ✈ €
19 Hoopers Way, Torrington,
Devon, EX38 7NS
Ⓣ (01805) 624739
Ⓔ thereallywildnursery@yahoo.co.uk
Ⓦ www.thereallywildnursery.co.uk
Also sells wholesale
Contact: Kathryn Moore
Opening Times: Not open.
Min Mail Order UK: £10.00 + p&p
Min Mail Order EU: £20.00 + p&p
Cat. Cost: 3 x 1st class
Specialities: Wildflowers, bulbs & seeds. Note: mail order all year round, grown to order (plants in pots or plugs). Credit card payment accepted in person only.

CSam **SAMPFORD SHRUBS** ⊠ €
Sampford Peverell, Tiverton,
Devon,
EX16 7EN
Ⓣ (01884) 821164
Ⓔ martin@samshrub.co.uk
Ⓦ www.samshrub.co.uk
Contact: M Hughes-Jones & S Proud
Opening Times: 0900-1700 Thu-Sat, Feb. 0900-1700 7 days, Mar-Jun. 0900-1700 Thu-Sat Jul-15 Nov. Mail order Oct-mid Mar.
Min Mail Order UK: £15.00 + p&p*
Cat. Cost: A5 34p stamps sae
Credit Cards: All major credit/debit cards.
Specialities: Large displays of *Pulmonaria & Crocosmia*. Nat. Coll. of *Helenium*. *Note: mail order is for herbaceous only from Oct-mid Mar.
Map Ref: C, B4 **OS Grid Ref:** ST043153

CSBt **ST BRIDGET NURSERIES LTD** ⊠ ♿
Old Rydon Lane, Exeter,
Devon, EX2 7JY
Ⓣ (01392) 873672
Ⓕ (01392) 876710
Ⓔ info@stbridgetnurseries.co.uk
Ⓦ www.stbridgetnurseries.co.uk
Contact: Garden Centre Plant Advice
Opening Times: 0800-1700 Mon-Sat, 1030-1630 Sun, 0900-1700 Bank Hols. Closed Xmas Day, Boxing Day, New Year's Day & Easter Sunday.
Min Mail Order UK: Nmc
Cat. Cost: Free
Credit Cards: Visa MasterCard Switch Solo
Specialities: Large general nursery, with two garden centres. Note: mail order available between Nov & Mar.
Map Ref: C, C4 **OS Grid Ref:** SX955905

CSdC **SHERWOOD COTTAGE** €
Newton St Cyres, Exeter, Devon,
EX5 5BT
Ⓣ (01392) 851589
Ⓔ vaughan.gallavan@connectfree.co.uk

Contact: Vaughan Gallavan
Opening Times: By appt. only.
Cat. Cost: 2 x 1st class
Credit Cards: None.
Specialities: Magnolias, trees & shrubs. Nat. Coll. of Knap Hill azaleas. Ghent & species deciduous azaleas. Sherwood Garden new Nat. Coll. of *Magnolia*. Stock in limited quantities.
Map Ref: C, C3

CSec SECRET SEEDS ⊠ ✈ ⌂ € ♿
(office) Turnpike Cottage, Trow, Salcombe Regis, Sidmouth, Devon, EX10 0PB
Ⓣ (01395) 515265
Ⓜ 07870 389889
Ⓕ (01395) 515265
Ⓔ pf@secretseeds.com
Ⓦ www.secretseeds.com
Also sells wholesale
Contact: Mike Burgess
Opening Times: 1000-1700 Tue-Sun, Mar-Dec.
Min Mail Order UK: Nmc
Min Mail Order EU: Nmc
Cat. Cost: 2 x 1st class
Credit Cards: All major credit/debit cards.
Specialities: *Echium*. Note: mail order seeds only. Nursery at Popplefords, Newton Poppleford, Sidmouth, Devon, EX10 0DE.
Map Ref: C, C4 **OS Grid Ref:** SY071896

CSev LOWER SEVERALLS NURSERY ⊠ ♿
Crewkerne, Somerset, TA18 7NX
Ⓣ (01460) 73234
Ⓕ (01460) 76105
Ⓔ mary@lowerseveralls.co.uk
Ⓦ www.lowerseveralls.co.uk
Contact: Mary R Pring
Opening Times: 1000-1700 Fri-Wed 1st Mar-mid-Oct & Sun 1400-1700 May & Jun.
Min Mail Order UK: £20.00
Cat. Cost: 4 x 1st class
Credit Cards: None.
Specialities: Herbs, herbaceous & conservatory plants. Note: Mail order perennials only.
Map Ref: C, B5 **OS Grid Ref:** ST457111

CSil SILVER DALE NURSERIES € ◆
Shute Lane, Combe Martin, Devon, EX34 0HT
Ⓣ (01271) 882539
Ⓔ silverdale.nurseries@virgin.net
Contact: Roger Gilbert
Opening Times: 1000-1800 7 days.
Cat. Cost: 4 x 1st class
Credit Cards: Visa MasterCard Eurocard
Specialities: Nat. Coll. of *Fuchsia*. Hardy fuchsias (cultivars and species).
Map Ref: C, B3

CSim SIMPSON'S SEEDS LTD ⊠ ♿
The Walled Garden Nursery, Horningsham, Warminster, Wiltshire, BA12 7NT
Ⓣ (01985) 845004
Ⓕ (01985) 845052
Ⓔ sales@simpsonsseeds.co.uk
Contact: Jane Simpson
Opening Times: 1100-1700 Wed-Sun Apr-end Jun. Other times, please phone first.
Min Mail Order UK: Nmc
Min Mail Order EU: Nmc
Credit Cards: Visa MasterCard Switch
Specialities: Large range of hardy perennials, limited quantities of each. Large range of seeds & vegetable plants. Specialities tomato & pepper. Note: mail order catalogue currently only for seed & veg plants.

CSLe SILVER LEAF NURSERIES ⊠ ⌂ ♿
Charmouth Road, Lyme Regis, Dorset, DT7 3HF
Ⓣ (01297) 444655
Ⓕ (01297) 444655
Ⓔ woodberry@fsbdial.co.uk
Ⓦ www.silverleaf@woodberrydown.com
Also sells wholesale
Contact: Chris Hughes
Opening Times: Please phone first.
Min Mail Order UK: £25.00
Cat. Cost: 4 x 1st class
Credit Cards: None.
Specialities: Silver- & grey-leafed plants, incl. many lavenders. Will propagate to order.
Map Ref: C, C4 **OS Grid Ref:** ST932343

CSli SLIPPS GARDEN CENTRE ♿
Butts Hill, Frome, Somerset, BA11 1HR
Ⓣ (01373) 467013
Ⓕ (01373) 467013
Also sells wholesale
Contact: James Hall
Opening Times: 0900-1730 Mon-Sat, 1000-1630 Sun.
Cat. Cost: None issued
Credit Cards: Visa Access MasterCard Delta Switch
Specialities: *Achillea*.
Map Ref: C, B5

CSna SNAPE COTTAGE
Chaffeymoor, Borton, Dorset, SP8 5BY
Ⓣ (01747) 840330 (evenings only).
Ⓕ (01747) 840330

KEY		
	⊠ Mail order to UK or EU	⌂ Delivers to shows
	✈ Exports beyond EU	€ Euro accepted
	♿ Accessible by wheelchair	◆ See Display advertisement

C

Ⓔ ianandangela@snapecottagegarden.co.uk
Ⓦ www.snapestakes.com
Contact: Mrs Angela Whinfield
Opening Times: Last 2 Sun in Feb for snowdrops and hellebores. 1030-1700 Wed, Apr-Sep. Closed Aug.
Cat. Cost: None issued
Specialities: *Galanthus* & *Helleborus*. 'Old' forms of many popular garden plants. Plantsman's garden open same time as nursery.

CSpe SPECIAL PLANTS ⊠ ∩ € ♿
Hill Farm Barn, Greenways Lane,
Cold Ashton, Chippenham,
Wiltshire, SN14 8LA
Ⓣ (01225) 891686
Ⓔ derry@specialplants.net
Ⓦ www.specialplants.net
Contact: Derry Watkins
Opening Times: 1030-1630 7 days Mar-Sept. Other times please ring first to check.
Min Mail Order UK: £10.00 + p&p
Min Mail Order EU: £20.00 + p&p
Cat. Cost: 5 x 2nd class (sae only for seed list)
Credit Cards: MasterCard Visa Delta Switch Electron Maestro
Specialities: Tender perennials, *Mimulus, Pelargonium, Salvia, Streptocarpus*. Hardy geraniums, *Anemone, Erysimum, Papaver, Viola* & grasses. Many varieties prop. in small numbers. New introductions of S. African plants. Note: mail order Sep-Mar only.
Map Ref: C, A5 **OS Grid Ref:** ST749726

CSPN SHERSTON PARVA NURSERY ⊠ ✈ ∩ € ♿
Malmesbury Road, Sherston, Wiltshire,
SN16 0NX
Ⓣ (01666) 841066
Ⓕ (01666) 841132
Ⓔ sales@sherstonparva.com
Ⓦ www.sherstonparva.com
Contact: Martin Rea
Opening Times: 1000-1700 7 days 1st Feb-31th Dec. Closed Jan.
Min Mail Order UK: Nmc
Min Mail Order EU: Nmc
Cat. Cost: Free
Credit Cards: MasterCard Delta Visa Switch
Specialities: *Clematis*, wall shrubs & climbers.
Map Ref: C, A5

CSto STONE LANE GARDENS ⊠ ♿
Stone Farm, Chagford, Devon, TQ13 8JU
Ⓣ (01647) 231311
Ⓕ (01647) 231311
Ⓔ kenneth_ashburner@talk21.com
Ⓦ www.mythicgarden.com
Also sells wholesale
Contact: Kenneth Ashburner
Opening Times: By appt. only.
Min Mail Order UK: £5.00
Cat. Cost: £3.00 for descriptive catalogue
Credit Cards: None.
Specialities: Wide range of wild provenance *Betula* & *Alnus*. Interesting varieties of *Rubus, Sorbus* etc.
Map Ref: C,C3 **OS Grid Ref:** SX709909

CStr SUE STRICKLAND PLANTS ⊠ ∩
The Poplars, Isle Brewers, Taunton,
Somerset, TA3 6QN
Ⓣ (01460) 281454
Ⓕ (01460) 281454
Ⓔ sues@stricklandc.freeserve.co.uk
Contact: Sue Strickland
Opening Times: 0930-1430 Mon-Wed Mar-Jul & Sep-Oct, some Sun, please phone first. Other times by appt.
Min Mail Order UK: 4 plants
Cat. Cost: 2 x 1st class
Credit Cards: None.
Specialities: *Salvia* & unusual herbaceous perennials incl. *Nepeta, Helianthus, Origanum* & grasses. Note: mail order to UK mainland only.
Map Ref: C, B4

CStu STUCKEY'S ALPINES ∩
38 Phillipps Avenue, Exmouth,
Devon,
EX8 3HZ
Ⓣ (01395) 273636
Ⓔ stuckeysalpines@aol.com
Contact: Roger & Brenda Stuckey
Opening Times: As NGS dates or by appt.
Cat. Cost: None issued
Credit Cards: None.
Specialities: Alpines in general. Hardy & half-hardy bulbs. NZ *Clematis* hybrids. Extensive choice of plants, many in small quantities.
Map Ref: C, C4

CSut SUTTONS SEEDS ⊠
Woodview Road, Paignton, Devon,
TQ4 7NG
Ⓣ 0870 220 2899
Ⓕ 0870 220 2265
Ⓦ www.suttons-seeds.co.uk
Contact: Customer Services
Opening Times: (Office) 0830-1700 Mon-Fri. Also answerphone.
Min Mail Order UK: Nmc
Cat. Cost: Free
Credit Cards: Visa MasterCard Switch Delta
Specialities: Over 1,000 varieties of flower & vegetable seed, bulbs, plants & sundries.

CSWC **SOUTH WEST CARNIVOROUS PLANTS** ⊠ ♠
2 Rose Cottages, Culmstock, Cullompton, Devon, EX15 3JJ
Ⓣ (01884) 841549
Ⓕ (01884) 841549
Ⓔ flytraps@littleshopofhorrors.co.uk
Ⓦ www.littleshopofhorrors.co.uk
Contact: Jenny Pearce & Alistair Pearce
Opening Times: By appt.
Min Mail Order UK: £10.00 + p&p
Min Mail Order EU: £20.00 + p&p
Cat. Cost: 2 x 2nd class
Credit Cards: All major credit/debit cards.
Specialities: *Cephalotus, Nepenthes, Dionea, Drosera, Darlingtonia, Sarracenia, Pinguicula* & *Utricularia*. Specialists in hardy carnivorous plants & *Dionea muscipula* cvs.
Map Ref: C, B4

CSWP **SONIA WRIGHT PLANTS** ⊠ ✈ ♿
Buckerfields Nursery, Ogbourne St George, Marlborough, Wiltshire, SN8 1SG
Ⓣ (01672) 841065
Ⓕ (01672) 541047
Contact: Anyas Simon, Sonia Wright
Opening Times: 1000-1800 Wed-Sat, Mar-Oct. 1000-1600 Fri-Sat, Nov-Feb.
Min Mail Order UK: £15.OO primulas only*
Min Mail Order EU: £15.00 primulas only
Cat. Cost: 4 x 1st class
Credit Cards: All major credit/debit cards.
Specialities: Barnhaven polyanthus & primroses. Grasses, grey-leaved plants, *Iris, Euphorbia, Penstemon*, old roses. *Note: mail order primroses only despatched autumn. Nursery has moved to above address.
Map Ref: C, A6

CTbh **TREBAH ENTERPRISES LTD**
Trebah, Mawnan Smith, Falmouth, Cornwall, TR11 5JZ
Ⓣ (01326) 250448
Ⓕ (01326) 250781
Ⓔ mail@trebah-garden.co.uk
Ⓦ www.trebah-garden.co.uk
Contact: Plant Sales Staff
Opening Times: 1030-1700 all year.
Cat. Cost: None issued
Credit Cards: All major credit/debit cards.
Specialities: Tree ferns, *Camellia, Gunnera* & conservatory climbers.
Map Ref: C, D1 **OS Grid Ref:** SW770276

CTho **THORNHAYES NURSERY** ⊠
St Andrews Wood, Dulford, Cullompton, Devon, EX15 2DF
Ⓣ (01884) 266746
Ⓕ (01884) 266739
Ⓔ trees@thornhayes-nursery.co.uk
Ⓦ www.thornhayes-nursery.co.uk
Also sells wholesale
Contact: K D Croucher
Opening Times: 0800-1600 Mon-Fri.
Min Mail Order UK: Nmc
Min Mail Order EU: Nmc
Credit Cards: None.
Specialities: A broad range of forms of ornamental, amenity & fruit trees incl. West Country apple varieties.
Map Ref: C, C4

CTrC **TREVENA CROSS NURSERIES** ⊠ € ♿
Breage, Helston, Cornwall, TR13 9PS
Ⓣ (01736) 763880
Ⓕ (01736) 762828
Ⓔ sales@trevenacross.co.uk
Ⓦ www.trevenacross.co.uk
Contact: Graham Jeffery, John Eddy
Opening Times: 0900-1700 Mon-Sat, 1030-1630 Sun.
Min Mail Order UK: Nmc
Min Mail Order EU: Nmc*
Cat. Cost: A5 Sae with 2 x 1st class
Credit Cards: Access Visa Switch
Specialities: South African, Australian & New Zealand plants, incl. *Aloe, Protea*, tree ferns, palms, *Restio*, hardy succulents & wide range of other exotics. *Note: mail order to EU by negotiation.
Map Ref: C, D1 **OS Grid Ref:** SW614284

CTrh **TREHANE CAMELLIA NURSERY** ⊠ ♠ € ♿
J Trehane & Sons Ltd, Stapehill Road, Hampreston, Wimborne, Dorset, BH21 7ND
Ⓣ (01202) 873490
Ⓕ (01202) 873490
Also sells wholesale
Contact: Lorraine or Jeanette
Opening Times: 0900-1630 Mon-Fri all year (excl. Xmas & New Year). 1000-1600 Sat-Sun in spring & by special appt.
Min Mail Order UK: Nmc
Min Mail Order EU: Nmc
Cat. Cost: £1.70 cat./book
Credit Cards: Visa Access MasterCard
Specialities: Extensive range of *Camellia* species, cultivars & hybrids. Many new introductions. Evergreen azaleas, *Pieris, Magnolia* & blueberries.
Map Ref: C, C6

KEY
⊠ Mail order to UK or EU ♠ Delivers to shows
✈ Exports beyond EU € Euro accepted
♿ Accessible by wheelchair ◆ See Display advertisement

C

CTri **TRISCOMBE NURSERIES** ⊠ ♿ ◆
West Bagborough, Nr. Taunton,
Somerset, TA4 3HG
Ⓣ (01984) 618267
Ⓔ triscombe.nurseries2000@virgin.net
Ⓦ www.triscombenurseries.co.uk
Contact: S Parkman
Opening Times: 0900-1300 & 1400-1730 Mon-Sat. 1400-1730 Sun & B/hols.
Min Mail Order UK: Nmc
Cat. Cost: 2 x 1st class
Credit Cards: None.
Specialities: Trees, shrubs, roses, fruit, *Clematis*, herbaceous & rock plants.
Map Ref: C, B4

CTrw **TREWITHEN NURSERIES** ⊠ €
Grampound Road, Truro, Cornwall,
TR2 4DD
Ⓣ (01726) 882764
Ⓕ (01726) 882301
Ⓔ gardens@trewithen-estate.demon.co.uk
Ⓦ www.trewithengardens.co.uk
Also sells wholesale
Contact: L Hazelton
Opening Times: 0800-1630 Mon-Fri.
Min Mail Order UK: Nmc
Cat. Cost: £1.25
Specialities: Shrubs, especially *Camellia* & *Rhododendron*.
Map Ref: C, D2

CTuc **EDWIN TUCKER & SONS** ⊠
Brewery Meadow, Stonepark,
Ashburton, Newton Abbot, Devon,
TQ13 7DG
Ⓣ (01364) 652233
Ⓕ (01364) 654211
Ⓔ seeds@edwintucker.com
Ⓦ www.edwintucker.com
Contact: Geoff Penton
Opening Times: 0800-1700 Mon-Fri, 0800-1600 Sat.
Min Mail Order UK: Nmc
Min Mail Order EU: Nmc
Cat. Cost: Free
Credit Cards: Visa MasterCard Switch
Specialities: Over 100 varieties of seed potatoes. Wide range of vegetables, flowers, green manures & sprouting seeds in packets. All not treated. Over 200 varieties of organically produced seeds.

CWan **WANBOROUGH HERB NURSERY**
Callas Hill, Wanborough, Swindon,
Wiltshire, SN4 0AG
Ⓣ (01793) 790327 (answering machine)
Ⓔ Biggs@wanbherbnursery.fsnet.co.uk
Contact: Peter Biggs
Opening Times: 1000-1700 Tue-Fri (closed 1300-1400), w/ends 1000-1600, Mar-Oct. 1000-1600 (closed 1300-1400) Thu-Sun, Nov & Dec. Other times by appt.
Cat. Cost: 2 x 1st or A4 Sae
Credit Cards: None.
Specialities: Herbs, Herbaceous, esp. culinary. Available in limited numbers.
Map Ref: C, A6 **OS Grid Ref:** SU217828

CWat **THE WATER GARDEN** ⊠ ♿
Hinton Parva, Swindon, Wiltshire, SN4 0DH
Ⓣ (01793) 790558
Ⓕ (01793) 791298
Ⓔ watergarden@supanet.com
Contact: Mike & Anne Newman
Opening Times: 1000-1700 Wed-Sun.
Min Mail Order UK: £10.00 + p&p
Cat. Cost: 4 x 1st class
Credit Cards: Visa Access Switch
Specialities: Water lilies, marginal & moisture plants, oxygenators & alpines.
Map Ref: C, A6

CWCL **WESTCOUNTRY NURSERIES (INC. WESTCOUNTRY LUPINS)** ⊠ ⌂ € ◆
Donkey Meadow, Woolsery, Bideford,
Devon, EX39 5QH
Ⓣ (01237) 431111
Ⓕ (01237) 431111
Ⓔ SarahConibear@westcountry-nurseries.co.uk
Ⓦ www.westcountry-nurseries.co.uk
Also sells wholesale
Contact: Sarah Conibear
Opening Times: 1000-1600 7 days.
Min Mail Order UK: £15.00
Min Mail Order EU: £50.00
Cat. Cost: 2 x 1st class + A5 Sae for full colour cat.
Credit Cards: None.
Specialities: *Lupinus, Lewisia, Hellebore*, cyclamen, lavender, select perennials & grasses.

CWDa **WESTDALE NURSERIES** ⊠ ☑ ⌂ ♿
Holt Road, Bradford-on-Avon,
Wiltshire, BA15 1TS
Ⓣ (01225) 863258
Ⓕ (01225) 863258
Ⓔ westdale.nurseries@talk21.com
Ⓦ www.westdalenurseries.co.uk
Also sells wholesale
Contact: Louisa Bernal
Opening Times: 0900-1800 7 days.
Min Mail Order UK: £10.00 + p&p
Min Mail Order EU: £10.00 + p&p

Cat. Cost: 4 x 1st class
Credit Cards: All major credit/debit cards.
Specialities: *Bougainvillea, Geranium,* conservatory plants. Note: export beyond EU by arrangement.
Map Ref: C, A5

CWdb WOODBOROUGH GARDEN CENTRE LTD € ♿
Nursery Farm, Woodborough, Nr. Pewsey, Wiltshire, SN9 5PF
Ⓣ (01672) 851249
Ⓕ (01672) 851465
Ⓔ clanparker@aol.com
Contact: Alison Parker
Opening Times: 0900-1700 Mon-Sat, 1100-1700 Sun.
Cat. Cost: None issued
Credit Cards: All major credit/debit cards.
Specialities: Wide range of shrubs, trees, herbaceous, alpines & herbs. Large selection of climbers esp. *Clematis*, & spring bulbs. PYO fruit & daffodils.
Map Ref: C, A6 **OS Grid Ref:** SU119597

CWGr WINCHESTER GROWERS LTD. ⊠ ✈ ♿
Varfell Farm, Long Rock, Penzance, Cornwall, TR20 8AQ
Ⓣ (01736) 851033
Ⓕ (01736) 851033
Ⓔ dahlias@wgltd.co.uk
Ⓦ www.wgltd.co.uk
Also sells wholesale
Contact: Sarah Thomas
Opening Times: 1300-1630 Thu, Fri & Sat, 15th Jul 2004-28th Aug 2004. Open w/end 1000-1600, 21st & 22nd Aug 2004.
Min Mail Order UK: Nmc
Min Mail Order EU: Nmc
Cat. Cost: Free
Credit Cards: Visa Delta MasterCard Switch
Specialities: Nat. Coll. of *Dahlia*. Due to large number of varieties, stock of some is limited.
Map Ref: C, D1

CWib WIBBLE FARM NURSERIES ⊠ ✈ ⛺ ♿
Wibble Farm, West Quantoxhead, Nr. Taunton, Somerset, TA4 4DD
Ⓣ (01984) 632303
Ⓕ (01984) 633168
Ⓔ sales@wibblefarmnurseries.co.uk
Ⓦ www.wibblefarmnurseries.co.uk
Also sells wholesale
Contact: Mrs M L Francis
Opening Times: 0800-1700 Mon-Fri, 1000-1600 Sat. All year excl. B/hols.
Min Mail Order UK: Nmc
Min Mail Order EU: Nmc
Cat. Cost: 2 x 1st class
Credit Cards: All major credit/debit cards.
Specialities: Growers of a wide range of hardy plants, many rare & unusual.
Map Ref: C, B4

CWil FERNWOOD NURSERY ⊠ ✈ € ♿
Peters Marland, Torrington, Devon, EX38 8QG
Ⓣ (01805) 601446
Ⓔ hw@fernwood-nursery.co.uk
Ⓦ www.fernwood-nursery.co.uk
Contact: Howard Wills & Sally Wills
Opening Times: Any time by appt. Please phone first.
Min Mail Order UK: Nmc
Min Mail Order EU: Nmc
Cat. Cost: Sae for list.
Credit Cards: None.
Specialities: Nat. Coll. of *Sempervivum, Jovibarba, Rosularia* & *Phormium.*
Map Ref: C, C3 **OS Grid Ref:** SS479133

CWin WINFRITH HOSTAS ⊠ € ♿
5 Knoll Park, Gatemore Road, Winfrith Newburgh, Dorchester, Dorset, DT2 8LD
Ⓣ (01305) 851996
Ⓔ plantman35187681@aol.com
Ⓦ www.winfrithhostas.co.uk
Contact: John Ledbury
Opening Times: 1000-1600, daily.
Min Mail Order UK: Nmc
Cat. Cost: 3 x 1st class
Credit Cards: None.
Specialities: *Hosta.*
Map Ref: C, C5

CWiW WINDRUSH WILLOW ⊠ ✈ €
Higher Barn, Sidmouth Road, Aylesbeare, Exeter, Devon, EX5 2JJ
Ⓣ (01395) 233669
Ⓕ (01395) 233669
Ⓔ windrushw@aol.com
Ⓦ www.windrushwillow.com
Also sells wholesale
Contact: Richard Kerwood
Opening Times: By appt.
Min Mail Order UK: Nmc
Min Mail Order EU: Nmc
Cat. Cost: 2 x 1st class

KEY
⊠ Mail order to UK or EU ⛺ Delivers to shows
✈ Exports beyond EU € Euro accepted
♿ Accessible by wheelchair ◆ See Display advertisement

C

Credit Cards: None.
Specialities: *Salix*. Unrooted cuttings available Dec-Mar.

CWoo **Ian and Rosemary Wood** ⊠
Newlands, 28 Furland Road,
Crewkerne, Somerset,
TA18 8DD
Ⓣ (01460) 74630
Ⓔ ianwood@ukgateway.net
Contact: Ian and Rosemary Wood
Opening Times: By appt. only. Primarily mail order service.
Min Mail Order UK: Nmc
Cat. Cost: 2 x 1st or 2nd class
Credit Cards: None.
Specialities: *Erythronium, Cyclamen* species & dwarf *Narcissus* species. Note: some species may only be available in small quantities, see catalogue.
Map Ref: C, B5

CWrd **Ward Alpines** ⊠ ☒ ⌂ €
Newton Farm Nursery, Hemyock,
Cullompton, Devon, EX15 3QS
Ⓣ (01823) 680410
Ⓕ (01823) 680410
Ⓦ www.wardalpines@btopenworld.com
Also sells wholesale
Contact: J.F. & S.M. Ward
Opening Times: By appt only & when garden open under NGS.
Min Mail Order UK: Nmc
Min Mail Order EU: Nmc
Cat. Cost: 3 x 1st class
Specialities: Wide range of *Gentiana sino-ornata, Rhodohypoxis/Rhodoxis, Iris sibirica* & *I. ensata.*
Map Ref: C, B4 **OS Grid Ref:** ST140123

CWri **Nigel Wright Rhododendrons** ♿
The Old Glebe, Eggesford,
Chulmleigh, Devon, EX18 7QU
Ⓣ (01769) 580632
Also sells wholesale
Contact: Nigel Wright
Opening Times: By appt. only.
Cat. Cost: 2 x 1st class
Credit Cards: None.
Specialities: *Rhododendron* only. 200 varieties field grown, root-balled, some potted. For collection only. Specialist grower.
Map Ref: C, B3 **OS Grid Ref:** SS6171

CWSG **West Somerset Garden Centre** ⊠ ♿
Mart Road, Minehead, Somerset, TA24 5BJ
Ⓣ (01643) 703812
Ⓕ (01643) 706470
Ⓔ wsgc@btconnect.com
Ⓦ www.westsomersetgardencentre.co.uk
Contact: Mrs J K Shoulders
Opening Times: 0800-1700 Mon-Sat, 1000-1600 Sun.
Min Mail Order UK: Nmc
Cat. Cost: Not available
Credit Cards: Access Visa Switch Solo
Specialities: Wide general range. *Ceanothus.*
Map Ref: C, B4

CWVF **White Veil Fuchsias** ⊠ ♿
Verwood Road, Three Legged Cross,
Wimborne, Dorset, BH21 6RP
Ⓣ (01202) 813998
Contact: A. C. Holloway
Opening Times: 0900-1300 & 1400-1700 Mon-Fri Jan-Dec, & Sat Jan-Aug. 0900-1300 Sun Jan-Jul, closed Sun Aug, closed Sat & Sun Sep-Dec.
Min Mail Order UK: 8 plants
Cat. Cost: 4 x 1st class
Credit Cards: None.
Specialities: Fuchsias.

Eastern

EAll **Allen's Nurseries** ⊠ ⌂
Barton Road, Wisbech,
Cambridgeshire,
PE13 4TG
Ⓣ (01945 580433
Ⓕ (01945) 463389
Ⓔ allensnurseries@msn.com
Ⓦ www.allensnurseries.co.uk
Contact: Richard Allen
Opening Times: Not open. Mail order only.
Min Mail Order UK: £10.00
Cat. Cost: 4 x 1st class
Credit Cards: All major credit/debit cards.
Specialities: *Clematis.*

EAmu **Amulree Exotics** ⊠ ⌂ ♿
(Office) Katonia Avenue,
Maylandsea, Essex,
CM3 6AD
Ⓣ (01245) 425255
Ⓕ (01245) 425255
Ⓔ SDG@exotica.fsbusiness.co.uk
Ⓦ www.turn-it-tropical.co.uk
Also sells wholesale
Contact: S Gridley
Opening Times: 0930-1730 7 days spring-autumn, 1000-1630 7 days autumn-spring.
Min Mail Order UK: Nmc
Cat. Cost: 1 x 2nd class
Credit Cards: Visa MasterCard Electron Solo Switch

Specialities: Hardy & half-hardy plants for home, garden & conservatory. Palms, bamboos, bananas, tree ferns, cannas, gingers & much more. Note: nursery is at Tropical Wings, Wickford Road, South Woodham Ferrers.
Map Ref: E, D2

EBak **B & H M BAKER**
Bourne Brook Nurseries, Greenstead Green, Halstead, Essex, CO9 1RJ
Ⓣ (01787) 476369/472900
Also sells wholesale
Contact: B, HM and C Baker
Opening Times: 0800-1630 Mon-Fri, 0900-1200 & 1400-1630 Sat & Sun.
Cat. Cost: 2 x 1st class + 33p
Credit Cards: MasterCard Delta Visa Switch
Specialities: *Fuchsia* & conservatory plants.
Map Ref: E, C2

EBee **BEECHES NURSERY** ⊠ ♠ ♿
Village Centre, Ashdon, Saffron Walden, Essex, CB10 2HB
Ⓣ (01799) 584362
Ⓕ (01799) 584421
Ⓦ www.beechesnursery.co.uk
Contact: Alan Bidwell/Kevin Marsh
Opening Times: 0830-1700 Mon-Sat, 1000-1700 Sun & B/hols.
Min Mail Order UK: £10.00
Min Mail Order EU: £20.00
Cat. Cost: 6 x 2nd class heraceous list
Credit Cards: Visa Access MasterCard Eurocard Switch
Specialities: Herbaceous specialists & extensive range of other garden plants. Note: mail order generally from Oct-Feb, Mar-Sep where conditions permit. Trees NOT available by mail order.
Map Ref: E, C2 **OS Grid Ref:** TL5842

EBla **BLACKSMITHS COTTAGE NURSERY** ⊠ ♠ €
Langmere Green Road, Langmere, Diss, Norfolk, IP21 4QA
Ⓣ (01379) 740982, (01379) 741917 (nursery)
Ⓕ (01379) 741917
Ⓔ Blackcottnursery@aol.com
Also sells wholesale
Contact: Ben or Jill Potterton
Opening Times: 1000-1700 Fri-Sun Mar-Oct & B/hols, or by appt.
Min Mail Order UK: Nmc
Min Mail Order EU: Nmc
Cat. Cost: 3 x 1st class
Credit Cards: All major credit/debit cards.
Specialities: Hardy *Geranium, Digitalis, Heuchera, Crocosmia, Polygonatum, Tricyrtis* & Siberian *Iris*. Over 2000 species grown. Large selection of shade plants.
Map Ref: E, C3

EBls **PETER BEALES ROSES** ⊠ ✈ ♿
London Road, Attleborough, Norfolk, NR17 1AY
Ⓣ (01953) 454707
Ⓕ (01953) 456845
Ⓔ sales@classicroses.co.uk
Ⓦ www.classicroses.co.uk
Contact: Customer Advisers
Opening Times: 0900-1700 Mon-Sat, 1000-1600 Sun & B/hols.
Min Mail Order UK: Nmc
Min Mail Order EU: Nmc
Cat. Cost: Free
Credit Cards: Visa MasterCard Access Switch Solo Delta JCB
Specialities: Old fashioned roses & classic roses. Nat. Coll. of Species Roses.
Map Ref: E, C3

EBrs **BRESSINGHAM GARDENS (INCORP. VAN TUBERGEN UK)** ⊠ ♿
Bressingham, Diss, Norfolk, IP22 2AG
Ⓣ (01379) 688282
Ⓕ (01379) 687227
Ⓔ info@bressinghamgardens.com
Ⓦ www.bressinghamgardens.com
Also sells wholesale
Contact: General Manager
Opening Times: Gardens only 1030-1730 1st Apr-31st Oct 2004. Foggy Bottom 1230-1630.
Min Mail Order UK: £10.00
Min Mail Order EU: £30.00
Cat. Cost: 2 x 1st class
Credit Cards: Visa Access MasterCard Switch
Specialities: Bulbs, perennials. Nat. Collection of *Miscanthus*.
Map Ref: E, C3 **OS Grid Ref:** TM08800780

EBur **JENNY BURGESS** ⊠ ✈ € ♿
Alpine Nursery, Sisland, Norwich, Norfolk, NR14 6EF
Ⓣ (01508) 520724
Contact: Jenny Burgess
Opening Times: Any time by appt.
Min Mail Order UK: £5.00 + p&p
Min Mail Order EU: £10.00 + p&p

KEY
⊠ Mail order to UK or EU ♠ Delivers to shows
✈ Exports beyond EU € Euro accepted
♿ Accessible by wheelchair ◆ See Display advertisement

E

E

Cat. Cost: 3 x 1st class
Credit Cards: None.
Specialities: Alpines, *Sisyrinchium* & *Campanula*. Nat. Coll. of *Sisyrinchium*. Note: *Sisyrinchium* only by mail order.
Map Ref: E, B3

ECGP **CAMBRIDGE GARDEN PLANTS** ♿
The Lodge, Clayhithe Road, Horningsea, Cambridgeshire, CB5 9JD
Ⓣ (01223) 861370
Contact: Mrs Nancy Buchdahl
Opening Times: 1100-1730 Thu-Sun mid Mar-31st Oct. Other times by appt.
Cat. Cost: 4 x 1st class
Credit Cards: None.
Specialities: Hardy perennials incl. wide range of *Geranium, Allium, Euphorbia, Penstemon, Digitalis*. Some shrubs, roses & *Clematis*.
Map Ref: E, C2 **OS Grid Ref:** TL497637

ECha **THE BETH CHATTO GARDENS LTD** ⊠ ♿
Elmstead Market, Colchester, Essex, CO7 7DB
Ⓣ (01206) 822007
Ⓕ (01206) 825933
Ⓔ info@bethchatto.fsnet.co.uk
Ⓦ www.bethchatto.co.uk
Contact: Beth Chatto
Opening Times: 0900-1700 Mon-Sat 1st Mar-31st Oct. 0900-1600 Mon-Fri 1st Nov-1st Mar. Closed Sun.
Min Mail Order UK: £20.00
Min Mail Order EU: Ask for details
Cat. Cost: £3.00 incl. p&p
Credit Cards: Visa Switch MasterCard
Specialities: Predominantly herbaceous. Many unusual for special situations.
Map Ref: E, D3 **OS Grid Ref:** TM069238

ECho **CHOICE LANDSCAPES** ⊠ ⊠ ♠ € ♿
Priory Farm, 101 Salts Road, West Walton, Wisbech, Cambridgeshire, PE14 7EF
Ⓣ (01945) 585051
Ⓕ (01945) 580053
Ⓔ info@choicelandscapes.org
Ⓦ www.choicelandscapes.org
Contact: Michael Agg & Jillian Agg
Opening Times: 1000-1700 Tue-Sat 3rd Feb-30th Oct 2004. Not open on show dates, please phone. Other times by appt.
Min Mail Order UK: £10.00
Min Mail Order EU: £10.00 + p&p
Cat. Cost: 6 x 1st class or 6 IRC
Credit Cards: Visa MasterCard Switch Solo
Specialities: Dwarf conifers, alpines, acers, rhododendrons, hostas, bulbs, pines & lilies.
Map Ref: E, B1

EChP **CHOICE PLANTS** ⊠ ♠ € ◆
83 Halton Road, Spilsby, Lincolnshire, PE23 5LD
Ⓣ (01790) 752361
Ⓕ (01790) 752524
Ⓔ jgunson@spilsby94.fsnet.co.uk
Ⓦ www.choiceplants.net
Contact: Joan Gunson
Opening Times: 1000-1700 Wed-Sun & B/hol Mon Mar-Sep.
Min Mail Order UK: £20.00 + p&p*
Cat. Cost: 2 x 1st class
Credit Cards: None.
Specialities: Hardy *Geranium, Crocosmia, Hemerocallis, Iris* & a good selection of unusual hardy perennials. *Note: mail order Feb-May & Sep-Nov only.
Map Ref: E, B1

ECnt **CANTS OF COLCHESTER** ⊠⊠
Nayland Road, Mile End, Colchester, Essex, CO4 5EB
Ⓣ (01206) 844008
Ⓕ (01206) 855371
Ⓔ finder@cantsroses.co.uk
Ⓦ www.cantsroses.co.uk
Contact: Angela Pawsey
Opening Times: 0900-1300, 1400-1630 Mon-Fri. Sat varied, please phone first. Sun closed.
Min Mail Order UK: Nmc
Min Mail Order EU: Nmc
Cat. Cost: Free
Credit Cards: Visa MasterCard Delta Solo Switch
Specialities: Roses. Unstaffed rose field can be viewed dawn-dusk every day from end Jun-end Sep. Note: mail order end Oct-end Mar only.
Map Ref: E, C3

ECot **THE COTTAGE GARDEN** ♿
Langham Road, Boxted, Colchester, Essex, CO4 5HU
Ⓣ (01206) 272269
Ⓔ enquiries@thecottage-garden.co.uk
Ⓦ www.thecottage-garden.co.uk
Contact: Alison Smith
Opening Times: 0800-1700 7 days spring & summer. 0800-1700 Thu-Mon Sep-Feb.
Cat. Cost: Free leaflet
Credit Cards: Visa Access Connect Switch Delta
Specialities: 400 varieties of shrubs, 500 varieties of herbaceous. Huge range of trees, grasses, alpines, herbs, hedging, all home grown. Garden antiques.
Map Ref: E, C3 **OS Grid Ref:** TM003299

ECou **COUNTY PARK NURSERY**
Essex Gardens, Hornchurch, Essex,
RM11 3BU
Ⓣ (01708) 445205
Ⓦ www.countyparknursery.co.uk
Contact: G Hutchins
Opening Times: 0900-dusk Mon-Sat excl. Wed, 1000-1700 Sun Mar-Oct. Nov-Feb by appt. only.
Cat. Cost: 3 x 1st class
Credit Cards: None.
Specialities: Alpines & rare and unusual plants from New Zealand, Tasmania & Falklands. Nat. Coll. of *Coprosma*. Many plants in small quantities only.
Map Ref: E, D2

ECre **CREAKE PLANT CENTRE** ♿
Nursery View, Leicester Road,
South Creake, Fakenham,
Norfolk, NR21 9PW
Ⓣ (01328) 823018
Contact: Mr T Harrison
Opening Times: 1000-1300 & 1400-1730 7 days excl. Xmas.
Cat. Cost: None issued
Credit Cards: None.
Specialities: Unusual shrubs, herbaceous, conservatory plants. Huge selection of hardy *Geranium*.
Map Ref: E, B1

ECri **CRIN GARDENS** ⊠
79 Partons Road, Kings Heath,
Birmingham, B14 6TD
Ⓣ 0121 443 3815
Ⓕ 0121 443 3815
Contact: M Milinkovic
Opening Times: Not open.
Min Mail Order UK: Nmc
Cat. Cost: 2 x 1st class
Credit Cards: None.
Specialities: Lilies. Limited stock available on first come, first served basis.

ECrN **CROWN NURSERY** ⊠ ♿
High Street, Ufford, Woodbridge,
Suffolk, IP13 6EL
Ⓣ (01394) 460755
Ⓕ (01394) 460142
Ⓔ enquiries@crown-nursery.co.uk
Ⓦ www.crown-nursery.co.uk
Also sells wholesale
Contact: Jill Proctor
Opening Times: 0900-1700 (or dusk if sooner) Mon-Sat.
Min Mail Order UK: Nmc
Cat. Cost: 2 x 1st class
Credit Cards: Visa Delta MasterCard Eurocard JCB Switch
Specialities: Mature & semi-mature native, ornamental & fruit trees.
Map Ref: E, C3 **OS Grid Ref:** TM292528

ECtt **COTTAGE NURSERIES** ⊠ ♿
Thoresthorpe, Alford, Lincolnshire,
LN13 0HX
Ⓣ (01507) 466968
Ⓕ (01507) 463409
Ⓔ bill@cottagenurseries.net
Ⓦ www.cottagenurseries.net
Also sells wholesale
Contact: W H Denbigh
Opening Times: 0900-1700 7 days 1st Mar-31st Oct, 1000-1600 Thu-Sun Nov-Feb.
Min Mail Order UK: Nmc
Cat. Cost: 3 x 1st class
Credit Cards: None.
Specialities: Wide general range.
Map Ref: E, A2 **OS Grid Ref:** TF423716

EDAr **D'ARCY & EVEREST** ⊠ ⛺ € ♿
(Office) PO Box 78, St Ives, Huntingdon,
Cambridgeshire, PE27 4UQ
Ⓣ (01480) 497672
Ⓜ 07715 374440/1
Ⓕ (01480) 466042
Ⓔ richard@darcyeverest.co.uk
Ⓦ www.darcyeverest.co.uk
Also sells wholesale
Contact: Angela Whiting, Richard Oliver
Opening Times: By appt. only.
Min Mail Order UK: £10.00 + p&p
Min Mail Order EU: £50.00 + p&p
Cat. Cost: 6 x 1st class
Credit Cards: None.
Specialities: Alpines, herbs & selected perennials. Note: nursery is at Pidley Sheep Lane (B1040), Somersham, Huntingdon.
Map Ref: E, C2 **OS Grid Ref:** 533276

EDsa **DARASINA NURSERY** ♿
Ingatestone Hall, Hall Lane, Ingatestone,
Essex, CM4 9NR
Ⓣ (01277) 353235
Also sells wholesale
Contact: Stephen Nelson
Opening Times: 1130-1730 Sat, Sun & B/Hol, Easter Sat-end Sep. Other times by appt.
Cat. Cost: Free list
Credit Cards: None.

KEY
⊠ Mail order to UK or EU ⛺ Delivers to shows
✈ Exports beyond EU € Euro accepted
♿ Accessible by wheelchair ◆ See Display advertisement

Specialities: Courtyard style & container planting. Hardy & half-hardy shrubs incl. figs, *Pittosporum, Melianthus*. Many uncommon perennials, ferns, herbs & veg. plants.
Map Ref: E, D2 **OS Grid Ref:** TQ653987

E

EEls ELSWORTH HERBS ⊠ ♿
Avenue Farm Cottage,
31 Smith Street, Elsworth, Cambridgeshire,
CB3 8HY
Ⓣ (01954) 267414
Ⓕ (01954) 267414
Ⓔ john.twibell@talk21.com
Contact: Drs J D & J M Twibell
Opening Times: By appt. only.
Min Mail Order UK: £10.00
Cat. Cost: 3 x 1st class
Credit Cards: None.
Specialities: Nat. Colls. of *Artemisia* (incl. *Seriphidium*) & *Nerium oleander*. Wide range of *Artemisia* & *Seriphidium, Nerium oleander*. Ltd. stocks. Orders may require propagation from Collection material, for which we are the primary reference source.
Map Ref: E, C2

EExo THE EXOTIC GARDEN COMPANY ♿
Hall Farm, Saxmundham Road, Aldeburgh, Nr. Ipswich, Suffolk, IP15 5JD
Ⓣ (01728) 454456
Ⓕ (01473) 787158
Ⓦ www.theexoticgardenco.co.uk
Also sells wholesale
Contact: Matthew Couchy
Opening Times: 1000-1700 Mon-Sat, 1000-1600 Sun.
Cat. Cost: A4 Sae
Credit Cards: MasterCard Visa Switch
Specialities: Palms (hardy & half-hardy), bamboos, tree ferns & other exotics.
Map Ref: E, C3

EFer THE FERN NURSERY ⊠ ♿
Grimsby Road, Binbrook,
Lincolnshire,
LN8 6DH
Ⓣ (01472) 398092
Ⓔ richard@timm.984fsnet.co.uk
Ⓦ www.fernnursery.co.uk
Also sells wholesale
Contact: R N Timm
Opening Times: 0900-1700 Sat & Sun Apr-Oct or by appt.
Min Mail Order UK: Nmc
Min Mail Order EU: Nmc
Cat. Cost: 2 x 1st class
Credit Cards: None.
Specialities: Ferns & hardy perennials. Note: only plants listed in the mail order part of the catalogue will be sent mail order.
Map Ref: E, A1 **OS Grid Ref:** TF212942

EFEx FLORA EXOTICA ⊠ ✈ €
Pasadena, South-Green, Fingringhoe,
Colchester, Essex,
CO5 7DR
Ⓣ (01206) 729414
Contact: J Beddoes
Opening Times: Not open, mail order only.
Min Mail Order UK: Nmc
Min Mail Order EU: Nmc
Cat. Cost: 4 x 1st class
Credit Cards: None.
Specialities: Exotic flora incl. orchids.

EFly THE FLY TRAP PLANTS ⊠ ⌂
160 Kimberley Road, Lowestoft,
Suffolk, NR33 0UA
Ⓣ (01502) 584689
Ⓜ 07765 061629
Ⓕ (01502) 584689
Ⓔ sales@tftplants.co.uk
Ⓦ http://tftplants.co.uk
Contact: Pauline Steward
Opening Times: By appt. only.
Min Mail Order UK: Nmc
Cat. Cost: 1 x 1st class sae
Credit Cards: None.
Specialities: All kinds of carnivorous plants.
Map Ref: E, C3

EFpt FILLPOTS NURSERY ⊠
52 Straight Road, Boxted,
Colchester, Essex, CO4 5RB
Ⓣ (01206) 272389
Ⓕ (01206) 272389
Ⓔ plants@fillpots.fsnet.co.uk
Ⓦ www.fillpots.com
Also sells wholesale
Contact: Richard, Mary or Les Brann
Opening Times: 0900-1700 Mon-Sat, 1000-1600 Sun.
Min Mail Order UK: £6.60 + p&p
Cat. Cost: 3 x 1st class
Credit Cards: Switch Solo MasterCard Visa
Specialities: *Fuchsia* & bedding plants. Limited access for wheelchair users.
Map Ref: E, C3 **OS Grid Ref:** 337997

EFtx FERNATIX ⊠ ⌂
Ivy Cottage, Ixworth Road, Honington,
Suffolk, IP31 1QY
Ⓣ (01359) 269373
Ⓔ fernatix@supanet.com
Ⓦ www.fernatix.co.uk
Contact: Steven Fletcher & Kerry Robinson

Opening Times: By appt. only.
Min Mail Order UK: £15.00
Cat. Cost: 5 x 1st class for cat., or sae for plant list.
Credit Cards: None.
Specialities: Ferns, hardy & greenhouse species & cultivars. Some available in ltd. numbers only.
Map Ref: E, C2

EFul FULBROOKE NURSERY ⊠
Home Farm, Westley Waterless,
Newmarket, Suffolk, CB8 0RG
Ⓣ (01638) 507124
Ⓕ (01638) 507124
Ⓔ fulbrook@clara.net
Ⓦ www.fulbrooke.co.uk
Contact: Paul Lazard
Opening Times: By appt. most times incl. w/ends.
Min Mail Order UK: £5.50 + p&p
Min Mail Order EU: £6.00 + p&p
Cat. Cost: 3 x 1st class
Credit Cards: None.
Specialities: Bamboos & grasses.
Map Ref: E, C2

EGFP GRANGE FARM PLANTS ⊠ ♿
Grange Farm, 38 Fishergate Road, Sutton St James, Spalding, Lincolnshire, PE12 0EZ
Ⓣ (01945) 440240
Ⓜ 07742 138760
Ⓕ (01945) 440355
Ⓔ ellis.family@tinyonline.co.uk
Contact: M C Ellis
Opening Times: By appt. only.
Min Mail Order UK: Nmc
Cat. Cost: 1 x 1st class
Credit Cards: None.
Specialities: Rare trees & shrubs, esp. *Juglans, Fraxinus*. Some species in ltd supply.
Map Ref: E, B2 **OS Grid Ref:** TF3818

EGln GLENHIRST CACTUS NURSERY ⊠ ✈
Station Road, Swineshead, Nr. Boston, Lincolnshire, PE20 3NX
Ⓣ (01205) 820314
Ⓕ (01205) 820614
Ⓔ info@cacti4u.co.uk
Ⓦ www.cacti4u.co.uk
Contact: N C & S A Bell
Opening Times: Visitors welcome, but by telephone appt. only.
Min Mail Order UK: Nmc
Min Mail Order EU: Nmc
Cat. Cost: 2 x 1st class
Credit Cards: Visa MasterCard Switch Solo Electron
Specialities: Extensive range of cacti & succulent plants & seeds, incl. Christmas cacti & orchid cacti. Hardy & half-hardy desert plants. Display gardens. Palms, *Cordyline, Phormium* & other hardy architectural plants. Note: exports plants & seeds to EU, seeds only outside the EU.
Map Ref: E, B1 **OS Grid Ref:** TF245408

EGlv GLENVILLE NURSERIES ⊠ ♿ ◆
King John Bank, Walpole St Andrew, Wisbech, Cambridgeshire, PE14 7LD
Ⓣ (01945) 780020
Ⓕ (01945) 780078
Ⓔ brtowler@btopenworld.com
Ⓦ www.glenvillenurseries.co.uk
Also sells wholesale
Contact: B R Towler
Opening Times: 1000-1600 Mon-Fri, Sat by arrangement, closed Sun.
Min Mail Order UK: £6.00 + p&p
Min Mail Order EU: £30.00 + p&p
Cat. Cost: 2 x 2nd class
Credit Cards: MasterCard Switch Delta Visa
Specialities: Young flowering, ornamental & climbing shrubs. Also conifers.
Map Ref: E, B1 **OS Grid Ref:** TF487188

EGol GOLDBROOK PLANTS ⊠ ✈
Hoxne, Eye, Suffolk, IP21 5AN
Ⓣ (01379) 668770
Ⓕ (01379) 668770
Contact: Sandra Bond
Opening Times: 1000-1700 or dusk if earlier, Thu-Sun Apr-Sep, Sat & Sun Oct-Mar or by appt. Closed during Jan, Chelsea & Hampton Court Shows.
Min Mail Order UK: £15.00 + p&p
Min Mail Order EU: £100.00 + p&p
Cat. Cost: 4 x 1st class
Credit Cards: None.
Specialities: Very large range of *Hosta* (1100+), *Hemerocallis*.
Map Ref: E, C3

EGoo ELISABETH GOODWIN NURSERIES ⊠ ⛟ ♿
Elm Tree Farm, 1 Beeches Road, West Row, Bury St Edmunds, Suffolk, IP28 8NP
Ⓣ (01638) 713050
Ⓔ mail@e-g-n.co.uk
Ⓦ www.e-g-n.co.uk
Also sells wholesale

KEY
⊠ Mail order to UK or EU — ⛟ Delivers to shows
✈ Exports beyond EU — € Euro accepted
♿ Accessible by wheelchair — ◆ See Display advertisement

E

Contact: Elisabeth Goodwin
Opening Times: The nursery will hopefully be re-opening in 2004. Please see website or phone for details.
Min Mail Order UK: £15.00
Cat. Cost: 6 x 1st class or sae for list.
Credit Cards: None.
Specialities: Drought tolerant plants for both sun & shade esp. *Helianthemum, Sedum, Teucrium, Vinca,* grasses, *Aquilegia, Digitalis, Achillea, Agastache* & *Onosma*. Some plants grown in ltd. quantities.
Map Ref: E, C2

EGra GRASMERE PLANTS ⊠ ♿
Grasmere, School Road, Terrington St John, Wisbech, Cambridgeshire, PE14 7SE
Ⓣ (01945) 880514
Contact: Roger Fleming
Opening Times: 1000-1700 Fri-Wed, closed Thu, Mar-late Oct, other times by appt. Please phone first. Garden open.
Min Mail Order UK: £15.00 + p&p*
Cat. Cost: 2 x 2nd class
Credit Cards: None.
Specialities: Hardy perennials incl. *Geranium* & crocosmias, shrubs & dwarf conifers. Some stock available in small quantities only. *Note: mail order perennials only.
Map Ref: E, B1 **OS Grid Ref:** 537143

EHan HANGING GARDENS NURSERIES LTD € ♿
Ongar Road West, A414 Writtle, Chelmsford, Essex, CM1 3NT
Ⓣ (01245) 421020
Ⓕ (01245) 422293
Ⓔ @hangingardens.co.uk
Ⓦ www.hangingardens.co.uk
Contact: Jim Drake, Bob Teasell, Nick Mennie
Opening Times: 0900-1730, 7 days.
Cat. Cost: None issued
Credit Cards: All major credit/debit cards.
Specialities: *Clematis*, David Austin roses, basket & patio plants, excellent range of hardy nursery stock. Note: (office) 15 Further Meadow, Writtle, Chelmsford CM1 3LE.
Map Ref: E, D2

EHoe HOECROFT PLANTS ⊠ € ♿ ◆
Severals Grange, Holt Road, Wood Norton, Dereham, Norfolk, NR20 5BL
Ⓣ (01362) 684206
Ⓕ (01362) 684206
Ⓔ hoecroft@acedial.co.uk
Ⓦ www.hoecroft.co.uk
Contact: Jane Lister
Opening Times: 1000-1600 Thu-Sun 1st Apr-1st Oct or by appt.
Min Mail Order UK: Nmc
Min Mail Order EU: Nmc
Cat. Cost: 5 x 2nd class/£1coin
Credit Cards: None.
Specialities: 240 varieties of variegated and 300 varieties of coloured-leaved plants in all species. 270 grasses. Note: nursery 2 miles north of Guist on B1110.
Map Ref: E, B3 **OS Grid Ref:** 008289

EHol HOLKHAM GARDENS
Holkham Park, Wells-next-the-Sea, Norfolk, NR23 1AB
Ⓣ (01328) 711636
Ⓔ info@holkhamgardens.com
Contact: Peter Gill, Trevor Gill
Opening Times: 1000-1700 7 days Mar-Oct. 1100-dusk 7 days Nov-Feb. Closed mid Dec-early Jan.
Cat. Cost: 3 x 1st class
Credit Cards: Access Visa Switch MasterCard
Specialities: Wide range of shrubs, herbaceous perennials, alpines, wall plants, climbers, roses, conservatory plants and herbs, both common & unusual. Some plants in ltd. supply.
Map Ref: E, B1

EHon HONEYSOME AQUATIC NURSERY ⊠
The Row, Sutton, Nr. Ely, Cambridgeshire, CB6 2PF
Ⓣ (01353) 778889
Ⓕ (01353) 777291
Also sells wholesale
Contact: Mrs L S Bond
Opening Times: At all times by appt. only.
Min Mail Order UK: Nmc
Cat. Cost: 2 x 1st class
Credit Cards: None.
Specialities: Hardy aquatic, bog & marginal.
Map Ref: E, C2

EHrv HARVEYS GARDEN PLANTS ⊠ ń € ♿
Mulberry Cottage, Bradfield St George, Bury St Edmunds, Suffolk, IP30 0AY
Ⓣ (01284) 386777
Ⓕ (01284) 386777 & answerphone
Ⓔ roger@harveysgardenplants.co.uk
Ⓦ www.harveysgardenplants.co.uk
www.hellebore.co.uk
Contact: Roger Harvey
Opening Times: 0930-1700 Thu & Fri, 0930-1300 Sat, 15th Jan-30th Jun & 1st Sep-31st Oct. Other times by arrangement.
Min Mail Order UK: 6 plants + p&p
Min Mail Order EU: Please enquire.
Cat. Cost: 7 x 2nd class
Credit Cards: All major credit/debit cards.

Specialities: *Helleborus, Anemone, Epimedium, Euphorbia, Eryngium, Astrantia, Pulmonaria* & other herbaceous perennials. Woodland plants, heleniums. Nat. Coll. of *Helenium* being set up with NCCPG.
Map Ref: E, C2

EHul HULL FARM ⊠
Spring Valley Lane, Ardleigh, Colchester, Essex, CO7 7SA
Ⓣ (01206) 230045
Ⓕ (01206) 230820
Also sells wholesale
Contact: J Fryer & Sons
Opening Times: 1000-1600 7 days excl. Xmas.
Min Mail Order UK: £30.00 + p&p
Cat. Cost: 5 x 2nd class
Credit Cards: MasterCard Visa
Specialities: Conifers, grasses.
Map Ref: E, C3 **OS Grid Ref:** GR043274

EHyt HYTHE ALPINES ⊠ € ♿
Methwold Hythe, Thetford, Norfolk, IP26 4QH
Ⓣ (01366) 728543
Ⓕ (01366) 728543
Contact: Mike Smith
Opening Times: 1000-1700 Tue & Wed Mar-Oct. Also every w/end Apr-Jun.
Min Mail Order UK: Nmc
Min Mail Order EU: Nmc
Cat. Cost: 6 x 1st class, 4 x IRCs
Credit Cards: None.
Specialities: Rare & unusual alpines, rock garden plants & bulbs for enthusiasts & exhibitors.
Map Ref: E, C2

EJRN JOHN RAY NURSERY ♿
36 Station Road, Braintree, Essex, CM7 3QJ
Ⓜ 07866 296531
Ⓕ (01376) 322484
Also sells wholesale
Contact: Brian James
Opening Times: 0900-1730 Sat, 1030-1630 Sun & B/Hol.
Cat. Cost: None issued.
Credit Cards: None.
Specialities: *Pittosporum.*
Map Ref: E, D2

EJWh JILL WHITE ⊠
'St Davids', Recreation Way, Brightlingsea, Essex, CO7 0NJ
Ⓣ (01206) 303547
Also sells wholesale
Contact: Jill White
Opening Times: By appt. only.
Min Mail Order UK: Nmc
Cat. Cost: Sae
Credit Cards: None.
Specialities: *Cyclamen* species esp. *Cyclamen parviflorum*. Also seed. Note: small quantities only.
Map Ref: E, D3

EKen KENWICK FARMHOUSE NURSERIES ◆
Kenwick Road, Louth, Lincolnshire, LN11 8NW
Ⓣ (01507) 606469
Ⓕ (01507) 606469
Ⓔ info@kenwicknursery.co.uk
Ⓦ www.kenwicknursery.co.uk
Contact: Janet Elmhirst
Opening Times: 0930-1700 (dusk in winter)Tue-Sat, closed Mon except B/hol. 1000-1600 Sun. Closed Jan.
Cat. Cost: 2 x 1st class
Credit Cards: None.
Specialities: Hardy plants.
Map Ref: E, A2 **OS Grid Ref:** TF342853

EKMF KATHLEEN MUNCASTER FUCHSIAS ♿
18 Field Lane, Morton, Gainsborough, Lincolnshire, DN21 3BY
Ⓣ (01427) 612329
Ⓔ jim@smuncaster.freeserve.co.uk
Ⓦ www.kathleenmuncasterfuchsias.co.uk
Contact: Kathleen Muncaster
Opening Times: 1000-dusk Thu-Tue. After mid-Jun please phone to check.
Cat. Cost: 2 x 1st class
Credit Cards: None.
Specialities: *Fuchsia.* Nat. Coll. of Hardy *Fuchsia* (full status).
Map Ref: E, A1

ELan LANGTHORNS PLANTERY ⊠ ♿
High Cross Lane
West, Little Canfield, Dunmow, Essex, CM6 1TD
Ⓣ (01371) 872611
Ⓕ (01371) 872611
Ⓔ info@langthorns.com
Ⓦ www.langthorns.com
Contact: E Cannon
Opening Times: 1000-1700 or dusk (if earlier) 7 days excl. Xmas fortnight.
Min Mail Order UK: Nmc
Cat. Cost: £1.50

KEY
⊠ Mail order to UK or EU — Delivers to shows
Exports beyond EU — € Euro accepted
♿ Accessible by wheelchair — ◆ See Display advertisement

Credit Cards: Visa Access Switch MasterCard Delta
Specialities: Wide general range with many unusual plants. Note: mail order 9cm perennials, 2 & 3 litre shrubs.
Map Ref: E, D2 **OS Grid Ref:** 592204

E

ELau LAUREL FARM HERBS ⊠ ♿
Main Road, Kelsale,
Saxmundham,
Suffolk, IP13 2RG
Ⓣ (01728) 668223
Ⓔ laurelfarmherbs@aol.com
Ⓦ www.theherbfarm.co.uk
Contact: Chris Seagon
Opening Times: 1000-1700 Wed-Mon 1st Mar-31st Oct. 1000-1500 Wed-Fri 1st Nov-28th Feb.
Min Mail Order UK: 6 plants + p&p
Min Mail Order EU: 12 plants
Cat. Cost: Online only.
Credit Cards: Visa MasterCard Switch Delta
Specialities: Herbs esp. rosemary, thyme, lavender, mint, comfrey & sage. Note: mail orders accepted by email, phone or post.
Map Ref: E, C3

EMag MAGPIES NURSERY ♿
Green Lane, Mundford,
Norfolk,
IP26 5HS
Ⓣ (01842) 878496
Ⓔ magpies@eidosnet.co.uk
Contact: Patricia Cooper
Opening Times: 0900-1700 Tue-Fri, 1000-1700 Sat & Sun. Closed Mon.
Min Mail Order UK:
Min Mail Order EU:
Cat. Cost: Free
Credit Cards: None.
Specialities: Unusual hardy perennials, grasses & foliage plants.
Map Ref: E, C2

EMan MANOR NURSERY ♿
Thaxted Road, Wimbish,
Saffron Walden, Essex,
CB10 2UT
Ⓣ (01799) 513481
Ⓕ (01799) 513481
Ⓔ flora@gardenplants.co.uk
Ⓦ www.gardenplants.co.uk
Contact: William Lyall
Opening Times: 0900-1700 summer. 0900-1600 winter. Closed Xmas.
Cat. Cost: 4 x 2nd class
Credit Cards: Visa Access Switch Eurocard MasterCard
Specialities: Uncommon perennials, grasses, hardy *Geranium, Sedum* & cottage garden plants. Variegated & coloured foliage plants. Many newly introduced cultivars.
Map Ref: E, C2

EMar LESLEY MARSHALL ⊠ ♿
Uncommon Garden Plants,
Islington Lodge Cottage,
Tilney All Saints, King's Lynn,
Norfolk, PE34 4SF
Ⓣ (01553) 765103
Ⓔ lesley.marshall@amserve.net
Contact: Lesley & Peter Marshall
Opening Times: 0930-1800 Mon, Wed, Fri-Sun Mar-Oct.
Min Mail Order UK: 6 plants
Cat. Cost: £1 refundable. £1 coin/4 x 1st class
Credit Cards: None.
Specialities: Uncommon garden plants, hardy perennials & plants for foliage effect. *Hemerocallis* & *Crocosmia*. Choice seed list. Some plants available in ltd. quantities. Note: mail order Feb-Apr (spring list) & Sep-Nov (autumn list).
Map Ref: E, B1

EMcA S M MCARD (SEEDS) ⊠
39 West Road, Pointon, Sleaford,
Lincolnshire, NG34 0NA
Ⓣ (01529) 240765
Ⓕ (01529) 240765
Ⓔ seeds@smmcard.com
Ⓦ www.smmcard.com
Also sells wholesale
Contact: Susan McArd
Opening Times: Not open, mail order only.
Min Mail Order UK: Nmc
Min Mail Order EU: Nmc
Cat. Cost: 2 x 2nd class
Credit Cards: None.
Specialities: Unusual & giant vegetables esp. tree (Egyptian) onion. Seeds & plants.

EMFP MILLS' FARM PLANTS & GARDENS ⊠
Norwich Road, Mendlesham, Suffolk,
IP14 5NQ
Ⓣ (01449) 766425
Ⓕ (01449) 766425
Ⓔ sue@millsfarmplants.co.uk
Ⓦ www.millsfarmplants.co.uk
Contact: Peter & Susan Russell
Opening Times: 0900-1730 Wed-Sun Mar-Nov & B/hol Mon.
Min Mail Order UK: Nmc
Min Mail Order EU: Nmc
Cat. Cost: 5 x 2nd class
Credit Cards: All major credit/debit cards.

Specialities: Pinks, old roses, scented plants, wide general range.
Map Ref: E, C3 **OS Grid Ref:** TM119650

EMFW MICKFIELD WATERGARDEN CENTRE LTD ⊠ ✈ € ♿
Debenham Road, Mickfield, Stowmarket, Suffolk, IP14 5LP
Ⓣ (01449) 711336
Ⓕ (01449) 711018
Ⓔ mike@mickfield.co.uk
Ⓦ www.watergardenshop.co.uk
Also sells wholesale
Contact: Mike & Yvonne Burch
Opening Times: 0930-1700 7 days.
Min Mail Order UK: Nmc
Min Mail Order EU: £25.00 + p&p
Cat. Cost: £1.00
Credit Cards: Visa Access MasterCard Switch
Specialities: Hardy aquatics, *Nymphaea* & moisture lovers.
Map Ref: E, C3

EMic MICKFIELD HOSTAS ⊠ ⛺ € ♿
The Poplars, Mickfield, Stowmarket, Suffolk, IP14 5LH
Ⓣ (01449) 711576, m. 07720 380361
Ⓕ (01449) 711576
Ⓔ mickfieldhostas@btconnect.com
Ⓦ www.mickfieldhostas.co.uk
Contact: Mr & Mrs R L C Milton
Opening Times: For specified dates see catalogue or website.
Min Mail Order UK: Nmc
Min Mail Order EU: Nmc
Cat. Cost: 4 x 1st class*
Credit Cards: Visa MasterCard
Specialities: *Hosta*, over 1000 varieties (some subject to availability) mostly from USA. New varieties become available during the season. *Note: catalogue cost refunded on order.
Map Ref: E, C3

EMil MILL RACE NURSERY € ♿
New Road, Aldham, Colchester, Essex, CO6 3QT
Ⓣ (01206) 242521
Ⓕ (01206) 241616
Ⓔ admin@millracenursery.co.uk
Ⓦ www.millracenursery.co.uk
Also sells wholesale
Contact: Bill Mathews
Opening Times: 0900-1730 7 days.
Cat. Cost: Sae + 2 x 1st class
Credit Cards: Access Visa Diners Switch
Specialities: Over 400 varieties of herbaceous & many unusual trees, shrubs & climbers.
Map Ref: E, C2 **OS Grid Ref:** TL918268

EMon MONKSILVER NURSERY ⊠ €
Oakington Road, Cottenham, Cambridgeshire, CB4 8TW
Ⓣ (01954) 251555
Ⓕ (01223) 502887
Ⓔ plants@monksilver.com
Ⓦ www.monksilver.com
Contact: Joe Sharman & Alan Leslie
Opening Times: 1000-1600 Fri & Sat 1 Mar-30 Jun, 20 Sep + Fri & Sat Oct 2002.
Min Mail Order UK: £15.00 + p&p
Min Mail Order EU: £30.00 + p&p
Cat. Cost: 8 x 1st class
Credit Cards: None.
Specialities: Herbaceous plants, grasses, *Anthemis, Arum, Helianthus, Lamium, Nepeta, Monarda, Salvia, Vinca,* sedges & variegated plants. Many NCCPG `Pink Sheet' plants. Ferns.
Map Ref: E, C2

ENBC NORFOLK BAMBOO COMPANY ⊠
Vine Cottage, The Drift, Ingoldisthorpe, Kings Lynn, Norfolk, PE31 6NW
Ⓣ (01485) 543935
Ⓕ (01485) 543314
Ⓔ Lewdyer@hotmail.com
Contact: Lewis Dyer
Opening Times: 1000-1800 Fri, Apr-Sep, or by appt.
Min Mail Order UK: £12.00 + p&p
Cat. Cost: 1 x 1st class sae for price list
Credit Cards: None.
Specialities: Bamboos.
Map Ref: E, B2 **OS Grid Ref:** 683331

ENot NOTCUTTS NURSERIES ⊠ ✈ € ♿
Woodbridge, Suffolk, IP12 4AF
Ⓣ (01394) 445400
Ⓕ (01394) 445440
Ⓔ sales@notcutts.co.uk
Ⓦ www.notcutts.co.uk
Also sells wholesale
Contact: Plant Adviser
Opening Times: Garden centres 0900-1800 Mon-Sat & 1030-1630 Sun. Check for local variations and late night openings.
Min Mail Order UK: £250.00 + p&p (£30.00 if collected from a Notcutts Garden Centre)
Min Mail Order EU: £1000.00 + p&p
Cat. Cost: £5.00 + £1.25
Credit Cards: Visa Access Switch Connect

KEY
⊠ Mail order to UK or EU ⛺ Delivers to shows
✈ Exports beyond EU € Euro accepted
♿ Accessible by wheelchair ◆ See Display advertisement

Specialities: Wide general range. Specialist list of *Syringa*. Nat. Coll. of *Hibiscus*.
Map Ref: E, C3 **OS Grid Ref:** TM268487

EOas OASIS ⊠
42 Greenwood Avenue, South Benfleet, Essex, SS7 1LD
Ⓣ (01268) 757666
Ⓔ paul@oasisdesigns.co.uk
Ⓦ www.oasisdesigns.co.uk
Contact: Paul Spracklin
Opening Times: Strictly by appt. only.
Min Mail Order UK: Nmc
Cat. Cost: None issued, see website.
Credit Cards: None.
Specialities: Small nursery offering exciting new range of cold-hardy bromeliads & succulents. Most items held in ltd. quantities. Note: mail order sent by overnight courier only.
Map Ref: E, D2

EOHP OLD HALL PLANTS ⊠ €
1 The Old Hall, Barsham, Beccles, Suffolk, NR34 8HB
Ⓣ (01502) 717475
Ⓔ info@oldhallplants.co.uk
Ⓦ www.oldhallplants.co.uk
Contact: Janet Elliott
Opening Times: By appt. most days, please phone first.
Min Mail Order UK: Nmc
Min Mail Order EU: Nmc
Cat. Cost: 4 x 1st class
Credit Cards: None.
Specialities: Herbs, over 500 varieties grown. *Mentha, Plectranthus, Streptocarpus*. Partial wheelchair access.
Map Ref: E, C3 **OS Grid Ref:** TM395904

EOrn ORNAMENTAL CONIFERS ◆
22 Chapel Road, Terrington St Clement, Kings Lynn, Norfolk, PE34 4ND
Ⓣ (01553) 828874
Ⓕ (01553) 828874
Contact: Peter Rotchell
Opening Times: 0930-1700 Thu-Tue, closed Wed. Closed 20th Dec-2nd Feb.
Credit Cards: None.
Specialities: Conifers.
Map Ref: E, B1

EPem PEMBROKE FARM NURSERY ⊠ ♠ € ♿
Pembroke Farm, Barway, Ely, Cambridgeshire, CB7 5UB
Ⓣ (01353) 722903
Ⓕ (01353) 722903
Ⓔ Pemcacti@aol.com/enquiries@cactiandsucculents.co.uk
Ⓦ www.cactiandsucculents.co.uk
Also sells wholesale
Contact: Richard & Sheena Drane
Opening Times: Please phone or check website for opening times.
Min Mail Order UK: Nmc
Cat. Cost: 1 x 1st class
Credit Cards: None.
Specialities: Cacti & succulents incl. *Agave, Aloe* & *Sempervivum*. Many plants are available in limited quantities. Note: mail order sempervivums only.
Map Ref: E, C2

EPfP THE PLACE FOR PLANTS € ♿
East Bergholt Place, East Bergholt, Suffolk, CO7 6UP
Ⓣ (01206) 299224
Ⓕ (01206) 299224
Ⓔ sales@placeforplants.co.uk
Contact: Rupert & Sara Eley
Opening Times: 1000-1700 (or dusk if earlier) 7 days. Closed Easter Sun. Garden open Mar-Oct.
Cat. Cost: 2 x 1st class
Credit Cards: Visa Access MasterCard Eurocard Delta Switch
Specialities: Wide range of specialist & popular plants. 15 acre mature garden.
Map Ref: E, C3

EPGN PARK GREEN NURSERIES ⊠ ✈
Wetheringsett, Stowmarket, Suffolk, IP14 5QH
Ⓣ (01728) 860139
Ⓕ (01728) 861277
Ⓔ nurseries@parkgreen.fsnet.co.uk
Ⓦ www.parkgreen.co.uk
Contact: Richard & Mary Ford
Opening Times: 1000-1600 Mon-Fri & 1000-1300 Sat, 1 Mar-25 Sep.
Min Mail Order UK: Nmc
Min Mail Order EU: Nmc
Cat. Cost: 4 x 1st class
Credit Cards: Visa MasterCard Delta Switch
Specialities: *Hosta,* ornamental grasses & herbaceous.
Map Ref: E, C3 **OS Grid Ref:** TM136644

EPla P W PLANTS ⊠ ♠ ♿
Sunnyside, Heath Road, Kenninghall, Norfolk, NR16 2DS
Ⓣ (01953) 888212
Ⓕ (01953) 888212
Ⓔ pw.plants@paston.co.uk
Ⓦ www.hardybamboo.com

Contact: Paul Whittaker
Opening Times: Every Fri & last Sat in every month, plus all Sats Apr-Sep.
Min Mail Order UK: Nmc
Min Mail Order EU: Nmc
Cat. Cost: 5 x 1st class
Credit Cards: Visa MasterCard Switch JCB Solo
Specialities: Bamboos, grasses, choice shrubs & perennials. Note: does not deliver to Chelsea Show.
Map Ref: E, C3

EPot **POTTERTONS NURSERY** ⊠ ✈ ♠ € ♿
Moortown Road, Nettleton, Caistor, Lincolnshire, LN7 6HX
Ⓣ (01472) 851714
Ⓕ (01472) 852580
Ⓔ rob@pottertons.co.uk
Ⓦ www.pottertons.co.uk
Contact: Robert Potterton
Opening Times: 0900-1630 7 days.
Min Mail Order UK: Nmc
Min Mail Order EU: Nmc
Cat. Cost: £1.00 in stamps
Credit Cards: MasterCard Switch Visa
Specialities: Alpines, dwarf bulbs, conifers, shrubs & woodland plants. Hardy orchids & *Pleione*. Seed list sent out in Nov.
Map Ref: E, A1 **OS Grid Ref:** TA091001

EPPr **THE PLANTSMAN'S PREFERENCE** ⊠ ♠ ♿
(Office) Lynwood, Hopton Road, Garboldisham, Diss, Norfolk, IP22 2QN
Ⓣ (01953) 681439 (office) (07799) 855559 (nursery)
Ⓔ info@plantpref.co.uk
Ⓦ www.plantpref.co.uk
Contact: Jenny & Tim Fuller
Opening Times: 0930-1700 Fri, Sat & Sun Mar-Oct. Other times by appt.
Min Mail Order UK: £15.00
Min Mail Order EU: £30.00
Cat. Cost: 5 x 1st class/IRCs. Also Online.
Credit Cards: All major credit/debit cards.
Specialities: Hardy *Geranium* (450), grasses & sedges (600+). Unusual & interesting perennials. Nat. Coll. of *Molinia*. Note: nursery is at Hall Farm, Church Road, South Lopham, Diss.
Map Ref: E, C3 **OS Grid Ref:** TM041819

EPts **POTASH NURSERY** ⊠ ♠ ♿
Cow Green, Bacton, Stowmarket, Suffolk, IP14 4HJ
Ⓣ (01449) 781671
Ⓔ enquiries@potashnursery.co.uk
Ⓦ www.potashnursery.co.uk
Contact: M W Clare
Opening Times: 1000-1700 Fri-Sun & B/hol Mons mid Feb-mid Jun.
Min Mail Order UK: £10.00
Cat. Cost: 4 x 1st class
Credit Cards: Visa Delta MasterCard
Specialities: *Fuchsia.*
Map Ref: E, C3 **OS Grid Ref:** TM0565NE

EPyc **PENNYCROSS PLANTS**
Earith Road, Colne, Huntingdon, Cambridgeshire, PE28 3NL
Ⓣ (01487) 841520
Ⓔ plants@pennycross99.freeserve.co.uk
Also sells wholesale
Contact: Janet M Buist
Opening Times: 0900-dusk Thu, 1400-dusk Fri, 1st Mar-31st Oct. Other times by appt.
Cat. Cost: 4 x 2nd class
Credit Cards: None.
Specialities: Hardy perennials. Grasses. Some plants available in ltd. quantities only.
Map Ref: E, C2 **OS Grid Ref:** TL378759

EPza **PLANTAZIA** ⊠ ♿
Woodford Farm, Weston Green Road, Weston Longville, Norwich, Norfolk, NR9 5LG
Ⓣ (01603) 880757
Ⓕ (01603) 880757
Ⓔ plantazia.co@virgin.net
Ⓦ Plantazia-nursery.co.uk
Contact: Mike Read
Opening Times: 1000-1700, 7 days, 1st Mar-31st Oct. 1000-1600 Sat & Sun only Nov-Dec. Closed Jan & Feb. Mail order all year round.
Min Mail Order UK: Nmc
Cat. Cost: 2 x 1st class
Credit Cards: ALL
Specialities: Grasses, *Gunnera, Bamboo.*
Map Ref: E, B3 **OS Grid Ref:** TG090153

ER&R **RHODES & ROCKLIFFE** ⊠ ✈ €
2 Nursery Road, Nazeing, Essex, EN9 2JE
Ⓣ (01992) 451598 (office hours)
Ⓕ (01992) 440673
Ⓔ RRBegonias@aol.com
Contact: David Rhodes or John Rockliffe
Opening Times: By appt.
Min Mail Order UK: £2.50 + p&p
Min Mail Order EU: £5.00 + p&p
Cat. Cost: 2 x 1st class

KEY
⊠ Mail order to UK or EU ♠ Delivers to shows
✈ Exports beyond EU € Euro accepted
♿ Accessible by wheelchair ◆ See Display advertisement

Credit Cards: None.
Specialities: *Begonia* species & hybrids. Nat. Coll. of *Begonia*. Plants propagated to order. Note: mail order Apr-Sep only.
Map Ref: E, D2

ERea **READS NURSERY** ⊠ ✈ ♿
Hales Hall, Loddon, Norfolk, NR14 6QW
Ⓣ (01508) 548395
Ⓕ (01508) 548040
Ⓔ plants@readsnursery.co.uk
Ⓦ www.readsnursery.co.uk
Contact: Stephen Read
Opening Times: 1000-1630 (dusk if earlier) Mon-Sat, 1100-1600 Sun & B/hols Easter-end Sep & by appt.
Min Mail Order UK: Nmc
Min Mail Order EU: £10.00 + p&p
Cat. Cost: 4 x 1st class
Credit Cards: Visa Access Switch
Specialities: Conservatory plants, vines, *Citrus*, figs & unusual fruits & nuts. Wall shrubs & climbers. Scented & aromatic hardy plants. UK grown. Nat. Colls. of *Citrus*, figs, vines. Mostly accessible by wheelchair (some gravel paths).
Map Ref: E, B3 **OS Grid Ref:** TM369960

ERob **ROBIN SAVILL CLEMATIS SPECIALIST** ⊠ ✈
(Office) 2 Bury Cottages, Bury Road, Pleshey, Chelmsford, Essex, CM3 1HB
Ⓣ (01245) 237380
Ⓕ (01245) 603882
Also sells wholesale
Contact: Robin Savill
Opening Times: Visitors by appt. only.
Min Mail Order UK: 1 plant + p&p
Min Mail Order EU: 1 plant + p&p
Cat. Cost: £2.50 or 10 x 1st class
Credit Cards: None.
Specialities: Over 800 varieties of *Clematis* incl. many unusual species & cvs from around the world. Nat. Coll. of *Clematis viticella*.
Map Ref: E, D2

ERod **THE RODINGS PLANTERY** ⊠ ✈ ⌂ €
Anchor Lane, Abbess Roding, Essex, CM5 0JW
Ⓣ (01279) 876421
Ⓔ andy@bamboo100.fsnet.co.uk
Contact: Jane & Andy Mogridge
Opening Times: By appt. only. Occasional open days, please phone for details.
Min Mail Order UK: £15.00 + p&p
Min Mail Order EU: £500.00 + p&p
Cat. Cost: 3 x 1st class
Credit Cards: None.
Specialities: *Bamboo*. Rare & unusual trees.
Map Ref: E, D2

ERom **THE ROMANTIC GARDEN** ⊠ ✈ € ♿ ◆
Swannington, Norwich, Norfolk, NR9 5NW
Ⓣ (01603) 261488
Ⓕ (01603) 864231
Ⓔ enquiries@romantic-garden-nursery.co.uk
Ⓦ www.romantic-garden-nursery.co.uk
Also sells wholesale
Contact: John Powles/John Carrick
Opening Times: 1000-1700 Wed Fri & Sat all year.
Min Mail Order UK: £5.00 + p&p
Min Mail Order EU: £30.00 + p&p
Cat. Cost: 4 x 1st class
Credit Cards: Visa Access Amex
Specialities: Half-hardy & conservatory. Buxus topiary, ornamental standards, large specimens.
Map Ref: E, B3

ERos **ROSEHOLME NURSERY** ⊠ ✈ ♿
Roseholme Farm, Howsham, Market Rasen, Lincolnshire, LN7 6JZ
Ⓣ (01652) 678661
Ⓕ (01472) 852450
Ⓔ Pbcenterpr@aol.com
Also sells wholesale
Contact: P B Clayton
Opening Times: By appt. for collection of orders.
Min Mail Order UK: Nmc
Min Mail Order EU: Nmc
Cat. Cost: 2 x 2nd class
Credit Cards: None.
Specialities: Underground lines – bulbs, corms, rhizomes & tubers (esp. *Crocus*, *Iris*).
Map Ref: E, A1

ERou **ROUGHAM HALL NURSERIES** ⊠ ✈ ⌂ € ◆
Ipswich Road, Rougham, Bury St Edmunds, Suffolk, IP30 9LZ
Ⓣ 0800 970 7516
Ⓕ (01359) 271149
Ⓔ hardyperennials@aol.com
Ⓦ www.roughamhallnurseries.co.uk
Also sells wholesale
Contact: A A & K G Harbutt
Opening Times: 1000-1600 7 days, 1st Mar-31st Oct. 1000-1600 Mon-Fri 1st Nov-28th Feb.
Min Mail Order UK: Nmc
Min Mail Order EU: Nmc
Cat. Cost: 5 x 1st class
Credit Cards: All major credit/debit cards.

Specialities: Hardy perennials esp. *Aster* (n-a, n-b & species), *Delphinium, Hemerocallis, Iris, Kniphofia, Papaver* & *Phlox*. Nat. Colls. of *Delphinium* & gooseberry. Note delphiniums for collection only, no mail order.
Map Ref: E, C2

ESCh SHEILA CHAPMAN CLEMATIS ⊠ ♠ ♿
Crowther Nurseries, Ongar Road, Abridge, Romford, Essex, RM4 1AA
Ⓣ (01708) 688090
Ⓕ (01708) 688090
Ⓦ www.sheilachapman.co.uk
Contact: Sheila Chapman
Opening Times: 0930-1700 (or dusk in winter) all year excl. Xmas week.
Min Mail Order UK: Nmc
Cat. Cost: 4 x 1st class
Credit Cards: All major credit/debit cards.
Specialities: Over 600 varieties of *Clematis*.
Map Ref: E, D2 **OS Grid Ref:** TL548197

ESgI SEAGATE IRISES ⊠ € ♿
A17 Long Sutton By-Pass, Long Sutton, Lincolnshire, PE12 9RX
Ⓣ (01406) 365138
Ⓕ (01406) 365447
Ⓔ Sales@irises.co.uk
Ⓦ www.irises.co.uk
Contact: Julian Browse or Wendy Browse
Opening Times: 1000-1800 daily May-Sep. Please phone for appt. Oct-Apr.
Min Mail Order UK: £30.00
Min Mail Order EU: Nmc carriage at cost.
Cat. Cost: £2.50 or €5, no stamps pls.
Credit Cards: Visa Access MasterCard Switch
Specialities: Bearded *Iris*, over 600 varieties, modern & historic tall bearded, medians & dwarfs. Many container grown available.
Map Ref: E, B1 **OS Grid Ref:** TF437218

EShb SHRUBLAND PARK NURSERIES
⊠ ♠ € ♿ ◆
Coddenham, Ipswich, Suffolk, IP6 9QJ
Ⓣ (01473) 833187
Ⓜ 07890 527744
Ⓕ (01473) 832838
Ⓔ gill@shrublandparknurseries.co.uk
Ⓦ www.shrublandparknurseries.co.uk
Also sells wholesale
Contact: Gill Stitt
Opening Times: 1000-1700 (dusk if earlier) Wed-Sun or by appt. Please ring first during Dec & Jan. Enter Shrubland Park via gate opposite Sorrel Horse pub, 1 mile north of Claydon.
Min Mail Order UK: £10.00
Min Mail Order EU: £25.00
Cat. Cost: 3 x 1st class, free by email
Credit Cards: All major credit/debit cards.
Specialities: An increasing range of conservatory plants, houseplants & tender perennials, incl. passion flowers, unusual succulents & architectural foliage plants. 500+ hardy perennials. Groups welcome.
Map Ref: E, C3 **OS Grid Ref:** TM128524

ESis SISKIN PLANTS ⊠
30 Jackson Road, Newbourne, Woodbridge, Suffolk, IP12 4NR
Ⓣ (01394) 448068
Ⓕ (01394) 448502
Ⓔ info@siskinplants.co.uk
Ⓦ www.siskinplants.co.uk
Contact: Tricia Newell
Opening Times: Open by appt.
Min Mail Order UK: Nmc
Cat. Cost: 3 x 2nd class
Credit Cards: None.
Specialities: Alpines, sempervivums, small perennials, grasses & dwarf shrubs esp. plants for troughs and dwarf hebes. Some stock only in small quantities.
Map Ref: E, C3

ESlt SCARLETTS QUALITY PLANTS ⊠ ♠ ♿
Nayland Road, West Bergholt, Colchester, Essex, CO6 3DH
Ⓣ (01206) 240466
Ⓕ (01206) 242530
Ⓔ info@scarletts.co.uk
Ⓦ www.scarletts.co.uk
Also sells wholesale.
Contact: Kate Backhouse
Opening Times: By appt. only.
Min Mail Order UK: Nmc
Cat. Cost: Free list
Credit Cards: MasterCard Eurocard Visa Delta
Specialities: Conservatory plants. *Citrus*.
Map Ref: E, C2

ESou SOUTHFIELD NURSERIES ⊠ ♠ ♿
Bourne Road, Morton, Nr. Bourne, Lincolnshire, PE10 0RH
Ⓣ (01778) 570168
Also sells wholesale
Contact: Mr & Mrs B Goodey
Opening Times: 1000-1215 & 1315-1600 7 days. Nov-Jan by appt. only.
Min Mail Order UK: Nmc

KEY
⊠ Mail order to UK or EU ♠ Delivers to shows
✈ Exports beyond EU € Euro accepted
♿ Accessible by wheelchair ◆ See Display advertisement

E

Min Mail Order EU: Nmc
Cat. Cost: 3 x 1st class
Credit Cards: None.
Specialities: A wide range of cacti & succulents incl. some of the rarer varieties, all grown on our own nursery.
Map Ref: E, B1 **OS Grid Ref:** TF094234

ESty STYLE ROSES ⊠ ♠ ♿
10 Meridian Walk, Holbeach, Spalding, Lincolnshire, PE12 7NR
Ⓣ (01406) 424089,
Ⓜ 07932 044093/07780 860415
Ⓕ (01406) 424089
Ⓔ styleroses@aol.com
Ⓦ www.styleroses.co.uk
Also sells wholesale
Contact: Chris Styles, Margaret Styles
Opening Times: Vary, please phone.
Min Mail Order UK: Nmc
Min Mail Order EU: Nmc
Cat. Cost: Free
Credit Cards: None.
Specialities: Roses: standard & bush roses. Note: export subject to countries' plant health requirements, carriage & export certificates where required charged at cost.
Map Ref: E, B1

ESul BRIAN & PEARL SULMAN ⊠ ♠ ♿
54 Kingsway, Mildenhall, Bury St Edmunds, Suffolk, IP28 7HR
Ⓣ (01638) 712297
Ⓕ (01638) 712297
Ⓔ pearl@sulmanspelargoniums.co.uk
Ⓦ www.sulmanspelargoniums.co.uk
Contact: Pearl Sulman
Opening Times: Not open, mail order only. Open w/end 15/16 May 2004 & 5/6 Jun 2004. Phone for information on 2005 dates.
Min Mail Order UK: £20.00
Min Mail Order EU: £20.00
Cat. Cost: 4 x 1st class
Credit Cards: Visa MasterCard
Specialities: *Pelargonium*. Some varieties only available in small numbers.
Map Ref: E, C2 **OS Grid Ref:** TL715747

ETho THORNCROFT CLEMATIS NURSERY ⊠ ✈ ♿
The Lings, Reymerston, Norwich, Norfolk, NR9 4QG
Ⓣ (01953) 850407
Ⓕ (01953) 851788
Ⓔ sales@thorncroft.co.uk
Ⓦ www.thorncroft.co.uk
Contact: Ruth P Gooch
Opening Times: 1000-1600 Tue-Sat all year, closed Sun & Mon. Open B/hol Mon.
Min Mail Order UK: Nmc
Min Mail Order EU: £16.00
Cat. Cost: 6 x 2nd class
Credit Cards: MasterCard Solo Visa Delta Switch
Specialities: *Clematis*. Note: does not export to USA, Canada or Australia.
Map Ref: E, B3 **OS Grid Ref:** TG039062

ETow TOWN FARM NURSERY ⊠ ♿
Street House, The Street, Metfield, Harleston, Norfolk, IP20 0LA
Ⓣ (01379) 586189
Ⓔ david.baker@themail.co.uk
Ⓦ www.madaboutplants.co.uk
Contact: F D Baker
Opening Times: Feb-Oct by appt. only.
Min Mail Order UK: £5.00 + p&p
Min Mail Order EU: £20.00 + p&p
Cat. Cost: Sae
Credit Cards: None.
Specialities: Unusual alpines, border perennials. Also seed. Limited stocks available.
Map Ref: E, C3 **OS Grid Ref:** 62942805

EUJe URBAN JUNGLE ⊠
The Nurseries, Ringland Lane, Old Costessey, Norwich, Norfolk, NR8 5BG
Ⓣ (01603) 744997
Ⓕ (0709) 2366869
Ⓔ liz@urbanjungle.uk.com
Ⓦ www.urbanjungle.uk.com
Contact: Liz Browne
Opening Times: 1000-1700 Tue-Sun, closed Mon, Mar-Oct, 1000-1600 Fri-Sun, Nov-Feb. Open B/Hols except Xmas Day & Boxing Day.
Min Mail Order UK: Nmc
Min Mail Order EU: Nmc
Cat. Cost: 2 x 1st class
Credit Cards: All major credit/debit cards.
Specialities: Exotic plants, gingers, bananas and aroids.
Map Ref: E, B3

EUnu UNUSUAL HERBS AND EDIBLES ⊠
39 Oxford Road, Lowestoft, Suffolk, NR32 1TN
Ⓣ (01502) 502001
Ⓔ laurenrayner@aol.com
Ⓦ www.unusualherbsandedibles.co.uk
Contact: Lauren Rayner
Opening Times: By appt. only. Please email or phone first.
Min Mail Order UK: Nmc
Cat. Cost: Free

Specialities: Much stock available in small quanitites only. Credit card payment available Online through PAYPAL and NOCHEX.

EVFa VALLEY FARM PLANTS
Hillington, Kings Lynn, Norfolk, PE31 6DW
Ⓣ (01485) 600288
Ⓕ (01485) 601211
Ⓔ olineave@freeuk.co.uk
Contact: Oliver Neave
Opening Times: 1000-1700 Wed-Sun 2nd week Mar-3rd week Oct.
Specialities: Variegated & interesting foliage plants. Mainly perennials, shrubs & grasses.
Map Ref: E, B1

EWes WEST ACRE GARDENS
West Acre, Kings Lynn, Norfolk, PE32 1UJ
Ⓣ (01760) 755562
Contact: J J Tuite
Opening Times: 1000-1700 7 days 1st Feb-30th Nov. Other times by appt.
Min Mail Order UK: Nmc
Cat. Cost: 4 x 1st class
Credit Cards: Visa MasterCard Delta Switch
Specialities: Unusual shrubs, herbaceous & alpines. Large selection of *Rhodohypoxis* & grasses. Note: mail order Oct-Mar only.
Map Ref: E, B1 **OS Grid Ref:** TF792182

EWin WINTER FLORA PLANT CENTRE
Hall Farm, Weston, Beccles, Suffolk, NR34 8TT
Ⓣ (01502) 716810
Ⓜ 07771 882613
Ⓕ (01502) 716666
Ⓔ retail@goosegreennurseries.co.uk
Ⓦ www.goosegreennurseries.co.uk
Also sells wholesale
Contact: Stephen Malster
Opening Times: 1000-1700 Mon-Sun all year except 25th-27th Dec & 1st Jan.
Cat. Cost: Online only.
Credit Cards: All major credit/debit cards.
Map Ref: E, C3 **OS Grid Ref:** TM423878

EWll THE WALLED GARDEN ◆
Park Road, Benhall, Saxmundham, Suffolk, IP17 1JB
Ⓣ (01728) 602510
Ⓕ (01728) 602510
Ⓔ jim@thewalledgarden.co.uk
Ⓦ www.thewalledgarden.co.uk
Contact: Jim Mountain
Opening Times: 0930-1700 Tue-Sun Mar-Oct, Tue-Sat Nov-Feb.
Cat. Cost: 2 x 1st class
Credit Cards: All major credit/debit cards.
Specialities: Tender & hardy perennials & wall shrubs.
Map Ref: E, C3 **OS Grid Ref:** TM371613

EWoo WOOTTEN'S PLANTS
Wenhaston, Blackheath, Halesworth, Suffolk, IP19 9HD
Ⓣ (01502) 478258
Ⓕ (01502) 478888
Ⓔ sales@woottensplants.co.uk
Ⓦ www.woottensplants.co.uk
Contact: M Loftus
Opening Times: 0930-1700 7 days.
Min Mail Order UK: Nmc
Min Mail Order EU: Nmc
Cat. Cost: £2.50 illus. + £1.50 p&p
Credit Cards: Access Visa Amex Switch
Specialities: *Pelargonium, Hosta, Auricula* & *Iris*. Grasses.
Map Ref: E, C3 **OS Grid Ref:** TM42714375

EWsh WESTSHORES NURSERIES
82 West Street, Winterton, Lincolnshire, DN15 9QF
Ⓣ (01724) 733940
Ⓕ (01724) 733940
Ⓔ westshnur@aol.com
Ⓦ www.westshores.co.uk
Contact: Gail & John Summerfield
Opening Times: 0930-1800 (or dusk) Wed-Sun & B/hols 1st Mar-mid Nov.
Min Mail Order UK: £15.00
Cat. Cost: 2 x 1st class
Credit Cards: All major credit/debit cards.
Specialities: Ornamental grasses & herbaceous perennials. Note: mail order grasses only.
Map Ref: E, A1

EWTr WALNUT TREE GARDEN NURSERY €
Flymoor Lane, Rocklands, Attleborough, Norfolk, NR17 1BP
Ⓣ (01953) 488163
Ⓕ (01953) 483187
Ⓔ info@wtgn.co.uk
Ⓦ www.wtgn.co.uk
Contact: Jim Paine & Clare Billington
Opening Times: 0900-1800 Tue-Sun Feb-Nov & B/hols.
Min Mail Order UK: £30.00
Cat. Cost: 4 x 1st class
Credit Cards: Visa MasterCard Switch Solo
Map Ref: E, B1 **OS Grid Ref:** TL978973

KEY
Mail order to UK or EU — Delivers to shows
Exports beyond EU — € Euro accepted
Accessible by wheelchair — ◆ See Display advertisement

EZes **ZEST EXOTICS** ⊠
262 Aylsham Road,
Norwich, Norfolk,
NR3 2RG
Ⓣ (01603) 452740
Ⓕ (01603) 452740
Ⓔ plants@zestexotics.co.uk
Ⓦ zestexotics.co.uk
Contact: Ben Blake
Opening Times: Not open. Mail order only.
Min Mail Order UK: Nmc
Cat. Cost: 2 x 1st class
Credit Cards: None.
Specialities: Hardy & unusual *Citrus, poncirus trifoliata* varieties, unusual plants and exotics. We are a new & small nursery, so plants are only available in limited numbers. Growing to order may be possible on request. Check website for stock levels.

SCOTLAND

GAbr **ABRIACHAN NURSERIES** ⊠
Loch Ness Side, Inverness, Scotland,
IV3 8LA
Ⓣ (01463) 861232
Ⓕ (01463) 861232
Ⓔ info@lochnessgarden.com
Ⓦ www.lochnessgarden.com
Contact: Mr & Mrs D Davidson
Opening Times: 0900-1900 daily (dusk if earlier) Feb-Nov.
Min Mail Order UK: Nmc
Min Mail Order EU: Nmc
Cat. Cost: 4 x 1st class
Credit Cards: None.
Specialities: *Herbaceous, Primula, Helianthemum, hardy Geranium, Sempervivum* & *Primula auricula.*
Map Ref: G, B2 **OS Grid Ref:** NH571347

GBar **BARWINNOCK HERBS** ⊠ €
Barrhill, by Girvan, Ayrshire,
Scotland,
KA26 0RB
Ⓣ (01465) 821338
Ⓔ herbs@barwinnock.com
Ⓦ www.barwinnock.com
Contact: Dave & Mon Holtom
Opening Times: 1000-1700 7 days 3rd Apr-3rd Oct.
Min Mail Order UK: Nmc
Min Mail Order EU: Nmc
Cat. Cost: Free
Credit Cards: All major credit/debit cards.
Specialities: Culinary, medicinal, fragrant-leaved plants & wildflowers organically grown.
Map Ref: G, D2 **OS Grid Ref:** NX309772

GBBs **BORDER BELLES** ⊠ ♘ ♿
Old Branxton Cottages, Innerwick,
Nr. Dunbar, East Lothian, Scotland,
EH42 1QT
Ⓣ (01368) 840325
Ⓕ (01368) 840325
Ⓔ borderbelles@whsmithnet.co.uk
Ⓦ www.borderbelles.com
Also sells wholesale
Contact: Gillian Moynihan & Kirstie Wenham
Opening Times: Please phone before visiting.
Min Mail Order UK: Nmc
Min Mail Order EU: On request
Cat. Cost: 3 x 1st class
Credit Cards: None.
Specialities: *Anemone, Allium, Campanula, Diplarrhena*, hardy geraniums, *Hosta, Trillium, Tricyrtis*, woodland plants incl. *Actaea, Mertensia* & *Mitchella.* Note: mail order Oct-Mar only.
Map Ref: G, C3

GBin **BINNY PLANTS** ⊠ €
West Lodge, Binny Estate,
Ecclesmachen Road, Nr. Broxbourn,
West Lothian, Scotland,
EH52 6NL
Ⓣ (01506) 858931
Ⓕ (01506) 858155
Ⓔ binnyplants@aol.com
Ⓦ www.binnyplants.co.uk
Also sells wholesale
Contact: Billy Carruthers
Opening Times: 1000-1700 7 days 1st Mar-31st Oct.
Min Mail Order UK: Nmc
Min Mail Order EU: £25.00
Cat. Cost: 3 x 1st class
Credit Cards: Visa MasterCard Switch Eurocard
Specialities: Perennials incl. *Euphorbia, Geranium, Hosta, Paeonia* & *Iris.* Plus large selection of grasses & ferns. Note: Mail order Oct-Mar only.
Map Ref: G, C3

GBon **BONHARD NURSERY** ⊠ ♿
Murrayshall Road:Scone, Perth,
Scotland, PH2 7PQ
Ⓣ (01738) 552791
Ⓕ (01738) 552939
Contact: Mr C Hickman
Opening Times: 0900-1700, or dusk if earlier, 7 days.
Cat. Cost: Free (fruit trees & roses)
Credit Cards: Access Eurocard MasterCard Switch Visa

Specialities: Herbaceous, conifers & alpines. Fruit & ornamental trees. Shrub & species roses.
Map Ref: G, C3

GBri BRIDGE END NURSERIES ♠ ♿
Gretna Green, Dumfries & Galloway, Scotland, DG16 5HN
Ⓣ (01461) 800612
Ⓕ (01461) 800612
Ⓔ enquiries@bridgendnurseries.co.uk
Ⓦ www.bridgendnurseries.co.uk
Contact: R Bird
Opening Times: 0930-1700 all year. Evenings by appt.
Cat. Cost: None issued
Credit Cards: All major credit/debit cards.
Specialities: Hardy cottage garden perennials. Many unusual & interesting varieties.
Map Ref: G, D3

GBuc BUCKLAND PLANTS ⊠ € ♿
Whinnieliggate, Kirkcudbright, Scotland, DG6 4XP
Ⓣ (01557) 331323
Ⓕ (01557) 331323
Ⓦ www.bucklandplants.co.uk
Contact: Rob or Dina Asbridge
Opening Times: 1000-1700 Thu-Sun 1st Mar-1st Nov.
Min Mail Order UK: £15.00 + p&p
Min Mail Order EU: £50.00 + p&p
Cat. Cost: 3 x 1st class
Credit Cards: All major credit/debit cards.
Specialities: A very wide range of scarce herbaceous & woodland plants incl. *Anemone, Cardamine, Crocosmia, Erythronium, Helleborus, Lilium, Meconopsis, Primula, Tricyrtis* & *Trillium.*
Map Ref: G, D2 **OS Grid Ref:** NX719524

GBut BUTTERWORTHS' ORGANIC NURSERY ⊠
Garden Cottage, Auchinleck Estate, Cumnock, Ayrshire, KA18 2LR
Ⓣ (01290) 551088
Ⓜ 07732 254300
Ⓔ butties@webage.co.uk
Ⓦ www.webage.co.uk/apples/
Contact: John Butterworth
Opening Times: By appt. only.
Min Mail Order UK: £5.00
Cat. Cost: 2 x 1st class
Credit Cards: None.
Specialities: Fruit trees. Scottish apple varieties. Much of stock is limited. Nursery partially accessible for wheelchairs.
Map Ref: G, D2 **OS Grid Ref:** 502231

GCai CAIRNSMORE NURSERY ⊠ ♠ ♿
Chapmanton Road, Castle Douglas, Kirkcudbrightshire, DG7 2NU
Ⓜ 07980 176458
Ⓔ cairnsmorenursery@hotmail.com
Ⓦ www.cairnsmorenursery.co.uk
Contact: Valerie Smith
Opening Times: 1000-1700, Tue-Sat, Mar-Oct.
Min Mail Order UK: Nmc
Min Mail Order EU: Nmc
Cat. Cost: 4 x 1st class
Credit Cards: Visa MasterCard
Specialities: Primulas for the garden and cold greenhouse, incl. auriculas, heucheras and tiarellas.
Map Ref: G, D2 **OS Grid Ref:** NX756637

GCal CALLY GARDENS ⊠ ♿
Gatehouse of Fleet, Castle Douglas, Scotland, DG7 2DJ
Ⓕ (01557) 815029. Also information line.
Ⓦ www.callygardens.co.uk
Also sells wholesale
Contact: Michael Wickenden
Opening Times: 1000-1730 Sat-Sun, 1400-1730 Tue-Fri. Easter Sat-last Sun in Sept.
Min Mail Order UK: £15.00 + p&p
Cat. Cost: 3 x 1st class
Credit Cards: None.
Specialities: Unusual perennials. *Agapanthus, Crocosmia, Eryngium, Euphorbia,* hardy *Geranium* & grasses. Some rare shrubs, climbers & conservatory plants.
Map Ref: G, D2

GCed CEDAR COTTAGE PLANTS ⊠
Aberfoyle Road, Balfron Station, Glasgow, Scotland, G63 0SQ
Ⓣ (01360) 440701
Ⓕ (01360) 440933
Ⓔ rkpgreen@aol.com
Contact: Richard Green
Opening Times: Mail order only.
Min Mail Order UK: Nmc
Cat. Cost: 3 x 1st class
Credit Cards: None.
Specialities: Herbaceous perennials.
Map Ref: G, C2 **OS Grid Ref:** NS532918

GCoc JAMES COCKER & SONS ⊠ ♿
Whitemyres, Lang Stracht, Aberdeen, Scotland, AB15 6XH

KEY
⊠ Mail order to UK or EU ♠ Delivers to shows
✈ Exports beyond EU € Euro accepted
♿ Accessible by wheelchair ◆ See Display advertisement

G

Ⓣ (01224) 313261
Ⓕ (01224) 312531
Ⓔ sales@roses.uk.com
Ⓦ www.roses.uk.com
Also sells wholesale
Contact: Alec Cocker
Opening Times: 0900-1730 7 days.
Min Mail Order UK: Nmc
Min Mail Order EU: £4.90 + p&p
Cat. Cost: Free
Credit Cards: Visa MasterCard Delta Switch
Specialities: Roses.
Map Ref: G, B3

GCra CRAIGIEBURN CLASSIC PLANTS
Craigieburn House, by Moffat, Dumfrieshire, Scotland, DG10 9LF
Ⓣ (01683) 221250
Ⓕ (01683) 221250
Contact: Andrew Wheatcroft
Opening Times: 1030-1800 Fri, Sat, Sun, Easter-17 Oct 2004. Plus all English & Scottish public holidays. Other times by appt.
Cat. Cost: £1.00
Credit Cards: None.
Specialities: *Meconopsis* plants for damp gardens, herbaceous perennials.
Map Ref: G, D3

GCrs CHRISTIE'S NURSERY ⊠ € ◆
Downfield,Westmuir, Kirriemuir, Angus, Scotland, DD8 5LP
Ⓣ (01575) 572977
Ⓕ (01575) 572977
Ⓔ ianchristie@btconnect.com
Ⓦ www.christiealpines.co.uk
Contact: Ian & Ann Christie
Opening Times: 1000-1700 Mon, Wed-Sat 1st Mar-31st Oct. Closed Tue & Sun. By appt. only at other times.
Min Mail Order UK: 5 plants + p&p
Min Mail Order EU: On request
Cat. Cost: 4 x 1st class
Credit Cards: All major credit/debit cards.
Specialities: Alpines, esp. gentians, *Cassiope, Primula, Lewisia*, orchids, *Trillium* & ericaceous.
Map Ref: G, B3

GEdr EDROM NURSERIES ⊠
Coldingham, Eyemouth, Berwickshire, Scotland, TD14 5TZ
Ⓣ (01890) 771386
Ⓕ (01890) 71387
Ⓔ info@edromnurseries.co.uk
Ⓦ www.edromnurseries.co.uk
Contact: Mr Terry Hunt
Opening Times: 0900-1700 Mon-Sun, 1 Mar-30 Sep. Other times by appt.
Min Mail Order UK: Nmc
Min Mail Order EU: £20.00
Cat. Cost: 3 x 2nd class
Credit Cards: Visa MasterCard
Specialities: *Trillium, Arisaema, Primula, Gentiana, Meconopsis, Anemone* & other alpines.
Map Ref: G, C3 **OS Grid Ref:** NT8866

GEve EVELIX DAFFODILS ⊠ €
Aird Asaig, Evelix, Dornoch, Sutherland, Highland, Scotland, IV25 3NG
Ⓣ (01862) 810715
Ⓔ dugaldmacarthur@lineone.net
Contact: D C MacArthur
Opening Times: By appt. only.
Min Mail Order UK: Nmc
Min Mail Order EU: Nmc
Cat. Cost: 3 x 1st class, available end May
Credit Cards: None.
Specialities: New *Narcissus* cultivars for garden display & exhibition. Many cultivars are in ltd. supply.
Map Ref: G, A2

GFai FAIRHOLM PLANTS ⊠
Fairholm, Larkhall, Lanarkshire, Scotland, ML9 2UQ
Ⓣ (01698) 881671
Ⓕ (01698) 888135
Ⓔ james_sh@btconnect.com
Contact: Mrs J M Hamilton
Opening Times: Apr-Oct by appt.
Min Mail Order UK: Nmc
Cat. Cost: 1 x 2nd class for descriptive list.
Credit Cards: None.
Specialities: *Abutilon* & unusual half hardy perennials esp. South African. Nat. Coll. of *Abutilon* cvs. Note: mail order for young/small plants.
Map Ref: G, C2 **OS Grid Ref:** NS754515

GFle FLEURS PLANTS ⊠
2 Castlehill Lane, Abington Road, Symington, Biggar, Scotland, ML12 6SJ
Ⓣ (01899) 308528
Ⓔ jell.flrs@tiscali.co.uk
Contact: Jim Elliott
Opening Times: Please phone to arrange a visit.
Min Mail Order UK: £8.00 + p&p
Min Mail Order EU: £20.00 + p&p
Cat. Cost: Sae
Credit Cards: None.
Specialities: *Primula, Meconopsis.*
Map Ref: G, C3 **OS Grid Ref:** 010353

GFlt **Floreat Plants** ⊠ ⊠ ⊠
9 Station Road, Bardowie, Glasgow, Scotland, G62 6ET
Ⓣ (01360) 620241
Ⓜ 07802 482253
Ⓕ (01360) 620241
Ⓔ floreatplants@ic24.net
Also sells wholesale
Contact: Sue Bell
Opening Times: 1030-1230 Wed & Thu, 1400-1600 Sun, Mar-Sep or by appt. at any other time.
Min Mail Order UK: Nmc
Cat. Cost: 3 x 1st class
Credit Cards: None.
Specialities: Unusual range of alpines, bulbs & herbaceous plants. Some stock available in small quantities. Note: nursery at different location, please phone for directions.
Map Ref: G, C2 **OS Grid Ref:** NS541809

GFor **Fordmouth Croft Ornamental Grass Nursery** ⊠ ⊠
Fordmouth Croft, Meikle Wartle, Inverurie, Aberdeenshire, AB51 5BE
Ⓣ (01467) 671519
Ⓔ Ann-Marie@fmcornamentalgrasses.co.uk
Ⓦ www.fmcornamentalgrasses.co.uk
Contact: Robert & Ann-Marie Grant
Opening Times: Strictly by appt. only.
Min Mail Order UK: Nmc
Cat. Cost: 2 x 1st class
Credit Cards: None.
Specialities: Grasses, sedges, rushes. Small orders available.
Map Ref: G, B3 **OS Grid Ref:** NJ718302

GGar **Garden Cottage Nursery** ⊠
Tournaig, Poolewe, Achnasheen, Highland, Scotland, IV22 2LH
Ⓣ (01445) 781777
Ⓕ (01445) 781777
Ⓔ sales@gcnursery.co.uk
Ⓦ www.gcnursery.co.uk
Contact: Ben Rushbrooke
Opening Times: 1030-1800 Mon-Sat mid Mar-mid Oct or by appt.
Min Mail Order UK: £10.00 + p&p
Cat. Cost: 4 x 2nd class
Credit Cards: None.
Specialities: A wide range of plants esp. those from the southern hemisphere, Asiatic primulas & plants for coastal gardens.
Map Ref: G, A2 **OS Grid Ref:** NG878835

GGGa **Glendoick Gardens Ltd** ⊠ ⊠
Glencarse, Perth, Scotland, PH2 7NS
Ⓣ (01738) 860205
Ⓕ (01738) 860630
Ⓔ sales@glendoick.com
Ⓦ www.glendoick.com
Also sells wholesale
Contact: P A, E P & K N E Cox
Opening Times: 2004:1000-1600 Mon-Fri only, mid- Apr-mid-Jun, otherwise by appt. 1400-1700 1st & 3rd Sun in May. Garden centre open 7 days.
Min Mail Order UK: £40.00 + p&p
Min Mail Order EU: £100.00 + p&p
Cat. Cost: £2.00 or £1.50 stamps
Credit Cards: Visa MasterCard Delta Switch JCB
Specialities: Rhododendrons, azaleas and ericaceous, *Primula* & *Meconopsis*. Plants from wild seed. Many catalogue plants available at garden centre. Limited wheelchair access.
Map Ref: G, C3

GGre **Greenhead Roses** ⊠
Greenhead Nursery, Old Greenock Road, Inchinnan, Renfrew, Scotland, PA4 9PH
Ⓣ (0141) 812 0121
Ⓕ (0141) 812 0121
Ⓔ greenheadnursery@aol.com
Also sells wholesale
Contact: C N Urquhart
Opening Times: 1000-1700 7 days.
Min Mail Order UK: Nmc
Min Mail Order EU: Nmc
Cat. Cost: Sae
Credit Cards: Visa Switch
Specialities: Roses. Wide general range, dwarf conifers, trees, heathers, rhododendrons & azaleas, shrubs, alpines, fruit, hardy herbaceous & spring & summer bedding. Note: mail order for bush roses only, Oct-Mar.
Map Ref: G, C2

GIBF **Iain Brodie of Falsyde** ⊠
(Office) Cuilalunn, Kinchurdy Road, Boat of Garten, Invernesshire, Scotland, PH24 3BP
Ⓣ (01479) 831464
Ⓕ (01479) 831672
Ⓔ plants&seeds@falsyde.sol.co.uk
Contact: Iain Brodie of Falsyde
Opening Times: Please phone first.
Min Mail Order UK: £20.00
Min Mail Order EU: £30.00
Cat. Cost: 3 x 1st class (only available from Oct)

KEY
⊠ Mail order to UK or EU — Delivers to shows
Exports beyond EU — € Euro accepted
Accessible by wheelchair — ◆ See Display advertisement

Credit Cards: None.
Specialities: *Betulaceae*, *Rosaceae* & *Ericaceae*. Note: nursery is at Auchgourish Gardens, Boat of Garten. Anchgourish Gardens are open Apr-Sep.
Map Ref: G, B2

G

GKev KEVOCK GARDEN PLANTS & FLOWERS ⊠ ☒ ♠ €
16 Kevock Road, Lasswade,
Midlothian, EH18 1HT
Ⓣ 0131 454 0660
Ⓜ 07811 321585
Ⓕ 0131 454 0660
Ⓔ info@kevockgarden.co.uk
Ⓦ www.kevockgarden.co.uk
Also sells wholesale
Contact: Stella Rankin
Opening Times: Not open.
Min Mail Order UK: Nmc
Min Mail Order EU: Nmc
Cat. Cost: 4 x 1st class
Credit Cards: Visa MasterCard Switch
Specialities: Chinese & Himalayan plants. *Primula*, *Meconopsis*, *Iris*.

GKir KIRKDALE NURSERY ⊠
Daviot, Nr. Inverurie,
Aberdeenshire, Scotland,
AB51 0JL
Ⓣ (01467) 671264
Ⓕ (01467) 671282
Ⓔ kirkdalenursery@btconnect.com
Ⓦ www.kirkdalenursery.co.uk
Contact: Geoff or Alistair
Opening Times: 1000-1700 7 days (summer), 1000-1600 7 days (winter).
Min Mail Order UK: £20.00 + p&p
Cat. Cost: None issued
Credit Cards: Visa Access Switch
Specialities: Trees, herbaceous, grasses. Note: mail order strictly mid-Oct to mid-Mar, carriage at cost.
Map Ref: G, B3

GLbr LADYBRAE FARM NURSERY ⊠ ◆
Ladybrae Farm, Ladysbridge,
Banff, Scotland,
AB45 2JR
Ⓣ (01261) 861259 (after 1800)
Ⓔ sales@justfuchsia.co.uk
Ⓦ www.justfuchsia.co.uk
Contact: Frances Beasley
Opening Times: 1000-1800 Mon-Sat, 1100-1600 Sun.
Min Mail Order UK: £7.95
Cat. Cost: 2 x 1st class
Credit Cards: None.
Specialities: Hardy ornamentals, esp. hardy geraniums, hebes. Note: mail order Nov-Mar. *Clematis* & *Fuchsia* only.
Map Ref: G, B3

GLil LILLIESLEAF NURSERY ⊠ €
Garden Cottage, Linthill,
Melrose, Roxburghshire,
Scotland, TD6 9HU
Ⓣ (01835) 870415
Ⓕ (01835) 870415
Ⓔ lleafnursery@aol.com
Contact: Teyl de Bordes
Opening Times: 1000-1700 Mon-Sat, 1000-1600 Sun. Dec-Feb, please phone first.
Min Mail Order UK: Nmc*
Min Mail Order EU: Nmc
Cat. Cost: 2 x 1st class
Credit Cards: Visa Access
Specialities: *Epimedium* & wide range of common & uncommon plants. Nat. Coll. of *Epimedium*. *Note: mail order of *Epimedium* only.
Map Ref: G, C3 **OS Grid Ref:** NT547262

GMac ELIZABETH MACGREGOR ⊠ ☒
Ellenbank, Tongland Road,
Kirkcudbright, Scotland,
DG6 4UU
Ⓣ (01557) 330620
Ⓕ (01557) 330620
Ⓔ elizabeth@violas.abel.co.uk
Contact: Elizabeth MacGregor
Opening Times: 1000-1700 Mon, Fri & Sat May-Sep, or please phone.
Min Mail Order UK: 6 plants £13.20
Min Mail Order EU: £50.00 + p&p
Cat. Cost: 4 x 1st class or 5 x 2nd class
Credit Cards: Visa MasterCard
Specialities: Violets, violas & violettas, old and new varieties. *Campanula*, *Geranium*, *Penstemon*, *Aster*, *Primula*, *Iris* & other unusual herbaceous.
Map Ref: G, D2

GMaP MACPLANTS ♠
Berrybank Nursery, 5 Boggs Holdings,
Pencaitland, E Lothian, Scotland,
EH34 5BA
Ⓣ (01875) 341179
Ⓕ (01875) 340842
Ⓔ sales@macplants.co.uk
Ⓦ www.macplants.co.uk
Also sells wholesale
Contact: Claire McNaughton
Opening Times: 1030-1700 7 days mid Mar-end Sept.
Cat. Cost: 4 x 2nd class

Credit Cards: MasterCard Switch Visa
Specialities: Herbaceous perennials, alpines, hardy ferns, violas & grasses. Nursery partially accessible to wheelchairs.
Map Ref: G, C3 OS Grid Ref: 447703

GPoy **POYNTZFIELD HERB NURSERY** ⊠ ✈ € ♿
Nr. Balblair, Black Isle, Dingwall,
Ross & Cromarty, Highland,
Scotland, IV7 8LX
Ⓣ (01381) 610352*
Ⓕ (01381) 610352
Ⓔ info@poyntzfieldherbs.co.uk
Ⓦ www.poyntzfieldherbs.co.uk
Contact: Duncan Ross
Opening Times: 1300-1700 Mon-Sat 1st Mar-30th Sep, 1300-1700 Sun Apr-Aug.
Min Mail Order UK: £5.00 + p&p
Min Mail Order EU: £10.00 + p&p
Cat. Cost: 4 x 1st class
Credit Cards: All major credit/debit cards.
Specialities: Over 400 popular, unusual & rare herbs esp. medicinal. Also seeds. *Note: phone between 1200-1300 & 1800-1900 only.
Map Ref: G, B2 **OS Grid Ref:** NH711642

GQui **QUINISH GARDEN NURSERY** ⊠ ◆
Dervaig, Isle of Mull, Argyll, Scotland,
PA75 6QL
Ⓣ (01688) 400344
Ⓕ (01688) 400344
Ⓔ quinishplants@aol.com
Ⓦ Q-gardens.org
Contact: Nicholas Reed
Opening Times: By appt. only.
Min Mail Order UK: Nmc
Min Mail Order EU: Nmc
Cat. Cost: 2 x 1st class
Credit Cards: None.
Specialities: Choice garden shrubs & conservatory plants.
Map Ref: G, C1

GSki **SKIPNESS PLANTS** ⊠ ♿
The Gardens, Skipness, Nr. Tarbert, Argyll,
Scotland, PA29 6XU
Ⓣ (01880) 760201
Ⓕ (01880) 760201
Ⓔ info@plants-scotland.co.uk
Ⓦ www.plants-scotland.co.uk
Also sells wholesale
Contact: Bill & Joan McHugh
Opening Times: 0900-1800 Mon-Fri, 0900-1600 Sat-Sun end Mar-Oct.
Min Mail Order UK: Nmc
Min Mail Order EU: Nmc
Cat. Cost: £1.00*

Credit Cards: Visa MasterCard Delta
Specialities: Unusual herbaceous perennials, shrubs, climbers & grasses. *Note: Catalogue cost refunded on first order.
Map Ref: G, C2

GTou **TOUGH ALPINE NURSERY** ⊠
Westhaybogs, Tough, Alford, Aberdeenshire,
Scotland, AB33 8DU
Ⓣ (01975) 562783
Ⓕ (01975) 563561
Ⓔ info@tough-alpines.co.uk
Ⓦ www.tough-alpines.co.uk
Also sells wholesale
Contact: Fred & Monika Carrie
Opening Times: 1st Mar-31st Oct. Please check first.
Min Mail Order UK: Nmc
Min Mail Order EU: Nmc
Cat. Cost: 3 x 2nd class
Credit Cards: MasterCard Access Switch Delta Visa
Specialities: Alpines.
Map Ref: G, B3 **OS Grid Ref:** 610114

GTSp **THE TREE SHOP** ⊠ ♿ ◆
Ardkinglas Estate Nurseries Ltd.,
Cairndow, Argyll, Scotland,
PA26 8BH
Ⓣ (01499) 600263
Ⓕ (01499) 600348
Ⓔ tree.shop@virgin.net
Ⓦ www.scottishtrees.co.uk
Contact: Glyn Toplis or Sally Hall
Opening Times: 0930-1800 Apr-Sep, 0930-1700 Oct-Mar.
Min Mail Order UK: Nmc
Min Mail Order EU: Nmc
Cat. Cost: 2 x 1st class
Credit Cards: All major credit/debit cards.
Specialities: Native species. Rare & unusual conifers. Rhododendrons, plus an interesting range of trees, shrubs & perennials. Many plants available in small numbers only.
Map Ref: G, C2 **OS Grid Ref:** NN189127

GTwe **J TWEEDIE FRUIT TREES** ⊠
Maryfield Road Nursery, Nr. Terregles,
Dumfries, Scotland, DG2 9TH
Ⓣ (01387) 720880
Contact: John Tweedie
Opening Times: Please ring for times. Collections by appt.

KEY
⊠ Mail order to UK or EU — Delivers to shows
✈ Exports beyond EU — € Euro accepted
♿ Accessible by wheelchair — ◆ See Display advertisement

Min Mail Order UK: Nmc
Cat. Cost: Sae
Credit Cards: None.
Specialities: Fruit trees & bushes. A wide range of old & new varieties.
Map Ref: G, D2

G

GUzu **UZUMARA ORCHIDS** ⊠ ✈ €
9 Port Henderson, Gairloch, Ross-shire, Scotland, IV21 2AS
Ⓣ (01445) 741228
Ⓕ (01445) 741228
Ⓔ i.la_croix@virgin.net
Ⓦ www.uzumaraorchids.com
Contact: Mrs I F La Croix
Opening Times: By appt only.
Min Mail Order UK: Nmc
Min Mail Order EU: Nmc
Cat. Cost: Sae
Credit Cards: None.
Specialities: African & Madagascan orchids.

GWCH **WOODSIDE COTTAGE HERBS** ⊠
Woodside Cottage, Longriggend, Airdrie, Lanarkshire, Scotland, ML6 7RU
Ⓣ (01236) 843826
Ⓕ (01236) 842545
Ⓔ mail@herbscents.co.uk
Ⓦ herbscents.co.uk
Contact: Brenda Brown
Opening Times: By appt. only.
Min Mail Order UK: Minimum 10 plants.
Cat. Cost: 4 x 1st class
Credit Cards: Visa MasterCard Switch Solo
Specialities: Herbs, wild flowers & hardy plants incl. shrubs, grasses & cottage garden flowers.
Map Ref: G, C2 **OS Grid Ref:** NS824708

N. IRELAND & REPUBLIC

IArd **ARDCARNE GARDEN CENTRE** €
Ardcarne, Boyle, Co. Roscommon, Ireland
Ⓣ 00 353 (0)7196 67091
Ⓕ 00 353 (0)7196 67341
Ⓔ ardcarne@indigo.ie
Ⓦ www.ardcarnegc.com
Contact: James Wickham, Mary Frances Dwyer, Kirsty Ainge
Opening Times: 0900-1800 Mon-Sat, 1400-1800 Sun & B/hols.
Credit Cards: Access Visa Amex
Specialities: Coastal plants, native & unusual trees, specimen plants & semi-mature trees. Wide general range.
Map Ref: I, B1

IBal **BALI-HAI MAIL ORDER NURSERY** ⊠ ✈ € ♿
42 Largy Road, Carnlough, Ballymena, Co. Antrim, N. Ireland, BT44 0EZ
Ⓣ 028 2888 5289
Ⓕ 028 2888 5976
Ⓔ ianwscroggy@btopenworld.com
Ⓦ www.balihainursery.com
Also sells wholesale
Contact: Mrs M E Scroggy
Opening Times: Mon-Sat by appt. only.
Min Mail Order UK: Nmc
Min Mail Order EU: Nmc
Cat. Cost: £1.50
Credit Cards: None.
Specialities: *Hosta, Phormium*. Note: export beyond EU restricted to bare root perennials, no grasses.
Map Ref: I, A3

IBlr **BALLYROGAN NURSERIES** ⊠ ✈ € ♿
The Grange, Ballyrogan, Newtownards, Co. Down, N. Ireland, BT23 4SD
Ⓣ (028) 9181 0451 (evenings)
Ⓔ gary.dunlop@btinternet.com
Also sells wholesale
Contact: Gary Dunlop
Opening Times: Only open by appt.
Min Mail Order UK: £10.00 + p&p
Min Mail Order EU: £20.00 + p&p
Cat. Cost: 2 x 1st class
Credit Cards: None.
Specialities: Choice herbaceous. *Agapanthus, Celmisia, Crocosmia, Euphorbia, Meconopsis, Rodgersia, Iris, Dierama, Erythronium, Roscoea* & *Phormium*. Note: ltd. exports beyond EU.
Map Ref: I, B3

ICro **CROCKNAFEOLA NURSERY** €
Killybegs, Co. Donegal, Ireland
Ⓣ 00 353 (0)74 97 51018
Ⓕ 00 353 (0)74 97 51095
Ⓔ crocknafeola@hotmail.com
Contact: Fionn McKenna
Opening Times: 0900-1800 Mon, Tue, Thu-Sat, closed Wed. 1200-1800 Sun.
Cat. Cost: None issued
Credit Cards: None.
Specialities: Bedding plants, herbaceous perennials, rhododendrons, plants for containers, roses, plus shrubs & hedging for coastal areas.
Map Ref: I, D2

IDee **DEELISH GARDEN CENTRE** ⊠ €
Skibbereen, Co. Cork, Ireland
Ⓣ 00 353 (0)28 21374
Ⓕ 00 353 (0)28 21374

Ⓔ deel@eircom.net
Ⓦ www.deelish.ie
Contact: Bill & Rain Chase
Opening Times: 1000-1300 & 1400-1800 Mon-Sat, 1400-1800 Sun.
Min Mail Order UK: 100 Euros + p&p
Min Mail Order EU: 100 Euros + p&p
Cat. Cost: Sae
Credit Cards: Visa Access
Specialities: Unusual plants for the mild coastal climate of Ireland. Conservatory plants. Sole Irish agents for Chase Organic Seeds.
Map Ref: I, D1

IDic **DICKSON NURSERIES LTD** ☒ ✈
Milecross Road, Newtownards, Co. Down, N. Ireland, BT23 4SS
Ⓣ (028) 9181 2206
Ⓕ (028) 9181 3366
Ⓔ mail@dickson-roses.co.uk
Ⓦ www.dickson-roses.co.uk
Also sells wholesale
Contact: A P C Dickson OBE, Linda Stewart
Opening Times: 0800-1230 & 1300-1700 Mon-Thu. 0800-1230 Fri. Closes at 1600 Mon-Thu Dec-Jan.
Min Mail Order UK: One plant
Min Mail Order EU: £25.00 + p&p
Cat. Cost: Free
Credit Cards: None.
Specialities: Roses esp. modern Dickson varieties. Note: most varieties are available in ltd. quantities only.
Map Ref: I, B3

IFro **FROGSWELL NURSERY** €
Clooncoulon, Straide, Foxford, Co. Mayo, Ireland
Ⓣ 00 353 (0)94 903 1420
Ⓕ 00 353 (0)94 903 1420
Ⓔ jane@frogswell.com
Ⓦ www.frogswell.com
Contact: Jane Stanley
Opening Times: Please phone first. Garden open by appt., group bookings welcome.
Cat. Cost: 3 x 1st class
Credit Cards: None.
Specialities: A small nursery growing unusual perennials & shrubs, many from seed sourced in Japan & South America, often in small quantities.
Map Ref: I, B1

IGor **GORTKELLY CASTLE NURSERY** ☒ €
Upperchurch, Thurles, Co. Tipperary, Ireland
Ⓣ 00 353 (0) 504 54441
Contact: Clare Beumer
Opening Times: Not open to the public.
Min Mail Order UK: Nmc
Min Mail Order EU: Nmc
Cat. Cost: 5 x 1st class (UK), 5 x 48c (Rep. of Ireland)
Credit Cards: None.
Specialities: Choice perennials.
Map Ref: I, C2

IHMH **HUBERT MCHALE** ☒ €
Foghill, Carrowmore-Lacken, Ballina, Co. Mayo, Ireland
Ⓣ 00 353 (0)96 34996
Ⓔ hubertmchale@eircom.net
Also sells wholesale
Contact: Hubert McHale
Opening Times: By appt. only.
Min Mail Order UK: Nmc
Min Mail Order EU: Nmc
Cat. Cost: 2 x 1st class
Credit Cards: None.
Specialities: Perennial herbs, aquatics, foliage & rockery plants.
Map Ref: I, B1

ILis **LISDOONAN HERBS** ☒ € ♿
98 Belfast Road, Saintfield, Co. Down, N. Ireland, BT24 7HF
Ⓣ (028) 9081 3624
Ⓔ b.pilcher@dial.pipex.com
Contact: Barbara Pilcher
Opening Times: Wed & Sat am. For other times, please phone to check.
Min Mail Order UK: Nmc
Min Mail Order EU: Nmc
Cat. Cost: 2 x 1st class
Credit Cards: None.
Specialities: Aromatics, herbs, kitchen garden plants, period plants, some native species. Freshly cut herbs & salads. Some stock available in limited quanities only.
Map Ref: I, B3 **OS Grid Ref:** J390624

ILsc **LISCAHANE NURSERY** € ♿
Ardfert, Tralee, Co. Kerry, Ireland
Ⓣ 00 353 (0)667 134222
Ⓕ 00 353 (0)667 134600
Contact: Dan Nolan/Bill Cooley
Opening Times: 1000-1800 Tue-Sat (summer), 1000-1700 Thu-Sat (winter). Sun please phone. Closed Mon.

KEY
☒ Mail order to UK or EU — Delivers to shows
✈ Exports beyond EU — € Euro accepted
♿ Accessible by wheelchair — ◆ See Display advertisement

Cat. Cost: None issued
Credit Cards: Visa Access Laser
Specialities: Coastal shelter plants.
Map Ref: I, D1

IMGH **M G H NURSERIES** € ♿
50 Tullyhenan Road,
Banbridge, Co. Down,
N. Ireland, BT32 4EY
Ⓣ (028) 4062 2795
Contact: Miss M G Heslip
Opening Times: 1000-1800 Thu, Fri & Sat & B/Hol Mons.
Cat. Cost: 3 x 1st class
Credit Cards: None.
Specialities: Grafted conifers, holly, maples, box, ornamental trees & flowering shrubs.
Map Ref: I, B3

IOrc **ORCHARDSTOWN NURSERIES** ⊠ ✈ € ♿
4 Miles Out, Cork Road,
Waterford,
Ireland
Ⓣ 00 353 (0)513 84273
Ⓕ 00 353 (0)513 84422
Ⓔ info@orchardstown.com
Ⓦ www.orchardstown.com
Contact: Ron Dool
Opening Times: 0900-1800 Mon-Sat, 1400-1800 Sun.
Min Mail Order UK: Nmc
Min Mail Order EU: Nmc
Cat. Cost: None issued
Credit Cards: Visa MasterCard
Specialities: Unusual hardy plants incl. shrubs, shrub roses, trees, climbers, Rhododendron species & water plants. Note: only some plants mail order.
Map Ref: I, D2

IPot **THE POTTING SHED** ⊠ ⌂ €
Bolinaspick, Camolin, Enniscorthy,
Co. Wexford, Ireland
Ⓣ 00 353 (0)548 3629
Ⓕ 00 353 (0)548 3629
Ⓔ sricher@iol.ie
Ⓦ www.camolinpottingshed.com
Contact: Susan Carrick
Opening Times: 1100-1800 Wed-Sat, 1300-1800 Sun, 31st Mar-2nd Oct 2004. Other times by appt.
Min Mail Order UK: Nmc
Min Mail Order EU: Nmc
Cat. Cost: 3 x 1st class
Credit Cards: MasterCard Visa
Specialities: Herbaceous & ornamental grasses.
Map Ref: I, C3

IRhd **RINGHADDY DAFFODILS** ⊠ ✈ €
Ringhaddy Road, Killinchy,
Newtownards, Co. Down,
N. Ireland, BT23 6TU
Ⓣ (028) 9754 1007
Ⓕ (028) 9754 2276
Ⓔ ringdaff@nireland.com
Contact: Nial Watson
Opening Times: Not open.
Min Mail Order UK: £20.00 + p&p
Min Mail Order EU: £30.00 + p&p
Cat. Cost: £2.50 redeemable on order.
Credit Cards: None.
Specialities: New daffodil varieties for exhibitors and hybridisers. Limited stock of some varieties.

IRya **RYANS NURSERIES** €
Lissivigeen, Killarney, Co. Kerry, Ireland
Ⓣ 00 353 (0)64 33507
Ⓕ 00 353 (0)64 37520
Ⓔ tlryan@eircom.net
Ⓦ www.ryansnurseries.com
Contact: Mr T Ryan
Opening Times: 0900-1800 Mon-Sat 1400-1800 Sun.
Cat. Cost: None issued
Credit Cards: Visa LA:MasterCard
Specialities: *Camellia, Pieris, Acacia, Eucalyptus, Dicksonia*, azaleas & many tender and rare plants.
Map Ref: I, D1

ISea **SEAFORDE GARDENS** ⊠ ✈ ⌂ € ♿
Seaforde, Co. Down, N. Ireland,
BT30 8PG
Ⓣ (028) 4481 1225
Ⓕ (028) 4481 1370
Ⓔ plants@seafordegardens.com
Ⓦ www.seafordegardens.com
Also sells wholesale
Contact: P Forde
Opening Times: 1000-1700 Mon-Fri all year. 1000-1700 Sat & 1300-1800 Sun mid Feb-end Oct.
Min Mail Order UK: Nmc
Min Mail Order EU: Nmc
Cat. Cost: Free
Credit Cards: None.
Specialities: Over 600 varieties of self-propagated trees & shrubs. Nat. Coll. of *Eucryphia.*
Map Ref: I, B3

ISsi **SEASIDE NURSERY** ⊠ € ♿
Claddaghduff, Co. Galway, Ireland
Ⓣ 00 353 (0)95 44687
Ⓕ 00 353 (0)95 44761

Ⓔ seaside@anu.ie
Ⓦ www.anu.ie/seaside/
Also sells wholesale
Contact: Tom Dyck
Opening Times: 1000-1300 & 1400-1800 Mon-Sat, 1400-1800 Sun. Closed Sun 1 Nov-31 Mar.
Min Mail Order UK: Nmc
Min Mail Order EU: Nmc
Cat. Cost: €3.50.
Credit Cards: Visa MasterCard
Specialities: Plants & hedging suitable for seaside locations. Rare plants originating from Australia & New Zealand esp. *Phormium, Astelia.*
Map Ref: I, B1

ITer **TERRA NOVA PLANTS** ⊠ ✈ €
Dromin, Kilmallock,
Co. Limerick,
Ireland
Ⓣ 00 353 (0)63 90744
Ⓔ terranovaplants@eircom.net
Ⓦ http://homepage.eircom.net/~terranovaplants
Contact: Deborah Begley
Opening Times: Garden & nursery open by appt.
Min Mail Order UK: Nmc
Min Mail Order EU: Nmc
Cat. Cost: 1 x IRC
Credit Cards: None.
Specialities: Bulbous aroids, variegated plants, unusual plants grown from seed. Large seedlist in autumn.
Map Ref: I, C2

ITim **TIMPANY NURSERIES & GARDENS** ⊠ ✈ ♠ ♿
77 Magheratimpany Road,
Ballynahinch, Co. Down,
N. Ireland, BT24 8PA
Ⓣ (028) 9756 2812
Ⓕ (028) 9756 2812
Ⓔ timpany@alpines.freeserve.co.uk
Ⓦ www.alpines.freeserve.co.uk
Also sells wholesale
Contact: Susan Tindall
Opening Times: 1030-1730 Tue-Sat, Sun by appt. Closed Mon excl. B/hols.
Min Mail Order UK: Nmc
Min Mail Order EU: £30.00 + p&p
Cat. Cost: £1.50
Credit Cards: Visa MasterCard
Specialities: *Celmisia, Androsace, Primula, Saxifraga, Helichrysum, Dianthus, Meconopsis, Primula auricula* & *Cassiope.*
Map Ref: I, B3

LONDON AREA

LAma **JACQUES AMAND** ⊠ ♿ ♠ € ♿
The Nurseries,145 Clamp Hill, Stanmore, Middlesex, HA7 3JS
Ⓣ (020) 8420 7110
Ⓕ (020) 8954 6784
Ⓔ bulbs@jacquesamand.co.uk
Ⓦ www.jacquesamand.com
Also sells wholesale
Contact: Stuart Chapman & John Amand
Opening Times: 0900-1700 Mon-Fri, 1000-1400 Sat-Sun. Limited Sun opening in Dec & Jan.
Min Mail Order UK: Nmc
Min Mail Order EU: Nmc
Cat. Cost: 1 x 1st class
Credit Cards: Visa Access
Specialities: Rare and unusual species bulbs esp. *Arisaema, Trillium, Fritillaria,* tulips.
Map Ref: L, B3

LAst **ASTERBY & CHALKCROFT NURSERIES** ♿
The Ridgeway, Blunham, Bedfordshire, MK44 3PH
Ⓣ (01767) 640148
Ⓕ (01767) 640667
Ⓔ sales@asterbyplants.co.uk
Ⓦ www.asterbyplants.co.uk
Contact: Simon & Eva Aldridge
Opening Times: 1000-1700 7 days. Closed Xmas & Jan.
Cat. Cost: 2 x 1st class
Credit Cards: Visa MasterCard Switch
Specialities: Hardy shrubs & herbaceous. *Clematis* & trees.
Map Ref: L, A3 **OS Grid Ref:** TL151497

LAyl **AYLETT NURSERIES LTD** ♿
North Orbital Road, London Colney,
St Albans, Hertfordshire,
AL2 1DH
Ⓣ (01727) 822255
Ⓕ (01727) 823024
Ⓔ info@aylettnurseries.co.uk
Ⓦ www.aylettnurseries.co.uk
Also sells wholesale
Contact: Roger S Aylett
Opening Times: 0830-1730 Mon-Fri, 0830-1700 Sat, 1030-1630 Sun.
Cat. Cost: Free
Credit Cards: All major credit/debit cards.

KEY
⊠ Mail order to UK or EU ♠ Delivers to shows
✈ Exports beyond EU € Euro accepted
♿ Accessible by wheelchair ◆ See Display advertisement

Specialities: *Dahlia*. Note: trial grounds at Bowmans Farm nr Jct. 22 M25, at MacDonalds roundabout take B556 to Colney Heath on left hand side 500m.
Map Ref: L, B3 **OS Grid Ref:** TL169049

LBBr **Bell Bar Nursery** ⌂ ♿
Bulls Lane:Bell Bar, Nr. Hatfield, Hertfordshire, AL9 7BB
Ⓣ (01707) 650007
Ⓕ (01707) 650008
Ⓔ swener@globalnet.co.uk
Ⓦ www.bellbarnursery.co.uk
Also sells wholesale
Contact: S Wener
Opening Times: 0900-1630 Fri & Sat Mar-Nov. 1000-1600 Sun, Mar-Oct. Other times by appt.
Cat. Cost: 2 x 1st class
Credit Cards: None.
Specialities: Hardy perennials, grasses, bulbs, ferns & bamboos. *Euphorbia, Geranium, Carex, Miscanthus,* & *Penstemon.*
Map Ref: L, B4 **OS Grid Ref:** TL243053

LBee **Beechcroft Nursery** ♿
127 Reigate Road, Ewell, Surrey, KT17 3DE
Ⓣ (020) 8393 4265
Ⓕ (020) 8393 4265
Also sells wholesale
Contact: C Kimber
Opening Times: 1000-1600 Mon-Sat, 1000-1400 Sun and B/hols. Closed Xmas-New Year week.
Cat. Cost: None issued
Credit Cards: All major credit/debit cards.
Specialities: Conifers & alpines.
Map Ref: L, C3

LBmB **Bloms Bulbs** ⊠ ☒ €
Primrose Nurseries, Melchbourne, Bedford, MK44 1ZZ
Ⓣ (01234) 709099
Ⓕ (01234) 709799
Ⓔ chrisblom@blomsbulbs.com
Ⓦ www.blomsbulbs.com
Contact: R J M Blom
Opening Times: 0900-1700 for phone enquiries or to collect orders. Nursery not open to the public, mail order only.
Min Mail Order UK: Nmc
Min Mail Order EU: Nmc
Cat. Cost: Free
Credit Cards: Visa MasterCard Switch
Specialities: Spring & summer flowering bulbs, hardy border plants. Note: exports bulbs only worldwide.

LBuc **Buckingham Nurseries** ⊠ ☒ € ♿ ◆
14 Tingewick Road, Buckingham, MK18 4AE
Ⓣ (01280) 822133
Ⓕ (01280) 815491
Ⓔ enquiries@buckingham-nurseries.co.uk
Ⓦ www.buckingham-nurseries.co.uk
Contact: R J & P L Brown
Opening Times: 0830-1730 (1800 in summer) Mon-Fri, 1000-1600 Sun. Late night opening Thu 1930 (2000 in summer). 0900-1700 Sat.
Min Mail Order UK: Nmc
Min Mail Order EU: Nmc
Cat. Cost: Free
Credit Cards: Visa MasterCard Switch
Specialities: Bare rooted and container grown hedging. Trees, shrubs, herbaceous perennials, alpines, grasses & ferns.
Map Ref: L, A2 **OS Grid Ref:** SP675333

LBut **Butterfields Nursery** ⊠
Harvest Hill, Bourne End, Buckinghamshire, SL8 5JJ
Ⓣ (01628) 525455
Also sells wholesale
Contact: I Butterfield
Opening Times: 0900-1300 & 1400-1700. Please phone beforehand in case we are attending shows.
Min Mail Order UK: Nmc
Min Mail Order EU: £30.00 + p&p
Cat. Cost: 2 x 2nd class
Credit Cards: None.
Specialities: Nat. Coll. of *Pleione. Dahlia* for collection. Scientific Award 1999. Note: only *Pleione* by mail order.
Map Ref: L, B3

LCha **Chase Organics (GB) Ltd** ⊠ ♿
Riverdene Business Park, Molesey Road, Hersham, Surrey, KT12 4RG
Ⓣ 0845 130 1304
Ⓕ (01932) 252707
Ⓔ enquiries@chaseorganics.co.uk
Ⓦ www.organiccatalogue.com
Contact: S Bossard
Opening Times: 0930-1630 Mon-Fri. Customer service 0800-2000 Mon-Fri orderline, 0900-1700 Sat orderline.
Min Mail Order UK: £1.00 handling charge for orders under £20.00
Min Mail Order EU: No minimum charge (seed only).
Cat. Cost: Free
Credit Cards: Visa Access Switch MasterCard

Specialities: 'The Organic Gardening Catalogue' offers vegetable, herb & flower seeds & garden sundries especially for organic gardeners. Note: mail order plants only to UK, seeds to EU. Outside EU by arrangement.
Map Ref: L, C3

LChw **CHADWELL SEEDS** ⊠ ✈
81 Parlaunt Road, Slough,
Buckinghamshire, SL3 8BE
Ⓣ (01753) 542823
Ⓕ (01753) 542823
Contact: Chris Chadwell
Min Mail Order UK: Nmc
Min Mail Order EU: Nmc
Cat. Cost: 3 x 2nd class
Credit Cards: None.
Specialities: Seed collecting expedition to the Himalayas. Separate general seed list of Japanese, N. American & Himalayan plants.

LCla **CLAY LANE NURSERY** ⊠ ⌂
3 Clay Lane, South Nutfield,
Nr. Redhill, Surrey, RH1 4EG
Ⓣ (01737) 823307
Ⓔ ken.claylane@talk21.com
Contact: K W Belton
Opening Times: 1000-1700 Tue-Sun 1st Feb-30th Jun. Other times by appt. Please phone before travelling.
Min Mail Order UK: £6.00*
Cat. Cost: 3 x 1st class
Credit Cards: None.
Specialities: *Fuchsia*. Note: mail order by telephone pre-arangement only. Limited stock of many varieties.
Map Ref: L, C4

LCon **THE CONIFER GARDEN** ⊠ ⌂
Herons Mead, Little Missenden,
Amersham, Buckinghamshire,
HP7 0RA
Ⓣ (01494) 862086 (0900-1800 hrs)
Ⓕ (01494) 862086
Ⓔ info@conifergarden.co.uk
Ⓦ www.conifergarden.co.uk
Contact: Mr & Mrs M P S Powell
Opening Times: Open by appt. only.
Min Mail Order UK: Nmc
Cat. Cost: 2 x 1st class for list only
Credit Cards: None.
Specialities: Conifers only, over 400 varieties always available. Note: mail order to UK only, by overnight carrier.

LCtg **COTTAGE GARDEN NURSERY** ◆
Barnet Road, Arkley, Barnet,
Hertfordshire, EN5 3JX
Ⓣ (020) 8441 8829
Ⓕ (020) 8531 3178
Ⓔ nurseryinfo@cottagegardennursery-barnet.co.uk
Ⓦ www.cottagegardennursery-barnet.co.uk
Contact: David and Wendy Spicer
Opening Times: 0930-1700 Tue-Sat Mar-Oct, 0930-1600 Tue-Sat Nov-Feb, 1000-1600 Sun & B/hol Mon all year.
Cat. Cost: None issued.
Credit Cards: Visa Access MasterCard Switch Solo Delta
Specialities: General range of hardy shrubs, trees & perennials. Architectural & exotics, *Fuchsia*, seasonal bedding, patio plants.
Map Ref: L, B3 **OS Grid Ref:** TQ226958

LDai **DAISY ROOTS** ⊠ ⌂
(offic) 8 Gosselin Road,
Bengeo, Hertford,
Hertfordshire,
SG14 3LG
Ⓣ (01992) 582401
Ⓕ (01992) 582401
Ⓔ anne@daisyroots.com
Ⓦ www.daisyroots.com
Contact: Anne Godfrey
Opening Times: 0900-1700 Fri only Mar-Oct, or by appt.
Min Mail Order UK: Nmc
Cat. Cost: 3 x 1st class
Credit Cards: None.
Specialities: Ever-increasing range of choice & unusual perennials, particularly *Agastache, Anthemis, Digitalis, Erysimum, Salvia* & *Sedum*. Note: nursery is at Jenningsbury, London Road, Hertford Heath.
Map Ref: L, B4

LDea **DEREK LLOYD DEAN** ⊠ ✈ ⌂
8 Lynwood Close,
South Harrow, Middlesex,
HA2 9PR
Ⓣ (020) 8864 0899
Ⓦ www.dereklloyddean.com
Contact: Derek Lloyd Dean
Opening Times: Not open, mail order only.
Min Mail Order UK: £2.50 + p&p
Min Mail Order EU: £2.50 + p&p
Cat. Cost: 2 x 1st class
Credit Cards: None.
Specialities: Regal, angel, ivy & scented leaf *Pelargonium*. Nat. Coll. of Angel *Pelargonium*.

KEY
⊠ Mail order to UK or EU ⌂ Delivers to shows
✈ Exports beyond EU € Euro accepted
♿ Accessible by wheelchair ◆ See Display advertisement

LEar **Earlstone Nursery** ⊠
Earlstone Manor Farm,
Burghclere,
Newbury, Berkshire,
RG20 9NG
Ⓣ (01635) 278648
Ⓕ (01635) 278672
Ⓔ earlstonenursery@wistbray.com
Ⓦ www.earlstoneboxandtopiary.co.uk
Also sells wholesale
Contact: B C Ginsberg or G MacPherson
Opening Times: By appt.
Min Mail Order UK: £30.00 + p&p
Cat. Cost: Free
Credit Cards: None.
Specialities: Some varieties of *Buxus. Buxus sempervirens* topiary. Large orders of *Taxus* & *Ilex* can be sourced.

LEdu **Edulis** ⊠ ♁ € ♿
(office) 1 Flowers Piece,
Ashampstead, Berkshire,
RG8 8SG
Ⓣ (01635) 578113
Ⓕ (01635) 578113
Ⓔ edulis.nursery@virgin.net
Ⓦ www.edulis.co.uk
Also sells wholesale
Contact: Paul Barney
Opening Times: By appt. only.
Min Mail Order UK: £30.00 + p&p
Min Mail Order EU: £50.00 + p&p
Cat. Cost: 6 x 1st class
Credit Cards: None.
Specialities: Unusual edibles, architectural plants, permaculture plants. Note: nursery is at Bere Court Farm, Tidmarsh Lane, Pangbourne, RG8 8HT.
Map Ref: L, B2

LExo **Exotic-Gardening UK** ⊠ ♁ ◆
30 Stamford Road,
Maidenhead,
Berkshire,
SL6 4RT
Ⓔ richard@exotic-gardening.co.uk
Ⓦ www.exotic-gardening.co.uk
Contact: Richard Evans
Opening Times: Not open to the public.
Min Mail Order UK: Nmc
Cat. Cost: 2 x 1st class
Credit Cards: All major credit/debit cards.
Specialities: Banana, *Heliconia, Datura, Hedychium* & other hardy exotics. Also seed. All plants are UK propagated so some stock is available in small quantities only. Note: mail order seeds all year, plants (Mar-Oct). Credit cards accepted only for online orders.

LFol **Foliage Scented & Herb Plants**
Walton Poor, Crocknorth Road, Ranmore Common, Dorking, Surrey, RH5 6SX
Ⓣ (01483) 282273
Ⓕ (01483) 282273
Contact: Mrs Prudence Calvert
Opening Times: Open during Apr-Sep, please phone for appt. if possible.
Cat. Cost: 3 x 2nd class
Credit Cards: None.
Specialities: Herbs, aromatic & scented plants.
Map Ref: L, C3

LFox **Foxgrove Plants** ⊠ ♁ ♿
Foxgrove, Enborne, Nr. Newbury, Berkshire, RG14 6RE
Ⓣ (01635) 40554
Ⓕ (01635) 30555
Contact: Mrs Louise Peters
Opening Times: 1000-1300 & 1400-1600 Thu-Sat. Closed Sun-Wed & Aug.
Min Mail Order UK: Nmc
Min Mail Order EU: Nmc
Cat. Cost: £1.00
Credit Cards: None.
Specialities: Hardy & unusual plants, incl. *Galanthus*, hellebores, grasses, *Penstemon*, alpines. Note: Mail order for *Galanthus* only.
Map Ref: L, C2

LGod **Godly's Roses** ⊠ ♿
Redbourn, St Albans,
Hertfordshire, AL3 7PS
Ⓣ (01582) 792255
Ⓕ (01582) 794267
Also sells wholesale
Contact: Colin Godly
Opening Times: 0900-1900 summer, 0900-dusk winter, Mon-Fri. 0900-1800 Sat & Sun, summer. 0900-1600 Sat & Sun, winter.
Min Mail Order UK: Nmc
Cat. Cost: Free
Credit Cards: Visa Amex Switch MasterCard
Specialities: Roses. Note: standard roses not sent mail order.
Map Ref: L, B3 **OS Grid Ref:** TL096137

LGro **Growing Carpets** ⊠ ♁ € ♿
Christmas Tree House, High Street,
Guilden Morden, Nr. Royston,
Hertfordshire, SG8 0JP
Ⓣ (01763) 852705
Contact: Mrs E E Moore
Opening Times: Mail order only.
Min Mail Order UK: Nmc
Min Mail Order EU: Nmc
Cat. Cost: 5 x 2nd class
Credit Cards: None.

Specialities: Wide range of ground-covering plants. Note: to avoid bad weather conditions, mail order plants are only dispatched in Apr, Sep-Oct on a first-come first-served basis. Some plants available in small numbers only.
Map Ref: L, A4 **OS Grid Ref:** TL278438

LHew HEWITT-COOPER CARNIVOROUS PLANTS ⊠ ♠
76 Courtney Crescent,
Carshalton on the Hill, Surrey,
SM5 4NB
Ⓣ (020) 8643 9307
Ⓕ (020) 8661 6583
Ⓔ nigel@nigelandpolly.fsnet.co.uk
Ⓦ www.hccarnivorousplants.co.uk
Contact: Nigel Hewitt-Cooper
Opening Times: By appt.
Min Mail Order UK: £10.00 + p&p
Min Mail Order EU: £50.00
Cat. Cost: 1 x 1st class/1 x IRC
Credit Cards: Visa MasterCard
Specialities: Carnivorous plants. Some species ltd. Note: mail order May-Nov. Credit cards not accepted for mail order.
Map Ref: L, C4

LHyd HYDON NURSERIES ⊠ € ◆
Clock Barn Lane, Hydon Heath,
Godalming, Surrey, GU8 4AZ
Ⓣ (01483) 860252
Ⓕ (01483) 419937
Also sells wholesale
Contact: A F George, Rodney Longhurst & Mrs A M George
Opening Times: 0930-1700 Mon-Sat (closed for lunch 12.45-1400), Feb-mid Jun & Oct-mid Nov. Other months 0930-1600 Mon-Fri, 0930-1300 Sat. Sun by appt.
Min Mail Order UK: Nmc
Min Mail Order EU: £25.00 + p&p
Cat. Cost: £2.00 or 7 x 1st class or 10 x 2nd class
Credit Cards: None.
Specialities: Large and dwarf *Rhododendron, yakushimanum* hybrids, azaleas (deciduous & evergreen), *Camellia* & other trees & shrubs. Specimen Rhododendrons. Conservatory: scented tender rhododendrons & winter-flowering camellias.
Map Ref: L, C3

LIck LOWER ICKNIELD FARM NURSERIES ♿
Lower Icknield Way, Great Kimble, Aylesbury, Buckinghamshire, HP17 9TX
Ⓣ (01844) 343436
Ⓜ 0780 3979993
Ⓕ (01844) 343436
Contact: S Baldwin, D Baldwin
Opening Times: 0900-1730 7 days excl. Xmas-New Year.
Credit Cards: None.
Specialities: Patio & basket plants. Tender & hardy perennials. Salvias. Grasses. *Argyranthemum.*
Map Ref: L, B3 **OS Grid Ref:** SP814058

LKna KNAP HILL & SLOCOCK NURSERIES ⊠ ✈ ♿
Barrs Lane, Knaphill, Woking,
Surrey, GU21 2JW
Ⓣ (01483) 481214/5
Ⓕ (01483) 797261
Ⓦ www.knaphillrhododendrons.co.uk
Also sells wholesale
Contact: Mrs Joy West
Opening Times: 0900-1700 Mon-Fri by appt. only.
Min Mail Order UK: Nmc
Min Mail Order EU: Nmc
Cat. Cost: 3 x 1st class
Credit Cards: Visa Access MasterCard
Specialities: Wide variety of rhododendrons & azaleas.
Map Ref: L, C3

LLin LINCLUDEN NURSERY ⊠ ✈ ♠ € ♿ ◆
Bisley Green, Bisley, Woking, Surrey, GU24 9EN
Ⓣ (01483) 797005
Ⓕ (01483) 474015
Ⓔ sales@lincludennursery.co.uk
Ⓦ www.lincludennursery.co.uk
Also sells wholesale
Contact: Mr & Mrs J A Tilbury
Opening Times: 0930-1630 Tue-Sat all year excl. B/hols. Closed Chelsea week & Xmas.
Min Mail Order UK: Nmc
Min Mail Order EU: Nmc
Cat. Cost: 3 x 1st class
Credit Cards: Visa MasterCard Solo Switch
Specialities: Dwarf, slow-growing & unusual conifers.
Map Ref: L, C3
OS Grid Ref: SU947596

LLWP L W PLANTS ⊠ ♠
23 Wroxham Way, Harpenden,
Hertfordshire, AL5 4PP
Ⓣ (01582) 768467
Ⓔ lwplants@waitrose.com
Ⓦ www.thymus.co.uk

KEY
⊠ Mail order to UK or EU ♠ Delivers to shows
✈ Exports beyond EU € Euro accepted
♿ Accessible by wheelchair ◆ See Display advertisement

Contact: Mrs M Easter
Opening Times: 1000-1700 most days, but please phone first.
Min Mail Order UK: £15.00 + p&p
Cat. Cost: A5 Sae + 5 x 2nd class
Credit Cards: None.
Specialities: Plants from a plantsman's garden, esp. *Geranium*, grasses, *Penstemon* & *Thymus*. Nat. Colls. of *Thymus, Hyssopus* & *Satureja*. Note: mail order late Sep-Apr, *Thymus* all year round & no minimum charge.
Map Ref: L, B3 **OS Grid Ref:** TL141153

L

LMil **MILLAIS NURSERIES** ⊠ ♿ ◆
Crosswater Lane, Churt, Farnham,
Surrey, GU10 2JN
Ⓣ (01252) 792698
Ⓕ (01252) 792526
Ⓔ sales@rhododendrons.co.uk
Ⓦ www.rhododendrons.co.uk
Also sells wholesale
Contact: David Millais
Opening Times: 1000-1300 & 1400-1700 Mon-Fri. Sat spring & autumn. Daily in May and early Jun.
Min Mail Order UK: £30.00 + p&p
Min Mail Order EU: £60.00 + p&p
Cat. Cost: 4 x 1st class
Credit Cards: Visa Switch Delta MasterCard
Specialities: Rhododendrons, azaleas, magnolias & acers. Note: mail order Oct-Mar only.
Map Ref: L, C3 **OS Grid Ref:** SU856397

LMor **MOREHAVENS** ⊠ ♿
Sandpit Hill, Buckland Common,
Tring, Hertfordshire, HP23 6NG
Ⓣ (01494) 758642
Ⓦ www.camomilelawns.co.uk
Also sells wholesale
Contact: B Farmer
Opening Times: Only for collection.
Min Mail Order UK: £14.95
Min Mail Order EU: £64.95
Cat. Cost: Free
Credit Cards: None.
Specialities: *Camomile* 'Treneague'.
Map Ref: L, B3

LNCo **NATURE'S CORNER** ⊠
11 Bunyan Close, Pirton,
Nr. Hitchin, Hertfordshire,
SG5 3RE
Ⓣ (01462) 712519
Ⓔ DouglasCrawley@Naturescorners.co.uk
Ⓦ www.Naturescorners.co.uk
Contact: Douglas Crawley
Opening Times: Not open. Mail order only.
Min Mail Order UK: Nmc
Cat. Cost: 1 x 1st class
Credit Cards: None.
Specialities: *Nymphaea*.

LPBA **PAUL BROMFIELD – AQUATICS**
⊠ ✈ € ♿
Maydencroft Lane,
Gosmore, Hitchin,
Hertfordshire, SG4 7QD
Ⓣ (01462) 457399
Ⓜ 07801 656848
Ⓔ info@bromfieldaquatics.co.uk
Ⓦ www.bromfieldaquatics.co.uk
Also sells wholesale
Contact: P Bromfield
Opening Times: 1000-1700 Mon-Sat Feb-Oct. Please ring first. Order online at website.
Min Mail Order UK: £15.00 incl.
Min Mail Order EU: £100.00 incl.
Cat. Cost: Available online only.
Credit Cards: Visa MasterCard Delta JCB Switch
Specialities: Water lilies, marginals & bog.

LPen **PENSTEMONS BY COLOUR**
76 Grove Avenue, Hanwell, London,
W7 3ES
Ⓣ (020) 8840 3199
Ⓕ (020) 8840 6415
Ⓔ debra.hughes1@virgin.net
Also sells wholesale
Contact: Debra Hughes
Opening Times: Any time by appt.
Cat. Cost: Free
Credit Cards: None.
Specialities: *Penstemon*.
Map Ref: L, B3

LPhx **PHOENIX PERENNIAL PLANTS** ń € ♿
Paice Lane, Medstead,
Alton, Hampshire,
GU34 5PR
Ⓣ (01420) 560695
Ⓕ (01420) 563640
Ⓔ GreenFarmPlants.Marina.Christopher@Care4free.net
Contact: Marina Christopher
Opening Times: 1000-1800 Thu-Sat, 25th Mar-23rd Oct 2004.
Cat. Cost: 4 x 1st class
Credit Cards: All major credit/debit cards.
Specialities: Perennials, many uncommon. *Sanguisorba, Thalictrum, Achillea, Eryngium, Monarda, Phlox, Verbascum,* bulbs & grasses. Note: formerly Green Farm Plants, co-located with Select Seeds LSss.
Map Ref: L, C2 **OS Grid Ref:** SU657362

LPio **PIONEER NURSERY** ⊠ ⌂ € ♿
Baldock Lane, Willian, Letchworth, Hertfordshire, SG6 2AE
Ⓣ (01462) 675858
Ⓔ milly@pioneerplants.com
Ⓦ www.pioneerplants.com
Also sells wholesale
Contact: Nick Downing
Opening Times: 0900-1700 Tue-Sat 1000-1600 Sun, Mar-Oct, 1000-1600 Tue-Sat Nov, Dec & Feb.
Min Mail Order UK: £15.00 + p&p
Min Mail Order EU: € 30.
Cat. Cost: Free
Credit Cards: MasterCard Visa
Specialities: *Salvia,* tender perennials. Wide range of hard-to-find perennials & bulbs.
Map Ref: L, A3

LPJP **PJ'S PALMS AND EXOTICS** ⊠ €
41 Salcombe Road, Ashford, Middlesex, TW15 3BS
Ⓣ (01784) 250181
Contact: Peter Jenkins
Opening Times: Mail order only 1st Mar-30th Nov. Visits by arrangement.
Min Mail Order UK: Nmc
Min Mail Order EU: Nmc
Cat. Cost: 2 x 1st class
Credit Cards: None.
Specialities: Palms, bananas & other exotic foliage plants, hardy & half-hardy. *Trachycarpus wagnerianus* seeds available. Note: plants available in small quantities.
Map Ref: L, B3

LRav **RAVEN VALLEY PLANT NURSERY**
Mayfields, Whitmore Lane, Woking, Surrey, GU4 7QB
Ⓣ (01483) 234605
Ⓜ 07887 925945
Ⓔ ravenvalley@aol.com
Ⓦ www.plantzalive.com
Contact: Maria & Terry Milton
Opening Times: 1000-1600 (1700 in summer), Sat, Sun & B/hols only. Or by arrangement, please phone first. Closed Jan & Feb.
Cat. Cost: On floppy disc only. Sae.
Credit Cards: None.
Specialities: *Eucalyptus*, grasses.
Map Ref: L, C3

LRHS **WISLEY PLANT CENTRE (RHS)** ♿ ◆
RHS Garden, Wisley, Woking, Surrey, GU23 6QB
Ⓣ (01483) 211113
Ⓕ (01483) 212372
Ⓔ wisleyplantcentre@rhs.org.uk
Opening Times: 1000-1800 Mon-Sat 1100-1700 Sun summer, 1000-1730 Mon-Sat 1000-1600 Sun winter. Closed 25-26 Dec & Easter Sun.
Cat. Cost: None issued
Credit Cards: MasterCard Access Amex Switch Visa
Specialities: Very wide range, many rare & unusual.
Map Ref: L, C3

LSiH **SINO-HIMALAYAN PLANT ASSOCIATION** ⊠ ✈
81 Parlaunt Road, Slough, Buckinghamshire, SL3 8BE
Ⓣ (01753) 542823
Ⓕ (01753) 542823
Contact: Chris Chadwell
Min Mail Order UK: Nmc
Cat. Cost: None issued
Credit Cards: None.
Specialities: Seed available for exchange to members. Please apply for membership.

LSou **SOUTHON PLANTS** ⊠ ♿ ◆
Mutton Hill, Dormansland, Lingfield, Surrey, RH7 6NP
Ⓣ (01342) 870150
Contact: Mr Southon
Opening Times: 0900-1700 Mar-Oct, closed Wed in Jul, Sep & Nov. Dec, Jan & Aug please phone first.
Min Mail Order UK: Nmc
Cat. Cost: £2.00 or free with sae.
Credit Cards: All major credit/debit cards.
Specialities: New & unusual hardy & tender perennials, incl. herbs. Also hardy ferns, alpines, grasses, shrubs & climbers incl. many variegated plants. Note: mail order Oct-Feb.
Map Ref: L, C4

LSpr **SPRINGLEA NURSERY** ♿
Springlea, Seymour Plain, Marlow, Buckinghamshire, SL7 3BZ
Ⓣ (01628) 473366
Ⓜ 07761 213779
Contact: Mary Dean
Opening Times: Apr-Sep. Please check before visiting. Garden open, see NGS for details.
Cat. Cost: None issued
Credit Cards: None.

KEY
⊠ Mail order to UK or EU ⌂ Delivers to shows
✈ Exports beyond EU € Euro accepted
♿ Accessible by wheelchair ◆ See Display advertisement

Specialities: Wide range of rare & unusual shrubs & perennials incl. hardy *Geranium, Pulmonaria, Primula*, bog plants, ground cover & shade loving plants.
Map Ref: L, B3

LSRN **SPRING REACH NURSERY** ◆
Long Reach, Ockham,
Guildford, Surrey, GU23 6PG
Ⓣ (01483) 284769
Ⓜ 07884 432666
Ⓕ (01483) 284769
Ⓔ n.hourhan@btopenworld.com
Also sells wholesale
Contact: Nick Hourhan
Opening Times: 7 days. Mon-Sat 1000-1700, Sun 1030-1630. Closed Wed 1st Jul-1st Feb.
Cat. Cost: 2 x 1st class
Credit Cards: All major credit/debit cards.
Specialities: Shrubs, grasses, bamboos, climbers, perennials, trees & *Clematis*. Nursery partially accessible for wheelchair users.
Map Ref: L, C3

LSss **SELECT SEEDS** ⊠ € ♿
Paice Lane, Medstead, Nr. Alton, Hampshire, GU34 5PR
Ⓣ (01420) 560695
Ⓕ (01420) 563640
Ⓔ GreenFarmPlants.Marina.Christopher@Care4free.net
Contact: Marina Christopher
Opening Times: Not open. Mail order only.
Min Mail Order UK: £10.00
Cat. Cost: 3 x 1st class
Credit Cards: All major credit/debit cards.
Specialities: Seeds. *Aconitum, Eryngium, Thalictrum, Sanguisorba* & *Angelica*. Note: co-located with Phoenix Perennial Plants LPhx.
Map Ref: L, C2 **OS Grid Ref:** SU657362

LStr **HENRY STREET NURSERY** ⊠ ♿
Swallowfield Road, Arborfield, Reading, Berkshire, RG2 9JY
Ⓣ (0118) 9761223
Ⓕ (0118) 9761417
Ⓔ info@henrystreet.co.uk
Ⓦ www.henrystreet.co.uk
Also sells wholesale
Contact: Mr M C Goold
Opening Times: 0900-1730 Mon-Sat, 1030-1630 Sun.
Min Mail Order UK: Nmc
Min Mail Order EU: Nmc
Cat. Cost: Free
Credit Cards: Visa Access Switch
Specialities: Roses.
Map Ref: L, C3

LToo **TOOBEES EXOTICS** ⊠ ✈ € ♿
(Office) 20 Inglewood,
St Johns, Woking, Surrey,
GU21 3HX
Ⓣ (01483) 797534 (nursery), (01483) 722600 (evenings)
Ⓕ (01483) 751995
Ⓔ bbpotter@compuserve.com
Ⓦ www.toobees-exotics.com
Contact: Bob Potter
Opening Times: 1000-1700 Thu-Sun & B/hol Mons, 18 Apr-26 Sep 2004. Other times by appointment.
Min Mail Order UK: Nmc
Min Mail Order EU: Nmc
Cat. Cost: Sae
Credit Cards: MasterCard Visa Delta Switch
Specialities: South African & Madagascan succulents, many rare & unusual species. Palms, tree ferns, air plants, carnivorous plants, *Euphorbia, Pachypodium*. Note: nursery is at Blackhorse Road, Woking.
Map Ref: L, C3

LTwo **TWO JAYS ALPINES** ◆
(Office) 35 Greenways, Luton, Bedfordshire, LU2 8BL
Ⓣ (01442) 864951
Ⓕ (01442) 864951
Ⓔ john.spokes@talk21.com
Contact: John Spokes
Opening Times: 0930-1730 or dusk if earlier, 7 days.
Cat. Cost: 3 x 2nd class
Credit Cards: Visa MasterCard
Specialities: Large range of alpines, herbaceous, shrubs, many in small quantities. Note: nursery is at Little Heath Farm, Little Heath Lane, Potten End, Berkhamstead.
Map Ref: L, A3

LVER **THE VERNON GERANIUM NURSERY** ⊠ ♿
Cuddington Way, Cheam,
Sutton, Surrey, SM2 7JB
Ⓣ (020) 8393 7616
Ⓕ (020) 8786 7437
Ⓔ mrgeranium@aol.com
Ⓦ www.geraniumsuk.com
Contact: Philip James & Liz Sims
Opening Times: 0930-1730 Mon-Sat, 1000-1600 Sun, 1st Mar-30th Jun.
Min Mail Order UK: Nmc
Min Mail Order EU: Nmc
Cat. Cost: £2.00 UK, £2.50 EU
Credit Cards: All major credit/debit cards.
Specialities: *Pelargonium* & *Fuchsia*.
Map Ref: L, C4

MIDLANDS

MAJR **A J ROBINSON** ⊠
Sycamore Farm, Foston,
Derbyshire,
DE65 5PW
Ⓣ (01283) 815635,(01283) 815635
Ⓕ (01283) 815635
Contact: A J Robinson
Opening Times: By appt. for collection of plants only.
Min Mail Order UK: £12.50
Cat. Cost: 2 x 1st class for list.
Credit Cards: None.
Specialities: Extensive collection of tender perennials. Salvias. National Collection of *Argyranthemum*. Note mail order argyranthemums & heliotrope only.
Map Ref: M, B2

MAln **L A ALLEN** ⊠
178 Hill Village Road, Four Oaks, Sutton Coldfield, W Midlands, B75 5JG
Ⓣ (0121) 308 0697
Ⓦ www.fidalgo.freeserve.co.uk
Also sells wholesale
Contact: L A Allen
Opening Times: By prior appt.
Min Mail Order UK: Nmc
Min Mail Order EU: Nmc
Cat. Cost: 4 x 1st class
Credit Cards: None.
Specialities: Nat. Coll. of *Primula auricula*. Type: alpine auricula, show edged, show self, doubles, stripes. Surplus plants from the Collection so ltd. in numbers. Occasionally only 1 or 2 available on some cvs.

MAnH **ARN HILL PLANTS** ⊠ €
62 West Lockinge, Wantage,
Oxfordshire, OX12 8QE
Ⓣ (01235) 834312
Ⓜ 07879 862749
Ⓕ (01235) 862361
Ⓔ sally@arnhillplants.com
Ⓦ www.arnhillplants.com
Contact: Sally Hall
Opening Times: By appt. only.
Min Mail Order UK: Nmc
Cat. Cost: Free
Credit Cards: None.
Specialities: Wide range of unusual & traditional hardy perennials and grasses.
Map Ref: M, D2 **OS Grid Ref:** SU423878

MArl **ARLEY HALL NURSERY**
Arley Hall Nursery, Northwich, Cheshire,
CW9 6NA
Ⓣ (01565) 777479/777231
Ⓕ (01565) 777465
Contact: Jane Foster
Opening Times: 1100-1730 Tue-Sun Easter-end Sep. Also B/hol Mons.
Cat. Cost: 4 x 1st class
Credit Cards: All major credit/debit cards.
Specialities: Wide range of herbaceous incl. many unusual varieties. Wide range of pelargoniums.
Map Ref: M, A1

MAsh **ASHWOOD NURSERIES LTD** ⊠
Greensforge, Kingswinford,
W Midlands,
DY6 0AE
Ⓣ (01384) 401996
Ⓕ (01384) 401108
Ⓔ ashwoodnurs@hotmail.com
Ⓦ www.ashwood-nurseries.co.uk
Contact: Mark Warburton & Philip Baulk
Opening Times: 0900-1800 Mon-Sat & 0930-1800 Sun excl. Xmas & Boxing Day.
Min Mail Order UK: Nmc
Min Mail Order EU: Nmc
Cat. Cost: 6 x 1st class
Credit Cards: Visa Access MasterCard
Specialities: Large range of hardy plants & dwarf conifers. Nat. Colls. of *Lewisia* & *Cyclamen* species. *Hellebores, Hepatica, Salvia.* Note: mail order seeds, special packs only.
Map Ref: M, C2

MAus **DAVID AUSTIN ROSES LTD** ⊠ €
Bowling Green Lane, Albrighton,
Wolverhampton,
WV7 3HB
Ⓣ (01902) 376377
Ⓕ (01902) 372142
Ⓔ retail@davidaustinroses.co.uk
Ⓦ www.davidaustinroses.com
Also sells wholesale
Contact: Retail Dept
Opening Times: 0900-1700 Mon-Fri, 1000-1800 Sat, Sun & B/hols. Until dusk Nov-Mar.
Min Mail Order UK: Nmc
Min Mail Order EU: Nmc
Cat. Cost: Free
Credit Cards: Switch Visa MasterCard
Specialities: Roses. Nat. Coll. of English Roses.
Map Ref: M, B1

KEY
⊠ Mail order to UK or EU — Delivers to shows
Exports beyond EU — € Euro accepted
Accessible by wheelchair — ◆ See Display advertisement

M

MAvo **AVONDALE NURSERY**
(Office) 3 Avondale Road,
Earlsdon, Coventry,
Warwickshire,
CV5 6DZ
Ⓣ (024) 766 73662
Ⓜ 07979 093096
Ⓕ (024) 766 73662
Ⓔ enquiries@avondalenursery.co.uk
Ⓦ www.avondalenursery.co.uk
Contact: Brian Ellis
Opening Times: 1000-1230, 1400-1700 7 days 1st Mar-15th Oct. Closed Sun pm Jul-Aug. Other times by appt.
Cat. Cost: 4 x 1st class
Credit Cards: None.
Specialities: Rare & unusual perennials esp. *Campanula, Eryngium, Leucanthemum, Geum, Crocosmia, Pulmonaria* & grasses. Note: nursery is at Smith's Nursery, 3 Stoneleigh Road, Baginton, Nr. Coventry.
Map Ref: M, C2

MBar **BARNCROFT NURSERIES**
Dunwood Lane, Longsdon,
Nr. Leek, Stoke-on-Trent,
Staffordshire, ST9 9QW
Ⓣ (01538) 384310
Ⓕ (01538) 384310
Ⓦ www.barncroftnurseries.co.uk
Also sells wholesale.
Contact: S Warner
Opening Times: 0930-1730 or dusk if earlier Fri-Sun all year, plus Mon-Thu 0930-1730 Mar-Dec. Closed Xmas to New Year.
Min Mail Order UK: £20.00 + p&p
Cat. Cost: £2.50 incl. p&p
Credit Cards: None.
Specialities: Extensive range of over 2000 heathers, conifers, shrubs, trees, climbers, dwarf grasses & rhododendrons. Display garden containing 400 heather cvs.
Map Ref: M, B1 **OS Grid Ref:** SJ948552

MBct **BARCOTE GARDEN HERBACEOUS PLANTS**
Barcote Garden, Faringdon,
Oxfordshire,
SN7 8PP
Ⓣ (01367) 870600
Contact: Christine Smith
Opening Times: By arrangement Apr-Sep. Closed Oct-Mar.
Cat. Cost: Sae for plant list.
Credit Cards: None.
Specialities: Herbaceous perennials. Ferns. Small quantities of all plants listed.
Map Ref: M, D2 **OS Grid Ref:** SU322977

MBlu **BLUEBELL ARBORETUM & NURSERY**
€
Annwell Lane, Smisby,
Nr. Ashby de la Zouch,
Derbyshire, LE65 2TA
Ⓣ (01530) 413700
Ⓕ (01530) 417600
Ⓔ sales@bluebellnursery.com
Ⓦ www.bluebellnursery.com
Contact: Robert & Suzette Vernon
Opening Times: 0900-1700 Mon-Sat & 1030-1630 Sun Mar-Oct, 0900-1600 Mon-Sat (not Sun) Nov-Feb. Closed 24th Dec-4th Jan. Closed Easter Sun.
Min Mail Order UK: Nmc
Min Mail Order EU: Nmc
Cat. Cost: £1.30 + 2 x 1st class
Credit Cards: Visa Access Switch
Specialities: Uncommon trees & shrubs. Display garden & arboretum.
Map Ref: M, B1

MBnl **BENSLEY NURSERIES**
(office) 7 Bramble Way, Kilburn, Derbyshire, DE56 0LH
Ⓣ (01332) 781961
Ⓜ 07968 951019
Ⓕ (01332) 690546
Ⓔ info@bensleynurseries.co.uk
Ⓦ www.bensleynurseries.co.uk
Contact: Mairi Longdon
Opening Times: 1000-1630 Mon-Thu, 1st Mar-31st Oct. Other times by appt. Closed B/hols.
Min Mail Order UK: Nmc
Cat. Cost: 4 x 1st class
Credit Cards: None.
Specialities: Choice & unusual perennials esp. *Achillea, Geranium, Geum, Helenium, Heuchera, Pulmonaria* & grasses. Note: nursery is at White Gables, Dale Road, Stanley, Derbyshire.
Map Ref: M, B2 **OS Grid Ref:** SK417398

MBNS **BARNSDALE GARDENS**
Exton Avenue, Exton, Oakham, Rutland, LE15 8AH
Ⓣ (01572) 813200
Ⓕ (01572) 813346
Ⓔ office@barnsdalegardens.co.uk
Ⓦ www.barnsdalegardens.co.uk
Contact: Nick or Sue Hamilton
Opening Times: 0900-1700 Mar-May & Sep-Oct, 0900-1900 Jun-Aug, 1000-1600 Nov-Feb, 7 days. Closed 23th & 25th Dec.
Min Mail Order UK: Nmc
Min Mail Order EU: Nmc
Cat. Cost: A5 + 5 x 1st class

Credit Cards: Visa Access MasterCard Switch Delta Amex
Specialities: Choice & unusual garden plants. Over 70 varieties of *Penstemon*, over 170 varieties of *Hemerocallis*.
Map Ref: M, B3

MBow BOWDEN HALL NURSERY ⊠
(Office) Malcoff Farmhouse,
Malcoff, Chapel-en-le-Frith,
High Peak, Derbyshire,
SK23 0QR
Ⓣ (01663) 751969
Ⓜ 07867 502775
Ⓔ info@bowdenhallnursery.co.uk
Ⓦ www.bowdenhallnursery.co.uk
Contact: Julie Norfolk
Opening Times: 1000-1700 Wed-Sun & B/hols from 1st Mar. Other times by appt.
Min Mail Order UK: £12.00 + p&p*
Cat. Cost: 6 x 1st class or £1.95.
Credit Cards: All major credit/debit cards.
Specialities: Herbs, wild flowers & hardy cottage garden plants & some old roses. Plants grown in peat-free compost using organic fertilisers. *Note: mail order excl. roses. Nursery at Bowden Hall, Bowden, Chapel-en-le-Frith, High Peak.
Map Ref: M, A2 **OS Grid Ref:** SK065817

MBPg BARNFIELD PELARGONIUMS ⊠
Barnfield, Off Wilnecote Lane,
Belgrave, Tamworth, Staffordshire,
B77 2LF
Ⓣ (01827) 250123
Ⓕ (01827) 250123
Ⓔ brianandjenniewhite@hotmail.com
Contact: Jennie & Brian White
Opening Times: Not open to the public.
Min Mail Order UK: £4.00
Min Mail Order EU: £6.50
Cat. Cost: 4 x 2nd class
Credit Cards: None.
Specialities: Over 190 varieties of scented leaf pelargoniums.

MBri BRIDGEMERE NURSERIES € ♿ ◆
Bridgemere, Nr. Nantwich,
Cheshire, CW5 7QB
Ⓣ (01270) 521100
Ⓕ (01270) 520215
Ⓔ info@bridgemere.co.uk
Ⓦ www.bridgemere.co.uk
Contact: Keith Atkey, Roger Pearce
Opening Times: 0900-1800 7 days, except Xmas Day & Boxing Day.
Cat. Cost: None issued
Credit Cards: Visa Access MasterCard Switch
Specialities: Perennials, shrubs, trees, roses, climbers, rhododendrons & deciduous azaleas, alpines, heathers, bamboos, ferns, grasses, aquatics, houseplants.
Map Ref: M, B1 **OS Grid Ref:** SJ727435

MBrN BRIDGE NURSERY € ♿
Tomlow Road, Napton-on-the-hill,
Nr. Rugby, Warwickshire,
CV47 8HX
Ⓣ (01926) 812737
Ⓔ pmartino@beeb.net
Ⓦ www.Bridge-Nursery.co.uk
Also sells wholesale.
Contact: Christine Dakin & Philip Martino
Opening Times: 1000-1600 Fri-Sun 1st Feb-22nd Dec. Other times by appt.
Cat. Cost: 4 x 1st class
Credit Cards: None.
Specialities: Ornamental grasses, sedges & bamboos. Also range of shrubs & perennials.
Map Ref: M, C2 **OS Grid Ref:** SP463625

MBSH BRITISH SEED HOUSES LTD ⊠ ✈ €
Camp Road, Witham St Hughs, Lincoln,
LN6 9QJ
Ⓣ (01522) 868714
Ⓕ (01522) 868095
Ⓔ seeds@bshlincoln.co.uk
Ⓦ www.britishseedhouses.com
Also sells wholesale.
Contact: Simon Taylor
Opening Times: 0800-1730 Mon-Fri excl. B/hols.
Min Mail Order UK: £50.00 + p&p
Min Mail Order EU: £50.00 + p&p
Cat. Cost: 2 x 1st class
Credit Cards: All major credit/debit cards.
Specialities: Seed.

MCCP COLLECTORS CORNER PLANTS ⊠ 🚚
33 Rugby Road, Clifton-upon-Dunsmore,
Rugby, Warwickshire, CV23 0DE
Ⓣ (01788) 571881
Contact: Pat Neesam
Opening Times: By appt. only.
Min Mail Order UK: £10.00
Cat. Cost: 6 x 1st class
Credit Cards: None.
Specialities: General range of choice herbaceous perennials, grasses, shrubs, palms, ferns & bamboos.
Map Ref: M, C3

KEY
⊠ Mail order to UK or EU — 🚚 Delivers to shows
✈ Exports beyond EU — € Euro accepted
♿ Accessible by wheelchair — ◆ See Display advertisement

MChe **CHESHIRE HERBS** ⊠ ⌂ € ♿ ◆
Fourfields, Forest Road,
Nr. Tarporley, Cheshire,
CW6 9ES
Ⓣ (01829) 760578
Ⓔ info@cheshireherbs.com
Ⓦ www.cheshireherbs.com
Contact: Ted Riddell
Opening Times: 1000-1700 7 days 3rd Jan-24th Dec.
Min Mail Order UK: Nmc
Min Mail Order EU: Nmc
Cat. Cost: 2 x 1st class
Credit Cards: Access Visa Switch
Specialities: Display herb garden & Elizabethan knot garden. Note: mail order seeds only (not plants).
Map Ref: M, B1 **OS Grid Ref:** SJ580673

MCls **COLES PLANT CENTRE** ♿
624 Uppingham Road, Thurnby,
Leicestershire, LE7 9QB
Ⓣ (0116) 241 8394
Ⓕ (0116) 243 2311
Ⓔ info@colesplantcentre.co.uk
Ⓦ www.colesplantcentre.co.uk
Also sells wholesale.
Contact: Mark Goddard
Opening Times: 0800-1700 Mon-Fri, 0900-1700 Sat & Sun.
Credit Cards: MasterCard Switch
Specialities: Fruit, Ornamental Trees & Shrubs.
Map Ref: M, B3

MCoo **COOL TEMPERATE** ⊠
39 Maple Avenue, Beeston,
Nottinghamshire, NG9 1PU
Ⓣ (0115) 917 0416
Ⓕ (0115) 917 0416
Ⓔ philcorbett53@hotmail.com
Ⓦ www.cooltemperate.co.uk
Also sells wholesale.
Contact: Phil Corbett
Opening Times: Not open, mail order only.
Min Mail Order UK: Nmc
Min Mail Order EU: Nmc
Cat. Cost: 2 x 1st class
Credit Cards: None.
Specialities: Tree fruit, soft fruit, nitrogen-fixers, hedging, own-root fruit trees.

MCre **CRESCENT PLANTS** ⊠ ⌂
34 The Crescent, Cradley Heath,
W Midlands, B64 7JS
Ⓣ (0121) 550 2628
Ⓕ (0121) 550 2732
Ⓔ Goddarius@hotmail.com
Ⓦ www.auriculas.co.uk
Also sells wholesale.
Contact: Ian Goddard
Min Mail Order UK: Nmc
Min Mail Order EU: Nmc
Cat. Cost: 2 x 1st class
Credit Cards: None.
Specialities: Named varieties of *Primula auricula* incl. show, alpine, double, striped & border types. Also seed. Anomalous polyanthus eg hose-in-hose, Jack in the Green.

MDHE **DHE PLANTS** ⊠ ⌂
(Office) Rose Lea, Darley House Estate,
Darley Dale, Matlock, Derbyshire,
DE4 2QH
Ⓣ (01629) 732512
Contact: Peter M Smith
Opening Times: By appt. only. The nursery will be closing during 2004.
Min Mail Order UK: Nmc
Cat. Cost: 2 x 1st class
Credit Cards: None.
Specialities: Alpines esp. *Erodium* (70+), *Helianthemum* & *Saxifraga*. Notes: mail order Oct-Mar only. Nursery stock is at Robert Young Floral Centre, Bakewell Rd, Matlock.
Map Ref: M, B1

MDKP **D K PLANTS** ⌂
(Office) 19 Harbourne Road,
Cheadle, Stoke on Trent,
Staffordshire, ST10 1JU
Ⓣ (01538) 754460
Ⓜ (daytime) 07779 545015
Ⓔ daveknoxc@aol.com
Contact: Dave Knox
Opening Times: 0900-2000 (or dusk if earlier) Mon-Tue & Thu-Fri. Other times by appt.
Cat. Cost: 4 x 1st class A4 Sae plus 42p 1st or 34p 2nd class stamps.
Credit Cards: None.
Specialities: Unusual hardy alpines & perennials. All grown on the nursery. Note: nursery is at new roundabout across from Queen's Arms pub, Freehay Crossroads, Cheadle.
Map Ref: M, B1

MDun **DUNGE VALLEY GARDENS** € ♿
Windgather Rocks, Kettleshulme, High Peak,
Cheshire, SK23 7RF
Ⓣ (01663) 733787
Ⓕ (01663) 733787
Ⓔ plants@dungevalley.co.uk
Ⓦ www.dungevalley.co.uk
Also sells wholesale.
Contact: David Ketley

Opening Times: 1030-1700 Thu-Sun Mar, Tue-Sun Apr-Jun, Thu-Sun Jul & Aug. Open B/Hols. Otherwise by appt.
Cat. Cost: 2 x 1st class
Credit Cards: All major credit/debit cards.
Specialities: *Rhododendron* species & hybrids. Magnolias, acers, *Meconopsis*, trilliums, trees, shrubs & perennials, some rare & wild collected.
Map Ref: M, A2 **OS Grid Ref:** SJ989777

MEHN **Elizabeth House Nursery** ⛟ € ♿
Weedon Lois, Towcester,
Northamptonshire,
NN12 8PN
Ⓣ (01327) 860056
Ⓕ (01327) 860779
Also sells wholesale.
Contact: Lindsey Cartwright
Opening Times: 1000-1700 Thu-Sat, Mar-Oct. Closed Aug.
Cat. Cost: 2 x 1st class
Credit Cards: None.
Specialities: Wide range of hardy perennials.
Map Ref: M, C3 **OS Grid Ref:** SP604472

MFie **Field House Nurseries** ⊠
Leake Road, Gotham, Nottinghamshire,
NG11 0JN
Ⓣ (0115) 9830278
Ⓕ (0115) 9831486
Ⓔ dlvwjw@field-house-alpines.fsbusiness.co.uk
Contact: Doug Lochhead & Valerie A Woolley
Opening Times: 0900-1600 Fri-Wed or by appt.
Min Mail Order UK: Min. order 4 plants*
Min Mail Order EU: £30.00
Cat. Cost: 4 x 1st or 4 x IRCs
Credit Cards: Visa Access
Specialities: *Primula*, auriculas, alpines & rock plants. 3 Nat. Colls. of *Primula* and *P. auricula*. *Note: mail order for *Primula*, auriculas & seeds only.
Map Ref: M, B3

MFOX **Fox Cottage Plants** ⛟ ♿
Yew Tree Farm, Thatchers Lane,Tansley,
Matlock, Derbyshire, DE4 5FD
Ⓣ (01629) 57493
Ⓜ 07787 963966
Ⓕ (01629) 57493
Ⓔ avril@yewtreefarm1.fslife.co.uk
Contact: Mrs Avril Buckley
Opening Times: 1200-1700 Mon-Sat, Feb-Oct. Nov-Jan by appt. Please ring to confirm.
Cat. Cost: 2 x 1st class
Credit Cards: None.
Specialities: Unusual hardy & tender perennials. Stock available in small quantities only.
Map Ref: M, C2 **OS Grid Ref:** SK324594

MFry **Fryer's Nurseries Ltd** ⊠ ✈ € ♿
Manchester Road, Knutsford, Cheshire,
WA16 0SX
Ⓣ (01565) 755455
Ⓕ (01565) 653755
Ⓔ garethfryer@fryers-roses.co.uk
Ⓦ www.fryers-roses.co.uk
Also sells wholesale.
Contact: Gareth Fryer
Opening Times: 0900-1730 Mon-Sat & 1030-1630 Sun & 1000-1730 B/hols.
Min Mail Order UK: Nmc
Min Mail Order EU: Nmc
Cat. Cost: Free
Credit Cards: All major credit/debit cards.
Specialities: Extensive rose nursery & garden centre producing over half a million bushes annually. Rose fields in bloom Jun-Sep.
Map Ref: M, A1 **OS Grid Ref:** SJ738803

MGag **Gaggini's Plant Centre** ⊠ ✈ ♿
Glebe House, Glebe Road, Mears Ashby,
Northamptonshire, NN6 0DL
Ⓣ (01604) 812371/811811
Ⓕ (01604) 812353
Ⓦ www.gagginis.co.uk
Also sells wholesale.
Contact: John B & Mrs J E Gaggini
Opening Times: 0800-1730 Mon-Fri. 0900-1730 Sat & Sun.
Min Mail Order UK: £8.00 + p&p
Cat. Cost: £1.00 (please state retail)
Credit Cards: Visa Access Switch MasterCard
Specialities: Specialist growers of container trees, shrubs, conifers & fruit, esp. Wisteria. Note: mail order for *Wisteria* only.
Map Ref: M, C3

MGan **Gandy's (Roses) Ltd** ⊠
North Kilworth, Nr. Lutterworth,
Leicestershire, LE17 6HZ
Ⓣ (01858) 880398
Ⓕ (01858) 880433
Ⓔ sales@gandys-roses.co.uk
Ⓦ www.gandys-roses.co.uk
Also sells wholesale.
Contact: Miss R D Gandy

Opening Times: 0900-1700 Mon-Sat & 1400-1700 Sun.
Min Mail Order UK: Nmc
Min Mail Order EU: £25.00 + p&p
Cat. Cost: Free
Credit Cards: None.
Specialities: 580 rose varieties.
Map Ref: M, C3

MGGn THE GREEN GARDEN ⊠ ⌂
Dewsnaps, Chinley, High Peak, Derbyshire, SK23 6AW
Ⓣ (01663) 751175
Ⓕ (01663) 751332
Contact: Sally Williams
Opening Times: Please phone for appt.
Min Mail Order UK: No minimum charge
Cat. Cost: 4 x 1st class
Credit Cards: None.
Specialities: Nat. Coll. of *Ballota* & *Stachys*.
Map Ref: M, A2

MGol GOLDEN COTTAGE PLANTS ⊠ ✈
Golden Cottage, Scarcliffe Lanes, Upper Langwith, Mansfield, Nottinghamshire, NG20 9RQ
Ⓜ 07952 804077
Contact: C Coleman
Opening Times: By appt. only.
Min Mail Order UK: Nmc
Min Mail Order EU: Nmc
Cat. Cost: 2 x 1st class
Credit Cards: None.
Specialities: Ethnobotanical plants and seeds. Hardy, tropical & sub-tropical. All plants & seeds only available in ltd. quantity ie 2 plants/person/species.

MGos GOSCOTE NURSERIES LTD € ♿ ◆
Syston Road, Cossington, Leicestershire, LE7 4UZ
Ⓣ (01509) 812121
Ⓕ (01509) 814231
Ⓔ sales@goscote.co.uk
Ⓦ www.goscote.co.uk
Contact: Derek Cox, James Toone
Opening Times: 7 days, closed between Xmas & New Year.
Cat. Cost: 5 x 1st class
Credit Cards: Visa Access MasterCard Delta Switch
Specialities: Japanese maples, rhododendrons & azaleas, *Magnolia, Camellia, Pieris* & other *Ericaceae*. Ornamental trees & shrubs, conifers, fruit, heathers, alpines, *Clematis* & unusual climbers. Show Garden to visit.
Map Ref: M, B3

MHar HARTS GREEN NURSERY
89 Harts Green Road, Harborne, Birmingham, B17 9TZ
Ⓣ (0121) 427 5200
Contact: B Richardson
Opening Times: 1400-1730 Wed Apr-Jul & Sep. Other times, excl. Aug, by appt.
Cat. Cost: None issued.
Credit Cards: None.
Specialities: Hardy perennials. Some in small quantities only.
Map Ref: M, C2 **OS Grid Ref:** SP030845

MHer THE HERB NURSERY ♿ ◆
Thistleton, Oakham, Rutland, LE15 7RE
Ⓣ (01572) 767658
Ⓕ (01572) 768021
Contact: Peter Bench
Opening Times: 0900-1800 (or dusk) 7 days excl. Xmas-New Year.
Cat. Cost: A5 Sae.
Credit Cards: None.
Specialities: Herbs, wild flowers, cottage garden plants, scented-leaf pelargoniums. Especially *Thymus, Mentha, Lavandula.*
Map Ref: M, B3

MHom HOMESTEAD PLANTS ⊠
The Homestead, Normanton, Bottesford, Nottingham, NG13 0EP
Ⓣ (01949) 842745
Ⓕ (01949) 842745
Contact: Mrs S Palmer
Opening Times: By appt.
Min Mail Order UK: Nmc
Cat. Cost: 4 x 2nd class
Credit Cards: None.
Specialities: Unusual hardy & half-hardy perennials, especially *Helleborus* & *Paeonia* species. *Hosta, Jovibarba, Sempervivum* & *Heliotrope*. Most available only in small quantities.
Map Ref: M, B3 **OS Grid Ref:** SK812407

MHrb THE HERB GARDEN ♿
Kingston House Estate, Race Farm Lane, Kingston Bagpuize, Oxfordshire, OX13 5AU
Ⓣ (01865) 823101
Ⓕ (01865) 820159
Ⓔ vcjw37@yahoo.com
Ⓦ www.KingstonHerbGarden.co.uk
Contact: Val Williams
Opening Times: As for Kingston Bagpuise House Open Days, or phone for appt. See website for details.
Cat. Cost: 2 x 1st class
Credit Cards: None.

Specialities: Small nursery specialising in the more unusual lavenders. Herbs, dye plants, olive & citrus fruit trees according to season displayed in a walled garden setting.
Map Ref: M, D2

MIDC IAN AND DEBORAH COPPACK ⊠ ♿ ◆
Woodside, Langley Road, Langley, Macclesfield, Cheshire, SK11 0DG
Ⓣ (01260) 253308
Ⓕ (01260) 253308
Ⓔ coppack@worldonline.co.uk
Also sells wholesale.
Contact: Ian & Deborah Coppack
Opening Times: 0900-1700 Mar-Sep.
Min Mail Order UK: Nmc
Cat. Cost: 2 x 1st class
Credit Cards: None.
Specialities: *Hosta.*
Map Ref: M, A2 **OS Grid Ref:** 938715

MInt INTAKES FARM
Sandy Lane, Longsdon, Stoke-on-Trent, Staffordshire, ST9 9QQ
Ⓣ (01538) 398452
Contact: Mrs Kathleen Inman
Opening Times: By appt. only.
Cat. Cost: None issued
Credit Cards: None.
Specialities: Double, variegated & unusual forms of British natives & cottage garden plants.
Map Ref: M, B1

MJac JACKSON'S NURSERIES
Clifton Campville, Nr. Tamworth, Staffordshire, B79 0AP
Ⓣ (01827) 373307
Ⓕ (01827) 373307
Also sells wholesale.
Contact: N Jackson
Opening Times: 0900-1800 Mon Wed-Sat, 1000-1700 Sun.
Cat. Cost: 2 x 1st class
Credit Cards: None.
Specialities: *Fuchsia.*
Map Ref: M, B1

MJnS JUNGLE SEEDS AND GARDENS ⊠
PO Box 45, Watlington SPDO, Oxfordshire, OX49 5YR
Ⓣ (01491) 614765
Ⓕ (01491) 614765
Ⓔ enquiry@junglegardens.co.uk
Ⓦ www.junglegardens.co.uk
Contact: Penny White
Opening Times: By appt. only to collect plants.
Min Mail Order UK: Nmc
Cat. Cost: 2 x 1st class
Credit Cards: Visa MasterCard Switch
Specialities: Hardy, semi-hardy & conservatory exotics. Some items ltd. availability.

MJon C & K JONES ⊠ ✈ ⌂ €
Golden Fields Nurseries, Barrow Lane, Tarvin, Cheshire, CH3 8JF
Ⓣ (01829) 740663
Ⓕ (01829) 741877
Ⓔ keith@ckjones.freeserve.co.uk
Ⓦ www.jonestherose.co.uk
Also sells wholesale.
Contact: Keith Jones/P Woolley
Opening Times: Office hours 0930-1600 Fri-Mon. 1st w/end in each month only & the Fri & Mon either side. Closed Jan & Feb.
Min Mail Order UK: 1 plant + p&p
Min Mail Order EU: Nmc.
Cat. Cost: £1.00
Credit Cards: MasterCard Delta Switch Visa
Specialities: Roses.
Map Ref: M, B1

MKay KAYES GARDEN NURSERY ♿
1700 Melton Road, Rearsby, Leicestershire, LE7 4YR
Ⓣ (01664) 424578
Ⓔ hazelkaye.kgn@nascr.net
Contact: Hazel Kaye
Opening Times: 1000-1700 Tue-Sat & B/hols 1000-1200 Sun Mar-Oct. By appt. Nov, Dec & Feb. Closed Jan.
Cat. Cost: 2 x 1st class
Credit Cards: None.
Specialities: Herbaceous, climbers & aquatic plants. Grasses.
Map Ref: M, B3 **OS Grid Ref:** SK648140

MLan LANE END NURSERY
Old Cherry Lane, Lymm, Cheshire, WA13 0TA
Ⓣ (01925) 752618
Ⓔ sawyer@laneend.u-net.com
Ⓦ www.laneend.u-net.com
Contact: I Sawyer
Opening Times: 0930-1730 Thu-Tue Feb-Dec.
Cat. Cost: None issued
Credit Cards: None.

KEY
⊠ Mail order to UK or EU ⌂ Delivers to shows
✈ Exports beyond EU € Euro accepted
♿ Accessible by wheelchair ◆ See Display advertisement

M

Specialities: Award of Garden Merit plants with a wide range of choice & unusual shrubs, trees, perennials & ferns.
Map Ref: M, A1 **OS Grid Ref:** SJ664850

MLea LEA RHODODENDRON GARDENS LTD ⊠ ✈ ♿
Lea, Matlock, Derbyshire, DE4 5GH
Ⓣ (01629) 534380/534260
Ⓕ (01629) 534260
Contact: Peter Tye
Opening Times: 1000-1730 7 days 20 Mar-30 Jun. Out of season by appt.
Min Mail Order UK: £15.00 + p&p
Min Mail Order EU: £15.00 + p&p
Cat. Cost: 30p + Sae
Credit Cards: All major credit/debit cards.
Specialities: Rhododendrons & azaleas.
Map Ref: M, B1 **OS Grid Ref:** SK324571

MLLN LODGE LANE NURSERY & GARDENS ⌂
Lodge Lane, Dutton, Nr. Warrington, Cheshire, WA4 4HP
Ⓣ (01928) 713718
Ⓕ (01928) 713718
Ⓔ rod@lodgelanenursery.co.uk
Ⓦ www.lodgelanenursery.co.uk
Contact: Rod or Diane Casey
Opening Times: 1000-1700 Wed-Sun & B/hols, mid Mar-mid Sep. By appt. outside these dates.
Cat. Cost: 3 x 1st class
Credit Cards: None.
Specialities: Unusual perennials & shrubs incl. *Allium, Campanula, Digitalis, Penstemon, Euphorbia, Geranium, Heuchera, Inula, Kniphofia, Penstemon, Salvia* & ornamental grasses. National Collection of *Inula*.
Map Ref: M, A1 **OS Grid Ref:** SJ586779

MLod LODGE FARM ⊠ ⌂ ♿
Case Lane, Fiveways,
Hatton,
Warwickshire,
CV35 7JD
Ⓣ (01926) 484649
Ⓜ 07977 631368/07870 851924
Ⓔ richard.a.cook@btinternet.com
Also sells wholesale.
Contact: Janet Cook & Nick Cook
Opening Times: 1000-1700 Tue-Sun (closed Mon), Mar-end Oct.. If travelling a long way, please phone to check availability & directions. Nov-Feb by appt. only, please phone first
Min Mail Order UK: Nmc
Cat. Cost: 2 x 1st class
Credit Cards: None.
Specialities: Wildflowers, herbs and sensual plants. Vegetable plants, fruit, topiary. Native trees & hedging. Old fashioned cottage garden plants. Note: larger nursery at Herb.E.Flowers, Kungla Nursery, Red Lane, Burton Green, Kenilworth, CV8 1PB.
Map Ref: M, C2

MLul LULWORTH PLANTS ⌂ ♿
28 Gladstone Street, Wigston Magna, Leicestershire, LE18 1AE
Ⓜ 07814 042889
Contact: Chris Huscroft
Opening Times: By appt. only.
Cat. Cost: Sae
Credit Cards: None.
Specialities: *Arisaema*, plus small selection of shade-loving plants, small quantities only.
Map Ref: M, B3

MMat MATTOCK'S ROSES ⊠
Notcutts Ltd, Ipswich Road, Woodbridge, Suffolk, IP12 4AF
Ⓣ (01865) 343454
Ⓕ (01865) 343166
Ⓔ roses@mattocks.co.uk
Ⓦ www.mattocks.co.uk
Contact: Plant Adviser
Opening Times: 0900-1800 Mon-Sat, 1030-1630 Sun.
Min Mail Order UK: £30.00 if collected from a Notcutts garden centre.
Credit Cards: Visa MasterCard Switch
Specialities: Roses. All Mattocks roses are part of the Notcutts range of plants and available from Notcutts garden centres. Note: mail order only available at Notcutts garden centres.
Map Ref: M, D3

MMHG MORTON HALL GARDENS ⊠ ⌂ ♿
Morton Hall, Ranby, Retford,
Nottinghamshire,
DN22 8HW
Ⓣ (01777) 702530
Ⓔ mortonhall@business77.freeserve.co.uk
Contact: Gill McMaster
Opening Times: By appt.only
Min Mail Order UK: £5.00 + p&p
Cat. Cost: 3 x 1st class
Credit Cards: None.
Specialities: Shrubs & perennials.
Map Ref: M, A3

MMil MILL HILL PLANTS ♿
Mill Hill House, Elston Lane, East Stoke, Newark, Nottinghamshire, NG23 5QJ
Ⓣ (01636) 525460

Ⓜ 07713 176507
Ⓔ millhill@talk21.com
Ⓦ http://come.to/mill.hill.plants&garden
Contact: G M Gregory
Opening Times: By appt. only. See also NGS dates.
Cat. Cost: none issued
Credit Cards: None.
Specialities: Hardy perennials, many unusual. Nat. Coll. of *Berberis.*
Map Ref: M, B3

MMoz MOZART HOUSE NURSERY GARDEN
84 Central Avenue, Wigston, Leicestershire, LE18 2AA
Ⓣ (0116) 288 9548
Contact: Des Martin
Opening Times: By appt. only.
Cat. Cost: 5 x 1st class
Credit Cards: None.
Specialities: *Bamboo,* ornamental grasses, rushes & sedges, ferns.
Map Ref: M, C3

MNFA THE NURSERY FURTHER AFIELD ⊠
Evenley Road, Mixbury,
Nr. Brackley, Northamptonshire,
NN13 5YR
Ⓣ (01280) 848808
Ⓕ (01280) 848808
Contact: Gerald & Mary Sinclair
Opening Times: 1000-1700 Wed-Sat Mar-early Oct. Open days 1400-1700 11th & 18th July 2004.
Min Mail Order UK: Nmc
Cat. Cost: 2 x 1st class
Credit Cards: None.
Specialities: Hardy perennials, many unusual, incl. *Anemone, Aster, Campanula, Geranium, Hemerocallis & Iris sibirica.* Nat. Coll. of *Hemerocallis.* Note: mail order for *Hemerocallis* only.
Map Ref: M, C3 **OS Grid Ref:** SP608344

MNHC THE NATIONAL HERB CENTRE
Banbury Road, Warmington,
Nr. Banbury,
Oxfordshire, OX17 1DF
Ⓣ (01295) 690999
Ⓕ (01295) 690034
Ⓦ www.herbcentre.co.uk
Contact: Nick Turner
Opening Times: 0900-1730 Mon-Sat, 1030-1700 Sun.
Credit Cards: All major credit/debit cards.
Specialities: Herbs, culinary & medicinal. Extensive selection of rosemary, thyme & lavender, in particular.

MNrw NORWELL NURSERIES ⊠ ◆
Woodhouse Road, Norwell, Newark,
Nottinghamshire, NG23 6JX
Ⓣ (01636) 636337
Ⓔ wardha@aol.com
Also sells wholesale.
Contact: Dr Andrew Ward
Opening Times: 1000-1700 Mon, Wed-Fri & Sun (Wed-Mon May & Jun). By appt. Aug & 20th Oct-1st Mar.
Min Mail Order UK: £12.00 + p&p
Cat. Cost: 3 x 1st class
Credit Cards: None.
Specialities: A large collection of unusual & choice herbaceous perennials & alpines esp. *Penstemon,* hardy *Geranium, Geum,* summer bulbs, *Hemerocallis,* grasses & woodland plants. Gardens open.
Map Ref: M, B3

MOak OAKLAND NURSERIES ⊠
147 Melton Road, Burton-on-the-Wolds,
Loughborough, Leicestershire, LE12 5TQ
Ⓣ (01509) 880646
Ⓕ (01509) 889294
Ⓔ tim@joakland.freeserve.co.uk
Ⓦ www.oaklandnurseries.co.uk
Also sells wholesale.
Contact: Tim & John Oakland
Opening Times: Strictly by appt. Apr-Sep.
Min Mail Order UK: £15.00 + p&p
Min Mail Order EU: £15.00 + p&p
Cat. Cost: 4 x 1st class
Credit Cards: MasterCard Visa
Specialities: Tender perennials, *Canna, Coleus, Caladium, Abutilon, Streptocarpus,* conservatory & exotic plants. Some *Canna* ltd. quantity, *Coleus* propagate to order. Note: export *Canna/Caladium* only as dormant plants.
Map Ref: M, B3 **OS Grid Ref:** SK615214

MOne ONE HOUSE NURSERY ⊠ ◆
Buxton New Road, Macclesfield, Cheshire,
SK11 0AD
Ⓣ (01625) 427087
Contact: Miss J L Baylis
Opening Times: 1000-1700 Tue-Sun & B/hol Mons Mar-Oct, Nov-Feb ring for opening times.
Min Mail Order UK: Nmc*
Cat. Cost: 3 x 1st class
Credit Cards: None.

KEY
⊠ Mail order to UK or EU — Delivers to shows
Exports beyond EU — € Euro accepted
Accessible by wheelchair — ◆ See Display advertisement

M

Specialities: Alpines & perennials. Good range of *Primula auricula, Sempervivum* & bulbs. *Note: mail order for *Sempervivum* & double primroses only.
Map Ref: M, A2 **OS Grid Ref:** SJ943741

MPet **PETER GRAYSON (SWEET PEA SEEDSMAN)** ⊠ ☒
34 Glenthorne Close, Brampton, Chesterfield, Derbyshire, S40 3AR
Ⓣ (01246) 278503
Ⓕ (01246) 278503
Also sells wholesale.
Contact: Peter Grayson
Opening Times: Not open, mail order only.
Min Mail Order UK: Nmc
Min Mail Order EU: Nmc
Cat. Cost: C5 Sae, 1 x 2nd class
Credit Cards: None.
Specialities: *Lathyrus* species & cvs. Large collection of old-fashioned sweet peas & over 100 Spencer sweet peas incl. own cultivars and collection of old-fashioned cottage garden annuals & perennials.

MPhe **PHEDAR NURSERY** ⊠ ☒ €
Bunkers Hill, Romiley, Stockport, Cheshire, SK6 3DS
Ⓣ (0161) 430 3772
Ⓕ (0161) 430 3772
Ⓔ mclewin@phedar.com
Ⓦ www.phedar.com
Also sells wholesale.
Contact: Will McLewin
Opening Times: Frequent esp. in spring but very irregular. Please phone to arrange appt.
Min Mail Order UK: Nmc
Min Mail Order EU: Nmc
Cat. Cost: 2 x A5 AE or address labels + 4 x 1st class
Credit Cards: None.
Specialities: *Helleborus, Paeonia*. Note: non-EU exports subject to destination & on an ad hoc basic only. Please contact nursery for details. Limited stock of some rare items.
Map Ref: M, A2 **OS Grid Ref:** SJ936897

MPkF **PACKHORSE FARM NURSERY** ♿
Sandyford House, Lant Lane,Tansley, Matlock, Derbyshire, DE4 5FW
Ⓣ (01629) 57206, m. 07974 095752
Ⓕ (01629) 57206
Contact: Hilton W. Haynes
Opening Times: 1000-1700 Tues & Wed, 1st Mar-31st Oct. Any other time by appt. only.
Cat. Cost: £1.50
Credit Cards: None.
Specialities: *Acer*, rare stock is limited in supply. Other more unusual hardy shrubs, trees & conifers.
Map Ref: M, B2 **OS Grid Ref:** SK322617

MRav **RAVENSTHORPE NURSERY** ⊠ ♿
6 East Haddon Road, Ravensthorpe, Northamptonshire, NN6 8ES
Ⓣ (01604) 770548
Ⓕ (01604) 770548
Ⓔ ravensthorpenursery@hotmail.com
Contact: Jean & Richard Wiseman
Opening Times: 1000-1800 (dusk if earlier) Tue-Sun. Also B/hol Mons.
Min Mail Order UK: Nmc
Min Mail Order EU: Nmc
Cat. Cost: None issued.
Credit Cards: Visa MasterCard
Specialities: Over 2,600 different trees, shrubs & perennials with many unusual varieties. Search & delivery service for large orders, winter months only.
Map Ref: M, C3 **OS Grid Ref:** SP665699

MRod **RODBASTON COLLEGE** ⊠
Rodbaston, Penkridge, Staffordshire, ST19 5PH
Ⓣ (01785) 712209
Ⓕ (01785) 715701
Also sells wholesale.
Contact: Yoke van der Meer
Opening Times: By appt.
Min Mail Order UK: £10.00
Min Mail Order EU: £15.00
Cat. Cost: 2 x 1st class
Credit Cards: None.
Specialities: Salvias. Nat. Coll. of 'New World' *Salvia*. Note: mail order small size plugs only. Stock available in ltd. quantities only.
Map Ref: M, B1

MS&S **S & S PERENNIALS** ⊠
24 Main Street, Normanton Le Heath, Leicestershire, LE67 2TB
Ⓣ (01530) 262250
Contact: Shirley Pierce
Opening Times: Afternoons only, otherwise please phone.
Min Mail Order UK: Nmc
Cat. Cost: 2 x 1st class
Credit Cards: None.
Specialities: *Erythronium, Fritillaria*, hardy *Cyclamen*, dwarf *Narcissus, Hepatica* & *Anemone*. Note: stock available in small quantities only.
Map Ref: M, B1

MSal **SALLEY GARDENS** ⊠ ✈ € ♿
32 Lansdowne Drive,
West Bridgford, Nottinghamshire,
NG2 7FJ
Ⓣ (0115) 9233878 evenings
Ⓜ 07811 703982
Contact: Richard Lewin
Opening Times: 0900-1700 Sun-Wed, 1st Apr-30th Sep and by appt.
Min Mail Order UK: Nmc
Min Mail Order EU: Nmc
Cat. Cost: Sae
Credit Cards: None.
Specialities: Medicinal plants esp. from North America & China. Dye plants, herbs, spices, seeds. Some species available in limited quanitities only. Note: nursery is at Simkins Farm, Adbolton Lane, West Bridgford, Notts.
Map Ref: M, B3

MSGs **SHOWGLADS** ⊠
105 Derby Road, Bramcote,
Nottingham, NG9 3GZ
Ⓣ (0115) 925 5498
Ⓔ rogerbb@lineone.net
Contact: Roger Braithwaite
Opening Times: Not open.
Min Mail Order UK: £4.00
Cat. Cost: 2 x 1st class
Credit Cards: None.
Specialities: *Gladiolus.*

MSph **SPRINGHILL PLANTS** ⛫
(Office) 18 Westfields, Abingdon,
Oxfordshire, OX14 1BA
Ⓣ (01235) 530889 after 1800
Ⓜ 07790 863378.
Contact: Caroline Cox
Opening Times: Apr-Jun by appt. only. Please phone first.
Credit Cards: None.
Specialities: Small nursery offering a wide range of unusual & garden-worthy perennials & shrubs. Many AGM & rare plants available. Some stock available in small quantities. Note: nursery is at Buildings Farm, Gozzard's Ford, Nr. Marcham, Abingdon.
Map Ref: M, D2

MSte **STEVENTON ROAD NURSERIES** €
Steventon Road, East Hanney, Wantage,
Oxfordshire, OX12 0HS
Ⓣ (01235) 868828
Ⓕ (01235) 763670
Ⓔ johngraham.steventonroadnursery@virgin.net
Ⓦ www.steventonroadnurseries.co.uk
Contact: John Graham
Opening Times: 0900-1700 Mon-Fri, 1000-1700 Sat Mar-Nov. Winter by appt. Closed Sun.
Cat. Cost: 4 x 1st class
Credit Cards: None.
Specialities: Tender & hardy perennials.
Map Ref: M, D2

MSwo **SWALLOWS NURSERY** ⊠
Mixbury, Brackley,
Northamptonshire, NN13 5RR
Ⓣ (01280) 847721
Ⓕ (01280) 848611
Ⓔ enq@swallowsnursery.co.uk
Ⓦ www.swallowsnursery.co.uk
Also sells wholesale.
Contact: Chris Swallow
Opening Times: 0900-1300 & 1400-1700 (earlier in winter) Mon-Fri, 0900-1300 Sat.
Min Mail Order UK: Nmc
Cat. Cost: 2 x 1st class
Credit Cards: Visa MasterCard Switch
Specialities: Growing a wide range, particularly shrubs, trees, roses and heathers. Note: trees not for mail order unless part of larger order.
Map Ref: M, C3 **OS Grid Ref:** SP607336

MTho **A & A THORP**
Bungalow No 5, Main Street,
Theddingworth, Leicestershire,
LE17 6QZ
Ⓣ (01858) 880496
Contact: Anita & Andrew Thorp
Opening Times: 1000-1700.
Cat. Cost: 4 x 1st class
Credit Cards: None.
Specialities: Unusual plants or those in short supply.
Map Ref: M, C3

MTis **TISSINGTON NURSERY** ⛫ ♿
Tissington, Nr. Ashbourne,
Derbyshire, DE6 1RA
Ⓣ (01335) 390650
Ⓕ (01335) 390693
Ⓔ info@tissingtonnursery.co.uk
Ⓦ www.tissingtonnursery.co.uk
Contact: Mrs Sue Watkins
Opening Times: 1000-1800 daily 1st Mar-30th Sep incl. Easter Sun & B/hols.
Cat. Cost: 3 x 1st class
Credit Cards: Visa MasterCard

KEY
⊠ Mail order to UK or EU ⛫ Delivers to shows
✈ Exports beyond EU € Euro accepted
♿ Accessible by wheelchair ◆ See Display advertisement

Specialities: Perennials, shrubs & climbers incl. unusual varieties. Some available only in very ltd. numbers.
Map Ref: M, B1 **OS Grid Ref:** SK176521

MWar **WARD FUCHSIAS** ⊠
5 Pollen Close, Sale, Cheshire, M33 3LS
Ⓣ (0161) 282 7434
Contact: K Ward
Opening Times: 0930-1700 Tue-Sun Feb-Jun incl. B/hols.
Min Mail Order UK: Nmc
Cat. Cost: Free
Credit Cards: None.
Specialities: *Fuchsia*. Available in small quantities.
Map Ref: M, A2

MWat **WATERPERRY GARDENS LTD** ⊠ ♿
Waterperry, Nr. Wheatley,
Oxfordshire, OX33 1JZ
Ⓣ (01844) 339226/254
Ⓕ (01844) 339883
Ⓔ office@waterperrygardens.fsnet.co.uk
Ⓦ www.waterperrygardens.co.uk
Contact: Mr R Jacobs
Opening Times: 0900-1730 Mon-Fri, 0900-1800 Sat & Sun summer. 0900-1700 winter.
Min Mail Order UK: Nmc
Cat. Cost: None issued.
Credit Cards: Visa MasterCard Switch Amex
Specialities: General, plus Nat. Coll. of *Saxifraga* (*Porophyllum*). Reasonable wheelchair access. Note: ltd. mail order, please phone for information.
Map Ref: M, D3 **OS Grid Ref:** SP630064

MWgw **WINGWELL NURSERY** ⊠
Top Street, Wing,
Oakham, Rutland, LE15 8SE
Ⓣ (01572) 737727
Ⓕ (01572) 737788
Ⓔ rosedejardin@btinternet.com
Ⓦ www.wingwellnursery.com
Contact: Rose Dejardin
Opening Times: 1000-1700 daily Mar-Dec.
Min Mail Order UK: Nmc
Cat. Cost: £1.00 for descriptive cat.
Credit Cards: All major credit/debit cards.
Specialities: Herbaceous perennials. Note: mail order Oct-Mar for herbaceous plants, grasses & ferns only.
Map Ref: M, B3 **OS Grid Ref:** SP892029

MWhe **A D & N WHEELER** ⌂
Pye Court, Willoughby, Rugby,
Warwickshire, CV23 8BZ
Ⓣ (01788) 890341
Ⓕ (01788) 890341
Contact: Mrs N Wheeler
Opening Times: 1000-1630 7 days mid Feb-late Jun. Other times please phone for appt.
Cat. Cost: 3 x 1st class
Credit Cards: None.
Specialities: *Fuchsia, Pelargonium* & hardy *Geranium*.
Map Ref: M, C3

MWhi **WHITEHILL FARM NURSERY** ⊠ € ♿
Whitehill Farm, Burford, Oxfordshire, OX18 4DT
Ⓣ (01993) 823218
Ⓕ (01993) 822894
Ⓔ whitehill.farm@virgin.net
Contact: P J M Youngson
Opening Times: 0900-1800 (or dusk if earlier) 7 days.
Min Mail Order UK: £5.00 + p&p
Min Mail Order EU: £5.00 + p&p
Cat. Cost: 4 x 1st class*
Credit Cards: All major credit/debit cards.
Specialities: Grasses & bamboos, less common shrubs & perennials. *Note: £1.00 of catalogue cost refunded on 1st order.
Map Ref: M, D2 **OS Grid Ref:** SP268113

MWht **WHITELEA NURSERY** ⊠ ♿
Whitelea Lane, Tansley, Matlock, Derbyshire, DE4 5FL
Ⓣ (01629) 55010
Ⓔ whitelea@nursery-stock.freeserve.co.uk
Ⓦ www.nursery-stock.freeserve.co.uk
Contact: David Wilson
Opening Times: By appt.
Min Mail Order UK: No minimum charge*
Cat. Cost: 2 x 1st class
Credit Cards: None.
Specialities: *Bamboo*, ivies. Substantial quantities of 30 cvs & species of bamboo, remainder stocked in small numbers only. *Note: palletised deliveries only at present.
Map Ref: M, B1 **OS Grid Ref:** SK325603

MWrn **WARREN HILLS NURSERY** ⊠ ⌂ ♿
Warren Hills Cottage,
Warren Hills Road, Coalville,
Leicestershire, LE67 4UY
Ⓣ (01530) 812350
Ⓔ warrenhills@tinyworld.co.uk
Ⓦ www.warrenhills.co.uk
Contact: Penny Waters or Bob Taylor
Opening Times: By appt. only, please phone. See NGS for open days.
Min Mail Order UK: £10.00 + p&p
Cat. Cost: 4 x 1st class
Credit Cards: None.

Specialities: *Astrantia*. Genuine hardy & unusual perennials. Nat. Coll. *Astrantia*.
Map Ref: M, B1

MWya WYATTS ⌂ € ♿
Hill Barn Farm, Great Rollright,
Chipping Norton, Oxfordshire, OX7 5SH
Ⓣ (01608) 684835, (01608) 684990
Ⓕ (01608) 684990
Ⓔ wyatts@callnetuk.com
Ⓦ www.cotswoldgardenplants.co.uk or www.wyattscountry.com
Contact: John Wyatt or Christine Chittenden
Opening Times: 0900-1700 7 days 21st Oct-1st Mar, 0930-1800 2nd Mar-20th Oct.
Cat. Cost: 2 x 1st class
Credit Cards: MasterCard Switch Delta Visa
Specialities: Many unusual, rare & exotic plants, shrubs & trees incl. *Daphne, Euonymus, Viburnum, Magnolia, Clematis, Cornus* & *Acer*. Alpines, fruit trees & cane fruit. Please check availability list.
Map Ref: M, C2 **OS Grid Ref:** SP317313

NORTHERN

NArg ARGHAM VILLAGE NURSERY ✉ ♿
Argham Grange, Grindale, Bridlington,
East Yorkshire, YO16 4XZ
Ⓣ (01723) 892141
Ⓕ (01723) 892141
Ⓔ geoffpickering@arghamvillage.co.uk
Ⓦ www.arghamvillage.co.uk
Contact: Geoff Pickering
Opening Times: 1000-1700 Mar-Oct, 1130-1500 Nov-Feb, 7 days.
Min Mail Order UK: £50.00 + p&p
Cat. Cost: 4 x 1st class
Credit Cards: Visa MasterCard Delta
Specialities: Herbaceous perennials. Aquatic plants, marginals, bog, alpines, rock plants.
Map Ref: N, C3

NAsh ASHTONS NURSERY GARDENS ♿
Mythop Road, Lytham, Lytham St Annes,
Lancashire, FY8 4JP
Ⓣ (01253) 736627/794808
Ⓕ (01253) 735311
Ⓔ info@ashtons-lytham.co.uk
Ⓦ www.ashtons-lytham.co.uk
Also sells wholesale.
Contact: T M Ashton
Opening Times: 0900-1700 daily.
Cat. Cost: None issued
Credit Cards: MasterCard Visa Switch Delta Amex
Specialities: Herbaceous plants. Hardy shrubs.
Map Ref: N, D1

NBat BATTERSBY ROSES ✉ €
Peartree Cottage, Old Battersby,
Great Ayton, Cleveland,
TS9 6LU
Ⓣ (01642) 723402
Ⓔ battersbyroses@lineone.net
Ⓦ www.battersbyroses.8m.com
Contact: Eric & Avril Stainthorpe
Opening Times: 1000-dusk most days.
Min Mail Order UK: Nmc
Min Mail Order EU: Nmc
Cat. Cost: Sae
Credit Cards: None.
Specialities: Exhibition roses incl. some American & Canadian miniatures.
Map Ref: N, C2

NBea BEAMISH CLEMATIS NURSERY € ♿
Burntwood Cottage, Stoney Lane, Beamish,
Co. Durham, DH9 0SJ
Ⓣ (0191) 370 0202
Ⓕ (0191) 370 0202
Ⓦ www.beamishclematisnursery.co.uk
Contact: Colin Brown or Jan Wilson
Opening Times: 0900-1700 Wed-Mon, closed Tue. Closed Easter Sun & Xmas week.
Cat. Cost: Available Online only.
Credit Cards: None.
Specialities: *Clematis*, climbers, shrubs & ornamental trees.
Map Ref: N, B2

NBee BEECHCROFT NURSERIES ✉ ♿
Bongate, Appleby-in-Westmorland,
Cumbria, CA16 6UE
Ⓣ (01768) 351201
Ⓕ (01768) 351201
Contact: Roger Brown
Opening Times: 0900-1700 Tue-Sun, closed Mon.
Min Mail Order UK: Nmc
Cat. Cost: Sae for tree list.
Credit Cards: None.
Specialities: Hardy field-grown trees. Note: mail order trees Nov-Mar only.
Map Ref: N, C1

NBid BIDE-A-WEE COTTAGE GARDENS ✉ ♿
Stanton, Netherwitton, Morpeth,
Northumberland, NE65 8PR
Ⓣ (01670) 772262
Ⓔ bideaweecg@aol.com
Contact: Mark Robson

KEY
✉ Mail order to UK or EU ⌂ Delivers to shows
✈ Exports beyond EU € Euro accepted
♿ Accessible by wheelchair ◆ See Display advertisement

N

Opening Times: 1330-1700 Sat & Wed 24th Apr-28th Aug 2003.
Min Mail Order UK: Nmc
Cat. Cost: 3 x 1st class
Credit Cards: None.
Specialities: Unusual herbaceous perennials, *Primula*, ferns, grasses. Nat. Coll. of *Centaurea*.
Map Ref: N, B2 **OS Grid Ref:** NZ132900

NBir BIRKHEADS COTTAGE GARDEN NURSERY ⊠ ♿
Nr. Causey Arch, Sunniside,
Newcastle upon Tyne, NE16 5EL
Ⓣ (01207) 232262
Ⓜ 07778 447920
Ⓕ (01207) 232262
Ⓔ birkheads.nursery@virgin.net
Ⓦ www.birkheadsnursery.co.uk
Contact: Mrs Christine Liddle
Opening Times: 1000-1700 every day Mar-end Oct. Closed Nov-Feb. Groups by appt.
Min Mail Order UK: £30.00
Cat. Cost: None issued
Credit Cards: None.
Specialities: Hardy herbaceous perennials, grasses, bulbs & herbs. *Allium, Campanula, Digitalis, Euphorbia, Geranium, Primula.* Max. 30 of any plant propagated each year. Note: mail order Nov-Feb only. Orders taken all year for winter deliveries.
Map Ref: N, B2 **OS Grid Ref:** NZ220569

NBlu BLUNDELL'S NURSERIES ♿
68 Southport New Road, Tarleton,
Preston, Lancashire, PR4 6HY
Ⓣ (01772) 815442
Ⓔ jerplusjeff@aol.com
Also sells wholesale.
Contact: Any member of staff
Opening Times: 0900-1700 daily excl. Weds. Closed Dec-Feb.
Cat. Cost: None issued
Credit Cards: None.
Specialities: Trees, shrubs, incl. topiary & large specimens, conifers. Perennials, alpines, ferns, heathers, herbs, hanging basket/bedding/conservatory plants, aquatics, hedging, roses. Garden design service available.
Map Ref: N, D1

NBPC THE BARN PLANT CENTRE & GIFT SHOP ♿
The Square, Scorton, Preston,
Lancashire, PR3 1AU
Ⓣ (01524) 793533
Ⓕ (01524) 793533
Ⓔ neil.anderton@virgin.net
Ⓦ www.plantsandgifts.co.uk
Contact: Neil Anderton, Karen Macleod
Opening Times: 0900-1700 Mon-Sat, 1000-1800 Sun.
Cat. Cost: 2 1st class
Credit Cards: All major credit/debit cards.
Specialities: 600 varieties of perennials. Old roses.
Map Ref: N, C1 **OS Grid Ref:** GR501487

NBre BREEZY KNEES NURSERIES ⊠ ♿
Common Lane, Warthill,
York, YO19 5XS
Ⓣ (01904) 488800
Ⓦ www.breezyknees.co.uk
Contact: Any member of staff
Opening Times: 0930-1600 Mon-Fri mid-March-Sep.
Min Mail Order UK: Nmc
Cat. Cost: Free.
Credit Cards: All major credit/debit cards.
Specialities: Wide range of perennials from popular favourites to something decidedly different.
Map Ref: N, C3 **OS Grid Ref:** SE675565

NBrk T H BARKER & SON ⊠ ♿
Baines Paddock Nursery, Haverthwaite,
Ulverston, Cumbria, LA12 8PF
Ⓣ (015395) 58236
Ⓔ rachel@thbarker.demon.co.uk
Ⓦ www.ukclematis.co.uk
Contact: W E Thornley
Opening Times: 1000-1700 Wed-Mon 15th Feb-15th Nov. Closed Tue. Winter – please ring for appt.
Min Mail Order UK: 3 plants
Cat. Cost: 5 x 1st class (*Clematis* only.)
Credit Cards: None.
Specialities: *Clematis, Lonicera* & other climbers. Cottage garden plants. Many rare. Most stock grown on the nursery. Note: mail order *Clematis* only.
Map Ref: N, C1

NBro BROWNTHWAITE HARDY PLANTS ⊠ ♿
Fell Yeat, Casterton,
Kirkby Lonsdale, Lancashire,
LA6 2JW
Ⓣ (015242) 71340 (after 1800).
Contact: Chris Benson
Opening Times: Tue-Sun 1st Apr-30th Sep.
Min Mail Order UK: Nmc
Cat. Cost: 3 x 1st class*
Credit Cards: None.
Specialities: Herbaceous perennials & grasses incl. *Geranium, Hosta, Iris*, especially *I. ensata*

& *I. sibirica, Heucherella, Tiarella, Primula auricula* & *P. sieboldii*. *Note: sae for *P. auricula* mail order list, also ltd *Iris* list.
Map Ref: N, C1

NBtw **Braithwell Nurseries** €
2 Holywell Cottages, Braithwell, Rotherham, South Yorkshire, S66 7AB
Ⓣ (01709) 812093
Contact: Philip Yardley
Opening Times: 1000-1800 Mar-Nov, times vary Dec-Feb, please phone first. Closed Xmas & New Year.
Cat. Cost: None issued
Credit Cards: None.
Specialities: Wide range incl. shrubs, perennials, grasses, climbers, alpines, bamboos, palms, agave. Many seasonal plants. Small stocks of some. Note: nursery on B6427 between Braithwell & Maltby.
Map Ref: N, D2 **OS Grid Ref:** SK535938

NBur **Burton Agnes Hall Nursery** ⊠ ♿
Burton Agnes Hall Preservation Trust Ltd, Estate Office, Burton Agnes, Driffield, East Yorkshire, YO25 0ND
Ⓣ (01262) 490324
Ⓕ (01262) 490513
Ⓔ burton.agnes@farmline.com
Ⓦ www.burton-agnes.com
Contact: Mrs S Cunliffe-Lister
Opening Times: 1100-1700 Apr-Oct.
Min Mail Order UK: £15.00 + p&p
Min Mail Order EU: £15.00 + p&p
Cat. Cost: 4 x 1st class
Credit Cards: None.
Specialities: Large range perennials & alpines. Many unusual varieties esp. *Penstemon, Osteospermum, Digitalis, Anemone, Geranium*. Nat. Coll. of *Campanula*. Note: mail order Nov-Mar only.
Map Ref: N, C3

NCGa **Cath's Garden Plants** ⊠ ♿
Eriskay, Sea View, Nether Kellet, Carnforth, Lancashire, LA6 1EG
Ⓣ (01524) 735567 office, (015395) 61126 nursery
Ⓕ (01524) 735567
Ⓔ cath@cathsgardenplants.fsbusiness.co.uk
Ⓦ www.cathsgardenplants.gbr.cc
Also sells wholesale.
Contact: Bob Sanderson
Opening Times: 1030-1700 Fri-Mon, Apr-Oct.
Min Mail Order UK: Nmc
Min Mail Order EU: £25.00
Cat. Cost: 4 x 1st class
Credit Cards: All major credit/debit cards.
Specialities: Wide variety of perennials, incl. uncommon varieties & selections of grasses, ferns, shrubs & climbing plants. Note: nursery is at Heaves Hotel, Levens, Nr. Kendal, Cumbria.
Map Ref: N, C1 **OS Grid Ref:** SD497867

NChi **Chipchase Castle Nursery** ♿
Chipchase Castle, Wark, Hexham, Northumberland, NE48 3NT
Ⓣ (01434) 230083
Ⓦ www.northernperennials.co.uk
Contact: Suzanne Newell & Janet Beakes
Opening Times: 1000-1700 Thu-Sun & B/hol Mons Easter (or 1st Apr)-mid Oct.
Cat. Cost: A5 sae for list
Credit Cards: None.
Specialities: Unusual herbaceous esp. *Erodium, Eryngium, Geranium* & *Viola*. Some plants only available in small numbers. Suitable for accompanied wheelchair users.
Map Ref: N, B2 **OS Grid Ref:** NY880758

NChl **Chiltern Seeds** ⊠ ✈ € ◆
Bortree Stile, Ulverston, Cumbria, LA12 7PB
Ⓣ (01229) 581137 (24 hrs)
Ⓕ (01229) 584549
Ⓔ info@chilternseeds.co.uk
Ⓦ www.chilternseeds.co.uk
Opening Times: Normal office hours, Mon-Fri.
Min Mail Order UK: Nmc
Min Mail Order EU: Nmc
Cat. Cost: 3 x 2nd class
Credit Cards: Visa Access Amex Switch MasterCard Eurocard
Specialities: Over 4,600 items of all kinds – wild flowers, trees, shrubs, cacti, annuals, houseplants, vegetables & herbs.

NCiC **Cicely's Cottage Garden Plants**
43 Elmers Green, Skelmersdale, Lancashire, WN8 6SG
Ⓣ (01695) 720790
Ⓔ maureen.duncan@ic24.net
Contact: Maureen Duncan
Opening Times: Please phone to avoid disappointment as opening times vary.
Cat. Cost: Free plant list
Credit Cards: None.
Specialities: Hardy, half-hardy & tender perennials incl. *Penstemon*. Traditional &

KEY
⊠ Mail order to UK or EU — Delivers to shows
✈ Exports beyond EU — € Euro accepted
♿ Accessible by wheelchair — ◆ See Display advertisement

N

unusual cottage garden plants & pelargoniums. Stock available in small quantities.
Map Ref: N, D1

NCob **COBBLE HEY GARDENS** ♿
Off Hobbs Lane, Claughton-on-Brock, Garstang, Nr. Preston, Lancashire, PR3 0QN
Ⓣ (01995) 602643
Ⓔ cobblehey@aol.com
Contact: Edwina Miller
Opening Times: 1030-1630 every Sun from 11th Apr-end Sep, or by appt.
Credit Cards: None.
Specialities: *Phlox paniculata*. Unusual plants.
Map Ref: N, C1

N

NCot **COTTAGE GARDEN PLANTS** ⊠
1 Sycamore Close, Whitehaven, Cumbria, CA28 6LE
Ⓣ (01946) 695831
Ⓔ jnprkss@aol.com
Ⓦ www.cottagegardenplants.com
Contact: Mrs J Purkiss
Opening Times: By appt. only. For garden, consult local press & radio for charity openings.
Min Mail Order UK: Nmc
Cat. Cost: 3 x 1st class sae
Credit Cards: None.
Specialities: Hardy perennials incl. *Geranium, Polemonium, Primula* & bog plants. Small quantities only.
Map Ref: N, C1

NCro **CROSTON CACTUS** ⊠ ♿
43 Southport Road, Eccleston, Chorley, Lancashire, PR7 6ET
Ⓣ (01257) 452555
Ⓔ desert.plants@lineone.net
Ⓦ www.CROSTON-CACTUS.CO.UK
Contact: John Henshaw
Opening Times: 0930-1700 Wed-Sat & by appt.
Min Mail Order UK: £5.00 + p&p
Min Mail Order EU: £10.00 + p&p
Cat. Cost: 2 x 1st or 2 x IRCs
Credit Cards: None.
Specialities: Mexican cacti, *Echeveria* hybrids & some bromeliads & *Tillandsia*.
Map Ref: N, D1

NDlv **DALESVIEW NURSERY** ⊠ ♿
24 Braithwaite Edge Road, Keighley, West Yorkshire, BD22 6RA
Ⓣ (01535) 606531
Also sells wholesale.
Contact: David Ellis & Eileen Morgan
Opening Times: 1000-1700 Wed-Sun & B/hols, Feb-Oct. Nov-Jan by appt. please telephone.
Min Mail Order UK: Nmc
Min Mail Order EU: Nmc
Cat. Cost: 4 x 1st class
Credit Cards: None.
Specialities: Dwarf *Hebe, Saxifraga, Primula, Rhododendron, Fuchsia* & conifers.
Map Ref: N, C2

NDov **DOVE COTTAGE NURSERY** ♿
23 Shibden Hall Road, Halifax, West Yorkshire, HX3 9XA
Ⓣ (01422) 203553
Ⓔ dovecottage.nursery@virgin.net
Ⓦ www.dovecottagenursery.co.uk
Contact: Stephen & Kim Rogers
Opening Times: 1000-1800 Wed-Sun & B/hols Feb-Sep. Closed Sun Aug & Sep.
Cat. Cost: Free
Credit Cards: All major credit/debit cards.
Specialities: *Helleborus* & selected perennials & grasses for naturalistic planting.
Map Ref: N, D2 **OS Grid Ref:** SE115256

NDvn **DEVINE NURSERIES** ⊠ €
Withernsea Road, Hollym, East Yorkshire, HU19 2QJ
Ⓣ (01964) 613840
Ⓕ (01964) 613840
Ⓔ devinenurseries1@another.com
Also sells wholesale.
Contact: Tony Devine
Opening Times: Not open.
Min Mail Order UK: Nmc
Min Mail Order EU: Nmc
Cat. Cost: 4 x 1st class
Credit Cards: Visa MasterCard
Specialities: *Gladiolus*, alliums, *Eremurus* , bulbous.

NEgg **EGGLESTON HALL** ⊠ €
Garden Cottage, Eggleston, Barnard Castle, Co. Durham, DL12 0AG
Ⓣ (01833) 650115
Ⓕ (01833) 650971
Ⓔ mbhock@btinternet.com
Ⓦ www.egglestonhallgardens.com
Also sells wholesale.
Contact: Malcolm Hockham, Gordon Long
Opening Times: 1000-1700 7 days.
Min Mail Order UK: £12.95
Cat. Cost: Online only.
Credit Cards: Eurocard Maestro Visa Electron Switch Solo JCB

Specialities: Rare & unusual plants with particular emphasis on flower arranging. Note: mail order *Celmisia spectabilis* Oct-Mar only.
Map Ref: N, C2 **OS Grid Ref:** NY997233

NEqu EQUATORIAL PLANT CO. ✉ ✈ ⛟ €
7 Gray Lane, Barnard Castle,
Co. Durham, DL12 8PD
Ⓣ (01833) 690519
Ⓕ (01833) 690519
Ⓔ equatorialplants@teesdaleonline.co.uk
Ⓦ equatorialplants.com
Also sells wholesale.
Contact: Dr Richard Warren
Opening Times: By appt. only.
Min Mail Order UK: Nmc
Min Mail Order EU: Nmc
Cat. Cost: Free
Credit Cards: Visa Access
Specialities: Laboratory raised orchids only.

NFir FIR TREES PELARGONIUM NURSERY
✉ ⛟ ♿
Stokesley, Middlesbrough,
Cleveland,
TS9 5LD
Ⓣ (01642) 713066
Ⓕ (01642) 713066
Ⓦ www.firtreespelargoniums.co.uk
Contact: Helen Bainbridge
Opening Times: 1000-1600 7 days 1st Apr-31st Aug, 1000-1600 Mon-Fri 1st Sep-31st Mar.
Min Mail Order UK: £3.00 + p&p
Cat. Cost: 4 x 1st class or £1.00 coin
Credit Cards: MasterCard Visa Switch
Specialities: All types of *Pelargonium* – fancy leaf, regal, decorative regal, oriental regal, angel, miniature, zonal, ivy leaf, stellar, scented, dwarf, unique, golden stellar & species.
Map Ref: N, C2

NFla FLAXTON HOUSE NURSERY
Flaxton, York, North Yorkshire,
Y060 7RJ
Ⓣ (01904) 468753
Contact: Mrs H Williams
Opening Times: 1000-1700 Tue-Sun 1st Mar-mid-Oct.
Cat. Cost: 2 x 1st class
Credit Cards: None.
Specialities: Wide general range of herbaceous & alpines with many unusual plants. Selection of climbers & shrubs. Ltd. quantities so phone before travelling. Accessible for wheelchair users with assistance.
Map Ref: N, C2 **OS Grid Ref:** SE467462

NFor FORD NURSERY ✉ ♿
Castle Gardens, Ford,
Berwick-upon-Tweed,
TD15 2PZ
Ⓣ (01890) 820379
Ⓕ (01890) 820594
Ⓔ Ford.nursery@which.net
Ⓦ www.FordNursery.co.uk
Contact: Sarah Glass & Roy Harmeston
Opening Times: 1000-1730 7 days Mar-Oct, 1000-1630 Mon-Fri Nov-Feb.
Min Mail Order UK: £10.00
Cat. Cost: None issued
Credit Cards: All major credit/debit cards.
Specialities: Over 1200 different species of container grown hardy ornamental shrubs, perennials, trees & herbs, climbers & grasses.
Map Ref: N, A2

NGby GILBEY'S PLANTS ✉ ⛟ € ♿
(office) 42 Park Street, Masham, Ripon,
North Yorkshire, HG4 4HN
Ⓣ (01765) 689927:(01845) 525285
Ⓕ (01765) 689927
Ⓔ gilbeyplants@aol.com
Also sells wholesale.
Contact: Giles N Gilbey
Opening Times: 1000-1700 Mon-Sat, 1400-1700 Sun, 1st Mar-1st Oct. Winter by appt. only.
Min Mail Order UK: Nmc
Min Mail Order EU: Nmc
Cat. Cost: 4 x 1st class
Credit Cards: All major credit/debit cards.
Specialities: Unusual hardy perennials & ferns. Notes: mail order Oct-Mar only. Nursery at The Walled Garden, Cemetery Road, Thirsk YO7 4DL.
Map Ref: N, C2

NGdn GARDEN HOUSE NURSERIES ♿
The Square, Dalston, Carlisle,
Cumbria, CA5 7LL
Ⓣ (01228) 710297
Ⓔ david@gardenhousenursery.co.uk
Ⓦ www.gardenhousenursery.co.uk
Contact: David Hickson
Opening Times: 0900-1700 7 days Mar-Oct.
Cat. Cost: None issued, plant list on web
Credit Cards: None.
Specialities: *Geranium, Hosta, Hemerocallis, Iris,* grasses & bamboos.
Map Ref: N, B1 **OS Grid Ref:** NY369503

KEY
✉ Mail order to UK or EU ⛟ Delivers to shows
✈ Exports beyond EU € Euro accepted
♿ Accessible by wheelchair ◆ See Display advertisement

N

NGHP **GREEN GARDEN HERBS & PLANTS** ⊠ ♠ ♿ ◆
13 West Bank, Carlton, North Yorkshire, DN14 9PZ
Ⓣ (01405) 860708
Ⓔ green@gardenherbs.fsnet.co.uk
Also sells wholesale.
Contact: Sarah Clark, Stefan Vida
Opening Times: 1000-1700 Wed-Mon, Mar-Sep. Other times by appt.
Min Mail Order UK: £10.00
Min Mail Order EU: £10.00
Cat. Cost: 5 x 2nd class
Credit Cards: MasterCard Visa
Specialities: Herbs, aromatic, culinary, medicinal & ornamental, incl. *Salvia, Monarda, Thymus* & wide selection of *Lavandula.*
Map Ref: N, D3 **OS Grid Ref:** SE626242

N

NHal **HALLS OF HEDDON** ⊠ ✈ ♿
(Office) West Heddon Nurseries, Heddon-on-the-Wall, Northumberland, NE15 0JS
Ⓣ (01661) 852445
Ⓕ (01661) 852398
Ⓔ orders@hallsofheddon.co.uk
Ⓦ www.hallsofheddon.co.uk
Also sells wholesale.
Contact: Judith Lockey
Opening Times: 0900-1700 Mon-Sat 1000-1700 Sun.
Min Mail Order UK: Nmc
Min Mail Order EU: £25.00 + p&p*
Cat. Cost: 3 x 2nd class
Credit Cards: MasterCard Visa Switch Delta
Specialities: *Chrysanthemum* & *Dahlia.* Wide range of herbaceous. *Note: mail order *Dahlia* & *Chrysanthemum* only. EU & export *Dahlia* tubers only.
Map Ref: N, B2

NHar **HARTSIDE NURSERY GARDEN** ⊠ ✈ ♠
Nr. Alston, Cumbria, CA9 3BL
Ⓣ (01434) 381372
Ⓕ (01434) 381372
Ⓔ Hartside@macunlimited.net
Contact: S L & N Huntley
Opening Times: 0930-1630 Mon-Fri, 1230-1600 Sat, Sun & B/hols, mid Mar-31st Oct. By appt. 1st Nov-mid Mar.
Min Mail Order UK: Nmc
Min Mail Order EU: £50.00 + p&p
Cat. Cost: 4 x 1st class or 3 x IRC
Credit Cards: Visa Access Switch
Specialities: Alpines grown at altitude of 1100 feet in Pennines. *Primula,* ferns, *Gentian* & *Meconopsis.*
Map Ref: N, B1

NHaw **THE HAWTHORNES NURSERY** ⊠ ♠ ♿
Marsh Road, Hesketh Bank, Nr. Preston, Lancashire, PR4 6XT
Ⓣ (01772) 812379
Ⓦ www.hawthornes-nursery.co.uk
Contact: Irene & Richard Hodson
Opening Times: 0900-1800 7 days 1st Mar-30th Jun, Thu-Sun July-Oct. Gardens open for NGS.
Min Mail Order UK: £10.00
Cat. Cost: 5 x 1st class
Credit Cards: None.
Specialities: *Clematis,* honeysuckle, choice selection of shrub & climbing roses, extensive range of perennials, mostly on display in the garden.
Map Ref: N, D1

NHer **HERTERTON HOUSE GARDEN NURSERY**
Hartington, Cambo, Morpeth, Northumberland, NE61 4BN
Ⓣ (01670) 774278
Contact: Mrs M Lawley & Mr Frank Lawley
Opening Times: 1330-1730 Mon Wed Fri-Sun 1st Apr-end Sep. (Earlier or later in the year weather permitting.)
Cat. Cost: None issued
Credit Cards: None.
Specialities: Country garden flowers.
Map Ref: N, B2

NHHG **HARDSTOFT HERB GARDEN**
Hall View Cottage, Hardstoft, Pilsley, Nr. Chesterfield, Derbyshire, S45 8AH
Ⓣ (01246) 854268
Contact: Lynne & Steve Raynor
Opening Times: 1000-1700 daily 15th Mar-15th Sep. Closed Tue excl. Easter & B/hol weeks.
Cat. Cost: Free
Credit Cards: MasterCard Switch Delta Visa
Specialities: Wide range of herbs. Over 40 lavenders & 12 rosemary. Scented pelargoniums. Nat. Coll. of *Echinacea.*
Map Ref: N, D2

NHor **HORN'S GARDEN CENTRE** ♿
Dixon Estate, Shotton Colliery, Co. Durham, DH6 2PX
Ⓣ (0191) 526 2987
Ⓕ (0191) 526 2889
Contact: G Horn & Theresa Horn
Opening Times: 0900-1730 Mon-Sat 1000-1600 Sun, all year excl. Easter Mon.
Cat. Cost: 3 x 1st class
Credit Cards: All major credit/debit cards.

Specialities: *Fuchsia*, pelargoniums. Wide range of trees, shrubs & perennials.
Map Ref: N, B2

NJOw JOHN OWEN NURSERIES
20 West Bank, Carlton, Nr. Goole, East Yorkshire, DN14 9PZ
Ⓣ (01405) 861415
Ⓜ 07762 650131
Ⓕ (01405) 861415
Ⓔ johnowen-nurseries@njow.fsnet.co.uk
Also sells wholesale.
Contact: John D W Owen
Opening Times: 1000-1700 Thu-Sat, 1st Mar-31st Oct. Please phone first.
Cat. Cost: 3 x 2nd class
Credit Cards: None.
Specialities: Alpines & perennials, especially *Allium, Campanula, Dianthus, Oxalis, Primula* & *Saxifraga*. A few varieties available in small quantities only.
Map Ref: N, D3 **OS Grid Ref:** SE629243

NLan LANDLIFE WILDFLOWERS LTD ⊠ ♿
National Wildflower Centre, Court Hey Park, Liverpool, L16 3NA
Ⓣ (0151) 737 1819
Ⓕ (0151) 737 1820
Ⓔ gill@landlife.org.uk
Ⓦ www.wildflower.org.uk
Also sells wholesale.
Contact: Gillian Watson
Opening Times: 1000-1700, 7 days, 1 Apr-30 Sep only.
Min Mail Order UK: £30.00 (plants), no min. for seeds.
Cat. Cost: Sae + 2 x 2nd class
Credit Cards: Visa Delta Access Switch Solo
Specialities: Wild herbaceous plants & seeds. Cafe & shop. Visitor centre, admission charge.
Map Ref: N, D1

NLAp LANESIDE ALPINES ⊠ ⛺ ♿
74 Croston Road, Garstang, Preston, Lancashire, PR3 1HR
Ⓣ (01995) 605537
Ⓜ 0794 6659661
Ⓔ jcrhutch@aol.com
Contact: Jeff Hutchings
Opening Times: 1000-1700 Fri-Sun, 1st Mar-30th Sep (except when at shows), please phone to check.
Min Mail Order UK: Nmc
Cat. Cost: Sae
Specialities: Alpines, incl. gentians, *Penstemon* species, primulas, show auriculas, *Saxifraga*, dwarf evergreen shrubs, celmisias, New Zealand plants, planted bowls & planted tufa. Many species available in small numbers only.
Notes: nursery located at Bells Bridge Lane, Nateby, Nr. Gastang. Mail order auriculas, primulas, saxifrage & trough plants.
Map Ref: N, D1

NLar LARCH COTTAGE NURSERIES ⊠ € ♿ ◆
Melkinthorpe, Penrith, Cumbria, CA10 2DR
Ⓣ (01931) 712404
Ⓕ (01931) 712727
Ⓔ plants@larchcottage.freeserve.co.uk
Ⓦ www.larchcottagenurseries.co.uk or www.larchcottagenurseries.com
Contact: Joanne McCullock/Peter Stott
Opening Times: Daily from 1000-1730.
Min Mail Order UK: Nmc
Min Mail Order EU: Nmc
Cat. Cost: £3.50
Credit Cards: Visa Access Switch Delta Solo
Specialities: Unusual & old fashioned perennials. Rare & dwarf conifers. Unusual shrubs & trees.
Map Ref: N, C1 **OS Grid Ref:** NY315602

NLLv LEEDS LAVENDER ⊠
Greenscapes Nursery, Brandon Crescent, Shadwell, Leeds, LS17 9JH
Ⓣ (0113) 2892922
Ⓦ www.leedslavender.co.uk
Also sells wholesale.
Contact: Ruth Dorrington
Opening Times: 1000-1630, Mon-Fri, 1000-1700 Sat & Sun all year round, or by appt.
Min Mail Order UK: Nmc
Cat. Cost: 2 x 1st class
Credit Cards: None.
Specialities: *Lavandula*. Limited numbers of particular varieties available at certain times, especially at end of summer. Wheelchair access difficult in some areas.
Map Ref: N, D2

NLon THE LONGFRAMLINGTON CENTRE FOR PLANTS & GARDENS ⊠ ◆
Swarland Road, Longframlington, Morpeth, Northumberland, NE65 8DB
Ⓣ (01665) 570382
Ⓕ (01665) 570382
Ⓔ info@longframlingtongardens.co.uk
Ⓦ www.longframlingtongardens.co.uk
Also sells wholesale.
Contact: Hazel Huddleston

KEY
⊠ Mail order to UK or EU ⛺ Delivers to shows
✈ Exports beyond EU € Euro accepted
♿ Accessible by wheelchair ◆ See Display advertisement

N

Opening Times: 0900-1700 (or dusk) 7 days all year, or by appt.
Min Mail Order UK: Nmc
Cat. Cost: £2.50 incl.
Credit Cards: Access Visa
Specialities: Hardy ornamental trees, shrubs, perennials, herbs, ground cover & alpines.
Map Ref: N, B2 **OS Grid Ref:** 145008

NLRH LITTLE RED HEN NURSERIES ⊠
91 Denholme Road, Oxenhope, Keighley, West Yorkshire, BD22 9SJ
Ⓣ (01535) 643786
Ⓔ louise@redhens.co.uk
Ⓦ www.redhens.co.uk
Also sells wholesale.
Contact: Louise Harris
Opening Times: Please phone first.
Min Mail Order UK: Nmc
Cat. Cost: Free
Credit Cards: None.
Specialities: Small nursery with ltd. stock. Details in catalogue or on website.
Map Ref: N, D2 **OS Grid Ref:** SE045343

N

NLsd LANESIDE NURSERY
Stocks Lane, Middop, Nr. Gisburn, Clithero, Lancashire, BB7 4JR
Ⓣ (01200) 445404
Ⓕ (01200) 445404
Ⓔ helen@middop.freeserve.co.uk
Also sells wholesale.
Contact: Helen Hamer
Opening Times: 1400-1900 Wed, 1400-1700 Fri, 1000-1700 Sat, mid-Apr to mid-Sep. Other times by appt. Groups welcome by prior arrangement.
Cat. Cost: 2 x 1st class
Credit Cards: None.
Specialities: Cottage garden perennials. Stock in small quantities. Tough plants grown on a north-facing slope in the Pennines at 750ft.
Map Ref: N, D2

NMen MENDLE NURSERY ⊠ ♁ ♿
Holme, Scunthorpe, Lincolnshire, DN16 3RF
Ⓣ (01724) 850864
Ⓔ annearnshaw@lineone.net
Ⓦ www.mendlenursery.com
Contact: Mrs A Earnshaw
Opening Times: 1000-1600 Tue-Sun.
Min Mail Order UK: Nmc
Min Mail Order EU: Nmc
Cat. Cost: 3 x 1st class
Credit Cards: All major credit/debit cards.
Specialities: Many unusual alpines esp. *Saxifraga* & *Sempervivum*.
Map Ref: N, D3 **OS Grid Ref:** SE925070

NMir MIRES BECK NURSERY ⊠ ♿
Low Mill Lane, North Cave, Brough, East Riding Yorkshire, HU15 2NR
Ⓣ (01430) 421543
Also sells wholesale.
Contact: Irene Tinklin & Martin Rowland
Opening Times: 1000-1600 Wed-Sat 1st Mar-30th Sep. 1000-1500 Wed-Fri 1st Oct-30th Nov & by appt.
Min Mail Order UK: Nmc
Min Mail Order EU: Nmc
Cat. Cost: 3 x 1st class
Credit Cards: None.
Specialities: Wild flower plants of Yorkshire provenance. Note: mail order for wild flower plants, plugs & seeds only.
Map Ref: N, D3 **OS Grid Ref:** SE889316

NMoo MOOR MONKTON NURSERIES ⊠ ♿
Moor Monkton, York Road, Nr.York, Yorkshire, YO26 8JJ
Ⓣ (01904) 738770
Ⓕ (01904) 738770
Ⓔ sales@bamboo-uk.co.uk
Ⓦ www.bamboo-uk.co.uk
Contact: Peter Owen
Opening Times: 0900-1700.
Min Mail Order UK: Nmc
Min Mail Order EU: £20.00
Cat. Cost: 5 x 2nd class or email for details.
Credit Cards: None.
Specialities: Bamboos, palms, ferns, unusual trees, shrubs & perennials. Note: Mail order for bamboo only.
Map Ref: N, C2

NMRc MILLRACE NURSERY ⊠ ♿
84 Selby Road, Garforth, Leeds, LS25 1LP
Ⓣ (0113) 286 9233
Ⓕ (0113) 286 9908
Contact: C Carthy
Opening Times: 1000-1700 Mon, Tue, Thu-Sun, Mar-May & Mon, Tue, Thu-Sat Jun-Sep.
Min Mail Order UK: Nmc
Cat. Cost: 4 x 1st class
Credit Cards: None.
Specialities: Unusual perennials, especially drought-resistant, incl. hardy geraniums, alliums, campanulas, penstemons, potentillas & veronicas. Some plants in small numbers only.
Map Ref: N, D2

NMyG MARY GREEN ⊠ ♁
The Walled Garden, Hornby, Lancaster, Lancashire, LA2 8LD
Ⓣ (01257) 270821
Ⓜ 07778 910348

Ⓕ (01257) 270821
Ⓔ Marygreenplants@aol.com
Contact: Mary Green
Opening Times: By appt. only.
Min Mail Order UK: £10.00
Cat. Cost: 4 x 1st class
Credit Cards: None.
Specialities: Choice herbaceous perennials, incl. hostas, astilbes & geraniums.
Map Ref: N, C1 **OS Grid Ref:** SD588688

NNew NEWTON HILL ALPINES € ♿
335 Leeds Road, Newton Hill, Wakefield, West Yorkshire, WF1 2JH
Ⓣ (01924) 377056
Ⓔ newtalp@aol.com
Also sells wholesale.
Contact: Sheena Vigors
Opening Times: 0900-1700 Fri-Wed all year. Closed Thu. Please phone first.
Cat. Cost: 2 x 1st class
Credit Cards: None.
Specialities: Alpines esp. *Saxifraga*, also *Erica*, conifers & dwarf shrubs.
Map Ref: N, D2 **OS Grid Ref:** SE328229

NNor NORCROFT NURSERIES ♿
Roadends, Intack, Southwaite, Carlisle, Cumbria, CA4 0LH
Ⓣ (016974) 73933
Ⓜ 07789 050633
Ⓕ (016974) 73969
Ⓔ stellaandkeithbell@sbell44.fsnet.co.uk
Also sells wholesale.
Contact: Keith Bell
Opening Times: Every afternoon excl. Mon but open B/hols.
Cat. Cost: 2 x 2nd class
Credit Cards: None.
Specialities: Hardy herbaceous, ornamental grasses, hostas, *Lilium, Hemerocallis, Penstemon.*
Map Ref: N, B1 **OS Grid Ref:** NY474433

NOaD OAK DENE NURSERIES ⊠
10 Back Lane West, Royston, Barnsley, South Yorkshire, S71 4SB
Ⓣ (01226) 722253
Ⓕ (01226) 722253
Also sells wholesale.
Contact: J Foster or G Foster
Opening Times: 0900-1800 1st Apr-30th Sep, 1000-1600 1st Oct-31st Mar. (Closed 1230-1330.)
Min Mail Order UK: Please phone for further info.
Cat. Cost: None issued.
Credit Cards: None.
Specialities: Cacti, succulents & South African *Lachenalia* bulbs.
Map Ref: N, D2

NOak OAK TREE NURSERY ⊠ ⛟
Mill Lane, Barlow, Selby, North Yorkshire, YO8 8EY
Ⓣ (01757) 618409
Contact: Gill Plowes
Opening Times: By appt. only.
Min Mail Order UK: £10.00 + p&p
Cat. Cost: 2 x 1st class
Credit Cards: None.
Specialities: Cottage garden plants, grasses & ferns.
Map Ref: N, D3

NOGN THE ORNAMENTAL GRASS NURSERY ⊠ ⛟ ♿
Church Farm, Westgate, Rillington, Malton, North Yorkshire, YO17 8LN
Ⓣ (01944) 758247
Ⓜ 07813 327886
Ⓕ (01944) 758247
Ⓔ sales@ornamentalgrass.co.uk
Ⓦ www.ornamentalgrass.co.uk
Also sells wholesale.
Contact: Angela Kilby
Opening Times: 0930-1600 Tue-Sun. Closed Mon. Easter-mid Oct.
Min Mail Order UK: Nmc
Cat. Cost: 4 x 1st class
Credit Cards: MasterCard Visa
Specialities: Ornamental grasses, bamboos, ferns, hostas & herbaceous perennials, alliums, *Eremurus.* Note: mail order bulbs only.
Map Ref: N, C3

NOrc ORCHARD HOUSE NURSERY
Orchard House, Wormald Green, Nr.Harrogate, North Yorkshire, HG3 3NQ
Ⓣ (01765) 677541
Ⓕ (01765) 677541
Also sells wholesale.
Contact: Mr B M Corner
Opening Times: 0800-1630 Mon-Fri.
Cat. Cost: 4 x 1st class
Credit Cards: None.
Specialities: Herbaceous perennials, ferns, grasses, water plants & unusual cottage garden plants.
Map Ref: N, C2

KEY
⊠ Mail order to UK or EU ⛟ Delivers to shows
✈ Exports beyond EU € Euro accepted
♿ Accessible by wheelchair ◆ See Display advertisement

NPal **THE PALM FARM** ⊠ € ♿
Thornton Hall Gardens, Station Road, Thornton Curtis, Nr.Ulceby, Humberside, DN39 6XF
Ⓣ (01469) 531232
Ⓕ (01469) 531232
Ⓔ bill@thepalmfarm.com
Ⓦ www.thepalmfarm.com
Also sells wholesale.
Contact: W W Spink
Opening Times: 1400-1700 7 days.
Min Mail Order UK: £11.00 + p&p*
Min Mail Order EU: £25.00 + p&p*
Cat. Cost: 1 x 2nd class
Credit Cards: None.
Specialities: Hardy & half-hardy palms, unusual trees, shrubs & conservatory plants. Some plants available only in small quantities. Notes: euro payment accepted only if purchaser pays bank commission. *Mail order only if small enough to go by post (min. charge £12.50 p&p) or large enough to go by Palletline (min. charge £35.00 p&p).
Map Ref: N, D3 **OS Grid Ref:** TA100183

NPar **GERRY PARKER PLANTS** ⊠ ⌂ € ♿
9 Cotherstone Road, Newton Hall, Durham, DH1 5YN
Ⓣ (0191) 386 8749
Ⓔ gerryparker@btinternet.com
Contact: G Parker
Opening Times: Open by appt.
Min Mail Order UK: Nmc
Min Mail Order EU: Nmc
Cat. Cost: 3 x 1st class
Credit Cards: None.
Specialities: Woodland plants, bulbs, border plants, all suited to clay soils. Many in small quantities.
Map Ref: N, B2

NPen **PENTON MILL RHODODENDRONS** ⊠ ✈ € ♿
Penton, Carlisle, Cumbria, CA6 5QU
Ⓣ (01228) 577336
Ⓕ (01228) 577336
Ⓔ info@pentonmill.com
Ⓦ www.pentonmill.com
Contact: Amanda Cullen
Opening Times: Vary, due to off-site working. Please phone first.
Min Mail Order UK: Nmc
Min Mail Order EU: Nmc
Cat. Cost: 6 x 1st class
Credit Cards: None.
Specialities: Rhododendrons & azaleas & moisture loving primulas.
Map Ref: N, B1 **OS Grid Ref:** NY434764

NPer **PERRY'S PLANTS** ♿
The River Garden, Sleights, Whitby, North Yorkshire, YO21 1RR
Ⓣ (01947) 810329
Ⓕ (01947) 810940
Ⓔ perry@rivergardens.fsnet.co.uk
Contact: Pat & Richard Perry
Opening Times: 1000-1700 mid-March to Oct.
Cat. Cost: Large (A4) Sae
Credit Cards: None.
Specialities: *Lavatera, Malva, Erysimum, Euphorbia, Anthemis, Osteospermum* & *Hebe*. Uncommon hardy & container plants & aquatic plants.
Map Ref: N, C3 **OS Grid Ref:** NZ869082

NPoe **POETS COTTAGE SHRUB NURSERY** ♿
Lealholm, Whitby, North Yorkshire, YO21 2AQ
Ⓣ (01947) 897424
Ⓕ (01947) 840724
Contact: Ilona J McGivern
Opening Times: 0900-1700 Mar-Christmas, 1300-1530 Jan & Feb, 7 days.
Cat. Cost: None issued.
Credit Cards: All major credit/debit cards.
Specialities: Dwarf conifers, *Acer* & herbaceous.
Map Ref: N, C3

NPol **POLEMONIUM PLANTERY** ⊠ ⌂ ♿
28 Sunnyside Terrace, Trimdon Grange, Trimdon Station, Co. Durham, TS29 6HF
Ⓣ (01429) 881529
Ⓔ DANDD@Polemonium.co.uk
Ⓦ www.polemonium.co.uk
Also sells wholesale.
Contact: David or Dianne Nichol-Brown
Opening Times: Open for NGS 30 May 2004. Other times by appt. only. Donation to NGS please.
Min Mail Order UK: £10.00
Cat. Cost: Sae for list
Credit Cards: None.
Specialities: Nat. Coll. of *Polemonium* & related genera, plus some rare North American plants. The collection holds scientific status.
Map Ref: N, B2 **OS Grid Ref:** NZ369353

NPri **PRIMROSE COTTAGE NURSERY** ♿ ◆
Ringway Road, Moss Nook, Wythenshawe, Manchester, M22 5WF
Ⓣ (0161) 437 1557
Ⓕ (0161) 499 9932
Ⓔ info@primrosecottagenursery.co.uk
Ⓦ www.primrosecottagenursery.co.uk
Contact: Caroline Dumville

Opening Times: 0830-1730 Mon-Sat, 0930-1730 Sun (summer). 0830-1700 Mon-Sat, 0930-1700 Sun (winter).
Cat. Cost: 2 x 1st class
Credit Cards: All major credit/debit cards.
Specialities: Hardy herbaceous perennials, alpines, herbs, roses, patio & hanging basket plants. Shrubs.
Map Ref: N, D2

NPro PROUDPLANTS ⌂
East of Eden Nurseries,
Ainstable, Carlisle,
Cumbria, CA4 9QN
Ⓣ (01768) 896604
Ⓕ (01768) 896604
Contact: Roger Proud
Opening Times: 0900-1800 7 days Mar-Nov. Other times by appt.
Cat. Cost: None issued
Credit Cards: None.
Specialities: Interesting & unusual shrubs & perennials esp. dwarf & ground cover plants.
Map Ref: N, B1 **OS Grid Ref:** HA1336186

NRar RARER PLANTS ♿
Ashfield House, Austfield Lane, Monk Fryston, Leeds, LS25 5EH
Ⓣ (01977) 682263
Contact: Anne Watson
Opening Times: 1000-1600 Sat & Sun 20th Feb-1st Apr.
Cat. Cost: Sae
Credit Cards: None.
Specialities: *Helleborus* & *Galanthus*.
Map Ref: N, D2

NRib RIBBLESDALE NURSERIES ♿
Newsham Hall Lane, Woodplumpton, Preston, Lancashire, PR4 0AS
Ⓣ (01772) 863081
Ⓕ (01772) 861884
Contact: Mr & Mrs Dunnett
Opening Times: 0900-1800 Mon-Sat Apr-Sep, 0900-1700 Mon-Sat Oct-Mar. 1030-1630 Sun.
Credit Cards: Visa MasterCard Delta Switch
Specialities: Trees, shrubs & perennials. Conifers, hedging, alpines, fruit, climbers, herbs, aquatics, ferns & wildflowers.
Map Ref: N, D1 **OS Grid Ref:** SD515351

NRnb RAINBOW PLANTS
Springvale Nursery,
Springvale, Penistone,
Sheffield, Yorkshire, S36 6HJ
Ⓜ 07798 691853
Contact: Brian Cockerline

NRob W ROBINSON & SONS LTD ⊠ ✈ € ♿
Sunny Bank, Forton, Nr.Preston, Lancashire, PR3 0BN
Ⓣ (01524) 791210
Ⓕ (01524) 791933
Ⓔ info@mammothonion.co.uk
Ⓦ www.mammothonion.co.uk
Also sells wholesale.
Contact: Miss Robinson
Opening Times: 0900-1700 7 days Mar-Jun, 0800-1700 Mon-Fri Jul-Feb.
Min Mail Order UK: Nmc
Min Mail Order EU: Nmc
Cat. Cost: Free
Credit Cards: Visa Access Amex Switch
Specialities: Mammoth vegetable seed. Onions, leeks, tomatoes & beans. Range of vegetable plants in the spring.

NRya RYAL NURSERY ⊠ ⌂ ♿
East Farm Cottage, Ryal, Northumberland, NE20 0SA
Ⓣ (01661) 886562
Ⓕ (01661) 886918
Ⓔ alpines@ryal.freeserve.co.uk
Also sells wholesale.
Contact: R F Hadden
Opening Times: Mar-Jul 1300-1600 Mon-Tue but please phone first, 1000-1600 Sun & other times by appt.
Min Mail Order UK: £10.00 + p&p
Min Mail Order EU: £10.00 + p&p
Cat. Cost: Sae
Credit Cards: None.
Specialities: Alpine & woodland plants. Mainly available in small quantities only.
Map Ref: N, B2 **OS Grid Ref:** NZ015744

NScw SCAWSBY HALL NURSERIES ⊠ ♿
Barnsley Road, Scawsby, Doncaster, South Yorkshire, DN5 7UB
Ⓣ (01302) 782585
Ⓕ (01302) 783434
Ⓔ mail@scawsbyhallnurseries.co.uk
Ⓦ www.scawsbyhallnurseries.co.uk
Contact: David Lawson
Opening Times: 0930-1730 Mon-Sat, 1100-1700 Sun, Mar-Sep, 0930-1630 Mon-Sat 1100-1630 Sun, Oct-Feb.
Min Mail Order UK: Nmc
Min Mail Order EU: Nmc
Cat. Cost: None issued
Credit Cards: Visa MasterCard Switch Solo

KEY
⊠ Mail order to UK or EU ⌂ Delivers to shows
✈ Exports beyond EU € Euro accepted
♿ Accessible by wheelchair ◆ See Display advertisement

N

Specialities: A wide range of herbaceous perennials, hardy trees, shrubs & indoor plants.
Map Ref: N, D3 **OS Grid Ref:** SE542049

NShi SHIRLEY'S PLANTS ⊠ ⌂
6 Sandheys Drive, Church Town, Southport, Merseyside, PR9 9PQ
Ⓣ (01704) 213048
Ⓜ 07951 834066
Ⓦ www.stbegonias.com
Contact: Shirley & Terry Tasker
Opening Times: By appt. only.
Min Mail Order UK: Nmc
Cat. Cost: 2 x 1st class
Credit Cards: None.
Specialities: Nat. Coll. of *Begonia* species & hybrids.
Map Ref: N, D1 **OS Grid Ref:** SD355183

N

NSla SLACK TOP ALPINES ⌂ €
Hebden Bridge, West Yorkshire, HX7 7HA
Ⓣ (01422) 845348
Also sells wholesale.
Contact: M R or R Mitchell
Opening Times: 1000-1700 Wed-Sun 1st Mar-30th Sep & B/hol Mons 1st Mar-31st Oct.
Cat. Cost: Sae
Credit Cards: None.
Specialities: Alpine & rockery plants. *Gentiana, Saxifraga, Primula Hepatica, Paeonia* & *Pulsatilla.*
Map Ref: N, D2 **OS Grid Ref:** SD977286

NSpr SPRINGWOOD PLEIONES ⊠ ⌂ € ♿
35 Heathfield, Leeds, LS16 7AB
Ⓣ (0113) 261 1781
Ⓔ ken@pleiones.com
Ⓦ www.pleiones.com
Contact: Ken Redshaw
Opening Times: By appt. only.
Min Mail Order UK: £3.00 + p&p
Min Mail Order EU: £3.00 + p&p
Cat. Cost: 1 x 1st class
Credit Cards: None.
Specialities: *Pleione.*
Map Ref: N, D2 **OS Grid Ref:** SE265400

NSti STILLINGFLEET LODGE NURSERIES ⊠ ♿
Stillingfleet, North Yorkshire, YO19 6HP
Ⓣ (01904) 728506
Ⓕ (01904) 728506
Ⓔ vanessa.cook@still-lodge.freeserve.co.uk
Ⓦ www.stillingfleetlodgenurseries.co.uk
Contact: Vanessa Cook
Opening Times: 1000-1600 Tue Wed Fri & Sat 1st Apr-18th Oct. Closed Sat in Aug.
Min Mail Order UK: Nmc
Cat. Cost: 8 x 2nd class
Credit Cards: None.
Specialities: Foliage & unusual perennials. Hardy *Geranium, Pulmonaria*, variegated plants & grasses. Nat. Coll. of *Pulmonaria.* Note: mail order Nov-mid Mar only.
Map Ref: N, C2

NTay TAYLORS CLEMATIS NURSERY ⊠ ⌂ ♿ ◆
Sutton Road, Sutton, Nr. Askern, Doncaster, South Yorkshire, DN6 9JZ
Ⓣ (01302) 700716
Ⓕ (01302) 708415
Ⓔ info@taylorsclematis.co.uk
Ⓦ www.taylorsclematis.co.uk
Also sells wholesale.
Contact: John Taylor
Opening Times: 1000-1600, 15th Feb-15th Nov. Phone for opening times 16th Nov-14th Feb.
Min Mail Order UK: 1 plant + p&p
Cat. Cost: free
Credit Cards: All major credit/debit cards.
Specialities: *Clematis* (over 300 varieties).
Map Ref: N, D2 **OS Grid Ref:** SE552121

NTHB TAVISTOCK HERB NURSERY ⊠ ⌂
Tavistock, Preston Old Road, Clifton, Lancashire, PR4 0ZA
Ⓣ (01772) 683505
Ⓕ (01772) 683505
Ⓔ tavistockherbs@themail.co.uk
Also sells wholesale.
Contact: Mrs C Jones
Opening Times: By appt. only.
Min Mail Order UK: Nmc
Cat. Cost: 2 x 1st class stamps
Credit Cards: None.
Specialities: Herbs. *Mentha* & *Thymus* species. Note: main nursery at Garstang Road, Barton, near Preston, Lancs.
Map Ref: N, D1

NVic THE VICARAGE GARDEN ⊠ ♿
Carrington, Manchester, M31 4AG
Ⓣ (0161) 775 2750
Ⓔ info@vicaragebotanicalgardens.co.uk
Ⓦ www.vicaragebotanicalgardens.co.uk
Contact: Paul Haine
Opening Times: 0900-1700 Mon-Sat, closed Thu. 1000-1630 Sun all year.
Min Mail Order UK: Nmc
Cat. Cost: 2 x 2nd class for list
Credit Cards: All major credit/debit cards.
Specialities: Herbaceous, alpines, grasses, ferns. Free admission to 7 acre gardens.
Map Ref: N, D2 **OS Grid Ref:** SJ729926

NWCA **White Cottage Alpines** ⊠ ♞ ♿
Sunnyside Nurseries, Hornsea Road,
Sigglesthorne, East Yorkshire,
HU11 5QL
Ⓣ (01964) 542692
Ⓕ (01964) 542692
Ⓔ plants@whitecottagealpines.co.uk
Ⓦ www.whitecottagealpines.co.uk
Contact: Sally E Cummins
Opening Times: 1000-1700 (or dusk) Thu-Sun & B/hol Mon 1 Mar-30 Sep. If travelling far, please phone first. In winter by appt. only.
Min Mail Order UK: £7.50 + p&p
Min Mail Order EU: £15.00 + p&p by card only.
Cat. Cost: 4 x 1st class
Credit Cards: Visa MasterCard Switch
Specialities: Alpines & rock plants. 500+ species incl. American, dwarf *Salix* & *Helichrysum*, also increasing range of *Penstemon*. Note: euro payments by card only.
Map Ref: N, C3

NWea **Weasdale Nurseries Ltd.** ⊠ €
Newbiggin-on-Lune,
Kirkby Stephen, Cumbria,
CA17 4LX
Ⓣ (01539) 623246
Ⓕ (01539) 623277
Ⓔ sales@weasdale.com
Ⓦ www.weasdale.com
Contact: Andrew Forsyth
Opening Times: 0830-1730 Mon-Fri. Closed w/ends, B/hols, Xmas-New Year.
Min Mail Order UK: Nmc
Min Mail Order EU: Nmc
Cat. Cost: £1.50 or 6 x 1st class, £2 by credit/debit card
Credit Cards: Visa MasterCard Switch Delta Access Solo
Specialities: Hardy forest trees, hedging, broadleaved & conifers. Specimen trees & shrubs grown at 850 feet. Mail order a speciality. Note: mail order Nov-Apr only.
Map Ref: N, C1

NWit **D S Witton** ⊠
26 Casson Drive, Harthill,
Sheffield, Yorkshire,
S26 7WA
Ⓣ (01909) 771366
Ⓕ (01909) 771366
Ⓔ donshardyeuphorbias@btopenworld.com
Ⓦ www.donshardyeuphorbias.btinternet.co.uk
Contact: Don Witton
Opening Times: By appt. only.
Min Mail Order UK: Nmc*
Cat. Cost: 1 x 1st class + sae
Specialities: Nat. Coll. of Hardy *Euphorbia*. Over 130 varieties. *Note: mail order *Euphorbia* seed only.
Map Ref: N, D2 **OS Grid Ref:** SK494812

NWoo **Woodlands Cottage Nursery** ♿
Summerbridge, Harrogate, North Yorkshire,
HG3 4BT
Ⓣ (01423) 780765
Ⓔ annstark@btinternet.com
Ⓦ www.woodlandscottagegarden.co.uk
Contact: Mrs Ann Stark
Opening Times: By appt. only, mid Mar-mid Sep.
Cat. Cost: 2 x 1st class
Credit Cards: None.
Specialities: Herbs, plants for shade & hardy perennials. Plants available in small quantities only.
Map Ref: N, C2 **OS Grid Ref:** SE195631

S

Southern

SAdn **Ashdown Forest Garden Centre & Nursery** ♿
Duddleswell, Ashdown Forest, Nr. Uckfield, East Sussex, TN22 3JP
Ⓣ (01825) 712300
Ⓦ www.ashdownforestgardencentre.co.uk
Also sells wholesale.
Contact: Victoria Tolton
Opening Times: 0900-1730 winter, 0900-1900 summer.
Credit Cards: All major credit/debit cards.
Specialities: *Lavandula* & ornamental grasses.
Map Ref: S, C4

SAft **Afton Park Nursery** ♞ ♿
Newport Road, Afton, Freshwater, Isle of Wight, PO40 9XR
Ⓣ (01983) 755774
Ⓜ 09665 43031
Ⓔ chris@aftonpark.co.uk
Ⓦ www.aftonpark.co.uk
Contact: Chris Barnes
Opening Times: 0930-1700 7 days1st Mar-end Nov. Winter, please phone first.
Cat. Cost: 4 x 1st class
Credit Cards: Visa MasterCard
Specialities: Wide general range, emphasis on unusual perennials, grasses, coastal shrubs & plants for Mediterranean gardens.
Map Ref: S, D2 **OS Grid Ref:** SZ349864

KEY
⊠ Mail order to UK or EU ♞ Delivers to shows
✈ Exports beyond EU € Euro accepted
♿ Accessible by wheelchair ◆ See Display advertisement

SAga **AGAR'S NURSERY** € ♿
Agars Lane, Hordle, Lymington,
Hampshire, SO41 0FL
Ⓣ (01590) 683703
Contact: Diana Tombs, Debbie Ursell
Opening Times: 1000-1700 Fri-Wed Mar-Oct, 1000-1600 Fri-Wed Nov, Dec & Feb.
Credit Cards: None.
Specialities: *Penstemon* & *Salvia*. Also wide range of hardy plants incl. shrubs, climbers & herbaceous.
Map Ref: S, D2

SAin **AINSWORTH DISPLAYS** ⊠ ⌂
5 Kentidge Road, Waterlooville,
Hampshire, PO7 5NH
Ⓣ (023) 92 255057
Ⓔ Britishpalms@aol.com
Also sells wholesale.
Contact: Mark Ainsworth
Opening Times: Not open.
Min Mail Order UK: £10.00 + p&p
Cat. Cost: 2 x 1st class for price list.
Credit Cards: Visa MasterCard
Specialities: Palm trees.

SAll **ALLWOOD BROS** ⊠ ⌂ ♿
London Road, Hassocks, West Sussex,
BN6 9NB
Ⓣ (01273) 844229
Ⓕ (01273) 846022
Ⓔ info@allwoodbros.co.uk
Ⓦ www.allwoodbros.co.uk
Contact: David James or Emma
Opening Times: 0900-1630 Mon-Fri. Answer machine all other times.
Min Mail Order UK: Nmc
Min Mail Order EU: Nmc
Cat. Cost: 2 x 1st class
Credit Cards: Access Visa MasterCard Switch
Specialities: *Dianthus* incl. hardy border carnations, pinks, perpetual & *Allwoodii*, some available as seed. Note: exports seed only.
Map Ref: S, D4

SAPC **ARCHITECTURAL PLANTS (CHICHESTER) LTD** ⊠ ✈ ⌂ € ♿ ◆
Lidsey Road Nursery, Westergate,
Nr. Chichester, West Sussex,
PO20 6SU
Ⓣ (01243) 545008
Ⓕ (01243) 545009
Ⓔ chichester@architecturalplants.com
Ⓦ www.architecturalplants.com
Also sells wholesale.
Contact: Christine Shaw
Opening Times: 1000-1600 Sun-Fri all year. Closed Sat & B/hol Mons. Open Good Fri.
Min Mail Order UK: Nmc
Min Mail Order EU: £150.00 + p&p
Cat. Cost: Free
Credit Cards: All major credit/debit cards.
Specialities: Architectural plants & hardy exotics esp. evergreen broadleaved trees & seaside exotics, trees & spiky plants, yuccas/agaves. Note: second nursery near Horsham, Code SArc.
Map Ref: S, D3

SApp **APPLE COURT** ⊠ € ◆
Hordle Lane, Hordle, Lymington,
Hampshire, S041 0HU
Ⓣ (01590) 642130
Ⓕ (01590) 644220
Ⓔ applecourt@btinternet.com
Ⓦ www.applecourt.com
Contact: Angela & Charles Meads
Opening Times: 1000-1700 Fri, Sat, Sun & B/hol 1st Mar-31st Oct. Closed Nov-Feb.
Min Mail Order UK: £15.00 + p&p
Min Mail Order EU: £50.00 + p&p
Cat. Cost: 4 x 1st class
Credit Cards: All major credit/debit cards.
Specialities: *Hemerocallis, Hosta*, grasses & ferns.
Map Ref: S, D2 **OS Grid Ref:** SZ270941

SArc **ARCHITECTURAL PLANTS** ⊠ ✈ ⌂ € ♿ ◆
Cooks Farm, Nuthurst, Horsham,
West Sussex, RH13 6LH
Ⓣ (01403) 891772
Ⓕ (01403) 891056
Ⓔ enquiries@architecturalplants.com
Ⓦ www.architecturalplants.com
Also sells wholesale.
Contact: Sarah Chandler
Opening Times: 0900-1700 Mon-Sat, closed Sun.
Min Mail Order UK: Nmc
Min Mail Order EU: £150.00 + p&p
Cat. Cost: Free
Credit Cards: All major credit/debit cards.
Specialities: Architectural plants & hardy exotics. Note: second nursery near Chichester, code SAPC.
Map Ref: S, C3

SBai **STEVEN BAILEY LTD** ⌂ ♿
Silver Street, Sway, Lymington,
Hampshire, SO41 6ZA
Ⓣ (01590) 682227
Ⓕ (01590) 683765
Ⓦ www.steven-bailey.co.uk
Also sells wholesale.
Contact: Stef Bailey
Opening Times: 1000-1600 all year.

Credit Cards: Visa MasterCard Switch
Specialities: Carnations, pinks, *Alstroemeria* & penstemons.
Map Ref: S, D2

SBch **Birchwood Plants** ♿
(office) 10 Westering, Romsey, Hampshire, SO51 7LY
Ⓣ (01794) 502192
Ⓔ lesleybaker@lycos.co.uk
Contact: Lesley Baker
Opening Times: By appt. only at nursery. Plants also available at Mottisfont Abbey (NT) but ring first to check availability.
Cat. Cost: Free by email or 5 x 1st class.
Credit Cards: None.
Specialities: Wide range of plants, mainly herbaceous, many unusual. Good selection of salvias, geraniums, grasses & herbs. Grown in peat-free compost. Happy to propagate to order. Some stock limited. Note: nursery at Gardener's Lane, Nr. Romsey, SO51 6AD.
Map Ref: S, D2 **OS Grid Ref:** SU333190

SBig **Big Plant Nursery** ⊠ ◆
Hole Street, Ashington, West Sussex, RH20 3DE
Ⓣ (01903) 891466
Ⓕ (01903) 892829
Ⓔ info@bigplantnursery.co.uk
Ⓦ www.bigplantnursery.co.uk
Also sells wholesale.
Contact: Bruce Jordan
Opening Times: 0900-1700 Mon-Sat, 1000-1600 Sun & B/hols.
Min Mail Order UK: Please phone for further info.
Cat. Cost: A5 sae with 2 x 1st class
Credit Cards: All major credit/debit cards.
Specialities: Bamboos, hardy exotics & palms.

SBir **Birchfleet Nursery**
Nyewood, Petersfield, Hampshire, GU31 5JQ
Ⓣ (01730) 821636
Ⓕ (01730) 821636
Ⓔ gammoak@aol.com
Ⓦ www.birchfleetnurseries.co.uk
Also sells wholesale.
Contact: John & Daphne Gammon
Opening Times: By appt. only. Please phone.
Cat. Cost: 2 x 1st class
Credit Cards: None.
Specialities: Oaks. Beech. *Carpinus*. Nat. Coll. of *Liquidambar*. Note: nursery accessible for wheelchairs in dry weather.
Map Ref: S, C3

SBla **Blackthorn Nursery** € ♿
Kilmeston, Alresford, Hampshire, SO24 0NL
Ⓣ (01962) 771796
Ⓕ (01962) 771071
Contact: A R & S B White, M Ellis
Opening Times: 0900-1700 Fri & Sat only, 5th Mar-26th Jun & 3rd-25th Sep 2004. 0900-1700 Fri & Sat only, 4th Mar-25th Jun 2005.
Cat. Cost: Plant list for 3 x 1st class
Credit Cards: None.
Specialities: Choice perennials & alpines, esp. *Daphne, Epimedium, Helleborus* & *Hepatica.*
Map Ref: S, C2 **OS Grid Ref:** SU590264

SBLw **Brian Lewington** ⊠ ♿
(office) 9 Meadow Rise, Horam, Heathfield, East Sussex, TN21 0LZ
Ⓣ (01435) 810124
Ⓕ (01435) 810124
Ⓔ BHLewington@aol.com
Ⓦ www.treesandhedges.co.uk
Also sells wholesale.
Contact: Brian Lewington
Opening Times: 0800-1700 Sat. Other times by appt. only.
Min Mail Order UK: Nmc
Specialities: Larger size trees and hedging. Note: nursery is at Leverett Farm, Dallington, Nr. Heathfield, Sussex.
Map Ref: S, D4 **OS Grid Ref:** TQ578172

SBod **Bodiam Nursery** ♿
Cowfield Cottage, Bodiam, Robertsbridge, East Sussex, TN32 5RA
Ⓣ (01580) 830811
Ⓕ (01580) 831989
Contact: Danielle Seymour
Opening Times: 1000-1700 7 days. Closed Mon, Nov-Feb.
Cat. Cost: 4 x 1st class
Credit Cards: Visa MasterCard Solo JCB
Specialities: Herbaceous perennials, grasses, conifers, *Camellia* & climbers. Acers.
Map Ref: S, C5

SBra **J Bradshaw & Son** ⊠ ⌂ ◆
Busheyfield Nursery, Herne, Herne Bay, Kent, CT6 7LJ
Ⓣ (01227) 375415
Ⓕ (01227) 375415
Also sells wholesale.
Contact: D J Bradshaw & Martin Bradshaw

KEY
⊠ Mail order to UK or EU ⌂ Delivers to shows
✈ Exports beyond EU € Euro accepted
♿ Accessible by wheelchair ◆ See Display advertisement

S

Opening Times: 1000-1700 Tue-Sat 1st Mar-31st Oct & B/hol Mons. Other times by appt. only.
Min Mail Order UK: 2 plants + p&p
Cat. Cost: Sae + 2 x 1st class
Credit Cards: Visa MasterCard Switch
Specialities: *Clematis, Lonicera*, other climbers & wall shrubs.
Map Ref: S, C5 **OS Grid Ref:** TR174646

SBri **BRICKWALL COTTAGE NURSERY** ⊠ ♿
1 Brickwall Cottages,
Frittenden, Cranbrook,
Kent, TN17 2DH
Ⓣ (01580) 852425
Ⓔ suemartin@brickcot.fsnet.co.uk
Contact: Sue Martin
Opening Times: By appt. only.
Min Mail Order UK: Nmc
Credit Cards: None.
Specialities: Hardy perennials. Stock ltd. in quantity. *Geum, Potentilla*, herbaceous. Note: mail order geums only.
Map Ref: S, C5 **OS Grid Ref:** TQ815410

S

SBrm **BRAMBLY HEDGE** ⊠
Mill Lane, Sway,
Hampshire, SO41 8LN
Ⓣ (01590) 683570
Ⓔ swaystreps@lineone.net
Contact: Kim Williams
Opening Times: 1000-1400 certain Sats, Jun-Oct, phone or write for dates.
Min Mail Order UK: Nmc
Cat. Cost: 9"x 7" sae
Credit Cards: None.
Specialities: National Collection of *Streptocarpus*. Note: mail order Mar-Oct, small quantities only available.
Map Ref: S, D2 **OS Grid Ref:** SZ294973

SBrw **BROADWATER PLANTS** ⊠ ◆
Fairview Lane,
Tunbridge Wells, Kent,
TN3 9LU
Ⓣ (01892) 534760
Ⓕ (01892) 534760
Ⓔ Broadwaterplants@aol.com
Contact: John Moaby
Opening Times: 0900-1600 Mon-Sat.
Min Mail Order UK: Nmc
Cat. Cost: 3 x 1st class
Credit Cards: MasterCard Visa
Specialities: Rare & exciting plants, in addition to a range of rhododendrons & ericaceous plants. Limited stocks of some varieties. Limited wheelchair access.
Map Ref: S, C4 **OS Grid Ref:** TQ558377

SCac **CACTI & SUCCULENTS**
Hammerfield, Crockham Hill,
Edenbridge, Kent, TN8 6RR
Ⓣ (01732) 866295
Contact: Geoff Southon
Opening Times: Flexible. Please phone first.
Cat. Cost: None issued.
Credit Cards: None.
Specialities: *Echeveria* & related genera & hybrids. *Agave*, haworthias, aloes, gasterias, crassulas. (Large range of plants available in small quantities.)

SCam **CAMELLIA GROVE NURSERY** ⊠ ✈ ⌂ € ♿
Market Garden, Lower Beeding,
West Sussex, RH13 6PP
Ⓣ (01403) 891143
Ⓕ (01403) 891336
Ⓔ rhs20@camellia-grove.com
Ⓦ www.camellia-grove.com
Also sells wholesale.
Contact: Chris Loder
Opening Times: 1000-1600 Mon-Sat, please phone first so we can give you our undivided attention.
Min Mail Order UK: Nmc
Min Mail Order EU: £100.00 +p&p
Cat. Cost: 2 x 1st class
Specialities: Camellias & azaleas.
Map Ref: S, C3

SChr **JOHN CHURCHER** ⊠ ✈
47 Grove Avenue, Portchester, Fareham,
Hampshire, PO16 9EZ
Ⓣ (023) 9232 6740
Ⓔ John@plants-palms.freeserve.co.uk
Contact: John Churcher
Opening Times: By appt. only. Please phone.
Min Mail Order UK: Nmc
Min Mail Order EU: Nmc
Cat. Cost: 4 x 1st class
Credit Cards: None.
Specialities: Hardy *Opuntia, Agave, Aloe*, succulents, palms, treeferns, plus small general range of attractive species for the exotic garden, hardy & half-hardy.
Map Ref: S, D2 **OS Grid Ref:** SU614047

SChu **CHURCH HILL COTTAGE GARDENS** € ♿
Charing Heath, Ashford, Kent,
TN27 0BU
Ⓣ (01233) 712522
Ⓕ (01233) 712522
Contact: Mr M & J & Mrs M Metianu
Opening Times: 1000-1700 1st Feb-30th Sep Tue-Sun & B/hol Mons. Other times by appt.
Cat. Cost: 4 x 1st class
Credit Cards: None.

Specialities: Unusual hardy plants, *Dianthus*, *Hosta*, ferns, *Viola*, & alpines.
Map Ref: S, C5

SCnR COLIN ROBERTS ⊠
Tragumna, Morgay Wood Lane, Three Oaks, Guestling, East Sussex, TN35 4NF
Ⓜ 07718 029909
Ⓕ (01424) 814308
Contact: Colin Roberts
Opening Times: Not open.
Min Mail Order UK: £20.00
Cat. Cost: 2 x 1st class
Credit Cards: None.
Specialities: Dwarf bulbs & woodland plants incl. many rare & unusual, in small numbers.

SCog COGHURST CAMELLIAS ⊠ € ♿
Ivy House Lane, Near Three Oaks,
Hastings, East Sussex,
TN35 4NP
Ⓣ (01424) 756228
Ⓕ (01424) 428944
Ⓔ rotherview@btinternet.com
Ⓦ www.rotherview.com
Also sells wholesale.
Contact: R Bates & W Bates
Opening Times: 0930-1600 7 days.
Min Mail Order UK: Nmc
Min Mail Order EU: Nmc
Cat. Cost: 4 x 1st class
Credit Cards: All major credit/debit cards.
Specialities: *Camellia*. Note: nursery is on the same site as Rotherview Nursery.
Map Ref: S, D5

SCoo COOLING'S NURSERIES LTD ♿
Rushmore Hill, Knockholt, Sevenoaks, Kent, TN14 7NN
Ⓣ (01959) 532269
Ⓕ (01959) 534092
Ⓔ Plantfinder@coolings.co.uk
Ⓦ www.coolings.co.uk
Contact: Mark Reeve & Gary Carvosso
Opening Times: 0900-1700 Mon-Sat & 1000-1630 Sun.
Cat. Cost: None issued
Credit Cards: Visa Access Switch Electron Delta MasterCard
Specialities: Large range of perennials, conifers & bedding plants. Some unusual shrubs & trees.
Map Ref: S, C4

SCrf CROFTERS NURSERIES € ♿
Church Hill, Charing Heath,
Near Ashford, Kent,
TN27 0BU
Ⓣ (01233) 712798
Ⓕ (01233) 712798
Ⓔ crofters.nursery1@virgin.net
Contact: John & Sue Webb
Opening Times: 1000-1700. Closed Sun-Tue. Please check first.
Cat. Cost: 3 x 1st class
Credit Cards: None.
Specialities: Fruit, ornamental trees & conifers. Old apple varieties. Small number of *Prunus serrula* with grafted ornamental heads.
Map Ref: S, C5 **OS Grid Ref:** TQ923493

SDay A LA CARTE DAYLILIES ⊠ € ◆
Little Hermitage,
St Catherine's Down,
Nr. Ventnor,
Isle of Wight,
PO38 2PD
Ⓣ (01983) 730512
Ⓔ andy@ukdaylilies.com
Ⓦ www.ukdaylilies.com
Also sells wholesale.
Contact: Jan & Andy Wyers
Opening Times: By appt. only.
Min Mail Order UK: Nmc
Min Mail Order EU: Nmc
Cat. Cost: 3 x 1st class
Credit Cards: None.
Specialities: *Hemerocallis*. Nat. Colls. of Miniature & Small Flowered *Hemerocallis* & Large Flowered *Hemerocallis* (post-1960 award-winning cultivars).

SDix GREAT DIXTER NURSERIES ⊠ ♿
Northiam, Rye, East Sussex,
TN31 6PH
Ⓣ (01797) 253107
Ⓕ (01797) 252879
Ⓔ nursery@greatdixter.co.uk
Ⓦ www.greatdixter.co.uk
Contact: K Leighton
Opening Times: 0900-1230 & 1330-1700 Mon-Fri, 0900-1200 Sat all year. Also 1400-1700 Sat, Sun & B/hols Apr-Oct.
Min Mail Order UK: £15.00 + p&p
Min Mail Order EU: £15.00 + p&p
Cat. Cost: 4 x 1st class
Credit Cards: Access Switch Visa MasterCard Solo Delta
Specialities: *Clematis*, shrubs and plants. Gardens open. Note: plants dispatched Sep-Mar only.
Map Ref: S, C5

KEY
⊠ Mail order to UK or EU — Delivers to shows
Exports beyond EU — € Euro accepted
♿ Accessible by wheelchair — ◆ See Display advertisement

S

SDnm **DENMANS GARDEN, (JOHN BROOKES LTD)** ♿
Clock House, Denmans, Fontwell,
Nr. Arundel, West Sussex, BN18 0SU
Ⓣ (01243) 542808
Ⓕ (01243) 544064
Ⓔ denmans@denmans-garden.co.uk
Ⓦ www.denmans-garden.co.uk
Contact: Michael Neve & Clare Scherer
Opening Times: 0900-1700 7 days 1st Feb-24th Dec.
Cat. Cost: None issued
Credit Cards: Visa MasterCard
Specialities: Rare and unusual plants.
Map Ref: S, D3

SDow **DOWNDERRY NURSERY** ⊠ ⊠ ♠ € ♿
Pillar Box Lane, Hadlow, Nr. Tonbridge,
Kent, TN11 9SW
Ⓣ (01732) 810081
Ⓕ (01732) 811398
Ⓔ info@downderry-nursery.co.uk
Ⓦ www.downderry-nursery.co.uk
Contact: Dr S J Charlesworth
Opening Times: 1000-1700 Tue-Sun 1st May-31st Oct & by appt.
Min Mail Order UK: Nmc
Min Mail Order EU: Nmc
Cat. Cost: 3 x 1st class
Credit Cards: Delta MasterCard Switch Visa
Specialities: Nat. Colls. of *Lavandula* and *Rosmarinus.*
Map Ref: S, C4 **OS Grid Ref:** TQ625521

SDys **DYSONS NURSERIES** ⊠ ♠ ♿
Great Comp Garden, Platt, Sevenoaks, Kent,
TN15 8QS
Ⓣ (01732) 886154
Ⓔ dysonsnurseries@aol.com
Ⓦ www.greatcomp.co.uk
Also sells wholesale.
Contact: William T Dyson
Opening Times: 1100-1730 7 days 1st Apr-31st Oct. Other times by appt.
Min Mail Order UK: £9.00 + p&p
Cat. Cost: 4 x 1st class
Credit Cards: None.
Specialities: Salvias, especially New World species and cultivars.
Map Ref: S, C4

SECG **THE ENGLISH COTTAGE GARDEN NURSERY** ⊠
Herons, Giggers Green Road,
Aldington, Kent,
TN25 7BU
Ⓣ (01233) 720907
Ⓕ (01233) 720907
Ⓔ enquiries@englishplants.co.uk
Ⓦ www.englishplants.co.uk
Also sells wholesale.
Contact: Teresa Sinclair
Opening Times: 7 days, please phone first.
Min Mail Order UK: Nmc
Cat. Cost: Free
Credit Cards: MasterCard Visa Solo Electron Switch
Specialities: Small nursery offering variety of traditional cottage garden plants, wildflowers & herbs. Notes: ltd. stock of some wildflowers. Plants can be ordered & paid for online.

SEND **EAST NORTHDOWN FARM** ⊠ € ♿ ◆
Margate, Kent, CT9 3TS
Ⓣ (01843) 862060
Ⓕ (01843) 860206
Ⓔ friend.northdown@ukonline.co.uk
Ⓦ www.botanyplants.com
Also sells wholesale.
Contact: Louise & William Friend
Opening Times: 0900-1700 Mon-Sat, 1000-1700 Sun all year. Closed Xmas week & Easter Sun.
Min Mail Order UK: Nmc
Cat. Cost: Available Online only.
Credit Cards: Visa Switch MasterCard
Specialities: Chalk & coast-loving plants.
Map Ref: S, B6

SFam **FAMILY TREES** ⊠ ♿
Sandy Lane, Shedfield, Hampshire,
SO32 2HQ
Ⓣ (01329) 834812
Contact: Philip House
Opening Times: 0930-1230 Wed & Sat mid Oct-end Apr.
Min Mail Order UK: Nmc
Min Mail Order EU: Nmc
Cat. Cost: Free
Credit Cards: None.
Specialities: Fruit & ornamental trees. Trained fruit tree specialists: standards, espaliers, cordons. Other trees, old- fashioned & climbing roses, evergreens. Trees, except evergreens, sold bare rooted. Large specimens in pots.
Map Ref: S, D2

SGar **GARDEN PLANTS** ⊠ ♠
Windy Ridge, Victory Road,
St Margarets-at-Cliffe, Dover, Kent,
CT15 6HF
Ⓣ (01304) 853225
Ⓔ GardenPlants@GardenPlants-nursery.co.uk
Ⓦ www.GardenPlants-nursery.co.uk

Also sells wholesale.
Contact: Teresa Ryder & David Ryder
Opening Times: 1000-1700 (closed Wed).
Min Mail Order UK: Nmc
Cat. Cost: 2 x 1st class + A5 sae
Credit Cards: None.
Specialities: Unusual perennials, *Penstemon* & *Salvia*. Plantsman's garden open to view. Map essential for first visit.
Map Ref: S, C6 **OS Grid Ref:** TR358464

SGSe GARDEN SECRETS ⊠ ♿ ◆
8 Holly Lane, Ashley, New Milton, Hampshire, BH25 5RF
Ⓜ 07779 084245
Contact: Tim Woodford
Opening Times: 0900-1700 Sat & Sun, Mar-Jan. Other times by appt. only. Please phone first.
Min Mail Order UK: £15.00
Cat. Cost: 3 x 1st class
Credit Cards: None.
Specialities: Perennials, grasses and ferns. Note: nursery is at Green Pastures, Pitmore Lane, Sway, Hampshire SO41 8LL.
Map Ref: S, D2 **OS Grid Ref:** SZ296972

SHaC HART CANNA ⊠ € ♿
27 Guildford Road West, Farnborough, Hampshire, GU14 6PS
Ⓣ (01252) 514421
Ⓕ (01252) 378821
Ⓔ plants@hartcanna.com
Ⓦ www.hartcanna.com
Also sells wholesale.
Contact: Keith Hayward
Opening Times: Visitors by arrangement.
Min Mail Order UK: Nmc
Min Mail Order EU: Nmc
Cat. Cost: Free.
Credit Cards: All major credit/debit cards.
Specialities: *Canna*. National Collection of *Canna*.
Map Ref: S, C3

SHar HARDY'S COTTAGE GARDEN PLANTS ⊠ ⌂ ♿
Freefolk Priors, Freefolk, Whitchurch, Hampshire, RG28 7NJ
Ⓣ (01256) 896533
Ⓕ (01256) 896572
Ⓔ hardy@cottagegardenplants.fsnet.co.uk
Ⓦ www.hardys-plants.co.uk
Contact: Rosy Hardy
Opening Times: 1000-1700 7 days 1st Mar-31st Oct.
Min Mail Order UK: Nmc
Cat. Cost: 8 x 1st class.
Credit Cards: Visa Access Electron Switch Solo
Specialities: Hardy *Geranium* & other herbaceous both old & new. Collection of *Viola odorata* & Parma violets now available. Note: a charge of £2.00 is made for delivery of pre-ordered plants to shows.
Map Ref: S, C2

SHay HAYWARD'S CARNATIONS ⊠
The Chace Gardens, Stakes Road, Purbrook, Waterlooville, Hampshire, PO7 5PL
Ⓣ (023) 9226 3047
Ⓕ (023) 9226 3047
Also sells wholesale.
Contact: A N Hayward
Opening Times: 0930-1700 Mon-Fri.
Min Mail Order UK: £10.00 + p&p
Min Mail Order EU: £50.00 + p&p
Cat. Cost: 1 x 1st class
Credit Cards: None.
Specialities: Hardy pinks & border carnations (*Dianthus*). Greenhouse perpetual carnations.
Map Ref: S, D2

SHBN HIGH BANKS NURSERIES ♿
Slip Mill Road, Hawkhurst, Kent, TN18 5AD
Ⓣ (01580) 754492
Ⓕ (01580) 754450
Also sells wholesale.
Contact: Jeremy Homewood
Opening Times: 0800-1700 (1630 in winter) daily.
Cat. Cost: £1.50 (stamps) + A4 Sae
Credit Cards: All major credit/debit cards.
Specialities: Wide general range with many unusual plants. Minimum of 250,000 plants on site at any one time. Many unusual plants. Open ground stock ltd. between Nov and Feb.
Map Ref: S, C5

SHDw HIGHDOWN NURSERY ⊠ ✈ ⌂ €
New Hall Lane, Small Dole, Nr. Henfield, West Sussex, BN5 9YH
Ⓣ (01273) 492976
Ⓕ (01273) 492976
Ⓔ highdown.herbs@btopenworld.com
Also sells wholesale.
Contact: A G & J H Shearing
Opening Times: 0900-1700 7 days.
Min Mail Order UK: £10.00 + p&p

KEY
⊠ Mail order to UK or EU ⌂ Delivers to shows
✈ Exports beyond EU € Euro accepted
♿ Accessible by wheelchair ◆ See Display advertisement

S

Min Mail Order EU: £10.00 + p&p
Cat. Cost: 3 x 1st class
Credit Cards: Visa MasterCard Delta JCB Eurocard
Specialities: Herbs. Partial wheelchair access.
Map Ref: S, D3

SHel HELLYER'S GARDEN PLANTS ⊠
Orchards, off Wallage Lane*,
Rowfant, Nr. Crawley, West Sussex,
RH10 4NJ
Ⓣ (01342) 718280
Ⓕ (01342) 718280
Ⓔ penelope.hellyer@hellyers.co.uk
Ⓦ www.hellyers.co.uk
Contact: Penelope Hellyer
Opening Times: 1300-1700 Wed-Sat Mar-Oct & by prior appt.
Min Mail Order UK: Nmc
Cat. Cost: 4 x 1st + A5 Sae (1st class).
Credit Cards: None.
Specialities: Hardy plants for sun/shade. Small selection of climbers, shrubs. 100+ varieties of hardy *Geranium*. Some stock in ltd. quantities; small numbers available through propagation service. *Notes: Wallage Lane is off the B2028 equidistant Crawley Down & Turners Hill. Mail order mainland Britain only.
Map Ref: S, C4 **OS Grid Ref:** TQ334373

SHFr SUE HARTFREE
25 Crouch Hill Court, Lower Halstow,
Nr. Sittingbourne, Kent, ME9 7EJ
Ⓣ (01795) 842426
Contact: Sue Hartfree
Opening Times: Any time by appt. Please phone first.
Cat. Cost: A5 Sae + 4 x 1st class
Credit Cards: None.
Specialities: Rare & unusual plants for the garden & conservatory incl. many varieties of *Salvia*. Some plants available in small quantities, but can be propagated to order. Garden open.
Map Ref: S, C5 **OS Grid Ref:** TQ860672

SHGC HAMBROOKS GROWING CONCERN ♿
Wangfield Lane, Curdridge, Southampton,
Hampshire, SO32 2DA
Ⓣ (01489) 780505/779993
Ⓕ (01489) 785396
Ⓔ timedwards@hambrooks.co.uk
Ⓦ www.hambrooks.co.uk
Also sells wholesale.
Contact: Tim Edwards
Opening Times: 0730-1800 Mon-Fri.
Cat. Cost: 2 x 1st class
Credit Cards: All major credit/debit cards.
Specialities: Specimen stock, herbaceous, conifers, shrubs, grasses, climbers & hedging.
Map Ref: S, D2 **OS Grid Ref:** SU523141

SHGN HILL GARTH NURSERY ♿
Woodgreen Road, Godshill,
Fordingbridge, Hampshire,
SP6 2LP
Ⓣ (01425) 657619
Ⓕ (01425) 657619
Contact: Mrs S J Giddins
Opening Times: 0930-1700 Thu & Sun, Mar-end Oct.
Cat. Cost: None issued
Credit Cards: None.
Specialities: Small nursery offering a range of rare, unusual & traditional hardy perennials, shrubs & trees. Some stock may be limited.
Map Ref: S, D1

SHHo HIGHFIELD HOLLIES ⊠ ◆
Highfield Farm, Hatch Lane,
Liss, Hampshire,
GU33 7NH
Ⓣ (01730) 892372
Ⓕ (01730) 894853
Ⓔ louise@highfieldhollies.com
Ⓦ www.highfieldhollies.com
Contact: Mrs Louise Bendall
Opening Times: By appt.
Min Mail Order UK: £30.00
Cat. Cost: £3.50 for illustrated cat.
Credit Cards: None.
Specialities: 150+ species & cultivars *Ilex* incl. specimen trees, hedging & topiary. Some in short supply.
Map Ref: S, C3 **OS Grid Ref:** SU787276

SHmp HAMPSHIRE CARNIVOROUS PLANTS
⊠ ☒ €
Ya-Mayla, Allington Lane, West End,
Southampton, Hampshire,
SO30 3HQ
Ⓣ (023) 8047 3314
Ⓜ 07703 258296
Ⓕ (023) 8047 3314
Ⓔ matthew@msoper.freesave.co.uk
Ⓦ www.hampshire-carnivorous.co.uk
Also sells wholesale.
Contact: Matthew Soper
Opening Times: By appt. only.
Min Mail Order UK: Nmc
Min Mail Order EU: £50.00 + p&p
Cat. Cost: 2 x 2nd class
Credit Cards: Visa MasterCard
Specialities: Carnivorous plants esp. *Nepenthes, Heliamphora, Sarracenia Pinguicula & Utricularia.*

SHom **HOME PLANTS**
52 Dorman Ave North,
Aylesham, Canterbury, Kent,
CT3 3BW
Ⓣ (01304) 841746
Contact: Stuart & Sue Roycroft
Opening Times: By appt. only, please phone first.
Cat. Cost: SAE for list
Credit Cards: None.
Specialities: *Phygelius.* Limited stock, please phone first.

SHop **HOPALONG NURSERY** ♿
Crabtree Close, Fairseat,
Sevenoaks, Kent, TN15 7JR
Ⓣ (01732) 822422
Ⓕ (01732) 822422
Ⓔ jon@hopalong.fsworld.co.uk
Ⓦ www.hopalongnursery.co.uk
Contact: Jon Clark
Opening Times: 1000-1700 Wed-Sat, 1100-1600 Sun, 1st Mar-31st Oct. Open B/hols.
Cat. Cost: £2.00 or free Online
Credit Cards: None.
Specialities: Unusual hardy herbaceous perennials, grasses, ferns, *Cistus*. Some plants in small quantities.
Map Ref: S, C4 **OS Grid Ref:** TQ632613

SHvs **HARVEST NURSERIES** ⊠ €
Harvest Cottage, Boonshill Farm,
Iden, Nr. Rye, East Sussex,
TN31 7QA
Ⓣ (01797) 230583
Ⓔ harvest.nurseries@virgin.net
Contact: D A Smith
Opening Times: Not open, mail order only.
Min Mail Order UK: Nmc
Min Mail Order EU: £20.00 + p&p
Cat. Cost: 2 x 1st class
Credit Cards: None.
Specialities: *Epiphyllum* & wide range of succulents. Descriptive catalogue.

SHyH **HYDRANGEA HAVEN** ⊠ ✈ 🚚 € ♿
Market Garden, Lower Beeding,
West Sussex, RH13 6PP
Ⓣ (01403) 892580
Ⓕ (01403) 891336
Ⓔ rhspf@hydrangea-haven.com
Ⓦ www.hydrangea-haven.com
Also sells wholesale.
Contact: Chris Loder
Opening Times: 1000-1600 Mon-Sat, please phone first, so we can give you our undivided attention.
Min Mail Order UK: Nmc
Min Mail Order EU: £100.00 + p&p
Cat. Cost: 2 x 1st class
Credit Cards: Visa
Specialities: *Hydrangea.*
Map Ref: S, C3

SHzl **HAZEL COTTAGE** ⊠ 🚚
Land of Nod, Headley Down, Bordon,
Hampshire, GU35 8SJ
Ⓣ (01428) 717979
Ⓕ (01428) 717020
Ⓔ info@hazelcottagenursery.co.uk
Ⓦ www.hazelcottagenursery.co.uk
Also sells wholesale.
Contact: Trudy Thompson
Opening Times: Not open to the public.
Min Mail Order UK: £15.00
Cat. Cost: Free.
Credit Cards: All major credit/debit cards.
Specialities: Ornamental grasses.

SIde **IDEN CROFT HERBS** ⊠ ♿ ◆
Frittenden Road, Staplehurst, Kent,
TN12 0DH
Ⓣ (01580) 891432
Ⓕ (01580) 892416
Ⓔ idencroftherbs@yahoo.co.uk
Ⓦ www.herbs-uk.com
Contact: Tracey Pearman
Opening Times: 0900-1700 Mon-Sat & 1100-1700 Sun & B/hols during summer. Open all winter with reduced hours – please phone to confirm prior to visit.
Min Mail Order UK: £10.00
Min Mail Order EU: £25.00
Cat. Cost: 2 x 1st class for descriptive list.
Credit Cards: All major credit/debit cards.
Specialities: Herbs, aromatic & wild flower plants & plants for bees & butterflies. Nat. Colls. of *Mentha, Nepeta* & *Origanum.* Wheelchairs available at nursery. Note: exports seed only.
Map Ref: S, C5

SIFN **IAN FITZROY NURSERYMAN** ⊠ 🚚
(Office) 2 Moor Cottages,
Moor Lane, Marsh Green,
Edenbridge, Kent, TN8 5RA
Ⓣ (01342) 851179
Ⓕ (01342) 851179
Ⓔ sales@ianfitzroy.com
Ⓦ www.ianfitzroy.com
Also sells wholesale

KEY
⊠ Mail order to UK or EU — 🚚 Delivers to shows
✈ Exports beyond EU — € Euro accepted
♿ Accessible by wheelchair — ◆ See Display advertisement

S

Contact: Ian FitzRoy
Opening Times: By appt. only.
Min Mail Order UK: Nmc
Min Mail Order EU: Nmc
Cat. Cost: 4 x 1st class
Credit Cards: Switch Visa MasterCard
Specialities: Japanese maple. Rare and unusual trees and shrubs. Note: nursery is at Scarlets, Smithers Lane, Cowden, Kent TN8 7EG.
Map Ref: S, C4

SIgm TIM INGRAM ⌂ € ♿
Copton Ash, 105 Ashford Road,
Faversham, Kent, ME13 8XW
Ⓣ (01795) 535919
Contact: Dr T J Ingram
Opening Times: 1400-1800 Tue-Fri & Sat-Sun Mar-Oct. Nov-Feb by appt.
Cat. Cost: 4 x 1st class
Credit Cards: None.
Specialities: Unusual perennials, alpines & plants from Mediterranean-type climates incl. *Lupinus, Penstemon, Salvia* & umbellifers. Ltd. stock of some rarer plants.
Map Ref: S, C5 **OS Grid Ref:** TR015598

S

SIng W E TH. INGWERSEN LTD ⌂
Birch Farm Nursery, Gravetye,
East Grinstead, West Sussex,
RH19 4LE
Ⓣ (01342) 810236
Ⓔ info@ingwersen.co.uk
Ⓦ www.ingwersen.co.uk
Contact: M P & M R Ingwersen
Opening Times: 0900-1600 daily excl. Sun & B/hols, Mar-Sep. 0900-1600 Mon-Fri Oct-Feb.
Cat. Cost: 2 x 1st class
Credit Cards: None.
Specialities: Very wide range of hardy plants mostly alpines. Also seed.
Map Ref: S, C4

SIoW ISLE OF WIGHT LAVENDER ⊠ ♿
Staplehurst Grange, Newport,
Isle of Wight, PO30 2NQ
Ⓣ (01983) 825272
Ⓕ (01983) 825272
Ⓔ sales@lavender.co.uk
Ⓦ www.lavender.co.uk
Contact: Paul Abbott
Opening Times: 1000-1800 daily. Closed Xmas week.
Min Mail Order UK: Nmc
Cat. Cost: 1st class sae
Credit Cards: All major credit/debit cards.
Specialities: Lavender.
Map Ref: S, D2

SIri IRIS OF SISSINGHURST ⊠ € ♿ ◆
Plummers Farmhouse, Biddenden Road,
Sissinghurst, Kent, TN17 2JP
Ⓣ (01580) 715137
Ⓔ irisofs@aol.com
Contact: Margaret Roberts
Opening Times: 1000-1700 following w/ends: 10th-11th Apr, 15th-16th May, 5th-6th, 12th-13th Jun, 4th-5th Sep 2004. Other times by appt.
Min Mail Order UK: Nmc
Min Mail Order EU: Nmc
Cat. Cost: 2 x 1st class
Credit Cards: None.
Specialities: *Iris*, short, intermediate & tall bearded, *ensata, sibirica* & many species.
Map Ref: S, C5

SJoh VIC JOHNSTONE AND CLAIRE WILSON
43 Winchester Street, Whitchurch,
Hampshire, RG28 7AJ
Ⓣ (01256) 893144
Contact: Vic Johnstone, Claire Wilson
Opening Times: By appt. Please telephone first.
Cat. Cost: 2 x 1st class
Credit Cards: None.
Specialities: National Collection of *Verbascum. Verbascum* only.
Map Ref: S, C2 **OS Grid Ref:** SU463478

SKee KEEPERS NURSERY ⊠
Gallants Court, Gallants Lane, East Farleigh,
Maidstone, Kent, ME15 0LE
Ⓣ (01622) 726465
Ⓕ 0870 705 2145
Ⓔ info@keepers-nursery.co.uk
Ⓦ www.keepers-nursery.co.uk
Contact: Hamid Habibi
Opening Times: All reasonable hours by appt.
Min Mail Order UK: Nmc
Cat. Cost: 2 x 1st class. Free by email.
Credit Cards: Visa MasterCard Amex Switch Solo
Specialities: Old & unusual top fruit varieties. Top fruit propagated to order.
Map Ref: S, C4

SKen KENT STREET NURSERIES ⊠ €
Sedlescombe, Battle, East Sussex, TN33 0SF
Ⓣ (01424) 751134
Ⓔ peter@1066-countryplants.co.uk
Ⓦ www.1066-countryplants.co.uk
Also sells wholesale.
Contact: P Stapley
Opening Times: 0900-1800 7 days.
Min Mail Order UK: £6.50
Min Mail Order EU: £6.50

Cat. Cost: 2 x 1st class, email, or on web
Credit Cards: All major credit/debit cards.
Specialities: *Pelargonium*, bedding & perennials. Note: mail order *Pelargonium* list only. Nursery partially accessible for wheelchair users. Credit cards not accepted for mail order.
Map Ref: S, D5 OS Grid Ref: 790155

SLau **THE LAURELS NURSERY** ⊠ ♠ €
Benenden, Cranbrook, Kent,
TN17 4JU
Ⓣ (01580) 240463
Ⓕ (01580) 240463
Ⓦ www.thelaurelsnursery.co.uk
Also sells wholesale.
Contact: Peter or Sylvia Kellett
Opening Times: 0800-1700 Mon-Thu, 0800-1600 Fri, 0900-1200 Sat, Sun by appt. only.
Min Mail Order UK: £20.00
Cat. Cost: Free
Credit Cards: None.
Specialities: Open ground & container ornamental trees, shrubs & climbers incl. flowering cherries, birch, beech & *Wisteria*. Note: mail order of small *Wisteria* only.
Map Ref: S, C5 **OS Grid Ref:** TQ815313

SLay **LAYHAM GARDEN CENTRE & NURSERY** ⊠ ♿
Lower Road, Staple,
Nr. Canterbury, Kent,
CT3 1LH
Ⓣ (01304) 813267
Ⓕ (01304) 814007
Ⓔ layham@gcstaple.fsnet.co.uk
Also sells wholesale.
Contact: Ellen Wessel
Opening Times: 0900-1700 7 days.
Min Mail Order UK: Nmc
Min Mail Order EU: £25.00 + p&p
Cat. Cost: Free
Credit Cards: Visa Switch MasterCard
Specialities: Roses, herbaceous, shrubs, trees & hedging plants.
Map Ref: S, C6 **OS Grid Ref:** TR276567

SLBF **LITTLE BROOK FUCHSIAS** ♿
Ash Green Lane West,
Ash Green, Nr. Aldershot,
Hampshire, GU12 6HL
Ⓣ (01252) 329731
Ⓔ carol.gubler@business.ntl.com
Ⓦ www.littlebrookfuchsias.co.uk
Also sells wholesale.
Contact: Carol Gubler
Opening Times: 0900-1700 Wed-Sun 1st Jan-4th Jul.
Cat. Cost: 50p + Sae
Credit Cards: None.
Specialities: Fuchsias, old & new.
Map Ref: S, C3

SLdr **LODER PLANTS** ⊠ ✈ ♠ € ♿
Market Garden, Lower Beeding, West Sussex, RH13 6PP
Ⓣ (01403) 891412
Ⓕ (01403) 891336
Ⓔ rhspf@rhododendrons.com
Ⓦ www.rhododendrons.com
Also sells wholesale.
Contact: Chris Loder
Opening Times: 1000-1600 Mon-Sat, please ring first so we can give you our undivided attention.
Min Mail Order UK: Nmc
Min Mail Order EU: £100.00 + p&p
Cat. Cost: 2 x 1st class
Credit Cards: Visa Access
Specialities: Rhododendrons & azaleas in all sizes. *Camellia, Acer, Hydrangea* & ferns.
Map Ref: S, C3

SLim **LIME CROSS NURSERY** ♿ ◆
Herstmonceux, Hailsham, East Sussex,
BN27 4RS
Ⓣ (01323) 833229
Ⓕ (01323) 833944
Ⓔ LimeCross@aol.com
Ⓦ www.Limecross.co.uk
Also sells wholesale.
Contact: J A Tate, Mrs A Green
Opening Times: 0830-1700 Mon-Sat & 1000-1600 Sun.
Cat. Cost: 2 x 1st class
Credit Cards: Visa MasterCard Delta Switch
Specialities: Conifers, trees & shrubs, climbers.
Map Ref: S, D4

SLon **LONGSTOCK PARK NURSERY** ⊠ ♿
Longstock, Stockbridge, Hampshire,
SO20 6EH
Ⓣ (01264) 810894
Ⓕ (01264) 810924
Ⓔ longstocknursery@leckfordestate.co.uk
Ⓦ www.longstocknursery.co.uk
Contact: David Roberts
Opening Times: 0830-1630 Mon-Sat all year excl. Xmas & New Year, & 1100-1700 Sun Mar-Oct.

KEY
⊠ Mail order to UK or EU ♠ Delivers to shows
✈ Exports beyond EU € Euro accepted
♿ Accessible by wheelchair ◆ See Display advertisement

S

Min Mail Order UK: Min. postal charge £8.50 for parcels up to 10kg mainland UK.
Cat. Cost: £2.00 cheque incl. p&p
Credit Cards: Visa Access Switch MasterCard
Specialities: A wide range, over 2000 varieties, of trees, shrubs, perennials, climbers, aquatics & ferns. Nat. Colls. of *Buddleja* & *Clematis viticella*. Note: no trees over 2m high sent by mail order.
Map Ref: S, C2

SLPl LANDSCAPE PLANTS ⊠ ✈ ♿
Cattamount, Grafty Green,
Maidstone, Kent,
ME17 2AP
Ⓣ (01622) 850245
Ⓕ (01622) 858063
Ⓔ landscapeplants@aol.com
Also sells wholesale.
Contact: Tom La Dell
Opening Times: 0800-1600 Mon-Fri, by appt. only.
Min Mail Order UK: £100.00 + p&p
Min Mail Order EU: £200.00 + p&p
Cat. Cost: 2 x 1st class
Credit Cards: None.
Specialities: Garden & landscape shrubs & perennials.
Map Ref: S, C5 **OS Grid Ref:** TQ772468

SMac MACGREGORS PLANTS FOR SHADE ⊠ ⌂ ♿
Carters Clay Road, Lockerley, Romsey, Hampshire, SO51 0GL
Ⓣ (01794) 340256
Ⓔ plants@macgregors-shadeplants.co.uk
Ⓦ www.macgregors-shadeplants.co.uk
Also sells wholesale.
Contact: Irene & Stuart Bowron
Opening Times: 1000-1600 most days Mar-Oct, or by appt. Please phone before travelling to confirm nursery open.
Min Mail Order UK: Nmc
Cat. Cost: 3 x 1st class
Credit Cards: MasterCard Visa
Specialities: All types of shade plants & other less usual shrubs & perennials. Limited stock of rarer plants. Note: mail order usually restricted to small numbers of mature plants sent by 24hr carrier. Other arrangements by negotiation.
Map Ref: S, C2 **OS Grid Ref:** SU308239

SMad MADRONA NURSERY ⊠ ⌂ € ♿
Pluckley Road, Bethersden, Kent, TN26 3DD
Ⓣ (01233) 820100
Ⓕ (01233) 820091
Contact: Liam MacKenzie
Opening Times: 1000-1700 Sat-Tue 15th Mar-28th Oct. Closed 7th-20th Aug.
Min Mail Order UK: Nmc
Cat. Cost: Free
Credit Cards: Visa MasterCard Amex JCB Switch
Specialities: Unusual shrubs, conifers & perennials. Eryngiums, *Pseudopanax*.
Map Ref: S, C5 **OS Grid Ref:** TQ918419

SMar THE MARKET GARDEN ⌂ ◆
Ganders Gate Pig Farm, Glasshouse Lane, Kirdford, West Sussex, RH14 0LW
Ⓣ (01403) 820634
Ⓜ 0771 404 4024
Ⓔ foxglove_garden_design@hotmail.com
Contact: Sally Welch, Terri Lefevre
Opening Times: 1000-1600 Fri & Sun Mar-end Sep, or by appt.
Cat. Cost: 2 x 1st class
Credit Cards: None.
Specialities: Herbaceous perennials & grasses. A small nursery propagating all our plants, some grown in small quantities. Partly accessible for wheelchairs.
Map Ref: S, C3 **OS Grid Ref:** TQ014253

SMeo MEON VALLEY PLANTS ⊠ ⌂
(office) PO Box 155, Petersfield, Hampshire, GU32 1XQ
Ⓣ (office) (01730) 828079
Ⓜ 07818 088019,
Ⓔ camillamoreton@meonvalleyplants.co.uk
Ⓦ www.meonvalleyplants.co.uk
Contact: Camilla Moreton
Opening Times: 1000-1700 2nd Fri & Sat, Mar-Oct and by appt.
Min Mail Order UK: £20.00
Cat. Cost: 4 x 1st class.
Credit Cards: None.
Specialities: Unusual bulbs & perennials. Nursery is located on private land in Froxfield, near Petersfield. Please phone or email for details. Many plants produced in small quantities.
Map Ref: S, C2 **OS Grid Ref:** SU713259

SMer MERRYFIELD NURSERIES (CANTERBURY) LTD ⊠ ♿
Stodmarsh Road, Canterbury, Kent, CT3 4AP
Ⓣ (01227) 462602
Ⓔ merry-field@tinyonline.co.uk
Contact: Mrs A Downs
Opening Times: 1000-1600 Mon, 0900-1730 Tue-Sat, 1000-1700 Sun B/hol Mons.
Min Mail Order UK: £10.00 + p&p
Cat. Cost: None issued
Credit Cards: Access Visa Switch

S

Specialities: Wide range of shrubs, conifers, herbaceous, many unusual.
Map Ref: S, C5

SMHT **MOUNT HARRY TREES** € ♿ ◆
Offham, Lewes, East Sussex, BN7 3QW
Ⓣ (01273) 474456
Ⓕ (01273) 474266
Contact: A Renton
Opening Times: By appt.
Cat. Cost: 2 x 1st class
Credit Cards: None.
Specialities: Deciduous trees, specialising in heavy-standard to semi-mature sizes, incl. *Sorbus* varieties.
Map Ref: S, D4 **OS Grid Ref:** TQ313913

SMHy **MARCHANTS HARDY PLANTS** ♿
2 Marchants Cottages, Ripe Road, Laughton, East Sussex, BN8 6AJ
Ⓣ (01323) 811737
Ⓕ (01323) 811737
Contact: Graham Gough
Opening Times: 0930-1730 Wed-Sat, 10th Mar-23rd Oct 2004.
Cat. Cost: 4 x 1st class
Specialities: Uncommon herbaceous perennials. *Agapanthus, Kniphofia, Sedum*, choice grasses, *Miscanthus, Molinia.*
Map Ref: S, D4 **OS Grid Ref:** TQ506119

SMrm **MERRIMENTS GARDENS**
Hawkhurst Road, Hurst Green, East Sussex, TN19 7RA
Ⓣ (01580) 860666
Ⓕ (01580) 860324
Ⓔ alanasharp@beeb.net
Ⓦ www.merriments.co.uk
Contact: Alana Sharp
Opening Times: 0930-1730 Mon-Sat, 1030-1730 Sun (or dusk in winter).
Cat. Cost: Online only
Credit Cards: Visa Access Amex
Specialities: Unusual shrubs. Tender & hardy perennials.
Map Ref: S, C4

SMur **MURRELLS PLANT & GARDEN CENTRE** ♿
Broomers Hill Lane, Pulborough, West Sussex, RH20 2DU
Ⓣ (01798) 875508
Ⓕ (01798) 872695
Contact: Clive Mellor
Opening Times: 0900-1730 summer, 0900-1700 winter, 1000-1600 Sun.
Cat. Cost: 3 x 1st class
Credit Cards: Switch MasterCard Visa Solo
Specialities: Shrubs, trees & herbaceous plants incl. many rare & unusual varieties.
Map Ref: S, D3

SNew **NEW FOREST PALMS & EXOTICS** ♿
Pauls Lane, Sway, Lymington, Hampshire, SO41 6BR
Ⓣ (01590) 683864
Ⓜ 07870 483972
Ⓔ Paulsnursery@farmersweekly.net
Ⓦ www.newforestpalms.co.uk
Also sells wholesale.
Contact: F R Toyne
Opening Times: 1000-1700 Tue-Sun Mar-Oct. 1000-1500 Tue-Sun Nov-Feb. Closed Mon. Closed Jan.
Cat. Cost: 2 x 1st class
Credit Cards: Visa MasterCard
Specialities: Ornamental grasses & plants for the Mediterranean look, incl. bamboos, tree ferns etc.
Map Ref: S, D2 **OS Grid Ref:** SZ292978

SNut **NUTLIN NURSERY** ♿
Crowborough Road, Nutley, Nr. Uckfield, East Sussex, TN22 3HU
Ⓣ (01825) 712670
Ⓕ (01825) 712670
Contact: Mrs Morven Cox
Opening Times: Phone in evening (before 2100) before visiting.
Cat. Cost: 1 x 1st class
Credit Cards: None.
Specialities: *Hydrangea, Wisteria*, hardy ferns. Largely grown peat free.
Map Ref: S, C4 **OS Grid Ref:** TQ4428

SOkd **OAKDENE NURSERY** ⊠ ✈
Street End Lane, Broad Oak, Heathfield, East Sussex, TN21 8TU
Ⓣ (01435) 864382
Ⓔ sampson500@aol.com
Contact: David Sampson
Opening Times: 0900-1700 Wed-Sat excl. B/hols. Sun by appt.
Min Mail Order UK: £10.00
Min Mail Order EU: £25.00
Cat. Cost: 3 x 1st class
Credit Cards: None.
Specialities: Rare & unusual alpines. Woodland plants. Herbaceous perennials. Bulbs.
Map Ref: S, C4

KEY
⊠ Mail order to UK or EU — Delivers to shows
✈ Exports beyond EU — € Euro accepted
♿ Accessible by wheelchair — ◆ See Display advertisement

S

SOkh **OAKHURST NURSERY** ⌂
Mardens Hill, Crowborough, East Sussex, TN6 1XL
Ⓣ (01892) 653273
Ⓕ (01892) 653273
Ⓔ stephanie@colton2648fsnet.co.uk
Contact: Stephanie Colton
Opening Times: Most days, mid Apr-mid Sep, but please phone for appt.
Cat. Cost: 2 x 1st class
Credit Cards: None.
Specialities: Common & uncommon herbaceous perennials in small quantities to enable as wide a range as possible.
Map Ref: S, C4 **OS Grid Ref:** TQ324501

SPav **PAVILION PLANTS** ⊠ ⌂
18 Pavilion Road, Worthing, West Sussex, BN14 7EF
Ⓣ (01903) 821338
Ⓜ 07881 876037
Ⓔ rewrew18@hotmail.com
Also sells wholesale.
Contact: Andrew Muggeridge
Opening Times: Please phone for details.
Cat. Cost: 4 x 1st class
Credit Cards: None.
Specialities: Perennials and bulbs.
Map Ref: S, D3

SPer **PERRYHILL NURSERIES LTD** ⊠ ⌂ ♿
Hartfield, East Sussex, TN7 4JP
Ⓣ (01892) 770377
Ⓕ (01892) 770929
Ⓔ sales@perryhillnurseries.co.uk
Ⓦ www.perryhillnurseries.co.uk
Contact: P J Chapman
Opening Times: 0900-1700 7 days 1st Mar-31st Oct. 0900-1630 1st Nov-28th Feb.
Min Mail Order UK: Nmc
Cat. Cost: £2.00 or on web
Credit Cards: Visa Access MasterCard Switch
Specialities: Wide range of trees, shrubs, conifers, *Rhododendron* etc. Over 1300 herbaceous varieties, over 500 rose varieties. Will deliver to small number of non-RHS shows. Note: mail order despatch depends on size & weight of plants.
Map Ref: S, C4 **OS Grid Ref:** TQ480375

SPet **PETTET'S NURSERY** ⊠ € ♿
Poison Cross, Eastry, Sandwich, Kent, CT13 0EA
Ⓣ (01304) 613869
Ⓕ (01304) 613869
Ⓔ terry@pettetsnursery.fsnet.co.uk
Ⓦ www.pettetsnursery.co.uk
Also sells wholesale.
Contact: T & EHP Pettet
Opening Times: 0900-1700 daily Mar-Jun. 1000-1600 daily Jul-Oct.
Min Mail Order UK: Nmc
Credit Cards: None.
Specialities: Climbers, shrubs, herbaceous perennials, alpines, pelargoniums, fuchsias.
Map Ref: S, C6

SPin **JOHN AND LYNSEY'S PLANTS**
2 Hillside Cottages, Trampers Lane, North Boarhunt, Fareham, Hampshire, PO17 6DA
Ⓣ (01329) 832786
Contact: Mrs Lynsey Pink
Opening Times: By appt. only.
Cat. Cost: None issued
Credit Cards: None.
Specialities: Mainly *Salvia* with a wide range of other unusual perennials. Ltd. stock, be will be happy to propagate to order. Garden design & consultation service also available.
Map Ref: S, D2 **OS Grid Ref:** SU603109

SPla **PLAXTOL NURSERIES** ⊠ ♿
The Spoute, Plaxtol, Sevenoaks, Kent, TN15 0QR
Ⓣ (01732) 810550
Ⓕ (01732) 810149
Ⓔ info@plaxtol-nurseries.co.uk
Ⓦ www.plaxtol-nurseries.co.uk
Contact: Alan Harvey
Opening Times: 1000-1700 7 days. Closed 2 weeks from Xmas Eve.
Min Mail Order UK: £10.00 + p&p
Min Mail Order EU: £30.00 + p&p
Cat. Cost: 2 x 1st class
Credit Cards: Visa Amex MasterCard
Specialities: Hardy shrubs & herbaceous esp. for flower arrangers. Old-fashioned roses, ferns & climbers.
Map Ref: S, C4 **OS Grid Ref:** TQ611535

SPlb **PLANTBASE** € ♿
Lamberhurst Vineyard, Lamberhurst Down, Lamberhurst, Kent, TN3 8ER
Ⓣ (01892) 891453
Ⓔ graham@plantbase.freeserve.co.uk
Contact: Graham Blunt
Opening Times: 1000-1700 7 days Mar-Oct.
Cat. Cost: 2 x 1st class
Credit Cards: Visa Switch Access MasterCard Delta
Specialities: Wide range of alpines, perennials, shrubs, climbers, waterside plants, herbs, Australasian shrubs & South African plants.
Map Ref: S, C5

SPoc POCOCK'S ROSES ⊠ ♿
Jermyn's Lane, Romsey,
Hampshire,
SO51 0QA
Ⓣ (01794) 367500
Ⓕ (01794) 367503
Ⓔ sales@pococksroses.co.uk
Ⓦ www.pococksroses.co.uk
Also sells wholesale.
Contact: Stewart Pocock
Opening Times: 1000-1600 Tue-Sun Mar-Sep, 1000-1600 Thu-Sun Oct-Feb.
Min Mail Order UK: Nmc
Min Mail Order EU: Nmc
Cat. Cost: 2 x 1st class
Credit Cards: All major credit/debit cards.
Specialities: Roses.

SPoG THE POTTED GARDEN NURSERY
Ashford Road, Bearsted,
Maidstone,
Kent, ME14 4NH
Ⓣ (01622) 737801
Ⓕ (01622) 632459
Ⓔ pottedgarden@btconnect.com
Contact: Robert Brookman
Opening Times: 0900-1730 (dusk in winter) 7 days. Closed Xmas, Boxing Day & New Year's Day.
Credit Cards: Visa MasterCard Switch Electron Delta Solo
Specialities: Nursery partially accessible for wheelchair users.
Map Ref: S, C5

SPol POLLIE'S PERENNIALS AND DAYLILY NURSERY ⊠
Lodore, Mount Pleasant Lane,
Sway, Lymington,
Hampshire,
SO41 8LS
Ⓣ (01590) 682577
Ⓕ (01590) 682577
Ⓔ terry@maasz.fsnet.co.uk
Contact: Pollie Maasz
Opening Times: 0930-1730 w/ends only Apr-Sep, any other time by appt, especially during the daylily season mid-May to mid-Aug.
Min Mail Order UK: £4.50
Cat. Cost: Free
Credit Cards: None.
Specialities: *Hemerocallis*, also less commonly available hardy perennials. Stock available in small quantities only. Nat. Collection of spider & unusual form *Hemerocallis* applied for. Notes: mail order, daylilies only. Nursery partially accessible for wheelchair users.
Map Ref: S, D2

SPop POPS PLANTS ⊠ ✈ ⛫ €
Pops Cottage, Barford Lane,
Downton, Salisbury, Wiltshire,
SP5 3PZ
Ⓣ (01725) 511421
Ⓔ mail@popsplants
Ⓦ www.popsplants.com
Contact: G Dawson or L Roberts
Opening Times: By appt. only.
Min Mail Order UK: Nmc
Min Mail Order EU: Nmc
Cat. Cost: £2.00 for colour brochure.
Credit Cards: None.
Specialities: *Primula auricula*. Some varieties in ltd. numbers. Nat. Collection of Show, Alpine & Double Auriculas.

SPur PURE PLANTS
Blackboys Nursery, Blackboys,
Uckfield, East Sussex,
TN22 5LS
Ⓣ (01825) 890858
Ⓕ (01825) 890878
Contact: Brian Fidler
Opening Times: 0900-1700 Tue-Sat. Closed Sun & Mon except B/hol Sun 1000-1600 & B/hol Mon 0900-1700.
Cat. Cost: 2 x 1st class
Credit Cards: All major credit/debit cards.
Specialities: Trees, shrubs, herbaceous, grasses & ferns. Many unusual varieties offered.
Map Ref: S, C4 **OS Grid Ref:** TQ515206

SReu G REUTHE LTD ⊠
Crown Point Nursery,
Sevenoaks Road, Ightham,
Nr. Sevenoaks, Kent,
TN15 0HB
Ⓣ (01732) 810694
Ⓕ (01732) 862166
Contact: C & P Tomlin
Opening Times: 0900-1630 Mon-Sat (closed Wed). 1000-1630 Sun & B/hols Apr & May only, occasionally in Jun, please check. Closed Jan, Jul & Aug.
Min Mail Order UK: £30.00 + p&p
Min Mail Order EU: £500.00
Cat. Cost: £2.00
Credit Cards: Visa Access
Specialities: Rhododendrons & azaleas, trees, shrubs & climbers. Note: mail order certain plants only to EU.
Map Ref: S, C4

KEY
⊠ Mail order to UK or EU ⛫ Delivers to shows
✈ Exports beyond EU € Euro accepted
♿ Accessible by wheelchair ◆ See Display advertisement

S

SRGP **ROSIE'S GARDEN PLANTS** ⊠ ✈ ⌂ ♿
Rochester Road, Aylesford, Kent, ME20 7EB
Ⓣ (01622) 715777
Ⓕ (01622) 715777
Ⓔ JC Aviolet@aol.com
Ⓦ www.rosiesgardenplants.bis
Contact: J C Aviolet
Opening Times: Please phone for opening hours.
Min Mail Order UK: Nmc
Min Mail Order EU: Nmc
Cat. Cost: 2 x 1st class
Credit Cards: Visa MasterCard Switch
Specialities: Hardy *Geranium, Buddleja* & *Aster.*
Map Ref: S, C4 **OS Grid Ref:** TQ7460

SRiv **RIVER GARDEN NURSERIES** ⊠ € ♿
Troutbeck, Otford, Sevenoaks, Kent, TN14 5PH
Ⓣ (01959) 525588
Ⓕ (01959) 525810
Ⓔ box@river-garden.co.uk
Ⓦ www.river-garden.co.uk
Also sells wholesale.
Contact: Jenny Alban Davies
Opening Times: By appt. only.
Min Mail Order UK: £10.00 + p&p
Min Mail Order EU: £50.00 + p&p
Cat. Cost: 2 x 1st class
Credit Cards: All major credit/debit cards.
Specialities: *Buxus* species, cultivars & hedging. *Buxus* topiary.
Map Ref: S, C4 **OS Grid Ref:** TQ523593

S

SRkn **RAPKYNS NURSERY** ⌂ ♿
Scotsford Farm, Street End Lane, Broad Oak, Heathfield, East Sussex, TN21 8UB
Ⓣ (01825) 830065
Ⓜ 07771 916933
Ⓕ (01825) 830065
Also sells wholesale.
Contact: Fiona Moore, Steven Moore
Opening Times: 1000-1700 Tue , Thu & Fri, Mar-Oct.
Cat. Cost: 2 x 1st class
Credit Cards: None.
Specialities: Unusual shrubs, perennials & climbers. *Azaleas, Campanulas, Ceanothus*, geraniums, lavenders, lobelias, *Clematis*, penstemons & grasses. New collections of *Phormium, Phygelius, Agastache, Anemone, Heuchera, Heucherella* & Salvias.
Map Ref: S, C4 **OS Grid Ref:** TQ604248

SRms **RUMSEY GARDENS** ⊠ ♿ ◆
117 Drift Road, Clanfield, Waterlooville, Hampshire, PO8 0PD
Ⓣ (023) 9259 3367
Ⓔ info@rumsey-gardens.co.uk
Ⓦ www.rumsey-gardens.co.uk
Contact: Mr N R Giles
Opening Times: 0900-1700 Mon-Sat & 1000-1700 Sun & B/hols. Closed Sun Nov-Feb.
Min Mail Order UK: Nmc
Cat. Cost: Online only
Credit Cards: Visa MasterCard Switch
Specialities: Wide general range. Nat. & International Coll. of *Cotoneaster.*
Map Ref: S, D2

SRob **ROBINS NURSERY** ♿
Coldharbour Road, Upper Dicker, Hailsham, East Sussex, BN27 3PY
Ⓜ 07798 527634
Ⓔ stuart@robnurse.free-online.co.uk
Ⓦ www.robnurse.free-online.co.uk
Contact: Stuart Dye
Opening Times: 1100-1700 Sat & Sun, Mar-Oct.
Cat. Cost: Free
Credit Cards: None.
Specialities: Small retail nursery specialising in herbaceous plants, incl. *Euphorbia* & *Echium.* All plants are grown at nursery in peat-free compost.
Map Ref: S, D4 **OS Grid Ref:** TQ561109

SRos **ROSEWOOD DAYLILIES** ⊠
70 Deansway Avenue, Sturry, Nr. Canterbury, Kent, CT2 0NN
Ⓣ (01227) 711071
Ⓕ (01227) 711071
Ⓔ Rosewoodgdns@aol.com
Contact: Chris Searle
Opening Times: By appt. only. Please phone.
Min Mail Order UK: Nmc
Cat. Cost: 2 x 1st class
Credit Cards: None.
Specialities: *Hemerocallis*, mainly newer American varieties. *Agapanthus.*
Map Ref: S, C5

SRot **ROTHERVIEW NURSERY** ⊠ ⌂ € ♿
Ivy House Lane, Three Oaks, Hastings, East Sussex, TN35 4NP
Ⓣ (01424) 756228
Ⓕ (01424) 428944
Ⓔ rotherview@btinternet.com
Ⓦ www.rotherview.com
Also sells wholesale.
Contact: Ray Bates
Opening Times: 1000-1700 Mar-Oct, 1000-1530 Nov-Feb, 7 days.

Min Mail Order UK: £10.00 + p&p
Min Mail Order EU: £20.00 + p&p
Cat. Cost: 4 x 1st class
Credit Cards: All major credit/debit cards.
Specialities: Alpines. Note: nursery is on same site as Coghurst Camellias.
Map Ref: S, D5

SSea SEALE NURSERIES ⊠ ♿ ◆
Seale Lane, Seale, Farnham,
Surrey, GU10 1LD
Ⓣ (01252) 782410
Ⓔ plants@sealesuperroses.com
Ⓦ www.sealesuperroses.com
Contact: David & Catherine May
Opening Times: Tue-Sun & B/hol Mons. Closed 25th Dec-8th Jan 2004.
Min Mail Order UK: £10.00 + p&p
Cat. Cost: 5 x 1st class
Credit Cards: Visa Switch Access Delta
Specialities: Roses & *Pelargonium*. Some varieties in short supply, please phone first.
Map Ref: S, C3 **OS Grid Ref:** SU887477

SSpe SPELDHURST NURSERIES ♿
Langton Road, Speldhurst,
Tunbridge Wells, Kent,
TN3 0NR
Ⓣ (01892) 862682
Ⓕ (01892) 862682
Ⓔ StephenLee@speldhurstnurseries.co.uk
Ⓦ www.speldhurstnurseries.co.uk
Contact: Christine & Stephen Lee
Opening Times: 1000-1700 Wed-Sat excl. Jan. 1000-1700 Sun Mar-Jul & Sep-Oct.
Cat. Cost: 4 x 1st class for list.
Credit Cards: MasterCard Visa Switch Delta
Specialities: Herbaceous.
Map Ref: S, C4

SSpi SPINNERS GARDEN €
School Lane, Boldre, Lymington,
Hampshire, SO41 5QE
Ⓣ (01590) 673347
Ⓕ (01590) 679506
Ⓔ kevin@hughes83.fsnet.co.uk
Ⓦ www.spinnersgarden.com
Contact: Kevin Hughes
Opening Times: 1000-1700 Tue-Sat. Sun & Mon by appt. only.
Cat. Cost: 3 x 1st class
Credit Cards: None.
Specialities: Less common trees & shrubs esp. *Acer, Magnolia*, species & lace-cap *Hydrangea*. Woodland & bog plants. Nat. Coll. of *Trillium*. Wide range of bulbs incl. *Narcissus, Erythronium, Fritillaria* & *Lilium*.
Map Ref: S, D2 **OS Grid Ref:** SZ323981

SSta STARBOROUGH NURSERY ⊠ ♿
Starborough Road, Marsh Green,
Edenbridge, Kent, TN8 5RB
Ⓣ (01732) 865614
Ⓕ (01732) 862166
Contact: C & P Tomlin
Opening Times: 0900-1600 Mon-Sat (closed Wed & Sun). Closed Jan, Jul & Aug.
Min Mail Order UK: £30.00 + p&p
Min Mail Order EU: £500.00
Cat. Cost: £2.00
Credit Cards: Visa Access
Specialities: Rare and unusual shrubs especially *Daphne, Acer*, rhododendrons & azaleas, *Magnolia* & *Hamamelis*. Note: certain plants only to EU.
Map Ref: S, C4

SSth SOUTHEASE PLANTS € ♿
Corner Cottage, Southease,
Nr. Lewes, East Sussex, BN7 3HX
Ⓣ (01273) 513681
Ⓕ (01273) 513681
Contact: Adrian Orchard
Opening Times: 1100-1700 Wed-Sat, 1400-1700 Sun & by appt.
Cat. Cost: 2 x 1st class
Credit Cards: None.
Specialities: A small nursery concentrating on hellebores, with a small range of herbaceous perennials, biennials & annuals in ltd. quantities.
Map Ref: S, D4 **OS Grid Ref:** TQ422052

SSto STONE CROSS GARDEN CENTRE ♿ ◆
Rattle Road, Pevensey, Sussex, BN24 5EB
Ⓣ (01323) 763250
Ⓕ (01323) 763195
Ⓔ gardencentre@stone-cross-nurseries.co.uk
Ⓦ www.stone-cross-nurseries.co.uk
Also sells wholesale.
Contact: Mrs J Birch
Opening Times: 0830-1730 Mon-Sat & 1000-1600 Sun & B/hols.
Cat. Cost: None issued
Credit Cards: Visa Access Switch
Specialities: *Hebe* & *Clematis*, evergreen shrubs. Lime tolerant & coastal shrubs & plants.
Map Ref: S, D4 **OS Grid Ref:** 6104

SSvw SOUTHVIEW NURSERIES ⊠ 🚐 ◆
Chequers Lane, Eversley Cross, Hook,
Hampshire, RG27 0NT

KEY
⊠ Mail order to UK or EU — 🚐 Delivers to shows
✈ Exports beyond EU — € Euro accepted
♿ Accessible by wheelchair — ◆ See Display advertisement

S

Ⓣ (0118) 9732206
Ⓕ (0118) 9736160
Ⓔ Mark@Trenear.freeserve.co.uk
Ⓦ www.southviewnurseries.co.uk
Contact: Mark & Elaine Trenear
Opening Times: Mail order only. Orders for collection by prior arrangement.
Min Mail Order UK: Nmc
Cat. Cost: Free
Credit Cards: None.
Specialities: Unusual hardy plants, specialising in old fashioned pinks & period plants. Nat. Coll. of Old Pinks. Orders by prior arrangement only. Pinks Collection open in June. Please ring for details.
Map Ref: S, C3

STes TEST VALLEY NURSERY ⌂ €
Stockbridge Road, Timsbury, Romsey, Hampshire, SO51 0NG
Ⓣ (01794) 368881
Ⓕ (01794) 368493
Ⓔ jbenn@onetel.net.uk
Ⓦ www.testvalleynursery.co.uk
Contact: Julia Benn
Opening Times: 1000-1700 Tue-Sun Mar-Oct, or by appt.
Cat. Cost: 3 x 2nd class
Credit Cards: MasterCard Visa
Specialities: Small nursery with range of herbaceous perennials, specialising in unusual & new varieties. Ltd. quantities of some varieties. Phone first to avoid disappointment.
Map Ref: S, C2

STil TILE BARN NURSERY ⊠ ☒ €
Standen Street, Iden Green, Benenden, Kent, TN17 4LB
Ⓣ (01580) 240221
Ⓕ (01580) 240221
Ⓔ tilebarn.nursery@virgin.net
Ⓦ www.tilebarn-cyclamen.co.uk
Also sells wholesale.
Contact: Peter Moore
Opening Times: 0900-1700 Wed-Sat.
Min Mail Order UK: £10.00 + p&p
Min Mail Order EU: £25.00 + p&p
Cat. Cost: Sae
Credit Cards: None.
Specialities: *Cyclamen* species.
Map Ref: S, C5 **OS Grid Ref:** TQ805301

STre PETER TRENEAR ⊠ ♿
Chantreyland, Chequers Lane, Eversley Cross, Hampshire, RG27 0NX
Ⓣ (0118) 9732300
Ⓔ peter@babytrees.co.uk
Ⓦ www.babytrees.co.uk
Contact: Peter Trenear
Opening Times: 0900-1630 Mon-Sat.
Min Mail Order UK: £5.00 + p&p
Cat. Cost: 1 x 1st class
Credit Cards: None.
Specialities: Trees, shrubs, conifers & *Pinus*.
Map Ref: S, C3 **OS Grid Ref:** SU795612

SUsu USUAL & UNUSUAL PLANTS ⌂ €
Onslow House, Magham Down, Hailsham, East Sussex, BN27 1PL
Ⓣ (01323) 840967
Ⓕ (01323) 844725
Ⓔ jennie@onslow.clara.net
Contact: Jennie Maillard
Opening Times: 0930-1730 Wed-Sat & B/Hol Mons 17 Mar-16 Oct. Other times strictly by appt. only.
Cat. Cost: Sae + 75p
Credit Cards: None.
Specialities: Small quantities of a wide variety of unusual perennials esp. *Erysimum, Euphorbia*, hardy *Geranium, Salvia* & grasses.
Map Ref: S, D4 **OS Grid Ref:** TQ607113

SVal VALE NURSERY ⊠
Heath Cottage, Hayes Lane, Stockbury Valley, Sittingbourne, Kent, ME9 7QH
Ⓣ (01795) 844004
Ⓕ (01795) 842991
Ⓔ info@valenursery.co.uk
Ⓦ www.valenursery.co.uk
Contact: Anthony Clarke
Opening Times: Not open, mail order only.
Min Mail Order UK: £10.00
Cat. Cost: Free
Specialities: Herbaceous perennials. Ltd. quantities of some stock.

SVil THE VILLAGE NURSERIES ⌂ € ♿ ◆
Sinnocks, West Chiltington, Pulborough, West Sussex, RH20 2JX
Ⓣ (01798) 813040
Ⓕ (01798) 817240
Ⓔ petermanfield@aol.com
Ⓦ www.village-nurseries.co.uk
Contact: Peter Manfield
Opening Times: 0900-1800 or dusk, 7 days.
Cat. Cost: None issued
Credit Cards: Visa Delta MasterCard Switch Solo
Specialities: Wide range of hardy perennials & grasses, incl. many new varieties. Selected shrubs, conifers, climbers & trees. Japanese maples.
Map Ref: S, D3 **OS Grid Ref:** TQ095182

SWal **WALLACE PLANTS** ⛫
Lewes Road Nursery, Lewes Road, Laughton, East Sussex, BN8 6BN
Ⓣ (01323) 811729
Ⓔ sjk@wallaceplants.fsnet.co.uk
Contact: Simon Wallace
Opening Times: 0930-1800 or dusk 7 days incl B/hols.
Cat. Cost: 3 x 1st class
Credit Cards: None.
Specialities: Ornamental grasses, hebes, hardy fuchsias, salvias, penstemons, unusual plants.
Map Ref: S, D4 **OS Grid Ref:** TQ513126

SWCr **WYCH CROSS NURSERIES** ♿
Wych Cross, Forest Row, East Sussex, RH18 5JW
Ⓣ (01342) 822705
Ⓕ (01342) 825329
Ⓔ roses@wychcross.co.uk
Ⓦ www.wychcross.co.uk
Contact: J Paisley
Opening Times: 0900-1730 Mon-Sat.
Cat. Cost: Free
Credit Cards: All major credit/debit cards.
Specialities: Roses.
Map Ref: S, C4 **OS Grid Ref:** TQ42133190

SWvt **WOLVERTON PLANTS LTD** € ♿ ◆
Wolverton Common, Tadley, Hampshire, RG26 5RU
Ⓣ (01635) 298453
Ⓕ (01635) 299075
Ⓔ Julian@wolvertonplants.co.uk
Ⓦ www.wolvertonplants.co.uk
Also sells wholesale.
Contact: Julian Jones
Opening Times: 0900-1800 (or dusk Nov-Feb), 7 days. Closed Xmas/New Year.
Cat. Cost: Online
Credit Cards: All major credit/debit cards.
Map Ref: S, C2 **OS Grid Ref:** SU555589

SYvo **YVONNE'S PLANTS**
66 The Ridgway, Woodingdean, Brighton, Sussex, BN2 6PD
Ⓣ (01273) 300883
Ⓔ yvonne@yvonnesplants.co.uk
Ⓦ www.yvonnesplants.co.uk
Contact: Mrs Yvonne Law
Opening Times: Mar-Oct by appt. only and Open Day 1000-1600 Sat 24 Apr 2004.
Cat. Cost: None issued, plant list online
Credit Cards: None.
Specialities: Conservatory, tender & herbaceous perennials, incl. *Cestrum, Agapanthus, Canna, Fuchsia, Hedychium* & grasses.
Map Ref: S, D4 **OS Grid Ref:** TQ360056

WALES AND THE WEST

WAba **ABACUS NURSERIES** ✉ €
Drummau Road, Skewen, Neath, West Glamorgan, Wales, SA10 6NW
Ⓣ (01792) 817994
Ⓔ plants@abacus-nurseries.co.uk
Ⓦ www.abacus-nurseries.co.uk
Also sells wholesale.
Contact: David Hill
Opening Times: Not open to the public. Collection by arrangement.
Min Mail Order UK: Nmc
Min Mail Order EU: Nmc
Cat. Cost: 1 x 2nd class
Credit Cards: None.
Specialities: *Dahlia*. Note: euros only accepted as cash.
Map Ref: W, D3

WAbb **ABBEY DORE COURT GARDEN** € ♿
Abbey Dore Court, Abbey Dore, Herefordshire, HR2 0AD
Ⓣ (01981) 240419
Ⓕ (01981) 240419
Contact: Mrs C Ward
Opening Times: 1100-1730 27th Mar-3rd Oct. Closed Mon, Wed & Fri. Open B/hol Mons.
Cat. Cost: None issued
Credit Cards: None.
Specialities: Shrubs & hardy perennials, many unusual, which may be seen growing in the garden. *Astrantia, Crocosmia, Helleborus, Paeonia, Pulmonaria* & *Sedum.*
Map Ref: W, C4

WAbe **ABERCONWY NURSERY** ⛫ ♿
Graig, Glan Conwy, Colwyn Bay, Conwy, Wales, LL28 5TL
Ⓣ (01492) 580875
Contact: Dr & Mrs K G Lever
Opening Times: 1000-1700 Tue-Sun mid-Feb-mid-Oct.
Cat. Cost: 2 x 2nd class
Credit Cards: Visa MasterCard
Specialities: Alpines, including specialist varieties, esp. autumn gentians, *Saxifraga* & dwarf ericaceous. Shrubs, incl. large range of *Cistus*, & woodland plants incl. *Helleborus* & smaller ferns.
Map Ref: W, A3 **OS Grid Ref:** SH799744

KEY
✉ Mail order to UK or EU ⛫ Delivers to shows
✈ Exports beyond EU € Euro accepted
♿ Accessible by wheelchair ◆ See Display advertisement

W

WAct **ACTON BEAUCHAMP ROSES** ⊠ ✈
Acton Beauchamp, Worcestershire, WR6 5AE
Ⓣ (01531) 640433
Ⓕ (01531) 640802
Ⓔ enquiries@actonbeaurose.co.uk
Ⓦ www.actonbeaurose.co.uk
Contact: Lindsay Bousfield
Opening Times: 1400-1700 Wed-Sun Mar-Oct, 1000-1700 B/hol Mon. Note: Nov-Feb mail order, visitors by appt.
Min Mail Order UK: Nmc
Min Mail Order EU: Nmc
Cat. Cost: 3 x 1st class
Credit Cards: Visa MasterCard
Specialities: Species roses, old roses, modern shrub, English, climbers, ramblers & ground-cover roses.
Map Ref: W, C4 **OS Grid Ref:** SO683492

WAul **AULDEN FARM** ⊠ ⌂ ♿
Aulden, Leominster, Herefordshire, HR6 0JT
Ⓣ (01568) 720129
Ⓔ pf@auldenfarm.co.uk
Ⓦ www.auldenfarm.co.uk
Contact: Alun & Jill Whitehead
Opening Times: 1000-1700 Tue & Thu Apr-Aug.
Min Mail Order UK: Nmc
Cat. Cost: 2 x 1st class
Credit Cards: None.
Specialities: Hardy herbaceous perennials, with a special interest in *Hemerocallis* & *Iris*. Note: limited mail order for *Hemerocallis & Iris* only.
Map Ref: W, C4

WBad **BADSEY LAVENDER FIELDS** ⊠ ♿
Badsey Fields Lane, Evesham, Worcestershire, WR11 5EX
Ⓣ (01386) 832124
Ⓕ (01386) 832124
Also sells wholesale.
Contact: Phil Hodgetts
Opening Times: 0900-1800 Mon-Sat, closed Sun.
Cat. Cost: 2 x 1st class
Credit Cards: None.
Specialities: Lavenders.
Map Ref: W, C5

WBan **THE GARDEN AT THE BANNUT** ♿
Bringsty, Herefordshire, WR6 5TA
Ⓣ (01885) 482206
Ⓕ (01885) 482206
Ⓔ everettbannut@zetnet.co.uk
Ⓦ www.bannut.co.uk
Contact: Daphne Everett
Opening Times: 1400-1700 Wed, Sat, Sun & B/hols Easter-end Sep & by appt.
Specialities: *Penstemon, Calluna, Erica* & *Daboecia*.
Map Ref: W, C4 **OS Grid Ref:** SO691546

WBar **BARNCROFT NURSERIES** ♿
Olden Lane, Ruyton-xi-Towns, Shrewsbury, Shropshire, SY4 1JD
Ⓣ (01939) 261619
Also sells wholesale.
Contact: Mrs R E Eccleston
Opening Times: 1000-1730 Tue-Sat 1000-1600 Sun. Closed throughout Jan. Open B/hols.
Cat. Cost: None available
Credit Cards: None.
Specialities: Wide range of unusual herbaceous plants, shrubs, water plants, water lily ponds & ferns, as well as cottage garden favourites.
Map Ref: W, B4

WBcn **BEACON'S NURSERIES** ⊠ ✈ ♿
Tewkesbury Road, Eckington, Nr. Pershore, Worcestershire, WR10 3DE
Ⓣ (01386) 750359
Ⓔ Jon@Beaconsnurseries.com
Ⓦ www.beaconsnurseries.com
Also sells wholesale.
Contact: Jonathan Beacon
Opening Times: 0900-1300 & 1400-1700 Mon-Sat & 1400-1700 Sun. (Closed 25th Dec-1st Jan.)
Min Mail Order UK: Nmc
Min Mail Order EU: Nmc
Cat. Cost: 2 x 1st class
Credit Cards: None.
Specialities: Shrubs, camellias, herbaceous, aquatics, conifers, climbing plants & hollies. Note: mail orders processed by Cotswold Garden Mail Order. All major credit cards accepted for mail order.
Map Ref: W, C5

WBGC **BURFORD GARDEN COMPANY** ⊠ € ♿
Burford House Gardens, Tenbury Wells, Worcestershire, WR15 8HQ
Ⓣ (01584) 810777
Ⓕ (01584) 810673
Ⓔ info@burford.co.uk
Ⓦ www.burford.co.uk
Contact: Hilary Simons
Opening Times: 0900-1800 7 days. Gardens close at dusk if earlier.
Min Mail Order UK: Nmc
Min Mail Order EU: Nmc
Cat. Cost: 4 x 1st class stamps
Credit Cards: Visa Access Switch

Specialities: *Clematis* and herbaceous, trees & shrubs. Nat. Coll. of *Clematis.* Formerly Treasures of Tenbury.
Map Ref: W, C4

WBor **Bordervale Plants**
Nantyderi, Sandy Lane, Ystradowen, Cowbridge, Vale of Glamorgan, Wales, CF71 7SX
Ⓣ (01446) 774036
Ⓔ nyd@btopenworld.com
Ⓦ www.bordervale.co.uk
Contact: Claire E Jenkins
Opening Times: 1000-1700 Fri-Sun & B/hols mid Mar-mid Oct. Other times by appt.
Cat. Cost: 2 x 1st class large sae or on website.
Credit Cards: None.
Specialities: Unusual herbaceous perennials trees & shrubs, as well as cottage garden plants, many displayed in the 2 acre garden.
Map Ref: W, D3 **OS Grid Ref:** ST022776

WBou **Bouts Cottage Nurseries**
Bouts Lane, Inkberrow, Worcestershire, WR7 4HP
Ⓣ (01386) 792923
Ⓦ www.boutsviolas.co.uk
Contact: M & S Roberts
Opening Times: Not open to the public.
Min Mail Order UK: Nmc
Min Mail Order EU: Nmc
Cat. Cost: Sae
Credit Cards: None.
Specialities: *Viola.*

WBrE **Bron Eifion Nursery**
Bron Eifion, Criccieth, Gwynedd, Wales, LL52 0SA
Ⓣ (01766) 522890
Ⓔ gardencottage@onetel.com
Contact: Suzanne Evans
Opening Times: 1000-dusk 7 days 1st Mar-31st Oct. 1st Nov-29th Feb by appt. only.
Min Mail Order UK: £30.00 + p&p
Min Mail Order EU: £50.00 + p&p
Cat. Cost: 4 x 2nd class
Credit Cards: None.
Specialities: *Kalmia, Daphne, Embothrium,* plants for coastal regions & wide and interesting range of hardy plants.
Map Ref: W, B2

WBrk **Brockamin Plants**
Brockamin, Old Hills, Callow End, Worcestershire, WR2 4TQ
Ⓣ (01905) 830370
Ⓔ dickstonebrockamin@tinyworld.co.uk
Contact: Margaret Stone
Opening Times: By appt. only.
Cat. Cost: Free.
Credit Cards: None.
Specialities: Hardy perennials, especially hardy geraniums and some asters. Sells at Gardeners' Markets. Stock available in small quantities only.
Map Ref: W, C5 **OS Grid Ref:** SO830488

WBuc **Bucknell Nurseries**
Bucknell, Shropshire, SY7 0EL
Ⓣ (01547) 530606
Ⓕ (01547) 530699
Also sells wholesale.
Contact: A N Coull
Opening Times: 0800-1700 Mon-Fri & 1000-1300 Sat.
Min Mail Order UK: Nmc
Cat. Cost: Free
Credit Cards: None.
Specialities: Bare rooted hedging conifers & forest trees.
Map Ref: W, C4 **OS Grid Ref:** 737355

WBVN **Banwy Valley Nursery**
Foel, Llangadfan, Nr. Welshpool, Powys, Wales, SY21 0PT
Ⓣ (01938) 820281
Ⓕ (01938) 820281
Contact: Syd Luck
Opening Times: 1000-1700 Tue-Sun. Open B/hols.
Cat. Cost: 2 x 1st class
Credit Cards: None.
Specialities: Perennials, shrubs, incl. climbers, ornamental & fruit trees. Ever expanding range of magnolias & rhododendrons. All grown on the nursery.
Map Ref: W, B3 **OS Grid Ref:** SH993107

WBWf **British Wildflowers**
Marked Ash Cottage, Rushbury, Church Stretton, Shropshire, SY6 7EL
Ⓣ (01584) 841539
Also sells wholesale.
Contact: Spencer Stoves
Opening Times: By appt. only.
Min Mail Order UK: Nmc
Cat. Cost: 1 x 1st class stamp
Credit Cards: None.
Specialities: British wildflowers of known British origin only.
Map Ref: W, B4 **OS Grid Ref:** SO516908

KEY

Mail order to UK or EU — Delivers to shows
Exports beyond EU — Euro accepted
Accessible by wheelchair — See Display advertisement

W

WCAu **CLAIRE AUSTIN HARDY PLANTS**
⊠ € ♿ ◆
The Stone House, Cramp Pool, Shifnal, Shropshire, TF11 8PE
Ⓣ (01952) 463700
Ⓕ (01952) 463111
Ⓔ enquiries@claireaustin-hardyplants.co.uk
Ⓦ www.claireaustin-hardyplants.co.uk
Contact: Claire Austin
Opening Times: 1000-1600 7 days, Mar-Oct. By appt. Nov-Feb.
Min Mail Order UK: Nmc
Min Mail Order EU: £50.00 + p&p
Cat. Cost: Free
Credit Cards: MasterCard Visa Switch
Specialities: *Paeonia, Iris, Hemerocallis* & hardy plants.
Map Ref: W, B4

W

WCel **CELYN VALE EUCALYPTUS NURSERIES**
⊠ ✈ €
Carrog, Corwen, Clwyd, Wales, LL21 9LD
Ⓣ (01490) 430671
Ⓕ (01490) 430671
Ⓔ info@eucalyptus.co.uk
Ⓦ www.eucalyptus.co.uk
Also sells wholesale.
Contact: Andrew McConnell & Paul Yoxall
Opening Times: 0900-1600 Mon-Fri Jan-Nov. Please phone first outside these days.
Min Mail Order UK: 3 plants + p&p
Min Mail Order EU: 3 plants + p&p
Cat. Cost: 2 x 1st class
Credit Cards: Switch Delta Solo Electron MasterCard Visa
Specialities: Hardy *Eucalyptus* & *Acacia*.
Map Ref: W, A3 **OS Grid Ref:** SJ116452

WCFE **CHARLES F ELLIS & SON** €
(Office) Barn House, Wormington, Nr. Broadway, Worcestershire, WR12 7NL
Ⓣ (01386) 584077 (nursery)
Ⓕ (01386) 584491
Contact: Charles Ellis
Opening Times: 1000-1600 7 days 1st Apr-30th Sep.
Cat. Cost: None issued.
Credit Cards: None.
Specialities: Wide range of more unusual shrubs, conifers & climbers. Note: Nursery is at Oak Piece Farm Nursery, Stanton, Broadway.
Map Ref: W, C5

WCHb **THE COTTAGE HERBERY** ⌂
Mill House, Boraston, Nr. Tenbury Wells, Worcestershire, WR15 8LZ
Ⓣ (01584) 781575
Ⓕ (01584) 781483
Ⓦ www.thecottageherbery.co.uk
Contact: K & R Hurst
Opening Times: By appt. only. Order collection service available.
Cat. Cost: 5 x 1st class
Credit Cards: None.
Specialities: Over 600 varieties of herbs. Aromatic & scented foliage plants, esp. *Symphytum, Monarda, Ajuga, Lobelia, Rosmarinus, Campanula*, alliums & seeds. Soil Assoc. licence no. 96475.
Map Ref: W, C4

WChG **CHENNELS GATE GARDENS & NURSERY** ♿
Eardisley, Herefordshire, HR3 6LT
Ⓣ (01544) 327288
Contact: Mark Dawson
Opening Times: 1000-1700 7 days Mar-Oct.
Cat. Cost: None issued.
Credit Cards: None.
Specialities: Interesting & unusual cottage garden plants, grasses, hedging & shrubs.
Map Ref: W, C4

WCot **COTSWOLD GARDEN FLOWERS**
⊠ ✈ ⌂ € ◆
Sands Lane, Badsey, Evesham, Worcestershire, WR11 5EZ
Ⓣ nursery: (01386) 833849, mail order: (01386) 49671
Ⓜ 07966 589473.
Ⓕ nursery: (01386) 49844, mail order: (01386) 49671
Ⓔ info@cgf.net
Ⓦ www.cgf.net
Also sells wholesale.
Contact: Bob Brown/Vicky Parkhouse/Andy Houghton (mail order)
Opening Times: 0900-1730 Mon-Fri all year. 1000-1730 Sat & Sun Mar-Sep, Sat & Sun Oct-Feb by appt.
Min Mail Order UK: Nmc
Min Mail Order EU: Nmc
Cat. Cost: £1.50 or 6 x 1st class.
Credit Cards: MasterCard Access Visa Switch
Specialities: A very wide range of easy & unusual perennials. Nat. Coll. of *Lysimachia*.
Map Ref: W, C5 **OS Grid Ref:** SP077426

WCra **CRANESBILL NURSERY** ⊠ € ♿
White Cottage, Stock Green, Nr. Redditch, Worcestershire, B96 6SZ
Ⓣ (01386) 792414
Ⓕ (01386) 792280
Ⓔ smandjbates@aol.com

Contact: Mrs S M Bates
Opening Times: 1000-1700 19th Mar-30th Sep. Closed Wed & Thu. Aug by appt. only. Please contact for w/end opening.
Min Mail Order UK: Nmc
Min Mail Order EU: Nmc
Cat. Cost: 4 x 1st class
Credit Cards: All major credit/debit cards.
Specialities: Hardy geraniums & other herbaceous plants.
Map Ref: W, C5

WCru CRÛG FARM PLANTS ♿
Griffith's Crossing, Nr. Caernarfon, Gwynedd, Wales, LL55 1TU
Ⓣ (01248) 670232
Ⓔ bleddyn&sue@crug-farm.co.uk
Ⓦ www.crug-farm.co.uk
Also sells wholesale.
Contact: B and S Wynn-Jones
Opening Times: 1000-1800 Thu-Sun last Sat Feb-last Sun Sep, plus B/hols.
Cat. Cost: 3 x 2nd class
Credit Cards: Visa Access Delta MasterCard
Specialities: Shade plants, climbers, hardy *Geranium, Pulmonaria*, rare shrubs, *Tropaeolum*, herbaceous & bulbous incl. self-collected new introductions from the Far East. Nat. Colls. of *Coriaria, Paris* & *Polygonatum.*
Map Ref: W, A2 **OS Grid Ref:** SH509652

WCwm CWMRHAIADR NURSERY ☒
Glaspwll, Machynlleth, Powys, Wales, S♿ 20 8UB
Ⓣ (01654) 702223
Ⓕ (01654) 702223
Ⓔ glynne.jones@btinternet.com
Contact: Glynne Jones
Opening Times: By appt. only. Please phone. Garden open under NGS.
Min Mail Order UK: Nmc
Cat. Cost: Sae for list
Credit Cards: None.
Specialities: *Acer* species. Camellias & rhododendrons. Rarer conifer species & clones. Note: mail order Nov & Mar only.
Map Ref: W, B3

WDav MARTIN DAVIS PLANTS ☒ ✈ ⌂ €
Osric, 115 Calton Road, Gloucester, GL1 5ES
Ⓣ (01452) 539749
Ⓔ martin@osrics.freeserve.co.uk
Contact: Martin Davis
Opening Times: By appt. only.
Min Mail Order UK: Nmc
Min Mail Order EU: Nmc
Cat. Cost: 4 x 1st class
Credit Cards: None.
Specialities: *Allium, Lilium, Canna*, dwarf bearded *Iris* & other bulbous/rhizomatous subjects. Note: mail order for bulbs Oct-Jan, for plants Mar-May, ltd. stock.
Map Ref: W, D5

WDib DIBLEY'S NURSERIES ☒ ⌂ € ♿ ◆
Llanelidan, Ruthin, Denbighshire, LL15 2LG
Ⓣ (01978) 790677
Ⓕ (01978) 790668
Ⓔ sales@dibleys.com
Ⓦ www.dibleys.com
Also sells wholesale.
Contact: R Dibley
Opening Times: 1000-1700 7 days Mar-Oct.
Min Mail Order UK: Nmc
Min Mail Order EU: Nmc
Cat. Cost: Free
Credit Cards: Visa Access Switch Electron Solo
Specialities: *Streptocarpus, Columnea, Solenostemon* & other gesneriads & *Begonia.* Nat. Coll. of *Streptocarpus.*
Map Ref: W, A3

WDin DINGLE NURSERIES € ♿
Welshpool, Powys, Wales, SY21 9JD
Ⓣ (01938) 555145
Ⓕ (01938) 555778
Ⓔ kerry@dinglenurseries.co.uk
Ⓦ www.dinglenurseries.co.uk
Also sells wholesale.
Contact: Kerry Hamer
Opening Times: 0900-1700 Wed-Mon, 1400-1700 Tue.
Cat. Cost: Free plant list
Credit Cards: MasterCard Switch Eurocard Delta Visa
Specialities: Largest range of trees & shrubs in Wales. Wide seasonal selection of garden plants incl. roses, herbaceous perennials, conifers & barerooted forestry, hedging & fruit. All sizes incl. many mature specimens.
Map Ref: W, B4 **OS Grid Ref:** SJ196082

WDyf DYFFRYN NURSERIES ☒ ⌂ € ♿
Home Farm, Dyffryn, Cardiff, Wales, CF5 6JU
Ⓣ (02920) 592085
Ⓕ (02920) 593462
Ⓔ sales@dyffryn-nurseries.co.uk
Ⓦ www.dyffryn-nurseries.co.uk
Also sells wholesale.

KEY
☒ Mail order to UK or EU ⌂ Delivers to shows
✈ Exports beyond EU € Euro accepted
♿ Accessible by wheelchair ◆ See Display advertisement

W

Contact: Victoria Hardaker
Opening Times: 0800-1600 Mon-Fri, 1100-1600 Sat & Sun.
Min Mail Order UK: £25.00
Min Mail Order EU: £25.00
Cat. Cost: Information on request
Credit Cards: MasterCard Access Switch Delta Visa
Specialities: Native & exotic mature, hardy specimen & architectural plants.
Map Ref: W, D3

WDyG DYFFRYN GWYDDNO NURSERY ⊠ ⌂
Dyffryn Farm, Lampeter Velfrey, Narberth, Pembrokeshire, Wales, SA67 8UN
Ⓣ (01834) 861684
Ⓔ sally.polson@virgin.net
Ⓦ www.pembrokeshireplants.co.uk
Also sells wholesale.
Contact: Mrs S L Polson
Opening Times: 1000-1700 Mon-Thu Apr-Oct & many Sun. Phone for details or an appt. for other times.
Min Mail Order UK: Nmc
Cat. Cost: 2 x 2nd class
Credit Cards: None.
Specialities: Eclectic, yet wide-ranging, from tender salvias & grasses to bog. Peat free & principled. Note: mail order via website.
Map Ref: W, D2 **OS Grid Ref:** SR138148

W

WEas EASTGROVE COTTAGE GARDEN NURSERY ♿
Sankyns Green, Nr. Shrawley, Little Witley, Worcestershire, WR6 6LQ
Ⓣ (01299) 896389
Ⓦ www.eastgrove.co.uk
Contact: Malcolm & Carol Skinner
Opening Times: 1400-1700 Thu-Sun 8th Apr-31st Jul & B/hol Mons. Closed Aug. 1400-1700 Thu-Sat 2th Sep-16th Oct plus Sun 26 Sep.
Cat. Cost: On web
Credit Cards: None.
Specialities: Unique cottage garden & arboretum. Many varieties of *Viola, Iris, Dianthus* & *Aquilegia*, plus a wide range of old favourites & many unusual plants. RHS Partnership garden.
Map Ref: W, C5 **OS Grid Ref:** SO795644

WEll ELLWOOD PENSTEMONS ⊠
Ellwood House, Fern Road, Ellwood, Coleford, Gloucestershire, GL16 7LY
Ⓣ (01594) 833839
Contact: Yvonne Shorthouse
Opening Times: Visitors very welcome at most times Mon-Sat May-Oct, please phone first.
Min Mail Order UK: Nmc
Cat. Cost: 3 x 1st class
Credit Cards: None.
Specialities: Penstemons. Will propagate to order. Stock ltd. as propagated on site. Personal visit strongly recommended. Note: mail order very limited.
Map Ref: W, D4 **OS Grid Ref:** SO591082

WEve EVERGREEN CONIFER CENTRE ⊠ ♿ ◆
Tenbury Road, Rock, Nr. Kidderminster, Worcestershire, DY14 9RB
Ⓣ (01299) 266581
Ⓕ (01299) 266755
Ⓔ brian@evergreen-conifers.co.uk
Ⓦ www.evergreen-conifers.co.uk
Contact: Mr B Warrington
Opening Times: 0900-1700 (dusk in winter) Mon-Sat.
Min Mail Order UK: Nmc*
Cat. Cost: 4 x 1st class for list
Credit Cards: Electron Visa MasterCard Switch Solo
Specialities: Conifers mainly but also acers, heathers, trees, evergreen shrubs. *Note: mail order conifers only.
Map Ref: W, C4

WFar FARMYARD NURSERIES ⊠ ✈ ♿ ◆
Llandysul, Dyfed, Wales, SA44 4RL
Ⓣ (01559) 363389:(01267) 220259
Ⓕ (01559) 362200
Ⓔ richard@farmyardnurseries.co.uk
Ⓦ www.farmyardnurseries.co.uk
Also sells wholesale.
Contact: Richard Bramley
Opening Times: 1000-1700 7 days excl. Xmas, Boxing & New Year's Day.
Min Mail Order UK: Nmc
Min Mail Order EU: Nmc
Cat. Cost: 4 x 1st class
Credit Cards: Visa Switch MasterCard
Specialities: Excellent general range esp. *Helleborus, Hosta, Tricyrtis* & *Schizostylis*, plus shrubs, trees, climbers, alpines & esp. herbaceous. Nat. Coll. of *Tricyrtis*.
Map Ref: W, C2

WFFs FABULOUS FUCHSIAS
The Martins, Stanley Hill, Bosbury, Nr. Ledbury, Herefordshire, HR8 1HE
Ⓣ (01531) 640298
Ⓔ afuchsia@excite.com
Contact: Angela Thompson
Opening Times: By appt. only. Sells at local plant fairs.
Cat. Cost: 3 x 1st class
Credit Cards: None.

Specialities: *Fuchsia*: hardy, bush, trailing, species, triphyllas, unusual varieties, many available in small quantities only.

WFib FIBREX NURSERIES LTD ⊠ ✈ ⛺
Honeybourne Road, Pebworth, Stratford-on-Avon, Warwickshire, CV37 8XP
Ⓣ (01789) 720788
Ⓕ (01789) 721162
Ⓔ sales@fibrex.co.uk
Ⓦ www.fibrex.co.uk
Also sells wholesale.
Contact: U Key-Davis & R L Godard-Key
Opening Times: 1030-1700 Mon-Fri, 1200-1700 Sat & Sun Mar-Jul. 1030-1600 Mon-Fri Aug-Feb. Office hours 0930-1700 Mon-Fri all year excl. last 2 wks Dec/1st wk Jan.
Min Mail Order UK: £10.00 + p&p
Min Mail Order EU: £20.00 + p&p
Cat. Cost: 2 x 2nd class
Credit Cards: Switch MasterCard Visa
Specialities: *Hedera*, ferns, *Pelargonium* & *Helleborus*. National Collections of *Pelargonium* & *Hedera*. Note: plant collections subject to time of year, please check by phone. Restricted wheelchair access.
Map Ref: W, C5 **OS Grid Ref:** SP1246

WFoF FLOWERS OF THE FIELD
Field Farm, Weobley, Herefordshire, HR4 8QJ
Ⓣ (01544) 318262
Ⓕ (01544) 318262
Ⓔ flowerofthefield@tesco.net
Also sells wholesale,
Contact: Kathy Davies
Opening Times: 0900-1900 7 days.
Cat. Cost: 2 x 1st class
Credit Cards: None.
Specialities: Traditional & unusual perennials, grasses, shrubs, trees & herbs. Summer & winter hanging baskets & bedding. Nursery partially accessible for wheelchairs.
Map Ref: W, C4

WGei W G GEISSLER
Winsford, Kingston Road, Slimbridge, Gloucestershire, GL2 7BW
Ⓣ (01453) 890340
Ⓕ (01453) 890340
Ⓔ geissler.w@virgin.net
Ⓦ www.t.mann.taylor.clara.net/ptero.html http://freespace.virgin.net/geissler.w/
Contact: W G Geissler
Opening Times: 0900-1700 Mar-Nov.
Cat. Cost: None issued.
Credit Cards: None.
Specialities: Hardy cacti & succulents & related books. Nat. Colls. of *Opuntia* (sect. *Tephrocactus*) & *Pterocactus*.
Map Ref: W, D4

WGer FRON GOCH GARDEN CENTRE ♿
Pant Road, Llanfaglan, Caernarfon, Gwynedd, Wales, LL54 5RL
Ⓣ (01286) 672212
Ⓕ (01286) 678912
Ⓔ info@frongoch-gardencentre.co.uk
Ⓦ www.frongoch-gardencentre.co.uk
Contact: RA & Mrs V Williams
Opening Times: 0900-1800 Mon-Sat, 1030-1630 Sun all year.
Cat. Cost: None issued
Credit Cards: All major credit/debit cards.
Specialities: Wide range of trees, shrubs, conifers & herbaceous perennials, ferns & grasses; emphasis on plants for coastal & damp sites.
Map Ref: W, A2

WGHP GREEN HILL PLANTS ⊠ ♿
Goodrich Court Stables, Goodrich, Ross-on-Wye, Herefordshire, HR9 6HT
Ⓣ 0845 458 1164
Ⓜ 07977 555089
Ⓔ greenhillplants@hotmail.com
Also sells wholesale.
Contact: Darren or Elizabeth Garman
Opening Times: 0930-1500 Wed-Sat, Mar-Oct and other times, please phone for details.
Min Mail Order UK: Nmc
Min Mail Order EU: Nmc
Cat. Cost: 2 x 1st class
Credit Cards: None.
Specialities: Herbs, grasses, herbaceous perennials & willows. Note: *Salix* cuttings only, winter months.
Map Ref: W, C4 **OS Grid Ref:** SO569200

WGor GORDON'S NURSERY ⊠ ♿
1 Cefnpennar Cottages, Cefnpennar, Mountain Ash, Mid-Glamorgan, Wales, CF45 4EE
Ⓣ (01443) 474593
Ⓕ (01443) 475835
Ⓔ gordonsnursery@compuserve.com
Ⓦ http:\\ourworld.compuserve.com/homepages/gordonsnursery
Contact: D A Gordon

KEY
⊠ Mail order to UK or EU ⛺ Delivers to shows
✈ Exports beyond EU € Euro accepted
♿ Accessible by wheelchair ◆ See Display advertisement

W

Opening Times: 1000-1800 7 days 1st Mar-31st Oct. 1100-1600 Sat & Sun 1st Nov-28th Feb.
Min Mail Order UK: Nmc
Cat. Cost: 3 x 1st class
Credit Cards: Visa MasterCard Switch Solo Electron
Specialities: Shrubs, perennials, alpines & dwarf conifers. Note: mail order only available in some cases, please check for conditions in catalogue.
Map Ref: W, D3 **OS Grid Ref:** SO037012

WGwG GWYNFOR GROWERS ⊠ € ♿
Gwynfor, Pontgarreg, Llangranog, Llandysul, Ceredigion, Wales, SA44 6AU
Ⓣ (01239) 654151
Ⓔ info@gwynfor.co.uk
Ⓦ www.gwynfor.co.uk
Also sells wholesale.
Contact: Steve & Angie Hipkin
Opening Times: 1000-1700 every Sun & most Wed-Sat.
Min Mail Order UK: Nmc
Min Mail Order EU: Nmc
Cat. Cost: 4 x 1st class, free by email.
Credit Cards: None.
Specialities: Plants for wildlife, herbs & intriguing perennials for everyone from novice gardeners to specialist plantsmen. We use organic, peat-free compost.
Map Ref: W, C2 **OS Grid Ref:** SN331536

WGWT GRAFTED WALNUT TREES ⊠ € ♿
The Manse, Capel Isaac, Llandeilo, Camarthenshire, Wales, SA19 7TN
Ⓣ (01558) 669043
Ⓔ sales@graftedwalnuts.co.uk
Ⓦ www.graftedwalnuts.co.uk
Also sells wholesale.
Contact: Gary Wignall
Opening Times: 0900-1800 Mon-Fri. Nursery visits by appt. only.
Min Mail Order UK: Nmc
Min Mail Order EU: Nmc
Cat. Cost: 3 x 1st class
Credit Cards: None.
Specialities: Grafted walnut trees incl. nut bearing varieties of English walnut, ornamental forms of English & black walnut, minor species & hybrids. Ltd. supply of ornamental varieties.
Map Ref: W, C3 **OS Grid Ref:** SN580266

WHal HALL FARM NURSERY €
Vicarage Lane, Kinnerley, Nr. Oswestry, Shropshire, SY10 8DH
Ⓣ (01691) 682135
Ⓕ (01691) 682135
Ⓔ hallfarmnursery@ukonline.co.uk
Ⓦ www.hallfarmnursery.co.uk
Contact: Christine & Nick Ffoulkes-Jones
Opening Times: 1000-1700 Tue-Sat 2nd Mar-9th Oct 2004.
Cat. Cost: 4 x 1st class
Credit Cards: None.
Specialities: Unusual herbaceous plants incl. hardy *Geranium, Pulmonaria*, grasses, bog plants & pool marginals, late-flowering perennials, foliage plants. Nursery partially accessible for wheelchairs.
Map Ref: W, B4 **OS Grid Ref:** SJ333209

WHar HARLEY NURSERY ♿
Harley, Shropshire, SY5 6LP
Ⓣ (01952) 510241
Ⓕ (01952) 510570
Ⓔ Harleynurseries@farmersweekly.net
Contact: Duncan Murphy, Moira Murphy, Michael Birt
Opening Times: 0900-1730 Mon-Sat, 1000-1750 Sun & B/hols. Winter hours 1000-1600 Sun & B/hols.
Cat. Cost: 2 x 1st class
Credit Cards: All major credit/debit cards.
Specialities: Wide range of ornamental & fruit trees. Own grown shrubs, climbers, wide range of hedging plants year round. Conservation & wildlife plants & native trees a speciality.
Map Ref: W, B4

WHCG HUNTS COURT GARDEN & NURSERY ♿
North Nibley, Dursley, Gloucestershire, GL11 6DZ
Ⓣ (01453) 547440
Ⓕ (01453) 549944
Ⓔ keith@huntscourt.fsnet.co.uk
Contact: T K & M M Marshall
Opening Times: Nursery & garden 0900-1700 Tue-Sat excl. Aug. Also by appt. See NGS for Sun openings.
Cat. Cost: 5 x 2nd class
Credit Cards: None.
Specialities: Old roses species & climbers. Hardy *Geranium, Penstemon* & unusual shrubs.
Map Ref: W, D4

WHCr HERGEST CROFT GARDENS
Kington, Herefordshire, HR5 3EG
Ⓣ (01544) 230160
Ⓕ (01544) 232031
Ⓔ gardens@hergest.co.uk
Ⓦ www.hergest.co.uk
Contact: Stephen Lloyd

Opening Times: 1230-1730 7 days Apr-Oct, 1200-1800 7 days May-Jun.
Cat. Cost: None issued
Credit Cards: All major credit/debit cards.
Specialities: *Acer, Betula* & unusual woody plants. Limited wheelchair access.
Map Ref: W, C4

WHer THE HERB GARDEN & HISTORICAL PLANT NURSERY ⊠
Pentre Berw, Gaerwen, Anglesey, Gwynedd, Wales, LL60 6LF
Ⓣ (01248) 422208
Ⓜ 07751 583958
Ⓕ (01248) 422208
Ⓦ www.HistoricalPlants.co.uk
Contact: Corinne & David Tremaine-Stevenson
Opening Times: By appt. only.
Min Mail Order UK: £15.00 + p&p
Min Mail Order EU: £50.00 + p&p sterling only.
Cat. Cost: List £2.00 in stamps
Credit Cards: None.
Specialities: Wide range of herbs, rare natives & wild flowers; rare & unusual & historical perennials & old roses.
Map Ref: W, A2

WHil HILLVIEW HARDY PLANTS ⊠ ✈ ⌂ € ♿ ◆
(off B4176), Worfield, Nr. Bridgnorth, Shropshire, WV15 5NT
Ⓣ (01746) 716454
Ⓕ (01746) 716454
Ⓔ hillview@themutual.net
Ⓦ www.hillviewhardyplants.com
Also sells wholesale.
Contact: Ingrid Millington, John Millington
Opening Times: 0900-1700 Mon-Sat Mar-mid Oct. At other times, please phone first.
Min Mail Order UK: £15.00 + p&p
Min Mail Order EU: £15.00 + p&p
Cat. Cost: 5 x 2nd class
Credit Cards: All major credit/debit cards.
Specialities: Choice herbaceous perennials incl. *Aquilegia, Astrantia, Auricula, Primula, Crocosmia, Eucomis, Phlox, Schizostylis, Verbascum, Acanthus.* Nat Collection of *Acanthus.*
Map Ref: W, B4 OS Grid Ref: SO772969

WHlf HAYLOFT PLANTS ⊠
Manor Farm, Pensham, Pershore, Worcestershire, WR10 3HB
Ⓣ (01386) 554440
Ⓕ (01386) 553833
Ⓔ hayloftplants@talk21.com
Ⓦ www.hayloftplants.co.uk
Contact: Yvonne Walker
Opening Times: Not open, mail order only.
Min Mail Order UK: Nmc
Min Mail Order EU: Nmc
Cat. Cost: Free
Credit Cards: All major credit/debit cards.

WHoo HOO HOUSE NURSERY € ◆
Hoo House, Gloucester Road, Tewkesbury, Gloucestershire, GL20 7DA
Ⓣ (01684) 293389
Ⓕ (01684) 293389
Ⓔ nursery@hoohouse.co.uk
Also sells wholesale.
Contact: Robin & Julie Ritchie
Opening Times: 1000-1700 Mon-Sat, 1100-1700 Sun.
Cat. Cost: 3 x 1st class
Credit Cards: None.
Specialities: Wide range of herbaceous & alpines – many unusual, incl. *Campanula, Geranium* & *Penstemon.* Nat. Colls. of *Platycodon* & *Gentiana asclepiadea* cvs.
Map Ref: W, C5 OS Grid Ref: SO893293

WHrl HARRELLS HARDY PLANTS
(Office) 15 Coxlea Close, Evesham, Worcestershire, WR11 4JS
Ⓣ (01386) 443077
Ⓕ (01386) 443852
Ⓔ enicklin@evesham11.fsnet.co.uk
Ⓦ www.harrellshardyplants.co.uk
Contact: Liz Nicklin & Kate Phillips
Opening Times: By appt. only. Please phone before visiting.
Cat. Cost: 3 x 1st class
Credit Cards: None.
Specialities: A developing nursery offering wide range of hardy plants, new & old, many unusual. Note: nursery located off Rudge Rd, Evesham. Please phone for directions or see catalogue.
Map Ref: W, C5 OS Grid Ref: SP033443

WIvo IVOR MACE NURSERIES ⊠
2 Mace Lane, Ynyswen, Treorci, Rhondda, Mid-Glamorgan, Wales, CF42 6DS
Ⓣ (01656) 302680 day, (01443) 775531 evening
Ⓔ ivormace@hotmail.com

KEY
⊠ Mail order to UK or EU | ⌂ Delivers to shows
✈ Exports beyond EU | € Euro accepted
♿ Accessible by wheelchair | ◆ See Display advertisement

W

Ⓦ www.ivormace.netfirms.com
Contact: I Mace
Opening Times: Not open. Plants can be seen growing. By appt.
Min Mail Order UK: £5.00 + p&p
Cat. Cost: Sae
Credit Cards: None.
Specialities: Large exhibition chrysanthemums. Note: delivery by mail order or collection during Feb & Mar only.
Map Ref: W, C3

WIvy **Ivycroft Plants** ⊠ ♿
Upper Ivington, Leominster, Herefordshire, HR6 0JN
Ⓣ (01568) 720344
Ⓔ rogerandsue@ivycroft.freeserve.co.uk
Ⓦ www.ivycroft.freeserve.co.uk
Contact: Roger Norman
Opening Times: 0900-1600 Wed & Thu Mar-Sep. Other times by appt., please phone.
Min Mail Order UK: Nmc
Cat. Cost: 2 x 1st class
Credit Cards: None.
Specialities: *Cyclamen, Galanthus, Salix*, alpines & herbaceous. Note: mail order Feb/Mar *Galanthus* & *Salix* only.
Map Ref: W, C4 **OS Grid Ref:** SO464562

WJas **Paul Jasper Trees** ⊠
The Lighthouse, Bridge Street, Leominster, Herefordshire, HR6 8DX
Ⓕ (01568) 616499 for orders.
Ⓔ enquiries@jaspertrees.co.uk
Ⓦ www.jaspertrees.co.uk
Also sells wholesale.
Contact: Paul Jasper
Opening Times: Mail order only.
Min Mail Order UK: £40.00 + p&p
Cat. Cost: 2 x 1st class
Credit Cards: None.
Specialities: Full range of fruit & ornamental trees. Over 100 modern and traditional apple varieties + 220 others all direct from the grower. Many unusual varieties of *Malus domestica*.

WJek **Jekka's Herb Farm** ⊠ ✈ ⌂ €
Rose Cottage, Shellards Lane, Alveston, Bristol, BS35 3SY
Ⓣ (01454) 418878
Ⓕ (01454) 411988
Ⓔ farm@jekkasherbfarm.com
Ⓦ www.jekkasherbfarm.com
Also sells wholesale.
Contact: Jekka McVicar
Opening Times: 4 times a year. Please check website for dates.
Min Mail Order UK: Nmc
Min Mail Order EU: Nmc*
Cat. Cost: 4 x 1st class
Credit Cards: Visa MasterCard Delta Switch
Specialities: Culinary, medicinal, aromatic, decorative herbs. *Note: individual quotations for EU Sales. Soil Association licensed herb farm.
Map Ref: W, D4

WJun **Jungle Giants** ⊠ ✈ €
Ferney, Onibury, Craven Arms, Shropshire, SY7 9BJ
Ⓣ (01584) 856481
Ⓕ (01584) 856663
Ⓔ bamboo@junglegiants.co.uk
Ⓦ www.junglegiants.co.uk
Also sells wholesale.
Contact: Michael Brisbane
Opening Times: 7 days. By appt. only please.
Min Mail Order UK: £25.00 + p&p
Min Mail Order EU: £100.00 + p&p
Cat. Cost: 2 x 1st class
Credit Cards: Access MasterCard Visa
Specialities: *Bamboo.*
Map Ref: W, C4 **OS Grid Ref:** SO430779

WKif **Kiftsgate Court Gardens** ♿
Kiftsgate Court, Chipping Camden, Gloucestershire, GL55 6LW
Ⓣ (01386) 438777
Ⓕ (01386) 438777
Ⓔ kiftsgte@aol.com
Ⓦ www.kiftsgate.co.uk
Contact: Mrs J Chambers
Opening Times: 1400-1800 Wed, Thu & Sun 1st Apr -30th Sep & B/hol Mons. Also Mon & Sat in Jun & Jul.
Cat. Cost: None issued
Credit Cards: None.
Specialities: Small range of unusual plants.
Map Ref: W, C5

WKin **Kingstone Cottage Plants** ⊠ ♿
Weston-under-Penyard, Ross-on-Wye, Herefordshire, HR9 7PH
Ⓣ (01989) 565267
Contact: Mr M Hughes
Opening Times: By appt. and as under NGS.
Min Mail Order UK: Nmc
Min Mail Order EU: Nmc
Cat. Cost: 2 x 1st class
Credit Cards: None.
Specialities: Nat. Coll. of *Dianthus*.
Map Ref: W, C4

WLav THE LAVENDER GARDEN ⊠ ⌂ €
Ashcroft Nurseries, Nr. Ozleworth, Kingscote, Tetbury, Gloucestershire, GL8 8YF
Ⓣ (01453) 860356 or 549286
Ⓔ Andrew007Bullock@aol.com
Ⓦ TheLavenderG.co.uk
Also sells wholesale.
Contact: Andrew Bullock
Opening Times: 1100-1700 Sat & Sun. Weekdays variable, please phone.
Min Mail Order UK: £30.00 + p&p
Min Mail Order EU: £30.00 + p&p
Cat. Cost: 2 x 1st class
Credit Cards: None.
Specialities: *Lavandula, Buddleja,* plants to attract butterflies. Herbs, wild flowers.
Map Ref: W, D5 **OS Grid Ref:** ST798948

WLeb LEBA ORCHARD – GREEN'S LEAVES ⊠ ⌂
Lea Bailey, Nr. Ross-on-Wye, Herefordshire, HR9 5TY
Ⓣ (01989) 750303
Also sells wholesale.
Contact: Paul Green
Opening Times: By appt. only, w/ends preferred.
Min Mail Order UK: £10.00 + p&p
Cat. Cost: 4 x 2nd class
Credit Cards: None.
Specialities: Ornamental grasses, sedges & phormiums. Increasing range of rare & choice shrubs, also some perennials.
Map Ref: W, C4

WLFP LINNETT FARM PLANTS ⊠ ✈ ♿
Ullingswick, Hereford, Herefordshire, HR1 3JQ
Ⓣ (01432) 820337
Contact: Basil Smith
Opening Times: Not open.
Min Mail Order UK: £15.00 + p&p
Min Mail Order EU: £15.00 + p&p
Cat. Cost: Free
Credit Cards: None.
Specialities: Hardy *Cyclamen* for the garden, named *Helleborus, Dierama* & *Schizostylis*. Also seeds. Note: nursery formerly CTDA.

WLHH LAWTON HALL HERBS
Lawton Hall, Eardisland, Herefordshire, HR6 9AX
Ⓣ (01568) 709215
Ⓔ herbs@lawtonhall.co.uk
Ⓦ www.LawtonHall.co.uk
Contact: Alexandra Fox
Opening Times: 1030-1830 Wed-Mon, closed Tue.
Cat. Cost: 3 x 1st class
Credit Cards: None.
Specialities: Herbs, culinary, aromatic & medicinal.
Map Ref: W, C4 **OS Grid Ref:** SO445595

WLin LINGEN NURSERY AND GARDEN ⊠ ⌂
Lingen, Nr. Bucknell, Shropshire, SY7 0DY
Ⓣ (01544) 267720
Ⓕ (01544) 267720
Ⓔ kim&maggie@lingen.freeserve.co.uk
Ⓦ www.lingennursery.co.uk
Also sells wholesale.
Contact: Kim W Davis
Opening Times: 1000-1700 Thu-Mon Feb-Oct. Closed Tue-Wed all year.
Min Mail Order UK: Nmc
Min Mail Order EU: £20.00 + p&p
Cat. Cost: 3 x 1st class
Credit Cards: Visa MasterCard
Specialities: Alpines, rock plants, herbaceous esp. *Androsace, Aquilegia, Campanula, Iris, Primula, auriculas* & *Penstemon.* Nat. Coll. of *Herbaceous Campanula* & housing *Iris sibirica.* Partially accessible for wheelchair users.
Map Ref: W, C4 **OS Grid Ref:** SO366669

WMnd MYND HARDY PLANTS ⊠
Delbury Hall Estate, Diddlebury, Craven Arms, Shropshire, SY7 9DH
Ⓣ (01547) 530459
Ⓕ (01547) 530459
Ⓔ sales@myndplants.co.uk
Ⓦ www.myndplants.co.uk
Also sells wholesale.
Contact: Steve Adams
Opening Times: 1000-1700 Mon, Wed-Sat, closed Tues, 1100-1700 Sun, Mar-end Sep. Other times phone for appt.
Min Mail Order UK: £10.00 + p&p
Min Mail Order EU: £10.00 + p&p
Cat. Cost: 4 x 2nd class
Credit Cards: Visa MasterCard
Specialities: Herbaceous plants.
Map Ref: W, B4 **OS Grid Ref:** SO510852

WMoo MOORLAND COTTAGE PLANTS ⊠ ♿
Rhyd-y-Groes, Brynberian, Crymych, Pembrokeshire, Wales, SA41 3TT
Ⓣ (01239) 891363
Ⓔ jenny@moorlandcottageplants.co.uk
Ⓦ www.moorlandcottageplants.co.uk

KEY
⊠ Mail order to UK or EU ⌂ Delivers to shows
✈ Exports beyond EU € Euro accepted
♿ Accessible by wheelchair ◆ See Display advertisement

W

Contact: Jennifer Matthews
Opening Times: 1000-1800 daily excl. Wed end Feb-end Sep.
Min Mail Order UK: See cat. for details.
Cat. Cost: 4 x 1st class
Credit Cards: None.
Specialities: Traditional & unusual hardy perennials. Many garden-worthy rarities. Cottage garden plants; ferns & many shade plants; moisture lovers; ornamental grasses & bamboos; colourful ground cover. Display garden open for NGS.
Map Ref: W, C2 **OS Grid Ref:** SN091343

WMou MOUNT PLEASANT TREES €
Rockhampton, Berkeley,
Gloucestershire,
GL13 9DU
Ⓣ (01454) 260348
Also sells wholesale.
Contact: P & G Locke
Opening Times: By appt. only.
Cat. Cost: 3 x 2nd class
Credit Cards: None.
Specialities: Wide range of trees for forestry, hedging, woodlands & gardens esp. *Tilia, Populus & Platanus.*
Map Ref: W, D4

W

WMow COTTAGE GARDEN PLANTS ⊠
Barley Mow House,
Aston Rogers,
Nr. Westbury, Shropshire,
SY5 9HQ
Ⓜ 07779 936006
Contact: Tony Faulkner
Opening Times: 1200-1700 Wed, Thu & Sat Mar-Oct. Other times by appt.
Min Mail Order UK: Nmc
Cat. Cost: None issued.
Credit Cards: None.
Specialities: *Campanula, Sidalcea* & other hardy herbaceous perennial plants.
Map Ref: W, B4 **OS Grid Ref:** SJ3406

WMul MULU NURSERIES ⊠ ✈ ♠ € ♿
Longdon Hill, Wickhamford,
Evesham, Worcestershire,
WR11 7RP
Ⓣ (01386) 833171
Ⓕ (01386) 833136
Ⓔ plants@mulu.co.uk
Ⓦ www.mulu.co.uk
Also sells wholesale.
Contact: Andy Bateman
Opening Times: 1000-1800 or dusk 7 days.
Min Mail Order UK: Nmc
Min Mail Order EU: £25.00 + p&p
Cat. Cost: free
Credit Cards: Visa MasterCard Delta Switch
Specialities: Exotic plants, hardy & tender incl. bananas, gingers, palms, tree ferns, aroids.
Map Ref: W, C5 **OS Grid Ref:** SP060417

WNor NORFIELDS ⊠ ✈ ♠ €
Llangwm Arboretum, Usk,
Monmouthshire,
NP15 1NQ
Ⓣ (01291) 650306
Ⓕ (01291) 650577
Ⓔ andrew@norfields.co.uk
Ⓦ www.Norfields.co.uk
Also sells wholesale.
Contact: Andrew Norfield
Opening Times: Not open.
Min Mail Order UK: £3.00 + p&p
Min Mail Order EU: £3.00 + p&p
Cat. Cost: 2 x 1st class
Credit Cards: None.
Specialities: Wide range of tree seedlings for growing on. *Acer, Betula, Stewartia* & pre-treated seed.

WOFF OLD FASHIONED FLOWERS ⊠ ✈
Cleeway, Eardington, Bridgnorth,
Shropshire, WV16 5JT
Ⓣ (01746) 766909
Ⓔ jand.cm@virgin.net
Contact: John Snocken
Opening Times: By appt. only.
Min Mail Order UK: Nmc
Min Mail Order EU: Nmc
Cat. Cost: 2 x 2nd class
Credit Cards: None.
Specialities: Show pansies, fancy pansies & exhibition violas. Nat. Coll. of Florists' Violas & Pansies. Some bedding violas.
Map Ref: W, B4 **OS Grid Ref:** 723907

WOld OLD COURT NURSERIES ⊠ ✈ € ♿
Colwall, Nr. Malvern, Worcestershire,
WR13 6QE
Ⓣ (01684) 540416
Ⓔ picton@dircon.co.uk
Ⓦ www.autumnasters.co.uk
Contact: Paul & Meriel Picton
Opening Times: 1100-1700 Fri-Sun May-Oct, 7 days 2nd week Sep-2nd week Oct.
Min Mail Order UK: Nmc
Min Mail Order EU: Nmc
Cat. Cost: 1 x 1st class
Credit Cards: None.
Specialities: Nat. Coll. of Michaelmas Daisies. Herbaceous perennials. Note: mail order for *Aster* only.
Map Ref: W, C4 **OS Grid Ref:** SO759430

WOrn **ORNAMENTAL TREE NURSERIES** ⊠ ♿
Broomy Hill Gardens,
Cobnash, Kingsland, Herefordshire,
HR6 9QZ
Ⓣ (01568) 708016
Ⓕ (01568) 709022
Ⓔ enquiries@ornamental-trees.co.uk
Ⓦ www.ornamental-trees.co.uk
Also sells wholesale.
Contact: Russell Mills
Opening Times: 0900-1800 Mon-Sat. 1000-1600 Sun.
Min Mail Order UK: £9.95
Cat. Cost: 3 x 1st class
Credit Cards: Visa Switch MasterCard Access Delta Amex
Specialities: Ornamental trees. Fruit trees.
Map Ref: W, C4

WOut **OUT OF THE COMMON WAY** ⊠ ⌂
(Office) Penhyddgan, Boduan, Pwllheli,
Gwynedd, Wales, LL53 8YH
Ⓣ (01758) 721577 (Office):(01407) 720431 (Nursery)
Ⓔ penhyddgan@tiscali.co.uk
Contact: Joanna Davidson (nursery) Margaret Mason (office & mail order)
Opening Times: By arrangement.
Min Mail Order UK: Nmc
Min Mail Order EU: Nmc
Cat. Cost: A5 sae 34p (2nd class)
Credit Cards: None.
Specialities: *Aster, Lobelia, Nepeta, Geranium, Salvia, Digitalis, Lavandula* & *Stachys*. Notes: some plants propagated in small quantities only. Nursery is at Pandy Treban, Bryngwran, Anglesey.
Map Ref: W, A2 **OS Grid Ref:** SH370778

WOVN **THE OLD VICARAGE NURSERY** ⊠ ⌂
Lucton, Leominster, Herefordshire,
HR6 9PN
Ⓣ (01568) 780538
Ⓕ (01568) 780818
Contact: Mrs R M Flake
Opening Times: By appt.
Min Mail Order UK: Nmc
Cat. Cost: 2 x 1st class
Credit Cards: None.
Specialities: Roses: old roses; climbers & ramblers; species & ground cover. *Euphorbia* & half-hardy *Salvia*.
Map Ref: W, C4

WP&B **P & B FUCHSIAS** ⊠ ⌂ € ♿
Maes y Gwaelod, Penclawdd Road,
Penclawdd, Swansea, West Glamorgan,
Wales, SA4 3RB
Ⓣ (01792) 851669
Ⓔ sales@gower-fuchsias.co.uk
Ⓦ www.gower-fuchsias.co.uk
Contact: Paul Fisher
Opening Times: 0900-1800 7 days 1 Mar-30 Sep.
Min Mail Order UK: £9.00 (6 plants @ £1.50 incl. P&P)
Cat. Cost: 3 x 1st class
Credit Cards: None.
Specialities: Fuchsias. Hybrid & species. Note: cuttings only available Mar-May. Very ltd. quantities of each.
Map Ref: W, D3

WPat **CHRIS PATTISON** ⊠ ⌂ €
Brookend, Pendock,
Gloucestershire, GL19 3PL
Ⓣ (01531) 650480
Ⓕ (01531) 650480
Ⓔ cpplants@redmarley.freeserve.co.uk
Ⓦ www.chrispattison.fsnet.co.uk
Also sells wholesale.
Contact: Chris Pattison
Opening Times: 0900-1700 Mon-Fri. W/ends by appt. only.
Min Mail Order UK: £10.00 +p&p
Cat. Cost: 3 x 1st class
Credit Cards: None.
Specialities: Choice, rare shrubs & alpines. Grafted stock esp. Japanese maples & *Liquidambar*. Wide range of *Viburnum, Phormium*, dwarf willows & dwarf ericaceous shrubs. Note: mail order Nov-Feb only.
Map Ref: W, C5 **OS Grid Ref:** SO781327

WPen **PENPERGWM PLANTS** ♿
Penpergwm Lodge,
Abergavenny, Gwent,
Wales, NP7 9AS
Ⓣ (01873) 840422/840208
Ⓕ (01873) 840470/840208
Ⓔ boyle@penpergwm.co.uk
Ⓦ www.penplants.com
Also sells wholesale.
Contact: Mrs J Kerr/Mrs S Boyle
Opening Times: 25th Mar-26th Sep 2004, 24th Mar-25th Sep 2005, Thu-Sun 1400-1800.
Cat. Cost: 2 x 1st class
Credit Cards: None.
Specialities: Hardy perennials.
Map Ref: W, D4 **OS Grid Ref:** SO335104

KEY
⊠ Mail order to UK or EU ⌂ Delivers to shows
✈ Exports beyond EU € Euro accepted
♿ Accessible by wheelchair ◆ See Display advertisement

WPer **PERHILL NURSERIES** ⊠ €
Worcester Road, Great Witley,
Worcestershire,
WR6 6JT
Ⓣ (01299) 896329
Ⓕ (01299) 896990
Ⓔ PerhillP@aol.com
Ⓦ www.hartlana.co.uk/perhill/
Also sells wholesale.
Contact: Duncan Straw
Opening Times: 0900-1700 Mon-Sat, 1000-1600 Sun, 1st Feb-15th Oct & by appt.
Min Mail Order UK: Nmc
Min Mail Order EU: £10.00
Cat. Cost: 6 x 2nd class
Credit Cards: MasterCard Delta Switch Eurocard Visa Maestro
Specialities: 2500+ varieties of rare, unusual alpines & herbaceous perennials incl. *Penstemon, Campanula, Salvia, Thymus,* herbs, *Veronica.*
Map Ref: W, C4 **OS Grid Ref:** 763656

W

WPGP **PAN-GLOBAL PLANTS** ⊠ ♿
The Walled Garden, Frampton Court,
Frampton-on-Severn,
Gloucestershire, GL2 7EX
Ⓣ (01452) 741641
Ⓜ 07801 275138
Ⓕ (01453) 768858
Ⓔ info@panglobalplants.com
Ⓦ www.panglobalplants.com
Contact: Nick Macer
Opening Times: 1100-1700 Wed-Sun 1st Feb-31st Oct. Also B/hols. Closed 2nd Sun in Sep. Winter months by appt., please phone first.
Min Mail Order UK: £50.00
Cat. Cost: 4 x 1st class
Credit Cards: MasterCard Visa Solo Delta Amex
Specialities: A plantsman's nursery offering a wide selection of rare & desirable trees, shrubs, herbaceous, bamboos, exotics, climbers, ferns etc. Specialities incl. *Magnolia, Hydrangea* & *Bamboo.*
Map Ref: W, D5

WPic **THE PICTON CASTLE TRUST NURSERY** ♿
Picton Castle, Haverfordwest,
Pembrokeshire, Wales, SA62 4AS
Ⓣ (01437) 751326
Ⓕ (01437) 751326
Ⓔ pct@pictoncastle.freeserve.co.uk
Ⓦ www.pictoncastle.co.uk
Contact: D L Pryse Lloyd
Opening Times: 1030-1700 7 days except Mon Apr-Sep. Other times by arrangement.
Cat. Cost: 1 x 1st class
Credit Cards: None.
Specialities: *Rhododendron.* Myrtle and relatives. Woodland & unusual shrubs.
Map Ref: W, D2 **OS Grid Ref:** SN011135

WPnn **THE PERENNIAL NURSERY**
Rhosygilwen, Llanrhian Road,
St Davids, Pembrokeshire, Wales,
SA62 6DB
Ⓣ (01437) 721954
Ⓕ (01437) 721954
Ⓔ pdsymons@tiscali.co.uk
Contact: Mrs Philipa Symons
Opening Times: 1030-1730 Mar-Oct. Nov-Feb by appt.
Credit Cards: None.
Specialities: Herbaceous perennials & alpines. Tender perennials. Coastal plants.
Map Ref: W, C1 **OS Grid Ref:** SM775292

WPnP **PENLAN PERENNIALS** ⊠ ✈ € ♿
Penlan Farm, Penrhiwpal,
Llandysul, Ceredigion, Wales,
SA44 5QH
Ⓣ (01239) 851244
Ⓕ (01239) 851244
Ⓔ rcain@penlanperennials.co.uk
Ⓦ www.penlanperennials.co.uk
Contact: Richard & Jane Cain
Opening Times: 0930-1730 Wed-Sun Mar-Sep & B/hols. Oct-Feb by appt.
Min Mail Order UK: Nmc
Min Mail Order EU: Nmc
Cat. Cost: 4 x 2nd class or free online
Credit Cards: All major credit/debit cards.
Specialities: Aquatic, marginal & bog plants. Shade-loving & woodland perennials, ferns & grasses, all grown peat free. Note: mail order all year, next day delivery.
Map Ref: W, C2 **OS Grid Ref:** SN344457

WPop **POPPINGER NURSERIES** ⊠
Woodsend, Ashperton,
Ledbury,
Herefordshire,
HR8 2RR
Ⓣ (01432) 890295
Ⓕ (01432) 890388
Ⓔ poppinger.nurseries@virgin.net
Ⓦ www.wetlandplants.co.uk & www.poppinger.co.uk
Contact: Carola Girling
Opening Times: Not open. Mail order only.
Min Mail Order UK: No minimum charge
Specialities: Herbaceous plants, wildflowers, herbs, water lilies, marginals, deep water and bog plants.

WPrP **Prime Perennials** ⊠ ♠
Llety Moel, Rhos-y-Garth, Llanilar,
Nr. Aberystwyth, Ceredigion, Wales,
SY23 4SG
Ⓣ (01974) 241505
Ⓜ 07890 708142
Ⓔ liz@prime-perennials.co.uk
Contact: Elizabeth Powney
Opening Times: Open by appt. only.
Min Mail Order UK: Nmc
Min Mail Order EU: Nmc
Cat. Cost: 4 x 1st class
Credit Cards: None.
Specialities: Unusual & interesting perennials, bulbs & grasses. *Tulbaghia, Kniphofia, Tricyrtis* & many others grown in peat free compost. Nursery 650ft above sea level. Note: mail order Apr-Dec.
Map Ref: W, C3

WPtf **Pantyfod Garden Nursery** ⊠
Llandewi Brefi, Tregaron, Ceredigion,
SY25 6PE
Ⓣ (01570) 493564
Ⓕ (01570) 493585
Ⓔ pantyfodgarden@btopenworld.com
Ⓦ www.pantyfodgarden.co.uk
Contact: Susan Rowe
Opening Times: 1100-1600 Sat only, 17th Apr-18th Sep 2004.
Min Mail Order UK: Nmc
Min Mail Order EU: Nmc
Cat. Cost: £2.00 cheque redeemable against first order.
Credit Cards: None.
Specialities: Hardy geraniums, unusual hardy perennials, woodland plants, plants for moist soil, all grown largely peat-free. Some plants are in small quantities. Nursery at 950ft.
Map Ref: W, C3 **OS Grid Ref:** SN654540

WRai **Rails End Nursery**
Back Lane, Ashton under Hill, Evesham,
Worcestershire, WR11 7RG
Ⓣ (01386) 881884
Ⓕ (01386) 881884
Ⓔ salski@quinweb.net
Contact: Sally Skinner
Opening Times: 1000-1700 7 days, mid-Feb-end Oct. Nov-Jan by appt. only.
Cat. Cost: 2 x 1st class sae.
Credit Cards: All major credit/debit cards.
Specialities: Family-run nursery, specialising in hardy herbaceous perennials, with an extending range of the unusual. All stock in small quantities. Partially accessible for wheelchair users.
Map Ref: W, C5 **OS Grid Ref:** SO999375

WRha **Rhandirmwyn Plants**
2 Tremcecynog, Rhandirmwyn, Nr.
Llandovery, Carmarthenshire,
Wales, SA20 0NU
Ⓣ (01550) 760220
Contact: Sara Fox/Thomas Sheppard
Opening Times: Open most days, but please ring first to avoid disappointment.
Cat. Cost: 2 x 1st class for seed list.
Credit Cards: None.
Specialities: 1000+ varieties & species incl. aquilegias, campanulas, chrysanthemums, *Digitalis*, geraniums, geums, *Lychnis, Mentha, Monarda, Origanum*, primulas, *Rosmarinus*, salvias & violas. Stock ltd in quantity but not variety!
Map Ref: W, C3 **OS Grid Ref:** SN796428

WRHF **Red House Farm** ♿
Flying Horse Lane, Bradley Green, Nr.
Redditch, Worcestershire, B96 6QT
Ⓣ (01527) 821269
Ⓕ (01527) 821674
Ⓔ contact@redhousefarmgardenandnursery.co.uk
Ⓦ www.redhousefarmgardenandnursery.co.uk
Contact: Mrs Maureen Weaver
Opening Times: 0900-1700 Mon-Sat all year. 1000-1700 Sun & B/Hols.
Cat. Cost: 2 x 1st class
Credit Cards: None.
Specialities: Cottage garden perennials.
Map Ref: W, C5 **OS Grid Ref:** SO986623

WRic **Rickard's Hardy Ferns Ltd** ⊠ €
Carreg y Fedwen, Sling, Tregarth,
Nr. Bangor, Gwynedd, LL57 4RP
Ⓣ (01248) 602944
Ⓕ (01248) 602944
Contact: Richard Hayward
Opening Times: 1000-1700 Mon-Fri, 1100-1700 Sat & Sun Mar-Oct. 1100-1600 Nov-Mar by appt. only.
Min Mail Order UK: £30.00 + p&p*
Min Mail Order EU: £50.00 + p&p*
Cat. Cost: 5 x 1st class or 6 x 2nd class
Credit Cards: None.
Specialities: Ferns, hardy & half-hardy, tree ferns. *Note: UK customers order with ltd. cheque. EU customers confirm availability before ordering. Rare items in ltd. numbers, year round availability not guaranteed.
Map Ref: W, A3 **OS Grid Ref:** GR592667

KEY
⊠ Mail order to UK or EU ♠ Delivers to shows
✈ Exports beyond EU € Euro accepted
♿ Accessible by wheelchair ◆ See Display advertisement

WRos **Rosemary's Farmhouse Nursery** ♿
Llwyn-y-moel-gau, Llanfihangel,
Llanfyllin, Powys, Wales,
SY22 5JE
Ⓣ (01691) 648196
Ⓕ (01691) 648196
Ⓔ rosemary@farmhouse-nursery.fsnet.co.uk
Contact: Rosemary Pryce
Opening Times: 1000-1700 most days all year, but advisable to phone to confirm.
Cat. Cost: None issued.
Credit Cards: None.
Specialities: Unusual perennials & ornamental grasses. Hardy geraniums.
Map Ref: W, B3 **OS Grid Ref:** SJ083149

WSAf **SAflora Plant Nursery** ⊠ €
Pen-y-Lan, North Road, Lampeter,
Ceredigion, SA48 7JA
Ⓣ (01570) 422924
Ⓕ (01570) 422924
Ⓔ nursery@safloraplants.co.uk
Ⓦ www.safloraplants.co.uk
Contact: Tricia Carter
Opening Times: Not open.
Min Mail Order UK: Nmc
Min Mail Order EU: Nmc
Cat. Cost: Free of charge
Credit Cards: All major credit/debit cards.
Specialities: South African and Australian plants, in particular Proteaceae, also *Clivia miniata* 'Citrina'.

W

WSan **Sandstones Cottage Garden Plants** ⊠ ń € ♿
58 Bolas Heath, Great Bolas, Shropshire,
TF6 6PS
Ⓣ (01952) 541657
Ⓜ 07801 338133
Ⓕ (01952) 541657
Ⓔ brelsforths@supernet.com
Ⓦ www.sandstoneplants.co.uk
Contact: Joanne Brelsforth/Paul Brelsforth
Opening Times: By appt. only.
Min Mail Order UK: £10.00 + p&p
Min Mail Order EU: £25.00 + p&p
Cat. Cost: 4 x 1st class
Credit Cards: All major credit/debit cards.
Specialities: Unusual & interesting hardy perennials. Specialing in plants for shade & moist areas.
Map Ref: W, B4

WSel **The Selsley Herb Nursery** ń ♿
Hayhedge Lane, Bisley, Stroud,
Gloucestershire, GL6 7AN
Ⓣ (01452) 770073
Ⓕ (01452) 770879
Contact: Rob Wimperis
Opening Times: 1000-1700 Tue-Sat, 1400-1700 Sun & B/hols Mar-Oct. Nov-Feb variable, please phone to check. only.
Cat. Cost: 4 x 1st class
Credit Cards: MasterCard Visa
Specialities: Culinary, aromatic & medicinal herbs & selected garden plants.
Map Ref: W, D5 **OS Grid Ref:** SO058906

WSHC **Stone House Cottage Nurseries** ♿
Stone, Nr. Kidderminster,
Worcestershire,
DY10 4BG
Ⓣ (01562) 69902
Ⓕ (01562) 69960
Ⓔ louisa@shcn.co.uk
Ⓦ www.shcn.co.uk
Contact: L N Arbuthnott
Opening Times: 1000-1730 Wed-Sat. By appt. only Oct-Mar.
Cat. Cost: Sae
Credit Cards: None.
Specialities: Small general range esp. wall shrubs, climbers & unusual plants.
Map Ref: W, C5

WShi **Shipton Bulbs** ⊠ ✈ €
Y Felin, Henllan Amgoed,
Whitland, Dyfed, Wales,
SA34 0SL
Ⓣ (01994) 240125
Ⓕ (01994) 241180
Ⓔ bluebell@zoo.co.uk
Ⓦ www.bluebellbulbs.co.uk
Contact: John Shipton & Alison Foot
Opening Times: By appt. only.
Min Mail Order UK: Nmc
Min Mail Order EU: Nmc
Cat. Cost: Sae
Credit Cards: None.
Specialities: Native British bulbs, & bulbs & plants for naturalising.
Map Ref: W, D2 **OS Grid Ref:** SN188207

WSPU **Pershore College of Horticulture** ♿
Specialist Plant Unit & Plant Centre,
Avonbank, Pershore, Worcestershire,
WR10 3JP
Ⓣ (01386) 561385
Ⓕ (01386) 555601
Also sells wholesale.
Contact: Jo Yates (Plant Centre)
Opening Times: (Plant centre) 0900-1700 Mon-Sat, 1030-1630 Sun.
Cat. Cost: £1.00
Credit Cards: Visa Access

Specialities: Nat. Coll. of *Penstemon*. Open for viewing 0800-1630 Mon-Fri.
Map Ref: W, C5

WSSM SOUTH SHROPSHIRE MEADOW ⊠
Brays Tenement, Marton Hill, Welshpool, Powys, Wales, SY21 8JY
Ⓣ (01938) 580030
Ⓕ (01938) 580030
Ⓔ SouthShropshireM@aol.com
Ⓦ www.southshropshiremeadow.co.uk
Contact: Kate Nicholls
Opening Times: Not open to the public.
Min Mail Order UK: Nmc
Cat. Cost: 5 x 1st stamps
Credit Cards: All major credit/debit cards.
Specialities: Quality hardy perennials and cottage garden plants. Stock available in limited quanitites, please contact for details.

WSSs SHROPSHIRE SARRACENIAS ⊠ ✈ ♠ ♿
5 Field Close, Malinslee, Telford, Shropshire, TF4 2EH
Ⓣ (01952) 501598
Ⓔ mike@carnivorousplants.uk.com
Ⓦ www.carnivorousplants.uk.com
Contact: Mike King
Opening Times: By appt. only.
Min Mail Order UK: Nmc
Min Mail Order EU: Nmc
Cat. Cost: 2 x 1st class
Credit Cards: None.
Specialities: *Sarracenia*. Some stock limited. National Collection of *Sarracenia*.
Map Ref: W, B4 **OS Grid Ref:** SJ689085

WSuV SUNNYBANK VINE NURSERY ⊠ ✈
King Street, Ewyas Harold, Herefordshire, HR2 OEE
Ⓣ (01981) 240256
Ⓔ vinenursery@hotmail.com
Ⓦ http://vinenursery.netfirms.com
Also sells wholesale.
Contact: B R Edwards
Opening Times: Not open, mail order only.
Min Mail Order UK: £8.00 incl. p&p
Min Mail Order EU: £10.00 incl. p&p
Cat. Cost: Sae
Credit Cards: None.
Specialities: Vines. National Collection holder status applied for. Note: EU sales by arrangement.
Map Ref: W, C4

WTel TELLING AND COATES ⊠
64A Church Street, Charlton Kings, Cheltenham, Gloucestershire, GL53 8AS
Ⓣ (01242) 514472
Ⓔ tellingandcoates@freenet.co.uk
Ⓦ www.tellingandcoates.freeola.net
Contact: John Coates
Opening Times: By appt. only.
Min Mail Order UK: Nmc
Cat. Cost: 3 x 1st class or 4 x 2nd class
Credit Cards: None.
Specialities: A traditional hardy plant nursery offering a wide range of shrubs, climbers, heathers, alpines & herbaceous plants at reasonable prices.
Map Ref: W, C5 **OS Grid Ref:** SO966205

WThu THUYA ALPINE NURSERY ⊠
Glebelands, Hartpury, Gloucestershire, GL19 3BW
Ⓣ (01452) 700548
Contact: S W Bond
Opening Times: 1000-dusk Sat & Bank hol. 1100-dusk Sun, Weekdays appt. advised.
Min Mail Order UK: £4.00 + p&p
Min Mail Order EU: £4.00 + p&p
Cat. Cost: 4 x 2nd class
Credit Cards: None.
Specialities: Wide and changing range including rarities. Partially accessible for wheelchair users.
Map Ref: W, C5

WTin TINPENNY PLANTS ♿
Tinpenny Farm, Fiddington, Tewkesbury, Gloucestershire, GL20 7BJ
Ⓣ (01684) 292668
Ⓔ Tinpenny@btinternet.com
Contact: Elaine Horton
Opening Times: 1200-1700 Tue-Thu or by appt.
Cat. Cost: 2 x 1st class
Credit Cards: None.
Specialities: Wide range of hardy garden-worthy plants esp. *Helleborus, Iris* & *Sempervivum*. Small nursery will propagate to order rare plants from own stock.
Map Ref: W, C5 **OS Grid Ref:** SO919318

WTMC TIR MAB CYNAN NURSERY ⊠ ♿
Brithdir, Dolgellau, Gwynedd, Wales, LL40 2RW
Ⓣ (01341) 450339
Ⓕ (01341) 450339
Ⓦ www.tirmabcynan.nursery@btopenworld.com

KEY
⊠ Mail order to UK or EU ♠ Delivers to shows
✈ Exports beyond EU € Euro accepted
♿ Accessible by wheelchair ◆ See Display advertisement

W

Also sells wholesale.
Contact: Jim Haunch
Opening Times: 1000-1700, 7 days, Easter-1st Sep. Other times by appt.
Min Mail Order UK: Nmc
Cat. Cost: None issued
Specialities: Hardy *Geranium, Hemerocallis,* hostas, ferns, *Iris*, a wide range of hardy perennials & sought after plants. Provision National Collection holder status for *Geranium phaeum* cvs.
Map Ref: W, B3

WVaB VALDUCCI BRUGMANSIAS ⊠ ń € ♿
61 Green Lane, Bayston Hill,
Shrewsbury, Shropshire, SY3 0NR
Ⓣ (01743) 236246
Ⓕ (01743) 246716
Ⓔ brugmansias:hotmail.com
Contact: Luigi Valducci
Opening Times: 0900-1700 by appt. only.
Min Mail Order UK: Nmc
Credit Cards: All major credit/debit cards.
Specialities: Brugmansias. Note: nursery main site at Meole Brace Garden Club, Vicarage Road, Shrewsbury.

WWeb WEBBS OF WYCHBOLD € ◆
Wychbold, Droitwich, Worcestershire,
WR9 0DG
Ⓣ (01527) 861777
Ⓕ (01527) 861284
Ⓔ olly@webbsofwychbold.co.uk
Ⓦ www.webbsofwychbold.co.uk
Also sells wholesale.
Contact: Olly Spencer
Opening Times: 0900-1800 Mon-Fri winter. 0900-2000 Mon-Fri summer. 0900-1800 Sat & 1030-1630 Sun all year. Closed Xmas Day, Boxing Day & Easter Sun.
Cat. Cost: None issued
Credit Cards: Visa Access Amex
Specialities: Hardy trees & shrubs, climbers, conifers, alpines, heathers, herbaceous, herbs, roses, fruit & aquatics. Nat. Coll. of Shrubby *Potentilla.*
Map Ref: W, C5

WWes WESTONBIRT ARBORETUM ⊠
(Forest Enterprise),
The National Arboretum,
Tetbury, Gloucestershire,
GL8 8QS
Ⓣ (01666) 880544
Ⓕ (01666) 880386
Ⓔ plant.centre@forestry.gsi.gov.uk
Ⓦ www.westonbirtarboretum.com
Contact: Rose Birks, Sarah Landers
Opening Times: 1000-1700 7 days all year.
Min Mail Order UK: Nmc
Cat. Cost: None issued.
Credit Cards: Visa Access Switch Solo Delta
Specialities: Japanese maples & general range of trees & shrubs, many choice & rare. Specimen trees. Most plants available in small numbers only. Note: mail order Dec-Mar only.
Map Ref: W, D5

WWFP WHITEHALL FARMHOUSE PLANTS ⊠
Sevenhampton, Cheltenham,
Gloucestershire,
GL54 5TL
Ⓣ (01242) 820772
Ⓜ 07711 021034
Ⓕ (01242) 821226
Ⓔ wfplants@btopenworld.com
Contact: Victoria Logue
Opening Times: By appt. only.
Min Mail Order UK: Nmc
Cat. Cost: 2 x 1st class
Credit Cards: None.
Specialities: A small nursery producing a range of interesting & easy perennials for the garden. Some plants held in small quantities only.
Map Ref: W, C5 **OS Grid Ref:** SP018229

WWhi WHIMBLE NURSERY ♿
Kinnerton, Presteigne, Powys,
Wales, LD8 2PD
Ⓣ (01547) 560413
Ⓔ whimble@btopenworld.com
Contact: Liz Taylor
Opening Times: 1030-1730 Wed-Sun (closed Mon & Tue except B/hol Mons) Apr-mid Oct.
Cat. Cost: 5 x 1st class*
Credit Cards: None.
Specialities: Mainly herbaceous, some unusual. Small collections of *Achillea, Crocosmia, Geranium, Viola.* *Note: send sae for plant list (no descriptions).
Map Ref: W, C4

WWHy WELSH HOLLY ⊠ ♿
Llyn-y-gors, Tenby Road,
St Clears, Carmarthenshire,
Wales, SA33 4JP
Ⓣ (01994) 231789
Ⓕ (01994) 231789
Ⓔ info@welsh-holly.co.uk
Ⓦ www.welsh-holly.co.uk
Also sells wholesale.
Contact: Philip Lanc
Opening Times: By appt. only.
Min Mail Order UK: Nmc
Cat. Cost: 2 x 1st class

Credit Cards: None.
Specialities: Hollies. Note: limited stock of less common plants.

WWlt **WOLLERTON OLD HALL GARDEN** ♿
Wollerton, Market Drayton, Shropshire, TF9 3NA
Ⓣ (01630) 685760
Ⓕ (01630) 685583
Ⓔ info@wollertonoldhallgarden.com
Ⓦ www.wollertonoldhallgarden.com
Contact: Mr John Jenkins
Opening Times: 1200-1700 Fri, Sun & B/hols Easter-end Aug. Sun only in Sep.
Cat. Cost: None issued
Credit Cards: All major credit/debit cards.
Specialities: Perennials.
Map Ref: W, B4 **OS Grid Ref:** SJ624296

WWol **WOOLMANS PLANTS LTD** ⊠ €
Knowle Hill, Evesham, Worcestershire, WR11 7EN
Ⓣ (01386) 833022
Ⓕ (01386) 832915
Ⓔ sales@woolman.co.uk
Ⓦ www.woolman.co.uk
Also sells wholesale.
Contact: John Woolman
Opening Times: 0900-1700 Mon-Fri.
Min Mail Order UK: Nmc
Min Mail Order EU: Nmc
Cat. Cost: Free
Credit Cards: MasterCard Visa Switch
Specialities: *Chrysanthemum*, hanging basket & patio plants, perennials & *Dianthus*.
Map Ref: W, C5

WWpP **WATERPUMP PLANTS** ⊠
Waterpump Farm, Ryeford, Ross-on-Wye, Herefordshire, HR9 7PU
Ⓣ (01989) 750177
Ⓔ liz@sugden2.freeserve.co.uk
Contact: Mrs E Sugden
Opening Times: 1200-1700 Wed-Sat Apr-Sep or by appt.
Min Mail Order UK: £15.00
Cat. Cost: 4 x 1st class
Credit Cards: None.
Specialities: Hardy geraniums, aquatics, moisture loving and many unusual herbaceous plants. Organically grown. Some stock in limited quantities, but can be grown to order.
Map Ref: W, C4 **OS Grid Ref:** SO642226

WWst **WESTONBIRT PLANTS** ⊠ ✈ €
9 Westonbirt Close, Worcester, WR5 3RX
Ⓣ (01905) 350429 (answerphone)
Ⓕ (01905) 350429
Contact: Garry Dickerson
Opening Times: Not open, strictly mail order only.
Min Mail Order UK: Nmc
Min Mail Order EU: Nmc
Cat. Cost: 3 x 1st class
Credit Cards: None.
Specialities: *Iris, Fritillaria, Erythronium*, particular interest in Juno *Iris* species, + *Crocus, Corydalis, Lilium, Arisaema, Trillium, Arum* & tulip species. Many rare plants in ltd. numbers.

WWye **THE NURTONS GARDEN & NURSERY** ♿ ◆
Tintern, Chepstow, Gwent, Wales, NP16 7NX
Ⓣ (01291) 689253
Ⓕ (01291) 689253
Ⓔ elsa.adrian@thenurtons.fsnet.co.uk
Ⓦ www.thenurtons.co.uk
Contact: Adrian & Elsa Wood
Opening Times: 1030-1700 Wed-Mon, mid Feb-mid Oct. Other times by appt. (closed Tue).
Cat. Cost: 3 x 1st class
Credit Cards: None.
Specialities: Wide range of garden-worthy perennials to suit many garden situations; herbs, *Salvia*, grasses, hostas. Soil Association symbol. Cert UK 5.
Map Ref: W, D4 **OS Grid Ref:** SO536011

ABROAD

XB&T **B & T WORLD SEEDS** ⊠ ✈ €
Paguignan, 34210 Olonzac, France
Ⓣ 00 33 (0) 4689 12963
Ⓕ 00 33 (0) 4689 13039
Ⓔ lesley@b-and-t-world-seeds.com
Ⓦ www.b-and-t-world-seeds.com
Also sells wholesale.
Contact: Lesley Sleigh
Min Mail Order UK: £14.00 inc. carriage
Min Mail Order EU: £14.00 inc. carriage
Cat. Cost: £10 Europe, £14 elsewhere.
Credit Cards: Visa MasterCard
Specialities: Master list contains over 30,000 items. 700 sub-lists available. Exports seed only. Catalogue/botanical reference system available on CD Rom. SeedyRom (TM) catalogue £20 worldwide.

KEY
⊠ Mail order to UK or EU — Delivers to shows
✈ Exports beyond EU — € Euro accepted
♿ Accessible by wheelchair — ◆ See Display advertisement

X

XBlo **TABLE BAY VIEW NURSERY** ⊠ ✈
(Office) 60 Molteno Road, Oranjezicht, Cape Town 8001, South Africa
Ⓣ 00 27 21 683 5108/424 4854
Ⓕ 00 27 21 683 5108
Ⓔ info@tablebayviewnursery.co.za
Contact: Terence Bloch
Opening Times: No personal callers.
Min Mail Order UK: £15.00 + p&p
Min Mail Order EU: £15.00
Cat. Cost: £3.40 (cheque/postal order)
Credit Cards: None.
Specialities: Tropical & sub-tropical ornamental & fruiting plants.

XDoo **IGNACE VAN DOORSLAER** ⊠ € ♿
Kapellendries 52, B 9090, Melle Gontrode, Belgium
Ⓣ 0032 (09) 252 11 23
Ⓕ 0032 (09) 252 44 55
Also sells wholesale.
Contact: Ignace van Doorslaer
Opening Times: 6 days per week, by appt.
Min Mail Order UK: Depends on weight*
Min Mail Order EU: Depends on weight*
Cat. Cost: Free
Credit Cards: None.
Specialities: *Agapanthus*. *Note: invoice sent when transport charges known. £ stirling accepted. Located 12km south of Gent. Will deliver to shows in Belgium, France & Holland.

XFro **FROSCH EXCLUSIVE PERENNIALS** ⊠ ✈ €
Lindener Str. 5, D-83623 Dietramszell-Lochen, Germany
Ⓣ 00 49 172 842 2050
Ⓕ 00 49 8027 9049975
Ⓔ info@cypripedium.de
Ⓦ www.cypripedium.de
Also sells wholesale.
Contact: Michael Weinert
Opening Times: Not open, mail order only. 0700-2200.
Min Mail Order UK: £120.00 + p&p
Min Mail Order EU: £120.00 + p&p
Cat. Cost: None issued.
Credit Cards: None.
Specialities: *Cypripedium* hybrids. Hardy orchids.

XJel **JELITTO PERENNIAL SEED** ⊠ ✈ € ◆
Postfach 1264, D-29685 Schwarmstedt, Germany
Ⓣ 00 49 50 71-98 29-0
Ⓕ 00 49 50 71-98 29-27
Ⓔ info@jelitto.com
Ⓦ www.jelitto.com
Also sells wholesale.
Contact: Ulrich Schamp, Georg Uebelhart
Opening Times: Not open. Mail order & Online shop.
Min Mail Order UK: €40 + p&p
Min Mail Order EU: €40 + p&p
Cat. Cost: €5
Credit Cards: Visa MasterCard JCB
Specialities: Alpines, perennials, herbs, wild flowers, ornamental grass seed, 2700+ varieties. UK Agent: Meadows (Fenton) Ltd, PO Box 78, St Ives, PE27 6ZA (Richard Oliver) tel: (01480)463570 fax: (01480) 466042 email: richard@jelitto.com

XPep **PÉPINIÈRE FILIPPI** ⊠ €
RN 113, 34140 Meze, France
Ⓣ 04 67 43 88 69
Ⓕ 04 67 43 84 59
Ⓔ olivier.filippi@wanadoo.fr
Ⓦ www.jardin-sec.com
Also sells wholesale.
Contact: Olivier Filippi
Opening Times: 0900-1200 & 1330-1730 Mon-Fri, 0900-1200 Sat, Sep-Jun. Closed Sun & B/hols. 0830-1200 Mon-Sat, Jul-Aug.
Min Mail Order UK: €30
Min Mail Order EU: €30
Cat. Cost: €10 or free online
Credit Cards: Visa MasterCard
Specialities: *Cistus* and botanical range of mediterranean plants. CCVS, French National Collection of *Cistus*.

XRut **RUTA PIANTE DEL CAV. GIORGIO RUTA** ⊠ ✈ €
(office) Via Carducci, 188, 97100 Ragusa (RG), Italy
Ⓣ (0039) 0932 230252
Ⓕ (0039) 0932 616324
Ⓔ sruta@mac.com
Also sells wholesale.
Contact: Sergio Ruta
Opening Times: 0800-1300 & 1400-1700
Min Mail Order UK: £50.00
Min Mail Order EU: £50.00
Cat. Cost: £5.00
Credit Cards: All major credit/debit cards.
Specialities: Mediterranean, subtropical and tropical plants. Note: nursery address is Km.1, S.P. Marina di Ragusa, S. Croce, 97010 Marina di Ragusa.

NURSERY INDEX BY NAME

Nurseries that are included in the *RHS Plant Finder* for the first time this year (or have been reintroduced) are marked in **bold type**. Full details of the nurseries will be found in **Nursery Details by Code** on page 788. For a key to the geographical codes, see the start of **Nurseries**.

Nursery	Code
Dickson Nurseries Ltd	IDic
Dingle Nurseries	WDin
Samuel Dobie & Son	CDob
Ignace van Doorslaer	XDoo
Dorset Water Lilies	CDWL
Dove Cottage Nursery	NDov
Downderry Nursery	SDow
Duchy of Cornwall	CDoC
Dulford Nurseries	CDul
Dunge Valley Gardens	MDun
Dyffryn Gwyddno Nursery	WDyG
Dyffryn Nurseries	WDyf
Dysons Nurseries	SDys
Earlstone Nursery	LEar
East Northdown Farm	SEND
Eastgrove Cottage Garden Nursery	WEas
Edrom Nurseries	GEdr
Edulis	LEdu
Eggleston Hall	**NEgg**
Elizabeth House Nursery	MEHN
Charles F Ellis & Son	WCFE
Ellwood Penstemons	WEll
Elm Tree Nursery	**CElm**
Elsworth Herbs	**EEls**
Elworthy Cottage Plants	CElw
Endsleigh Gardens	CEnd
English Cottage Garden Nursery, The	SECG
Equatorial Plant Co.	NEqu
Evelix Daffodils	GEve
Evergreen Conifer Centre	WEve
Exotic Garden Company, The	**EExo**
Exotic-Gardening UK	**LExo**
Fabulous Fuchsias	WFFs
Fairhaven Nursery	CFai
Fairholm Plants	GFai
Family Trees	SFam
Farmyard Nurseries	WFar
Feebers Hardy Plants	CFee
Fentongollon Farm	**CFen**
Fern Nursery, The	EFer
Fernatix	EFtx
Fernwood Nursery	CWil
Fibrex Nurseries Ltd	WFib
Field House Nurseries	MFie
Fillan's Plants	CFil
Fillpots Nursery	**EFpt**
Fir Tree Farm Nursery	CFir
Fir Trees Pelargonium Nursery	NFir
Margery Fish Gardens	CFis
Ian FitzRoy Nurseryman	**SIFN**
Flaxton House Nursery	NFla
Fleurs Plants	GFle
Flora Exotica	EFEx
Floreat Plants	GFlt
Flower Bower, The	CFwr
Flowers of the Field	WFoF
Fly Trap Plants, The	**EFly**
Foliage Scented & Herb Plants	LFol
Ford Nursery	NFor
Fordmouth Croft Ornamental Grass Nursery	**GFor**
Fox Cottage Plants	MFOX
Foxgrove Plants	**LFox**
Frogswell Nursery	IFro
Fron Goch Garden Centre	WGer
Frosch Exclusive Perennials	XFro
Fryer's Nurseries Ltd	**MFry**
Fulbrooke Nursery	EFul
Rodney Fuller Helianthemum Collection, The	CFul
Gaggini's Plant Centre	**MGag**
Gandy's (Roses) Ltd	**MGan**
Garden at the Bannut, The	WBan
Garden Cottage Nursery	GGar
Garden House Nurseries	NGdn
Garden Plants	SGar
Garden Secrets	**SGSe**
W G Geissler	WGei
Gilbey's Plants	NGby
Glendoick Gardens Ltd	GGGa
Glenhirst Cactus Nursery	EGln
Glenville Nurseries	EGlv
Global Orange Groves UK	**CGOG**
Godly's Roses	LGod
Goldbrook Plants	EGol
Golden Cottage Plants	MGol
Elisabeth Goodwin Nurseries	EGoo
Gordon's Nursery	WGor
Gortkelly Castle Nursery	IGor
Goscote Nurseries Ltd	MGos
Grafted Walnut Trees	WGWT
Graham's Hardy Plants	CGra
Grange Farm Plants	EGFP
Grasmere Plants	EGra
Peter Grayson (Sweet Pea Seedsman)	MPet
Great Dixter Nurseries	SDix
Green Garden, The	**MGGn**
Green Garden Herbs & Plants	NGHP
Green Hill Plants	WGHP
Mary Green	NMyG
Greenhead Roses	GGre
C W Groves & Son	CGro
Growing Carpets	LGro
Gwynfor Growers	WGwG
Hadspen Garden & Nursery	CHad
Hall Farm Nursery	WHal
Halls of Heddon	NHal
Halsway Nursery	CHal
Hambrooks Growing Concern	SHGC
Hampshire Carnivorous Plants	SHmp
Hanging Gardens Nurseries Ltd	EHan
Hardstoft Herb Garden	NHHG
Hardy Exotics	CHEx
Hardy Orchids	CHdy
Hardy's Cottage Garden Plants	SHar
Harley Nursery	WHar

M & M Plants	CM&M
M G H Nurseries	IMGH
Ivor Mace Nurseries	WIvo
Elizabeth MacGregor	GMac
MacGregors Plants for Shade	SMac
Macpennys Nurseries	CMac
Macplants	**GMaP**
Madrona Nursery	SMad
Magpies Nursery	EMag
Mallet Court Nursery	CMCN
Manor Nursery	EMan
Marchants Hardy Plants	SMHy
Market Garden, The	**SMar**
Lesley Marshall	EMar
Marwood Hill Gardens	CMHG
Mattock's Roses	MMat
S M McArd (Seeds)	EMcA
Hubert McHale	IHMH
Mead Nursery, The	CMea
Meadow Cottage Plants	CMCo
Meadows Nursery	CMdw
Mendip Bonsai Studio	CMen
Mendle Nursery	NMen
Meon Valley Plants	**SMeo**
Merriments Gardens	SMrm
Merryfield Nurseries (Canterbury) Ltd	SMer
Mickfield Hostas	EMic
Mickfield Watergarden Centre Ltd	EMFW
Mill Cottage Plants	CMil
Mill Hill Plants	MMil
Mill Race Nursery	EMil
Millais Nurseries	LMil
Millrace Nursery	NMRc
Mills' Farm Plants & Gardens	EMFP
Mires Beck Nursery	NMir
Monksilver Nursery	EMon
Monocot Nursery	**CMon**
Moor Monkton Nurseries	NMoo
Moorland Cottage Plants	WMoo
Morehavens	LMor
Morton Hall Gardens	MMHG
Mount Harry Trees	SMHT
Mount Pleasant Trees	WMou
Mozart House Nursery Garden	MMoz
Mulu Nurseries	WMul
Kathleen Muncaster Fuchsias	EKMF
Murrells Plant & Garden Centre	SMur
Mynd Hardy Plants	WMnd
Naked Cross Nurseries	CNCN
National Herb Centre, The	MNHC
Natural Selection	CNat
Nature's Corner	LNCo
New Forest Palms & Exotics	SNew
Newport Mills Nursery	CNMi
Newton Hill Alpines	NNew
Nicky's Rock Garden Nursery	CNic
Norcroft Nurseries	NNor
Norfields	WNor
Norfolk Bamboo Company	**ENBC**
Norwell Nurseries	MNrw
Notcutts Nurseries	ENot
Nursery Further Afield, The	MNFA
Nurtons Garden & Nursery, The	WWye
Nutlin Nursery	SNut
Oak Dene Nurseries	NOaD
Oak Leaf Nurseries	COkL
Oak Tree Nursery	NOak
Oakdene Nursery	SOkd
Oakhurst Nursery	SOkh
Oakland Nurseries	MOak
Oasis	EOas
Old Court Nurseries	WOld
Old Fashioned Flowers	WOFF
Old Hall Plants	EOHP
Old Mill Herbary, The	COld
Old Vicarage Nursery, The	WOVN
Old Withy Garden Nursery, The	COlW
One House Nursery	MOne
Orchard House Nursery	NOrc
Orchardstown Nurseries	IOrc
Ornamental Conifers	EOrn
Ornamental Grass Nursery, The	NOGN
Ornamental Tree Nurseries	WOrn
Otter Nurseries Ltd	COtt
Out of the Common Way	WOut
John Owen Nurseries	NJOw
P & B Fuchsias	WP&B
P M A Plant Specialities	CPMA
P W Plants	EPla
Packhorse Farm Nursery	MPkF
Palm Farm, The	NPal
Palm House, The	CPHo
PJ's Palms and Exotics	LPJP
Pan-Global Plants	WPGP
Pantyfod Garden Nursery	**WPtf**
Parham Bungalow Plants	CPBP
Park Green Nurseries	EPGN
Gerry Parker Plants	NPar
Parks Perennials	CPar
Chris Pattison	WPat
Pavilion Plants	**SPav**
Pembroke Farm Nursery	EPem
Penlan Perennials	WPnP
Pennard Plants	CPen
Pennycross Plants	EPyc
Penpergwm Plants	WPen
Penstemons by Colour	LPen
Penton Mill Rhododendrons	NPen
Pépinière Filippi	XPep
Perennial Nursery, The	WPnn
Perhill Nurseries	WPer
Perry's Plants	NPer
Perryhill Nurseries Ltd	SPer
Pershore College of Horticulture	WSPU
Pettet's Nursery	SPet
Peveril Clematis Nursery	CPev

Nursery	Code
Speldhurst Nurseries	SSpe
Spinners Garden	SSpi
Spring Reach Nursery	**LSRN**
Springhill Plants	MSph
Springlea Nursery	LSpr
Springwood Pleiones	NSpr
Starborough Nursery	SSta
Steventon Road Nurseries	MSte
Stillingfleet Lodge Nurseries	NSti
Stone Cross Garden Centre	SSto
Stone House Cottage Nurseries	WSHC
Stone Lane Gardens	CSto
Sue Strickland Plants	CStr
Stuckey's Alpines	CStu
Style Roses	ESty
Brian & Pearl Sulman	ESul
Sunnybank Vine Nursery	WSuV
Suttons Seeds	CSut
Swallows Nursery	MSwo
Table Bay View Nursery	XBlo
Tavistock Herb Nursery	NTHB
Taylors Clematis Nursery	NTay
Telling and Coates	WTel
Terra Nova Plants	ITer
Test Valley Nursery	STes
Thorncroft Clematis Nursery	ETho
Thornhayes Nursery	CTho
A & A Thorp	MTho
Thuya Alpine Nursery	**WThu**
Tile Barn Nursery	STil
Timpany Nurseries & Gardens	ITim
Tinpenny Plants	WTin
Tir Mab Cynan Nursery	WTMC
Tissington Nursery	MTis
Toobees Exotics	LToo
Tough Alpine Nursery	GTou
Town Farm Nursery	ETow
Trebah Enterprises Ltd	CTbh
Tree Shop, The	GTSp
Trehane Camellia Nursery	CTrh
Peter Trenear	STre
Trevena Cross Nurseries	CTrC
Trewithen Nurseries	CTrw
Triscombe Nurseries	CTri
Edwin Tucker & Sons	**CTuc**
J Tweedie Fruit Trees	GTwe
Two Jays Alpines	LTwo
Unusual Herbs and Edibles	**EUnu**
Urban Jungle	EUJe
Usual & Unusual Plants	SUsu
Uzumara Orchids	GUzu
Valducci Brugmansias	WVaB
Vale Nursery	SVal
Valley Farm Plants	**EVFa**
Vernon Geranium Nursery, The	LVER
Vicarage Garden, The	NVic
Village Nurseries, The	SVil
Wallace Plants	SWal
Walled Garden, The	EWll
Walnut Tree Garden Nursery	EWTr
Wanborough Herb Nursery	**CWan**
Ward Fuchsias	MWar
Ward Alpines	CWrd
Warren Hills Nursery	MWrn
Water Garden, The	CWat
Waterperry Gardens Ltd	MWat
Waterpump Plants	WWpP
Weasdale Nurseries Ltd.	NWea
Webbs of Wychbold	WWeb
Welsh Holly	WWHy
West Acre Gardens	EWes
West Harptree Nursery	CHar
West Somerset Garden Centre	CWSG
Westcountry Nurseries (inc. Westcountry Lupins)	CWCL
Westdale Nurseries	CWDa
Westonbirt Arboretum	WWes
Westonbirt Plants	WWst
Westshores Nurseries	EWsh
A D & N Wheeler	MWhe
Whimble Nursery	WWhi
White Cottage Alpines	NWCA
Jill White	EJWh
White Veil Fuchsias	CWVF
Whitehall Farmhouse Plants	**WWFP**
Whitehill Farm Nursery	MWhi
Whitelea Nursery	MWht
Wibble Farm Nurseries	CWib
Winchester Growers Ltd.	CWGr
Windrush Willow	CWiW
Winfrith Hostas	CWin
Wingwell Nursery	MWgw
Winter Flora Plant Centre	**EWin**
Wisley Plant Centre (RHS)	LRHS
D S Witton	NWit
Wollerton Old Hall Garden	**WWlt**
Wolverton Plants Ltd	SWvt
Ian and Rosemary Wood	CWoo
Woodborough Garden Centre Ltd	CWdb
Woodlands Cottage Nursery	NWoo
Woodside Cottage Herbs	GWCH
Woolmans Plants Ltd	WWol
Wootten's Plants	EWoo
Nigel Wright Rhododendrons	CWri
Sonia Wright Plants	CSWP
Wyatts	MWya
Wych Cross Nurseries	SWCr
Yvonne's Plants	SYvo
Zest Exotics	**EZes**

SPECIALIST NURSERIES

Nurseries have classified themselves under the following headings where they *exclusively* or *predominantly* supply this range of plants. Plant groups are set out in alphabetical order. Refer to **Nursery Details by Code** on page 788 for details of the nurseries whose codes are listed under the plant group which interests you. See page 785 for a fuller explanation.

ACID LOVING PLANTS

CMen, CRow, CTrh, CWCL, CWrd, CWri, ECri, GCrs, GGGa, GWCH, LHyd, LMil, MBar, MGos, MLea, NLAp, NPen, SBrw, SCam, SHmp, SHyH, SLdr, SRot, WAbe, WCru, WPic, WThu

ALPINE/ROCK PLANTS

CAvo, CBrm, CCha, CFul, CGra, CLyd, CM&M, CMea, COkL, CPBP, CPMA, CWil, CWrd, ECho, EEls, EHyt, EPot, ESis, ETow, GCrs, GFle, GKev, GTou, ITim, LBmB, LPVe, MCre, MDHE, MOne, MS&S, NArg, NBro, NDlv, NHar, NJOw, NLAp, NMen, NPol, NRya, NSla, NWCA, NWoo, SIgm, SIng, SPop, SRot, SScr, WAbe, WGor, WHoo, WLin, WOBN, WPat, WThu, XFro

AQUATIC PLANTS

CBen, CDWL, COld, CRow, CWat, EHon, EMFW, LNCo, LPBA, NArg, NOrc, WPnP, WRic, WWpP, XBlo

BAMBOOS

CBct, CBig, CDul, EAmu, ENBC, EPla, ERod, EZes, GBin, LEdu, MBrN, MMoz, MWhi, MWht, MWod, NGdn, NMoo, NOGN, NPal, SAPC, SArc, SBig, WAbb, WJun, WMul, WPGP

BRITISH WILD FLOWERS

CArn, CKin, COld, CRea, CRWN, GBar, GWCH, MGas, MHer, MLod, MSal, NCWG, NHHG, NLan, NMir, NPol, NTHB, SECG, WBWf, WCHb, WHer, WJek, WLav, WShi

BULBOUS PLANTS

CAvo, CBro, CElm, CLAP, CMea, CPou, CQua, CWoo, ECri, EHyt, EPot, ERos, GCrs, GEve, IBal, LBmB, LBow, LPhx, MS&S, NDvn, NOaD, NOGN, SHaC, WDav, WOBN, WShi, WWst, XBlo

CACTI & SUCCULENTS

CPhi, CWil, EGln, EOas, EShb, ESou, LSou, LToo, NCro, NMen, NOaD, SChr, SHvs, CSec

CARNIVOROUS PLANTS

CSWC, EFly, LHew, SHmp, WSSs

CHALK-LOVING PLANTS

CBot, CKel, CSev, CSpe, LGro, LPhx, SJoh, SLon, SMHT, SYvo

CLIMBERS

CPlN, CRHN, CSPN, CTri, CWhi, ECot, EHan, ELan, EOrc, ESCh, ETho, MBar, MCad, NBea, NBrk, NSti, SBra, SLau, SLay, SRkn, WAct, WCru, WFib, WSHC

COASTAL PLANTS

CSLe, CTbh, CTrC, GGar, IBal, SAft, SChr, WPnn

CONIFERS

CKen, CLnd, CMen, CRob, CTho, ECho, EOrn, ERom, GTre, LCon, LLin, MBar, MGos, MPkF, SLim, WEve, WGor, WMou, WThu

CONSERVATORY PLANTS

CBrP, CGOG, CPlN, CRHN, CRoM, CSpe, CTbh, CWDa, EBak, ECot, EEls, EOHP, ERea, EShb, GFai, LDea, LExo, LHyd, LToo, MJnS, MOak, NFir, NPal, SAin, SHaC, SYvo, WDib, WRic, WSAf, XBlo

DROUGHT TOLERANT

CBot, CKno, CSLe, ECha, ECri, EGln, EGoo, EOas, LLWP, LSss, SAft, SChr, SHzl, SIgm, SIoW, SJoh, SUsu, WBad, WKin, WWye, XPep

FERNS

CFwr, CLAP, CRWN, CTrC, ECha, EFer, EFtx, EMon, GBin, LPBA, MMoz, NBid, NHar, NMar, NMoo, NMyG, NOGN, NOrc, NWoo, SApp, SArc, SHmp, SNut, SRot, WAbe, WFib, WHal, WMoo, WRic

FRUIT

CAgr, CCAT, CGOG, CTho, CTri, ECrN, ERea, EUnu, EZes, GBut, GTrc, GTwe, LBuc, LEdu, MCoo, SBdl, SCrf, SFam, SKee, WHar, WJas, WOrn, WSuV, XBlo

GRASSES

CBig, CBrm, CFwr, CKno, CM&M, CMea, COld, CPen, CRWN, CStr, EBrs, ECha, ECot, EHoe, ELan, EPla, EPPr, EPyc, EWsh, GBin, GCal, GDea, GFor, GIBF, LEdu, LLWP, LPhx, LSss, MBrN, MMoz, MNrw, MWhi, MWod, NBea, NBid, NBro, NCWG, NGdn, NOGN, NOrc, NSti, SAft, SApp, SHel, SHzl, SMar, SRkn, SUsu, SWal, SYvo, WAbb, WHal, WLeb, WMoo, WPGP, WPrP, WRus, WWye

HEDGING

CCVT, CDul, CKin, CLnd, CTri, ECot, ECrN, ERom, GTre, IClo, IMGH, LBuc, LEar, MCoo, MHrb, NBee, NCWG, SAft, SBLw, SCam, SHHo, SIoW, SRiv, WAct, WBad, WCel, WDin, WEve, WHar, WLav, WMou, WOrn, WWeb

HERBS

CAgr, CArn, CBod, CCha, CHby, COld, CSev, CWan, ELau, EOHP, EUnu, GBar, GDea, GPoy, GWCH, ILis, LFol, LLWP, MChe, MHer, MHrb, MLod, MSal, MWhi, NCWG, NGHP, NHHG, NLan, NLLv, NTHB, NWoo, SECG, SHDw, SIoW, WBad, WCHb, WJek, WLav, WLHH, WSel, WWye

MARGINAL/BOG PLANTS

CBig, CDWL, CLAP, COld, CRow, CWat, CWrd, GGar, GKev, LNCo, LPBA, NBid, SHzl, WHal, WMoo, WPnP, WShi, WWpP

ORCHIDS

CBur, CHdy, CRea, EFEx, EFly, EPot, GCrs, GUzu, LBut, NEqu, NSpr, XFro

ORGANIC

CBig, CHby, COld, CRow, CSec, CWan, GBar, GBut, GDea, GPoy, ILis, LEdu, LLWP, MSal, NPol, NTHB, WCHb, WGWT, WJek, WShi, WWpP, WWye

ORNAMENTAL TREES

CBdw, CCAT, CDul, CEnd, CLnd, CM&M, CMen, CPMA, CTho, CTri, ECot, ECrN, EGFP, ELan, EPla, ERod, ERom, GIBF, GTre, IMGH, LBuc, MGos, MPkF, NBea, NBee, SAin, SBir, SBLw, SCrf, SHHo, SLau, SLay, SMHT, WCel, WEve, WHar, WJas, WMou, WNor, WOrn, WPGP

PALMS

CBrP, CPHo, CRoM, EAmu, EGln, EZes, NPal, SAin, SAPC, SArc, SBig, WMul

PEAT FREE

CBot, CBrP, CElw, CHby, CHea, CKno, CKob, CMdw, CMea, CPen, CPom, CRHN, CRWN, CSam, CSev, CWan, EBla, ECri, EDsa, EGoo, ERea, GCai, ILis, LEdu, LLWP, MBNS, MEHN, MGas, MLod, MMoz, MPhe, MRod, MSal, NBid, NGby, NLan, NLRH, NOGN, NPol, SAft, SBch, SECG, SFam, SRob, SYvo, WCHb, WDyG, WGWT, WHoo, WJek, WMou, WPnP, WPrP, WRha, WSel, WShi, WWpP, WWye

PERIOD PLANTS

CArn, CKel, CWGr, EMFP, IBal, ILis, NFir, SAll, SFam, SSvw, WAct, WHer, WKin

PROPAGATE TO ORDER

CBig, CBre, CDul, CElw, CHdy, CKel, CMdw, CMen, CRHN, CRow, CRWN, CTho, CWan, CWCL, CWGr, EBla, ECtt, EEls, EGFP, EOHP, EPla, EPyc, ERea, EShb, EZes, GBin, GBut, GFai, GKev, ILis, LHyd, LLWP, MDHE, MLod, MMoz, MOak, MRod, MSph, NCot, NCro, NGHP, NLLv, NPol, NRya, NShi, NTHB, NWoo, SAft, SAga, SBch, SBdl, SCrf, SECG, SHDw, SHel, SHyH, SJoh, SLau, SLdr, SLon, SRiv, SSea, WBad, WCHb, WEll, WFFs, WFib, WHer, WHil, WJek, WLav, WOBN, WP&B, WPrP, WSSs, WTin, WVaB, WWHy, WWpP, WWye, XBlo

ROSES

CPou, EBls, ECnt, EMFP, ESty, GCoc, IDic, LGod, MFry, MMat, SFam, SPoc, SSea, SWCr

SEED

CAgr, CDob, CElm, CHby, CKin, CRea, CSec, CSpe, CSut, CTuc, EMcA, GDea, GIBF, LCha, LExo, LSss, MGol, MJnS, MSal, NChl, NLan, NOGN, NRob, SAft, SHel, SPop, WJek, WLFP, WNor, WSAf, XJel

SPECIMEN SIZED PLANTS

CBig, CBrP, CCVT, CDul, CGOG, CKel, CMen, CPhi, CPMA, CTho, CTrC, CTrh, EAmu, EBla, ECot, ECrN, EGol, EHan, ELan, ELau, ENBC, ERom, ESou, GGGa, GIBF, GTre, IMGH, LBuc, LPBA, LPVe, LRav, MBar, MBrN, MHrb, MLod, MOak, NArg, NCro, NOrc, NPal, NPol, SAft, SAin, SBig, SBLw, SBrw, SCam, SEND, SFam, SHGC, SHHo, SHmp, SHyH, SLdr, SMHT, WBad, WCel, WDin, WEve, WJek, WOrn, WRic, WWeb, WWye

TOPIARY

ECot, ERom, LEar, SHHo, SRiv, WWeb

TROPICAL PLANTS

CDWL, CGOG, CPlN, CRoM, CTrC, CWDa, EAmu, EOas, ERea, EShb, EUJe, EUnu, LExo, LToo, MJnS, MOak, NDvn, SAPC, SBig, SHaC, SHmp, WCru, WDib, WMul, XBlo, XRut

INDEX MAP

The maps on the following pages show the approximate location of the nurseries whose details are listed in this directory.

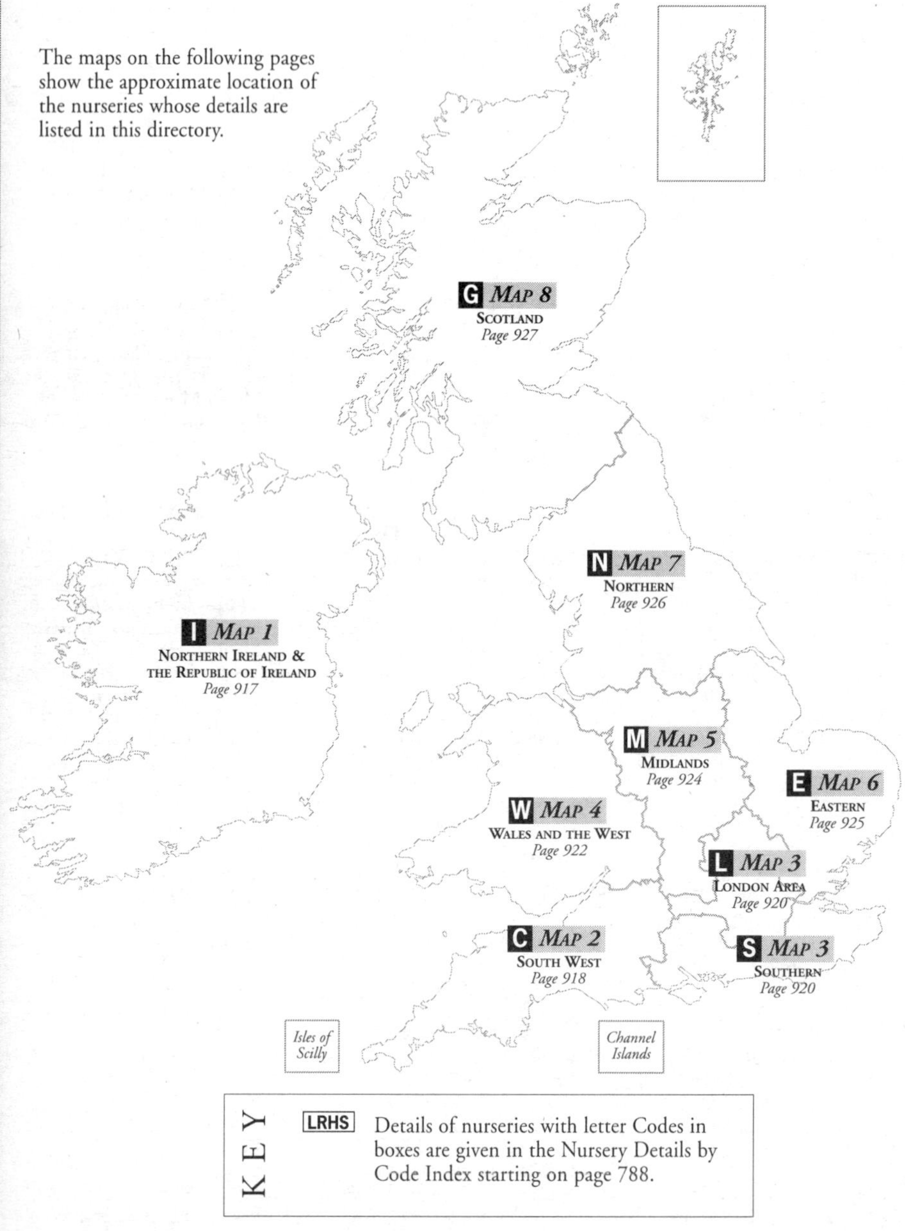

KEY

LRHS Details of nurseries with letter Codes in boxes are given in the Nursery Details by Code Index starting on page 788.

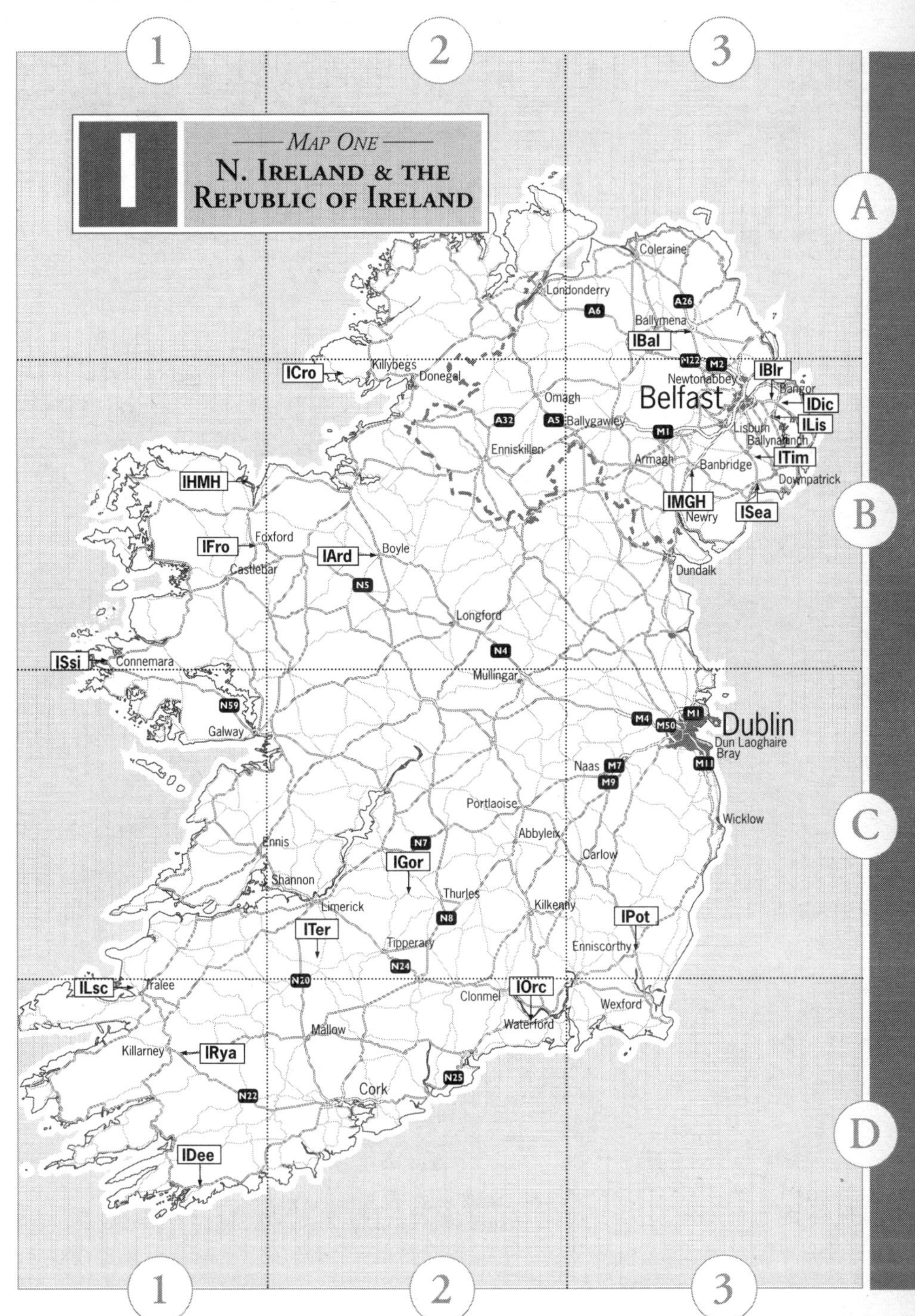
I
Map One
N. Ireland & the Republic of Ireland
1
2
3
A
B
C
D
Coleraine
Londonderry
A26
A6
Ballymena
IBal
Killybegs
ICro
Donegal
M22
M2
IBlr
Newtonabbey
Bangor
Belfast
IDic
Omagh
A32
A5
Ballygawley
M1
Lisburn
ILis
Ballynahinch
Enniskillen
ITim
Armagh
Banbridge
Downpatrick
IHMH
IMGH
ISea
Newry
IFro
Foxford
IArd
Boyle
Castlebar
N5
Dundalk
Longford
N4
ISsi
Connemara
Mullingar
N59
M1
M4
M50
Dublin
Dun Laoghaire
Galway
Bray
Naas
M7
M11
M9
Portlaoise
Wicklow
Ennis
N7
Abbyleix
IGor
Carlow
Shannon
Thurles
Limerick
Kilkenny
N8
IPot
ITer
Tipperary
Enniscorthy
N24
N20
ILsc
Tralee
IOrc
Clonmel
Wexford
Waterford
Mallow
Killarney
IRya
N25
N22
Cork
IDee

C
MAP TWO
SOUTH WEST
1
2
3
A
B
C
D
Llanelli
M4
Neath
Swansea
Port Talbot
Bridgend
CSil
Ilfracombe
Combe Martin
CMHG
Barnstaple
CRoM
Bideford
CAni
CHid
CFai
CM&M
CAlb
CKen
CPne
CBig
CWri
A39
A377
Bude
CWil
CCha
CBdn
CSdC
CSto
Okehampton
CLyd
CPev
Launceston
CRow
CCge
CBre
CPla
CEnd
Newton Abbot
COld
CRez
Tavistock
CPle
Wadebridge
CBct
CTuc
CPin
CHll
CBod
Bodmin
Liskeard
CDev
CFil
CBrm
CDoC
Newquay
Plymouth
CPrp
A38
A30
CMCo
CHVG
CTrw
CPou
St Austell
CPLG
CRHN
CRob
Truro
CBos
Redruth
St Ives
CHex
Camborne
CBcS
CFen
CTrC
CCtw
CFir
Falmouth
Penzance
Helston
CTbh
CWGr
COlW
CQua

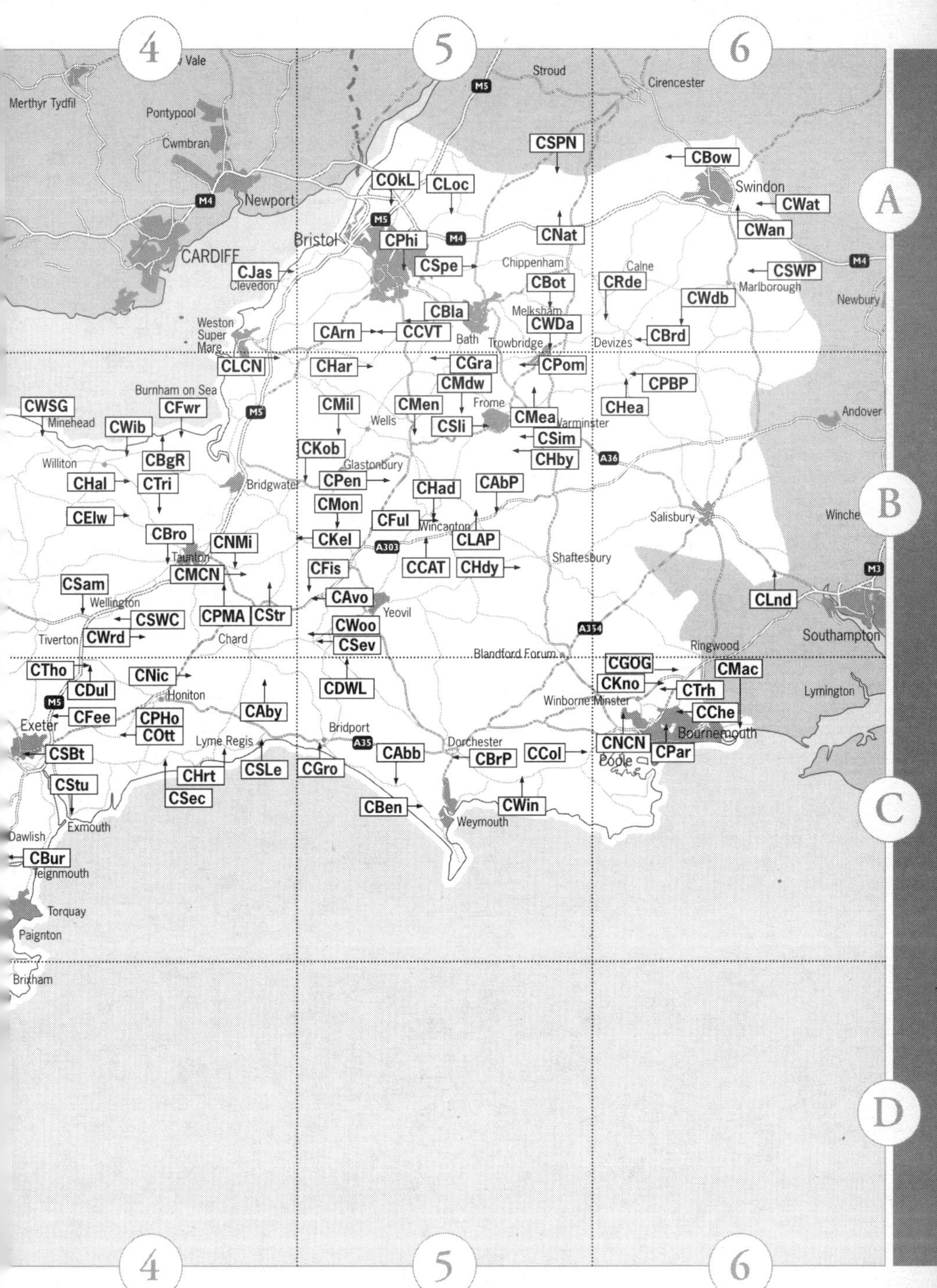
4
5
6
A
B
C
D
Merthyr Tydfil
Pontypool
Cwmbran
Newport
CARDIFF
Bristol
Clevedon
Weston Super Mare
Stroud
Cirencester
Swindon
Chippenham
Calne
Marlborough
Newbury
Melksham
Bath
Trowbridge
Devizes
Frome
Warminster
Andover
Burnham on Sea
Minehead
Williton
Wells
Glastonbury
Bridgwater
Wincanton
Salisbury
Taunton
Shaftesbury
Wellington
Yeovil
Southampton
Tiverton
Chard
Ringwood
Blandford Forum
Honiton
Wimborne Minster
Lymington
Exeter
Bridport
Lyme Regis
Dorchester
Bournemouth
Poole
Weymouth
Exmouth
Dawlish
Teignmouth
Torquay
Paignton
Brixham
M4
M5
M3
A36
A303
A354
A35
CSPN
CBow
COkL
CLoc
CWat
CWan
CNat
CPhi
CJas
CSpe
CSWP
CBot
CRde
CWdb
CBla
CWDa
CArn
CCVT
CBrd
CLCN
CHar
CGra
CPom
CMdw
CPBP
CWSG
CFwr
CMil
CMen
CMea
CHea
CWib
CSli
CSim
CBgR
CKob
CHby
CHal
CTri
CPen
CHad
CAbP
CMon
CElw
CFul
CBro
CNMi
CKel
CLAP
CCAT
CHdy
CFis
CMCN
CSam
CAvo
CLnd
CSWC
CPMA
CStr
CWoo
CWrd
CSev
CTho
CGOG
CMac
CNic
CDul
CDWL
CKno
CTrh
CAby
CFee
CPHo
CChe
COtt
CNCN
CSBt
CAbb
CCol
CPar
CBrP
CHrt
CSLe
CGro
CStu
CSec
CBen
CWin
CBur

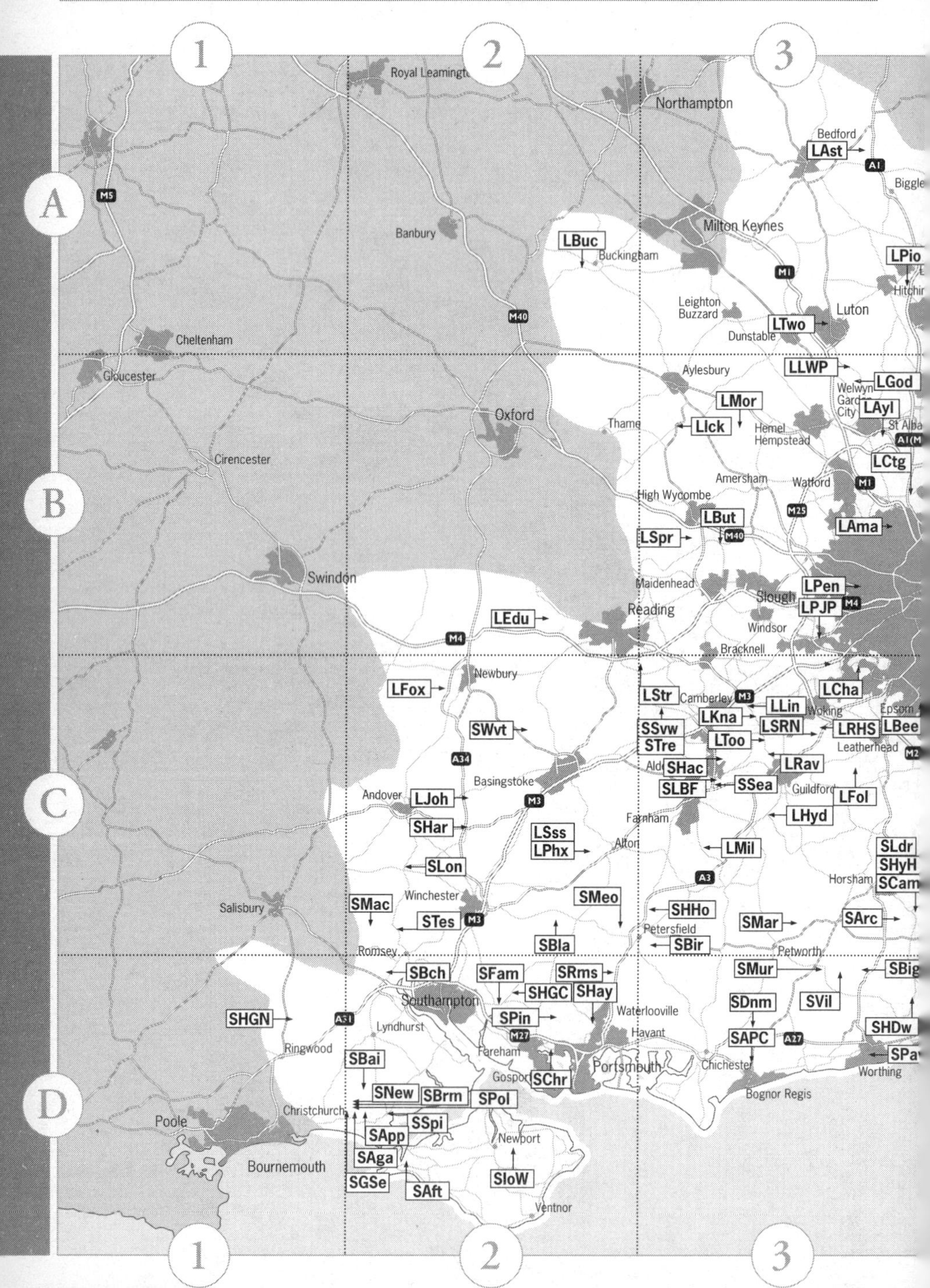
1
2
3
A
B
C
D
Royal Leamington
Northampton
Bedford
LAst
Biggle
Banbury
LBuc
Buckingham
Milton Keynes
LPio
Hitchin
M5
M40
M1
A1
Leighton Buzzard
Luton
LTwo
Dunstable
Cheltenham
Gloucester
Aylesbury
LLWP
LGod
Welwyn Garden City
LAyl
St Alba
LMor
Oxford
Thame
LIck
Hemel Hempstead
A1(M)
Cirencester
LCtg
Amersham
Watford
High Wycombe
M25
LBut
LSpr
LAma
Swindon
Maidenhead
LPen
Slough
LPJP
M4
LEdu
Reading
Windsor
Bracknell
Newbury
LFox
LStr
Camberley
M3
LLin
LCha
Woking
Epsom
LKna
SSvw
LSRN
LRHS
LBee
SWvt
STre
LToo
Leatherhead
A34
SHac
LRav
Basingstoke
SLBF
SSea
Guildford
Andover
LJoh
LFol
Farnham
SHar
LHyd
LSss
LPhx
Alton
LMil
SLdr
SHyH
SLon
A3
Horsham
SCam
SMac
Winchester
SMeo
SHHo
Salisbury
STes
SArc
SMar
Petersfield
SBla
SBir
Romsey
Petworth
SBch
SFam
SRms
SMur
SBig
SHGC
SHay
Southampton
SVil
SDnm
SHGN
A31
SPin
Waterlooville
Lyndhurst
Havant
SHDw
M27
SAPC
A27
Ringwood
Fareham
SPa
SBai
Portsmouth
Chichester
Worthing
Gosport
SChr
SNew
SBrm
SPol
Bognor Regis
Christchurch
Poole
SSpi
SApp
Newport
SAga
Bournemouth
SGSe
SAft
SIoW
Ventnor

Cambridge
Ipswich
LGro
Colchester
Braintree
Hertford
LDai
Harlow
Chelmsford
Clacton on Sea
Billericay
Brentwood
Rayleigh
Basildon
Southend on Sea
Canvey Island
Grays
Sheerness
Gravesend
SEND
Margate
Herne Bay
Ramsgate
LHew
SHop
SRiv
SDys
SRGP
SHFr
SBra
SReu
Maidstone
Sittingbourne
SRos
Canterbury
SLay
Sandwich
SCoo
SKee
SPoG
SIgm
SMer
SPet
SLPi
SChu
LCla
SPla
SPlb
SCrf
LSou
SSta
SSpe
SDow
SMad
Ashford
SGar
SIde
SHel
SBrw
SIri
Dover
SIFN
Royal Tunbridge Wells
SBri
Crawley
STil
Folkestone
SIng
SPer
SOkh
SLau
SNut
SMrm
SWCr
SAdn
SOkd
Hurst Green
SDix
SBod
SRkn
Maresfield
SPur
SHBN
SKen
SAll
SWal
SMHy
SBLw
Hastings
SMHT
Lewes
SRob
Hailsham
SCog
SUsu
Bexhill
SRot
SSth
SSto
SYvo
Eastbourne
LONDON
M25
M11
A10
M20
M26
M2
A2
M23
4
5
6
A
B
C
D
L&S
Map Three
London Area & Southern

MAP FOUR
WALES & THE WEST
W
1
2
3
A
B
C
D
WOut
WHer
WAbe
Llandudno
A55
Bangor
WCru
WRic
A470
WGer
Caernarvon
A5
Betws-y-coed
WDib
WCel
WBrE
Porthmadog
A470
A494
Dolgellau
WRos
WTMC
WBVN
A470
A458
Machynlleth
WCwm
Aberystwyth
A44
Llangurig
A483
WPrP
A487
A470
WPtf
Builth Wells
WGwG
WRha
A470
Cardigan
WPnP
A483
WMoo
WFar
Fishguard
Llandovery
WGWT
WPnn
St David's
Llandeilo
WPic
WShi
Carmarthen
Haverfordwest
A40
St Clears
A48
WIvo
Mer thy
Tydfil
WDyG
Milford Haven
Pembroke Dock
Tenby
WGor
Llanelli
Neath
WAba
WP&B
Swansea
Port Talbot
WBor
Bridgend
WDyf
Barry

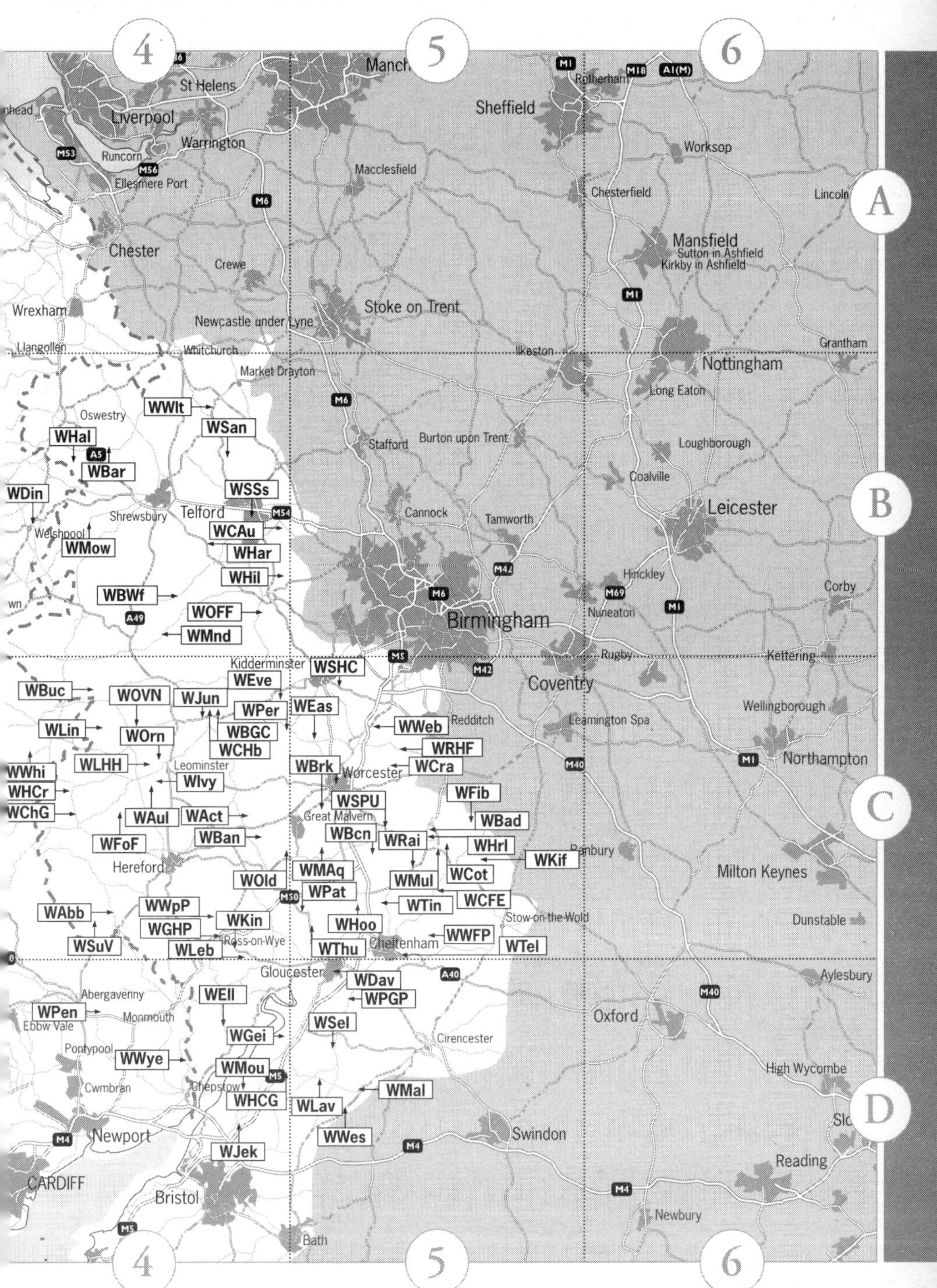

4
5
6
A
B
C
D
Liverpool
St Helens
Warrington
Runcorn
Ellesmere Port
Chester
Crewe
Wrexham
Llangollen
Whitchurch
Newcastle under Lyne
Stoke on Trent
Macclesfield
Sheffield
Rotherham
Worksop
Chesterfield
Mansfield
Sutton in Ashfield
Kirkby in Ashfield
Lincoln
Grantham
Nottingham
Ilkeston
Long Eaton
Loughborough
Coalville
Leicester
Market Drayton
Oswestry
Stafford
Burton upon Trent
Shrewsbury
Telford
Welshpool
Cannock
Tamworth
Hinckley
Corby
Birmingham
Nuneaton
Rugby
Kettering
Coventry
Kidderminster
Redditch
Leamington Spa
Wellingborough
Northampton
Leominster
Worcester
Great Malvern
Banbury
Milton Keynes
Hereford
Stow-on-the-Wold
Dunstable
Ross-on-Wye
Cheltenham
Gloucester
Aylesbury
Abergavenny
Monmouth
Ebbw Vale
Oxford
Pontypool
Cirencester
Cwmbran
Chepstow
High Wycombe
Newport
Swindon
Reading
CARDIFF
Bristol
Newbury
Bath
M1
M18
A1(M)
M53
M56
M6
M54
M42
M69
M5
M40
M50
A40
A5
A49
M4
WWlt
WSan
WHal
WBar
WDin
WSSs
WCAu
WMow
WHar
WHil
WBWf
WOFF
WMnd
WSHC
WEve
WBuc
WOVN
WJun
WPer
WEas
WLin
WOrn
WBGC
WWeb
WCHb
WRHF
WLHH
WBrk
WCra
WWhi
WIvy
WHCr
WSPU
WFib
WChG
WAul
WAct
WBad
WBan
WBcn
WRai
WFoF
WHrl
WKif
WMAq
WOld
WMul
WCot
WPat
WCFE
WWpP
WTin
WAbb
WKin
WHoo
WGHP
WWFP
WSuV
WLeb
WThu
WTel
WDav
WEll
WPGP
WPen
WSel
WGei
WWye
WMou
WHCG
WMal
WLav
WWes
WJek

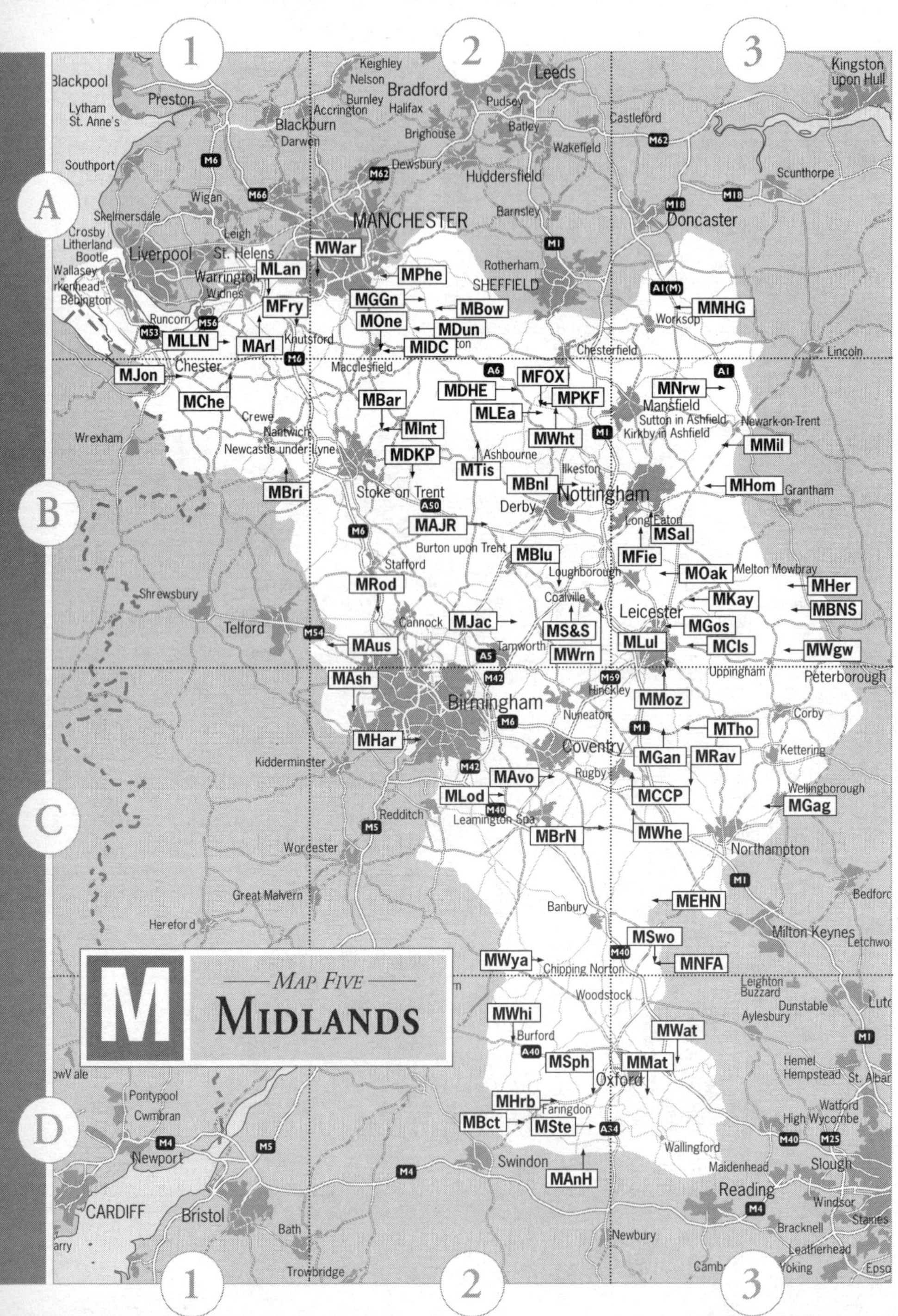
MAP FIVE
MIDLANDS
M
1
2
3
A
B
C
D
Blackpool
Preston
Lytham St. Anne's
Southport
Blackburn
Leeds
Bradford
Kingston upon Hull
Wigan
MANCHESTER
Doncaster
Liverpool
St. Helens
Warrington
Widnes
Runcorn
Knutsford
Chester
Macclesfield
SHEFFIELD
Rotherham
Chesterfield
Worksop
Lincoln
Mansfield
Crewe
Nantwich
Newcastle under Lyne
Wrexham
Stoke on Trent
Derby
Nottingham
Ashbourne
Ilkeston
Grantham
Newark-on-Trent
Stafford
Burton upon Trent
Loughborough
Long Eaton
Melton Mowbray
Shrewsbury
Telford
Cannock
Coalville
Leicester
Tamworth
Uppingham
Peterborough
Birmingham
Hinckley
Nuneaton
Coventry
Corby
Kettering
Kidderminster
Rugby
Wellingborough
Redditch
Leamington Spa
Worcester
Northampton
Great Malvern
Banbury
Bedford
Hereford
Milton Keynes
Chipping Norton
Woodstock
Leighton Buzzard
Dunstable
Aylesbury
Burford
Oxford
Hemel Hempstead
Faringdon
Watford
High Wycombe
Pontypool
Cwmbran
Newport
Swindon
Wallingford
Maidenhead
Slough
Reading
CARDIFF
Bristol
Bath
Newbury
Windsor
Bracknell
Trowbridge
Leatherhead
MWar
MLan
MPhe
MFry
MGGn
MBow
MOne
MDun
MLLN
MArl
MIDC
MJon
MChe
MMHG
MDHE
MFOX
MPKF
MNrw
MBar
MLEa
MInt
MWht
MMil
MDKP
MTis
MBnl
MHom
MBri
MAJR
MSal
MBlu
MFie
MOak
MHer
MRod
MKay
MBNS
MJac
MS&S
MGos
MAus
MLul
MCls
MWgw
MWrn
MAsh
MMoz
MTho
MHar
MGan
MRav
MAvo
MLod
MCCP
MGag
MBrN
MWhe
MEHN
MSwo
MWya
MNFA
MWhi
MWat
MSph
MMat
MHrb
MBct
MSte
MAnH

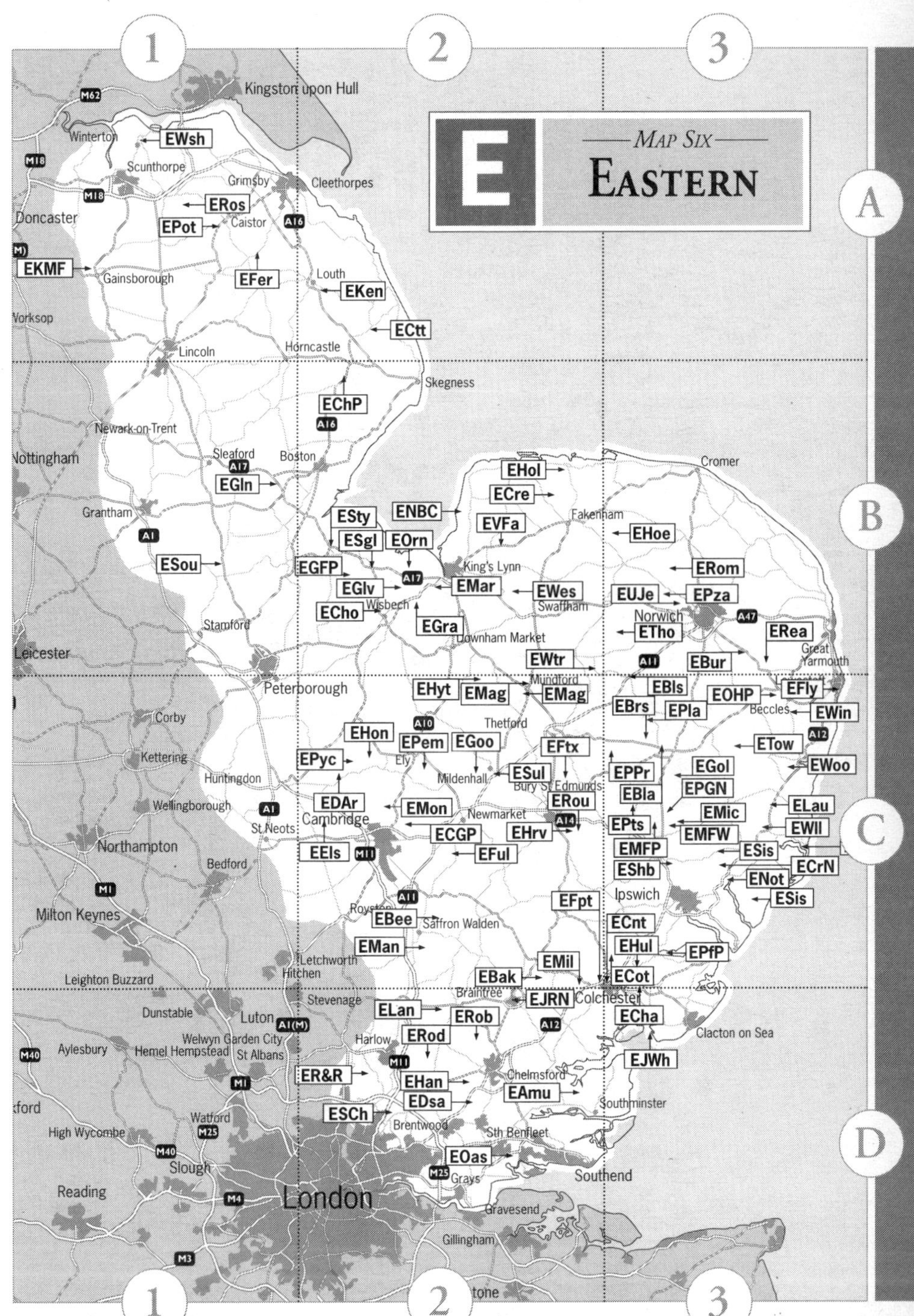
E
Map Six
Eastern
1
2
3
A
B
C
D
Kingston upon Hull
Winterton
EWsh
Scunthorpe
Grimsby
Cleethorpes
Doncaster
ERos
EPot
Caistor
EKMF
Gainsborough
EFer
Louth
EKen
Worksop
ECtt
Lincoln
Horncastle
Skegness
EChP
Newark-on-Trent
Nottingham
Sleaford
Boston
EGln
Grantham
ESty
ENBC
EHol
ECre
EVFa
Fakenham
Cromer
EHoe
ESgl
EOrn
ESou
EGFP
King's Lynn
ERom
EGlv
EMar
EWes
Swaffham
EUJe
EPza
ECho
Wisbech
Norwich
EGra
Downham Market
ETho
ERea
Stamford
Great Yarmouth
Leicester
EWtr
EBur
Peterborough
EHyt
EMag
Mundford
EMag
EBls
EOHP
EFly
EBrs
EPla
Beccles
EWin
Corby
Thetford
EHon
EPem
EGoo
EFtx
ETow
Kettering
EPyc
Ely
EGol
EWoo
Huntingdon
Mildenhall
ESul
Bury St Edmunds
EPPr
EBla
EPGN
Wellingborough
EDAr
EMon
ERou
ELau
EMic
Cambridge
Newmarket
EPts
St Neots
ECGP
EHrv
EMFW
EWll
Northampton
EMFP
ESis
EEls
EFul
ECrN
Bedford
EShb
ENot
Ipswich
ESis
Milton Keynes
EFpt
Royston
EBee
Saffron Walden
ECnt
EMan
EHul
EPfP
Letchworth
Hitchin
EMil
Leighton Buzzard
EBak
ECot
Braintree
EJRN
Colchester
Stevenage
Dunstable
Luton
ELan
ERob
ECha
Clacton on Sea
Welwyn Garden City
Harlow
ERod
Aylesbury
Hemel Hempstead
St Albans
EJWh
ER&R
Chelmsford
EHan
EAmu
EDsa
Southminster
Watford
ESCh
High Wycombe
Brentwood
Sth Benfleet
EOas
Slough
Grays
Southend
Reading
London
Gravesend
Gillingham

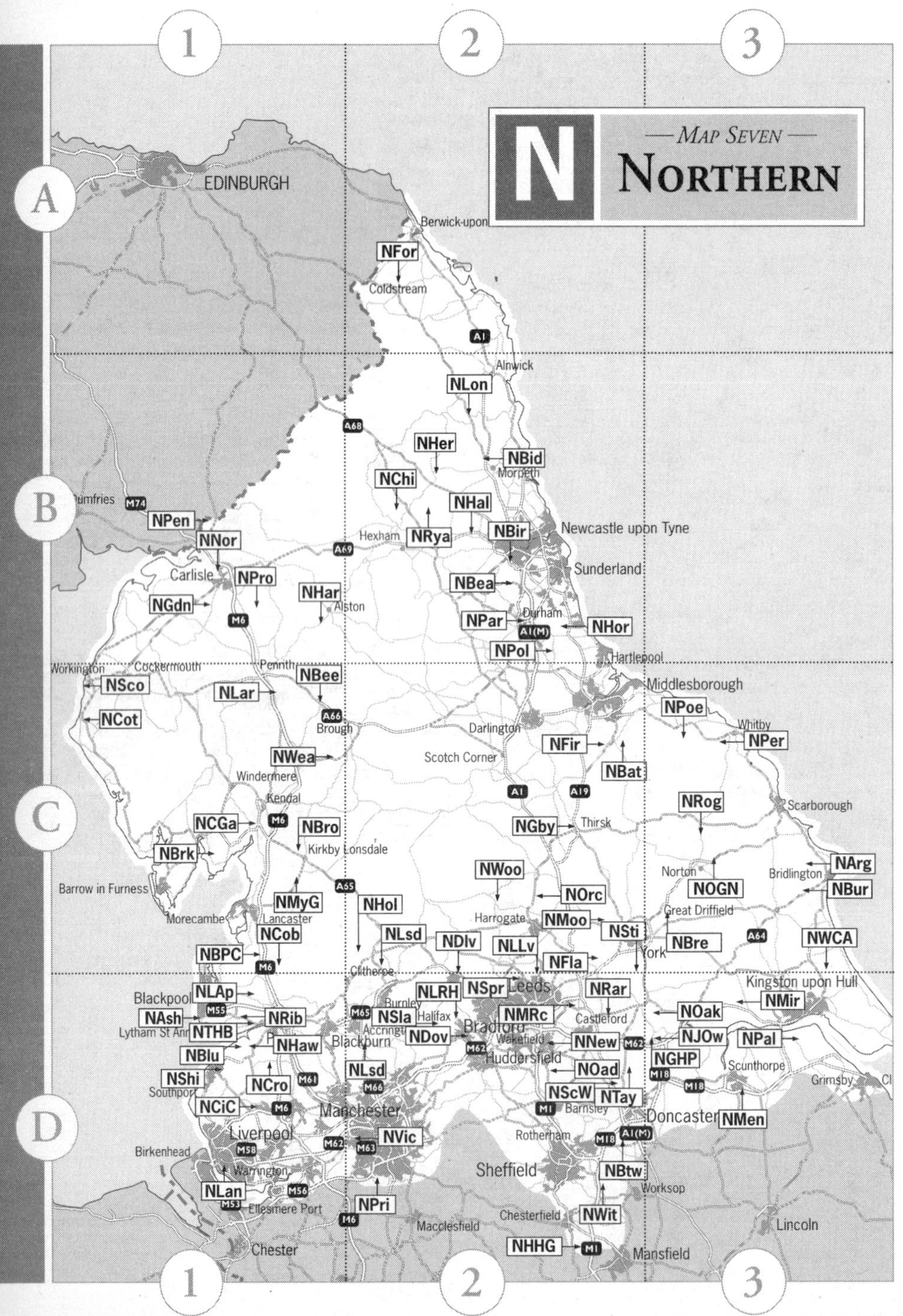

N
— MAP SEVEN —
NORTHERN
1
2
3
A
B
C
D
EDINBURGH
Berwick-upon
Coldstream
Alnwick
Morpeth
Dumfries
Hexham
Newcastle upon Tyne
Sunderland
Carlisle
Alston
Durham
Hartlepool
Workington
Cockermouth
Penrith
Middlesborough
Brough
Darlington
Whitby
Scotch Corner
Windermere
Kendal
Thirsk
Scarborough
Kirkby Lonsdale
Barrow in Furness
Norton
Bridlington
Great Driffield
Morecambe
Lancaster
Harrogate
York
Clitheroe
Leeds
Kingston upon Hull
Blackpool
Burnley
Halifax
Bradford
Castleford
Lytham St Ann
Accrington
Blackburn
Wakefield
Huddersfield
Scunthorpe
Grimsby
Southport
Barnsley
Manchester
Doncaster
Liverpool
Rotherham
Birkenhead
Warrington
Sheffield
Worksop
Ellesmere Port
Macclesfield
Chesterfield
Lincoln
Chester
Mansfield
NFor
NLon
NHer
NBid
NChi
NHal
NPen
NNor
NRya
NBir
NPro
NHar
NBea
NGdn
NPar
NHor
NPol
NBee
NSco
NLar
NCot
NPoe
NFir
NPer
NWea
NBat
NRog
NCGa
NBro
NGby
NBrk
NWoo
NArg
NOGN
NBur
NMyG
NHol
NOrc
NMoo
NCob
NLsd
NDlv
NSti
NBre
NWCA
NBPC
NLLv
NFla
NLAp
NLRH
NSpr
NRar
NMir
NAsh
NRib
NSla
NMRc
NOak
NTHB
NHaw
NDov
NNew
NJOw
NPal
NBlu
NGHP
NShi
NCro
NLsd
NOad
NCiC
NScW
NTay
NMen
NVic
NBtw
NLan
NPri
NWit
NHHG
A1
A68
M74
A69
M6
A1(M)
A66
A19
A65
A64
M55
M65
M62
M61
M66
M1
M18
M58
M56
M53
M63
M6

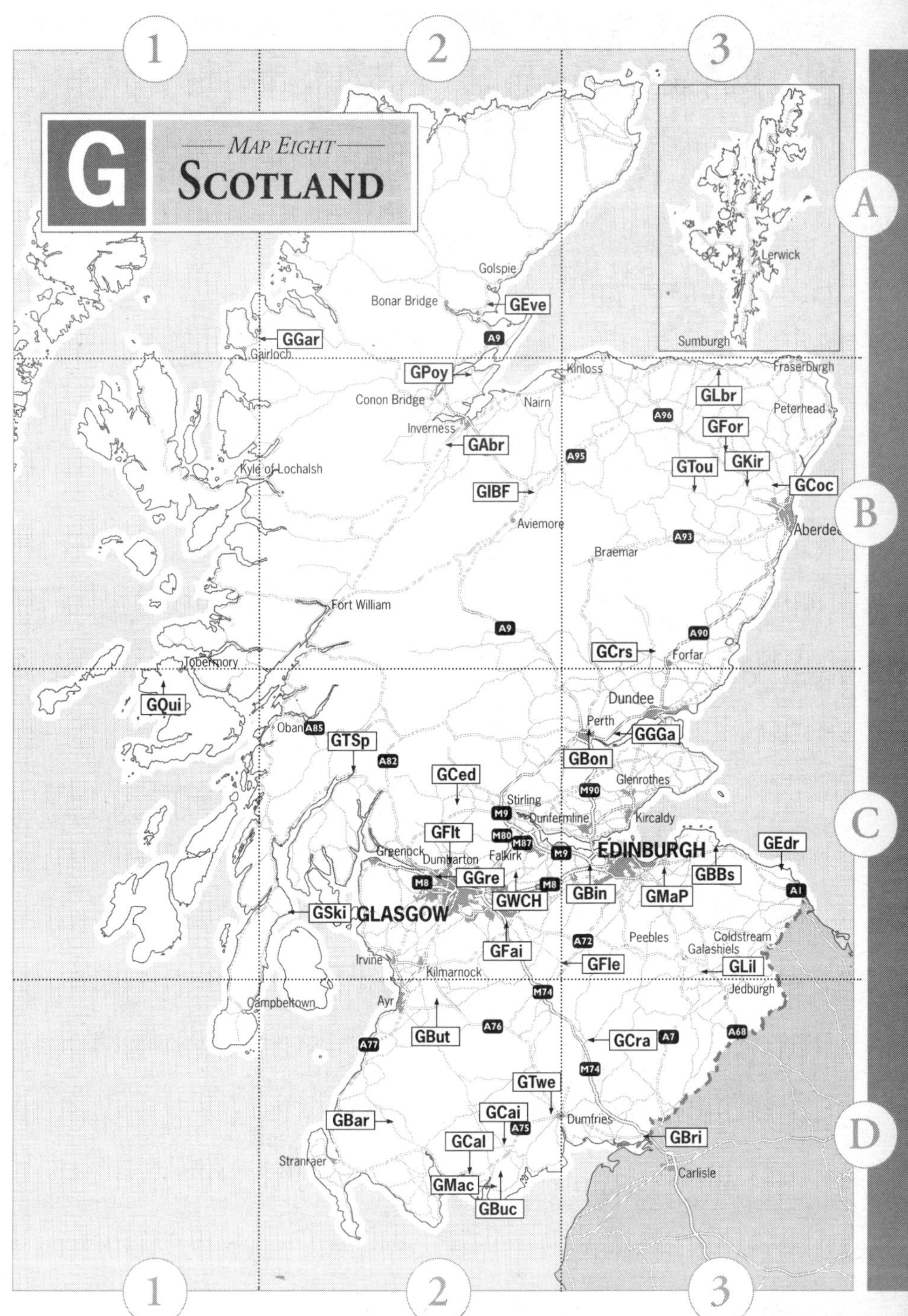

G
MAP EIGHT
SCOTLAND
1
2
3
A
B
C
D
Lerwick
Sumburgh
Golspie
Bonar Bridge
GEve
GGar
Gairloch
A9
GPoy
Kinloss
Fraserburgh
GLbr
Conon Bridge
Nairn
Peterhead
A96
GFor
Inverness
GAbr
A95
GKir
GTou
Kyle of Lochalsh
GCoc
GIBF
Aviemore
Aberdee
A93
Braemar
Fort William
A9
A90
GCrs
Forfar
Tobermory
Dundee
GQui
Perth
GGGa
Oban
A85
GTSp
GBon
A82
GCed
Glenrothes
M90
Stirling
M9
Dunfermline
Kircaldy
GFlt
GEdr
M80
M87
Greenock
Dumbarton
Falkirk
M9
EDINBURGH
GGre
GBBs
M8
M8
GWCH
GBin
GMaP
A1
GSki
GLASGOW
A72
Peebles
Coldstream
Galashiels
GFai
Irvine
GFle
GLil
Kilmarnock
Jedburgh
M74
Campbeltown
Ayr
A76
GBut
GCra
A7
A68
A77
M74
GTwe
GBar
GCai
Dumfries
A75
GBri
GCal
Stranraer
Carlisle
GMac
GBuc

The
GARDEN ROOM
CaféRestaurant

Webbs
OF WYCHBOLD

Grange Farm Nursery

**GUARLFORD
MALVERN
WORCESTERSHIRE**

SPECIALIST PLANT CENTRE

A small Nursery with an emphasis on Hardy Shrubs and Trees, Climbing Plants, Roses, Conifers and Seasonal Bedding.

WINTER FLOWERING PLANTS

Acer, Cornus, Betula, Sorbus, Magnolia, Hydrangea, Philadelphus, Viburnum, Skimmia, Pieris, Helleborus, Hostas, Phormiums, Grasses, Wisteria.

HERBACEOUS PLANTS

This tiny Nursery, personally run by Carol Nicholls since 1980 is beautifully arranged in seasonal displays, making it a pleasure to visit. The Nursery is set within old farm buildings, located in the beautiful area of the Malvern Hills east on the B4211 in the centre of Guarlford. Open every day except for two weeks after Christmas.

MALVERN

Email: sales@grangefarmnursery.freeserve.co.uk
National Garden Gift Tokens Bought and Exchanged

CHRISTIE'S NURSERY

THE ALPINE PLANT SPECIALISTS

**Downfield, Main Road, Westmuir,
Kirriemuir, Angus DD8 5LP
Telephone and Fax: (01575) 572977**

Our range of plants is ideally suited for Rock Gardens, peat and raised beds, screes, troughs, gems for the Alpine House or cold frame. Also in stock a selection of hardy orchids and woodland plants.

Open 5 days from 1st March to 31st October
10.00am to 5.00pm
Closed Tuesdays and Sundays.
Outwith the above times and dates by appointment only.

*Mail order service available from September to March.
Plant list available on receipt of four first class stamps.
All major credit cards accepted.*

**Email us at: ianchristie@btconnect.com
or look us up at our
Web site: http://www.christiealpines.co.uk**

Ornamental Conifers
Japanese Garden

We specialise in true dwarf and unusual Conifers, with growth rates from 6 inches in 10 years, many suitable for sinks, troughs and screes.

Many Japanese plants in stock.

Our established display gardens look good throughout the year, free entry.

P. & S. ROTCHELL

22 CHAPEL ROAD
TERRINGTON ST CLEMENT
KING'S LYNN • NORFOLK PE34 4ND
TEL/FAX: 01553 828874

*Open: 9.30 am-5.00 pm (dusk if earlier)
2nd February-20th December
CLOSED WEDNESDAYS*

EVERGREEN CONIFER CENTRE

Extensive collection of miniature, dwarf, slow growing and unusual conifers. Mature conifers and hedging conifers. Topiary, trees, shrubs, heathers etc.

CLOSED SUNDAYS

For further details including mail order see code WEVE.

Tel: 01299 266581

Email: brian@evergreen-conifers.co.uk
Web Site: evergreen-conifers.co.uk
Tenbury Road, Rock, Kidderminster, Worcs DY14 9RB

Over 500 varieties of Flowering, Ornamental & Climbing shrubs. Many new and unusual, despatched in 7 cm pots hardened off ready for re-potting or planting. Send 2 x 2nd class stamps for descriptive catalogue.

Glenville Nurseries (PF)

P.O. Box 2, Walpole St Andrew, WISBECH, Cambs PE14 7LD
Website: www.glenvillenurseries.co.uk

CONSERVATORY PLANTS & HARDY PERENNIALS

EShb

Our growing Suffolk nursery now offers over 1000 species/varieties. Mature conservatory plants on display in greenhouse & hardy perennial display beds in adjoining walled garden. Group visits to Nursery & Shrubland Gardens welcome. Mail Order.

SHRUBLAND PARK NURSERIES

www.shrublandparknurseries.co.uk
IPSWICH, SUFFOLK IP6 9QJ. 01473 833187

Nursery in grounds of Shrubland Park: From A14 (Junction 52) follow road through CLAYDON, take right turn into Park through gate opposite Sorrel Horse Pub, follow drive ½ mile, take sharp right turn opposite hall & follow signs.

OPEN: WED to SUN 10am-5pm (dusk if earlier)

TREE SHOP

Ardkinglas Estate Nurseries
Cairndow, Argyll PA26 8BL
Tel: (01499) 600263
tree.shop@virgin.net

Plants by mail order throughout the UK from Scotland's West Coast

Native species, unusual conifers, rhododendrons and a plantsman's choice of trees and shrubs.

Contact us by phone, post or email for catalogue (2 x 1st class stamps appreciated) or visit:

www.scottishtrees.co.uk

EAST NORTHDOWN FARM

Family Run Garden Centre/Nursery

Specialising in coast & chalk loving plants.
Comprehensive online plant list/catalogue

www.botanyplants.com

MARGATE KENT CT9 3TS
Tel: 01843 862060 Fax: 01843 860206

HOPLEYS

Code: LHop
Growers of Choice Garden Plants
Established 1968

You've seen us at the shows, now come and visit our nursery and garden! You've been meaning to do so for years, so this year put a date in your diary now - we would be delighted to see you.

You will find over a thousand varieties of choice garden plants, many of which can be seen growing as specimens in our 4 acre display garden. As an incentive, bring this advert with you and we will give you free entry to the garden! Now there's no excuse!

If you really cannot come, you may like to know that we offer mail order all year and are also happy to bring orders to shows.

See our website **www.hopleys.co.uk** for full details, or send 5 first class stamps for a catalogue to:

HOPLEYS PLANTS Ltd
High St, Much Hadham, Herts, SG10 6BU

Picnics allowed - No Dogs - Refreshments - Parking

A miscellany of plants - reflective of our interests and of plants that will grow (even thrive) in wet clay; our ¾ acre garden is open to visitors.

FEEBERS HARDY PLANTS

(PROP: MRS E. SQUIRES)

1 FEEBERS COTTAGE, WESTWOOD
BROADCLYST, DEVON EX5 3DQ
Telephone: 01404 822118

Open March/July and September/October on Wednesday 10am - 5pm.
Saturday and Sunday by prior appointment.
Limited mail order.

From B3181 Dog Village, Broadclyst, take Whimple Road for 1.25m; take left turn (signed Westwood) continue further 1.25m; Nursery on right entering Westwood.

INDEX OF ADVERTISERS

The Hardy Plant Society

Explores, encourages and conserves all that is best in gardens

The Hardy Plant Society encourages interest in growing hardy perennial plants and provides members with information about familiar and less well known perennial plants that flourish in our gardens, how to grow them and where they may obtained. This friendly society offers a range of activities locally and nationally, giving members plenty of opportunity to meet other keen gardeners to share ideas and information in a convivial atmosphere. The activities and work of the Society inform and encourage the novice gardener, stimulate and enlighten the more knowledgeable, and entertain and enthuse all gardeners bonded by a love for, and an interest in, hardy perennial plants.

Local Groups

There are over 40 local groups across the UK and national members are invited to join the group nearest to them. Each group offers a wide range of gardening activities including informative lectures, garden visits and plant plus educational and social events throughout the year. Most groups produce their own newsletters. Full details of how to join a local group are sent out to new members.

Specialist Groups and Gardening by Post

Specialist Groups produce their own newsletters and organise meetings and events for fellow enthusiasts. The Correspondents Group ensures that members who are unable to attend meetings can exchange gardening ideas and information.

Seed Distribution

Every member can join in the annual Seed Distribution Scheme by obtaining or donating hardy perennial seed. The Seed List offers over 2,500 tempting varieties of rare, unusual and familiar seeds and is sent to every member in December.

Please see overleaf for an application form

Shows and Events

Exhibits at major shows throughout the country let visitors see hardy plants in bloom and leaf in their natural season and more information about the work of the Society is available. Events hosted by local group members are also organised, from plant study days to residential weekends to garden visits. The Society also organises overseas garden tours.

Conservation

The Hardy Plant Society is concerned about the conservation of garden plants and is working towards ensuring that older, rarer and lesser-known perennial plants are conserved and made available to gardeners generally.

Publications and the Slide Library

The Society's journal, *The Hardy Plant*, is published twice a year and regular newsletters provide information on all the Society's events, activities, interests and group contacts. The Society also publishes a series of booklets on special plant families which include Hardy Geraniums, Pulmonarias, Hostas, Grasses, Iris, Epemendiums, Success with Seeds, Euphorbias, Phlox, Campanulas for the garden and Umbellifers. Other publications for members include a B&B list and a gardens to visit list. The Slide Library has a wide range of hardy plant slides available on loan.

Information about the Society is available from:

The Administrator
Mrs Pam Adams
The Hardy Plant Society
Little Orchard
Great Comberton
Pershore
Worcestershire WR10 3DP

Tel: 01386 710317
Fax: 01386 710117
E-mail: admin@hardy-plant.org.uk
Website: www.hardy-plant.org.uk

MEMBERSHIP APPLICATION FOR 2004

The Annual Subscriptions are:
Single **£13.00** per year (one member)
Joint **£15.00** per year (two members at the same address)

• Subscriptions are renewable annually on **1 January**.
• Subscriptions of members joining after 1 October are valid until the end of the following year.
• Overseas members are requested to pay in pounds sterling by International Money Order or by credit card. An optional charge of £10.00 is made for airmail postage outside Western Europe of all literature, if preferred.

Please fill in the details in BLOCK CAPITALS, tear off this form and send it with your payment to the Administrator or telephone the Administrator with details of your credit card.

Please tick the type of membership required

☐ Single £13.00 per year (one member)

☐ Joint £15.00 per year (two members at one address)

☐ Airmail postage £10.00 per year (optional for members outside Western Europe)

NAME/S ....

ADDRESS ....

....

.... POST CODE ....

TELEPHONE NUMBER ....

I enclose a cheque/postal order* payable to THE HARDY PLANT SOCIETY (in pounds sterling ONLY) for £............

OR
Please debit my Visa/Master Card* by the sum of £ ....
(* delete as required)

CARD NUMBER ☐☐☐☐ ☐☐☐☐ ☐☐☐☐ ☐☐☐☐

EXPIRY DATE ☐☐☐☐

Name as embossed on card ....

Signature ....

Please print your name and address clearly, tear out the page and send it to The Administrator at the address overleaf

The Hardy Plant Society is a Registered Charity, number 208080

MEMBERSHIP APPLICATION

Title (e.g. Mr, Mrs) | | Name | |

Address

Postcode | | Tel | |

College (*if applying for Student Membership*)

I/We wish to apply for national membership of The National Council for the Conservation of Plants & Gardens (The Company) and wish to receive copies of The Plant Heritage Journal.

I/We enclose subscription of £ made payable to: **'The National Council for the Conservation of Plants & Gardens'** *or*

I/We wish to pay by direct debit and enclose completed mandate form for £

I/We wish to be sent information about our local group. (place tick ✓ in box)

I/We would like to receive details of the following to support the work of NCCPG:

● Donation ● Legacies (place tick ✓ in box(es))

Instruction to your Bank or Building Society to pay by Direct Debit

DIRECT Debit

Originators Identification Number | NCCPG use only

9	7	4	2	1	2

Name and full postal address of your Bank or Building Society

The Manager, (BLOCK CAPITALS, PLEASE)

Bank/Building Society

Address

Postcode

Name(s) of Account Holders

Bank sort code (top right hand corner of your cheque)

Bank/Building Society account no.

Signature | Date

Instruction to your Bank or Building Society

Please pay The National Council for the Conservation of Plants & Gardens Direct Debits from the account detailed in the instruction subject to the safeguards assured by the Direct Debit Guarantee. I understand that this instruction may remain with the NCCPG and if so, details will be passed electronically to my Bank/ Building Society.

Banks & Building Societies may not accept Direct Debit instructions for some types of account.

This Guarantee is offered by all Banks and Building Societies that take part in the Direct Debit Scheme. The efficiency and security of the scheme is monitored and protected by your own Bank or Building Society.

If the amounts to be paid or the payments dates change, you will be told of this at least six weeks in advance.

If an error is made by The National Council for the Conservation of Plants and Gardens or your Bank or Building Society, you are guaranteed a full and immediate refund from your branch of the amount paid.

You can cancel a Direct Debit at any time, by writing to your Bank or Building Society. Please also send a copy to NCCPG National Office.

National Membership Fees: **(Group rates vary)**
Individual £10.00 **Corporate 50.00**
Student (in full time education) £4.00

Credit Card Payments - if you prefer your Credit/Debit card please fill in the following:

Card No

Expires end | Amount £

Name on Card

Signature | Date

GIFT AID

In April 2000 measures were introduced to help charities reclaim the tax that supporters have already paid on their contributions.

Please complete the Gift Aid Declaration below to increase the value of your support for the NCCPG at no additional cost to yourself.

I would like the NCCPG (Reg. Charity No 1004009) to reclaim the tax on all contributions I make on or after the date of this declaration.

I understand that I must pay an amount of income tax or capital gains tax at least equal to the tax the charity reclaims on my donation in the tax year.

Signature

Date

(Please note that Gift Aid is only applicable if you are a UK tax payer)

Please complete this membership form and send with remittance to:

NCCPG National Office,
RHS Garden, Wisley, Woking, Surrey GU23 6QP